Joy of Cooking

JOY OF COOKING

Irma S. Rombauer

Marion Rombauer Becker

Illustrated by Ginnie Hofmann and Ikki Matsumoto

SCRIBNER
Published by Simon & Schuster
New York London Toronto Sydney Tokyo Singapore

SCRIBNER
1230 Avenue of the Americas
New York, NY 10020

First Scribner Edition 1995

Originally published by the Bobbs-Merrill Company, Inc.,
a subsidiary of Macmillan, Inc., New York

Manufactured in the United States

55 54

Library of Congress Cataloging-in-Publication Data

Rombauer, Irma von Starkloff
Joy of cooking

Includes index.
1. Cookery, American. I. Becker, Marion Rombauer,
joint author. II. Title
TX715.R75 1975 641.5 75-10772

ISBN: 0-02-604570-2

To friends of the **Joy** who over the years through their countless letters and words of appreciation have made us feel that our efforts are worthwhile.

"That which thy fathers have bequeathed to thee, earn it anew if thou wouldst possess it."

Goethe: *Faust*

ACKNOWLEDGMENTS

Joy has always been a family affair. Written by my mother, Irma Starkloff Rombauer, a St. Louisan, it was tested and illustrated by me, with technical assistance from my mother's secretary, Mary Whyte Hartrich. It was privately printed in 1931 and distributed from the home. The responses **Joy** evoked were collected and published on its thirtieth birthday in a celebratory account entitled *Little Acorn*. Now over forty, **Joy** continues to be a family affair, revealing more than ever the awareness we all share in the growing preciousness of food.

Since his retirement from architectural practice, my husband, John, has given constant and unstinting effort toward **Joy's** enrichment. My sons—Ethan, with his Cordon Bleu and camping experiences, and Mark, with nis interest in natural foods—have reinforced **Joy** in many ways, as has my own sensitivity over the years to a oneness with the environment, culminating in the highly satisfying experience of writing *Wild Wealth* with ecologists Frances Jones Poetker and Paul Bigelow Sears.

As the scope of **Joy** has increased, so have other generous sources of proffered knowledge—too many and too specialized to mention in detail. Ever-ready understanding has continued to come from Jane Brueggeman, our valued co-worker for thirty years; from our competent home economics consultants Lolita Harper and Lydia Cooley; from our legal literary aide, Harriet Pilpel; from our guide to the New York cooking world, Cecily Brownstone; and from our kitchen mainstay, Isabell Coleman. More recently we have received thorough testing help from Joan Woerndle Becker, devoted editorial advice from Marian Judell Israel, and perfectionist secretarial assistance from Nancy Swats. Throughout the years Leo Gobin, now president of Bobbs-Merrill, has guarded for us great freedom in our work, and Eugene Rachlis, the editor-in-chief, has lent a sympathetic ear. Thanks also to Gladys Moore, our copy editor, for unending patience; to William Bokermann for the excellent book design; and to John van Biezen for his care in the physical production of this edition. We are sure our readers are as grateful as we are to Ginnie Hofmann and Ikki Matsumoto, whose drawings so skillfully enhance our text.

But **Joy,** we hope, will always remain essentially a family affair, as well as an enterprise in which its authors owe no obligation to anyone but themselves and you.

Marion Rombauer Becker

ACKNOWLEDGMENTS

CONTENTS

Foreword **xi**
The Foods We Eat **1**
Entertaining **15**
Menus **25**
Beverages **36**
Drinks **48**
Canapés and Tea Sandwiches **66**
Hors d'Oeuvre **77**
Salads **92**
Fruits **123**
The Foods We Heat **145**
Soups **167**
Cereals and Pastas **198**
Egg Dishes **220**
Griddle Cakes and Fritter Variations **235**
Brunch, Lunch and Supper Dishes **250**
Vegetables **276**
Savory Sauces and Salad Dressings **336**
Stuffings and Forcemeat **370**
Shellfish **375**
Fish **394**
Poultry and Wildfowl **417**
Meat **442**
Game **513**
Know Your Ingredients **519**
Breads and Coffee Cakes **599**
Pies and Pastries **638**
Cakes, Cupcakes, Torten, and Filled Cakes **664**

Cookies and Bars **700**
Icings, Toppings and Glazes **721**
Desserts **734**
Frozen Desserts and Sweet Sauces **758**
Candies and Confections **777**
The Foods We Keep **798**
Canning, Salting, Smoking and Drying **802**
Freezing **819**
Jellies and Preserves **832**
Pickles and Relishes **841**
Index **850**

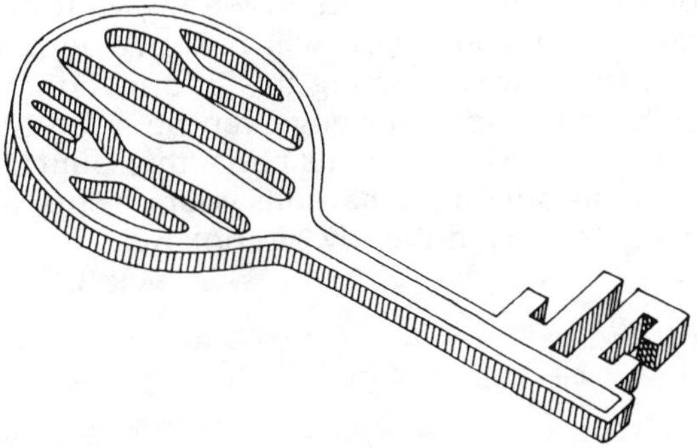

FOREWORD

We present you first with the front-door key to this book. Whenever we emphasize an important principle, we insert a pointer to success ➤. We use other graphic symbols, too—✱, ▲, ( ), ⊗, ⅄, ▤, ★—described on the **next page** to alert you quickly to foods appropriate for certain occasions or prepared by certain methods. Among the symbols is the parenthesis, which indicates that an ingredient is optional. Its use may enhance, but its omission will not prejudice the success of a recipe. ➤ Note, too, the special meanings of the following terms as we use them. Any meat, fish, or cereal, unless otherwise specified, is raw, not cooked. Eggs are the 2-ounce size; milk means fresh whole milk; butter is sweet and unsalted; chocolate means bitter baking chocolate; flour denotes the unbleached all-purpose variety; spices are ground, not whole; condensed canned soup or milk is to be used undiluted. In response to many requests from users of the **Joy** who ask "What are your favorites?" we have indicated some by adding to a few recipe titles the word "Cockaigne," which in medieval times signified "a mythical land of peace and plenty" and which we chose as the name for our country home. Where a recipe bears a classic title, you can be assured that it contains the essential ingredients or methods that created its name in the first place. And for rapidity of preparation we have grouped in Brunch, Lunch and Supper Dishes many quickly made recipes based on cooked and canned food.

There is a back-door key, too—the Index. This will open up for you and lead you to such action terms as simmer, casserole, braise, and sauté; such descriptive ones as printanière, bonne femme, rémoulade, allemande, and meunière; and to national culinary enthusiasms such as couscous, Devonshire cream, strudel, zabaglione, rijsttafel and gazpacho.

Other features of this book which we ask you to investigate include the chapter on Heat, which gives you many clues to maintaining the nutrients in the food you are cooking. Know Your Ingredients reveals vital characteristics of the materials you commonly combine, how and why they react as they do, how to measure them and, when feasible, how to substitute one for another. Then, in the paragraphs marked "About," you will find information relating to those food categories, including the amounts to buy.

But, even more important, we hope that in answering your question "What shall we have for dinner?" you will find in Foods We Eat a stimulus to combine foods wisely. Using this information, you may say with Thomas Jefferson, "No knowledge can be more satisfactory to a man than that of his own frame, its parts, their functions and actions." Choose from our offerings what suits your person, your lifestyle, your pleasure; and join us in the joy of cooking.

M.R.B.

WATCH FOR THESE SYMBOLS

- POINTERS TO SUCCESS
- FROZEN FOODS
- ( ) OPTIONAL
- PRESSURE COOKING
- BLENDER
- OUTDOOR COOKING
- ★ CHRISTMAS
- ▲ ALTITUDE COOKING

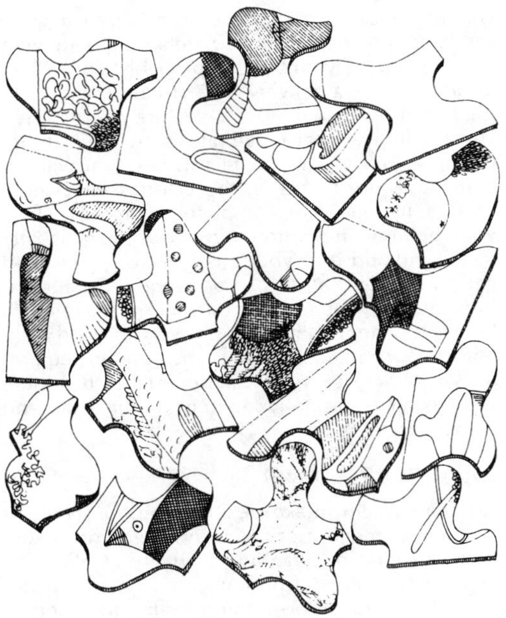

FOODS WE EAT

Put this puzzle together and you will find milk, cheese and eggs, meat, fish, beans and cereals, greens, fruits and root vegetables—foods that contain our essential daily needs.

Exactly how they interlock and in what quantities for the most advantageous results for every one of us is another puzzle we must try to solve for ourselves, keeping in mind our age, body type, activities, the climate in which we live, and the food sources available to us. How we wish someone could present us with hard and fast rules as to how and in what exact quantities to assemble the proteins, fats and carbohydrates as well as the small but no less important enzyme and hormone systems, the vitamins, and the trace minerals these basic foods contain so as best to build body structure, maintain it, and give us an energetic zest for living!

Where to turn? Not to the sensational press releases that follow the discovery of fascinating bits and pieces about human nutrition; nor to the oversimplified and frequently ill-founded dicta of food faddists that can lure us into downright harm. ➤ First we must search for the widest variety of the best grown unsprayed foods we can find in their freshest condition, and then look for foods with minimal but safe processing and preservatives and without synthetic additives. While great strides have been made in the storage of foods commercially and in the home, ➤ if fresh foods in good condition are available to you, choose them every time. To compare the nutritive values in frozen, canned and fresh vegetables, see 798.

Next we can find in the *U.S. Handbook on the Composition of Foods* some of the known calorie, protein and other values based on the edible portions of common foods. Recent mandatory labeling information, 7, is of some help, although the U.S. Recommended Daily Allowances are based on information from a nongovernmental agency, the National Research Council, a source not acceptable to some authorities. But no one chart or group of charts is the definitive answer for most of us, who are simply not equipped to evaluate the complex relationships of these elements, or to adapt them to the practicalities of daily living. Such studies are built up as averages, and thus have greater value in presenting an overall picture than in solving our individual nutrition problems.

Nevertheless, by applying plain common sense to available mass data, we as well as the experts are inclined to agree that many Americans are privileged to enjoy superabundance ➤ and that our nutritional difficulties have to do generally not with under- but with overeating. Statistics on consumption also bear out other trends: first, that we frequently make poor choices and eat too much of the wrong kinds of foods; second, that many of us overconsume drugs as well as foods. Medication, often a lifesaver, may, when used habitually, induce an adverse effect on the body's ability to profit fully from even the best dietary intake.

Individually computerized diagnoses of our lacks may prove a help in adjusting our deficiencies to our needs. But what we all have in our bodies is one of the greatest of marvels: an already computerized but infinitely more complex built-in system that balances and allocates with infallible and almost instant decision what we ingest, sending each substance on its proper course to make the most of what we give it. And since nutrition is concerned not only with food as such but with the substances that food contains, once these essential nutrients are chosen, their presentation in the very best state for the body's absorption is the cook's first and foremost job. Often taste, flavor and color at their best reflect this job well done. Read The Foods We Heat, 145, and follow our pointers to success for effective ways to preserve essential nutrients during cooking. And note at the point of use recommendations for optimum storage and handling conditions, for one must always bear in mind the fragility of foods and the many ways contaminants can affect them, and consequently us, when they are carelessly handled or even when such a simple precaution as washing the hands before preparing foods is neglected.

But now let's turn to a more detailed view of nutritional terms: calories, proteins, fats, carbohydrates, accessory factors like vitamins, minerals, enzymatic and hormonal fractions—all of which are needed—and see how they interact to maintain the dietary intake best suited to our individual needs.

ABOUT CALORIES

A too naïve theory used to prevail for explaining regeneration through food. The human system was thought of as an engine, and you kept it stoked with foods to produce energy. Food can be and still is measured in units of heat, or calories. A **Calorie,** sometimes called a kilocalorie or K Calorie, is the amount of heat needed to raise one kilogram of water one degree Centigrade. Thus translated into food values, each gram of protein in egg, milk, meat or fish is worth four calories; each gram of carbohydrate in starches and sugars or in vegetables, four calories; and each gram of fat in butters, in vegetable oils and drippings, and in hidden fats, 5, about nine calories. The mere stoking of the body's engine with energy-producing foods may keep life going in emergencies. But to maintain health, food must also have, besides its energy values, the proper proportions of biologic values. Proteins, vitamins, enzymes, hormones, minerals and their regulatory functions are still too complicated to be fully understood. But fortunately for us the body is able to respond to them intuitively.

What we really possess, then, we repeat, is not just a simple stoking mechanism, but a computer system far more elaborate and knowledgeable than anything that man has been able to devise. Our job is to help it along as much as possible, neither stinting it nor overloading it. Depending on age, weight and activity the following is a rough guide to ➤ the favorable division of daily caloric intake: a minimum of 15% for proteins, under 25% for fats, and about 60% for carbohydrates. These percentages are relative: some people with highly efficient absorption and superior metabolism require both lower intake and the lesser amount of protein. No advice for reducing is given here, nor are the vaunted advantages of unusually high protein intake considered —as again such decisions must be highly individual, see About Proteins, at right. In general, and depending also on age, sex, body type and amount of physical activity, adults can use 1700 to 3000 calories a day. Adolescent boys and very active men under fifty-five can utilize close to 3000 calories a day. At the other extreme, women over fifty-five need only about 1700 calories. Women from eighteen to thirty-five need about 2000 calories daily. During pregnancy they can add 200 calories and, during lactation, an extra 1000 calories. Children one to six need from 1100 to 1600. Before a baby's first birthday, his diet should be closely watched, and parents should ask their pediatricians about both the kinds and the amounts of food to give their baby.

Given your present weight, perhaps a more accurate way to calculate your individual calorie requirement is to consider your activity rate. If you use a car to go to work and have a fairly sedentary job, or even if you are a housewife with small children, your rate is probably only 20%; 30% if you are a delivery man or patrolman working out of doors, and 50% if you are a dirt farmer, construction worker or athlete in training. If you multiply your weight by 14 calories, you will get your basal need, that is, the calories you would require if you were completely inactive. When you multiply this amount by your own activity factor and add it to your basal needs, you should get an approximation of your required daily caloric intake. If you reduce your caloric intake much below this approximate norm, you may be lacking in your mineral, vitamin and protein requirements. Whatever your caloric intake, distribute your choices properly among protein, fat and carbohydrate values.

ABOUT PROTEINS

On our protein intake depends the constant virtual replacement of self. And nowhere in the diet is the relation of quantity to quality greater. The chief components of proteins are 22 amino acids. They form an all-or-nothing team, for food is utilized by the body only in proportion to the presence of the scarcest of them. Fourteen of the 22 aminos are both abundant and versatile. If they are not present when food is ingested, the body is able to synthesize the missing ones from those present. The remaining 8 aminos, however, cannot be synthesized and must be present in the food when ingested. These eight are known as the **essential aminos.** Four of them—leucine, valine, phenylalanine and threonine—are relatively abundant in foods, but the other four—isoleucine, lysine, methionine and tryptophan—are more scarce. And because utilization of protein by the body depends in each instance on the least abundant member of the essential aminos, these latter four are known as the **key aminos.**

Generally speaking, proteins from animal sources like egg, meat, fish, and dairy products are valued because their total protein content is high, and they are referred to as **complete** because they are rich in the essential aminos, and therefore more of the total protein present is utilizable. Those from vegetable sources such as whole grains, nuts, seeds, and legumes—with the exception of soybeans—are less valuable because their total protein content is low. They are referred to as **incomplete** because they are also low in one or more of the eight essential amino acids, meaning that less of their total protein can be utilized by the body. The terms "complete" and "incomplete" are somewhat misleading, however, because of their absolute connotations. It is still possible to fulfill your daily requirements for protein from incomplete vegetable sources, provided you are willing and able to consume large enough quantities of the incomplete protein item in question. But the utilizable protein content of most cereals is so poor that consuming enough to satisfy protein requirements would be a practical impossibility.

Take corn, for example. It has little protein and many starch calories. A diet based exclusively on corn would require consumption of enormous quantities of corn to establish the needed essential aminos. A complete protein source like eggs would therefore be more realistic and desirable in satisfying the same protein requirement with far less caloric intake. In fact, for 10 grams of egg protein at 125 calories, you would have to eat 16.5 grams of corn protein at 500 calories to get an equivalent amount of usable protein. But since no one wants to live on corn or eggs alone, a more reasonable way to approach the problem is to note how complete and incomplete proteins complement each other.

There are various ways of expressing protein values—net protein utilization, or NPU; protein efficiency ratio, or PER; and biologic value, or BV. Another unit of measure used on product labels is protein value in relation to casein, 7. Although these terms are all derived by different methods, they correlate well with each other. Whatever the method of expressing this utilization efficiency, one fact remains: that is, the body requires certain kinds and amounts of essential amino acids which must be supplied each day.

Any excess intake of amino acids not compensated for is metabolized away and thus not used for growth or maintenance of the body. Eggs, with a BV of 94, may be considered the most ideal protein from the point of view of utilization to replace body protein. But we can't survive on one food alone.

If we combine durum wheat, with a BV of 60, and lima beans, with a BV of 50, we get through their complementarity of utilizable protein a score of 60. But a BV of 60 is marginal for body replacement, and so a more complete protein such as that contained in milk or eggs should be added to such a meal. Combine, for instance, 1 tablespoon of peanut butter, with a BV of 43, and **one slice of white bread, with a BV of 52. If you** add 4 ounces of milk, with a BV of 86, the combination stabilizes at a BV of approximately 80.

In countries dependent mainly on beans and rice or other cereal combinations, the beneficial effects of adding to the diet even small amounts of meat, fish, eggs or dairy products is well recognized. And when various pastas are the staple foods, the inclusion of at least one-third in the form of a complete protein is considered the minimal amount to bring the meal up to acceptable levels. Furthermore, it should be stressed that any meal or snack which fails to include sufficient complete protein, although it may temporarily stay one's hunger, will not replenish all of the metabolic losses of the body.

In regions where only vegetable protein is available, grains combined with pulses such as beans and peas are classic. It has been found that increments of about one-third complete protein reinforce incomplete protein to form a total that is greater than the sum of its parts.

Even more significant differences are found between processed and unprocessed foods. Brown rice has a BV of 75, as opposed to white rice with a BV of 65. Whole wheat bread has a BV of 67; white bread, 52.

To meet the needs of underdeveloped areas and the threat of worldwide protein shortages, in recent years experiments involving grain, seed and legume combinations, 198, have been undertaken which may one day prove valuable to all of us. Gross nutritional deficiencies are more conspicuous in areas where protein imbalances are drastic and prolonged, and the effects of improved diet are easier to evaluate than in areas like ours, where such deficiencies are less severe and thus harder to detect. Until recently, we have relied on animal experimentation, and although dietary results thus achieved are valuable, they are not always applicable to man, and, for the most reliable results, data must be based on human reactions.

➤ Since vegetable proteins are incomplete except as noted above, it is wise to draw two-thirds of the daily protein intake or 10% of your caloric intake from animal sources. Preferably, meats should be fresh—not pickled, salted or highly processed. ➤ Protein foods when cooked should not be subjected to too high heat, for then they lose some of their nutrients. Familiar danger signals are curdling in milk, "stringiness" in cheese and dryness in meat and fish.

Protein requirements generally are slightly higher in colder climates ➤ but no matter what the climate, growing children, pregnant women and nursing mothers need a larger proportion of protein than the average adult. The elderly, whose total caloric intake often declines with age, should consume a relatively larger percentage of protein to reinforce their body's less efficient protein metabolism. Again, absolute amounts cannot be given, because needs will depend on the efficiency of utilization by your own body. If your protein supply is largely from meats, fish, fowl and dairy products, a useful formula for calculating average daily protein intake is to allow .4 gram of protein per pound of body weight for adults, and for children from one to three years, 1 gram of protein per pound of body weight. In vegetarian diets structured on vegetable sources alone, with no animal by-products such as eggs and milk, careful balancing is needed to ensure enough complete protein. It is also suggested that the protein content of such a diet be upped from .4 to .5 gram per pound of body weight.

Experiments have shown variations in protein utilization between individuals to be as high as two to one. They have also demonstrated that an individual's protein needs may rise by one-third when he is under great physical or emotional stress. A natural luster in hair, firmness of nails, brightness of eyes and speed of healing are superficial indications of a well-being that comes from adequate protein intake. For a listing of approximate protein content—complete, incomplete and mixed—in average servings of individual foods, see 8.

Today, we cannot mention protein and protein sources without looking beyond our own frontiers. With overpopulation a world problem, can we continue our upward trend in meat consumption? Amounts of land required to produce protein increase by a ratio of one to ten as we proceed from the beginning to the end of the food chain: that is, from the growing plant to meat-eating man. To put it another way, the herbivorous animal must consume about 10 pounds of vegetable or cereal matter to turn it into 1 pound of meat. Or, as another example, the same amount of land is required to produce 10 pounds of soybeans as 1 pound of beef. You can readily see that there is protein waste in this type of food production.

As long as chickens scratched more or less on their own; as long as pigs scavenged family wastes; as long as cattle ingested grasses from lands often too rough or too dry for efficient grain harvesting, a something-for-nothing process existed. Today's animal husbandry competes in the main for crops that could also be utilized by humans. Chickens fed in batteries, pigs and cattle concentrated in feed lots need preprocessed foods and drugs to prevent the diseases these abnormal living conditions encourage. And their droppings, once recycled on the land, are too often uselessly burned or channeled into our streams, thus initiating gross pollution of air and water.

But should conditions be changed to allot greater quantities of grains, seeds and pulses to human consumption, we would still be faced with the problem of incomplete vegetable protein. As the growing of soybeans, the only complete-protein plant, is limited to certain climates, other vegetable protein sources must be improved or compensated for by combinations of grains and pulses or by the addition of some complete animal protein.

However, amazing genetic advances have been made in the development of grain hybrids, 548, higher both in protein content and in yield than the older types: short, sturdy, storm-resistant, heavy-headed wheat and rice hybrids, rich in protein and quick-maturing; high-lysine corns; and the intergeneric rye-and-wheat hybrid, triticale, are among the recent developments that promise primary improvements in natural sources of vegetable protein. Vegetable protein mixtures, see 3, combined with dry milk or fish meals, now mainly used for animal feeding, would find greater human acceptance if they were made more palatable, which in turn would guarantee a tremendous advance in protein availability at low cost for all. Protein has also been developed from yeasts, algae, kelp and petroleum products, and there is even the possibility of recycling the proteins in animal wastes; but, again, unpalatability has kept most of these newer protein sources from the table.

It is of the utmost importance that we guard our ecological soundness with all the knowledge we have at hand—knowledge that in some fields is far in advance of our willingness to apply it. It is essential that we consider new methods of utilizing and conserving land, for many of our soils are exploited to the point of depletion and are yielding crops with reduced protein and mineral content. Other soils produce only when saturated with chemical fertilizers and develop an inability to recover crop yields without revitalization through either animal or green manuring.

We must also be on the alert for various air pollutants. Spinach and romaine, for instance, will not grow where the air-sulfur content is high, and acreage yields of grains and other vegetables in such areas are adversely affected as well. Further research is needed to explain why saltwater fish die in waters made up from our formula for seawater but will thrive in natural seawater. Readings of chromatograms of synthetic as opposed to natural vitamins reveal startling differences which are as yet unexplained. These instances would indicate there are present in natural substances certain micronutrients—as yet not completely identified—which an organism needs in order to carry on vital internal chemical processes and which are lacking in engineered or synthetically produced foods, 535.

Further research and development of genetic seedbanks, now in their infancy, are needed to maintain efficient seed strains as the wild areas where natural hybridization has taken place are impinged on. For many of our best strains still come from fortuitous rather than man-induced selection. There is an unfortunate tendency to utilize these new seed strains in all areas before their climatic and soil adaptability has been proved, procedures that make them vulnerable to massive failure.

Again, just as variety in the selection of the foods we eat is necessary for our health, a variety of seed sources is essential to maintain the health of our foods. The breeding of plants resistant to disease, drought and insects, and tolerant of varying climates, is as important as hybridization aimed at protein increase. We like to keep in mind the wise old Indian who, when asked why he continued to grow three strains of corn when only one was his favorite for food, yield and flavor, answered that he was hedging his bets; the other two strains would always protect him against a too dry or too cold season or against insect infestation, while his favorite would succumb unless conditions were ideal.

We cannot leave our ecological musings without stressing the importance of these fundamental interrelationships, as complex and subtie in the world of edible plants as are those of the protein combinations and their subsequent utilization by the body, as discussed at left.

Although most grains are wind-pollinated, few of us realize how large and often unexpected a role insect life plays in pollination, and how insecticides can destroy this vital link in the food chain. The current abundance of fruit and vegetables in America can be traced in large part to the importation of the honeybee. The Indians had an excess of arable land, but for many of their crops they had to rely on much less efficient native pollinators such as noncolonizing bees, wasps and flies. Today, guarding against losing helpful insects is as important as destroying insect enemies—a fact stressed less often than is the need to solve the equally knotty problem of pesticide poisons in the food chain. We can no longer afford to ignore the interrelationships on which global food supplies depend.

ABOUT FATS

While fats have acquired a bad image of late, we must not forget how essential they are. As part of our body fabric ➤ they act as fuel and insulation against cold, as cushioning for the internal organs, and as lubricants. Without fats there would be no way to utilize fat-soluble vitamins. Furthermore, the fats we eat that are of vegetable origin contain unsaturated fatty acids which harbor necessary growth factors and help with the digestion of other fats. An important consideration in fat intake is the percentage of saturated to unsaturated fats. We hear and read much about cholesterol—that essential constituent of all body cells. It is synthesized, and its production regulated, by the liver. Cholesterol performs a number of indispensable body functions. Up to a limit, the more of it we eat, the less the liver produces. Excess cholesterol intake, however, like other excesses, is to be avoided, since a surplus of cholesterol may have serious consequences. The fatty acids in the **saturated fats,** which are derived from dairy products, animal fats, coconut oil and hydrogenated fats, 541, tend to raise the amount of cholesterol in the blood, while the fatty acids in **polyunsaturated vegetable oils** tend to lower cholesterol levels if taken in double proportion to saturated fats. To differentiate between these types of fat, see 539.

Few of us realize that much of the fat we consume—like the great mass of an iceberg—is hidden. Hamburgers and doughnuts, all-American classics, contain about one-fourth fat; chocolate, egg yolk and most cheeses about a third; bacon and peanut butter, as much as one-half. And in pecans and certain other nuts and seeds, the fat content can be almost three-fourths! These proportions are graphically suggested below.

All fats are sensitive to high temperatures, light and air. For best nutritive values store them carefully; and when cooking with them be sure that you do not let them reach the smoking point, 541. If properly handled they have no adverse effect on normal digestion. Favorable temperatures are indicated in individual recipes. Fats are popular for the flavor they impart to other foods, and for the fact that, being slow to leave the stomach, they give a feeling of satiety.

➤ We suggest, again, the consumption of a variety of fats from animal and vegetable sources, but remind you that fat consumption in the United States has climbed in twenty years from the recommended minimum of 20% to more than 40% today.

ABOUT CARBOHYDRATES

Carbohydrates, found largely in sugars, fruits, vegetables and cereals, are classed as starches or sugars. The sugars include monosaccharides, such as fruit sugars, 557, and honey, 558, which are sweeter than the disaccharides, such as common table sugar, and the polysaccharides, such as starch. The latter two types must be broken down into simple sugars before they are available for body use. This action is initiated by an enzyme in the saliva, which means that these complex starch carbohydrates should be carefully chewed. So dunking is not only bad manners but bad practice.

The caloric value of fruits and vegetables is frequently lower than that of cereals, while that of all concentrated sweets is higher. Children and athletes can consume larger amounts of sugars and starches with less harm than can relatively inactive people; but many of us tend to eat a

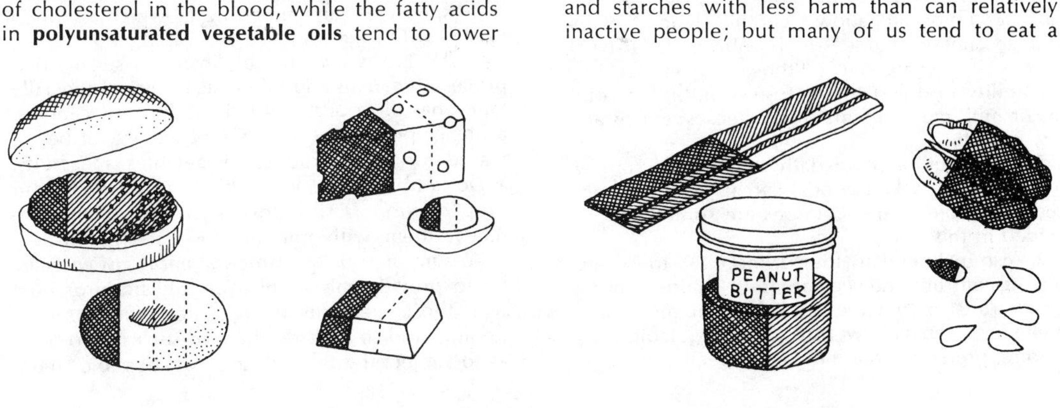

greater amount of carbohydrates than we can handle. Our consumption of sweet and starchy foods, to say nothing of highly sweetened beverages, is frequently excessive. Since the 1900s U.S. sugar consumption has increased by 25%, mainly in foods commercially prepared before they come into the home, making our per capita intake of these empty calories 103 pounds annually. The imbalance that results is acknowledged to be one of the major causes of malnutrition, for the demands excess carbohydrates make on the system may cause, among other dietary disturbances, a deficiency in its supply of the vitamin B complex. For itemized Calorie Values, see 8.

ACCESSORY FACTORS

Besides those already described, there are some fifty-odd important known nutrients required by the body, including minerals, vitamins, and other accessory factors. The body can store a few of these, such as the fat-soluble vitamins A, D, E and K, but others, such as the water-soluble vitamins B complex and C, must continually be replaced. The latter occur in those fragile food constituents that are lost through indifferent handling, excessive processing, and poor cooking. For instance, ➤ if you fail to utilize vegetable cooking waters, you are throwing out about one-third the minerals and water-soluble vitamins of the vegetable. To retain as much of them as possible, please follow the cooking suggestions given in subsequent chapters, and see About Stocks, 520.

If you maintain an adequate intake in such a way as to achieve the complete-protein and fat and carbohydrate balance described above, and if you choose from the following food groups, you will probably include all the necessary accessory factors. So fill your market basket first ➤ so as to assure two 3-ounce servings of complete-protein foods daily—meat, fish, fowl or eggs. Or, if you use combinations of incomplete proteins such as cereals and legumes, seeds, peanuts or gelatin, make sure you plan for the inclusion of some complete-protein food at the same meals, see 8.

➤ Drink daily or use in cooking 2 cups of fresh milk or reconstituted dry milk, 531, or allow enough of the following milk equivalents: for each ½ cup of milk allow 1 cup ice cream, ⅓ cup cottage cheese or one 1-inch cube cheddar-type cheese. If you are one of those persons lacking the ability to digest the lactose in milk, get your major milk requirements from cheeses, which are low in lactose.

➤ Plan four or more daily servings of starchy foods such as baked goods, cereals or pastas, accenting whole grains. Potatoes are sometimes included in this group.

➤ Also include daily four or more ½- to ¾-cup servings of fruits and vegetables distributed among citrus fruits or tomatoes and three or more dark green or deep yellow fruits and vegetables, including preferably one raw leafy green vegetable.

➤ Also check the constituents of each meal for the bulk found in vegetables and fruits to make sure there are more high- than low-residue foods.

Foods abundant in accessory values include: eggs, cheese, butter, whole milk, egg yolks, fish—especially herring, salmon, tuna and shellfish; beans, peas, nuts, seeds and whole grains; red meats and pork, variety meats, 499; fresh vegetables—especially the yellow and leafy green types—including white and sweet potatoes, brown rice and yellow corn; fresh fruits and berries and their juices; tomatoes and tomato juice; cabbage, spinach and cauliflower, as well as watercress, lettuces and other salad greens, and vegetable oils, 541. Bake with whole grains and flavor with brown sugars, molasses, wheat germ and butter. Don't forget to ingest one of the important accessory values, vitamin D, which you can get through exposure to sunlight, and remember that although outdoor exercise will tone your muscles and increase your oxygen intake—and perhaps your calorie needs—it will not necessarily make greater demands on your store of protein, vitamins or minerals.

If you have chosen wisely from the above substances, you may not need additional vitamin supplements. We all know from practical experience and statistical evidence that a well-nourished body has greater resistance to disease than a poorly nourished one. Recent research tends to support the thesis that adequate intake of accessory factors can contribute not only to disease resistance but also to disease prevention.

Other incidentals to bear in mind are: drink 5 to 7 glasses of fluid a day, including water, and, if you live in a region that calls for it, use iodized salt, see About Salt, 569.

The schedule outlined above is not necessarily a costly one. It is nearly always possible to substitute cheaper but equally nutritious items from the same food groups. Vegetables of similar accessory value, for example, may be differently priced. Seasonal foods, which automatically give us menu variations, are usually higher in food value and lower in cost. You can also profitably grow your own. Whole-grain cereals are no more costly than highly processed ones. Fresh fruits are frequently less expensive than canned fruits, which are often loaded with sugar.

If you are willing to cut down on sugar-laden processed cereals and other sugar items, especially fancy baked goods, bottled drinks, and candies, a higher percentage of the diet dollar will be released for dairy products, vegetables and fruits. ➤ Do not buy more perishable foods than you can properly store. Use leftovers cold, preferably. To reheat them with minimal loss, see 281.

To sum up, our fundamental effort always must be to provide this highly versatile body of ours with those elements it needs for efficient functioning, and to provide them in such proportions as to subject the body to the least possible strain.

However, not realizing the importance of variety in the selection of foods, some people are guided by calorie values alone. For instance, with bread and potatoes, almost equal in carbohydrates, you will find that bread scores higher in protein and fat factors but potatoes are greatly superior in iron, provitamin A, vitamin C and thiamin, all valuable accessory factors. Some help in making choices is available through product labeling. If any prepared and packaged food shipped in interstate commerce makes nutritional claims as to protein, fat, carbohydrate, calories, vitamins, minerals or enrichment, it must have labels declaring certain nutrient contents and giving both serving size and servings per container. The food processor has the option of declaring fatty acid and/or cholesterol content. He may also indicate the sodium content in the food. Because of differences in protein quality, two levels of protein intake are shown according to the protein efficiency ratio, 8, of casein: foods with levels equal to or greater than casein, and foods with less than casein values. ➤ If a food has less than 20% of the PER of casein, its label cannot declare that it is a source of protein. Sometimes labels indicate the percentages of available nitrogen instead of protein. Given the nitrogen percentage, you may approximate the protein content by multiplying the nitrogen figure by six.

Well-grown minimally processed foods are usually our best sources for complete nourishment; and a well-considered choice of them should in most cases meet our dietary needs.

You will find in this book, along with the classic recipes, a number which remain interesting and palatable even though they lack some everyday ingredient such as eggs or flour. These may be used by those people who have allergies. But we do not prescribe corrective diets; we feel that such situations demand special procedures in consultation with one's physician. As to the all-too-prevalent condition of overweight, it is now generally recognized that on-and-off crash diets are dangerous, and that a reeducation in moderate and varied eating habits is the only safe and permanent solution to this problem.

We stress again that the cook who has the responsibility for supplying the family with food will do well to keep alert to advances in the field of nutrition.

Take an active part in working toward consumer protection, for more and more food processors are gaining control over the condition and content of foods as we buy them. Take an interest, too, in legislative changes affecting labeling. The FDA's original intent for foods included under "standards of identity" ensured that terms like "mayonnaise" or "ice cream" would guarantee the same basic ingredients required in the government-established recipe no matter who manufactured it. But since the manufacturer is free to disclose or reveal as he pleases a wide variety of added ingredients, the consumer is at a loss to know just what he is buying. And there is a further, more recent loophole. While formerly the word "imitation" was required on labels for any deviations from the original substance, such as variations in taste, smell, color, texture, melting quality, or method of manufacture, today the term "imitation" may be omitted if the government considers the substitute to be nutritionally equal to the original. This so-called equality of the substitute food may be chemically induced or may be achieved by additives or enrichments. "Buyer, beware!"

But in planning menus and cooking, there are considerations other than mere percentages of intake in relation to fats, carbohydrates, proteins, minerals and vitamins. Peoples have learned over the centuries how to cope with poisonous elements that exist in some of the most basic foods. They know sprouting potatoes are heavy in glycoalkaloids; that cassava must be washed in a complicated fashion to rid it of its hydrocyanic content; that soy products must be either heated or fermented to destroy their trypsin- and urease-inhibiting factors; that cabbage, if it plays a large part in the diet, should be cooked in quantities of water to release its goiterogenic factors even at the expense of vitamin losses, just as wild greens frequently need several blanchings and discardings of the cooking water to rid them of their toxic content, 305. But peoples have also discovered a twentyfold increase in calcium content in limewater-soaked corn for tortillas; that oatmeal, if left wet and warm overnight, will with subsequent cooking release the phytin which otherwise inhibits the body's calcium absorption from other ingested food. Recently it has been noted that the phytins in soy depress the absorption of zinc. To ensure a control factor against these and various other food pollutants, it would be wise to vary your choice of foods.

So we come back to our puzzle. Unless and until greater and more practical advice about food properties becomes common knowledge, each of us must choose a wide variety from the basic food groups to make us feel well and to furnish our bodies with the components they need for growth and for maintaining stamina.

APPROXIMATE CALORIE AND PROTEIN VALUES IN AVERAGE SERVINGS

"Personal size and mental sorrow have certainly no necessary proportions. A large, bulky figure has as good a right to be in deep affliction as the most graceful set of limbs in the world. But, fair or not fair, these are unbecoming conjunctions, which reason will patronize in vain—which taste cannot tolerate—which ridicule will seize."—Jane Austen

We have tried, from data currently furnished by the U.S. Department of Agriculture and other authoritative sources, to give you in the first column below as accurate a calorie count as possible for the total edible portion of each serving of food as it comes to you at the table. Our soup figures are for canned soups diluted with the same amount of water—or whole milk, in the case of cream soups—unless we specify them as homemade. A cup is the standard 8-ounce measure, and a tablespoon or teaspoon is always a level one. Since we do not expect you to weigh your food at table, this chart should give you a fairly accurate guide to normal servings for a healthy adult. Remember, however, that two martinis before dinner count as much as a generous slice of pie for dessert, and, if you are watching your weight, second thoughts may be better than second helpings.

To use the protein values in the second column on the charts which follow, determine how many grams of protein you require each day, 3. Remember that adequate protein is vital for body maintenance and repairs. Note that with some foods you get too many calories per gram to make that food desirable as a protein source, 3. What is the price in calories you have to pay for a given gram of protein? To find out, divide the number of calories given in a portion of food by the grams of protein in that same portion of food. Foods with less than 35 calories per gram of protein are considered acceptable. Those with 35 to 70 calories are considered marginal, and those with 70 or more calories per gram are usually considered unacceptable. But it must be pointed out that the above figures apply only to protein values. While the apple, for instance, is clearly unacceptable for its protein value, it is treasured for its vitamins and minerals and its carbohydrates, mainly in the form of natural sugars. Again there must be a balancing of interrelationships in your intake of basic requirements.

In calculating protein content for the foods below, we have followed those values as suggested by government laws on labeling expressed as to whether the Protein Efficiency Ratio is greater or less than that of casein, the chief protein of milk. You will need 45 grams if the PER is equal to or greater than casein, in which case the figure is in bold-face type, and 65 grams of protein if the PER is less than the value of casein, in which case the figure is in light-face type. If the protein has a value of less than 20% of casein, it cannot be considered a significant source of protein and should not be included in your protein calculations. If the figure appears in italics, there is a mixture of foods. A "T" indicates only a trace of protein, and where a dash appears, reliable information on the protein value is not presently available.

Food	Calories	Protein Grams
Almonds, 1 cup shelled	850	26.0
Apple, 1 raw, 3" diam.	117	.4
Apple, 1 medium-sized, baked with 2 tablespoons sugar	200	.3
Apple butter, 1 tablespoon	37	.1
Apple dumpling, 1 medium-sized	235	*3.0*
Apple juice, 1 cup	120	.3
Apple pie, 1/6 of 9" pie	400	*3.0*
Applesauce, sweetened, ½ cup	127	.3
Applesauce, unsweetened, ½ cup	50	.2
Apricot nectar, canned, ½ cup	70	.4
Apricots, canned, sweetened, 4 halves, 2 tablespoons juice	80	.8
Apricots, dried, stewed, sweetened, 4 halves, 2 tablespoons juice	123	1.4
Apricots, 3 whole fresh	55	1.0
Artichoke, globe, 1 large, cooked	51	2.8
Artichoke, Jerusalem, 4 small	70	—
Asparagus, 8 stalks	20	2.2
Asparagus soup, cream of, 1 cup	160	5.9
Avocado, ½ medium-sized	190	2.5
Bacon, 1 crisp 6" strip	45	**1.8**
Banana, 1 medium-sized	100	1.3
Banana cream pie, 1/6 of 9" pie	300	*6.1*
Barley, pearled, light, uncooked, 1 cup	700	**16.5**
Beans, baked, canned, ½ cup	155	8.1
Beans, green or snap, cooked, ½ cup	15	1.0
Beans, kidney, cooked, ½ cup	115	7.2
Beans, lima, cooked or canned, ½ cup	95	5.4
Beans, navy, cooked, ½ cup	112	7.5
Bean soup, homemade, 1 cup	170–260	7.6
Bean sprouts, Mung, cooked, ½ cup	18	2.1
Bean sprouts, raw, ½ cup	10	1.1
Beef, corned, cooked, 3 oz., 3 slices, 3" x 2½" x ¼"	185	**22.9**
Beef, corned, hash, 3 oz.	155	7.6
Beef, dried, 2 oz.	115	**19.4**

Food	Calories	Protein Grams
Beef, 1 filet mignon, 4 oz.	400	**63.0**
Beef, hamburger, lean to average fat, 1 patty, 3 oz.	185–245	**21.8**
Beef, rib roast, 3 oz.	375	**19.9**
Beef, roast, lean round, 3 oz.	140	**23.3**
Beef heart, 3 oz.	160	**21.0**
Beef loaf, 1 slice, 2½″ x 2¼″ x ⅝″	115	*6.7*
Beef potpie, 4¼″ diam.	560	*23.0*
Beef soup with meat, 1 cup	113	**18.3**
Beef steak, sirloin, lean to average fat, 3 oz.	**172–330**	**20 to 26**
Beef stew, 1 cup	260	*18.6*
Beef tongue, 3 slices, 3″ x 2″ x ⅛″	160	**12.7**
Beer, 12 oz.	150	1.6
Beet greens, cooked, ½ cup	12	1.1
Beets, ½ cup	30	1.1
Berry pie, 1/6 of 9″ pie	400	*4.0*
Biscuit, baking powder, 2½″ diam.	150	*3.0*
Blackberries, fresh, ¾ cup	62	1.3
Blueberries, fresh, ¾ cup	64	.7
Bologna sausage, 1 slice, 3″ diam. x ⅛″	40	*2.*
Boston cream pie, 1/12 of 8″ dia.	210	*3.5*
Bouillon, 1 cup	32	.8
Bouillon cube, 1	5	.8
Braunschweiger sausage, 1 slice, 2″ diam. x ¼″	33	*1.5*
Brazil nut, 1 shelled	30	.7
Bread, commercial, rye, 1 slice, ½″ thick	55	2.1
Bread, commercial, white, 1 slice, ½″ thick	60–65	2.0
Bread, commercial, whole wheat, 1 slice, ½″ thick	60	2.3
Bread, gluten, 1 slice, 4″ x 4″ x ⅜″	64	7.0
Bread pudding, ½ cup	200	*6.0*
Broccoli, cooked, 1 large stalk or ⅔ cup	29	3.3
Brown Betty, ½ cup	160–250	*1.7*
Brownie with nuts, 1 piece	95	*1.3*
Brussels sprouts, ½ cup, approx. 5	30	3.0
Butter, 1 square, ¼″ thick	70	.8
Buttermilk, 1 glass, 8 oz.	90	**9.0**
Cabbage, chopped, raw, ½ cup	10	.5
Cabbage, cooked, ½ cup	15	.8
Cake, angel, plain, 3″ slice	150	*4.0*
Cake, cheese, 2″ wedge	**250**	*25.0*
Cake, chocolate layer, 2″ square	356	*4.1*
Cake, coffee, 1 piece, 3″ x 2½″ x 2″	133	*2.6*
Cake, cup, 1 frosted, 2½″ diam.	130	*1.5*
Cake, fruit, dark, 1 small slice, ½″ thick	142	*1.8*
Cake, pound, 1 slice	473	*5.7*
Cake, sponge, 2″ slice	145	*3.7*
Cake, white, 2-layer, with chocolate icing, 1 slice	375	*3.3*
Cake, yellow, 2-layer, with chocolate icing, 1 slice	365	*4.2*
Cantaloupe, ½ of 5″ melon	60	1.4
Caramel, 1 medium	42	.4
Carbonated water	0	0
Carrots, cooked, ½ cup	25	.7
Cashew nuts, 11 to 12	100	3.0
Catsup, 1 tablespoon	17	.3
Cauliflower, cooked, 1 cup	25	2.5
Caviar, granular sturgeon, 1 tablespoon	66	**6.7**
Celeriac, 1 medium-sized	40	1.8
Celery, raw, 3 small inner ribs	9	.5
Charlotte Russe, 1 serving	265	*5.5*
Cheese, American, 1″ cube	65	4.1
Cheese, Camembert, 1⅓-oz. wedge	115	7.5
Cheese, cheddar, 1″ cube	70	4.4
Cheese, cottage, creamed, ½ cup	106	**13.6**
Cheese, cottage, plain, ½ cup	86	**17.0**
Cheese, cream, ½ 3-oz. cake	160	**4.0**
Cheese, Edam, 1 oz.	87	7.7
Cheese, Liederkranz, 1 oz.	85	4.6
Cheese, Parmesan, 1 tablespoon, grated	25	2.3
Cheese, Roquefort or Blue, 1″ cube	65	3.6
Cheese, Swiss, 1″ cube	55	3.8
Cheese soufflé, 1 cup	238	*10.8*
Cheese straws, 3	100	2.5
Cherries, canned, sweetened, ½ cup	100	1.0
Cherries, fresh, sweet, 15 large	61	1.1
Chicken, broiler, small	136	**23.8**
Chicken, canned, boned meat, 3 oz.	170	**18.6**
Chicken, fried, ½ breast	155	**24.7**
Chicken, fried, drumstick	90	**12.5**
Chicken, roasted, dark meat, 3½ oz.	184	**29.3**
Chicken, roasted, light meat, 3½ oz.	182	**32.3**
Chicken livers, 1 medium-large liver	74	**10.3**
Chicken pie, 1 individual pie, 4¼″ diam.	535	*23.0*
Chicken salad, ½ cup	200	*17.4*
Chicory, or curly endive, 15 to 20 inner leaves	10	.5
Chocolate, bitter, 1 oz.	144	*3.1*
Chocolate, made with milk, 1 cup	245–277	*3.6*
Chocolate, sweet, 1 oz.	155	*1.3*
Chocolate, semisweet, 1 oz.	147	*1.2*
Chocolate bar, milk, 1 oz.	145	*1.2*

Food	Calories	Protein Grams
Chocolate creams, 1 small	51	*.5*
Chocolate éclair, custard filling, 1 average-sized	316	*8.2*
Chocolate fudge, 1″ cube	85	*.8*
Chocolate malted milk, made with 8 oz. milk and ice cream	502	*14.1*
Chocolate milk shake, made with 8 oz. milk and ice cream	421	*11.2*
Chocolate soda	255	*2.7*
Chocolate syrup topping, 1 fl. oz.	90	*1.0*
Cinnamon bun, 1 average	200	*3.9*
Clam chowder, Manhattan, 1 cup	87	*2.4*
Clams, canned, solids and liquid, 3 oz.	45	**6.8**
Clams, raw, 3 oz.	65	**11.2**
Cocoa, made with milk and water, 1 cup	150	*7.0*
Cocoa, made with whole milk, 1 cup	245	*10.0*
Coconut, shredded, dried, firmly packed, 1 cup	450	4.9
Coconut custard pie, 1/6 of 9″ pie	311	*7.9*
Codfish, creamed, ½ cup	200	**28.5**
Codfish balls, 2 of 2″ diam.	200	**17.1**
Cod liver oil, 1 tablespoon	100	0
Coffee, clear, 1 cup	0	.3
Coffee, with 1 lump sugar, 1 cup	27	.3
Coffee, with 1 tablespoon cream, 1 cup	30	.6
Cola beverages, 1 glass, 12 oz.	145	0
Coleslaw, with mayonnaise, ½ cup	85	*2.9*
Consommé, canned, 1 cup	35	*5.7*
Cookies, chocolate chip, 1, 2½″ diam.	50	*.5*
Cookies, sugar, 1, 3″ diam.	64	*.9*
Corn, canned, ½ cup drained solids	70	**2.2**
Corn bread, 1 square, 2″ x 2″ x 1″	139	*5.0*
Corn on cob, 1 medium, 7″ long	100	**3.7**
Corn soup, cream, ½ cup	100	*3.5*
Corn syrup, 1 tablespoon	57	0
Cornflakes, ¾ cup	75	1.5
Cornmeal, cooked, ⅔ cup	80	1.8
Cornstarch blancmange, ½ cup	152	.1
Crab meat, canned, 3 oz.	85	**14.8**
Crab meat, fresh, ½ cup	54	**9.3**
Cracker, butter, 1	16	*.2*
Cracker, graham, 1, 2½″ square	27	.6
Cracker, oyster, 12, 1″	50	*1.2*
Cracker, saltine, 1, 2″ square	17	*.4*
Cracker, soda, 1, 2½″ square	24	*.5*
Cranberry jelly, 2 tablespoons	47	T

Food	Calories	Protein Grams
Cranberry sauce, 2 tablespoons	21	T
Cream, coffee, 18.5% fat, 1 tablespoon	30	**.5**
Cream, half-and-half, 1 tablespoon	20	**.5**
Cream, sour, cultured, 1 tablespoon	25	**.4**
Cream, sour, imitation, 1 tablespoon	12	.2
Cream, whipped topping of vegetable oil, 1 tablespoon	10	T
Cream, whipping, 1 tablespoon	45–55	**.4**
Cream soups, canned, 1 cup	175–250	*7.0*
Cream of wheat, cooked, ¾ cup	100	*3.1*
Creamers of vegetable oil, 1 tablespoon	15	.3
Creamers of vegetable oil, powdered, 1 teaspoon	2	T
Cucumber, 12 slices	10	.6
Custard, ½ cup	153	*7.2*
Custard pie, 1/6 of 9″ pie	325	*9.1*
Daiquiri cocktail, 3 oz.	130	.1
Dates, 3 or 4	85	*.7*
Deviled ham, canned, 1 tablespoon	45	**1.8**
Divinity, 1½″ cube	102	—
Doughnut, cake type, plain, 1, 3¼″ diam.	165	*1.9*
Doughnut, sugared, 1, 3¼″ diam.	180	*1.8*
Doughnut, yeast, plain, 1, 3¾″ diam.	175	*2.7*
Duck, roast, 1 medium piece	300	**15.0**
Dumpling, 1 small	100	*1.0*
Egg, boiled or poached, 1 whole	80	**6.3**
Egg, 1 fried with 1 teaspoon butter	105	**6.7**
Egg, 1 scrambled with 2 tablespoons milk and 1 teaspoon butter	110	**7.1**
Egg yolk, 1 raw	60	**2.7**
Egg white, 1 raw	15	**3.5**
Eggnog, ½ cup	196	*10.5*
Eggplant, breaded and fried, 2 slices, ½″ thick	210	10.1
Farina, cooked, ¾ cup	80	*2.3*
Fig, 1 large dried	55	.9
Fig, 3 small fresh	95	1.4
Figbars, 1 small	50	*.5*
Fishsticks, breaded, cooked, frozen, 10 sticks or 8-oz. package	400	*37.8*
Flounder, baked, average serving	204	**30.2**
Frankfurter, 1	170	*7.2*
French dressing, commercial, 1 tablespoon	65	*.1*

Food	Calories	Protein Grams
French dressing, homemade, no sugar, 1 tablespoon	86	*.7*
French toast, 1 piece	170	*5.4*
Frog legs, fried, 2 large	140	**8.6**
Fruit cocktail, canned, drained, ½ cup	50	*.7*
Fruit cocktail, canned with heavy syrup, ½ cup	100	*.5*
Fruit cocktail, fresh, ½ cup	50	*.7*
Gelatin, dry, 1 tablespoon	25	6.4
Gelatin dessert, ½ cup	70	*1.8*
Gin, 1½-oz. jigger	105	0
Ginger ale, 12 oz.	115	0
Gingerbread, 1, 2″ square	170	*2.0*
Gingersnap, 1	20	*.3*
Goose, roast, 3½-oz. serving	426	**23.7**
Gooseberries, cooked, sweetened, ½ cup	100	2.0
Grape juice, 1 glass, 8 oz.	165	1.0
Grapefruit, ½ medium	45	.7
Grapefruit juice, unsweetened, 1 cup	100	1.0
Grapes, green seedless, 60	66	.5
Grapes, Malaga or Tokay, ½ cup	55	.5
Gravy, thick, 3 tablespoons	180	*1.3*
Green pepper, 1 whole	20	1.0
Griddle cakes, 2 of 4″ diam.	150	*4.5*
Grits, hominy, cooked, ¾ cup	90	*2.1*
Guavas, 1 medium	70	.9
Gum drop, 1 large	35	0
Haddock, 1 fillet, breaded, fried, 3 oz.	140	**16.6**
Halibut steak, sautéed, 3″ x ½″ x 1″	125	**18.4**
Ham, baked, medium fat, 3 oz.	245	**26.3**
Ham, boiled, 2 oz.	135	**14.5**
Hamburger—*see* Beef		
Hard candy, 1 oz. (3 or 4 balls, ¾″ diam.)	110	0
Hard sauce, 1 tablespoon	50	T
Herring, fresh, 3 oz.	128	**9.1**
Herring, pickled Bismarck, 3½″ x 1½″ x 1¼″	218	**19.5**
Herring, smoked, 3 oz.	200	**21.0**
Hickory nuts, about 12	100	2.1
Hollandaise sauce, 1 tablespoon	65	*1.4*
Honey, 1 tablespoon	65	.1
Honeydew melon, 1 wedge, 2″ x 7″	50	1.2
Horseradish, grated, 1 tablespoon	12	.4
Ice cream, commercial, plain, ½ cup	125–165	**1.9–2.9**
Ice milk, commercial, plain, ½ cup	65–100	**2.0–3.0**
Icing, chocolate, with milk and butter, 1 cup	1,035	*9.7*
Icing, coconut, boiled, 1 cup	605	*3.2*
Icing, white, boiled, 1 cup	300	*1.3*
Jam or jelly, 1 tablespoon	50–60	.1
Kale, cooked, 1 cup	30	3.3
Kidneys, beef, braised, 3½ oz.	159	**20.9**
Kohlrabi, cooked, ½ cup	23	1.6
Kumquats, 3	35	.5
Ladyfingers, 1	37	*.8*
Lamb, roast leg, lean to average fat, 3 oz.	156–235	**11.7–22.8**
Lamb, roast shoulder, lean to average fat	170–285	**11.7–15.8**
Lamb chop, broiled, 4 oz.	400	**20.2**
Lamb stew with vegetables, 1 cup	250	*14.8*
Lard, 1 tablespoon	115	0
Leek, 1	10	.5
Lemon, 1 medium-sized	20	.8
Lemonade, 1 cup	88	*.3*
Lemon gelatin, ½ cup	100	*2.0*
Lemon ice, ½ cup	116	*1.0*
Lemon juice, 1 tablespoon	5	.1
Lemon meringue pie, 1/6 of 9″ pie	345	*5.0*
Lentil soup, homemade, 1 cup	150–260	*5.0*
Lettuce, iceberg, ¼ large head	18	1.2
Lettuce, 6 large leaves	30	2.2
Lime juice, 1 tablespoon	5	.1
Liver, beef, fried, 2 oz.	130	**13.2**
Liver, calf, fried, 2 oz.	110	**15.1**
Liverwurst or liver sausage, 2 slices, 3″ diam. x ¼″	160	*8.5*
Lobster, 1 cup	105	**19.5**
Lobster, whole, small, baked or broiled with 2 tablespoons butter	308	**10.6**
Loganberries, canned, ½ cup	55	.6
Macaroni, cooked, plain, ½ cup	80	2.7
Macaroni and cheese, ½ cup	215	*8.4*
Mackerel, broiled, 3 oz.	200	**20.0**
Malted milk, 8 oz.	245	*11.1*
Mangoes, tropical, 1 large	85	.9
Manhattan cocktail, 3 oz.	160	T
Maple syrup, 1 tablespoon	50	0
Margarine, 1 tablespoon	100	.1
Marmalade, 2 tablespoons	120	*.2*
Marshmallows, 5	125	*.8*
Martini cocktail, 3 oz. 3:1	145	.1
Mayonnaise, 1 tablespoon	65–109	*.2*
Meat loaf, beef and pork, 1 slice, 4″ x 3″ x ⅜″	264	*12.2*
Melba toast, 1 slice, 4″ x 4″	39	*1.2*
Milk, condensed, sweetened, ½ cup	490	**12.3**

Food	Calories	Protein Grams
Milk, dry, nonfat instant, water added, 1 cup	82	**8.2**
Milk, evaporated, ½ cup	173	**8.8**
Milk, half-and-half, ½ cup	163	**3.9**
Milk, partly skimmed, 2%, 1 cup	145	**14.5**
Milk, powdered, whole, 1 tablespoon	40	**2.2**
Milk, skimmed, 1 cup	90	**9.3**
Milk, whole fresh, 3.5% fat, 1 cup	160	**8.0**
Mincemeat pie, 1/6 of 9″ pie	417	*3.8*
Minestrone, 1 cup	105	*5.0*
Mints, chocolate cream, 3 small	100	.9
Molasses, 1 tablespoon	55	—
Muffin, 2″ diam.	55	*1.6*
Muffin, corn, 2⅜″ diam.	125	*2.5*
Muffin, English, 1 large	140	*3.7*
Mushrooms, canned, ½ cup	20	**2.2**
Mushrooms, fresh, 10 small	16	**1.5**
Mushrooms, sautéed, 7 small	78	**1.7**
Mustard greens, cooked, 1 cup	35	3.3
Mutton—*see* Lamb		
Nectarine, 1	40	.4
Noodles, egg, cooked, ½ cup	100	3.3
Oatmeal, cooked, ½ cup	65	**3.4**
Okra, sliced, ½ cup	25	1.7
Old-fashioned cocktail, 1 glass	185	0
Olive oil, 1 tablespoon	124	0
Olives, green, 2 small or 1 large	8	.1
Olives, ripe, 2 small or 1 large	10	.1
Onion soup, 1 cup	100	*8.1*
Onions, 4 small	100	4.0
Onions, creamed, ⅓ cup	100	*12.0*
Onions, raw green, 5 medium	23	.6
Orange, 1 average-sized	65	1.1
Orange ice, ½ cup	110	*1.0*
Orange juice, 1 cup	110	1.4
Oxtail soup, 1 cup	100	—
Oyster stew, with milk, 1 cup	275	*15.8*
Oysters, raw, 1 cup	160	**21.2**
Pancake, 1, 4″ diam.	60	*1.8*
Papaya, ½ medium	72	1.1
Parsley, chopped, 2 tablespoons	2	.1
Parsnips, cooked, ½ cup	50	1.1
Peach, fresh, 1, 2″ diam.	35	.5
Peaches, canned, 2 halves with 2 tablespoons syrup	85	.4
Peanut butter, 2 tablespoons	190	8.5
Peanuts, 20 to 24 nuts	100	4.5
Pear, fresh, 1, 2½″ diam.	60	.8
Pears, canned, 2 halves with 2 tablespoons juice	85	.2
Pea soup, cream, 1 cup	270	*13.3*
Peas, canned, ½ cup	65	3.7
Peas, dried, cooked, ½ cup	103	7.2
Peas, fresh, cooked, ½ cup	56	3.8
Pecans, 6 halves	52	.7
Pepper, green, 1 medium-sized	15	.7
Perch, breaded and fried, 3 oz.	195	**22.5**
Persimmons, 1 medium-sized	78	.7
Pickles, cucumber, 1 large dill	15	.5
Pickles, cucumber, 1 sweet-sour	20	1.0
Pigs' feet, pickled, ½ foot	125	*10.5*
Pineapple, fresh, diced, ½ cup	40	.3
Pineapple, with syrup, canned, 1 slice	78	.3
Pineapple ice, ½ cup	120	*1.0*
Pineapple juice, 1 cup	135	1.0
Pizza (cheese), ⅛ of 14″ pie	185	*9.4*
Plums, canned, 3 or 4 with syrup	150	.7
Plums, fresh, Japanese, 2″ diam., 3 or 4	100	1.0
Pimiento, canned, 1 medium	10	.3
Popcorn, no butter, 1 cup	25	.8
Popover, 1	100	*3.9*
Pork chop, rib, broiled, 3½ oz.	260	**21.4**
Pork roast, 3 oz.	310	**18.9**
Pork tenderloin, 2 oz.	200	**12.2**
Potato, baked, 1 medium-sized	90	2.5
Potato, boiled, 1 medium-sized	90	2.5
Potato, sweet, baked, 1 medium-sized	155	1.5
Potato, sweet, candied, 1 potato, 3½″ x 2¼″	295	*2.3*
Potato chips, 8 to 10 large	100	.9
Potato salad, ½ cup	125–180	*4.9*
Potatoes, French-fried, 10 pieces	155	2.4
Potatoes, hash-browned, ½ cup	175	2.4
Potatoes, mashed, milk and butter added, 1 cup	185	*4.1*
Potatoes, pan-fried, ½ cup	230	3.4
Potatoes, scalloped, no cheese, ½ cup	125	*3.6*
Praline, 1	300	—
Preserves, 1 tablespoon	55–75	*.1*
Pretzels, 5 small sticks	5	*.1*
Prune juice, 1 cup	200	1.0
Prunes, dried, cooked, ½ cup	125	1.0
Prunes, dried, cooked, sweetened, ½ cup	205	1.0
Prunes, stewed, 4 medium with 2 tablespoons juice	120	.6
Pudding, chocolate, home recipe, 1 cup	385	*8.1*
Pudding, mix, 4-oz. package	410	*3.0*
Pumpkin, 1 cup	76	4.0
Pumpkin pie, 1/6 of 9″ pie	315	*6.0*
Rabbit, baked, 3½ oz.	177	**22.7**
Radishes, 5 medium	6	.4
Raisins, seedless, ¼ cup	107	.9
Raspberries, red, fresh, ½ cup	35	.7
Raspberries, red, frozen, sweetened, ½ cup	120	.9
Red snapper, baked, 3″ x ½″ x 4″	183	**39.0**
Rhubarb, fresh, diced, 1 cup	20	.7

Food	Calories	Protein Grams
Rhubarb, stewed, sweetened, ½ cup	192	.7
Rice, brown, cooked, ½ cup	100	**2.1**
Rice, white, cooked, ½ cup	100	1.8
Rice, wild, cooked, ⅔ cup	103	**2.2**
Roll, hard, white, 1 average-sized	155	*4.9*
Roll, Parker House, 1	81	*2.0*
Root beer, 12 oz.	105	0
Rum, 1½-oz. jigger	150	0
Rutabagas, cooked, ½ cup	25	.6
Salami, dry, 1 oz.	130	*6.9*
Salmon, fresh, poached, 3½ oz.	200	**29.7**
Sardines, canned, in oil, 3 oz.	175	**19.6**
Sauerkraut, ⅔ cup	27	1.5
Sauerkraut juice, ½ cup	4	.3
Sausage, pork link, 2 oz.	125	*2.3*
Scallops, fried, 5 to 6 medium-sized	427	**39.5**
Shad roe, sautéed, average serving	175	**32.6**
Sherbet, ½ cup	135	*1.0*
Sherry, dry, 3 oz.	110	.3
Sherry, sweet, 3 oz.	150	.3
Shortcake with ½ cup berries and cream, 1 medium-sized biscuit	350	*4.0*
Shredded wheat biscuit, 1 large	100	2.8
Shrimp, boiled, 5 large	70	**15.5**
Shrimp, canned, 3 oz.	100	**20.8**
Shrimp, fried, 4 large	259	**23.5**
Smelts, baked or broiled, 4 or 5 medium-sized	91	**17.3**
Smelts, fried, 4 to 5 medium-sized	448	**17.3**
Snow pudding, ⅔ cup	114	—
Soft drinks, fruity, 12 oz.	140–170	0
Sole, Dover, baked, 3½ oz.	202	**30.0**
Sole, fillet—*see* Flounder		
Soybeans, dried, cooked, ½ cup	120	**9.9**
Spaghetti, plain, cooked, 1 cup	155	5.2
Spareribs, meat from 6 average-sized ribs	246	**14.9**
Spinach, cooked and chopped, ½ cup	23	2.8
Spinach soup, cream, homemade, 1 cup	240	*7.0*
Split pea soup, 1 cup	145	*9.0*
Split peas, dried, cooked, 1 cup	290	19.0
Squab, 1 whole, unstuffed, 2½ oz. meat	149	**10.0**
Squash, Hubbard or winter, cooked, ½ cup	65	2.3
Squash, summer, cooked, ½ cup	15	1.0
Starch, cornstarch, etc., 1 tablespoon	29	T
Strawberries, fresh, ½ cup	30	.6
Strawberries, frozen, sweetened, ½ cup	120	.5
Strawberry shortcake with cream, average serving	350	*3.7*

Food	Calories	Protein Grams
Succotash, canned, ½ cup	85	*3.8*
Sugar, brown, 1 tablespoon	50	0
Sugar, confectioners', 1 tablespoon	30	0
Sugar, granulated, 1 tablespoon	48	0
Sweetbreads, broiled, ½ medium pair	185	**15.0**
Swordfish, broiled in butter, 3 oz.	150	**24.0**
Syrup, corn, 1 tablespoon	57	0
Syrup, sorghum, 1 tablespoon	55	0
Tangerine, 1	35	.6
Tangerine juice, ½ cup	55	.5
Tapioca pudding, ½ cup	133	*4.9*
Tartare sauce, 1 tablespoon	100	*.2*
Tea, clear, unsweetened, 1 cup	0	.1
Thousand Island dressing, 1 tablespoon	80	*.1*
Tomato, fresh, 1, 3″ diam.	40	2.0
Tomato catsup, 1 tablespoon	17	.3
Tomato juice, 1 cup	50	2.4
Tomato purée, 1 tablespoon	6	.3
Tomato soup, clear, 1 cup	90	*2.0*
Tomato soup, cream, homemade, 1 cup	175–250	*7.0*
Tomatoes, canned, 1 cup	60	.3
Tripe, cooked in milk, average serving	150	*28.6*
Trout, brook, broiled, 3 oz.	216	**19.2**
Trout, lake, broiled, 3 oz.	290	**21.5**
Tuna fish, canned, water-packed, ½ cup	165	**36.4**
Tuna fish, canned, in oil, 3 oz.	170	**25.8**
Turkey, roast, dark meat, 3½ oz.	203	**30.0**
Turkey, roast, light meat, 3½ oz.	176	**32.9**
Turnip greens, cooked, 1 cup	30	3.2
Turnips, cooked, 1 cup	40	1.4
Vanilla wafer, 1	20	*.2*
Veal chop, loin, fried, 1 medium-sized	186	**21.0**
Veal cutlet, 3 oz.	185	**23.0**
Veal roast, 3 oz.	230	**23.3**
Veal stew, 1 cup	242	*23.9*
Vegetable cooking fats, 1 tablespoon	110	0
Vegetable juice, 1 cup	48	*2.5*
Vegetable soup, 1 cup	80–100	*5.0*
Venison, baked, 3 slices, 3½″ x 2½″ x ¼″	200	**34.5**
Vienna sausage, canned (7 per 5-oz. can), 1 sausage	40	*2.3*
Vodka, 1½-oz. jigger	105	0
Waffles, 1, 7″ diam.	210	*5.0*
Waldorf salad, average serving	137	*1.3*
Walnuts, English, 4 to 8 halves	50	1.1

Food	Calories	Protein Grams
Watercress, 10 sprigs	5	.6
Watermelon, 1 slice, ¾″ thick, 6″ diam.	90	1.7
Welsh rarebit, 4 tablespoons on 1 slice toast	200	*9.1*
Wheat germ, 1 tablespoon	25	**1.8**
Whisky, bourbon, 1½ oz.	120	0
Whisky, Scotch, 1½ oz.	105	0
White sauce, ¼ cup	106	*2.6*
Whitefish, average serving	100	**13.4**
Wines, dry, 3 oz.	65–95	T
Wines, sweet or fortified, 3 oz.	120–160	.2
Yams—*see* Potatoes, sweet		
Yeast, brewer's, 2 teaspoons	18	2 5
Yeast, compressed, 1 cake	10	1.4
Yogurt, fruit-flavored, ½ cup	130	*4.4*
Yogurt, plain, ½ cup	65	**4.4**
Yogurt, whole milk, ½ cup	75	**3.6**
Zucchini, cooked, 1 cup	40	2.8
Zwieback, 1 slice	35	*.9*

ENTERTAINING

When you are entertaining, try not to feel that something unusual is expected of you as a hostess. It isn't. Just be yourself. Even eminent and distinguished persons are only human. Like the rest of us, they shrink from ostentation; and nothing is more disconcerting to a guest than the impression that his coming is causing a household commotion. Confine all noticeable efforts for his comfort and refreshment to the period that precedes his arrival. Satisfy yourself that you have anticipated every possible emergency—the howling child, the last-minute search for cuff links, your husband's exuberance, your helper's ineptness, your own qualms. Then relax and enjoy your guests.

If, at the last minute, something does happen to upset your well-laid plans, rise to the occasion. The mishap may be the making of your party. Capitalize on it, but not too heavily. Remember that 'way back in Roman times the poet Horace observed, "A host is like a general: it takes a mishap to reveal his genius."

We are frequently asked what is the ideal number for a dinner party. Estimates vary. On the absurd side, we are reminded of the response made to this question by a less-than-gregarious nineteenth-century gourmet: "Myself and the headwaiter"; and of Aubrey Menen's Ceylonese grandmother, who regarded the act of eating as so vulgar that she practiced it only when alone, in complete seclusion. Seriously speaking, there is no ideal answer to the question. Some of the reasons will become apparent in the discussion that follows. Yet there is probably a workable minimum; and unless the guests are very close friends, that minimum much exceeds two. Back in the living room afterward, first-time acquaintances must be able to exercise options and establish small centers of mutual interest; and we suggest that this can only be engineered with any degree of success among groups of at least eight. Twelve is an even happier number.

The procedures below represent simple, dignified current practice in table service. If you plan to serve cocktails or nonalcoholic beverages before a meal, have glasses ready on a tray. With the apéritif, you may pass some form of cracker, canapé or hors d'oeuvre. If you and your guests are discriminating diners, you will keep this pickup light. Too generous quantities of food and drink beforehand will bring jaded palates to the dinner on which you have expended such effort. Should you have the kind of guests who enjoy a long cocktail period and varied hors d'oeuvre, be sure to season your dinner food more highly than usual. You may politely shorten the cocktail preliminaries, which have a bad habit these days of going on indefinitely, by serving a delicious hot or cold consommé or soup, either near the bar area or from a tureen on a cart.

Never forget that your family is really the most important assembly you ever entertain. Whether for them or for friends ➤ always check the freshness of the air, the temperature of the dining area, and the proper heat or chill for plates, food and drinks—especially hot ones. If warming oven space is limited, use the heat cycle of your dishwasher; or, if you entertain often, you may wish to install an infrared heating unit which can be raised or lowered above a heatproof counter. Be sure that each diner has plenty of elbow room, about 30 inches from the center of one plate service to the center of the next.

Formal meals, given in beautifully appointed homes, served by competent, well-trained servants—who can be artists in their own right—are a great treat. We cannot expect to have ideal conditions at all times in the average home. However, no matter what the degree of informality, always be sure that the table is attractive and immaculately clean—and always maintain, as nearly as possible, an even rhythm of service.

TABLE DÉCOR

As to the table itself, a top that is heat- and stain-resistant lends itself to the greatest ease of service and upkeep. You can expose as much or as little of its surface as you like. If you have a tabletop of natural hardwood, you must protect it against heat at all times with pads or trivets.

For versatility and effective contrast, keep your basic flatware and dishes simple in form and not too pronounced in pattern or color. Then you can combine them, without fear of clashing, with varied linens, fruits and flowers and—most importantly—varied foods. You will find that changes in décor and accessories stimulate the appetite as much as changes in seasoning.

It is pleasant to vary table presentations by serving soup not only in cups and bowls, but from a tureen; or by making use of a crescent-shaped salad plate designed to fit at the side of a round dinner plate and so give the table a less crowded feeling. Individual serving dishes for vegetables may be replaced by an outsized platter holding several kinds of vegetables attractively garnished.

Also, small raw vegetables and fruits may be substituted for garnishes of parsley and cress to give a meat platter a festive air. Instead of using pairs of matching dessert dishes, try contrasting bowls of glass or bright pottery. For a rustic effect, serve a hearty menu on your everyday dishes and use bright linens and wooden salad bowls with a centerpiece of wooden scoops filled with pears and hazelnuts in the husk.

For a more elegant effect, serve a dainty meal on porcelain and crystal dishes, against a polished board decorated with fragile glasses and flowers. See sketch below.

Whatever your decorative scheme, flower arrangements should be low or lacy. Tall arrangements that obstruct the view discourage across-the-table conversation. There is nothing more distracting than dodging a floral centerpiece while trying to establish an intimate relationship among your guests. For the same reason, candles should be placed strategically. On a formal buffet or tea table, which is viewed from above, the decorations may be as tall as you wish. In fact, food or flower accents that are elevated on epergnes or stemmed dishes add a note of drama.

Lacking an antique epergne, you can still expand the impact of flowers and fruit on a framework structured from tumblers, tinware or silverware, as shown in the chapter heading. Leaves and bloom clusters, vines and fruits bind these disparate elements and disguise or expose their origins. There, as suggested by my friend and one of my coauthors of *Wild Wealth,* Frances Jones Poetker, is an opulent arrangement made on a bare structure she suggested of a reversed wide bowl surmounted by a flat plate on which a stemmed compote is centered—and centered on that, in turn, a stemmed glass.

Several harmonious small containers of flowers or fruit—similar or varied—can be effectively grouped around a central element or scattered along the length of a table to replace a single focal point such as the one described above. One of these small units could be long-needled pine tufts bracing snowdrops; or clematis, as illustrated in the semiformal luncheon service, below.

A piece of sculpture scaled to your table makes a charming base for a centerpiece. Surround it with an ivy ring and vary the décor from time to time with other greenery or any elements that suggest borders or garlands. If the sculpture is slightly raised on a base, it can be enjoyed to great advantage. Whatever you use, don't overcrowd the table. One of the most important things to remember is that ➤ no matter what the decoration, it should be suited in color and scale to the foods served to enhance it. Don't make your effects so stagey that your guests' reactions will be, "She went to a lot of trouble." Make them say, rather, "She had a lot of fun doing it!"

Consider, too, the colors of the flowers, food and linens available to you, and plan your menu accordingly. Beets or beet soup may be just the strengthening note you want on a cold day; grapefruit and avocado may bring that chill delicacy of palette you need for a torrid summer lunch. The sources at your command are really legion.

Cramped dining quarters can be eased by unconventional service distribution—a bar in the study, soup on the patio or on a traveling tea cart, a long, narrow buffet to facilitate traffic flow. But whether the party is large or intimate, you can stretch your normal equipment with unconventional use of trays, baskets, pumpkin soup tureens, watermelon fruit bowls, or ice punch bowls, 62.

TABLE SETTING

There are certain time-honored positions for tableware and equipment that result from the way food is eaten and served. So keep in mind these basic placements. ➤ Forks to the left except the very small fish fork, which goes to the right. ➤ Spoons, including iced-tea spoons, and knives to the right, with the sharp edge of the knife toward the plate. There is, of course, a practical reason for placing the knife at the diner's right, since right-handed persons, who predominate, commonly wield the knife with their favored hand, and do so early in the meal. Generally, having cut his food, the diner lays down his knife and transfers his fork to the right hand. Formal dining makes an exception to this rule; and with left-handed or ambidextrous persons the transfer seems superfluous to us, on any occasion. ➤ Place flatware that is to be used first farthest from the plate. It is also better form never to have more than three pieces of flatware at either side. Bring in any other needed table utensils on a small tray as the course is served. The server is always careful to handle tableware by the handles only, including carving and serving spoons and forks, which are placed to the right of the serving dish.

If you look at some of the place settings illustrated, you can, with a few exceptions, practically predict the menu. Let's consider the semiformal luncheon setting, 16. Line up the bases of the handles about one inch from the edge of the table. Some people still consider it important to supply a knife at luncheon, even if that knife is not needed for the actual cutting of meat. Others omit the knife if a typical luncheon casserole is passed or is served in individual containers. For a formal luncheon, a butter plate is placed to the left on a level with the waterglass. The butter knife is usually located as shown, and a butter ball or curl, 541, is already in place before the guests are seated. Later, the butter plate is removed simultaneously with the salad plate. Both are taken from the left side. The butter plate is picked up with the left hand, the salad plate with the right.

At semiformal luncheons, you may have the dessert spoon and fork in place above the plate, as sketched opposite. This indicates that no finger bowl will be supplied. Or you may, as in the dinner service, bring the dessert silver to the table with the finger bowl, as sketched on 20.

Water and wine glasses are already in place as sketched left. The water is poured in the former to about two-thirds capacity; the wineglasses are left empty. ➤ Glasses are filled from the right and are never lifted by the server when pouring. Goblet types are always handled by the stem in presentation, replacement or removal, by the diner or server; tumbler types are always held well below the rim.

When it is time to serve coffee, empty cups and saucers are placed to the right. There is a spoon on the saucer, behind the cup and parallel to the cup handle, which is turned to the diner's right. After all the cups are placed, they are filled by the server, and afterward sugar and cream are offered from a small tray from the left. But the entire coffee service may be offered, even for luncheon, in the living room, after the dessert.

Individual ashtrays and cigarettes may be placed on the table. Fortunately, a host or hostess is not required to press his conviction that smoking is injurious to either health or gastronomy. But if you are a strong-willed hostess, you may prefer to have the ashtrays and cigarettes placed on the table just after the dessert is served.

At informal dinner parties, place cards may be omitted and the hostess may indicate where guests are to sit. When the diners number six, ten or fourteen, the host is at one end of the table, the hostess at the other. If the guests number eight or twelve and you want to alternate men and women guests, place the host at one end and the hostess to the left of the other end.

The honor guest, if a woman, is seated to the right of the host; if a man, to the left of the hostess. At a formal meal, a dish is presented, but ➤ not served, to the hostess first. Food is actually offered first to the woman guest of honor. The other women are then all served. Finally, the men are served, beginning with the guest of honor. If there is no special guest of honor, you may want to reverse the direction of service every other course, so that the same people are not always served last.

While it is not the best form, some people prefer to have the hostess served first. She knows the menu, and by the way she serves herself she sets the pattern for the other guests. This is a special help if the guest of honor is from another country. In America it is customary for guests to wait until everyone is served and the hostess begins to eat. In Europe, however, where each course is usually served complete on one plate, it is permissible to start eating as soon as one is served.

➤ Plates are usually removed from the right and placed or passed from the left. Service and dinner plates are frequently of different patterns. For the purpose of clarity in the illustrations following, service plates are sketched with a solid banding, plates on which cold food is being served are shown with a thin double-banded edge, and plates for hot food are unadorned.

FORMAL ENTERTAINMENT

Most of us moderns look with amazement, not to say dismay, at the menus of traditionally formal dinners. Such meals are a vanishing breed, like the whale—but, like the whale, some manage to survive. They begin with both clear and thick soups. Then comes an alternation of **entrées** and **relevés,** each with its accompanying vegetables. The relevés are lighter in quality and fewer in number than the hefty joints and whole fish which make up the entrées; but by current standards many of them amply qualify as main dishes in their own right.

However, in the parlance of the haute cuisine, the term "entrée" had a quite different significance. Classic entrées commonly occurred immediately after the main entrée as we now define it, and consisted of timbales, seafoods and variety meats, served in rich pastes and with delicate sauces—tidbits distinguished for their elegance.

A salad takes next place in this stately procession and is usually made of a seasoned cooked vegetable such as asparagus, with greens doing garnish duty only. After this, the diner may choose from a variety of cheeses.

Entremets—hot or cold sweets—succeed the cheese course; and these are topped off, in turn, by both hot and cold fruits. Thus, in outline—if "outline" can be regarded as *le mot juste*—a dinner in the grand manner; except, of course, to add that each course is accompanied by a choice and sympathetic wine.

We marvel at the degree of sophistication required to appreciate so studied and complex a service—to say nothing of the culinary skills needed to present the menu in proper style. But, more critically, we ask, "Where do the guests stow away all that food?" Granted that a truly formal dinner lasts for hours and that each portion may be a dainty one, the total intake is still bound to be formidable. Such an array is seldom encountered in this casual and girth-conscious era. But a semiformal dinner with traces of classic service still graces the privileged household.

When the guests come into the dining room, the table is all in readiness. Again the setting forecasts the menu through the first three courses. If more silver is required, it is always brought in separately later. The water glasses are about two-thirds full; the wineglasses, though empty, stand in place, see illustrations at right.

At formal and semiformal dinners, butter plates are seldom used. Melba toast or crackers are served with the appetizer or soup, and hard rolls without butter later, with the roast. The setting indicates a seafood cocktail, a soup, a meat course, 19, a salad course, water and two wines. Water and wine are poured from the right. The glasses may stay in place throughout the meal, but it is preferable to remove each wineglass after use. A third wineglass may be strung out on a line with the others or placed to form a triangle slightly forward toward the guest and just above the soup spoon. However, if more than three wines are to be served, fresh glasses replace the used glasses as the latter are removed.

Once the guests are seated, the server's steady but unobtrusive labor begins. There is a plate, filled or unfilled, before each guest throughout the meal. The server usually removes a plate from the right and replaces it immediately with another from the left, so that the courses follow one another in unbroken succession. At such a dinner, second helpings are seldom offered.

When a platter is presented, it is offered from the left to the guest by the server, who holds it on a folded napkin on the palm of his left hand, and may steady it with the right. The server should always make sure that the handles of the serving tools are directed toward the diner.

The passing of crackers, breads and relishes, the refilling of water glasses, and the pouring of wines take place during, not between, the appropriate courses. When the party is less formal, the host may prefer to pour the wines himself from a decanter or from a bottle. If the wine is chilled, he will wrap it in a napkin, and hold a napkin in the left hand to catch any drip from the bottle. The hostess on such occasions may pass relishes to the guest at her right, and the guests may continue to pass them on to one another. Also, relishes may be arranged at strategic places on the table, but must be removed with the soup. However, even with these slight assists, the work of the server is one that calls for nicely calculated timing. It is easy to see why one server should not be called on to take care of more than six or eight guests—at the most—if smooth going is expected.

Let us go back to our dinner, which begins—as forecast by the setting sketched below—with a seafood cocktail, and goes on to the soup. The seafood, served in a specially iced glass, is in place when the guests enter the dining room.

After the seafood has been eaten, the empty seafood cocktail glasses are removed—leaving the service plate intact. The soup plate is placed on it —served from the left. Crackers and relishes are presented.

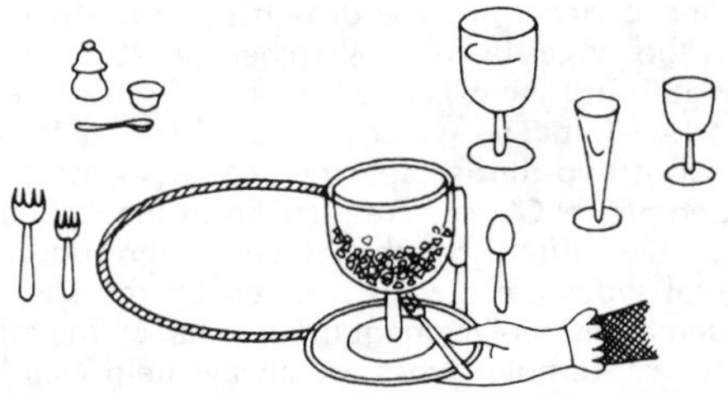

The service plate is now removed, along with the empty soup plate, from the right. If a platter of hot food is to be passed, an empty hot plate is placed before the guest—from the left.

However, if the meat course is to be carved and served in the dining room, the soup plate only is removed, leaving the service plate before the guest. The meat platter is put before the host, who carves enough meat for all the guests before any further serving takes place. The server, who has replaced the host's service plate with a hot one, stands to the left of the host, holding an extra hot plate on a napkin. When the host has filled the individual plate before him, the server removes it and replaces it with the empty hot plate he has been holding. Then, after taking the service place in front of the guest of honor from the right, the server gives him the filled hot plate from the left, returns to the host via the buffet for the next hot plate, and waits to replace the plate being filled by the host for another guest.

When all guests have been attended to, the server passes the gravy and then the vegetables—with a serving spoon and fork face down on the platter and the handles directed toward the guest. The hot breads come next. During this course, the server replenishes water and wine.

The menu we have been serving has consisted of three courses: seafood cocktail, soup, meat-and-vegetable. A salad and dessert course will follow; but first let us consider a different menu—one that omits the cocktail and introduces a fish course.

Obviously, a different setting of flatware is in order for this alternate menu. The illustration will show you that it consists of soup, first. After that, there is a fish course, followed by meat, salad and so on. You will notice that there are one water

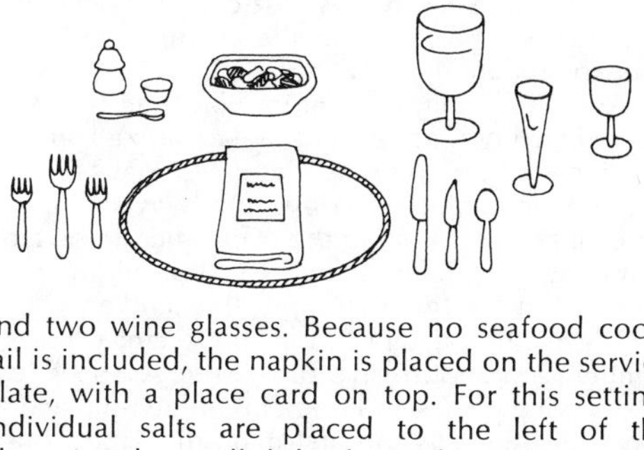

and two wine glasses. Because no seafood cocktail is included, the napkin is placed on the service plate, with a place card on top. For this setting, individual salts are placed to the left of the glasses, and a small dish of mixed nuts is centered above the service plate. No other food is on the table when the guests are seated.

For this second menu, plates of soup are passed from the left and placed directly on the service plates—after guests have removed napkins and place cards.

After the soup has been relished, the soup plate and service plate are removed together from the right and the fish course, arranged in the pantry

on individual plates, is presented next from the left. If sherry accompanied the soup, the sherry glass is removed at this time.

After the server has removed the empty fish plate from the right, a hot plate is put before the guest from the left, as shown next.

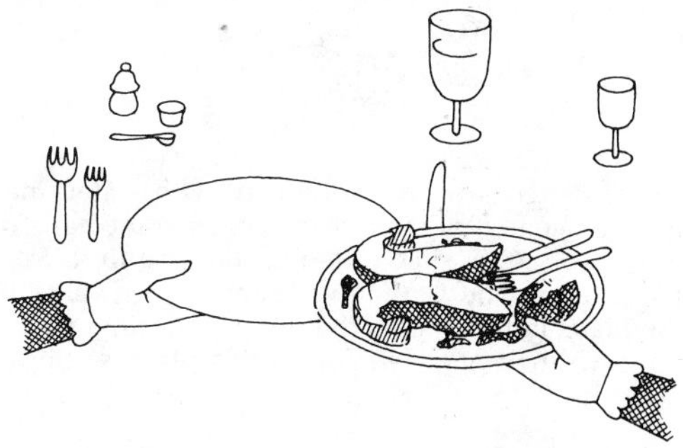

The meat course follows—either carved by the host, or previously arranged in the pantry. A vegetable placed on a narrow so-called bone plate shown to the left of the meat plate may follow. With such vegetables as asparagus and artichokes, or salads with vinegar dressings, no wines are served.

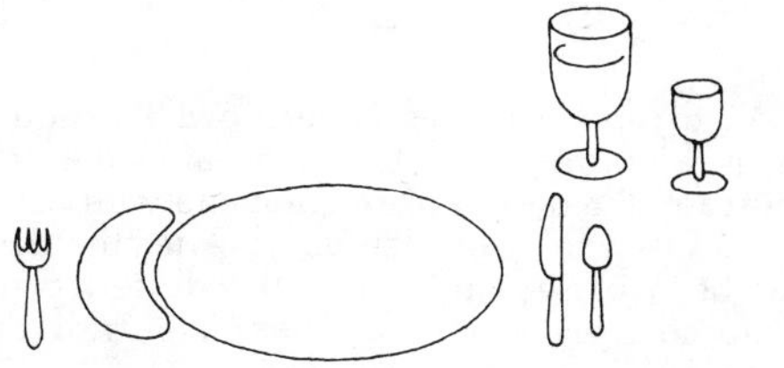

A handsomely arranged fruit compote, passed during the meat course, can be used as an alternate to a salad. If a compote is substituted for a salad, a spoon is put on the right of the setting, instead of a salad fork on the left, as illustrated.

The next illustration shows a separate salad set-up after the meat course is removed. After

the salad course is removed, the table is denuded for a short time. Any unused flatware, salts and peppers and relishes are taken away. The table is crumbed. The server uses a folded napkin and brushes the crumbs lightly onto a plate or a crumb tray.

Now, the dessert setting with the finger bowl and doily is placed in front of each guest.

The finger bowl, partially filled with water, may have a scented geranium leaf, a fragrant herb or flower, or a thin slice of lemon floating in it. Each guest places the fork and spoon to either side of the plate and then puts the doily, with finger bowl on it, to the upper left side of his place setting—opposite the water glass.

An exception to this finger bowl procedure is made when fruit is to be served after dessert. In this case, the dessert plate complete with flatware is placed in front of each guest. After the dessert has been passed and eaten, the dessert plate is removed. Next comes a fruit plate with doily, finger bowl, fruit knife and fork.

Should coffee be served at the table, empty demitasse cups and saucers are, at this time, placed to the right of the diners. Demitasse spoons are on the saucers, behind the cup and parallel to the handle. Coffee is poured from the right and cream and sugar passed on a small tray from the left. Liqueur may be served with the coffee or passed on a tray later, in the living room.

Women's liberation works both ways. A host or hostess may still welcome a lull of 15 minutes or more after dinner, during which the sexes are segregated and free to develop conversational topics of special and specific interest. The traditional—and entirely suitable—time for such a break is between dessert and coffee. The men may remain in the dining room to converse over glasses of port or brandy; or the entire company, after the English custom, may first share a savory, 755. The hostess may then retire to the drawing room with the ladies and later pour coffee for her reassembled guests there. By this time, good food, wine and conviviality have usually broken down the minor social inhibitions, and the coffee service may be completely informal.

INFORMAL ENTERTAINMENT

Your chances for a successful informal dinner party are much greater if you key your efforts to your own belongings and service rather than struggling to meet the exacting demands of the kind of dinner just described. ➤ Plan a menu that will make advance preparation and last-minute serving feasible. Offer fewer courses and put several kinds of food on one platter. But please do not let your guests sit, trying to make conversation, with a rapidly congealing slice of meat before them, waiting with embarrassment for a seemingly shipwrecked gravy boat to follow.

There are actually two kinds of informal company meals—and by informal we mean those which can be successfully carried off by a hostess acting more or less alone. The first is a small sit-down affair; and when we say small we mean one limited to eight guests—six is a more confidence-inspiring number. Such a dinner flourishes not on spur-of-the-moment activity but on careful forethought and now and then some nimble footwork. Main dishes should be limited to two or three: a casserole, for instance, an aspic and a pôt-de-crème. Many such dishes that can be prepared in advance will be found in the chapters on Lunch, Brunch and Supper Dishes; Salads; and Frozen Desserts. Five minutes before your guests are expected, everything should be organized and in readiness: hors d'oeuvre and cocktails—which may be simple—on a conveniently available side table, plates warming in the oven, and dining table completely set, needing only that last-minute ceremonial touch—the lighting of the candles.

One of the hostess's more important roles is a deliberately unobtrusive one. After she sees to it that serving dishes and implements are in place on the table, she sets the first main dish and a stack of heated plates in front of the host, whose responsibility it becomes to fill them and pass them along to the guests. She then promptly takes her own seat at table, determined not only to remain graciously installed there until the time comes for main-dish replenishment or for bringing on another course, but to be generally at ease throughout the rest of the meal.

When the guests have finished the first course, serving initiatives are largely hers. She gathers the plates left over from the first course, removes them from the dining area, and reappears with whatever serving dishes and implements are needed for the next course. These she sets at her own place at table; she seats herself again and serves each guest in turn, repeating the host's previous procedure. The main objective here is to ensure that guests and hosts remain at table: nothing disrupts a little sit-down dinner so much as the inclination of anyone present to execute a series of disappearing acts and U-turns.

The hostess's continuing presence may be further assured by arranging to serve the wine in a decanter, which can be passed from hand to hand during the meal, like the relishes and the bread. The bread, incidentally, may be of the crusty-loaf variety cut into thick slices and buttered, then warmed in the same oven used to heat the dinner plates.

For removing relishes and odd items, a small tray is handy. "Crumbing" may be dispensed with. But do resist the messy and quite intolerable practice of stacking plates as you remove them from the table.

While we deplore the kind of pinch-hitting that often turns the maidless dinner into a volunteer free-for-all, we do not in the least reject an unobtrusive dependable assist from the host, or from a close friend of the hostess who knows her way around the house and is cooperatively disposed. The host may help by carrying out such far-flung responsibilities as mixing salads and drinks, greeting the guests and taking care of their wraps, inquiring about and distributing "seconds," and in general seeing to it that the company is kept promptly and well supplied. The help that a close friend can proffer is less thoroughgoing and less well defined: it may vary from filling water glasses to clearing the table. Whatever its extent, it should stop short of officiousness. A hostess who wants to keep her sanity should resolutely resist the invasion of her kitchen by a guest who is inspired to "keep her company" while she makes her final preparations for the meal.

In order for food to reach the table at the right temperature, it is wise to use such aids as covered dishes—in which case, remember to allow a place to put hot lids; double dishes with provision underneath for ice or hot water; and a samovar arrangement for hot drinks.

For both service and removal, a cart may facilitate matters, unless there are children trained to lend unobtrusive help. Impromptu deputization of your guests may invite chaos and should be avoided except in extreme emergencies or in deliberate plans such as those described in participatory menus, 34.

BUFFET SERVICE

Obviously, from the hostess's standpoint, buffet service is the most satisfactory way to take care of large groups informally. However, under no circumstances should you expect your guests to eat without enough chairs or table space for all.

Plan a menu from foods that hold well, keeping hot foods above 140° and cold foods below 40°. The best way to keep an attractive buffet looking that way is to concentrate on individual portions. These can be replenished easily, thus preserving the looks of the table. For instance, rather than a large aspic, use individual fancy molds—even if released from paper cups. Use sea shells or vegetable cups, 98, as individual containers for seafood or other mixtures. You may cut turkey, ham and salmon into individual portions. Also see About Stuffed Vegetables, 280, and Cases for Food, 250. For garnishes see 98 and 99.

Types of food especially suitable for buffet service are a risotto or jambalaya, a goulash, a seafood Newburg, moussaka, empanadas, a cheese tray. Meats served **en croûte,** 448, and as **chaud-froid,** 369, make dramatic features of buffet service. Both types of preparation keep buffet food from drying out. Avoid soups and other sloshy food that may prove hazardous for diners in motion.

If the servings are not individual, cater generously, as guests are apt to take larger portions at buffets. Layouts below and on 22 show typical buffet settings. The first one represents a dinner at which the host or hostess serves the guests, who then proceed to tables which are already set. The menu includes duck with orange cups, wild rice, podded peas and a green salad. The serving platters are later removed and replaced by the dessert; or individual desserts may be served at table.

Note again that height in candles or flowers is often a distinct asset in buffet service, as is the use of tiered dishes.

The drawing on 22 shows a buffet at which the guests serve themselves and proceed to sit at small

tables. If there are no tables, individual trays may be used. For tray service, plan food that does not call for the use of a knife.

Shown are a meat or fish casserole dish; artichokes vinaigrette filled with masked hard-cooked eggs with herbs; relishes and rolls. A dessert may be on the table at the beginning of the service. If the serving table seems too crowded, place the water and hot drinks on another serving surface.

TEA SERVICE

The institution of afternoon tea is going out of fashion—menaced on the one hand by the cocktail party and on the other by the "coffee break," which in America is beginning to assume the proportions of a compound fracture. We still find tea or coffee in the afternoon—whether of the formal or the informal type—a revivifying event, even if an occasional one. When it is informal, the hostess does the honors alone. However, when the tea is formal, friends of the hostess sit at each end of the table and consider it a privilege to pour.

The drawing opposite shows a handsome, formal tea set-up with a coffee service at one end. Tea may be served at the other. It is wise to instruct a supplier to keep in frequent touch with the pourers to anticipate their need for additional hot water, coffee or cups. It is also canny to have additional platters ready to replace those at the table that have become rather ragged-looking. Medium-sized rather than large platters are easier to keep in trim.

CASUAL ENTERTAINING FOR ONE OR FOR MANY

Tray meals can be a delightful stimulant if they include a surprise element in the form of a lovely pitcher, a small flower arrangement or some seasonal delicacy. Make sure, especially if the recipient is an invalid, that all needed utensils are present, that the food is hot or cold as required, sufficient in amount and fresh and dainty looking.

A cookout, whether a mere wienie roast or a luau, can be—although it seldom is anymore—one of the least complicated ways to entertain. Unless your equipment is equal to that of a well-appointed kitchen and you can assure your guests of comparably controlled cooking, we suggest that you choose menus that are really enhanced by outdoor cooking procedures, 155.

Have enough covered dishes on hand to protect food from flies. Give your guests a tray or a tray-like plate if there are no regular places set or normal seating arrangements. And prepare an alternate plan of accommodation in case of bad weather.

We recall an informal party that was really too big for our quarters and whose pattern might provide a substitute for a weather-beleaguered barbecue. The guests arrived to find no evidence of entertaining, only a most gorgeous arrangement of colchicum, those vibrant fall blooms, 25, that resemble vast, reticulated crocuses. After drinks were served and hors d'oeuvre passed, the host circulated a cart with soup tureen and cups. In its wake followed tray baskets containing white paper bags, each fitted out with individual chicken salad, olives, endive filled with avocado, cocktail tomatoes, cress and cheese sandwiches, bunches of luscious grapes and foil-wrapped brownies. Coffee was served, again from the circulating cart.

In order to get an informal after-supper party rolling, young hostesses are often so eager to present the fruits of their labors that refreshments are served too early for the comfort of the guests, most of whom have rather recently dined. Instead of hustling in solid food and alcoholic or carbonated drinks, it might be pleasant to open the proceedings with a tisane, 40.

Here are a few parting reminders as we wind up this chapter on entertaining. In cooking for more people than you are normally accustomed to, allow yourself enough extra time both for preparing the food and for heating or cooling it. Please read the comments on the enlarging of recipes, 590. Be sure that your mixing and cooking equipment is scaled to take care of your group, and ➤ most important of all, that you have the refrigerator space to protect chilled dishes and the heated surfaces to maintain the temperature of the hot ones. Don't hesitate to improvise steam tables or iced trays. Utilize insulated picnic boxes or buckets either way, and wheelbarrows or tubs for the cracked ice on which to keep platters chilled.

If you often entertain casually, it may be worthwhile to make—as one of our friends did—a large rectangular galvanized deep tray on which the dishes of a whole cold buffet can be kept chilled. Or try confecting an epergne-like form such as that shown on 60 for chilling seafoods, hors d'oeuvre or fruit.

For camping trips or boating parties, consider the safety factor when choosing the menu. No matter what the outing ➤ don't transport perishable foods in hot weather in the even hotter trunk of a car.

Not all types of entertaining—formal or casual or in-between—can be detailed here. But, whatever the occasion, assemble your tried skills in menu planning so as to reflect the distinctive character of your home. Flavor the occasion with your own personality. And keep handy somewhere, for emergency use, that cool dictum attributed to Colonel Chiswell Langhorne of Virginia: "Etiquette is for people who have no breeding; fashion for those who have no taste."

COOKING FOR LARGE PARTIES

Most of the recipes in this book make 4 to 6 servings and will double satisfactorily for 8 to 12. But at times all of us are called on to produce meals for larger groups, and it is then that we must be on our guard. For unexpected surprises are apt to pop up just when we want everything to go particularly well. No matter how rich or how simple the menu, remember, first, that for special occasions it is preferable to cook from recipes with which you are familiar. Secondly, cook in several moderate-sized batches, rather than in one big chunk, because, mysterious as it sounds—but true, even for the experts—quantity cooking is not just a matter of indefinite multiplication, 590. If you overexpand, too, you may run into a number of other problems.

Take into account the longer time needed in preparation—not only for paring and washing of vegetables or drying salad greens, but for heating up large quantities. Even more important, you may be confronted with a sudden pinch of refrigerator space—discovering that the shelves are needed for properly chilling large aspics or puddings just when they should be doubling to keep other sizable quantities of food at safe temperatures. ➤ This warning is of great importance if you are serving stuffed fowl, creamed foods, ground meat, mayonnaise, cream puffs, custards or custard pies: these foods spoil readily without showing any evidence of hazard. Before completing the menu for larger groups, assess equipment for mixing, cooking, refrigerating and serving.

If the meal is a hot one, plan to use recipes involving both the oven and top burners. Increase your limited heating surfaces by supplementing them with electric skillets, steam tables or hot trays to hold food in good serving condition above 140°. But do check the electric capacity of your system.

If serving individual casseroles, see that you have enough oven space; or, if the casseroles are large, that they will fit. In fact, stage a dress rehearsal—from the cooking equipment requirements right through to the way the service dishes

and table gear will be placed. Then, satisfied that the mechanical requirements are met, schedule the actual work on the menu so that enough can be done in advance to relieve the sink and the work surfaces of last-minute crowding and mess.

Stick not only to those dishes you are confident you can handle without worry, but to those that make sense for the time you can spare for them. If one dish is going to require much last-minute hand work and fiddling, balance it against others that can be preassembled or are easy to serve: casseroles, baked or scalloped dishes, gelatins or frozen foods. See Menus for further suggestions, 32.

One of the hardest things in mass cooking is to give the food that personalized and cherished look that is achieved in intimate dinners. Do not hesitate to serve simple foods for company. Choose seasonal ingredients and cook them skillfully. Then wind up with a home-baked cake or pastry—nothing is more delicious or more appreciated. Guests are really captives, so build a menu, in any case, that is not too restrictive. If you decide on octopus pasta, be sure you know the guests are adventurous enough or have sophisticated enough palates to enjoy it—or that they know you well enough to be able to ask for an egg instead.

MENUS

When to eat what is a matter of ever-changing habit and custom. Think of an epicure's diet in pre-Communist China: the constant nibbling of small rich confections, interspersed with light, irregularly spaced meals. Think of the enormous breakfast, late dinner and bedtime repasts of early nineteenth-century England, with a little sherry and biscuit served at lunchtime to guarantee survival. And, if you imagine for a moment that we have triumphantly freed ourselves from the excesses of the Groaning Board, think of the multitude of strange hors d'oeuvre that are downed during a typical big cocktail party in the Age of Anxiety.

Present-day nutritionists are divided, the majority sticking to three square meals a day, while others advocate scrapping this custom in favor of a sort of Chinese dietary of intermittent snacks. ➤ For the sheer amounts of food that, according to statistics, hold the average American body and soul together, see 799. More importantly, check The Foods We Eat, 1. Whichever menu practice we decide to follow, there is in the combining of foods a perennial fascination; and we can still on all occasions respond sympathetically to Brillat-Savarin's aphorism: *"Menu malfait, diner perdu."*

Below are some suggestions for assembling meals. They are suggestions only. Your tastes, girth, circumstances, market, mood—and, we hope, imagination—will modify them considerably. ➤ For further service suggestions, please read the previous chapter on Entertaining. Note also that individual recipes frequently carry recommendations for congenial or time-honored accompaniments. ➤ If the party is to include more people than you usually cook for, see 23 for important suggestions both for the safe handling of food and ease of preparation, and do check the availability of cooking and serving equipment and sufficiency of heating power.

BREAKFAST AND BRUNCH SUGGESTIONS

Breakfast can be the most exciting meal of the day, whether it is shared with those you love, or served in seclusion with time to contemplate ways to make the day meaningful. Or it can be delayed into that charming social hour called brunch. Whatever the setting, proteins are better utilized if they are eaten at breakfast time than at any other time of day, and nutritionists advise that one-third of our daily protein intake be allotted to this meal. If tea, coffee, hot chocolate or milk, all favorite breakfast beverages, fail to appeal to you with the menus below, try a tisane, 40. Remember that hot chocolate and milk will add both calories and protein.

Banana slices and orange sections, 135
Scrambled Eggs, 222, and Bacon, 486
Hot Whole Wheat Biscuits, 633, and honey

Papaya, 139, garnished with lime
French Omelet, 226
Bacon in Muffins, 630

Sliced fresh peaches, 139, on hot cereal, 199,
with milk and brown sugar

Chilled Tomato and Clam Juice, 43
Bagels, 617, and Cream Cheese, 71
Eggs with Smoked Salmon, 222

Orange and grapefruit sections, 135
Boiled Smoked Tongue, 507,
and Scrambled Eggs, 222
Brioches, 615

Prunes in Wine, 141
Broiled Stuffed Mushrooms Cockaigne, 308,
garnished with watercress, 93
Toasted Cheese Bread, 604

Orange and Lime Juice, 43
Pecan Waffles, 241,
with Brown-Sugar Butter Sauce, 773,
and Rich Cream Cheese, 537

Chilled fresh pears, 139
Eggs Poached in Wine, 221
Toasted Panettone, 619

Poached plums, 126
Buttered Hominy Grits, 200
Eggs Baked in Bacon Rings, 224

Broiled grapefruit, 136, with sherry
Grilled Kippers, 408, on toast
with Scrambled Eggs, 222

Pork Scrapple or Goetta, 499
Hot Applesauce, 131, or hot Poached Rhubarb, 142
Quick Drop Biscuits, 633

Eggs Poached in Tomato Soup, 221
Baked Winter Squash, 330
Melba Toast, 636, and Bel Paese Cheese, 756

Dry cereal: wheat or bran biscuit topped with
Baked Custard, 734, or Yogurt, 533,
and Sugared Strawberries, 133

Broiled Pineapple Rings, 127
Souffléed Omelet, 227, with cheese
Whole-Grain Muffins, 630

Chilled Concord grapes, 137
Sautéed Sausage Meat Patties, 498,
topped with Poached Eggs, 221
Croissants, 615, and Orange Marmalade, 839

Fresh black raspberries, 133
Creamed Chipped Beef, 260,
on Toasted Oat Bread Cockaigne, 608

Baked Fresh Fruit Compote, 126
French Toast Waffles, 242, with Maple Syrup, 558
Canadian Bacon, 486

Blueberries, 133, with sweet cream
Sautéed Ham and Eggs, 485
Quick Sour Cream Coffee Cake, 627
Paradise Jelly, 834

Fresh Pineapple Cup, 141
Broiled Fresh Scrod, 406, with lemon garnish
Fried Cornmeal Mush, 201

Macedoine of Pears and Melon Balls in Port, 124
Oyster and Chicken Croquettes, 248
Brioches, 615, and Five-Fruits Jam Cockaigne, 836

Pared rounds of honeydew melon filled with
red raspberries, 139
Ham and Potato Cakes, 258
Shirred Eggs, 223

Sliced mango, 138
Sautéed Chicken Livers on Toast, 500,
with Grilled Tomato Slices, 332

Cranberry Juice, 44
Corned Beef Hash and Potatoes, 261
with Poached Eggs, 221

Canteloupe Melon Baskets, 138
Broiled Veal Kidneys, 506
Whole-Grain Toast, 607
Lime Marmalade, 839

Ripe or Poached Cherries, 135
Baked Brains and Eggs, 504
No-Knead Yeast Coffee Cake, 619

LUNCHEON SUGGESTIONS

Although various luncheon menus are listed below, you may turn to Brunch, Lunch and Supper Dishes, 250; Pastas, 198; and Eggs, 220, where you will also find many combination dishes that need only a simple salad or bread to form a complete meal. If speed is your object, remember, too, that many fish and ground meat dishes are quickly prepared from scratch. Also, if attractive presentation is your goal, remember that tomatoes, avocados or cucumbers are handy ever-ready containers for meat and fish salads, 107, and that small eggplant, squash and cucumbers make attractive cases for sauced meat and fish fillings. To make, see Vegetables, 280.

LUNCHEONS WITH MEATS

If you are tight on time, turn to meat salads, 107, or Sandwiches, 269, for quick solutions to the problem. But if you are turning lunch into a luncheon—with leisure to prepare and to enjoy—consider some of the menus below.

Jellied Ham Mousse, 120
Fresh Corn Pudding Cockaigne, 300
Sliced fresh cucumbers, 102, and basil
Brownies Cockaigne, 701

Tomato Aspic Ring II, 114,
filled with Chicken Salad, 108,
with Curry Mayonnaise, 365
Corn Dodgers, 628
Lemon and Orange Ice, 766

Sausage and Millet Casserole, 259
Celeriac Salad, 101
Apples Cockaigne, 131

Chicken Soufflé II, 230, with Suprême Sauce, 344,
and cress garnish
Sautéed Okra, 311
Filled Pineapple, 141
Pecan Drop Cookies, 706

Turkey Divan, 264, on toast
Flambéed Peaches, 127
Curled Nut Wafers, 720,
filled with chocolate cream cheese

Pot-au-Feu, 170
Melba Cheese Rounds, 635
Chicory-Beetroot Salad, 96
Plum Cake Cockaigne, 661

Club sandwiches, 274
Fennel Sticks, 304,
and Bread and Butter Pickles, 842
Poached Cherries, 135, with Yogurt, 533

Clear Watercress Soup, 171
Tripe à la Mode, 509
Boiled New Potatoes, 317, with parsley
Blender Fruit Whip, 746

Pineapple Tidbits, 140
Lamb Patties, 488
Broccoli Timbale, 231
Cloverleaf Rolls, 611
Floating Island, 735

Ham Noodles, 214
Watercress Salad, 93, with raw mushrooms
Quick Cherry Crunch, 662

Garnished English Mixed Grill, 473
Tomato Pudding Cockaigne, 333
Asparagus Salad, 100
Hard Rolls, 616
Baked Fruit Compote, 126, using rhubarb

Cold Sliced Roast Beef, 454
Tomato Stuffed, 105, with Russian Salad, 99
Sourdough Rye Bread, 609, and cheese
Flan with Fruit, 655

LUNCHEONS WITH FISH

Although Lent no longer controls the spring dietary as in ages past, and church strictures against meat have relaxed, appreciation of their protein and unsaturated fat values and the sheer deliciousness of truly fresh seafoods have brought about a resurgence in their consumption.

Shrimp Pilaf, 209
Tossed Green Salad, 94,
with Chutney Dressing, 361
Bread Sticks, 606
Banana Pineapple Sherbet, 768

Frog Legs Forestière, 416,
garnished with Green Peas and fresh mint, 314
Melon Salad, 111
Corn Zephyrs Cockaigne, 628
Cream Meringue Tart Cockaigne, 689

Onion Soup, 171
Omelet, 226, filled with seafood
Seedless Grape and Celery Ring, 118
Angel Cake, 668, with Lemon Filling, 697

Bouillabaisse, 188, with French Bread, 605
Black olives, 85, and Finocchio, 304
Spiked Melon, 139

Cream of Asparagus Soup, 182
Paella, 210
Escarole Salad, 93
Crème Caramel, 735

Jellied Tomato Bouillon, 174
Scallop Kebabs, 382
Sautéed Summer Squash, 329
Deep-Fried Parsley, 314
Date Spice Cake, 679

Crab Louis, 107,
garnished with avocado slices, 110
Parker House Rolls, 611
Lemon and Orange Ice, 766, with a cherry liqueur

Clam Broth, 186
Cheese Popovers, 632
Butterfly Shrimp, 391
Cooked Celery Salad, 101,
with Boiled Salad Dressing, 366
Chocolate Charlotte, 748

Jambalaya with Fish, 211
Oakleaf lettuce, 93,
with Thousand Island Dressing, 364
Melba Toast, 636
Orange Chiffon Pie, 658

Leek-Potato Soup, 184
Fillets of Sole Florentine, 400
Corn Sticks, 627
Spiked Honeydew Melon, 139

Tomato Bouillon, 170
Fish Fillets Baked in Seafood Sauce Marguéry, 400
Baked Green Rice, 208
Crêpes, 236, with Tutti-Frutti Cockaigne, 840

◇◇◇◇◇◇◇◇◇◇

Stuffed French Pancakes, 236,
with Creamed Oysters, 377
Celery, 84, and olives, 85
Chilled fresh figs, 137
Nut Bars, 703

◇◇◇◇◇◇◇◇◇◇

Quick Cucumber Soup Cockaigne, 192
Crab or Lobster Salad, 106,
with Herb Mayonnaise, 364
Chilled green grapes, 137
Quick Coffee Cake, 626

◇◇◇◇◇◇◇◇◇◇

Mushrooms Stuffed with Clams, 309
Purée of Peas, 315
Bibb lettuce salad, 92,
with Green Goddess Dressing, 364
Overnight Rolls, 612
Caramel Custard, 735, with Sauce Cockaigne, 770

◇◇◇◇◇◇◇◇◇◇

Waffles, 241, with Seafood à la King, 264
French Tomato Salad, 105
Frozen Lemon Surprise, 766
Pecan Puffs, 706

◇◇◇◇◇◇◇◇◇◇

Sautéed Shad Roe, 412
Glazed Celery, 298
Podded Peas, 315
Corn Zephyrs Cockaigne, 628
Frozen Orange Surprise, 766,
with Marzipan leaf decorations, 781

◇◇◇◇◇◇◇◇◇◇

Consommé Madrilène, 169
Artichokes Stuffed with Crab Meat Salad, 100
Buttermilk Crackling Corn Bread, 628
Pineapple Snow, 746

◇◇◇◇◇◇◇◇◇◇

Quick Tomato-Corn Chowder, 192
Cucumbers Stuffed, 102,
with Tuna or Shrimp Salad, 108
Seeded Crackers, 636
Lemon Meringue Pie, 657

◇◇◇◇◇◇◇◇◇◇

Smelts, 412
Buttered Peas and Carrots, 315
Scalloped Potatoes, 319
Poached Apricots, 126
Sand Tarts, 711

Scallops Mornay, 383
Corn Creole, 301
Blender Coleslaw, 97, with Mayonnaise, 363
Bran Muffins, 630
Coffee Cream Tarts, 656

◇◇◇◇◇◇◇◇◇◇

Seafood à la King, 264
Grilled Tomatoes, 332
Watercress, 93, with Sour Cream Dressing, 367
Rhubarb Pie, 652

◇◇◇◇◇◇◇◇◇◇

Poached Quenelles, 206,
with Newburg Sauce, 359
Green Peas and Mushrooms, 315
Wilted Cucumbers, 102
Cloverleaf Rolls, 611
Velvet Spice Cake, 678

◇◇◇◇◇◇◇◇◇◇

Chilled Cream of Spinach Soup, 185
Shrimp Sandwiches with Cheese Sauce, 275
Avocado and Fruit Salad, 110,
with Curry Dressing for Fruit Salad, 367
Rich Roll Cookies, 711

◇◇◇◇◇◇◇◇◇◇

Tomatoes Stuffed, 105, with Crab Salad, 106
Pepper Slices, 103,
filled with Cream Cheese Spread, 71
Whole-Grain Bread, 607
Orange Fruit Soup, 128

◇◇◇◇◇◇◇◇◇◇

Gazpacho, 171 or 191
Fillets of Fish Florentine
with Shrimp and Mushrooms, 400
French Bread, 605
Seedless grapes, 137, and assorted cheese, 756

◇◇◇◇◇◇◇◇◇◇

Lobster or Seafood Curry, 388,
in a Rice Ring, 207,
served with Chutney, 846
Celery and spinach, 94, with French Dressing, 360
Pears in Liqueur, 140

◇◇◇◇◇◇◇◇◇◇

LUNCHEONS WITH EGGS AND CHEESE

Called by some "meatless" menus, those below are comparable nutritionally to meals which include meat and fish. Strict vegetarians exclude egg and dairy products. Since the structuring of such restricted diets, 3, needs constant care and skill to maintain sufficient proteins and accessory factors, they are not included in these cursory suggestions.

◇◇◇◇◇◇◇◇◇◇

Eggs in Aspic Cockaigne, 117, on watercress, 93
Brioche Loaf Cockaigne, 605
Macedoine of Fresh Fruit, 124
Molasses Crisps Cockaigne, 716

Ratatouille Provençale, 304
Cannelloni, 216, with cheese filling, 219
Dandelion Salad, 94, with oil and vinegar, 95
Wine Gelatin, 745, with Custard Sauce, 771

Bean Soup with Vegetables, 177
Puffed Bread Blocks, 635
Tossed Green Salad, 94
Prune Whip, 741

Bulgarian Cold Cucumber Soup, 183
Curried Eggs, 224
Refrigerator Bran Rolls, 619
Fresh Cherry Pie, 651

Cheese Custard Pie, 255
Tomato Aspic, 114, on mixed salad greens, 94
Strawberries with Kirsch, 133, on Meringues, 649

Quick Spinach Soup, 193, with Tofu, 535
Creamed Eggs and Asparagus Cockaigne, 224
Ambrosia, 124
Anise Drop Cookies, 707

Soupe Paysanne, 175
Cheese Soufflé Cockaigne, 229
French Bread, 605
Citrus Fruit Salad, 111,
with French Dressing, 360
Devil's Food Cake Cockaigne, 676

Quick Consommé Fondue Cockaigne, 191
Cold Stuffed Tomatoes II
with Eggs and Anchovies, 105
Swedish Rye Bread, 608,
with assorted cheeses, 756
Angel Cup Cakes, 694

Cheese Casserole, 253
Waldorf Salad, 109, on watercress, 93
Apricot Whip, 741

Quick Onion Soup, 193
Deviled Eggs in Sauce, 225
Rye Rolls, 614
Snap Bean Salad, 101, with French Dressing, 360
Florentines, 706

ONE-PLATE LUNCHEONS

This is the most convenient way to serve food easily to a large number of people, especially if the menu is planned for what in England is called a "fork" luncheon. If hot and cold foods are to be served on the same plate, be sure that the hot is in a ramekin and the cold in a container that will not be affected by a heated plate.

Beef Stroganoff, 458
Rice Ring or Mold, 207
Grilled Tomatoes, 332, with watercress garnish, 93

Small Eggplant Stuffed with Lamb or Ham, 304
Molded Vegetable Gelatin Salad, 115,
with Boiled Salad Dressing, 366

Ham Timbales, 232, or Ham Croquettes, 248,
with Mushroom Sauce, 348
Molded Pineapple Ring, 119
Popovers, 631

Quick Chicken Pot Pie, 252
Romaine or cos salad, 93,
with Lorenzo Dressing, 360

Fish Paupiettes, 400, with Oyster Sauce, 343
Podded Peas, 315
Hard Rolls, 616

Blanquette de Veau, 470, on Boiled Noodles, 213
Panned or Sicilian Spinach, 327

Stuffed Eggs on Rosettes with Savory Sauce, 225
Asparagus Tip and Green Pepper Salad, 100,
with bibb lettuce, 92

Honeydew or canteloupe melon, 138,
filled with creamed cottage cheese, 536,
garnished with seedless green grapes, 137
Quick Nut Bread, 623

DINNERS FOR FAMILY OR FRIENDS

We have preferred not to sort these into family and company categories, but to leave the choice to you. First, our families can be our best company; second, almost any menu can be for guests, depending on who's coming to dinner and what you do particularly well. The most important quality of a "company" dinner should be the excitement of the unusual—for them. This need by no means be a matter of fancy versus plain, nor a selection as far out as that of the Franklin Roosevelts when they entertained the King and Queen of England at Hyde Park with hot dogs as the unforgettable pièce de résistance. At a recent spectacular dinner in Lyons for the top-flight chefs of France, hosted by one of them, the multi-course menu included among its openers wild strawberries and Caspian caviar—foods appropriate enough for these jaded palates. But the main and surprise course consisted of six magnificent American prime ribs of beef grilled on the spit before a natural charcoal fire and served with baked Idaho potatoes.

Don't forget that with any of the following meals a salad of seasonal greens is not amiss. Serve it as many Europeans do—the mixed greens in a large bowl, ready to be dressed, with a double cruet such as that shown on 92 standing by—to which the Italians have given the inimitable name of *nuora e suocera*—mother- and daughter-in-law.

Prosciutto and Fruit, 80
Lasagne, 215
Tossed salad, 94, with French Dressing, 360
Zabaglione, 736

German Meatballs, 489
Noodle Rings III, 214
Tomato Aspic, 114
Linzertorte, 686

Small Tomatoes filled with
Coleslaw de Luxe VI, 105
Roast Cornish Hen, 434, with Rice Dressing, 373
Braised Leeks, 306
Hard Rolls, 616
Strawberry Bombe, 764

Crown Roast of Lamb, 472,
with Tangerine-Rice Dressing Cockaigne, 373
Steamed Zucchini, 328
Belgian endive, 93, Vinaigrette, 360
Sour Cream Apple Cake Soufflé Cockaigne, 741

Stuffed Veal Roast, 467
Green Bean Casserole, 285
Cold Beet Cups, 101
Rice Flour Muffins, 631
Profiteroles, 647

Fillet of Beef, 454,
with Marchand de Vin Sauce, 347
Potatoes Anna, 320
Stuffed Baked Artichokes, 283
Peach Ice with Cassis, 766

Tiny Broiled Sausages, 86
Sautéed Mushrooms, 308
Summer Squash Casserole Cockaigne, 330
Prunes in Wine, 141
Molasses Nut Wafers, 706

Sweetbreads on Skewers with Mushrooms, 503
Braised Celery, 298
Sliced tomatoes, 104, with French Dressing, 360
Cheese Straws, 641
Coffee Chocolate Custard, 735

Liver Lyonnaise, 500
Shoestring Potatoes, 322
Sweet-Sour Beans, 286
Blueberries, 133, and cream

Shrimp Casserole with Snail Butter, 391
Pheasant in Game Sauce, 439
Wild Rice Ring, 212, with Spinach, 326
Strawberries Romanoff, 133

Braised Lamb Shanks, 474, with vegetables
Boiled Noodles, 213
Cucumber Salad, 102
Jelly Tot Cookies, 717

Veal Roast, 467
Kohlrabi, 306
Wilted Greens, 96
Riced Potatoes, 318
Mocha Gelatin, 745

Onion Soup, 171
Roast Wild Duck, 437
Oranges in Syrup, 136
Chestnut Dressing, 372, with sausage
Celeri-Rave Rémoulade, 102
Almond Torte Cockaigne, 685

Baked Ham, 483
Green Soybeans, 286
Crusty Soft-Center Spoon Bread, 629
Applesauce, 131,
with crushed pineapple and ginger

Baked Green Rice, 208
Scallops Meunière, 382
Belgian endive, 93, with French Dressing, 360
Champagne Sherbet, 768
Pecan Wafers, 706

Broiled Steak, 456, with watercress garnish
Never-Fail French Fries, 322
Cauliflower, 297, with Polonaise Sauce, 351
Applesauce Cake, 678

Cold Sliced Roast Beef, 454
Peppers, 316, stuffed with Corn Creole, 301
Popovers, 631
Persimmon Pudding, 753

Chicken Broth with Egg, 170
Lamb Shish Kebabs, 473
Baked Kasha with Almonds, 201
Bibb lettuce salad, 92, with Yogurt Dressing, 367
Baklava, 794

Romanian Noodle and Pork Casserole, 215
Coleslaw, 96
Uncooked Cranberry Relish, 134
Gingersnaps, 707

Fresh Cod à la Portugaise, 405
Corn Pudding Cockaigne, 300
Deep-Fried Zucchini, 330
Fresh peaches, 139, in Marsala

Tarama, 87, on lettuce
Moussaka, 491
Roasted chestnuts, 79
Dried figs, 137
Vin Brûlé, 61

Artichokes Vinaigrette, 282
Coq au Vin, 425
Boiled New Potatoes, 317
Boston lettuce salad, 92
Beignets, 246, with Sauce Cockaigne, 770

Cold Borsch, 175
Broiled Salmon Steak, 410
Potatoes with parsley, 317
Broccoli, 291, with Polonaise Sauce, 351
Lemon Soufflé, 740

Gänseklein, 434
Apples Stuffed with Sauerkraut, 131
Nockerln, 203
Rote Grütze, 749

Beef Goulash, 465
Spätzle, 205
Lettuce and watercress, 93
Lemon Sponge Custard, 737

Cucumber Aspic, 114, on tomato slices, 104
Couscous, 476
Pomegranate, 142, with Yogurt, 533

Belgian Beef Stew, 461
Mashed Potatoes, 318
Brussels sprouts, 292,
with lemon juice and nutmeg
Belgian endive salad, 93
Strawberry Bavarian Crearn, 747

Winter Melon Soup, 185
Chinese Egg Rolls, 250
Stir-Fried Chicken Breasts, 430, with almonds
Sweet and Sour Pork, 480
Boiled Rice, 206
Oriental Bean Sprout Salad, 96
Litchi nuts, 138

New England Clam Chowder, 190
Swordfish Steaks, 414
Corn on the Cob, 300
Creamed Onions, 312
Cranberry Sherbet, 768

Iced Poached Shrimp in Shell, 390,
with Quick Pink Chaud-Froid, 369
Fish Fillets Sautéed Palm Beach, 404
Tiny New Potatoes Sautéed, 318
Steamed Asparagus, 284,
with buttered bread crumbs
Baked Bananas II, 132

Meatless Dolmas, 492
Persian Chicken, 425, and Flat Bread, 609
Young spinach leaves, 326,
with Yogurt Dressing, 367
French Pancakes, 236
Currant Jelly, 834

Avocado slices, 110, with French Dressing, 360
Turkey Casserole Mole, 428, with Tortillas, 629
Orange and Onion Salad, 111
Crème Frite, 739

Braised Oxtails, 511
Noodles, 213
Carrots Vichy, 297
Cold Green Beans à la Grecque, 281
Date Spice Cake, 679

Roast Duckling, 432
Apple Dressing, 372
Polenta, 201
Peas and Mushrooms, 315
Ginger Crisp, 662

Potage St. Germain with Croutons, 178
Veal Scallopini, 467, with Marsala and mushrooms
Risotto alla Milanese, 209
Sicilian or Panned Spinach, 327
Fresh tangerines, 135

Shrimp Tempura, 391
Sukiyaki, 458, with Boiled Rice, 206
Curried Fruit, 128

Chestnut Soup, 182
Rabbit à la Mode, 514, with Gnocchi, 204
Creamed Lettuce, 306
Compote of Greengage Plums, 126

Baked Pork Chops, 479
Sweet Potato Puffs, 325
Creamed Spinach, 327
Gingerbread, 681

Boeuf Bouilli, 461, with Horseradish Sauce, 343
Boiled New Parsley Potatoes, 317
Mulled Cucumbers, 302
Raspberry Trifle, 688

AFTERNOON TEA SUGGESTIONS

The essentials of this gracious interlude are embodied in the comment of a kindergartner who volunteered to us, "Mommy's having friends over this afternoon and we're serving tea and 'sordid' cookies." Assorted small sandwiches, as well, go with this cozy type of sociability, and even a delicious cake like Poppy Seed Custard Cake, 689, served with tea, coffee or hot chocolate. "High" tea, that old British custom more like a late-day brunch, fortifies the urbanite before the theater or a very late dinner; for the country-dweller it is often the last meal of the day. Formal afternoon teas haven't changed much in character since Brillat-Savarin dubbed them "an extraordinary form of entertainment—offered," he added, "to people who have already dined well and therefore feel neither thirst nor hunger, so that its purpose is solely of passing the time and its foundation is no more than a display of dainties." Be that as it may, we all still enjoy teas at special times.

Dry sherry
Seeded Crackers, 636
Creamed Seafood, 264, in Timbale Cases, 247
Orange Tea Rolls, 616
Almond Torte, 685, with Sauce Cockaigne, 770
Individual Babas au Rhum, 689
Chocolate Éclairs, 647
Glazed Mint Leaves, 794

Dubonnet
Salted Almonds, 79
Eggs in Aspic Cockaigne, 117
Small Choux-Paste Shells, 646,
filled with Chicken Salad, 108
Sandwiches of Cream Cheese Spread, 71,
and Persimmon Purée, 140
Lemon and Orange Ice, 766
Madeleines, 695
Molasses Crisps Cockaigne, 716
Bourbon Balls, 790
Glazed Fresh Fruits, 794

Claret Cup, 64
Flower Canapés, 67
Crêpes, 236, with Creamed Oysters, 377
Rolled Cress Sandwiches, 67
Dobos Torte, 685
Pecan Slices, 703
Candied Citrus Peel, 795

May Wine, 64
Fish Quenelles, 206
Toasted Mushroom Canapés, 73
Cucumber Lilies, 84
Peach Ice Cream, 760
Macaroons, 709
Small Mohrenköpfe, 688
Turkish Fruit Paste, 791

COCKTAIL AND BUFFET SUGGESTIONS

Today the cocktail party is the favored mode of repaying social obligations. In some areas, when you are invited for cocktails, it may be strictly a prelude to dinner. Elsewhere the custom is to provide a sturdier assortment that carries you into the later hours of the evening. In the first type of party, choose delicate, rich, spicy morsels that are drink-inducers and appetite-stimulators, see Hors d'Oeuvre, 77, and Canapés, 66, and note particularly the illustrations in these chapters and in Salads, 92–122, for decorative ways to present them. The other kind of gathering calls for some blander types of food, which may include large joints or fowl and salads, and turns into a light buffet. In either case, your menu should include foods such as butter, cheese, nuts and rich dips that absorb the impact of the alcohol, with raw vegetable tidbits as a foil. Often a hot soup or a few nonalcoholic drinks are welcomed by nondrinkers.

Seafood in Creole Sauce, 265
Seviche, 88, in avocado halves, 110
Cold Fillet of Beef, 454
Mushroom Ring Mold with Sweetbreads, 234
Cold Fried Chicken, 424
Manicotti, 216

Lobster or Seafood Curry, 388
Beef Kebabs, 459
Jellied Chicken Mousse, 120
Veal Terrine, 496
Spiced Beef, 463
Lasagne, 215

Mousseline of Shellfish, 122
Cold Baked Ham, 483
Tongue in Aspic, 508
cont.

Gaston Beef Stew, 459
Sliced turkey, 422
Cannelloni, 216

Cold Glazed Salmon, 411
Standing Rib Roast of Beef, 454
Souffléed Liver Pâté Cockaigne, 496
Shrimp in the shell, 390
Chicken à la Campagne, 428
Fondue, 254

Swedish Smorgasbord, 79

FORMAL MENUS

There are Occasions—with a capital O—when nothing but perfection will do. The menus in this section are all in what we might call the champagne class. Incidentally, don't overlook the Champagne Fountain, 56, as a preliminary, on a day when an outpouring of joy and congratulations is in order. For other appropriate wines, see chart on 57. Celery, olives and hard rolls are the usual accompaniments of such menus and may be placed on the table before the guests are seated. In this day and age when the pink-cheeked domestic is on the endangered species list, all but the most formal meals may, with advance planning, be served buffet style. And you need not sacrifice a premeditated seating arrangement—or even the use of place-cards if you are a true-blue perfectionist. Follow the meal, if you like, with coffee and assorted liqueurs.

LUNCHEON

Quick Clam and Chicken Broth, 193
Cheese Straws, 641
Fish Soufflé with Lobster, 230
Broiled Lamb Chops, 472,
garnished with Stuffed Baked Artichokes, 283
Tomato Olive Casserole, 332
Bibb, watercress and endive salad, 92,
with Avocado Dressing, 362
Assorted cheeses, 756
Cabinet Pudding, 746

DINNER

Consommé, 169, with Royale, 172
Bread Sticks, 617
Lobster Parfait, 389
Filet Mignon, 456, with Béarnaise Sauce, 359
Soufflé or Puffed Potatoes, 321
Creamed Spinach, 327
Belgian endive, 93, Vinaigrette, 360
Lemon Sponge Custard, 737

HOLIDAY DINNERS

Clear Soup, 169, and Marrow Balls, 196
Christmas Canapés, 68
Hearts of Finocchio, 304
Goose, 433,
stuffed with Sweet Potatoes and Apple, 374
Turnip Cups, 335, filled with peas, 314
Corn Zephyrs Cockaigne, 628
Fresh Cherry Pie, 651

Oysters Rockefeller, 378
Roast Stuffed Turkey, 422,
with Chestnut Dressing, 372
Glazed Onions, 312
Brussels sprouts, 292, with Hollandaise Sauce, 358
Filled Pimientos or Christmas Salad, 103,
on watercress, 93
Mince Pie, 652

Hot Consommé, 169
Roast Suckling Pig, 478, with Onion Dressing, 372
Duchess Potatoes, 323
Red cabbage, 295
Escarole and romaine, 93,
with Thousand Island Dressing, 364
Hazelnut Soufflé, 741

Mushroom Broth I, 171
Pâté de Foie de Volaille, 495
Rib Roast of Beef, 454
Stuffed Baked Potatoes, 319
Green beans, 285, with Amandine Garnish, 553
Tossed Salad, 94, with Roquefort Dressing, 367
White Fruit Cake, 683
Pulled Mints, 786

WEDDING BUFFET

Hot Consommé Brunoise, 169
Mushrooms à la Schoener, 308
Rolled Sandwiches, Cress and Cucumber, 67
Pastry Cheese Balls, 82
Galantine of Turkey, 431
Lobster Newburg, 388, in Patty Shells, 645
Bibb lettuce salad, 92,
with Sour Cream Dressing, 367
Stuffed Endive, 84, and olives
Macedoine of Fruits with Kirsch, 124
Wedding Cake, 667
Petits Fours, 695
Spiced Nuts, 79
Peppermint Cream Wafers, 780

HUNT BREAKFAST

Bloody Marys, 53
Hot Buttered Rum, 61
Café Brûlot or Diable, 38
Blended Fruit Juice, 44
Baked fresh fruit, 126
Steak and Kidney Pie, 465
Pheasant in Game Sauce, 439
Broiled Bacon, 486
cont.

Pan-Broiled Sausage, 498
Scambled Eggs, 222
Grilled Tomatoes, 332
Prunes and Chestnuts in Wine, 142
Toasted English Muffins, 617
Croissants, 615
Red Red Strawberry Jam, 835
Orange Marmalade, 839
Scandinavian Pastry, 621

SUGGESTIONS FOR PARTICIPATORY MENUS

Many guests offer to be where the action is, and the hostess, in conventional gatherings, is often hard pressed to find more to suggest than the last-minute pouring of the ice water. The setups listed below can utilize willing manpower to good effect either in helping serve or in doing some at-table cooking, and in exploiting the guests' special talents to add to the conviviality.

I. Have a soup tureen filled with a hearty protein-rich lentil soup, 177, with Sausage Balls, 196; or a clear soup, 169–171, with Farina Balls, 203; an assortment of salad makings and dressings or a large salad plate as illustrated on 98, from which guests can select their choice. Have nearby an assortment of pastries and cheeses.

II. With guest chefs in charge, have two chafing dishes or skillet setups such as those illustrated on 235 for omelet- or crêpe-making. Read About Omelets, 226, for suggestions, and have on hand an assortment of fillings such as creamed seafood, 264, or poultry, 263; a piquant cheese or mushroom sauce, 342 or 348; a large tossed salad, 94, with generous vegetable components; and an Almond Torte Cockaigne, 685, with fresh strawberries and whipped cream or Sauce Cockaigne, 770, or Hot Fudge Sauce, 772.

III. Have all the makings for open-faced sandwiches similar to those described and illustrated on 270, with a "sampler" tray as your buffet decoration, flanked by baskets of assorted fresh fruits that can serve as dessert.

IV. Prepare the ingredients for one of the following recipes which give guests a choice of combinations: Rijsttafel, 211; Chinese Firepot, 462; Boeuf Fondu Bourguignonne, 457.

V. And for teens, set up a hamburger stand serving the less usual hamburgers, 487–488, with varied buns and fixings, and a platter of iced raw vegetables. For dessert, serve assorted ice cream in cones, or sundaes or malts, 42.

PICNIC SUGGESTIONS

Picnics are fun; but picnic food is subject to hazards not all of which are ants and sand. Transport perishables in the coolest part of your car, covering them against the sun. If you use a cold box, pack it with well-prechilled foods. If you have no cold box or insulated plastic bags, carry frozen juices. Use them en route to cool such perishables as mayonnaise and deviled eggs. Or fill a plastic bag with ice cubes and put it in a coffee can to improvise a chilling unit that will last out transportation time. Or insulate the sandwich boxes with damp newspapers. ➤ Do not repack in your cold box or carry over to a second picnic meal during the day any foods that spoil easily. ➤ Should you use dry ice, be sure the container and the car windows are partially open to allow the gas to escape. ➤ To wrap sandwiches for easy identification, see 701. ➤ To mix picnic salads conveniently, see 95.

Most important of all, if it's a basket picnic ➤ plan the kind of food that holds well and is easily served, so everyone can enjoy every minute of the outing. If it's to be a cookout, please read About Outdoor Cooking and Pit Cooking, 155. All **Joy** recipes marked ⊟ are suitable for outdoor preparation. Check also Clambake, 380, and Fish Baked in Clay, 399.

Sandwiches, salads, fruits and cookies are naturals for picnics. Consult these sections; or for slightly fancier combinations, see the menus below.

Grilled Frankfurters, 258
Potatoes baked in embers
Bread and Butter Pickles, 842
Buttermilk Rolls, 612
Cheddar cheese, 756
Gingerbread, 681
Pears and grapes, 139, 137

Lamb Kebabs, 473
Flat Bread, 609
Tossed Salad, 94,
with Thousand Island Dressing, 364
Pound Cake, 675
Blue plums, 141

Cold Fried Chicken, 424
Potato Salad Nicoise, 104
Oat Bread Cockaigne, 608
Marble Cake, 672
Watermelon, 138

Fried Fish, 403
Grilled or Roasted Corn, 300
Coleslaw, 96
Quick Oatmeal Cookies, 708
Peaches, 139

Hot or Cold Barbecued Ribs, 481
Carrot and celery sticks, 296
cont.

Black olives, 85
Dill Batter Loaf, 604
Gold Layer Cake, 674, with Caramel Icing, 726
Apples, 129

Baked Ham, 483
Nut Creams Rolled in Chives, 82
Picnic Tossed Salad, 95
Rye Rolls, 614
Brownies Cockaigne, 701
Bananas, 132

BACKPACKING MENU SUGGESTIONS

If you intend to travel by shank's mare far from civilization, you should be interested in food and equipment that are light in weight and low in bulk. Choose food that cooks in little or no time to conserve fuel, whether it be fuel hauled on your back or that provided by nature on the spot. For ways to build fires, see 155. But in case of inclement weather, it is wise to carry a solid-fuel stove. Solid fuel, a variety of hexamethylene tetramine, can be purchased in bulk from a chemical supply house in granules or in tablets at outfitters'. This fuel is practical only for emergencies or for traveling light.

Pretest your meals at home first; what tastes good at home will be excellent fare on the trail. Menu planning and prepackaging are essential for fast and foolproof trail cooking. Each meal for each person should be prepackaged with seasonings in polyethylene bags with excess air removed, sealed with heat or rubber bands. One day's meals, along with that day's munchies and extra beverage mixes, vitamin pills and sundries should be placed in a large marked bag. Try to provide at least one course in each meal—or a large part of the main course—in a form that can be eaten without cooking, in case of a weather or fuel emergency or some other disaster. Always include the welcome extra munch items in a separate bag. If you are in very dry country where water is likely to be in short supply, remember that proteins require fairly large amounts of water to be utilized by the body, so increase carbohydrates in the expedition diet. In cold weather you will notice a craving for foods heavy in fats. Also during cold weather you may wish to serve soups more often and coffee or tea less. Dried fruits, nuts, chocolate bars and the conglomeration of raisins, nuts and chocolate drops known to climbers as "gorp" make good desserts and trail munchies. See Fruit-Nut Pemmican, 125, for a nourishing mixture with honey. If you plan your initial meals around sandwiches and later ones around tinned fish, freeze-dried meats, jerked meat—see beef Jerky, 814—instant rice, instant potatoes, vegetable flakes and Japanese-style quick-cooking noodles, you will have more time to enjoy the outdoors. At high altitudes, be certain that all foods are easy to digest and blander than usual, for altitude sickness seems to be more prevalent when the expedition diet is highly spiced or difficult to digest.

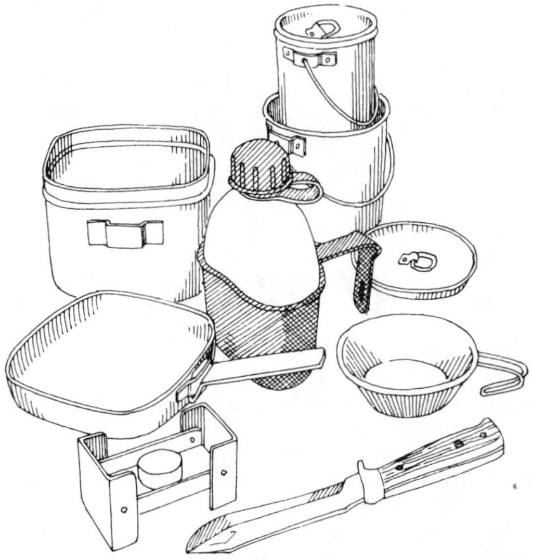

Pick outdoor cooking utensils that can also serve for storage of water or food. Shown above are the GI canteen and GI stainless steel cup—aluminum cups burn the lips—as well as a square aluminum storage box for pot and frypan, and the French army cook kit. Some campers prefer the shallow Sierra cup. Basic outdoor cooking tools are a sharp hunting knife and stainless steel soup spoon. One person can easily scrape by on two canteens and two canteen cups—one cup for beverages and the other to cook the main course in.

After meals, be sure to carefully scrape clean and rinse all cooking and eating utensils and then dunk them first in soapy boiling water and then in clear boiling rinse water; or if water or fuel is scarce, scorch the insides and food-bearing surfaces over an open flame. Remember that even a mild case of dysentery can be disabling far from civilization. Wilderness water supplies should be treated with suspicion. If you have the slightest doubt as to the water's purity, boil it for at least five minutes, or treat it with halazone or iodine tablets according to the instructions which come with them.

BEVERAGES

As our friend the late Edgar Anderson pointed out in his stimulating book, *Plants, Man and Life,* primitive man located the only sources of caffeine known to this day: tea, coffee, cola, cocoa and yerba maté and its relatives. Subsequent generations have adopted social rituals and created special equipment to enhance the cheer and communicativeness that these plants release. Shown here is a massive Russian samovar with its charcoal pipe, the tea essence above, the hot water container below, and a few typical metal-encircled serving glasses: a strong cultural contrast to the Japanese teabowl and whisk nearby. Illustrated, too, is a charming porcelain coffee mill from Central Europe which makes a much coarser grind than does its tall Turkish counterpart. Rounding out the assembly are two examples from south of the border. From Mexico comes a wooden chocolate-stirrer, or molinillo; from South America, carved gourds for yerba maté. The gourd is supported on a silver stand, but after it has been filled with maté leaves and boiling water it becomes a communal cup and is passed from hand to hand, each guest taking a sip through the bombilla, a metal "straw," finely perforated at its bulbous base to strain out the herbs.

Other less rousing brews have been traditionally made from leaves, roots, bark, blossoms and seeds. In France, for example, the tisane mentioned so lovingly by Colette is frequently served as a comforting after-dinner drink, 40. Grow your own herbs, 577, if possible, and use them frequently, fresh or dried, as infusions. If you buy them, you will find them on your grocers' shelves, more and more of them freeze-dried, a process which helps somewhat to preserve essential oils and savor.

The recipes in this chapter are nonalcoholic, except for a few variations under Coffee and Tea and one or two composite party drinks. Even these are very low-power—even lower than the kind of potation that an outrageous punster once declared "took two pints to make one cavort." For alcoholic liquors of all kinds, their preparation and use, see Drinks, 48. Remember that, in any beverage you may brew, the quality of the water greatly affects results.

ABOUT COFFEE

Coffee has always thrived on adversity—just as people in adversity have thrived on coffee. When this beverage began its highly successful career, Islamic leaders identified it with wine—a new kind of wine which was all the more offensive to Koranic teaching because it did not merely loosen men's tongues but sharpened their critical faculties.

Thanks especially to vacuum-packed cans—with freeze-dried instants running a fairly respectable second among those in pressing need—making good coffee at home has become a surefire delight, although some people still prefer to blend and grind their own for each making in a small mill, a picturesque example of which is shown in the chapter-head illustration.

Of the several ways of preparing this beverage, we prefer the drip method. Vacuum preparation and the percolator have their advocates, too; but we regard them as, respectively, more troublesome and less apt to produce fresh flavor. The steeped-coffee recipe which follows is suggested for campers or others who happen to lack any equipment more specialized than a saucepan. Illustrated on the next page are several devices for making filtered coffee: one type employs a metal or plastic filter; another, which is made of chemical glass, uses a paper filter folded into conical shape. The latter gives a pure essence with no sediment—which a coffee connoisseur demands in a perfect brew. Also sketched is the proper equipment for Caffè Espresso and Turkish coffee.

Whatever device you choose ➤ follow the directions of its manufacturer carefully, especially as to the grind recommended—regular, drip or fine. In each case, to assure a full-bodied brew, ➤ use not less than 2 level tablespoons of coffee to each ¾ cup of freshly drawn water. Other things to remember are: use soft, not softened or hard, water; when brewing coffee, keep the coffeemaker almost full; time your method consistently; keep the coffeemaker scrupulously clean, rinsing it with water in which a few teaspoons of baking soda have been dissolved and always scalding it before reuse. If cloth filters are required, do not allow them to become dry but keep them immersed in cold water. ➤ Never boil coffee, since boiling brings out the tannic acid in the bean and makes for a bitter as well as a cloudy brew. Remember that any moisture activates coffee; and that water between 200° and 205° is ideal for extracting flavor without drawing acids. Never, of course, reuse coffee grounds.

If coffee is ground in the household, it should be ground in small quantities in a meticulously clean grinder. Open only one can at a time. Store ground coffee in a tightly closed jar in the refrigerator.

For those who love coffee but are highly sensitive to caffeine or in whom it induces insomnia, we suggest the use of a decaffeinized product rather than a coffee substitute. However, tests show that nondecaffeinated instants, due to a processing factor called hydrolization, contain up to 50 percent less caffeine than freshly brewed coffee. It may be helpful to remember also that certain varieties of coffee—such as those grown in Puerto Rico—have a substantially lower caffeine content than the typical Brazilian or Colombian bean.

For those who hanker after coffee like the kind their German grandmother used to make or a brew which reminds them of that little brasserie on the Left Bank, the answer may be to add an ounce of ground chicory—the root of the wild plant, *Cicoria entybus*—to a cup of ground coffee before brewing. ➤ When cream is used in coffee, allow it to reach room temperature beforehand, so as to cool the drink as little as possible. For coffee-chocolate combinations, see About Chocolate, 41, Brazilian Chocolate, 41, and Cocomoka, 46.

DRIP COFFEE OR CAFÉ FILTRÉ

Place finely ground coffee in drip filter. Allow:

2 tablespoons coffee for each ¾ to 1 cup water

Pour freshly boiled water over the coffee. When the dripping process is complete, serve coffee at once. Dripping coffee more than once through a filter, contrary to popular belief, does not strengthen the brew. Serve with a:

Twist of lemon peel

VACUUM-METHOD COFFEE

This needs special equipment.
Allow:

2 tablespoons regular- or fine-grind coffee for every
¾ to 1 cup water

Measure water into lower bowl. Place on heat. Place a wet filter in upper bowl and add the ground coffee. Insert upper bowl into lower one with a light twist to ensure a tight seal. If your equipment has a vented stem, you may place it, already assembled, on the heat. If it does not have this small hole on the side of the tube above the hot-water line, wait until the water is actively boiling before putting the upper bowl in place. When nearly all the water has risen into the upper bowl —some of it will always remain below—stir the water and coffee thoroughly. In 1 to 3 minutes, the shorter time for the finer grinds, remove from heat.

PERCOLATED COFFEE

Place in the percolator:

¾ to 1 cup cold water for every
2 tablespoons regular-grind coffee you have measured into the percolator basket

When water boils, remove percolator from heat. Put in the basket. Cover percolator, return to heat and percolate slowly 6 to 8 minutes. Remove the coffee basket and serve. ➤ Over-percolating does not make coffee stronger. It impairs its flavor.

STEEPED COFFEE

Place in a pot:

2 tablespoons regular- or fine-grind coffee to each ¾ to 1 cup freshly boiling water

Stir the coffee for at least ½ minute. Let it stand covered in a pan of boiling water 5 to 10 minutes, depending on the grind and the strength of brew desired. Pour the coffee off the grounds through a strainer.

COFFEE IN QUANTITY

40 to 50 Servings

Put in a cheesecloth bag large enough to allow for double expansion:

1 lb. medium-grind coffee

Shortly before serving, have ready a kettle holding:

5 to 7 quarts water

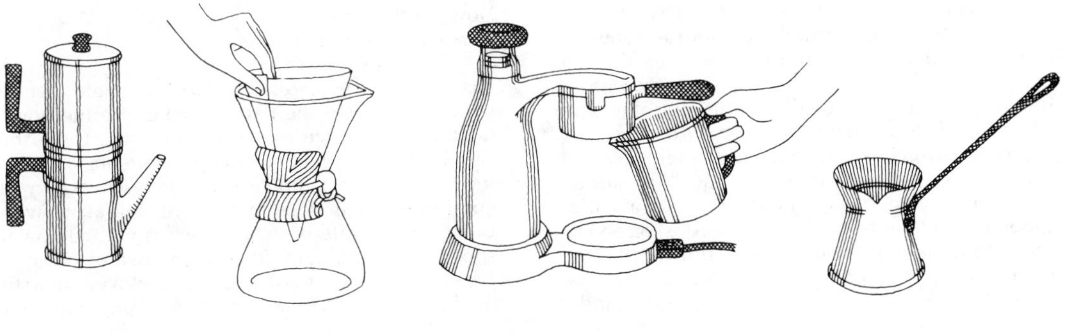

Bring the water to a boil. Place the coffee-filled bag in it. Let stand in a warm place 7 to 10 minutes. Agitate the bag several times during this period. Remove bag, cover kettle and serve at once.

INSTANT COFFEE

The polls are against us, but we really can't yet regard the jiffy product as equal to the one that takes a few minutes longer to prepare. Instant coffee, whether regular or freeze-dried, begins to deteriorate in flavor after about 2 weeks' storage. Use for each serving:

1 teaspoon instant coffee
5½ oz. boiling water

For 6 servings:

6 teaspoons instant coffee
1 quart boiling water

Add the water to the instant coffee to avoid foaming. A better flavor is obtained by simmering gently about 2 minutes.

ESPRESSO COFFEE

This Italian specialty, which, of course, is called Caffè Espresso on its home grounds, must be carefully distinguished from any brew made by filtering, no matter how concentrated. The Espresso machine works by an entirely different "steam pressure" principle, uses a very dark, very powdery grind identified as "Espresso" on the package, and delivers a powerful drink with the consistency of light cream. Use the recipe for Espresso which comes with your equipment and serve it after dinner, in a demitasse or Espresso glass, with or without lemon peel. Vary the brew with a dash of Tía Maria, Strega or apricot brandy and a dollop of whipped cream.

COFFEE CAPUCCINO

Combine equal parts of:

Espresso Coffee, above
Hot milk

with a:

Dash of cinnamon or cardamom or a grating of nutmeg

TURKISH COFFEE

As Turkish coffee settles very rapidly, it is made at the table, over an alcohol lamp. The average content of the long-handled metal pot is about 10 ounces of liquid, and it should never be filled to more than ⅔ capacity. The pot is narrowed before it flares at the top, to allow the swishing and swinging of its contents between "frothings"—a procedure which keeps the very finely divided grains in suspension until the liquid is sipped from tiny stemmed cups holding about a tablespoon of fluid. In the Near East it is considered impolite to drink more than three of these, although more may be served in the United States. The glass of ice water and the Rahat Loukoum candy, 791, served on the side for nonhabitués are often welcome additions. The connoisseur adds no sweetening to the brew itself. Serve the coffee so that a little of the lighter frothy top goes into each cup first and is followed on the next round by some of the heavier liquid on the bottom. No commercial grind available in America proves fine enough for Turkish coffee, so take the finest you can get and pulverize it further in an electric blender. For each serving, place in a Turkish coffeemaker:

⅓ cup water
1 teaspoon to 1 tablespoon finely pulverized coffee
(2 teaspoons sugar)

Heat until the coffee rises to a boil. Remove at once from heat but only momentarily. Repeat this process a second and third time. ➤ Never allow the coffee to boil. Serve at once as described above.

CAFÉ AU LAIT

The milk coffee of France.
Combine equal parts of:

Strong coffee
Hot milk

Add:

(Sugar to taste)

CAFÉ BRÛLOT, DIABLE OR ROYAL

8 Servings

This festive coffee bowl requires a darkened room. Prepare:

1 small orange

by studding it with:

20 whole cloves

Place in a deep silver bowl:

Thinly sliced peel of 1 orange
Thinly sliced peel of 1 lemon
2 sticks cinnamon
10 small cubes sugar

Heat but ➤ do not boil, and pour over these ingredients:

¾ cup brandy or ¼ cup Cointreau

Place bowl on a tray and bring bowl, orange and a ladle to the table. Ignite the brandy and ladle the mixture repeatedly over the spices until the sugar melts. Pour into the bowl:

4 cups freshly made coffee

Now fill the ladle with:

¼ cup warm brandy or ¼ cup Cointreau

Tip the orange carefully into the ladle, ignite liquid, and lower the flaming ladle into the bowl, floating the orange as shown opposite. Ladle the café brûlot into demitasse cups. Here are 2 miniature versions: for individual servings put a small cube of sugar in a coffee spoon, saturate it with brandy and ignite it. When sugar is melted, lower spoon into a partially filled demitasse of hot coffee. Add a lemon twist and 1 or 2 cloves, and stir mixture with a cinnamon stick. Also, you may simply stir a teaspoonful of warmed light rum or whisky into a small cup of hot coffee—adding a twist of lemon peel and sweetening to taste. While brandy and Cointreau are the usual fireworks, you may want to try white crême de menthe, curaçao, or kümmel.

CAFÉ CONTINENTAL

4 Servings

Prepare, using 3 tablespoons coffee to 1 cup water, and keep very hot:

4 cups Coffee, 36

Just before serving add:

½ teaspoon coriander
1 tablespoon sugar
½ cup warmed sweet red wine
(1 tablespoon powdered ginger)

Pour into mugs topped with:

A quartered slice of orange

IRISH COFFEE

Individual Serving

Some people hold that Irish coffee can only be made "proper" with Demerara sugar, 557. It does make a difference.

Heat ➤ but do not boil and place in a prewarmed 7-ounce goblet or coffee cup:

1 jigger Irish whisky
1 or 2 teaspoons sugar

Fill to within ½ inch of top with:

Freshly made hot coffee

Stir until sugar is dissolved. Float on top of liquid:

Chilled whipped cream

ICED COFFEE

Prepare Coffee, 36, any way you wish, using:

2½ to 3 tablespoons coffee to ¾ cup water

Chill it or pour it hot over cubed ice in tall glasses. You may sweeten the drink with:

(Sugar or Sugar Syrup, 48, to taste)

Stir in:

(Cream)

or top with:

(Whipped cream or vanilla ice cream)

ICED COFFEE VIENNOISE

Individual Serving

Prepare:

Iced Coffee, above

in a tall glass. Add:

1 small jigger light rum or brandy

topping it with:

Whipped cream

⅄ BLENDER FROZEN COFFEE

Place in electric blender for each drink:

¼ cup coffee

prepared as for Iced Coffee, above.
Add:

1 tablespoon sugar
1/16 teaspoon ground cloves
(1 small jigger medium rum)

Add not less than:

1 cup crushed ice

Blend thoroughly and serve in chilled tall glasses.

ABOUT TEA

In one of Lin Yutang's books, he tells of the infinite care with which a certain sage living in the second or Classical period of Chinese tea-making procured from a famous spring, in just the proper sort of earthen pot, sufficient water for a brew with which he intended regaling an honored guest; how, on a clear, calm evening, taking pains to keep the water undisturbed, he sailed with it cautiously across an arm of the sea to his home; and how, before steeping the choice leaves, he brought the water to precisely the critical boil. There were other refinements, too, most of them equally unthinkable in our less leisurely age.

However, no matter how we abridge the tea-making ritual today, it is well to keep in mind the importance of the water we use and its temperature. It should be freshly drawn, soft—not softened and not hard—and heated, if possible, in a glass or enameled vessel. When the leaves are dropped into it, the water should only just have arrived at a brisk rolling boil—so the tea will not have a flat flavor and the leaves will describe a deep wheel-like movement, each one opening up for fullest infusion.

Tea brewers who do not wish to trouble with a strainer and are willing to compromise may use a tea ball. In any case ➤ stirring the brew just before serving in a scalded, preheated pot is imperative, since it circulates through the liquid the essential oils that contribute so much to tea's characteristic flavor.

There is only one tea plant, but there are many commercial varieties of tea, depending on soil, locality, age of leaf, manufacture, grading, blending and the addition of blossoms, zests or spices. The two chief basic types are green and black. The former is dried immediately after plucking; the latter—by all odds the more favored—is allowed to ferment before further processing.

Oolong, a semi-fermented leaf, is in a class by itself.

Chinese teas, which less than a century ago dominated the world market, have now largely yielded to the more robustly aromatic varieties of India, Ceylon and Southeastern Asia. There are also any number of blends in which teas of several regions are mingled. Unfortunately, tea producers have not yet followed the example of coffee manufacturers, by putting up tea in vacuum packages. Therefore, when it reaches your kitchen, we suggest you place it at once in a tightly sealed jar.

TEA

Place tea leaves in a preheated pot. Allow:

1 teaspoon tea leaves

for each:

5 to 6 oz. water

Proceed as indicated above, permitting the leaves to steep not less than 3 and not more than 5 minutes. Serve the tea promptly, stirring, for the ultimate touch, with a small bamboo whisk, as shown at the chapter head. Strain. Sugar or lemon? Yes, if you wish—the earliest tea-makers, curiously enough, added salt! On a chilly afternoon we sometimes like to put a small decanter of rum or brandy on the tea tray for the cup that cheers. But we draw the line at tea bags and cream. The bag container or the fat in the cream will adulterate the flavor of this subtle beverage. Milk is frequently added in England. Never steep tea leaves more than once.

SPICED TEA

8 Servings

Prepare an infusion by bringing to a boil:

½ cup water
¾ cup sugar

Remove from heat and add:

¼ cup strained orange juice
½ cup strained lemon juice
6 cloves
1 stick cinnamon

Meanwhile, prepare:

Tea, above

Use, in all, 10 teaspoons tea and 5 cups water—in a regular measuring cup. Put the hot, spiced infusion in a heavy crystal bowl. Pour the steeped tea over the mixture and serve at once in punch or tea cups.

ICED TEA

We swell with patriotic pride when we recall that this beverage originated in our native town, St. Louis—even though the inventor was actually an Englishman who arrived at the concoction as an act of desperation. The year was 1904; the place, the St. Louis World's Fair; the provocation, the indifference of the general public, in the sweltering midwestern heat, to Richard Blechynden's tea concession. In brewing iced tea, avoid China teas—they lack the requisite "body." Hard water produces murky iced tea due to precipitation. Prepare:

Tea, above

➤ Use twice the quantity of leaves indicated for making the hot beverage. Stir, strain and pour over cubed ice. Serve with:

Lemon slices
(Sprigs of mint)
(Sugar to taste)

Instant tea is now available, sometimes sweetened with sugar, and lemon-flavored. If speed of preparation is a real factor, it makes a convenient, if not superior, iced tea.

ICED TEA WITH COLD WATER

This effortless brew has a fine flavor, will keep for several days, and never clouds. Combine in a glass jar:

4 teaspoons tea
1 quart water

Refrigerate covered overnight. Strain out the leaves before serving over ice cubes.

FLAVORINGS FOR ICED TEA

I. Pour hot, steeped tea over:

Bruised mint leaves
Lemon rind

Chill the tea. Remove leaves and rind. Pour the tea into tall glasses. Add ice cubes and:

Sugar to taste
(Sprigs of mint)

II. Add to each serving of iced tea:

1 teaspoon rum

Garnish the glasses with:

Slices of lemon or lime
(Sprigs of lemon thyme)

ABOUT TISANES AND OTHER INFUSIONS

From time immemorial various plants, less stimulating than tea or coffee, have been used the world over as restoratives. An old herbalist recommended them "for wamblings of the stomach." Today, the French often serve them shortly after dinner. They range all the way from such homely makings as rose hips and alfalfa to that Paraguayan tea shrub, maté, the leaves of which are commercially obtainable in some North American localities.

Some of the homegrown herbs which, singly or in combination, may become interesting beverages are the fresh or dried leaves of angelica, bergamot, comfrey, hyssop, lemon verbena, mints, sages, thymes; the blossoms of camomile, clover, linden, orange, lemon, wintergreen and elderberry; the seeds of anise and fennel. There is a good general rule for quantity per cup of water in preparing these infusions.

For strong herbs, allow:

½ to 1 tablespoon fresh material
¼ to ½ teaspoon dried material

For mild herbs, allow:

Twice the above amounts

➤ Never use a metal pot. Before straining and serving, steep for 3 to 10 minutes in water brought to a rolling boil. Serve with:

(Honey or lemon)

Habitués say "never use cream." Try one of the following dried herbs, allowing for each cup:

1 star anise cluster
6 camomile flowers
1/8 teaspoon powdered mint
1/4 teaspoon powdered fennel
1/2 teaspoon linden blossom
1/2 teaspoon verbena

ABOUT CHOCOLATE AND COCOA BEVERAGES

Chocolate, an Aztec drink, comes to us via Spain with the addition of sugar and spice. It really pains us to speak evil of so distinctively delicious a drink. But chocolate, with its high fat and sugar content, if habitually substituted for milk, may create an imbalance in the diet. In some places, unless you ask for French chocolate, the base will be water and the drink garnished with whipped cream. In France you can count on a milk base and cream incorporated into the drink. In Vienna they add a generous topping of whipped cream. In America you may have to face a marshmallow or a piece of cinnamon-stick candy; in Russia and Brazil, coffee is added; and in modern Mexico we find in it cinnamon and even orange rind and sherry. For more information about chocolates and cocoas, see 565.

Cocoa does not always combine easily with liquid. To remove any lumps before cooking, combine it with the sugar or mix it in the blender with a small quantity of the water called for in the recipe. You may want to keep on hand homemade cocoa or chocolate syrups, below. ➤ Both cocoa and chocolate scorch easily, so brew them over hot water as suggested below. In Mexico a special wooden stirrer or whipper called molinillo, illustrated at the chapter head, is used to fluff chocolate drinks just before serving. This also inhibits the formation of the cream "skin" which often appears on top. If you want this aerated effect, try a wire whisk or a rotary beater. Serve the hot beverage in a deep narrow chocolate cup so as to retain the heat.

COCOA

About 4 Servings

Combine, stir and boil for 2 minutes in the top of a double boiler over direct but low heat:

1 cup boiling water
1/4 cup cocoa
1/8 teaspoon salt
2 to 4 tablespoons sugar

Then add:

1/2 teaspoon cinnamon
1/16 teaspoon cloves and/or nutmeg

Place the top of the boiler ➤ over boiling water. Add:

3 cups scalded milk

Stir and heat the cocoa. Cover and keep over hot water 10 more minutes. Add:

1 teaspoon vanilla

Beat with a wire whisk before serving.

CHOCOLATE

About 6 Servings

Melt ➤ in the top of a double boiler until thoroughly dissolved:

1 1/2 to 2 oz. chocolate
1/2 cup boiling water

Scald:

3 1/2 cups milk

with:

1 vanilla bean, or add just before serving
1 teaspoon vanilla

Dissolve in the hot milk:

1/4 to 1/3 cup sugar
(1/8 teaspoon salt)

If you have used the vanilla bean, remove it. Pour the milk mixture while hot over the smooth chocolate mixture and beat well with a wire whisk. In each heated cup, place:

(A stick cinnamon)

Before serving, top each cup with:

1 tablespoon whipped cream at room temperature

BRAZILIAN CHOCOLATE

About 4 Servings

Melt in a double boiler ➤ over hot water:

1 oz. chocolate
1/4 cup sugar
1/8 teaspoon salt

Add and stir in:

1 cup boiling water

Continue to heat 3 to 5 minutes. Add:

1/2 cup hot milk
1/2 cup hot cream
1 1/2 cups freshly made hot strong coffee

Beat mixture well and add:

1 teaspoon vanilla
(A grating of cinnamon)

ICED CHOCOLATE

Prepare and then chill:

Chocolate, or
Brazilian Chocolate, above

Serve over crushed ice. Top with:

Whipped cream or coffee ice cream

Garnish with:

Grated sweet chocolate

CHOCOLATE OR CHOCOLATE MALT SHAKE SYRUP

About 20 Servings

First, make the following syrup which you may keep on hand in the refrigerator about 10 days.

Melt in the top of a double boiler ➤ over hot water:

7 oz. chocolate

Stir slowly into the melted chocolate:

15 oz. sweetened condensed milk
1 cup boiling water

Stir in until dissolved:

½ cup sugar

Cool and store the syrup.

To make up an individual shake, use:

2 tablespoons chocolate syrup, above
1 cup chilled milk

Beat the mixture well or blend it. For increased food value, add:

(½ cup milk solids or malt)
(2 teaspoons nutritional yeast)

Serve at once blended with:

A dip of vanilla, chocolate or mint ice cream

or over:

Cracked ice

COCOA SHAKE SYRUP

About 8 Servings

In the top of a double boiler make a lumpless paste of:

1 cup sugar
½ cup cocoa
¼ cup cold water
(½ cup malt)

Bring this mixture just to a boil over low direct heat, stirring constantly. Then continue to heat ➤ over hot water 3 to 5 minutes. Cool mixture. You may store it covered and refrigerated 2 to 3 weeks.

HANDY HOT CHOCOLATE OR COCOA

About 1 Serving

Prepare:

Chocolate Shake Syrup or
Cocoa Shake Syrup, above

For each 8-ounce cup of cocoa desired, use:

2 tablespoons syrup

Stir in slowly:

¾ cup scalding milk

and heat thoroughly without boiling before serving.

MILK EGGNOG

4 Servings

The following three recipes, as well as the fruit eggnog, 45, can serve as liquid-diet meals. See note on uncooked eggs, 743.

I. Combine in a shaker:

4 cups chilled milk
4 eggs
4 tablespoons confectioners' sugar or honey
1 teaspoon vanilla, grated orange or lemon rind
(½ cup orange juice)
½ cup cracked ice

Shake well. Sprinkle the top with:

Freshly grated nutmeg

Of course it will do no harm to add a jigger or two of whisky, cognac or rum.

II. To enrich or change the flavor of I, above, add one or more of the following:

Ice cream
3 tablespoons carob powder
1 tablespoon nonfat milk solids
¼ to ½ cup nutritional yeast
1 to 3 teaspoons smooth peanut or other nut butter

FRUIT MILK SHAKE

4 Servings

Combine in a shaker or blender:

1⅓ cups chilled sweetened apricot, prune, strawberry or raspberry juice
2⅔ cups cold milk

Serve over cracked ice.

ABOUT JUICES AND FRUIT BEVERAGES

Fresh herbs and fruits, when available, make attractive garnishes for cold or hot fruit beverages. For examples, see the illustration below: a sprig of mint, intense blue borage blossoms, lemon balm, strawberries, cherries, sweet woodruff or waldmeister, pineapple, apple mint, and fancy-shaped or clove-studded citrus.

Another way to heighten the charm of cold beverages is to spruce them up with decorative ice cubes. Fill a freezer tray with water. Place in each section one of the following: a maraschino cherry, a preserved strawberry, a piece of lemon or pineapple, a sprig of mint, etc. You may flavor the cubes, before freezing, with sherry or whisky —using not more than 2 tablespoons per tray.

The short recipes that immediately follow are designed mainly to whet the appetite. They are dedicated to two kinds of people—those who cannot take cocktails because of their alcoholic content and those who like to appear convivial but who are convinced that a stiff alcoholic drink before dinner blunts the flavor of good food. The basic liquid ingredients may, of course, be served without our suggested modifiers. To make rich vegetable juices, blend vegetables, but be sure to cook and strain first any fibrous ones such as celery. Don't forget the convenience of frozen concentrates, especially for strongly flavored, quick-chilling drinks.

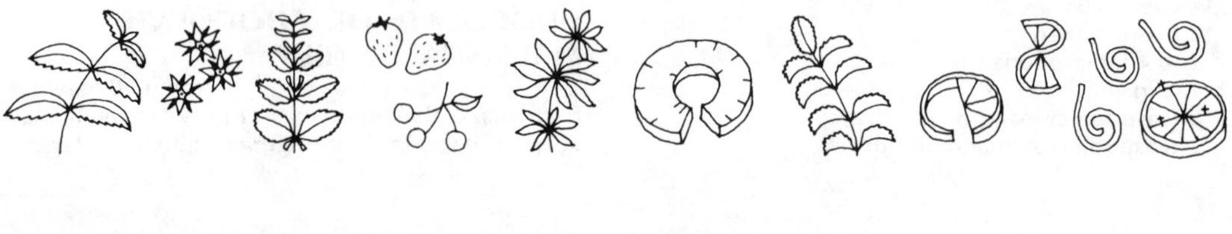

TOMATO JUICE

I. From Fresh Tomatoes — **4 Servings**

Simmer ½ hour:

12 medium-sized raw ripe tomatoes

with:

½ cup water
1 slice onion
2 ribs celery with leaves
½ bay leaf
3 sprigs parsley

Strain these ingredients. Season with:

1 teaspoon salt
¼ teaspoon paprika
¼ teaspoon sugar

Serve thoroughly chilled.

II. From Canned Tomatoes — **4 Servings**

Combine in a shaker:

2½ cups tomato juice
½ teaspoon grated onion
1 teaspoon grated celery
½ teaspoon horseradish
1½ tablespoons lemon juice
A dash of Worcestershire or hot pepper sauce
⅛ teaspoon paprika
¾ teaspoon salt
¼ teaspoon sugar

This juice may be served hot or chilled. Curry powder, a few cloves, a stick of cinnamon, tarragon, parsley or some other herb may be steeped in the cocktail and strained out before it is served.

CHILLED TOMATO CREAM

4 Servings

Combine in a pitcher:

1½ cups chilled tomato juice
¾ cup chilled cream
1 teaspoon grated onion
⅛ teaspoon salt
⅛ teaspoon celery salt
A few drops hot pepper sauce
A few grains cayenne
¼ cup finely cracked ice

TOMATO JUICE AND CUCUMBER

4 Servings

Combine in a pitcher:

2 cups tomato juice
2 tablespoons vegetable oil
1 tablespoon vinegar
½ teaspoon salt
⅛ teaspoon paprika
(¼ teaspoon basil)
½ cup cracked ice

Peel, seed, grate and add:

1 cucumber

ORANGE AND TOMATO JUICE

4 Servings

Combine in a pitcher:

1½ cups tomato juice
1 cup orange juice
1 teaspoon sugar
1 tablespoon lemon or lime juice
½ teaspoon salt
½ cup crushed ice

SAUERKRAUT JUICE

4 Servings

The straight article is—like brandy—a decoction for heroes; modifications like those which follow will encourage the rest of us.

I. Combine and chill:

1 teaspoon lemon juice
⅛ teaspoon paprika
2 cups sauerkraut juice

II. Chill, then combine:

1 cup sauerkraut juice
1 cup tomato juice
(½ teaspoon prepared horseradish)

CLAM JUICE

4 Servings

Combine:

2 tablespoons lemon juice
1½ tablespoons chili sauce
2 cups clam juice
A drop hot pepper sauce
Salt if needed
(½ teaspoon grated onion)
¼ teaspoon celery salt

Chill these ingredients. Strain before serving. This is a tasty combination, but there are many others. Horseradish may be added; so may Worcestershire sauce. The cocktail may be part clam juice and part tomato juice. Serve sprinkled with:

Freshly ground pepper

ORANGE AND LIME JUICE

4 Servings

Combine in a pitcher:

2 cups orange juice
1 tablespoon lime juice or 2 tablespoons lemon juice
⅛ teaspoon salt
½ cup cracked ice

FRESH PINEAPPLE JUICE

About 1½ Cups of Juice

A very refreshing drink.

Peel and core, 140:

A pineapple

Cut it into cubes. Extract the juice by putting the pineapple through a food grinder or a ⅄ blender. There will be very little pulp. Strain the juice and serve it iced with:

Sprigs of mint

PINEAPPLE AND TOMATO JUICE

4 Servings

Combine in a pitcher:

1 cup pineapple juice
1 cup tomato juice
¼ teaspoon salt
½ cup crushed ice

PINEAPPLE AND GRAPEFRUIT JUICE

4 Servings

Boil together 3 minutes:

1/3 cup sugar
1/3 cup water

Add:

1 1/4 cups grapefruit juice
2/3 cup pineapple juice
1/4 cup lemon juice

Serve chilled.

FRUIT SHRUBS OR VINEGARS

These are most refreshing in hot weather. Try adding rum in the winter.

Prepare:

Fruit juice

Depending on the sweetness of the juice, simmer until the sugar is dissolved:

1 cup juice
1 to 1 1/2 cups sugar

For every cup of juice, add:

1/4 cup white wine vinegar

Use at once or bottle in sterile jars. Serve the shrub over shaved ice.

CITRUS FRUIT JUICE MEDLEY

4 Servings

Combine in a pitcher:

3/4 cup grapefruit juice
1/4 cup lemon juice
1/2 cup orange juice
1/3 to 1/2 cup sugar
1 cup cracked ice

Pour into glasses and serve garnished with:

Sprigs of mint

★ HOT OR MULLED CIDER

Great on a frosty night, with canapés or sandwiches. Heat well, but do not boil:

Apple cider
A few cloves or cardamom seeds
A stick of cinnamon

CRANBERRY JUICE

4 Servings

Cook until skins pop open, about 5 minutes:

1 pint cranberries
2 cups water

Strain through cheesecloth. Bring the juice to a boil and add:

1/4 to 1/3 cup sugar
(3 cloves)

Cook for 2 minutes. Cool. Add:

1/4 cup orange juice or
1 tablespoon lemon juice

Serve thoroughly chilled. Garnish with:

A slice of lime

★ HOT CRANBERRY JUICE

Heat well, but do not boil:

Cranberry juice
A thinly sliced lemon
A few cloves
A cracked nutmeg
(Honey to taste)

Strain out the spices. Serve in mugs, with cinnamon stick stirrers.

FRUIT JUICE TWOSOMES

Good combinations are equal parts of:

Orange juice and pineapple juice

or:

Loganberry juice and pineapple juice

or:

White grape juice and orange juice

or:

Cranberry juice and sweetened lime, pineapple or grapefruit juice

⅄ ABOUT BLENDED JUICES

The blender transforms many kinds of fruit and vegetables into rich and delicious liquid food. The only trouble in using it is that the enthusiast often gets drunk with power and whirls up more and more weird and intricate combinations—some of them quite undrinkable. Resist the temptation to become a sorcerer's apprentice.

Sometimes, too, a gray color results. If so, gradually stir in lemon juice, a little at a time. Serve immediately after adding the lemon juice, as the clear color may not last long. A few suggestions follow. Each recipe yields 2 to 3 cups.

I. Combine in a blender:

1 1/2 cups chilled seeded orange pulp
1 cup chilled melon meat: cantaloupe or honeydew
2 tablespoons lemon juice
1/8 teaspoon salt
1/2 cup finely crushed ice

II. Made with fresh fruit, this is almost like a sherbet.

Combine in a blender:

1 1/2 cups chilled apricot or peach pulp
1/2 cup milk
1/2 cup cream
2 tablespoons sugar
1/2 cup finely crushed ice
(1 tablespoon lemon juice)

III. Combine in a blender:

1 cup chilled unsweetened pineapple juice
1 cup peeled seeded chilled cucumber
1/2 cup watercress
2 sprigs parsley
1/2 cup finely crushed ice

IV. Combine in a blender:

1 1/2 cups chilled unsweetened pineapple juice
1 ripe banana
2 teaspoons honey
Juice of 1/2 lime
1/2 cup finely crushed ice

Garnish with:

(Sprigs of mint)

PINEAPPLE OR ORANGE EGGNOG

4 Servings

For other drinks that serve as liquid meals, see 42. Please see note on uncooked eggs, 743.
Combine in a shaker or blender:

2 cups chilled pineapple or orange juice
1 tablespoon confectioners' sugar or honey
1½ tablespoons lemon juice
1 egg or 2 egg yolks
A pinch of salt
¼ cup cracked ice

Shake or blend well.

ABOUT PARTY BEVERAGES

As with Party Drinks, each of the following recipes, unless otherwise indicated, will yield about 5 quarts and accommodate approximately 20 people. For "ice-bowl" containers and other suggestions for attractively serving large groups of people, see Party Drinks, 62.

GALA TOMATO PUNCH

For a summer brunch in a shady corner of the patio.
Combine:

4 quarts tomato juice, 808
1 quart canned beef consommé

Season to taste with:

Lemon juice
(A chiffonade of herbs)

Chill and pour into a bowl that has been rubbed with:

(Garlic)

Adorn with:

Decorative ice ring, 62

in which has been set:

An herb bouquet

LEMONADE OR LIMEADE

For each cup of water, add:

1½ tablespoons lemon or lime juice
3 to 4 tablespoons sugar
⅛ teaspoon salt

The sugar and water need not be boiled, but the quality of the lemonade is improved if they are. Boil the sugar and water for 2 minutes. Chill the syrup and add the fruit juice. Orange, pineapple, raspberry, loganberry, white grape juice and other fruit juices may be combined with lemonade. Chilled tea added to these fruit combinations, about ⅓ cup for every cup of juice, gives lemonades an invigorating lift. Quite acceptable are frozen lemonade and limeade concentrates, diluted a little less than prescribed by the processor.

LEMONADE FOR 100 PEOPLE

Boil for 10 minutes:

4 cups water
8 cups sugar

Cool the syrup. Add:

7½ cups lemon juice

Stir in the contents of:

7 cups crushed pineapple: 2 No. 2½ cans, or
6 to 8 cans frozen juice concentrate: 6-oz. size

Add:

8 sliced seeded oranges
4 gallons water

Chill. Serve over ice.

LEMONADE SYRUP

About 4½ Cups

I. Boil for 5 minutes:

2 cups sugar
1 cup water
Rind of 2 lemons, cut into thin strips
⅛ teaspoon salt

Cool and add:

Juice of 6 lemons

Strain the syrup. Store in a covered jar. Add:

2 tablespoons syrup

to:

1 glass ice water or carbonated water

II. Add:

1 tablespoon syrup, above
2 tablespoons orange, apricot or pineapple juice

to:

1 glass ice water or carbonated water

ORANGEADE

Serve undiluted:

Orange juice

over:

Crushed ice

or add to the orange juice, to taste:

(Water, lemon juice and sugar)

PINEAPPLE PUNCH

Place in a large bowl:

2 cups strong tea

Add and stir well:

¾ cup lemon juice
2 cups orange juice
2 tablespoons lime juice
1 cup sugar
Leaves from 12 sprigs mint

Place these ingredients on ice for 2 hours. Shortly before serving, strain the punch and add:

8 slices canned pineapple, including juice
5 pints chilled ginger ale
4 pints chilled carbonated water
Crushed ice

RED RASPBERRY COOLER

Pour:

3 tablespoons Red Raspberry Vinegar, 527

over:

Crushed ice

and dilute to taste with water. Or, you may add:

1 or more tablespoons Red Raspberry Vinegar, 527

to:

Lemonade, 45

FRUIT PUNCH

Boil for 10 minutes:

1¼ cups sugar
1¼ cups water

Add:

2½ cups strong hot tea

Cool the mixture. Add:

1 cup crushed pineapple
2½ cups strawberry juice or other noncitrus fruit juice
Juice of 6 lemons
Juice of 7 oranges

Chill these ingredients for 1 hour. Add sufficient water to make 4 quarts of liquid. Immediately before serving, add:

1 quart carbonated water

Pour over large pieces of ice in punch bowl.

FRUIT PUNCH FOR 50 PEOPLE

Make a syrup by boiling for 10 minutes:

1¼ cups water
2½ cups sugar

Reserve ½ cup. Add to the remainder, stir, cover and let stand 30 minutes or more:

1 cup lemon juice
2 cups orange juice
1 cup strong tea
2 cups white grape juice, grapefruit juice, pineapple juice or crushed pineapple
(1 cup maraschino cherries with juice)
2 cups fruit syrup

This last—the fruit syrup—is the key ingredient. It may consist of strawberry or raspberry jam diluted with hot water; or canned berry juice thickened by boiling. Strain the syrup. Add ice water to make about 1½ gallons of liquid. Add at the last minute:

1 quart carbonated water

If you find the punch lacking in sugar, add part or all of the reserved sugar syrup.

STRAWBERRY FRUIT PUNCH

Boil for 5 minutes:

4 cups water
4 cups sugar

Cool the syrup. Combine:

2 quarts hulled strawberries
1 cup sliced canned or fresh pineapple
1 cup mixed fruit juice—pineapple, apricot, raspberry, etc.
Juice of 5 large oranges
Juice of 5 large lemons
(3 sliced bananas)

Add the syrup, or as much of it as is palatable. Chill these ingredients. Immediately before serving, add:

2 quarts carbonated water
3 cups or more crushed ice

The basic mix is a concentrated one, to offset dilution through icing. Water may be added later if desired.

COCOMOKA HOT

Prepare and combine, using 3 tablespoons coffee to 1 cup water:

9 cups Coffee, 36
9 cups Cocoa, 41

Bring to just under the boiling point and add immediately before serving:

¾ cup warmed rum
1 cup warmed crème de cacao
4 tablespoons cinnamon or 2 tablespoons cardamom
2 tablespoons almond extract
(¼ cup honey)

Stir, test for desired sweetness, and pour into hot mugs. Top with:

Whipped cream

sprinkled with:

Grated nutmeg or grated sweet chocolate

COCOMOKA COLD

Prepare, then chill well:

7 cups freshly made coffee

Whip until stiff:

2 cups whipping cream

You may whip an additional ½ cup heavy cream and then reserve it to garnish the tops. Have in readiness:

2 quarts chocolate ice cream

Pour the chilled coffee into a large chilled bowl. Add ½ the ice cream. Beat until the cream is partly melted. Add:

¼ cup rum or 1 teaspoon almond extract
¼ teaspoon salt

Fold in the remainder of the ice cream. Pour into tall glasses. Garnish the tops with the reserved cream. Sprinkle with:

Freshly grated nutmeg or grated sweet chocolate

ABOUT "SOFT DRINKS"

We cannot resist, as a postscript, a few words of caution regarding the increased use of certain types of beverages commonly and loosely classified as "soft drinks." Not the least of our concern is the hard-core fact that colas, carbonates and synthetic fruit concoctions make up a disturbingly large fraction of the juvenile intake, and that this fraction almost everywhere stands in inverse proportion to the size of the household food budget. With cola beverages the family provider finds himself between devil and deep blue sea. The "normal" bottled or canned cola drink is a blend of caffeine, sugar, flavoring and water; caloric, unless you use a sugarless counterpart, both devoid of nutritional value.

As to canned or bottled "fruit drinks," the government has seen fit to identify no less than six categories, ranging from those in which genuine fruit juice—with certain preservatives—predominates, to those in which the product is entirely or almost entirely artificial. Close attention to the list of ingredients printed on the container—sometimes in very small lettering—is urgently recommended. Our suggestion is to make a practice of offering children unsweetened unadulterated fruit juice, or on occasion, if the going gets really rough, sugar-sweetened juice.

DRINKS

The preceding chapter on Beverages has to do with nonalcoholic drinks. This one takes up the subject of liquor, from cocktails to what the host or hostess offers late in the evening, either to give the dinner party a new lease on life or—hopefully in the rarest emergencies—to mark the passage of time and allow it to dawn on at least some members of an ill-chosen guest list that leave-taking might be an act of extreme unction.

Because when to serve what drinks is as important as any other aspect of menu building, and because to so many hostesses the intricacies of mixing drinks are pretty much a total mystery, this section of the text remains explicit and detailed. Always in the back of our minds, spurring us on, is the memory of a cartoon which depicted a group of guests sitting around a living room, strickenly regarding their cocktail glasses, while the hostess, one of those inimitable Hokinson types, all embonpoint, cheer, and fluttering organdy, triumphantly announces, "A very dear friend gave me some wonderful old Scotch and I just happened to find a bottle of papaya juice in the refrigerator!"

COCKTAILS AND OTHER BEFORE-DINNER DRINKS

The cocktail is probably an American invention, and most certainly a typically American kind of drink. Whatever mixtures you put together—and part of the fascination of cocktail making is the degree of inventiveness it seems to encourage—hold fast to a few general principles. ➤ The most important of these is to keep the quantity of the basic ingredients—gin, whisky, rum, etc.—up to about 60% of the total drink, never below half. ➤ Remember, as a corollary, that cocktails are before-meal drinks—appetizers. For this reason they should be neither oversweet nor overloaded with cream and egg, in order to avoid spoiling the appetite instead of stimulating it.

Illustrated below are some of the tools included in basic bar equipment. To the left of the ice bucket and tongs are a strainer, jigger and muddler; next left, the only corkscrew we know that doesn't induce complete frustration; above it is an ingenious substitute which raises the air pressure inside the bottle by means of a hand-operated tube-and-piston device, and so gently pushes out the cork—a real boon if the cork is in crumbly condition. Next to these are a combination bottle-cap remover and can puncturer and, at far left, a lemon peeler guaranteed to get only the colored part of the rind. To the right of the ice bucket we show a martini pitcher and bar spoon, a heavy glass cocktail shaker, and, at the far right, a bitters bottle with a dropper-type top. Not illustrated here are an ice crusher or a heavy canvas bag and wooden mallet for converting cubes to crushed ice; a blender, 337, indispensable for preparing frozen summer concoctions, and the squeezer, ice pick and sharp knife your equipment probably includes if you mix drinks in your kitchen.

A simple **Sugar Syrup** is a useful ingredient when making drinks. Boil for 5 minutes 1 part water to 2 parts sugar, or half as much water as sugar. Keep the syrup in a bottle, refrigerated, and use it as needed.

In addition to various liquors, it is advisable for the home bartender to have on hand a stock of: bitters, carbonated water, tonic water, bitter lemon, dry ginger ale, cola and tomato juice; lemons, oranges, limes, olives and cherries. For

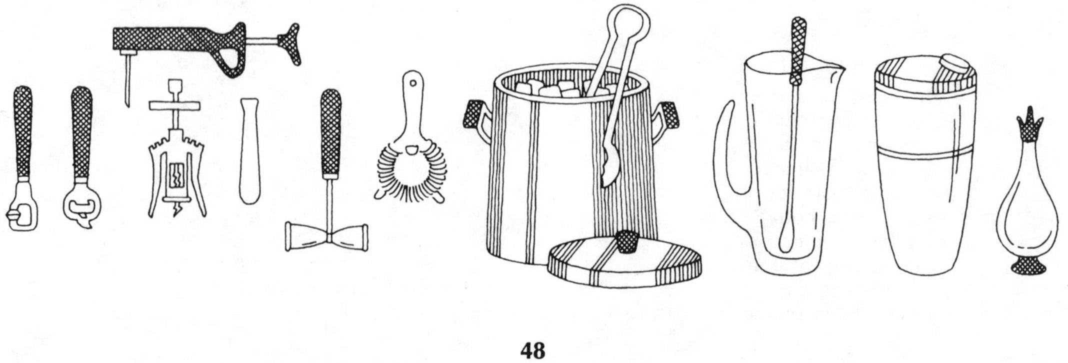

garnishes, see 42. See also the chapters on Canapés and Hors d'Oeuvre for suitable accompaniments for cocktails—besides a steady head.

Note the two types of cocktail glasses illustrated on the left below. Both are so designed that the heat of the hand is not transferred to the contents of the glass. These hold about 3 ounces each. The old-fashioned glass featured next holds about 6 ounces and retains its chill by reason of a heavy base. This type of container is increasingly used these days by people who prefer their martinis "on the rocks" instead of "up"—that is, in the rather more fussy and more precise cocktail-glass type of presentation. The next drawing shows a typical "sour" glass. It holds about 4 ounces. Champagne cocktails are often served in such a glass, rather than in the more traditional sauce-bowl stem glass at the end of the line, the better to retain bubbles. The little glass in between is for straight whisky.

➤ Mix only one round at a time. Your stock as a bartender will never go up on the strength of your "dividend" drinks. The cocktails that follow are some fundamental ones, listed according to their basic ingredients. ➤ Each recipe, unless otherwise noted, makes about 4 drinks. When cracked—not crushed—ice is indicated, use about ¾ cup. ➤ All "shaken" cocktails should be shaken and strained into the glasses just before serving.

ABOUT MEASUREMENTS FOR DRINKS

1 dash	= 6 drops
3 teaspoons	= ½ ounce
1 pony	= 1 ounce
1 jigger	= 1½ ounces
1 large jigger	= 2 ounces
1 standard whisky glass	= 2 ounces
1 pint	= 16 fluid ounces
1 fifth	= 25.6 fluid ounces
1 quart	= 32 fluid ounces

ABOUT GIN AND GIN COCKTAILS

Gin is a spirit—that is, a distilled liquor. Much of its distinctive flavor comes from the juniper berry. Victorian novelists tended to assume that only the lower classes—footmen, scullery maids and the like—had a taste for gin; just as they implied that rum was an equally vulgar tipple and might be relegated to the common seaman. The "bathtub" concoctions of the Roaring Twenties did nothing to enhance gin's repute. Recent generations, however, have recognized the fact that this liquor, regardless of its shady past and its possibilities as a straight drink, is probably the best mixing base ever invented.

Of the three general gin types, Geneva and Holland are somewhat bitter and highly aromatic. They appeal to a small minority and should be taken "neat." By far the most popular kind of gin is the dry London type, which can be found in all liquor dispensaries. More perhaps than is the case with most other liquors, the quality of commercial gin varies: its cost is a rough measure of its worth. Certain brands of gin, which we happen to prefer, are aged for a time in sherry casks, a process which imparts a golden color.

ALEXANDER

Shake with ¾ cup cracked ice:

1 jigger sweet cream
1½ jiggers crème de cacao
5 jiggers gin

Strain into chilled glasses.

BRONX

Shake, using ¾ cup cracked ice:

1 jigger dry vermouth
1 jigger sweet vermouth
1 jigger orange juice
5 jiggers gin

Strain into chilled glasses. Add a twist of orange peel to each glass.

GIMLET

Shake, using ¾ cup cracked ice:

1 tablespoon Sugar Syrup, 48
2 large jiggers lime juice
5 jiggers gin

Strain into chilled glasses.
Substituting orange juice for ½ the lime juice changes a Gimlet into an **Orange Blossom.** Vodka is becoming increasingly popular as a base for both.

GIN BITTER

1 Serving

With bourbon or rye whisky this becomes a **Whisky Bitter.**
Half-fill an old-fashioned glass with cracked ice. Shake, using ¾ cup cracked ice:

2 jiggers gin
2 dashes angostura or orange bitters

Pour into glass. Top with twist of orange peel or a thin slice of cucumber, unpeeled.

GIN OR WHISKY SOUR

This recipe becomes a **Whisky, Rum** or **Brandy Sour** if the base is changed.
Shake, using ¾ cup cracked ice:

1 jigger Sugar Syrup, 48
2 jiggers lemon or lime juice
5 jiggers gin or whisky

Strain into chilled glasses.

MARTINI

With a small onion in each glass, this cocktail becomes a **Gibson.** Try also a hazelnut and name it yourself. Changing the base makes a **Vodka Martini**. How the "Gibson" got its name, incidentally, makes an engaging if perhaps apocryphal story. As a skillful and popular American diplomat, Hugh Gibson found himself obliged to attend a stupefying number of cocktail parties. What impressed his fellow corpsmen was his apparently unlimited capacity for dry martinis, although they considered rather peculiar his insistence that his own glass contain a pickled onion instead of the protocol-hallowed olive. What they did not know, of course, was that by prearrangement with cooperative waiters Gibson's glass, pickled onion intact for ready identification, was brought in at each fresh round replenished simply with cold clear water. True martinis follow.

I. Stir well, using 3/4 cup cracked ice:

1 to 2 jiggers dry vermouth
6 to 7 jiggers gin

Twist over the top:

Lemon peel

or add:

A small seeded olive

II. A formula we happen to prefer, and which would be more nearly recognizable by Signor Martini who—presumably—invented this world-renowned concoction three-quarters of a century or so ago.

Stir well, using 3/4 cup cracked ice:

1 jigger dry vermouth
1 jigger sweet vermouth
6 jiggers gin

Add to each drink:

1 dash orange bitters

Serve with olive in bottom of glass.

PINK LADY

Shake, using 3/4 cup cracked ice:

1/2 jigger grenadine
1 jigger lemon or lime juice
1 jigger apple brandy
2 egg whites
4 1/2 jiggers gin

Strain into chilled glasses.

WHITE LADY

Shake, using 3/4 cup cracked ice:

1 1/2 jiggers lemon juice
1 jigger Cointreau
2 egg whites
4 1/2 jiggers gin

Strain into chilled glasses.

ABOUT WHISKY AND WHISKY COCKTAILS

There are, as everyone knows, several kinds of whisky; but two in particular, bourbon and Scotch, far outrank all others in popularity. Bourbon is of American—that is, United States—manufacture, distilled chiefly from corn. Scotch—as might be expected—is made in Scotland, of barley. Its characteristic taste is achieved by smoking the barley malt on a porous floor, over peat fires, before distillation.

Government regulations have required that before a manufacturer can label his whisky "bourbon," the mash from which it is made must be at least 51% corn. But no restrictions are put on the kinds of grain which make up the remainder. The freedom of choice which results, plus the distillers' option of using a "sweet" or a "sour" mash, gives bourbons their distinctive "body," aroma and flavor. These qualities are often impaired if it becomes necessary to overdilute a given whisky in compliance with federal requirements that overall proof not exceed 110. Proof simply designates alcoholic content: a 100-proof liquor has 50% alcohol, 200-proof 100%, and so on.

In addition, if the mash is less than 80% corn, the whisky can be labeled "straight" bourbon, even if blended, as long as the components are distilled more or less at the same time and come from the same distillery. Otherwise, the bourbon must be labeled "blended." If, in any case, another kind of spirit is used than whisky itself, the resulting product cannot be called bourbon at all, but simply "blended whisky," or "whisky—a blend."

A word as to "bond." Bonded bourbon, like other high-class bourbons, is at least 4 years old, sometimes older, and then so acknowledged on the bottle. Bonding is also a guarantee of the whisky's "straightness" and its proof. Otherwise, "bottled in bond" has no qualitative connotations whatever. We suggest, however, that in selecting bourbons you choose from among straight and bonded brands only.

An American whisky that has a limited but steady popularity is rye, based on a mash that is predominantly made up of that cereal rather than corn. It also comes in various degrees of quality, including "bondage," and can be used interchangeably with bourbon in most formulas. "Tennessee" is another nonbourbon whisky, but most tasters can detect little difference between it and various bourbon types.

A few years ago the government relaxed some of the rather arbitrary standards it had applied to the manufacture of domestic whisky. The result has been a proliferation of "light" whiskies. These are usually aged in used barrels to reduce "hardness." They are paler in color and "drier," to suit the prevailing taste, by reason of their dilution with neutral spirits; and at once smoother and somewhat less flavorsome than traditional bourbons. Light whiskies range in color from crystal clear to a brown somewhere between that of old-fashioned bourbons and Scotch.

Coming back to Scotch whiskies, almost all are

blended, several varieties being expertly combined before bottling; and they are always blended "straight"—that is, without the admixture of neutral spirits, i.e., alcohol. As with bourbons, Scotches are not acceptable unless at least 4 years old.

Which is "better," bourbon or Scotch? This is a little like asking whether a peach or a pear is better. It depends, like the appreciation of a good many other kinds of liquor, on one's personal taste. It can certainly be said that in concocting mixed drinks—cocktails, old-fashioneds, sours, etc.—bourbon is immeasurably superior to Scotch, the smoky taste of which tends to balk successful mergers.

Incidentally, a fifth kind of whisky, Irish, which makes a rather offbeat choice—except in Irish Coffee, 39—is manufactured in both smoky and nonsmoky types. It benefits by at least 7 years of aging.

MANHATTAN

Scotch may replace the bourbon or rye in this formula and the one following, in which case the cocktail is called a **Rob Roy.** When a dash of Drambuie is added, a **Rob Roy** becomes a **Bobbie Burns.** Try substituting Peychaud bitters as a variation.

I. Stir well with ice cubes:
1 to 2 jiggers dry vermouth
6 to 7 jiggers bourbon or rye
Add to each drink:
1 dash angostura bitters
A twist of lemon peel

II. A more nostalgic version.
Stir well with ice cubes:
1 jigger dry vermouth
1 jigger sweet vermouth
6 jiggers bourbon or rye
Add to each drink:
1 dash angostura bitters
(Maraschino cherry)

OLD-FASHIONED

1 Serving

Put into an old-fashioned glass and stir:
½ teaspoon Sugar Syrup, 48
2 dashes angostura bitters
1 teaspoon water
Add:
2 ice cubes
Fill glass to within ½ inch of top with:
Bourbon or rye
Stir. Decorate with a twist of lemon peel, a thin slice of orange and a maraschino cherry. Serve with a muddler.

The above formula, like that for the Julep, 59, is a rock-bottom affair. Some like their old-fashioneds on the fancy side, adding a squeeze of lemon juice, a dash of curaçao, kirsch or maraschino liqueur or a spear of fresh pineapple; or substituting a fresh ripe strawberry for the time-honored cherry. Try also, if you care to, a Scotch old-fashioned.

SAZERAC

Stir with ice cubes:
4 teaspoons Sugar Syrup, 48
4 dashes Peychaud bitters
4 dashes anisette or Pernod
7 jiggers bourbon or rye
Pour into chilled glasses. Add a twist of lemon peel to each glass.

ABOUT RUM AND RUM COCKTAILS

Another spirit, this, as blithe and potent as whisky and gin and, next to gin, perhaps the most versatile of "mixers." Rum is distilled from sugar cane—or, rather, molasses. Generally the rum available to the American consumer is of two fairly sharply differentiated types: Puerto Rican, or light-bodied, and Jamaican, a heavier-bodied, darker and quite dissimilar-tasting product. Only the light type and of the highest quality should be used for cocktails: that marked "white label" for dry drinks, "gold label" for sweeter ones. Save the heavier, more pungent types of rum for long drinks, punches, nogs, colas and shakes.

Some people like the taste and look of a frosted glass and consider it the final fine touch to cocktails of the rum type.

➤ To frost a cocktail glass: cool the glass and swab the rim with a section of lemon or lime from which the juice is flowing freely. Swirl the glass to remove excess moisture, then dip the rim to a depth of ¼ inch in powdered or confectioners' sugar. Lift the glass and tap it gently upside down to remove any excess sugar. To frost a julep glass, see 60.

BÉNÉDICTINE

Shake with ¾ cup cracked ice:
1½ jiggers lime juice
1½ jiggers Bénédictine
5½ jiggers rum
Strain into chilled glasses.

CUBANA

Shake with ¾ cup cracked ice:
½ jigger Sugar Syrup, 48
1½ jiggers lime juice
2 jiggers apricot brandy
4 jiggers rum
Strain into chilled glasses.

DAIQUIRI

With grenadine substituted for sugar syrup, this cocktail becomes a **Pink Daiquiri** or **Daiquiri Grenadine.**
Stir well with ¾ cup cracked ice:
½ jigger Sugar Syrup, 48

1½ jiggers lime juice
6 jiggers rum
Strain into chilled glasses.

BLENDER FROZEN DAIQUIRI

Spectacular and delicious frozen cocktails may be made by using an electric blender. In the Daiquiri recipe, for instance, by increasing the amount of crushed ice to between 2 and 3 cups, substituting 2 tablespoons confectioners' sugar for each jigger of syrup and blending the ingredients until they reach a snowy consistency, you will achieve a hot-weather triumph. Serve it in champagne glasses. This is a formula that can be interestingly varied. For a group, try using more ice, more rum and, instead of the lime juice and sugar, a chunk of frozen concentrated limeade fresh out of the can.

EL PRESIDENTE

Shake with ¾ cup cracked ice:
1½ jiggers dry vermouth
1½ jiggers lemon juice
2 dashes grenadine
2 dashes curaçao
5 jiggers rum
Strain into chilled glasses and decorate with a twist of orange peel.

KNICKERBOCKER

Shake with ¾ cup cracked ice:
½ jigger raspberry syrup
½ jigger pineapple syrup
1½ jiggers lemon juice
5½ jiggers rum
Strain into chilled glasses and serve with a twist of orange peel.

MAI TAI

Shake well:
1 jigger orgeat syrup
1½ jiggers curaçao
1½ jiggers dark rum
1 jigger light rum
3 jiggers lime or lemon juice
½ teaspoon powdered ginger
Half-fill outsized old-fashioned glasses, add finely crushed ice, garnish with pineapple sticks and serve with straws. It will be observed that a Mai Tai comes close to the rococo limit for a cocktail. Substituting Southern Comfort for the rum will push this drink over the line and into the warm-weather after-dinner period.

ABOUT BRANDY AND BRANDY COCKTAILS

Here is a spirit distilled from fruit, most commonly from grapes. Except for apple brandy, known in America as **applejack** and in France as **Calvados,** virtually no brandy is produced in America. Most alleged fruit brandies made in this country are cordials, not true distillates. In the formulas which follow, references always apply to grape brandy, although experimentation with a superior grade of applejack is encouraged. Incidentally, the name "cognac" does not by any means apply to all grape brandies—only to the top-level French product.

Aging is of great importance in the quality of this liquor, but, due to a variety of circumstances, most brandies sold over American counters neither boast of nor confess to their true age. The only sure signs, in order of increasing seniority, are these: Three-Star, V.O., V.S.O., V.S.O.P., and V.V.S.O.P. While we firmly adhere to the belief that "the better the liquor, the better the drink," no one in his right mind and of sound palate should use brandies more venerable than V.O. for any purpose other than reverential sipping.

Brandy cocktails, too, may be served in frosted glasses, see 51, with grenadine substituted for the lemon juice in preparing the glass for frosting.

CHAMPAGNE COCKTAIL

1 Serving

Pour into a large champagne glass:
½ teaspoon Sugar Syrup, 48
½ jigger chilled brandy
Fill glass almost to top with:
Chilled dry champagne
Add:
2 dashes yellow Chartreuse
2 dashes orange bitters

CURAÇAO COCKTAIL

Shake well with ¾ cup cracked ice:
1½ jiggers curaçao
½ jigger lemon juice
6 jiggers brandy
Add to each drink:
1 dash angostura bitters
Strain into chilled glasses and add a twist of lemon peel.

SCARLETT O'HARA

Shake well with ¾ cup cracked ice:
4 jiggers Southern Comfort
3 jiggers cranberry juice
1 jigger lime juice
Strain into chilled glasses and serve with a twist of lime peel.

SIDECAR

The use of apple brandy changes a Sidecar into a **Jack Rose.** Shake with ¾ cup cracked ice:
½ jigger Cointreau
1½ jiggers lemon juice
6 jiggers brandy
Strain into chilled glasses and serve with a twist of lemon peel.

STINGER

Shake with ¾ cup finely crushed ice:
1½ jiggers white crème de menthe
6 jiggers brandy
(½ jigger lime juice)
Strain into chilled glasses.

ABOUT VODKA, AQUAVIT, TEQUILA AND THEIR COCKTAILS

The spirits mentioned above just about complete the roster of those normally obtainable in the American market. They are strikingly different in character. Vodka and aquavit look—deceptively, we hasten to add—like branch water. But whereas vodka is almost tasteless while going down and almost odorless afterwards, aquavit has a strong aroma of caraway. It follows that while vodka is often used instead of gin or whisky in mixed drinks—particularly sours—aquavit is almost invariably drunk straight and very cold. Occasionally, it is combined with tomato juice as a cocktail. Tequila, which a friend of ours has dubbed "the Gulp of Mexico," appeals to a very limited number of aficionados. Try it before you buy it.

MARGARITA

Stir well with ¾ cup cracked ice:

5 jiggers tequila
2½ jiggers lime or lemon juice
½ jigger Triple Sec

Pour into glasses, the rims of which have been rubbed with citrus rind and then spun in salt.

TOVARICH

Shake well with ¾ cup cracked ice:

3½ jiggers vodka
2½ jiggers kümmel
2 jiggers lime juice

Strain into chilled glasses draped with a small sprig of parsley.

BLOODY MARY

This and the cocktail below are noticeably less aggressive than the usual run. In fact, they are widely recommended for the morning after, as well as the night before. When gin takes the place of vodka, we have a **Ruddy Mary.**

Shake well or blend with ¾ cup crushed ice:

3 jiggers vodka or aquavit
6 jiggers or 1 cup chilled tomato juice
1 teaspoon lemon juice
1 teaspoon Worcestershire sauce
2 drops hot pepper sauce
¼ teaspoon celery salt
¼ teaspoon salt
Pinch garlic salt

Serve without straining in whisky sour glasses.

SCREWDRIVER

Shake well with ¾ cup cracked ice:

2 jiggers vodka
6 jiggers very fresh orange juice

Strain into chilled glasses decorated with a small slice of orange. If the orange juice is bland, this drink benefits from a small quantity of sweetened lemon juice to taste.

ABOUT WINES

All this talk about the wine explosion in America goes with our conviction that the Revolution is here with a bang. And high time, too, that we blew up the wall of snobbery shutting out the Common People from the sanctum haunted by such characters of fact and legend as Dumas père, who declared that certain wines should only be drunk kneeling, with head bared; the French general who ordered his troops to present arms each time they marched past his favorite vineyard; and the Feinschmecker in the *New Yorker* story who could remark with perfect aplomb to a fellow diner sharing first sips of a new vintage: "Ah, an obscene little wine!"

The obvious reason for the explosion is the number of traveling Americans exposed to the boons of the Old World, where wine is a staple like bread. Another sign of the times is the spectacular progress in the development of better and better wines on this side of the Atlantic. We rejoiced when one of the last bastions of snobbery came tumbling down in the spring of 1974. Two top French gastronomic critics began with a kind word for a certain wine available by the half gallon in our supermarkets. This was no news: all the cognoscenti have been in agreement that our wines in this class far outrank their Old World counterpart, the workingman's *vin ordinaire*. But then these two experts dropped their bombshell: A certain scarce vintage-marked California varietal was the rival of one of the finest French Bordeaux!

So as the Grape Revolution gains ground, we join the cause, gently proclaim the appreciation of wine as one of the Rights of Man, and make a few primer remarks that may serve as a preamble for those learning to develop an individual taste. To those far head of us, we cite Rabelais: *"Fays ce que vouldras"*—which, from fifteenth-century French to twentieth-century English, means "Do your own thing"—still the best advice about wine drinking. For the whole point of wine, as our ancestors well knew, is that it should be enjoyed—whether you pour it from a raffia-skirted chianti bottle like the one illustrated in the chapter heading; or the hand-blown flacon with the built-in ice chamber, on its left; or the crystal and silver walrus reminiscent of the many animal-shaped vessels of antiquity and after; or the more familiar Burgundy bottle at ease in its willow cradle.

Whatever pomp and trappings surround it, wine is basically the product of the grape and the airborne yeast that turns the sugar of the grape juice into alcohol. Wine is alive. Unlike soft drinks—or hard liquor—it can't be bottled up by its makers and forgotten. From the time the grape is picked until the wine is poured, it is responding to its surroundings with an almost feminine waywardness. Consider, for instance, the process called "racking"—transferring the clear young wine from one barrel to another: to produce the happiest results, this must be done when the moon is full, the wind from the north, and the weather clear.

The color of wine is due not to the color of the grape but to the length of time the skins remain with the juice. White wines may be made from red or black as well as from white grapes, but for white wine the skins are removed at the earliest possible moment. For the rosés—"pink" in French—red or black grapes are used, and the skins remain one to three days. For red wine, the skins remain for varyingly longer periods.

How to describe wine has always been a problem. **Dry** in wine parlance—not sour—is the opposite of sweet; all table wines—those of lower alcoholic content we drink with our meals as distinguished from the fortified types—are dry in varying degrees. All of this has more to do, of course, with taste than with quality. For **body** the best definition is substance. A full-bodied wine is not necessarily higher in alcohol, but it gives an impression of weight rather than lightness, and a sort of afterglow we associate with alcoholic drinks. Full body is far from always being a virtue. One wine can have flavor and alcoholic content similar to another's, yet be relatively more light-bodied and "delicate." You may like one or the other—or you may like both, though with different foods. When delicacy and body exist together, the balance is there that is one of the requisite qualities of a fine wine. The professional winetasters' accolade of "great" is reserved for the rarest combination of traits, for great wines, like great men and women, are few and far between.

As with man, age in wine can be a merit but often is not. Every wine has a youth, a prime and an old age. All table wines improve more in the bottle than in the cask, but some of them for only six or eight months, while others—especially among the reds—if properly stored, go on improving for years and years. Most wine, however, is as good when a year old as it will ever be, and will go downhill after its third birthday. Wines that should be consumed by the time they are three years old, and certainly by five, include most of the lesser reds in the world, most whites, and all the rosés. These include, in short, most of the wines that most of us will be drinking most of the time.

If wine, like art, is a matter of taste, we owe it to ourselves to become as discriminating as we can. Voltaire put it more graphically: "Beauty to the toad is the she-toad." How, then, do you go about training your palate? You taste all you can; you read all you can—or can stand to; and, when you get that far, you cultivate someone who knows wine and knows you—it could be your friendly wine seller. Sooner or later you will probably want to sample one of the fine, aged wines of the Old World to understand the meaning of the standards of excellence.

Many countries of the world produce good wines, and everywhere the quality depends on four factors: soil, grape type, man and climate. The last is, naturally, what enters most into the custom of marking on the bottle a wine's vintage; that is, the date of the specific harvest. The more unpredictable the summer weather in a particular part of the world, the more important is the vintage labeling; where summers are invariably hot, vintage ratings are of little or no importance. And, for a number of reasons, vintage years taken out of context can mislead. Even in colder and variable climates, a year designated poor does not exclude the possibility of fine wines in some vineyards where microclimates may have protected the crop. Charted vintage ratings on the whole represent a consensus on how good the wines are going to be at their peak—which may be in five years, maybe in ten, or maybe in two. Putting such subtleties aside, there are nevertheless years to remember, and in the last ten years in France and Germany there are many, though not necessarily in both countries at one time: '66, '69, '70, '71, '72, '73. Memorable wine years are coming thicker and faster than ever before—a fact due not only to climate but also, in part, to the increase of knowledge and skill among growers.

One can't stay for very long on the subjects of food and wine—those pleasures of life on which, with love included, the French are often considered authorities—without lapsing into their tongue and opening the atlas to France. For more than half the world's fine wines come from there, and in America and elsewhere some French regional names like Burgundy and Chablis have been appropriated as broad terms for wine classification. French precision has developed a legal system of controlled place-names—*appellation contrôlée*—that guarantees not only the place of origin but the quality of a wine. The more specific the locale indicated on the label, the higher the quality. The system closes in like a series of concentric circles. For example, all the wines produced within a wide radius of the city of Bordeaux or blended with wines of the same general area can call themselves Bordeaux. Within that section are the smaller areas—townships such as St. Emilion or Graves—within which the legal requirements are higher. Wines grown within the district and meeting the standards have the right to use the specific district name, and the buyer can expect certain distinctive characteristics of wines grown there. Then comes a series of still smaller place names—specific parishes or communes within which the minimum requirements for quality are still more stringent.

Wine bottled at the *château* or *domaine* where it is grown, and not blended with wines from elsewhere, is labeled *Mise en bouteilles au château,* and often bears the name of the grower himself. A specific vineyard and its product may be marked as a certain *cru*—or growth—which implies that the wine is among the élite of its kind. One needn't add that the more specific the label, the more expensive the wine. As on all imported-wine labels, the French bottle often carries the name of the shipper or dealer first; the contents represent his choice or his blend.

The Bordeaux region in the southwest is by far the major wine-producing section of France, and the *cabernet sauvignon* is the most important grape type for Bordeaux wines—whose English synonym is claret. Despite its fame, the old province of Burgundy, southeast of Paris, produces only about 2% of the wines of France. But there are as many place "appellations" as there are separate and distinct wines, and the system reaches its logical conclusion when it zeroes in on the tiny parcels that produce the superb wines of the Côte d'Or—some of them only a few acres. This "Golden Slope" of scrubby hills has long produced the unparalleled wines that have given Burgundy its international name. The Burgundy grape types are chiefly *pinot noir* and *Chardonnay*, and all the wines carry the name of their village. The vineyards of the Beaujolais district produce a lighter and fruitier red wine from the *Gamay* grape; this wine, unlike the classic Burgundies, has to be drunk very young. The red wines of the Rhone Valley, considered sidekicks of the Burgundies, are grown in a sunnier region.

Moving northeast on the map of France, we come to Alsace, that ancient border province whose wines, like the names of its inhabitants, have a strong German accent. Its vineyards, among the world's loveliest, produce mostly white wines that, like those produced across the Rhine, are known for their pleasant lightness. They are usually named after the grape from which they are made, and sometimes carry the village name as well. Across the border in Germany, all the wines of consequence—many of them outstanding—are white and of varying degrees of sweetness. As in France there are two main districts, Rhine and Moselle, and two chief grape types, *Riesling* and *Sylvaner*. There are nongeographic names such as Liebfraumilch and Moselblümchen that include all qualities. The German labeling system, prior to 1971, was a monument to the thoroughness of the Teutonic mind, and, after a pointer or two, we will leave you on your own in its orderly thicket.

The less favorable northern climate with its unpredictable doses of sunshine made the vintage year on German wines very important. The names on the labels reflected how much sun was available and how man manipulated the degree of sweetness: Spätlese—wine from ripened grapes picked after the main vintage is over; Auslese—from very ripe grapes in perfect bunches, some of them afflicted by the cultivated illness that the French call "noble rot"; Beerenauslese—only the finest, ripest grapes, picked out one by one; Trockenbeerenauslese—an echt-German term meaning piled together like a ten-car collision on the Autobahn, but here, grapes picked individually and left on the vine until practically raisined. Today, one need only look for the terms Qualitätswein or Qualitätswein mit Prädikat to assure a fine German wine.

When we've talked about wines from the hand-embroidered-handkerchief plots of Burgundy and those that come in minuscule amounts from German grapes chosen lovingly one by one, we have arrived—but where? In those very rarefied reaches we had wanted to avoid. It's time we headed home. For meantime, back at the ranch, things are happening to brighten the horizon for every wine amateur.

In California—whence come 85% of our domestic wines—and in the East, too, the new watchword is **varietals.** This refers to wines named after the grape variety from which they are made —as against the **generics,** those tagged with the old misappropriated European regional names—like California claret or New York State Burgundy —and which are often available as jug wines. Varietal grapes—among many others are *cabernet sauvignon, pinot noir, Chardonnay, Riesling*—are more expensive and have a smaller yield per acre than those used in the generics, and are more complex in taste and aroma. Dedicated growers are planting more of the top grape varieties in the microclimates that suit them. Law requires only 51% of the name grape in a varietal bottle, but with more prime grapes available, more wineries are using from 75% to 100% varietals, blending for consistent flavor and other qualities rather than for economic reasons alone. And the red wines that need aging are being held longer. In short, wine-making in America is developing some overtones of the Old Country, where wines of individually distinctive character have been gradually differentiated over the centuries by nuances of geography, method and aging. It's a heartening trend.

The one great havoc that all but "did in" the European wines was wrought last century by a devastating plant louse, phylloxera. The phylloxera story is a curious series of vines-across-the-seas exchanges that hasn't ended yet. It began when the louse was transported to Europe by accident on some American vine cuttings exported for experimentation. Vines native to the eastern United States had apparently always been host to the louse, to which they had grown resistant, thanks to their tough, heavy roots. But in Europe, the more tender *Vitis vinifera,* from which almost all the good wines of the world are made, was almost fatally vulnerable. The remedy *in extremis* was for us to send over our resistant stocks, on which the agonizing vinifera—"the wine-bearer" —was grafted. Practically all the wines of Europe now come from these vines grafted on American roots—and so do most American wines. The moral of the tale: Cast your vines on the water and they come back varietals.

But, strictly speaking, the only really American

wines are from New York State—from such varieties as the Delaware and the Elvira—and, in much smaller amounts, from Ohio, where the grape type is the Catawba that had its heyday on the Rhinelandish Cincinnati hillsides in the 1890s. These varieties are from that entirely different breed, the native *labrusca* that could face up to the depredations of the plant louse and the North American winters. The sturdy *labrusca* harks back to the wild "fox" grapes that Viking explorers found growing in such profusion on these shores that they named their discovery Vineland. But non-foxy varietals are also now grown in these New York and Ohio vineyards, and white wines of the Riesling and Chardonnay types have met with increasing favor.

Our American champagnes—as well as their stepsisters the sparkling wines—come from vineyards both east and west. Whether or not they are in any way relatives of their French namesake is the question asked by some experts about all American wines of legitimate or illegitimate lineage. In any case, champagne the world over keeps its aura of felicitation. One of its French discoverers exclaimed that it tasted like stars, while Art Buchwald says he likes it because it tastes as though his foot's asleep. In buying imported champagne, the brand is—for once—more important than the vineyard, for virtually all champagne is a blend. By law, French champagne must be made by the laborious and expensive process of bottle-fermenting and must come from the Champagne country to the east of Paris. In America, any sparkling wine—even red—can legally call itself champagne if it's bottle-fermented and clearly labeled with its geographical origin—New York State, California or American. Sweetness in all champagne is produced by artificial "dosage" with small percentages of sugar. Beginning with the driest, the degrees are brut, extra-dry, and dry or sec. Champagne and sparkling wines come with a wired-down cork that has to be eased out gently—➤ the bottle thoroughly chilled, to 35° or 40°, and held away from you and anyone else nearby. Devotees of champagne find it a good accompaniment to any meal, including breakfast. For those events in life which call for celebration with a gala, nothing equals a champagne fountain.

A single pouring from a jeroboam takes care of 34 glasses placed in fountain form. Shown here is a glorious fountain for 31. For smaller parties, 11 glasses will work. Whether you pour champagne or punch, the effect is memorable. Better practice first, though, with tap water!

In the non-table-wine category come the sherries; their Italian cousins the Marsalas; the ports and the Madeiras—all again bearing Old World generic names from the towns of Jerez in Spain, Marsala in Sicily, Oporto in Portugal, and the Portuguese island of Madeira. These are "made" rather than natural wines: that is, they are fortified with alcohol while young to stop fermentation

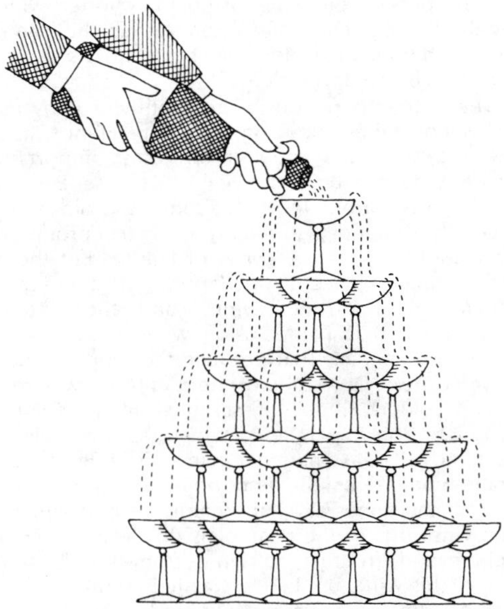

and preserve sweetness. In sherries, any sweetness and color is added, and neither is in any degree accidental. The drier sherries, like the drier Marsalas, are often used in cooking. They are distinguished by their nutlike flavor and make excellent apéritifs, as does a rare dry Madeira. They may be served chilled or at room temperature, as you prefer—here again controversy has raged. The darker, heavily sweetened sherries, including cream sherry, are, like the ports and most of the Madeiras, best enjoyed at the dessert end of a meal—or alone. Their relatives the fortified apéritif wines, sold under proprietary names such as Byrrh, Pernod, Dubonnet and Cinzano, are—except for some of the vermouths—really too sweet to be appetite stimulators, but they fill their niche as late-afternoon socializers.

The chart following is a bare-bones outline of suggestions as to what goes with what. It reflects the experience of generations in combining those traditional good marriages of food and wine. Their

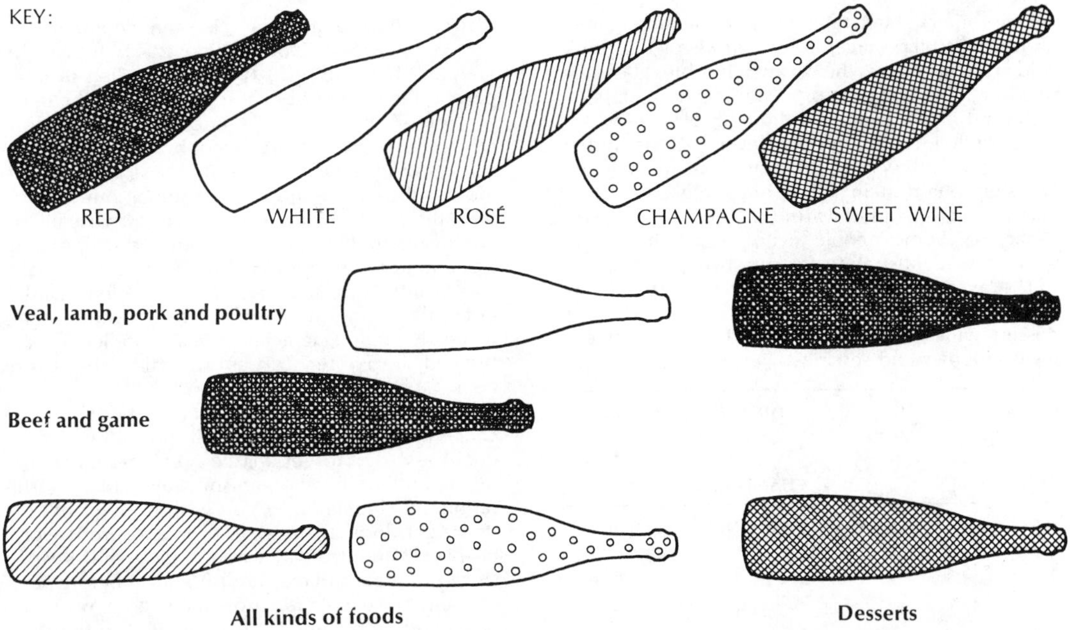

principles were sound and may still be followed, but one should leave some leeway for infidelity. For example, the purist dictum that wine served at a meal be preceded by the product of the grape —not the grain—will no doubt be more honored in the breach; it limits happy-hour intake to dry sherry or Madeira, dry white wine or champagne, or dry vermouth. The rest is common sense. If more than one wine is being served, white goes better before red. Sweet wines should be reserved for dessert. As a rule, the heavier the food, the heavier the wine: neither should overpower the other. And some foods fight with wine like cat and dog, so beware of any showdowns with vinegary salads, fishy hors d'oeuvre, onions, garlic, curries and strongly flavored sauces.

While the rosés do not usually compare with the reds or whites as dinner companions, they can be useful in bringing together the various flavors of a cold buffet, a barbecue, a picnic or a sandwich at lunch—or perhaps at dinner on a hot summer night, whatever the menu. Which brings us to the matter of temperature. The whites and rosés are served chilled; as for the reds, let the climate, the quality of the wine, and your own preference be your guide. If it bothers you to be told you can serve red wine only at room temperature, think of the European peasant and cool it: he drinks his *vin ordinaire*—red or white—cooled in the brook in the summer and at the prevailing temperature in the winter. You might follow his style for an everyday wine. But for the Sunday red chosen for its special character, chilling could be a dirty trick. Bear in mind, too, that the "room temperature" rule came before central heating, and 72° is the top limit.

A few hints about serving and storing, and we will leave you with your corkscrew and your friends. The old custom of pouring a small amount of wine into the host's glass first—a sensible gesture that allowed him to check its quality—is less often observed today. In formal serving, wine is poured from the diner's right—where the glass is. The bottle should at all times be handled as little as possible. Wine bottles should be stored horizontally so that the wine covers the cork. If they are "laid away," the storage space should have some ventilation and as even a temperature as possible, with 45° and 70° as permissible extremes. A fine red wine should be stood upright to settle for a few hours and the cork removed for a time before serving. For how long? Again there is controversy. So, we repeat, put hidebound rules aside, and above all, enjoy!

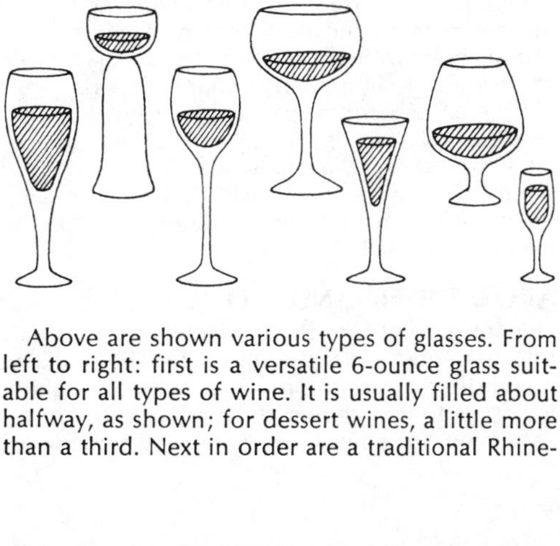

Above are shown various types of glasses. From left to right: first is a versatile 6-ounce glass suitable for all types of wine. It is usually filled about halfway, as shown; for dessert wines, a little more than a third. Next in order are a traditional Rhine-wine röhmer; a tall tulip glass for champagne—preferable to the saucer type, as it keeps the drink cold and preserves the fizz; a bubble glass for sparkling Burgundy; a pipe-stem sherry glass; a balloon brandy snifter; a liqueur glass. All are shown filled to the proper levels at the initial pouring. All except the brandy glass are held by the stem for drinking. The brandy glass is held cradled in the hand to warm the liquor and release its aroma. Some people even like their brandy warmed, see illustration for café brûlot, 39.

The average serving of dinner wine or champagne is 3 to 3½ fluid ounces; of cocktail or dessert wine, 2 to 2½ ounces. The chart below gives volumes and servings:

		DINNER WINE AND CHAMPAGNE	COCKTAIL AND DESSERT WINE
SIZE	OUNCES	SERVINGS	SERVINGS
Fifth—4/5 qt.	25.6	8	8-12
Tenth—4/5 pt.	12.8	4	4-6
Split	6.4	2	
Quart	32	10	10-14
Pint	16	5	5-7
½ Gallon	64	20	20-30
Gallon	128	40	40-60

ABOUT LIQUEURS AND CORDIALS

A common characteristic of almost all liqueurs and cordials is their sweetness. This quality relegates them as straight drinks to the after-dinner hour, along with a second demitasse. With some, such as kümmel, curaçao, Cointreau, Grand Marnier, anisette, crème de menthe or crème de cacao, a single flavor predominates. In others—Chartreuse, Bénédictine, Vieille Cure, Drambuie, for example—the flavor is more intricate. Those of still a third category are used almost entirely as components of mixed drinks. Of these the following are perhaps the best known: falernum and orgeat, both with an almond flavor; kirsch/wild cherry; maraschino/cherry; crème de cassis/currant; grenadine/pomegranate. However, do not overlook the "mixing" potential of other liqueurs: a few drops, experimentally added, have touched off many a brave new cocktail. By themselves, serve liqueurs at room temperature or a little below, and in small quantities.

ABOUT BEER AND ALE

The storied nut-brown ale of old was a prosaic drink—cloudy, yeasty and unstable. The sparkling brews of today are the result of complex technological advances during the past century and a half. Those we now enjoy are brewed from barley malt and hops, chiefly, and vary in alcoholic content from around 3 to a little over 4% by weight. They are basically of 3 types, depending in large part on the degree of heat in processing: the light-bodied—"champagne"—and medium-bodied types, both greatly preferred by American consumers, and a heavy type. The last tends to be more substantial, more flavorsome, more bitter than the first two. Except for "Bock," virtually all the heavy-bodied beers currently distributed in this country are imported from Germany, Holland and Scandinavia and are usually labeled "Dark." Bock, the domestic manufacture of which seems to be dwindling, is a fairly heavy-bodied variant brewed in winter for spring sale—an "Easter beer."

Whether you purchase beer in bottles or in cans—and we have detected no difference in quality—never forget that despite pasteurization it is still full of living organisms, subject to deterioration and shock. So, if you wish to savor beer at its height, look at the date to make sure it won't be over 2 months old when it is served. Keep it stored in a dark place. Chill it slowly before serving and once cold do not allow it to warm up again and be rechilled. Never allow it to freeze.

Like the wine connoisseur, the beer expert is most particular about the temperatures at which he serves his brew. Forty degrees is favored as producing the fullest flavor, a not too great contrast between the temperature of the drink and that of the taste buds.

A slightly higher serving temperature is suggested for ale. This drink is made from the same ingredients as beer, except for the strain of the yeast. It is fermented rapidly and at room temperature rather than at the almost freezing temperatures modern beer demands, in its long, slow and intricately controlled processing.

Here are the traditional beer and ale glasses and mugs: a sentimental-looking stein, a Pilsner glass for light beer and an ale glass and mug. The true enthusiast is probably happiest drinking from an opaque container. It does not allow him to see

the small imperfections in the appearance of the beer, which are visible when it is served in improperly washed glasses. Grease is the natural enemy of beer, for it kills the foam. So wash glasses with detergent, not with soap. The glasses should never be dried, but allowed to drain on a soft cloth. Glasses may be chilled, but in any case they should be rinsed in cold water just before using and the beer poured into a tilted wet glass.

You may like a high or a low collar. The usual size is one-fourth the height of the glass or mug. A bottle of beer, despite popular superstition, is not so caloric as the average cocktail, but since it lacks the disembodied quality of table wines it is usually served with snacks and suppers.

ABOUT MIXED DRINKS

In the foregoing pages of this chapter we have dealt with our material on the "basic ingredient" principle and have attempted a chronological résumé of the drinks, simple or compound, which are likely to precede, go along with or follow meals—from the ceremonious to the completely informal. The following sections describe a number of between-meal or special-occasion drinks of such variety as to defy systematic listing—at least as far as their components are concerned.

Glasses and cups for mixed drinks vary greatly in size and shape. Collins glasses and lemonade and highball glasses, shown at the left, are similar in shape and vary in content from 8 to 16 ounces. The one illustrated is a 12-ouncer.

Silver cups with a handle, so that the frost remains undisturbed, are highly favored for such drinks as mint juleps. Some persons dislike drinks served in metal, but if straws are used no metallic taste is noticeable. Juleps without straws should be served in very thin glassware. To frost the glasses, see below.

Tom and Jerry mugs, shown next, hold about 8 ounces; punch glasses or cups, 3 or 4 ounces. These are frequently made of porcelain, an advantage when serving mulled or flaming drinks.

ABOUT TALL DRINKS

King-size drinks are commonly served in glasses holding 8 ounces or more. When mixers such as carbonated water—seltzer, club soda, Vichy, etc.—or ginger ale are used, refrigerate them if possible before adding them to the drink. To make decorative ice cubes for tall drinks, see 42.

HIGHBALLS AND RICKEYS

Individual Servings

Use bourbon, Scotch, rye, or gin.
Into a 6-oz. glass, put 2 large ice cubes and add:
1 jigger of liquor chosen
Fill the glass with:
Carbonated water
Stir lightly with bar spoon and serve.
For a rickey, add before the carbonated water:
Juice of ½ large lime
With dry liquors, you may add:
½ teaspoon Sugar Syrup, 48

A luxurious rickey can be concocted by adding a teaspoon or so of liqueur to the lime juice. Interesting effects in the tall-drink categories above are possible by further varying the basic ingredient. Try an applejack highball or one made with Dubonnet. The three following drinks are classic results of using one's imagination freely in this area: **Vermouth Cassis,** with a base consisting of 1 pony crème de cassis and 1 jigger dry vermouth; **Horse's Neck** or **Cooler,** with a long spiral of lemon peel draped over the edge of the glass and ginger ale substituted for carbonated water; and **Spritzer**, with half Rhine wine and half carbonated water.

TOM COLLINS

1 Serving

Collinses, like rickeys, are a large family. But this one is the granddaddy of all the rest.
Combine in a 14- or 16-oz. glass with 4 ice cubes:
1 tablespoon Sugar Syrup, 48
Juice of medium-sized lemon
2 jiggers gin
Fill glass with:
Carbonated water
Stir and serve immediately.

GIN FIZZ

1 Serving

Fizzes may be made with whisky, rum or brandy as a base.
Combine in a bar glass:
1 tablespoon Sugar Syrup, 48
Juice of medium-sized lemon or lime
1½ jiggers gin
Shake well with ½ cup crushed ice and strain into prechilled 8-oz. glass. Fill with:
Carbonated water
Stir and serve.
A **Silver Fizz** is made by beating into the above Gin Fizz ingredients:
1 egg white

MINT JULEP

1 Serving

This drink can be superlative. And it is well, at this point, to remember that, as Voltaire put it, "The good is the enemy of the best." Use only the best bourbon; tender, terminal mint leaves for bruising; and very finely crushed or shaved ice. Chill a 14- or 16-oz. glass or silver mug in refrigerator.
Combine in a bar glass:
2 teaspoons Sugar Syrup, 48

6 medium-sized mint leaves
(1 dash angostura bitters)

Bruise leaves gently with muddler and blend all ingredients by stirring together. Pour into bar glass:

1 large jigger bourbon whisky

Stir again. Remove serving glass from refrigerator, pack it with ice and strain into it the above mixture. With a bar spoon, churn ice up and down. Add more ice to within ¾ inch of top. Add:

1 pony whisky

Repeat churning process until glass begins to frost. Wash and partially dry:

A long sprig of fresh mint

and dip it in:

Powdered sugar

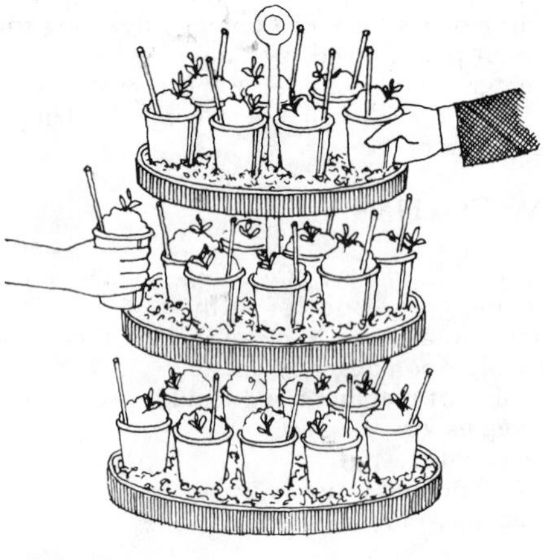

Decorate glass with the sugared mint sprig. Insert long straws and serve.

When making a number of mint juleps, a less nerve-racking way to frost the glasses is to omit prechilling them. After churning, instead of waiting for them to frost in the open, place them in the refrigerator for 30 minutes. ➤ Be careful throughout this whole process not to grasp glasses with bare hands.

The stand illustrated, with its tiers of ice and carrying ring, makes a julep server par excellence. If the number of glasses required is not enough to fill all the shelf space, use the ones at the top for hors d'oeuvre. A deep tray, packed with finely crushed ice, will make an acceptable substitute for the julep stand.

CUBA LIBRE

1 Serving

Combine in bar glass:

Juice of 1 lime
½ squeezed lime
1 large jigger rum

Put ingredients into 12- or 14-oz. glass. Add 3 large ice cubes. Fill with:

Cola

Stir and serve.

MAPLED RUM

1 Serving

Combine in 10-oz. glass:

Juice of 1 lemon or lime
1 tablespoon pure maple syrup
1 jigger rum
2 dashes grenadine

Fill glass with finely crushed ice and churn up and down with bar spoon. Have ice within ¾ inch of top. Add:

1 pony rum

Churn again, insert straws and decorate before serving with:

Pineapple stick
Slice of orange
Cherry

TONIC

1 Serving

Into a 12-oz. glass place 3 ice cubes and add:

1 large jigger gin or vodka

Fill glass with:

Quinine water or bitter lemon
(Lime or lemon juice to taste)

ABOUT PLUGGED FRUIT

We had no luck when, much younger, we plugged a watermelon and cautiously tried to impregnate it with rum. We never quite solved the problem of distribution. Later we discovered we had been too impatient. Time does the trick—about 8 hours. For those fortunate ones who can easily come by an abundance of other kinds of fruit, we give the following formulas for a couple of picturesque and delightfully refreshing drinks. Shown below are watermelon, coconut and pineapple.

COCONUT EXTRAVAGANZA

1 Serving

This rather beguiling specialty, as well as the one which follows, is only feasible if you have at hand a fairly plentiful supply of the featured container.

To hold a coconut upright for serving, see 60. Cut or saw off the top of:

A coconut

This should produce a hole about 2½ inches in diameter. Drain and reserve the milk and add to it that of a second coconut. Pour into the hollow:

1 large jigger light rum
3 teaspoons apricot liqueur or Cointreau
3 teaspoons coconut cream, 566
The coconut milk

Add ¾ cup finely crushed ice, stir, insert straws and serve.

PINEAPPLE TROPIC

1 Serving

Slice off the top of:

A ripe pineapple

Hollow out a cavity about the size of a highball glass. Pour into it:

1 large jigger light rum
3 teaspoons Bénédictine

Fill cavity with finely crushed ice; stir well, bruising the inside of the pineapple, and garnish with:

Fresh fruit

Serve lidded, or cut a notch in the lid to insert the straw.

SHORT DRINKS

"Some like it hot, some like it cold." The drinks which follow are of both varieties, in that order.

GROG

1 Serving

In an 8-oz. mug, stir together:

1 teaspoon Sugar Syrup, 48
1 tablespoon strained lemon juice
1 jigger dark rum

Fill mug with:

Very hot tea or water

Garnish with a twist of:

Lemon peel

Try this drink using maple syrup instead of sugar syrup. Dust top with a little:

Ground nutmeg or cinnamon

HOT BUTTERED RUM

1 Serving

Place in a hot tumbler:

1 teaspoon powdered sugar

Add:

¼ cup boiling water
¼ cup rum
1 tablespoon butter

Fill glass with boiling water. Stir well. Sprinkle on top:

Freshly grated nutmeg

This is an old-time New England idea of an individual portion. It may be modified. Curious, isn't it, that the Puritans made drinks like this one, which has been said to make a man see double and feel single.

TODDY

1 Serving

In an 8-oz. mug, place:

1 teaspoon Sugar Syrup, 48
1 stick cinnamon
1 jigger whisky, rum or brandy

Fill mug with:

Very hot water

Impale over edge of mug:

½ lemon slice

studded with:

3 cloves

★ HOT TOM AND JERRY

4 Servings

Beat to a stiff froth:

3 egg whites

Beat separately until light in color:

3 egg yolks

Beat into yolks gradually:

3 tablespoons powdered sugar
½ teaspoon each ground allspice, cinnamon and cloves

Fold yolks into whites and pour 2 tablespoons of this mixture into each of four 8-oz. china mugs. Add to each mug:

½ jigger lukewarm brandy
1 jigger lukewarm dark rum

Fill mugs with very hot water, milk, or coffee. Stir well and sprinkle the tops with:

Grated nutmeg

★ VIN BRÛLÉ

4 Servings

This winter-evening cheer, outdoors or in, offers a bonus before and after. When touched with a match, it bursts briefly into a tall blue flame—worth extinguishing the lights for. And the French say this grateful potion is better than aspirin to ward off the grip of a cold as well as the night chill.

Place in a saucepan, covered, over high heat:

1 bottle dry red wine
4 sticks cinnamon
Peel of 1 orange
3 or 4 tablespoons sugar

When the mixture comes to a boil, uncover and ignite. When the flame has died down, remove mixture from heat and ladle at once into mugs.

★ EGGNOG

1 Serving

If you are preparing this drink for an invalid, see note on uncooked eggs on 743.

In a small bowl, beat until light:

1 egg yolk

Beat in slowly:

1 tablespoon sugar
¼ cup cream
⅛ to ¼ cup rum, brandy or whisky
A few grains salt

Whip separately until stiff:

1 egg white

Fold white lightly into other ingredients. Transfer mixture to punch glass. For eggnog in quantity, see About Party Drinks, following.

FLIP

1 Serving

Shake in bar glass with cracked ice:

1 whole egg
1 teaspoon sugar
1 jigger sherry, brandy or port

Strain into 6-oz. glass. Sprinkle over top:

Grated nutmeg

SANGRIA

6 Servings

An adaptation of a favorite Spanish summer thirst-quencher, to be served iced from a pitcher.

Mix:

¾ cup brandy
½ cup Cointreau
4 cups red wine
Juice of 3 lemons
Sugar to taste

Add:

2 thinly sliced oranges
1 thinly sliced lemon
¾ cup seeded sweet cherries
1 cup sliced fresh or canned peaches

SYLLABUB OR MILK PUNCH

2 Servings

Beat together in bar glass:

1 tablespoon Sugar Syrup, 48
1 jigger top milk
1 large jigger heavy cream
½ cup sherry, port, Madeira or bourbon whisky

Serve at once in punch glasses.

ABOUT PARTY DRINKS

Most of the formulas in this section are of the punchbowl variety. In each instance, the ➤ quantity of liquid will amount to approximately 5 quarts and will serve about 20 persons—each one having two 4-oz. cups. When the word "bottle" is used, it means a fifth of a gallon or 25 ounces.

Fruit juices used in the concoction of party drinks should preferably be fresh; but frozen, unsweetened concentrates are quite acceptable, as long as you dilute them only about half as much as the directions on the container prescribe. Canned and bottled juices vary in quality—the best, in our opinion, being pineapple, apricot, cranberry, raspberry and grape. Ideally, punch mixes should be allowed to blend for an hour or so and, if served cold, chilled in the refrigerator before carbonated water or ice is added. With cold punches, be on the alert for dilution. Ice only two-thirds of the liquid at the outset and add the remainder just before the guests come back for seconds. Speaking of ice, avoid small pieces. At the very least, remove the cube grid from your ice trays and freeze a full unit. However, the two chilling devices illustrated are a lot more fun.

Before taking leave of cold party drinks, we want to remind you that any of the "sour" type cocktails—those made of an alcoholic base plus fruit juice—may serve as the foundation for delectable punches and cups. See Cocktails, 48–53.

DECORATIVE ICE MOLDS

Set aside in a bowl the amount of water to be frozen. Stir it well 4 or 5 times during a 10- or 15-minute period to break up and expel the air bubbles with which newly drawn tap water is impregnated. Otherwise, the ice mold you build will be cloudy instead of crystal clear.

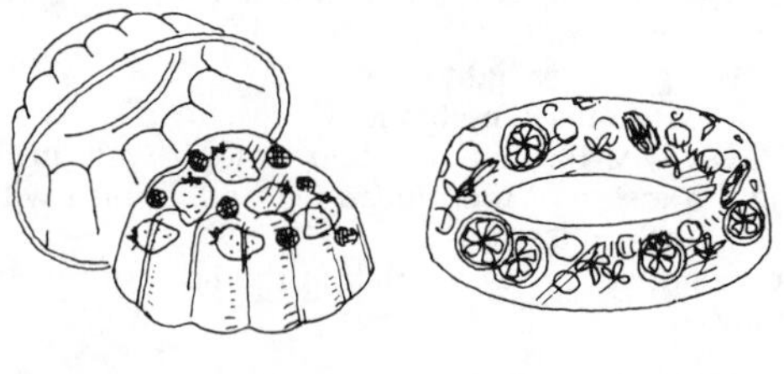

Have at hand such decorative ingredients as whole limes, lemons, oranges, slices of citrus fruit, large fresh cherries or strawberries, clusters of grapes, sprigs of mint, sweet woodruff, lemon thyme or other herbs and a few handsome fresh grape or bay leaves, etc.

Select a decorative metal mold of the tubular or ring type. Avoid vessels which are so deep as to induce top-heaviness in your final product and risk its turning turtle later.

Begin operations by partially freezing a layer of water in the container—proceeding much as you would in making a fancy gelatin salad, 560. In this case, of course, successive hardenings are frozen instead of being chilled. On the first slushlike layer, arrange a wreath of fruit and greenery. Cover the decoration carefully with a second layer of very cold water, returning the mold to the freezer, so that with renewed freezing the decoration is completely surrounded by clear ice. Repeat this procedure if the depth of the mold permits. Allow the contents to become thoroughly frozen. When the refrigerated drink has been transferred to the punch bowl, reverse the ice mold container, wrap a hot wet towel around the metal until the ice is disengaged, and float it in this position on the drink.

To make decorative ice cubes for individual drinks, see 42.

ICE PUNCH BOWLS

Next, we show a punch bowl which is ice itself—particularly useful if you wish to dilute a cold drink as little as possible. Place in the kitchen sink a 50-pound cube of ice. Choose a round metal bowl of at least 3-quart capacity. Chip out a small depression in the center of the ice block and set the bowl over it. Fill the bowl with boiling water, being careful not to spill any on the ice beneath. As the heat of the bowl melts the ice, stir the water; and as the water cools, empty and refill the bowl, each time bailing out the depression in the ice, until the desired volume is displaced. Now, set the ice block where you wish to dispense the drink, moving it onto a waterproof tray or a leakproof square of heavy-duty aluminum foil. The foil square should be a couple of inches larger than the block, with the edges turned up about 1½ inches all around to form a channel. Any crudities can be masked by greenery or flowers. The "ice bowl" may, of course, be utilized equally well for serving sherbets and mixing cocktails.

A subtle flavor can be imparted to punches by steeping in the basic mix, during the lagering period, slices of peeled seeded cucumber, then removing them before the drink is further processed. Sometimes a few dashes of bitters will confer "the old one-two" on an otherwise flabby punch. However you serve party drinks, go easy on decorative heavy fruit trimmings in the bowl itself.

PLANTER'S PUNCH

The difficulty with this drink, we have discovered, is that—in the ideal form we now present it—it has become complicated for single-drink construction. Accordingly, we have moved it to this part of the chapter: first, because it really should be shared with others; second, because we hope, having done so, you may go to the trouble of putting together, on occasion, an improvised approximation just for yourself.

Mix in a large pitcher or bowl:

2 cups dark Jamaica rum
2 cups curaçao
8 cups light rum
6-oz. can frozen pineapple juice concentrate
6-oz. can frozen orange juice concentrate
6-oz. can frozen limeade concentrate
10-oz. frozen lemonade concentrate

Test for sweetness, using, if desired, remaining:

(2 oz. lemonade)

Fill tall glasses three-fourths full with crushed ice. Pour punch mixture to within ¾ inch of top. Decorate with pineapple chunk, slice of orange, strawberry or maraschino cherry. Serve with straws. The above formula makes a little more than a gallon and, being hefty to start with, should make 20 servings.

FISH HOUSE PUNCH

Mix in punch bowl:

1 cup Sugar Syrup, 48
1 cup lemon juice
1 bottle dark rum
1 bottle light rum
1 bottle brandy
7 cups water
½ cup peach brandy

If peach liqueur is used instead of peach brandy, the amount of syrup should be reduced to taste. Some recipes for this famous punch use strong tea instead of water.

BOWLE

A German favorite that may be made with any of a variety of fruits.

Slice and place in a large bowl one of the following fruits:

6 ripe unpeeled peaches or 8 ripe unpeeled apricots or 1 sliced pineapple or 1 quart strawberries

Sprinkle over the fruit:

1 cup powdered sugar

Pour over mixture:

1½ cups Madeira or sherry

Allow to stand 4 hours or longer. Stir, then pour over a block of ice in a bowl. Add:

4 bottles dry white wine

CHAMPAGNE PUNCH

Most punches are traditionally mixed with plain rather than carbonated water. When carbonated water is a component, the drink becomes a **cup.** Champagne Punch, sacred to weddings, occupies middle ground.

Peel, slice, crush and place in a large bowl:

3 ripe pineapples

Cover pineapple and juice with:

1 lb. powdered sugar

Let mixture stand, covered, for 1 hour. Add:

2 cups lemon juice
½ cup curaçao
½ cup maraschino
2 cups brandy
2 cups light rum

Stir and let stand for 4 hours. Place in a punch bowl with a block of ice. Stir to blend and chill. Just before serving, add:

4 bottles chilled champagne

WHISKY OR BRANDY CUP

Slice, place in a large bowl and crush:

2 cups fresh pineapple

Add:

1 quart fresh strawberries

Sprinkle over the fruit:

¾ lb. powdered sugar

Pour over mixture:

2 cups dark rum

Allow mixture to stand, covered, for 4 hours. Add:

2 cups lemon juice
1½ cups orange juice
1 cup grenadine
2 bottles bourbon or brandy

Place in punch bowl with block of ice. Stir to blend and chill. Just before serving, add:

2 quarts chilled carbonated water or dry ginger ale

If you like a predominant rum flavor, substitute for the fruit-steeping ingredient above:

1½ cups brandy

and for the basic ingredient:

2 bottles light rum

In this as in other punch bowl drinks, it is wise to test the mix for flavor and sweetness before adding the diluent.

RUM CASSIS CUP

Mix in a punch bowl:

2½ bottles light rum
2½ cups dry vermouth
2½ cups crème de cassis

Add block of ice. Pour over the ice:

2 quarts carbonated water

CLARET CUP

Slice, place in large bowl and crush:

1 cup fresh pineapple

Peel, halve and add:

4 ripe peaches
½ cup brandy

Sprinkle over mixture:

1 cup powdered sugar

Let stand for 4 hours. Add:

1 cup lemon juice
2 cups orange juice
½ cup maraschino
½ cup curaçao
2 bottles claret or other red wine

Chill the mixture for 1 hour; remove peaches and pour over a block of ice in a punch bowl. Stir and add:

2 quarts carbonated water

RHINE WINE CUP

Mix in punch bowl:

1 cup Sugar Syrup, 48
2 cups lemon juice
1 cup brandy
2 cups dry sherry
1 cup strong tea
3 bottles Rhine wine or other dry white wine
2 cups thinly sliced, peeled, seeded cucumbers

After 20 minutes, remove cucumber. Add a large block of ice and pour over it:

1 quart carbonated water

MAY WINE

Another German drink, dedicated to springtime and featuring fresh waldmeister or sweet woodruff, 587, which, incidentally, may be grown in a shady corner of your backyard.

Place in a bowl:

12 sprigs young waldmeister
1¼ cups powdered sugar
1 bottle Moselle or other dry white wine
(1 cup brandy)

Cover this mixture for 30 minutes, ➤ no longer. Remove the waldmeister. Stir contents of bowl thoroughly and pour over a block of ice in a punch bowl. Add:

3 bottles Moselle
1 quart carbonated water or champagne

Thinly sliced oranges, sticks of pineapple and, most appropriately of all, sprigs of waldmeister may be used to decorate the "Maitrank."

★ EGGNOG IN QUANTITY

I. A rich and extravagant version that is correspondingly good. Some people like to add a little more spirit to the following recipes, remembering Mark Twain's observation that "too much of anything is bad, but too much whisky is just enough." See note on uncooked eggs, 743. Beat separately until light in color:

12 egg yolks

Beat in gradually:

1 lb. confectioners' sugar

Add very slowly, beating constantly:

2 cups dark rum, brandy, bourbon or rye

These liquors may each form the basic ingredient of the nog or may be combined to taste. Let mixture stand covered for 1 hour to dispel the "eggy" taste. Add, beating constantly:

2 to 4 cups of liquor chosen
2 quarts whipping cream
(1 cup peach brandy)

Refrigerate covered for 3 hours. Beat until stiff ➤ but not dry:

8 to 12 egg whites

Fold them lightly into the other ingredients. Serve the eggnog sprinkled with:

Freshly grated nutmeg

II. Less powerful, less fluffy than the preceding nog, and a boon to the creamless householder. Beat until light in color:

12 eggs

Beat in gradually:

1 lb. confectioners' sugar
½ teaspoon salt
¼ cup vanilla

Stir in:

8 cups evaporated milk

diluted with:

3 cups water

Stir in:

4 cups dark rum, brandy, bourbon or rye

Cover the nog closely and let it ripen in the refrigerator for 24 hours. Stir again and serve sprinkled with:

Freshly grated nutmeg

★ TOM AND JERRY IN QUANTITY

See note on uncooked eggs, 743. Beat until stiff ➤ but not dry, cover and set aside:

1 dozen egg whites

Beat separately until light in color:

1 dozen egg yolks

Into the yolks, beat gradually:

¾ cup powdered sugar
2 teaspoons each ground allspice, cinnamon and cloves

Fold seasoned yolks into whites. Into each of twenty 8-ounce china mugs, place 2 tablespoons egg mixture and:

½ jigger lukewarm brandy
1 jigger lukewarm dark rum

Fill each mug with:

Very hot water, milk or coffee

Stir vigorously until drink foams. Dust top with:

Grated nutmeg

★ GLOGG

Twenty 6-Ounce Servings

Heat separately in stainless steel pans ➤ but do not boil:

2 quarts claret
2 quarts aquavit

Place in the hot claret:

Peel of 1 orange

and also a silver tea ball holding:

Seeds from 4 cardamom pods
12 whole cloves

In a silver punch bowl, place:

16 lumps sugar

Pour over it 2 cups of the heated aquavit and ignite it. While it is still burning, pour in, so as to extinguish the flame, the rest of the aquavit and the hot wine. Meanwhile place in individual heated mugs:

3 or 4 whole blanched almonds
3 or 4 seeded raisins

Fill the mugs with the hot mixture and serve at once.

★ MULLED WINE OR NEGUS IN QUANTITY

Make a syrup by boiling for 5 minutes:

2½ cups sugar
1¼ cups water
4 dozen whole cloves
6 sticks cinnamon
3 crushed nutmegs
Peel of 3 lemons, 2 oranges

Strain syrup. Add to it:

4 cups hot lemon or lime juice

Heat well ➤ but do not boil, and add:

4 bottles red wine or Madeira, port or sherry

Serve very hot with slices of:

Lemon and pineapple

★ WASSAIL

The best time to "come a-wassailing" is, of course, Christmas week.

Core and bake, 130:

1 dozen apples

Combine in a saucepan and boil for 5 minutes:

1 cup water
4 cups sugar
1 tablespoon grated nutmeg
2 teaspoons ground ginger
½ teaspoon ground mace
6 whole cloves
6 allspice berries
1 stick cinnamon

Beat until stiff ➤ but not dry:

1 dozen egg whites

Beat separately until light in color:

1 dozen egg yolks

Fold whites into yolks, using large bowl. Strain sugar and spice mixture into eggs, combining quickly. Bring almost to boiling point separately:

4 bottles sherry or Madeira
2 cups brandy

Incorporate the hot wine with the spice and egg mixture, beginning slowly and stirring briskly with each addition. Toward the end of this process, add the brandy. Now, just before serving and while the mixture is still foaming, add the baked apples.

Wassail can also be made with a combination of beer and wine, preferably sherry, in which case the proportion should be roughly 4 of beer to 1 of sherry.

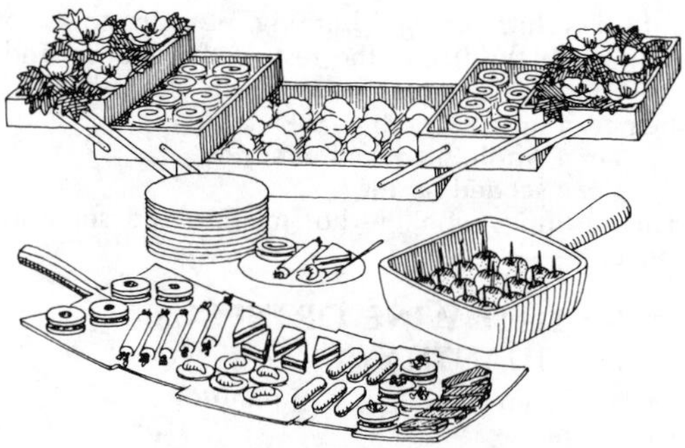

CANAPÉS AND TEA SANDWICHES

In contrast to hors d'oeuvre, which follow in the next chapter, canapés have their own built-in bread or pastry component and often resemble very small tea sandwiches. Since the making is similar, they are discussed here together. For additional fillings in sandwiches served as luncheon entrées and for heartier large sandwiches, see 269.

Illustrated above on the long leaf-tray is a varied assortment. Beginning at the handle end are, first, several two-tiered sandwiches, the top layer of which is doughnut-shaped, so that the filling is partially revealed. Next come those perennial favorites—watercress sandwiches—rolled in the thinnest of buttered bread; followed by some two-toned triangles and open-faced cucumber disks garnished with tiny shrimp and seafood-filled barquettes; crab-meat sandwiches garnished with parsley; and, finally, strips of toasted bread filled with mushrooms. Although a set piece like this laden big leaf creates a sensation when initially presented, it loses effect if some of its contents manage to survive the first round. For this reason it is often better practice to serve on smaller platters which can be quickly replenished. This is especially true for heated or toasted items, as shown on the right in an attractive heatproof ceramic dish with a handle for easy passing.

The upper tiers of the extended oriental box are filled with mayapple blossoms and ivy for double duty as a centerpiece. In the other trays are small cream puff shells, 646, filled with pâté, and filled sandwiches rolled like snails, 69.

Because a gay and festive presentation of canapés and tea sandwiches is so desirable, we suggest ways in which breads and pastries can be made to look their best, by methods either fast and furious or more leisurely and elaborate.

It is often easier to make small sandwiches in quantity ➤ by working with a whole loaf rather than with individual slices. A number of methods of cutting and combining different breads are illustrated. In several instances the crusts have been removed and the bread cut horizontally. It is possible to get six or seven long slices from the loaf and then spread the entire surface before stacking and shaping. A variety of forms cut economically from a single big sandwich base is sketched below. Parti-colored sandwiches can be produced by combining white, whole wheat, rye and brown bread.

Rolled sandwiches may be made quickly from long thin slices. A number of other shapes are illustrated at left. Lower left are two-layer sandwiches, the top layer of which is doughnut-shaped to allow the color of the filling to show through. On 67, lower right, successive thin bread or sausage slices are shown bound with a filling and cut in pie-shaped wedges, 86.

When making sandwiches of any kind in quantity ➤ time is saved by setting up an assembly line and using mass-production techniques. Line up bread slices in rows. Place dabs of seasoned butters or mayonnaise on one row, filling on the next. Then do the final spreading by bringing the fillings and butters well out to the edges. Put hard butter or mayonnaise twice through a grinder with other ingredients and use a coarse blade. For closed sandwiches, do all the assembling, stacking, cutting and packaging in turn. For open-faced sandwiches, cut garnishes just before serving and keep them from drying out by placing them in plastic bags. After the base is spread, complete the garnishing of one type, then of another, before arranging for presentation.

PREPARING AND KEEPING SANDWICHES

➤ A few preliminary steps help toward serving sandwiches in prime condition. Have ready foil; moistened, wrung-out cloths; transparent self-sealing tissue, or plastic bags. Refrigerate double sandwiches, wrapped, without delay.

Open-faced sandwiches, if made of materials heavy in fat, may be quick-frozen and can then be wrapped without damage to their decorations or surfaces. Store in boxes to keep them free from the weight of other foods. Also place them away from freezer coils or fast-freeze area. For more details, see 829. ➤ It is often preferable to freeze the fillings alone and make up these fancy sandwiches shortly before serving.

When preparing in advance sandwiches that include watery materials like lettuce not suitable for freezing, be sure that any moist or juicy filling is put on bread well spread with a firm layer of butter or heavy mayonnaise, so that the bread will not get soggy. If tomato or cucumber slices are used, see that they are cut and allowed to drain well on a rack before putting them in the sandwiches.

To avoid excessively dry bread in preparing canapés on toast, proceed as follows for open-faced types: toast bread on one side under broiler; apply spread or topping to toasted side; and return to oven until topping is warmed through. For double-toasted sandwiches, toast under broiler one side only of each slice; spread topping between toasted sides; return to oven to toast the top untoasted surface; and serve—toasted side up. For toasted canapés which must be prepared more than a few minutes in advance, use Melba toast, 636, and heat briefly in a moderate oven just before serving.

BREAD FOR SANDWICHES

The number of sandwiches to a loaf of bread is hard to gauge because of shape variations, but from a 1-pound loaf of sandwich bread you can expect at least 20 slices. Allow about 1 pound butter for 3 to 4 pounds of sandwich loaf. Do not have the loaf presliced, but slice it thin yourself. The number of sandwiches to allow for each guest is even harder to judge, although 8 to 10 small snacks, either sandwiches or canapés, are not too much to count per person.

➤ To avoid raggedy sandwiches, use a finely textured bread. Otherwise, try chilling or freezing ordinary bread before cutting. This procedure makes for more practical handling throughout, particularly in preparing rolled shapes, which should be very thin and made of very fresh bread. Other sandwiches are easier to make if the bread is one day old. Cut fresh or frozen bread with a very sharp hot knife. Remember, though, that all bread which has been frozen dries out quickly after thawing and that precautions should be taken to keep the sandwiches as moist as possible. Have spreads at about 70° to protect bread from pulling or tearing. If the spread happens to be an aspic, keep it in place by applying to the bread a very thin preliminary coating of mayonnaise.

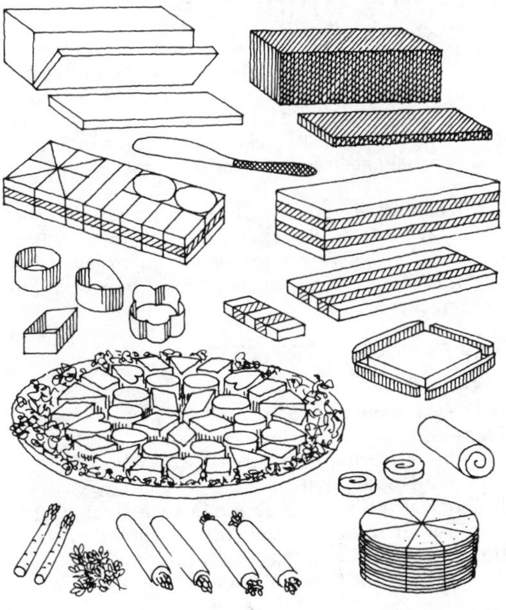

SANDWICH SHAPES

It is surprising how a few fancy sandwiches with attractive garnishes, 269, will help to perk up a platter. A combination of open and closed sandwiches gives variety to the tray. Sometimes medium-sized oblong trays filled with alternating rows of similarly cut but contrastingly spread open-faced sandwiches—placed closely together—make a quick and pleasant change from large platters more sparsely arranged with fancy sandwiches. Rolled sandwiches with sprigs of cress or parsley projecting—placed like the spokes of a wheel—make a charming border for a platter.

ROLLED SANDWICHES

Freeze:

Fresh unsliced sandwich bread

Remove crusts and slice as thin as possible with a hot sharp knife. Spread the bread with:

A softened filling

We particularly enjoy as a filling:

(Cream cheese mixed with cucumber and onion juice)

Be sure the filling goes out to the edges, so the roll will be well sealed. When the bread is completely thawed, roll the sandwiches. Tuck into the ends, but allow to protrude:

Cress or parsley sprigs

➤ Wrap firmly and refrigerate, so the sandwiches will hold their cylindrical shape when served.

RIBBON SANDWICHES

Cut the crusts from:

White bread
Dark bread

Spread the slices with:

Butter or Cream Cheese Spreads, 70, 71

Place 3 to 5 slices of bread alternately in stacks. Cut them into bars, squares or triangles, see illustration, above left.

FLOWER CANAPÉS

If you have an herb garden, many enchanting sandwiches can be made from the small-scaled leaves and blossoms. Or in winter, cut:

Small rounds or squares of bread

Flatten with a rolling pin before spreading with:

Soft cream cheese

Place across each sandwich a very narrow:

Strip of green pepper or stem of chive or parsley

This represents a stem. Place at the top to form the flower:

A slice of stuffed olive or a fancy cut of carrot or radish

Cut into lengthwise slices to form leaves:

Small sweet-sour pickles

Place the pickle slices opposite each other on the green pepper stem.

★ CHRISTMAS CANAPÉS

I. Cut into 2-inch rounds:

Thin bread slices

Spread the rounds with:

A cream cheese mixture, 71

Cut into tiny rounds, about ⅛-inch:

Maraschino cherries, pimiento, cranberries—or use tiny red decorettes

Chop until fine:

Parsley

Make a narrow ring of the parsley around each piece of bread. Dot it at intervals with the red rounds to suggest a holly wreath.

II. Or, use:

A sprig of parsley

shaped like a tree and dot it with the small red "balls" described above.

ZOO SANDWICHES

For very young children's parties, make closed double or triple sandwiches in animal shapes using fancy cookie cutters. Triple-layered sandwiches can be made to stand upright on the plate as shown below.

SANDWICH LOAVES

These can even be a meal by themselves—an excellent luncheon dish with coffee and a dessert, and, when made in individual sizes, real charmers. As a decorative center for a birthday buffet, use one large loaf, as shown above; or make an individual loaf for each guest, seen above on the right, and group the loaves around a pile of gaily wrapped gifts.

I. Cut the crusts from:

A loaf of unsliced white or whole wheat bread

Cut the loaf into 3 or 4 lengthwise slices. Butter the inner sides of the slices and spread them with a layer of:

Chicken, shrimp, ham, egg or salmon salad

a layer of:

Drained crushed pineapple and cream cheese

a layer of:

Drained sliced tomatoes, lettuce or watercress

or any appetizing combination of salad or sandwich ingredients. If it suits your filling, add some:

Anchovy paste or curry powder

to the cream cheese. Be sure to cut the bread thin enough and spread the fillings thick enough to keep the bread from dominating. Wrap the loaf firmly in a moist towel, chill well, unwrap and place on a platter. Cover with:

Softened cream cheese, smooth cottage cheese, or Mayonnaise Collée, 368

Individual slices cut from the finished loaf are shown above.

II. This holds well if prepared in advance. Cut the top and bottom from:

An unsliced large round rye loaf

and reserve them as the base and lid for a crust container. Using as much of the bread as possible, carefully cut out in one piece a straight-sided cylinder from the soft center, leaving a crust ring. Then slice this cylinder of bread horizontally into 6 thin slices. Coat the tops of the second, fourth and sixth slices with butter and with not too moist:

Seasoned fillings

Cover the spread slices with the first, third and fifth slices. Keeping the shape of the large cylinder orderly, cut it into narrow wedges. Now, carefully place the cut cylinder on the bottom crust and surround with the crust ring. Insert picks around the outer edge of the crust bottom to impale the crust ring and keep it from sliding. Cover with the top crust as a lid. Wrap and refrigerate until ready to serve.

BREAD OR OTHER BASES FOR CANAPÉS

Use coarse ryes, whole wheats and cheese breads from the Yeast and Quick Bread section, 599, and suggestions from Uses for Ready-Baked Breads, 635. There are good cracker suggestions in Soups, 195, and suggestions for various pastries in Pies, 638–649.

Or use small versions of luncheon sandwiches, 269; Ravioli, 216; Bouchées, 645; or Tarts or Barquettes, below. Don't forget the many available "ethnic" bases, like tortillas or crisp thin Japanese rice crackers.

TARTS AND TARTLETS FOR CANAPÉS

I. Preheat oven to 425°.

Prepare:

Biscuit Dough, 632, or Pie Dough, 640

Roll or pat it until it is about ⅛ inch thick. Cut it into 3-inch squares. Place in the center of each square one of the fillings listed under:

Fillings for Pastry Canapés, 70

Moisten the corners of the dough lightly with water. Fold up the sides of the dough and pinch the corners to make a tart shape. Bake tarts about 10 minutes.

II. Or, fill the tart with:

A thin slice of cheese, 1½ x 2 inches

Top this with:

½ slice tomato

Season the tomato with:

A grating of pepper
A little salt
(A sprinkling of brown sugar)

Sprinkle the top with:

Cooked diced bacon

Bake as in I, above.

III. Fill with:

Hot spicy puréed spinach

Lay on it:

A smoked oyster

Brush with:

A little White Sauce I, 341

to which has been added:

Grated Swiss cheese

Bake as in I, above.

RICH COCKTAIL TART OR QUICHE

A physician in our family once took to task a scandalously obese patient. "But, doctor," said the patient plaintively, "one must offer the stomach something from time to time." This is a favorite offering in our family.

Preheat oven to 400°.

Prepare any unsweetened:

Pie Dough, 640

Shape into tiny tarts and bake about 5 minutes. Remove from oven. ➤ Lower heat to 325°. Fill each tart with 1 tablespoon of the following mixture:

1 beaten egg
¾ cup cream
2 teaspoons grated Parmesan cheese
(2 tablespoons sautéed mushrooms or crab meat)
½ teaspoon salt
A small pinch coriander

Bake the tarts 15 minutes or until the quiche has set. Keep them hot and toasty in an electric skillet. For other Quiche recipes, see 254.

BARQUETTES FOR CANAPÉS

I. Preheat oven to 425°.

Prepare:

Biscuit Dough, 632, or
Pie Dough, 640

Roll until it is about ⅛ inch thick. Since barquettes are shaped like a scow or flat-bottomed boat, but with pointed ends, use either a barquette mold or something similarly shaped to form the pastry. Place in the barquettes a:

Filling for Pastry Canapés, 70, suitable for heating

Bake 10 to 12 minutes.

II. Line the bottoms of the baked barquette shells with a coating of:

Mayonnaise

Make a pattern of:

Chilled caviar
Pearl onions

Coat the top with:

Aspic Glaze, 368

The aspic should be based on fish or chicken stock. Flavor with:

Lemon

Refrigerate several hours before serving.

STUFFED CHOUX, PUFF PASTE OR PÂTE SHELLS

I. Bake:

1-inch Choux Paste Shells, 646, or
Bouchées, 645

Split them on one side. Fill with one of the softer fillings, see:

Fillings for Pastry Canapés, 70

Reheat the puffs in a 425° oven.

II. Put into the base of a small cream puff shell a layer of:

Sweetened whipped cream

Lightly insert with the pointed end up:

A flawless ripe strawberry

III. Or, fill the puffs with:

Soft cream cheese
A dab of bright jelly

TURNOVERS, RISSOLES OR FRIED PIES

These triangular or crescent-shaped pastries make attractive canapés. If baked, they are **turnovers.** If deep-fat-fried, you may apply the homely title of **fried pies** or the more exotic one of **rissoles** or **empañadas.**

Roll to the thickness of ⅛ inch any:

Pie Crust, 640

Cut it into 2½-inch rounds or squares. Place in the center of each round any of the:

Fillings for Pastry Canapés, 70

Brush the edges of the rounds lightly with water. Fold the dough over into crescents. Be sure to seal the pastries very firmly if you are deep-fat frying, so that none of the filling escapes into and ruins the frying fat. Fry in deep fat heated to 365° until golden. For turnovers the tops of the pastries may be brushed with:

(1 egg yolk, diluted with 2 tablespoons cream)

Bake in a 400° oven until brown. Serve them around a large garnish of:

Fried Parsley, 314, or chervil

CANAPÉ SNAILS

If the approval of guests is to be taken as a criterion of excellence, this is the prize-winning canapé. It reminds us of a fellow guest who hesitated to help himself, saying, "Well, I shouldn't

—I've had two already." Which remark was capped by his hostess's brisk and crushing reply: "You've had six, but who's counting?"
Preheat oven to 425°.
Cut into very thin oblongs any:

Pie Crust, 640, or crustless soft bread

The bread will be easier to cut if wrapped in foil and chilled thoroughly. Spread the oblongs with:

Fillings for Pastry Canapés, right

Roll them like a jelly roll. Chill; cut in ½-inch slices and bake on a greased pan until light brown.

TACOS

This popular Mexican snack is called by many names in different parts of the country. Tacos are toasted tortillas cut into thirds and filled with hot or mildly seasoned ingredients. This mix is fairly mild. Sauté until golden brown:

1 finely chopped onion

in:

2 tablespoons butter

Add and simmer about 3 minutes:

½ cup tomato juice
3 peeled minced green chilis
1 cup shredded cooked chicken or cooked pork sausage meat
⅛ teaspoon thyme
1 teaspoon salt
Dash of cayenne

Set this filling aside. Now fry in deep fat heated to 380° until golden:

About 18 Tortillas, 629

Remove them from the fat and drain. Cut into thirds. Place 1 teaspoon of the above filling on each piece. Fold in half, secure with a pick and bake until almost crisp in a 450° oven.

GLAZED CANAPÉS AND SANDWICHES

Small glazed canapés are very showy for cocktail service and in larger sizes make a lovely luncheon plate when garnished with a salad. ➤ But they must be kept refrigerated, as they have a natural tendency to turn soggy.
Use:

Choux Paste Shells, 646, tartlets or fancy-shaped thin toasts

Coat these canapé bases first with:

Mayonnaise

Then spread them with:

Well-seasoned fish paste, turkey, drained tomato slices, ham strips or asparagus tips

You may sprinkle with:

(Chopped dill)

or any combination suitable for open-faced sandwiches. Cover with a ¼-inch to ⅜-inch layer of:

Well-seasoned Aspic Glaze, 368

using 1⅓ cups stock or vegetable juice, 1 tablespoon gelatin and 1 tablespoon lemon juice. Place the canapés on a rack. The aspic should be jelled to the thickness of heavy cream partially beaten. Allow it to coat the surface of the tart or envelop the canapé. Refrigerate at once and let the gelatin set 1 to 2 hours. Then serve as soon as possible.

FILLINGS FOR PASTRY CANAPÉS

Place in the center of the preceding pastry cases 1 teaspoon or more of one of the following ingredients:

Cheese Spreads, 71
Anchovy paste and soft cream cheese
Well-seasoned or marinated oysters
Mushrooms, heavily creamed and seasoned
Chicken or other croquette mixtures, highly seasoned
Chicken, lobster, crab or fish salad
Caviar and soft cream cheese
Liver sausage or braunschweiger, seasoned with catsup
Cooked sausage meat, seasoned with mustard
Sliced link sausages and stuffed olives
Deviled ham, cream cheese and catsup
Minced cooked clams or crab meat
Cooked calf brains with Hollandaise Sauce, 358
Curried shrimp or poultry
Thin slices of ham, smoked tongue or smoked sausage and cheese

BUTTER SPREADS

There are many ways of preparing flavorsome, quick sandwich spreads with a butter base. Beat the butter until soft. Add other ingredients gradually. Chill the butter mixture until it is of spreadable consistency or shape it attractively. For Butter Shapes, see 540.

Use one of the simple suggestions in this recipe or in the more elaborate Seasoned Butters, 349.
Beat until soft:

¼ cup butter

Add to the butter slowly one or more of the following:

½ teaspoon lemon juice
½ teaspoon Worcestershire sauce or ½ teaspoon dry mustard
½ teaspoon grated onion or minced garlic
(⅛ teaspoon lemon rind)

Additions to the butter mixture may be chosen from these fresh herbs and other ingredients—either chopped or made into a paste by using your mortar and pestle:

2 tablespoons parsley
2 tablespoons chives
1 tablespoon dill or fennel
1 tablespoon mixed herbs: basil, tarragon, burnet and chervil
2 tablespoons watercress
1 tablespoon nasturtium leaves
¼ cup soft or grated cheese: Parmesan or Romano
1 tablespoon anchovy or other fish paste
1 tablespoon horseradish
1 tablespoon olive paste

2 tablespoons Catsup, 847, or Chili Sauce, 847
1 tablespoon chutney
¼ teaspoon curry powder
Season to taste

⅄ SEAFOOD BUTTER

For a more economical form, see 351.
Put through a sieve or blender, or chop:
1 cup cooked shrimp, lobster, lobster coral, fish roe, etc.
¼ lb. butter
1 teaspoon or more lemon juice
A fresh grating of white pepper
Mold and chill to serve on an hors d'oeuvre platter or use as a spread.

DRIED HERBS IN WINE FOR BUTTER SPREADS

Combine:
2 tablespoons crushed dried herbs: thyme, basil, tarragon, chervil
½ cup dry white wine or lemon juice
Permit the herbs to soak for 2 hours or more. Follow the above recipe for Butter Spreads, adding the herb mixture to taste. Keep the rest to use combined with melted butter as a dressing for vegetables.

⅄ BLENDER MUSHROOM BUTTER

Sauté until golden brown:
½ lb. sliced mushrooms
in:
¼ cup butter
Put the mushrooms and butter into an electric blender and add:
½ cup soft butter
¼ teaspoon pepper
¼ teaspoon salt
3 tablespoons dry sherry or brandy
Blend until smooth.

NUT BUTTERS

I. Cream until soft enough to stir:
½ cup butter
Stir in:
1 cup finely ground pecans or walnuts
2 tablespoons Worcestershire sauce

II. ⅄ In electric blender combine:
1 to 2 tablespoons salad oil
1 cup salted peanuts, cashews or pecans

CREAM CHEESE SPREADS

What would we do without cream cheese?—the perfect emergency binder for one of the many taste-provokers listed below.
Rub a bowl with:
(Garlic)
Mash until soft and combine:
1 package cream cheese: 3 oz.
1 tablespoon cream or cultured sour cream
Add one or more of the following:
½ teaspoon onion juice
1 teaspoon chopped onion or chives
1 tablespoon lemon or lime juice
1 tablespoon finely chopped Fines Herbes, 572
1 tablespoon finely chopped parsley
1 tablespoon finely chopped celery or green pepper
¼ cup chopped ripe or pimiento-stuffed olives
1 tablespoon horseradish
3 tablespoons chopped crisp bacon, minced chipped beef or ground cooked ham
½ tablespoon anchovy or fish paste
½ cup shredded salted almonds or other nuts
1 tablespoon caviar
1 tablespoon chopped fresh marigold petals
Season with:
Salt, paprika or red pepper, if needed
For a tea canapé, use a:
Bar-le-Duc mixture, 757

CUCUMBER CREAM CHEESE SPREAD

Mash with a fork:
2 packages cream cheese: 6 oz.
Into a fine sieve or cheesecloth bag, grate:
1 medium-sized cucumber
1 onion
Press out the juice and combine with the cream cheese. Add:
Salt to taste
⅛ teaspoon hot pepper sauce
Add to spreading consistency:
Mayonnaise

CHEESE PUFF CANAPÉS

Preheat broiler.
Beat until very stiff:
2 egg whites
Fold in:
1 cup shredded American cheese
1 teaspoon Worcestershire sauce
½ teaspoon paprika
½ teaspoon dry mustard
Toast on one side:
Small rounds of bread or crackers
Spread the untoasted side with the cheese mixture. Place the canapés under a broiler for about 6 minutes, until the cheese is well puffed and brown.

ROQUEFORT SPREAD

This delicious spread keeps well and improves with age—better when 1 week old than when newly made.
Combine to a paste:
½ lb. Roquefort cheese
2 packages soft cream cheese: 6 oz. or use an 8-oz. package
2 tablespoons soft butter
(1 small grated onion)
1 tablespoon Worcestershire sauce

2 tablespoons dry sherry
Salt as needed

Keep the spread in a closely covered jar in the refrigerator. May be spread on crisp potato chips, crackers or toast rounds. Decorate with:

Radish slices and capers

PUFFED ROQUEFORT STICKS

Preheat broiler.
Remove crusts from:

4 slices bread several days old

Cut each slice into 4 strips and coat with:

Butter

Prepare:

3/4 cup White Sauce II, 341

Combine with:

2 oz. Roquefort cheese
1 beaten egg
Season to taste

Spread the sauce on the bread and run under the broiler about 5 minutes. Serve at once.

CHEESE SPREADS FOR TOASTED SANDWICHES OR CHEESE DREAMS

I. This practical sandwich spread will keep refrigerated a week or more.
Scald in a double boiler:

1/2 cup milk

Add:

1 beaten egg
1/4 teaspoon dry mustard
1/2 teaspoon salt
3/4 lb. diced American cheese

Cook these ingredients ➤ over, not in, boiling water 15 minutes. Stir constantly. When ready to use, spread the mixture between:

Rounds of bread

Place on each side of the canapés or sandwiches a generous dab of:

Butter

Toast in a 350° oven or under a broiler until crisp.

II. ⅄ This filling is more quickly made, but not so bland as the preceding one. Combine and stir to a smooth paste or blend in the electric blender:

2 cups soft shredded sharp cheese
1/2 teaspoon salt
A few grains cayenne
1 teaspoon prepared mustard
3 tablespoons cream or 1 to 2 tablespoons soft butter

Cut the crusts from:

Thin slices of white bread

Spread and roll the slices. Toast as in I. Serve the rolls very hot.

BACON AND CHEESE CANAPÉS

Preheat broiler.
Toast on one side:

Rounds of bread

Spread the untoasted side thickly with a mixture of:

2 cups shredded sharp cheese
2 slices minced crisp bacon
1/4 teaspoon dry mustard
A few grains cayenne
1 tablespoon Worcestershire sauce

Broil the canapés until cheese is melted.

CHUTNEY AND CHEESE CANAPÉS

Preheat broiler.
Cover:

Round crackers or toast

with:

Chutney, 846
A thin slice of American cheese

Broil the crackers to melt the cheese.

TOASTED CHEESE LOGS OR ROLLS

Preheat oven to 350°.
Trim the crusts from:

Thin slices of bread

Place on each slice, not quite covering it:

A thin slice of cheese

or, place on each slice of bread:

An oblong block of cheese

Spread the cheese lightly with:

Anchovy paste, prepared mustard or horseradish

Gather up 2 opposite corners and fasten them with a pick, or roll the bread. Brush the outsides of the logs with:

Melted butter

Toast them in the oven until light brown. Serve piping hot on picks.

SWEET TEA SPREADS

For those of us equipped with a "sweet tooth," it is always a welcome sight to behold on the canapé tray something less acid, spicy or tart than the usual fare. And for less venturesome nibblers, don't forget Nut Butters, 71, and Cinnamon Toast, 636.

I. Moisten:

Cream cheese

with:

Cream

Add:

Chopped ginger or dried apricots
Chopped almonds

This makes a great partner for:

Brown or whole wheat bread

II. Spread on small toasts:

Bar-le-Duc, 757

III. Combine:

1 package soft cream cheese: 3 oz.
Grated rind of 1 orange or 2 tablespoons orange or ginger marmalade
1/4 teaspoon salt
1/8 teaspoon paprika

Spread:
Thin slices of bread
with:
Mayonnaise or butter
Cover with the cheese and:
Toasted chopped pecan meats

IV. Combine:
Equal parts soft butter and honey

V. Spread toast with:
Butter
Apple butter
Sprinkle with:
Grated cheese
Run under the broiler until the cheese is toasted.

HARD-COOKED EGG SPREADS

I. Combine and mix to a paste with a fork:
2 hard-cooked eggs
1 tablespoon or more cultured sour cream
¼ teaspoon salt
⅛ teaspoon paprika
1 tablespoon chopped chives
(1 teaspoon lemon juice)
Garnish the canapé with a row of:
(Sliced stuffed olives)

II. Combine:
4 chopped hard-cooked eggs
1 cup chopped pecan meats
2 dozen chopped stuffed olives
Well-seasoned mayonnaise

III. Combine:
Chopped hard-cooked eggs
Minced anchovies
Minced celery
Moisten these ingredients with:
Mayonnaise

IV. Marinate 30 minutes:
Shrimp or crab meat
in:
French dressing or lemon juice
Drain, chop and combine, by making into a paste with:
Mayonnaise
A dash Worcestershire sauce
Hard-cooked eggs

V. Combine:
Finely chopped hard-cooked eggs
A liver pâté, 495–496

ROLLED ASPARAGUS CANAPÉS OR SANDWICHES

Cut the crusts from:
Thin slices of bread
Spread them thinly with:
Butter and mayonnaise
Sprinkle lightly with:
Chopped chives
Place on each slice a well-drained:
Asparagus tip
Roll the canapés. Wrap the rolls in foil until ready to serve. These sandwiches may be toasted.

MUSHROOM CANAPÉS

Sauté:
Mushrooms, 308
Mince the mushrooms. Prepare:
White Sauce II, 341
Make half as much sauce as mushrooms. Season with:
Salt and paprika
Freshly grated nutmeg
Combine sauce and mushrooms. When cold, add a little:
Whipped cream
Heap these ingredients on:
Small rounds of bread or toast
Garnish the canapés with:
Paprika and parsley
Serve immediately or run under the broiler.

ONION AND PARSLEY CANAPÉS

Parsley tends to neutralize onion odors. Use it profusely in this decorative sandwich and preserve group charisma.
Make a filling of:
1 grated onion
1 cup stiff mayonnaise
¼ teaspoon Worcestershire sauce
A few drops hot pepper sauce
⅛ teaspoon turmeric
Put the filling between small rounds of:
Brioche-type bread
or a bread that will not become soggy. Spread the outside edges of the sandwich with:
Mayonnaise
and roll these edges in:
Finely chopped parsley

BLACK RADISH CANAPÉ

Peel and mince:
2 black radishes
Combine with:
1 small minced onion
2 tablespoons cultured sour cream or yogurt
1 tablespoon lemon juice
⅛ teaspoon salt
Just before serving, spread on thin slices of:
Pumpernickel

TOMATO OR CUCUMBER SANDWICHES

Very attractive for a spring tea party. To keep these sandwiches from becoming soggy, drain the sliced tomatoes and cucumbers well in advance of use.
Cut:
Small rounds of bread
Spread them lightly with:
Butter

Place on each round, covering it completely:

Small round of peeled sliced tomato or a large round of pared sliced cucumber or both

or you may hollow out the cucumber before slicing and fill each hollow slice with:

(A tiny shrimp)

Decorate each sandwich with a generous:

Dab of mayonnaise

Garnish the mayonnaise with a tiny sprig of:

Lemon thyme

CAVIAR AND ONION CANAPÉS

I. Sauté in butter:

Rounds of thin toast

Combine and spread on the toast equal parts of:

Caviar
Finely chopped onion

Season with:

Lemon juice

Garnish the edges of the canapés with:

Riced hard-cooked egg yolks

Top with:

(Tiny shrimp or prawns)

II. Sauté:

Chopped onions

in:

Butter

Make a mound of the chopped onions on a round of:

Pumpernickel

In the scooped-out center, put some:

Cultured sour cream

and a dab of:

Caviar

CAVIAR AND CUCUMBER CANAPÉS

Dip:

Slices of cucumber

in:

French Dressing, 360

Drain them. Prepare:

Small rounds of buttered toast

Peel, then slice crosswise:

Mild onions

Separate the slices into rings. Place a ring on each round of toast, so that it will form a curb. Place a slice of cucumber in each ring. Cover the cucumber with:

Small mounds of caviar, seasoned with lemon and onion juice or chives

Garnish the canapés with:

Capers
Riced hard-cooked egg

SMOKED TONGUE CANAPÉ

Cut thin slices of:

Smoked tongue

to fit squares of:

Melba or rye toast

Spread toast with:

Bercy Butter, 350

Place on it one of the tongue slices and cap with a dab of:

Freshly grated horseradish

DEVILED OR POTTED CHICKEN SPREAD

About 2½ Cups

Grind together 3 times, using a fine blade:

2 cups cooked chicken
¼ cup boiled or baked ham
⅛ teaspoon nutmeg
A pinch of white pepper
½ teaspoon salt
3 tablespoons butter
1 tablespoon lemon juice or
½ teaspoon lemon zest, 571

You may further press this through a fine wire sieve or knead gently before storing, covered and refrigerated. It will keep longer if the top is coated with Clarified Butter, 349. When serving, garnish with:

Chopped fresh herbs

DEVILED OR POTTED HAM SPREAD

About 3 Cups

Preheat oven to 350°.

Grind 3 times with a fine blade:

1 lb. lean ham
¼ lb. ham fat

Season with:

A pinch of cayenne
⅛ teaspoon each mace, nutmeg and pepper

Put the mixture in a buttered 5 x 9-inch bread pan. Cover with foil. Bake about 45 minutes. When cool, cover top with Clarified Butter, 349, and store refrigerated. Remove butter before serving.

CHICKEN OR HAM SALAD SPREAD

Chop until fine:

1 cup cooked chicken or ham

Add:

2 tablespoons finely chopped celery
¼ cup chopped blanched almonds or other nutmeats
(¼ cup chopped pineapple or ½ cup finely chopped green olives)

Combine these ingredients with sufficient:

Highly seasoned mayonnaise

to make a paste that will spread easily.

SMALL PIZZA CANAPÉ

Preheat broiler.

Serve sectioned pizzas, 610, as canapés. If you are in a hurry, substitute for pizza dough:

Biscuits or small English muffins

Tear either in two horizontally and toast the flat sides under the broiler; spread on the reverse a mixture of:

1½ teaspoons Chili Sauce, 847
Strips of sharp cheddar or grated Mozzarella or Gruyère cheese
⅛ teaspoon oregano

Top with an:
Anchovy fillet
and drizzle over all:
A little olive oil
Toast 5 inches below broiler element until the cheese is thoroughly melted.

FOIE GRAS AND LIVER CANAPÉS

You may serve pâté in a crust, sliced, as a canapé, 494; cut it into rondelles on toast; or incorporate it into Brioches, 615, Bouchées, 645, pastry, barquettes or turnovers. See 493–496 for a number of versions of liver pastes, soufflés and pâtés—simple and complex.

LIVER SAUSAGE CANAPÉS

I. Combine and mix to a paste:
¼ lb. liver sausage
1 or more tablespoons cream
(1 tablespoon brandy)
Fold in lightly:
¼ cup or more chopped watercress
Serve on rye bread or toast.

II. Make a paste of:
½ cup liver sausage
2 tablespoons tomato paste
(A few drops Worcestershire sauce)
Spread on thinly cut crustless bread, then roll and toast.

CLAM PUFFS

Try also some of the dips on 89 as ingredients in this recipe.
Preheat broiler.
Combine:
1 package cream cheese: 3 oz.
2 tablespoons whipping cream
1 cup minced clams
¼ teaspoon mustard
1 tablespoon Worcestershire sauce
¼ teaspoon salt
½ teaspoon grated onion or onion juice
Heap the mixture on toast rounds and run under broiler.

CRAB OR LOBSTER PUFF BALLS

Serve these only if you have time to whip the cream and fill the puff shells at the last minute. The charm of this canapé lies in the bland creaminess of the filling and the dry crunchiness of the casing.
Shred or dice:
Cooked crab or lobster meat
Combine lightly 2 parts of the chilled seafood with:
1 part stiffly whipped seasoned cream
Put the mixture into:
Small cream puff shells, 646
Sprinkle the tops with:
Chopped parsley and basil
Serve open or put puff lid on top after filling. Good hot or cold, but serve promptly—and we mean at once.

SHRIMP PUFFS

24 Puffs

Preheat broiler.
Chop:
12 cooked shrimp
Whip until stiff:
1 egg white
Fold in:
¼ cup shredded cheese
⅛ teaspoon salt
⅛ teaspoon paprika
A few grains red pepper
½ cup mayonnaise
and the shrimp. Heap these ingredients lightly onto crackers or rounds of toast. Broil the puffs until light brown. Serve hot.

LOBSTER CANAPÉ

Combine:
Chopped cooked lobster meat
Chopped hard-cooked eggs
Chopped cucumbers
Well-seasoned mayonnaise
Serve on:
Barquettes, 69

CREAMED SEAFOOD CANAPÉS

A little messy, but definitely in the class of what the French call **amuse-geules** or, freely translated, palate-teasers.
Preheat broiler.
Combine:
½ lb. cooked oysters, lobster, crab or tuna meat
½ lb. Sautéed Mushrooms, 308
1 cup rich White Sauce II, 341
1 tablespoon finely chopped green pepper
1 tablespoon chopped pimiento
¼ teaspoon curry powder or
1 teaspoon Worcestershire sauce
3 tablespoons dry white wine
Salt and pepper
Heap the mixture on rounds of:
Toast
which may be spread with:
Anchovy paste
Sprinkle the tops with:
Au Gratin II, 553
Broil the canapés until slightly brown. Serve at once.

MARINATED HERRING AND ONIONS ON TOAST

Drain:
Marinated herring
Place fillets on:
Squares or rounds of toast

Cover with:
Thin slices of Bermuda onion
Sprinkle with:
Chopped parsley or watercress
Serve promptly.

ANGELS ON HORSEBACK

May also be served as a savory, see 755.
Preheat oven to 400°.
Toast lightly and butter:
Small rounds of bread
Wrap:
Large drained oysters
with:
Very thin pieces of bacon
You may lightly spread the inner surface of the bacon with:
(Anchovy paste)
Secure with picks and place the canapés in a pan. Bake about 3 minutes or long enough to crisp the bacon. Drain well. Remove the picks and serve on the toast.

SMOKED SALMON CANAPÉS

If the salmon you are served is pale pink and not salty, it has been truly smoked; but if it is a strong red in color and very salty, smoke salt extract, 570, has been used in the processing. Salmon for canapés should be sliced across the grain as thinly as possible. It is delicious when served garnished with cucumber or egg. The thin slices make an ideal lining for tarts or barquettes.

I. Place on crackers or squares of toast very thin slices of:
Smoked salmon
Dust with:
Freshly ground pepper
Sprinkle with:
Lemon juice
Serve at room temperature.

II. Or, top with a slice of:
Stuffed olive
Brush the canapés with:
Mustard or Aspic Glaze, 368

III. Or, top the salmon with:
Guacamole, 83
and serve on toasted rounds.

IV. Or, garnish with a mixture of:
Hard-cooked egg yolk, grated onion and capers

SARDINE CANAPÉ ROLLS

Preheat oven to 400°.
Mash with a fork:
12 skinless, boneless sardines
Add:
½ teaspoon Worcestershire sauce
½ teaspoon Tomato Catsup, 847
1 tablespoon finely cut celery or onion
1 tablespoon chopped stuffed olives
Moisten these ingredients until they are of spreading consistency with:
Mayonnaise or French Dressing, 360
Season with:
Salt and pepper
Cut the crusts from:
Thin slices of white bread
Spread the sardine mixture on the bread. Roll the slices and secure them with picks. Toast the canapés until lightly browned and serve very hot.

HORS D'OEUVRE

Hors d'oeuvre and canapés are types of food served with drinks. The canapé, 66, sits invitingly on its own little couch of crouton or pastry tidbit, while the hors d'oeuvre is a free agent, so to speak, gregarious and ready to meet up with whatever bread or cracker is presented separately.

If hors d'oeuvre and canapés are served at a cocktail party, they become an end in themselves, and so may be more varied and substantial than when they are designed as appetizers. The illustration above shows an assemblage of such hors d'oeuvre. What a fillip to festivity when you get out an heirloom caviar server like the one above, or the compartmented dishes you triumphantly bid on at last month's antiques auction, and fill them with smoked salmon curls, toasted nuts, olives, cheese-stuffed celery or green pepper slices, marinated mushrooms and buttered radishes! Hot hors d'oeuvre are represented by the candle-warmed dish of quenelles, 205. And you may lighten the effect of more formal containers by including on the buffet table a handsome big Savoy cabbage—a "centerpiece" all in itself—scooped out, 78, to hold a shellfish dip, 91, and festooned with small shrimp. When you add a few canapés of your choice, and put within easy reach some of the delightful breadstuffs now commercially available, you will already have gone a long way toward confounding that jaded circuit-goer who characterized the cocktail party as "a fête worse than death."

When intended for appetizers, many hors d'oeuvre are rich in fat or are combined with an oil or butter base to buffer the impact of alcohol on the system. If, during preprandial drinking, the appetizer intake is too extensive, any true enjoyment of the meal itself is destroyed. The palate is too heavily coated, too overstimulated by spices and dulled by alcohol. For these reasons and on most occasions, don't hesitate to simplify your appetizer list; nuts, olives, and a few interesting spreads usually suffice. A very hot, light soup between hors d'oeuvre and dinner is often a help in clearing the palate for the more delicate and subtle flavors of the meal.

While hors d'oeuvre, freely translated, means "outside the main works," and while we approve of serving imaginative combinations, it is important to remember that, unlike the opera overture, the hors d'oeuvre course should not forecast any of the joys that are to follow. Should you serve—either in the living room or at table—caviar in pickled beets or anchovy eggs on tomatoes, forget the very existence of beet and tomato when planning the dinner. This is not a superfluous caution, for one encounters many such carelessly repetitious meals. ➤ Choose for living room service bite-sized self-contained canapés or hors d'oeuvre, unless you are furnishing plates. Serve hot hors d'oeuvre fresh from the oven. If they are the type that will "hold," use a hibachi, 156, a chafing dish, or an electrically heated tray. ➤ Cold hors d'oeuvre may be transferred directly from refrigerator to serving point, or set first on chilled platters over cracked ice. Cheeses should be presented at a temperature around 70°. ➤ Allow 6 to 8 hors d'oeuvre per person.

Here are a few types of food which are particularly appropriate for the hors d'oeuvre course: caviar, 87; pâtés and terrines, 494; Vegetables à la Grecque, 281; Stuffed Artichokes, 100; Stuffed Brussels Sprouts and Beets, 83, and Cherry Tomatoes, 84; and Marinated Mushrooms, 84. You may also use spreads and dips, 89; deviled, pickled, truffled or chopped eggs, 82; skewered or bacon-wrapped tidbits, 80; sauced smoked seafood; quenelles, 205; and timbales, 231; choice hot and cold sausages; glazed or jelled foods; nuts, olives or cheeses. From the Salad chapter, choose individual aspics; a filled ring of aspic, 115; one of the mousses, 120; or an Italian, Viennese or Russian salad. From the Vegetable chapter, choose Ratatouille, 304.

WAYS TO SERVE HORS D'OEUVRE AND CANAPÉS

Food often looks more dramatic if some of it can be presented on several levels. Sometimes, unfortunately, this technique can be exhibited in quite alarming ways. Look at the complex, inedible architectural underpinnings by which the glories of ancient chefs used to be supported—and still are today, on celebratory occasions—in some large hotels and restaurants. Artificial coloring, fussy detailing, slick surfaces abound. Don't torture and mortify buffet food. Instead, play up its gustatory highlights and allow its subtle natural colors and textures to glow. And set off hors d'oeuvre with plenty of attractively cut vegetables and garnishes of fresh herbs and greens, 99.

Keep in mind, too, what the hors d'oeuvre platter will look like as it begins to be demolished: it is often more sensible to arrange several small plates which are easily replaced or replenished than one big one which may be difficult to restore to its pristine glory.

Illustrated below are a few effortless constructions designed to give the hors d'oeuvre platter a focus of interest. Simplest are a big red apple cut off at the bottom for stability; stud it with delicacies on picks for a small impromptu children's party; or, for an outdoor grill, use a big potato. The grapefruit "pincushion" will look more attractive if it consists of a three-quarter round, as shown, instead of a mere half. Larger and more ambitious are the pair of pineapple halves at center; the shrimp-studded eggplant pictured on 375; and the cabbage-container on 77. While Savoy cabbages make perhaps the most elegant receptacles, red cabbages harmonize colorfully with foods like stuffed beets and slices of pâté. Even plain, everyday cabbages can be made interesting if you can persuade your greengrocer to let you have one from which the outer leaves have not been hacked, or if you can get one intact straight out of the garden. Curl the leaves back carefully, so as not to bruise them. Into the center of these and other cabbages you may cut a cavity into which you can insert a sauce bowl, deep enough so the curled leaf edges will conceal its rim.

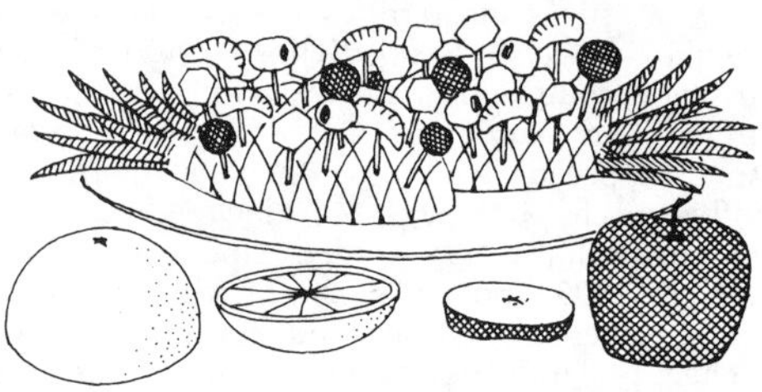

Just by the adroit placement of food on an hors d'oeuvre platter, you can bring about height variations and attractive color relationships. On an oblong plate, for instance, try centering some dainty triangular toasts or breads, peaks up like a long mountain range. Place small well-drained marinated shrimp along the base of the range on either side, and accent the watercress-garnished edge of the platter with French endive or celery filled with Guacamole, 83, and smoked salmon wrapped around individual marinated asparagus tips.

If platters need not be passed, you may also achieve height contrasts by placing cold hors d'oeuvre on crushed ice on a layered tray similar to that shown on 66, or on a simple épergne. If you use a silver or metal tray ➤ you may want to protect it from food acids by an undergarnish of lettuce, grape leaves, croutons or diced aspic, 113.

We saw a chef friend rapidly arrange a tray almost entirely from stored foods—a gala quickie you can reproduce when a merry mob descends on you with short or no warning. Garnish a large platter with lettuce. For the center, make a large mound of Russian Salad, 99, using canned drained vegetables; or one of shrimp salad; or a Spiced Cabbage Mound, 83. Garnish it with slices of tomato as a base for hard-cooked egg slices and top with a tiny tip cluster of tarragon, thyme or parsley. Or cut the eggs and tomatoes into wedges and border the mound by placing the wedges against it, with the yolk side against the salad, see 82.

Other possibilities—depending on the state of your larder—are a mound of creamed cottage cheese decorated with tender stalks of burnet pressed into the mound to resemble coarse fern fronds and accented with borage blossoms; a double spiral of overlapping radish disks, the interstices filled in with chopped chives. The platter may be garnished at each end with lemon slices and a cluster of canned white asparagus tips bound together with onion or lemon rings, or green pepper cups holding caviar or a Liver Sausage Pâté, 75. Another expedient is to open a fresh crock of cheddar or Liptauer cheese and press it into instant service as the principal feature; or prepare a filled Edam or Gouda, 81. Even the contents of a can of good white-meat tuna, coated with mayonnaise and attractively garnished with ripe olives or capers, looks good when surrounded by canned drained artichoke hearts or hearts of palm and filled in with shrimp or mussels. These may be sprinkled with a vinaigrette, sour cream and chili sauce, or mayonnaise; or you may place a few small bowls of sauces on the platter. Don't forget an occasional garnish of anchovy or pimiento strip. And remember that a plate of interesting breads and crackers is a most attractive foil and accessory.

ABOUT ANTIPASTO

Antipasto—or "what comes before the pasta course"—can be a snack with drinks or the base of an entire luncheon. This ever-present constituent of Italian menus is an assortment of hard sausages; prosciutto with melon or figs; fish, such as anchovies, sardines and Mediterranean tuna; pickled onions, beets, peppers, artichokes, cauliflower and mushrooms; highly seasoned garbanzos; and cold eggplant in tomato purée. It also includes fresh tomatoes, fennel, 304, cheeses—the hard types, as well as Mozzarella and ricotta—fine crusty breads, and deep-fat-fried fish, meat, fowl or game, which goes under the name of Fritto Misto, 243, when encased in a light batter.

Some suggestions for antipasto are listed below. Serve them on platters or make them up on individual plates.

Tomato slices cut lengthwise
Vegetables à la Grecque, 281
Anchovies
Seviche, 88
Smoked Salmon Rolls, 88

Rollmops, 88
Pickled Oysters, 89
Marinated Mushrooms, 84
Stuffed Celery, 84
Pickled Beets and Caviar, 87
Ratatouille, 304
Sardines
Slices of salami
Hard-Cooked Eggs, 220
Masked Eggs, 225
Garlic Olives, 85
Cucumber and green pepper sticks
Stuffed Leeks, 84
Black Radishes, 84
Artichoke Hearts à la Grecque, 281

ABOUT SMORGASBORD

This Scandinavian spread has been so thoroughly adapted in this country to the casual cocktail hour that some of us have lost sight of its original importance. Smorgasbord in its home territory is a square meal in itself, not the prelude to one. Its mainstays of meat and fish—and the aquavit which washes them down—are climatic imperatives when subarctic weather hovers for months outside the door. Like all native dishes, it closely reflects a country's ecology and its people's way of life.

The foods of which a smorgasbord is traditionally composed are sufficiently dissimilar to require at least three plates and silver services per person, so that the flavors of one course do not disturb those of the next. Typical of those first presented are herring, hot and cold, smoked eel, salmon or shellfish—all served with small boiled potatoes, seasoned with dill—and at least three kinds of bread with small mountains of butter balls. In fact, it is its bread and butter that gives this kind of meal its name.

With the first change of plate come cheeses, deviled eggs, pancakes and omelets with lingonberries, sausages, marinated and pickled vegetables, and aspics.

With the next, hot foods are in order, such as meatballs, ham with apples, goose with prunes, tongue and baked beans. Although many of these foods are prepared in advance, their true charm lies in the freshness of their garnish and arrangement. Do not leave the platters with their cut meats exposed too long on the buffet table.

To assemble a smorgasbord from some of the recipes in this book, see Herring, 407 and 408, Swedish Rye Bread, 599, salmon hors d'oeuvre, 88, Cold Glazed Salmon, 411, Swedish Meatballs, 489, Crêpes with Lingonberries, 237, and shrimp dishes.

CRACKERS AND BREADS TO SERVE WITH HORS D'OEUVRE

Bought crackers and breads can be dressed up into delightful additions to the hors d'oeuvre table with the cut of a knife, a few aromatic seeds, a bit of cheese and an oven. See fancy Breads and Crackers for Soup, 195, and bread and cracker recipes on 635–637.

You may also bake small Biscuits, 632, Beaten Biscuits, 634, Corn Dodgers, 628, and Corn Zephyrs Cockaigne, 628. Bake Grissini, 606, or some good rye, cheese or French breads. Make Potato Chips, 323, and don't forget Cheese Straws, 641, and unsweetened pastries in variety, 638 to 641.

NUTS AS HORS D'OEUVRE

These can be roasted or shallow-fried.

I. Preheat oven to 300°.
To roast, put in a greased shallow pan:
Blanched or unblanched nuts, 562: almonds, pecans, peanuts, pistachios or cashews
Bake until golden, 15 to 20 minutes.
Sprinkle during baking with:
(Melted butter)
seasoned lightly with:
(Celery salt, onion salt, cayenne, chili powder or paprika)

II. Have ready:
Blanched or unblanched nuts, 562
For every cup of nuts, allow:
½ cup vegetable oil
Cook the nuts in oil heated to 365° until golden. Test so as not to overcook—pecans and Spanish peanuts will need about 2 minutes. Drain nuts on paper toweling. After salting, store tightly covered.

CURRIED NUTS

Combine in a skillet:
¼ cup olive oil
1 tablespoon curry powder
1 tablespoon Worcestershire sauce
⅛ teaspoon cayenne
When this mixture is very hot, add:
2 cups nuts
Stir until well coated. Line a baking pan with brown paper, pour in the nuts and bake at 300° about 10 minutes or until crisp.

SKEWERED CHESTNUTS

Prepare:
Boiled Chestnuts I, 298
by boiling in milk. Omit the vinegar. When the chestnuts are cooked until soft enough to penetrate with a fork, roll them in a mixture of:
Au Gratin III, 553
Place on a greased baking dish and run under a hot broiler for a few moments. Dust with:
Chopped parsley
Serve at once on picks.

⊟ ROASTED CHESTNUTS

Preheat oven to 425°
➤ Prick the shells of:
Chestnuts
with a fork before putting them in the oven for

15 to 20 minutes—or they may explode. More hazardous, but more fun, is to roast the chestnuts in a pan such as that shown below, on a cold winter's evening, on the coals of an open hearth. A childhood game was for each of us to cheer on our own chestnut to pop first.

TOASTED SEEDS

Separate the fiber from:

Melon, pumpkin, squash, sunflower or watermelon seeds

Cover with:

Salted water

Bring to a boil and ➤ simmer 2 hours. Drain and dry on brown paper. Then:

I. Fry as for Nuts as Hors d'Oeuvre II, 79.

II. Spread the seeds in a shallow pan. Coat with:

Vegetable oil
(Salt)

Bake in a 250° oven until golden brown. Stir from time to time.

PUFFED CEREALS FOR COCKTAILS

Melt in a skillet, over low heat:

¾ cup butter

Add:

(1 clove garlic, pressed)

Stir in lightly:

12 cups crisp small cereals
1½ teaspoons curry powder
1 teaspoon celery salt
1 tablespoon Worcestershire sauce
(1 cup pumpkin seeds or nuts)

Mix gently until the cereal has absorbed the seasoned butter. Drain on paper toweling and serve at once.

SEASONED POPCORN OR POPPED WILD RICE

Prepare:

Popcorn, 790, or wild rice as for popcorn

Season with:

Melted butter
(Squeeze of garlic or onion juice)
(Grated sharp cheese)

STUFFED DRIED FRUIT APPETIZERS

Highly decorative surroundings for Glazed Cocktail Ribs, 85.

Prepare well in advance, as described in Prunes in Wine, 141:

Dried apricots, dates or prunes

Drain the fruit and reserve the liquor for sauces, gravies, etc. Place in each cavity 1 or 2 of the following:

A walnut or other nutmeat
A canned water chestnut
A sautéed chicken liver
Chutney
Cheddar or Roquefort cheese

The fruit may be served cold or hot. You may also wrap each piece with:

A narrow strip of bacon

Secure it with a pick and bake in a 375° oven until the bacon is crisp.

COLD SKEWERED TIDBITS

Alternate on cocktail picks:

Small onions with pieces of cocktail sausages and gherkins
Squares of cheese with pickle slices, stuffed olives or small onions
Slices of raw carrot and blocks of tongue or ham
Shrimp, lightly flavored with mustard and pieces of celery, or Celeri-Rave Rémoulade, 102
Squares of cheese and slices of green onion, topped with a ripe olive
Chilled balls of cream cheese, sprinkled with paprika or mixed with chopped olives and anchovy or smoked herring or salmon sections
Pieces of ham and watermelon pickle
Cubes of smoked turkey and honeydew melon

PROSCIUTTO AND FRUIT

On small picks alternately interlace:

Prosciutto or Virginia ham slices

around:

Melon balls
Pineapple, pear or peach chunks
Fresh figs

The fruit may be marinated in:

(Port wine)

At the very tip of the pick, impale a clustered tip of:

Mint leaves

▤ HOT SKEWERED TIDBITS OR TIDBITS EN BROCHETTE

Hors d'oeuvre en brochette may be broiled with or without wraps. Attractive skewer combinations of the unwrapped kind include: bacon and blanched sections of onion; scallops, mussels, shrimps or oysters with bacon and firm miniature tomatoes; chicken livers or pieces of calf liver or kidney alternating with cocktail sausages and mushrooms; diced eggplant or squash, blanched small onions, cherry tomatoes and bacon; shrimp or diced lobster, diced cucumber and stuffed

olives; pieces of fish, sections of blanched celery and bacon; sections of sausage and pickled onions; bacon and small chunks of unpeeled apple. See also Skewered Chestnuts, 79.
Any of the following may be surrounded by:

Thin strips of bacon or ham

secured to them with picks, impaled on skewers, and broiled until the bacon is crisp:

Pineapple chunks
Spiced cored crab apples
Prunes stuffed with almonds
Watermelon pickles
Dates stuffed with pineapple
Skinned firm grapefruit sections
Large stuffed olives
Pickled onions
Smoked oysters or mussels
Raw scallops or oysters
Cooked shrimp
Sautéed chicken livers

RUMAKI

Cut into bite-sized pieces:

Chicken livers

Sprinkle with:

(Soy sauce)

Prepare an equal number of:

¼-inch canned water chestnut slices

Marinate the chestnuts in:

(Port wine)

Wrap a piece of liver and one of water chestnut together in:

½-inch-wide slice of bacon

Secure with a wooden pick or small metal skewer and broil slowly until the bacon is crisp. Serve hot.

FILLED EDAM CHEESE

Fine for a buffet meal. Hollow:

A small Edam or Gouda cheese

Crumble the removed part. Combine it with:

2 teaspoons or more Worcestershire sauce or red wine
1 tablespoon prepared mustard
A few grains cayenne
1 or 2 tablespoons fresh or dried minced herbs

Or, to preserve its lovely characteristic flavor, blend just enough:

Whipping cream

with the cheese to make it easy to spread. Refill the cheese shell. Serve it surrounded by toasted crackers.

EDAM NUGGETS

About 16

Combine:

1 cup shredded Edam cheese
2 tablespoons finely chopped celery
⅛ teaspoon dry mustard
2 tablespoons cream or ale

Make into small balls and roll in:

Finely chopped parsley

VICKSBURG CHEESE ROLL OR BALL

Blend with a fork until smooth:

⅓ Roquefort cheese
⅓ cheddar cheese
⅓ soft cream cheese

Sprinkle thickly a large piece of waxed paper with:

Paprika

Roll the cheese mixture into a sausage shape, then on the paper until it has a generous coating of paprika. You can cut it into slices later. You may also shape the mixture into a large ball, which can be rolled in:

(Chopped nuts or finely chopped dried beef)

Place in refrigerator to chill.

NUT CHEESE BALLS

About 16

Work to a paste:

1 cup Roquefort cheese, or part Roquefort and part cream cheese
2 tablespoons butter
1 teaspoon Worcestershire sauce or 1 tablespoon brandy
1 teaspoon paprika
A few grains cayenne

Shape into 1-inch balls. Roll them in:

½ cup ground nutmeats
Chopped herbs or watercress

Chill. This is also effective made into one large cheese ball.

TOMATO ASPIC WITH TASTY CENTERS

8 Servings

I. Prepare:

Tomato Aspic, 114

When it is about to set, pour into wet individual molds or ice cube molds and fill them to one-third of their capacity. Combine and roll into balls:

1 package soft cream cheese: 3 oz.
1 tablespoon anchovy paste
2 drops Worcestershire sauce

Drop a ball into each mold and cover it with aspic. Chill the aspic until firm. Unmold on lettuce leaves. Serve with:

Mayonnaise

II. Use for the filling:

Any small pieces of well-seasoned cooked meat, fowl or fish

ANCHOVY CHEESE OR KLEINER LIPTAUER

See also Liptauer Cheese, 757.
Work until smooth:

2 packages cream cheese: 6 oz.

Work in:

3 tablespoons soft butter
2 minced anchovies
1½ tablespoons grated onion or 1 minced shallot

1½ teaspoons chopped capers
½ teaspoon caraway seed
¾ teaspoon paprika
2 drops Worcestershire sauce
Salt as needed

Shape the mixture into small patties. Chill thoroughly.

NUT CREAMS

Roll into ¾-inch balls:

Soft cream cheese
(Squeeze of garlic or lemon juice)

Flatten balls slightly between:

2 salted English walnuts or pecans

CHEESE CARROTS

Grate:

Yellow cheese

Moisten with:

Cream or salad dressing

until it is of a good consistency to handle. Shape into small carrots. In the blunt end, place:

A sprig of parsley

DEEP-FAT-FRIED HORS D'OEUVRE

If you can lick the service problem and offer this type of hors d'oeuvre while hot and just out of the fryer, nothing is more delicious. Consider the other suggestions in this chapter, as well as Tempura, 243, and Fritto Misto, 243.

CHEESE BALLS FLORENTINE

About 30

➤ Please read about Deep-Fat Frying, 147.

Measure by packing closely:

1 cup well-drained cooked spinach

Put it through a purée strainer or chop it in the ⅄ blender until fine. Stir in:

2 beaten eggs
1½ cups fine dry bread crumbs
1 tablespoon grated onion
½ cup shredded cheese
1 teaspoon salt
1 tablespoon lemon juice

Shape this mixture into 1½-inch balls. Coat with a Bound Breading, 552. Fry in deep fat heated to 375° until brown and crisp. Drain on paper toweling. Serve with:

Thickened Tomato Sauce, 352, or
Hollandaise Sauce, 358

FRIED CHEESE DREAMS

About 36

➤ Please read about Deep-Fat Frying, 147.

Mix:

½ lb. shredded Swiss cheese
3 well-beaten eggs
1 teaspoon double-acting baking powder
1 tablespoon sherry
⅛ teaspoon paprika

Put some flour in a narrow glass or cup. Drop a tablespoon of the mixture into the flour and swirl until it is coated with flour. Fry in deep fat heated to 375° until golden brown.

PASTRY CHEESE BALLS

About 36

Preheat oven to 450°.

Prepare dough for:

Cheese Straws, 641

Pinch off pieces of dough and form into ¾-inch balls. Chill for 2 hours, if possible, and bake about 10 minutes. Serve hot or cold.

ABOUT EGGS AS HORS D'OEUVRE

Perhaps no other single food plays such a varied role in hors d'oeuvre as eggs do. You find them plain hard-cooked as a bland foil for the many spicy items surrounding them; deviled in the most complex ways, with anchovies, curry, capers, caviar; truffled and En Gelée, 117, or pickled. They are particularly useful cut into fancy shapes as garnishes for other hors d'oeuvre—or with the whites and yolks chopped very finely.

Overlap slices of hard-cooked egg as shown in the clay casserole at the top on the right, or pink the whites with an hors d'oeuvre cutter—second from the top on the left. Garnish egg slices with caviar, olive, small shrimp, herbs or rolled anchovy fillets shown bottom left and on the far right in the second row. Deviled or plain hard-cooked eggs may be similarly garnished, and the deviled ones may be further decorated by using a pastry tube filled with the softened yolk. On the bottom right are 3 cuts for deviled egg cups. Pictured lower left center is a molded salad garnished with sliced egg sections in a pinwheel and wreathed with parsley or chervil. Another mold to the right shows a center of sieved egg yolk and sections of white forming a casual chrysanthemum motif. To make the border on the top left, alternate wedges of tomato and hard-cooked egg.

GARNISHED ASPARAGUS SPEARS

Marinate:

Canned white asparagus tips

in:

French Dressing, 360

Wrap around the base of each spear:

Thinly sliced ham, smoked salmon or prosciutto

Serve chilled.

AVOCADO SPREAD OR GUACAMOLE

★ A holiday touch here is a bit of pimiento or a slice of stuffed olive for garnish. Guacamole makes a great celery stuffer.

I. Peel:

1 or 2 ripe avocados

Mash the pulp with a fork. Add:

Onion juice and lemon juice
Salt
(Tomato pulp—a very small amount)

Heap this on small crackers or toast. Garnish with:

Paprika and parsley or a touch of peeled, seeded, chopped green chili peppers

II. Have ready a combination of:

1 peeled, seeded, chopped ripe tomato
1 finely chopped scallion with 2 inches of the green
(½ seeded, chopped green pepper)
½ teaspoon chili powder
1 teaspoon olive oil
1 tablespoon lemon or lime juice
½ teaspoon coriander
Salt and pepper

Add to the above, just before spreading:

2 peeled mashed ripe avocados

AVOCADO AND CHUTNEY

Peel just before serving and slice lengthwise into 4 to 6 thick slices:

Avocado

Fill the hollow at the base of each slice with:

Chutney, 846

MARINATED BEANS

Drain:

2 cups canned garbanzo beans or freshly cooked haricots blancs

Prepare the following marinade and soak the beans in it 4 hours:

2 tablespoons lemon juice
2 tablespoons red wine vinegar
½ cup olive oil
Garlic clove
Various herbs

Drain and serve chilled.

STUFFED BEETS COCKAIGNE

I. Prepare, leaving them whole, very small and shapely:

Cooked or canned beets

If small beets are not available, shape large ones with a melon scoop. Hollow the beets slightly. Fill the hollows with:

Caviar

sprinkled with a very little:

Lemon juice

Garnish with:

A sprig of parsley or lemon thyme

II. Fill the beet cups with:

Frozen Horseradish Sauce, 357

III. Or fill them with a combination of:

Chopped hard-cooked eggs
Mayonnaise
Herbs, preferably chives and tarragon

IV. You may also fill them with:

Chopped vinaigretted cucumbers

and garnish with:

Anchovy

STUFFED BRUSSELS SPROUTS

Drain well:

Cooked or canned Brussels sprouts

Cut a small hollow in each one, preferably from the top. Drop into each hollow:

½ teaspoon French Dressing, 360

Chill them. Fill with any:

Sandwich spread or salad mixture

Use liver sausage and tomato paste, cream cheese and chives or anchovy, adding the chopped center portion of the sprouts to the spread. Garnish with:

A sprig of parsley, savory, basil, etc.

Serve several as a salad or use as hors d'oeuvre.

SPICED CABBAGE MOUND

A decorative platter for a buffet or first course. Shred:

White cabbage

Dress it with equal parts of:

Mayonnaise
Chili Sauce, 847

Arrange it in a mound. Cover the top with:

Marinated shrimp

Surround the mound with:

Deviled eggs, topped with caviar

MARINATED RAW VEGETABLES OR CRUDITÉS VINAIGRETTE

Slice julienne, 296, and arrange in groups on a large platter a combination of some of the following:

Raw sweet green peppers, carrots, zucchini, turnips, Florence fennel, cucumber, celery, green and red cabbage, very fresh large mushrooms

Coat each pile with:

Herbed French Dressing, 360

Serve chilled.

MARINATED CARROTS

Slice as thin as soup noodles:

Carrots

Marinate the slices in:

Lemon or orange juice
A little sugar

Serve well chilled.

RADISH HORS D'OEUVRE

I. Dip whole or strips of:

White or red radishes

in:

Whipped cream

seasoned with:

Salt
Vinegar

II. Or serve red radishes cut in rose shapes, illustrated below, filled with:

Anchovy Butter or other Seasoned Butters, 349

III. Remove the rind from solid black radishes and slice thinly across the grain. Soak them covered in a little salted water about 15 minutes. Drain. Marinate in a mixture of:

Oil
Vinegar
White pepper

Serve chilled.

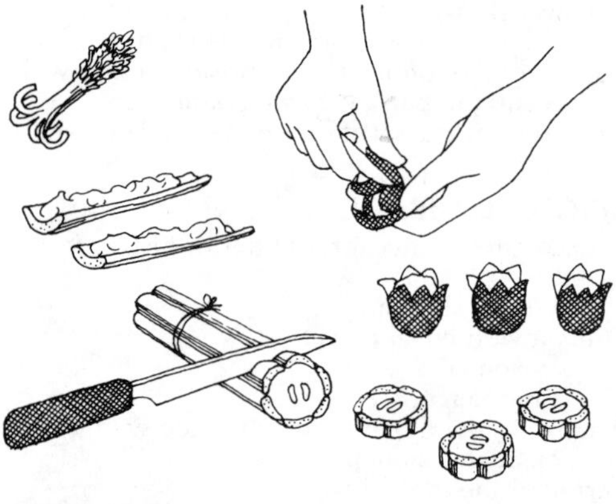

CELERY CURLS

Separate, then wash the inner smaller:

Stalks of celery

Trim leaves. Cut several long gashes in each rib. Soak in ice water until crisp and curled, as sketched above, and serve on a tray with buttered radish roses, see II, above.

STUFFED CELERY, FINOCCHIO, FRENCH ENDIVE OR BAMBOO SHOOTS

I. Combine:

1 tablespoon butter
1 tablespoon Roquefort cheese
1 package cream cheese: 3 oz.
Salt
(1 teaspoon caraway, dill or celery seed)

Place this mixture in:

Dwarf celery or finocchio ribs, the leaves of French endive, or separated canned bamboo shoots

If you want them to look very elegant, force the cheese mixture through a large pastry tube onto small individual ribs or endive. Sprinkle with:

Paprika

Chill.

II. Fill vegetable with:

Guacamole, 83

III. Or with:

Caviar and cultured sour cream, with a little lemon juice

STUFFED CHERRY TOMATOES

Cut off tops and with a melon scoop hollow out:

Large cherry tomatoes

Fill with crab meat or any salad mixture or sandwich spread.

STUFFED LEEKS

18 to 24 Pieces

Cut into 1½-inch cross sections the white portions of:

3 large cooked leeks

When chilled, cut the cross sections in two, lengthwise. Stuff the leeks with Shrimp or Shad Roe Salad, 108. Coat the top with more:

(Mayonnaise)

or garnish with a tiny sprig of:

(Fresh lemon thyme)

CUCUMBER LILY

Have ready:

Thin slices unpeeled cucumber
3-inch carrot sticks

Gently fold the cucumber slice around the base of the carrot stick. Fold a second slice around the stick from the other side. These form the lily petals, with a carrot stamen in the center. Fasten with a pick, being careful to catch all four lapped edges of the cucumber as well as piercing the carrot stick. Wrap flowers lightly in a moistened paper towel and refrigerate until ready to use as garnish for the hors d'oeuvre or salad tray.

MARINATED MUSHROOMS

Be sure to include in your repertoire Stuffed Mushrooms, 308–309.

Marinate 1 hour or more:

Small button-type mushrooms or thinly sliced large mushrooms
French Dressing, 360
(Dash herb vinegar)
Chopped chives or onion juice

Chopped parsley
Serve on:
Lettuce or watercress
or on picks.

ABOUT OLIVES

While the grading and typing of olives is taken very seriously by the processors, what should matter most to the cook is that size does not necessarily have anything to do with quality. You don't have to be a connoisseur to know that the big, woody dull-green queen olives can't compare in flavor or in texture with the small, succulent, yellowish Manzanilla fines.

Try various types in making up your hors d'oeuvre tray. The green ones, picked unripe, are treated with a potassium or ash solution and then pickled in brine. Since they have not been heat-treated, a film sometimes forms after the bottle is opened. If this happens, you may float olive oil on the surface of the liquid in the bottle before storing again, or rinse the olives in cold water, drain, place in a clean jar and re-cover with a solution of 1 teaspoon salt and 1 tablespoon white vinegar to a cup of water. Black olives are picked ripe, put in a boiling brine and sold dried, pickled or in oil. To reduce the saltiness of dried or pickled olives, store them in olive oil that you can later use for dressing.

There are many stuffings for olives: a sliver of almond or pimiento, a slice of anchovy, smoked salmon, prosciutto, etc. For a real treat, put in a little foie gras and close with a pistachio nut.

GARLIC OLIVES

Drain the liquid from:
Green or ripe olives
Add:
12 peeled cloves garlic
Cover with:
Olive oil
Let stand 24 hours or more under refrigeration. Drain. Remove the garlic and use the oil for salad dressing. You may dust the olives with:
Chopped parsley

PASTRY-WRAPPED OLIVES

About 4 Dozen

Preheat oven to 400°.
Prepare the dough for:
Cheese Straws, 641
Wrap individually with about 1 teaspoon of this dough, depending on size of fruit:
50 stuffed olives
so as to cover each fruit completely.
Arrange the covered olives on ungreased baking sheets. Bake until dough is golden.

✻ If you want to reserve these nuggets for later use, freeze until firm, then place at once in plastic bags. Do not defrost before baking about 15 minutes and serving promptly.

MARINATED ONIONS

Skin, then slice:
Bermuda onions
Soak 30 minutes in:
Brine: ⅔ cup water to 1 tablespoon salt
Drain. Soak 30 minutes in:
Vinegar
Drain, then chill. They are then ready to be served side by side with celery, radishes, olives, etc.

PEPPER HORS D'OEUVRE

Remove skins from:
Sweet green or red peppers
by roasting under a broiler until soft and pliable. Also remove top and bottom, core and seeds. Marinate 15 minutes in:
Olive oil
Lemon juice
Slice the peppers vertically into thirds. On each strip, put:
1 tablespoon Tuna Salad, 108, or anchovies with capers
seasoned with the marinade and:
Chopped parsley
Form the strips into small sausagelike rolls and hold closed with a pick.

STUFFED SNOW PEA PODS

Scrub:
Snow pea pods
Blanch the pods in boiling water for 30 seconds. Drain, rinse in cold water and drain well again. Refrigerate covered. Just before serving, cut off the stem end of the pod diagonally. Fill a pastry bag with:
Vicksburg Cheese, 81, and very finely chopped nuts
or:
Finely chopped filling for Crab Puff Balls, 75
thinned down with:
Whipping cream
to a consistency that passes easily through the bag without splitting the pod. Allow about 1 teaspoon of filling for every pod.

MARROW HORS D'OEUVRE

Bake:
Beef marrowbones, 471
Serve the marrow with long spoons. It is delicious.

GLAZED COCKTAIL RIBS

Allow 2 to 3 Ribs per Person

Preheat oven to 350°.
Cut into 1-rib sections:
2 spareribs: about 5 lb.
Season with:
Salt and pepper
Place in a pan. Roast about 40 minutes. Drain the fat. Reduce oven heat to 300°. During the next 35 minutes of cooking, brush the ribs frequently and lightly with a marinade of:

3 tablespoons catsup or Chili Sauce, 847
4 tablespoons honey or molasses
1 tablespoon grated fresh gingerroot
2 crushed garlic cloves
4 tablespoons soy sauce
2 tablespoons sherry

When crisp and well glazed, serve at once.

STEAK TARTARE OR CANNIBAL BALLS

Forty-Eight 1-Inch Balls

We always tender this recipe with some misgiving because of the risks run in eating uncooked meat and eggs. Cannibal balls are a mini-version of the classic **Steak Tartare** or **Cannibal Mound:** a clump of raw beef with a shallow indentation on top into which a raw egg yolk is broken, garnished with chopped onion, caviar or anchovy, and capers. The amounts indicated here will serve six persons. Both for the cocktail hors d'oeuvre below and for steak tartare the meat is prepared just before serving as follows:

Scrape with the back of a knife, turning the meat several times until only the fibers remain, or grind at home using a medium blade:

3 lb. top sirloin

If you grind, the fibrous muscle will periodically choke the grinder, allowing only the velvety portion of the meat to get through. Whether you scrape or grind, you will end with about 2 pounds of meat. Mix with the meat:

2 egg yolks
½ cup very finely minced Bermuda onion

Reserve about one-fourth of the meat and arrange the rest in 48 shapes similar to Jelly Tots, see illustration on 717. Into each depression put:

1 caper
⅛ teaspoon caviar: 2½ oz. in all; or
½ mashed anchovy

Close the tops of the balls with the reserved meat. Dip them in:

2 unbeaten egg whites

Roll them in:

¾ cup very finely chopped parsley

Arrange on a platter surrounded by small:

Sandwiches of buttered pumpernickel

Garnish the platter with radish roses, 84, and sprigs of parsley.

MEATBALL HORS D'OEUVRE

Prepare:

Tiny meatballs, hamburgers, nutburgers, Königsberger Klops, 489, or small-sized Dolmas, 492

Season them well. Serve very hot on picks or between small biscuits.

TONGUE, CHIPPED BEEF OR BOLOGNA CORNUCOPIAS

Prepare one of the following spreads:

Seasoned creamed cheese, 71
Hard-Cooked Egg Spread, 73
Piccalilli, 844
Cultured sour cream and horseradish

Spread the mixture on very thin slices of:

Smoked boiled tongue, chipped beef or bologna

Roll into cornucopias. Or stack 6 slices, wrap them in waxed paper, chill and cut into 6 or more pie-shaped wedges.

TINY BROILED SAUSAGES

Heat on a hibachi or broil:

Very small sausages

Serve them hot on picks with:

Mustard Sauce, 357

or grouped on skewers, flambéed in:

Jamaica rum

SHERRIED CHICKEN BITS

Stew and place while still warm in a large jar:

Breasts of fat stewing hens

Leave the meat on the bone and cover with:

Sherry

Cover the jar closely and refrigerate 10 days before using. Skin, bone and cut the meat into bite-sized pieces. Serve cold on picks between:

Salted walnut meats

ABOUT CHICKEN AND GOOSE LIVERS AS HORS D'OEUVRE

Both these delicacies may be cut to bite size and briefly sautéed; overcooking, as usual, is disastrous. The centers should remain pink. Simply seasoned with salt, the livers may be served on picks, or they may be wrapped in thin slices of bacon and run under the broiler until the bacon is crisp. See Rumaki, 81. You may prefer a liver pâté, 495 and 496, and use it for stuffing olives, artichoke hearts or mushroom caps; or roll it up like small cheroots in the thinnest slices of prosciutto. Use liver pastes also in individual molds, glazed with port or an aspic, 368. For pâté surrounded by pâte, see Foie Gras Canapés, 75.

CHOPPED GOOSE OR CHICKEN LIVERS

Drop into boiling seasoned water and simmer until barely done:

1 lb. chicken or goose livers

Drain and cool them. Cook until hard, shell, chop and add:

2 eggs

Chop coarsely, then sauté:

2 medium-sized onions

in:

2 tablespoons butter

Chop or blend these ingredients to a fine paste.

Season to taste

adding:

(2 tablespoons chopped parsley)
(1 oz. cognac or brandy)

SMOKED TURKEY OR PHEASANT HORS D'OEUVRE

Roll:

Thin slices of smoked turkey or pheasant

around:

Large pitted green olives

Serve on small picks.

ABOUT CAVIAR AND OTHER ROES

A lady was once moved to ask plaintively why caviar is so expensive; to which a helpful maître d' replied: "After all, madam, it is a year's work for a sturgeon." The best caviar is the roe of the sturgeon, and the most sought-after caviar comes from Iran and Russia as **Beluga** and **Oscietre.** A third type, smaller because taken from a smaller Caspian sturgeon, is called **Sevruga** and is the kind usually obtainable in this country. None of these is either fishy in taste, or briny—as only 2% salt by weight is added as a preservative before transshipment to America. The eggs should be shiny, translucent, gray and large grained. ➤ As imported fresh caviar spoils in a few hours in temperatures of 40° or above, always serve it on ice. Its high oil content keeps it from freezing.

To serve individual portions attractively, heat the back of a metal spoon, press it into an ice cube and fill the depression with the caviar—using a plastic spoon. ➤ Never allow the caviar itself to touch metal or to be served on it. If you spread it on canapés or in barquettes, see 69, or stuff beets with it, 83, be careful not to bruise the eggs. The classic accompaniments are lemon wedges, parsley, black bread, pumpernickel or not-too-dry toast. Although hard-cooked egg whites and yolks and onions—all very finely minced and separately arranged—are more frequently used as a garnish, connoisseurs consider them less suitable than the simpler lemon and parsley. Other favored ways to serve caviar are in blinis with sour cream, 238, or simply mixed half and half with sour cream. Caviar should be accompanied by either slightly chilled white wines or—preferably—champagne or vodka.

Other types of caviar are the roes of salmon, carp, cod, herring, lumpfish, pike, tuna and gray mullet. Those of cod, salmon, carp, pike and tuna are red or pink, and all are more gelatinous than sturgeon roes. To cook roes, see 411. For a sauce made of roe, see Caviar Butter, 350, and the recipe just below. To preserve caviar, see 814.

TARAMA

About 2½ Cups

This coral-pink roe mixture is served throughout Greece as a salad dressing. We use it most often as a dip, or to give added color and flavor to other hors d'oeuvre.

Prepare:

1 cup riced potatoes, 318

Keep them hot and toss promptly with:

2 tablespoons olive oil

Let this mixture cool. Beat in a mixer:

½ cup smoked salmon or carp roe

1 tablespoon chopped onion

Combine with the potato and:

3 tablespoons lemon juice

Add slowly as for Mayonnaise, 363:

⅓ to ½ cup olive oil

The whole mixture should thicken to the consistency of a heavy cream sauce; no more. You may incorporate:

(1 tablespoon finely chopped parsley)

(A small amount of tomato purée)

Season to taste

and refrigerate until ready to serve.

ABOUT SEASIDE TIDBITS

When you go collecting at the shore, you can often find edible treats. Those sketched below can be eaten raw as hors d'oeuvre. Reading from top to bottom on left are **Nuttall's Cockle** and at the

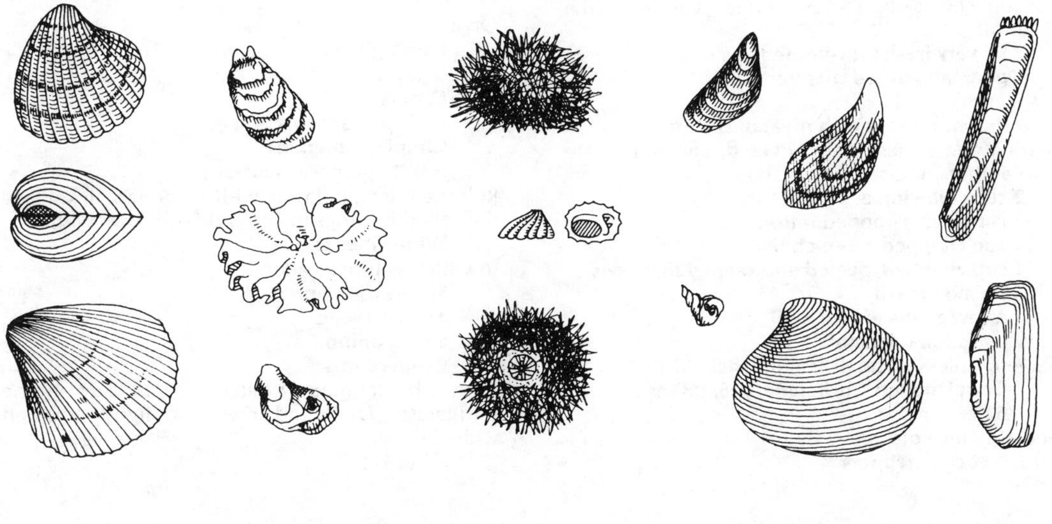

base the **Giant Atlantic Cockle,** with a side view between of the heart shape that gives them their name. Next are the **Eastern** and the native **Pacific Oyster,** with a bit of **Laver,** one of the large edible purple seaweeds, centered between them. The bristly **Sea Urchin** follows, shown at top as it hugs the rocks, and at the bottom revealing the unprotected edible contents. ➤ Always be certain to wear leather gloves when handling urchins. To prepare for eating raw or for cooking, free the tangerinelike sections from the gut. Cook as for Poached Eggs II, 221. The flavor is much like that of brains. If eaten raw with a spoon, both roe and milt—the creatures are bisexual—are highly prized. In Japan the flesh is served as a fermented paste. In Latin America it frequently finds it way into an omelet. Between the urchins is the keyhole **Limpet.** You eat the foot, shown shaded, and discard the visceral hump. Second at top right is the **Californian Mussel** and beside it the **Common Mussel**—more about these on 379. Below them is the **Periwinkle,** which can be extracted with a pin or a fine crochet hook. Below the "winkle" is a **Clam,** and top and bottom at extreme right are the long **Atlantic Jack Knife** and the shorter **Pacific Razor Clam;** more about these on 379. For other sea tidbits try small shellfish, 375, in spicy sauces. Serve hot or cold. ➤ Due to red tides, mollusks may be poisonous during the summer months. Be sure to check local conditions.

SEVICHE

Raw fish marinated in lime juice is very popular as an hors d'oeuvre in South America and Japan. If you are squeamish ➤ or if you are not sure your fish comes from unpolluted waters, you may prefer—as Europeans often do—to poach the fish lightly and pour over it a hot marinade of olive oil and vinegar, rather than relying merely on the acidulous action of lime juice. The poached and marinated fish is refrigerated covered 24 hours and served cold. This dish is called **escabèche.**

For seviche, skin, remove bones and dice the meat of:

2 lb. very fresh firm-fleshed raw sole, pompano or red snapper

Or you may dice:

(2 lb. raw lobster, crab meat or scallops)

Marinate in a glass dish, covered, and refrigerate 3 to 4 hours, entirely immersed in:

2 cups lime juice
½ cup finely chopped onions
¼ cup chopped green chilis
1 cup chopped, peeled and seeded tomatoes
2 teaspoons salt
A few grains of cayenne
⅛ teaspoon oregano

Serve on picks in small scallop shells with:

Corn Dodgers Cockaigne, 628, or Tortillas, 629

and a garnish of:

Hot chili peppers

FISH BALLS

Prepare very small:

Codfish Balls, 405, or Gefilte Fish Balls, 402

Serve them hot on picks with:

Tartare Sauce, 364

ANCHOVY, EEL OR SMOKED SALMON ROLLS

I. Cut into ½-inch strips:

Smoked salmon, eel or anchovies

Roll the strips around small:

Sweet-sour or other gherkins or thin strips of cucumber

Secure and serve the rolls with picks.

II. Cut into very thin slices:

Smoked salmon

Spread on the slices:

Cream cheese seasoned with cucumbers, horseradish, chopped chives, parsley or caviar

Roll the strips. Secure and serve them on picks.

HERRING OR SARDINE HORS D'OEUVRE

Have all ingredients very cold.

Place on plates:

Lettuce leaves

Build up into a small cone:

Finely shredded coleslaw

Pour over the cone:

Cultured sour cream

The cream may be thinned with a few tablespoons of the liquor from the pickled herring. Top the cone with:

Small pieces of pickled herring, sardine or anchovy

ROLLMOPS

On a:

Herring fillet

Place a layer of:

Capers
Chopped shallots
Chopped gherkins
A little prepared mustard

Roll the fillet and fasten with a wooden pick. Place the rolled herrings in jars and cover well with:

Wine vinegar

to which you have added:

Slivers of lemon peel
Mustard seed
Sliced onion
Peppercorns

Allow the rollmops to steep for 10 days in the refrigerator. Drain and serve cold, lightly brushed with:

Olive oil

COLD OYSTER OR MUSSEL HORS D'OEUVRE

Prepare:

Sour Cream Dip, below

Coat with this sauce:

18 oysters or mussels in the half shell

Decorate tops with:

Red caviar

Serve on a bowl of ice.

PICKLED OYSTERS

Combine in the top of a double boiler:

1 quart oysters
1 quart oyster liquor

If needed, supplement the liquor with canned clam juice. Heat until the oysters are plump. Drain and wipe them. Reserve the liquor and simmer it 15 minutes with:

1 tablespoon peppercorns
1 tablespoon whole allspice
1 thinly sliced lemon
2 tablespoons vinegar
Dash of hot pepper sauce
Season to taste

Pour the sauce over the oysters and refrigerate at least 24 hours before serving.

PICKLED SHRIMP

For your most fiery guests.

Cover:

5 lb. shrimp

with:

Flat draft beer or 2/3 vinegar and 1/3 water

Add:

1 tablespoon bruised peppercorns
1/4 cup salt
3 bay leaves
1 teaspoon hot pepper sauce or 1/8 teaspoon cayenne pepper
1/4 cup chopped celery tops

Bring to a boil and simmer 15 minutes. Remove from the heat and let shrimp stand in the liquor at least 1 hour in the refrigerator. Drain and place on a platter of crushed ice on artichoke leaves.

ASPIC-GLAZED SHRIMP

Clean and devein, 389:

1 1/2 lb. boiled shrimp

Cut them lengthwise down the center, as shown on 389. Prepare:

Aspic Glaze, 368

Chill the glaze until it begins to set. Spear the shrimp on picks. Dip them into the glaze. When partly set, dip again. Chill well and serve cold.

⊟ BROILED SHRIMP COCKAIGNE

Without cutting into the meat, shell, clean and devein, leaving the tails on, 389:

2 lb. jumbo shrimp

Marinate the shrimp in the refrigerator for several hours in:

1 pressed clove garlic
1 cup olive oil
1/2 cup sauterne wine
Juice of 1/2 lemon
3 tablespoons parsley and basil, chopped together
1 teaspoon salt
1/4 teaspoon pepper

Grill or broil the shrimp about 10 minutes, being careful not to scorch them. Serve at once with:

Lemon Butter, 350

flavored with:

1 large pressed clove of garlic

or for a touch of the Orient use:

Chinese Low-Calorie Dressing, 362

FRIED SHRIMP BALLS

Mix and shape into balls:

1 1/4 lb. shelled, deveined, minced shrimp
6 finely chopped canned water chestnuts
1 piece ginger, finely chopped
1 small onion, chopped
1 egg white
1 teaspoon cornstarch
3 teaspoons wine
1 teaspoon sesame or other vegetable oil
Dash of pepper

Fry in deep fat heated to about 365° until golden brown.

ABOUT DIPS

Dangerously close to overimmersion, perhaps, dipped dainties are still the most popular types of hors d'oeuvre, and the easiest to prepare. They are versatile, too: entirely acceptable not only just before dinner, but as afternoon and late-evening snacks. Don't forget to use for dipping some of the spreads listed in Canapés; Welsh Rarebit, 252; Cheese Fondue, 254; Guacamole, 83; or the sauce which accompanies Bagna Cauda, 90. Make them juicier ➤ but still on the firm side, with a little cream, lemon juice or mayonnaise; and choose additional seasonings to your own taste. When serving ➤ it is wise to set the dip container over crushed ice.

FOOD DIPPERS

Crackers or strips of pumpernickel or rye toast
Potato or corn chips
Small wheat biscuits
Toast sticks
Fried oysters
Cooked seafood chunks
Chilled vegetables
Meatballs and small sausages

SOUR CREAM DIPS

I. Combine:

2 cups thick cultured sour cream
2 tablespoons chopped parsley

2 tablespoons chopped chives
1 teaspoon dried herbs
1/8 teaspoon curry powder
1/2 teaspoon salt
1/4 teaspoon paprika

II. Combine:
1 cup cultured sour cream
1 or more tablespoons horseradish
1/2 teaspoon salt
1/4 teaspoon paprika

CHEESE DIPS

The mania for cheese dips, cold, has replaced that for cheese dips, hot—without which no party used to be complete.
Try serving the following dips in a hollowed-out:
Round loaf of dark rye bread
Slice off the top of the loaf; then with a curved serrated knife remove the soft inner part of the loaf, leaving about 1 inch of thickness at sides and bottom. Use the removed bread later as chunks for dipping. ➤ Fill the hollow loaf with the dip just before serving.

I. Combine:
3/4 lb. cheddar cheese
1/4 lb. Roquefort cheese
2 tablespoons butter
1/2 teaspoon Worcestershire sauce
1/2 teaspoon prepared mustard
1/4 teaspoon salt
1/2 pressed clove of garlic
and melt over heat with:
1 cup beer

II. Beat until smooth:
2 packages cream cheese: 6 oz.
1 1/2 tablespoons mayonnaise
1 tablespoon cream
1/4 teaspoon salt
1 teaspoon grated onion or chives
1 teaspoon Worcestershire sauce

LONG-LIVED CHEESE SPREAD OR DIP

About 1 1/2 Cups

This concoction, if refrigerated, keeps for a week or so and makes excellent toasted cheese sandwiches or a sauce. Thin it as needed with a little milk in a double boiler.
Cut into small pieces and stir over very low heat, or over—not in—boiling water until melted:
1/2 lb. cheese
We find a soft cheese or a processed one preferable for this recipe. Add:
1 cup evaporated milk
3/4 teaspoon salt
3/4 teaspoon dry mustard
1/4 teaspoon curry powder
1/2 teaspoon caraway seeds
Remove from heat and stir in:
1 beaten egg
Stir and cook the cheese mixture very slowly until the egg thickens a bit. Remove from heat. Pour into a dish. Cool it slowly, beating as it cools, to keep a crust from forming. Cover and chill.

BAGNA CAUDA

Place in a heavy fondue pot, shown on 254:
1/2 cup butter
1/2 cup olive oil
8 mashed anchovy fillets
2 cloves garlic, pressed
and simmer about 5 minutes, stirring occasionally. Add:
1/2 teaspoon freshly ground black pepper
Have ready a platter of bite-sized young vegetables, thinly sliced if the vegetables are fibrous, and peeled or seeded if necessary. Suitable are:
Carrots, Florence fennel, Belgian endive or celery, young artichoke hearts, cherry tomatoes, green peppers and zucchini
Let the guests dip their choices into the warm sauce on fondue forks.

ORIENTAL DIP

Good with raw mushrooms and raw cauliflower. Combine:
1/2 cup finely chopped green onions
1/2 teaspoon fresh coriander
1/4 cup chopped parsley
2 tablespoons chopped fresh ginger
1 tablespoon soy sauce
2 tablespoons chopped canned water chestnuts
1 cup cultured sour cream
2 tablespoons mayonnaise

HUMMUS

About 3 1/2 Cups

Combine in a ⅄ blender:
2 cups strained cooked chick-peas
2/3 cup Tahin, 564
3/4 cup lemon juice
2 pressed cloves garlic
1/4 cup seeded black olives
1 teaspoon salt
After removing this mixture from blender, add:
3 tablespoons finely chopped parsley
Serve as a dip with:
Rye toast fingers
Strips of unleavened bread

CAVIAR DIP

Whip:
1/2 cup whipping cream
Fold in:
2 to 3 tablespoons caviar
1 to 2 tablespoons finely chopped onion
Place in the center of a dish and garnish with:
Sliced hard-cooked eggs and small rounds of toast

CLAM DIP

Drain:

1 cup minced clams

Combine with:

1 package soft cream cheese: 3 oz.
1 tablespoon Worcestershire sauce
1/8 teaspoon mustard
Salt, as needed
1 tablespoon, more or less, onion juice
1/4 cup whipping cream

CRAB MEAT OR TUNA DIP

Flake:

1 cup cooked crab meat or tuna

Stir in:

2 tablespoons mayonnaise
1 to 2 tablespoons tomato paste, catsup, or Chili Sauce, 847
Juice of 1 lemon
Seasoning, as needed
(Chopped celery or olives)

SHRIMP DIP

Combine:

1 can cooked cleaned shrimp: 5 oz.
1 cup creamed fine-curd cottage cheese
3 tablespoons Chili Sauce, 847
1/2 teaspoon onion juice
2 teaspoons lemon juice
1 to 2 tablespoons cream, if needed for consistency

SALADS

We remember the final scene of a Maeterlinck play. The stage is strewn with personages dead and dying. The sweet young heroine whimpers, "I am not happy here." Then the head of the house—or what remains of it—an ancient noble, asks quaveringly, "Will there be a salad for supper?"

With virtually everyone, from the youngest commoner to the most palsied of patricians, salad nowadays has assumed a legitimately high priority, as well as—increasingly—first place on the menu. We are still inclined to prefer it in its traditional location—between entrée and dessert—mainly because a green salad makes a clean break between meat and sweet. But the initial presentation of a light salad at dinner can be a life-saver for a host or hostess whose pièce de résistance has, in fact, resisted and is not so ready as the guests.

All salads were once light salads: the edible parts of various herbs and plants, seasoned solely with salt—from which the word "salad" comes. In more or less this form they play a cooperative role in reducing diets, always assuming that further sprucing up is limited to a sprinkling of lemon juice, a touch of spiced vinegar, or at most a low-calorie dressing, 362.

For those who can be more expansive, salads mean all sorts of combinations of chilled fruit, vegetables, herbs, meat, cheese, fish—even, we acknowledge with less than whole-hearted enthusiasm, cereals and pasta—served with some kind of moist dressing. At informal luncheons they may not only accompany the entrée but actually stand in for it. However, the chief danger in the present-day embarrassment of salad riches is that in carelessly planned meals the salad often tends to compete with the main dish, whenever or however served.

Keep the rest of the menu well in mind when preparing your salad and its dressing. A rich, heavy entrée demands a tart green salad. Slaws go well with casual meals, cookouts and impromptu suppers at which hearty, uncomplicated foods are served. Elaborate salads beautifully arranged and garnished, brilliant aspics, and decorative chaud-froids all look well on formal buffet tables or at special summer luncheons. In some cases these are served individually rather than as a single glittering showpiece.

We have suggested suitable dressings for the individual salads in this chapter and want you to try some of the variations listed. See also Sauces, 336–369. Don't go overboard, however; an undiluted heavy dressing will make any lettuce except iceberg collapse just when you want to keep it crisp. Your dressing should enhance the salad by summoning forth its special flavor and texture and by adding a delicate piquancy. Don't overlook, incidentally, the possibility of using a salad such as Celeri-Rave Rémoulade, 102, as an appetizer; and, conversely, an appetizer like Vegetables à la Grecque, 281, as a salad.

ABOUT CULTIVATED SALAD GREENS

Enjoy the full range of cultivated greens, a number of which are sketched opposite. In successive rows at top, left to right, are crisphead or iceberg lettuce, Boston, bibb, Oakleaf, and Matchless; on the next row, witloof chicory, curly endive, watercress, and corn salad or mâche; at the bottom, Chinese cabbage, celtuce, roquette, escarole, and cos or romaine.

CRISPHEAD OR ICEBERG LETTUCE

Large firm head, crisp, brittle, tightly packed. Outer leaves medium green, inner pale green and chunky. Can be torn, shredded or sliced like cabbage. Adds "crunch" and does not readily wilt. Improved recent varieties are Imperial, Great Lakes, Vanguard and Western.

BUTTERHEAD LETTUCE

Smaller, less compact, softer than crisphead. Delicate leaves, of which the outer are dark green, the inner light green to yellowish and "buttery" to the taste. **Boston** and **buttercrunch** are the time-honored cultivars, but the aristocrat of the line is undoubtedly **bibb.** A Hawaiian-bred variety, **Manoa,** holds up in warm weather and is slow to bolt.

LOOSE-LEAF LETTUCE

Some of these much more fragile, delicious and highly diversified kinds of lettuce can be occasionally and fleetingly bought at market or at roadside stands. If they are not purchasable, they are well worth bringing on early in the spring or fall in the family garden patch. The loose leaves branch from a single stalk, do not bunch, and vary in color. They are frequently used as an undergarnish for molded salads, aspic, or arrangements of salad vegetables and fruits.

Green and bronze **Oakleaf** is one of these types; **Salad Bowl,** which looks like a curly pale-green nosegay, another. **Matchless** is a deer's-tongue variety developed to resist heat and drought. **Prizehead** has a red-pigmented leaf that adds dash to a tossed salad.

FIELD OR CORN SALAD, LAMB'S LETTUCE OR MÂCHE

Roughly also in the loose-leaf category, these plants, found wild in America, have been extensively cultivated in France and Italy. The clusters are small, made up of smooth green leaves; they may be grown in cold weather with little mulching. Like other varieties of lettuce, they are sometimes used as cooked greens.

COS OR ROMAINE LETTUCE

Elongated head, with long stiff leaves which are usually medium dark to dark green on the outside and become greenish-white near the center. Its more pungent flavor enlivens a tossed salad.

STEM LETTUCE

A Chinese variant in which the stem, rather than the leaves, furnishes the edible portion. It is used in Chinese cookery rather like the water chestnut, the taste of which it resembles when raw. Although easy to grow, it is rarely found in this country. Much more familiar to us is a close relative, **celtuce,** which may be eaten uncooked or braised like celery and which has a very high vitamin C content.

RED-LEAVED CHICORY OR ARUGULA

A lettucelike sparker-up of salads, much favored in northern Italy. Its spectacular crimson color, much showier than that of Prizehead, above, is characteristic only of the young growth that is carefully shielded from sunlight.

CURLY ENDIVE OR CHICORY

Spiky leafage from a yellow-white stem. It adds a bitter flavor and a somewhat prickly texture to a tossed salad. Occasionally used as a garnish.

ESCAROLE OR CHICORY ESCAROLE

Also known as **Batavian endive.** The leaves are broader, paler, less highly crimped than curly endive, above, and the taste is less bitter.

BELGIAN OR FRENCH ENDIVE OR WITLOOF CHICORY

Another bitterish salad component, although highly variable: its freshly harvested heads are quite bland in flavor. They look rather like young unshucked corncobs. The outer of the closely packed greenish-white leaves may, like celery ribs, serve as receptacles for hors d'oeuvre.

ROQUETTE

The kind of salad material that sets up a love-hate relationship but which an impassioned minority contends it cannot do without. There are a number of varieties, all coarse-leaved, fuzzy, aggressive in flavor. To avoid a mixed reception, we advise its use only in a mixed salad.

WATERCRESS

Dime-sized dark green glossy leaves on sprigged stems. The leaves and the tender portions of the stems are spicy and peppery additions to any tossed salad. They contain twice the protein, four times the vitamin C and much more calcium than lettuce.

In France, watercress is the invariable accompaniment to a roast chicken. In America it is one of our most interesting greens, frequently available in the wild. Its consumption, however, is often discouraged, because it may be growing in polluted water. To settle any doubts you may have, soak the cress first in 2 quarts of water in which 1 tablet of water purifier has been dis-

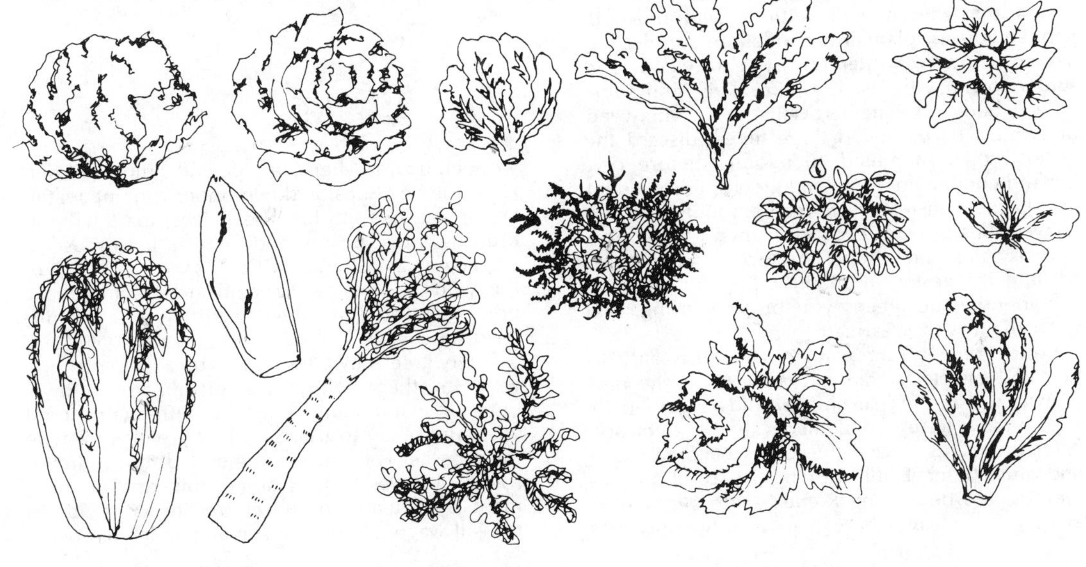

solved. Then rinse in clear water. Dry and chill before serving.

➤ To store watercress, cut off ½ inch of the stems. Loosen the tie and set in a container which does not press it on the sides or top. Fill the container with 1 inch of cold water, cover and set in the refrigerator. Wash thoroughly when ready to use. Cut off the tough ends before tossing.

SEA KALE

Although this plant grows wild along European coasts, it also flourishes in inland gardens, where its thick, glaucous basal leaves, cropped from February to June, make a nutty-flavored salad component.

CELERY AND SPINACH

The tender yellow tops of the celery as well as the sectioned ribs lend color and flavor to salads. So do the smaller leaves of spinach.

CABBAGES

Not all types, of course, are candidates for salad. **Chinese** and **celery cabbage** very definitely are. Slaw, 96, it is important to remember, can be made of the **red** and the Chinese variety as well as the conventional "white" cabbage.

GARDEN CRESS

Do not confuse with watercress. Garden cress has very tiny leaves which are picked 14 days after sowing. In sandwiches and hors d'oeuvre they are frequently combined with baby mustard greens. To grow, see 565.

WHITE MUSTARD

A European annual, with small tender green leaves, usually cut about a week after the seeds have been sown and used with garden cress in salads or for garnish.

ABOUT WILD SALAD GREENS

Young **purslane, miner's lettuce, wild mustard, pepper grasses, plantains, dandelion, sorrels, Canadian burnet, winter cress, chickweed** and **spiderwort** may be used raw in salads; and some flower buds, like **hemerocallis,** 235. **Milkweed** buds must be parboiled three times (discard the waters), then simmered 10 minutes before drying and cooling. In using wild greens, it is prudent to add them in relatively small amounts to more conventional greens, because many of them contain oxylates and other substances that may be harmful if ingested in quantity. Be very sure you can identify the greens you propose using, and wash them with great care.

Dandelion, or *Taraxacum officinale,* is easy to find and easy to handle if it is cut off at the root crown so that the leaf cluster holds together. Its slightly acid taste complements that of beetroot. After the plants flower, the leaves become tough and quite bitter. Edible varieties of sorrel are numerous, the best being *Rumex acetosella* and *R. acetosa.* The leaves have a pleasantly sour taste and when cooked make an esteemed garnish for seafood. Winter cress, or *Barbarea vulgaris,* is, as its name implies, highly resistant to cold and is widely distributed. The rosette of smooth dark-green leaves may be gathered as new growth either in early spring or late fall.

ABOUT TOSSED SALADS

Salad ingredients prepared long in advance suffer a loss of nutritive value and arrive at table looking discouragingly limp. Take care in washing not to bruise them; see that they are well chilled, crisp and—especially—dry. It is usual to tear rather than cut greens, except iceberg lettuce, which, if you desire smaller pieces, can be sliced or shredded.

➤ To prepare lettuce, separate the leaves and wash them thoroughly. With iceberg lettuce this is difficult unless you core the solid part of the stem, either by using a sharp knife or by pounding the bottom of the head quite hard on a

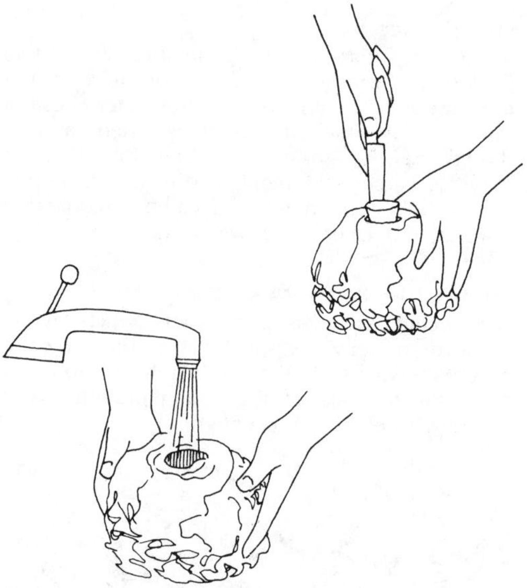

wooden board, when the core will simply fall out. Hold the head upside down under running water. Water pressure pushes the leaves apart without bruising them. Boston and field lettuces must be inspected carefully for grit and sand. Try some of the wild as well as the cultivated salad greens previously listed, for their texture and flavors differ distinctively.

➤ Dry greens by letting them drip in a colander, wrapping them lightly in a soft absorbent towel until dry, and chilling in the refrigerator until crisp and ready to use. Whirling greens in a wire salad basket is often recommended, but a Breton friend observes that, at home, this kind of treatment is contemptuously referred to as "a ride in the jail wagon," because it manhandles the occupants. If you like to whirl, try doing it in a tea towel. To dry such lettuces as bibb, which may be cleaned while still in head form, invert to drain, then place in the refrigerator on a turkish towel, cover with another plain towel and chill for several hours. Gravity and capillary action render them dry and crisp.

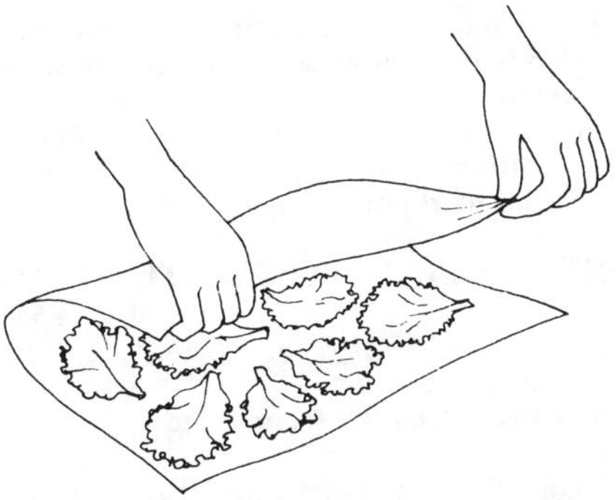

Place the greens in an ample bowl and give them a preliminary light coating of oil. About 1 tablespoon of salad oil will suffice for a medium-sized head of lettuce. Toss repeatedly by lifting the leaves gently with a large fork and spoon until each leaf is completely coated. This conditions the greens against the wilting actions of the vinegar. Follow up with more oil, vinegar—in all, about ¼ the amount of oil—salt to taste, and further tossing. If the salad is mixed on this principle it will stay crisp, although it is usually eaten too quickly to prove it.

Since vinegar and salt release juices and impair vitamin content, add them as close to serving time as possible. ▤ For a picnic or barbecue, prepare the greens, wash and drain them, and put them in a large plastic bag. Take the dressing along in a separate container. Just before serving, pour the dressing into the bag and gently work it until the salad greens are coated. Serve from the bag or turn out into a large bowl.

The choice of salad oil is important. First in order of excellence is virgin-press olive oil, slightly unsaturated, light in color and with a faint aroma. Also available are mixtures of bland polyunsaturated oils, 5, preferred by some for dietetic reasons. You will also encounter an occasional gourmet who uses nothing but sesame oil, or a cholesterol-conscious person who will eat only oil of safflower. An economical and effective substitute for straight safflower oil is a mixture of 20% safflower and 80% of another polyunsaturated oil such as peanut or cottonseed. If you find the taste of olive oil too strong, try combining it with any one of the blander, more highly polyunsaturated salad oils.

Your choice of a sour ingredient will depend on your own taste, but a good wine vinegar or lemon juice is the usual accompaniment to oil. Various kinds of herb vinegars are frequently chosen, but you may prefer to add these herbs separately later when you add the other seasonings. For a discussion of vinegars, see page 526. The classic oil-to-vinegar proportions are 3 or 4 to 1. Remember the old admonition: "Let the salad-maker be a spendthrift for oil, a miser for vinegar, a statesman for salt, a madman for mixing." To which we would add: an abolitionist for moisture.

Additional dressings, condiments and trimmings may be added after oil and vinegar to produce that infinite variety in flavor that is one of the chief charms of a tossed salad. Garlic is perhaps the most influential seasoning. There are two ways of giving to a salad a delicate touch of this pungent herb. Split a clove of garlic and rub the inside of the salad bowl with it. Or rub a rather dry crust of bread on all sides with a split clove of garlic; this is called a **chapon.** Place the bread in the bowl with the salad ingredients. Add the dressing and toss the salad lightly to distribute the flavor. Remove the chapon and serve the salad at once. If you wish to have a slightly stronger flavor, you may mash the garlic at the bottom of your salad bowl with other seasonings before adding oil and vinegar. This seems to modify its heavy pungency. ➤ Never leave a whole clove of garlic in any food brought to the table. Salting your salad may be unnecessary. If, after a cautious taste-test, you decide that it will improve your mix, sprinkle it on very sparingly and give the salad a final thorough tossing.

Additions to tossed salads may include sliced hard-cooked eggs, radishes, chopped olives, nut meats, pimiento or green pepper, sardines, anchovy, slivered cheese, julienned ham, chicken, tongue, grated carrots, cubed celery, onions—pickled, grated or as juice—and horseradish. Even a bit of cream or catsup may transfigure an otherwise lackluster mayonnaise, French or boiled dressing. In particular, the use of fresh herbs, 579, may make a salad the high point of a meal. For already made-up dressings suitable for tossed salads, see variations on French Dressings, 360, 361, Low-Calorie Dressings, 362, and Mayonnaise Dressings, 363, 368. The last may be used as indicated or slightly thinned with cream or yogurt.

➤ It is unwise to add cut-up tomatoes to a tossed salad; their juices will thin the dressing. Prepare them separately and use them for garnishing the salad bowl. The French cut tomatoes into vertical slices, 106, since they bleed less this way. Another nice last-minute addition is small hot Croutons, 551, sprinkled over a tossed salad just before serving.

Well-seasoned wooden salad bowls have acquired a sacred untouchability with some gourmets which we think is misplaced. If the surface of a wooden salad bowl is protected by a varnish, as many are nowadays, the flavors of the oil, vinegar and herbs will not penetrate it, and you might just as well wash it in the usual way. An untreated wooden surface will certainly absorb some of the dressing used, but the residue left after wiping the bowl tends to become rancid, since we house our utensils in quarters warmer than they do abroad. This rancidity can noticeably affect the flavor of the salad. We prefer a bowl made of glass, of pottery with a glazed surface, or of hard, dense, greaseproof plastic.

CAESAR SALAD

4 Servings

Steep:

1 clove garlic, peeled and sliced

in:

½ cup olive oil: none other

for 24 hours. Sauté:

1 cup cubed French bread

in 2 tablespoons of the garlic oil, above.
Break up into 2-inch lengths:

2 heads washed, dried romaine

Place the romaine in a salad bowl. Sprinkle over it:

1½ teaspoons salt
¼ teaspoon dry mustard
A generous grating of black pepper
(5 fillets of anchovy, cut up small or mashed to a paste, 570)
(A few drops of Worcestershire sauce)

Add:

3 tablespoons wine vinegar

and the remaining 6 tablespoons of garlic oil. Cook gently in simmering water for 1 to 1½ minutes, or use raw, 743:

1 egg

Drop the egg from the shell onto the ingredients in the bowl. Squeeze over the egg:

The juice of 1 lemon

Add the croutons and:

2 to 3 tablespoons Parmesan cheese

Toss the salad well. Serve at once.

WESTERN SALAD

4 Servings

Prepare:

Caesar Salad, above

omitting the anchovies and adding:

2 tablespoons crumbled blue cheese

WILTED GREENS

4 Servings

Exceptions prove the rule, and we justify the formulas for wilted greens in this section as applying to semicooked rather than raw salads—and thus outside our previous insistence on crispness of leaf.

Sauté:

4 or 5 slices bacon

Remove from pan, drain on absorbent paper and cut or crumble into small pieces. Heat:

2 tablespoons melted butter, bacon drippings or oil

Add:

¼ cup mild vinegar
(1 teaspoon chopped fresh herbs, 579)

Add the bacon, and also at this time if you choose:

(1 teaspoon grated onion)
(1 teaspoon sugar)

Pour the dressing while hot over:

1 head lettuce, separated; shredded cabbage; dandelion, young spinach leaves or other greens

Serve at once from a warm bowl onto warm plates, garnished with:

Sliced hard-cooked eggs

CHICORY AND BEETROOT SALAD

4 Servings

A favorite winter salad in France. Cut in ½-inch slices into a salad bowl:

6 heads Belgian or French endive

Add:

2 cups drained sliced canned or cooked beets

Toss in:

French Dressing, 360, or
Watercress Dressing, 360

ORIENTAL BEAN SPROUT SALAD

6 Servings

Place in a salad bowl:

4 cups crisp salad greens
1 cup drained bean sprouts
½ cup thinly sliced water chestnuts
¼ cup toasted slivered almonds

Toss, just before serving, in:

¼ to ⅓ cup Oriental Dip, 90

thinned with:

2 tablespoons cream

COLESLAW

6 Servings

For those who wonder why cabbage is way out in front as the American vegetable crop, the answer is a rude four-letter word: slaw. Use "white" or red cabbage alone, or combine them for more interesting color. Or substitute Chinese cabbage, or bok choi, 94. Pared and diced pineapple or apple may be added, and bean sprouts are a welcome addition. Remove the outer leaves and the core from:

A small head of cabbage

Shred or chop the remainder, cutting only as much as is needed for immediate use. Chill. Just before serving, moisten with:

French Dressing, 360, or Boiled Dressing, 366
Sour Cream Dressing, 367, or equal parts mayonnaise and chili sauce, or sweet or cultured sour cream

If you choose the cream, be sure to season with a little vinegar, salt and sugar. You may add to any of the above dressings:

(Dill, caraway or celery seed)
(Chopped parsley, chives or other herbs)

COLESLAW DE LUXE

8 Servings

Shortly before serving time, remove the core from:

A small head of cabbage

Cut it into the thinnest shreds possible. Place in a deep bowl. Add:

1 to 2 tablespoons lemon juice
(Fresh herbs: chopped parsley, chives, etc.)

Beat until stiff:

¾ cup whipping cream

Fold in:

½ teaspoon celery seed
½ teaspoon sugar
¾ teaspoon salt
¼ teaspoon freshly ground white pepper
1 cup seedless green grapes
½ cup finely shredded blanched almonds

Pour this mixture over the cabbage. Toss quickly until well coated. Serve at once with:

Tomatoes, or in an Aspic Ring, 113

ROQUEFORT COLESLAW

4 Servings

Based on a recipe from Herman Smith. His engaging little books, *Stina* and *Kitchens Near and Far,* have appealed to all lovers of good eating and reading.

Shred finely:

1½ cups young white or red cabbage

Peel and cut into long, narrow strips:

1 cup apples

In order to keep them from discoloring, sprinkle with:

Lemon juice

Toss salad lightly with:

Roquefort Sour Cream Dressing, 367

Serve at once, garnished with:

Parsley

⊟ COLESLAW FOR BARBECUE

6 Servings

The tangy dressing in this slaw goes well with meat broiled or barbecued outdoors. If you are cooking farther from home than your own backyard or patio, try the plastic bag method of "tossing" the slaw described on 95.

Combine:

1 cup Mayonnaise, 363
4 chopped scallions
2 teaspoons vinegar
⅛ teaspoon Worcestershire sauce
¼ teaspoon salt
⅛ teaspoon pepper
¼ teaspoon sugar

Add this mixture to:

3 cups shredded cabbage
3 cups salad greens
1 thinly sliced carrot
½ green pepper, cut into strips

Toss salad lightly and serve.

HOT SLAW WITH APPLE

6 Servings

Place in a skillet:

½ lb. finely diced salt pork

Render it slowly, then remove the crisp browned pieces, drain on absorbent paper and reserve. Add to the rendered fat in the skillet:

3 tablespoons vinegar
2 tablespoons water
1 tablespoon sugar
1 teaspoon caraway or celery seed
1 teaspoon salt

Cook and stir these ingredients over high heat until they boil. ➤ Reduce heat to a simmer. Stir in:

3 cups shredded cabbage
1 large pared, grated apple

Simmer the slaw about one minute longer and serve garnished with the tiny browned cubes of salt pork.

⅄ BLENDER SLAW

4 Servings

Quarter and core:

1 small head of cabbage

Core, seed and remove membrane of:

½ green pepper

Peel:

½ medium-sized onion
1 carrot

Chop these vegetables coarsely into the blender container until it is half filled. Add to within 1 inch of the top:

Cold water

➤ Cover and blend for 2 seconds—no longer—using the chopping speed. Empty the vegetables into a sieve to drain, and repeat the process until all the vegetables are shredded. Place them in a salad bowl and sprinkle with:

(1 teaspoon caraway seeds)

Toss lightly in:

Mayonnaise, 363, or
Sour Cream Dressing, 367

thinned with:

2 tablespoons lemon juice

GINGHAM SALAD WITH COTTAGE CHEESE

4 Servings

Place in a mixing bowl and toss:

1½ cups coarsely chopped young spinach leaves
2 cups shredded red cabbage
⅓ teaspoon salt
¼ teaspoon celery seed
3 tablespoons chopped olives or chives
1 cup cottage cheese

Place these ingredients on:

4 large lettuce leaves

Serve the salad with:

Mayonnaise, 363, Sour Cream Dressing, 367, or Green Mayonnaise, 364

ABOUT TOSSED COMBINATION SALADS

Serve combination salads as a luncheon main dish, accompanied by Toasted Cheese Rolls, 72, or savory sandwiches, 269. Practically every restaurant serves some kind of combination salad, often named after its own inventive chef, but all have the distinction of containing some form of protein such as meat, chicken or cheese in addition to the greens and vegetables. Here are variations:

COMBINATION SALADS

I. Rub a salad bowl with:

Garlic

Place in it:

Lettuce or spinach leaves
Chopped, pitted ripe olives
Sliced radishes
Sliced hard-cooked eggs
Shredded Swiss cheese
(Chopped anchovies or bits of sautéed bacon or salami)

Toss the salad with:

French Dressing, 360

Garnish it with:

Skinned and quartered tomatoes

For a **Greek Salad,** add sliced cucumbers, cubes of the crumbly white cheese known as feta, and a sprinkling of oregano.

II. **About 30 Servings**

This makes a showy platter for a luncheon buffet. On an oblong tray, make a base of salad greens:

Lettuce
Endive
Romaine
Watercress

Prepare, but do not overcook:

1 whole cooked cauliflower
3 cups cooked green beans
2 cups cooked beets
4 bunches cooked asparagus tips

Add:

3 cups bean sprouts
1 cup raw sliced mushrooms
1 cup raw julienned celeriac

Marinate all the above several hours in:

French Dressing, 360, or Italian Dressing, 361

Use about 1/4 cup of dressing to 2 cups of vegetables. Drain well. Arrange the vegetables around the cauliflower center as shown, garnished with:

Deviled Eggs, 225
Radishes
Red pepper lobster cutouts

Other garnishes might include:

(Olives)
(Sardines or anchovies)
(Cherry tomatoes)

III. **2 Servings**

What various chefs call their **Maurice Salad** has spread like a brushfire all over America and abroad. Ours is not the original version, which was put together by a Cincinnatian; but at least the ingredients, except for the optional ones, remain fairly orthodox.

Place in each of 2 sizable salad bowls:

A bed of shredded crisphead lettuce

Divide and arrange on the top of each:

1/2 cup julienned cooked chicken
1/2 cup julienned baked ham
(10 or 12 strips julienned Swiss cheese)

Add to each bowl:

(1 or 2 chopped anchovies)
(A few capers)

Garnish with:

2 sections skinned, quartered tomatoes
2 quarters hard-cooked egg

Toss with a dressing made of:

1/2 chopped hard-cooked egg
1 teaspoon finely chopped chives
3/4 cup Mayonnaise, 363
1 teaspoon lemon juice
1 teaspoon Worcestershire sauce
1 tablespoon chopped dill pickle or pickle relish
(1 pressed clove garlic)

CUTTING VEGETABLE GARNISHES AND CASES

Use vegetables as cases for piquant fillings as sketched at the top of following page: a hollowed-out pepper which can be lidded with its own handsomely fat stem portion; next, a trimmed cooked artichoke, with core removed to form a cup; an onion sliced to produce rings which will hold vinaigretted asparagus upright—center—on an hors d'oeuvre tray; to right of center, citrus rind rings or green or red pepper rings which can be used in the same manner to sup-

port food; onion cups made from raw or slightly blanched onions; a cucumber slashed and hollowed out to hold olives or gherkins; and, last in line, a scored cucumber cup.

Try your hand at carving vegetables and see what fun you can have and how attractive your trays can look with a little effort. Don't force effects. Use them sparingly. Begin with a choice of assorted herbs, below, left—thyme, burnet, tarragon, chives and garlic chives, fennel and watercress—above carrots cut in scrolls, radishes made into roses, and pickles into fans. Provide geometric accents with hors d'oeuvre cutters and scoops, shown at center left and at the top on the right. Shape flowers and borders of red, yellow or green peppers; olives, at right of center, with twists of cucumber at lower right. Make an ingenuous turnip or egg white and carrot daisy, gay for spinach dishes, or small daffodil blooms of carrots and turnips, shown at center right. The flowers can have fernlike stems and leaves of chive or other herbs, as you like. Try for some asymmetric drawinglike effects, such as shrimps suggested by thin lines of red pepper. One of the loveliest decorations we've ever seen were 2 small lobsters cut in conventionalized style from red peppers and placed casually on the side and the top of a cream-covered mousse. Seaweed, indicated by fennel leaves, partially crowned the top. See also 571 for varied lemon garnishes.

ABOUT VEGETABLES FOR SALAD

A welcome summertime alternative to crisp green salads or slaws is a vegetable salad, attractively arranged and dressed. Try the marinated Combination Salad, 98; simply prepare chilled cooked vegetables and serve them with a light vinaigrette or chiffonade dressing; or use Vegetables à la Grecque, 281, including snow peas. All the vegetables should be lightly cooked so as to retain some "bite."

GARNISHES FOR SALADS

To garnish salads, use the following:

Tomato slices dipped in finely chopped parsley or chives
Parsley or watercress in bunches or chopped lettuce leaves, cress, endive or romaine
Heads of lettuce cut into slices or wedges
Lemon slices with pinked edges, dipped in chopped parsley
Shredded olives or sliced stuffed olives
Cooked beets cut into shapes or sticks
Carrots cut into shapes
Pearl onions
Pickles
Capers
Pomegranate seeds
Seedless or seeded table grapes
Fennel slices
Cucumber or Cucumber Slices, 102
Green and red peppers, shredded
Pepper slices
Mayonnaise or soft cream cheese forced through a decorating tube
Aspic jellies in small molds, or chopped aspic
Eggs—hard-cooked, sliced, riced or stuffed
Small-sized tomatoes, halved, and stuffed with cottage cheese
Cherry tomatoes
Slices of Spanish or Bermuda onion
Fresh herbs, sprigs or chopped
Mint leaves
Nasturtium leaves
Nutmeats
Chopped truffles
Shaped truffles

RUSSIAN SALAD

6 Servings

This recipe can be made quickly with canned vegetables, although it is not quite so good. If you

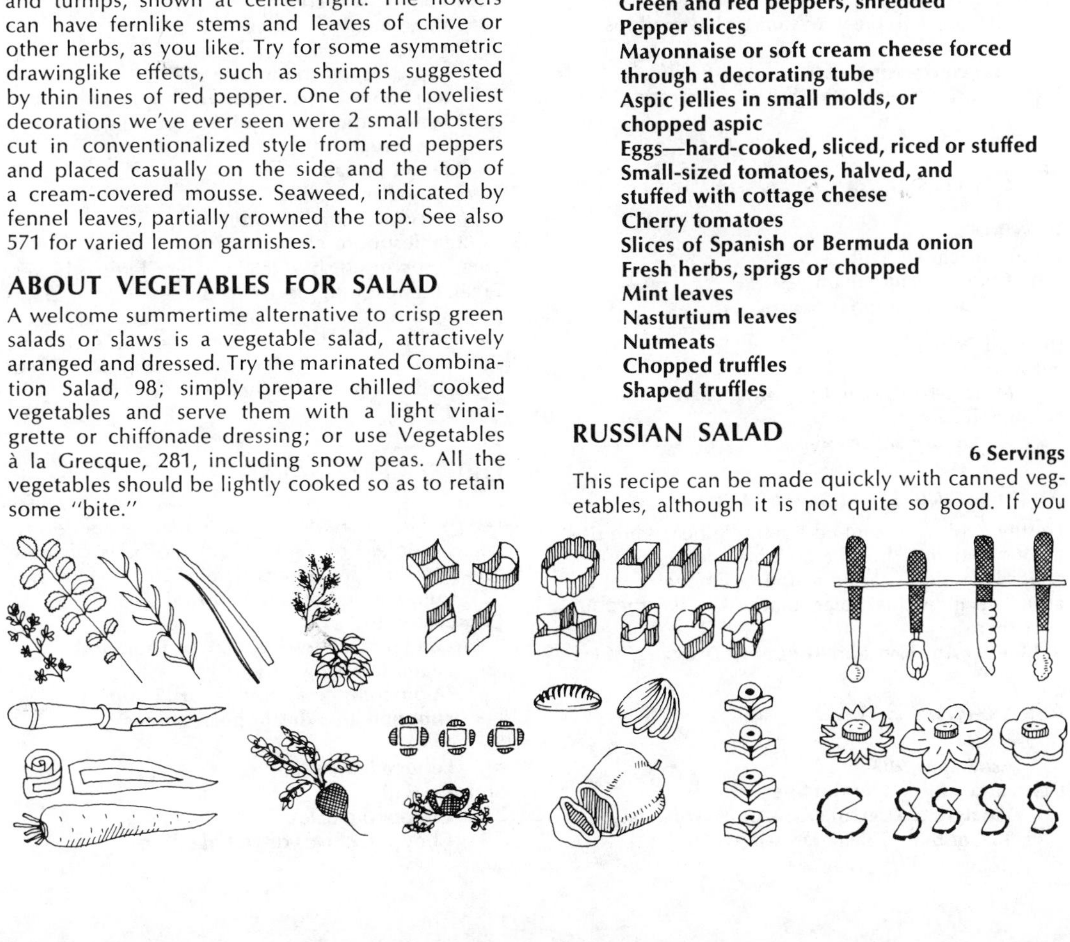

wish, you may marinate your vegetables for 1 hour in French dressing, then drain and toss them in the mayonnaise. Prepare and dice in ¼-inch cubes:

1 cup cooked carrots
1 cup cooked waxy potatoes
1 cup cooked beets
½ cup cooked green beans

Add:

½ cup cooked peas

Toss the vegetables in:

Mayonnaise, 363

Serve in mounds on lettuce leaves, garnished with:

(A few capers)
(Julienned strips of ham)

For a more elegant occasion, after incorporating the mayonnaise—which should be a stiff one—mold the salad into a fish shape and cover with thin overlapping slices of cucumber, suggesting fish scales.

STUFFED ARTICHOKE SALAD

I. With Seafood

Cook:

Artichokes, 282

Chill, and remove the inedible choke. Marinate:

Shrimp, crab meat, oysters or bay scallops

in:

French Dressing, 360

Fill the artichokes with the seafood and serve with:

Mayonnaise, 363

on a bed of:

Shredded lettuce

II. With Caviar

Fill the artichokes with:

Cultured sour cream
Caviar or salmon roe

III. With Meat

Fill with:

Minced ham, veal, tuna or chicken

combined with:

Andalouse Sauce, 364

ARTICHOKE HEART SALAD

Freshly cooked or canned artichoke hearts are delicious and may be cut up and added to green salads or aspics, or used as the groundwork for an attractive individual salad plate. We like to pour over them:

⅄ Blender Anchovy and Roquefort Dressing, 361

ASPARAGUS SALAD

Cook:

Asparagus, 283

Drain and chill. Cover the tips with:

Vinaigrette Dressing, 360, or Mayonnaise, 363, or Boiled Salad Dressing, 366

thinned with a little:

Cultured sour cream

Add:

(Chopped tarragon, parsley or chives)

ASPARAGUS TIP AND GREEN PEPPER SALAD

Drain the contents of a can of:

Asparagus tips

Place around 4 or 5 tips a ring of:

Red or green pepper

Place the asparagus in the ring on:

Shredded lettuce

Serve the salad with:

French Dressing, 360, Italian Dressing, 361, or Mayonnaise, 363

ASPARAGUS AND EGG SALAD

6 Servings

Chill in a dish:

2 cups well-drained, cooked asparagus cut into pieces
3 sliced hard-cooked eggs
6 sliced stuffed olives

Wash, drain and place in refrigerator to crisp:

1 bunch watercress
1 small head of lettuce

When ready to serve, combine:

½ cup cultured sour cream
2 teaspoons grated onion or chopped chives
2 tablespoons lemon juice, caper liquor or vinegar
1 teaspoon salt
¼ teaspoon paprika
1/16 teaspoon curry powder
(2 tablespoons capers)

Line a serving dish with the larger lettuce leaves. Break the rest into pieces. Add these to the asparagus mixture. Cut up coarsely and add the watercress. Pour the dressing over these ingredients. Toss lightly. Place them in the serving dish. Serve the salad at once, garnished with:

Parsley

DRIED BEAN SALAD

4 to 6 Servings

Lentils, kidney, navy, lima or miniature edible soybeans, cooked or canned, are the basis of these "stick-to-the-ribs" salads. Drain well and chill:

2½ cups canned or cooked beans

Combine with:

¼ cup French Dressing, 360, or Thousand Island Dressing, 364
(A pinch of curry powder or ¼ cup chopped gherkins or pearl onions)

Serve on:

Lettuce leaves

Sprinkle with:

Chopped parsley
Chopped chives or grated onion

⊟ GREEN BEAN SALAD

4 to 6 Servings

Prepare:
3 cups cooked Green Beans, 285
Drain well and toss while warm in:
French Dressing, 360, or
Lorenzo Dressing, 360
Chill thoroughly, then add:
Chopped or grated onions, chives or pearl onions
Serve on:
Lettuce leaves

HOT GREEN BEAN SALAD

6 Servings

Prepare:
3 cups cooked Green Beans, 285
Drain them. Combine them with the dressing for:
Wilted Greens, 96
Season as desired or with:
(Summer savory)
Serve from a warm bowl onto warm plates.

COLD BEET CUPS

Cook:
Large Beets, 290
and chill. Hollow out the beets and fill them with:
Chopped Wilted Cucumbers II, 102, with cultured sour cream, or Russian Salad, 99, Coleslaw, 96, or Deviled Eggs, 225
Garnish with:
Curly endive

PICKLED BEET SALAD

5 to 6 Servings

Drain:
2½ cups cooked or canned beets
Reserve the juice. Slice the beets. Place them in a fruit jar. Boil:
½ cup sharp vinegar
½ cup beet juice
Add and heat to boiling:
2 tablespoons sugar
2 cloves
½ teaspoon salt
3 peppercorns
¼ bay leaf
(1 sliced green pepper)
(1 sliced small onion)
(½ teaspoon horseradish)
Pour these ingredients over the beets. Cover the jar. Refrigerate at least 12 hours before serving on:
Watercress
with:
Quartered hard-cooked eggs

CARROT SALAD WITH RAISINS AND NUTS

4 Servings

Scrape well:
4 large carrots
Place them on ice for 1 hour. Grate them coarsely into a bowl. Add and mix lightly:
½ cup raisins
½ cup coarsely chopped pecans or peanuts
¾ teaspoon salt
Freshly ground black pepper
2 teaspoons grated lemon peel
1 tablespoon lemon juice
Place the salad in a bowl. Pour over it:
1 cup or more cultured sour cream, or half sour cream and half mayonnaise
Toss the salad and serve.

CELERY CABBAGE SALAD

Use celery cabbage in any recipe for hot or cold slaw, 96, or in the following colorful recipe.
Wash well, then crisp:
1 stalk celery cabbage
Cut it crosswise into shreds. Serve very cold with:
French Dressing, 360, o
Curry Mayonnaise, 365
This cabbage combines superbly with:
Watercress
Use any convenient proportion. Garnish the salad with:
Pickled Beets, left

COOKED CELERY OR ENDIVE SALAD

I. Prepare:
Braised Celery or Endive, 298
and serve cold on:
Lettuce leaves

II. Simmer until tender:
Trimmed, halved dwarf celery or endive heads
in a quantity of:
Veal or chicken stock
Drain. Refrigerate the juices for use in sauces. Marinate the vegetable in:
French Dressing, 360
to which you may add:
(1 teaspoon anchovy paste)
Chill and serve on:
Lettuce

CELERIAC OR CELERY ROOT SALAD

Prepare:
Celeriac, 298
Chill it. Toss it in:
Mayonnaise, 363, well seasoned with mustard, or Salsa Verde, 361
or, best of all, in:
French Dressing, 360
to which you may add:
(Minced shallots or chives)
Serve on:
Endive or watercress

CELERIAC OR CELERI-RAVE RÉMOULADE

5 to 6 Servings

This also makes an interesting hors d'oeuvre. Wash well and pare as for Cooked Turnips, 335, in ¼-inch rounds:

2 celeriac, about 4 inches in diameter

Blanch, 154, in boiling salted water 3 to 4 minutes. Drain at once. Cool and dry. Cut into a fine julienne, 296. Cover with:

Rémoulade Sauce, 364

allowing about ½ cup sauce for each 2 cups of celeriac strips. Chill well and serve on:

Watercress

TURNIPS RÉMOULADE

4 Servings

Wash well, pare, 335, and slice julienned, 296:

2 cups turnips

Cover with:

Rémoulade Sauce, 364

allowing about ½ cup sauce for each 2 cups of julienned turnips. Serve chilled on:

Chicory

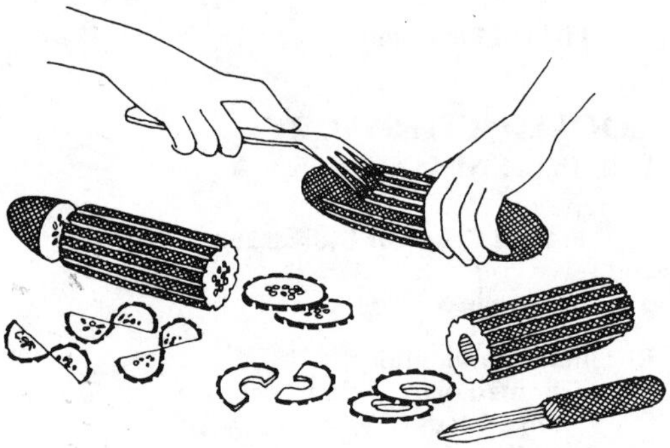

CUCUMBER SALAD

Be sure to select firm, hard cucumbers. Unless you are dealing with the roundish "apple" cucumber, yellowness is an undesirable trait, as is flabbiness. Both signify age, a pithy interior, and a tough skin. Otherwise the skin is edible, sometimes even by allergics who cannot tolerate the pulp alone. The skin should have a slight sheen; if highly polished, however, it has probably been waxed and should then be discarded. If you wish to make the cucumbers more decorative, leave them unpared and score them with a fork, as sketched, before slicing.

Chill, pare and slice:

Cucumbers

Combine them with:

French Dressing, 360, or
Sour Cream Dressing, 367

to which you may add:

(Finely minced parsley)

Serve at once.

WILTED CUCUMBERS

As with other wilted salad materials, nutritive value declines; but heightened delicacy of flavor and appealingly smooth texture go far to compensate.

I.

Pare and slice very thin:

Cucumbers

A potato peeler, left, does a fine job. Place the slices in a bowl. Salt each layer and place a weighted plate over the whole. Cover and refrigerate 3 to 6 hours. Drain and toss in:

Cultured sour cream or yogurt

Garnish with:

Chopped dill, basil or tarragon

Serve chilled at once.

II. **3 Servings**

Slice, leaving the skins on if very young and unwaxed:

1½ to 2 cups cucumbers

Salt and weight as above. Refrigerate 2 hours. Rinse in cold water, drain and dry. Place the cucumbers in a bowl and toss them in:

¼ cup vinegar

and:

1 tablespoon sugar

dissolved in:

1 tablespoon water
Season to taste

Chill 1 to 2 hours and serve garnished with:

Chopped dill or burnet or very thinly sliced Bermuda onion rings

COLD STUFFED CUCUMBERS

Refreshing on a luncheon plate or as hors d'oeuvre.

Chill:

Small, shapely cucumbers

Pare them. Cut them in halves lengthwise or cut off a slice lengthwise and remove the seeds. The cucumber boats may be wrapped in waxed paper and chilled. Fill with:

Chicken Salad, 108, a fish salad, 107

or anything suitable that you can think of, such as:

Nutmeats or green grapes in seasoned cream cheese, minced ham, etc.

These ingredients may be moistened with or served with:

Mayonnaise, 363, Beet and Anchovy Dressing, 361, or Chutney Dressing, 361

Serve the cucumbers on:

Shredded lettuce or watercress

LOTUS ROOT SALAD

Peel and slice thin, crosswise:

1 lb. lotus root

Soak 10 minutes in:

Acidulated Water, 520

Drain and dip slices into:

Fresh, boiling acidulated water

Plunge quickly into:

Cold water

and drain again. Combine and heat:

2 tablespoons sesame oil
1 to 2 drops hot pepper sauce
1½ tablespoons sugar
2½ tablespoons soy sauce

Pour this sauce over the drained lotus root and let stand about 1 hour. Serve chilled in the sauce.

OKRA SALAD

A hot-weather salad. The marinated pods are slightly reminiscent of oysters, even more so if white-podded okra is used.

Prepare:

Stewed Okra, 310

Drain. Place in a dish and cover with:

Well-seasoned French Dressing, 360, Horseradish Dressing, 362, or Mayonnaise, 363

Chill. Serve very cold on:

Lettuce

HEARTS OF PALM SALAD

I. Cut into strips lengthwise:

Chilled canned hearts of palm

Serve on:

Romaine

garnished with:

Stuffed olive slices
Green or red pepper rings

Sprinkle with:

Chopped parsley
Paprika

Serve with:

French Dressing, 360, or Roquefort or Blue Cheese Dressing, 361, or Mayonnaise, 363

II. If you live in Florida, you can have fresh:

Hearts of Palm

but see page 313. Be sure to eat them as soon as peeled, for they discolor quickly. Cut them into dice and sprinkle with:

Lemon juice

and serve with:

French Dressing 360, made with lime juice, or Sauce Louis, 365

Another way to serve them is to treat the hearts as for Coleslaw, 96.

SALAD NIÇOISE

4 Servings

This recipe from the South of France is often carried to the point of agreeable anarchy, when it becomes a **salmagundi,** and is apt to include strips of cooked chicken, seedless grapes or little onions, and hard-cooked eggs. In compounding, keep in mind the law of diminishing returns.

Rub your salad bowl with garlic, then place in it:

2 skinned and quartered tomatoes
1 pared and finely cut cucumber
6 coarsely chopped fillets of anchovy
12 coarsely chopped pitted black olives
1 cup bibb lettuce
1 cup romaine

Toss in:

French Dressing, 360, or Italian Dressing, 361

PEPPER SLICES WITH FILLINGS

8 to 10 Slices

Highly decorative. These make a pretty salad and are bracing as canapés on toast or crackers.

Wash:

2 medium-sized red or green peppers

Cut a piece from the stem end and remove the seeds and membranes. Stuff the peppers with a Cream Cheese Spread, 71, or Ham Salad, 109, and chill 12 hours. Slice, not too thinly, with a sharp hot knife and replace on ice. You may serve the slices on:

Lettuce

with:

French Dressing, 360, or Mayonnaise, 363, or Curry Mayonnaise, 365

★ FILLED PIMIENTOS OR CHRISTMAS SALAD

6 Servings

Cheery as Santa's chuckle; but do not expect the peppers to look like fresh ones. They are simply a gift-wrap for the soft filling.

Drain:

6 large canned pimientos

Dice:

2½ cups drained canned pineapple

Add to it:

1½ cups diced celery
1 tablespoon pickled tiny pearl onions

Whip until stiff:

¼ cup whipping cream

Combine with:

1 cup Mayonnaise, 363

Fold into these liquid ingredients the pineapple, celery and onions. Stuff the pimientos with the mixture. Chill. Bed on a nest of:

Shredded lettuce

POTATO SALAD

Potato salad is best prepared from potatoes cooked in their jackets and peeled and marinated while still warm. The small red waxy potatoes hold their shape and don't crumble when sliced or diced, but medium-sized mature Idahos are also entirely satisfactory. Do not try to make do with yesterday's cold boiled potatoes; they will have lost much of their down-to-earth savor. ➤ For hot weather picnics, use an eggless dressing to avoid dangerous spoilage.

I. **4 Servings**

Prepare as described above:

2 cups sliced boiled potatoes

Marinate in:

½ cup heated French Dressing, 360

Mix in gently with a wooden spoon, just before serving:

1 tablespoon chopped parsley
1 tablespoon chopped chives or
1 tablespoon finely grated onion

Serve tepid.

II. **4 Servings**

Marinate the potatoes well with:

½ cup French Dressing, 360, soup stock or canned bouillon

Chop or slice and add discreetly a mixture of any of the following:

Hard-cooked eggs, onions, olives, pickles, celery with leaves, cucumbers, capers
1 to 2 teaspoons salt
Paprika
A few grains cayenne
(2 teaspoons horseradish)

After one hour or more of refrigeration, add:

Mayonnaise, 363, Boiled Salad Dressing I, 366, or cultured sour cream

Refrigerate about 1 hour longer. Shortly before serving, you may toss in:

(Coarsely chopped watercress)

POTATO AND HERRING SALAD

6 Servings

Place in a large bowl and toss gently:

2 cups diced boiled potatoes
1¼ cups diced marinated or pickled herring fillets
¾ cup chopped celery with leaves
1 tablespoon minced parsley
1 tablespoon minced chives
6 tablespoons cultured sour cream
1½ tablespoons lemon juice
¾ teaspoon paprika

Serve the salad chilled in:

Lettuce cups

GERMAN HOT POTATO SALAD

6 Servings

Cook in their jackets, in a covered saucepan, until tender:

6 medium-sized potatoes

Peel and slice while hot. Heat in a skillet:

4 strips bacon, minced, or 2 tablespoons bacon drippings

reserving bacon. Sauté until golden:

¼ cup chopped onion
¼ cup chopped celery

Add:

1 chopped dill pickle

Heat to the boiling point:

¼ cup water or stock
½ cup vinegar
½ teaspoon sugar
½ teaspoon salt
⅛ teaspoon paprika
(¼ teaspoon dry mustard)

Combine all ingredients in skillet, stir gently with the potatoes, and serve at once with chopped parsley or chives. Leftovers are good served cold.

POTATO SALAD NIÇOISE

12 Servings

Cook:

3 cups Boiled New Potatoes, 317

in water to which a clove of garlic has been added. Peel and slice and, while still warm, sprinkle potatoes with:

½ cup heated white wine or ¼ cup wine vinegar and ¼ cup stock

Let stand 1 hour at 70°. Have ready:

3 cups chilled cooked green beans
6 skinned quartered tomatoes

which have been marinating in:

French Dressing, 360

To serve, mound the potatoes in a volcano shape in the center of a platter garnished with:

Salad greens

Garnish the potatoes with:

Capers
Small pitted black olives
1 dozen anchovy fillets

Alternate the tomato quarters and small heaps of the green beans around the potatoes.

RICE SALAD

6 Servings

A variation of this theme with bulgar or cracked wheat as the cereal is called **tabuli**.

Prepare:

2 cups Boiled Rice, 206

The grains must be dry and fluffy. While the rice is warm, mix in:

½ to ¾ cup Herbed French Dressing, 360
¼ cup finely chopped celery
(¼ cup coarsely chopped green pepper)
(10 black olives, pitted and halved)
1½ cups chopped Poached Scallops, 382, or 2 cans white tuna: 7 oz. each

Garnish with:

Skinned, quartered tomatoes or strips of red pepper

in a bowl lined with:

Leaf lettuce or watercress

or in:

Halves of avocado

If the fish is omitted, this dish teams up very successfully with cooked chicken or cooked smoked tongue. Serve tepid.

ABOUT TOMATOES FOR SALAD

Please read About Tomatoes, 331. In preparing tomatoes for salad, always cut out the stem-end core, which is tough and may be bitter. Good texture is as important as good flavor. Vine-ripened tomatoes are infinitely superior to those picked green and allowed to mature on their way to the supermarket. Use the latter for Stuffed Tomatoes, below, where they can be somewhat redeemed with a spicy filling. If available, the pear-shaped Italian variety, which has a distinctive mellow flavor, makes an excellent substitute. Another way to cope with this problem is to choose, instead, small cherry tomatoes, which, because of their proportionately large skin area, are pleasantly sharp in flavor. Halved or whole, they also lend themselves to dainty decorative uses.

FRENCH TOMATO SALAD

Cut into very thin vertical slices, 106:

6 medium-sized unskinned tomatoes

Place them so that they overlap around a cold platter or across it. Pour over them a dressing made of:

French Dressing, 360
1/4 cup minced parsley
2 minced shallots or green onions

CANNED TOMATO SALAD

Chill the contents of a can of:

Whole tomatoes

or use the firm part of any canned tomatoes. Place them in individual dishes. Sprinkle with:

Celery salt
Salt
Lemon juice
Brown sugar

or a garnish of your own improvisation. The main thing is to serve them very cold.

ABOUT COLD STUFFED TOMATOES

A bit of tomato skin was once as much out of place at a dinner table as a bowie knife. The discovery that tomato skins contain highly valued vitamins makes them *salon-fähig*—so whether to serve tomatoes skinned or unskinned rests with the hostess's sense of delicacy or her nutritional single-mindedness.

To skin tomatoes, first wash them, and then use one of the following methods: stroke the skin with the dull edge of a knife blade until the skin wrinkles and can be lifted off; or immerse in boiling water for 1 minute, then immediately in cold water, then drain and skin; or pierce with a fork and rotate over a burner until the skin is tight and shiny, plunge into cold water and peel.

To prepare tomato cases, first skin the tomatoes as described above, then hollow them out. Invert the tomatoes to drain for 20 minutes. Chill them and fill the hollows with one of the fillings suggested below.

Tomatoes cut and stuffed in a variety of attractive ways provide a gay splash of color for buffet salads. If you do not wish to serve large portions, cut the tomatoes into halves or slices. Place on each slice a ring of green pepper 1/2 inch or more thick. Fill the ring.

You may also cut tomatoes crosswise in zigzag fashion, fill them sandwich-style and top them with a mint leaf. Or, fill deeply gashed halves separately. Fill a whole tomato, which can have small or large gashes, and garnish with an olive slice or pimiento star; or cover with a pepper lid. Or, slice horizontally in thirds and fill like a double sandwich. All these cuts are shown below.

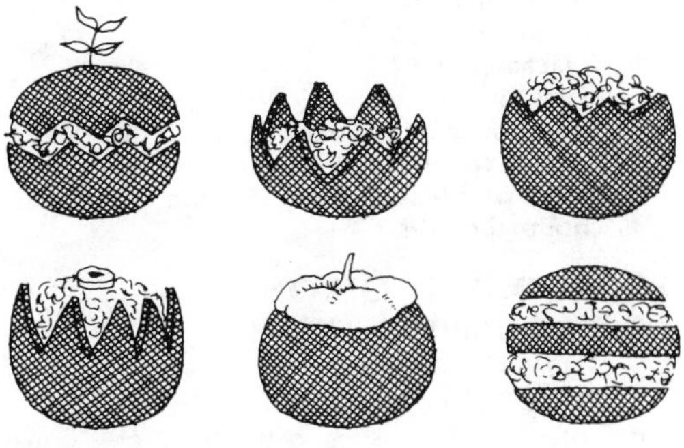

FILLINGS

I. Pineapple and Nutmeats

Combine equal parts of:

Chopped celery
Shredded fresh pineapple
A few walnut meats
Mayonnaise, 363

II. Eggs and Anchovies

Combine:

Chopped hard-cooked eggs
Chopped anchovies or anchovy paste
Onion juice or grated onion
Chopped parsley or other herb
Mayonnaise, 363, or cultured sour cream

III. Eggs and Ham

Combine:

2 chopped hard-cooked eggs
1 cup ground or minced ham
1/2 cup chopped celery
12 sliced olives
Fresh or dried savory
2 chopped sweet pickles
Sour Cream Dressing, 367, or
Mayonnaise, 363

IV. Deviled Eggs

Place in each tomato hollow:

1/2 Deviled Egg, 225

Serve on:

Lettuce

with:

Anchovy Sauce, 343

V. Aspic

For about 6 tomato cases prepare:

1 1/2 cups aspic, 113

This may also be an Aspic Salad, 113, to which chopped meat or fish and vegetables may be added. When the aspic is about to set, fill the tomato cases. Chill until firm. Garnish with:

Olives, parsley, etc.

and serve with:

Mayonnaise, 363

VI. Some other good fillings are:

Wilted Cucumbers I, 102
Crab Meat Salad, 106, or
a Fish Salad, 108
Chicken Salad, 108
Guacamole I, 83
Coleslaw, 96
Shrimp with Mayonnaise, 363
Cottage cheese or soft cream cheese
mixed with Mayonnaise, 363, and
chopped chives

TOMATO AND ONION OR CUCUMBER SALAD

Skin and chill:

Medium-sized tomatoes

Cut 5 or 6 vertical gashes in the tomatoes, equal distances apart. Place in each cut, as shown below, a thin slice of:

Bermuda onion or cucumber

Or, cut the slices through, and arrange them alternately on a so-called bone plate, shown above. Serve on:

Lettuce or watercress

with:

French Dressing, 360, or
Sour Cream Dressing, 367, or
Avocado Dressing II, 362

MOLDED EGG AND CAVIAR SALAD

Also notable as an hors d'oeuvre. Crush with a fork:

8 hard-cooked eggs

Stir into them:

3 tablespoons soft butter
1/3 teaspoon dry mustard
2 oz. caviar or salmon roe
3 tablespoons lemon juice
1 tablespoon Worcestershire sauce

Pack these ingredients into an oiled tall glass. Chill. Unmold and cut into ½- to 1-inch slices. Serve on:

Skinned thick tomato slices

cut in the French manner, as shown at left, or use to decorate a salad platter. Cover with a dab of:

Mayonnaise, 363
(A rolled anchovy)

STUFFED LETTUCE ROLLS

Add to:

Creamed cottage cheese

all or some of the following:

A sprinkling of chives or grated onion
Chopped boiled ham
Seedless raisins
Chopped celery
Chopped green peppers
Chopped nutmeats

Spread a thick layer of the cheese mixture on:

Large lettuce leaves

Roll the leaves and secure with toothpicks. Chill. Allow 2 or 3 rolls to a person. When set, remove the toothpicks and serve with:

Mayonnaise, 363, or French Dressing, 360

Garnish with a fancy-cut vegetable as sketched on 99.

MACARONI OR SPAGHETTI SALAD OR CALICO SALAD

5 Servings

Prepare:

2 cups cooked elbow macaroni, 213

Drain. Beat well:

1½ tablespoons lemon juice or
2 tablespoons vinegar
1 tablespoon salad oil

Combine this with the cooked macaroni. Chill the salad several hours. Toss with it a mixture of:

1 teaspoon grated onion or
2 tablespoons chopped chives
1 cup diced celery with leaves
1 cup minced parsley
½ cup chopped stuffed olives
¾ teaspoon salt
Freshly ground black pepper
3 tablespoons cultured sour cream
2 tablespoons chopped pimiento

Try substituting for the mixture above:

Basil Pesto, 570

Serve on:

Lettuce

or in:

A Tomato Aspic Ring, 115

CRAB OR LOBSTER SALAD

4 Servings

Dice:

1 cup canned or cooked crab or lobster meat

Add:

(Grated onion)

Marinate in:
¼ cup French Dressing, 360
Chill 1 hour. Combine with:
1 cup chopped celery
Place on:
Lettuce
Cover or combine with:
½ cup Mayonnaise, 363
to which you may add:
(2 tablespoons dry sherry)
Garnish with:
Lobster or crab claws
Olives and radishes
Hard-cooked eggs
Capers and pickles
Or prepare:
Tomato Aspic, 114
in a ring or in individual molds.
Invert the aspic on:
Lettuce or very tender cabbage
Fill the ring or surround the aspics with the shellfish.

CRAB LOUIS

4 Servings

A version from the West Coast, where the magnificent Dungeness or Pacific crab, or the Alaskan King crab is frequently served in this way. Arrange around the inside of a bowl:
Lettuce leaves
Place on the bottom:
¾ cup shredded lettuce leaves
Heap on these:
2 cups cooked crab meat
Pour over the crab:
1 cup Sauce Louis, 365
Slice:
(2 hard-cooked eggs)
Place them on top of the crab. Sprinkle over them:
Chopped chives

★ HERRING SALAD

About 20 Servings

Herring is traditional for our family at Christmastime. The rich color, thanks to the red beets, and elaborate garnishing make this dish an imposing sight.
Soak in water 12 hours:
6 milter herring
Skin and remove the milt and the bones. Rub the milt through a colander with:
1 cup dry red wine or vinegar
Cut into ¼-inch cubes the herring and:
1½ cups cold cooked veal
2 hard-cooked eggs
1½ cups Pickled Beet Salad, 101
½ cup Spanish or Bermuda onions
½ cup pickles
2 ribs celery
½ cup diced cold boiled potatoes
3 cups peeled diced apples
1 cup blanched, shredded almonds
Combine the milt mixture with:
1 cup sugar
2 tablespoons horseradish
2 tablespoons chopped parsley
Pour this over the other ingredients. Mix well. Shape the salad into a mound or place it in a bowl. Garnish with:
Riced hard-cooked eggs
Pickles and olives
Anchovies and sprigs of parsley

★ VIENNESE BEAN AND HERRING SALAD

20 Servings

Drain the juice from:
2 cups pickled beets: 1-lb. jar
reserving the juice. Dice the beets.
Combine and set aside:
¼ cup beet juice
2 tablespoons prepared mustard
2 to 4 tablespoons sugar
Drain the following vegetables and combine them with the beets in a large bowl:
1 cup baked beans
½ cup canned or cooked kidney beans
1 cup canned or cooked lima beans: 8½ oz. can
1 cup diced boiled potatoes
1 cup cooked or canned peas and carrots: 8½ oz. can
2 cups diced, peeled and cored tart apples
1 cup finely diced sweet gherkins
1 large diced, peeled dill pickle
Drain, dice and add:
2 cups canned herring in wine sauce
Toss the salad thoroughly with the sweetened mustard sauce and refrigerate at least 2 hours. Mound onto a large platter of lettuce and surround with:
Curly endive
Onion rings

SHRIMP OR LOBSTER MOLD

4 Servings

This makes a lovely center for an hors d'oeuvre tray. Chop and combine:
1 lb. cooked shrimp or lobster
1 tablespoon capers
⅓ small onion
Add and mix well:
⅓ cup softened butter
3 tablespoons whipping cream
2 tablespoons Pernod
A dash of hot pepper sauce
1 teaspoon salt
1 teaspoon fresh tarragon
Pack into a mold. Refrigerate 3 to 4 hours before serving. For a special occasion, mold the mixture flat in either individual molds or one large mold.

Cover with a thin icing of:

Whipped cream

Cut large crescents from pieces of:

Red peppers

and arrange them on the salads to suggest the tails, claws and antennae of lobster or shrimp. For an added touch of realism, garnish with seaweed made of:

Wisps of finocchio leaf

and a few:

Seedless green grapes

TUNA FISH, SHRIMP OR SHAD ROE SALAD

4 Servings

Have ready:

1 cup canned fish or canned or cooked roe

Flake it with a fork. Add:

½ to 1 cup diced celery or cucumber

Make a French dressing using:

2 tablespoons olive oil
2 tablespoons lemon juice

or use:

¼ cup Mayonnaise, 363

Add:

(1 tablespoon chopped chives)
(1 tablespoon chopped parsley)

Serve very cold on:

Lettuce

FISHERMAN'S SALAD

12 Servings

Have ready raw or unshucked:

1 lb. medium-sized shrimp
1½ lb. squid
24 cherrystone clams
3 lb. mussels

To prepare them, rinse shrimp, mussels and clams, scrubbing if necessary to remove weed and scum. If fishmonger has not done so, lift out beak, eyes and backbone of squid; remove ink sac and pull off brown skin, 408.

Simmer uncovered 40 minutes:

1 cup sliced onions

in:

2 cups Fish Stock, 524
2 cups dry white wine
2 cups water
1 bay leaf
1 rib celery

Add successively to the above the following seafood, first simmering uncovered 7 minutes:

The shrimp

Remove shrimp, let cool, shell and devein. Add to liquid, simmering uncovered 17 minutes:

The squid

Remove squid, let cool, and cut into ¼-inch slices. Add to liquid, simmering uncovered until shells open—about 5 minutes:

The clams

Remove clams; remove meat, discarding shells; let meat cool. Add to liquid, simmering uncovered until shells open—about 7 minutes:

The mussels

Remove mussels; remove meat, discarding shells; let meat cool.

Mix in a large bowl:

¾ cup olive oil
3 tablespoons wine vinegar
1½ tablespoons Dijon mustard
1 teaspoon crushed garlic
1 teaspoon salt
1 tablespoon chopped parsley
1 tablespoon capers
¼ teaspoon white pepper

Toss this dressing with the fish and let marinate 10 to 12 hours in refrigerator, retossing once or twice. Serve on bed of:

Curly endive or watercress

Garnish with:

Lemon wedges

CHICKEN SALAD

4 Servings

A traditional party dish, chicken salad should taste of chicken, the other ingredients being present only to enhance flavor and add variety of texture. So always keep the proportions of at least twice as much chicken as the total of your other ingredients. Since the meat is usually combined with mayonnaise, be careful to ➤ refrigerate this salad, particularly if you make it in advance.

Dice:

2 cups cooked chicken
1 cup celery
(¼ cup salted almonds)

Chill these ingredients. They may be marinated lightly with:

French Dressing, 360

When ready to serve, combine with:

1 cup Mayonnaise, 363

Season the salad to taste with:

Salt and paprika

Serve it on:

Lettuce

Garnish with:

Pimiento and olives
(Sliced hard-cooked eggs and capers)

Quantity note: Generous main-dish servings for 50 will require:

1 gal. cooked cubed chicken

To obtain this amount, you need about 17 pounds ready-to-cook chicken. If you substitute turkey, you need only a boneless 12-pounder.

CHICKEN SALAD VARIATIONS

Follow the preceding recipe. You may substitute cooked duck, turkey or veal for the chicken, remembering to keep the proportions of 2 of meat or fowl to 1 of the other ingredients.

Chicken, celery and hard-cooked eggs
Chicken, bean sprouts and water chestnuts

Chicken, cucumber and English walnut meats
Chicken, Boiled Chestnuts, 298, and celery—pimiento may be added
Chicken and parboiled oysters
Chicken and fruit such as seedless grapes, fresh chopped pineapple and pomegranate seeds

You may add to the mayonnaise:

(Chili Sauce, 847)

See also Chicken Mousse, 120.

HAM, CORNED BEEF, VEAL OR BEEF SALAD

I. Let this be largely a matter of inspiration. Dice:

Cooked ham, corned beef, veal or beef
Hard-cooked eggs
Celery with the youngest leaves
(Green peppers or pickles)

Combine these ingredients with:

Tart Mayonnaise, 363, or French Dressing, 360

Garnish with:

Chopped chives, parsley or other herbs

Surround the meat with tomatoes, sliced or whole.

II. Serve, garnished as above:

Thinly sliced cooked beef, veal or ham

covered with:

Sauce Gribiche, 365

ABOUT FRUIT SALADS

Somehow the contrast between fresh and canned components seems to become more pronounced whenever we address this topic, but perhaps we have been obliged too often to confront the syrupy peach-half, the scoop of cottage cheese, the blob of mayonnaise and—crown and anticlimax of the whole sorry construction—that maraschino cherry. With the increasing wealth and diversity of fresh materials available, and the scope they afford the designer, fruit salads can in fact be utterly irresistible and, when skillfully arranged on a platter, can substitute for flowers as a buffet centerpiece.

With protein such as chicken, meat, cheese or fish, fruits make wonderful summer luncheon dishes. As a general rule, keep the dressings for pre-dessert fruit salads fairly tart, so that the appetite is not dulled. As a change from the usual base of salad greens, serve them where suitable in baskets, cups or cases made from fruit as described on 138. In advance preparation, to avoid browning, bananas, peaches and other fruits that discolor quickly should be covered during storage with the acid dressing you plan using.

BIRD OF PARADISE SALAD

This exotic Hawaiian hybrid makes a festive appearance at a luncheon or supper table. For two individual servings, split in two lengthwise:

A green-tufted ripe pineapple

Scoop out the center of each half, discarding the tough pulp; reserve and chop the remainder, keeping enough intact to form a bird's head, see illustration below. The birds in the foreground contain either mixed fruits or a fruited chicken salad. The bird in the background with the more flamboyant tail holds enough pineapple for 4 servings and is suggested as a centerpiece for an intimate dinner. Combine:

1 cup finely diced cooked chicken

with the pineapple and:

½ cup Cream Mayonnaise, 365

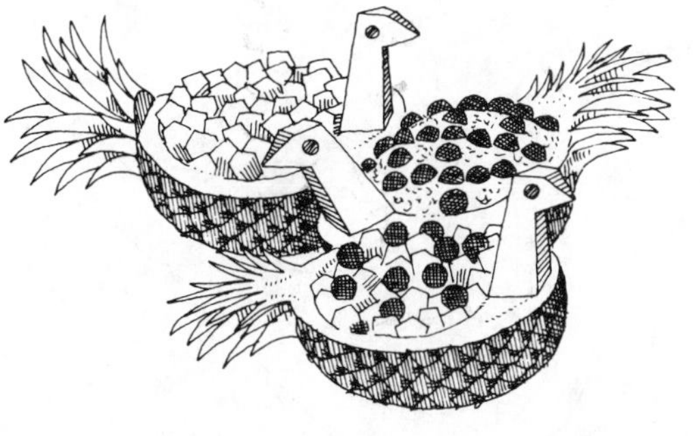

Fill the hollow in the bird's back with the chicken mixture and round it slightly. Attach the pineapple head with a countersunk toothpick. Embroider the bird's back with a pattern of halved grapes or pomegranate seeds, using a portion of the garnish on countersunk toothpicks for bird's eyes. As can be readily imagined, this *rara avis* easily evolves into an all-fruit salad when the major fillers are seedless grapes or pitted Queen Anne cherries and of course pineapple, and when the dressing is hopped up with a liberal dash of fruit liqueur. See About Fruit Salads, opposite.

APPLE, PEAR OR PEACH SALAD

Try this with an omelet, French bread and coffee. Pare, core, slice and sprinkle with lemon juice to keep them from discoloring:

Well-flavored apples, pears, or peaches

Serve on:

Lettuce

with:

Yogurt Dressing, 367
or French Dressing, 360

Garnish the salad with:

Vicksburg Cheese, 81, or
Nut Cheese Balls, 81

The apples may be cut into rings and the cheese balls placed in the center.

WALDORF SALAD

6 Servings

Prepare:

1 cup diced celery
1 cup diced apples
(1 cup Tokay grapes, halved and seeded)

Combine with:

½ cup walnut or pecan meats
¾ cup Mayonnaise, 363, or Boiled Salad Dressing III, 367

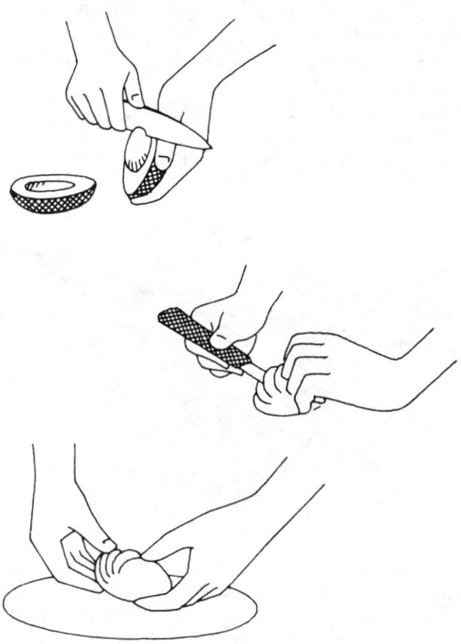

ABOUT AVOCADO SALADS

Please read About Avocados, 131. To prepare avocado cups, cut the fruit in half lengthwise, place between the palms of the hands and gently twist the halves apart. Tap the large seed with the edge of a knife and lift or pry it out, as shown at top, above. ➤ To prevent the fruit from darkening after cutting, sprinkle with lemon juice. ➤ To store a cut avocado, allow the seed to remain embedded, spread the edges with mayonnaise, soft butter or cream, cover well with wax paper or plastic, and refrigerate. Avocado has a soft, buttery texture and taste which combines best with citrus fruits or tomatoes and a sharp or tangy dressing. It also has an unexpected affinity for shrimp, crab or lobster. All of these combinations offer a pleasing contrast of color as well as texture and taste—the hallmark of a delectable salad.

Illustrated center and at bottom in the sketch above are steps in cutting avocado into a charming fan-shape.

Select only ripe fruit; lay the peeled halves cup side down on a flat surface; then, using a sharp knife inserted at a slight angle, and with a slight spiraling motion, slice thinly from one end to about ¾ inch from the other. You will find that the slices may be splayed out in an overlapping pattern. The finished product is shown at left in the sketch opposite, amplified by the addition of cherry tomatoes and watercress. On the right are variations of avocado and orange or grapefruit slices.

AVOCADO SLICES

These may also be used as a garnish for meats and fish.

Chill:

Avocados

Pare and slice them. Marinate about 5 minutes in highly seasoned, chilled:

French Dressing, 360

You may also add:

(Hot pepper sauce, Chili Sauce, 847, or Catsup, 847)

Sprinkle with:

Chopped parsley or chopped mint

Try these avocado slices in:

(Tomato Aspic, 114)

AVOCADO AND FRUIT SALAD

Pare:

Avocados

Slice them lengthwise and arrange them with skinned sections of:

Orange and grapefruit or pineapple slices

in wheel shape, on:

Lettuce

as shown below, or make a rounded salad by alternating the fruit with the green avocado slices into an approximate half globe on the lettuce as pictured lower right.

Serve with:

Celery Seed Dressing, 362, or
French Dressing for Fruit Salad, 361

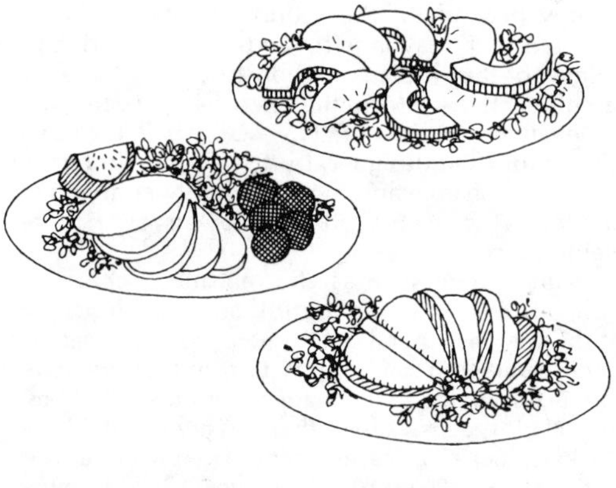

AVOCADO SALAD CUPS

Cut into halves and remove the seeds from:

Chilled avocados

You may then fill the hollows with:

I. Chili Sauce, 847, seasoned with horseradish

II. Marinated seedless grapes, 111

Garnish with:

A sprig of parsley, mint or watercress

III. Dress up:
Crab meat, chicken or fruit salad
with:
Mayonnaise, 363
thinned with a little:
Lemon or lime juice
and fill the avocado cup.

IV. Fill with a **Tomato Ice** which can be made like:
Fruit Ice, 765
substituting tomato juice for the fruit juice.

V. Scoop the pulp out of the skin instead of paring the avocado. Turn it into:
Guacamole, 83
Put the mixture back in the half shell and garnish with:
A slice of stuffed olive

BANANA, ORANGE AND NUT SALAD

For each serving, peel and split lengthwise:
1 banana
Arrange the 2 halves on either side of:
Skinned orange sections, 135
or:
Dates stuffed with cheese, 137
Sprinkle with:
Chopped peanuts or English walnuts
Garnish with:
Tender lettuce leaves
Serve with:
Honey Dressing, 361

CHERRY AND HAZELNUT SALAD

Drain and pit:
Canned white cherries
Insert in each cherry:
A hazelnut meat
Serve very cold with:
Cottage cheese
Mayonnaise, 363, or
Fruit Salad Mayonnaise, 365

ABOUT GRAPE SALADS

Ever peel a grape? Well, it takes time, but what is more luxurious than a lovely mound of peeled, seeded table grapes—seedless green, or Tokay, Malaga, olivette, etc.—lightly tossed in a mild olive oil and vinegar dressing, served in lettuce cups or as the center for a clear gelatin salad ring mold, 112? To make a baroque grape finish on a gelatin top, see 561. Or mix seedless grapes with cultured sour cream, yogurt or creamed cottage cheese as a fruit salad garnish.

CITRUS FRUIT SALAD

I. **4 Servings**

Prepare:
Sections of 2 grapefruit or 4 oranges, 136 and 135, or a combination of the two
Arrange them on individual plates on:
Lettuce, witloof chicory, or watercress
You may place between alternate sections of the citrus fruit:
Strawberries or cooked cranberries
Serve with:
French Dressing, 360

II. When the entrée is game, prepare the above salad with oranges only and dress with a mixture of:
2 tablespoons brandy
2 tablespoons olive oil
1 teaspoon sugar
¼ teaspoon salt
A few grains cayenne
Sprinkle the tops of the fruit with:
Chopped tarragon

MELON SALAD

Prepare:
Melon Baskets, 138, or
Melon Rounds, 139
Fill with:
Hulled berries
Diced pineapple or seedless grapes
Moisten with chilled:
French Dressing, 360, or Cream Mayonnaise, 365, or cultured sour cream

ORANGE AND ONION SALAD

Arrange:
Skinned orange sections or peeled, sliced oranges
Thin slices of Bermuda onion
(Pink grapefruit sections)
on:
Lettuce leaves, endive or escarole
Serve with:
Celery Seed Dressing, 362
An Italian version of this salad adds:
Pitted black olives

FRESH PEACH AND CHEESE SALAD

6 Servings

Cut into 6 parts:
3 oz. cream cheese
Roll the cheese into balls, then in:
Chopped nutmeats
Pare, cut into halves and pit:
6 ripe peaches
Place a ball of cheese between 2 peach halves. Press the peach into shape. Roll it in lemon juice to enhance flavor and prevent discoloration. If the peaches are not to be served at once, chill them in closed containers. Serve on:
Watercress
with:
French Dressing for Fruit Salad, 361
A bit of cress may be placed in the top end of

each peach. Decorative—though it may puzzle a horticulturist.

PEAR SALAD

Chill and pare:

Ripe fresh pears or drained canned pears

Follow the preceding recipe for Peach Salad. Or fill the hollows with:

Cream cheese

combined with:

Chopped Candied Ginger, 796

Brush the side of each pear with:

Red vegetable coloring

Insert in the base:

A clove

and at the top, simulate leaves with:

A bit of watercress

Serve with:

French Dressing, 360

PEAR AND GRAPE SALAD

Pare:

Fresh pears

or drain:

Canned pears

Place half a pear cut side down on a plate. Thin:

Cream cheese

to spreading consistency with:

Cream

Cover each pear half with a coating of cheese. Press into the cheese, close together to look like a bunch of grapes:

Stemmed halved seedless grapes

Add a leaf of some kind, preferably grape.
Serve with:

Mayonnaise, 363, or French Dressing, 360

JAPANESE PERSIMMON SALAD

An opportunity for color. If you wish to skin the fruit, rub it first with the blunt side of a knife and peel with the sharp edge.
Chill:

Ripe Japanese persimmons

Leave them whole or cut them lengthwise almost to the base and insert in the slashes:

Slices of peeled orange, grapefruit and avocado

and serve with:

Boiled Salad Dressing III, 367

PINEAPPLE SALAD

Drain:

Slices of canned pineapple

Serve them on:

Lettuce with French Dressing, 360

Add to the French Dressing:

A little confectioners' sugar

Or cover the slices with:

Riced soft cream cheese

topped with:

A spoonful of currant jelly

Serve the salad with:

French Dressing, 360, or Mayonnaise, 363

ABOUT MOLDED SALADS

For utilizing leftovers, an aspic is second only to a soufflé. Any clever person can take a few desolate-looking refrigerator scraps and glorify them into a tempting molded salad or mousse. This kind of dish has two further advantages. One is that it can be prepared a day or so in advance and kept chilled in the refrigerator. The other is built in, so to speak, and has to do with gelatin's properties as a protein-extender, see Ingredients, 560. Each of these salads depends on gelatin to hold its shape, so please read About Gelatin, 560. Molds may be filled dry, but a jellied mixture is more readily removed when the molds have been moistened with water. If the mixture is not a clarified one, you may lightly brush the mold with oil. Be sure to sample your salad before molding and season to taste. ➤ Undersalt if it is to be held 24 hours. ➤ Never freeze gelatin salads.

Many of the recipes that follow may be made either in a large mold or in individual small ones like those shown below. Use ring molds if you wish to fill centers with some other kind of salad, such as chicken, Vegetables à la Grecque, 281, fruit, or a cream cheese mixture, dressed and garnished to your fancy. Fish-shaped molds can make a seafood aspic appear very professional. For large groups, you may even use small paper drinking cups for individual portions: simply tear off the cup when the aspic has congealed, and behold—

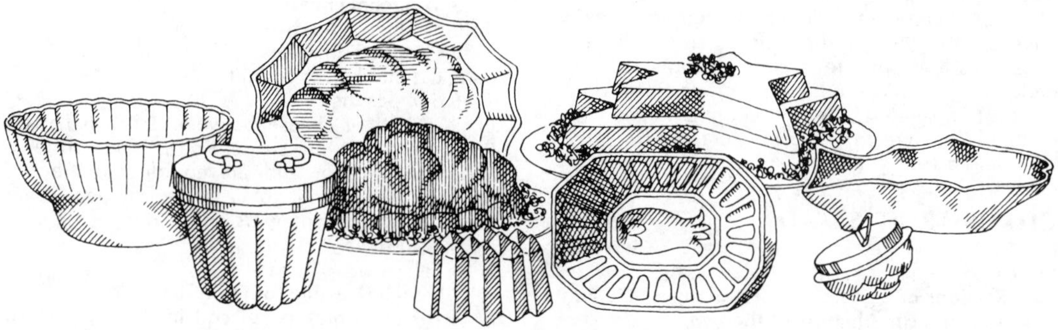

jiffy jelly! Or use large No. 2½ cans and cut around the bottom of the can when ready to turn out the cylinder. Push the salad out of the can, slice, and serve the rounds on lettuce.

Aspics and other molded salads with a clear body lend themselves to highly decorative treatment, although their preparation can be time-consuming. However, certain ingredients naturally come to rest either at the top or bottom of a jelling salad, and you can achieve interesting layered effects by manipulating "floaters" and "sinkers." See on 561 a list of the ingredients that can be incorporated into your salad simultaneously and which will more or less automatically layer themselves.

ABOUT ASPICS

Nothing gives a cooler, lovelier effect on a hot summer night and nothing is easier to prepare than a brilliantly clear aspic. The problem, of course, is to keep the jelly properly chilled when serving. For small groups, chilled plates, individually served, will do if you can control the timing. For large groups, if you want to use a quivery aspic, serve it molded in a crystal-clear glass bowl set in another larger glass bowl with crushed ice between, or on a handsome, well-chilled platter set on ice.

The most delicious aspics of all are reduced chicken and veal stocks, cooked down from the clarified gelatinous portions of these animals, 522. Clarified strong meat, fish and fowl stocks with added gelatin are next in favor—but the average home cook seldom clarifies her own. She depends largely on canned bases for her jellies. ➤ Canned consommés, if over a year old, tend to lose some of their jelling power, so it is wise to refrigerate the can before using to test for texture. The consommé is still good to eat even if it fails to jell fully out of the can, but when used for aspic it will need about 1 teaspoon of gelatin per cup of consommé to firm it. To add gelatin, see 560. If you save vegetable stocks, 520, you can add them to meat or fish stocks to modify and enrich the otherwise easily identifiable canned flavors. It is wise to choose a stock that has the same general base as the food to be molded: fish stock for fish, meat stock for meat. For gelatin salads made with eggs or cream—that is, unclear types—see Mousses, 120.

One package of unflavored gelatin is the equivalent in strength to 1 tablespoon gelatin. To make aspics, allow 1 tablespoon gelatin to 1¾ to 2 cups liquid. Use the lesser amount of liquid if the solids to be incorporated are juicy or watery. ➤ Never reduce aspic made with added gelatin with the idea of thickening it. It only wastes your good stock and never thickens. If you run into trouble, start the gelatin process over again, making a guesstimate as to the added fresh gelatin required.

➤ The addition of wine or liqueur to your aspics can make them something rather special. Don't add too much, ➤ one or two tablespoons per cup of liquid being sufficient to heighten the flavor significantly. Substitute the wine for part of the liquid called for in the recipe ➤ and add it when the gelatin has been dissolved and is beginning to cool. Dry white wine or a dry sherry goes well with savory aspics such as chicken and veal. Sweeter wines, such as sauterne or fruit-flavored liqueurs, are good for molded fruit salads.

Aspic should be made of clarified stocks, 522, unless you want to serve up something that resembles a molded London fog. If you decide to skip this process, be sure to plan to mask your mold, see Mayonnaise Collée, 368, or Sauce Chaud-Froid, 369.

➤ To make decorative molds, see 560. Clear aspic jelly can serve as an attractive garnish for a meat or chicken salad. Chill it in a refrigerator ➤ but do not freeze, and when ready to serve, cut in squares or fancy shapes or chop it rather fine and arrange it around the center.

Many salads can become full-fledged luncheon dishes with the addition of various types of chopped meat, chicken or flaked fish. For other recipes including meat, fish and shellfish and Chicken Mousses see 120, 121.

A choice or a combination of the following ingredients may be included in a molded salad, but always keep in mind that fresh or frozen—but not canned—pineapple must be brought to a boil before you use it in a gelatin-based salad.

Cooked diced meat or poultry
Cooked flaked fish
Hard-cooked eggs
Cooked sweetbreads
Shredded cabbage
Diced celery
Diced cucumbers
Cooked celeriac
Sliced green peppers
Raw or cooked carrots
Cooked beets
Canned asparagus
Canned drained fruit
Halved cranberries
Seedless grapes
Peeled seeded table grapes: Tokay or Malaga
Skinned grapefruit, orange or tangelo sections
Stuffed ripe or green olives
Pickles
Nutmeats
Chopped parsley, chives or other herbs

BASIC ASPIC OR GELATIN SALAD

5 Servings

Please read About Gelatin, 560.

Soak:

1 tablespoon gelatin

in:

¼ cup cold water

Dissolve it in:

¼ cup boiling stock

Add this to:

1½ cups cold stock or 1¼ cups stock plus ¼ cup tomato juice
2 tablespoons vinegar or 1½ tablespoons lemon juice
Salt and paprika
Celery salt
(1 tablespoon grated onion)

If the aspic is to cover unseasoned food, make the gelatin mixture more piquant. Chill it, and when it is about to set, combine it with:

1½ to 2 cups solid ingredients

Pour the aspic into a wet mold and chill until firm. Unmold. Surround with:

Lettuce leaves

Serve with or without:

Mayonnaise, 363, Sour Cream Horseradish Dressing, 356, or yogurt

JELLIED VEAL STOCK

4 to 6 Servings

Sometimes it is rewarding—and fun—to make an aspic without added gelatin.

Place in a soup kettle:

A knuckle of veal
¼ cup cut-up onion
½ carrot
6 ribs celery with leaves
1 teaspoon salt
¼ teaspoon pepper

Cover the veal with:

Boiling water

Simmer the meat until tender. Strain and reserve the liquid. Remove the veal. When cold, cut the meat into small cubes. After removing the fat, reheat the stock. Add the veal or reserve it for other dishes, and use the stock after clarifying it, 522, to mold other ingredients.

Season to taste

Add:

(1 teaspoon dried herbs—basil, tarragon, etc.)

Rinse a mold in cold water. Pour in the veal mixture. Cover and keep in a cold place to set. Unmold and slice.

ASPIC GARNISH

Prepare:

Basic Aspic or Jellied Veal Stock, above

When firm and just before serving, chop the aspic so the light catches its many facets, and use it to garnish salads or meats.

CUCUMBER ASPIC

8 Servings

Fine for a meat platter or a ring mold.

➤ Please read About Gelatin, 560.

Pare and seed:

Cucumbers

Grate them. There should be 4 cups of pulp and juice. Soak:

2 tablespoons gelatin

in:

½ cup cold water or chicken stock

Dissolve it in:

¾ cup boiling water or chicken stock

Add:

6 tablespoons lemon juice
2 teaspoons grated onion

Add the gelatin mixture to the cucumber pulp with:

1 teaspoon sugar
Salt, as needed
¼ teaspoon paprika

Strain the jelly. Place it in small wet molds. When firm invert onto:

Thick slices skinned tomatoes

Garnish the slices with:

Watercress

Serve the salad with:

Mayonnaise, 363

Or place it in a wet 9-inch ring mold. Chill the jelly. When firm, invert onto a platter. Fill the center with:

Marinated shrimp

Garnish the edge with:

Tomato slices

Serve the ring with:

Green Mayonnaise, 364, or Watercress Dressing, 360

TOMATO ASPIC

8 Servings (without the addition of solid ingredients)

I. ➤ Please read About Gelatin, 560.

Simmer 30 minutes, then strain:

3½ cups tomatoes
1 teaspoon salt
½ teaspoon paprika
1½ teaspoons sugar
2 tablespoons lemon juice
3 tablespoons chopped onion
1 bay leaf
4 ribs celery with leaves
(1 teaspoon dried basil or tarragon)

Soak:

2 tablespoons gelatin

in:

½ cup cold water

Dissolve it in the strained hot juice. Add water to make 4 cups of liquid. Chill the aspic. When it is about to set you may add 1 to 2 cups of solid ingredients—a choice or a combination of:

Sliced olives
Chopped celery
Chopped green peppers or grated carrots
Sliced avocados
Chopped meat
Flaked fish or chopped shellfish
Well-drained oysters

Chill the aspic until firm. Unmold and serve with:

Mayonnaise, 363, or Boiled Salad Dressing II, 366

II. If you prefer a clear ring, keep the aspic simple and fill the center with:

Coleslaw, marinated cucumbers or avocados, chicken or shrimp salad, or cottage cheese and chives

Serve with:

Chiffonade Dressing, 360

III. **8 Servings**

Not quite up to the preceding basic recipe in clarity, but delicious, unusual and much simpler. Soak:

1 tablespoon gelatin

in:

2 tablespoons cold water

Dissolve it in:

2 tablespoons boiling water

Add the contents of:

1 can condensed tomato soup: 10½ oz.

Heat:

2 cups tomato juice

Dissolve in it:

1 package lemon- or lime-flavored gelatin

Combine the two mixtures. Add:

⅛ teaspoon salt

Mold and chill the aspic.

CANNED TOMATO OR VEGETABLE JUICE ASPIC

8 Servings

➤ Please read About Gelatin, 560.

Soak:

2 tablespoons gelatin

in:

½ cup cold canned tomato juice

Dissolve it in:

3½ cups hot tomato juice or canned tomato and vegetable juice

Tomato juice varies. It is wise to taste the aspic to see whether additional seasoning is required. Lemon juice is good; so is a teaspoon of chopped or dried herbs, 579, preferably basil. Add, if desired:

(1 or 2 cups solid ingredients)

See Tomato Aspic, opposite. Mold, chill, unmold and serve the aspic as directed.

MADRILÈNE RING WITH SHAD ROE COCKAIGNE

A fine summer dish.

Fill a ring mold with:

Canned Madrilène aspic or tomato-seasoned meat stock aspic

Chill. Invert on:

Shredded lettuce

Place in the center:

Chilled canned shad roe

Garnish with:

Mayonnaise, 363, or Curry Dressing, 367
Lemon wedges or parsley

MOLDED VEGETABLE GELATIN SALAD

6 Servings

Dissolve the contents of:

1 package lime- or lemon-flavored gelatin

in:

2 cups hot water

Prepare and add, when the jelly is about to set:

1½ cups finely diced vegetables: cucumber, carrot, celery, sliced unpeeled radishes, olive, pimiento
½ diced green pepper
2 teaspoons grated onion
¾ teaspoon salt
¼ teaspoon paprika

Place the salad in wet individual ring molds. Chill thoroughly. Unmold on:

Lettuce or watercress

Fill the centers with:

Boiled Salad Dressing II, 366

GOLDEN GLOW GELATIN SALAD

8 to 10 Servings

Good in flavor and lovely in color.

Grate or grind:

2 cups raw carrots

Drain, reserving the juice:

1 cup canned crushed pineapple

Heat to the boiling point:

⅞ cup pineapple juice
⅞ cup water
½ teaspoon salt

Dissolve in the hot liquid:

1 package lemon-flavored gelatin

Chill, and when the gelatin mixture is about to set, combine it with the carrots, the pineapple and:

(½ cup chopped pecans)

Place in a wet mold. Chill until firm. Unmold on:

Lettuce

Serve with:

Mayonnaise, 363

ASPARAGUS AND CELERY ASPIC

10 Servings

Another refreshing warm-weather salad.

➤ Please read About Gelatin, 560.

Drain the contents of:

3 cups canned asparagus tips

Reserve the liquor. The tips may be cut in two or they may be used whole as a garnish around the edge of the mold. Soak:

1 tablespoon gelatin

in:

3 tablespoons asparagus liquor

Heat the remaining asparagus liquor and dissolve

the gelatin in it. Add to make 2 cups of liquor in all:

Chicken bouillon or canned bouillon

Season these ingredients with:

Salt and paprika

Chill them. When they are nearly set, combine them with:

2 cups chopped celery

and the cut asparagus tips in a wet mold.
Chill the salad until firm. Unmold and serve with:

Cream Mayonnaise, 365

BEET GELATIN SALAD

8 Servings

Wash well, then ⊗ pressure-cook:

8 medium-sized beets, or use canned beets

Drain and reserve the beet juice. Peel the beets and dice them. There should be about 1 cup. Prepare:

¾ cup diced celery

Dissolve the contents of:

1 package lemon-flavored gelatin

in:

1 cup boiling water

Add to it:

¾ cup beet juice
3 tablespoons vinegar
½ teaspoon salt
2 teaspoons grated onion
1 tablespoon prepared horseradish

Chill these ingredients until they are about to set. Fold in beets and celery. Place the salad in a wet mold. Chill until firm. Unmold on:

Lettuce or endive

Serve with:

Boiled Salad Dressing II, 366, or
cultured sour cream

JELLIED CLAM RING

8 Servings

➤ Please read About Gelatin, 560.
Dilute:

Clam juice or minced clams

with:

Water or vegetable juices

to make a palatable mixture. There should be 4 cups. Season with:

Lemon juice and paprika
A few drops Worcestershire sauce

Soak:

2 tablespoons gelatin

in ½ cup of the liquid.
Heat ➤ just to the boiling point 1 cup of the liquid. Dissolve the soaked gelatin in it. Return it to the remaining liquid with the minced clams, if they were used. Pour into a wet 9-inch ring mold. Chill until firm. Invert the jelly onto a plate. Fill the center with:

Marinated vegetables

Surround the ring with:

Tomato slices

Serve with:

Watercress Sauce, 365, or
Chiffonade Dressing, 360

JELLIED SEAFOOD MOLD

6 Servings

➤ Please read About Gelatin, 560.
Prepare:

Basic Aspic, 113

using a fish fumet, 524, or light meat stock.
Dice:

Celery

Pare, seed and dice:

Cucumbers or green peppers

Drain and flake:

Salmon, crab or tuna fish: 1½ cups fish and vegetables in all

Add:

(2 chopped hard-cooked eggs)
(Sliced stuffed olives)

When the jelly is nearly set, combine it with the solid ingredients. Pour it into a wet mold and chill until firm. Unmold and serve on:

Lettuce

with:

Boiled Dressing I or II, 366, or
Green Goddess Dressing, 364

LUNCHEON ASPIC SALAD

8 Servings

➤ Please read About Gelatin, 560.
Drain, reserving the juices:

2½ cups grapefruit sections
¼ cup green or white cooked asparagus tips
1 cup canned or cooked crab meat or shrimp

Cut the asparagus into pieces. Pick over the crab meat or remove the intestinal vein from the shrimp. Add to the juices, to make 2¾ cups of liquid:

Chicken broth, Stock, 523,
canned consommé or dissolved
chicken bouillon cubes

Soak:

1½ tablespoons gelatin

in ½ cup of this liquid. Dissolve it in 1 cup of hot liquid. Combine the gelatin and the remaining liquid. Season well with:

Juice of 1 or more lemons or
with ¼ cup dry white wine

Add, if needed:

Salt

Add:

(3 or more tablespoons capers)

Chill the gelatin until it begins to thicken. Have ready a mold which has been rinsed in cold water. Pour part of the gelatin into it, sprinkle some grapefruit, crab meat and asparagus over it, then alternate layers of gelatin and the other ingredients. Wind up with gelatin on top. Chill the aspic until very cold. Serve on:

Lettuce

with:

Green Mayonnaise, 364

CHICKEN SALAD IN ASPIC

6 to 8 Servings

Soak:
1 tablespoon gelatin
in:
1/4 cup cold water
Dissolve it in:
2 cups boiling chicken broth or stock
Add:
Seasoning, if needed
Chill, and when the gelatin begins to set, rinse a mold in cold water and fill it with 1/2 inch of the jelly. Build up layers of:
3 cups cooked diced chicken
and the jelly. Ornament the layers with:
1 cup canned mushroom caps
2 hard-cooked eggs, chopped or sliced
12 sliced stuffed olives
Chill the jelly until firm. Unmold and serve with or without:
Mayonnaise, 363, or Curry Mayonnaise, 365

MOLDED EGG RING

4 Servings

A one-platter luncheon if the center of the mold is filled with crab meat or chicken salad.
Rice:
8 hard-cooked eggs, 220
Add:
1 tablespoon finely chopped onion
2 tablespoons finely chopped parsley
A dash of hot pepper sauce
1/2 cup Mayonnaise, 363
Pack into a 7-inch ring mold and refrigerate until firm. Unmold just before serving and garnish with:
Tomato quarters and artichoke hearts
or surround the ring with:
Watercress
and frost it lightly with:
Chutney, 846

EGGS IN ASPIC OR OEUFS EN GELÉE

Make:
Basic Aspic, 113, or Jellied Veal Stock, 114, flavored with port or brandy
Have ready:
Poached Eggs, 221
Swish cold water in individual molds until they are cold and wet. Drain but do not dry. Coat the interior with the congealing aspic so that it adheres to the sides. Chill until jelled. Place an egg in the center of each mold and fill with more aspic. Chill. Serve masked with:
Mayonnaise Collée, 368, or cold Mayonnaise, 363

EGGS IN ASPIC COCKAIGNE

Molded with one-half hard-cooked or deviled egg, this makes a pleasant hors d'oeuvre. With three halves, it makes enough for a luncheon salad.
Prepare:
Eggs in Aspic, left
using rich chicken stock for the aspic base and replacing the poached eggs with:
Deviled Eggs, 225
Place the molds on a bed of:
Watercress
Mask the eggs with a coating of:
Cultured sour cream
Garnish with:
Finely chopped chives, basil and chervil
Red caviar and tomato slices
"for pretty," as the Pennsylvania Dutch put it.

BASIC GELATIN FOR FRUIT SALADS

6 Servings

➤ Please read About Gelatin, 560. It is well known that fresh or frozen pineapple cannot be added to a gelatin salad without ruining it. This also applies to frozen pineapple juice, alone or combined with other frozen juices such as orange or grapefruit. The pineapple or the juice must be brought to ➤ a boil. Canned pineapple has been cooked and may be used as is.
Soak:
1 tablespoon gelatin
in:
1/2 cup cold water
Dissolve it in:
1 cup boiling water or fruit juice
Add:
4 to 6 tablespoons sugar, less if sweetened fruit juice is used
1/8 teaspoon salt
1/4 cup lemon juice
Chill the aspic, and when it is about to set, combine with:
1 1/2 cups prepared drained fruit
Place it in a wet mold and chill until firm. Serve with:
Cream Mayonnaise, 365

MINT GELATIN FOR FRUIT SALADS

Pour:
1 cup boiling water
over:
1/4 cup crushed mint leaves
Let steep 5 minutes. Drain this infusion. Add:
A few drops of green vegetable coloring
Prepare, by the recipe above:
Basic Fruit Salad Gelatin
substituting the mint infusion for the boiling water.

MOLDED AVOCADO SALAD

3 to 4 Servings

➤ Please read About Gelatin, 560.
Soak:
1 tablespoon gelatin
in:
2 tablespoons water

Dissolve it in:

1 cup boiling water

When cooled somewhat, add:

¼ cup lemon juice
1 cup mashed avocado
¼ teaspoon celery salt
1 teaspoon salt
½ teaspoon Worcestershire sauce
A few grains cayenne
¼ cup chopped pimiento

Mold and serve.

MOLDED CRANBERRY SALAD

6 to 8 Servings

➤ Please read About Gelatin, 560.

Soak:

1 tablespoon gelatin

in:

3 tablespoons water

Cook until the skins pop:

2 cups cranberries

in:

1 cup boiling water or fruit juice

Use the cranberries strained or unstrained. If the former, strain them at this time. Add and cook for 5 minutes:

½ cup sugar
¼ teaspoon salt

Add the soaked gelatin. Chill the jelly. When it is about to set, fold in:

⅔ cup diced celery
(½ cup chopped nutmeats)
(1 cup drained canned crushed pineapple)

Place in a wet mold and chill until firm. Serve with:

Mayonnaise, 363

MOLDED CRANBERRY AND APPLE SALAD

8 to 10 Servings

➤ Please read About Gelatin, 560.

Put through a food grinder:

1 lb. cranberries

Add:

The grated rind of 1 orange
½ cup orange juice
3½ tablespoons lemon juice
1½ cups sugar

Refrigerate overnight. Soak:

1 tablespoon gelatin

in:

3 tablespoons cold water

Dissolve:

1 package lemon-flavored gelatin

in:

1 cup boiling water

Add the soaked gelatin. Stir until dissolved. Combine these ingredients with the cranberry mixture. Pare, then chop and add:

3 tart apples

Place the salad in a wet mold. When firm, unmold and serve on:

Watercress

with:

Cream Mayonnaise, 365

SEEDLESS GRAPE AND CELERY RING

8 to 10 Servings

Prepare:

1 package lemon- or orange-flavored gelatin or Basic Fruit Gelatin, 117

When about to set, add to it:

3 cups halved seedless grapes and diced celery, combined in any proportion

Place the jelly in a wet 9-inch mold and chill. Unmold on:

Lettuce

Fill the center with:

Cream Mayonnaise, 365

GRAPEFRUIT SHERRY ASPIC

10 Servings

➤ Please read About Gelatin, 560.

Soak:

2½ tablespoons gelatin

in:

½ cup cold water

Stir over heat until the sugar is dissolved:

½ cup water
1 cup sugar

Dissolve the gelatin in the hot syrup. Cool. Add:

2 cups and 6 tablespoons fresh grapefruit juice
3 tablespoons lemon juice
½ cup dry sherry
¼ teaspoon salt

Pour these ingredients into a wet 9-inch ring mold. Chill until firm. Turn it out on a platter. Fill the center with:

Soft cream cheese balls rolled in chopped nuts

Garnish the outer edge of the platter with:

Avocado slices

alternating with skinned:

Grapefruit or orange sections

on:

Watercress or shredded lettuce

Sprinkle with:

Pomegranate seeds

Serve the salad with:

Mayonnaise, 363, or French Dressing, 360

GINGER ALE GELATIN SALAD

10 Servings

➤ Please read About Gelatin, 560.

Soak:

2 tablespoons gelatin

in:

¼ cup cold water

Dissolve it in:

½ cup boiling fruit juice

Add:

1/2 cup sugar
1/8 teaspoon salt
2 cups ginger ale
Juice of 1 lemon

Chill these ingredients until nearly set. Combine with:

1/2 lb. skinned, seeded table grapes
1 peeled, sliced orange
1 grapefruit in skinned sections
6 slices drained canned pineapple, cut in pieces
3 teaspoons chopped preserved ginger

Place the salad in a wet 9-inch ring mold. Chill and unmold on:

Lettuce

Serve with:

Cream Mayonnaise, 363

FRUIT SALAD MOLDED WITH CHEESE BALLS

8 Servings

➤ Please read About Gelatin, 560.

Soak:

2 1/2 tablespoons gelatin

in:

1/2 cup water

Drain and reserve the juice from:

3 1/2 cups canned peaches, apricots or pears
(1 cup seedless grapes)

Combine and boil:

2 cups of the juice
1 1/2 cups sugar

Dissolve the gelatin in it. Add these ingredients to the remaining juice with:

3/4 cup lemon juice
3 tablespoons lime juice
1/4 teaspoon ginger

Add water or other fruit juice to make up 4 cups of liquid in all. Chill the gelatin. Soften:

1 package cream or pimiento cheese: 3 oz.

with a little:

Mayonnaise, 363

Roll it into balls. Roll the balls in:

Chopped nutmeats

When gelatin is about to set, incorporate the fruit with it; place the cheese balls evenly around the bottom of a ring mold and surround them with the fruit and gelatin mixture. Chill well and invert onto:

Watercress

Serve with:

Mayonnaise, 363

CHEESE RING

8 Servings

Drain and reserve the liquid from:

1 can crushed pineapple: 8 1/4 oz.

Should there not be enough, add water to make 1/2 cup of reserved liquid in all.

Soak:

2 teaspoons gelatin

for 5 minutes in:

1/2 cup cold water

Boil the reserved pineapple juice and water and dissolve the gelatin in it. Cool. Meanwhile mix together:

2 cups small-curd cottage cheese
8 oz. crumbled blue cheese
1 finely chopped green pepper
2 teaspoons onion juice
1/2 cup Mayonnaise, 363
(1/2 cup blanched almonds)

and the reserved crushed pineapple. When the gelatin is almost set, add the cheese mixture and pack into a ring mold that has been rinsed in cold water. Refrigerate until ready to serve.

MOLDED PINEAPPLE RING

8 Servings

➤ Please read About Gelatin, 560.

Soak:

2 tablespoons gelatin

in:

1/2 cup cold water

Strain and reserve the juice of:

2 1/2 cups canned crushed pineapple

Add to the juice:

1/2 cup hot water

Bring these ingredients to the boiling point. Stir in the soaked gelatin until dissolved. Add:

5/8 cup sugar: 1/2 cup plus 2 tablespoons

Cool the mixture. Add the pineapple and:

(2 cups grated cabbage)
The grated rind of 1 orange or lemon
3/4 cup orange juice
5 tablespoons lemon juice

Pour these ingredients into a wet 9-inch ring mold. Chill the gelatin. Unmold on a bed of:

Lettuce or watercress

Fill the center with:

Cottage cheese, soft cream cheese balls rolled in chopped nutmeats, or chicken salad

Serve with or without:

Mayonnaise, 363

ASPIC-FILLED MELON

6 Servings

It is perfectly possible to serve this dish as a dessert; in which case, of course, the lettuce bed and the dressing are omitted. For the latter, try instead a garnish of Cold Sabayon Sauce, 771.

Pare:

1 large melon

leaving it whole. Cut off enough from one end so you can scrape out the seeds. Reserve the cap. Fill the cavity with water, then pour the water into a measuring cup; this is to guide you for the amount of gelatin you have to prepare. Stand the melon upside down to drain. Then fill, depending on the color of the melon flesh, with:

Fruit-flavored gelatin
(Diced or small fruits)
Try a combination of:
Orange-flavored gelatin, canned crushed pineapple, canned mandarin oranges or sliced bananas
or:
Raspberry gelatin with fresh raspberries
Refrigerate, and after the center is set, replace the cap, toothpicking it in place. Slice the melon horizontally, being careful not to dislodge the gelatin. On individual plates, bed it down on:
Leaf lettuce
Top it with a spray of fresh herbs. Keep chilled until ready to serve with:
Cream Mayonnaise, 365

STRAWBERRY AND RHUBARB SALAD MOLDS

8 to 10 Servings

Dissolve:
3 packages strawberry-flavored gelatin
in:
3 cups hot water
Drop in:
2 packages frozen rhubarb: 10 oz. each
Stir to separate the rhubarb. When the jelly begins to set, add:
1 quart sliced fresh strawberries
Pour into individual wet molds and chill until set. Unmold on:
Watercress
Garnish each with:
A fresh whole strawberry
Serve with:
Cream Mayonnaise, 365, or
Fruit Salad Mayonnaise, 365

ABOUT SAVORY MOUSSES

This kind of salad gelatin differs from the aspic in its lack of transparency—or, putting it more positively, in its inclusion of two additional ingredients: cream and egg. We qualify the "mousse" with "savory" to distinguish the recipes that follow from the sweet mousses you will find further along under Desserts, 734. A **mousseline** may be either a kind of pastry or, as in this section, a mousse confected with whipped cream.

JELLIED HAM MOUSSE

10 Servings

Soak:
1 tablespoon gelatin
in:
¼ cup cold water
Dissolve it in:
1½ cups boiling Stock, 520
Chill the jelly. When it is nearly set, combine it with:
3 cups cooked ground or chopped ham
¼ cup chopped celery
1 tablespoon grated onion
½ cup Mayonnaise, 363
¼ cup chopped sour or sweet-sour pickles
Add, if required:
Worcestershire sauce
Season to taste
Seasonal variation: omit onion and pickles and add:
(1 cup seedless green grapes)
Moisten a mold with cold water. If desired, and if the grapes have been omitted, decorate the sides and bottom with:
Stuffed olives and sliced hard-cooked eggs
Add the other ingredients. Chill the mousse until firm.

JELLIED CHICKEN OR VEAL MOUSSE

I. **10 Servings**

Use the recipe for Jellied Ham Mousse, above. Use chicken stock. Substitute cooked ground chicken or veal for the ham, or use part chicken and part ham.

II. **8 Servings**

Soak:
1½ tablespoons gelatin
in:
¼ cup Chicken Stock, 523
Dissolve it in:
½ cup hot stock
Beat:
3 egg yolks
Add:
1½ cups milk
Cook these ingredients in a double boiler until they are smooth and fairly thick. Stir in the dissolved gelatin. When the mixture is cool, add:
2 cups cooked minced or ground chicken or veal
(½ cup diced seeded cucumber)
Season with:
Salt, white pepper and paprika
Chill the jelly. When it is about to set, fold in:
1 cup whipped cream
Place the mousse in a wet mold and chill it until firm. Unmold it.

CUCUMBER MOUSSE

I. **4 Servings**

➤ Please read About Gelatin, 560.
Soak:
2 teaspoons gelatin
in:
3 tablespoons cold water
Dissolve these ingredients over heat. Add:
2 teaspoons vinegar, or lime or lemon juice
1 teaspoon grated onion
¾ teaspoon salt
¼ teaspoon paprika
Chill until about to set. Drain well:
1 cup pared, seeded, chopped cucumbers
Whip until stiff:
½ cup whipping cream

Beat the gelatin mixture gradually into the cream. Fold in the cucumbers. Rinse individual molds. Fill them with the mousse. When they are thoroughly chilled, invert onto a garnished platter.

II. **5 to 6 Servings**

Dissolve:

1 package lime-flavored gelatin

in:

¾ cup hot water

Add:

¼ cup lemon juice
1 tablespoon grated onion

Chill until about to set, then stir in:

1 cup cultured sour cream
1 cup finely chopped unpared cucumber

Pour into 6 small wet molds and chill until firm.

SEAFOOD MOUSSE

6 Servings

➤ Please read About Gelatin, 560.

Soak:

2 teaspoons gelatin

in:

¼ cup cold water

Dissolve it in:

¼ cup boiling water

Add it to:

¾ cup Mayonnaise, 363

Combine it with:

1 cup flaked crab meat or flaked tuna fish
½ cup chopped celery or carrots
2 tablespoons chopped parsley
½ cup chopped cucumber
2 tablespoons chopped stuffed or pitted black olives
1 tablespoon or more lemon juice
Season to taste

Place these ingredients in an oiled mold. Chill them until firm. Unmold on:

Cress or shredded lettuce

Serve with:

Cucumbers in sour cream

If you want a mousse based on whipped cream, see Lobster Mousse, next.

LOBSTER MOUSSE

6 Servings

An attractive salad made in a 9-inch ring mold.

➤ Please read About Gelatin, 560.

Soak:

1 tablespoon gelatin

in:

¼ cup water

Dissolve it over boiling water. Combine:

¾ cup minced celery
1½ cups canned or cooked lobster meat
(⅔ cup minced apple)

Season these ingredients with:

Salt and paprika

Stir the gelatin into:

¾ cup Mayonnaise, 363
3 tablespoons lemon juice
(1 teaspoon dry mustard)
(½ clove garlic, pressed)
(A few drops hot pepper sauce)

Whip until stiff, then fold in:

⅓ cup whipping cream

Fold this mixture into the other ingredients. Place the mousse in an oiled 9-inch ring mold. Chill thoroughly. Unmold on a platter, garnished with:

Watercress
Marinated cucumbers

Serve with:

Cold Quick Tomato Sauce, 352, or
Mayonnaise Collée, 368

MOLDED CREAMED FISH

I. **6 Servings**

➤ Please read About Gelatin, 560.

Soak:

¾ tablespoon gelatin

in:

2 tablespoons water

Combine in a double boiler, then stir constantly ➤ over—not in—boiling water until thickened:

2 egg yolks
1½ tablespoons soft butter
½ tablespoon flour
1½ teaspoons salt
2 teaspoons sugar
1 teaspoon Worcestershire sauce or ¾ teaspoon curry or 1 teaspoon dry mustard
1 teaspoon grated onion
A few grains red pepper
1 tablespoon chopped pimiento
¼ cup lemon juice
¾ cup milk or tomato juice

Add gelatin and stir until dissolved. Refrigerate. Prepare:

1½ cups seafood: cooked or canned shrimp, salmon, etc.

Or use part fish and part chopped celery. When the gelatin is nearly set, place some of it in the bottom of an oiled ring mold, add some of the fish, then more gelatin. Repeat this until all ingredients have been used, finishing with gelatin on top. Chill the salad until firm. Serve on:

Watercress

Fill the ring with:

Wilted Cucumbers, 102

Surround it with:

Sliced tomatoes

II. **6 Servings**

A quick version of the above.

Soak:

1½ teaspoons gelatin

in:

3 tablespoons cold water

Dissolve it in:

1 can heated condensed cream of chicken soup: 10¾ oz.

When the gelatin mixture begins to set, add:

1 teaspoon Worcestershire sauce
½ cup finely chopped celery
2 tablespoons chopped parsley
1 tablespoon chopped chives
1 can shredded white meat tuna fish: 6½ oz.

Chill until set. Serve garnished with:

Halved, cored, very thinly sliced Cucumbers, 102

which have been marinated briefly in:

Herb vinegar

MOUSSELINE OF SHELLFISH

6 Servings

Line a 1½-quart fish mold with half-set:

Fish- or chicken-flavored Basic Aspic, 113

Refrigerate it. Prepare, using a fumet, 524:

2 cups Velouté Sauce, 343

to which has been added:

1 tablespoon gelatin

soaked until dissolved in:

¼ cup cold stock or water

Combine the cooled sauce with:

1 lb. chopped cooked shellfish meat

Add:

½ cup partially whipped cream
Season to taste

and pour into the fish mold over the aspic. Chill before unmolding onto a cold serving platter.

CHILLED FRUIT SALAD MOUSSE

4 Servings

Dissolve:

1 package lime-flavored gelatin

in:

1 cup hot water

Add:

½ cup cold water
½ cup Mayonnaise, 363
2 tablespoons lemon juice
¼ teaspoon salt

Whip with a rotary beater until well blended. Pour into a refrigerator tray and chill until firm at the edge but still soft in the center. Turn into a bowl and whip in the same manner until fluffy. Fold in:

1 cup peeled and diced apples
¼ cup chopped pecans
¾ cup seeded Tokay grapes

Pour into a mold and refrigerate until firm.

TWENTY-FOUR-HOUR FRUIT SALAD WITH CREAM

12 to 14 Servings

Cook in a double boiler ➤ over—not in—hot water until thickened:

2 egg yolks
¼ cup sugar
¼ cup cream
Juice of 2 lemons
⅛ teaspoon salt

Stir these ingredients constantly. Chill them and add:

6 diced slices canned pineapple
2 cups pitted canned Queen Anne cherries
1 cup shredded blanched almonds
½ lb. marshmallows, cut in pieces
2 cups whipped cream
(½ lb. peeled, seeded grapes)

Chill the salad 24 hours. Serve on:

Lettuce

with:

Mayonnaise, 363

or as a dessert, garnished with:

Whipped cream

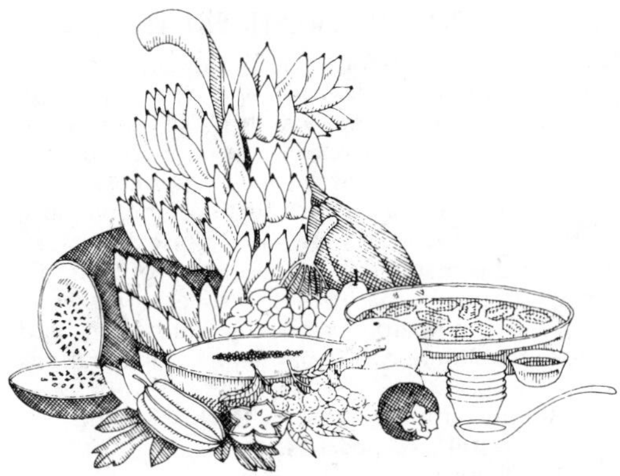

FRUITS

"It was not a watermelon that Eve took," observed Mark Twain. "We know it because she repented." There is something about "a piece of fruit"—no matter which—so tidy, shapely, self-contained and full of promise as to appeal to the larcenous instincts in all Eve's children.

Shown above, in addition to Twain's irresistible watermelon, are such staples of the world's diet as bananas and dates—and in more northerly climes, the pear; a papaya, whole and halved, next to a compote of kiwi. A spray of litchi and a Japanese persimmon contrast with the sweet-sour carambola, shown whole and in starry cross-section.

Today's menu-builder often takes herself too seriously and tops off an impressive edifice with a disastrously rich dessert, forgetting that fresh fruit, with perhaps a cheese, would be a far happier conclusion of the meal for all concerned. Well worth exploiting, too, are the virtues of fruit —in either cup, compote, salad or sherbet form— as a "lightener" during as well as after a big meal.

If fruits lack flavor, serve them or prepare them with candied peels, ginger, zest or spices; or add a little lemon or lime juice to cooked fruits and fruit fillings. Vary the flavor of a particular fruit by steeping it in the juices of other fruits or in wine, or by blending it with others in a purée. You may glaze poached fruit with contrasting fruit jellies, especially those of apple and quince, which are high in pectin; or combine canned, frozen and fresh fruits—cold or slightly heated—in what the French call a **compôte composée.** Try presenting your "composed compote" in a giant lidded snifter, laced with brandy or liqueur, and serve it to your guests in smaller individual snifters.

Serve Fruit with Custards, 734, or Creams, 696; Fruit Brûlé, 127, or Flambé, 127. For dried or preserved fruits used as garnishes, see About Candied and Glazed Fruits, 794. For fresh fruit combinations, see below, and also consult the Salad chapter, 92–122. For frozen and canned fruits, see 822 and 805. Recipes involving fruit used as an ingredient in desserts will be found in the Dessert chapter, 734–757.

ABOUT FRESH FRUITS

Pomologists have been working tirelessly—never more than now—to hybridize the most popular domestic fruits in order to lengthen the harvest season early and late; to produce plants more resistant to disease and adverse climate; and to improve shipping and keeping characteristics. In fact, much of this effort has been carried forward with little regard for retaining juiciness and flavor. Furthermore, crossbreeding within varieties has proceeded so rapidly, and the new cultivars have been so casually styled, that among apples, for example, 20 or 30 descendants may be traced to McIntosh and Winesap, but never through their names, which reveal not the slightest hint of their ancestry. In view of so confusing a situation, it is often advisable to sample fruit before buying it— a precaution that is a little difficult to arrange for in the average supermarket.

Should you undertake to grow your own fruit, choose catalog stock expressly labeled "for the home garden." Such fruit has been developed with an eye to immediate consumption, and so comprises varieties more delicate in flavor and texture than those commercially propagated.

Most ripe fresh fruit may be stored under refrigeration at temperatures between 35° and 40°. Most fruit varieties, too, including tangerines, benefit from the protection of a sealed plastic bag—exceptions being other citrus fruits, melons and pineapples. Mature bananas will keep chilled for a day or two.

Be wary of "fruit specials." Such produce may include pieces that are below standard in either quality or size and could prove to be no bargains at all. U. S. Government standards are of necessity variable, but you can judge for yourself as to size: ➤ the smaller the number of fruits per box or basket, obviously, the larger the individual fruit.

Not all varieties of fruit ripen satisfactorily after plucking. Those which do are apricots, avocados, bananas, melons, mangoes, medlars, nectarines, pawpaws, peaches, pears, persimmons, sapodillas, tamarinds, strawberries to a limited extent, and pineapples; none of these grow sweeter, however. If purchased underripe, these fruits should be stored at room temperature in a dark place. Keep each variety in a partly closed paper bag, the individual pieces—except for strawberries, bananas and melons—separated by loose wraps of paper toweling. Examine them twice daily, keep from bruising and, as soon as ripened, chill in the refrigerator before serving.

There is a persistent but mistaken belief that all fruits abound in vitamin C. Many do, notably the citrus family; but in others, like apples, pineapples, pears, figs and bananas, the C content is conspicuously low. Virtually all fresh fruits lose their flavor rapidly when soaked in water, so always ➤ wash them quickly in gently flowing water just before using and dry at once. If peaches, plums, apricots and cherries are cooked with the seeds in, be careful ➤ that the inner kernel of the pit which looks nutlike is not eaten. Eight to ten such kernels, if chewed, can release enough hydrogen cyanide to prove fatal.

ANTI-BROWNING SOLUTION FOR FRESH FRUITS

Solutions that prevent the browning of fruits and certain vegetables on exposure to air are used in both canning and freezing and can be successfully applied to fresh fruits peeled slightly in advance of serving. For fresh fruits we like to use Acidulated Water II, 520, or to combine pared fruits with citrus fruits to prevent darkening.

FRUIT CUPS

Sweetened fresh fruit may be served in attractive small bowls or glass cups, in melon baskets, see 138, or in a Caramel Cornflake Ring, 690. ➤ To frost containers, see 51. Use seedless grapes, citrus sections, and watermelon and green and yellow melons cut into balls with a French potato cutter, see 99.

Chill and prepare for serving:

Fresh fruit

Five minutes before serving, sprinkle lightly with:

Confectioners' sugar

Immediately before serving, flavor with:

Lime juice, lemon juice, sherry, a liqueur, or lightly sweetened fruit juice

Garnish with:

Glazed Mint Leaves, 794, or sweet woodruff

AMBROSIA

4 Servings

A versatile old favorite, especially popular in the South.

Peel carefully, removing all membrane:

2 large Valencia or navel oranges

Peel and cut into thin slices:

3 ripe bananas

Pineapple is sometimes added, or other fruits: seeded grapes, apples, etc. Combine and stir:

¼ cup confectioners' sugar
1½ cups shredded coconut

Arrange alternate layers of oranges and bananas in individual serving dishes or in a bowl. Sprinkle each layer with part of the coconut mixture, reserving some for the top. Pour over the fruit:

A little orange juice

Chill well before serving. Instead of the coconut topping, try a garnish of:

(Crushed mint, a cherry or a strawberry)

MACÉDOINE OF FRESH FRUITS

The following fruit and wine or liqueur combinations should be made with ripe, perfect, pared, seeded and sliced seasonal fruits. Favorites for this dessert are strawberries, raspberries, peeled seedless green grapes, peaches, apricots, kiwi slices, orange and grapefruit sections, melon balls, cherries and nectarines. Be sure to prick the fruits to allow the marinade to soak in. If you use raw apples or pears, marinate the slices for several hours in wine or liqueur or they will be too hard in texture. Some good marinating combinations are:

Brandy with oranges or with cherries and clove-studded peaches
Port with melon balls
Kirsch with strawberries
Grand Marnier with peeled seedless grapes

A macédoine is usually served cold, but you may flambé it, see 127, if the fruit is at room temperature—and if you add extra liqueur, slightly warmed.

Place in layers in a crystal bowl:

Prepared fruit, see above

Sprinkle each layer with:

Confectioners' sugar

Stir the fruit gently until the sugar is almost dissolved, then add for each quart of fruit:

2 to 4 tablespoons brandy, kirsch, Grand Marnier or Southern Comfort

Serve very cold over:

Vanilla ice cream, 759

or with:

Cake

FRUIT FOOLS

4 Servings

Long ago the word "fool" was used as a term of endearment. We have an old-fashioned fondness for the recipes in which fruit is combined with cream.

I. With Fresh Fruit

Prepare:

Raspberries or strawberries

Add to taste:

Confectioners' sugar

Let the mixture stand 10 minutes. Combine it with an equal amount of:

Whipping cream

flavored with:

(3 tablespoons kirsch, port or Madeira wine)

Chill well before serving.

II. With Cooked Fruit

Whip until stiff:

½ cup sweetened whipping cream

Fold in:

1 cup applesauce, rhubarb, berry, apricot, currant or other fruit purée
1½ teaspoons grated lemon rind or ¼ teaspoon almond extract

Place the mixture in the bowl from which it is to be served. Chill thoroughly. Sprinkle the top with:

Crumbled Macaroons, 709

or serve with:

Ladyfingers, 695

ABOUT RAISINS AND OTHER DRIED FRUITS

The high caloric and nutritive values of dried fruits can be readily grasped if you realize that it takes 5½ pounds of fresh apricots to yield 1 pound when dried. When fruits are dried without cooking, their subsequent contact with the air—as well as the enzymatic activity that takes place within them—tends to darken the pulp. A sulfur dioxide solution is often used to lessen darkening. If you are interested in drying your own fruits, see 816.

Dates, figs, apples, peaches, pears, plums, apricots, currants and grapes are among the fruits most often dried. They must all be ➤ stored tightly covered in a cool, dark place. Under most household shelf conditions, they are likely to deteriorate in a matter of months. This is especially true of the increasingly numerous dried fruits that are treated and tightly packaged so as to remain plump and soft. All varieties must be watched for the insect infestation that develops in them with age.

Raisins, which of course are simply dried grapes, divide into **seedless,** those which grow without seeds; and **seeded,** which have had the seeds removed. As their flavors are quite different, it is wise to use the types called for in the recipes —without interchanging. White raisins, often called **muscats,** are especially treated to retain their lovely color.

Currants and raisins both profit, unless they are very fresh, by plumping, especially when used in short-cooking recipes. This can be done by soaking them in the liquid in which they are to be cooked—such as the liquid called for in cakes—for 10 to 15 minutes before use. Raisins and currants may also be plumped by washing briefly, draining, spreading on a flat pan and then heating, closely covered, in a 350° oven until they puff up and are no longer much wrinkled.

In cooking dried fruits, do not soak them first unless the processor so directs on the package. The less water used, the more natural sugars will be retained within the fruit. If you must soak fruit such as dried apples, cover with boiling water and soak until tender. Use this water in further preparation. Allow 1 pound dried for 3½ to 4 pounds fresh apples and proceed as for any apple recipe.

Small dried fruits are often messy to cut or chop. If they are sticky, flour them, ➤ using for this purpose, when baking, a portion of the flour called for in the recipe. They may also be more easily cut if the scissors or the knife blade is heated. Handle the knife as for chopping nuts. But if you are chopping in quantity, you may want to use a meat grinder instead. ➤ Heat the grinder very thoroughly in boiling water before feeding in the fruit.

Candied and preserved fruits are sometimes substituted for dried fruits. If large amounts of candied fruits are used, allow for their extra sugar content. With preserved fruits, compensate for both sugar and liquid.

Fine-quality dried dessert fruits are an elegant note on the cheese platter, especially dried Malaga grapes. Should any of the fruits have become unpleasantly dried out, steam them lightly—sprinkled with wine or water—in the top of a double boiler ➤ over—not in—boiling water; or prepare them for stuffing by steaming 10 to 15 minutes in a colander ➤ over boiling water, until tender enough to pit. Stuff with a hazelnut or with fillings suggested under confections, 793.

FRUIT-NUT PEMMICAN

This quite palatable albeit gooey substance is the modern outdoorsman's version of the old suet–parched corn–fruit concoction that sustained both Indians and frontiersmen in earlier times. Grind in a meat grinder, using the coarse plate:

⅓ cup each: raisins, dried apricots, dried apples, pecans, toasted soybeans and Spanish peanuts

Combine with:

2 tablespoons honey

These ingredients may be changed to fit individual preferences. For a tasty variation, use pecans as the only nuts. Package for the trail in wide-mouth plastic bottles or plastic bags.

ABOUT COOKED FRUITS

A good reason for serving fruits uncooked is to retain fully their high vitamin content. But if we do cook them, we can minimize the loss of vitamins and natural sugars by using as little water as possible and by cooking briefly. Fruits may be poached, puréed, baked, broiled, sautéed or pickled, see Spiced Syrup, 126.

Fruits should always be poached rather than stewed. ➤ Drop them into a boiling liquid, ➤ reduce the heat at once and simmer until barely tender. Remove from the heat and drain them immediately, so they will not continue to cook in the pan and get mushy. Soft, juicy fruits, like ripe peaches, are best poached by putting them for a few moments into heavy boiling syrup and then plunging the pan into a larger pan of cold water to arrest the cooking. Apples and other hard fruits should be poached in simmering water. Watch closely to guard against overcooking. If necessary, add sugar, but only after poaching. A baked fruit compote or a mixture of cooked fruits makes a refreshing addition to a meat course, provided that fruit juices have not been used in basting the meat. Always pare fruit with a ➤ stainless steel knife to avoid discoloration.

SYRUPS FOR FRUITS

I. Thin Syrup

For apples, grapes and rhubarb.
Combine and heat:

1 cup sugar
3 cups water
1/16 teaspoon salt

II. Medium Syrup

For apricots, cherries, grapefruit, pears and prunes.
Combine and heat:

1 cup sugar
2 cups water
1/8 teaspoon salt

III. Heavy Syrup

For berries, figs, peaches and plums.
Combine and heat:

1 cup sugar
1 cup water
1/8 teaspoon salt

SPICED SYRUP FOR FRESH FRUITS

Enough for 1 to 1½ Pints Fruit

Tie in a cheesecloth bag:

1½ teaspoons each whole cloves, whole allspice
1 stick cinnamon

Add and boil 5 minutes:

1½ cups white or brown sugar
or 2 cups honey
1 cup cider vinegar
1 cup water

Remove the spice bag and discard. Drop whole, sliced, pared or unpared fruit into the boiling syrup. Cool and serve.

SPICED SYRUP FOR CANNED FRUITS

Drain and reserve the syrup from:

Canned peaches, apricots, pears or pineapple

Measure the syrup and ➤ simmer until slightly reduced with:

¼ to ½ as much wine vinegar

Allow for every 2 cups of juice and vinegar:

1 stick cinnamon
½ teaspoon cloves without heads
(2 or 3 small pieces gingerroot)

After simmering about 10 minutes, add fruit. Remove pan from heat and let fruit cool in the liquid. Strain out the spices and serve hot or cold with meat.

POACHED OR "STEWED" PARED FRUIT

Please read About Cooked Fruits, 125.
Boil 3 minutes:

A Syrup for Fruit, above

Drop into the boiling syrup about:

1 quart peeled or pared fruit

➤ Reduce the heat at once. Simmer gently until tender. You may season the syrup with any of the following:

(Spices)
(Crème de menthe)
(Wine)
(Stick cinnamon)
(Slice of lemon)

Drain fruit and reduce syrup. Pour syrup over fruit and chill before serving.

POACHED OR "STEWED" THIN-SKINNED FRUIT

By adding the sugar late in the cooking as suggested here, you will need less of it to sweeten the same quantity of fruit than if you had used it from the start. This method will also keep the skin soft.
Boil:

2 cups water

Prepare and add:

1 quart unpared fruit: peaches, pears, apricots or nectarines

Reduce heat at once. Simmer fruit until nearly tender. Add:

½ to ¾ cup sugar

During the last few minutes of cooking, add:

(A vanilla bean, 577)

POACHED OR "STEWED" THICK-SKINNED FRUIT

Use whole or cut into halves and if necessary remove the seeds from:

4 cups thick-skinned fruit: plums, blueberries or cherries

You may prick the fruit before dropping it into:

1 to 1½ cups boiling water

Reduce heat at once. Simmer until nearly tender. Add:

½ to 1 cup sugar

Cook a few minutes longer. ➤ After cooking blueberries, to which lemon juice is a good addition, shake the container to avoid clumping.

BAKED FRESH FRUIT COMPOTE

4 Servings

Use this also as a garnish for custard or blancmange.
Preheat oven to 350°.
Pare:

8 small peaches, apples or pears

Place them whole or in thick slices in a baking dish. Combine, heat but do not boil, stir and pour over them:

⅔ cup red wine or water
⅔ cup sugar
½ stick cinnamon
4 whole cloves

1/8 teaspoon salt
1/2 thinly sliced seeded lemon or lime

Bake the fruit either covered or uncovered until tender when tested with a fork. If cooked uncovered ➤ it must be basted every 10 minutes. For more rapid and even cooking, some people prefer to turn the fruit over after the first two bastings.

ADDITIONS TO BAKED FRUITS

I. To be served as a meat garnish. After baking, fill centers of fruits with:

Mint, currant or cranberry jelly, or a mixture of pearl onions, shredded candied ginger and seasoned cream cheese

II. As dessert. Fill centers with:

A mixture of Roquefort or blue cheese, cream cheese and chopped almonds, pecans, hickory nuts or walnuts

ABOUT PURÉED FRUITS

Puréed fruits are most delicate if cooked covered over gentle heat. ➤ We do not recommend pressure-cooking of any fresh fruits. Apples, rhubarb and cranberries, especially, tend to sputter and obstruct the vent. They are almost explosive unless every vestige of steam is expelled before removal of the cover. ➤If you want to purée canned fruit, you should know that, after draining, a No. 2½ can will yield 1¼ to 1½ cups.

GARNISHES FOR PURÉED FRUITS

Serve puréed fruit hot or cold with one of the following toppings:

Grated lemon rind or cinnamon
Whipping cream and nutmeg
Chopped Glazed Chestnuts, 796, and marmalade
6 crushed dry macaroons to 1 cup whipped cream
Cultured sour cream or yogurt with sugar, rum and nuts
Bread or cake crumbs browned in butter with chopped slivered almonds
Freshly chopped mint

BROILED FRUITS

Drain:

Poached or canned peaches, pears or pineapple rings

Place peaches or pears, hollow side up, in a shallow pan. Place on the centers:

A dab of butter

Plug up the pineapple hole with:

A preserved cherry

Sprinkle each piece of fruit lightly with:

Salt and cinnamon

Broil under moderate heat until light brown. You may garnish the fruits with:

(Cranberry or other jelly)

FRESH FRUIT KEBABS

8 Servings

Serve with meat course or as a dessert. Marinate about 30 minutes:

6 canned peach halves—drained and cut in half
3 thickly sliced bananas
2 apples, cut in sections
1 cubed fresh pineapple
3 sectioned grapefruits

in a mixture of:

1 cup grapefruit juice
1/2 cup honey
2 tablespoons Cointreau
(1 teaspoon chopped mint)

Broil on skewers about 5 minutes, basting often with the marinade.

FLAMBEED FRUITS

For best results, use at least 2 ounces of alcoholic liquor, and remember that ➤ unless the temperature of the fruit is at least 75°, you may not get any effect at all. Heat the fruit ➤ mildly in a ➤ covered chafing dish or electric skillet. ➤ Warm the liquor, too, but do not boil it. Sprinkle the fruit lightly with sugar and, after pouring the warm liquor over the warm fruit, re-cover the pan for a moment before lighting. Stand back!

The following recipe makes 6 servings as a sauce, but only 3 if used as a main dessert dish. Caramelize, 559, lightly over low heat:

3 tablespoons sugar

Add:

3 tablespoons butter

or, if you are lazy, melt the butter first and substitute brown sugar, stirring until dissolved. Cook over very low heat for 4 to 5 minutes. Add 2 of the following:

3 split bananas, mangoes, peaches or pears or 3 slices pineapple

Simmer until tender, basting occasionally. Since the banana will cook more rapidly than the rest of the fruit, it should be added later. Flambé the fruit with:

2 oz. brandy, dark rum or liqueur

FRUIT BRÛLÉ

4 to 5 Servings

This recipe is most often made with seedless green grapes but lends itself equally well to strawberries, raspberries and peaches.

Fill the bottom of a 9-inch ovenproof baker or glass pie pan with an even layer of one of the above-mentioned:

Fruits

Cover the fruit with:

1 cup cultured sour cream

mixed with:

1 teaspoon vanilla

Cover and refrigerate until thoroughly chilled. Preheat broiler.
Just before serving, dust the cream evenly with:
About 1 cup light brown sugar
so that none of the cream shows through. Place the filled pan over a pan of equal size filled with:
Cracked ice
Put the stacked pans under the hot broiler until the sugar caramelizes, 559. This is a moment for watchfulness, as the sugar must fuse but not scorch. Serve at once.

SAUTÉED FRUITS

6 Servings

Core and slice or cut into rings:
6 tart, well-flavored apples; or peaches, apricots, or pineapple slices
Melt in a skillet over high heat:
2 tablespoons butter or bacon drippings
When the fat is hot to the point of fragrance stir in the fruit. Cover until the fruit steams. Sprinkle with:
½ cup white or brown sugar
⅛ teaspoon salt
Cook uncovered over gentle heat until tender. Add, if needed:
(Butter or drippings)
Serve with a meat course or with:
Bacon
To serve with meat, you may begin making this dish by placing a layer of finely sliced onions, about 1 cup, in the butter. Cook slowly in the fat 5 minutes. Season with salt and paprika. Add the fruit and proceed as directed.

CURRIED FRUIT FONDUE

8 Servings

Fruit in season may be dipped into or served in a two-way hot sauce—hot with both spice and cooking.
Combine and simmer covered ½ hour:
1 cup chicken broth
1 cup dry white wine
1 tablespoon curry powder
Add:
1 tablespoon quick-cooking tapioca
soaked in:
3 tablespoons water
Stir the sauce until thickened. Add:
1 cup freshly grated coconut
1 cup slivered, toasted almonds
½ cup white raisins
While the sauce is cooking, cut into cubes or finger-sized sections a combination of:
About 4 cups fresh fruit: pineapple, mangoes, papayas, bananas and melons
Keep the sauce hot in a chafing dish. Dip the fruits in the fondue; or pour sauce over individual fruit portions just before serving. For other fruit fondue sauces, see 769, 770.

ABOUT FRUITS FOR MEATS AND ENTRÉES

Fruit Compotes, 126, Fruit Kebabs, 127, Sautéed Fruits, left, or pickled or spiced fruits served with meat are delights we may have a tendency to neglect. Consider using as occasional decorative fruit garnishes:
Apple Rings, 129
Glazed Stuffed Apricots, 794
Kumquats
Orange slices with cranberry or other jelly
Cranberries

FRUIT SOUPS

In Scandinavia, fruit soups are served as a dessert, but in Germany they constitute a chilled summertime prelude to the entrée. Mix fresh and dried fruits; use one variety or a combination, cooked until they can be puréed easily. If served at the beginning of the meal, go easy on the sugar. Fruit soups are also refreshing when made from frozen fruits, in winter, as a dessert. Rote Grütze II, 749, will serve in the dessert capacity, or use the cherry, orange or rose hip recipe below.

I. CHERRY SOUP

4 Cups

Prepare:
1 lb. stoned sour cherries
Place in an enamel pan and cover with:
2 cups water
1 cup red wine
Cook until the fruit is soft, about 10 minutes. Add and stir until dissolved:
¼ cup sugar
½ teaspoon grated orange rind
Blend or sieve the fruit and thicken the juice with:
1 teaspoon arrowroot
mixed with a little of the cooled syrup. Return the mixture to the soup and cook about 2 minutes. Serve hot or cold. Garnish with:
Unsweetened whipped cream, croutons or Dumplings, 202

II. ORANGE SOUP

6 Servings

Scrub and remove the orange-colored peel in shreds from:
1 Valencia or navel orange
Add these peelings to a syrup of:
1 cup sugar
½ cup currant jelly
¼ cup water
Simmer about 15 minutes. Meanwhile, section the peeled orange, 135, and also:
5 more peeled Valencia or navel oranges
➤ Cool the syrup to about 85°. Pour it over the orange sections. Add:
2 tablespoons brandy
Refrigerate, covered, about 12 hours, before serving with:

A crisp thin refrigerator cookie, 715,
or a curled cookie, 718
Also good with:
Cinnamon toast

ROSE HIP SOUP

Crush in a stainless steel or enamel pot:
2 cups fresh rose hips
➤ but be sure the bushes from which they are gathered were not sprayed. Cover with:
1 quart water
Bring to a boil, then simmer, covered, about 45 minutes. Strain through a sieve lined with several thicknesses of cheesecloth. Add enough:
Fruit juice: raspberry, peach, orange
to make about 1 quart liquid in all. Mix:
1 tablespoon arrowroot
with a small quantity of the liquid and:
1/3 cup honey
Simmer and stir until the mixture begins to thicken. Chill well and serve garnished with:
Whipped cream
Slivered Spiced Nuts, 789

INDIVIDUAL FRUITS

Already familiar and now seasonably obtainable in most American markets are the fruits shown below: the fresh fig with its renowned leaf; a decorative spray of kumquats; a mango, shown cut to reveal its large fiber-covered seed. Next is a pomegranate; then the ugly duckling of the apple family, the quince; and finally the prickly pear.

ABOUT APPLES

A predecessor of ours, Amelia Simmons, in her pioneering *American Cookery*—circa 1845—had this to say: "If every boy in America planted an apple tree (except in our compactest cities) in some useless corner, and tended it carefully, the net saving would in time extinguish the public debt." A century or so later it is becoming evident that a solid layer of applesauce a half-mile thick would not suffice to "extinguish the public debt." And we are even beginning to wonder, in these days of office visits only, just how politic we were more recently to invent the adage about the apple a day and the doctor.

Although apples are in the market the year around, they are not at their peak from January to June. There is probably no flavor superior to that of the Greenings or Transparents that fleetingly initiate the harvest. If you plan canning or freezing, do try to get the first picking for prompt preservation of this unusual tart flavor.

So-called dessert apples—firm, long-keeping types always eaten uncooked—include Yellow and Red Delicious and Newtown Pippin. We find most varieties of Delicious too dry and their somewhat corky aftertaste faintly unpleasant.

All-purpose apple varieties—good for eating, for salads and for most cooking—are Northern Spy, Spitzenburg, Baldwin, Jonathan, Stayman, Winesap, Wealthy, McIntosh, Gravenstein, Grimes Golden, Melrose, Russet, and Rhode Island Greening—which cooks best of all. Wealthys and McIntoshes are not good bakers. ➤ Best for this purpose are Spitzenburgs, Northern Spys, Cortlands, York Imperials, Staymans, Winesaps, Baldwins and Rome Beautys, unless the latter are overripe. In that condition they become mealy.

Mealiness in apples, to which larger varieties are more prone, may also denote too long or improper storage. Browning near the core means that the fruit has been stored at too low a temperature.

If you wonder why the apple in commercial pies has a firmer texture than yours, it is due to added calcium. An apple of poor flavor can be improved in cooking by the addition of lemon juice, but remember that nothing can really compensate for natural tartness. After paring, should apples seem dry, simmer their cores and skins, reduce the liquid and use it to moisten them during cooking.

If you receive a windfall from a friend's orchard and want to reserve some of it, let it stand in a cool, shady place for 24 hours. Inspect for blemishes. Wrap each fruit in paper and store in slotted boxes in a cool, dark, airy place.

For apple recipes, see below and the Index.

APPLE RINGS

Wash, core and cut crosswise into slices:
3 large, perfect cooking apples
Heat in a skillet:
3 tablespoons bacon fat or butter
Place in it a single layer of apple rings.
Sprinkle lightly with:
Confectioners' sugar
Add to the skillet:
2 tablespoons water

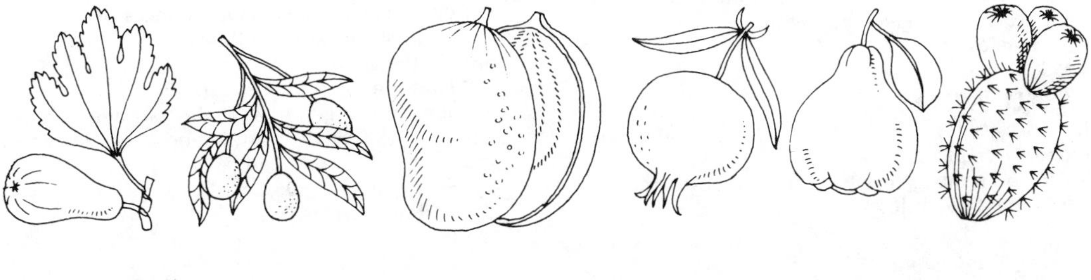

Cover the skillet and ➤ simmer the apples until tender. Remove cover and brown rings on both sides. Serve hot, the centers filled with:
Bright red jelly
or dust the rings with:
Cinnamon

GLAZED APPLES

6 Servings

Recommended only for tart apples. If the only ones at hand are listless, try the next recipe below instead.
Preheat oven to 350°.
Pare, core and slice thinly:
4 cups tart apples
Place them in a 6 x 9-inch pan. Pour over them:
3 tablespoons melted butter
Bake 15 to 30 minutes, or until tender. Remove from oven and dust with:
¾ to 1 cup white or brown sugar
(2 to 3 tablespoons dark rum)
Run under a broiler, leaving the oven door ajar, until the sugar and rum glaze the surface. ➤ Watch carefully. Serve at once.

HONEY APPLES

An excellent way to use a dull-flavored apple. Heat in a small porcelain or stainless steel pan:
1 cup honey
½ cup vinegar
Pare, core and slice thinly:
2 cups apples
Drop the apples a few at a time into the simmering, bubbling honey mixture. Skim them out when transparent. Serve chilled or hot as a relish with pork, as a tart filling, or as a dessert with cream.

SAUTÉED APPLES AND BACON

4 Servings

A fine breakfast or luncheon dish.
Pare and core:
Tart cooking apples
Cut them into cubes. There should be about 4 cups. Sauté in a heavy skillet:
8 slices bacon
Remove the bacon when crisp. Keep it hot. Leave about 2 tablespoons of fat in the skillet. Add:
2 tablespoons vegetable oil
Add the apples. Sauté uncovered over high heat until translucent. Sprinkle with:
2 tablespoons white or brown sugar
Place apples on a hot platter. Surround them with the bacon. Serve garnished with:
Parsley

BAKED APPLES

I. **4 Servings**

Preheat oven to 375°.
Wash and remove core to ½ inch of bottoms of:
4 large tart apples
Combine:
¼ cup white or brown sugar
(1 teaspoon cinnamon)
If the apples are bland, add:
(⅛ teaspoon grated lemon rind)
Fill the centers with this. Dot the filled cores with:
Butter
Put the apples into an 8 x 8-inch pan with:
¾ cup boiling water
(2 tablespoons sugar)
Bake about 30 minutes—or until tender but not mushy. Remove from the oven and baste the apples several times with the pan juices. Should the juices be thin, remove the apples to a serving dish and reduce the pan juices before glazing the apples with them. Serve hot or chilled.

II. **6 Servings**

Obviously a richer dish than that produced by the above recipe.
Preheat oven to 425°.
Pare and core:
6 large baking apples
Fill the cores with a mixture of:
½ cup chopped blanched almonds or pecans
½ cup sugar
2 tablespoons raisins, chopped figs or prunes, or mincemeat
(1 egg white)
Make another mixture of:
½ cup fine bread crumbs
2 tablespoons sugar
1 teaspoon cinnamon or ½ teaspoon powdered ginger
Coat the apples with:
6 tablespoons melted butter
Roll them in the bread crumbs. Bake the apples in individual buttered bakers about 25 minutes. Serve hot, covered with:
Caramelized Sugar, 559
or cold with:
Cream

BAKED APPLES FILLED WITH SAUSAGE MEAT

6 Servings

A three-star winter dish.
Preheat oven to 375°.
Wash:
6 large tart baking apples
Cut a slice from the tops. Scoop out the cores and pulp, leaving shells ¾ inch thick. Cut the pulp from the cores and chop it. Combine it with:
1 cup well-seasoned sausage meat or small sliced sausage links
Sprinkle the shells with:
(2 tablespoons brown sugar)
Fill them heaping full with the sausage mixture. Bake in a baking dish until tender. Serve with a mound of:
Steamed Rice, 206, or
Boiled Noodles, 213

APPLES STUFFED WITH SAUERKRAUT

4 Servings

Preheat oven to 375°.
Pare the tops of:
4 large baking apples
Remove the pulp and discard the core, leaving a ½-inch shell. Chop the pulp and add to it:
2 cups drained canned or cooked sauerkraut
⅛ teaspoon pepper
¼ teaspoon caraway seeds
Salt, as needed
Fill the shells. Place them in a baking dish with ¼ cup water or dry wine. Bake until tender. Baste frequently with pan juices.

APPLES COCKAIGNE

4 to 5 Servings

Wash, core and pare down to about 1 to 1½ inches from the top:
4 or 5 medium-sized baking apples
Place them in a heavy 8-inch pan with a mixture of:
2½ cups water
1 cup sugar
2 tablespoons red-hots or cinnamon drops
The red-hots give the apples a spicy tang and a beautiful color. The fruit should be submerged to a level just below the upper edge of the peel. Simmer about 20 minutes, or until the steeped portion of the apples gives slightly at the pressure of a spoon. Turn them over and simmer about 3 minutes longer. Remove the fruit carefully from the syrup and place on a rack in a broiler pan. Preheat the broiler.

Reduce the syrup to about 1 cup. Ladle a tablespoon of syrup over each apple. Broil the apples about 3 minutes, at least 5 inches from heat source. Repeat the ladling and broil 2 minutes longer. Baste with remaining syrup. Place the apples in individual dishes and spoon the syrup from the bottom of the baking pan into the cored centers. Serve warm or cold, with or without:
Cream

APPLESAUCE

➤ Please read About Puréed Fruits, 127.

I. **About 1 Quart**

Wash, cut into quarters and core:
2½ lb. apples: preferably Early Transparents, Northern Spys or Russets
Place them in a saucepan and partly cover with water. Old apples require more water than new ones. ➤ Simmer the apples until tender. Put them through a food mill or ricer, or ⅄ blend, skin and all. Return the strained apple pulp to the saucepan. Add enough:
Sugar
to make it palatable. Cook gently about 3 minutes. Add to tasteless apples:
Lemon juice or Zest, 571

Canned applesauce may be seasoned in the same way. Sprinkle it, if desired, with:
(Cinnamon)
Serve hot or cold. If hot, add:
1 or 2 teaspoons butter
If cold, add:
½ teaspoon vanilla or a few drops almond extract
When served with pork, you may add:
(1 or 2 tablespoons horseradish)

II. Combine:
2 cups applesauce as cooked above
with:
1 cup puréed apricots or raspberries
or with:
1 cup crushed pineapple
1 teaspoon finely crushed preserved ginger
or with:
2 cups Cranberry Sauce, 133
sprinkled with:
Grated orange rind

ABOUT APRICOTS

Fresh apricots have a beautiful blush and should be firm in texture. If they appear wilted or shriveled, they lack flavor and will decay quickly. Apricots may be eaten raw or cooked in a very light syrup and serve flambéed in Meringues, 649.

As a purée made from the dried fruit—a modification of the recipe below—the apricot is a frequent addition in the European cuisine. Especially, in a more or less cooked-down or glazed state, it enlivens a whole galaxy of filled cakes, open tarts, torten and frozen desserts.

COOKED DRIED APRICOTS

10 Servings

Place in a heavy pan:
1 lb. dried apricots
3 cups water
Simmer the fruit about 35 minutes. Add:
½ to 1 cup sugar
Heat until the sugar is dissolved, about 5 minutes longer. You may purée the fruit.

ABOUT AVOCADOS

A native of America, this valuable fruit harbors no less than 11 vitamins. Two varieties are usually available, depending on the season: a smooth green-skinned type, and a much darker one with pebbled skin. Like the banana, the avocado is never allowed to mature on the tree. Buy it slightly underripe and ripen it at 70°, hastening the process, if you like, by enclosing it in a paper bag. Test an avocado not by poking it with a finger, but by applying gentle pressure with the entire hand. When the fruit yields slightly it is ready to eat.

The flesh of the avocado discolors rapidly when exposed, and becomes bitter if cooked. To forestall browning, sprinkle with citrus juice. When combining avocado with cooked foods ➤ add it at the last moment, away from heat, to keep it from turning bitter. If using only half an avocado, keep the unused part unpeeled, with the seed still embedded in it; wrap it in foil and store at a temperature between 40° and 70°. For salad combinations and ways to cut avocado, see 110.

BAKED AVOCADOS STUFFED WITH CREAMED FOOD

Cut into halves:

Avocados

Place in each half:

1 tablespoon Garlic Vinegar, 527

Let stand 30 minutes. Discard vinegar. Fill them with well-seasoned, hot creamed:

Cooked crab, lobster, shrimp, chicken, or ham

Use one-fourth as much sauce as filling. Place the avocados on waxed or buttered paper.
Preheat oven to 375°.
Cover the tops with:

Grated cheese, buttered crumbs or cornflakes

Bake until ➤ just heated through.

ABOUT BANANAS

Bananas have been called "the humblest fruit": nobody takes them quite seriously. Yet in this country they happen to be the fruit most frequently eaten—not surprisingly, for they are by and large the most easily digestible and the least expensive. Indeed, for nutritive value they probably rank as the cheapest of all foods, including milk—despite their low protein content.

Bananas, when ready to eat, vary in size and in skin color, which ranges from a pale creamy yellow to russet red. Cook all bananas called **plantains,** 317. Commercial varieties, always picked unripe, are matured by special moist processing, before reaching the point of sale. They should not be eaten until further ripened by holding them at 70° in a closed paper bag until yellow in color. Once cut, they darken rapidly unless sprinkled with citrus juice. As a rule use slightly underripe bananas for cooking, except in Banana Bread, 624.

For decades we were warned, to music, "never, never" to refrigerate bananas. We find, however, that although the skins darken ominously, the interiors remain palatable even after 2 or 3 days of refrigeration. Bananas may also be successfully frozen if, after partially thawing in the refrigerator, they are used immediately. In fact, there are a number of ways in which we may prepare frozen bananas and enjoy them even without thawing. One is simply to cut them into chips, spread the chips out on a piece of foil, wrap them securely, freeze, and munch them as occasional snacks. Or mash up the pulp, if ripe, with a palatable mixture of lemon juice, honey and cinnamon before freezing. Another freezing process—which really turns the youngsters on—is conversion into Chocolate-Dipped Bananas, opposite.

⊟ BAKED BANANAS

I. Preheat oven to 375°.
Bananas may be baked in their skins in an oven or on an outdoor grill about 20 minutes. On opening, sprinkle with:

Lemon juice
Salt or confectioners' sugar

II. **2 Servings**

A candied version.
Preheat oven to 375°.
In a small saucepan, melt together and boil about 5 minutes:

½ cup dark brown sugar
¼ cup water

Peel, slice in half the long way and then once laterally and place in a buttered shallow dish:

1½ to 2 slightly underripe bananas

Sprinkle with:

Salt

Add to the cooled syrup:

Juice of ½ lemon or 1 lime

Pour the syrup over the bananas and bake about 30 minutes, turning the fruit after the first 15 minutes. Serve on hot dessert plates, sprinkled with:

Rum
Chopped candied ginger

BANANAS IN BLANKETS

Prime as a breakfast dish or served with a meat course.
Preheat broiler.
Peel and cut into lengthwise halves:

Firm ripe bananas

Place between the halves:

Canned pineapple sticks

Wrap the bananas with:

Slices of bacon

Broil in a pan, turning frequently until the bacon is crisp.

CARIBBEAN BANANA

For each serving, melt in a skillet:

1 tablespoon butter

Peel and split lengthwise:

A moderately ripe banana

Simmer the banana gently in the butter, first on one side, then on the other. Baste with:

2 tablespoons Sauce Cockaigne, 770
(A dash of lime juice)

Serve on a hot plate, flambé, 127, with:

Rum

and garnish with:

(A candied kumquat and a sprig of lemon thyme)

or, after flambéing the bananas, garnish with:

Vanilla ice cream

* CHOCOLATE-DIPPED BANANAS

12 Sticks

Peel and cut in half crosswise:

6 perfect ripe bananas

Insert firmly in the flat end of each half a wooden meat skewer about 6 inches long—or, better still, a tongue-depressor. Store the bananas in the freezer, on a sheet of foil, at least 1 hour.
Prepare:

Quick Chocolate Fondue Sauce II, 773

making up half the recipe. Pour the coating from the double boiler while still warm into a small shallow pan. Remove bananas from freezer and dip them one by one into the chocolate, twirling to assure complete coverage. Serve at once; or return to freezer in a plastic bag for later use.

ABOUT BERRIES

Good color, firm flesh and plumpness in berries denote prime condition. Remember, in preserving, 832, that the less ripe berries contain more pectin. Store ripe berries immediately in the refrigerator, covered, unwashed and unstemmed. Do not crowd or press.

For an attractive way to serve berries out of doors, make some berry cones. We saw them first in the shadows of the rain forest in Puerto Rico, where we were greeted beside a waterfall by children with wild berries in leaf cones held in punctured box tops. Glorify your box top with foil.

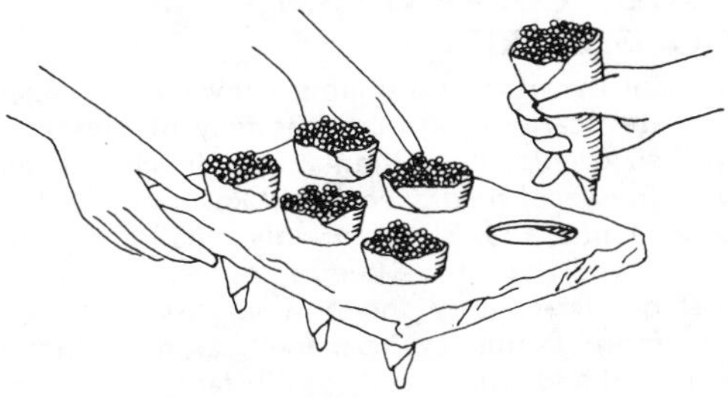

FRESH SELF-GARNISHED BERRIES

Clean:

1 quart berries

Reserve two-thirds and chill. Rub the remaining third through a sieve or ⅄ blend if using strawberries. Sweeten the pulp and juice with:

Powdered sugar

and stir until well dissolved. Serve the whole berries chilled and garnished with the sweetened pulp.

BERRIES COCKAIGNE

Serve:

Unhulled berries

Arrange them on the plate around mounds of:

Brown sugar or shaved maple sugar

Pass a dish of:

Cultured sour cream, yogurt or whipped cream

ABOUT STRAWBERRIES

It is hard to reconcile so luscious a fruit with its absurdly arid name—a fruit so constantly in demand that growers' catalogs offer not infrequently a choice among twenty-five or thirty varieties, and which has now become a fresh "fruit for all seasons." Most varieties are a ruddy red, and most very large cultivated fruit is less flavorsome than that of medium size. No one, however, has really experienced paradise on earth until he has plucked and eaten a clutch of tiny fully ripe wild strawberries, warmed by mountain sunshine.

FRESH STRAWBERRY VARIATIONS

Serve sliced strawberries in fruit cocktail glasses with one of the following variations.
Simmer 10 minutes equal parts of:

Orange juice
Strawberry juice

with:

¼ as much sugar or as much as is palatable

Chill the syrup. Season well with:

(Sherry or kirsch)

Or cover:

Chilled strawberries

with:

Chilled pineapple juice

Add, if needed:

Confectioners' sugar

Or, sprinkle berries lightly with:

Lemon juice
Confectioners' sugar

Decorate fruit with:

Mint leaves

STRAWBERRIES ROMANOFF

Prepare:

2 quarts sugared strawberries

Whip slightly:

1 pint ice cream

Fold into the ice cream:

1 cup whipped cream

Add:

6 tablespoons Cointreau

Blend the cream and the strawberries together ➤ very lightly with a spoon. Serve immediately.

ABOUT BLUEBERRIES AND HUCKLEBERRIES

If the seeds are small it's blueberries you have. If they are many and large, it's huckleberries. The difference is why the blueberry is preferred, both for eating out of hand and for cooking.
Pick before the dew is off:

Blueberries or huckleberries

To cook, see Poached Thick-Skinned Fruit, 126.

CRANBERRY SAUCE AND CRANBERRY JELLY

Pioneer New England sea captains knew the value of the vitamin C content of cranberries as a preventive against scurvy. Color differences in the fresh fruit have to do with the variety, not relative age.

Wash and pick over:

4 cups cranberries: 1 lb.

Place them in a saucepan. Cover with:

2 cups boiling water

As soon as the water begins to boil again, cover the saucepan with a lid. Boil the berries 3 or 4 minutes or until the skins burst. Put them through a strainer or ricer. Stir into the purée:

2 cups sugar

Place over heat and bring to a rolling boil. If you want cranberry sauce, remove from heat at once. If you want to mold cranberry jelly, boil about 5 minutes, skim, then pour into a wet mold. The cooking periods indicated are right for firm berries. Very ripe berries require a few minutes longer.

SPICED CRANBERRY JELLY

Prepare:

Cranberry Jelly, above

adding to the water:

2 inches stick cinnamon
2 whole cloves
¼ teaspoon salt

WHOLE CRANBERRY OR ROSELLE SAUCE

I. Place in a saucepan and stir until the sugar is dissolved:

2 cups water
2 cups sugar

Boil the syrup 5 minutes. Pick over, wash and add:

4 cups cranberries: 1 lb.

Simmer the berries in the syrup ➤ uncovered, very gently without stirring, until the berries are translucent, about 5 minutes. Skim off any foam. Add:

(2 teaspoons grated orange rind)

Pour the berries into 1 large or several individual molds which have been rinsed in cold water. Chill until firm. Unmold to serve.

II. A pleasant substitute for cranberries in this recipe makes use of the tropical **roselle.** Cut off the red part and discard the green pod of:

2 cups well-washed roselles

➤ Simmer, uncovered, about 10 minutes in:

1 cup water

Mix and add:

1½ cups sugar
2 tablespoons cornstarch

Cook about 5 minutes longer or until the cornstarch cannot be tasted. Serve cool with meat or dessert.

UNCOOKED CRANBERRY RELISH

To be served like a compote.

Grind:

4 cups cranberries: 1 lb.

Remove the seeds, then grind:

1 whole orange

You may prefer to use only the yellow portion of the orange skin, as the white is often bitter. Stir into the cranberries the orange and:

2 cups sugar

Place these ingredients in covered jars and refrigerate. Let them ripen 2 days before using. Serve the relish with meat or fowl or with a hot bread.

ABOUT RASPBERRIES

With the exception of mulberries, all the fruits under this heading belong to one species—*Rubus*—and have similar characteristics. **Raspberries** proper come in four colors: red, amber, purple and black. **Dewberries** are simply cultivars of the **blackberry; loganberries** and **boysenberries** are, in all probability, crosses between the dewberry and the tarter and more distinctively flavored red raspberry. Rarely encountered in this country is a small acid-tasting red raspberry of oriental origin usually called **wineberry.** The **mulberry,** despite its close resemblance to members of the *Rubus* family, is not in the least related. As everyone knows, the leaves of the white-fruited tree make up the traditional diet of the silkworm. Purple-fruited mulberry trees are best suited, in our opinion, for varying the diets—and flexing the muscles—of marauding schoolboys.

ABOUT CURRANTS AND GOOSEBERRIES

Both of these fruits are almost invariably cooked and are nearly always used as jelly or preserves. In their dried state, currants taste delicious when used in sweet breads: see About Raisins and Other Dried Fruits, 125. Black currants, small and bitter in the wild state, have been improved during the past quarter-century and now appear with more and more frequency at market, along with the usual red and white varieties. Currants and gooseberries, being of the same species, hybridize; and the cross has produced some interesting new cultivars. For those who like "dessert" gooseberries, look for large, completely ripe fruit with a slight tawny blush. To cook gooseberries, see Poached Thick-Skinned Fruit, 126. Even the homely **elderberry**—a fruit which should not be used in its uncooked state—has been taken in hand recently by the experts, who promise continuing selectivity, systematic cultivation, larger size and better flavor.

ABOUT CHERRIES

Mark Twain claimed that women, if given enough time and hairpins, could build a battleship. Hairpins, also mighty useful as cherry-pitters, are growing scarce. You may prefer to substitute a fresh, strong pen point inserted in a clean holder—although these accessories, too, we regret to report, are harder and harder to come across, as is a cherry-pitter like the one shown on 798.

The best sour or "pie" cherries derive from the **Morello** strain. **Montmorency** is the one most frequently available in the United States. Cultivated sweet cherries are either very deep red in color, or pale yellow flushed with red; favored varieties are **Black Tartarian** and **Napoleon,** respectively. Included in this fruit category—by courteous extension—is the **Surinam cherry:** not a cherry at all but a Brazilian fruit which resembles it and is now grown rather extensively in California and Florida. It makes a spicy and delicious jelly.

POACHED CHERRIES

I. For preparing a compote of sour cherries, see Poached Thick-Skinned Fruit, 126.

II. Cook until tender but still shapely, see Poached Thick-Skinned Fruit, 126:

Pitted sweet cherries

For each pound cherries, have ready:

½ cup currant jelly

melted in:

¼ cup kirsch or other liqueur

Drain the cherries. Reserve the juice for pudding sauce or use it in basting meats or in baking. Shake the drained cherries in the jelly mixture until well coated. Chill and serve.

ABOUT CITRUS FRUITS

Citrus fruits are so delightful in and of themselves that it almost seems a shame to dissect them into their nutritional components. But it must be pointed out that they are a potent source of vitamin C, as well as furnishing several other dietary essentials.

When they appear at market, citrus fruits are usually equipped with a thin coating of wax to protect them during distribution. The wax is harmless, but it is undesirable if you are grating the skin and may be removed by lightly scrubbing with detergent and water. ➤ In grating, do not take off more than the highly colored outer coating: the white skin beneath may be bitter. To extract citrus juice easily, first roll the fruit on a hard surface, exerting pressure.

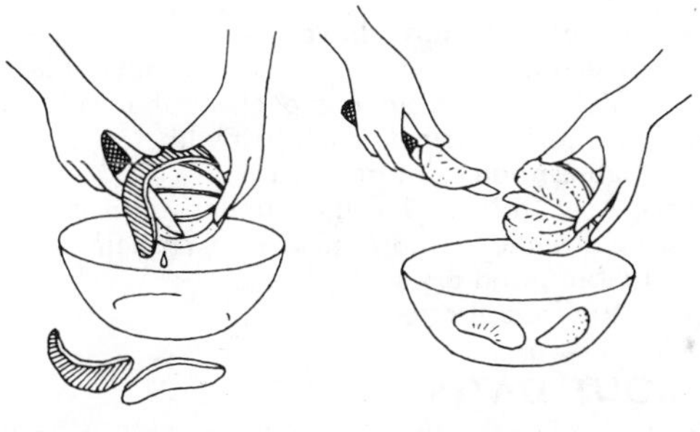

To section a small or average-sized citrus fruit, hold it over a bowl to catch all the juices, and use a sharp knife to remove the rind, including the pulpy white skin. Pare it around and around like an apple so that the cells are exposed. Loosen the sections by cutting between the fruit and the membrane. Lift out each segment in one piece, as shown, and remove any seeds.

To section larger fruits like grapefruit, remove the outer skin, pull into halves, and split the membrane as shown. Pull the membrane down and around the outer edge to the base of the section. Let the released membrane hang loose. With your thumb, separate the section from the remaining membrane. The segment may break, but virtually none of the juice is lost. You may prefer the method shown for smaller citrus, opposite.

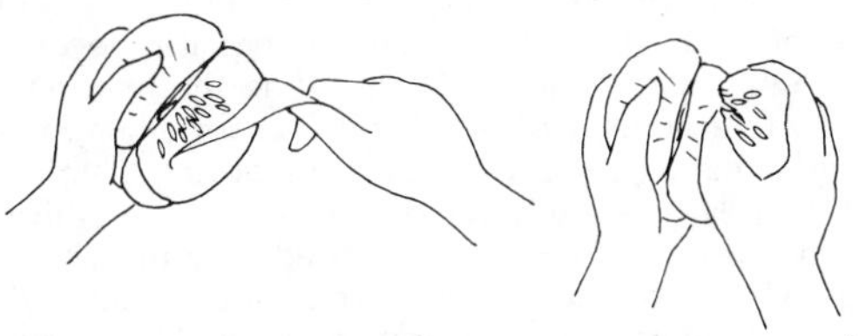

ABOUT LEMONS AND LIMES

Both of these fruits are quite indispensable, but for obvious reasons we discuss them more fully under Ingredients, 571. In buying lemons, choose yellow-colored ones. If tinged with green, they are not properly "cured." In choosing limes, the dark green ones are usually stronger in acid and preferable to the yellowish types. Many uses for lemon and lime juice and rind are indicated in individual recipes. For their use in beverages, see 42; for use to arrest discoloration of fresh fruits and vegetables, see 823; as decoration and garnish, see 571.

ABOUT ORANGES

For many of us the day begins with oranges, which we often casually classify as "juicers" or "eaters" —more accurately as varieties of **Valencia** on the one hand and **navel** on the other. In our household—and strictly en famille—if we have fruit of interesting flavor in either category, we often cut it in half right across the middle and section each half into thirds or fourths, then proceed to eat the slices at table, as if we were handling those of a Lilliputian watermelon. This untidy approach is encouraged by the recent proliferation of seedless oranges of all types. And it lets us ingest the fibrous parts of the valuable pulp as well as its juice. For the same reason, when we ream oranges for juice, we prefer not to use a fine strainer.

Highly desirable for table use is the **blood orange,** with dark red meat. For special uses no variety can equal the **Seville** or **bitter orange,** although it is not often available. Bitter oranges make superb components of marmalade and lend piquancy to meat and fish dishes and to various drinks.

An orange variant is the **tangerine** or **mandarin.** A **calamondin** is a strain of tangerine; and **Murcott** and **Temple** oranges result from an orange and tangerine cross. The **kumquat,** which has become as definitely associated with Christmas holidays as plum pudding, closely resembles the tangerine, but is actually in its botanical classification not a citrus fruit at all, though a close relative. Just the opposite applies to **citron**—a true citrus derivative which doesn't taste like one, at least in the processed form we find it packaged at market. See Candied Citrus Peel, 795.

The skins of ripe oranges often remain greenish in color. Growers and packers bring them closer to the conventionally acceptable warm yellow in two ways. One is by the use of ethylene gas, which breaks down the chlorophyll component present in the skin. Ethylene, incidentally, has also become a highly useful agent in controlling the maturization of a number of other fruits, especially apples and bananas. The second coloring device is simply a skin-dye, carefully restricted as to its chemical makeup by the USDA, prohibited in some citrus-growing states, and in any case applied to the fruit for a limited period during the year. All oranges so treated must bear the stamp "color added."

A word about frozen orange juice: why it all tastes alike, and why it doesn't taste anything like fresh orange juice. The juice to be frozen may come from several varieties. It is boiled to a high viscosity in a vacuum, separated into several component batches, reassembled, flavored—at which time fresh juice may be added—and at long last frozen solid. Finally, note that something labeled "orange drink" under federal regulations need contain no natural orange at all.

ORANGES IN SYRUP

8 Servings

Wash:

6 large well-flavored navel oranges

Peel the fruit, leaving no white showing, and cut the peel from three of the oranges into slices about ¼ inch thick. Boil these peels 3 minutes in:

1 cup water

Strain and discard the water. Combine:

1 cup sugar
⅓ cup water

When boiling and clear, add the orange peel. Cook about 5 minutes over low heat. Arrange the orange slices in a dessert bowl. Pour the peels and sauce over the oranges and chill at least 2 hours.

KUMQUAT COMPOTE

Calamondins and kumquats may be eaten raw without paring, and make beautiful garnishes. They may also become a dessert or may accompany a meat dish, as below.

Parboil, unpeeled, 5 minutes:

Kumquats

Drain and cool. Slice the top off each. Remove seeds and fill each fruit with:

½ to 1 teaspoon sugar

Stand upright in a shallow buttered pan. Bake about 15 minutes in a preheated 350° oven, basting frequently with:

Pineapple juice

For Preserved Kumquats, see 795.

ABOUT GRAPEFRUIT

The main types are whitish or pink-fleshed, with a few varieties ruby-red. Late in the season, the skin may change in tint from yellowish to greenish, a sign of real maturity and high sugar content. But beware of late-season grapefruit if it seems unduly light in weight or if the skins are puffy, for the flesh may then be dry. Offbeat and piquant grapefruit hybrids are the **tangelo** and the aptly named **ugli**—both crosses with the ever-promiscuous tangerine. ➤ Always chill grapefruit at once. It will not ripen after picking and keeps better at lower temperatures.

SWEETENED GRAPEFRUIT

4 Servings

Peel, section, see 135, and chill:

2 large grapefruit

Place the fruit in glass compotes. Fifteen minutes before serving, sprinkle lightly with:

Confectioners' sugar or honey

Immediately before serving, add to each compote:

(1 tablespoon Cointreau)

or fill each compote one-fourth full of:

Chilled orange juice

GRAPEFRUIT CUPS

I. Chill:

Grapefruit

Cut into halves. Loosen the pulp from the peel with a sharp-toothed, curved grapefruit knife, see 307, or remove the seeds and cut out the tough fibrous center with a grapefruit corer. Five minutes before serving, sprinkle the grapefruit with:

Confectioners' sugar

Add to each half immediately before serving:

1 tablespoon curaçao or a Crystallized Mint Leaf, 794

II. Preheat broiler.

Prepare:

Grapefruit Cups, above

When grapefruit is very ripe it is inadvisable to loosen the pulp from the peel, as it makes the fruit too juicy. Sprinkle each half with:

1 tablespoon or more sugar

Place the fruit under the broiler until heated through. Remove and pour over each half:

1 tablespoon dry sherry

Serve the fruit at once.

ABOUT DATES

In desert regions the date palm was traditionally put to almost total use—for food and fibers. It dominated a culture as exclusively as the bison did among the Plains Indians in the New World—shaping, regulating and limiting a life-style. Date varieties now cultivated in the United States—**Medjool, Deglet Noor** and **Khadrawy**—are all, as their names indicate, of Arabic origin. About half the fruit consists of sugar, which accounts for the grayish crystallization that frequently shows up on both fresh and dried dates. It also explains why eating only a few brings on a surfeit; and why, served as a garnish for a fruit dessert tray, see 793, they are often stuffed with cream cheese and nuts, with a fondant made piquant with almond paste and spices, or with a tangy marmalade. ❄ Dates freeze successfully and, refrigerated, may be kept for an extended period. For other uses of dates, see Index.

ABOUT FIGS

When Cato advocated the conquest of Carthage, he used as his crowning argument the advantage of acquiring fruits as glorious as the North African figs, specimens of which he pulled from his toga as exhibits in the Roman Senate. These fruits have become so popular in America that many varieties —purplish, brownish and greenish—are grown in profusion. Even when shipped, they must be tree-ripened.

Fresh figs are very different from the dried ones we get from Smyrna and our South. They are ripe when soft to the touch and overripe when sour in odor, indicating a fermentation of the juice. For figs with prosciutto, see 80; for dried fig confections, see 793.

STUFFED FRESH FIGS

Fill stemmed fresh:

Figs

with:

Cultured sour cream and grated orange peel

or with:

Ham Salad Spread, 74

POACHED FIGS

Wash and remove the stems from:

1 lb. dried figs

Add:

Cold water to cover well
1½ tablespoons lemon juice
A piece of lemon rind
(A large piece of gingerroot)

Stew the figs, covered, until they are soft. Drain and sweeten the juice with:

Sugar: about 1 cup

Simmer the syrup until thick. Add:

1 tablespoon lemon juice

Replace the figs in the syrup. Cool. Add:

(1 tablespoon dry sherry)

Chill and serve with:

Cream

ABOUT GRAPES

Table grapes—as distinguished from wine grapes —can be grouped into three classes. Of these the *labruscan*, or slip-skin types, all of which have at least some trace of native American "blood," and the *vinifera* are most important. The distinction between the two is best pointed up by citing Concord as the *labruscan* with which we are most familiar and Tokay as the prototype of *vinifera*.

Tokay types—we are temped to call them "non-slip" varieties—grow only in California, and in a rather limited area. Their flesh is solid, and their shipping and keeping qualities are so outstanding that those in commercial production are available all winter long. A new variety of **Tokay** is **Flame Tokay,** a very beautiful purplish-red. **Malaga** ripens several weeks earlier than the true Tokays. Among the "white" *vinifera* are **Olivette,** with—as the name indicates—oval berries, and **Thompson Seedless. Ribier** heads the "black" *vinifera,* which are actually a very deep blue.

In contrast to *vinifera,* all *labruscans* are more perishable and for this reason seasonal, their availability being limited more or less to the four months between July 1 and the end of October. A seedless **Concord** has been developed—look for it and many other hybrids ranging in color from palest green or yellow through red to darkest purple. Most widely distributed, perhaps, and in order of ripening are **Ontario, Early Giant, Interlaken Seedless, Delaware, Caco, Catawba, Fredonia, Van Buren, Worden, Niagara, Kenka** and **Steuben.**

Table grapes of a third and much smaller class are the spicy **muscadines** from the American South —technically *Vitis rotundifolia*—of which **scuppernong** is an ancestor, and **Golden Muscat,** one of the finest new hybrids. Here again, as in all other categories of grape, seedless varieties have been recently developed that will modestly revolutionize grape cookery, especially—we speak with feeling—pie-making. From the muscadines come the seedless packaged **raisins.** Only three varieties in this country are used in the production of raisins: Thompson Seedless, Muscat, and **Black Corinth.** All canned grapes are seedless.

In buying grapes, choose clusters with green stems, plump berries and full color. "Whites" will taste better if they have acquired a slightly tawny blush. See grape recipes in Salads, 92; Desserts, 734; and Pies, 638. To frost grapes, see 794.

GUAVAS

When ripe, guavas vary in color from white to dark red and in size from that of a walnut to that of an apple. They may be served puréed, baked or fresh, alone or in combination with other fruits such as bananas or pineapple. They have an exceptionally high vitamin content. Sprinkle:

Peeled and sliced guavas

lightly with:

Sugar

Chill and serve with:

Cream

or bake in a 350° oven about 30 minutes and then serve with the cream. See also Apple Cake Cockaigne, 661, and prepare guava jelly with cream cheese, as for Bar-le-Duç, 757.

LITCHIS

A little like jellied incense, these most oriental of fruits are protected by an exquisitely fragile shell, as shown on 123. The fresh fruit is white; when dried it becomes much smaller and turns dark brown. Serve 3 to 5 nuts on a green leaf, or use them to garnish a fruit bowl. Litchis are also available canned, but the flavor is not so hauntingly aromatic.

MANGOES

These delicious flattish oval fruits are about 8 inches long, of a yellowish-green color and sometimes flecked with red or black. When chilled and eaten raw, they are as good as any peach-pineapple-apricot mousse you can concoct—rich and sweet but never cloying. If unchilled, they sometimes have the faintest savor of turpentine. The seed, which extends the length of the fruit, makes eating somewhat awkward, and special holders, not unlike those which bring corncobs under control, may be used. Pare, slice and serve mangoes on vanilla ice cream. Sauté ripe fruits. Use them when just mature in chutneys and when unripe for poaching or baking. If you want to freeze mangoes, see Frozen Puréed Fruits, 824.

MEDLARS

In the South of Europe and in southern United States these 2-inch fruits, which resemble crab apples, are eaten fresh-plucked. In England, quite far north in their range, they are always overtaken by frost and look shabby indeed, although their flavor is desirable, especially for jellies.

ABOUT MELONS

Melons are being developed into so many delicious strains that it is difficult to list them all by name. A distinction is usually made between **muskmelons** and **winter melons.** The skins of the former are variously netted, the reticulations being raised and of a paler color. Muskmelons are aromatic even before being opened—and short-lived. In America—but not abroad—the **cantaloupe** is in this group, the name being reserved here for a smallish, very heavily and regularly netted melon with pale orange colored flesh. The flesh of a new hybrid named **Ogen,** however, developed in Israel, is green.

Winter melons are usually smooth-skinned, sometimes striated, and lack netting; they have little or no aroma and keep over a much longer period. Some of the best-known varieties are **Casaba, Persian, Crenshaw** and **honeydew. Watermelons** are rather a race apart: their size and their festive red interior suggest merry group eating; the small round ones of recent introduction never quite generate the meltingly sweet succulence of the old-time giants.

Melons are usually eaten raw. The varieties can be served singly or in combination. Try a palette ranging from the pale greens of the honeydews, through the golden peach tones of the cantaloupes, to the blue-reds of the watermelon. They can be served from one end of a meal to the other in many attractive ways.

In order for it to be genuinely sweet—and this is one's perennial hope as he bites into each fresh specimen—the fruit must have matured on the vine. If it did, you will see that the scar at the stem end is slightly sunken and well calloused. The more fragrant the melon, the sweeter it will be. A watermelon, if truly ripe, will respond by giving up a thin green shaving if scraped with a fingernail.

If you want to store melons for several days, keep them at between 50° and 70°, away from sunlight; and chill just before serving. To protect other food in your refrigerator from taking on a melon taste, seal the fruit in plastic or foil. Melons respond favorably to lime or lemon juice or a sprinkling of powdered ginger, and can be cut into highly decorative shapes. For an aspic-filled melon, see 119. For fancy melon cuts see below.

MELON BASKETS OR FRUIT CUPS

8 Large Servings

Cut into halves or make into baskets, as shown above:

4 cantaloupes or other melons

Remove the seeds. Scallop the edges. Chill the fruit. Combine the following ingredients:

2 cups peeled, sliced seeded or seedless oranges
2 cups peeled, sliced fresh peaches
2 cups diced pineapple: fresh or canned
1 cup sliced bananas
(1 cup sugar, dissolved in the various fruit juices)

Chill thoroughly. Just before serving, fill the melon cups with the fruit. Pour over each cup:

(1 tablespoon Cointreau or rum)

Top with:

(Orange and Lemon Ice, 766, or Sherbet, 767)

MELON ROUNDS FILLED WITH RASPBERRIES OR STRAWBERRIES

Cut into 1- to 2-inch crosswise slices:

Chilled pared honeydew melons or cantaloupe

Allow 1 slice for each person. Remove seeds. Fill the centers with:

Chilled, sugared raspberries or strawberries

Serve on individual plates with:

Lime or lemon wedges
(A sprinkling of ginger)

SPIKED MELON

Cut a plug in the upper side of a:

Melon

Dig out seeds with a long-handled spoon. Pour in:

3/4 to 1 cup port wine

Chill melon in ice in the refrigerator at least 8 hours. Slice and serve with rind removed and use the marinating wine as a dressing.

PAWPAWS

These smoky-tasting native fruits should be picked—and eaten—after the first heavy frost. Wrap them individually in tissue paper and store in a cool place until soft. A taste for them, we feel, is an acquired one.

PAPAYAS

Papayas grow up to 20 inches in length. When fully ripened, the flesh develops orangey tones and the greenish rind turns soft and yellow. They are eaten like melons. Their milky juice, when chilled, makes a pleasant drink, and their black seeds, which contain pepsin, are used for garnish, eaten raw or used as for capers. Many of us know this plant only by its derivative papain, the tenderizer made from the enzymes of its leaves, 444.

Use underripe fruits for cooking. Process them as for summer squash types, 328. If serving papayas raw, chill and sprinkle with lime or lemon juice. See sketch in the chapter heading, 123.

ABOUT PEACHES AND NECTARINES

As fruits so often curiously do—but queens seldom if ever—the "queen of fruits" leads a double life. The mostly yellow-fleshed **freestones** are favorites at table and for canning and drying; **clingstones,** with white flesh and somewhat sharper flavor, make excellent "poachers."

Choose firm but well-colored fruit without the flattened brownish bruises which betray areas of decaying flesh underneath. If plucked green, peaches will not ripen. They merely soften and wither, gaining nothing in flavor. ➤ Discard peach seeds, as their almondlike kernels are high in deadly prussic acid.

Although their smooth skin and their flavor strongly suggest a cross between peach and plum, **nectarines** are in fact simply a variety of peach, resulting from what botanists call "bud variation."

FILLED PEACHES

8 Servings

Peel, halve and pit:

4 chilled peaches

Place them in a bowl. Combine and stir:

2 cups chilled berries
6 tablespoons sugar
1 1/2 tablespoons lemon juice

Pour the berries over the peaches. Serve with:

Sweetened Whipped Cream, 696

STUFFED PEACHES

8 Servings

Preheat oven to 350°.
Peel, halve and pit:

4 peaches, or use 8 canned halves

Chop until fine:

1/3 cup blanched toasted almonds
1 tablespoon glazed orange peel

Blend thoroughly with:

1/4 cup confectioners' sugar

Fill the fruit with the above mixture and place in a baking pan. Sprinkle with:

1/2 cup dry sherry
1/4 cup confectioners' sugar

and if canned peaches are used:

(A little lemon juice)

Bake 10 minutes and serve warm.

ABOUT PEARS

All types of pears seem to keep congenial company with cheese. Follow the season, beginning with the **Bartletts,** of which **Max Red Bartlett** is an interesting all-red-skinned variety. **Seckels** are apt to come next: tiny, sugar-sweet and unprepossessing-looking, but much in demand, along with the **Kiefers,** for cooking and pickling. The Bartletts, highly flavored but perishable, have vanished by November—except for the **Winter Bartletts**—but they are succeeded by a dazzling array of hardier fall varieties, some of which can still be purchased far into the winter months: the ruddy **comices,** the green-skinned **Anjous,** the **Winter Nellises,** and the russet **Boscs,** among others.

Pears are picked when they are approaching maturity but haven't reached full ripeness. They may then be ripened at 60° to 65°. If you plan to cook them, make sure to use them while they are still firm. To store for eating, wrap the fruit in paper and put them away in a slotted box in a cool place. If pears or peaches that look sound have become brown inside, they have been held too long at a too-low temperature.

STUFFED PEARS

4 Servings

Preheat oven to 350°.
Pare, core and halve:

4 firm pears

Mix together and stuff into the hollows:

¼ cup white raisins
2 tablespoons chopped walnuts
2 tablespoons sugar
1 tablespoon lemon juice

Place the pears in a baking dish with:

2 tablespoons water

Pour over them:

½ cup light corn syrup

Cover and bake until tender, about 30 minutes. You may baste during the cooking with:

(Pineapple juice and brown sugar)

or remove the cover and sprinkle the fruit lightly with:

(Granulated sugar)
(A light dusting of cinnamon)

then place under the broiler until golden brown and serve immediately.

PEARS IN LIQUEUR

4 Servings

Pare, quarter, core and prick lightly:

4 pears

Combine:

1 cup chilled orange juice
1 tablespoon confectioners' sugar
2 tablespoons curaçao or kirsch

Cover the pears with the juice. Chill until ready to serve.

PERSIMMONS

Be sure, in the recipes, to distinguish between our native *Diospyros virginiana* and Kaki, the oriental type, the latter seen on 123. Ours are small, full of seeds and ➤ inedible until after frost. In fact, we wonder how we survived the many we consumed as children, because the skins resist digestion and can form waddy balls, as obstructive as hair-balls in animals.

Both native and oriental persimmons sometimes tend to be puckery, even when ripe—depending on variety. The orientals lose their astringency if stored for 2 to 4 days in a plastic bag with a ripe apple. The natives do not always prove so amenable. Eat as fresh fruit, in salads or puréed, fresh or frozen, combined in ice creams, custards or sherbets.

ABOUT PINEAPPLES

So beloved was this fruit that on many southern mansions it was carved above the door as a symbol of hospitality. In fact, the first fruits grown in England in a nobleman's "stove-house" were graciously rented to his friends for their table decorations.

A small compact crown usually denotes the finest type of fruit. As neither skin nor fruit color indicates ripeness, a dull solid sound when the finger is snapped against the side of the fruit, along with protruding "eyes" and a delicious aroma, is perhaps the most reliable test for ripeness.

Store at 70° away from sunlight. Pineapple lends itself magnificently to all kinds of combinations, but watch for one thing: ➤ be sure to cook fresh pineapple before combining it with any gelatin mixture, see 113. For pineapples as decorative containers for other foods, see 78, 109 and 141.

To prepare pineapple slices, trim the sharp points of the tuft. Grasp the tuft firmly and pare the skin with wide downward strokes. Then further remove the "eyes" by grooving the pineapple diagonally. Cut off the tuft. The fruit may then be sliced crosswise or in wedges or flat thin slices from top to bottom. Trim out the core if it is tough.

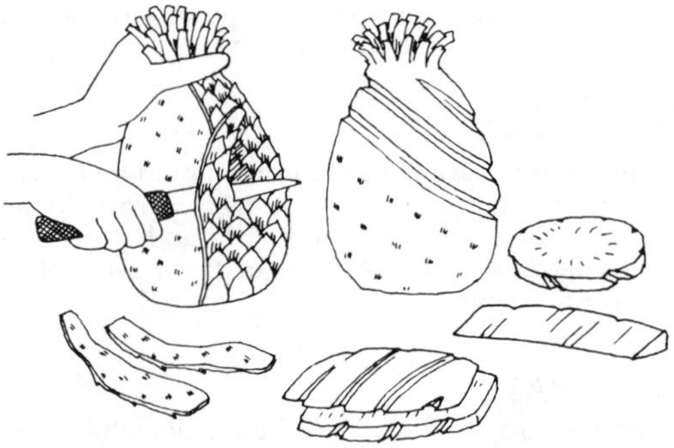

PINEAPPLE TIDBITS

I. **8 Servings**

This dish is alluring in appearance, but must be made with very ripe pineapple. Trim two-thirds from the leafy top of:

1 chilled ripe pineapple

Cut the fruit into 8 lengthwise wedges. Cut off the core and place each part so that it will resemble a boat, as sketched. Pare the skin in 1 piece, leaving it in place, and cut the pulp downward into 5 or 6 slices, retaining the boat shape as shown 141, top right. Serve each boat on an individual plate, with a small mound of:

Confectioners' sugar

Add:

5 or 6 large unhulled strawberries for each serving

II. A Texas girl taught us to prepare a pineapple this way. Divide a chilled pineapple into small sections by cutting it down to the core, diagonally, with a sharp knife as seen 141, top left. Impale each section with a pick and let the guests serve themselves.

III. Pineapple can make an attractive edible centerpiece. Cut off the top and bottom of a ripe pineapple and reserve them. Insert a long sharp knife about ½ inch from the outer edge so the fruit is entirely loosened but the pineapple as a whole retains its shape. Leaving the fruit in this cylindrical shell, cut it in about 12 long pie-shaped wedges. Set it back on its base and use the top for a lid as shown on right below. Let guests remove the long spears with a two-pronged fork.

FILLED PINEAPPLE

For a more elaborate version, see 109.
Cut in half, hollow out and chill:

A fresh pineapple

Cube the cut-out pineapple and some:

Slices of melon

Fill the chilled pineapple shells with the cubed fruit and add:

A few raspberries

Sprinkle with:

Chopped mint leaves
(2 tablespoons liqueur)

FRESH PINEAPPLE CUP

6 Servings

Pare, core and dice:

1 fresh pineapple

Chill it. Boil for 1 minute:

1 cup sugar
⅓ cup water

Chill this syrup. Add:

½ cup chilled orange juice
3 tablespoons lime juice

Place the pineapple in glasses and pour the syrup mixture over it.

GRILLED PINEAPPLE

4 Servings

Drain:

8 pineapple spears

Wrap around them:

8 slices bacon

Fasten the slices with picks and broil the bacon under moderate heat.

ABOUT PLUMS

As with many fruits under centuries-old cultivation, plum varieties from the Old World still predominate—with modern improvements. These **European plums** are green- or yellow-fleshed. They include the **greengage,** or **Reine Claude,** from which, by an incredibly complicated procedure, authentic sugar plums are still produced in Portugal; the **blue plum;** the **yellow egg plum;** the darker **Lombards** and **Italians;** as well as a host of larger more recent introductions. A European variety with special characteristics is the **Damson,** very dark, tart and thick-skinned. It is not, like the others, suitable for table use or for canning and drying, but it makes superb conserves, 837.

The earliest native varieties of the **American plum,** such as the **red plum,** the **wild goose,** the **Pacific** and the **beach plum,** are now, after decades of neglect, in the hands of breeders who have introduced some interesting variants and combinations. American plums are smaller than the European favorites; their flesh is yellow to pale orange; and they are by and large best suited to jam, desserts, and sweet sauces. Similar uses are recommended for the less often encountered **Oriental** or **Japanese plum,** whose fruits are even more ruddy in color, and spicier. A non-plum with plumlike characteristics, available now and then at market, is the tropical **Carissa,** or **Natal plum.** ➤ To cook plums, see Poached or Stewed Thick-Skinned Fruit, 126.

Prunes are simply small purplish-black freestone plums sufficiently high in sugar content and firm enough to battle successfully the twin hazards of drying out and of interior decay.

STEWED PRUNES

8 Servings

➤ If the label calls for soaking, please read About Raisins and Other Dried Fruits, 125. Otherwise, cover with cold water:

1 lb. dried prunes

Bring to the boiling point. ➤ Reduce the heat and simmer gently about 20 minutes. Add:

(¼ cup or more sugar)

Cook about 10 minutes longer. You may add to the prunes, during this second cooking period:

(½ sliced lemon)
(1 stick cinnamon)

PRUNES IN WINE

4 Servings

Cook by the above method until almost tender:

½ lb. dried prunes

Add:

3 tablespoons sugar

Cook 5 minutes longer. Remove from heat and add:

½ cup or more dry sherry or ½ to ¾ cup port
(6 very thin slices lemon)

Place in a covered jar. Chill thoroughly. Shortly before serving, the prunes may be pitted and filled with:

Halves of walnuts or blanched almonds

PRUNES AND CHESTNUTS

4 to 6 Servings

Drain and place in a casserole:

1½ cups canned chestnuts
¾ cup pitted stewed or canned prunes

Combine, heat and pour over the above:

1 tablespoon butter
¼ teaspoon salt
(1 tablespoon sugar)
½ cup dry white wine

Heat thoroughly and serve with ham or fowl.

PICKLED PRUNES

Keep this delightful compote on hand, for it makes a decorative meat garnish and may be drained and pitted and used in Stuffings, 370. Place in a heavy pan:

3 cups water
1 cup cider vinegar
2 cups brown sugar
2 cups dried prunes
1 teaspoon whole cloves, with heads removed
1 teaspoon whole allspice
1½ sticks cinnamon

➤ Simmer about 45 minutes or until fruit is plump. Place the prunes in a jar. Straining out the spices, pour the liquor over the prunes to cover. Keep refrigerated.

POMEGRANATES

By eating a single seed of the pomegranate offered her by the wily Pluto, Proserpine was obliged to return periodically to the infernal regions, leaving earth for six months in the cheerless embrace of winter. We have always wondered—since our own first encounter with the crimson cells enclosing seed and luscious pulp—how Proserpine managed to eat only one. These jewel-like morsels make a most beautiful garnish. Use them in French dressing, or roll them in small cream cheese balls. Or, if you live where the fruit is available ripe and in abundance, you may feel it is sacrilegious to eat them any way but plain—or chilled, with yogurt. If you use them for jelly, do not bruise the seed kernels, for then an unpleasant flavor develops. See illustration on 129.

PRICKLY PEARS

A cactus also known as **Indian** or **Barbary fig** or **tuna,** the so-called prickly pear, illustrated on 129, is now as much at home on the shores of the Mediterranean as in its native America. The red and yellow fruits, which are eaten raw, have sharp spines which can be removed by singeing before peeling.

BAKED QUINCES

4 Servings

These hard uncooperative-looking fruits, illustrated on 129, turn pink when cooked and make delicious preserves and confections. See Index.

Preheat oven to 350°.

Wash:

4 large whole quinces

Rub with:

Butter

and bake about 45 minutes until almost tender. Core and hollow out about two-thirds of the remaining fruit and mix this pulp with:

⅓ cup fine bread crumbs
¼ cup chopped nuts
¼ cup brown sugar
Grating of lemon rind
Salt

Return mixture to the partially hollow rind and bake about 15 minutes longer or until tender. Serve hot or cold.

RHUBARB

Only by the wildest stretch of the imagination can rhubarb be included in this chapter, but its tart flavor and its customary uses make it a reasonable facsimile, when cooked, of fruit. Hothouse-grown rhubarb is tenderer and sweeter and needs no peeling. If the hardier type is used, the reddish young shoots are preferred. Should the stalks be tough, peel them back like celery and remove the coarsest strings before cooking. In any case, use as little water as possible. ➤ Never cook the leaves, as they are heavy in poisonous oxalic acid.

POACHED RHUBARB

4 Servings

Wash and cut, without peeling, into 1-inch pieces:

1 lb. rhubarb

Place in heavy pan. Sprinkle lightly with water. Simmer over medium heat until segments can be easily pierced with fork. Add and stir:

½ to ¾ cup sugar

Continue poaching until rhubarb is soft. Dot with:

(Butter)
(Cinnamon or powdered ginger)

BAKED RHUBARB AND JAM

Preheat oven to 350°.

To give color to rhubarb and keep it whole, have ready:

¼ cup seedless red jam
½ cup sugar

Coat a small baking dish with one-third of the jam. Cut into 2-inch slices:

1 lb. rhubarb

Lay the slices in the jam base in close patterns and sprinkle with half the sugar and:

(½ teaspoon powdered ginger)

Add another layer of rhubarb and cover with the rest of the jam and sugar. Bake covered for about 15 minutes.

TROPICAL EXOTICS

The fruits listed below are occasionally or more often available at "ethnic" groceries or plain ordinary fruiterers with a well-traveled or novelty-struck clientele. Illustrated are passion fruit, far left; cherimoyas, next left; the fruit and the great cut leaves of monstera, right, close to the trim **mangosteen, shown whole and in cross section. Rounding out the picture are akee, below center, and tamarind.**

ACEROLA

The size and habitat of this tart fruit are indicated by its aliases: **Barbados** and **West Indian cherry.** Acerolas contain much greater quantities of ascorbic acid, even when cooked, than do fresh citrus fruits.

AKEE

Blighia sapida, named after the infamous Captain Bligh, is one of the most strikingly beautiful and delicious of fruits; however, ➤ unless it has ripened to the point of voluntary opening, it is a deadly poison. No overly ripe, fallen, discolored or unripe fruit dare be eaten, and the greatest care must be used to ➤ remove all seeds before cooking, as these are always poisonous. When picked ripe, hulled and completely seeded, the akee may be eaten raw or cooked. Parboiled it may be used hot or cold, customarily with a main dinner course. See illustration, below.

PURÉED AKEE

3 Servings

Remove the white pods from:

6 firm unbruised open akees

➤ Discard every seed. Place the pods in:

Boiling water

to cover. ➤ Reduce the heat at once and simmer gently until soft. Strain and mash them until coarsely crushed. Season with:

Salt and pepper
(Grated Parmesan cheese)
(Toasted chopped cashews)

CARAMBOLA

Yellow, translucent, juicy and refreshing, this lobed fruit, shown in the chapter heading, may be eaten unpeeled and the seeds disregarded. It is a versatile addition to a southern menu. Serve it raw as a vegetable or salad. When fully ripe it is delicious as a dessert.

CERIMAN

Shown below, this fruit is known to most of us as **monstera,** a desirable house plant with great cut and holey leaves. Unless we are in subtropical climates, we seldom see the 8- to 10-inch cylindrical pine-conelike fruit with its pineapple-banana flavor. A single fruit ripens over a 3- to 4-day period, and the lower sections, which break apart first at the base of the stem, should be eaten only as the shell ripens to a yellow color. To keep the top sections unbruised until ripened, place the fruit, stem end up, in a jar and pluck as the segments ripen.

CHERIMOYA

The nineteenth-century traveler Humboldt, who left his scientific imprint over South America and Mexico, declared that this fruit, shown below, is worth a trip across the Atlantic. It must be tree-ripened but still firm when picked and should be handled carefully so as to avoid bruising. Sometimes called **sherbet fruit,** the cherimoya shows on its light green skin jacquarded engravings or longish bumps. Discard the hard black seeds which occur at random in the pulp. Eat raw or use to make drinks and sherbets. Other less widely known fruits of the *Annona* or custard apple family are the **sweetsop** or **sugar-apple,** and the **soursop,** which has an acidulous taste.

DURIAN

Fruits of this famous tree, native to Southeast Asia, weigh up to 20 pounds and have been described as "smelling like Hell, and tasting like Heaven." They are highly favored by certain wild animals; and tales abound of Malays who gather durians,

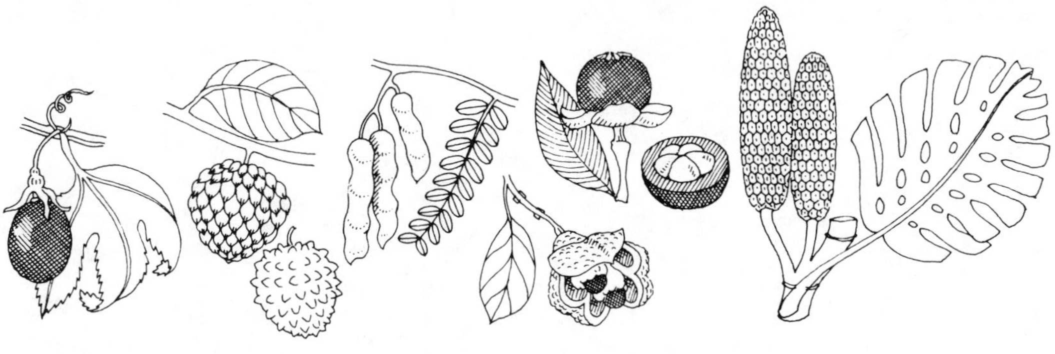

only to be gathered up in turn by elephants. The large seeds are roasted and eaten like nuts.

FEIJOA

Often called **pineapple guava**—a sobriquet which aptly reflects the feijoa's delicious and complex flavor—this fruit is dark green, about 2 inches long, with a white interior; it is used chiefly for jellies and preserves.

GENIP

Sometimes called **Spanish limes** because of their taste only, these 1-inch round Caribbean fruits are eaten fresh, like grapes.

KIWI

Also known as **Chinese gooseberry,** this fruit comes from New Zealand. The hairy, soberly brown exterior of kiwis does not prepare one in the least for their vivid green translucency when sectioned, or the lovely intricacies of pattern the seeds reveal when the fruit is sliced as shown in the chapter heading, 123. Kiwis are not only highly decorative but may be served with a little lime juice as a table fruit; or peeled, poached and garnished with lemon juice and kirsch. Remove the hairs by hand-friction.

LOQUATS

These olive-sized fruits, yellow and loosely clustered, mature in the springtime. New cultivars have a larger ratio of flesh to seeds, and so are beginning to lift the loquat out of the mere garnish and jelly-making categories. They may be eaten fresh or stewed. When cooked, their flavor is rather similar to that of poached plums.

MANGOSTEENS

This 2- to 3-inch-diameter fruit has a most exquisite milky juice. Its sections—5 to 6 in number—may be easily scooped out and eaten with a spoon, see illustration, 143.

PASSION FRUITS

Sometimes called the **purple granadilla,** this tropical American fruit, shown on 143, is egg-sized and is at its best when a little overripe and wrinkled-looking. As the sweet aromatic pulp is inseparable from the seeds, passion fruit is used mainly as a table ornament or for its quite delicious juice.

SAPODILLAS

Sapodilla is the tree whose sap produces **chicle gum.** The fruit has a rather grainy but entirely edible flesh, with somewhat the texture of moist brown sugar. The seeds must be removed, after which the raw pulp may be eaten fresh or used in puddings and other desserts. A sprinkling of lemon juice helps. A close relative, the **sapote,** has similar traits and makes an excellent sherbet.

TAMARINDS

The 2- to 6-inch pods of this graceful tree are shown on 143. When fresh and tender, they can be either cooked with rice and fish or sucked raw for their spicy pulp with its date-apricot flavor. This spicy pulp is also preserved for use in curries and chutneys, as well as a medicinal drink. If you wish to preserve tamarinds, remove the seeds and pack the pulp into a jar with alternate layers of sugar. Refrigerate.

THE FOODS WE HEAT

We are told that a hard-boiled professional cook, when asked what she regarded as primary briefing for a beginner, tersely replied: "Stand facing the stove." While our own first cooking lesson would substitute the gradual approach for the frontal assault, it is perfectly true that somewhere along the line, in perhaps ninety-five out of a hundred kitchen sequences, heat will have been applied. This has been so from ages past.

The chapter head illustration shows the contemporary metal counterpart of a clay kebab-roasting pan unearthed from the Palace of Nestor. In an equally time honored tradition is the three-legged cast-iron pot behind it, which has accompanied military campaigns for three millennia, and with its rimmed lid is still in use in Appalachia. On a more sophisticated level is the elegant Chinese fire-pot, primarily intended for the gentle poaching in delicious stocks. The aventador, or fan, right front, encourages a draft; behind it the salamander, when heated, helps to brown omelets and casseroles. Neither, needless to say, is required to operate today's efficient electric skillet, shown left.

Yet from Charles Lamb's legendary Bobo—you will remember him from your high school English classes as the boy who couldn't make roast pig without burning down the house—to the bride described by her matron of honor as incapable of boiling an egg, heating food, despite a wealth of equipment, has often turned into a frustrating, sometimes even disastrous, experience.

It needn't be. We have tried throughout our book, but especially in this chapter, to identify and explain the various types of cooking heat; to tell you simply and clearly how these heats are initiated, controlled and arrested to ensure highest nutritive value and best flavor, texture and color. We have tried also to indicate what processes, when followed, will bring cooked food to the table in that ideal state of readiness the French call **à point.**

Asking a cook why he heats food at all is, of course, like asking an architect why men do not live in caves. The obvious answer is that it usually tastes better that way. There are other reasons, too. Some are prosaic. Cooking destroys unwanted and sometimes unfavorable microorganisms. Contrary to some remarkably persistent notions, it makes many categories of food more digestible, more nutritious, and less—to toss in a stylish term—allergenic.

Cooking, again, can seal up in food most of those natural juices which nourish and delight us. For some kinds of preparation—stocks and soups are examples—the objective is just the reverse. It is true, also, that certain salted and variety meats, as well as a good many vegetables, profit by a pre-cooking or blanching which modifies texture or releases disagreeable odors and off-flavors.

Many cooks, like the rest of humankind, are born innovators, too. And they often introduce stimulating refinements in the heating of food, some of which—like the smoking process—emphasize taste at the expense of nutritional integrity.

▲ HIGH-ALTITUDE COOKING

Cooking in mountainous country is an art all in itself. If high altitudes are new to you, watch for the high-altitude cooking symbol ▲ which will give you formulas for adjusting ingredients or temperatures. Roasting procedures do not differ materially from those at sea level. Adjustments required in using sea-level baking recipes at high altitudes are indicated where necessary for each baking category. Basic cake recipes for high altitudes and their baking temperatures, marked ▲, may be found on page 692. But any process involving liquid will be proportionately lengthened as altitude increases: see the chart below showing the boiling point of water at different levels.

	F.	C.
Sea level	212°	100°
2,000 ft.	208°	98°
5,000 ft.	203°	95°
7,500 ft.	198°	92°
10,000 ft.	194°	90°
15,000 ft.	185°	85°
30,000 ft.	158°	70°

If these hints are not sufficiently specialized for your area, write the home economics department of your state college or call on your county home demonstration agent for more information. And if you are doing any pressure cooking, the accuracy of the gauge is vital. These agencies can also tell you where to have gauges tested.

ABOUT HEATS

Let us consider first how heats are transferred to food, whether in air or in moisture, in fat or through a pan. Results in each case will be quite astonishingly different. Cooking heats are generally known as **dry** or **moist.** In the following text, we shall list types of each separately.

ABOUT DRY HEATS

Truly dry heats are achieved in a number of ways Grilling over coals is one, broiling or roasting in a ventilated oven another. When we say "barbecue," we may be referring to Pit-Cooking, 155, in which case we refer to a moist-heat process. Or we may mean skewer-cooking with its variants—spit, brochette or rotisserie—which are dry processes and are themselves forms of grilling. Parenthetically, the word "barbecue" has been traced back by some philologists to the Spanish "barbacoa," a raised platform for cooking; but we like to think of it, with other authorities, as originating among the French settlers in Florida, who roasted the native goats whole, *de barbe en queue*—from beard to tail. Some further remarks on barbecuing will be found later in this chapter, see Outdoor Cooking, 155.

Baking is a dry-heat process, too. In addition to the reflected and radiant heat of the oven, heat is transferred from the pan to the food and may be further diffused by the use of paper liners, temporary covers of foil, or a dusting of flour between food and pan-bottom. Since, in baking, moisture is released from the food itself and continues to circulate as warm vapor in the closed oven chamber, this process is less dry than those previously mentioned.

Oddly enough, deep-fat frying is still another kind of dry-heat cooking. Here the heat is transferred not only by the oil or fat used as a cooking medium, but by the moisture in the food itself, some of the steam from the food juices being forced into the fat and then out into the atmosphere. Among dry-heat pan processes, sautéing uses the smallest amount of fat. Pan-broiling and pan-frying are successive steps beyond sautéing and away from the driest heat. In pan-broiling and pan-frying, the food develops a greater amount of rendered fat than in sautéing and absorbs a larger share of it. In doing so, it gives up proportionately more of its juices. To keep both pan-frying and pan-broiling at their best, excess fat should be poured off during cooking.

Among dry-heat processes which may be described as "partial" are planking and flambéing—or flaming. Either way, the food is heated beforehand, and these processes only give it its finishing touch.

BROILING

Whether you broil on a grill or in a range, the principle is identical. The heat is a radiant glow; and the process differs from roasting or baking in that only one side of the food at a time is exposed to the heating source—unless you happen to use the rather special kind of equipment shown on 403.

However, all three of these types of dry heat depend, for their effectiveness, on proper ventilation. In the great majority of modern ranges, either gas or electric, you are given no selectivity in broiling temperatures. And individual variations in wattage —coil or burner area—as well as venting capacity make it necessary that you become familiar with the special requirements of your own equipment. Some ranges, for example, must be preheated before broiling can begin; in others, broiler heat is almost instantaneous. Likewise, in some electric ranges, broiling takes place with the oven door ajar; in others, the door may, or even must, be kept closed.

When the heat indicator on a household range is turned to a ➤ broil position, the temperature is around 550° or slightly above and should remain constant. If you wonder why you cannot always match the results you admire in some restaurant cookery, remember that commercial installations deliver much higher heats which are quite beyond the reach of home equipment.

Under the limitations of the household range ➤ as much temperature control in broiling is exerted by the placement of the oven rack as by any other means. It is usually adjusted so that there is a 3-inch space between the source of heat and the top of the food. ➤ To lower the broiling heat for browning fragile sauces or delicate dishes like sweetbreads or for cooking very thick meats—where the heat must have time to penetrate deeply without charring—lower the broiling rack to make a 4- to 6-inch space between the food and broiler. Place food on a cold rack to prevent sticking. If the rack is hot, grease it—or grease the food. For details of broiling and pan-broiling meats, see 445; fowl, 158 and 423; fish, 402; vegetables, 256, 282.

SKEWER COOKING

From a marshmallow impaled on a stick, to the most delicate bay scallops, skewer-grilled food never seems to lose its charm for young or old. A most important first step is to ➤ choose items that will cook at the same rate of speed, or to make the proper adjustment if they do not. When the meat or fish selected is a quick-cooking one, see that the onions, peppers or other more resistant vegetables which alternate with it are blanched in advance, so that the food will all be done at the same time. Should the meat need relatively longer cooking, skewer delicate alternates like tomatoes and mushrooms separately and mingle meat and vegetables in serving. Protect delicate meats such as sweetbreads and liver with breading or a wrapping of thinly sliced bacon. Choose skewers, whether of metal or wood, that are either square or oval, so that, as the food softens in cooking, it will not slip while revolving. Soak bamboo or wood skewers in water for several hours before using.

If using a grill, grease it and place the skewered food on the grill over medium heat. Turn the skewers often. Food grilled in this way may take anywhere from 6 to 12 minutes. For skewered food combinations, see 80.

If cooking in a range, broil on a greased grill about 3 inches from the source of heat, or adjusted on a pan as shown in the chapter heading. You may, of course, prefer to use the skewer element on your rotisserie. For more details about rotisserie and spit-cooking, see 158–159. Should you decide to precook any sort of skewered food, you may do so on the skewers themselves in a skillet, provided, of course, the skewers are no longer than the pan bottom. Sometimes partially precooked, skewered foods are coated with a sauce or with a bound breading and then cooked to completion in deep fat. When handled in this way, they are called **attereaux.** In flambéing skewered foods, 155, provide some protection for your hand.

DEEP-FAT FRYING

Deep-fat frying, like a number of other accomplishments in cooking, is an art in itself—an art in which experience is the best teacher. Even a novice, however, who follows our instructions to the letter can succeed in turning out delicious dishes in this ever-popular category—and, what's more, food fried without excessive fat absorption. A serving of French fried potatoes properly cooked may have a lower calorie count than a baked potato served with butter. Remember, too, that fat-absorption increases with the length of cooking time and with the amount of surface exposed to the fat.

Equipment such as that shown below need not be elaborate, for equally good French fried potatoes can come out of a black iron kettle as from the latest model electric fryer. This is not to underestimate the value of the fryer, which offers the convenience of a built-in thermostat, but any deep kettle or saucepan, preferably a heavy one, serves nicely for deep frying. Use in a 3- or 4-quart kettle about 3 pounds of fat. It isn't wise to try to skimp on the amount, for there must always be enough to cover the food and to permit it to move freely in the kettle. ➤ There must also be room for the quick bubbling up of the fat which occurs naturally in frying potatoes, onions and other wet items. ➤ Never fill any container more than half full of fat. ➤ Remember also to heat the fat gradually, so that any moisture in it will have evaporated by the time it reaches the required temperature.

The kettle should have a flat bottom, so that it will sit firmly on the heating unit. Keep the handle of the kettle turned inward to avoid knocking against it. A short handle is desirable, to avoid the danger of accidentally overturning the hot fat and causing a small conflagration. In case fat should ever catch fire, have a metal lid handy to drop over the kettle. You may also smother the flame with salt or baking soda. ➤ Never use water, as this will only spread the fire.

For frying certain types of food such as doughnuts and fritters where bubbling is not a problem, a heavy skillet, an electric frypan or a tempura pan is sometimes preferred to a deep kettle because of the wider surface, which allows more pieces to be fried at one time.

A wire basket is practically a necessity for successful results in frying any quantity of small-sized material. The food is raised and lowered more easily and uniform browning is assured.

For judging the temperature of the fat, use a frying thermometer, no other. Have the thermometer ready in a bowl of hot water to lessen the chance of breakage; but ➤ never plunge it into the fat without wiping it very dry. Nothing is more important in frying than proper temperatures. As that wise old gourmet, Alexandre Dumas, so aptly put it, the food must be "surprised" by the hot fat, to give it the crusty, golden coating so characteristic and so desirable. The proper temperature in most instances is 365°, as easy to remember as the number of days in a year.

When no thermometer is available, a simple test for temperature can be made with a small cube of bread about 1 inch square. When you think the fat is hot enough, drop in the bread cube and count slowly to sixty, or use a timer for sixty seconds. If the cube browns in this time, the fat will be around 365°. A few foods—soufflé potatoes, for instance—may require higher or lower tempera-

tures, but these will always be noted in the specific recipes.

Above all, do not wait for the fat to smoke before adding the food. Not only is this hard on the fat, since smoke indicates that it is breaking down and may be spoiled for reuse; but the crust that forms on the food is likely to be overbrowned before the product is cooked through, and the food will be burned on the surface and raw inside. On the other hand, food introduced into fat that isn't hot enough to crust immediately will tend to become grease-soaked.

After frying one batch ➤ let the temperature come up again to the required heat, so that you may continue to "surprise" each additional one. ➤ Skim out bits of food or crumbs frequently as they collect in the fat during frying. If allowed to remain, they induce foaming, discolor the fat, and affect the flavor of the food. Have ready a supply of paper toweling on which to drain the cooked food and so rid it of excess fat before serving.

At the end of the frying, and after the fat has cooled somewhat and become safe to handle, strain it to remove all extraneous particles, then store it well covered and refrigerated for future use. To clarify fats before reusing, see 542. Adding some fresh fat for each new frying materially lengthens the life of the fat. When it becomes dark and thickish-looking, it will no longer be satisfactory for frying. At this stage, the smoking point has dropped too low; the flavor that it contributes to the food will be unpleasant and absorption high. Discard it.

Fats known simply as **shortenings** are favorites for deep frying. These include suitable solid fats such as lard and the hydrogenated fats; and the liquid oils, among which corn, cottonseed, safflower, soybean and peanut are most commonly available. Except for lard, which has a characteristic odor and flavor, these fats are bland and very similar in appearance and composition. Most of them are 100% vegetable in origin. These all have smoking points well above those needed for deep frying. For more details, see About Oils, 541.

➤ Butter and margarines, also known as shortenings, and valuable as they are for other purposes, are not considered suitable for deep frying because of their low smoking points.

Various other fats are sometimes used for deep frying. Olive oil is popular where locally produced, and rape and sesame oils are widely used where they are commonly grown and processed.

For special purposes and in certain circumstances, chicken and goose fat are rendered in the home for frying, as are also veal, pork, suet and beef-kidney fats. These are inclined to have low smoking points, but when handled with care they can be used to produce acceptable fried foods. If it seems desirable, the smoking point of these animal fats can be brought up to the required limit by blending them with any one of the cooking oils. To render these fats, see 542.

➤ Whenever possible, foods should be at room temperature and as dry as possible when introduced into the kettle. ➤ Always immerse gently with long-handled tongs or a slotted spoon or in a frying basket. ➤ Always dip these utensils into the hot fat first, so that the food will release quickly from them without sticking. And have a pan ready in which to rest the utensils when they come dripping from the fat.

➤ For good results, the food to be fried must be properly prepared. So that they will all cook in the same length of time, pieces should be uniform in size and preferably not thicker than 1½ inches. Small pieces, obviously, will cook through faster than large ones. It is difficult here to give advice about length of cooking. When in doubt, it is wise to remove one piece and try for doneness.

Raw foods, ➤ especially wet ones, should be patted between towels or paper toweling before cooking, to remove excess surface moisture. This reduces the amount of bubbling when the food is introduced into the fat. In adding a batch of raw food, always lower the basket gradually so that you can observe the amount of bubbling and be ready to lift it up if it looks as though the fat might be going over the top. Do not try to put too many pieces into the basket; fry several small batches rather than one large one. The cooked food may be kept hot on a paper-lined pan in an oven set at very low heat.

Certain types of food, such as croquettes, eggplant and fish, need special coating for proper browning and crust formation. For Breading, see 552. The coating may be simply flour, cornmeal or finely crushed dry cereal. Or it may be a Fritter Batter, 242, an egg and crumb mixture, or even a pastry envelope. Whatever it is, it should cover the surface evenly.

Foods to be coated with batter—shrimp, for instance, or pineapple slices—should be surface-dried beforehand. Doughnuts, fritters and other batter foods need no extra coating, as the egg-starch mixture browns nicely by itself when lowered into the hot fat. Many cooks do not realize that ➤ the richer a dough or batter mixture, the more fat it will absorb during frying. By adding even a little too much shortening or sugar to the mix, a doughnut may become so rich that it will end up grease-soaked. Or a fritter may simply disintegrate in the hot fat, or a too-rich batter slide off onion rings altogether.

✲ Frozen foods already breaded and deep-fat-fried need only defrosting and reheating in the oven. They should be defrosted outside the package to avoid the formation of surface moisture that would interfere with the crisping of the outer coating. Uncooked frozen foods that have to be coated should be dried on the surface after defrosting, and the coating applied as usual.

▲ In deep-fat frying at high altitudes, you will find that moist foods will require lower fat temperatures because of the lower boiling point of the water within them. For instance, French fries, which call for 365° in their final frying period, might need only a 355° fat temperature at high altitudes.

SAUTÉING OR PAN-FRYING

Sauter literally means "to jump," and this is just about what happens to the food you cook by sautéing. The cooking is done in an ➤ open pan which is kept in motion. The process is rapid, the food is usually thin or minced, and the ➤ heat must be kept up from the moment cooking starts until the food is tender.

There are other requirements, too. The pan and the ➤ small quantity of fat used must be hot enough, when the food is added, to sear the food at once, to prevent the loss of juices and to prevent sticking. The food at the start should be 70° or more, cut to a uniform thickness and size, and dry on the surface. If the food is too cold it will lower the heat, and if it is wet it will not brown properly. Worst of all, steam will form and break the seal holding the juices. To ensure a dry surface, food is frequently floured or breaded, see 552. ➤ Steam will also form if the pan is crowded. There must be space between the pieces of food you are sautéing.

For the best sauté, use a Clarified Butter, 349, or a combination of 3 parts butter and 4 parts oil When the combined fats reach the point of fragrance, add the 70° food, but not so much at a time as to reduce the heat in the pan. To keep the food from too quick browning, agitate the pan constantly. Too much turning of the food delays the quickness of heating. But food with a bound breading, especially if the coating has not been dried long enough before cooking, may steam. In this case, turning will help to release some of that steam more rapidly. Meat not floured or breaded is browned or cooked on one side until the juice comes up to the surface of the exposed side, then turned and browned on the other side. Proceed in the same way for fish, but the cooking time is apt to be considerably shorter.

To serve sautéed food with a sauce, remove the food from the pan and keep it warm on a hot serving dish. Quickly deglaze the delicious residue in the sauté pan—unless you have been cooking a strongly flavored fish—with stock or wine. Reduce the sauce and pour it over the sautéed food. ➤ If you heat or keep sautéed food hot in a sauce, you steam it too much.

SKILLET-PANNING OR SHALLOW- OR STIR-FRYING

If you are an American housewife you may have added to your wanted-for-Christmas list a **wok,** shown with its conical- or round-bottomed pan on 279, and its supporting and heat-concentrating metal ring. Ironically enough, most of the East Asian brides living in our area happily substituted for it some while ago a good old-fashioned skillet with a tight-fitting lid, even though the cooking period involved is slightly longer. With either utensil the vegetables are prepared the same way: that is, subjected to high heat in an open pan at the outset, and steamed, lidded, at the finish. In anywhere from 3 to 8 minutes, depending on material, you have tender but still crunchy vegetables and thin strips of fresh-tasting meat—all for immediate consumption.

Preparing the food is the slowest part of this procedure. If the meat is cooked along with vegetables—a popular practice—it is uniformly sliced to a thickness of about ⅛ inch and partially cooked first, until red changes to bright pink. Then it is removed from the frypan and reserved for addition later to the half-cooked vegetables for final cooking. For further details about vegetable stir-frying, see 279; for meats, see Sukiyaki, 458.

ABOUT MOIST HEATS

What a number of processes can be assigned to the moist-heat category! There are complete ones like boiling, pressure cooking, scalding, simmering, poaching, stewing, fricasseeing, braising, casseroling, cooking in wraps, double-boiler cookery and steaming. Just as with dry heats, there are partial moist-heat processes, like those in blanching and fireless cookery. We may as well mention here and now—although not on the side of simplification—that certain classic terms for kinds of moist-heat cookery are broadly interpreted, even by the most knowledgeable cooks. Also a number are neither moist nor dry, but a combination of both. Some stews, for example, may be begun in a pan by browning, while others, like the Irish variety, never see the inside of a skillet. Similarly, a braise, a fricassee and a "smother" may all, like a browned stew, have their origin in dry-heat sautéing and then are finished by cooking in a little stock.

BOILING

Discussing this process tempts us to mention stews again, in connection with the old adage, "A stew boiled is a stew spoiled." And we may point out that the same sentiment can be applied to almost every other kind of food. While recipes often call for foods to be brought to the boiling point—that is, in liquid which has reached 212°F. —or to be plunged into boiling water, they hardly ever demand boiling for a protracted period. Even "boiled" eggs, so-called, should be simmered.

Quick evaporation—seldom advisable except in parboiling—is one of the few justifications for keeping a food at boiling point. When evaporating, never boil covered, as steam condenses on the lid and falls back into the pot, reducing the amount of liquid very little, if at all.

Adding foods to boiling water will lower the boiling point, unless the quantity of water is at least three times as much as will cover the food—to offset its lower temperature. Such compensation is recommended in Blanching, 154, and in the cooking of cereals and pasta. When the pores of food are to be sealed, it may be plunged into rapidly boiling liquid, after which the temperature is usually reduced to a simmer.

✪ PRESSURE COOKING

We often wonder what is done with the moments saved by the purchase and preparation of "convenience foods." Something, we assume, of major importance, to compensate for their second-hand flavor. For the cook in a terrible hurry, but who still hankers after taste and nutritional value, we offer the pressure pan as a kind of consolation prize.

No matter how high the heat source, boiling in water in the presence of air can never produce a temperature over 212°. But, because in pressure cooking the air in the pan is withdrawn first, heat as high as 250° can be maintained at a 15-pound gauge reading. Some home cookers are geared to a range of from 3¾ to 20 pounds, although 15 pounds is commonly used. Cooking at 15 pounds pressure takes only about one-third the total time—from the lidding of the pressure cooker through the capping of the vent and the release of pressure—that it takes to cook food in conventional ways at boiling temperatures. In pressure-cooking vegetables over short periods at these higher temperatures, more than time is saved. Nutrients and flavor are also conserved, see Pressure-Cooking and Pressure-Steaming Vegetables, 278, 281.

In the pressure cooking of meats and soups, however, the higher heats involved tend both to toughen the protein and to affect flavor adversely. Therefore, we recommend this method only when time is more important to you than choice results.

In the canning of all nonacid foods, the higher heat of pressure cooking is essential to kill unwanted organisms, see 802.

Pressure cooking of ➤ beans and cereals and dried or puréed fruits, which may sputter and clog the vent, is not recommended.

It is essential in any pressure cooking to know your equipment well. ➤ Follow manufacturer's directions to the letter, observing the following general principles: ➤ Never fill a pressure cooker with more food than half its capacity if there is much liquid, or two-thirds if the contents are mainly solids. ➤ Be sure the required amount of liquid has been put into the cooker. ➤ Season lightly, as there is less liquid to dilute the flavor than in more traditional types of cooking.

If you have a timer, use it. If not, watch the time carefully, as overcooking results very quickly. As soon as the time is up, to arrest further cooking and reduce the pressure in your cooker instantly, place it in cool water or let cool water run over the sides. Exceptions are steamed puddings, many meats, and soups, which should be allowed to cool gradually.

➤ The cover must not be removed until all the steam is out of the pressure cooker. Here again, handle your particular type of appliance exactly as you are instructed. ➤ When the cover is difficult to remove, do not force it; there is still steam in the container which will be exhausted if you wait a few minutes.

When cooking foods that require different periods of cooking, begin with the ingredient that requires the longest time. Always reduce the pressure, as directed in the manufacturer's booklet, before opening the lid to add the ingredient that requires the shorter period of cooking. Readjust the cover, place the cooker again over high heat and proceed as before. When the desired degree of pressure has been reached, recap the cooker, reduce the heat and begin to count the rest of the cooking time.

Or, when cooking together vegetables that require an unequal period of cooking, equalize them by cutting into small dice those that require the longer period, such as potatoes and turnips.

▲ A general rule for pressure cooking at high altitudes, whether you are cooking at 10, 15 or 20 pounds pressure, is to maintain the same timing as at sea level, but to increase the pressure by ½ pound for every 1,000-foot rise, using a specially calibrated gauge.

For additional details about high-altitude pressure cooking, see Vegetables, 282; Meat, 448; and Canning, 804. To use a pressure-cooker as a steamer, see Steamed Puddings, 753.

SIMMERING

This ranks as one of the most important moist heats. The temperatures range from about 140° to 185°. Simmering protects fragile foods and tenderizes tough ones. The French verb for the slow simmer is *mijoter,* and the French engagingly refer to low simmers—between 130° and 135°—as "making the pot smile." When food is simmering, bubbles come gently to the surface and barely seem to break. It is the heat best used for soups—uncovered; and for stews, braises, pot roasts and fricassees—covered; and for food prepared *à l'étouffée,* 151—covered.

POACHING

This kind of moist-heat cooking is one that most people associate only with eggs, but its range is much wider. The principle of poaching never varies. The heat source is a liquid just under the boiling point, and a distinguishing feature of the process is the basting or self-basting which is constant during the cooking period.

When an egg is properly poached, it is floated on simmering water and then either basted with this simmering liquid or covered with a lid, so that steam accumulates to perform a self-basting action. Because the egg cooks in just a few minutes, the lid does not allow the formation of excess steam. In poaching meat or fish, where the cooking period is lengthened, entrapped steam may become too heavy. For these and delicate foods, therefore, a lid is not recommended. Instead, substitute a poaching paper, see sketch opposite.

A poaching paper permits excess steam to escape through its small top vent and around the sides. The narrow vent also maintains better color in the food than when air is excluded altogether—as in other more tightly confined moist-heat processes, such as casseroling. ➤ To make a poaching paper, take a piece of square cooking parchment, the sides of which are a little larger than the diameter of the pan you wish to cover. Fold it in fourths and roll it diagonally: begin at the folded tip, as sketched. Hold it over the pan to

determine the radius. Then snip off the part that projects beyond the edge of the pan. Cut a tiny piece off the pointed end to form a vent. When you unfold the paper, you will have a circle just the area of your pan, with a perforation at its center. Place it over the food to form a self-baster.

If the cooking process is a short one, or if the food to be cooked is in small units, the liquid may be at simmering point when the food is added. If the food is chunky, like a whole chicken, the water is put on cold, the food added and the water brought to a simmer ➤ uncovered. The liquid may then be skimmed and the poaching paper applied. If the liquid becomes too greatly reduced during the cooking process, it must be replenished. This type of poaching is often miscalled boiling or stewing.

CASSEROLING

The term casserole has been bandied about so carelessly that it is time we took stock of its meaning—or, rather, all its meanings. In correct parlance, a "casserole" is both a utensil—usually a lidded one—and the process used for cooking a raw food in that utensil. But it has also come to mean a favorite type of self-service dish which graces so many American buffets but is not in the least the real McCoy. This mock casserole is a mixture of several foods, one of which may be a pasta or rice in a sauce. The mixture is often precooked or consists of a combination of precooked and quick-cooking food; and it is served in the baking dish in which it was heated. ➤ Such mock casseroles are usually cooked uncovered in a moderate oven to avoid building up too much steam and breaking down the sauce in which they are served. They often have a gratinéed top to protect the food and absorb excess fat. ➤ It is wise to wipe off the edges and exposed surfaces of these "prefabricated" casserole dishes after filling and before heating, so they will not show any browned spilled-over areas on the outside surfaces when served. Often, for large groups, a rather shallow dish is used, both to ensure its heating through quickly and to provide plenty of gratinéed top for each serving. If topping with biscuit or corn pone, heat in a 375° to 400° oven.

The basic character of the casserole as a utensil has hardly altered since men learned to shape clay into pots. The typical earthenware casserole is squat, with bulging sides, easily grasped round handles and a slightly arched lid. Clays used in some unglazed pots have been found to be heavy in lead and are not recommended. ➤ To season an unglazed casserole and to prevent an "earthy" taste or the subsequent retention of unwanted flavors, rub it well, inside and out, with cut cloves of garlic. Then fill it with boiling water, add onion skins, celery and leek tops, put in a low oven, let the water come to a boil, and simmer covered about 4 hours. Finally, discard the water and wash the dish and lid, after which the casserole is ready for use. ➤ To avoid cracking, never set a clay casserole directly on a heating element. If your burner is not thermostatically controlled, it is wise to use an asbestos pad or wire trivet.

Today the word casserole is applied to any deepish pot in which cooking actually goes on, or even to pots more rightly called *sautoirs,* or straight-sided deep skillets. ➤ In true casseroling, as distinguished from "mock" casseroling, a tight lid is integral to the process. Generous quantities of butter, fat or oil are added, and sometimes—but not always—a small amount of stock; the stock, as well as the juice from the food, condenses on the lid and supplies a measure of self-basting, although some hand-basting with the pan fats may be necessary. The very slow cooking goes on in about a 300° oven and develops a bare simmer, condensing the food juices into a delicious residue. After the food is removed, the residue, when degreased if necessary and then deglazed, forms the sauce for the dish. This method of cooking, if in a lidded pot, is also called cooking **à l'étouffée.**

FIRELESS AND OTHER SLOW MOIST-HEAT COOKING PROCESSES

If fuel is scarce and a long heating period is needed in certain foods, there is a possible advantage in using a fireless cooker. This appliance is enclosed on all sides by material that is a non-conductor of heat and is preheated to a desired temperature by an electric coil or by hot stones. Hot food set in it continues to cook without the addition of further heat.

Deep-wells, pots countersunk in range tops, and pots thermostatically controlled for low, slow heat are also favored at times of fuel shortage or when the cook cannot keep check on a stew over a long period. Some models have electric coils built into the sidewalls as well as the base of the container to give a very consistent low heat.

WRAP COOKERY

Wrapping food before introducing it into direct heat is almost as old as cooking itself. Primitive societies to this day surround pieces of food with various materials to tenderize them and to protect them from burning. In the Caribbean, petate mats serve this tenderizing purpose, just as papaya leaves do in the Pacific islands. One of the most mouth-watering sights we've ever seen was shown in a documentary movie of an Indonesian tribe on the march. When mealtime came, everyone, from oldster to tot, stopped to devise a case for cooking his food in the coals—an intricately folded leaf, a stoppered section of bamboo, a reed basket. You knew at once that in each "case" the steam produced would give special flavor and succulence to the food. Our American Indians baked fish, see 399, small animals and birds in clay. Drawn but not skinned, the animal was completely packaged in mud and bedded in coals—up to several hours if the size required it. Removal of the clay brought along with it skin and feathers, leaving the skinned game ready to eat.

More sophisticated methods of exploiting the wrap principle are the dough-encased meat pastries of English kiln workers and the esteemed French en croûte, 448, and en papillote, 153, methods, in which pastry and paper are the respective casings. And one could consider the prized product of a New England clambake, 380—with seaweed the incomparable flavoring agent—as a glorified example of wrap cookery. But in any true wrap cookery, the enclosing material allows some steam to escape. If you use aluminum foil, 153, in indoor or outdoor cooking, remember that the food is actually steamed, and far removed in taste and texture from food cooked either by direct heat or in a less impervious wrapping.

LEAF-WRAPPINGS

Certain fresh green unblemished leaves such as lettuce, cabbage, grape and papaya give an edible coating to food, while banana skins, palm leaves and corn husks only furnish protection during cooking. Preparation of suitable leaves and the wrapping and timing of the food for cooking are described below.

Cabbage Leaves: Cut the stem from a head of cabbage deep enough to start a separation of the very outer leaves from the core. Dip the head in boiling water. This will loosen three or four leaves. Dip again and continue to remove the loosened leaves. Blanch, 154, the leaves 2 minutes, drain and plunge into cold water. Wrap a meat mixture in the leaves as shown in the illustration below. Either tie the leaf packet as shown, or place it, if left untied, seam side down. Cook as follows.

I. Melt in a casserole:

2 tablespoons butter

Add:

2 cups boiling water or stock

Put packets in a single layer on bottom of casserole. Place a heavy plate directly on top of the food as a weight during cooking. If the leaf-filling is uncooked, bake or simmer the packets, ➤ covered, 35 to 40 minutes—longer for pork. If the wrapped filling is precooked, 10 minutes is enough to heat the packet through.

II. If packets are tied, they may be dropped into simmering broth and cooked, ➤ covered, gently until done. See timing under I.

III. Or, steam the tied packets in a vegetable steamer. See timing under I.

Lettuce Leaves: Soak them very briefly in boiling water. Drain, dry and fill. Wrap as for cabbage leaves and cook only as for I or III. The leaves are not strong enough to cook as for II.

Fresh Grape Leaves: for Dolmas, 492. Drop young pale-green leaves into boiling water and blanch till color darkens—about 4 to 5 minutes. Remove leaves. Drain them on a rack. Should you have to use large leaves, remove the tough part of the central rib. Place shiny side down on a board. Roll the filling into ¾-inch balls. If the filling is of rice, use not more than 2 teaspoons, as the rice will swell. Set a ball of stuffing near the broad end of a leaf and fold over the left and right segments, as sketched below. Then roll the enclosed ball toward the leaf-tip. Place the packet loose side down, and cook as directed in I above.

Canned Grape Leaves: Place them briefly in hot water to separate, then drain and dry. Fill and cook as above.

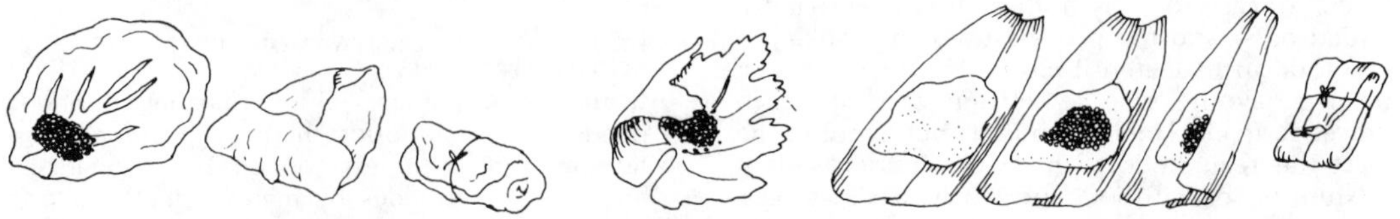

Papaya Leaves: Cover them with cold water. Bring ➤ just to the boiling point, uncovered, to remove any bitterness. Drain. Plunge into boiling water to cover and ➤ simmer, uncovered, until tender.

Banana Leaves: Cut away the central rib and carefully tear sections about 10 inches square by pulling along the veins. Sponge off the leaves on both sides with cold water, always keeping the action along the leaf veins. Dry the leaves gently with paper toweling or a soft cloth. Center the filling as for tamales, illustrated at right opposite, but fold first against the veining, and then secure the loose ends by folding them up and securing them with a string. When filled, cook as for III, opposite.

Corn Husks: Place them in boiling water, remove from heat and allow to stand 30 to 45 minutes before draining. To roll food in them, overlap two or three corn husks. Fold the leaves first lengthwise from one side to slightly past the center and then overlap from the other side, as shown left. Fold up the ends so they can be tied with one string. For use in Tamales, see 201.

FOIL COOKERY

Aluminum foil solves many kitchen problems, but if you cook food wrapped in foil, please consider the following: Foil is impervious to air and moisture from the outside. Therefore, it traps within its case all the moisture released from the food during the cooking period. So even if the heat source is dry, like that of an oven, the result will always be a steamed food, never a roasted one. Since the foil also has high insulating qualities, foil-wrapped food will require ➤ longer cooking periods at the same temperatures indicated in non-foil cookery. An exception is poultry, see 422.

You may be willing to pay for both the foil and extra heat needed to enjoy the convenience of, for example, the practically effortless Pot Roast described on 463. If you are cooking outdoors, see Campfire Vegetables, 282, and the comments in Outdoor Cooking, 155.

❄ Frozen food may be cooked in foil by leaving the ends of the foil-wrap open, in which case a four-pound frozen rolled beef roast will require about 3 hours in a 400° oven, a five-pound frozen chicken the same time at 450°, and a three-pound frozen fish more than 1 hour, again at 450°. The foil may then be turned back altogether to brown the food: about 20 minutes for the chicken or roast, 10 for the fish. You may prefer, after opening the foil, to insert a meat thermometer instead, and cook to the recommended internal temperature.

COOKING EN PAPILLOTE

This is a delightful way to prepare delicate, quick-cooking, partially cooked or sauced foods. The dish, served in the parchment paper in which it was heated, retains the aromas until ready to eat. As the food cooks, some of the unwanted steam it generates evaporates through the paper. Just the same, the paper rises and puffs as heating progresses, putting considerable strain on the folded seam. So note the following directions and sketches carefully.

To make a papillote: fold in half, crosswise, a piece of cooking parchment, ➤ not foil, of appropriate size. Starting at the folded edge, cut a half-heart shape, so that when the paper is unfolded the full heart shape materializes, as shown below.

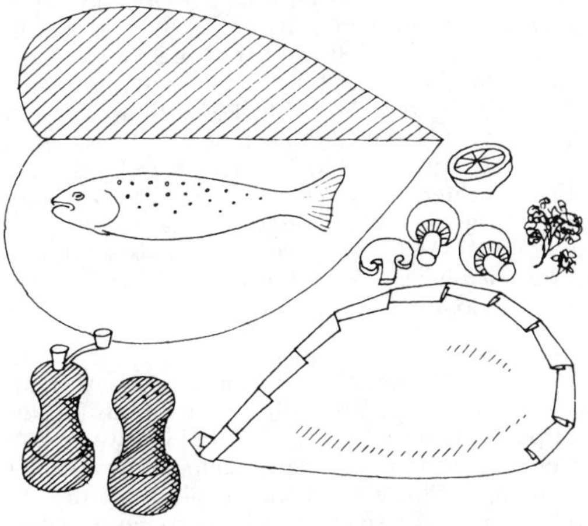

Be generous in cutting, allowing almost twice again as much paper as the size of the object to be enclosed. Place the food near the fold—but not too near. Turn the filled paper with the folded edge toward you. Holding the edges of the paper together, make a fold in a small section of the rim. Crease it with your fingers and fold it over again. Hold down this double fold with the fingers of one hand, and with the other start a slightly overlapping and again another double overlapping fold. Each double fold overlaps the previous one. Repeat this folding, creasing and folding around the entire rim, finishing off at the pointed end of the heart with a tight twist of the parchment—locking the whole in place.

Now butter the paper well. Place the papillote in a buttered ovenproof dish in a 400° preheated oven for 5 to 6 minutes or until the paper puffs. In serving, snip about three-fourths of the paper on the curved edge just next to the fold to reveal the lovely food and release the aroma.

Because of the varied and doubtful chemical composition of the paper, we do not recommend the brown paper bag of the supermarket type as a substitute for the cooking parchment in papillote cookery.

DOUBLE-BOILER COOKING

For those foods which are quickly ruined beyond hope of resurrection if overheated, even for a short period—especially egg, cream or chocolate dishes—we recommend the use of a double boiler. Sometimes food may be started over direct heat in the top of a double boiler and finished ➤ over—not in—boiling water. For sauces, we like a double boiler that is rather wide. Deep and narrow vessels tend to overheat the sauce at the bottom even when it is stirred—if it is held for any time at all. ➤ The material of which the upper portion of the double boiler is made is very important. When it is too thin, it transmits heat too fast. If it is too thick, it absorbs and retains too much heat.

For years we made magnificent Hollandaise in a stoneware bowl that fit the base of an aluminum double boiler. It was a completely effortless procedure. Then the bowl broke and the magic fled. We found stainless steel and aluminum too quick. A deluxe saucière of stoneware, deep set in a copper base, was too reluctant and, when it finally heated, too retentive of heat. A heat-resistant glass double boiler, 358, has been a reliable substitute for our favorite old makeshift, and it does allow us to keep track easily of the over—not in—boiling water factor.

STEAMING

For cooking vegetables, steaming is an excellent process. On 278 we describe two methods for this purpose: direct steaming over boiling water and pressure steaming at greater temperatures. Direct steaming is also a good way to plump raisins, to release salt from smoked meats and, more importantly, to cook fish and to prepare delicate vegetables for freezing.

ABOUT PARTIAL HEAT PROCESSES

Certain processes involve heating but are not in themselves complete methods of cooking. They extend from the driest, like **toasting,** which adds color and flavor, to complete immersion, in **steeping,** which may plump foods or remove unwanted flavors.

BLANCHING AND PARBOILING

These terms are among the most carelessly used in a cook's vocabulary. To introduce some order into traditional confusion, we describe and differentiate among four different types of blanching.

BLANCHING I

This means pouring boiling water over food to remove outer coverings, as in loosening the brown hulls of almonds or making the skins of peaches and tomatoes easier to peel off. This process is also used to soften herbs and vegetables for more flexible and longer-lived decoration.

BLANCHING II OR PARBLANCHING

This involves placing food to be blanched into ➤ a large quantity of cold water, bringing it slowly to a boil, uncovered, and continuing to simmer it for the length of time specified for blanching. Following this hot bath, the food is drained, plunged quickly into cold water to firm it and to arrest further hot-water cooking, and then finished as directed in the recipe. This is the process used to leach excess salt from tongue, cured ham or salt pork and to remove excess blood or strong flavors from variety meats. The cold-water plunge after blanching effectively firms the protein in the more fragile variety meats, like brains and sweetbreads.

BLANCHING III OR PARBOILING

This means that food is plunged into ➤ a large quantity of rapidly boiling water—a little at a time so as not to disturb the boiling—and then boiled for the blanching period indicated in the recipe. The purpose of this particular kind of blanching or parboiling may be to set color or—by partial dehydration—to help preserve nutrients and to firm the tissues of vegetables. If further cooking follows immediately, the blanched food need not be chilled as above, but merely drained. Should an interval elapse before final cooking and serving, use the cold water plunge, drain and store the food refrigerated. Blanching vegetables in this way preparatory to canning or freezing is described in greater detail on 803. Small amounts of the vegetable are plunged into ➤ boiling water just long enough to retard enzymatic action and to shrink the product for more economical packaging. Then the vegetables are drained and quickly plunged into ice water, so that cooking is arrested at once.

BLANCHING IV, STEAM-BLANCHING OR PARSTEAMING

Similar to steaming, left, but of shorter duration. An alternate method for food to be frozen or canned is described on 803.

REDUCING LIQUIDS

This process is used mainly to intensify flavor: a wine, a broth or a sauce is evaporated and condensed over lively heat. A so-called double consommé is made in this way, the final product being half the original in volume. Naturally, reducing applies only to sauces without egg. And those which have a cream or flour base must be watched carefully and stirred often to avoid scorching. For further details, see 339.

PLANKING

Why bother about planking? One reason is the attractive appearance of a planked meat, surrounded with a decorative band of duchess potatoes beautifully browned on their fluted edges and garnished with colorful vegetables. Another reason is the delicious flavor a hardwood slab can give to meat. Planks are usually 1-inch-thick kiln-dried oak ovals. They often have a tree design cut down their length to drain juices into a shallow depression toward one end.

If all the cooking is done on the plank, the plank will char rapidly. Usually steaks are broiled on an oven grill fully on one side and partially on the other before being planked. To season a new plank, brush it with cooking oil and heat in a 225° oven for at least one hour before using. To protect it when cooking, oil well any exposed part, or cover, as suggested above, with a decoration of mashed potatoes or other puréed vegetables.

FLAMING OR FLAMBÉING

Flaming always comes at a dramatic moment in the meal, sometimes a tragi-comical one if you manage to get only a mere flicker. To avoid anti-climax, remember that ➤ food to be flamed should be warm and that the brandy or liqueur used in flambéing should also be warm—but well under the boiling point. For meat, do not attempt this process with less than one ounce of liquor per serving. For nonsweet food served from a chafing dish or electric skillet, pour the warmed liquor over the surface of the food and ignite by touching the edge of the pan with the flame of a match or taper. For hot desserts in similar appliances, sprinkle the top surface with granulated sugar, add the warm liqueur and ignite as above. Or, ignite brandy-dipped sugar cubes. To flambé fruits, see 127.

SCALDING

As the term is used in this book, scalding means cooking at a temperature of about 185° or just below boiling. You will find this process discussed in relation to Milk, 530, the food for which it is most frequently used.

OUTDOOR COOKING

Cooking out of doors may put to use all kinds of heat, but its enthusiasts do best when they stick to simple methods. As soon as cookouts get complicated, the whole party—in our perhaps jaundiced opinion—will do well to move back into the kitchen, where equipment is handy, controls positive, and effects less problematical. We never attend a patio barbecue featuring paper chef's hats, aprons with printed wisecracks, striped asbestos gloves, an infrared broiler on white-walled wheels, and yards and yards of extension cord and culinary red tape without entertaining the possibility of a heavy thunderstorm.

Speaking of easy outdoor cooking devices, we once went on a picnic with some friends in a beech woods. Our host, toward suppertime, made crisscross fires, just big enough for each individual steak. First, he set up log-cabinlike cribs about four layers high with twigs approximately one inch thick. In these he laid a handful of dry leaves and fine brush. On top of the cribs, he continued to build for about three inches an additional structure of pencil-like material. When, after firing, the wood had been reduced to a rectangular framework of glowing rods, he unlimbered some thin steaks from a hamper and, to our consternation, laid them calmly and directly on the embers. In a few moments he removed them with tongs, shook off whatever coals had adhered, turned the steaks over and repeated the process on the other side. They were delicious.

There is no law, of course, against availing oneself of ready-made instead of improvised cooking gear, and as much of it as the traffic will bear. There are even available, for the Davy Crocketts of the New Frontier, various solar-heat cookers; but it is suggested that they be given homeside tryouts in advance. Various solid fuels based on hexamethylene tetramine can be purchased in granular form, in bulk, from a chemical supply house, or in tablets at outfitters. This fuel is only adequate for emergencies or when traveling light. For fancy or long-cooking camp foods, gas, either liquid or vapor, is the preferred fuel. Liquid-gas stoves have many adherents but may be a bit cranky. Bottled-gas stoves are easier to use but do not work so well at very low temperatures.

For campers, al fresco cooking is a necessity rather than a pleasant indulgence. But fires in wilderness areas carry for the builder perhaps his greatest responsibility. Before starting your fire, dig or scrape a narrow trench around the area to stop roots under the fire pit from catching fire and smoldering, sometimes for days, then suddenly bursting into flame many yards away. Through the duration of the fire, watch for sparks on surrounding vegetation.

To start a wood fire, collect a few small dead branches with the twigs attached and break up the branches into categories, beginning with matchstick thickness, then pencil thickness, then thumb size and larger. Make a loose untidy pile about 3 or 4 inches high of the smallest size, thrust a burning match into the center, and, as it blazes up, slowly add the next thickness, and then the thumb size. Add fuel on the downwind side of the fire, and remember to let it breathe—air is as important as fuel! Hardwoods smoke less and provide much more heat than do most of the softwoods. Those preferred are oak, beech, maple, ash and then the evergreens. Beech wood will burn green; aspen will not burn at all. If the wood is wet, split it; the interior portions are usually drier, and if a fire is started and is hot, it will use all but soaking-wet wood—albeit with a great deal of smoke. Take a tip from the Indians and keep your fire small: it takes less wood for cooking, it is less bothersome and cozier, and in winter it is easier to cuddle up to for warmth.

➤ Never leave a fire untended. Be sure to watch for overhead branches as fire hazards. When you finally leave a fire, drown it, mix it with mud, stir into it non–vegetation-carrying dirt, stomp on it, mix it with snow or sand, and leave it ➤ dead.

➤ Before bringing any sort of cooking container into close contact with a wood fire, remember to cover the pan's undersurface with a film of soap or detergent. This precaution will greatly facilitate the removal of soot later, when the pan is cleaned.

Pit-Cooking is the most glamorous of all primitive types because it is so largely associated with picturesque places, hearty group effort and holiday spirit. Pits may be small holes of just sufficient depth and width to take a bean pot, a three-legged kettle or a true braising pot with a depression on top for coals, as sketched in the chapter heading. Or the pit may be big enough to accommodate all the makings of a king-sized luau, replete with suckling pigs. In direct pit-fire cooking, hardwood embers are left in the pit, and steel rods are put across it, a few inches above the fire on rocks or logs set around its periphery; the rods, in turn, support a wire mesh grid on which the food is cooked.

A switch from direct pit-firing to fireless pit-cooking can achieve a completely different range of culinary effects. Fairly large-scale cookery of the latter type requires digging a pit not less than 2 feet deep, 3 feet across and 4 feet long. If pit-cooking is more than occasional and the locale does not vary, you may find it more convenient to build a surface pit by constructing a hollow rectangle of concrete blocks, about the same height as a true pit is deep.

The next step is to line the bottom and sides of the pit with medium-sized flat rocks, ➤ never with shale, which may explode when heated. Toss in another loose layer of rock. Now spread over the rocks a substantial bonfire of hardwood deadfall or driftwood. Hickory, beech, maple and ironwood are prime for this purpose. And grapevine cuttings lend grilled food special distinction. The French, incidentally, regard food broiled over grape wood, or *sarments de vigne,* as extraordinarily choice. When the fire has completely burned down—this should take not less than 2 hours—rake out the red embers and the top rocks. Now, sprinkle a quart or so of water over the hot rocks remaining and add a two-inch layer of fresh leaves—grape, beech, pawpaw—or of corn husks or seaweed for a shore dinner. If you have remembered to bring along some handfuls of aromatic herbs, add them too.

➤ Work quickly at this point, so that the rocks do not lose their stored heat. On the bed of packed foliage, arrange the elements of your meal: fish, cuts of meat, green peppers, onions, corn in its husks, unpeeled potatoes, acorn squash. Pile over them a second layer of green leafage, then a second grouping of food, and finally a third layer of green leafage. Cap off the stratification with the remaining hot rocks, a tarpaulin or canvas cover, and four inches of earth or sand to weight things down and to keep heat and steam at work inside—cooking your meal. How long this will take depends, of course, on what's cooking—maximum time will probably be required for a small pig; it should test 190° when done and takes about 20 minutes per pound. The whole pit-cookery operation, whether it is carried out on the beach or in the woods, has a distinctly adventurous character. And periodic tests for doneness performed on the foods closest to the edge of the pit are an essential part of the process. In lifting the tarp and in removing it altogether when you are ready to serve, be extremely careful not to get food fouled up with sand or earth.

A modified form of pit-cookery is described in Smoking Food, 814.

For shore dinners, with seaweed as filler, wire mesh is often placed over at least one layer to better support small crustaceans, clams and oysters. For details of a Clambake, see 380.

Far and away the most popular technique for outdoor cookery involves direct heat from reduced charcoal. We prefer portable rather than built-in cookers. ➤ **If using any charcoal-fired equipment indoors, be sure to put it within a fireplace where the carbon monoxide fumes can be carried off completely. Do not use charcoal burners ever in a tent, cabin, garage or any enclosed area: insufficient ventilation may prove fatal.**

The most common cookout stove is a portable brazier-type, of which the **hibachi,** shown below, is the Far-Eastern representative. But, to accommodate a main dish for groups of four or more,

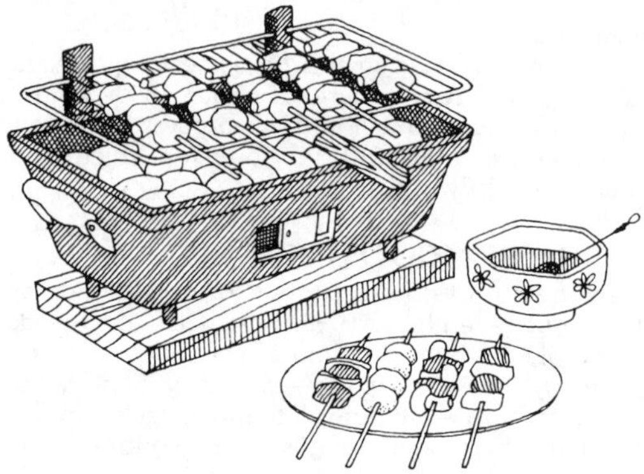

only the larger westernized brazier offers an adequate cooking surface. A hibachi-type broiler or two will supplement this larger grill in the preparation of side dishes such as hors d'oeuvre and vegetables. The circular grills shown at right have fairly good-sized wheels for easy transport, as well as a lid or a collar to shield the grill surface from wind. The grills may be turned to expose food to the most active areas of heat, and both are equipped with a device which raises and lowers the grill for varied exposures. The lidded model can double as a device for smoke-flavored cooking. Before use, soak wood chips of hickory, apple, oak or cherry about two hours in water and add a few at a time to the charcoal during the cooking period.

Some braziers with horizontal grills have superimposed over them additionally a spit, in which case they are commonly protected from wind by a three-sided metal shield with a roof. Without an electrical connection or the use of a cumbersome counterweight system, the only practical way to turn a spit is by hand; and this—make no mistake—is a real chore. On the whole, should you go in extensively for spit-cooking, we advise either an electric oven equipped with a spit, or a separate rotisserie. If you do cook out of doors electrically, you may want to make use of a vertical broiler similar to that shown on 403, which exposes a maximum of food surface to the heat source. Whatever brazier equipment you use, pay close attention to the directions furnished by its manufacturer.

Remember that in all spit-cooking, the weight losses due to shrinkage are great, and flare-up from lost fats and juices may be frequent. Flare-ups can be avoided in part by careful trimming of surplus fat. Some short flare-ups may be desired for browning; slight unwanted ones can be doused with a sprinkle of water from a sprinkling bottle or a water gun. To minimize the fall of fat onto

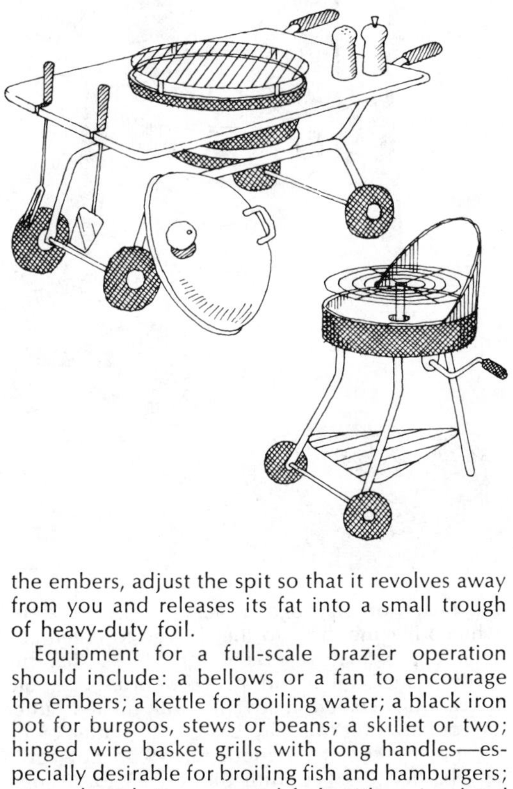

the embers, adjust the spit so that it revolves away from you and releases its fat into a small trough of heavy-duty foil.

Equipment for a full-scale brazier operation should include: a bellows or a fan to encourage the embers; a kettle for boiling water; a black iron pot for burgoos, stews or beans; a skillet or two; hinged wire basket grills with long handles—especially desirable for broiling fish and hamburgers; some sharp knives; a metal fork with an insulated handle; a spatula; tongs; a long pastry brush for glazing; a chopping block; skewers—these must be nonrusting, ➤ square or oval, not round and sharp-pointed; a roll of heavy-duty aluminum foil; a supply of pot holders or a couple of pairs of asbestos mitts; individual serving trays; a pail of water and, with it, a flare-up quencher. If you plan to roast a fowl or a joint, you will need also a baster, 446, and a meat thermometer.

➤ To prepare a brazier fire with charcoal, be sure that you build a big enough bed of coals to last out the cooking operation. We find prepared hardwood briquets most uniform and convenient. They should be put into the brazier approximately two deep—preferably over a layer of gravel, enough to level the bed out to the edge of the bowl.

A circle of aluminum foil, cut to size and put down under the gravel, will protect the brazier from grease. To ready fuel for an extended firing period, arrange an extra circle of briquets around the edge. As the center of your fire burns to embers, these may be pushed inward. For short-term cookery you may group briquets at about two-inch intervals. To help ignite the charcoal, put a few briquettes in a dry waxed milk carton along with a few scraps of paper. ➤ When the charcoal is covered with a fine white ash, you are ready to begin cooking. Flick off the ash, which acts as insulation.

Judging the heat of a brazier fire is strictly a matter of manual training. Hold your hand above the grill at about the same distance from the coals that the food will be while cooking, and think of the name of a four-syllable state—"Massachusetts" or "Mississippi" will do nicely. If you can pronounce it once before snatching your hand away, your coals are delivering high heat; twice, medium heat; if three times, low heat.

What food should be cooked out of doors? Just as we recommend simple cooking equipment in the open, so we now urge simple outdoor menus. Do remember to have your meat at 70° before cooking, and protect it and the other foods against insects. For further menu suggestions, see 34 and 35.

Also throughout this book you will find recipes which we regard as suitable for outdoor cookery marked with this grill-like symbol ⊟. While, obviously, pan-broiled and pan-cooked food may be prepared over a brazier out of doors, you will not find such recipes singled out by the distinctive outdoor cookery symbol. We have, in large part, selected only those in which the flavor is actually improved by the outdoor cooking medium. ⊟ For cooking vegetables, see 282. ⊟ For cooking on skewers, see 146.

Steaks and chops are extraordinarily well suited to flat-broiling on a brazier. ➤ Choose well-marbled meat, 442. But by this we definitely do not mean meat that has a rim or collar of fat. On the contrary, it is important ➤ to trim off all excess fat before broiling to reduce the risk of flare-ups. Also, cut through encircling sinew—being careful not to slice into the meat itself—so that the meat does not curl up under the high heat which initiates its cooking. ➤ Avoid excessively thick cuts: an inch and a half should be the limit for individual servings. Grease the grill first with some of the meat fat or with a vegetable oil. ➤ To sear the meat and seal in its juices, lower the grill close to the coals before laying the meat on it or use a bellows to increase the heat momentarily.

Searing to seal is even more essential in flat-broil grilling than in pan or oven broiling, because the meat juices, once lost, are irrecoverable. After searing, raise the grill to about three inches from the fire and broil the meat until done. No specific time schedule for doneness can be set up, because so much depends not only on the degree of heat itself, but on the age of the animal, how long the meat has been hung, the nature of the cut and, of course, individual preference.

Here are a few things to keep in mind: Just as in any meat cookery, large cuts take, weight for weight, proportionately less cooking time. If the cut is large, testing for doneness with a thermometer is safer than testing with a knife or fork or with your thumb, 447. We would like to spare you the ordeal of an old friend of ours whose enthusiasm for outdoor grilling is repeatedly dampened by his wife's low-voiced but grim injunction: "Remember, Orville, medium-burned, not well-burned."

➤ If you flat-broil chicken or other fowl, restrict the weight of the bird to two pounds or under. Split it in half, coat both sides with cooking oil, and set the halves on the grill, cavity side down. The bony structure of the bird will transmit heat to the flesh above and at the same time provide insulation. Finish the cooking with the fleshy side down; but ➤ to keep the skin from sticking, make sure to cook farther from the heat source.

Spit and **rotisserie** cooking are best for very small or large fowl; for joints, like leg of lamb; and for other chunky cuts of meat. Here again, consult the directions that come with your equipment to determine maximum weight, which will probably be in the neighborhood of ten pounds for roast meat and up to fifteen for fowl. Smaller birds should be strung transversely on the spit, larger ones head to tail along the spit's axis, as illustrated below.

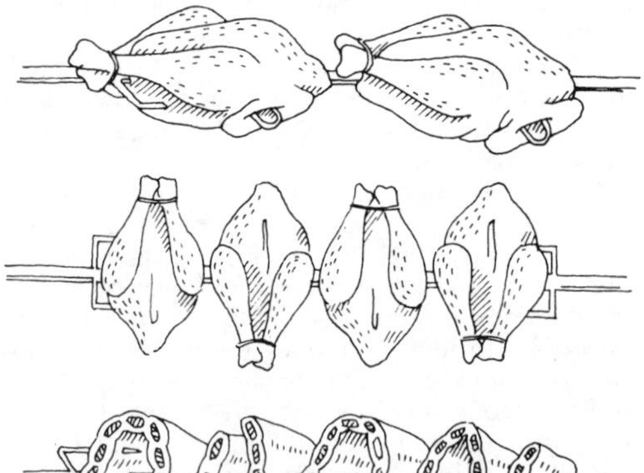

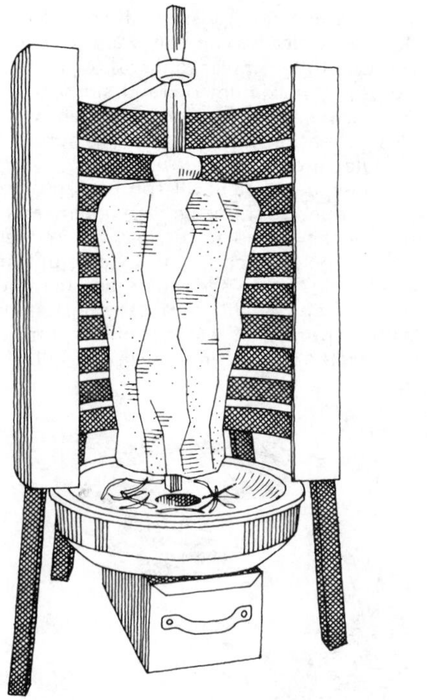

For spareribs, get your butcher to cut them in half crosswise, forming two long strips; prebake or parboil them in the kitchen and then string them like an accordion on your outdoor spit, as shown. Fowl and certain other types of meat must be trussed, 419, before spitting. Especially if they are heavy or of irregular shape, it is necessary, while adjusting them to the skewer, to determine their approximate center of gravity so that the birds balance well in turning. Fowl on a spit should be carefully coated in advance with melted butter or cooking oil. You may baste with butter or oil during the cooking period, but ➤ do not apply any barbecue sauce until the last 15 to 20 minutes of cooking. For Barbecue Sauces, see 354.

The **yiro,** illustrated above, is a strikingly functional method of large-scale barbecueing we observed some years ago at the American Farm School in Thessalonica. Common in the Near East, it is an updated descendant of ember-roasting techniques as old as that part of the world. An electrically powered merry-go-round rotates an impaled mass of compressed meat before a vertical half-cylinder of "ember" coils. As the outside of the tall chunk reaches perfect succulence, very thin slices are cut off lengthwise with a razor-sharp knife. The slices are cut into a scoop and each individual portion is inserted with relishes into a pocket of flat bread. With its cut surfaces successively exposed, the meat continues to turn, to brown—and to diminish happily.

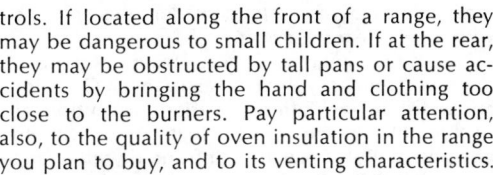

ABOUT INDOOR COOKING EQUIPMENT

Certain cooking effects we have admired overseas and would like to bring back with us seem to defy stateside domestication. Part of the difficulty may have to do with the way food is grown elsewhere or with the fact that it is sometimes impossible to buy ingredients of comparable freshness. But, just as often, the loss in translation may be traced to special techniques which simply cannot be duplicated in the average American kitchen. This is true of the following: the quick, intense, short-lived fires and the huge pans that are essential to Chinese stir-frying; the very low, long-retained-heat chamber called *étuve* in old French kitchens—so ideal for drying out meringues or for simmering foods in covered pots; and, for that matter, the open-air charcoal grilling in our own country, which imparts its distinctive aroma to a steak, or the seaweed-smother which gives that authentic touch to lobsters pit-cooked at the shore. Conditions like these may be approximated in cooking on modern ranges, but never completely reproduced.

If you grew up using gas for cooking heat, you appreciate its dynamic flexibility of control. If your experience has been with electric ranges, you value the evenness of their broiling heat and the stored warmth of their surface units. The relatively new electronic devices have attracted favorable attention because of their ability to reduce heating time to a fraction of its former length. If you are considering investing in this type of equipment, you would do well to see first the section on microwave cooking, 160; and if you do invest, be sure to read the manufacturer's booklet with care.

Indeed, whatever your source of cooking heat, learn thoroughly the characteristics of your range. Find out if the broiling elements need a preheating period; if broiling in the oven requires an open or a closed door. Some new electric ovens have a double unit for broiling in which the racked meat is placed midway between the heating elements—a horizontal version of the outdoor double broiler shown 403. A dripping pan is inserted below the lower coils. This broiling unit cuts timing by about half.

In purchasing, consider the safety value of controls. If located along the front of a range, they may be dangerous to small children. If at the rear, they may be obstructed by tall pans or cause accidents by bringing the hand and clothing too close to the burners. Pay particular attention, also, to the quality of oven insulation in the range you plan to buy, and to its venting characteristics.

For loading ovens, we make the following suggestions: ➤ Place oven racks where you want them before heating, not after. To brown a sauce or a gratinéed casserole, place the pan—briefly—close under the broiler, as shown first on the left below. Few cooks realize the importance of air circulation in ovens: overcrowding results in uneven baking. Make sure that the pans or sheets you are using fit the oven shelf comfortably, with at least two inches of space between the pans as well as between pans and oven walls. Never use two shelves if you can avoid it, but if you must, stagger the pans as shown second from the left. For a discussion of heat and pan-size relationships, see 666.

For cake baking in general, the best position for the pan is just above center. But for angel food cakes, torten or soufflés, the placement is below center, as shown third in the sketch; for often, in modern ovens, the slight heat provided by a top element is enough to harden the surface of a soufflé, if it is set too close, preventing expansion.

Some commercial ovens feature devices for introducing moisture into an oven as needed. In the home range, a practical substitute, should the recipe require it, is a shallow pan partially filled with water, as shown on the right.

In baking, set the oven thermostat to the desired temperature. Preheat 10 to 15 minutes if there is no indicator light to inform you when the temperature is reached. Insert the pans as quickly as possible. Try not to peek until the time is up—or almost up.

If you use a thermostatically controlled gas or electric oven, don't think you are speeding things up by setting the thermostat higher than the recipe indicates. You will get better results at the specified temperature. And don't, incidentally, press a thermostatically controlled oven into service as a kitchen heater. This will throw the thermostat out of gear. Ovens vary, however, and even under normal use, thermostats need frequent adjustment—at least once every 12 or 14 months.

Keep in mind always that a clean oven will maintain temperature and reflect heat more accurately than an untidy one, and in buying a new

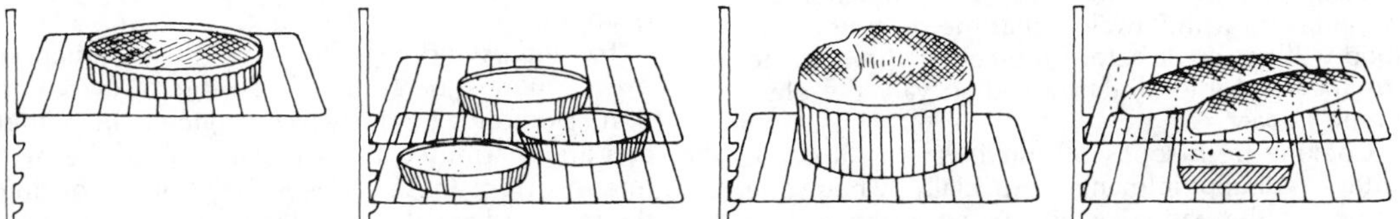

range, you may want to consider one equipped with a self-cleaning system.

As to the range top, here again, as with its interior, familiarity breeds assurance. Questions about its use are almost without exception answered fully in the booklet that comes with the equipment. But if you are confronted with a range for which printed instructions are lacking, or if special problems arise, call your local utility company. They frequently maintain a staff of obliging and well-trained consultants, prepared to give you advice free of charge. A most important determination to make in electric ranges is whether your surface heating units—one or several—are thermostatically controlled to level off disconcertingly when you most need sustained heat for a sauté. Also, learn if they are so differentiated as to provide all the potentials of an electric skillet.

In using gas burners, watch the relation of flame to pan. ➤ The flame should never come closer than ½ inch to the outer edge of the pan-bottom.

Before using such a specialized utensil as a wok or any utensil that would concentrate unusual heat onto the surface of a range, check with the manufacturer as to its practicality; enamel may craze or chrome discolor.

One-piece ceramic range-tops are now available. One has its own ceramic cookware engineered to exactly fit the heating areas; the pots are so flat-bottomed that no heat is lost. Other ceramic tops use any flat-bottomed cookware. Another even more revolutionary concept has been developed: a one-piece ceramic range-top with magnetic coils beneath that leave the cooking surface cool. Energy is generated only in the iron or magnetic stainless steel pans in which the cooking is done.

MICROWAVE COOKING

Our experience with microwave has followed a familiar contemporary pattern: inadequate response to great expectations. For who among us, on the long summer afternoons, has not harbored the recurring and roseate dream of prolonging to the very last minute the joys of gardening—or of tennis, or beachcombing with the children—before returning to the kitchen and putting dinner together in a trice? Even microwave's most obvious advantage—defrosting and reheating frozen foods—has proved of limited value, and in any case it takes care of only an inconsequential fraction of our cooking schedule. Because no matter what particular microwave equipment you own, you may have to be on hand during much of the reheating period—to rotate the dish, to alternate cooking and withdrawal so that the outside of the food will not cook before the center thaws, or to stir the food intermittently and so vary the electronic impact.

Cooking fresh foods by microwave is also not without disappointments, especially when one compares the eating quality or appearance with that of more conventionally cooked foods. In order to arrive at fair conclusions, we divided into two equal parts each category of food—fresh vegetables, refrigerated or frozen casseroles and leftovers, fresh or frozen meats and fish, pie doughs and cakes—then cooked each by microwave and conventional method respectively. Formulas for cakes and cookies, which, baked by microwave, require less riser, were properly adjusted. We found that timing varied greatly from that prescribed in the manuals of microwave instruction, and almost all types of food tended to toughen. Meats have been shown to dry out and lose more nutrients than when properly roasted by conventional methods. Microwave-baked cakes turned out coarse in texture and over-moist, with pallid tops; those in which egg is the sole riser can only be regarded as failures. If milk or milk-mixtures are cooked in a microwave oven, they must be constantly watched, as they tend to boil over very quickly.

Browning—which in many traditional cooking processes is responsible for both the flavor and the aesthetic pleasure of the food—is not truly achievable with microwave equipment. Attempts have been made through the use of special browning dishes or pre- and post-browning techniques with a unit combining conventional electric heat, but they often complicate procedures or add to the cooking time so that the microwave cooking period may be longer than that of the older methods. Even expedients like dusting with paprika or brushing with soy sauce must often for best results be combined with the use of conventional equipment.

Other limitations of microwave cookery are freely acknowledged by its partisans. Only those tender meat, 442, and fowl cuts which cook by dry heat respond adequately, and only those that have been boned—like rolled roasts—prove really trouble-free. For bony or uneven cuts, metal foil, which is not penetrated by the microwaves, must be used for part of the cooking time to cover the thinner portions; but the foil must be kept at least two inches away from the walls of the unit to prevent arcing, as described later. Many microwave cooks make a practice of covering food in the oven with plastic or paper wrapping to hold in steam and prevent spatter. Cooking whole hams, except for the reheating of fully cooked types, is not recommended. As we have implied, meat cuts and fowl requiring moist heat are apt to be more tender when cooked by conventional methods—and take no more time. The time factor is similar for foods like rice or pasta, which require large quantities of liquid in cooking.

To understand why the foregoing limitations exist, you must be aware of how microwaves function. Electromagnetic waves originate in a tube and are distributed to all metal parts of the oven interior; from these surfaces they bounce off into the food and are absorbed by it, provided the food is on or in certain materials discussed below. These penetrating waves cause the water molecules in the food to vibrate at an intense rate, and the resulting friction produces the heat, which in turn cooks the food. Since this friction continues after the food is removed from the oven—sometimes in a roast for as long as 30 minutes—microwave-cooked food is in effect undercooked, then allowed to stand outside the oven afterward to complete the process. Care must be exercised in choosing the material on which food is microwave-cooked. The molecular structure of glass, some plastics, ungreased white paper, and some ceramics is such that energy input is not impaired; the food cooked in or on such materials absorbs the waves without adverse effects on them or on the oven. A simple test for cookware suitability is to set it in the oven empty: if it is hot to the touch after 15 seconds of "cooking," it should be discarded. In any event ➤ metal or metal-trimmed dishes must be avoided, as they cause an arcing interaction with the oven walls which damages the magnetron tube. Very shallow freezer containers and TV trays made of foil, however, may be used, provided the cooking period is relatively short and they are kept at least two inches from oven sidewalls.

It is true that microwave ovens do not heat up the kitchen, and that the cookware indicated above remains cool during the cooking procedure itself, almost all heat being absorbed by the food. But at the end of the cooking period the hot food very quickly transfers its heat to the dish, and—especially if the dish is quite full—pot holders may be necessary to remove it, and lids or wrappings should be cautiously removed to avoid steam burns.

Because foods of varying types cook at different rates, it is usually necessary to microwave such dishes in succession, holding those finished until the rest have had their turn. In any case, in most portable ovens no more than four servings of any given food can be cooked at one time, nor more than one layer of cake. With the latter handicap, it will readily be seen, the microwave model loses the layer-cake race to the old-fashioned oven in which three or four layers can be simultaneously accommodated.

There are many safety factors one must keep aware of. To avoid danger, door mechanism and switches should be in flawless working order. Air filters must be clean and the oven interior unpitted. Any sign of irregularity should be occasion enough for a service call.

There are available in stationary and professional sizes combination microwave and conventional ovens which dispel some of the disadvantages described earlier. Also to shorten cooking time there are new **convector ovens** which by the use of fans force electrically heated air into oven areas for more rapid baking and roasting. But neither of these is apt to bring to the average household cook the freedom she dreams of via a kitchen robot, for heat is a subtle medium that for best results will always demand intelligent human attention.

So, all things considered—and at the risk of being put down as unadventurous or just plain not with it—we still prefer conventional techniques over those involved in microwave cookery. We find them less demanding, more flexible, and productive of more nutritious and appealing food.

ABOUT THE TIME ELEMENT IN COOKING

How long to heat food? There are many answers. They lie in the interaction of the heat source, the equipment and the medium—air, liquid or fat.

Consider the following rates of heat transferral. A dough that either bakes at 400° or steams at 212° for 20 minutes will cook in deep fat heated to 400° in 3 minutes. A hard-cooked egg will cool off in 5 minutes if plunged into ice water, but will need 20 minutes to cool in 32° air. A vegetable that will cook in 20 minutes in water at 212° will need only 2 minutes steaming under 15 pounds pressure at 250°.

In timing, a great deal depends on the freshness of food—this is especially true of vegetables; on the aging and fat content of meat; and on the size of the food unit. Large, thick objects like roasts need lower heat and a longer cooking period than do cutlets, to allow the heat to penetrate deep into the center. The amount of surface exposed is also a factor, as you have learned from experience with whole as compared with diced vegetables.

Still another determinant is the reflective and absorptive quality of the pan. Recent tests have shown that a whole hour can be cut from the roasting time of a ten- or twelve-pound turkey if it is cooked in one of those dark enamel pans that absorb heat rather than in a shiny metal one that reflects it. And we have discussed elsewhere, 153, the insulative qualities of foil when used in wrap-cooking. Personal preference affects timing, of course, as well as the idiosyncrasies of equipment. Even placement in an oven, 159, makes a difference and, last but not least, the temperature of food at the onset of heating. For all these reasons it is with some trepidation that we have indicated cooking periods in our individual recipes. We know from our fan mail that timing is among the most worrisome of all problems for the beginning cook. Therefore, if our timing and yours do not jibe, we beg you to look for solutions in the facts we have set down above, before you take pen in hand.

HOLDING FOOD AT SERVING TEMPERATURES AND REHEATING FOOD

Everyone knows that food which is held hot or reheated is not so tasty or nutritious as that served immediately after preparation. Unfortunately, laggards and leftovers are frequently a cook's fate. Here are a few hints on the best procedures:

There are two ways to reheat dishes that are apt to curdle when subjected to direct high temperatures. These include au gratin, egg or creamed dishes or any other dish rich in fat. One way is to put them in the oven in a container of hot water about two-thirds the depth of the cooking pan. Or place under the pan a cookie tin or a piece of foil—shiny side down—so that the heat is deflected. The latter suggestion is particularly handy to avoid overbrowning when reheating pies or cakes.

Reheat other cream and egg-sauced foods in a double boiler ➤ over—not in—boiling water.

To retain color in vegetables reheated in a double boiler, use a vented lid.

If reheating whole roasts, bring them to room temperature and then heat through in a moderate oven.

If reheating roasted meat, slice it paper thin and put it on hot plates just before pouring over it boiling-hot gravy. ➤ Any other method of reheating will toughen it and make it taste second-hand.

To reheat deep-fat-fried foods, spread them on racks ➤ uncovered, in a 250° oven.

To hold pancakes, place them on and between cloth towels in a 200° oven.

To reheat casseroles, make certain the container is ovenproof before placing it in a 325° oven directly from the refrigerator.

To reheat creamed or clear soups or sauces, heat to boiling point and serve immediately.

Other devices that hold foods for short periods are electrically controlled trays, individual retractable infrared lamps, the age-old chafing dish, and the bain-marie or steam table. None of these should be used for a protracted period, however, if you hope to preserve real flavor and avoid bacterial growth. ➤ Holding temperatures should be at about 140°.

ABOUT UTENSILS

The material of which pots and pans are made, as well as their sizes and shapes, frequently determines success or failure. So, often in this book we not only caution about too high heat, but especially warn against combining it with thin cooking pans. The latter may develop hot spots and cause sticking, or they may require an undue amount of stirring to avoid scorching. ➤ Choose a pan, then, of fairly heavy gauge—not so heavy as to make for difficult handling, but heavy enough to diffuse heat evenly. Note, too, that we distinguish in recipes between **flame- or heatproof ware** that can be used on direct heat—except for heatproof glass, which needs a trivet—and **ovenproof ware,** which is designed for oven use only.

HEAVY ALUMINUM

The advantage here is good diffusion, but aluminum will pit—no matter how expensive. And it will not only tend to become discolored itself but will adversely affect the color of some foods. Don't clean aluminum with harsh soaps, alkalis or abrasives. To remove discoloration, boil in aluminum pans for 5 to 10 minutes a solution of 2 teaspoons cream of tartar to 1 quart of water.

COPPER

Best in heavier gauges. It gives a quick, even heat distribution if kept clean. But ➤ unless well tinned, or lined with stainless steel on surfaces contacting the food, it is affected by acids and can prove poisonous. To clean, keep handy a squeeze bottle filled with a vinegar-and-salt mixture. Place some on a cloth and rub discolored copper until bright, then rinse in hot water.

STAINLESS STEEL

Of course, this is the easiest material of all to keep clean. Its poor heat-conductivity is usually offset by thinning down the gauge, so that hot spots develop and food cooked in it is apt to burn easily. But stainless steel with an inner core of aluminum or copper which increases heat diffusion makes one of the choicest of utensils for surface cooking.

IRON

Heavy but low in conductivity, iron rusts easily and discolors acid foods. To treat new commercially preseasoned skillets or Dutch ovens, wash with soapy water, rinse and dry. Coat frequently with unsalted vegetable oil, and just before using, wipe with paper toweling. To reseason an old iron skillet, scour and wash with ➤ soap—not detergent. Dry; then coat with an unsalted shortening, and place in a 350° oven about 2 hours.

TEMPERED GLASS AND PORCELAIN ENAMEL

Both are poor heat conductors. The glass is apt to crack and the enamel scratches and chips. Unless of best quality and treated to resist acid foods, the glaze of enamel ware is quickly affected by them. It also is marked by metal utensils; only wooden or nylon hand tools should be used with it. High heat may make the enamel stick to the heating element, so a trivet is advisable.

EARTHENWARE

While a poor conductor of heat, glazed or unglazed earthenware holds heat well and doesn't discolor foods. But it is heavy and breaks easily with sudden temperature changes. There are recent discoveries that indicate some danger of lead transference to food from soft glazes and even from certain unglazed earthenwares. To season and use an earthenware casserole, see 151.

TINWARE

This has good conductivity but is apt to mar, and it rusts quickly. It turns dark after use and is affected by acid foods.

GREASELESS PANS

These are a delight to people suddenly put on fat-free diets. The soapstone griddle illustrated, 235, is age-old. There is newer equipment with non-sticking silicone and fluorocarbon resin surfaces which can withstand temperatures up to 450°. These surfaces do not affect heat distribution but will help to keep food from sticking. As some scratch easily, use a nylon or wooden paddle for turning, and a nylon or wooden spoon for stirring. When cooking eggs, breaded fish and meat you may need added fat.

If you are on a fat-free diet and tired of broiling or of using greaseless utensils, poach food in skim milk, fruit juice, stock or wine for variety in flavor.

PLASTICS

There are plastics which can stand relatively high heat but not high enough for cooking or ➤ even for containing hot liquids that may dissolve the plastic and seriously burn the cook. Many storage containers, funnels and other kitchen utensils cannot even be washed in water over 140°. Others are ruined by oil and grease. The surfaces of all plastic utensils retain grease, ➤ so don't try to get egg whites to whip in a plastic bowl, 544.

You will wonder after reading these pros and cons what pan materials to choose. Fortunately there are on the market today a number of brands of cooking ware with good flat bottoms made of alloys that take advantage of the superior diffusion of aluminum, the quick conductivity of copper, and the noncorrodible quality of stainless steel. But while we are speaking of combinations of metal, let us say that ➤ pots of copper, even when tin-lined, and of iron must not be covered with aluminum foil if the food to be cooked is very acid, as the foil can be dissolved into it. In fact, it is usually best to avoid dissimilar metal pots and lids when cooking any very acid foods. In the final analysis, you may still prefer a heavy iron Dutch oven for stews, an earthenware casserole for fondues, a heatproof glass vessel for saucemaking. ➤ Don't invest in large pan sets of a single material until you know what your preference really is. Be sure the pot handles are metal-reinforced at the jointure and are replaceable.

When you cook, choose a pan that fits the size of the heat unit. This correlation gives better cooking results and is more economical of fuel. Be certain, too, that the lid, if the process calls for one, is tight-fitting. ➤ Be sure the cooking pan is appropriate in size to its contents. Especially in braising and baking, the relation of pan size to contents is vital, see 447 and 666.

In baking, round pans will give you more even browning; square pans tend to cause heavier browning at the corners. Note, too, that shiny metal baking pans deflect heat and that dark enamel or glass ones both catch and hold the heat more. ➤ Therefore, food cooked in glass or enameled pans needs at least a 25° reduction in the oven temperatures given in our recipes. While vitreous or dark metal materials may brown cookies too rapidly, they will ensure better browning for pies and puff pastes. If cooking fuel is scarce, a great saving can be effected by the use of these heat-retaining pans.

In pan-broiling or using a griddle, utensils should be brought up slowly to cooking temperature. ➤ Do not place an unfilled pan on high heat unless it has fat or liquid in it.

And should you scorch food by some unlucky chance, the scorched taste is greatly lessened by plunging the pan first into cold water before transferring the food to a clean container. To clean scorched pots, except those coated with silicone or a similar material, use a nylon pouff or a nylon brush with a built-in detergent container. If that is not sufficient, soak overnight with some detergent in the water. If that still isn't enough, in the scorched pot bring to a boil 1 teaspoon washing soda or cream of tartar for each quart of water.

There is a certain pace in food preparation that an experienced cook learns to accept. This doesn't mean she scorns short cuts, but she comes to know when she has to take the long way 'round to get proper results. She senses not only the demands of her equipment but the reactions of her ingredients.

A man once summed up his wife's life with the epitaph, "She died of things." It might have happened to any of us. We are constantly encouraged to buy the latest gadget that will absolutely, positively make kitchen life sublime. No kitchen can ever have enough space at convenient levels to take care of even a normal array of equipment. So think hard before you buy so much as an extra skewer.

Get pans that nest well. And if you can't resist a bulky mold, see that it hangs on an out-of-the-way pegboard panel, or make it a decorative feature for an odd, unused nook. Buy square rather than round canisters for economical use of storage space. Keep canisters with spices and staples in alphabetical arrangement for quick identification. And place these close to the areas where you will be using them most.

BASIC KITCHEN EQUIPMENT

We all enjoy and expect shining, easily cleaned kitchen surfaces. Some traditional ones like cross-cut or laminated wood chopping blocks, even when sanded daily, can harbor harmful bacteria. It is hard but wise to toss out slightly crazed or chipped pottery, but you can relegate it to the flower department. Choose shapes that are free from grooves and jointures that catch food, and select materials that are impervious to acids and rust.

Kitchens today are fairly scientifically laid out. Everyone is aware that the big kitchen is a time and energy waster; and that a U-shape or a triangular relationship of sink, stove and refrigerator —with their accompanying work spaces—is a step-saver. We may have to live with the kitchens we have, but it pays occasionally to think about your work habits. See if you can make them more efficient.

Well-designed nonrusting hand tools save your towels and your temper. The following is a reasonably comprehensive basic equipment list for which illustrations can be found as noted.

4 saucepans of assorted sizes with lids, 172
2 frying pans—large and small—with lids, 205
Large stewing or soup kettle, 167
Double boiler, 358
Pressure cooker, 278
Mold for steaming, 112
Deep-fat-frying equipment, 147
3 strainers, 198, 278, 337
Steamer, 278
Colander, 538
Coffee maker, 37
China teapot and teakettle, 63
Candy thermometer, 781
Deep-fat-frying thermometer, 147
Griddle, 236
Bean pot, 250
Oven roasting pan with rack, 420
3 round 9-inch cake pans, 666
2 square 9-inch cake pans, 666
2 loaf or bread pans, 601
2 cake racks for cooling, 552
Muffin tins, 611
2 pie pans—tin or glass, 639
2 cookie sheets, 711
Small ovenproof dish, 250
Large ceramic or glass casserole, 417
6 custard cups, 735
9-inch tube pan, 668
Shallow 9 x 12-inch pan, 721
8-inch soufflé baking dish, 220
Set of mixing bowls, 544
Set of metal measuring cups, 546
8-oz. dry-measure glass cup, 546
8-oz. liquid-measure glass cup, 539
Set of measuring spoons, 337
Large and small metal spoons, 665
Slotted wooden spoon, 278
Large fork, 454
Small fork, 317
2 paring knives, 84
Serrated bread knife, 551
Carving and slicing knives, 449
French chopping knife, 562
Grapefruit knife, 282
Knife sharpener, 449, 550
Spatula, 711
Eggbeater, 337
Ladle, 167
A 4-sided and a rotary grater, 336, 337
Meat grinder, 798
Sugar or flour scoop, 546
Funnel, 780
Tongs, 147
Kitchen shears, 168
Flour sifter, 546
Potato ricer and food mill, 204
Potato masher, 317
Wooden chopping bowl and chopper, 370
Salad bowl, 92
Doughnut cutter, 147
Biscuit cutter, 634
Pastry blender, 639
Pastry board, 600
Pastry brush, 639
Vegetable brush, 279
Rolling pin, 639
Pastry cloth and cover for rolling pin, 639
Pancake turner, 236
Apple corer, 99
Vegetable slicer or parer, 296
Rubber scraper, 600
Weighing spoon or scales, 543
Ice cream freezer, 759
Citrus fruit juicer, 60
Electric mixer, 664
Blender, 336
Waffle iron, 240
Impervious cutting board, see 562
Asbestos pad or trivet, 358
Bottle openers, below
Corkscrew, below
Can openers, below
Nutcracker, 562
Salt shaker and pepper grinder, 153
Pot holders, opposite
Plastic detergent dispenser with nylon brush, below, and nylon pouf, opposite
Jar unscrewers, below

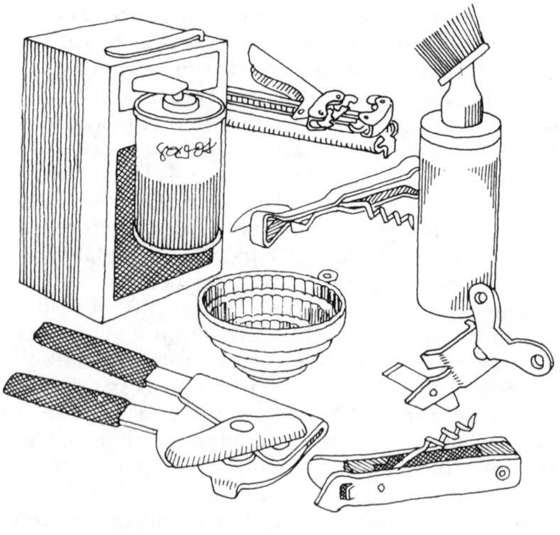

OTHER USEFUL ACCESSORIES

4 or more canisters
Cake cover and carrier
Dish drainer
Dutch oven or enameled metal-lidded casserole
Garbage can
Wastebasket
Meat thermometer

Toaster
Vegetable bin
1 or more trays
Bucket
Wooden picks for testing cakes
Refrigerator containers
Waxed paper and paper toweling
Plastic storage bags
Aluminum foil
Dishpan
12 dishtowels
4 dishcloths
Plastic sponges

Small kitchen amenities for which we are enduringly grateful are those extensions of power like can openers, lid lifters, jar unscrewers and the nylon brush-topped detergent dispenser, left, and the jar lifter and pot holders below.

We end these lists with a reminder. ➤ Always clean off tops before opening cans, as they may be dusty or may have been sprayed with poisonous insecticides while in the store. Also in opening a can ➤ avoid metal slivers by starting beyond the side seam and stopping before you cut through it. Food may be stored safely in opened cans, covered and refrigerated, for a few days.

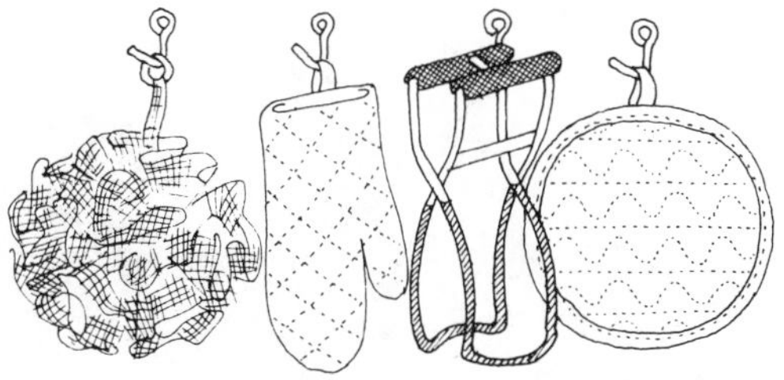

ABOUT BURNS AND BURNING

In the foregoing pages we have supplied, among other information, enough facts to keep our readers from ever burning the food they heat. Now a few safeguards against burning the cook—and what to do should such an emergency occur.

Never throw water on a grease fire. Use salt or soda, or if the area is a small one, cover with a metal lid.

Choose a range, if you can find one, on which the burners are level with the surrounding platform so pots cannot tip.

Use flat-bottomed, well-balanced pans that are steady when empty. Be sure handles are not so heavy that the pot will tip, or so long that they can catch on a sleeve.

When deep-fat frying, please note the precautions given on 147.

Put boiling liquid to the back of the stove, out of reach of small children.

In pan-frying, keep a colander handy to place over the pan should the fat begin to sputter.

Keep heavy pot holders and metal tongs near the range for removing hot objects and hot foods.

Watch that your hands or the cloths you are to use are not damp when touching or wiping electrical equipment or hot handles or lids.

Have polarized attachments put on your electrical appliances to avoid shock.

Should you receive an extensive or painful burn, seek immediate help from your physician or the emergency room of your local hospital. Lie down, remain calm, and keep warm until skilled help is available.

The first aid treatment of the wound itself is much the same for large or small burns. Loosen clothing or other material over or near the wound and remove it. Take care not to cut or remove the burned skin or any material adhering to the burned surface. If blisters are present, they should not be broken or cut.

Submerge the burned area in cold water or apply cold water as soon as possible after injury for periods up to one or two hours. This will help to relieve the pain. Then apply a dry sterile gauze dressing as a protective bandage. If sterile gauze is not readily available, clean linen can be used. Larger burn wounds should be covered by a clean sheet for protection and comfort until medical help is provided.

Do not use antiseptic preparations, ointments, sprays, butter, or home remedies on the burn wound, since these substances may interfere with treatment by the physician later.

Individuals with face burns should be observed continuously to assure that they are breathing normally.

After first aid treatment has been initiated, further medical care should be under the direction of a physician.

STAIN REMOVAL

We give here a partial list of removal instructions for those stains most encountered in the kitchen and dining room. These directions are for natural linens and cotton. If wool or synthetic fibers are involved, avoid hot water and bleaches. For other stains we recommend consulting the Home and Garden Bulletin No. 62 of the USDA, Washington, D.C.

Alcoholic Beverages: Sponge stain with cool water or soak 30 minutes or longer. Wash with soap or detergent.

Butter, Margarine or Mayonnaise: Regular washing removes some stains; others will need soap or detergent rubbed into the stain, then rinsing with warm water. For large stains use a commercial grease solvent and follow manufacturer's directions.

Catsup and Chili Sauces: See Alcoholic Beverages.
Chocolate and Cream: Sponge with cool water or soak 30 minutes or longer. Rub gently with soap and rinse. If stain remains, apply a commercial grease solvent.
Coffee and Tea: Boiling water poured from a height of 2 feet is good for fresh stains. Stretch stained material over a washbowl and ➤ be very careful not to scald yourself.
Fruit, Fruit Juices and Wines: Boiling water as for coffee stains; or try bleaching in sun after moistening with lemon juice and salt.
Lipstick: Apply undiluted detergent to stain, rub well and rinse. Repeat if necessary.
Mustard: See Lipstick, above.
Soft Drinks: See Alcoholic Beverages, above.
Wax or Paraffin: Scrape cloth to remove hardened wax. Place blotting paper or facial tissues both over and under the cloth and press with warm iron. Sponge with a commercial grease solvent.

SOUPS

In the good old days, when a "soup bunch" cost a nickel and bones were lagniappe, pounds and pounds of meat trimmings and greenstuff were used in the household to concoct wonderful essences for everyday consumption. The best soups are still based on homemade stocks. ➤ Please read About Stocks, the foundation of soup, meat and sauce cookery, and therefore found under Ingredients, 520. Note the suggestions offered for the long slow cooking of meat stocks or the rapid cooking of fish fumets and vegetable stocks, which also apply to soup making. Fish and vegetable stocks are especially important in *au maigre* or meatless cooking.

Because not everyone wants to bother with the painstaking methods often required to extract soup stock, and because soups are such an interesting addition to or base for meals, we suggest toward the end of this chapter a large number of time-saving prepared soup combinations. Have on hand a supply of canned, dried or frozen bases to bring quick and revivifying soups into the range of even the most casual cook. No one can afford to be without a varied store of these consistently good, and often excellent, products. Learn to use herbs and seasonings, 579 and 567. Keep your own economical stockpot to dilute condensed soups and to enrich them with added minerals and vitamins. Astound your friends with effortlessly made and unusually flavored soup sensations!

To minimize cooking time, use your ⅄ blender for the processing of raw vegetables, and your ❂ pressure cooker for suitable meat scraps, fresh or leftovers. See Quick Household Stock, 523.

No matter by what method it is made, soup should complement or contrast with what is to follow; and however enticing its name, it will fit into one of the categories below:

Bouillon—concentrated brown stock 170
Consommé—clarified double-strength brown stock 169
Broths—clear liquors from fish, meat, fowl and vegetables . . . . .523 and 524
Jellied Soups—made from gelatinous knuckle bones, clarified and used as they are or with added gelatin 173
Vegetable Soups—all vegetable or prepared with meat or fish stocks in which vegetables predominate 174–175
Purées of Vegetables and Legumes—with or without cream added 175–176
Cream Soups—cream, butter, cereal- or egg-thickened soups, often on a vegetable base .181
Bisques—shellfish-based cream soups 187
Chowders—thick fish, meat and vegetable soups, to which salt pork, milk, diced vegetables, even bread and crackers may be added 190
Fruit Soups 128

Some of the above are served hot, some cold, some either way, like bouillons, borsch, vichyssoise and fruit soups. ➤ To serve soups piping hot, use tureens, lidded bowls or well-heated cups. Especially if drinks and hors d'oeuvre have been offered first, a hot soup helps to recondition the palate.

➤ Cold soups should be very well chilled, and served in chilled dishes—especially jellied soups, which tend to break down more rapidly, being relatively light in gelatin. Cold soups, when not jellied, may be prepared quickly by using a ⅄ blender and chilling briefly in the freezer. On informal occasions, they may be chilled in a tall jug and served directly from it into chilled cups or bowls.

You should be able to count on about 6 servings from a quart of soup unless it is the mainstay for a lunch, as is frequently the case with a soup rich in solids. ➤ The quantities noted in the individual recipes are consistently given in standard 8-ounce cups; servings in about 6-ounce cups.

There are some classic dishes—Petite Marmite, 170, New England Boiled Dinner, 466, and Goulash, 464—that occupy middle ground between soups and stews.

▲ Above 2500 feet, soups need longer cooking periods than called for in the regular recipes, as the liquids boil at a lower temperature.

SOUP SEASONINGS

Soup is as flavorful as the stock on which it is based. Please read About Stocks, 520, and Seasonings for Stocks, 521.

The addition of wine to soup frequently enhances its flavor, but ➤ do not oversalt soups to which wine is added, as the wine intensifies saltiness. A not-too-dry sherry or Madeira blends well with veal or chicken soup. A strongly flavored soup prepared with beef or oxtail is improved by the addition of dry red table wine—½ cup wine to 1 quart soup. A dry white table wine adds zest to a fish, crab or lobster bisque or chowder. Add 1/4 to 1/2 cup unfortified wine to 1 quart soup. Fortified wines should be added to the hot soup shortly before it is served. To add wine to soups containing cream or eggs, see individual recipes. ➤ Do not boil the soup after adding the wine.

Beer adds a tang to bean, cabbage and vegetable soups. Use 1 cup for every 3 cups soup. Add the beer just before serving. Reheat the soup well, but ➤ do not boil.

COLORING SOUP

If soup has been cooked with browned onion skins or browned onions, and if the amount of meat used is substantial, it should have a good, rich color. Tomato skins also lend color interest. Caramelized Sugar III, 559, may be added if necessary. We prefer it to commercial soup coloring, which is apt to overwhelm a delicately flavored soup with its own pervasive, telltale aroma. Also read About Vegetable Stock-Making, 524.

REMOVING FAT FROM SOUP

I. Chill the soup. The fat rises at once and will solidify when cold. It is then a simple matter to remove it.

II. Float a paper towel on the surface of the soup, and when it has absorbed as much fat as it will hold, discard; or roll a paper towel and use one end to skim over the soup surface to remove the fat. When the end becomes coated with fat, cut off the used part with scissors and repeat the process as shown below.

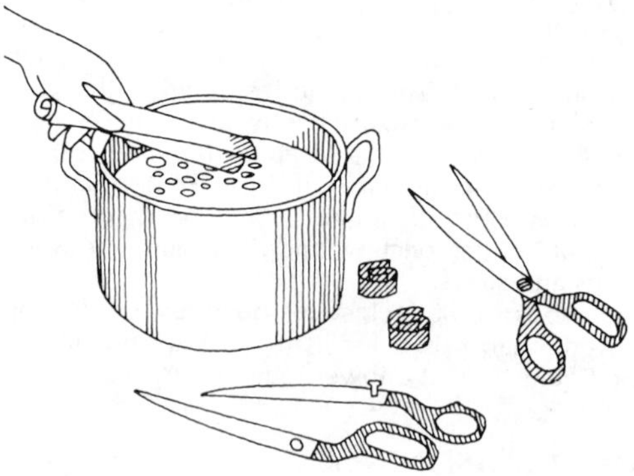

III. Use your meat baster, 446, with the bulb as a suction device for grease removal.

ABOUT CEREALS FOR THICKENING SOUPS

Noodles and dumplings and precooked cereal garnishes such as rice give an effect of body to a clear soup. But for intriguing texture and elegance of flavor, they do not compare to the thickeners added raw and cooked as an integral part of the soup.

To add any of the following, bring the soup to a boil and then reduce the heat to a simmer as soon as the addition has been made. Stir ➤ raw cereals into soup for the last hour of cooking. For a light thickening, allow to the original amount of liquid approximately:

1 teaspoon barley to 1 cup liquid
1 teaspoon green kern to 1 cup liquid
1 teaspoon rice to 1 cup liquid
1 teaspoon oatmeal to 1 cup liquid
2 tablespons wheat germ flour to 1 cup liquid
2 tablespoons peanut flour to 1 cup liquid
2 tablespoons soya flour to 1 cup liquid
1/2 teaspoon quick-cooking tapioca to 1 cup liquid

If you wish to thicken cooked soup with flour, allow:

1 1/2 teaspoons flour to 1 cup soup

Make a paste of the flour with about:

Twice as much cold stock, milk or water

Pour the paste slowly into the boiling soup, while stirring. Simmer and stir 5 to 10 minutes.

Or, make a roux, 338. To 1 cup soup allow:

1 1/2 teaspoons butter
1 1/2 teaspoons flour

Pour the soup over this mixture, stirring constantly until smooth and boiling.

Or add in the same proportions as above:

Flour and butter

to cooled soup in a ⅄ blender—then reheat the soup. Bring to a boil, lower heat and simmer 5 minutes.

Additional thickenings for soup are dry, crustless French bread or Panades, 179. Also, thick cream or a White Sauce, 341, may be used.

ABOUT OTHER THICKENINGS FOR SOUPS

I. Egg yolks are one of the richest and best of soup thickeners—but they must be added just before serving. ➤ Take care that the soup is not too hot when this is done.
Allow for each cup of soup:

1 egg yolk, beaten with 1 tablespoon cream or sherry

To avoid curdling, it is wise to add to this beaten mixture a small quantity of the hot soup before incorporating it into the soup pot. ➤ When using egg or cream-based thickeners, it is always essential that the soup, after their addition, be kept below the boiling point.

II. Or, allow for each cup of soup:

2 riced hard-cooked egg yolks

Add at the last minute and, of course, do not allow the soup to boil.

III. A good soup thickener, for those whose diet does not include flour, consists of:

3 tablespoons grated raw potato

for each cup of soup. Grate the potato directly into the soup about 15 minutes before it has finished cooking. Then simmer until the potato is tender, when it will form a thickener.

IV. Soups cooked with starchy vegetables ➤ such as dried beans, peas or lentils, will separate and must be bound. To do this, blend:

1 tablespoon melted butter
1 tablespoon flour

with a small amount of:

Cold water, stock or milk

This mixture will thicken about:

3 cups strained boiling soup

Stir in and simmer at least 5 minutes before serving.

V. Miso

This favorite Japanese seasoning, heavy in salt, is used in many dishes as a protein extender. Made from fermented soybeans, which may be combined with rice or barley, it ranges in color and taste from beige and sweet to dark brown and savory. For each cup of clear soup, stir in as it heats:

1 tablespoon Miso

It will hold well, sealed and refrigerated.

ABOUT SOUP MEAT

Any meat that is ➤ immersed in cold water and simmered for a long period is bound to give its best flavor to the cooking liquor. But some food values remain in the meat, and it may be heightened in flavor by serving it, when removed from the soup, with one of these sauces:

Horseradish Sauce, 343
Hot Mustard Sauce, 345
Quick Tomato Sauce, 352
Brown Onion Sauce, 346

ABOUT CLEAR SOUPS

Because so much valuable material and expert time go into the making of clear soups and because they taste so delicious, most of us assume that they have high nutritive value. It disappoints us to have to tell you that, while they are ➤ unsurpassed as appetite stimulators, the experts give them an indifferent nutritional rating. We suggest, therefore, combining them with egg garnishes, 171.

I. For chicken broth use:

Light Stock from Poultry, 523

II. For game broth use:

Fowl, Rabbit or Game Stock, 523

III. For fish broth use:

Fish Fumet or Stock, 524

IV. For vegetable broth use:

Vegetable Stock, 524

➤ Be sure to see Garnishes for Soups, 194.

CONSOMMÉ

Prepare:

Brown Stock I, 522

and clarify it by Method I, 522. This will give you a clear, thin consommé. For double strength, clarify the stock by the second method. Before serving add:

(3 tablespoons Marsala, 56)

CONSOMMÉ BRUNOISE

3 Cups

Make a mixture of the following finely diced vegetables:

1 rib of celery
1 small carrot
½ small turnip
½ small onion

Sauté them gently in:

1 tablespoon heated butter

Enough time should be allowed to let the vegetables absorb the butter, but ➤ do not let them brown. Add:

1 cup consommé

and continue cooking, covered, until the vegetables are tender. Pour the above into:

2 cups hot consommé

Remove fat and:

Season to taste

Just before serving, add:

1 tablespoon finely chopped chervil
1 tablespoon cooked peas
1 tablespoon finely diced cooked green beans

CONSOMMÉ MADRILÈNE

About 4 Cups

Heat to the boiling point and strain:

2 cups tomato juice
½ teaspoon grated onion
2 cups Light Stock from Poultry, 523
A piece of lemon rind
Salt and pepper

Flavor with:

Lemon juice, dry sherry or Worcestershire sauce

Or garnish with:

Cultured sour cream

dotted with:

Red caviar

CHICKEN OR TURKEY BROTH

➤ See the many cream soups, 181, and egg-garnished soups, 171, based on this simple broth. Prepare:

Fowl, Rabbit or Game Stock, 523

or use canned stock. When it is boiling, remove from heat. You may add for each 4 cups:

½ cup cream

Reheat but ➤ do not boil. Serve with Chiffonade of Herbs, 195, or with Dumplings, 202.

CHICKEN BROTH OR BOUILLON WITH EGG

Individual Serving

A good dish for a convalescent, but not to be scorned by those in the best of health.

Remove fat, clarify, and heat:

Chicken Broth, 169
Season to taste

For every cup add:

(1 teaspoon lemon juice)
(1 tablespoon chopped parsley)

When the soup is hot, add:

An egg drop, 171

allowing 1 egg per serving. Serve at once.

POT-AU-FEU, POULE-AU-POT OR PETITE MARMITE

About 10 Cups Broth

A marmite is an earthenware lidded pot, higher than it is wide. Its material accounts in part for the flavor of the soup. This pot is conditioned by boiling clear water in it 12 hours. Traditionally, it is always washed out only with clear water. In pot-au-feu, another name for petite marmite, the major meat is beef, with an addition of chicken wings and gizzards. In making poule-au-pot, a juicy hen—the chicken which Henri IV wanted for every pot—is substituted for the giblets. Marrowbones are usually included, tied in cheesecloth. The vegetables may be seasonally varied. Blanched cabbage is often served as a side dish.

Put into a marmite:

2½ quarts cold water
2 lb. shank or chuck beef, cut into chunks, chicken wings and giblets

Tie in cheesecloth and add:

(1 marrowbone)

Bring this mixture ➤ slowly to a boil and ➤ skim off both foam and fat. Cut Parisienne style, 277, and add:

2 carrots
1 small turnip
3 leeks: white parts only
3 small ribs celery
1 whole onion stuck with 3 cloves
1 teaspoon salt
1 Bouquet Garni II, 572

Bring these ingredients to a boil. ➤ Skim again. Cover and cook slowly about 3 hours in a 350° oven. The bouillon should be clear and amber in color.

To serve, start with the clear soup and offer the meat and vegetables on the side with the marrowbone and:

Small pieces toasted French Bread, 605

BOUILLON

Bouillon is an unsalted strong beef stock, not so sweet as consommé.

Clarify and reduce by one-third:

Brown Stock I or II, 522
Season to taste

Serve with:

A Garnish for Clear Soups, 195

TOMATO BOUILLON

About 3 Cups

Bring to the boiling point and simmer 5 minutes:

3 cups strained tomato juice
½ small bay leaf
¼ cup cut-up celery, with leaves
2 tablespoons chopped fennel
2 whole cloves
1 tablespoon fresh basil
(1 small skinned, chopped and sautéed onion)

Strain.

Season to taste

Serve hot or cold in cups, topped with a teaspoon of:

Whipped cream or cultured sour cream

BEEF TEA

About ¾ Cup

Grind twice:

1 lb. lean round steak or neck bone meat

Place in a quart mason jar and add:

1 cup cold water
½ teaspoon salt

Cover the jar lightly. Place it on a cloth in a pan containing as much cold water as possible without upsetting the jar. Bring the water slowly to a gentle boil and continue boiling 1 hour. Remove the jar. Place on a cake rack to cool as quickly as possible. Strain the juice. Store it in a covered container in the refrigerator until ready to heat and serve.

BROTH ON THE ROCKS

For the guest who shuns an alcoholic drink, offer a clear broth such as:

Chicken broth or bouillon

combined with:

(Tomato and orange juice)

poured over ice cubes. ➤ Be sure the broth is not too rich in gelatin, or it may suddenly congeal.

VEGETABLE BROTH

About 6 Cups

Quickly made and very good. Serve strained or unstrained, hot or chilled.

Chop:

3 cups or more Vegetables for Stock-Making, 524

Sauté them gently and slowly 5 minutes in:

3 tablespoons butter

➤ Do not let them brown. Add:

4 cups boiling water or part water and tomatoes or tomato juice

Simmer the soup partially covered about 1 hour.

You may add:

(1 bouillon cube)

Season to taste

MUSHROOM BROTH

I. **About 6 Cups**

⅄ Blend or chop until fine:

¾ lb. mature mushrooms

Add them to:

6 cups Light Stock from Poultry, 523, or beef consommé

Simmer partially covered about 15 minutes, or only 5 if you have used the blender. Strain, if you like, or thicken, see 168. Serve very hot. Add to each cup:

1 tablespoon dry sherry

II. **About 6 Cups**

Prepare:

¾ lb. diced mature mushrooms
2 ribs celery, diced
½ skinned and diced carrot
¼ skinned and diced onion

Cover these vegetables with:

3 cups water

➤ Simmer partially covered 45 minutes. Strain the broth. Add to make 6 cups of liquid:

Light Stock from Poultry, 523, or beef consommé

Add, if needed:

Salt and paprika

Serve as for I, above.

ONION SOUP

6 Cups

Onion soup, with vegetable stock, fish fumet or water substituted for meat stock, is used for meals *au maigre*.

Sauté until very well browned, but not scorched:

1½ cups thinly sliced onions

in:

3 tablespoons butter

Add:

6 cups beef or chicken broth
¼ teaspoon freshly ground black pepper

Cover and cook over low heat 30 minutes. The soup is now put into a casserole. Add:

(A dash of cognac or dry sherry)

Cover with:

6 slices toasted French bread

The toast should be crisp. Sprinkle over the toast:

1 cup mixed grated Parmesan and Gruyère cheese

Heat in a 275° oven about 5 minutes or until the cheese is melted.

CLEAR WATERCRESS SOUP

About 5 Cups

Simmer together:

5 cups hot chicken broth
1½ cups chopped watercress

about 4 to 6 minutes or until watercress is just dark green—not an olive green. Serve at once.

COLD TOMATO SOUP OR GAZPACHO

About 6 Cups

Chilled clear soup full of fresh vegetables with fresh herbs—a summer delight from the caves of Spain, where it is held cooled. Just before serving, a few cubes of ice are added.

Peel and seed:

2 large ripe tomatoes

Seed and remove membrane from:

1 large sweet green pepper

Peel:

1 clove garlic

Wash:

½ cup or more fresh mixed herbs: chives, parsley, basil, chervil, tarragon

Place all ingredients in a wooden chopping bowl. Chop them. Stir in gradually:

½ cup olive oil
3 tablespoons lemon or lime juice
3 cups chilled consommé or light beef stock

Add:

1 peeled, thinly sliced sweet Spanish onion
1 cup peeled, seeded, diced or grated cucumber
1½ teaspoons salt, or more if needed
½ teaspoon paprika

Some cooks prefer to use their ⅄ blender for the vegetables. Others like to serve the soup unblended with a bowl of additional chilled, finely diced vegetables. Chill the soup about 2 hours or more before serving.

To serve, place in each bowl:

2 ice cubes
1 tablespoon chopped parsley

Add the soup and sprinkle the tops with:

½ cup crumbled dry bread

EGG DROPS FOR CLEAR SOUPS

If your travels have led you to the Mediterranean or China, you probably know the trick of turning a cup of broth into a midmorning pickup or a light nourishing lunch. Our friend Cecily Brownstone gave us these infallible directions for Egg Drops.

I. **2 Servings**

Heat in a quart pan, until boiling vigorously:

2 cups chicken broth or beef stock

Reduce the heat, so the broth ➤ simmers. This means that the bubbles form slowly and collapse below the surface of the liquid. Break into a cup:

1 egg at room temperature

➤ Beat it with a fork, just long enough to combine yolk and white. When the egg is lifted high, it should run off the tines of the fork in a watery stream. Now, with the broth ➤ simmering, hold the cup with one hand, 5 inches above the rim of the saucepan. Pour a little of the beaten egg slowly in a fine stream into the broth. With a fork in the other hand, describe wide circles on the surface of the broth to catch the egg as it strikes and draw it out into long filmy threads. Rather than pour the egg in one fell swoop, break its fall 3 or 4 times, so as not to disturb the simmering. If you have a helper he can pour the egg through a strainer instead of from a cup. Simmer about 1 minute.

Season to taste

Add:

(A generous squeeze of lemon)

Serve at once in hot cups.

II. Greek Lemon Soup **6 Servings**

The egg drops in this Avgolemono do not "flower" so profusely. Heat to a rolling boil:

3 cups chicken broth
¾ cup cooked rice or cooked fine noodles

Beat in a large bowl, just long enough to combine and be uniform in color:

2 eggs
2 to 3 tablespoons lemon juice or wine

Stir in 2 tablespoons of the hot broth; then from on high ➤ gradually, so as not to curdle the eggs but to allow them to shred, pour the eggs into the hot ➤ but not boiling soup, stirring constantly. Serve at once in hot cups.

III. **8 Servings**

A still stauncher mix is made in Germany and is called **Baumwollsuppe.**

➤ Simmer:

4 cups strong brown stock

Mix together:

2 eggs
1 tablespoon flour
¼ cup cream
(1 tablespoon butter)
(Pinch of nutmeg)

Mix and cook as described in I. Serve in hot cups.

IV. **4 Servings**

In Italy a ragged, fluffy drop is made by beating until well combined:

1 egg
1½ teaspoons grated Parmesan cheese
1 tablespoon grated dry bread crumbs
(½ pressed clove garlic)

Stir this mixture rapidly into:

3 cups ➤ simmering consommé

Continue to simmer and stir until egg is set. Serve at once.

HARD-COOKED EGG DROPS

Crush with a fork:

2 hard-cooked egg yolks

Add to them and blend well:

1 tablespoon soft butter
1 raw egg yolk
A few grains of cayenne
A light grating of nutmeg
⅛ teaspoon salt

Form these ingredients into ½-inch balls. Roll them in:

Flour

Cook the drops in ➤ simmering consommé about 1 minute.

SOUP CUSTARD OR ROYALE

These tender drops are used in clear soups. Bake them as for Cup Custard, 734, poured to ½-inch thickness into a well-buttered 9-inch pie pan. Because of their fragile consistency, they must always be ➤ well cooled before handling. Any slight crusting may be trimmed.

Preheat oven to 325°.

Beat well:

½ cup milk or stock
⅛ teaspoon each salt, paprika, and nutmeg
1 egg
(1 egg yolk)

Bake about 25 minutes, then ➤ cool before cutting into dice or fancy shapes. Simmer the soup and drop the royales into it, just long enough to heat them through. Serve at once, allowing 3 or 4 small drops to each cup of broth.

KREPLACH SOUP

About 6 Cups

Prepare:

Noodle Dough, 213

This will make about 20 pastries. Do not allow the dough to dry, however, before cutting it into 3-inch squares. Put about 1½ tablespoons of one of the following fillings in the center of each square, as shown left on the next page.

I. Sauté in:

1 tablespoon vegetable oil
½ cup minced onions
½ lb. ground beef

Add:

¾ teaspoon salt
¼ teaspoon pepper

II. Or combine:

1½ cups minced cooked chicken
¼ cup minced sautéed onion

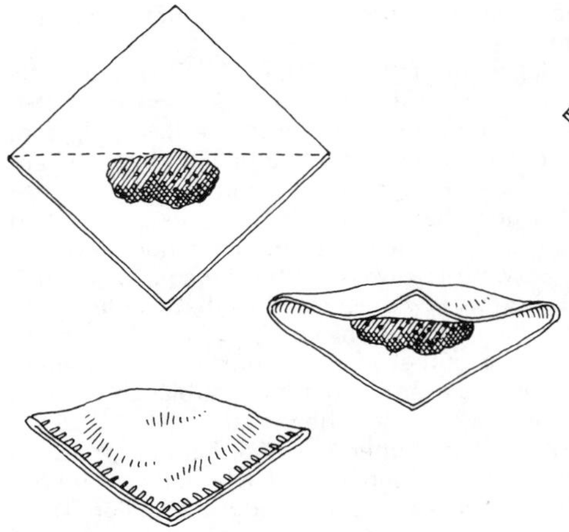

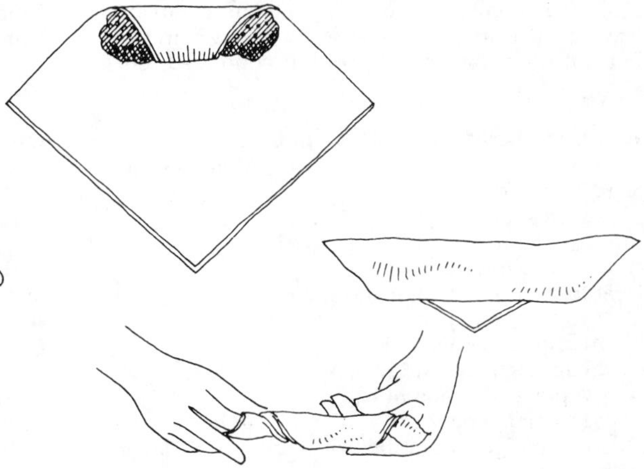

1 egg yolk
¾ teaspoon salt
1 tablespoon chopped parsley

Fold the dough over the filling into a triangular shape. Press the open edges carefully with a fork to seal them completely. Before cooking ➤ allow the kreplach to dry on a flour-dusted towel 30 minutes on each side. Then drop them into:

About 1 gallon rapidly boiling broth or salted water

and ➤ simmer gently 7 to 10 minutes. Drain well and serve in:

6 cups strong broth

WON TON SOUP

About 4 Cups

Prepare:

Noodle Dough, 213

Cut into 3½-inch squares. The fillings may be of cooked pork, veal, chicken, shrimp, crab meat or Chicken Farce, 374.

Combine:

½ lb. cooked meat, see above
2 finely chopped green onions, white parts only
1 cup chopped spinach
1 beaten egg

There are many fancy wrappings for won tons, which in most cases produce a high proportion of paste to meat. If truly Chinese, won tons emerge with a rather loose shape and fluttery outline. Try the one illustrated top right. Place cylindrically shaped filling well above the diagonal. Roll until contained. Insert index finger first in one end and then in the other to give a twist that seals the ends. Cook by putting all the won tons at once into:

About 1 gallon rapidly boiling water

Now ➤ lower the heat to medium. When the water again comes to a boil, add:

2 cups cold water

to temper the dough. About 10 minutes should elapse from the time the won tons are first added to the boiling water until they are ready to serve. Put 5 won tons for each serving into a soup bowl. Sprinkle them with:

(Soy sauce)

Have ready and pour over them:

3 cups seasoned, hot, clear chicken broth or bouillon

A few prettily cut Chinese vegetables or partially cooked spinach leaves with center stems removed usually garnish the broth.

ABOUT JELLIED CLEAR SOUPS

These delicious warm-weather soups may be more highly seasoned than hot soups, but ➤ watch their salt content. If you prepare them in advance, their saltiness is intensified.

Serve with:

A lemon and parsley garnish

You may add to the soup before jelling:

A few drops of Worcestershire sauce

Or allow per cup:

1 tablespoon sherry or 1 teaspoon lemon juice

If you add more lemon juice, be sure you have allowed sufficient gelatin. Stock made from veal knuckle and beef bone may jell enough naturally to be served without added gelatin. We have learned that if canned consommé is from a new pack, it too has enough gelatin in it to respond favorably to mere chilling. If the pack is as old as two years, it must be treated as though it had no gelatin. ➤ Do not freeze it, but try it out by refrigerating for at least 4 hours, to see how much additional thickening it will need. Keep in mind that if too stiff, soup jellies are not very attractive. Allow, if necessary:

1½ teaspoons gelatin

to each:

2 cups consommé or broth

For rapid chilling, you may place clear soups in

a bowl over cracked ice, or give them a start by leaving them in the freezer ➤ for a few minutes but not longer, as intense cold, if continued, destroys the texture.

JELLIED TOMATO BOUILLON

About 5 Cups

Soak 5 minutes:

2 tablespoons gelatin

in:

½ cup cold water

Heat to the boiling point and strain:

2 cups tomato juice
½ teaspoon grated onion
2 cups Light Stock, 522
A piece of lemon rind
Salt and pepper

Dissolve the gelatin in the hot stock. Cool. Flavor with:

Lemon juice, dry sherry or Worcestershire sauce

Pour stock into a wet mold. Chill. The bouillon may be beaten slightly before serving garnished with:

Lemon slices, chopped chives, mint, small nasturtium leaves, chopped olives, hard-cooked riced eggs, relish, horseradish, parsley, watercress or dill

JELLIED BEET CONSOMMÉ

4 Servings

Combine and heat:

1 cup beet juice
1 cup consommé

Add:

1 tablespoon gelatin dissolved over hot water, 560
Season to taste

When about to jell, add:

1 cup minced cooked beets
(1 tablespoon lemon juice)

Pour gelatin mixture into cups. In serving, garnish each cup with:

(1 teaspoon caviar)
A slice of lemon decorated with minced fresh tarragon or basil, or a dab of cultured sour cream

ABOUT THICK SOUPS

Purée, cream, bisque, velouté, potage—to the connoisseur each of these is a quite distinctive embodiment of the indispensable thick soup.

If you like to attach a label to your creations, know that a **purée** is a soup which gets its major thickening from the vegetable or other food put through a sieve or blender and has butter swirled into it at the very last moment. By omitting the butter or lessening the amount of it and adding cream and sometimes egg yolk, you get—guess what?—a **cream soup!** If that soup is on a shellfish base—and only if it is—you may call it a **bisque.** If you add both eggs and cream and a Velouté Sauce, 345, to a purée base, you achieve a **velouté soup.**

Potages, the most variable of soups, are likely to have the phrase *du jour* added, meaning that they are both the specialty of the day and, from the cook's point of view, seasonal and convenient to compose. Potages, which tend to be hefty, taste best when their vegetables are first braised in butter and are then put through a fine sieve before serving. For ways to thicken soups, see 168.

Here are a few practical hints that will help you make the most of thickened soups. Be sure to scrape the purée off the bottom of the strainer. ➤ If you use a ⅄ blender, first parblanch or cook any vegetables with strings, like celery, or skins, like peas. After butter, cream or eggs are ➤ added never allow the soup to reach a boil. If you are not serving at once, heat it in a double boiler. Thick soups should not be served as the first course of a heavy meal. The wonderful thing about them is that they are nearly a meal in themselves. Balanced by a green salad or fruit, they make a complete luncheon.

BARLEY SOUP

I. **About 8 Cups**

A favorite of French farmers. For the best flavor use stock from country-cured hams, but not aged ones like Smithfield, Kentucky, or Virginia.

Melt in a skillet:

2 tablespoons salt pork

Add and cook until translucent:

3 tablespoons diced shallots or onions

Add:

½ cup barley

Agitate the pan to coat the barley well in the hot fat. After about 5 minutes, add:

1 quart hot stock from country-cured ham

Cook the mixture, covered, until the barley is tender, about 1 hour. Bind or not as you like, depending on how rich and thick you want the soup, with:

(3 well-beaten egg yolks)
(1 cup cream)

➤ Heat, but do not boil, after adding the eggs and cream. Before serving, add as a garnish:

2 tablespoons finely chopped parsley
1 cup sautéed, coarsely chopped mushrooms

II. Scotch Broth

About 15 Cups

Soak 12 hours:

½ cup pearl barley

in:

2 cups water

If you use other barley, soak it 1 hour. Add this to:

3 lb. mutton or lamb with bones
10 cups water

Simmer, covered, 2 hours or until the meat is tender. Add for the last half hour of cooking:

2 cups sautéed vegetables, see Consommé Brunoise, 169
(A dash of curry)

Remove the meat from the soup. Dice it. You may use a flour or egg thickener, 168, to bind the soup. Return the meat to the soup. Reheat it.

Season to taste

Serve garnished with:

Chopped parsley

GREEN KERN SOUP

About 15 Cups

If you are English, corn means wheat; if you are Scottish it means oats; if you come from "down under" or are American, you know corn grows on a cob. Kern sounds as though it too might be somebody's word for corn, but it isn't. It's dried green wheat and makes a favorite European soup.

Soak for ½ hour:

½ to 1 cup green kern

in:

4 cups water

Then cook as for Barley Soup II, opposite, replacing the lamb with beef.

VEGETABLE SOUP OR SOUPE PAYSANNE

5 Cups

Place in a large kettle or pressure cooker:

2 tablespoons bacon fat or butter

Sauté briefly in the fat:

¼ cup diced carrots
½ cup diced onions
½ cup diced celery

Add:

3 cups hot water or stock
1 cup canned tomatoes
(½ cup pared, diced potatoes)
(½ cup pared, diced turnips)
1 tablespoon chopped parsley
½ teaspoon salt
⅛ teaspoon pepper

Cover and cook about 35 minutes; then add:

(½ cup chopped cabbage, spinach or lettuce)

Cook about 5 minutes more. If using a pressure cooker, cook at 15 pounds pressure 3 minutes. Remove from heat and let stand 5 minutes, then reduce pressure instantly.

Season to taste

and serve with:

Melba Cheese Rounds, 635

BLENDER VEGETABLE SOUP

About 4 Cups

Blend in:

¼ cup stock
2 cups coarsely cut mixed vegetables

If cucumbers, celery, asparagus or onions are used, blanch them first to soften seeds or fibers and to make the onion flavor more agreeable.

Heat the blended vegetables until tender in:

3 cups boiling stock

Serve at once.

VEGETABLE CHOWDER

About 6 Cups

Cut the stems from:

1 quart okra

Slice the okra. Prepare:

2 cups diced celery

Seed, remove membrane and dice.

1 green pepper

Skin and chop:

1 small onion

Sauté the vegetables 5 minutes in:

¼ cup butter or bacon drippings

Skin, chop and add:

2 large ripe tomatoes or 1 cup canned tomatoes

and:

1 teaspoon brown sugar
¼ teaspoon paprika
4 cups boiling water

Simmer the vegetables gently until they are tender, about 30 minutes. Add, if required:

Salt and paprika

Cooked chicken, meat, fish or crisp bacon may be diced and added to the chowder. Serve with:

Boiled Rice, 206

BEET SOUP OR BORSCH

About 5 Cups

There are probably as many versions of borsch as there are Russians. For good quick versions, see 191.

Chop until very fine:

½ cup pared carrots
1 cup skinned onions
2 cups pared beets

Barely cover these ingredients with boiling water. Simmer gently, covered, about 20 minutes. Add and simmer 15 minutes more:

1 tablespoon butter
2 cups beef or other stock
1 cup very finely shredded cabbage
1 tablespoon vinegar

Place the soup in bowls. Add to each serving:

1 tablespoon cultured sour cream

mixed with:

(Grated cucumber)
Season to taste

and serve hot or cold with:

Pumpernickel bread

CABBAGE SOUP

About 6 Cups

This superb cabbage soup, quick and inexpensive, is from Herman Smith's book, *Kitchens Near and Far.* You will find it, as well as his incomparable *Stina,* most rewarding.

Sauté gently in a saucepan until tender and yellow:

1 large minced onion
1½ tablespoons butter

Grate or shred and add:

1 small head green cabbage: about ¾ lb.

Bring to a boil:

4 cups Brown Stock I, 522

Add the stock to the vegetables. Season as needed with:

Salt and pepper

Simmer the soup about 10 minutes. If you wish, use this delicious topping:

½ cup cultured sour cream
1 tablespoon minced parsley
(½ teaspoon caraway seeds)

Place a spoonful of the sour cream mixture on the top of each serving of soup.

CHICKEN CURRY OR SENEGALESE SOUP

About 4 Cups

Melt:

2 tablespoons butter

Add to it:

1½ to 2 teaspoons curry powder

Stir in, until blended:

1½ tablespoons flour

Stir in slowly:

3 cups chicken broth

When the soup is boiling, season it with:

Paprika

Reduce the heat. Beat:

2 egg yolks
½ cup cream

When the soup is no longer boiling, stir these ingredients into it. Stir over low heat until the egg yolks have thickened slightly ➤ but do not boil. Add also, still not allowing the soup to boil:

½ cup slivers of cooked white chicken meat
(3 to 4 tablespoons chutney)

Serve hot or chilled, garnished with:

Chopped chives

CHICKEN GUMBO

About 12 Cups

Cut into pieces and dredge with flour:

1 stewing chicken

Brown it in:

¼ cup bacon drippings

Pour over it:

4 cups boiling water

Simmer, uncovered, until the meat falls from the bones. Strain the stock and reserve, and chop the meat. Place in the soup kettle and simmer, uncovered, about 30 minutes or until the vegetables are tender:

2 cups skinned seeded tomatoes
½ cup fresh corn cut from the cob
1 cup sliced okra
(1 large green pepper, seeds and membrane removed, or 2 small red peppers)
½ teaspoon salt
¼ cup diced onion
¼ cup rice
5 cups water

Combine these ingredients with the chicken meat and stock.

Season to taste

Classic gumbo recipes then read—

Add:

(1 to 2 teaspoons filé powder, moistened with a little water)

After adding the filé ➤ do not boil the soup, as it will become stringy. Today, we are told filé powder, based on sassafras, is a carcinogen. So, for a similar texture, a tapioca thickening may be substituted. Two tablespoons of quick-cooking tapioca may be added when you start to cook the vegetables.

ABOUT LEGUME SOUPS

Lentils, Beans, Peas

➤ Please read About Dried Legumes, 286.

Some packaged dried legumes do not require soaking. Follow directions on the label. Cook legumes in ham or other stock to which tomato juice or purée may be added, along with ham scraps, bacon or fresh pork fat. Try out the pork, 542. Brown an onion in the fat. The cracklings may be added to the soup or used as garnish. For vegetables and seasonings, see the following recipes.

For easy removal of fat, chill the soup, see 168. Legume soups may be served unstrained, although they are usually more digestible if strained. They may be thinned with stock, tomato juice or milk. Navy bean soup always calls for milk.

Legume soups, whether made of fresh or dried materials, should be bound. See Thickenings for Soups IV, 169.

⊗ We do not recommend the use of a pressure cooker for legume soups.

DRIED BEAN SOUP

4 Cups

If you use marrow beans and add the optional mashed potato, you will have come close to reproducing the famous United States Senate Bean Soup.

Soak, see above:

½ cup dried navy, kidney, lima or marrow beans

Add:

A small piece of ham, a ham bone or ⅛ lb. salt pork
4 cups boiling water
½ bay leaf
3 or 4 peppercorns
3 whole cloves

Cook the soup slowly until the beans are soft, 2½ to 3 hours. For the last 30 minutes, add:

1 diced carrot
3 ribs celery with leaves, chopped
½ sliced onion
(1 minced clove garlic)
(⅛ teaspoon saffron)
(½ cup freshly cooked mashed potatoes)
(½ cup chopped sorrel)

Remove and mince the meat. Put the soup through a food mill, ⅄ blender or sieve. Thin the soup, if required, with boiling water or milk.

Season to taste

Serve with the meat and garnish with:

Croutons, 197
Chopped chives or parsley

BLACK BEAN SOUP

About 9 or 10 Cups

Follow the recipe for Split Pea Soup, below. Substitute for the peas:

2 cups black beans

As this soup is drier, add:

3, instead of 2, tablespoons butter

Just before serving, you may add:

(1 tablespoon dry sherry for each cup)

Serve garnished with:

2 teaspoons deviled or Smithfield ham for each cup
Thin slices of lemon
Thin slices of hard-cooked eggs

BEAN SOUP WITH VEGETABLES OR GARBURE

About 10 Cups

A highly variable soup. Perhaps the most famous version comes from Béarn. It includes preserved goose and is cooked in a glazed casserole. Exotic? It is made in season with freshly hulled haricot beans. Soak overnight:

1 cup dried haricot or navy or fava beans

You may blanch, 154, or not, depending on its maturity:

2 lb. green or white cabbage

Shred the cabbage finely the length of the leaf. Peel and slice:

1½ cups potatoes
1 cup carrots
1 cup white turnips
¼ cup leeks, using white portion only
½ cup onion
1 sprig thyme
(A ham bone)

Place all the above ingredients in a heavy pan and cover with:

Liquid

Use water if you plan to add salt pork; game stock, 523, with game.

Add:

1 lb. diced salt pork or sausage or boneless game or veal

➤ Simmer, partially covered, 2½ hours or until the meat is tender.

Season to taste

Pour the soup over:

Garlic-buttered croutons, 551

MINESTRONE

About 3 Quarts

An Italian soup made with many kinds of vegetables, even zucchini blossoms. Sometimes elbow macaroni or other pasta and sometimes rice is added instead of dried beans. Sweet sausages and smoked spareribs may also be put in at the end. Soak and cook until tender, see 286:

½ cup dried kidney beans
½ cup lentils or chick-peas

Drain the beans. Sauté in:

3 tablespoons olive oil
¼ lb. diced salt pork

When the cracklings are crisp, remove and reserve them. Then sauté in the remaining fat:

¼ cup diced white onion

When the onion is golden, add and continue to sauté briefly:

1 cup chopped Savoy cabbage
1 diced leek
½ cup diced carrots
1 cup diced zucchini or vegetable marrow
1 pressed clove garlic

Remove from heat and add:

½ cup fresh peas
1 cup diced Italian tomatoes
1 teaspoon salt

Have ready:

2 quarts Brown Stock, 522

Add the drained legumes. Bring slowly to a boil. Reduce heat and simmer about 30 minutes. Add the mixed vegetables and continue to cook about 15 minutes longer. Add:

A generous grating of black pepper
Season to taste

Serve garnished with the reserved cracklings and pass:

Grated Parmesan or Asiago cheese

LENTIL SOUP

About 8 Cups

Wash well and drain:

2 cups lentils

Add:

10 cups boiling water
¼ lb. salt pork or a piece of ham or a ham bone

➤ Simmer about 4 hours. During the last hour, add:

1 large minced onion

which has been sautéed in:

3 tablespoons butter
Season to taste

and serve puréed or not, as you prefer. If you purée, bind the soup with Thickenings for Soup IV, 169.

SPLIT PEA OR LENTIL SOUP

About 8 Cups

Try this on a cold winter day.

Wash and soak, 286:

2 cups split peas or lentils

Drain the peas, reserving the liquid. Add enough water to the reserved liquid to make 10 cups. Adding peas again, cook, covered, 2½ to 3 hours with:

A turkey carcass, a ham bone or a 2-inch cube salt pork

Add and simmer, covered, 30 minutes longer until tender:

½ cup chopped onions
1 cup chopped celery with leaves
½ cup chopped carrots

Add:

(1 clove garlic)
(1 bay leaf)
(1 teaspoon sugar)
(A dash of cayenne or a pod of red pepper)
(¼ teaspoon thyme)

Remove bones, carcass or salt pork. Put the soup through a sieve. Chill. Remove fat. To bind the soup, melt:

2 tablespoons butter or soup fat

Stir in it until blended:

2 tablespoons flour

Slowly add a little of the soup mixture. Cook and stir until it boils, then stir it into the rest of the reheated soup.

Season to taste

Serve with:

Croutons, or sour black bread and Jellied Pigs' Feet, 511

⅄ BLENDER SPLIT PEA SOUP

About 1 Quart

Simmer about 45 minutes or until tender:

½ cup split peas

in:

2½ cups water

When slightly cooled, pour into a blender and add:

1 cup chopped luncheon pork sausage
1 small sliced onion
1 diced rib celery with leaves
1 clove garlic
1 teaspoon salt
2 teaspoons Worcestershire sauce
A pinch of rosemary
⅛ teaspoon pepper

Blend until smooth. Return the soup to saucepan to heat. Rinse the blender with:

1 cup water

Add this to the soup and simmer about 10 minutes. Garnish with:

Pieces of crisp bacon
Cultured sour cream

SPLIT PEA SOUP AU MAIGRE

Use the recipe for Split Pea Soup to make either a thick or a thin soup. During the last 20 minutes of cooking, substitute for the fowl or ham bone any clean fish scraps—such as heads, tails and fins.

GREEN PEA SOUP OR POTAGE ST. GERMAIN

About 6 Cups

We never hear the French name of this soup without being reminded of the *New Yorker* vignette of lunchtime at prison—and the disconsolate cry of one of the zebra-striped inmates on the arrival of the inevitable steaming tub: "Aw, shucks, purée St. Germain aux croutons again!" It's a comment you're not likely to hear if the soup is made with fresh peas—which are in fact the first essential; do not try to make it with canned or frozen peas. If you do not have fresh peas, it is better to try the good Quick Pea Soup, 192.

Hull:

3 lb. green peas

There should be about 3 cups hulled peas.

Sauté gently until tender:

1 head Boston lettuce, shredded
1 peeled diced onion
½ cup or more chopped celery with leaves
2 sprigs parsley, chopped

in:

2 tablespoons butter

Add:

2½ cups chicken stock
2 cups of the hulled peas
10 or 12 pea pods
(⅓ bay leaf)

Simmer these ingredients, covered, until the peas are very soft. Put the soup through a food mill or a potato ricer. Simmer until tender the remaining:

1 cup hulled peas

in:

1½ cups chicken stock

Add them to the strained soup. To bind the soup, see Thickenings for Soups IV, 169.

Season to taste

You may color the soup with a drop or two of:

Green vegetable coloring

and serve it with:

Butter Dumplings, 203, or Croutons, 551
(2 teaspoons chopped mint, or 1 tablespoon horseradish and slices of water chestnut)

BOULA-BOULA

5 Cups

➤ Simmer in boiling water until tender:

2 cups green peas

Purée them through a fine sieve or in a ⅄ blender. Reheat and add:

2 tablespoons sweet butter

Add:

2 cups canned green turtle soup
1 cup dry sherry

Heat ➤ but do not boil the soup. Spoon soup into heated cups. Top each serving with:

2 tablespoons whipped cream

Place briefly under broiler. Serve at once.

MULLIGATAWNY SOUP

About 7 Cups

Sauté lightly, but do not brown:

½ cup diced onion
1 diced carrot
2 diced ribs celery

in:

¼ cup butter or tried-out lamb fat

Stir in:

1½ tablespoons flour
2 teaspoons curry powder

Stir and cook these ingredients about 3 minutes. Pour in and simmer 15 minutes:

4 cups chicken or lamb broth
1 bay leaf

Add and simmer 15 minutes longer:

¼ cup diced tart apples
½ cup Boiled Rice, 206
½ cup diced cooked chicken or lamb
1 teaspoon salt
¼ teaspoon pepper
⅛ teaspoon thyme
½ teaspoon grated lemon rind

Immediately before serving, stir in:

½ cup hot cream or coconut milk, 566

OXTAIL SOUP

I. **About 7 Cups**

Brown:

1 disjointed oxtail or 2 veal tails: about 2 lb.
½ cup sliced onions

in:

2 tablespoons butter or fat

Add to the above and ➤ simmer, uncovered, about 4½ hours:

8 cups water
1½ teaspoons salt
4 peppercorns

Strain, chill, remove fat, and reheat the stock. The meat may be boned and diced and added to the soup later. Add to the stock and simmer ½ hour longer or until the vegetables are tender:

¼ cup chopped parsley
½ cup diced carrots
1 cup diced celery
½ bay leaf
¼ cup barley
½ cup tomato pulp
1 teaspoon dried thyme, marjoram or basil

Brown in a skillet:

1 tablespoon flour

Add and stir until blended:

2 tablespoons butter

Add the stock slowly, then the reserved meat and vegetables.

Season to taste

When thoroughly heated, add:

(¼ cup dry sherry or Madeira or ½ cup red wine)

Serve the soup with:

Fritter Garnish, 196, or slices of lemon

II. ⊗ **About 3 Cups**

Brown in a pressure cooker:

1 oxtail, joints separated
1 small diced onion

in:

3 tablespoons fat

Add:

4 cups hot water or ½ water, ½ tomato juice
1 teaspoon salt
2 peppercorns

Adjust cover. Cook at 10 pounds pressure 1 to 1¼ hours. Reduce pressure quickly. Remove the cover. Remove ox joints. Add to liquid in cooker:

1 diced carrot
4 ribs celery, diced

Readjust cover. Pressure-cook the soup 5 minutes longer. Remove fat after chilling the soup. Reheat and:

Season to taste

You may add:

(2 tablespoons dry sherry or tomato catsup)

Separate meat from the joints. Add to soup. Reheat and serve with:

Chopped parsley

PANADES

About 4 Cups

These filling vegetable soups are a very good way to utilize leftover bread. Panades combine well with leeks, celery and sorrel; but leafy vegetables like watercress, spinach, lettuce and cabbage may be substituted.

Cook slowly until soft, but not brown:

1 cup finely chopped celery, leeks or onions

in:

1 tablespoon butter

Cover. If a leafy vegetable is used, add it to the butter, cover and cook slowly until wilted and reduced to about one-fourth. Add:

2 cups hot water or milk
½ teaspoon salt
3 cups diced fresh or dry bread

Stir well and let the mixture boil. Then ➤ simmer ½ hour. Beat it well until smooth with a wire whisk or in a ⅄ blender. Combine:

1 cup light cream
1 egg

Stir this slowly into the hot soup. Heat until the egg thickens but ➤ do not let the soup boil. Serve with:

Chopped parsley
Freshly grated nutmeg

PEPPER POT

About 10 Cups

Cut into small pieces and sauté in a heavy saucepan until translucent:

4 slices bacon

Add and simmer about 5 minutes:

⅓ cup minced onion
½ cup minced celery
2 minced green peppers, seeds and membranes removed
(1 teaspoon marjoram or summer savory)

Wash, cut into fine shreds and add:

¾ lb. cooked honeycomb Tripe, 509

Add:

8 cups Brown Stock, 522
1 bay leaf
½ teaspoon freshly ground pepper

Bring these ingredients to the boiling point. Add:

1 cup pared and diced raw potatoes

Gently ➤ simmer the soup, uncovered, until the potatoes are tender. Melt:

2 tablespoons butter

Stir in until blended:

2 tablespoons flour

Add a little of the soup. Bring these ingredients to the boiling point, then pour them into the rest of the soup.

Season to taste

Shortly before serving, reheat and add:

½ cup warm cream

COCK-A-LEEKIE

5 to 6 Cups

Old recipes for this leek, chicken and cream soup start with a fowl or cock simmered in strong stock, and wind up with the addition of prunes. The following version is delicious, if not traditional.

Remove and discard the dark green part of the tops and the roots from:

6 leeks

Wash carefully—they may be sandy. Cut them in half lengthwise, then crosswise in ⅛-inch slices. There should be about 4 cups. Place in a pan with:

3 cups boiling water
1½ teaspoons salt

Simmer from 5 to 7 minutes or until tender but not mushy. Add and heat to a boil:

2 tablespoons chicken fat or butter
1½ cups well-seasoned strong chicken broth

Reduce heat and stir in:

½ cup cream
Season to taste

Serve the soup at once.

GHANIAN PEANUT OR GROUNDNUT SOUP

About 3 Quarts

Cut up and place in a soup kettle:

A 5½- to 6-lb. stewing chicken
2 skinned whole medium-sized onions
4 pared whole carrots
1 teaspoon salt
2 quarts water

Bring slowly to a boil, then reduce heat and ➤ simmer, partially covered, about 50 minutes or until chicken is tender. Remove the chicken and reserve for other use or cut up into bits to serve in the soup. Strain the stock. Blend together with a small amount of stock:

6 oz. tomato paste
1 cup smooth peanut butter
1 pinch cayenne
¼ teaspoon pepper

Add the remaining stock and simmer slowly until oil rises to the top, about 20 minutes. Skim off the oil, see 168, and add:

¼ cup diced cooked pimientos
Season to taste

and serve hot or well chilled, with or without the bits of chicken.

SAUERKRAUT SOUP

About 7 Cups

Sauté until golden brown:

½ cup chopped onion

in:

3 tablespoons bacon fat

Add:

½ clove minced garlic
½ lb. diced lean pork

Cover and cook over low heat about 20 minutes. Add:

1 lb. chopped sauerkraut
6 cups stock

Cook until soft, about 45 minutes. Melt:

1½ tablespoons butter

Stir in:

1½ tablespoons flour

Stir in slowly a little of the hot soup, blend and return the mixture to kettle. Add:

(1 teaspoon sugar)
Season to taste

and garnish with:

Diced ham or salami

SPINACH SOUP

About 6½ Cups

Pick over, wash, drain thoroughly, then chop fine or blend:

2 lb. tender young spinach

You may use instead 4 cups cooked or two 14-ounce packages of frozen spinach, defrosted and drained. Melt in a saucepan:

¼ cup butter

Sauté in it until golden brown:

¼ cup minced onion

Add the spinach. Stir to coat it well with the butter. Cover and cook gently till the spinach is just tender. ⅄ Blend or put the spinach through a food mill or sieve. Return to pan and add:

4 cups chicken stock
A grating of nutmeg
Salt or paprika

Bring the soup slowly to a boil and serve; or you may serve it cold, garnished with:

Diced, seeded cucumbers or chives and cultured sour cream

NETTLE SOUP

About 5 Cups

Using rubber gloves to protect you from the stinging nettles, remove the central stem from:

1 quart young nettle tops

Have boiling:

5 cups stock

Blend in:

2 tablespoons cooked rice or oatmeal

Add the nettles and simmer about 10 to 15 minutes, during which period any sting from the nettles is eliminated.

Season to taste

and serve.

GREEN TURTLE SOUP

About 8 Cups

It is a timesaver to buy canned or frozen turtle meat. But if you can turn turtles, feel energetic and want to prepare your own, see 393.

Place in a saucepan and bring to the boiling point:

1 lb. green turtle or terrapin meat, cut into pieces
3 cups water
3 cups Brown Stock, 522
1 bay leaf
1 sprig fresh thyme
2 cloves
¼ teaspoon ground allspice
Juice and thinly sliced peel of ½ lemon
A few grains cayenne
¼ teaspoon freshly ground black pepper
½ teaspoon salt
4 whole corianders

These latter pods will rise to the top by the end of the cooking period and can be skimmed out before serving. Simmer the soup, covered, until the meat is tender, at least 2 hours.

Heat:

2 tablespoons vegetable oil

Sauté in this 2 minutes:

2 chopped medium-sized onions

Stir in:

1 tablespoon flour

Add:

1½ cups skinned, seeded fresh tomatoes

Let these ingredients cook 10 minutes. Combine them with the turtle mixture and add:

1 tablespoon chopped parsley
2 minced cloves garlic

You may add a few drops of caramel coloring. Add to each serving:

1 tablespoon dry sherry

Garnish the soup with:

2 chopped hard-cooked eggs
Lemon slices

MOCK TURTLE SOUP

About 16 Cups

This full-bodied, nourishing soup, served with crusty rolls, can be the main dish for any meal.

Cover:

5 lb. veal bones

with:

14 cups water

Bring to the boiling point. Add and ➤ simmer, covered, about 3½ hours:

6 chopped celery ribs with leaves
5 coarsely cut carrots
1 cup chopped onion
2 cups canned tomatoes
1 small can tomato paste: 6 oz.
6 crushed peppercorns
1 tablespoon salt
6 whole cloves
2 bay leaves
½ teaspoon dried thyme

Remove bones and fat. Sauté about 5 minutes in a greased skillet:

2 minced cloves garlic
2 lb. ground beef
2 teaspoons salt

Add the meat to the stock with:

¼ teaspoon Worcestershire sauce
4 teaspoons sugar

Bring to a boil, reduce heat and ➤ simmer about 30 minutes. Blend:

6 tablespoons Browned Flour, 339
1 cup cooled stock

Stir this paste into the simmering soup. Let it simmer 5 minutes more. Add:

2 thinly sliced lemons
1 set chopped, parboiled calf brains, 504

Reheat but do not boil. Serve the soup garnished with:

3 sliced hard-cooked eggs

NEW YEAR'S SOUPS

Served just before parties break up, these are also known as hangover soups, or Lumpensuppe, and are sometimes helpful for the morning after.

I. Onion Soup, 171, with the addition of:
1 cup red wine

II. Lentil Soup, 177, with sour cream and sausage.

ABOUT CREAM SOUPS

These favored luncheon soups are also sometimes served at dinner. In this latter role, they satisfy, as often as not, a functional rather than a nutritional need. Like hors d'oeuvre, they act as a stabilizer for the cocktails that have just been drunk or as a buffer against the wines that are about to come.

For the richest of cream soups—the veloutés—first, sauté the vegetables in butter, purée them and combine the purée in equal parts with Velouté Sauce, 345. Bind with egg yolk, allowing 2 to 4 yolks for each pint of soup. Simpler cream soups may be made on a White or Béchamel Sauce base, 341, or on this quick Béchamel: use 2 tablespoons butter to 1½ tablespoons flour, plus 2 cups cream and ¾ to 1 cup vegetable purée. Should you wish to thin these ingredients, use a little well-flavored stock.

For everyday cream soups, we find we can purée the tender vegetables raw, or cook the more mature, fibrous ones and process them in a ⅄ blender. The soup is served without straining. ➤ If seafood or fowl is blended it tends to be unpleasantly stringy; and the entire soup will need straining before serving.

➤ All cream soups, whether bound with egg or not, are ruined by boiling, so be sure to heat just to the boiling point, or cook them in the top of a double boiler ➤ over—not in—boiling water. Reheat them this same way.

CREAM OF ASPARAGUS SOUP

About 6 Cups

Wash and remove the tips from:

1 lb. fresh green asparagus

Simmer the tips, covered, until they are tender, in a small amount of:

Milk or water

Cut the stalks into pieces and place them in a large saucepan. Add:

6 cups Veal or Poultry Stock, 523
¼ cup chopped onion
½ cup chopped celery

Simmer these ingredients, covered, about ½ hour. Strain them through a sieve. Melt in the top of a double boiler:

3 tablespoons butter

Stir in until blended:

3 tablespoons flour

Stir in slowly:

½ cup cream

Add the asparagus stock. Heat the soup, adding the asparagus tips. Season immediately before serving with:

Salt, paprika and white pepper

Garnish with:

A chopped hard-cooked egg

CREAM OF CAULIFLOWER SOUP

About 8 Cups

Prepare:

1 large Steamed Cauliflower, 297

Drain it, reserving the water and about one-third of the florets. Put the remainder through a food mill, blender or sieve. Melt:

¼ cup butter

Sauté in it, until tender:

2 tablespoons chopped onion
3 minced celery ribs

Stir in:

¼ cup flour

Stir in slowly and bring to the boiling point:

4 cups Veal or Poultry Stock, 523, and the reserved cauliflower water

Add the strained cauliflower and:

2 cups milk or cream

Reheat but do not boil. Add the florets and:

A grating of nutmeg
Salt and paprika

Garnish with:

(Grated cheese)

CREAM OF CELERY SOUP

About 4 Cups

Melt:

1 tablespoon butter

Add and sauté 2 minutes:

1 cup or more chopped celery with leaves
(⅓ cup sliced onion)

Pour in and simmer about 10 minutes:

2 cups Veal or Poultry Stock, 523

Strain the soup. Add and bring to the boiling point:

1½ cups milk

Dissolve:

1½ tablespoons cornstarch

in:

½ cup cold milk

Stir these ingredients gradually into the hot soup. Bring to the boiling point. Stir and simmer about 1 minute. Serve with:

(2 teaspoons chopped fresh dill or 2 tablespoons chopped parsley)

CHESTNUT SOUP

About 4 Cups

Prepare:

1 lb. Boiled Chestnuts, 298

Mash and beat them until smooth in:

2 cups milk

Melt:

¼ cup butter

Add and simmer until soft and golden:

1 minced onion

Sprinkle with:

1 tablespoon flour
1 teaspoon salt
⅛ teaspoon each nutmeg and white pepper
½ cup chopped celery leaves

Stir and slowly add the chestnut and milk mixture. ➤ Simmer about 10 minutes. Pour in:

1 cup cream

Heat ➤ but do not boil. Serve immediately, garnished with:

Chopped parsley
Croutons, 551

CREAM OF CHICKEN SOUP

About 4½ Cups

Simmer:

3 cups Poultry Stock, 523
½ cup finely chopped celery

When the celery is tender, add and cook 5 minutes:

½ cup Boiled Rice, 206

Add:

½ cup hot cream
1 tablespoon chopped parsley
Salt and paprika

➤ Do not boil the soup after adding the cream. For a fresh approach, see Cream of Watercress Soup II, 186.

CREAM OF CORN SOUP

About 5 Cups

Put through a food mill or coarse sieve:

2½ cups cream-style canned corn or 2½ cups corn, cut from the ear and simmered until tender in 1 cup milk

Melt:

3 tablespoons butter

Simmer in it until translucent:

½ sliced medium-sized onion

Stir in:

3 tablespoons flour
1½ teaspoons salt
A few grains freshly ground white pepper
(A grating of nutmeg)

Stir in the corn and:

3 cups milk, or 2½ cups milk and ½ cup cream

Serve the soup sprinkled with:

3 tablespoons chopped parsley or chives
(Grated Parmesan cheese)

CORN CHOWDER

About 7 Cups

Sauté slowly until lightly browned:

½ cup chopped salt pork

Add and sauté until golden brown:

3 tablespoons chopped onion
½ cup chopped celery
3 tablespoons chopped green pepper, seeds and membrane removed

Add and simmer:

1 cup diced pared raw potatoes
2 cups water
½ teaspoon salt
¼ teaspoon paprika
½ bay leaf

When the potatoes are tender, in about 45 minutes, combine until blended, bring to the boiling point, and add to the above:

3 tablespoons flour

and:

½ cup milk

Heat about 5 minutes and add:

1½ cups hot milk
2 cups whole-kernel corn

Reheat but do not boil the soup Serve it sprinkled with:

Chopped parsley

BULGARIAN COLD CUCUMBER SOUP

About 3 Cups

"*Nazdrave*," as the Bulgarians say for "*Bon appétit.*"

Two to 6 hours before serving, refrigerate, covered:

1½ cups pared seeded cucumbers

marinated in a mixture of:

1 teaspoon salt
¼ teaspoon white pepper
¼ to 1 cup chopped walnuts
2 tablespoons olive oil
1 minced clove garlic
2 tablespoons chopped fresh dill

➤ The fresh dill is the essential touch. When ready to serve, add:

1 to 1½ cups thick yogurt or cultured sour cream

Place 1 or 2 ice cubes in each soup bowl. Pour in the mixture. It should have the consistency of chilled borsch. If not thin enough, it can be thinned with a small amount of light stock. Serve at once.

CHILLED CUCUMBER-HERB CREAM SOUP

6 Cups

Pare, seed and slice into a saucepan:

2 medium-sized cucumbers

Add:

1 cup water
2 slices onion
¼ teaspoon salt
⅛ teaspoon white pepper

Cook the cucumbers, covered, until very soft. Put them through a fine strainer or an ⅄ electric blender. Stir until smooth:

¼ cup flour
½ cup chicken stock

Stir into this flour paste:

1½ cups Poultry Stock, 523

Add the cucumber purée and:

¼ bay leaf or 2 cloves

Stir the soup over low heat. Simmer 2 minutes. Strain and chill in a covered jar. Before serving, stir in:

¾ cup chilled cream, cultured sour cream, or yogurt
1 tablespoon finely chopped dill, chives or other herb, or grated lemon rind
Season to taste

Serve the soup very cold.

CREAM OF MUSHROOM SOUP

About 4½ Cups

The flavor of mushrooms is more pronounced if they have begun to color. Prepare for cooking:

½ lb. mushrooms with stems

Sauté lightly in:

2 tablespoons butter

Add them to:

2 cups Poultry Stock, 523, or water
½ cup chopped tender celery
¼ cup sliced onion
2 tablespoons shredded parsley

Simmer, covered, 20 minutes. Drain the vegetables, reserving the stock. ⅄ Blend or put them through a food chopper. Prepare:

White Sauce I, 341

Pour the liquid slowly into the cream sauce, cook and stir until the soup just reaches a boil. Add the ground vegetables. Heat ➤ but do not boil. Season the soup with:

½ teaspoon salt
⅛ teaspoon paprika
(⅛ teaspoon nutmeg)
(3 tablespoons dry white wine)

Serve topped with:

(Whipped cream)

Garnish with:

Paprika
Sprigs of parsley or chopped chives

CREAM OF ONION SOUP OR ONION VELOUTÉ

About 4 Cups

Melt:

3 tablespoons butter

Add and sauté till a golden brown:

1½ cups thinly sliced onions

Stir in:

1 tablespoon flour
½ teaspoon salt

Add:

4 cups milk or cream and Light Stock, 522

Simmer, covered, until the onions are very tender. Add a small amount of hot soup to:

4 beaten egg yolks

Add the egg mixture to the soup. Heat but ➤ do not boil. Season with:

Salt and paprika
Freshly grated nutmeg or Worcestershire sauce

Place in each cup:

1 teaspoon chopped parsley

Pour the hot soup over it.

POTATO SOUP

About 5 Cups

Pare and slice:

2 medium-sized potatoes

Chop:

2 medium-sized onions
4 ribs celery

Sauté these ingredients in:

1½ tablespoons butter

Add:

Boiling water to cover
½ teaspoon salt
(½ bay leaf)

Boil the vegetables until the potatoes are tender, or ⚙ pressure-cook them 3 minutes at 15 pounds pressure. Put them through a ricer or ⅄ blender. Beat into them:

2 tablespoons butter

Thin the soup to the desired consistency with:

Light cream and/or Poultry Stock, 523

Add if required:

Salt and paprika
A dash Worcestershire sauce

Serve with:

Chopped parsley, chives or watercress
1 cup sliced frankfurters or chopped cooked shrimp or diced cooked ham

POTATO SOUP WITH TOMATOES

About 12 Cups

A more sophisticated version of the previous recipe.

Sauté very gently until translucent:

2 cups sliced onions

in:

¼ cup butter

Add the onions to:

2 cups sliced potatoes
6 cups boiling water

Simmer about 30 minutes. Add and simmer, covered, about 20 minutes:

5 cups seeded sliced tomatoes or 3 cups canned tomatoes
2 teaspoons sugar
1 teaspoon salt
⅛ teaspoon paprika
A pinch of chervil

Put the soup through a fine strainer or ⅄ blender. Reheat and:

Season to taste

Scald:

1 cup cream

Stir the tomato mixture into the cream. Serve at once.

VICHYSSOISE OR LEEK-POTATO SOUP

This leek soup may be served hot or very cold. Yes, the last "s" *is* pronounced, like a "z," but most Americans shun it, in a "genteel" way, as though it were virtuous to ignore it. Be sure to serve the soup reduced to a velvety smoothness.

I. About 8 Cups

Mince:

3 medium-sized leeks: white part only
1 medium-sized onion

Stir and sauté them 3 minutes in:

2 tablespoons butter

Pare, slice very fine and add:

4 medium-sized potatoes

Add:

4 cups Poultry Stock, 523

Simmer the vegetables, covered, 15 minutes or until tender. Put them through a very fine sieve, food mill or ⅄ blender. Add:

1 to 2 cups cream
(¼ teaspoon mace)
Salt and white pepper
Chopped watercress or chives

II. About 4 Cups

Superlative! Less rich and made in about 20 minutes by using a ⅄ blender and a ⚙ pressure cooker. Serve it hot or chill it quickly by placing it briefly in the freezer.

Prepare as above:

Vichyssoise

using half the amount of ingredients given. After adding the potatoes and stock, pressure-cook the soup 3 minutes at 15 pounds. Cool. Add:

1 cup pared, seeded and diced cucumbers

Blend covered until smooth, about 1 minute. Place the soup in a jar. Chill it thoroughly. You may add the cream called for above, but you may just like the result as well without it. Hot or cold, serve it sprinkled with:

Chopped chives

PUMPKIN SOUP

About 6 Cups

A flavor that keeps your guests guessing. Place:

3 cups canned or 2 lb. cooked fresh pumpkin

in:

3 cups scalded milk or chicken broth

Knead together and add:

1 tablespoon butter
1 tablespoon flour

Add:

1 tablespoon sugar or 2 tablespoons brown sugar
Salt and pepper
(Ginger and cinnamon)
½ cup finely julienned ham
(¾ cup light cream if you have used the chicken broth)

Heat ➤ but do not boil. Serve at once.

WINTER MELON SOUP

About 4 Servings

In China, the outside of a winter melon is laced with delicate carvings. Steamed with the broth in it, the melon serves as the soup tureen. Although not so appealing to the eye, the following recipe is as appealing to the taste.

Reconstitute in warm water 20 minutes:

4 dried mushrooms, 306

Combine and heat in a large saucepan:

4 cups Poultry Stock, 523
⅓ cup diced cooked chicken breasts
1 cup shelled cleaned shrimp
1 lb. peeled, seeded winter melon cut into 1-inch squares
1 small diced leek
1 diced bamboo shoot
¼ teaspoon grated fresh ginger

and the drained chopped mushrooms. Bring the soup to a boil, cover and lower the heat. Simmer about 15 minutes. Before serving, add:

⅓ cup diced cooked ham

CREAM OF SORREL SOUP

5 to 6 Cups

Also known as **Potage Germiny** and a favorite combination with veal and fish dishes. Because of the oxalic acid in sorrel ➤ use a stainless steel or enamel pan, and do not increase the proportion of sorrel to lettuce as given below.

Clean, shred from the midrib and chop:

½ cup sorrel leaves
1½ cups leaf lettuce

Sauté them until wilted in:

1 to 2 tablespoons butter

When they are sufficiently wilted, there will be only about 3 tablespoons of leaves. Add:

5 cups Poultry Stock, 523
(1 tablespoon fresh green pea purée)

Simmer about 2 minutes. Remove from the heat and add a small amount of the soup to:

½ cup cream
3 beaten egg yolks

Combine all ingredients and heat until the soup thickens slightly ➤ but do not boil. Serve garnished with:

Chopped chervil

CREAM OF SPINACH, ESCAROLE OR LETTUCE SOUP

About 5 Cups

Pick over and wash:

1 lb. spinach or escarole or 1 lb. leaf lettuce

Or you may use:

(1 cup frozen spinach)

Place it, while moist or frozen, in a covered saucepan. Cook about 6 minutes. Drain. Put through a strainer or ⅄ blender. Melt in a saucepan:

2 tablespoons butter

Add and sauté 3 minutes:

1 tablespoon grated onion

Stir in and cook until blended:

2 tablespoons flour

Stir in gradually:

4 cups milk and/or stock

Season with:

¾ teaspoon or more salt
¼ teaspoon paprika
(A grating of nutmeg)

Add the spinach or lettuce. Heat the soup well. Serve sprinkled with:

(Grated Parmesan cheese or sieved egg yolk)

CREAM OF TOMATO SOUP

About 5½ Cups

Simmer, covered, about 15 minutes:

2 cups canned or seeded, skinned, cut-up fresh tomatoes
½ cup chopped celery
¼ cup chopped onion
2 teaspoons white or brown sugar

Prepare:

4 cups White Sauce I, 341

Strain into this the tomato and vegetable stock.

Season to taste

and serve with:

Croutons, 197
Chopped parsley, burnet or basil

If served chilled, garnish with:

Chopped chives or whipped cream and paprika

CREAM OF WATERCRESS OR PURSLANE SOUP

I. **About 4 Cups**

Sauté until just wilted:

1 cup chopped watercress or purslane

in:

1 tablespoon butter

Add and cook gently about 3 minutes:

Salt, white pepper and paprika
½ cup white wine

Remove from heat and add:

4 cups light cream

Heat but do not boil. Serve at once

II. **About 5 Cups**

To:

5 cups hot Cream of Chicken Soup, 182

add:

1½ cups chopped or ⅄ blended watercress or purslane

The latter was Gandhi's favorite vegetable.
Simmer the soup about 5 minutes. Add and stir a small quantity of the soup into:

2 well-beaten eggs

Add this to the rest of the soup, stirring it in slowly. Heat the soup ➤ but do not boil. Serve at once.

An interesting taste variation results by adding:

2 slices fresh ginger

which have been lightly sautéed in:

Butter
Salt

Remove ginger after reheating and before serving the soup.

MILK TOAST OR SOUP

Individual Serving

While not exactly a soup, this dish can bring something like the same cozy comfort to the young or the ailing.
Toast lightly on both sides:

A slice of bread ¾ inch thick

Spread it lightly with:

Butter

Sprinkle it with:

(Salt)

Place it in a bowl and pour over it:

1 cup hot milk

ABOUT FISH SOUPS

Making a broth or fumet of fish, 524, is like making a stock of any kind of meat in that the process toughens the meat. It differs in that it takes a good deal less time. Extraction is limited to a ➤ 20- to 30-minute period ➤ over relatively high heat, instead of the slow simmering recommended for warm-blooded meat. ➤ As a consequence, most fish soups are quick soups. When fisherman's stews are served, the meat is often presented on the side; and in the preparation of delicate bisques based on shellfish, the shrimp or lobsters are often poached separately, then pounded in a mortar or minced before incorporation into a separate stock, cream and egg base.

The original stock may be used as a court bouillon for cooking other fish or reduced for use in *au maigre*, or meatless, sauces. Bisques, as well as oyster, clam and mussel soups and stews, need so little heat that the stock bases are warmed first and the shellfish then just heated through in them, preferably in a double boiler ➤ over—not in—boiling water. Serve fish soups at once. If you must hold or reheat, be sure to do so ➤ over—not in—boiling water.

CLAM BROTH OR SOUP

About 4 Cups

Clams are of various types, see About Clams, 379. The broth is delicious when fresh. It may also be frozen until mushy and served in small glasses or on the shells with wedges of lemon. The meat of the clams themselves may be used in various seafood dishes, 380–381.
Prepare as described on 379, then place in a kettle:

2 quarts clams in shells

Add:

1¾ cups water, chicken broth or tomato juice
3 cut-up ribs celery with leaves
A pinch of cayenne

➤ Cover the kettle closely. ➤ Steam the clams until the shells open. Strain the liquor through wet double cheesecloth to remove any sand. It may be heated and diluted with warm cream or rich milk.

Season to taste

Each cup of broth may be topped with a spoonful of:

(Unsweetened whipped cream)

sprinkled with:

(Chopped chives)

COQUINA BROTH

If you are lucky enough to be on a beach in Florida, collect in a sieve at ebb tide:

Coquinas

the little native periwinkle clams, in their rainbow-hued shells. Rinse them clean of sand, then barely cover with:

Water

Bring slowly to a boil and ➤ simmer about 10 minutes. Pour the broth through a fine sieve. When you imbibe it, remember the advice of an old German who urged, when serving a fine vintage, "Don't gullop it, just zipp it!"

SPINACH SHELLFISH SOUP

About 4 Cups

Sauté until golden in:

3 tablespoons butter
1 tablespoon finely chopped shallots

Add and cook until reduced by one-half:

1 cup dry white wine

Gradually stir in until smooth:

3 tablespoons flour
1½ cups clam or oyster broth
(A pinch of dry mustard)

After the mixture thickens, add and heat but ➤ do not boil:

1½ cups light cream
¼ cup cooked puréed spinach
Season to taste

Serve in ovenproof soup bowls. Garnish each bowl with a topping of:

1 tablespoon whipped cream
1 teaspoon Parmesan cheese

and place the bowls under the broiler about 2 minutes until the cheese browns lightly.

SHE-CRAB SOUP

6 Servings

Steam and remove the meat and roe from:

2 blue she-crabs

Reserve the roe. Prepare a roux by melting in a saucepan:

2 tablespoons butter

Blend in:

1 tablespoon flour

Gradually add, stirring constantly:

4 cups milk or half cream and half milk

When the sauce is heated through, add the crab meat with:

½ teaspoon onion juice
½ teaspoon Worcestershire sauce
⅛ teaspoon mace
Season to taste

When ready to serve, divide the roe and place it in the bottom of 6 heated bowls.
Pour the soup into the bowls. Garnish the soup with:

Freshly chopped chervil

CRAWFISH BISQUE

About 6 Cups

Wash and scrub with a brush under running water:

3 dozen live crawfish

Soak 30 minutes in salted water, using 1 tablespoon salt to 4 cups of water. Repeat once or twice. Rinse thoroughly. Place the crawfish in a saucepan with:

6 cups boiling water
A few grains of cayenne
½ teaspoon salt

Bring to a boil, then ➤ simmer 15 minutes. Drain, reserving the stock. Separate the heads and tails. Remove the fat from the heads. Devein the tails and remove the meat. Clean the remaining foreign matter from 18 heads and refrigerate the meat, the fat and the cleaned heads. Return all remaining heads to the stock. Bring to a boil. Add:

4 ribs celery, chopped
2 tablespoons chopped parsley
½ carrot, diced
⅛ teaspoon thyme or a sprig of fresh thyme

➤ Simmer 30 minutes. Strain, discarding the cooked heads. Meanwhile, prepare the stuffing for the chilled heads. Mince the refrigerated crawfish meat. Sauté until golden:

2 tablespoons minced onion

in:

2 tablespoons butter

Add and cook 3 minutes:

2 tablespoons finely minced celery
1 tablespoon finely minced parsley

Remove from heat and add half the crawfish meat and:

½ cup bread crumbs

Beat and add:

1 egg
Salt and paprika as required

Stir lightly with a fork. Stuff the chilled heads with this mixture. Place them on a greased shallow pan. Dot each head with butter. For 10 minutes, before serving the soup, bake the heads in a preheated 325° oven. Melt:

2 tablespoons butter

Sauté in it until delicately browned:

¼ cup minced onion

Add and stir until lightly browned:

2 tablespoons flour

Add the fish stock slowly, stirring until smooth. Add the remaining crawfish meat and the fat from the heads.

Season to taste

➤ Simmer the bisque about 5 minutes, stirring it often. To serve, place the heated heads in hot soup plates, then pour the bisque over them.

LOBSTER BISQUE

About 8 Cups

Remove the meat from:

2 medium-sized boiled lobsters, see 385

Dice the body meat and mince the tail and claw meat. Reserve it. Crush the shells. Add to them the tough end of the claws and:

2½ cups Poultry Stock, 523, or Fish Fumet, 524
1 sliced onion
4 ribs celery with leaves
2 whole cloves
1 bay leaf
6 peppercorns

Simmer these ingredients for 30 minutes. Strain the stock. If there is coral roe, force it through a fine sieve. Combine it with:

¼ cup soft butter

Blend in:

¼ cup flour

Gradually pour into this mixture:

3 cups heated milk
¼ teaspoon nutmeg

When the sauce is smooth and boiling, add the lobster and the stock. ➤ Simmer the bisque, covered, 5 minutes. Turn off the heat. Stir in:

1 cup ➤ hot but not boiling cream
Season to taste

Serve at once with:

Minced parsley
Paprika

MUSHROOM AND CLAM BISQUE

About 3 Cups

Sauté:

½ lb. chopped mushrooms

in:

2 tablespoons butter

Stir in:

2 tablespoons flour

Stir in slowly:

2½ cups clam broth

Simmer 5 minutes. Remove from the heat. ➤ Heat but do not boil:

¾ **cup cream**

Add to the other ingredients.

Season to taste

and serve with:

Chopped parsley or chives

SHRIMP BISQUE

About 5 Cups

Remove shells and intestines from:

1½ lb. Poached Shrimp, 390

Put the shrimp through a meat grinder or ⅄ blender. Cook, covered, in the top of a double boiler ➤ over—not in—boiling water 5 minutes:

6 tablespoons butter
2 tablespoons grated onion

Add the ground shrimp and:

3 cups warm milk

Cook 2 minutes. Stir in slowly and heat ➤ but do not boil:

1 cup cream

Add:

Salt, if needed, and paprika or freshly ground white pepper
A grating of nutmeg
2 tablespoons parsley or chives

Serve at once.

OYSTER STEWS AND BISQUES

Here are two good recipes which differ in nutritive value and effort of preparation. The first calls for milk and cream and is unthickened; the second, a bisque, calls for milk, cream and egg yolks. To clean oysters, see 375.

I. **About 4 Cups**

Our instructions are foolproof, as the use of a double boiler prevents overcooking the oysters. Combine in the top of a double boiler and sauté lightly over direct heat:

2 to 4 tablespoons butter
½ teaspoon or more grated onion or leek, a sliver of garlic or ½ cup cooked celery

Add:

1 to 1½ pints oysters with liquor
1½ cups milk
½ cup cream
½ teaspoon salt
⅛ teaspoon white pepper or paprika

Place the pan ➤ over—not in—boiling water. When the milk is hot and the oysters float, add:

2 tablespoons chopped parsley

II. **About 4 Cups**

This is a true oyster bisque.

Prepare:

Oyster Stew I, above

Before adding the parsley, remove the soup from the heat and pour a small quantity over:

2 beaten egg yolks

After mixing, add them slowly to the hot bisque. Heat slowly for 1 minute but ➤ do not allow to boil. Serve at once.

MUSSEL STEW

Clean the mussels and remove the beard, 379. Steam them. Strain and reserve the liquor. Use either recipe for Oyster Stew, left, substituting mussels for oysters.

LOBSTER STEW

About 5 Cups

Sauté 3 or 4 minutes:

1 cup diced fresh lobster meat

in:

3 tablespoons butter

Add slowly:

4 cups scalded milk or 3 cups milk and 1 cup cream
2 teaspoons onion juice

➤ Do not allow to boil. A Maine correspondent writes that this stew is much improved by the addition, at this time, of:

(½ cup clam broth)
Season to taste

and serve.

SHRIMP, CRAB AND OYSTER GUMBO

About 8 Cups

Melt:

1 tablespoon butter

Stir in and cook until golden:

¼ cup chopped onion

Stir in until blended:

2 tablespoons flour

Add and stir until smooth:

1½ cups strained tomatoes
4 cups Light Stock, 522, or Fish Fumet, 524
1 quart thinly sliced okra

Break into small pieces and add:

½ lb. shelled, cleaned shrimp
½ lb. crab meat

➤ Simmer these ingredients until the okra is tender. Add:

16 shelled oysters
Season to taste

and serve the gumbo as soon as the oysters are plump. Sprinkle with:

Chopped parsley

Pass:

Hot Boiled Rice, 206

which may be spooned into the gumbo.

ABOUT BOUILLABAISSE AND OTHER FISHERMAN'S STEWS

Necessity is the mother of invention; and convenience gave birth to the can and the frozen package. Use frozen or canned fish, if you must, but remember that ➤ the fragrant, distinctive and elusive charm of fisherman's stew can only be captured if the fish which go into them are themselves freshly caught. Curnonsky reminds us of the legend that bouillabaisse, the most celebrated of these stews, was first brought by angels to the Three Marys of the Gospels when they were shipwrecked on the bleak shores of the Camargue.

Divinely inspired or not, it is true that bouillabaisse can only be approximated in this country, even if its ingredients are just off the hook. For its unique flavor depends on the use of fish native to the Mediterranean alone: a regional rockfish, high in gelatin content, for example, which gives a slightly cloudy but still thin texture to the soup, and numberless finny tidbits, too small for market. We offer a free translation of bouillabaisse into American, realizing fully that we have succeeded only in changing poetry to rich prose.

A similar accommodation has been made for matelote or freshwater fish stew, in which eel, carp, bream, tench and perch are combined with wine. A certain amount of freewheeling must be the rule, too, in concocting chowders and stews of both sea and fresh fish, which are milk-based and often have potatoes added. Whatever fish you use, see that it is as ➤ fresh as possible and experiment with combinations of those that are most easily available.

BOUILLABAISSE

8 Cups

➤ Please read About Bouillabaisse, above.

Have ready:

1/4 cup finely chopped onion
4 finely julienned leeks, white portions only

Squeeze out the seeds, 331, and then dice:

4 medium-sized skinned tomatoes

Combine:

5 minced cloves garlic
1 tablespoon finely chopped fresh fennel
1/2 to 1 teaspoon saffron
2 crushed bay leaves
1 teaspoon grated orange rind
2 tablespoons tomato paste
1/8 teaspoon celery or fennel seed
3 tablespoons chopped parsley
1 teaspoon freshly ground white pepper
1 to 2 teaspoons salt

Heat in a large casserole:

1/4 to 1/2 cup olive oil

When the oil is hot, add the ingredients above and cook until the vegetables are transparent. Meanwhile, cut into 1-inch dice and add:

4 lb. very fresh fish in combination: red snapper, halibut, pompano, sea perch, scallops. Also—all in the shell and well-scrubbed—clams and mussels, whole shrimp and 1-inch pieces of lobster

You may prefer to leave the fish in 2-inch-thick slices and use some of the smaller fish whole. If so, add the thinner pieces or small scrubbed shellfish to the pot slightly later than the thicker ones ➤ but do not disturb the boiling. Cover the fish with:

4 cups hot Fish Fumet, 524, or water

➤ Keep the heat high and force the boiling, which should continue to be rapid for 15 to 20 minutes.

Season to taste

To serve, have already arranged in the bottom of 8 hot bowls:

3/4-inch slices French bread

which has been dried in the oven and brushed with:

Garlic butter

When the bouillabaisse is ready, arrange attractively some of each kind of fish on and around the bread. You may remove the lobsters from the shell and remove the upper shells from the clams and mussels. Then pour the hot broth into the bowls and serve at once. Or, you may strain the broth onto the bread and pass the seafood on a separate platter. Plan the meal with a beverage other than wine.

MATELOTE

8 Cups

Depending upon the amount of stock and wine used, this dish can be either a soup or a stew.

Cook separately and have ready to add as a garnish, just before serving the matelote:

12 small Steamed Onions, 312
1/2 lb. Sauteed Mushrooms, 308
1/2 lb. shelled Poached Shrimp, 390

Now, clean and cut into 1-inch slices:

3 lb. freshwater fish: eel, carp, tench, bream or perch

Cover first the fish that need the longest cooking with a combination of one-half:

Good red wine

and one-half:

Fish Fumet, 524, or meat stock, 522

If you are serving the matelote as a soup, you will need about 3 quarts of liquid, for this will be reduced by one-third later on. Add:

2 teaspoons chopped parsley
1/2 cup chopped celery
1 small bay leaf
2 cloves garlic
1/4 teaspoon thyme
1 teaspoon salt

Bring the mixture to a boil, remove from heat and float on the surface:

2 tablespoons warm brandy

Ignite the brandy, and when the flame dies down, return the mixture to heat, add the remaining fish, cover the pan and simmer the soup about 15 minutes. Now, remove the fish to a serving dish and keep it warm. Strain the liquid into another pan. Reduce the liquid by one-third. Thicken the soup with a Beurre Manié, 340, of:

3 tablespoons butter
2 1/2 tablespoons flour

adding it a little at a time to the hot soup. Bring the soup just to a boil, stirring constantly. It should be creamy in texture, but will go thin if boiled.

Season to taste

To serve, put the fish into soup bowls and cover first with the onions and mushrooms, then with the sauce; garnish the whole with the shrimp. Be sure to serve over:

Sautéed Soup Croutons, 197

MANHATTAN CLAM CHOWDER

About 8 Cups

Chowder should be allowed to ripen refrigerated; it is always better the following day.
Prepare as described, 379:

1 quart quahog clams

Then wash them in:

3 cups water

Drain through cheesecloth. Reserve liquid. Cut the hard part of the clams from the soft part. Chop finely:

The hard part of the clams
A 2-inch cube of salt pork
1 large onion

Sauté the salt pork very slowly. Remove and reserve the cracklings. Add the minced onions and hard part of the clams to the fat. Stir and cook slowly about 5 minutes. Sift over them and stir until blended:

3 tablespoons flour

Heat and stir in the reserved liquid. Prepare and add:

2 cups pared raw potatoes, diced
3 cups cooked or canned peeled tomatoes
(½ cup diced green pepper)
(½ bay leaf)
(¼ cup catsup)

Cover the pan and simmer the chowder until the potatoes are done, but still firm. Add the cracklings, the soft part of the clams and:

3 tablespoons butter

Simmer 3 minutes more. Place the chowder in a hot tureen.

Season to taste

Serve with:

Oyster crackers

You may substitute for the fresh clams:

(2½ cups canned minced clams)

to be added with the cracklings, above. Strain the juice. Add water to make 3 cups of liquid. Use this liquid in place of the water measurement given above.

NEW ENGLAND CLAM CHOWDER

About 8 Cups

Most New Englanders consider the above recipe an illegitimate child. They omit the tomatoes, green peppers and catsup, but pour in:

4 cups hot, ➤ not boiling, milk

after the cracklings have been added. ➤ Do not let the mixture boil. Serve with large crackers.

CONCH CHOWDER

Prepare:

Manhattan Clam Chowder, above

using conch meat to replace the clams. ➤ To prepare conch in the shell, cover:

5 to 15 conchs or large whelks

with cold water and ➤ simmer 20 to 30 minutes. Remove from shell and beat the white body meat in a canvas bag until it begins to disintegrate. Marinate 2 hours in:

¼ cup lime juice

After adding the conch meat to the chowder, simmer 3 to 5 minutes longer than directed for Manhattan Clam Chowder.

ABOUT QUICK SOUPS COCKAIGNE

When we were very young, we were more appalled than edified by *Struwwelpeter*, a book of rhymed fables for children, which had been written in Germany by a Korpsbruder of our great-grandfather. We are still haunted by the story of Suppenkaspar, a little boy who resolutely refused to eat his soup, wasted away for his stubbornness and was buried with a tureen as his headstone. Looking back and taking note of our wonderful present-day battery of canned, frozen and dried soups, we can see that Kaspar was born a century too soon and, beyond a doubt, in this generation would have chosen to live.

We suggest here a process rather than a recipe for achieving very special effects. Mingle canned and frozen soups in your repertory with the vegetable stocks that are precious by-products of daily cooking. And, if you have on hand some leftover bones, lean fowl or meat trimmings, put your ⊗ pressure cooker to work at building a soup base, see Quick Household Stock, 523. Remember in this connection that most fish soups, 186, are quick soups, even when you start with raw materials. There is also the possibility that you are harboring some refrigerator scraps that could constructively respond to ⅄ blender treatment. Before processing, add to them a few mushrooms or a few leaves of spinach, lettuce or cress and a small amount of milk and cream. Lacking these, do not scorn a bouillon cube. And if you have a plot or some pots of fresh herbs, now is the time to commandeer a clipping. Or use parsley lavishly, or dried herbs discreetly.

Words of caution: ➤ Normally, we dilute ready-prepared soups considerably less than their manufacturers recommend, whether we use home-cooked stocks, milk or—less desirably—just plain water. But we find that the more concentrated the soup, the more likely it is to taste oversalted. Test your mix and correct this tendency, see 568. ➤ Be sure, too, if you blend uncooked vegetables, that they are tender enough not to spoil the texture of your soup with stringy fibers or bits of hull. Add to a clear soup a canned consommé or chicken broth, diluted as suggested above, or one of several quickly confected egg drops, 171. If you fancy a more filling dish, serve Blender Borsch, 191, or Quick Cucumber Soup Cockaigne, 192. For other sturdy potages and casseroles, see suggestions in Brunch, Lunch and Supper Dishes, 250. Then perhaps a naïve house guest will say, as did a restaurant diner: "I like your soup du jour, but why is it different every day?"

QUICK CANNED CONSOMMÉ VARIATIONS

I. A clear soup is supposed to be as bracing as a clear conscience.
Add to each serving of consommé, hot or cold:

A slice of lemon, or 1 tablespoon sherry or Madeira, or some diced avocado
A dollop of cultured sour cream

Or add to hot consommé:

Egg Drops, 171, Marrow Balls, 196, or Noodles, 213

II. **About 4½ Cups**

For a cold-day pick-me-up, serve piping hot in mugs; and for a hot-day refresher, serve well chilled in old-fashioned glasses, see 49, garnished with sprigs of fresh herbs.
Mix together:

2 cups tomato juice
1 can condensed consommé
1 can condensed chicken broth
Juice of one lemon

III. **About 3 Cups**

A cool drink with a tropical tang.
Combine and heat:

1 can condensed consommé
1 can condensed Madrilène

Stir in:

The juice of 1 large orange

Serve chilled on the rocks.

⅄ QUICK CONSOMMÉ FONDUE COCKAIGNE

About 2 Cups

Blend together:

1 can condensed consommé
8 oz. cream cheese
1 pressed clove garlic

Chill and garnish with:

Chopped parsley

Pass a bowl of:

Toasted French bread cubes

and dip as for fondue.

⅄ BLENDER GAZPACHO

About 1 Cup

Blend together 2 or 3 minutes:

¼ cup pared, seeded cucumbers
¾ cup skinned, seeded tomatoes
¼ cup condensed consommé or water
½ teaspoon chopped red pimiento

Add and blend for a shorter time:

1 teaspoon to 1 tablespoon olive oil

Add, but do not blend, as the flavor would be too strong:

1 teaspoon chopped chives
Season to taste

and serve by pouring the broth over 2 ice cubes. A good garnish is:

Garlic croutons

QUICK VEGETABLE SOUP

About 2½ Cups

Melt:

2 tablespoons butter

Add and stir until blended:

1¼ tablespoons flour

Add and stir until smooth:

1½ cups vegetable stock

You may utilize the water in which vegetables, below, have been cooked. Bring to a boil and cook 2 minutes. Lower the heat and add:

½ cup cream or stock

Add:

½ cup cooked, diced or strained vegetables
2 tablespoons chopped parsley
(A dash of celery salt)
Season to taste

Heat thoroughly ➤ but do not boil if you have chosen to add the cream.

⅄ BLENDER CREAM OF VEGETABLE SOUP

4 to 5 Cups

Blend:

1 can condensed cream of vegetable soup
1 can condensed chicken rice soup
1 cup canned or strong asparagus stock
(¼ cup cream)

Heat ➤ but do not boil and serve at once.

QUICK CREAM OF ASPARAGUS SOUP

5 to 6 Cups

Combine:

1 can condensed cream of asparagus soup
1 can condensed chicken broth
(1 can condensed cream of mushroom soup)
1½ cups milk

Heat, stirring until smooth.

⅄ QUICK CHILLED CREAM OF AVOCADO SOUP

3 Cups

Combine in a blender:

2 cups condensed cream of chicken soup
½ cup puréed avocado

When ready to serve, stir in:

¾ cup chilled milk
⅛ teaspoon white pepper

Serve in cups, sprinkled with:

1 teaspoon chopped chives or chervil

⅄ BLENDER BORSCH

I. **4 to 5 Cups**

Combine in a blender:

1 can condensed consommé
1 can condensed cream of chicken soup

1 can beets: No. 2½
(1 minced clove garlic)

Half of the liquid from the beets may be drained if a thick soup is desired. Blend until smooth and chill. Serve with a garnish of:

Cultured sour cream and chopped Fines Herbes, 572

II. **About 4 Cups**

Combine in a blender:

2 cups tomato juice
2 cups canned beets
3 small dill pickles
3 tablespoons finely grated onion
1 drop hot pepper sauce
(1 minced clove garlic)

Chill the soup and serve garnished with:

4 thinly sliced hard-cooked eggs
Cultured sour cream
Chopped fresh dill or fennel

QUICK PEA SOUP

About 6 Cups

Combine and bring to the boiling point:

1 can condensed consommé
1 can clear chicken broth
1 can condensed pea soup

Add:

1⅓ cups water or stock
¼ cup finely diced cooked ham
1 teaspoon grated onion
(4 oz. fine Boiled Noodles, 213)
(1 tablespoon Worcestershire sauce)
(1 tablespoon chili sauce)

Simmer, covered, until hot.

QUICK CREAM OF CHICKEN SOUP

Easy to make and very good.

Heat in a double boiler ➤ over—not in—boiling water:

Chicken bouillon
Cream—about ¼ the amount of the bouillon

Add if you wish:

A dash of nutmeg
Chopped parsley

And if you want to be really luxurious add:

Ground blanched almonds—use about 2 tablespoons to 1 cup soup

QUICK CUCUMBER SOUP COCKAIGNE

About 5 Cups

Bring to a boil:

2½ cups strong chicken broth

Drop in about:

1½ cups pared, seeded and diced cucumbers

Simmer until translucent, about 15 minutes. Add:

1 can condensed cream of chicken soup

Again bring to a boil. Now add:

½ cup canned crab meat, shrimp or minced clams
1 teaspoon fresh parsley or chervil

Heat ➤ but do not boil, and serve at once.

QUICK COLD CUCUMBER SOUP

About 5 Cups

Combine in a saucepan:

1 can frozen condensed cream of potato soup
An equal amount of milk
1 chicken bouillon cube
1¾ cups finely chopped pared cucumber

Heat slowly, stirring until very hot and until the cucumber is partially cooked, about 10 minutes. ⅄ Blend or put through a food mill and refrigerate, covered, until chilled. Shortly before serving, stir in:

1 cup light cream

QUICK CREAM OF CAULIFLOWER SOUP

About 3½ Cups

Heat:

2 tablespoons butter

Cook in the butter about 4 minutes:

¼ cup sliced onion
2 minced small ribs celery with leaves

Add:

1½ cups chicken broth
1 cup mashed or riced cooked cauliflower

Heat to the boiling point. Add:

1 cup light cream

➤ Do not let the soup boil after adding the cream.

Season to taste

and serve with:

1 tablespoon chopped parsley
A light grating of nutmeg or a pinch of coriander

QUICK CHEESE SOUP

About 4 Cups

Combine and stir over low heat until the cheese is melted:

1 can condensed cream of celery soup
1 can condensed consommé
1¼ cups water or milk
½ cup shredded cheddar or pimiento cheese

Add:

(1 tablespoon chopped onion)
(¼ teaspoon Worcestershire sauce)

➤ Do not let the soup boil. Serve with:

Chopped parsley

QUICK TOMATO CORN CHOWDER

3 Cups

Combine and heat, but ➤ do not boil:

1 can condensed tomato soup
An equal amount of milk
½ cup cream-style corn
½ teaspoon sugar
(¼ teaspoon curry powder)
Season to taste

and serve.

QUICK MUSHROOM SOUP

I. **About 4 Cups**

Combine, stir and heat:

1 cup condensed cream of mushroom soup
1 cup condensed beef or chicken bouillon or consommé
1¼ cups water or milk

II. **5 Cups**

Reconstitute:

1 oz. dried mushrooms, 306

in:

2 cans condensed consommé

Add:

1 can condensed mushroom soup
1 cup milk

Heat and serve.

QUICK ONION SOUP

About 2 Cups

Heat:

1 can condensed onion soup

Add:

2 teaspoons lemon juice
A grating of lemon rind
½ pressed clove garlic
⅛ teaspoon nutmeg
(¼ cup sherry)
Season to taste

Top each serving with:

Melba Cheese Rounds, 635

QUICK OXTAIL SOUP WITH WINE

About 2½ Cups

Combine:

1 cup water
1 can condensed oxtail soup
1 teaspoon grated onion
3 strips lemon rind: 2 inches each

➤ Simmer these ingredients for 5 minutes. Remove the lemon rind and:

Season to taste

Reduce the heat. Stir in:

½ cup claret or ¼ cup very dry sherry
1 tablespoon minced parsley

Serve at once with:

Toasted crackers

QUICK SPINACH SOUP

About 2 Cups

Combine:

½ cup puréed Boiled Spinach, 326
1 can condensed cream of chicken soup

If the spinach has already been creamed, use instead:

(1 can chicken broth)

You may thin the soup with:

Spinach water, stock or milk
Season to taste

Heat and serve.

QUICK TOMATO SOUP

About 4 Cups

➤ Simmer, covered, 15 minutes:

2½ cups canned tomatoes
¼ cup sliced onion
½ cup chopped celery with leaves

Strain and reserve the tomato stock. Melt:

2 tablespoons butter

Add and stir until blended:

2 tablespoons flour

Add, cook and stir until smooth and boiling:

2 cups Brown Stock, 522, or canned bouillon
½ teaspoon sugar
⅛ teaspoon paprika
The strained tomato stock
Season to taste

and add, just before serving:

(1 tablespoon chopped fresh basil or ¾ teaspoon anchovy paste or a dollop of whipped cream)

QUICK CHILLED FRESH TOMATO CREAM SOUP

I. **About 3 Cups**

One way to use surplus garden tomatoes. Peel, seed and chop coarsely into a blender:

2½ cups very ripe fresh tomatoes

Blend briefly with:

1 cup cream
1 tablespoon parsley
1 tablespoon basil
Season to taste

Chill and serve with:

Lemon slices

II. **About 3 Cups**

Combine in a cocktail shaker:

2 cups chilled tomato juice
1 cup chilled cream
4 or more ribs raw celery, grated
1 teaspoon grated onion
A few drops hot pepper sauce
A few grains cayenne

Or, you may omit the onion and use:

(¼ teaspoon dry ginger)
(⅛ teaspoon allspice)
Season to taste

and add:

¼ cup chopped ice

Shake well.

QUICK CLAM AND CHICKEN BROTH

Combine equal parts of:

Clam broth
Chicken stock

If the clam broth is very salty, you may have to use more chicken stock or water. Season lightly with:

White pepper

When the soup reaches a boil, remove from heat and place in hot cups. Top each cup with:

1 tablespoon whipped cream

Have the cream at room temperature. For color, sprinkle the top with:

Paprika or chopped chives or parsley

Serve at once.

QUICK CRAB OR LOBSTER MONGOLE

About 4 Cups

Sprinkle:

3 tablespoons dry white wine or
1 teaspoon Worcestershire sauce

over:

1 cup flaked canned crab or lobster

Combine and heat to the boiling point:

1 can condensed cream of tomato soup
1 can condensed cream of green pea soup

Stir the above mixture slowly into:

1¼ cups hot light cream or part cream and part bouillon

Add the crab. Heat the soup ➤ but do not let it boil.

QUICK LOBSTER SUPREME

About 5 Cups

Combine and heat:

1 can condensed asparagus soup
1 can condensed cream of mushroom soup
3 tablespoons dry sherry

Add:

2 cups light cream

Pick over and add:

6 to 8 oz. canned lobster meat

Heat this soup ➤ but do not let it boil.

QUICK LOBSTER CHOWDER

About 8 Cups

An easy-to-get soup meal.

Sauté in a saucepan about 5 minutes:

¼ cup finely diced onion
½ cup finely diced celery

in:

2 tablespoons butter

Add:

1½ cups water
1 small bay leaf
1 package frozen mixed vegetables, defrosted

➤ Cover and bring to a boil. Cook the vegetables until barely tender, about 5 minutes. Remove the bay leaf. Drain, but reserve the liquor from:

1 can chopped broiled mushrooms: 3 oz.

Stir into the liquor until smooth:

1 tablespoon cornstarch

Add this to the mixture in the saucepan, stirring constantly until it thickens. Add the drained mushrooms and:

1 cup tomato sauce
2 cups milk
1 cup canned lobster
Season to taste

and heat slowly ➤ but do not boil. Serve with an assortment of:

Cheese

or, as they do in France, with:

Crusty bread and sweet butter

QUICK SEAFOOD TUREEN

About 6 Cups

Melt in a saucepan:

¼ cup butter

Add:

2 cups flounder fillets, cut into pieces
1½ cups dry white wine

➤ Cover and simmer about 10 minutes. Add:

1 cup cooked shrimp
1 cup cooked lobster meat
1 small can sliced mushrooms
1½ cups condensed cream of mushroom soup
2 tablespoons chopped canned pimientos
1 crushed clove garlic
⅛ teaspoon saffron

Simmer about 5 minutes longer. Add:

(½ cup dry sherry)
Season to taste

Serve in a tureen with:

Buttered toast or French bread

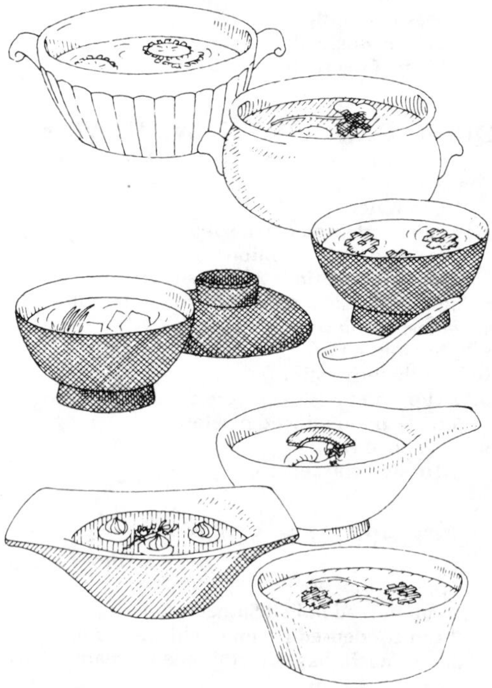

ABOUT GARNISHES FOR SOUP

Adding marrow balls instead of a chiffonade of cress to the same clear soup can change the temper of a meal. Scan the parade of breads and garnishes below to determine your pace-setter du jour. If serving an informal buffet, arrange a group of garnishes around a tureen to give your guests a choice among rich, lean or green. Whip up some satisfying dumplings, 202, for hungry children or pass a rice ring. Tempt a finicky appetite with an egg drop, 171. ➤ Be sure none of the garnishes is chilled, unless the soup is an iced one.

To turn individual servings into added visual and taste treats, decorate soup bowls as illustrated or as described below. The most popular soup garnish for clear or thick soups is lemon—shown first, with a notch-edged slice. For other lemon cuts, see 571. Flowers such as calendula and nasturtium lend color to pale cream soups; a small nasturtium and its piquant leaf floated on vichyssoise are shown next. Japanese clear broths are endlessly fascinating with their bits of vegetables and greens swirling across the top. Usually minimal in material like the turnip rosettes shown next, or the tofu barge with its herb cargo, they add inexpressible charm. Strengthen the color of a shrimp bisque with a whole shrimp garnished with an avocado slice and parsley. Float on a spinach soup tiny raw mushroom caps filled with sour cream amid a few sprigs of young burnet. Or as shown next, carved-carrot flowers with stems made of blanched chives.

FOR CLEAR SOUPS

Drop into the soup:

Thin slices of lemon or orange
Thin slices of avocado drenched in lemon
Minced parsley, chives, watercress, onion, mint, basil or chervil floated on the surface or concentrated on a dab of whipped cream
Podded or snow peas
Thin slices of cooked root: parsley, chervil or celeriac
Consommé Brunoise, 169
Cucumber balls
Noodles, 213
Gnocchi, 204
Won Ton, 213
Kreplach, 213
Dumplings, see many varieties, 202 and 205
Ravioli, 216
Farina Balls, 203
Spätzle, 205
Nockerln, 203
Quenelles, 205
Meatballs, Marrow Balls, Sausage Balls, 196
Cheese Balls, 197
Pesto, 570
Bean Curd or Tofu, 535
Bean Sprouts, 565

FOR CREAM SOUPS

Garnish with:

Salted whipped cream or sour cream and a dusting of finely chopped mixed herbs
Chiffonade of Herbs for Soup, right
Blanched, shredded, toasted almonds or cashews
Flavored popcorn or puffed cereals

FOR THICK SOUPS

Use:

Thin slices of orange, lemon or lime
Sliced small sausages or thin slices of hard sausages
Sliced hard-cooked eggs
Croutons, 197 and 551
Sour cream
Meatballs, 196
Gnocchi, 204
Julienned strips of ham, tongue, chicken or bits of seafood
Grated cheeses
Pesto, 570

BREADS TO SERVE AS A SIDE DISH WITH SOUPS

Fancy shapes in toasted white, rye or whole wheat
Melba toast, 636
Toasted rye sticks
Plain or toasted garlic bread, 636, or other herbed breads
Crackers, hot and plain or spread with herb butters, cheese spreads or fish pastes
Cheese Wafers or Straws, 641
Pastry Snails, 69
Hush Puppies, 629
Corn Dodgers, 628, or Zephyrs, 628
Croutons, 197 and 551
Small Choux Paste Puffs, 646
Rissoles, 69
Turnovers, 69
Seeded Crackers, 636

CHIFFONADE OF HERBS FOR SOUPS

For a chiffonade, always use the freshest and most tender of greens—being sure ➤ to remove stems and coarse midribs of lettuce, sorrel or parsley—alone or in combination with whatever fresh herbs you have on hand that are compatible with the flavor of your soup. Allow:

1 or 2 tablespoons fresh herbs or greens

to:

1 pint soup

Add the herbs to a small quantity of broth and chop in a ⅄ blender until fine. Combine the blended herbs with the remaining broth. If you have no blender, mince a combination of herbs very, very fine.

CHOUX PASTE GARNISH

About 1½ Cups

For either of these garnishes, you may add:

(4 to 6 tablespoons grated Parmesan cheese)

to the dough.

I. Use a pastry bag with a ¼-inch-diameter tube. Fill with:

Unsweetened or cheese-flavored Choux Paste, 646

Squeeze onto a greased baking tin pea-sized bits of dough. Bake in a preheated 400° oven about 10 minutes. Add these to the soup the instant before serving.

II. Fill a pastry bag with:

Unsweetened Choux Paste, 646

Make 1-inch rounds. Flatten carefully with a moistened finger any points remaining after the bag is lifted off. Glaze with:

French Egg Wash, 731

Bake in a preheated 400° oven about 10 minutes. Be sure the puffs are well dried out before removing them from the oven. ➤ Fill them, the last minute before serving, with a farce that combines well with the soup. ➤ Place in soup the instant before serving to avoid sogginess.

FRITTER GARNISH

About ¾ Cup

➤ Please read About Deep-Fat Frying, 147.

Beat until light:

1 egg

Add:

¼ teaspoon salt
⅛ teaspoon paprika
½ cup flour
2 tablespoons milk

Drop the batter through a colander into deep fat heated to 365°. Fry until the garnish is brown. Drain on paper toweling. Place in the soup just before serving.

LIVER DUMPLINGS OR LEBERKLÖSSE

Please read About Dumplings, 202.

Being the descendants of South Germans, we cannot well compile a cookbook without including a recipe typical of that neck of the woods—not exactly a handsome dish, but it has qualities.

I. **About 3 Cups**

Skin and remove the fiber from:

1 lb. calf liver or chicken livers

Grind or chop until very fine. Slightly frozen liver is easy to grind. Soak in water 3 minutes, then wring the water from:

2 slices white bread

Mix bread and liver thoroughly, then add and beat:

2 egg yolks
¼ cup soft butter
2 teaspoons chopped onion
2 tablespoons chopped parsley
1½ teaspoons salt
½ teaspoon pepper
2 tablespoons flour

Beat until stiff ➤ but not dry, then fold in:

2 egg whites

Shape this mixture into 1½-inch balls. Drop them into gently boiling soup or stock. ➤ Simmer 5 or 6 minutes. Serve them with the soup.

II. LIVER SAUSAGE DUMPLINGS

About 1 Cup

Combine and work with a fork:

¼ lb. liver sausage
½ egg or 1 egg white or yolk
½ cup cracker crumbs
1 tablespoon chopped parsley or chives
(1 tablespoon catsup)

Shape the mixture into 1-inch balls. ➤ Simmer gently about 2 minutes in soup stock.

MEATBALLS FOR SOUP

A superb main dish may be had by adding these to vegetable soup. Make up half the recipe for:

German Meatballs, 489

You may use more bread if desired. Mix the ingredients lightly with a fork. Shape them without pressure into 1-inch balls and drop into boiling soup or stock. ➤ Simmer them until done, about 10 minutes.

SAUSAGE BALLS FOR SOUP

About 1½ Cups

Good in pea, bean or lentil soup. Combine:

½ lb. raw sausage meat
1 egg white
2 teaspoons chopped parsley
½ teaspoon fresh basil
¼ teaspoon fresh rosemary
3 tablespoons toasted bread crumbs

Roll this mixture into 1-inch balls. Drop them into boiling stock. Reduce the heat at once and ➤ simmer the soup until the balls are done, about 30 minutes. Skim the fat from the soup before serving.

MARROW BALLS

About ¾ Cup

These delicate drops may be prepared several hours in advance and refrigerated.

Combine and beat until creamy:

¼ cup fresh marrow
2 tablespoons butter

Add:

3 egg yolks
¼ teaspoon salt
⅛ teaspoon paprika
2 tablespoons chopped parsley
Cracker crumbs

Use at least ½ cup cracker crumbs to make the mixture of a stiff consistency to shape into balls with:

3 stiffly beaten egg whites

Cook the balls in ➤ simmering soup about 15 minutes or until they rise to the surface.

CHEESE BALLS FOR SOUP

About 1½ Cups

Combine:

2 beaten egg yolks
2 tablespoons grated cheese, preferably Parmesan
2 tablespoons dry bread crumbs
⅛ teaspoon paprika
½ teaspoon dried herbs or 1 teaspoon chopped fresh chives or parsley

Beat until stiff ➤ but not dry, then fold in:

2 egg whites
⅛ teaspoon salt

Drop the batter from a spoon into ➤ simmering soup. Simmer only 1 or 2 minutes.

SOUP CROUTONS

For other croutons, see 551.

To retain the crispness of these ever-popular diced toasts, serve them in individual dishes and let the guests add them to their soup. Or, use them diced small, so they are much like buttered toasted crumbs, to garnish spinach, noodles or game. They may be flavored by sautéing in:

Butter and olive oil

or dusting them with:

Grated cheese

while still hot.

CEREALS AND PASTAS

On a train trip from Palermo to Syracuse, a stranger leaned toward us to say in the most casual tones that this was the field from which Pluto abducted Proserpina and rushed her to his dark abode. True or false, this brought to mind the lamentations of her mother, Ceres, and the surprises in store for her should she survey her domain today. She might rightly mourn that her noble way of grinding grain between stones is scorned, and, instead, grains divested of their rich germs are mercilessly swirled and crushed between high-speed hot rollers. But she might rejoice in some of the new higher protein hybrids, 4, and the fact that four-fifths of the world now relies on grains for nourishment. There are some recent discoveries in cereal research, both in plant breeding and in the combining of cereals when serving, that we cannot help but feel are hopeful for man's future. Cereals—including the high-durum wheats—when eaten alone lack certain essential aminos present in complete-protein foods, 2. But they do contain varying amounts of incomplete-protein elements, and when cereals are skillfully combined, 2, or are served with the addition of meat, fish, egg, cheese or soy products, the protein elements of the cereal itself are enhanced. Note that such combinations have for centuries been instinctively and skillfully used in lands where cereals form the overwhelming staple of the diet. Without benefit of science, the Orientals have realized the importance of incorporating into rice bits of seafood or soybean substances; the North Africans add to their couscous morsels of meat or fish; and in Italy a thousand forms of pasta based on high-durum wheat have proliferated since the days of Ceres, and are customarily served with sauces or fillings containing meat, seafood or cheese. From Italy, too, come fanciful and melodic names: fettucine, lasagne, macaroni, mostaccioli, spaghetti, linguine, vermicelli. The glass jars shown above contain a few of these, with a ravioli roller in the foreground. To cook pastas, see 212; for the rice ring, left, see 207.

In America, ready-to-eat cereals, our classic morning eye-openers, are found in mountainous piles of boxes in every supermarket and are shouted about daily from the mountaintops on TV. They are either exploded into puffs under high steam, pressed and dried in myriad forms from moist pastes, or malted, sugared and shattered into flakes. You pay as much for all this processing and for the expensive packaging to retain crispness as you pay for the cereals themselves. It takes more time to cook whole grains yourself or to make up cereal snacks, see below, but there is no question of the increased nutritive value and economy.

All cereals should be stored covered against insect or rodent infestation and moisture absorption. Raw whole cereals also require storage in a cool place, as even mild heat promotes development of rancidity. Some cereals like rice and oats are sold partially precooked to destroy the enzymes that hasten spoilage. If using precooked cereals, finish the cooking according to the directions on the label.

ABOUT COLD WHOLE-GRAIN MIXTURES AND SNACKS

Grain combinations supplemented with seeds, nuts and dried fruits—raisins, dates, prunes and apricots—for their iron content, and fruit sugar for sweetening, have long been popular in health and vegetarian circles and prized by campers and climbers for their high energy potential. Snackers love them for their delicious flavors but must watch their intake because of the heavy caloric content. If the grains are toasted before being added to the other ingredients, the mix is often called **granola;** and if the grains are mixed raw the term is usually **müsli,** see 199. There is some vitamin loss in the toasting, but some people find the untoasted grains indigestible. Whatever mixture you decide suits your taste, balance it by drinking milk or eating cheese with it; or include enough soybean substances, milk solids and wheat germ to furnish adequate complete protein, 2.

GRANOLA

I. **About 6 Cups**

Preheat oven to 300°.

Stirring frequently, toast in a 13 x 9-inch pan 10 minutes:

1 cup buckwheat groats

Add and continue to stir frequently for 15 minutes:

1 cup rolled oats or cornmeal
1 cup wheat flakes

mixed with:
½ cup heated vegetable oil
Add:
½ cup sesame seeds
½ cup hulled sunflower seeds
1 cup coarsely chopped almonds, pine nuts or walnuts
Stir and toast 10 minutes longer. Remove from oven and add:
½ cup wheat germ
1 cup chopped dates or apricots
Store covered and refrigerated. Serve with:
Milk or yogurt

II. **About 7 Cups**
A sweetened version.
Preheat oven to 300°.
Scatter in a 13 x 9-inch pan and toast about 15 minutes, stirring frequently:
3 cups rolled oats
Mix in a large bowl:
1½ cups wheat germ
½ cup dry milk solids
1 cup coarsely chopped almonds
1 cup shredded or flaked coconut
½ cup sesame seeds
1 cup hulled sunflower seeds
Heat slowly and combine with the above:
½ cup vegetable oil
½ cup honey or maple syrup
Combine with the toasted oats and spread thinly in the pan, continuing to toast and to stir frequently another 15 minutes or until the ingredients are all toasted. Cool and store tightly covered and refrigerated.

III. **About 10 Cups**
An easier formula but with somewhat more loss of nutrient value.
Preheat oven to 300°.
Heat slowly in a 9 x 13-inch pan:
½ cup vegetable oil
½ cup honey or molasses
Mix into the oil and honey:
3 cups rolled oats
½ cup rye flakes
2 cups wheat germ
1 cup hulled sunflower seeds
½ cup sesame seeds
2 cups coarsely chopped mixed nuts: pecans, hazelnuts or peanuts
1 cup dry milk solids
½ cup soy flour
Toast about 35 minutes, stirring frequently. Remove from oven and mix in:
1 cup raisins
Cool and store as above.

MÜSLI OR SWISS OATMEAL

4 Servings

Soak overnight covered:
1 cup rolled oats
(¼ teaspoon salt)
1 cup boiling water
Before serving, combine the oat and water mixture with:
2 to 3 tablespoons honey
½ cup raisins
¼ cup chopped pitted prunes
¼ cup chopped dried apricots
⅓ cup chopped nuts
½ cup grated apple
2 tablespoons lemon juice
Serve with:
Milk or cream

ABOUT COOKING CEREALS

Scientists tell us that cereals are edible as soon as the starch granules have swollen to their full capacity in hot liquid. This state they speak of glibly as gelatinization, although it remains something of a chemical mystery. To cooks, this phenomenon is evident in the thickening of cereals and sauces. While the technical-minded insist that the starch and protein in cereals are adequately cooked in a short period of time, many cooks claim that the results are not so nutty and sweet as when the older, slow-heat methods are used. Whether you back the cook or the scientist, on these points they agree: cereals must be added ➤ slowly to ➤ sufficient rapidly boiling water and ➤ stirred in, so that each individual grain is surrounded and quickly penetrated by the hot liquid. The boiling point of the water ➤ 212°, must be maintained throughout as the cereal is added. If you cook cereals or starches in an acid liquid like fruit juice, the thickening power is lowered.

With cereals that tend to gumminess, this slow addition to the boiling water allows the outer starch layers to stabilize and keeps the granules separated after swelling. The cereal is done when it looks translucent. The granules should still be separated, retaining their individual shape even though they are soft. Serve at once.

Cereals increase in bulk depending on the amount of water they absorb. You may count 4 to 6 servings for each cup of uncooked cereal. For particulars see equivalents, 593. If you cook cereal in advance of serving ➤ cover it at once while it is still hot from the first cooking, so no crust forms on the top. If you plan to use it more than an hour after the first cooking, refrigerate it. ➤ To avoid lumps on reheating, place the cereal over—not in—boiling water and allow the cereal to heat thoroughly before stirring.

To make a **gruel** for the baby or an invalid, cook the cereal with 3 times the amount of water or milk called for and cook twice as long. Strain and serve.

To cook finely ground, coarsely ground, and whole-grain cereals, see 200. For more details about some individual cereals, see Ingredients, 593.

FINELY MILLED CEREALS

About 4 to 6 Servings

➤ Please read About Cooking Cereals, 199. To prepare fine-granule cereals, have water boiling in the bottom of a double boiler. In the top of the boiler, over direct heat, bring to a rolling boil:

4 to 6 cups water or milk or a mixture of both
1 teaspoon salt

Use the lesser amount of water for finest grains. Very slowly, ➤ without disturbing the boiling point, sprinkle into the liquid:

1 cup dry cornmeal, farina or hominy grits

Continue to cook over direct heat 2 to 3 minutes, then cook over—not in—boiling water 5 to 20 minutes. To avoid gumminess ➤ do not stir. During the last few minutes of cooking, you may fold in:

3 tablespoons dry skim-milk solids
2 teaspoons Nutritional Yeast, 554

for each cup dry cereal. These ingredients make no noticeable change in taste and are a great addition in food value. You may at this time also add:

Dates, figs, raisins or cooked dried fruits

Or serve with:

Cold or hot sliced canned or fresh fruits
A cinnamon-sugar mixture
Sugar and cream
Maple syrup
Jams and preserves

COARSELY MILLED AND WHOLE CEREALS

About 4 to 6 Servings

Coarsely ground or cracked grains have many different names, but all are cooked the same way. The wheats, whole-grain and cracked, also include **triticale,** 548, and **bulgur,** a parboiled, dried and cracked whole-grain wheat. **Groats** may be **cracked wheat, buckwheat** or **oats.** Coarsely ground **buckwheat, barley** or **millet** is also called **kasha.** Millet can replace rice in most recipes. **Cracked corn** is called **samp. Coarse oats** come in a number of forms, steel-cut or rolled. It is best to presoak all these cereals, covered, from 4 to 8 hours. To cook, use:

2 to 4 cups water, milk or fruit juice
1 teaspoon salt

for every:

1 cup dry cereal

Use the lesser amount of water for finer grains. Using the same method as given above for Finely Milled Cereals, cook, covered, 40 to 60 minutes or until translucent and tender.

HOMINY

Yield 1 Quart

Hominy is corn with the hull and germ removed. In an attempt to give it calcium values, it is sometimes also soaked in wood ash lye It has recently gained favor as an antistrontium absorbent. Hominy can be dried and ground into a coarse flour for baking, cooked as a cereal, or used in any recipe calling for corn. **Hominy grits,** also called **corn grits,** are the broken grains.

To prepare hominy from corn, shell and wash:

1 quart dried corn

Put it into an enamel or stainless steel pan. Cover with:

2 quarts water

Add:

2 tablespoons baking soda

Cover the pan and let this mixture sit 12 hours. Then bring it to a boil in the liquid in which it has soaked. Simmer about 3 hours or until the hulls loosen. If necessary, add water. Drain and plunge into cold water. Rub corn until hulls are removed. Bring to a boil in:

2 quarts cold water

Drain and rub again. Repeat this boiling process again in fresh water, adding:

1 teaspoon salt

Drain once more and serve. Season with:

Melted butter

BAKED HOMINY

I. With Ham — **4 Servings**

Preheat oven to 375°.

Combine:

½ cup water
1 can condensed tomato soup

Or you may use:

(2 cups White Sauce I, 341)

Add:

1 cup diced cooked ham
½ teaspoon salt
½ teaspoon sugar
⅛ teaspoon paprika or pepper

Drain and add:

2½ cups canned or cooked hominy, above

Heat these ingredients. Combine:

1 cup soft bread crumbs
1 cup shredded cheese
⅛ teaspoon paprika
¼ teaspoon salt

Place half the hominy mixture in a greased baking dish; cover it with half the bread mixture. Dot the top with:

1 tablespoon butter

Repeat the process. Bake until the top is brown, about 12 minutes.

II. With Bacon — **6 Servings**

Preheat oven to 400°.

Combine and place in a greased baking dish:

2 cups drained, cooked hominy, above
1 cup Cheese Sauce, 342
½ cup minced green pepper, seeds and membrane removed

Cover the top with:

Strips of bacon

Bake about 20 minutes.

HOMINY GRITS CHEESE CASSEROLE

Preheat oven to 325°.
Bring to a boil:
1 cup quick-cooking hominy grits
3 cups milk
1 teaspoon salt
Add and cook until thickened:
2 beaten eggs
3/4 cup milk
Stir in and blend well:
1 cup shredded cheddar or garlic-flavored cheese
1/2 cup butter
(1/4 cup chopped chives)
Bake in a buttered baking dish 45 to 50 minutes. Serve hot.

CORNMEAL MUSH

4 Servings

Combine and stir:
1 cup white or yellow cornmeal
1/2 cup cold water
1 teaspoon salt
Place in the top of a double boiler:
4 cups boiling water or water and milk
Stir cornmeal mixture in gradually. Cook and stir the mush over quick heat from 2 to 3 minutes. Steam, covered, over—not in—hot water 25 to 30 minutes. Stir frequently. Serve with:
Maple syrup, honey, molasses, milk or cream
Or pour the mush into a loaf pan to chill. When firm, slice and sauté in cooking fat until slightly crisp and browned. Serve with:
Honey, maple syrup or molasses

POLENTA

Just as our greatest architectural surprise in Italy was to find St. Francis's first church a log cabin, so were we amazed to discover that even more delicious and interesting things are done with cornmeal in Italy than in our deep South.

Cheese is sometimes cooked with it or served sprinkled over it. Or serve cornmeal with a tomato sauce or meat sauce.

I. Prepare:
Cornmeal Mush, above
Add to it for the last 15 minutes of cooking:
1/8 teaspoon paprika
A few grains red pepper
(1/2 cup shredded cheese)

II. Prepare as above and sauté sliced mush in:
Olive oil or butter

TAMALES

24 Tamales

A curious call used to rend the air on hot summer nights, one that brought a sense of adventure to our limited childhood world. It was the cry of the Mexican tamale man, whose forbidden, hence desirable, wares long remained a mystery. These varied leaf-wrapped confections, like individual puddings, may be filled with spicy mole, with cheese and peppers, or with almond, citron and coconut.

Tamales steam slowly to allow the wrapping, either corn husks or banana leaves, to both protect and flavor the contents. Most tamales have two components not easily obtained north of the Rio Grande. First, a pastate or tortilla base—that moistened mixture of unslaked lime and dried corn which is ground into flour in a matate; and second, a combination of tequesquite and transparent green tomato parings which makes the puddings puff up. The procedure that follows makes a concession to Gringo ingredients.
Remove outer husks from:
10 ears fresh or dried corn
Soak the leaves 5 minutes in hot water and drain.
Combine:
2 cups fine-ground cornmeal, preferably masa harina
2 teaspoons double-acting baking powder
1 teaspoon salt
Cream in an electric mixer:
1/3 cup lard
When it is very fluffy, beat the corn mixture in gradually, about 2 tablespoons at a time, until well combined. Slowly add, beating constantly:
1 1/2 cups meat or poultry stock
until a small bit of dough is light enough to float in a glass of water. Lay out enough 4 x 9-inch softened leaves to make 24 tamales, or, if the leaves are narrow, overlap them, see 153. Using a spatula, spread on each leaf about 1 tablespoon of the dough in a rectangle about 3 inches wide and 4 inches long. Have ready as a filling:
1 1/2 cups Turkey Casserole Mole, 428
dicing the turkey finely after deep-frying. Or use uncooked:
(1 1/2 cups filling for Sloppy Joes, 490)
Drop a tablespoon of the filling in the center of each dough-lined leaf. Wrap by overlapping the edges of the leaves lengthwise and folding up the ends as shown, 152. Layer the folded husks seam side down in a flat-bottomed steamer colander, 278.

Fill the lower pan of the steamer with water to within about 1 inch of the colander base. Bring to a rolling boil and cover tightly. Reduce the heat so the tamales continue to steam 1 to 1 1/2 hours or until the dough is firm enough to pull away easily from the leaves. Serve the tamales in the leaves on a heated platter, allowing about 3 to a person; the leaves are discarded. If tamales are made in advance, resteam them for 1/2 hour. If frozen, bring to room temperature before resteaming.

BUCKWHEAT GROATS OR KASHA

I. **4 Servings**

Brown in a hot skillet with:
2 tablespoons hot chicken fat or butter
1 cup kasha, 200

Using a fork, stir until each grain is coated. Add:

2½ cups boiling water

Cover and simmer about 30 minutes

II.

Combine in a bowl:

1 cup buckwheat groats or kasha
1 egg
2 teaspoons salt

Brown this mixture in:

2 tablespoons hot chicken fat or butter

Add:

2½ cups boiling water

Cover and simmer 15 minutes.
Preheat oven to 350°.
Sauté:

1 medium-sized chopped onion

in:

1 tablespoon chicken fat or butter

Add:

1 cup stock or chicken broth

and the cooked kasha. Pour into a 2-quart casserole and bake 15 to 20 minutes.

BULGUR PILAF

4 Servings

Bulgur wheat, sometimes called parboiled wheat, has had some bran removed before being cracked into coarse angular fragments. It makes a fine substitute for rice or potatoes.

Sauté until translucent:

½ cup sliced onions

in:

2 tablespoons vegetable oil

Stir in until the granules are coated:

1 cup bulgur

Slowly add and bring to a boil:

2 cups Poultry Stock, 523, or canned chicken broth
(½ cup chopped celery)
¼ teaspoon sweet marjoram

Cover and simmer about 40 minutes or until tender and fluffy. Add:

Chopped parsley
Season to taste

ABOUT DUMPLINGS

This category of cereal dish, sometimes reinforced with protein, is one of winter's comforts when combined with soups or stews. We have also included here dumpling types based on potatoes.

The secret of making light dumplings is to keep them steaming on top of ➤ simmering liquid. And be sure the temperature of the stock, gravy or water in which you are cooking them never exceeds a simmer. Most dumplings are bound together by egg, and the protein in the egg must not be allowed to toughen. Use ample liquid in a wide-topped cooking vessel, giving each ball or drop a chance to expand. ➤ Never crowd the pan. The minute the batter is floating in the liquid ➤ cover the pot, so the steam can begin functioning. ➤ Do not lift the lid until the dumpling is done. This is not so hard as it sounds if you cover the pan with a tight-fitting heat-resistant glass pie pan or lid, illustrated below, left, so you can watch the swelling of the batter. When the dumplings look fluffy, test them for doneness as you would a cake, by inserting a wooden pick. If it comes out clean, the dumplings are done. Once

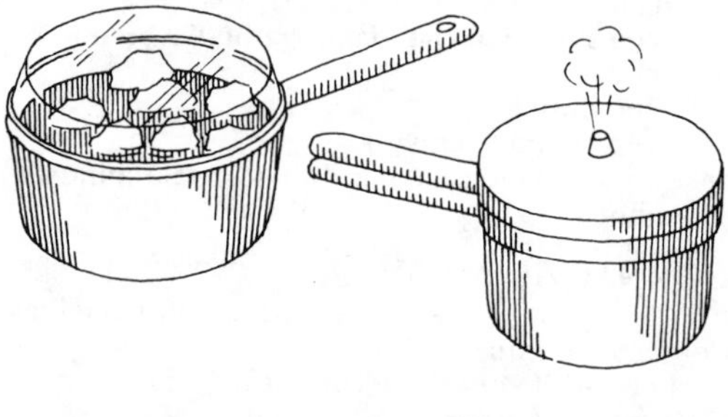

you are expert at timing, try simmering dumplings in a ✪ pressure pan. Drop the batter from a spoon into at least 3 cups hot stock or water. Instead of the glass cover, use the pressure pan lid. ➤ Keep the vent open as shown right, and cook about 5 minutes. Some good additions to dumpling dough are parsley or other herbs, cheese or grated onion.

We give dumpling amounts in cups, for some people like large dumplings, others small. ➤ A cup of dough will usually yield about eighteen to twenty 1-inch balls, but marrow, liver and meatballs do not expand as do those high in cereal and egg.

DUMPLINGS

2 Cups

➤ Please read About Dumplings, above. Measure, then sift:

1 cup cake flour
2 teaspoons double-acting baking powder
½ teaspoon salt

Break into a measuring cup:

1 egg

Add until the cup is half full:

Milk

Beat well and stir the liquid slowly into the sifted ingredients. Add more milk if necessary but keep the batter as stiff as possible. You may add:

(¼ cup finely chopped parsley, or 1 tablespoon fresh chopped herbs, or ½ teaspoon grated onion and 3 tablespoons minced green peppers)

Bring just to a boil in a 9-inch saucepan:

2 or 3 cups stock

To drop dumpling batter from a spoon easily, dip the spoon in stock first; then dip the spoon in the batter, fill it and drop the batter into the stock. Continue doing this until the dumplings are barely touching. Then cover them and simmer 10 minutes. They should be served at once.

CHEESE DUMPLINGS

To the above recipe for:

Dumplings

Add:

2 tablespoons shredded cheese

Cook the dumplings in:

Tomato juice

BUTTER DUMPLINGS OR BUTTERKLÖSSE

About 3/4 Cup

Beat until soft:

2 tablespoons butter

Beat and add:

2 eggs

Stir in:

6 tablespoons flour
1/4 teaspoon salt

Drop the batter from a spoon into ➤ simmering soup and simmer the dumplings, covered, about 8 minutes. You may also simmer them in the soup about 4 minutes in a ✪ pressure cooker, keeping the vent open the entire time.

NOCKERLN

About 1 Cup

Beat until creamy:

1/4 cup soft butter
1 egg

Stir in:

1 cup all-purpose flour
1/8 teaspoon salt

Add gradually, until a firm batter is formed, about:

6 tablespoons milk

Cut out the batter with a teaspoon to form small balls. Drop them into boiling water or directly into the clear soup in which they will be served. Reduce the liquid to a ➤ simmer and continue to simmer, covered, for about 10 minutes. For a stew, cook nockerln in water, drain, and drop them into the meat mixture just before serving.

MATZO MEAL OR CRACKER MEAL DUMPLINGS

About 2 Cups

These light Passover soup drops are made with the finely crushed crumbs of special unleavened crackers.

Beat until thick and well blended:

2 egg yolks
3 tablespoons soft chicken fat

Pour over them and beat well:

1/2 cup hot stock

Stir in gently a mixture of:

3/4 cup matzo meal or cracker meal
1/2 teaspoon salt
(1/8 teaspoon ginger)
(1/8 teaspoon nutmeg)
(1 tablespoon finely chopped parsley)
(1 tablespoon finely grated onion)

Beat until ➤ stiff, but not dry:

2 egg whites

Fold the egg whites into the cracker mixture and chill, covered, 1/2 to 1 hour. About 1/2 hour before you are ready to serve, form this dough lightly into small balls. If you will wet your hands with cold water, the job will be easier. Drop them into:

6 cups boiling stock

Reduce heat at once to a ➤ simmer and cook, covered, about 15 minutes.

FARINA BALLS COCKAIGNE

6 Servings

Please read About Dumplings, 202.

These remain after many tests the queen of dumplings. Though usually served in soup, they may be simmered in stock or boiling water, then served with meat gravy. Or they may be drained, placed in a greased baking dish and covered with a cup of White Sauce I, 341, to which you may add onion juice and parsley, or chopped chives. Sprinkle the top with 1/4 cup grated Parmesan cheese, dot it with butter and bake the dish in an oven about 15 minutes.

Heat to the boiling point:

2 cups milk

Add, stir and simmer until thick:

1/2 cup farina
1 tablespoon butter
1/2 teaspoon salt
1/8 teaspoon paprika
(1/8 teaspoon nutmeg)

Remove the batter from the heat and beat in vigorously ➤ one at a time:

2 eggs about 70°

The heat of the mixture will thicken the eggs. Drop the batter, a generous teaspoon at a time, into ➤ simmering soup stock. Cook, covered, about 2 minutes and serve.

CORNMEAL DUMPLINGS

Cooking in the United States is undoubtedly up-and-coming, but it seemed to us that a peak was reached in a small Kentucky town where we were served chicken with dumplings—the latter light as thistledown. "Oh, yes!" said the hotel proprietress wearily when we exclaimed over them. "They are always like that when our cook is drunk."

Far be it from us to limit your sources of inspiration, but we are convinced that the following recipe will give you superlative results without prior dissipation.

Set a steamer rack into:

5 or 6 cups simmering corned beef stock, consommé or any clear soup or stock

Sift together:

1/2 cup cornmeal
3/4 cup all-purpose flour
2 teaspoons double-acting baking powder
1/2 teaspoon salt

Cut in with a fork or pastry blender:

1 tablespoon butter

Beat together:

1 egg
⅓ cup milk

Combine all ingredients until just blended. Drop teaspoonfuls of batter onto the hot, steaming rack. Cover the pan closely. Simmer the dumplings about 20 minutes. Serve them while hot with the soup.

POTATO DUMPLINGS OR KARTOFFELKLÖSSE

These are light and tender, especially good with beef à la mode or other roast with gravy. It is traditional to serve them with Sauerbraten.

Boil uncovered in their jackets until tender:

6 medium-sized mature baking potatoes

Peel and rice them, see ricer below. Add:

2 eggs
1½ teaspoons salt
½ cup flour

Beat the batter with a fork until it is fluffy. Roll it lightly into balls 1 inch in diameter. Many cooks prefer to put a crouton in the center of each ball. Drop the balls into gently boiling salted water and cook about 10 minutes. Drain them well. Melt:

½ cup butter or drippings

Stir in:

¼ cup dry bread crumbs

Or, if you did not place croutons in the dumplings, prepare:

(½ cup Croutons, 551)

Pour the crumbs or croutons over the dumplings.

GNOCCHI

Serve in place of potatoes or as a soup garnish.

I. With Flour — 4 Servings

Scald:

1 cup milk

Melt in a skillet:

2 tablespoons butter

Stir and blend in until smooth:

2 tablespoons flour
2 tablespoons cornstarch
½ teaspoon salt

Stir in the scalded milk. Reduce the heat and add:

1 egg yolk
(½ cup shredded cheese)

Beat the batter until the egg has thickened and the cheese has melted. Pour it onto a shallow greased platter or pan.

Preheat oven to 375°.

When the batter is cool, cut it into strips 2 inches long. Place the strips in a pan and pour over them:

Melted butter

Sprinkle with:

(Grated cheese)

Heat them in the oven.

We prefer poaching to baking the batter after it has been cut into strips. Poach in gently boiling water or stock 1 or 2 minutes. Drain the strips and serve with melted butter.

II. With Farina — 4 Servings

Scald:

2 cups milk

Stir in, all at once:

¾ cup farina

Stir the mush over low heat until thick. Remove from heat and beat in until smooth:

1 tablespoon butter
1 egg yolk
¼ teaspoon salt

You may spread the mixture evenly in an 8 x 8-inch pan lined with foil for easier handling. Chill about 3 hours.

Preheat oven to 425°.

Cut the farina mixture into 1½-inch squares. Place the squares in a well-greased ovenproof dish, letting them overlap slightly. Dot with:

2 tablespoons butter

Pour over them slowly:

1 cup Hunter's Sauce, 347,
or Aurore Sauce, 344

Sprinkle the top with:

6 tablespoons grated Parmesan cheese

Bake about 10 minutes.

III. With Potatoes — 6 Servings

➤ The potatoes must be freshly cooked and used at once. Boil, then put through a ricer as shown above, in the foreground:

2 medium-sized peeled potatoes

Heat to the boiling point:

½ cup milk
5 tablespoons butter

Stir in, until the dough forms a ball:

1 cup flour

Remove from heat. Beat in:

2 eggs
1 teaspoon salt

¼ teaspoon paprika
(3 tablespoons grated cheese)

and the potatoes. Sprinkle the dough with flour. Roll it into sticks ½ inch thick. Cut into 1-inch lengths. Drop the gnocchi into simmering salted water. Or force the dough through a pastry bag, cutting into desired lengths as shown at left, as the gnocchi fall into the water. Simmer, uncovered, 3 to 5 minutes. Drain. You may place them on a greased pan in a hot oven about 3 minutes; the baking is optional. Serve the gnocchi dressed with melted butter and grated cheese.

SPATZEN, SPÄTZLE OR GERMAN EGG DUMPLINGS

4 Servings

Spatzen are good at any time, but they are particularly good served with roast veal or in soup.
Beat:

2 eggs

Combine them well with:

1½ cups all-purpose flour
½ cup water
½ teaspoon salt
¼ teaspoon double-acting baking powder
(A small grating of nutmeg)

Drop small bits of the batter from a spoon into simmering salted water or stock. Or put the batter through a colander or a spätzle cutter, opposite left, or use a pastry bag as shown. Spatzen should be very light and delicate. Try a sample; if it is too heavy, add water to the batter. Simmer until they are done. When served with meat, drain, place them in a dish and cover with:

Croutons, or ¼ cup bread crumbs sautéed in ½ cup butter

ABOUT QUENELLES

Once encountered, never forgotten is the texture of a well-made quenelle. Success lies not only in the mixing but in the very shaping. The ground mixture—of fish, chicken, veal or game—is placed in a large bowl ➤ set in ice, see below, and worked into a smooth paste with a wooden spoon.

To shape, you may roll quenelles in flour, but this is not the best method. We suggest the following classic spoon-molding, illustrated opposite; the size of the spoon determines the size of the quenelles. They will expand to about double their original size. Have ready a well-buttered cooking pan and 2 spoons of equal size. Put one spoon in a bowl of hot water. With the other spoon, lightly scoop out enough of the quenelle mixture to just fill it. Invert the other hot, moist spoon over the filled spoon, shaping as shown. ➤ Do not press hard; only smooth the surface. After shaping the point, invert the little egg shapes into the buttered pan. Continue to shape and place the quenelles in neat rows, allowing for expansion space.

To poach the quenelles, pour almost boiling salted water or stock very gently into the pan from the sides so as not to dislodge them. The stock should half cover the quenelles. ➤ Simmer gently 8 to 10 minutes; the water should be barely quivering. As the undersides cook, the quenelles become light, rise and turn over; but the weight of the uncooked portion will keep them half submerged until they are thoroughly done, and floating.

Although not quite so delicate as when served at once, quenelles may be held several hours, poached as described above. Place them gently in a bowl of cold water to cool, then drain off onto a cloth and place on a plate. ➤ Butter the surfaces to keep them from crusting.

If you want very small quenelles for a garnish, cut a parchment paper the size of the pan in which you plan to poach them. Use a decorating bag with a small round tip, fill with the quenelle mixture and force out small units onto the parchment paper in uniformly spaced rows. Lift the whole paper into the pan and, as with larger quenelles, pour the water gently from the side of the pan until the quenelles are only half-covered. As they simmer for 5 to 8 minutes, they will float free and roll over. When floating, skim them off and place in a bowl of warm, mildly salted water until ready to use.

If fancy shapes are desired, pack the quenelle mixture into buttered decorative individual molds. To poach, place the molds in a pan of hot water so that they are completely covered. When the quenelles are cooked, they will release themselves and rise to the surface and then can be removed for serving.

Reheat quenelles by ➤ simmering them in the sauce or soup in which they are to be served.

POACHED OR BAKED QUENELLES

6 Servings

➤ Please read About Quenelles, 205.
Run through the finest blade of a food chopper 3 times:

1½ lb. fresh pike, sole, shrimp or lobster

Place the ground mixture in a large bowl ➤ set in a bowl of ice. With a wooden spoon, work it to a smooth paste. Gradually work in ➤ by small additions:

2 egg whites

Season with:

Grated fresh nutmeg
Salt
White pepper
Dash of cognac
Dash of cayenne or hot pepper sauce

Mix well. At this point the quenelle mixture should be very firm. Still over ice, add ➤ very, very gradually and mix well with a wooden spoon:

2 to 2½ cups well-chilled whipping cream

The consistency now should be that of a firm whipped cream. To form and poach, follow directions above. Serve with:

Newburg Sauce, 359
Poulette Sauce, 345

YORKSHIRE PUDDING COCKAIGNE

Six 3-Inch Squares

It was customary to cook this delicious dish in the pan with the roast, letting the drippings fall upon it. As many of us no longer want extravagant drippings, we recommend cooking Yorkshire pudding separately in the hot oven required to puff it up almost instantly. Serve it from the dish in which it was cooked, cut into squares. In Yorkshire it is served before the meat course as a hefty pudding. We substitute it for the usual starch served with a main course.

➤ Have all ingredients at 75°.
Stir into a bowl:

⅞ cup flour
½ teaspoon salt

Make a well in the center, into which pour:

½ cup milk
½ cup water

Stir in the liquid. Beat until fluffy and add:

2 eggs

Continue to beat until large bubbles rise to the surface. Let stand covered and refrigerated at least 1 hour and beat again ➤ after bringing it back to 70°.
Preheat oven to 400°.
Have ready a hot ovenproof dish about 9 x 13 inches, containing about ¼ cup ➤ hot beef drippings or melted butter. Pour in the batter. It should be about ½ inch high. Bake the pudding 20 minutes. ➤ Reduce the heat to 350° and bake about 10 to 15 minutes longer. Serve at once.

ABOUT RICE

"May your rice never burn" is the New Year's greeting of the Chinese. "May it never be gummy" is ours. So many people complain to us about the variability of their results in rice cookery. Like flour, the rice itself may have more or less moisture in its makeup. In Japan the standard ratio is 8 cups of water to 8 cups of rice for the first six weeks after harvest. The amount of water then rises steadily. And when the rice is 11 months old, 8 cups of rice need 10 cups of water.

Not only is there moisture variability in rice, but the type must also be reckoned with. Brown rice, which retains its bran coat and germ, is much slower to tenderize, although more valuable nutritionally, than highly polished white rice.

There are also differences in the grain hybrids. Use short- or medium-grain types—which cook up tender and moist—in recipes calling for sauces, rings, croquettes and puddings. Long-grain types are best for salads, soups and main dishes, where each grain should be separate and fluffy. Also on the market are preprocessed rices; follow the directions on the label. Some of these that are parboiled before milling have greater nutritive value than polished white rice. Wild rice is not a true rice. The seed comes from a strictly American plant and needs its own recipes, see 212.

➤ To keep rice white when cooking in hard water, add 1 teaspoon lemon juice or 1 tablespoon vinegar to the cooking water.

➤ One cup raw rice equals 3 cups when cooked. One cup brown rice yields 3 to 4 cups cooked rice. If using preprocessed rice, the volume will be less, about 1 to 2 cups cooked for 1 cup uncooked. This is also true for recipes in which rice is browned in a skillet, with or without fat, prior to cooking it with moisture. But this browning helps to keep the grains separate and does contribute to good flavor.

BOILED RICE

6 to 7 Servings

I. Bring to a ➤ rolling boil:

2 to 2½ cups water, stock or consommé

Use the larger amount for brown rice. Add:

¾ teaspoon salt

You may add:

(1 tablespoon melted butter)

to the rice, before cooking, to keep it from sticking to the pot. Stir slowly into the water, so as not to disturb the boiling:

1 cup white or brown rice

Cover and cook over slow heat. White rice will take from 25 to 30 minutes, brown from 40 to 50. If the rice becomes too dry, add ¼ cup or more ➤ boiling water. When the grains have swelled to capacity, uncover the pot for about the last 5 minutes of cooking. Continue to cook the rice over ➤ very low heat, shaking the pot from time to time until the grains have separated. Or fluff the cooked rice with a fork. Enliven the above by cooking with the rice:

(Chopped celery)
(Chopped scallions)
(Chopped spinach)
(Grated carrots)

II. A moist oriental-type rice. **3 Servings**

Wash and drain:

½ cup short- or medium-grain rice

Place in a deep, heavy kettle with:

1½ cups cold water

Boil 5 minutes or until most of the surface water is gone and air bubbles can be seen on the surface of the rice. ➤ Reduce the heat and continue to cook ➤ covered about 20 minutes longer. Remove from heat and let the rice stand covered about 20 minutes more. It is then ready to serve.

RICE RING OR MOLD

A molded rice ring, shown filled in the chapter heading, is a handsome way to enclose the food comprising your main course. For color, include chopped parsley with the cooked rice.

I. **6 Servings**

Preheat oven to 350°.

Boil:

1 cup short- or medium-grain rice, 206

Season with:

½ teaspoon grated nutmeg

Place in a well-greased 7-inch ring mold. Melt and pour over it:

¼ cup butter

You may add:

(¾ cup coarsely chopped blanched almonds)

Set the mold in a pan of hot water. Bake the rice for about 20 minutes. Loosen the edges and invert the contents of the mold onto a platter. Fill the center with:

Creamed Chicken, 263
Creamed Mushrooms, 308, or
a creamed or buttered vegetable

II.

We have had success packing hot cooked rice firmly into a well-buttered ring mold. Rest it 3 or 4 minutes and then turn it out onto the serving platter to be filled with the hot entrée. Do not use this method if egg is called for in the recipe—use instead I, above.

MUSHROOM RICE RING

6 Servings

No need to bake this mold.

Boil:

1 cup short- or medium-grain rice, 206

Grind, chop fine or ⅄ blend:

½ to 1 lb. mushrooms

Sauté them 2 or 3 minutes in:

2 tablespoons butter

Add:

¼ cup hot stock or water

Combine the mushrooms and rice. Add:

(¾ cup coarsely chopped blanched almonds)
Season to taste

Press the rice firmly into a greased 7-inch ring mold and let stand 3 or 4 minutes. Invert the rice onto a platter. Fill the center with a buttered vegetable, creamed fish, etc.

CHEESE RICE RING

3 Servings

Preheat oven to 350°.

Combine:

1½ cups Boiled Rice, 206
1 beaten egg
2 tablespoons olive oil or melted butter
¼ cup milk
⅓ cup shredded sharp cheese
¼ tablespoon grated onion
1 teaspoon Worcestershire sauce
¼ teaspoon salt
3 tablespoons chopped parsley

Grease a 7-inch ring mold. Fill it with the rice mixture. Bake it, set in a pan of hot water, about 45 minutes.

RICE AND HAM RING

6 Servings

Preheat oven to 375°.

Combine:

2 cups Boiled Rice, 206
1 cup diced cooked ham

Combine and beat:

1 egg
⅔ cup condensed mushroom soup
½ cup milk
¼ teaspoon salt
(½ teaspoon dried basil)

Grease a 9-inch ring mold. Place in it layers of rice and ham. Pour the liquid ingredients over them. Sprinkle the top with:

1 cup crushed potato chips or bread crumbs

Bake the mold in 1 inch of hot water about ½ hour. Invert it onto a platter. Fill the center with:

A cooked vegetable: carrots and peas,
or green beans

RICE BAKED IN CHICKEN STOCK

6 to 7 Servings

Preheat oven to 375°.

Sauté:

½ chopped onion

in:

¼ cup butter

until translucent. Add and stir until well coated:

1 cup long-grain rice or brown rice

Add:

2 cups boiling chicken stock or broth

Cover and bake 20 to 25 minutes.

Gently mix with the rice:

2 tablespoons melted butter

Serve the rice at once.

BAKED GREEN RICE

3 Servings

Outstanding alone or as a stuffing for breast of veal. This amount will fill a 7-inch ring mold.
Preheat oven to 325°.
Beat:
1 egg
Add and mix well:
1 cup milk
½ cup finely chopped parsley
1 finely chopped clove garlic
1 small minced onion
2 cups Boiled Rice, 206
½ cup shredded sharp cheese or
2 tablespoons butter
⅛ teaspoon curry powder
Salt to taste
Place these ingredients in a baking dish, into which has been poured:
2 tablespoons olive oil
Bake about 30 minutes.

BAKED PINEAPPLE RICE

6 Servings

This versatile dish may be served with baked ham or fried chicken or as a dessert with cream.
Preheat oven to 350°.
Boil:
1 cup rice, 206
Drain, then cut into pieces:
3½ cups cubed pineapple
Place one-third of the rice in a buttered baking dish. Cover with half the pineapple. Repeat the layer of rice and pineapple. Place the last third of the rice on top. Dot each layer with:
1½ tablespoons butter
¼ cup brown sugar
Use in all 5½ tablespoons butter and ¾ cup sugar.
Pour over all:
¾ cup pineapple juice
Bake the rice covered about 30 minutes.

CURRIED RICE

3 Servings

An unusual and delicious rice dish. Its popularity is undoubtedly due to the restraint with which the spice is used.
Pour:
2 cups hot water
over:
½ cup rice
Place the rice where it will remain hot, but will not cook, about 45 minutes.
Preheat oven to 350°.
Add to the rice:
½ cup drained, chopped tomatoes
¾ teaspoon salt
¼ cup finely sliced onion
¼ cup sliced green peppers
2 tablespoons melted butter
¾ teaspoon curry powder
Bake these ingredients in a baking dish 1½ hours or until done. Stir them from time to time. At first, there will be a great preponderance of liquid, but gradually the rice will absorb it. Remove the dish from the oven while the rice is still moist. Good served with beer.

CHEESE RICE

6 to 7 Servings

A good dish to serve with a cold supper.
Boil:
1 cup rice, 206
When the water is nearly absorbed, add:
½ to ¾ cup or more shredded cheese
¼ teaspoon paprika
A few grains cayenne
Add:
1 cup condensed tomato or mushroom soup
Stir the rice over low heat until the cheese is melted.

RICE WITH SPINACH AND CHESTNUTS

6 to 8 Servings

Preheat oven to 350°.
Combine:
1 cup Boiled Rice, 206
1 cup cooked chopped spinach
1 cup cooked chestnuts, 298
½ to 1 cup shredded cheese
Cover with:
Au Gratin II, 552
Bake about 35 minutes or until thoroughly heated.
Before serving, garnish with:
Sprigs of watercress and ribbons of pimiento

BACON AND RICE CUSTARD

4 Servings

Preheat oven to 325°.
Sauté until partly done:
8 slices bacon
Line each of 4 muffin tins with 2 slices of bacon. Fill them with the following mixture. Combine:
2 cups Boiled Rice, 206
1 beaten egg
2 tablespoons cream
1 tablespoon melted butter
1 tablespoon grated onion
1 tablespoon chopped parsley
⅛ teaspoon salt
⅛ teaspoon paprika
Bake until the custard is firm, about ½ hour.
Serve with:
Tomato or other sauce

CHINESE FRIED RICE

6 Servings

The rice for this recipe must be ➤ cooked, fluffy, and prepared at least one day before use. Heat in a heavy skillet:
¼ cup vegetable oil
Toss in it:
3 cups Boiled Rice, 206
until hot and golden. Add:
4 minced scallions

3/4 teaspoon salt
(1/2 cup julienned cooked roast pork or ham or 1 cup diced cooked shrimp)
When these ingredients are well mixed, hollow a center in the rice. Break:
3 eggs
into the hollow and scramble until semicooked, then stir into the rice mixture. Sprinkle with:
1 1/2 tablespoons soy sauce
(1/4 cup minced coriander leaves)
and serve with:
Podded Peas, 315

ITALIAN RICE OR RISOTTO ALLA MILANESE

8 to 10 Servings

This dish needs fairly constant watching for about 20 minutes and ➤ must be served at once to prevent gumminess. Melt in a heavy pan:
1/4 cup Clarified Butter, 349
Sauté in it, until golden:
1 small minced onion
Add and stir well with a wooden spoon until all the butter is absorbed:
2 cups rice
Have ready:
8 to 10 cups hot beef or chicken stock
(1/2 cup Italian white wine)
After the rice is well coated with the fat, add 1 cup of the stock. Continue to stir, adding about two-thirds of the hot stock over a 10-minute period. Dissolve in a little of the stock:
(A pinch of saffron or 1/2 teaspoon fennel seed)
Continue to stir and add stock about 5 to 8 minutes longer, when the rice should have absorbed all of the liquid. ➤ Do not let it dry out.
Season to taste
Place the rice in a hot serving dish. Pour over it and mix:
1/4 cup melted butter
(Sautéed chicken livers and giblets)
Sprinkle over it:
1 cup grated aged Parmesan cheese

SPANISH RICE

3 to 4 Servings

Sauté until crisp:
3 slices bacon, minced
Remove the bacon. Stir and cook in the drippings until browned:
1/2 cup rice
Add and cook until golden:
1/2 cup thinly sliced onions
Add the bacon and:
1 1/4 cups canned tomatoes
1/2 teaspoon salt
1 teaspoon paprika
1 seeded and minced green pepper
(1 pressed clove garlic)
Steam the rice in a double boiler about 1 hour. Stir it frequently. Add water or stock if the rice becomes too dry. It may be served with:
Cheese Sauce, 342

ROMBAUER RICE DISH

4 Servings

Freely varied each time it is made, but in such demand that we shall try to write a general rule for it.
Boil:
1/2 cup rice, 206
Prepare:
Veal stew: 1 1/2 lb. meat, 469
Pare, slice and add the last 20 minutes of cooking:
1/2 parsnip
2 carrots
2 onions
and:
6 ribs celery, sliced
3 sprigs parsley
Drain the stew. To make the gravy, see 341. There should be about 3 cups of stock. If there is not enough, add chicken bouillon, a bouillon or vegetable cube and water, rice water, or sweet or sour cream to make up the difference. If there is not enough fat, add butter. The better the gravy, the better the dish. Combine rice, meat, vegetables and gravy and reheat. Garnish with:
Parsley
You may add a dash of curry powder and some herbs—thyme, basil, etc., 579. You may use leftover meat, gravy and vegetables. You may serve the stew in a baking dish, au gratin or in individual baking dishes.

A deluxe dish is this recipe made with rice, chicken, sauce—with cream and chicken gravy—and blanched slivered almonds. An everyday dish is this recipe made with corned beef and some canned soup to substitute for gravy.

PILAF

4 Servings

A rice dish combined with shrimp or chicken livers, etc. It has many variations, some with grits, millet, or dried or split peas to replace the rice.
Boil:
2/3 cup long-grain rice, 206
Sauté until golden and add to the rice:
3 tablespoons chopped onion
in:
1 to 2 tablespoons butter
In a separate pan, simmer:
2 1/2 cups tomatoes
1/3 teaspoon salt
1/4 teaspoon paprika
1/2 teaspoon brown sugar
and a bouquet garni, 572, of:
1/2 bay leaf
3 ribs celery with leaves
When the tomato mixture is thick, remove the bouquet garni. Add to the tomato mixture:
1 cup cooked shrimp, lobster meat, crab meat, or sautéed chicken livers

(½ cup chopped pecans)
Combine these ingredients with the rice.
Season to taste
Place the rice in a greased baking dish. Sprinkle with:
¼ cup grated cheese and bread crumbs
Place under a heated broiler to brown.

PAELLA

8 Servings

If you do not own a paellero, the vessel to which this dish gives its name, you will need a generous lidded casserole in which to cook and serve it.
Preheat oven to 350°.
Have ready:
2 cups cooked chicken, cut in 1- to 1½-inch pieces
4 cups hot chicken stock
Heat until golden in the casserole:
¼ cup olive oil
½ cup thinly sliced onions
Over moderate heat add, stirring until lightly browned:
2 cups rice
Add the hot stock, in which has been dissolved a small quantity of:
Saffron—or up to 2 teaspoons if you are Spanish
Add:
2 pressed cloves garlic
2 sliced sweet red peppers, seeds and membranes removed
1 teaspoon paprika
¼ teaspoon oregano
Thin slices chorizo or hard Spanish sausage
Season to taste
Also put in the chicken, arranging it toward the top of the mixture. Cover and bake in a 350° oven about 15 minutes. Add, arranging them attractively on the top:
Raw shrimp
Well-scrubbed clams in their shells
Cover and steam about 10 minutes longer. Serve at once.

FRUIT, NUT AND RICE CASSEROLE

10 Servings

Cover with water and soak ½ hour:
2 cups dried apricots
1 cup white raisins
In the meantime, boil:
1 cup rice, 206
Preheat oven to 375°.
In a skillet, melt:
½ cup butter
Sauté:
1 cup minced onion
½ cup chopped green pepper, seeds and membrane removed
(½ teaspoon curry powder)
Add:
(1 cup toasted almonds)
and the drained, chopped apricots and raisins and cooked rice.
Season to taste
Put into a greased baking dish to bake covered about 30 minutes.

RICE AND NUT LOAF

4 Servings

Serve with broccoli or any green leafy vegetable.
Preheat oven to 375°.
Melt:
3 tablespoons butter
Sauté in it until soft:
1 minced onion
1 seeded chopped green pepper, seeds and membrane removed
Add:
1 cup Boiled Rice, 206
⅓ cup bread crumbs
1 cup drained, chopped tomatoes
1 cup chopped or ground walnuts or other nutmeats
1 beaten egg
2 tablespoons chopped parsley
¾ teaspoon salt
¼ teaspoon paprika
(1 teaspoon grated lemon peel)
Bake these ingredients in a greased baking dish about 30 minutes. Cover the top with:
Au Gratin II, 552
Brown under a broiler. Serve the loaf with:
A tomato sauce

RICE LOAF OR CASSEROLE

I. **5 Servings**

Boil:
⅔ cup rice, 206
Line a buttered mold with it. Reserve ½ cup for the top. Cook:
1 cup White Sauce II, 341
Stir in and thicken slightly over low heat:
1 egg yolk
Add:
1 cup diced canned salmon, cooked fish or meat
½ cup bread crumbs
1 tablespoon chopped parsley
1 tablespoon chopped onion
½ cup chopped celery
1 teaspoon lemon juice or 1 teaspoon Worcestershire sauce
Salt, paprika, nutmeg
Preheat oven to 375°.
Fill the rice mold and place the reserved rice over the top. Cover with a piece of buttered paper. Set the mold in a pan of hot water and bake or steam until set, about 30 minutes. Invert the loaf onto a platter. Garnish it with:
Sprigs of parsley
Serve it with:
A tomato sauce, or
Mushroom Sauce, 348

II. **6 Servings**

Boil:

⅔ cup rice, 206

There should be about 2 cups cooked rice.

Drain:

1 cup canned tuna fish

Break the tuna into pieces with a fork.

Cook:

2 cups White Sauce II, 341

Add:

½ teaspoon salt—more if rice is unsalted
½ teaspoon paprika
A few grains red pepper

Reduce the heat to low. Stir in until melted:

2 cups shredded cheese

Preheat oven to 400°.

Place in a baking dish alternate layers of rice, fish and sauce. Dot the top with:

Au Gratin II, 552

Bake the dish until the crumbs are brown. If preferred, bake the ingredients in a ring, invert and serve with the center filled with Sautéed Mushrooms, 308.

VEGETABLE RICE OR JAMBALAYA

4 Servings

Ideal for a picnic supper.

Boil:

⅔ cup rice, 206

Sauté lightly in butter:

¾ to 1 lb. mushrooms

Chop and add:

2 medium-sized green peppers, seeds and membrane removed
1 medium-sized onion
1 rib celery
2 diced pimientos
1¼ cups fresh or drained canned tomatoes

Season these ingredients with:

¾ teaspoon salt
A few grains cayenne
½ teaspoon paprika

Add:

¼ cup melted butter

These proportions may be varied.

Preheat oven to 300°.

Combine the rice and other ingredients. Place in a greased baking dish. Bake ➤ covered 30 to 40 minutes. The sautéed mushroom caps and the pimientos may be used to garnish the top of the dish. They are highly decorative with a bunch of parsley in the center.

JAMBALAYA WITH MEAT OR FISH

6 to 8 Servings

Have ready:

3 cups Boiled Rice, 206

Sauté lightly in a saucepan:

2 diced slices bacon

Add and sauté until golden:

¼ cup chopped onion

Stir in:

1 tablespoon flour

Add:

1 cup tomato pulp
⅓ cup water

Bring these ingredients to the boiling point. Stir in the rice and:

2 cups coarsely diced cooked ham, chicken, sausage, tongue, shrimp or crab, alone or in combination

Add:

¼ teaspoon thyme
(Worcestershire sauce)
Season to taste

Stir over very low heat about 10 minutes or heat over boiling water about ½ hour. Serve sprinkled with:

Chopped parsley

CHICKEN JAMBALAYA

4 to 6 Servings

Cut into pieces:

A young chicken

Sauté about 5 minutes in:

¼ cup vegetable oil or butter

Remove meat from pan. Sauté in the fat, about 3 minutes:

⅓ cup minced onion
½ cup skinned, seeded and chopped tomato

Stir in:

1 diced green pepper, seeds and membrane removed
½ cup diced celery
1 cup rice

When the rice is well coated with fat, stir in the sautéed chicken. Cover these ingredients well with:

About 3 cups boiling water

Add:

1 bay leaf
¼ teaspoon thyme
¼ cup chopped parsley
1 teaspoon salt
¼ teaspoon pepper

Simmer these ingredients until the chicken is tender and the rice almost done. Add:

½ lb. finely diced cooked ham
Season to taste

Dry out the jambalaya by placing it about 5 or 10 minutes in a 350° oven.

RICE TABLE OR RIJSTTAFEL

8 Servings

As this Javanese dish is very filling, it is ideal for suppers served with ice-cold beer, followed by salad. It may be made as elaborate or as simple as you wish. If you object to coconut or do not like the flavor of curry, do not discard this dish. Instead, carry out the idea of the rijsttafel by substituting creamed chicken, ragoût fin or a lamb stew you do like, followed by vegetables and condiments served in some attractive way.

Grate:

A fresh coconut, or use about 2 cups unsweetened canned coconut

Heat but do not scald:

4 cups milk or coconut milk, 566

Add the coconut. Let these ingredients stand 2 hours in a cool place. Melt:

1 tablespoon butter

Sauté in it, until light brown:

½ cup finely chopped onion

Add:

Chopped gingerroot: 2-inch length
1 chopped clove garlic
1½ tablespoons curry powder

Strain and add the coconut. Add to the cooled, strained milk:

1 cup milk or Poultry Stock, 523

With 3 tablespoons of this liquid, mix:

1 tablespoon flour
1 tablespoon cornstarch

Heat the remaining liquid and stir the starch paste into it. Cook and stir the sauce until it is hot and thickened.

Season to taste

Place half the sauce in the top of a double boiler. Add the coconut-curry mixture and:

3 cups cooked diced chicken, shrimp, fish, veal, sweetbreads or mushrooms, either alone or in combination

Heat remaining sauce in another double boiler. Have ready and rather dry and flaky:

2 cups Boiled Rice, 206

The ceremony of serving this dish is part of its charm. In Java one refers to it by the separate dishes, as a "One-boy curry" or a "Twenty-two-boy curry," each boy representing one dish. Pass the rice first. Spread it generously over your plate, forming a base or "table." Pass the food in the sauce next. Follow this with:

Onion rings
Sieved hard-cooked eggs
Grated peanuts or toasted almonds
Grated coconut, if there is none in the sauce
Relish
Chutney, raisins, preserved ginger or kumquats
Halved fried bananas
Mixed pickles

Now pass the extra heated sauce.

To simplify matters, the last four or five may be served from one large condiment dish. Servings from these various dishes are placed on the rice table. Cut through the layers and proceed to feast.

ABOUT WILD RICE

Wild rice is the seed from a grass growing wild in the northern United States, and nutritionally it is closer to wheat than to rice. It remains a luxury because of the difficulty of harvesting. For economy you may combine cooked wild rice with cooked white or brown rice.

One cup of wild rice equals 3 to 3½ cups of cooked wild rice.

WILD RICE

4 Servings

Wash well in several waters, pouring off the foreign particles from the top:

1 cup wild rice

Drain it. Stir it slowly into:

4 cups boiling water
1 teaspoon salt

Cook without stirring about 40 minutes or until tender.

WILD RICE RING

4 Servings

Cook as directed above:

1 cup wild rice

You may add:

1 pressed clove garlic

When the rice is tender, add:

¼ cup butter
½ teaspoon poultry seasoning or freshly grated nutmeg
(1 cup sautéed onions and mushrooms)
(¼ cup dry sherry)

Preheat oven to 350°.

Place rice in a well-greased 7-inch ring mold set in a pan of hot water in the oven. Bake about 20 minutes. Loosen the edges with a knife, invert the contents onto a platter and fill the center with one or more of the following:

Creamed Mushrooms, 308
Chicken Livers Lyonnaise, 500
Sautéed Onions, 312
Snow Peas, 315, and Water Chestnuts, 335

"LONG RICE" OR HARUSAME

This is not a rice at all, but an oriental pasta made of soybean powder, also known as bean thread noodles, Saifun, or dried cellophane noodles. We infinitely prefer its native name of "Spring Rain."

To prepare, pour:

Boiling water

over:

Harusame

Let stand 15 minutes or until it is limp. Cut into desired lengths and drain. Add as a garnish for soup, meat or vegetables. It should then ➤ simmer during the last 15 minutes of the cooking of these foods.

COOKING PASTAS

Freshly made pastas are an incomparable treat. Noodles are those most frequently made in the home, as they do not require the difficult-to-purchase high-gluten flours that other pasta forms demand. To make noodles and casings for filled pastas like Ravioli, 216, Kreplach, 172, and Won Ton, 173, see Noodle Dough, opposite.

Because pasta shapes are so variable we give the weight rather than the volume for amounts to be cooked. And at meals where pasta is the predominant ingredient of the main dish, the individual serving is more generous than the usual meat or vegetable serving, so we allow ➤ 1/4 pound of dry pasta per serving. For more detailed information, please see Equivalents and Substitutions, 593.

All pastas should be added ➤ gradually to a large quantity of rapidly boiling water so that the boiling is not disturbed. As in the cooking of all cereals, it is essential that the outer surfaces be penetrated as quickly as possible. This requires a kettle large enough to accommodate about 7 quarts of rapidly boiling water for a pound of pasta. Add 1 tablespoon salt and 1 tablespoon olive oil. Long pastas are immersed as shown below; the dry material softens as it is gradually lowered into continuously boiling water, until all

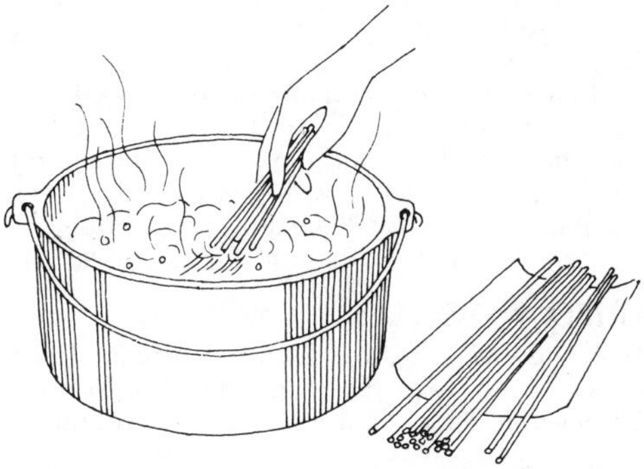

the pasta floats free. No matter which pasta you are cooking ➤ do not overcook. The timing can be gauged only by tasting—not once, but several times. If the noodles are very thin or freshly made, a few minutes suffice. The perfect state any Italian recognizes as *al dente* is reached when ➤ no taste of raw flour remains and the pasta still offers slight resistance to the bite. Thick forms of commercial pastas with uncertain shelf histories may need cooking as long as 15 or 20 minutes. When the *al dente* state is reached, remove the pasta from the water with a pasta scoop similar to the one shown in the chapter heading and let the pasta drip-dry momentarily over the pot before releasing it into a large warm buttered bowl or spooning it with a pasta server, shown also in the chapter heading in the foreground. When all the pasta is drained and tossed in butter, portion it into hot bowls; served thus without a sauce, it is called *al burro*. Pass the grated cheese. For ways to garnish and serve pastas, see suggestions for Boiled Noodles, below, Pasta Sauces, 219, and Pasta Fillings, 218.

WHITE OR GREEN NOODLE DOUGH OR FETTUCINE

About 1/2 Pound Dry or 4 Cups Cooked Noodles

If you are a beginner, do not try to make noodles in damp weather. This dough may be used for Won Ton, Ravioli or Kreplach cases, but cut it into squares without allowing it to dry, and fill at once. To fold and cook, see individual recipes. On a large pastry board or marble tabletop make a well, 643, of:

2/3 cup all-purpose flour

Drop into it:

1 egg

barely combined with:

1 tablespoon water
1/2 teaspoon salt
1 teaspoon oil

Work the mixture with your hands, folding the flour over the egg until the dough can be rolled into a ball and comes clean from the hands. If you want to make green noodles, add at this point:

(2 to 4 tablespoons very well drained and dried, finely chopped cooked spinach)

Knead the dough as for bread, 600, about 10 minutes. Then let it stand, covered, about 1 hour. Now roll the dough, stretching it a little more with each roll. Between each rolling and stretching, continue to sprinkle it with flour to keep the dough from sticking to the pin or board or developing holes. Repeat this procedure about 10 times or until the dough is paper-thin and translucent. Let it dry about 30 minutes. You can hang it as the Neapolitans do, like laundry, with a piece of foil or plastic underneath. Before it becomes brittle, roll it into a scroll and cut it on the bias as shown below into strips of any width you prefer: 1/8 inch for soup or 2 inches for lasagne. Allow about 3 tablespoons uncooked noodles for each quart

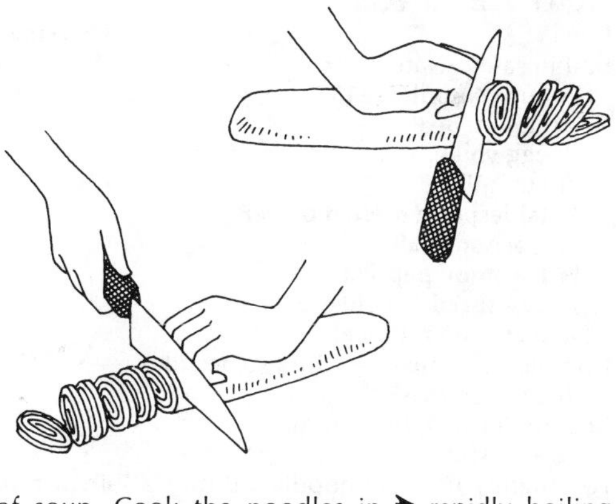

of soup. Cook the noodles in ➤ rapidly boiling salted water about 10 minutes. Drain and add them to the soup before serving.

BOILED NOODLES, SPAGHETTI, MACARONI AND OTHER PASTAS

5 Servings

Please read about Cooking Pastas, 212.
Drop:

2 cups Pasta

into:

3 quarts boiling, salted water—½ teaspoon salt to the quart—or chicken stock, consommé, etc.

Boil 8 to 10 minutes, depending on size and your taste preference. Drain in a colander and immediately put back into cooking pot, set over very low heat and toss generously in:

Melted butter

I. If served at once without sauce, they may be called **Fettucine al Burro.** With the pasta, pass:

(Grated Asiago, Romano or Parmesan cheese)

II. You may prefer instead of the butter to mix with them:

¾ cup cultured sour cream

Add:

(3 tablespoons chopped parsley)
(2 tablespoons poppy seed)

or:

(½ cup blanched slivered almonds sautéed in 1 tablespoon butter)

III. Or make **Good Friday Noodles.** Add:

Buttered Croutons, 551

and pass a bowl of:

Stewed prunes

IV. Or prepare:

Welsh Rarebit I or II, 252

and when hot, stir in:

½ lb. freshly cooked, drained noodles
1 to 2 cups diced cooked ham or cooked smoked tongue

NOODLE RINGS

I. **4 Servings**

Boil in salted water:

1½ cups Noodles, 213

Drain them. Beat:

2 egg yolks
½ cup milk
¾ tablespoon melted butter
¼ teaspoon salt
⅛ teaspoon paprika
(½ cup shredded cheese)
(⅛ teaspoon nutmeg)

Combine this mixture with the noodles.
Preheat oven to 350°.
Beat until stiff ➤ but not dry:

2 egg whites

Fold lightly into the noodles. Butter a 7-inch ring mold or individual ring molds. Fill with the noodle mixture. Place in a pan of hot water and bake until done, about 45 minutes for a large mold or 30 minutes for the small ones. Invert the contents of the molds on hot plates and fill the centers with:

Creamed spinach, peas, mushrooms, hash, stewed tomatoes or Chicken à la King, 263

II. Made with cheese, this is our favorite. Follow the recipe above. Use in all:

¾ cup milk

Add to the noodle mixture before folding in the egg whites:

1½ teaspoons Worcestershire Sauce, 848
½ tablespoon catsup or sautéed onions
¾ cup grated cheddar cheese or cottage cheese

III. **10 Servings**

Use a 9-inch ring. For 5 servings prepare half the recipe and use a 7-inch ring. Boil in salted water:

2 cups fine Noodles, 213

Drain. Beat and pour over the noodles:

4 egg yolks
¼ teaspoon paprika
½ cup melted butter

Preheat oven to 350°.
Whip until stiff:

4 egg whites
¼ teaspoon salt

Beat until stiff:

1 cup whipping cream or 1 cup cultured sour cream

Fold the egg whites and the cream lightly into the noodle mixture. Fill a well-greased ring. Place it in a pan of hot water. Bake until firm, about 1 hour or more. Invert the ring and fill as above.

FRIED NOODLES

To be served instead of a starchy vegetable or as a garnish on vegetables or other dishes, notably Chinese. Boil in salted water about 5 minutes:

Thin noodles

Place them in a colander and rinse with cold water to rid them of surface starch. Drain, separate and dry well. In deep fat heated to 390°, fry, a small amount at a time, until they are a delicate brown. Drain on paper toweling. Sprinkle lightly with:

Salt

Keep them hot or reheat in a 400° oven.

NOODLE BASKETS

For these you need a tea strainer about 3 inches in diameter and a second strainer about ⅜ inch smaller that fits into it but leaves space for the swelling of the noodles. Prepare:

Noodle Dough, 213

Before the dough is dry, fold it over and cut it into ¼-inch strips. Dip the strainers in hot fat to keep the noodles from sticking. Line the larger strainer with 2 layers of noodles in crisscross effect. Snip off the ragged edges. Place the smaller strainer over the noodle basket. Fry the noodle basket in deep fat heated to 390° until lightly browned. Remove it carefully from the strainers and fry the next one. You may fill the fried baskets at once with creamed food, etc., or you may cool and reheat them later by dipping briefly in hot fat without the strainers. Drain on paper toweling.

HAM NOODLES

6 Servings

This recipe is capable of wide interpretation and its proportions may be varied.

Preheat oven to 350°.
Have ready:
3 cups Boiled Noodles, 213
Grease a baking dish. Place in it layers of noodles sprinkled with:
3/4 cup diced or ground cooked ham
(1/2 cup shredded cheese)
(1/2 cup shredded green pepper and diced celery)
Combine:
1 1/2 cups milk
1 or 2 eggs
1/4 teaspoon paprika
1/4 to 1/2 teaspoon salt—omit if the ham is very salty
Pour this over the noodles. Cover with:
Bread or cracker crumbs
Bake about 45 minutes.

LEFTOVER NOODLE DISH

I. Follow the previous recipe. Substitute for the ham:
Diced cooked roast beef, chicken, crab, shrimp, chipped beef, mushrooms and other vegetables

TUNA, NOODLE AND MUSHROOM SOUP CASSEROLE

4 Large Servings

An excellent emergency dish.
Preheat oven to 450°.
Have ready:
2 cups Boiled Noodles, 213
Drain:
1 can tuna fish: 7 oz.
Separate it with a fork into large flakes. Do not mince it. Grease an ovenproof dish. Arrange a layer of noodles, then sprinkle it with fish and so on, with noodles on top. Pour over this mixture:
1 cup condensed mushroom soup
Season the soup with:
Worcestershire sauce, curry powder or dry sherry
1/4 cup chopped parsley
Cover the top with:
Buttered cornflakes or cracker crumbs
Bake until the top is brown.

ROMANIAN NOODLE AND PORK CASSEROLE

8 Servings

Preheat oven to 350°.
Have ready:
1 lb. fine Boiled Noodles, 213
Combine:
1 lb. cooked ground pork
1 slice bread, soaked in milk and wrung out
1 minced leek
1/2 to 1 teaspoon fennel seeds
1/4 cup chopped parsley
1 teaspoon salt
1/2 teaspoon pepper
In a shallow large baking pan, arrange alternate layers of noodles and pork mixture, ending with noodles. Beat together:
4 eggs
2/3 cup cream
1/4 cup grated hard cheese
Pour this mixture over the noodles and dot with:
1/4 cup butter
Bake about 45 minutes.

QUANTITY NOODLE AND CHEESE LOAF

18 Servings

Boil in salted water:
5 cups Noodles, 213
and drain them. Have ready:
1 lb. shredded sharp cheese
1 1/2 cups dry bread crumbs
Mix together half the cheese and 1 cup of the crumbs with:
1/4 cup melted butter
Mix the rest of the crumbs, the cheese and the noodles with:
7 beaten eggs
1 3/4 cups milk
3 tablespoons grated onion
1/3 cup chopped pimiento
1/3 cup chopped green pepper, seeds and membrane removed
1 teaspoon salt
1/2 teaspoon white pepper
(1 cup finely chopped celery)
(1/2 cup sliced stuffed olives)
Preheat oven to 325°.
Divide the mixture into two parts and place in two 9 x 9-inch baking pans. Cover with the cheese, butter and crumb mixture. Bake about 25 minutes or until the custard sets and the top is golden brown. To test the custard for doneness, see 734.
Serve with:
Quick Mushroom Sauce, 348, Marinara Sauce, 353, or Creole Sauce, 348

LASAGNE

16 Servings

These 2-inch wide, rather thick noodles often have a wavy ridge along one or both edges.
➤ Please read about Cooking Pastas, 212. Have ready a double portion of:
Italian Meat Sauce for Pasta I, 352
Also have ready:
3/4 lb. Ricotta cheese
1/3 lb. thinly sliced or crumbled Mozzarella cheese
1/2 lb. grated Parmesan cheese
Cook barely to the *al dente* stage, 213, in salted water:
3/4 lb. lasagne noodles
using about 2 tablespoons olive oil in the boiling water. Stir occasionally. Drain and separate the lasagne strips.

Preheat oven to 350°.
Spread a thin layer of the sauce, then a layer of pasta, in each of two 13 x 9 x 2-inch baking dishes. Cover with a sprinkling of each of the three cheeses. Spoon another layer of sauce over all, then another layer of pasta placed crisscross, and a layer of cheeses. Continue to build layers, reserving enough sauce to cover the final layer of pasta and enough Parmesan cheese to dust the top. Bake about 30 to 40 minutes. Let stand briefly before cutting and serving.

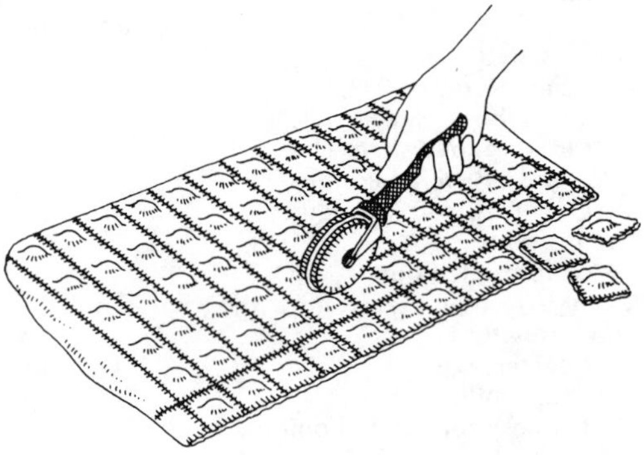

RAVIOLI

If you make this filled pasta often, use a wooden roller such as the one shown in the foreground of the chapter heading, 198. Otherwise roll out a sheet of:

Noodle Dough, 213

Place the sheet on a floured board and divide into 2 equal oblongs. Depending on how large you prefer your ravioli, partly score half the strips to indicate 2-inch or 3-inch squares. Place in the center of each square:

2 to 3 teaspoons Pasta Filling I, II or III, 218–219

Place the unscored strips of pasta over the scored strips and with your fingers press down to seal the filling firmly on four sides in separate little mounds. With a pie jagger, first cut along the lengthwise edges of the strips to reinforce the closures. Then cut between the strips to separate the ravioli as shown above. Put the squares on a rack to dry about 1½ to 2 hours, turning once. Have ready a pot of:

Boiling water or chicken stock
1 tablespoon salt

Without disturbing the boiling, place about 6 ravioli in the pot. Reduce the heat at once and simmer until the pasta is *al dente,* 213. Remove with a skimmer and place them in a heated bowl. Continue cooking the remaining ravioli. Serve covered generously with:

Melted butter
Freshly grated Parmesan cheese or a tomato sauce

CANNELLONI OR MANICOTTI

4 to 5 Servings

When they are wrapped around fillings and baked in a sauce, the charm of these "channels" or "little muffs" lies in the delicacy and freshness of the dough. The pasta, however, can be made a few hours in advance and refrigerated in foil or plastic to cover and separate the pieces.
Prepare a double portion of:

Noodle Dough, 213

After kneading the dough until very smooth, rest it ➤ covered with a cloth 10 minutes. Divide the dough in half. Roll each portion to a ⅛-inch thickness. For Cannelloni, cut into 4 x 4½-inch pieces. For Manicotti, cut into 4 x 6-inch oblongs. In either case, dry thoroughly on a cloth-covered surface; cover with a cloth about 1 hour.

To cook this pasta, have ready a kettle with at least:

5 quarts boiling salted water

Drop about 3 pieces at a time into the water so as not to disturb the boiling, and cook almost to the *al dente* stage, 213. Remove with a skimmer and dry quickly on a cloth-covered surface.
Preheat oven to 350°.
Place in the center of each piece of cooked pasta:

A heaping tablespoon Pasta Filling, 218–219

For Cannelloni, roll into pipelike "channels." For Manicotti, fold up the ends before rolling to make the "little muffs." In either case place them seam side down in a buttered ovenproof dish. Cover generously with:

A tomato sauce

or:

Melted butter
A sprinkling of fresh basil
Grated Parmesan cheese or Velouté Sauce, 345

Bake about 10 minutes and serve at once with additional:

(Grated Parmesan cheese)

PASTA WITH EGG AND CHEESE

8 to 10 Servings

Not the usual cheese sauce, but an Italian version.
➤ Please read about Cooking Pastas, 212
Boil in salted water:

1 lb. spaghetti, macaroni or noodles, 213

In the meantime, cook in a small skillet:

2 tablespoons olive oil
6 slices finely cut bacon

until the bacon is crisp. Add:

⅓ cup dry white wine

and reduce until the wine has evaporated. Beat together:

3 eggs
⅔ cup grated mixed Parmesan and Romano cheese

Drain the pasta and return it to the hot saucepan. Add the egg and cheese mixture and the hot bacon fat and bits, stirring them in quickly. The heat of the pasta will cook the egg mixture.

Season to taste
Serve immediately.

BOILED MACARONI WITH CHEESE

4 to 6 Servings

➤ Please read about Cooking Pastas, 212.
Boil in salted water until tender:
1/2 lb. macaroni: 2 cups, 213
Drain. Return it to the saucepan.
Over low heat stir in:
1/2 cup light cream
Place the macaroni in a dish and sprinkle with:
1/2 cup or more grated cheese
Serve with any of the Pasta Sauces on 219.

BAKED MACARONI

4 Servings

➤ Please read about Cooking Pastas, 212.
Boil in salted water:
4 oz. macaroni: 1 cup, 213
Drain it.
Preheat oven to 350°.
Place layers of macaroni in a buttered baking dish.
Sprinkle the layers with:
1 cup shredded cheddar cheese
Beat until blended:
1 or 2 eggs
2/3 cup milk
1/4 teaspoon salt
1/8 teaspoon paprika
A few grains cayenne
(1 sliced pimiento)
(1/4 cup chopped green peppers or 2 tablespoons chopped parsley)
(1 tablespoon grated onion)
Pour this mixture over the macaroni. Sprinkle the top with:
Au Gratin III, 553
Bake the macaroni about 40 minutes.

MACARONI WITH TOMATOES, LIVERS, MUSHROOMS AND CHEESE

About 1 1/2 Quarts

➤ Please read about Cooking Pastas, 212.
Boil in salted water:
1/2 lb. macaroni: 2 cups, 213
Drain. Place in a deep casserole. While the macaroni is cooking, sauté:
1/2 lb. mushrooms, 308
Sauté or boil until tender:
1/2 cup chicken livers or calf liver
Chop the mushrooms and the liver. Simmer until fairly thick:
4 cups canned tomatoes
Strain them. Season with:
3/4 tablespoon salt
1 teaspoon brown sugar
A few grains cayenne
(1 teaspoon dried basil)
Sauté:
1 minced onion
(1/2 minced clove garlic)
in:
2 tablespoons butter
Combine these with the other ingredients and pour them over the macaroni. Mix them well with 2 forks. Sprinkle the top with:
Grated cheddar cheese
Preheat oven to 400°.
Bake the macaroni until the cheese is golden.

MACARONI WITH SHELLFISH

4 Servings

➤ Please read about Cooking Pastas, 212.
Boil in salted water:
1 1/2 cups macaroni
Drain it. Sauté:
1 tablespoon minced onion
in:
3 tablespoons butter
Stir in until blended:
1 1/2 tablespoons flour
Stir in until smooth:
1 1/2 cups milk
3/4 cup shredded cheese
1 teaspoon Worcestershire sauce
1/2 teaspoon lemon juice
1 teaspoon salt
1/4 teaspoon paprika
A few grains cayenne
Preheat oven to 350°.
Have ready:
1 1/2 to 2 cups cleaned shrimp, oysters or clams
Place layers of macaroni and fish in a baking dish. Pour the sauce over them. Cover the top with:
Au Gratin III, 553
Bake about 30 minutes.

QUICK SPAGHETTI MEAT PIE

4 Servings

Preheat oven to 375°.
Sauté lightly:
2 cups cubed or ground cooked meat
2 teaspoons grated onion
in:
2 tablespoons butter
Add:
1/4 cup cream
Season it with:
Salt and pepper
(1/2 teaspoon basil)
Place in a greased baking dish:
1 can spaghetti: 24 oz.
Make a depression in the center. Place the meat in it. Sprinkle the top with:
Au Gratin III, 553
Bake about 25 minutes.

QUICK SPAGHETTI WITH TUNA, SALMON OR BEEF

4 Servings

Drain and reserve the oil from:
1 can tuna fish or salmon: 7 oz.

Sauté in the oil and add to the fish:
1/3 cup chopped onion
Or if you are preparing a meat dish, sauté the onion and:
(1/2 lb. ground beef)
in:
(1/4 cup shortening)
Combine:
1 cup condensed tomato soup
2 1/2 cups canned spaghetti
Fold in the flaked fish or beef. Season with:
1/2 teaspoon sugar
A few grains cayenne
Salt and paprika
Cook until thoroughly heated. You may rub a bowl with:
(A cut clove garlic)
Add the spaghetti mixture. Garnish it with:
2 tablespoons chopped parsley

CHICKEN OR TURKEY TETRAZZINI

8 to 10 Servings

A fan writes that she prefers using 1/4 pound macaroni and 1 pound mushrooms. A bit more extravagant but very good. ➤ Please read about Cooking Pastas, 212.
Cut the meat from the bones of:
A boiled chicken
There should be 2 to 3 cups shredded meat. Boil in salted water:
1/2 lb. macaroni or spaghetti: 2 cups, 213
Drain and add to this:
(1/2 cup blanched, slivered almonds)
1/2 to 3/4 lb. Sautéed Mushrooms, 308
When sautéing the mushrooms, add to the pan:
3 tablespoons dry white wine
Make a sauce of:
3 tablespoons butter or chicken fat
2 tablespoons flour
2 cups chicken broth
Season to taste
Remove from heat. Stir in:
1 cup heated whipping cream
Preheat oven to 375°.
Add half the sauce to the chicken and half to the macaroni and mushrooms. Place the macaroni in a greased baking dish. Make a hole in the center. Place the chicken in it. Sprinkle the top with:
Grated Parmesan cheese
Bake until lightly browned and heated through.

SEAFOOD TETRAZZINI

8 Servings

➤ Please read about Cooking Pastas, 212.
Boil in salted water:
1/2 lb. spaghetti: 2 cups, 213
Sauté until golden:
6 tablespoons chopped onion
in:
2 tablespoons olive oil
Add:
2 cups cream of mushroom soup
1 1/3 cups water
1/4 cup grated Romano cheese
Stir in and heat thoroughly:
2 cups chopped drained tuna, shrimp or clams
2/3 cup sliced pitted ripe olives
Add:
2 tablespoons chopped parsley
2 teaspoons lemon juice
1/8 teaspoon each thyme and marjoram
Preheat broiler.
In a buttered casserole, mix the sauce and the drained spaghetti. Top with another:
1/4 cup grated Romano cheese
Heat under the broiler until golden brown.

MOSTACCIOLI

5 Servings

Manicotti are little muffs, cannelloni are pipes, linguine are tongues, fettucine are ribbons, vermicelli are wormlets; but we think these "little mustaches" have the most fetching name of all.
➤ Please read about Cooking Pastas, 212.
Reconstitute:
1/4 lb. dried mushrooms, 573
Melt:
1 tablespoon butter
Stir and brown in it:
3/4 to 1 lb. ground round steak
1 large chopped onion
1 clove garlic cut into halves
Cover these ingredients with boiling water. Add:
3/4 teaspoon salt
1/8 teaspoon pepper
Simmer covered until almost dry. Fish out the garlic. Add:
2 cups canned tomatoes
(1/2 teaspoon each basil and oregano)
Continue to simmer, stirring frequently. Cook until the sauce is thick, from 1 to 1 1/2 hours. As it thickens, add mushrooms, and when the sauce is almost done, add:
1/4 cup olive oil
Boil in salted water until tender:
1/2 lb. mostaccioli: about 2 cups
Serve the mostaccioli on a hot platter: first a layer of the pasta, then a layer of sauce, then a layer of the pasta and again a layer of sauce. Sprinkle each meat sauce layer generously with:
Grated Parmesan cheese
Freshly grated black pepper

PASTA FILLINGS AND TOPPINGS

There can be much leeway in the makeup of pasta fillings, with combinations of meats and vegetables of your preference. Use for Cannelloni, Ravioli, Tortellini, Manicotti, large seashells, and other pastas.

I. **About 2 Cups**

Our favorite Ravioli filling.
Combine:
1/2 cup cooked puréed spinach

1 cup cooked meat: ground veal and lean pork
2 eggs
1/4 cup lightly toasted bread crumbs
1/2 cup grated Romano or Parmesan cheese
1/2 teaspoon dried basil or marjoram
(1/2 minced clove garlic)
2 teaspoons finely chopped parsley
Salt and pepper
and enough:
Stock, cream or gravy to form a stiff paste

II. **About 2 1/2 Cups**
Beat:
1 lb. Ricotta cheese
Add, one at a time, and continue to beat:
2 eggs
Add:
1 tablespoon chopped parsley
1/2 cup grated Parmesan cheese
Salt and pepper to taste

III. **About 4 Cups**
Our favorite Cannelloni filling.
Lightly sauté together:
2 tablespoons butter
1/4 cup finely chopped onion
1/4 lb. finely chopped mushrooms
Add and simmer about 5 minutes:
1 cup drained, chopped cooked spinach
2 cups minced cooked white chicken meat
1/4 teaspoon nutmeg
Salt and pepper
After the mixture has cooled somewhat, add:
3/4 cup Ricotta or dry cottage cheese
2 tablespoons cream
Mix thoroughly and:
Season to taste

IV. **About 2 Cups**
Combine thoroughly after putting through a fine grinder:
1/4 lb. Italian bologna
2 oz. prosciutto
1/8 lb. lean beef
1/8 lb. pork
Sauté the mixture over medium heat in:
2 tablespoons olive oil
When thoroughly cooked, remove from heat and mix in enough:
Dry seasoned bread crumbs
to make a stiff mixture. Add:
1/4 cup chopped parsley
1/4 teaspoon nutmeg
Salt and pepper
Chill for easier handling before filling pasta.

EGG AND CHEESE TOPPING FOR PASTA

About 1 Cup

This is a good topping for spaghetti or noodle casserole dishes which have to wait for tardy guests, as it prevents the spaghetti from drying out.
Beat until light yellow and foamy:
3 eggs
Stir in, to form a thick paste:
2/3 cup grated Parmesan cheese
Spread over the top of the dish and bake in a 400° oven until the eggs and cheese are set and browned.

CHICKEN LIVER TOPPING FOR PASTA

Sauté until just done:
1 cup chicken livers
in:
1/4 cup vegetable or olive oil
Remove the livers from the pan and cut up coarsely. In the same pan, sauté 5 minutes:
1 cup sliced mushrooms
then add:
1/2 cup halved pitted ripe olives
and the chicken liver pieces. Stir and deglaze the pan with:
1/2 cup dry sherry
Spread the topping over the pasta in an even layer and sprinkle as evenly as possible with:
1/2 cup chopped hard New York cheese
Place under the broiler until the cheese is toasted, about 2 minutes.

SUGGESTED PASTA SAUCES

The following are not the only sauces to enhance a pasta, so search our Sauce chapter for others that may appeal to your ingenuity.

Unthickened Tomato Sauce, 351
Thickened Tomato Sauce, 352
Quick Tomato Sauce, 352
Blender Tomato Sauce, 352
Italian Meat Sauce for Pasta I and II, 352
Bolognese Pasta Sauce, 353
Spaghetti Sauce with Liver, 353
Marinara Sauce, 353
Octopus Pasta Sauce, 353
Quick Shrimp and Clam Sauce for Pasta, 354

EGG DISHES

For a philosopher or a mathematician, the sphere is the most satisfactory of all forms. But for humankind in general, the ovoid—or egg-shape—exerts an even greater fascination. Ovoids crop up in architecture, from the earliest Greek moldings to the latest of Late Renaissance cartouches. The egg's significance as a symbol of the Resurrection and its importance to the Eastern Church led to the wildly extravagant, exquisitely wrought golden Easter eggs which the Imperial Russian Court commissioned during the decades preceding the Revolution. While the results of our American efforts to paint eggs may prove more homely, they are made easier if the eggs are held in a wire treelike form, shown above.

It is not surprising that so elegant a package should turn out to hold a small treasure of balanced nutrients—proteins, fats and minerals. Eggs and egg dishes may be acceptably served at any meal, fried, scrambled, boiled, poached, baked, or incorporated into omelets or into a soufflé, as shown above. And, almost unlimited variations of meat, vegetables or fish may accompany or be folded into them. For more about eggs, see Ingredients, 543.

No egg dish really succeeds, however, unless the eggs are "strictly fresh" and are cooked with due respect for their delicacy and sensitive response to heat. ➤ In only one type of preparation should the heat be high and brief—for omelets. ➤ Otherwise, dishes in which eggs predominate invariably do best if gently cooked and carefully timed, see the egg timer illustrated on 543. In combining eggs in custards, soufflés and sauces, let them partially cook on the stored heat in the pan. Do not put them back on direct heat, because they never will have so satisfactory a texture.

SOFT-COOKED, HARD-COOKED AND CODDLED EGGS

The difference among these three is more a matter of timing than of method.

For soft- and hard-cooked eggs, place in a saucepan, preferably glass or enamel:

Unshelled eggs

Cover them with:

Cold water

Put the pan over medium heat and bring the water to the boiling point. ➤ Lower heat to a simmer. Now watch your time, which will depend on how large and how cold your eggs are. The following timings are for 70° eggs. Right out of the refrigerator, they will require at least 2 minutes more. After the heat is reduced, eggs will be **soft-cooked** in 2 to 3 minutes; **medium-cooked** in about 4; **hard-cooked** in 10 to 15. Hard-cooked eggs should be plunged into cold water at once to arrest further cooking and to prevent the yolks from discoloring.

To **coddle** eggs, lower them carefully into boiling water with a tablespoon. Cover the pan and remove from the heat. Allow 6 to 8 minutes for delicately coddled eggs. If you want the eggs to remain shapely when opened, turn them several times within the first few minutes of coddling so that the white of the egg solidifies evenly in the air space and the yolk is centered.

➤ To shell hard-cooked eggs, crack the shell and roll the egg between the palms of the hands to free the thin tough skin from the egg and make shelling easier. If eggs are very fresh, they are more difficult to shell. If you want to slice the eggs smoothly, dip a knife into water before slicing.

Soft-cooked eggs may be served shelled, in the various ways suggested for Poached Eggs, opposite.

Recipes and suggestions for serving hard-cooked eggs follow. Others will be found in Hors d'Oeuvre and Salads.

SAUTÉED OR FRIED EGGS

4 Servings

Melt in a skillet over low heat:

1 or 2 tablespoons butter

Break carefully into the skillet:

4 eggs

Baste the eggs with the hot butter. Cook them over a very low heat until done. To get a firm white ➤ cover the pan with a lid at once. If you like a softer white, you may at once pour over the eggs:

1 tablespoon boiling water

then cover the skillet and cook about 1 minute. When the eggs are firm, serve them seasoned with:

Salt and pepper

If you prefer "once-over-lightly" to "sunny-side-up," proceed as above; but when the whites are firm, insert a slotted spatula under the egg, supporting the yolk area, and cautiously reverse it in the skillet. Cooking the second side should take only a matter of moments.

ADDITIONS TO SAUTÉED EGGS

It is often the extras that give punch to eggs, especially in brunch and luncheon dishes. Try eggs on a small mound of:

Boiled rice, noodles or potatoes, or on rounds of toast

Pour over any of these:

A mushroom, tomato or onion sauce, see Index
A canned soup sauce, 348
White sauce seasoned with mustard or curry powder, herbs, onion, celery, green peppers, capers, anchovies or cheese
Black Butter, 350, or Brown Butter, 349

POACHED EGGS

Individual Serving

I. Poached eggs, unless made in individual molds —in which case cook them over—not in—boiling water—are apt to produce "streamers" that you may trim off with scissors before serving.
Grease the bottom of a 6- to 8-inch pot. Put in enough slightly salted water to fill to twice the depth of an egg. While the water is coming to a boil, break into a small bowl:

1 egg

Swirl the water into a mad vortex with a wooden spoon. Drop the egg into the well formed in the center of the pot. ➤ The swirling water should round the egg. ➤ Reduce the heat. ➤ Simmer 4 to 5 minutes or let stand off the heat for 8 minutes. By this time the white should be firm and the yolk soft. Remove with a skimmer and drain well. If not using the egg immediately, plunge it at once into cold water to stop the cooking. Repeat the process for each egg. To store, see II, below. To reheat the eggs, drop them into hot—not boiling —water.

II. **4 Servings**

Have ready:

4 eggs

Place in a skillet 1½ inches of water. Bring it to a rolling boil, then reduce heat until water is quiet. Break an egg into a cup and bring the edge of the cup level with the surface of the water. Slide the egg in gently. Do this with each egg. Simmer eggs from 3 to 5 minutes or until the whites are firm and yolks appear pink. With practice, you will be able to judge the right degree of doneness. With a slotted spoon or pancake turner, lift out the eggs. Let drain well before serving. Eggs may be poached in a small amount of milk, cream or stock. For other additions, see below. To store for later use—but not later than 24 hours after the original cooking—put the poached eggs in a bowl of ice-cold water in the refrigerator. This is the professional way to prepare eggs in advance for use the following day in Eggs Benedict, 222, or any other recipe calling for poached eggs. The heat from the platter, toast and sauce warms up the egg.

ADDITIONS TO POACHED EGGS

I. Poached Eggs Mornay

Arrange poached eggs in a shallow buttered baking dish.
Cover with:

Mornay Sauce, 342

Sprinkle with:

Grated cheese
Bread crumbs

and brown quickly under a hot broiler.

II. Cover the bottom of a shallow buttered baking dish with:

Creamed Spinach, 327

Arrange the poached eggs on the spinach and proceed as for Poached Eggs Mornay, above, to produce **Eggs Florentine.**

III. Hollow out a hard roll, insert egg, cover with:

Quick Seafood Spaghetti Sauce, 349

and garnish with:

Cooked shrimp, mussels and oysters

IV. Serve on toast, covered with:

Hunter's Sauce, 347, or Aurore Sauce, 344

V. Poach eggs in:

Creole Sauce, 348

EGGS POACHED IN SOUP

4 Servings

The following recipe makes an attractive light meal, prepared in a few minutes. Combine in an 8-inch skillet and heat to the boiling point over low heat:

1 can condensed tomato soup: 10½ oz.

diluted with:

½ cup water

Add:

(½ teaspoon dried basil)
(¼ teaspoon sugar)

➤ Reduce the heat and keep the liquid below boiling point. Slide into the soup from a saucer, one at a time:

4 eggs

➤ Simmer 4 to 5 minutes or until the eggs firm up.
Serve on:

Rounds of toast

covered with the soup. Sprinkle with:

Chopped parsley or basil

EGGS POACHED IN WINE

6 Servings

Combine in a skillet:

1 cup dry red wine
1 crushed clove garlic
2 tablespoons minced onion or shallot
¼ teaspoon salt
⅛ teaspoon pepper
A Bouquet Garni, 572

Heat to boiling point, ➤ reduce heat and simmer about 3 minutes, then remove the bouquet. Slide into the wine from a saucer, one at a time:

6 eggs

Poach them until the whites are firm. Remove and put them on:

Slices of fried bread (rubbed with garlic)

Strain the wine, put it back into the skillet and thicken with:

Kneaded Butter, 340

Pour the sauce over the eggs.

EGGS BENEDICT

6 Servings

Try this substituting oysters for eggs.
Have ready:

6 Poached Eggs, 221

Toast:

6 rounds of bread or halves of English muffins

Cover each with:

A thin slice of hot ham, minced cooked bacon or deviled ham

Top each with one of the poached eggs.
Serve them hot, covered with:

Hollandaise Sauce, 358

POACHED EGGS BLACKSTONE

6 Servings

Have ready:

6 Poached Eggs, 221

Sauté, then mince:

3 slices bacon

Reserve the drippings. Cut:

6 slices tomato, ½ inch thick

Season them with:

Salt and white pepper

Dip the slices in flour and sauté them in the bacon fat. Sprinkle with the minced bacon. Cover each slice with a poached egg.
Pour over the eggs:

Hollandaise Sauce, 358

EGGS WITH SMOKED SALMON

A genial winter breakfast or luncheon dish.
Prepare:

Buttered toast or slices of pumpernickel bread

Dip into boiling water:

Very thin slices of smoked salmon

Dry them. Place them on the toast. Cover with:

Poached or sautéed eggs

Sprinkle with:

(Dill seed)

HUEVOS RANCHEROS OR COWBOY EGGS

4 Servings

A traditional Spanish and Latin American dish. These eggs can be baked in the following sauce, or poached or sautéed with the sauce poured over afterward. Heat in a skillet:

¼ cup olive oil

and sauté in it for 5 minutes:

1 crushed clove garlic

Remove the garlic and add, sautéeing until soft:

2 medium-sized finely chopped onions
1 large finely chopped green pepper

Add:

1 cup peeled, seeded and chopped fresh tomatoes
½ teaspoon salt
¼ teaspoon freshly ground black pepper
2 teaspoons chili powder
¼ teaspoon oregano
⅛ teaspoon powdered cumin

Simmer covered until thick and well blended.

Season to taste

The sauce should be very hot and well flavored.
Pour it over:

8 poached or sautéed eggs

allowing 2 eggs per serving.
Or, to bake, preheat oven to 450°.
Pour the sauce into a heatproof shallow dish or 4 individual casseroles and nest the uncooked eggs in the same. Garnish with:

Strips of red pimiento

Sprinkle with:

A little grated cheese

Bake until eggs are set.

SCRAMBLED EGGS

For proper results, eggs should be not below room temperature. To achieve more fluffiness, beaten whites may be added to whole eggs in the proportion of 1 additional white to 3 whole eggs.

I. **2 Servings**

Melt in a skillet over low heat:

1 to 2 tablespoons butter

Have ready by the time the butter is hot and add the following mixture, beaten with a fork until the eggs are uniform in color:

3 eggs
¼ teaspoon salt
⅛ teaspoon paprika
(2 tablespoons milk or cream)

As the eggs heat through, increase the heat somewhat, and with a spoon shove the eggs about gently but with accelerating speed, turning them if necessary, until they have thickened but are still soft.

II. **2 Servings**

A slower but quite foolproof alternative. Melt in a double boiler ➤ over—not in—boiling water:

1 tablespoon butter

Have ready:

The seasoned egg mixture in I, above

When the butter is hot, pour in the egg mixture. Stir repeatedly with a wooden spoon until eggs have thickened into soft creamy curds.
You may serve the eggs on:

Hot toast lightly buttered or spread with fish paste, deviled ham or liver sausage; or in a hollowed-out hard roll

Another attractive way to present scrambled eggs is to put them in warm, well-buttered individual ring molds while the eggs are still rather creamy in consistency. Let them finish cooking in their own heat, which will set them. Turn them out and fill the centers with any of the additions listed below.

ADDITIONS TO SCRAMBLED EGGS

Small amounts of the following may be stirred into the egg mixture before scrambling. Ingredients should be about 70°.

Freshly ground mace
Grated or crumbled cheese
Chopped, peeled, seeded, sautéed tomatoes flavored with basil
Cultured sour cream and chives
Canned chopped sardines
Crab meat, seasoned with curry powder
Capers
Chopped canned anchovies
Chopped sautéed onions
Crisp bacon bits
Small pieces of broiled sausage
Sautéed mushrooms
Poached calf brains and parsley

EGGS SCRAMBLED WITH CREAM CHEESE

4 Servings

Melt in a double boiler over simmering water:
1 package cream cheese: 3 oz.
1 tablespoon butter
Scald and stir in:
1 cup cream
Add:
½ teaspoon salt
¼ teaspoon paprika
Break into the sauce:
6 eggs
Before the egg whites are firm, stir the eggs gently with a fork until thick. Add:
1½ tablespoons sherry

SCOTCH WOODCOCK

2 Servings

Toast:
2 slices bread
Butter well and spread with a thin layer of:
Anchovy paste
Cut the toast into fingers. Beat together:
3 or 4 egg yolks
½ cup cream
⅛ teaspoon pepper
⅛ teaspoon salt
Melt in a double boiler:
2 tablespoons butter
Add the egg mixture and scramble until creamy. Arrange the anchovy toast on a hot dish and cover with the egg mixture. Garnish with:
Chopped parsley

SHIRRED OR BAKED EGGS OR EGGS EN COCOTTE

Individual Serving

Baked eggs always have great "eye appeal" served in little ramekins, casseroles or cocotte dishes. Care must be taken not to overcook them, for the ramekin will retain the heat and continue to cook the egg after it is removed from the oven. If you put a poaching paper, 151, over the ramekin, it will return enough heat to the top side of the egg to set it. The yolks should be soft, the whites just set. Don't try to hurry baked eggs.
Preheat oven to 350°.
Grease small bakers or ramekins. Break carefully into each one:
1 egg
Add lightly:
Salt
Sprinkle over the top:
1 teaspoon cream or melted butter
Place ramekins in a pan of hot water. Bake about 6 to 7 minutes, depending on the thickness of the ramekin. You may garnish with:
Chopped sautéed chicken livers, well-seasoned
or serve covered with:
A tomato sauce, 351–354

BAKED EGGS ON TOAST

Individual Serving

Carefully prepared, this makes a delectable dish.
Preheat oven to 325°.
Grease warmed individual molds with:
Butter
Place in each one:
1 teaspoon chopped celery, chives or parsley
Break into each one:
1 or 2 eggs
Season with:
Salt and paprika
Cover each mold with a small poaching paper, 151. Place the molds in a pan of hot water, to a depth of ½ inch from the top of the mold. Bake until the eggs are firm. Turn them out on:
Rounds of hot buttered toast
Serve with well-seasoned:
White Sauce I, 341, with a little mustard added, or Sauce Dijonnaise, 342
or with one of the Additions to Baked Eggs listed below.

ADDITIONS TO BAKED EGGS

For interesting variations to baked eggs try adding: cooked mushrooms, asparagus tips, tomatoes or other vegetables, such as creamed spinach. Or add chicken hash, small bits of bacon, sausage or anchovy. Or place a round of toast covered with Gruyère cheese in the bottom of the baker before the eggs are added. You may cover the eggs with a cheese or tomato sauce before baking. Other tasty additions are: Creamed Mushroom Caps, 308, or Creamed Onions, 312.

EGGS IN A NEST

1 to 2 Servings

A gala-looking dish.
Preheat oven to 350°.
Beat until very stiff:
2 egg whites
Heap them in a greased ovenproof dish. Make 2 cavities equally distant from but not too near the edge. Slip into them:
2 unbroken egg yolks
Bake 10 minutes or until the eggs are set. Season with:
Salt and white pepper
Sprinkle with:
(Chopped chives)

EGGS BAKED IN BACON RINGS

Individual Servings

Preheat oven to 325°.
Sauté or broil lightly:
Strips of bacon
Grease the bottoms of muffin pans. Line the sides with the bacon. Place in each pan:
(1 tablespoon chili sauce)
Drop into it:
1 egg
Pour over the egg:
1 teaspoon melted butter
Sprinkle with:
Salt and paprika
Bake about 10 minutes or until the eggs are set. Turn them out onto:
Rounds of toast or warm slices of drained pineapple
Garnish with:
Parsley

EGGS IN HAM CAKES

4 Servings

Preheat oven to 325°.
Combine:
1 cup ground cooked ham
1 egg
1 tablespoon water
1/8 teaspoon paprika or pepper
Press these ingredients into 4 greased muffin tins. Leave a large hollow in each one. Drop into the hollows:
4 eggs
Bake the cakes until the eggs are firm. Turn out the cakes on:
Rounds of toast
Garnish with:
Parsley or chopped chervil

HARD-COOKED EGG AND VEGETABLE CASSEROLE

5 Servings

Preheat oven to 350°.
Combine:
1 cup cooked vegetables
1 cup White Sauce I, 341, or Creole Sauce, 348
You may add:
(2 teaspoons chopped fresh parsley, thyme or basil)
A sprinkling of dill or celery seed is wonderful.
Prepare:
5 Hard-Cooked Eggs, 220
Slice them. Grease a baking dish. Place alternate layers of vegetables and eggs in the dish. Top with:
Au Gratin III, 553
Bake about 15 minutes.

CURRIED EGGS

4 Servings

Cook:
6 Hard-Cooked Eggs, 220
Shell and slice or cut them in half lengthwise.
Prepare:
2 cups Curry Sauce, 345
You may chop and add:
(1/4 cup blanched almonds)
Add the eggs. Heat well and serve on:
Hot buttered toast
garnished with:
Parsley

CREAMED EGGS AND ASPARAGUS COCKAIGNE

We use both versions, depending on the time available. The texture is lovely if the asparagus is well drained and the sauce not overheated.

I. **6 Servings**

Drain well, reserving the liquid, and cut in 1-inch pieces:
2 cups cooked or canned asparagus tips
Have ready:
6 Hard-Cooked Eggs, 220
Prepare:
2 cups Quick White Sauce, 342
using milk and the reserved asparagus liquor. When the sauce is hot, gently fold in the asparagus and sliced eggs. Either heat this mixture further in the top of a double boiler ➤ over—not in—boiling water, or preheat oven to 350° and place in a greased baking dish. Cover with:
Au Gratin I, 553
and bake until the eggs and asparagus are heated through, about 10 minutes. Serve with:
Slices of ham
Hot French Bread, 605

II. **4 Servings**

Preheat oven to 350°.
Reserve the asparagus liquor and have ready:
4 to 6 sliced Hard-Cooked Eggs, 220
1 1/2 cups well-drained canned asparagus, cut in 1-inch lengths
1 can condensed cream of chicken soup: 10 1/2 oz., diluted with 1/4 cup asparagus liquor

In 4 individual baking dishes place alternate layers of eggs and asparagus. Top each dish with equal amounts of soup mixture. Cover with:

Au Gratin III, 553

and bake about 15 minutes or until thoroughly heated.

CREAMED EGGS AU GRATIN

4 Servings

Preheat broiler.
Slice into a baking dish:

4 Hard-Cooked Eggs, 220

Combine:

1½ cups White Sauce II, 341
¼ cup Chili Sauce, 847

Pour this mixture over the eggs. Top with:

Au Gratin III, 553

Place the dish under the broiler until the crumbs are golden.

MASKED EGGS

Allow 1 Egg to a Person

Chill:

Hard-Cooked Eggs, 220

Cut them into halves lengthwise. Place them cut side down on:

Watercress or shredded lettuce

Pour over them:

Mayonnaise, 363, thinned with a little lemon juice or cream; Mayonnaise Collée, 368; or Sauce Chaud-Froid, 369

Sprinkle them with:

Capers, chopped anchovies, or bits of cooked ham or cooked bacon

STUFFED EGGS ON ROSETTES WITH SAVORY SAUCE

8 Servings

This dish is elaborate but capable of prefabrication. The rosettes and the sauce may be made and the eggs cooked the day before.
Prepare:

8 Hard-Cooked Eggs, 220

Cut them crosswise into halves. Remove the yolks, and mash. Combine the yolks with an equal part of:

Finely chopped seasoned cooked spinach or Creamed Spinach, 327

Fill the egg whites with the mixture. Prepare:

2 cups White Sauce I, 341

Season it with:

1 tablespoon Worcestershire Sauce, 848
2 tablespoons dry sherry
¾ cup Chili Sauce, 847
Salt and pepper

When the sauce is smooth and hot, add:

2 cups cooked or canned shrimp or diced cooked sweetbreads

Prepare:

16 Rosettes, 246

Place a stuffed egg half on each rosette and cover with sauce. Serve at once while the rosettes are crisp. If you have made the sauce and the rosettes ahead of time, reheat the sauce in a double boiler, and the rosettes briefly in a 400° oven.

DEVILED OR STUFFED EGGS

The blandness of hard-cooked eggs is a challenge to adventurous cooks. Here are a few suggestions to enliven this basic ingredient with supplies from your pantry shelves.
Prepare:

Hard-Cooked Eggs, 220

Cut the eggs in half lengthwise or slice off both ends, which leaves a barrel-shaped container. Remove yolks carefully so as not to damage the whites. Crush the yolks without packing them and moisten them pleasantly with:

French dressing or mayonnaise; sweet or cultured sour cream; soft butter with vinegar and sugar; lemon juice or sweet pickle juice

Season to taste with:

Salt and paprika

or one or more of the following:

(A little dry mustard)
(Catsup)
(A dash of cayenne, curry, or hot pepper sauce)
(Worcestershire Sauce, 848)

Exotic additions to the yolks are:

Anchovy or sardine paste
Liver sausage paste or Foie Gras, 494
Chopped sautéed chicken livers
Chopped ginger and cream cheese
Chutney
Caviar
Smoked salmon
Deviled ham or tongue
Grated Roquefort cheese
Chopped chives, tarragon, chervil, parsley, burnet or basil

Put the filling back in the whites. You may use a pastry tube for elaborate effects. For improved flavor and texture, remove the eggs from the refrigerator ½ hour before serving.
Garnish with:

Olives, capers or truffles

DEVILED EGGS IN SAUCE

4 Servings

Preheat oven to 425°.
Prepare:

4 Deviled Eggs, above

Place the halves in a greased dish. Pour over them:

1 cup Quick Tomato Sauce, 352, or Mornay Sauce, 342, Béchamel Sauce I, 341, or Mushroom Sauce, 348, or Tomato Shrimp Sauce, 343

Coat the sauce with:

Au Gratin II or III, 553

Bake until the top is brown

ABOUT OMELETS

The name "omelet" is loosely applied to many kinds of egg dishes. In America, you often get a great, puffy, soufflélike, rather dry dish in which the egg whites have been beaten separately and folded into the yolks. In France an entire mystique surrounds a simple process in which the yolks and whites are combined as unobtrusively as possible to avoid incorporating air, and this marbleized mixture is quickly turned into a twofold miracle. In an Italian frittata, the food is often mingled at once with the stirred egg, and this thin pancake-like disk is cooked in a little oil, first on one side and then on the other, with a result not unlike a large edition of Eggs Fooyoung, 228.

Since omelet-making is so rapid, see that you have ready everything you are going to serve the omelet with or on, and be sure you have your diners captive. For more details about equipment, see About Omelet Pans, right.

The success of all of these so-called omelets demands that ➤ the pan and the fat be hot enough to bind the base of the egg at once so as to hold the softer egg above, but not so hot as to toughen the base before the rest of the egg cooks.

➤ Eggs, therefore, and any food incorporated with them, must be at least 70° before being put into the pan. More omelet failures are due to eggs being used direct from the refrigerator than to any other cause. There is always, too, the problem of salting. As salt tends to toughen the egg structure, it should, in general, be added to the fillings or garnishes you choose to fold into the omelet.

Glazing omelets makes them look prettier but also tends to toughen them. ➤ To glaze an omelet, brush it with butter. Or, if it is a sweet omelet, sprinkle it with sugar and run it under the broiler briefly, or use a hot salamander, 145, or brander. If you want a really sophisticated job, put the omelet on a warm ovenproof server, coat it lightly with a thin Mornay Sauce, 342, and run it under a broiler 2 minutes.

To fill a 3-egg omelet, have ready about ½ to ¾ cup cooked or creamed mushrooms, seafood, ham or tongue. Place one-fourth on the upper surface of the omelet while still in the pan and fold. Reserve the remainder for a final garnish on top. Or, a simple method is to fold the omelet as sketched below, then cut an incision along the top and insert the hot food. Herbs or finely grated cheese may be added to the beaten eggs before cooking. For other fillings, see Additions to Scrambled Eggs, 223.

ABOUT OMELET PANS

Omelet pans generate more tempests than teapots do. Doctrinaire omelet-makers contend that one pan should be used solely for their specialty and that it should never be washed—simply rubbed with soft toweling and a handful of salt. The argument for the exclusive pan goes further. Any pan used for frying or braising is apt to develop hot spots. Yet those of us who resent giving kitchen space to a pan for a single function find an all-purpose skillet—cleaned with modern detergents—entirely feasible for omelet preparation ➤ provided the pan surface remains smooth so the eggs can slide freely over it. For this reason coated pans are preferred by some cooks, but if this type of pan is used in omelet-making, you may reduce the butter by not more than one-third. The pan should be moderately heavy, and slowly but thoroughly heated. Otherwise the egg cannot stand what one French authority calls "the too great brutality" of the quick heat that is so essential.

The next thing to consider is the omelet in relation to pan size. Since French omelets are made so quickly, we never try more than 2 to 3 eggs at a time—cooked in 1 tablespoon of sweet butter. If more than one omelet is needed, have some extra butter already melted to save preparation time. We use a skillet with a long handle and a 5-inch base flaring gently to a 7-inch top, as shown in the sketches. For larger omelets—and they can be made successfully with up to 8 or 10 eggs—see that the similarly shaped pan is big enough to keep the egg, when poured, no deeper than ¼ inch; and add a proportionate amount of butter.

FRENCH OMELET

Andrew Carnegie once counseled: "Put all your eggs in one basket. Then watch that basket!" When the container is a skillet and the objective an omelet, his advice is especially apt.

➤ Please read About Omelets, above. Remember that an omelet of the French type takes only 30 to 50 seconds to make, depending on your pref-

erence for soft or firm results. Mix briefly in a bowl with a dinner fork:

3 eggs

Put in a 7-inch omelet pan:

1 tablespoon clarified sweet butter, 349

To avoid sticking, clarified butter is best. Roll it over the bottom and sides of the pan. When it is hot and ➤ has reached the point of fragrance, but is not brown, pour in the eggs. Meanwhile, agitate the pan forward and backward with the left hand. Keep the egg mass sliding as a whole over the pan bottom. With a dinner fork, quickly swirl the eggs with a circular motion, as shown on the preceding page. Hold the fork so the tines are parallel to, but not scraping, the base of the pan. At this point the heat in the pan may be sufficient to cook the eggs, and you may want to lift the pan from the heat as you gently swirl the eggs, as illustrated, in circular scrolls from the edges to the center. Pay no attention to the ridges formed by the fork. The rhythm of the pan and the stirring is like a child's trick of patting the head while rubbing the stomach. ➤ Have ready a hot serving plate, which helps to inflate the omelet; choose a heat-resistant one if you plan to glaze, see About Omelets, above. Whether you fill your omelet or leave it plain, grasp the handle of the pan so the left palm is up, as shown. Tip the pan down away from the handle and, with the fork, flip about one-third of the omelet over, away from the handle, as shown in the center. If the omelet shows any tendency to stick, discard the fork and give the pan handle a sharp rap or two with the fist, as sketched. The omelet will flip over without the use of a fork and will start to slide. Slant the pan to 90° or more until the omelet makes a second fold in sliding out of the pan and lies with its ends folded under on the plate—ready to serve. Glaze and garnish, if you wish, and serve at once. For fillings, see About Omelets, opposite.

FLUFFY OR SOUFFLÉED OMELET

4 Servings

If you have 1 or 2 extra egg whites, add these and omit the baking powder. You may add some grated Parmesan cheese or chopped parsley, chives and chervil to the egg mixture before cooking it, or sprinkle these on top before putting the omelet in the oven.

Combine and beat with a fork:

¼ cup milk
4 egg yolks
1 teaspoon double-acting baking powder

Beat until stiff, but not dry:

4 to 6 egg whites

Melt in a heavy skillet over slow heat:

1 tablespoon clarified sweet butter, 349

Fold the yolk mixture lightly into the egg whites. Pour the batter into the skillet. Cover the skillet with a lid. As the omelet cooks, slash through it several times with a knife to permit the heat to penetrate the lower layer. When the omelet is half done—after about 5 minutes—it may be placed uncovered on the center rack of a 350° oven until the top is set. Jet-propel this to the table as it comes out of the oven, because it will collapse quite quickly.

Cut the omelet in pie-shaped wedges, serving single segments garnished with any of the fillings or sauces suggested under About Omelets, opposite. Or double the omelet over the fillings, sandwich-style. Sprinkle with:

Chopped parsley

FIRM OMELET

4 Servings

For the beginner, the texture of this omelet is a little more manageable.

Beat with a fork until blended:

4 eggs

Beat in:

¼ cup milk, cream or stock
½ teaspoon salt
⅛ teaspoon paprika

Melt in a skillet:

1½ tablespoons clarified sweet butter, 349

When the butter is fairly hot, add the egg mixture. Cook over low heat. Lift the edges with a pancake turner and tilt the skillet to permit the uncooked mixture to run to the bottom, or stick the egg mixture with a fork in the soft spots to permit the heat to penetrate the bottom layer. When it is all an even consistency, fold the omelet over and serve it. For a festive occasion, fold into the omelet before serving:

(3 tablespoons cultured sour cream)
(1½ tablespoons red caviar)

SWEET OMELET

See 742 for other sweet omelets.

I. Follow the recipe above for:

Fluffy Omelet

Add to the yolk mixture:

1 tablespoon sugar

Just before serving, spread the omelet with:

Jam or jelly

Sprinkle the top with:

Confectioners' sugar

Fruit juice may be substituted for the milk and the omelet spread with cooked or raw sweetened fruit instead of jelly.

II. Prepare:

Fluffy Omelet, left

Add to the egg yolks:

1 tablespoon brandy
1 tablespoon curaçao

When finished, sprinkle with:

Confectioners' or castor sugar

and flambé, 155.

EGGS FOOYOUNG WITH SHRIMP

Fooyoung is really a rich omelet made with additions of cooked vegetables, fish and meat.
Clean or drain:

2 cups bean sprouts

Heat:

A little vegetable oil

in a skillet and stir-fry, 279, until translucent and crisp:

1 minced slice gingerroot
6 chopped green onions
1 rib celery, thinly sliced
1 cup chopped cooked fish, shrimp or finely diced cooked meat

Have ready and combine the above ingredients and the sprouts with:

6 well-beaten eggs
1 teaspoon salt
½ teaspoon pepper

Heat an additional:

1 tablespoon vegetable oil

in another small skillet. Drop the above mixture into it to form small omelets, golden brown on both sides. Serve with:

Soy sauce

SPANISH OMELET

2 Servings Without Potatoes
4 Servings With Potatoes

A true Spanish omelet always includes potatoes. We find that we get best results by cooking them separately, keeping them warm, and adding them to the rest of the vegetables at the last moment. Without potato, and with the addition of a dozen or so julienned strips of cooked ham, this omelet becomes a **piperade,** or **Basque omelet.**
If using potatoes, heat in a 10-inch skillet until it reaches the point of fragrance:

½ cup olive oil

Add:

1 cup thinly sliced potatoes

Turn them constantly until well coated with the oil. Reduce the heat and, turning occasionally, continue to cook the potatoes about 20 minutes. After starting the potatoes, heat in a heavy skillet to the point of fragrance:

2 tablespoons olive oil

Add, stirring constantly, and cook about 5 minutes:

½ cup thinly sliced onions
½ cup julienned green pepper strips

Add:

1 pressed garlic clove
Salt and pepper to taste
⅓ cup peeled, seeded, drained, chopped tomatoes

Continue to cook about 15 minutes. If you are adding potatoes, combine them now with the above and keep the mixture hot. When the filling is ready, prepare a French Omelet, 226. When the omelet is cooked, do not fold, but slide onto a heated plate so that it retains the flat shape it assumed in the pan. Cover with the hot vegetables and serve at once.

FRITTATA

3 Servings

This Italian omelet usually has the filling mixed into the eggs before they are cooked. You may use any of the suggested fillings under About Omelets, 226, except the creamed or sauced ones, allowing about 1 cup of filling to 3 eggs.
Prepare and keep warm:

2 cups diced cooked vegetables, chicken, seafood or ham—in any desired combination

Beat with a fork until blended:

6 eggs

Stir in the filling and:

Season to taste

How much salt and pepper you add will depend on how highly seasoned your filling is. Have ready a 10-inch greased omelet pan. Into another 10-inch pan which has been heated, put:

1½ tablespoons olive oil

Pour in the egg mixture and proceed as in the basic French Omelet, 226, until the bottom of the frittata is set and the top is still like creamy scrambled eggs. Place the greased skillet with the greased side over the frittata like a lid. Reverse the position of the skillets so the frittata falls into the "lid," which is then heated to complete the cooking of the dish, a matter of 1 to 2 minutes more. Serve at once on a hot platter.

ABOUT SOUFFLÉS

The soufflé is considered the prima donna of the culinary world. The timbale, 231, is her more even-tempered relative. With closer cultivation both become quite tractable and are great glamorizers for leftover foods. ➤ Cooked foods are best to use in both soufflés and timbales, as they release less moisture into the mixture than do raw ones.

Soufflés have a duration as evanescent as the "breath" for which they are are named; some last a bit longer than others, but all have a built-in limit for holding their puff. If the soufflé is well made, you can count on about 10 short minutes in a holding oven ➤ but beware of drafts. Since they depend on egg white and steam for their ascent ➤ not a second should be wasted from the beating of the whites until the soufflé is popped quickly into the ➤ preheated oven. With very few exceptions, every action, including ➤ immediate serving after baking, should contribute to holding their "breath" as long as possible. These tours de force, often based on a white sauce with egg yolks and whipped whites, are easy to make if the pointers are carefully heeded. The white sauce should be a rather firm one ➤ heated just to a boil. Remove it from the heat for ½ minute before the 70° eggs and any other ingredients—also at 70°—are added. The egg whites should be ➤ stiff, but not dry, 544. ➤ Soufflés can always be made lighter if an extra egg white is added for every 2 whole eggs.

➤ To prepare a soufflé dish for baking, use a straight-sided ovenproof baking dish, shown in the chapter heading, 220. Grease the bottom and sides well with butter and then coat the buttered surface with a thorough dusting of flour, sugar or dry grated cheese, depending on the flavor of your soufflé. It will also climb up the sides of an ungreased baker, but it will not rise so high, and the lovely brown crust will stick and have to be scraped off the sides rather than forming the glossy coating that adds so much to the look of the individual serving.

Next, be sure the oven is heated to the indicated temperature. ➤ A soufflé needs quick bottom heat. ➤ If your electric oven is an old model, you may need to remove the top element, as the heat in it is often enough to stiffen the top surface of the soufflé too quickly and not allow for its fullest expansion during the baking period. ➤ For oven placement of soufflé baking dishes, see sketch on 159. Some recipes suggest making soufflés in the top of a double boiler ➤ over—not in—boiling water. This is advisable only if an oven is not available, as the resulting texture is closer to that of a timbale than a soufflé. To make a soufflé with a crown—a "high-hat soufflé"—just before putting the soufflé into the oven, take a large spoon or a rubber scraper and run a groove about 1½ inches deep all around the top, about 1¼ inches from the edge of the dish. A crown may also be made by extending the height of the baking dish with a piece of parchment paper tied firmly around the dish. We find this satisfactory only with so-called cold soufflés based on cream gelatins.

CHEESE SOUFFLÉ COCKAIGNE

4 Servings

➤ Please read About Soufflés, above.
Preheat oven to 350°.
Prepare:

1 cup White Sauce II, 341

Bring to a boil. Remove from heat ½ minute. Add, stirring well:

5 tablespoons grated Parmesan cheese
2 tablespoons shredded Gruyère cheese
3 beaten egg yolks

Beat until stiff, but not dry:

4 egg whites

Fold into the cheese mixture. Pour into one 7-inch or four individual prepared soufflé baking dishes. You may decorate the soufflés before baking with:

Paper-thin slices of aged Swiss cheese cut into fancy shapes

Bake 25 to 30 minutes or until set.

ϒ BLENDER CHEESE SOUFFLE

4 or 5 Servings

A somewhat firm but very acceptable soufflé.
➤ To prepare baking dish, please read About Soufflés, above.
Preheat oven to 325°.
Dice into cubes:

6 oz. sharp cheddar cheese

Heat to just below boiling:

1½ cups milk

Pour milk into blender container and quickly add:

2 tablespoons butter
6 to 8 pieces crustless bread, torn into large pieces
½ teaspoon salt
⅛ teaspoon pepper or a few grains of cayenne
(⅛ teaspoon dry mustard)

Blend until thickened. Add the cubed cheese. Beat in a large bowl until lemon-colored:

4 egg yolks

Add the cheese mixture ➤ very slowly, beating constantly. Beat until stiff, but not dry, and fold in gently:

4 egg whites

Place the mixture in a prepared 8-inch soufflé baking dish and bake about 50 minutes or until set.

ADDITIONS TO CHEESE SOUFFLÉS

For a more complete dish, consider adding one of the following to cheese soufflé:

½ cup ground or finely chopped cooked ham
½ to 1 cup well-drained chopped or ground cooked vegetables, such as celery or carrots
3 tablespoons Italian tomato paste

VEGETABLE SOUFFLÉ

4 Servings

Please read About Soufflés, 228.
Cooked oyster plant, eggplant, cauliflower, peas, onions, carrots, canned or fresh scraped corn, or asparagus may be used alone or in chosen combinations. The addition of small quantities of finely minced raw carrots, celery, onions, olives and pimiento freshens the flavor.
Preheat oven to 350°.
Prepare and bring to a boil:

1 cup White Sauce II, 341, using ⅓ cup cream and ⅔ cup vegetable stock

Stir in:

1 cup minced drained vegetables

When the vegetables are hot, reduce the heat and add:

3 beaten egg yolks

Cook and stir 1 minute longer to let the yolks thicken. Season as required with:

Salt and pepper
(Nutmeg)

Cool this mixture slightly. Whip until stiff, but not dry:

3 egg whites

Fold them lightly into the vegetable mixture. Bake the soufflé in a prepared 7-inch baking dish about

40 minutes or until firm. If you would like a dish that is a course in itself, serve the soufflé with one of the following:

Mushroom Wine Sauce, 347
Soubise Sauce, 344
Paprika Sauce, 344
Sauce Indienne, 344

ONION SOUFFLÉ

4 Servings

One of our pet accompaniments to a light meal. Please read About Soufflés, 228.
Preheat oven to 325°.
Prepare:

1 cup Steamed Onions, 312

Drain and mince them. Melt:

2 tablespoons butter

Stir in until blended:

2 tablespoons flour

Combine and stir in slowly:

½ cup milk
½ cup evaporated milk or cream

When the sauce is smooth, add the minced onion and heat thoroughly. ➤ Remove onions from heat and stir in:

3 beaten egg yolks

Cook ➤ but do not boil, and stir about 1 minute longer to let the yolks thicken. Season with:

Salt, paprika and nutmeg
2 tablespoons chopped parsley or ½ teaspoon dried basil

Cool these ingredients slightly. Whip until stiff, but not dry:

3 egg whites

Fold them lightly into the onion mixture. Bake the soufflé in a prepared 7-inch baking dish until it is firm, about 40 minutes.

SWEET POTATO AND PINEAPPLE OR APPLESAUCE SOUFFLÉ

6 Servings

Superlative with cold or hot ham. Please read About Soufflés, 228.
Preheat oven to 350°.
Prepare:

3 cups Boiled Sweet Potatoes, 324

While still warm, add and beat with a fork until the potatoes are fluffy:

3 tablespoons butter
½ teaspoon salt
½ teaspoon grated lemon rind
2 beaten egg yolks

Fold in:

½ to ¾ cup drained crushed pineapple or tart applesauce

Cool these ingredients slightly. Whip until stiff and fold in:

2 egg whites

Bake the soufflé in a prepared 7-inch baking dish about 35 minutes.

CHICKEN SOUFFLÉ

I. **5 Servings**

Please read About Soufflés, 228.
Preheat oven to 325°.
Prepare:

1 cup White Sauce II, 341

using chicken stock and cream for the liquid. When the sauce is hot, add:

1 cup solids: minced cooked chicken, nutmeats, minced and drained cooked vegetables

Remove from heat and add:

3 beaten egg yolks

Season with:

Salt and pepper
Freshly grated nutmeg

Let cool slightly. Whip ➤ until stiff, but not dry:

3 or 4 egg whites

Fold them lightly into the chicken mixture. Bake in a prepared 8-inch soufflé baking dish until firm, about 35 minutes.

II. **16 Individual Soufflés**

A favorite luncheon soufflé, having more "body" than most others. Serve in individual baking dishes.
➤ Please read About Soufflés, 228.
Preheat oven to 325°.
Mince:

2¼ cups cooked chicken

Prepare:

3 cups White Sauce II, 341

using chicken fat to replace the butter, and stock or cream as the liquid. Stir in the minced chicken and:

1 cup chopped nutmeats
1 cup chopped cooked vegetables or raw celery, carrots and onions

When these ingredients are hot, remove from the heat and add:

9 beaten egg yolks

Season with:

Salt and pepper
Nutmeg

Let cool slightly. Whip ➤ until stiff, but not dry:

9 egg whites

Fold them lightly into the chicken mixture. Fix prepared soufflé baking dishes, 220, two-third full. Bake until firm, 20 to 25 minutes. Serve the soufflés with:

Mushroom Wine Sauce, 347, or
Poulette Sauce, 345

MEAT OR FISH SOUFFLÉ

4 Servings

➤ Please read About Soufflés, 228.
Preheat oven to 325°
Prepare:

1 cup White Sauce II, 341

When it is smooth, stir in:

¾ to 1 cup flaked cooked fish: tuna, crab,

clams, lobster or shrimp, or finely chopped cooked meat
¼ cup each finely chopped raw carrots and celery
(2 tablespoons chopped parsley)

When these ingredients are hot, remove from the heat and stir in:

3 beaten egg yolks

Season with:

Salt and paprika
Nutmeg
Lemon juice, Worcestershire Sauce, 848, or Tomato Catsup, 847
(⅓ cup sliced stuffed olives)

Let cool slightly. Whip ➤ until stiff, but not dry:

3 to 4 egg whites

Fold them lightly into the mixture. Bake in a prepared 7-inch soufflé baking dish until firm, about 35 minutes. Serve the soufflé with:

A tomato sauce, 351, 352, or Nantua Sauce, 343, or Anchovy Sauce, 343

OYSTER SOUFFLÉ

4 Servings

Please read About Soufflés, 228.
Preheat oven to 325°.
Drain, but save the liquor from:

½ to 1 pint oysters

Dry them on a towel. Prepare:

1 cup White Sauce II, 341, using part cream and part oyster liquor

When it is hot, remove from heat and add the oysters. Add:

3 beaten egg yolks

Season with:

Salt and pepper
Nutmeg
(Lemon juice)

Let cool slightly. Whip ➤ until stiff, but not dry:

3 to 4 egg whites

Fold them lightly into the oyster mixture. Bake in a prepared 7-inch soufflé baking dish until firm, about 35 minutes.

ABOUT TIMBALES AND TIMBALE RING MOLDS

A virtually indispensable mainstay of that sterling American institution, the ladies' luncheon, the timbale is a soufflé with a more equable disposition and greater stamina because of the steaming of the molded custardlike dish—often referred to as a **savory mousse.** The recipes that immediately follow include those in which a timbale mixture is incorporated into a custard, as well as those in which the custard is baked separately in a ring mold to surround a vegetable or meat combination. Or, the mold can be reversed onto a hot dish or into a previously baked pastry shell. It is often coated or served with a sauce.

Butter individual or larger molds lightly, and fill them about two-thirds full with the timbale mixture. ➤ Place on a rack in a pan of hot, but not boiling, water. The water should be as high as the filling in the molds. If a rack is not available, fold several thicknesses of paper and place the molds on them. ➤ Check the heat occasionally to make sure the water around the mold never boils—just simmers. It is wise to protect the top of the timbale with a poaching paper, 151.

Bake the timbales in a ➤ moderate oven, about 325°, 20 to 50 minutes, depending on the size of the mold. They are done when a knife blade inserted in the center of the mold comes out uncoated. They are then ready to invert onto a serving platter.

BASIC TIMBALE CUSTARD

4 Servings

Preheat oven to 325°.
Combine and beat with a wire whisk:

1½ cups warm cream or ½ cup cream and 1 cup chicken stock
4 eggs
¾ teaspoon salt
½ teaspoon paprika
(⅛ teaspoon grated nutmeg or celery salt)
(1 tablespoon chopped parsley)
(A few drops onion or lemon juice)

To bake and unmold, see About Timbales, left.
Serve with:

Creamed vegetables or Mushroom Wine Sauce, 347

For a brunch, garnish with:

Crisp bacon
Parsley

VEGETABLE TIMBALES

I. SPINACH, BROCCOLI OR CAULIFLOWER TIMBALE

5 or 6 Servings

Preheat oven to 325°.
Prepare:

Basic Timbale Custard, above

Add to the custard:

1 to 1½ cups well-drained cooked spinach, broccoli or cauliflower, chopped or put through a food mill
(½ cup grated cheese)

Add seasoning if required. To bake, see About Timbales, left. Garnish with:

Hollandaise Sauce, 358

II. MUSHROOM TIMBALE

5 or 6 Servings

Preheat oven to 325°.
Prepare:

Basic Timbale Custard, above

Add:

2 cups drained, chopped, sautéed mushrooms

To bake, see About Timbales, left.

III. ASPARAGUS TIMBALE

4 Servings

Preheat oven to 325°.
Grease 4 deep custard cups or a 7-inch ring mold.
Place around the sides of each container:

3 to 5 well-drained canned or cooked asparagus tips, heads down

Fill the cups with:

Basic Timbale Custard, 231

To bake, see About Timbales, 231. Place between the inverted timbales:

Hollandaise Sauce, 358

Garnish them with:

Parsley

and surround with:

Broiled or boiled link sausages

EGGPLANT TIMBALE

Preheat oven to 325°.
Prepare for stuffing:

An eggplant, 304

Cut it lengthwise and hollow out the pulp, leaving shells about ½ inch thick.
Combine the cooked mashed pulp with:

¾ cup soft bread crumbs
2 beaten egg yolks
1 tablespoon melted butter
½ cup chopped nutmeats or shredded cheese
Salt and pepper
Grated nutmeg

If the filling seems stiff, add:

1 tablespoon or more milk

Whip until ➤ stiff, but not dry:

2 egg whites

Fold them lightly into the other ingredients. Fill the eggplant shells. Cover the tops with:

Buttered crumbs or cornflakes

Place them in a pan with a little water and bake about 30 minutes.

CELERIAC RING MOLD

6 Servings

➤ Please read About Timbales, 231.
Preheat oven to 325°.
Cook:

4 medium-sized celery roots, 298

Drain well. Put them through a grinder, using a coarse blade, or through a ricer. Soak:

2 slices white bread

in:

3 tablespoons milk

Stir this into the celery and add:

2 tablespoons melted butter
1 teaspoon grated onion
2 tablespoons cream
4 beaten egg yolks
¾ teaspoon salt
½ teaspoon paprika
A fresh grating of nutmeg or 1 teaspoon horseradish

Whip until ➤ stiff, but not dry:

4 egg whites

Fold them into the celery mixture. Bake the mixture in a greased ring mold set in a pan of hot water about 45 minutes. Invert the mold onto a hot plate. Fill the center with:

Buttered peas or sautéed mushrooms

MEAT-AND-VEGETABLE TIMBALE

5 or 6 Servings

Use any interesting combination of cooked vegetables and cooked meat.
Preheat oven to 325°.
Follow the rule for:

Basic Timbale Custard, 231

using milk instead of cream. Omit the seasoning.
Cut into small pieces and add:

1 to 1½ cups leftover food
(Chopped parsley)
(Grated onion)
(¼ cup ground ham)
(A few chopped stuffed olives)

After the above have been added to the timbale mixture, season it to taste. If the food is dry, no additional thickening is needed. If it is slightly moist, add to the leftovers, before combining them with the custard, until they form a moderately thick paste:

Cracker crumbs or bread crumbs

To bake, see About Timbales, 231. Serve with:

A tomato sauce, 352, Sauce Albert, 343, or Ravigote Sauce, 345

CHEESE TIMBALE OR CRUSTLESS QUICHE

For a classic Quiche, see 254.
Preheat oven to 325°.
Prepare the filling for:

Cheese Custard Pie, 255

To bake, see About Timbales, 231. Good served with:

Green peas, spinach or broccoli

CHICKEN OR HAM TIMBALES

6 Servings

Preheat oven to 325°.
Grind twice or blend:

2 cups cooked white chicken meat or 1 cup each chicken and cooked ham

Stir in very slowly to form a paste:

¾ cup cold cream
¼ teaspoon salt
⅛ teaspoon paprika

Whip until stiff:

4 egg whites

Fold them lightly into the meat mixture. Line 6 greased timbale molds with:

(Pieces of truffles, ripe olives or pimiento)

Add the timbale mixture. To bake, see About Timbales, 231. Serve with:

Mushroom Wine Sauce, 347, or chicken gravy with chopped parsley

CHICKEN LIVER TIMBALE

4 Servings

Very light and delicate.
Preheat oven to 325°.
Put through a ricer, grinder or ⅄ blender:
¾ cup cooked chicken livers
½ cup Boiled Rice, 206
Add:
A scant ¼ teaspoon salt
A few grains cayenne and nutmeg
½ teaspoon prepared mustard
Whip until stiff:
2 egg whites
In a separate bowl, whip until stiff:
¼ cup whipping cream
Fold these ingredients lightly into the chicken-liver mixture. To bake, see About Timbales, 231. Serve with:
Caper Sauce, 345, Poulette Sauce, 345, or Smitane Sauce, 345

VEAL TIMBALE

4 Servings

Preheat oven to 325°.
Grind twice or blend:
1¼ cups cold cooked veal
Beat slightly and add:
3 egg yolks
Stir the ingredients well. Continue to stir while adding:
⅓ cup whipping cream
¼ cup dry white wine or 2 tablespoons lemon juice
⅛ teaspoon paprika
Salt, as needed
Beat until stiff:
3 egg whites
(¼ teaspoon mace)
Fold these into the other ingredients. To bake, see About Timbales, 231. Serve with:
Mushroom Wine Sauce, 347, or a tomato sauce, 351–354

FISH TIMBALE

I. **6 Servings**

Cooked fish may be substituted as in III, but uncooked fish gives a better result. Pike is preferred, but a combination of pike and sole is more than acceptable.
➤ Please read About Timbales, 231.
Preheat oven to 350°.
Grind, put though a ricer or ⅄ blend:
1 lb. uncooked fish: 2 cups
Over low heat, melt:
1½ tablespoons butter
Stir in until blended:
1 tablespoon flour
then add:
¼ cup milk
➤ Remove from heat. Beat and stir in:
2 egg yolks
Season the egg mixture with:
½ teaspoon salt
⅛ teaspoon white pepper
⅛ teaspoon nutmeg
Stir the yolks 1 or 2 minutes. Add the ground fish. Cool. Whip ➤ until stiff, but not dry:
2 egg whites
Whip until stiff:
1 cup whipping cream
Fold these ingredients lightly into the fish mixture. Garnish a greased 9-inch ring mold with:
Strips of pimiento
(Strips of green pepper)
Pour the mixture into the mold. Set the mold in a pan of hot water. Bake about 45 minutes, or until set. Let stand 5 minutes. Unmold. Serve with:
Hollandaise Sauce, 358, Horseradish Sauce, 343, or Oyster Sauce, 343

II. **4 Servings**

A less rich version. This recipe is highly recommended for conversion into a ring mold.
Preheat oven to 350°.
Combine and cook to a paste:
1 cup bread crumbs
½ cup cream
When the mixture is hot, add:
½ lb. finely chopped raw halibut or salmon
Season with:
¼ teaspoon salt
⅛ teaspoon paprika
Cool these ingredients slightly. Whip until ➤ stiff, but not dry:
2 egg whites
Fold them lightly into the fish mixture. Place the mixture in a 7-inch buttered baking dish and set it in a pan of hot water. Bake about 40 minutes. Serve with:
Oyster Sauce, 343, Nantua Sauce, 343, or Anchovy Sauce, 343
Garnish with:
Tomatoes
Watercress

III. **5 or 6 Servings**

Preheat oven to 325°.
Flake and chop until very fine:
2 cups cooked fish
Season it with:
¼ teaspoon salt
⅛ teaspoon paprika
½ teaspoon grated lemon rind
1½ teaspoons lemon juice
Whip until stiff:
½ cup whipping cream
In a separate bowl, whip until stiff:
3 egg whites
Fold the cream into the fish mixture, then fold in the egg whites. To bake, see About Timbales, 231. Serve with:
Béchamel Sauce, 341, or Tartare Sauce, 364

SHAD ROE TIMBALE

4 Servings

➤ Please read About Timbales, 231.
Preheat oven to 375°.
Poach 3 to 5 minutes:

1 fresh shad roe

Remove outer integument and veins. Crumble the roe and combine it with:

2 beaten eggs
1 cup whipped cream
A grating of nutmeg
Season to taste

Fill individual molds three-fourths full of this mixture. Set molds in a pan of hot water. Bake about 25 minutes. Serve with:

Allemande Sauce, 345, or
Béarnaise Sauce, 359

CHESTNUT RING MOLD

4 Servings

A delightful way to use chestnuts. The egg white lightens the consistency of the mixture.
➤ Please read About Timbales, 231.
Preheat oven to 325°.
Combine:

2 tablespoons flour
1 teaspoon salt
¼ teaspoon paprika
1 cup riced Boiled Chestnuts, 298
½ teaspoon grated onion

Add gradually:

½ cup milk

Stir and cook these ingredients over low heat about 5 minutes. Cool slightly. Whip until ➤ stiff, but not dry, then fold in:

3 egg whites

Bake the mixture about ½ hour in a 7-inch ring mold set in a pan of hot water. Invert it onto a hot plate. Fill it with:

Buttered green peas
Chopped parsley

It may be served with:

Mushroom Wine Sauce, 347

MUSHROOM RING MOLD WITH SWEETBREADS OR CHICKEN

8 Servings

➤ Please read About Timbales, 231.
Preheat oven to 325°.
Blanch, 502:

1 pair sweetbreads, or use 1 cup cooked minced chicken

Remove the skin and membrane and mince the sweetbreads. Prepare:

1 cup White Sauce II, 341

Melt in a pan:

2 tablespoons butter

Add and sauté about 3 minutes:

2 slices onion

Remove the onion. Add to the pan:

1½ cups finely minced mushrooms

and the sweetbreads or chicken. Heat the white sauce to the boiling point and combine it with the mushroom mixture. Remove from heat and stir in:

¼ cup dry bread crumbs
1 chopped pimiento
¼ teaspoon salt
2 beaten egg yolks

Cook and stir about 1 minute longer to let the yolks thicken. Cool these ingredients slightly. Whip until ➤ stiff, but not dry:

2 egg whites

Fold them lightly into the mushroom mixture. Place the mixture in a greased ring mold set in a pan of hot water and bake covered with a piece of buttered paper 35 minutes or until firm. Invert the mold onto a platter and serve filled with:

Asparagus spears or peas

and pass with:

Suprême Sauce, 344

GRIDDLE CAKES AND FRITTER VARIATIONS

Perhaps no foods lend themselves to more occasions than those in this chapter, which can be served as hors d'oeuvre; as breakfast, luncheon or supper treats; or as desserts. What's more, they are an ideal way to glamorize leftovers. Many people like to cook these delicacies at table, using auxiliary heat so that they reach the diner in peak condition. Waffle irons, 240; electric skillets, 145; or a double crêpe pan set, shown in the heading, left rear, where the crêpes can be both cooked and sauced, are all tableside conveniences; while in the kitchen, both iron and soapstone griddles have their adherents. The soapstone, which needs no greasing, is shown in the left foreground, filled with small-sized so-called silver-dollar pancakes from the batter in the pitcher upper left. Above and below it are elderberry and hemerocallis blossoms, both delicious when deep-fat-fried in batters, 243. In the right foreground is a rosette iron on which several shapes can be inserted; a honey dipper and a pancake turner. At the right rear are honey and molasses dispensers, jellies and nuts on a lazy-susan stand near liqueurs for flambéing, 155.

ABOUT PANCAKES, GRIDDLE CAKES OR BATTER CAKES

No matter what your source of heat—a hot rock or an electric skillet; no matter how fancy the name—blintzes, crêpes or Nockerln—all these confections are easily mixed and made from simple batters.

There are three equally important things to control in producing pancakes and waffles: the consistency of your batter, the surface of your griddle or pan, and the evenness of its heat. Mix the liquid ingredients quickly into the dry ingredients. ➤ Don't overbeat. Give just enough quick strokes to barely moisten the dry ingredients. ➤ Ignore the lumps. Superior results are gained if most pancake doughs are mixed and ➤ rested, covered, refrigerated, 3 to 6 hours or longer before cooking. This resting period does not apply to recipes which include separately beaten egg whites, or to yeast-raised cakes that have the word "raised" in the title. Variation in moisture content of flours, 545, makes it wise to test the batter by cooking one trial cake first. Adjust the batter ➤ if too thick, by diluting it with a little water, ➤ if too thin, by adding a little flour. You may also use a pancake dough for waffles provided you ➤ add for each recipe at least 2 extra tablespoons of butter or oil to keep the dough from sticking.

If your griddle is a modern one or is of soapstone, you may not need to use any type of fat. Nor should you need to grease any seasoned pan surface if you have at least two tablespoons of butter for every cup of liquid in the recipe. If you are using a skillet or crêpe pan, you may grease it lightly and continue to do so between batches. ➤ Before cooking, test the griddle by letting a few drops of cold water fall on it. If the water bounces and sputters, the griddle is ready to use. If the water just sits and boils, the griddle is not hot enough. If the water vanishes, the griddle is too hot. See illustration on 236.

➤ To assure a well-rounded cake, don't drop the batter from on high but let it pour from the tip of a spoon. Make the cakes large or small. It will be two to three minutes before the cakes are ready to turn. When bubbles appear on the upper surfaces, but before they break, lift the cakes with a spatula to see how well they have browned. ➤ Turn the cakes only once and continue cooking them until the second side is done. Cooking this side takes only about half as long, and the second side never browns as evenly. Serve the cakes at once. If this is not possible, keep them on a toweled baking sheet—well separated by the tea towel—in a 200° oven. Or fold for yourself a sort of cloth file in which to store them. ➤ Never stack one on the other without the protection of cloth—for the steam they produce will make the cakes flabby.

▲ In high altitudes, use about one-fourth less baking powder or soda than indicated in the following recipes.

Several egg dishes approximate pancakes, see Eggs Fooyoung, 228, and Frittata, 228.

Pancakes are delicious stuffed, rolled or glazed with a sauce and run under the broiler. Try filling with prunes and cinnamon or with creamed seafood, 264. The batter may be seasoned with sautéed chopped onions and, when cooked, filled with seafood, creamed sweetbreads or chicken. Or you may incorporate in the batters finely chopped nuts and candied fruits or currants; or wheat germ, soy flour or flaked bran. To do this, let the cereal or fruit rest in the liquid called for in the recipe about half an hour before making up the batter. For additional garnishes and sauces, see Dessert Sauces, 769.

PANCAKES, GRIDDLE CAKES OR BATTER CAKES

About Fourteen 4-Inch Cakes

Sift before measuring:
1½ cups all-purpose flour
Resift with:
1 teaspoon salt
3 tablespoons sugar
1¾ teaspoons double-acting baking powder
Combine:
1 or 2 slightly beaten whole eggs
3 tablespoons melted butter
1 to 1¼ cups milk
Mix the liquid ingredients quickly into the dry ingredients. ➤ To test griddle and cook, see About Griddle Cakes, 235. Serve the cakes with:
(Sausages and syrup)

WHOLE-GRAIN GRIDDLE CAKES

About Fourteen 4-Inch Cakes

Sift before measuring:
½ cup all-purpose flour
Resift with:
½ teaspoon salt
½ teaspoon double-acting baking powder
¾ teaspoon baking soda
Stir in:
1 cup finely milled whole wheat flour
Combine and beat:
2 tablespoons sugar, honey or molasses
1 egg
2 cups buttermilk or yogurt
2 tablespoons melted butter or bacon drippings
➤ To test griddle and cook, see About Griddle Cakes, 235.

WHOLE-GRAIN AND SOY GRIDDLE CAKES

Prepare:
Whole-Grain Griddle Cakes, left
Substitute for the all-purpose flour:
¼ cup soy flour
¼ cup cornmeal
1 cup finely milled whole-grain flour

FRENCH PANCAKES OR CRÊPES

Fourteen to Sixteen 5-Inch Cakes

Sift:
¾ cup all-purpose flour
Resift with:
½ teaspoon salt
1 teaspoon double-acting baking powder
2 tablespoons powdered sugar
Beat:
2 eggs
Add and beat:
⅔ cup milk
⅓ cup water
½ teaspoon vanilla or ½ teaspoon grated lemon rind
Make a well in the sifted ingredients. Pour in the liquid ingredients. Combine them with a few swift strokes. Ignore the lumps; they will take care of themselves. You may rest the batter refrigerated 3 to 6 hours. Heat a 5-inch skillet. Grease it with a few drops of oil. Add a small quantity of batter. Tip the skillet and let the batter spread over the bottom. Cook the pancake over moderate heat. When it is brown underneath, reverse it and brown the other side. Use a few drops of oil for each pancake. Spread the cake with:
Jelly
Roll it and sprinkle with:
Confectioners' sugar

STUFFED FRENCH PANCAKES OR CRÊPES

I. With Seafood

Prepare but omit the sugar:
French Pancakes, above
Prepare:
Creamed Oysters, 377
or cream any available canned or frozen seafood. Spread the pancakes with the creamed mixture. Roll them. Cover with the remaining sauce. Sprinkle with:
(Grated cheese)
Brown lightly under a broiler.

II. With Meat or Vegetables

Follow the above recipe, filling the pancakes with:
Hash with gravy, or creamed vegetables, chicken, ham, chipped beef or other precooked meat
The cream sauce may be made from a condensed cream soup.

III. Roll in the pancakes:
Precooked pork sausages
Serve very hot with:
Applesauce

GÂTEAU CRÊPE

10-Inch Skillet

Prepare batter for:
French Pancakes, opposite
Make four or five large pancakes. Cool them. Stack and spread between the layers:
Lemon, Orange or Lime Sauce, 769, or Lemon or Orange Filling, 697, 698
You may spread over the top layer:
Caramelized sugar, see Clear Caramel Glaze, 732
or simply sprinkle the top with:
Powdered sugar

FRUIT PANCAKES

Four Large (9-Inch) Cakes

Prepare batter for:
French Pancakes, opposite
Prepare and have ready:
1 cup or more thinly sliced, lightly sugared, sautéed apples, peaches, bananas or blueberries
Also have ready two 9-inch skillets. Melt in each:
2 teaspoons butter
2 teaspoons shortening
When the fat is hot, pour one-fourth the batter into each skillet. Turn the cakes when they are lightly browned and cook the other side. Place one of the cakes on a hot platter. Sprinkle over it half of the still-warm fruit. When the other cake is browned on the second side, slide it over the fruit. Cook the other two griddle cakes for the remaining warm fruit. Serve hot, dusted with:
Powdered sugar
or a mixture of:
½ teaspoon cinnamon
½ cup sugar

BLINTZES OR COTTAGE CHEESE PANCAKES

4 Servings

Prepare:
French Pancakes, opposite
Use a 5-inch skillet. Cook very thin cakes on one side only, until the top is bubbly. Place them on a damp tea towel, cooked side down. Prepare the following filling.
Mix well:
1½ cups smooth, rather dry cottage cheese: 12 oz.
1 egg yolk
1 teaspoon soft butter
1 teaspoon vanilla or grated lemon rind
Place about 2 tablespoons of filling on the center of each cake. Roll the edges up and over from either side. At this point the blintzes may be cooked at once; or, if you are not ready to serve them, they may be placed seam side down in a closely covered dish and chilled for several hours.
Melt in a large skillet:
½ tablespoon oil
½ tablespoon butter
Place several blintzes in it, seam side down. Fry them to a golden brown, turning them once. Repeat, adding more oil or butter to the skillet, as needed, until all are done. Serve them hot, sprinkled with:
Sugar and cinnamon
You may pass:
(Cultured sour cream)

CRÊPES SUZETTE

4 Servings

At an early age the famous Franco-American cook, Henri Charpentier, invented Crêpes Suzette—a glorified French pancake.

One day when he was composing a complicated crêpe sauce for his patron, Albert, Prince of Wales, the cordials accidentally caught fire, and the poor boy thought both he and his sauce were ruined. Quickly he plunged the crêpes into the boiling liquid, added more of the cordials and let the sauce flame again. The dish was a triumph. Below is an approximation of Henri's crêpe batter and sauce.

Combine and stir until the ingredients are the consistency of thin cream:
3 eggs
2 tablespoons all-purpose flour
1 tablespoon water
1 tablespoon milk
A pinch of salt
We recommend keeping this batter 3 hours to overnight, covered and refrigerated. Place in a 5-inch crêpe pan:
1 tablespoon butter
When this bubbles, pour in enough batter to cover the bottom with a thin coating. Keep the pan moving, for this is a delicate substance. A minute of cooking and the job is three-fourths done. Turn the cake and keep turning it until it is well browned. Fold it twice so it will be triangular in shape. The cakes may be stacked with a cloth between them and reheated in sauce much later. Although they may be frozen and reheated, we do not feel that freezing improves them.

BUTTER SAUCE FOR CRÊPES SUZETTE

This may be made in advance and kept for months refrigerated. Cut into very thin strips a piece of:
Lemon rind, ¾ inch square
Orange rind, ¾ inch square
using only the colored portion of the rind. Add:
1 teaspoon Vanilla Sugar, 557

Or substitute a few drops of vanilla and 1 teaspoon sugar. Let these ingredients stand closely covered 12 hours or more. Melt in a large skillet:

½ cup butter

When it starts to bubble, add:

1 pony maraschino
1 pony curaçao
1 pony kirsch

Put a lighted match to the sauce. As the flame dies down, add the lemon and orange mixture. Place the sauce in a cool place until ready to use, if you wish. Make the crêpes. You may place in each crêpe before rolling:

(1 tablespoon Hard Sauce, 775)

Plunge the cakes into boiling sauce. Turn them. Again, add:

1 pony each maraschino, curaçao and kirsch

Put a lighted match to the sauce. Let it flame. Serve the cakes at once. The final performance—plunging the folded crêpes into the hot sauce, adding and burning the liquor—is done at table just before serving the crêpes on a hot plate.

PFANNKUCHEN OR GERMAN PANCAKES

1 Large Pancake—2 Servings

Henriette Davides, the German counterpart of the fabulous English Mrs. Beeton, says that the heat under this pancake must be neither "too weak nor too strong," that it is advisable to put "enough butter in the skillet, but not too much," and that the best results are obtained in making this simple great pancake with not more than 4 eggs. Henriette's recipes make mouth-watering reading. But on Henriette's terms, only a strongly intuitive person with a madly active imagination has a chance of success. Firming up Henriette's rule, will you try our version of this famous pancake?

Combine and stir until smooth:

4 beaten egg yolks
2 tablespoons cornstarch
¼ cup lukewarm milk
¼ cup lukewarm water
¾ teaspoon salt
1 tablespoon sugar
Grated rind of 1 lemon

Beat until very stiff:

4 to 5 egg whites

Fold them into the yolk mixture. Melt in a heavy 10-inch skillet:

2 tablespoons butter

When the skillet is hot, pour in the pancake batter. Cook it over low to medium heat, partly covered with a lid, for about 5 minutes. Or the batter may be cooked until it begins to set and then be placed briefly in a preheated 400° oven until it is puffed and firm. Cooking time in all is about 7 minutes. It should puff up well, but it may fall. So serve it at once with:

Confectioners' sugar and cinnamon or lemon juice; covered with jam or jelly and rolled; or with wine, fruit or rum sauce

AUSTRIAN PANCAKES OR NOCKERLN

6 Cakes

In Salzburg, when we were last there, few visitors failed to indulge in one or more of these souffléed globular puffs between the delights of the annual Musical Festival. Make them immediately before serving.

Preheat oven to 225°.

Beat until very light:

4 egg yolks

Beat in:

¼ cup cake flour

Whip until stiff:

6 to 8 egg whites

and add gradually while continuing to beat:

½ to ¾ cup sugar
½ teaspoon vanilla

Fold the yolk mixture lightly into the egg whites. Melt in a 9-inch skillet:

2 to 3 tablespoons butter

The butter should coat the bottom and sides of the pan and be bubbling when the soufflé mixture is put into it. Heap the soufflé into the hot skillet in 6 even mounds and cook until the undersides color lightly. Place the skillet in the oven and bake until the puffs are golden, about 8 to 10 minutes. The center should remain soft. If you are serving the Nockerln without fruit or sauce, sprinkle them with:

Confectioners' sugar

➤ Serve at once on heated plates.

RUSSIAN RAISED PANCAKES OR BLINI

About Twenty-Four 2-Inch Cakes

Dissolve:

1 cake compressed yeast

in:

2 cups scalded milk which has cooled to 85°

Stir in until well blended:

1½ cups sifted all-purpose flour
1 tablespoon sugar

Cover the bowl and set this sponge to rise in a warm place about 1½ hours. Beat until well blended:

3 egg yolks
1 tablespoon melted butter

Stir in:

½ cup sifted all-purpose flour
1 teaspoon salt

Beat these ingredients into the sponge and let it rise again about 1½ hours or until almost doubled in bulk. Whip until stiff, but not dry:

3 egg whites

Fold them into the batter. After 10 minutes, cook the batter, a very small quantity at a time, in a greased skillet or on a griddle. See About Griddle

Cakes, 235. Turn to brown lightly on the other side. Serve each blini rolled and filled with:

1 tablespoon caviar

and garnished with:

Cultured sour cream

BUTTERMILK PANCAKES

About Ten 4-Inch Cakes

Sift before measuring:

1 cup cake flour

Resift with:

1 teaspoon sugar
½ teaspoon salt
¾ teaspoon double-acting baking powder
½ teaspoon baking soda

Beat until light:

1 egg

Add:

1 cup buttermilk
1 to 2 tablespoons melted butter

Combine the sifted and the liquid ingredients with a few swift strokes. To test griddle and çook, see About Griddle Cakes, 235.

CORNMEAL PANCAKES

About Twelve 4-Inch Cakes

Measure and place in a bowl:

1 cup white or yellow cornmeal
1 teaspoon salt
1 to 2 tablespoons honey, syrup or sugar

Stir in slowly:

1 cup boiling water

Cover these ingredients and let stand 10 minutes. Beat:

1 egg
½ cup milk
2 tablespoons melted butter

Add these ingredients to the cornmeal mixture. Sift before measuring:

½ cup all-purpose flour

Resift with:

2 teaspoons double-acting baking powder

Stir the sifted ingredients into the batter with a few swift strokes. To test griddle and cook, see About Griddle Cakes, 235.

⊟ CRISP CORN FLAPJACKS

About 20 Thin 2-Inch Cakes

If you make up this traditional camp treat without the eggs, the pancakes become lacy.

Place in a bowl:

1⅓ cups white cornmeal
1¼ teaspoons salt
½ teaspoon baking soda
¼ cup sifted all-purpose flour

Cut into this with a pastry blender:

¼ cup butter

Combine and beat:

2 cups buttermilk
(1 to 2 eggs)

Stir the liquid into the sifted ingredients with a few swift strokes. Make the cakes small for easier turning. The batter settles readily, so beat it between spoonings. To test griddle, cook and serve, see About Griddle Cakes, 235.

JOHNNYCAKES

About 2 Dozen 4-Inch Cakes

Heat in a double boiler ➤ over—not in—boiling water:

1 cup stone-ground cornmeal
½ teaspoon salt

To avoid lumping, stir constantly and scald the cornmeal by adding in a thin stream:

1¼ cups boiling water

Continue to stir about 10 minutes more, then add:

2 tablespoons butter
1¼ to 1½ cups milk

to make the batter easy to drop, a tablespoon at a time, onto a greased hot griddle. Cook over low heat about 10 minutes, or until the underside is golden brown. Turn and cook until the other side is golden brown. Serve with:

Maple syrup and butter

HOMINY CAKES

5 Servings

Drain:

2½ cups cooked or canned hominy

Combine it with:

2 tablespoons flour
1 egg
Salt and pepper

Form these ingredients into flat cakes. Sauté them until they are brown in:

Butter or drippings

Serve them hot—plain or with:

Honey or syrup

RICE-CORNMEAL GRIDDLE CAKES

Twelve 4-Inch Cakes

Sift before measuring:

½ cup all-purpose flour

Resift with:

1 teaspoon salt
½ teaspoon baking soda
1 tablespoon sugar

Add:

½ cup stone-ground cornmeal
1 cup cold boiled rice

Combine, beat, then stir into the sifted ingredients with a few swift strokes:

2 cups buttermilk
2 egg yolks
2 tablespoons melted, cooled shortening

➤ Beat until stiff, but not dry:

2 egg whites

Fold them into the batter. To test griddle and cook, see About Griddle Cakes, 235.

RICE FLOUR GRIDDLE CAKES

About Eighteen 4-Inch Cakes

Mix, then sift:

2 cups rice flour

4½ teaspoons double-acting baking powder
2 teaspoons maple sugar
2 teaspoons salt

Beat the mixture while adding:

2 cups milk

Add and barely blend:

1 beaten egg
1 tablespoon melted butter

To cook and serve, see About Griddle Cakes, 235.

OATMEAL GRIDDLE CAKES

About Twelve 4-Inch Cakes

Sift before measuring:

½ cup all-purpose flour

Resift with:

1 teaspoon double-acting baking powder
½ teaspoon salt

Beat:

1 egg

Stir in:

1½ cups cooked oatmeal
½ cup evaporated milk
¼ cup water
2 tablespoons melted butter or bacon drippings

Stir this mixture into the sifted ingredients. To cook and serve, see About Griddle Cakes, 235.

BUCKWHEAT CAKES

About Forty 3-Inch Cakes

Mix together thoroughly:

1 cup buckwheat flour
1 cup sifted all-purpose flour or whole wheat flour
2 teaspoons double-acting baking powder
1 teaspoon baking soda
2 teaspoons sugar
1 teaspoon salt

You may substitute 2 teaspoons molasses for the sugar. If so, add it to the buttermilk, below. Stir into the flour mixture:

2 beaten egg yolks
¼ cup melted butter
2 cups buttermilk

Whip until ➤ stiff, but not dry:

2 egg whites

Fold them into the batter until it is blended only. Cook on a greased hot griddle, see About Griddle Cakes, 235.

RAISED BUCKWHEAT CAKES

About Eighteen 2½-Inch Cakes

Scald, then cool to 105° to 115°:

2 cups milk

Add and stir until dissolved:

1 package active dry yeast

Add and stir to a smooth batter:

1¼ cups buckwheat flour
½ cup all-purpose flour or ¼ cup flour and ¼ cup cornmeal
1 teaspoon salt

Cover the batter with a cloth and place in refrigerator overnight. In the morning, stir in:

1 tablespoon molasses
½ teaspoon baking soda dissolved in ¼ cup lukewarm water
1 egg or ¼ cup melted shortening

Let stand at room temperature 30 minutes. To cook, see About Griddle Cakes, 235. Serve with:

Maple syrup

ABOUT WAFFLES

You don't have to be told how good these are with syrup, honey, marmalade or stewed fruit. But you may not realize what attractive cases they make for serving creamed foods, shown center, and for leftovers and ice creams. You can even cook raw bacon placed directly on the batter, as shown below, and have it come out crisp and nut brown. But be sure to treat your iron with care. Manufacturer's directions should be followed exactly in seasoning a new electric waffle iron. Once conditioned ➤ the grids are neither greased nor washed. You may brush the iron out to remove any crumbs. ➤ The iron itself is never immersed in water. After use, merely wipe down the outside with a cloth well wrung out in hot water.

Heat a waffle iron until the indicator shows it is ready to use. If it has been properly conditioned, it will need no greasing, as most waffle batters are heavy in butter. Have the batter ready in a pitcher. Cover the grid surface about two-thirds, as sketched on the left. Close the lid and wait about 4 minutes. When the waffle is ready, all steam will have stopped emerging from the crack of the iron. If you try to lift the top of the iron and the top shows resistance, it probably means the waffle is not quite done. Cook slightly longer and try again.

The richer the waffle dough, the crisper the

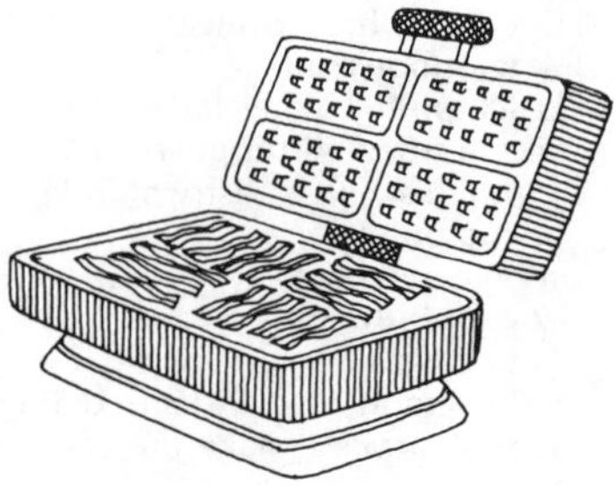

waffle becomes. With the butter flavor baked in, there is then no reason for ladling butter on top of the waffle. We also suggest ➤ beating egg whites separately for a superbly light result. Since waffles are made from a batter ➤ keep them tender by not overbeating or overmixing the dough.

▲ In high altitudes, use about one-fourth less baking powder or soda than indicated in our recipes.

WAFFLES

6 Waffles

➤ If used with savory foods, omit the sugar.
Sift before measuring:
1¾ cups cake flour
Resift with:
2 teaspoons double-acting baking powder
½ teaspoon salt
1 tablespoon sugar
Beat well:
3 egg yolks
Add:
2 to 7 tablespoons melted butter or vegetable oil
1½ cups milk
Make a hole in the center of the sifted ingredients. Pour in the liquid ingredients. Combine them with a few swift strokes. The batter should have a pebbled look, similar to a muffin batter. At this time, superb as these waffles are "as is," you may want to include for variety one of the following:
(½ cup fresh fruit or berries)
(¼ cup raisins or puréed dried fruit)
(¼ cup finely chopped nuts or coconut)
(¼ cup grated semisweet chocolate)
(½ cup shredded sharp cheese)
(1 cup finely diced cooked ham)
➤ Beat until stiff, but not dry:
3 egg whites
Fold them into the batter until they are barely blended. To cook, see About Waffles, above. Good served with:
Maple syrup or Honey Sauce, opposite, or sweetened fruit or a dessert sauce, 769

GOLDEN YAM OR SQUASH WAFFLES

6 Waffles

Prepare:
½ cup boiled mashed yams, 324, or winter squash, 330
Add:
3 well-beaten eggs
1½ cups milk
2 tablespoons melted butter or shortening
Sift together and add to the yam mixture:
1 cup sifted all-purpose flour
½ teaspoon salt
2 teaspoons double-acting baking powder
2 tablespoons sugar
(⅛ teaspoon cinnamon or nutmeg)
➤ Stir only enough to moisten. To cook, see About Waffles, 240. Serve with:
Honey and butter or Sauce Cockaigne, 770
The sauce makes this a dessert waffle.

BUTTERMILK WAFFLES

6 Waffles

Sift before measuring:
2 cups all-purpose flour
Resift with:
¼ teaspoon baking soda
1½ teaspoons double-acting baking powder
1 tablespoon sugar
½ teaspoon salt
Beat in a separate bowl until light:
2 egg yolks
Add and beat:
1¾ cups buttermilk
6 tablespoons melted butter
Combine the liquid and the dry ingredients with a few swift strokes. ➤ Beat until stiff, but not dry:
2 egg whites
Fold them into the batter. To cook, see About Waffles, 240.

SOUR CREAM WAFFLES

About 4 Waffles

Sift before measuring:
1 cup cake flour
Resift with:
1¼ teaspoons double-acting baking powder
⅛ teaspoon salt
1 teaspoon sugar
1 teaspoon baking soda
Beat in a separate bowl until light:
3 egg yolks
Add:
2 cups thick cultured sour cream
Combine the liquid and the dry ingredients with a few swift strokes. ➤ Beat until stiff, but not dry:
3 egg whites
Fold them into the batter. To cook, see About Waffles, 240.

BACON-CORNMEAL WAFFLES

6 Waffles

Don't worry about too much grease from the bacon, as this is all absorbed in the cooking.
Beat slightly:
2 eggs
Add:
1¾ cups milk
Sift:
1 cup cake flour or ⅞ cup all-purpose flour
2½ teaspoons double-acting baking powder
1 tablespoon sugar
½ teaspoon salt
Add:
1 cup yellow stone-ground cornmeal
Combine these ingredients with the eggs and milk in a few quick strokes. Add:
¼ cup melted bacon fat or other shortening

Cut into halves or quarters:

6 to 12 very thin slices bacon

Place pieces of bacon on each waffle iron section after pouring the batter, see illustration, 240. To cook, see About Waffles, 240.

CHOCOLATE WAFFLES

6 Waffles

Delectable with ice cream.

Sift before measuring:

1½ cups cake flour

Resift with:

2 teaspoons double-acting baking powder
¼ teaspoon salt
(¼ teaspoon cinnamon)
(¼ teaspoon nutmeg)

Cream:

½ cup butter

with:

1 cup sugar

Beat in, one at a time:

2 eggs

Add:

1 teaspoon vanilla

Melt ➤ cool and add:

2 oz. unsweetened chocolate

Add the sifted ingredients in about three parts, alternately with:

½ cup milk

To cook, see About Waffles, 240.

FRENCH TOAST WAFFLES

Combine:

1 beaten egg
¼ cup milk
2 tablespoons melted butter
⅛ teaspoon salt

Cut into pieces to fit a waffle iron:

Sliced bread

Coat the bread well in the batter. Toast it on a hot waffle iron.

ABOUT FRITTERED FOODS

The term fritter is rather confusingly used to cover three quite different types of food. We think of a true fritter as a delicately flavored batter, heavy in egg and deep-fat-fried. While they are not called fritters, crullers and doughnuts, 244–246, are very closely related to them—the crullers usually richer in fat, the doughnuts heavier in flour. The success of these batters depends on the care and skill with which they are mixed and fried, so please read About Deep-Fat Frying, 147.

➤ Don't confuse the texture of any of the aforementioned fritters with certain pan- or shallow-fried mixtures like corn fritters, 301. The term fritter may also apply to bits of meat, fish, vegetable or fruit dipped in a batter and dried before deep-fat frying. In this last type, the fritter batter acts as a protective coating. Other examples of fritterlike foods are Deep-Fat-Fried Vegetables, 279, and Croquettes, 247.

Variations of this completely encased food are rosettes, illustrated in the chapter heading, 235, and timbale cases or *cassolettes* in which the deep-fat-fried casing is a free-standing affair, so shaped that it may be filled. ➤ Be sure to choose fillings that are rather on the stable side with these types, and put them in just before serving, so the fritterlike casing will stay crisp.

Either cooked or uncooked foods may be fried in batter, although uncooked meats are more satisfactory if minced. ➤ But veal, pork and pork products should always be cooked, and brains and sweetbreads must be parboiled before deep frying. To prepare frittered vegetables, use almost any leftover or raw vegetables. Seafood and sliced, firm tomatoes are also delectable served this way.

To cook fritters, please read About Deep-Fat Frying, 147. One at a time ➤ slide the fritters into the heated fat at the side of the kettle. If using a spoon, first dip it into the hot fat before picking up the fritter. Time depends on the size of the fritter. If slightly smaller than doughnut size, precooked food requires only 2 to 3 minutes at about 365° to 375°. Uncooked food in larger units is better at 350° to 360° and will need from 5 to 7 minutes. This allows more time for thorough cooking of the interior.

▲ Batters for deep-fat-fried fritters and doughnuts must be adjusted and the temperature of the fat usually must be lowered when cooking at high altitudes.

ABOUT FRITTER BATTERS

These are really much like simple pancake mixtures, but they ➤ must have the consistency that makes them stick to the food to be fried. As in all recipes involving flour, measurements can only be approximate. If the surface of the food you are frying is as dry as possible, the dough will adhere if it follows this easy test: ➤ Take a generous spoonful of batter and hold it above the mixing bowl. Instead of running from the spoon in a broad shining band, a consistency that the French call *au ruban,* the batter should start to run for about a 1½-inch length, then drop in successive long triangular "splats." When the batter is this consistency ➤ beat it until very smooth. ➤ Cover it refrigerated at least two hours. It may even be stored overnight. This resting period allows a fermentation which breaks down any rubberiness of the batter—a process that is further activated if beer or wine forms part of the liquid used.

➤ If you do not have time to let the batter rest, mix it to smoothness with as few strokes as possible so as not to build up the gluten in the flour. Batters heavy in egg yolk resist fat penetration during frying. Use whole eggs if you wish, but if you separate them and plan to rest the batter, fold in the whites beaten ➤ stiff, but not dry, at the last minute before coating the food.

ABOUT FRUIT FRITTERS

Fritter batter for fruit, like any other batter, profits by resting at least 2 hours after mixing. ➤ Please read About Fritter Batters, above.

It is very important that fruit used in these desserts be ripe but not mushy. Keep fruit slices about ½ inch thick. Use apples—cored and cut crosswise—pineapple and orange wedges, halves of canned or stewed apricots, or bananas cut in 3 or 4 diagonal pieces. In season, even try fuzzy white elderberry blossoms, 235. Dusted with powdered sugar and sprinkled with kirsch, they are dreamy.

The fruit is often marinated in advance in a little wine, kirsch, rum or brandy. This marinade may also be used in the batter, but in this case you must marinate and drain prior to mixing the batter and adjust the amount of liquid to that called for in the recipe. Even beer can be used as a liquid. Both beer and wine help to break down the gluten and make a tender batter. After marination of about 2 hours, be sure to ➤ drain the fruit well and dust it with confectioners' sugar just before immersing it in the batter. To cook, please read about Fritter Batter for Fruit, below. Either dust fritters with sugar or serve with a sauce.

If a variety of fruits are served in this way, they are called a **Fritto Misto.**

FRITTER BATTER FOR FRUIT

About 8 to 10 Servings

This batter can be used either to encase about 2 cups diced fruit or to hold the same amount of small fruits and berries that are mixed directly and gently into it. See About Fruit Fritters, above.

I. Beat together:

2 egg yolks
⅔ cup milk or the liquid from the fruit marinade
1 tablespoon melted butter

Sift before measuring:

1 cup all-purpose flour

Resift with:

¼ teaspoon salt
1 tablespoon sugar

Combine liquid and dry ingredients. If you have the time, rest the dough at least 2 hours, covered and refrigerated. Then beat this mixture well, until smooth. Otherwise, stir until just blended. Just before using the batter, whip ➤ until stiff, but not dry:

2 egg whites

Fold them into the batter. Dip into the batter or mix with it the well-drained sugared fruit. To cook, have deep fat heated to 375°. The fritters will take from 3 to 5 minutes to brown. Drain them on paper toweling. Dust with:

Confectioners' sugar

II. Prepare:

Fritter Batter for Vegetables, right

omitting the pepper and adding:

1 to 2 tablespoons sugar

Follow directions given in I, above.

III. Mix together and beat until smooth:

1¼ cups sifted all-purpose flour
1 cup white wine
1 tablespoon sugar
½ teaspoon grated lemon rind
¼ teaspoon salt

Rest the batter refrigerated and covered 3 to 12 hours. Just before using ➤ whip until stiff, but not dry, and fold in:

1 egg white

Follow directions given in I, above.

BLOOMS IN BATTER

There is a chichi revival of the age-old custom of eating flowers. If you are an organic gardener and if you know your flowers, all is well. A lily of the valley which always looks good enough to eat is very poisonous, and the sprays used on roses are lethal not only to pests but to you. From sprayed gardens, save petals for fragrance only—not eating. Wash and drain well any kind of blooms and leaves you use for garnish.

➤ To make fritters of blossoms, please read About Fritter Batters, opposite. Pick with the dew on them and dry well:

Unsprayed elderberry, squash, pumpkin, lilac, yucca or hemerocallis blooms

Dip them in:

Fritter Batter for Fruit II, above

Fry them in deep fat heated to 350°.

UNSWEETENED CHOUX PASTE FRITTERS

Prepare:

Choux Paste, 646

Omit the sugar. Add:

(¼ cup grated Parmesan cheese)
(½ teaspoon prepared mustard)

Shape dough with greased spoons or a small greased self-releasing ice cream scoop. Fry in 370° deep fat about 6 minutes.

FRITTER OR TEMPURA BATTER FOR VEGETABLES, MEAT AND FISH

Enough to Coat About 2 Cups Food

➤ Please read About Fritter Batters, 242.

Put in a bowl and mix well:

1⅓ cups all-purpose flour or rice flour
1 teaspoon salt
¼ teaspoon pepper
1 tablespoon melted butter or vegetable oil
2 beaten egg yolks

Add gradually, stirring constantly:

¾ cup flat beer

Allow the batter to rest covered and refrigerated 3 to 12 hours. Just before using, you may add:

(2 stiffly beaten egg whites)

PURÉED VEGETABLE FRITTERS

3 Servings

➤ Please read About Frittered Foods, 242.

Beat until light:

1 egg

Add and beat well:

1 cup mashed or puréed cooked carrots, parsnips or butter beans

Stir in:

¼ teaspoon salt
1½ tablespoons melted butter
1½ tablespoons all-purpose flour
6 tablespoons milk
1 teaspoon Worcestershire sauce or
2½ teaspoons onion juice
½ teaspoon dried herb, or
2 tablespoons chopped parsley

Spread these ingredients on a greased platter. When they are chilled, shape into 1-inch balls. Flour and roll the balls in:

Bound Breading, 552

Fry the balls in deep fat heated to 365°.

EGGPLANT FRITTERS

6 Servings

➤ Please read About Frittered Foods, 242.

Pare and slice:

A small-sized eggplant

Cook until tender in:

Boiling water to cover
1 teaspoon vinegar

Drain the eggplant. Mash it. Beat in:

1 egg
½ teaspoon salt
3 tablespoons all-purpose flour
½ teaspoon double-acting baking powder

Drop the batter from a spoon into deep fat heated to 365°.

RICE FRITTERS

About 10 Fritters

➤ Please read About Frittered Foods, 242.

Combine:

2 cups Boiled Rice, 206
2 tablespoons all-purpose flour
1 tablespoon finely chopped parsley
½ teaspoon paprika
½ teaspoon salt
(1 teaspoon onion juice)
(½ cup grated sharp cheese)

Beat and add:

2 egg yolks
2 tablespoons milk

Beat until stiff:

2 egg whites

and fold into the rice mixture. Drop into deep fat heated to 365° and cook until golden. Serve with:

Mushroom Wine Sauce, 347, or a tomato sauce

CALF BRAIN FRITTERS

3 Servings

➤ Please read About Frittered Foods, 242.

Prepare and blanch:

1 set calf brains, 504

Dry them between towels. Pull them into small pieces. Sift:

1 cup all-purpose flour
1 teaspoon double-acting baking powder
¼ teaspoon salt

Beat until light and add to flour mixture:

2 egg yolks

Beat in:

1 tablespoon melted butter
1 teaspoon grated lemon rind
A grating of nutmeg
½ cup milk
(1 tablespoon wine or brandy)

Beat until stiff ➤ but not dry:

2 egg whites

Fold them into the batter with the brains. Drop the batter from a spoon into deep fat heated to 365°. Serve when golden.

COOKED MEAT FRITTERS

Prepare and deep-fry as for:

Calf Brain Fritters, above

substituting for the brains about:

1½ cups chopped cooked meat

Add to the meat, if desired:

(2 tablespoons chopped parsley)
(1 tablespoon lemon juice or 1 teaspoon Worcestershire sauce)

Serve the fritters with:

A tomato sauce or
Horseradish Sauce, 343

CORN AND HAM FRITTERS

6 Servings

➤ Please read About Frittered Foods, 242.

Beat until light:

2 egg yolks

Add and combine with a few swift strokes:

½ cup milk
1⅓ cups sifted all-purpose flour
2 teaspoons double-acting baking powder
¾ teaspoon salt
¼ teaspoon paprika

Fold in:

2 tablespoons minced parsley or onion
¼ cup drained cream-style corn
¾ cup cooked minced ham
2 stiffly beaten egg whites

Drop the batter from a spoon into deep fat heated to 365° and cook until golden brown.

ABOUT DOUGHNUTS, CRULLERS AND BEIGNETS

Crullers are richer than doughnuts, and beignets richer than both. For tender cakes ➤ have all ingredients at about 70°, so the dough can be mixed quickly. This prevents the development of gluten in the flour, which would tend to toughen the batter. Keep the mix just firm enough to be easy to handle. Chill the dough slightly to shape it, before cutting, so that the board won't have to be too heavily floured. Roll or pat the dough to about

½-inch thickness. ➤ Cut with a well-floured double cutter, or 2 sizes of biscuit cutters. ➤ If you allow the dough to dry 10 or 12 minutes on a very lightly floured board or paper toweling, the doughnuts will absorb less fat while frying. The richer and sweeter the dough, the more fat they absorb.

➤ Please read About Deep-Fat Frying, 147. For delicate flavor, the frying fat must be impeccable. Bring the fat to 375° unless otherwise stated. Then, one at a time ➤ slide the doughnuts into the fat at the side of the kettle. They will keep their shapes if you transfer them to the fat with a pancake turner which has already been dipped into the kettle.

Each cake takes 2 to 3 minutes to a side to cook, depending on size. ➤ Never crowd the frying kettle. You can develop a machinelike precision by adding one at a time at about 15-second intervals. Turn each as soon as it browns on one side. It will usually rise at this point. When done, remove with a fork or tongs and place on paper toweling to drain. Replace it immediately with an uncooked cake to keep the fat at an even temperature.

When the cakes cool, dust with powdered, spiced or flavored sugar. For an easy method, use a paper bag as shown on 552. Or glaze them with Milk or Lemon Glaze, 731. Beignets may also be served hot with a sauce.

▲ Yeast-based doughnuts require no adjustment for high altitudes. For quick leavened doughnuts, reduce the baking powder or soda by one-fourth. ➤ But do not reduce soda beyond ½ teaspoon for each cup if sour milk or sour cream is used.

SWEET MILK DOUGHNUTS

About 36 Doughnuts

➤ Please read About Doughnuts, above.

Beat:

2 eggs

Add slowly, beating constantly:

1 cup sugar

Stir in:

1 cup milk
5 tablespoons melted shortening

Sift before measuring:

4 cups all-purpose flour

Resift with:

4 teaspoons double-acting baking powder
½ teaspoon cinnamon or 1 teaspoon grated lemon rind
½ teaspoon salt
(¼ teaspoon nutmeg)

Mix moist and dry ingredients. Fry in deep fat heated to 375° until golden brown.

SOUR CREAM DOUGHNUTS

About 36 Doughnuts

➤ Please read About Doughnuts, above.

Beat well:

3 eggs

Add slowly, beating constantly:

1¼ cups sugar

Stir in:

1 cup cultured sour cream

Sift before measuring:

4 cups all-purpose flour

Resift with:

1 teaspoon baking soda
2 teaspoons double-acting baking powder
½ teaspoon cinnamon or nutmeg
½ teaspoon salt

Stir the sifted ingredients and the egg mixture until blended. Fry in deep fat heated to 375° until golden brown.

YEAST DOUGHNUTS

About 48 Doughnuts

➤ Please read About Doughnuts, above.

Prepare dough for:

Buttermilk-Potato Roll, 613, or
No-Knead Yeast Coffee Cake, 619

After dough has risen to double its bulk, place on a lightly floured board and pat or roll to ½-inch thickness. Cut into rings or into strips ½ x 3½ inches. Twist the strips gently. You may bring the ends together to form twisted wreaths. Allow the twists to rise ➤ uncovered about 30 minutes. Fry in deep fat heated to 375° until golden brown. While still warm, shake in a bag filled with:

Sugar or sugar and cinnamon

BUTTERMILK-POTATO DOUGHNUTS

About 36 Doughnuts

➤ Please read About Doughnuts, above.

Prepare:

1 cup freshly riced boiled potatoes

Beat well:

2 eggs

Add very slowly, beating constantly:

⅔ cup sugar

Stir in the potatoes and:

1 cup buttermilk
2 tablespoons melted butter

Sift before measuring:

4 cups all-purpose flour

Resift with:

2 teaspoons double-acting baking powder
1 teaspoon baking soda
⅔ teaspoon salt
¼ teaspoon nutmeg or
¼ teaspoon cinnamon

Stir in the sifted ingredients and the potato mixture until they are blended. Chill the dough until it is easy to handle and cut. Fry in deep fat heated to 375° until golden brown.

DOUGHNUT VARIATIONS

I. Berlin or Jelly Doughnuts

Prepare Yeast Doughnuts, above. Cut the dough into ¼-inch-thick 2½-inch rounds instead of rings. Place on one round:

1 heaping teaspoon jelly or preserves
Brush the edges of the round with:
Egg white
Cap it with another round. Press the edges together. Repeat the process. After allowing the doughnuts to rise, fry them as directed in About Doughnuts, 244.

II. Orange Doughnuts
Prepare any of the recipes for Doughnuts. Substitute for ¼ cup of the milk:
The grated rind of 1 orange and
¼ cup orange juice

III. Chocolate Doughnuts
Prepare any one of the recipes for Doughnuts, adding:
5 tablespoons flour
Melt:
1½ oz. unsweetened chocolate
Add it to the melted shortening plus:
¼ cup additional sugar
1½ teaspoons vanilla

IV. Pecan or Date Doughnuts
Prepare any recipe for Doughnuts. Add:
½ cup broken nutmeats or diced pitted dates

V. Drop Doughnuts
While devoid of the characteristic hole, these are lighter in texture. Prepare any recipe for doughnuts not requiring yeast, using ¼ to ½ cup less flour. Slide a tablespoon of dough at a time into the hot fat.

BEIGNETS OR FRENCH FRITTERS

I. **4 to 6 Servings**
These are light as air. ➤ Please read About Doughnuts, 244.
Combine in a saucepan and boil and stir over low heat about 5 minutes:
6 tablespoons water
1 tablespoon butter
6 tablespoons all-purpose flour
Remove the pan from the heat. Beat in one at a time:
4 eggs
Beat the batter about 3 minutes after each addition. Add:
1 teaspoon vanilla
Drop the batter from a teaspoon into deep fat heated to 365°. Cook until golden. Drain. Dust with:
Confectioners' sugar
Serve at once with:
Lemon Sauce, 769, or
Gooseberry Preserves, 838

II. Prepare dough for:
Cream Puff Shells, 646
Add:
(½ teaspoon grated lemon or orange rind)
but instead of baking, drop a teaspoon of dough at a time into deep fat heated to 365°. As soon as they are cooked enough on one side, they will automatically turn themselves over. Remove when brown on both sides. Drain and sprinkle with:
Powdered sugar
Serve with:
Vanilla Sauce, 774, or Sauce Cockaigne, 770

CRULLERS

This recipe makes a lot—it is hard to gauge the exact amount! ➤ Please read About Doughnuts, 244.
Beat until light:
4 eggs
Add gradually:
⅔ cup sugar
Blend until mixture is creamy. Add:
¾ teaspoon grated lemon rind
⅓ cup melted shortening
⅓ cup milk
Sift before measuring:
3½ cups all-purpose flour
Resift with:
1½ teaspoons cream of tartar
½ teaspoon soda
¼ teaspoon salt
(½ teaspoon nutmeg or ¼ teaspoon cardamom)
Stir the sifted ingredients into the egg mixture. Roll the dough to the thickness of ¼ inch. With a pie jagger, cut it into strips of about ½ x 2½ inches. To make a fancier shape, twist the strips slightly. Fry in deep fat heated to 365° until golden brown. Drain and sprinkle with:
Confectioners' sugar

RICE CRULLERS OR CALAS

4 or 5 Servings
➤ Please read About Doughnuts, 244.
Mix together:
2 cups cold Boiled Rice, 206
3 beaten eggs
½ cup sugar
½ teaspoon vanilla
½ teaspoon nutmeg or grated lemon rind
2¼ teaspoons double-acting baking powder
And add only enough flour to bind the batter. You may need:
½ to 1 cup all-purpose flour
Drop the batter from a teaspoon into deep fat heated to 365°. Fry the cakes until they are golden brown—about 7 minutes. Drain on paper toweling. Sprinkle with:
Confectioners' sugar
Serve with:
Tart jelly

ROSETTES

About Thirty-Six 2½-Inch Rosettes
Rosettes are shaped with a small iron made for the purpose and shown in the chapter heading, 235. Onion or garlic salt, paprika and other seasonings enliven the rosettes when used as a base for creamed chicken or sweetbreads. For dessert, add

the sugar and vanilla and serve with a sweet sauce or stewed fruit or alone with coffee.

➤ Please read About Deep-Fat Frying, 147.

Beat until blended:

2 eggs
1/4 teaspoon salt
(1 tablespoon sugar)
(1 teaspoon vanilla)

Stir alternately into the egg mixture

1 1/4 cups sifted all-purpose flour

and:

1 cup milk

Beat until smooth. If you are using a thin 3/4-inch-high rosette mold, the frying fat need be only about 2 1/2 inches deep. When using taller molds, increase the depth of the fat. Heat the fat to between 325° and 350°. Prepare the iron by dipping first in the hot fat; then dip in the batter, but do not let it run over the top of the iron, for then it is difficult to remove the rosette when cooked. Hold the batter-coated iron over the fat a moment before completely immersing 20 to 35 seconds. Remove the rosette with a fork. Reheat the iron in the deep fat and repeat the process. Drain the rosettes on paper toweling and, if served as a dessert, dust with:

Confectioners' sugar

TIMBALE CASES FOR FOOD

Select a timbale iron that is fluted, like the one shown in the chapter heading, 235. It is easier to handle than a plain one.

➤ Please read About Deep-Fat Frying, 147.

Sift:

3/4 cup all-purpose flour
1/2 teaspoon salt

Combine and beat:

1 egg
1/2 cup milk

Combine the liquid and the sifted ingredients with a few swift strokes. Add:

1 teaspoon olive oil or melted butter

Let the batter stand for 1 hour to avoid bubbles which disfigure the cases. For a crisper, thinner case, rest the batter 2 hours or longer, covered and refrigerated. To fry timbale cases, prepare the iron by immersing its head in deep fat. Heat the deep fat to 365°—hot enough to brown a cube of bread in 1 minute. Wipe the iron with a cloth wrapped around a fork. Plunge the iron into the batter, within 3/4 inch of the top. Remove it. Allow the batter to dry slightly on the iron. Fry the timbale in the hot fat until it is golden brown, about 1 to 1 1/2 minutes. Remove it from the iron and drain it on a paper towel. Repeat the process.

ABOUT CROQUETTES

Well made, these are literally crunchy on the outside, as their name implies, but should retain a creamy interior texture whether they are of a sweet or a savory type. Because their cooking time is short—3 to 4 minutes—the recipes nearly always call for already cooked minced foods. With seafoods such as oysters and mussels and with brains and sweetbreads, parboiling is called for. ➤ Beef, pork and pork products should always be precooked. ➤ Use about 3/4 cup of heavy White Sauce III, 341, or Brown Sauce, 346, to 2 cups of cooked ground or minced solids, meat or fish and vegetables. ➤ The solids should never be watery—always well drained. You may add to the hot sauce 1 to 2 egg yolks and let them thicken slightly off the heat. Add enough sauce to the solids so they are well bound. There is a good deal of leeway in this relationship, provided—after chilling—the mixture can be handled. Spread it in a greased pan to about 1-inch thickness. You may also brush the top of the mixture lightly with butter or cover with waxed paper to avoid crusting. Chill at least 2 hours or freeze for 1 hour. When cool, it is best to cut the chilled mixture into squares or bars, not larger than 1 1/2 x 2 1/2 inches. Have ready a flour-covered paper. Put the croquette shapes, one at a time, on it and shape into a cylinder or round by manipulating the paper. Then coat thoroughly with a Bound Breading, 552. ➤ Let the coated croquettes dry on a rack at least 1 hour. ➤ Or if the mixture is a very soft one, dry for 10 minutes, after breading, and recoat with a bound breading again. This time allow a full hour for the drying period. ➤ Should the outer coating not be all-enveloping and very dry when it meets the hot fat, the croquette mixture may leak into the fat and cause boiling over. ➤ Please read About Deep-Fat Frying, 147. Immerse the croquettes, a few at a time, in a basket in deep fat heated to 365°. They will be golden in 2 to 4 minutes, unless otherwise indicated. Drain on paper toweling. You may hold them briefly on a rack in a 350° oven before serving. ➤ To reheat croquettes, once they have cooled, use a 400° oven.

CROQUETTES OF MEAT, FISH, FOWL OR VEGETABLES

About 12 Croquettes

➤ Please read About Croquettes, above.

Prepare:

White Sauce III, 341

When the sauce is smooth and hot, remove from heat and add:

1 to 2 egg yolks

allowing them to thicken slightly. Add to the sauce until it binds:

2 cups minced solid food: cooked meat, fish, fowl or vegetables
2 teaspoons grated onion or onion juice
2 tablespoons chopped parsley

Return the pan to very low heat and season the food well with a choice of one of the following:

(Salt, pepper or paprika)
(Freshly grated nutmeg or celery salt)
(2 teaspoons lemon juice)
(1 teaspoon Worcestershire sauce)
(1/2 teaspoon hot pepper sauce)

(2 teaspoons sherry)
(1/2 teaspoon dried or 1 tablespoon fresh herbs)
(1/2 teaspoon curry powder)

Cool and shape as directed above and, in shaping, place in the center of each croquette either:

(A sautéed mushroom)
(A piece of cooked chicken liver)
(A pimiento-stuffed olive)

Bread, dry and deep-fat-fry the croquettes as directed. Drain on paper toweling. You may serve the croquettes with one of the following if suitable to your croquette mixture:

(Onion Sauce, 344, Mushroom Sauce, 348, Piquant Sauce, 347, a tomato sauce, or leftover gravy)

CHEESE CROQUETTES COCKAIGNE

12 Croquettes

➤ Please read About Croquettes, 247.

Melt:

1/4 cup butter

Stir in:

5 tablespoons all-purpose flour

Stir in gradually until thickened:

1 cup milk
1/3 cup cream

Stir in, over low heat:

1/2 lb. shredded Swiss cheese

Cool slightly. Stir in:

3 beaten egg yolks
3/4 teaspoon salt
1/8 teaspoon paprika

Pour the custard into a well-greased pan, about 6 x 9 inches. Chill well. When ready to use, immerse pan for a moment in hot water, reverse it and turn the custard onto a flat surface. Cut into shapes. Bread and dry twice as directed. Fry in deep fat heated to 365°. Drain on paper toweling. Serve with:

Mexican Tomato Sauce, 352

HAM AND CORN CROQUETTES

8 Croquettes

➤ Please read About Croquettes, 247.

Combine and mix well:

1 1/4 cups cream-style corn
2 tablespoons finely chopped green pepper
1 cup ground or minced cooked ham
1 beaten egg
1/2 cup dry bread crumbs

Chill, shape, bread, dry and deep-fat-fry as directed. Drain on paper toweling. Serve the croquettes with:

A tomato sauce

MUSHROOM CROQUETTES

About 6 Croquettes

➤ Please read About Croquettes, 247.

Prepare:

1/2 cup White Sauce III, 341

Remove it from the heat. Add:

1/2 teaspoon Worcestershire sauce
1/8 teaspoon curry powder
1 slightly beaten egg
2 tablespoons cracker crumbs
1 cup chopped mushrooms
1/2 teaspoon salt
1/4 teaspoon paprika

Chill, shape, bread, dry and deep-fat-fry the croquettes as directed. Drain on paper toweling. Serve at once.

SWEET RICE CROQUETTES

About 12 Croquettes

➤ Please read About Croquettes, 247.

Combine:

1 cup chopped walnuts or butternuts
1/2 cup toasted white bread crumbs
2 cups cold cooked rice
1 teaspoon sugar
1/2 teaspoon salt
1 beaten egg
1 teaspoon grated lemon rind or vanilla

Chill, shape, bread, dry and deep-fat-fry as directed. Drain on paper toweling. Serve with:

Tart jelly

CHICKEN OR VEAL CROQUETTES

➤ Please read About Croquettes, 247. Try adding poached sweetbreads or brains.

Combine:

1 1/2 cups finely minced cooked chicken or veal

with:

1/2 cup chopped sautéed mushrooms, minced celery or minced nuts

Add, until these ingredients are well bound:

About 3/4 cup hot Velouté Sauce, 345

Chill, shape, bread, dry and deep-fat-fry the croquettes as directed. Drain on paper toweling. Serve with:

Mushroom Wine Sauce, 347, or
Poulette Sauce, 345

OYSTER AND CHICKEN CROQUETTES

About 12 Croquettes

➤ Please read About Croquettes, 247.

The addition of whole oysters in a chicken croquette mixture is interesting. Heat in their liquor until they are plump:

1 pint oysters

Drain but reserve the liquor. Dry them.

Melt:

2 tablespoons butter

Sauté slowly in the butter until golden:

(3 tablespoons minced onion)

Stir in, until blended:

1/4 cup flour

Slowly add:

1 cup oyster liquor and Chicken Stock, 523
Season to taste

and add:

A few grains cayenne
A few grains nutmeg

Stir in:

½ cup minced cooked chicken

Reduce the heat and add:

3 beaten egg yolks
1 tablespoon minced parsley

Allow mixture to thicken. Whip until stiff and fold into the chicken mixture:

½ cup whipping cream

Spread the mixture on a platter. Chill. Dip the oysters one at a time in the chicken mixture until they are well coated. Shape, bread, dry and fry the croquettes in deep fat as directed. Drain on paper toweling. Serve garnished with:

Lemon slices
Parsley or watercress

SALMON CROQUETTES

About 12 Croquettes

➤ Please read About Croquettes, 247.

Mix:

2 cups flaked cooked or canned salmon
2 cups mashed potatoes
1½ teaspoons salt or anchovy paste
⅛ teaspoon pepper
1 beaten egg
1 tablespoon minced parsley
1 teaspoon lemon juice or Worcestershire sauce

Chill, shape, bread, dry and fry the croquettes in deep fat as directed. Drain on paper toweling before serving.

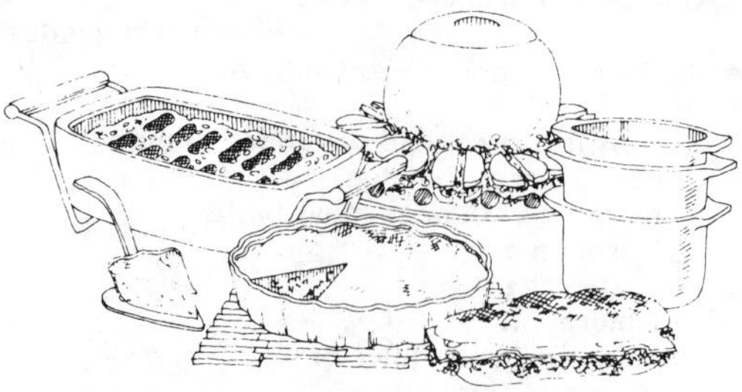

BRUNCH, LUNCH AND SUPPER DISHES

How we love this grab-bag chapter—for the ease and speed with which most of its dishes, elegant or plebeian, may be prepared; for its tricks with already cooked foods, and for the stimulus it gives to the attractive serving of leftovers. Shown on the left is a sausage and millet casserole, 259; next to it, in the rear, a bean pot containing a quick bean-and-fruit mixture, 288, surrounded by buttered brown bread. In the foreground are a tempting Quiche Alsacienne, 254, and a hefty Reuben Sandwich on a well-seeded rye roll, 272. The nesting flame-proof, lidded casseroles, right, are great storage-space and serving-time savers. In this chapter, too, are last-minute ways to combine staples from your larder—dried, preserved, canned or frozen—many of them perked up with onions, cheese, herbs and fruit—great emergency fare for unexpected guests!

Do not neglect other combinations in the egg, cereal and griddle-cake chapters. From many of these recipes attractive meals may be prepared in less than half an hour's time. Keep in mind that many fresh fish and shellfish recipes are almost as rapidly cooked as those involving a preprocessed food. For other quick dishes, refer also to the section on Ground Meats, 486, and Variety Meats, 499. For the quickest of sauces, see soup-based sauces, 348.

Care in cooking and skill in seasoning and presentation can make even a tin of tuna memorable. The large gratinéed casserole, the individual lidded baking dish or one of the following cases for food—as well as garnishes made from simple materials—all lend distinction in making a quick dish a gracious one.

CASES FOR FOOD

We have left behind the era of trenchers, those coarse, gravy-soaked loaves that served as both dishes and food—and whence came the word "trencherman." But none of us has lost a taste for sauce-flavored pastry, pancake, tortilla or toast. All manner of creamed foods—meat, vegetable or fish mixtures, cheese concoctions, as well as farces and stews—can be placed in one of the following cases and served with a sauce.

Patty Shells, 645
Popovers, 631
Brioches, 615
Rounds of buttered and toasted bread or French Toast, 636
A loaf of bread that has been hollowed, buttered lightly and toasted in a 300° oven
A Rice Loaf, 210
Large or individual Rice Rings, 207
Pies or Tart Shells, 640
Large or individual Noodle Rings, 214
Noodle Baskets, 214, or Potato Baskets, 323
Biscuits or Shortcakes, 633
A Mashed Potato Ring, 318
A Bread Dressing Ring, 262
Stuffed Pancakes, 236
Waffles, 241
Stuffed vegetables, 280
Sandwich Loaf, 68
Barquettes, 69
Turnovers, 69 and 251
Leaf Wrappings, 152
Coconut shells, 567
Sea shells, 375

See also the recipes that follow.

ROLL CASES

Preheat oven to 300°.
Hollow out:
Small rolls
Spread the hollows with:
Melted butter
Toast in the oven until crisp.

BREAD CASES OR CROUSTADES

Preheat oven to 300°.
With a biscuit cutter make rounds from:
1¼-inch-thick slices of bread
With a smaller cutter, press out an inner round, but do not cut deeper than 1 inch. Hollow out these smaller rounds and brush the hollows with:
Melted butter
Toast the cases in the oven until crisp and golden, or make them into croustades by deep-frying them, 147, at 350°.

MELBA TOAST BASKETS

Preheat oven to 275°.
Lightly butter on both sides:
Thin crustless bread slices
Press them into muffin tins, letting the corners of the bread protrude slightly. Toast in the oven until crisp and golden.

CHINESE EGG ROLLS

12 Egg Rolls

Egg rolls are frequently used for hors d'oeuvre, or you may serve them as the main dish at luncheon.

The pancakelike skins are available at Chinese grocery stores, or you may make the following dough.
Sift into a bowl:

1 cup all-purpose flour

Add gradually to make a thin, smooth batter:

2 cups water

Beat in:

2 eggs
½ teaspoon salt

Grease a 6-inch-diameter skillet and put over ➤ low heat. Beat the batter again and pour 1 tablespoon into the pan. Let it spread over the surface of the pan to form a very thin, flexible pancake. When it shrinks away from the sides, turn it and let it set on the other side. Do not let it become brown or crisp. Remove pancakes to a dish when done and cover with a damp cloth until ready to use.
Heat in a skillet or wok:

3 tablespoons vegetable oil

Stir-fry in it briefly:

½ cup finely chopped celery
¾ cup shredded cabbage
4 finely chopped scallions

Add and stir-fry for 3 minutes:

½ cup diced shrimp
½ cup diced cooked pork

Add and stir-fry 5 more minutes:

½ cup drained, finely chopped water chestnuts
½ cup bean sprouts
1 minced clove garlic
¼ cup soy sauce
A grating of gingerroot
½ teaspoon sugar

Cool the filling. Place 4 tablespoons of filling in rectangular shape on the center of each pancake and fold up envelope-style, sealing the last flap with a paste made of:

1 tablespoon flour
2 tablespoons cold water

Fry until golden brown in deep fat heated to 375°. Or use oil about 1 inch deep in a skillet and fry the egg rolls until golden brown. Serve with:

Chinese mustard
Soy sauce
Oriental Sweet-Sour Sauce, 355

TURNOVERS, PIROSHKI, OR MEAT-FILLED PASTRIES

6 Servings

➤ Please read About Meat Pie Toppings, 449.
This recipe and the following one make excellent hot canapés. For canapés, cut the dough into small, attractive shapes. For hot luncheon sandwiches, make them a more generous size. If prepared in advance, keep chilled until ready to bake.
Preheat oven to 450°.
Prepare, using about 2 cups flour:

Biscuit Dough, 632, or Pie Dough, 640, or Vienna Pastry Dough, 641

Pat or roll it until thin. This is a matter of taste—about ¼ inch for biscuit dough, ⅛ inch for Vienna pastry dough. Cut 3 x 3-inch squares, or cut into rounds. Place on each piece of dough as much filling, below, as will fit. Moisten the edges, fold over and pinch together with a fork. Place the triangles or crescents in a pan. Brush lightly with:

(Soft butter)

Bake until the dough is done, about 20 minutes. This may be served with:

Brown Sauce, 346

Fillings

I. Lightly moisten:

Ground or minced cooked meat

with:

Gravy or cream, Brown Sauce, 346, or a canned soup sauce, 348

Season well with:

Salt and pepper
Worcestershire sauce or chili sauce

II. Moisten braunschweiger sausage with chili sauce or tomato soup.

III. Use:

1½ cups cooked ground ham
½ cup White Sauce II, 341, thick cream or evaporated milk
2 tablespoons chopped pickles or olives
1 tablespoon chopped onion
1½ tablespoons catsup
Salt and pepper, if needed

IV. Sauté gently until yellow:

2 cups chopped onion

in:

3 tablespoons olive or anchovy oil

Add:

¼ cup or more chopped ripe olives
6 or 8 chopped anchovies

V. Use any good cooked seafood filling; taste before seasoning.

MEAT PIE ROLL OR PINWHEELS

4 Servings

This is a palatable, quickly made everyday dish—an attractive way to serve a small quantity of left-over meat.
➤ Please read About Meat Pie Toppings, 449.
Preheat oven to 450°.
Prepare, using 2 cups flour:

Biscuit Dough, 632, or Pie Dough, 640

If you use biscuit dough, make it a little drier than for ordinary biscuits or it will be difficult to handle. Roll the dough until very thin. Cut it into an oblong. To prevent sogginess, use a pastry brush and brush it lightly with:

1 egg white or soft butter

Spread the dough with:

A cooked meat filling, above

Leave about 1 inch at the sides uncovered. Roll it loosely. Moisten the end with water to bind it together. Moisten the sides and pinch them together. This roll may be prepared in advance and placed in the refrigerator until ready for use. Bake the roll on a greased cookie sheet until done, about 20 minutes. Or cut the roll into 3/4-inch pinwheel slices. Dot the tops with:

Butter

Bake the pinwheels until the dough is done, about 20 minutes. Serve the roll or pinwheels with:

Brown Sauce, 346, or a tomato sauce

QUICK CHICKEN OR BEEF POT PIE

➤ Please read About Meat Pie Toppings, 449.
Preheat oven to 400°.
Have ready:

A lightly baked pie shell and baked pie crust top, 640

formed to fit your casserole or individual baking dishes. We find the prebaked shell more convenient and tastier than the prefilled unbaked crust which has to be exposed to longer, slower cooking. Heat:

Creamed chicken, Chicken or Turkey Hash, 263, or Beef Hash, 261

Fill the shell with the meat filling and cover with the baked pie topping. Bake until the filling is thoroughly heated and the top is light brown.

CORN BREAD TAMALE PIE

6 Servings

Sauté in a lightly greased skillet:

1 pound ground beef
1 chopped onion

When the meat is highly browned and the onion translucent, add:

1 cup cream of tomato soup
1 cup water or stock
1/4 teaspoon pepper
1 teaspoon salt
1 tablespoon chili powder
1 cup drained whole-kernel corn
1/2 cup chopped green pepper, seeds and membrane removed

Simmer 15 minutes.
Preheat oven to 425°. Meanwhile, sift and mix together:

3/4 cup cornmeal
1 tablespoon flour
1 tablespoon sugar
1/2 teaspoon salt
1 1/2 teaspoons double-acting baking powder

Moisten with:

1 beaten egg
1/3 cup milk

Mix lightly and stir in:

1 tablespoon vegetable oil

Place meat mixture in a greased 2-quart casserole and cover with the corn bread topping. The topping will disappear into the meat mixture, but will rise during baking and form a layer of corn bread. Bake about 20 to 25 minutes or until corn bread is brown.

ENCHILADAS

About 2 Dozen

Preheat oven to 350°.
Have ready:

Hot Tortillas, 629

In a heavy saucepan, heat:

2 tablespoons olive oil

Sauté until golden:

1/2 cup chopped onion
1 minced clove garlic

Add:

2 teaspoons to 1 tablespoon chili powder
1 cup tomato purée
1/2 cup chicken or beef stock

Season with:

Salt and pepper
1 teaspoon cumin

Spread some sauce over the tortillas and fill the centers with equal quantities of:

Finely minced raw onion
Shredded Mozzarella or longhorn cheese

Roll the tortillas and place them ➤ seam side down in an ovenproof dish. Pour more sauce over the tops and sprinkle with:

Shredded Mozzarella or longhorn cheese

Heat thoroughly in the oven about 15 minutes.

QUICK TOMATO TART

6 Servings

Preheat oven to 350°.
Have ready:

6 baked unsweetened 2 1/2-inch tart shells, 640

Slice 1/2 inch thick:

6 skinned seeded fresh tomatoes

Mix and heat well:

1/4 cup sautéed sliced mushrooms
1/4 cup canned cream of chicken soup
1/4 cup Italian tomato purée
1/4 teaspoon sugar
1/4 cup softened liver sausage
4 large chopped stuffed olives
2 teaspoons fresh chopped basil
1/4 teaspoon salt

First place a layer of heated sauce in each tart shell, then a tomato slice. Cover with the remaining hot mixture. Dust each tart with:

Grated Parmesan cheese

Heat the filled tarts on a baking sheet in the oven about 15 minutes.

WELSH RAREBITS

Our correspondence is closed on the subject of rarebit vs. rabbit. We stick to rarebit because rabbit already means something else. But we can only answer the controversy with a story. A stranger mollifying a small crying boy: "I wouldn't cry like that if I were you!" Small boy: "You cry your way and I'll cry mine."

I. With Beer **6 to 8 Servings**

Grate or shred:

1 lb. aged yellow cheese

Melt in a double boiler over—not in—boiling water:

1 tablespoon butter

Stir in:

1 cup beer

When the beer is warm, stir in the cheese. Stir constantly with a fork until the cheese is melted. Beat slightly and add:

1 egg

Season the rarebit with:

1 teaspoon Worcestershire sauce
1 teaspoon salt
(½ teaspoon paprika)
A few grains red pepper
(¼ teaspoon curry powder or a pinch of saffron)
¼ teaspoon dry mustard

Serve the rarebit at once on:

Crackers, hot toast or Grilled Tomatoes, 332

II. With Milk **4 Servings**

Melt in a double boiler over—not in—boiling water:

1 tablespoon butter

Stir in and melt:

1½ cups diced aged yellow cheese

Add:

¼ teaspoon salt
¼ teaspoon dry mustard
A few grains cayenne
1 teaspoon Worcestershire sauce

Stir in slowly:

½ to ¾ cup cream

When the mixture is hot, remove the pan from the heat. Beat in:

1 egg yolk

Serve the rarebit at once over:

Hot toasted crackers or bread

TOMATO RAREBIT OR WOODCHUCK

I. **4 Servings**

Combine and bring to the boiling point:

1 cup condensed tomato soup
½ cup water

You may add:

(¾ cup thinly sliced Sautéed Onions, 312)

Add and stir until melted:

¾ lb. or more shredded aged yellow cheese

Remove pan from heat. Combine, beat and add:

2 egg yolks
1 teaspoon Worcestershire sauce
1 teaspoon dry mustard
1 teaspoon salt
¼ teaspoon paprika
⅛ teaspoon white pepper

Stir these ingredients over low heat 1 or 2 minutes to let the yolks thicken slightly. Whip until ➤ stiff, but not dry:

2 egg whites

Fold them into the hot cheese mixture. Serve the rarebit on:

Hot toast or crackers

II. **4 Servings**

Stir and melt over low heat:

½ lb. shredded aged cheddar cheese: 2 cups

Add, stir and heat:

1 cup condensed tomato soup
3 tablespoons water
½ teaspoon salt
A few grains cayenne

Serve the rarebit on:

Toast or toasted crackers

CHEESE CASSEROLE

A most appetizing luncheon or supper dish when balanced by a green vegetable, a salad, or orange and grapefruit cups.

I. **4 Servings**

Preheat oven to 350°.

Cut ½ inch thick:

7 slices bread

Spread the slices lightly with:

Butter

Cut 2 of the slices twice across on the bias, making 8 triangular pieces. Cut the remaining bread into cubes. There should be about 4 cups of diced buttered bread. Place layers of diced bread in a buttered baking dish. Sprinkle the layers with:

1 cup shredded cheese

Combine and beat:

2 eggs
1 cup milk
1 teaspoon salt
¼ teaspoon paprika
A few grains cayenne
½ teaspoon dry mustard

Pour these ingredients over the cheese. Place the triangles of bread upright around the edge to form a crown. Bake about 25 minutes. Serve at once.

II. **4 Servings**

Trim the crusts from:

8 slices bread

Cut them in half on the bias. Place half of them in the bottom of a greased 8-inch ovenproof dish, spiral fashion, not letting them overlap. They should resemble a pinwheel. Cut into slices ¼ inch thick:

6 oz. aged cheddar cheese

Cover the bread layer with the cheese slices, not letting them overlap. Cover the cheese with the rest of the bread, again in spiral fashion.

Beat lightly:

3 eggs

Add and beat well:

¼ teaspoon salt
⅛ teaspoon paprika
A few grains cayenne
2 cups cream
(1 teaspoon grated onion, 1 tablespoon parsley or chives, or ¼ teaspoon dry mustard)

Pour this mixture over the bread. ➤ Let the dish stand 1 hour. Bake in a 350° oven about 1 hour or until well browned. Serve hot.

CHEESE, NUT AND BREAD LOAF

6 Servings

Preheat oven to 350°.
Combine well:

2 cups fresh bread crumbs
1 cup minced walnut or pecan meats
1 cup shredded American cheese
1 cup milk
¾ teaspoon salt
½ teaspoon paprika
1 tablespoon finely chopped onion
1 tablespoon minced parsley
1 beaten egg

Shape these ingredients into a loaf in a greased bread pan. Bake about 25 minutes. Serve it with:

Quick Tomato Sauce, 352, Quick Mushroom Sauce, 348, or White Onion Sauce, 344

ABOUT CHEESE FONDUE

For so simple an affair, the controversy involved in the making of this dish is vast indeed. Its confecting is a ritual that varies with each Swiss household. Experiment has led to the following conclusions, no matter how simple or how complex a version you choose to make. Use a heavy pot and both high and low heat. The cheese or combination of cheeses used must be ➤ natural cheeses, not pasteurized types. The wine must be ➤ a dry white wine. Although kirsch is traditionally de rigueur, you may substitute a nonsweet liqueur like slivovitz, cognac or applejack. ➤ Measure all ingredients and have them ready to add

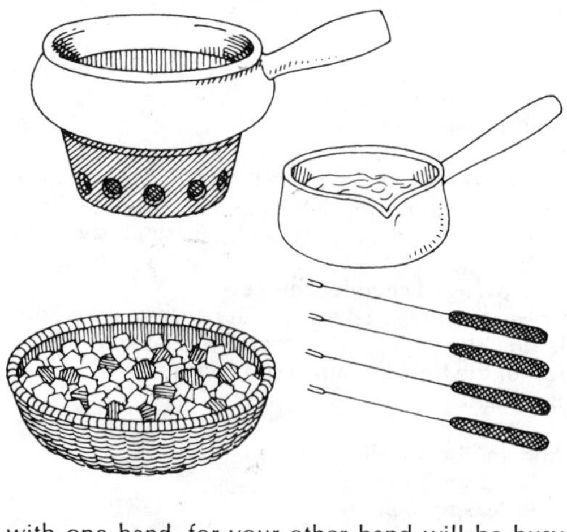

with one hand, for your other hand will be busy stirring the mixture with a wooden spoon—from the time the wine is hot enough for the cheese until the fondue is ready to eat. Altogether, this is a matter of about 10 minutes of cooking. ➤ Never make this dish in advance.

Have ready a breadbasket or bowl filled with crusty French or Italian bread cut into 1 x 1 x ¾-inch pieces, making sure that each piece has one side of crust. The guests, each equipped with a heatproof-handled fork—preferably two- or three-tined—spear the bread from the soft side and dip the impaled bit into the well-warmed cheese. The fondue will at first be on the thin side, but will thicken as the process progresses. There is seldom much left by the time another 10 minutes has elapsed. Serve with fresh fruit and tea.

FONDUE

4 Servings

Shred:

1 lb. Emmenthaler, or ½ lb. Emmenthaler and ½ lb. Gruyère cheese

Rub a heavy saucepan with:

A clove of garlic

Put into the pan:

2 cups dry white wine

While this is heating ➤ uncovered, over moderately high heat, pour into a cup:

3 tablespoons kirsch

This is the classic flavoring, although one of the other dry liqueurs mentioned above may be used. Stir into the kirsch until well dissolved:

1 teaspoon cornstarch

By this time the wine will begin to show small foamy bubbles over its surface. When it is almost covered with this fine foam ➤ but is not yet boiling, add the coarsely shredded cheese gradually ➤ stirring constantly. Keep the heat high, but do not let the fondue boil. Continue to add the cheese until you can feel a very slight resistance to the spoon as you stir. Then, still stirring vigorously, add the kirsch and cornstarch mixture. Continue to cook until the fondue begins to thicken. Add to taste:

Nutmeg, white pepper or paprika

Quickly transfer it to a heatproof heavy pan and place the container over an alcohol lamp or in a fondue pot or a chafing dish. Or use an electric skillet adjusted to ➤ low heat. After this transferral the cooking continues on low heat and the guests take over as described above.

ABOUT QUICHES

Early recipes for Quiche called for bacon and cream, but later cheese was added. When sautéed onions were included, the dish was dubbed **Alsacienne.** Cool the onions before adding them.

Other ingredients have found their way into this delicious custard base: tomatoes, nuts, and cooled, well-drained braised endive.

Quiche makes a hefty brunch or an hors d'oeuvre baked in tiny tarts no larger than the lining of muffin tins. As it is always served lukewarm, time it accordingly. Following are several variations on a Quiche theme.

QUICHE LORRAINE

6 Servings

Preheat oven to 375°.
Prepare a 9-inch pie shell of:
Pâte Brisée, 641, or any rich pie dough
Brush it with:
The white of an egg
and prick it well. Chop into 1-inch lengths:
1/4 lb. sliced bacon
Cook the bacon in a heavy skillet, stirring constantly, until the fat is almost rendered out, but the bacon is not yet crisp. Drain on paper toweling. Scald to hasten the cooking time:
2 cups milk or cream
Cool slightly, then beat together with:
3 eggs
1/4 teaspoon salt
1/8 teaspoon white pepper
A fresh grating of nutmeg
1 teaspoon chopped chives
Sprinkle in the bottom of the pie shell the bacon and:
1/2 cup diced Swiss cheese
Pour the custard mixture over it. Bake 35 to 40 minutes or until the top is a golden brown. For doneness, you may test as for Custard, 734.

CHEESE CUSTARD PIE OR FLAN

4 Servings

Preheat oven to 325°.
Prepare:
An 8-inch baked pie crust shell, 640
at least 2 inches deep. When cool, brush with:
Egg white
Scald:
1 3/4 cups milk or cream
Reduce the heat and add:
1 cup shredded cheese
Stir until the cheese is melted. Add:
1/2 teaspoon salt
1/4 teaspoon paprika
1/2 teaspoon grated onion
A few grains cayenne
Remove the mixture from the heat and beat in, one at a time:
3 eggs
You may add:
(3/4 cup diced cooked seafood)
Fill the pie crust and bake it until the custard is firm, about 45 minutes.

ONION SHORTCAKE

6 Servings

Preheat oven to 425°.
Peel and slice:
10 medium-sized white onions
Sprinkle them with:
1/2 teaspoon salt
Melt in a saucepan:
3 tablespoons butter
Add the onions, cover and simmer until tender. Add:
1/4 teaspoon paprika
2 teaspoons chopped parsley
(1/2 cup diced cooked ham)
A grating of nutmeg or white pepper
Place the mixture in a casserole and cover with:
1 cup White Sauce I, 341
into which you have beaten:
1 egg
(1/4 cup grated cheese)
Prepare half the amount of:
Fluffy Biscuit Dough, 633
omitting the sugar. Spread the dough over the onion mixture. Bake about 20 minutes or until the dough is done.

ONION OR LEEK PIE

Preheat oven to 450°.
Line a 9-inch pie pan with:
Pie Dough, 640
Prick and chill it. Skin and slice thinly:
2 1/2 lb. Bermuda onions or leeks
Melt in a heavy saucepan:
3 tablespoons butter
Add the onions. Stir and cook over low heat until they are translucent. Cool them well. Combine and heat slowly until blended:
3 eggs
1 cup cultured sour cream
1 teaspoon salt
1/4 teaspoon freshly ground pepper
(1 tablespoon minced fresh herb or 1 teaspoon dill or celery seed)
Stir this mixture into the onions. Brush the bottom of the cooled pie shell with:
1 slightly beaten egg white
Fill it with the slightly cooled onion mixture. Place over the top:
(4 strips bacon, diced, or crumbled cooked sausage)
Bake the pie in a 450° oven 10 minutes. ➤ Reduce the heat to 300° and bake until the crust is light brown, about 1/2 hour. Serve it piping hot with a:
Tossed green salad

SOY OR LIMA BEAN CASSEROLE

4 Servings

Preheat oven to 325°.
Have ready:
2 1/2 cups cooked lima beans or 1 1/2 cups lima beans and 1 cup cooked soybeans
Stir into them:
1/2 cup chicken stock
Or melt:
(2 tablespoons butter)
You may add and sauté 3 minutes:
(1/4 cup minced onion)
Stir into the stock or butter, over low heat, until melted:
1/2 lb. shredded cheese
Add the beans and:
1/2 teaspoon salt

¼ teaspoon pepper
1 teaspoon dried basil or thyme
A few grains cayenne
(1 cup chopped nutmeats)

Bake the beans about ½ hour. Serve with:

Quick Tomato Sauce, 352

SOY CAKES

4 Servings

Sauté in:

3 tablespoons butter or vegetable oil
¼ cup chopped onion
¼ cup finely chopped green pepper, seeds and membrane removed
¼ cup finely diced celery

Mix with:

1 cup cooked dried soybeans, 286
1 cup Boiled Rice, 206
1 or 2 eggs
Season to taste

Form into 4 patties and roll in:

Sesame seeds

Sauté gently in:

2 tablespoons sesame or vegetable oil

until the seeds are golden.

MIXED VEGETABLE GRILL

Preheat broiler.
Cut into slices:

Tomatoes

Brush them with:

Melted butter

Season them with:

Salt and pepper
Brown sugar

Prepare for cooking:

Sliced mushrooms
Sliced green peppers, seeds and membrane removed

Brush them with:

Melted butter

Season lightly with:

Salt
(Lemon juice)

Grease the broiler. Place on it the tomato slices, and on the slices the mushrooms, peppers and:

(Sliced bacon)
(Sausages)

Broil these ingredients until done. Meanwhile sauté or poach:

Eggs

Serve the eggs on a hot platter on:

Toast rounds

surrounded by the grilled food. Garnish the platter with:

Parsley and olives

CREAMED LEFTOVER VEAL

6 Servings

Melt in a chafing dish or electric skillet:

¼ cup butter

Add and sauté about 5 minutes:

½ lb. sliced mushrooms
¼ cup diced green pepper, seeds and membrane removed

Add and stir well:

¼ cup flour

Pour over the mixture and stir until thickened:

½ cup cream
1 cup veal or chicken stock

Add:

2 cups diced cooked veal
2 tablespoons minced pimiento
¼ teaspoon marjoram
½ cup dry white wine
Season to taste

Simmer about 5 minutes longer and serve over:

Rice, noodles or macaroni

Garnish with:

Chopped parsley

VEAL OR LAMB AND SPINACH CASSEROLE

Preheat oven to 425°.
Place in a casserole a 1-inch layer or more of:

Creamed Spinach, 327

which has been delicately flavored with a little:

Grated onion

Place over it:

Slices of roast veal or lamb

If you have gravy, pour a little of it over the meat, or use some thick cream. Cover the top with:

Au Gratin III, 553

Bake until the top is brown. Garnish with:

Parsley

COOKED CURRIED VEAL OR LAMB AND RICE

4 Servings

Peel and slice:

1 cup onions
(½ cup diced celery)

Core, pare and slice:

2 medium-sized apples

Melt in a saucepan:

3 tablespoons butter

Add:

½ to 1 teaspoon curry powder

Caution: use only ½ teaspoon curry to begin with if you are unfamiliar with it. Add the onions and apples and sauté until the onions are tender. Remove them from the pan. Brown lightly in the pan about:

2 cups sliced or diced cooked veal or lamb

Remove from the pan. Stir into the pan juices:

2 teaspoons flour

Stir in slowly:

1 cup stock
(½ cup raisins)

When the sauce is smooth and boiling, add the onions, apples and meat. Stir in:

1 tablespoon lemon juice
Season to taste

and serve with:

Boiled Rice, 206

LAMB TERRAPIN

4 Servings

Chop or rice:
2 hard-cooked eggs
Combine the eggs with:
2 cups diced cold cooked lamb
2 tablespoons olive oil
1 tablespoon lemon juice
Melt:
2 tablespoons butter
Stir in until blended:
3 tablespoons flour
1 teaspoon dry mustard
Stir in slowly:
2 cups lamb stock or milk
Add:
1 teaspoon Worcestershire sauce
Season to taste
Cook and stir the sauce until it is boiling. Add the lamb and egg mixture. Reduce heat and simmer until reheated. Serve on:
Hot toast
Garnish with:
Mint

CHOP SUEY OR CHOW MEIN

4 Servings

These vaguely Chinese dishes which can be made with cooked pork, chicken or seafood differ in that Chop Suey is served over steamed rice, and Chow Mein over fried noodles. Both are—like some of the old Chinese porcelain patterns—strictly for export. To get the feeling of true Chinese food, read Mrs. Buwei Yang Chao's delightful *How to Cook and Eat in Chinese*. To prepare the dish below please read about Stir-Frying, 149.
Cut into 2-inch julienne strips about 1/4 inch wide:
2 cups cooked pork roast
Slice diagonally, see 277:
1/2 cup celery with tender leaves
1/2 cup green onions
Chop coarsely:
1 green pepper, seeds and membrane removed
1 cup mushrooms
Drain:
1 cup bean sprouts
Heat well in a deep heavy skillet:
2 tablespoons cooking oil
Stir-fry the onion and celery about 3 minutes. Then add the mushrooms, pork, peppers and bean sprouts. Continue to stir-fry 2 to 3 minutes longer.
Add:
(1/2 cup peeled, seeded and slivered fresh tomatoes)
Jellied juices from the roast or a bit of Meat Glaze, 368
1 cup strong consommé
Season with:
Salt and pepper
1 tablespoon soy sauce
3 tablespoons dry sherry
You may thicken the juices with cornstarch, 339.
Serve at once.

POLYNESIAN PORK OR CHICKEN

4 Servings

Prepare and keep warm:
Oriental Sweet-Sour Sauce II, 355
Stir-fry, 149, in a wok or skillet:
1 tablespoon vegetable oil
1 cup finely diced cooked chicken or pork
When thoroughly heated, put meat into a heated dish. In the wok, stir-fry briefly:
1 cut-up orange
1 small cubed banana
(1/4 cup grated coconut)
in:
1 tablespoon vegetable oil
Add the meat and the warm sauce. Mix lightly until all ingredients are coated and hot. Serve at once over:
Chow Mein noodles

LEFTOVERS IN BACON

Preheat oven to 450°.
Moisten lightly three parts of:
Cooked ground meat or meat loaf
and one part of:
Boiled Rice, 206
with:
Gravy or cream
Season well with:
Salt and pepper
Minced onion or onion juice
Roll the mixture into small balls, flatten slightly and wrap around them:
Slices of bacon
Secure the bacon with wooden picks. Place the patties in a greased baking dish and bake until the bacon is crisp, about 15 minutes. Serve with:
A tomato sauce

COOKED GROUND HAM LOAF

6 Servings

Preheat oven to 350°.
Combine:
2 cups cooked ground ham
1 cup bread or cracker crumbs or crushed cornflakes
2 eggs
2 tablespoons grated onion
1/8 teaspoon pepper
1 cup milk
2 tablespoons chili sauce
2 to 4 tablespoons chopped parsley or celery
Bake these ingredients in a greased loaf pan about 30 minutes. Serve the loaf with:
Horseradish Sauce, 343, Hot Mustard Sauce, 345, Mushroom Wine Sauce, 347, or a tomato sauce

STUFFED HAM ROLLS

I. **4 Servings**

Make these when you have leftover rice.
Preheat oven to 400°.
Trim:

8 thin slices baked or boiled ham

Spread them lightly with:

Mustard

Place on each slice part of the following filling. Combine:

1½ cups cooked rice
⅓ cup chopped raisins
1 beaten egg
¼ teaspoon paprika
½ teaspoon Worcestershire sauce
(¼ cup chopped celery)
(½ teaspoon basil)

Roll the slices and secure them with wooden picks. Brush with:

Milk

Bake the rolls until they are thoroughly heated. Serve with:

Hot Cumberland Sauce, 356

II. Prepare, as for above:

Slices of ham or prosciutto

Place on each slice:

4 asparagus tips

Roll, brush and heat the ham as directed above. Serve the rolls with:

1½ cups Cheese Sauce, 342

III. **4 Servings**

Preheat oven to 350°.
Prepare, as for above:

8 large slices ham

Combine and mix well:

¾ cup cultured sour cream
1 cup sieved creamy cottage cheese
1 slightly beaten egg
¼ cup minced onions
½ cup drained chopped cooked spinach
½ teaspoon dry mustard
¼ teaspoon salt

Place about 2 tablespoons filling on each slice of ham. Roll and tuck in the edges. Put in a shallow baking dish and cover with a mixture of:

1 cup cream of mushroom soup
¼ cup cultured sour cream

Bake 20 to 25 minutes.

GROUND HAM ON PINEAPPLE SLICES

4 Servings

Preheat oven to 400°.
Combine:

1 cup ground cooked ham
1 teaspoon prepared mustard
2 tablespoons mayonnaise

Spread this mixture on:

4 slices drained pineapple

Bake the slices in a greased pan about 10 minutes.

HAM AND POTATO CAKES

4 Servings

Combine:

1 cup mashed potatoes
1 cup ground cooked ham
1 tablespoon chopped parsley
½ teaspoon grated onion
⅛ teaspoon pepper
Salt, if needed

Shape this mixture into flat cakes. Dip lightly in:

Flour

Sauté in:

Bacon drippings or other fat

HAM CAKES WITH PINEAPPLE AND SWEET POTATOES

6 Servings

Prepare:

3 large Boiled Sweet Potatoes, 324

Preheat oven to 375°.
Combine:

2 cups chopped or ground cooked ham
½ cup dry bread crumbs
2 eggs
⅛ teaspoon salt
(1 teaspoon prepared mustard)

Shape these ingredients into 6 flat cakes. Melt in in a skillet:

5 tablespoons bacon drippings

Brown lightly in the skillet:

6 slices drained pineapple

Remove them and brown the ham cakes in the skillet. Place the pineapple slices in a baking dish and cover each slice with a ham cake. Skin the sweet potatoes. Cut them lengthwise into halves. Combine and sprinkle over them:

¼ teaspoon cloves
¼ cup brown sugar

Cook the potatoes slowly in the skillet until well caramelized. Place them over the ham cakes in the baking dish. Baste with:

Pineapple juice

Bake about 10 minutes.

HAM À LA KING

6 Servings

Prepare:

2 cups White Sauce I, 341

When the sauce is boiling, add:

2 cups diced cooked ham
2 diced hard-cooked eggs
1 cup Sautéed Mushrooms, 308, or canned mushrooms with sliced stuffed olives
1 tablespoon chopped green pepper
1 tablespoon chopped pimiento

Serve the ham very hot on:

Rounds of toast, on rusks, in bread cases or on corn bread squares

Garnish with:

Chopped parsley

⊟ BARBECUED FRANKFURTERS, WIENERS OR HOT DOGS

I. Preheat broiler or grill.
Grill:

Frankfurters, wieners or hot dogs

or put under the broiler on a rack in a roasting pan. During the cooking baste them ➤ constantly with:

A Barbecue Sauce, 354

II. Cut lengthwise:

Frankfurters, wieners or hot dogs

Fill with:

A strip of sharp cheese

Wrap spirally with:

A strip of bacon

Grill, turning often, until bacon is crisp. Serve with:

A Barbecue Sauce, 354

⊟ FRANKFURTER KEBABS

8 Servings

Cut into about 4 pieces each:

8 frankfurters

Marinate about 30 minutes in:

French Dressing, 360

Preheat grill or broiler.
Skewer the pieces alternately with bits of:

Bacon
Small canned pickled onions
Green pepper

Grill or broil, turning often.

FRANKFURTERS OR SAUSAGES IN SAUCE

I. **3 Servings**

Preheat oven to 400°.
Place in a shallow pan:

6 frankfurters

Prepare:

1 cup Quick Tomato Sauce, 352
or Barbecue Sauce, 354

You may add:

(Chopped green peppers, seeds and membranes removed)
(Grated onions or chives)

Pour these ingredients over the sausages. Bake them until they swell and the sauce thickens.

II. Prepare, using no salt:

Quick Tomato Sauce, 352

Season it well with:

Paprika

Sauté, 149:

Vienna Sausages

Drain them. Heat them in the sauce. Serve with:

Boiled Rice, 206, Noodles, 213,
or Mashed Potatoes, 318

SAUSAGE BAKED WITH APPLES

4 Servings

Preheat oven to 400°.
Arrange in a baking dish:

8 partly sautéed pork sausages

Core:

6 tart apples

Cut them into ¼-inch slices and place around the sausages. Sprinkle with:

¾ cup brown sugar

Bake at 400° for 10 minutes. ➤ Reduce the heat to 350° and continue baking about 15 minutes longer. Baste with the drippings.

SAUSAGES AND MUSHROOMS

Prepare:

Mashed Potatoes, 318, or
Mashed Boiled Chestnuts, 298

Heap them in a mound on a hot platter. Keep them hot. Sauté:

Sausages, 496

Place them around the potatoes. Sauté in the drippings:

Sliced Mushrooms, 306

Garnish the platter with them and:

Sprigs of parsley

Pour drippings over the potatoes or chestnuts.

SAUSAGE AND ONIONS

4 Servings

Heat in a skillet:

2 tablespoons vegetable oil or shortening

Add:

1½ cups sliced onions

Cook and stir over low heat about 15 minutes or until golden. Cut a lengthwise slit in:

8 hot dog sausages or frankfurters

Fill them with the onions. Fasten with wooden picks. Broil slowly on both sides. Remove picks and place stuffed sausages on:

Toast or toasted buns

SAUSAGE AND MILLET CASSEROLE

Using millet, prepare:

Rice or Millet Spoon Bread, 629

While the spoon bread is baking, sauté:

Small link sausages

Fry long enough to remove most of the fat. About 10 minutes before the spoon bread is done, place the sausages on top. Coat with:

Chili Sauce, 847, or
Quick Tomato Sauce, 352

Continue to bake about 10 minutes longer.

CANNED BAKED BEANS WITH BACON OR FRANKFURTERS

6 Servings

Preheat oven to 350°.
To put zing into this dish, and to make it moist and palatable, add to:

2½ cups canned beans: 21-oz. can

approximately:

¼ cup catsup
2 tablespoons molasses
2 tablespoons brown sugar
2 tablespoons bacon drippings
Minced onion, celery and green pepper
Salt, if needed
(3 drops hot pepper sauce, a few grains of red pepper, or 1 tablespoon prepared mustard)

Place the beans in a greased shallow ovenproof dish. Cover the top with:

Bacon or skinned sliced frankfurters

Bake covered about 30 minutes. Uncover and bake 30 minutes more.

LENTIL OR LIMA BEAN SAUSAGE CASSEROLE

4 Servings

This dish, puréed, makes a fine stuffing for peppers or onions.

Preheat oven to 375°.

To:

1 cup cooked or canned lima beans or lentils

add:

6 sliced frankfurters or cooked sausages
1 chopped green pepper, seeds and membrane removed
2 chopped tomatoes

You may wish to purée the beans or lentils. Place these ingredients in a baking dish and cover with:

Au Gratin II, 553

Bake about 15 minutes.

PIGS IN POTATOES

3 Servings

➤ Please read about Deep-Fat Frying, 147.

Combine and beat well:

1 teaspoon minced onion
1 teaspoon minced parsley
2 cups Mashed Potatoes, 318
1 egg yolk

Sauté:

6 small Vienna sausages

or use:

Precooked pork sausages

Coat them with the potato mixture. Roll in:

Finely crushed bread crumbs

then in:

1 egg diluted with 1 tablespoon water or milk

then again in the crumbs. Fry the piggies in deep fat heated to 375° until they are a golden brown.

CREAMED CHIPPED BEEF

4 Large Servings

➤ Do not salt this dish.

Pull apart:

8 oz. chipped beef

Melt:

3 tablespoons butter

Sauté until the onions are golden:

3 tablespoons minced onion
3 tablespoons minced green pepper

Sprinkle with:

3 tablespoons flour

Add slowly, stirring constantly:

2 cups milk

Add the beef. Simmer these ingredients until they thicken. Remove from the heat and season with:

1 tablespoon chopped parsley or chives
¼ teaspoon paprika
2 tablespoons dry sherry
(2 tablespoons capers or chopped pickles)

Serve the beef on:

Hot buttered toast

CHIPPED BEEF IN CREOLE SAUCE

3 Servings

➤ Do not salt this dish.

Prepare and keep hot:

Quick Creole Sauce, 352

Melt:

1 tablespoon butter

Sauté 1 minute:

4 oz. shredded chipped beef

Add the sauce. Serve on:

Buttered toast

CHIPPED BEEF IN CHEESE SAUCE

2 Servings

➤ Do not salt this dish.

Prepare:

1 cup Cheese Sauce, 342

Add to it:

4 oz. or more shredded chipped beef

Heat it. Serve over:

Hot corn bread squares or pancakes

CHIPPED BEEF AND SWEET POTATO CASSEROLE

5 Servings

Preheat oven to 375°.

➤ Do not salt this dish.

Cut into cubes:

5 cooked or canned sweet potatoes

Shred:

4 oz. dried beef

Prepare:

¼ cup grated onion
1½ cups White Sauce I, 341, or a canned cream soup

Place these ingredients in layers in a greased casserole. Cover the top with:

Crushed cornflakes

Dot with:

Butter or cheese

Bake about 20 minutes.

CHIPPED BEEF OR CORNED BEEF IN CANNED SOUP

4 to 5 Servings

➤ Do not salt this dish.

Combine and heat:

1 cup cream soup—mushroom, celery or asparagus
6 tablespoons milk or stock
⅛ teaspoon freshly ground nutmeg
A grating of black pepper

Add:

8 oz. shredded chipped beef or 1 cup diced canned corned beef
(1 cup leftover vegetables: onions, artichoke hearts or asparagus)

Heat these ingredients. Serve on:

Toast or hot biscuits

sprinkled with:

Chopped parsley, chives or grated cheese

CORNED BEEF HASH AND POTATOES

6 Servings

Grind, using coarse blade, or dice:

1½ lb. cooked or canned corned beef: about 3 cups

Dice:

2 cups boiled potatoes

Melt in a large saucepan:

2 tablespoons butter

Stir in and simmer until tender:

½ cup chopped onion
1 diced green pepper, seeds and membrane removed
2 ribs celery, chopped
(1 clove garlic)
(1 cup mushrooms)

Add the beef and potatoes and:

1 teaspoon Worcestershire sauce
2 tablespoons minced parsley or chives

Stir lightly over medium heat while adding gradually:

⅓ to ⅔ cup White Sauce III, 341
Season to taste

Stir and cook till well blended and thoroughly heated. Place on a hot platter and serve topped with:

6 Poached Eggs, 221

CANNED CORNED BEEF HASH PATTIES

4 Servings

Sauté:

3 tablespoons chopped onion

in:

2 tablespoons butter

Add:

2 tablespoons horseradish
½ teaspoon thyme
2 cups canned corned beef hash

Form patties of this mixture. Sauté them on both sides in:

Hot butter or drippings

Sauté in the same pan:

(Sliced firm tomatoes)

Season with:

Brown sugar
Salt and pepper

Arrange the tomatoes and patties on a platter, garnished with:

Parsley

Or, if you omit the tomatoes, serve the patties with:

1½ cups White Sauce I, 341

to which you may add:

(2 chopped hard-cooked eggs)
(2 tablespoons chopped pickles)

ABOUT HASH

The Irish cook, praised for her hash, declared: "Beef ain't nothing. Onions ain't nothing. Seasoning's nothing. But when I throw myself into my hash, that's hash!" The usual way to make hash is to cut the meat from a chicken or turkey carcass or from a beef roast, combine it with leftover gravy, reheat it briefly and season it acceptably. ➤ Never allow it to boil or overcook once the meat is added. There should be about half as much gravy as other ingredients. Have sauce or gravy at the boiling point. Put in the solids, then ➤ reduce the heat at once and let them warm through thoroughly. If heating hash in the oven, be sure to use a topping to prevent the drying out of the top layer of meat or vegetables. Covering with a lid may develop steam, which will thin the gravy. See Au Gratins, 552.

You may add to the meat cooked mushrooms, celery or potatoes, chopped olives, green peppers, parsley or some other herb. The proportions may be varied; this is a matter of taste and expediency. In the absence of gravy, sweet or sour cream or a sauce—white, tomato or creole—may be substituted. Or you may add a sauce or cream to the gravy to obtain the desired amount. When using cream, reheat the hash in a double boiler, because boiling thins it. Sherry or Madeira may be added, or, for each 2 cups of gravy, a tablespoon each of vinegar and sugar to give a sweet-sour effect. Serve hash in a pastry shell or a rice or noodle ring or in individual bread cases, 250.

BEEF HASH WITH POTATOES AND MUSHROOMS

Cut into cubes equal parts of:

Cooked roast beef
(Diced cooked ham)
Pared raw potatoes

Reserve the beef. Place in a saucepan the potatoes, plus the ham if used. Cover with:

Brown Sauce, 346

Cover the pan and simmer 15 minutes. Add:

½ lb. or more sliced mushrooms

Simmer covered 15 minutes longer. Add the beef. Reheat the hash, but do not let it boil. Season with:

A pinch of basil, thyme or savory
Dry sherry
Salt or garlic salt

Serve the hash on:

Hot toast

garnished with:

Chopped parsley

SAUTÉED OR BROWNED HASH

4 Servings

Combine and grind:

1½ cups cooked meat
½ cup cubed raw potatoes with or without skins
1 medium-sized onion

Season with:

Salt, pepper, celery seed

Turn these ingredients into a skillet in which you have melted:

2 tablespoons butter
1 tablespoon vegetable oil

Cook the hash over medium heat until a crust forms on the bottom; turn it and brown the other side. Stir from time to time to let the hash brown throughout. Shortly before it is done, pat it down firmly to form an unbroken cake. This mixture requires about ½ hour's cooking in all. Serve the hash with:

Catsup or a tomato sauce

QUICK HASH

4 Servings

Heat and stir over very low heat:

1 cup cream of mushroom soup
¼ cup milk

Add:

1 cup cubed cooked meat: ham, frankfurters, hamburgers, etc.
2 sliced hard-cooked eggs

Season the hash with:

A pinch dried basil or thyme
Salt and pepper
(Chopped parsley)

Serve it over:

Hot corn bread or toast

HASH WITH VEGETABLES

6 Servings

This is an excellent combination.
Preheat oven to 350°.
Combine:

½ cup diced cooked potatoes
⅓ cup diced cooked onions
⅓ cup parboiled sliced green peppers
⅓ cup parboiled chopped celery
3 tablespoons diced pimiento
2 cups cold cooked meat, cut into ⅓-inch cubes

Combine and heat just to the boiling point:

1 cup leftover gravy or canned cream soup
⅓ cup tomato puree
1 tablespoon butter
1 teaspoon Worcestershire sauce

Add the meat and vegetables.

Season to taste

Pour the hash into 1 large baking dish or into 6 individual baking dishes. Sprinkle the top with:

Au Gratin III, 553

Brown in the oven.

HASH IN CREAMED CABBAGE

Preheat oven to 400°.
Prepare:

Creamed Cabbage II, 293

Place half the cabbage in a greased ovenproof dish. Place on top of it a layer of:

Hash moistened lightly with gravy or cream

Cover with the remaining cabbage. Sprinkle the top with:

Au Gratin II or III, 553

Bake the cabbage until the topping is light brown.

SHEPHERD'S PIE

Preheat oven to 400°.
Prepare:

Hash

Spread it in one large baking dish or in smaller individual ones. Cover with fresh hot:

Mashed Potatoes, 318

Coat with:

Melted butter

Bake until the potatoes are browned.

BREAD DRESSING IN A RING FILLED WITH HASH

Preheat oven to 400°.
Grease a ring mold. Fill it with:

Bread Dressing, 370, or Apple and Onion Dressing, 372

Bake until brown. Invert it onto a hot plate. Fill the center with:

Hash or stewed creamed fresh or leftover vegetables

Serve with:

Leftover gravy or some other sauce

ROAST BEEF IN SAUCE

I. **4 Servings**

Cut into ½-inch cubes:

2 cups cooked roast beef

Prepare:

Hot Cumberland Sauce, 356

Add the beef and heat in the sauce, but do not boil. Serve at once on:

Hot toast

II. Prepare:

Quick Creole Sauce, 352, or Curry Sauce, 345

Arrange very thin slices of:

Cooked roast beef

on a hot platter. Pour the hot sauce over them. Sprinkle the top with:

Chopped parsley or chopped chives

BOEUF MIROTON

Melt:

2 tablespoons butter

Sauté in it until golden:

1 coarsely sliced onion

Sprinkle over all and mix rapidly with a wooden spoon:

1 tablespoon flour

Add and stir until boiling:

1 cup bouillon
Season to taste

Reduce the heat and add:

1 to 2 teaspoons vinegar

Simmer about 15 minutes. Arrange on a hot platter:

Thin slices of boiled or roasted beef

Cover the slices with the above hot sauce and serve.

CHICKEN OR TURKEY HASH

4 Servings

➤ Please read About Hash, 261.

Combine and heat:

1½ cups diced cooked chicken or turkey
½ cup drained cooked celery or boiled potato cubes
1 cup leftover chicken or turkey gravy or other sauce
1 tablespoon chopped parsley or chives
Season to taste

CREAMED CHICKEN OR VEAL

4 Servings

Prepare:

1 cup White Sauce I, 341

using cream and chicken stock or vegetable water for the liquid, or use part gravy and part milk. Add:

2 tablespoons chopped parsley
2 cups minced cooked chicken or veal
(½ cup Sautéed Mushrooms, 308, or cooked peas)

Season these ingredients with:

1 teaspoon lemon juice or ½ teaspoon Worcestershire sauce or 2 teaspoons dry sherry
(3 tablespoons chopped pickle or olives)
¼ teaspoon celery salt or salt and pepper as needed

Grease a baking dish and put the creamed mixture in it. Sprinkle the top with:

Au Gratin II or III, 553
(½ cup shredded blanched almonds)

Place the dish under the broiler until the crumbs are brown. Or serve the creamed ingredients unbreaded on:

Hot Waffles or in a Noodle or Rice Ring, 214 or 207

CHICKEN À LA KING

4 Servings

Dice:

1 cup cooked chicken
½ cup Sautéed Mushrooms, 308
¼ cup chopped pimiento

Melt:

3 tablespoons chicken fat or butter

Stir in and blend:

3 tablespoons flour

Add slowly:

1½ cups Chicken Stock, 523, or cream

When the sauce is smooth and boiling, add the chicken, mushrooms and pimiento. Reduce the heat. Pour some sauce over:

1 beaten egg yolk

and return mixture to pan. Stir until it thickens slightly. Add:

Seasoning, if required
(¼ cup blanched slivered almonds)
(1 tablespoon dry sherry)

Fill:

Patty Shells, 645

with the chicken and serve at once.

TURKEY OR CHICKEN CASSEROLE WITH VEGETABLES

4 Servings

Prepare by cutting into cubes:

2 cups cooked turkey or chicken

Melt:

3 tablespoons butter

Stir in and sauté gently until onions are golden:

½ cup diced celery
⅓ cup thinly sliced onions
⅓ cup thinly sliced green pepper, seeds and membrane removed

Sprinkle over the top, stir in and cook slowly 5 minutes:

3 tablespoons flour

Stir in gradually:

1½ cups turkey or chicken stock

Remove the pan from the heat. Stir in:

2 lightly beaten egg yolks

and the turkey meat. Stir over low heat just long enough to let the sauce thicken slightly. You may add:

(3 tablespoons dry white wine)
Season to taste

Place the mixture in one large or in individual casseroles. Sprinkle the top with:

Minced chives, parsley, or nutmeats

Serve at once. Good with rice or spoon bread or on toast.

QUICK CHICKEN CREOLE

8 Servings

Melt:

3 tablespoons chicken fat

Sauté in it:

2 tablespoons chopped onion
(1 minced clove garlic)

Stir in:

3 tablespoons flour
¼ teaspoon salt
¼ teaspoon paprika

Add:

½ cup tomato purée or strained tomatoes
1 cup chicken broth

Stir and cook these ingredients until they boil. Add:

1 teaspoon lemon juice
½ teaspoon horseradish
2 cups diced cooked chicken meat
½ cup sliced Sautéed Mushrooms, 308
½ cup chopped pimiento
Season to taste

Serve the chicken in a:

Rice Ring, 207, or Noodle Ring, 214

COOKED TURKEY, CHICKEN OR VEAL LOAF

4 to 6 Servings

Preheat oven to 350°.
Cook and stir 1 minute:

1½ tablespoons grated onion

in:

1 tablespoon butter

Add it to:

2 cups diced cooked turkey, chicken or veal
½ teaspoon salt
1 cup cracker crumbs
¾ cup gravy or thickened Chicken Stock, 523
¾ cup milk
2 beaten eggs
(½ cup finely chopped celery)
(¾ teaspoon chili powder)

Place these ingredients in a well-greased loaf pan set in a pan of hot water. Bake about 40 minutes. Serve with:

Leftover gravy with chopped olives,
Quick Mushroom Sauce, 348, or
White Sauce IV, 341, with lots of chopped parsley or chives

CHICKEN OR TURKEY DIVAN

4 Servings

Preheat oven to 400°.
Butter a 9 x 12-inch shallow heatproof dish. Place on the dish:

(4 slices hot buttered toast)

Next place a layer of:

Sliced cooked chicken or turkey

The white meat is best. Allow 2 or 3 slices per serving. Cook until almost done and lay on top the contents of:

1 package frozen broccoli or asparagus spears, well drained

Or use leftover cooked broccoli or asparagus. Cover the whole with:

2 cups Mornay Sauce, 342

Sprinkle with:

Grated Parmesan cheese

and heat in the oven until the sauce is browned and bubbling. Serve at once.

HOT CHICKEN SALAD

4 Servings

This recipe enlarges well for quantity service.
Preheat oven to 350°.
Combine:

2 cups cubed cooked chicken
1 cup finely diced celery
½ teaspoon salt
¼ teaspoon tarragon
½ cup toasted almonds
1 tablespoon chopped chives
2 tablespoons lemon juice
½ cup mayonnaise
½ cup White Sauce I, 341

Bake in very shallow individual baking dishes 10 to 15 minutes or until heated through. Garnish with:

Parsley or small sprigs of lemon thyme

QUANTITY CHICKEN LOAF

16 to 24 Servings

This is a wonderfully stretchable recipe to serve at group meetings. It is rather firm, slices well and is attractive covered with a sauce.
Preheat oven to 350°.
Remove meat carefully from:

A 4- to 5-lb. stewed chicken

Dice it. Combine lightly with a fork:

2 to 4 cups dry bread crumbs
1 to 3 cups cooked rice
1½ to 2 cups chicken broth, depending on how much rice and crumbs are added
3 to 4 lightly beaten eggs
Season to taste
(½ cup chopped ripe olives)
(½ cup slivered pistachio nuts)

Bake ➤ uncovered in a 9 x 13-inch ovenproof pan 25 to 30 minutes. Serve with:

Chicken pan gravy, 341, seasoned with a little lemon rind, parsley and
1/16 teaspoon saffron

or with:

Quick à la King Sauce, 348, or
Quick Mushroom Sauce, 348, or
Poulette Sauce, 345

SEAFOOD À LA KING

4 Servings

Combine:

1 cup canned lobster, crab meat or tuna
3 diced hard-cooked eggs
1 chopped pimiento

Sauté and add:

½ cup chopped mushrooms, 306

Cook in boiling water until tender; drain and add:

¼ cup chopped sweet red peppers, seeds and membrane removed

Prepare:

White Sauce I, 341

When the sauce is smooth and boiling, add the above ingredients.

Season to taste

and add:

1 teaspoon Worcestershire sauce,
1 tablespoon lemon juice or 2 tablespoons dry white wine

Serve the seafood over:

French Toast, 636, or rusks, or in patty shells, or au gratin in ramekins

Or garnish with toast triangles spread with:

Mashed avocado and lemon juice

CREAMED SEAFOOD

4 Servings

Prepare:

1½ cups White Sauce I, 341, or
Poulette Sauce, 345

Add:
1 cup canned tuna, shrimp or clams
Just before serving, heat the seafood through and add:
½ to 1 cup coarsely chopped watercress
1 diced avocado
Serve over:
Toast or rusks

CREAMED SEAFOOD AU GRATIN

6 Servings

Preheat oven to 350°.
Combine 3 or 4 kinds of raw fish or shellfish, for example:
½ lb. chopped lobster meat
1 cup drained oysters
1 cup minced fillet of haddock
Prepare:
1½ cups Sautéed Mushrooms, 308
4 cups White Sauce I, 341
using cream as the liquid. When the sauce is smooth and hot, fold in the fish. Add the mushrooms.
Season to taste
Fill ramekins or shells with the mixture. Cover the tops with:
Au Gratin II, 553
Bake the fish about 25 minutes.

CREAMED SEAFOOD WITH VEGETABLES

4 Servings

Preheat broiler.
Cook one or more of the following:
1 cup chopped celery, eggplant or cucumber
Drain well. Prepare:
¾ cup White Sauce I, 341
When the sauce is boiling, add the vegetable and:
¾ lb. cooked shrimp, crab meat or tuna
Season with:
Salt, if needed
⅛ teaspoon paprika
(½ teaspoon Worcestershire sauce)
Place these ingredients in greased ramekins. Cover with:
Au Gratin I, 552, or unsweetened grated coconut
Heat under the broiler until golden.

KEDGEREE OF LOBSTER OR OTHER FISH

6 Servings

Combine:
2 cups cooked rice
1 lb. cooked flaked lobster, cod fillets or skate
4 minced hard-cooked eggs
¼ cup butter
¼ cup cream
2 tablespoons minced parsley
Salt and cayenne
Heat these ingredients in a double boiler.

SEAFOOD CASSEROLE IN CREOLE SAUCE

4 Servings

Prepare:
¾ lb. cooked shrimp or other seafood
Melt in a skillet:
2 tablespoons butter
Toss the seafood in the hot butter about 2 minutes. Add:
2 cups Creole Sauce, 348
¼ cup dry white wine
Simmer the shrimp covered about 5 minutes. You may add:
(Salt and pepper)
(A few grains cayenne)
(3 diced hard-cooked eggs)
Serve the shrimp with:
Boiled Rice, 206

WEST AFRICAN TUNA CASSEROLE

6 Servings

Have ready:
2 cups cooked dried black-eyed peas, 286
Preheat oven to 350°.
Place peas in an ovenproof baking dish. Sauté:
½ cup finely chopped onions
in:
3 tablespoons vegetable oil
Add to the peas with:
1 large chopped tomato
2 teaspoons crushed hot red peppers
Bake covered 15 minutes. Add:
2 cans flaked tuna: 7 oz. each
2 tablespoons tomato paste
½ teaspoon salt
Cover dish, return to oven and bake 10 minutes without stirring. Remove cover, stir, sprinkle with:
Au Gratin II, 553
and bake 5 minutes longer uncovered. Serve with:
Baked Bananas, 132
omitting the sugar.

QUICK SEAFOOD DIVAN

4 Servings

Preheat oven to 325°.
Prepare and heat:
1½ cups White Sauce I, 341, or Quick Canned Soup Sauce II or III, 348, or Quick Creole Sauce, 352
Have ready:
1 cup cooked shrimp, crab meat or tuna
Season to taste
Put into a hot baking dish:
2 cups cooked asparagus, broccoli or cauliflower
½ cup Sautéed Mushrooms, 308
2 teaspoons diced pimientos
Cover the vegetables with the seafood. Pour the hot sauce over the seafood. Garnish with:
Grated cheese
Bake about 25 minutes.

QUICK CRAB MEAT OR LOBSTER MONGOLE

4 Servings

For a perfect luncheon or supper, serve with rice and a salad.

Combine and heat in a double boiler ➤ over—not in—boiling water:

¾ cup canned tomato soup
¾ cup canned pea soup
¾ cup cream
1 cup canned crab or lobster meat

When hot, serve as a thick soup over:

Croutons

or pour the Mongole over:

Boiled Rice, 206

Garnish with:

Parsley

CRAB MEAT CUSTARD

8 Servings

Preheat oven to 325°.

In the bottom of a large buttered casserole place:

4 slices crustless bread

Place on top of the bread:

2 cups canned flaked crab meat
½ cup shredded cheddar cheese
Season to taste

Beat together:

4 eggs
3 cups milk
½ teaspoon salt
Dash of cayenne

Pour this mixture over the fish and top with:

½ cup shredded cheddar cheese

Bake as for a Custard, 734, until done. Serve with:

A mixed green salad

DEVILED CRAB

4 Servings

Flake and pick over:

1½ cups canned or cooked crab meat

Sauté:

¼ cup finely chopped onions
¼ cup finely chopped green peppers, seeds and membrane removed
¼ cup finely chopped celery

until onions are golden in:

2 tablespoons butter

Add:

¼ cup cracker crumbs
¾ cup milk, cream or clam broth

Cook these ingredients until thick. Remove from the heat. Beat and add:

2 eggs
¼ teaspoon salt
1½ teaspoons prepared mustard
A few grains cayenne or ⅛ teaspoon hot pepper sauce

Add the crab meat. Pack these ingredients into crab shells or ramekins. Brush the tops with:

Melted butter

Brown in a 400° oven or under a broiler.

INDIVIDUAL FISH PIES

6 Servings

Bake 6 individual Pie Shells, 640. Combine and heat:

1 cup flaked cooked tuna or salmon
1 or 1½ cups thick White Sauce II, 341, or canned cream soup slightly diluted with milk

Season with:

2 tablespoons fresh chopped parsley or chervil
¼ teaspoon curry powder
½ teaspoon Worcestershire sauce

Just before serving, place the hot mixture in the hot pie shells. Serve garnished with:

Chopped chives

QUICK FISH LOAF

4 Servings

Preheat oven to 400°.

Drain, then flake:

1 lb. cooked or canned fish: 2 cups

Combine and beat:

1 egg
¼ cup undiluted evaporated milk or whipping cream
¾ cup soft bread crumbs
½ teaspoon salt
¼ teaspoon paprika
2 teaspoons lemon juice or 1 teaspoon Worcestershire sauce
1 tablespoon melted butter
3 tablespoons minced parsley
2 tablespoons chopped celery, onion, green pepper or olives

Add the fish. Place these ingredients in a greased baking dish. Bake about 30 minutes. This loaf may be served hot with:

Quick Tomato Sauce, 352, Cheese Sauce, 342, or Caper Sauce, 345

or cold with:

Mayonnaise

EMERGENCY FISH CAKES

Excellent cakes may be made quickly by combining cooked seafood with canned cream soup. Keep your mixture rather stiff. Treat it as you would any other fish ball or cake. See recipes below.

FISH BALLS OR CAKES

About 4 Servings

Also use as a hot hors d'oeuvre.

Combine and mix well:

1 cup grated or flaked canned tuna or salmon
1 cup mashed potatoes
6 chopped olives
8 capers
½ minced clove garlic or 1 teaspoon grated onion
1 tablespoon minced parsley
Salt and paprika
1 teaspoon brandy or dry sherry

(1 teaspoon dried or 1 tablespoon freshly chopped basil)

Shape the mixture into 1-inch balls or into flat cakes. Sauté them 2 or 3 minutes in:

1/2 cup hot olive oil or butter

Drain, then roll in:

3/4 cup ground nutmeats

SEAFOOD POTATO CAKES

6 Servings

Prepare:

Leftover Potato Cakes, 324

Use the egg and 2 cups mashed potatoes.
Add in small flakes:

1 cup or more canned salmon or tuna

Season with:

Chopped parsley, onion juice or celery seed

Shape the mixture into cakes. Roll in:

Crushed cornflakes or bread crumbs

Sauté them slowly in:

Butter or vegetable oil

CRAB, CLAM OR OYSTER CAKES

Six 3-Inch Cakes

Melt:

2 tablespoons butter

Add, stir and simmer 3 minutes:

2 tablespoons minced onion

Combine and add:

2 beaten eggs
1/2 cup cream
1/2 cup soft bread crumbs
2 cups minced oysters, canned clams or flaked crab meat—separately or combined
1/2 cup finely minced celery
1/2 teaspoon dry mustard or 1 tablespoon lemon juice
2 tablespoons chopped parsley
1/2 teaspoon salt
1/2 teaspoon paprika

Chill this mixture 2 hours. Shape into cakes. Lightly dust with:

Flour or bread crumbs

Melt in a skillet:

1 tablespoon butter

Quickly brown the cakes on both sides. ➤ Lower the heat and cook the cakes slowly about 6 minutes longer. Or you may deep-fat-fry the cakes, first coating with:

Bound Breading à l'Anglaise, 552

Let dry, then fry until golden in fat heated to 375°, about 15 minutes.

SALMON CAKES

6 Servings

Drain and flake:

2 cups canned salmon

Stir in:

1/2 cup cracker crumbs
2 beaten eggs
1/2 teaspoon salt
1/8 teaspoon paprika

Form these ingredients into cakes. Sauté until brown in:

Butter

Serve the cakes with:

Quick Mushroom Sauce, 348, or Celery Soup Sauce, 348

to which you have added:

Chopped fresh fennel

SALMON PUFFS

6 Servings

Preheat oven to 350°.
Remove skin and bones, drain, then flake:

2 cups canned salmon

Add and stir lightly to blend:

1/2 cup fresh bread crumbs
2 tablespoons grated onion
1 tablespoon lemon juice
1 tablespoon melted butter
Season to taste

Beat together:

1 egg
1/2 cup milk

Combine with the salmon mixture. Place in 6 well-greased baking cups set in hot water. Bake about 45 minutes. Unmold onto a hot platter. Serve with:

Velouté Sauce, 345, or Quick Tomato Sauce, 352

SEAFOOD AND CHEESE LOAF

6 Servings

Preheat oven to 350°.
Prepare:

1 cup Cheese Sauce, 342

Grease a baking dish and spread in it:

1 1/2 cups Mashed Potatoes, 318

Cover them with half the sauce. Drain, skin, then flake:

2 cups canned salmon or tuna

Place it over the sauce. Cover with the remaining sauce. Bake about 30 minutes. Serve with:

Quick Tomato Sauce, 352

SEAFOOD POT PIE

8 Servings

Prepare:

Biscuit Dough, 632

Prepare:

1 cup chopped cooked celery
1 cup cooked peas

Drain the vegetables, reserving the liquid.
Preheat oven to 425°.
Drain and flake if necessary:

2 cups canned salmon, shrimp or tuna

Melt:

1/4 cup butter

Sauté in it about 2 minutes:

1 1/2 tablespoons minced onion

Stir in until smooth:

6 tablespoons flour

Stir in until boiling:

¾ cup vegetable water
1½ cups milk

Add:

1 teaspoon salt
⅛ teaspoon paprika
1 tablespoon lemon juice or 1 teaspoon Worcestershire sauce
1 teaspoon or more chopped parsley or chives

Fold the vegetables and the seafood into the cream sauce.

Season to taste

Place the mixture in a large casserole. Roll the biscuit dough ¼ inch thick. Cut it into rounds. Top the salmon mixture with biscuits. Bake until done, about 12 minutes.

SEAFOOD AND TOMATO SCALLOP

4 Large Servings

Preheat oven to 375°.
Drain:

2 cups canned salmon, tuna or shrimp

Combine them with:

3 cups soft bread crumbs
2 tablespoons butter
¼ cup chopped onion
½ teaspoon salt
1 teaspoon sugar
¼ teaspoon paprika or pepper
2½ cups chopped, drained tomatoes
(1 chopped seeded green pepper, membrane removed)
(1 beaten egg)
(1 teaspoon Worcestershire sauce or lemon juice)
(¼ cup white wine)

Place these ingredients in a greased baking dish. The top may be sprinkled with:

Grated cheese

Bake until the top is golden and the interior heated.

SEAFOOD IN PARSLEY SAUCE WITH RICE OR NOODLE RING

6 Servings

Drain:

2 cups canned salmon, tuna or other seafood

Remove skin and bones. Break into large flakes. Combine:

1½ teaspoons dry mustard
½ teaspoon salt
⅛ teaspoon pepper
½ teaspoon paprika
3 tablespoons flour

Combine and beat into the dry ingredients:

1 cup milk
¾ cup light stock

Place in double boiler ➤ over—not in—boiling water and beat with a wire whisk:

1 egg
2 tablespoons lemon juice

Add the milk mixture and stir and cook until the sauce has thickened. Add the salmon and:

2 tablespoons butter
½ cup finely minced parsley
1 teaspoon Worcestershire sauce

Heat well and serve in:

Rice Ring, 207, or Noodle Ring, 214

PROSCIUTTO STUFFED WITH LOBSTER OR CRAB MEAT

6 Servings

Have ready:

6 large thin slices prosciutto

Melt in a skillet to the point of fragrance:

¼ cup butter

Add and cook 2 minutes:

2 tablespoons finely chopped shallots
2 tablespoons finely chopped celery

Add:

2 cups canned crab meat or lobster in small chunks

Heat the mixture until blended. Remove skillet from heat and add:

2 teaspoons finely chopped tarragon
3 tablespoons chopped parsley
Salt and pepper to taste

Spoon the mixture on half of each ham slice and fold the other half over it. Garnish the tops with:

A sprig or two of watercress

Serve with:

Crisp hot Rye Rolls, 614

CREAMED SHAD ROE

2 Servings

Sauté:

1 cup canned shad roe

in:

Butter

with:

½ teaspoon curry powder

Add:

Salt and paprika
¾ cup cream

Reheat but do not boil the roe. Serve on:

Toast

See other roe recipes on 411.

BROILED SHAD ROE

2 Servings

Preheat broiler.
Separate into pieces:

1 cup canned shad roe or other canned fish roe

Dry with paper toweling. Brush with:

Melted butter

Sprinkle with:

Lemon juice
Paprika

Place roe in a shallow greased pan or on a greased broiler. Broil gently about 10 minutes, turning once. Baste frequently with:

Melted butter

Serve on toast, garnished with:

Slices of lemon
Chopped parsley

FISH ROE IN RAMEKINS

3 Servings

Preheat oven to 325°.
Combine:

1 cup drained canned fish roe
1½ teaspoons bread crumbs
1½ teaspoons butter
1 beaten egg
Salt, if needed
¼ teaspoon paprika
2 teaspoons chopped parsley
½ cup milk

Fill three greased ramekins. Bake them in a pan of hot water until firm—about 20 minutes. Serve the roe with:

Slices of lemon

ABOUT SANDWICHES

Innumerable hostesses—not to mention quick-lunch stands—keep green the memory of Lord Sandwich, whose mania for gambling, from which he didn't want to be disturbed long enough to eat, gave the world the convenient concoction that bears his name.

Sandwiches range widely in size and complexity. ➤ Don't neglect the Canapé chapter, where many delectable smaller versions are found. To keep sandwiches fresh, wrap in wax paper, foil or a well-wrung-out dampened cloth.

GRILLED OR SAUTÉED SANDWICHES

Especially good when a thin slice of cheese spread with mustard, salt and paprika is put between the bread slices; or use deviled ham, meat mixtures, jam or jelly.
Melt in a small skillet large enough to accommodate one sandwich:

1½ teaspoons butter

Sauté a sandwich ➤ slowly on one side until browned. Add to the skillet:

1½ teaspoons butter

Brown the second side slowly and serve at once.

TOASTED OR WAFFLE SANDWICHES

Cut into thin slices:

White or dark bread

Spread it lightly with:

Soft butter

Cut off the crusts and spread between the slices:

Cheese Spread or other sandwich fillings, 72 and 73

Cut the sandwiches to fit the sections of a waffle iron. Wrap them in a moist cloth until ready to toast. Heat a waffle iron, arrange the sandwiches upon the iron, lower the top and bake until crisp.

TOASTED SANDWICHES

These are offered as luncheon suggestions. Many of the sandwich fillings given in the chapter on Canapés may be spread between slices of toast. The sandwiches may be served with a hot sauce or a cold dressing.
Put between:

2 slices of toast

any of the following combinations:

Sliced chicken
Sautéed bacon
Shredded cheese
Quick Mushroom Sauce, 348

Creamed chicken
Parmesan cheese
Grilled tomatoes and bacon

Sliced baked ham
Creamed chicken and mushrooms

Sliced ham
Sliced chicken
Mayonnaise
Lettuce

Braunschweiger
Sliced tomatoes
Lettuce
Tart mayonnaise

Sliced tongue
Sliced tomatoes or cucumbers
Sautéed bacon
Mayonnaise

Lettuce, French dressing
Sliced tomato and avocado
Crisp sautéed bacon

Asparagus tips
Crisp bacon
Welsh Rarebit, 252

Sliced chicken
Lettuce, sliced tomato
Crumbled Roquefort cheese
Crisp bacon

OPEN-FACED SANDWICHES

These have great appeal, especially when glazed, 70, and attractively garnished like those shown below. Vary the bread shapes as well as the bread varieties. For other toppings see Canapés, 66. Reading from left to right in the drawing are:
1. Scallions or tiny hearts of celery or Florence fennel stalks with slices of caviar-covered hard-cooked egg
2. Halves of radish or cucumber slices unpeeled or partially peeled as shown, with slices of stuffed olives in the center
3. Asparagus tips mounted by cooked shrimp

4. A thick slice of tomato topped with seafood salad on lettuce leaves taken from the heart of the head
5. Bamboo shoots with grapefruit sections and sliced pimiento
6. A parsley fringe surrounding a tomato slice, topped by a cucumber slice, topped by a dab of Andalouse Sauce, 364
7. Belgian endive hearts spread generously with Guacamole, 83
8. Small caviar-filled beets, 83, accented with watercress
9. Artichoke heart garnished with parsley or lemon and filled with Tartare Sauce, 364, or with Crab Salad, 106

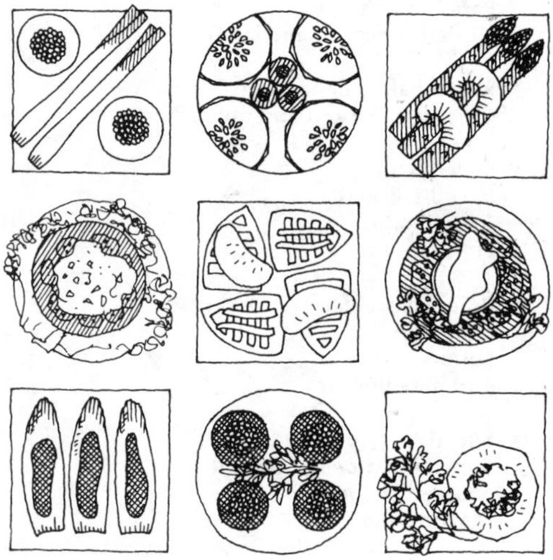

BREAD ROLL FILLINGS

Recommended for picnic sandwiches, as they are easy to handle.
Cut into lengthwise halves:
Soft rolls
Hollow them slightly. Fill the hollows with any palatable sandwich spread, such as:
Chicken Salad, 108
Tuna Fish Salad, 108
Braunschweiger sausage
Canapé Fillings, 70 to 75
Chopped celery, nuts and mayonnaise
Chopped olives and cream cheese

HOT BISCUITS BAKED WITH FILLINGS

About Eighteen 2½-Inch Biscuits

Combine:
1 cup shredded cooked meat: chicken, fish, ham, veal, or beef
½ cup thick gravy, White Sauce I, 341, or condensed cream soup
1 tablespoon grated onion
1 chopped hard-cooked egg
2 tablespoons chopped pickles or olives
Season to taste
Preheat oven to 450°.
Prepare:
Rolled Biscuit Dough, 632
Roll it to the thickness of ¼ inch. Cut it into rounds. Place on one round 1 tablespoon of the meat mixture. Moisten the edges and cover with another round. Seal the edges by pressing with a fork. Prick the tops. Place the biscuits on a baking sheet and bake until brown. You may serve these with:
(Quick Mushroom Sauce, 348)

MEAL-IN-ONE SANDWICH

4 Servings

On your toes when you make this. It's easy if you have all your ingredients ready before you poach the eggs.
Prepare:
4 large slices of toast
8 sautéed bacon slices
4 skinned and sliced large tomatoes
½ cup French Dressing, 360
1 cup White Sauce I, 341
1 cup shredded cheese
Place the toast on a baking sheet; cover it with the bacon, tomatoes and dressing. Poach:
4 eggs
Place an egg on each piece of garnished toast and cover with the white sauce and grated cheese. Place the toast under the broiler until the cheese melts and the sauce begins to color. Serve piping hot.

HOT ROAST BEEF SANDWICH

4 Servings

Slice:
Cold roast beef
Prepare:
1 cup Brown Sauce, 346
Add to it:
1 tablespoon finely minced sour pickle or ½ cup chopped olives
Cut:
6 thin slices of light or dark bread
Beat until soft:
2 tablespoons butter
¼ teaspoon prepared mustard or 1 teaspoon horseradish
Spread the bread with this mixture. Dip the beef slices in the hot sauce. Place them between the slices of bread. Serve on a hot platter and garnish with remaining sauce.

CORNED BEEF OR CHIPPED BEEF AND CHEESE SANDWICHES

6 Servings

Cream well together:
¼ cup shredded sharp cheddar cheese
2 tablespoons mayonnaise
Shred finely and add:
4 oz. canned corned beef or chipped beef

Add:

¼ cup finely chopped sweet-sour pickles
1 tablespoon grated onion
(2 tablespoons minced celery or parsley)

Season the spread, as needed, with:

Salt and pepper
Prepared mustard or Worcestershire sauce

Spread it between:

Slices of bread

The sandwiches may be toasted or served with sliced tomatoes and lettuce between the layers.

SAVOYARDE SANDWICH

1 Serving

Preheat boiler.

Place on a shallow baking dish or cookie sheet:

½ English muffin

topped with:

A large thin slice of ham

Make a:

French Omelet, 226, using 2 eggs

large enough to cover the ham. Do not fold the omelet, but slip it flat onto the ham. Sprinkle with:

Shredded Gruyère or Swiss cheese

Place under broiler until cheese melts. Serve at once.

WESTERN SANDWICH

1 Serving

For each sandwich, mix the following ingredients:

1 beaten egg
2 tablespoons milk
2 tablespoons chopped cooked ham
1 tablespoon finely minced onion
1 tablespoon finely chopped green pepper
Season to taste

In a 9-inch skillet melt:

2 teaspoons butter

Pour the egg mixture into the hot pan and cook until almost set, then turn and cook 1 minute longer. Serve on:

A large warm hard roll

CROQUE MONSIEUR SANDWICH

1 Serving

Make a sandwich of:

2 slices white bread

Place between them, trimmed to the same size as the bread:

A ⅛-inch slice Gruyère cheese
A ¼-inch slice baked ham

You may spread the ham lightly with:

(Dijon mustard)

Top with another:

Slice Gruyère cheese

Melt in a skillet just large enough to hold the sandwich:

2 tablespoons butter

Generously brush the upper side of the sandwich with melted butter; then place the sandwich with the unbuttered side in the skillet and brown it slowly. Turn and brown the other side. Place the skillet in a 350° oven and let the sandwich heat until the cheese is thoroughly melted. Serve at once.

To make a **Croque Madame Sandwich,** substitute thinly sliced chicken for the ham, and Emmenthaler for the Gruyère.

HAM OR TONGUE SALAD SANDWICHES

I. Combine:

Ground cooked ham or tongue
Chopped onion or chives
Chopped celery or bean sprouts

Moisten with:

Cream or salad dressing

If cream is used, season with:

Paprika and salt, if needed

Spread the filling between:

Thin slices of bread

II. Combine and mix:

2 tablespoons chopped onion
2 tablespoons catsup
2 tablespoons chopped green pepper
2 tablespoons chopped pickles
½ lb. chopped sharp cheese
3 oz. deviled ham or ½ cup finely cut cooked ham
¼ cup cream or a little melted butter

Serve in hollowed hard rolls.

HAWAIIAN TOAST WITH BACON SANDWICH

4 Servings

Cut:

4 to 6 slices dry bread, ½ inch thick

Beat until light:

2 eggs

Beat in:

1 cup pineapple juice
½ teaspoon salt

Dip the bread in the egg mixture. Soak it well. Sauté in a skillet:

8 slices bacon

Remove them to a hot platter. Keep them hot. Fry the bread in the bacon drippings, browning one side, then the other. Remove the bread to the hot platter. Sauté in the bacon drippings:

4 slices drained pineapple, cut into halves

Garnish the platter with the bacon and the pineapple. Serve toast at once.

HAM AND PINEAPPLE FRENCH TOAST SANDWICH

Combine equal parts:

Ground ham
Drained crushed pineapple

Season these ingredients with:

Dijon mustard

Spread this filling between slices of:

Buttered bread

Prepare an egg mixture as for French Toast, 636;

spread on the outside of the sandwiches and sauté as directed.

HAM, TOMATO AND EGG SANDWICH

Slice and butter:
Rye bread
Place on it:
Boiled ham slices
Lettuce leaves
Sliced tomatoes
Garnish the sandwiches with:
Hard-cooked egg slices
Parsley sprigs
Serve with:
Cream Horseradish Dressing, 357, or
Russian Dressing, 364

TOAST ROLLS WITH HAM AND ASPARAGUS

4 Servings

A fine luncheon or supper dish with a molded grapefruit salad and coffee.
Preheat oven to 400°.
Drain and reserve liquid:
12 to 16 asparagus tips
Remove the crusts from:
8 thin slices of bread
Brush lightly on both sides with:
Melted butter
Place on each piece of bread:
A slice of boiled ham
and three or four of the asparagus tips. Roll the bread around the tips or bring 2 corners together. Fasten the bread with wooden picks. Bake these rolls on a baking sheet until lightly browned. Use the asparagus liquor and cream to make:
White Sauce I, 341
Serve the rolls piping hot with the sauce.

TOASTED DEVILED HAM AND CHEESE SANDWICHES

Cover:
Thin slices of toast
with a paste made of:
Deviled ham
Dijon mustard or horseradish
Cover the ham with thin slices of·
Cheddar cheese
Dot with:
Capers
Press the sandwiches and sauté until heated through, in:
Butter
Serve hot.

POOR BOY OR SUBMARINE OR HERO SANDWICH

4 Servings

Native to New Orleans, where you can find in the filling fried oysters, chili sauce and chicken, as well as the ingredients below. Similar also is the Italian Hero Sandwich served with a tomato-meat sauce.
Cut in half lengthwise a long loaf of:
French Bread, 605
Spread both cuts with:
Butter
On the bottom half, arrange layers of:
Sliced salami sausage
Sliced sharp cheese
Thinly sliced boiled ham
(Thinly sliced tomato)
Put on the top half of the loaf to make a sandwich, and cut into 4 pieces. Mix together:
¼ cup dry mustard
1 tablespoon dry white wine
Serve this with the sandwich.

REUBEN SANDWICH

1 Serving

Preheat oven to 400°.
Lightly butter on one side only:
2 slices sour rye bread or a cut rye roll
Layer between the slices of bread or roll:
Thinly sliced corned beef
Sauerkraut
1 slice Swiss or Gruyère cheese
Spread generously with:
Russian Dressing, 364
Wrap in foil and heat in oven until cheese is melted and sandwich is heated through. You may also grill this sandwich under the broiler or brown in a skillet.

TOASTED BRAUNSCHWEIGER SANDWICH

Braunschweiger is a refined version of the rather heavy smoked liver sausage.
Combine and stir to a smooth paste:
Braunschweiger sausage
Canned cream of tomato soup or tomato paste
(A few drops of cream or Worcestershire sauce)
Cut the crusts from:
Thin slices of bread
Spread them with the sausage mixture. Roll the bread or make double-deck sandwiches. Toast and serve very hot.

BACON AND CHEESE SANDWICH

4 Servings

Preheat broiler.
Toast either on one or on both sides, or use untoasted:
4 slices of bread
Place on each slice:
(A thick slice tomato)
(Chopped onion and green peppers)
(Sliced olives or pickles)
A slice of cheddar cheese

Spread with:
Mustard or Chili Sauce, 847
Cover each sandwich with:
2 slices crisp broiled bacon

EGG AND CHEESE SANDWICH WITH TOMATO SAUCE

4 Servings

Rub:
4 slices French Bread, 605
with:
(Garlic)
Dip them quickly in:
Milk seasoned with a pinch of salt
Brown in a skillet in:
Olive oil
Place them on a hot ovenproof plate. Cover with:
4 chopped hard-cooked eggs
6 or more chopped olives
1 cup or more grated cheese
Place the open-faced slices under a broiler until the cheese is melted. Serve with:
Quick Tomato Sauce, 352

FRENCH TOAST AND CHEESE

4 Servings

Preheat oven to 350°.
Prepare, omitting the sugar:
French Toast, 636
Then toast the bread in the oven on a buttered ovenproof plate about 5 minutes. Stir over very low heat until smooth:
½ lb. shredded or minced cheese
½ teaspoon salt
A few grains cayenne
¼ cup milk
3 tablespoons butter
Spread the toast with the cheese mixture. Return it to the oven to brown lightly.

TOMATO FRENCH TOAST

6 Servings

Beat until light:
2 eggs
½ teaspoon salt
¼ teaspoon paprika
½ cup canned cream of tomato soup
Dip in this:
6 bread slices
Sauté the bread in hot:
Butter or drippings
When brown, serve with:
Cheese Sauce, 342
Minced parsley or chives

CHEESE SANDWICH WITH MUSHROOM SAUCE

Trim the crusts from:
Light or dark bread slices
Spread with:
Butter
Place on each piece:
Slices of cheese
Lettuce leaves
Tomato or cucumber slices
Hard-cooked egg slices
Olive or pickle slices
Serve the sandwiches open-faced with:
Quick Mushroom Sauce, 348

PUFFED CHEESE WITH MUSHROOMS ON TOAST

6 Servings

Preheat oven to 375°.
Melt in a saucepan:
1 tablespoon butter
Add and sauté until tender:
½ cup finely sliced mushrooms
1 teaspoon grated onion
Combine and heat:
2 egg yolks
½ lb. shredded Swiss or Gruyère cheese: 2 cups
¾ teaspoon salt
¼ teaspoon pepper
A few grains cayenne
Stir in the mushroom and onion mixture. Beat until stiff ➤ but not dry:
2 egg whites
Fold them into the mixture. Toast on one side:
6 slices bread
Place them untoasted side down on a cookie sheet. Spread the toasted sides lightly with:
(Butter)
Heap the cheese mixture on the bread. Bake the slices until firm to the touch and well puffed.

PEANUT BUTTER AND TOMATO SANDWICH

Preheat broiler.
Toast on one side:
A slice of bread
Spread the untoasted side with:
Peanut butter
mixed with:
Chopped cooked bacon
Bacon drippings
Top this with:
A thick slice of tomato
Season the tomato with:
¼ teaspoon brown sugar
Salt and paprika
Put the sandwich under a broiler for a minute or two.

PEANUT BUTTER AND BACON SANDWICH

4 Servings

Virtue, however admirable, is frequently dull. Peanut butter needs enlivening. Try this mixture on the unconverted.
Preheat broiler.

Combine:

3/4 cup peanut butter
1/4 cup mayonnaise
1/4 teaspoon salt
2 tablespoons pickle relish or chili sauce
1/4 cup cooked minced bacon

Toast on one side:

4 slices bread

Spread the untoasted side with the mixture. Broil the sandwiches until the tops are golden. Slice them diagonally.

FRUIT STICKS

I. Cut into strips 3 x 1 x 1 inch thick:

White bread

Toast them on 3 sides. Place them on a baking sheet with the untoasted side up. Drain:

Pineapple or apricot slices

Place on the untoasted sides. Sprinkle them well with a mixture of:

Brown sugar and cinnamon

Dot with:

Butter

Brown lightly under a broiler.

II. Preheat oven to 450°.

Prepare:

Pie Dough, 640

Roll it until very thin. Cut it into oblongs. Sprinkle:

Drained pineapple or apricot slices

with:

Cinnamon and brown sugar

Wrap the slices in the oblongs. Moisten the edges with water. Bake the slices about 20 minutes.

CLUB SANDWICH

Individual Serving

Spread:

3 large square slices of toast

on one side only with:

Butter, mayonnaise or Russian Dressing, 364

Cover the spread side of slice 1 with:

A lettuce leaf
3 crisp slices hot bacon
Tomato slices
(Drained pineapple slices)

Over this place slice 2, its spread side covered with:

Slices of cold cooked chicken

Place the spread side of slice 3 over the chicken. Cut the sandwich on the bias.

LAMB OR CHICKEN SANDWICH

Trim the crusts from:

Large slices rye bread

Spread them with:

Butter

Place on each piece:

Cold lamb or chicken slices
Lettuce leaves
Tomato slices
Hard-cooked egg slices

Serve the sandwich with:

Russian Dressing, 364, or Mayonnaise

CHICKEN AND CREAM CHEESE SANDWICHES

Spread:

Slices of whole wheat bread

with:

Cream cheese softened with cream

Add:

Slices of cooked chicken
Chopped green olives
Salt, if needed

HOT CHICKEN SANDWICHES

I. Cut into slices:

Cold cooked chicken

Dip the slices in:

Mayonnaise

Prepare:

Biscuits, 632

While hot, open and spread with:

Butter

Place the chicken slices in the biscuits. Serve hot with:

Chicken gravy, Cheese Sauce, 342,
or Quick Mushroom Sauce, 348

II. Using biscuits as in the previous recipe, fill with:

Chicken Salad, 108

or combine:

1/2 cup cooked minced chicken
1 chopped hard-cooked egg
6 chopped stuffed olives
1/4 cup mayonnaise
(2 tablespoons chopped parsley)

Serve hot with one of the sauces mentioned previously.

III.

Preheat oven to 375°.

Prepare:

Buttered toast

Cover the toast with:

Sliced chicken

Sprinkle with:

Crumbled Roquefort cheese

Cover with:

Strips of bacon

Bake about 10 minutes, until the bacon is crisp.

TOASTED ROLLS WITH CRAB MEAT AND CHEESE

4 Servings

Preheat broiler.

Cut into halves:

4 rolls

Cover the 4 lower halves with:

Lettuce leaves

Combine:

3/4 cup canned crab meat
1/4 cup mayonnaise

Spread this on the lettuce. Spread the remaining halves with:

Butter
Slices of cheese
(Mustard)

Toast the cheese halves under a broiler until the cheese is soft. Combine the halves.

LOBSTER SANDWICHES

Flake:

6 oz. canned lobster or other seafood

Sprinkle over it:

1 teaspoon lemon juice

Add:

½ cup minced celery
1 tablespoon minced onion or chives
½ cup mayonnaise

Mayonnaise, if too thick, may be thinned with sour cream. Season with:

(Worcestershire sauce or curry powder)

Add:

(Capers, chopped olives, pickles or parsley)

Spread these ingredients on:

Buttered rye bread

You may add:

(Crisp lettuce leaves)

SHRIMP SANDWICHES WITH CHEESE SAUCE

6 Servings

Clean and chop:

1½ cups cooked shrimp

Melt:

2 tablespoons butter

Add:

1 tablespoon grated onion
(1 sliced pimiento)

and the shrimp. Stir over low heat for 1 minute. Prepare:

6 slices toast

Heap the shrimp on the toast. Serve with:

Cheese Sauce, 342

VEGETABLES

Rumor has it that the Baron Éduard de Rothschild never sent word to his gardener what vegetables he had chosen for dinner until an hour before mealtime to ensure their appearing at table absolutely fresh. If you "grow your own" you don't have to be one of the richest men in the world to know how spectacularly delicious corn on the cob can be if gathered while the water for it is coming to a boil. To preserve true, delicate flavor as well as natural sugars and nutrients, and to enjoy green vegetables at their wholesome best, wash them just before cooking. Cook only to the point of doneness, not a moment more, and transfer them at once from cook to consumer.

If you grow your own vegetables, you can choose seeds specifically listed for the home garden, seeds that usually produce a harvest of superior texture and flavor. Grow them in organically enriched soil, and control their moisture requirements through mulching and watering during dry periods when they need a boost. The longer it takes vegetables to mature, the coarser their cellulose. These slowpokes and overdeveloped vegetables will demand a longer cooking period and incur consequent loss of nutritive value, color and eating quality.

Some unusual vegetables are shown above. Reading left to right, in the foreground are a lotus pod, okra and kohlrabi; in the front of the basket is a bamboo shoot to the left, salsify to the right. Behind these, from left to right, are Florence fennel or finocchio, Jerusalem artichokes and celeriac or knob celery. But vegetables don't have to be unusual to be of the utmost importance in your diet. They are essential for many vitamin, enzyme and mineral factors and often furnish a surprising amount of protein, see 2.

While few things could make us happier than to branch out at this point with how our readers might successfully produce for themselves at least the basic repertory of garden vegetables, the subject is too broad for inclusion here. If you live in the Northeast you might consult Catherine Osgood Foster's *The Organic Gardener*, and for more generalized information *The Basic Book of Organic Gardening* by E. R. Rodale or *Growing Food the Natural Way* by Ken and Pat Kraft.

Because, on the other hand, the growing of a dozen-odd culinary herbs can be achieved in small outdoor areas or even in window pots on an all-year 'round basis; because fresh herbs are so rarely obtainable at market, and since they so greatly enhance the savor of vegetables as well as that of other foods, we have given explicit instructions for their culture on pages 577 to 588.

Newly in vogue but almost as old as the hills is the collecting of "greens," 305, and of wild fruits, roots and blossoms. This enterprise is not without peril for the uninitiated. Indeed, in looking into the "bag" of the bolder explorers we are sometimes reminded, unfairly we know, of Oscar Wilde's description of a fox-hunt: "The unspeakable in pursuit of the inedible." For the fact that the birds and the beasts seem to be thriving on certain kinds of native verdure does not necessarily prove them fit for human consumption.

We have included in the pages which follow those "far-out" vegetables we have found, on close inspection, to be most palatable and trouble-free. Even some of these have toxic elements when raw which must be carefully dispersed by heating or leaching: see, for example, About Mushrooms, 306, and About Wild Greens, 305. Where the use of regional names might produce dangerous confusion, we have identified edible varieties by supplying scientific names and specific descriptions. In the field be sure that plants taken from roadside habitats have not been coated with poisonous sprays.

On your more conventional quests—trips to market—use the tests for ripeness we describe under individual vegetable listings. If store stocks are uneven, give preference to a fresh garden-type lettuce over a pale green watercress, or a crisp bunch of carrots over darkened leathery artichokes. Care in cooking, piquancy in seasoning and ingenuity in combining familiar varieties can compensate for the more commonplace choice. But the choices are constantly increasing. It is amazing how many airborne "out-of-season" and exotic vegetables are becoming available almost all year 'round from the controlled-temperature bins of our "fancier" grocers. While most of these novelties are identified in the pages which follow, the inquisitive reader is referred to D. Hawkes's *A World of Vegetable Cookery* for an even more comprehensive count-down.

Should fresh vegetables of any description be in drastically short supply or altogether unavailable, the next best bets are—in order of preference—those frozen, canned or dried. To compare nutritive values in these categories, see 798.

In all vegetable cookery involving moisture, be sure to utilize the resulting liquids in sauces or as stocks. Otherwise, nutritional losses are great. For vegetable combinations, often protein-enriched, consult Brunch, Lunch and Supper Dishes, 250, where you will discover a host of recipes in which cooked vegetables make up the principal ingredient.

STORING VEGETABLES

Certain vegetables and fruits should not be stored together. Apples give off an ethylene gas that makes carrots bitter, and onions hasten the spoilage of potatoes. Watch for other such relationships. Do not wash vegetables until you are ready to use them. Cut the leaves from all root vegetables at once, for the flow of sap continues to the leaf at the expense of the root. We have found that even in the vegetable-keeper of the most modern refrigerators lettuces, celery and beans, for example, hold over much better if encased in plastic bags. For storing watercress and mushrooms, see 94 and 307. Vegetables like salad greens, including celery and endive, are best held in moderate humidity at about 35°—as are salsify, turnips and parsnips. Between 35° and 40° is best for most other vegetables, including the cabbage family. Potatoes and tomatoes are best around 40°. Potatoes should always be stored in a dark place to keep them from turning green and so activating poisonous qualities. Held under dry conditions between 35° and 40° are dried peas and beans. Onions and garlic, also stored in dry air, need about 35°. To ripen sweet potatoes and tomatoes, store in warm dry air at about 60° to 70°.

PREPARING VEGETABLES FOR COOKING

Prepare vegetables as close to cooking time as possible. Most thin-skinned vegetables may be rinsed, scrubbed if necessary, and cooked unpared. If vegetables are to be pared before cooking, trim them as thinly as possible unless the individual recipe indicates otherwise. Also, unless the individual processing requires it, never soak vegetables after paring or slicing if conserving nutrients is of prime importance. Should vegetables tend to brown after paring, sprinkle them with lemon juice or ascorbic acid, 124. Whether you cook vegetables whole or pared and sliced, see that the pieces are uniform in size so they will all cook through in the same length of time.

You will avoid trouble if, when slicing round vegetables like onions, you first cut them in half and place the flat side down on the cutting surface. Whatever the object to be sliced, hold it as sketched right. Many chopping and slicing devices are advertised, but nothing can replace a skilled relaxed wrist and a sharp knife. Acquire this indispensable trick and you will be forever grateful. Practice with a mushroom, which is yielding and not slippery when placed cap down, and work up to an onion, which can be both resistant and evasive.

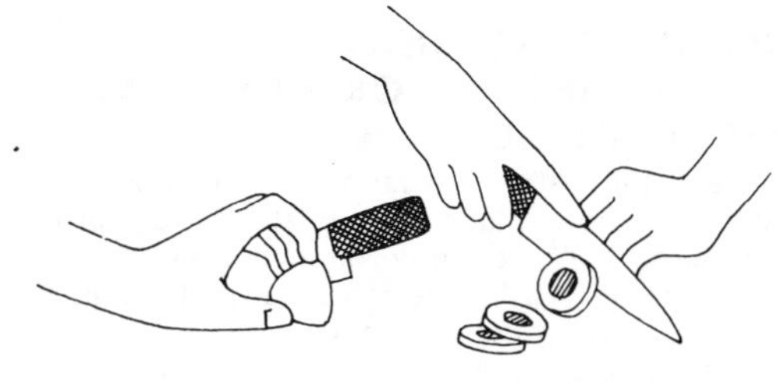

➤ The point of the knife is never lifted from the cutting board but forms a pivot. The cutting edge, in turn, is never lifted above the first joint of the left forefinger, as shown above. The handle end of the knife is raised high enough to be eased gently up and down, its wide blade guided by the perpendicular left forefinger and mid-finger. As the slicing progresses, inch a slow retreat with the left hand without releasing a firm grasp on the object.

Should a vegetable like celery or Chinese cabbage be sliced on the diagonal, the two guide fingers are set at an angle, as shown next. But the knife in the right hand continues its relaxed accurate slicing, while the left makes way without losing control of the stalks. To pare very hard, round vegetables, see 335.

In making a really determined effort to lure your family into eating vegetables, you will find that they will respond more readily if the vegetables are appealing in shape. Think of the irresistible charm of vegetables floating like flowers in a Japanese lacquered bowl. The French are also very adept at presentation, if more lavish, and they disguise the same old carrots, beans and potatoes under a mass of impressive modifiers. As **printanière** they are spring-grown, young, tender and thinly sliced. As **brunoise, salpicon, mirepoix** and **macédoine** they are ageless, and sliced respectively from 1/8 to 1/4 to 3/8 inch, which latter size we call just plain **diced.** As **jardinière, julienne** or **allumette,** they are taller and thinner, about 2 to 3 inches long and 1/8 inch through. When they are round in shape and small, you may call them

pearls; if they are elliptical, **olivette** at 3/8 inch, **noisette** at 1/2 inch, and **Parisienne** if about 1 inch at their narrowest diameter. Utilize whatever scraps are left over in ⅄ blender soups or, unless they are starchy ones, in the stockpot.

RETAINING NUTRIENTS, FLAVOR AND COLOR DURING VEGETABLE COOKING

Some enthusiasts go so far as to insist that vegetables are best if not cooked at all. But carrots and spinach, for example, among a good many other varieties, will have more nutrients available for body absorption when cooked, despite the inevitable losses due to heating. No one method of vegetable cookery can claim complete superiority. Some vegetables may be scrubbed, then steamed or baked unpeeled, minimizing vitamin loss—provided the cooking is not overly prolonged. Pressure steaming, below, like stir-frying and pan-steaming, is both quick and efficient; as is steaming with only the water which adheres to the vegetables after rinsing, plus a small quantity of butter or oil. Other methods are discussed at length in the following pages.

Probably the greatest loss of vitamins, especially of vitamin C—from one-fourth to one-half—occurs in mashing and puréeing. The water-soluble vitamins, C and the B-complex group, are the hardest to retain during the application of any type of heat; and this points up again the importance of utilizing all the vegetable juices which result, unless they are bitter or off-flavored. Be sure to drain these stocks as shown opposite, and store refrigerated for later use.

Both steaming and stir-frying help to retain good color, provided the vegetables are not kept covered after the point of palatable tenderness. Color should never be maintained by the addition of baking soda, for this procedure not only destroys nutrient values but makes the vegetable mushy. Color may also be lost through cooking in hard water, 519. Retention of color as well as flavor can be helped along by salting just after the onset of cooking. Allow about 1/4 teaspoon salt to each cup of water.

Since older vegetables tend to lose their natural sugars, they often profit by a pinch of sugar during cooking, as well as by dressing with seasoned butters, herbs, spices and sauces. Dried legumes and canned vegetables in particular profit greatly by bold seasoning. But vegetables in their prime may simply be tossed in butter, allowing not more than one to two teaspoons per cup, so that the full flavor of the vegetable still prevails.

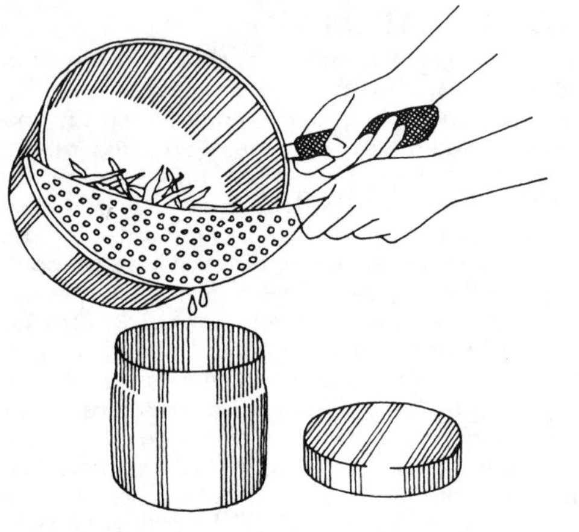

PRESSURE-COOKING AND PRESSURE-STEAMING VEGETABLES

The use of a pressure cooker saves both time and nutrients, especially if you pressure-steam, a process involving a rack as illustrated below. Allow a minute or two longer than the times given for pressure-cooked vegetables in the individual recipes. Also please read About Pressure Cooking, 150.

STEAMING VEGETABLES

Some cooks find the supervision of a pressure cooker worrisome. If you are of this number, use

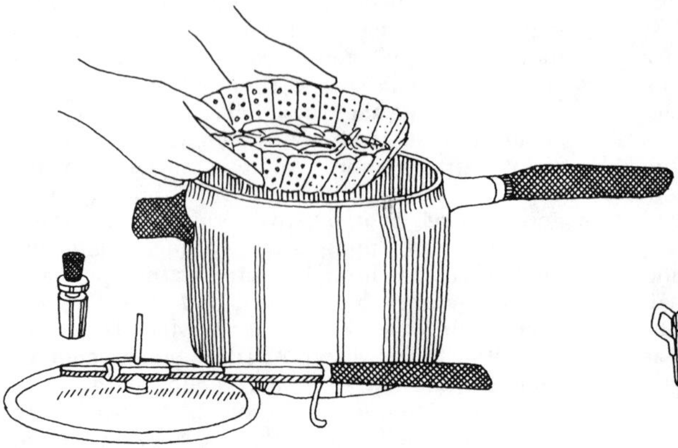

the special steaming pan shown at right opposite. Be sure the water in the lower element is boiling briskly before setting in place the perforated top with its vegetables. Cover at once and cook the vegetables until tender.

SKILLET-PANNING AND STIR-FRYING VEGETABLES

Oriental cooks are justifiably partial to these methods of cooking vegetables, which preserve freshness of flavor and crisp texture. Please read about Stir-Frying, 149, and see drawing below.

The slow part of both of these similar methods is the preparation. For best results the vegetables must be finely sliced to uniform thickness. Those that tend to stringiness are cut on the diagonal. Stem ends and midribs should be removed from coarse-leaf vegetables and sliced separately. The vegetables are then grouped so the tougher ones go into the pan first. For 4 servings allow about 1 pound of kale, cabbage, okra, celery or celery cabbage; about 1½ pounds of spinach or chard, and about ¾ pound of beans. Cucumber, tomato, zucchini, spinach, Chinese cabbage and salad greens need no water during the cooking period. Have ready for green beans and young root vegetables about ¾ cup boiling water per pound and allow 5 to 8 minutes for cooking. Maturer root vegetables are better steamed, as discussed above.

Use about 1 to 2 tablespoons of cooking oil—sesame is a great favorite—or oil and butter combined, per pound of vegetables. Heat the pan well, put in the cooking oil and heat to the point of fragrance. You may add a slice or two of garlic or fresh gingerroot briefly and discard before the vegetables are put into the pan. Stir the vegetables rapidly with a large flat spatula, coating them with oil until they show signs of wilting slightly. Some cooks like to season at this point with a dash of soy sauce and stock before clapping on the lid to maintain succulence. Lower the heat. When the vegetables are just tender, you may stir in a small quantity of additional stock if needed, or Chinese Sauce for Vegetables, 349. ➤ Cover the pan briefly until the sauce reaches the boiling point, and serve at once.

If meat and vegetables are to be cooked together, the meat, 149, is cooked first. Remove it from the pan and add it again with the vegetables for reheating. If cooking vegetables in the pod either in a skillet or wok, no oil is needed. Allow for 4 servings 1½ to 2 pounds per person, depending on how full the pods are. Depending also on the thickness of the pods, have ready ½ to ¾ cup boiling water for each pound of vegetable and cook, covered, 5 to 15 minutes or until tender. Shell after cooking and butter before serving. For snow peas, see 315. To ensure crispness, serve immediately. Make certain also that lidded dishes from which the food is served are preheated.

DEEP-FAT-FRYING VEGETABLES

The French have made the fried potato famous as **French fries,** 322; the English as **chips,** 323. The Italians, by using either a beaten-egg coating or a batter, produce their famous fried vegetable and other mixtures as **fritto misto,** 243; and the Japanese, who learned this trick from Portuguese sailors way back in the sixteenth century, prepare them today under the term **tempura,** 243.

Since success depends so largely on the ➤ quality of the fat and avoiding its excess absorption, please read About Deep-Fat-Frying, 147. After preparing the vegetables, be sure to sprinkle with lemon juice any that may discolor. Check to see that the vegetables are ➤ dry before applying a coating. It is also best to let the coating dry for about 10 minutes before immersing the food in fat heated to between 350° and 375°. Cook until the vegetables are golden.

Vegetables suitable for this type of cooking are long green beans; ⅓-inch-thick eggplant slices barely nicked with tiny knife marks at ½-inch intervals all around the bands of skin; mushrooms and tiny green peppers, whole or cut in half vertically; cucumber, squash, zucchini or sweet potato rounds; sliced lotus roots or bamboo shoots;

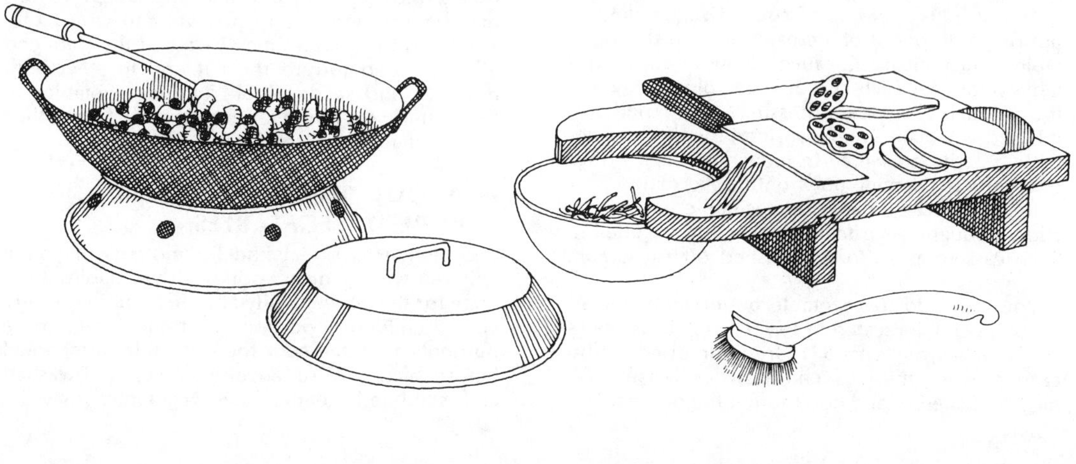

small bundles of julienned onions or very young green onions; asparagus tips; cauliflower or broccoli florets, artichoke hearts or stems.

GLAZED ROOT VEGETABLES

Vegetables produced by this method are suitable for garnishing and require no further saucing. Choose:

2 cups young vegetables: onions, carrots, turnips or potatoes

Simmer, covered, in a very heavy pan with:

1 cup veal or chicken stock
½ teaspoon salt
2 teaspoons sugar
2 tablespoons butter

When the vegetables are nearly done and the liquid has been almost absorbed, ➤ uncover and continue to cook, shaking the pan continually over brisk heat until they are coated with a golden glaze.

ABOUT VEGETABLES FOR A ROAST

To cook vegetables for a roast, it is better on several scores to process them separately. For one thing, if they are placed in the roasting pan, the steam they release tends to give a moister oven heat than is desirable for meat roasting. For another, typical root vegetables such as potatoes, carrots, onions and turnips profit by separate cooking. Steam them, 278, until partially tender, then drain and dry. Finish cooking them in butter in a ➤ heavy, covered pan until tender, and complete the browning uncovered.

ABOUT CREAMED, BUTTERED AND SAUCED VEGETABLES

Practically any vegetables may be served in or with a sauce. They may be steamed or even deep-fried before saucing. ➤ Drain them well before combining with sauces or butter. The amount to allow for garnishing will depend largely on the richness of the sauce, from 1 teaspoon to 1 tablespoon of butter per cup of cooked vegetables, on up to 4 tablespoons of a cream sauce. If the vegetable is heated in the sauce, allow about 2 to 3 tablespoons for each cup of vegetables, using less if it is a rich sour cream dressing—more, perhaps, if based on cream soup. Consider, too, if the vegetable is to be presented in individual deep dishes or from a big serving bowl onto a flat plate.

If you are casseroling the vegetable in a sauce, allow enough sauce to just cover the vegetables. Such casseroles are often finished off Au Gratin, 552.

You may add to vegetable butters and sauces, if not already indicated in the recipe, citrus juices and pinches of zests, 571, fresh or dried herbs, curry powder, mustard, chili powder, horseradish or grated cheese; and don't forget the onions, 583.

ABOUT STUFFED VEGETABLES

Tomatoes, peppers, squashes, cucumbers, onions, mushrooms, all make decorative and delicious vegetable cases. For a "new dimension," fill them with other vegetables, contrasting in color or flavor; or point up the bland ones with a farce of cooked food, with buttered, crumbed, cooked vegetables or with creamed mixtures. Raw foods that need long cooking should not be used in vegetable stuffings.

Since vegetable cases need different timing when blanched, see recipes under individual vegetables for this information. Other factors remain the same. After draining, place the filled cases on a rack in a pan containing about ¼ inch of water.

Heat the cases through in a 400° oven, unless otherwise indicated, before serving. Or, if you want to serve them Au Gratin I or II, 553, you may find they have better color if you run them first under a broiler and then bake as above. With Au Gratin III, the cheese will probably brown the tops sufficiently in the baking alone without the use of a broiler at all.

ABOUT VEGETABLE FONDUES

Although the term fondue is usually associated with cheese, 254, it applies if you are French to Boeuf Fondu Bourguignonne, 457, or if Spanish to Bagna Cauda, 90. The term is also used for vegetables reduced to a pulp by very, very slow cooking in butter, as for Tomato Pudding II, 333. Some other vegetables that lend themselves well to such dishes are carrots, celery, eggplant, sweet peppers, onions, leeks and lettuce.

To prepare vegetables for fondueing, first rid them of excess moisture in one of the following ways. Except for tomatoes, they may be parblanched, 154, from 3 to 5 minutes. Eggplant and cucumber may be sliced, salted generously and allowed to drain on a rack. Salting clears them of the rather unpleasant astringent quality they sometimes acquire. They may also be thinly sliced, salted, placed in a bowl and weighted to force out excess moisture. Mushrooms and green onions may be wrapped in a dish towel and wrung out. Tomatoes for fondues may be cut at the stem end and squeezed toward the cut end to eject both moisture and seeds. Cook fondue vegetables in the butter, covered, over very low heat until they reach a naturally puréed state.

⅄ ABOUT BLENDED PURÉED VEGETABLES

The blender is a real find for mothers of young children who want to cook fresh vegetables all at once for the whole family and then purée the very young children's portion. In either case, more nutrients are retained if the vegetables are cooled before blending. As an alternative, well-washed and scrubbed, tender raw vegetables may be blended and then cooked to the boiling point. Tough ones should be parboiled, cooled and then blended. You may reheat briefly in butter or cream before serving.

VEGETABLES À LA GRECQUE

These mixed vegetables, left whole if small or cut into attractive shapes, 277, become aromatic as the result of simmering in a court bouillon of highly seasoned oil and water. ➤ They are served at between 70° and 90°, so that the oil will not be evident. They make convenient hors d'oeuvre, meat tray or salad garnishes, as they keep well if covered and refrigerated. They are excellent, too, for an antipasto tray. Prepare one of the following court bouillons or hot marinades in which to cook:

1 lb. mixed vegetables

Suitable varieties include artichoke hearts, julienned carrots, cauliflower florets, celery, fennel, green beans, leeks, mushrooms, pearl onions, peppers and whole olives. Cucumber and eggplant slices or strips are delicious, but these should have excess moisture removed, 302.

Squeeze over the cut vegetables, to prevent browning:

Juice of 2 lemons

I. Place in a 3-quart stainless or enamel pan:

4 cups water
1/3 to 1/2 cup olive oil
1 teaspoon salt
2 peeled cloves garlic
(3 peeled shallots)

and the following herbs and spices, tied in a cheesecloth bag:

6 sprigs parsley
2 teaspoons fresh thyme
12 peppercorns
(3 coriander seeds or 1/4 teaspoon oregano)
(1/8 teaspoon fennel or celery seeds)

Add for flavor 2 of the squeezed lemon halves. Bring the mixture to a boil, then remove from the heat to season for about 15 minutes. Remove the spice bag and garlic. Bring the court bouillon again slowly to a simmer. Add in turn the most delicately flavored of the prepared vegetables. Once more bring the liquid just to a boil, reduce the heat and let the vegetables heat through and then cool in the marinade. Drain and place them in a jar, using a slotted wooden spoon. Now, cook the next most delicately flavored vegetable. Continue till each one has been cooked and cooled in the marinade. When they are all in the jar, mixed or separate, cover them with the marinade to store. After the vegetables have been eaten, use the marinade for sauces.

II. Combine in a stainless or enamel pan:

1 cup wine
2 cups olive oil
1/2 cup vinegar
1/2 to 3/4 cup water
2 cloves garlic
3 sprigs parsley
6 peppercorns
2 sliced lemons
1/4 teaspoon salt

Cook the vegetables in the heated mixture, as in I.

III. This rather offbeat version is a pleasant change.

Combine in a stainless or enamel pan:

3/4 cup olive oil
1/2 cup wine vinegar
3/4 cup catsup
1/2 cup chili sauce
1 clove garlic
1 teaspoon Worcestershire sauce

Cook the vegetables in the heated mixture, as in I.

* COOKING FROZEN VEGETABLES

Please read About Thawing and Cooking of Frozen Foods, 822. To cook these convenience foods so they lie flat and are all heated through at the same time, we prefer using a rectangular frozen-food steamer.

⊗ To pressure cook frozen vegetables, allow about 1/2 as long as for the regular pressure cooking times given in individual recipes, but use the same amounts of water.

If using an electric skillet, place the hard-frozen vegetables—except for spinach and corn on the cob, which must be partially thawed—in the skillet and then cover. Set at 350° until steam escapes. Reset to 300° until the vegetable is tender.

ABOUT REHEATED AND CANNED VEGETABLES

Delicious, often, are the uses of leftovers, but reheated vegetables have lost much of their nutritive value. If you do reheat them, put them in the top of a covered double boiler with a few teaspoons of water or stock, or reheat or bake them in a hot sauce. Allow about 1/4 to 1/2 as much sauce as vegetables. ➤ Be sure to retain the canning or cooking water for use in soup or sauce or as the medium in which to reheat. Making leftover vegetables into soufflés, 229, timbales, 231, omelets and frittatas, 228, both glamorizes and stretches them. The sautéing and browning of cooked vegetables diminish vitamin content. Try serving leftover vegetables vinaigretted in a salad, remembering—contrary to at least one precept we learned at mother's knee—that cold food is as nutritious as hot. Canned or frozen vegetables have, of course, already suffered some loss of flavor and vitamins. Reheating before serving increases this loss.

➤ Always clean off tops before opening cans, as they may be dusty or may have been sprayed with poisonous insecticides while in the store. ➤ Once opened, cans should not be used to store food. Lead may leach from the cans into the contents, especially if the food is acid.

COOKING VEGETABLES BY MICROWAVE

Please read About Microwave Cooking, 160. In electronic cooking, most vegetables are casseroled with a small quantity of water and are cooked covered. Because they need moisture, the cooking periods are generally comparable to pressure steaming, 278. If the vegetable can be baked like a potato, cooking time is saved. Scientific tests seem to show that nutrients are well retained, although the majority of taste panels rate vegetables cooked by other methods superior in flavor and texture. For timing follow manufacturer's directions.

⊟ ABOUT CAMPFIRE AND BARBECUE VEGETABLES

Here are 2 simple, potless ways to cook vegetables for an outdoor barbecue. For the first, use frozen or sliced and washed vegetables. Place them on heavy-weight aluminum foil and season them. Use the drugstore wrap, 821. Place the foil-wrapped vegetables on a grill or under or on hot coals for 10 to 15 minutes. For the second method, place—directly on a greased grill above the coals—thick slices of tomato, mushroom, pepper, parboiled onion. Cover with an inverted colander. Cook until tender.

▲ COOKING VEGETABLES AT HIGH ALTITUDES

In baking vegetables at high altitudes, use approximately the same temperatures and timing given for sea-level cooking. In cooking vegetables at high altitude by any process involving moisture, both more liquid and a longer cooking time are needed, as the vegetables boil at lower temperatures. Frequently, the longer time can be reduced if the vegetables are thinly sliced or cut into small units. To avoid tough stems and overcooked leaves on leafy vegetables, remove the midrib and use it in the stock pot.

Make these adjustments as an approximate time guide: for each 1000 feet of elevation, add to the cooking time given in the recipes about 10% for whole beets, carrots and onions and about 7% for green beans, squash, green cabbage, turnips and parsnips. ✻ In cooking frozen vegetables at high altitudes, whole carrots and beans may require as much as 5 to 12 minutes of additional cooking, while other frozen vegetables may need only 1 to 2 more minutes.

The extension division of most land grant colleges will test the gauge of your pressure cooker and probably provide a pressure chart for your area free of charge.

⊗ In pressuring vegetables at high altitude, you will have to increase the liquid in your cooker 1/4 to 1/2 cup for every 2 cups of vegetables, depending on their respective length of cooking time. As with other vegetable-cooking at high altitudes, sliced or shredded vegetables, as well as peas, corn and spinach may cook almost as rapidly as at sea level, at 15 lbs. pressure. But you may find that, with some of the leafy greens, 10 lbs. of pressure and a slightly longer cooking period give a better result. This has been found true for asparagus, celery, turnips and cauliflower. Don't be surprised if whole potatoes, beets, yams and beans need considerably more time than at sea level.

ABOUT ARTICHOKES

Artichokes of the globe type, sketched below, differ in shape, taste and method of cooking from Jerusalem artichokes, right. If the leaves are spreading or discolored, artichokes are not tender. Sometimes, when immature, they are cooked, pickled, 841, and eaten whole. The mature vegetable, after cooking, is most frequently served one to each diner and eaten with the fingers. The leaves are removed singly and dipped into a sauce, the lower end of the leaf being simply drawn through the teeth to extract the tender edible portion, and the leaf then discarded. Continue this procedure until a light-colored cone of young leaves appears. Pull this up with one movement. Then, with a knife, cut out cleanly the fuzzy center below and discard it. Eat the remaining heart with a fork, dipping each piece first into a sauce. Artichoke hearts, with bottoms neatly trimmed, make delicious salad material, as well as bases for stuffing, 283, and see below.

UNCORED ARTICHOKES

To wash, hold by the stem end and dash up and down quickly in a deep bowl of water. To prepare:

Artichokes

cut off the stems with scissors. Trim the top leaves by one-fourth. Snap off the tough bottom row of leaves by bending them back from the core. To avoid discoloration, dip the trimmed base in:

Lemon juice

Place the artichokes top down on a trivet over 1 to 2 inches of boiling water. Add to the water:

1 sliced onion or 1 mashed clove garlic
2 celery ribs with leaves
1½ tablespoons lemon juice, wine or vinegar
(2 tablespoons vegetable oil)
(A bay leaf)

Steam, 278, covered 45 minutes or until tender. Drain and serve hot with:

Melted butter, Mayonnaise, 363, Hollandaise Sauce, 358, Béchamel Sauce, 341, or Sauce Vinaigrette, 360

Cooked artichokes may be served chilled.

⊗ Pressure cook large artichokes at 15 lbs. about 15 minutes, small ones 8 minutes.

CORED ARTICHOKES

Clean and trim as described above:

Artichokes

Turn them upside down. Press hard to force the leaves apart. Reverse and insert a curved knife, as shown left, to cut out and remove the choke. Tie artichokes into shape with string. Cook as in previous recipe but upright on the trivet. Drain well, untie and serve warm, the centers filled with:

Hollandaise Sauce, 358

If the artichokes are too hot when filled, the Hollandaise may separate. Or fill the centers with:

1 cup cooked cocktail shrimp or small chunks of lobster

heated in:

Newburg Sauce, 359

You may also serve these cored artichokes cold and stuffed as salad. Incidentally, the very tender leaves usually discarded in the coring, if trimmed and cooked, make delectable flavorings for an omelet or a casserole.

ARTICHOKE HEARTS

For a good way to stuff cold artichoke hearts, see Salads, 100.

I. Remove all leaves and chokes, as shown on the opposite page center right, from:

Artichokes

Steam the hearts, 278, or drop them into 1 inch of:

Boiling water

to which you may add:

Lemon juice

Simmer covered for 20 minutes or until tender. Serve with:

Brown Butter, 349, or
Hollandaise Sauce, 358

II. Cooked or canned artichoke hearts, well drained, may be sautéed until hot in:

Butter or drippings

to which you may add:

Garlic, shallots or onions

Season with:

Salt and paprika
Lemon juice

Serve hot or cold.

STUFFED BAKED ARTICHOKES

Preheat oven to 350°.

I. Roman Style

Clean, trim and blanch, 154:

Artichokes

Drain well. Make a dressing of:

Bread crumbs
Minced garlic or onion
Chopped celery
Chopped anchovies or anchovy paste
Grated Parmesan cheese
Chopped parsley
Salt and paprika

Push the dressing down between the leaves. The choke may be removed, as described previously, if desired, and the center filled with the dressing. Pour over the artichokes a little:

Olive oil

Place them on a rack in a baking dish and cover the bottom of the dish with 1 inch of:

Boiling water or stock

Bake covered about 1 hour.

II. Or fill the artichokes with either:

Ham or sausage stuffing, 371

JERUSALEM ARTICHOKES

Vegetable nomenclature abounds in double or doubtful terms—endive, chicory, pepper, yam and "wild rice" being examples; but "Jerusalem artichoke," seen in the chapter heading, center rear, should get some sort of prize in the misnomer sweepstakes. It is not even a thistle, like the true artichoke, but the tuber of a sunflower; and "Jerusalem" is a corruption of the Italian "girasole," or "turn-to-the-sun," as the sunflowers, like heliotropes, are obliged to do. They may be eaten raw, peeled, or may be prepared as for Saratoga Chips, 323, or as below.

Wash:

1½ lb. Jerusalem artichokes

Steam, 278, or drop them into:

Boiling water

To prevent discoloration, add:

1 teaspoon mild vinegar or white wine

Cook covered until ➤ tender only. If permitted to cook beyond this point, they will again become tough. Test with a fork after 15 minutes. Drain. Rub off the peel. Melt:

2 to 3 tablespoons butter

Add:

2 drops hot pepper sauce
2 tablespoons chopped parsley

Pour these ingredients over the artichokes or cream them, 280. Or cut into halves and ⊗ pressure cook 10 minutes at 15 lbs.

ASPARAGUS

The Romans used to say if they wanted something in a hurry, "Do it in less time than it takes to cook asparagus." Hilled, blanched asparagus, grown by heavy fertilization and deep mulching, is now available in American markets. This is a thick white variant which, though less nutritious than the green, has a distinctive succulence all its own. "Whites"—familiar to us all in their canned state—must be peeled, cutting from below the head and increasing the depth of cut as you go downward. This is also sometimes necessary with the larger older "greens" to eliminate bitterness in the skins.

I. **4 to 6 servings**

Wash:

2 lb. asparagus

Snap off the lower part of the stalks where they break easily. Keep the trimmings for soup. Tie the asparagus in serving bunches with white string. Place them upright in an asparagus steamer or in the bottom part of a double boiler, the lower ends in:

½ cup boiling water

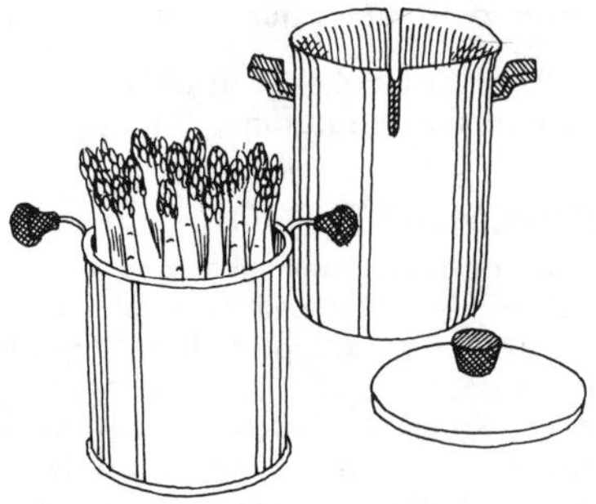

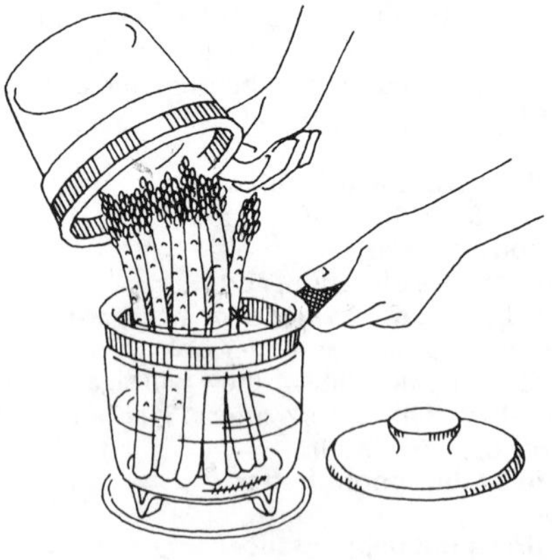

Cook the asparagus ➤ closely covered 12 minutes or until tender. An inverted double boiler top may be used. The steam will cook the tips. Drain well, reserving the liquid. Add:

½ teaspoon salt

Melt:

⅓ cup butter or Brown Butter, 349

Sauté in it, for 1 minute:

1 cup bread crumbs

Pour this mixture over the tips of the asparagus, or serve them with:

1 cup White Sauce I, 341, made with half cream and half asparagus liquid, or Hollandaise Sauce, 358

II. For real speed, slice diagonally ¼ inch thick:

Asparagus

Stir-fry, 279, and garnish with:

Buttered bread crumbs

III. Sometimes, if asparagus must be held, both the color and the texture are improved if this recipe is used—although we do not guarantee nutritive value.

Arrange in a flat pan:

2 lb. cleaned asparagus

Place them not more than 3 or 4 deep. Add:

½ teaspoon salt

Cover with cold water, then with a poaching paper, 151. Bring to a boil, reduce heat at once and ➤ simmer about 15 minutes. Keep lukewarm until ready to serve, then drain before serving.

BAMBOO SHOOTS

In oriental dishes, these slightly acid shoots complement mushrooms and meat. They must be young and tender and from an edible bamboo plant. See illustration in chapter heading on 276. If fresh, boil:

Bamboo shoots

in:

Water

about 10 to 15 minutes. Texture should remain somewhat crisp. Discard the water. If using canned shoots, scrape off the calcium deposits. If using only part of a can, store the remainder by pouring off the original liquid, replacing it with cold water and refrigerating, covered, for not more than a few days.

ABOUT FRESH BEANS

Fresh beans are of many varieties. **Snap beans,** seen first at left, opposite, can be eaten whole. Formerly called **string,** because their strings had to be removed, they have in many instances been hybridized so that they snap clean and need only have the ends snipped off. True **haricots verts,** with their okralike overtones, shown next, are a tenderer and slimmer version of snap beans. **Kentucky Wonders** and **wax beans,** not shown, still require both snipping and stringing. **English runner beans,** third from the left, respond to the same cooking procedures as snap beans. Any stringy portions should be cut off, and, before cooking, the bean should always be sliced into pieces no bigger than ½ inch. If they do not snap easily, they should be hulled and their red-streaked seeds cooked as for **lima beans,** 289, seen third from the right. Hulled also if they are larger than a pea are **fava beans** or **European broad beans,** second from the right, which are then cooked as for

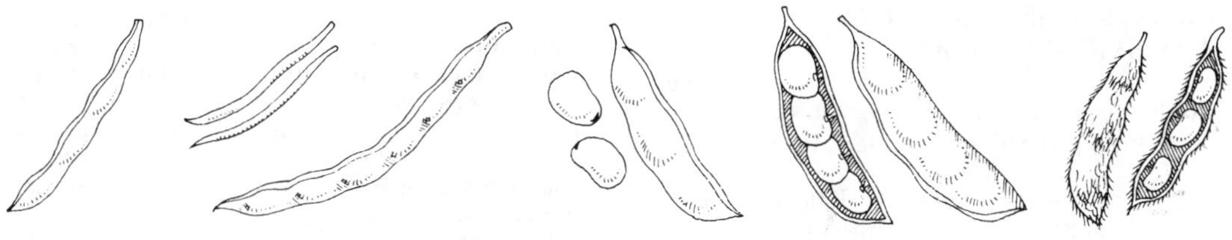

limas. If under pea size, the filled pods may be sliced two or three times and prepared as for snap beans. Cook **edible soy beans,** shown at far right, as described, 286. To avoid toughening any fresh beans, add salt when cooking is half finished.

GREEN OR SNAP BEANS

5 Servings

This vegetable is available fresh the year 'round and lends itself to endless variations.

1 lb. green beans

Snip off the ends. You may then sliver them, French them on the diagonal or leave them whole. If the last, tie them in individual bunches before cooking. When cooked and drained, arrange them on a platter and cover with one of the garnishes or sauces suggested below. To cook green beans, steam, 278, or drop them into:

Boiling water or part water and part stock

Reduce the heat at once. Cook partially covered if you wish to preserve the color; or covered if you wish to preserve more nutrients. Simmer until barely tender, no longer—about 20 minutes. Drain and:

Season to taste

Cover with:

1 tablespoon melted butter

✪ Pressure cook 3 minutes at 15 lbs.

We note here that one of our very favorite ways of second-guessing a quantity of cooked green beans is to make them into a salad, 98.

ADDITIONS TO GREEN BEANS

To further flavor beans during the cooking, add:

1 small cut-up onion
1- to 2-inch cube of salt pork

To garnish or sauce, use for 1 lb. of beans:

1 tablespoon butter or Brown Butter, 349,
or 1/4 cup buttered crumbs,
or 2 tablespoons brown onion butter,
or 2 tablespoons crumbled bacon and drippings

Add to the above fats:

1/2 teaspoon celery or dill seed, or
1 teaspoon fresh summer savory or basil,
or 2 teaspoons chopped chives

Or garnish with:

Anchovy Butter or Oil, 350, or
Almond Garnish, 553

Or add:

1/2 cup Sautéed Mushrooms, 308
1/3 to 1/2 cup cultured sour cream
2 tablespoons chopped parsley

Or add:

2 tablespoons wine vinegar
1/4 teaspoon mustard
1 tablespoon Worcestershire sauce
A drop of hot pepper sauce

Or add:

2 tablespoons butter
1/4 cup toasted slivered almonds
1/4 cup sliced water chestnuts

If the beans are not served at once, reheat in:

A White Sauce variation, 341, or
canned cream of chicken or mushroom soup seasoned with herbs, or
Quick Tomato Sauce, 352

GREEN BEAN CASSEROLE

I. **6 Servings**

What becomes of the onions and peppers? They frequently disappear, leaving marvelously seasoned beans. An easy dish for the hostess who cooks her own dinner.

Preheat oven to 350°.

Trim:

1 lb. green beans

Skin and chop:

4 medium-sized white onions

Remove the seeds and membrane from:

2 medium-sized green peppers

Chop the peppers. Butter a baking dish. Place in it alternate layers of the vegetables, beginning and ending with a layer of beans. Sprinkle each layer with:

Salt and paprika

Dot each layer with:

Butter

Bake the vegetables covered for about 1 hour, or until the beans are tender. Before serving, garnish with:

Au Gratin II, 553

II. **6 Servings**

Preheat oven to 350°.

Prepare for cooking:

1 lb. green beans

Place them in a buttered casserole. Cover with:

1 can cream of tomato soup: 10 1/2 oz.
3 tablespoons prepared horseradish
1 teaspoon Worcestershire sauce
1/4 teaspoon salt
1/4 teaspoon paprika

Bake covered about 1 hour or until tender. Remove the lid and garnish with:

Au Gratin III, 553

Serve when the cheese is melted.

GREEN BEANS, POTATOES AND SMOKED MEAT

8 Servings

Cook until nearly tender in water to cover:

A small piece of smoked meat: ham, Canadian bacon or link sausage

Or if using already cooked or leftover ham or bone, bring just to a boil before adding:

1 lb. green beans
4 halved, pared, medium potatoes
(1 onion)

Simmer, covered, about 20 to 25 minutes. Drain.

Season to taste

Serve from a large platter, garnished with:

Lemon wedges

SWEET-SOUR BEANS

5 Servings

Trim and shred lengthwise:

1 lb. green beans

Steam them, 278, or drop them into:

Boiling water

to barely cover. Cook covered about 20 minutes. Now render the fat slowly from:

3 pieces lean bacon

Cook with it:

2 tablespoons chopped onion

When the bacon is lightly browned, remove it and swirl in the pan:

1 tablespoon white wine vinegar
1 tablespoon sugar
½ teaspoon salt

Drain the liquid from the beans and add it to the skillet mixture. Then combine with the beans and cut-up bacon and serve. A happy variation is the addition of:

(Bean Sprouts, right)

PURÉED GREEN BEANS, PEAS OR LIMAS

4 Servings

Puréed, these lend a fresh note if used as a base for soup, as a ring in serving sautéed mushrooms, or as a vegetable garnished with parsley.

Purée:

2 cups cooked fresh beans or peas

Use a ⅄ blender or a food mill. Add:

2 tablespoons butter
Season to taste

and serve as soon as possible after puréeing. If the purée must be held over, cover it while hot with whipping cream and, in reheating in a double boiler ➤ over hot water, beat in the cream before serving.

GREEN SOYBEANS

Use the edible vegetable type, not field varieties of beans. The fuzzy pods, shown on 285, should still be green. They can be eaten hot or as an informal cold snack. Let the diner pop them from the pod. To serve hot, immerse them in boiling water. Cover the pot. Cook in boiling water until tender, approximately 10 to 15 minutes. Use the shelled beans as in any recipe for lima beans, 289.

The cooked beans may also be spread in a greased pan, dotted with butter and roasted in a 350° oven until brown; or they may be browned in deep fat, 147.

Soy milk, 535, and bean curd, 535, can also be made from the raw beans.

COOKED BEAN SPROUTS

8 Servings

Sprouted beans eaten raw, just after sprouting, see 289, have more vitamin C than when cooked.

Bring to a boil:

¾ cup water

Add:

4 cups sprouted beans, Mung or edible soybeans or lentils

Simmer, covered, until almost soft, just long enough to remove the raw bean flavor. Season with:

Salt
(Soy sauce)

Bean sprouts, fresh or cooked, immediately recall the Chinese-American cuisine, and suggest such added ingredients as chicken, shrimp, scallions, mushrooms or water chestnuts.

ABOUT DRIED LEGUMES

Dried peas and beans, being rather on the dull side, respond readily—like a good many dull people—to the right contacts. Do not upstage them, for they have valuable, if incomplete, proteins, 2. Mix them with tomatoes, onions, chili, meat and cheese. They are also much more temperamental than one would think. Their cooking time depends on the locality in which they were grown and on their age—usually two unknowns for the cook; plus the type of water used in cooking them, see About Water, 519. Wash, unless the package states otherwise. Do not use soda, see 278. Soak in 3 to 4 times as much water as beans. Remove any that float or that ➤ may be moldy. If not preprocessed, the beans are usually soaked overnight. Bring them to a slow boil in the water in which they were soaked, unless it is bitter, as happens sometimes with soybeans. Reduce the heat and ➤ simmer. All beans should be cooked until tender. One test, provided you discard the beans you have tested, is to blow on a few of them in a spoon. If the skins burst, they are sufficiently cooked.

If you have forgotten to soak, a quick method to tenderize for cooking is to cover beans with cold water, bring to a boil and simmer for 2 minutes. After removing them from heat let them stand, tightly covered, 1 hour. Alternatively, blanching for 2 minutes is almost equivalent to 8 hours of soaking.

You may use preprocessed beans which require

no soaking. But remember that some nutrients have been lost in the preparation. Lentils and split peas are the better for soaking but do not require it. Remember, too, that 1 cup of dried beans, peas or lentils will expand to 2 to 2½ cups after cooking.

There are over 25 types of beans and peas available in our stores. They include broad, black or turtle, cranberry, scarlet runner, red, kidney, black-eyed peas or beans, edible soys, pinto, cowpeas or Mexican frijoles, chick-peas or garbanzos, flageolets—which are the French haricots, dried—and adzuki beans from which oriental bean paste is made. Each variety has, for the connoisseur, its own slightly different but satisfyingly hefty charm.

White beans, which the white man learned of from the Indians and then took sailing, became our navy beans. They are usually the toughest of the lot and take up to 3 hours simmering. Dried limas, after soaking for 8 hours, may cook almost as rapidly as fresh ones—in about ½ hour. Lentils take about 1½ hours to cook.

PURÉE OF DRIED LEGUMES

Please read About Dried Legumes, opposite.
Cook until tender:
Dried lentils, beans or peas, see above
You may add:
(A clove of garlic)
After draining the lentils, put them through a fine sieve, a purée strainer or ⅄ blender. Allow to every cup of purée:
1 tablespoon butter
¼ to ½ teaspoon salt
¼ teaspoon pepper or paprika or
⅛ teaspoon cloves
You may brown in the butter:
1 tablespoon flour
Whip the purée over a high heat. Serve in a mound, garnished with:
Sautéed Onions, 312, or chutney
Chopped parsley

HOPPING JOHN

Eaten on New Year's Day, this dish is supposed to bring good luck.
Bring to a boil in a large covered saucepan:
1¼ cups dry black-eyed peas
4 cups water
After boiling 2 minutes, remove pan from heat and let stand 1 hour. Add:
1½ cups chopped onions
½ teaspoon pepper
¼ teaspoon crushed dried red pepper
1 minced clove garlic
1 bay leaf
After bringing to a boil, cover and simmer 1 hour, stirring occasionally. Stir in:
8 oz. coarsely chopped salt pork
Simmer another hour, uncovered, stirring frequently. Remove the salt pork and the bay leaf. Slightly mash the pea mixture.
Season to taste
Serve with:
Boiled Rice, 206

REFRIED BEANS OR FRIJOLES REFRITOS

4 Servings

Melt in a heavy skillet:
4 tablespoons lard or vegetable oil
Add:
2 cups cooked pinto beans
If they are very dry you may add several tablespoons of:
(Hot stock)
While the beans are frying, stir to heat them through and then shape them, with the back of a wooden spoon, into a large cake. Cook until they are glazed enough to shake loose as one mass. Move the mass to one side of the pan and flip over in pancake style. Continue to turn and heat until a glazed loaf is formed. Top with cubes of:
Mild cheddar
Let the beans stay in the pan until the cheese is melted. Serve garnished with:
Shredded lettuce
on triangles of:
Tortillas

DRIED BEAN PATTIES

4 Servings

Grind and mash:
2 cups cooked dried beans: soy, lima, or navy
Add to them:
1 small chopped onion
¼ cup chopped parsley
Beat and add:
2 egg yolks
2 tablespoons cream or evaporated milk
¼ teaspoon pepper
1 teaspoon salt
Shape these ingredients into balls. Flatten them. Dip them in:
Flour
Chill the patties for 1 hour or more. Sauté slowly, until brown, in:
Butter, drippings or other fat
Serve with any:
Barbecue Sauce, 354

DRIED BEAN CASSEROLE

4 Servings

Preheat oven to 350°.
Combine:
1 cup cooked corn
1 cup cooked navy beans
1 cup lightly drained canned tomatoes
¾ teaspoon salt
¼ teaspoon paprika

½ teaspoon brown sugar
1 teaspoon grated onion

Place in a greased casserole. Sprinkle the top with:

Browned bread crumbs or grated peanuts

Bake covered about 45 minutes.

BAKED BEANS

Did you know that baked beans are as traditional in Sweden as they are in Boston? Please read About Dried Legumes, 286.

6 Servings

If quick-cooking or precooked beans are used, follow directions on the package. Otherwise, soak:

1½ cups dried beans

Cover them with water. Bring to a boil, then simmer slowly for ½ hour or more, until tender.
Preheat oven to 250°.
Drain the beans, reserving the cooking water, and add:

¼ cup chopped onion
2 tablespoons or more dark molasses
2 or 3 tablespoons catsup
1 tablespoon dry mustard
1 teaspoon salt
½ cup boiling bean water or beer
(½ teaspoon vinegar)
(1 teaspoon curry powder)
(1 tablespoon Worcestershire sauce)

Place beans in a greased baker, decorate them with:

¼ lb. sliced salt pork

and bake covered 6 to 9 hours. If they become dry, add a little:

Well-seasoned stock or reserved bean water

Uncover the beans for the last hour of cooking.

CANNED BAKED BEANS WITH FRUIT

6 Servings

Preheat oven to 300°.
Arrange:

2½ cups canned beans

in layers in a casserole with:

2 sliced apples
2 sliced oranges or 6 canned apricot halves or pineapple slices
(2 large onions, sliced)

Top with:

¼ lb. salt pork

Cover with:

¼ to ½ cup molasses or brown sugar

Bake 1 to 1½ hours, depending on how dry you like baked beans.

BOILED BEANS

5 Servings

Soak, 286, then drain:

1 lb. dried beans: kidney, navy, or marrowfat

Place them in a heavy saucepan. Cover with water. Add:

6 tablespoons butter
⅓ cup chopped onion
3 whole cloves
2 teaspoons salt
¼ teaspoon freshly ground pepper
¼ teaspoon dried thyme

Simmer the beans, covered, from 1 to 1½ hours. Stir from time to time. Add and cook for about 20 minutes longer:

1 cup dry red wine or stock

When the beans are tender, serve hot, garnished with:

Chopped chives or parsley

✪ We do not recommend the pressure cooking of dried beans because of the danger of frothing and blocking the vent.

▤ CAMPFIRE BEANS

Have ready at least 2 to 3 quarts of hot coals. Dig a hole deep enough and wide enough to hold a covered iron kettle, allowing about 4 extra inches to the depth of the hole. Get ready for cooking:

Baked Beans, left

Put half the coals in the bottom of the hole. Sink the covered kettle. Cover the lid with a large piece of foil to keep out dirt. Put the rest of the coals on the kettle lid. Now, fill in the rest of the hole with dirt and put at least 3 inches of dirt on top of the kettle. Don't dig in to peek for at least 4 hours.

CANNED KIDNEY BEANS AND TOMATOES

4 Large Servings

The mixture below may be used to stuff green peppers, 316.
Preheat oven to 350°.
Grease a baking dish. Have ready:

2½ cups canned red kidney beans
1 cup canned tomatoes or diluted tomato soup
¼ cup chopped onion
¼ lb. chopped bacon

Cover the bottom of the dish with a layer of beans. Sprinkle it with some of the bacon and onions. Repeat the process. Pour the tomatoes over the whole. Cover the top with:

Bread crumbs or crushed cornflakes

Dot with:

Butter

or sprinkle with:

Grated cheese

Bake the dish until the top is browned, about 30 minutes.

PINTO BEANS AND RICE

4 Servings

A combination relished in South American countries.
Soak, see 286:

½ cup pinto beans

in:

3 cups ham stock

Gently boil the beans in the stock until almost done. Add:

1/2 cup chopped cooked ham
1/2 cup rice
Cover and cook 20 to 30 minutes until the rice is tender.

LENTILS

I. **8 Servings**
Please read About Dried Legumes, 286.
Combine:
2 cups lentils
3 sprigs parsley or a celery rib with leaves
1/4 cup sliced onions
1/2 bay leaf
(A piece of fat corned beef, ham skin or bacon rind, tried-out pork fat or smoked sausage)
(2 cloves without heads)
(A slice of garlic)
Cover with:
4 cups water
Simmer covered about 1 1/2 hours. Stir occasionally and add boiling water if necessary. Drain the lentils and serve with:
Quick Tomato Sauce, 352
Or serve as a Purée, 280. If you omit the bacon or pork flavorings above, serve the lentils with:
Roast Pork, 477
Applesauce, 131

II. **4 Servings**
Wash but do not soak:
1 cup lentils
Sauté until golden brown:
1 minced onion
in:
1/4 cup olive oil
Add the lentils and let them absorb the oil. Pour over them:
3 1/2 cups boiling water
Cover the pan and simmer about 1 1/2 hours.
Season to taste
and serve hot or cold. If used for a salad, garnish with French dressing and hard-cooked egg slices.

LENTILS AND PRUNES

4 Servings
Please read About Dried Legumes, 286. Wash and prepare:
1 cup cooked lentils
Pit and mash:
1 cup cooked dried prunes, 125
Add them to the lentils with:
1/4 cup dry sherry
1 teaspoon salt
(Lemon juice and spices)
Stir over low heat until thoroughly heated.

ABOUT LIMA, BUTTER OR BROAD BEANS

The following cooked beans, whether canned, frozen, fresh or dry, may be substituted for one another in most recipes: Fordhooks or baby limas; Sieva types or fava, the European broad beans, shown on 285—which really taste more like peas. Both limas and favas have poisonous properties when eaten raw.

If you are hulling fresh limas, cut a thin strip along the inner edge of the pod to which the beans are attached. The beans will pop out easily. One pound in the pods will yield 2 servings.

For that famous combination called Succotash, see 301.

LIMA BEANS

I. **6 Servings**
Steam, 278, or cover:
1 quart shelled fresh lima beans
with:
1 inch boiling water
Add:
1 tablespoon butter
Simmer the beans for 15 minutes. Add:
1 teaspoon salt
Simmer covered until tender, about 20 minutes more, depending on the age of the beans. Add:
1 tablespoon butter or olive oil
1 1/2 tablespoons lemon juice
1 tablespoon chopped parsley, chives or dill
Or dress them with:
Warm cultured sour cream and freshly ground white pepper
Or serve them with:
Sautéed onions, creamed mushrooms, or a sprinkling of crisp bacon
⊗ Pressure cook fresh lima beans about 2 minutes at 15 lbs.

II. **6 Servings**
Place in a heavy saucepan:
1 quart fresh shelled lima beans
1 small clove garlic
2 tablespoons skinned, seeded, finely diced tomatoes
Barely cover with:
1 inch water, or half water and half olive oil
Cover and simmer about 15 minutes. Remove garlic. Add:
2 tablespoons butter
1/2 teaspoon salt
1 tablespoon chopped parsley
Continue cooking covered until beans are tender.

CHILI LIMA BEANS

6 Servings
Preheat oven to 300°.
Drain:
2 cups cooked lima beans
Add:
1/4 lb. salt pork cut into strips
1 large minced onion
1 tablespoon molasses
2 cups drained cooked tomatoes
1 tablespoon brown sugar

¼ teaspoon chili powder or pepper
1 teaspoon salt
Bake these ingredients in a greased casserole about 1 hour.

LIMA BEANS AND MUSHROOMS

6 Servings

Serve this with crisp bacon and grapefruit salad. Have ready:
2 cups freshly cooked or canned lima beans
Drain and reserve the bean liquor.
½ lb. Sautéed Mushrooms, 308
Place in a skillet:
1 tablespoon butter
Stir in:
2 tablespoons flour
Cook and stir these ingredients until they are well blended. Stir in slowly:
½ cup chicken stock, or stock and bean liquor
½ cup cream
Season to taste
Add the beans and mushrooms. Heat them.
Add before serving:
(1 tablespoon sherry)
(½ teaspoon chopped fresh basil
The dish may be served with:
Au Gratin II, 553
Place it under a broiler until the crumbs are brown.

BEETS

4 Servings

Cut the tops from:
1 lb. beets
leaving 2 inches of stem. If the tops are young, reserve and cook. See Beet Greens, 291. Wash the beets. Steam them, 278, or half cover with:
Boiling water
Lid the pot and cook gently until tender. Allow 30 to 40 minutes for young beets, as much as 2 hours for old beets. Add boiling water if needed. When the beets are done, cool them slightly and slip off the skins. If small, serve whole. If larger, slice.
Season to taste
Then either pour over them:
Melted butter
Chopped parsley
or serve the beets in:
White Sauce II, 341
seasoned with:
Mustard, curry powder, horseradish or ¼ cup sautéed onions
Or prepare:
White Sauce II, 341
using in place of the milk half orange juice and half water. Add:
3 tablespoons brown sugar
2 teaspoons grated orange rind
⊗ Pressure cook small beets 12 minutes, large beets 18 minutes at 15 lbs.

CASSEROLED BEETS

8 Servings

Preheat oven to 400°.
Pare, then slice or chop fine:
2 lb. medium-sized beets
Grease a 7-inch baking dish. Place the beets in it in layers. Season them with:
(2 tablespoons sugar)
¾ teaspoon salt
¼ teaspoon paprika
Dot them with:
3 tablespoons butter
Add:
1 tablespoon lemon juice or a sliver of fresh ginger
⅓ cup water
(1 tablespoon grated onion)
Cover the dish closely and bake the beets for 30 minutes or until tender. Stir twice.

SWEET-SOUR OR HARVARD BEETS

6 Servings

For a cold version of sweet-sour, see Pickled Beet Salad, 101.
Slice or dice:
3 cups freshly cooked or canned beets
Stir in a double boiler until smooth:
½ cup sugar
1 tablespoon cornstarch
½ teaspoon salt
2 whole cloves
½ cup mild cider vinegar or dry white wine
Cook and stir these ingredients until they are clear. Add the beets and place them ➤ over hot water for about 30 minutes. Just before serving, heat but do not boil the beets and add:
2 tablespoons butter
(1 tablespoon orange marmalade)

BOILED BEETS IN SOUR CREAM

6 Servings

Combine in a double boiler:
3 cups cooked or canned sliced beets
½ cup cultured sour cream
1 tablespoon prepared horseradish
1 tablespoon chopped chives
Salt as needed
(1 teaspoon grated onion)
Heat these ingredients ➤ over hot water.

SWEET-SOUR APPLE BEETS

4 Servings

Preheat oven to 325°.
Grease a casserole. Mix together and put into it:
2 cups chopped cooked beets
2 cups chopped tart apples
¼ to ½ cup thinly sliced onions
1½ teaspoons salt
A generous grating of nutmeg
If the apples are very tart, add:
(1 tablespoon sugar)

If they are bland:
(2 tablespoons lemon juice)
Dot with:
2 to 3 tablespoons butter
Cover and bake about 1 hour.

BAKED BEETS

I. Beets may be baked like potatoes—in their jackets.
Preheat oven to 325°.
Wash, taking care not to break the skin:
Beets
Trim the tops, leaving 2 inches of stem. Place them on a pan and bake until tender. Allow at least ½ hour for young beets and 1 hour for old. Slip off the skins. Season the beets with:
Salt and paprika
Serve them with:
Melted butter

II. Have ready a preheated 325° oven or ⊟ hot coals in the grill. Pare and slice:
Beets
Season to taste
and add:
Butter
to individual servings before wrapping each one in aluminum foil. Bake until tender.

BEET GREENS

I.
Beet greens may be prepared like Spinach, 326. If you are serving the greens with the beets, put the beets in a ring and serve the greens in the center, dressed with melted butter, and garnish with Horseradish Sauce, 343.

II. **4 Servings**
Heat in a frying pan:
2 tablespoons butter or cooking oil
Add and simmer until tender:
2 cups cooked chopped beet greens
1 teaspoon grated onion
¼ teaspoon salt
½ tablespoon prepared mustard
1 tablespoon grated horseradish
Remove from the heat and add:
½ cup cultured sour cream
✪ Pressure cook beet greens 3 minutes at 15 lbs.

BREADFRUIT

If ever your fate is that of Robinson Crusoe, remember that you can eat raw any breadfruit that has seeds. All seedless varieties must be cooked.

Breadfruit is 6 to 8 inches in diameter and greenish brown or yellow when ripe. The slightly fibrous meat is light yellow and sweet. You may remove the center core with its seed, if it has one, before or after cooking. Season and serve as you would sweet potato.

I. **6 Servings**
To boil, choose mature firm fruit, with rind still green in color. Core and dice:
4 cups peeled breadfruit
Drop into:
3 cups boiling water
and simmer covered about 1 hour, until tender. Drain, season and serve.

II. Preheat oven to 375°.
To bake, place in a baking pan:
1 unpeeled breadfruit
Have enough water in the pan to prevent burning. Bake until tender, about 1 hour, when the stem and core will pull out easily. Discard them. Cut fruit in half. Season with:
Salt and pepper or sugar and butter

III. To steam, skin and core:
1 breadfruit
Cut into halves or quarters and place the pieces in a pan to steam, covered, 278, 2 hours. Drain. Season with:
Butter
Salt and pepper
You may steam ¾-inch-thick breadfruit slices, roll them in flour and fry in deep fat until golden brown.

BREADFRUIT SEEDS

These are so close to chestnuts in flavor and texture that they may be substituted in any chestnut recipe.
Wash well:
1 lb. breadfruit seeds
Drop them into:
1 quart boiling water
3 tablespoons salt
Cook covered about 45 minutes. Drain and serve hot.

BROCCOLI

4 Servings

Choose heads that are all green. If yellow appears, the bloom is coming up and the broccoli is apt to be tough. Remove the large leaves and the tough parts of the stalks. Cut deep gashes in the bottoms of the stalks. It is worth remembering, in general, that broccoli leaves have a much higher vitamin A content than either the buds or the stalks and may be set aside and prepared like Greens, 305. If the broccoli is mature, cook it like Cabbage, 292. If it is young, steam it, 278, or place it upright so that only the stems are in water and the heads steam, see Asparagus, 283. Or, to retain excellent color, use a poaching paper, 151.
Soak in a cooking pot 10 minutes in cold water:
2 lb. broccoli
Drain well. Add:
1 inch boiling water or chicken stock
Cook the broccoli closely covered until barel[y] tender, 10 to 12 minutes. Drain and sprinkle w[ith]

½ teaspoon salt
Serve with:
Buttered crumbs, melted butter or lemon juice
to which add:
(¼ cup chopped salted almonds or walnuts)
or try serving it:
Au Gratin II, 553
or with one of the following sauces:
Hot Vinaigrette Sauce, 360
Hollandaise Sauce, 358
Cheese Sauce, 342
Onion Sauce, 344
Sour Cream Dressing, 367
Allemande Sauce, 345
⊗ Pressure cook broccoli about 2 minutes at 15 lbs.

QUICK CREAMED BROCCOLI

4 Servings

Preheat broiler.
Prepare:
2 cups cooked broccoli
Drain. Either cover it with:
Quick Canned Soup Sauce, 348
or dice the broccoli and fold it gently into the sauce. Place in a buttered casserole and sprinkle with:
Crushed cornflakes
(Grated Romano cheese)
Run it under the broiler until golden.

DEEP-FRIED BROCCOLI

Prepare:
Cooked broccoli
Drain before it is tender; dry and cool it. Cut it into quarters. Dip into:
Batter for Vegetables, 243
Fry the broccoli in deep fat, 147, heated to 375°, until golden brown.

BRUSSELS SPROUTS

6 Servings

These are among the most prevalent of winter cabbage types and all too often suffer from simplistic treatment.
If wilted, pull the outer leaves from:
1 lb. Brussels sprouts
Cut off the stems. Soak the sprouts for 10 minutes in cold water to which a little salt has been added. Drain. Cut crosswise gashes into the stem ends. Steam, 278, or drop them into a quantity of rapidly boiling:
Water
Reduce heat and simmer uncovered until they are barely tender, about 10 minutes. ➤ Do not overcook. Drain and serve with:
1 tablespoon melted butter
(Grated Parmesan cheese and chopped parsley, or 1 tablespoon lemon juice, or a grating of nutmeg)
or sauté in the butter:
1 tablespoon grated onion, or
2 tablespoons bread crumbs and
¼ teaspoon dried mustard
or serve with:
Quick Canned Soup Sauce III, 348
into which you may put at the last moment:
(½ cup finely chopped fresh celery)
or, serve with:
Sicilian Garnish for Vegetables, 366
or, best of all, with lots of:
Hollandaise Sauce, 358
⊗ Pressure cook Brussels sprouts about 3 minutes at 15 lbs.

BAKED BRUSSELS SPROUTS AND CHESTNUTS

6 Servings

Preheat oven to 350°.
Have ready:
2 cups cooked Brussels sprouts
½ lb. whole Boiled Chestnuts, 298
Butter a baking dish. Fill it with alternate layers of sprouts and chestnuts. Dot the layers with:
Butter
Season to taste
Moisten lightly with:
Stock
Cover with:
Au Gratin II, 553
Bake uncovered 20 to 30 minutes.

ABOUT CABBAGE

Cabbage types are as different as the uses of the word. In France, "mon petit chou" is a term of endearment; but it is highly politic never to call a German a "Kraut." The recipes below—which, you will note, are many, as befits a vegetable so available, versatile and inexpensive—are guaranteed to give a boost to international good will.

Shown from left to right is a range of cabbages: that firm old standby **head cabbage,** green or red; the soft-leaved crinkly **Savoy;** the clustered **cauliflower** and **broccoli;** columnar-fruiting **Brussels sprouts;** leafy **collards** and the similarly shaped **kale,** not illustrated; the stemmed **Swiss chard;** the elongated **bok-choi** and its better-known cousin **Chinese cabbage,** or **pe tsai.**

All cabbage types, if fresh, are a plentiful source of vitamin C, if you use the cooked cabbage water in sauces and soups. Choose firm cabbage heads and allow 1 lb. raw cabbage for 2 cups cooked. Old cabbage recipes called for long boiling, see 7. We recommend quartering a cabbage head and cooking it gently, uncovered, about 15 minutes; Savoy types about 20 minutes. Better still, shred the cabbage first, 277, and cook only 7 to 10 minutes respectively. You may prefer to stir-fry shredded cabbage, 279. And don't forget that cabbage lends itself to stuffing, as do the leaves, see Dolmas, 492. ⊗ Pressure cook 2- to 3-inch wedges of cabbage 3 to 5 minutes at 15 lbs.

I. **6 Servings**

Remove the outer leaves from:

A 2-lb. head cabbage

Drop it into a quantity of rapidly boiling:

Water

Reduce heat to a simmer. Cook ➤ uncovered until tender but still crisp. Drain. Add:

1 teaspoon salt

Place in a serving dish and pour over it:

¼ cup melted butter
(Bread crumbs or caraway, chilis, or poppy seeds, or a few drops lemon juice and 1 tablespoon chopped parsley)

or place the cooked cabbage in a baking dish and cover with:

Creole Sauce, 348, or Au Gratin III, 553

Heat through in a 350° oven.

II. **4 Servings**

All rules have exceptions, so try out this cabbage dish, which calls for little water. Cut into wedges:

A 2-lb. head cabbage

Trim off part of the core. Drop the wedges into:

½ inch boiling water

Cover and cook about 10 minutes. Drain well. Dress with:

1 cup White Sauce, 341

to which has been added:

½ teaspoon freshly grated nutmeg or
2 teaspoons prepared mustard or
½ cup shredded cheese

or use:

1 cup Horseradish Sauce, 343
or 1 cup creamed canned condensed soup
or Allemande Sauce, 345

III. **6 Servings**

This method makes young cabbage very delicate and is a great help in disguising the age of a mature one, but you may be losing some nutrients. Cut into very fine shreds:

3 cups cabbage

Drop gradually into:

¾ cup boiling milk

Boil for 2 minutes. Drain, and discard the milk. Drop the cabbage into hot:

White Sauce I, 341

Simmer 3 minutes longer and serve at once with:

(Broiled sausages)

CABBAGE, POTATOES AND HAM

4 Servings

Cook until nearly tender in water to cover:

A piece of smoked ham: picnic, butt, shank or cottage ham or roll

If using already cooked or leftover ham, bring the water just to a boil before adding:

1 large quartered cabbage
4 halved and pared medium-sized potatoes

Simmer covered about 20 to 25 minutes. Drain.

Season to taste

Serve from a large platter, garnished with:

Lemon wedges

BAKED CABBAGE

4 Servings

Preheat oven to 325°.
Put in a buttered baking dish:

3 cups shredded cabbage

Pour over it a mixture of:

¾ cup cream
2 well-beaten eggs
1 tablespoon sugar
½ teaspoon salt
½ teaspoon paprika
(½ cup chopped nuts or 1 cup seedless green grapes)

Sprinkle the top with:

Au Gratin III, 553

Bake about 45 minutes.

SAUTÉED CABBAGE

4 Servings

Preheat oven to 375°.
Shred:

A 2-lb. head cabbage

Sauté it lightly in:

Butter or bacon drippings

Season with:

½ teaspoon salt
¼ teaspoon paprika
Minced garlic or onion

Place the cabbage in a greased baking dish. Pour over it:

1 cup cultured sour cream

Bake about 20 minutes.

FRENCH-FRIED CABBAGE

➤ Please read About Deep-Fat Frying, 147.

Crisp in cold water:

Finely shredded cabbage

Drain and dry it. Dip in:

Milk

then in:

Flour

Rest it for 10 minutes.

Fry a small amount at a time in deep fat heated to 365°. Drain on paper toweling.

Season to taste

CABBAGE OR LETTUCE AND RICE DISH

6 Servings

This is a "gleaner's" dish to make on the trail of a salad luncheon, using outer leaves. Melt:

2 tablespoons bacon drippings
2 tablespoons butter or 3 tablespoons other fat

Stir in, cover and cook gently about 10 minutes:

3 cups finely shredded cabbage or lettuce
½ cup finely chopped onion
1 chopped green pepper, seeds and membrane removed

Stir these ingredients frequently. Stir in and cook until well heated:

1 cup cooked rice
2 cups tomato pulp or thick stewed tomatoes
Salt and pepper

This is enhanced by serving with it:

Crisp bacon or cold ham

CABBAGE OR SAVORY STRUDEL

12 to 14 Servings

Prepare:

Strudel Dough, 648

Steam blanch, 154, for 5 minutes:

4 lb. shredded cabbage

Press out any excess moisture and place on the dough with:

1½ cups cultured sour cream
(1 teaspoon caraway seed)
(4 chopped hard-cooked eggs)

To roll and bake the strudel, see 648.

SCALLOPED CABBAGE

8 Servings

Shred and prepare by any method for cooked cabbage:

A 4-lb. head cabbage

Drain it well. Prepare:

1½ cups White Sauce I, 341

Prepare:

2 tablespoons chopped seeded green pepper
2 tablespoons chopped pimientos

Sauté and mince:

(6 slices bacon)

Preheat oven to 375°.

Melt:

2 tablespoons bacon fat or butter

Toss lightly in this:

½ cup bread crumbs

Place layers of drained cabbage in a greased baking dish. Sprinkle with the minced bacon and peppers and:

1 cup or less shredded cheese

Cover with the cream sauce. Top with the bread crumbs. Bake about 10 minutes.

CABBAGE OR BRUSSELS SPROUTS WITH TOMATO

6 Servings

Preheat oven to 325°.

Cook for 5 minutes:

3 cups finely shredded cabbage or whole Brussels sprouts

Drain well. Have ready:

1 can condensed tomato soup: 10½ oz.

mixed with:

¼ teaspoon paprika
2 teaspoons brown sugar

Butter a baking dish. Place in it alternate layers of cabbage and the soup mixture. Sprinkle the top with:

Au Gratin III, 553

Bake the dish about ½ hour.

CABBAGE STUFFED WITH CORNED BEEF HASH

4 Servings

Trim the outer leaves and the stem from:

A 2-lb. head cabbage

Cook it uncovered in:

2 quarts boiling water

until barely tender and slightly crisp. Drain well. Scoop out the inside, leaving a 1½-inch shell. Place the shell in a greased ovenproof dish. Keep it hot. Chop the removed part. Add it to the contents of:

1 can minced corned beef hash: 16 oz.
¼ cup or more Sautéed Onions, 312
A pinch of thyme

Moisten it with a little:

Cream, evaporated milk or bacon drippings

Heat these ingredients. Fill the shell. Cover the top with:

Buttered cornflakes

The cabbage may be heated in a 425° oven about 10 minutes and served with:

A Quick Canned Soup Sauce, 348

CABBAGE STUFFED WITH HAM

6 Servings

Preheat oven to 325°.

Cook and scoop out as for the above recipe:

A firm 2-lb. head cabbage

Combine:

2 cups cooked ground or chopped ham
1 cup bread crumbs
3/4 cup grated American cheese
1/2 teaspoon dried mustard
Salt, depending on saltiness of ham
1/2 teaspoon paprika
A few grains cayenne

Place the cabbage on a rack in a greased ovenproof dish with 1/4 inch chicken stock in the bottom. Fill the hollowed cabbage with the ham mixture, cover closely, and bake about 30 minutes until heated through. Serve with:

Cheese Sauce, 342

RED CABBAGE

4 Servings

An old favorite to serve with game—cooked either as in this recipe or for a shorter time as in the next.
Pull off and discard the outer leaves from:

A head of red cabbage: about 2 lb.

Cut the head into sections. Remove the hard core, shred the cabbage and soak briefly in cold water. Cook over low heat until some fat is rendered out:

4 slices bacon, chopped, or use 3 tablespoons melted butter

Sauté in the fat until golden:

3 or 4 tablespoons finely chopped onion

Lift cabbage from the water, leaving it moist. Place it in an enameled iron casserole, cover, and let it simmer 10 minutes. Then add:

2 thinly sliced apples
(1/8 teaspoon caraway seeds)
1/4 teaspoon salt if bacon is used, or
1 teaspoon salt if unsalted butter is used
1/4 cup vinegar or 1/2 cup red wine or a mixture of 2 tablespoons honey and 2 tablespoons vinegar

Add the sautéed onion and stir these ingredients. Cover pan and simmer the cabbage very slowly about 1 hour. Add boiling water during cooking if necessary. If liquid is left when the cabbage is done, uncover the pot and cook gently until it is absorbed.

RED CABBAGE AND CHESTNUTS

6 Servings

A colorful dish when served in green peppers, see Stuffed Peppers, 316.
Have ready:

1 cup chopped Boiled Chestnuts I, 298

Shred until very fine:

1 small head red cabbage: 1 lb.

Place it in a bowl. Cover with:

Boiling water

Add:

1/4 cup dry white wine or vinegar

Let it soak for 15 minutes. Drain well. Heat in a saucepan:

2 1/2 tablespoons bacon drippings or butter

Add the cabbage. Sprinkle it lightly with:

Salt and pepper

Sauté the cabbage until it is limp. Cover and simmer for ten minutes. Sprinkle it with:

1 tablespoon flour

Add the chestnuts and:

1 cup water
1 1/2 tablespoons sugar
1/4 cup dry white wine or vinegar
1/3 cup seedless raisins
1 peeled, cored, thinly sliced apple

Simmer until well blended.

Season to taste

and serve hot.

CHINESE OR CELERY CABBAGE

6 to 8 Servings

Use this vegetable raw as a salad or prepare it by any of the recipes for cabbage; or stir-fry it as the Chinese do, 279. If young, it may require only a few minutes' cooking.
Steam, 278, or place a stalk of:

Whole or shredded celery cabbage

in:

1/2 cup boiling water

Cook until barely tender. Drain thoroughly. Add:

1/2 teaspoon salt

Serve with:

Melted butter or Hollandaise Sauce, 358

or season with:

1/2 teaspoon turmeric

and garnish with:

1/4 cup freshly grated coconut

SAUERKRAUT

6 Servings

The healthful quality of sauerkraut was recognized in 200 B.C. when, history records, it was doled out to the laborers working on that largest and longest of public works—the Great Wall of China. To retain its full flavor, sauerkraut should be served raw or barely heated through. Cooking makes kraut milder.
Melt in a skillet:

2 tablespoons butter or bacon drippings

Add and sauté until clear:

1/2 cup sliced onion or shallots

Add and sauté for about 5 minutes:

1 quart fresh or canned sauerkraut

Peel, grate and add:

1 medium-sized potato or tart apple

Cover the kraut with:

Boiling stock or water
(1/4 cup dry wine)

Cook uncovered 30 minutes; cover and bake in a 325° oven about 30 minutes longer. You may season with:

1 or 2 tablespoons brown sugar
1 teaspoon caraway or celery seed

Serve with:

Frankfurters, roast pork or spareribs

SAUERKRAUT AND TOMATO CASSEROLE

8 Servings

Preheat oven to 350°.
Drain well:

4 cups canned or fresh sauerkraut

Put through a strainer:

3½ cups canned tomatoes

Melt:

2 tablespoons bacon or other fat

Add, cook and stir about until golden:

1 small chopped onion

Add the strained tomatoes and:

¼ cup brown sugar
Freshly ground pepper

Add the drained sauerkraut. Place the mixture in a covered casserole and bake about 1 hour. ➤ Uncover the last 20 minutes of cooking. Garnish the top with:

Crumbled crisp bacon

CARDOONS

A vegetable of the thistle family, like artichoke—but the tender stalks and root are eaten, rather than the fruiting head. Often used for soups. Allow 1 lb. to 2 persons. Wash well. Discard outside stalks; trim the strings as for celery. Leave the heart whole. Cut into 3-inch pieces:

Tender stalks of cardoon

Parblanch, 154, in:

Court Bouillon Blanc, 525

for 5 to 7 minutes to prevent discoloration. Drain and rinse at once in cold water to remove bitterness. Simmer covered for about 1¼ hours or until tender in:

Boiling Acidulated Water, 520, to cover

Drain and serve with:

Cream, butter or White Sauce I, 341
Season to taste

Slice the heart and arrange it as a garnish.

CARROTS

Carrots continue to suffer from the jibes of people who like to dispense what H. W. Fowler called "worn-out humor." Their unsavory reputation is ill deserved. Look for the delicious "baby" carrots, now more and more beginning to appear at market. For jaded palates, combine carrots with onions, celery, green peppers, olives or mushrooms. Peel or scrape them, using the tool shown above: by far the most effective we have found for taking the hide off a coarse or bumpy vegetable. Or use them unpeeled, cut into slices or diced. If small, they may be served whole. If large, they may be more attractive if cut Parisienne, 278, or julienned as shown above left.
Wash and scrape:

Carrots

Steam, 278, or place them in a small quantity of:

Boiling water or stock

Cook covered until tender, 20 to 30 minutes. Allow a shorter cooking period for cut-up carrots. Let them absorb the water in which they are cooked. If necessary add a small quantity of boiling water. Serve with:

(Seasoned chopped parsley)
Bercy Butter, 350, or
White Sauce I, 341

or add to 2 cups cooked carrots:

1 or 2 tablespoons butter
1 to 2 tablespoons sugar, honey or orange marmalade
(¼ teaspoon cinnamon or nutmeg)

Simmer the carrots in this mixture until well glazed. Or use the glaze for:

Candied Sweet Potatoes, 325

⊗ Pressure cook carrots whole 4 minutes—sliced, 2½ minutes—at 15 lbs.

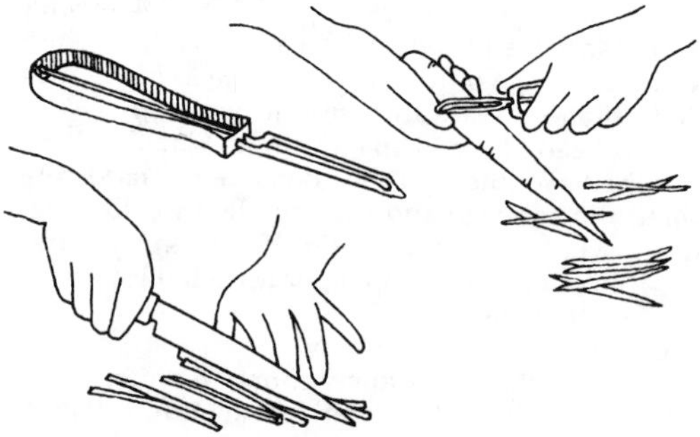

CARROTS IN BUNCHES

Steam or cook as in preceding recipe:

Small, shapely carrots in their jackets

Cool and skin them. Reheat by placing them over steam or by sautéing briefly in a little butter. Serve in 2 bunches—one at each end of a meat platter. Place at the blunt ends, to represent carrot greens:

Sprigs of parsley

Pour over them:

Melted butter seasoned with a dash of cloves

MASHED CARROTS OR CARROT RING

4 Servings

Cook as above:

2 bunches young carrots in their jackets

Skin the carrots and mash or rice them or use a ⅄ blender. Beat in:

1 tablespoon butter
Salt and pepper
1 tablespoon chopped parsley, dillweed or chives

Add:

½ cup sliced green grapes

and heap the carrots in a mound with:

Sprigs of parsley

Or, to make a ring, beat in:

1 to 2 egg yolks

Place in a greased mold and heat ➤ over hot water in a 350° oven until set, 20 to 30 minutes. Invert mold. Fill center of the ring with:

Green Peas, 314

CARROTS VICHY

4 Servings

Place in a saucepan:

2 cups thinly sliced scraped carrots
½ cup boiling water
2 tablespoons butter
1 tablespoon sugar
¼ teaspoon salt
(1 teaspoon lemon juice)

Cover the pan closely. To form a glaze with the butter and sugar, simmer the carrots until the water is absorbed. Serve sprinkled with:

Chopped parsley

BAKED CARROTS

4 Servings

Preheat oven to 350°.
Melt:

3 tablespoons butter

Sauté in it for about 3 minutes:

¼ cup chopped onion

Add and stir in:

2 cups shredded peeled carrots

Place these ingredients in a baking dish. Combine and pour over the carrots:

¾ teaspoon salt
1 tablespoon brown sugar
1 teaspoon dry mustard or ¼ teaspoon cloves
(A few drops hot pepper sauce)
½ cup stock

Cover the dish. Bake until tender.

STEAMED CAULIFLOWER

4 Servings

Mostly white, these delicately flavored clustered "curds"; but occasionally encountered in green, or even purple, with no very noticeable difference in taste. Select firm heads lacking in brownish discoloration, although such blemishes may be pared off with only cosmetic damage.
Cut off the tough end of the stem, removing the leaves, and soak in cold salted water, head down, for 10 minutes:

A 2-lb. cauliflower

Drain it. You may break it into florets. Cut deep gashes into the stalks. Steam, 278, or place uncovered, head up, in about 1 inch of:

Boiling water or milk

The milk will help keep it white, as will:

(Juice of ½ lemon)

Reduce the heat to a simmer and cook ➤ partially covered, until the stalk is barely tender—about 12 minutes. Drain well and place in a serving dish. For **Cauliflower Polonaise,** cover it with:

Brown Buttered Bread Crumbs, 551
(Chopped nuts sautéed in butter)

Or cover with:

Hollandaise Sauce, 358
Quick White Sauce, 342 (with crumbled bacon or chopped ham)
Creole Sauce, 348
Lemon Butter, 350

⊗ Pressure cook whole cauliflower about 7 minutes at 15 lbs.

SAUTÉED CAULIFLOWER

4 Servings

Cook as above:

Boiled or steamed cauliflower

Break it into florets. Heat:

2 tablespoons butter
2 tablespoons vegetable oil

Add and cook for 2 minutes:

½ clove garlic or 2 teaspoons grated onion

Remove the garlic. Sauté the florets in the fat until they are well coated. Cover and cook for several minutes. Season with:

Salt and paprika
A fresh grating of nutmeg

or serve the cauliflower with:

Chopped parsley or chives

DEEP-FRIED CAULIFLOWER

➤ Please read About Deep-Fat Frying, 147.
Drain:

Cooked cauliflower

Separate the florets.
Dip each section of cauliflower into:

Fritter Batter for Vegetables, 243

Drain, rest 10 minutes and deep fry in fat heated to 365° until golden. Serve with:

Hollandaise Sauce, 358, or
Sour Cream Dressing, 367

CAULIFLOWER AND MUSHROOMS IN CHEESE SAUCE

6 Servings

Cook, see Steamed Cauliflower, above:

A 3-lb. cauliflower

Drain well and put it in a greased baking dish. Keep it hot. Melt in a skillet:

2 tablespoons butter

Sauté in it for 2 minutes:

½ lb. mushrooms

Cook:

1½ cups White Sauce I, 341

Stir into the hot sauce ➤ off the heat:

¾ cup shredded cheese

When the cheese is melted, add the sautéed mushrooms and pour the sauce over the cauliflower. Serve at once.

CELERY

4 Servings

The unbleached green variety—Pascal, so-called—is growing in popularity and, like all unbleached vegetables, has a higher vitamin content than its paler counterpart. The golden leafage, usually discarded, is well worth reserving: chopped fine, it makes a delicate component of an Omelet aux Fines Herbes, 572; dried carefully in a slow oven and rubbed through a sieve, it makes a powder for flavoring sauces. For Celery Root, or Celeriac, see below.

Wash:

2 cups chopped celery

Steam, 278, or drop it gradually into:

½ inch boiling water

Cook covered until tender, about 8 minutes, allowing it to absorb the water. Should there be any liquid, drain the celery and reserve the liquid for the sauce. Brown the celery in:

Seasoned butter

Or drop the celery into:

1 cup White Sauce I, 341, made with cream and celery liquor

Season the sauce with:

Curry powder, or celery, dill or sunflower seeds, or freshly grated nutmeg, or herbs, 579

⊗ Pressure cook celery 1½ minutes at 15 lbs.

BRAISED OR GLAZED CELERY OR ENDIVE

4 Servings

Not only celery and Belgian endive but Boston lettuce is choice prepared in this way. Do blanch the endive and lettuce briefly first.

Wash and trim:

1½ lb. celery

Cut into 3- to 4-inch lengths. Arrange them attractively in the bottom of a ➤ flameproof glass or enamel casserole. Pour over them:

3 tablespoons lemon juice
½ cup chicken or veal stock
½ teaspoon salt
1 tablespoon sugar
2 tablespoons butter

Bring the liquid to a boil, then cover with a poaching paper, 151. Now, cover the casserole with a lid and simmer for about 25 minutes or until tender. Place the celery on a heated serving dish and keep warm. Reduce the pan liquid to about ½ cup. Add:

1 tablespoon butter or Beurre Manié, 340

Pour this glaze over the celery.

CELERY ROOT OR CELERIAC

4 Servings

This knobby tough root, also called **celeri-rave,** is often woody if too old, but can be one of the most subtly flavored of vegetables, see illustration in the chapter heading on 276. It is difficult to peel, so cut it into slices first, as shown on page 277. To make the flavor more delicate for use in salads and hors d'oeuvre, and to keep it white, blanch 1 to 2 minutes after peeling by using lemon juice in the water.

Scrub well and peel:

1½ lb. celery root

Steam, 278, or cover with:

Boiling water

Simmer uncovered until tender—about 25 minutes. Drain. Cover with:

1½ cups White Sauce II, 341

or serve with:

Au Gratin III, 553

⊗ Pressure cook about 5 minutes at 15 lbs.

SWISS CHARD

Prepare:

Chard

by washing carefully and removing the midribs. Cook the leaves by any recipe for Spinach, 326. Cook the ribs as for Asparagus, 283.

CHAYOTES

4 Servings

This pear-shaped vegetable belongs to the gourd family. Treat chayotes much as you would any squash, 328, after removing the long flattish central seed. They may be served with meats and seafoods and may even be used, like pumpkin, in desserts.

Pare and cut crosswise into ¾-inch slices:

1 lb. chayotes

Drop into:

Boiling water to cover

Reduce the heat at once and simmer 45 minutes, if young, or as long as 1 hour if mature. Drain. Dress with:

Butter, salt and pepper, or Black Butter, 350, Amandine, 553, or a cream sauce and grated cheese

Chayotes are delicious if halved and steamed and stuffed with:

Mushrooms and cheese

⊗ Pressure cook whole chayotes at 15 pounds 6 to 8 minutes; if diced, 2 minutes.

BOILED CHESTNUTS

I. **4 Servings**

To prepare as a vegetable, shell and skin, 563:

1 lb. chestnuts

or ½ lb. shelled dried chestnuts that have been soaked overnight. Use this water. Drop the chestnuts into:

Boiling water or milk

To which add:

3 chopped ribs celery
1 small peeled chopped onion
(1 tablespoon vinegar)
(⅛ teaspoon anise)

Cook until tender. Drain well. Mash with:

1 tablespoon butter
Season to taste

Add:

2 or more tablespoons warm cream

Beat the chestnuts until fluffy. Keep them hot over hot water.

II. To prepare as a compote, shell, skin, cook as above:

1 lb. chestnuts

in:

Boiling water or milk

Drain. Save the liquid and add enough to make about 2 cups. Prepare a syrup by adding:

2 cups sugar
Juice and grated rind of 2 lemons
Juice and grated rind of 1 orange
4 whole cloves
1 stick cinnamon
1/4 teaspoon ground ginger
(1/2 cup raisins)
(1/2 cup chopped nuts)

Simmer the syrup gently until slightly reduced, add chestnuts and serve hot or chilled.

BAKED CHESTNUTS

6 Servings

Prepare and cook:

3 cups chestnuts, above

Preheat oven to 325°.

Grease a baking dish. Place the drained whole chestnuts in it. Pour over them:

1 3/4 cups chicken stock
(2 tablespoons or more brown sugar)

Cover and bake about 3 hours. Pour off the stock and reserve. Melt:

2 tablespoons butter

Stir in until blended:

1 tablespoon flour

Stir the stock in slowly. When the sauce is smooth and boiling, pour it over the chestnuts and serve.

STEAMED CHESTNUTS

Our French friend Max Lachaux describes with contagious nostalgia a time-consuming method of preparing chestnuts that was used in his childhood home and which is traditional in his native Périgord.

Authenticity demands three pieces of equipment. First, the écuradour, a kind of wooden shears as illustrated. This would make a good project for a whittling boy. Each arm is about 16 inches in length and 1 1/2 inches square; the arms are attached at the center with a nut, like scissors. The so-called blades have hand-carved sawtoothing on all edges for removing the inner skins of the chestnuts. Second, the oule, seen in the drawing opposite, a 10- to 20-quart round-bottomed three-legged cast-iron pot with a narrower neck, made especially for the chestnut-steaming process. Third, a sieve made of wire mesh on a wooden frame with sides a few inches high, the mesh slightly finer than the chestnut size.

Prepare by removing the outer shells with a knife. Place chestnuts in the oule after soaking them in water a few moments, and immediately place the oule over hot coals and leave it for about 10 minutes. The inner skin softens, swells and separates from the nuts. Take the oule from the fire and, without removing the chestnuts, "scissor" them in all directions with the écuradour. The nuts are not cooked and remain whole as the teeth of the shears pull off the skin. When almost all of it has come off, the chestnuts are placed in the sieve and the bits of skin pass through. Wash the chestnuts, removing any remaining pieces of skin.

Line the oule with fig leaves and raves—a long French variety of turnip. Small potatoes may be substituted but are not as good. Place the wet chestnuts in the oule, adding no more water. Cover with muslin cloth in layers forming a thickness of at least an inch at the neck of the oule. Place the oule on hot fire until steam begins to escape from underneath the lid. Then move to low heat and cook slowly and continuously until no more steam appears.

The chestnuts must be eaten very hot and may be served with sweet cider or new white wine. Those at the bottom of the pot have been roasted—a children's favorite, to be eaten as an after-school snack. The turnips or potatoes are perfumed with absorbed fragrances.

If you do not have an oule and if you have not found in your grandmother's attic a three-legged iron pot similar to that shown in the illustration on 167, try a Dutch oven elevated on bricks. Have fun—we did—and bon appétit!

CHICORY

Witloof chicory, the **French** or **Belgian endive,** may be prepared by any recipe for cooked lettuce or celery. Differentiate it from the sunburst-centered, highly ruffled or frisée endive, or chicory, 93, common in our stores and usually used raw, and the wild chicory, 305.

ABOUT CORN

One of the comic inventions of the late Ed Wynn was a corn-on-the-cob-eating machine, put together along the lines of a typewriter, with the ear of corn itself constituting the carriage. In truth, any device which speeds sweet corn to the "chomping" stage is to be encouraged, because its "bouquet," like that of a newly plucked ripe tomato, is fleeting.

The corn we usually find in our markets comes from two progenitors: "Country Gentleman" and "Golden Bantam"—white and yellow, respectively —the latter hybrids having a more robust flavor. But many years ago, when we were very young, we were captivated by the great diversity of color we encountered in the delicious "Indian corn" of northern Minnesota: kernels in red, brown, blue and purple.

When cooked corn is called for in the following recipes, it can be canned, fresh cooked or frozen. Try cutting fresh corn for puddings and fritters by scraping with the tool shown enlarged on the right below—and notice the superior results this kind of preparation gives. If you must use a knife

to cut off the kernels, do not cut deeply. Then press down along the rows with the dull side of the knife to retrieve the richly flavored juice and heart of the kernel. ➤ To avoid toughness in cooking corn, add salt when the cooking period is half over.

If ⊗ pressure cooking ✱ frozen corn on the cob ➤ be sure to thaw partially before cooking about 4 minutes at 15 lbs.

CORN ON THE COB

I. Remove the husks and silk from:

Ears of fresh corn

Steam, 278, or drop them, ear by ear, so as not to disturb the boiling, into:

Boiling water to cover

Boil the corn rapidly until tender, from 3 to 5 minutes, depending on maturity. Drain and serve with:

Butter
Salt
Freshly ground pepper

II. Remove the husks and silk from:

Very young freshly picked corn

In a large kettle which you can cover tightly, bring to a rolling boil:

Enough water to cover corn generously

Slip the ears into the water one by one. Cover the kettle and remove from the heat at once. Allow the corn to remain in the hot water for about 5 minutes or until tender. Drain and serve at once.

FRESH CORN CUT FROM THE COB

Cut or grate from the cob:

Fresh corn

Simmer it covered for several minutes, until tender, in its own juice and a little:

Butter

Season with:

Salt and white pepper

Moisten with:

Milk or cream

You may devil it by adding:

Worcestershire sauce
Minced garlic

⊟ GRILLED OR ROASTED CORN

Preheat oven to 475° or have ready a generous bed of coals.

I. Pull down husk to remove silk and any damaged portions of the ear on:

Young roasting corn

Replace the husk. Run into the husk as much:

Water

as it will hold. Drain and close the husk by twisting it. Put the ears on a rack over the hot coals or in the preheated oven and bake 20 to 25 minutes. Husk before serving.

II. Strip the husk and silk from:

Roasting ears

Remove any damaged portions. Rub with:

Butter
Salt and white pepper

Wrap in foil and roast 20 to 30 minutes, depending on the size of the ears.

FRESH CORN PUDDING COCKAIGNE

4 Servings

This is a luscious dish, but it is a little difficult to give an exact recipe for it because the corn differs with the season. Early on, should the corn be watery, it is sometimes necessary to add a beaten egg. Later more cream may be required—up to 1 cup. When the corn mixture is right, it looks, after scraping, like thick curdled cream.

Preheat oven to 325°.

Scrape as shown left, but ➤ do not cut:

2 cups fresh corn

Add:

(1 teaspoon sugar)
½ to ¾ cup cream
Salt and white pepper

Place these ingredients in a generously buttered flat baking dish. Dot the top with:

Butter

Bake the pudding for about 1 hour. ✱ This dish may be frozen, 828.

SOUFFLÉED CORN PUDDING

5 Servings

Sturdy and satisfying.
Drain:
1 No. 2 can kernel corn: 2½ cups
Reserve the liquid. Melt:
2 tablespoons butter
Stir in until blended:
2 tablespoons flour
Combine and stir in slowly:
The corn liquid and enough cream to make 1 cup
When the sauce is smooth and hot, stir in the drained corn and:
¼ cup chopped seeded green pepper with membrane removed
1 chopped pimiento
When this mixture reaches a boil ➤ reduce heat.
Beat well:
2 egg yolks
Pour part of the corn mixture over them off the heat. Beat it and return to corn mixture. Stir and cook for several minutes ➤ over very low heat to let the yolks thicken slightly.
Add:
¾ teaspoon salt
¼ teaspoon paprika
(¼ cup minced ham or crumbled cooked bacon)
Preheat oven to 350°.
Place on a platter and whip ➤ until stiff but not dry:
2 egg whites
Fold them lightly into the corn mixture.
Bake the pudding in a baking dish prepared as for a soufflé baker, 229, for about 30 minutes.

SCALLOPED CORN

4 Servings

Preheat oven to 325°.
Combine:
2 cups uncooked corn, scraped or cut from the ear
2 beaten eggs
½ teaspoon salt
(¼ cup minced seeded green peppers with membrane removed, or chopped stuffed green olives)
¾ cup cream
Place in a baking dish prepared as for a soufflé baker, 229. Sprinkle with:
Au Gratin II, 553
Bake the corn for about ½ hour.

SUCCOTASH

4 Servings

This is entirely acceptable made with canned or frozen vegetables.
Combine, then heat in a double boiler ➤ over—not in—boiling water:
1 cup cooked fresh corn
1 cup cooked fresh lima or finely shredded green beans
2 tablespoons butter
½ teaspoon salt
⅛ teaspoon paprika
Chopped parsley

CORN CREOLE

4 Servings

Seed, remove membranes and chop:
¼ cup green pepper
Skin and chop:
1 small onion
Melt:
2 tablespoons butter
Sauté the vegetables in the butter until translucent. Heat in the top of a double boiler:
1 cup drained canned or fresh cooked tomatoes
Add the sautéed vegetables and:
½ teaspoon salt
⅛ teaspoon pepper
A few grains cayenne
Cook and stir these ingredients ➤ over—not in—boiling water about 5 minutes. Add:
⅔ cup cooked corn
Heat 2 minutes longer. Stir in until melted:
1⅓ cups shredded cheese

CORN FRITTERS WITH FRESH CORN

4 Servings

The author of the following account graciously permitted us to use it when we told him how much it pleased us.

"When I was a child, one of eight, my father frequently promised us a marvelous treat. He, being an amateur arboriculturist, would tell us of a fritter tree he was going to plant on the banks of a small lake filled with molasses, maple syrup or honey, to be located in our backyard. When one of us children felt the urge for this most delectable repast, all we had to do was to shake the tree, the fritters would drop into the lake, and we could fish them out and eat fritters to our hearts' content.

"Mother was a good cook and she duly developed this fabulous fritter." The following is, we hope, a faithful transcription of her recipe.
Scrape:
2½ cups fresh corn
Add:
1 well-beaten egg yolk
(2 teaspoons flour)
¼ teaspoon salt
Whip until ➤ stiff but not dry:
1 egg white
Fold the corn mixture into it. Sauté as for pancakes, 235, until light brown and fluffy. Do not overcook.

CORN OYSTERS

About Sixteen 1½-Inch Fritters

For best results, make the batter immediately before using it. Have ready:

1 cup freshly scraped corn or drained canned cream-style corn

Add:

2 well-beaten eggs
6 tablespoons flour
½ teaspoon double-acting baking powder
¼ teaspoon salt
⅛ teaspoon nutmeg

Melt in a small skillet:

3 tablespoons butter

When it has reached the point of fragrance, add a tablespoon of batter at a time. Let the bottom of the cakes brown, reverse them and brown the other side. Serve at once with:

Quick Creole Sauce, 352, or maple syrup

ABOUT CUCUMBERS

How often the Japanese draw these highly decorative plants! And from the opposite corner of Asia the prophet Isaiah lamented their absence in bitter weather: "desolate as . . . a cottage cucumber garden abandoned in winter."

Among the varieties of this almost endlessly fascinating fruit are a very long virtually seedless Japanese type, and the round, yellowish "apple cucumbers," which are somewhat mellower to the taste than the greenskins.

A cucumber fit for use is rigid. It should have a lustrous skin—but do not be misled by the heavy, waxy, man-applied finish on some of those now in the markets. If the skin is not waxed, it is edible. Some people who are allergic to cucumbers find they can enjoy them if they are seeded and cooked. Use any recipe for summer squash or one of the following.

MULLED CUCUMBERS

I. **4 Servings**

Pare, seed and cut into strips:

2 cups cucumbers

Drop them into:

1½ cups boiling water

➤ Simmer until nearly tender—but no longer, so as to retain their color. Drain well. While still in the pan, season the cucumbers with:

Salt and white pepper
Freshly grated nutmeg or 1 teaspoon chopped fresh herbs or dill or celery seeds

and stir in:

2 tablespoons heavy cream

Reheat briefly and serve at once.

II. Prepare:

Mulled Cucumbers I, above

Drain and serve with:

Lemon Butter, 350, with capers; or a tomato sauce with basil; or Soubise or Onion Sauce, 344

CUCUMBER ANCHOVY CASSEROLE

4 Servings

Preheat oven to 400°.
Prepare:

2 cups Mulled Cucumbers, above

Drain well. Prepare:

1 cup White Sauce, 341

seasoned with:

1 tablespoon anchovy paste

Place the vegetable in a baking dish. Pour the hot sauce over it. Cover with:

Au Gratin III, 553

Bake the dish until the top is brown.

CUCUMBER CREOLE CASSEROLE

6 Servings

Pare and seed:

3 cups cucumbers

Cut them into ¼-inch slices. Combine with half the recipe for:

Creole Sauce, 348

Preheat oven to 375°.
Place in the bottom of a greased ovenproof dish:

½ cup dry bread crumbs

Add the cucumbers. Pour the sauce over them. Cover with:

Au Gratin I, 552

Bake about 35 minutes.

ABOUT EGGPLANT OR AUBERGINE

These vegetables, lovely when stuffed, also make beautiful individual servings with their green caps against the polished purple of the cases. We have tried alternating them with green and red stuffed peppers for an effective buffet platter.

There are several important things to keep in mind in cooking eggplant. It may become very watery. Get rid of excess moisture by salting and draining on a rack before using it in unthickened recipes; or stack the slices, cover with a plate, place a heavy weight on top and let stand until moisture is squeezed out. ➤ Eggplant discolors quickly when cut and should be sprinkled or rubbed with lemon juice. Also, because of discoloration ➤ cook in pottery, enamel, glass or stainless steel. One pound of eggplant equals 3 cups diced.

Eggplant has a blotterlike capacity for oil or butter, well pointed up by this Near East tale. The imam or priest was so fetched by the eggplant dish his fiancée prepared that he asked that her dowry be the oil in which to cook it. Great Ali Baba jars of oil were stored in their new home. The first night the eggplant was delicious, also the second; but on the third night his favorite dish was not waiting for him. "Alas," said the wife, "the first two nights have exhausted the supply of oil." And then the priest fainted! If the newly wedded housewife had taken the precaution to keep the oil well heated, it would have lasted a great deal longer.

Imam Baaldi, the classic dish which caused the priest's downfall and carries his name, calls for halved eggplant, stuffed, soaked in oil and casseroled covered for 1½ hours.

EGGPLANT SLICES

After frying, 279, sautéing, 149, or baking, eggplant slices can be used in the following ways.

I. Top with:
Creamed Spinach, 327
Sprinkle with:
Grated Gruyère cheese
and run under broiler.

II. Put in a casserole and cover with:
Creole Sauce, 348, and
Au Gratin I, 552
Run under broiler.

III. Place on each slice:
A slice of Tomato Provençale, 332

IV. Place on eggplant slice:
A grilled tomato slice
Cover with:
A poached egg and Cheese Sauce, 342

V. Place on an eggplant slice:
Creamed ham or hash

BAKED EGGPLANT SLICES

4 Servings

Preheat oven to 400°.
Pare:
A 1½- to 2-lb. eggplant
Cut it crosswise into slices ½ inch thick. Spread the slices on both sides with a mixture of:
Soft butter or vegetable oil
seasoned with:
Salt and pepper
Grated onion or lemon juice
Place on a baking sheet and bake until tender, about 12 minutes, turning once. Garnish with:
Chopped parsley or chervil

BAKED EGGPLANT HALVES

4 Servings

Preheat oven to 325°.
Wash, dry, then cut into halves lengthwise:
A 2-lb. eggplant
Crisscross the flat cut sides with gashes about 1 inch deep. Sauté the halves cut side down about 10 minutes in:
3 tablespoons hot olive oil
Set them skin side down in a shallow ovenproof dish. Make a paste by mashing together until well blended:
8 minced anchovy fillets
2 chopped cloves garlic
¼ cup bread crumbs
2 tablespoons beef stock
⅛ teaspoon freshly ground pepper
Spread this over the tops of the eggplant. Sprinkle them with:
Au Gratin II or III, 553
Bake about 20 minutes.

SCALLOPED EGGPLANT

4 Servings

Pare and cut into dice:
A 1½- to 2-lb. eggplant
Simmer it until tender in:
½ cup boiling water
Drain well. Sprinkle with:
(2 tablespoons chopped parsley)
Chop until very fine:
1 small onion
Melt:
1 tablespoon butter
Sauté the onion in this until it is golden. Add it to the eggplant with:
½ cup milk
(2 well-beaten eggs)
Melt:
3 tablespoons butter
Stir into it, until the butter is absorbed:
¾ cup cracker crumbs or ½ cup bread crumbs
Preheat oven to 375°.
Place layers of eggplant and layers of crumbs in a baking dish. Season them, if the crackers are unsalted, with:
¼ teaspoon salt
¼ teaspoon paprika
Wind up with a top layer of crumbs. Place on it:
(Thin slices of cheese or grated cheese)
Bake the eggplant for ½ hour. Garnish with:
Crisp crumbled bacon or
thin strips of pepperoni

DEEP-FRIED EGGPLANT SLICES

4 Servings

➤ Please read About Deep-Fat-Fried Vegetables, 279.
Pare and cut into ½-inch slices or sticks:
An eggplant
Dip them in:
Fritter Batter for Vegetables, 243
Fry them in deep fat heated to 365° until golden. Drain on paper toweling and serve after adding:
Salt

SAUTÉED EGGPLANT SLICES

4 Servings

Peel and cut into ½-inch slices, cubes or sticks:
A 1½- to 2-lb. eggplant
Dip the pieces in:
Milk
Dredge them in:
Seasoned flour, crumbs or cornmeal
For easier handling, place slices on a rack to dry for 15 minutes before cooking. Melt in a skillet:
Butter or oil

Sauté the pieces until tender. Serve while very hot with:

Chopped parsley or tarragon
A sliced lemon or a tomato sauce,
or a garnish of green pepper strips and
pitted black olives

EGGPLANT CASSEROLE OR RATATOUILLE PROVENÇALE

8 Servings

This ends up looking in color like a very successful Braque still-life.

Peel, slice and salt to get rid of excess moisture, 302:

2½ cups diced eggplant

Put in a deep skillet:

⅓ cup olive oil

Sauté until golden:

¾ cup thinly sliced onions
2 cloves garlic

Add:

½ cup whole pitted black olives
4 julienned green peppers, seeds and membrane removed
3 cups zucchini in ½-inch slices
2 cups skinned, seeded, quartered tomatoes

Add the drained eggplant. Sprinkle the mixture with:

Olive oil

Add:

(½ teaspoon oregano or 2 teaspoons chopped fresh basil)

Simmer covered over very low heat about 45 minutes. ➤ Uncover and continue to heat 15 minutes longer to reduce the amount of liquid. Add:

Salt and a grating of fresh pepper

Serve hot or cold with:

Cultured sour cream

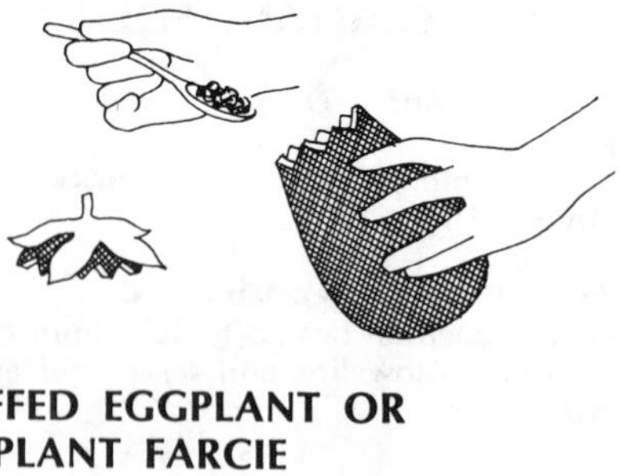

STUFFED EGGPLANT OR EGGPLANT FARCIE

4 Servings

Eggplant makes a wonderful "background" food due to its color and shape. Cut eggplant just under and following the lines of the leafy green cap, which then forms an attractive lid. Large cases may be filled with any desired combination of food, to which the cooked eggplant pulp is added. Smaller ones may be served individually.

Cut as described:

A 2-lb. eggplant

Scoop out the pulp, leaving a ½-inch shell. Drop the pulp into a small quantity of boiling water or stock and cook until tender. Drain well and mash it. Combine with:

Farce, 374, of chopped or
ground cooked meat: lamb or ham
or rice and shrimp

Preheat oven to 400°.

Fill the shell. Cover with the cap. Bake in a small amount of water until filling is heated.

STUFFED EGGPLANT CREOLE

4 Servings

Cut into halves:

A small eggplant

Scoop out the pulp and chop it. Leave a shell ½ inch thick. Mince and heat in a skillet:

2 strips bacon

Add to it and sauté until the bacon is cooked:

¼ cup minced onion
¼ cup minced seeded green pepper with membrane removed

Add the eggplant pulp and:

2 cups drained canned tomatoes
¼ cup diced celery

Simmer these ingredients until the eggplant is tender. Beat them with a fork until well blended. Thicken with:

⅓ cup bread crumbs

Season with:

Salt and freshly ground pepper

Add:

½ cup Sautéed Mushrooms, 308

Preheat oven to 350°.

Fill the eggplant shells with the mixture. Cover the tops with:

Au Gratin III, 553

Place the eggplant on a rack in a pan with very little water and bake until thoroughly heated, about 15 minutes.

ABOUT FENNEL OR FINOCCHIO

The anise-flavored root and stalks of the Florence fennel, illustrated in the chapter heading on 276, which can be found in season at Italian markets, may be eaten raw as a choice hors d'oeuvre, used as a substitute for celery in stuffings, or braised as for celery, 298. The leaves can also be used discreetly for seasoning, but the usual plant for this purpose is *Foeniculum vulgare*, 581.

FERN SHOOTS

Since we are now all dedicated environmentalists, we remind you that if fern clumps occur in any but very plentiful communities they should not be harvested at all. We might add that many people are allergic to ferns, and that ostrich fern fiddleheads are least likely to irritate.

In the spring, cut ferns while the shoots are still curled in crosiers. Wash and tie in bundles of 6 to 8 fronds. Stand upright and steam as for Asparagus, 283, about 20 minutes or until just tender. Serve with:

Hollandaise Sauce, 358

Fiddleheads may also be deep-fat-fried in a batter, 242.

ABOUT CULTIVATED GREENS

Greens such as turnips, mustard, kale, collards, corn salad, comfrey and borage are seldom creamed. However, there is no reason why they should not be. The old-fashioned custom is to cook them to death, for an hour or more, with bacon, salt pork or ham hocks and to serve them with vinegar. We prefer to retain color and nutrients by the following methods. To reduce cooking time—when the green is unusually large and mature—strip the leafage from the midrib, which can then be cooked separately, much like Asparagus, 283. Collard greens, incidentally, are sweetest after the frost has hit them.

I. Prepare greens by washing carefully to remove grit and cut out any blemished areas or tough stems. Simmer for 2 hours in water to cover:

A 1-lb. piece side meat: salt pork or cottage ham

Add:

2 to 3 lb. greens

and simmer 25 to 40 minutes, until just tender.

II. If the greens are very young, prepare as for:

Panned Spinach, 327

allowing about 10 minutes cooking time.

ABOUT WILD GREENS, SHOOTS, ROOTS, SEEDS AND BERRIES

If you are in earnest about collecting edible wild foods, try to find a local expert. If such a person is not available, the best advice comes from the *U.S. Armed Services Survival Manuals* and *Poisonous Plants of the United States and Canada* by John M. Kingsbury.

Many wild greens harbor large concentrations of oxalates, nitrates and other as yet unidentified but definitely toxic elements. Such irritants can be lessened by parboiling before final cooking. Generally, avoid all plants with milky or colored juices; all unknown plants with white or red berries; all unknown seeds, especially those which are three-angled or three-lobed; and any bulbs that do not smell like onion. Sample all wild greens sparingly, especially if your diet has been deficient. Remember, too, that all plants have seasons when they are succulent and periods when they are inedible; and that they all need careful washing to remove grit.

COOKING WILD GREENS

Although many of them have been found to contain toxins, the greens listed below are those most popularly collected. Prepare as for Spinach, 326: young chickweeds, lamb's quarters, purslane, yellow rocket cress, mustards, miner's lettuce, tiny plantains, bladder campion, cleavers, cheese mallows, shepherd's purse, sheep sorrel, spiderwort and nettles. All these will cook down by at least half. Nettles, which have to be handled before cooking with tongs or impervious gloves, may be used as blanched shoots all winter if the roots are dug and grown on in boxes of soil in a cool cellar. Prepare these also as for spinach.

Parboil the plants listed below for about 5 minutes; then, after discarding the water, cook again for 10 minutes or so in fresh boiling water: dandelion leaves picked before the plant flowers, young sour and curly dock, young chicory leaves, evening primrose and escaped comfrey. Most of these, even after parboiling and cooking, will remain slightly bitter. Unless you are working up a real or imaginary survival program, their continued use is of questionable benefit.

COOKING WILD SHOOTS

There are certain wild shoots that bring rave reviews—wild asparagus, of course, and stalks of bellwort. The latter are usually too scarce to consider cropping. In fact their own survival is due in large part to the difficulty of finding them, for it is often necessary to spot the clumps first in full leaf and mark them for the following season's devouring. This does not hold for such prevalent shoots as cattails, fireweed, burdock and the escaped Japanese butterbur, which grow in such thriving colonies that they are easy to locate. The roots of burdock and butterbur, or fuki, see below, may be used, as well as the stems, which should be very carefully peeled prior to cooking. All the above may be prepared as for Asparagus, 283.

Then there are poke shoots, which must be cut very young, for both leaf and root are poisonous. The shoot should be parblanched, 154, in two waters, and the waters discarded, before cooking a third time until tender.

COOKING WILD ROOTS

For survival, again, or if you still like to feel the squish of mud between your toes, are the gathering and preparation of certain watergrown roots. Bulrushes and cattails can be dug the year around. Use the root stalks. Scrape and remove the hairs. Parboil at least ten minutes, then boil for over an hour. Roasting in coals takes from 2 to 3 hours. Arrowhead tubers, dug in the fall, are treated as for bulrushes. All need lemon juice to prevent discoloration after peeling. Boil the long spongy roots of the yellow spatterdock water lily about 30 minutes. You may also eat the unopened flowers of the fragrant white water lily, boiled very briefly, or the boiled green seeds of our beautiful native yellow lotus, which are really too precious to plunder. Among water plants, the root shoots of pickerelweed are the quickest to prepare, needing only about 8 minutes of boiling.

Among the land-based roots, Jerusalem artichokes, also found in cultivated forms, 283, are favorites. Cooked like them are groundnut roots, butterbur and burdock roots, and—after their runners are removed—the roots of the day lily. To prepare the buds and flowers, see 845. The first-year roots of evening primrose may also be prepared as for Jerusalem artichokes if they are parboiled ten minutes first. Spring beauty roots, which are sometimes found as sods in old lawns, may be treated as for potatoes; but patience and Lilliputian appetites are necessary prerequisites.

JICAMA

A Mexican tuber with the crispness and whiteness of a turnip. Use it raw, sliced in hors d'oeuvre or salads, or slice thinly and cook as for or with Pan-Fried Potatoes, 320.

KOHLRABI

4 Servings

These "knobs"—actually thickened stems—are superb in flavor, but, unless young, are frequently too fibrous in texture to be worth preparing, see illustration in chapter heading on 276.

Wash:

16 small kohlrabi

Cut off the tops and pare the knobs. Slice the knobs and drop into a quantity of rapidly:

Boiling water

Cook uncovered until barely tender, about 20 minutes, and drain. Boil the tops separately in the same manner. After draining well, chop the tops until very fine or purée and combine them with the knobs.

Prepare:

White Sauce I, 341

Add:

(A grating of nutmeg)

When the sauce is smooth and hot, add the kohlrabi.

ABOUT LEEKS OR POIREAUX

How we wish that leeks were as common here as in France, where they are known, all too modestly, as the "asparagus of the poor." Leeks, like other onion types, 583, make a wonderful seasoning. When cooked as a vegetable, they must be carefully washed to free the interlacing leaves from grit; and only the white portion is used. Cook as for Asparagus, 283, or braise as for Celery, 298.

PURÉE OF LEEKS

4 Servings

Very special as a side dish with meat, or as a stuffing for tomatoes.

Prepare and cook as suggested opposite:

8 leeks

Drain them well. Chop them coarsely. For each cup add:

2 tablespoons butter
½ cup fresh bread crumbs
Salt and pepper

Stir and simmer them gently until blended. If they become too thick, add:

A little cream

Serve the purée very hot with:

Finely chopped parsley

COOKED LETTUCE

Home gardeners in their enthusiasm often find themselves with sudden surpluses of lettuce and wish they had rabbits instead of children—failing to realize that a crisp nibble is not the only approach to this vegetable. Try these delectable alternatives after making sure that the leaves at hand are not bitter: cook lettuce as a Cream Soup, 181; cream it like Spinach, 327; cook with peas; stuff it like Cabbage, 294; cook and smother it with stewed tomatoes, or braise as for Celery, 298, allowing the lettuce to simmer only a few minutes before reducing the sauce; or cook, drain and casserole it in a Curry Sauce, 345, garnished with chopped filberts.

LOTUS

The handsome seed pod of lotus shown first on the left in the chapter heading, 276, is symbolic of the fragrant delicacy of all parts of this majestic, versatile plant. The leaves, either fresh or dried, make vegetable, meat or rice wrappings. The peeled 2- x 8-inch jointed underwater stems can be sliced and stir-fried or stuffed and steamed. Soak them first in acidulated water, 520, to avoid discoloration. The blanched ½-inch oval seeds may be eaten, but push out the bitter center portion first with a wooden pick. Also use these vitamin-rich seeds in soups or stews; or dried like Amandine, 553, or in sweet dishes.

ABOUT MUSHROOMS

Who would expect a lot of sunshine vitamin D in plants like these, which flourish in cellars, woods and caves? Another amiable trait of mushrooms is their ability to lend an air of elegance to every dish of which they become a part. They gratify many of us, too, with their almost total lack of calories. But they trick us, while cooking, with

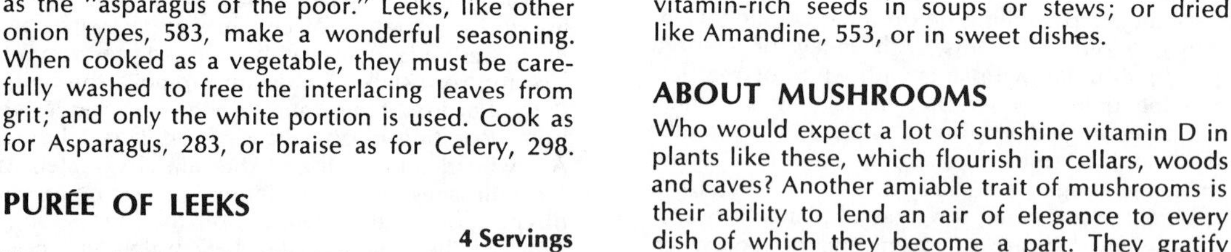

their sly habit of absorbing considerable amounts of butter, oil and cream.

Some of their trickery is, of course, of a very serious order. A number of poisonous mushroom types, during various stages of development, resemble edible forms. The quite innocent-looking and rather widely distributed **amanitas** are white-gilled and include varieties so deadly that they are frequently assumed to have furnished the murderous potions so useful to the princely houses of the early Renaissance. In sober truth, there is no simple way to identify harmless mushrooms and other related fungi. Even the experts often prefer to examine up to ten specimens of a single variety before announcing a verdict.

The novice should remember that there are bold mushroom hunters and old mushroom hunters, but no bold old mushroom hunters, and begin his collecting with a safe and obvious—if not very thrilling—family like the **puffballs,** which have neither stems nor gills. They are edible if they grow above ground and the flesh inside is white throughout. **Lycoperdon giganteum,** shown first on the left, varies from marble to watermelon size, and **Lycoperdon craniforme,** not shown, resembles a skull slightly shriveled even when in prime eating condition.

Agaricus campestris, shown in the center, is the type most often found fresh at market. The young pale buttons are succulent; the older drier ones are best for sauces, as the flavor intensifies as the gills darken. The dried **Gyromitra esculenta,** not shown, usually imported from Europe, is very strong in flavor when reconstituted, see opposite. Strangely enough, it can never be eaten raw, as it has a poisonous alkaloid which disappears entirely in drying or parboiling—a quality which also characterizes most varieties of **morel,** shown second from left, opposite. ➤ But cooking will not destroy the toxins within most poisonous types.

Morels grow in the spring. Second from the right is **chanterelle,** which appears in summer. On the far right is **Boletus edulis,** a great European favorite known to gourmets as **cèpe** or **Steinpilz.** For **truffles,** those black diamonds of the kitchen, see 310.

➤ Never use any mushroom that shows signs of decay. It harbors ptomaines and toxins just like any other decaying vegetation. ➤ Never cook light-colored mushrooms in aluminum, as it darkens them. Don't worry about mushrooms packaged by reputable firms, who guard their beds intensively against harmful invading spores. And don't bother to buy spawn blocks to grow your own mushrooms if your cellar is warmer than about 55°. To preserve seasonal mushrooms, see 809.

In preparing fresh mushrooms, brush or wipe them with a cloth. If they must be washed, dry thoroughly. As the skins harbor much of the flavor, do not remove them. Some people use only the caps, since the stems tend to be tougher Should you be so extravagant, turn the mushroom on its side and cut the stem so enough is left within the cap to prevent subsequent shrinkage at the center during cooking. Be sure to use the stems in Stock Making, 520, in Farces, 370, or in Duxelles, 573. Another way to keep the mushrooms plump and to use most of the stem is to turn them, as sketched, and slice lengthwise.

One of the best-looking food garnishes is the channeled mushroom. Shown also are decorative mushrooms under glass. To carve curving lines on the rather firm but spongy-textured mushroom evenly with a sharp knife requires considerable skill, but we find the point of a curved grapefruit knife quick and easy for the amateur. We have even been tempted to use a V-shaped linoleum-carving tool.

To store mushrooms temporarily, keep them refrigerated in a ventilated container. To keep mushrooms light in color, sprinkle with lemon juice or white wine, or cook à blanc, 447. To reconstitute dried mushrooms, soak from ½ to 4 hours in tepid water to cover. Drain and use as for fresh mushrooms. Use the water, if not gritty, for sauces or soups.

Store dried mushrooms uncovered in a glass container in a light but not sunny place. ➤ Three ounces dried mushrooms reconstituted equal 1 pound fresh. To keep fresh mushrooms or truffles impaled on food as a garnish, use tiny branches of fresh lemon thyme as picks.

STEAMED MUSHROOMS

4 Servings

This is a fine way to prepare very large mushrooms for stuffing.

➤ Please read About Mushrooms, above.

Prepare:

1 lb. mushrooms

Place them in the top of a double boiler ➤ over—not in—boiling water. Dot with:

2 tablespoons butter

Add:

¼ teaspoon salt
⅛ teaspoon paprika
½ cup milk

Cover closely. Steam about 20 minutes or until tender. The broth that results is superlative. Serve it with salt or use in sauces.

SAUTÉED MUSHROOMS

4 Servings

Prepare for cooking, using caps or pieces sliced to uniform thickness:

1 lb. mushrooms

Melt in a skillet over moderately high heat until they reach the point of fragrance:

2 tablespoons butter
1 tablespoon vegetable oil

or use:

(3 tablespoons clarified butter, 349)

Add the mushrooms and ➤ shake the pan, so the mushrooms are coated without scorching. Drop in:

(1 clove garlic)

Continue to cook over moderately high heat ➤ uncovered, shaking the pan frequently. At first the mushrooms will seem dry and will almost invisibly absorb the fat. Continue to shake the pan for 3 to 4 minutes, depending on the size of the pieces. Remove garlic. If you are holding the mushrooms to add to other food, do not cover, as this will draw out their juices. If using as a garnish or vegetable, serve at once on:

Toast rounds
Grilled tomatoes or eggplant

or on a bed of:

Puréed Peas, 315

CREAMED MUSHROOMS

4 Servings

Sauté as for Sautéed Mushrooms, above:

1 lb. sliced mushrooms
1 tablespoon finely chopped onion

Add:

2 tablespoons dry white wine

Cook briefly, remove from heat and combine the above with:

1 cup hot White Sauce II, 341
or Velouté Sauce, 345

Season with:

Salt and paprika
A pinch of herbs

Marjoram is the traditional touch. Chives and parsley are also recommended. Serve over a baked potato or in a casserole, covered with:

Au Gratin III, 553

MUSHROOMS À LA SCHOENER

4 Servings

A Viennese specialty.

➤ Please read About Deep-Fat-Frying Vegetables, 279.

Wipe off with a clean cloth:

1 lb. button mushrooms

Choose mushrooms with about a 1- to 1½-inch cap and cut off the stems ¼ to ½ inch below the caps. Sprinkle with:

Lemon juice
Salt

Dip in:

Fritter Batter for Vegetables, 243

and deep-fat-fry them in oil heated to 365° until golden brown. You may hold them, covered with a paper towel, for a very short time in a 200° oven. Just before serving, dust with:

Chopped parsley or chervil

Serve with:

Tartare Sauce, 364

BROILED MUSHROOMS

Preheat broiler.

Wipe with a dry cloth and remove the stems from:

Mushrooms

Brush generously with:

Butter or oil

Broil stem side down on a hot greased broiler about 2½ minutes. Turn and put in each cap a small lump of:

Butter or a dab of ground ham

Season the mushrooms with:

Salt and paprika
Chopped parsley and lemon juice

Continue to broil, stem side up, until tender. Serve at once on:

Hot toast

BROILED STUFFED MUSHROOMS COCKAIGNE

4 Small Servings

Farces in which the main ingredient is finely chopped sweetbreads, ham, or sausage make wonderful mushroom stuffing; or just seasoned puréed peas, garnished with a sprig of lemon thyme. The mushroom stems may be incorporated into the stuffing. Our favorite formula is given below.

Remove stems. Wipe with a damp cloth:

12 large mushroom caps

Chop the stems and simmer them for 2 minutes in:

1 tablespoon butter

Add:

1½ cups dry bread crumbs
¼ cup chopped pecans or other nutmeats
(1 pressed clove garlic)
1½ tablespoons chopped chives, basil or tarragon

Bind these ingredients with:

2 tablespoons cream, stock or part stock and part sherry

Season with:

Salt and paprika

Preheat broiler.

Brush the mushroom caps with:

Butter or olive oil

Fill them with the above dressing and sprinkle with:

Grated Parmesan cheese

to which you have added a pinch of:

Paprika

Place them stem side up on a well-greased pan. Broil about 5 minutes and serve sizzling hot on:

Toast

MUSHROOMS STUFFED WITH CLAMS OR OYSTERS

Preheat broiler.
Prepare as for Broiled Mushrooms, above:

Large mushrooms

After cooking, stem side down, place in each one:

A clam or oyster

Cover each clam with:

1 teaspoon or more mayonnaise

seasoned with:

Horseradish and Worcestershire sauce

Continue to broil about 6 inches from the source of heat until the sauce begins to color. Serve hot.

MUSHROOMS FLORENTINE

4 Servings

Preheat broiler.
Prepare as for Broiled Stuffed Mushrooms Cockaigne, left:

12 large mushrooms

Add to the stems and the juice in the pan:

2 teaspoons grated onion
2 tablespoons chopped parsley
(1 teaspoon anchovy paste)

Cook these ingredients gently about 3 minutes Add:

½ to ¾ cup Creamed Spinach, 327

Brush the caps with:

Butter or olive oil

Fill them with the above mixture and broil stem side up on a greased pan about 5 minutes. Serve as a garnish for individual steaks or scrambled eggs.

MUSHROOMS STUFFED WITH SEAFOOD OR SNAILS

8 Servings

Preheat broiler.
Remove the stems from:

24 large mushrooms

Wipe caps and stems with a dry cloth. Chop the stems. Shell, then chop:

½ lb. cooked shrimp, snails or crab meat

Melt:

2 tablespoons olive oil or butter

Stir in:

2 tablespoons flour

Add:

1 cup shrimp, chicken or clam stock

Add the mushroom stems. ➤ Lower the heat. Stir and simmer the sauce for 2 minutes. Add the seafood or snails and:

2 teaspoons chopped chives or other herbs

Stir gently until well blended and add:

⅛ teaspoon curry powder or 1 tablespoon sherry
Season to taste

Brush the mushroom caps with:

Butter or olive oil

Fill them with the above dressing, place stem side up on a well-greased pan and broil about 5 minutes. Prepare:

8 rounds buttered toast, each large enough to hold 3 mushrooms

Place the cooked caps on the toast. Serve garnished with:

Parsley and broiled bacon

MUSHROOMS AND ONIONS IN WINE

4 Servings

Fine for a chafing dish.
Prepare for cooking, 307:

1 lb. mushrooms

Melt:

½ cup butter

Skin, add, stir and sauté 5 minutes:

16 tiny white onions

Add the mushrooms. When they are coated with butter, add:

2 tablespoons flour
¼ cup chopped parsley
½ bay leaf
¼ teaspoon freshly grated nutmeg
½ cup bouillon or stock

Cook and stir these ingredients until the onions are tender. Add:

¼ cup Madeira or dry sherry

Serve garnished with:

Croutons, 551

MUSHROOM RING OR MOUSSE

6 Servings

Chop finely:

1 lb. mushrooms

Melt:

2 tablespoons butter

Stir in:

2 tablespoons flour

Brown the flour slightly. Sauté the mushrooms in this mixture for 2 minutes. Cool them. Beat in:

4 beaten egg yolks
½ teaspoon salt
¼ teaspoon paprika

Preheat oven to 325°.
Whip until stiff:

½ cup whipping cream

In another bowl ➤ whip until stiff, but not dry:

2 egg whites

Fold the cream lightly into the mushroom mixture. Fold in the egg whites. Butter a 9-inch ring mold. Pour in the mousse. Cover it with a piece of buttered paper. Place the ring mold in a pan of hot water. Bake about 1 hour. Remove paper. Invert the mousse onto a platter. Fill center with:

Buttered peas and parsley

MUSHROOMS UNDER GLASS

4 Servings

This supposedly "posh" specialty, shown as served on 307, is quite within the reach of anyone with an ovenproof glass bowl that fits closely over a baking dish.

Preheat oven to 350°.

Trim the stems from and channel, see 307:

1 lb. mushrooms

Beat until creamy:

¼ cup butter

Stir in very slowly:

2 teaspoons lemon juice

Add:

1 tablespoon chopped parsley

⅓ teaspoon salt

¼ teaspoon paprika

Cut with a biscuit cutter and toast:

4 rounds bread, ½ inch thick

When cold, spread both sides with half the butter mixture. Spread the rest on the tops of the mushroom caps. Place the toast in the bottom of a small baking dish and heap the mushrooms upon it. Pour over them:

½ cup cream

Cover closely with a glass bowl. Bake about 20 minutes. Add more cream if the mushrooms become dry. Just before serving, add:

2 tablespoons dry sherry

Serve the mushrooms—still under the glass—garnished with:

Parsley

ABOUT TRUFFLES

So precious are these nubbly unattractive-looking fungi that in Southern Europe, where they are exclusively found—or rather strip-mined—they are locked up in hotel safes. On the other hand, they have become so widely distributed in the canned state that we are reminded of a friend of ours who asked the proprietor of a small fruit store in her neighborhood if he had any truffles; at which the fruiterer, who was a little hard of hearing, shrugged his shoulders eloquently and replied: "And who hasn't?"

Truffles defy cultivation. The French type—the blacks—like the rest of the genus, grow underground. As in Italy, where a "white" variety occurs, they are rooted out by trained pigs or dogs. Too bad for us humans that we haven't invented a truffle Geiger counter; but at least we know in general where to start digging: truffles are symbiotic with oaks. And—another hint—the "season" is October to March!

The terms **Périgourdine, Piémontaise** and **Lucullus** are often applied to truffled dishes. Dishes frequently seasoned with truffles are: pâté de foie in pastry; scrambled eggs; garnishes for hors d'oeuvre; farce for artichokes.

To prepare fresh truffles, wash in several waters. As the skin is rough, you may have to scrub them clean. Pare them with care, or rub off the skin, which should be saved for seasoning sauces or for the garnish below. Truffles should be sliced very thin, for their aroma is overpowering. To take advantage of it, place thin slices on food and store overnight in a closed container in the refrigerator. Add truffles to dishes at the end of the cooking period to avoid overcooking. If you are working with canned truffles, merely heat them with the food or use them as a garnish. If you open a can and use only a portion, place the remainder, covered with oil or sherry, in a tightly lidded glass container. It will keep refrigerated about a month.

✻ Truffles may be frozen in their own juice; or add some Madeira wine if juice is lacking.

⅄ TRUFFLE GARNISHES

I. To produce black truffles in economical quantity for decorating, put in a blender:

7 tablespoons truffle bits, peelings, rubbings and juice

1 tablespoon gelatin

dissolved in:

¾ cup water

If this blended mixture is not dark enough to suit you, heat it over hot water until it colors to your satisfaction. Spread the mixture thin on a cookie tin and cool it in the refrigerator. Cut into any desired form and use on cold food, see Chaud-froid, 369. This same process may be used for pimientos.

II. Bits of white truffle may be used raw over risotto or fondue, puréed for canapés, processed in foie gras or cooked 2 to 3 minutes in butter.

OKRA

This vegetable, see illustration in chapter heading on 276, is often combined in stews, where its gluey sap helps thicken the sauce and gives to such dishes the name of **Gumbo.** See Chicken Gumbo, 176.

STEWED OKRA

3 Servings

Wash:

2 cups young okra

If the pods are small, leave them whole, in which case less sap is released. If large, cut off the stems and slice into 1-inch pieces. Drop into a small amount of:

Boiling water

enough to cover the bottom of the pan by ⅛ inch. Simmer covered until tender, if whole about 8 minutes, if cut about 5. Drain if necessary.

Season to taste

Serve hot with:

2 tablespoons melted butter

or with:

Hollandaise Sauce, 358

or if cooled with:

Vinaigrette, 360

⊗ Pressure cook okra cut into 1-inch slices 4 minutes at 15 lbs.

SAUTÉED OKRA

6 Servings

Wash:

1 quart okra: 1 lb.

Dry it well, cut off the stem ends and slice crosswise thinly. Melt:

2 tablespoons butter

Add the okra, cover and simmer gently about 5 minutes. Stir frequently. Add:

1/4 cup finely chopped green peppers
1/2 cup finely chopped onion
1 cup skinned, seeded, chopped tomatoes
1/2 teaspoon sugar
1/2 teaspoon fresh basil

Simmer covered about 20 minutes longer. Remove the cover and continue cooking until tender.

ABOUT ONIONS

An elderly cousin of ours maintained that onions are the secret of health; to which our grandfather liked to rejoin, "But how on earth can you keep the secret?" For various suggestions to disguise their outspokenness and exploit their potential, please read About Onions as Seasoning, 583, where you will also find a full discussion of this marvelous family with the qualities each member contributes.

Carl Sandburg contended that life itself is like an onion: it has a bewildering number of layers; you peel them off, one by one, and sometimes you cry. To prepare onions without tears, you may drop them into rapidly boiling water for about 8 seconds, then drain and chill them; after which the skins should slip off easily. Or you may work under running water as shown, to keep the irritants diluted. For the unskilled there is the closed chopping device, but this, of course, must be cleaned. Also shown is a special grater. But, again, a skilled wrist and a sharp knife as shown above right are the quickest approach. Peel the onion, leaving the tuft at the root end intact.

Cut the onion in half from stem to stern. Place one half cut side down. Start slicing it perpendicular to the root end in 1/8-inch parallels but leave about 1/2 inch of the root end in one piece. Then turn your knife so the blade is parallel to the table surface and again make 1/8-inch parallel incisions to the 1/2-inch demarcation at the root end. Finally make 1/8-inch slices from the top perpendicular to the longitudinal slices starting at the stem end of the onion. When you reach the demarcation line your onion will fall into dice. To remove onion odors you may rub your hands—and the cutting board—with a slice of lemon or a little powdered mustard; then rinse them in water.

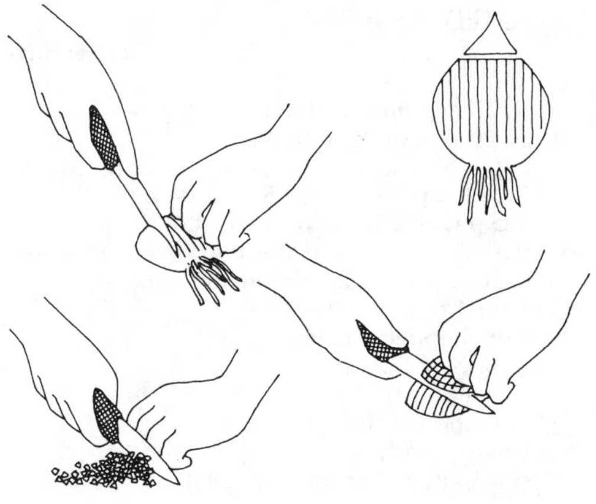

Onions all rebel under high heat or too long a cooking period by discoloring and giving off an unpleasant odor caused by the breakdown of their sulfur component. In sautéing them, be sure they are evenly sliced so they all cook golden at the same time and none remains raw and harsh in taste.

Several kinds of onions are generally available: the small whites, ideal for creaming and stews; the big full-flavored "globes," yellows, and red and white Creoles; as well as the Bermudas, the sweet Spanish and the Italian reds, which are so much milder that they can be used raw in salads and sandwiches.

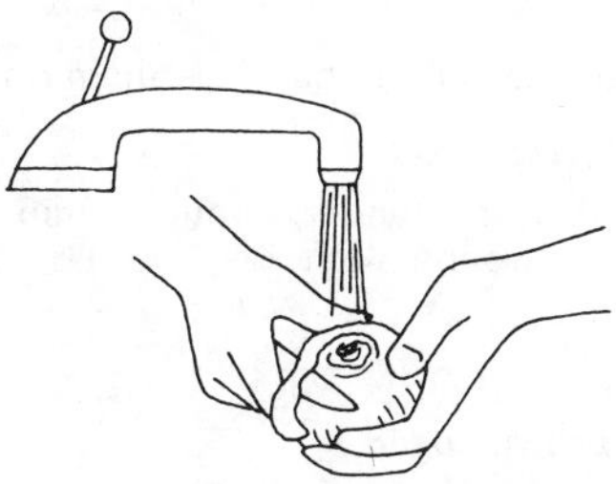

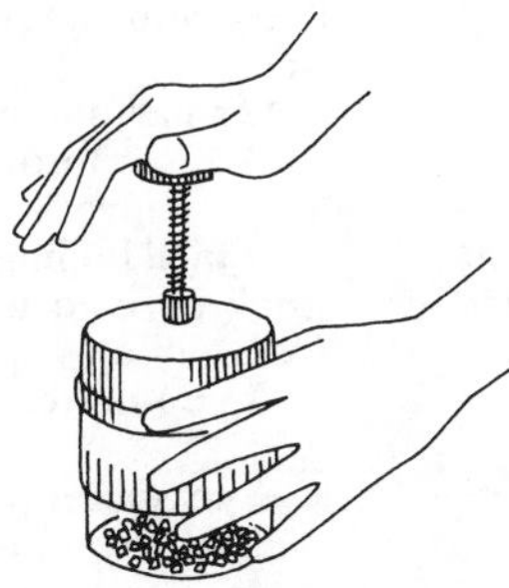

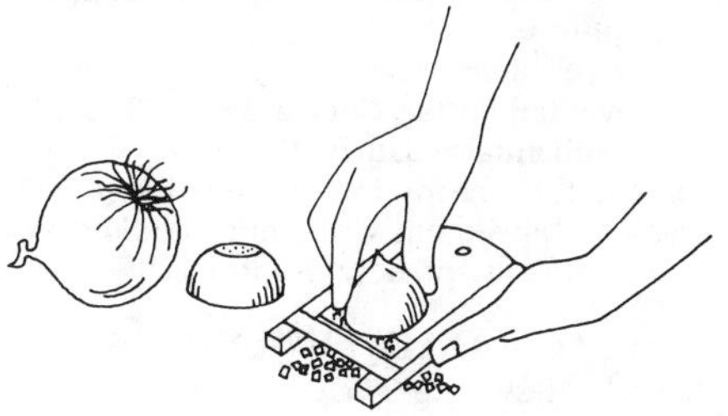

STEAMED ONIONS

5 Servings

We prefer this method to stewing because it avoids the dangers of overheating.
Place on a rack ➤ over—not in—boiling water:

10 medium-sized dry unpeeled onions: about 1½ lb.

Cover the pan and cook until tender, 30 minutes or more. Peel and serve them with:

(1 cup browned buttered bread crumbs)

or dress them with:

¼ cup melted butter
½ teaspoon salt
½ teaspoon cinnamon or cloves
(1 teaspoon sugar)

CREAMED ONIONS

5 Servings

Prepare:

Steamed Onions, above

Cover with one of the following:

1 cup White Sauce I, 341, and Au Gratin III, 553; 1 cup Allemande Sauce, 345; or 1 cup Quick Tomato Sauce, 352

You may use ¼ onion water and ¾ cream in the white sauce. Cook the onions and the sauce together for 1 minute. Add:

¼ cup chopped parsley
A dash of cloves
¼ teaspoon paprika
(2 tablespoons sherry)

You may also add:

(½ cup Sautéed Mushrooms, 308)

or:

(Minced celery, cooked or raw)

Serve the onions on:

(Toast)

YOUNG GREEN ONIONS OR SCALLIONS

4 Servings

Rinse and trim, allowing 3 inches of green:

3 bunches scallions

Place them in a heavy skillet with:

½ cup boiling water
2 tablespoons butter

Cook covered until nearly tender, about 5 minutes. Drain well. Place them in rows on:

4 very thin slices toast

Season with:

Salt and freshly grated white pepper or nutmeg

Pour over them:

Melted butter, Cheese Sauce, 342, or Hollandaise Sauce, 358

Or cut the onions into small pieces, cook them and combine them with other cooked vegetables—peas, beans, or new potatoes.

WHOLE BAKED ONIONS

I. Preheat oven to 375°.
Wash:

Medium-sized onions: 8 oz. each

Bake on a rack in a pan above ¼ inch water about 1½ hours. Cut a slice from the root end. Discard the outer shells. Pour over the onions:

Melted butter

Season with:

Salt and paprika

Cover with:

(Grated Parmesan cheese or chopped parsley)

II. ⊟ Cook, as you would potatoes, in a bed of coals about 45 minutes:

Whole onions

The outer skin forms a protection. When the onions are tender, puncture the skin to let the steam escape. Scoop out the centers and serve with:

Salt and pepper

SAUTÉED ONIONS

2 Servings

These can be useful also as a garnish for a greater number than two.
Skin:

4 medium-sized onions

Cut them into very thin slices or chop them. Melt in a skillet:

2 tablespoons butter or bacon drippings

Add the onions and sauté until golden brown. Stir frequently to prevent burning. Before serving, season with:

Salt
(Worcestershire sauce)

SMALL BRAISED ONIONS

Skin:

Small onions

Pour over them to the depth of ½ inch:

Boiling stock

Simmer covered over low heat. Let them absorb the liquid until they are tender, about 25 minutes. Add additional stock if necessary. When the onions are almost tender:

Season to taste

and add:

(Seeded white raisins)

GLAZED ONIONS

4 Servings

Boon companions for a pork roast.
Skin:

12 small onions

Prick them through the center and place them on a rack above:

1 inch boiling water

Cook covered until nearly tender, about 25 minutes. Dry on paper toweling. Melt:

¼ cup butter

Add:

½ teaspoon salt
2 tablespoons brown sugar

Cook this syrup 1 minute. Add the onions and move them about until they are well coated. Cook over low heat 15 minutes, using an asbestos mat under the pot, if needed, to prevent scorching.

SCALLOPED ONIONS WITH CHEESE

6 Servings

Peel, slice crosswise and poach in:
Milk
until tender:
6 large white onions: about 4 lb.
Drain them well.
Preheat oven to 350°.
Place in a buttered baking dish:
4 slices buttered toast
Arrange the onions on the toast. Sprinkle with:
½ cup grated American cheese
Beat well:
1 egg
1 cup milk
½ teaspoon salt
⅛ teaspoon paprika
Pour this mixture over the onions. Dot the top with:
1 tablespoon butter
Bake about 15 minutes. Serve with:
Crisp bacon
Parsley

FRENCH-FRIED ONION RINGS

4 Servings

➤ Please read About Deep-Fat Frying, 147.
Skin and cut crosswise into ¼-inch slices:
4 large white onions: about 3 lb.
Combine:
1 cup milk
1 cup water
Soak the onions in the liquid for 1 hour. Drain them, spread on paper toweling and dredge in:
Fritter Batter for Vegetables, 243
Pick up a group of the rings on a fork and let excess batter drip off before frying them in deep fat heated to 365° until light brown. Drain on paper toweling before serving.

STUFFED ONIONS

Onions make attractive garnishes or individual servings when filled. Orientals often give very special dishes fanciful names, like "Phoenix Bursting Through Clouds" or "Lady's Grace." We call this one "Cultured Pearls."
➤ Please read About Stuffed Vegetables, 280.
Skin and parboil, 154, about 10 minutes:
Large onions
Drain well. Cut a slice from the top and remove all but ¾ inch of shell. Chop the removed pulp with:
Seasoned bread crumbs or cooked rice, chopped cooked fish, meat or sausage, baked beans, mushrooms and bacon, or Deviled Ham, 74, and nutmeats
Moisten these ingredients with:
White Sauce I, 341, a tomato sauce, melted butter, stock, cream or gravy
Season to taste
and add:
Chopped fresh herbs
Fill the onion cases. Cover the tops with:
Au Gratin III, 553
Place the filled onions in a pan on a rack with enough water below to keep them from scorching, and bake in a preheated 375° oven until tender, about 30 to 40 minutes, depending on size.

ONIONS STUFFED WITH SAUERKRAUT

4 Servings

Not for a ladies' luncheon.
Prepare:
6 onion cases, above
Preheat oven to 400°.
Combine the chopped onion pulp and:
1 cup drained sauerkraut
½ cup soft bread crumbs
¼ teaspoon salt
(¼ teaspoon caraway or celery seed or a few juniper berries)
Heap the mixture into the onion cases. Sprinkle the tops generously with:
Buttered crumbs
Bake the onions in a pan with a very little water until well heated and tender, about 35 minutes.

ONION AND APPLE CASSEROLE

4 Servings

Preheat oven to 375°.
Peel and cut crosswise into ⅛-inch slices:
4 large onions: about 3 lb.
Peel, core and cut in the same way:
4 medium-sized apples
Sauté, remove from the pan and mince:
8 slices bacon
Take out all but 2 tablespoons of the bacon fat.
Toss in the fat left in the pan and reserve:
½ cup soft bread crumbs
Grease a baking dish. Arrange the onions, apples and bacon in alternate layers. Combine and pour over them:
¾ cup hot stock or water
½ teaspoon salt
Bake the dish covered 30 minutes. Uncover and dot the top with the reserved bread crumbs. Bake about 15 minutes longer.

ABOUT HEARTS OF PALM

Not all palm "hearts" are edible. Most of those eaten in this country are taken from the palmetto, and the same variety furnishes almost all the canned product, which comes from Florida or Brazil. Since the plant is of slow growth and cannot survive removal of the heart, conservation-minded cooks are presented with a problem.

Hearts generally weigh between 2 and 3 pounds when trimmed. They must be prepared quickly to preserve color and flavor.

➤ To boil, remove the outer covering of the heart, leaving a cylindrical portion, the base of which should be tested for bitterness. Remove fibrous upper portion. Slice thin and soak for 1 hour. Use the same water to blanch the palm à blanc, 447, 5 minutes—if there is any trace of bitterness. Now drain and plunge into boiling water again. Cook covered about 45 minutes. Drain and serve with:

Hollandaise Sauce, 358

or in:

White Sauce I, 341

➤ To roast, leave the heart in its sheath. Roast in a 400° oven until tender. Lay back the sheath. Slice the heart crosswise and serve with:

Lemon juice and salt

PARSLEY

During the earlier years of this century parsley, in most American households, was regarded as a purely decorative plant—like asparagus fern or smilax—except for an occasional light sprinkling over boiled potatoes. Now, nutritionally, it has come into its own, 586. The so-called turnip-rooted or Hamburg parsley can be occasionally found at market. It makes an interesting change from other types of root vegetable and is cooked similarly.

DEEP-FRIED PARSLEY

➤ Please read About Deep-Fat Frying, 147. When parsley takes the following form it is really quite irresistible. Care is the watchword, though: it becomes limp if the fat is not hot enough and olive green if the fat is too hot. The finished product should be at once crisp and a bright dark green. To achieve both objectives, have at least 2 to 3 inches of fat per cup of parsley. The parsley must first be carefully stemmed, washed and placed between towels until absolutely dry. Put in a frying basket:

1 cup fresh curly parsley

Immerse the basket in deep fat which has been heated to between 400° and 425° and leave it 1 to 2 minutes or until no hissing noise is heard. Remove and drain on paper toweling. Serve immediately!

PARSNIPS

4 Servings

To bring out the best flavor of parsnips, store them for several weeks at temperatures just above 32°. Parsnips discolor easily. To avoid this see Salsify, 326.

Preheat oven to 375°.

Pare, then cut into halves, discarding cores if woody:

4 medium-sized parsnips: 1 lb.

Place them in a buttered ovenproof dish.

Brush with:

2½ tablespoons butter

Sprinkle with:

½ teaspoon salt

Add:

¾ cup stock or water

Cover the dish and bake until the parsnips are tender, about 30 to 45 minutes. Serve with:

Chopped parsley and butter, or
Lemon Butter, 350

✪ Pressure-cook parsnips 7 minutes at 15 pounds.

FRENCH PARSNIPS

Prepare as for:

Carrots Vichy, 297

GREEN PEAS

2 Servings

Young peas, with good reason, have always brought forth paeans of praise; but how to cope with the older ones, with their often dismayingly tough skins? Try salting when cooking is about half over, or try Purée of Peas, below. One pound of well-filled pea pods will yield about 1¼ to 1½ cups hulled peas. Wash, then hull:

1 lb. green peas

Steam them, 278, or cook covered in:

⅛ inch boiling water or light stock

to keep them from scorching. Add:

½ teaspoon lemon juice

to help preserve color. There is a tradition that one must add to peas:

(A pinch of sugar)

Two or three pods may be cooked with the peas for flavor. Simmer 7 to 10 minutes. When the peas are tender, drain them if there is any water left. Remove the pods. Season with:

Melted butter or hot cream

to which you may add:

Chopped parsley or mint

✪ Pressure cook peas 2 minutes at 15 lbs.

GREEN PEAS COOKED IN LETTUCE

4 Servings

Steaming in a lettuce casing tenderizes peas and imparts to them a subtly delicious flavor.

Wash and remove the heart from:

A head of lettuce

leaving a deep shell reinforced by 3 or 4 thicknesses of leaves. Reserve the heart for salad. Wash, then hull:

2 cups green peas

Season with:

Salt
Pinch of sugar

Fill the head of lettuce with the peas and place it in a heavy pan narrow enough to support the lettuce case. Add a small quantity of:

Boiling water or light stock

Simmer covered until the peas are tender, about

30 minutes. Drain off any liquid. The lettuce leaves may be chopped and served with the peas. Dress with:

Melted butter or cream

PURÉE OF PEAS

This makes a lovely base on which to place stuffed mushrooms.

Prepare:

2 cups cooked frozen peas

⅄ Blend when tender with:

3 tablespoons cream

Season to taste

and serve at once.

PEAS AND CARROTS

Disdainfully dubbed "Keys and Parrots" by a cousin of ours, a devout anti-vegetarian; but a classic just the same.

Combine in any proportion:

Hot drained cooked Carrots, 296

Hot canned or cooked green peas

Drain the vegetables well.

Season to taste

Pour over them:

Melted butter

Chopped parsley

Serve at once.

PEAS AND MUSHROOMS

Prepare as for:

Peas and Carrots, above

substituting for the carrots:

Sautéed Mushrooms, 308

but omit additional butter.

PODDED PEAS

4 Servings

These sought-after varieties, known also as **sugar peas, snow peas** and **mange-tout,** are often available in Chinese shops. If they are mature, slice the pods diagonally.

Wash, cut off the ends and any strings adhering to:

1 lb. podded peas

Cook as for:

Green Beans, 285

or you may stir-fry about 1½ minutes. Serve while still crisp.

ABOUT PEPPERS OR PIMIENTOES

"Pepper" is one of those confusing designations so frequent in the world of vegetable cookery. The term "pimiento" is commonly used to describe the cooked, fully ripened sweet pepper, which turns red in color and which is used as a garnish or seasoning, 586. The recipes that follow all basically refer to the less mature fruits known as **sweet, green, globe** or **bell** peppers—sometimes, to add to the confusion, called **mangoes** in the Midwest—and have nothing to do with the fruit, the condiment, or the red-hot chili pepper. For more details, see 586. Peppers of all types are chock-full of vitamin C. To peel peppers, put under the broiler and turn often until they blister.

These are one of the few vegetables that can be ✻ frozen without blanching. So buy when they are plentiful. Small packets of frozen chopped peppers can be counted on to add zest to any number of dishes. ➤ Never overcook peppers, as they become bitter.

Illustrated are the mild bell peppers, which vary in shape from the long reds to the squat porcelain greens, and similar yellow types so well shaped for stuffing, shown on the left, and also shown cut to reveal the fibrous membrane and seeds common to all *capsicum* peppers. These portions must be removed before eating. They also cause severe discomfort if they come in contact with eyes or lips. From rather sharp to mild are the next two peppers used for **paprika** and **ancho,** a favorite for chili powder. The really hot ones next, like **Tabasco,** the small **Japanese santaka** and **cayenne,** are treasured as condiments.

GREEN PEPPERS IN SAUCE

Stewed green peppers combine well with other vegetables—for example, tomatoes, celery or onions. Remove stem, seeds and fibrous membranes from:

Green peppers

Cut them into oblongs or strips. Drop into:

½ inch boiling water

Boil until tender, about 10 minutes. Drain well. Serve in:

Cheese Sauce, 342, or a Canned Soup Sauce, 348

Allow about half as much sauce as peppers.

ONIONS AND GREEN PEPPERS

4 Servings

A sterling accompaniment to cold meat.

Skin, then cut into thin slices:

6 medium-sized onions

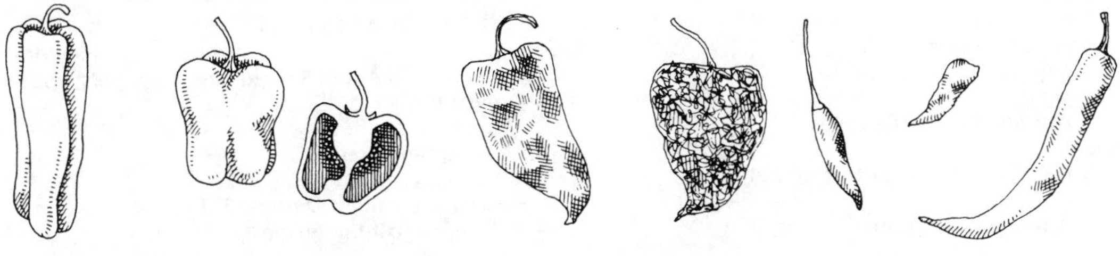

Cut coarsely, after removing seeds and membranes:

3 green peppers

Melt in a large skillet:

3 tablespoons butter, ham fat or olive oil

Sauté the onions about 10 minutes. Add the peppers and sauté 5 minutes longer. Add:

2 tablespoons stock or water
Season to taste

Cover the skillet. Simmer the vegetables until the onions are tender, about 10 minutes. Serve with:

Quick Tomato Sauce, 352

ABOUT STUFFED GREEN PEPPERS

Should you wish to fill peppers with heated precooked food, remove seeds and membranes. Parboil them, 154, until nearly tender, about 10 minutes. Fill and serve. Or cover the filling with Au Gratin I, II, or III, 552, and run briefly under a broiler until the crumbs are golden. You may fill pepper cases with any of the fillings suggested for Stuffed Tomatoes, 333, or one of the following: parslied, buttered lima beans; creamed spinach, peas or celery; creamed asparagus with shredded almonds; or any stuffings of precooked food such as macaroni and cheese, Corn Creole, 301, Tomatoes Creole, 332, or those in the recipes which follow.

GREEN PEPPERS STUFFED WITH ANCHOVY DRESSING

4 Servings

➤ Please read About Stuffed Green Peppers, above.
Preheat oven to 350°.
Prepare for stuffing:

4 pepper cases

Fill cases with a mixture of:

1⅔ cups dried bread crumbs
2 tablespoons melted butter
6 crushed anchovy fillets
2 tablespoons capers
½ cup sliced green olives
½ teaspoon salt
1¼ cups drained canned tomatoes

Bake 10 to 15 minutes.

GREEN PEPPERS STUFFED WITH RICE

4 Servings

➤ Please read About Stuffed Green Peppers, above.
Preheat broiler.
Prepare for stuffing:

4 pepper cases

Have ready:

1 cup hot Boiled Rice, 206

Add:

½ cup stock, cream or tomato pulp
Salt and pepper
A few grains cayenne
½ teaspoon curry powder or a small pinch of oregano
½ cup or more grated cheese

Fill the pepper cases. Cover the tops with:

Au Gratin I or II, 552

Brown briefly under a broiler.

GREEN PEPPERS STUFFED WITH MEAT AND RICE

4 Servings

➤ Please read About Stuffed Green Peppers, left.
Preheat oven to 350°.
Prepare for stuffing:

4 pepper cases

Melt:

2 tablespoons drippings or butter

Add, stir and sauté until light-colored:

½ lb. ground beef
3 tablespoons minced onions

Add:

1 cup hot Boiled Rice, 206
2 well-beaten eggs
½ teaspoon salt
⅛ teaspoon paprika
¼ teaspoon celery seed, curry powder, dried herbs or Worcestershire sauce

Fill the pepper cases. Bake 10 to 15 minutes.

GREEN PEPPERS STUFFED WITH CORN À LA KING

6 Servings

➤ Please read About Stuffed Green Peppers, above.
Prepare for stuffing:

6 pepper cases

Place in a double boiler ➤ over—not in—boiling water:

2½ cups drained corn niblets: 1 No. 2 can
1 chopped canned pimiento

You may add:

(4 slices sautéed minced bacon)
(2 tablespoons minced onion that has been sautéed in the bacon fat and drained)

Combine, beat and add to the above:

1 egg
½ cup milk
1 tablespoon soft butter
¾ teaspoon salt
⅛ teaspoon paprika

Cook until the mixture is slightly thickened, about 15 minutes. Fill the peppers and serve.

GREEN PEPPERS STUFFED WITH CREAMED OYSTERS

4 Servings

➤ Please read About Stuffed Green Peppers, above.
Preheat broiler.
Prepare for stuffing:

4 pepper cases

Have ready:

½ pint Creamed Oysters, 377 using half the recipe

Add:

2 tablespoons chopped parsley

Fill the pepper cases with the hot oysters.
Cover the tops with:

Au Gratin II or III, 553

Brown briefly under a broiler.

PLANTAIN

These 9- to 12-inch bananas, unlike their ubiquitous smaller cousins, must be cooked before eating, but never overcooked, since high heat releases an objectionable tannin component. They can be prepared in their green state, as well as when semi-ripe or quite mature, when the skins often become black and mottled. Cooked chopped ripe plantains also make a more than acceptable component of soups, stews and omelets.

Remove the fibrous strings from plantains before cooking, as they darken. Peel green plantains under running water to keep from staining the hands. Cut across into 2-inch-thick pieces; place at once in rapidly boiling water. Simmer 30 minutes. Season and serve with butter. If plantains are ripe, slice fine and cook in deep fat heated to 365°; or cook as for Candied Sweet Potatoes, 325. The purple bud end of plantain can be roasted in its husk. Only the heart is eaten. Serve with crumbled bacon or cracklings.

ABOUT POTATOES

Anyone who has visited Hirschhorn, in the sweetly romantic Neckar Valley, and who has climbed the hill to the partly ruined castle that dominates the little village will remember being confronted by a monument dedicated piously, if unhistorically, "To God and Francis Drake, who brought to Europe for the everlasting benefit of the poor—the Potato."

Potatoes come in all shapes and sizes, but the two types generally found in markets across the country are the thin-skinned round "white" Katahdins, and the oblong russet Burbanks, or Idahos, higher in starch, and for this reason a better bet for baking and French frying and for pommes soufflés. Rising in popularity is a rather newly developed variety known as California long white, almost "eyeless," smooth-skinned, and moderate in starch content. Whatever the type, the older the potato the starchier.

In recent years, potatoes have been maligned as over-caloric—although they are only equal in this respect to the same-sized apple or a baking powder biscuit. They are full of B, C and G vitamins, plus many minerals and even some high-class protein. Don't use sprouted potatoes that are green from exposure to light, as the green portions as well as sprouts are poisonous; or frost-bitten ones, which are watery and have a black ring under the skin when cut in cross sections.

If you wonder why there are no recommendations for ✻ freezing potatoes in this chapter, let us say that this operation is not feasible with home equipment. Potatoes purchased frozen have all been treated to quick-vacuum partial dehydration and instant freezing, to which home equipment does not lend itself.

In the following recipes we have tried to give these delicious vegetables a renewed status. ➤ Be sure, if a potato type is specified, to use that type only—and remember that ➤ once a potato is cold, mealiness can never be returned to it.

Potatoes are often combined and mashed with other cooked vegetables, as: ⅔ celeriac to ⅓ potato, or in equal parts with turnips, or ¼ fresh avocado to ¾ potato.

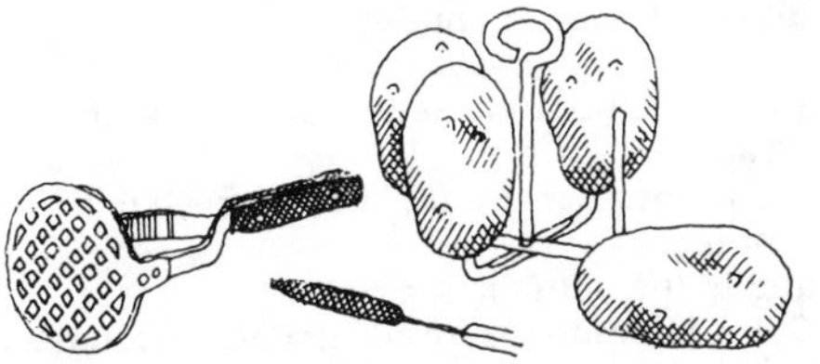

Illustrated above are three implements we have found useful in preparing potatoes of various types. At left is a potato masher. Centered is a pickle spearer with tines of almost needlelike slenderness—an invaluable help in peeling new potatoes. The rack on the right has heavier tines on which potatoes may be impaled for baking. The inserted metal causes rapid penetration of heat, and at the same time releases steam, which assures a desirable flakiness.

BOILED MATURE POTATOES OR POMMES ANGLAISE

6 Servings

Wash well, remove sprouts and blemishes, then pare:

6 medium-sized potatoes: 2 lbs.

When in haste, cut them into quarters. Cook covered 20 to 40 minutes in:

4 cups boiling water
½ teaspoon salt

When they are tender, drain well. Reserve the **Potato Water** for a thick soup base or for use in bread making.

To make the potatoes mealy, place a folded towel over the pot for 5 minutes. Shake the pot well. Remove the towel, which will have absorbed excess steam. Roll the potatoes in:

2 to 3 tablespoons melted butter
3 to 4 tablespoons chopped parsley or chives

⊗ Pressure cook large potatoes about 15 minutes at 15 lbs.

BOILED NEW POTATOES

4 Servings

Few vegetables are as ingratiating as small new—which is to say, young—potatoes, especially when they are served in their tender skins, so that all their delicate goodness is held until the very moment they are eaten. We are put in mind of the character in *Patience* who developed "a passion à la Plato for a bashful young potato."

In the illustration, 317 center, is a pickle fork useful when peeling hot new potatoes.

Wash well:

12 small new potatoes

Drop them into:

Boiling water to cover

Cook covered until tender, 20 to 30 minutes. Remove the skins and serve with:

Chopped parsley, mint or chives

Or melt in a skillet:

3 to 6 tablespoons butter

Add the potatoes and shake them gently over low heat until well coated. Serve sprinkled with:

Salt

Chopped parsley or chopped fresh dill or fennel

Or add to the butter in the pan:

3 to 4 tablespoons freshly grated horseradish

and shake the potatoes until coated. This last is particularly choice with cold cuts.

⊗ Pressure cook small new potatoes about 2½ minutes at 15 lbs.

TINY NEW POTATOES, SAUTÉED

4 Servings

Scrub and scrape well:

24 very small whole new potatoes

Heat in a heavy saucepan:

2 to 3 tablespoons olive oil or clarified butter

Turn the potatoes in the oil, cover closely and cook slowly until tender. Shake the pan from time to time. Sprinkle the potatoes with:

Salt and paprika

(Chopped chives or parsley)

RICED POTATOES

6 Servings

A fine foil for meat with a rich gravy.

Prepare:

Boiled Mature Potatoes, 317

When they are tender and dried, put them through a food mill or a ricer, seen 204. Heap them on a dish and pour over them:

(2 tablespoons melted butter)

MASHED POTATOES

6 Servings

Mashed potatoes should be served at once but in a pinch can be kept warm by placing the pan in a larger pan of hot water. Or put them in a greased casserole, run a slight film of cream over the top and keep in a warm oven. The cream should brown to an attractive color.

Prepare:

Boiled Mature Potatoes, 317

You may add to the water a small onion or a cut clove of garlic, a piece of bay leaf and a rib of celery with leaves. Remove these ingredients before mashing potatoes with a fork or a potato masher, seen 317, or putting them through a food mill, ⅄ blender or electric mixer. Add to them:

3 tablespoons butter

1 teaspoon salt

⅓ cup hot milk or cream

Beat with a fork or heavy whisk until the potatoes are creamy. Grated or sautéed onions with the drippings, minced crisp bacon, chopped parsley, caraway seeds, chives or watercress may be added to mashed potatoes. To help fluff the potatoes, cover the pan after they are mashed and place over very low heat about 5 minutes.

MASHED POTATO CHEESE PUFFS

6 Puffs

This is a tempting potato dish and a good-looking one.

Preheat oven to 350°.

Beat:

2 egg yolks

Add and beat until fluffy:

1⅓ cups hot or cold Mashed Potatoes, above

3 tablespoons hot milk

⅓ cup grated cheese

Season these ingredients with:

¼ teaspoon paprika

¼ teaspoon celery salt

(½ teaspoon finely grated onion)

(1 teaspoon chopped green pepper or parsley)

Beat until stiff, then fold in:

2 egg whites

Place the mixture in mounds in a greased pan. Brush the tops with:

1½ tablespoons soft butter

Bake the puffs about 20 minutes.

Should you want them evenly browned, turn once during the baking period.

CHANTILLY POTATOES

6 Servings

The use of whipping cream is what makes a dish **Chantilly.**

Prepare:

3 cups Mashed Potatoes, above

Preheat oven to 375°.

Whip until stiff:

½ cup whipping cream

Season it with:

Salt and white pepper

A few grains cayenne

Combine it with:

½ cup grated hard cheese

Shape the potatoes into a mound on an ovenproof plate. Cover the mound with the whipped cream mixture. Bake until the cheese is melted and the potatoes are lightly browned.

CREAMED POTATOES

Prepare:

Boiled New Potatoes, 317

Drain and dry off potatoes over very low heat. Peel and cut into ½-inch dice. Serve at once in:

White Sauce II, 341

flavored with:

(Dill seed)

Should you wish to delay serving this dish, place the potatoes in a buttered casserole. Cover with Au Gratin III, 553, and bake in a 400° preheated oven until heated through.

SCALLOPED POTATOES

I. **6 Servings**

Preheat oven to 350°.

Drop into boiling water:

3 cups pared, very thinly sliced potatoes
1 teaspoon salt

Parboil about 8 minutes. Drain well. Grease a 10-inch baking dish. Place the potatoes in it in 3 layers, sprinkling each layer with flour and dotting with butter. Use in all:

2 tablespoons flour
3 to 6 tablespoons butter

There are many tidbits you can put between the layers. Try:

(¼ cup finely chopped chives or onions)
(12 anchovies or 3 slices minced crisp bacon—but then reduce the salt in the recipe)
(¼ cup finely sliced sweet peppers)

Heat:

1¼ cups milk or cream

Season with:

1¼ teaspoons salt
¼ teaspoon paprika
(¼ teaspoon dry mustard)

Pour the mixture over the potatoes. Bake about 35 minutes, testing for tenderness with a fork.

II. **6 Servings**

Preheat oven to 350°.

Pare and slice thin:

3 cups potatoes

Heat:

1¼ cups hot condensed mushroom or celery soup

Stir in:

¼ cup grated cheese
(½ cup Steamed Mushrooms, 307)

Pour the mixture over the potatoes. Bake about 1 hour, testing for doneness with a fork.

BAKED POTATOES

We have always liked the snug phrase "baked in their jackets" to describe this process. But we are told that at least one young cook, after encountering it, called a home economist at the local utility company and complained that her grocer was unable to supply her with potato-jackets!

The best baked potatoes are flaky when served—so start with mature baking types like Idahos. Although new potatoes can be used and will need only about half as much baking time, they will never have the desired quality. The present rage for wrapping potatoes in foil inhibits flakiness, because too much moisture is retained. In fact, to draw moisture out of bakers, they are often placed on a bed of rock salt. See the potato baking rack shown on 317.

Preheat oven to 400°.

Wash and scrub even-sized, shapely:

Baking potatoes

Dry them and grease lightly with:

Butter

Bake for 40 to 60 minutes, depending on size. When potatoes are half done, pull out rack; quickly puncture skin once with a fork, permitting steam to escape. Return to oven and finish baking. When done, serve at once with:

Butter or thick sweet or cultured sour cream, or chopped chives or parsley, or
1 tablespoon Deviled Ham, 74, or
Cheese Sauce, 342

▤ POTATOES COOKED IN ROSIN

6 Servings

Coming upon this sensational setup after an hour or two of skating or skiing will send the spirits soaring—and no other method turns out a potato so distinctively flaky. Allow a minimum of three hours for this recipe; because of the fumes, never try it indoors. Rosin can be purchased at athletic and dance supply stores. Place in a 3-gallon iron kettle or galvanized bucket:

15 to 25 lb. rock rosin

The rosin may be used repeatedly. Heat it to 275°F. over a grill or hotplate. Carefully lower into it on a large slotted wooden-handled spoon, one at a time:

6 large baking potatoes

After about 45 minutes in the simmering rosin they will float to the surface. Simmer them 30 minutes longer. Remove one potato and wrap in heavy brown paper, twisting the ends tightly. Let cool 10 minutes and serve. If the texture is not exceptional, cook the remaining potatoes ten minutes more before testing. Serve with:

Butter, salt, and freshly ground pepper

Avoid eating the rosin-covered skins.

STUFFED POTATOES

6 Servings

Prepare:

6 Baked Potatoes, above

Cut them in halves crosswise, lengthwise like boats, or leave them whole, cutting a small ellipse on the flat top. Scoop out the pulp. Add to it:

3 to 4 tablespoons butter
3 tablespoons hot milk or cream
1 teaspoon salt
(2 tablespoons sautéed grated onion)

Or, if you plan to serve these with fish, add for piquancy:

(1 tablespoon horseradish)
along with the butter and cream. Beat these ingredients until they are smooth. Whip until stiff:
(2 egg whites)
Fold them into the potato mixture. Fill the potato shells. Sprinkle the exposed potato with:
½ cup grated hard cheese
Paprika
Broil under low heat until the cheese is melted.

BAKED POTATOES STUFFED WITH VEGETABLES

8 Servings

Preheat oven to 400°.
Prepare:
4 Baked Potatoes, 319
Have ready:
1 cup White Sauce I, 341
Mix into the sauce:
¼ teaspoon salt
½ cup grated hard cheese
½ cup cooked peas
½ cup cooked chopped carrots
¼ cup diced green peppers, seeds and membrane removed
2 tablespoons diced pimientos
Cut the potatoes lengthwise into halves. Remove the pulp without breaking the skin. Mash the pulp and fold in the sauce and vegetables. Heap the potato shells with the mixture. Cover with:
Au Gratin II, 553
Place the potatoes on a pan in the oven until the tops are brown. Serve with:
(Hot or cold meat)

LYONNAISE OR PAN-FRIED POTATOES

4 Servings

Prepare:
6 medium-sized Boiled New Potatoes, 317
While hot, peel and slice thinly and evenly. Sauté to an even brown in a heavy skillet in:
2 tablespoons butter
2 tablespoons vegetable oil
Meanwhile, sauté until golden in another pan:
½ cup finely sliced onions
in:
2 tablespoons butter or beef drippings
Mix onions and potatoes together gently.
Season to taste
Sprinkle with:
Parsley
and serve at once.

FRANCONIA OR BROWNED POTATOES

4 Servings

We love browned potatoes but have an aversion to the hard-crusted, grease-soaked variety so often served. To ensure a tender crust, we suggest preparing:
6 boiled mature potatoes: about 2 inches in diameter
Cook them until they are ➤ not quite done, so that there is still resistance to the testing fork.
Preheat oven to 350°.
Melt in a small heavy skillet a mixture of:
Butter and vegetable oil
to a depth of about ¼ inch. When the fat is hot but not quite to the point of fragrance, put in the potaoes. Let them cook ➤ covered in the oven about 20 minutes, turning them for even coloring. On the last turn put in:
2 tablespoons finely chopped parsley
Bake ➤ uncovered about 10 minutes longer.

POTATOES ANNA

6 Servings

A beautiful ware for a beautiful dish is the lidded copper Potatoes Anna pan, shown above, about 8 inches in diameter and 3½ inches high. The lid, which has side handles, fits down over it to a 1½-inch depth during the oven period, but is reversed to hold the potatoes for serving. You may substitute a heavy lidded skillet.
Peel and cut large mature baking potatoes into even 3/16-inch slices; then with a small biscuit-cutter cut them into enough equal-sized rounds to make:
4 cups potatoes
Soak them in ice water for 10 minutes. Drain. Dry carefully in a towel.
Preheat oven to 375°. Heat in the Anna pan:
2 to 3 tablespoons butter
2 tablespoons vegetable oil
Do not brown the fats, but let them just reach the point of fragrance. Put the potatoes in the butter in slightly overlapping spirals until the base of the pan is filled. Shake occasionally while filling to make sure the potatoes are not sticking. Add a sprinkling of:
Salt
Grated onion
Parmesan cheese

The butter will bubble up. But make sure, before adding another layer of slightly overlapping potato slices, that the first layer is coated with additional:

Melted butter

Continue this process for the first 2 layers, letting the potatoes color slightly. Be sure the layers are welded together. Add a sprinkling of salt, onion and butter each time. It is not necessary to continue adding butter if you have used about ½ cup. The moisture from the cooking potatoes will make it continue to bubble up so that in building the next layer or two you may omit the butter. Continue to shake the pan now and then to prevent sticking. Cover the pan and bake 45 minutes to 1 hour. Just before the potatoes are done, turn the entire mass over into the lid—to brown the upper side. Serve in the lid or turned out onto a platter.

HASH BROWN POTATOES

4 Servings

Combine with a fork:

3 cups finely diced raw potatoes
1 teaspoon grated onion
1 tablespoon chopped parsley
½ teaspoon salt
¼ teaspoon black pepper

Heat in a 9-inch skillet:

3 tablespoons bacon drippings, oil or other fat

Spread the potato mixture over the fat. Press it with a broad knife into a cake. Sauté the potatoes slowly, shaking them from time to time to keep them from sticking. When the bottom is brown, cut the potato layer in half and turn each half with 2 spatulas. Pour slowly over the potatoes:

¼ cup cream

Brown the second side and serve the potatoes piping hot.

POTATO PANCAKES

About Twelve 3-Inch Cakes

➤ This recipe demands mature potatoes.

Pare and grate coarsely until you have:

2 cups grated potatoes

Fold the gratings into a muslin towel and wring the towel to extract as much moisture from the potatoes as possible. Place them in a bowl. Beat well:

3 eggs

Stir them into the potatoes.

Combine and sift:

1½ tablespoons all-purpose flour
1¼ teaspoons salt

Add the flour to the potato mixture with:

1 to 3 teaspoons grated onion

Heat in a heavy skillet:

¼ inch or more beef drippings or oil

Place spoonfuls of the potato mixture in the skillet, forming them into patties ¼ inch thick and 3 inches in diameter. Brown, then turn and brown the second side until crisp. These are usually served hot with:

Applesauce, 131

If you must hold until all the batter is cooked, place them on a rack above a baking sheet in a 200° oven. Then serve all of them at once after draining on paper toweling to remove any excess fat.

PAN-BROILED GRATED POTATOES

4 Servings

Very good, quick—next best to a potato pancake.

Wash, then grate on a medium grater, skin and all:

3 medium-sized mature baking potatoes
2 tablespoons grated onion

Melt in a skillet to the point of fragrance:

2 tablespoons butter
2 tablespoons vegetable oil

Spread the potatoes in the skillet to a depth of about ¼ inch. Cook covered over medium low heat until the bottom is brown. Reverse and brown the other side.

Season to taste

SOUFFLÉ OR PUFFED POTATOES

6 Servings

According to legend—which we like to believe—Louis XIV, on campaign against the Dutch and, as major monarchs of the 17th century were wont to do, traveling in an exquisite little palace on wheels, had sent a courier ahead to his chef, detailing just what he desired for dinner. The roads were nearly impassable; the hour grew late; and the chef, who had managed to keep most of the elaborate menu in reasonably prime condition, found to his consternation as the King's party clattered into the courtyard that his *pommes frites* had gone utterly limp. In a frenzy, he immersed the potatoes in the hot fat a second time, madly agitated the pan, and behold!—the dish which was to make him rich and famous.

There were several more coincidences that the cook may not have been aware of. His potatoes must have been old, so that the starch content was just right to make them puff. He must have had a very systematic apprentice who cut the potatoes all with the grain and to a very uniform thickness, as sketched 322. In his relief at having something to serve, he evidently didn't mind a 10% failure, for even experts who make this dish daily count on that great a percentage of spud-duds. All this is just to encourage you if, like us, you expect a 100% return on your efforts. The duds, by the way, are acceptable as French fries, even if they are not so glamorous as the puffs.

➤ Please read About Deep-Fat Frying, 147.

Choose:

8 large mature potatoes

Restaurants famous for this dish age their own to the point where you can no longer pierce or scrape the skin off with your fingernail, but must use a knife to pierce it. There should be about 80% starch in the potato. Pierre Adrian, who was very expert, maintained that there is nothing like

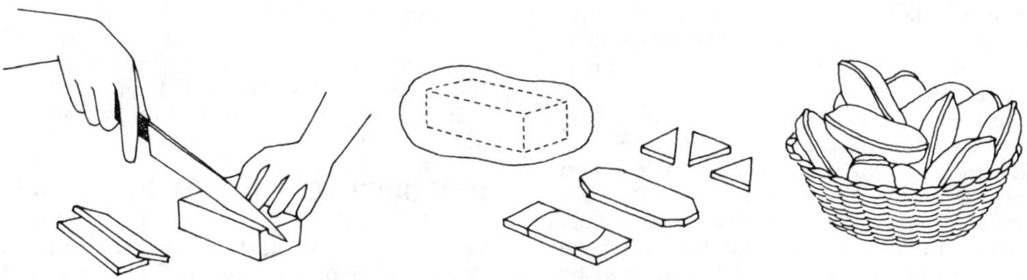

a Holland potato, grown on Spanish soil; but we have been obliged to content ourselves with Idahos or Burbanks. Cut from the unpared potato the largest possible oblong ➤ with the grain—that is, the long way, as sketched—into ➤ ⅛-inch slices that are of uniform thickness from one end to the other. In restaurants this accuracy is produced by a slicing machine. Once you have these long even slices, you can cut them into the classic polygonal shape, as sketched, or even into triangles, circles or fancy ovals with crimped edges. Soak the slices for at least 25 minutes in:

Ice water

Dry them thoroughly. Have ready a deep-fat-frying kettle one-third filled with:

Rendered beef kidney fat or vegetable oil

heated to 275°. Drop the slices in separately. ➤ Do not crowd the pan. The slices will sink. This next admonition is not without danger for the unskilled. ➤ When, after a few seconds, they rise, use a continuous shaking motion with the pan, which will set up a wavelike action to keep the floating strips bathed in the fat. Continue to cook them at 275°, turning them at least once, until they begin to clarify toward the centers and show a marked difference in texture at the cut edges, to a depth of about 1/16 inch. Drain on paper toweling. If you do not want to use them at once, they may be refrigerated before the second cooking, but ➤ bring them to room temperature befo·e immersing in the hot fat the second time. If you want to proceed at once, let them cool off and drain for about 5 minutes before the second cooking.

Just before you are ready to serve, drop them again one by one into a fryer filled ⅓ full with the fat at 385°. Again agitate the pan as described. The once-fried slices should puff at once, although they always retain a seam wherever you have made an original perimeter cut. Cook to a golden brown. Drain. Dry on paper toweling. Salt and serve the puffed ones at once, preferably in a basket as shown above, to keep them crisp. If they are not crisp enough, return them to the fat for a few seconds. Drain again. Sometimes it is worth trying the duds once more, after they have cooled.

NEVER-FAIL FRENCH FRIES

The following recipe, like Soufflé Potatoes, calls for a two-stage frying operation. After the first stage, you may drain and cool the potatoes on paper toweling. Cook the second stage just before serving.

➤ Please read About Deep-Fat Frying, 147.

As with all successful potato frying, much depends on the maturity of the potato, so choose:

Mature baking potatoes

Pare and slice them into strips about 2¼ inches long and about ⅜ inch through. If you are using cold-storage potatoes and want a light-colored result, soak the slices for 15 minutes in 90° water. Wipe well with a towel to remove surface moisture and excess starch. Slowly heat to between 300° and 330°:

Vegetable oil or rendered beef kidney fat

Drop the potatoes in—about 1 cup at a time—and cook about 2 minutes, until all sputtering ceases. Skim out the rather limp potatoes, drain on paper toweling and cool at least 5 minutes before starting the second stage. ➤ Heat the oil to 365°. Place the potatoes in a frying basket. This will assure quick and easy removal. Fry them for about 3 minutes. They should be golden brown and will be crisp when drained on paper toweling. ➤ Never cover them, as they will get flabby. Serve at once in a napkin-lined basket.

SHOESTRING POTATOES

Cut into very thin strips, not more than 3/16 inch thick:

Mature baking potatoes

Cook as for:

Never-Fail French Fries, above

OVEN "FRENCH-FRIED" POTATOES

4 Servings

Preheat oven to 450°.

Pare:

4 medium-sized potatoes

Cut them lengthwise into strips about ½ inch thick. You may soak them in cold water for 10 minutes. Dry well between towels. Spread in a single layer in a flat ovenproof dish. Pour over them:

¼ cup melted butter, bacon drippings or vegetable oil

Stir them until coated. Bake about 30 to 40 minutes, turning several times during this period. Drain on paper toweling. Sprinkle with:

½ teaspoon salt
¼ teaspoon paprika

POTATO PUFFS

3 to 4 Servings

➤ Please read About Deep-Fat Frying, 147.
Combine:

½ cup sifted flour
1 teaspoon double-acting baking powder
¼ teaspoon salt

Add and mix:

1 cup Mashed Potatoes, 318

The potatoes should be soft and at room temperature. If they are not, add a little hot milk or water and beat. Add:

1 slightly beaten egg
1 teaspoon minced parsley

Drop by spoonfuls into deep fat heated to 365° Fry to a golden brown. Drain on paper toweling.

POTATO OR SARATOGA CHIPS

➤ Please read About Deep-Fat Frying, 147.
As with Soufflé Potatoes, 321, and French Fries, 322, it is very important to have properly aged potatoes. Use these chips as a vegetable, a garnish or a cocktail snack.
With a vegetable slicer, slice as thinly as possible:

Peeled Idaho potatoes

Soak the slices 2 hours in cold water, changing the water twice. Drain and dry well. ➤ Very slowly heat to 380° in a deep fryer:

Vegetable oil

If you want a good luster on your cooled chips, allow the cooking oil to reach 75° before heating. Place a frying basket in the oil and drop the slices in one by one. Shake the basket or stir the potatoes several times to prevent the chips from sticking together. Cook until golden. Drain and place on paper toweling to get rid of excess fat.

POTATO BASKETS

➤ Please read About Deep-Fat Frying, 147.
Use a shredder to cut into long ¼-inch strips:

Peeled potatoes

Soak them for 30 minutes in ice water. Drain well and dry between towels. To form the baskets, please read About Noodle Baskets, 214.
Heat to 380°:

Vegetable oil

Deep-fry the potato baskets 3 to 4 minutes. Remove from the fat and drain. Bring the fryer up to 380° again and immerse basket for 1 minute more. Drain on paper toweling and serve at once.

DUCHESS POTATOES

8 Servings

Prepare:

4 cups Riced Potatoes, 318

Add while still hot:

¼ cup butter
2 beaten egg yolks
(A dash of dry mustard)
Season to taste

and allow this mixture to cool briefly.
Preheat oven to 400°.
Shape the potato mixture into flat cakes on a floured board. Place the cakes on a buttered baking sheet. Brush with:

A slightly beaten egg

Bake until golden and serve at once.
If you are using the above mixture decoratively, do not allow it to cool before inserting it into a pastry tube and fluting it at once in wavy scallops around the edge of a plank or a heat-resistant platter, then browning it in the oven.

DAUPHINE POTATOES

If you add about 2 tablespoons of grated Gruyère cheese to each cup of potatoes called for in this recipe, you will have **Potatoes Lorette.**
➤ Please read About Deep-Fat Frying, 147.
For every cup:

Freshly Mashed Potatoes, 318

add:

⅓ to ½ cup Pâte à Choux, 646

made without sugar and seasoned with:

A grating of nutmeg

Form the potato mixture by hand into 1- to 1½-inch balls or insert in a pastry bag with a large plain tube, shaping as for Spätzle, 205.
Roll in:

(Dry white bread crumbs)

Heat to 350°:

Vegetable oil

Deep fry the balls 3 to 4 minutes and allow the heat of the fat to increase to 370° until they are golden. Drain on paper toweling. Add:

Salt

and serve at once.

FRIED POTATO BALLS

6 Servings

A simpler version, not unlike Dauphine Potatoes, above.
➤ Please read About Deep-Fat Frying, 147.
Prepare:

2 cups hot Riced Potatoes, 318: 4 medium-sized potatoes

Add to them:

2 tablespoons butter
½ cup grated cheese
½ teaspoon salt
A few grains cayenne
2 tablespoons cream
2 beaten egg yolks
½ teaspoon any baking powder

Whip these ingredients until light. Shape into balls. Roll the balls in:

Flour

then in:

1 egg beaten with 2 tablespoons water

and in:

Fine bread crumbs

Heat to 380°:

Vegetable oil

Deep fry the balls until golden. Drain on paper toweling. Serve at once.

ABOUT LEFTOVER POTATOES

Not inappropriately is an unresponsive person called a "cold potato." Held over after cooking, potatoes lose their mealiness and that subtle down-to-earth flavor. They are probably most effective when ⅄ blended into a soup base, in which the combining liquid should be hot. We give the following additional suggestions as better-than-nothing bargains.

LEFTOVER GERMAN-FRIED POTATOES

4 Servings

Melt in a skillet:

2 or more tablespoons vegetable oil

Add:

2 cups sliced leftover boiled potatoes
Salt and paprika
1 or more teaspoons minced onion

Sauté the potatoes slowly until light brown. Turn frequently.

LEFTOVER POTATOES O'BRIEN

6 Servings

Preheat oven to 350°.
Dice:

6 medium-sized leftover boiled potatoes

Add:

1 chopped seeded green pepper with membrane removed
1 minced onion
1 tablespoon flour
Salt and pepper
A few grains cayenne
(3/4 cup grated cheese)

Place these ingredients in a greased baking dish. Pour over them:

1 cup hot milk

Cover with:

Au Gratin II, 553

Bake about 30 minutes.

LEFTOVER POTATO CAKES

Shape into little cakes:

Leftover mashed potatoes

Add for each cupful:

(A beaten egg)
(Chopped parsley)
(Chopped celery or celery seed)
(Grated onion or 1/4 cup chopped sautéed onions)
(A grating of nutmeg)

Dip the cakes in:

Flour, bread crumbs or crushed cornflakes

Melt in a skillet:

Butter or other fat

Brown the cakes on one side, reverse and brown the other.

LEFTOVER AU GRATIN POTATOES

Preheat oven to 400°.
Cut into dice:

Leftover boiled potatoes

Prepare:

White Sauce I, 341, or Cheese Sauce, 342

Make half as much sauce as there are potatoes. Combine potatoes and sauce. Add:

(Chopped parsley, minced onion or chives)

Put the mixture in a greased baking dish. Cover with:

Au Gratin II, 553

Bake until browned.

ABOUT SWEET POTATOES OR YAMS

There are two quite distinct types of "sweet potato": a rather dry type with pinky-yellow flesh, and a sweeter, softer, much more moist and vividly orange-colored kind affectionately if mistakenly called **yam** in many parts of the country. Sweet potatoes are extremely high in vitamin A, while yams contain only a trace. Buy only enough of either type for immediate use, as they do not store well.

Sweet potatoes lend themselves to most of the cooking methods used for white potatoes and are delightfully enhanced by fruits and fruit flavoring. They reheat better than leftover white potatoes.

BOILED SWEET POTATOES

To prepare sweet potatoes in their jackets, drop them into boiling water to cover and cook ➤ covered until tender, about 25 minutes. Peel and salt before serving.

MASHED SWEET POTATOES

4 Servings

Prepare:

5 medium-sized Boiled Sweet Potatoes, above: 2 cups

Skin and put them through a ricer, or mash with a potato masher. Add:

2 tablespoons butter
1/2 teaspoon salt
A little hot milk, cream, lemon juice or dry sherry
(2 teaspoons brown sugar)

Beat the potatoes with a fork or whisk until very light. Sprinkle with:

Grated orange or lemon rind, cloves or cinnamon

Chopped dates and nutmeats may be added. To make attractive individual servings, heap the mixture into hollowed-out orange halves. Place these cups in a covered buttered baking dish and heat through in a 375° oven.

BAKED SWEET POTATOES

Follow the recipe for:

Baked Potatoes, 319

➤ Be sure to cut a small slice off one end or to puncture a sweet potato when half cooked as a safety valve to prevent its bursting.

STUFFED SWEET POTATOES

6 Servings

Preheat oven to 375°.

I. Prepare and bake as for Baked Potatoes, 319:

3 large shapely sweet potatoes

Cut lengthwise into halves and scrape out most of the pulp. Add to the pulp:

2 tablespoons butter
¼ cup hot cream or ¾ cup crushed pineapple
½ teaspoon salt
(1 tablespoon dry sherry)

Southern people say "use lots of butter, some brown sugar, nutmeg and black walnut meats; and replace the sherry with 2 tablespoons bourbon whisky."

Beat these ingredients with a fork until fluffy. Fill the shells and cover the tops with:

Au Gratin, 552

Marshmallows may be substituted for the bread crumbs and butter. These are a matter of taste, or —in our strongly biased view—lack of it. Bake the potatoes until browned.

II. These make a heartening cold weather touch. Bake as for Baked Potatoes, 319.

Sweet potatoes

Just before serving, insert in each potato:

1 tablespoon warm Deviled Ham, 74

CANDIED SWEET POTATOES

4 Servings

Cook covered in boiling water to cover until nearly tender:

5 medium-sized sweet potatoes

Preheat oven to 375°.

Pare and cut the potatoes lengthwise in ½-inch slices. Place in a shallow greased baking dish. Season with:

Salt and paprika

Sprinkle with:

¾ cup brown sugar or ⅓ cup maple syrup
(½ teaspoon grated lemon rind)
1½ tablespoons lemon juice or
⅛ teaspoon ginger

Dot with:

2 tablespoons butter

Bake uncovered about 20 minutes, until glazed.

CARAMELIZED SWEET POTATOES

4 Servings

Slice:

5 medium-sized Boiled Sweet Potatoes, above

Melt:

3 tablespoons orange marmalade or
Sauce Cockaigne, 770

Cook the potatoes gently in the sauce until glazed and brown.

DEEP-FRIED SWEET POTATOES

➤ Please read About Deep-Fat Frying, 147.

Wash, then parboil for 10 minutes:

Large sweet potatoes

Pare and cut them into strips. Heat to 365°:

Vegetable oil

Deep-fry the strips until golden brown. Drain on paper toweling. Sprinkle with:

Brown sugar
Salt
Freshly grated nutmeg

SWEET POTATO PUFFS

4 Servings

Preheat oven to 500°.

Have ready:

2 cups riced cooked sweet potatoes

Peel, mash and add:

1 large ripe banana

Combine and add, stirring well:

1½ tablespoons melted butter
1 beaten egg yolk
1½ teaspoons salt
3 to 4 tablespoons hot milk or cream
(⅛ teaspoon nutmeg or ginger)

Beat until stiff:

1 egg white

Fold it lightly into the potato mixture. Drop the batter from a tablespoon in mounds—well apart— on a greased tin, or place the mixture in buttered ramekins. Bake about 12 minutes.

SWEET POTATOES AND FRUIT

6 Servings

This tart dish is exceptionally good with roast pork, baked ham or game. Cook covered until nearly done in boiling water to cover:

6 medium-sized sweet potatoes

Peel and cut them into ½-inch slices. Cook covered until nearly done in a very little boiling water:

1½ to 2 cups thinly sliced apples

If the apples are not tart, sprinkle them with:

Lemon juice

Preheat oven to 350°.

Grease a baking dish and place in it alternate layers of apples and sweet potatoes. Sprinkle the layers with:

½ cup or more brown sugar
A dash cinnamon or grated lemon rind
(2 tablespoons seedless raisins)
(2 tablespoons chopped pecans)

Dot with:

¼ cup butter

Pour over the top:

½ cup of the apple water or water

Bake about 30 minutes.

Or you may omit the sugar and substitute for the apples:

½ cup puréed, sweetened apricots, 127, Sauce Cockaigne, 770, or crushed pineapple

RADISHES

Transforming red or white radishes into clever garnishes fascinates the young; and the allure endures. If you've read Pepys, you know that he ate buttered radishes at William Penn's—worth trying, too, especially with black ones. The jumbo-sized **daikon** sometimes exceeds 3 feet in length. It is so plastically promising that the Japanese, to whose country it is native, sometimes carve it into a fantastically intricate net, with which they cover a sizable baked fish. Daikon can be cooked by any recipe for Turnips, 334. So can any other radish, for that matter; or prepared as for Celeriac Rémoulade, 298. To store radishes before using, cut off the leaves.

BOILED RUTABAGAS OR SWEDES

4 Servings

Look for a new Laurentian hybrid of rutabaga developed in Canada and superior in texture and flavor. Rutabagas, also called **yellow turnips,** may be French-fried as for Shoestring Potatoes, 322, or baked like Potatoes, 319.

To boil, pare and dice:

2 medium-sized rutabagas: 2 cups

➤ Do not use the leaves. Drop the pieces into:

Boiling water

Cook uncovered until tender, 20 to 30 minutes. Drain well. Add:

½ teaspoon salt

Serve with:

Melted butter

to which you have added generously:

Lemon juice
Chopped parsley

Or mash the turnips and add them in any proportion to mashed potatoes with lots of:

Chopped parsley or cultured sour cream and nutmeg

ABOUT SALSIFY OR OYSTER PLANT

The salsify commonly found in the market is the white-skinned variety, see chapter heading, 276. But, if available, choose **scorzonera,** the black-skinned type, which is better flavored. Best results are obtained if the vegetable is stored for several weeks at temperatures just above 32°.

To avoid discoloration, cook this root unpeeled, or, if peeled, à blanc, as below.

SALSIFY À BLANC

Have ready:

3 cups boiling water

in which you have dissolved:

1 tablespoon flour
2 teaspoons lemon juice
½ teaspoon salt

Drop in:

2 cups peeled salsify

and cook 7 to 10 minutes. Serve in:

White Sauce I, 341

or with:

2 tablespoons melted butter
(Chopped chives or parsley)
(A grating of nutmeg)

SAUTÉED SALSIFY

Wash and peel:

Salsify

Dip at once in:

Milk

Drain and season with:

Salt and pepper

Roll in:

Flour, bread crumbs or crushed cornflakes

Sauté slowly until golden in:

Butter

SKIRRET

Cook as for any recipe using carrots, but always peel after boiling to retain flavor. Be sure also to remove the inner hard core before serving.

SORREL

Because it is heavy in oxalic acid, this vegetable is usually parblanched, 154, for 3 minutes and drained before being cooked as for spinach or chard and combined with them rather than being served by itself. Alone, as a garnish, it lends itself to flavoring with meat glaze, eggs and cream; or puréed and seasoned with mustard and tarragon, it may form a bed for fish.

ABOUT SPINACH

One of the more controversial greens, this is believed—with some scientific justification—to inhibit the body's absorption of calcium. It is also the most delectable of greens. We recommend throwing caution to the winds and enjoying it in moderation. Spinach is a special treat as a garnish with other foods, where its presence is usually heralded by the title **Florentine.**

Yield per pound varies from 2 servings if young, to 3 if old. Spinach requires little salt. Its astringent taste may be counteracted by a pinch of sugar.

⊗ Pressure cook spinach 1 minute at 15 lbs.

BOILED SPINACH

3 to 4 Servings

Pick over and cut the roots and tough stems from:

¼ peck spinach: 1 lb.

Wash it quickly in several waters until it is free from sand and soil. If young and tender, cook as for Panned Spinach, opposite. If old, place the spinach in:

2 cups rapidly boiling water

➤ Reduce heat and simmer covered until tender, about 10 minutes. Discard the water if it is strong in flavor. If not, keep it for use in soups and sauces. Drain the spinach well. ⅄ Blend briefly or cut up the spinach with 2 sharp knives or a triple chopper until it is as fine as you like it.

Sauté:

2 tablespoons diced sweet red pepper,
2 tablespoons minced onion or a clove of garlic

in:

Butter or drippings

Add:

Lemon juice
Season to taste

➤ being careful not to oversalt. Serve the seasonings over the spinach. Other garnishes for spinach include:

Hard-cooked egg
Crumbled bacon
Fine buttered croutons
Hollandaise Sauce, 358
Au Gratin III, 553

CREAMED SPINACH

I. **3 Servings**

Prepare:

2 cups Boiled Spinach, above

⅄ Blend, rice or chop to a fine purée. Melt in a skillet which may be rubbed lightly with a clove of garlic:

1½ to 2 tablespoons butter

Add and cook until golden:

(1 tablespoon or more very finely chopped onion)

Stir in until blended:

1 tablespoon flour or 2 tablespoons Browned Flour, 339

Stir in slowly:

½ cup hot cream or stock
½ teaspoon sugar

When the sauce is smooth and hot, add the spinach. Stir and cook 3 minutes. Season with:

Salt and pepper
(Freshly grated nutmeg or grated rind of ½ lemon)

Serve garnished with slices of:

1 hard-cooked egg

II. **3 Servings**

Cook and drain:

Boiled Spinach, opposite

⅄ Put it very briefly through a blender with:

¼ cup cultured sour cream or condensed cream of chicken soup
A grinding of nutmeg or ⅛ teaspoon prepared mustard
(1 teaspoon horseradish)
Season to taste

Heat briefly and serve.

III. **4 Servings**

⅄ Place in blender:

¾ cup milk
(1 thin slice onion)
3 tablespoons soft butter
2 tablespoons flour
½ teaspoon salt
⅛ teaspoon paprika
A fresh grating of nutmeg or lemon rind
(½ peeled clove garlic)

Blend in small amounts, lidding blender after each addition:

12 oz. spinach, coarse stems removed

When smooth, put this mixture into a heavy skillet and stir over low heat about 3 minutes until it bubbles and the flour is cooked. Serve with:

Buttered crumbs
4 slices cooked crumbled bacon
2 sliced hard-cooked eggs

PANNED OR SICILIAN SPINACH

3 Servings

The seasonings in this dish help to enliven even canned spinach.

Wash well and remove the coarse stems from:

1 lb. spinach

Shake off as much water as possible. Heat in a large heavy skillet:

1 tablespoon butter
2 tablespoons olive oil

Add:

(1 clove minced garlic)

Add the spinach. Cover skillet and cook over high heat until steam appears. Reduce the heat and simmer until tender, 5 to 6 minutes in all.

Season to taste

To turn this into **Sicilian Spinach,** add:

(2 or more chopped anchovies)

SPINACH WITH TOMATOES

3 Servings

Prepare:

Boiled Spinach, opposite

Drain. ⅄ Blend or chop fine with:

½ cup Italian tomato paste or tomato purée

Sauté:

1 pressed clove garlic

in:

(2 tablespoons olive oil)

Add the spinach mixture and heat.

Season to taste

SPINACH, TOMATO AND CHEESE LOAF

8 Servings

Preheat oven to 350°.

Place in a bowl:

2 cups cooked drained spinach
2¼ cups drained canned tomatoes
¼ cup chili sauce
½ lb. grated hard cheese or crumbled feta
1 cup cracker crumbs
Juice of ½ onion
¼ teaspoon salt
¼ teaspoon freshly ground pepper

Toss these ingredients until blended. Place in a greased loaf pan. Bake the dish about 35 minutes. Serve garnished with:

Crisp Bacon, 486

SPINACH IN PANCAKES

Prepare:

Creamed Spinach, above

Prepare:

French Pancakes, 236
Chopped Sautéed Mushrooms, 308

Place the spinach and mushrooms on the pancakes. Roll them like a jelly roll. The tops may be sprinkled with:

Grated cheese

Place the rolls under a broiler until the cheese is melted. Serve at once.

ABOUT SQUASHES

Easy cross-pollenization accounts for the myriad diversity of this family. It probably also accounts for occasional bitterness in the cultivated types, which may have interbred with their very bitter wild forebears. Unless squashes are to be stuffed, always choose the smaller specimens.

These plants divide into summer and winter types. We often call for special varieties of each type in the recipes which follow, but others may be substituted, as long as they belong to the respective type.

SUMMER SQUASHES

Whether green, yellow, white; long, round or scalloped, these are all thin-skinned and easily punctured with a fingernail—the shopper's furtive assurance and the proprietor's despair. They should be firm and heavy. Avoid them if the rind is tough or the stem dry or black. If they are young, there is no need to pare them or to discard the seeds. Should only hard-rinded ones be available, do both. Summer squash do not store well, but a limited number of varieties can be found all year 'round at the "fancier" markets.

Our own favorite is zucchini. Try also the closely related cocozelle and vegetable marrow. Prepare these squash as for any cucumber and eggplant. Shown below in top row from left to right are **straight neck, crooked neck, cymling** or **pattypan, cocozelle** and **zucchini.** To stuff summer squash or squash blossoms, see below.

WINTER SQUASHES

These, again, are of many colors and shapes and remain on the market from fall to early spring. Except for butternut, they have hard-shelled skins. Choose the others for their hard rinds. Watery spots indicate decay. The winter types, sketched below in the lower row, are **Golden Delicious acorn, buttercup** or **turban, butternut** and **Hubbard.** For ways to cook **pumpkin,** the most famous of all winter varieties, see 330. Unless you bake squash whole, remove the seeds and stringy portions. Peel and cut into small pieces. Winter squashes need from 10 to 45 minutes of cooking.

Because squash is so bland in flavor, it will benefit from imaginative treatment. It may be cut lengthwise into "boats," scooped out, or cooked and the centers loaded with a succulent cargo. For fillings, see Stuffings, 370. If the squash is a tender summer type, you may combine the removed portion with the filling, which may include vegetables, bread crumbs, nuts, mushrooms or cooked meat.

STEAMED SUMMER SQUASH

4 Servings

➤ Please read About Squashes, above.

I. Wash and cut into small pieces:

2 cups any summer squash: zucchini, yellow crooked neck, etc.

If very tender, the squash may even be left whole.

Steam it covered, 278, until tender. Drain very well. Sprinkle generously with:

Grated Parmesan cheese and melted butter

II. Prepare the squash as above, then mash it with a fork. Beat until fluffy. Beat in:

2 tablespoons cream
2 tablespoons butter or olive oil
1/8 teaspoon white pepper
(2 teaspoons grated onion or chopped fresh herb or a touch of saffron)
1/2 teaspoon salt

Reheat the squash briefly and serve.

STUFFED SQUASH BLOSSOMS

If you grow squashes, you may wonder why so many blossoms fall off without maturing. These are male flowers not retained for seed development. After they close and drop they make decorative as well as edible cases for Forcemeat, 374. Open each flower and put in only enough of the forcemeat to allow the petals to close again. Place stuffed blossoms side by side on a greased baking dish in a moderate oven until thoroughly heated. Serve alone or as a platter garnish.

Partially opened squash flower buds may be sautéed in butter or olive oil. Do not brown.

BAKED SUMMER SQUASH

4 Servings

➤ Please read About Squashes, above.
Preheat oven to 350°.
If summer squash is young, it need not be pared. Cut into strips and place in a greased baking dish:

3 cups any summer squash

Cover it with:

1/4 cup milk

Dot with:

2 tablespoons butter

Sprinkle with:

1 teaspoon salt
1/4 teaspoon paprika
(A grating of nutmeg or 1 teaspoon fresh lemon thyme)

Cover the dish. Bake for about 1/2 hour or until tender. Garnish with:

Crisp crumbled bacon

SAUTÉED SUMMER SQUASH

4 Servings

➤ Please read About Squashes, above.
Wash and dice:

3 cups any summer squash

Melt in a skillet:

3 tablespoons butter or olive oil

Add and sauté in it until golden:

1 cup minced onion

Add the squash and:

1/2 teaspoon salt
1/4 teaspoon freshly ground white pepper

Cover the pan and cook until tender, about 6 minutes, shaking the pan occasionally to prevent sticking. Remove lid and cook 3 minutes longer. Serve sprinkled with:

Chopped parsley or basil
Grated Parmesan cheese or Quick Tomato Sauce, 352

STEAMED STUFFED SUMMER SQUASH

I. **4 Servings**

➤ Please read About Squashes, opposite.
Wash thoroughly, then cut the stem ends from:

4 small summer squashes

Steam as for Steamed Summer Squash, above, but leave whole. When almost tender, drain and cool. Scoop out the centers, leaving a shell about 1/2 inch thick. Chop the removed pulp. Add to it:

1/4 teaspoon paprika
1/2 teaspoon Worcestershire sauce
Minced garlic or onion
1/4 teaspoon salt
1 tablespoon butter
3 tablespoons dry bread crumbs
1/4 cup grated cheese
A few grains cayenne
1/8 teaspoon curry powder or dry mustard

Preheat oven to 400°.
Refill the shells. Place them in a pan on a rack above 1/4 inch of water. Bake until hot, about 10 minutes.

II. Or fill these cooked squash cases while hot with:

Heated creamed chicken, ham, fish or spinach

Garnish with:

Parsley or tiny sprigs of lemon thyme

STUFFED BAKED SUMMER SQUASH

4 Servings

➤ Please read About Squashes, opposite.
Preheat oven to 350°.
Wash:

4 small summer squashes

Cut them down the middle, either crosswise or horizontally. Scoop out the pulp, leaving a 1/2-inch shell. Sauté in:

2 tablespoons butter
2 tablespoons chopped onions

Add the squash pulp and:

1/2 teaspoon salt
1/4 teaspoon paprika
A dash of nutmeg or cloves

Stir and cook these ingredients until hot. Remove from the heat. Add:

1 beaten egg
1/2 cup dry bread crumbs
1/2 cup grated cheese

You may rub the squash shells with:

Butter or drippings

Fill them with the stuffing. Place in an ovenproof

dish on a rack over 1/8 inch of water or stock. Sprinkle the tops with:

Au Gratin II, 553

Bake the squashes until tender, about 20 to 25 minutes, depending on their size.

SUMMER SQUASH CREOLE

➤ Please read About Squashes, 328.

Have ready:

2½ cups well-drained cooked zucchini, yellow crooked neck or pattypan squash

Place it in a greased baking dish and proceed as for:

Stuffed Eggplant Creole, 304

substituting squash for eggplant.

DEEP-FRIED ZUCCHINI

➤ Please read About Deep-Fat Frying, 147, and About Squashes, 328.

Wash, dry and cut into ¼- to ½-inch slices:

Zucchini

Dry well. Dip in:

Fritter Batter for Vegetables, 243

Heat in a deep fryer to 365°:

Vegetable oil

Fry the squash until golden. Serve at once.

SUMMER SQUASH CASSEROLE COCKAIGNE

4 Servings

We are particularly fond of zucchini in this dish.

➤ Please read About Squashes, 328.

Preheat oven to 375°.

Drain:

2 cups cooked zucchini, 328, or other squash, cut into ¾-inch slices

Place zucchini in 4 buttered flat ramekins. Cover with a mixture of:

1 can condensed cream of chicken soup: 10 oz.
½ cup cultured sour cream or yogurt

Top with:

Au Gratin III, 553
(Chopped nuts)

Bake about 7 minutes or until thoroughly heated.

SPAGHETTI SQUASH

For those on wheat-free diets, try this as a base for pasta sauces. Bake like potatoes, 319. Crack open the peeling and scoop out strings and seeds. Add butter, salt and pepper. Or boil without peeling in water to cover 20 to 30 minutes. Cut in half and remove seeds. Sauce and toss as for spaghetti.

MASHED WINTER SQUASH

➤ Please read About Squashes, 328.

I.

Preheat oven to 375°.

Scrub:

A Hubbard or other winter squash

Place it on a rack and bake until it can be pierced easily with a wooden pick. Cut it in halves; remove the seeds. Peel the squash and mash the pulp. To:

1 cup squash

add:

1 tablespoon butter
1 teaspoon brown sugar
¼ teaspoon salt
⅛ teaspoon ginger

Beat this well with enough:

Warm cream or orange juice

to make it a good consistency. Place in a serving dish. Sprinkle with:

Raisins or nutmeats
¼ cup crushed pineapple

II. ✻ If using frozen or canned squash, you may season with:

Sautéed onions
Cultured sour cream
A pinch allspice
Chopped parsley

Heat in a double boiler over—not in—boiling water.

BAKED WINTER SQUASH

➤ Please read About Squashes, 328.

Preheat oven to 375°.

If the squash is small, like:

Acorn or butternut squash

it may be washed, dried, greased and treated just like Baked Potatoes, 319. Bake at least 1 to 1½ hours. Season as in the above recipe and garnish with:

(Pimiento strips or Au Gratin II, 553)

The smaller baked winter squashes make attractive cases for the stuffings in the recipe below.

STUFFED WINTER SQUASH

Small acorn or butternut squash are ideal for individual service. You may fill the raw shell, or bake it first as in Baked Winter Squash, above, and then fill it with the hot creamed foods suggested below.

➤ Please read About Stuffed Vegetables, 280, and About Squashes, 328.

Prepare cooked:

Acorn squash cases, see above

Fill them with:

Creamed oysters, chicken, chipped beef, crab, fish, or mushrooms; spinach, hash, hash and vegetables, hot applesauce or crushed pineapple; cooked sausage meat or Ham à la King, 258

Garnish the tops with:

Parsley

Reheat in an ovenproof dish 10 to 15 minutes in a 350° oven.

PUMPKIN

We Americans think of this squash first as pie, 654, and next as soup, 185, but it is also surprisingly satisfactory as a vegetable. Cook by any recipe calling for a winter squash, or see page 654. About ½ pound will serve 1 person.

TAMPALA OR CHINESE SPINACH

When the leaves of this tropical amaranth are about 6 inches tall, it is cooked as for Spinach, 326.

ABOUT TARO OR DASHEEN

This versatile plant has leaves similar in form to the inedible elephant ears we grow decoratively, and a potatolike root that becomes grayish or violet when cooked. It is used as a vegetable or as a base for puddings and confections. The spinach-flavored leaves, if young, are cooked as for spinach; when mature, they may need about 45 minutes.

To bake, remove loose fibers and parboil the unpared root 15 minutes, then time as for potato baking, but make sure the oven is not over 375°. Uncooked taro may prove irritating to the skin, so handle it in water to which you add 1 tablespoon baking soda for every quart of water. To boil taro, treat as for Boiled Potatoes, 317. Taro may also be fried as for Saratoga Chips, 323. Do not soak the slices—merely dry for 30 minutes on paper toweling.

POI

About 5 Cups

Dice into 1-inch cubes:

2½ lb. boiled, peeled taro roots, above

Mash in a wooden bowl with a wooden potato masher until a starchy paste forms. Work in gradually with the hands:

2½ cups water

To remove lumps and fiber, force the poi through several thicknesses of cheesecloth. Serve promptly or let it stand 2 to 3 days in a cool place until it ferments and has a sour taste.

ABOUT TOMATOES

Those of us accustomed to having the highest court in the land pronounce upon paramount issues of our national life will not be surprised to learn that as long ago as 1893 the Justices resoundingly declared the tomato a vegetable, not a fruit. Either way, it ranks with lemon as a perennial inspiration for culinary uplift—fresh or canned or as juice, purée, paste, catsup or chili sauce. To process for canning, see 808.

In many sections of the country fresh large-sized field-grown tomatoes are not available during the colder months, being supplanted by hydroponic or hothouse-grown kinds. We find most of these disappointingly mushy in texture. Try occasionally the meaty pear-shaped **Italian tomatoes,** which are sweeter than the American types.

When you use fresh tomatoes in cooking, their juiciness is seldom an asset. To avoid watery results, slit the stem end and remove it; then, holding your hand palm down above a bowl, squeeze the tomato to eject excess juice and seeds. When recipes call for strained canned tomatoes, be sure to force the pulp through the sieve well, to make the most of its thickening and seasoning power; and watch your brands—the cheaper ones are apt to be diluted. To skin fresh tomatoes, see 105.

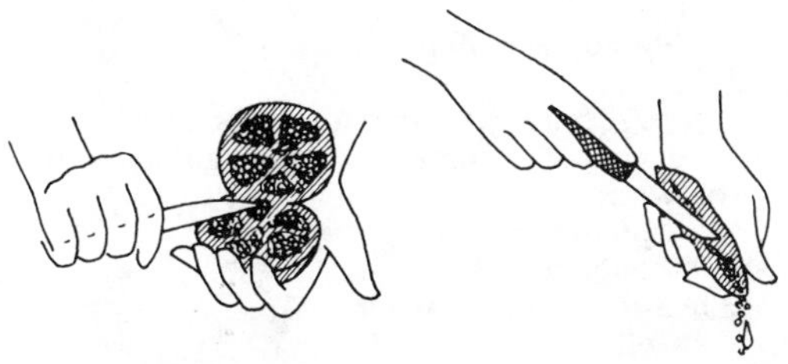

Tomatoes have run the usual checkered gamut of vegetable introductions: they were regarded at one time or another as purely decorative, poisonous, and aphrodisiac. Now that they have become staples, it is nice to emphasize their solid virtues, one of which is high vitamin A and C content. These values as well as good color and condition may be preserved in ripe—not overripe—fruit for as long as 5 to 6 days after picking if stored in light—not sunlight—unwrapped, at between 65° and 75°, and upside down. Best practice, though, is to make use of only vine-ripened fruit and to store it at once in the refrigerator. Similarly, to assure maximum food value, prepare tomatoes just before serving. Fruit of mature size but still green in color may be ripened on a windowsill but will lack the flavor and some of the nutritive value of its vine-ripened counterpart. Immature small-sized tomatoes will not ripen satisfactorily after harvesting. Use them, if at all, for pickling, 844. Do not attempt to freeze tomatoes: no effective process has yet been developed.

Prepare tomatoes stuffed, not only for Salads, 105, but as cases for vegetables; see recipes on 333–334.

STEWED TOMATOES

4 Servings

Wash, skin and quarter:

6 large tomatoes or 2½ cups canned tomatoes

Place them in a heavy pan over slow heat—about 20 minutes for the fresh tomatoes, 10 for the canned. You may add:

(1 teaspoon minced onion)
(½ cup chopped celery)
(2 or 3 cloves)

Stir occasionally to keep them from scorching. Season with:

¾ teaspoon salt
¼ teaspoon paprika
2 teaspoons white or brown sugar

1/8 teaspoon curry powder or 1 teaspoon chopped parsley or basil
1 tablespoon butter

The tomatoes may be thickened with:

(1/2 cup bread crumbs)

STEWED GREEN TOMATOES

4 Servings

Sauté until light brown:

2 tablespoons minced onion

in:

2 tablespoons butter

Add:

2 cups sliced large green tomatoes

Stir and cook the tomatoes slowly until tender. Season with:

3/4 teaspoon salt
1/4 teaspoon paprika
1/2 teaspoon curry powder

Garnish with:

1 tablespoon chopped parsley

CREAMED CANNED TOMATOES

4 Servings

Simmer gently about 3 minutes:

2 cups drained canned tomatoes
1 pressed clove garlic or 2 teaspoons onion juice
3/4 teaspoon salt
1/4 teaspoon paprika
2 teaspoons brown sugar
(1/2 cup chopped celery)

Combine until smooth and bring just to a boil:

1 tablespoon flour
1/2 cup cream or milk

➤ To avoid curdling, add the tomato mixture slowly to the cream or milk, never vice versa. Stir constantly over very low heat until the raw-flour taste is gone, about 3 to 5 minutes.

TOMATO PROVENÇALE

This dish looks very professional as a platter-garnish. Choose:

Firm ripe tomatoes

Slice off a deep enough section horizontally on the stem end to get an even surface. Do the same on the base. Divide the rest of the tomato horizontally. Place these thick slices on a rack to drain. Sprinkle on top of each:

Salt and black pepper
Chopped basil
A slight pinch of oregano

Melt enough:

Butter

to coat the tomato slices. Place in the butter:

A split clove of garlic

Or, as an alternative to the butter, squeeze a little garlic juice on a thin square of:

(Parmesan cheese)

that will almost cover the tomato slice. Allow the seasoned tomatoes to remain at 70° for 1 hour. Preheat both broiler and oven to 350°. Put the slices on a greased baking sheet. Run them under a broiler first to brown slightly and then bake 15 minutes. Serve at once.

GRILLED TOMATOES

4 Servings

Preheat broiler.
Wash:

4 large firm tomatoes

Cut them crosswise into even 1/2- to 1-inch slices. Season well with:

1 teaspoon salt
1/4 teaspoon pepper
A pinch of white or brown sugar
(Celery salt)

Place in a greased pan and cover closely with

About 1 cup Au Gratin III, 553
(2 tablespoons or more grated onion)

Broil about 10 minutes ➤ approximately 5 inches from the heat source.
Or dip them in:

Bound Breading III, 552

Bake on a greased sheet until nearly soft, then broil as above, until brown, turning once.

TOMATOES CREOLE

4 Servings

Sauté until golden in:

2 tablespoons butter
1 large minced onion

Add:

6 skinned, sliced, seeded tomatoes or 2 cups drained canned tomatoes
2 tablespoons minced celery
1 shredded green pepper

Cook the vegetables until tender, about 12 minutes. Add:

3/4 teaspoon salt
1/4 teaspoon paprika
2 1/2 teaspoons brown sugar
(3/4 teaspoon curry powder)

Strain the juice from the vegetables and add to it enough:

Cream

to make 1 1/2 cups of liquid. Stir in:

Beurre Manié, 340

Simmer and stir the sauce until thick and smooth. Combine with the vegetables and serve hot on:

Toast

with:

Sautéed bacon

Or use the mixture to fill pepper or squash cases.

TOMATO OLIVE CASSEROLE

4 Servings

If you have any prejudice against tapioca, please dismiss it long enough to try out this fine dish. Serve with ham, scrambled eggs or omelet.
Discard as many seeds as possible and place in the top of a double boiler:

1 1/2 cups canned tomatoes

Sauté until golden:

1/4 cup minced onion

in:

1 tablespoon butter

Add it to the strained tomatoes with:

3 tablespoons quick-cooking tapioca
½ teaspoon salt
½ teaspoon sugar
⅛ teaspoon paprika

Cook and stir these ingredients in the double boiler ➤ over—not in—hot water about 7 minutes. Chop coarsely and add:

18 stuffed or ripe olives

Preheat oven to 350°.
Grease a baking dish. Fill it with the mixture.
Cover the top with:

Au Gratin III, 553

Bake about 30 minutes.

TOMATO CUSTARD

6 Servings

Preheat oven to 325°.
Skin and squeeze well, 331, to expel excess liquid and seeds and put through a coarse sieve:

Enough tomatoes to make 2 cups

Beat together with:

3 eggs
1 cup milk
¼ cup sugar
½ teaspoon salt
⅛ teaspoon nutmeg

Bake in custard cups about 30 minutes or until set. Serve hot or cold.

TOMATO PUDDING COCKAIGNE

Either of these recipes should serve six, but we find the demand for this favorite makes four servings a safer count.

I. Preheat oven to 375°.
In winter, place in a saucepan:

1¼ cups Tomato Purée, 806
¼ cup boiling water

Heat to the boiling point and add:

¼ teaspoon salt
6 tablespoons brown sugar
½ teaspoon dried basil

Place in a 9-inch baking dish:

1 cup fresh white bread crumbs, 551

Pour over them:

¼ cup melted butter

Add the tomato mixture and:

(2 tablespoons chopped stuffed olives)

➤ Cover the dish closely. Bake the pudding about 30 minutes. Do not lift the lid until ready to serve.

II. Preheat oven to 325°.
In summer, substitute for the dried basil:

1½ to 2 teaspoons fresh chopped basil
1 teaspoon chopped chives
1 teaspoon chopped parsley

and for the tomato purée and water substitute:

14 skinned, seeded, sliced tomatoes

Bake the dish 2½ to 3 hours until it has cooked down to a pastelike consistency.

SCALLOPED TOMATOES

6 Servings

Preheat oven to 350°.
Drain:

3 cups canned Italian-type tomatoes or peeled, diced fresh tomatoes

Sauté until golden in:

3 tablespoons butter
¼ cup finely chopped onions

Add:

1 tablespoon brown sugar
1 teaspoon salt
¼ teaspoon pepper
(A grating of nutmeg)
1¾ cups toasted bread crumbs

Place the tomatoes in a buttered baking dish alternately with layers of the bread crumb mixture, ending with a layer of crumbs. Bake about 30 minutes.

TOMATO TART

6 Servings

Have ready:

6 baked 2-inch Tart Shells, 640

Prepare a filling of:

¾ cup Tomato Purée, 806
¾ cup White Sauce III, 341
3 tablespoons sautéed chopped onions
½ cup sautéed chopped chicken livers
2 tablespoons chopped stuffed olives

Just before serving, preheat the oven to 400°. Fill the tarts and bake until thoroughly heated. Serve at once.

ABOUT HOT STUFFED TOMATOES

To prepare cases for hot food, cut large hollows in the stem ends of very firm unpeeled tomatoes. Salt and invert them on a rack to drain about 15 minutes. Fill the tomato cases with any of the following cooked foods and cover with:

Au Gratin I, II, or III, 552

Place the cases on rack in a pan with enough water to keep them from scorching and bake in a preheated 350° oven 10 or 15 minutes. If they are very ripe, you may bake them in well-greased muffin tins to keep them shapely. For fillings, try:

Creamed ham or cooked sausage and mushrooms
Bread crumbs and deviled ham
Chestnuts and rice or wild rice, seasoned with salt and brown sugar
Creamed green peas or mushrooms with parsley
Mashed potatoes and nuts
Creamed Spinach, 327

Or use one of the following recipes.

TOMATOES STUFFED WITH PINEAPPLE

4 Servings

➤ Please read About Stuffed Tomatoes, above.
Preheat oven to 350°.

Prepare:
4 medium-sized tomato cases
Sprinkle each hollow with:
1 teaspoon brown sugar
Place in each hollow some of the following mixture:
1 cup drained crushed pineapple
2 tablespoons dry bread crumbs
A grating of fresh ginger
Sprinkle the tops with:
Au Gratin II, 553
Bake as for Hot Stuffed Tomatoes, 333, and serve on:
Toast rounds

TOMATOES STUFFED WITH CORN

4 Servings

➤ Please read About Stuffed Tomatoes, 333.
Preheat oven to 350°.
Prepare:
4 tomato cases
Sauté, then crumble:
4 slices bacon
Combine:
1 cup cooked drained corn
1 chopped pimiento
½ chopped green pepper, seeds and membrane removed
2 tablespoons chopped celery
½ cup bread crumbs
2 tablespoons corn liquor or cream
½ teaspoon salt
¼ teaspoon paprika
½ teaspoon sugar, if the corn is green
Add the bacon. Fill the tomato cases. Sprinkle the tops with:
Au Gratin I or III, 552
Bake as for Hot Stuffed Tomatoes, 333.

TOMATOES FILLED WITH ONIONS AND ANCHOVIES

6 Servings

➤ Please read About Stuffed Tomatoes, 333.
Preheat oven to 350°.
Prepare:
6 tomato cases
Melt:
2 tablespoons bacon drippings or butter
Add and sauté until golden:
½ cup finely chopped onion
Chop the pulp taken from the tomatoes and combine it with the onions. Add:
1½ teaspoons brown sugar
½ teaspoon salt
1 tablespoon celery seed
Simmer these ingredients for about 10 minutes. Add:
2 tablespoons sautéed chopped peppers
4 chopped anchovies
If the filling is too moist, it may be thickened with:
(Bread crumbs)
If too dry, it may be moistened with:
(Stock)
Fill the tomato cases. Cover the tops with:
Au Gratin I or III, 553
Bake as for Hot Stuffed Tomatoes, 333.

TOMATOES STUFFED WITH CREAMED SWEETBREADS

8 Servings

➤ Please read About Stuffed Tomatoes, 333.
Prepare:
8 large tomato cases
Have ready:
½ cup chopped Sautéed Mushrooms, 308
Have ready:
1 cup Poached Calf Sweetbreads, 502
Bring to the boiling point:
1 cup White Sauce I, 341
Add the other ingredients to the sauce. Thicken with:
(¼ cup bread crumbs)
Preheat oven to 350°.
Fill the tomato cases. Cover the tops with:
Au Gratin II or III, 553
Bake as for Hot Stuffed Tomatoes, 333.

TOMATOES STUFFED WITH SEAFOOD

6 Servings

➤ Please read About Stuffed Tomatoes, 333.
Preheat oven to 350°.
Prepare:
6 tomato cases
Melt over low heat:
1½ tablespoons butter
Add and cook for 3 minutes:
3 tablespoons minced green pepper
3 tablespoons minced onion
Stir in until blended:
1½ tablespoons flour
Stir in slowly:
1½ cups milk
When sauce is thick and hot, add:
1½ cups crab meat, chopped shrimp or lobster
⅓ teaspoon salt
A few grains red pepper
2 teaspoons Worcestershire sauce
(1 cup grated cheese)
Simmer and stir these ingredients until the cheese is melted. Fill the tomato cases with this mixture. Bake as for Hot Stuffed Tomatoes, 333.

ABOUT TURNIPS

Children often enjoy these spunky, time-honored vegetables well-washed and raw, like apples; and the knowing choose them as an accompaniment to game. They make a good change, if browned, to serve instead of potatoes around a roast, 454. A favorite peasanty dish, **Himmel und Erde,** is made of mashed turnips, potatoes and seasoned apples, combined in any proportion.

Discard woody turnips and parblanch old ones

3 to 5 minutes before cooking. One pound of turnips will yield about 2 cups cooked.

Cut off the tops at once and store turnips in a dark cool place. The tops, if tender, may be used as greens, 305.

⊗ Pressure cook whole turnips 8 to 12 minutes at 15 lbs.

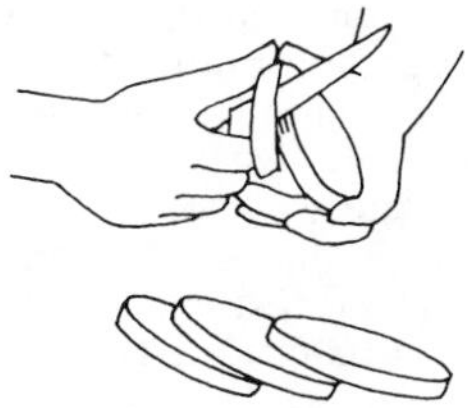

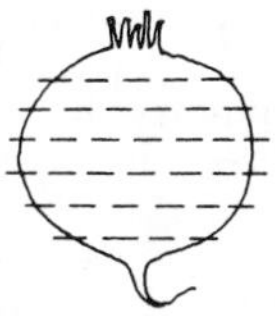

COOKED TURNIPS

I. **4 Servings**

Wash, slice as shown above, and to avoid bitterness pare past the dark line separating rind from the white center:

1 lb. young turnips

Steam, 278, 15 to 20 minutes. Drain.

Season to taste

and dress with:

Butter

Lemon juice and vinegar or Quick Tomato Sauce, 352

or mash or cream as for potatoes.

II. If turnips are mature, you may parblanch, 154, 3 to 5 minutes:

Pared sliced or whole turnips

Drop them into rapidly boiling water to cover. Add:

½ teaspoon salt

½ teaspoon sugar

Cook uncovered 15 to 20 minutes if sliced, 20 to 25 minutes if whole, or until tender. Serve as in I.

GLAZED TURNIPS

Cook as directed above:

Young turnips

Drain and dry them well. Brown in:

Hot melted butter

Season with:

Paprika and sugar or a little Meat Glaze, 368

which helps with the browning.

Season to taste

Serve at once, rolled in:

Chopped parsley

SCALLOPED TURNIPS

Prepare as for:

Scalloped Potatoes, 319

substituting for the potatoes turnips alone or turnips and sliced onions or turnips and apples.

STUFFED TURNIP CUPS

I. **8 Servings**

➤ Please read About Stuffed Vegetables, 280.

Preheat oven to 350°.

Pare, then blanch, 3 to 5 minutes:

8 medium-sized turnips

Hollow into cups, reserving and chopping the pulp. Melt:

1 tablespoon butter

Sauté in it about 3 minutes:

1 tablespoon grated onion

2 tablespoons seasoned cooked peas

Combine the pulp with the onion and peas. Season with:

Salt and white pepper

Thicken slightly with:

Cracker crumbs or bread crumbs

Fill the turnip cups with this mixture. Place them in a greased baking dish. Pour around them:

½ cup milk

Bake until tender, about 15 minutes.

II. Proceed as above, using a filling of leftover sauced foods, or a cooked stuffing, 370.

WATER CHESTNUTS

Please read About Water Chestnuts, 563.

These crisp vegetables are added usually as a garnish to other vegetables.

➤ Add for the last 2 or 3 minutes of cooking only.

WATERCRESS

Usually thought of only as salad and sandwich material, watercress not only adds a distinctive flavor to soups and vegetables but lends piquancy to other cooked greens. Never overcook it, as it becomes stringy. Serve it puréed as a garnish with grills, chops or scallops.

SAVORY SAUCES AND SALAD DRESSINGS

When Voltaire chose to contrast his native country with England by observing that France was a land of forty-two sauces and one religion, whereas Britain was a land of one sauce and forty-two religions, he was wrong on both counts. But the witticism throws an interesting light on which two cultural consolations even a free-thinking Frenchman instinctively brackets as enjoying top international priority.

Some sauces complement the food with which they are served: that is, they supply either the blandness or the piquancy which that food lacks. Others compliment it, so to speak: they enhance or heighten its intrinsic flavor. All sauces, of whatever character, should be so perfectly smooth, so skillfully blended that, like successful soups, they can be eaten all by themselves. Basic prerequisites in sauce-making are ➤ never to use high heat; ➤ to remove sauces-in-progress from the heat before stirring in fresh ingredients; and ➤ always, if such ingredients are cold, to **temper** them by mixing them first in a separate container with a small quantity of the original hot liquid before returning both to the cook-pot. This last injunction is especially important for egg-based sauces. Other pointers to infallible sauce-making will be found in each sauce category, with suggestions for adding herbs, especially fresh herbs such as basil, above, rear right; and chervil, near the blender—which do not dry well—or a grating of lemon rind or gingerroot and a few minced shallots, all shown in chapter heading.

By designating the sauces in this chapter as **savory**, we mean to differentiate them from the **sweet** types which are dealt with on pages 769 to 776. The savory sauces that follow are themselves grouped into two general classes, hot and cold, although a few can be served both ways. It must be noted here, too, that Europeans—sensibly, we think—do not carry temperatures to extremes, their "cold" savory sauces being served, for the most part, cool, never chilled; the "hot" ones generally lukewarm. As to content, the sequence runs as follows: white sauces; brown sauces, or gravies; soup-based sauces, which are simpler to make and less caloric than the classic *sauces brunes,* as well as surprisingly satisfactory; butter sauces, including seasoned butters; sauces in which tomato dominates; barbecue sauces; sweet-sours; cream sauces; hot egg-based sauces; those based on French dressing, or vinaigrettes—with a trail of other non-egg, non-cream sauces; cold egg-based sauces; some cold cream-based salad dressings; and decorative thick sauces, like glazes and glaçage.

After a number of these groups, we have set down formulas for low-calorie substitutes—or, to use a more appropriate term—makeshifts. Such sauces are based on gelatin, evaporated milk, bread crumbs, cream of rice, strong stocks, tomato juice, walnut and mustard catsup, etc. Slimmers might keep in mind that almost any zesty salad dressing may be pretty much defused if its butter, egg or flour content is sharply cut back or eliminated altogether; also that dressings made with lemon juice or yogurt, or *au maigre* constituents, such as fish fumet—indeed, all the boiled or sweet-sour sauces—make helpful allies for anybody who happens to be "thick and tired of it."

For Marinades, see 528; Au Gratin, 552; Tomato and other Catsups, 847; Chili Sauce, 847; Worcestershire Sauce, 848; Pickled Horseradish, 848. For sweet sauces of all types, see Dessert Sauces, 769.

ABOUT SAUCE TOOLS

Handy-sized simple tools hanging near the stove encourage the addition of interesting ingredients to sauces. ➤ The three hand beaters sketched on the left, opposite, make lumps vanish. The third is particularly useful for beating an egg in a cup. ➤ If the recipe calls for beating over ice, see illustration, 205. For adding flavorings, keep measuring spoons handy. For a quick grating of cheese, onion or bread crumbs, try the rotary grater shown next. Kitchen shears with a self-releasing hinge are easy to keep clean and unrusted. Snip herbs quickly, right into the sauce.

A garlic press, center, will squeeze enough juice to give an ineffable flavor to your sauces, and the hand grater is convenient for a touch of shaved lemon rind or a grating of nutmeg. Also have ready a bar-type strainer for the quick clearing of very small quantities of sauce. For larger ones, use a Chinese hat or conical strainer, illustrated last, and for very careful straining, line this with muslin.

By all means use very hard wooden spoons for the fragile sauces that may be broken down by the more vigorous metal tools. A sauce spoon with one pointed end, shown next to last, will easily scrape the pan edges clean and will help avoid lumping. If you should use a metal spoon, make sure it is stainless steel, so as not to discolor a delicate mixture.

Electric beaters and ⅄ blenders are great labor-savers in the kitchen and will beat out lumps very quickly. They do, however, change the texture and flavor of the sauce somewhat, as they whip in a good deal of air, which will tend to make a thickened sauce foamy and less tasty and a brown sauce rather lighter in color. At high speed they also are likely to overmacerate herbs and so sharpen their flavor.

ABOUT HOT SAVORY SAUCES

There are certain old dowagers who try to dominate "sauciety." Call them the mother sauces, as the French do, if you like. Each has her strong peculiarities of individual makeup; each traditionally queens it over a whole coterie of dishes. The leanest member of the clan, but one capable of much highly successful cross-breeding, is pan gravy.

Her roux-based cousins have more solid and dependable backgrounds and take greater abuse in heating, reheating and storing, for their flour and butter base combines into as stable an alliance as any in the kitchen. There are the delicate pale members of the roux family, descended from Béchamel, who accept the company of eggs, cream and even shallots. There are the robust characters, originating in browned flours, who have picked up acquaintanceships with strange foreign spices, who love tomatoes, and who, on occasion, set their caps for garlic. Both rely for authenticity on two principles: ➤ Their roux base must be cooked to rid it and them of any trace of plebeian floury origin, and it must always be hot when added to cold liquids or cold when added to hot.

There are the plush sauce aristocracy who scorn flour altogether and derive their stamina from eggs. Like a lot of other sauces for cold food, the mayonnaise branch performs this elegant trick without requiring heat. While its cousins, the Hollandaise-Béarnaise group, must have heat, they need it only in small doses and only for short periods.

Most showy and demonstrative of all are the wine sauces, the vinaigrettes, the playful tenderizing sweet-sours or agrodolces, the barbecues, and of course the truly sweet dessert sauces, 769, which are the simpering sentimentalists of the whole colony.

Do not limit your acquaintanceship with this far-flung family until you have met them all; and until you are clever enough even to spot a rare nonidentical twin—with arrowroot as thickener—or an occasional reveler in fancy dress, tricked out with Beurre Manié, 340, or Butter Swirls, 339. These wayward collaterals are among the most treasured, if fleeting, personalities of all.

When you once feel at home in sauce circles, you will learn rapidly how to make their charmed members your partners in a day-to-day campaign of culinary enhancement. You will learn how to skillfully blend the hot ingredients, so that they receive food without thinning. You will discover that ➤ adding the wine before—not after—the eggs and cream will avoid curdling, and that ➤ a mixture can be stabilized with that extra bit of cream when separation threatens.

Of course, there is always the ⅄ blender to fall back on in a crisis of this kind, but the texture of the sauce can never be so smooth or so thick as if it had been properly made in the first place. In sauces based on cornstarch ➤ overbeating itself can disturb consistency—and this factor alone may cause thinning, see Cornstarch, 548. The use of a light whisk or a wooden spoon is a help in avoiding this condition. Another reason for thinning in sauces may be the addition of acid in the form of fruit juice or wine. ➤ Sauces will also lose body if covered and held heated, for the excess steam created thins them and tends to cause separation. ➤ To lessen separation in frozen sauces, see Waxy Rice Flour, 549. ➤ In preparing sauced foods, allow half as much sauce as solid ingredients

COLOR IN SAUCES

The vast majority of sauces, if well prepared, need no artificial coloring; the various ways ➤ to maintain and develop their natural color are described above. Rich beef stock combined with some tomato, browned meat—in the case of a stew—browned onions and carrots and a brown roux will result in a rich brown sauce needing no addition

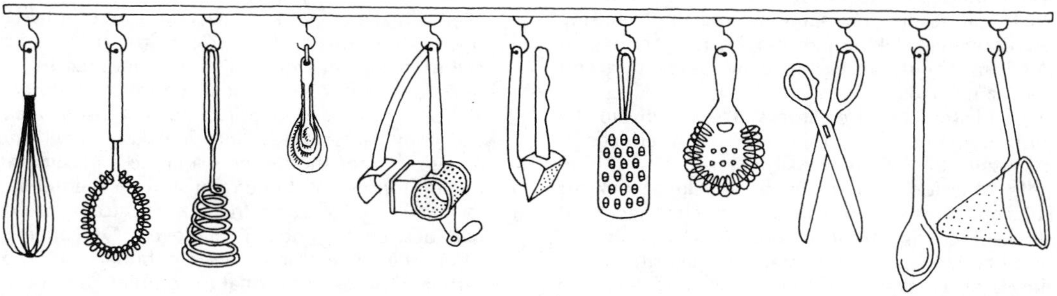

of caramel to bring up the color. If you feel obliged to add caramel, soy sauce or vegetable-based dyes to gravies, add them sparingly. Some cooks use yellow coloring for chicken gravies and sauces to try to hide the omission of chicken fat and egg yolks. Should you use saffron, do beware of its overpowering flavor. A tomato sauce will keep good color if you do not cook it too quickly or too long.

SAUCES IN QUANTITY

➤ If you are making gravies or sauces in large amounts, it will take considerably longer to get rid of the raw flour taste after the liquid has been added to the roux than when you are making only 1 or 2 cups for immediate family use. We advise heating these large amounts ➤ uncovered in a slow oven ½ to ¾ hour and straining the sauce before serving, to remove any crusting or lumps. But if you will stir the sauce from time to time, it may not be necessary to strain it.

➤ When doubling the ingredients in sauce recipes, taste before adding the full amount of seasoning. It is easy to overdo it.

KEEPING SAUCES

You may keep Béchamel, Velouté, tomato and brown sauces in the refrigerator about a week. To store, strain the sauce, pour it into a container and cover with a thin layer of fat or sherry.

You can also ✻ freeze the sauces mentioned above in ice-cube trays and keep the cubes in your freezer in a plastic bag, taking out as many as you need for immediate use. They may be melted in a double boiler—4 large cubes melt down to about ½ cup of sauce. You may also freeze Hollandaise Sauce, 358, and Béarnaise Sauce, 359, but be very careful when reheating. Do not try to freeze mayonnaise; it will break. And, in general, do not try to keep sauces made with eggs, cream or milk for more than 2 or 3 days in the refrigerator.

ABOUT SAVORY SAUCE INGREDIENTS

Many savory sauces depend on some sort of pan gravy, because pan residues, unless derived from less-than-fresh fish or from strong variety meats like kidneys, are most desirable sauce ingredients. They may result from sautéing, roasting, braising or browning. Making pan gravies is described in detail in About Sauces Made by Degreasing and Deglazing, 340.

Good strong, fat-free Stocks, 520, are invaluable sauce ingredients, too, especially when reduced to a Glaze, 367. Where possible, the stock should reflect the food it is to flavor: chicken stock for chicken, lamb stock for lamb, etc. Although meat stocks, including those of poultry and game, are often combined in sauce-making—favorites being those of chicken and veal—fish and shellfish Fumets, 524, should be reserved only for fish and shellfish dishes. Meat broths always make better sauce ingredients if refrigerated 24 hours and then defatted.

When pan residues or stocks are scanty, turn—with discretion—to wine. ➤ Please read About Wine for Cooking, 525. Use, as a rule of thumb, dry white wines in sauces for fish or white meats; dry red wines for red meats. Strong game sauces sometimes support stronger liquors such as rum, brandy or Madeira, but whisky is not recommended. ➤ In any wine sauce, add egg, milk, cream or Butter Swirls, 339, after the wine has been incorporated.

ABOUT THICKENERS FOR SAUCES

Sauces not made by deglazing with liquids, as described above, are generally thickened just enough to coat food lightly. Suggestions for thickening—other than those below—are found in Thickeners for Soups, 168.

ROUX

The most common thickeners for savory sauces are the roux—white or brown. All of them are made of the same ingredients to begin with but change in character as heat is applied. These mixtures of flour and fats are blended gently ➤ over very low heat from 5 minutes to a considerably longer period, depending on your available time and your patience. White roux should not color; those to which stock is added, barely; while brown ones should reach the color of hazelnut and smell deliciously baked. ➤ Unless a roux is cooked long enough to dispel the raw taste of flour, this unpleasant flavor will dominate the strongest stocks and seasonings. And unless the flour and butter are stirred to distribute the heat and to allow the starch granules to swell evenly, they will later fail to absorb the liquid, and the sauce will be thin. ➤ This heated blending period is most important. Using excessive heat to try hurrying it will burn the flour, giving it a bitter taste; and it will shrink the starch, making it incapable of continuing to swell.

For white roux-based sauces, see Béchamel, 341; for those made of white sauce to which stock is added, see Velouté, 343; for brown sauces, see Sauce Espagñole, 346. Since most cooks use some form of roux every day, you may find it a timesaver to make one in advance and store it in tablespoon-sized units under refrigeration. It will keep in the ✻ freezer, too, for several months if you proceed as follows. When the roux has been cooked to the desired color and is still soft, measure it by tablespoons onto a baking sheet and freeze. Transfer the frozen wafers to a plastic bag or wide-topped container and store in the freezer. To thicken sauce, drop the wafers into the sauce until desired thickness is achieved. Or you may soften the wafers in a double boiler over hot water and proceed as usual to complete the sauce.

BROWNED FLOUR

A variant used in gravies to enhance color and flavor. The slow but inexpensive procedure by which it is made is worth trying. The flour, when ready, should smell nutty and baked. Place:

1 cup flour

in a dry heavy skillet. ➤ Stir constantly over very low direct heat, scraping the flour from the sides and bottom of the pan. Or, heat the flour in a very slow oven, 200° to 250°, in a very heavy pan. Shake the pan periodically so the flour browns evenly. Do not let it get too dark or, as with brown roux, it will become bitter and lose its thickening power altogether. ➤ Even properly browned flour has only about half the thickening power of all-purpose flour. It may be stored in a tightly covered jar in a cool place.

FLOUR PASTE

Sometimes pressed into service to thicken emergency gravies and sauces, but the results are never so palatable as when even a quick roux is used. Make a paste of flour and cold water or stock. Use about two parts water and one part flour. Stir as much of the paste as needed into the boiling stock or drippings. Let the sauce heat until it thickens and ➤ simmer at least 3 minutes more to reduce the raw taste of the flour. Stir frequently with a wire whisk.

CORNSTARCH

Cornstarch, see 548, is often used where translucency is desirable, as in some Chinese sauces. It should be mixed with a little cold water before being added to the hot liquid. One tablespoon cornstarch will thicken 1½ to 2 cups of liquid. Most Chinese sauces are finished over direct heat. ➤ Overbeating cornstarch-based sauces thins them.

ARROWROOT

Of all the thickeners, this makes the most delicately textured sauces. ➤ But use it only when the sauce is to be served within 10 minutes of preparation. It will not hold, nor will it reheat. Since the flavor of arrowroot is neutral and it does not have to be cooked to remove rawness, as do flour and cornstarch, and since it thickens at a lower temperature than either of them, it is ideal for use in egg and other sauces which should not boil. Allow 2½ teaspoons to 1 cup liquid.

POTATO STARCH OR FECULA

Preferred by some cooks to flour as a thickener in certain delicate sauces. When it is used, less simmering is required and the sauce gains some transparency. ➤ If heated beyond 176°, the sauce will thin out. Serve soon after it has thickened, as it has no holding power. One tablespoon of potato starch will moderately thicken 1 cup of liquid.

EGG YOLKS

Egg yolks not only thicken but also enrich a sauce. ➤ Never add them directly to hot liquid. Stir them into a little cream, then incorporate with them some of the hot sauce in preparation. Stir this mixture into the remainder of the hot liquid and continue to stir over low heat until the sauce thickens. ➤ Do not allow the sauce to boil, or it will curdle. If this happens, plunge pot into cold water and stir; or beat in a small amount of chilled cream. It is generally safer to add egg yolks to a mixture in a double boiler ➤ over—not in—boiling water, unless you can control the heat source very exactly. Two or three egg yolks with a little cream will thicken 1 cup of liquid. Egg yolks added very slowly to melted butter or oil with constant stirring will produce an emulsion that is quite thick. Suitably seasoned, this becomes the base for Hollandaise or mayonnaise. Hard-cooked egg yolks and oil will also emulsify, see Sauce Gribiche, 365.

BLOOD

Blood from the animal or bird the sauce will accompany is a desirable thickener. To save the blood from a freshly killed hare, rabbit or chicken, see 810. You may store it refrigerated a day or two, mixed with 1 or 2 tablespoons vinegar to prevent clotting. Strain it and add it to the sauce at the last minute just before serving, swirling it in as you would butter, below. Simmer gently, but ➤ never allow the sauce to boil after the blood is added.

REDUCTION

Another classic way to thicken sauces. Béchamel and Espagñole may be thickened during very slow simmering by the evaporation of liquid to achieve more richness and subtlety. If you intend to thicken a sauce by reducing it, season ➤ after you have brought it down to the right viscosity; otherwise you may find it highly overseasoned or unpleasantly salty. There are a good many recipes for tomato sauces which demand long cooking and reducing. Unless you can keep these sauces—or, in fact, any thickened sauces—on very low heat, they will cook too fast, and flavor and color will be impaired. In the case of roux-thickened sauces which call for reducing, do use an oven. It is a great labor-saver, and the heat can be controlled much more exactly. ➤ Almost all reduced sauces, to be perfect in texture, should be strained before serving.

BUTTER SWIRLS

These finish off many fine, rich sauces, both white and brown, after straining and final heating. But after swirling, the sauce must be served at once ➤ nor can it be reheated. In addition to improving the flavor, the butter swirl also very slightly thickens the sauce. To make a sauce *finie au beurre* after straining and heating, add ➤ unsalted, unmelted butter bit by bit, moving the pan in a circular motion, so that the butter makes a visible spiral in the hot sauce as it melts. Remove the pan from the heat before the butter is fully melted and continue to swirl. ➤ Do not use a spoon to stir it and do not try to reheat it. About 1 tablespoon butter is generally used to "finish" 1 cup of sauce.

KNEADED BUTTER OR BEURRE MANIÉ

A magic panacea for rectifying sauces or thickening thin ones at the end of the cooking process. Avoid using it, though, for those which require long simmering. After adding kneaded butter ➤ do not boil the sauce. Simmer only long enough to dispel the floury taste. Manipulate with your fingers, as though you were rubbing for fine pastry, 2 tablespoons butter and 2 tablespoons flour. Form into small balls and drop into the hot liquid, stirring constantly until the ingredients are well blended and the sauce thickens. This amount will be sufficient for 1 cup of thin liquid.

FILÉ

Filé powder, the classic thickener of Creole gumbos, has been banned by the FDA as carcinogenic. To reproduce its mucilaginous texture, use Tapioca Flour, 550.

WAYS TO SERVE SAUCES

See above various containers for hot or cold sauces, but there are other attractive ways to serve them. Cold sauces and dips with a mayonnaise or sour cream base may be presented in a crisp hollowed-out cabbage, 77, or individually in tomato or pepper cases, 105. Suggest the sea habitat of cold shrimp or poached salmon with a delicate pink Mayonnaise, 363, or Rémoulade Sauce, 364, by serving them in a large seashell.

Hot sauces may be served in ramekins, tiny tin-lined copper saucepans, and other small heatproof containers. The doll house instinct rises in all of us at the sight of these miniature individual pitchers and pots that are so appropriate when hot lobster, artichokes or asparagus is on the menu. Sauces on the buffet table may be kept hot in small three-legged French saucepans, placed over a candle, in chafing dishes, or in an enameled iron pot over heat, shown in the chapter heading on 336. Like the food it accompanies, sauce, if it is meant to be hot, must be kept hot. However, ➤ any sauce that is worth its salt won't keep indefinitely on a steam table or in a casserole. There is a point of maximum goodness at which it should be served.

Cold sauces and Seasoned Butters, 349, may be kept chilled on a mound of crushed ice; molds and pats of seasoned butter placed directly on the ice. Don't use ice cubes—the butter slips down between them.

ABOUT SAUCES MADE BY DEGREASING AND DEGLAZING

These are a welcome change after the heavier and more familiar roux-based types. Residues and scrapings from sautéing, broiling, roasting and browning constitute the precious base for many delectable pan gravies that are to be served with sautéed or roasted fowl, meat dishes and fish. It is always best, if you sauté with butter—and the butter should be sweet, not salted—to clarify it, 349, or to combine it with a little cooking oil to raise its smoking point, and so prevent scorching. If margarine has been substituted for butter, you may wish to improve the flavor of the final product by finishing off the sauce with a Butter Swirl, 339. In roasting meat, be sure to grease the pans lightly at the start to keep from burning any juices which may drip into the bottom of the roasting pan before it receives a protective covering of rendered fat. Browning lends attractive color, and the incorporation of some fat from the pan will intensify the characteristic meat flavor. Even more effective in this respect is to add to the pan, after browning the meat, a cup of Mirepoix, 572. When the meat is done, remove it from the pan and pour off the fat. There are several ways to do this quickly. One is to pour all the juices into a heatproof glass container and submerge it in cold water. The fat will rise at once and can be spooned off. Another, if there is more fat than stock, is to use a baster, 446: tip the pan and siphon off the good juices from underneath the top layer of grease. Pour off the grease. Return juices to roasting pan. Add 1/4 cup or more hot water, wine or stock and cook on top of the stove, stirring and scraping the solidified juices from the bottom and sides. The addition of wine or dry sherry will hasten the deglazing process and heighten aroma. Use the stock appropriate to your meat or fowl and the kind of wine you would normally drink with it. This, with a Butter Swirl, 339, Beurre Manié, 340, or a little cream, can make the finest of all sauces.

MEAT PAN GRAVY

1 Cup

If you use drippings for sauces, you may want to strain them first and remove excess fat. Reheat some of the fat because it will absorb the flour better. Remove the meat from the pan. Place it where it will remain hot. Pour off all but:

2 tablespoons drippings

Blend into them:

1 or 2 tablespoons flour

Stir with a wire whisk until the flour has thickened and until the mixture is well combined and smooth. Continue to cook slowly and stir constantly, while adding:

The degreased pan juices and milk, water, stock, cream, wine or beer to make 1 cup

The beer may be "flat." Season the gravy with:

Salt
Pepper
Fresh or dried minced herbs
Grated lemon rind

Color, if necessary, with:

A few drops Caramel, 559

You may strain the gravy; reheat before serving. If you are using a thickener other than flour, please read About Thickeners, 338, for the correct amount of cornstarch or arrowroot to be added for the above amount of liquid.

POULTRY PAN GRAVY

About 2 Cups

Strain the juices from the roasted fowl. Pour off and reserve the fat. Heat in a saucepan:

1/4 cup of the fat

Add and stir until blended:

1/4 cup flour

Stir in slowly:

Pan juices and enough Chicken or Poultry Stock, 523, to make 2 cups

Cook and stir the gravy until smooth and ➤ simmer 5 minutes. Add:

Chopped cooked giblets
(1/4 cup or more cream)

➤ If the gravy is very rich, it may separate. Add the cream slowly. Stir it constantly. This will usually forestall any difficulty. Should you wish to add the brown material in the original pan, pour a small quantity of the gravy into the pan to dislodge it, heating slightly if necessary. Stir well and return this liquid to the rest of the gravy.

Season to taste

and serve.

WHITE SAUCE I OR BÉCHAMEL

1 Cup

Very basic: used not only for creaming foods like vegetables and fish but as a base for many other sauces. Melt over low heat:

2 tablespoons butter

For a delicate flavor, even commercial establishments have found no substitute for butter. Add and blend over low heat for 3 to 5 minutes:

1 1/2 to 2 tablespoons flour

Stir in slowly:

1 cup milk

For better consistency, you may scald the milk beforehand; but be sure—to avoid lumping—that the roux is cool when you add it. Add:

1 small onion studded with 2 or 3 whole cloves
1/2 small bay leaf

Cook and stir the sauce with a wire whisk or wooden spoon until thickened and smooth. Place in a 350° oven for 20 minutes to cook slowly. The oven interval also saves your time and hands for other kitchen jobs. Strain the sauce.

Season to taste

Add:

A grating of nutmeg

and serve. For creamed dishes, use about one-half as much sauce as solids.

WHITE SAUCE II OR HEAVY BÉCHAMEL

1 Cup

Used in soufflés.
Prepare:

White Sauce I, above

Use in all:

3 tablespoons butter
3 tablespoons flour
1 cup liquid

WHITE SAUCE III OR BINDING BÉCHAMEL

1 Cup

For croquettes.
Prepare:

White Cream Sauce I, above

Use in all:

3 tablespoons butter
1/3 cup flour
1 cup liquid

WHITE SAUCE IV OR ENRICHED BÉCHAMEL

For poached lean fish.
Reduce:

1 cup White Sauce I, above

to three-fourths of its volume. Stir in:

1/4 cup heavy cream

and bring to boiling point. If the sauce is for fish, add:

(1/2 to 1 teaspoon lemon juice)

QUICK WHITE SAUCE

This base can be flavored and modified in many ways. Melt over low heat:

2 tablespoons butter

Add ➤ still over low heat, stirring about 3 to 4 minutes or until well blended and the taste of raw flour has vanished:

1½ to 2 tablespoons flour

Stir in slowly:

1 cup milk, milk and light stock, light stock, or light stock and cream
Season to taste

and vary the flavor with one or more of the following:

Celery salt
A grating of nutmeg
1 teaspoon lemon juice
½ teaspoon Worcestershire sauce
1 teaspoon sherry
1 teaspoon onion juice
2 tablespoons chopped parsley
2 tablespoons chopped chives

➤ Simmer and stir the sauce with a wire whisk until it has thickened and is smooth and hot. Combine it with other ingredients just as it boils, so that it will not become watery. For creamed dishes, use about half as much sauce as there are solids.

WHITE SAUCE WITH HARD-COOKED EGG

1¼ cups

Delicious when made with half chicken stock and half cream.
Prepare:

White Sauce I, 341

Add to it:

2 chopped hard-cooked eggs
1 tablespoon capers or chopped pickle

FLORENTINE SAUCE

About 2 Cups

Combine:

1 cup White Sauce I, 341
A dash of hot pepper sauce
2 drops Worcestershire sauce
1 cup finely chopped spinach
A fresh grating of nutmeg
1 tablespoon finely chopped parsley

If using the sauce cold for fish, do not thin. If using it hot, you may thin with:

(Cream or dry white wine)

MORNAY SAUCE

About 1¼ Cups

Excellent for masking fish, egg and vegetable dishes. If you are using it in a dish to be browned in the oven or under the broiler, sprinkle a little grated cheese over the top first. Prepare:

1 cup White Sauce I, flavored with onion or shallots, 341

Beat until blended:

1 egg yolk
2 tablespoons cream

➤ Add a little of the sauce to the egg yolk and cream, stirring constantly, then return the mixture to the rest of the sauce and cook until well heated. Then add:

2 tablespoons grated Parmesan cheese
2 tablespoons grated Gruyère cheese

Keep stirring with a small whisk to help melt the cheese and to keep the sauce smooth while it thickens.

Season to taste

with:

Salt and a few grains of cayenne

SAUCE DIJONNAISE

About 2 Cups

For baked or boiled ham or a rather coarse-grained fish.
Prepare:

1 cup White Sauce III, 341

omitting the whole onion. Reserve. Sauté in:

2 tablespoons butter
⅓ cup finely chopped onions

until onions are translucent. Add to skillet:

¼ teaspoon thyme
¼ teaspoon crushed garlic
½ bay leaf
1 teaspoon basil

stirring constantly. Put into a separate pan:

1 can condensed chicken broth
1 cup drained canned tomatoes

and simmer until these ingredients are reduced by half. Remove bay leaf and combine all ingredients. Put them through a sieve, if you like. Bring mixture to a boil, remove from heat and stir in:

1 tablespoon prepared Dijon-type mustard, 582
2 tablespoons Madeira
Season to taste

When ready to serve, add:

A Butter Swirl, 339

CHEESE SAUCE

About 2 Cups

Prepare:

White Sauce I, 341

When it is smooth and hot, reduce the heat and stir in:

1 cup or less mild grated cheese

Season with:

½ teaspoon salt
⅛ teaspoon paprika
A few grains cayenne
(½ teaspoon dry mustard)

Stir the sauce until the cheese is melted.

WHITE WINE SAUCE FOR FISH

About 1¼ Cups

Reduce by half over medium heat a mixture of:

¼ cup white wine
1 bay leaf
2 cloves

2 black peppercorns
(1½-inch piece gingerroot)
¼ cup Fish Stock, 524
1 teaspoon chopped shallots or mild onions
Strain and add to:
1 cup strained White Sauce I, 341
To make a sauce that coats well and browns beautifully, add:
(2 tablespoons whipped cream)

NANTUA OR SHRIMP SAUCE

About 1½ Cups

For fish.
Prepare:
1 cup White Sauce I, 341
Add:
½ cup whipping cream
Rub through a fine sieve:
2 tablespoons Shrimp Butter, 351
Instead of the shrimp butter, you may add 1 tablespoon finely ground shrimp made into a smooth paste with 1 tablespoon butter. Heat to boiling point.
Season to taste
Garnish with:
Finely chopped shrimp

TOMATO SHRIMP SAUCE

3½ Cups

This sauce may be poured over a platter of baked or steamed fish, or may accompany either. It may also be served with a soufflé or a simple omelet.
Prepare:
2 cups Thickened Tomato Sauce, 352
Season the sauce well. Add and heat to the boiling point:
1 teaspoon Worcestershire Sauce, 848, or
2 teaspoons Chili Sauce, 847
2 tablespoons chopped parsley
¼ cup chopped olives
½ cup boiled or canned shrimp
½ cup sautéed or canned mushrooms
¼ cup finely chopped celery

OYSTER SAUCE

About 2 Cups

For fish.
Prepare:
1 cup White Sauce II, 341
Season it well with:
Salt
(1 teaspoon Worcestershire sauce)
Shortly before serving, bring the sauce to the boiling point and add:
3 tablespoons chopped parsley
1 cup finely chopped poached oysters and juice

ANCHOVY SAUCE

1 Cup

For fish and bland vegetables.
Prepare:
White Sauce I, 341
Add to it:
3 fillets of anchovy, washed and pounded to a paste
Blend it well with the sauce.

HORSERADISH SAUCE OR SAUCE ALBERT

1 Cup

A happy complement to boiled or corned beef.
Prepare:
White Sauce I, 341
Remove it from the heat. Add:
3 tablespoons prepared horseradish
2 tablespoons whipping cream
1 teaspoon sugar
1 teaspoon dry mustard
1 tablespoon vinegar
Reheat but do not boil. Serve immediately.

LOW-FAT WHITE SAUCE

About 2 Cups

Combine and scald:
2 cups skim milk
½ teaspoon salt
A dash of white pepper
Sprinkle over the surface and stir in for 1 minute:
3 tablespoons cream of rice
Remove from heat, cover and let stand 4 minutes. Beat well until smooth. Reheat and serve, or store refrigerated and reheat for future use.

BREAD SAUCE

About 3 Cups

The bread crumbs here substitute for flour. This sauce is usually served with small roasted wild birds or roast meat.
Skin:
A small onion
Stud it with:
3 whole cloves
Place the onion in a saucepan with:
2 cups milk
2 tablespoons butter
Bring the milk to a boil. Add:
1 cup fresh white bread crumbs
Simmer for 15 minutes. Remove the onion. Beat the sauce smooth and stir in until blended:
3 tablespoons cream

WHITE SAUCE WITH STOCK OR SAUCE VELOUTÉ

1½ Cups

Another basic: a white sauce made from a roux in which a light stock usually takes the place of milk or cream. The stock may be chicken, veal or fish, depending on the dish the sauce is to accompany. A quick Velouté may be made like White Sauce I, 341, using stock in place of milk, but for a classic sauce of fine texture, proceed as directed below. ➤ The sauce should never be cooked in aluminum pans because they discolor it badly. Melt in the top of a double boiler:

2 tablespoons butter

Stir in:

2 tablespoons flour

When blended, add gradually:

2 cups chicken, veal or fish stock

and stir over low heat until well combined and thickened. Add:

¼ cup mushroom peelings

Place in the double boiler and simmer ➤ over—not in—boiling water about 1 hour, stirring occasionally. Strain through a fine sieve, then add:

A pinch of nutmeg
Season to taste

and stir occasionally during the cooling process to prevent a crust from forming. You may enliven a Velouté by adding combinations of very finely chopped fresh herbs.

AURORE SAUCE

About 2 Cups

A sole-mate—Dover sole.
Prepare:

Velouté Sauce, above

Add:

2 tablespoons tomato purée

to the sauce and mix. Let boil a little before pouring through a sieve and adding:

A Butter Swirl, 339

SOUBISE OR WHITE ONION SAUCE

About 1½ Cups

A delicate onion-flavored sauce for fish, poultry or vegetables.
Prepare:

1½ cups Velouté Sauce, 343

Sauté until transparent:

2 chopped medium-sized onions

in:

2 tablespoons butter

Add the onions to the Velouté Sauce and simmer over low heat 30 minutes, stirring occasionally. Rub the whole sauce through a fine sieve, and finish it off with:

2 tablespoons whipping cream
Season to taste

SUPRÊME SAUCE

About 2 Cups

For fish, poultry and eggs. Its special characteristics are its perfect whiteness and delicacy.
Prepare:

1½ cups Velouté Sauce, 343, made with chicken stock

Add:

1 cup strong light chicken stock
¼ cup mushroom peelings

Bring to a boil, reduce the heat and simmer, stirring occasionally, until the sauce is reduced to 1½ cups. Strain through a fine sieve and add, stirring constantly:

½ cup whipping cream

Stir in:

1 tablespoon butter
Season to taste

CHAMPAGNE SAUCE

About 1¼ Cups

Not every householder has to worry about what to do with leftover champagne, but should this appalling dilemma be yours, there is no better way than this to solve it and make a light but rich sauce for fish or chicken.
Prepare:

¾ cup Velouté Sauce, 343

using fumet to replace the stock if the dish is fish. Have ready:

½ cup butter divided into six portions

Cook together until the mixture reduces almost to a glaze:

1 cup champagne
½ cup minced shallots or mild onions

Remove the mixture from the heat and add the butter, piece by piece, so that it softens but does not liquefy and retains the texture of a Béarnaise sauce. Add:

1½ teaspoons freshly chopped tarragon

and combine the above with the heated but not boiling Velouté. Have the warm cooked fillets of fish or breast of chicken ready on a hot dish. Cover them with the sauce and serve at once.

PAPRIKA OR HUNGARIAN SAUCE

About 1½ Cups

For fish, poultry or veal.
Sauté until golden in:

1 tablespoon butter
1 finely chopped medium-sized onion

Add:

2 tablespoons mild Hungarian paprika

and stir for 1 minute. Add gradually, stirring constantly:

1 cup cream
⅓ cup Velouté Sauce, 343
Season to taste

SAUCE INDIENNE

About 2 Cups

Sauté slowly until tender in:

¼ cup butter
¼ cup finely chopped onion

Stir in and cook, without browning, for 4 or 5 minutes:

2½ tablespoons flour
½ to 2 teaspoons curry powder
A pinch to ¼ teaspoon saffron

Add slowly, stirring constantly, and simmer until well blended:

1 cup chicken broth
1 cup cream
½ teaspoon grated lemon peel

If you wish to have a perfectly smooth sauce, add the chicken broth and grated lemon peel only, cook 10 minutes, strain through a sieve, add the cream and bring back to a boil. You may liven up this sauce, if you like a hot curry, with dashes of:

(Hot pepper sauce)
(Cayenne)
(Ginger)
(Dry sherry)

or by adding:

(Chopped chutney)
(Very small gherkins)

RAVIGOTE SAUCE

Served lukewarm over variety meats, fish, light meats and poultry. Chop until very fine:

2 shallots

Add:

1 tablespoon tarragon vinegar

Cook these ingredients rapidly about 3 minutes, stirring constantly. Add:

1 cup Velouté Sauce, 343

to the shallots and simmer about 10 minutes. Stir frequently. Add:

Salt and freshly ground pepper

Cool the sauce to lukewarm. Add:

1 tablespoon chopped parsley
1 tablespoon chopped chervil
1 tablespoon chopped capers
½ teaspoon chopped chives
½ teaspoon chopped tarragon

Quaintly enough, the classic cuisine also includes a cold "Ravigote" sauce which is not based on Velouté at all, but is in essence an Herbed French Dressing, 360.

SMITANE SAUCE

About 2 Cups

For roast poultry or wildfowl—especially pheasant —and for game if the brown base is used.
Melt in a saucepan:

1 tablespoon butter

Add:

¼ cup finely chopped onions

and cook until transparent, then add:

½ cup dry white wine

and cook until the mixture is reduced to one-half. Add:

1 cup Velouté, 343, or Brown Sauce, 346

Blend and simmer 5 minutes, then add:

1 cup cultured sour cream
Season to taste

For a tarter effect, add:

(A little lemon juice)

After adding the sour cream, do not allow the sauce to boil or it will curdle.

WHITE WINE SAUCE

About 1 Cup

Serve over Sautéed Brains, 504, Sweetbreads, 502, or other light meats. If using with a fish dish, substitute a fumet, 524, for the stock, below.
Heat:

2 tablespoons butter

Add and sauté until light yellow:

1 tablespoon chopped onion or shallots

Stir in until smooth:

1½ tablespoons flour

Stir in gradually, until the sauce is smooth and very hot:

½ cup chicken or veal stock
½ cup dry white wine

You may add:

(1 tablespoon chopped parsley or chives)
Salt, as needed

ALLEMANDE SAUCE OR EGG-THICKENED VELOUTÉ

1½ Cups

An enriched Velouté Sauce, to be used with poached chicken or vegetables. It becomes **Poulette** if, as a final step, you add finely chopped parsley. If, at the last minute, you add a generous tablespoon of drained chopped capers, you have **Caper Sauce,** which goes well with fish or mutton. ➤ Do not let an Allemande boil after the egg is added, or it will curdle.
Prepare:

1½ cups Velouté Sauce, 343

Stir in:

¾ cup strong chicken stock

Blend well and reduce to two-thirds its original volume, stirring occasionally. Remove from the heat and add:

1 egg yolk mixed with 2 tablespoons cream

Stir the sauce until slightly thickened. Just before serving, stir in:

1 tablespoon lemon juice
1 tablespoon butter

CURRY SAUCE

1½ Cups

Pour over whole poached fish or fish fillets.
Prepare:

1½ cups Allemande Sauce, above

adding:

1 teaspoon curry powder

and replacing the ¾ cup chicken stock with:

¾ cup coconut milk, 566

HOT MUSTARD SAUCE

1½ Cups

For poached or broiled fish.
Prepare:

1½ cups Allemande Sauce, above

Add, just before serving:

½ teaspoon dry mustard or 1 teaspoon prepared mustard
¼ teaspoon salt
½ teaspoon freshly ground black pepper

SAUCE FOR WILDFOWL

After roasting the game bird which has been barded with salt pork or bacon and basted with equal quantities of butter and white wine, flambé it in:

⅛ cup brandy: 1 oz.

Remove the game and keep warm. Degrease the pan juices and reduce them over low heat for 1 minute. Then add, for each small bird:

1 egg yolk

Beat in:

½ cup whipping cream

Stir until thickened ➤ but do not allow the sauce to boil. Season well.

PEANUT PEPPER SAUCE

About 1¼ Cups

Use over chicken or beans to enrich their protein content.

Combine in a heavy saucepan over low heat and stir constantly until the ingredients thicken:

½ cup milk
½ cup chicken broth or vegetable stock
4 tablespoons peanut butter
1 teaspoon soy sauce
½ clove garlic, pressed
2 tablespoons finely shredded green pepper or pimiento
(1 teaspoon sugar)
Season to taste

Serve at once.

BROWN SAUCE OR SAUCE ESPAGÑOLE

About 6 Cups

Legion are the children of this mother-sauce, and only the cook's clumsiness or lack of ingenuity need convert them into the changelings we lump together as "gravy." Espagñole is the fundamental brown sauce, but its classic preparation is time-consuming, often involving slow reduction over an 8- to 12-hour period. Today many illustrious restaurants are basing their brown sauces on canned condensed soups, a heresy we have for years happily practiced. The decline in quality, we often think, is balanced by infinitely greater speed of preparation and a welcome drop in caloric content. The recipe below is a kind of compromise short-cut requiring 2 to 2½ hours.

Melt in a heavy saucepan:

½ cup beef or veal drippings

Add:

1 cup Mirepoix, 572

When this begins to color, add:

½ cup flour

and stir until the flour is thoroughly browned.

Add:

10 black peppercorns
2 cups drained, peeled tomatoes or 2 cups tomato purée
½ cup coarsely chopped parsley

Stir and mix well, then add:

8 cups rich beef stock

Simmer 2 to 2½ hours or until reduced by one-half. Stir occasionally and skim off the fat as it rises to the top. Strain and stir occasionally as the sauce cools to prevent the formation of a skin. The sauce should be the consistency of whipping cream, no thicker. If you are using this sauce "as is":

Season to taste

Herbs, spices and mushrooms are frequent additions to any brown sauce.

DEMI-GLAZE SAUCE

About 4½ Cups

The Espagñole, above, reduced to the *n*th degree. Serve with filet mignon or any meat with which Madeira Sauce, below, is generally used.

Combine in a heavy saucepan:

4 cups Brown Sauce, above
4 cups rich beef stock, flavored with mushroom trimmings

Simmer slowly until reduced by half. Strain into a double boiler and keep warm over hot water while adding:

½ cup dry sherry

MADEIRA SAUCE

About 1 Cup

A dry sherry may be substituted. Highly sympathetic to game or fillet of beef.

Reduce:

1 cup Brown Sauce, above

to three-fourths its volume, then add:

¼ cup Madeira
(1 teaspoon Meat Glaze, 368)

Finish with a:

Butter Swirl, 339

and another:

2 tablespoons Madeira

Keep hot, but do not let boil after adding the butter. You may also make this in the pan in which you have cooked the meat. Remove meat and pour off fat. Deglaze the pan with the above quantity of Madeira until the wine is reduced by half, then add the Brown Sauce and cook 10 minutes before finishing, as described above.

LYONNAISE SAUCE OR BROWN ONION SAUCE

1¼ Cups

An inspired choice for leftover meat.

Melt in a saucepan:

2 tablespoons butter

Add:

2 finely chopped onions

and cook until golden brown. Add:

⅓ cup dry white wine or 2 tablespoons vinegar

If you use the wine, simmer until reduced by half. Then add:

1 cup Brown Sauce, above

and simmer for 15 minutes. Just before serving, add:

1 tablespoon finely chopped parsley

HUNTER'S SAUCE OR SAUCE CHASSEUR

About 2 Cups

Sauté gently until very tender:

2 tablespoons minced onion or shallots

in:

2 tablespoons butter

Stir in and sauté gently for about 2 minutes:

1 cup sliced mushrooms

Add:

½ cup dry white wine
(2 tablespoons brandy)

Simmer until reduced by half. Add:

½ cup tomato sauce or purée
1 cup Brown Sauce, 346

Cook 5 minutes, then:

Season to taste

and add:

1 teaspoon chopped parsley
(¼ cup pine nuts)

BORDELAISE SAUCE

For sweetbreads, chops, steaks, grilled meats.
Cook together in a saucepan:

½ cup dry red wine
4 or 5 crushed black peppercorns

until reduced to three-fourths, then add:

1 cup Brown Sauce, 346

Simmer 15 minutes. Add, just before serving:

¼ cup diced beef marrow, poached for a few minutes and drained
(½ teaspoon lemon juice)
½ teaspoon chopped parsley

MARCHAND DE VIN OR MUSHROOM WINE SAUCE

About 2 Cups

Serve with broiled steak.
Sauté:

1 cup finely sliced mushrooms

in:

2 tablespoons butter

Add:

½ cup hot beef stock

➤ Simmer 10 minutes. Add:

1 cup Brown Sauce, 346
½ cup dry red wine or Madeira

➤ Simmer 20 minutes, then:

Season to taste

You may add:

(Juice of ½ lemon)

ROSEMARY WINE SAUCE

1 Cup

Serve with Calf's Head, 510, or turtle meat, 393. Aptly enough, the strongly flavored combination of herbs which gives this sauce its special tang is known in France as herbs à *tortue*.
Heat to boiling point:

½ cup Madeira or dry sherry

Add:

1 teaspoon mixed dried marjoram, rosemary, sage, bay leaf, thyme and basil

Remove from heat and let stand 5 to 10 minutes. Strain off the herb-flavored wine and add it to:

1 cup hot Brown Sauce, 346

SAUCE PÉRIGUEUX

1 Cup

For croquettes, shirred eggs and chicken.
Prepare:

Madeira Sauce, 346

Just before adding the butter swirl, stir in:

1 tablespoon chopped truffles

Very similar is **Sauce Périgourdine,** but the truffles are finely diced instead of chopped and a dice of foie gras is added.

PIQUANT SAUCE

About 1¼ Cups

Excellent for giving extra zip to bland meats and for reheating leftover meat. A good sauce, too, for pork and pigs' feet.
Lightly brown:

2 tablespoons minced onions

in:

1 tablespoon butter

Add:

2 tablespoons dry white wine or
2 tablespoons vinegar or lemon juice

and cook until the liquid is almost evaporated. Add:

1 cup Brown Sauce, 346

and simmer 10 minutes. Just before serving, add:

1 tablespoon chopped parsley or chopped mixed parsley, tarragon and chervil
1 tablespoon chopped sour pickles
1 tablespoon chopped capers
Season to taste

SAUCE ROBERT

1¼ Cups

Prepare:

Piquant Sauce, above

doubling the amount of onion and omitting the parsley, chervil and tarragon. Just before serving, stir in:

1 teaspoon prepared Dijon-type mustard
A pinch of powdered sugar

POIVRADE OR PEPPER SAUCE

3 Cups

The traditional sauce to serve with venison. It constitutes the basis of several other game sauces.
Heat:

¼ cup vegetable oil

Sauté in it, until brown:

1 chopped carrot
1 chopped onion
(Game bones, trimmings and giblets, if available)

Add:

3 sprigs parsley
1 bay leaf
A pinch of thyme
¼ cup vinegar or ¼ cup marinade liquid, if the game has been marinated before cooking

Simmer until reduced to one-third original quantity. Add:

3 cups Brown Sauce, 346

Bring to a boil ➤ reduce heat and simmer 1 hour. Add:

10 peppercorns

and simmer 5 more minutes. Strain the sauce into another saucepan and add again:

¼ cup marinade liquid

Cook slowly 30 minutes more, then add:

½ cup dry red wine
Season to taste

adding enough:

Freshly ground black pepper

to make a hot sauce.

CREOLE SAUCE

About 2 Cups

Melt over low heat:

2 tablespoons butter

Add and cook covered about 2 minutes:

¼ cup chopped onion
1 minced clove garlic
6 minced green olives

Add and cook until the sauce is thick, about 50 minutes:

1½ cups canned tomatoes or ½ cup tomatoes and 1 cup Brown Sauce, 346
½ chopped green pepper, with seeds and membranes removed
½ bay leaf
A pinch of thyme
1 teaspoon chopped parsley
1 teaspoon white or brown sugar
⅓ teaspoon salt
A few grains cayenne
(1 tablespoon dry sherry)
(¼ cup chili sauce)
(2 tablespoons diced ham)
(½ cup sliced mushrooms)

ABOUT QUICK CANNED SOUP SAUCES

Not only do unconcentrated canned consommés and broths perform a valuable impromptu role as strengtheners and flavoring for sauces: condensed canned soups may be used to furnish the very foundations for sauce as well. The results, of course, are not so subtle and delicate as roux-based sauces carefully constructed from fresh meat or poultry stock. But an impressive saving in time and a substantially lower caloric content go far toward offsetting loss of quality. Taste these mixtures before salting and final seasoning.

I. **1¼ Cups**

For chicken, veal and fish.
Heat:

1 cup condensed cream of chicken soup
2 tablespoons butter
2 to 4 tablespoons rich chicken or vegetable stock
A grating of lemon rind

II. **1¼ Cups**

For beef hash.
Heat:

1 cup condensed cream of mushroom soup
2 to 4 tablespoons strong beef stock
½ teaspoon Meat Glaze, 368
Few drops garlic juice
1 tablespoon butter

III. **1¼ Cups**

For creaming vegetables.
Heat:

1 cup condensed cream of celery soup
2 tablespoons butter
2 to 4 tablespoons chicken stock
1 tablespoon chopped chives

QUICK BROWN SAUCE

About 1 Cup

You may rub your pan with:

½ clove garlic

Melt:

2 tablespoons butter

Stir in until blended:

2 tablespoons flour

Stir in:

1 cup canned bouillon, or 1 or 2 bouillon cubes dissolved in 1 cup boiling water

Permit the gravy to reach the boiling point. Stir constantly. Season as required with:

Salt and pepper or paprika
Dry sherry or Worcestershire sauce
Lemon juice, catsup or chili sauce
Dried herbs

QUICK MUSHROOM SAUCE

About 2 Cups

For roast meat, chicken and casseroles.
Sauté:

¼ lb. sliced mushrooms

in:

2 tablespoons butter

Remove the mushrooms from the skillet. Add to the drippings:

Quick Brown Sauce, above

When the sauce is heated, add the sautéed mushrooms.

QUICK À LA KING SAUCE

About 1½ Cups

The stout stanchion under many a quickly trumped-up luncheon-bridge.
Sauté until tender:

1 minced green pepper

in:

1 tablespoon butter

Add:

1 cup condensed cream of mushroom soup
¼ cup milk

Heat the sauce and add:

1 pimiento, cut into strips
(2 tablespoons dry sherry)

QUICK TOMATO CHEESE SAUCE

About 1½ Cups

Good over eggs.
Heat in a double boiler:

1 cup condensed tomato soup

Add:

¼ teaspoon salt
¼ teaspoon pepper or paprika

Stir and cook these ingredients until they are hot. With a wire whisk beat in:

1 cup or more grated cheese

until the cheese is melted.

QUICK SEAFOOD SPAGHETTI SAUCE

About 1 Quart

Heat:

1½ cups condensed tomato soup

Melt in a saucepan over low heat:

¼ cup olive oil or butter

Stir in and cook until transparent:

¼ cup or more chopped onion
¾ cup chopped green pepper

Stir in slowly the hot soup and:

½ cup Fish Stock, 524

When the sauce is hot, add very slowly, stirring constantly:

½ lb. cooked or canned diced lobster, crab, shrimp or tuna

Remove from heat and add:

½ lb. diced cheese: Mozzarella, Parmesan or Scamorza
Season to taste

and stir in cheese until melted. Pour over cooked spaghetti.

DRIED SOUP SAUCES

4 Servings

Not so speedy as canned ones, but they can provide a well-flavored base when reconstituted with half the amount of liquid called for normally: the dried vegetable components swell during cooking. Combine and heat:

1 package dried cream of leek, cream of mushroom or smoky pea soup
1½ cups light cream or top milk

Use with leftover chicken or veal, with rice or noodles in a casserole. Or combine and heat:

1 package dried onion soup
1½ to 2 cups water

and add to meat and vegetables in a casserole. Again, do not salt—and go easy on other seasonings—until these sauces have cooked about 20 minutes and you have tasted them.

CHINESE SAUCE FOR VEGETABLES

For About 1 Pound Vegetables

Blend until smooth:

1 tablespoon cornstarch
3 tablespoons cold water

Add:

½ teaspoon salt
1 tablespoon soy sauce
(½ teaspoon finely grated gingerroot)

Pour over vegetables that are cooking. Stir well until the whole mixture comes to a boil.

ABOUT SEASONED BUTTERS AND BUTTER SAUCES

These garnishes are quick, tasty and simple to make. The main thing is to use fresh, high-quality butter, preferably unsalted. For other seasoned butters used as Spreads, see 70. For Seafood Butters, see 71.

Allow about 1 tablespoon butter per serving. A few butter sauces are melted, but most of them are creamed and reach the table in solid form, being allowed to melt on the hot fish, meat or vegetables for which they are designed. You may form the butter into fancy shapes and molds, see 541. Most solid seasoned butters may be prepared more quickly and taste almost as good as melted butter sauces. If you use melted butter, dress the food in the kitchen. Make sure you spoon out the seasonings with the butter. They will sink to the bottom if you serve the melted butter at table in a sauce boat. There are some butters, such as shrimp and lobster, which are used to flavor and finish sauces but are rarely served by themselves as sauces.

Seasoned butters may be ✲ frozen for several weeks. But they ➤ should not be refrigerated longer than 24 hours, as the herbs deteriorate quickly.

DRAWN OR CLARIFIED BUTTER OR GHEE

There need be neither mystery nor mystique about this substance: it is merely melted butter with the sediment removed. But, as it is used in so many different ways—among others as a sauce for cooked lobster, to make brown and black butter and as a baking ingredient—here is the recipe. Melt completely over low heat:

Butter

Remove from heat and let stand a few minutes, allowing the milk solids to settle to the bottom. Skim the butter fat from the top and strain the clear yellow liquid into a container.

BROWN BUTTER OR BEURRE NOISETTE

4 Servings

Brown or so-called black butters can only be made successfully with clarified butter, since otherwise the sediment always present in "raw" butter will

tend to burn and make the resultant sauce speckled and bitter. Use for asparagus, broccoli and brains.
Melt in a saucepan and cook slowly until light brown:
¼ cup Clarified Butter, 349

BLACK BUTTER OR BEURRE NOIR

4 Servings

For fish, eggs, vegetables, sweetbreads and brains.
Melt and cook very slowly, until dark brown:
¼ cup Clarified Butter, 349
Stir in at once:
1 teaspoon vinegar or lemon juice
If served with brains or fish, you may add:
1 tablespoon chopped capers
Serve immediately.

MEUNIÈRE OR LEMON BUTTER

4 Servings

Prepare:
Brown Butter, 349
Add:
1 tablespoon finely chopped parsley
1 teaspoon lemon juice
Season to taste

BURGUNDY SAUCE OR SAUCE BOURGUIGNONNE

1 Cup

For snails and egg dishes.
Reduce by half a mixture of:
2 cups dry red wine, preferably red Burgundy
2 minced shallots or mild onions
A few sprigs parsley
A pinch of thyme
¼ bay leaf
(Mushroom peelings)
Strain the mixture. When ready to serve, heat and add:
1 to 1½ tablespoons Kneaded Butter, 340
(A dash of cayenne)

ALMOND BUTTER

⅓ Cup

Often used in cream sauces, for sautéed chicken and other "amandine" dishes. Another version is Amandine Garnish, 553.
Cream:
¼ cup butter
Blanch:
¼ cup almonds, 562
Remove the skins and pound the almonds to a paste with:
1 teaspoon water
Add gradually to the butter, blending well. Rub through a fine sieve.
Season to taste

ANCHOVY BUTTER

4 Servings

Fine spread over hot broiled fish, a steak or canapés.
Cream until soft:
¼ cup butter
Beat in:
1 teaspoon anchovy paste
⅛ teaspoon onion juice
¼ teaspoon lemon juice
A few grains cayenne

BERCY BUTTER

About ¼ Cup

For broiled meats.
Cook together until reduced to about one-fourth the original quantity:
2 teaspoons finely chopped shallots
⅔ cup dry white wine
Cool. Cream:
4 tablespoons butter
and add:
2 teaspoons finely chopped parsley
Combine the two mixtures and:
Season to taste

CAVIAR BUTTER

6 to 8 Servings

A lovely fish garnish.
Cream:
½ cup butter
Add:
1 tablespoon lemon juice
¼ cup black caviar or salmon roe
Salt, if necessary
Chill slightly, mold or cut into shapes and serve.

MAÎTRE D'HÔTEL BUTTER

4 Servings

Good over broiled steak.
Cream until soft:
¼ cup butter
Add:
½ teaspoon salt
⅛ teaspoon white pepper
1 teaspoon finely chopped parsley
Add very slowly, stirring the sauce constantly:
¾ to 1½ tablespoons lemon juice

COLBERT BUTTER

4 Servings

Use on fish and roasted meats.
Cream together:
¼ cup Maître d'Hôtel Butter, above
½ teaspoon melted beef extract or Meat Glaze, 368
¼ teaspoon finely chopped fresh tarragon

SNAIL BUTTER

About 1 Cup

Should any of this remain after stuffing the snails ✱ freeze for a short period for use on steaks, fish or vegetables.
Cream until soft:
¾ cup butter

Work into it:

1 to 2 tablespoons minced shallots or mild onions
1 to 2 well-pressed cloves garlic
(1 tablespoon minced celery)
1 tablespoon minced parsley
½ teaspoon salt
Freshly ground pepper
(1 tablespoon lemon juice)

DEVILED BUTTER FOR SEAFOOD

4 Servings

Work until soft:

¼ cup butter

Combine it with:

½ teaspoon dry mustard
2 teaspoons wine vinegar
2 teaspoons Worcestershire sauce
¼ teaspoon salt
1/16 teaspoon cayenne
2 egg yolks

Beat well.

GARLIC BUTTER

4 Servings

For steak, if you are a garlic fancier, or for garlic bread. Boil in a little water 5 or 6 minutes:

1 to 3 cloves garlic

Drain, crush and pound well in a mortar with:

¼ cup butter

GREEN BUTTER

About ¼ Cup

Use for broiled fish and to give white or cream sauces a green color.
Blanch the following ingredients 5 minutes, then plunge into cold water, drain and dry in a towel:

2 shallots or 1 tablespoon mild onion
1 teaspoon fresh tarragon
1 teaspoon fresh chervil
1 teaspoon fresh parsley
6 to 8 spinach leaves

Chop until fine and pound them in a mortar. Work in gradually:

¼ cup butter
Salt, if needed

SHRIMP OR LOBSTER BUTTER

½ Cup

Delicately pink and deliciously flavored. Use for finishing cream sauces served with fish or by itself with the shellfish you have used in making the butter.
Dry the shells from:

1 lb. shrimp or 1 large lobster

in a low oven for a short time. Pound in a mortar or put them through the food grinder, breaking them up as finely as possible. Melt:

½ cup butter

in a double boiler ➤ over—not in—boiling water. Add the shells and:

2 tablespoons water

Simmer 10 minutes. ➤ Do not let the butter boil. Line a sieve with cheesecloth or fine muslin and strain the hot butter into a bowl of ice water. Refrigerate and skim off the butter when it hardens.

WHITE BUTTER

4 Servings

For poached fish. The fumet required is from the same type of fish. If you lack a fumet, a surprisingly effective alternative is an equal amount of clam juice, canned or fresh. Simmer until reduced to one-fourth its original volume:

1 teaspoon finely chopped shallots
¼ cup wine vinegar
¼ cup Fumet, 524

Cool this mixture and add, a little at a time:

¼ cup softened butter

beating constantly with a sauce whisk until the sauce is creamy and whitened, rather like whipped cream.

Season to taste

Add:

2 tablespoons mixture of very finely chopped fresh fennel, parsley, chives, basil, chervil or tarragon, or 1 tablespoon of the dried herbs

POLONAISE OR BROWNED BUTTER CRUMB SAUCE

4 Servings

A topping for vegetables.
Brown:

⅓ cup fine dry bread crumbs

in:

Meunière Butter, 350

If you wish, you may sauté:

(1 tablespoon minced onion)

in the butter, until transparent, before adding the bread crumbs. Garnish the vegetable with:

Finely chopped hard-cooked egg

and pour the sauce over it.

BUTTER SAUCE FOR CANNED OR COOKED VEGETABLES

Drain the vegetables. Let the stock or juice boil until reduced by half. Add:

Melted butter
Seasonings and lemon juice

UNTHICKENED TOMATO SAUCE

About 4 Cups

Place over low heat:

3 tablespoons olive oil

Add and stir about 3 minutes:

1 large Bermuda onion, chopped
2 chopped celery ribs with leaves
1 carrot cut in small pieces

(½ chopped green pepper, seeds and fibrous portions removed)
(1 pressed clove garlic)

Add:

4 cups drained canned tomatoes or 6 large fresh tomatoes

If the latter are very juicy, peel and squeeze slightly to get rid of excess liquid and seeds. Add:

1 sprig thyme, basil or tarragon
1 teaspoon salt
⅛ teaspoon pepper
1 teaspoon sugar

Cook gently, uncovered, until the mixture is thick, about 45 minutes. ➤ Watch it, so that it does not burn. Put it through a fine strainer. Add seasoning, if needed. This sauce will keep several days.

THICKENED TOMATO SAUCE

About 1½ Cups

Bring to a boil and then ➤ simmer 30 minutes before sieving:

2 cups canned tomatoes
1 onion, stuck with 3 cloves
2 chopped celery ribs with leaves
1 diced carrot
1 Bouquet Garni, 572
1 bay leaf
(½ chopped green pepper)

➤ Be sure to pass through all the pulpy residue when sieving, so that only cloves, leaves and seeds remain behind. This well-flavored pulp helps thicken the sauce. Melt in a saucepan:

3 tablespoons butter

Stir in, until blended:

2 tablespoons flour

Add the strained thickish stock slowly with:

¼ teaspoon sugar

➤ Simmer and stir the stock 5 to 10 minutes.

Season to taste

including, if desired:

(1 tablespoon fresh basil)

QUICK TOMATO SAUCE

About 2½ Cups

Strain:

1 large can Italian tomatoes: 16 oz.

Add:

3 oz. canned tomato paste
½ teaspoon salt
1 tablespoon onion juice or 2 tablespoons finely grated onion
½ teaspoon sugar

Bring to a boil and simmer gently 15 to 20 minutes.

QUICK CREOLE SAUCE

2½ Cups

To:

2 cups Quick Tomato Sauce, above

Add:

½ cup very finely chopped green pepper, onion, celery, olives and pimiento

COCKTAIL SAUCE

About 1 Cup

For dunking or garnishing shellfish, small sausages or other hors d'oeuvre.

Combine:

¾ cup Catsup, 847
⅛ to ¼ cup prepared horseradish
Juice of 1 lemon
1 dash hot pepper sauce

MEXICAN TOMATO SAUCE

About 1 Cup

Just what you might expect. You will feel hot inside, down to your toes. Use with Cowboy Eggs, 222.

Place in a small saucepan and simmer until fairly thick:

¾ cup drained canned tomatoes or about 3 large, skinned and quartered, peeled and seeded fresh tomatoes
6 tablespoons Chili Sauce, 847
2 teaspoons prepared mustard
3 tablespoons grated or prepared horseradish
½ teaspoon sugar
¾ teaspoon salt
¼ teaspoon pepper
A few grains cayenne
¾ teaspoon curry powder
6 tablespoons vinegar
1 teaspoon onion juice
1 sliced clove garlic

Strain the mixture. Add:

1 teaspoon dried or 1 tablespoon fresh herbs

This sauce may be served—in discreet quantities—by itself, but it combines excellently with hot cream sauce or hot or cold mayonnaise. Add as much of it to these as you find palatable.

BLENDER TOMATO SAUCE

About 1 Cup

Serve over bland foods, sweetbreads, cold veal, hot or cold fish, or salads.

Combine and blend:

¾ cup tomato purée or 2 large skinned tomatoes—the juice and seeds pressed from them
1 medium-sized onion
1 green pepper, seeds and membrane removed
¼ cup celery, or 1 teaspoon celery and/or dill seeds
2 tablespoons chopped parsley or chives
½ teaspoon salt
¼ teaspoon freshly ground pepper
(2 tablespoons French Dressing, 360)

Chill the sauce about ½ hour.

ITALIAN MEAT SAUCE FOR PASTA I.

About 1 Quart

Heat:

½ cup olive oil

Add:

1 pressed clove garlic

1 lb. ground round steak
¼ lb. ground lean pork
2 cups Italian tomatoes
½ cup Italian tomato paste
½ cup beef or veal stock
1½ teaspoons salt
¼ teaspoon pepper
1 bay leaf

Simmer the sauce uncovered about 1 hour. Add for the last 15 minutes:

(½ cup sliced mushrooms)

Season with:

1 to 2 tablespoons fresh basil or oregano

Serve over:

Cooked spaghetti or noodles

with:

Grated Parmesan or Romano cheese

II. **About 1½ Quarts**

Mince and cook over very slow heat:

3 slices bacon

Stir in and sauté:

¼ cup chopped onion
½ lb. ground round steak

When the meat is nearly done, add:

2½ cups skinned tomatoes, pressed to expel seeds and juice
½ cup chopped green pepper
1 cup chopped canned mushrooms or ½ to 1 lb. sliced fresh Sautéed Mushrooms, 308

Season with:

1 teaspoon chopped basil
2 cups shredded cheese: ½ lb.
Salt, cayenne or paprika

Simmer ➤ uncovered 20 or 30 minutes. If more liquid is needed, add:

½ cup hot stock or canned bouillon

BOLOGNESE PASTA SAUCE

About 2 Cups

An interesting variation, involving cream.
Reconstitute, 573:

6 dried mushrooms

reserving them and the liquor.
Melt in a large saucepan:

⅓ cup butter

Add:

¼ cup minced lean ham or Canadian bacon
¼ cup finely chopped carrot
¼ cup finely chopped onion

Stir and cook for 1 or 2 minutes. Add:

1 cup chopped lean beef

and brown over medium heat, stirring occasionally, then add the mushrooms, their liquor and:

2 tablespoons tomato paste
1 strip lemon peel
A pinch of nutmeg
1 cup beef stock
(½ cup dry white wine)

Partially cover and simmer slowly 1 hour. Remove from heat, take out lemon peel and stir in:

¼ cup whipping cream

just before serving with:

Green Noodles, 213

SPAGHETTI SAUCE WITH LIVER

4 Servings

Melt:

2 tablespoons butter or drippings

Sauté in it until light brown:

½ cup chopped onions

Add and sauté very lightly:

1 cup cubed calf liver or chicken livers

Add and simmer about 15 minutes:

½ cup any tomato sauce for pasta

Season with:

1 teaspoon salt
⅛ teaspoon pepper
(¼ teaspoon basil)

Serve over noodles, spaghetti, etc., garnished with:

Parsley

MARINARA SAUCE

About 1½ Cups

Use a little on green beans or a lot over spaghetti.
Sauté lightly:

1 minced clove garlic

in:

2 tablespoons olive oil and the oil from the anchovies

Add slowly:

2½ cups canned pressed and drained whole or Italian tomatoes

Stir in:

6 finely chopped anchovies
½ teaspoon oregano
1 tablespoon chopped parsley

Bring to a boil, then ➤ reduce heat and simmer uncovered 15 to 20 minutes, stirring occasionally. If served with spaghetti, pass with:

Grated Parmesan or Romano cheese

Try omitting the oregano and adding:

(5 chopped canned artichoke hearts)

Simmer 3 or 4 minutes more.

OCTOPUS PASTA SAUCE

For 1 Pound Linguini Pasta

See About Octopus, 408.
Heat in a large saucepan:

1 to 1¼ cups olive oil

Add:

1¼ cups seeded, peeled fresh tomatoes
⅔ to 1 cup finely chopped parsley
1 teaspoon salt
2 cloves garlic

Simmer the mixture 15 to 20 minutes. Remove the garlic. Add:

1½ cups cooked octopus, cut into bite-sized pieces

Simmer another 15 to 20 minutes. Toss with the cooked, drained pasta and serve at once.

QUICK SHRIMP AND CLAM SAUCE FOR PASTA

Enough for 1 Pound Pasta

This sauce goes down well with seafood addicts who don't care for the usual tomato sauces.
Heat in a skillet:

6 tablespoons olive oil

Add:

3 minced cloves garlic

and cook gently 5 minutes. Add:

¾ cup finely chopped parsley
1 cup minced clams or mussels with liquid
½ lb. shelled raw shrimp, cut into bite-sized pieces
(⅛ teaspoon oregano)

Heat until bubbling and the shrimp is pink. Serve at once over hot cooked seashell pasta—conchiglie—to complete the marine effect. Pass with:

Grated Parmesan or Romano cheese

LOW-CALORIE TOMATO SAUCE

About 1 Cup

Try this over raw or cooked vegetables or seafood.
Combine:

¾ cup Italian tomato paste
1 teaspoon dry mustard
1 tablespoon sugar
½ teaspoon salt
1 tablespoon vinegar
1 tablespoon drained horseradish
(1 tablespoon chopped onion, chives or fresh herbs)

BARBECUE SAUCES

Please read About Skewer Cooking, 146. It is important to ➤ baste with barbecue sauces only during the last 15 minutes of cooking. Longer cooking will make the spices bitter.

I. **About 2 Cups**

Sauté until brown:

¼ cup chopped onion

in:

1 tablespoon drippings or other fat

Add and simmer for 20 minutes:

½ cup water
2 tablespoons vinegar
1 tablespoon Worcestershire sauce
¼ cup lemon juice
2 tablespoons brown sugar
1 cup Chili Sauce, 847
½ teaspoon salt
¼ teaspoon paprika
¼ teaspoon pepper
1 teaspoon mustard, or chili or curry powder

II. **About 1½ Cups**

Simmer 15 minutes, stirring frequently:

12 to 14 oz. Tomato Catsup, 847
½ cup distilled white vinegar
1 teaspoon sugar
A few grains cayenne pepper
¼ teaspoon black pepper
⅛ teaspoon salt

FEROCIOUS BARBECUE SAUCE

Combine and heat:

1½ cups Barbecue Sauce II, above
¼ of a seeded lemon, diced fine
½ teaspoon ground cumin
1 teaspoon ground coriander
⅛ teaspoon paprika
⅛ teaspoon saffron
¼ teaspoon ground ginger

BARBECUE SAUCE FOR FOWL

I. **For 1 Fowl**

Combine and heat:

4 teaspoons lemon juice
1 teaspoon Worcestershire Sauce, 848
1 teaspoon Tomato Catsup, 847
1 tablespoon butter

II. **About 2½ Cups**

Cook slowly until golden:

1 medium-sized onion, chopped
1 minced clove garlic

in:

3 tablespoons drippings or other fat

Add and simmer for 30 minutes:

3 tablespoons soy or Worcestershire sauce
1 cup water
1 chopped red pepper
2 tablespoons vinegar
2 to 4 tablespoons brown sugar
1 cup Tomato Catsup, 847
1 teaspoon prepared mustard
½ cup diced celery
½ teaspoon salt

Then add:

¼ cup lemon juice

SWEET-SOUR BACON SAUCE

About 1 Cup

Fine for green beans.
Slowly render until crisp:

4 thin slices bacon, cut up

At the same time, you may cook until transparent:

(1 teaspoon minced onion)

Remove the bacon and onion and pour off all but:

2 tablespoons bacon fat

Add to the fat:

¾ cup of the bean or other stock
2 tablespoons vinegar
1 to 2 tablespoons sugar

Heat and pour over the vegetables. Garnish with the bacon and onion bits.

AGRODOLCE SAUCE

About 1¼ Cups

For sweetbreads, calf's head or diced meat.
Slightly caramelize in:

1 tablespoon vinegar
1 tablespoon sugar

Add and cook until shallots are soft:

½ cup white wine
1 tablespoon minced shallots or mild onion

Mix in:

½ cup Demi-Glaze Sauce, 346

and heat briefly with:

½ cup chopped seeded Malaga grapes or
2 tablespoons chopped parsley

ORIENTAL SWEET-SOUR SAUCE

For Chinese-type vegetables and shellfish.

I. **1 Cup**

Heat:

½ cup pineapple juice
3 tablespoons vegetable oil
2 tablespoons brown sugar
1 teaspoon soy sauce or salt
½ teaspoon pepper
¼ cup mild vinegar

II. **2½ to 3 Cups**

A Polynesian version, for luau food, Chinese Meatballs, 489, or Sweet-Sour Pork, 480.

Have ready a paste of:

2 tablespoons cornstarch
½ cup chicken broth
2 tablespoons soy sauce

Melt in a heavy pan:

2 tablespoons butter

Add:

1 cup chicken broth
¾ to 1 cup diced green peppers
6 slices diced canned pineapple

Cover and simmer 5 minutes. Add the cornstarch paste and the following ingredients to the peppers and pineapple:

½ cup vinegar
¾ cup pineapple juice
½ cup sugar
½ teaspoon salt
¼ teaspoon ginger

Simmer, stirring constantly, until the mixture thickens.

SWEET-SOUR MUSTARD SAUCE

About 2½ Cups

For ham or tongue.

Combine in a double boiler ➤ over—not in—boiling water:

½ cup sugar
1 tablespoon flour
4 teaspoons dry mustard

Add gradually:

2 cups cream

mixed with:

2 egg yolks

Cook until thick. Stir in gradually:

½ cup vinegar

SWEET-SOUR ORANGE SAUCE

About 2 Cups

For duck or goose turn this into a true **Bigarade Sauce** by using the rind and juice from the Seville or bitter orange, and omitting the lemon juice.

Pour off the fat from the pan in which you have roasted the bird. Deglaze the pan with:

1 cup Game Stock, 523

Thicken with:

1 teaspoon arrowroot or cornstarch

mixed first with a little of the stock. In another pan, cook together until light brown:

2 tablespoons vinegar
2 tablespoons sugar

Add the sauce from the roasting pan and cook 4 or 5 minutes, then add:

2 tablespoons julienned and blanched navel orange rind
½ cup hot orange juice
1 tablespoon lemon juice
2 tablespoons curaçao
Season to taste

Serve immediately over goose or wild or domestic duck and garnish with:

Orange sections

SWEET-SOUR CREAM DRESSING

About 1 Cup

For green beans or cabbage.

Combine and stir over very low heat until the sauce thickens slightly:

1 beaten egg
½ cup cultured sour cream
2 tablespoons sugar
¼ cup vinegar
½ teaspoon salt
¼ teaspoon paprika

Serve hot over hot vegetables or cold over chilled ones.

CARAWAY SAUCE

Really a garnish to enhance plain vegetables.

Cook until the water is absorbed:

1 tablespoon caraway seeds

in:

2 tablespoons water

Melt in a skillet:

4 tablespoons butter

Sauté seeds and:

1 tablespoon grated onion

in the butter just a few moments, until seeds brown slightly. Remove from heat.

Season to taste

Add:

1 teaspoon lemon juice

Pour sauce over hot vegetables.

MINT SAUCE

About 1 Cup

The usual accompaniment to roast lamb.

Heat:

3 tablespoons water

Dissolve in it:

1½ tablespoons confectioners' sugar

Cool the syrup and add:

⅓ cup finely chopped mint leaves
½ cup strong vinegar

This is best made ½ hour before serving.

PLUM, PEACH OR APRICOT SAUCE

About 3/4 Cup

For spareribs and Chinese dishes.

⅄ Blend:

1/2 cup plum, peach or apricot preserves
1/4 cup Chutney, 846

To use as a marinade, dilute with a small quantity of vinegar.

CHERRY SAUCE

About 1 Cup

For ham and roast pork.

⅄ Blend:

1 cup drained, pitted canned sour red cherries
1/2 cup plum preserves
2 teaspoons soy sauce
1/4 teaspoon dry mustard

Stir in:

(1/4 cup finely chopped walnuts)

Serve hot or cold.

RAISIN SAUCE

About 1 1/2 Cups

For ham or tongue.

Combine in a saucepan:

2 tablespoons butter
2 tablespoons flour

Add:

1 1/2 cups cider or fruit juice
1/2 cup seedless raisins

Cook until mixture boils, stirring constantly. Simmer about 10 minutes, until thickened. Add:

1 teaspoon grated lemon rind
(3/4 teaspoon prepared mustard)
(1 tablespoon sherry)

CIDER OR BEER RAISIN SAUCE

About 1 1/2 Cups

For hot or cold ham or smoked tongue.

Combine in a saucepan:

1/4 cup firmly packed brown sugar
1 1/2 tablespoons cornstarch
1/8 teaspoon salt

Stir in:

1 cup fresh cider or beer
1/4 cup raisins, cut in halves

Put in a cheesecloth bag and suspend the bag in the sauce as it heats:

8 whole cloves
2-inch stick cinnamon
1/4 diced lemon

Cook and stir about 10 minutes. Remove the spices. Add:

1 tablespoon butter

Serve the sauce very hot.

CUMBERLAND SAUCE

I. **About 2 Cups**

A classic formula for cold ham and game. The sauce may be served cold. For quicker currant jelly sauces, see opposite.

Combine:

1 teaspoon dry mustard
1 tablespoon brown sugar
1/4 teaspoon powdered ginger
A few grains cayenne
1/4 teaspoon salt
1/4 teaspoon ground cloves
1 1/2 cups red wine, preferably port
(1/2 cup seedless raisins)
(1/2 cup slivered blanched almonds)

Simmer the sauce, covered, 8 minutes. Dissolve:

2 teaspoons cornstarch

in:

2 tablespoons cold water

Stir this into the sauce. Let it simmer about 2 minutes. Stir in:

1/4 cup red currant jelly
1 tablespoon grated orange and lemon rind
1/4 cup orange juice
2 tablespoons lemon juice

For a rather exquisite final touch you may add:

(2 tablespoons Grand Marnier)

II. **About 3/4 Cup**

Combine and blend well:

Grated rind of 1 lemon
Juice of 1 lemon
Grated rind of 1 orange
1 tablespoon confectioners' sugar
1 teaspoon prepared mustard
1/2 cup melted red currant jelly
1 tablespoon port wine

If the jelly is very stiff, it may have to be diluted over heat with:

(1 or 2 tablespoons hot water)

III. **About 1 1/4 Cups**

For cold meats.

Heat in a double boiler just before serving:

3/4 cup currant jelly

Stir in:

1/2 cup Indian chutney
1 teaspoon lemon juice
1 tablespoon brandy
Salt

IV. **About 1/2 Cup**

Make a quickie version by mixing:

1/2 cup currant jelly
2 tablespoons horseradish
1/2 teaspoon dry mustard

SOUR CREAM HORSERADISH DRESSING OR DRESDEN SAUCE

1 Cup

A fine change from the well-liked but often monotonous butter or cream sauce. Usually served with smoked or braised fish.

Combine and stir:

1 cup cultured sour cream
1/2 teaspoon prepared mustard
1/2 teaspoon grated horseradish
1/4 teaspoon salt

CREAM HORSERADISH DRESSING

About 1¼ Cups

Another cold-meat dressing.
Beat until stiff:

½ cup heavy cream

Add slowly, beating constantly:

3 tablespoons lemon juice or vinegar
¼ teaspoon salt
⅛ teaspoon paprika
A few grains cayenne
2 tablespoons grated horseradish
(3 tablespoons mayonnaise)

FROZEN HORSERADISH SAUCE

About 1½ Cups

This comes out rather like a sherbet and is delicious with boiled beef.
Combine:

¼ cup grated horseradish
¼ cup fresh orange juice
1 teaspoon sugar

and fold into:

1 cup stiffly whipped cream

Freeze about 3 to 4 hours in a tray and spoon out into a bowl to serve. Do not hold frozen for long periods.

CUCUMBER ALMOND SAUCE

About 1½ Cups

Mostly for aspics and mousses; but also for cold meat or fish, especially salmon.
Beat until stiff:

¾ cup heavy sweet or cultured sour cream

If the cream is sweet, add slowly:

2 tablespoons vinegar or lemon juice

Season the sauce with:

¼ teaspoon salt
⅛ teaspoon paprika

Pare, seed, cut finely and drain well:

1 large cucumber

Add it to the sauce with:

Slivered almonds
(2 teaspoons finely chopped chives or dill)

SOUR CREAM SAUCE FOR BAKED POTATOES

1 Cup

Do not chill before serving—keep at room temperature.
Combine:

1 cup cultured sour cream
1 teaspoon Worcestershire sauce
A dash of hot pepper sauce
½ teaspoon salt
Freshly ground black pepper

Garnish with:

Chopped chives

CAVIAR SAUCE

About 1⅓ Cups

Try as a dip for cold vegetables, in hors d'oeuvre, or on salads or baked potatoes.
Combine:

1 cup cultured sour cream
1 teaspoon onion or shallot juice
2 teaspoons capers
¼ cup red caviar

COLD MUSTARD SAUCE

I. **About ¼ Cup**

For boiled or cold meats or fish. This sauce is in the nature of a relish.
Combine:

2 teaspoons grated onion
1 tablespoon Dijon- or Düsseldorf-type mustard
1½ teaspoons sugar
1 to 2 tablespoons vegetable oil
2 tablespoons vinegar or lemon juice
(2 hard-cooked egg yolks)
(1 tablespoon cream)

II. **About ½ Cup**

A highly seasoned sauce lower in calories than I. For cold meats or broiled sausages.
Blend gradually:

2 tablespoons or more dry mustard

with a little:

Water

until it is the consistency of thick cream. Fold this paste into:

½ cup evaporated milk, whipped, 532

Season, if desired, with:

Salt and paprika

ABOUT HOLLANDAISE AND OTHER HOT EGG-THICKENED SAUCES

Delicious and loaded with calories, these transform into a superb dish the plainest and simplest cooked vegetables or broiled or roasted meat. But they have their maddening caprices, too. To circumvent them, we offer some stratagems. Don't try to make Hollandaise or Béarnaise on a very humid day, unless you use Clarified Butter, 349. Cook these sauces ➤ over—not in—hot, but not boiling, water. If you use a heatproof glass double boiler you can see when the water begins to boil, at which time add 1 or 2 tablespoons of cold water to lower temperature slightly. Keep stirring the sauce constantly and ➤ add the melted butter very, very slowly at first. Scrape the mixture away from the sides and bottom of the pan as you stir, to keep the sauce smooth. As with Mayonnaise, 363, a wooden spoon or a whisk is the best tool for making Hollandaise. A professional chef will make it over a low direct heat, but don't try this unless you are prepared to act out a new definition of "stir-crazy." Some of our friends freeze Hollandaise just as they do roux-based sauces. If frozen, it must be reheated in a double boiler ➤ over—not in—hot water, stirring briskly to preserve consistency. Should any of these egg sauces break, beat into them at once 1 to 2 tablespoons chilled cream. A slightly curdled sauce can be rescued in a blender, although its texture will not be so smooth as that of an originally well made sauce. Or it can be reconstituted, using a fresh egg yolk, as for Mayonnaise, 363.

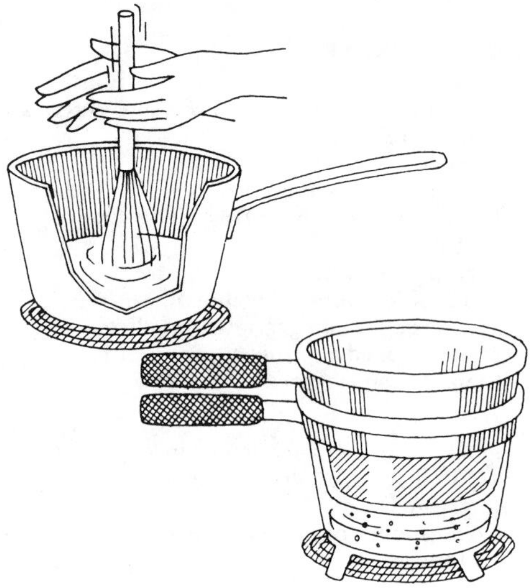

HOLLANDAISE SAUCE

1 Cup

➤ Please read About Hollandaise Sauce, above. Our cook calls this "holiday sauce"—isn't that a grand name for it? If directions are carefully followed, it never fails.

Melt slowly and keep warm:

½ cup butter

Barely heat:

1½ tablespoons lemon juice, dry sherry or tarragon vinegar

Have ready a small saucepan of boiling water and a tablespoon with which to measure it when ready. Place in the top of a double boiler ➤ over —not in—hot water:

3 egg yolks

Beat the yolks with a wire whisk until they begin to thicken. Add:

1 tablespoon boiling water

Beat again until the eggs begin to thicken. Repeat this process until you have added:

3 more tablespoons water

Then beat in the warm lemon juice. Remove double boiler from heat. Beat the sauce well with a wire whisk. Continue to beat while slowly adding the melted butter and:

¼ teaspoon salt
A few grains cayenne

Beat until the sauce is thick. Serve at once.

⅄ BLENDER HOLLANDAISE

About 1 Cup

Easy, but less flavorful and paler in color than handmade Hollandaise. ➤ Do not make it in a smaller quantity than given here: there will not be enough heat to cook the eggs properly.

Have ready in your blender:

3 egg yolks
2 tablespoons lemon juice
A pinch of cayenne
¼ teaspoon salt

Heat to bubbling stage, do not brown:

½ cup butter

Cover container and turn motor on "High." After 3 seconds, remove the lid and pour the butter over the eggs in a steady stream. By the time the butter is poured in—about 30 seconds—the sauce should be finished. If not, blend on "High" about 5 seconds longer. Serve at once or keep warm by immersing blender container in warm water. This sauce may also be frozen and reconstituted over hot water.

QUICK WHOLE-EGG HOLLANDAISE

About 1 Cup

Even paler in color than the sauce in the preceding recipe; but it does, once and for all, solve the problem of what to do with those extra whites.

Place in a mixing bowl and whip with a fork until thoroughly blended and pale yellow:

3 whole eggs
4 or 5 teaspoons lemon juice
3 tablespoons water

In a heavy ➤ nonstick coated skillet melt ➤ over low heat:

6 or 7 tablespoons butter

Add egg mixture slowly, stirring continuously until sauce has thickened. ➤ Do not overcook. Before serving add:

½ teaspoon salt
Season to taste

HOLLANDAISE VARIATIONS

For less rich versions, try one of the following; or if you are in a hurry, prepare Hot Mayonnaise, below.

I. **About 1¼ Cups**

Mix in the top of a double boiler:

1 cup cultured sour cream
Juice of 1 lemon
2 egg yolks
½ teaspoon salt
¼ teaspoon paprika

Stir ➤ over—not in—hot water until thick.

II. **4 Servings**

Good over vegetables such as Brussels sprouts and cauliflower.

Place in a double boiler ➤ over—not in—hot water:

2 beaten eggs
¼ cup cream
⅛ teaspoon salt
⅛ teaspoon freshly ground nutmeg
1 tablespoon lemon juice

Cook and stir these ingredients until they are thick, then add a little at a time:

2 tablespoons butter

Serve at once.

HOT MAYONNAISE SAUCE

About 1 Cup

See Mayonnaise, 363. If you have mayonnaise on hand but no Béarnaise, try it sometime on steak or fish.

Heat in a double boiler and stir:

1 cup Mayonnaise, 363

Add:

Lemon juice and capers

SOUFFLÉD MAYONNAISE

Enough for a 3-Pound Fish

See Mayonnaise, 363. For fish or as a masking for broiled tomatoes.

Combine and beat well:

½ cup Mayonnaise, 363
¼ cup pickle relish
2 tablespoons chopped parsley
1 tablespoon lemon juice
¼ teaspoon salt
A few grains cayenne

Beat until stiff, but not dry:

2 egg whites

Fold them into the mayonnaise mixture. Spread the sauce evenly on hot cooked fish or tomatoes. Broil until the sauce is puffed and golden.

MOUSSELINE SAUCE

1¼ Cups

Use with vegetables or fish as a change from Hollandaise.

Just before serving, add:

½ cup whipped cream

to:

1 cup Hollandaise Sauce, 358

Serve hot or cold.

CHORON SAUCE

1¼ Cups

We have known adults who, understandably enough, used this sauce with as much abandon as a child with a bottle of restaurant catsup.

Prepare:

1 cup Hollandaise Sauce, 358

Beat in very slowly:

¼ cup warm tomato purée, reduced until very thick

Add:

(1 to 2 tablespoons chopped parsley)
Season to taste

and serve.

MALTAISE SAUCE

About 1 Cup

Interesting on asparagus.

Add:

2 to 3 tablespoons orange juice
1 teaspoon grated orange rind

to:

1 cup Hollandaise Sauce, 358

BÉARNAISE SAUCE

About 1½ Cups

Heavenly on most broiled red meat, especially beef tenderloin. It is also quite at home with fish and eggs.

Combine in the top of a double boiler:

¼ cup white wine
2 tablespoons tarragon vinegar
1 tablespoon finely chopped shallots or onion
2 crushed white peppercorns
2 sprigs tarragon, chopped
1 sprig chervil, finely chopped
(1 sprig parsley, minced)

Cook over direct heat until reduced by half. ➤ If you have used dried tarragon or coarsely chopped onion, strain the mixture. Allow it to cool. Then, beating briskly ➤ over—not in—hot water, add alternately a little at a time and beat steadily so that they are well combined:

3 egg yolks
¾ cup melted butter
Season to taste

When you have added all the butter, the sauce should have the consistency of Hollandaise.

⅄ BLENDER BÉARNAISE SAUCE

About 1 Cup

➤ Do not make in a lesser quantity than given here, as there is then not enough heat to cook the eggs properly.

Prepare as in the above recipe:

The seasoned wine vinegar mixture

Have ready in your blender the above mixture and:

3 egg yolks
½ teaspoon salt

Heat to the bubbling stage but do not brown:

¾ cup butter

Cover container and turn motor on "High." After 3 seconds, remove lid and pour the butter over the eggs in a steady stream. By the time the butter is poured in—about 30 seconds—the sauce should be finished. If not, blend on "High" about 5 seconds longer. Serve at once or keep warm by placing blender container in warm water. This sauce may be frozen and reconstituted over hot water.

FOYOT SAUCE

Prepare:

1 cup Bearnaise Sauce, above

Add:

1 teaspoon melted Glace de Viande, 368, or
¼ teaspoon concentrated meat extract

Serve with grilled meats, chicken and eggs.

NEWBURG SAUCE

About 1 Cup

I.

Melt in the top of a double boiler:

½ cup Lobster Butter, 351

Add and cook gently until translucent:

1 teaspoon finely chopped shallots or mild onions

Add and continue to cook about 3 minutes:

¼ cup sherry or Madeira

Into:

1 cup cream

beat:

3 egg yolks

Add the two mixtures, stirring constantly until the sauce thickens. Use at once.

II. To turn this sauce a seductive pink, add:

1 tablespoon tomato paste
(1 tablespoon brandy)

ABOUT COLD SAVORY SAUCES

These are salad and fruit dressings of two very different types, and there is a widely cherished notion that those in the first category—the French-dressing type, or vinaigrettes, as opposed to those based on the mayonnaise principle—are virtually noncaloric. The fact is that although a salad is in itself an unimpeachable slenderizer, a salad dressing most definitely is not. Commercial mayonnaise must by law consist of 65% fat, but the fat content even of commercial French dressings runs about 35 to 40%; and these amounts are almost always exceeded by their homemade counterparts. Whether simple or rich and complex, salad dressings, with the rarest exceptions, should never repeat in their composition the materials they grace. Please read About Salads, 95, About Oil, 541, and About Vinegar, 526. For heavier dressings, see Dips, 89.

FRENCH DRESSING OR SAUCE VINAIGRETTE

About 1 Cup

This dressing is best made just before use and can become part of the salad-making if you like. See Tossed Salad, 94. The classic proportions are 3 to 4 parts of oil to 1 part lemon juice, lime juice or vinegar, and salt and pepper to taste. However, you may find it satisfactory—and less caloric—to use a dry red wine instead of vinegar, wholly or in part: since the wine is less tart, the amount of oil may be substantially reduced. Many other condiments are often added to the time-honored ingredients in the recipe; including Worcestershire sauce, chili sauce, chutney, Roquefort cheese, spices, sweet and sour cream and, of course, herbs and garlic. Garlic cloves and herbs should be removed after 24 hours.

Place in the bottom of a jar:

½ teaspoon salt
⅛ teaspoon freshly ground pepper
¼ cup vinegar or lemon juice
¼ to ½ teaspoon prepared mustard

Lid and shake jar until these ingredients are blended. Add gradually, shaking between additions:

¾ cup olive or walnut oil

If made in advance, cover jar and refrigerate. Shake well before using.

HERBED FRENCH DRESSING

About ½ Cup

➤ Fresh herbs should be added only when the sauce is to be used at once, because they become strong and unpleasant if left in the oil for any length of time. This is also true for grated onions and capers.

Prepare and place in a jar with a screw top:

½ cup French Dressing, above

using tarragon vinegar. Add:

½ teaspoon dry mustard
¾ teaspoon each of the following fresh herbs: basil, thyme, sweet marjoram and chervil
¼ teaspoon salt
⅛ teaspoon pepper

Lid and shake well and serve promptly.

CHIFFONADE DRESSING

About 1½ Cups

Prepare:

½ cup French Dressing, above

Add to it:

2 chopped hard-cooked eggs
2 tablespoons julienned cooked beetroot
2 tablespoons chopped parsley
2 teaspoons chopped chives
1 teaspoon chopped onion

SPINACH OR WATERCRESS DRESSING

About 2 Cups

Excellent over salad greens or Cucumber Gelatin Salad, 114, and Shrimp, 107.

Combine:

2 tablespoons lemon juice
1 tablespoon tarragon vinegar
½ cup olive oil
1 teaspoon salt
⅛ teaspoon pepper

Chop finely and stir in:

2 cups watercress or very young spinach leaves

Use at once.

⅄ BLENDER CRESS DRESSING

Blend to a paste in an electric blender:

2 hard-cooked eggs
2 tablespoons olive oil
¾ cup cut watercress, packed lightly

Dilute this paste with:

French Dressing, left

to the consistency you prefer. Use at once.

LORENZO DRESSING

About ¾ Cup

For cold meat or fish.

Combine:

½ cup French Dressing, opposite
3 tablespoons Chili Sauce, 847
3 tablespoons chopped watercress

FRENCH DRESSING FOR FRUIT SALAD

About ½ Cup

Prepare:
½ cup French Dressing, 360
substituting for the vinegar:
3 tablespoons grapefruit or lemon juice

ANCHOVY DRESSING

About ½ Cup

For a leaf lettuce salad.
Prepare:
½ cup French Dressing, 360
Beat into it:
1 tablespoon or more anchovy or other fish paste

ANCHOVY AND BEET DRESSING

About 1 Cup

For endive or crisp leaf lettuce salads.
Place in a jar with a screw top:
½ cup French Dressing, 360
3 or 4 chopped anchovies
2 small chopped cooked beets
1 chopped hard-cooked egg
Season the dressing highly.

SALSA VERDE OR ANCHOVY CAPER SAUCE

About 1¼ Cups

To be used with salads and fish.
Prepare:
French Dressing, 360
Soak in it:
1 crustless slice white bread or
1 small riced boiled potato
Add:
½ cup chopped parsley
1½ tablespoons capers
2 garlic cloves
3 anchovy fillets or ½ teaspoon anchovy paste
2 tablespoons sugar
Season to taste
Any of the following may be added:
(Horseradish or chopped pickles, green olives or green peppers)
Beat well and serve at once.

ROQUEFORT OR BLUE CHEESE FRENCH DRESSING

About ⅔ Cup

Prepare:
½ cup French Dressing, 360
Beat into it:
2 tablespoons or more crumbled Roquefort or blue cheese

BLENDER ANCHOVY AND ROQUEFORT DRESSING

About 1½ Cups

Place in electric blender and blend until smooth:
⅔ cup olive or walnut oil
1 can anchovies with oil: 2 oz.
3 tablespoons vinegar
3 tablespoons lemon juice
¼ teaspoon paprika
(1 clove garlic)
½ teaspoon prepared mustard
½ teaspoon sugar
½ teaspoon celery salt
A dash of Worcestershire sauce and hot pepper sauce
A 3-inch wedge Roquefort cheese

FRENCH DRESSING WITH CREAM CHEESE

About ⅞ Cup

Serve this dressing over a green salad or one made with vegetables.
Mash with a fork and beat until smooth:
1 package cream cheese: 3 oz.
Beat in:
1 teaspoon finely minced onion
½ teaspoon prepared mustard
1 teaspoon salt
Freshly ground black pepper
2 tablespoons chopped parsley
Beat in gradually:
¼ cup vegetable oil
1½ tablespoons vinegar

CHUTNEY DRESSING

About 1 Cup

Combine in a jar and chill:
1 tablespoon chopped hard-cooked egg
1 tablespoon chopped chutney
¼ teaspoon curry powder
1 tablespoon lemon juice
½ cup olive oil
3 tablespoons vinegar
¼ teaspoon salt
1 teaspoon sugar
A few grains black pepper
Shortly before serving this dressing, beat it well with a fork.

HONEY DRESSING

1 Cup

For fruit salads.
Combine:
½ cup honey
½ cup lime juice
(A pinch of ground ginger)

ITALIAN DRESSING

About 1 Cup

Its pedigree is shaky, this sauce being basically a French dressing with a strongly Neapolitan accent; but in recent years it has become highly popular.
Steep 1 hour—no more—in:
⅓ cup white wine vinegar
2 sliced cloves garlic
½ teaspoon oregano
¼ teaspoon basil

¼ teaspoon dill
(¼ teaspoon fennel)
Strain the above mixture into:
⅔ cup olive or walnut oil
1½ teaspoons lemon juice
Chill. Shake well before using.

AVOCADO DRESSING

I. **About ¾ Cup**

Great for sliced tomatoes.
Peel and mash:
½ avocado
Add gradually:
½ cup French Dressing, 360
and beat until smooth. Use immediately.

II. Use this variant as a heavy dressing or as a filling for tomatoes, cucumbers, celery or endive. See Salads, 92, and Hors d'Oeuvre, 77.
Mash:
A ripe avocado
with:
Lemon juice or vinegar
and:
Season to taste

HORSERADISH DRESSING

About ½ Cup

Prepare:
½ cup French Dressing, 360
Beat into it:
1 tablespoon or more fresh or prepared horseradish

CELERY SEED DRESSING

About 2 Cups

Add to fruit salad just before serving. This dressing may be made with an electric ⅄ blender or mixer. Constant beating, in any case, is a prerequisite.
Combine:
½ cup sugar
1 teaspoon dry mustard
1 teaspoon salt
1 to 2 teaspoons celery seed
Add:
1 tablespoon grated onion
Gradually add, beating constantly:
1 cup vegetable oil
⅓ cup vinegar
Garnish with:
(A few finely cut sprigs lemon thyme)

LOW-CALORIE FRENCH DRESSING

About ½ Cup

No, it isn't a special treat, but it may be eaten by the bulging with a clear conscience.
Soak:
1 teaspoon gelatin
in:
1 tablespoon cold water or tomato juice
Dissolve it in:
¼ cup boiling water
Add:
1 tablespoon sugar
½ teaspoon salt
Cool this mixture. Add:
1 teaspoon grated lemon rind
¼ cup lemon juice
⅛ teaspoon prepared mustard
¼ teaspoon paprika
A few grains cayenne
⅛ teaspoon pepper
¼ teaspoon onion juice
(⅛ teaspoon curry powder)
Shake the dressing. Chill it. Before serving, beat well with a wire beater. Add, if you wish:
(2 tablespoons minced parsley)
(1 tablespoon minced chives)

SWEET-SOUR LOW-CALORIE DRESSING

1 Cup

For a green salad.
Combine:
⅓ cup lemon juice
⅔ cup water
1 teaspoon sugar
¼ teaspoon salt

CHINESE LOW-CALORIE DRESSING COCKAIGNE

About ½ Cup

Good on sliced cucumber and tomato.
Combine:
4 tablespoons lemon or lime juice
¼ cup condensed bouillon or reduced stock
2 tablespoons soy sauce
½ to 1 teaspoon sugar
(1 teaspoon grated fresh gingerroot)

LOW-CALORIE SALAD DRESSING WITH TOMATO

I. **About 1¼ Cups**

Combine in a glass jar:
1 cup tomato juice
2 tablespoons tarragon vinegar
1 teaspoon Worcestershire sauce
1 teaspoon onion juice
½ teaspoon salt
½ teaspoon fresh dill
½ teaspoon fresh basil
Beat into the above ingredients:
Yolks of 2 hard-cooked eggs
Shake well after making and before using. Chill.

II. **1¼ Cups**

Blend in a saucepan, using a wire whisk:
¼ cup water
2 teaspoons cornstarch
When the paste is smooth, add, beating constantly:
½ cup water
Simmer and stir over low heat until thickened—about 3 minutes. Cool. Add:

2 tablespoons lemon juice
1½ teaspoons sugar
2 tablespoons vegetable oil
1 teaspoon grated horseradish
1¼ teaspoons prepared mustard
1 teaspoon salt
¼ cup Catsup, 847
½ teaspoon paprika
½ teaspoon garlic powder or chili sauce

Beat well. Chill.

MAYONNAISE

Mayonnaise is at its best when made by hand. But, with care, we can now abridge the process fairly satisfactorily in an electric mixer or a ⅄ blender. Blender mayonnaise is made more quickly and has greater volume and fluffier texture, but it cannot duplicate the smooth, rich-looking glisten of the hand-beaten product. We believe it is also slightly less adaptable to some mayonnaise variations, such as Mayonnaise Collée, 368. See also Hot Mayonnaise, 359. In making mayonnaise by any method ➤ eggs, oil and bowl or mixer must all be at room temperature, 70°. Warm the oil slightly if it has been refrigerated, rinse your bowl in hot water first and dry it. ➤ Don't try to make mayonnaise if a thunderstorm threatens or is in progress, as it simply will not bind.

Care must be used in ➤ storing all mayonnaise combinations under refrigeration, as they are subject to bacterial activity which may be very toxic without any evidence of spoilage. Cooked foods to be mixed with mayonnaise keep much better and help deter bacteria if they have been marinated in vinegar or lemon juice or are mixed with pickle. But, even if they have this added acid content, they must be kept thoroughly refrigerated. Freezing mayonnaise combinations is chancy, as the spoilage is only arrested, not destroyed, and accelerates when the food is defrosted.

If you have to resort to bottled mayonnaise, beating in 1 to 2 tablespoons good olive oil until all trace of it has disappeared will make it stiffer and heavier and will improve flavor. Sour cream, according to taste, can also do wonders for commercial mayonnaise—if well incorporated. Please note that commercial "Salad Dressing" is not mayonnaise, and the above suggestions will not work if it is used.

I. **About 1¼ Cups**

Place in a medium-sized bowl and beat with a wire whisk or wooden spoon until lemon-colored:

2 egg yolks

Beat in:

¼ to ½ teaspoon dry mustard
½ teaspoon salt
A few grains cayenne
½ teaspoon vinegar or lemon juice
½ teaspoon confectioners' sugar

Beat in, very slowly, ½ teaspoon at a time:

½ cup olive oil

The mixture will begin to thicken and emulsify. Now you can relax! Combine in a cup or small pitcher:

1½ tablespoons vinegar
2 tablespoons lemon juice

Have ready:

½ cup olive, safflower, walnut or sesame oil

Alternate the oil ➤ drop by drop, with a few drops of the lemon and vinegar mixture. If the oil is added slowly during constant beating, this will make a good thick sauce. The sauce will break if you have either added your oil too fast toward the end or added too much of it—figure no more than ½ to ¾ cup oil to each large yolk. It may also break if your oil has been cold and your egg yolks warm. Do not despair. Try first stirring in a teaspoon of warm water. If this doesn't work, the mayonnaise can be salvaged by placing another egg yolk in a fresh bowl and adding the curdled sauce to it very, very slowly, beating the mixture all the while, until it again thickens. If the dressing becomes too heavy, it may be thinned with cream.

II. **About 1½ Cups**

You may make the above recipe following exactly the same procedure, in the same order, using an electric mixer on medium speed or the speed indicated for whipping cream.

III. ⅄ **About 1¾ Cups**

Blender mayonnaise differs from the first recipe in that it uses a whole egg. If your beating arm is rather weak, we suggest you try this method, as the emulsifying is produced by the action of the blender.

Put in blender container:

1 egg
1 teaspoon dry mustard
1 teaspoon salt
A dash of cayenne
1 teaspoon sugar
¼ cup olive or vegetable oil

Cover and blend on "High" until thoroughly combined. With blender still running, take off the cover and slowly add:

½ cup vegetable oil

and then:

3 tablespoons lemon juice

until thoroughly blended. Add slowly:

½ cup vegetable oil

and blend until thick. You may have to stop and start the blender to stir down the mayonnaise.

MAYONNAISE GRENACHE

About 2 Cups

Serve with smoked turkey or smoked tongue.

Combine:

1 cup Mayonnaise, above
½ cup red currant jelly
3 tablespoons grated horseradish
¼ teaspoon salt
⅛ teaspoon freshly ground pepper
2 tablespoons dessert sherry or Madeira

Fold in:
½ cup whipped cream

HERB MAYONNAISE

About 1¼ Cups

Combine:
1 cup Mayonnaise, 363
with:
1 pressed clove garlic
1 teaspoon Worcestershire sauce
and ½ teaspoon of any 3 of the following:
Chopped basil, chervil, dill, burnet, tarragon or parsley

GREEN GODDESS DRESSING

About 2 Cups

For fish or shellfish or vegetable salads.
Combine:
1 cup Mayonnaise, 363
1 minced clove garlic
3 minced anchovy fillets
¼ cup finely minced chives or green onions
¼ cup minced parsley
1 tablespoon lemon juice
1 tablespoon tarragon vinegar
½ teaspoon salt
Ground black pepper
½ cup cultured sour cream

GREEN MAYONNAISE OR SAUCE VERTE

1 Cup

For cold shellfish or vegetables.
Chop, blanch, 154, 2 minutes and drain in a sieve:
2 tablespoons parsley
2 tablespoons tarragon, fennel or dill
2 tablespoons chives
2 tablespoons spinach or finely chopped cucumber
2 tablespoons watercress
Rub through sieve and combine to make a paste with:
2 hard-cooked egg yolks
Add to:
1 cup stiff Mayonnaise, 363

RÉMOULADE SAUCE

About 1⅓ Cups

For cold meat and poultry—also shellfish, with which it is especially appropriate.
Combine:
1 cup Mayonnaise, 363
1 tablespoon drained, finely chopped cucumber pickle
1 tablespoon drained, chopped capers
2 teaspoons French mustard
1 teaspoon finely chopped parsley
½ teaspoon chopped fresh tarragon
½ teaspoon chervil
(½ teaspoon anchovy paste)

RUSSIAN DRESSING OR RUSSIAN MAYONNAISE

About 1¾ Cups

Use on arranged salads, eggs and shellfish; or in chicken sandwiches, instead of butter or a plainer mayonnaise.
Combine:
1 cup Mayonnaise, 363
1 tablespoon grated horseradish
(3 tablespoons caviar or salmon roe)
(1 teaspoon Worcestershire sauce)
¼ cup Chili Sauce, 847, or Catsup, 847
1 teaspoon grated onion

TARTARE SAUCE

About 1⅓ Cups

A good old standby for fried fish.
Combine:
1 cup firm Mayonnaise, 363
1 teaspoon French mustard
1 tablespoon finely chopped parsley
1 teaspoon minced shallots
1 tablespoon chopped, drained sweet pickle
(1 tablespoon chopped, drained green olives)
1 finely chopped hard-cooked egg
1 tablespoon chopped, drained capers
Season to taste
You may thin the sauce with:
A little wine vinegar or lemon juice

THOUSAND ISLAND DRESSING

About 1½ Cups

Serve over iceberg lettuce wedges, eggs, etc.
Combine:
1 cup Mayonnaise, 363
¼ cup Chili Sauce, 847, or Catsup, 847
2 tablespoons minced stuffed olives
1 tablespoon chopped green pepper
1 tablespoon minced onion or chives
1 chopped hard-cooked egg
2 teaspoons chopped parsley

LOW-CALORIE MOCK THOUSAND ISLAND DRESSING

About 2 Cups

Combine in a large screw-top jar:
¾ cup tarragon vinegar
1 cup condensed tomato soup
1 minced garlic clove
A few grains cayenne
2 tablespoons chopped dill pickle
2 tablespoons finely chopped celery
2 tablespoons finely chopped parsley
1 tablespoon Worcestershire sauce
1 teaspoon paprika
1 teaspoon prepared mustard

ANDALOUSE SAUCE

2 Cups

For vegetable salads, cold fish or egg dishes.
Combine:
2 cups Mayonnaise, 363

1 chopped tomato with seeds and juice removed, or ½ cup tomato purée
¼ julienned red pimiento

FRUIT-SALAD MAYONNAISE

1½ Cups

Combine:
1 cup Mayonnaise, 363
½ cup pineapple juice
1 teaspoon grated orange rind
1 tablespoon orange curaçao

CREAM OR CHANTILLY MAYONNAISE

2 Cups

Serve with fruit salad.
Prepare:
1 cup Mayonnaise, 363
Shortly before serving, blend in:
1 cup whipped cream

CURRY MAYONNAISE

About 1 Cup

This dressing makes an interesting binder for a fruit, molded chicken or shellfish salad.
Combine:
1 cup Mayonnaise, 363
¼ teaspoon ginger
½ to 1 teaspoon curry powder
1 mashed clove garlic
1 teaspoon honey
1 tablespoon lime juice
You may add:
(1 tablespoon chopped chutney)
(1 tablespoon chopped kumquats)
(1 tablespoon blanched slivered almonds)

WATERCRESS SAUCE OR SAUCE AU CRESSON

About 1 Cup

Excellent with cold fish dishes.
Combine:
¼ cup finely chopped watercress
¾ cup Mayonnaise, 363
1 tablespoon lemon juice
Season to taste

SAUCE LOUIS

About 2 Cups

Especially relished with stuffed artichokes, shrimp or crab. It is the sauce used for Crab Louis, 107.
Combine:
1 cup Mayonnaise, 363
¼ cup heavy cream
¼ cup chili sauce
1 teaspoon Worcestershire sauce
¼ cup chopped green pepper
¼ cup chopped green onion
2 tablespoons lemon juice
Season to taste

HALF-AND-HALF DRESSING

About 2½ Cups

Serve on tossed salad, combination salads or hearts of lettuce.
Combine:
1 cup Mayonnaise, 363
1 cup French Dressing, 360
1 minced garlic clove
1 teaspoon mashed anchovies
½ cup grated Parmesan cheese

SAUCE GRIBICHE OR MAYONNAISE WITH HARD-COOKED EGG

About 3 Cups

For fish and cold meat.
Mash in a bowl until smooth:
3 hard-cooked egg yolks
Add:
½ teaspoon salt
A dash of pepper
1 teaspoon Dijon-type mustard
Add very gradually and beat constantly:
1½ cups olive oil
½ cup vinegar
The mixture will thicken. Then stir in:
3 finely julienned hard-cooked egg whites
½ cup mixed finely chopped sour pickles and capers, with the moisture squeezed out
2 tablespoons finely chopped mixed parsley, chervil, tarragon and chives

AIOLI OR GARLIC SAUCE

1 Cup

Very popular in France, where it is sometimes known as **Beurre de Provence.** Serve over fish, cold boiled potatoes, beet rounds and boiled beef.
Skin, then chop very finely the:
4 garlic clove sections
that give the sauce its original name. Beat in:
2 egg yolks
⅛ teaspoon salt
(1 slice dry French bread without crust, soaked in milk and wrung out)
Add, as for mayonnaise, very slowly and beating constantly:
1 cup olive oil
As the sauce thickens, beat in:
½ teaspoon cold water
1 teaspoon lemon juice
In case the sauce fails to thicken, treat as a defeated Mayonnaise, 363.

SKORDALIA

1 Cup

For soups.
Prepare:
Aioli Sauce, above
omitting the optional bread and adding, after the sauce has thickened:
¼ cup ground almonds
¼ cup fresh bread crumbs or 1 small riced boiled potato

3 teaspoons lemon juice
2 tablespoons chopped parsley

LOW-CALORIE MOCK MAYONNAISE

About 2½ Cups

On the gelatin principle.
Mix:
2 tablespoons unflavored gelatin
in:
1 tablespoon cold water
Combine in a saucepan and bring to a boil:
½ cup herb vinegar
1 teaspoon prepared mustard
½ teaspoon salt
¼ teaspoon white pepper
3 teaspoons liquid artificial sweetener
Add gelatin to above mixture, stirring until completely dissolved. Add, continuing to stir:
2 cups buttermilk
1 tablespoon onion flakes
Cover and refrigerate until set. You may flavor this dressing with:
(¼ cup or more tomato purée)

EGGLESS MOCK MAYONNAISE

About ¾ Cup

Combine in a mixing bowl:
3 tablespoons evaporated milk
¼ teaspoon salt
¼ teaspoon paprika
¼ teaspoon prepared mustard
A few grains white pepper
Beat in gradually:
½ cup vegetable oil
then:
3 to 4 teaspoons lemon juice
Keep covered in refrigerator.

ROUILLE SAUCE

About 1 Cup

Strongly flavored, served with fish soups or bouillabaisse. Pound together in a bowl or mortar to make a smooth paste:
1 blanched, seeded, skinned red pimiento or 1 canned pimiento
1 small red chili, boiled until tender, or a dash of hot pepper sauce
¼ cup white bread crumbs soaked in water and squeezed dry
2 mashed cloves garlic
Beat in, very slowly, as in Mayonnaise, 363:
¼ cup olive or vegetable oil
Thin the sauce just before serving with:
2 to 3 tablespoons of the soup you are serving
Pass with the soup.

MOCK ROUILLE SAUCE

About 1 Cup

For fish soups, bland meats and vegetables. Lower in calories than the genuine article. Prepare as above:
Rouille Sauce
omitting the oil and substituting for the soup an equal amount of:
Canned condensed consommé

SICILIAN GARNISH

6 Servings

For vegetables.
Sauté until golden:
1 finely sliced large onion
in:
¼ cup olive oil
Add and cook briefly:
½ crushed clove garlic
Add:
¼ cup chopped black olives
4 mashed anchovy fillets
A grating of black pepper
Pour over vegetables just before serving and finish off with a grating of:
Parmesan or Romano cheese

BOILED SALAD DRESSINGS

Note that the term "boiled," while traditionally used, is inaccurate: "double-boiled" comes closer. Of the three versions, I is the most economical, and more than acceptable for vegetable and potato salads; II is recommended for slaw, tomato salad and aspics; III for fruit salad. Keep all of them refrigerated.

I. **About 1¼ Cups**

Mix together:
½ to 1 teaspoon dry mustard
1 to 2 tablespoons sugar
½ teaspoon salt
2 tablespoons flour
¼ teaspoon paprika
in:
½ cup cold water
Beat in the top of a double boiler:
1 whole egg or 2 yolks
¼ cup vinegar
Add the above ingredients. Cook and stir the dressing ➤ over—not in—boiling water until thick and smooth. Add:
2 tablespoons butter
Chill the dressing. It may be thinned with:
Sweet or cultured sour cream

II. **About 1½ Cups**

Beat in the top of a double boiler:
2 egg yolks
2 teaspoons sugar
1 tablespoon melted butter
⅔ cup milk
¼ cup vinegar
2 teaspoons salt
A few grains cayenne
1 teaspoon dry mustard
Dissolve:
2 teaspoons cornstarch

in:

⅓ cup milk

Add it to the ingredients in the double boiler. Cook and stir the dressing ➤ over—not in—boiling water until thick. Cool it. You may add chopped parsley, chives or other herbs, celery or dill seeds, etc. Fold the sauce into:

2 stiffly beaten egg whites

III. **About 1¼ Cups**

Beat in the top of a double boiler:

1 teaspoon salt
⅓ teaspoon paprika
¼ to ½ cup sugar
2 tablespoons melted butter
6 tablespoons cream
3 eggs
(½ teaspoon prepared mustard)

Stir and cook the dressing ➤ over—not in—boiling water until thick. Add slowly:

6 tablespoons lemon juice

The dressing may be thinned with:

Fruit juice or cream

ROQUEFORT SOUR CREAM DRESSING

About 1½ Cups

Combine in a bowl or ⅄ blender:

¼ lb. Roquefort or blue cheese
1 tablespoon vinegar
1 tablespoon onions or chives
1 cup cultured sour cream

SOUR CREAM DRESSING FOR VEGETABLE SALAD

About 1 Cup

Beat until smooth:

1 cup thick cultured sour cream

Add to it:

1 teaspoon grated onion or fresh onion juice
1 teaspoon celery or dill seed
½ teaspoon salt
A fresh grating of white pepper
(2 tablespoons chopped green or sweet red pepper)

CREAM CHEESE DRESSING FOR FRUIT SALAD

About 1¼ Cups

Mash with a fork and beat until smooth:

1 package cream cheese: 3 oz.

Beat in slowly:

1 tablespoon lemon juice
2 tablespoons currant jelly
¾ cup cream

Chill the dressing 1 hour or more before serving.

CURRY DRESSING FOR FRUIT SALAD

About 1 Cup

Combine:

2 tablespoons mild vinegar
1 tablespoon lemon juice
¼ to ½ teaspoon curry powder
1 teaspoon sugar

Stir in:

1 cup cultured sour cream

See also Curry Mayonnaise, 365.

YOGURT DRESSING

Yogurt, 533, simple and unadorned, is excellent on honeydew and cantaloupe melon balls in a lettuce cup. Try it, too, with other fresh fruits or over crisp salad greens on hot summer days. Good for dieters, too.

LOW-CALORIE YOGURT AND CUCUMBER DRESSING

About 1½ Cups

For salads.

⅄ Blend:

1 large peeled seeded cucumber

Fold in:

1 cup Yogurt, 533
Salt and pepper to taste
Chopped fresh herbs

ABOUT GLAZES AND GLAÇAGE

These terms are among the trickiest in the cooking vocabulary. However, take heart: we have postponed the explanation of sweet glazes—by all odds the more confusing—to Desserts, Icings, Pastries, Ice Creams, Fruits and Candies. We shall deal here only with the somewhat simpler topic of savory glazes: those nonsweet maskings and coatings which impart so much color and glamor to meats, fish, salads and vegetables.

Savory glazing—particularly with meats and vegetables—can have, as we have warned it might, several connotations. Before sorting them out, we may as well remind you of "deglazing," which has already been described in this chapter, 340. The fat-free juices extracted in this effortless way from sautéed or braised foods, or those prepared à l'étouffée, 151, may be used just as they are, reduced, or as the liquid in roux-based sauces. But meats may be glazed also by the use of Glace de Viande, or Meat Glaze, described below—a substance yielded by a lengthy process of reduction. It is potent and delectable, but, like all other powerful essences, it must be used with moderation.

You may "glaze" vegetables by letting the butter in which they have been cooked combine with their reduced juices. This is best done over carefully controlled heat; often a little sugar or honey is added, see 280.

To glaze a sauce may mean to run it under a broiler until it turns golden brown. To glaze a tongue, an hors d'oeuvre or an open-faced sandwich may mean to apply an aspic coating to it. You may coat eggs or fish with a rich White Sauce,

341—a procedure which is then referred to as napping or glazing them.

TO GLAZE A SAUCE ON A CASSEROLE

Try this only if you have preheated the broiler well. Then run your dish quickly under the heat, until it browns delicately. Should the sauce boil before it colors, it will separate into an oily, watery mass. ➤ Be sure the sauce does not touch the edge of the casserole. Allow an empty area all around for expansion. It is also a wise precaution to protect the casserole by putting it in a pan of hot water. Do not leave it longer than 3 minutes. A perfect all-over brown glaze on a sauce used to coat fish or chicken dishes can be achieved by the following method: Reserve some of a Béchamel or other white sauce and fold in whipped cream, at least 4 tablespoons to 1 cup of sauce. The more whipped cream, the smoother the browning. Put under a hot broiler and watch closely.

MEAT GLAZE OR GLACE DE VIANDE

What a convenience and delight this substance is if you have the patience to make it.
Prepare:

Brown Stock, 522

Reduce slowly until the stock forms an even coating on a spoon inserted into it. Remove from heat and cool, at which point the mass solidifies and becomes very glutinous. Covered and refrigerated, a meat glaze will last for several weeks.

Or you may cut it in squares equivalent to 1 tablespoon or more and freeze them in individual packets for use in preparing sauces.

SPIRIT GLAZE FOR HAM

Combine:

½ to 1 cup dry red wine
½ to 1 cup bourbon whisky
1 cup brown sugar
6 bruised cloves
2 tablespoons grated orange peel

Spread on the ham after it is skinned and continue to baste during the last ½ hour of cooking.

CRANBERRY GLAZE FOR FOWL

Combine:

1 cup canned cranberry sauce
½ cup brown sugar
2 tablespoons lemon juice

HONEY GLAZE FOR MEAT OR ONIONS

Combine:

¼ cup honey
¼ cup soy sauce
1 teaspoon prepared mustard

ASPIC GLAZE

Spoon this over the flat surfaces of cold sliced meat or open-faced sandwiches.
Soak:

1 tablespoon gelatin

in:

½ cup meat or vegetable stock

Dissolve it over hot water. Add it to:

1½ cups clarified stock

Season mildly. Chill until the glaze thickens somewhat. ➤ Be sure you have the food to be glazed and the tools you are working with well chilled. Apply a thin even coat of aspic which has begun to jell. Chill the food. Repeat, if needed, with a second layer and chill again.

MAYONNAISE COLLÉE OR GELATIN MAYONNAISE

This coating, also known as **Mayonnaise Chaud-Froid,** is ordinarily used to coat or mask aspics, cold fish, meat or fowl dishes. But if you make it fairly stiff, it can be piped through a pastry tube, and you can achieve the same rococo flights of fancy as when icing a wedding cake. You may also use delicately tinted Mayonnaise Collée, made from Green Mayonnaise, 364, but please avoid highly colored low-relief effects, which look unappetizingly artificial. Note that this stiffened mayonnaise serves much the same purpose as the Béchamel-based Chaud-Froid Sauce, below, but it does not hold well or long, for the heavy oil content may cause oozing. ➤ The dish you wish to coat should be well chilled and dry.

I. Soak:

1½ to 2 teaspoons gelatin

in:

1½ to 2 tablespoons water

Beat this mixture into:

1 cup heavy Mayonnaise, 363

To color the mayonnaise pink, you may add:

(Tomato purée or Lobster Butter, 351)

To color it green:

(Spinach purée)

II. Or beat:

¼ cup Aspic Glaze, above

into:

1 cup Mayonnaise, 363

The Aspic Glaze should be at about 70°—tepid and still liquid. Once it has begun to jell, it will not incorporate with the mayonnaise properly. Spread the mayonnaise as you would frosting, with firm strokes of a spatula, working quickly, for it tends to congeal even at room temperature. Chill the dish, then decorate as described below. After the decorations have also set, place the whole dish on a rack with a platter under it and glaze it with aspic glaze, which should be about the consistency of thick syrup. Your food must be very cold, so that the aspic sets almost at the moment of contact. Use a ladle which holds about 1 cup glaze and pour it on with the motion illustrated for Petits Fours, 695, giving the whole dish two or three coats, which should be perfectly smooth, with no streaks or lumps. The aspic which has fallen through the rack onto the platter may be reused, after straining, for the second and third coats.

SAUCE CHAUD-FROID

Chaud-Froid is so called because it begins as a heated sauce and is served as a cold one. It differs from Mayonnaise Collée in emphasizing the flavor of the dish to which it is applied, since it is made with the selfsame stock. Chaud-Froid is often used to coat whole cooked chickens, ham or veal roasts, fish or other cold buffet items.
Prepare:

2 cups Béchamel Sauce, 341, slightly overseasoned

substituting for the milk Light Stock or Fumet, 522, 523—according to the dish you intend to mask. Chaud-Froid may also be made with a Brown Sauce, 346, for meats or chicken. Many people find the dark color more appetizing. Add:

2 tablespoons gelatin

softened in:

3 or 4 tablespoons stock

again using the appropriate flavor for the dish. Stir constantly over medium heat until thoroughly combined. Remove from heat and cool, stirring from time to time to keep a skin from forming. ➤ When cool enough to coat a spoon, but not set, ladle it over the cold chicken or fish in the manner described above. Chill to set. The dish may need more than one coat of the sauce. Decorate and glaze.

QUICK PINK CHAUD-FROID

1½ Cups

Especially good as a sauce or glaze for fish.
Combine, stir, then chill:

1 cup mayonnaise
½ cup catsup
1½ tablespoons lemon juice
A few drops hot pepper sauce
Salt to taste

ABOUT DECORATIONS FOR CHAUD-FROID

Decorations on dishes masked with Sauce Chaud-Froid or Mayonnaise Collée can be as fanciful as you wish. And professional chefs achieve masterful effects. With a little practice, you can produce the same elegantly curving sprays of flowers, leaves and stems, using as basic material leeks, chives, eggplant skin or green peppers. To make them pliable, they must be blanched about 3 minutes in salted water, then cooled immediately on crushed ice to retain color. Chives form the stems, and leeks, etc., can be cut into leaf shapes—freehand or with the fancy cutters shown on 99.

Lemon rind, carrot and red pepper, blanched as above, can be used for flower petals—or paper-thin slices of ham. Other materials suitable for decoration are: truffles or black olives—you can use the skins of ripe olives as a truffle substitute; pickles, hard-cooked eggs and grapes; parsley and other herbs, blanched 1 minute; peas, capers and wilted cucumber slices.

These decorations are first dipped in clear Aspic Glaze, 368, then applied to the dish to be ornamented as described on 368. If they slip after the first application of clear glaze, replace them carefully with tweezers. If the decorating proves slow, be sure to chill periodically so that the Chaud-Froid does not darken.

Chaud-Froids are often garnished with aspic jelly, chopped or cut in fancy shapes. For Chaud-Froid poultry dishes, decorate the platter with foie-gras balls rolled in chopped nuts or Truffles, 310. Lemon wedges sprinkled with finely chopped parsley and other fancy lemon shapes are shown on 571. To garnish with hard-cooked eggs, see 82.

LOW-FAT TOFU DRESSING

About 1 Cup

This base makes a fine medium for several seasonings—add pickles, nuts, raisins or various herbs and spices. Perishable! Use within one or two days.
⅄ Purée in a blender:

⅔ cup drained Tofu, 535
3 tablespoons lemon juice or wine vinegar
3 to 4 tablespoons oil or olive oil
½ teaspoon salt or 2 teaspoons soy sauce
Pepper

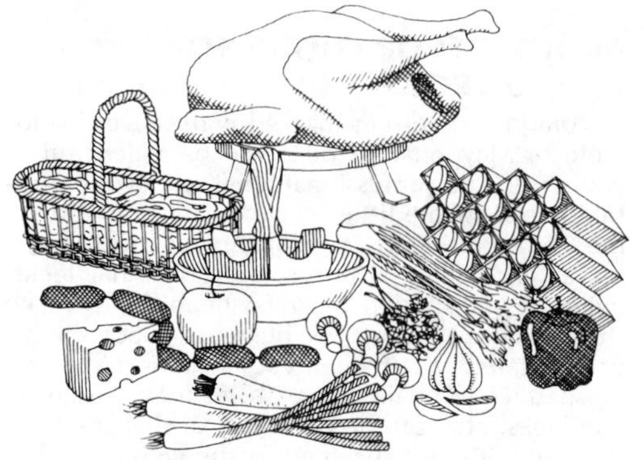

STUFFINGS AND FORCEMEAT

"No more turkey," announced the little boy at the Thanksgiving dinner table, "but I'd like another helping of that bread he ate." Not all stuffings are made of bread; but all, if delicately and interestingly put together, are quite delicious enough to lure a budding gourmet away from even the most tradition-hallowed main dish. Some of the "makings," which may include those shown above, are celery, spices, herbs, oysters, giblets, sausage, mushrooms, olives, nuts and fruits, as well as the essential members of the onion family. They enrich the bread crumbs, rice, chestnuts and other cereals that bind stuffings, dressings and **farces** together.

Many foreign and old-fashioned stuffing recipes call for bread soaked in a liquid and then pressed before using. We find that most commercial American breads are already so soft in texture that soaking produces too pasty a dressing. For best results we recommend day-old bread in any case, and, unless otherwise indicated, the use of home-made white, whole wheat or corn bread.

The quality of the crumbs used is very important, so check page 551 to differentiate between fresh and dry. ➤ Never grind bread, as the stuffing will be too compact. It is important, too, ➤ to stuff food just before cooking; ➤ to handle stuffings lightly so as not to compact them; and ➤ to allow space when stuffing, so the mixture can swell and stay light. Should there be extra dressing that does not fit the cavity of fish, fowl or roast, cook it separately in a greased baking dish.

A useful rule of thumb in judging the amount of stuffing needed is ➤ to allow ½ cup of stuffing for each pound of bird or fish.

➤ Never use raw pork in dressings. Dressings are done when they reach an internal temperature of 165° to 170°.

For stuffings for vegetables, see individual stuffed vegetable recipes and pages 280 and 218.

Make dressings just before cooking stuffed foods to achieve superior texture, but particularly to ➤ avoid danger from spoilage. If made in advance, stuffings should be refrigerated separately from the meat, fowl or fish. To take off the chill, remove the dressing from the refrigerator about 20 minutes before stuffing and cooking. Remember too ➤ to allow extra cooking time for stuffed food, see for fish, 398, for meat, 770; for poultry and game, 421. Should there be any stuffing left after serving, remove it promptly from the cavity of the meat, fish or fowl and refrigerate it separately.

BREAD DRESSING WITH MUSHROOMS, OYSTERS, NUTS, GIBLETS, ETC.

About 5 Cups

There are no set proportions for ingredients in bread dressing. It should be palatable, light and slightly moist, well flavored but bland. Chopped green peppers, nutmeats, sautéed mushrooms and drained or slightly sautéed oysters may be added to it. Stock or oyster liquor may be substituted for milk.

Chop:

Giblets

Melt:

¼ cup butter

Add and sauté about 2 minutes:

(2 tablespoons or more chopped onion)

and the chopped giblets. Combine these ingredients with:

4 cups crustless day-old or slightly toasted, diced white, whole wheat or corn bread crumbs
¼ cup chopped parsley
¼ to 1 cup chopped celery
1 teaspoon crushed dried tarragon or basil
¾ teaspoon salt
½ teaspoon paprika
⅛ teaspoon nutmeg
Milk, stock or melted butter to moisten the dressing very lightly
(2 or 3 eggs)

You may add:

1½ cups nutmeats: Brazil, pine, pecan or walnut

and one of the following:

1 cup browned sausage meat
1 cup or more sliced mushrooms, sautéed with onion
1 cup chopped or whole drained oysters
1 cup chopped or whole soft-shell clams
1 cup cooked chopped shrimp

DRY DRESSING

About 5 Cups

This name was given by our cook, Sarah Brown, to a dressing she frequently made, which is by no means dry when served. Chopped pecans, oysters and olives may be added to it.

Make of day-old white or whole wheat bread:

About 3½ to 4 cups soft bread crumbs, 551

Combine with:

About 1 cup chopped celery
About ½ cup chopped sautéed onion

Season with:

Salt and paprika

Partly fill chicken or turkey with the dressing. Melt:

¾ to 1 cup butter

Pour half of it onto the dressing in the cavity. Fill it lightly with the remaining dressing and pour the remaining butter on it. Sew up the opening.

SHERRY BREAD DRESSING

1½ Cups

Soak 10 minutes:

1 cup bread crumbs, 551

in:

½ cup dry sherry

Wring the wine from the bread. Stir and sauté 3 minutes:

¼ cup finely chopped green pepper
½ cup finely chopped onion

in:

3 tablespoons butter

Add the bread crumbs and:

2 teaspoons Chili Sauce, 847

OYSTER BREAD DRESSING

2½ Cups

Enough for a 4-pound fish or the crop of a turkey. Melt:

6 tablespoons butter

Sauté in the butter until brown:

¼ cup chopped onion

Add:

1 tablespoon chopped parsley
2 cups dry bread crumbs, 551
1 cup drained whole or chopped oysters: ½ pint
¾ teaspoon salt
¼ teaspoon paprika
2 tablespoons capers
(½ cup drained chopped spinach)

BREAD DRESSING FOR FISH

2 Cups

A fine but plain, unsophisticated dressing. Combine:

1½ cups soft bread crumbs, 551
2 tablespoons chopped onion
½ cup chopped celery
2 tablespoons chopped parsley
1 or 2 beaten eggs

Season these ingredients well with:

½ teaspoon salt
⅛ teaspoon paprika
½ teaspoon dried tarragon or dill seed
2 tablespoons capers
(¼ teaspoon nutmeg)

Use enough:

Milk, melted butter or soup stock

to barely bind the ingredients.

GREEN DRESSING FOR FISH OR FOWL

About 1½ Cups

This has a tempting pistachio-green color. Sauté until transparent:

2 tablespoons chopped shallots

in:

2 tablespoons butter

Cool slightly. Place this in a blender and ⅄ blend to a paste with:

1 egg
½ cup tender celery with leaves
½ cup parsley tops
¼ cup watercress tops
½ cup crumbled crustless bread
½ teaspoon salt
⅛ teaspoon dried basil

Blend in with a fork:

½ cup pulled crustless bread crumbs, 551
¼ cup pistachio nuts, sliced water chestnuts or seeded peeled grapes

SEAFOOD DRESSING

For filling fish or for use in Vegetable Cases, 280. Combine:

1 cup flaked crab meat, drained oysters or mussels
2 slightly beaten eggs

Melt:

2 tablespoons butter

Sauté in it:

½ cup chopped onion
¾ cup chopped celery
2 slices bacon, minced
1 cup fresh bread crumbs

Combine with the seafood.

Season to taste

Add:

(1 teaspoon Worcestershire sauce, 1 tablespoon dry sherry, ⅛ teaspoon ginger or ½ teaspoon grated lemon rind)

SAUSAGE DRESSING

About 2½ Cups

Heat and stir in a skillet until done:

½ cup sausage meat

Drain off the surplus fat. Add:

½ cup chopped celery
2 cups cracker crumbs or 1 cup soft bread crumbs and 1 cup corn bread crumbs
¼ teaspoon minced onion
¼ teaspoon salt
⅛ teaspoon paprika
(½ cup chopped tart apple)

Moisten the dressing with:

½ cup stock or water

STUFFING FOR CROWN ROAST OF PORK

This stuffing is added for the last hour of the baking of the roast, 477.

Combine:
2½ lb. cooked pork sausage
½ cup dry bread crumbs, 551
¼ cup chopped onions
½ cup chopped celery
Moisten these ingredients with a very little:
Milk
Season with:
Savory
Paprika
Fill the crown with this dressing.

CHESTNUT DRESSING FOR GAME

About 4 Cups

Rice:
2½ cups Boiled Chestnuts, 298
Combine them with:
½ cup melted butter
1 teaspoon salt
⅛ teaspoon pepper
¼ cup cream
1 cup dry bread or cracker crumbs
2 tablespoons chopped parsley
½ cup chopped celery
(1 tablespoon grated onion or ¼ cup seedless raisins)
You may add, but remember this will increase the amount:
(½ cup liver sausage, ¼ cup chopped Chipolata sausage or 2 cups raw or creamed oysters)

ONION DRESSING

About 4 Cups

Prepare:
2 cups chopped onions
Drop them into:
4 cups boiling salted water
Simmer for 10 minutes. Drain. Mix the onions and:
3 cups dry bread crumbs, 551
1 beaten egg
½ cup melted butter
¾ teaspoon salt
⅛ teaspoon paprika
½ teaspoon poultry seasoning
(1 cup chopped tart apple or ½ cup sliced olives)
Moisten the mixture slightly with:
Stock, 522

ONION AND SAGE DRESSING

About 4¼ Cups

Prepare:
Onion Dressing, above
Add:
¼ cup cooked pork sausage
2 teaspoons chopped fresh sage leaves or ¾ teaspoon dried sage

FENNEL DRESSING

About 1 Cup

Brown:
1 cup bread crumbs, 551
in:
1 tablespoon butter
1 teaspoon Meat Glaze, 368
Cut into julienned strips:
1 carrot
1 white base of leek
2 ribs celery
Add the above to the butter mixture. Add:
2 drops garlic juice
and simmer until coated. Add:
1 sprig of chopped fresh fennel
1 small pinch thyme
¼ teaspoon salt
Mix with the crumbs:
Freshly ground pepper

APPLE DRESSING

About 4 Cups

Pare and slice:
6 cups tart cooking apples
Combine them with:
1 cup currants or raisins
(2 tablespoons lemon juice)
You may steam the currants or raisins in 2 tablespoons of water in the top of a double boiler 15 minutes before combining them with the apples.

APPLE AND PRUNE DRESSING

About 4½ Cups

Combine lightly:
3 cups diced crustless bread
½ cup melted butter or drippings
1 cup diced apples
¾ cup drained chopped cooked prunes
½ cup chopped nutmeats
1 teaspoon salt
½ teaspoon paprika
1 tablespoon lemon juice

APPLE AND ONION DRESSING

About 12 Cups

Place in boiling water for 5 minutes:
1 cup raisins
Drain well. Add them to:
7 cups soft bread crumbs
Melt:
¾ cup butter
Sauté in it 3 minutes:
1 cup chopped onion
1 chopped clove garlic
1 cup chopped celery
Add these ingredients to the bread crumbs with:
3 cups diced tart apple
¼ cup finely chopped parsley
1½ teaspoons salt
¼ teaspoon paprika

HAM DRESSING FOR TURKEY

About 7 Cups

Combine:
1 to 1½ cups ground cooked ham
4 cups soft bread crumbs, 551
1 cup crushed pineapple

1 cup plumped white raisins
1 cup chopped walnuts
¼ to ½ cup honey

LIVER DRESSING

About 4 Cups

Chop:
½ lb. calf or baby beef liver
Sauté it lightly in:
1½ tablespoons butter
(1 tablespoon grated onion)
Combine these ingredients with:
2 cups soft bread crumbs, 551
¾ cup chopped nutmeats
2 beaten eggs
½ cup cream or cream and stock
1 teaspoon salt
½ teaspoon paprika
1½ tablespoons mixed minced chives and parsley
1 teaspoon chopped fresh tarragon
½ teaspoon lemon juice
(2 tablespoons dry sherry)

RICE DRESSING

About 5 Cups

Mince:
6 slices bacon
Sauté lightly 5 minutes with:
3 tablespoons chopped onion
Pour off all but 2 tablespoons of the fat. Combine the contents of the skillet with:
4 cups Boiled Rice, 206
1 cup dry bread crumbs, 551
1 cup chopped celery
¾ teaspoon salt
¼ teaspoon pepper
⅛ teaspoon sage or nutmeg
½ cup milk
½ cup cream
(¼ cup grated cheese)

WILD RICE DRESSING FOR GAME

About 3 Cups

Chop:
Giblets
Bring to the boiling point:
4 cups water, stock or tomato juice
1 teaspoon salt
Drop the giblets into the water and simmer about 15 minutes. Remove giblets from the water and bring it to a rolling boil. Stir into it:
1 cup wild rice, 212
➤ Simmer until nearly tender, about 30 minutes.
Melt in a skillet:
¼ cup butter
Sauté in it about 3 minutes:
2 tablespoons chopped shallots
1 tablespoon chopped green pepper
¼ cup chopped celery
Add the hot drained rice and the chopped giblets. You may also use one or two of the following ingredients, but remember that the quantity of dressing will be increased:
(1 cup sautéed mushrooms)
(½ cup chopped ripe or green olives)
(¼ cup tomato paste)
(½ cup chopped nuts)
(½ cup sliced water chestnuts)

RICE DRESSING FOR CORNISH HEN OR PIGEON

About 4½ Cups

Soak 10 minutes:
½ cup white raisins
in:
¼ cup cognac
Drain, reserving cognac, and sauté them in:
6 tablespoons butter
Add:
¼ cup chopped shallots
Combine with the above and toss lightly:
½ teaspoon salt
1½ cups Boiled Rice, 206
¼ cup chopped pistachio or pine nuts
Grating of fresh nutmeg
Moisten until just softened:
2 cups soft bread crumbs
in:
1½ to 2 cups milk
Add the bread crumbs to this mixture with the drained cognac.

TANGERINE OR PINEAPPLE RICE DRESSING COCKAIGNE

2 Cups

Try this for chicken or squab.
Combine:
6 chopped ribs pascal celery with leaves
¼ cup chopped parsley
1 cup dry cooked rice, lightly sautéed in chicken fat or butter
Sections and julienned strips of
1 tangerine and some of its rind, or
1 cup drained crushed pineapple
⅓ cup lightly sautéed shallots
⅓ cup lightly sautéed mushrooms
(⅓ cup pine nuts)
(2 tablespoons brandy)

APRICOT OR PRUNE DRESSING

About 5 Cups

Cut into strips:
1½ cups cooked apricots or seeded prunes
Combine with:
4 cups dry bread crumbs or 3 cups Boiled Rice, 206
¼ cup melted butter
½ teaspoon salt
⅛ teaspoon pepper
½ cup chopped green pepper or celery
Moisten lightly with:
Stock or apricot or prune water

SWEET POTATO AND SAUSAGE STUFFING

About 7 Cups

Sufficient for a 10-pound turkey.
Prepare:

4 cups Mashed Sweet Potatoes or Yams, 324

Sauté until thoroughly cooked:

½ lb. sausage meat: 1 cup

Break it up with a fork. Remove it from the pan. Add to the pan and sauté 3 minutes:

3 tablespoons chopped onion
1 cup chopped celery

Add the sausage meat, the sweet potatoes and:

2 cups dry bread crumbs, 551
(3 tablespoons chopped parsley)
Season to taste

Mix these ingredients well.

SWEET POTATO AND APPLE DRESSING

About 5 Cups

Prepare:

Sweet Potatoes and Fruit, 325

using apples and replacing the apple water with light or dark stock.

CHICKEN FARCE OR FORCEMEAT

Enough for 3 Six-Pound Chickens

A gala stuffing for boned chicken or galantines.

Grind 3 times:

About 3½ lb. raw chicken meat
3 cups mushrooms

Add to this mixture:

2 cups pistachio nuts
1⅓ cups dry sherry
¼ cup sliced truffles
1 teaspoon grated onion
8 or 9 slightly beaten eggs
1⅓ cups butter, cut in small dice
1½ tablespoons salt
¼ teaspoon freshly ground pepper
½ cup canned or Sautéed Mushrooms, 308
2 tablespoons chopped parsley

SAUERKRAUT DRESSING FOR GAME

Mix:

1 quart chopped drained sauerkraut

with:

1 clove garlic
¼ cup chopped onion
1 tart pared and chopped apple
(2 tablespoons brown sugar)
(¼ cup dried currants)
(1 cup chopped water chestnuts)
(⅛ teaspoon thyme)
Season to taste

SHELLFISH

Connoisseurs used to dispute as to which stretches of the world's seacoasts provided the best breeding grounds for shellfish and were ready to do battle over the relative merits of oysters and mussels versus lobsters and crabs. Today they worry that the too-efficient factory methods of capture, plus mounting pollution of the oceans, will increasingly deprive them of these high-protein delicacies. We must sidestep most of these controversies in the pages that follow, but hope to clarify the distinctions among lobster, 385, langouste, 385, and langoustine, 385, and between crevettes, 389, and scampi, 385—sneaking in freshwater relatives like crayfish or écrevisses, as well as the snapping turtle and the land-based snail. And we will put our chief emphasis on how to cook so as to retain a just-caught flavor. Details for handling are given in each category.

For ways to serve seafood that exploit their decorative qualities, consider colorful pink and white shrimp impaled against the purplish soft glaze of an eggplant, shown at rear in the chapter heading. Next, to the right, is a large shell heaped with iced stone crab claws; and varied dips in small shells or in glass bowls are shown nearby. Heat scallops or seafood mixtures in beautiful large scallop shells, 381, seen in the center foreground. Alternated in a snail dish on the left are two ways of serving snails: tucked into the shell or nestled in mushroom caps.

If sea treats are to be served raw, they should be properly chilled. For a great variety of delectable small shellfish that may be gathered live along the seashore and eaten on the spot, see About Sea Tidbits, 87. Keep in mind that commercial shellfish collection is permitted only in areas where waters are unpolluted. ➤ If you collect on your own, be sure the water in the area is safe.

Recipes for mussels, oysters and clams are fairly interchangeable, and exciting dishes may be created by combining mollusks and crustaceans. Seafood is often seasoned with wine. For every 6 servings, allow 2 tablespoons dry sherry, 4 tablespoons white wine or 1 tablespoon brandy. Incidentally, what looks like bits of glass in canned seafoods usually turns out to be "struvite," a harmless crystal. If in doubt, test in a little vinegar; struvite will melt; glass will not.

SHELLFISH COCKTAILS

Serve these well chilled, preferably in glasses embedded in ice. If serving individually, allow about 1/3 cup seafood per person, with about 1/4 cup sauce. You may pour the sauce over the seafood, present it separately for dipping, or toss the seafood in the sauce and serve it on lettuce, endive or cress. For appropriate sauces, see:

Russian Dressing, 364, or seafood dips and sauces, 91 and 353

Serve with these cocktails:

Oyster crackers
Cheese crackers
Matzos
Crackers: rye, rice, seaweed or soy
Garlic bread toast

ADDED COLOR AND FLAVOR IN SEAFOOD DISHES

To 3 well-crushed lobster shells and 2 pounds shrimp shells, add 1/2 bottle dry white wine. Reduce by boiling, 339, to half or one-third. A bright red sauce results which, when tepid, can be added with puréed shrimp or lobster to Hollandaise sauce. A few tablespoons of purée of pimiento may also be used to add color.

ABOUT OYSTERS

These shellfish, edible at any time, are best in flavor when they are not spawning. As southern oysters spawn all during the year, they do not have the fine flavor of northern types and are therefore often served highly condimented. These bivalves have one shallow and one deep shell, and it is in the deeper shell that they are served raw or baked. Some canny diners have been known to ask for them in restaurants on the shallow shell, in the hope of getting them absolutely freshly opened. Oysters in the shell should be alive. If they gape and do not close quickly in handling, discard them, as well as those with broken shells.

"He was a bold man," declared Dean Swift, "that first eat an oyster." In our own prejudiced opinion, once opened, this bivalve must have been found quite irresistible; only the shucking needed hardihood. ➤ To open oysters, provide yourself first with a strainer and a bowl in which to catch the juices. Later you may pour the strained liquor over the oyster before serving it on the bottom half shell—bedded down in coarse salt if served hot or on cracked ice if cold. When preparing oysters in a sauce, add the oyster liquor to it.

Now back to the actual opening of the shells. Hold a well-scrubbed oyster, deep shell down, in a folded napkin in the palm of one hand, working over a strainer with a bowl beneath it. Insert the edge of an oyster knife into the hinge of the shells. Turn the knife to pry and lift the upper shell enough to cut through the hinge muscle. Then run the knife between the shells to open.

Until you develop a knack, shucking is not easy. Should you grow slightly desperate, you may be willing to sacrifice some flavor for convenience. If so, place the oysters in a 400° oven for 5 to 7 minutes, depending on size, drop them briefly into ice water and drain. They should open easily.

However you open an oyster, complete the release of the flesh from the shell by using a knife, and examine each oyster with your fingers to be sure no bit of shell is adhering to it. If you are using the oysters off the shell, drop them into a strainer, reserving the rest of the juice. If the oysters are sandy, you may rinse them in a separate bowl, allowing ½ cup cold water to each quart of shucked oysters. Pour it over the oysters and reserve the water. Before using the oyster liquor and the water mixture in sauces, be sure to strain it through fine muslin to free it from grit. ➤ Before using oysters in any fried or creamed dish, dry them carefully in an absorbent towel.

If oysters have been bought in bulk, already opened, be sure, again, to free them of bits of shell. They should be plump and creamy in color; the liquor clear, not cloudy, and free from sour or unpleasant odor. If oysters burst during cooking, they have been previously soaked in fresh water to plump them, and their flavor as well as their texture has been ruined. ➤ Allow 1 quart undrained, shucked oysters for 6 servings. It is hard to estimate amounts for oysters on the shell, as they vary in size—6 moderate-sized eastern oysters would equal about 20 of the tiny Olympia West Coast oysters.

➤ To store oysters in the shell, refrigerate at 39°, not directly on ice. Keep dry. Store shucked oysters at the same temperature, covered by their liquor, in a closed container. The container may be set in crushed ice, up to about three-fourths its height. If you received them fresh, oysters may be stored in this way up to 3 days.

For other oyster suggestions, see Hors d'Oeuvre, 75, and Canapés, 89. For cooked oyster suggestions and oyster cakes, see Lunch Dishes, 267. Champagne is a fine accompaniment.

OYSTERS ON THE HALF SHELL

Allow 5 to 6 Oysters per Serving

➤ Please read About Oysters, 375.
Scrub well, chill and ➤ open just before serving:

Oysters

Arrange them in cracked ice on serving plates. You may place in the center a small glass of:

Cocktail Sauce, 352, or
Lorenzo Dressing, 360

or serve them with:

Lemon wedges and ground, flavored horseradish

and:

Buttered brown bread

BROILED OYSTERS

Allow 6 Oysters per Serving

➤ Please read About Oysters, 375.
Preheat broiler.
Shuck, drain and dry in a towel:

Oysters

Place them on a well-buttered baking sheet. Broil about 3 minutes, until lightly browned, turning once. Serve with:

Lemon wedges, parsley or Lemon Butter, 350

⊟ GRILLED OYSTERS

Allow 6 Oysters per Serving

You may grill western oysters—except Olympias—right on the coals without toughening them, but if you have eastern oysters, put them on a piece of foil in which you have punched holes, before placing them on your grill over a bed of coals.

I. Put on the foil:

Scrubbed, unopened oysters in their shells

Grill until the shells pop. Season and serve with:

Lemon wedges
Melted butter

II. Open:

Scrubbed oysters

Sprinkle them with a:

Gremolata, 572

Heat for a few minutes on the grill over moderate coals.

DEEP-FAT-FRIED OYSTERS

2 Servings

➤ Please read About Deep-Fat Frying, 147.
Drain:

12 large shucked oysters

Dry them well between towels. Beat together:

1 egg
2 tablespoons water

Inserting a fork in the tough muscle of the oysters, dip them in the egg, then in:

Seasoned bread crumbs

once more in the egg and again in the crumbs. Let them dry on a rack for 30 minutes. Fry them about 4 minutes in deep fat heated to 375°. Serve with:

Andalouse Sauce, 364, Tartare Sauce, 364, or Sauce Indienne, 344

SAUTÉED OYSTERS

2 Servings

Bread, as above for Deep-Fat-Fried Oysters:

12 large shucked oysters

When they are dry, sauté them until golden in a combination of:

3 tablespoons vegetable oil
2 tablespoons butter

Serve at once with:

Watercress Sauce, 365, or Aurore Sauce, 344

BAKED OYSTERS ON THE HALF SHELL

Allow 6 Oysters per Serving

Preheat oven to 475°.
Have ready:

Oysters on the half shell

Cover each with:

1 tablespoon sauce as prepared for Creamed Oysters, right

Sprinkle them with:

Bread crumbs

Bake about 10 minutes or until golden.

SCALLOPED OYSTERS

I. **6 Servings**

Preheat oven to 350°.
Have ready:

1 quart shucked oysters in their liquor

and a deep buttered casserole. Mix together:

2 cups coarsely crushed soda cracker crumbs
1 cup dry bread crumbs, 551
¾ cup melted butter

Place in the bottom of the casserole a thin layer of the crumb mixture. Cover it with half of the oysters. Pour over the oyster layer half of the following mixture:

1 cup cream

seasoned lightly with:

Nutmeg or mace
Salt and pepper
(Celery salt)

Follow with three-fourths of the remaining crumbs and the rest of the oysters. Pour the other half of the seasoned cream over the oysters and cover with the remaining bread crumbs. Bake 20 to 25 minutes.

II. **6 Servings**

Preheat broiler.
Drain and dry, reserving the liquor:

1 pint shucked small oysters: 2 cups

Combine:

1 cup dry bread or cracker crumbs
3 tablespoons melted butter
¼ teaspoon salt
1 teaspoon minced parsley

Heat to the boiling point:

1 cup cream of celery, mushroom or chicken soup
The oyster liquor or ¼ cup clam juice or water

or replace 1 tablespoon of the liquor with:

(Catsup)

Add the oysters. Heat until the edges begin to curl. Place half the buttered crumbs in a hot casserole; add the oyster and soup mixture. Top with the remaining crumbs. Place the dish under a broiler until the top is golden brown.

CREAMED OYSTERS

4 Servings

➤ Please read About Oysters, 375.
Drain and dry:

1 pint shucked oysters

Reserve the liquor. Melt in a saucepan:

2 tablespoons butter

Add and stir until blended:

2 tablespoons flour

Stir in slowly:

1 cup oyster liquor, or oyster liquor and cream, milk or chicken stock

Add:

½ teaspoon salt
⅛ teaspoon paprika or cayenne
(½ to 1 teaspoon curry powder)

When the sauce is smooth and hot, add the drained oysters. Heat them to the boiling point, but not above it. When the oysters are thoroughly heated, season with:

1 teaspoon lemon juice or ½ teaspoon Worcestershire sauce

Serve them at once in:

Bread Cases, 250, or patty shells, or on hot buttered toast

Sprinkle generously with:

Chopped parsley

OYSTERS CREAMED WITH CELERY

4 Servings

Preheat oven to 350°.
Prepare:

Creamed Oysters, above

Before adding the oysters, thicken the sauce with:

2 egg yolks

Place in a baking dish:

¾ cup peeled, diced white celery

Cover with the creamed oysters and dust with:

Parmesan cheese

Bake until golden, about 15 minutes.

BAKED CREAMED OYSTERS AND SEAFOOD

6 Servings

Do not take these proportions too literally. Change them, add or subtract to suit yourself. It's a grand basic dish with which to work.
Preheat oven to 375°.
Prepare:
Creamed Oysters, 377
seasoned with:
1 tablespoon chopped fresh marjoram
Add:
1 cup chopped cooked shrimp, lobster, crab meat, tuna, scallops or leftover fish
Cover with:
Au Gratin II or III, 552
Bake about 10 minutes.

OYSTERS IN MUSHROOMS AU GRATIN

I. **4 Servings**

Preheat oven to 375°.
Sauté:
20 large mushroom caps, 308
in:
3 tablespoons butter
Place the mushrooms, cavity side up, in a greased baking dish. Fill them with:
20 drained shucked medium-sized oysters
and cover them with:
1 cup hot White Sauce I, 341
seasoned with:
Dry sherry
Sprinkle the top with:
Grated Parmesan cheese
Place the dish in the oven until the top is browned.

II.
Or proceed as above, omitting the cream sauce and dotting each oyster in its mushroom cap with:
¼ teaspoon butter
A few drops lemon juice
Bake about 10 minutes, until the oysters are plump. Serve on:
Creamed Spinach, 327

OYSTER RAREBIT

4 Servings

Cook in their liquor until plump:
2 cups shucked oysters: 1 pint
Drain. Keep them warm and reserve the liquor. Cook in a double boiler ➤ over—not in—boiling water, and stir until smooth:
2 tablespoons butter
¼ lb. diced Swiss or Gruyère cheese
½ teaspoon salt
A few grains cayenne
Add:
The oyster liquor: about ¾ cup
and enough:
Milk to make 1 cup of liquid
and:
2 beaten egg yolks
Continue to cook and beat until the sauce thickens. Add the warm oysters and season with:
Salt
1 teaspoon Worcestershire sauce
Serve on:
Toast
Garnish with a sprinkling of:
Paprika

OYSTERS ROCKEFELLER

6 Servings

Best with oysters in the shell. The dish may also be approximated using bulk oysters in clean shells previously set aside for the purpose.

I.
Preheat oven to 475°.
Have ready:
36 medium-sized oysters on the half shell
Put through a food grinder a mixture of:
2 cups cooked spinach
¼ cup chopped onion
½ cup dry bread crumbs
2 tablespoons chopped cooked bacon
1 tablespoon parsley
1 teaspoon salt
6 drops hot pepper sauce
Stir into this mixture:
6 tablespoons melted butter
2 teaspoons anisette
Spread the mixture over the oysters. Embed the filled shells in pans of rock salt to steady them and to protect the seafood from too high heat. Bake about 10 minutes, or until plump; run under broiler to brown. Serve at once.

II. A simpler version.
Half-fill a shell with:
Creamed Spinach, 327
Place on spinach:
1 large shucked oyster
Cover with:
1 teaspoon chopped parsley
A few drops lemon juice and Worcestershire sauce
A square inch of partly cooked bacon
Bake as in I.

III. Fill half the shell, as above, with:
Creamed Spinach, 327
Place the oyster on the spinach and cover with:
1 teaspoon well-seasoned White Sauce I, 341
1 teaspoon grated Parmesan cheese
Bake as above.

OYSTERS CASINO

4 Servings

➤ Please read About Oysters, 375.
Preheat oven to 450°.
Prepare:
24 oysters on the half shell

Embed them in pans of rock salt. Cream together:

½ cup sweet butter
⅓ cup finely chopped shallots
¼ cup finely chopped parsley
¼ cup finely chopped green pepper
¼ cup finely chopped white celery
Juice of 1 lemon

Put a piece of the butter mixture on each oyster, plus:

½ teaspoon chopped pimiento
A small square partly cooked bacon

Bake until the bacon is browned, from 5 to 8 minutes.

ABOUT MUSSELS

Mussels are sometimes called "the oysters of the poor," which goes to show that poverty can be not only dignified, as some people claim, but for brief periods even endurable. These delicious mollusks do, however, deteriorate rapidly and, if uncooked, may be the cause of infections.

➤ To test mussels for freshness, try to slide the two halves of the shell across each other. If they budge, the shell is probably filled with mud, not mussel. Discard any mussels with broken shells or shells that will not close after placement in the freezer a minute or two. Mussels are distinguished by a beard which is usually clipped off with a scissors just before cooking.

Wash mussels in a colander under running water. Scrub them with a stiff brush and prepare as for clams, below: both fresh and canned mussels may be sandy. Mussels may be steamed, removed from the shell, debearded and served much like oysters or clams; or served with a sauce, shell and all. It is permissible—no doubt because it is necessary—to separate the shells by hand. Gourmets suggest that a half shell be used to spoon up the liquor to the last drop. ➤ For 4 servings allow about 1 quart undrained shucked or 3 quarts unshucked mussels. **Cockles,** 87, and **periwinkles** may also be cooked as for mussels.

STEAMED MUSSELS OR MOULES MARINIÈRE

3 to 4 Servings

➤ Please read About Mussels, above.

Sauté until golden in:

¼ cup butter
6 chopped shallots
1 clove garlic

Cook in a deep, heavy skillet about 2 minutes:

¼ cup dry white wine
⅓ bay leaf

Add the sautéed shallots and:

3 quarts scrubbed, bearded unshucked mussels

Cook ➤ closely covered over high heat 6 to 8 minutes. Agitate the pan sufficiently during this time to cook the mussels evenly, but ➤ remove from heat the moment the shells open. Pour the mussels, shells and all, into heated bowls. Then pour in the sauce, as is or thickened with:

(2 tablespoons fresh bread crumbs or Rémoulade Sauce, 364)

Serve garnished with:

¼ cup chopped parsley

BAKED BUTTERED MUSSELS

Preheat oven to 450°.

Place in a large pan:

Well-cleaned mussels
2 tablespoons olive oil

Heat in the oven until the shells open. Do not overcook. Remove the upper shell and beard or fringe. Reserve the liquor. If any has escaped to the pan, strain and add it to the reserved liquor from the shell. Serve the mussels on the lower shell with:

Melted butter or melted Garlic Butter, 351

and the liquor in small cups or glasses. See Steamed Clams, 381.

ABOUT CLAMS

All clams are sandy, especially surf clams. Before shucking, they should be scrubbed and washed in several waters, then soaked in a cold brine of ⅓ cup salt to 1 gallon of water; and it may even be necessary later to put the cooked clams under cold running water to rid them completely of sand. Clams are sold in the shell or shucked. If in the shell ➤ test to see that they are tightly closed or, if slightly open, that they close tightly at once upon being touched. ➤ Discard any that float or have broken shells.

➤ Eight quarts of clams in the shell will yield about 1 quart shucked. ➤ Allow about 1 quart of unshucked clams per person for steamed clams, 6 to 8 medium-sized clams if served shucked.

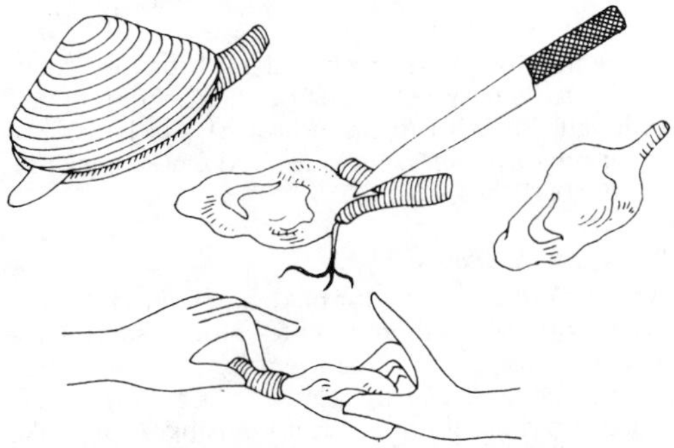

SOFT-SHELL OR LONGNECK CLAMS

Found mostly north of Cape Cod, these are the preferred East Coast type for eating raw or steamed whole. They are easily opened by running a short sharp knife along the edge of the top shell. Work over a bowl, as for oysters, illustrated on 376, so as to trap the juices. Cut the meat from the bottom shell. Slit the skin of the neck, or siphon, as sketched, and pull off the neck skin. This skin is too tough to eat as it is, but may be chopped or ground and used in chowders or creamed dishes with other clam meat.

HARD-SHELL CLAMS

These include **butter clams** and **quahogs,** which in turn are called **cherrystones** or **littlenecks.** The **Pacific butter clam** is distinguished from its Atlantic counterpart by its small size—even when adult—and its rarity, but makes up for both in succulence. Two other choice West Coast varieties are the aptly named **razor clam** and the **Pismo.**

The large, strongly flavored hard-shells are preferred for chowders, the smaller sizes for eating on the half shell. If in the shell, you may wash them in several waters, then cover with a cold brine of 1/3 cup salt for each gallon of water and sprinkle on the top 1/4 cup cornmeal to every quart clams. Leave them in this bath 3 to—preferably—12 hours. This whitens them, rids them of sand, and causes them to eject the black material in their stomachs. After soaking, wash again in clear water.

Quahogs are difficult to open, but if they are covered 5 minutes with water and then gently picked up, you may be able to insert a knife quickly in the opening. Or, if you are using them in a cooked dish and do not mind a small loss in flavor, you may place them in a pan in a moderate oven until they open. After opening, cut through the muscle holding the shells together. If they have not had a cornmeal bath, open the stomachs with sharp shears and scrape out and discard the contents. Large hard-shelled clams have a tough upper portion which may be separated from the tender portion, chopped or ground and used in various dishes, creamed, scalloped, in fritters, chowders, etc., following any of the recipes for oysters, or any of the following clam recipes.

SURF CLAMS

These may be used in chowders, broth or cocktails, but their sweetness should be counteracted with salt. They are the sandiest of all clams.

For other recipes, see Soups and Chowders, 186, or Lunch Dishes, 267.

ABOUT CLAMBAKES

Whatever the size of your bake, dig your clams the day before. Scrub them well to remove sand. Give them the cornmeal treatment as for hard-shell clams, above. Leave the clams in a ➤ cool place. Rinse and drain them just before using. A big bake is described in I; a smaller one, often more practical, in II, with amounts proportionately cut.

⊟ CLAMBAKE

I. **20 Servings**

Allow:

200 soft-shell clams
(50 hard-shell clams)

Start preparations at least 4 hours before you plan to serve. Dig a sand pit about 1 foot deep and 3½ feet across. Line it with smooth round rocks. Have ready a wet tarpaulin larger than the pit area by 1 foot all around, and a few stones to weight the edges. Build a fire over the rock lining using hardwood, and keep feeding it for the next 2½ to 3 hours while the rocks are heating. Gather and wash about 4 bushels of wet rock seaweed. In fact, it is wise to soak the seaweed for at least 45 minutes before use. Have a pail of sea water at hand. Partially husk about:

4 dozen ears sweet corn

Do not pull them quite clean but leave on the last layer or two of husks. Rip these back far enough to remove the silk. Then replace them, so the kernels are fully protected. Reserve the pulled husks. Quarter:

5 broiling chickens

Have ready:

10 sweet potatoes
(20 frankfurters)

You may wrap the chicken pieces in cheesecloth or divide the food into 20 individual cheesecloth-wrapped servings, so that each person's food can later be removed as one unit. Scrub:

Twenty 1½-lb. lobsters or 5 pecks soft-shell crabs

Now you are ready to arrange for the "bake." Rake the embers free of the hot stones, remove them from the pit and line it with the wet seaweed. The lining should be about 6 inches deep. Put over it, if you wish, a piece of chicken wire. If you haven't wrapped the individual servings in cheesecloth, now pack the pit in layers. For added flavor, put down first a layer of hard-shell clams, then the frankfurters, if you use them, and after that, in succession, the sweet potatoes, the lobsters or crabs, the chicken, the corn and the soft-shell clams. You may also put seaweed between the layers. Cover the layered food with the reserved corn husks and sprinkle the whole with the bucket of sea water. Quickly cover with the wet tarp. ➤ Weight the tarp down well with rocks. The whole should steam ➤ covered, about 1 hour. During the steaming, the tarp will puff up, which is a sign of a satisfactory "bake." To test, lift the tarp carefully at one corner ➤ so as not to get sand into the pit, and see if the clams have opened. If so, the whole feast should be cooked just to the right point. Have handy plenty of towels and:

Melted butter

Serve with the bake:

Beer or ale

and afterward:

Watermelon
Coffee

II. **8 Servings**

A more domesticated bake in a new wash boiler or lard can on a stove or outdoor grill.

Soak for 45 minutes and remove sand from seaweed in several rinsings. Line the bottom of the boiler with a 4-inch layer of the seaweed. Add about:

1 quart water

When water boils, add:

8 foil-wrapped potatoes

2 cut-up broiler chickens wrapped in cheesecloth

➤ Cover boiler and cook gently 30 minutes. Add:

8 well-scrubbed 1½-lb. lobsters

Cover and cook 8 minutes more, then place on top of the lobsters:

8 shucked foil-wrapped ears of corn

Cook 10 minutes, still covered, and add:

48 well-scrubbed soft-shell clams

Cover and steam until the clams open, from 5 to 10 minutes longer. In serving, use:

Melted butter

STEAMED SOFT-SHELL CLAMS WITH BROTH

Allow 7 to 9 Medium-Sized Unshucked Clams per Serving

Scrub thoroughly with a brush and wash in several waters:

Soft-shell clams

Place them close together in the top of a steamer, as sketched 278, or on a rack in a stock pot with a spigot, as shown on 521. Place in the bottom of the steamer or stock pot:

½ inch water

Cover the kettle closely. Steam the clams over moderate heat until they open, but no longer—5 to 10 minutes. Overcooking makes clams tough. Place them in individual soup bowls. Serve each bowl garnished with:

Lemon wedges

and accompanied by a small dish of:

Melted butter

The broth is served in cups along with the clams or used for clam juice cocktail later. ➤ To eat clams, pick them up from the shell by the neck with the fingers, dip into broth to remove possible sand, then into butter. All of the clam except the neck sheath is edible. The broth is delicious to drink, but, to avoid any residue of sand, don't entirely drain the cup. To prepare clam broth separately, see 186.

BAKED SOFT-SHELL CLAMS

4 Servings

Preheat oven to 425°.

Scrub with a brush and wash in several waters:

36 soft-shell clams

To keep them steady, place them in a pan on a bed of rock salt or crumpled foil. Bake about 15 minutes until the shells open. Remove the top shell carefully to avoid spilling the juices. Serve on individual plates with:

A Seasoned Butter, 349, or

Sour Cream Horseradish Sauce, 356

and garnish with:

Lemon wedges

CLAMS BROILED ON THE HALF SHELL

Allow 6 to 8 Medium-Sized Clams per Person

Preheat broiler.

Place on an ovenproof dish in which foil has been crumpled to keep shells steady:

Cherrystone clams on the half shell

Cover each clam with:

A dash of Worcestershire sauce

A square of bacon

Broil the clams until the bacon is done.

FRIED CLAMS

Allow 6 to 8 Medium-Sized Clams per Person

➤ Please read About Clams, 379.

Shuck and wash well in a colander under running water:

Soft-shell clams

Dry them between towels. Cut away the black skin of the neck or siphon. Dip the clams in a:

Bound Breading, 552

Sauté until golden in a combination of:

3 parts vegetable oil

2 parts butter

Serve with:

Tartare Sauce, 364, Curry Sauce, 345, or Hot Mustard Sauce, 345

ABOUT SCALLOPS

These beautiful mollusks known on menus as Coquilles St. Jacques are emblematic of the pilgrims who visited the shrine of St. James of Compostella. They ate the mollusks as penance—surely not a rigorous one—and afterward fastened the cockle shells to their hats. Scallops are also responsible for the cooking term "scalloped," which originally meant seafood creamed, heated and served in a shell. Scallops available at market are almost never the whole mollusk but are instead the edible sections of its adductor muscle, which controls its very spectacular movement.

If you do get scallops in the shell, wash and scrub them thoroughly. Place in a 300° oven, deep shell down, until they open. Remove, trim and wash the hinge muscle. In Europe, both the handsome beanlike coral and the beard are used, as well as the meat. The former is treated as for any roe; the latter is cut up, sautéed briefly, and then simmered ➤ covered, in white wine 30 minutes. Many people prefer the small, tender, creamy pink or tan **bay scallops,** shown right, 382, to the larger, firmer, whiter, but also quite delicious **sea scallops,** shown on the left. If only the large ones are available, slice them—after cooking—into 3 parts, against the grain, for use in salads and creamed dishes or sauces.

➤ To test scallops for freshness, see that they have a sweetish odor. If in bulk, they should be free of liquid. For sautéing or broiling, allow about ⅓ pound of sea scallops or ¼ pound of bay scallops per serving. Cooked scallops may be used in any recipe for fish salads or creamed fish, or they may be skewered and grilled, see right. The blandness of scallops suggests combining them in sauced dishes with more robustly flavored shellfish like shrimp and crab. See also seafood suggestions in Lunch Dishes, 264.

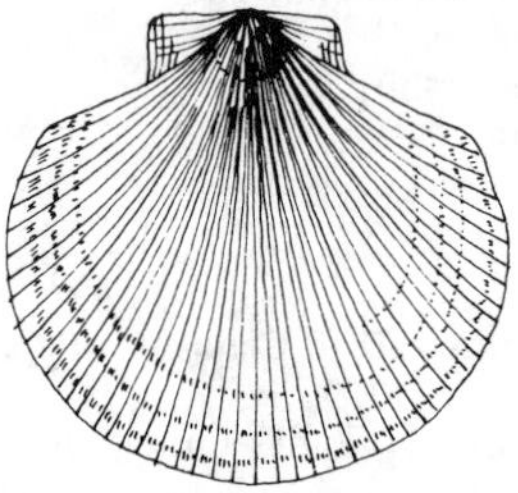

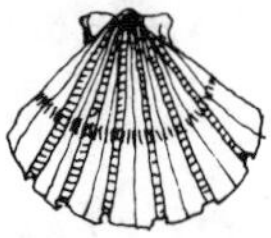

POACHED SCALLOPS

6 to 8 Servings

Poach, 3 to 5 minutes:
4 cups bay or sea scallops
in a mixture of enough:
Water and white wine or light stock
to cover, adding to the liquid:
A bay leaf
3 sprigs parsley
After poaching, remove herbs, drain the liquid and reduce it to serve, further seasoned to taste, as a **sauce.**

SCALLOPS MEUNIÈRE

4 Servings

Dry between towels:
1 lb. shucked, drained bay or sea scallops
Dip them in a:
Bound Breading, 552
Let them dry on a rack about 15 minutes. Sauté one layer deep, using a large heavy skillet, in:
2 tablespoons butter
2 tablespoons vegetable oil
➤ agitating frequently; about 5 minutes for bay scallops, 8 minutes for sea scallops. Just before cooking time is over, sprinkle with:
Lemon juice
Finely chopped parsley
Serve with:
Tomatoes Provençale, 332

BAY SCALLOPS FONDU BOURGUIGNONNE

4 Servings

➤ Please read about Boeuf Fondu Bourguignonne, 457, using instead of beef:
1 lb. poached bay scallops, above
Serve as sauces:
Sweet-Sour Orange Sauce, 355, replacing game stock with clam broth; or Aurore Sauce, 344; or Quick Creole Sauce, 352

⊟ SCALLOP KEBABS

Allow ¼ Pound Bay or ⅓ Pound Sea Scallops per Person

Preheat broiler or grill.
If shucked scallops are large or old, drop into boiling water and allow them to stay immersed, but removed from heat, 1 minute. Drain and dry. If tender, simply brush:
Shucked scallops
with:
Vegetable oil
Dip in:
Fine bread crumbs
Skewer alternately with:
1-inch squares of bacon
Grill over moderate heat 10 minutes or until golden brown, or broil 4 inches from the source of heat, turning several times during the cooking period. Serve with:
Sauce Dijonnaise, 342, or Curry Sauce, 345
and garnish with:
Lemon wedges
Fried Parsley, 314

DEEP-FAT-FRIED SCALLOPS

6 to 8 Servings

Wash and pick over:
1 quart shucked scallops: about 2 lb.
Drain. Dry between towels. Season with:
White pepper
Celery salt
Dip them in a:
Bound Breading, 552
Fry 2 minutes in deep fat heated to 385°. Drain on paper toweling. Serve with:
Tartare Sauce, 364, Mousseline Sauce, 359, or a tomato sauce, 351

SCALLOPS IN WINE

6 to 8 Servings

Wash well:
2 lb. shucked scallops
➤ Simmer them until tender, about 5 minutes, in:
2 cups dry white wine
Drain and reserve the liquid. Melt:
¼ cup butter
Sauté:
4 finely chopped shallots
24 finely sliced mushroom caps
2 tablespoons minced parsley
Stir in, until blended:
2 tablespoons flour
Add the reserved liquid and:
2 to 4 tablespoons whipping cream
Add the scallops to the hot ➤ but not boiling sauce. Place in a shallow casserole. Cover with:
Au Gratin II, 552
and run under a broiler until golden brown. For an unusual variation which stretches this recipe to 10 or more servings, add:
2 cups minced cooked ham
to the above mixture.

SCALLOPED SCALLOPS OR SCALLOPS MORNAY

6 Servings

Scallops served in the shell are called **St. Jacques,** even when—as might happen in the recipe below—you substitute Creole Sauce, 348, for Mornay. Preheat broiler.

Prepare:

Mornay Sauce, 342

Poach:

3 cups shucked scallops

in:

1½ cups dry white wine or Light Stock, 522, or Fumet, 524

Drain and slice the scallops. Coat each of the deep halves of 12 scallop shells with 1 tablespoon of the Mornay Sauce. You may edge the shell, using a pastry tube or bag, with a decorative rim of:

(Duchess Potatoes, 323)

Almost fill the shell with the sliced scallops. Coat each shell, staying within the rim of the potatoes, with:

Mornay Sauce

Dust the sauce coating with:

Grated Parmesan or Gruyère cheese

Run under a broiler until the sauce is lightly browned. Serve at once.

ABOUT ABALONE

The foot of this delicious shellfish—contraband if shipped from California—comes to our markets canned or frozen from Mexico and Japan, shelled, pounded and ready to cook. If you get it in the shell, remove the edible portion by running a knife between the shell and the meat. Trim off the dark portion. Abalone, like inkfish, needs prodigious pounding to tenderize it, if it has died in a state of tension. Leave it whole or cut it in ¼-inch strips for pounding with an even, not too hard, motion. The meat is ready to cook when it looks like Dali's limp watch. ➤ For steaks, slice against the grain. Bread it if you like in dry crumbs or in a Bound Breading, 552, and sauté. Or you may "boil," 400, as for any fish. Beat and chop abalone for chowder or for Fritters, 243. Allow 1 pound for 2 to 3 servings.

SAUTÉED ABALONE

2 to 3 Servings

Cut into ⅜-inch-thick steaks across the grain and pound:

1 lb. abalone

Dip in a:

Bound Breading, 552

Melt in a heavy skillet:

2 tablespoons vegetable oil or clarified butter

When the fat reaches the point of fragrance, sauté the abalone steaks, allowing 1½ to 2 minutes to each side.

ABOUT CRABS

Recipes for cooking crab meat apply to almost all species of edible crab, but either the type of crab or the part of the crab from which the meat is taken may make a difference in color, taste and texture. ➤ Crabs must be both alive and lively when cooked. If mucky or slimy, they should be scrubbed. ➤ Freshly cooked crab meat in partially aerated cans must be under constant refrigeration until used. It should have no ammonialike odor. The completely sealed canned crab meats, Japanese and Korean, are all nonperishable until the cans are opened. ➤ For crab dishes made with cooked or canned crab, see 267. In using canned meat, be sure to pick it over for small bits of shell and bone.

To prepare crab shells for restuffing, select large, perfect shells and scrub them well with a brush until clean. Place them in a large kettle and cover with hot water. Add one teaspoon baking soda. Cover the kettle closely. Bring to a boil and simmer 20 minutes. Drain, wash and dry. The shells are now ready for refilling.

BLUE CRABS

These denizens of the Atlantic furnish most of the fresh crab meat in the market. Lump or back-fin meat, taken from the body, is white in color and choice for looks. Flake meat, while less shapely, is also white. Claw meat is brownish, but very choice.

If taken live, blue crabs fall into two classifications: hard-shell and soft-shell, which are prepared and eaten quite differently.

I. Hard-shell crabs designate those caught between their periodic sheddings of carapace, or "lid," when the carapace has hardened. To cook and eat them, see Poached Hard-Shell Crabs, 384. To prepare them for crab meat, first place them upside down in a large bowl and cover with very hot water until no air bubbles rise. Remove large claws at body. Turn the crab on its back and lift the pointed apron at the base away from the body. Shown right, 384, is a female with a wider fringed apron than the male on the left. With a firm hold at the wide end, slowly twist and pull so as to remove the apron and the intestinal vein simultaneously. Discard both. Scrub the crab under cold running water, using a vegetable brush. Grasping the legs in your fist, pull the entire chest section free of the hard carapace. Cut out and discard the feathery lung sections which lie as shown on the soft-shell crab, top. Next to the lungs lies the soft tomalley or liver. Remove the liver from the carapace with a small spoon and put it into a sieve to drain as for oysters, 376, reserving the strained liquid and the tomalley for later use as directed in crab recipes.

With a wooden mallet, lightly crack the crab shells, being careful not to pound any shell bits into the meat. Remove easily accessible meat with a curve-bladed knife, 282. Take each removed leg at the ends and bend it to break at the joint, while pulling the cartilage from the upper leg meat. Cut the lower section of the legs into small pieces and reserve them for a shellfish butter, 351.

II. Soft-shell crabs are those freshly molted whose carapace is still tender and flexible. Molting, incidentally, occurs often in a crab's career, but the carapace remains pliable only a few days. Since almost every part of a soft-shell crab is edible, it is usually broiled, breaded and sautéed, or deep-fat-fried, as in the specific recipes below.

➤ To prepare soft-shell crabs for cooking, wash them in several waters. Place live crab face-down on a board. Make an incision just back of the eyes and cut out the face. Lift the tapering points on each side of the back shell to remove sandbag and spongy gills, as shown in sketch. Turn crab on its back and with a pointed knife remove the small pointed apron at the lower part of the shell, pulling it, as described above in Hard-Shell Crabs, to release the intestinal vein.

DUNGENESS AND ROCK CRABS

Both packaged in one grade, combining body and claw meat. The rock crab flesh is brownish. Dungeness is native to the West Coast and is best in 2½- to 3-pound size.

KING CRABS

Mostly from Alaskan waters, pinkish in tone, and consisting mainly of leg meat. Slit the underside of the leg shell with a cross-shaped cut before broiling.

STONE CRABS

From Florida, with pale flesh, and very delicate in texture and flavor. Stone crabs have become so rare that the authorities now insist that when one is caught only one claw may be removed, and the crab must be returned to its habitat, where, hopefully, it will see fit to grow another claw—as crabs are quite capable of doing.

OYSTER CRABS AND HERMIT CRABS

There are two edible types of miniature crabs. Oyster crabs are crispy ½-inch pinkish "boarders" found living right in the shell with live oysters; they may be eaten raw, sautéed or deep-fat-fried. When deep-fat-fried, several dozen may be served with several dozen fried whitebait, 415, as one portion. Tiny hermit crabs are found in vacated univalve shells and respond to deep-fat frying and sautéing. They should not be eaten raw.

To deep-fat-fry either of these crabs or whitebait, keep them on ice until the last minute. Wash and dry carefully and put into a bag to dust with flour, 552, then in a sieve to bounce off as much flour as possible. Place a few at a time in a frying basket in deep fat heated to 390° and cook only 2 to 3 seconds until crisp.

DEEP-FAT-FRIED SOFT-SHELL CRABS

Allow 2 to 3 per Serving

➤ Please read About Deep-Fat Frying, 147.
Dry between towels:
Cleaned soft-shell crabs
Dip them in a :
Bound Breading, 552
Fry 3 to 5 minutes or until golden brown in deep fat heated to 375°. Turn once while frying. Drain on paper toweling. Sprinkle well with:
Salt and pepper
Serve at once with:
Tartare Sauce, 364, or Rémoulade Sauce, 364, with parsley

BROILED SOFT-SHELL CRABS

Allow 2 or 3 per Serving

Preheat broiler.
Prepare for cooking:
Soft-shell crabs
Combine:
¼ cup butter
2 tablespoons lemon juice
A few grains cayenne
A small grating of white pepper
Roll the crabs in the butter mixture, then lightly in:
Flour
Place them on the broiling rack 2 inches from the heat. Broil about 10 minutes. Turn once.

SAUTÉED SOFT-SHELL CRABS

Allow 2 to 3 per Serving

To prepare the crabs for cooking, follow the above recipe for:
Broiled Soft-Shell Crabs
Sauté in butter or vegetable oil over moderate heat. Place on a platter. Serve with:
Fried Parsley, 314

POACHED OR "BOILED" HARD-SHELL CRABS

Have ready a large pot of:
Boiling salted water

Allow for each quart of water:

1 tablespoon salt

Handling with a tongs, slide, one at a time, into the water so as not to disturb the boiling:

Washed hard-shell crabs

➤ Reduce heat at once to a simmer and cook about 25 minutes more.

To eat hard-shell crabs, open the tail flap on the bellyside and pull it against the carapace, removing both. Sometimes a sharp knife will be necessary to complete this job. Take out and discard the spongy substance under the shell and split the bodies to pick out the meat, discarding the gills, intestines and sandbags. Claw meat can be released with a nutcracker. ➤ From a 5-ounce hard-shell crab you can expect about 1½ ounces of meat. The preparation recommended above is basic. Relax and serve the crabs whole, with a side dish of melted butter and lemon juice. Or choose one of the many recipes using cooked crab meat in Lunch Dishes, 267, and Salads, 106, or indexed under Seafood.

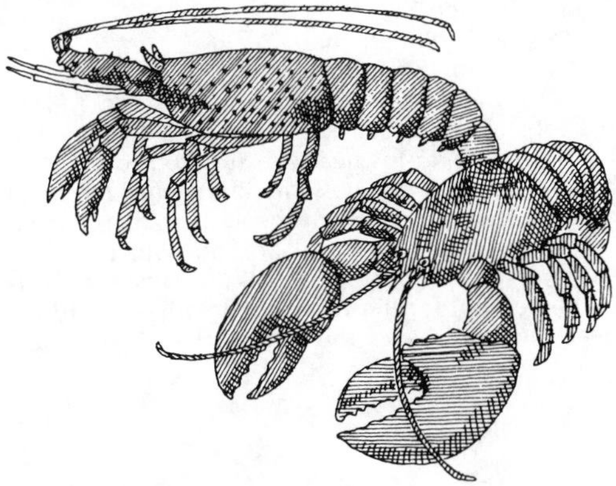

ABOUT LOBSTERS

The **American** or **Northern lobster,** with its great delicious claw meat, is sketched above. It is caught from Maine to the Carolinas. Very similar, but somewhat smaller, is the **European lobster,** which is also found not infrequently along our own more southerly American coasts.

Called crayfish in Australia and New Zealand, this **spiny rock lobster,** or **langouste,** is shipped from Florida, California, Australia, South Africa and the Mediterranean. It has extra-long antennae but no claws; and most of the meat is in the heavy tail, as you can also see above.

The Americans and Europeans, when caught, are a mottled dark blue-green, most delicious we think, served hot. The spinys, which usually reach us frozen, may be tough, especially if they weigh over 10 ounces. They vary in color from tan through reddish orange to maroon, with lighter spotting and variable spininess. If fresh they are often preferred in cold dishes.

Still a third kind of lobster, more rarely encountered on this side of the Atlantic because exclusively native to European waters, is the **Norwegian,** a relative of the spinys, known in France as **langoustine,** and famous in Italy as **scampo.**

Of whatever kind, lobsters require about the same cooking time and may be cut and cleaned as shown on 386. But as lobster ritual is more complicated in the American type, we will discuss it in further detail below.

Among connoisseurs the female lobster is considered finer in flavor. Look for the soft, leathery, finlike appendages on the underside, just where the body and tail meet. In the male, these appendages are bony. In opening the female lobster, you may find a delicious roe or **coral** that reddens in cooking. Use it as a garnish or to color a sauce. The flesh of the male stays firmer when boiled. The greenish substance in both of them is the liver or **tomalley.**

➤ Allow ½ large lobster or 1 small lobster per serving. Buy active live lobsters weighing from 1¼ to 2½ pounds. Lobsters weighing 3 pounds and over are apt to be coarse and tough. A 2½-pound lobster will yield about 2 cups of cooked meat.

➤ To store live lobsters until ready to use, place them in the refrigerator, but not directly on ice. The claws should be plugged with a small piece of wood and held together with rubber bands. Before cooking, test to make sure your lobsters are active and that the tail snaps back if it is stretched out flat when you pick up the lobster. Make sure, too, that your crustacean is clean. Grasp it firmly at the back and rinse claws, body and back under a faucet.

POACHED OR "BOILED" LOBSTER

I. To poach lobster for hot family-type table service, place in a large heavy cook-pot enough:

Water

so the lobster will be completely covered when you plunge it in. Allow for each quart of water:

1 tablespoon salt

Bring water to a rolling boil. Because of splashing, carefully immerse head first:

Lobster

and allow the water to return to a boil. ➤ Reduce the heat at once and simmer the lobster about 5 minutes for the first pound and about 3 minutes for each additional pound, slightly less time if the lobsters have recently shed and the shells are soft. Drain. Serve with small bowls filled with a mixture of:

The juices from the pot or melted butter
Lemon wedges

And provide each person with a finger bowl, a bib and an abundance of napkins. The uninitiated are sometimes balked by the intractable appearance of a lobster at table. They may take comfort from the little cannibal who, threading his way through the jungle one day at his mother's side, saw a strange object flying overhead. "Ma, what's that?" he quavered. "Don't worry, sonny," said Ma. "It's an airplane. Airplanes are pretty much like lobsters. There's an awful lot you have to throw away, but the insides are delicious."

When a whole lobster is served, it lies on the plate with head and tail intact, arched shell up. The claws, detached before serving, rest cracked beside it, drained of excess moisture. Shielded by your lobster bib, you are ready to take the offensive. Pick up the lobster in your fingers, turn it soft side up and arch it until the tailpiece separates from the body, as shown in the upper part of the drawing below. Remove the tail flippers by bending them back until they too crack off.

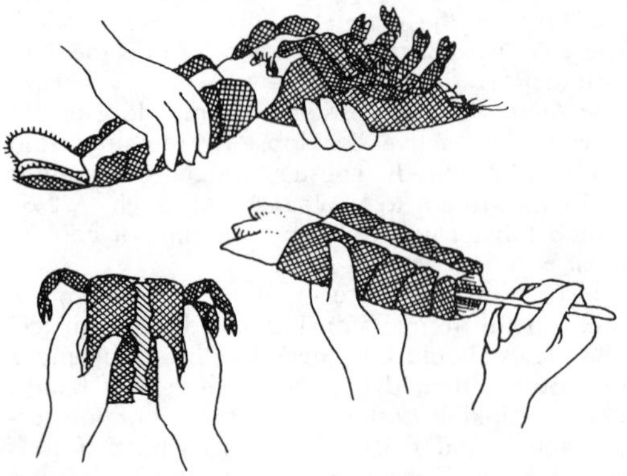

Now lift the tailpiece downside up, insert the lobster fork at the point where the flippers broke off, and push the meat out through the open end, as shown at the right.

Having freed the tail meat, grasp the chest portion in both hands to release the contents as shown to the left. Edible are the small quantity of meat, the greenish tomalley or liver, and the coral or roe, if there is any. Before turning your attention to the finger bowl, break off the legs one at a time, insert the broken end in your mouth and suck out the contents—quietly.

II. To cook lobster for salads, hors d'oeuvre or sauced dishes, prepare as for I, using:

A 2½- to 3-lb. lobster

Larger ones are apt to be tough. After the cooking period, drain and plunge into cold water to arrest further cooking. When cool, ➤ to remove the meat from the shell, place the lobster on its back. With sharp scissors cut a lengthwise gash in the soft underside as sketched on 388. Draw out the tail meat in one piece. Remove and discard the lady, or sandbag, and the intestinal vein, as well as the spongy lungs, which, while harmless, are tough. Add the red coral, if any, and the green liver, or tomalley, to the lobster meat or reserve it for use in sauces.

If you buy preboiled lobster in the shell, see that the color is bright red and that it has a fresh seashore aroma. ➤ Most important of all—as with the uncooked lobster—the tail, when pulled, should roll back into place under the body. This means the lobster was alive, as it should have been, when cooked.

To remove lobster meat from the large claws, crack them with a nutcracker or a mallet. If you want them in a single piece for garnish, break off the claw at the first joint. Place it on a flat surface, the lighter underside up. Using a mallet, hit the shell at the inner hump. This will crack it so that the meat in the entire larger pincer claw is released. Crack off the small pincer shell, and its meat will slide out. For attractive service, you may want to keep the lobster shell to refill with the seasoned sauced meat or use it to make Lobster Butter, 351.

For recipes which make use of lobster meat already cooked, see Lunch Dishes, 264, and the Index.

⊟ BROILED LOBSTER

1 Serving

Preheat broiler.
Prepare for broiling:

A 1¼-lb. live lobster

severing the vein at the base of the neck. Place the lobster on his back. Hold him with your left hand firmly over his head. Be sure to protect your hand with a towel. Draw the knife from the head down through the base of the abdomen, as shown below, so the lobster will lie flat, with the meat evenly exposed to the heat. All the lobster meat is edible, except for the stomach, or lady—a hard sac near the head—and the intestinal vein that runs

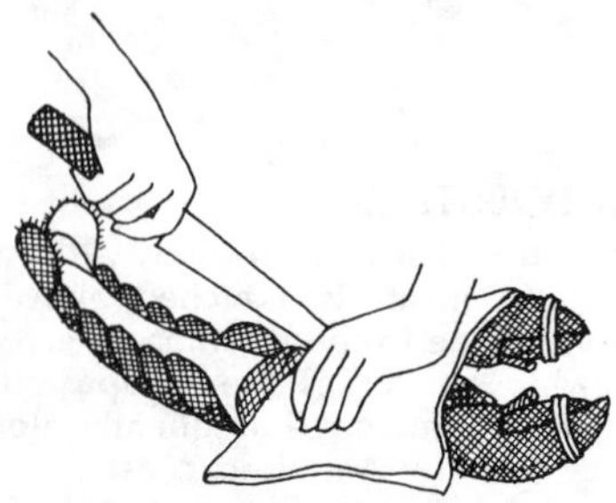

through the middle of the underside of the tail meat. Remove and discard these inedible parts. The spongy substance to either side of the body—the lungs—is harmless. It may or may not be removed when the lobster is cooked in the half shell. Beyond a doubt edible are the delicious black roe, which turns into the so-called red coral in cooking, and the greenish-brown liver or tomalley. You may prepare a stuffing by removing and mixing together:

The coral
The tomalley
1 tablespoon toasted bread crumbs
1 teaspoon lemon juice or dry sherry

Replace in the cavity and brush it and the exposed lobster meat with:

Melted butter

➤ If broiling stuffed, place shell side down on the oven grill and broil about 16 minutes. If broiling unstuffed or grilling over charcoal, place shell side toward heat 7 to 8 minutes; then turn and broil, flesh side to heat, about 8 minutes more. In either case, serve with:

Lemon wedges and melted butter

➤ To eat broiled lobster served to you on the half shell, begin with the tail meat first, using the sharp-pronged small lobster or oyster fork, see sketches below. You may twist off bite-sized pieces with the fork. This needs some skill, and when dining out, we often wish for a good European fish knife. Dip the pieces in the sauce. You

may also squeeze lemon juice from the garnish wedges over the lobster meat. Twist off a large claw with the fingers and, if necessary, also use the cracker which should always be provided. Crack the claw, as shown, to release the delicate rich meat. You may then pull off the small side

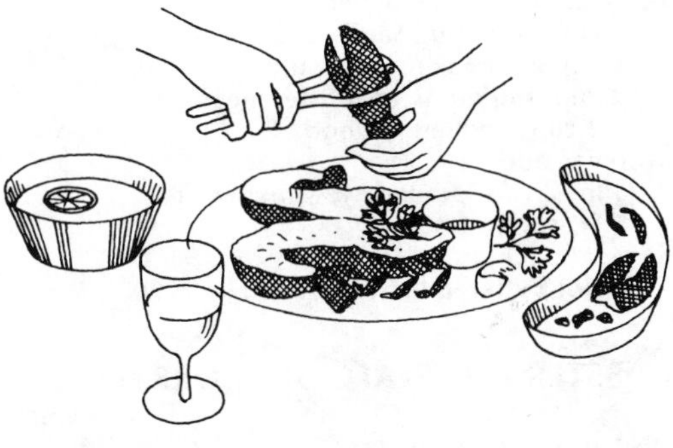

claws, one by one, with the fingers, and suck out the meat. As you empty the shells, place them on the bone tray or extra plate, and make use of the finger bowl when needed. Continue to eat the contents of the shell: it is good to the last shred. Some people even suck the knuckle after releasing it from the gray gristle.

LOBSTER AMERICAINE OR ARMORICAINE

2 Servings

Who really cares how it's spelled? This method of cooking lobster is good enough to credit regional inventiveness on both sides of the Atlantic. Have ready:

½ cup Fish Stock or Fumet, 524

Place on a flat pan, so as to be able to reserve any juice that results from cutting:

2 live 1½-lb. hen lobsters

With a sharp knife, sever the vein at the base of the neck. Cut off the claws. Divide the body at the tail and cut the tail into 3 or 4 pieces at the segmentations. Divide the shell in half, lengthwise. Remove and discard the sac. Reserve the coral, if any, and the tomalley for the sauce. Have ready two heavy skillets. In one, sauté:

3 tablespoons butter
1 cup Mirepoix, 572
½ cup chopped shallots

Heat in the other, to the point of fragrance:

½ cup olive oil
1 clove garlic

Sauté in the oil about 4 minutes ➤ still in the shell, the cut-up lobster. Keep the pan moving. When the lobster shell is red and the flesh firm, add it to the mirepoix in the first skillet. Flambé, 155, the lobster mixture in:

1 oz. brandy

Place in the second skillet and simmer about 5 minutes:

½ cup tomato purée
1 cup white wine
3 skinned, seeded, chopped tomatoes

In winter use the small Italian-type canned tomatoes. Add the sautéed lobster pieces still in the shell, the fumet and:

1 teaspoon chopped fresh tarragon
The juice or "blood" of the lobster
The coral and tomalley

to the tomato mixture. Simmer about 15 minutes.

Season to taste

Thicken the sauce slightly with:

(Beurre Manié, 340)

Serve the lobster with the hot sauce poured over it, garnished with:

Chopped parsley

⊟ GRILLED LOBSTER TAILS

4 Servings

Marinate several hours:

4 spiny lobster tails

in a mixture of:

¼ cup lemon or lime juice
¼ cup vegetable oil
1 teaspoon each salt and paprika
¼ cup minced shallots

Preheat broiler or grill.

Remove with scissors the soft under-cover of the lobster tails, as sketched, 388. Slightly crack the hard upper shell with a cleaver so that the tails will lie flat, and grease the meat lightly. Broil about 4 inches from coals or heating source about

5 minutes to a side, basting well with the marinade. These make an attractive plate served with:

Asparagus spears

placed to either side and:

Meunière or Lemon Butter, 350, or
Béarnaise Sauce, 359

BAKED STUFFED LOBSTER

2 Servings

Split in half, as for Broiled Lobster, 386:

A freshly Boiled Lobster, 385:
about 2½ lb.

Remove the meat. Chop it. Melt:

¾ tablespoon butter

Stir in until blended:

¾ tablespoon flour

Stir in slowly:

½ cup Chicken or Fish Stock, 523, 524

Season the sauce with:

1¼ teaspoons dry mustard
1 teaspoon chopped onion
Salt
Paprika

Melt in a separate saucepan:

2 tablespoons butter

Sauté the lobster meat in the butter only until it is heated through. Add the boiling sauce. Simmer these ingredients about 2 minutes. Remove from the heat.
Preheat broiler.
Beat, then stir into the above:

1 tablespoon cream
2 egg yolks

Add:

(½ cup chopped Sautéed Mushrooms, 308)

Fill the lobster shells with the mixture. Cover them with:

Au Gratin I or II, 552

Broil the lobster until the crumbs are brown. Season it, as it is removed from the oven, by pouring over it:

(2 tablespoons sherry)

LOBSTER THERMIDOR

2 Servings

Prepare:

2 Poached Lobsters, 385, about 1 or
1½ lb. each

Remove and crack claws; extract meat. Remove entire tail portion, body meat, tomalley and coral, if present, keeping tail shell intact, and discarding lower membrane: see illustration for Spiny Lobster, 386. Cut tail and claw meat into ½-inch chunks. Have ready:

Mornay Sauce, 342

omitting cheese, and adding:

1 teaspoon prepared mustard
The sieved tomalley and coral
(1 to 2 tablespoons sherry)

Fill tail shells with one-third of the sauce, add meat and cover it with the rest of the sauce. You may sprinkle the tops with a mixture of:

(Grated Parmesan cheese and melted butter)

Run the lobsters under a broiler until the sauce is golden brown. Serve with:

Wilted Cucumbers, 102

LOBSTER OR SEAFOOD NEWBURG

4 Servings

I.
Melt in a double boiler ➤ over—not in—boiling water:

4 tablespoons butter

Add, stir and cook 3 minutes:

2 cups boiled diced lobster meat

Add:

¼ cup dry sherry or Madeira

Cook gently about 2 minutes more. Add:

½ teaspoon paprika
(⅓ teaspoon nutmeg)

Beat and add:

3 egg yolks
1 cup cream

Cook and stir these ingredients until they thicken

Season to taste

Serve the lobster at once on:

Hot buttered toast

II. Heat in a double boiler:

2 cups Newburg Sauce, 359

Add, stir and cook for 3 minutes:

2 cups boiled diced lobster meat or
2 cups cooked seafood

You may add:

(1 lb. sliced Sautéed Mushrooms, 308)
Season to taste

Serve at once on:

Hot buttered toast or Boiled Rice, 206

LOBSTER OR SEAFOOD CURRY

4 Servings

Heat in a double boiler ➤ over—not in—boiling water:

2 cups Curry Sauce, 345

Add, stir and cook about 3 minutes:

2 cups boiled diced lobster meat or
2 cups cooked seafood

You may add:

(3 sautéed chopped ribs celery)

(½ sautéed chopped green pepper, seeds and membrane removed)
(1 teaspoon grated sautéed onion)
Season to taste

Cook until well heated. May be served at once with:

Boiled Rice, 206, Chutney, 846, or slivered almonds

⅄ LOBSTER PARFAIT

6 Servings

This is an exceedingly elegant way of presenting cold lobster. Consider serving it with iced champagne.

Purée in the ⅄ blender:

The meat of 1 freshly killed and cooked 2½-lb. lobster, or 2 cups cooked meat from frozen lobster tails

with:

3 tablespoons tomato purée
2 tablespoons lemon juice
1 tablespoon dry sherry
2 teaspoons brandy
½ cup water

Mix in:

1 minced clove garlic
1 finely chopped shallot

Cook the mixture over low heat until reduced by one-third. Cool, then add:

1½ tablespoons whipping cream
2 cups mayonnaise
½ teaspoon paprika
1 teaspoon salt

Chill 1½ hours. Arrange an additional chilled:

4 oz. lobster meat per serving

in 6 parfait glasses. Cover the meat with the above sauce, letting it trickle down in parfait style. Garnish with:

Chilled whipped cream
Watercress

Serve at once.

HOT LOBSTER RING

5 Servings

Preheat oven to 325°.

Melt:

2 tablespoons butter

Stir in, until blended:

3 tablespoons flour

Stir in gradually:

2 cups chicken bouillon or 1 cup bouillon and 1 cup cream

Add:

1 tablespoon minced parsley
½ cup grated bread crumbs—not toasted
4 beaten egg yolks
2 cups cooked diced lobster meat
Salt and white pepper to taste

Whip until stiff ➤ but not dry:

4 egg whites

Fold lightly into the other ingredients. Bake the lobster mixture in a well-oiled 9-inch ring mold until firm, about 20 minutes. Unmold and serve with:

White Wine Sauce for Fish, 342

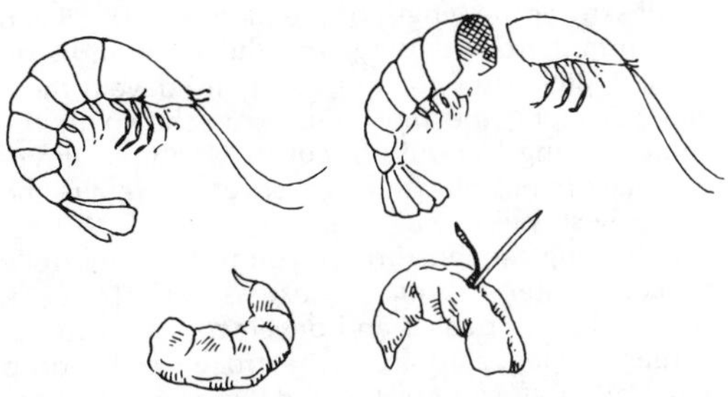

ABOUT SHRIMP

Formerly our southern shrimp or **crevette** was the only one available in most of our markets. Today we can buy many members of this family. So let us remind you of the miniature ones from our West Coast and from Scandinavia—now widely used as hors d'oeuvre; and those jumbo-sized varieties often called **prawns**—shrimp so large that two or three suffice for a serving. In spite of slight differences in flavor and texture, all may be substituted for one another if size is taken into consideration for serving amounts and cooking time.

➤ To test shrimp for freshness, see that they are dry and firm. For 3 servings allow about 1 pound of shrimp in the shell—these are called "green" shrimp—or ½ pound of cooked shrimp without shells. In buying, remember that 2 to 2½ pounds of shrimp in the shell gives only about 1 pound cooked, shelled shrimp, or 2 cups. While shrimp may be cooked in the shell or unshelled, the shells add considerable flavor. To prevent curling and toughening, ➤ drain them at once after cooking. Shucking is easy, either before or after cooking. A slight tug releases the body shell from the tail.

Devein before or after cooking, using a small pointed knife or the end of a pick, as sketched above. This is essential. Large shrimp may be made more decorative by slicing them lengthwise after cleaning.

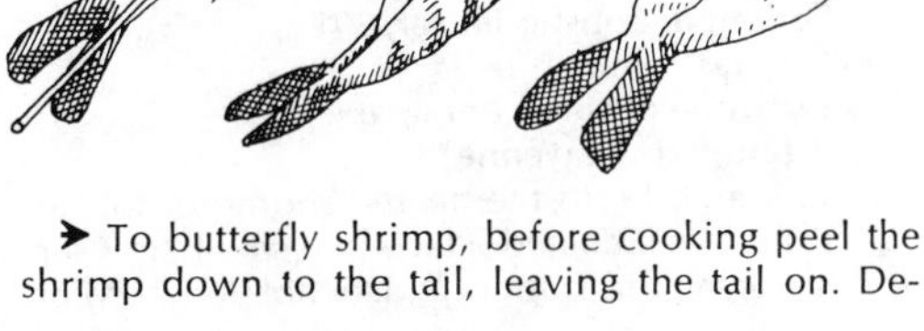

➤ To butterfly shrimp, before cooking peel the shrimp down to the tail, leaving the tail on. Devein. Holding so the underside is up, slice down its length, almost to the vein. Spread and flatten to form the butterfly shape. To butterfly after cooking, it is wise to begin by running a toothpick or small skewer the length of the inner curve to keep the shrimp from curling, see the illustration on the left, 389. After cooking, peel and devein them and cut along the inner curve, as shown in the center, being careful to cut only about three-fourths of the way through so as to retain the butterfly shape.

➤ If using canned shrimp, you may rinse briefly in cold water to remove excess salt. To cook frozen shrimp, peeled and deveined, and also the "green" types, start from the frozen state, drop into boiling stock or water, and begin counting the time when the stock comes up to a simmer.

For other shrimp recipes, see the chapters on Hors d'Oeuvre, Salads, and Lunch Dishes.

POACHED SHRIMP

6 Servings

We prefer this basic procedure to "boiling" shrimp.

Simmer about 5 minutes:

8 cups water
¼ cup sliced onion
1 clove garlic
1 bay leaf
2 celery ribs with leaves
1½ tablespoons salt

Wash, drain and add:

2 lb. green shrimp

Slice and add:

½ lemon

Simmer the shrimp about 5 minutes or until pink but not tightly curled. Drain immediately and chill. Serve the shrimp very cold in their shells—if they are to be shucked at table—with a bowl of:

Russian Dressing, 364, or
Rémoulade Sauce, 364

or shell them, removing the intestinal vein, and use the shrimp in a hot dish as desired.

POTTED SHRIMP OR LOBSTER

This terrine can be used as a luncheon or hors d'oeuvre spread. Cook:

Raw shrimp or lobster, see above

Drain and remove meat from shells. Chop coarsely. Reserve shells. Allow for every cup of seafood:

2 to 3 tablespoons butter

To half of the butter, add the reserved shells to make:

Shrimp or Lobster Butter, 351

Season to taste with:

⅛ teaspoon mustard or mace
A few grains cayenne

Stir the seafood into the heated shrimp or lobster butter until well coated. Place in a small jar. Clarify the remaining butter. ➤ Do not let it color. Pour it while hot over the seafood, making sure the food is well covered. Refrigerate lidded.

MOLDED SHRIMP

Put through a coarse food chopper:

1½ lb. cooked cleaned shrimp
2 tablespoons capers
Juice of 1 very small onion

Combine the above ingredients in a mixing bowl with:

¼ lb. soft butter
¼ cup whipping cream

Season with:

Salt
Hot pepper sauce
Tarragon
Chopped parsley

Mix well until mixture has the consistency of whipped cream. Pack in a pretty mold which has been rinsed in cold water, and refrigerate covered 3 or 4 hours. Unmold and garnish with:

Cherry tomatoes, parsley or fennel

▤ SHRIMP TERIYAKI

3 Servings

Marinate:

1 lb. shelled, deveined raw shrimp

about 15 minutes in:

½ cup pineapple juice
2 to 4 tablespoons soy sauce
½ cup bland vegetable oil

Drain and broil or grill 3 or 4 minutes on each side, 4 inches from heat. Serve with:

Boiled Rice, 206, or Curried Rice, 208

NEW ORLEANS SHRIMP

4 to 6 Servings

Poach, see left:

2 lb. raw shrimp

Shell and devein them. Rub a bowl with:

Garlic

Mix together in the bowl:

½ cup finely chopped celery
1 green onion, finely chopped
1 tablespoon chopped chives
6 tablespoons olive oil
3 tablespoons lemon juice
¼ teaspoon hot pepper sauce
5 tablespoons horseradish
2 tablespoons prepared mustard
¼ teaspoon paprika
¾ teaspoon salt
½ teaspoon white pepper

You may marinate the shrimp in this sauce up to 12 hours. Keep refrigerated until ready to serve on:

Lettuce

SHRIMP NEWBURG

3 to 4 Servings

Prepare:

1 lb. Poached Shrimp, above

Serve with:

Newburg Sauce, 359

using 1 to 1½ cups of sauce, in a:

Rice Ring, 207

or over:

Baked Green Rice, 208

SHRIMP CASSEROLE WITH SNAIL BUTTER

4 Servings

Prepare:

1½ lb. Poached Shrimp, above

Have ready in refrigerator:

Colbert or Snail Butter, 350

Preheat oven to 400°.

Put a ¼-inch layer of the butter in the bottom of a shallow casserole. Lay shrimp in rows and press into the butter. Cover the shrimp with the remaining butter and bake about 10 minutes. Broil a few minutes to let top brown. Serve at once.

DEEP-FAT-FRIED SHRIMP

3 Servings

➤ Please read About Deep-Fat Frying, 147.

Shell:

1 lb. raw shrimp

Remove the intestinal vein. Combine:

⅔ cup milk
⅛ teaspoon paprika
¼ teaspoon salt

Soak the shrimp in the milk 30 minutes. Drain the shrimp well. Sprinkle with:

Lemon juice
Salt

Roll in:

Cornmeal

Let them dry on a rack for 15 minutes before frying in deep fat heated to 375° until golden brown. Drain on paper toweling. Serve hot with:

Lemon juice or Mayonnaise, 363, seasoned with puréed chutney

DEEP-FAT-FRIED STUFFED SHRIMP

14 Large Shrimp

Shell and devein:

10 jumbo-sized raw shrimp

Chop them into a pulp and add:

6 water chestnuts

which have been smashed with a cleaver and finely chopped. Now shell, leaving the tails intact, and devein:

14 jumbo-sized raw shrimp

Split lengthwise along the deveined edge ➤ but not far enough to separate. Spread the shrimp flat and lay along each crevice:

A thin julienne of prosciutto or Westphalian ham

Spread the shrimp and chestnut mixture in the crevices over the ham and mold it into a rounded smooth surface when you partially reclose the shrimp for breading. Dip each shrimp into:

Beaten egg

then into:

Flour

Allow to dry on a rack 15 to 20 minutes.

➤ Please read About Deep-Fat Frying, 147.

Heat deep fat to 370°. Lift the shrimp by the tails and slide them gently into the heated fat. Fry about 5 minutes or until golden. Drain on paper toweling. Serve at once with:

Oriental Sweet-Sour Sauce, 355

adding some:

Plum jam

BUTTERFLY SHRIMP

➤ Please read About Deep-Fat Frying, 147. To cut for butterfly shape, see About Shrimp, 389.

Don't flour or crumb the tails, but do coat the body of the shrimp with:

Bread crumbs or grated coconut, or flour or egg or both; or in a Fritter Batter for Fish, 243

Fry in deep fat heated to 370° for 8 to 10 minutes or until golden. Drain on paper toweling. Serve at once with:

Soy sauce, Tartare Sauce, 364, or Oriental Sweet-Sour Sauce, 355

SHRIMP TEMPURA

➤ Please read About Deep-Fat Frying, 147.

Prepare:

Butterfly Shrimp, above

Dip them in:

Fritter Batter for Fish, 243

Fry in deep fat heated to 350° until golden.

Serve with:

Hot Mustard Sauce, 345,
Oriental Sweet-Sour Sauce, 355, or
Sauce Dijonnaise, 342

SHRIMP FRIED IN BATTER

➤ Please read About Deep-Fat Frying, 147.

Shell and clean, 389:

1 lb. raw shrimp

You may leave the tails on. Prepare:

Fritter Batter for Fish, 243

Dip a few shrimp at a time in the batter, holding them by the tail. ➤ Do not cover the tail with batter. Fry in deep fat heated to 370° until golden brown. Drain on paper toweling. Serve with:

Lemon wedges or Mayonnaise, 363, seasoned with catsup and mustard

ABOUT CRAYFISH, CRAWFISH, OR ÉCREVISSES

➤ Allow About One Dozen per Serving

One of the thrills of our grandparents was to find in Missouri streams the crayfish they had so relished in Europe. These crustaceans, looking like miniature lobsters, were brought to the table in great steaming crimson mounds, garnished with

dill or swimming in their own juices; that is, *à la nage*. By the way, a single Australian "crayfish" suffices for one serving!
To cook, wash well in several waters:

Crayfish

If they have been kept in fresh running water for several days, they need not be eviscerated. If they have not, clean them while still alive. Grasp the middle tail fin, as sketched; give a long firm twist, and pull to remove the stomach and intestinal vein. Have ready a large pot of:

Boiling water

seasoned with:

A leek—white part only
Parsley
1 chopped carrot
(3 tablespoons vinegar)

Drop the crayfish one by one into the boiling water at a rate that will not disturb the boiling. Cook not longer than 5 to 7 minutes. Serve in the shell. Have on the side plenty of:

Melted butter

seasoned with:

Fresh dill

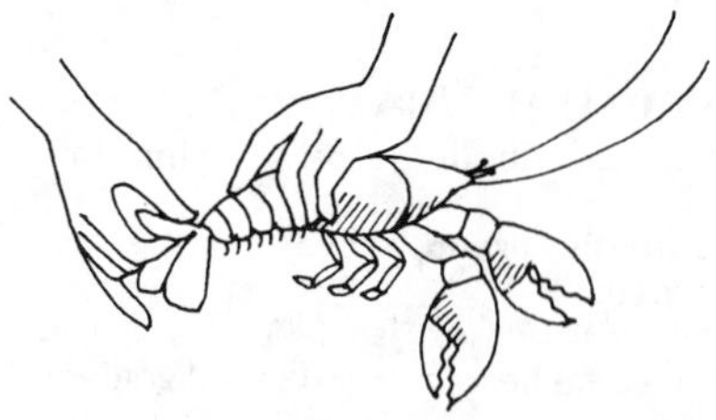

Crayfish are eaten with the fingers. Separate tail from body. Crack open tail by holding between thumb and finger of both hands and force it back against the curve of the shell. Be sure to serve with finger bowls. If you are preparing these crustaceans for hors d'oeuvre, cook only until the water is boiling well, after they are all immersed. Then remove from heat. Let them cool in the liquid. Shelled, they lend themselves to all kinds of combinations and sauces, but the connoisseur usually wants them for themselves alone.

ABOUT SNAILS

The Romans, who were addicted to snails, grew them on ranches where they were fed special foods like bay, wine and spicy soups as preseasoning.

Before they hibernate, snails contract into their shells and tightly close their opercula. It is usually at this phase that snails are available in markets. When they feed in late spring and summer, they may indulge in some foliage inimical to humans and, if used during this period, must be placed in a covered basket in a cool place and starved for 48 hours. For the next ten days to two weeks, feed them on lettuce leaves, removing the old leaves and furnishing new ones every few days. Then, in any season, scrub until all slime is removed. Cut out the opercula and put the snails into a large stainless steel or enamel pot. To prepare enough acidulated water to cover about 50 snails, mix:

Water
¼ cup vinegar
½ cup salt

Rinse them and repeat this entire process two more times or until the acidulated water is clear. Discard any snails whose heads have not by this time popped out of their shells. Drain. Cover with boiling water and cook for 5 minutes. Drain, cool and remove the snails from shells with an oyster fork. Hold the upper part of the snail with the thumb and forefinger and score the lower part of the body to pull out the swollen intestinal tube. Discard it. Reserve shells. Simmer the snails in a court bouillon of:

½ water or light stock and ½ white wine

about 3 hours or until they are tender, adding during the last half hour of cooking:

A Bouquet Garni, 572
2 cloves garlic

Allow them to cool in the court bouillon. Drain.

I. Allow 6 to 9 Snails per Serving

Prepare snails and shells as described above. Dry the snails and shells with a cloth. Place in each shell a dab of:

Snail Butter, 350

Replace the snails. Pack them firmly in the shell, so generously covered that only the lovely green herbed butter is visible at the opening. You may chill the snails for later use, or bake them at once on a pan lightly sprinkled with water in a 425° oven just long enough to get them piping hot—a matter of a few minutes only. Have ready heated, grooved snail dishes as shown in the chapter heading. Also shown is the snail shell holder which has a spring handle to adjust its viselike grip to the size of the snail. The long, closely tined fork is used with a slight twist to remove the meat.

II. For canned snails, the following effects a small miracle of resuscitation.
Prepare enough to fill 48 snail shells:

Snail Butter, 350

Reduce to 1 cup over high heat:

1 cup canned condensed consommé
1 cup dry white wine

cooked with:

½ bay leaf
1 clove garlic

Put in a colander:

48 canned snails

Pour over them:

1 quart warm water

Drain well. Simmer the snails briefly in the hot reduced consommé and wine. Wash the snail shells well and drain. Pack as described above with:

Snail Butter, 350

Heat and serve as for I.

III. Or, replace the shells with:

Sautéed Mushroom Caps, 308

Fill the mushrooms with one or more snails, depending on size. Coat the snails with:

Snail Butter, 350

and run under a broiler briefly until heated.

ABOUT TURTLES AND TERRAPIN

Sea or **green turtles** are peaceable and sagacious. Their habits are nowhere more fascinatingly described than in *The Windward Road* by Archie Carr. Handling and cooking these monsters, some of which weigh over 300 pounds, is not a usual household procedure. Therefore most of us are content to enjoy their highly prized, highly priced gelatinous meat ready-diced and in cans. The greenish meat from the top shell is considered the best—that taken from the bottom is whitish.

While sea turtles are tropical in habitat, those most frequently caught and consumed in temperate North America are freshwater types, such as **snapping turtles,** which abound in streams and lakes from North Dakota to Florida. As to disposition, they are again a quite different kettle of fish: short-tempered and capable of inflicting nasty bites.

Choicest of all turtle meat is furnished by the **terrapin,** which inhabits salt-marshes along the East Coast. But this holds good only for the female of the species—the males being unacceptably tough—and to those weighing not much more than 3 pounds.

Regardless of the turtle's size, sectioning it for cooking is an irksome job, even if you overcome the worst of the opposition—as old hands are wont to do when dealing with snappers—by instantly chopping off the head.

Before preparation, however, it is advisable to rid turtles of wastes and pollutants. Put them in a deep open box, with well-secured screening on top; give them a dish of water; and feed them for a week or so on 3 or 4 small handouts of ground meat.

➤ To cook, place in a pan of cold water:

A 7-inch turtle

Bring water slowly to a boil and parblanch at least 10 minutes. Drain. Plunge into cold water and leave until cool enough to handle. Scrub well. Place the turtle in rapidly boiling water and add:

(A Bouquet Garni, 572)
(An onion stuck with cloves)
(3 stalks celery)

➤ Reduce the heat at once and simmer 35 to 45 minutes or until the claws can be removed by pulling. Drain, reserving the stock. Allow the turtle to cool on its back in order to trap the juices as it cools. When cool, pry the flat plastron free from the curved carapace—easier said than done. Near the head you will find the liver. ➤ Free it carefully from the gall. Discard the gall. Slice the liver thin and reserve it, as well as the eggs, if any. You may or may not want to reserve the small intestines, which may be chopped and added to the meat or sauce. Remove the meat from both the carapace and the skinned legs. When ready to serve, you may toss the meat, including the ground liver and intestines, in:

6 tablespoons hot melted butter

Garnish with:

Parsley

Serve with:

Sherry, as a drink

or you may heat the meat briefly over very low heat or in the top of a double boiler ➤ over—not in—boiling water in a sauce made by combining:

1 cup Brown Sauce, 346
The chopped, cooked eggs, if any
1 teaspoon mixed herbs: including basil, sweet marjoram and thyme, with a touch of rosemary, bay and sage
3 tablespoons Madeira or dry sherry

Garnish with:

Watercress

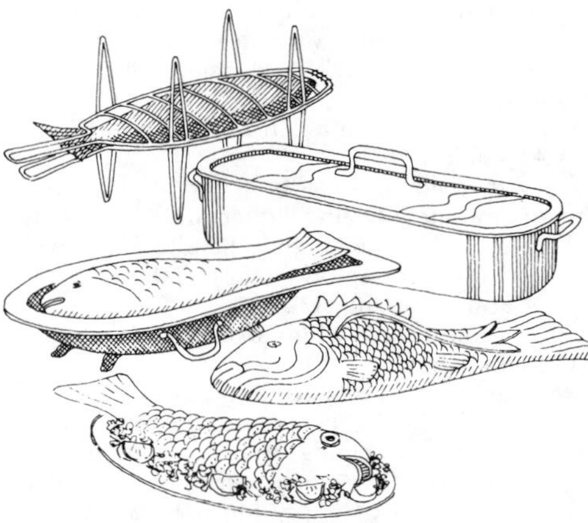

FISH

ABOUT FISH

One of the ill winds ruffling late-twentieth-century waters is the belated discovery that many of our lakes and ocean estuaries have become nearly incapable of supporting life. But in compensation, this bad news has blown us a host of scientists determined to reverse the situation, to systematically create new spawning beds for the fish and crustaceans we already know, and to launch research into the possibility of reaping even the tiny, fantastically numerous and exotic creatures we call plankton after the Greek word for "wanderer."

Fish of all kinds provide high-grade protein, most of it considerably less fatty than most meats. For those concerned with lean and fat fish, the following are considered in the not-so-lean category: albacore, bloaters, butterfish, bluefish, chub, eel, herring, mackerel, pompano, salmon, sardine, shad, smelt, sprat, tuna, trout and whitefish—the fat content ranging from 15% to about 30% with eel.

➤ If you have any reason to believe that the fish you are using harbors objectionable amounts of DDT or other chemicals, filleting is the safest approach. Chemical residues tend to be concentrated in the fatty tissues, namely the belly flesh and the dark areas at the sides. These areas may all be cut away during the filleting process, see 396.

Now, a few more general comments. Fish of many kinds respond favorably to deep-fat frying or sautéing. Those with naturally dry flesh—pike, pickerel and muskellunge are freshwater examples—often profit by baking and by preliminary marination, marination being also a corrective for too strong a flavor; while fish of moister texture are better suited to broiling. And there are fish that steam or poach well: cod, buffalo fish, hake, haddock, sheepshead, red snapper, grouper, pollock, halibut and salmon. Some very oily fish may be smoked or may be bought smoked. Some others are available fresh or salted. For fish timbales and soufflés, see 233 and 230.

Many fish are seasonal delicacies. Available all year round are rock bass, carp, cod, eel, flounder, grouper, haddock, hake, halibut, herring, mullet, red snapper, salmon, sole and tuna.

If you are adventuring with eel, herring, some types of sole, or an officious stranger like octopus, consult the Index to see if we have some extra-special suggestions for preparing, cooking or seasoning them; and also look at the individual recipes for ways to use the cooking and serving equipment shown in chapter heading opposite.

SEA FISH

These include: albacore, amberjack, sea bass, bluefish, bonito, butterfish, chub, cod, croaker, cusk, the small dolphin, flounder, grouper, haddock, hake, halibut, Atlantic herring, Pacific herring, kingfish, lingcod, mackerel, mullet, pilchard, plaice, pollock, pompano, porgy, red snapper, rosefish, sailfish, sand dab, sardines, smelt, the soles, sprat, swordfish, tuna, turbot, weakfish, whitebait and whiting.

FRESHWATER FISH

These include: bass, buffalo, carp, catfish, crappie, lake herring, mullet, muskellunge, perch, pickerel, pike, sheepshead, sucker, sunfish, brook trout, lake trout and whitefish.

Either sea or freshwater fish—depending on age and season—are eel, elver and shad. Some fish are changelings, as witness the recent effortless conversion of certain types of salmon, like the Coho, and of sea-trout, notably the steelhead, from a life-cycle requiring freshwater infancy and salt-water adulthood to a cycle entirely accomplished in the Great Lakes and their tributaries.

TESTING FOR AND MAINTAINING FRESHNESS OF FISH

With America gone fishing-crazy, no housewife knows when she will answer a knock at the kitchen door and be suddenly faced with a neighbor's surplus catch in all its chill, scaly impersonality. This need not be a moment of consternation. If it happens to you, judge the gift—after, of course, enthusiastically thanking the donor—as critically as you would judge a fish offered at market. To test its freshness ➤ make sure that its eyes are bulging and its gills are reddish, that the scales are adhering firmly to the skin, and that the flesh, when you press it, is firm to the touch. The scales should have a high sheen. Also be certain that the fish has no offensive odor—especially around the gills or the belly. If it is very fresh, and you cannot use it at once but plan to do so in a day or two, store it at 39°, preferably lidded, so that its penetrating odor does not permeate other foods in the refrigerator. Fish may be kept directly on ice if drainage is provided to prevent it from soaking up water. Length of fish storage depends largely on the condition in which it reaches you. The sooner it can be used the better, for its fragile gelatinous substances break down and dry out quickly as the fish ages, destroying flavor as they dry.

If you must hold fish for a longer period, see directions for freezing fish and for cooking frozen fish, 827. When buying fish, remember that a whitish surface indicates excessive dehydration, and that in some stores ➤ thawed frozen fish is sold with no sign or comment to indicate the important fact that it should be used at once and never refrozen. If you are in doubt about the freshness of a fish, place it in cold water. A newly caught fish will float.

PREPARING FISH FOR COOKING

The most important factor in fish cookery is to have or keep fish fresh. Whether your fish is large or small, choose the cooking method best suited to retain its juiciness, and no matter what its size or type ➤ never overcook it.

SMALL FISH

To clean fish like smelts, sardines or sprats, spread open the outer gills, take hold of the inner gills with the forefinger and pull gently. The parts unfit for food are all attached to these inner gills and come out together, leaving the fish ready to cook after rinsing. These respond to deep-fat frying and pan-frying.

Small fish may be **butterfly-filleted.** In this technique, head and tail are removed, after which the flesh is cut cleanly away on both sides of the backbone and the dorsal fin; the ventral or belly fin is removed by slot-cutting around it. The meat is then cut off in a single piece, freeing it from the backbone, and flattened out ready for rinsing, drying and cooking.

LARGE FISH

If fish are two pounds or over, bake, steam, poach or "steak" them as described below. Fish of this size and somewhat smaller ones both may be filleted.

You will sometimes see suggestions for slashing the skin of large fish before cooking. This expedient is adopted chiefly for firm-fleshed fish, to hasten heat-penetration; or when, as with a whole turbot, the skin area is extensive and might otherwise burst.

To prepare a fish which is to be cooked in one piece, begin by spreading on a firm work surface several layers of newsprint covered with 3 thicknesses of brown paper. If the fish needs scaling, cut off the fins with scissors so they will not nick you while you are working. Wash the fish briefly in cold water—scales are more easily removed from a wet fish. Grasp the fish firmly near the base of the tail as shown below. If it is very slippery, you may want to hold it in a cloth. Begin at the tail, pressing a rigid sharp knife blade or scaler at a

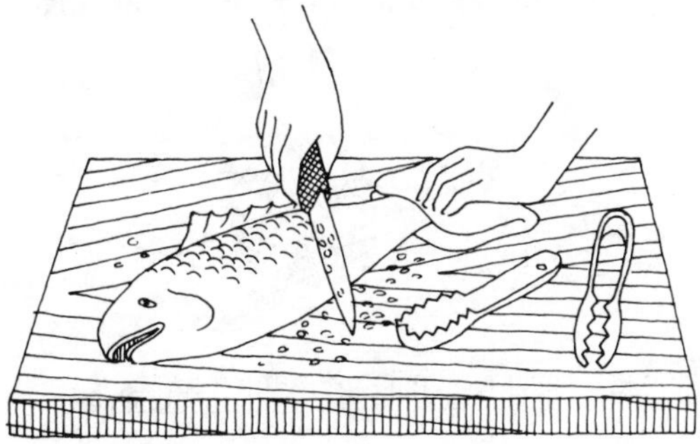

slight angle from the vertical position to raise the scales as you strip them off. Work against the "nap"—up toward the head. Be sure to remove the scales around the base of the head and the fins. After scaling, discard the first layer of brown paper with the scales on it.

Next, draw the fish. Cut the entire length of the belly from the vent to the head as shown below,

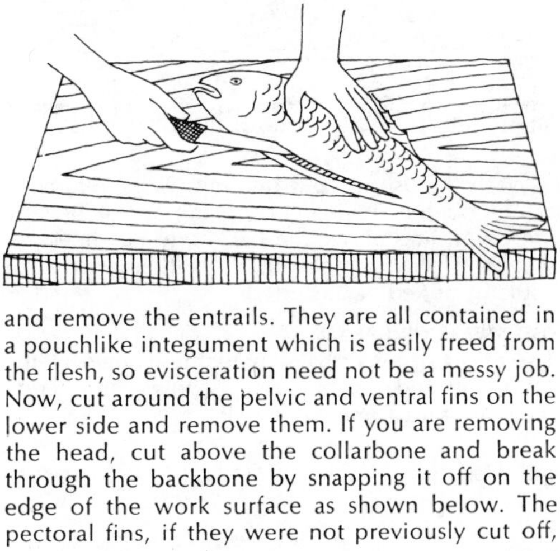

and remove the entrails. They are all contained in a pouchlike integument which is easily freed from the flesh, so evisceration need not be a messy job. Now, cut around the pelvic and ventral fins on the lower side and remove them. If you are removing the head, cut above the collarbone and break through the backbone by snapping it off on the edge of the work surface as shown below. The pectoral fins, if they were not previously cut off,

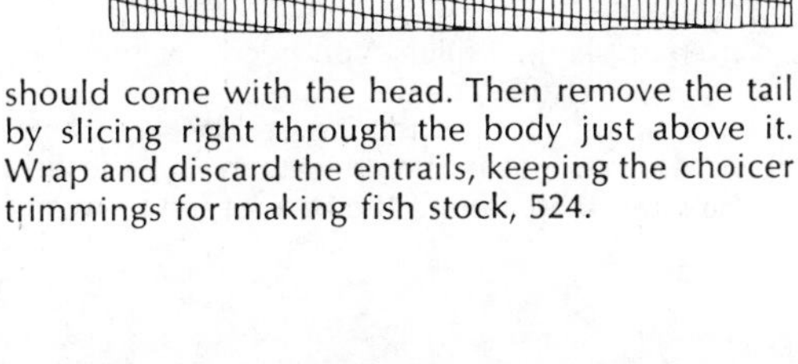

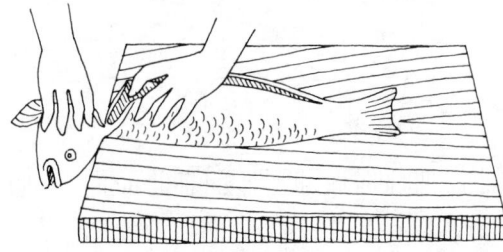

should come with the head. Then remove the tail by slicing right through the body just above it. Wrap and discard the entrails, keeping the choicer trimmings for making fish stock, 524.

If the fish has been scaled and you are preparing it for stuffing, you can remove the dorsal fin in such a way as to release unwanted bones. Cut first down to either side of it for its full length.

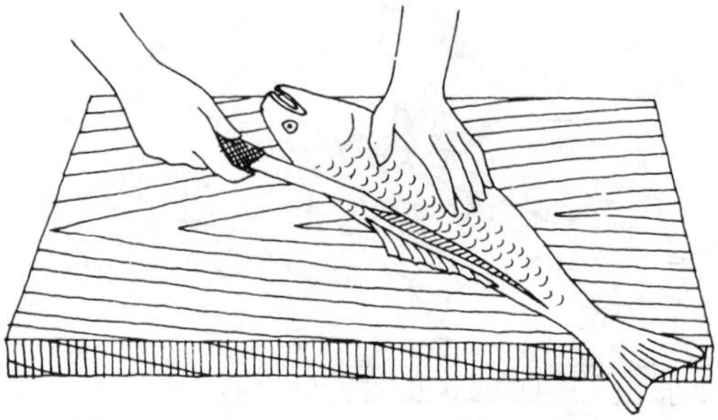

Then give a quick pull forward toward the head end to release it, and with it the bones that are attached to it, as sketched below.

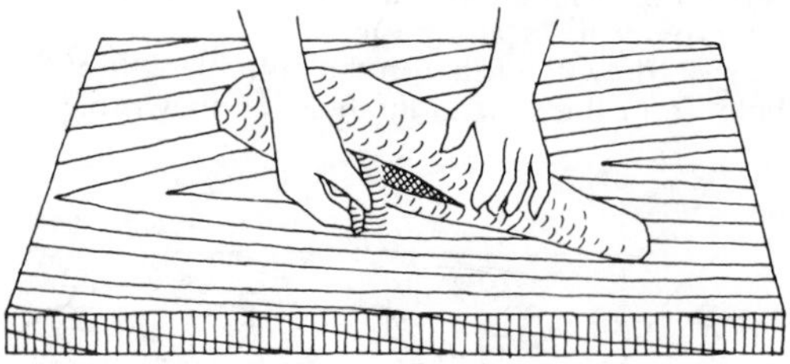

Wash the fish in cold running water, removing any blood, bits of viscera or membrane. ➤ Be sure the blood line under the backbone has been removed. Dry the fish well. It is then ready for cooking stuffed or unstuffed.

FISH STEAKS OR DARNES

To cut a fish into steaks, or darnes, begin at the head end and cut evenly, as shown, into cross sections at least one inch thick.

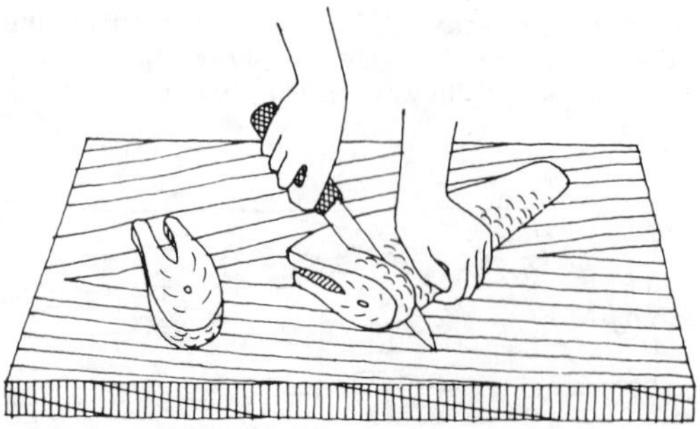

FILLETING FISH

To prepare skinned fillets, you need not scale the fish, remove its fins, or draw it.

Place on the work surface several thicknesses of newsprint covered by brown paper. Cut the fish, as shown, first all around the base of the head and just above the tail, then all along the back ridge. Now slice down at a slight angle behind the collarbone beyond the gill, until you feel the backbone against the knife. Turn the knife flat, with the cutting edge toward the tail and the point toward the cut edge of the backbone. Keep the blade flat and in the same plane with the backbone. Now, cut with a sliding motion along the backbone until you have freed the fillet all the way to the tail, see below. It should come off in one piece.

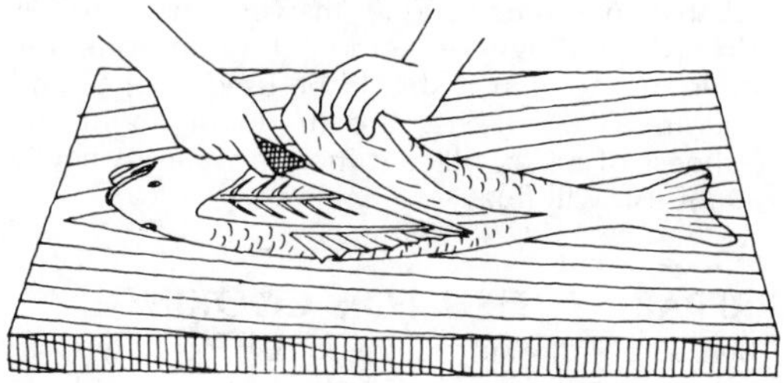

To skin, place the fillet skin side down. Hold the tail firmly with your free hand as shown. Cut through the flesh of the fillet about ½ inch above the tail. Flatten the knife against the skin with the blade pointing toward the top of the fillet. Work the knife forward, keeping in the same plane and close against the skin while your left hand continues to hold the skin taut.

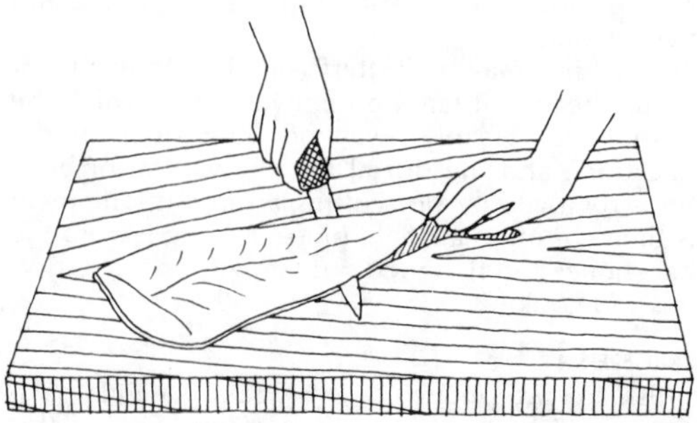

An exception to the above procedure must be made with a certain group of very flat fish, some of which, rather disconcertingly, have both eyes on their upper surface. All of them are skinned and filleted in a special way; and all of them, including turbot, which is less flat than most, may be cooked by recipes for sole or flounder.

The true English or Dover sole, whose eyes are situated normally, has the most delicate flavor and texture of them all. But fillets of flounder, plaice, dab, and lemon or gray sole are often palmed off on the unsuspecting purchaser as the genuine article.

➤ To fillet these flat varieties, first skin the fish by cutting a gash through the skin above the tail.

Peel back the skin for about 3/4 inch. Grasp the released skin firmly in the right hand as shown. Hold the tail flat in the left hand while pulling steadily toward the head with the right. When skinned, a flat fish reveals a lengthwise indentation down the center which separates a set of fillets—two on the dark-skinned side and two on the light side. Cut through the flesh on either side of the spine. Slip the knife under the fillet, close to the bone, and cut the fillet loose from the backbone toward the outside edge of the fish. Having freed the fillets, refrigerate them, discarding all the unusable entrails. You may keep the bone structure, skin, heads and tails for fish stock, 524, unless the fish is a strong-flavored or oily one.

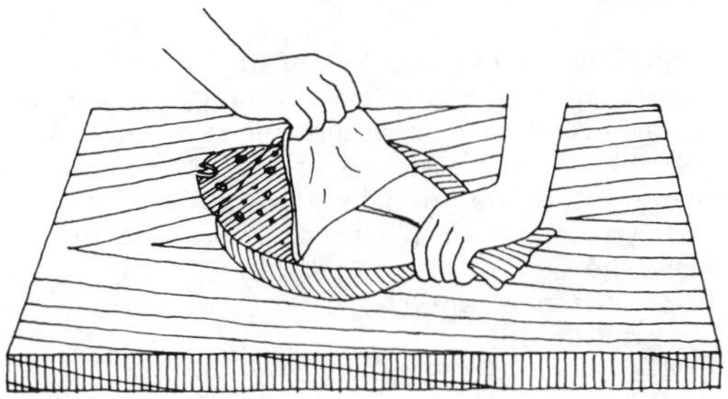

COOKING FISH

Most of our fish recipes call for cooking in ovenproof dishes. Service is simplified if such dishes are attractive enough to appear at table. This way, fish—which is fragile—undergoes less handling, and you have fewer "fishy" dishes to clean up later.

➤ Allow per serving 1 pound whole small fish, 3/4 pound if entrails, head, tail and fins are removed; 1/2 pound fish steaks; or 1/3 pound fish fillets.

➤ To test a fish for doneness, you may insert a thermometer at an angle into the thickest portion of the flesh. Fish is edible when the internal heat reaches 140°. At 150° its tissues begin to break down, allowing both juices and flavors to escape. Remove the fish from the heat, surely by 145°. ➤ Remember that because fish needs so little heat to cook, it will continue to do so on a hot platter.

If you have no thermometer, stick a wooden pick into the thickest part of the fish; if it meets little resistance and comes away clean, it is in all likelihood done. A "rule of finger" for doneness in a soft-fleshed fish is to press it as you would a cake to see if the flesh returns to its original shape. Another more reliable yardstick is the disappearance of translucency: a fish is done when its flesh flakes readily. A good cook knows through experience how long to cook her fish; but even she will watch the proceedings with a vigilant eye to guard against overdoneness.

Many fish are bland in flavor and profit by a sauce. If, on the contrary, the fish is strong in flavor, many expert cooks ➤ discard the butter or cooking oil in which it has been cooked. Otherwise, deglaze the pan, 340.

➤ To keep a whole fish warm, put it on a heated serving platter in a very low oven. Leave the door ajar. For fillets, treat as for a whole fish, but cover them with a damp warm paper towel or cloth. ➤ Be sure that any sauce served on the fish is very hot.

➤ To keep a sauced fish warm, use an uncovered double boiler, or place the baking dish in which you plan to serve the fish in a pan of boiling water and hold uncovered.

➤ If cooked fish is to be served cold, keep refrigerated until the very last minute. If served buffet-style, place it over cracked ice.

➤ To minimize fish tastes and odors, use lemon, wine, vinegar, ginger, spring onions, or garlic in the marinating or cooking. To remove the odor of fish from utensils and dishcloths, use a solution of 1 teaspoon baking soda to 1 quart water. Pans may be washed in hot suds, rinsed and dried, and then scalded with a little vinegar. To remove the odor of fish from the hands, rub them with lemon juice, vinegar or salt before washing.

To prepare fish dishes based on cooked fish and shellfish, see Brunch, Lunch and Supper Dishes, 250–275; Hors d'Oeuvre, 77; and Canapés, 66. To prepare Fish Stews and Soups, see 186–190. To cure and smoke fish, see 816. A great variety of sauces suitable for fish are coupled with individual recipes in this chapter. Others may be found in the Sauce chapter, 336.

There are any number of attractive ways to serve and garnish fish. Handsome foundations for cold dishes are salmon, lake trout, chicken halibut, turbot, filleted Dover sole, walleyed pike and carp.

A tasty way to prepare a hot fish in summer is to ⊟ broil it on a fish grill, as shown in the chapter heading, upper left, on 394. Then flambé it several seconds before serving over a dry bed of fennel stalks. Another addition to fish is Fried Parsley, 314, both delicious and decorative.

FROZEN FISH

Frozen fish should be thawed, refrigerated, before cooking, or cooked while still frozen, unless stuffed or rolled. Also, fish sticks or individual portions should not be thawed before cooking. ➤ Use thawed fish immediately, and do not refreeze; it may be cooked in the same way as its fresh counterpart. ➤ If cooked frozen, it is best baked, broiled, or cooked *en papillote* or in aluminum foil. Double the cooking time given for fresh fish, and in foil cooking add another 15 minutes to allow the heat to penetrate the foil. Freezing processes for fish have improved greatly in the last few years, bringing us varieties hitherto not available. But we still think that frozen fish cannot compare with fresh fish for flavor and texture. As the gelatins lose their delicate quality, it is apt to be dry and thus needs a well-flavored sauce or a good deal of moisture or fat in the cooking process. ➤ If you are buying frozen fish from frozen food cabinets, buy only solidly frozen packages. They should not be torn or misshapen or show evidence of refreezing. Follow the processor's directions. ➤ Skin frozen fish before cooking it.

Following below are the descriptions of cooking procedures especially appropriate for fish, such as sautéing, baking, steaming, poaching, braising and broiling, each followed by some typical recipes. Recipes devised for specific kinds of fish arranged in alphabetical order complete the chapter. We include those for octopus—really a mollusk—and for frogs—i.e., frog legs—even though these agile amphibians have a disconcerting habit in cookbooks of leaping back and forth between the fish and the shellfish sections. Cooking times in individual recipes apply to fresh fish—including thawed fish—at 70°, but no warmer.

BAKING FISH

Baking is a highly recommended way of cooking fish: it preserves nearly intact the subtle, distinctive and delicate fresh flavor of a soft-fleshed fish. Temperature in the preheated oven should reach 350°—no more. The unskinned and lightly greased fish is set in an amply large baking dish on an oiled rack high enough to clear not only the juices the fish itself may yield, but also those which may accumulate if it is basted; and the dish is placed a little higher than the oven center. Firmer-fleshed fish will, of course, require longer baking, as will stuffed fish. Try to turn your fish only once, if at all, and if necessary with two spatulas, to minimize the risk of its breaking apart. To test for doneness, see Cooking Fish, 397.

BAKED UNSTUFFED FISH

Allow ½ Pound per Person

Preheat oven to 325°.
Scale, remove the entrails and clean:
A 3-lb. fish
A larger fish may be used, but it will require longer, but not proportionately longer, baking, see testing for doneness, 397. If the fish has a tough skin, slash it in several places. Place it on a greased rack in an ovenproof baking dish. Rub generously with:
Clarified Butter, 349
If the fish is lean, you may bard it, 420. If it is not barded, baste it frequently with:
Clarified butter
Bake about 30 minutes or until done. Serve on a hot platter garnished with:
Slices of lemon
Sprigs of parsley or basil
Stuffed Tomatoes, 333
Suitable sauces are:
Almond Garnish, 553, Shrimp Sauce, 343, or Hot Mustard Sauce, 345
and, for very bland fish:
Lorenzo Dressing, 360, or Salsa Verde, 361
➤ To carve an unstuffed fish, remove the skin and cut a line down the middle of the exposed side from head to tail. To either side of this line, cut pieces 2½ to 3 inches wide. Lift them off above the bone structure and serve. Pry up the backbone, beginning at the tail, letting it break at the neck, and lift it to one side. The exposed lower fillet will then be ready to carve just as the upper one was.

BAKED STUFFED FISH

6 Servings

Stuffing for fish should not be so bold in seasoning as to destroy the naturally delicate fish flavor. Scandinavians would object to this counsel; they make lavish use of fennel in preparing many of their traditional seafood dishes.
➤ If you bone a fish before stuffing, be sure to leave the skin intact.
Scale, eviscerate and clean:
A 3-lb. fish
Preheat oven to 325°.
Stuff fish with:
1½ cups Oyster Bread Dressing, 371, Bread Dressing for Fish, 371, Green Dressing, 371, or Fennel Dressing, 372
or with a combination of:
Pressed cucumbers, bread crumbs and almonds
Bake about 40 minutes or until done. Serve with:
Soubise Sauce, 344, Suprême Sauce, 344, or Colbert Butter, 350
and:
Lime wedges

PLANKED FISH

6 Servings

➤ Please read about Planking, 154.
Preheat oven to 350°.
Scale, clean, wash in running water and dry:
A 3- to 4-lb. fish
Brush with:
Clarified Butter, 349, or vegetable oil
Place the fish on a well-greased ovenproof or metal platter, about 18 x 13 inches. A seasoned plank may be used ➤ but, if used, should in the future be reserved solely for fish. Bake the fish 40 to 60 minutes; ➤ if stuffed, about 10 minutes longer.
Preheat broiler.
Garnish the platter with a decorative edging of:
Duchess Potatoes, 323
Broil 6 to 8 minutes, 8 inches from the source of heat, or until the potato garnish is delicately browned. Further garnish the plank with:

A stuffed vegetable
Parsley, fennel or watercress
and serve.

FISH BAKED IN A COVERED DISH

4 Servings

This is a simple way to bring out the flavor of a delicate fish.
Preheat oven to 350°.
Combine:

2 tablespoons Clarified Butter, 349
1/8 teaspoon pepper or paprika
A fresh grating of nutmeg

Rub the mixture over:

2 lb. fish, preferably in 1 chunky piece

Place the fish in an ovenproof dish. Cover with a closely fitting lid. Bake 20 to 25 minutes, or until done. The time depends largely on the shape of the fish. You may add while cooking:

(2 tablespoons dry white wine)

Place the fish on a hot platter. Melt:

3 tablespoons butter

Add:

2 tablespoons capers
1 teaspoon chopped parsley
1 teaspoon chopped chives
2 teaspoons lemon juice
Season to taste

Pour sauce over the fish.

⊟ FISH BAKED IN FOIL

Individual Serving

Please read about Foil Cookery, 153.
Preheat oven to 350°.
Scale and clean a small fish. Rub with:

Seasoned Butter, 349

Place on a piece of buttered aluminum foil large enough to make a generous fold at the edges. Do not include more than 1 pound in each packet. Bake 35 to 40 minutes to the pound.

FISH BAKED IN CLAY

Scoop out of the ground a hole about twice as big as the fish you are going to cook. Either wet and tamp the ground or line the area with stones, see 155. Prepare a bed of coals in the pit, and lay more flat stones on top of it to heat for 1 to 2 hours. After cleaning the fish and removing its gills, season the cavity with onions or herbs, or wipe with lemon. Close openings so that mud cannot get inside. Have ready a batch of "mudpie" clay, preferably blue clay, with which to coat the fish. Continue to lay on layers of mud until the covering is 1½ to 2 inches thick. Now clear away the top rocks and the coals from the pit. Place the "clay" fish on the hot lining stones and cover with earth and the rest of the hot stones you have set aside. Rebuild the fire over all and cook 1 to 3 hours, depending on size of fish. A 2½- to 3-pound fish will take about 2 hours. When it is done, uncover and crack open the clay mold. Skin and scales, head and tail will come off with the mold, revealing a delicious result. Needless to say, serve at once with corn roasted in the husks, 300.

BAKED FISH FILLETS SPENCER

4 Servings

This method produces a tender crust outside and a tender and moist interior.
Preheat oven to 550°.
Have ready:

4 skinned fillets of carp or other fish

and a plate of:

Dry bread crumbs

Fill a shallow pan with:

1/2 cup warm milk
1/2 teaspoon salt

Dip the fillets into the milk and the crumbs, in that order, making sure they are well coated. Place them in a well-greased ovenproof pan and gently pour over them:

3 tablespoons melted butter or bacon fat

Place pan on top shelf of oven and bake 10 to 12 minutes, transferring at once to a hot platter garnished with parsley and lemon wedges. You may serve with:

Tartare Sauce, 364, Florentine Sauce, 342,
or Sauce Dijonnaise, 342

BAKED FILLETS OF FISH

4 Servings

Preheat oven to 350°
Place in a greased ovenproof dish:

1½ lb. skinned fillets of sole or other fish

If the fillets are large they may be cut in half. Pour over them:

1 cup dry white wine
(2 tablespoons dry sherry)

Bake until just done, see 397. Serve covered with the liquid from the dish, which you may reduce slightly. Garnish with:

Lemon wedges
Sautéed mushroom caps

Or, you may omit the wine, baste with a fish stock, 524, or a small quantity of canned clam juice, and serve under:

Curry Sauce, 345, Champagne Sauce, 344,
or Aurore Sauce, 344

BAKED FISH WITH SOUR CREAM

8 Servings

Preheat oven to 350°.
Scale, clean, split and remove the bones from:

A 4-lb. whitefish or other fish

Flatten it out. Rub inside and out with:

Paprika and butter

Place on an ovenproof dish. Cover with:

2 cups cultured sour cream

Cover the dish. Bake about 45 minutes, or until done, see 397. Before serving, sprinkle with:

Chopped parsley

BAKED SMALL FISH FILLETS OR STICKS AU GRATIN

Allow About ⅓ Pound per Serving

Prepare for cooking:

Small drawn, boned, skinned fish, pieces of fish or fish fillets

Dip them in:

¼ cup whole milk or cream

then in:

Seasoned bread crumbs or crushed cornflakes

Let the fish dry on a rack for at least 20 minutes Preheat oven to 350°. Bake in an ovenproof dish until firm and golden. Baste twice during the cooking period with:

Melted butter

QUICK BAKED FILLETS OF FISH

3 Servings

Preheat oven to 350°.

Place in a small ovenproof dish:

1 lb. small, skinned fish fillets

Stir and heat until smooth:

⅔ cup condensed cream soup: tomato, celery, mushroom or asparagus

2 tablespoons milk or light stock

Add:

A few grains cayenne

(3 tablespoons finely chopped ham or prosciutto)

Pour the sauce over the fish. Bake ➤ uncovered 10 minutes. Serve with:

Boiled Rice, 206

FISH STEAKS OR FILLETS MARGUÉRY

6 Servings

Place in a mixture of boiling water and wine and simmer until nearly tender:

6 skinned fillets or 3 steaks

This will be a quick process if the pieces are thin. Drain the fish. Place in a greased baking dish. Keep them where they will remain warm. Melt:

¼ cup butter

Stir and sauté in it until done:

½ lb. sliced mushrooms

Stir in:

¼ cup all-purpose flour

Stir in gradually:

1 cup milk

¾ cup cream

Simmer in their liquor until plump:

½ pint oysters: 1 cup

Strain and reserve the liquor. Dry in a towel and add the oysters to the hot cream sauce. Stir in:

¼ lb. cooked shelled deveined shrimp, split lengthwise

Remove the sauce from the heat. Add the oyster liquor.

Season to taste

Pour the sauce over the fillets. Run under a broiler until the sauce colors.

FILLETS OF FISH FLORENTINE WITH SHRIMP AND MUSHROOMS

3 Servings

Cook, 326, drain and chop:

1 lb. spinach

Poach, see below:

1 lb. skinned fish fillets

Cook, then shell and devein, 389:

½ lb. shrimp cut lengthwise

Sauté:

½ lb. sliced mushrooms

Place the spinach on a buttered ovenproof dish, with the fillets on top. Pour over them:

White Wine Sauce, 345, Aurore Sauce, 344, or Mousseline Sauce, 359

Surround them with the mushrooms and shrimp. Place the dish in a preheated 400° oven just long enough to heat.

MOLDED FILLED FILLETS OF FISH, OR PAUPIETTES

4 Servings

Preheat oven to 350°.

Have ready:

8 skinned fillets of Dover sole or bluefish, or other very thin fillets

Butter 4 individual molds. Line each mold with 2 fillets crisscrossing at the bottom and extending up the sides, making sure that the fillets are long enough, when doubled back, to overlap at the top. Fill the center with the farce below, or with a fish quenelle mixture, 206, and fold the ends of the fillets to make a casing. With a fork, combine and stir a farce made of:

¼ cup melted butter

1½ cups soft bread crumbs

¼ cup chopped celery

1 teaspoon grated onion

1 tablespoon chopped parsley

(⅛ teaspoon dried burnet or basil)

¼ teaspoon salt

Fill the cases with this filling. Place the molds in a pan of hot water. Bake about 30 minutes. Unmold on a hot platter. Garnish with:

Lemon wedges

Parsley or watercress

Serve with:

Lemon Butter, 350, Oyster Sauce, 343, or Anchovy Sauce, 343

STEAMING, POACHING OR BRAISING FISH

Steaming is one of the better ways to treat a delicate lean fish if you want to retain flavor; although—unlike meat—fish will lose more weight processed in this way than in poaching. Poaching

—sometimes also called braising in fish cookery—runs steaming a close second.

A steamer has a perforated tray designed to hold the fish above the water level. Shown in the chapter heading is a poacher—the tray is not elevated and allows the fish to be immersed in the liquid. ➤ A poaching tray is always greased before the fish is placed on it. Fish may be poached in Fumets, 524, in Court Bouillons, 525, in Light Stocks, 522, or à blanc, 447—depending on the flavor you wish to impart or the degree of whiteness you desire. If you are chiefly concerned with preserving the true flavor of the fish, salted water may be all you care to use. Allow 1 tablespoon of salt for every 2 quarts of water. For details, see individual recipes.

If fumet or light stock is used for the steaming or poaching liquid, you may want to use some of it either as is, or reduced, in the fish sauce. ➤ Court bouillons are not used in this way, nor are à blanc liquids, because they are both apt to contain too much vinegar and salt.

➤ Please read the general principles of Poaching, 150, which apply here. Small fish or cut pieces are started in a boiling liquid, large pieces in cold liquid—especially important—because ➤ immersing a fish of any considerable size in boiling water causes the skin to shrink and burst. In either case, when the liquid reaches the boiling point ➤ reduce it immediately to a simmer for the remainder of the cooking period, allowing 5 to 8 minutes per pound, depending on the size of the fish.

Without a poacher, there is the problem of keeping the top of the fish constantly bathed in liquid or steam. This problem can be solved by the use of a poaching paper, 151, or by tying the fish loosely in muslin. The latter procedure is a great help, after cooking, in lifting fish out of the pan without breaking them.

If a large pan is not available, cut the fish in two and place it in a smaller pan, with the halves dovetailed. The fish can be reassembled on a platter later. If served hot or cold, it can be masked with a sauce without anyone's being the wiser for your subterfuge. Whatever pan you are using, put into it several onion and lemon slices, a chopped carrot and a few ribs of celery. Fill the pan with Court Bouillon, 525, to within an inch of the top. If you have used a cloth wrap, baste the fish with the court bouillon in which the fish is cooking as it simmers on the stove or in the oven. ➤ See that the cloth is always completely soaked. The top of the fish will then cook as quickly as the bottom.

After the cooking period the fish is sometimes allowed to cool in the water. We do not recommend this practice, as it leads to overcooking and waterlogging. ➤ If the fish is to be served cold, it is easier to remove the skin and trim the fish while it is still warm.

Another "hot-water" procedure—cooking **au bleu**—is fully described later in this chapter under the heading Blue Trout, 414.

POACHED FISH STEAKS

3 Servings

Cut into pieces suitable for individual servings:

1½ lb. halibut or other fish steak

Place them in a skillet. Cover with:

Boiling water

Season with:

4 whole peppercorns
½ bay leaf
2 teaspoons lemon juice

Simmer about 10 minutes, or until tender. Remove to a hot platter. Strain the stock and use it to make the sauce. Try:

Sauce Indienne, 344, Allemande Sauce, 345, or Anchovy Sauce, 343

FISH FILLETS BONNE FEMME

4 Servings

The tag **Bonne Femme** suggests the simple and straightforward flavor of this pleasing dish.

Cut, wipe with a damp cloth and dry:

4 skinned flat fish fillets, 396

Place in a buttered heavy skillet. Cover with:

¾ cup finely sliced mushrooms
1 minced shallot
1 teaspoon chopped parsley

Pour gently into the dish:

⅔ cup dry white wine

Cover with a poaching paper, 151, and ➤ simmer 10 to 15 minutes. Remove the fish onto a hot shallow ovenproof serving dish. Reduce the wine mixture by half. Stir into it gradually until well blended:

⅔ cup Velouté Sauce, 343

using fish stock. You may swirl in:

2 tablespoons butter

Pour the sauce over the fillets and run them under a broiler until sauce is lightly browned. Serve with:

Boiled New Potatoes, 317

FISH IN ASPIC COCKAIGNE

About 5 Servings

Scale and clean, leaving head and tail on, then cut into 4 or 5 pieces:

A fish weighing about 2½ lb.

Bring to the boiling point:

5 cups water
3 or 4 ribs celery with leaves
1 small sliced onion
4 or 5 sprigs parsley
3 tablespoons lemon juice
1 inch lemon rind
3 peppercorns
½ teaspoon dried herbs: tarragon, basil, etc.
½ teaspoon paprika
1 teaspoon salt

Drop the fish into the boiling stock. ➤ Simmer until tender. Do not let it boil again at any time. This is a quick process, requiring only 12 to 15 minutes or so. To test for doneness, see 397. Remove the fish from the stock. Strain the stock.

There should be about 3½ cups. If there is not, add water or chicken stock to make up the difference. Soak:

2 tablespoons gelatin

in:

¼ cup cold fish stock

Dissolve it in the hot stock. Add:

2 tablespoons or more capers
2 or 3 tablespoons lemon juice or dry white wine
Season to taste

Chill until stock begins to thicken. Remove the head, tail, skin and bone from the fish. Divide it into large flakes or pieces. Place a layer of aspic, 560, in a wet mold, cover it with flaked fish and repeat this process, winding up with aspic on top. Chill. Serve the aspic very cold with:

Mayonnaise, 363, or cultured sour cream

to either of which you may add:

1 to 2 tablespoons chopped herbs: chives, tarragon or parsley
Diced cucumbers

or with:

Andalouse Sauce, 364, or Cold Mustard Sauce, 357

Decorate the platter with watercress or shredded lettuce, and surround it with deviled eggs, radishes and olives. Serve with:

Brioche Loaf Cockaigne, 605, or Garlic Bread, 636

GEFILTE FISH

10 Servings

In times gone by, this homely favorite was everywhere prepared in orthodox fashion, just as the name indicates: that is, a fish skin was stuffed with a mixture of ground-up raw fish, vegetables, eggs and spices, then cooked until tender in a rich fish broth. These days many of the good Jewish cooks we know dispense with this nerve-wracking ritual, and we follow suit.

Clean thoroughly, bone and skin:

3 lb. mixed lean and fat fish, 394: whitefish, bluefish, jack salmon, pike, carp or buffalo

Prepare a stock using the head, skin and bones, covered with a small amount of water. Simmer, covered, 30 to 40 minutes with:

1 medium-sized sliced onion
3 chopped ribs celery, with leaves
3 sliced carrots
1 teaspoon salt
¼ teaspoon pepper

If the broth cooks down too much, add more water. While the stock is cooking, grind the fish, using a medium blade, with:

1 small onion
1 rib celery
¼ cup chopped parsley

Put the fish mixture in a bowl and stir into it until fluffy:

2 beaten eggs
¼ cup matzo meal or crushed crackers
½ teaspoon salt
¼ teaspoon pepper
¾ to 1 cup chilled water

Cover the fish mixture and refrigerate until the stock has cooked. Dip hands in chilled water and shape fish into 1-inch balls. Strain fish stock and bring to a boil, adding more water if necessary to float the balls. Gently drop the balls into the stock: there should be enough room for them to puff up. Cover and barely simmer 2 hours; then simmer uncovered 30 minutes longer. Remove balls with slotted spoon. Thoroughly chill balls and stock. Chop the jelled stock as for aspic, 114, and serve as a garnish with:

Grated horseradish

PICKLED FISH OR ESCABÈCHE

Allow ½ Pound per Serving

For a similar raw fish, see Seviche, 88.

➤ Please read About Deep-Fat Frying, 147. Use smelts, fresh anchovies, sardines, whitings or mullets not over ½ inch thick.

Clean, wash, dry and flour:

1 lb. small whole fish

Plunge them into:

Hot cooking oil

heated to 375°, for 5 to 10 seconds, according to size. Remove them, drain, and arrange in a shallow ovenproof glass or earthenware dish. Using 3 tablespoons of the oil, sauté until the onion is translucent:

2 tablespoons finely minced carrot
1 small finely minced onion
4 whole cloves garlic

Add:

⅔ cup wine vinegar
¼ cup water
A small bay leaf
A sprig of thyme
Salt
2 small red hot peppers

Simmer 10 minutes, then pour sauce over the fish. When cooled, refrigerate 24 hours. Serve the fish in the same dish in which it was marinated.

⊟ BROILING FISH

"Ruling a large kingdom," observed Lao-tzu, "is like cooking a small fish." What he meant was that both should be discreetly handled, and the treatment never overdone. We have usually respected the old philosopher's advice. But in broiling fish, we have discovered that they taste even better when they can be subjected to quite high and intense, rather than gentle, heat. The following cooking procedure, for instance, is most effective.

For a 2½-pound fish, cleaned, scaled but unskinned, broil in the bottom of a preheated broiler at 400° for 5 minutes, then move to a top broiler for 5 minutes more at a preheated 800°. The 800° is not a misprint. But it requires coil or burner capacity that most household ranges are simply not equipped to supply, see 159. The closest practical home approach is to use a pair of vertical charcoal grills—set as sketched—which produce what is known in France as a *rôti* rather than a grill. Most of us, however, must be content with

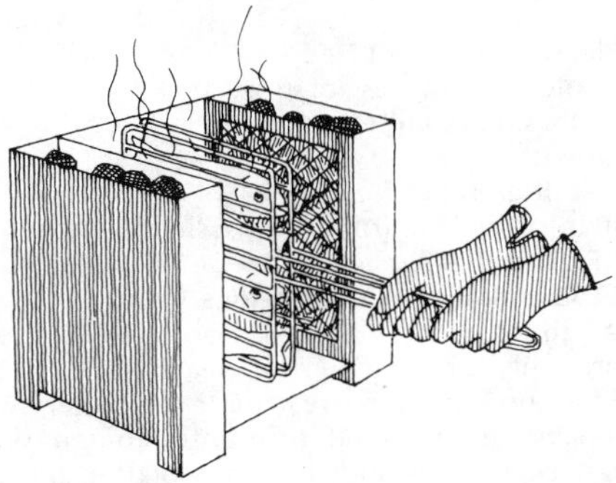

our range broilers preheated to 550°. ➤ It helps to warm up the broiling rack in advance, thus transferring some heat at once to the fish; but be sure to ➤ grease the rack after preheating so the fish will not stick. If the fish is to be turned, the double wire rack which fits into the vertical grill, as sketched, may also be conveniently used in the oven broiler pan. Grease it with cooking oil, and the fish with clarified butter. A lean fish may be floured before dotting with butter.

Fillets, flat and split fish are usually placed about 2 inches from the source of heat. If unskinned, place them skin side down. It is not necessary to turn them, but it is advisable to baste several times during the cooking period.

If thick fish steaks or large fish are being broiled, place the rack about 6 inches from the source of heat. They may take as long to cook as 5 or 6 minutes to a side.

Types of fish good for broiling include: halibut or salmon steaks, sole, and its cousins, split herring, mackerel and sea trout. For swordfish steaks, be sure to baste with plenty of butter, as they tend to become dry. Melted butter, lemon wedges and parsley adequately garnish broiled fish. If the fish is fat, try a spicy tomato sauce, 352–353, Cold Mustard, 357, Tartare, 364, or Allemande Sauce with capers, 345; if lean, Hollandaise, 358, Béarnaise, 359, or one of the seasoned butters. You will find specific sauce suggestions following some individual recipes.

⊟ FISH BROILED ON SKEWERS, OR FISH KEBABS

6 Servings

Prepare:

2 lb. skinned firm-fleshed fish: swordfish, halibut, cod or haddock

Cut into 1-inch cubes. Place in a glass, enamel or stainless steel pan and marinate 30 minutes in:

½ cup cooking oil
½ cup lemon juice
¼ teaspoon powdered bay leaf
4 drops soy sauce

Stir once or twice to coat fish thoroughly.
Preheat broiler.
Thread on skewers, alternating with thick slices of:

2 marinated cucumbers, 102, and stuffed olives

Broil or grill 10 minutes, turning frequently and basting with the marinade.

SAUTÉED OR PAN-FRIED AND DEEP-FAT-FRIED FISH

In pan-frying sizable fish, it is important to use Clarified Butter, 349, but equally important to ➤ combine it about half and half with cooking oil, since the butter may otherwise burn. To keep the fat from spattering your hands, you may cover the pan with an inverted colander. The fish is placed in the pan when the fat mixture begins to sizzle. Reduce the heat slightly. When the bottom side is completely cooked, turn the fish and cook until the second side is done. Quite large fish may be sautéed on both sides until seared, then placed in a preheated 375° oven about 10 minutes for finishing.

To prepare deep-fat-fried fish, please read About Deep-Fat Frying, 147, and then follow the recipes below with care.

SAUTÉED OR PAN-FRIED FISH

I. Scale, if necessary, and clean, 395:

A large fish or several small pan fish: crappie, brook trout, sunfish, perch, etc.

Cut the large fish into steaks or darnes before rolling them or the smaller fish in:

Seasoned flour or cornmeal or Bound Breading, 552

Melt in a skillet to the depth of ⅛ inch:

Clarified Butter, 349, and cooking oil

When the fat is hot, place the fish in the pan. Reduce the heat slightly and cook until done, from 3 to 5 minutes.

II. **2 Servings**

Scale if necessary and clean, 395:

A small fish—1 lb. or less: trout, sunfish, bream, crappie, perch, etc.

Dip it into a mixture of:

½ cup milk
1 teaspoon salt

Sauté until flaky, turning once, in:

2 tablespoons Clarified Butter, 349, and
2 tablespoons bacon fat, or use
1 tablespoon each butter and olive oil

Transfer fish to a hot plate and pour over it the pan drippings, seasoned with:

A little dry white wine or light stock
Chopped dill or tarragon
(A few minced capers)

Garnish with sprigs of parsley.

SAUTÉED FILLETS OF FISH AMANDINE

Allow 1/3 Pound per Serving

Dip:

Skinned fillets of sole, perch, brook trout, haddock, etc.

in:

Milk

Dust with:

Flour

Melt in a skillet:

Butter

Use enough to cover the bottom well. Sauté the fillets in the pan. Turn once. Place on a hot platter. Melt additional:

Butter

Brown in it lightly:

Shredded blanched almonds

Pour them over the fillets. Garnish the dish with:

Lemon and parsley

SAUTÉED FISH FILLETS PALM BEACH

2 Servings

Bread if you like:

2 small skinned fish fillets

Sauté until golden brown in:

2 tablespoons Clarified Butter, 349

Serve with 3 or 4 alternate sections of:

Grapefruit and orange

on each fillet. Pour the pan gravy over the garnished fillets and serve at once.

DEEP-FAT-FRIED FISH

Allow About 1/3 Pound per Serving

➤ Please read About Deep-Fat Frying, 147. Have fish at 70°. Clean and prepare for cooking:

Small fish or 1-inch pieces of fish

Dip them in:

Fritter Batter for Fish, 243, or
Bound Breading, 552

Fry in deep fat heated to 370° for 5 to 8 minutes, or until a golden brown. The fish will rise to the surface when done. Drain on absorbent paper. Serve very hot with:

Lemon Butter Sauce, 350, Tartare Sauce, 364, or Sour Cream Horseradish Dressing, 356

MARINATED DEEP-FAT-FRIED FISH

3 Servings

➤ Please read About Deep-Fat Frying, 147. Skin and cut into pieces:

1 1/2 lb. fish steaks: cod, halibut, catfish, whitefish, etc.

Marinate 30 minutes in:

6 tablespoons dry white wine or
2 tablespoons lemon juice

Drain dry and dip each piece separately in:

6 tablespoons cream

then in:

Flour

Fry the fish in deep fat heated to 370° about 7 minutes. Serve with:

Tartare Sauce, 364

FISH AND CHIPS

4 Servings

➤ Please read About Deep-Fat Frying, 147.
Cut into uniform serving pieces:

1 1/2 lb. skinned fillet of flounder

Coat with:

Fritter Batter for Fish, 243

Cut into thick uniform strips slightly larger than for French fries:

1 1/2 lb. mature baking potatoes

Soak in cold water for 1/2 hour. Drain and dry thoroughly. Fry in deep fat heated to 375° until golden brown. Remove, drain and keep warm. Deep-fry the breaded fish until golden brown. Arrange potatoes and fish on a platter and serve on the side as a dip:

Hot cider vinegar

or serve with:

Ravigote Sauce, 345

SOUTHERN-FRIED CATFISH

Clean and skin:

A catfish

Dredge with:

Seasoned white cornmeal

Fry in deep fat heated to 370° until golden brown. Serve with:

Hush Puppies, 629
Sliced Tomatoes, 105

and:

Sauce Dijonnaise, 342, or Allemande Sauce with capers, 345

ABOUT CARP

These great, languid soft-finned fish whose portraits we admire on Chinese scrolls can be admirable eating too. But be sure to hold them alive for several days in clear running water to rid them of the muddiness they acquire in their native haunts. To enjoy carp at their best, kill them just before cooking. If you cannot appoint a Lord High Executioner and must perform the act yourself, we recommend a preliminary perusal of the chapter called "Murder in the Kitchen" in Alice B. Toklas's weird and wonderful *Cookbook*.

Carp lend themselves to cooking Au Bleu, 414; are delicious baked, stuffed or braised; in red wine, 525; and may be eaten hot or cold. If cold, try Sauce Gribiche, 365, or Aioli Sauce, 365. Serve hot with new potatoes and Celeriac, 298.

ABOUT COD

Fabulous were the early voyagers' tales about the plenitude of cod, which gave its name to America's most curiously shaped and best-known cape. Because it was the mainstay of the colonists' diet, cod assumed many variations which persist today. **Scrod** is a term for cod weighing 2 pounds or under but may refer to pollock and haddock.

Salt cod, often very tough, is pounded before desalting. To freshen salt cod, leave it under running water for 6 hours; or soak it up to 48 hours in several changes of water in a glass, enamel or stainless steel pan. Salt cod is most often used flaked. To prepare for flaking, put the desalted fish in cold unsalted Court Bouillon, 525, to cover, then bring it to a boil and ➤ simmer 20 to 30 minutes. Drain, skin, bone and flake it. One pound dried salt cod will yield about 2 cups cooked flaked fish.

SCALLOPED COD

4 Servings

Preheat oven to 375°.
➤ Please read about Salt Cod, above.
Cook and flake:
1 lb. dried salt cod
Combine:
1 tablespoon flour
2 cups milk
1 well-beaten egg
Cook and stir these ingredients until they are thick, in the top of a double boiler ➤ over—not in—boiling water.
Season to taste
Prepare:
1½ cups bread crumbs
1½ cups finely chopped celery
Grease a baking dish. Place in it half the fish and a layer of one-third the crumbs and celery. Cover with half the sauce and repeat the process. Sprinkle the remaining crumbs on the top. Dot with:
Butter or grated cheese
Bake about 20 minutes, or until the crumbs are golden brown.

CODFISH BALLS OR CAKES

4 Servings

➤ Please read about Salt Cod, above.
Prepare:
1 cup desalted, flaked salt cod
Rice or mash:
6 medium-sized boiled potatoes, or half potatoes and half parsnips
Combine the fish and vegetables. Beat in one at a time:
2 eggs
Beat in until fluffy:
2 tablespoons cream
(1 teaspoon grated onion)
(1 teaspoon dry mustard)
(1 teaspoon Worcestershire sauce)
Season to taste
Shape the mixture into balls or patties, and use one of the following cooking methods.

I. Form the mixture into 2-inch cakes, dip in flour and sauté in butter until brown. Serve at once.

II. Form into 1-inch balls, dip in milk, roll in flour. Fry until golden brown in deep fat heated to 375°.

III. Preheat oven to 375°.
Form into patties and bake in a greased pan about 30 minutes. Dot with butter and serve.

With all of the above versions you may enjoy:
Hot Mustard Sauce, 345, Anchovy Sauce, 343, or Aurore Sauce, 344

FRESH COD À LA PORTUGAISE

4 Servings

Season:
4 thick cod fillets
with:
Pepper
Place the fish in a heavy saucepan. Add:
1 finely chopped onion
1 crushed clove garlic
¼ cup coarsely chopped parsley
A sprig of thyme
3 peeled, seeded and coarsely chopped tomatoes
½ cup dry white wine
Bring to boiling point, ➤ reduce the heat and simmer gently, covered, about 10 minutes. Remove the fish carefully. Arrange it on a hot serving dish and keep warm. Reduce the cooking liquid by one-third.
Season to taste
and finish with a:
Butter Swirl, 339
Pour the sauce over the fish and serve at once.

⅄ BRANDADE DE MORUE

10 Servings

Suitable for serving hot as a main dish or cold as an hors d'oeuvre, a brandade is in either case beaten to a mousselinelike consistency.
➤ Please read about Salt Cod, above.
Prepare for flaking and poach about 30 minutes in water to cover:
1½ lb. freshened salt cod
Have ready:
2 cups freshly boiled, riced potatoes
Drain and flake the fish and combine it with:
⅓ cup warm olive oil
in which you have sautéed, then removed:
2 cloves garlic
Have ready:
1 cup warm milk or cream
Put the fish and oil mixture into a blender alternately with the potatoes and the warm milk, and blend at moderate speed until it is smooth and fluffy. Serve it hot on a platter garnished with:
Grilled Tomatoes, 332, and
Buttered Croutons, 551
or chilled, garnished with:
Parsley and black olives

COD SOUNDS AND TONGUES

Allow About ¼ Pound per Serving

Sounds—or cod cheeks—and tongues, really the meat at the base of the tongue, may come fresh or salted. If salted, they must be soaked overnight,

drained, simmered 5 minutes in water started cold, then drained again.
To poach, cover with boiling water, reduce the heat and simmer about 5 minutes. Drain. You may serve them with:

Mornay Sauce, 342, or Allemande Sauce, 345

Or you may bread, 552, and sauté them until golden brown and serve with:

Maître d'Hôtel Butter, 350

FRESH COD BOULANGÈRE

4 Servings

Preheat oven to 350°.
Parboil in separate pans:

16 small peeled potatoes
12 small white onions

Place in a buttered shallow ovenproof dish:

A center cut of cod or a whole small cleaned cod

Arrange the onions and potatoes around it and sprinkle with:

A pinch of thyme
Season to taste

Brush frequently during the baking process with:

Melted butter

Bake about ½ hour. Serve in the same dish garnished with:

Chopped parsley
Slices of lemon

BROILED FRESH SCROD

Allow ½ Pound per Serving

Split, then remove the bones from:

A young codfish

Leave it whole, flatten it out, or cut it in pieces. Broil as described on 402.

ABOUT EEL

The eel is a fish that believes in long journeys. It is spawned in the Sargasso Sea in the western Atlantic, and from there will travel back to its freshwater haunts in this country or in Europe to feed and grow up in the rivers and streams frequented by its parents. The young eel or elver is still only 2 or 3 inches longer after its immense journey, and is transparent and yellowish. Little eels can be cooked and larger ones smoked or pickled to make a delicious addition to hors d'oeuvre or Antipasto, 78.

As with cats, there is more than one way to skin a fresh eel. We prefer the following. Keep the eel alive until ready to skin. Kill it with a sharp blow to the head. Slip a noose around the eel's head and hang the other end of the cord on a hook, high on the wall. Cut the eel skin about 3 inches below the head all around, so as not to penetrate the gallbladder, which lies close to the head. Peel the skin back, pulling down hard—if necessary with a pair of pliers—until the whole skin comes off like a glove. Clean the fish by slitting the white belly and removing the gut, which lies close to the thin belly skin.

Eel may be sautéed as for:

Trout à la Meunière, 414

poached 9 to 10 minutes and then served with a:

Velouté Sauce, 343

or one of its variations, made from the eel stock.

Skinned, cleaned, boned and cut into 3-inch pieces and dried, eel may be dipped in:

Batter, 243, or Bound Breading, 552

and deep-fried until golden brown. Serve this way with:

Fried Parsley, 314, and lemon wedges, or Tartare Sauce, 364, or a tomato sauce

Eel may also be broiled as for any fat fish, 402.

MARINATED FLOUNDER FILLETS

6 Servings

Marinate 10 minutes:

2 lb. flounder fillets

in:

1 cup tarragon vinegar

Drain, and coat with a mixture of:

½ cup yellow cornmeal
½ cup flour
¼ teaspoon salt
⅛ teaspoon freshly ground pepper

Sauté the fillets in:

¼ cup butter

until golden brown, about 4 minutes on each side. Serve with:

Ravigote Sauce, 345, or Nantua Sauce, 343

ABOUT HADDOCK

Fresh haddock may be prepared as in any recipe for cod, flounder or other lean white fish. It may be baked plain or stuffed, its fillets fried, sautéed, or poached. Smoked haddock—or **finnan haddie**—may be broiled, well basted in butter, or baked, as in the recipes below.

BAKED FILLETS OF FRESH HADDOCK IN CHEESE SAUCE

4 Servings

Preheat oven to 350°.
Place on an ovenproof dish:

4 haddock or other lean fish fillets

Prepare:

2 cups Mornay Sauce, 342

Season the sauce well, adding:

1 teaspoon Worcestershire sauce, or ½ teaspoon dry mustard, or 1 teaspoon fennel, dill or celery seed

Pour it over the fillets. Bake the fish until done, see 397. You may sprinkle over the top:

(1 cup or more freshly cooked or canned shrimp or crab meat)

Place the dish under a broiler until thoroughly warmed. Garnish with:

Chopped parsley

BAKED FILLETS OF FRESH HADDOCK WITH MUSHROOMS AND TOMATOES

6 Servings

Preheat oven to 375°.
Using a large saucepan, sauté about 5 minutes:
½ cup chopped onion
¼ cup chopped celery
½ cup chopped fresh mushrooms
in:
3 tablespoons butter
Stir into the sautéed vegetables:
2 cups soft bread crumbs
1 teaspoon salt
⅛ teaspoon pepper
A pinch of dried tarragon
(A pinch of dried rosemary)
Arrange in a layer on a large shallow greased baking dish:
2 lb. haddock fillets
Sprinkle the fish with:
Lemon juice
and spread the dressing over it. Cover with:
3 or 4 skinned sliced tomatoes
Bake uncovered 35 to 40 minutes. Serve with:
Boiled Potatoes, 317

BAKED FINNAN HADDIE

6 Servings

Preheat oven to 350°.
Prepare for cooking:
2 lb. smoked haddock
by soaking it in warm water for 30 minutes, skin side down. Pour off the water. Put the fish on a greased ovenproof pan and cover with:
1 cup cream
Dot generously with:
Butter
Sprinkle with:
¼ cup chopped onions
Paprika
Bake about 40 minutes. If cream evaporates, use additional cream. The dish may be served with:
Florentine Sauce, 342, or a tomato sauce, 352

CREAMED FINNAN HADDIE

Barely cover:
Smoked haddock
with:
Milk
Soak 1 hour. Bring slowly to the boiling point. Simmer 20 minutes. Drain. Flake and remove the skin and bones. Place the fish in very hot:
White Sauce I, 341
Use about two-thirds as much sauce as you have fish. Add for each cup of flaked fish:
1 chopped hard-cooked egg
1 teaspoon chopped green pepper, seeds and membrane removed
1 teaspoon chopped pimiento
Serve fish on:
Rounds of toast
sprinkled with:
Lemon juice
Chopped chives or parsley

CURED FISH

You may smoke your own fresh fish, 816, if you like, in which case they must be cooked before serving. Some commercially cured fish—smoked, dried, salted or pickled—come both preserved and prepared for serving. Haddock and several kinds of herring are usually Cold-Smoked, 814. They have been salted and smoked over a smoldering fire to the dry stage, but have not been cooked. Whitefish, chub and salmon are usually Hot-Smoked, 814, so that they cook in the heat of the smoking fire, and so can be used without further cooking. Haddock, when smoked, becomes **finnan haddie.** A smoked herring is known as a **kipper**—actually, a general term for any smoked fish. ➤ Store all smoked fish refrigerated in covered containers to lengthen their keeping period.

Cod, mackerel and herring are often salted and air-dried, and before cooking should be soaked in water for several hours—skin side down. If soaking in fresh running water is not practical, change the water frequently during the soaking period. For ways to cook, see Salt Cod, 404. Fish was often pickled in the days before refrigeration, and in eighteenth-century English and American cookbooks you will find recipes for "caveaching" fish in spices, oil and vinegar. We imagine there is a relationship between the French *escabèche,* and its Spanish variant, **seviche,** in word derivation and method. Nowadays, herring and mackerel are usully reserved for pickling, although Escabèche, 402, can be used for small fish, like fresh anchovies, sardines, young mullet and whiting.

ABOUT HERRING

Herring is one of the least expensive, most nutritious and readily obtainable fish one can buy. It is very fat, with a calcium content twice that of milk. "Kippering" originally referred to the reddening of certain types of salmon when salted and smoked at spawning time. Reddish color induced in other kinds of similarly processed fish is due to artificial coloring. Split, salted and smoked, a herring of any hue today is known as a **kipper;** smoke-cured without salt, as a **bloater.** Bloaters are very perishable and should be eaten right after curing. Perhaps the reason herring is not more popular is that it has innumerable tiny, fine bones. If you split a herring down the center of the back with a sharp knife, lever up the backbone and carefully pull it out, most of these small bones will come with it. After cleaning, 395, you may then cook the herring in one piece or split it in two.

Marinated herring comes in various disguises.

Rollmops, 88, are fresh herring fillets seasoned and rolled—like Paupiettes, 400—around a pickle or cucumber. **Bismarck herring** is the flat fillet in a sour marinade; **matjes** or virgin herring can be sour or salted. Commercially available, too, are female herring containing the "hard" roe, or egg-cluster, and male herring caught before the dispersal of their fertilizing fluid, or **milt**—sometimes also referred to as "soft" roe. Usually, when processed, both of these roes are extracted, thinned, and mixed with sour cream or a vinegar-based additive as the sauce in which the herring is packed. For more roe information, see 411.

BAKED HERRING AND POTATOES

4 Servings

I. Preheat oven to 375°.
To prepare salt herring, soak overnight in water or milk to cover:
2 large salt herring
Drain and split them. Remove and discard skin and bones. Cut fillets into 1-inch-wide pieces. Pare and slice very thinly:
6 raw potatoes
2 medium-sized onions
Butter a baking dish. Place in it alternate layers of potatoes, onions and herring, beginning and ending with potatoes. Cover the top with:
Au Gratin II, 552
Bake 45 minutes or more.

II. A Yorkshire version substitutes:
Sour apples
for the onions, and uses:
Fresh herring
In this case, prepare as above, but season with:
Salt and pepper
after each layer of herring.

MARINATED HERRING

12 Servings

Soak for 3 hours in water to cover:
24 milter herring
Change the water twice. Cut off the heads and tails. Split the herring. Remove the milt, see above. Reserve it. Remove the bones as described, 407. Discard them. Cut the fillets into pieces about 3 inches long. Place in a crock in alternate layers with the herring:
½ the milt
2 very thinly sliced lemons
2 skinned and thinly sliced onions
⅓ cup mixed pickle spices
1 tablespoon sugar
Cover these ingredients with:
Malt or other vinegar
Soften with a fork and add:
The remaining milt
Dilute the vinegar with a little water if it is very strong. ➤ Cover the crock and keep refrigerated. The herring will be ready to serve after one week.

SWEET AND SOUR HERRING

Allow 1 Herring per Serving

Prepare as for Marinated Herring, above:
6 milter herring
using only 1 lemon, 1 onion, 2½ tablespoons mixed spices and ¼ cup vinegar. Add:
1 cup cultured sour cream
Keep in a cool place. Serve after 48 hours.

SCOTCH FRIED HERRING

Allow 1 Herring per Serving

This dish must be made with:
Fresh-caught herring
You may fry them whole, but they are better split down the backbone and boned, as described, 407. Cut off head, tail and fins. Roll in:
Medium-ground seasoned Scotch oatmeal
pressing a little to make it stick. Fry the herring on both sides in:
Bacon fat or olive oil
Serve with:
Lemon wedges
A pat of butter
or with:
Hot Mustard Sauce, 345
Garnish with:
Parsley

GRILLED OR BAKED KIPPERS OR BLOATERS

Allow ½ Pound per Serving

An excellent breakfast dish with scrambled eggs. Do not try to grill canned kippers; they are too wet.
Preheat broiler.
Place:
Kippers or bloaters
skin side down on a hot oiled grill. Dot with:
Butter
Grill 5 to 7 minutes. Serve very hot. You may also bake them in a 350° oven 10 minutes, or En Papillote, 153, 15 minutes at the same temperature. Season with:
A little lemon juice
Pepper

ABOUT OCTOPUS AND SQUID

Both of these **inkfish** belong emphatically to the large category of horrendous-looking sea creatures that must be eaten to be appreciated. These mollusks are not dissimilar in shape and taste, having long edible arms, a tail portion that can be formed into a natural sack for stuffing if desired, as well as an ink-expelling sac which furnishes the pigment known as sepia. The latter is used in recipes just as blood is used, 339, to color, flavor and give body to sauces, often seasoned with nutmeg and garlic. When the ink is not available, it is sometimes faked by the use of chocolate, as in the sauce for Turkey Mole, 428.

Octopus, which has eight arms, grows to enormous size but is apt to be very tough if over 2 to

2½ pounds in weight. These and squid that are longer than 8 inches after cleaning need tenderizing. Pound them mercilessly on a solid surface.

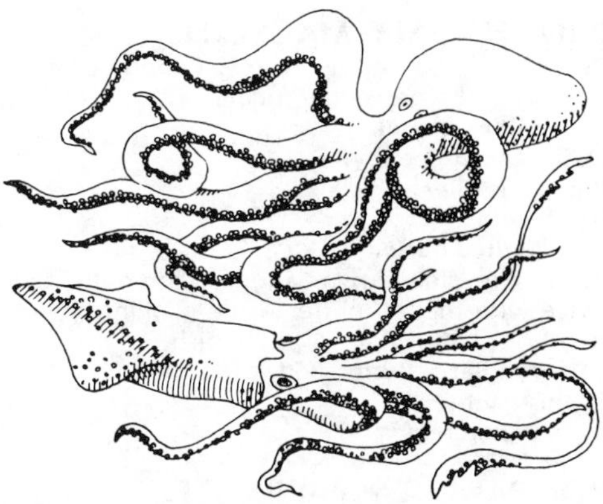

To prepare fresh octopus for cooking, make sure first that your victim is dead—by striking it a conclusive blow on the head. Remove the beaklike mouth, the anal portion and the eyes, taking care in doing so not to pierce the ink sac, which lies close by. Reserve this for later use. If the inkfish is small, these operations may be performed with a pair of scissors; if larger, you will need a knife to penetrate far enough to slip the creature inside out and remove and discard the yellowish pouch and the attached membranes. With octopus the very ends of the tentacles are also discarded. Cut out all cartilage and wash the fish well in running water to remove gelatinous portions.

Preparation procedure for fresh squid differs somewhat. After the same advance precautions—squid bite, too—grasp the head section firmly at a point just below the eyes. You can then pull free from the rest of the body the outer portion of the tail and fin section. Also revealed will be the grayish ink sac. Remove it carefully to a sieve. Next, cut the tentacles free just above the eye section. Discard the eye section along with the innards and a small roundish cartilage at the base of the tentacles which can be popped out with the fingers. Discard also the icicle-shaped pen or cuttlebone inside the tail. This slim bone, when dried, becomes the bone one sees in bird cages. You will also encounter a red membrane which covers much of the squid. This should be as nearly removed as possible by rubbing, or by parblanching briefly 1 to 2 minutes. Arrest further cooking by plunging into cold water. When plunging octopus into boiling water, drop it in with a sliding motion head first so its tentacles won't spread out. Remaining then, as edible, are the tentacles and the peeled tail section and fins, as well as the ink sac fluid, which, like that of the octopus, makes a flavorsome seasoning for a sauce.

With both types of inkfish, arms and tentacles are cut crosswise in 1- to 1¼-inch rounds, and to equalize the cooking time, the white portions of the body meat are often cut into squares or diamond shapes of about the same size. Octopus need long, slow cooking. Even after marinating, the simmering time may run close to 3 hours, unless the specimens are very young, when about 50 minutes should suffice. For squid cooking times, see individual recipes.

Squid is available in cans ready to use and is sometimes found frozen or dried. ➤ To use dried squid, marinate in a combination of water, gin and ginger for 45 minutes, and then use in recipes as for the fresh meat.

➤ Allow about ½ pound of fresh squid or octopus per serving.

CASSEROLED OCTOPUS OR SQUID

Allow ½ Pound per Person

Clean, pound, and cut up as described above and place in a flameproof casserole:

6 small octopus or squid
½ cup olive oil
⅓ cup vinegar or ½ cup dry wine
2 cups julienned mushrooms
1 cup chopped onions
1 pressed clove garlic
1 tablespoon each fresh chopped parsley, chervil and basil
⅓ bay leaf

Cover and bring just to a boil. ➤ Reduce the heat at once and simmer, very tightly covered, 2½ to 3 hours. You may add the ink to the pan drippings just before serving. ➤ Do not boil. Serve with:

Creamed Spinach, 327

FRIED SQUID

Allow ½ Pound per Person

Clean and wash as described above. Leave whole or cut into 1- to 1½-inch pieces:

Small squid

Some sophisticates discard the tentacles. Clean the pouch well, removing the cuttlebone in the flesh at the back and using only the remaining flesh, cut into narrow strips. Dry well and dust with:

Flour

Deep-fry at 365° until golden brown. Serve at once sprinkled with:

Salt, white pepper and lemon juice

STUFFED SQUID

Allow 2 per Person

Choose:

Twelve 5-inch squid

Cut below the eyes and discard the head and tentacles. Without splitting, clean the pouch thoroughly, removing the bone. Cut out the fins and pull off the black skin.
Preheat oven to 325°.
Prepare half of the recipe for:

Rice Dressing for Cornish Hen, 373

and stuff each squid and tie each pouch at the top.

Place them in a single layer in an ovenproof baking dish and cover with a mixture of:

1/4 cup olive oil
1/4 cup tomato sauce
1/2 cup white wine
1/2 cup water
1/4 cup finely chopped parsley

Sprinkle this sauce with a heavy coating of:

Dry bread crumbs

Bake about 1 hour and 15 minutes or until the squid is tender. Serve hot or cold.

SQUID IN INK SAUCE

4 Servings

➤ Please read About Squid, 408.

Clean and cut up:

2 lb. squid

Place the ink sacs in a sieve and press the ink into a bowl beneath it. To extract more ink, pour over the ink sacs while continuing to press:

1 cup water

Add to the ink mixture and beat until smooth:

1 1/2 tablespoons flour
A grating of nutmeg

and reserve this mixture. Heat in a heavy skillet:

3/4 cup olive oil

When hot, sauté until translucent:

3/4 cup chopped onions
1 pressed clove garlic

Then add the cut-up squid. Reduce heat at once. Simmer covered about 20 minutes. Add the ink mixture. Stir constantly over low heat at least 5 minutes until the sauce thickens. ➤ Do not allow the sauce to boil.

Season to taste

and serve at once over:

Pasta, 213, or Boiled Rice, 206

BROILED FRESH MACKEREL

Preheat broiler.

Split and bone, see 395:

A fresh mackerel

Place it skin side down in a greased pan. Sprinkle with:

Paprika

Brush with:

Melted butter or olive oil

Broil slowly on one side only until firm, about 20 minutes. Baste with the drippings while cooking. Remove to a hot platter. Spread with:

Anchovy Butter, 350

Garnish with:

Parsley and lemon slices

BOILED SALT MACKEREL

Allow 1/3 to 1/2 Pound per Serving

Soak overnight, skin side up, well covered with cold water:

Salt mackerel

Drain, place in a shallow pan, cover with water and simmer until tender, about 12 minutes. Drain well. Place on a hot platter. Pour over the fish:

Melted butter

to which add:

Chopped chives or parsley, lemon juice or Worcestershire sauce

BROILED SALT MACKEREL

Allow 1/3 to 1/2 Pound per Serving

Soak as in the preceding recipe:

Salt mackerel

Drain, then wipe dry.

Preheat broiler.

Brush with:

Melted butter

Broil, skin side down, about 20 minutes. Baste twice with melted butter while cooking. Remove to a hot platter. Pour over the fish:

1/2 cup Bercy Butter, 350

Garnish with:

Watercress

POMPANO EN PAPILLOTE

Individual Serving

Preheat oven to 450°.

Place on heart-shaped parchment paper, 151:

2 medium-sized skinned pompano fillets

Cover with:

Shrimp Sauce, 343

Close the parchment paper, fold the edge and bake about 15 minutes until the paper is browned and puffed. Serve immediately. For a party, make individual packets ahead of time, refrigerate and, before baking, allow them to reach about 60°. Preheat oven and bake as above.

ABOUT SALMON

Atlantic salmon, pink and prized, comes to our markets mainly fresh, pink—and prized. In England it wasn't always so. Indentured apprentices petitioned that they should not be forced to eat fresh salmon more than twice a week!

Pacific salmon reaches us in many forms. These include the choice King or Chinook from Alaska and the Columbia River areas. They may be pink or white-fleshed and are about 17% fat. Included also are the red-fleshed sockeye, the pinkish silver Coho and the yellowish-fleshed, almost fat-free dog salmon. ➤ All smoked salmon, including the delicious **lox,** is highly perishable and should be kept refrigerated. For other salmon dishes, see Brunch, Lunch and Supper Dishes, 264–268.

BROILED SALMON STEAKS OR DARNES

Allow 1/2 Pound per Serving

Preheat broiler.

To cut steaks or darnes, see 396.

Brush preheated broiler rack and:

3/4-inch-thick salmon steaks

well with:

Clarified Butter, 349

Place rack 6 inches from the source of heat. Broil 5 minutes. Baste, turn, baste again and continue to broil 5 to 8 minutes. To test for doneness, see if you can lift out the central bone without bringing any of the flesh with it. Serve with:

Freshly grated horseradish

The steak shape lends itself to attractive service, as the hollow may be filled with:

A stuffed tomato, or a mound of vegetables, or potatoes garnished with parsley

More elaborate dressings for this dish are:

(Sour Cream Horseradish Dressing, 356, or Hot Mustard Sauce, 345)

COLD GLAZED SALMON

Allow ½ Pound per Serving

This method of preparation applies to any fish you wish to glaze and serve cold.

Poach, 400, leaving head and tail on:

1 large cleaned salmon

Remove from the poaching water when done. Leaving the head and tail, and working with the grain, skin and trim the rest of the fish, removing the fins and the gray, fatty portions until just the pink flesh is left. Place on a large serving platter and refrigerate. If time is limited, the fish may be eaten just this way with mayonnaise. But to glaze—and build up to a culinary event—read on. ➤ Work quickly to prevent the glaze from darkening, and keep chilling between processes. Coat the visible pink portion of the fish evenly and smoothly with:

Mayonnaise Collée, 368, or
Sauce Chaud-Froid, 369

Rechill until this sauce has set. Decorate as described in the Sauce Chaud-Froid recipe. Chill again. Coat the whole surface, head and tail too, with:

Aspic Glaze, 368

Chill and continue coating and chilling until you have built up an even clear ¼ inch of aspic. Clean the platter by removing aspic dribbles. Save any leftover aspic and chill it in sheet form. Chop it fine and surround the fish with an edging of little sparkling tidbits. Serve the fish with:

Andalouse Sauce, 364, or
Green Mayonnaise, 364

The classic garnish is:

Tiny tomatoes stuffed with Russian Salad, 105

We suggest also:

Cold leeks marinated, 306

ABOUT SARDINES

Sardines were to us something that came out of a can on laundry day—until one summer we entertained a Breton guest. Her family had for centuries lived an amicably divided life in seaside castles on opposite sides of a river inlet. Her uncle's fleets dredged seaweed from which chemicals were produced. Her father's fleet sailed from Maine to Spain—following those Atlantic sardines which were fit even for the Czar of Russia himself, to whom they were purveyed. But fish, like people, may change habits suddenly. For three years the fleet failed to find the sardine runs. Sonar might have changed Odette's fate, but Brittany's loss was our vivacious and warmhearted gain.

True sardines are types of herring, and those caught in the Pacific are much larger—up to 10 or 12 inches long—than those taken in Atlantic or Mediterranean waters, which are known in Britain and the Dominions as **pilchard. Anchovies** and **sprats** are closely related. Treat fresh sardines as for smelts, 412.

If you want to present canned sardines in an interesting way, skin and bone:

12 canned sardines

Mash 6 of them with:

1 teaspoon minced onion
2 teaspoons butter
½ teaspoon prepared mustard
1 teaspoon lemon juice

Spread:

6 narrow toast strips

with this mixture. Place a whole sardine on each toast and run under the broiler. Before serving, garnish with:

Finely chopped fennel
A grating of black pepper

ABOUT SEA SQUAB OR BLOWFISH

These puffers are related to the sought-after Japanese fugu. As the ovaries and liver are very poisonous, be sure to discard all but the back flesh before cooking. Prepare as for any delicate fish.

ABOUT ROE AND MILT

The eggs of the female fish are known as **roe** or hard roe; the male fish's sperm is known as **milt** or soft roe, as its texture is creamy rather than grainy. Both types are used in cooking, and the roe of certain fish is more valued than the fish itself, see Caviar, 87.

Shad roe is considered choice. You may serve the roe or milt of other fish such as herring, mackerel, flounder, salmon, carp, or cod as in the following recipes for shad roe. The milt of salmon must have the vein removed.

Hard roe, to be cooked and served alone, should be pricked with a needle to prevent the membrane from bursting and splattering the little eggs. Cook roe gently with very slow heat. Overcooked, it is hard, dry and tasteless. If pepper is used in seasoning, use only white pepper. Roe may be served as a luncheon dish; as a savory; as stuffing or garnish for the fish from which it comes. Or it may be used raw, as in Marinated Herring, 408, or as an hors d'oeuvre. Also see canned roe dishes, 268.

➤ Allow 6 oz. per serving.

PARBOILED SHAD ROE

➤ Please read About Roe, above.

Prick with a needle in several places and cover with boiling water:

Shad roe

Add to it:

2 tablespoons lemon juice or
3 tablespoons dry white wine

Simmer from 3 to 12 minutes, according to size. Drain and cool. Remove the membrane. Add salt if needed. The roe is now ready to be sautéed, sauced, or used in a garnish or hors d'oeuvre.

BAKED SHAD ROE

Preheat oven to 375°.
Parboil, see above:

Shad roe

Place in a buttered pan. Cover with.

Creole Sauce, 348
Mushroom Wine Sauce, 347

Bake 15 or 20 minutes, basting every 5 minutes.

SAUTÉED SHAD ROE

Heat until light brown:

2 tablespoons Clarified Butter, 349

Sauté in this until delicately browned on both sides:

Parboiled Shad Roe, above
Season to taste

Remove to a hot platter. Add to the drippings and heat:

2 teaspoons lemon juice
½ teaspoon chopped chives
½ teaspoon chopped parsley
1 minced shallot
½ teaspoon dried tarragon, chervil or basil

Pour the sauce over the roe. Sautéed roe may also be served with:

(Mornay Sauce, 342, or Suprême Sauce, 344, or Brown Butter, 349)

sprinkled with:

(Lemon juice and chopped parsley)

and surrounded by:

(Peeled orange sections)

BROILED SHAD ROE

Preheat broiler.
Parboil, see above, wipe dry and place on a greased rack:

Shad roe

Sprinkle with:

Lemon juice

Bard, 420, with:

Bacon

Broil from 5 to 7 minutes. If the roe is large, you may have to turn it, baste with drippings and cook until firm. Serve on toast garnished with:

Maître d'Hôtel Butter, 350
Parsley

ABOUT BONING AND CARVING SHAD

These are painstaking procedures. Sometimes the fishmonger can be inveigled into boning: an ounce of expertise in this difficult area is worth a pound of private initiative. Otherwise boning is a catch-as-catch-can affair: even tweezers may be necessary, since every effort must be made to remove as many bones as possible before cooking. When carving time comes, the fish is sliced completely through its entire thickness in about 4-inch parallel widths. Any exposed bones may again be removed with tweezers before the cut pieces are put on the individual plates.

BAKED SHAD WITH CREAMED ROE

6 to 8 Servings

Preheat oven to 350°.
Bone, see above:

A 3- or 4-lb. shad

Place it skin side down on a well-greased broiler rack or a flat pan. Brush with:

Melted butter

Bake, allowing about 8 minutes per pound. While the shad is baking, parboil, see above:

Shad roe

➤ Simmer 15 minutes. Drain. Remove the outside membrane. Mash the roe. Melt in a saucepan:

2 tablespoons butter

You may add and sauté about 3 minutes:

(1 tablespoon grated onion)

Add the roe and stir in:

2 tablespoons flour
½ cup cream

When these ingredients begin to boil, remove from heat. Stir in:

2 egg yolks

Season the roe mixture well with·

2 tablespoons lemon juice

Spread the creamed roe over the baked fish and cover with:

Au Gratin II, 552

Return to the broiler and brown evenly. Serve at once garnished with:

Lemon slices
Parsley or watercress
Pickled beets or cucumbers

ABOUT SHARK

If you are an adventurer—or adventuress—you will find that shark meat that is close to and along the backbone responds to recipes for Fish Fillets, 399, or to Poaching, 400. The belly sections need long simmering.

SMELTS

2 Servings

Clean, 395, rinse thoroughly and wipe dry:

12 smelts

Leave whole. Season with:

Lemon juice

Let them stand covered for 15 minutes. Roll the smelts in:

Cream

Dip in:

Flour or cornmeal

and cook by one of the following methods

I. Melt:

¼ cup butter

Sauté the smelts gently in the butter until done.

II. Bake smelts in a buttered pan in a 450° oven about 8 to 10 minutes. Place them on a hot platter. Add to the butter in the pan:

Juice of 1 lemon
2 tablespoons chopped parsley or chives

Pour the sauce over the smelts.

III. ➤ Please read About Deep-Fat Frying, 147. Smelts may be dipped in crumbs or in egg and crumbs and fried about 3 minutes in deep fat heated to 370°. Serve with:

Tartare Sauce, 364

BAKED RED SNAPPER WITH SAVORY TOMATO SAUCE

4 to 6 Servings

Preheat oven to 350°.
Prepare for cooking:

A 3-lb. red snapper or other large fish

Dredge it inside and out with:

Seasoned flour

Place in a baking pan. Melt:

6 tablespoons butter

Add and simmer 15 minutes:

½ cup chopped onion
2 cups chopped celery
¼ cup chopped green pepper, seeds and membrane removed

Add and simmer until the celery is tender:

3 cups drained canned tomatoes
1 tablespoon Worcestershire sauce
1 tablespoon catsup
1 teaspoon chili powder
½ finely sliced lemon
2 bay leaves
1 minced clove garlic
1 teaspoon salt
A few grains red pepper

Press these ingredients through a potato ricer or food mill. Pour the sauce around the fish. Bake about 45 minutes, basting frequently with the sauce. To test for doneness, see 397.

ABOUT FILLETS OF SOLE

The recipes which follow call for fillets of English or lemon sole—European flat fish flown fresh into better markets or available frozen. ➤ If frozen, the fish must be thawed completely before proceeding. These recipes are often prepared from more easily available fillets of flounder, freshwater trout, bluefish, brill or other fish that flake readily. For this reason the fish is usually served sauced in the baking dish in which it was cooked. ➤ Do not overcook. For other recipes for fish fillets, see 399–401.

SOLE VÉRONIQUE

4 Servings

Marinate for about 1 hour in:

1 cup dry white wine
1½ cups skinned seedless grapes

Drain grapes, reserving the wine.
Preheat oven to 350°.
In a large skillet, place:

2 lb. skinned fillets of sole

which have been carefully dried between paper towels. Heat the reserved wine and add to the fillets. Cover with a buttered poaching paper, 151, and simmer about 10 minutes or until fillets are opaque. Then, keeping the fish warm, place them in an ovenproof baking dish. If necessary reduce the fish stock to 1 cup for use in preparing:

White Wine Sauce, 345

Fold into the sauce the marinated grapes and:

½ cup whipping cream
(1 tablespoon curaçao)

Coat the fish with this mixture and run the dish under a preheated broiler until the sauce colors. Serve at once, garnished with crescents and diamonds of egg-glazed:

Puff Paste, 643

SOLE AMBASSADEUR

Allow ½ Pound per Person

Prepare for poaching:

10 skinned fillets of sole—lemon or English—trout or halibut

Place in a buttered heatproof dish or skillet and sprinkle with:

1 tablespoon finely chopped shallot or onion
Salt and pepper

Add:

½ cup dry white wine
Juice of 1 lemon

Cover with a buttered poaching paper, 151, and simmer until the fillets are done, see 397. While they are cooking, melt in a heavy saucepan:

1 tablespoon butter

Sauté in the butter:

1 cup finely chopped mushrooms
Juice of ½ lemon
Salt and pepper

Cook over high heat about 3 minutes, until the juices disappear. Reduce heat. Add:

½ cup whipping cream

➤ Simmer until reduced by a third. Remove from the heat and beat in:

1 egg yolk

Drain and save the stock from the fish. Spread the mushroom mixture on a heatproof serving platter and arrange the fillets over it. Heat the fish stock and add:

Kneaded Butter, 340

Beat in well until thickened. Add:

½ cup whipping cream

Heat to the boiling point. ➤ Remove from the heat and add:

3 egg yolks

Strain the sauce and pour it over the fish fillets. Glaze under the broiler until brown. Serve at once.

SOLE DUGLÉRÉ

4 Servings

Preheat oven to 350°.
Prepare and dry well between paper towels:
2 lb. skinned fillets of sole
Sprinkle with:
2 tablespoons lemon juice
Sauté in a skillet:
¼ cup finely chopped shallots
¼ cup finely chopped mushrooms
2 tablespoons very finely chopped parsley
in:
3 tablespoons butter
Add the fish and:
1 cup dry white wine
Bring to a boil. Reduce heat at once and cover pan with a buttered poaching paper, 151. Remove pan to oven and bake about 10 minutes or until fish is opaque. Prepare, meanwhile, a fresh tomato purée by skinning and dicing:
1 lb. tomatoes
from which you have scraped out the seeds, 331. Place the fish in a buttered ovenproof baking dish, reserving the stock. If necessary reduce the stock to about 1 cup and use it in preparing:
White Wine Sauce, 345
to replace the stock and wine in that recipe. When the sauce thickens, add the puréed tomatoes. Pour the sauce over the fish. Sprinkle the top generously with:
Grated Parmesan cheese
mixed with:
A dash of paprika
Run under a broiler until the sauce colors.

FILLETS OF SOLE FLORENTINE

6 Servings

Poach, 400:
6 fillets of sole or other fish
In the bottom of an ovenproof platter, put a layer of:
1½ cups Creamed Spinach, 327
Arrange the poached, drained fillets on top. Cover with:
1 cup seasoned White Sauce II, 341
Sprinkle over it:
Au Gratin III, 552
Run under the broiler to heat through until the sauce is glazed.
To prepare **Sole Marguéry,** see Fish Steaks Marguéry, 400.

SWORDFISH STEAKS

Prepare as for:
Salmon Steaks, 410
This fish dries out even when in prime condition; be sure to use plenty of butter in the cooking.

BROOK TROUT MEUNIÈRE

4 Servings

Clean and wash:
4 brook trout: 8 inches each
Cut off the fins. Leave the heads and tails on. Dip in:
Seasoned flour
Melt:
¼ cup Clarified Butter, 349
Sauté the trout until they are firm and nicely browned. Remove to a hot platter. Add to the drippings in the pan:
3 tablespoons clarified butter
Let it brown. Cover the fish with:
Chopped parsley
Pour the browned butter over the fish. Garnish with:
Lemon wedges

BROILED LAKE TROUT OR WHITEFISH

Allow About ½ Pound per Serving

Preheat broiler.
Bone, 396:
A large lake trout or whitefish
Flatten it out or cut it into pieces. Rub a saucer with:
Garlic
Mix in it:
1 or 2 tablespoons olive oil
¼ teaspoon white pepper
Rub the fish on both sides with these ingredients. Place it in a greased shallow pan. Broil until brown, turning once. Spread with.
Maître d'Hôtel Butter, 350
or Lemon Butter, 350
Garnish with:
Parsley
Wilted Cucumbers, 102

BLUE TROUT OR TRUITE AU BLEU

Allow One 4- to 6½-Ounce Trout or Other Freshwater Fish per Person

It is only the skin that turns so brilliant a blue under this procedure, not—of course—the whole fish. But this startling achievement is only possible if your fish is alive when brought to the kitchen and if, in cleaning, it is handled so carefully that its natural coating of slime is left undisturbed. We ate these first in the Black Forest at an inn bordering a stream, but we think of them always in connection with Joseph Wechsberg's zestful book, *Blue Trout and Black Truffles.*
Have ready and boiling:
Court Bouillon for Fish, 525, using vinegar rather than wine
Kill the fish with one sharp blow on the head. Split and clean it with a single stroke if possible. Plunge it at once into the boiling water. Let the water come to a boil again, then remove the pan from the heat and cover it, allowing it to stand about

5 minutes, although the larger-sized fish may need another 2 or 3 minutes. The white eyeballs pop out when the fish is done. Remove the fish and drain well. Serve, if hot, with a flourish and a garnish of:

Parsley

and:

Boiled or steamed potatoes and sweet butter balls, or melted butter

You may also serve other fancy butters or:

(Hollandaise Sauce, 358)

If you serve the fish cold, pass:

Sauce Gribiche, 365, or
Watercress Sauce, 365

ABOUT TUNA

Very widely distributed and of widely differing characteristics, tuna range in size from the **bluefin** or **tunny**—a magnificent game fish which may weigh up to 1500 pounds—to the much smaller **albacore,** which furnishes the whitest and choicest meat. Most of us come by our tuna in prosaic tins. The label on the can must now show whether the fish is "white," "light," or "dark"—the darker grades being of inferior flavor; and designate the nature of the packing medium: olive oil, vegetable oil or water. It must also indicate whether the contents are "solid pack," that is, mostly in one piece; "chunk," or made up of irregular pieces; "flake," of less desirable irregular pieces; or "grated," pieces cut to small uniform size. Smoked canned tuna must also be so identified. To find additional recipes for canned tuna, see Index.

FRESH TUNA OR BONITO

Allow ½ Pound per Serving

Clean:

A fresh tuna or bonito

Braise or roast as for veal, or brush the delicate stomach sections with:

Vegetable oil

and broil.

POACHED TURBOT

Allow ½ Pound per Serving

This firm-fleshed, very white flat fish may be skinned and filleted, 396, and poached in Court Bouillon, 525, with part wine—or part milk to reinforce its whiteness—and cooked as for any recipe for Sole, 413. As both the skin and the gelatinous areas near the fins are considered delicacies, turbot is often cooked and served unskinned. To keep it from curling or bursting, cut a long gash down the center of the brown underside before poaching.

To cook in the skin, place the fish in a greased pan; float it in a cool:

Court Bouillon, 525

Cover with a poaching paper, 151. Bring the liquid to a boil. ➤ Reduce the heat at once. Barely simmer about 30 minutes, basting several times during the cooking. Be sure to seal the paper after each basting. Serve with:

Soubise Sauce, 344, or
Champagne Sauce, 344

WHITEBAIT OR BLANCHAILLE

Whitebait are really minnows, or the small fry of fresh or saltwater fish. Pick over, and wash only if necessary:

Whitebait

Roll them in:

Seasoned Flour I, 552

Fry 2 to 3 minutes, depending on size, in deep fat heated to 375°. Garnish with:

Lemon slices

ABOUT FROG LEGS

Frog legs resemble chicken in texture and flavor. They are usually bought skinned and ready to use. Allow 2 large or 6 small frog legs per person. If the frogs are not prepared, cut off and discard the feet; then cut off the hind legs—the only part of the frog used—close to the body. Separate and wash the legs in cold water. Begin at the top and strip off the skin like a glove. Through an experiment with a twitching frog leg, Galvani discovered the electric current that bears his name. Should you prefer keeping your kitchen and your scientific activities separate and distinct, chill the frog legs before skinning.

BRAISED FROG LEGS

4 Servings

Clean:

8 large frog legs

Roll them in:

Seasoned flour

Melt in a skillet:

6 tablespoons Clarified Butter, 349

Add to it:

½ cup chopped onions

Brown the frog legs in the butter. Reduce the heat and add:

¾ cup boiling Light Stock, 523

Cover skillet closely and cook the frog legs until tender, about 10 minutes. Melt:

6 tablespoons butter

Sauté in the butter:

1¼ cups seasoned bread crumbs
(¾ cup finely chopped hazelnuts)

Add:

1 teaspoon lemon juice

Roll the frog legs in the bread crumbs and serve them garnished with:

Fennel

or, if you have used the hazelnuts, with:

Parsley

DEEP-FAT-FRIED FROG LEGS

➤ Please read About Deep-Fat Frying, 147.

Clean:

Frog legs

Dip them in:

A Bound Breading, 552

Let dry for 1 hour. Fry the frog legs in deep fat heated to 375° until golden. Drain. Serve with:

Tartare Sauce, 364

FROG LEGS IN MUSHROOM SAUCE

3 Servings

Clean:

6 large frog legs

Cut the meat from each leg into 3 or 4 pieces. Place the meat in a saucepan. Cover with:

Boiling water or Light Stock, 523

Add:

2 thin slices lemon
1/8 teaspoon white pepper
(Celery, parsley, onion or vegetables suitable for soup)

Simmer the frog meat, covered, until tender. Drain well. Melt in a saucepan:

3 tablespoons butter

Add to it and sauté until light brown:

1 cup sliced mushrooms

Stir in:

1 1/2 tablespoons flour

Stir in slowly:

1 1/2 cups chicken stock or stock in which the frog legs were cooked
Season to taste

When the sauce is hot, add the frog meat. Reduce the heat to low. Beat well:

3 egg yolks
3 tablespoons rich cream

Stir these ingredients into the sauce. Let the entire mixture thicken off the heat. Serve the meat at once, covered with the sauce.

FROG LEGS FORESTIÈRE

Allow 5 per Serving

Sprinkle:

Small frog legs

with:

Brandy

Let stand about 2 hours refrigerated and wipe dry. Sauté them in:

Clarified Butter, 349

During the last few minutes of cooking, when the frog legs become firm to the touch, sauté with the meat for each portion:

2 thinly sliced mushrooms
1 tablespoon chopped parsley
1 teaspoon lemon juice
(1 tablespoon very finely sliced fresh sweet red pepper)
Season to taste

POULTRY AND WILDFOWL

The chicken is a world citizen; duck, turkey and geese cosmopolites. Along with a number of the game birds that migrate from continent to continent, they are international favorites. And each nation has learned to cook them in a manner distinctively its own. The worldly wise cook will not be content with chicken and dumplings, roast turkey, or quail served on a crouton, but instead will welcome into the kitchen some of the specialties that have enlivened a global cuisine: from Italy, chicken caccicatore, illustrated above left; pressed duck from France, for which the equipment is shown at the rear; from Mexico, turkey mole; from Germany, Gänseklein. The principles of cooking poultry and game birds are just sufficiently different to warrant separate treatment, wildfowl having its own peculiarities in handling even before cooking. There is the need to keep wild birds aired after shooting, and to the hunter interested in bringing home his booty in prime condition, a carrying strap such as that shown in the center foreground above is as important a piece of equipment as the wooden decoy shown behind it. Then there are determinations to be made as to the age of the bird and how long it should be hung—the results of which establish the specific method of cooking.

Whether you shoot your bird or buy it, you will always have to assess its quality and potential, sizing it up for the application of the cooking techniques that will be suitable and rewarding. ➤ See, for example, under the Dry Heat processes, 146, ways to cook young birds. For birds of questionable age, consult the Moist Heat processes, 149, or cook them in milk, or marinate them to tenderize them.

The preliminary steps are similar for all fowl, whether barnyard variety or rara avis.

ABOUT POULTRY

That poultry served immediately after slaughtering is not a delicacy was brought home to me early when my father and I would go down to check Grandfather's holdings at Brickeys on the Mississippi. As the local landlady at whose abode my grandfather kept quarters saw us get off the train —for everyone looked out for newcomers and talked to the engineer while the engine was "watered"—she would dash to the yard behind her house, grab for the axe and behead the nearest chicken. The less said about lunch the better. So we learned early that quick cooling and hanging in a cool place from 8 to 24 hours will avoid stringiness and develop flavor. Cut-up poultry is more perishable than whole birds, and turkey and duck more perishable than chicken. All poultry is difficult to keep well in home refrigerators. When you buy poultry in an airtight wrapping, loosen the wrapping before refrigerating. Dressed poultry should be washed in running water before cooking. If you have to hold it more than a day or two, cook it, then reheat it in a sauce before serving.

Poultry must be cooked thoroughly at one time—never partially cooked and then stored for finishing later. Cooked poultry, stuffing and broth should be used within 2 days. ➤ Always remove the stuffing and store it in a separate container before refrigerating the loosely wrapped cooked meat.

For amounts of bird to allow per serving, see individual recipes; but if a large number of people are to be fed, turkey meat is the least expensive and turkey breast yields the greatest amount of protein per pound. The net amount of edible meat, minus fat or skin, is about 46% for turkeys, 41% for chicken and 22% for duckling.

A federal inspection stamp for dressed poultry sold in interstate commerce is mandatory, but as the stamp is placed on the carton rather than the bird, the consumer has no way of knowing whether he is purchasing inspected poultry.

ABOUT FROZEN POULTRY

We are less than one hundred percent advocates of frozen poultry. Sometimes the fowl have been watered before freezing, and the weight loss on thawing may make them more expensive as well as less flavorful. Watch too for "freezer burn"—brownish skin areas that are telltale evidence of dehydration or improper storage. We do not advocate purchasing ready-stuffed frozen fowl, but if you should buy one ➤ never thaw it before cooking, but transfer it directly from freezer to hot oven. And ➤ read packer's directions carefully. Also available frozen are the so-called self-basting turkeys, in which butter or oil has been inserted into the breast meat before freezing. The fat bubbles out during the roasting process to baste the skin.

➤ Unstuffed frozen birds should be thawed before cooking. Thawing a large bird in the refrigerator may take several days, so buy your fowl well in advance. Leave the bird in its original bag, place it on a tray in the refrigerator and thaw 1 to 2 days for a bird weighing 4 to 12 pounds; 2 to 3 days for 12 to 20 pounds; 3 to 4 days for 20 to 24 pounds. A faster way to thaw is to leave poultry well sealed in original bag and place in cold water for 2 to 7 hours, depending on size. Change the water frequently. When the flesh is pliable, the bird is ready to cook. ➤ Thawed poultry must be cooked at once.

PLUCKING AND SINGEING POULTRY

Poultry is usually plucked and drawn when purchased. Buy dry-picked poultry whenever possible. If not already done, pluck it at once—except for those game birds which must hang and are easier to pluck later. It is much easier to pluck and draw a bird that is thoroughly chilled. After plucking the bird, remove all pinfeathers. Use a pair of tweezers, or grasp each pinfeather between forefinger and the tip of a knife, then pull.

After removing the coarser feathers, if those remaining are downy or small, you may use the paraffin method. Make up a mixture of 3/8 pound melted paraffin and 7 quarts boiling water. Brush enough of this mixture over the bird to cover. Allow it to harden. Pull off the paraffined coating, and it will carry the feathers with it.

➤ To singe a bird, hold it by the legs and singe the pinfeathers over a gas flame or a candle. Turn it so that all parts of the skin are exposed to the heat. ➤ But do not singe a bird that is to be frozen until you are just ready to use it, because the heat of singeing breaks down the fat and hastens rancidity.

DRAWING AND DRESSING A BIRD

Cut off the head so that the neck is as long as possible, and at once catch hold of and bind the 2 tubes attached to the crop, to prevent contamination. Draw down the neck skin. Cut or twist off the neck, close to the body, ➤ being careful not to tear or cut through the tubes or the neck skin. The skin should then be loose enough to allow you to reach in at the base of the neck and draw out the bound tubes and the crop.

In large domestic fowl and in game birds the leg tendons are apt to be tough and should be removed. Most butchers use a clever gadget that breaks the foot, holds the carcass securely and draws the tendons as the foot separates from the body. Amateurs have a somewhat harder time. It is easier to get the tendons out if the feet have not been cut off. Cut through the skin 1½ inches above the knee joint. Be careful not to cut the tendons. Lay the fowl down on its back, with the cut in the skin just at the edge of a table or board and the rest of the leg projecting beyond it. Press the foot and ankle down, sharply, to snap the bone at the knee joint. Pull steadily. The tendons should all come away with the foot and lower leg bone as seen in the foreground below. If they do not, remove those that are left by forcing a skewer crosswise under each and pulling them out one by one. If the bird is young, there is no need to remove the tendons. Simply cut off the feet as shown below.

➤ Taking great care not to pierce the innards, make a shallow incision through the skin from the tip of the breastbone to and around the vent as shown in the center drawing. Insert the hand, palm down, into the cavity between the organs and the breastbone. Feel for the gizzard, which is firm and roundish, and pull it out steadily. It will bring with it most of the other entrails except the kidneys. These lie in the hollows near the base of the backbone. To either side of the spine between the ribs you will find the spongy red lungs. Take them out. Explore carefully to ensure the removal of every bit of the viscera from the cavity, as well as surplus fat, which may prove to be too strong in flavor. ➤ Among the edible viscera of a fowl are the valuable giblets: heart, liver and gizzard. Remove veins, arteries, thin membrane and blood from around the heart and discard them. Cut the green sac or gallbladder away from the liver very carefully and discard it. It is better to leave a small piece of liver attached to the sac than to cut the sac so close to the liver as to risk puncturing it, for the bitterness of its fluid will ruin whatever it touches. Cut away any portion of the liver that may be discolored. ➤ Discard the liver of a fryer if it is yellow; however, it may be normal to find a yellow liver in a stewer. Sever the intestines from the gizzard and remove membrane and fat from it. Then cut a shallow slit along the indented curve of the gizzard, being

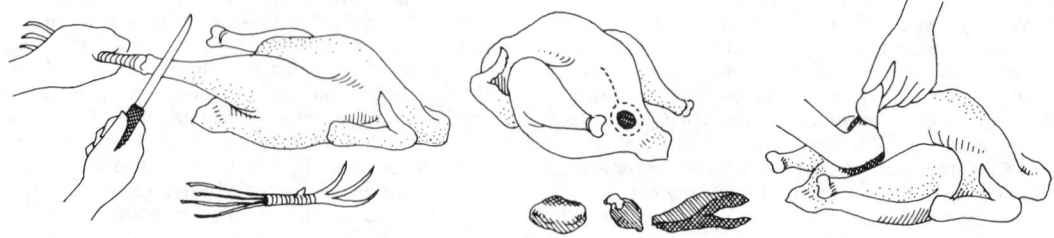

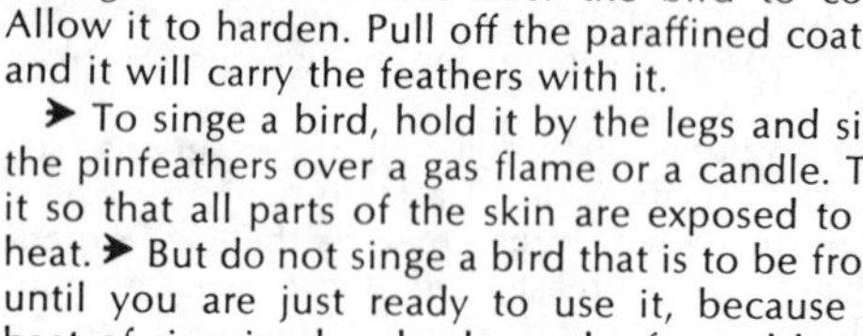

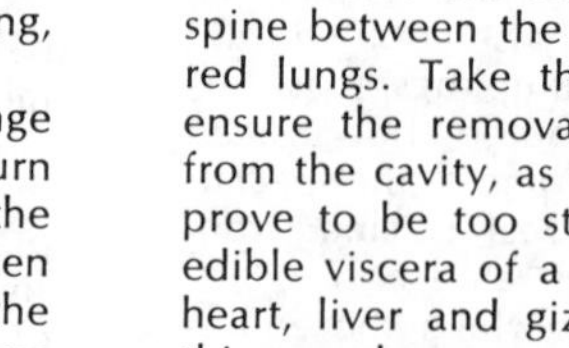

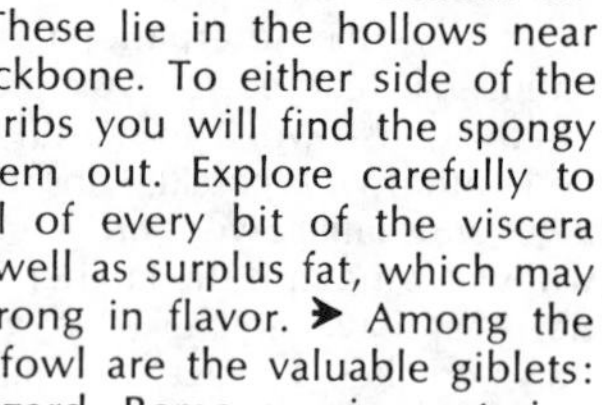

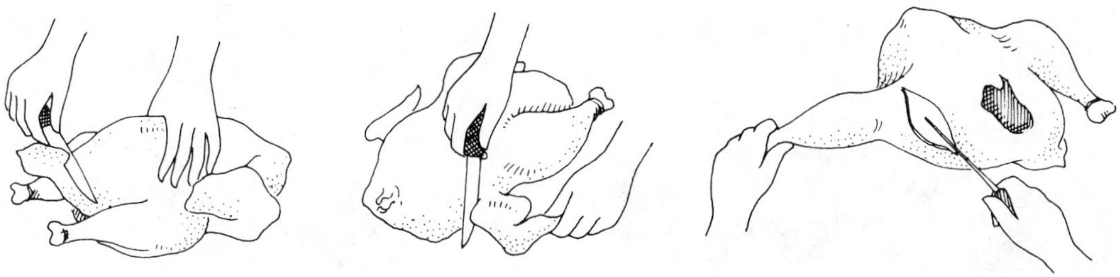

careful not to cut so deeply as to pierce the lining of the inner sac. Push against the outside of the opened gizzard with the thumbs to force out the sac. Discard it. Wash and dry giblets. Seen in the foreground, 418, are the gizzard, heart and liver. Keep them well refrigerated, and use or cook them as soon as possible. See Variety Meats, 499, Stuffings, 370, and Sauces, 336–360, for the many ways to use giblets. If the chicken is a hen, you may find some egg yolks in varying sizes which can be simmered in water and used in sauces and dressings.

Turn the chicken over and cut out and discard the oil sac at the base of the tail, as shown on the left above, by scooping out an oyster shape above the heart-shaped area called the croupion or—by the irreverent—the pope's nose.

➤ Do not soak the bird in water at any time. Wipe it well with a damp cloth after drawing. Should it be necessary to wash the bird, hold it briefly under running water to cleanse the inside, and ➤ dry it well with a cloth. It is then ready for stuffing or for cutting up for sautéeing or for a fricassee.

CUTTING UP A DRAWN BIRD

Grasp the drawn bird by a wing, letting its weight tug against the skin at the wing joint, as shown above. Clip through the skin, flesh and joint, severing the wing from the body. Use the same method to sever the second wing. For easier eating, you may want to transform the wings into mock legs. Just cut off the wing tips and straighten the two remaining sections with the hands. You may have to cut through the skin to do this. Pull them into a straight line to look like a small double leg. Silly, but the wings seem to taste better this way.

To cut off the legs, force them outward and down, as shown above. Where the leg joins the body, insert a knife to release the ligaments. When the leg has loosened, cut a long gash and continue to cut toward the back, allowing as much skin as possible to remain on the leg. Cutting off the neck is described previously on 418. With the neck, wings and legs severed, you are ready to cut up the carcass. To cut the body apart, place the carcass flat on its back. Make a diagonal cut as shown on the left, below.

With a young chicken, it is possible to pry the body apart by cracking the backbone, as shown on the right, below. Leave the breast in one piece, or cut it in two to four pieces with poultry shears, shown in the chapter heading. The back has little meat except for two choice "oysters" that lie above the croupion. Save the rest of the back and the neck for stock.

STUFFING AND TRUSSING A BIRD

➤ Always wait to stuff a bird until just before roasting. This may not be convenient, but it is the only safe procedure. Contamination is frequent in prestuffed fowl, for even when the dressing is refrigerated, the cold may not fully penetrate it.

➤ Fill the bird only three-fourths full, as the dressing will expand. Stuff it loosely, as sketched, 420. Your task will be easier if you place the bird in a large pan. The crop cavity may be stuffed, too. You may also loosen the breast skin with a spoon and fill out the breast between the skin and the flesh. Close the openings with small skewers and a crisscrossed string. Or use a spiral skewer as

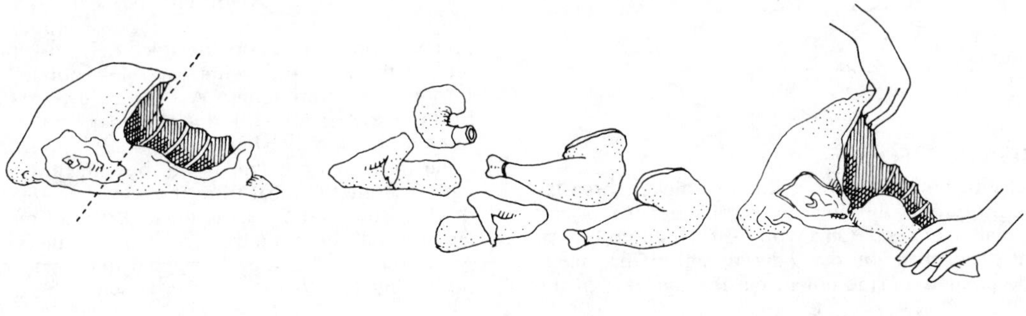

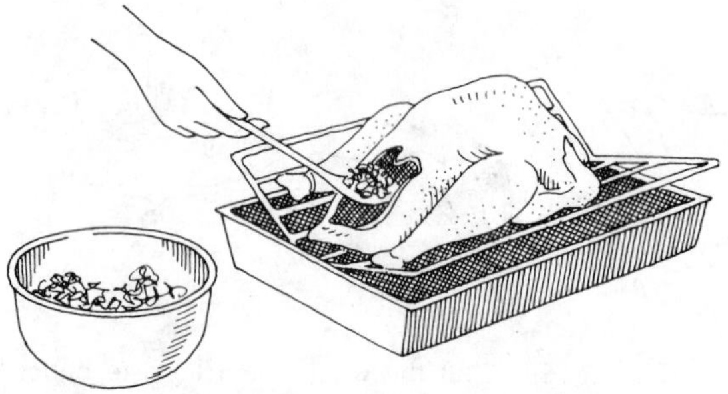

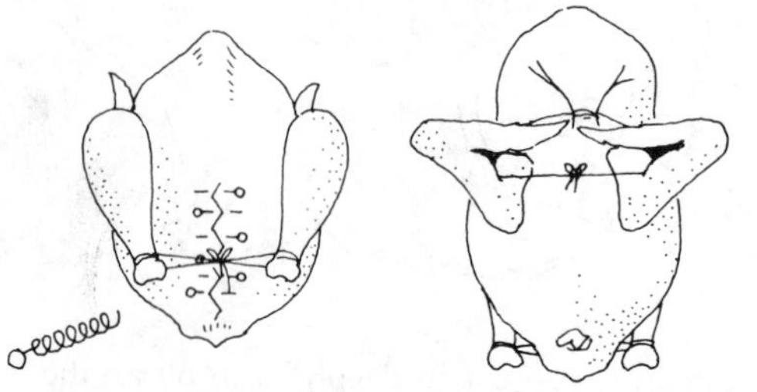

shown in the center drawing. Fasten the legs close to the body by tying the ends of the drumsticks together, as shown in the center. Tie a piece of string around the skin of the neck. Leave two long ends. Turn the wings back, as shown on the right, and pass the string around them and secure it.

BARDING FOWL

Guinea hen as well as partridge—very lean birds of any description—and birds from which the skin has been removed greatly benefit by barding before roasting; that is, by covering completely with a ¼-inch layer of salt pork or bacon, as shown on the left, below. Use pieces about 3 or 3½ inches square. As you truss the fowl, slip 2 pieces into place on either side between the legs and breast, as shown at center right. Cover the bird—legs and all—with other pieces, and tie securely, as shown at left, making certain that all exposed surfaces are blanketed. After cooking, discard the barding. This procedure may be used also for pieces cut from larger fowl. Also see Larding, 444.

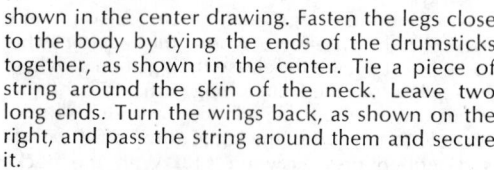

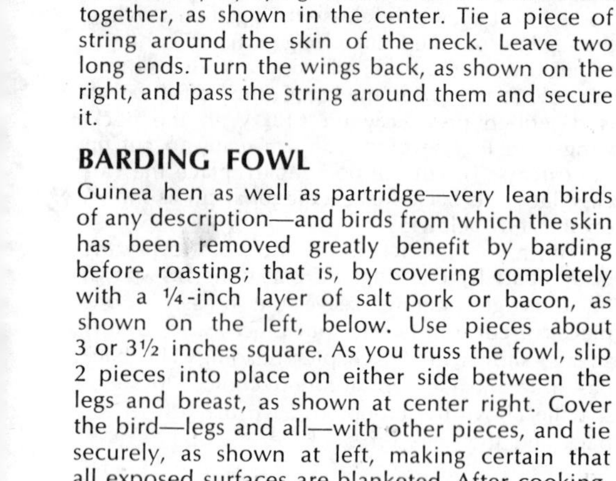

BONING FOWL

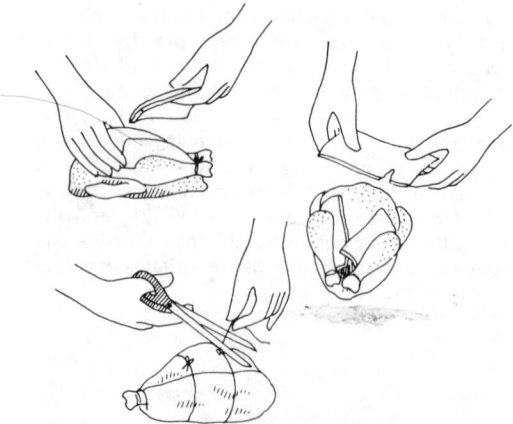

Let's begin with boning up on chicken breasts, because that's the only boning maneuver most of us will ever need. Once you start, you'll find it's a lot easier than you may have thought. First, place the breast skin side down; cut through the gristle and keel bone at the top center of the breast. This allows you to flatten the breast and remove the keel bone. Cut the meat free from the long rib-cage bone on both sides of the breast and then cut around the upper edge of the breast, up to and through the joint. Scrape the rest of the meat away from the bones. Loosen the tendons and pull them out. You may also remove the skin if desired. This gives you a butterflied whole breast. It is easier to bone the breasts singly by cutting free one side at a time.

As for the major boning operation on a whole bird that is to be restuffed and shaped into an impressive facsimile of its original self for a special occasion, the trick is again much less difficult than you might suspect. But do not attempt this plastic surgery on a dressed bird, because the previously cut openings, usually carelessly done, make success impossible. The bird to be boned, then, is neither dressed nor drawn. At the very end of the operation, you will be able to remove everything intact—innards, skeleton and all. ➤ During the entire boning job, be careful not to pierce the skin except for the initial incision. An unpierced skin will act as protection, encasement and insulation all through the cooking period. ➤ Always keep the tip of the knife toward the skeleton and close to the bone. When all the bones are out and you hold up the result, it looks—glory be!—like a small romper with wings. Pull the legs and sleeves into the lining.

Begin the boning by placing the bird breast down on the board. Make an incision the entire length of the spine, through both skin and flesh. Using a sharp-pointed short boning knife, follow as close to the frame as you can cut, pushing the skin and flesh back as you cut. Work the skin of the neck down so that the neck protrudes as much as possible. Chop the neck off short, protecting the skin and being careful ➤ not to cut through the crop tubes. Work first toward the ball-and-socket joint of the shoulder, cutting it free and boning the shoulder blade. Pull the wing bone through from the inside, bringing the skin with it. Bone the meat from the wing and reserve it. Then strike for the ball-and-socket joint of the leg and pull the bone through. Reserve the meat. After you have freed and reserved the meat from both wings and legs, continue to work the meat free, first from one side of the body, then from the other, until the center front of the breastbone is reached. ➤ Here great care is needed to free the skin without piercing it, as it is very thin at this point. You should now be able to get the whole skeleton out with its contents all in one mass. Leave the severing of the opening into the intestine until the last. Then, with the innards removed, wash the skin and flesh in cold running water and pat with a towel ➤ until very dry. For a farce for boned chicken, see 374.

ROASTING FOWL

There are differences of opinion as to whether to salt poultry before roasting. We prefer to salt after the browning—if at all—and never salt the interior. For small birds, see Barding, 420. For larger birds, rub them well with melted unsalted shortening and place on a greased rack in an ➤ uncovered roasting pan. Cover the entire top surface of the fowl with a coarsely woven cloth that has been soaked in melted unsalted butter or vegetable oil. This procedure, we have learned by experience, is the best method of solving the problem built into the roasting of every bird—and especially of turkeys: that is, how to cook to moist tenderness two kinds of meat at the same time—the softer meat of the breast and the tougher, fatter leg meat. Basting is done both over and under the cloth. If necessary for browning, the cloth may be removed during the last half hour of cooking.

Directly upon removal from the refrigerator, place the bird in a preheated 450° oven. Reduce the heat immediately to 350°, or to 325° for large turkeys. After the first half hour of cooking, for birds of all sizes, ➤ baste frequently with pan drippings or additional fat—about every 10 minutes.

Timing involves many factors: the age of the bird and its fat content, its size, and whether it was frozen. If using a thermometer, insert it into the center of the inner thigh muscle, taking care that the tip is not in contact with the bone. Cook to an internal temperature of 180° to 185°. The center of the stuffing should reach at least 165°. If not using a thermometer, allow 20 to 25 minutes per pound for birds up to 6 pounds. For larger birds, allow 15 to 20 minutes per pound. For turkeys weighing over 16 pounds, allow 13 to 15 minutes per pound. In any case, add about 5 minutes to the pound if the bird you are cooking is stuffed. Other popular tests for doneness are to prick the skin of the thigh to see if the juice runs clear or to jiggle the drumstick to see if the hip joint is loose. This latter response, we find, usually means that the bird is not only done but overdone. Sometimes with a young bird the meat close to the bone remains reddish brown even after adequate cooking. The bone marrow in immature fowls has not yet fully hardened, and the red blood cells frequently seep into the adjacent meat.

Some people like to use an even, slow heat throughout the cooking period, placing the bird in a preheated 325° oven and not basting at all. This method has gained popularity because it is carefree and has been rumored to entail much less shrinkage. We have found the flavor remarkably superior when the meat is sealed by high temperature at the outset—and the difference in shrinkage is negligible.

CARVING FOWL

After removing a chicken from the oven, allow it to rest about 10 minutes, a turkey about 20 minutes, to make slicing easier. If the bird is to be carved at table, be sure the heated serving platter is large enough, and garnish it lightly with parsley or watercress. There is a subtle art to carving. Keeping the knife keen-edged and using with it a 2-tined handle-guarded fork are fundamentals in mastering it.

Place the bird, breast side up, on a platter. Insert the fork firmly into the knee joint, as sketched below, pulling the leg away from the body of the bird. Slice the thigh flesh away from the body until the ball-and-socket hip joint is exposed. To sever the thigh joint, make a twisting movement with the knife and continue to hold the knee joint down firmly with the fork. Cut the joint between the thigh and drumstick, as shown. Repeat the above, cutting off the other leg. Arrange pieces attractively on the serving platter.

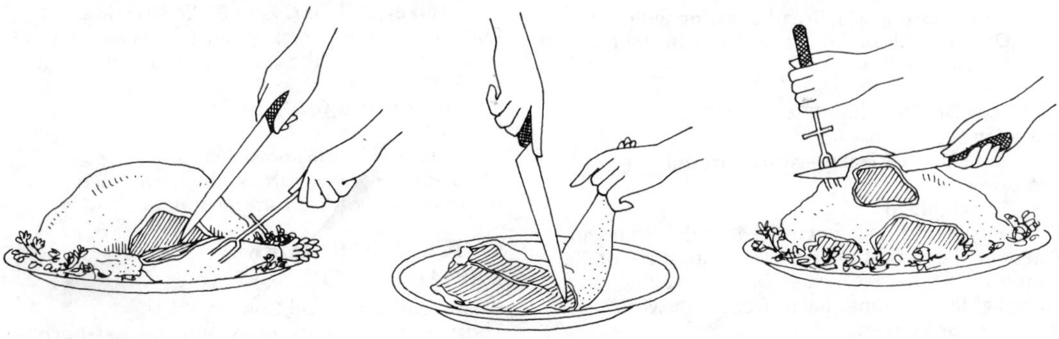

If a large bird is being carved, some slices of meat may be cut from the thigh and the drumstick at this point. Proceed to remove the wings in a similar manner and, if the bird is large, divide the wings at the second joint. To slice the breast, begin at the area nearest the neck and slice thinly across the grain, the entire length of the breast. With a large bird such as a turkey, carve only one side unless more is needed at the first serving.

In carving a duck, you will find the leg joint more difficult to sever because it is attached much farther under the bird and is somewhat recessed at the joint. Here, as in general, for the inexperienced carver or the impatient one, poultry shears are an inspired addition to his weaponry.

ABOUT CHICKEN

Young chickens of either sex are called **broilers** if they weigh about 2½ pounds and **fryers** if they weigh 2½ to 3½ pounds. **Roasters,** also of either sex, are under 8 months old and weigh 3½ to 5 pounds. Roasters are an appropriate choice for rotisseries or for Suprêmes, 426. **Stewing chickens,** usually over 10 months, are pretty much what their name implies. **Capons,** or castrated males, weigh 6 to 8 pounds. Their loss is the epicure's gain, capon flesh being exceptionally tender. Fowl is a broadly polite *nom de plume* for hens aged 10 months or more and **stag** and **cock** for males that are too old to roast but make well-flavored adjuncts for the stock pot.

To size up a chicken, look for moist skin, soft legs and feet, bright eyes, a red comb, a wing tip that yields readily if pressed back and, most importantly ➤ a flexible breastbone. If the tip of the bone bends easily, the bird is young; if it is stiff, the bird is past its prime. ➤ Beware of skin that is dry, hard, purplish, broken, bruised or scaly, or that has long hairs sprouting from it.

ROAST CHICKEN

6 Servings

➤ Please read about Roasting Fowl, 421.
Preheat oven to 450°.
➤ Draw, singe, stuff and truss, 418 to 420:

A 4- to 5-lb. chicken or capon

Use for the stuffing one-half the recipe for:

Rice Dressing, 373, Bread Dressing with Oysters, Nuts or Giblets, 370, or Chestnut Dressing, 372

or make:

2 cups Dry Dressing, 370

replacing the onion with:

½ cup chopped leeks—white part only

and using:

French bread

Put the bird on a rack, uncovered, in the oven and ➤ reduce the heat at once to 350°. Roast about 20 minutes per pound. Chicken without stuffing may take slightly less time. Baste frequently with pan drippings. Serve with:

Gravy or any Velouté Sauce variation, 343 to 345, or White Wine Sauce, 345, or Quick Mushroom Sauce, 348

ABOUT TURKEY

Benjamin Franklin wrote in a letter to his daughter: "I wish the bald eagle had not been chosen as the representative of our country. . . . The turkey is a much more respectable character and, withal, a true original native of America." Presumably Ben would have been delighted at the turkey's subsequent success story: its domestication, its genetic adaptability, its supplanting even the goose as the mainstay of Christmas dinner. Indeed, the turkey has taken first place in the feasts of his countrymen. Hens and toms are about equal in tenderness, although the butcher charges more per pound for the female. Look for plump white birds, well-rounded over the breastbone, and fresh rather than frozen. ➤ For turkeys less than 12 pounds, allow ¾ to 1 pound per serving, and ½ to ¾ pound per serving for those weighing over 12 pounds. With modern feeding methods, turkeys up to 25 pounds need not be older than 6 months. Certain white turkey types bred for heavy breasts and small bone structure cook more rapidly, if bought unfrozen, than the dark-feathered types. Boned, rolled turkey is sometimes a good buy economically, but the flavor developed with long, slow roasting may be lacking here. Ground turkey, too, is available. Prepare as for Chicken Patties, 488.

ROAST TURKEY

12 Servings

➤ Please read about Roasting Fowl, 421.
Preheat oven to 450°.
➤ Draw, singe, and truss, 418 to 420:

A turkey

If you stuff the turkey, 5 cups of one of the following stuffings should fill a 10-pound bird:

Dry Dressing, 370, Apple Onion Dressing, 372, or Chestnut Dressing, 372

Or you may want to use two kinds of dressing: in the crop a richer one like:

Sausage Dressing, 371

and in the cavity:

Bread Dressing, 370, Ham Dressing for Turkey, 372, or Oyster Bread Dressing, 371

Put the bird on a rack in an uncovered roasting pan and follow the directions under Roasting Fowl, 421. Make:

Poultry Pan Gravy, 341

adding:

Sautéed Mushrooms, 308

Or flavor the gravy with the finely chopped giblets if they were not used in the stuffing.

CHICKEN OR TURKEY BAKED IN FOIL

Please read about Foil Cookery, 153.
Today, "roasting" in aluminum foil has become popular because no basting is needed. So, if you

decide, despite our Cassandra warnings about this method, that you'd rather clean the attic, improve your serve, or write Chapter IX of the Great American Novel than to baby-sit a bird, go ahead with the foil and take the consequences—which will be steamed rather than roasted. Roasting can go on only under ventilation. Remember that foil insulates against heat, so your oven will have to be hotter. And any attempt to brown your bird by removing the foil during the last half hour of cooking will just dry out the meat—although you can compensate somewhat by repeated bastings with pan drippings after taking off the foil.
Preheat oven to 450°.
Season the fowl well, and add a little butter and fresh herbs, such as tarragon or rosemary. Or use one of the barbecue sauces on 354. Wrap the fowl in heavy-duty or double foil. Bake a 5-pound stuffed chicken about 2½ hours at 350°; parts or halves, 1¾ to 2 hours. A 10- to 12-pound stuffed turkey will take 3¼ to 3¾ hours, and a 14- to 18-pound stuffed turkey will need 3¾ to 4 hours. A 3- to 4-pound turkey quarter will take 2 to 2½ hours.

ROASTED TURKEY BREAST

Allow ⅓ Pound per Serving

When the family prefers all white meat, serve whole turkey breasts, ranging in size from 3½ to 7 pounds.
Preheat oven to 450°.
Rinse and dry:

A turkey breast

You may stuff the cavity with any suitable:

(Dressing, 372 to 374)

If possible, skewer the skin flaps together to hold the dressing; or cover the filled cavity with foil. Place the breast on a rack in a shallow pan and brush with:

Butter or margarine

Reduce the heat to 325° and roast uncovered, basting frequently, about 20 minutes per pound.

BROILED CHICKEN

Allow ¾ Pound per Person

Broiling or barbecueing chicken should be a slow process—keeping meat at least 5 to 6 inches from the heat source.
Preheat broiler.
Clean and cut into halves or quarters:

Broilers, 422

Rub on both sides with:

Butter or vegetable oil

Place them in a pan, skin side down. Broil the chickens until brown, 15 to 20 minutes for each side, basting with more fat as you turn the pieces. For excellent flavor we suggest basting with a mixture of:

2 tablespoons butter
1 tablespoon lemon juice
A grind of fresh pepper
(Fresh or dry herbs)

Or, for an accent on beautiful color:

2 tablespoons butter
¼ teaspoon paprika

Allow these amounts for each half broiler. Or, when the broilers are ready, flambé them, 155, with:

1 oz. warmed brandy

for each broiler. Or make:

A thickened Poultry Pan Gravy, 341, using tarragon; or an unthickened one, deglazing with dry white wine

⊟ BARBECUED CHICKEN

Follow directions for:

Broiled Chicken, above

but place broilers cavity side down on the grill over moderate heat. Cook from 15 to 25 minutes per side or until fork-tender. Brush the birds with:

A Barbecue Sauce, 354

during the last 10 minutes.

⊟ CURRIED BARBECUE CHICKEN

About 6 Servings

Disjoint:

2 broilers, 422

Marinate chicken pieces overnight in refrigerator in a mixture of:

1½ cups plain yogurt
½ cup lime juice
1 teaspoon grated lime peel
1 to 2 crushed cloves garlic
2 teaspoons finely chopped ginger
1½ teaspoons paprika
2 teaspoons ground coriander
1 teaspoon ground cayenne
1 teaspoon ground curry
1 teaspoon salt

Preheat broiler or grill and follow directions in:

Broiled Chicken, above

basting frequently with the strained marinade.

⊟ BROILED MARINATED CHICKEN

I. With Tarragon and Wine — **4 Servings**

Disjoint:

2 broilers, 422

Marinate the pieces at least 1 hour in:

¼ cup fresh or 2 tablespoons dried tarragon leaves
4 finely minced shallots
1 cup dry white wine

Preheat broiler or grill. Follow the directions for:

Broiled Chicken, above

basting with:

Melted butter

and the heated strained marinade. If oven broiling, save some of the marinade to deglaze the broiler pan.

Season to taste

and serve the chicken on a hot platter with some of the marinade poured over it.

II. Teriyaki
Follow recipe I, above, using:
Teriyaki Marinade, 529

III.
Follow directions under:
Marinade for Chicken, 529

PAN-FRIED OR SAUTÉED CHICKEN

Allow 3/4 Pound per Person

Please read About Sautéing, 149.
Clean and cut into pieces:
Young chickens
You may dredge them lightly with:
(Seasoned flour or cornmeal)
Melt in a skillet:
A mixture of butter and vegetable oil
allowing for each half chicken 2 or more tablespoons of fat. When the fat has reached the point of fragrance, add the chicken. Cook and turn it in the hot fat until brown. Reduce the heat and continue cooking uncovered, turning the chicken frequently until done, from 25 to 40 minutes, according to size. ➤ Cook only until tender, as further cooking will dry and toughen the meat. Remove the chicken from the pan and make:
Poultry Pan Gravy, 341
Season to taste
Serve at once, garnished with:
Parsley

OVEN-FRIED CHICKEN

I. **2 Servings**

Preheat oven to 350°.
Disjoint:
A broiler, 422
Wipe dry. Dredge it in:
Seasoned flour
Heat to the point of fragrance in a heavy skillet:
1/4 cup butter
Sauté the chicken lightly. Remove from the skillet to a rack in a shallow baking pan. Baste with the skillet pan drippings. Bake uncovered until tender, 30 to 40 minutes, basting with added fat if necessary and turning occasionally. Serve with:
Poultry Pan Gravy, 341, or Sauce Périgueux, 347, or Quick Canned Soup Sauce I, 348

II. **2 Servings**

A simpler version but not quite so tasty.
Preheat oven to 400°.
Prepare as for I, above:
A broiler, 422
In a shallow 9 x 12-inch baking pan, melt in the preheated oven:
1/4 cup butter
Remove the butter from the oven when melted and hot. Place the dredged chicken in it ➤ skin side down. Baste the upper surface with melted butter from the pan. Bake the chicken uncovered 25 minutes. Turn it skin side up. ➤ Reduce the heat to 350° and bake until tender, 30 to 35 minutes, basting often with the pan drippings. ➤ Do not overcook. White meat portions may be removed and kept warm while dark meat is cooked slightly longer. Serve at once. For gravy and other sauces, see I, above.

OVEN-FRIED CHICKEN WITH FRUIT, OR CHICKEN TAHITI

6 Servings

Prepare and cook as for Oven-Fried Chicken I, above:
2 frying chickens
Meanwhile combine in a saucepan, stirring constantly:
1 cup orange juice
2 tablespoons lemon juice
1/2 cup brown sugar
2 tablespoons soy sauce
1 tablespoon cornstarch
Bring the mixture to a boil. When thickened and clear, add:
1 fresh pineapple cut into cubes
1 fresh papaya cut into cubes
Pour the sauce over the baked chicken. Place it in the oven and bake 10 minutes longer. Serve with:
Boiled Rice, 206, and Green Peas, 314
For more glamor, serve the chicken and fruit in warmed scooped-out pineapple halves cut lengthwise, see 109.

MARYLAND CHICKEN

4 to 5 Servings

Cut into pieces for serving:
A frying chicken, about 3 1/2 lb.
Bread it by dipping each piece into:
Milk
and rolling it in:
Flour
Let dry for 1 hour. Heat in a heavy skillet until it reaches the point of fragrance:
1/2 to 1 inch combination of cooking oil and bacon drippings
Add the chicken. Brown it on all sides.
Preheat oven to 375°.
Place the browned chicken in a fresh pan and bake, covered, until steamed through, about 1/2 hour. This Border dish is usually served with a cream gravy made from the drippings to which flour and milk are added, see Poultry Pan Gravy, 341. You may further enrich the gravy with:
(Egg Yolks, 339)
Serve with:
Ham and Corn Fritters, 244

CHICKEN IN BATTER

4 Servings

➤ Please read About Deep-Fat Frying, 147.
Cut into pieces:
A 3-lb. roasting chicken
Dip into:
Fritter Batter for Meat, 243
Place the dipped pieces on a rack and let them dry 15 to 30 minutes. Immerse a few pieces at a

time in deep fat heated to 365° and cook 10 to 15 minutes. Drain on paper towels. Serve hot or cold.

BRAISED CHICKEN WITH FRUIT

Allow ¾ Pound per Person

Preheat oven to 350°.
Clean and quarter:
Frying chickens
Heat in a skillet:
Butter
Add chicken pieces and sauté until brown. Dip the browned chicken into a sauce of:
1 cup orange juice
¼ cup honey
2 tablespoons lemon juice
½ teaspoon ground curry powder
1 teaspoon salt
Arrange the chicken in a baking dish, skin side down, cover with the sauce and bake uncovered 20 minutes. Turn the chicken over and add one of the following or in combination:
Whole preserved kumquats, peaches, pears or plumped prunes, apricots or raisins
Strips of orange rind
Baste the fruit with the sauce and bake 30 minutes longer or until the chicken is tender.

CHICKEN BRAISED IN WINE OR COQ AU VIN

4 Servings

We are often asked why this recipe turns out a rich medium brown rather than the very dark brown sometimes served in restaurants. Abroad, in country places where chickens are locally butchered, the blood is often kept and added to the gravy at the last minute as a thickener, see 339. After this addition, the sauce is not allowed to boil. Here in America, this effect is imitated by adding caramel coloring, 559.
Disjoint, wash and dry:
A broiler or roasting chicken
Use the back and neck for the stock pot.
Melt in a large heavy skillet:
3 tablespoons butter or olive oil
Add and brown lightly:
¼ lb. minced salt pork
¾ cup chopped mild onions or ½ cup peeled pearl onions
1 sliced carrot
3 minced shallots or scallions
1 peeled, finely chopped garlic clove
Push the vegetables aside. Brown the chicken in the fat. Add and stir:
2 tablespoons flour
2 tablespoons minced parsley
1 tablespoon fresh chervil or marjoram
½ bay leaf
½ teaspoon thyme
1 teaspoon salt
⅛ teaspoon freshly ground pepper
(1 tablespoon brandy)
Stir in:
2 cups dry red wine
Simmer the chicken covered over low heat until done, about 1 hour. Add for the last 5 minutes of cooking:
½ lb. sliced mushrooms
Skim off excess fat.
Season to taste
Serve the chicken on a hot platter, with the sauce and vegetables poured over it.

CHICKEN PAPRIKA

3 Servings

Disjoint:
A frying chicken: about 2½ lb.
Melt in a heavy pot:
1½ tablespoons butter
1½ tablespoons vegetable oil
Add and simmer until glossy and red:
1 cup finely chopped onions
2 teaspoons to 2 tablespoons sweet Hungarian paprika
Add:
½ teaspoon salt
2 cups well-seasoned chicken stock
As soon as these ingredients have reached boiling point, add the chicken. ➤ Simmer covered until tender, about 1 hour. Stir:
2 teaspoons flour
into:
1 cup cultured sour cream
Stir it slowly into the pot and simmer until thickened and smooth, about 5 minutes, but ➤ do not boil. Serve at once. Good with noodles or rice.

SMOTHERED CHICKEN

6 to 7 Servings

Preheat oven to 350°.
Prepare for cooking:
A 4-lb. roasting chicken
Disjoint it. Place the chicken in a paper bag with:
¼ cup Seasoned Flour, 552
Close the bag and shake vigorously. Brown the chicken in:
¼ cup olive or vegetable oil
Place it in a casserole. Cook in the fat for 10 minutes:
1 small sliced onion
1 sliced clove garlic
3 or 4 chopped celery ribs
1 medium-sized carrot
Put the vegetables in the casserole. Pour over the mixture:
1½ cups hot chicken stock
Bake ➤ covered about 1½ hours or until tender. Add to the dish 5 minutes before it is done:
(1 cup sliced Sautéed Mushrooms, 308)
(12 sliced stuffed olives)

PERSIAN CHICKEN

4 Servings

Disjoint and cut into pieces:
A broiler or roasting chicken

Sauté the chicken until brown and almost done in:

Butter or vegetable oil

Heat in a large saucepan or casserole:

2 tablespoons butter

Sauté until soft and golden:

1 finely chopped onion

Add and stir well:

1 cup ground walnuts

Add:

½ cup fresh pomegranate juice or the juice of 2 lemons
2¼ cups chicken stock

Stir while sauce heats and thickens somewhat.

Season to taste

and, if necessary, add:

1 to 2 teaspoons sugar

Add the chicken pieces and simmer gently, covered, 30 minutes. Serve with:

Boiled Rice, 206

CHICKEN OR TURKEY STEW OR FRICASSEE

A fricassee is a simmered meat, usually chicken, veal or rabbit. Whether this meat is to be simmered in stock or in water; whether it is to be sautéed first in butter or put directly into boiling liquid; whether it is to be simmered first and browned afterward; what the additions are to be; whether or not a thickening of flour is to be used; whether the stock is to be thickened at the last with cream and eggs—these are all matters of tradition, personal taste and convenience. Typical fricassees are the following.

I. **5 Servings**

Clean and cut into pieces:

A 5-lb. stewing chicken or pieces of turkey

Place the chicken in a stewing pan and bring to the boiling point with:

3 cups water
1 sliced carrot
2 ribs celery with leaves
1 small sliced onion

Reduce heat and simmer the fowl about 15 minutes and remove scum. Continue to ➤ simmer covered until the meat is tender, 2 hours or more. ➤ Do not boil at any time. At the end of the first hour of cooking, add:

3 or 4 peppercorns

Remove the meat and strain the stock. If a very concentrated gravy is desired, boil the stock before thickening until reduced to 1½ cups. Thicken with:

Flour, see Poultry Pan Gravy, 341

Pour the gravy over the chicken. Garnish with:

Parsley

Serve with:

Noodles, 213, Dumplings, 202, or Boiled Rice, 206

II. **4 to 5 Servings**

Cook à Blanc, 447, until tender, and reserve:

1 dozen mushrooms
1 dozen small onions

Cut into pieces:

A 5-lb. stewing chicken or pieces of turkey

reserving the neck and back for stock. Dust the meat with:

Flour

Melt in a heavy pan:

2 tablespoons butter

When the butter reaches the point of fragrance, add the floured chicken. Cook until the flour crusts but does not color. Add just enough to cover:

Water or Chicken Stock, 523
An onion stuck with 3 cloves
1 teaspoon salt

Bring the liquid to a boil. ➤ Reduce heat at once. ➤ Simmer, uncovered, about 45 minutes. Remove the meat and the clove-studded onion from the liquid. Discard the onion. Keep the meat warm. Melt in the top of a double boiler over direct heat:

3 tablespoons butter

Add:

3 tablespoons all-purpose flour

Make a sauce by adding to this roux the liquid from the meat. Simmer, stirring, about 5 minutes. Have everything else ready to serve, because the sauce does not hold well once the eggs are added. Stir some of the sauce into:

3 beaten egg yolks
¾ cup cream or milk

Pour the egg sauce into the rest of the sauce and place ➤ over—not in—boiling water, stirring until the eggs thicken. Add the reserved mushrooms and onions. Place the chicken on a hot platter, inside a:

Rice Ring, 207

Pour the garnished sauce over the meat. You may decorate the platter with small bunches of:

Cooked carrots
Parsley

so arranged as to look like fresh carrots with tops.

FRENCH CASSEROLE CHICKEN

5 Servings

Whenever we see one of our contemporaries trying to regain her youthful allure with gaudy sartorial trappings, we think of a dish we found in a collection of college alumnae recipes, called: "Suprême of Old Hen." We all know that "suprême," in chef's parlance, simply means a breast of fowl. But in this case it really lives up to its billing and makes such a good dish out of a poorish bird that the old girl is still an acceptable morsel.

Disjoint:

A 5-lb. stewing chicken

Sear the pieces in:

¼ cup butter

Add:

¼ cup dry white wine

Remove the chicken from the pot. Place in the pot:

2 pared, cored, sliced tart apples
6 chopped celery ribs with leaves
1 minced or grated onion
3 sprigs parsley
½ teaspoon salt
¼ teaspoon paprika

Cover and cook these ingredients gently until tender. Stir in:

2½ tablespoons flour
2 cups Stock, 523

Cook and stir the sauce until it boils. Add the chicken. Cover and simmer until tender, 1 hour or more. Remove the chicken to a hot ovenproof serving dish. Strain the sauce. Reheat it in the top of a double boiler ➤ over—not in—boiling water and add to the strained sauce:

⅓ cup sweet or cultured sour cream
Season to taste

Add:

1 tablespoon fresh tarragon or basil

Pour the sauce over the chicken. Sprinkle it generously with:

Grated Parmesan cheese

Place the dish under a broiler until the cheese is melted.

BRUNSWICK STEW

8 Servings

This southern specialty has many variations: combinations of chicken and pork, in equal amounts, or squirrel and pork. Chili peppers and mustard are optional seasonings.

Disjoint for cooking:

A 5-lb. chicken

Sauté it slowly until light brown in:

¼ cup shortening

Remove from the pan. Brown in the fat:

½ cup chopped onions

Place in a large stewing pan the chicken, onions and:

1½ to 2 cups skinned, seeded, quartered tomatoes
3 cups fresh lima beans
1 cup boiling water
A few grains cayenne
(2 cloves)

➤ Simmer these ingredients, covered, until the chicken is nearly tender. Add:

3 cups corn, cut from the cob

Simmer the chicken and vegetable mixture covered until tender.

Season to taste

Add:

2 teaspoons Worcestershire sauce

Stir in:

(1 cup toasted bread crumbs)

CHICKEN CACCIATORE OR HUNTER'S CHICKEN

4 Servings

Hunters who cook always seem to have tomatoes and mushrooms handy. Cut into individual pieces:

A 4-lb. chicken

Dredge with:

2 to 3 tablespoons flour

Sauté until golden brown in:

¼ cup olive oil

with:

2 tablespoons chopped shallots
(1 minced clove garlic)

Add:

¼ cup Italian tomato paste
½ cup dry white wine
1 teaspoon salt
¼ teaspoon white pepper
¾ cup Chicken Stock, 523
½ bay leaf
⅛ teaspoon thyme
½ teaspoon basil
⅛ teaspoon sweet marjoram
½ to 1 cup sliced mushrooms
(2 tablespoons brandy or ¼ cup Muscatel)

Simmer the chicken covered for 1 hour or until tender. Serve with:

Boiled Pasta, 213, or sautéed tiny new potatoes, 318

CHICKEN MARENGO

8 Servings

This was the dish served to Napoleon after he had fasted through his victory at Marengo. Composed of findings from the nearby countryside, the dish was such a success that from there on in, Napoleon's chef had to prepare it after every battle. It is a good buffet casserole which profits by a day's aging, refrigerated.

Cut into quarters:

2 frying chickens

Sauté until delicately colored:

1 thinly sliced onion

in:

½ cup olive oil

then remove. Add the chicken pieces and brown on all sides. Add:

½ cup dry white wine
2 crushed garlic cloves
½ teaspoon thyme
1 bay leaf
Sprigs of parsley
1 cup Chicken Stock, 523
2 cups Italian-style tomatoes

Cover the pot and simmer about 1 hour, until tender. When meat is done, remove it to a platter. Strain the sauce and reduce it about 5 minutes and:

Season to taste

Sauté:

16 to 20 small white onions
1 lb. sliced mushrooms

in:

¼ **cup butter**
Juice of 1 lemon

Arrange chicken quarters, mushrooms, onions and:

1 cup pitted black olives

in a deep earthenware casserole. Sprinkle over all:

1 jigger brandy

Add the sauce and reheat in a 350° oven.
Garnish with:

Chopped parsley

Serve with:

Boiled Rice, 206, or Wild Rice, 212

COUNTRY CAPTAIN OR EAST INDIA CHICKEN CURRY

4 Servings

This dish has become a favorite in America, although it probably got its name not from the sea captain who brought the recipe back to our shores, but from the Indian officer who first made him acquainted with it. So says Cecily Brownstone, a great friend; this is her time-tested formula. For still another oriental chicken curry, see Rijsttafel, 211.
Preheat oven to 350°.
Cut into pieces:

A fryer

Coat them with:

Seasoned Flour, 552

Brown the chicken in:

¼ **cup butter**

Remove, drain and place in a casserole. Simmer gently in the pan drippings until golden:

¼ **cup finely diced onions**
½ **cup finely diced green pepper, seeds and membrane removed**
1 minced garlic clove
1½ to 3 teaspoons curry powder
½ **teaspoon thyme**

Add:

2 cups stewed or canned tomatoes

and simmer until the pan is deglazed. Pour this sauce over the chicken and bake uncovered about 40 minutes or until the chicken is tender. During the last 5 minutes of cooking add:

3 tablespoons currants

Serve with:

Boiled Rice, 206

garnished with:

Toasted slivered almonds

CHICKEN OR TURKEY À LA CAMPAGNE

10 to 12 Servings

Roast, uncovered, 2 hours at 350°:

A 5-lb. chicken

Remove meat from bones. Use bones and skin in your stock pot. Sauté, 308:

1 lb. small button mushrooms

Have ready:

1 cup cooked green peas
(3 cups canned artichoke hearts)

Prepare à la Parisienne, 278:

1 cup each cooked carrots and white turnips

Arrange these ingredients in a 3-quart casserole, alternating layers of chicken and vegetables until all are used, with chicken on the top layer. Make the sauce by melting in a saucepan:

½ **cup butter**

Add and stir until smooth over low heat:

½ **cup flour**

Continue to stir over low heat and add:

2 cups strong Chicken Stock, 523
1½ cups dry white wine
1 cup cream
½ **cup chopped parsley**

Season to taste with:

Salt
Freshly ground white pepper

Continue to cook over low heat 10 minutes. Pour sauce over the food in the casserole. Shake the dish well, so the sauce penetrates all layers. You may cover the top with:

(Au Gratin I, 552)

and heat about 30 minutes in a 350° oven.

TURKEY CASSEROLE MOLE

This Mexican recipe combines the native bird with chocolate and a few varieties of native peppers.
➤ Please read About Deep-Fat Frying, 147.
Cut up:

A 12- to 14-lb. turkey

Dip the pieces first in:

Milk

then in:

Flour

and put them on a rack to dry, about 15 minutes.
Prepare by removing seeds and membrane of:

6 Chimayo peppers
6 broad bell peppers
3 chili peppers

If the chilis are dry, drop them into hot water about 10 minutes before removing seeds and veins. Deep-fry the peppers about 5 minutes in fat heated to 370°. Drain and reserve them.
Preheat oven to 325°.
Slide the turkey pieces gently into the 370° pepper-flavored fat and deep-fry about 5 minutes. Drain the pieces and put them into a large casserole. Cover with:

Turkey or Game Stock, 523

Cover the casserole and bake the turkey about 1 hour. Toast in a dry pan, over gentle heat:

1 tablespoon sesame seeds
½ **cup pine nuts**
½ **cup blanched almonds**

Grind together with the fried peppers:

2 tortillas

Cook:

3 minced garlic cloves

in:

2 tablespoons vegetable oil or lard

Add:

2 cups skinned, seeded tomatoes
1 bay leaf
½ teaspoon coriander
3 cloves
1 teaspoon cinnamon
(2 tablespoons vinegar)

Combine the above ingredients with the nuts and pepper mixture and simmer 15 minutes. Pour this thick sauce with about:

2 cups turkey stock

over the cut-up turkey and simmer, covered, about 2½ hours more. This dish may be made a day or two before serving, but its most characteristic ingredient is reserved for the very last. Just before serving, add to the heated sauce:

1 to 2 oz. grated unsweetened chocolate
(A pinch of sugar)

BREAST OF CHICKEN COCKAIGNE

Allow a Whole Breast per Serving

This delicate recipe does not work with frozen chicken.

Skin, bone, divide in halves, see 420:

Chicken breasts

Cook up a flavorful stock from the skin and bones of the chicken. When ready to cook, dust the chicken breasts, which should be 70°, lightly with:

Flour

For each breast, heat in a heavy skillet to the point of fragrance:

½ tablespoon butter
½ tablespoon vegetable oil

Put the floured pieces of chicken into the hot oil. Shake the pan constantly so the flour crusts but does not color. Cover and poach in the butter over very low heat 10 to 15 minutes, depending on the thickness of the meat. Turn the meat occasionally. Remove pan from heat and allow to stand covered about 10 minutes more. This rather unorthodox procedure makes breasts puff up and keeps the meat both tender and moist. Remove chicken from pan and keep warm. Prepare a gravy of the pan drippings and the stock made from the bones and skins, see:

Poultry Pan Gravy, 341

STUFFED CHICKEN BREASTS

Individual Serving

These are quickly prepared in a chafing dish or electric skillet.

Have ready:

A boned, skinned breast of chicken

beaten with a cleaver until very thin, 444. Heat to the point of fragrance:

1½ to 2 tablespoons butter

Quickly move the chicken about in this hot fat until it is no longer pink, ➤ about 2 to 3 minutes in all. Fold this thin piece over once to hold:

1 thin slice Virginia ham
1 very thin small piece Swiss cheese
(1 preserved kumquat or cooked apricot, sliced nearly in half)

Remove chicken from pan and keep warm. Sauté in pan drippings:

1 tablespoon finely minced shallots
3 mushroom caps

When mushrooms have cooked about 3 minutes, add:

¼ cup dry white wine
2 tablespoons freshly skinned, chopped, seeded tomato

Simmer about 3 minutes again. Add to this sauce:

2 tablespoons cream

Heat the chicken breasts in the sauce slowly, but ➤ do not let them boil. Turn once or twice. When heated through, add:

1 tablespoon chopped parsley
Season to taste

Serve at once, over:

Boiled Rice, 206, with saffron, or
Buttered Noodles, 213

CHICKEN BREASTS IN QUANTITY FOR CREAMING OR SALAD

This recipe is particularly useful in preparing large quantities of chicken meat for such dishes as Chicken à la King, 263, or Chicken Pot Pies, 252. Many knowledgeable cooks consider poaching an ideal approach, but we would like to suggest the following method, which we find more flavorful. After the chicken is baked, save the pan juices and make a stock of the skin and bones. Combine these two defatted by-products in making sauce if the chicken is to be served hot or in an aspic. Or use the juices and defatted stock for broth or other cooking if the chicken is served as salad.

Preheat oven to 300°.

Place on a rack in a large shallow pan, skin side up:

Chicken breasts

Brush them, allowing for each whole breast:

1½ tablespoons butter

Bake about 40 minutes, basting frequently. When slightly cooled, remove the skins and bone the breasts. Cover and refrigerate the meat until ready to use.

CHICKEN KIEV

4 Servings

Bone, skin, cut in halves and pound, 420, to a ¼-inch thickness:

4 chicken breasts

Form into 8 rolls about 2 inches long and ½ inch in diameter:

Butter

Roll butter lightly in a mixture of:

2 tablespoons chopped chives
2 tablespoons chopped parsley or tarragon
(1 minced clove garlic)
½ teaspoon salt
¼ teaspoon white pepper

Place one of the seasoned butter pieces in the center of each half breast and roll so that the butter is completely enclosed. Secure with a wooden pick, if necessary. Dust with:

Flour

Brush with:

Beaten egg

Roll in:

Dry bread crumbs

Fry in deep fat heated to 360° until golden brown. Drain on paper toweling before serving.

BRANDIED CHICKEN BREASTS

4 Servings

Skin, bone and divide into halves:

4 chicken breasts

Rub with:

Brandy

Let them stand about 10 minutes. Season with:

Salt, pepper and marjoram

Heat to the point of fragrance:

6 tablespoons sweet butter

Sauté the breasts over medium heat, 6 to 8 minutes on each side. Remove to a heated ovenproof platter and keep warm. To the remaining butter in the pan, add:

½ cup dry sherry

Simmer over ➤ low heat until the liquid is reduced to half. Add, stirring constantly:

2 cups cream

beaten with:

4 egg yolks

Season with:

Salt and pepper

(Nutmeg)

Stir and cook until slightly thickened. Pour the sauce over the chicken breasts. Sprinkle with:

Shredded Swiss cheese

mixed with equal parts of:

Fine buttered crumbs

Glaze under the broiler.

CHICKEN AND SWEETBREADS

8 Servings

➤ Please read About Sweetbreads, 502.

Blanch, firm, dry, trim and poach 25 minutes:

2 pairs calf sweetbreads

In the meantime, prepare and cook:

Brandied Chicken Breasts, above

coarsely chopping the chicken after it is sautéed. When the sweetbreads are cooked, coarsely chop and add them to the chicken and sauce with:

1 cup blanched button mushroom caps, 307

Instead of garnishing with Swiss cheese, use:

Chopped parsley

and serve in coquille dishes or warmed patty shells, 645.

QUICK CREAMED CHICKEN BREASTS

6 Servings

Preheat oven to 350°.

Place in a shallow baking dish:

6 boned whole chicken breasts

Combine and pour over the chicken:

1 cup canned cream of mushroom soup

1 cup cultured sour cream

(½ cup chopped mushrooms)

¼ cup chopped parsley

Sprinkle with:

Paprika

and bake, uncovered, about 1 hour.

CHICKEN BREASTS CHAUD-FROID

6 Servings

Prepare and cook in advance as for Chicken Stew, 426:

3 large split chicken breasts

Simmer only 30 minutes or until tender, then refrigerate. Make certain to have on hand at least 2 cups well-seasoned chicken stock to make:

Sauce Chaud-Froid, 369

Coat the chicken as directed on 368. After decorating, serve with:

Rice Salad, 104

STIR-FRIED CHICKEN BREASTS

6 Servings

➤ Please read about Stir-Frying, 149.

If you plan serving this dish with fluffy rice, cook:

Boiled Rice, 206

while preparing the following. Skin and bone, see 420:

3 whole chicken breasts

Cut the meat into strips 1½ to 2 inches long and ⅛ inch wide. Simmer the bones and skin of the chicken in a little water to make a stock. Mix the chicken strips thoroughly with:

1 teaspoon salt

2 teaspoons cornstarch

1 tablespoon dry sherry or Chinese rice wine

1 lightly beaten egg white

Have ready:

½ cup sliced onions

1 cup shredded green or red sweet pepper, seeds and membrane removed

½ cup diced water chestnuts

½ cup diagonally sliced celery

Pour into a wok or a large skillet over medium-high heat:

2 tablespoons peanut or vegetable oil

When hot, add half the chicken and briskly stir about 1 minute. The meat will turn white when done. Push to one side and cook the rest of the chicken, adding more oil if necessary. Add the vegetables and:

½ cup chicken stock

Cover and steam about 2 minutes. Combine in a bowl:

2 tablespoons soy sauce

2 tablespoons cornstarch

¾ cup chicken stock

and stir into chicken and vegetable mixture. Heat and stir about 1 minute or until sauce is slightly thickened. Serve over the rice.

▤ CHICKEN KEBABS

I. Yakitori **6 Servings**

Cut into bite-sized pieces:

3 whole boned and skinned chicken breasts, 420
1 lb. chicken livers

Marinate the pieces about 1 hour in:

Teriyaki Marinade, 529

Preheat broiler or grill.
Cut into 1-inch pieces:

5 leeks, white part only

Alternate on skewers the chicken, leeks and livers. Grill 5 minutes; turn and grill 5 minutes more, basting with the marinade. When done, serve immediately, sprinkled with:

Cayenne pepper

II. A good kebab combination is:

Pieces of chicken or chicken breasts

marinated in:

Marinade for Chicken, 529

wrapped in:

Bacon

and grilled on skewers with:

Cherry tomatoes

Broil each side about 3 minutes.

★ STUFFED BONED CHICKEN

See about Boning Fowl, 420.
This recipe, which we enjoyed on many holiday occasions with our friend Clara Kupferschmid, is one she brought close to perfection over the years.
Choose a very fresh, dry-picked, undressed:

6-lb. chicken

Be sure the skin is intact. Bone it. Allow for the filling 1/3 of the recipe for:

Chicken Farce, 374

Before stuffing the chicken "romper," tie it off securely at the neck, wing ends and legs. Sew shut the vent under the tail. Be sure not to pack the farce or fill the skin too tightly or it may burst during the cooking as the stuffing swells. In filling, "make like" a taxidermist or a sculptor, shaping the stuffing so that, when you have sewn the seam down the back, the bird will resemble its former self. Preheat oven to 450°.
Brush the bird generously all over with:

Clarified Butter, 349

For this and for subsequent basting, allow about 1/2 pound of butter. Prick the chicken all over with a darning needle and repeat this operation after every basting. Place the bird on a rack in a pan in the hot oven and ➤ reduce the heat at once to 350°. After 40 minutes of cooking, baste it at 10-minute intervals and continue until done, about 2 hours in all. Boned stuffed chickens may be served hot but are unusually delicious when served cold. Chill at least 24 hours to allow the seasonings to develop. To serve, slice very thin with a hot serrated knife.

GALANTINE OF TURKEY

If Served Hot, 15 Servings
If Served as an Hors d'Oeuvre, 30

A galantine of fowl is a white-tie-and-tails production that begins with the boning process. The skin of the bird eventually becomes the covering of an oversized sausage that contains the meat of the bird combined with eggs, spices and other meats. When a galantine finally appears in all its glazed and truffled splendor, no one could suspect how it began, for in no way does it resemble any avifauna. For this reason, it is possible to start with a ready-dressed bird—but if you do, be sure to choose one with the smallest possible precut opening. For either dressed or undressed turkey, follow the boning instructions on 420. After making the first slit down the spine ➤ it is vital to keep the rest of the skin intact. Any cuts must be patched by sewing.
Bone:

A 12- to 15-lb. turkey

Reserve the meat, including that cut from the drumsticks and the breast. Make a Stock, 522, of the bones. Reserve half the breast meat for filling and cut it into 1/2-inch strips. Grind 3 times and put into a large bowl:

1 lb. lean white veal
1 lb. lean pork

as well as the turkey meat, except the reserved strips. Season the mixture with:

1/4 cup brandy, dry sherry or Madeira
1 teaspoon freshly grated nutmeg
Ground black pepper
2 teaspoons Worcestershire sauce
1 tablespoon salt
A dash hot pepper sauce

Add:

8 eggs
1/2 cup finely chopped parsley

Mix these ingredients into a smooth paste. Spread a large piece of clean linen or cheesecloth on the table. Place in the center of the cloth the turkey skin, outer side down, as shown in the center, 432. Pat the meat mixture onto it in an even rectangular shape, extending it all the way to the edges of the skin. Arrange in neat alternating rows down the center, as shown:

Strips of cooked ham or tongue

and the reserved strips of turkey breast. Arrange a center row of:

Small whole truffles, 310, or seeded black olives

Over the whole, sprinkle:

3/4 cup pistachio nuts
1/4 cup finely chopped parsley

Starting at the long side farthest away from you, pull the cloth toward you gently—rolling the filled turkey skin into a sausagelike shape. You do not want the cloth to be inside the turkey roll, but keep manipulating it until it forms an outside casing. You may need an extra helping hand. Tie the cloth securely at both ends. The roll should be smooth and even. Also tie it lengthwise, as sketched. Place it on a rack, seam side down, in a large poaching kettle over:

Mirepoix, 572

and in:

Enough turkey or poultry stock to cover, 523

Cover the kettle and bring to a boil, then ➤ reduce the heat and simmer very gently 1½ to 2 hours until the roll is firm to the touch. Carefully remove it from the broth. You may serve it—unwrapped—hot, sliced, with buttered toast. Or let it cool—wrapped—on a large platter. You may weight it if you wish. When it has cooled to at least 70°—not before—remove the outside wrapping and refrigerate the galantine thoroughly. To decorate, either use:

Sauce Chaud-Froid, 369

or cover with a savory:

Aspic Glaze, 368

made from the poaching broth. Serve thinly sliced with:

Buttered toast

as an hors d'oeuvre or an entrée.

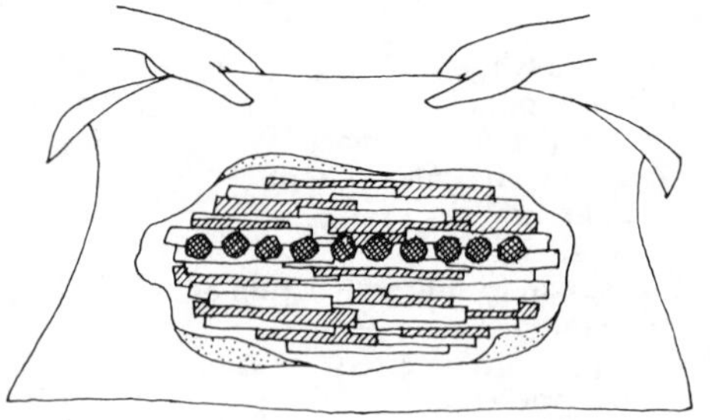

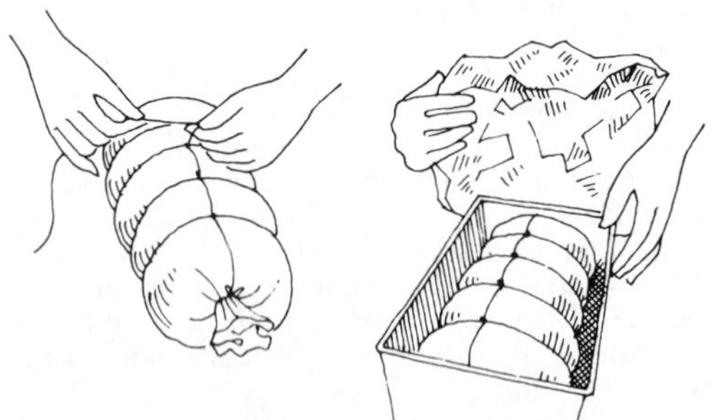

ABOUT DUCK

As it happens these days, we ordinarily dine not on duck but on **duckling,** if we dine on the domesticated bird. Most such ducks, like the members of other prominent American families, grow up on Long Island. Unlike their human counterparts, however, the ducks exhibit very uniform characteristics. When we make their acquaintance at market, dressed for the occasion, they are commonly 7 to 8 weeks old and weigh 3 to 5 pounds. As duck has both a heavy frame and a high fat content, we allow about 1⅓ to 1½ pounds per serving. The only trouble with these otherwise superlative young birds is that one is too little for two persons, and two are too much. A practice followed by some prudent ménagères is to serve a whole duckling to each person anyway, but to remove the legs beforehand for subsequent mincing. For a far more attractive presentation, serve duck as a Salmi, 436. In purchasing, look for a white skin and a plump body. Remember to save the carcasses for conversion to stock. Duck livers furnish excellent material for pâtés, 494.

ROASTING DUCK OR GOOSE

➤ Please read About Duck, above. Pluck, singe, draw and truss as described on 418. Remove the oil sac at the base of the tail, see 419. Since these birds are so fat, we often prefer to prepare a separate stuffing in a baking dish, so that the dressing will not be overpowered by the flavor and slickness of the fat. These birds ➤ must be pricked frequently, but lightly, all over to allow excess fat to escape. If they are not stuffed, you may rub the cavity with lemon juice, or place a cored and peeled apple, a carrot, an onion, celery ribs or a potato in the body cavity to attract off-flavors. Discard these vegetables before serving. You may also hasten the cooking with the old Chinese trick of placing several heated metal forks in the cavity to intensify the heat at that point. Place the bird in a 450° preheated oven, lower the heat to 350° and proceed as for chicken, allowing about 20 minutes to the pound for an unstuffed duck, 25 minutes per pound for a gosling. Larger geese take about 15 minutes per pound. Add 20 to 30 minutes if the duck or goose is stuffed.

ROAST DUCKLING

3 Servings

➤ Please read About Duck and Roasting Duck, above.

Preheat oven to 450°.

Pick, clean and singe, if necessary:

A 4½- to 5½-lb. duckling

Dry with paper toweling and rub with:

(Garlic)

or sprinkle evenly with:

(Paprika)

Place it on a rack in a roasting pan. If stuffing is used, try:

Sausage Dressing with apples, 371, or
Apple and Prune Dressing, 372, or
Sauerkraut Dressing for Game, 374

Put the bird, uncovered, into the oven and ➤ reduce the heat at once to 350°. Cook until tender, allowing about 20 minutes to the pound for an unstuffed bird, longer for a stuffed one, see above. Make:

Poultry Pan Gravy, 341

Serve with:

Polenta, 201

or, if the duck has not been stuffed, with:

Crushed pineapple, Sweet-Sour Orange Sauce, 355, or Cranberry Glaze for Fowl, 368, or Fruit and Honey Glaze, see below

FRUIT- AND HONEY-GLAZED DUCKLING

3 Servings

For those who like sweet with meat.
Preheat oven to 450°.
Prepare and cook:

Roast Duckling, above

Remove from oven just before done.
Make a thick glaze to pour over the duck. Combine and mix well:

1 cup apricot, cherry or peach preserves
½ cup clover honey
1 tablespoon brandy
1 tablespoon Grand Marnier or other orange-flavored liqueur

Coat the duck with this glaze and return it to the oven 10 to 15 minutes until the glaze caramelizes.

ROAST DUCK BIGARADE OR À L'ORANGE

This famous recipe depends for its flavor on the Seville or bitter orange, 135, which gives the dish its name.
Prepare:

An unstuffed Roast Duckling, above

When it is done, remove it from the roasting pan and keep warm. Prepare:

Sweet-Sour Orange Sauce, 355

using Seville or bitter oranges and omitting the lemon. Degrease the pan juices and deglaze the pan as described on 340.

DUCKLING ROUENNAISE

4 to 5 Servings

Unless you choke your duck, pluck the down on its breast immediately afterward and cook it within 24 hours, you cannot lay claim to having produced an authentic Rouen duck. The first two steps assure the dark red flesh and the special flavor of this dish. If, as is likely, duck-strangling will bring you into local disrepute, you may waive the sturdy peasant preliminaries and serve a modified version, garnished with quotation marks. First of all ➤ please read About Salmi of Wildfowl, 436.
Clean:

A 5-lb. duckling

reserving the liver. Free it from the gall. Tuck the liver into the body cavity. Use a spit or rotisserie to roast the duck, only 20 to 22 minutes in all. Only the breast and legs, if tender, are reserved and kept warm. The rest of the carcass and skin is pressed as described on 436.
Meanwhile melt:

2 tablespoons butter

When the fat reaches the point of fragrance, add and simmer:

1 finely minced small onion
¾ cup Burgundy

When the duckling is done, remove and crush the liver and add it to the reduced wine mixture. Poach it gently in the wine with the drippings from the pressed carcass. Add several tablespoons of:

(Pâté de Foie de Volaille, 495)
Season to taste

Slice the breast lengthwise into about 20 thin strips and put them in a chafing dish. Should you want to serve the legs, they must at this point be removed and grilled, as they are too raw without further cooking. We prefer to utilize them later in some other dish.

➤ Cover the sliced meat quickly with the hot liver sauce and serve ➤ immediately from the chafing dish at table.

DUCK PILAF

4 Servings

Remove the meat from:

Roast Duckling, 432

There should be about 2 cups. Break the carcass apart. Add to it:

4 cups water
1 chopped onion
Some celery leaves

Simmer this stock covered for 1 hour. Strain. Bring to boiling point. Stir in slowly, not disturbing the boiling:

⅔ cup rice

Cook the rice until it is tender, about ½ hour. Strain it. Reserve the liquor. Melt:

2 tablespoons butter

Add and sauté covered for 5 minutes:

¾ cup finely chopped celery
1 teaspoon grated onion

Add the duck meat, the rice and:

1 cup liquid: leftover gravy, duck liquor or cream

Mix these ingredients well with a fork. Season them, if needed, with:

Salt and paprika

Serve the pilaf hot with:

Stewed plums or apricots

ABOUT GOOSE

Among the reasons for the decline in the popularity of goose are its high fat content and the toughness of a fully matured bird. The first drawback is being constantly reduced by breeders; the second may be lessened by buying no goose weighing over 12 to 14 pounds, dressed. Braise rather than roast any bird larger than this or one you suspect is older than 6 months. All goose meat is dark. Goose fat should be rendered and saved as a flavoring. It is especially good with braised cabbage or sauerkraut. Allow approximately 1 pound for each individual serving.

★ ROAST GOSLING OR GOOSE

Allow 1 Pound for Each Serving

Since goose is roasted like duck, ➤ please read about Roasting Duck or Goose, 432.

Preheat oven to 450°.
Pick, clean and singe, if necessary:

An 8-lb. gosling or a 10- to 14-lb. goose

Fill the cavities or a separate baking dish with:

Apple, Prune, Chestnut or Sauerkraut Dressing for Game, 372 to 374

Allow 1 cup dressing to each pound of bird. If not stuffing the bird, try filling the cavity with:

(Quartered oranges, pricked to release juices)

Place the goose on a rack in an uncovered pan, allowing 25 minutes to the pound for a gosling and about 15 minutes to the pound for larger birds. Reduce the heat at once to 350° and pour off the fat as it accumulates. Make:

Poultry Pan Gravy, 341

Season it with:

Pearl onions
Ginger

Or, if unstuffed, serve with:

Prunes in Wine, 141, Gooseberry Preserves, 838, Red Cabbage, 295, Curried Fruit, 128, or Chestnut Purée, 298

BRAISED TRIMMINGS OF GOOSE OR GÄNSEKLEIN

Rub with garlic:

Goose back, neck, gizzard, wings and heart

Place in a heavy pot. Add:

Mirepoix, 572

Half cover with boiling water. Simmer ➤ closely covered, until nearly tender, about 1½ hours.

Season to taste

and add:

(A pinch of ginger)

Cover and simmer the meat until tender, about ½ hour longer. Remove from the pot. Strain the stock, removing the grease. Make:

Poultry Pan Gravy, 341

Pour it over the meat. Garnish with:

Chopped parsley

Serve with:

Apples Stuffed with Sauerkraut, 131, or Dumplings, 202, and applesauce

POTTED GOOSE OR CONFIT D'OIE

Draw, pluck, singe, 418, and cut up:

A 10-lb. goose

Cut off, reserve and refrigerate the heavy fat. Salt the pieces of goose well on all sides. Place in an earthenware crock and weight with a nonresinous hardwood board. Cover and leave in a cool, dry place, not over 40°, 6 to 8 days. When ready to cook, place the refrigerated fat in the bottom of a large heavy pan.
Put on top of it:

A Bouquet Garni, 572

Wipe the salt from the meat and put the pieces on the fat layer. Simmer slowly 2 to 4 hours. ➤ Be sure, as the fat melts, that there is enough to cover the meat completely. If not, add, as needed:

Lard

Use at once or store in a cool place, again making sure that the meat is ➤ well covered with the fat. This dish will keep for months and can be served cold or reheated in the fat. If hot, a good accompaniment is:

Franconia Potatoes, 320

which are cooked in the goose fat. Or use in:

Cassoulet, 475

ABOUT ROCK CORNISH HENS, GUINEA FOWL, AND SQUABS

Like iced tea and peanut butter, **Rock Cornish hens** are, so to speak, an American invention, and a surprisingly recent one, the result of patient crossbreeding of Cornish gamecocks and Plymouth Rock hens. They are plump little birds with all white meat and an attractive gamy flavor, due partly to their ancestry and partly to a diet that usually includes acorns and cranberries. Choose young birds, 5 to 7 weeks old, weighing about 2 pounds dressed.

Guinea fowl came originally from Africa—hence their name. The hens are much tenderer than the cocks. Because their meat is naturally very dry, it is of prime importance ➤ to bard them, 420, and not to overcook.

Squabs, originally wildfowl, are now raised on farms, like chickens. When young—about ¾ pound—they are called **doves;** when grown up—1¼ pounds or so—**pigeons.** No one in the least hungry has ever been satisfied with fewer than two doves.

ROAST CORNISH HENS, GUINEA FOWL AND SQUABS

Allow 1 Small Bird per Person

➤ Please read about these birds, above.
Preheat oven to 450°.
Pick and draw:

Small guinea fowl, squabs or Cornish hens

Either bard, 420, or brush with:

Melted butter

and dredge with flour. They may be loosely stuffed with:

Wild Rice Dressing for Game, 373, or Rice Dressing for Cornish Hen, 373, or a fruit dressing, 373, adding some green grapes

Place the birds breast side up, with legs tied, uncovered, in the oven. ➤ Reduce the heat at once to 350° and roast until tender: 1 hour or more if stuffed, about 45 minutes if not. They may be basted while cooking. If barded, remove the salt pork and allow them to brown. Make:

Poultry Pan Gravy, 341, with mushrooms

or serve with:

Bar-le-Duc Preserves, 838

BREASTS OF GUINEA HEN

Allow 1 Breast per Person

Preheat oven to 425°.
Bard, 420, each:

Breast of guinea hen

Put into the oven and ➤ reduce the heat at once

to 350°. Baste the breasts frequently. Cook about 45 minutes or until they are tender. Serve *sous cloche*, a fancy way to say under a glass bell, with:

Colbert Butter, 350

Or serve with:

White Wine Sauce, 345, or Champagne Sauce, 344

and:

Sautéed Mushrooms, 308

BRAISED SQUABS

4 Servings

➤ Please read about Squabs, above.

Preheat oven to 350°.

Cut into pieces or leave whole:

4 pigeons or 8 doves

Dredge them with:

Seasoned Flour, 552

Melt:

¼ cup butter

Sauté the birds slowly in the butter until they are just seared. Place them in a casserole. Add to the fat in the pan:

¼ cup chopped onion
1 diced carrot
¼ cup chopped celery

Stir these ingredients about 3 minutes. Add:

1 cup boiling Chicken Stock, 523

Pour this over the birds. Cover closely. Bake about 45 minutes or until tender. You may add for the last ½ hour:

1 cup sliced mushrooms

Do not let birds become dry. If they do, add more stock. Make:

Poultry Pan Gravy, 341

to which you may add:

Cultured sour or sweet cream
(Chopped olives)

Serve the squabs within a ring of:

Boiled Rice, 206

Sprinkle them with:

Chopped parsley or chives

BROILED SQUABS

Preheat broiler.

Pick, draw and clean:

Squabs

Split down the back and flatten them. You may cut out the backbone with shears. Put them on a greased broiler, skin side up. Brush well with:

Melted butter

Place the birds 4 inches from the heat. Broil 15 to 30 minutes, turning once. Season with:

Salt and paprika

Serve on:

Buttered toast

Pour the drippings over them. Garnish with:

Chopped parsley

Serve with:

Cranberry Jelly or Sauce, 133
Crusty Soft-Center Spoon Bread, 629

ABOUT WILDFOWL

The opening of the season for grouse—that very British bird which dwells in and feeds on heather—stirs up a degree of knowledgeable excitement equaled only by a *vendange* in the Côte d'Or. All over Southern Europe, each autumn, small birds, spicy with berries, are netted by the hundreds. And along the shores of Chesapeake Bay, the canvasback duck—which in October feeds on the wild celery of the shoreline—is preferred above all others.

We lived for years under one of the major flyways of the world and looked forward to the days when the males in our family sought out the bird-blinds in the surrounding marshes and rich fields. On their return, dinner parties were held in profusion. The children usually clamored for the plump little quail, leaving the rare, well-hung ducks to their more sophisticated elders.

To a large extent, proper care immediately after shooting determines the ultimate excellence of flavor in wild birds. While the bird is still warm, the neck is split and the carcass bled. To keep the blood for use in sauces, see 339. Check the neck for any undigested food and remove it.

Some birds—snipe, woodcock and plover—are cooked with the trail still inside, see 440. Although quail and a few other smaller birds should be plucked, drawn and cooked within 24 hours of killing, it is important in general not to pluck or draw any wildfowl until you are ready to cook it, since the added surface exposure of the carcass to air will induce spoilage before tenderization can be accomplished.

To tenderize and improve flavor, it is advisable to hang many wild birds, specifically partridge, prairie fowl, ducks, plover, grouse and hazel hen. How long to hang depends first on age. Old birds can be held longer than young ones. A second consideration is the weather. In muggy periods, ripening is accelerated. The third—and perhaps the most important—is personal preference. Some hunters go to extremes, holding a bird until the legs stiffen, even until head and body part company. A more moderate and acceptable state of maturity is reached when the feathers just above the tail can be drawn out easily or when a slight bluish-green tinge appears on the thin skin of the abdomen. However long birds are to be hung, suspend them, undrawn, by the feet ➤ in a cool, dry, airy place. If the weather is very warm, dust the feathers with charcoal. In any season, the birds should be protected with cheesecloth or screening.

➤ Dry-pluck all fowl. This is easier to do if the bird is chilled. Scalding or soaking preparatory to plucking breaks down the fatty tissues in the skin too rapidly if they are subsequently to be held for even a short time or are to be frozen.

Before cooking, look the birds over carefully and remove any shot with a pointed utensil. Do not use any livers or gizzards that have been penetrated by shot. Cut out meat that has discolored near the shot or any dog-damaged areas. Remove the oil sac at the base of the tail. After plucking, wildfowl should never be washed before cooking, merely wiped with a damp cloth. Safe exceptions are fish-feeding ducks which, if they must be used, should be parblanched for ½ hour before cooking.

➤ Singe all fowl just before cooking, including those which have been frozen. The interior of the bird may first be salted or rinsed with 2 tablespoons of brandy or sherry. Should it be necessary to counteract a too gamy taste, we suggest cooking with sauerkraut or using a marinade. Never try to soak out the taste with water. If the bird is to be cooked unstuffed, placing in it an apple, an onion, a carrot, parsley, a few celery ribs or some juniper berries helps attract off-flavors. These fillers are, of course, discarded before serving.

➤ Age determines how wildfowl should be cooked. If you are at all doubtful that a bird is young or prime, do not hesitate ➤ to use a moist-heat method of cooking, 149, or roasting in foil, 422. Very old birds are fit only for the stock or soup pot or for making hash, forcemeat and sauces.

On many occasions only the breasts of wildfowl are served, as the legs are often tough and full of tendons. If you use the legs, remove the tendons, see 418. Otherwise, simmer the legs with the wings, necks and giblets for game stock, 523. This is most useful, for in no cooking is less gravy naturally produced than in that of game. Therefore, it is doubly important to increase the stock of the game you are cooking, in order to bring up the flavor of a sauce or aspic. If game stock is not available, veal stock is the most sympathetic substitute.

Before roasting or marinating wildfowl, break down the breastbone by a blow with the flat side of a cleaver. This not only makes carving easier, but reduces the amount of marinade needed. To prepare a wildfowl for broiling, split the back and spread the breasts flat, using poultry shears for small birds.

Whether roasted or broiled, wild birds are, without exception, leaner than domestic varieties and for this reason should be cooked for shorter periods. Barding, 420, is usually advisable. Sometimes a flour and butter paste is used to coat them before barding. The barding may be removed halfway through the cooking process, but, if so, basting with butter or pan drippings should continue until the bird is taken from the heat. If a paste has not been applied you may, after the removal of the barding, want to dust the bird with flour to hasten its browning.

Most light-fleshed wildfowl is cooked well done and most dark fowl is cooked *vert-cuit* or *saignant*, that is, roasted brown on the outside under high heat, but still rare and running with juice and blood within. With these differences in mind, you can prepare most larger wildfowl by the recipes suggested for chicken, 422 to 431.

With smaller birds the situation is more complex. Ideally, the criterion for doneness should be internal temperature; but the flesh of such birds is shallow, and the usual meat thermometers are too bulky for practical use. Instead, the cook is advised to choose a time somewhere within the suggested limits we recommend and, if necessary, cut into the meat carefully toward the end of the period to determine how much more time it requires.

Suggestions are given in individual wildfowl recipes for those combinations of foods which are classic with game. Let us also recommend, as compatible accompaniments, a dressing of chestnuts or wild rice; a salad of chicory or cress; a dish of gooseberry or quince conserve; and a sour cream or wine sauce, not too powerfully seasoned.

ABOUT SALMI OF WILDFOWL

A true salmi has two major characteristics. The meat is roasted—barely so, if the game is dark. And the meat from the breasts and the legs, if choice, is sliced and put to one side and kept warm. Preparation is concluded at table, much as in Duck Rouennaise, 433, where the skin and the chopped carcass are put through a duck press, shown in the chapter heading. If the game is a water bird, the skin may be too oily to use. The pressed juices are combined with the flambéed livers, the sauce enhanced with a mirepoix and then reduced and strained. It is then reinforced by a Demi-Glaze Sauce, 346, or Sauce Espagñole, 346, based on the same kind of game as that being served. Salmis may also be enriched with mushrooms or truffles. The meat is just heated through at table in a chafing dish with this very rich sauce, given a swirl of butter, 339, and served at once.

Obviously, a classic salmi, fully accoutered, is only foı the skilled cook whose husband is a Nimrod and has presented her with more than a single bird. If she is less well endowed, she will have to base her sauce on the backs, wings and necks of the bird that is being presented and eke out her Espagñole Sauce with veal stock. Needless to say, the dish is rarely presented in its original form. And the salmis that appear on menus are usually made from reheated meat, with sauces which have been previously confected. They can still be delicious, especially if care is taken ➤ not to boil the sauce and thereby toughen the meat. Another simpler way to serve precooked game is to make up a mixture similar to Pheasant in Game Sauce, 439, which lends itself even to ❄ freezing.

MARINATED WILDFOWL

Serves 2

➤ Please read About Wildfowl, 435. Clean and disjoint a:

Pheasant, partridge or grouse

Place in a casserole and cover with a marinade of:

1 small quartered onion
1 small bay leaf
1 clove garlic
2 cups port wine
1½ teaspoons salt
½ teaspoon pepper

Be sure the wine covers the pieces. Let stand refrigerated 24 hours. Remove the meat from the marinade, and dry with a towel. Reserve the marinade.
Preheat oven to 375°.
Put into a heatproof casserole:

2 tablespoons butter

Add the cut-up pieces of bird and bake, uncovered, about 45 minutes, turning several times. Strain the marinade and pour it over the pieces. Return to the oven for another 30 minutes or until tender. Take the pieces from the casserole. Keep them warm. Reduce the sauce and:

Season to taste

Serve with:

Wild Rice, 212, Kasha, 201, or Noodles, 213

ABOUT WILD DUCKS

Flavor depends so much on the way ducks have been feeding. The shallow-water types may have been feasting in nearby grain fields and may be very succulent. These include **mallard, black duck, pintail, baldpate, gadwall, teal, widgeon, shoveler** and **wood duck.** The deep-water or diving ducks thrive on aquatic vegetation. They include **canvasback, redhead, ruddy, bufflehead, golden eye, scaup** and **ring-neck.** Sometimes these varieties feed on fish or shellfish, a diet which alters their flavor. The red and American mergansers or other habitual fish eaters should be used only in emergencies.

Wild ducks are usually not stuffed, but their interiors may be greased to help retain juices. If gamy, they may be rubbed with ginger or lemon. Celery, grapes or sliced apples in the cavity also help minimize a too pronounced taste. Discard these additions before serving.

Cooking times vary with types. They may be as long as 20 minutes for canvasback and mallard or just 12 minutes for teal. The livers of most ducks, as well as those of coot, see under Small Game Birds, 440, are especially choice and make delectable pâtés, 494.

ROAST WILD DUCK

4 Servings

To draw, pluck, singe and truss ➤ please read About Wildfowl, 435, and About Wild Ducks, above. This cooking method seems to be the hunter's ideal. The juices are red and flow freely when the duck is carved.
Preheat oven to 500°.
Prepare:

2 wild ducks

Have them at room temperature. Dry thoroughly inside and out. Rub the insides with:

Butter

Fill cavities loosely with:

A few skinned onions or peeled, cored and chopped apples, or drained sauerkraut

Bard, 420. Place the ducks on a rack in a roasting pan. ➤ Reduce heat to 350° and roast, uncovered, 18 to 20 minutes. Degrease the drippings and add:

Wine and stock

Reduce, then remove from heat and add:

Cultured sour cream

Reheat, but ➤ do not boil. Serve the ducks at once with the sauce and:

Braised Celery, 298

▤ BROILED OR BARBECUED WILD DUCK

A good way to cook wild duck and an easy way to serve it.
Preheat broiler.
Split down the back, clean well and wipe until dry:

A wild duck

Rub it with:

(Garlic)

Spread with:

Unsalted butter

seasoned with:

Paprika

Broil about 4 inches under the broiler or 4 inches above charcoal. Baste frequently with:

An unsalted fat or oil and wine

Cook until tender. Remove to a hot platter.

Season to taste

Make a sauce with the drippings, 542.
Serve with:

Oranges in Syrup, 136, or
Kumquat Compote, 136

Fried hominy is a well-known accompaniment to wild ducks. So are grilled sweet potatoes, or apples stuffed with sweet potatoes.

BRAISED WILD DUCK

Draw, pluck, singe and truss:

A wild duck

Melt in a heavy flame-proof casserole:

4 tablespoons butter

When it reaches the point of fragrance, put in the duck and brown on all sides. Add, when browned:

1 leek—white part only—or 6 button onions
4 tender turnips
1 Bouquet Garni, 572

➤ Simmer, covered, 25 to 35 minutes or until the duck is tender. Degrease the drippings and garnish the casserole with:

Green Peas, 314

Serve at once with:

Citrus Salad II, 111

WILD GOOSE AND WILD TURKEY

1 Pound per Person

These birds are only table-worthy if under a year old—preferably between 6 and 9 months. Whatever the age, both types of birds should be hung, from 24 hours to a week, and cooked with moist heat, 149. Weights fluctuate, depending on variety and age, from about 4 to 9 pounds. ➤ To draw, pluck, singe and truss, see 418–419. For wild goose and wild turkey proceed as for turkey, 422, or cut into pieces:

A 5- to 6-lb. wild goose

In a heavy casserole, heat to the point of fragrance:

1/3 cup butter
1 1/2 cups small white whole onions

Add:

1/4 lb. finely diced salt pork

and continue to cook until onions are golden. Lift out onions and pork and discard. In the remaining fat, brown the cut-up bird. Add:

Juice of 1/2 lemon
1/2 teaspoon allspice
(A few slivers gingerroot)

➤ Simmer, covered, about 30 minutes. Stir if necessary. Add:

2 cups dry red wine

➤ Simmer, covered, about 45 minutes longer or until tender. Thicken the pan gravy slightly with:

Toasted dry bread crumbs

Serve with:

Noodles, 213
Spiced apricots or crab apples

POTTED WILD FOWL

Allow 1 Pound per Person

A good way to preserve any extra wildfowl.
➤ Please read about Wild Goose, above.
Draw, pluck, singe and cut into pieces:

A young wild goose or other wildfowl

Prepare as for:

Potted Goose, 434

Serve either hot or cold.

HAZEL HEN

Allow 1 Pound per Person

Please read About Wildfowl, 435.
Since this bird is apt to be resinous, it is best to poach it first in milk for 15 minutes. Bone, and grill about 12 minutes in all.

ABOUT PHEASANT

➤ Please read About Wildfowl, 435. We hope your pheasant is young, with a flexible breastbone, gray legs and a large pointed terminal feather in its wings. If it is a cock, it should have rounded, not sharp or long, spurs. Then you may roast or broil it even without hanging. With pheasant, barding is usually advisable. These young birds can be used as in any recipe for chicken.

Otherwise, to give the bird both flavor and tenderness, about a 3-day hanging period is advised, during which the color of the breast will change somewhat and there will be a slight odor.

An old bird should be barded and either braised or used in another moist heat recipe.

ROAST PHEASANT

3 Servings

➤ Please read About Wildfowl, 435, and About Pheasant, above.
Preheat oven to 400°.
Bard, 420:

A young pheasant

You may stuff it with:

Chestnut Dressing, 372, or Sausage Dressing, 371

Place in oven. ➤ Reduce heat at once to 350°. Cook about 25 minutes per pound or until tender. If unstuffed, serve with:

Fried Croutons, 551, or Bread Sauce, 343; currant jelly and Braised Celery, 298; or Rice Pilaf, 209, and Gooseberry Preserves, 838

or, classically, with:

Smitane Sauce, 345

BRAISED PHEASANT

3 Servings

This recipe comes from a hunting fan.
➤ Please read About Wildfowl, 435, and About Pheasant, above.
Preheat oven to 400°.
Prepare:

A 3 1/2- to 4-lb. pheasant

Pound:

A thin slice salt pork

Separate the skin from the breast flesh of the pheasant and insert the salt pork. Place in the body cavity the pheasant liver and:

A small peeled tangerine

Lace the opening tightly. Truss the pheasant, 419.
Melt in a heavy pan:

1/4 cup lard

Brown the bird, turning it and basting until it is golden all over. Place in a casserole. Add and turn in the fat:

12 sliced mushroom caps

Pour these over the pheasant. Melt in a saucepan:

1/4 cup butter

Stir in, cook, but do not let brown:

3 shallots or 1 small minced onion
2 tablespoons flour

Stir in gradually:

1/4 to 1/3 cup Marsala or Madeira
1/2 teaspoon salt and freshly ground pepper

Pour this into the casserole. Our correspondent adds a sprig of fresh fennel and 2 crushed juniper berries. ➤ Cover the casserole and bake the pheasant about 1/2 hour. Serve it from the casserole with:

Fried Hominy, 200, and currant jelly
A green salad

* PHEASANT IN GAME SAUCE

10 to 12 Servings

➤ Please read About Wildfowl, 435.
Preheat oven to 400°.
Prepare for roasting:

5 or 6 pheasants

Bard, 420, with:

Bacon or salt pork

Fill the cavity, if you wish to reduce the gamy taste, with:

Apple or onion slices

Discard them after birds are roasted. Roast at 400° for 20 minutes. Remove meat from bones and reserve, keeping the meat in as large pieces as possible. Cook for 2 hours, or until reduced about a third, a stock made from the bones, skins, drippings and barding, using:

2 large chopped onions
2 cloves garlic
2 bay leaves
1 tablespoon black peppercorns
1 teaspoon thyme
1 small pinch rosemary
1 cup chopped parsley
(6 juniper berries)
¼ lb. ham trimmings
1 quart dry red wine
2 quarts water or Chicken Stock, 523
Stems from 2 lb. of mushrooms
3 fresh tomatoes

Strain the stock an add it to:

¾ cup White Sauce I, 341

Add to this sauce:

Caps of 2 lb. of mushrooms
¾ cup red wine

Simmer about 25 minutes.

Season to taste

Reduce by one-third, strain and add:

¼ cup brandy

Simmer another 10 minutes. Arrange meat in a 3-quart casserole. You may put it on a bed of:

(Cooked wild rice)

Pour sauce over it. To serve, reheat, uncovered, in a 350° oven 45 to 55 minutes. If frozen, thaw and bring to room temperature before reheating.

PHEASANT SMITANE

3 Servings

Bard, 420:

A 3½- to 4-lb. pheasant

with:

Sliced salt pork or bacon

Brown the pheasant in:

Butter

in a heavy pan. Then place it in a deep casserole with the drippings. Cover tightly and let simmer over low heat until tender, about 45 minutes. Add:

4 cups diced tart apples
2 tablespoons brandy or Calvados
2 cups cultured sour cream
Season to taste

and cook over low heat until the apples are tender. ➤ Do not boil. Serve with:

Wild Rice, 212, or Gnocchi, 204

ABOUT PARTRIDGE

French restaurant menus list young partridge as *perdreau*—masculine; older ones, invariably and ungraciously, as *perdrix*—feminine. Hang an old bird the better part of a week. Marinate it before cooking, preferably by braising. An old partridge in full feather may be recognized by the conspicuous red ring on the eye circle, its yellow beak and its dark legs. If a partridge is under six months old, it still has its pointed first-flight feather, and its legs will be plump. The red-legged French partridges are larger and not considered so delicate as the English. There is some confusion in America about the very name of partridge. No true partridge is native, but the name is given in the north to the ruffed grouse and in the south to quail.

If the bird is fresh, it has a rigid vent. ➤ A true partridge can be cooked by any recipe for chicken if larded; or, if barded, as for pheasant. But, if it is old, a longer cooking period will be necessary. It may be served in a Salmi, 436, as for duck. Some people like it braised with Sauerkraut, 295, allowing 2 pounds of the sauerkraut to three 3-pound birds. Add the sauerkraut the last ½ hour of cooking. Others shudder at so strongly flavored an accompaniment. A more delicate one is Braised Endive, 298. Or wrap the partridge in grape leaves, simmer it in wine and stock for 35 minutes; then roast it in a 350° oven 25 minutes. Allow 1 pound per person. Make Poultry Pan Gravy, 341, and serve the partridge with Boiled New Potatoes, 317, and watercress.

GROUSE, PTARMIGAN OR PRAIRIE CHICKEN

Allow 1 Pound per Person

Young grouse which feeds on the tender shoots of the heather is one of the most coveted of all game. To test for youth, hold the bird aloft by the lower mandible. If this breaks, failing to support the weight of the bird, you have a young specimen. Roast or broil if young. Braise if old. The same treatments apply to **Canadian Grouse** or **Black Game,** also known as **Black Grouse** or **Coq de Bruyère.** Resinous in flavor, this species is not quite so delicious as true grouse. Both must be dry-plucked, because of the birds' soft feathers and tender skin. We do not recommend broiling grouse, as the meat is too dry.
Preheat oven to 300°.
Prepare for cooking as you would a chicken:

Young grouse

You may lard the breast, 445, with thin strips of:

Salt pork

or bard it, 420. Or you may stuff it with:

A small apple, a skinned onion or ribs of celery

Grouse is served rare, cooked to a pale pink tone.

Allow 30 to 45 minutes' cooking in all. Baste frequently with:

Melted butter or drippings

Remove the bacon. Brush the bird with:

Butter

Dredge it lightly with:

Flour

Place it in a hot 500° oven until brown. Make:

Poultry Pan Gravy, 341

Serve with:

Rowanberries or cranberry sauce

ABOUT SMALL GAME BIRDS

Birds here discussed are of many kinds: **quail, woodcock, ortolans, figpeckers, coots or mudhens, wild doves, snipe, rails, curlews, plover, larks, reed birds, thrushes, moorhens** and **gallinules.** They are bracketed on the basis of similar treatment, although coots should be skinned rather than plucked, and the fact that they are served one or more to a person. Small birds are usually used as fresh as possible, although they remain edible as long as the legs are flexible. Quail, which is about the largest discussed here, should not be hung longer than 24 hours. ➤ All small birds, except coots, should be dry-plucked. You may clean as for chicken. In fact, some, like snipe, plover, ring doves and woodcock, may be cooked undrawn, although the eyes and crop are discarded before roasting. To use the entrails after cooking, sieve or chop the intestines and flambé them, 155, briefly in brandy. Mix with pan drippings and spread on a crouton or over the bird as a glaze before serving. Or, if you draw the bird before cooking, reserve the intestines, chop them, sauté them briefly in butter, then proceed as above.

Small birds should be barded, 420, or you may wrap them first in fig or grape leaves. All lend themselves to roasting and skewering or broiling from 3 to 10 minutes. Blackbirds and crows, if eaten as a matter of necessity, must be parblanched 10 to 15 minutes first, 154.

Small birds produce very little pan drippings. Pour what there is on a crouton, or on a piece of crisp scrapple. Or combine the drippings with a Demi-Glaze Sauce, 346, and wine or lemon, or use them to make Smitane Sauce, 345, Hunter's Sauce, 347, Bread Sauce, 343, or White Wine Sauce, 345; or use any recipe for braised chicken—allowing in the timing for difference in size. Any special peculiarities or classic combinations are listed in individual recipes.

ROASTED SMALL GAME BIRDS

➤ Please read About Small Game Birds, above.

Preheat oven to 450°.

Bard, 420:

6 small game birds

It is not necessary to stuff them, although a few peeled grapes or bits of celery or parsley may be tucked inside and discarded later. Place in the pan with the birds:

1 tablespoon butter

Bake the birds about 5 minutes, ➤ reduce the heat to 350° and bake them 5 to 15 minutes longer, according to their size. Timing in general varies from woodcock, 8 to 10 minutes, to quail, unstuffed, 10 to 15 minutes; to stuffed, 15 to 18 minutes.

BROILED SMALL GAME BIRDS

➤ See About Small Game Birds, above.

Preheat broiler.

Bard, 420:

6 small game birds

Place them on a broiler. Cook from 12 to 20 minutes, according to size. Turn frequently. The barding may be removed toward the end of the cooking period and the birds browned briefly by further broiling. Add the juice of:

1 lemon

to:

Stock or wine

if there is an insufficient amount of drippings.

Season to taste

Serve the birds on:

Croutons, 551

Pour the gravy over them. Garnish with:

Parsley

BRAISED SMALL GAME BIRDS

➤ Please read About Small Game Birds, above.

Preheat oven to 350°.

Prepare for cooking:

6 small game birds

Melt in a saucepan:

2 tablespoons butter

Add the birds and sauté them until lightly browned. Add:

½ cup boiling stock or wine

A Mirepoix, 572

Cover the birds with a poaching paper, 151, and bake 15 to 20 minutes. Make:

Poultry Pan Gravy, 341

Add to the gravy:

(2 tablespoons lemon juice or cultured sour cream or brandy)

Serve on:

Croutons, 551

Garnish with:

Parsley

⊟ SKEWERED SMALL BIRDS

➤ See About Small Game Birds, above.

Wrap in buttered grape or fig leaves:

Small birds

or bard them, 420, with very thin slices of:

Salt pork

Roast skewered over coals 10 to 15 minutes. To finish for serving, you may remove the barding, roll the birds in bread crumbs, baste with drippings and heat in a moderate oven 5 minutes longer.

DOVES OR WOOD PIGEONS

1 to 2 pe Person

➤ Please read About Small Game Birds, 440

A dark meat with a fine flavor. Dove is usually tenderer than pigeon. Unless the birds a·e very young, prepare as for:

Braised Small Game Birds, above

Serve the sauce garnished with:

Almond-stuffed olives

or with a compote of:

Red Sour Cherries, 135

QUAIL

1 per Person

Somtimes called partridge in our deep South. ➤ Please read About Small Game Birds, opposite. Quail has a delicious white meat. If the fat of the bird is hard rather than firm before cooking, the flesh will be tough and must be prepared by a moist heat method. If the bird is young, roast or broil. ➤ Never overcook. Serve with:

Quince preserves and curried rice.
or watercress and lemon wedges

or with:

Smitane Sauce, 345, and green grapes; or a baked pear, the center stuffed with a pimiento

If you have broiled the quail, brush it with:

(Anchovy Butter, 350)

SNIPE OR WOODCOCK

Allow 1 to 2 Birds per Person

These fowl are highly prized by some epicures in the autumn when they are fat and meaty. At other seasons the more critical connoisseurs claim that the only part worth bothering with is the cooked entrail, au jus, on a few croutons.

➤ Please read About Small Game Birds, opposite.

Prepare and cook as for:

Small Game Birds

or use the recipe for Grouse, 439. You may use the trail, see 440. Skin the head, but leave it on. Remove the eyes and crop. Bring the long, curved beak down to pierce and hold the legs in place. Bard, 420, and roast 10 to 15 minutes.

MEAT

ABOUT MEATS

A reappraisal of meat and its role is due in this protein-hungry world. With milk, eggs and fish, meat is still the source of our most complete protein, and, coming at the end of the food chain, it provides as well a richness of minerals and trace elements, many of which are increasingly recognized as essential to our physical development. In this period of world inflation, however, many see meat as a wasteful commodity whose production costs far exceed those of grains, which, if skillfully combined and supplemented, can furnish us with adequate nourishment. For many, too, meat eating provokes ethical considerations. For whatever reasons vegetarianism may be adopted, see page 1 for a discussion of its potential nutritional pitfalls.

With these factors in mind, our meat shopping is done with a greater awareness than ever of the need for intelligence in the use of this valuable element in menu building, whether we serve hamburger or splurge with a crown roast of lamb, 472, or a piglet, 478, or blend meat and innards in a pâté, 494, all illustrated above.

A novice approaching the meat counter may also approach a state of panic. The friendly, informative butcher of a good while back has often been succeeded by a presence that mysteriously slices, grinds and wraps behind a glass partition; or, more recently, by binfuls of boxed meat-cuts straight from the processing plant, where new procedures of boning and packing save transportation costs and safeguard sanitation. Whatever the merits of prepackaging—and skillful aging is not likely to be one of them—the cuts look bafflingly similar, but often react to cooking in totally unexpected ways. If you are a rank amateur, we hope that this chapter will give you the skill of an expert in choosing the right cut for the type of dish in mind. Note, too, that meat recipes are grouped consistently, first for tender and then for tougher cuts.

Tender cuts generally, you will see on the chart, 451, lie in those sections of the animal where the least movement and stress occur, and respond to ➤ dry-heat processes: roasting, broiling, pan-broiling, sautéing and stir-frying. For further details, see the chapter on Heat, 145, for these processes and those for the tougher cuts. The latter, with more connective tissue, demand long, slow cooking with moisture or with ➤ moist-heat processes: braising, stewing, fricasseeing, pot-roasting, poaching and deep-fat frying. In all but the last named, the temperature of the cooking liquid ➤ should never go above 180°. For this reason, we do not recommend the pressure cooking of meats, although expediency sometimes overcomes our better judgment. But if you should pressure-cook meat, follow the directions given by the manufacturer of your equipment.

For ways to counteract toughness, see about Cooking Tough Meats, 444; about Marinating, 445; about Grinding and Pounding, 444; and About Larding, 444. For a discussion of microwave cooking of meat, see 160.

But there is more about meat than cuts, grades and cooking methods that must be learned the hard way. How the animal was fed—whether on grass or corn; how long meat has been held and at what temperatures; whether it is watered or treated with preservatives; when it was packaged—all are factors for which you must rely partly on your experience but mostly on the integrity of the butcher.

ABOUT MEAT GRADES AND BUYING

Most American consumers benefit from two forms of protection offered in the meat market by the U.S. Department of Agriculture. First, all meats sold in interstate commerce are subject to government inspection for wholesomeness and cleanliness; but do be cautious in purchasing ➤ locally butchered meats not subject to these rigid federal sanitation regulations. Second, meats sold by the wholesale packing companies are graded and stamped by government-employed "graders" according to nationally uniform federal standards of quality for tenderness, juiciness and flavor. We are especially concerned here with grading, for the quality of the meat is as important in our choice of cooking method as is the cut—or where the meat lies on the animal's body. U.S. grading falls into six main classes, as follows—although **Choice** and **Good** are the two grades of major interest to most consumers:

PRIME

A scarce grade generally commandeered by hotels and clubs and rarely available in neighborhood markets. From young, specially fed cattle, Prime is abundantly marbled or flecked with fat; it is tender, well-flavored, fine-textured and usually aged; the encasing fat is white.

CHOICE

Meat of high quality but with somewhat less marbling than prime. There are now five subcategories of the Choice grade, of increasing degrees of leanness; the tenderer cuts may be dry-roasted or broiled.

GOOD

Still a relatively tender grade, but with a higher ratio of lean. The encasing layer of fat may be thin; there is less juiciness and flavor. Oven-roasting by the constant-heat method may be satisfactory for tenderer sections, but moist-heat cooking should usually prevail.

STANDARD

From low-quality young animals, with a very thin fat covering and virtually no marbling. The youth of the animals gives this grade a bland flavor, but tenderness cannot be counted on; there may also be a tendency toward dryness. Use moist-heat cooking methods only.

COMMERCIAL AND UTILITY

Meat from old animals. By reason of maturity and fat content, these meats have better flavor than Standard grade, but are tough and coarse in texture—even when carefully cooked—because of their great proportion of connective tissue.

Although we are always being assured that ➤ the protein value of meat from older animals is comparable to that from the younger, more tender ones, we know that they rarely match in eating quality. Definite exceptions apply to meats for stocks, 520, and for soups, 169. Both have more flavor if made from the meat of more mature animals.

Sometimes you will see a further USDA inspection stamp—K for **Kosher** or "clean" meat. This is meat from which the jugular vein has been removed to facilitate the drainage of blood at the time of slaughtering. The Kosher stamp should also guarantee freshness, as ritual demands consumption within 72 hours of slaughter.

Besides being graded, meats are sometimes marked with a second USDA stamp, a **Yield** number, which indicates in increasing proportion from 1 to 5 the amount of excess fat content or waste. The usual yield number available in most markets is Yield 2. In purchasing meat, bear in mind that cuts with the smallest percentage of bone and fat make the best buys, and that while price per pound may go down for bonier cuts with more fat, the amount you need per serving goes up. It may surprise you to know that the cost of sirloin steak is comparable per portion to unboned chuck, that center-cut pork chops are cheaper per serving than loin or rib chops, and that spareribs can be twice as expensive per serving as center-cut pork chops.

In buying trimmed meats, allow for boneless cuts 1/4 to 1/3 pound per serving. This category includes ground beef, lamb and veal, boneless stew, boned roasts and steaks, flank, tenderloin and most variety meats. ➤ In buying meat with some bone, allow 1/3 to 1/2 pound per serving. These cuts include rib roasts, unboned steaks, chops and ham. ➤ For bony cuts, allow 3/4 to 1 pound per serving. In this bracket are short ribs, spareribs, lamb shanks, shoulder, breast and plate cuts, brisket and hock. The chart on 451 will give you an additional appraisal of the proportion of bone as a cost factor in various meat cuts.

STORING MEAT BEFORE COOKING

Raw meat should be stored at once at 35° to 40°, loosely wrapped; or, if encased in fat, uncovered. You will see a typical butcher wrap illustrated on 821. If you will simply pull out the ends of the paper and loosen them, adequate protection and proper ventilation are usually ensured. As a general rule, the larger the piece of meat, the longer it will store.

Ground meat, fresh sausage and variety meats are among the most perishable kinds, both as to flavor-retention and safety. Cook them within 24 hours of purchase; and, if the ground meat is to be stored in amounts over a pound, make sure it is loosely covered and so placed in a container that it is no more than 2 inches thick, thereby allowing the chill of the refrigerator to penetrate it quickly. Uncooked diced and cubed meats should be used within 48 hours or so. Roasts will hold 3 to 5 days; steaks 2 to 4.

Pork, lamb and veal are slightly less stable than beef. Prepackaged cured or smoked meat and sausages may be stored refrigerated for a week in the original wrapper. Once meat is opened, exposed surfaces should be protected. In checking for spoilage, be sure meat is not slimy to the touch; that there is no off-odor on the surface of beef, or in pork where the bone meets the flesh. To freeze meat for storage, see 826.

SEASONING MEAT

If you add salt to meat, it is best to do so at or toward the end of cooking, whether by dry- or moist-heat methods, because salting before browning draws the juices, with their considerable natural salt content, out of the meat and into the pan. There are other ways to accent flavor. In dry-heat methods, meat may be rubbed with garlic, onion, herbs or spices about a half hour before cooking; or slivers of garlic or onion may be inserted near the bone of a roast. Any bits of garlic remaining on the surface of the meat should be discarded before cooking, as its scorched flavor is objectionable. In moist-heat methods, the addition of herbs or wine to the stock will lessen the need for salt. For flavoring meat by marination, see 445. Delicacy of flavor may be preserved in meat heavy with fat by pouring off excess grease after the first half hour of cooking.

COOKING TOUGH MEATS

Tenderness in raw meats depends not only on the comparative youth of the animal, but on the strain of cattle to which it belongs and the way it was fed. Toughness is due both to the presence of connective tissues and to a lack of fat in the muscle. Larding, below, and Barding, 420, can help to make up somewhat for lack of fat. But the best way to convert stringy to tenderer tissue is by very long and very slow covered cooking in the presence of moisture. See Pot-Roasting, Stewing and Braising, 447. Grinding and mincing, too, make chewing easier. The texture of the meat, however, if basically tough, remains so, and it should never be used in luxury dishes like galantines or, for that matter, even in those so commonplace as hamburger.

Any meat can be made more palatable by seasonings and by added fats or dressings. Pounding and scoring are a help in cuts that are normally treated by dry-heat methods, like sautéing and pan-frying. Another favorite technique is marination, 445.

Chemical tenderizing is a modern development. One controversial innovation of this type is beyond the control of the consumer. The live animal is given an injection of vegetable enzyme, the effects of which are carried throughout the body before butchering. Special aging and storing techniques must accompany this method. The enzyme is reactivated at 130° and reduces cooking time. Unfortunately all meat tissues—those which need it and those which do not—are affected by enzyme injection. As a result, the tender portions may become flabby and somewhat tasteless, and the meat generally has a jellied consistency which we find unpleasant.

Nor can we say much for the home method of sprinkling the meat with papain, a derivative of papaya, which also tenderizes but adversely affects the flavor. If you care to try out a papain derivative of the household type, sprinkle it on both sides of the meat, allowing 1 teaspoon of tenderizer per pound. Prick the meat all over with a fork after applying the tenderizer. Recent studies seem to indicate that papain enzymes function as meat warms up to between 140° and 176°, so the tenderizer may be applied just before the meat is put on to cook.

MINCING, GRINDING, POUNDING AND MACERATING MEAT

The effects of the first two processes are quite different. Particles of minced meat remain separate in further preparation; but ground meat, especially if ground 2 or 3 times, tends to pack. ➤ Always handle ground meat lightly to avoid a dense finished texture.

Pounding, which breaks down the tough fibers of meat, may be done with a wooden or rubber mallet or the flat side of a cleaver. If you are inexperienced, hold the cleaver in both hands and ➤ be sure the handle projects beyond the board or table surface—so that you don't bang your fingers. Or use a macerating mallet such as shown in the foreground.

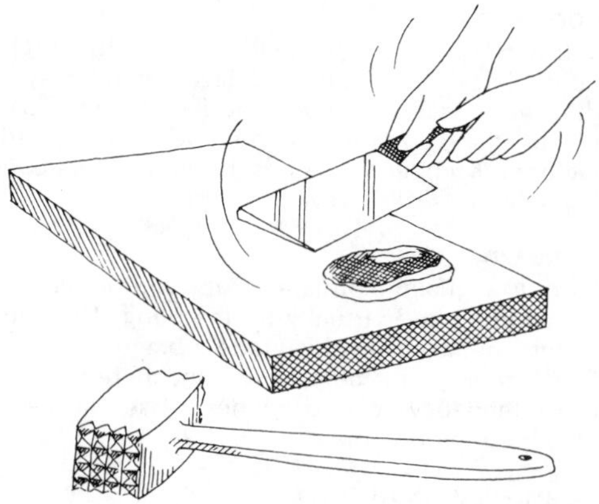

If you slightly moisten the cleaver or mallet, and strike with a glancing motion, the meat is not so apt to stick. In pounding something delicate, like a capon breast, put it first into a fold of oiled parchment paper. These precautions will keep the meat intact, even when pounded paper-thin. A chef friend has suggested that if you find a very thin piece of meat too measly-looking, it can be pounded and then folded over for the cooking to make it more presentable when served.

➤ All working surfaces in these procedures—especially those of wood—should be carefully cleansed with hot water and detergent afterward and carefully dried, since *salmonella* and other dangerous bacteria thrive in equipment not properly sanitized.

ABOUT LARDING

Larding, or the insertion of strips of pork fat into lean cuts, helps give meat juiciness and flavor. This process has become more useful now that the trend in meat production is toward less marbled meat. To prepare lardoons, see directions on the recipe opposite. Use short ones inserted near the surface, and put them in across the grain of the meat or fowl. Cut long ones so they protrude slightly at either end of a chunk of meat, and force them in parallel to the grain so they show up when the meat is sliced. It is important for attractiveness to cut all lardoons in uniform square-cut thicknesses varying from ⅛ to ½ inch. Larding needles are of two types. Those used in surface larding are very thin pinpointed models with a flexible top which can easily be pried open to insert the lardoon and then pressed tightly against the lardoon to hold it as the needle is drawn completely through the meat at a shallow angle as shown below. Sometimes these shallow lardoons are so placed that their ends form decorative rosettes. Allow about 2 to 3 ounces of pork fat for one pound of meat.

For internal larding, use the handled lardoire. Its blade is like a pen point, the base of which elongates the entire length of the shaft and remains open all along the top. Use this type to make, as well as insert, the lardoon. To fill, run it along the top of a long piece of salt pork. Then insert the point of the lardoire into the meat.

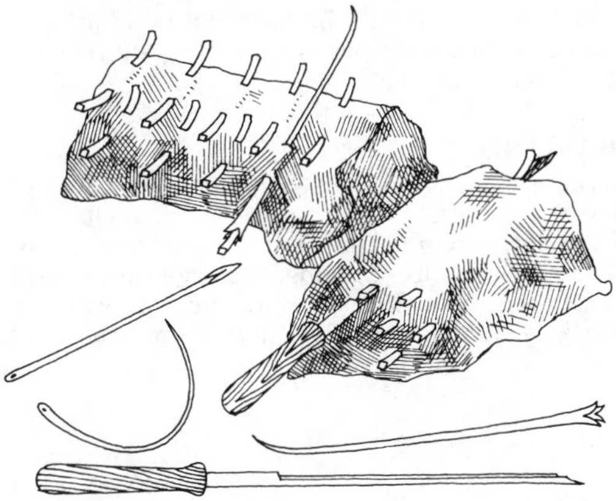

With a slow motion, push the lardoire through the meat, turning it continuously in one direction until at least ½ inch of the lardoon projects at either end of the meat. With the still-filled lardoire at rest, release the exposed lardoon from the lardoire, both top and bottom, with the tip of a knife. With the thumb of one hand, hold the released top portion of pork fat firmly against the top of the meat so as to keep the lardoon from coming out of the meat as you withdraw the lardoire with the other hand. Pull the lardoire gently, twisting it from side to side, so the lardoon releases along its entire length. Allow about one lardoon for every inch of the diameter of the meat.

For another method of preventing the drying out of meat, see Barding, 420.

LARDOONS

Enough for 2½ Pounds of Meat

Please read About Larding, above. Lardoons may be blanched briefly to release salt; then dried. They may also be frozen just long enough to stiffen them before insertion into meat, or you may proceed as follows.

I. Rub:

¼ lb. pork back fat, salt pork or bacon

with a cut:

(Clove of garlic)

Cut into small uniform strips varying in cross section from ⅛- to ½-inch squares. Dip into:

Freshly ground pepper
Ground cloves

II. Marinate:

¼ lb. salt pork lardoons

in:

A few tablespoons of brandy

Just before using, sprinkle with:

Nutmeg
Chopped parsley or chives

MARINATING MEAT

This is a process which enhances tenderness and flavor in meat by soaking it in a liquid containing some form of seasoning and almost always an acid, such as vinegar, wine, lemon juice, buttermilk or yogurt. Using this process involves nutritive losses unless the marinade is subsequently used to sauce the meat. Because marination is also used for foods other than meat, it is discussed fully in Ingredients, 528.

SAUTÉING OR PAN-FRYING MEAT

Since this process is often used for foods other than meat, a full description will be found on 149. It is a popular and quick method of cooking thin or breaded cuts of meat.

PAN-BROILING MEAT

This method of broiling may be convenient for cooking steaks or chops about an inch or less in thickness or for hamburgers. Slowly heat a heavy—preferably iron—skillet until the edge of a steak lightly touched to the skillet will sizzle briskly—not hiss sharply. Greasing the pan is unnecessary for meats that are marbled or for hamburger with normal fat content; for lean meat you may rub the skillet with a very small amount of fat. Let meat cook uncovered, sizzling briskly, for about 5 minutes. When the meat is seared and brown on the bottom, turn at once and sear for a few minutes on the other side. Avoid long cooking, which toughens the meat. ➤ Pour off any fat that may accumulate, or the meat will wind up fried or sautéed rather than pan-broiled. We do not recommend the old technique of pan-broiling on a salt base, which extracts meat juices. Fat-free broiling may be done in a coated skillet or on a soapstone griddle; in either case, follow manufacturer's instructions.

BROILING MEAT

Please read about Broiling, 146, and about spit-cooking and outdoor grilling, 155. Choose tender cuts, see Chart, 451, such as beef steak or lamb chops. Flank steak or London Broil, 457, is also broiled, but must be cooked rare. The broiling of veal and fresh pork is not recommended; instead, sauté or pan-fry such cuts. Kebabs are frequently marinated before broiling. For broiling frozen meats, see 826.

Consult your range manufacturer's instructions as to whether preheating is required and whether or not the oven door is to be left ajar. Remove meat from refrigerator about an hour before cooking. Cut off excess fat and score the remaining fat about every 2 inches around the edge, to keep the meat from curling. Center the meat on the grid—which should be cold to prevent sticking—and adjust the broiler rack so that the top surface of the meat is 3 to 5 inches from the heat source. If grid is hot, grease it or the meat. Without seasoning the meat, broil the top side until well browned; then turn and broil until the second side is browned. Only one turning is required for a 1-inch steak or chop. For 2-inch thickness lower the rack so the surface of the meat is 4 inches from the heat source and turn more frequently. Broiling time depends on thickness, fat content, whether the meat was aged, and the degree of doneness desired. Approximate timings for various meats are given under the individual broiling recipes.

ROASTING MEAT

Please see the chart on 451, and About Meat Grades and Buying, 442, for types of meat appropriate for dry-heat roasting. In choosing meat for this process and deciding what variation of the procedure to follow, the important factors are the tenderness of the cut and the amount of marbling. Temperatures and timings are given in the individual recipes. Please read about Timing and Doneness, 447. For gravy-making methods, please read about Sauces Made by Degreasing and Deglazing, 340, or about Meat Pan Gravy, 341.

In all cases, the meat should be removed from the refrigerator about 2 hours before cooking. For Prime and Choice grades, place roast—not less than about 3 ribs in thickness—on a rack, fat side up, in an open shallow greased pan in a preheated oven. As soon as you close the oven door, reduce the heat and time the cooking from that point, depending on the size of the roast and degree of doneness wanted. For Prime meats, the fat content makes basting unnecessary. Choice-grade meats are subdivided into five categories, depending on the amount of marbling, but ➤ all Choice-grade cuts profit by basting, see right; and the last two categories—which are quite lean—may benefit from larding, 444, or barding, 420.

If you are dealing with the next lower grade, U.S. Good, be forewarned that you may be taking a chance if you dry-roast rather than pot-roast meat of this type, and that dry-roasting is not recommended for pieces weighing less than 4 pounds.

For Good-grade, use the following constant-heat, dry-roasting method as an alternative to the initial high-heat procedure used in **Joy** recipes. Place meat in a preheated oven—350° for pork, 325° for beef and lamb—and keep temperature steady during the entire roasting process. Larding, barding and basting may prove helpful. In short, everything possible should be done to accentuate whatever tenderness the leaner grades may have. One of the tricks is never to roast the less tender cuts more than medium rare—except for pork, which must be cooked until all pink color disappears—and to carve the meat in very thin slices, diagonally, across the grain.

Another constant-heat roasting method for meats other than pork, see above, uses lower heat for a longer period. The oven should remain ➤ at least 275° at all times, for unwanted organisms may not otherwise be destroyed, no matter how long the cooking. Dry-roasting is not recommended for meat lower than Good-grade. These tougher meats should be prepared by long, slow moist-heat cooking. See Pot-Roasting, Stewing and Braising, 447.

BASTING

Basting is a method of retaining the juiciness of meat by moistening its surface with melted fat from time to time during the roasting process. Since roasting, like broiling, is a dry-heat process, the meat remains uncovered and no water or stock is used, for these liquids form steam and

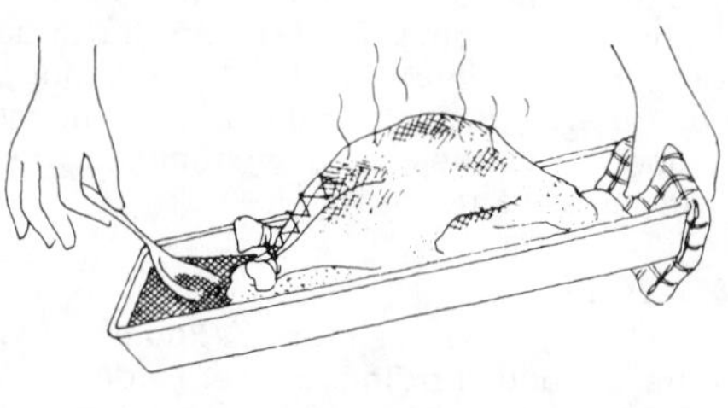

change the process to moist-heat cooking. No basting is necessary for well-marbled meats with a high intrinsic fat content. But all the less marbled cuts profit by basting. ➤ Before roasting brush the pan with a small bit of fat to prevent charring the drippings, which results in a bitter taste in the juices used later for gravy. Basting should begin after about the first half hour of cooking and should be repeated as often as necessary to prevent drying—at intervals of 10 minutes or more, depending on the size of the roast, its leanness, the oven temperature, and the stage of the roasting process. The best utensil for basting is a bulb-type baster, illustrated opposite, that suctions pan drippings, to which other melted fat may be added if necessary. Or a spoon may be used as shown opposite. Very lean meats profit by larding, 444; and barding, 420, produces an effective form of self-basting.

ABOUT POT-ROASTING, STEWING AND BRAISING MEAT

All three procedures benefit the less tender cuts such as chuck, shoulder, bottom round and brisket. These moist-heat methods cook by simmering meat in varying amounts of liquid in a closed pot or casserole for relatively long periods. Pot-roasting may be used for pieces up to 4 or 5 pounds, and stewing for meat in smaller chunks. Cuts of various sizes may be braised, using less liquid than for a stew, and a somewhat longer simmering period. Braising is invariably preceded by browning. The ideal type of container for all three methods is a heavy pan like a Dutch oven, with a tight-fitting cover.

For moist-heat cooking in general, and especially on an electric range, we recommend the following procedure. Before it is browned, the meat may simply be wiped dry, or it may be dredged with flour, 552, or it may be marinated, 445. For browning, we prefer rendered fat from the meat itself—or fat that complements its flavor—and only enough to cover the bottom of the pan and to prevent charring, which imparts a bitter taste to gravy. In a heavy skillet or Dutch oven, heat the fat slowly until a piece of meat sizzles briskly when it touches the pan. Turn the meat frequently so that it browns slowly. It is important not to crowd the pan—which lowers the heat, causes steam to form, and results in graying rather than browning. For flavoring, diced vegetables such as onions, celery and carrots may be added to the fat when the meat is partially colored. Or, to control the heat more easily, the vegetables may be sautéed separately until they have a translucent quality and then combined with the meat. Separately sautéed onions may be sprinkled with a very small amount of sugar; the caramelizing that results adds attractive color to a stew.

After browning meat, pour off excess fat. You may leave 1 or 2 tablespoons of fat in the pan and set the meat on a bed of Mirepoix, 572. Or, for pot-roasting, place the meat on a rack or on a piece of pork rind. Then add boiling stock. For a stew, the liquid should barely cover the meat. In pot-roasting and braising, add liquid in the bottom of the pan to a depth of 1/4 to 1/2 inch. As soon as the liquid reaches a boil, reduce the heat at once to maintain a simmer ➤ and cover the pan tightly. If necessary, replenish the liquid from time to time, adding boiling stock or water. Turn the meat occasionally to keep it moist. After browning, you may place the pan in a preheated slow oven for the remainder of the cooking, ➤ keeping the temperature constant throughout. The temperament of your oven and the degree of heat retention of your pan will determine the correct temperature—300° to 325°—for long, slow, steady cooking.

If cooking is done on top of the stove, the vegetables you will serve with the meat may be added to the casserole during the last 45 minutes of cooking—about 1/4 pound of vegetables to 3/4 pound of meat. Very mature vegetables may profit by a brief blanching beforehand. For oven stews, it is preferable to cook the vegetables separately on top of the stove and add them to the casserole toward the very end of the cooking period.

You can, of course, short-cut the entire process above by ✪ pressure cooking, but the necessarily high heat produces a less desirable result.

There is a method known as cooking **à blanc**—sometimes used for veal, pork or poultry in stews and pot roasts—in which raw meat is placed directly in boiling water and the heat reduced ➤ almost at once to a simmer as the meat changes color. Also cooked without browning are the **Chinese red stews,** but because the liquid used is half soy sauce and half water, the meat is colored during the cooking. In red-stewing, season with ginger, scallions and sherry.

Gravy served with a stew should not be thick but should have good body—what the French call *du corps.* Always allow a stew or pot roast to stand at least 5 minutes off the heat so that the fat will rise and can be skimmed off before serving. If the stew is made some hours in advance, the meat may be drained and the gravy cooled and defatted more easily. You may thicken the gravy with a small amount of flour paste, 339. To reheat leftover stews, see 449.

TIMING AND DONENESS

Timings and temperatures for varying degrees of doneness are given in the individual meat recipes. But, at best, meat timings are approximate, for there are many factors that make precision impossible—the temperature of the meat at the outset of cooking, its shape and thickness, the fat and bone content, the matter of aging. We recommend, therefore, the use of a meat thermometer for more accurate results. Insert the thermometer into the center of the meat, away from fat or bone, with the top of the thermometer as far as possible from the heat source.

If you have no thermometer, there are a couple of time-honored tests for doneness. Press the surface of the roast with your finger; if the meat is soft yet resilient, if it dents easily and at once resumes its shape, it is cooked to medium rare.

If it remains firm under finger pressure, it is well done. Another test is to prick or cut into roasted or broiled meats, though you thus lose valuable juice. Rare meat produces red juice; medium-rare, pink; well-done, colorless juice. ➤ Because of the danger of trichinosis, it is vital that pork, see 476, be cooked thoroughly, to the stage when juices run clear. Most other meats—with the exception of white meat of fowl—will be overdone at this stage.

The following are some general rules related to the timing of meats. Ovens must be preheated for roasting; in broiling, consult range manufacturer's instructions. Take roasts from the refrigerator about 2 hours before cooking; steaks or chops about 1 hour. To ensure internal temperatures high enough to destroy bacteria, 275° is the minimum oven heat for roasting meats, except for pork, see 476, no matter how long the meat is cooked—even up to 12 hours of roasting. For comparative periods of moist-heat cooking, a simmering temperature of 180° suffices because of the more penetrating quality of the heat.

If a household product for tenderizing is used, the papain derivative, see 444, greatly shortens the cooking period. The insertion of metal pins in roasting conserves energy to the extent that cooking time is shortened while juiciness is retained; but the meat will not be quite so tender. We recommend the ✪ pressure cooking of meats only if saving time is important; but tests show that the flavor is better retained at 10 pounds pressure; in any case, consult manufacturer's instructions. ▲ In high altitudes, roasting meat needs no time adjustment up to 7000 feet; after that, a longer cooking period may be needed. For the thawing and cooking of frozen meats, please see 826.

COOKING MEAT EN CROÛTE

Meat in a crust, or en croûte, lends itself particularly to buffet service: hot, it remains in good serving condition for half an hour; and, hot or cold, it is a conversation piece. There are two ways to proceed. Roasted meat—which may be beef, lamb, fowl or ham—may be precooked to within 30 to 45 minutes of doneness and cooled somewhat before the encasing dough is applied; the wrapped meat is then baked only long enough to brown the pastry and conclude the cooking of the meat, see Beef Wellington, 455. An alternate method applies the dough to uncooked meat, and the whole encased roast or ground-meat pâté is baked long enough to cook the meat thoroughly while the crust browns; see Pâté en Croûte, 494. For meats not precooked, it is essential that the dough covering be vented in several places when applied, to allow the escape of steam and to prevent buckling of the crust.

Following the French tradition, the tough croûte or dough covering is not eaten, but serves merely as a medium to preserve aroma and juices. If you prefer a latter-day American variety of edible crust, you may use a Pâte Brisée, 641; a Brioche Dough, 615; a Puff Paste, 643; or a stiff bread dough—which will need to be punched down once before rolling out. The recipe given here is for the traditional nonedible croûte—heavy in egg to lend the tensile strength necessary to cover big pieces of meat securely.

I. For Partially Cooked Meats

Preroast meat to within 30 or 45 minutes of doneness. Remove meat from oven and let it cool to room temperature. Make a covering of one of the doughs mentioned above, or the following:

Have all the ingredients at 70°. Mix together, to the consistency of coarse cornmeal:

4 cups all-purpose flour
1 cup shortening
1½ teaspoons salt

Make a well, 643, of these ingredients and work in, one at a time:

3 to 4 eggs

and:

½ cup water

Knead the dough until well bound. Roll into a ball and rest covered for several hours at 70°. Preheat the oven to 450°. Roll the dough into a large sheet about 3/16 inch thick. Place the meat on the dough, top surface down. Then fold the dough over it neatly, pressing it to take the form of the meat. Be careful to keep the covering intact. Bring the edges of the dough together and seal the seam with egg white. Then turn the covered meat right side up. Brush any excess flour off the dough with a dry brush.

Now the fun begins. From the pastry scraps that remain, cut rounds, flowers and leaves, or any decorations that suit your mood. If you like, score them with a fork to give their surfaces a variation that will show up markedly after baking. You may even use Puff Paste, 643, for such trimmings. Space them on the dough up to three thicknesses by applying French Egg Wash, 731, to each as a glue. When you are satisfied with your design—and don't make it too cluttered—brush the surfaces with egg wash again. Put the meat in a preheated 450° oven. Reduce the heat at once to 350°. Allow the crust to bake until it is delicately browned. For an even effect, repeat the egg glazing at the end of the baking. You may also brush the crust with butter on removal from the oven.

II. For Uncooked Meats

Prepare the dough as in I above; or use one of the previously mentioned doughs. Coat the meat to be covered with Egg Wash, 731. Fold the pastry around the meat and decorate as described in I above. ➤ Cut a series of decorative gashes—steam vents—in the dough casing, as for a covered pie. Bake the meat in a preheated 300° oven 2 to 3 hours, depending on size. Hams and legs of lamb may be boned and stuffed before wrapping. ➤ Precook any stuffing you may use, as the heat may not penetrate it sufficiently to cook it through.

ABOUT MEAT PASTRIES AND MEAT PIE TOPPINGS

How we'd relish judging an international competition of housewives turning out their native meat pastries! The doughs would range from the resilient to the flaky, with fillings running a full gamut of flavor. They would include: Won Ton, Ravioli, Kreplach, Piroshki, Rissoles, Enchiladas, Pot Pies. It is in such homely functional dishes, varied according to the season and by the individual cook, that the true cuisine of a country dwells. Many of the small-sized specialties call for precooked fillings which, already encased, need only a brief cooking of the dough and reheating of the filler, either by simmering in a broth, deep-fat frying, sautéing or baking. Pastry-covered meats can fit into the menu in many ways, depending on their size—from hors d'oeuvre or soup garnishes to a one-dish meal. The prize for the heartiest would go to the English with their Steak-and-Kidney Pie, 465. Usually the one most common on American tables is the Pot Pie, 252—pre-stewed meat heated in gravy, sometimes with vegetables, covered in various fashions with a dough topping.

One method is to place unbaked biscuits or dumplings on top of a stew, spacing them widely enough to allow steam to escape. The two essentials in making a meat pie are: first, to have enough tastily seasoned gravy to almost cover the cooked meat, and, second, to ensure that steam does not produce a soggy crust. One surefire procedure to prevent sogginess is the following.

I. Use:

Any unsweetened Pie Dough, 640

and prebake separately on a baking tin dough cut to cover the casserole or smaller individual dishes in which you will serve the meat pie. Since pie dough shrinks in baking, you must cut it slightly larger than the dish and prick the dough with a fork. Bake the pastry separately at 425° for 15 or 20 minutes, until golden brown. Remember that this separate baking means you will have to cover your casserole in some other way as the stew itself heats—with a piece of foil placed lightly on top, or with a loose-fitting lid. Just before serving, when the casserole has been heated through, place the prebaked crust on top and serve at once.

II. If you prefer to put an unbaked dough topping on the stew and heat the meat mixture and the dough at the same time, proceed as follows:
Preheat oven to 350°.
Fill baking dish with cooked stew and gravy to one inch from the top. Place over it a generous round of dough to allow for shrinkage, brushing the undersurface with white of egg to help make it impervious to steam. ➤ Be sure to slash vents in the dough covering. Heat the dish 45 minutes to 1 hour, when the stew should be thoroughly heated and the crust golden. You may brush the crust with butter before serving.

STORING COOKED MEAT

It is wise to promptly cover meat that is left over and to refrigerate it, covered, as soon as it has cooled slightly.

Do not store ➤ meat in hot gravy in quantities larger than 3 cups. Drain off the gravy and allow it to cool separately if the amounts are larger. If meats are ➤ stuffed, unstuff them and store the stuffing separately.

REHEATING MEAT

For convenience one is sometimes obliged to prepare roasted meat in advance, to be reheated just before serving. Although this procedure is not always satisfactory because of the tendency of meat—especially large roasts—to become dry on reheating, it can be done if there is no other solution to your problem of time. Simply bring the preroasted meat to room temperature and warm through in a ➤ preheated moderate oven.

Reheat sliced or sauced meats or hash by first heating the sauce separately, just to the point of boiling. Add the meat. ➤ Reduce heat to low at once. When the meat is thoroughly heated, serve immediately. Another method for warming sliced roasted meat is suggested on 161.

SHARPENING KNIVES FOR CARVING

A dull knife is a lazy servant that requires you to do more than your share of the work. But a sharp knife allows you to make neater, less ragged slices; it permits greater precision; it requires less cutting pressure, and therefore you are less likely to slice yourself. We recommend two implements for sharpening knives. One is a 6- to 10-inch sharpening stone with coarse and fine sides. Place

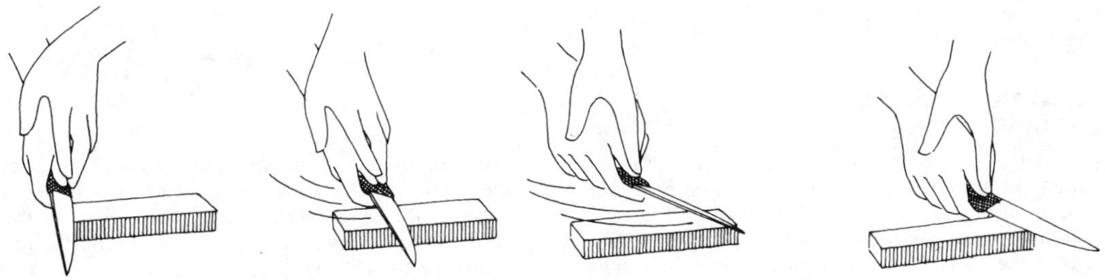

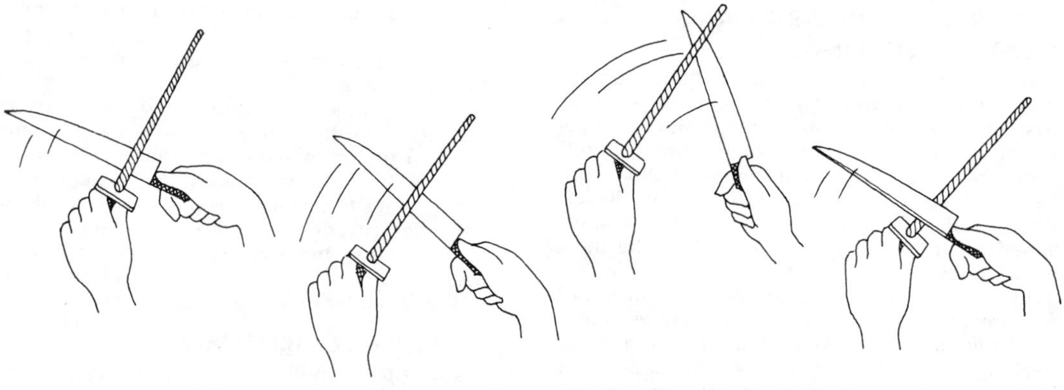

this stone in front of you lengthwise on a countertop. Lay the knife against the stone first on the coarse side at about a 15° to 20° angle and draw it in a curved sweeping motion toward you, as shown in the first three drawings on the left, ten times for each side. Then turn the stone over to the fine side, increase the angle of the blade very slightly, as shown on the right, and repeat. Be sure to clean from the blade the excess grit which you will have removed from the stone.

If you are sharpening your knife with a steel, you should do so before each carving period. The steel, which must be kept magnetized, realigns the molecular structure of the blade.

➤ To true the blade, hold the steel firmly in the left hand, thumb on top of the handle. Hold the knife in the right hand, point upward, the blade away from you, and the hand slightly away from the body. Place the heel of the blade against the far side of the base of the steel and begin to draw it along the length of the blade as illustrated in the first two sketches. The steel and blade should meet at about a 15° to 20° angle. ➤ Draw the blade across the steel, bringing it up from the left hand, with a quick swinging motion of the right wrist. ➤ The entire blade should pass lightly over the steel.

To start the second stroke, shown above right, bring the knife into the same position as in the first, but this time the blade should lie in front of the steel, away from you. About twelve strokes are enough to true the edge.

If you will get into the habit of sharpening your knife at frequent intervals, you will find that chopping, slicing and carving chores will go incredibly faster, and you will have a truly useful, extremely snappy servant at your command.

TO MAKE A FRILL FOR A SHANK BONE

To make a frill for a shank ham, a lamb bone or drumsticks, fold in half dinner-sized stiff paper napkins, about 12 x 8 inches. Cut through the fold at ½-inch intervals to within 1 inch of the open edge. Reverse the fold, bringing the open edges together. Begin to roll the uncut portion of the newly folded paper, leaving an opening at the folded open edge big enough to slip over the bone. Fasten this roll with scotch tape and slide the frill over the bone.

ABOUT MEAT CUTS

If you are doing your own butchering, you need to know intimately every bone in the body of the animal. We show, 451, the skeleton of a beef, which is very similar to that of other quadrupeds, except for proportion of bone to meat.

With all quadrupeds, the areas along the central spine portion which more or less hangs between the shoulder blade and the hip socket—areas with the least active musculature—are the tenderest. They can be counted on to cook by the dry-heat methods: roasting, broiling and pan-frying. Those areas just contiguous sometimes respond to dry heat by the constant-heat method, 146, but, like all the rest of the meat up through the shoulder and foreshank in front and from the rump to the hind shank, where muscles are active, they will need slow, moist cooking to break down the connective tissues. This is particularly true as you descend from Prime to Utility grades, 442.

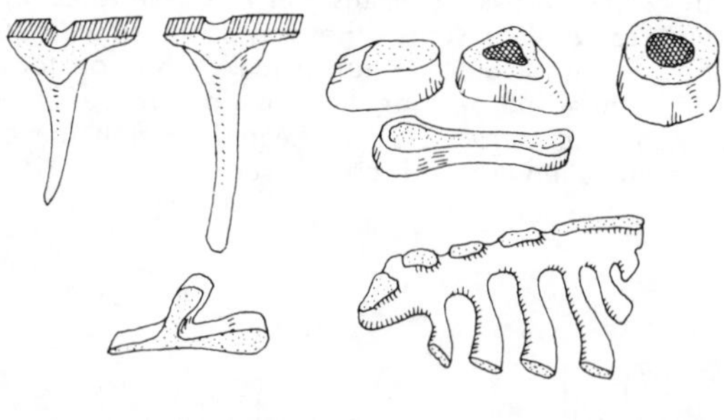

If you buy your meat ready cut and prepackaged, you need a different kind of knowledge of these same bones—what they look like as they lie cut and trimmed ready to use in see-through wraps. Familiarity with the bone structure is your

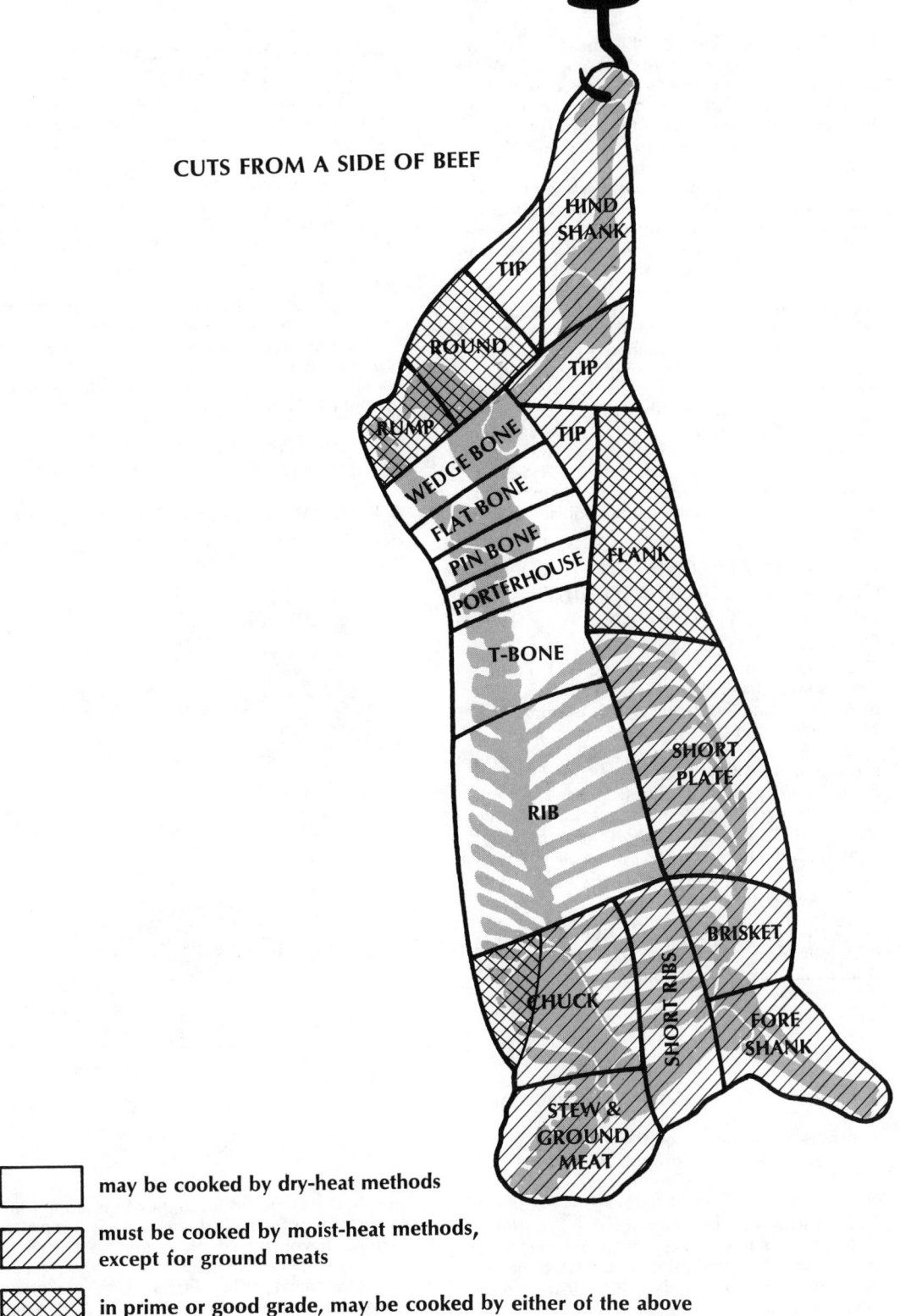

CUTS FROM A SIDE OF BEEF

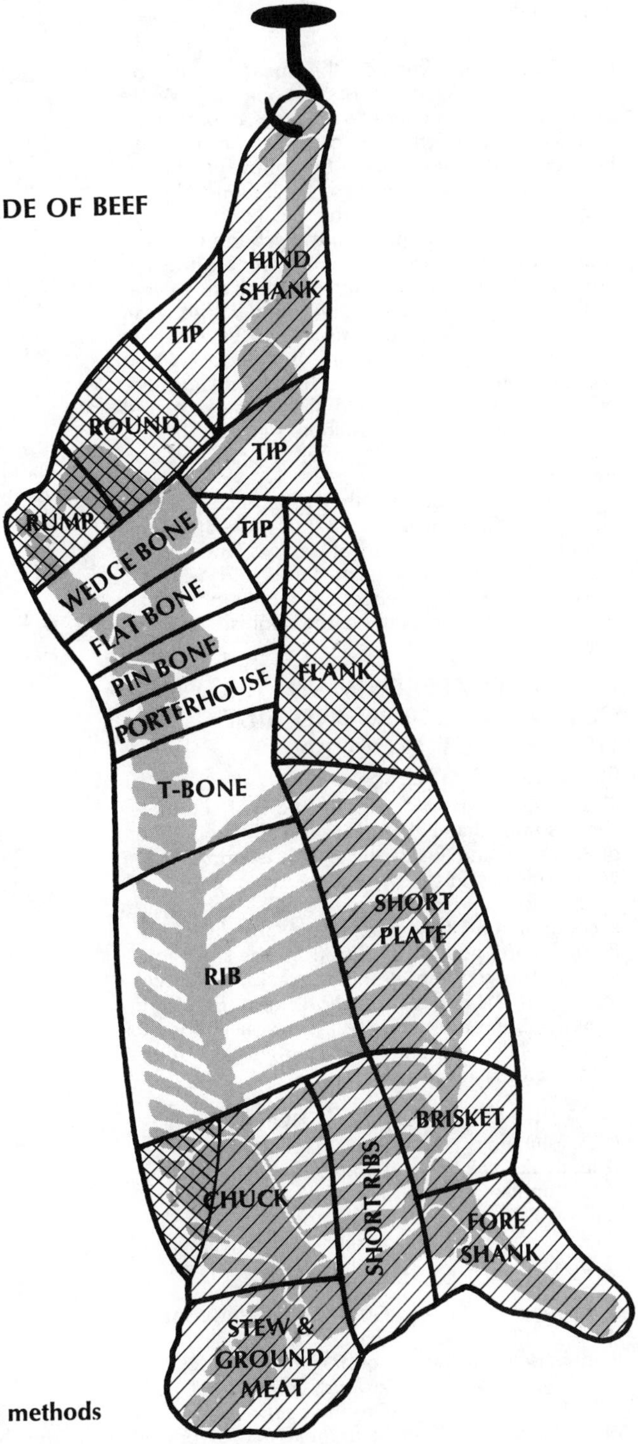

may be cooked by dry-heat methods

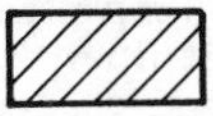
must be cooked by moist-heat methods, except for ground meats

in prime or good grade, may be cooked by either of the above

best clue as to whether the meat should be cooked by a dry- or moist-heat method. While there are slight variations of shape among beef, veal, lamb and pork, you can roast, broil, panbroil or pan-fry all cuts with the following shapes. Reading from left to right are the T-bone, the rib bone and three types of the wedge bone. The first of the wedge bones is the pin bone near the short loin; in the front of this group is the flat bone which is in the center cut, and above that is the wedge bone near the round. With veal, pork and lamb you may also cook by dry-heat methods if they show a round bone such as that seen last on the right above. If it is not ground, beef with this type of bone should be prepared by a moist-heat method, as should any cut having a blade bone or a brisket bone, grouped left and right in the foreground.

There are, of course, other differences in cuts and major differences in cooking procedures, all carefully noted in the meat recipes and in the Abouts on beef, veal, pork, lamb and venison. Taste and flavor preferences are highly individual, depending in large part on the sophistication of one's palate.

GUIDE TO APPROXIMATE YIELD OR CUTS FROM 250-POUND SIDE OF BEEF, CUT FROM AN 800-POUND STEER

Please see Chart, 451, for location of alternate choices immediately below; and read About Fillet of Beef, 454, and Steaks, 455. As an example, from 26 pounds of short loin you will have a choice of club, sirloin and porterhouse steaks—which are a combination of T-bone, sirloin and fillet. But, if you want 5 pounds of fillet from the short loin, you must forgo the porterhouse steaks, which will leave you 21 pounds of short loin for sirloin steaks, T-bone and club steaks. If you choose to have the fillet, see the illustration, 454, to utilize it to the best advantage.

FROM	CHOICE OF
21 lb. loin end	Butt steaks and roasts
2 lb. flank steak	Ground beef—flank steak
45 lb. boneless round	Top and bottom, Swiss steak, pot roasts, hamburger, cubed steak
23 lb. rib	7-rib roast, rolled roast, rib steaks
42 lb. boneless chuck	Ground beef, stew, pot roast
10 lb. boneless brisket	For braising, stewing, ground, corned beef
17 lb. plate	Ground beef, stew
10 lb. shank	Soup meat, marrowbones

Usable also will be the tripe, tongue, liver, heart, sweetbreads, brains, kidneys, oxtail and head. But you will have 49 pounds of unusable fat, bone and waste, and about 5 pounds will be lost in trimming.

ABOUT ECONOMICAL USE OF LARGE CUTS OF MEAT

If you are shopping for a household of two, there are times when you may look longingly at the "weekly special" on meat. How tempting the standing rib roast of beef, the rump of beef, the leg of spring lamb, the loin of pork, the round of veal or the half or whole ham! But unless you are planning to have guests, it looks like far more meat than you care to buy. But by taking advantage of special sale prices and planning ahead to freeze a part of the cut for future use, it is an economy to buy the larger piece. You can still have your delicious small roast—or steaks from the ham or veal, chops from lamb or pork, short ribs from beef. Then the remainder of the roast may be used in many interesting leftover dishes, see Brunch, Lunch and Supper Dishes, 250.

SUGGESTIONS FOR THE ECONOMICAL USE OF LARGE CUTS

6 RIBS OF BEEF—18 TO 20 POUNDS

Have the butcher cut a roast of 6 ribs as shown below.

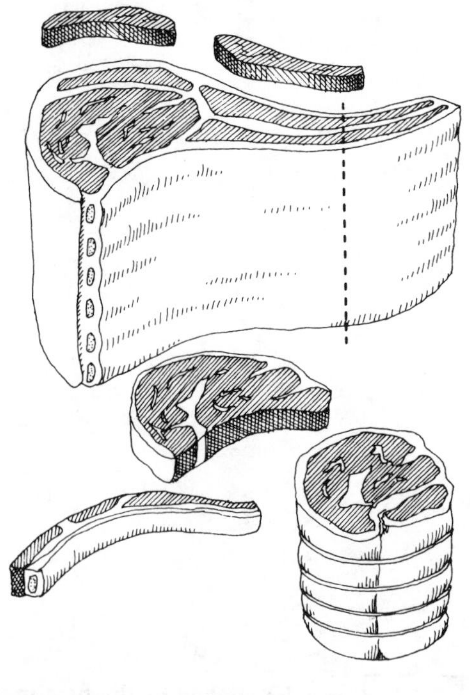

The **short ribs** are on the right of the dotted line. Baked, 464, or barbecued, these ribs will serve two persons. If you then look at the roast from the top, you will see two long, rather coarse-grained pieces of meat called **lifters.** They are shown above the roast and sliced, although they extend for the full depth of the roast. These are best cooked by moist heat in a beef stew, 459–462, and will serve four to five persons.

The **eye of the rib** removed next is tied into a roast which will produce about 24 slices; or, sliced horizontally, about ten 1-inch Delmonico or Spencer steaks; and the six bones will serve two persons.

2 RIBS OF BEEF—5 POUNDS

Have butcher cut off:

Short Ribs	464
Beef Roast	454

The leftover beef can be reheated in Cumberland Sauce, 356.

Or use it in:

Hot Roast Beef Sandwich with Brown Sauce and olives	270
Shepherd's Pie	262
Leftovers in Bacon	257
Peppers Stuffed with Meat and Rice	316
Cold Roast Beef and Tomato Sauce	352
Acorn Squash Filled with Creamed Food	330

RUMP OF BEEF—4 TO 5 POUNDS

Have butcher cut off a piece about 2 inches thick and dice it into 1-inch cubes for:

Beef Stew with Wine	460

Or use it in 1 piece for:

Pot Roast	459

Use the leftovers as:

Cold Roast Beef and Curry Sauce	345

or hot as hash, or in:

Hot Roast Beef Sandwich	270
Turnovers Filled with Meat	251

LOIN OF PORK—9 TO 10 POUNDS

Have butcher cut off 4 chops from center of loin for:

Pork Chops	479
Deviled Pork Chops	480
Braised Pork Chops	479

Use one end for:

Pork Roast	477

Freeze the other end for:

Pork Roast Stuffed with Sauerkraut	478

Use leftovers in:

Meat Pie Roll	251
Chop Suey	257
Shepherd's Pie	262
Pizza	610
Scrapple or Goetta	499

LEG OF LAMB, VEAL, FRESH PORK OR HAM

The bone structure of the leg in veal, lamb and pork is similar to that of beef shown on the chart, 451. In all these leg cuts, the center can be sliced separately for lamb steaks, veal cutlets or ham slices. The veal and lamb center cuts can be sautéed, as can pork, if smoked. Legs of lamb can be roasted. Similar veal and pork cuts demand moist-heat cooking. To cut or carve, see illustrations on 471 and 484, and the suggestions below.

LEG OF LAMB—5 TO 6 POUNDS

Have butcher cut off 4 loin chops for:

Broiled Lamb Chops II	472

Also a slice about 2 inches thick, diced into 1-inch cubes, for:

Curried Lamb	475
Lamb Stew	474

Roast the remaining shank end. 471

Leftovers may be used in:

Veal or Lamb and Spinach Dish	256
Eggplant Filled with Leftover Food	304
Lamb Terrapin	257
Lamb Sandwich	274
Scotch Broth	174

ROUND OF VEAL

Have butcher cut off 1 or 2 thin slices of veal for:

Veal Birds	469
Mexican Veal Steak with Noodles	470
Wiener Schnitzel	468

Have another slice cut off to dice into 1-inch cubes for:

Blanquette de Veau	470
Casseroled Veal with Sour Cream	470

Use the remainder for:

Veal Roast	467

Use leftovers in:

Curried Veal and Rice	256
Creamed Veal	256
Veal and Spinach	256
Veal Timbales	233

HALF HAM—4 TO 7 POUNDS

Have butcher cut off 1 or 2 slices to use for:

Broiled Ham	484
Stuffed Ham Rolls III	258
Ham with Fruit	485

Use remainder as:

Baked Ham	483

Use leftovers for:

Ham and Corn Croquettes	248
Ham à la King	258
Stuffed Ham Rolls II with Asparagus	258
Jellied Ham Mousse	120
Ham Cakes with Pineapple and Sweet Potatoes	258
Ham Loaf with Cooked Ham	257
Split Pea or Lentil Soup	177
Waffles and Ham in à la King Sauce	348

ABOUT BEEF

Beef, far and away the most popular American meat, is from mature cattle usually older than 9 months. There are other beef terms, such as **bullock beef,** which denotes meat from male cattle under 24 months; **calf,** usually between 3 and 8 months; and **veal,** see 466. Please read the general remarks About Meats, 442; and, to identify the various beef cuts, see the beef illustrations, 452, 455 and 456; for Economical Use of Large Cuts, see 452. The recipes that immediately follow are those involving ➤ dry-heat first, then moist-heat methods. For ground beef recipes, see 486 to 493; for cooked and leftover beef recipes, see Luncheon Dishes, 250.

ROAST BEEF

2 to 3 Servings to the Pound

These directions are for the large, tender cuts we think of as Sunday dinner roast beef. The most tender are the standing rib roast and rolled rib roast. The sirloin-tip roast, eye of round or rolled rump may be cooked the same way if they are of Prime or Choice grade. If you choose a standing rib roast, have your butcher remove spinal cord, shoulder bone and chine, and have him tie the chine back on to keep the contour of the meat and to protect the eye of the roast during cooking.

Preheat oven to 550°.

Having removed the roast from the refrigerator about 2 hours before, place meat fat side up on a rack in a shallow greased roasting pan. Do not cover. Add no liquid. Insert meat thermometer, 447, so that the tip is in the center of the thickest

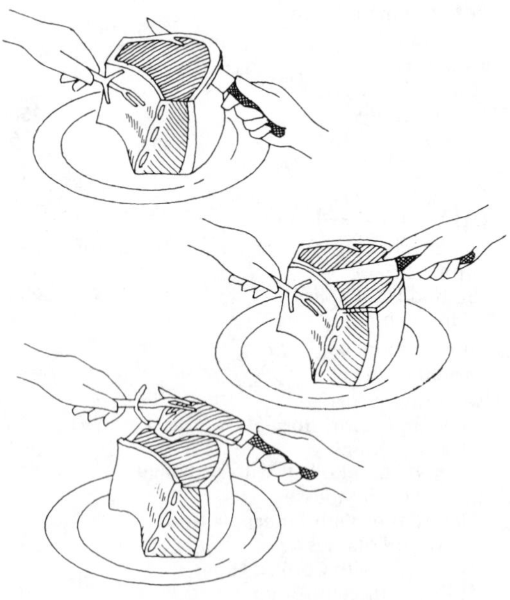

part and not touching fat or bone. ➤ Immediately reduce heat to 350° and roast 18 to 20 minutes to the pound for medium-rare. A rolled roast will require 5 to 10 minutes longer to the pound. Thermometer reading should be between 140° rare and 170° well-done. To make gravy, see Sauces Made by Degreasing and Deglazing, 340, or About Meat Pan Gravy, 341. Serve the roast with:

Baked Macaroni, 217, or
Yorkshire Pudding, 206, or
Tomato Pudding Cockaigne, 333

To carve, see left below.

ROAST STRIP SIRLOIN

24 to 30 Servings

Preheat oven to 550°.

Having removed meat from refrigeration about 2 hours before, trim excess top fat from:

An 18- to 22-lb. eye of the strip sirloin

Place fat side up on a rack in a greased shallow pan in the oven. ➤ Reduce heat at once to 350°. Roast uncovered, about 1 hour for rare meat, or until thermometer registers between 130° and 140°.

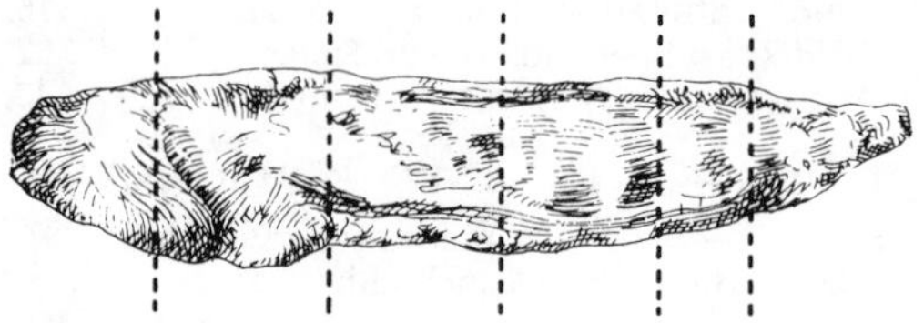

ABOUT FILLET OF BEEF

This choicest, most tender cut can be utilized in many ways. First trim off fat and sinew. Loosen fat at the small or tail end and tear this off, as well as the clods of fat near the thicker end. With a sharp pointed knife, remove the thin, tough, bluish sinew underneath. To cook the fillet whole, tuck the thin end under to equalize thickness; or you may simply cut off about 6 inches of the tail end and save it for Beef Stroganoff, 458; Sukiyaki, 458; Kebabs, 459; or Steak Tartare, 86. There is some dissension about classic fillet cuts for steaks. Perhaps the drawing above will help clarify the situation. Beginning and extending not quite halfway through the heavy end of an entire fillet is the head, or tenderloin butt. In the second half of the heavy end lies the **Chateaubriand** section, usually cut thick enough for a double or triple portion. If you divide the remainder of the fillet into four sections, as shown, you have first the **fillet** steaks, next the **tournedos,** then the **filet mignons,** or small fillets, and finally a tip section that is usually cubed for Beef Stroganoff, 458, or brochettes or beef kebabs, 459. The cuts vary from 2 to 3 inches in thickness for Chateaubriand, 1½ to 2 inches for fillets, and 1 inch for tournedos. Cooking times, therefore, vary proportionately.

FILLET OR TENDERLOIN OF BEEF

Allow ⅓ Pound per Serving

Remove meat from refrigerator about 1 hour before.

Preheat oven to 500°.
Remove the surplus fat and skin from:

A fillet of beef, at least 5 lb.

You may lard, 444, with narrow strips of:

(Salt pork or bacon)

Fold over the thin end of the fillet and secure with string. If not larded, spread the meat generously with butter or tie strips of bacon over it. Place on a rack in a greased roasting pan in the oven. Do not cover or baste it. ➤ Reduce the heat immediately to 400° and bake 30 minutes in all. A fillet is usually cooked rare when the internal temperature reaches 130°. Season when done. You may surround the fillet with:

Broiled Mushrooms, 308

Garnish the platter with:

Sprigs of parsley
Soufflé Potatoes, 321

Serve with:

Marchand de Vin Sauce, 347
Bordelaise Sauce, 347
Béarnaise Sauce, 359

BEEF WELLINGTON OR FILET DE BOEUF EN CROÛTE

About 12 Servings

If time is no object and your aim is to out-Jones the Joneses, you can serve this twice-roasted but rare beef encased in puff paste—but don't quote us as devotees.
Double the recipe for:

Puff Paste, 643

which can be prepared the day before and reserved in the refrigerator.
Preheat oven to 425°.
Rub with butter:

A 5-lb. fillet of beef

Roast on a rack 25 minutes or until thermometer reads 120°—very rare. On taking meat from oven, you may flambé with:

(1/3 cup brandy)

➤ Let meat cool to room temperature. You may then thinly coat with:

(Pâté de foie gras or de volaille, 495)

Now roll out part of the puff paste into a rectangle about 1 1/2 inches larger in width and length than the fillet. Spread the rectangle with:

Duxelles, 573

that have been well cooled. Preheat oven again to 425°. Center the fillet on the rolled-out dough. Roll out remaining dough and shape it over the entire fillet. Secure top and bottom pieces together, finger-pinching all around after brushing edges with:

White of egg

Use any excess dough for decorations, which you can stick to the surface with more of the egg white. Brush exposed surfaces with:

French Egg Wash, 731

Place the covered fillet on a greased baking sheet. Bake 10 minutes. ➤ Reduce heat to 375° and bake until crust is golden, about 20 minutes more. Allow to stand 15 minutes before serving on a garnished platter. Carve with a very sharp knife into slices about 3/4 inch thick. Serve with:

Sauce Périgueux, 347, or
Bordelaise Sauce, 347

ABOUT BEEF STEAK CUTS

As the growth of steak houses has shown, no meat is more popular, and at home when celebrating, the cry is usually, "Let's have steak." This word covers many cuts, the most desirable in the white section of the chart, 451. Coming from the sirloin section are the **wedge bone,** the **flat bone,** and the **pin or hip bone,** illustrated below. The pin bone, closest to the short loin, has a large tenderloin or fillet portion. The **sirloins** coming from the end near the hip are leaner than the porterhouse and T-bones that lie in the short loin section described next. Again see the chart, 451.

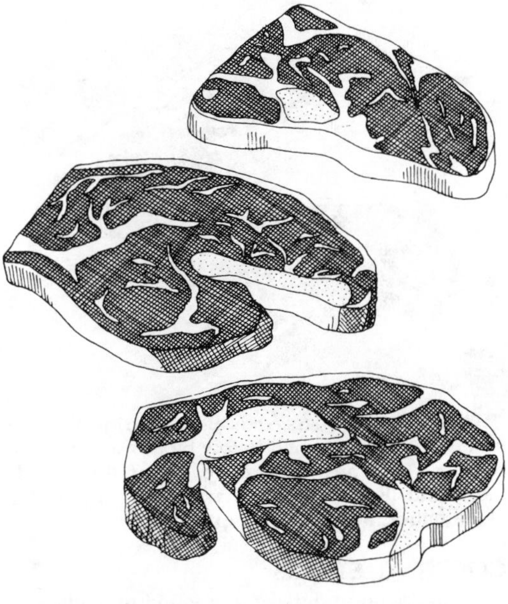

From the short-loin section comes the **porterhouse,** 456, which has a larger section of tenderloin and a longer tail than the **T-bone** below it. Still another cut in this area, shown last, 456, is the **club** or **minute** or, when trimmed, **Delmonico** steak, which has no tenderloin.

When steaks from the loin section are cut whole or in individual servings with the tenderloin removed, they are called **strip** or **shell** steaks. When cooked in individual portions they are broiled; in one piece they may be roasted, 454. For the sectioning of a whole **tenderloin** or **fillet** into steaks, see 454. For **Spencer** or **rib eye** or **rib** steaks from the rib section shown next on the chart, 451, please see illustrations in Economical Use of Large Cuts of Meat, 452.

By courtesy and custom the term steak is applied to the following beef cuts. Some, like **Salisbury** steak and **hamburger,** 486; **cube,** if macerated; and **flank** when prepared as for London Broil, 457, are treated by dry-heat methods. Hamburger patties made of ground meat, and Salisbury steak patties made of minced meat, are from trimmings of round or chuck and sometimes from the **hanging tender.** For scraped fillet of tender beef called **Steak Tartare,** which is eaten raw, see 86.

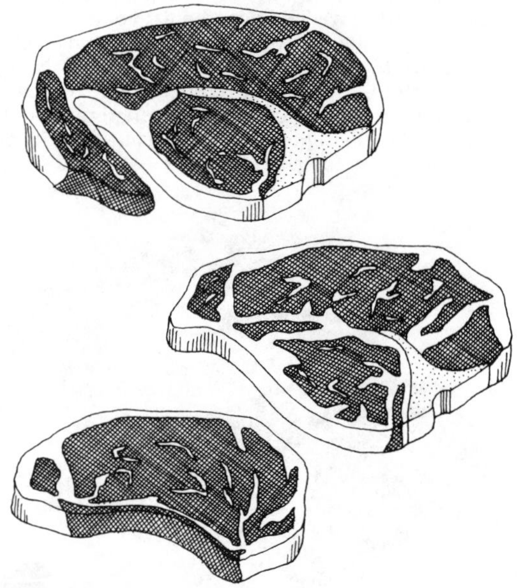

To avoid toughness, it is best to cook the so-called steaks mentioned below by moist-heat procedures. They are **flank, cube, tip of the round,** the **round** itself, with its characteristic bone, the **blade chuck, Swiss** and **rump steaks.**

COOKING STEAKS

A roving friend of ours who dropped into a tavern in upstate New York not long ago tells us that the management had chosen to preface a rather limited menu list with the proud claim: "All steaks broiled to your likeness." Few cooks anywhere would attempt such feats of portraiture, but steak—from charcoal grilled to planked Châteaubriand, 454—does duty for so many different occasions that we think it worthwhile to discuss steak varieties below. Unless special directions are given, all types of steak may be broiled, 456, or pan-broiled, 457. The meat should be removed from refrigeration about an hour before cooking. The grid should be cold; or, if it is hot, either grid or meat should be oiled to prevent sticking. The broiling compartment should be preheated and the oven door left slightly ajar if the range manufacturer so recommends. Season steak at the end of cooking, not before. Hot or cold, steak is sometimes enhanced by a sauce such as one of the following:

Garlic Butter, 351
Maître d'Hôtel Butter, 350
Colbert Butter, 350
Mushroom Wine Sauce, 347
Béarnaise Sauce, 359
Bordelaise Sauce, 347
Sour Cream Horseradish Dressing, 356

BROILED STEAK

➤ Please read About Beef Steak Cuts, 455. Remove meat from refrigeration about an hour before cooking.
Preheat broiling compartment.
Prepare for cooking:

Sirloin, T-bone, strip or porterhouse steak, 1½ to 2 inches thick

You may rub the steak with:

(A cut clove of garlic)

Or, an hour before cooking, spread it with:

(Olive oil)

Put steak on a cold grid—or on a greased hot grid—over a shallow greased pan, the top surface of the meat 3 inches from the heat source for a 1½-inch-thick steak. Brown the meat on one side, then turn once and brown the other side, allowing about 7 minutes per side for rare and about 8 minutes for medium. For a 2-inch steak, place meat 4 inches from heat source; turn more frequently, allowing in all about 9 minutes per side for rare and about 10 minutes for medium. When done, spread with butter or degreased pan drippings. Add:

Chopped parsley or chives

Serve the steak garnished with:

Sautéed Mushrooms, 308
French Fried Onion Rings, 313

BROILED FILLET STEAK

For fillet steak cuts, please see About Fillet of Beef, 454. The thickness of the steak varies, and therefore the cooking times vary proportionately. These steaks are usually served quite rare.
Flatten slightly:

Fillet steaks: 1 to 2 inches thick

Or have the butcher shape and surround them with a strip of bacon secured by a wooden pick.
Spread with:

Butter

Broil as for:

Broiled Steak, above

When done, remove the bacon. Serve steak on:

A toasted crouton, 551

with:

Béarnaise Sauce, 359
Lemon and parsley
Broiled Mushrooms, 308
Potatoes Anna, 320, or Duchess Potatoes, 323

PLANKED STEAK

It seems to us a regrettable state of affairs that this way of serving broiled steak in high style has become "dated." If you can come by one of those special hardwood planks incised with well-and-tree design to catch the juices, you're in. ➤ Follow directions for seasoning a plank, 154, if it's new. Prepare:

Duchess Potatoes, 323

Brush the plank with:

Vegetable oil

and preheat it. Broil, 456, ➤ to rare only:

A 1½- to 2-inch steak

Brush the steak with:

Melted butter

and season with:

Salt and pepper

Place steak in center of plank. Using a fluted pastry tube, ruffle a border of potatoes around the edge of the plank. Now place the filled plank briefly under the broiling element, just long enough for the potatoes to color. Remove from oven and garnish with several of the following, arranged between the steak and potatoes:

Green Peas, 314
Grilled Tomatoes, 332
Broiled Mushrooms, 308
Young Carrots in Bunches, 296
Parsley or watercress

PAN-BROILED STEAK

Please read About Beef Steak Cuts, 455, and about Pan Broiling, 445. This method is not recommended for steaks more than about 1 inch thick. Prepare for cooking:

A beef steak

Heat a heavy frying pan over lively heat until meat sizzles briskly as it touches the pan. If the meat is very lean, rub the pan lightly with:

A bit of beef fat

Put the steak into the pan and sear uncovered about 5 minutes Turn and sear the other side. Reduce heat and continue cooking until done, about 8 or 10 minutes in all. Pour off any fat that may have accumulated in the pan, for, if it is allowed to remain, the steak will be "fried," not "broiled." Season with:

Salt and freshly ground pepper

Make with the drippings:

Pan Gravy, 341

or use:

Maître d'Hôtel Butter, 350

For suggestions for steak sauces, see 456. Serve with:

Franconia Potatoes, 320

PAN-BROILED FILLET STEAK

Pan-broil, as above:

Four 1-inch fillet steaks

using, to prevent sticking, a small amount of:

Butter

When meat is done—not more than 3 minutes to a side—deglaze pan, 340, with:

¼ cup dry red wine
2 tablespoons beef stock
1 teaspoon Meat Glaze, 368

Serve with:

Artichoke hearts, stuffed with Creamed Spinach, 327

STEAK AU POIVRE OR PEPPERED STEAK

Use:

Trimmed 1-inch-thick strip sirloin, club or filet mignon steaks

Crush ➤ don't grind:

Peppercorns

coarsely on a board with a pressing, rolling movement, using the bottom of a pan. Press the steaks into the crushed pepper and work it into both sides of the meat with the heel of your palm or with the flat side of a cleaver. Sprinkle the bottom of a 9-inch skillet with:

2 teaspoons salt

When it begins to brown, put the steaks into the pan and brown ➤ uncovered over high heat. ➤ Reduce to medium heat, turn steaks and cook to desired degree of rareness. In a separate pan, prepare:

¼ cup butter
1 teaspoon Worcestershire sauce
2 tablespoons lemon juice

Remove steaks from the pan in which they have been cooked and discard the pan drippings. If you wish to flambé the steaks, 155, do so with:

(2 oz. brandy)

Serve the butter mixture separately.

LONDON BROIL OR FLANK STEAK

4 Servings

Have the butcher score the meat crosswise on both sides. It may be rubbed before cooking with a mixture of:

(1 tablespoon vegetable oil)
(1 finely chopped shallot)
(1 clove garlic, crushed)

Preheat broiler.
Place on greased broiler rack:

A 2- to 3-lb. flank steak

Broil within 2 to 3 inches of heat—the hotter the better—about 5 minutes on one side and 4 minutes on the other, ➤ making sure meat is kept rare. If flank steak is cooked medium or well done, it becomes extremely tough. ➤ Carve in ¼-inch slices and cut diagonally across the grain. Serve with:

Bearnaise Sauce, 359
Bordelaise Sauce, 347

BOEUF FONDU BOURGUIGNONNE

6 Servings

This dish is cooked at table in a special deep metal pot which narrows at the top to keep the butter from spattering. It can also be cooked in an electric skillet ➤ if the butter is sweet and clarified, which keeps it from popping. We love this dish inordinately. It gives the hostess an easy time, both from the cooking angle and from the entertaining one—as the guests quickly reveal their individual characteristics. They are all there—hoarder, cooperator, kibitzer, boss. ➤ Don't try to get more than 5 or 6 guests around one heat source. Allow for each person ⅓ to ½ pound fillet of beef.

Cut into 1-inch dice and bring to the table on a platter garnished with parsley:

About 3 lb. fillet of beef

Have ready at room temperature or slightly warmed several of the following accompaniments:

Mustard with capers
Sour Cream Horseradish Dressing, 356
Andalouse Sauce, 364
Herb or Curry Mayonnaise, 364, 365
Watercress Dressing, 360
Chutney Dressing, 361
Orange Marmalade, 839
Marchand de Vin Sauce, 347

Melt in an electric skillet or in a fondu pot:

1 cup clarified butter or peanut oil

When the butter is brownish, announce the rules of the game. Ask each guest to limit himself to two pieces of meat at a time, so as not to crowd the pot and lower the cooking temperature. If a skillet is used, each person impales the cubes on his fork, releases the meat into the pan and worries it around in the hot fat until it's done to his liking; if he prefers rare, the time is very short. If a deep fondu pot is used, the meat must stay on the fork during the cooking, or it will be irretrievably lost—but, according to an old Swiss custom, the loser gets a consolation prize: the right to kiss the Swiss miss on his left! Meantime, each guest has arranged on his plate an assortment of sauces—like oils on an artist's palette—into which he dips the hot browned meat. Serve with crusty French bread or rolls and a tossed salad with green grapes or avocado slices.

BEEF STROGANOFF

delicious!!

4 Servings

This dish ✻ freezes well and can be made with fillet ends, shown on 454.

Cut into ½-inch slices across the grain:

1½ lb. fillet of beef

Pound them until thin. Cut into strips about 1 inch wide. Melt in a pan:

1 tablespoon butter

Sauté in the butter about 2 minutes:

¾ tablespoon grated onion

Sauté beef quickly in the butter about 5 minutes, until browned evenly. Remove and keep hot. Add to the pan:

2 tablespoons butter

Stir and sauté in the butter:

¾ lb. sliced mushrooms

Drain and add the beef. Season with:

Salt and pepper
A grating of nutmeg
(½ teaspoon basil)

Add and heat briefly:

¼ cup dry white wine

Then add:

1 cup warm whipping cream or cultured sour cream

Serve with:

Green Noodles, 213

SUKIYAKI

6 Servings

Japan's famous "friendship dish" is winning more and more Stateside friends. It's a one-plate meal prepared ceremoniously at table in an electric skillet—or, less festively, in the kitchen in a heavy skillet or wok. The orderly cooking ritual lasts about 15 minutes, as one after another the uniformly sliced ingredients are taken from a beautifully arranged platter and sautéed. Have ready on platter:

2 lb. beef: sirloin tip, eye of round or fillet, sliced ⅛ inch thick

The meat is easy to slice if put in the freezer for 20 minutes. Cut against the grain. But meat and all other ingredients should be ➤ at room temperature for cooking. Have ready:

2 strips beef suet, about 1 oz. each, or
3 tablespoons vegetable oil

Also arrange attractively on the platter, in diagonally cut uniform slices:

½ cup thinly sliced onions
6 scallions with 2 inches of green
Canned bamboo shoots
2 cups thinly sliced mushrooms
½ cup Chinese cabbage or watercress, or
¼ cup Chinese chrysanthemum leaves
½ cup ¾-inch cubes soybean curd, 535

If a single skillet is used, it is best to cook only half the amount on the platter at one time, sharing that batch and then cooking the "seconds" later. Put the suet or oil into the hot skillet over medium heat. When the point of fragrance is reached, remove unmelted bits—if you have used suet—and add the thin beef slices. Sauté ➤ without browning, turning frequently, about 3 minutes. Push the meat to one side and sauté in sequence the onions, scallions, mushrooms and Chinese cabbage. The sautéing of the onions to almost golden, followed by the gradual addition of the other vegetables, should take about 7 minutes in all. As the other vegetables are being added, pour in, a little at a time, a mixture of:

¼ cup soy sauce
½ cup stock
1 teaspoon sugar

This procedure produces a fast-rising steam but not enough moisture to waterlog the vegetables. Push the meat into the center of the skillet, add the bamboo shoots and bean curd and stir about

4 minutes more. The vegetables should retain crispness and color.

Season to taste

Serve this mixture at once over:

Boiled Rice, 206

As an authentic detail, you may have at room temperature in individual dishes:

(Raw eggs)

to coat the bits of the Sukiyaki as the food is dipped into it with chopsticks.

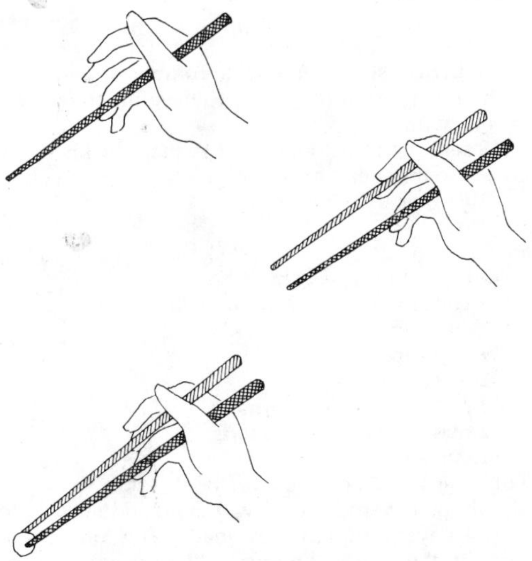

To eat with chopsticks, hold them by the upper square portion. Although the two are alike in shape, the functions of the chopsticks differ in that the lower stick remains stationary; the upper one, which is pressed against the lower, moves up and down to complete a tonglike action in grasping the food. First place the lower stick in the crease of the thumb as shown upper left, with the lower end of the chopstick braced firmly against the soft inner surface of the last joint of the ring finger as shown. Then position the upper stick much as you would hold a pencil but with the point of the stick protruding about one-third of its entire length and approximately equalized with the lower stick when pressed together at the point. For westerners these tools at first automatically bring on a leisured pace of consumption, and it is a comfort to know that in eating rice and noodles it is not bad form to bring the bowl up just under the chin—a maneuver which facilitates matters greatly for the uninitiated.

⊟ BEEF KEBABS

4 Servings

➤ Please read about Skewer Cooking, 146, and About Marinades, 528.

Cut into 1½-inch cubes:

1½ lb. good-quality round, flank or chuck

Marinate and cook as for:

Lamb Kebabs, 473

using one of the marinades listed in that recipe; or use:

Teriyaki Marinade, 529, or
Beer Marinade, 529

BEEF POT ROAST

6 Servings

➤ Please read About Pot-Roasting, 447.

Prepare for cooking one of the following in this general order of preference:

3 to 4 lb. chuck, shoulder, top or bottom round, brisket, blade or rump

If the meat is lean, you may lard it, 444. Rub meat with:

(Garlic)

Dredge in:

(Flour)

Heat in a heavy pan:

2 tablespoons rendered suet or vegetable oil

Brown the meat on all sides in the fat. ➤ Do not let it scorch. Add to pot when the meat is half browned:

1 chopped carrot
1 diced rib celery
(1 diced small white turnip)
(¼ cup chopped green pepper, seeds and membrane removed)

When the meat is browned, spoon off excess fat. Add:

1 small onion stuck with 3 cloves
2 cups boiling meat or vegetable stock or part stock and part dry red wine
1 bay leaf

Cover and bake 3 to 4 hours in a 300°–325° oven, or simmer on top of the stove. During this time turn the meat several times and, if necessary, add additional:

Hot stock
Season to taste

When the meat is tender, spoon off excess fat, remove bay leaf and serve with the pot liquor as it is or slightly thickened with:

Kneaded Butter, 340, or ¾ cup cultured sour cream

You may, if you wish, add to the pot roast drained boiled vegetables. Serve with:

Potato Pancakes, 321; Kasha, 201; or Green Noodles, 213, sprinkled with poppyseed

and:

Blue Plum or Cherry Compote, 126

BEEF STEW GASTON

4 to 6 Servings

This one-dish meal seems to taste better when cooked a day ahead.

Cut into small pieces and, if very salty, parblanch, 154, briefly:

½ lb. salt pork

Dry and sauté the pork slowly in a large skillet. Cut into pieces:

2 lb. boneless stewing beef

Brown the beef in the hot drippings over high heat. Spoon off most of the accumulated fat. Sprinkle the meat with:

Seasoned Flour, 552

Combine and heat until boiling:

1½ cloves garlic, chopped
1 large chopped onion
1 cup bouillon
1 cup canned tomato sauce
12 peppercorns
3 whole cloves
¼ cup chopped parsley
⅓ bay leaf

Place the meat in a heavy saucepan. Pour above ingredients over it. Simmer covered 2 to 3 hours or until meat can be easily pierced with a fork. During the last hour of cooking, add:

½ cup dry white wine

Cook separately until nearly tender:

6 medium-sized pared quartered potatoes
6 pared quartered carrots
1 rib celery, chopped

Add these vegetables to the stew for the last 15 minutes of cooking.

BEEF STEW WITH WINE OR BOEUF BOURGUIGNONNE

4 to 6 Servings

For added bouquet, the meat may be marinated and refrigerated overnight in dry red wine. Drain and reserve wine for use in cooking the stew. Preheat oven to 300°.
Try out, 542:

½ lb. thinly sliced blanched salt pork

You may substitute 3 tablespoons butter for the pork, but don't expect the same subtle flavor. Peel, add and sauté lightly:

12 small onions or 4 shallots

Remove pork and onions from pan and reserve. Cut into 1-inch dice and sauté in the hot fat until light brown:

2 lb. lean boneless stewing beef

Sprinkle meat with:

(1½ tablespoons flour)

Place it in an ovenproof dish with:

1 teaspoon salt
4 peppercorns
½ bay leaf
1 or 2 cloves garlic, minced
(½ teaspoon thyme or sweet marjoram)

Using the reserved wine if you marinated the meat, bring to the boiling point enough dry red wine and water to cover the meat:

¾ wine to ¼ water

Simmer ➤ covered in a 300° oven for 2 hours. Place pork and onions on top of the meat and continue to simmer covered another hour or until beef is tender. For the last 10 minutes of cooking you may add:

(1 cup sautéed mushrooms)
Season to taste

Serve the stew sprinkled with:

Chopped parsley

You may flambé, 155, at the last minute with:

(¼ cup brandy)

Serve with:

French Bread, 605, or Noodles, 213, or Mashed Potatoes, 318

SAUERBRATEN

6 Servings

Prepare for cooking:

3 lb. beef shoulder, chuck, rump or round

If the meat does not appear to have much fat, lard it, 444, with:

(18 seasoned Lardoons, 445, ¼ inch thick)

Rub into the meat thoroughly:

Pepper
(Garlic)

Place the meat in a deep crock or glass bowl. Heat together ➤ but do not boil:

2 cups mild vinegar or wine vinegar
2 cups water
½ cup sliced onions
2 bay leaves
1 teaspoon peppercorns
(2 teaspoons caraway seeds)
¼ cup sugar

Pour the hot marinade over beef; more than half should be covered. Cover with a lid and refrigerate 2 to 4 days, turning occasionally. The longer you leave it, the sourer the meat. When ready to cook, drain the meat, saving the marinade. Heat in a heavy pan:

2 tablespoons vegetable oil or other fat

Brown the meat on all sides and cook as for:

Pot Roast, 459

using the heated marinade in place of stock. When the meat is tender, sprinkle it with:

¼ cup brown sugar

and roast 5 to 10 minutes more or until sugar is dissolved. Remove meat from the pot. Thicken stock with:

Flour, see Pan Gravy, 341

Add:

1 cup sweet cream or cultured sour cream

We like the gravy "straight." Some cooks add:

(Raisins, catsup and ground gingersnaps)

Serve roast with:

Potato Dumplings, 204, or Potato Pancakes, 321

and you will have a treat. ➤ This dish does not freeze successfully.

BOEUF À LA MODE

6 Servings

A pot roast de luxe, because so elegantly presented. The meat is sliced very thin and even, covered with a sauce, and the platter garnished with beautifully arranged vegetables.
Prepare the beef as for:

Sauerbraten, above
larding it but marinating for only 4 to 5 hours in a mixture of:

1½ to 2 cups dry red wine
¼ cup brandy

When ready to cook, add:

2 boned blanched calves' feet

Use Blanch II, 154, simmering 10 minutes. ➤ Then simmer covered 3½ to 4 hours. Toward the last hour of cooking, add to the degreased sauce and cook with the meat:

1 cup sliced carrots
1 cup sliced onions

Just before serving, heat with the dish.

1 cup sautéed mushrooms

Cut the meat as described above and serve garnished with the vegetables and with the calves' feet cut into one-inch squares.

GLAZED BOEUF A LA MODE OR DAUBE GLACÉ

Showy on a buffet table.
Prepare:

Boeuf à la Mode, above

➤ So as to get a clear stock, do not add the vegetables. When the beef is tender, drain the liquid through a cloth. Degrease it as much as possible. Allow it to cool until it starts to jell. Meanwhile, cut the meat from the calves' feet into 1-inch squares, and cut the beef into thin, even slices. Arrange the slices in an overlapping pattern on a platter, surrounded by the cubed calf meat. When the stock begins to congeal, pour it over the meat. Refrigerate covered. When the stock has completely jellied, serve the glazed beef surrounded with cooked vegetables at room temperature:

Artichokes à la Grecque, 281
Marinated Raw Carrots, 83

and garnished with:

Parsley or watercress

BOILED BEEF OR BOEUF BOUILLI

6 to 8 Servings

Joseph Wechsberg reminds us in *Blue Trout and Black Truffles* of the Viennese enthusiasm for boiled beef—in no less than 24 local variations. Its superiority there can be credited in large part to the beef itself—from cattle bred selectively and fed a diet of sugar beets—comparable in quality to the Kobe beef of Japan and the Charolais of France.
Bring to a boil in a heavy pot:

6 cups water

Put in:

3 lb. lean stewing beef in one piece

Bring to a boil and skim the pot. Add:

1 onion stuck with 3 cloves
1 bay leaf
½ cup sliced carrots
½ cup sliced celery with leaves
1 teaspoon salt
(1 sliced turnip)

Cover and simmer the meat until tender, 3 to 4 hours. Drain and reserve the stock. Melt:

¼ cup butter

Brown lightly in the butter:

¼ cup chopped onions

Stir in until blended:

2 tablespoons flour

Stir in slowly 2 cups of the degreased stock. Season the sauce with:

2 tablespoons horseradish
Salt
(Sugar)
(Vinegar or lemon juice)

If using prepared horseradish, use less vinegar or lemon juice, and:

Season to taste

Cut the meat into thin slices against the grain and reheat ➤ very briefly in the hot gravy. Garnish with:

Chopped parsley

Serve with:

Spätzle, 205, or Boiled New Potatoes in their jackets, 317
Sauerkraut, 295

BEEF BRISKET WITH SAUERKRAUT

6 Servings

Tie into a compact shape:

3 lb. beef brisket or other boneless stewing beef

Melt in a deep kettle:

3 tablespoons bacon fat or other fat

Add and brown lightly:

(¼ cup chopped onions)

Add the meat and place over it:

2 lb. sauerkraut
(1 large apple, cored and quartered)
2 cups boiling water or beef stock

Simmer the meat covered about 2½ hours or until tender. Season with:

Salt and pepper
(Caraway seed)

Serve with:

Boiled Potatoes, 317

garnished with:

Cultured sour cream
Chopped parsley or chives

BELGIAN BEEF STEW OR CARBONNADE FLAMANDE

4 to 6 Servings

Cut into 1½-inch cubes and coat in seasoned flour, 552:

2 lb. boneless stewing beef

Sauté lightly in:

1 tablespoon butter
¼ cup thinly sliced onions

Reserve the onions. Add:

1 tablespoon butter

and brown the floured meat. Drain off any excess fat. Combine and bring to a boil:

1 cup flat beer

1 clove garlic, pressed
½ teaspoon sugar
½ teaspoon salt

Pour this over the meat and add the onions. Cover and simmer 2 to 2½ hours. After straining the sauce, you may add:

½ teaspoon vinegar

Serve meat with:

Boiled New Potatoes, 317, garnished with parsley or dill

Use sauce as gravy.

WEST AFRICAN BEEF STEW

8 Servings

Cut into cubes:

2 lb. boneless stewing beef

Brown it in:

4 tablespoons hot butter or other fat

Remove meat from pan and add:

1 cup chopped onions

When golden in color, add:

2 tablespoons flour
2 to 3 tablespoons curry powder
¼ cup peanut butter

Slowly add to the above mixture and stir until thickened:

2 cups beef stock, or 1 cup water and 1 cup coconut milk, 566

Add the meat and simmer covered about 2 hours or until tender. Twenty minutes before end of cooking time, add:

½ lb. trimmed whole okra

Serve over:

Boiled Rice, 206

Garnish with:

4 quartered hard-cooked eggs

Have ready to pass in small individual dishes:

Grated toasted coconut, preferably fresh
Chutney
Fresh or broiled banana and pineapple chunks
Fresh orange, mango or melon slices
Fresh or broiled tomato slices
Fried onion rings
Roasted peanuts
Croutons

⊟ CHINESE FIREPOT

A participatory complete-meal simmered dish for which equipment can be improvised if the conventional firepot shown to the left rear in the chapter heading, 145, is not available. But there are caveats. If the heat source is charcoal, it is mandatory ➤ to enjoy this ritual out-of-doors. It is also necessary to have the broth or water in which the food is to be simmered ➤ piping hot and in the firepot before the charcoal, ➤ heated to grayness in advance, is tucked into the firepot base just before the diners assemble. This precaution keeps the soldered seams of the pot from melting. There should be enough charcoal in the pot to provide heat for the entire process.

Allow at least ½ pound of food and 1 to 1½ cups of liquid per person. All food to be simmered by the guests is previously cut and trimmed. Some stalk vegetables need to be parblanched; noodles and the dried mushrooms require soaking in advance. Sometimes the raw food is lightly marinated. Condiment containers at hand should include soy sauce, vinegar, tomato paste, hot pepper oil, Chinese mustard, sugar, salt and pepper, and herb leaves such as coriander, 581, gingerroot and various onions, 583. The food is grouped on platters. You may use meat or fish and shellfish, or a combination with the white meat of poultry. Allow about 2 minutes' cooking time for meat cut into thin strips—diagonally against the grain—except for pork, which, after cutting, needs to be cooked until it is no longer pink. Shellfish cook in a minute or less. Fish fillets are cut into cubes or strips thicker than the meat to prevent their disintegrating. Have ready at each diner's place a plate; 2 sets of chopsticks—one for cooking, the other for eating; or one set of chopsticks for eating and a small strainer for cooking; a bowl for the broth; and a small sauce bowl for each diner's choice of condiments in which to make his own flavorful sauce. The order of cooking is meat or fish first, then noodles and vegetables. Broth is the only liquid served with the meal. Should the broth run low, add more preheated broth to the firepot. If it should go above simmering, guests are asked to simultaneously immerse a vegetable for cooking to reduce the heat somewhat. The broth may be ladled out early but is usually reserved for the end as the customary finish for a Chinese meal.

9 to 10 Servings

Allow for:

2½ quarts chicken broth

at least three of the following:

1 lb. sliced beef tenderloin
1 lb. shelled deveined shrimp
1 lb. bite-sized chicken breasts
1 lb. fish fillets in thick strips
½ lb. chicken livers or oysters

and two of the following vegetables:

1 lb. washed spinach with stalks removed
½ lb. watercress
1 lb. celery cabbage sliced into stalks and blanched, 154, briefly

Add also:

¼ cup scallions or other green onion types, 584, cut into 1-inch pieces
9 dried mushroom caps, soaked 1 hour in warm water, drained and cut into 1-inch cubes
3 cakes tofu cut into 1-inch cubes
½ cup canned Chinese chestnuts or
½ cup bamboo shoots

and:

2 oz. Chinese noodles

soaked for 30 minutes, then drained and cut into 4-inch lengths.

CASSEROLED BEEF WITH FRUIT

6 Servings

A complete meal with a Near East flavor.
Soak until soft:

2 cups chopped mixed dried fruit: apricots, pears, prunes

in:

2 cups water
Juice and rind of 1 lemon

Cut into small cubes:

2 lb. lean stewing beef

Preheat oven to 300°.
Melt in a heavy skillet:

3 tablespoons butter
2 tablespoons vegetable oil

When the fat is fragrant, add the diced meat. When well browned, stir in the fruit mixture and:

(1 tablespoon cinnamon or 2 teaspoons curry)

Put this mixture into a covered casserole and bake about 1½ hours. Add:

2 lb. shredded spinach

Cover and bake ½ hour longer or until the meat is tender. Serve over:

Boiled Rice, 206

SOUP MEAT

Even though many of a meat's nutrients are dissolved into the stock in soup making, the meat may be served as a separate dish—with an assertive sauce as a fillip for its bland flavor. Remove meat from soup kettle before the vegetables are added, and serve the meat with:

Horseradish Sauce, 343; Cold Mustard Sauce, 357; Thickened Tomato Sauce, 352; or Brown Onion Sauce, 346

SPICED BEEF

8 to 10 Servings

Good served hot. Fine for a cold meat platter.
Place in a large bowl:

4 to 5 lb. chuck, shoulder or round roast

Cover with:

Dry red wine or cider
2 sliced onions
½ bay leaf
1 teaspoon each cinnamon and allspice
½ teaspoon cloves
1½ teaspoons salt
1 teaspoon pepper

Cover bowl and refrigerate in this marinade 12 hours or more. Drain and reserve the marinade.
Preheat oven to 275°.
Place the meat in a roasting pan. Heat to the boiling point and pour over it half the marinade and:

1 cup boiling water

Cover and ➤ simmer about 3 hours. Mince and sauté in butter:

2 onions
4 large carrots
1 medium-sized yellow turnip
1 rib celery

Add these ingredients to the roast for the last half hour of cooking.

Season to taste

You may thicken the sauce with:

(Flour, see Gravy, 341)

or reduce it, 339. Add to the stock at the very end:

6 to 8 preserved kumquats

sliced into ¼-inch pieces.

CHUCK ROAST IN FOIL

12 Servings

Foil-cooked meats often have a pasty look about them, but the use in this recipe of dehydrated onion soup gives great vigor of color and flavor, in spite of the fact that the meat is not browned first. Try this for informal company.
Preheat oven to 300°.
Place:

A 7-lb. chuck roast

on a double thickness of heavy-duty foil large enough to envelop it. Sprinkle the meat with:

½ to 1 package dehydrated onion soup

Turn the meat over and sprinkle the other side with:

½ to 1 package dehydrated onion soup

Now wrap the roast carefully with the foil, seaming so that no juices can escape. Place the package in a pan and bake 3½ to 4 hours. If your company is informal, do not cut the foil until you are at table and ready to carve. The sudden burst of fragrance adds to the anticipation. Serve with:

Spätzle, 205, or with a Rice Ring, 207, filled with fresh peas

SWISS STEAK

6 Servings

Preheat oven to 300°.
Trim the edges of a ¾-inch thick:

2-lb. bottom round steak

Rub with:

½ clove garlic

Pound, 444, into both sides of the steak with a mallet:

As much seasoned flour as the steak will hold

Cut into serving pieces or leave whole. If left whole, gash the edges to prevent curling. Heat in a large heavy casserole:

¼ cup bacon drippings or ham drippings

Sear steak on one side until brown. Turn it over and add:

½ cup finely chopped onions
1 cup finely mixed chopped carrots, peppers and celery

Do not allow vegetables to brown.

Season to taste

Add:

1 cup hot stock
(½ cup hot tomato sauce)

Cover casserole and place in the oven 1½ to 2 hours or more. Remove steak to a hot platter. Strain and degrease drippings. Make:

Pan Gravy, 341

Pour gravy over the steak and serve with:

Mashed Potatoes, 318

STEAK AND GREEN PEPPERS

8 Servings

Cut into ½-inch strips:

2 lb. round steak, ½ inch thick

Combine:

¼ cup soy sauce
1 cup beef bouillon
2 cloves garlic, mashed
½ teaspoon ginger

Pour this marinade over the meat and refrigerate covered 2 to 12 hours. Drain meat, discarding the garlic and reserving ½ cup marinade. Dry meat strips on paper toweling. In a large skillet sauté meat until light brown in:

3 tablespoons vegetable oil

Add heated reserved marinade and:

1 cup boiling water

➤ Cover skillet and simmer meat about 45 minutes. Add:

3 large green peppers, cut into ½-inch strips, seeds and membrane removed
(1 cup sliced water chestnuts)

Simmer 15 minutes more or until meat is tender. Mix until smooth:

3 tablespoons cornstarch
¼ cup water

and gradually stir this mixture into skillet until gravy has thickened slightly. Serve with:

Boiled Rice, 206

FLANK STEAK WITH DRESSING

4 to 6 Servings

The sharper the seasonings, the more "deviled" the total effect.

Have ready:

A 2- to 3-lb. flank or round steak, 456

Trim the edges. Season with and pound in:

1 teaspoon salt
⅛ teaspoon paprika
¼ teaspoon mustard
(⅛ teaspoon ginger)
(1 teaspoon Worcestershire sauce)

Melt:

¼ cup butter or bacon drippings

Add and sauté until golden:

2 tablespoons chopped onion

Add:

1 cup rye or white bread crumbs
¼ teaspoon salt
A few grains paprika
2 tablespoons chopped parsley
3 tablespoons chopped celery
1 slightly beaten egg

Spread this dressing over the steak, roll loosely and tie it. For variety, try Sausage Dressing with apples, 371.

Preheat oven to 300°.

Heat in a skillet:

3 tablespoons vegetable oil

Sear the rolled steak on all sides in the hot oil. Place it in a casserole. Stir into the oil in the skillet:

2 tablespoons flour

Add:

1 cup water or stock
1 cup tomato juice or dry red wine
¼ teaspoon salt

When thickened, pour this mixture over the steak. Bake covered about 1½ hours. Add seasoning if required.

SHORT RIBS OF BEEF

2 to 3 Servings

This is a two-step recipe. Tenderizing the meat may be done ahead of time, and the oven crisping just before serving.

Cut into about 3-inch pieces:

2 lb. lean short ribs of beef

Place in a heavy pot with a lid:

5 cups water
1 small sliced onion
1 small sliced carrot
4 or more ribs celery with leaves

Bring these ingredients to the boiling point. Add the meat. Simmer covered until ➤ nearly tender, about 2 hours. Take out meat. Strain and degrease the stock. Make about 3 cups of thin gravy, 341, using:

¼ cup fat
¼ cup flour
3 cups stock
Season to taste

Preheat oven to 325°.

Heat in a heavy skillet:

¼ cup fat

Slice, add and stir until golden:

1 small onion

Brown the meat in the hot fat. Pour over it half the gravy. Bake ➤ uncovered about 45 minutes until brown and crisp. You may baste occasionally with the drippings. Reheat remaining gravy. Add to it:

1 teaspoon marjoram, preferably fresh
Season to taste

Place the meat on a hot platter. Garnish with:

Mashed Potatoes, 318

Serve piping hot with gravy.

ABOUT GOULASH, GULYAS OR PÖRKÖLT

This Hungarian specialty is a thick stew that may be cooked in many ways; it is always highly spiced—usually, but not always, seasoned with sweet paprika. Some epicures insist that only the imported Rosen paprika will do, while others use freshly ground black pepper instead. In Beef Goulash, the meat is always browned before simmering. A knowing friend claims that shinbone meat with its high gelatin content makes a glorious goulash. But variations using veal, pork or lamb alone or in combination, on 475 and 481, may be cooked à blanc—that is, without browning. Versions containing lamb or pork may be called Pörkölt. The liquid is sometimes water, sometimes stock or dry red wine. Vegetables may be added for the last hour of cooking.

BEEF GOULASH

6 Servings

Cut into 1-inch cubes:
2 lb. stewing beef, or 1 lb. beef and 1 lb. lean veal
Melt in a heavy pot:
¼ cup butter, vegetable oil or bacon drippings
Brown meat on both sides in the hot oil. Add and sauté until transparent:
1½ cups chopped onions
Add:
1 cup boiling Stock, 522, or tomato juice
1 diced green pepper, seeds and membrane removed
1 teaspoon salt
1 teaspoon to 1 tablespoon paprika
Use just enough stock to keep the meat from scorching, adding more gradually during cooking, if necessary. Cover the pot and simmer the meat for 1½ hours. Six small peeled potatoes may be added for the last half hour of cooking, but they soak up the gravy, which is apt to be the best part of the goulash. Remove the meat from the pot and thicken the stock for:
Pan Gravy, 341
It may be necessary to add more stock or tomato juice.
Season to taste
If potatoes have not been included, serve the goulash with:
Polenta, 201, or Noodles, 213

ABOUT BEEF ROLLS, ROULADES OR PAUPIETTES

Thin strips of pounded meat or poultry or fish rolled around vegetables or other fillings are known also as roulades or paupiettes. They may be further wrapped in salt pork or bacon. To make them with beef, use:
Thin strips of pounded round or flank steak, 3 x 4 inches
Season with:
Salt and pepper
Place on each strip about 2 tablespoons of one of the following fillings:

I. Well-seasoned smoked or cooked sausage with chopped parsley or dill pickle

II. Minced ham, julienned carrot and celery

III. Seasoned cooked rice, chopped stuffed olives, or seedless green grapes with lemon zest

Roll meat and tie with string near both ends, or wrap as for cabbage leaves, shown 152. Dredge in:
Flour
Brown in bacon drippings or rendered salt pork. Place in a casserole and use for every 6 rolls:
1½ cups stock or dry wine
1½ to 2 tablespoons tomato paste
Cover and cook slowly in a preheated 300° oven, or simmer on direct heat about 1 hour and 15 minutes.

STEAK-AND-KIDNEY PIE

4 Servings

Classic recipes for this old English favorite often call for beef kidneys. If they are used, they must be blanched, 154, and cooking time must be increased to assure tenderness. Rather than encasing the stew in dough, we recommend a topping only.
Preheat oven to 350°.
Cut into half-inch-thick slices:
1½ lb. round or other beefsteak
Wash, skin and slice thin:
¾ lb. veal or lamb kidneys
Melt in a skillet:
3 tablespoons butter or beef fat
Sauté the kidneys over high heat for 1 to 2 minutes. Shake constantly. Add and sauté lightly:
⅓ cup onions
Shake the beef in a bag of:
Seasoned Flour, 552
Lightly grease an ovenproof baker. Place in it a layer of meat, then a layer of kidneys and onions. Or you may reserve the kidneys and add them the last 15 minutes before placing the pastry cover.
Add:
2 cups Brown Stock, 522
1 cup dry red wine or beer
Cover the dish and bake 1 to 1½ hours. Cool slightly. Increase oven heat to 425°. Cover the meat, see 449, with:
Pâte Brisée, 641
Bake 12 to 15 minutes.

⊟ KENTUCKY BURGOO

10 to 12 Servings

The accent is on the first syllable. This thick, long-simmered potpourri, a catch-as-catch-can mixture of meats, fowl and garden gleanings—with squirrel thrown in, in some authentic local versions—has an assortment of Old World forebears as numerous and far-flung as the Gypsies. In Spain it is known as **Olla Podrida;** in Ireland it surfaces as **Mulligan Stew.** But in Kentucky it came into its own as the local solution to feeding the multitudes; it used to be made, in amounts to serve several hundreds, in a huge hog-butchering kettle over an outdoor fire, providing an occasion for great socializing, a "stirring" overnight vigil. This simplified version can be varied according to

your preference or to what meat is available—lamb or veal may be used as well. It makes good sense, too, to freeze this seasonal dish in meal-sized packages.
Place in a heavy, lidded kettle:
3/4 lb. lean stewing beef, cubed
3/4 lb. pork shoulder, cubed
3 1/2 quarts water or stock
Bring slowly to a boil. ➤ Reduce heat at once and simmer about 1 1/2 hours. Add to the pot:
One 3 1/2-lb. chicken, disjointed
Bring ingredients again to a boil, ➤ reduce heat and simmer about 1 hour more or until meat falls from the bones. Cool the mixture enough to remove bones from meat. Return meat to the pot and bring to a boil. Add:
2 1/2 cups quartered, skinned ripe tomatoes
1 cup fresh lima beans
1/2 diced hot red pepper
2 diced green peppers, seeds and membrane removed
3/4 cup diced onions
1 cup diced carrots
1/2 cup diced celery
2 cups diced potatoes
1 cup diced okra
1 bay leaf
1 tablespoon Worcestershire sauce
Stirring frequently as it thickens, ➤ simmer the whole mixture 45 minutes or more over very low heat before adding:
2 cups corn, freshly cut from the cob
Simmer about 15 minutes more or until all vegetables are soft.
Season to taste
Garnish with:
Fresh parsley
Serve hot in deep bowls with squares of:
Salt-Rising Bread, 606, or
Corn Bread, 627

CORNED BEEF

I. Wash under running water to remove surface brine:
Corned Beef, 813
Cover with boiling water and simmer, allowing about 1 hour per pound, or until a fork can penetrate to center. Always slice corned beef very thin, diagonally across the grain. A classic accompaniment of corned beef served hot is:
Cabbage wedges
simmered with the beef the last 15 minutes of cooking. Serve hot with:
Horseradish Sauce, 343
Boiled Potatoes, 317, or Gnocchi with Farina, 204
Serve corned beef cold with:
Horseradish
➤ To press for slicing, cool the meat and force it into a deep pan; cover and refrigerate weighted. The moisture pressed from the meat should form a jellied coating.

II. After cooking corned beef as in I, above, you may coat it with the following glaze and bake in a preheated 350° oven 15 minutes or until the topping is set.
Combine and mix well:
1 tablespoon brown sugar
1 tablespoon water
1 teaspoon soy sauce
2 teaspoons paprika
1/2 teaspoon ginger

III. Tenderized corned beef can now be bought for oven roasting; follow manufacturer's directions.

CORNED BEEF AND CABBAGE OR NEW ENGLAND BOILED DINNER

10 to 12 Servings

This is a delectable dinner if composed only of beef, onions and cabbage. But for authenticity, additional vegetables are included.
Cook until tender:
Corned Beef I, above
Meantime, cook separately until tender, then skin and reserve:
10 to 12 medium-sized beets, 290
Some devotees of this dish add about:
(1/2 lb. salt pork)
to the corned beef for the last 2 hours of cooking. When done, remove the beef from the pot and cook in the simmering stock 30 minutes:
3 peeled, quartered small parsnips
6 peeled, quartered large carrots
3 peeled, quartered large yellow turnips
Skin and add:
10 small onions
Pare, quarter and simmer in the stock 15 minutes longer:
6 medium-sized potatoes
Cut into wedges, add and simmer until tender, about 10 to 15 minutes:
A head of cabbage
Reheat the meat in the stock. Serve it on a large platter, surrounded by the vegetables, including the beets. Garnish with:
Parsley
If there is enough of this dish left over, use for Red Flannel Hash, below.

RED FLANNEL HASH

New Englanders say that this hash, to be properly made, must be concocted from the leftovers of:
New England Boiled Dinner, above
Chop the leftover beets, cabbage, turnips, corned beef, etc., and brown the mixture in a skillet in:
2 tablespoons vegetable oil
until a brown crust forms.

ABOUT VEAL

A friend of ours at boarding school reports that one of the specialties served there with notorious frequency has been dubbed "Dreaded Veal Cutlet." Veal—young beef 3 to 8 months of age—

enjoys much more esteem in Europe than in America. This, we are convinced, is a pity; partly because veal has a superbly delicate and distinctive flavor, and partly because a number of classic dishes cannot be confected using a substitute. Occasionally still to be found is milk-fed veal—the very best; but in any case, top-quality veal should be tender and succulent and have a white or very pale pink color. The redder the meat, the older and tougher the veal. Veal over 225 pounds is known as calf. To improve older veal, blanch briefly, starting in cold water; or soak refrigerated in milk overnight; or marinate in lemon juice for 1 hour.

Veal needs a careful cooking approach, as it is lacking in fat and may toughen quickly. Since it also has a higher proportion of connective tissue, veal should not be broiled; ➤ long, slow, covered cooking is best. Large cuts of veal need some moisture, and the meat should be covered at least part of the cooking time. Abroad, certain dishes like Veal à la Meunière or à la Crême are served both rosy and juicy, but here veal is generally served well done or after reaching an internal temperature of 170°. For the Economical Use of Large Cuts, see 452. Also, see About Veal Scallops and Cutlets, below.

VEAL ROAST

Remove the meat from the refrigerator at least 1 hour before cooking. Veal roasts, both rolled and unrolled, need to be rubbed well with butter or oil. Or they may be barded, 420, with thin slices of salt pork or bacon which have been blanched to remove some of the salt.
Preheat oven to 425°. Season well:

A leg, shoulder, loin, saddle or rack of veal

with a choice of your favorite:

Herbs: garlic, dill, tarragon, chervil or thyme
Salt and pepper

or you may sprinkle the roast with:

(Lemon juice)

Place the oiled and seasoned meat on a rack in a greased shallow roasting pan. Add to the pan a:

Mirepoix, 572

Bake ➤ uncovered about 30 minutes. ➤ Reduce the heat to 325°, cover the roast loosely with foil or parchment, and continue cooking until the internal temperature reaches 170°, or approximately 15 to 20 minutes per pound. Baste occasionally with pan juices. If necessary, supplement these with a little:

Melted butter and white wine

You may add parboiled vegetables—potatoes, carrots, etc.—for the last half hour or so of cooking. Or you may spread over the roast for this last half hour a combination of:

(1 cup cultured sour cream)
(1 tablespoon flour)

Serve with:

Dumplings, 202, or Spätzen, 205
Pickled Prunes, 142

VEAL ROAST STUFFED OR FARCI

The meat may be rubbed first with garlic, or gashes may be cut in a shoulder roast, in which fine slivers of garlic, marjoram, peppercorns, anchovies or anchovy paste may be inserted. Remove the meat from the refrigerator at least 1 hour before cooking.
Preheat oven to 450°.
Cut a pocket in:

A breast or shoulder of veal

Rub with:

Garlic

Dust pocket lightly with:

Ginger

before filling with:

3 cups Dry Dressing, 370, plus 1 tablespoon chopped costmary; or Bread Dressing, 370, with 2 slices chopped salt pork added; or Oyster Dressing, 371; or Green Rice, 208, the cheese omitted

Sew up the pocket with a coarse needle and thread. Rub the meat with:

Butter

Dredge with:

Seasoned Flour, 552

Place in oven on a rack in a greased roasting pan and ➤ reduce the heat to 325°. Bake ➤ uncovered 25 to 30 minutes to the pound until done. Baste occasionally, or you may place on the roast several strips of:

(Blanched bacon, 154)

From the drippings left in the pan, make:

Pan Gravy, 341

When the gravy is done, you may remove it from the heat and add:

(1/4 cup cultured sour cream)

Heat the gravy but ➤ do not let it boil.

ABOUT VEAL SCALLOPS AND CUTLETS

The most prized meat for scallops comes from the long round muscle of the leg freed from its membrane and tough connective tissue; it is sliced thinly across the grain and pounded, 444, to 1/8- to 1/4-inch thickness. Cutlets, cut from the round of the leg, are usually cut 1/2 to 3/4 inch thick, with the small round bone intact. They are often pounded, especially if used in recipes calling for rolling or stuffing when the bone is removed. Sometimes veal from the rib section is treated in similar fashion. Whether you call them scallops, cutlets or **Schnitzels,** they may be sautéed with or without breading. Trim off any fat, and if any membrane adheres, slash it in a number of places so the meat will not curl up during cooking. Do not crowd the pan or you will get a steamed effect.

VEAL CUTLET OR SCALLOPINI

3 to 4 Servings

Please read About Veal Cutlets, above. Dredge lightly with flour on one side only:

1½ lb. pounded thin veal cutlets

Sauté them, floured side first, in:

¼ cup butter

heated until fragrant. In about 3 minutes, when juices begin to emerge on the upper side, turn the meat and continue to sauté about 3 minutes more. Shake the skillet vigorously from time to time until the meat is done. Remove from skillet and keep warm. Deglaze the pan juices with:

½ cup veal or chicken stock, or ¼ cup stock and ¼ cup Marsala or Madeira
Season to taste

You may swirl in at the end:

(1 tablespoon butter)

or add:

(½ lb. sautéed mushrooms, 308)

If you do not use the wine, you may add:

(1 tablespoon lemon juice)

Pour the sauce over the cutlets and serve.

VEAL SCALLOPINI WITH TOMATOES

3 to 4 Servings

Please read About Veal Cutlets, 467.
Preheat oven to 325°.
Cut into 1-inch squares:

1½ lb. veal cutlet cut thin, trimmed, boned and pounded

Dredge with:

Flour

Brown in a mixture of:

1 tablespoon butter
1 tablespoon olive oil

Add:

½ lb. thinly sliced mushrooms
½ to 1 clove garlic, pressed
2 tablespoons choppped parsley
2 tablespoons chopped fresh basil
½ cup skinned, seeded, diced fresh tomatoes
½ cup Marsala
2 tablespoons grated Parmesan cheese

Cover and bake about 45 minutes.

WIENER SCHNITZEL OR BREADED VEAL CUTLET

3 to 4 Servings

Viennese friends insist that the true Wiener Schnitzel is deep-fat-fried; others contend it is sautéed. But most typical Viennese recipes put up to ¾ cup of butter in the sauté pan, which virtually gives a deep-fat rather than a sautéed result anyway. Although there are many variations, we suggest the following. ➤ Please read About Veal Cutlets, 467. Before cooking, pound to about ¼ inch thick:

1½ lb. veal cutlet

Coat with:

Bound Breading, 552

Let cutlets stand at least 15 minutes.
Sauté them over low heat 2 minutes on one side in:

½ to ¾ cup butter

Turn and cook 2 minutes on the other side. Turn again and cook until done, not more than 10 minutes in all. Garnish with:

Lemon slices and rolled anchovies

If you cap the garnished cutlet with a fried egg, you may call it **Holstein.**

VEAL PARMIGIANA

3 to 4 Servings

Cut into 2 x 2-inch slices:

1½ lb. veal cutlets, ¼ inch thick

Pound thin until they reach about 3 x 3 inches. Dip into a:

Bound Breading, 552

Add to bread crumbs an equal amount of:

Grated Parmesan cheese

Allow the pieces to stand at least 15 minutes, then sauté them until crisp in:

Clarified Butter, 349

about 2 minutes on each side. Serve with:

Quick Tomato Sauce, 352

PAPRIKA SCHNITZEL OR CUTLET

3 or 4 Servings

Trim edges and remove bone from:

A ¼- to ½-inch-thick veal cutlet, 1½ lb.

Dredge one side only in:

Seasoned Flour, 552

Heat in a skillet:

¼ cup butter or shortening

Sauté lightly in the fat:

(½ cup or more sliced onions)

Remove and reserve the onions and sauté the meat, first on the seasoned side, in the hot fat, until lightly browned. Turn, then add until the fat becomes red:

Paprika

Remove pan from heat and add:

1 cup boiling vegetable or chicken stock

and the reserved onions. Cover and simmer the veal ➤ over very low heat until almost tender, about 15 minutes. Add:

½ cup cultured sour cream
Season to taste

Garnish with:

Parsley, capers, or anchovies

Serve with:

Applesauce, 131
Creamed Spinach, 327

VEAL SCALLOP OR ESCALOPE DE VEAU ORLOFF

3 to 4 Servings

Please read About Veal Cutlets, 467.
Preheat oven to 350°.
Cut into 2 x 2-inch slices:

1½ lb. scallops, ¼ inch thick

Pound until about 3 x 3 inches each. Sauté until barely frizzled on both sides in:

Clarified Butter, 349

Remove from pan and drain on paper toweling. To make a **Soubise,** mix and grind in a food chopper:

½ cup cooked rice
½ cup white onions
½ cup mushrooms
Season with:
Salt and pepper
Cover each scallop of veal with:
1 tablespoon liver paste
Then press firmly over each scallop the onion-rice mixture. Sprinkle over each:
1 teaspoon brandy or dry sherry
Dust generously with:
Grated Parmesan cheese
Place the meat on an ovenproof serving platter and bake about 15 minutes until the cheese is golden.

VEAL SCALLOPS WITH HAM

6 Servings

This recipe, also called **Cordon Bleu,** is good made with chicken breasts too.
Pound:
2 large veal cutlets
and slice into about 12 three-inch squares. Sauté until barely frizzled on both sides in:
Clarified Butter, 349
Remove from pan and drain on paper toweling. Cut into 6 thin slices:
Prosciutto or smoked ham
Place the ham on 6 slices of veal. Top with a similar sized slice of:
Swiss cheese
Cover the pieces with the remaining veal slices. Gently pat the meat in:
Bound Breading, 552
Let stand 15 minutes. Sauté in:
Clarified Butter, 349
until golden on each side, about 3 minutes. Or after breading you may bake the meat on an ovenproof platter in a 350° oven about 15 minutes, turning once.

BRAISED VEAL CHOPS

4 Servings

Veal chops may be cooked the same way as veal cutlets; or simply browned, then simmered slowly, covered, on top of the stove until done, about 15 to 20 minutes.
Preheat oven to 325°.
Brown on both sides in a large skillet:
4 veal chops, ¾ inch thick
in:
Butter and vegetable oil
Arrange the chops in an overlapping pattern in a casserole. Sauté in the hot fat until limp:
2 tablespoons chopped green onions or shallots
Add:
⅓ cup dry white wine
1 teaspoon each basil and tarragon
Salt and pepper
Pour the pan juices over the chops, cover and bake about 20 minutes, basting occasionally. Serve with a choice of:
Quick Tomato Sauce, 352, Mushroom Wine Sauce, 347, or Madeira Sauce, 346

VEAL BIRDS OR PAUPIETTES

Prepare:
Slices of veal from the round, ⅓ inch thick
as for:
Beef Rolls or Paupiettes, 465
Since veal is leaner than beef, you may prefer to bard or wrap the pounded paupiettes in blanched salt pork, 154. We suggest using Filling III. Cook about 45 minutes.

MOCK CHICKEN DRUMSTICKS OR CITY CHICKEN

6 Servings

Still popular, though the veal is now more costly than the chicken it used to mock.
Preheat oven to 325°.
Cut into 1 x 1½-inch pieces:
1 lb. veal
1 lb. pork
Arrange veal and pork cubes alternately on 6 skewers. Press pieces close together into the shape of a drumstick. Roll the meat in:
Seasoned Flour, 552
Beat:
1 egg
2 tablespoons water
Dip sticks in the diluted egg, then roll in:
Bread crumbs
Melt in a skillet:
¼ cup butter
Brown meat partially in the fat. Add:
1 tablespoon grated onion
Continue to brown meat. Cover bottom of skillet with:
Boiling Stock, 522
Cover skillet and bake in oven about 50 minutes or until meat is tender. Make:
Pan Gravy, 341

VEAL STEW MÉNAGÈRE

4 Servings

Cut into 1½-inch cubes:
1½ lb. veal with little bone or 2 lb. neck or shanks
Melt in a heavy pot:
3 tablespoons butter or shortening
Brown the meat in the hot fat with:
12 very small peeled onions
Remove meat and onions from the pan. Pour off all but 1 tablespoon of fat. Stir in:
1 tablespoon flour
Add and stir until smooth:
1½ cups consommé or stock
(½ cup dry red wine)
Add the meat and onions. Simmer covered until very tender, 1½ to 2 hours. Season and serve with:

Crusty Soft-Center Spoon Bread, 629, or Farina Balls, 203

or serve it in:

A Noodle Ring, 214

Veal stew is also good with a baked top crust. See About Meat Pies, 449.

BLANQUETTE DE VEAU

6 Servings

"Serenely full, the epicure may say, 'Fate cannot harm me: I have dined today.' " As the name suggests, this stew is cooked à blanc and enhanced with an egg sauce.

Cut into 1-inch pieces:

1½ lb. boneless veal shoulder
1½ lb. boneless veal breast

Parblanch, 154, the pieces of veal about 2 minutes in salted water. Drain and wash well under cold running water, removing all scum. Put meat in a heavy pan and add:

5 cups chicken or veal stock
1 large onion studded with 1 clove
1 peeled carrot
1 rib white celery, chopped
A Bouquet Garni, 572

Simmer uncovered 1¼ to 1½ hours, until veal is tender and can be pierced with a fork. Now skim out the vegetables and the bouquet. Add:

24 small white onions
2 cups fresh button mushroom caps

Simmer about 10 minutes. Combine:

¼ cup flour
¼ cup butter

Add this thickener to the stock and simmer another 10 minutes. Remove pan from heat. Mix together:

3 beaten egg yolks
½ cup warm whipping cream

Stir about 2 tablespoons of the hot veal stock into the eggs and cream; then return mixture to the pan. Add:

2 to 3 tablespoons lemon juice
Season to taste

Serve with:

Noodles or rice

garnished with:

Chopped parsley

VEAL AND PORK PIE

4 Servings

➤ Please read About Meat Pies, 449.

Cut into 1-inch pieces:

½ lb. veal
½ lb. lean pork

Stir and brown the meat lightly in:

2 tablespoons butter or vegetable oil

Add:

3 cups boiling water
1 teaspoon salt
½ teaspoon paprika
½ bay leaf
2 whole cloves

Simmer covered about 15 minutes. Remove bay leaf and cloves. Add:

¼ cup diced carrots
¾ cup diced celery
1 cup diced potatoes
12 small onions

Bring the stew to the boiling point ➤ then reduce heat and simmer covered until meat is tender, about 30 minutes longer.

Season to taste

Make:

Pan Gravy, 341

Preheat oven to 425°.

Place stew in a baking dish. Cool slightly. Top it with a vented:

Pie Crust, 449

Brush with the white of egg and bake 15 to 20 minutes.

MEXICAN VEAL STEAK WITH NOODLES

5 or 6 Servings

Cut into small sections:

1 lb. thin veal steak

Dredge with:

¼ cup flour

Heat:

3 teaspoons butter or olive oil

Sauté meat quickly on both sides until brown. ➤ Reduce heat. Cover meat with:

1½ cups sliced onions
6 tablespoons chili sauce
1¼ cups boiling stock

Simmer covered about ½ hour. Meanwhile, cook and drain:

2 cups Noodles, 213

Toss them in:

¾ cup canned condensed cream of chicken soup

Serve noodles mounded, covered with:

¼ cup buttered crumbs
2 tablespoons grated Parmesan cheese

Surround noodles with the veal. Garnish with:

(Parsley)

CASSEROLED VEAL WITH SOUR CREAM

4 Servings

This dish can be produced in quantity for large gatherings.

Preheat oven to 300°.

Cut into cubes:

1½ lb. boneless veal

Brown lightly in:

1½ tablespoons butter

Remove meat to an ovenproof baking dish. Add to butter, stir and sauté lightly:

1 tablespoon chopped onion
½ lb. sliced mushrooms

Remove from heat. Stir in slowly:

1 tablespoon flour
2/3 cup stock
1/2 teaspoon salt
1/8 teaspoon pepper

Pour sauce over meat. Cover and bake about 45 minutes. Degrease, 340, if necessary. Stir in:

1/2 cup warm cultured sour cream

Heat thoroughly before serving.

BAKED MARROWBONES OR OSSO BUCO

3 Servings

Preheat oven to 300°.

➤ To make this dish really delectable, the animal should be not more than 2 months old. Saw into 2-inch pieces:

2 lb. shin bone or knuckle of veal

Dip the bones first in:

Olive oil

then in:

Seasoned Flour, 552

Brown the bones very slowly for about 15 minutes in:

1/4 cup olive oil or half oil and half butter

Place the bones upright as close together as possible in a heavy pan just large enough to hold them. Cook until golden in the fat:

1/4 cup chopped onions

Add them to the bones. Heat and pour over bones:

1/2 cup white wine
1/2 cup skinned, diced, seeded fresh tomatoes
Seasoned stock—enough to cover the lower third of the bones

Cover and bake 1 to 1½ hours until any meat on the bones is tender. Before serving, sprinkle the tops of the bones with:

Gremolata, 572

Serve garnished with:

Fried Chipolata sausage and Boiled Chestnuts, 298, or Risotto, 209

and scoop the delicious marrow from the bones with marrow spoons.

ABOUT LAMB, MUTTON, KID AND GOAT MEAT

Since lamb is now shipped from various climates, young lamb is no longer referred to as spring lamb. When 3 to 5 months old, it is called baby or milk-finished lamb. From 5 months to a year, it is simply called lamb, and from there on out—mutton. Mutton, with its stronger flavor and tougher meat, may be substituted for lamb, but cooking time is usually increased from 5 to 10 minutes to the pound. Both lamb and mutton are covered with a papery whitish membrane called the fell, which is often removed before cooking, as it tends to make the flavor strong. Almost any cut of lamb may be cooked by dry-heat methods—including skewer cooking—for which recipes immediately follow; and many cuts are adaptable to the covered, moist-heat methods in the second group. To identify dry- and moist-heat cuts, please see chart, 451. For the Economical Use of Large Cuts, see 452. For ground lamb recipes, see 488, and for the use of leftover lamb, see Luncheon Dishes, 250. To carve, see below.

The meat of young goat, or kid, has an agreeable flavor that has long been appreciated in Southern Europe. It is sometimes available in U.S. markets, labeled **chevon** by government ruling. It may be cooked as for mutton—provided the animal is young, for it is always tougher than mutton; and the meat of a male goat must be eaten when the animal is very young indeed, not older than 4 months.

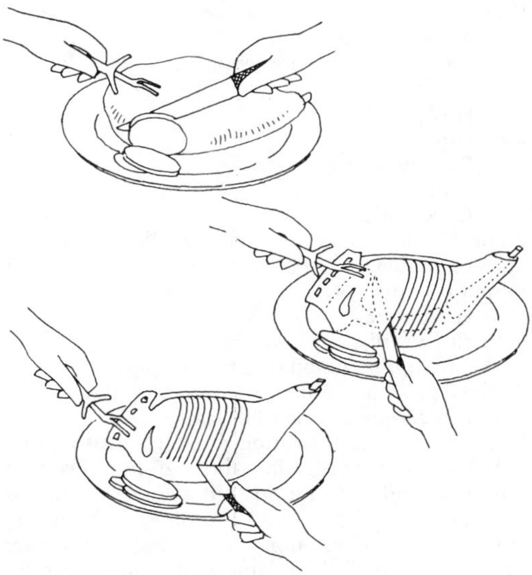

ROAST LEG OF LAMB OR MUTTON

About 8 Servings

➤ Please see Economical Use of Large Cuts, 452.

Remove from the refrigerator about 1 hour before cooking:

A 5-lb. leg of lamb or mutton

Preheat oven to 450°.

Remove the fell or papery outer covering. Rub the meat with:

(Cut garlic or lemon and rosemary)

Insert under the skin, using a pointed knife:

(Slivers of garlic or herbs)

or place on it as it goes into the oven:

(Lemon slices)

Place meat, fat side up, on a rack in an uncovered greased pan. Immediately ➤ reduce the heat to 325°. Roast it 30 minutes to the pound, or until the internal temperature reaches 175° to 180°, for meat well done. Most Europeans like lamb slightly rare or at an internal temperature of 160° to 165°.

➤ Do not cover or baste. Make:
Pan Gravy, 341, using cutured sour cream or milk
Or serve the roast with:
Deglazed drippings, 340
and:
Mint Sauce, 355
Instead of mint sauce you may prefer:
Cumberland Sauce, 356
To carve a lamb roast, see illustration, 471.

⊟ BARBECUED BUTTERFLY LEG OF LAMB

Please read about grilling and spit-cooking in Outdoor Cooking, 155.

I. Have butcher bone and flatten:
A leg of lamb
At least 2 hours before cooking, cover the leg with:
Fresh mint
Rub with:
Dry mustard
Pepper
Onion juice
Preheat grill or prepare coals. While charcoal is burning down to embers, cook gently about 5 minutes a sauce of:
1/4 cup butter
1/2 clove garlic, crushed
1 tablespoon grated onion
Remove garlic and add:
1/2 cup chopped fresh mint leaves
Place lamb on grill. During cooking, brush often with the warm sauce. After about 20 minutes, turn the meat, and continue to turn at intervals unless it is on a spit. If you like lamb pink, it should be ready in 35 to 45 minutes, depending on the heat of the coals. Well-done lamb will require 15 minutes more.

II. Marinate a boned, flattened leg of lamb refrigerated overnight in:
Lamb or Game Marinade, 528
Wipe dry before grilling as in I, above.

RACK OF LAMB

3 Servings

This is the rib end of the saddle or double loin, and has about six chops.
Preheat oven to 400°.
Remove the fell and excess fat from:
A rack of young lamb
If you French the rib bones as described in a Crown Roast, above, cover the ends with foil. Coat the rack with:
A cut garlic clove
Butter
Salt and pepper
Place it on a metal rack in a shallow pan and roast about 25 minutes or until the internal temperature reaches 145°. Carve into chops and serve.

CROWN ROAST OF LAMB

Allow 2 Ribs per Person

Preheat oven to 450°.
Wipe with a cloth:
A crown roast of lamb
French the ends of the bones by scraping clean from the end of the chops almost to the eye of the meat. Protect ends of bones by covering with aluminum foil. Proceed as directed for Roast Leg of Lamb, above, but remove meat from oven before the last hour of cooking and fill center with:
3 cups Bread Dressing, 370, or Dressing for Cornish Hen, 373
Return to oven and complete cooking. Remove covering from bones. Cover each with a paper frill, a slice of pickle or a stuffed olive. Top the dressing with a bunch of parsley or a pineapple crown, as in the illustration on 442. To carve into chops, see 477. Make:
Pan Gravy, 341
Serve with the gravy and:
Mint Sauce, 355, or currant jelly
An unfilled crown roast may be cooked upside down. Omit covering the bones. When done, fill the hollow of the roast with:
Green Peas, 314
or with:
Baked Chestnuts, 299, or
Brussels Sprouts, 292
Garnish with:
Parsley

LAMB SHOULDER ROAST

About 8 Servings

Preheat oven to 450°.
Prepare:
A 4- to 5-lb. cushion shoulder of lamb
by cutting a pocket in one side for inserting dressing. Rub meat with:
A cut clove of garlic
Fill cavity with:
Bread Dressing, 370, Tangerine Rice Dressing, 373, or Apricot Dressing, 373
Sew or skewer open side. Place roast uncovered on a rack in a greased pan in the oven. ➤ Reduce heat immediately to 325° and cook about 30 minutes to the pound. Serve with:
Pan Gravy, 341

ABOUT LAMB CHOPS

There are several kinds of lamb chops; those from the loin and rib are the tenderest and most costly; they are cooked by broiling. Large leg chops of varying shapes—sometimes called lamb steaks—often have a fine flavor and are also cooked by dry heat. Shoulder chops are the least tender, but they can be broiled and are excellent breaded or braised.

BROILED LAMB CHOPS

2 Chops per Person

Trim the outer skin or fell from:
Loin or rib chops

I. Oven-broiled
Follow directions for:
Broiled Steak, 456
allowing a shorter time for cooking, according to thickness.

II. Pan-broiled
For chops an inch or less in thickness. Sear chops in a hot skillet which has been rubbed lightly with a small piece of lamb fat. Turn chops several times during cooking. Allow for well-done chops about 15 minutes in all. Pour off fat as it accumulates in the pan. Season with:
Salt and freshly ground pepper
Serve very hot, garnished with:
Parsley

BRAISED LAMB CHOPS

Shoulder chops, arm or blade, may be braised as for:
Pork Chops, 479
but reduce cooking time to about 40 minutes.

GARNISHED ENGLISH MIXED GRILL

1 to 2 Servings

While this is the classic serving for one, it does very well for two in our family.
Preheat broiling compartment.
Place on cold grid or greased hot grid:
2 lamb chops
2 small link sausages
2 chicken livers
½ blanched veal kidney
2 thin slices bacon
1 halved small tomato seasoned with salt, pepper and butter
½ cup mushroom caps dipped in butter
4 small whole blanched onions
Position broiler rack so that meat surface is about 3 inches from heat source. During cooking process, turn meats and mushrooms. Baste if necessary with clarified butter, 349. The chops may require a longer cooking than the other ingredients. Arrange on hot plates and serve with:
Béarnaise Sauce, 359

⊟ ABOUT KEBABS

Please read about Skewer Cooking, 146, and see example of a brazier for kebabs, 145, and the hibachi, 156. Kebabs lend themselves perfectly to picnics; the meat cubes, presoaked in a savory marinade, can be grilled over an open fire and served straight from the skewer onto a piece of Flat Bread, 609. The grilled cubes may be slipped off the skewers onto a bed of rice, kasha or bulgur, or served on parsley, watercress or shredded lettuce.

Though various kinds of meat and seafood can be used for kebabs, with a wide international choice of marinades, our own meat preference for tenderness and taste is lamb, which is traditional in the Near East—whence comes the term **shish kebab.** For any meat kebabs, the meat is cut into 1½-inch cubes, which are marinated refrigerated 2 to 3 hours, then wiped dry and threaded on skewers—close together if the meat is to be rare—widely spaced for well-done; bits of lamb fat or bacon or bay leaf may be inserted between the pieces of meat to add flavor. Kebabs are grilled or broiled about 3 inches from the heat source, the meat brushed frequently with melted butter or olive oil and turned to brown evenly; about 8 to 12 minutes according to taste.

The meat cubes may be alternated on skewers with an assortment of vegetables such as tomato chunks, green pepper slices, mushrooms and onions, or with pineapple slices or stuffed olives. But differences in cooking time require that firm vegetables such as onions and green peppers be parboiled; or, as we prefer, that the vegetables be skewered separately and cooked at the side of the grill where heat is less intense. For a dramatic effect, you may serve kebabs flambéed, see 155.

⊟ LAMB KEBABS

Follow procedure described in About Kebabs, above, using one of these marinades:
Yogurt or Buttermilk Marinade, 528
Apricot or Sassaties Marinade, 529
Lamb or Game Marinade, 528
Fish or Lamb Marinade I, II or III, 528

BRAISED SHOULDER OF LAMB

6 Servings

Melt in a heavy pot:
¼ cup vegetable oil or butter
Sear on all sides in the hot fat:
A rolled shoulder of lamb
Remove it from the pot. Sauté slowly in the fat 10 minutes:
½ cup chopped onions
¼ cup chopped carrots
¼ cup chopped turnips
½ cup chopped celery with leaves
(1 sliced clove garlic)
Return the meat to the pot. Add:
½ bay leaf
4 whole peppercorns
1 teaspoon salt
4 cups boiling vegetable stock or 3 cups stock and 1 cup tomato pulp
Cover the pot and simmer meat until tender, about 2 hours. When the meat is done, degrease and thicken stock slightly with:
Kneaded Butter, 340

BRAISED STUFFED SHOULDER OR FARCE OF LAMB

6 Servings

Rub:
A boned shoulder of lamb
with:
(Garlic)
or insert slivers of garlic under the skin. Prepare about:

3 cups Bread Dressing, 370

Spread it on the meat. Roll like a jelly roll Secure with string, or fasten with spiral skewers, 420. Brown in:

3 tablespoons vegetable oil or butter

Place in a roasting pan:

1 cup hot Vegetable Stock, 524

Put the browned roast in it and bake covered at 300°. Allow about 40 minutes to the pound. For added flavor you may put some of the bones in the pan. Meanwhile, prepare for cooking:

3 cups diced vegetables: celery, carrots, onions, potatoes

After the meat has cooked about 45 minutes, place the vegetables in the roasting pan with:

An additional cup vegetable stock

Cover and continue to cook meat about 1 hour after adding vegetables, or until the internal temperature of meat is 175° to 180°. Pour off and reserve most of the liquid, and allow meat and vegetables to glaze by baking them ➤ uncovered about 10 minutes longer. Meanwhile, make the sauce. Degrease reserved liquid and reduce it somewhat.

Season to taste

LAMB FORESTIÈRE OR MOCK VENISON

About 8 Servings

Wipe with damp cloth:

A 5-lb. leg of lamb or mutton

Marinate refrigerated 24 hours or more in:

Buttermilk or Yogurt Marinade, 528

turning occasionally.

Preheat oven to 450°.

Drain, wipe dry and lard meat, 444, with:

Blanched salt pork or bacon

Put roast on a rack in a pan in the oven and bake for 15 minutes. Add:

½ cup hot Vegetable Stock, 524
1 bay leaf
2 small whole peeled onions

Cover. ➤ Reduce heat at once to 325° and allow 35 minutes to the pound. When roast is nearly done, degrease, 340. Pour over roast:

1 cup Sautéed Mushrooms, 308
1 cup warm cultured sour cream

Cook ➤ uncovered 10 minutes. Make:

Pan Gravy, 341

Serve roast surrounded by:

Browned Potatoes, 320, or
Puréed Turnips, 280

Garnish with:

Parsley

BRAISED LAMB SHANKS AND TROTTERS

4 Servings

Use shanks for stews also. Cooked as for shanks, trotters or feet are not approved by the U.S. Government but are still served abroad.

Rub:

4 lamb shanks: 3½ to 4 lb.

with:

Garlic

Roll in:

Seasoned Flour, 552

Melt until fragrant:

2 tablespoons vegetable oil

Partially sear shanks and add:

2 tablespoons diced onions

Continue to cook meat until browned on all sides. Pour off fat. Place meat on a rack in a lidded pan. Add:

1½ cups boiling stock
(½ cup lemon juice)
⅓ teaspoon pepper
1½ teaspoons salt
½ bay leaf

Cover. ➤ Simmer meat or bake covered in a 325° oven about 1½ hours or until tender. You may add for the last ½ hour of cooking:

3 cups diced vegetables
½ cup boiling stock or water

The vegetables may be onions, carrots, celery, green peppers, turnips, tomatoes and potatoes—a matter of choice and expediency. Strain, degrease and reduce stock. Serve as it is or make:

Pan Gravy, 341

If you have not added the vegetables, you may serve the shanks with:

Creole Sauce, 348

LAMB STEW OR NAVARIN PRINTANIÈRE

8 Servings

This stew is called **printanière** because of its "springlike" host of ornately cut vegetables. Cut into 1½-inch pieces:

1 lb. boned shoulder of lamb
1 lb. boned breast of lamb

Brown the meat in a heavy skillet in:

2 tablespoons vegetable oil

Remove meat to a Dutch oven. Pour off fat and deglaze pan with:

2 cups light stock

to which you may add:

2 tablespoons tomato paste

Bring to a boil and pour over meat. Simmer covered. Meanwhile, peel and shape into ovals about 1½ inches long and reserve:

2 cups new potatoes
6 carrots
3 white turnips

Add:

18 small onions

After lamb has cooked about 1 hour, skim off fat, add vegetables to the pot and simmer covered about 1 hour longer or until vegetables are tender. Have ready to add:

1 cup cooked fresh peas
1 cup cooked sliced fresh green beans

When lamb and vegetables are tender, skim off

any fat and gently fold in cooked peas and beans. Serve at once, sprinkled with ½ cup finely chopped parsley.

LAMB OR PORK GOULASH À BLANC

6 Servings

Please read About Goulash, 464, and for another goulash using pork, see 475.

Sauté:

1½ to 2 cups chopped onions

in:

½ cup butter or vegetable oil

Mash in a mortar and add:

1 teaspoon caraway
2 teaspoons marjoram
A grating of lemon rind
1 clove garlic
1 tablespoon sweet paprika

Add and bring to a boil:

1 cup water or stock

Add:

2 lb. lamb or pork, cut into 1½-inch cubes

Simmer covered 1½ hours.

Garnish with:

Slivered red or green peppers

IRISH STEW

4 to 6 Servings

This famous stew is not browned.

Cut into 1½-inch cubes:

1½ lb. lamb or mutton

Peel and slice to ⅛-inch thickness:

¾ cup onions
2½ lb. potatoes

Put in the bottom of a heavy pan a layer of potatoes, a layer of meat, and a few slices of onion. Repeat this twice, ending with potatoes on top. Season each layer with:

Salt and pepper

Add to the pot:

1 bay leaf

Pour over the layers:

2 cups boiling stock or water
2 tablespoons finely chopped parsley

Bring to a boil. Cover and simmer gently about 2½ hours or until the meat is tender. Shake pot periodically to keep the potatoes from sticking. When done, all the moisture should have been absorbed by the potatoes.

CURRY OF LAMB WITH RICE

4 Servings

Remove gristle and fat from:

A 2-lb. lamb shoulder

Cut meat into 1-inch cubes. Heat:

3 tablespoons fat or vegetable oil

Brown meat in the hot fat with:

1 tablespoon chopped onion
1 tablespoon curry powder

Add:

1 cup Light Stock, 522
¼ cup or more chopped celery
2 tablespoons chopped parsley
(1 tablespoon chopped pimiento)
(¼ cup peeled, seeded, diced cucumbers)

Cover meat and simmer until tender, about ½ hour. Stir frequently.

Season to taste

Make:

Pan Gravy, 341

Place on a platter a mound of:

Boiled Rice, 206

Arrange meat and gravy around it. Garnish platter with:

Parsley

CASSOULET

About 15 Servings

With a thicker texture than a Pot-au-Feu, 170, this controversial dish from the South of France has one solid pivot—white beans. They are cooked usually with fresh pork and sausage, but often with mutton and duck, partridge or potted goose, 434. Goose fat is a frequent component; also an onion stuck with cloves. Vegetables vary seasonally. Garlic is essential. For this recipe you almost need a routing sheet. If, however, you follow directions, you may proceed with the self-confidence of the bullfighter who put mustard on his sword. The beans soak overnight and are cooked the next day with meat and other trimmings. The pork roasts for a while before the lamb joins it. Then the meats that have been cooking with the beans are taken from the bone and sliced before being returned to the beans. This way the flavors unite in a single casserole and make a final triumphant appearance under a crust of golden crumbs.

Soak overnight in cold water:

1 lb. dried marrowfat, broad or Great Northern beans

Roast in a preheated 350° oven about 2½ hours or until tender:

3 lb. boned Loin of Pork, 477

After the pork has been roasting for about 1 hour, brown in a heavy skillet:

3 lb. rolled lamb shoulder and the cut-out bones
1 tablespoon butter

Drain off any excess fat. Roast the lamb and the lamb bones about 1½ hours longer in the same pan with the pork roast. Meanwhile, blanch, 154, by placing in cold water and bringing just to a boil:

1 ham shank
1 lb. salt pork

Drain beans. Heat the water in which they were soaked, adding:

Enough water to make 4 quarts

Bring to a boil and skim the pot. Add drained, blanched ham shank, salt pork and:

A Bouquet Garni, 572
3 cloves garlic

Simmer covered about 1½ hours. Add:

6 small white onions
½ lb. hard Italian sausage, like Salcisetta

Simmer about 1 hour longer, until the beans are tender but still intact. Remove the lamb bones and, leaving the pork and lamb roasts in the same pan, reduce heat to 300°. Pour over the meat:

Thickened Tomato Sauce, 352

and bake covered about ½ hour more. Drain off and reserve sauce and drippings. Remove and slice the meat of both the lamb and the pork roast. Drain beans, adding the juice to the drained tomato sauce. Trim and slice the ham, the sausage and the salt pork in bite-sized pieces. Layer all these meats with the beans in a casserole and skim excess fat from the combined tomato and bean juices before adding them to the other ingredients. Top with:

1 cup buttered dry bread crumbs

Bake about 1 hour longer in the oven, when the crumbs should have turned a golden color.

COUSCOUS

6 Servings

Because this dish can be varied according to what ingredients are available and extended to serve any number, it is the classic main meal in North Africa, where the hospitality of the Arab people is legendary. The one constant ingredient is the cereal—fine-grained semolina—cooked so that each grain is separate and the mass light and fluffy. For perfect results, the cooking vessel should be a "couscoussier" of pottery or—a modern version—of stainless steel, shown here with its removable perforated top and its deep stewpot. A muslin-lined colander over a heavy double-boiler bottom makes a fair substitute, provided the two parts of the cooker may be fitted so closely that vapor can escape only through the colander perforations, and the colander does not touch the liquid below. Since the cereal, after steaming, has a very bland,

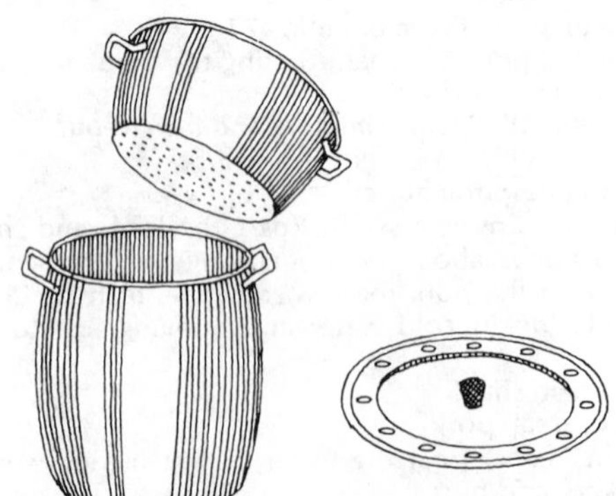

delicate flavor, the meat and vegetable mixture is frequently sharpened with additional seasonings like cayenne or chili pepper; or a portion of the sauce is reserved, fired up and passed around for the stimulation of the more able-bodied guests. And every Arab is able-bodied when it comes to consuming hot sauce!

Soak overnight, drain and reserve:

⅓ cup dried chick-peas
½ cup dried fava beans

Cut into a dozen or so good-sized chunks:

2 lb. lamb; or 1 lb. lamb, ½ lb. beef, ½ chicken

Place in the bottom element of the couscoussier the meat, beans and:

2 cups sliced turnips, 334
1½ cups sliced carrots
¾ cup chopped onions
¼ teaspoon black pepper
½ tablespoon salt
(¼ teaspoon saffron)
(½ teaspoon turmeric)
(¼ teaspoon ginger)
2 to 3 cups stock, to cover

Bring this mixture to a boil, ➤ reduce the heat, and simmer 40 minutes. Add:

2 cups sliced zucchini or yellow squash
2 quartered tomatoes or ½ cup tomato paste
1 small cabbage, quartered
(1 stalk finocchio, quartered)
(3 or 4 minced sweet peppers)
(¼ to ½ cup raisins)
¼ cup chopped parsley

and simmer 20 minutes longer. Ten minutes before the end of the above procedure, have ready in a large dish:

1 lb. semolina

Moisten the semolina slightly with a little cold water, working it with the fingers to keep it cohesive but not lumpy. The grains will swell. Place the cereal in the top or strainer element of the couscoussier and steam it, uncovered, over the simmering meat and vegetable mixture 30 minutes more.

Remove the couscoussier from the heat. Remove strainer and turn cereal into a large bowl. Sprinkle it with cold water to enlarge the grains further, stirring with a wooden spoon to break up any lumps. Return cereal to strainer, and strainer to pot, ➤ fitting it on tightly. Simmer an additional 30 minutes. Remove the cereal to a large heated platter, mixing with it 2 tablespoons of fat scooped from the top of the stew. You may at this point remove one cupful of the stew liquid and "inflame" it with:

(¼ teaspoon cayenne, or red or chili pepper)
(¼ teaspoon ginger)
(½ teaspoon harissa, or concentrate of red pimiento)

Arrange the meat and vegetable mixture around the cereal, and serve the dish with the fiery sauce in one pitcher and the remaining sauce—partially defatted—in another.

ABOUT PORK

Someone has observed that a pig resembles a saint in that he is more honored after death than during his lifetime. High-grade pork is fine-grained and firm, the shoulder cuts marbled, the fat white. Formerly, because of its heavy fat content, all parts of pork could be cooked by dry-heat methods, and the meat was virtually self-basting. Today, hogs are bred leaner, and some pork may require supplementary basting, or cooking by moist heat. ➤ An important word of caution. Incredible as it may seem at the end of the twentieth century, our government still has no requirement for the systematic microscopic inspection of pork. As long as this is true, the pork we buy as well as that from animals we raise ourselves may, under certain conditions, harbor the dangerous parasite that is passed on to man in the insidious disease called trichinosis. The only way to be certain that the parasite is destroyed is ➤ to cook pork thoroughly. The internal temperature must reach at least 137°. Judged by the eye, the meat must be white or grayish throughout, without a trace of pink, even in the very center of a large roast; the juices will run clear. Finally, ➤ never taste even a tiny bit of raw pork in any form, including bacon and sausage; and after handling it, carefully cleanse your hands and any knife, utensil or surface the pork may have touched. Slow cooking of pork is desirable, 30 to 45 minutes to the pound. Rolled and stuffed roasts require the longer cooking time. If you use a meat thermometer, the roasts of varying degrees of choiceness which come from the loin section—center cut, rib cut, loin end and blade or shoulder end—should be cooked to an internal temperature of 170°. The thicker roasts, which include leg of pork—known somewhat confusingly as fresh ham—and the shoulder, known as the picnic, are cooked to an internal temperature of 185°. Fresh ham may also be braised or pot-roasted. To identify those portions which cook by dry- or moist-heat methods, see chart, 451. Generally, the recipes for each cut of meat calling for dry-heat methods are given first, followed by the recipes for moist-heat methods. For Economical Use of Large Cuts, see 452. For uses of cooked pork, see Luncheon Dishes, 250. For hams, see 482.

PORK ROAST

Remove meat from refrigerator about 1 hour before cooking, and read About Pork, above.
Preheat oven to 450°.
Use a fine, juicy roast:

Loin or shoulder of pork

If boned or rolled, the roast will take 5 to 10 minutes more per pound than the timing given below.
Rub the roast well with:

A cut clove of garlic, fresh sage, dried rosemary, tarragon or thyme

Dredge with:

Seasoned Flour, 552

Place fat side up on a rack in a shallow greased pan in the oven. ➤ Reduce the heat at once to 325°. Cook ➤ uncovered 25 to 35 minutes to the pound, depending on cut and thickness of meat. The internal temperature should be 170° for a loin cut and 185° for a shoulder cut. Remove roast from oven and let rest 10 to 15 minutes before carving. In the meantime, make:

Pan Gravy, 341

You may roast alongside the meat for the last 35 minutes of cooking:

Peeled and parboiled sweet potatoes or parsnips

or on top of the roast:

Prunes and apricots or Orange Marmalade, 839

or serve the roast with:

Applesauce, 131, seasoned with 2 tablespoons horseradish and a grating of nutmeg
Sweet Potatoes and Fruit, 325
Apples with Sauerkraut, 131, or other sauerkraut variations
Onion and Apple Casserole, 313
Turnips and apples
Puréed Green Beans, Peas or Limas, 280

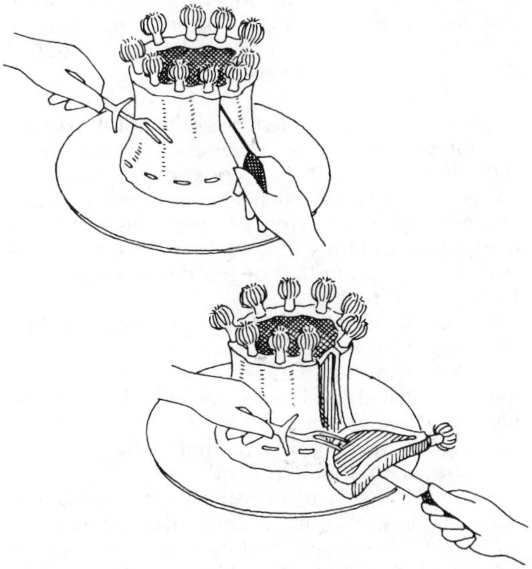

CROWN ROAST OF PORK

Allow 2 Ribs per Person

Remove meat from refrigerator about 1 hour before cooking.
Preheat oven to 450°.
Wipe with a cloth:

A crown roast of pork

Protect the ends of the bones by covering with aluminum foil. Immediately after putting the roast in the oven ➤ reduce the heat to 325°, allowing 25 to 30 minutes to the pound. If the crown is not to be filled with dressing, omit covering the bones and cook the roast upside down. Serve filled with a cooked vegetable; or, if the roast is to be stuffed, remove it 1 hour before it is done and fill the center with:

Stuffing for Crown Roast of Pork, 371, or
Sausage Dressing, 371, or
Apple and Onion Dressing, 372, or
Chestnut Dressing, 372

Return the roast to the oven and complete cooking. Make:

Pan Gravy, 341

Serve with:

Glazed Onions, 312
Apples Cockaigne, 131
Watercress or broiled canned apricots and crystallized ginger slices

To carve, see sketch, 477.

ROAST SUCKLING PIG

10 Servings

We never think of suckling pig without recalling our friend Amy, an American, long a resident of Mexico but determined to reconstruct in alien surroundings the traditional Christmas dinners of her youth. Describing the preparation of roast pig to her skilled Indian cook, she wound up with the announcement, "The pig is brought to table on plenty of greenery, with an apple in the mouth." The cook looked first baffled, then resentful, and finally burst out with a succession of "no's." Her employer persisted patiently with helpful gestures and increasing firmness. When the pig was served, she discovered that her cook could effect an entrée which surpassed her wildest expectations. There was plenty of greenery and a distinct air of martyrdom; but the apple was clenched, not in the pig's mouth, but in that of the desperate cook!

Preheat oven to 450°.

Dress, by drawing, scraping as for Opossum, 515, and cleaning as for Rabbit, 513:

A suckling pig

Remove eyeballs and lower the lids. The dressed pig should weigh about 12 pounds. Fill it with:

Onion Dressing, 372, or Stuffing for Crown Roast of Pork, 371

It takes 2½ quarts of dressing to stuff a pig this size. Multiply all your ingredients, but not the seasonings. Use these sparingly until dressing is combined, then taste it and add what is lacking. Sew up the pig. Put a block of wood in its mouth to hold it open. Skewer legs into position, pulling forelegs forward and bending hindlegs into a crouching stance. Rub the pig with:

Oil or soft butter
(A cut clove of garlic)

Dredge it with:

Flour

Cover ears and tail with aluminum foil. Place the pig in a pan ➤ uncovered, in the oven for 15 minutes. ➤ Reduce heat to 325° and roast until tender, allowing 20 minutes to the pound. Baste every 15 minutes with:

Pan drippings or additional vegetable oil if necessary

Remove foil from ears and tail. Rest 30 minutes before carving. Place pig on a platter. Remove wood from mouth. Replace with:

A small apple, lemon or carrot

Place in the eyes:

Raisins or cranberries

Drape around the neck a wreath of:

Small green leaves

or garnish the platter or board with:

Watercress

The pig may be surrounded with:

Apples Cockaigne, 131, Apples Stuffed with Sweet Potatoes, 324, Apples Stuffed with Mincemeat, 812, or Tomatoes Florentine, 342

Make:

Pan Gravy, 341

To carve, place head to left of carver. Remove forelegs and hams. Divide meat down center of back. Separate ribs. Serve a section of crackling skin to each person.

ROAST FRESH HAM OR LEG OF PORK

You may place a fresh leg of pork called:

A fresh ham

in a marinade, 528, and refrigerate covered for 24 to 48 hours.

Preheat oven to 450°.

Wipe the meat before roasting. Marinated or not, cook the ham as for:

Pork Roast, 477

basting every half hour with part of the marinade or with the traditional:

(Beer)

When done, the internal temperature should be 185°. Make:

Pan Gravy, 341

Serve with any of the accompaniments suggested in Pork Roast, 477. Leftover cold pork is a luxury to be used in many dishes, see Index.

PORK ROAST STUFFED WITH SAUERKRAUT

Preheat oven to 450°.

Have butcher remove bones from:

A pork shoulder

Also have one side left open for inserting:

Drained sauerkraut

Dredge with:

Flour

Close opening by sewing or skewering. Place the roast in the oven uncovered on a rack in a greased pan. ➤ Immediately reduce heat to 325° and bake about 40 minutes to the pound.

PORK TENDERLOIN

Preheat oven to 350°.

Split lengthwise:

A pork tenderloin

Flatten it with a cleaver, 444. Rub lightly with:

Butter
(Garlic)

Spread with:

Bread Dressing, 370, using ¼ the amount; or with Apple and Sweet Potato Dressing, 374, using about ⅓ the amount; or with stewed drained apricots or pitted prunes

Roll and tie it up. Dredge with:

Seasoned Flour, 552

or brush with unsalted fat. Place tenderloin on rack in greased pan. Bake 30 to 35 minutes to the pound. Make:

Pan Gravy, 341

You may add to the gravy:

(Cultured sour cream and cooked mushrooms, or sweet cream and currant jelly)

FRENCHED PORK TENDERLOIN

Cut crosswise into ¾-inch slices:

Pork tenderloin

Flatten slices slightly with a cleaver, as shown on 444. Dredge with:

Seasoned Flour, 552

Sauté as for:

Pork Chops, below

Add to the pan juices or the gravy:

½ teaspoon grated lemon rind

PORK TENDERLOIN WITH MUSHROOMS AND OLIVES

4 Servings

Cut into 1-inch crosswise slices and pound:

1 lb. or more pork tenderloin

Roll in:

Seasoned Flour, 552

Sauté until golden in:

2 tablespoons butter

with:

A sliced onion

Bring just to the boiling point:

½ cup dry white wine

Pour over the meat. Add at this time:

½ lb. sliced mushrooms
(⅛ teaspoon fresh rosemary, or ¼ teaspoon crushed coriander seed)

Cover the skillet closely. ➤ Simmer the rounds until done, about 45 minutes. Add:

6 sliced green olives, stuffed with almonds
(2 tablespoons lemon juice)

Serve garnished with:

2 tablespoons chopped parsley

PORK CHOPS

I. Sautéed

Brown in a hot pan in just enough vegetable oil or rendered pork fat to keep them from sticking:

Pork chops, 1 inch thick or less

Before searing, they may be rubbed with:

(Garlic or powdered rosemary)

After searing ➤ reduce heat. Cook the chops slowly, covered or uncovered, until done. Pour off excess grease as they cook. Season with:

Salt and pepper

Make:

Pan Gravy, 341

II. Baked

Recommended for thick chops.
Preheat oven to 350°.
After searing them as above, bake covered about 1 hour:

4 pork chops

During the last half hour, you may add for seasoning:

(3 tablespoons minced green pepper and celery)
(1 clove garlic)
(1 piece gingerroot mashed in 1 tablespoon vinegar)
(3 slices orange)
(½ cup orange juice)

BREADED PORK CHOPS

4 Servings

Rub with garlic:

4 half-inch-thick pork chops

Bread them, 552. Using a heavy hot pan, brown lightly in:

2 to 3 tablespoons rendered pork fat or vegetable oil

Reduce heat. Cook uncovered about 20 minutes longer or until tender. Make:

Pan Gravy, 341

BRAISED PORK CHOPS WITH FRUIT

Allow 1 Chop per Person

Preheat oven to 325°.
Sear in a lightly greased hot skillet:

Trimmed pork chops, ¾ inch thick or more

Season lightly with:

Salt and pepper
(⅛ teaspoon curry powder)

Place on the chops, skin side down:

Halved cored apples, pineapple slices or pitted apricots or prunes

Fill the centers of the fruit with:

Brown sugar

Cover the bottom of the skillet to ½ inch with

Chicken stock and/or some of the fruit juice

Cover the pan closely. Bake about 1 hour. Remove the chops from the pan carefully, so as not to disturb the fruit. Keep warm. Partially degrease and add to the pan juices:

¾ to 1 cup sweet cream or cultured sour cream

Serve this sauce with the chops and fruit.

BRAISED STUFFED PORK CHOPS COCKAIGNE

6 Servings

Preheat oven to 350°
Cut from the bone:

6 rib pork chops about 1 inch thick

Trim off excess fat and cut a large gash or pocket in the side of each chop. Prepare a dressing of:

1 cup bread crumbs
¼ cup chopped celery
¼ cup chopped onions
2 tablespoons chopped parsley
Milk to moisten the dressing
¼ teaspoon salt
⅛ teaspoon paprika

These proportions and ingredients may be varied. Fill the pockets with the dressing. Skewer them. Sear the chops in a hot skillet and place in a lidded ovenproof dish with:

Milk or stock, about ¼ inch deep

Cover and bake about 1 hour and 15 minutes or until tender. Make:

Pan Gravy, 341

or serve with:

Cranberry Sauce, 133

BRAISED PORK CHOPS WITH SAUERKRAUT

6 Servings

Preheat oven to 350°.
Have ready:

6 slices diced Sautéed Bacon, 486

Mix it in a casserole with:

2 lb. drained sauerkraut
2 cups Applesauce, 131
1 tablespoon brown sugar
¼ cup dry white wine
½ tablespoon dry mustard
¼ teaspoon freshly ground pepper

Sauté gently on both sides:

6 loin pork chops, 1 inch thick

Place them on top of the mixture. Cover and bake about 1 hour.

BRAISED PORK CHOPS CREOLE

6 Servings

Preheat oven to 350°.
Dredge:

6 pork chops, ½ inch thick or more

with:

Seasoned Flour, 552

Gently sauté them in:

Hot fat or vegetable oil

Place them in a baking dish. Combine, heat and pour around them:

1 can condensed tomato soup: 10½ oz.
½ can water or stock
½ cup chopped celery
1 chopped green pepper, seeds and membrane removed
¾ cup minced onions
½ teaspoon salt
¼ teaspoon paprika

Bake covered about 1 hour. Cook another 15 minutes ➤ uncovered and topped with:

Crushed cornflakes

BRAISED DEVILED PORK CHOPS

4 Servings

Using:

Pork Marinade, 529

marinate 3 to 6 hours, covered and refrigerated:

4 pork chops, 1 inch thick

Preheat oven to 325°.
Drain the chops, reserving the marinade. Wipe them dry. Brown them in a hot greased skillet. Heat the marinade and:

½ cup water or stock

Pour around the chops. Bake covered about 1 hour or until tender.

PORK BIRDS

6 Servings

Pound to the thickness of ¼ inch:

2 lb. pork steaks cut from the shoulder

Cut them into 6 oblong pieces. Spread them with half the recipe for:

Apricot or Prune Dressing, 373

Roll them. Secure the rolls with string or wooden picks. Dredge in:

2 tablespoons flour

Brown in:

2 tablespoons fat

Add:

1 cup boiling water or stock

Simmer covered about 50 minutes or until tender. Serve with the degreased and reduced pan juices, or thicken to make:

Pan Gravy, 341

SWEET AND SOUR PORK

6 Servings

I. Cut into ½-inch strips, 2 inches long:

2 lb. lean boneless pork loin or shoulder

In a wok or skillet, brown the meat in:

2 tablespoons hot vegetable oil

Drain the meat on paper toweling. Cook the following sauce until slightly thickened and clear:

1 cup pineapple juice
½ cup water or chicken stock
⅓ cup vinegar
¼ cup packed brown sugar
2 tablespoons cornstarch
2 tablespoons soy sauce
2 teaspoons Worcestershire sauce

Add the meat and simmer, covered, about 1 hour or until tender. Add:

1½ cups pineapple chunks
1 small sliced green pepper, seeds and membrane removed
(¼ cup onion slices)

Cook uncovered about 10 minutes. Serve over:

Boiled Rice, 206

II. Stir-Fried

This quick version is best used with very thinly sliced raw pork or larger pieces of cooked pork. Prepare:

Oriental Sweet-Sour Sauce II, 355

Cut into strips 1/4 inch thick and about 1/2 inch wide:

2 lb. lean boneless pork

Dust pieces with:

Seasoned Flour, 552

Sauté meat, a little at a time, in a wok or skillet in:

2 to 3 tablespoons vegetable oil

Return all the meat to the skillet and add the above sauce. Cover and simmer about 5 to 8 minutes. A good addition at this time would be:

(Cooked Podded Peas, 315)

Serve over:

Boiled Rice, 206

PORK AND VEAL GOULASH WITH SAUERKRAUT

4 Servings

Sauté until translucent:

6 tablespoons chopped onions

in:

2 tablespoons butter or vegetable oil

Add and sauté:

1/2 lb. 1-inch lean pork cubes
1/2 lb. 1-inch veal cubes

Heat and add:

1 lb. drained sauerkraut
1 teaspoon caraway seed

Simmer covered about 1 hour. Heat and add:

1 cup cultured sour cream
A generous grating of freshly ground pepper

Serve at once.

ABOUT SPARERIBS

There is much bone and little meat to spareribs—we love the self-explanatory name. ➤ Allow at least 1 pound per person. Country-style back ribs, also sold as spareribs, are meatier. Try using spareribs in some of the recipes calling for pork chops. These gloriously messy old favorites can simply be baked in a 325° oven about 1½ hours, but there are a good many more lively things to do with them. Before both baking and barbecueing, we recommend parboiling, 154, 2 to 4 minutes, which not only removes unwanted fat but makes the end result more palatable.

Comparatively little known but quite delicious are lamb spareribs. They need not be parboiled but in other respects may be prepared as for pork spareribs, except that cooking time should be reduced about one-third. For Glazed Cocktail Ribs, see 85.

BAKED SPARERIBS WITH APPLE-ONION DRESSING

4 Servings

Preheat oven to 500°.
Parboil 2 minutes:

4 lb. spareribs

Cut into 2 pieces. Spread 1 piece with:

Apple and Onion Dressing, 372

using only 4 cups of dressing. Cover the dressing with the other piece of meat. Tie the 2 pieces together. Rub the outside of the meat with:

2 tablespoons flour
1/8 teaspoon salt
A few grains pepper

Place on a rack in an uncovered roasting pan and ➤ reduce the heat at once to 325°. Bake about 1½ hours or until tender. Baste every 10 minutes with the fat in the pan.

SWEET-SOUR SPARERIBS

4 Servings

Preheat oven to 350°.
Have a butcher cut into 2-inch pieces:

4 lb. spareribs

Parboil, 154, 3 to 4 minutes. Drain and dry. Brush with:

Soy sauce

Bake uncovered on a rack in a pan in the oven 1 hour. Have ready the following sauce. Boil briefly:

1 cup vinegar
1 cup sugar
1/2 cup sherry
2 tablespoons soy sauce
2 teaspoons grated fresh ginger

Mix together and add:

4 teaspoons cornstarch
2 tablespoons water

Cook until cornstarch is transparent. Pour the sauce over the cooked spareribs and serve at once with:

Baked Green Rice, 208

⊟ BARBECUED SPARERIBS

I. Indoors

Bake spareribs in a 450° oven 15 minutes, covered with aluminum foil—do not seal. ➤ Reduce heat to 350° and pour a barbecue sauce over the meat. Bake 1 hour longer, basting frequently. Try one of the following sauces:

Barbecue Sauce I or II, 354
Oriental Sweet-Sour Sauce, 355
Ferocious Barbecue Sauce, 354
Mexican Tomato Sauce, 352
Plum Sauce, 356

II. Outdoors

Please read About Outdoor Cooking, 155, and also note illustration of ribs woven on a spit, 158.
Season:

2 sides spareribs

with:

Salt and pepper

Grill very slowly 30 minutes, then brush with one of the sauces above and continue to cook about 1 hour longer. Turn occasionally and brush with more sauce, until done.

BOILED SPARERIBS

Place:

Spareribs

in:

Boiling water to cover

Add:

Salt and pepper

Chopped onion, celery, parsley and carrots

(1 teaspoon caraway seed)

➤ Simmer the meat covered until tender, 1½ to 2 hours. If you care to crisp the ribs, drain well and just before serving sauté them in butter. Or simply drain and serve on a mound of hot:

Sauerkraut or Red Cabbage, 295

surrounded by:

Mashed Potatoes, 318, or

Purée of Lentils, 287

STEWED PORK NECK BONES

Partly cover with seasoned boiling water:

Pork neck bones

Simmer covered until tender, about 1½ hours. Vegetables may be added to the stew for the last ½ hour of cooking.

STEWED PORK HOCKS

Cover with seasoned boiling water:

Pork hocks

Simmer covered 1½ to 3 hours. You may add potatoes for the last ½ hour of cooking, or greens or cabbage for the last 20 minutes. Or marinate the cooled cooked hocks 2 hours or more in:

Herbed French Dressing, 360

and serve cold with a salad.

SALT PORK IN MILK GRAVY

4 Servings

Dip thin slices of:

1 lb. salt pork

in:

Boiling water

Drain and dip in:

Cornmeal

Brown slowly in a skillet, turning frequently until cooked through. Remove salt pork and all but 2 tablespoons drippings. Add and sauté until golden:

1 to 2 tablespoons chopped onion

Thicken drippings with:

2 tablespoons flour, see Pan Gravy, 341

Blend in slowly:

1 cup milk

Serve with:

Cornbread, 627, and Greens, 305

ABOUT DESALTING HAM AND OTHER CURED MEAT

Because of the prevalence of refrigeration, ham and Canadian bacon, tongue, corned beef, pastrami and salt pork are today subjected to much weaker brining than formerly. But all of these salted meats, while relished for their pungent flavors, are, like brined vegetables, less valuable nutritionally than when they are fresh. If the meats have been heavily pickled, 814, or aged—like "old" or country hams, 484—be sure to soak 12 hours, allowing 1 quart of water to 1 pound of cured meat. Or ➤ parblanch, 154, before cooking. After blanching, put the meat into rapidly boiling water, bring to a boil again and ➤ at once reduce heat to a simmer. Salted meats are always simmered à blanc, 447. Cook ➤ uncovered until tender. Time indications are noted in the individual recipes.

ABOUT HAMS

Someone defined eternity as a ham and two people. The definition probably dates from the days when the term applied only to the small mountain of meat we now call a whole ham—the cured and smoked hind of a hog. Now that there is a wide variety of cuts and sizes available, eternity has somewhat shortened. To identify cuts and use them economically, see 451 and 452.

Pork becomes ham after undergoing a thorough processing which includes curing with salt, smoking and sometimes aging. Years ago these processes were necessary to preserve the meat. Nowadays it is taste and convenience that govern processing, and often the packer keeps his method a well-guarded secret. Curing, a process that uses salt to retard the growth of bacteria, may be done by one or a combination of three methods: dry-curing—in which salt and spices are rubbed directly into the meat—the method recommended for home processing, 813; immersion of the pork in a brine and spice solution; or injection of a brine solution into the meat itself—the curing method usually used in commercial packing today.

The second step in processing—smoking—is what adds flavor, color and character to a ham. Smoking—often skipped for mild-tasting precooked hams—is done in a hot, airtight smokehouse, and flavor depends on the wood used, hickory being an old favorite. The U.S. Department of Agriculture requires that ham labeled "ready-to-eat" prior to being sold must have been exposed to an internal temperature of 140° for half an hour to destroy the dangerous trichina parasite. Light smoking accomplishes this, and produces a mildly flavored, juicy ham. Heavy and long smoking is used for such specialty hams as the domestic Smithfield and the European prosciutto and Westphalian, which are dryer and of a deeper color and richer flavor, having undergone, besides curing and smoking, a long and painstaking aging process—up to a year. These steps cause these "old" hams to shrink in size and to go up in price.

What pigs are fed produces nuances of flavor in hams from one area to another. Eighty percent of American hogs are corn-fed, but the mainstay of a porker's menu can also be acorns or peaches or peanuts—the last being the diet of the famous Smithfield hogs of Virginia and North Carolina. German pigs that produce the aged Westphalian hams thrive on a diet of sugar beets, while Italian pigs whose meat will in time become the delicacy called prosciutto are fed chestnuts or—in the Parma region—whey from the local cheese. These European hams are succulent and translucent and need no further preparation after their long aging; when sliced paper-thin they have a flavor and texture reminiscent of smoked salmon.

Fresh ham is a misnomer; it is in reality simply a pork roast—the hind leg which has not been cured or smoked. Today there are many cuts of ham with a confusing variety of names. Ham is usually labeled one of two ways: "Cook Before Eating" or "Ready to Eat." Whatever cut you buy, ➤ follow scrupulously the packer's instructions on the label. "Cook before eating" hams need roasting to an internal temperature of 160°. "Ready to eat" hams—also called "fully cooked" or "ready to serve"—may be eaten cold, as is, with no further preparation; but they will taste and look better if heated thoroughly, to an internal temperature of 140°, and glazed, 367, during the latter part of cooking.

Less frequently prepared in this instant-everything age is a third type of ham, the old-time **country ham,** or Virginia, Kentucky or Tennessee ham. The protoype of the country types is the Smithfield ham; all country hams are dry-cured and heavily salted and require soaking followed by long simmering, see Country Hams, 484. The flavor and aroma of these hams are worth the extra time and effort.

The wide assortment of **canned hams** now available offers the instant convenience one needs when the house is suddenly flooded with unexpected guests. When you buy canned ham, ➤ check the label for perishability and need of refrigeration. Most of the larger canned hams, including the superior qualities imported from Denmark, Holland and Poland, must be kept under refrigeration before opening, and can be stored thus for a few months. Some of the smaller canned hams can be stored without refrigeration. These hams have been sterilized in the canning process, but texture and taste are the losers in this overcooking process. Canned hams are usually sold under a manufacturer's label, and only by sampling various brands will you eventually reach the stage where purchasing one is not buying a pig in a poke.

A few basic cuts of ham to be found under various names in the market are described here with suggestions as to yield and uses. The whole ham, a 10- to 15-pound hind leg of pork, with bone intact, is the most flavorful and least wasteful cut. It will serve 20 to 30 people generously, probably with leftovers. A short plump shape, with a stubby rather than elongated shank or pointed end, is the better choice. For average families, it is more usual to buy a cut section of the whole ham, either the rounded part called the butt portion—the upper thigh of the animal—or the lower shank end. The butt half is somewhat more meaty but more difficult to carve. A 5- to 7-pound shank end will serve 10 to 12 people. From the flat cut end of either butt or shank, several slices or individual ham steaks may be removed for separate cooking.

Ham is available in many boneless forms—whole, in halves or in chunks of various sizes. After boning, the meat may be shaped by the packer or rolled and packaged in airtight wrappers or cans. These forms may lack the flavor of ham with the bone intact and are more expensive. ➤ Allow one-third pound per serving.

The smoked shoulder of pork, also known as picnic or Calais—"cally"—is a less expensive cut, but because it contains more fat, bone and skin in proportion to lean meat, you must figure ➤ almost a pound of roast shoulder per serving.

The smoked shoulder butt is a boneless cut from the neck and shoulder of the hog and may have several aliases: Boston butt, cottage ham or daisy ham. Though tender and tasty, it may be very fatty. A long narrow piece is usually preferable to a short plump selection, and ➤ will serve 3 or 4 people. Cut into slices, it makes a delicious alternative to bacon. It may be broiled, sautéed, roasted or simmered.

Ham should be served warm or cool, but never chilled. If a rainbow iridescence appears on sliced ham, it is merely due to light refraction on the fat film. To store ham, the rule is that all hams must be kept refrigerated, with two exceptions: small unopened canned ham not labeled perishable, and dry-cured ham—the country or Smithfield type—which can be kept in a cool, dry, dark place—or in the refrigerator. For best results, uncanned whole hams should not be stored longer than a week in the refrigerator before cooking; smaller portions not longer than 3 to 5 days. Sliced ham is best used within 2 days. Freezing any ham is not recommended because of rapid deterioration in quality and flavor, and canned ham is especially vulnerable because of its high water content.

BAKED HAM

➤ Please read About Hams to determine the type of ham and the number of servings.

I. Ham labeled "Cook Before Eating"

Preheat oven to 325°.

Place ham on a rack, uncovered, in a shallow pan. For a whole 10- to 15-pound ham, allow 18 to 20 minutes per pound; for a half—5 to 7 pounds—about 20 minutes per pound. For a shank or butt portion weighing 3 to 4 pounds, bake about 35 minutes to the pound. Or, in all cases, cook until internal temperature reaches 160°. Remove rind and excess fat and serve with:

Raisin Sauce, 356; Sour Cream Horseradish Dressing, 356; Barbecue Sauce, 354; Hot Cumberland Sauce I, 356; or Sauce Dijonnaise, 342

Or, if you prefer an attractive, quick finish, use:

Spirit Glaze for Ham, 368

Suggested accompaniments are:

Scalloped Potatoes, 319; or a barquette of Puréed Chestnuts, 280

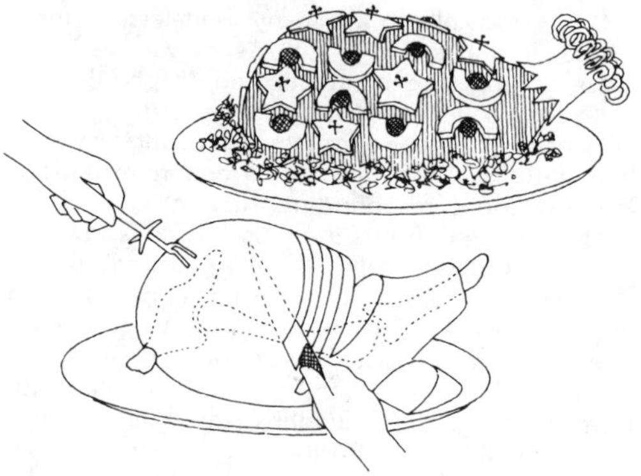

To decorate and carve a whole ham, see sketches above. To carve the butt end, see below.

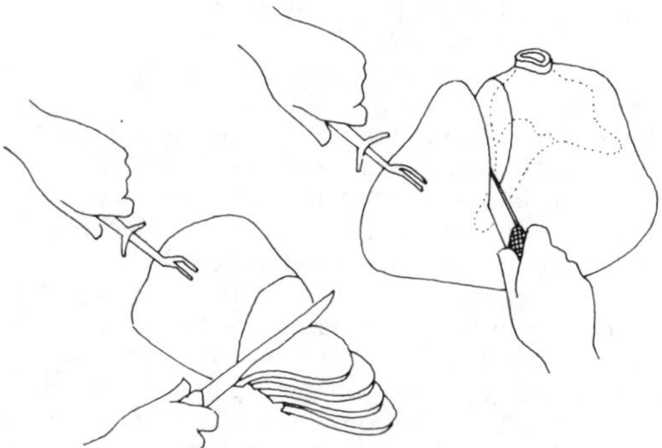

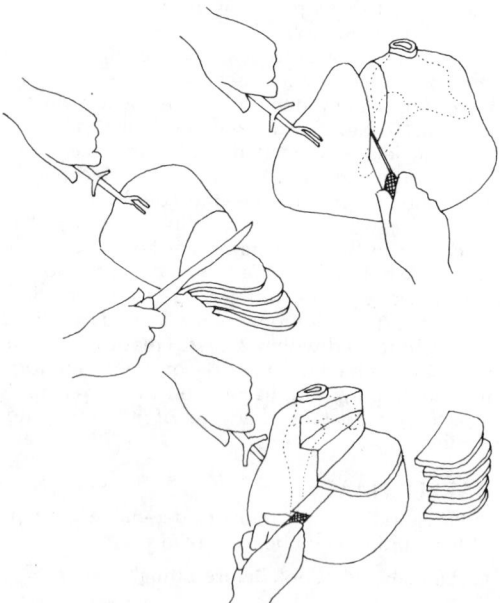

II. Ham labeled "Fully Cooked" or "Ready to Eat"

Preheat oven to 325°.

To heat the ham, place it on a rack, uncovered, in a shallow pan. For a whole ham, allow 15 to 18 minutes to the pound; for a half, 18 to 24 minutes per pound. The ham will be ready when internal temperature reaches 140°.

Remove ham from the oven about ½ hour before it is done. While preparing it for glazing, increase oven heat to 425°. Remove rind, all but a collar around the shank bone. Cut diagonal gashes across the fat top side of the ham, in diamond shapes, and cover this surface with:

1⅓ cups brown sugar
2 teaspoons dry mustard
⅓ cup fine bread crumbs

moistened with:

3 tablespoons cider vinegar, prune juice, wine, or ham drippings

Stud fat at intersections of each diamond with:

Whole cloves

Or decorate as shown opposite with:

Alternating ½ pineapple rings studded with cranberries and stars cut from preserved orange peels

➤ Reduce oven heat again to 325° and return ham to oven about 30 minutes. Place on platter. Garnish with:

Jellied cranberry slices topped with thin orange or pineapple slices

or with already cooked:

Apples filled with sweet potatoes, 324

COUNTRY HAMS: VIRGINIA, SMITHFIELD, KENTUCKY, ETC.

Please read about country hams, 483. To prepare a country ham, soak it in cold water to cover 24 to 36 hours. Then scrub it well, using a brush and yellow soap, if necessary, to remove the mold. Rinse thoroughly and place in a kettle of simmering well-seasoned water to cover. Simmer 20 minutes to the pound or until the meat reaches an internal temperature of 150°. Add to the water before the last quarter of cooking time:

1 quart cider
¼ cup brown sugar

Drain when cooking time has elapsed. Remove skin while ham is still warm, being careful not to tear fat. Trim fat partially. Dust the ham with a mixture of:

Freshly ground black pepper
Cornmeal
Brown sugar

Place ham in a preheated 425° oven long enough to glaze. Serve warm or cold. Be sure to slice ➤ very, very thin.

BROILED HAM

Allow ⅓ Pound per Person

Preheat broiler.

Slash in several places the fat edge of:

A piece of ham, about 1 inch thick

Place it on a broiler rack, 3 inches below heating unit. Broil 8 to 12 minutes to a side. After cooking it on one side and turning, you may brush it, toward the end of cooking, with a mixture of:

1 teaspoon dry mustard
1 tablespoon lemon juice
¼ cup grape jelly

If you do not use the glaze, a traditional accompaniment is:

Corn Fritters, 301
Tomato Slices, 106

SAUTÉED HAM AND EGGS

Trim the edges of:

A thin slice of smoked ham

Rub a skillet with ham fat. Heat it. Brown ham lightly on one side, then the other. Remove to a hot platter. ➤ Reduce the heat. Sauté gently in the tried-out ham fat:

Eggs, 220

CASSEROLED HAM SLICES

2 to 3 Servings

Appetizing dishes variously flavored are easily made from raw ham slices.
Preheat oven to 350°.
Place in a casserole:

A slice of smoked ham, about 1 inch thick

Pour over ham:

Barbecue Sauce I or II, 354, or
Hot Cumberland Sauce I, 356

Bake covered until tender, about 1 hour

HAM SLICE WITH FRUIT

2 to 3 Servings

Ham and fruit truly complement each other. You may arrange the fruit either between layers and on top of several ham slices or just on top of a single slice.
Preheat oven to 325°.
If the ham is not fatty, grease the bottom of a casserole lightly. Place in it:

A slice of ham, about 1 inch thick

sparingly seasoned with:

(Prepared mustard)

Cover ham with fruit seasoned to taste:

Cranberries, sliced apples or oranges

sprinkled with:

Brown sugar or honey

Or cover with drained:

Slices of canned pineapple, apricots, peaches, red plums, prunes, cherries or raisins

These may be sprinkled with:

Cinnamon, cloves or curry powder

Cover casserole. Baste several times with the pot juices or additional:

Fruit juice, sherry or cider

Bake about 45 minutes or until tender. Uncover for the last 10 minutes of cooking. Serve with:

Mashed Sweet Potatoes, 324

HAM BAKED WITH TOMATOES AND CHEESE

2 to 3 Servings

Preheat oven to 350°.
Place in a baking dish:

A slice of ham, about 1 inch thick

Pour over it:

1 cup seeded, chopped, drained canned tomatoes

Cover the dish. Bake the ham until tender, about 45 minutes. For the last 15 minutes of cooking, uncover the dish and sprinkle over ham:

¼ cup grated Parmesan cheese

HAM BUTT, SHANK OR PICNIC HAM

Use these comparatively small cuts of ham as a substitute for the corned beef in:

New England Boiled Dinner, 466

Cook ham until nearly tender or until the internal temperature reaches 160°. Add vegetables the last half hour of cooking.

SMOKED SHOULDER BUTT OR COTTAGE HAM

This cut may be boned. You may cut slices from this piece for broiling or sautéing, or roast or "boil" it.

HAM HOCKS WITH SAUERKRAUT

A tasty dish rather heavy in fat.
Rinse and put in a pot half filled with cold water:

4 smoked pork hocks

Add:

1 sliced onion
1 bay leaf

Cover the pot and ➤ simmer about 1½ hours. Turn the hocks several times during this period. Drain. Return the hocks to the pot with one cup of the drained, degreased liquid and:

1½ to 2 lb. drained sauerkraut
2 large cored sliced apples
1 teaspoon celery seed

Cover and simmer about 30 minutes more, stirring with a fork several times during this period. Serve with:

Mashed Potatoes, 318

ABOUT BACON

Thinly sliced bacon with a good proportion of lean striping, cured without excessive salt, is not easy to come by; the new packaging may help. But no matter how packaged, bacon remains flavorful for only about a week, even if refrigerated. It is a sobering fact that unless you use the rendered grease, you are eating only one-fifth of what you buy.

In separating raw bacon slices, sticking may be avoided if two or three slices are removed at a time and then subdivided into singles. ➤ Allow about 2 slices per person. To oven-broil bacon, begin with a cold grid; or, if you are sautéing it, place it in a cold skillet. We have found these methods prevent curling and work better than weighted covers or specialized gadgets. Keep heat low and check constantly: bacon burns in seconds, and old bacon twice as fast as fresh.

The usual bacon is the cured smoked sliced abdominal wall of pork; **Canadian bacon,** on the contrary, is the eye of the loin—which accounts for its leanness, its lack of layering and its high cost. It should be treated like ham. In England a side of bacon is called a **gammon,** and a slice or a portion is a **rasher.**

BAKED BACON

The preferred method for bacon in quantity.
Preheat oven to 350°.
Place on a cold grid over a drip pan:

Strips of bacon

If they are hard to separate, place in a slightly warm pan the entire block of strips you will need, and as they heat, slide them apart. Bake until crisp, 10 to 15 minutes. No turning is necessary. Drain on paper toweling.

SAUTÉED BACON

Place in a cold skillet:

Strips of bacon

Sauté slowly until done. You may spoon off the drippings while cooking. Turn frequently. Place between paper towels to drain.

CANADIAN BACON

I. Place in boiling water to cover:

1 lb. or more Canadian bacon

Simmer until tender, about 1 hour.

8 Servings

II. Preheat oven to 325°.
Bake uncovered 1 hour:

2-lb. piece of Canadian bacon

Baste every 15 minutes with:

½ cup pineapple or other acid fruit juice, dry sherry, cider or ginger ale

Combine:

½ cup brown sugar
½ teaspoon dry mustard
2 tablespoons fine bread crumbs
1 tablespoon cider vinegar

Spread the mixture over the bacon. Bake about 15 minutes more or until sugar has glazed.

III. Place in a heavy skillet:

⅛- to ¼-inch slices Canadian bacon

Cook them over low heat for 3 to 5 minutes. Turn frequently. When done, the lean part is a red brown and the fat a light golden brown. Serve with:

Hot Cumberland Sauce I, 356, or
Raisin Sauce, 356

ABOUT GROUND MEAT AND HAMBURGER

Merchants of the German port of Hamburg, through centuries of trade with Estonians, Latvians and Finns, had acquired the Baltic taste for scraped raw beef; but it was not until the St. Louis World's Fair in 1904 that broiled, bunned beef was introduced to the rest of the world by the Germans of South St. Louis as hamburger. Americans quickly latched on to the hamburger as their all-time favorite; for a bustling people it offered a combination of convenience, economy and tasty nourishment that seemed just what the doctor ordered. As a matter of fact, it was. Its more glamorous hotel-menu name, Salisbury steak, harks back to the end-of-the-century London physician, Dr. J. H. Salisbury, who invented a regimen based on broiled lean minced beef three times a day. Nowadays, alas, some American children are unconsciously such fans of Dr. Salisbury's diet that they will eat nothing else; one desperate mother we know has dubbed it "the daily grind."

According to federal ruling, ground beef sold as "hamburger" must contain no more than 30% fat, though most markets sell several grades labeled according to the degree of leanness, the leanest and most expensive grade containing perhaps 15% fat. This is an important consideration in buying hamburger, for the range reflects a drop in calories of more than a third. It may also affect your choice of cooking method. Federal statute further forbids the use of sodium sulfite, an additive which keeps the meat rosy. Recent surveys, however, indicate that the practice is far from dead. Should you find the color of ground meat too persistently red, expose a sample to bright sunlight. Untreated meat will darken.

➤ Do not store any uncooked ground meat longer than 24 hours. ➤ Be sure the mass is not more than 2 inches thick, so the cold can penetrate it quickly and thoroughly. ✲ To freeze beef for hamburger, see 826.

If you want very lean beef ground for hamburgers, use chuck, flank, shank, neck, heel, round or hanging tenderloin. ➤ Twice-ground meat will compact more than once-ground. You may be surpised at the apparently large amount of fat you didn't see go into the grinder. Grinders are so constructed that often as much as a fourth of every pound of meat that goes in stays in; the unexpected fat may come from the grinding of the previous order.

Good quality beef, freshly ground and used at once, needs only ➤ light shaping. You may want to incorporate into it some onion juice or finely chopped chives. ➤ If the beef has to be kept ground for 12 to 18 hours, it profits by having worked into it with a fork about 2 tablespoons beef stock for each pound of meat. This is done before shaping.

If beef is to be "stretched," see Additions to Hamburger, opposite. ➤ Incorporate these ingredients into the meat lightly with a fork and, with a light touch, shape the mixture into patties. Always decide before you put the meat into the pan how thick you want the finished hamburger.

➤ Never compact it in the pan by pressing down on it with a spatula.

ADDITIONS TO HAMBURGER AND MEAT LOAF

I. To Stretch

➤ The addition of root vegetables or cereals may require more seasonings.

To one pound of ground meat, you may mix in lightly with a fork any one of the following:

½ cup soft bread crumbs, 551

soaked briefly in:

⅓ to ½ cup milk or stock

or add:

½ cup finely grated raw carrots or potatoes or chopped raw mushrooms or bean sprouts

or add:

¼ cup ground nuts, dry cereals, wheat germ, ground sunflower seeds, presoaked cracked bulgur, or textured vegetable protein, up to 20%, 535

moistened with:

2 tablespoons beef stock, cream, tomato paste or lemon juice

Also, some of the piquant sauces found in the Sauce chapter, 336, will help stretch your main dish.

II. To Enrich

To one pound of ground meat, add one or more of the following:

1 egg
¼ cup dry milk solids
1 teaspoon dolomite or bone meal
1 tablespoon brewer's yeast

The above may need additional liquid.

III. To Flavor

About ½ hour before cooking, mix into one pound of ground meat one of the following combinations:

2 teaspoons chili sauce
1 teaspoon ground anchovy or anchovy paste
3 tablespoons sautéed mushrooms
1 tablespoon finely diced stuffed olives or 1 teaspoon capers

or:

¼ teaspoon thyme
1 garlic clove, pressed
1 teaspoon Worcestershire sauce

or:

2 tablespoons each chopped fresh parsley and chives, or 1 tablespoon grated chopped onions and 1 tablespoon coffee cream

or:

¼ cup crumbled Roquefort cheese or cultured sour cream
2 tablespoons chopped chives or green onion tops
A sprinkling of hot pepper sauce
¼ teaspoon dry mustard

SAUTÉED HAMBURGERS

4 Servings

➤ Please read About Hamburger, above.

Shape lightly into patties, allowing 2 for each serving:

1 lb. ground beef

Preheat an ungreased heavy skillet slowly, to the point where the meat when added will sizzle, not hiss sharply. If you use very lean beef, you will need to add to the pan:

1 tablespoon butter, beef fat or oil

Sauté over medium heat ➤ uncovered, for 3 or 4 minutes. During this time sufficient fat should come from the patty itself to permit the hamburger to be turned without sticking. Turn and cook on the other side another 3 minutes or even longer, depending on the thickness of the patty and the whims of your diners. Remove meat from the pan and season with:

Salt
Freshly ground pepper

Defat the pan drippings. Deglaze them with:

Stock

Reduce the juices slightly and pour them over the patties before serving. Or mix with the pan juices a little:

Barbecue or chili sauce, tomato catsup, red wine, horseradish, a few chopped olives or sautéed onions or mushrooms

Or spread over them:

Herb butters, 70–71, or mustard

You may garnish with:

Very thin raw or sautéed slices of sweet onion
A slice of tomato or cucumber

BROILED HAMBURGERS

4 Servings

Preheat broiler.

➤ Please read About Hamburger, above.

Shape lightly into ¾-inch-thick patties:

1 lb. ground beef

Place them on a broiler pan, 4 inches from source of heat, or place them so they cover the untoasted side of:

A piece of bread toasted on one side only

If on bread, broil about 12 minutes. If not, broil 6 minutes on one side, turn and broil about 4 minutes on the other. If the meat is very lean, you may brush it during broiling with:

Butter

⊟ GRILLED HAMBURGERS

We have watched with agony as good juices fed the flames and the guests were dealt dry chips. If you must grill ground meat, please see 157. To make the meat adhere well during handling and grilling, you may add to each pound:

(1 beaten egg)

Shape lightly into 1-inch-thick patties:

Hamburger

Grill each side 5 to 6 minutes for a medium-rare to medium-cooked hamburger.

CHEESEBURGERS

Although it is traditional to top hamburger with a piece of cheese, and broil until the cheese melts, we find the following method tastier.
Mix together with a fork:

1 lb. ground beef
½ cup shredded cheddar or Gruyère cheese
2 teaspoons Worcestershire sauce
½ teaspoon salt
(1 clove garlic, pressed)

Sauté or broil as directed in above recipes.

⊟ FILLED BEEF OR LAMBURGERS

6 Servings

➤ Please read About Hamburger, 486.
Preheat broiler or grill.
Divide into 12 portions and shape into flat patties:

1½ lb. ground beef or lamb

Sauté lightly:

(6 slices bacon)

Use one of the following fillings which you may vary with the addition of chopped avocados, celery, pickles, radishes, chili sauce, bread dressing or chopped leftover vegetables:

I.

6 tablespoons chopped nutmeats
3 tablespoons chopped parsley
2 tablespoons grated onion

II.

A mashed anchovy and a few capers for each patty

III.

Roquefort or cheddar cheese or braunschweiger
Prepared mustard

Spread the filling on 6 of the patties. Top them with those remaining. Bind the edges with the partially sautéed bacon strips and fasten with a wooden pick. Broil 10 to 15 minutes, turning once.

BEEF OR BIFF À LA LINDSTRÖM

4 to 5 Servings

Almost a meal in one dish.
Sauté until limp and transparent:

2 tablespoons finely chopped onions

in:

2 teaspoons butter

In a large bowl mix with a fork the onions and:

1 lb. lean ground beef: ground twice
2 egg yolks
1 to 2 tablespoons finely chopped capers
1 teaspoon salt
¼ teaspoon pepper
½ cup cream

Stir in:

¼ cup finely diced pickled beets
(1 cup diced boiled potatoes)

Form the mixture into round patties about 1 inch thick. Heat in a large skillet:

3 to 4 tablespoons butter and oil combined

Brown the meat quickly, turning only once. The patties should be pink inside and deep brown on the outside. In Sweden these hamburgers would be served garnished with:

(A fried egg)

but we prefer the pan juices instead.

CHICKEN, VEAL OR LAMB PATTIES

The French make many attractive dishes by grinding uncooked meat or fish, shaping it with other ingredients into patties, and poaching, broiling or sautéing them.

I. **About 15 Servings**

Preheat broiler.
Cut the meat from:

A 4½-lb. chicken, or use 3½ lb. veal or lamb

Pick over the carcass for all edible bits of meat. Put the meat through a grinder, using a coarse blade. Save the juices, if any. Combine the ground meat, the juices and:

¾ cup whipping cream
1½ cups soft bread crumbs
1 teaspoon salt
1 teaspoon dried basil or 1 tablespoon chopped parsley
A grating of lemon rind
¼ teaspoon paprika
A grating of nutmeg

Shape the mixture into 15 large patties. Roll them in a:

Bound Breading, 552

and let rest for 15 minutes. Place them in a ➤ shallow greased pan. Broil under moderate heat about 10 minutes to a side or until lightly browned. The patties may be left unbreaded and poached in a pan in the oven in a small amount of milk or stock, enough to cover the bottom of the skillet, until done. This means very low heat. Serve with:

Béarnaise Sauce, 359, or
Soubise Sauce, 344

II. **8 Servings**

Mix together:

2 lb. ground chicken, veal or lamb
½ cup soft bread crumbs
1 egg
½ cup chopped onions
1½ teaspoons grated lemon rind
1 teaspoon salt
1 teaspoon each ground coriander, nutmeg and curry powder
½ teaspoon pepper

Shape and broil as described in I, above. Serve with:

Curried Rice, 208, and mint

BAKED LIVER PATTIES

6 Servings

Preheat oven to 350°
Combine:
1 lb. ground beef liver
½ cup dry bread crumbs
¼ cup evaporated milk or cream
½ teaspoon salt
⅛ teaspoon pepper
2 teaspoons grated onion
2 tablespoons chopped parsley
Shape these ingredients into 6 flat patties. Wrap around them:
6 slices bacon
Secure the bacon with wooden picks. Place the patties in a lightly greased pan. Bake until well browned, about 6 minutes. Turn to ensure even baking.

GERMAN MEATBALLS OR KÖNIGSBERGER KLOPS

About Ten 2-Inch Balls

A good buffet dish if shaped into 1-inch balls.
Soak in water, milk or stock to cover:
1 slice of bread, 1 inch thick
Put through a meat grinder twice:
1½ lb. meat: ½ lb. beef, ½ lb. veal, ½ lb. pork or liver
Beat well and add to the meat:
2 eggs
Melt:
1 tablespoon butter
Sauté until golden:
¼ cup finely chopped onions
Add to the meat. Wring the liquid from the bread. Add bread to the meat and:
3 tablespoons chopped parsley
1¼ teaspoons salt
¼ teaspoon paprika
½ teaspoon grated lemon rind
1 teaspoon lemon juice
1 teaspoon Worcestershire sauce or a grating of nutmeg
A few minced anchovies or one-fourth herring may be added at this time to the mixture or later to the gravy. Combine these ingredients well. Do this lightly with the hands rather than with a fork or spoon. Shape lightly into 2-inch balls. Drop into:
5 cups boiling Vegetable Stock, 524
Simmer covered about 15 minutes. Remove from the stock. Measure the stock. Make gravy of it, 341, by using for every cup of stock:
2 tablespoons butter
2 tablespoons flour
Season to taste
Cook and stir until smooth. Add:
2 tablespoon capers, or 2 tablespoons chopped pickles, lemon juice or cultured sour cream
2 tablespoons chopped parsley
Reheat the meatballs in the gravy. Serve with a platter of:
Boiled Noodles, 213, or Spätzle, 205
Cover generously with:
Buttered Crumbs, 551

ITALIAN MEATBALLS

Preheat oven to 350°.
Follow the recipe for:
German Meatballs, left
but omit the Worcestershire sauce. Add to the meat mixture:
½ chopped clove garlic
3 tablespoons grated Parmesan cheese
¼ teaspoon oregano
Mix and form into balls. Brown lightly in:
2 tablespoons butter
Place in a casserole. Half cover with:
Unthickened Tomato Sauce, 351, or Marinara Sauce, 353
Bake covered about 30 minutes. Serve with:
Pasta, 212

SWEDISH MEATBALLS

About Eighteen 1½-Inch Balls

There are many recipes for this dish, all similar to, but in our opinion none superior to:
German Meatballs, left
Omit the Worcestershire sauce and add:
¼ teaspoon nutmeg
⅛ teaspoon allspice
Shape the meat into 1½-inch balls. Brown in:
2 tablespoons butter or drippings
Simmer closely covered until done, about 15 minutes, in:
2 cups consommé or other stock
Make:
Pan Gravy, 341
Season it with:
Sherry or 1 to 2 teaspoons finely minced fresh dill
Reheat the meat in the gravy. This is attractive served in a chafing dish, garnished with:
Small Potato Dumplings, 204

CHINESE MEATBALLS

6 Servings

➤ Please read About Deep-Fat Frying, 147.
Shape into 18 balls:
1½ lb. ground beef
Season with:
1½ teaspoons salt
2 teaspoons soy sauce
¼ teaspoon dry mustard
1 tablespoon finely chopped parsley
Coat the balls with:
Fritter Batter for Meat, 243
Let them dry on a rack 30 minutes. Deep-fry in fat heated to 365° until golden brown. Serve at once covered with:
Oriental Sweet-Sour Sauce II, 355

HAWAIIAN MEATBALLS

6 Servings

Combine in a large bowl:

1 lb. lean ground beef
½ cup soft bread crumbs moistened with milk
1 beaten egg
1 clove garlic, pressed
½ teaspoon dry mustard
¼ teaspoon ginger
½ teaspoon salt
1 tablespoon soy sauce

Form meat into 1-inch balls and sauté until brown in:

2 tablespoons vegetable or peanut oil

Pour over all:

Oriental Sweet-Sour Sauce II, 355

garnished with:

(Bean sprouts, 286)

Serve over:

Boiled Rice, 206

PORK BALLS IN TOMATO SAUCE

4 Servings

Soak in water to cover:

A slice of bread, 1½ inches thick

Wring the water from it. Add to the bread:

1 lb. ground pork
⅓ cup chopped onions
1 beaten egg
¾ teaspoon salt
¼ teaspoon paprika

Combine these ingredients lightly until well blended. Shape into 2-inch balls. Bring to a boil in a large pan:

1 can condensed tomato soup: 10½ oz.
An equal amount of water

Drop the balls into it. ➤ Reduce the heat at once. Cover the pan and simmer about 45 minutes.

SAUERKRAUT BALLS

4 Dozen 1¼-Inch Balls

➤ Please read About Deep-Fat Frying, 147.

Grind with a medium blade:

½ lb. each ham, corned beef and lean pork

Sauté the meat in:

3 tablespoons butter or fat

with:

⅓ cup finely chopped onions

To the above, add:

2 cups flour
½ to 1 teaspoon dry mustard
1 teaspoon salt
2 cups milk

Simmer the mixture until thickened, ➤ stirring constantly. Combine it with:

2 lb. cooked drained sauerkraut

Then regrind the entire mixture. Form into 1¼-inch balls. Roll them in:

Bound Breading, 552

Let stand about 15 minutes before deep-frying in fat heated to 365° until golden brown. Drain on paper toweling and serve at once.

PORCUPINES

6 Servings

Far too formidable a name for a dish without either pork or spines.

Combine:

1 lb. ground beef
½ cup bread crumbs
1 egg
¾ teaspoon salt
¼ teaspoon paprika
(2 tablespoons chopped green peppers)

Roll these ingredients ➤ lightly into balls. Press into flat cakes. Roll in:

¼ cup uncooked rice

Heat in a heavy pot:

Thickened Tomato Sauce, 352

Add:

(1 teaspoon chili powder)

Add the meat cakes. Cover and simmer about 45 minutes.

Season to taste

⊟ SLOPPY JOES

8 Sandwiches

Heat in a skillet:

2 tablespoons butter

Add and sauté:

½ cup minced onions
½ cup chopped celery
½ cup chopped green pepper, seeds and membrane removed

When these are limp, add:

1½ lb. ground beef

Cook and stir until meat is lightly browned. Add:

½ cup chopped mushrooms
4 tablespoons chili sauce
½ cup water
Season to taste

Simmer uncovered over low heat about 15 minutes until thickened enough to spoon onto:

8 slightly toasted sandwich buns

CHILI CON CARNE

(8 oz) 2 can tomato sauce

8 to 12 Servings

Melt:

2 — **2 to 3 tablespoons bacon drippings or butter**

Sauté in the fat:

1 med onion — **½ cup chopped onion and/or ½**
1 clove garlic — **clove garlic, chopped**

Add:

1 to 2 lb. ground beef or lamb

Stir and sauté the meat until well done. Add:

(14.5 oz) 1 can **1¼ cups canned tomatoes**
3 to 4 cups canned kidney beans (2) 15½ oz cans
1 tsp **¾ teaspoon or more salt**
½ bay leaf (1 bay leaf)
1 teaspoon sugar
(¼ cup dry red wine)
1 TBS — **2 teaspoons to 2 tablespoons chili powder**

depending on your taste and the strength of the chili powder. Cover and simmer about 1 hour or longer. The longer it cooks, the thicker it becomes and the better it tastes. Or make it a day ahead and reheat. Serve with:

Tortillas or crackers

or over:

Cooked spaghetti

garnished with:

(Chopped onions)
(Shredded cheese)

SPANISH CASSEROLE WITH RICE

6 Servings

A one-dish meal.
Steam:

2/3 cup rice, 206

Prepare:

1 cup chopped celery
1/4 cup chopped green pepper, seeds and membrane removed

Melt in a saucepan:

2 tablespoons butter or other fat

Sauté in the butter until golden:

1 chopped medium-sized onion

Add and sear:

1 lb. ground round steak or lean beef

Season with:

3/4 teaspoon salt
1/4 teaspoon paprika

Preheat oven to 350°.
Place in a greased baking dish one-third of the rice and half of the meat. Sprinkle over it half of the celery and pepper. Repeat this process. Place the last of the rice on top. Pour over all:

1 can condensed tomato soup: 10 1/2 oz.
Season to taste

Cover the dish and bake about 1/2 hour.

LAMB AND EGGPLANT CASSEROLE

4 Servings

Preheat oven to 350°.
Pare and chop until fine:

1 medium-sized eggplant

Combine with:

2 cups ground lamb: 1 lb.
1/2 cup chopped onions
3 tablespoons chopped parsley
1 teaspoon salt
1/4 teaspoon paprika
(1/2 teaspoon curry powder or 1/4 teaspoon oregano)
1 cup chopped drained tomatoes

Pour the mixture into a buttered casserole. Bake covered about 45 minutes. Remove the cover and let the top brown.

MOUSSAKA OR EGGPLANT CASSEROLE

8 to 10 Servings

For a large party, the quantity may be doubled or tripled to fill two or three casseroles.
Cut into lengthwise slices 1/4 to 1/2 inch thick:

3 peeled medium-sized eggplants

Salt the slices generously and let drain in a colander at least 45 minutes. Meanwhile, sauté until golden:

1 cup finely chopped onions

in:

1/4 cup olive oil or butter

Add and brown slowly:

2 lb. lean ground lamb

Add:

1 cup well-drained canned or fresh tomatoes or 3 tablespoons tomato paste
1/3 cup chopped parsley
1 cup white wine or stock
1/4 teaspoon nutmeg
A grating of black pepper

Simmer the above gently about 45 minutes. In the meantime, quickly sauté the drained eggplant slices until lightly browned on all sides in:

1/2 cup olive oil or butter

using only a little oil at a time, since eggplant soaks it up. Drain on paper toweling. Now, ➤ beat until stiff, but not dry:

3 egg whites

Fold the beaten whites into the cooked and cooled meat mixture with:

1/2 cup fine bread crumbs

Prepare a double portion of:

White Sauce II, 341

When hot, pour a small amount of the sauce into:

3 beaten egg yolks
A grating of nutmeg

Pour the yolk mixture into the sauce.
Preheat oven to 350°.
Assemble the ingredients in a 9 x 13-inch or larger baking dish, placing first a layer of eggplant, then the meat mixture, and ending with an eggplant layer. Cover the whole with the sauce. Sprinkle the top generously with:

Grated Parmesan cheese

Bake the casserole until thoroughly heated through, but do not allow the mixture to reach the boiling point.

The moussaka can be cut into squares if you will allow it to stand about 20 minutes before serving. This is the way moussaka is served all through Greece. The classic version omits the sauce, and the eggplant skins are used to line the dish and to protect the ingredients while cooking. The skins must be well oiled if they are to be used in this way.

STUFFED CABBAGE OR GEFÜLLTER KRAUTKOPF

6 Servings

➤ Please read About Leaf Wrappings, 152, and how to prepare and cook the leaves from:

A head of cabbage

Use one of the following meat fillings:

I. Soak in water for 2 minutes:

1 slice of bread, 1 inch thick

Press the water from it. Combine the bread with:

½ lb. ground pork
½ lb. ground beef
½ lb. ground veal
3 beaten eggs
¾ teaspoon salt
¼ teaspoon paprika

II. Or use a filling of:
1 lb. fresh pork sausage meat
3 slices of bread, ½ inch thick
1 beaten egg

III. Or cook until tender:
½ cup dried peas, 286
Drain the peas and combine with:
1 lb. ground lamb or beef
½ cup chopped onions
¼ cup chopped parsley
1 teaspoon grated lemon rind
½ teaspoon cinnamon
1 teaspoon salt
½ teaspoon pepper
You may make and simmer individual packets as described on 153, or line a bowl with a large napkin or cloth and fill it with alternate layers of the leaves and the meat dressing. Cover the top with 1 or 2 large leaves, gather up the cloth and tie it with a string. Place the bag in boiling water—the water in which the cabbage was boiled and as much fresh boiling water as needed to cover well. ➤ Simmer the cabbage gently for 2 hours if you are old-fashioned, but 45 minutes should be ample time. Drain it in a colander, untie the bag and place the cabbage in a hot serving dish. Serve with the following onion sauce. Brown in the top of a double boiler:
¼ cup butter
Add and stir until brown:
2 tablespoons flour
Have ready:
2 cups Stock, 520, or cabbage water
Stir ½ cup of this into the butter mixture. Add:
½ cup or more chopped onions
If required:
Season to taste
Cook the onions covered ➤ over—not in—boiling water, until very tender. Add the remainder of the stock gradually. The gravy is best when it is thick with onions.

BAKED STUFFED CABBAGE LEAVES

4 Servings

Preheat oven to 375°.
➤ Please read about Leaf Wrappings, 152, and how to wash and parblanch:
8 large cabbage leaves
Drain and dry them on a towel. Combine:
1 lb. ground beef or a mixture of beef, veal, pork and liver
3 tablespoons finely chopped onions
2 tablespoons finely chopped parsley
¾ teaspoon salt
½ teaspoon thyme
½ clove garlic, pressed
A few grains cayenne
If you want a sweet-sour effect, add:
2 tablespoons vinegar
3 tablespoons brown sugar
1 teaspoon capers
Divide the meat mixture into 8 parts. Put one part on each cabbage leaf. Roll the leaves as directed on 152. Tie or secure them with wooden picks. Place them seam side down and close together in a buttered baking dish. Dot each roll with:
½ teaspoon butter
Pour into the dish:
½ cup boiling stock
or you may use:
½ cup water, tomato juice or cultured sour cream and paprika
Bake the rolls covered about 50 minutes.

STUFFED GRAPE LEAVES OR DOLMAS

30 Dolmas

➤ Please read about Leaf Wrappings, 152, and prepare for stuffing:
30 fresh or canned grape leaves
Fill each one with a generous tablespoon of the following mixture:
2 cups finely chopped onions
½ cup uncooked rice
⅓ cup olive oil
2 tablespoons finely chopped parsley
2 tablespoons finely chopped dill
¼ cup pine nuts
¼ cup currants
(1 cup finely minced lamb)
Do not roll the leaves too tightly, as the rice will swell. Cook as for Cabbage Leaves I, 152, weighted with a plate, over low heat about 1½ hours. Serve chilled.

ABOUT MEAT LOAF

Although proportions of beef, veal and pork are specified in the following recipes, they may be varied, provided the total amount of meat remains the same. Be sure to ➤ cook thoroughly if pork is used. Handle ingredients for meat loaf ➤ lightly, mixing with a two-tined fork. Do not overcook; it should be firm but not dry. To stretch, see Additions to Hamburger, 487.

Meat loaf may be mounded on a flat greased pan or put into a greased ring mold or loaf pan. It may also be baked in 2 layers with a stuffing between. Individual meat loaves take only about 20 to 30 minutes and—for attractive service—may be baked in greased muffin tins and glazed. You may pour about ½ cup of catsup in the bottom of the pan before filling it with the meat; or you may pour about 2 tablespoons of chili sauce over the meat loaf when it is half baked. This gives it a good flavor and a light crust. You may cover the loaf with a piece of foil, but remove it the last quarter hour of baking.

If baked in a ring mold, it may be served hot, filled with green peas or some other vegetable and surrounded by browned potatoes. Or serve it cold, filled with potato or some other vegetable salad. Don't neglect to use for sandwiches and for picnics.

MEAT LOAF

4 Servings

I. Preheat oven to 350°.
Combine and shape into a loaf:
1 lb. ground beef: 1/4 this amount may be pork
(1 egg yolk)
2 tablespoons chopped parsley
1 tablespoon soft butter
1 tablespoon bread crumbs
1 teaspoon lemon juice
1 teaspoon salt
1/4 teaspoon pepper
1/2 teaspoon onion juice
Place the loaf in a lightly greased pan. Baste at intervals with the following sauce:
1/2 cup stock or 1/2 cup boiling water plus
1/4 package dried soup mix
Bake about 45 minutes.
Serve the loaf with:
Sweet Potato Puffs, 325

II. **4 Servings**
Preheat oven to 350°.
Place in a bowl:
1 lb. ground round steak
1 to 2 tablespoons horseradish
2 tablespoons catsup or chili sauce
1 teaspoon salt
1/4 teaspoon pepper
1/2 cup cream
Grind in a food chopper, then add:
6 slices bacon
2 medium-sized onions
1 cup broken crackers
Mix with a fork. Mold into a loaf. Roll in:
1/4 cup cracker crumbs
Place the loaf in a shallow baking pan. Pour into the pan:
1/2 cup stock
Bake the loaf about 50 minutes. Baste occasionally, adding more liquid if necessary. Make:
Pan Gravy, 341

MEAT LOAF COCKAIGNE

6 Servings

A favorite luncheon dish sliced and served cold.
Preheat oven to 350°.
Mix lightly:
1 1/2 lb. lean ground beef—be sure beef has been ground only once
1 can condensed cream of chicken or mushroom soup: 10 1/2 oz.
3/4 cup dry bread crumbs
1/4 cup mixed fresh tarragon, parsley, basil or chives
1 teaspoon salt
1 clove garlic, pressed
10 or more chopped stuffed olives or
1/4 cup chopped water chestnuts
(1/2 cup chopped nuts)
Bake in a 4 x 8 x 4-inch pan, about 45 minutes.
You may serve hot with:
(Thickened Tomato Sauce, 352)

VEAL LOAF

8 to 10 Servings

Preheat oven to 350°.
Grind:
2 lb. veal
1 lb. smoked ham or sausage
Add and ➤ mix very lightly:
1 tablespoon minced onion
1/4 cup chopped green pepper, seeds and membrane removed
2 beaten eggs
1/2 teaspoon salt
1/8 teaspoon paprika
3/4 cup dry bread crumbs
1 cup condensed mushroom soup
Place half of this mixture in a 4 x 8 x 4-inch loaf pan. You may then press whole mushrooms or hard-cooked eggs, stuffed olives or pistachio nuts into the meat in a pattern. Cover with the remaining meat. Bake about 45 minutes. Serve hot or cold.

LIVER LOAF

6 to 8 Servings

This makes a most appetizing everyday liver spread.
Preheat oven to 350°.
Boil for 5 minutes:
1 cup water
1 medium-sized chopped onion
3 chopped ribs celery with leaves
Prepare for cooking, 499, slice, add and simmer for 2 minutes:
1 lb. liver: beef, lamb or pork
Drain, reserving liquid. Put liver and vegetables through a meat chopper with:
2 slices bacon or a 1 1/2-inch cube salt pork
Add to mixture and blend well:
1 or 2 beaten eggs
3/4 teaspoon salt
1/8 teaspoon pepper
1 cup cracker or dry bread crumbs
1/2 teaspoon dried marjoram or thyme
1 cup liquid: reserved liver stock, milk, tomato juice, etc.
Pour into a greased loaf pan:
(1/2 cup catsup)
Place the meat in the pan. Bake about 40 minutes.

RAW SMOKED HAM LOAF

4 to 6 Servings

You may dress this up or down.
Preheat oven to 350°.

Try using:

(½ cup crushed pineapple)
(½ teaspoon dry mustard)

in the bottom of the pan. Grind:

1 lb. raw smoked ham
½ lb. lean pork
¼ cup chopped onion

Add and mix lightly with a fork:

2 well-beaten eggs
½ to 1 cup cracker or dry bread crumbs
An equal amount of milk
⅛ teaspoon pepper
3 tablespoons mixed fresh herbs

Shape the above ingredients and place in a greased loaf pan. Bake about 2 hours, basting frequently with:

Honey Glaze, 368, or Spirit Glaze for Ham, 368

ABOUT PÂTÉS AND TERRINES

Pâtés are the rich relatives of the meat loaf clan, and though they sometimes arrive at table dressed to the nines in their formal jacket of glazed pastry or glistening aspic, they are basically no harder to make than a meat loaf. What distinguishes them is the luxury quality of their ingredients, which may include some or all of the following: ground meat—veal, pork, liver; poultry or pork, often marinated in wine or brandy; diced fresh pork fat; sliced or cubed tongue, chicken, ham or game; cream, eggs, spices; perhaps pistachios, or, for the *ne plus ultra* touch, truffles. Endless combinations are possible to tempt you to eventually develop a pâté maison of your own. The texture may be smooth if all the meat is fine-ground, or patterned if the more colorful ingredients are diced or sliced to show decoratively when the loaf is cut as in Galantine, 431. The less formal terrine is baked in an enamel or earthenware dish, shown on 495, and is never enclosed in a crust.

Although many European countries have produced characteristic pâtés, the unrivaled queen of the traditional mixtures is France's now astronomically costly **pâté de foie gras,** made of goose liver marinated in cognac and flavored with truffles. The chief component of the genuine article is the liver of geese force-fed by hand until the liver has grown to one-fourth of the bird's total weight. American law forbids force-feeding, and chicken livers are a more than acceptable substitute. Recipes below give a few versions of chicken liver pâté. To serve a pâté coated with aspic, follow directions for the gelatin covering in Souffléed Liver Pâté Cockaigne, 496.

ABOUT PÂTÉ EN CROÛTE

A pâté presented in a pastry covering is called pâté en croûte—in a crust. Decorated and golden brown, the case does full justice to the pâté it encloses; sliced, it is even lovelier, revealing the smooth or patterned texture of the meat inside, with a clear gelatin top under the crust, see illustration opposite. The novice sometimes does not realize that the crust—in the traditional version—is not meant to be eaten but serves to protect the flavor and juices of the meat mixture. The late Chef Pierre Adrian, our good friend, worried so about his American diners' insistence on consuming the crust that he usually used Pâte Brisée, 641, a more appetizing if harder to handle pastry. He also warned us that the conventional hinged pâté molds, illustrated 442, nearly always leak, and if the crust breaks in any way, the delicious juices will run into the oven. If, instead, a 9 x 4½ x 4½-inch loaf pan is used, the juices as well as the characteristic shape are retained.

Pâte versus pâté: let's clarify once and for all the spelling that for most of us remains a "bafflement." With the "e" accented, we have seen that the word means a combination of meats and spices forming a kind of loaf; pâte with an unaccented "e" simply means dough—in this instance, the pastry used for the crust. The recipe that follows is for the traditional tough dough covering ➤ that is not to be eaten.

CRUST OR PÂTE FOR PÂTÉ

Work together with your fingers until you have achieved the consistency of coarse cornmeal:

6 cups sifted all-purpose flour
2 teaspoons salt
1½ cups lard or shortening

Make a well, 643, of these ingredients and break into the center, one at a time:

2 eggs

working them into the flour mixture from the inside and adding gradually:

About 3 cups water

You may need a little more water to make a dough that can be worked into a smooth mass and rolled into a ball. The dough is easier to handle if allowed to rest covered at about 70° for several hours. Then form about three-fourths of the dough into a thick oval approximately the size of the base of the mold or pan, and line the bottom. With the sides of the hands, in chopping motions, gradually work the dough from the base so that it thins out and creeps up the sides. Then, with the fingers patting it thin, form the rest of the crust. Let the excess hang over the sides, see opposite. Do not stretch or tear the dough. Next, line the mold with thin strips of blanched fat bacon in parallel U shapes, as sketched. Let the strips rest temporarily over the sides. Place the meat mixture in the mold; if you are aiming at a patterned texture, the diced or sliced ingredients are placed in alternate layers with the ground meat, to show a pattern in cross section when cut, as shown opposite. When the mold pan has been filled with the meat and the bacon strips folded over the meat filling, crimp the dough at the edges of the mold and cut off the excess. From the remaining fourth of dough, roll a 3⁄16-inch-thick piece for the lid. Apply the lid by pinching the dough into the already crimped edges of the pastry case, brushing the edges with Egg Wash, 731, as glue. Leave the dough lax enough so that it will not crack or distort in baking; trim edges. Cut from the scraps small geometric or floral shapes to ornament the top. Work your pattern around 2 or 3 circles which can hold pastry vents, as shown in the drawing. These will

later form openings for inserting the funnels when the aspic is carefully poured between the pâté and the upper crust. Apply the ornaments with egg wash and brush the top with it before baking. Vent the top crust with a few fancy cuts, as you would for a pie.

Preheat the oven to 400°.

To avoid too rapid browning of the crust, you may have ready a piece of foil to put loosely over the top. This will protect it in the early stages of baking. As soon as you put the pâté in the oven ➤ lower the heat to 325°. Pâtés are usually cooked 1½ to 2 hours. Test for doneness as for cake, 665.

Allow the pâté, still in the pan, to cool on a rack. Fill the space which will have formed at the top between filling and crust by pouring through the vents enough flavorful aspic that—when it solidifies—it will support the crust. Use a firm gelatin, allowing 1 tablespoon for each cup of meat stock. Hold a funnel in one of the vents and pour the mixture—being careful not to moisten the crust on the outside. Allow the pâté to remain in the pan refrigerated until the aspic is set. To unmold the pâté, proceed as for unmolding a gelatin, 560. Use a rack, however, on which to reverse it—to facilitate turning the pâté right side up onto a serving platter.

Pâtés should, of course, be stored refrigerated, and most pâtés profit by ➤ resting refrigerated for at least 48 hours before serving—so that the flavors blend and the contents are firm enough for even slicing. The whole pâté may be garnished with a border of chopped aspic jelly, parsley and lemon wedges. When serving, cut with a warm knife. An individual serving should be at least ⅜ to ½ inch thick and garnished with parsley and a lemon wedge, as shown left. For smaller servings, cut each slice in half on the diagonal.

CHICKEN LIVER PÂTÉ OR PÂTÉ DE FOIE DE VOLAILLE

Either of the following recipes may or may not be baked en croûte; please read About Pâtés and About Pâté en Croûte, opposite.

I. **About Twenty ½-Inch Slices**

Divide into 3 parts:

1½ lb. chicken livers

In a blender, mix one part with:

2 eggs

Blend the second part ➤ briefly with:

¼ cup whipping cream

Blend the third part with:

4 slices chopped bacon, blanched
1 egg
3 tablespoons brandy
2 tablespoons port wine
¼ cup flour

Mix these three blends together ➤ very lightly with:

1 teaspoon ginger
2 teaspoons salt
½ teaspoon freshly ground black pepper
1 teaspoon allspice or nutmeg
(¼ cup pistachio nuts or
1 to 2 minced truffles)

If you want to serve as pâté en croûte, follow directions opposite. If not, place mixture in a greased loaf pan and top with:

Thin-sliced blanched salt pork

Cover ➤ tightly with heavy foil and place baking pan up to about half its depth in a larger pan of boiling water. Bake at 325° about 1½ to 2 hours, or to an internal temperature of 180°. Serve cold, after removing some of the fat from the top surface if necessary. To store leftover pâté, be sure it is well covered with a layer of fat or clarified butter.

II. **About Forty ½-Inch Slices**

Should the veal be reddish, marinate it refrigerated overnight covered with milk.

Pound:

1 lb. white veal

Add and ➤ grind 3 times with the veal:

1½ lb. chicken livers
¼ lb. blanched salt pork
2 anchovy fillets

Mix in lightly until very smooth:

4 beaten eggs
½ cup whipping cream
3 tablespoons grated onions
2 tablespoons chopped parsley or chervil
⅛ teaspoon freshly ground black pepper
¼ cup brandy
1 tablespoon Madeira
(2 tablespoons chopped truffles)

If not served en croûte, top the pâté with

blanched salt pork and bake and serve as described in I, 495.

SOUFFLÉED LIVER PÂTÉ COCKAIGNE

Preheat oven to 350°.
Have ready two identical 9-inch bread pans. Prepare one of them as for a soufflé dish, 228. Grind:

1 lb. raw chicken livers

Beat in:

2 eggs
2 egg yolks
2 teaspoons onion juice
2 tablespoons chopped parsley
2 cups whipping cream

➤ You may use a ⅄ blender and ➤ very briefly blend liver and the above ingredients. Fold in:

2 stiffly beaten egg whites

Place the mixture in the prepared baking pan in a larger pan of boiling water and bake about 1 hour or until set. Refrigerate overnight.

To coat the soufflé with aspic, proceed as follows. Soak 3 minutes:

1 tablespoon gelatin

in:

¼ cup cold water

Bring to a boil:

2 cups well-seasoned Double Consommé, 169

and combine with the soaked gelatin, stirring until dissolved. Rinse the second 9-inch pan with cold water and pour in ½ inch of the gelatin mixture. Refrigerate until almost set. Reverse the chilled loaf onto the gelatin layer. Pour the remaining gelatin on the exposed surface, allowing it to coat the sides of the loaf as well. When the gelatin coating is well set, reverse the mold onto a platter and serve the gelatin-covered loaf garnished with:

Thinly sliced limes or stuffed olives and parsley

* TERRINE OF VEAL WITH CHICKEN, HAM OR PORK

The essential ingredient here is the fresh veal, which is responsible for jelling the whole as it cools. Please read About Terrines, 494.
Preheat oven to 300°.
Line the bottom and sides of an earthenware dish or a loaf pan with:

Strips of blanched bacon

overlapping the strips slightly and draping them as shown on 495—without the crust.
Sprinkle with:

1 tablespoon chopped parsley
1 tablespoon chopped onion

Pound, 444, very thin:

2 lb. veal scallops, cut ¼ inch thick

Have ready:

2 lb. finely sliced chicken, ham or pork or a combination of these

Overlay the bacon lining with a layer of the thin-pounded veal seasoned with:

Pepper
Thyme
Powdered bay leaf

Place a layer of chicken, ham or pork slices over the veal. Then continue to build up layers to the top of the casserole, alternating a layer of seasoned veal, parsley and onions with a layer of chicken, ham or pork. Pour:

1 cup dry white wine
1 to 2 teaspoons brandy

over the meat layers until all the crevices are filled with liquid. Fold the bacon strips over the top. Cover and set the pan in a larger pan of boiling water. Bake about 2 hours or until done. As soon as you remove the meat from the oven, cover with heavy aluminum foil and weight as in Cheese Making, 536. When the meat has cooled, a fatty jelly will have formed, which keeps the meat in prime condition. To serve, slice very thin. Store leftovers refrigerated and covered with:

Clarified butter

ABOUT SAUSAGE

One of our early European memories is that of the rapt stance of the citizenry as they gazed at window displays of German sausage. It made us aware for the first time of the wealth of choice. Sausage is one of the oldest of processed foods; 3000 years ago, grinding meat into sausage was an old Mediterranean custom. Around the world it has proliferated over the centuries into some 200 varieties from Alesandri to Kielbasa to Weiswurst. And any farm-bred American remembers early-winter butchering seasons when every family round about made its very own combination of the scrappier meat parts flavored with herbs.

Types of sausage fall into three main classes. First there is freshly ground sausage meat or so-called **country sausage,** which is very perishable and must be cooked and used at once; among these are Blood Sausage, or Boudin Noir, and Boudin Blanc, see 498. Added sometimes to this fragile category are spiced meats and innards such as liver loaf or braunschweiger, cooked ham and veal loaves—all of which need constant refrigeration. Next are the **lightly cured sausages,** often smoked precooked types such as frankfurters, wieners, vienna sausage, bologna, salami and mettwurst, all of which may be eaten as bought—unless the label reads to the contrary; but in all cases heating before serving improves taste. Federal regulation now requires that commercially available sausages be precooked before sale, to the point of safety for eating as is; or, if not precooked, they must be ➤ marked "fresh," which requires cooking them thoroughly before serving. They may be simmered, baked, or broiled, or cooked with beans or other vegetables or in pasta dishes. In broiling or pan-frying cased sausages, add a small amount of water to the pan. Puncture the sausages with a fork to keep the skins from bursting and to permit the fat to escape.

A third type, the partially dry or **dry sausage,** is delicious in sandwiches or as hors d'oeuvre or used to flavor bland dishes. These kinds are somewhat confusingly known as **summer sausage** because, though made in the winter, they keep through spring and summer without refrigeration, provided the casing is intact—which explains the traditional popularity of this highly seasoned meat in Southern European countries. Dry sausages include cervelat, salami, saucisson de Lyon, mortadella, pepperoni, chorizo and thuringer.

If you make your own sausage, you can be assured of lean, good quality meat. As for the commercial types, their contents can be a mystery wrapped in an enigma—despite government labeling regulations. The label must show the ingredients but not the exact proportions; they are listed in descending order, the largest content first. USDA limitations permit up to 30% fat, 10% added water, 20% corn syrup, and 3½% cereal or dry-milk fillers. If sausage is marked "all meat," its meat component must be muscle meat with its natural fat content only and no fillers. But beware! A label reading "all meat" and listing the ingredients as "beef, water, pork, seasonings," in that order, means that you are buying more water than pork. Chemical additives are usually responsible for bright pink or red color; choose the more muted tones. For a discussion of casings, see 812.

➤ Never taste raw or "fresh" sausage whether bought or homemade, because of the danger of trichinosis. After handling raw sausage, always carefully wash your hands and any knife, utensil, or surface you have used. ➤ For 4 servings, allow about 1 pound of freshly ground sausage meat, slightly less for the more aged and drier types. Once the sausage casing is cut open, smoked or cooked sausage can be stored refrigerated about 1 week; semidry and dry types, 2 weeks or more.

COUNTRY SAUSAGE

➤ Please read About Sausage, above.

At butchering time in our valley, the popular man is the one who knows how to flavor the sausage —not too much pepper or sage and just enough coriander. This process has to be played by ear, for ➤ uncooked meat cannot be tasted to correct the seasoning, and the strength of spices is so variable. The best way to learn is to mix a small batch and cook up a sample for the always hungry helpers to test.

I. Chill, then grind together:

2 parts lean ground pork
1 part firm diced lard

Season with a mixture of:

Thyme
Coriander
Summer savory
Sweet marjoram
Pulverized bay leaf
Freshly ground pepper

To sauté fresh sausage patties, start them in a ➤ cold ungreased pan over moderate heat, draining the fat as it accumulates in the pan. Cook until well done and medium brown on both sides.

II. **6 Medium Patties**

A convenient small-scale recipe. Grind ➤ twice with the finest blade:

½ lb. lean pork
½ lb. pork fat
½ lb. lean veal

Mix in a large bowl:

1 cup bread crumbs
Grated rind of 1 lemon
¼ teaspoon each sage, sweet marjoram and thyme
⅛ teaspoon summer savory
½ teaspoon freshly ground black pepper
2 teaspoons salt
A grating of fresh nutmeg

Add the ground meat and form this mixture into a 1½-inch layer. Store overnight refrigerated and covered to blend the seasoning. ➤ To cook, see I, above.

BLOOD SAUSAGE OR BLACK PUDDING

In France, known as **boudin noir;** in Germany, as **Blutwurst.**

➤ Please read About Sausage, above.

Have ready:

Sausage casings

Cook gently without browning:

¾ cup finely chopped onions

in:

2 tablespoons lard

Cool slightly and mix in a bowl with:

⅓ cup whipping cream
¼ cup bread crumbs
2 beaten eggs
A grind of fresh pepper
⅛ teaspoon fresh thyme
½ bay leaf, pulverized
1 teaspoon salt

Add:

½ lb. leaf lard diced into ½-inch cubes
2 cups fresh pork blood

Fill casings only three-fourths full; the mixture will swell during the poaching period. Without overcrowding, put the sealed casings into a wire basket. Bring to a boil a large pan half full of water or half milk and half water. ➤ Remove pan from heat and plunge the basket into the water. Now return pan to very low heat—about 180°—for 15 minutes. Test for doneness by piercing sausage with a fork: if blood comes out, continue to cook about 5 minutes more or until barely firm. Should any of the sausages rise to the surface of the simmering liquid, prick them to release the air that might burst the skins. To prepare, split and grill them very gently.

WHITE SAUSAGE OR BOUDIN BLANC

Delicate, perishable and the most costly of all.
➤ Please read About Sausage, 496.
Have ready and tied at one end:
Sausage casings, 1 inch wide, 812
Mince:
¼ lb. leaf lard or hard back fat
Grind once with the finest blade:
½ lb. pork loin
½ lb. chicken or rabbit breast
Combine meat with the minced fat. Add:
2 teaspoons salt
1 teaspoon freshly ground white pepper
⅛ teaspoon each cloves, nutmeg and ginger
¼ teaspoon cinnamon
Regrind with:
2 cups chopped onions
Soak in:
¼ cup warm cream
½ cup bread crumbs
Add to crumbs:
3 beaten eggs
and the meat mixture.
Fill casings only about three-fourths full, twisting and tying with white string at 6-inch intervals. Without overcrowding, put the sealed casings into a wire basket and plunge them into boiling water. ➤ Reduce heat at once to 190°, and continue to cook at this temperature about 20 minutes. Should any sausages rise to the surface of the liquid, puncture them to release air and prevent bursting. Cool. Brush with:
Melted butter
and grill until golden brown.

SAUTÉED SAUSAGE MEAT PATTIES

4 Servings

➤ Please read About Sausage, 496.
Combine:
1 lb. sausage meat
2 tablespoons flour
(¼ cup drained crushed pineapple or grated fresh apple)
Shape the meat into patties ½ inch thick. Sprinkle with:
Flour
Rub a skillet with melted suet or butter, and heat. Brown the patties quickly on both sides. Cover. ➤ Reduce the heat and cook about 10 minutes on one side. Pour off excess fat. Turn and cook 10 minutes on the other side until well done. Serve with:
Sautéed Onions, 312, or on Apple Rings, 129
garnished with:
(Parsley)

⊟ PAN-BROILED SAUSAGE

4 Servings

➤ Please read About Sausage, 496.
Cut apart and place in a skillet:
8 sausages
Add:
½ cup boiling water
Cover pan. Simmer gently, not over 190°, for 8 to 10 minutes or until almost done. Pour off liquid. Return sausages to the pan. Cook over low heat, shaking the pan constantly until they are an even brown. Drain. Serve with:
Prepared mustard

TOAD-IN-THE-HOLE

What's in a name? Don't let the toad in this one deter you! Prepare for baking:
Yorkshire Pudding, 206
Pan-broil, see above:
12 small pork sausage links
Preheat oven to 400°.
Melt in a 2-quart oblong ovenproof pan:
5 tablespoons beef drippings or butter
Pour pudding batter into pan and bake about 20 minutes. ➤ Reduce heat to 350°. Arrange the drained sausage links on top of batter. Continue to bake 10 to 15 minutes longer. Serve at once, with:
Honey Apples, 130

BAKED SAUSAGE MEAT RING

6 Servings

➤ Please read About Sausage, 496.
Preheat oven to 350°.
Grease lightly a 7-inch ring mold. Cover bottom with:
3 tablespoons cornflakes
Combine well:
1 lb. sausage meat
1 tablespoon minced onion
¾ cup fine bread crumbs
2 tablespoons chopped parsley
1 beaten egg
Place these ingredients in the mold. Bake the ring 15 minutes. Drain the fat and bake 15 minutes longer until well done. Invert the ring onto a hot platter and fill the center with:
8 Scrambled Eggs, 222
Garnish the top with:
Chopped parsley or paprika

SAUSAGE MEAT, SWEET POTATO AND FRUIT CASSEROLE

4 Servings

Doubled, this recipe makes a fine dish for an informal group.
➤ Please read About Sausage, 496.
Preheat oven to 350°.
Peel and cut into thin slices:
4 large boiled sweet potatoes, 324
Grease a baking dish. Cover the bottom with half the sweet potatoes. Shape into 4 flat cakes and brown lightly in a skillet:
1 lb. sausage meat
to which you may add:
(1 tablespoon minced bacon)

Pare and cut into thick slices:

4 large apples

or use:

(Canned pineapple slices)

Place the drained meat cakes on the sweet potatoes and cover with the bacon bits and fruit. Sprinkle lightly with:

Salt and brown sugar

Place the remaining sweet potatoes over the fruit. Brush with:

Milk

and sprinkle with:

Brown sugar

Bake about 45 minutes.

APPLE-STUFFED SAUSAGE ROLL

Serves 8 to 10

Try this nourishing dish doubled and serve it sliced for a teen-aged group on a winter evening.

➤ Please read About Sausage, 496.

Preheat oven to 350°.

Pat into an oblong about ½ inch thick:

2 lb. bulk pork sausage

Combine as a stuffing and mix well:

2 cups finely chopped apples
⅓ cup finely chopped onions
1 cup soft bread crumbs
1 cup wheat germ
2 tablespoons brown sugar

Spread apple mixture on sausage and roll up like a jelly roll. Bake in a shallow pan about 1 hour.

FRANKFURTER-SAUERKRAUT CASSEROLE

6 Servings

➤ Please read About Sausage, 496.

Preheat oven to 375°.

Toss lightly together and place in a 1½-quart baking dish:

1 lb. drained sauerkraut
½ cup flat beer
¼ teaspoon caraway seeds

Cover and bake about 10 minutes. Top with:

6 frankfurters

Return to oven and bake about 20 minutes longer.

BOILED SAUSAGE

➤ Please read About Sausage, 496.

Place in a kettle:

Smoked sausage

Cover with:

Boiling water

Simmer about 10 minutes. Drain, skin, slice and serve with:

Sauerkraut, 295

PORK SCRAPPLE OR GOETTA

About 6 Servings

➤ Please read About Sausage, 496.

If you use cornmeal, call it scrapple. If you use oats, call it goetta. Place in a pan:

2 lb. pork neck bones or other bony pieces

Add:

1½ quarts boiling water
1 sliced onion
6 peppercorns
(1 small bay leaf)

Simmer the pork until the meat falls from the bones. Strain, ➤ reserving the liquor. There should be about 4 cups. Add water or light stock if necessary to make this amount. Using this liquid in place of boiling water, prepare:

Cornmeal Mush, 201

You may substitute 1 cup oatmeal for the cornmeal, in which case, reduce liquid by one cup. Remove all meat from the pork bones and chop or grind it fine. Add it to the cooked mush. Season with:

Salt to taste
1 teaspoon or more grated onion
(½ teaspoon dried thyme or sage)
A grating of fresh nutmeg
A little cayenne

Pour the scrapple into a bread pan that has been rinsed with cold water. Let it stand until cold and firm. Slice it. To serve, sauté slowly in:

Melted butter or drippings

ABOUT VARIETY MEATS

Variety, we know, is the spice of life. And variety meats provide welcome relief from the weekly round of beef, pork, veal, chicken and fish. They include organ meats like sweetbreads, brains, lamb kidney, calf and chicken liver, shown from left to right in the upper row on 500; muscle meats like heart, tongue and tripe; and very bony-structured meats like oxtails and knucklebones and their delicious marrow centers, seen again from left to right in the lower row. Time was when most of these tidbits were ours almost for the asking simply because most Americans had built-in prejudices against them. But in recent years, the American passion for travel has developed more cosmopolitan tastes in food, and more of us have learned to appreciate the odds and ends from which European cooks prepare some of their most celebrated dishes. There are practical reasons, too, to serve these delectable oddments: with the exception of calf liver and sweetbreads, now in the higher-priced bracket, they are still gentle to a fragile budget; and last but not least, they contribute significantly to our well-being; although some of those formerly used, like lungs, are now outlawed. But even the muzzle of beef can be prepared as for tongue, 507. ➤ It is essential that variety meats be fresh. They are highly perishable; use them at once.

ABOUT LIVER

Chicken and calf livers are the tenderest and most desirable unless, of course, you can secure extra-fat goose livers—the kind which in Europe almost

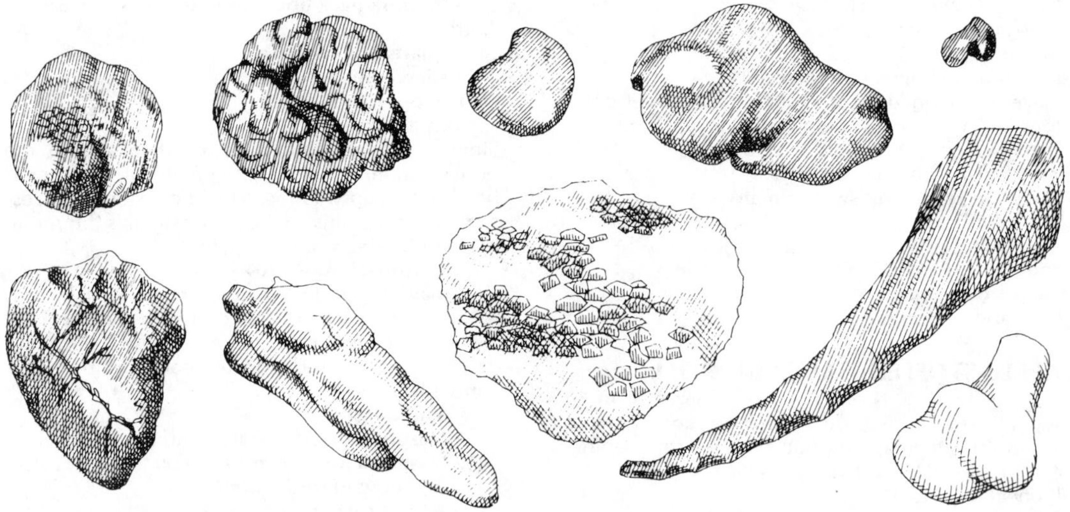

invariably find their way into Pâtés, 494. Baby beef liver comes next for quality. Lamb liver is also tender but less flavorful. Sheep, pork and older beef livers have a strong, distinctive flavor and should be soaked several hours in a spicy marinade or in milk, after which time the liquid is discarded. Pork liver is quite rich in vitamins and minerals and well worth the added effort of trimming out the tough fibers. Since it is pork, ➤ cook it until no pink shows, but try not to overcook, see below.

Most recipes call for 1/4-inch-thick sliced liver; however, thick slices over 1 inch may be successfully broiled as for steak.

➤ To prepare any liver for cooking, wipe it first with a damp cloth, then remove the thin outer skin and veining. The outer skin may be easily peeled from fresh liver. Except for the timing noted in individual recipes, the cooking method for liver generally is the same. ➤ Never toughen it by cooking too long or over excessive heat. ➤ Never cook beyond the point of tenderness. Sometimes the drippings in which liver has been cooked are bitter. Test them by tasting before you use them as sauce. Some good sauces to serve with liver are Béarnaise Sauce, 359, Barbecue Sauces, 354, Lyonnaise Sauce, 346, and Seasoned Butters, 349. ➤ Allow 1 pound liver for 4 servings.

SAUTÉED CALF OR CHICKEN LIVER OR LIVER LYONNAISE

2 Servings

➤ Please read About Liver, above.
Have sliced to a 1/4-inch even thickness:
1/2 lb. calf liver, or halved chicken livers
Coat lightly on both sides with:
Flour
In a skillet brown the slices quickly over moderate heat, about 1 minute to each side, in:
1 tablespoon butter
Add to taste:
Salt and pepper
In a separate skillet heat:
2 tablespoons butter
Add and sauté until golden:
1/4 cup sliced onions
(1/4 cup sliced mushrooms)
Put the liver on a hot plate, cover with the onions and serve with:
Chopped parsley
(Sautéed Bacon, 486)
The chicken livers may be served on toast.

⊟ BROILED LIVER

➤ Please read About Liver, 499.
Some epicures prefer liver "pure and simple," prepared the following way. We acknowledge its sterling qualities.
Place on a broiling rack, about 3 inches from the source of heat:
Slices of calf liver, 1/3 inch thick
You may brush them with:
(Butter or vegetable oil)
Broil the liver exactly 1 minute on each side.
Season to taste
and serve as is, or with:
Mushroom Wine Sauce, 347, or
Madeira Sauce, 346
Or serve with:
Sautéed Bacon, 486
Sautéed Bermuda onion slices, 312
garnished with:
Parsley
A lemon cut into quarters

BRAISED LIVER WITH VEGETABLES

6 Servings

➤ Please read About Liver, 499.
Cut into 1-inch slices:

1½ lb. calf or beef liver

If you use beef liver, you may lard it, 444. Dredge with:

Seasoned Flour, 552

Brown the liver in:

¼ cup hot bacon drippings

Combine and heap on the slices:

2 diced carrots
2 chopped green peppers, seeds and membrane removed
6 small onions
1 cup sliced celery

Add to the pan:

1 cup boiling water or stock

Cover and simmer until the liver is tender. If necessary, add more boiling stock. Calf liver will be tender in about 15 minutes, beef liver in about 30.

BRAISED LIVER COCKAIGNE WITH WINE

8 Servings

➤ Please read About Liver, 499.

Place:

2½ lb. calf or baby beef liver in 1 piece

in the following marinade refrigerated for 1 hour or more:

⅓ cup vegetable oil
1½ tablespoons lemon juice
¼ teaspoon salt
⅛ teaspoon paprika
¼ bay leaf

Turn it from time to time.

Preheat oven to 325°.

Melt in an ovenproof baking dish:

3 tablespoons butter

Add and stir about until lightly cooked:

1 small chopped onion or leek
1 diced carrot
2 or 3 diced ribs celery
2 or 3 minced sprigs parsley
1 tablespoon fresh basil or tarragon

Place the liver, marinade and all, in the ovenproof dish. Cover closely and bake until nearly tender, about 40 minutes. Baste from time to time. If you wish to serve the liver without further additions, continue cooking it until very tender.

The following ingredients are optional, but they complement the dish. While the liver is cooking, place in a heavy skillet and sauté over very slow heat:

4 slices diced bacon

Cook until the bacon is clear. Add and stir until well glazed:

18 small peeled shallots or onions
6 large or 8 small sliced carrots
3 ribs celery, sliced

Add:

1 cup Stock, 520, or canned consommé

Cover the skillet and cook the vegetables and bacon over direct low heat 15 minutes. Add them to the liver in the baking dish, cover and cook 15 minutes longer. Drain the contents of the baking dish, reserving the liquor. Place the liver on a hot platter. Add to the liquor:

½ cup dry white wine, or ¼ cup dry sherry

Cook and stir the sauce over low heat until hot. Pour the sauce over the liver. Serve with:

Boiled New Potatoes, 317, browned in butter

garnished with:

Parsley

BEEF LIVER CREOLE

4 Servings

➤ Please read About Liver, 499.

Cut into thin slices:

1 lb. beef liver

Dust lightly with:

Flour

Brown the liver in:

3 tablespoons hot butter or drippings

Add:

1¼ cups sliced onions
1½ cups canned tomatoes
½ cup diced celery
1 thinly sliced green pepper, seeds and membrane removed
½ teaspoon salt
A few grains cayenne

Cover the pan and simmer these ingredients about 20 minutes. Drain, reserving the liquid. Thicken with:

Flour, see Pan Gravy, 341

Add the liver and vegetables. Simmer 2 minutes longer. Serve with:

Boiled Rice, 206, or Noodles, 213

⊟ LIVER, PEPPER, ONIONS AND OLIVES ON SKEWERS

4 Servings

➤ Please read About Liver, 499.

Also see Hot Skewered Tidbits, 80.

Simmer covered in a little boiling water until nearly tender:

¾ lb. calf liver in 1 piece

Drain the liver. Cut it into 1-inch cubes. Peel and quarter:

4 medium-sized onions

Cut into 1-inch pieces:

6 strips bacon
2 green peppers, seeds and membrane removed

Alternate on skewers pieces of liver, onion, green pepper, bacon and:

Stuffed olives

Place them under a broiler or over heated coals until the bacon is crisp and the liver tender.

SKEWERED CHICKEN LIVERS

The Hors d'Oeuvre chapter has numerous suggestions for cooking chicken and goose livers en brochette, see About Chicken and Goose Livers as Hors d'Oeuvre, 86; Rumaki, 81; and Hot Skewered Tidbits, 80.

CHICKEN LIVERS À LA KING

Prepare:

1 cup or more Sautéed Chicken Livers, 500

Combine with:

1 cup Quick à la King Sauce, 348

Serve on rounds of toasted whole wheat bread.

CHICKEN LIVERS IN BATTER

Wipe with a cloth:

Chicken livers

Season them lightly with:

Salt and pepper

Dip them into:

Fritter Batter for Meat, 243

Fry them in deep fat, heated to 365° until well browned. Serve with:

An omelet, 226

or as a garnish for a hot vegetable plate.

CHICKEN LIVERS IN SOUR CREAM SAUCE

6 Servings

Cut into halves:

1 lb. chicken livers

Sauté until lightly browned in:

2 tablespoons butter
2 tablespoons vegetable oil

Remove the meat, add to the pan and sauté about 5 minutes:

¼ cup finely minced green pepper
½ cup minced onions
1 cup sliced mushrooms

Sprinkle over the vegetables and stir well:

2 tablespoons flour

Add:

1 cup cultured sour cream
¼ cup chicken stock

Stir and cook gently until mixture thickens. Add the livers and:

2 tablespoons chopped parsley
Season to taste

When thoroughly heated, serve over:

Boiled Rice, 206

or over small rounds of toast.

GOOSE LIVER

Remove the gallbladder, if attached. Soak in cold salted water for 2 hours:

A goose liver

Dry it with a cloth. Sprinkle it with:

⅛ teaspoon paprika
½ teaspoon sugar
⅛ teaspoon ginger

Sauté it in hot goose fat until tender. It is excellent served with sautéed onions and apples and with a litle dry sherry.

ABOUT SWEETBREADS

To paraphrase Puck: "What foods these morsels be!" Veal sweetbreads are those most favored. But beef sweetbreads are sometimes incorporated into mixtures like meat pies, pâtés and terrines. Sweetbreads, properly so-called, are the rounded, more desirable "heart" or "kernel" types, the pancreas. The thinner "throat" type is the thymus.

➤ Like all organ meats, sweetbreads are highly perishable and should be prepared for use as soon as purchased. First soak them at least 1 hour in a large quantity of cold water to release any blood, changing the water 2 or 3 times. Next they must be blanched: cover them with cold acidulated water, 520. Bring slowly to a boil and simmer uncovered from 2 to 5 minutes, depending on size. Drain. Firm them by plunging them at once into cold water. When cool, drain again and trim by removing cartilage, tubes, connective tissue and tougher membrane. Weight them refrigerated for several hours if you plan using them whole. If not, break them into smaller sections with your hands, being careful not to disturb the very fine membrane that surrounds the smaller units.

After these preliminary processes, ➤ to which all sweetbreads must be subjected, you may poach, braise, broil or cream or sauce them. ➤ Allow 1 pair for 2 servings.

SAUCED POACHED SWEETBREADS

2 Servings

➤ Please read About Sweetbreads, above.

Soak, blanch, firm, drain and trim:

1 pair veal sweetbreads

Bring to the boiling point:

Enough water to cover
¼ cup chopped onions
3 ribs celery with yellow leaves
2 peppercorns

Drop the sweetbreads into the liquid and ➤ lower the heat at once. Simmer covered with parchment paper, 151, 15 to 20 minutes, depending on size. ➤ Do not overcook. Serve in a delicate sauce such as:

Béchamel Sauce, 341, or Poulette Sauce, 345

made with some of the sweetbread liquor as stock, plus:

1 tablespoon dry sherry, Madeira, brandy or lemon juice

or use:

White Wine Sauce, 345

to any of which you may add:

(Chopped English walnuts or almonds)

Sauced sweetbreads are often served on:

A thin slice of Virginia ham or prosciutto or Canadian bacon

or in:

Patty shells, 645, or Bread Cases, 250

or with a:

Spinach Ring, 231; a Vegetable Soufflé, 229; or Wild Rice, 212

SAUTÉED SWEETBREADS

2 Servings

➤ Please read About Sweetbreads, above.

Blanch, firm, dry, trim and poach about 25 minutes:

1 pair veal sweetbreads

Bread with a:

Seasoned Bound Breading, 552

Sauté them in:

Hot butter

until they are a rich brown. Serve with one of the sauces in Poached Sweetbreads, opposite. Serve with:

Boiled New Potatoes, 317, and green peas

garnished with:

Watercress

BROILED SWEETBREADS

2 Servings

➤ Please read About Sweetbreads, opposite.

Soak, blanch, firm, drain, trim and poach about 25 minutes:

1 pair calf sweetbreads

Preheat broiler.

Place the broiling rack about 6 inches from the heat source. Break the sweetbreads into large pieces. Roll them in:

Seasoned Flour, 552

Surround them with:

Strips of bacon

Secure it with wooden picks. While broiling them, baste frequently with the juices that drip, and if they are rather dry, use additional:

Butter

Add to the drippings a small amount of:

(Sherry or lemon juice)

Serve with:

Madeira Sauce, 346, Poulette Sauce, 345, or broiled tomatoes

or on a bed of:

Creamed Spinach, 327

⊟ SWEETBREADS ON SKEWERS

2 Servings

➤ Please read About Sweetbreads, opposite.

Soak, blanch about 10 minutes, firm and trim:

1 pair calf sweetbreads

Break them into 1-inch chunks. Wrap the pieces with partially cooked:

Lean bacon, thinly sliced

Spread:

Mushroom caps

lightly with:

Butter

Place the wrapped sweetbreads and the mushrooms alternately on skewers. Grill over charcoal until the bacon is crisp. Or you may rest skewers on the edges of an ovenproof pan and bake at 400° about 10 minutes. Serve with:

Soufflé Potatoes, 321, or
Tomatoes Provencale, 332

GLAZED SWEETBREADS

2 Servings

➤ Please read About Sweetbreads, opposite.

Soak, blanch, firm, drain and trim:

1 pair calf sweetbreads

Melt in a heavy pan and sauté about 10 minutes or until the onions are translucent:

3 tablespoons butter
2 tablespoons finely julienned carrots
2 tablespoons finely chopped shallots or onions

Add the sweetbreads and stir with the vegetables. Add:

1½ cups veal stock

Simmer covered about 20 minutes. ➤ Make sure that the vegetables do not brown. Add more stock, if necessary. When the sweetbreads are cooked, transfer them to an ovenproof serving dish. Keep them warm. Deglaze the pan by the addition of:

½ cup dry white wine
Season to taste

Preheat oven to 400° for glazing. Reduce pan liquors to about ½ cup. Ladle 2 tablespoons of this glaze over each sweetbread and place the dish in the oven about 10 minutes, basting often. Meanwhile, melt in a skillet:

2 tablespoons butter

Sauté in it:

½ cup sliced mushrooms
¾ cup chopped cooked chestnuts

Serve the sweetbreads at once on:

Rounds of toast

garnished with:

Finely chopped chervil or parsley

and surrounded with the mushroom and chestnut mixture.

RAGOÛT FIN

4 Servings

A delicate and far-reaching dish.

➤ Please read About Sweetbreads, opposite.

Prepare and drain:

2 pairs poached sweetbreads, opposite

Drain:

2 cups halved cooked asparagus tips

Reserve the asparagus liquor. Melt in a heavy skillet:

¼ cup butter

Sauté in the butter about 3 minutes:

½ lb. mushrooms
(¼ cup chopped shallots)

Remove them from the skillet. Add to the fat in it:

6 tablespoons butter

Add and stir until blended:

6 tablespoons flour

Stir in slowly:

3 cups liquid: milk or cream, asparagus liquor or stock

When the sauce is smooth and boiling, gradually add the asparagus tips, the mushrooms and the sweetbreads. ➤ Reduce the heat. Put a small amount of sauce in a separate pan and beat in:

2 egg yolks

Add the egg mixture to the sauced sweetbreads and ➤ without letting it boil, stir for about 1 minute very gently, to avoid mashing the asparagus. Season with:

Salt and paprika
Freshly grated nutmeg
Just before serving, you may add:
(2 tablespoons dry sherry or
1 teaspoon Worcestershire sauce)
Serve the ragoût at once in:
Hot Patty Shells, 645; on hot buttered toast; in Bread Cases, 250; in a baked Noodle Ring, 214; or on hot Waffles, 241

ABOUT BRAINS

Calf, sheep, lamb, pork and beef brains are listed in order of preference. Brains may be used in all recipes calling for sweetbreads, but, as with sweetbreads, they must be very fresh. ➤ Keep refrigerated, for they are very perishable.

To prepare, give them a preliminary soaking of 1½ to 2 hours in cold acidulated water, 520. After skinning, soak them in several changes of cold water for 1 hour to free them from all traces of blood. Then, as they are rather mushy in texture, firm them by simmering in acidulated water to cover, about 20 minutes for calf brains, 25 for the others. ➤ Be sure the water does not boil. Let the brains cool in the cooking liquid about 20 minutes before draining. If not using immediately, refrigerate the drained brains. Brains are often combined with eggs or with sweetbreads in ragoût and soufflés. Because they are bland, be sure to give the dish in which they are used a piquant flavoring, as suggested below. ➤ Allow 1 pound of brains for 4 servings or 1 set for 2 servings.

SAUTÉED BRAINS

4 Servings

➤ Please read About Brains, above.
Prepare by soaking, skinning and blanching:
2 sets brains
Cut in two, lengthwise. Dry them between towels. Season with:
Salt and paprika
Roll them in:
Cornmeal or flour
Melt in a skillet rubbed with:
Garlic
⅓ cup butter or bacon drippings
When the fat reaches the point of fragrance, sauté the brains on each side about 2 minutes. Cover, reduce heat and complete the cooking, about 10 minutes in all. Serve with:
Lemon wedges
Thickened Tomato Sauce, 352, or Worcestershire sauce; or Brown Butter, 349, or Black Butter, 350

BAKED BRAINS

3 Servings

➤ Please read About Brains, above.
Preheat oven to 400°.
Prepare by soaking, skinning and blanching:
1 set brains
Chop coarsely and combine them with:
½ cup bread crumbs
2 chopped hard-cooked eggs
6 tablespoons cream
1 tablespoon catsup
2 peeled chopped green chilis
½ tablespoon lemon juice
Season to taste
Place in a greased baking dish or in individual dishes. Sprinkle the top with:
Au Gratin II, 553
Bake about 15 minutes.

BAKED BRAINS AND EGGS

4 Servings

➤ Please read About Brains, above.
Preheat oven to 350°.
Prepare by soaking, skinning and blanching:
2 sets brains
Cut into 1-inch dice and place them in 4 small greased casseroles. Skin, seed and dice:
4 tomatoes
Combine them with:
1½ tablespoons hot olive oil
1 teaspoon chopped parsley
1 teaspoon chopped onion or chives
Salt and paprika
1 teaspoon brown sugar
Pour these ingredients into the casseroles. Break into each one:
1 egg
Bake about 8 minutes, or until the eggs are firm. Melt and brown lightly:
¼ cup butter
Add:
2 teaspoons lemon juice
Pour this mixture over the eggs. Garnish with:
Parsley
Serve at once.

BROILED BRAINS

➤ Please read About Brains, above.
Prepare by soaking, skinning and blanching:
Brains
Preheat broiler.
Brush brains with:
Vegetable oil or melted butter
Dust with:
Paprika
Place broiler about 6 inches from heat source and broil the brains about 8 minutes on each side or until done. Baste with oil or butter. Serve piping hot with:
Broiled Bacon, 485
Chopped parsley and lemon wedges
or:
Grilled Tomato Slices, 332, and watercress

ABOUT KIDNEYS

Veal kidneys are the tenderest and most delicious. Those of lamb are somewhat soft and flat in flavor, but especially suitable for grilling. They should not be washed or soaked in water, as they absorb it. Simply split and remove the cores. Large beef kidneys tend to be hard and strong in flavor and need soaking first for 2 hours in cold salted water. Off-flavors may be withdrawn by blanching II, 154, in acidulated water for 20 minutes; or, after soaking and drying, the kidneys may be sautéed briefly over brisk heat and allowed to cool partially before further cooking.

The white membrane should be snipped from all kidneys before they are washed. Curved scissors are convenient for this. Removal of membranes is easier if you first sauté the kidneys in fat about 1 minute. Discard the fat.

➤ To prepare for broiling, almost halve the kidneys. Keep them from curling during cooking by skewering them open. Expose the cut side to the heat first.

Veal and lamb kidneys should be cooked as short a time as possible over medium heat. ➤ Do not overcook. The center should be slightly pink. The veal kidney may be left surrounded by its delicious delicate fat, or you can use it for seasoning or render it for deep-fat frying, 147. If kidneys are to be flambéed, never flame for more than 1 minute. Longer exposure to such high heat will toughen them. If kidneys are of the best quality, pan juices may be used. If not, discard the juices and use freshly melted butter or a wine sauce. In any case, ➤ never allow kidneys to boil in a sauce, as this only hardens them. Pour the hot sauce over them or toss them in it for a moment or two.

Beef, mutton and pork kidneys are most often used in terrines, braises and stews, and need the slow, moist cooking that is described in some of the following recipes.

➤ Allow 1 medium-sized veal kidney, 2 or 3 lamb kidneys, 1½ to 2 mutton, ½ beef or 1 small pork kidney per person.

BAKED VEAL KIDNEYS

Note for the lone householder: 1 veal kidney makes a fine little roast for 1 person.
➤ Please read About Kidneys, above.
Preheat oven to 300°.
Prepare, leaving the fat on, and place in a pan, fat side up:

Veal kidneys

Bake uncovered until tender, about 1 hour. Serve with:

Mushroom Sauce, 348, or
Quick Brown Sauce, 348, or
Marchand de Vin Sauce, 347

KIDNEY NUGGETS

2 Servings

➤ Please read About Kidneys, opposite.
Preheat oven to 375°
Prepare for cooking and slice in half:

4 lamb kidneys or 2 veal kidneys

Prepare:

Dressing for Braised Stuffed Pork Chops Cockaigne, 479

adding:

1 beaten egg

Spread the dressing on:

8 slices of thin lean bacon

Wrap the spread bacon around the kidney halves and fasten with a wooden pick. Bake about 20 minutes.

SAUTÉED KIDNEYS OR KIDNEYS BERCY

3 Servings

➤ Please read About Kidneys, opposite. Remove some of the fat from:

3 veal kidneys

Cut them crosswise into slices, removing all the white tissue. Rub a pan with:

(Garlic)

Melt in it:

¼ cup butter

Sauté in the butter until golden:

½ cup sliced onions or shallots

Remove onions and keep hot. Sauté the kidneys in the hot fat, a quick process, about 5 minutes. Add the onions and season with:

Salt and paprika
1 tablespoon lemon juice or ¼ cup dry white wine

You may serve this flambé, 155, with:

Mushrooms on toast

SAUTÉED KIDNEYS WITH CELERY AND MUSHROOMS

4 Servings

➤ Please read About Kidneys, opposite. Prepare:

8 lamb kidneys

Skin and quarter them. Sprinkle with:

Lemon juice

Heat in a skillet:

3 tablespoons butter or drippings

Sauté lightly in the fat:

1 cup chopped celery
¼ cup chopped onions

Add the kidneys. Simmer covered about 5 minutes. Stir in:

1 tablespoon flour
1 cup hot stock

When these ingredients are blended, add:

½ lb. chopped mushrooms

Season the kidneys lightly with:

Paprika
Worcestershire sauce

Simmer covered about 15 minutes. Add and allow to just boil up:

2 tablespoons dry sherry or Madeira
1 tablespoon chopped parsley
Season to taste

Serve in a:

Rice Ring, 207

or you may cut the caps off:

(4 Brioches, 615)

Scoop them out, warm in a 350° oven, insert the hot kidney mixture, cover with the caps and serve at once.

BROILED KIDNEYS

Allow 1 Kidney per Person

➤ Please read About Kidneys, 504.

Preheat broiler.

Remove most of the fat from:

Veal kidneys

Cut them crosswise into slices. Place 3 to 4 inches from source of heat and broil them about 5 minutes. Turn, and baste with:

Melted butter

Broil about 5 minutes longer or until done. Season with:

Lemon juice
Salt and paprika or freshly ground pepper

Serve with:

Chutney, 846, or Cold Mustard Sauce, 357

KIDNEYS EN BROCHETTE

Individual Serving

➤ Please read About Kidneys, 504. Prepare for cooking, allowing per serving:

1 veal or 3 lamb kidneys

Split the kidneys, remove the core and blanch 2 to 3 minutes in:

Milk or cold water and lemon juice

Dry. Cut in quarters. Wrap pieces in:

Bacon

Arrange on skewers and grill or broil 3 inches from heat source, about 3 minutes. Turn and broil 3 minutes more. Serve at once.

VARIETY MEAT PATTIES

4 Servings

➤ Please read About Kidneys, 504, About Liver, 499, or About Brains, 504. Prepare one of the following for cooking and then chop until fine:

2 pairs blanched brains; 1 lb. raw liver; or 1 beef, 2 pork or veal or 5 lamb kidneys

Sprinkle them with:

1 tablespoon lemon juice

Rub a skillet with:

Garlic

Heat in it:

2 tablespoons butter

Sauté in this lightly:

1 chopped onion or leek
½ cup minced celery
2 tablespoons minced green pepper, seeds and membrane removed

Remove from heat. Add the chopped variety meat and:

¼ cup dry bread crumbs
¼ cup milk
1 egg
¼ teaspoon salt
¼ teaspoon freshly ground pepper
4 drops Worcestershire sauce
(¼ teaspoon caraway or dill seed)

Drop this mixture by the tablespoon into a hot pan containing:

2 tablespoons hot bacon drippings

Brown the patties lightly on both sides. Serve with:

Quick Tomato Sauce, 352, Slaw, 96, or Vegetables à la Grecque, 281

VEAL KIDNEY CASSEROLE

4 Servings

➤ Please read About Kidneys, 504.

Preheat oven to 350°.

Prepare:

4 veal kidneys

Heat them about 1 minute in:

2 tablespoons vegetable oil or fat

Discard the fat. Skin and dice the kidneys and place them in a heated ovenproof dish. Heat in a skillet:

1 tablespoon butter

Sauté in the butter:

¼ to ½ lb. sliced mushrooms
2 tablespoons minced onion or ¼ clove garlic
1 tablespoon minced parsley

Stir and cook these ingredients about 2 minutes. Stir in:

3 tablespoons flour

Stir in:

1 cup boiling Veal or Light Stock, 522

Bring to the boiling point and add:

¼ cup dry white wine or ½ cup orange juice
Season to taste

Pour these ingredients over the kidneys in the casserole. Cover closely. Bake about 20 minutes or until tender. You may remove the kidneys and keep warm, reduce the sauce slightly if necessary, and then pour the thickened hot gravy over the kidneys. Have ready, by cutting into triangles:

4 thick slices bread

Sprinkle them with:

Grated cheese

Place bread on top of the kidneys. Broil until cheese is melted.

BEEF KIDNEY STEW

4 Servings

A favorite for Sunday breakfast, brunch or supper.

➤ Please read About Kidneys, 504. Soak, blanch and cut away all the white tissue from:

2 small beef kidneys

Drain and cool them. For easier slicing, you may place them in a covered dish in the refrigerator. When cold, cut the meat into wafer-thin slices. Dredge the slices with:

Seasoned Flour, 552

Melt:

1 or 2 tablespoons butter

Sauté the slices lightly in the hot butter. Remove and keep them warm. Sauté in the drippings:

½ cup thinly sliced onions

Add the meat and:

1 cup stock or red wine, or ½ cup stock and ½ cup flat beer

Simmer about 15 minutes. If the sauce is too thin, thicken with:

Beurre Manié, 340

Flavor by adding:

1 slice lemon or 2 tablespoons tomato paste
Salt and paprika, as needed

Serve with:

Boiled Potatoes, 317, or Noodles, 213;
or on toast or Cornmeal Waffles, 241

garnished with:

Chopped parsley

ABOUT TONGUE

Lucky indeed is the cook with the gift of tongues! No matter from which source—beef, calf, lamb or pork—the smaller-sized tongues are usually preferable. The most commonly used and best flavored, whether fresh, smoked or pickled, is beef tongue. For prime texture, it should be under 3 pounds.

➤ Scrub the tongue well. If it is smoked or pickled, you may wish to blanch it first, 154, simmering it about 10 minutes. Immerse the tongue in cold water. After draining, cook as for Boiled Fresh Tongue, below. If the tongue is to be served hot, drain, plunge it into cold water for a moment so you can handle it, skin it and trim it by removing the roots, small bones and gristle. Return it very briefly to the hot cooking water to reheat before serving.

If the tongue is to be served cold, allow it to cool just enough to handle comfortably. It skins easily at this point ➤ but not if you let it get cold. Trim and return it to the pot to cool completely in the cooking liquor. It is attractive served with Chaud-Froid Sauce, 369, or in Aspic, see below.

➤ To carve tongue, cut nearly through at the hump parallel to the base. But toward the tip, better-looking slices can be made if the cut is diagonal.

BOILED FRESH BEEF TONGUE

6 to 8 Servings

➤ Please read About Tongue, above. Place in a kettle:

A fresh beef or calf tongue, about 2 lb.

Peel and add:

2 medium-sized onions
1 large carrot
3 or more ribs celery with leaves
6 sprigs parsley
4 peppercorns
(4 whole cloves)
1 bay leaf

Barely cover these ingredients with boiling water. Skim off any scum after first 5 minutes. Simmer the tongue uncovered until tender, about 50 minutes per pound. Drain and reserve liquid. Skin and trim the tongue. Reheat in the cooking water before serving with:

Hot Mustard Sauce, 345;
Piquant Sauce, 347; or
Horseradish Sauce, 343

or with:

Harvard Beets, 290, or
capers or chopped pickle

BEEF TONGUE WITH RAISIN SAUCE

An undemanding dish to prepare while working on other things in the kitchen.

➤ Please read About Tongue, above.

Boil, as in previous recipe:

A fresh beef tongue

After it has been skinned and trimmed, place it where it will keep hot.

For the sauce, make:

Raisin Sauce, 356

to which you may add:

½ cup blanched almonds, 562
¼ cup crushed gingersnaps
(2 teaspoons Caramelized Sugar II, 559)
Season to taste

Serve the tongue with:

A Rice or Noodle Ring, 207, 214, filled with green peas

BOILED SMOKED, CORNED OR PICKLED TONGUE

6 to 8 Servings

➤ Please read About Tongue, left, and blanch as directed:

A 2-lb. smoked, corned or pickled beef tongue

Drain, then cover the tongue with:

Fresh water

Add:

1 whole onion stuck with 3 cloves
½ cup chopped celery with leaves
3 bay leaves
6 peppercorns

Simmer the tongue uncovered until tender, about 50 minutes per pound. Drain, skin and trim, as directed. Slice and serve hot with:

Creamed Spinach, 327
Boiled Potatoes, 317
Horseradish Sauce, 343

or cold with:

Cold Mustard Sauce, 357, or Sauce Gribiche, 365, or Cream Horseradish Dressing, 357

TONGUE BAKED IN CREOLE SAUCE

6 Servings

➤ Please read About Tongue, left.

Boil:

A fresh or smoked beef tongue, about 1½ lb., or 2 veal or 8 lamb tongues

Skin and trim as directed.
Preheat oven to 375°.
Prepare:

Creole Sauce, 348

Place the drained tongue, sliced or unsliced, in a casserole. Pour the sauce over it. Bake covered ½ hour. Serve with:

Chopped parsley

TONGUE IN ASPIC

8 Servings

A fine-looking dish.
Boil:

A Smoked Beef Tongue, 507

Drain, skin and trim the tongue, then leave it in the stock until it is cool. Make the following aspic. Soak:

1½ tablespoons gelatin

in:

½ cup cold beef stock

Dissolve this mixture in:

2½ cups boiling beef stock
½ cup dry white wine or the juice of 2 lemons
1 tablespoon sugar
Salt, if required
A few drops Caramelized Sugar II, 559, or commercial coloring
1 teaspoon Worcestershire sauce

Chill the aspic, and when it is about to set, add:

½ cup chopped sweet-sour pickles
1 cup chopped celery
½ cup chopped green peppers, seeds and membrane removed

Have ready a mold or bread pan moistened with cold water. Place a small amount of aspic in the bottom of the mold. If desired, add at this time small cooked carrots, beets, canned mushrooms, etc. Chill the aspic in the pan so it hardens somewhat. Then put the tongue into the mold and pour the remaining aspic around and over it. When well chilled, unmold the aspic onto a platter. Garnish it with:

Lettuce leaves
Deviled eggs
Parsley
Slices of lemon

Serve with:

Mayonnaise or Mayonnaise Collée, 368

ABOUT HEART

Heart, which is firm and rather dry, is best prepared by slow cooking. It is muscle, not organ meat, and so may be used in many recipes calling for ground meat. Before cooking, wash it well, removing fat, arteries, veins and blood, and dry carefully. ➤ A 4- to 5-pound beef heart will serve 6; a veal heart will serve one.

BAKED STUFFED HEART

3 Servings

➤ Please read About Heart, above.
Preheat oven to 325°
Prepare:

A small beef heart or 3 veal hearts

Tie with a string to hold its shape, if necessary, and wrap in muslin or foil and tie. Place on a rack in an ovenproof dish and pour over it:

2 cups stock or diluted tomato soup

Place over the heart:

4 slices bacon

Cover the dish closely and bake until tender—if beef, a matter of 3 to 4 hours, depending on size; if veal, about 2. Remove the heart to a plate and cool slightly. Heat in a double boiler, then fill the heart cavity with:

Apple and Onion Dressing, 372

You will need about 1 cup for a veal heart, about 3 for a beef heart. ➤ To allow for expansion, do not pack the dressing. Sprinkle the heart with:

Paprika

Return it to a 400° oven long enough to heat quickly before serving. The drippings may be thickened with:

Flour, see Pan Gravy, 341

BRAISED HEART SLICES IN SOUR SAUCE

6 Servings

A homey treat.
➤ Please read About Heart, above.
Prepare:

A 4- to 5-lb. beef heart or 6 veal hearts

If veal, you may halve the heart; if beef, cut it across the fiber into ¼-inch slices. Pour into a large saucepan or ovenproof dish to the depth of ¾ inch:

Boiling water

Add:

¼ cup diced carrots
¼ cup chopped celery with leaves
¼ cup sliced onion
½ teaspoon salt
(¼ cup diced green pepper)

Place the heart slices on a rack in the pan, well above the water. Cover closely. Steam the meat until tender, about 1½ hours for veal and 2½ hours for beef. Strain and reserve the stock. Chill and degrease it. Save the fat. Reserve the stock. Melt in the pan:

3 tablespoons butter or fat from the stock

Stir in:

3 tablespoons flour

Then add:

1½ cups stock

When it reaches a boil, add the meat and vegetables and ➤ reduce the heat. Add:

2 tablespoons lemon juice or dry red wine
½ teaspoon sweet marjoram or 2 tablespoons chopped parsley or olives
Season to taste

When heated through, serve with:

Spoon Bread, 629, Rice, 206, or Potato Dumplings, 204

ABOUT TRIPE

Tripe is the muscular lining of the four stomachs of ruminants. It includes *plain* tripe from the paunch or belly of the first stomach, the rumen; *honeycomb,* the most available, along with the fatter, partially honeycombed *gras double* near the belly end of the second stomach, or reticulum; *feuillet* or *manyplies* from the third stomach, the omasum; and *reed* from the fourth stomach, the abomasum.

Honeycomb tripe is the most delicate variety and today comes either in refrigerated plastic pouches or in large sheets, and fresh tripe usually comes already blanched and parboiled. After cutting into pieces, wash thoroughly. It is now ready to season and cook. ➤ Since tripe is very perishable, it should be kept refrigerated and used as soon as possible.

If you start from scratch, cooking tripe is a long-drawn-out affair. Fresh whole tripe calls for a minimum of 12 hours of cooking, some time-honored recipes demanding as much as 24. To prepare fresh tripe, trim if necessary. ➤ Wash it thoroughly, soaking overnight, and blanch, 154, for ½ hour in salted water. Wash well again, drain and cut for cooking. When cooked, the texture of tripe should be like that of soft gristle. More often, alas, ➤ because the heat has not been kept low enough, it has the consistency of wet shoe leather.

Sometimes tripe is pickled after cooking and served hot or cold in a marinade. Pickled tripe may also be found in the market.

COOKED FRESH TRIPE

4 to 5 Servings

➤ Please read About Tripe, above.

Trim, wash, soak, blanch, wash again and drain:

2 lb. fresh honeycomb tripe

Cut it into 1½- to 2-inch squares. Place it in a heavy pot that you can lid tightly later. Add:

Enough water to cover tripe
¼ teaspoon salt
¼ teaspoon sugar
1 clove garlic
⅔ cup chopped onions
1 cup chopped mixed celery and parsley
4 peppercorns

Bring to a boil. ➤ Reduce the heat at once. Seal the lid with a strip of pastry or tape and simmer 10 to 12 hours. When tender, you may serve the tripe with:

White Sauce I, 341

made with the drained liquid as stock, and adding:

Salt
½ teaspoon prepared mustard
1 teaspoon Worcestershire sauce
2 tablespoons chopped parsley

TRIPE À LA MODE DE CAEN

6 to 8 Servings

This classic Normandy dish demands a deep earthenware casserole and the inclusion of all 4 types of beef tripe. The second requirement is almost impossible to satisfy in America, where honeycomb tripe is the only kind usually available.

➤ Please read About Tripe, left.

Preheat oven to 250°.

Trim, wash, soak, blanch, wash again, drain and cut into 1½-inch squares:

3 lb. fresh tripe

Wash and blanch about 5 minutes:

2 calves' feet, split

Peel and slice:

2 lb. onions

Dice:

¼ lb. beef suet

Line the bottom of the casserole with a layer of onions, then a layer of tripe and a sprinkling of the beef suet. Sprinkle each layer with:

Salt and pepper

Continue to build successive layers, topping with the split calves' feet and:

An onion stuck with 3 cloves
A bay leaf
A Bouquet Garni, 572

Pour over this:

¼ cup brandy or Calvados or dry white wine

and enough:

Hard cider or cider

to cover all the ingredients. Seal the casserole with a strip of pastry dough, or cover with a double thickness of foil and tie securely. Cover with a lid. No steam should escape. Bring to a boil and transfer at once to the oven. Put a drip pan under the casserole just in case! Bake in the oven at least 12 hours. When ready to serve, break the seal on the casserole, remove the bouquet garni, the bay leaf and the whole onion. Degrease the sauce and pick the meat from the calves' feet. Return the meat to the casserole to heat through and serve the tripe in individual hot covered casseroles with:

Boiled Potatoes, 317

garnished with:

Chopped parsley and chives

FRIED TRIPE

➤ Please read About Tripe, left.

Cut into squares or strips:

Cooked Tripe, left

Or, you may use blanched and parboiled tripe, but it will need about 2½ hours of simmering first in salted water.

Sprinkle with:

Salt and paprika

Dip it into:

Fritter Batter for Meat, 243

Fry in deep fat heated to 365°. Serve with:

Tartare Sauce, 364

SPANISH TRIPE

6 Servings

➤ Please read About Tripe, 509.
Wash well, then cut into 1½-inch strips:
2 lb. tripe, blanched and parboiled
Boil the tripe, covered, about 2½ hours in:
Salted water
Drain. Heat in a skillet:
2 tablespoons vegetable oil or olive oil
Add and sauté until golden:
½ cup chopped onions
1 clove garlic, pressed
Add:
1 cup tomato purée
1 small diced green pepper, seeds and membrane removed
½ teaspoon thyme, basil or oregano
1 bay leaf
½ teaspoon salt
Freshly ground pepper
Cover and simmer about 15 minutes. Add the tripe and:
(½ cup cooked minced ham)
(½ cup sliced mushrooms)
Simmer 15 minutes more. If the sauce is too dry, add a small amount of:
Red wine
Good served with:
Boiled Rice, 206

LAMB FRIES

Also known as animelles, frivolitées or "mountain oysters," these testicles of young lambs are a great delicacy.

To prepare, first cut into the loose outer skin for the entire length of the swelled surface. Remove this skin and again cut into the two inner skins in the same manner, disturbing the flesh as little as possible in peeling off these skins. An oval flesh form will remain. Soak the peeled fries in enough cold water to cover for about 3 hours, refrigerated, changing the water several times during this period. Drain. Cover fries with fresh cold water. Bring to a boil. ➤ Reduce heat at once and simmer about 6 minutes. Drain again and plunge into cold water until cool.

I. **2 Servings**

Prepare as above and slice thinly crosswise:
4 lamb fries
Fry in deep fat heated to 365° until golden. Serve with:
Lemon slices
or combine with:
Scrambled Eggs, 222

II. **2 Servings**

Prepare as above and slice across in ⅓-inch slices:
4 lamb fries
You may marinate them about 1 hour in:
(¼ cup olive oil)
(2 tablespoons lemon juice)
(1 teaspoon tarragon)
If you have marinated them, dry before rolling them in:
(Bound Breading, 552)
Or, simply sauté them briskly until golden in:
¼ cup butter or butter and olive oil
Garnish with:
Fried Parsley, 314
and serve with:
Quick Tomato Sauce, 352

CALF OR LAMB HEAD

4 Servings for a Calf Head—
2 Servings for Lamb

It is always so easy to say, "Let the butcher prepare, etc." In this case, it is assumed that he has been more than duly accommodating: he has removed the eyes, and skinned the head, then split it the long way to facilitate removing the brains. These we prefer to cook separately, 504, as well as the tongue, 507. After scraping away blood clots, soak overnight refrigerated in salted cold water to cover:
1 calf or lamb head
Wash again in cold water. You may dry the head and brown it in butter or put in a large kettle and bring to a boil:
Enough water to cover the head
with:
1 carrot
1 onion
½ sliced lemon
1 bay leaf
4 cloves
1 tablespoon salt
¼ teaspoon pepper
You may also add, to keep the bones white:
(½ cup veal kidney fat or suet)
When this mixture reaches a boil, add the head. ➤ Reduce the heat at once and simmer uncovered until the meat is tender, about 1 hour for lamb, about 2 hours for calf. If you have included the tongue, it may take a little longer. When the meat is tender, drain and remove it from the bones and dice it. Keep the meat warm. Skin, trim and slice the tongue. Meanwhile prepare a double portion of:
Rosemary Wine Sauce, 347
using as stock the liquid in which the calf head was cooked.
Season to taste
You may wish to spice the sauce with:
(Mild white wine vinegar, lemon juice, or dry white wine)
Reheat the meat, the tongue and the cooked brains in the sauce. ➤ Do not boil. Serve this dish garnished with:
Chopped parsley

HEAD CHEESE OR BRAWN

4 Servings

A well-liked old-fashioned dish of jellied meat.
Have the butcher skin and quarter:

A calf head

Clean teeth with a stiff brush and remove ears, brains, eyes, snout and most of the fat. Soak the quarters about 6 hours in cold water to extract the blood. Wash them. Barely cover with fresh cold water, to which you may add:

(2 onions)
(5 cut-up celery ribs)

Simmer until the meat is ready to fall from the bones, about 2 to 3 hours. Drain but reserve stock. Chip the meat off the bones. Dice it. Reduce the stock by one-half. Cover the meat well with the stock. Reserve the brains. Now add:

1 tablespoon salt
1 teaspoon pepper
1/8 teaspoon hot pepper sauce
1/2 teaspoon mace or sage

Cook for 1/2 hour. Pour into a mold and cover with a cloth. Put a weight on top. Chill. Serve, cut into slices, with:

French Dressing, 360

to which you have added the diced cooked brains.

BRAISED OXTAILS OR OXTAIL STEW

6 Servings

Preheat oven to 350°.
Melt in a large heavy pan:

1/4 cup butter or beef drippings

Brown in the fat:

3 oxtails, joints separated

Add:

3 cups hot Brown Stock, 522, or
1/2 stock and 1/2 tomato juice
1 teaspoon salt
2 peppercorns

Bring these ingredients to a boil, then place them in a casserole, cover, and bake until oxtails are tender, 3 to 5 hours, adding more stock if needed. For the last 45 minutes or so of cooking add:

8 small peeled onions
1/2 cup diced celery
1/4 cup peeled diced carrots

Strain stock from the oxtails and skim off most of the fat. Thicken stock with:

Flour, see Pan Gravy, 341
Season to taste

Combine meat, vegetables and gravy. Serve with a platter of:

Boiled Noodles, 213

covered with:

Au Gratin II, 553

JELLIED PIGS' OR CALVES' FEET

6 Servings

Wash, leave whole or split in halves:

6 pigs' or calves' feet

You may wrap and tie them in cheesecloth to retain their shape. Cover them with water. Add:

1 large sliced onion
1 cut clove garlic
1 sliced lemon
2 bay leaves
3 or 4 whole black peppercorns
6 or 8 whole cloves

Bring this mixture to the boiling point. ➤ Reduce the heat and ➤ simmer uncovered about 4 hours. Add boiling water, if needed. Strain the stock through a sieve and cook until reduced by one-third. Remove the skin and the bones from the pigs' feet. Place the meat in the stock. Season to taste with:

White vinegar or dry white wine

Chop and add:

(1 pimiento, optional but decorative)

Pour the pigs' feet or calves' feet into a mold and chill until the stock is firm. Slice and serve cold with:

Rémoulade Sauce, 364

STEWED PIGS' FEET

6 Servings

Follow the recipe for:

Jellied Pigs' Feet, above

During the last 30 minutes of simmering, add:

1 1/2 to 2 lb. green beans, cabbage or sauerkraut

Cook the vegetables with the pigs' feet until tender.

Season to taste

and serve hot.

PIGS' KNUCKLES AND SAUERKRAUT

8 Servings

Combine in a large pot with a lid:

2 lb. sauerkraut
4 cleaned pigs' knuckles
1 onion stuck with 2 cloves
1 1/2 teaspoons caraway seeds
1 teaspoon pepper
2 cups beer, white wine or stock

Cover and ➤ simmer gently until the meat is tender, about 3 hours. Serve with:

Boiled Potatoes, 317, or
Mashed Potatoes, 318

PIGTAILS

Wash and blanch II, 154, about 3 to 5 minutes:

Pigtails

Skim the scum off and simmer 1 1/2 to 2 hours in a seasoned stock as suggested in:

Jellied Pigs' Feet, above

Drain. Cut into serving lengths and serve with:

Turnip Greens, 305

You may make a sauce from the reduced liquid in which the meat was cooked, adding a little:

Lemon juice

PIGS' EARS

Singe and clean the insides well:

Pigs' ears

Cover with:

Salted boiling water

seasoned with:

A Bouquet Garni, 572
An onion stuck with 3 cloves

➤ Reduce the heat at once to a simmer and cook about 50 minutes. Skin the ears and cut into coarse julienne strips, 296, or in halves. You may bread them with:

(A Bound Breading, 552)

and deep-fry them at 365°, or pan-fry them. Serve as a garnish for a pork roast or as an entrée with:

Mashed Potatoes, 318

CHITTERLINGS

6 to 7 Servings

We were well along in years before we discovered that the name of this dish had an "e," an "r," a "g"—and 3 syllables, and still farther along before we found these were the base for the sausage, **Andouillette,** the French set such store by. Just after slaughtering, empty the intestines of a young pig while still warm, by turning them inside out and scraping the mucous covering off completely. Wash in cold water, then soak 24 hours refrigerated in cold salted water to cover. Then wash again in 5 or 6 waters. Remove excess fat, but leave some for flavor.

Put in a large pot with enough water to cover:

10 lb. chitterlings cut into 2-inch lengths
1 garlic clove
2 teaspoons salt
½ teaspoon pepper
½ teaspoon each thyme, clove, mace and allspice
1 bay leaf
¼ cup sliced onions
(3 red pepper pods)
2 tablespoons fresh parsley
2 tablespoons white wine vinegar

Bring slowly to a boil. Cover and ➤ reduce the heat at once and simmer 3 to 4 hours. Stir occasionally to keep it from sticking. During the last 30 minutes of cooking, you may add:

(¼ cup tomato catsup)
Season to taste

and serve with:

Corn Bread, 627, or Black-Eyed Peas, 286

SAUTÉED CHITTERLINGS

Prepare previous recipe for:

Chitterlings

omitting the vinegar and catsup. When tender, drain and dry well. Dip them in:

Seasoned Flour, 552

Sauté gently in:

Butter

until a delicate brown.

CHICKEN GIBLET STEW

Dice, put into boiling water or stock, then ➤ reduce the heat at once and simmer until tender, about 1 hour:

Chicken giblets: gizzards and hearts

Add, for the last 15 minutes of cooking:

Chopped green pepper, seeds and membrane removed
Diced onion
Sliced carrot
Chopped celery

Drain these ingredients, reserving the stock. Make:

Gravy, 341

using:

2 tablespoons butter
2 tablespoons flour to 1 cup stock, or stock and dry white wine
Season to taste

Add the giblets and vegetables and simmer ➤ but do not boil. Serve on:

Toast

or with:

Rice or noodles

COCKSCOMBS

These have been used since the time of Apicius as a garnish for chicken dishes.

Blanch:

Cockscombs

Peel off the outer skin. ➤ Steam, covered, on a:

Mirepoix, 572

moistened with:

1 cup Light Stock, 522

until tender, about 45 to 50 minutes. Drain well, cut an incision and stuff with:

Duxelles, 573, or Chicken Farce, 374

Dip in:

Allemande Sauce, 345

then in crumbs and fry in deep fat heated to 365° until the crumbs color.

ABOUT MARROW

Spinal marrow may be substituted in any of the recipes for brains. Bone marrow may be removed from split large bones. ➤ It must not be overcooked, as it is very fat and simply disintegrates under too high heat. It may be cut into ½-inch slices and softened in the top of a double boiler over—not in—boiling water; or gently and briefly poached in a little stock 1½ to 2 minutes. Serve on small toast rounds as an appetizer. It may also be gently poached in the bone in water barely to cover, or baked in a 300° oven about 1 hour. If you have used spinal marrow, remove the filament before serving. See also Marrow Balls for Soup, 196, and Osso Buco, 471.

GAME

Through the ages every art lover has enjoyed vicariously the excitement of the chase. Those of us with sportsmen in the family have had more immediate gustatory pleasures. Venison has again become easily available to hunters in many sections of the country, and small creatures are still triumphantly pursued by the rural young. Friends from France have told us of stirring and fashionable boar hunts around Poitiers in their youth. Although we never expect to hear the hunting horn ourselves or to see the fierce tusks of this formidable foe on our own table, we have had the fun of the symbolic substitute, 517, during the holiday season. And with protein so sought after, we may all become more interested in having a colony of coneys nearby from which to make Hasenpfeffer in a handsome clay casserole, as shown above. May these recipes be a help.

ABOUT SMALL GAME

Small game should be dressed as soon as possible, see Preparing Game, 810. If you are a novice, the most important things to remember are the following: ➤ Never handle any wild meat without using gloves, because of the danger of tularemia infection. ➤ Always make sure the meat of wild animals is sufficiently cooked because any omnivorous warm-blooded animal may be harboring trichinosis. Be guided in your choice of recipe by the age of the animal, using a moist-heat process, 149, for older animals. Some of the most delicious game sauces use blood as a thickener. To trap and preserve the blood, see 810. To incorporate it into a sauce, see 339.

Small game such as rabbit, squirrel and muskrat may be substituted in most recipes calling for chicken. Here are some classic, and some not so classic, recipes which take into account the special characteristics of these small animals.

ABOUT RABBITS AND HARES

Rabbits weigh between 3 and 5 pounds, while hares may weigh up to 10 to 14 pounds. European hare is all dark meat, while American domestic hare is all white. When rabbit or hare is young and fresh, the cleft in the lip is narrow, the claws smooth and sharp. Test for the youth of the animal, also, by turning the claws sideways. If they crack, the animal is old. The ears should be soft and should bend easily. A young hare has a stumpy neck and long legs. To ensure tender meat, hang the animals by the feet from 1 to 4 days. They will be tender without hanging, however, if used before they have time to stiffen. Once stiffened, they are edible as long as the hind legs are rigid, but if the joint has become pliable, discard them.

➤ To dress rabbit or hare, don gloves to avoid possible tularemia infection. Sever the front legs at the joint as shown, 514, by the dotted line. Cut through the skin around the hind legs the same way. Tie the feet together securely. Hang the rabbit on a hook where tied. From the dotted line pull skin off the legs toward the hind feet, stripping it inside out like a glove. Then pull the remaining skin over the body and forelegs. Sever the head and discard it with the skin. Slit the rabbit down the front. Remove the entrails and discard them, except for the heart and liver. Wash the carcass inside and out with acidulated water—water to which 1 or 2 tablespoons of vinegar have been added. Rinse and dry carefully. Cook by any recipe calling for chicken, especially highly seasoned dishes like curries, or use any of the following recipes.

SAUTÉED RABBIT

If rabbit is very young, prepare as for:

Sautéed Chicken, 424

Serve with:

Elderberry preserves

ROAST RABBIT OR HARE

Preheat oven to 450°.

Skin and clean:

A young rabbit or hare

Stuff it with any recipe suitable for fowl, adding the rabbit's sautéed chopped liver. Truss it. Brush the rabbit all over with:

Melted butter or vegetable oil

Dredge with:

Seasoned Flour, 552

Place on a rack on its side in a roasting pan in the oven. ➤ Reduce the heat to 350°. Baste every 15 minutes with the drippings in the pan or, if necessary, with:

(Additional butter)

Turn the rabbit when cooking time is about half over. Cook until tender, about 1½ hours. Make:

Pan Gravy, 341

Serve with:

Grated fresh horseradish and Boiled Potatoes, 317

FRICASSEE OF RABBIT OR HARE

Skin, clean and cut into pieces:

A rabbit

Dredge with:

Seasoned Flour, 552

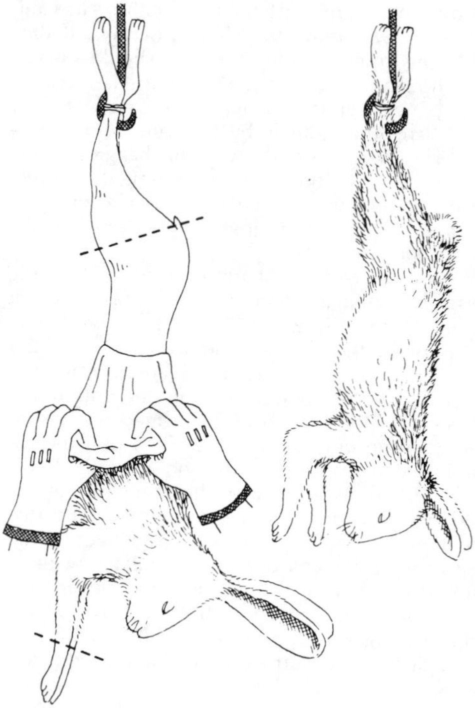

Melt in a skillet:

¼ cup butter

or you may use:

(¼ lb. diced, lightly rendered salt pork)

Add:

¼ cup chopped shallots or onions

(1 cup cut-up mushrooms)

Remove the shallots and mushrooms before sautéing the meat in the drippings until lightly browned. Flambé the rabbit by pouring over it:

(2 oz. brandy)

Add:

1½ cups stock or dry wine

and, in a cloth bag:

A piece of lemon rind

3 peppercorns

2 sprigs parsley

2 ribs celery with leaves

Cover the pot closely. Simmer the meat until done, 1 hour or more, or put it in a 300° oven covered for about 2 hours—but ➤ do not let it boil at any time. Ten minutes before you remove the rabbit from the pot, take out the seasoning bag and add the mushrooms and shallots. Place the rabbit on a hot serving dish. Remove the sauce from the heat and thicken with:

Beurre Manié, 340

BRAISED RABBIT OR HARE WITH ONIONS

Skin, clean and cut into pieces:

A rabbit

Dredge with:

Seasoned Flour, 552

Melt in a pot or skillet:

3 tablespoons drippings or butter

Sauté the rabbit in the drippings until browned. Cover thickly with:

Sliced onions

Pour over them:

1 cup cultured sour cream

Cover and simmer 1 hour, or place the pot in a 300° oven and bake the rabbit until tender, about 1½ hours.

RABBIT À LA MODE OR JUGGED HARE

In Germany this marinated stew of either hare or rabbit is known as **Hasenpfeffer;** in France, jugged rabbit is **civet de lapin,** jugged hare is **civet de lièvre.**

Skin:

A rabbit

Cut into pieces by severing the legs at the joints and cutting the back into 3 sections. Place the pieces in a crock or jar. Marinate refrigerated 24 to 48 hours in:

Cooked Marinade for Game, 529

Drain and reserve the marinade. Dry the pieces of rabbit. Dip them in:

Flour

Brown until golden in:

3 tablespoons bacon drippings

Remove the browned rabbit to an ovenproof casserole.

Preheat oven to 300°.

Sauté in the pan the rabbit was browned in:

1 cup finely chopped onions

2 tablespoons butter

Add the sauté to the casserole with the warmed marinade and bring to a boil on top of the stove. ➤ Remove at once, cover and place in the oven about 2 hours or until tender.

Season to taste

Place rabbit on a serving dish and pour sauce over it. Serve with:

Noodles, 213

CASSEROLED RABBIT AND SAUSAGE

4 Servings

Skin, clean and cut into pieces:

A rabbit

Place pieces in a large skillet and add:

1 lb. pork sausage or 3 smoked pork sausages

1 cup beer

¼ cup cider vinegar

1 cup consommé or stock

1 cup browned bread crumbs or ¼ cup rice

1 teaspoon caraway seeds

1 teaspoon grated lemon peel

1 teaspoon brown sugar

Salt and pepper

Bring to a boil, then ➤ reduce heat, cover and simmer gently 2 hours. Skim off fat before making:

Pan Gravy, 341

RABBIT WITH CHILI BEANS

4 Servings

Skin, clean and cut into pieces:

A rabbit

Brown the pieces in a large skillet in:

2 tablespoons olive oil

with:

1 clove garlic, pressed

Add:

1 cup hot water or light stock
½ teaspoon salt
½ teaspoon pepper
1 small can tomato paste: 6 oz.
1 teaspoon chili powder
2 cups kidney beans

Cover and simmer gently about 2 hours. Before serving, sprinkle with:

2 tablespoons grated cheese

Place under broiler until the cheese is golden.

SQUIRREL

➤ Please read About Small Game, 513.
Gray squirrels are preferred to red squirrels, which are quite gamy in flavor.

➤ To skin, don gloves to avoid possible tularemia infection. Cut the tail bone through from beneath, but take care not to cut through the skin of the tail. Hold squirrel by the tail and then cut the skin the width of the back, as shown center. Turn the squirrel over on its back and step on the base of the tail. Hold the hind legs in one hand and pull steadily and slowly, as shown in the center sketch, until the skin has worked itself over the front legs and head. While holding the squirrel in the same position, pull the remaining skin from the hind legs. Proceed then as for Rabbit, 513, cutting off the head and the feet and removing the internal organs, plus two small glands found in the small of the back and under each foreleg, between the ribs and the shoulders.

Stuff and roast squirrels as for Pigeons, 441, barding them, or as for Braised Chicken, 425, or use them in Brunswick Stew, 427. Season the gravy with:

Walnut Catsup, 848

and serve with:

Polenta, 201

OPOSSUM

Please read About Small Game, 513.
If possible, trap 'possum and feed it on milk and cereals for 10 days before killing. Clean, but do not skin. Treat as for pig by immersing the unskinned animal in water just below the boiling point. Test frequently by plucking at the hair. When it slips out readily, remove the opossum from the water and scrape. While scraping repeatedly, pour cool water over the surface of the animal. Remove small red glands in small of the back and under each foreleg between shoulder and ribs. Parblanch, 154, about 20 minutes each, in two or three changes of water, then roast as for pork, 477, or use recipes for rabbit. Serve with:

Turnip greens

PORCUPINE

➤ Please read About Small Game, 513. Skin by hanging back legs from hooks. Remove kernels in small of back and under forelegs. Hang in a cool dry place 48 hours. Soak overnight refrigerated in salted water:

1 porcupine

In the morning, bring this water to a boil. Drain and immerse porcupine again in cold water. Bring to a boil and again drain. Place the meat in a Dutch oven. Add:

3 cups water or light stock
1 rib celery, chopped
1 sliced medium-sized onion
¼ teaspoon pepper
1 teaspoon salt

Simmer until tender, about 2½ hours.

RACCOON

➤ Please read About Small Game, 513. Skin and remove glands in small of back and on either side of spine, and one under each foreleg of:

1 raccoon

Remove all fat, inside and out. Soak overnight refrigerated in:

Salt water

Blanch, 154, for 45 minutes. Add:

2 tablespoons baking soda

and continue to cook uncovered for 5 minutes.

Drain and wash in warm water. Put in cold water and bring to a boil. ➤ Reduce heat and simmer 15 minutes.
Preheat oven to 350°.
Stuff the raccoon with:

Sweet Potato and Apple Dressing, 374

Bake, covered, about 45 minutes. ➤ Uncover and bake 15 minutes longer before serving.

MUSKRAT

4 Servings

➤ Please read About Small Game, 513.
Skin and remove all fat from hams and shoulders of:

1 muskrat

These are the only edible portions. Remove musk glands under legs and belly and white stringy tissue attached to musk glands. Poach, 150, in salted water for 45 minutes. Drain. Place cut-up meat in Dutch oven and cover with:

Bacon strips

Add:

1 cup water or light stock
1 small sliced onion
1 bay leaf
3 cloves
½ teaspoon thyme

Cover and simmer until very tender. Serve with:

Creamed Celery, 297

WOODCHUCK

➤ Please read About Small Game, 513.
After field-dressing woodchuck and hanging it for 48 hours, skin as for rabbit, but watch for and remove 7 to 9 small kernel-like glands under the forelegs. Soak refrigerated overnight in salted water. Drain and wipe dry. Cook by any recipe for rabbit or chicken.

BEAVER

➤ Please read About Small Game, 513.
Use young animals only. Remove all surface fat when skinning, but avoid cutting musk glands, which must be removed from beneath the skin in front of the genital organs. Also remove kernels in small of back and under each foreleg. Hang in the cold for several days. Poach, 150, in salted water for 1 hour. Braise as for beef, 447, until tender.

BEAVER TAIL

To Indians and settlers alike, this portion of the animal was considered the greatest. Hold over open flame until rough skin blisters. Remove from heat. When cool, peel off skin. Roast over coals or ➤ simmer until tender.

ARMADILLO

Under its shell this small scaly creature has a light meat, porklike in flavor.
Draw and cut free from the shell:

1 armadillo

Discard fat and all but the back meat. Wash thoroughly in cold water and soak overnight refrigerated in cold water. Drain and dry. To cook, cut into pieces. Brush well with:

Butter or vegetable oil

Broil until the meat is a rich brown.

Season to taste

and serve at once.

ABOUT LARGE GAME

Today, when hunters are so aware of the need to treat their booty with care from the moment it is shot, joy can prevail. See About Preparing Game, 810. No matter what the method of handling, certain preparations are basic. Game shot in an unsuspecting moment is more tender and will also deteriorate less quickly than game that is chased. Avoid buying any trapped animals for food. Immediate and careful gutting, immediate removal of all hair near exposed flesh, and prompt skinning are essential. In dressing game, be careful not to cut into musk glands on lower belly.

➤ Care must be taken to remove all fat from any of these game animals, as it grows rancid quickly. ➤ Do not use it to grease pans or for sautéing or browning. The livers and heart, after cooling, are often eaten at the campsite. As with all game, the lushness of the season and the age of the animal contribute to the decision as to how to cook it. For Marinades for Game, see 529. Cultured Buttermilk Marinade, 528, will lessen the gamy flavor of the antlered animals.

For sauces for game, see 356. Cabbage, turnips, chestnuts and mushrooms are often suggested as classic game accompaniments, as are brandied fruits.

ABOUT VENISON

This romantic word can cover any of the edible animals taken in the chase, but we are discussing here only antlered types. A famous sportsman called venison a gift of joy to some, a matter of secret interment to others. ➤ Please read About Large Game, above.

The choice cuts of very young deer and of fat old bucks can be roasted or broiled as for beef. Since venison is lean, it needs larding, 444, or barding, 420. Other cuts should be marinated and cooked as for any moist-processed beef, 447. Reindeer meat also is cooked as for beef.

Moose meat, which is relatively fat, calls for cooking like pork and can also have the same sweet and sweet-sour garnishes and sauces. Elk is close to beef in taste and texture. Cook elk calf as for veal, but watch it for spoilage, as it sours quickly.

Mouffle, the loose covering around the nose and lips of the moose or elk, is prized for stewing or roasting. Cook as for Fresh Tongue, 507.

SADDLE OF DEER, MOOSE OR ELK

8 Servings

Preheat oven to 550°.
Lard, 444:
A 6- to 7-lb. saddle of venison
Rub it with:
A cut clove of garlic
Butter
Place the roast, fat side up, uncovered on a rack in the oven. ➤ Reduce the heat to 350° and bake, allowing in all 20 minutes to the pound. Make:
Pan Gravy, 341
Serve with:
Hot Cumberland Sauce, 356
Wild Rice, 212

ROAST LEG OF VENISON

Bard, 420, the roast. Cook as for Roast Beef, 454.

SAUTÉED VENISON STEAKS

I. Have ready:
Young venison steaks, ½ inch thick
Before cooking, rub with:
Garlic
To keep them crisp and brown on the outside, rare and juicy within, sauté them in:
1 tablespoon butter
2 tablespoons vegetable oil
5 to 6 minutes to the side. Serve with:
Hot Cumberland Sauce, 356
or with:
Maître d'Hôtel Butter, 350
or with:
Puréed celery with croutons and Sauce Poivrade, 347

II. Soak for 24 hours refrigerated:
Venison steaks, ¾ inch thick
in:
Lamb or Game Marinade, 528
Drain and dry. Sauté and serve as directed in I, above.

BRAISED VENISON

For this process, use the less tender cuts of meat either in 1 large piece or cut into small ones, but be sure to remove all fat. Place the meat in a marinade, 528, from 12 to 48 hours in the refrigerator. Turn it from time to time. Dry it. Prepare as for Pot Roast, 459. Use the marinade in the stock. Cook until tender; the length of time will depend on the age of the animal.

VENISONBURGER

To make this lean meat more interesting in ground form, combine:
2 parts ground venison
with:
1 part fresh sausage meat
Cook as for Hamburger, 487, but allow extra time ➤ to be sure the meat is no longer pink.

VENISON MEAT LOAF

Prepare:
Meat Loaf I, 493
using:
¾ lb. ground venison
¼ lb. ground sausage

BEAR

➤ Please read About Large Game, opposite.
Remove all fat and bone from bear meat. The fat turns rancid very quickly. If rendered at once, it is prized for cooking; if held, it is good only for boot grease. All bear is edible. Tough, strongly flavored bear may be improved by refrigerating at least 24 hours in an oil-based marinade before cooking. Cook, after marination, as for any recipe for Beef Pot Roast or Stew, 459. Bear cub will need about 2½ hours' cooking; for an older animal, allow 3½ to 4 hours. ➤ Bear, like pork, can carry trichinosis, so be sure the meat is always well cooked through.

PECCARY

Immediately after killing, remove the musk glands in the middle of the back. This meat needs marinating before cooking. After this, you may prepare it as in any moist-heat pork recipe, 479–482.

WILD BOAR

Use only very young animals, a year or under, and prepare as for:
Suckling Pig, 478
If older, prepare by a moist-heat process for:
Pork, 479–482

★ STUFFED BOAR'S HEAD

30 Servings

Among treasured Christmas traditions, like the gilded peacock, the boar's head ranks high, see illustration on 513. While this fierce creature may not be available, his domestic counterpart still subsists in Appalachia and can even be ordered in supermarkets throughout the U.S. during the holiday season. The separate ingredients for the stuffing can be prepared and refrigerated a day or two in advance, with the final mixing taking place immediately before stuffing and roasting the head.

After experiments with several different methods of preparing a boar's head, the following rather unconventional foil procedure was found to be most effective. It culminates in a gloriously glazed and garnished presentation. So gird up your loins for the fray and prepare to receive a hero's reward in gratitude from your assembled guests.

To loosen the head skin and to cook the head meat, place on a shallow rack in a large ham boiler:
A 15- to 18-lb. head of a young boar or pig
with eyes, teeth and brains intact. Pour into the boiler:
Water

deep enough to cover 1 inch of the base of the head, and keep the water ➤ simmering at that depth while steaming, covered, 2 to 3 hours.

After removing the head from the boiler, refrigerate it to chill thoroughly. When ready to remove the skin all in one piece, let the head reach a temperature warm enough on the outside so the skin is pliable. Put the head on a large cutting board. With a short thin knife, make a lengthwise incision from the base of the snout to the base of the neck skin. Beginning at the end of the incision, ➤ gently and carefully, especially around the eyes, cut upward under the skin on both sides to loosen the skin as you go. Continue to release the skin, being careful not to puncture it. Some fat will adhere to the skin; leave it on, as it will render away during the roasting and will help give the final brown and shiny look you want in the finished product. Fold and keep the skin chilled in a plastic wrapping until ready to stuff it.

Now start to remove the head meat. If it proves not to be tender enough to cut easily into bite-sized pieces, return the skinned head to the pot and steam 1 hour longer. When cutting, discard as much of the fat as possible. If meat still seems undercooked, you may sauté the small pieces very slowly until gray throughout. Discard the overcooked brains and eyes. Also discard the skull, and refrigerate the head meat until ready to prepare the stuffing.

STUFFING FOR BOAR'S HEAD

Have ready:

A 2- to 3-lb. cooked Boston butt pork roast, cut into bite-sized pieces
2 lb. cooked ground pork sausage
7 cups Boiled long-grain Rice, 206

Heat in a very large pot:

5 tablespoons butter

Add and sauté until golden, then cover and simmer until tender:

2 cups chopped onions
1 cup chopped celery
1 tablespoon poultry seasoning or Four Spices, 572
1 to 1½ teaspoons sage
½ teaspoon salt

Gently stir in:

1 cup dry white wine
1 cup Chicken Stock, 523
1 lb. coarsely chopped walnuts or Boiled Chestnuts, 298

and the cut-up cooked pork, the cooked sausage and the head meat. If there is excess fat, remove it. Take the pot off the heat and add:

6 cups seasoned coarse dry bread crumbs or cubes

The stuffing should have a ➤ moist, not wet, quality, as fat rendered from the skin will give it added cohesion. If you feel it needs more moisture, you may add:

(½ cup additional wine or stock)

Preheat oven to 325°.

Now to the stuffing of the skin, which needs two people. Have the skin at room temperature or warm enough so it is pliable. Prepare a large roasting pan with a rack. Cover the rack with heavy-duty foil, first lengthwise and then crosswise, allowing long enough pieces to eventually encompass the whole head and form a pyramid shape over the top. Neatly cut a lengthwise 5-inch gash through the center of the foil to allow excess fat to drain into the roaster. Place the skin "face up" in the middle of the foil, with the snout facing you. Should the skin have split at the bridge of the snout during the steaming, you can repair it with skewers or by sewing it with loose stitches, using a coarse thread and a meat or upholstery needle, 445. Do not tighten the stitches, as the stuffing will expand and damage the skin further. Or, you may even leave the split if you subsequently tighten the foil well when shaping up the head.

As one person lightly stuffs the hollow head, his helper carefully draws the foil up and around the head skin, letting it assume its own shape. You may have to lift the head slightly for it to shape up. When no more stuffing can be inserted without packing it, cover the open cavity with foil and crimp the foil tightly over the bridge of the snout and over eye openings, carefully pulling so it conforms to the head shape and also supports it. Protect the ears with additional foil so they will not burn.

Put any leftover stuffing in a separate ovenproof dish for the last hour of baking the head. Bake the head about 2 hours or until the skin is brown and lightly crisped. Serve on a large platter with the foil cut away. Surround with a lush bed of garnishes such as:

Glazed Vegetables, 280
Colorful drained poached fruits, 126, or greens

Place in each eye:

Halves of hard-cooked egg, 220

and under the snout:

An apple

For tusks, use:

Small scraped carrots

and, traditionally, a small flag is waving from the top of the head when it is brought to the table with a fanfare! The boar's head may be served with your favorite Christmas roast.

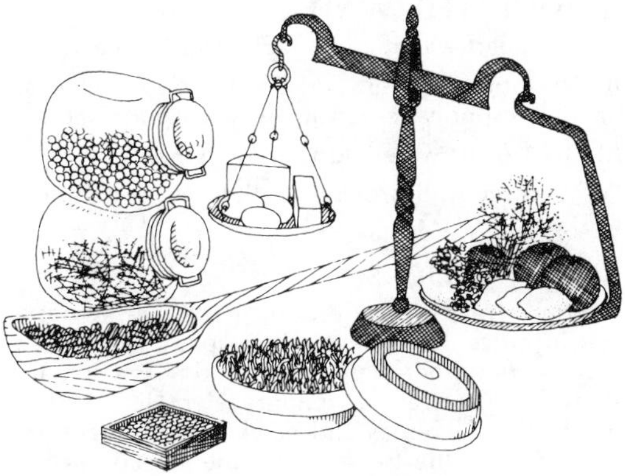

KNOW YOUR INGREDIENTS

What a wealth of materials we have to work with! Staples like milks and stocks, oils, beans, sprouts, honeys, gelatins, leavens, cheese and eggs, nuts, seeds, herbs, and exotics like chocolates and spices. Where do these supplies fit into your kitchen maneuvers? What qualities make them interchangeable? Which must you compensate for?

Oddly enough, many of the most basic cooking materials—those that go into ninety-nine out of a hundred recipes—are so familiar, or rather so constantly used, that their characteristics are taken for granted even by experienced cooks. And, by beginners, their peculiarities are often simply ignored. Yet success in cooking depends largely on one's becoming fully aware of how both common and uncommon ingredients react. Here and now we put them all—from water to weather—under the magnifying glass and point out just what it is that they contribute to the cooking process. With the knowledge gained in this chapter and the chapter on Heat, plus the information keyed by symbol and reference into our recipes at the point of use, we assure you a continuous and steady development from would-be to sure-fire cook.

ABOUT WATER

One of our family jokes involved an 1890 debutante cousin from Indianapolis who, when asked where her hometown got its water, replied: "Out of a faucet." Many of us have come to assume that there is a kind of nationwide standardization in tap water. As long as it runs clear, plentiful, hot and cold, and reasonably pleasant to the taste, few of us bother our heads further about its purity than did our pretty Victorian cousin. Yet there is a growing awareness that a galaxy of pollutants such as viruses, nitrates, heavy metals, pesticides, and asbestos and other carcinogens can and must be removed from our water supplies, just as purifying plants were set up earlier to control the bacteria that produced cholera, typhoid and dysentery. Both the quality and the composition of water remain essential to community health. And they are not irrelevant to the results we achieve in our kitchens.

In this book, when the word ➤ water appears in the recipes, we assume it has a 60° to 80° temperature. ➤ If hotter or colder water is needed, it is specified.

➤ Soft water is best for most cooking processes, although very soft water will make yeast doughs soggy and sticky. ➤ Hard water and some artificially softened waters affect flavor. They may toughen legumes and fruits and shrivel pickles. They markedly alter the color of vegetables in the cabbage family and turn onions, cauliflower, potatoes and rice yellow. If your water is hard, cooking these vegetables *à blanc,* 447, is a superior method of preparation. Hard water retards fermentation of yeast, although it strengthens the gluten in flour. Alkaline waters, however, have a solvent effect on gluten, as well as diminishing its gas-retaining properties—and, consequently, the size of the loaf.

Water hardness is due to various combinations of salts, and there are a number of ways by which it may be reduced. Passing hard water through a tank containing counteractive chemicals may be helpful, but most of these systems principally exchange sodium for calcium compounds and are more effective in treating water used in dishwashing than water used in cooking. If the salts happen to consist of bicarbonates of calcium and magnesium, simply boiling the water for 20 or 30 minutes will cause them to precipitate. But if the water originally held in solution large amounts of sulfates, boiling it will increase hardness rather than reduce it, because the sulfates are concentrated by evaporation. ➤ Certain types of hard water must be avoided by people who are on low-sodium or salt-free diets.

Sodium chloride, or common salt, may occur in inland as well as ocean waters. The Public Health Service's drinking water standards recommend that not more than .025% salt be permitted in a public drinking water supply. Should you be interested in finding out what type of water you have, call your local waterworks or health department if you live in a town, or your county agent if you live in the country.

Most old recipes recommend long soaking of food in water. But we know that fruits, salad greens and vegetables should be washed as quickly as possible. Soaking leaches out water-soluble vitamins. ➤ And, because of this leaching action, it is a good plan to utilize soaking and cooking waters, unless they have bitter or off-flavors or unless discarding is specified in a given recipe.

Occasionally recipes indicate ➤ water by weight, in which case use 1 tablespoon for ½ ounce, 1 cup for 8 ounces, 2 cups for 1 pound.

▲ The boiling temperature of water at sea level —212°—is increased in direct proportion to the number of particles dissolved in it. The amount of salt added in cooking is not enough to change the normal sea-level boiling point. With the addition of sugar, however, the boiling point is lowered appreciably. For boiling at high altitudes, see 145.

WATER PURIFICATION

In using or storing water, be sure of two things: that the source from which you get it is uncontaminated, and that the vessels you store it in are sterile. The color of water has nothing to do with its purity. As disease germs are more often derived from animal than from vegetable matter, a brown swamp water may be purer than a blue lake water. ➤ If water has been exposed to radioactive fallout, do not use it. Water from wells and springs, if protected from surface contamination, should be safe from this hazard. For water storage in shelters, use plastic bottles or glass ones that are surrounded by and separated from each other by excelsior or packing. Inspect the stored water periodically and replace any that is cloudy. Allow for each person, for drinking, a minimum of 7 gallons for each 2-week period; and for personal cleanliness, another 7 gallons.

If you are in doubt as to the purity of water, treat it in one of the following ways:

I. Boil water vigorously 3 minutes. Boiled water tastes flat but can be improved in flavor if aerated by pouring it a number of times from one clean vessel to another.

II. Use water purification tablets in the dosage recommended on the label.

III. Add to ➤ clear water, allowing 8 drops per gallon, any household bleach that contains hypochlorite in 5.25% solution. The label should give you this information. ➤ If the water is cloudy, increase to 16 drops per gallon. ➤ In either case, stir and allow the water to stand 30 minutes after adding the hypochlorite. ➤ The water should have a distinct chlorine taste and odor. This is a sign of safety, and if you do not detect it by smell, add another dose of the hypochlorite and wait 15 minutes. If the chlorine odor is still not present, the hypochlorite may have weakened through age, and the water is not safe for storage or drinking.

IV. ➤ Add to clear water, allowing 12 drops per gallon, 2% tincture of iodine. Stir thoroughly before storing. ➤ To cloudy water, allow 24 drops for each gallon. Stir thoroughly before storing or drinking. This method is not recommended for persons with thyroid disturbances.

ACIDULATED WATER

I. To 1 quart water, add 1 tablespoon vinegar.

II. To 1 quart water, add 2 tablespoons vinegar or 3 tablespoons lemon juice (1 teaspoon salt).

III. To 1 quart water, add ½ cup wine.

IV. Also see Anti-Browning Solutions for Canning, 805, and for Freezing, 823.

ABOUT STOCKS

Antique dealers may respond hopefully to dusty bits in attics, but true cooks palpitate over even more curious oddments: mushroom and tomato skins, fowl carcasses, tender celery leaves, fish heads, knucklebones and chicken feet. These are just a few of the treasures for the stockpot—that magic source from which comes the telling character of the cuisine. The juices made and saved from meat and vegetable cookery are so important that in France they are called bases or **fonds.** You will note in the recipes for gravies, aspics, soups or sauces the insistent call for stocks. While these need not always be heavily reduced ones ➤ do experiment by tasting the wonderful difference when these liquids replace water. ➤ When stocks are specified in long-cooking recipes, they are always meat stocks, as vegetable and fish stocks deteriorate in flavor if simmered longer than 30 minutes.

You will want to store separately, refrigerated, and use very sparingly certain strongly flavored waters like cabbage, carrot, turnip and bean or those from starchy vegetables, if the stock is to be a clear one. And you will certainly reserve any light-fleshed fish and shellfish residues for use in fish dishes exclusively. Fish and vegetable stocks with vegetable oils are important in **au maigre** cooking, on those days when religious observance calls for meatless meals, as contrasted with **au gras** or meat—and meat-fat-based—cooking.

Like us, you may look askance at the liquids in which modern hams and tongues have been cooked, because of the chemicals now used in curing. If you use cooking waters from salt meat, even a preliminary blanching, 154, may not reduce salt content sufficiently to allow its use in sauces. You will never, of course, want to use the cooking water from an "old" ham. But whether you are a purist who uses only beef-based stock with beef, and chicken with chicken, or whether you experiment with more complex combinations, for both nutrient values and taste dividends ➤ do make and save stocks.

MEAT STOCK MAKING

While we urge you to utilize the kitchen oddments described under Household Stock, 523, we become daily more aware that the neatly packaged meats and vegetables most of us get at the supermarket give us a decreasing minimum of trimmings. The rabbits, old pheasants and hens that make for such picturesque reading in ancient stock recipes—fairly thrusting the hunter and farmer laden with earthy bounty straight into the kitchen—have given way to a well-picked-over turkey carcass and a specially purchased **soup bunch** including celery stalks and leaves, carrots, green onions and parsley. But even these are worthwhile.

➤ Stock making is an exception to almost every other kind of cooking. Instead of calling for things young and tender ➤ remember that mature vegetables and meat from aged animals will be most flavorsome. Remember, too, that instead of making every effort to keep juices within the materials you are cooking, you want to extract and trap every vestige of flavor from them—in liquid form. So ➤ soaking in cold water and starting to cook in cold water—both of which methods draw juices—are the first steps to your goal; but have the ingredients to be cooked and the water at the same temperature at the onset of cooking. ➤ Bones are disjointed or crushed; meat is trimmed of excess fat and cut up; and vegetables, after cleaning, may even be ⅄ blended.

➤ In making dark stocks, browning a portion of the meat or roasting it until brown, but not scorched, will add flavor, but before proceeding, pour off any grease that develops. ➤ For a sturdy meat stock, allow only 2 cups of water to every cup of lean meat and bone. They may be used in about equal weights. When this much meat is used, only a few vegetables are needed to give flavor to the soup.

Bones, especially marrowbones and ones with gelatinous extractives, play a very important role in stock. But if a too large proportion of them is used, the stock becomes gluey and should be reserved for use in gravies and sauces. Raw and cooked bones should not be mixed if a clear stock is desired. Nor, for clear stock, should any starchy or very greasy foods be added to the stockpot. Starchy foods also tend to make the stock sour rapidly.

Essential to retaining the flavor of the extracted juices most is ➤ a steady low heat for the simmering of the brew. You may laugh at the following primitive suggestion. But it is our answer to the thinness of modern pots and the passing of that precious source of household heat, "the back of the stove," now found only in special equipment. ➤ If you do not have an asbestos pad to produce an evenly transmitted heat, get two or three bricks—depending on the size of your pot and the size of the heating area. Put them on your burner, set at low heat and place your soup pot on them, as shown in the sketch opposite. You need then have no worries about boiling over or about disturbing the long, steady simmering rhythm. Or, for a similar effect, use a double boiler. When choosing a heavy stockpot, avoid aluminum, as it may affect the clarity of the stock.

As the stock heats, quite a heavy scum rises to the surface. ➤ If a clear soup is wanted, it is imperative to skim this foamy albuminous material before the first half hour of cooking. After the last skimming, wipe the edge of the stockpot at the level of the soup. Some nutritionists advise against skimming stocks to be used for brown sauces.

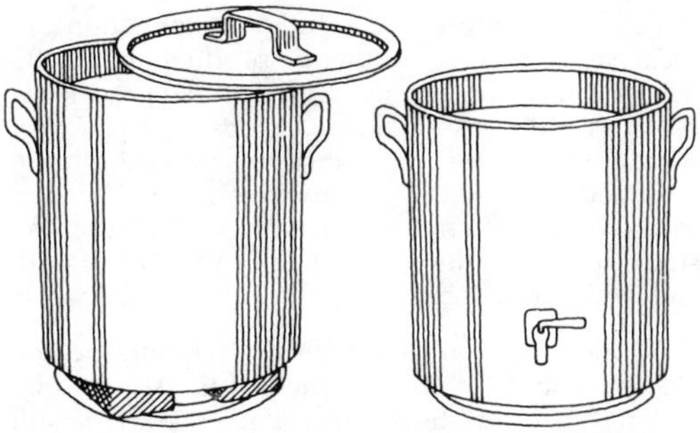

Add whatever seasoning vegetables are called for and simmer the stock ➤ partially covered, with the lid at an angle, until you are sure you have extracted all the goodness from the ingredients—at least 2 hours, and as long as 12 if raw bones are used. To keep the stock clear, drain it, not by pouring, but by ladling. Or use a stockpot with a spigot. Then strain the stock through 2 layers of cheesecloth that have been wrung out in water. Cool it ➤ uncovered. To cool quickly, place the stock in a tall container and partially immerse in cold water. Store it ➤ tightly covered and refrigerated. The grease will rise in a solid mass which is also a protective coating. Do not remove this until you are ready to reheat the stock for serving or use. For more about this coating, see About Drippings, 542.

Stocks keep 3 to 4 days refrigerated; for a longer period if frozen. The best practice is to bring them to a boil at the end of this period and cool partially before re-storing. It is also good practice to bring them to a boil if adding other pot liquors to them.

SEASONINGS FOR STOCKS AND SOUPS

These all-important ingredients ➤ should be added sparingly, about half an hour after the soup begins to simmer and the scum has been removed. The seasoning should be corrected again just before the soup is served.

➤ Never salt heavily at the beginning of stock making. The great reduction both in original cooking and in subsequent cooking—if the stock is used as an ingredient—makes it almost impossible to judge the amount you will need. And a little extra salt can so easily ruin your results. If stocks are stored, the salt and seasoning are apt to intensify, and if any wine is used in dishes made from stock, the salt flavor will be increased.

The discreet use of either fresh or dried herbs and spices is important. Use whole spices—peppercorns, allspice, cinnamon and coriander—and celery seeds and bay leaf, but not too much. Add mace, paprika and cayenne in the stingiest pinches. Be sure to use a Bouquet Garni, 572. For a quick soup, try a Chiffonade, 571. An onion stuck with two or three cloves is de rigueur, and, if available, add one or two leeks.

CLARIFYING STOCK

If you have followed carefully the directions in Meat Stock Making, 520, your product should be clear enough for most uses. But for extra-sparkling aspic, jellied consommé, or chaud-froid you may wish to clarify stock in one of two ways. Both are designed to remove cloudiness; the second method also strengthens flavor. ➤ Be sure the stock to be clarified has been well degreased, and never let it boil.

I. Allow to each quart of broth 1 slightly beaten egg white and 1 crumpled shell. If the stock to be clarified has not been fully cooled and is still lukewarm, also add a few ice cubes for each quart. Stir the eggs and the ice into the soup well. Bring the soup very, very slowly ➤ without stirring, just to a simmer. As the soup heats, the egg brings to the top a heavy, crusty foam more than an inch thick. Do not skim this, but push it very gently away from one side of the pan. Through this small opening, you can watch the movement of the simmering—to make sure no true boiling takes place. Continue simmering 10 to 15 minutes. Move the pot carefully from the heat source and let it stand 10 minutes to 1 hour. Wring out a cloth in hot water and suspend it, like a jelly bag, above a large pan. Again push the scummy crust to one side and ladle the soup carefully, straining it through the cloth. Cool ➤ uncovered. Store ➤ covered tightly and refrigerated.

II. This method of clarification produces a double-strength stock for consommé. Add to each quart of degreased stock 3 to 4 ounces of lean ground beef and 1 egg white and crumpled shell, and to the pot several uncooked fowl carcasses; and, if the stock is beef, fresh tomato skins. Some cooks also use a few vegetables. Beat these additions into the stock. Then ➤ very slowly bring the pot just to a simmer.

If the stock has boiled at any time during the process just described, the clarification is ruined. It will be necessary to start over again, proceeding as follows. After what should have been the simmering period in the second method, remove the pot from the heat and skim it. Allow the stock to cool to about 70°. Again add an egg white and a crumpled eggshell for each quart of stock. Then continue as for the first method above. Simmer up to 2 hours. Then remove the pot from the heat source and let it rest an hour or more. Ladle and strain it, as previously described. Cool ➤ uncovered. Store ➤ tightly covered and refrigerated.

REDUCING STOCKS OR GLAZES

Glazes are meat stocks cooked down very slowly, uncovered, until they have solidified and have formed a glutinous substance that will coat a spoon. Reduction usually involves condensing to about half the original amount of liquid. See Glazes and Glaçage, 367. When we have the patience to make them, these overpoweringly strong stocks from meat and fowl are most valuable for seasoning and finishing. They ✱ freeze very well, too.

BROWN STOCK

I. **About 2 Quarts**

➤ Please read About Stocks, 520.

Cut into pieces and brown in a 350° oven:

6 lb. lean shin bones and marrow bones

Place them in a large stockpot with:

4 quarts cold water

Bring slowly to a boil. ➤ Reduce heat and simmer, uncovered, about 30 minutes. Remove scum, see left, and add:

8 black peppercorns
6 whole cloves
1 bay leaf
1 teaspoon thyme
3 sprigs parsley
1 large diced carrot
3 ribs celery, diced
1 cup drained canned or fresh tomatoes
1 diced medium-sized onion
1 diced small white turnip

Bring to a boil and then simmer, partly covered, at least 6 hours. Strain the stock. Cool uncovered, and refrigerate covered.

II. **About 3½ Cups**

While Brown Stock I is more strongly flavored and clearer, do not scorn stocks made from cooked meats and bones. ➤ Please read About Stocks, 520.

Cut the meat from the bone. Place in a heavy stockpot:

2 cups cooked lean meat and bones
4 to 5 cups cold water

Bring the stock just to the boiling point, turn down the heat, and simmer, uncovered, 30 minutes. Remove the scum. Add:

¼ teaspoon salt
1 cup chopped vegetables: carrots, turnips, celery, parsley, etc.
1 small onion
1 cup tomatoes
½ teaspoon sugar
4 peppercorns
¼ teaspoon celery salt

Continue to simmer, partly covered, about 2 hours. Strain the stock and chill it. Remove the fat, reheat and season to taste before using.

LIGHT STOCK WITH VEAL

About 2 Quarts

➤ Please read About Stocks, 520.

Blanch 5 minutes, using method II, 154:

4 lb. veal knuckles or 3 lb. veal knuckles and 1 lb. beef

Drain, discard water, and add meat and bones to:

4 quarts cold water

Bring slowly to a boil. ➤ Reduce the heat at once and simmer, uncovered, about ½ hour. Remove scum. Add:

8 white peppercorns
1 bay leaf
1 teaspoon thyme
6 whole cloves
6 sprigs parsley
1 diced medium-sized onion
3 ribs celery, diced
1 diced medium-sized carrot

Continue to simmer, partly covered, 2½ to 3 hours or until reduced by about half. Strain stock and ➤ cool uncovered. Refrigerate covered.

LIGHT STOCK FROM POULTRY

I. From Poultry Parts **About 2 Quarts**

➤ Please read about soup stocks, 521.

Blanch 5 minutes, using method II, 154:

4 lb. poultry backs, necks, wings and feet

Drain, discard water and bring the poultry slowly to a boil in:

4 quarts cold water

➤ Reduce the heat at once and simmer, uncovered, about 30 minutes. Add:

8 white peppercorns
1 bay leaf
1 teaspoon thyme
6 whole cloves
6 sprigs parsley
1 diced medium-sized onion
3 ribs celery, diced
1 medium-sized diced carrot

Remove the scum and continue to simmer, partly covered, about 3 hours or until reduced by half. Strain stock. Cool uncovered, and refrigerate covered.

II. From Chicken Feet

A jellied, not too flavorful, but economical base. Cover with boiling water:

Chicken feet

Blanch them about 3 minutes. Drain. Strip away the skin and discard. Chop off the nails. Place the feet in a pan and cover with:

Cold water

Bring to a boil and ➤ reduce heat at once. Simmer, uncovered, about 30 minutes. Remove scum. Add:

Vegetables

as suggested under Fowl Stock I, below. Continue to simmer about 1½ hours, or use a ✪ pressure cooker, following directions in Quick Household Stock, below. Strain the stock and cool uncovered. Refrigerate covered.

FOWL, RABBIT OR GAME STOCK OR FUMET

When cold, this stock should solidify sufficiently to make a good aspic without additional gelatin.

I. **About 9 or 10 Cups**

Put into a heavy pot:

4 or 5 lb. cut-up fowl or rabbit
3 quarts cold water

Bring to a boil and ➤ reduce heat at once. Simmer uncovered, about 30 minutes. Remove scum. Add:

5 celery ribs with leaves
½ bay leaf
½ cup chopped onions
½ cup chopped carrots
6 sprigs parsley

Continue to simmer the stock for about 2½ hours, partly covered. Strain and season to taste. Cool uncovered, and refrigerate covered. Degrease before serving.

II. **1½ to 2½ Pints**

The housewife frequently meets up with the leavings of a party bird from which a good stock can be made. Try this simpler soup when you have leftover cooked chicken, duck or turkey.

Break into small pieces:

1 cooked chicken, duck or turkey carcass

Cover with:

4 to 6 cups water

The amount of liquid will depend on the size or number of carcasses you use. Bring slowly to a boil and ➤ reduce heat at once. Simmer, uncovered, about ½ hour. Remove scum. Add:

1 cup chopped celery with tender leaves
1 large onion, sliced
½ cup chopped carrots
Lettuce leaves
½ bay leaf
3 or 4 peppercorns
Parsley
A Bouquet Garni, 572

Continue to simmer, partly covered, 1 to 1½ hours. Strain and cool uncovered. Refrigerate covered. Degrease before serving.

✪ QUICK HOUSEHOLD STOCK

A careful selection of refrigerator oddments can often produce enough valid ingredients to make up a flavorful stock to use as a reinforcer for soups—canned, dried and frozen—and in gravies and sauces. If cooked and uncooked meats are combined, a darker, cloudier stock results. Put into a pressure cooker and use in all:

1 cup nonfat meat, bone and vegetables, cooked and uncooked
1 to 1½ cups cold water

Use the smaller amount of water if you are short on meat. For vegetables, see Vegetable Stock Making, 524. ➤ Do not fill the pressure cooker more than half full. If raw meat and bone are included, add:

(2 tablespoons vinegar)

and cook the raw ingredients first for 10 minutes at 15 pounds pressure. ➤ Reduce pressure and add the cooked meats and the vegetables and cook about 10 minutes longer at 15 pounds pressure. Reduce pressure. Strain the stock and cool uncovered. Refrigerate covered.

FUMET OR FISH STOCK

About 3 Cups

Most useful for cooking *au maigre*. Combine the fumet with vegetables and cream as a base for soup or use it in sauces or aspics. It will keep for several days, covered, in the refrigerator, or for several weeks frozen.

I. Place in a pan:

2½ cups cold water
½ cup chopped onions or shallots
¼ cup chopped carrots
½ cup chopped celery
6 white peppercorns
3 or 4 cloves
A Bouquet Garni, 572
A twist of lemon rind
½ cup dry white wine or 2 tablespoons lemon juice
1 to 1½ lb. washed lean fish bones, tails, skins, trimmings, and heads with the gills removed

The fish heads are particularly flavorful, but ➤ avoid trimmings from strong-flavored fish like mackerel, skate or mullet. Use salmon only for salmon sauce. Shells from crab, shrimp and lobster are delicious additions. Heat until the liquid begins to ➤ simmer, and continue simmering, uncovered, no longer than 15 minutes—or a bitter flavor may develop. Skim the surface to remove scum and foam. Add, at the last minute:

Any extra oyster or clam juices

Strain the stock and use in soups or sauces. To clarify fish fumet for aspic, proceed as for the first method of stock clarification, 522.

II. An emergency fish stock.
Combine and simmer, uncovered, until liquid is reduced to 2½ cups:

1 cup water
1 cup dry vermouth
1 cup bottled clam juice
2 diced celery ribs
1 diced small onion
3 sprigs parsley

Strain and before using.

Season to taste

VEGETABLE STOCK MAKING

In making vegetable stock, your goal is to draw all the flavor out of the vegetable. Use 1½ to 2 times as much water as vegetable. Prepare vegetables as you would for eating—wash, scrape or pare, as needed, and remove bruised or bad portions. Onions are the exception: the skins may be left on to give color to the stock.

➤ For quicker cooking and greater extraction, you may ⅄ blend the vegetables before cooking. But it is very important to taste the vegetable liquors you reserve. They vary tremendously, depending on the age of the vegetable and whether the leaves are dark outer ones or light inner ones. Green celery tops, for instance, can become bitter through long cooking in a stock, while the tender yellowish leaves do not. Often, too, celery is so heavily sprayed with chemicals that the outer leaves and tops taste strongly enough of these absorbed flavors to carry over into foods. Nutritionists recommend the outer leaves of vegetables because of their greater vitamin content. Eat these raw in salads, where the bitterness is not accented, as it is in soups or stocks.

Also balance the amounts and kinds of vegetables with other stock flavors. The cooking liquors from white turnips, cabbage, cauliflower, broccoli and potatoes, used with discretion, may be a real asset to a borsch but a real calamity in chicken broth. We find water from peas or pea pods, except in pea soups, a deadening influence. Carrots and parsnips tend to oversweeten the pot. Tomatoes, unless just the skins are used, can make a consommé too acid and yet be just the touch you want in a vegetable soup or a sauce. Some vegetable juices, like those from leeks, watercress and asparagus, seem ever welcome. ➤ Use any of these liquids, whether from fresh, canned or frozen vegetables, if they taste good.

You may also purée leftover cooked vegetables as thickeners for soup.

There are several ways to bring up the flavor of soup vegetables. One is to sauté them gently in butter, see Consommé Brunoise, 169. Another is to cook them in meat stocks.

Unlike the above ➤ when you add vegetables to soup as a garnish, the trick is not to soften them to the point where their cells break down and they release their juices, but to keep them full of flavor. However, if the vegetables you are using as a garnish are strong, like peppers or onions, blanch them first.

VEGETABLE STOCK

About 1 Quart

Sauté:

½ cup finely chopped onions

in:

2 tablespoons fat

Add:

A dash of white pepper
A dash of cayenne
½ teaspoon salt
A Bouquet Garni, 572
¼ cup each carrots, turnips, parsnips
2 cups diced celery ribs and yellow leaves
(1 cup shredded lettuce)
(Mushroom or tomato skins)

Add enough:

Cold water

to cover. Bring to a boil, ➤ cover partially with a lid and simmer about 1½ hours or until the vegetables are very tender. Strain and chill. Degrease before using, if necessary. If you prefer a more colorful stock, add a small amount of:

Caramelized Sugar, 559

STOCK REINFORCERS

I. BEEF JUICE

This is another rich stock item. To make it, see Beef Tea, 170.

II. BOUILLON AND CONSOMMÉ

These are both a great help. You may prefer canned bouillon—which is less sweet than canned consommé. Bouillon cubes and beef extracts, each diluted in ½ cup boiling liquid, are also useful.

III. CANNED, FROZEN AND DRIED SOUPS

Alone or combined with household stocks, these can produce very sophisticated results. Suggestions for their use appear in detail under Soups, Sauces, Aspics and Gravies.

IV. MILK AND CREAM

As a diluent, milk or cream is always preferable to plain water.

ABOUT COURT BOUILLON

Court bouillons are seasoned liquids which, as their name implies, are cooked only a short time. Their composition varies. They may simply be Acidulated Water, 520, acidulated water reinforced with braised or fresh vegetables, or even a hot marinade with oil.

They are not actual broths or stocks in themselves, but rather prototypes that may develop into them. Sometimes they are used only as a blanching or cooking medium. Then they are discarded, as in the cooking of vegetables, where their purpose is to preserve color in the vegetable or leach out undesirable flavors from it. Sometimes they are a liquid storage medium for food processed in them, as in Vegetables à la Grecque, 281. Or they may be used as a hot marinade in which fish is soaked before cooking. And sometimes, as in the cooking of delicately flavored fish, they become—after the fish is drained from them—a Fumet or Fish Stock, 524.

COURT BOUILLON FOR FISH

2 Quarts

Use this for any fish that is to be poached or "boiled." For court bouillon for trout, see Truite au Bleu or Blue Trout, 414.

Trim and clean:

3 lb. fish

and rub with:

Lemon juice

Meanwhile, in a large pan, bring to a boil:

2 quarts water

Add:

½ bay leaf
¼ cup chopped carrots
½ cup chopped celery
1 small onion stuck with 2 cloves
½ cup vinegar or 1 cup dry white wine
1 teaspoon salt
(Parsley or a Bouquet Garni, 572)

When the mixture is boiling, plunge the fish in and ➤ at once reduce the heat. Simmer the fish ➤ uncovered, 30 minutes or until tender. Drain and serve. You may keep and use this court bouillon for several days for poaching fish, but it should not be used in other soups, sauces and gravies, as is a fumet or fish stock.

COURT BOUILLON BLANC

For use in maintaining good color in variety meats and vegetables.

I. Allow to every:

1 quart boiling water
2 tablespoons lemon juice

Blend until smooth and add to the above:

2 tablespoons water
1 tablespoon flour
(3 tablespoons chopped suet)

Add:

Celery, carrot, leek, or an onion stuck with cloves

II. Or add the vegetables to a boiling mixture of:

½ water, seasoned with herbs
½ milk

Reduce to a simmer at once. The milk may curdle slightly, but this will not affect the food adversely.

ABOUT WINE AND SPIRITS FOR COOKING

There is no doubt that the occasional addition of wine—or of spirits and cordials—gives food a welcome new dimension. If yours is a wine-drinking household, you have probably always enjoyed cooking with "the butts." If wine is a stranger to your table, you may be hesitant about breaking open a new bottle for experimentation. When you do decide to take the plunge ➤ remember that the wine you choose need not be a very old or expensive one, but that it should at least be good enough to be drunk with relish for its own sake.

What kind of wine to use? The specific answer depends on the kind of food it is combined with; consult the list below. Start your purchasing with a dry white and a full-bodied red, and before you know it you will have developed a palate and a palette and will be well on the way to some strikingly colorful effects in a new medium. In general, however, keep wine away from very tart or very piquantly seasoned foods, unless you are using it as a Marinade, 528.

How much wine to use? That true sophisticate, Joseph Wechsberg, has observed: "*La cuisine alcoolisée* has no justification in serious cooking." ➤ Never add so much as to overbalance or drown out the characteristic flavor of the food itself. ➤ Count the wine as a part of any given sum total of liquid ingredients, not as an extra. A recipe for pot roast with wine may call for the addition of as much as a cup per pound. When you use it in such dishes, be sure it is warmed before adding, so as not to interrupt simmering. In meat or fowl recipes calling for both wine and salt pork, watch for too great saltiness. Season to taste ➤ at the end of cooking.

Fortified wine, 56, such as sherry and Madeira, is frequently used in dishes where a definite wine flavor is desirable; for example, to combat a too-fishy taste. Two tablespoons of fortified wine are equal in flavoring strength to about ½ cup of dry red or white table wine. Wines may be reduced to increase their flavoring power and to avoid overdilution in sauce-making; 1 cup of wine will reduce to about ¼ cup in 10 minutes of uncovered cooking. In aspic recipes, each cup of liquid indicated may be replaced by 1½ tablespoons fortified or 2 to 2½ tablespoons ordinary wine, and the wine should be added after the gelatin is dissolved.

When to add wine? This question is a hotly disputed one. If a wine sauce is heated, it loses not only its alcoholic content but, if cooked too long, its flavor. Fortified wines are usually added shortly before serving. Add wine to a sauce only during those periods when the dish can be covered, whether marinating, cooking, storing or chilling. While you may boil wine to reduce it ➤ never raise the heat to above a simmer when cooking food in wine. If you aim at mellow penetration or at tenderizing, the time to add wine is at the onset of cooking. ➤ To avoid curdling or separation, wine should always be added beforehand in any recipes which include milk, cream, butter or eggs. The wine should be reduced slightly and the ingredients just mentioned as likely to curdle should be added off the heat. If the dish cannot be served at once, it may be kept warm in a double boiler ➤ over—not in—boiling water.

To achieve a pronounced wine flavor, swirl reduced wine into food at the very end of the cooking process, after it has been removed from the heat. One of our favorite practices is to add wine to a pan in which meat has been cooking, deglazing, 340, the pan juices and so building up a pleasant substitute for roux-based gravy.

Spirits, liqueurs and cordials are most frequently used in flavoring desserts. Whisky is becoming increasingly popular, but, except for desserts, do not use bourbon, as it is too sweet. A spectacular use of spirits in cooking is flambéing—sometimes done at midpoint in preparation and sometimes as a final flourish in the dining room. ➤ Flambéing is surefire only if the liquor to be ignited, as well as the food, is previously warmed, see 155. To flambé fruits, see 127.

Exceptions not only prove the rule—they sometimes improve it. We list below certain time-tested combinations in wine cookery; but we encourage defiance and initiative.

For Soups: Cream sherry or semisweet white wines.

For Fish, Poultry and Eggs: Dry white wines; except, for Coq au Vin, dry red.

For Red Meat: Dry red wines or rosés.

For Pork, Veal, Lamb or Game: Red or white wines or rosés.

For Aspics and Wine Jellies: Any type—but red wines tend to lose their color. Brandy complements an aspic of game.

For Sauces: Dry or semisweet Bordeaux or Burgundy, champagne, Riesling, vermouth; see individual sauce recipes.

For Desserts: Sweet sherry, port, Madeira, Marsala, Tokay, muscatel, rum, liqueurs, cordials.

Beer and cider, as well as wine, have their own virtues in cooking, especially if the beer is flat and the cider hard, as their fermentative qualities help tenderize meats, doughs and batters. You will find them indicated in recipes where their use is appropriate.

ABOUT VINEGAR

Whether a vinegar is sharp, rich or mellow makes a tremendous difference in cooking. ➤ All vinegars are corrosive—with a 4% to 6% acidity—so be sure to mix pickled, vinaigretted or marinated foods in glass, enamel or stainless vessels. Keep away from copper, zinc, aluminum, and galvanized or iron ware. Be sure to store in glass with cork or noncorrodible tops.

Vinegars divide roughly into the following types:

DISTILLED WHITE VINEGAR

Based on dilute distilled alcohol fermented to a 4% acetic acid count. It is used in pickling when the pickle must remain light in color.

CIDER AND MALT-BASED VINEGARS

These are full-bodied and usually run between 5% and 6% acetic acid. Cider vinegar results from the fermentation of the juice of apples. Malt vinegars are the fermentations of an infusion of barley malt or cereals whose starch has been converted by malt.

WINE VINEGARS

These have about a 5% acetic acid content.

We have often admired the lovely light quality of dressings based on Italian wine vinegar. A friend told us his secret lies in fermenting a homemade unpasteurized red wine, but not allowing it to reach the point of bitterness. If you don't want to bother with this process, a substitute is to dilute sharp vinegars with red or white wine. Wine vinegars "mother," forming a strange, wispy residue at the base of the bottle. As they are of uncertain strengths, they are not recommended for pickling. If you plan to make spiced vinegars in quantity for gifts, please profit by our experience and mix in small batches: spices are tricky, see 575.

HERB VINEGARS

Make these with any of the above vinegars. Use individual herbs like tarragon or burnet or develop your favorite herb combinations—allowing not more than 3 tablespoons fresh herb leaves per quart of vinegar. If garlic is used, crush it and leave it in the jar only 24 hours. The reason for not overloading the vinegar with vegetable matter is that its preservative strength may not be great enough to prevent botulism, 802. After 2 to 4 weeks of steeping, filter the vinegar, rebottle it in sterilized containers and keep tightly corked.

FRESH HERB VINEGAR

A quantity recipe that serves well for making gifts. Heat slowly to just below the boiling point:

3 gallons cider or white wine vinegar

Combine:

2 dozen peppercorns
1 dozen sliced shallots
¾ cup tarragon
8 sprigs rosemary
8 sprigs thyme
4 branches winter savory
1 sprig chervil
1 well-cleaned, unpeeled, sliced celeriac root
½ cup parsley
1 sliced parsley root

Bottle these ingredients. After 2 weeks, strain the vinegar through cheesecloth. Place in sterile bottles and cork tightly.

SPICED VINEGAR

An excellent, if deceptive, mixture. It tastes like a delicious blend of herbs, but it is flavored with spices whole or ground.

Combine, stir and heat slowly until just under the boiling point:

¼ cup whole cloves
¼ cup allspice
2 tablespoons mace
3 tablespoons celery seed
¼ cup mustard seed
6 tablespoons whole black pepper
3 tablespoons turmeric
¼ cup fresh or dried gingerroot
1½ gallons cider vinegar
2 cups sugar

Place these ingredients in a covered noncorrodible container. Slice and add for 24 hours:

4 or more cloves garlic

Remove the garlic. Allow the other ingredients to steep 3 weeks. If ground spices are used, filter the vinegar before storing; otherwise strain and pour into sterile glass bottles. Cork tightly.

GARLIC VINEGAR

Heat to just below the boiling point:

1 cup vinegar

Cut into halves and add for 24 hours, then remove:

4 cloves garlic

Place the vinegar in a sterile glass bottle. Cork tightly. Use it in dressings or sauces.

QUICK HERB VINEGAR

About 1 Cup

Combine:

1 cup well-flavored vinegar: wine or cider
1 teaspoon dried crushed herbs: basil, tarragon, etc.

You may use this at once with salad oil. You may add ½ clove of garlic and fish it out within 24 hours. Shortly before serving, add:

2 tablespoons chopped parsley
1 tablespoon chopped chives

TARRAGON OR BURNET VINEGAR

About 2 Cups

Wash, then dry well:

1½ tablespoons fresh tarragon or burnet leaves

Bruise them slightly and add them to:

2 cups warmed cider vinegar
2 whole cloves
1 skinned, halved clove garlic

Place these ingredients in a covered jar. After 24 hours, remove the garlic. After 2 weeks, strain and store the vinegar in sterile, well-corked bottles. This makes a strong infusion that may be diluted later with more vinegar.

RED RASPBERRY VINEGAR COCKAIGNE

Would you believe this makes a marvelously refreshing summer drink served over crushed ice? See 45.

Put into a large enamel or stainless steel pan:

2 quarts ripe red raspberries

Cover them with:

1 quart cider vinegar

Let stand covered in a cool place about 48 hours. Then strain. Use this liquid to cover another:

2 quarts ripe red raspberries

Again, let stand 48 hours, then strain and measure the liquid into an enamel or stainless steel pan. Add an equal quantity, or slightly less, of:

Sugar

Bring to a boil and ➤ simmer 10 minutes. Skim and cool. Store in well-corked sterile bottles.

CHILI VINEGAR

You can make a really fiery French dressing with this. See also Chilis Preserved in Sherry, 845.

Steep:

1 oz. chilis

in:

1 pint vinegar

for 10 days. Shake daily. Then strain and bottle in sterilized containers.

GINGER VINEGAR

Combine:

1 cup cider vinegar
4 one-inch pieces dried gingerroot
2 tablespoons sugar

Strain after 1 week and bottle.

ABOUT MARINADES

Never underestimate the power of a marinade. These aromatic tenderizing liquids are easily abused. Every marinade contains varied amounts of seasonings, sometimes oil, and always an acid, ➤ so any marinade container should be of glazed ceramic, glass or an impervious metal like stainless steel. Less marinade is needed to cover if the meat is placed in a container just large enough to hold it. Use a wooden spoon to stir or turn the meat occasionally during the process.

Marinades are a means of spreading flavor by immersion. The soaking period may vary from only a few minutes to many hours. Stronger, spicier marinades may be devised to make bland food more interesting. But perhaps the most important function of a marinade is to tenderize tough foods. Sometimes marinades contain as one of their ingredients, extract of papaya, a tenderizing agent.

Marinades may be cooked or uncooked. The cooked ones more effectively impart their flavors to food, and are preferable if the soaking is to exceed 12 hours. The liquid should be cooked in advance and thoroughly chilled before the food is immersed. The amount of vinegar should be reduced slightly if meat is to be marinated longer than 24 hours.

The effects of marinating are hastened by higher temperatures, but so is the danger of bacterial activity. ➤ Refrigerate any foods in their marinade if the immersion period indicated is 1 hour or more.

Both cooked and uncooked marinades may be used in finishing sauces. So do not discard a marinade before deciding whether you want to incorporate it in your sauce. Poivrade Sauce, 347, for venison is an example. And dishes such as Hasenpfeffer, 514, and Sauerbraten, 460, are cooked in the marinade, which is then converted into a proper sauce just before serving.

Allow about ½ cup of marinade for every pound of food to be processed. Cubed meat is soaked just 2 to 3 hours; a whole 5- to 10-pound piece, overnight. Longer marination may be too pungent and may kill the flavor of the meat. Marinating 12 hours or more cuts the cooking time by one-third. In an emergency, try mixing oil and vinegar with packaged dried salad seasonings to achieve a quickly prepared marinade for meats or vegetables.

MARINADES FOR VEGETABLES

Marinated vegetables are usually served cold as hors d'oeuvre or salads. Suitable for the short-term marinating of vegetables are:

French Dressing, 360, seasoned with herbs
Ravigote Sauce, 345

See also Vegetables à la Grecque, 281.

FISH OR LAMB MARINADE

Enough for 1 Pound Lamb Kebabs

I. Combine:

2 tablespoons lemon juice
¼ cup olive oil
1 teaspoon salt
⅛ teaspoon pepper

Marinate the meat refrigerated and covered for 2 to 3 hours. Turn frequently.

II. Combine:

½ teaspoon turmeric
½ teaspoon powdered ginger
1 small pressed clove garlic
2 to 3 tablespoons lemon juice
½ teaspoon grated lemon rind

Toss the meat in this mixture, coating it thoroughly. Cover and refrigerate 2 hours.

III. Combine:

¼ cup pineapple juice
2 teaspoons soy sauce
2 teaspoons lemon juice
1 minced clove garlic

Marinate the meat covered and refrigerated for 2 hours. Turn it frequently.

LAMB OR GAME MARINADE

About 2 Cups

For marinated leg of lamb.
Combine:

1 cup dry red wine
¼ cup lemon juice
½ cup olive oil
3 or 4 juniper berries or 2 or 3 sprigs rosemary
A sprig of parsley
A sprig of thyme
2 bay leaves
1 to 2 crushed cloves garlic
A pinch of nutmeg
1 tablespoon sugar
1 teaspoon salt
A dash of hot pepper sauce

Marinate 24 hours, covered and refrigerated.

YOGURT OR BUTTERMILK MARINADE

About 2 Cups

This marinade can subsequently be incorporated into a sauce.
Add to:

2 cups yogurt or buttermilk
2 pressed cloves garlic

Season to taste with:
Salt and pepper or curry powder or cinnamon or ginger or cardamom

APRICOT OR SASSATIES MARINADE

Enough for 3 Pounds of Meat

Cook and purée:
½ lb. Dried Apricots, 131
Sauté until golden:
3 large sliced onions
1 minced clove garlic
in:
2 tablespoons butter
Add and cook for a minute longer:
1 tablespoon curry powder
Then add the apricot purée with:
1 tablespoon sugar
½ teaspoon salt
3 tablespoons vinegar
A few grains cayenne
2 tablespoons lemon or lime juice
Bring to a boil, then remove from heat and cool before pouring over raw meat.

COOKED MARINADE FOR GAME

About 8 Cups

This is a cooked marinade that can be stored in the refrigerator and used as needed for venison, mutton or hare.
Sauté a combination of:
1 cup chopped celery
1 cup chopped carrots
1 cup chopped onions
in:
1½ cups vegetable oil
until the onions are golden. Then add:
3 cups vinegar
2 cups water
½ cup coarsely chopped parsley
3 bay leaves
1 tablespoon thyme
1 tablespoon basil
1 tablespoon cloves
1 tablespoon allspice berries
A pinch of mace
1 tablespoon crushed peppercorns
6 crushed cloves garlic
Simmer for 1 hour. Strain and cool.

BEER MARINADE FOR BEEF OR PORK

I. **2 Cups**

Combine:
1½ cups flat beer
½ cup vegetable oil
stirring the oil in slowly. Then add:
1 clove garlic
2 tablespoons lemon juice
1 tablespoon sugar
1 teaspoon salt
3 cloves

II. **2 Cups**

More pungent.
Combine:
1½ cups flat beer
½ teaspoon salt
1 tablespoon dry mustard
1 teaspoon ground ginger
3 tablespoons soy sauce
⅛ teaspoon hot pepper sauce
2 tablespoons sugar or honey
4 tablespoons marmalade
2 minced cloves garlic

PORK MARINADE

Enough for 1 Pound of Pork Chops

Combine:
4 tablespoons Chili Sauce, 847
3 tablespoons lemon juice
1 tablespoon grated onion
¼ teaspoon dry mustard
2 teaspoons Worcestershire Sauce, 848
½ teaspoon salt
¼ teaspoon paprika

MARINADE FOR CHICKEN

¾ Cup

Use for chicken to be broiled or grilled.
Combine:
¼ cup vegetable oil
½ cup dry white wine
1 minced clove garlic
1 finely chopped medium-sized onion
½ teaspoon celery salt
½ teaspoon salt
½ teaspoon coarsely ground black pepper
¼ teaspoon dried thyme, tarragon or rosemary
Mix well. Chill several hours in covered jar or dish. Shake well, then pour over the chicken pieces. Chill about 3 hours, turning pieces at least once. Baste during cooking with any excess marinade.

TERIYAKI MARINADE FOR CHICKEN AND STEAK

About 2½ Cups

For Shrimp Teriyaki, see 390.
Combine and mix well:
½ cup vegetable oil
1 cup soy sauce
3 tablespoons brown sugar
3 mashed cloves garlic
1 tablespoon grated fresh gingerroot
2 tablespoons sherry
Marinate the meat 4 to 12 hours, refrigerated. Baste with the marinade during cooking.

ABOUT MILK AND CREAMS

"Drink your milk" has been a time-worn admonition at many an American family table, for the high food value of milk is an accepted fact. But nowadays many of our children almost automatically pour "down the hatch" considerably more than the 1½ to 2 pints they need daily—and thus cancel their appetite for other equally nourishing foods. Beware, incidentally, of assuming that chocolate milk is the nutritional equivalent of whole milk, see 41.

Most adults, including the middle-aged and their seniors, are well aware of the value of milk in their diet and manage to ingest their daily pint, if not as a drink, in soups, sauces or puddings. Expectant mothers should have at least 3 glasses of milk a day and nursing mothers 4. Sometimes adults may prefer to substitute cheeses. But if they do, they must be sure to get adequate B vitamins in the rest of their diet, for in cheese-making, more B vitamins are lost in the whey than can be subsequently re-created in the final product.

Milk is as perishable as it is valuable. Everything possible should be done ➤ to keep it constantly refrigerated at about 40°; ➤ to protect it from sunlight, which robs it quickly of vitamin B content; and ➤ not to hold milks of any type longer than 3 days, refrigerated. Milks vary in color, even when the animals from which they are taken have all been pastured in the same fields, on the same fodder. The milk of Jersey cows will be yellower than that of Holsteins; Holstein milk, in turn, will be yellower than the almost chalk-white milks of ewes and goats. Yellow coloring reveals the presence of a provitamin A factor called carotene, which some humans can convert better than others into vitamin A, which is almost colorless.

➤ In this book the word milk means pasteurized, fluid, whole milk unless otherwise specified. Such milk contains about 87% water, 4% milkfat, 3% protein, 5% lactose or carbohydrate, and 1% ash, plus minerals and vitamins. Examine labels for the milk components you want or need, and be sure you are not getting "nonmilks," 532.

PASTEURIZATION OF MILK AND CREAM

Milks sold in interstate commerce must by law be pasteurized, and most communities have enacted the same regulation for milk sold within their limits. Some people oppose pasteurization because of certain changes that occur in the milk as a result, such as losses of vitamin C and enzymatic changes affecting fermentation. But pasteurization, a mild, carefully controlled heating process, effectively halts many dreaded milk-borne diseases that the sanitary handling and certification of raw milk—no matter how scrupulously carried out—cannot always achieve.

Raw milk or cream may be pasteurized at home. Arrange empty, sterile, heatproof glass jars on a rack in a deep kettle. Allow an inch or two of headroom when you pour the raw milk or cream into the jars. Fill the kettle with water until it comes above the fill line of the milk in the jars. ➤ Put a sterile dairy thermometer in one of the jars. ➤ Heat the water and, when the thermometer registers 145°, hold the heat at that temperature 30 minutes. ➤ Cool the water rapidly until the milk is between 50° and 40°. ➤ Refrigerate, covered, at once.

If pasteurized milk develops an "off" or bitter flavor, it has been held too long after processing. Unpleasant flavor may also appear in milk when cows eat wild garlic or other strongly scented herbage. "Cowy" or cardboardy tastes are also due to improper feeding, and a fishy taste may be the result of processing in the presence of copper.

SCALDING MILK

Scalding is employed more often to hasten or improve a food process than to destroy bacteria. To a chemist, scalding is that point at which milk begins to come up to a light froth, just as it boils, around 212°. In practice, we rely on the age-old visual test for scalding, and in this book milk is scalded ➤ when tiny bubbles form around the edge of the pan and the milk reaches about 180°. Heating may be either over direct heat or in the top of a double boiler ➤ over—not in—boiling water. Before heating milk for scalding, it is a help in later cleaning to rinse out the pan with cold water.

ABOUT SWEET MILK

Milk is sold in many forms, some with added vitamins—especially D—to make its calcium and phosphorus more available to the body. For calorie count, see 8. Much milk is "standardized," which simply means that it comes from a milk pool covering a wide area and has cream or skim milk added to make it conform to the prevailing legally required balance between these two elements. Each of the following labels indicates the legally defined composition of the respective type of milk.

WHOLE MILK

A fresh, fluid milk typically contains at least 3.25% milkfat, and at least 8.25% protein, lactose and minerals. A cream line forms above the milk when the fat particles rise. The cream is plainly evident if the milk remains undisturbed for some time.

HOMOGENIZED MILK

Also a fresh, fluid milk, with the same percentage of ingredients as whole milk. However, it has no cream line, as during preparation the fat particles are broken up so finely that they remain uniformly dispersed throughout. Its finer curd is more easily digested than that of whole milk. Processors appreciate homogenization because it allows them to mix older and newer milks without the telltale evidence of curdling which characterizes milks beginning to stale.

In cooking, fresh homogenized milk gives a different texture from that produced by whole milk: Sauces may be stiffer and fat separation greater; cornstarch puddings more granular. Soups, gravies, cooked cereals, scalloped potatoes and custards tend to curdle. These texture changes are not present, however, when homogenized milks are evaporated.

SKIM, NONFAT AND LOW-FAT MILK

Skim and nonfat milks have only ½% or less of milkfat but all the protein and mineral value of whole milk. However, these milks are deprived of the valuable fat-soluble vitamins A, D, E and K. In "fortified" skim and low-fat milks, nonfat dry milk solids and vitamins A and D are added. Other examples of partly skimmed fortified milks are the 1% or 2% milks. The percentages refer to the small amount of fat retained to keep flavor and texture similar to those of whole milk.

EVAPORATED MILK

A canned whole milk freed of 60% of its moisture content and containing not less than 7.5% milkfat. Reconstitute by adding ½ cup water to the same quantity of evaporated milk and use to replace 1 cup fresh whole milk in any recipes except those calling for rennet. Because it can be preserved during times of excess production, it is sometimes less expensive than whole milk. It has a slightly caramelized taste due to the processing. The cans, which come in 5⅓-ounce and 13-ounce sizes, should be inverted every few weeks in storage to keep solids from settling. ➤ Do not hold condensed milk over 6 months before using. Once opened, the milk should be stored and treated as fresh milk. To make it flow easily from the can, punch two holes near the rim at opposite sides of the top. ➤ To whip, see Whipped Cream Substitute III, 532.

SWEETENED CONDENSED MILK

This process, used as early as Civil War days, reduces by about half the water content of milk and adds sugar. It contains not less than 8.5% milkfat. The 14-ounce can contains the equivalent of 2½ cups milk and 8 tablespoons sugar. It too settles during storage. The can should be inverted about every 2 weeks and ➤ held not longer than 6 months before using. Once opened, the can should be refrigerated. Because of the high sugar content, the milk will keep somewhat longer after opening than will evaporated milk.

DRY MILK SOLIDS

These are pasteurized milk particles, air-dried to eliminate all but about 5% moisture. In whole dry milk form they contain not less than 26% milkfat, and in nonfat dry milk form about 1.5% milkfat. Milk solids should always be stored in a cool place. Once opened, it is best to refrigerate them in a lightproof, airtight container. Discard them if they acquire any rancid, tallowy, scorched or soapy flavor.

➤ Be aware that some markets are selling reconstituted milk on the same shelves with fresh milk, so read the labels carefully.

➤ To reconstitute whole or skim dry milk solids, follow package instructions; or use 3 to 4 tablespoons powdered milk to 1 cup of water—which will be slightly more than a cup of fresh whole or skim milk in volume, and its equivalent in nutrition. For the best flavor, reconstitute at least 2 hours in advance of use and refrigerate.

Dry milk solids are useful in enriching the diet, but they need special handling. They scorch easily, requiring lower cooking and baking temperatures. To avoid scorching gravies and sauces made with dry milk, use a double boiler or very low heat. In preparing sauces, do not add more than 3 tablespoons of milk solids to each cup of liquid. To avoid lumping, mix the milk solids first with the flour and then with the melted fat, off the heat, and then add the warm, but not hot, liquid gradually.

In cooked cereals, add 3 tablespoons dry milk solids to each ½ cup of the dry cereal—before cooking—then use the same amount of water or milk called for in the regular recipe.

For cocoas, custards and puddings, add 3 tablespoons dry milk solids for each cup of liquid called for in the recipe.

To substitute reconstituted dry skim milk in recipes requiring fresh whole milk, add about 2 teaspoons butter for each cup reconstituted dry skim milk.

In baking, mix dry milk solids with the flour ingredients, see Cornell Triple-Rich Formula, 602, but be careful never to add more than ¼ cup of milk solids for each cup of flour, or the dough will have poor rising properties and the crumb will be too dense.

To whip nonfat dry milk, see Whipped Cream Substitutes IV, 532.

ABOUT SWEET CREAMS

Cream is that fatty part of whole milk that slowly rises to the surface on standing. The longer the milk stands, the richer it gets—up to a point, as described below.

The following terms are used throughout this book:

HALF-AND-HALF OR CEREAL CREAM

A mixture of milk and cream, frequently homogenized, containing 10½% to 18% milkfat, and often suggested as a drink in fattening diets.

LIGHT CREAM, COFFEE OR TABLE CREAM

Contains between 18% and 30% milkfat, which may be skimmed off after whole milk has stood 12 hours or longer.

WHIPPING CREAM

This is skimmed from milk that has been standing 24 hours or longer. **Light whipping cream** has 30 to 36% milkfat. Cream containing 36% to 40% milkfat is referred to as **heavy cream.**

WHIPPED CREAM

Whipping cream must be at least a day old; it expands to twice its volume by the incorporation of air. To get the right texture, bowl, beaters and cream should all be ➤ chilled in a refrigerator at least 2 hours before whipping, so that the milkfat stays firm during whipping rather than becoming oily from the friction involved. ➤ In warm weather beat over ice, see illustration, 205. If the cream is warmer than 45°, it may, on beating, quickly turn to butter. ➤ Never overwhip.

➤ To beat cream with an electric beater, turn to medium-high speed until the chilled cream begins to thicken, then lower the speed and watch like a hawk. ➤ Do not try to whip cream in a blender. We like our cream whipped just to the point where it falls in large globs and soft peaks, but still carries a gloss. This is a state almost comparable to the ➤ stiff, but not dry, of beaten egg white, 544. It is possible to use it in this desirably delicate state only if it is prepared the last split second before serving. If whipped cream is to be held for 24 hours or so, it sometimes is suggested that a small amount of gelatin be incorporated for stiffening, but we have never found this technique to be an advantage.

It does help, if the cream is to be flavored, to mix in a small quantity of confectioners' sugar, as the cornstarch in the sugar forms a stabilizer. For interesting ways to flavor whipped cream, see 696.

If whipped cream is to be used decoratively, bring it to the point where the cream molecules are about to become buttery. Should the cream really threaten to turn to butter, whip in 2 or more tablespoons of cream or evaporated milk and continue to beat. Cream at this stage may also be forced through a pastry tube for decorating. ➤ To freeze small decorative garnishes, shape them on foil. Freeze them uncovered on the foil, wrap when firm, and return to the freezer for future use.

CRÈME CHANTILLY

The French equivalent of our Sweetened Whipped Creams, 696. Unsweetened, it is called **Fleurette.** For Crème Fraîche, see 534.

WHIPPED CREAM SUBSTITUTES

First, let us say there are really no very satisfactory substitutes for whipped cream, but the following makeshifts are sometimes used. It is often wise to add vanilla, 1 teaspoon per cup, or one of the other flavors suggested in Sweetened Whipped Creams, 696, to mask the inferior flavor and texture of these substitutes.

I. If you allow light cream to stand refrigerated for 48 hours and skim it, the skimmed portion will sometimes—not always—whip. Handle as for whipped cream, above.

II. **About 2 Cups**

Soak:

1 or 1½ teaspoons gelatin

depending on heaviness of cream desired, in:

2 tablespoons cold water or fruit juice

When it is clear, dissolve it well in:

½ cup scalded light cream

Add:

1 cup light cream

1 tablespoon confectioners' sugar

Refrigerate. Stir from time to time. During the early part of the 4 to 6 hours needed to chill properly, add:

½ teaspoon vanilla

Then beat as for whipped cream, about 5 to 7 minutes.

III. Evaporated milk whips to 3 times its volume. Chill for 12 hours:

1 can evaporated milk

For each 13-ounce can, add:

3 tablespoons lemon juice

Whip until stiff.

IV. **About 1¾ Cups**

Dissolve:

½ cup nonfat dry milk

in:

⅓ cup cold water

Chill. Whip until mixture stands in soft peaks. Add:

1 tablespoon lemon juice

Whip again until peaks are soft. Beat in lightly:

2 to 4 tablespoons sugar

Refrigerate until served.

FILLED MILK

There are innumerable varieties of this imitation milk sold under a plethora of trade names. Ninety-seven percent of these products are made of skim or nonfat dry milk products or of soy products, 535. The remainder are composed of either vegetable or coconut oil or a combination of the two. Filled milk has approximately the same texture and caloric value as whole milk, but is not its nutrient equivalent.

MILK AND CREAM SUBSTITUTIONS

Sometimes it is convenient to substitute milk for cream. But if the substitution is made for baking, a different texture will result—unless the fat content of the cream is compensated for. ➤ To substitute for 1 cup light cream, use ⅞ cup milk and 3 tablespoons butter. To substitute for 1 cup whipping cream, use ¾ cup milk and ⅓ cup butter. This substitution, of course, will not whip.

SWEET AND SOUR MILK SUBSTITUTIONS

If recipes for baking specify sour or buttermilk and only sweet milk is available, you may proceed as follows: interchange sweet milk and baking powder with sour milk and soda. ➤ Use the same amount of liquid as is called for in the recipe. ➤ To sour sweet milk, have it at 70°. Place in the bottom of a measuring cup:

1 tablespoon lemon juice or distilled white vinegar

Then fill the cup with:

Fresh sweet milk or the equivalent amount of reconstituted evaporated or dried whole milk solids

Stir and let the mixture stand about 5 minutes to clabber. **Clabber,** much like cultured buttermilk or yogurt, is milk that has soured to the stage of a firm curd but not to a separation of the whey. ➤ If the leaven is baking powder or soda, be sure that it is added to the dry, not the liquid, ingredients. Make the following adjustments: for every teaspoon baking powder indicated in the recipe, use ¼ teaspoon baking soda plus ½ cup sour milk or buttermilk, or ¼ teaspoon baking soda and ½ tablespoon vinegar or lemon juice plus enough sweet milk to make ½ cup. For other substitutions, see 596.

ABOUT SOUR AND FERMENTED MILKS AND CREAMS

The longevity of certain groups of Arabs, Bulgars and other eastern peoples is often attributed to their diet of sour and fermented milks. The friendly bacteria in these milks settle in the intestines, where they break down the milk sugar into lactic acid, and where some are reported to manufacture B vitamins and to stimulate beneficial growth in the intestinal flora.

Known by many names—**yogurt** from ewe's milk, **kumiss** from mare's milk, **kefir** from camel's milk—they are often today made from cow's milk inoculated with various bacilli that create differences in acidity, flavor and content. The best known are the rather acid *Lactobacillus bulgaricus* used in yogurt and *L. acidophilus*. When yeast cells are also present—as in kumiss and kefir—fermentation takes place, producing a mild alcoholic content as well. Starters for these milk products are available at drug and health food stores. They come with full directions for their use and often produce more stable results than inoculation with the already made up yogurt or kefir, which will have been exposed to airborne contaminants or whose bacillus count may have been weakened through pasteurization.

Soured milks and creams also play an important part in cooking. The presence of lactic acid gives them all a tenderer curd, and this in turn makes for a tenderer crumb in baking and a smoother texture in sauces. In sauces, too, they contribute a slightly acid flavor that is highly prized. In cooking ➤ be sure to add these milks and creams at the very last and off the heat or over very low heat, or they will curdle. Stir constantly but gently. And in bread making, don't scald; just heat until warm. In any sour cream recipes, use salt sparingly, as salting also tends to cause curdling. None of these soured milks freezes well.

Milks and creams may be allowed to sour naturally, but yogurt and today's commercial buttermilk are processed by means of specially introduced bacterial cultures. In this book, for reasons of safety, we recommend souring or fermenting only milks and creams that have been pasteurized—and for best results use only the freshest of such products.

BUTTERMILK

Originally this was the residue left after butter making. Today it is usually made from pasteurized skim milk and contains about 8.5% milk solids other than fat. A culture is added to develop flavor and to produce a heavier consistency than that of the skim milk from which it is made. Buttermilk differs nutritionally from skim milk mainly in its greater amount of lactic acid. As its protein precipitate is in the form of a fine curd, it is also more quickly digested than skim milk. Commercial buttermilk frequently has added cream or butter particles. Try making buttermilk yourself.

Combine:

1 quart 70° to 80° skim milk
½ cup 70° cultured buttermilk
⅛ teaspoon salt

Stir well and cover. Let stand at 70° until clabbered. Stir until smooth. Refrigerate before serving. Store as for fresh milk. In recipes calling for sour milk, you may substitute buttermilk.

SOUR MILK

This is whole or skim milk that is allowed to sour naturally. ➤ It is good only if it results from unpasteurized or unscalded milk, because pasteurized or scalded milk will not sour, but simply spoil. Therefore, recipes which formerly called for sour milk now call for buttermilk. Or you may sour sweet milk still another way, see Sweet and Sour Milk Substitutions, 532.

YOGURT

Eastern yogurts are made with milk reduced by about one-third. Ours have the same milkfat percentage as the milk used. To make **yogurt cheese,** a substitute for sour cream, drip yogurt through cheesecloth in refrigerator 8 hours.

Like yeast, the activator in yogurt is a living organism sensitive to temperatures. For consistent results, test the milk with a cooking thermometer. Use milk from skim to half-and-half richness. Yogurt has the added idiosyncrasy that it doesn't care to be jostled while growing, so place all your equipment where you can leave it undisturbed. If you use one of the many electric devices for quick yogurt making, follow the directions carefully.

We make yogurt successfully, using either an insulated picnic cooler or an oven preheated to 100°. Have ready and keep warm a large sterile crock or enough sterile glass jars to receive the amount of milk you are preparing.

For the first batch, you will need a starter. Buy a jar of yogurt, get a small quantity from a friend, or buy a package of yogurt culture from a health food store. Heat a pint of milk to 180° or almost boiling. Cool it to between 105° and 110°. Stir into this milk very thoroughly a package of the culture or 2 to 3 tablespoons 70° yogurt. Do not allow the milk to register less than 106° when it is in the jars. Then place them in the warmed oven or insulated cooler. Cover the jars at once. The milk with the added yogurt should reach a custardy consistency in 3 to 4 hours; the milk with the yogurt culture may take 7 to 8 hours, depending on the weather. Check every half hour. Refrigerate when ready. Reserve from this first batch a small quantity to use for another batch. Preferably, yogurt should be not older than 5 days when used as a starter. Yogurt in general will keep 6 to 7 days.

You may wonder why so little starter is used and think that a little more will produce a better result. It won't. The bacillus, if crowded, gives a sour, watery product. But if the culture has sufficient *Lebensraum,* it will be rich, mild and creamy. If your yogurt does not coagulate within 8 hours, it may be because the temperature of the milk was too high and the culture was destroyed; or because your culture was a poor one; or there were antibiotics in the milk. Always remember ➤ don't eat every drop of your recent batch. Keep 2 to 3 tablespoons to form the starter for the next one.

If you wish to incorporate fruit when making yogurt, have the warm sweetened crushed fruit in the bottom of the jars before adding the milk and yogurt. When using yogurt in cooking, ➤ fold it gently into the other ingredients, as beating breaks down its texture.

CULTURED OR DAIRY SOUR CREAM

Many uses for this smooth semiplastic cultured cream are suggested in this book. If your dairy does not carry it, try making it yourself.
Place in a quart glass jar:

1 cup pasteurized 20% or light cream

➤ The cream must be at least this heavy and may be heavier—the heavier the better for the texture of the end product. Add:

5 teaspoons cultured buttermilk

The commercial type which is 1% acid and has carefully controlled bacteria is suggested rather than the less acid and less controlled homemade buttermilk. Cover the jar and shake these ingredients vigorously. Stir in:

1 cup pasteurized 20% or light cream

Cover the jar and allow this mixture to stand at 75° to 80° for 24 hours. The sour cream may then be used at once, although storage under refrigeration for another 24 hours makes a finer product. It does not freeze well. ➤ Add sour cream at the end of cooking processes over low heat and stir gently to avoid curdling. ➤ Do not overstir.

SOUR CREAM SUBSTITUTES

A low-calorie substitute to be used only in uncooked dressings or for garnish.

I. Mix for 2 or 3 seconds in a blender:

1 tablespoon lime or lemon juice
⅓ cup buttermilk
1 cup smooth cottage cheese

II. Mix:

1 cup 70° evaporated milk

with:

1 tablespoon vinegar

Allow the mixture to stand until it clabbers and thickens.

DEVONSHIRE OR CLOTTED CREAM

One of those regional specialties calling for certified unpasteurized cream. In winter, let fresh cream stand 12 hours; in summer, about 6 hours, in a heatproof dish. Then put the cream on to heat —the lower the heat, the better. It must never boil, as this will coagulate the albumen and ruin everything. When small rings or undulations form on the surface, the cream is sufficiently scalded. Remove at once from heat and store in a cold place at least 12 hours. Then skim the thick, clotted cream and serve it very cold as a garnish for berries.

CRÈME FRAÎCHE

A raw 30% cream which in France is allowed to mature until its flavor is nutty rather than acid. It tolerates higher temperatures in cooking than sour cream before it curdles. For a substitute, mix:

1 cup whipping cream
1 teaspoon cultured buttermilk

Heat to 85°. Let stand at a temperature between 60° and 85° until thickened. Stir gently and refrigerate until ready to use.

IMITATION MILK AND CREAM

Concocted in the laboratory of corn-syrup solids, vegetable fat, sodium caseinate or soybean protein, sugar, salt, chemical thickeners, colors, artificial flavors and water. The USDA is now working on a standard for this product. Read the labels with awareness.

ABOUT VEGETABLE AND NUT MILKS

These are all valuable nutritionally, but not comparable to animal milks, as their protein is of lower biologic value and their vitamin content is different.

NUT AND COCONUT MILKS

Almond and walnut milks have long been known to Europe's peasants. Our own Indians used hickory and pecan milk. These rather fragilely flavored milks, as well as coconut milk, are a great delicacy in sauces and puddings. ➤ They are as perishable as cow's milk and in storage and cooking should be treated like Coconut Milk, 566.

As nuts vary in weight, look up the measurement equivalent for almonds and blanch the nuts, if necessary. Then substitute accordingly in the following recipe. These milks are often used to substitute for milk in desserts, with sugar added. If using for sauces other than dessert sauces, you may combine them with stock as your liquid base.

ALMOND MILK

I. Blanch, 154:

⅔ cup almonds

Drain and discard the liquid. Cool the nuts. Remove skins. Pound the nuts in a mortar with:

¼ cup sugar

(1 tablespoon orange water)

If necessary, add from time to time a tablespoon or so of ice water to keep the nuts from becoming oily. When this mixture is quite smooth, stir in:

2 cups cold water

Cover and refrigerate about 2 hours. Strain the liquid through a cloth-lined sieve and refrigerate until ready to use.

II. ⅄ For a hurry-up version, use the above ingredients, but first blend the nuts with:

2 tablespoons water

(2 tablespoons orange water)

Proceed as above. Strain through a cloth-lined sieve. Refrigerate.

SOY MILK

About 4½ Cups

This milk can be substituted cup for cup for cooking and baking but should not be thought of as nutritionally equal to human milk or other animal milks. If used as a mainstay in infant feeding, it must be fortified. In Asia, drinks combined with soy milk are used to lure the populace from the consumption of nonnutrient cola drinks.

Soak 12 hours in:

Water to cover

½ lb. dried soybeans: 1¼ cups

After soaking, drain and rinse. ⅄ Purée beans in a blender with:

3 cups water

until the smooth consistency of whipped cream. In a 2-gallon heavy pot, have ready:

1 cup hot water

Add the blended soybean mixture and bring to a boil, stirring gently with a wooden spoon to avoid scorching. When foam suddenly rises, remove the pot from the heat. Have ready a large colander lined with a generous square of sterilized thin cotton muslin. Set the lined colander over a large bowl in the sink and pour the mixture into the colander. Tighten the cloth around the bean pulp—the *okara*—and press out as much milk as possible with the back of a spoon and, when cool enough, by wringing with the hands. Sprinkle over the pulp in the opened cloth:

¾ cup warm water

Press again and set aside the pulp, which is a nutritious filler used in Oriental dishes. Pour the milk into the cleaned 2-gallon pot and bring to a boil. ➤ Reduce the heat to low-medium and cook 10 minutes, stirring constantly to prevent sticking. ➤ The boiling is necessary to destroy the antinutritional factor trypsin. Cool the milk slightly and refrigerate before serving. ➤ But if you plan to make bean curd, use the milk at once while still hot, see following recipe.

TOFU OR SOYBEAN CURD

About 1½ Cups

Bean curd, a valuable complete-protein product of delicate cheeselike consistency, must be processed from the freshly made hot soy milk opposite. Have ready two 1-quart plastic freezer boxes of the type that nest. Perforate the bottom and lower portion of one with holes about ¼ inch in diameter as though on a 1-inch grid. For a solidifier, combine:

1 cup water

1½ teaspoons epsom salts or calcium sulfate; or use 2⅔ tablespoons lemon juice, or 2¼ tablespoons cider vinegar

Heat to boiling point, then remove from the heat:

4 cups soy milk, opposite

6 cups water

Add one-third cup of the solidifier solution. Stir gently and completely. Gently stir in another one-third cup of solidifier, and cover the pot for 3 minutes to await the forming of the curds. Sprinkle the remaining solution over the milk and gently stir the surface. Cover for 3 minutes, or for 6 minutes if using epsom salts or calcium sulfate. If curds do not form during this period, add:

(A little more dissolved solidifier)

Line the perforated quart container with a generous square of moist thin muslin and place the container in the sink. Gently ladle in the soy curd mixture and fold the ends of the cloth over the top. Partly fill the other plastic container with water to use as a 1-pound weight. Let set 10 to 15 minutes or until the whey no longer is expressed. The whey can be saved for stock. Submerge in cold water the perforated container with the wrapped curd. ➤ Very gently unwrap the curd under water and let it sit undisturbed for 3 to 5 minutes to firm up. It is highly perishable; store it refrigerated in water for only a few days. Use squares of drained Tofu as a soup garnish, in salads, or as a dressing, 369. For other suggestions, see *The Book of Tofu*, by William Shurtleff and Akiko Aoyagi.

SOYBEAN PASTE OR EXTENDER

This is used to stretch meat loaves and patties. Thoroughly drain cooked soybeans, 286, and when free from moisture, rice or press through a colander. Store covered and refrigerated. Season when adding to other foods.

ALTERNATE OR ENGINEERED FOODS

These are defined by the USDA as foods so processed that they improve nutrition, reduce cost, provide ease of preparation and improve stability. They include **Textured Vegetable Proteins,** a processor's answer to prayer, a backpacker's delight and a shopper's caveat. They are usually extractions of soy, wheat or cottonseed, although rape and yellow mustard seed and peanuts, field peas and beans, onions and oil seeds are all being experimented with. TVPs, as they are called, can be tailored in many forms, shapes, colors, textures and tastes. Those micronutrients naturally found in meat but lacking in TVPs and considered critical are added to TVPs to meet government specifications. Dehydrated TVPs are shelf-stable. As spun protein they must be kept frozen or refrigerated. In this so-called analog form they are about 16% to 20% protein, 12% to 18% fat, and 55% to 60% moisture.

Available separately or already combined with foods, Textured Vegetable Proteins are used to replace meat in patties up to 40%. In canned and prepared foods they sometimes replace meat altogether. In poultry and seafood combinations they usually substitute for about 30% of the flesh, in sausage products up to 30% of the lean meat; and although they are there, you may be unable to detect them in some salad dressings, pizzas, jerky, dips, sandwich spreads, cheeses, sour creams, yogurts and bakery goods. Since they absorb and retain moisture from the food with which they are combined and exude no fat during cooking, Textured Vegetable Proteins are shrinkproof.

Two other USDA-approved alternate foods are macaroni enriched with fortified protein, a blend of corn, soy and wheat with a fivefold increase over the protein in macaroni; and formulated grain-fruit products which provide both cereal and fruit juice components and are recommended to be eaten with milk to round out the protein.

Other engineered foods which have been distributed worldwide are a corn-soya-milk blend —**CSM**—of 64% gelatinized cornmeal, 24% soya flour, 5% nonfat dry milk, and a 2% premix of minerals and vitamins. Enough oil may be added to bring the minimum required fat level up to 6%. CSM has a protein minimum of 20% and a PER or protein efficiency rate nearly equal to the 2.5 of casein. **WSB** is a wheat-soy blend with nutritional values equal to CSM. Some of these cereal milks are combined with whey.

ABOUT CHEESE

We heartily agree with Clifton Fadiman, who called cheese "milk's leap to immortality." A bit of cheese as garnish, topping or dessert not only enlivens the taste but often adds those necessary aminos which round out the protein content to make a dish nutritionally satisfying as well. Like eggs, cheeses are very heat-sensitive, and individual recipes reflect their special needs. But unlike eggs, many cheeses depend for their flavor and cooking quality on skillful aging.

In some climates certain hard cheeses are cellared for years like wines, but the American housewife seldom has the kind of storage facilities to keep cheeses *à point*. Soft cheeses, like mozzarella and Petit Gervais, are best eaten the day they are made. Like wine, cheese is a substance constantly in the process of change. Cheeses do not freeze well, and refrigerate only on a short-term basis. They should be bought in small lots, brought to their peak of ripeness, and served promptly. There are special cheese-keepers with a cloche cover and a platform elevated above a vinegar-holding base. Another device for short-term preservation is to wrap cheese in cloths which have been wrung out in vinegar. Sometimes storing cheese in covered glass or enameled containers helps; and the separate wrapping of each variety of cheese under refrigeration is essential. The most drastic method —at which true turophiles wince—is to buy canned cheese; or to pot natural cheese in crocks, 756, with a sufficient addition of wine, brandy or kirsch to arrest enzymatic action.

MAKING UNRIPENED SOFT CHEESES

Time was when milk was allowed to rest in a warm place until clabbered, when the curds and whey were separated by draining through a cloth bag. When the curds were firm to the touch, they were refrigerated for several hours, after which they could be beaten with additional cream until smooth to make a cottage cheese or **Schmierkäse.**

Today, for safety reasons, the recipes that follow are given for ➤ pasteurized milk. But, because the milk is pasteurized, ➤ Cultured Buttermilk, 533, or Rennet, 561, must be added to all the recipes to activate the curdling process. In making these cheeses, use stainless steel, enamel or glazed crockery vessels. Have ready: a dairy thermometer, a long wooden spoon, a large pan, a rack, and a muslin sack or Chinese cap strainer, 337, for dripping the cheese. A long stainless knife is needed for cutting the curd. If you make these soft cheeses often, make yourself a curd cutter of a stainless wire looped into an elongated "U" with the arms from 1 to 2 inches apart, and deep enough to fit the pan in which you develop the curd. Make up the recipes as described. When the curd is ready, cut through it with your curd cutter, lengthwise and crosswise of the pan as shown on 538. Then cut from the bottom of the pan horizontally at 1-inch intervals to form cheese curd cubes. Process as described in the recipe. ➤ Store these cheeses refrigerated. Do not keep more than 4 or 5 days. Serve garnished with:

Chopped chives, burnet, basil or tarragon
Chopped olives or nuts

Use as a base for hors d'oeuvre and dips and to fill tomato cases. Or use them in:

Cottage Cheese Dessert, 756
Coeur à la Crème, 756

COTTAGE CHEESE

About 1½ Pounds

Commercially available today is a confusing variety of cottage cheese. If called **creamed,** they have been recombined so as to have the approximate fat value of whole milk. If called **bakers'** or **hoop** cheese, they are, like cottage cheese, made of skimmed milk but are more acid because the curd is not washed. If called **farmer's** cheese, they may

have been made with whole milk, but the curd has been pressed sufficiently so the cheese may be sliced.
➤ Please read about Making Unripened Soft Cheeses, above.
Have at 70° to 72°:

1 gallon pasteurized fresh skim milk

If whole milk is used, the cream is lost in the whey. Stir in:

½ cup fresh cultured Buttermilk, 533

Let this mixture stand at 70° to 75° temperature until clabbered, 12 to 14 hours. Cube the curd, as described previously. Let rest 10 minutes. Add:

2 quarts 98° to 100° water

Set the pan on a rack in a larger pan of water and heat until the curd reaches 98° to 100°. Hold at this temperature, ➤ not higher, 30 minutes to 1 hour, stirring gently every 5 minutes—or the curd will toughen. Do not break the curd. As the whey is forced out, the curds will settle. ➤ To test for doneness, squeeze them. They should break clean between the fingers and, when pressed, should not leave a semifluid milky residue. Pour the curds and whey ➤ gently into a scalded sack or Chinese cap strainer. Rough handling can cause as much as a 20% loss in bulk. Rinse the curds with:

(Cold water)

to minimize the acid flavor. Let drain in a cool place until whey ceases to drip; but the surface of the cheese should not become dry-looking. The cheese may then be combined with:

(Whipping cream)

To serve or store, see Making Unripened Soft Cheeses, above.

RICH CREAM CHEESE

About 1½ Pounds

➤ Please read about Making Unripened Soft Cheeses, above.
Combine:

1 gallon fresh pasteurized whole milk
½ cup fresh cultured Buttermilk, 533

Dissolve thoroughly in:

¼ cup cold water
¼ to ½ household rennet tablet—available at dairy supply houses

and mix with the milk, which should be at 85°. ➤ Stir gently 10 minutes and begin to watch for any thickening. ➤ Stop stirring the moment you sense the thickening. Put the filled bowl you are using into a larger one of warm water and maintain the milk at 80° to 85° until whey covers the surface and the curds break clean from the sides of the bowl when it is tipped. Cut into 1-inch curds as described above. Now put the curds and whey into a colander and, when nearly drained, press out any remaining whey. Reserve and chill the whey until you can skim off butterlike cream, and work it back into the curds. When the cheese is firm, add:

1½ teaspoons salt
(Additional seasoning)
(Additional cream)

To serve or store, see Unripened Soft Cheeses, opposite.

MAKING SEMIHARD AND HARD CHEESES

There are many variations, but the harder and more frequently you press the cheese during processing, the firmer the cheese will become. Except for a cheese press, which can be improvised as described below, hard cheeses can be made with regular sterile household equipment suggested in making soft cheeses, 536. The process described below is for about 1½ pounds of cheese. If you plan aging the cheese, you may want to make larger wheels to keep it from drying out.
Pour into a large stainless or enamel pan:

1 gallon milk: certified raw or homogenized, or goat's or ewe's milk

Add and stir in well:

3 tablespoons cultured Buttermilk, 533

If you have used goat's or ewe's milk, you may need to double the amount of buttermilk. Cover and let stand at 70° temperature at least 4 but not longer than 12 hours. If you care to color the cheese, use:

(A coloring tablet based on malt—available at dairy supply houses)

Dissolve the tablet well in:

2 tablespoons water

Now place the pan of prepared milk in a larger pan of hot water and slowly bring up the heat until the temperature of the milk is 86° F. If you are coloring the cheese, stir in the liquid color thoroughly at this time. While the milk is reaching the required temperature, prepare a coagulant by thoroughly dissolving:

1 household rennet tablet—available at dairy supply houses

in:

2 tablespoons cold water

Then allow the milk to reach 88° to 90° before stirring in the rennet solution. Continue stirring about 1 minute. Remove the pan from the hot water and allow the mixture to rest covered 30 minutes to 1 hour. If you have used certified raw milk or homogenized milk, it should coagulate during this period. If, however, you have used milk solids, it may be necessary to leave the pan immersed in the hot water, maintaining the 88° to 90° temperature of the milk. In either case, to test for the proper degree of coagulation, insert your well-washed finger in the curd at an angle as if to lift some out. If the curd breaks clean over your finger, it is ready for cutting.

Cut the curd lengthwise and crosswise at ½-inch intervals, as shown on 538, using a long stainless steel curd cutter or a stainless knife. Then cut diagonally at a 45° angle as shown. These repeated cuts will divide the curd into small, even bits. If these cuts have been carefully made from the top to the bottom of the pan, there should be no large lumps when you start to work the curd with your hand. Should there be some, however, cut them with the curd cutter rather than smashing them between your fingers. Then for 15 minutes work the curd with one well-washed hand, in long slow movements around the edge and up through the curd from bottom to top, letting the portion you bring to the surface gently recede into the mass. The curds will begin to shrink in size as they separate from the yellowish whey. Cook the curd a second time by returning the pan to its hot water bath and bringing the developing curds and whey to 102° over a 20- to 30-minute period. Hold at 102° for 30 to 40 minutes longer. During this time stir gently with a long wooden spoon every 3 to 5 minutes. The curd is ready for firming when it forms a loose mass in your hand. The individual curds will be of wheat-grain size and the entire mass will look like eggs scrambled over too high heat. To firm the curd, remove the pan from the hot water and let the curds-and-whey mixture stand, covered, 1 hour. During this period, stir every 5 to 10 minutes.

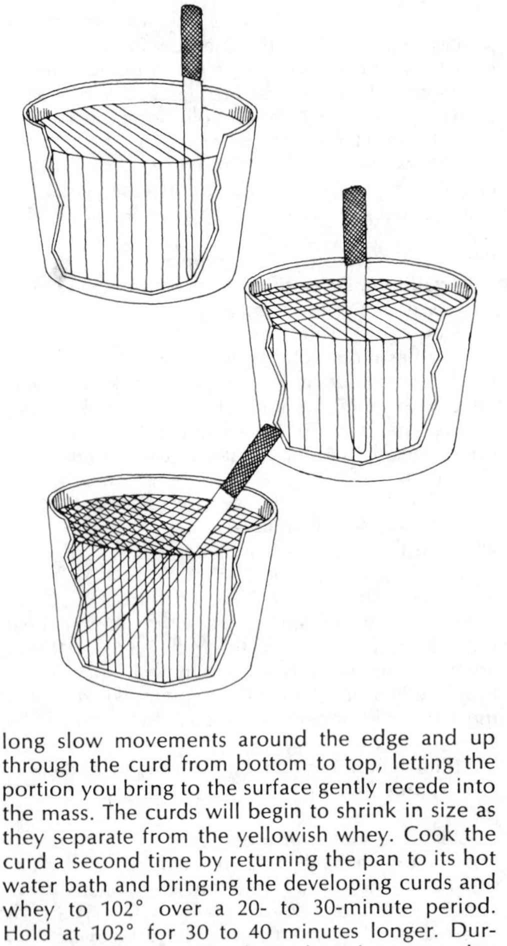

To drain the curd, line a colander with several thicknesses of cheesecloth that are large enough so the ends hang well over the sides of the colander. Pour the curds and whey into the lined colander, and drain off the whey by lifting the curds in the cloth and rolling the mass from one side of the cloth to the other. Now set the drained curd, still in the cloth, in the colander again. You may work into it with your well-washed hand about:

(5 teaspoons salt)

Then form the curd into a ball within the cloth and squeeze out as much whey as possible. Knot the cheesecloth around the ball to form a bag you can hang from your sink faucet, and let the cheese drain another 20 minutes. Just before pressing, you may add flavoring such as:

2 tablespoons caraway seed or preserved chopped peppers

Now prepare to press the cheese. As pressing is a drippy business, confine your activities to the sink area. If you have no press, improvise one by cutting a 7- to 8-inch-deep rim from a plastic container about 4 to 5 inches in diameter. Place it on a plate, as shown below. This will form your mold. Line it with a 15-inch square of boiled muslin. After heaping the curds into the lined mold, fold the muslin over the top so all the curds are wrapped. You will also need two 1-inch-thick oak disks, just smaller in diameter than the mold, and bricks for weighting them down. First, put on one disk and weight it down with the bricks. As

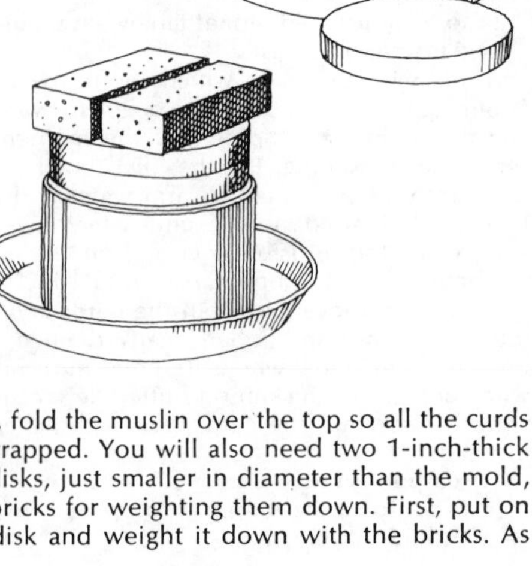

the whey rises and runs or is poured off and the curds contract, you may add the second disk under the bricks to allow pressure to continue.

During the next 20 minutes, increase the pressure by adding weight gradually with extra bricks. Be careful to add weight only to the point at which whey, and not curds, escapes. Then let the cheese rest in the press 12 to 24 hours in a cool place. Remove the cheese from the press, unfold the muslin and allow the cheese, again in a cool place, to air, unwrapped, on a rack from 12 to 36 hours. For an alternate way to make a mold and weight it, see 535.

This so-called new cheese is bland in flavor and suitable for cheese spread recipes, 71, and for some dessert cheeses, 756. To age this "new" cheese and allow it to develop its full flavor, dip it, when the exterior is absolutely dry, into a thin coat of melted paraffin, 833, to seal off the air and prevent mold. Refrigerate where the temperature drops no lower than 35°; or in the vegetable crisper of your refrigerator, where the temperature is about 40°. Temperatures above 55° cause the cheese to spoil. Date the wrapping with a masking-tape label. Flavor will develop within 2 weeks to 2 months or longer. ➤ If you have used unpasteurized or uncertified milk, age the cheese at least 6 months before serving. If any surface mold has formed, wipe it off; or if it has penetrated the cheese, cut it out. Mold-ripened cheese like Roquefort and blue which show a mold pattern throughout are specially impregnated with a bacillus during aging and are beyond the skills of most household operations. **Cheddaring** of cheese calls for still another cooking operation and elaborate cutting and layering of the cheese, as well as aging up to 3 years for a sharp cheddar.

ABOUT FATS IN COOKING

Nothing reveals the quality of a cuisine so unmistakably as the fat on which it is based. Bacon arouses memories of our South, olive oil evokes Mediterranean cooking, and sweet butter will bring forth memories of fine meals in many places. Not only flavors but food textures change with the use of different fats, whose characteristics are as individual as their tastes.

Let's take a bird's-eye view of fat versatility in cooking. Fats, when used with discretion and skill, have the power to force flavor in foods and to envelop gluten strands and "shorten" them into a more tender structure. Fats also form the emulsifying agent in gravies and mayonnaise and can act as a preservative in coating some foods like Stocks, 520, and Terrines, 494. And butter gives the most beautiful browning in breads and pastries.

Fats for cooking, of course, include both solid fats and liquid oils. ➤ Fats are solid at about 70°. ➤ Oils remain liquid at these temperatures, although they may become solidified when refrigerated. It is fashionable today to scorn fats for their calories and to fear "saturated" fats for their cholesterol. Examples of highly saturated fats are butter and the commercially hydrogenated shortenings. ➤ Other fats, like vegetable and nut oils, are polyunsaturated. Peanut and olive oils, called monounsaturated, are almost neutral in their effect. For more about the properties of fat, see 5.

MEASURING BULK FATS

We suggest measuring bulk fats by the displacement method. If you want ½ cup fat, fill the measuring cup half full of water. Put in fat until the water reaches the 1-cup calibration mark. Drain the cup of water. The amount of fat remaining in the container will then, of course, equal ½ cup.

Some people prefer to use a set of measuring cups, especially for solid shortenings. These hold respectively ¼, ⅓, ½ and 1 whole cup. ➤ But if you use them, push the solid shortening down well into the bottom of these measures or a considerable space may be left, which will make your measurement inaccurate.

ABOUT BUTTER

➤ Most of the recipes in this book call for **sweet butter**—first-grade butter made from sweet cream with no added salt. Sometimes amounts vary in a single recipe. In such instances, the lesser amount will give you a palatable result, while the larger quantity may produce a superlative one.

If you wonder why the lovely, pale, delicately fragrant, waxy curl on your Paris breakfast tray is so good, here is one reason. The Brittany cows are fed and milked so the butter making can be coordinated with the first possible transportation to Paris, where it is served at once. So use butter promptly.

All butter is made from fresh or soured cream and by law must have a fat content of 80%. The remaining 20% is largely water, with some milk solids. Small amounts of salt are sometimes added for flavor or for preservative action. **Salt butter** may be purchased or made at home from sweet or soured cream and keeps longer than sweet butter. Without the addition of color, most butter would be very pale rather than the warm "butter yellow" to which we are accustomed.

Processed butter, often sold in bulk, is made by rechurning less desirable butter with fresh milk to remove unwanted odors or flavors.

The word "creamery" which sometimes appears on both sweet and salt butter packages is a hangover from the days when cream went to a place called a creamery to be processed. The word now carries no standard or type significance—it's just meant to be reassuring!

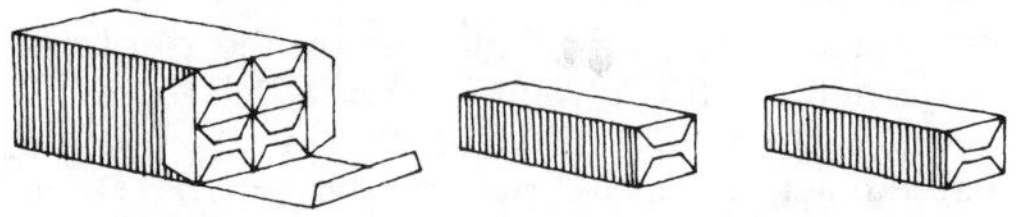

2 cups *½ cup or 8 tablespoons*

➤ All butter should be stored in the refrigerator and kept covered to prevent absorption of other food flavors. Two weeks is considered the maximum storage time for refrigerated butter.

✻ Freeze butter for no more than 6 months at 0° temperature. If no refrigeration is available, butter is best wrapped and kept in brine, 569, in a cool place.

➤ One pound of butter equals 2 cups, and when the pound is wrapped in quarters, each stick equals 8 tablespoons or ½ cup. See sketch above. ➤ To substitute butter for other fats, see 593. While these substitutions are satisfactory in cooking, flavor and nutritional factors are not necessarily similar. For seasoned butters, see 349; for nut butters, see 71 and 564. For Clarified or Drawn Butter, see 349.

CHURNED SWEET BUTTER

Butter is only as good as the cream from which it is made. Clean whole milk is kept cool and covered during separation, which takes about 24 hours by gravity. Skim the cream and pasteurize it, 530, stirring frequently to deter "skin" formation. Cool the cream at once to 50° or less and keep it at about 55° during the entire butter-making process. Start to churn after 3 to 24 hours of chilling. Most of us have inadvertently turned small quantities of cream into butter in an electric beater or ⅄ blender, see below. We may even have imitated churning by flipping a jar of cream rhythmically in a figure-8 motion. For larger quantities, use a churn and keep the cream between 55° and 60°. A higher temperature will produce a greasy consistency; a lower one, a brittle, tallowy one. A gallon of cream should yield about 3 pounds of butter.

Using at least 30% cream, fill a sterile churn one-third to one-half full. Depending on the quantity you are churning, the butter should "make" within 15 to 40 minutes. We used to visit a neighbor while she churned and were amazed at how much slower the process was in threatening or stormy weather. The cream usually stays foamy during the first half of churning. By and by it will look like cornmeal mush. At this point, proceed cautiously. It then grows to corn-kernel size. Now, stop churning. Drain off and measure the buttermilk. Wash the butter twice, with as much 50° to 70° pure water as you have buttermilk.

If you salt the butter, use ⅔ to 1 tablespoon salt to 1 pound butter, folding the salt into the butter with a wet paddle. Mold it in a form or fashion it into rolls, using a damp cloth. Wrap it in parchment or foil. To store, see About Butter, 539.

⅄ BLENDER SWEET BUTTER

Chill the blender. Blend at high speed about 15 seconds:

1 cup Light Whipping Cream, 531

or until the cream coats the blades. Add:

½ cup ice water

Continue to blend at high speed until the butter rises to the surface. Strain off the butter. Press out any additional moisture; mold and chill. Keep the liquid residue to add to soup; it is not rich enough to substitute for buttermilk.

GELATIN-EXPANDED BUTTER

For dieters and frugal housewives, there are two types of expanded butter. Whipped butter, a commercial product, has had air or some inert gas incorporated to increase volume and ease of spreading. The other type is increased by the addition of gelatin.

About 2 Pounds

Soak until dissolved:

¼ cup gelatin

in:

2 cups milk

Heat the milk and gelatin in a double boiler ➤ over, not in, boiling water. Cut into pieces and put into a deep bowl to soften:

1 lb. butter

Warm the butter bowl over hot water. Whip the gelatin mixture gradually into the butter. Add to taste:

(Salt)

Should milk bubbles appear, continue beating until they go away. Pour the butter into molds and chill well before serving.

ABOUT BUTTER SHAPES

Such a delicious staple deserves attractive presentation. Try using a butter curler, shown in use opposite on the right. It is our favorite because the light ⅛-inch-thick shells are such decorative assets and of just the right texture for spreading. Dip the curler into warm water before pulling it lightly over firm butter. If the butter is too cold, the curls will crack. Put the curls at once into cold water and store in the refrigerator until ready to drain and serve. The same procedure will keep intact the butter balls and molds described below.

Butter for molding is first cut into ½-inch-thick slices. It is most easily molded with a plunger, as shown lower center; or, if formed into balls, with

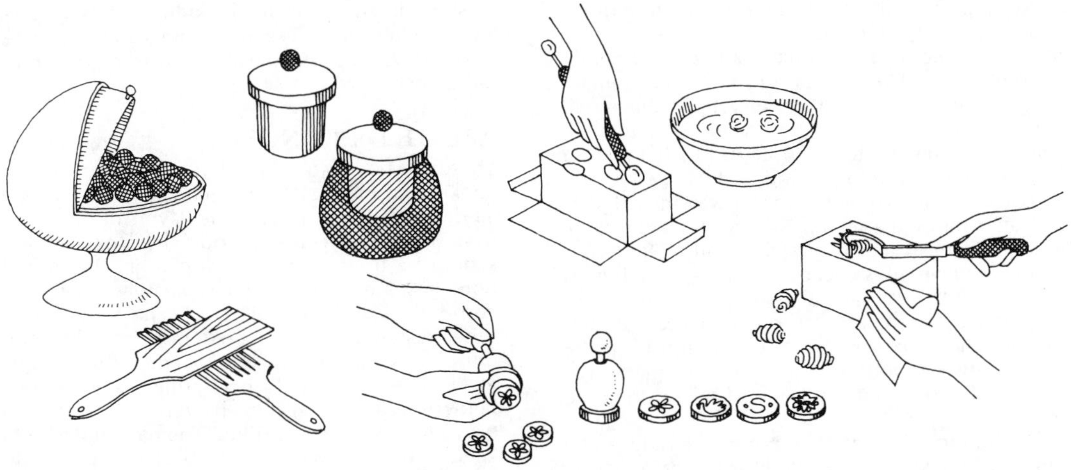

a pair of corrugated wooden paddles, shown lower left. Use the paddles so their striations form a crisscross pattern. Then treat as for butter curls, above. Both types of utensil must be conditioned for use by pouring over them a generous stream of boiling water, then submerging them in ice water. For an easier if less elegant way to make butter balls, try melon ballers, which come in various sizes. Dip ballers first into hot water. Scoop out the butter ball and drop it into a dish of ice water. Serve the balls piled on a rack over ice in a sliding-domed covered dish, shown top left. Another attractive way to serve butter is in small clay crocks. Our favorite, second on the left, is one that fits into a base that holds ice water. You may decorate evenly cut squares of butter with tiny herb leaves or flowers, lightly pressed into the surface.

ABOUT VEGETABLE SHORTENINGS

Frequently these have a polyunsaturated-oil base —soybean, corn, cottonseed, peanut—refined, deodorized and ➤ hydrogenated. This process, which adds hydrogen, solidifies the polyunsaturated vegetable oils, absorbing the oxygen in their free fatty acids and converting them to saturated fats. Often these oils also have some added animal fats or saturated vegetable fats such as coconut.

There may also be minute additions of emulsifiers and mono- and diglyceride fats. These and the air incorporated into them make these bland shortenings technically superior for baking: they add a greater volume than that achieved with other solid fats like butter, and they create a softer, spongier texture. If color has been added to any of these products, the label so states.

➤ Vegetable shortening may be stored covered in a tin at 70° over long periods.

➤ To substitute solid shortening for butter, replace measure for measure, as the water in the butter compensates for the air in the shortening.

➤ But, if substituting weight for weight, use 15% to 20% less shortening than butter.

ABOUT MARGARINES

Margarines, like butter, must by law contain 80% fat—the rest being water, milk solids and salt. Almost all margarines are enriched also with added vitamins and color, to try to make them comparable to butter. Margarines today are usually emulsions of milk and refined vegetable oils, some of which may be hydrogenated. Also, some may have added animal fats. Read the label for this information.

➤ Margarines, because of their similar moisture content, may be substituted for butter, weight for weight or measure for measure. They produce textures somewhat different from butter in both cooking and baking and lack the desirable butter flavor. They are perishable and must be kept covered, under refrigeration.

ABOUT OILS

Vegetable oils are pressed from various seeds, fruits and nuts. Nutrients are best retained by cold press processes. Among the oil sources are corn, cottonseed, olive, soybean, sesame, safflower, sunflower and peanut. There are also such nut oils as walnut, hickory and beechnut, which are better used for salad dressings than for cooking, as they break down under high heat.

After being pressed, the oils are refined, bleached and deodorized so thoroughly that, except for olive, the end products are rarely distinguishable one from the other by flavor or odor; but in cooking they differ greatly in their smoking points. Safflower, soybean, cottonseed and corn oil have higher smoking points than peanut and sesame oils. Soybean oil is not recommended for deep-fat frying, as it foams. Olive oil, the lowest, ranges around 400°.

Most oils for salad are further treated to remove cloudiness at refrigerator temperatures. Oils should not be held too long at 70° even if tightly closed and in dark bottles. Most of them remain in a liquid state under refrigeration. Olive oil, which becomes semisolid when refrigerated, should be allowed to stand at 70° to return to a liquid condition before using.

Olive oils are like wines in the way their flavors are affected by the soils in which they are grown. Greek, Spanish, Italian—try them all to find your favorite. Olive oil is cheaper by the gallon, but, as it is susceptible to rancidity—especially the cold-press type—when exposed to light and air, decant it into smaller containers. Use one and keep the other resealed bottles in a cool, dark place. For further discussion of the value of oils in the diet, see 5.

As oils are 100% fat, they ➤ must be reduced by 15% to 20% when substituted for butter, either by weight or by measure. However, there are additional complications when substituting them for solid fats, especially in baking, see 683. So in this book ➤ when oil is used in baking recipes, it is specifically indicated and the proper amounts and procedures are given.

ABOUT LARD

Lard, which is fat rendered from pork, is a softer, oilier fat than butter, margarine or the other solid shortenings. **Leaf lard**—whether bought or home-rendered—is a definitely superior type. It comes from the layered fat around the kidneys, rather than from trimmings and incidental fatty areas. Due to the more crystalline structure of this lard, it cuts into flour to create a flakier texture in biscuits and crusts, although this same crystalline character handicaps it for cake baking. This is less true for those lards which have been hydrogenated, refined and emulsified. Ordinary lards are offered in bulk or package form. ➤ All lards should be stored in covered containers in a cool place, preferably the refrigerator.

➤ To substitute lard for butter in cooking, use 15% to 20% less lard.

ABOUT POULTRY FATS

Fats from chicken, turkeys, ducks and geese, whether home or commercially rendered, are highly regarded for dietary reasons. When rendered from the leaf or cavity fat, they are firm, bland and light in color. From sources such as skimmed broth and other cooking, they are likely to be soft, grainy and darker in color. ➤ Store them covered in the refrigerator.

➤ To substitute, use 3/4 cup clarified poultry fat to 1 cup butter.

ABOUT PORK FAT

This is used in both fresh and salted form. Salt pork, which comes from the flank, is used to line Pâtés, 494; for Lardoons, 445; and for Barding, 420. Fresh pork fat, especially the kidney fat, is used as an ingredient in farces and sausages and in pâté mixtures. ➤ To remove excess salt from salt pork, see below.

ABOUT DRIPPINGS

These are fats that are rendered in the process of cooking fat meats. When making gravies, they are all desirable in reinforcing the flavors of the meats from which they come, although lamb and mutton should be used with great discretion. Bacon and pork fats are often stored separately for use in corn breads and meat pie crusts and for flavoring other dishes where salt pork may be called for. Other fats may be mixed together for storage. ➤ All these fats should be clarified, as described below, before storage in the refrigerator, to improve their keeping qualities. The natural desire to keep a container handy at the back of the stove to receive and reuse these drippings needs to be curbed. Exposed to varying degrees of warmth, these are subject to quick spoilage.

➤ To substitute drippings for butter, use 15% to 20% less drippings.

RENDERING OR TRYING OUT FATS

Trying out or rendering solid fats such as chicken, duck, suet and lard improves the keeping quality by removing all connective tissue, possible impurities and moisture. Dice the fat and heat it ➤ very slowly in a heavy pan with a small quantity of water. You may speed up this process by pressing the fat with the back of a slotted spoon or a potato masher. When the fat is liquid and still fairly warm, strain it through cheesecloth and store it ➤ refrigerated. The browned connective tissues in the strainer—known as **cracklings**—may be kept for flavoring.

CLARIFYING FATS

To clarify fats that have been used in frying and to rid them of burned food particles and other impurities ➤ heat them slowly. You may add to the fat during this heating 4 to 5 slices of potato per cup of fat to help absorb unwanted flavors. When the potato is quite brown, strain the fat while still warm through cheesecloth. ➤ Store refrigerated. To clarify butter, see 349.

REMOVING EXCESS SALT FROM FATS

To remove excess salt from bacon or salt pork, parblanch it before use for larding, 444, or in delicate braises and ragoûts. Put it in a heavy pan. Cover it with ➤ cold water. Bring the water slowly to a boil and ➤ simmer uncovered 3 to 10 minutes. Allow the longer time if the dice are as big as 1 x 1 x 1/2 inch. Drain and use.

To remove salt from cooking butter, heat it slowly to avoid browning it. Skim it. Allow it to cool in the pan and remove the fat cake. Any sediment and moisture should be in the bottom of the pan. Butter so clarified is used in a number of ways, especially to seal off potted meats and in cooking where a slower browning is wanted, as for boned chicken.

ABOUT EGGS

Nothing stimulates the practiced cook's imagination or the nutritionist's enthusiasm like a good fresh egg, for eggs contain all the balanced nutrients from which a complete organism develops.

Eggs can transform cake doughs by providing a structural framework for leaven, can thicken custards and make them smooth, can tenderize timbales and produce fine-grained ice creams. They bind gravies and mayonnaise, clarify or enrich soups, glaze rolls, insulate pie doughs against sogginess, create glorious meringues and soufflés, and make ideal luncheon and emergency fare.

Because fresh eggs do all these things better than old eggs and because there is no comparison in taste and texture between the two, ➤ always buy the very best quality you can find. It doesn't matter if their yolks are light or dark or if their shells are white or brown—as long as the shells are not shiny. While there is no test, except tasting, for good flavor, ➤ the relative freshness of eggs may be determined by placing them in a bowl of cold water. Those that float are not usable. Unshelled onto a plate as shown below ➤ a truly fresh egg has a yolk that domes up and stays up, and a thick and translucent white, containing a ropelike strand of material called chalaza which anchors the yoke in place. This is usable, as is the small dark fleck which indicates that the egg has been fertilized. Remove the fleck only if using the egg in a light-colored sauce or confection.

Strange as it may seem after stressing the purchase of fresh eggs, we now tack on an amendment. ➤ Do not use eggs fresher than three days old for hard-cooked eggs or for beating and baking. If you do, hard-cooked eggs will turn greenish and become difficult to peel, and cakes may fail to rise properly because the eggs will not beat to the proper volume.

➤ Never use a doubtful egg with any odor or discoloration, especially one that is cracked: here is where salmonella can develop, see 444.

Eggs should really be bought and measured by weight, but tradition is against this sensible approach. ➤ We assume in this book that you are using 2-ounce eggs. These are known in the trade as "large." They should carry a Grade A stamp as well as the date of grading. If in doubt about size, weigh or measure them. The yolk of a 2-ounce egg is just about 1 tablespoon plus a teaspoon; the white, about 2 tablespoons. For more equivalents, see 594 and 595. To realize how great a difference egg size has on volume, notice below that two large eggs give you about half a cup, but it takes three medium eggs to fill that same half-cup. When you decrease a recipe and want to use only part of an egg, beat the egg slightly and measure about 1½ tablespoons for half an egg and about 1 tablespoon for one-third.

Don't expect the same texture or flavor from eggs of other fowl—from lark to ostrich; one of the latter, by the way, will serve 24 for brunch. In using off-beat eggs be very sure of freshness.

✲ To freeze and thaw eggs, see 827. To preserve eggs, see 814.

DRIED EGGS

When fresh eggs are not available, dried eggs are a convenience, but they are not an economy. Because of bacterial dangers, they must always be used in recipes that call for thorough cooking, unless a large percentage of acid is indicated. Packaged dried eggs should be stored at 70° and, if opened, should be refrigerated in a tightly lidded glass container. To reconstitute the equivalent of 3 fresh eggs, sift ½ cup dried whole egg powder over ½ cup water. Whip until smooth. To substitute for 1 egg, use 2½ tablespoons sifted dry egg powder to 2½ tablespoons water. Beat until smooth. ➤ Use either of these mixtures within five minutes after combining. You may prefer to add the egg powder to the dry ingredients, and the water to the rest of the liquid called for in the recipe.

COOKING EGGS

It is possible, on a hot summer day, "they" say, to fry an egg on the sidewalk. We do not recommend this particular extravagance; we mention it to remind you that eggs cook quickly over any kind of heat—beginning to thicken at 144°.

Sometimes, even when eggs are cooking in a double boiler ➤ over—not in—boiling water, the heat of the pan will cause them to curdle. Be doubly careful then ➤ with all egg dishes, not to use excessive heat and not to prolong the cooking period. Should you suspect you have done either of these things, dump the egg mixture at once into a cold dish and beat vigorously, or add a tablespoon of chilled cream. You may thus save the mixture from curdling.

Only prior precautions, however, will produce smooth baked custard dishes. For, once the protein of the egg has shrunk, it can no longer hold moisture in suspension, and the results are bound to be watery. If you are combining eggs with a hot mixture, condition them first by adding a small quantity of the hot mixture to the beaten eggs. Then add the eggs to the remaining hot mixture. Often, too, at this point in egg cookery—if you are preparing a soufflé base or thickening soup or a sauce with yolks—there is enough stored heat in the pan to do the necessary cooking.

If you are going to cook an egg yolk and sugar mixture, beat the eggs, add the sugar, and continue to beat until the mixture runs in a broad ribbon from the side of the spoon. When this condition has been reached, the eggs will cook without graining. In preparing soft-cooked eggs, the use of an egg-timer, shown 543, is a safeguard against overcooking.

Now, armed with two more secrets, you can expect real magic from the rich, complete and tasty protein that is tidily packed inside an eggshell. For more details about the nutritive value of eggs, see 2. In baking and in making omelets or scrambled eggs, remember that eggs will give better texture and volume if they are about 65° to 75° at the outset. Also remember that because egg yolk is almost one-third fat, you can count on some slight thickening action as eggs cool in a pudding or sauce.

BEATING EGGS

➤ To beat whole eggs to their greatest volume, have them at 65° to 75°. Before adding them to batters and doughs, beat whole eggs and yolks vigorously—unless otherwise directed in the recipe—until they are light in color and texture.

For some recipes, whole eggs and yolks profit by as much as 5 minutes or more of beating in the electric mixer and will increase up to six times their original volume.

To describe the beating of egg whites is almost as cheeky as advising how to lead a happy life. But, because the success of a dish may rest entirely on this operation, we go into it in some detail. To get the greatest volume ➤ see that the egg whites are 65° to 75° and properly separated. We have already referred to the bride who couldn't boil an egg. But there are plenty of housewives who can't even break one. Here's how. Have 3 bowls ready, as sketched. Holding an egg in one hand, tap the center of the side of the egg lightly, yet sharply, on the edge of one of the bowls—making an even, crosswise break. Then take the egg in both hands with the break on the upper side. Hold it over the center of a small bowl and tip it so that the wider end is down. Hold the edges of the break with the thumbs. Widen the break by pulling the edges apart until the eggshell is broken into halves. As you do this, some of the egg white flows into the bowl underneath. The yolk and the rest of the egg white will remain in the lower half of the shell. Now pour the remaining egg back and forth from one half-shell to the other, letting some more of the white flow into the bowl each time until only the yolk remains in the shell. During this shifting process, you will be able to tell quickly, with each egg in turn, if there is any discoloration or off-odor. You can discard the dubious egg before it is put with the yolks on the left or with the whites in the large bowl on the right.

Should the yolk shatter during breaking, you can try to remove particles from the white by inserting the corner of a paper towel moistened in cold water and making the yolk adhere to it. Should you fail to clear the yolk entirely from the white, keep that egg for another use, because the slightest fat from the yolk will lessen the volume of the beaten whites and perceptibly change the texture.

➤ Choose a large deep bowl in which to beat, shaped as sketched on the right, below. Be sure it is not aluminum, which will gray the eggs; or plastic, which in spite of careful washing may retain a slight film of grease, deterring volume development. The French dote on copper. But if cream of tartar is used to give a more stable and tender foam, the acid present will turn the eggs greenish in a copper bowl.

In recipes for meringues and in some cakes, a portion of the sugar, about 1 teaspoon per egg, is beaten into the egg whites when they are foamy. Although this reduces volume slightly and means a longer beating period, it does give a much more upstanding foam.

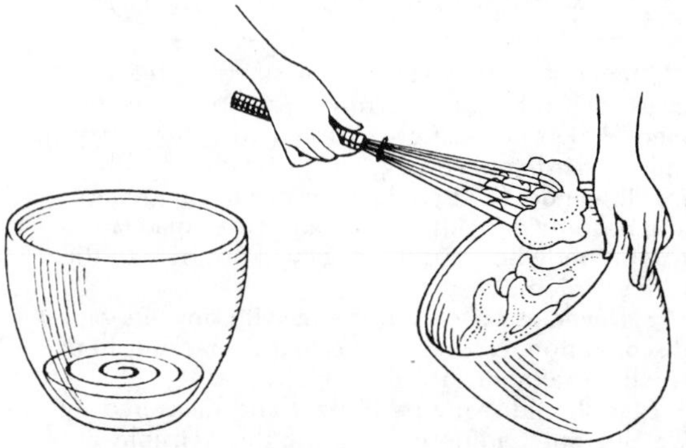

The lightness of the beating stroke, plus the thinness of the wire whisk used, also make an appreciable difference in building up the air capacity of egg-white cells. ➤ Choose as a beater a long many-thin-wired whisk, as shown. ➤ Be sure that bowl, beater and scraper are absolutely free of grease, but if made of plastic the equipment may not be greaseproof. To clean them, use a detergent or a combination of lemon juice and vinegar. Rinse and dry carefully.

If you are going to use the whites in baking, have the oven preheated. Start beating only when all other ingredients are mixed and ready. Be prepared to give about 300 strokes in 2 minutes to beat 2 egg whites. You can expect 2½ to 4 times the volume you start with. Begin slowly and lightly with a very relaxed wrist motion and beat steadily until the egg whites lose their yellowish translucency. They will become foamy. Then gradually increase the beating tempo. Beat without stopping ➤ until the whites are both airy and glossy and stand in peaks that are firm, but still soft and elastic, see opposite.

From start to finish, there should be no stopping until that state is reached that is best described as ➤ stiff, but not dry. Another test for readiness is the rate of flow when the bowl is tipped. Some cooks use the inverted bowl test in which the whites cling dramatically to the bottom of the upside-down bowl. Usually, when this is possible, the eggs have been beaten a trifle too long and are as a consequence too dry. Although they may have greater volume, their cells will not stretch to capacity in baking without breaking down. If using an electric mixer, follow the manufacturer's directions. We do not recommend the use of a blender for beating egg whites.

Folding in egg whites should always be a manual operation rather than a mechanical one, since it is essential again to retain as much air in the whites as possible. ➤ Work both quickly and gently. Add the heavier mixture to the lighter one. Then combine the two substances with two separate movements. Various special tools, like wire "incorporators" and spatulas, have been suggested for this process, but nothing can compare for efficiency with the human hand. First use a sharp, clean action, as though cutting a cake. Then, with a lifting motion, envelop the whites by bringing the heavier substance up from the bottom of the bowl. Repeat these slicing and lifting motions alternately, turning the bowl as you work, trying meanwhile not to break down the air in the beaten whites.

STORING EGGS

The storage of eggs is not difficult if you follow a few simple rules. ➤ Whether from nest or market ➤ eggs should not be washed until ready for use, as they are covered with a soluble film which protects the porous shell against bacterial entry. ➤ If there is no special storage area for them, place eggs still in their carton in the refrigerator. ➤ Raw eggs in the shell and foods containing eggs—like mayonnaise and custards in which the eggs are raw or only slightly cooked—should be kept covered, under refrigeration, and away from strong-smelling foods, as they absorb odors easily.

To store egg whites in the refrigerator, cover them closely and do not keep them longer than 4 days. Then ➤ use them only in recipes that call for cooking. To store unbroken egg yolks, cover them first with water, which you then drain off before using. Cover the storage dish before refrigerating. Yolks may be stored uncooked up to 4 days, or for a few days longer if poached in water until firm. Then ➤ they should only be used in recipes that call for cooking. If poached, sieve the eggs with a pinch of salt and use in sauces or as a garnish for vegetables. For other uses of extra whites or yolks, see 598.

Before we leave this subject, we pull out of our hat a conjurer's trick. Should you have any doubts about which eggs in your refrigerator are hard-cooked and which are not, a quick test is to twirl them on their pointed ends. The hard-cooked eggs will spin like a top; the others will simply topple over.

And a hint about washing egg-soiled dishes. Start with cold water, which releases rather than glues on the protein. Rub egg-stained silver with salt if polish is not handy.

ABOUT FLOURS

We have become so accustomed to our highly bleached white flours that we forget that earlier cooks knew only whole-kernel flours. These were not the so-called whole wheat of our commercial world, but the whole grain, which includes the germ. Even the fine manchet flour of tradition contained some germ. But many flours in general use today completely lack it. As Dr. A. J. Carlson, a leading investigator on foods and nutrition, says so graphically, "When rats and gray squirrels are given corn in abundance, they eat the germ and leave the rest. People leave the germ and eat the rest." This nutritious and tasty entity, the germ, is usually removed in modern milling, because flours made with it are harder both to mill and to keep. After the removal of the outer coats and germ, our flours may be "enriched," but the term is misleading. ➤ Enriched flour contains only some of the many ingredients known to have been removed from it in milling. You may further fortify your enriched all-purpose flour by combining it with some of the flours described below which may have as much as sixteen times the protein value of wheat along with other important substances lacking in the wheat and rye flours we commonly use. If you are interested in these cereal components, see *Composition of Foods*, published by the USDA.

Flours must meet rigid government specifications and, when manufactured, must contain not more than 15% moisture. But they often acquire more in careless storage. Keep flour in clean, airtight containers and store in a cool place. Flours tend to dry out in high altitudes or during the winter months. Varying moisture content affects the way flours "handle." So some recipes for breads and pastries may read "2½ to 2¾ cups flour." If they do, ➤ measure the smaller amount of flour first, then add enough of, or even more than, the remaining flour until the dough is no longer sticky and begins to clean the sides of the bowl. Moisture also affects volume, and therefore we recommend sifting white flours for cakes and cookies. But neither white flours nor coarser flours nor cornmeal need be sifted in bread making.

In our miraculously mechanical but standardized economy, the average housewife, oddly enough, usually finds at hand only two kinds of white flour, both the results of highly milled or "patent" processing. These two easily available flours, called "all-purpose" and "cake," are used as their names imply. ➤ The single word "flour" in **Joy** recipes always means all-purpose unbleached wheat flour. For various ways to use flours as thickeners, see 338 to 339. For Browned Flour, see 339.

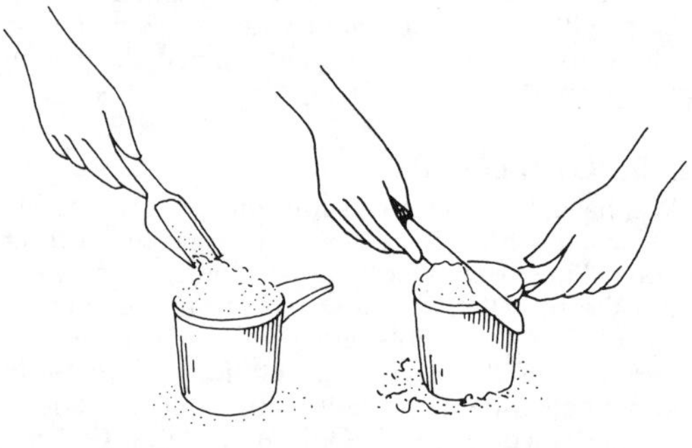

MEASURING FLOURS

It is particularly important that flour is not packed in measuring. Spoon the flour lightly into the cup so that it overflows the rim. Then level it off gently with a knife, as shown opposite.

➤ In baking, sifting-before-measuring is essential. There is a very easy way to do this neatly and quickly. Keep two 12-inch squares of stiff paper, foil or plastic on hand. Sift the flour onto the first square, as shown below, left. Rest your sifter on the second. Pick up the first sheet and curve it into a slide from which the flour can funnel itself into the measuring cup, which should be a dry measure shape, center. For very accurate measuring, cups designed for ¼, ⅓ and ½, as shown lower center, are also desirable. When the measure is filled, level the flour by running a knife across the top of the cup; see opposite. ➤ Never try to level the flour contents by shaking the cup, as this just repacks the sifted flour. Now you are ready to resift the flour with the other dry ingredients. Between siftings, move the sifter to the empty sheet and funnel the dry ingredients of the other sheet into the sifter top, as you did in measuring the flour in the center illustration.

Forgive us if we repeat, but always remember the important fact that ➤ flour can vary more than 20% in its ability to absorb moisture, depending on the type of wheat from which it was milled, its processing, and the amount of moisture absorbed during storage. For this reason, even the most accurate measurement may not always result in unqualified success, and sometimes adjustments must be made, on a purely experimental basis. Read about Flour Substitutions, 595.

ABOUT WHEAT FLOURS

Most grains are similar in their structure to the wheat kernel sketched in enlarged cross section. The outer or bran layers contain, with the germ—indicated by the darker swirl on the right—most of the grain's vitamins and minerals. The germ, which is only 2% of the entire kernel, contains the highest grade protein and all of the fat. The endosperm indicated on the left is largely starch, with some protein—different from but comple-

mentary to the protein of the germ. The outer coatings and the germ—small though they are compared with the whole kernel in this enlarged drawing—are of unchallenged importance in content and irreplaceable in flavor.

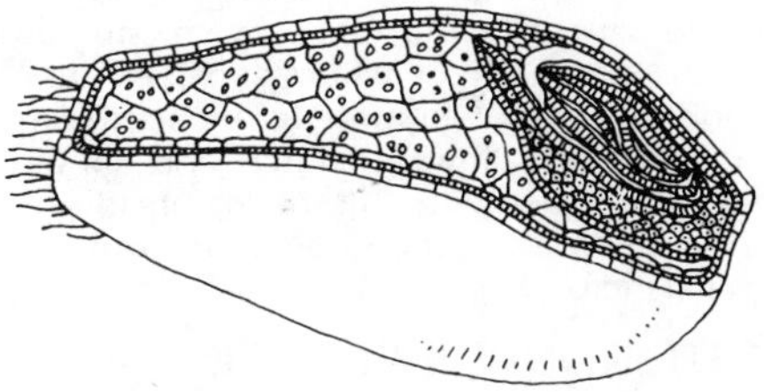

Older and slower methods of milling—such as stone grinding, which distributes the germ oil evenly and keeps the grain cooler during processing—prevent rancidity. High-speed steel milling produces greater heat and less even oil distribution, necessitating the removal of the germ to ensure longer shelf life. After buying very freshly ground unbleached flour, let it age about six weeks for best gluten development. However, try to use all flours containing gluten within 2 months of purchase, even though stored in the refrigerator or freezer, for gluten loses its strength with advancing age.

ALL-PURPOSE FLOUR

This is a blend of hard and soft wheat flours. The presence of more and tougher gluten in the hard wheat constituent results in a rather elastic and porous product. ➤ All-purpose flour, bleached or unbleached, can be used interchangeably, but unbleached has higher nutritional value. Some of the flours sold in our South as all-purpose are closer to cake flour in texture. In using them with yeast, give them only one rising period—to not quite double the volume—and then let the dough rise to normal, as indicated by the finger test sketched on 600. You may substitute for 1 cup of all-purpose flour 1⅛ cups of cake flour.

CAKE FLOUR

This is made of soft wheats, and their delicate, less expansive gluten bakes to a crumblier texture. Although you will not get the same result, in emergencies you may ➤ substitute 1 cup minus 2 tablespoons sifted all-purpose flour for 1 cup cake flour.

BREAD FLOUR

Although not easily come by, this flour is highly desirable for bread making, as its high proportion of gluten indicates a greater protein content. The gluten also gives elasticity to dough and allows it to expand and hold the gas liberated by the yeast. Bread flour feels almost granular or gritty when rubbed between the fingers.

PRESIFTED FLOURS

These are ground to a point of pulverization and, whether resifted or not, give a different texture to baking. Some of them also have a larger percentage of hard durum wheat, and although the manufacturers may suggest them to replace cake flour, the greater gluten content may tend to toughen cakes. If you use them for cakes, be sure to use 1 tablespoon less per cup than our recipes call for. ➤ We also suggest resifting.

PASTRY FLOUR

Soft, finely milled, low-gluten flour—often available in the South, where it is used for quick breads and pastries.

SELF-RISING FLOUR AND PHOSPHATED FLOURS

These contain the right amounts of leavens and salt for baking. Many people do not like to use them because, during delays in merchandising or storing, the leavens are apt to lose their potency. If used in pastry, these flours give a spongy, rather than flaky, texture. They should be used only for crusts where a low fat content is the objective and the fat in the recipe has been reduced. They are not recommended for making bread, but if you must use them, omit the salt called for in the recipe.

INSTANT FLOUR

A specialty flour used in the making of gravies and sauces. ➤ Never substitute for all-purpose flour.

SEMOLINA

A creamy-colored, granular, protein-rich durum wheat flour used commercially for all types of pasta. It is not your fault if homemade pastas and noodles fail to hold their shape no matter how carefully you have prepared and cooked them. The trouble lies in the lower gluten content of all-purpose flour on which housewives frequently depend.

FARINA

Also a creamy-colored, granular, protein-rich meal made from hard wheat other than durum, with the bran and most of the germ removed.

WHOLE-GRAIN, WHOLE WHEAT OR GRAHAM FLOUR

These and some commercial whole wheats retain their original vitamins, mineral salts, fats and other still unknown components—whether coarsely or finely milled. Scientists are aware of about twenty of these substances, even if they have so far failed to isolate them all or to produce them synthetically.

➤ You may substitute 1 cup of very finely milled whole-grain flours for 1 cup of all-purpose flour. For coarsely ground whole-grain flour, substitute 1 cup plus 2 tablespoons for 1 cup of all-purpose flour. This should be stirred lightly rather than sifted before measuring.

Yeast breads made from whole wheat flours do not have to be kneaded. They can be mixed and allowed to rise just once in the pan. However, if kneading is omitted, the texture will be coarser and denser.

BRAN FLOUR

This flour often gives a dry result unless you soften the bran by allowing the wet bread mixture, minus the yeast or baking powder, to stand for 8 hours or so. Bran flours are usually mixed with some all-purpose flour.

CRACKED WHEAT

Cut rather than ground, this flour gives up little of its starch as a binder. Therefore, it must be mixed with all-purpose or whole wheat flour in baking. We also prefer cooking it as for Coarse Cereals, 200, before adding it to the flour mixture.

GLUTEN FLOUR

This is a starch-free, high-protein flour made by washing the starch from hard wheat flour. The residue is then dried and ground. See Gluten Bread, 609. ➤ For 1 cup all-purpose flour, substitute 13 tablespoons gluten flour. Other flours lacking in gluten such as rye, soya and rice can be used in proportionately greater quantity if gluten flour instead of the usual all-purpose flour is added to them.

Gluten is found in its most complete form in wheat. Scientists think—but are not sure—that 2 substances, glutenin and gliadin, occurring separately in the wheat, interact to form gluten. Gluten can never develop except in the presence of moisture and when the grain is agitated, as in kneading. ➤ To prepare gluten from gluten flour, knead into a stiff dough:

4 cups whole-grain or unbleached flour
1½ to 3 cups lukewarm water

Roll it into a ball and submerge it in water for 2 hours. Then, still keeping the dough ball under water, work the starch out of it by kneading. At intervals, pour off the starchy water. Replace the water you pour off and continue to knead, repeating this operation until the water is almost clear. The gluten is then ready to cook. ➤ Form the starch-free dough into a loaf and cut it into ½-inch slices. Put into a 3-quart pan for which you have a tight lid:

¼ cup vegetable oil

You may flavor the gluten at this point by sautéing until clear and golden:

1 finely sliced medium-sized onion

Put the gluten slices into the pan and cover with:

Boiling water

Simmer, closely covered, for 1 hour and drain. Store refrigerated and closely covered. The gluten slices can then be further cooked by dipping them in egg and potato or rice flour and browning them slowly in an oiled pan. Or cover with undiluted tomato, mushroom or celery soup and place in a preheated 350° oven about 20 minutes or until thoroughly heated.

WHEAT-GERM FLOUR

This must be refrigerated after opening. It may be ➤ substituted by using ⅓ cup of powdered wheat germ and ⅔ cup of all-purpose flour for 1 cup of all-purpose flour. Be sure that the wheat germ, either powdered or whole, is very slightly toasted before combining it with the dough.

TRITICALE FLOUR

A nutritious sweet-tasting flour originally obtained from intergenetic hybridization by crossing durum wheat, hard red winter wheat and rye. Although the flour is higher in protein than all-purpose wheat flour, it is low in gluten and should be mixed with higher gluten flours for bread making. Use the grain as sprouts, 565, or cook as for Coarse Cereals, 200.

ABOUT NONWHEAT FLOURS

Some of the following nonwheat flours can be used alone. But in any bread recipe that fails to call for wheat flour at least in part, you must expect a marked difference in texture, as wheat gluten has a unique elastic quality. This protein gluten factor in wheat is activated when the flour is both moistened and handled, at which time the gluten is said to "develop." The flour is then able to absorb as much as 200 times its weight in moisture. In discussing nonwheat flours, some of which are richer in overall protein content than wheat, we give the closest substitutions we have been able to find, but ➤ we advise, if possible, using at least 1 cup wheat flour for every 2 cups other flour, or a very heavy dough results. For increased protein content, we suggest the use of Cornell Triple-Rich Formula, 602. ➤ Coarse flours need not be sifted before measuring. They do need more leavening than wheat types. ➤ Allow 2½ teaspoons baking powder for every cup of coarse flour.

CORN FLOUR

Yellow or white corn may be milled into corn flour, or the flour may be a by-product in the making of cornmeal. Use in baking, mixed with other flours.

CORNSTARCH

A refined starch obtained from the endosperm of corn, this is a very valuable thickener. ➤ Substitute one tablespoon cornstarch for 2 tablespoons all-purpose flour.

The new waxy starches made from certain varieties of corn are revolutionizing frozen sauces and fillings by their great stabilizing powers, ➤ but they are not to be used in baking. For thickening ➤ substitute 1 tablespoon waxy corn flour for 1 tablespoon all-purpose flour.

There is nothing more discouraging than the lumps any cornstarch can form or the raw taste it produces if it is badly handled or insufficiently cooked. Here are the things we have learned that help us to handle it more easily:

➤ Use a double boiler.

In recipes calling for sugar, avoid lumping by mixing cornstarch, sugar and salt together just before adding gradually to the ➤ cold liquid.

In recipes without sugar, make a paste of 1

tablespoon of cornstarch to 1 cup of the liquid called for in the recipe. Introduce this paste gradually into the ➤ hot, but not boiling, liquid.

Cornstarch, along with tapioca and arrowroot, is recommended for thickening very acid fruits because it does not lose its thickening power as quickly as flour does in the presence of acid. But if it is ➤ overcooked, it loses its thickening power very quickly, regardless of the presence of acid. These facts account for the countless letters we get on pie fillings. In the extra special care cooks lavish on fillings, they are apt to overcook, ➤ or overbeat them after cooking. Be very careful to check the cooking stages described later on.

Other causes for breakdown of thickening may come from a too high percentage of sugar in the recipe and, strangely, even from using too much cornstarch.

Also, tests have shown that ➤ the material from which the double boiler is made has a direct result on the thickening quality and the success of unmolding cornstarch puddings. Stainless steel and enamel are superior to heatproof glass or heavy crockery.

But to get on with the cooking. Once the cornstarch is properly added to the liquid, dispersed either in sugar or in a cold paste, it goes through 2 main cooking periods, 3 if eggs are added. To keep the temperature right for the timing given here, use an enamel or stainless steel pan. Fill the base of the double boiler so that the water just dampens the bottom of the liner. ➤ Bring the water to a bubbling boil before starting the timing. During the first period of about 8 to 12 minutes ➤ constant, gentle stirring is necessary to blend the mixture free from lumps and to hold the starch particles in suspension until gelatinization takes place and the mixture thickens. In this time, it should have reached at least 185°, the temperature that is essential for proper unmolding.

Then follows the second period of about 10 minutes when the mixture is ➤ covered and cooked undisturbed to complete gelatinization. Maintain the 185° temperature.

A third period, of about 2 minutes, follows the addition of the eggs. This adding procedure is just like any other when eggs or egg yolks must meet hot liquid. The eggs are well beaten first. A portion of the hot mixture is added to the eggs very gradually. This is returned to the original mass, which has temporarily ➤ been removed from the heat. ➤ The stirring is less constant and extremely gentle during the next 2 minutes. The pudding should thicken much more in cooling. Have ready molds rinsed out in cold water. Stir the mixture very gently into them—releasing steam which would condense and thin the mixture. Cool for about 30 minutes at room temperature. For successful unmolding, store individual molds 1 to 2 hours in refrigerator; larger molds, 6 to 12 hours.

▲ At altitudes of 5000 feet or higher, maximum gelatinization of cornstarch cannot be achieved in a double boiler. Use direct heat.

CORNMEAL

When stone-ground, cornmeal not only retains the germ but has a superior flavor. Yellow cornmeal has more vitamin A potential than has white cornmeal, but there is little difference in their nutritional or baking properties. Cornmeals can be used alone in Corn Dodgers, 628, or mixed with other flours in quick and yeast corn breads. To avoid graininess in corn breads, mix cornmeal and the liquid in the recipe, bring to a boil, and cool before mixing with the other ingredients.

RICE FLOUR

This makes a close but delicately textured cake in recipes heavy in egg. For recipes using rice flour, see Index. ➤ Substitute 1 cup minus 2 tablespoons rice flour for 1 cup all-purpose flour. But be sure, in baking, not to choose a waxy type of rice flour, also known as **mochika** or **sweet flour.** Instead, use these **waxy rice flours** in making sauces. They have remarkable stabilizing powers which prevent the separation of frozen gravies and sauces when reheated. They are also much less likely to lump.

RYE FLOUR

When used in most of the commercial rye breads, this flour is usually combined with a varying proportion of wheat flour. This is because the rye flour gluten factor provides stickiness but lacks elasticity. Breads made largely with rye flour are moist and compact and usually call for a sourdough leavener, 555. ➤ Substitute 1¼ cups rye flour for 1 cup all-purpose flour.

RYE MEAL

This is simply coarsely ground whole-rye flour. ➤ Substitute 1 cup rye meal for 1 cup all-purpose flour. See Rye Flour, above.

SOY FLOUR

This flour has both a high protein and a high fat content. However, some soy flour is made of beans from which the fat has been largely expressed, when it is known as **soybean low-fat flour.** It may be made from very lightly toasted beans or from raw beans, when it is known as **soybean flour.** Because of the fat, it is not mixed with the dry ingredients but is creamed with the shortening or blended with the liquids. Stir before measuring and substitute ➤ 2 tablespoons of soy flour plus ⅞ cup of all-purpose flour for 1 cup of all-purpose flour. But if you like the flavor, use up to 20% of the weight of the flour in the recipe. Soy flour causes heavy browning of the crust, so reduce baking temperatures about 25°.

SOY MEAL

This coarse meal should be soaked with 2 parts boiling water until all moisture is absorbed. Keep in the refrigerator and use as an extender for meats.

POTATO FLOUR OR POTATO STARCH

Made from cooked potatoes that have been dried and ground, this flour is used chiefly in soups, gravies, breads and cakes, in combination with other flours, or alone in Sponge Cakes, 669. To avoid lumping, blend it with sugar before mixing —or cream it with the shortening before adding a liquid. In bread recipes, it gives a moist, slow-staling loaf. ➤ To use as a thickener, substitute 1 tablespoon potato flour for 2 tablespoons all-purpose flour; in baking, 5/8 cup potato flour for 1 cup all-purpose flour.

SORGHUM FLOUR

Also called **milo maize,** this flour is often used to thicken soups.

TAPIOCA AND SAGO

These are similar in their uses. Tapioca is processed from the Brazilian cassava root and sago from certain Indian palms. Cassava is poisonous until heated to release the hydrocyanic acid. Sago and the so-called pearl tapioca must both be soaked for at least 1 hour before using. Soak 1/4 cup of the pearls in 1/2 cup water, which should be completely absorbed; if it isn't, the pearls are too old to use. If you have already embarked on mixing the recipe, you can substitute rice in equal parts for pearl tapioca. ➤ To substitute so-called minute or granular for pearl tapioca, allow 1 1/2 to 2 tablespoons of this finer form for 4 tablespoons of the soaked pearl. As a thickener, substitute 1 tablespoon quick-cooking tapioca for 1 tablespoon flour.

TAPIOCA FLOUR

Like the waxy rice and corn flours, above, these are popular for sauces and fruit fillings that are to be frozen. These sauces reconstitute without breaking down and becoming watery as do flour-thickened sauces after frozen storage.

➤ To use in freezing, substitute 1 tablespoon tapioca flour for 2 1/2 tablespoons all-purpose flour to 1 cup liquid. ➤ In nonfrozen sauces, substitute 1 1/2 teaspoons tapioca flour for 1 tablespoon all-purpose flour.

Tapioca flour is popular for making very clear glazes. Cook the tapioca and fruit juice or water only to the boiling point. ➤ Beware of overcooking, as the tapioca will become stringy. ➤ Never boil. When the first bubbles begin to break through the surface, remove the pan from the heat at once. The mixture will look thin and milky. Let it stand 2 or 3 minutes. Stir. Wait 2 or 3 minutes longer and stir again. If the recipe calls for butter, stir it in at this time. After 10 minutes more of undisturbed cooling, the glaze should be thick enough to apply to the food you are glazing.

ARROWROOT FLOUR OR STARCH

This is another popular base for cream sauces and clear and delicate glazes. It cooks by the same method as cornstarch, but ➤ substitutes in the amount of 1 1/2 teaspoons arrowroot to 1 tablespoon flour. To ensure an attractive consistency when arrowroot glaze is to be used on cold acid fruits, dissolve 1 1/2 teaspoons gelatin in 1 tablespoon cold water and add it to the hot glaze. Spoon the cooled, thickened glaze over the chilled fruit and keep cold until you serve.

BARLEY FLOUR

➤ To substitute, use 1/2 cup barley flour for each cup of all-purpose flour.

BUCKWHEAT FLOUR

This flour of high biologic value is best used in the proportion of 1/4 cup buckwheat to 3/4 cup other flour for good texture.

COTTONSEED FLOUR

With at least four times the protein value of wheat, this flour is often used to enrich breads. ➤ Substitute 2 tablespoons cottonseed flour plus 7/8 cup all-purpose flour for 1 cup all-purpose flour.

PEANUT FLOUR

Contains at least sixteen times the protein value of wheat. It may be ➤ substituted by using 2 tablespoons peanut flour plus 7/8 cup all-purpose flour for 1 cup all-purpose flour.

OAT FLOUR AND OATMEAL

These are ground to different consistencies to combine with wheat flours up to one-third. Oatmeal is better in baking if soaked in boiling water with the shortening and cooled before the yeast or other leaven is added.

ROLLED OATS

These are separate flakes formed by rolling the groats with hulls removed, and steaming them. The thinness of the flake determines regular or quick-cooking oats. They are popular for adding flavor to cookies. Steel-cut oats are obtained by passing the groats or kernels through special cutting machines. ➤ Substitute 1 1/3 cups rolled oat flakes for 1 cup all-purpose flour. To combine with wheat flours for breads, use 1/3 cup oat flakes for each cup flour.

BEAN FLOUR

➤ Substitute 4 to 5 cups bean flour for 1 cup all-purpose flour.

NUT MEAL

These finely ground dry nuts are used as a flour substitute in many Torten, 684.

CAROB FLOUR OR POWDER

A chocolate-flavored powder milled from the carob-tree pod which is also known as Saint-John's-bread. A nutritious substitute for chocolate for the allergic, low in fat and delicious in its own right.

➤ To substitute for flour, allow 1/8 to 1/4 cup carob powder plus 7/8 to 3/4 cup flour for every cup of flour. ➤ To substitute for chocolate, 3 tablespoons of carob flour plus 2 tablespoons liquid equals 1 ounce unsweetened chocolate. Use less sugar, as it is naturally sweet.

WHEAT-FLOUR ALLERGY SUBSTITUTE

This can be kept on hand for use in gravies and some quick breads, pancakes and biscuits. Sift together 6 times, ½ cup cornstarch and ½ cup of any of the following: rye flour, potato flour or rice flour. If you use this combination for baking, you will need 2 teaspoons baking powder for each cup of the flour mixture. ➤ If using cornstarch or rice flour in baking, be sure to avoid the waxy types.

COOKED CEREAL SUBSTITUTE

This may be ➤ substituted 1 cup cooked cereal for ¼ cup flour. But you must also cut the fluid in the recipe by 1 cup for each cup of cooked cereal used. To mix, stir the cooked cereal into the remaining fluid before combining with the other ingredients.

ABOUT CRUMBS

In reading recipes, note what kind of bread crumbs are called for. The results are very different, depending on whether they are dry, fresh, browned or buttered.

Finely crushed cracker crumbs or cornflakes, corn or potato chip crumbs are sometimes used in place of bread crumbs in breading and in au gratins, see below.

DRY CRUMBS

These are made from dry bread, zwieback or cake. If these materials are not sufficiently dry, crisp them on a baking sheet in a 200° oven before making the crumbs. Do not let the crumbs color. If only a few are being made, grind them in a rotary hand grater, as sketched on 562, or in a ⅄ blender. If making them in large quantities, put them through a meat grinder with a medium chopping blade. Tie a bag tightly over the mouth of the grinder to catch them all.

➤ Measure dry bread crumbs as you would sugar, 556. Store dry bread crumbs in a cool, dry place, not too tightly lidded, or they may mold.

SOFT BREAD CRUMBS

To prepare these, use two- to four-day-old bread. You may crumb it very lightly with your fingers. But a safer way to retain the light texture desired in such crumbs is to pull the bread apart with a fork—using a gingerly motion, as sketched. Do not crush the bread with the hand that is holding it.

➤ To measure soft bread crumbs, pile them lightly into a cup. Do not pack them down unless the recipe calls for soaking these fresh crumbs in water, milk or stock and pressing the moisture out before using, when they naturally compact. Use at once.

BROWNED OR BUTTERED BREAD CRUMBS

To prepare these, use dry bread crumbs, as described. Allow for each cup dry bread crumbs ½ teaspoon salt and brown them slowly in ⅓ cup butter. Use at once. You may enliven them with bits of chopped minced bacon, chopped nutmeats or grated cheese and paprika.

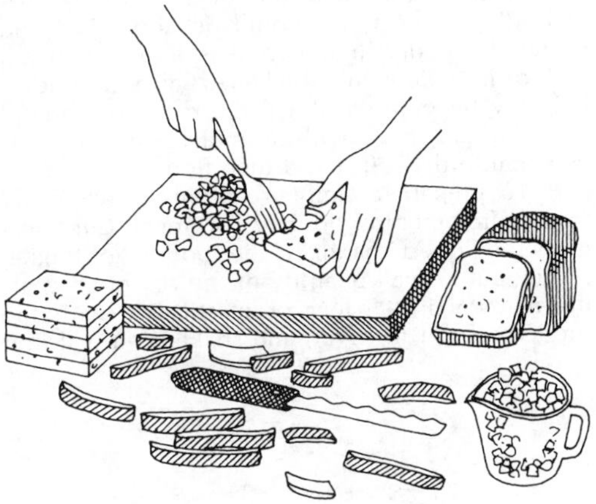

CROUTONS

These dry or fried seasoned fresh bread morsels come in all sizes. As coarse crumbs, they are an attractive garnish for noodles, dumplings or Spätzle. In small dice, they add glamour to pea and other soups. Use croutons in tiny dice and mound them around game, or, as larger toasts, under game or a chop. They can be spread with a pâté or be used as a spongy surface for the natural juices. In large size, they can also be placed under a dripping rack during the roasting of meats to catch and hold the juices.

I. Dice bread, fresh or dry, and sauté it in butter until it is an even brown. Or butter slices of bread, cut them into dice and brown them in a 375° oven.

II. When 2 cups croutons have been sautéed or browned in the oven, drop them while still hot into a bag containing:

1 teaspoon salt
1 teaspoon paprika
2 to 4 tablespoons ground Parmesan cheese or very finely minced fresh herbs

Close the bag. Shake it until the croutons are evenly coated. Add them to hot soup.

III. Use for soup, noodles or Caesar salad. Cut into ½-inch cubes:

Bread

Sauté the cubes in:

Hot butter or olive oil

You may rub the skillet with garlic or add grated onion to the butter. Stir them gently or shake the skillet until they are coated. Sprinkle with:

Grated cheese or herbs

FLOURING, BREADING AND CRUMBING FOODS

When **dredging** or lightly covering food with flour or crumbs or with a more elaborately bound coating, the main thing to remember is this: you want a thin, even and unbroken covering that will adhere. The food should be about 70° and should be ➤ dry. If the food is floury to begin with or is made with a thickened sauce, the flouring may be omitted. But for fish fillets, shrimp, meat, or anything with a moist surface, it is essential to dry it first and then flour it.

➤ To prepare a simple breading, have ready finely sifted crumbs, flour or cornmeal. Cornmeal gives the firmest coating. If the food is not fragile, simply put a small quantity of the seasoned coating material in a paper or plastic bag with the food you want to cover, and shake. You will find

this method gives a very even, quick and economical coating. Or prepare the following Seasoned Flour or Crumbs.

SEASONED FLOUR OR CRUMBS FOR BREADING

I. Mix:

1 cup all-purpose flour, finely sifted dry bread crumbs or finely crushed cornflakes
1 teaspoon salt
¼ teaspoon pepper or ½ teaspoon paprika
(⅛ teaspoon ginger or nutmeg)

II. Mix:

1 cup finely sifted dry bread crumbs or crushed cornflakes or crackers
3 tablespoons grated Parmesan cheese
½ teaspoon dried herbs, choosing from: savory, chervil, chives, basil or tarragon; or 1/16 teaspoon rosemary

BOUND BREADING OR COATING À L'ANGLAISE

Enough to Coat 8 Croquettes

To prepare a more adhesive bound breading—or coating à l'anglaise—begin by wiping the food dry. Then dip the dry food into a shallow bowl of seasoned flour. Have ready, aside from the flour, two other bowls. In the first bowl, put a mixture of:

1 slightly beaten egg
2 to 3 teaspoons water or milk
(2 teaspoons oil)

Stir these ingredients together with 10 or 12 mild strokes. ➤ Do not let the egg get bubbly, as this makes the coating uneven. In the other bowl, have ready:

¾ cup sifted seasoned dry bread crumbs

As each piece of food is floured, toss it lightly from one palm to the other, patting it gently all over and encouraging any excess flour to fall off, as sketched on the left. Then slide the flour-coated food through the egg mixture, making sure the entire surface is contacted, as shown at center. Allow any excess moisture to drip off. Then place the food in the crumb-lined bowl. See that the crumbs adhere evenly to all the edges of the food as well as to its larger surfaces. If you see any vacant places, sprinkle a few crumbs on them. Pat on any excess crumbs that might fall off and brown too rapidly, thus discoloring the frying fat. Handle the food very gently, so that the coating will not be cracked. ➤ Place on a rack to dry for about 20 minutes before frying. ➤ Do not chill this food before frying, as this will tend to make it absorb an undue amount of fat.

AU GRATIN

"Au gratin" is a term that, in America, is usually associated with cheese. But the term may merely refer to a light but thorough coating of fine fresh or dry bread crumbs or even crushed cornflakes, cracker crumbs or finely ground nuts placed on

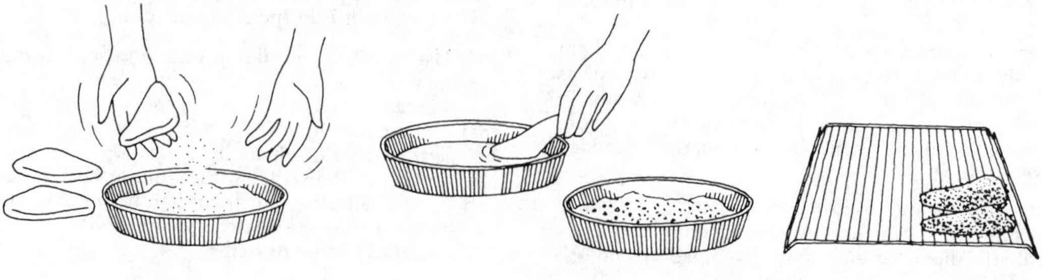

top of scalloped or sauced dishes. These are then browned in the oven or under the broiler to form a crisp golden crust. A sprinkling of paprika helps to induce browning. Such dishes are usually combinations of cooked shellfish, fish, meats, vegetables or eggs, bound by a white or brown sauce and served in the dish in which they were cooked. If the sauce is heavy in fat, it is wise to place the scalloped dish in a pan of hot water before running it under a broiler. Or you may set the casserole or baking dish on a piece of foil, shiny side down to deflect the heat. Or just set the casserole on a baking tin.

➤ To make the following au gratin mixtures quickly, put the ingredients in a ⅄ blender in the proportion and amount you need.

I. Place:

Dry bread crumbs

in a thorough, but light, covering over the sauced food. Bake in a 350° to 375° oven. Or place the dish under a preheated broiler 3 inches below the source of heat until a crisp, golden brown crust forms.

II. Place:

Dry bread crumbs and dots of butter
(Paprika—about ½ teaspoon per cup)

to make a thorough but light covering over the food, before baking it in a 350° oven. Or run the dish under a preheated broiler 5 inches from the source of heat, to produce a crisp golden crust.

III. Completely cover the food to be au gratined with:

Dry bread crumbs, dots of butter and grated cheese
(Paprika—about ½ teaspoon per cup)

Place the dish under a preheated broiler, 5 inches below the source of heat, to form a glazed golden crust. The finished result should be neither powdery nor rubbery but "fondant." It will be more "fondant" if you use natural-aged American or cheddar cheese, and drier if you use Parmesan or Romano.

ALMOND OR AMANDINE GARNISH

A Scant ½ Cup

This garnish is a classic. It glorifies the most commonplace dish:

Melt:

¼ cup butter

Stir and sauté in it over low heat, to avoid scorching, until lightly browned:

¼ cup blanched shredded almonds
Salt, as needed

As a variation on almonds as a vegetable garnish, try:

(Roasted pumpkin, squash or sesame seeds)

ABOUT LEAVENS

We are all so accustomed to light breads and cakes that we seldom question the part that leavens play.

Where does this rising power lie? First, the steam converted from the moisture, in any baking, may account for a third to four-fifths of the expansion of the dough. The greater amount is characteristic of popovers and cakes rich in egg white. So, to encourage the generation of this easily lost asset, ➤ preheat your oven.

We usually think of leavens as resulting from baking powders, 555, sour milk and soda, 555, and yeast—all of which expand with the steam to form gas as a major force. But we tend to forget the importance of the mechanical incorporation of air from which the rest of the rising power comes. To give a boost to the chemical reactions, be sure you know how to cream fat and sugar, 671; how to fold and mix batters, 664; how to beat eggs, 544; and, especially, how to beat egg whites to that state called "stiff, but not dry," 544. And who would ever guess that fresh-fallen snow—or even old snow from below the surface—makes an excellent substitute for eggs as a riser in puddings and pancakes—because of the snow's ammonia content?

ABOUT YEAST

Yeasts are living organisms with 3200 billion cells to the pound—and not one is exactly like another. They feed on sugars and produce alcohol and carbon dioxide—the "riser" we are after. But you may prefer, as we do, to accept a Mexican attitude toward yeast doughs. They call them almas, or souls, because they seem so spirited.

When flour is mixed with water to form a dough, which is then kept in a warm place, the wild yeast coming from the air and in the flour will start working and form a sourdough. There are enzymes in the flour to convert the wheat starch into the sugar on which the yeast feeds, making alcohol and carbon dioxide. Organic acids and other fragrant compounds are also created to give the sour effect. Sourdoughs, discussed below, are products of this primitive bacterial ferment. They are so primitive that they are recorded in Egyptian history in 4000 B.C. This leavened bread has been called the first "convenience" food, as its yeast content gives it excellent keeping quality.

The different yeasts, compressed and dried, activate at different temperatures, see below. These temperatures and the amount of food available limit the life span of the yeast. Its force, therefore, can be easily computed. One-half ounce raises 4 cups of flour in 1½ to 2 hours. One ounce raises 28 cups of flour in about 7 hours. For speedier raising, an excess of yeast is often added. But this is not necessary, and it often affects flavor and gives a porous texture. Small quantities of sugar also speed yeast activity, but too much will inhibit it. You may have noticed that it takes very sweet doughs longer to rise. As salt also inhibits yeast, ➤ never use salted water for dissolving yeast. In very hot weather, after the yeast is dissolved and added to the flour, salt may be added in small quantities to control too rapid fermentation.

Yeast dough is allowed to rise and fall a number of times during dough-making to improve the texture, but if allowed to overexpand, it can use up its energy. In this case, there is little rising power left for the baking period, when it is most needed.

For different methods of incorporating yeast in doughs, read about Mixing Bread Dough, 599. The liquids added to yeast, either alone or in combination, are water, which brings out the wheat flavor and makes a crisp crust; or skim milk, which not only adds to the nutritive value but also gives a softer crumb. The fat in whole and homogenized milk tends to coat the yeast and prevent its proper softening. Potato water may also be used, but it hastens the action of the yeast and gives a somewhat coarser, moister texture to dough. Both milk and potato water somewhat increase the keeping quality of bread.

To produce the best yeast bread, you must give the dough time to rise slowly; the entire process takes about 4 or 5 hours before baking. If you use 1 cake of yeast to 1½ cups of liquid and if the temperature is right, you can count on about 2 hours or more for the first rising; 1 or more for the second; and 1 hour for rising in the pans. You may increase the yeast content in any recipe and reduce your rising time considerably. Some successful quick recipes are given, but if you are going to the effort of using yeast, you might as well work for the superlative result which comes from the slower process.

COMPRESSED YEAST

This living organism is dependent on definite temperature ranges. It begins to activate at about 50° ➤ and is at its best between 78° and 82°. It begins to die around 120° and is useless for baking after 143°. We prefer using this moist cake weighing about 3/5 ounce. But it must be kept refrigerated. Although compressed yeast comes in larger sizes, when 1 cake is specified in this book it means the 3/5-ounce size. If bought fresh, it will keep about 2 weeks. Frozen, it will keep for 2 months. Take out only what is needed and let it defrost overnight in the refrigerator. When at its best it is a light grayish-tan in color. It crumbles readily, breaks with a clean edge and smells pleasantly aromatic. When old, it becomes brownish in color. To test for freshness, cream a small quantity of yeast with an equal amount of sugar. It should become liquid at once. You may let crumbled, compressed yeast dissolve in warm water or warm pasteurized skim milk at 80° to 90° for about 5 minutes before combining with the other ingredients called for in the recipes.

ACTIVE DRY YEAST

This granular form of yeast comes in airtight, moisture-proof packages measuring 1 scant tablespoon or in 4-ounce vacuum-packed jars. It is often preferred for its better keeping qualities. It comes dated and, if kept in a cool place, will hold for several months—and somewhat longer in a refrigerator. Greater heat and more moisture are needed to activate it than for compressed yeast. ➤ Use more water to dissolve it; but ➤ decrease by that amount the liquid called for in the recipe and ➤ heat the dissolving water to between 105° and 115°. To dissolve it readily, sprinkle the powdered yeast on the surface of the water. Or it may be mixed with the dry ingredients in the mixer method, 600, and activated by using 120° to 130° liquid. Since this yeast does not contain excess starch, it will not bubble when placed in water. For growth, add small quantities of flour and sugar.

➤ To substitute dry granular yeast for compressed yeast, use 1 package or 1 scant tablespoon active dry yeast granules for a 3/5-ounce cake of compressed yeast.

DEBITTERED BREWERS' OR NUTRITIONAL YEAST

Another form of dry yeast—but one without leavening power—which adds nutritive value to foods. It may be added to breads in the proportion of 1 to 3 teaspoons to 1 cup of flour without affecting flavor or texture adversely.

ABOUT SOURDOUGH

This term brings to mind at once the hardbitten pioneer whose sharing of the bread "starter" was a true act of friendship. Of course, the best French breads and many other famous doughs are also based on flour and water mixtures fermented in various ways to trap natural yeast. In kitchens where yeast baking has been going on for centuries, these organisms are plentiful in the air, and success is quickly assured, see II, below. But in an uninitiated streamlined kitchen, we recommend beginning a sourdough with a commercial yeast, especially in winter, see I, below.

Remember, the sourdough starter is just as fragile as the yeast and must be cosseted along. For a good method of fermenting and maintaining an 80° to 90° temperature during fermentation, see Potato Salt-Rising Bread, 607. Keep the starter away from drafts or too high heat. ➤ Two cups of this foamy mixture are substituted for 1 cake or package of yeast and the dissolving liquid. After you have made your starter, you can continue to use it for about 3 days at room temperature without reworking it and for about a week if it is refrigerated, then allowed to rest at 70° at least 1 hour before using. Try to use the sourdough at least once a week; you may freeze the starter if it is not to be used for several weeks. ➤ Allow at least 24 hours for the frozen starter to become active again at room temperature before using.

Keep at least 1½ to 2 cups starter on hand, covered loosely to allow escape of the gas which accumulates. If an alcoholic liquid forms on top, pour it off. To replenish, see opposite.

Expect the sourdough to have an odor very like salt-rising bread. Should it develop any abnormal coloration, discard it. To avoid spoilage, wash the starter crock about once a week with a detergent and warm water. Rinse well and dry carefully before returning the starter to the crock. Try the sourdough recipes listed in the Index if you are adventurous, persistent and leisurely.

SOURDOUGH STARTER

I. For kitchens lacking yeast spores in the air. Combine in a large wide-mouthed crockery or glass jar:

1 package active dry yeast
2 cups lukewarm water: 85°
2 cups all-purpose flour

Stir with a ➤ wooden spoon—never use any metal. Let stand uncovered at 80° to 90° for 4 to 7 days, or until it bubbles and emits a good sour odor. During this period, stir down once a day; if a crust develops, stir it down also. Use at once or refrigerate until ready to do so.

To replenish, discard all but 1 cup of the starter, because any excess, unless reactivated, may become rancid. Add the cupful to:

1 cup all-purpose flour
1 cup lukewarm water

Let stand overnight until fermented and bubbling, then use or refrigerate.

II. For kitchens laden with yeast spores from previous bread making, follow the directions in I, above, omitting the yeast, and using:

1 cup lukewarm milk
1 cup all-purpose flour
½ cup sugar

To replenish, add these 3 ingredients in these amounts to 1 cup starter.

ABOUT BAKING POWDERS AND BAKING SODA

When confronted with the questions growing out of the use of the various baking powders now on the market, the puzzled layman is apt to sigh for the good old days when this product was rather haphazardly mixed at home. ➤ Just in case you run out of baking powder, mix—for each teaspoon of baking powder called for in the recipe—½ teaspoon cream of tartar, ⅓ teaspoon bicarbonate of soda and ⅛ teaspoon salt. After adding the above ingredients, do not delay putting the batter into the oven. ➤ And don't try to store this mixture, as it has poor keeping qualities. If you doubt the effectiveness of any baking powder ➤ test by mixing 1 teaspoon of baking powder with ⅓ cup of hot water. Use the baking powder only if it bubbles enthusiastically.

There are three major kinds of baking powders, and you will find the ➤ type carefully specified on the label. For substitutions, see 593. In all of them there must be an acid and an alkaline material reacting with each other in the presence of moisture to form a gas—carbon dioxide—which takes the form of tiny bubbles in the dough or batter. In baking, these quickly expand the batter, which is then set by the heat to make a light-textured crumb. Before measuring any of these leavens, stir and break up any lumps, and use a dry measuring spoon.

▲ Because of the decrease in barometric pressure at high altitudes, the carbon dioxide gas expands more quickly and thus has greater leavening action. For this reason, the amount of baking powder should be decreased if you are using a recipe designed for low altitudes. You may select recipes designed especially for high altitudes if you wish; see 692.

▲ In high altitudes, baking soda is decreased as for baking powder, above; but in recipes using sour milk, where its neutralizing power is needed, never reduce soda beyond ½ teaspoon for every cup of sour milk or cream called for in the recipe.

TARTRATE BAKING POWDERS

In these, the soda is combined with tartaric acid or a combination of cream of tartar and tartaric acid. They are the quickest in reaction time, giving off carbon dioxide the moment they are combined with liquid. Therefore, if you are using this kind, be sure ➤ to mix the batter quickly and ➤ have the oven preheated so that too much gas does not escape from the dough before the cells can become heat-hardened in their expanded form. Especially ➤ avoid using tartrate powder for doughs and batters that are to be stored in the refrigerator or frozen before baking.

PHOSPHATE BAKING POWDERS

These use calcium acid phosphate or sodium acid pyrophosphate, or a combination of these, as the acid ingredient. They are somewhat slower in reaction but give up the greater part of their carbon dioxide in the cold dough. The remainder may be released when the mixture is baked.

DOUBLE-ACTING OR S.A.S. BAKING POWDERS

Often referred to as ➤ combination, or double-acting, baking powders, these are the baking powders we specify consistently in this book. They use sodium aluminum sulfate and calcium acid phosphate as the acid ingredients. They too start work in the cold dough, but the great rising impact does not begin until the dough contacts the heat from the hot oven.

SODIUM BICARBONATE OR BAKING SODA

Used alone, baking soda has no leavening properties. But used in combination with some acid ingredients such as sour milk or molasses, it gives one of the very tenderest crumbs. The proportion of baking soda to sour milk or buttermilk is usually 1 teaspoon soda to 1 cup sour milk. For more details about soda and sour milk or cream reactions, see 533. The reaction of the soda with the acid is essentially the same as that which takes place when the two ingredients in baking powder meet moisture, so always mix the baking soda with the dry ingredients first.

The acidity of chocolate, honey or corn syrup is not strong enough to be the only source of acid, so some recipes with these acid ingredients may call for both baking powder and baking soda. If they do, use about ½ teaspoon baking soda and ½ teaspoon baking powder for each 2 cups flour. The small amount of soda is desirable for neutralizing the acid ingredients in the recipe, while the main leavening action is left to the baking powder. The amounts of baking powder per cup of flour suggested above are for low altitudes, see About Baking Soda, above. To substitute baking soda for baking powder, see Substitutions, 593.

AMMONIUM BICARBONATE

This forerunner of our modern and more stable leaveners is also known as powdered baking ammonia, carbonate of ammonia, and **hartshorn.** Used for years in Europe to produce long-lasting crisp cookies, it must be pounded to a fine powder and then sifted with the dry ingredients or dissolved in a warm liquid such as water, rum or wine.

Substitute it for the baking powder and baking soda called for in cookie and cake recipes. Buy only small amounts from the drugstore, as it quickly evaporates if not very tightly contained.

ABOUT SOLID SUGARS

Most of our cooking is done with sugars made from beets or from cane. Both are so similar in their cooking reactions and taste that only the label gives us the clue to their source. But the various grinds of solid sugars affect not only their comparative volumes but their sweetening powers as well. Liquid sweeteners—again, according to type—react very differently in cooking combinations. Whichever type you use, more is needed to sweeten iced dishes or drinks.

Among other things, sugars, like fats, give tenderness to doughs. In small amounts, they hasten working of yeast. However, too much sugar at this early juncture will inhibit yeast activity. Sugar in bread, rolls and muffins produces a golden brown crust. Small pinches added to some vegetables bring up their flavor.

Sugars, whether solid or liquid, are not interchangeable. For a quick comparison of sugar weights and volumes, see 589. Many baking recipes call for the sifting of sugar before measuring. In America, where we are spoiled in having free-flowing, unlumpy granulated and powdered sugars, this initial sifting before measuring is usually ignored. But it is important to measure these and other sugars, except brown sugar, 557, by filling the measuring cup with a scoop or spoon to overflowing, taking care not to shake down the contents to even it, then leveling off the top with a knife, as shown for flour on 546.

➤ In substituting liquid for dry sweeteners, an adjustment in other liquid ingredients must be made, especially in baking, as discussed in About Liquid Sugars, opposite.

GRANULATED SUGAR

➤ In this book when the word sugar appears, the recipe calls for granulated sugar—beet or cane both being 99.5% pure sucrose. However, do not expect the same baking results if using a granulated sugar now on the market which is a combination of sucrose and dextrose. Its moisture-attracting characteristics will make baked goods softer—a disaster in some products. As we buy granulated sugar in America, it can be used for almost every purpose, even for meringues. The English granulated is too coarse for this, and their **castor sugar,** closer to our powdered, is used instead. ➤ One pound of granulated sugar equals approximately 2 cups.

LUMP OR LOAF SUGARS

These are granulated sugars molded or cut into convenient rectangular sizes for use in hot drinks. Rock Candy Crystals, 787, make an interesting stand-in for lump sugar and, when separated or crushed, a sparkling garnish for iced cakes.

SUPERFINE OR BERRY SUGAR

This finer grind of granulated sugar is still coarse enough so that the individual crystals are easily discernible. It is best used in meringues and for sweetening fruits and drinks. If it becomes lumpy, try rolling the sugar in a plastic bag with a rolling pin. ➤ It can be substituted cup for cup for granulated sugar.

CONFECTIONERS' OR POWDERED SUGAR

These two terms refer to the same product, known in the East as confectioners' and in the West as powdered sugar. In its finest form—10X—it may at a quick glance be mistaken for cake flour. Confectioners' sugar is the counterpart of the European or English **icing sugar.** In order to lessen

lumping, it comes with a small quantity of cornstarch added. But when it does lump, sieve it, as shown above. Measure confectioners' sugar as you would flour, 546. Since the cornstarch tends to give so-called uncooked icings a raw flavor, it is wise, before spreading this kind of mixture, to let it heat about 10 minutes ➤ over boiling water, see 726. The dense texture of confectioners' sugar also gives a different crumb to cakes in which it is used. ➤ Do not try to substitute it for granulated sugar in baking. However, in other uses, substitute 1¾ cups confectioners' for 1 cup granulated.

BROWN OR BARBADOS SUGAR

This is a moister beet or cane sugar which comes light or dark—the latter more strongly flavored with molasses. As both types harden and lump easily, keep them in tightly covered containers or in a tightly closed plastic bag in a cool, moist place. If sugar should become lumpy, sprinkle it very lightly with a few drops of water and heat in a low oven for a few moments or put it through a strainer as shown opposite, forcing the lumps out with a spoon. ➤ In this book the term brown sugar means the light form. If a stronger flavor is wanted, the term dark brown sugar appears.

Different forms of granulated brown sugar now appearing on the market may not be as sweet, so be sure you know what you are buying and follow directions on the package.

➤ To substitute brown sugar for granulated sugar, use 1 cup firmly packed brown sugar for each cup granulated sugar. Always, in measuring brown sugar, pack it firmly into a measuring cup and level it by pressing with the palm of the hand. Then unmold it, sand-castlewise, as shown.

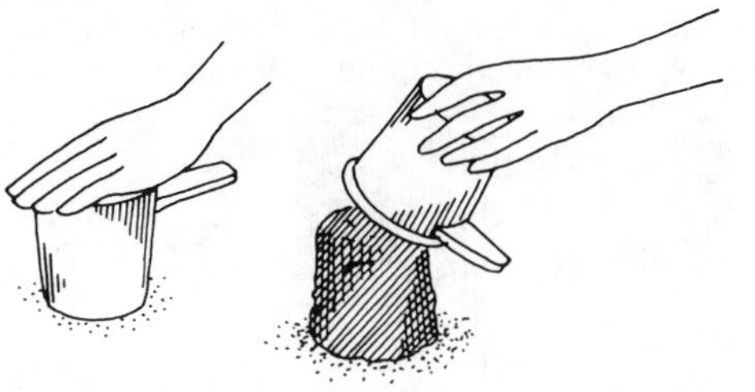

RAW AND TURBINADO SUGARS

Raw sugar is processed from cane, and the USDA notes that it is "unfit for direct use as a food ingredient because of the impurities it ordinarily contains." Turbinado is a partially refined, coarse, beige-toned crystal containing the molasses portion of the sugar. It is closest in character to the yellow or brownish **Demerara sugar** often called for in English recipes. ➤ Substitute cup for cup for granulated sugar, but be aware of its heavier molasses flavor.

CORN SUGAR

A crystallized dextrose-glucose obtained by hydrolizing cornstarch with acid.

FRUIT SUGARS

Fructose, the natural sugar in fruits, has the same caloric value as cane sugar, but because its sweetening power is 1.7 to 1 of sugar, use only about two-thirds as much.

MAPLE SUGAR

Evaporation of maple sap or syrup gives this sugar its distinctively strong, sweet taste, but, because of its high cost, it is often reserved just for flavoring. As it dissolves slowly, grate or sliver it before combining it with other ingredients. ➤ In substituting, allow about ½ cup for each cup of granulated sugar.

ABOUT SEASONED SUGARS

Keep these on hand for quick flavoring.

CINNAMON SUGAR

Mix 1 cup sugar with every 2 tablespoons cinnamon. Use for toast, coffee cake and yogurt toppings.

CITRUS FRUIT FLAVORED SUGARS

Extremely useful in custards and desserts. Mix 1 to 2 tablespoons grated citrus fruit rind for every cup of sugar. Store covered in a cool place.

VANILLA SUGAR

Make this by keeping 1 to 2 vanilla beans closed up in a canister with 2 cups of sugar. Or you may crush the beans with a few tablespoons of sugar before adding to the sugar you are storing. Then, you may strain the sugar before using, replace it with new sugar, and use until the beans lose their flavoring power.

ABOUT LIQUID SUGARS

There are a number of factors to contend with in substituting liquid for solid sweeteners: their sweetening powers vary greatly; their greater moisture content has to be taken into account; those that have an acid factor need neutralizing by the addition of baking soda. To measure liquid sugars, you may want to grease your measuring container first. Then pour or spoon these sticky substances into the measure, just to the level mark. Scrape out all the contents. ➤ Never dip a measuring cup into the honey or syrup container, for the added amount clinging to the outside may make your dough too sweet or too liquid.

CORN SYRUP

Corn syrup is dextrose and glucose and is generally used in canning and jelly-making. ➤ In this book the term corn syrup applies to the light type. If called for, the stronger-tasting dark is specified. ➤ For the same amount of sweetening power, you must substitute 2 cups corn syrup for 1 cup sugar. In cooking, for best results ➤ never use corn syrup to replace more than half the amount of sugar called for in a recipe. In baking, you are taking a chance in substituting corn syrup. But if you must, for each 2 cups of sugar in the recipe, reduce the liquid called for—other than syrup—by ¼ cup. For example: suppose you are baking a cake that calls for 2 cups of sugar. "Maximum syrup tolerance" here would be 1 cup sugar, 2 cups syrup. And for each 2 cups of sugar originally called for, you would reduce the other liquid ingredients by $\frac{1}{4}$ cup.

HONEY

This valuable ingredient has long been treasured because of its preservative qualities due to its high sugar content and an antimold enzyme. It is cherished by cooks for the remarkable keeping qualities, chewy texture and the browner color it gives to cakes, cookies and bread doughs. It is composed chiefly of levulose and dextrose. Its high liquid quality causes great variability in handling, and German cooks of old often refused to use it until it had aged for about a year. Variations in honey today are due in part to adulteration with additional glucose. Pasteurization, used to destroy the yeasts that may cause the honey to ferment, also reduces its nutrient value.

The varying flavors of thyme honey from Hymettos in Greece, of tupelo from Florida, and of orange blossom from California are easily distinguished, but honeys from the same plant taste markedly different when the plant is grown on different soils and in different climates. Very dark honeys may be disagreeably strong.

Honey is sold in two basic forms: comb and extracted. However, the extracted honey is in either liquid or crystallized form, and the latter may be labeled "creamed," "candied," "fondant" or "spread."

Warm the honey or add it to the other liquids called for to make mixing more uniform. To measure honey, oil the measuring cup or spoon so the honey will slip off easily, or measure the shortening first, then the honey in the same utensil.

➤ As honey has greater sweetening power than sugar, we prefer to substitute 1 cup honey for $1\frac{1}{4}$ cups sugar and to reduce the liquid in the recipe by $\frac{1}{4}$ cup. However, too much honey in a recipe may cause too brown a product. To neutralize the acidity of honey—unless sour milk or sour cream is called for in the recipe—add a mere pinch of baking soda. If honey is substituted in jams, jellies or candies, a higher degree of heat must be used in cooking. In candies, more persistent beating is needed and careful storage required against absorption of atmospheric moisture.

Honey is best stored covered in a dry place at room temperature. If it becomes crystallized, it can easily be reliquified by setting the jar on a trivet in a pan of ➤ warm water until the crystals are melted.

➤ Children under a year old should not be given honey, a suspected source of infant botulism.

MAPLE SYRUP

If so labeled, pure maple syrup must weigh not less than 11 pounds to the gallon. Largely sucrose with some invert sugar, the best grades are light in color. It is often stored covered at room temperature, but after it is opened it must be stored in the refrigerator to inhibit mold growth. If a mold develops, strain and bring the syrup to a rolling boil before rebottling. Should the syrup crystallize, set the jar in hot water; the syrup will quickly become liquid and smooth again.

➤ To substitute for sugar in cooking, generally use only $\frac{3}{4}$ cup maple syrup to each cup of sugar. ➤ To substitute maple syrup for sugar in baking, use these same proportions, but reduce the other liquid called for in the recipe by about 3 tablespoons for every cup of syrup substituted. One pint maple syrup has the same sweetening power as 1 pound maple sugar.

MAKING MAPLE SYRUP

Maple, that choicest of all syrups, is yours for the taking, with no harm to the trees that produce it. Collecting, however, is simpler than processing, for you will get only about one part syrup out of about forty to fifty parts of sap. The sugar maple, *Acer saccharum*, gives the sweetest sap. *Acer negrum* and *rubrum*, lower both in sugar and in yield, are also tapped, as are butternut, box elder, and some of the birches. The best months are late February, March and early April, when night temperatures are 20° and daytime 45°. Trees with diameters 10 to 30 inches at breast height can be hung with from one to four buckets. The taps can be on any area of the trunk from 2 to 5 feet from ground level, but if made late in the season should be on the north side. With a $\frac{7}{16}$-inch bit, bore a hole diagonally upward 2 to 3 inches. Insert a sap spout with a bucket hook attached, as shown below. Hammer the spout in gently but firmly so

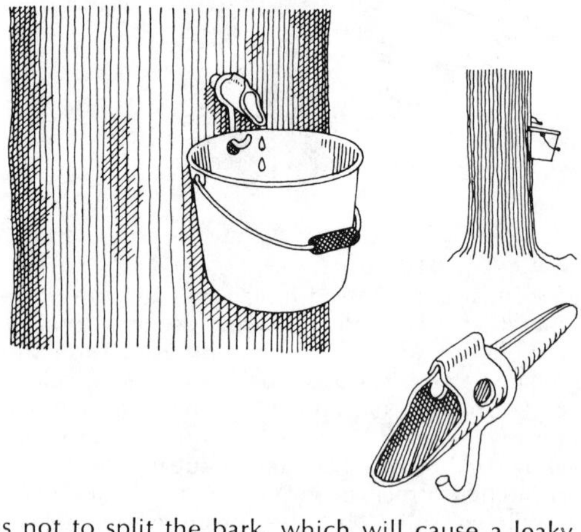

as not to split the bark, which will cause a leaky tap hole. If your bucket has a rim, make a small incision in the bucket beneath the rim so the bucket will be almost flush against the tree. Or use a special plastic collecting bag.

Within 12 hours you should find clear transparent sap in the bucket. Empty the buckets every day, strain the sap through a fine mesh strainer into sterile containers, and store under refrigeration until you have collected enough to boil. During cold weather you will probably not be bothered with microbial development at tap holes or in buckets. Should a mucouslike formation appear, scald or wipe both taps and buckets with a chlorine solution. Sap runs clear and usable until buds begin to swell, when an unpleasant odor and slight discoloration will warn you that the season is over.

When you have collected enough sap, it is advisable to start boiling it in shallow pans out of doors, as the boiling-off process produces quantities of sticky vapor. At first there is no danger of scorching the syrup, because of its great water content, but there is danger of its boiling over.

As the sap begins to thicken, you can move it to a more controlled heat source and cook it down in any heavy kettle whose capacity is three times the volume of the sap you are reducing. Maple sap, like water, boils at 212°. It becomes syrup at 219°. ▲ Adjust the temperature, therefore, at higher altitudes, depending on the boiling point of water at your altitude.

To make **maple cream,** boil to 225° to 227°; to make **maple sugar**, bring to 230° to 233°. Beat until it starts to thicken, then pour into molds. Before storing maple syrup and while it is still hot, filter it through a cloth-lined colander to rid it of sugar sand, a malate of lime. If sealed at 180°, the syrup will remain sterile for a year or more unrefrigerated.

MOLASSES

Rich in iron, molasses also improves the keeping qualities of breads and cakes. Molasses in this book means unsulfured or light molasses unless otherwise specified. There are 3 major types of molasses:

1. The best is unsulfured molasses deliberately made from the juice of sun-ripened cane which has grown from 12 to 15 months. 2. Sulfured molasses is a by-product of sugar making; the sulfur fumes used in the manufacturing of sugar are retained as sulfur in the molasses. Light molasses results from the first boiling of the cane. So-called dark molasses is a product of the second boiling. 3. Blackstrap molasses is a waste product. It is a rather unpalatable residue of a third boiling in which more sugar crystals are extracted but in which minerals such as iron remain.

Since molasses is not so sweet as sugar, use 1 cup molasses for ¾ cup granulated sugar. The molasses should replace no more than ½ the amount of sugar called for in the recipe. Add ½ teaspoon baking soda for each cup molasses added, and omit or use half the baking powder called for. Make sure also to reduce the other liquid in the recipe by 5 tablespoons for each cup of molasses used.

CANE SYRUP

A concentrated sap of sugar cane, this is substituted as for Molasses, above.

TREACLE, GOLDEN OR REFINER'S SYRUP

Golden syrup, a residual molasses, is clarified and decolorized, which makes it mild in flavor. Treacle is darker and heavier. Neither substitutes properly for molasses.

SORGHUM

Thinner and sourer in flavor than cane molasses, sorghum is substituted as for Molasses, above.

CARAMELIZED SUGAR

A marvelous flavoring which can be made in several ways. While its caramel flavor is strong, its sweetening power is reduced by about one-half.

I. For Hard Glazes

Heat in any ➤ very heavy, nonferrous pan over ➤ very low heat:

1 cup granulated sugar

Stir constantly with a long-handled spoon for 8 to 10 minutes until the sugar is melted and straw-colored. Remove the pan from the heat. Add:

¼ cup very hot water

➤ very slowly and carefully, for a quick addition might cause explosive action. This safeguard against the spurting of the hot liquid will also help make the syrup smooth. To make the syrup heavier, return the pan to low heat for another 8 to 10 minutes, continuing to stir, until the sugar mixture is the color of maple syrup. Toward the end of this process, to prevent its becoming too dark, you may remove the pan from the heat and let the caramelization reach a bubbling state from the stored heat of the pan. Store the syrup covered on a shelf for future use. The syrup hardens on standing but, if stored in a heatproof jar, is easily remelted by heating the jar gently in hot water. Should the sugar burn, use it for coloring, see below.

II. For a Croquant or Brown Nougat

Follow as in I, above, but at the beginning of the recipe, combine with the sugar:

1 tablespoon water

Proceed as directed.

III. For Coloring

If stored covered on a shelf, caramelized sugar will keep indefinitely. This can be used to replace the more highly seasoned commercial gravy colorings. The intense heat under which it is processed destroys all sweetening power.

Melt in a ➤ very heavy nonferrous pan over low heat:

1 cup sugar

Stir constantly until it is burned smoke-colored to black. ➤ Remove from the heat and be sure to let it cool. ➤ Quick addition of water to intensely hot sugar which is well over 300° can be explosive and very dangerous. Then, as in caramelizing above, add ➤ almost drop by drop:

1 cup hot water

After the water is added, stir over low heat until the burnt sugar becomes a thin dark liquid.

SYNTHETIC OR NON-NUTRITIVE SWEETENERS

There is some reason to question the systemic effect of all noncaloric sweeteners. ➤ Any of these sugar substitutes should be used on doctor's orders only and, in cooking or baking, according to manufacturers' directions. The FDA allows the saccharin-based substitutes to be sold without restrictions, but cyclamates alone or in combination with saccharin must be labeled as drugs. The saccharin types should not be cooked, as they produce a bitter flavor. Cyclamates can be heated, and in some cooked foods their sweetening power actually increases. But they do not give the same texture in baking as do true sugars and therefore should be used only in recipes specially developed for them. For amounts to be used in substitutions for sugars, see 597.

ABOUT GELATIN

To get the most nourishment out of gelatin, which is not a complete protein, see 2. Meat, fish, eggs, nuts or milk may be added to enrich its value. To get the most allure ➤ never use too much. The result is rubbery and unpleasant. The finished gelatin should be quivery—not rigid—when jostled. It is sympathetic to almost all foods ➤ except fresh or frozen pineapple, which contains a substance that inhibits jelling. Cooked pineapple presents no problem.

Gelatin is full of tricks. It can turn liquids into solids to produce gala dessert and salad molds. It makes sophisticated chaud-froid and ingenuous marshmallows. It also makes a showcase for leftovers and keeps delicate meats and fish in prime condition for buffet service. Chopped and used as a garnish, 114, or cut into fancy shapes, clear gelatins add sparkle to many dishes. Gelatin also gives a smoother texture to frozen desserts, to jellies and cold soups. It thickens cold sauces and glazes, 367, and, in sponge and whipped desserts, doubles the volume.

➤ Gelatin dishes must, of course, be refrigerated until ready to use. And, in buffets, they are best presented on chilled trays or platters set over crushed ice. While gelatin must be kept cold, it should ➤ never be frozen unless the fat content of the recipe is very high—as in certain ice creams.

Gelatin's power to displace moisture is due to its "bloom," or strength. In household gelatins this is rated at 150 and means that the contents of 1 package of unflavored gelatin or about 1 tablespoon can turn about 2 cups of liquid into a solid. Gelatin often comes ready to use in granules, but the most delicate fish and meat aspics are made with stocks reduced from bones, skin and fish heads. It also comes in sheets. For equivalents, see 595.

High sugar concentrations retard gelatinization and reduce thickening power. Unless a recipe is exceedingly acid, 1 tablespoon of gelatin to 2 cups of liquid should produce a consistency firm enough to unmold after 2 hours of chilling—if the gelatin is a clear one. But it must get 4 hours of chilling if the gelatin has fruits, vegetables or nuts added to it. Also, allow proportionately more jelling time for large, as opposed to individual, molds. If you prefer a less firm texture, use 1 tablespoon of gelatin to 2¼ to 2½ cups liquid. These gelatins will not mold but are delightful when served in cups or in coupes. If you are ➤ doubling a gelatin recipe that originally called for 2 cups of liquid, use only 3¾ cups in the doubled recipe.

For basic gelatin aspic recipes, see 113 to 120. For Gelatin Desserts, see 743 to 748. For an aspic glaze for hors d'oeuvre or open sandwiches, see 368. For interesting molds and gelatin combinations to fill them, see 112.

MIXING GELATIN

I. Sprinkle 1 tablespoon of gelatin granules over the surface of ¼ cup cold water and ➤ without stirring let it soak about 3 minutes until it has absorbed the moisture and is translucent. Have ready just at the boiling point 1¾ to 2 cups stock, fruit juice, milk, wine or water. Combine with the soaked gelatin and stir until dissolved.

You may allow the dissolved gelatin to cool at room temperature over a bowl of cracked ice, or in the refrigerator—but not in the freezer, as a gummy look is apt to develop, and the surface cracks miserably. It is interesting that gelatins that are slow to jell are also slow to break down when they are removed from the refrigerator, but any gelatin will begin to weep if exposed too long to high temperatures.

II. If you do not want to subject the liquid in the recipe to high heat or reduce its flavor and vitamin content, use a double boiler and sprinkle 1 tablespoon gelatin over ¼ cup cold water. Dissolve this mixture ➤ over—not in—boiling water. Add to the dissolved gelatin 1¾ to 2 cups 75° liquid and stir well.

III. If you are in a hurry and are making a gelatin that calls for 1 cup water and 1 cup stock or fruit juice, you can prepare the gelatin as in I above, boiling your cup of stock or fruit juice and then stirring about 8 large or 10 small ice cubes into the hot liquid to cool it. Stir the cubes constantly 2 to 3 minutes. Remove the unmelted ice. Let the mixture stand 3 to 5 minutes. Incorporate the fruit or other solids called for, and mold.

IV. For an even faster gelatin with frozen fruit, see Blender Fruit Whip, 746.

MAKING FANCY GELATIN MOLDS

➤ To prepare molds for clear gelatins, rinse them well in cold water, as shown opposite. Another method is to coat the mold with vegetable oil, but we do not recommend this for clear gelatin, because a blurred surface results. After filling an undecorated mold, run a knife through the mixture to release any air bubbles that might be trapped in it. Then refrigerate until ready to unmold.

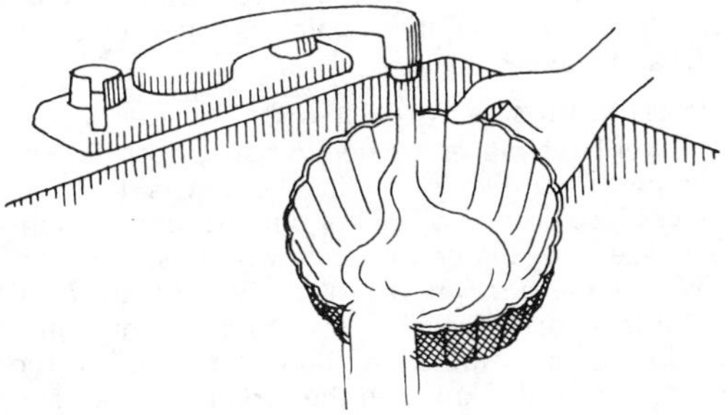

Before starting to make fancy designs in gelatin, have ready well-drained and chilled foods. Allow about 1¼ cups of solids for each cup of gelatin or aspic. Just as the gelatin thickens to about the consistency of uncooked egg white, put a small amount in a chilled mold or dish with sloping sides which has been rinsed in cold water. Roll and tip the mold in such a way that a thin layer of gelatin coats its inside surface. Refrigerate the mold to set the gelatin.

Now impale bits of food on a skewer or toothpick. Dip them one by one into the gelatin and place them just where you want them on the hardened layer in the mold, to form the design. When the decorations for one layer are in place, fill the spaces between with more gelatin. Return the mold to the refrigerator until this has set, and proceed with this method until the mold is filled.

When using a fish-shaped or other fancy mold, accent the lines of the design with slivers of egg white, cucumber or peppers, if for a salad; with citron, cherries, crystallized rinds or fruits, if for a dessert.

An easier way to make layered molds is to choose nuts, fruits and vegetables of different weights and porosity. Put them in a very slightly jelled mixture and let them find their own levels. The floaters are apple cubes, banana slices, fresh grapefruit sections or pear slices, fresh strawberry halves, broken nutmeats and marshmallows. The sinkers are fresh orange slices, fresh grapes, cooked prunes, and the following canned fruits: apricots, Royal Anne cherries, peaches, pears, pineapple, plums and raspberries. If you are making gelatins to serve in champagne coupes, you can decorate the tops with grape halves. Even though they are technically sinkers, you can wait until the gelatin is almost set and hold each grape for just a second until it makes enough contact not to turn wrong side up.

Another way to make fancy molds is to combine layers of clear and whipped or sponge gelatins, see About Gelatin Puddings, 743.

➤ To unmold aspics or gelatin puddings, have ready a chilled plate large enough to allow for a garnish. You may moisten the dish slightly. This will prevent the gelatin from sticking, and enable you to center the mold more easily. You may first use a thin knife at several points on the edge to release the vacuum. Then reverse the mold onto the plate. If necessary, place a warm damp cloth over the mold for a few seconds, as shown below. If the food is still not released, shake the mold lightly, bracing it against the serving dish. Some people dip the mold into hot water for just a second. We find this risky with delicate gelatins, as the heat must not go above 115°.

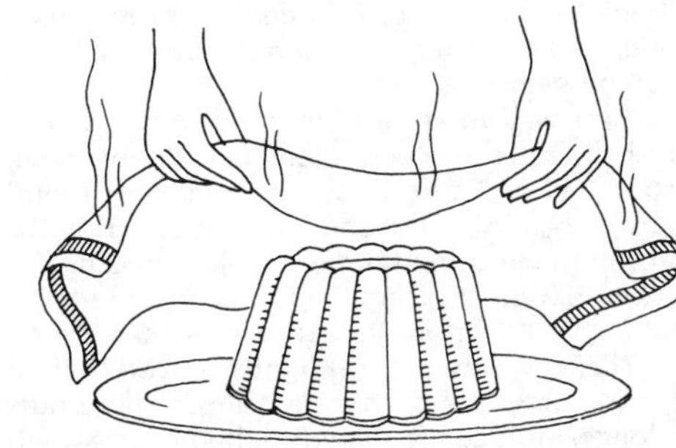

OTHER GELATINOUS THICKENERS

AGAR

This dried seaweed looks like transparent soup noodles. Its gel strength is not easily destroyed by heat or acid. For aspics or jelled desserts, allow 1 teaspoon agar for each cup of liquid to be jelled. Soften by first soaking in ¼ cup cold liquid, then dissolving in ¾ cup hot liquid. To avoid a weedy flavor, be sure the agar you buy is highly purified. If used as a salad garnish, soak 2 hours, changing the water 2 or 3 times. Cut into 2-inch lengths before serving.

IRISH MOSS OR CARRAGEENAN

Another seaweed which also needs to be well purified if a weedy odor is to be avoided. It is used as an emulsifier, stabilizer and thickener in a variety of foods. Allow from 6 to 10 grams powder per cup of liquid, depending on how stiff a gel you want. Prepare as for agar, above. It needs to be heated to 140° to dissolve, and becomes thin in the presence of acid.

GUM TRAGACANTH

Used in some icings to give pliability, and in salad dressings to add body. Use from 1 to 4 grams of powder for each cup liquid, depending on the thickness desired.

RENNET

Dioscorides said that rennet had the power to join things that were dispersed and to disperse things that came together. No chemist these days dares match such a claim! Rennet, an extract from the lining of the first stomach of calves, is the coagulant in cheese making, 536. See Rennet Pudding or Junket, 748.

ABOUT NUTS

Whether they are seeds, like pecans and walnuts; fruits, like lichees; or tubers, like peanuts—nuts contain concentrated protein and fats. Except for chestnuts, 563, they contain very little starch. But it is for their essential oils, which carry the flavor, and for the textural contrast that we treasure them so much. The reason they are so often listed as an optional ingredient in our recipes is merely that the recipes will carry without them—and with so much less cost and calorie value. Except for green almonds and pickled green walnuts, nearly all nuts are eaten when ripe.

The best way to store nuts is to keep them in their shells. This protects them from light, heat, moisture and exposure to air—factors which tend to cause rancidity in the shelled product. The difference in the keeping time for shelled pecans, for instance, may range from 2 months at about 70° to as long as 1 year in a freezer. So, if nuts are already shelled, store them tightly covered in a cool, dark, dry place or in a freezer. Unsalted nuts have longer storage life than do salted ones, which tend to rancidity. Refrigerate after opening. Some nuts, like pecans and Brazil nuts, are more easily shelled if boiling water is poured over them and they are allowed to stand in it 15 to 20 minutes. Be sure to discard any kernels that are moldy, shriveled or dry, as they may prove bitter or rancid.

As a rough rule, a pound of nuts in the shell yields about ½ pound shelled. For more detailed yields, see 597.

BLANCHING NUTS

In addition to the tough outer shell, some nuts have a thin inner lining or skin that may need removing. If so, just before using, pour boiling water over the shelled nuts. For large quantities, you may have to let them stand, but only for about 1 minute at the most. ➤ The briefer the length of time, the better. Drain. Pour cold water over them to arrest further heating and drain again. Pinch or rub off the skins.

For peanuts, filberts and pistachio nuts, you may prefer to roast in a 350° oven 10 to 20 minutes and then rub off the skins.

ROASTING OR TOASTING NUTS

This both crisps them and brings up the flavor. Unless otherwise specified, place them blanched or unblanched in a 300° oven and turn frequently to avoid scorching. ➤ To avoid loss of flavor and toughening, do not overtoast, as nuts tend to darken and become crisper as they cool.

SALTING NUTS

➤ Coat a bowl with egg white, butter or olive oil, add the nuts and shake them until they are coated. If you salt before cooking, allow not more than ½ teaspoon salt to one cup of nuts. Spread the nuts on cookie tins and heat in a 250° oven. Roast about 10 to 15 minutes, stirring frequently to achieve even browning. A more rapid way is to heat in a heavy iron skillet 2 tablespoons oil for every cup of nuts. Add nuts and stir constantly about 3 minutes. Drain on paper toweling. Salt and serve.

CHOPPING NUTS

If rather large pieces are needed, simply break nuts like pecans and walnuts with the fingers. For finer pieces, use a knife or a chopping bowl and chopper, see 370. Or chop as shown below. ➤ It is easier if the nuts are moist and warm and if the knife is a sharp French one. Group the nuts in a circle with a diameter of about the length of the blade. Grasp the knife on the top at both hilt and

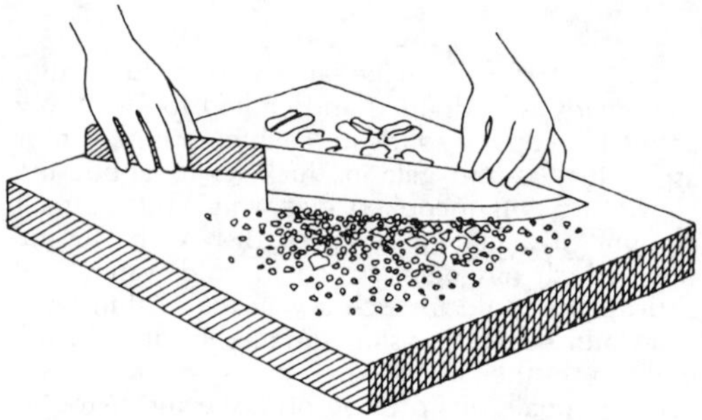

blade ends as shown. Rock the blade briskly from point to hilt, gradually turning the knife toward you in a semicircle. Gather the chopped bits together and repeat the rocking until the bits are as fine as you want them.

Almonds may be chopped in a ⅄ blender. ➤ Process no more than ½ cup at a time for 30 seconds at highest speed.

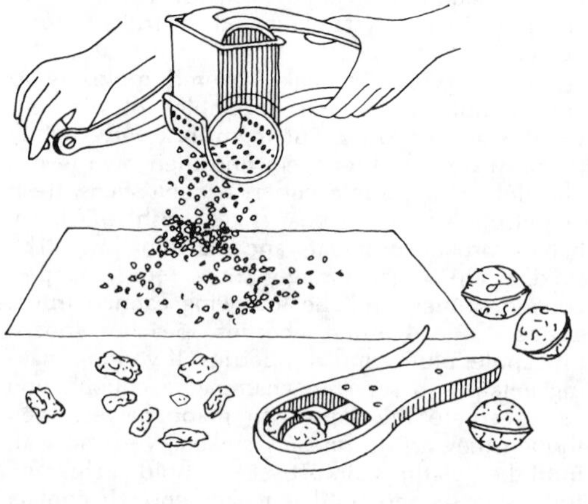

GRINDING NUTS

➤ Use a special type of grinder—one that shreds or grates them sharply to keep them dry, rather than a type that will crush them and release their oils. Do small quantities in a rotary grinder, as sketched. Light, dry, fluffy particles result, which become a binder in Torten, 684.

Sometimes, however, for butters and pastes, a a meat grinder or a ⅄ blender is used. We do not otherwise recommend a blender for grinding nuts, as it tends to make the nuts too oily—except for almonds, which should be done in small quantities.

Peanut butter is so popular that it has overshadowed the use of other nut butters. Try grinding almonds, pecans or walnuts into butter. These are so rich they need no additional oil. Use for every cup of nuts 1/3 teaspoon salt.

ALMONDS AND ALMOND OIL

Grown in Europe, Asia, Australia, South Africa and California, almonds are available in the shell or shelled and toasted with skins on or blanched with skins removed. Untoasted are best for baking, as toasted ones may become too brown. Look for a plump, smooth kernel, and buy in the shell for economy and freshness. Relatively high in balanced protein for a vegetable source, they are high in fat compared to beans. Almonds may be ground to make torten, marzipan, and almond paste, or slivered for toppings. As a garnish, see Amandine, 553. They may also be eaten while green and soft with cheese and wine. Almond oil is used like other vegetable oils, 541. It has a yellow-white appearance and is odorless, with a mild nutty flavor.

BITTER ALMONDS AND BITTER ALMOND OIL

Used as a flavoring and called for in some classic European recipes such as Orgeat syrup, bitter almonds are not available in the United States in concentrated form because they contain the poison prussic acid.

BEECHNUTS

A real treat—but just try to beat the squirrels to this harvest.

BRAZIL NUTS

The more delicate types do not ship well, and we must rely on a rather coarse, tough variety that does. To slice these large kernels, cover the shelled nuts with cold water and bring slowly to a boil. Simmer 5 minutes. Drain. Slice lengthwise or make curls with a vegetable slicer. You may toast the slices at 350° for about 12 minutes.

CASHEW NUTS

Cashews have an edible, fleshy fruit covering which can be eaten raw without harm. But between the outside shell and the kernel is a very irritating toxic oil related to poison ivy, which must be removed or destroyed by heat. Make cashew butter as for Peanut Butter, 564. For baking, use the untoasted cashew.

CHESTNUTS: MARRONS AND OTHER VARIETIES

The chestnuts in **Joy** recipes are not to be confused with the poisonous kind found in ornamental allées, or with the edible crisp Chinese water chestnuts, we usually know only in canned form and in oriental dishes, see below.

Chestnuts are frequently used as stuffing for fowl and traditionally combined with Brussels sprouts and red cabbage. One of our more knowing European friends insists that if navy beans are substituted for chestnuts in desserts strongly laced with coffee or almond paste, one cannot tell the difference.

To shell chestnuts, make two crosscut gashes on their flat side with a sharp pointed knife. The outer shell may come off when you do this, but the inner skin will still protect the kernel. To remove both the inner and outer coverings, place the nuts in a pan over high heat, dropping oil or butter over them—1 teaspoon to 1 pound of nuts. Shake them until coated, then place in a moderate oven until the shells and inner brown skin can be easily removed. This brown inside skin is bitter and must be peeled off while still warm.

Or, if you are using the chestnuts in a recipe calling for boiled chestnuts, they may be covered with boiling water, simmered 15 to 25 minutes and drained, after which the shells and skins may be removed. The meats may be tender enough to be put through a purée strainer. If not, again cover with boiling water and cook until tender. To boil, bake or steam chestnuts, see 298. To roast, see 79.

To reconstitute dried chestnuts, soak overnight in water to cover. Rinse and pick over. Simmer until they are tender and puffed up. ➤ Substitute them for cooked fresh chestnuts, cup for cup.

Allow about 1½ pounds in the shell for 1 pound shelled chestnuts. Thirty-five to 40 whole, fairly large chestnuts make about 2½ cups peeled. For the numerous uses of chestnuts, see Index.

The European blight that has almost destroyed *Castanea sativus* and its opulent hybrids such as the marron de Lyon, with its simple large kernel, has somehow spared the good Italian chestnuts that are still regularly imported to our American markets. And on our own American soil some blight-impervious oriental varieties are coming into their own: *crenata* from Japan and *mollissima* from China—not to mention the ever-sturdy little native chinquapin.

All chestnuts need long doses of tender loving care. In China they are roasted in hot sand which is continuously stirred, producing a constant moderate heat on all sides. For the French method which is also slow but produces delicious chestnuts, see Steamed Chestnuts, 299.

WATER CHESTNUTS

There are two types—both of which are crispy and delicious. In one type, the shell grows together into a horn at one end. The other is bulbous. Use water chestnuts in Hors d'Oeuvre, 79, Vegetables, 335, and Salads, 92.

FILBERTS AND HAZELNUTS

Varieties less rich than pecan, these are almost identical in their sophisticated flavor. Filberts are the more subtle European versions of our native hazelnuts.

HICKORIES AND BUTTERNUTS

Rich natives, like pecans, and they never need blanching.

MACADAMIA NUTS

Use these exotic, nutritious 1-inch-round nuts roasted or unroasted, in recipes calling for nuts; as cocktail snacks or as substitutes for Chinese chestnuts. As these nuts are hard to crack, try wrapping each one in heavy cloth and hammering it on a very hard surface. To roast, spread shelled nuts in a shallow pan and heat in a 250° oven 12 to 15 minutes, stirring often. Salt lightly and store in an airtight refrigerated container.

PINE OR INDIAN NUTS

Known also as piñon in Spain or pignola in Italy—where the variety is richer. These are good in Dolmas, 492, and in Pesto, 570.

PISTACHIO NUTS

These nuts, loved for their green color and haunting flavor, are often used in farces or pâtés. To skin, spread on baking sheets and heat at 400° for 4 minutes. Cool and slip off skins.

ENGLISH AND AMERICAN WALNUTS AND PECANS

Walnuts are highly polyunsaturated. Blanching for 3 minutes rids them of an acid which some people find indigestible. Then dry and toast as indicated above. The English or Persian walnut and the American or black walnut are perhaps the most familiar. Hull at once after harvesting. Pecans are probably the heaviest in fat of all our natives, with sometimes as much as three-fourths of their bulk in fat.

PEANUTS

These underground legumes—also called groundnuts or, in their larger form, goobers—are high in valuable, if incomplete, proteins. If the heart is left in, they make a real contribution to the diet. The small Spanish types will grow in the northern states. All peanuts are best eaten right after roasting, before they get limp. If roasting them in the shell at home, keep the oven at 300° and roast 30 to 45 minutes, or 20 to 30 minutes if shelled. Turn them constantly to avoid scorching. Check for doneness by removing skins. The inner skins, heavy in thiamin, are pleasantly flavored. But little is gained by home roasting, as a steam process used commercially for roasting peanuts in the shell gives superior results. ➤ Discard any peanuts that are moldy.

⅄ PEANUT BUTTER

Federal regulations require commercial peanut butter to contain 90% shelled roasted ground peanuts, with additions of no more than 10% of salt, sweeteners and oil. However smooth and satisfying commercial peanut butters may seem, they are often made without the germ of the nut. This valuable portion—as in grains—contains minerals, vitamins and proteins, yet it is literally fed to the birds. The commercial objection to the germ is twofold: 1. It gives the butter a somewhat bitter flavor, and 2., as with whole grains, the heat of processing and the heat in storage may cause the finished product to grow rancid. ⅄ If you are smart, you will make your own full-bodied peanut butter in an electric blender. Use:

Fresh roasted or salted peanuts

It is wise to start with a bland oil:

Safflower or vegetable oil

Allow 1½ to 2 tablespoons oil to 1 cup peanuts. If nuts are unsalted, add salt to taste:

About ½ teaspoon salt per cup

ABOUT SEEDS, GRAINS, BEANS AND PEAS

➤ Be certain to use only seeds which have not been fumigated or treated with pesticides or fungicides. **Sunflower, pumpkin, buckwheat, barley** and **squash** seeds should be hulled before eating or using in recipes. All of these are flavorful and nutritionally valuable. To roast, see the general rule under Nuts, 562. However, to roast **soybeans,** soak ¼ cup beans overnight, refrigerated, in 1 cup water. Drain and dry thoroughly. Roast in a shallow pan about 2 hours in a 200° oven, then put pan under broiler to brown the soybeans. Use as is or season and mix with oil.

Poppy seeds come from *Papaver somniferum,* but the seed has no narcotic properties. The most desirable is grown in Holland and is a slate-blue color. The seed is best when roasted or steamed and crushed before use in cooking—so its full flavor is released. If it is one of your favorite flavors, it is worth getting a special hand-mill for grinding it. Use it in baked items and try it on noodles.

Sesame or **benne seeds** are a favorite topping for breads, cookies and vegetables. Their nutty flavor is strongest when the unhulled seeds are lightly toasted about 20 minutes in a 350° oven and stirred frequently. If hulled, the seeds are white. Crushed, they may be made into an oily paste, called Tahin, see below. Crushed sesame, together with cooked chick-peas, also forms the base for Hummus, 90. Sesame oil from the seeds is desirable in salads. For other seeds, see About Spices, 574, and Herbs, 577.

⅄ TAHIN

A Mideast seed butter of yogurtlike consistency, used to dress salads or as a base for sweets. Combine in a blender:

4 tablespoons ground sesame seeds
1 teaspoon sesame oil
1 tablespoon lemon or lime juice
½ teaspoon salt

Add slowly while blending:

About ½ cup water

Remove from the blender and stir in if you wish:

(1 to 2 pressed garlic cloves)

SPROUTING GRAINS, BEANS AND PEAS

Sprouting seeds not only are one of the wonders of this world but probably produce by far the most nutritively valuable addition to the diet in relation to their cost. One-quarter cup of grain or beans expands into one pint of sprouts with rich protein content. The sprouting action greatly increases the already rich vitamin content. Soybeans, however, are the only seeds in which the protein is complete, 2.

Use or buy seeds, preferably organically grown, ➤ that have not been chemically pretreated for agricultural purposes. Remove any damaged or moldy seeds. For about a one-pint yield, wash and soak overnight in:

1 cup water
¼ cup seeds: alfalfa, red clover, fenugreek, mustard, radish, sesame, sunflower; any grains, beans or peas

➤ Avoid potato and tomato seeds, which, when sprouting, are poisonous, and fava and lima beans, which are extremely toxic when used raw. Next morning, drain, reserving the liquid for stock. Place the seeds in a one-quart wide-mouthed glass jar securely closed with nylon mesh or cheesecloth so that air can reach the seeds. If the jar is stored on its side the seeds can be shaken to spread over a larger area, which is desirable. Place the jar in a dark, warm cupboard or in an opaque bag so that light is excluded but air is still available. If this method is used, it is important to rinse and drain the seeds three times daily and to invert the jar to let it drain thoroughly after each rinsing. If you cannot rinse three times daily, place the seeds in a well-soaked new clay flower pot. The newness is important to discourage fungal development. The drain hole should be stopped up with a cotton wad or a cork. Place the pot in a saucer of water that you keep filled all during the process of sprouting. Place the pot in its saucer, loosely covered with a plate, in a dark, warm place. Whichever method you use, watch closely and discard if molding. Sprouts should develop in 3 to 5 days, although mung and soybeans may take 6 to 8 days.

A general rule is to serve the sprouted seeds when the sprout is at least as long as the seed, although sunflower and sesame are served when the sprout first appears. Chick-peas, flax, lentils and soybeans can be used with about half-inch sprouts, and mung bean sprouts can be more than 2 inches. If not served at once, refrigerate sprouted seeds in a covered colander or a loosely covered container. Do not hold more than a day or two. They can be frozen, but considerable nutritive value is lost. You may also add them to stir-fried dishes or to soups and stews just before serving, but for best nutritional results serve them raw, hulls and all, as a garnish or in salads or sandwich fillings. If you care to remove the hulls, stir the sprouts in a bowl of cold water until the husks rise and may be skimmed off. A famous tea sandwich combining sprouts of "cress"—not watercress but garden cress, *Lepidium sativum*—with sprouts of mustard, *Brassica nigra* or *Sinapsis alba,* takes advantage of an age-old English custom of producing fresh greens on a minuscule scale all year around in the kitchen. The sprouts, so tiny-leaved as to be reminiscent of doll houses, can be germinated between blotters or in a wrung-out piece of flannel or Turkish toweling in from 10 to 14 days. To have them ready simultaneously, sow the mustard 4 days later than the cress, as it germinates more rapidly. When sprouted, leave the sprouts on the germinating surface. Keep them moist and exposed to light until the two small leaves are green and about ⅛ inch long. Serve scattered on very thin, lightly sweet-buttered rounds of bread.

ABOUT CHOCOLATE AND COCOA

Both of these delights come from the evergreen trees of the genus *Theobroma,* "Food of the Gods." The manufacture of the two is identical up to the moment when the chocolate liquor is extracted from the nibs, or hulled beans, and molded into solid cakes. At this point, part of the "butter" is removed from some of the cakes, which become cocoa, and added to others, which, in turn, become the bitter chocolate we know as cooking or baking chocolate.

Cocoa butter is remarkable for the fact that, under normal storage conditions, it will keep for years without becoming rancid. There are many pharmaceutical demands for it, and in inferior chocolate it is sometimes replaced by other fat.

Ideal storage temperature for chocolate is 78°. The bloom that turns chocolate grayish after it has been stored at high temperatures is harmless—merely the fat content coming to the surface.

Semisweet chocolate, available in 8-ounce cakes or in bits or pieces, is good for candy dipping because of its sheen when melted. It is also good for icings, sauces and fillings. The best sweet chocolate is made by combining the melted bitter cake with 35% cocoa butter, finely milled sugar and such additions as vanilla and milk—depending on the type of chocolate desired. German's chocolate, which is conditioned against heat, refers not to the country but to a very canny person of that name who early realized there was a greater profit if the sugar was already added to the chocolate when it was sold. Milk chocolate—best known as candy bar chocolate—may be used for icings, pies and puddings.

An entire square of chocolate equals 1 ounce. Two-thirds cup of semisweet chocolate is 6 ounces by weight—or 10⅔ tablespoons by volume. But in any semisweet chocolate, you have about 60% bitter chocolate and 40% sugar. Should you want to substitute semisweet for bitter, make the adjustment in the recipe, using less sugar, more chocolate and a dash of vanilla.

➤ For exact substitution and equivalents of chocolate and cocoa, see 594. In some quick-cooking recipes, this substitution may not be successful, as the sugar doesn't crystallize properly with the chocolate. If semisweet chocolate stiffens when melted—in sauces, for instance—add a small amount of butter and stir well until smooth.

It is easy to substitute cocoa for chocolate in sauces: just add 1 tablespoon butter to 3 tablespoons cocoa for each ounce of chocolate. But in baking it is wiser to choose recipes written either for cocoa or for chocolate, as the cocoa has a flourlike quality that must be compensated for if chocolate is substituted, or the cake will become doughy. In cakes and cookies, soda is often used to give chocolate a ruddy tone. A few drops of vinegar serve the same purpose.

➤ All chocolate scorches easily, so melt it slowly over hot water. Do not use boiling water, as even a small amount of steam may harden or stiffen the chocolate. If this should happen, add for each ounce of chocolate ½ teaspoon or more of vegetable shortening—not butter—to reliquify the chocolate. If you don't like to clean the pot, float the chocolate on a small foil "boat" and discard the foil after use. Or place wrapped squares, folded edges up, in the top of a double boiler ➤ over—not in—hot water for 10 to 12 minutes. Cool chocolate to about 80° before adding it to cake, cookie or pudding mixtures.

To grate chocolate, chill it and try shaving or grating it in a rotary grinder, 562. Have a big bowl ready to receive it—or you may be annoyed by its flighty dynamism.

To make chocolate curls for decorating parfaits or cream pies, hold a wrapped square of chocolate in the hand to warm it slightly. Unwrap and shave chocolate with long thin strokes, using a vegetable peeler or a small sharp knife.

Cocoa is pulverized from the dry cocoa cakes, which, after processing, still contain from 10% fat for regular cocoa up to 22% to 24% fat for breakfast cocoa. The so-called Dutch type maintains the heavier fat content, and the small quantity of alkali introduced during the processing to neutralize the acids produces a slightly different flavor. Instant cocoa, which usually contains 80% sugar, is precooked and has an emulsifier added to make it dissolve readily in either a hot or a cold liquid.

For details about cocoa and chocolate as beverages, see 41. For Dipping Chocolate, see 781.

So-called **white chocolate** contains no chocolate at all but is prepared from vegetable fats, coloring and flavors. Should you be allergic to chocolate, try carob, 593, which tastes almost like chocolate, although not so strongly flavored.

ABOUT COCONUTS

If you live in coconut country, you know the delight of using the flower sap as well as the green and the mature fruit of this graceful palm. In cooking, you may substitute its "milk," "cream" and "butter" for dairy products. However, be aware that this exchange is not an equal one nutritionally, because the coconut is much lower in protein. ➤ Coconut products are very sensitive to high heat. For this reason they are added to hot sauces at the last minute or are cooked over hot water. They are especially treasured in preparing curries and delicate fish and fruit dishes.

The first thing to do with a coconut, of course, is to get at it. Lacking power tools, you drop the large fruit onto a rocklike substance. If it doesn't crack open enough so that the husk pulls away, use your trusty axe. Out comes a fiber-covered nut. Shake it. A sloshing noise means that the nut is fresh and that you can count on some watery liquid erroneously referred to as milk. If the husked coconut is green, the top can be lopped off with a large, heavy knife or a machete. The liquid within is clear, and the greenish jellylike pulp makes ideal food for small children and invalids. To open the harder shell of the mature nut, pierce the three shiny black dots which form a monkey face at the peak. Use a strong ice pick, and hammer it in. Reserve the drained liquid under refrigeration and be certain to use within 24 hours, or freeze it. Tap the nut briskly all over with a hammer. It usually splits lengthwise, and these halves can be used as containers for serving hot or cold food. See illustrations, opposite.

You may also open the shell with heat, but then the shell is useless for serving food. To do so, place the undrained husked coconut in a preheated 325° oven 15 to 20 minutes. ➤ Do not overcook, as this destroys the flavor. Remove from the oven and cool until the nut can be handled. Wrap it in a heavy cloth to prevent any pieces from flying off. Then crack it with hammer taps. ➤ Have a bowl ready to catch the milky liquid.

Coconut milk and cream, very rich in fat, are made from the grated, mature, stiff white meat of the nut. The grating is sometimes done while the meat is still in the shell. Note the illustration below of a grater given to us by a friend from

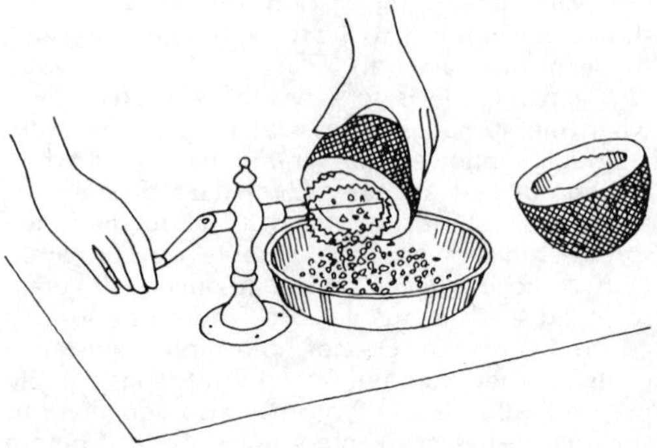

India which simplifies preparing coconut for cakes, garnishes or Coconut Dulcie, 774. Or you may leave the thin brown skin on and use it to

protect the fingers as you hand-grate. Use a vegetable parer to remove the skin. If the skin is removed, you may cut the meat into small chunks

and chop in the ⅄ blender, no more than ½ cup at a time. Add ¼ cup hot water to make coconut milk; hot milk to make coconut cream. Then strain and measure. If more milk is needed than results, add more hot water, reblend and strain again.

In the East Indies, they heat the grated coconut meat in its own natural liquid ➤ just to the boiling point, then remove it from the heat and cool. In the West Indies, they pour boiling water or milk over grated coconut and add the natural liquid—allowing in all about 1 pint liquid for a medium coconut. In either case, when the mixture has cooled, the coconut is drained through two thicknesses of cheesecloth, and the meat, retained in the cloth, is squeezed and kneaded until dry. The drained liquid is allowed to set, refrigerated; it solidifies into a cold butter and can be taken off in one piece. When the "cream" rises, it is skimmed off and refrigerated.

Coconut "butter," though vegetable in origin, contains completely saturated fatty acids. It is made from chilled coconut "cream"—also very rich in fat—by churning with a rotary beater or in a ⅄ blender. When the solid mass rises, force any excess water out of it with the back of a spoon. To utilize the coconut that remains, make **polvo de amor,** below. Use it as a garnish for breakfast foods and desserts.

Brown slowly in a heavy pan over low heat:

1 cup strained coconut pulp
2 tablespoons sugar

Grated fresh coconut may be soaked 6 hours refrigerated in milk to cover, and drained before use. This gives it about the same moisture content as the canned, shredded or flaked types—for which it may be substituted.

To toast grated coconut, spread it thinly on a baking sheet and heat about 10 minutes in a preheated 325° oven. Stir frequently. For a dessert or a spread made from grated coconut, see Coconut Dulcie, 774.

➤ To substitute flaked coconut, use 1⅓ cups firmly packed for 1 cup grated.

Coconut shells can make interesting food and drink containers. For a bowl, saw off the upper third of the shell. For a rack to hold this round-bottomed shell upright, cut off about one-half of the smaller piece as sketched on the left, opposite. For serving salads, cut the shell lengthwise. The shells can also be used to heat and serve sauced foods. Cut off the top third to serve as a lid. The food may be heated in a 350° oven by placing the lidded nutshell in a small custard cup or on an inverted canning jar lid in a pan of hot water. Baste the shell about every 10 minutes until the contents are hot. Or simply fill the shell with very hot food. The custard cup forms a base when you serve; or fold a napkin or ti leaf for support, as sketched opposite.

ABOUT FLAVORS AND SEASONINGS

"Season to taste." . . . How that time-tested direction stimulates the born cook! We know that seasonings, spices, herbs and condiments can complement and compliment food, but it is our own sense of taste that composes the symphony. Just how does it do so? The anatomy of taste is the tongue, and it differentiates between four basic sensations. The top of the tongue detects sweet and sour, the sides salt and sour, the back bitter. When we taste things, they pass so quickly over these areas that a fast sequence of tastes results, like an arpeggio or a chord. When we were young, lollipops were their sweetest—not without reason, because senses dull with age, and our taste buds were more impressionable then. Not only were we told to gulp our medicines fast, but we took them iced to reduce their impact. Conversely, as adults we hold chilled wine in our mouths until it has had a chance to warm up and release its flavor. And, to taste normally sweet, the ice cream we freeze must be sugared more than warm foods. It is relished more, too, when taken in small amounts and held in the mouth momentarily before swallowing. Heat seems to affect sourness and saltiness; lemon seems less acid when the tea is hottest, and soup saltier when hot than when cold. The best time to judge for salt adjustment is when food is just below 98°.

But sweet, sour, bitter and salt are only foundation tastes on which is built the complex and subtle structure whose charms are due much more to the sense of smell than to the sense of taste. Try tasting food while holding your breath; you will notice that a full and characteristic flavor is realized only when the breath is expelled through the nostrils. Since foods must be in solution for their flavors to be fully appreciated, texture plays a large part both directly and as contrast. Flavors that stand out in liquid may grow duller rather than sharper if some gumlike substance such as tragacanth or agar-agar is used as a thickener, with the intent of increasing tactile sensations related to taste. The peppers and ginger, because of their nonvolatile components, leave a somewhat painful burning sensation, along with a pleasant glow and tingle. In contrast, mint has the power to cool because of its high menthol content. Types of seasoning modify one another. Salt, for example, can make sugar less cloying and tone down acidity; as a corollary, sugar or vinegar may reduce saltiness. Ginger, brandy or sherry can lessen "gaminess" in fish and wildfowl while bringing a comforting warmth. Salt, pepper and parsley act as catalysts for other flavors. A reminder: prolonged drinking before and smoking during a meal tends to desensitize all the pathways along which food is appreciated.

The history of seasonings is an ironical one. Back in medieval days the spice routes to the Orient were fiercely contested, for spices were essential to render palatable the poorly preserved foods of Europe. Nowadays, many foods in our western world are so successfully and uniformly preserved that seasonings are needed to make them interesting enough to eat! The Greeks had recognized nine flavors: sweet, salty, sour, bitter, astringent, dry, pungent, vinous and oily. Even today no more generally acceptable categories exist. The infinite interplay of taste, aroma and texture combined with hereditary and national preferences defies exact classification, and only the familiar remains acceptable to the majority of people. Try setting your sails for new courses on this endlessly fascinating sea of taste.

➤ When adding seasoning, the greatest care must be used to enhance the natural or previously acquired flavor of the food at hand. The role of the seasoner is that of impresario, not actor: to bring out the best in his material, not to stifle it with florid, strident off-key delivery or to smother it with heavy trappings. First and best, of course, even before seasoning, are the built-in flavors of food grown in rich soils or from animals which have been nourished on flavor-inducing vegetation. Examples are the famous sea-marsh–grazed lamb of France, the heather-dieted grouse of Scotland, our own southern peach-fed pigs or northern game birds after they have taken their fill of juniper or other aromatic berries. Next come the flavors accentuated by heat: in the glazes on browned meats; in the essential roasting of coffee and cocoa beans; in the toasting of nuts, seeds and breads; in the highly treasured "ozmazome," as the gourmet calls it, which results from rich broths; as well as in the blending of tastes achieved generally through slow cooking.

Then there are the flavors induced by fermentation and bacterial activity, as in wines and cheeses; those created by distillation in extracts and liqueurs, and those brought about by smoking, 814, or marination, 528. Intensification of flavor in foods can be by purely mechanical means, too: the cracking and softening of seeds like those of poppy, anise, coriander and caraway to release their essential oils, the sources of aroma. This is also true during the mincing of herbs, the crushing of spices in a mortar, and the puréeing of pods to remove their more fibrous portions. Keep scissors handy to quickly add bits of flavorful foods such as herbs, celery, peppers and bacon.

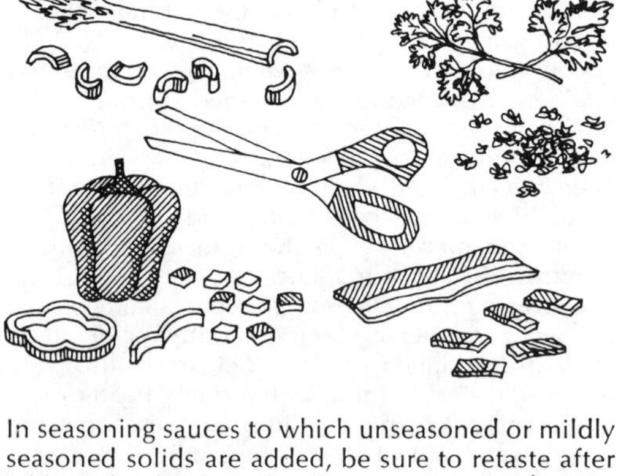

In seasoning sauces to which unseasoned or mildly seasoned solids are added, be sure to retaste after adding the food. Perhaps most important ➤ heat seasoned food with great care, since certain spices like cayenne, paprika and curry blends scorch easily, and others become bitter if overheated.

ABOUT SALTS

Salt has many powers. The interplay of salt and water is essential to life itself. The maintenance of a proper salt balance is vital to the system and different in every individual. Those for whom a low-salt or no-sodium diet has been recommended by their physician may replace the missing flavor by the skillful use of herbs, spices, lemon juice and wine. Also, they should be aware of the salt or sodium content of softened water. ➤ Salt's powers of preservation made possible our ancestors' survival in the waters, wastes and wilderness through which they forged the world's great trade routes. While its use in preserving food has become much less important with the advance of refrigeration, it is surprising how much we still depend on it: in food processing of various kinds; in the curing of meats; in the brining and pickling of vegetables; in freezing ice cream; even, now and then, for heating oysters and baking potatoes.

In food preservation, the action of salt is twofold. It draws out moisture by osmosis, thus discouraging the microorganisms which are always more active in moist than in dry food. Afterward, the brine formed by the salt and moisture in combination further prevents or retards the growth of surface microorganisms. To cook salted meats, see 482. To remove excess salt from bacon and salt pork, see 542; from anchovies, 570.

The power of salt to heighten the flavor of other foods is its greatest culinary asset. This is true even in candy making, when a pinch of salt often brings out a confection's characteristic best, and with uncooked food, as when salt is sprinkled on citrus fruits. Its reaction on cooked food is otherwise several-sided. It tends to dehydrate when added to water in which vegetables are cooked, and firms them. It draws the moisture from meats and fish in cooking processes. And it tends to deter the absorption of water by cereals, although it helps retain the shape of the grain. It toughens eggs. And it must be used cautiously in bread making, as too much inhibits the growth of yeast and adversely affects gluten formation. For the effects of salt water on cooking, see 519.

These diverse properties of salt have provoked arguments, from time to time, as to just when this very important ingredient should be added when cooking food. It must, of course, be used very sparingly, if at all, at the start of any cooking in which liquids will be greatly evaporated—such as the making of soups, stocks and sauces. But small quantities of salt, added early to soups and stews, will help in clarification. It is obviously good practice to sear grilled, broiled or roasted meat before adding salt, to retain juices and flavor—unless the meat is floured or breaded. And since it is almost impossible to get rid of excess salt in cooked foods—although occasionally a touch of sugar will make them more palatable—the amount must be calculated with care.

We know from long experience that the flavor-enhancing power of salt is most effective if it is added judiciously toward the end of the cooking process. Don't taste with the tip of the tongue only, but with the middle and sides as well, where the greatest response to salt-stimulus lies.

Salt occurs within foods in varying amounts, animal sources having a higher salt content than vegetable. Sea fish, especially shellfish, are heavier in salt than freshwater fish. Of course, pickled, cured or corned meats and sausages; broths, catsups and extracts; brine-processed frozen fish, sardines, herrings and anchovies, as well as canned soups unless labeled "salt-free," and canned fish and meats—all are high in salt. Do watch your salting arm when dealing with any of the foods mentioned above, and in cooking artichokes, beets, carrots, celery, chard, kale, spinach, dandelion greens, endive and corn—all of which are naturally more salty than most other vegetables. And also be cautious with dates, coconut and molasses.

Various kinds of salt are mentioned in this book. When the word salt is used without qualification, it means ➤ cooking or table salt. ➤ To keep it free-flowing, put a few grains of rice in the saltcellars.

COOKING OR TABLE SALT

This is a finely ground free-flowing type, about 90% sodium chloride—to which dehydrators are frequently added.

IODIZED SALT

This is recommended for certain areas where the water and soils are lacking in iodine, an essential trace element, 6.

COARSE, KOSHER OR SEA SALT

A squarish-grained salt, with natural iodine and other minerals. It is very flavorful when used in cooking and should be applied with a light touch. It is often served sprinkled over meats, after carving and just before serving, so that it does not have time to melt completely. It is also sprinkled over rolls, pretzels and bread before baking, as a sparkling garnish. ➤ Do not confuse this coarse salt with rock salt, see 570.

BRINE

Brine is a solution of salt and water—preferably soft water. Its purpose is to draw the natural sugars and moisture from foods and form lactic acids which protect them against spoilage bacteria. A **10% brine,** about the strongest used in food processing, is made by dissolving 1½ cups salt in 1 gallon of liquid or allowing 6 tablespoons salt to a quart of liquid. But after brining, as more liquid continues to be drawn from fruits and vegetables, the brine may be weakened. Always allow about 2 gallons of 10% brine plus enough food to fill a 4-gallon jar. ➤ A rule of thumb to test for 10% brine is that it will float a 2-ounce egg so the shell just breaks the surface of the liquid.

PICKLING OR DAIRY SALT

This is pure salt that is free from additives which might cloud the pickle liquid. It is available in both granulated and flake forms, which may be substituted pound for pound. But, if measuring by volume, use for every cup granulated salt about 1½ cups flake salt.

ROCK SALT
A nonedible, unrefined variety which is used in the freezing of ice cream—also as a base for baking potatoes or heating oysters on the half shell.

VEGETABLE SALTS
These are sodium chloride with added vegetable extracts—such as celery and onion. If you use them, cut down on the amount of salt called for in the recipes.

SEASONED SALTS
Usually a compound of vegetable salts, spices and monosodium glutamate. In using flavoring salts, be sure not to add regular cooking salt before tasting.

I.

10 tablespoons salt
3 tablespoons pepper
5 tablespoons white pepper
1 teaspoon red pepper
1 teaspoon each nutmeg, cloves, cinnamon, bay, sage, marjoram, rosemary

II.

4 tablespoons salt
1 tablespoon sugar
1 tablespoon paprika
1 teaspoon each mace, celery salt, nutmeg, curry, garlic powder, onion powder, mustard

HERB SALTS
I. Blend in a mortar for 3 or 4 minutes:

1 cup noniodized salt
1½ cups pounded fresh herbs

Spread the mixture on a heatproof tray. Preheat oven to 200°, then turn it off. Place the tray in the oven and allow salt mixture to dry.

II. You may also preserve some herbs by salting them down green in a covered crock, alternating ½-inch layers of salt with ½-inch layers of herbs. Begin and end with slightly heavier salt layers. After a few weeks, the salt will take on the flavor of the herbs you have chosen to combine and will be ready for use. The herbs which remain green may also be used.

MONOSODIUM GLUTAMATE
A concentrated form of sodium that is usually extracted from grains or beets. It is also present in bean curd and soy sauce. Long known as the magic powder of the East, where tons and tons of it are consumed annually, it is sometimes used in this country, especially in commercially processed foods, because of its power to intensify some flavors. It seems to have no effect on eggs or sweets. It may modify the acidity of tomatoes, the earthiness of potatoes and the rawness of onions and eggplant. It acts as a blending agent for mixed spices used in meat and fish cookery. It is soluble in water but not in fat. So, if you do use it, add it to the liquid ingredients. While it accentuates the saltiness of some foods, just as wine does, it lessens the saltiness of others. ➤ We detect a certain deadening similarity in foods flavored with monosodium glutamate and prefer, if a meat or vegetable is prime, to let its own choice character shine through unassisted.

Also known as MSG, this substance has recently been revealed as the cause of the allergic reaction known as Chinese Restaurant Syndrome which causes untoward physical side-effects in some people.

SOUR SALT
A citric acid which is sometimes used to replace a lemon flavoring or to prevent discoloration in fruits or canned foods.

SMOKED SALTS
Hickory and other scented smokes have been purified of tars and are chemically bound to these salts by an electrical charge.

SMOKY SALT MIXTURE
1 teaspoon smoked salt
½ cup catsup
¼ cup olive oil
2 tablespoons mustard

SALT SUBSTITUTES
These are chlorides in which sodium is replaced by calcium, potassium or ammonium. They should be used only on the advice of a physician.

ANCHOVIES AS SEASONING
Anchovies, sometimes referred to as sardelles, discreetly added to food, can bring a piquancy the source of which is most difficult to trace. About ⅛ of an anchovy to a cup of sauce will turn the trick, or ⅛ of a teaspoon of anchovy paste. The paste is both less strong in flavor and apt to be saltier than the whole anchovies, which may be treated in several ways:

I. For use in a salad, soak anchovies in cold water or milk ½ to 1 hour. Drain and dry on paper toweling before using.

II. For use in a sauce, soak them in warm water 5 to 10 minutes. Drain before using. Anchovies are sometimes used as lardoons to season meats, see 444.

ANCHOVY PESTO
Crush together:

1 anchovy fillet
2 tablespoons grated Parmesan cheese

Combine with an equal amount of:

Butter

BASIL PESTO
This uncooked seasoning can be made in advance. Use on pasta or on a baked potato, about 2 tablespoons to a portion, mixed with equal parts of butter. If you add a tablespoon or more per portion to Minestrone, 177, as is often done, you arrive

at a result close to the Provençal version called *Soupe au Pistou.*
Pound in a mortar about:
1½ cups fresh basil leaves
Parsley may be substituted, but of course the flavor is very different. Add and pound:
2 cloves garlic
¼ cup pine nuts
Add, until the mixture forms a thick purée:
About ¾ cup thinly grated Sardinia or Parmesan cheese
When the mixture is really thick, add very slowly, stirring constantly:
About ¾ cup olive oil
until of the consistency of creamed butter.
Put a film of olive oil over the top. Cover and refrigerate or freeze.

CHIFFONADE OF FRESH HERBS

One of our very favorite ways to disguise canned soup combinations is to use a freshly gathered bouquet of tender herbs. These we mince or, if we are in a hurry, ⅄ blend right in with the soup, except for chives, which we mince separately to keep them from being too pervasive. Also see Chiffonade of Herbs for Soup, 195.

CHILI POWDER

A chili blend may be based on a combination of spices as varied as cumin, coriander, oregano, black pepper, cloves and sweet and hot peppers; or it may be made up quickly from a combination of:
3 tablespoons paprika
1 tablespoon turmeric
⅛ teaspoon cayenne
But, no matter how simple or how complex the mix, use with it plenty of:
Pressed garlic
To heighten the flavor of chili powder, simmer the food at least 15 minutes after combining with the seasonings.

CITRUS ZESTS, JUICES AND GARNISHES

What better name than "zest" could be found for the gratings of the colorful outer coatings of lemons, oranges, tangerines and limes—those always available, valuable, yet somehow not fully appreciated ingredients! Zest is the very quality they add to baked items, stuffings, sauces, soups, meats and desserts. ➤ Zest must, however, be used with a light touch. If you keep an easily cleaned hand grater, fifth on the right, 337, hanging near the stove, you will be amazed at the subtlety you can add quickly to your seasoning. Use only the colored portions of the citrus skins; the white beneath is bitter. Citrus rinds are more intense in flavor than juice because of their heavy oil concentration. Fold them into icings, for instance, when the major beating is over, so as not to disturb the texture. Another way to get this oily residue for flavor is to grate the rinds coarsely, place them in a piece of cheesecloth and wring the oils onto sugar. Let stand about 15 minutes before using.

And enough can never be said in favor of the frequent use of small quantities of citrus juices—especially in salt-free diets where these flavors serve to obscure the lack of salt. Use them as a substitute for vinegar wherever delicacy is wanted. ➤ To get the greatest amount of juice out of citrus fruit, roll the whole fruit on a hard surface, gently but firmly pressing it with the palm while rolling, before cutting for juicing. Lemons and limes can be juiced quickly by holding the cut side against the palm and squeezing firmly. If the fruit is properly held, the seeds will be trapped.

➤ It is only the fresh rind and juice of these citrus fruits that hold the really magic seasoning power, but, if you must substitute, the following are approximations: 1 teaspoon freshly grated zest = 2 tablespoons fresh juice = 1 teaspoon dried zest = ½ teaspoon extract = 2 teaspoons grated candied peel.

Keep on hand for flavoring drinks and sauces Citrus-Flavored Sugars, 557. To make citrus peels for fruit sauces, take off just the colored portion of the peel with a sharp knife, a potato peeler or a special "zester" tool, shown lower right above. Blanch for 3 minutes to a limp stage. Wash in cold water. Shred and resimmer with the sauce. ➤ To use lemons as garnishes, cut them in one of the attractive ways shown above and on 42, or use juice from the practical pitcher also shown.

FINES HERBES

This classic phrase connotes a delicate blend of fresh herbs suitable for savory sauces and soups, and for all cheese and nonsweet egg dishes. Use equal parts of parsley, tarragon, chives and chervil—although some other mild herbs may be allowed to creep in. These mixed herbs, minced with a sharp knife and added ➤ at the last minute to the food being cooked, give up their essential oils but retain a lovely freshness.

BOUQUETS GARNIS OR FAGGOTS

Nothing helps a soup or stock so much as a combination of herbs and vegetables. They are best made of fresh materials and ➤ should be added for only the last half hour of cooking.

I. Bunch together:

3 or 4 sprigs parsley or chervil
⅓ to ½ bay leaf
2 sprigs fresh thyme
(1 leek, white portion only)
(2 cloves)

➤ To make removal easier, you may place them inside:

(Several overlapping celery ribs)

and bind tightly with a white string.

II. If you cannot get fresh materials, wrap dried herbs, still on the stem, or coarsely crumbled but not powdered, in 4-inch squares of cheesecloth tied into bags as shown, 579. Store them in a tightly covered container. Allow for 12 bags:

2 tablespoons dried parsley
1 tablespoon each thyme and marjoram
2 bay leaves
2 tablespoons dried celery leaves

FOUR SPICES OR SPICE PARISIENNE

Also called **Quatre Épices.** This is the mixture that is such a favorite for sweets and meats. It varies in composition according to the will of the épicier or the whim of his customer, and frequently exceeds four. Carême's formula for **épices composes** included dried thyme, bay leaves, basil, sage, a little coriander and mace, and—at the end—the addition of one-third ground pepper.

Mix:

1 teaspoon each cloves, nutmeg and ginger
1 tablespoon cinnamon

FIVE-SPICES POWDER

This pungent, slightly sweet mixture of ground spices is available ready-mixed in Chinese stores. Use sparingly when preparing red-stews, 447, and roasted meats or poultry.

Mix by grinding into a powder equal amounts of:

Chinese star anise, fennel, pepper,
cloves and cinnamon

GREMOLATA

A mixture of seasonings for sauces and pan gravies.

Mix:

2 tablespoons finely chopped parsley
1 minced clove garlic
½ teaspoon grated lemon rind

Sprinkle this mixture on sauce or gravy during the last 5 minutes of cooking. Simmer, covered, over very low heat so the flavors can be absorbed.

SEASONED LARD

This yellow lard is called **Sofrito** in the Caribbean, but in Italy the name is applied to Mirepoix, below. It gets its color from the annatto seed, a coloring often used to accentuate the yellow in pale butter. Seasoned lard is made in advance of use and stored refrigerated.

Wash, drain and melt ➤ uncovered over slow heat in a heavy pan, stirring occasionally:

1 lb. diced salt pork

Remove from heat and strain into another heavy pan. Wash and drain:

¼ lb. annatto seeds

Add them to the strained melted lard and heat slowly for about 5 minutes. Strain the colored lard into a large, heavy kettle. Grind and add:

1 lb. cured ham
1 lb. green peppers, seeds and membrane removed
¼ lb. sweet chili peppers, seeds and membrane removed
1 lb. peeled onions

Mash in a mortar and add:

15 fresh coriander leaves
1 tablespoon fresh oregano

Just before cooking, place in a small tea ball:

6 peeled cloves garlic

and add to the lard mixture. Simmer these ingredients over low heat, stirring frequently, for about 30 minutes more. After the mixture has cooled, remove garlic. Store ➤ covered and refrigerated.

SALT PORK, BACON AND HAM AS SEASONING

These give an interesting fillip to many bland foods. Bacon and salt pork are often blanched, 154, to remove excess salt. Although they may be used interchangeably, the flavors are quite distinct. Used as a garnish, the bits are called **grattons** or **cracklings.**

Dice:

Salt pork

Try it out, 542, in a skillet until brown and crisp, or place the dice in a very slow oven until golden brown.

MIREPOIX AND MATIGNON

About ⅔ Cup

Both of these terms refer to a blend of vegetables: diced in Mirepoix, minced in Matignon. The blend, always made just before use, is an essential of Sauce Espagñole, 346; and it can be used either as a base or as a seasoning for roasting meats and fowl or for flavoring shellfish.

Dice:

1 carrot
1 onion
1 celery heart: the inner ribs

Add:

½ crushed bay leaf
1 sprig thyme
(1 tablespoon minced raw ham or bacon)

Simmer the above in:

1 tablespoon butter

until the vegetables are soft. Deglaze the pan with:

Madeira

MUSHROOMS AS SEASONING

This family contributes one of the most coveted of all tastes. ➤ Never discard stems, and particularly not skins, for it is here that the greatest amount of flavor lies. Even the scrapings of their rarefied cousins, truffles, are sold at a good price and can be cooked with gelatin to form pungent garnishes for cold foods. To bring more flavor into canned mushrooms, sauté them in butter. Consider also, for seasoning, powdered or whole dehydrated mushrooms. And for a classic mushroom seasoning, see Duxelles, below. *Agaricus campestris,* the variety most commonly found in our markets, is strengthened in flavor as it withers but must be kept free of moisture in drying, so as not to mold.

➤ To dry mushrooms for storage, select fresh, firm specimens. You may wash them, then dry on paper toweling; or simply place them on a screen or thread them on a string to sun-dry. When thoroughly dry, put in sterile, tightly sealed glass jars. Keep from all moisture until ready to use. To reconstitute, see Dried Mushrooms, below.

For mushroom types and a discussion of the dangers of collecting, see 306. Mushroom spores are often sold in brick form for home culture, but unless conditions are ideal and temperatures constantly between 50° and 60°, experience has shown it is cheaper to buy your mushrooms full-grown.

DRIED MUSHROOMS

Reconstitute as follows. ➤ Wash in 3 waters to clean:

2 oz. dried mushrooms

Drain. Pour over them:

Boiling water to cover

and soak 15 to 30 minutes. Some types may need longer soaking, and some will still look like old leather. If they have swelled and softened somewhat, drain and use. If recalcitrant, bring them to a boil in:

Cold water to cover
3 teaspoons soy sauce
1 teaspoon salt
(2 teaspoons sugar)

Reduce heat and simmer 15 to 50 minutes, or until tender. Drain. Use as for fresh mushrooms. Utilize liquid in soups and sauces.

DUXELLES OR MUSHROOM SEASONING

This is a delicious and convenient way of using up mushroom stems and storing or preserving them for use whenever a mushroom flavor is wanted. Add to stuffings, sauces or gravies, or use in meat and fish cookery. You may strain before using. Allow 2 tablespoons for 1 cup chicken-flavored sauce.

Chop very fine:

½ lb. mushrooms

Squeeze in a cloth, twisting to extract as much moisture as possible. Reserve. Cook until golden:

¼ cup chopped onion or 2 tablespoons chopped shallots

in:

2 tablespoons butter
3 tablespoons olive oil

Add the mushrooms plus juice and:

¼ teaspoon grated nutmeg
Season to taste

Sauté on high heat until the mushroom moisture is absorbed. Refrigerate duxelles in a covered jar until ready to use, but do not hold longer than 5 days.

TOMATOES AS SEASONING

Whether fresh, canned, cooked, puréed, or as paste or catsup—and even as soup—the tomato weaves its way into innumerable dishes. To get the flavor without too much moisture, cut fresh tomatoes and squeeze to release extra moisture and seeds; then skin before using, as shown on 331. Canned and cooked ones are best drained, then strained so thoroughly that the tasty, pulpy part is forced through the sieve, leaving only the skin and seeds to discard. When making substitutions for purées, pastes and catsups, be sure to compensate for moisture differences and allow for the variations in strength of flavor.

TOMATO PASTE OR VELVET

About ¾ Cup

This makes a relish or a fine addition to sauces.

Wash, then mash:

6 large ripe tomatoes

Melt:

2 tablespoons butter

Add the tomatoes and:

1 teaspoon brown sugar
¼ teaspoon paprika
¾ teaspoon salt

Cook the tomatoes in a double boiler ➤ over—not in—boiling water, stirring occasionally, until they are the consistency of thick paste. Put the paste through a strainer. Store refrigerated.

ITALIAN TOMATO PASTE

This flavorful paste is diluted in a little boiling water or stock and added to sauces and soups. Fine in spaghetti and noodle dishes, as a dressing for cooked vegetables or salads, and as an addition to salad dressings.

Wash and cut into slices:

1½ pecks ripe Italian tomatoes: 6 quarts

Add:

1 large celery rib, cut up with some leaves
¾ cup chopped onion
3 tablespoons fresh herbs or 1 tablespoon dried herbs: basil, thyme, sweet marjoram or oregano
¾ teaspoon peppercorns
12 cloves
3 teaspoons salt
1 two-inch stick cinnamon
(1 minced clove garlic)

Simmer these ingredients until the tomatoes are soft. Stir frequently. Put the vegetables through a fine sieve. Simmer the pulp ➤ over—not in—boiling water, or over direct low heat with the use of an asbestos pad to prevent burning. Stir frequently. After several hours, when the pulp is thick and reduced by about half, spread the paste to a depth of ½ inch on moist plates. Cut into the paste to let air penetrate. Place the paste in the sun or in a 200° oven to dry. When the paste is dry enough, roll it into balls which you may dip in salad oil. Store refrigerated in airtight sterile jars.

SOYER'S UNIVERSAL DEVIL SEASONING

We have chosen this sauce from Alexis Soyer's *Culinary Campaign,* a fabulous account of the Crimean War, through which he cooked his way with abandon. No one brought more conviction to his work, whether changing the diet of the British armed forces, cooking at the Reform Club, or remolding the cooking habits of the English lower classes—which he attempted through his *Shilling Cook Book*. The original recipe called for a tablespoon of cayenne pepper. We have changed it to a small pinch, for in Soyer's day cayenne was baked into a sort of bread and then ground, making it about the same strength as a mild paprika. Rub any deviled food with the following mixture:

1 good tablespoon Durham mustard
¼ cup chili vinegar
1 tablespoon grated horseradish
2 bruised shallots
1 teaspoon salt
A few grains cayenne
½ teaspoon black pepper
1 teaspoon sugar
(2 teaspoons chopped chili peppers)
(2 raw egg yolks)

Soyer's instructions are to "broil slowly at first and end as near as possible the Pandemonium Fire."

ABOUT COMMERCIAL SAUCES

Ali Baab—in his great *Gastronomie Pratique*—refers to soy, Worcestershire, catsups, tabascos and other such frequently bought condiments as "sauces violentes" which mask out all other flavors. We find them useful as occasional accents, much too powerful to use unmodified; and we indicate suitable quantities as components in various sauces.

SOY SAUCE

Known as *shoyu* in Japan, the finest of all soy sauces are oriental types made from fermenting soybeans, roasted wheat, salt, yeast or malt, and sugar. They are sometimes fermented from 12 to 18 months and range from a light, thin variety which neither colors nor overwhelms chicken, seafood or light soups, through a darker type used in so-called red stewing, 447. A heavier bitter soy sauce made with molasses is almost black: it is better used as a coloring agent than for seasoning. Oriental soy sauces which are naturally fermented are preferable to domestic types produced by chemical means, which tend to be bitterer and saltier, due to additives, and may also include corn syrup or caramel and monosodium glutamate, 570.

WORCESTERSHIRE SAUCE

This sauce is claimed as original by the English. Its roots are said to be Roman and, not unlike their **Garum,** it has a base of anchovy. To make, see 848.

TABASCO SAUCE

This is made from hot tabasco peppers. ➤ Go easy—a few drops may be too much. Use in soups, cocktail sauce, piquant sauces.

ABOUT SPICES

Perhaps our interest in spices is the greater because of our descent from a sailing family, not in New England but in the old Hansa town of Lübeck, where ships with their cargoes of Kolonialwaren anchored at the wharves on the Trave. And the spices were stored in the mowlike corbie-stepped warehouses on the floors above the merchants' living quarters.

Spices, indeed, bring all the world together. Like wines and cheeses, their individuality is intense and their identification with places a vivid one. We associate the best bay leaves with Turkey; the best real cinnamon with Ceylon; the best red hot peppers with Louisiana. And there have been lively controversies over the relative merits of Spanish and Hungarian paprika; of Mexican and Malagasy vanilla beans.

Long before the first New England farm wife bought a wooden nutmeg, spice traders have known ways to camouflage their wares. We are lucky today that both government agencies and trade associations work hard to develop and maintain high standards for these relatively costly and still most important condiments.

Pepper, like salt, because of its preservative qualities, has been at times worth its weight in gold. And we are acquainted with a treasured bay leaf that on festive occasions—all during the last war—made the rounds of ten or fifteen beleaguered English households.

Since spices are used in such small quantities, we recommend that you purchase from impeccable sources. We also suggest that ➤ if you are using ground spices, they be replenished at least within the year, as they tend in powdered form to lose strength rapidly. Be sure to date your jars when you clean and fill them. Store spices in tightly covered nonabsorbent containers and in as dark and cool an area as your kitchen provides. But have them handy! Their discriminating use will pique many a dish from obscurity to memorableness.

In cooking, put whole spices in a cloth or in a stainless metal tea ball so you can remove them more readily when the dish is done. ➤ Do not overboil spices, in particular pepper and caraway, as they become bitter. And do not use high heat for paprika or curry, for they scorch easily. Some spices are available as distilled essences, and these clear additives are valuable in light Fruit Butters, 836, or Pickles, 841. Their flavor does not last as long as that of whole spices cooked with the food. ✻ In frozen foods, the flavors of the spices do not hold up well. And in ➤ quantity cooking, if you are enlarging household recipes, spice to taste rather than to measure. We suggest amounts considered pleasurable by the average person. You may wish to use more or less than we indicate. Spices, even when dry, can reactivate molds they may have had before, or developed during drying, so the government suggests you resist the temptation to sniff them. Below we describe spices and their uses.

ALLSPICE

In this book pimiento, the name for true peppers of the *Capsicum* family, see 586, is reserved for them. And pimento, *Pimenta dioica,* is kept for allspice only. Use allspice anywhere from soup to nuts, alone or in a combination with other spices. For within its single small reddish-brown berry lies a mixture of cinnamon, clove, nutmeg and juniper berry flavors. But do not confuse allspice with the mixture called in France Quatre Épices, or Four Spices, 572.

ANNATTO

Because of its color from the pulp surrounding the seed, annatto, *Bixa Orrellana,* is often used as a substitute for saffron.

THE CARDAMOMS

Powder the plump seeds of *Elettaria cardamomum* only as needed, for otherwise the aromatic loss is great. Use as for cinnamon and cloves, alone or in combination. Delicious in coffee. The smaller type, *Amamum cardamomum,* is used whole in barbecue-basting sauces and pickles.

THE CINNAMONS

True cinnamon, *Cinnamomum zeylanicum,* is the bark of a tree that flourishes in Ceylon and along the Malabar Coast. It is extremely mild whether rolled in a tight quill or stick or in powdered form. Most of the so-called cinnamon on the market is really cassia, *Cinnamomum cassia.* This is a similar bark that is not quilled, but formed as though a short scroll were rolled from both ends and left with its center portion flat. It has slightly bitter overtones compared to the warm, sweet, aromatic true cinnamon. The best forms of cassia come from Saigon. Use the stick form of either of these spices in hot chocolate, mulled wine, fruit compotes and pickles. We need hardly suggest trying cinnamon on toast, dusting it on cookie tops or incorporating it into desserts and baked items. But maybe its use in small quantities in meats and seafoods is new to you.

THE CLOVES

This spicy, dried, rich red, unopened bud of the clove tree, *Caryophyllus aromaticus,* contains so much oil that you can squeeze it out with a fingernail. Because its flavor is so strong, the heads of the cloves are sometimes removed so the seasoning will be milder. These milder portions are often used in the powdered form. Before serving a dish cooked with whole cloves, always remove them. The best cloves come from Madagascar and Zanzibar. Use in curries, stewed fruits, marmalades; in chutneys, pickles, marinades; and, in small quantities, with onions and meats; especially good with ham, as well as in spiced baked stews. An onion stuck with 3 or 4 cloves is a classic addition to stocks and stews. Oil of clove is available for use in light-colored foods, but watch out for its terrific pungency.

CURRY

We think of curry, which is really a highly seasoned sauce, mainly as a powder sitting on the shelf ready to be added when foods need a lift. But curry powders are best when the spices are freshly ground or incorporated into a paste with onion, garlic, fruits and vegetables as commonplace as apples and carrots and as exotic as tamarind and pomegranate.

The curry, in either powder or paste form, has its flavor developed in olive oil, or ghee, a clarified butter. The paste is then cooked in a low oven over a period of several hours before the final stage of preparation with the main food. Curries should be specially blended for each kind of dish: a dry one for coating meat; a sour one for marinated meats; and other mixtures for chicken or mutton, rice, beans, vegetables and fish. They range in strength from the fiercely hot curries of Madras to the mild ones of Indonesia. The mixtures below give you an idea of the variety and extent of curry bases. Amounts to use per portion are a matter of tolerance. Choose beer or a tart limeade as a beverage with curried foods. When making up the dish, use plenty of fresh garlic and onion and, if possible, fresh coconut milk, 566.

I.

1 oz. each ginger, coriander and cardamom
¼ oz. cayenne
3 oz. turmeric

II.

2 oz. each of the seeds of coriander, turmeric, fenugreek, black pepper
2½ oz. cumin seed
1½ oz. each poppy and cardamom seeds
½ oz. mustard seed
½ oz. dry ginger
2 oz. dry chilis
1 oz. cinnamon

III.

1 oz. each turmeric, coriander and cumin
½ oz. each dry ginger and peppercorns
¼ oz. each dried hot peppers and fennel seed
⅛ oz. each mustard, poppy seeds, cloves and mace

GINGER

The root of a bold perennial, *Zingiber officinale*—with the most heavenly scented lily—must be harvested at just the right moment or it will be fibrous and have a bitter aftertaste. Whole fresh or green ginger should have a smooth skin and be a uniformly buff color. It must be kept dry or it will sprout and be useless for flavoring. Refrigerated, in a plastic bag, it will keep about 3 weeks. Or you may wash the fresh ginger, cover with sherry and keep refrigerated. But it really tastes best unpeeled, sliced thin, and sautéed in oil to extract the flavor. To use in recipes, peel, grate, slice or mash.

When dry, it may be cut into ½-inch cubes and steeped for several hours in a marinade or in cold water, after which the liquid can be used as seasoning. Peeled or thinly sliced ginger can be added to stews or rubbed like garlic over duck or fish. It will do much to remove "fishy" flavors. Boiled and then preserved in syrup, it is known in this milder form as **Canton ginger** and is delicious in desserts, chopped fine and used with or without its syrup. And it is worth trying with bananas and even with tomatoes, squash, onions and sweet potatoes. Ginger is also candied or crystallized, 796, and may be used in baked goods and desserts. This form can, in a pinch, be washed of its sugar and substituted for fresh ginger. We all know the value of ground ginger for flavoring baked items. ➤ Equivalent flavoring strengths of the various forms are: ½ teaspoon ground equals 1 to 2 teaspoons thinly sliced preserved, equals 2 tablespoons syrup.

JUNIPER BERRIES

Berries from *Juniperus communis* are prized for seasoning game and bean dishes. Three to six berries suffice per serving. In fact, ½ teaspoon of these berries soaked for a long time in a marinade—or cooked long in a stew—gives a flavoring equivalent to ¼ cup gin, to which these berries lend their typical aroma.

MOCHA

This name is given to dishes flavored with a lightly roasted coffee bean. It is often paired with chocolate. We include it here, for coffee can be used profitably as a spice.

NUTMEG AND MACE

These flavors are so closely allied because they come from the same tough-husked fruit of *Myristica fragrans*. It is sun- or charcoal-dried and, when opened, has a lacy integument which is used whole in cooking fruits or desserts or ground into mace for seasoning. The hard inner kernel is the nutmeg. Use it sparingly but often, and, for its full flavor, grind it fresh from a handy nutmeg grinder that merely needs a twist—like a pepper mill. Try it not only in baked items but in spinach, with veal, on French toast—and always with eggnog. ➤ One grated whole nutmeg equals 2 to 3 teaspoons ground nutmeg.

THE WHITE AND BLACK PEPPERS

Both these peppers come from berry clusters of the vining *Piper nigrum,* the master spice. There is some difference in flavor, the white being slightly more aromatic, but their use is almost interchangeable.

The white is made from the fully ripe berry, from which the dark outer shell is buffed before the berry is ground. White pepper flavor holds up better in sausages and canned meats. This form is also used in all light-colored foods or sauces.

Black pepper is obtained from the underripe, fermented, sun-dried whole berries. The peppercorns themselves, when used in poivrade dishes, are crushed rather than ground, so the oils are not dispersed. And they are added the last few minutes before the sauce is strained. Also available for poivrade dishes are the more flavorful canned green peppercorns. Crush them before adding. But pepper, which can be used in any food except sweets—and here there is the further exception of Pfeffernüsse—is best freshly ground. It not only is a remarkable preservative but manages to strengthen food flavors without masking them as much as other spices do.

Unless otherwise specified, the word pepper in this book means black pepper. For cayenne pepper, see 586–587.

TURMERIC

This Indian rhizome—*Curcuma longa*—is bitterish, and its rather acrid fugitive fragrance warms the mouth, so it must be used with discretion. Its golden color gives the underlying tone to curry powders and to certain pickles. In small quantities it is used as a food coloring, often replacing saffron for this purpose.

VANILLA BEAN AND EXTRACT

Vanilla bean, before being marketed, is fermented and cured for 6 months. Vanilla extract is prepared by macerating the beans or pods in a 35% alcohol solution. To retain its greatest flavor, add it only when food is cooling. Try 2 parts vanilla to 1 part almond flavoring—a great Viennese favorite. Or try keeping vanilla beans in brandy and using the flavored brandy as a seasoning. ➤ Beware of synthetic vanillas whose cheap flavor is instantly detected and which ruin any dish that is frozen.

If you are curious about the little dark specks in a good vanilla ice cream, these are the seeds scraped from the vanilla bean, which is another way to use this flavoring. Allow about 1 inch of scraped bean for 1 teaspoon vanilla extract. For another way to flavor, see Vanilla Sugar, 557.

EXTRACTS AND FLAVORINGS USED WITH SWEETS

There are a number of other extracts, all of which should be used sparingly, such as lemon and almond. Derivatives of almond are: falernum, a syrup of lime, almond and spices dominated by ginger; grenadine, made from the juice of pomegranates; and rose and orange waters, both sweetened distillations. ➤ We do not recommend nonalcoholic liqueur flavorings.

GROWING CULINARY HERBS

Confucius, a wise man, refused to eat anything not in season. Everyone who has tasted the difference between foods served with fresh rather than dried herbs knows how wise he was. Few herbs can be bought in a fresh state at market, but the most important ones can be easily grown. We know, for we have raised and used all the culinaries in this section. Therefore, we beg you to exercise your green thumb at least on those whose evanescent oils deteriorate or almost disappear in drying. Chervil, borage, burnet and summer savory suffer the greatest losses. And the mainstays—chives, tarragon, parsley and basil—can never in their dry form begin to approach the quality of their fresh counterparts. Even the flavor of sage when fresh and discreetly used can be so delicate as to be a new sensation.

A hallmark of the Compleat Herb Grower is a love of sundials and armillary spheres—reflecting the herbs' own predilection for bright sunlight—frequently paralleled by a passion for symmetry. You might like to duplicate the sequences of plantings shown beginning at the right in the top layout on 578: in the end section is sage, followed by tarragon, parsley, dwarf basil and thyme, all partitioned by chives. You may prefer partitions of clipped lavender, santolina or fernlike burnet which, with the sage and thyme end sections, will give your garden in winter an indication of form.

We have tried growing herbs in many patterns. Since most herbs are sun-lovers that need air and dislike competition, bed layouts, such as those shown at center and below it, suit them well.

As long ago as the seventeenth century, the herbalist Parkinson in his *Paradisi in Sole* stressed the importance of proper drainage in herb growing. We too have discovered that good drainage, whether secured by boxing or simply by the selection of terraced ground, is a primary consideration. The upper and lower sketches show raised beds, the upper crescent-shaped held high by old granite street cobbles, the lower by flue-liners which also provide containment for rampant aggressors like the mints. Shown in the partially sunken flue-liners are squares of mints, calendulas and nasturtiums, and a combination of chives and parsley—all edible yet colorful. You might also try other annual or deciduous squares, or use alternate evergreen and deciduous herbs again to allow for some winter form. Try placing the liners in Greek fret designs or any pattern that adapts to your space.

You may prefer to use squared beds. A 15-inch to 2-foot unit area for each of most culinaries is more than enough to supply household demands. Sometimes, if we want only a single specimen—for instance, a sage or a lavender—we keep it pruned to a central shrub and use the edges around it for smaller plants. Sometimes we repeat a color accent—like the gray of sage or lavender—to unify the whole complex of squares. A more elegant solution is to use millstones which reflect the heat most herbs thrive on and which make ideal access points for the gardener to weed from. A millstone also gives the surrounding herbs freedom to spread over its edges, as well as over the flat stones that define the bed. Here in the centers are a pot of rosemary and a dwarf pepper plant, although a cherry tomato plant on a trellis would give more height to the layout. Camomiles and thymes are shown as bordering plants, but any of the dwarf creepers like dwarf savories could be used. Also to be considered, though not for patterned beds, are the unruly tousle-headed giants, the dills; the fennels, lovage, sorrel; the floppy borage and scraggly corianders; anises, sesames and mustards. If these mavericks are grown in unregimented fashion, borage, dill, fennel, chervil, coriander and parsley will self-sow. These all have less stability of condition as well as of structure, and profit by a background of fencing or a south-facing housewall which not only protects but lends unity to the plantings. These plants are always problems for the neat-minded, as are the treasured onion family shown 585, for with the exception of chives, they die back and yellow after ripening.

If you haven't room for the more extended layouts shown on 578, try setting out a few pots of annuals on your patio. Some evergreen perennials will weather the winter in a strawberry jar, 567. To prepare a jar for herbs, fill with a mixture of one-third rich friable soil and two-thirds

sand. Try the thymes, sweet marjoram, burnet and chervil on the shady side. You can dwarf fennel, borage and sage by root confinement. Replace the coarse marjorams with dittany of Crete, and coarse mints with *Mentha requienii*—both tender perennials.

Pots can be used, too, for growing herbs indoors in sunny windows. We have had moderate success with rosemary, sweet marjoram, the basils, dittany of Crete, lemon verbena and scented geranium—all from late summer cuttings—and with dill and bronze fennel from seed. If you plan bringing plants indoors, pot them up in late August and put them in a partially shaded area. Bring them in before frost. Tarragon dug after cold weather dormancy and potted up indoors may show six inches of green within ten days. A small potted sweet bay is both decorative and useful. ➤ But most houseplant herbs deteriorate in flavor, just as do hothouse tomatoes.

We find that the various thymes, pot marjoram and winter savories flourish in a rock garden. Treat them with neglect and reap them for twenty years. But we also find, with our hot midwestern summers and variable winters, that sage, burnet and tarragon are more apt to hold over in well-enriched garden soil. Most perennial herbs also hold over better if they have been clipped to about two-thirds their height several times during the season prior to early August. If they are creepers like thymes, bob them back at the base as well. Follow each clipping with a dose of liquid manure. If the herbs are evergreen varieties, treat them to a thorough watering prior to the first killing frosts.

HARVESTING, DRYING AND FREEZING HERBS

Our instinctive inclination toward the cultivation and use of herbs and our longing for a year-round supply put us in good company across the centuries: Alcuin, Charlemagne's tutor, called herbs "the friend of physicians and the praise of cooks." Which brings us to the matters of harvesting, drying and freezing of herbs—processes we must adopt to keep our kitchens in steady supply.

The first rule of harvesting herbs is to clip constantly through July; never allow the plants to reach the blossoming stage. Later heavy clipping may weaken perennials—not allowing recovery of the plant before winter. Unless otherwise indicated in the individual notes on cultivation, herbs are harvested ➤ just before their flowers emerge. At this time, when they are budding up, the leaves are at their most aromatic. Hose down the herbs the day before harvesting. Pick early next morning, as soon as the dew has dried off the leaves. If necessary, dry the leaves, without bruising.

Herbs are remarkably free from insect pests and should be grown where they are not subject to sprays. After gathering, you may tie them together and hang in small bunches until dry. You can expect about 1 pound dried herbs for every 8 pounds freshly gathered. The location traditionally recommended is a cool, airy attic. Since such spaces are becoming scarce, a shady breezeway will do. And lacking a breezeway, room-drying at temperatures preferably below 90° is preferable to oven-drying, for even when the oven is preheated as low as possible and the herbs inserted the moment the temperature drops below 90°, their flavor is weakened. For thick-leaved varieties, the oven process may have to be repeated several times until the herbs are bone-dry.

➤ To test for dryness before packaging, put a few of the brittle sprigs or leaves in a tightly stoppered glass jar and watch for condensation, mold development or discoloration. This is important, especially with basil. ➤ Store dried herbs in tightly stoppered lightproof glass or ceramic jars in a cool place. Should they show insect activity, discard them. You may want to strip leaves from the stems before drying or freezing herbs. If drying seeds, collect them in paper rather than plastic bags, and let them dry thoroughly before bottling in glass jars. ➤ Dried herbs retain their flavor best if pulverized in a mortar, shown opposite, just before using.

You may freeze herbs. If you do, use them before defrosting—in the same proportion as for fresh herbs. They are too limp for garnishes. Some herbs, like chives, get slimy when frozen ➤ so freeze or shot-freeze, parblanch, 154, for ten seconds, plunge into ice water for one minute and dry between towels. Put them up individually in recipe-sized packets for seasoning a salad dressing or a batch of stew, or freeze mixed bouquets garnis for soups and sauces. To preserve herbs by salting, see 570. The herbs and the salt, which has become savory, will be ready to use within two weeks.

USING HERBS

Handy as an herb chart might seem, we have refrained from compiling one, because some herbs are overpowering, and it is so difficult to indicate in a general way the amounts to use. Suitable quantities of herbs are listed in the individual recipes. Below we set down detailed characteristics and helpful horticultural tips for each culinary herb. Let us add that the delicately flavored types should be placed in sauces and soups only toward the end of preparation and left just long enough to release their volatile oils. And once again, while ➤ we advocate a constant use of herbs, we don't advise too many kinds at once or too much of any one kind.

To familiarize yourself with herb flavors, some "lazy day," when you feel experimental, blend ½ pound mild cheddar cheese with 2 tablespoons sour cream and 2 tablespoons vodka. Divide the mixture into small portions and add to each an herb or herb combination. Label the cheese samples as you mix them. Let them rest for about an hour to develop flavor. Then have a testing party with your spouse or friends.

➤ To substitute dried herbs for fresh, use ⅓ teaspoon powdered or ½ teaspoon crushed for every tablespoon fresh chopped herbs. ➤ To reconstitute dried herbs and develop their flavors, soak them in some liquid you can incorporate in the recipe—water, stock, milk, lemon juice, wine, olive oil or vinegar—for ten minutes to one hour before using. Or, simmer them in hot butter. For cooking, place nonpowdered dry herbs in a cloth bag or a stainless metal tea ball for subsequent easy removal. For blends, see 570 and 572.

ANGELICA

The leaves of this slightly licorice-flavored plant are candied as a garnish for desserts, 797; seeds may be added to pastry, young tips to rhubarb or gooseberries. *Angelica archangelica* grows to 4 to 8 feet. It dies after blooming but is perennial if blooming is inhibited. Seeds must be fresh, soil moist, and the locale shady.

THE ANISES

These have strangely subtle licorice overtones. Use seeds in Anise Cookies, 707; the oil as flavoring in sponge cake; or star anise in watermelon-rind pickle. To release the full flavor, crush seeds between towels with a rolling pin. *Pimpinella anisum* grows to 3 feet. Because of the long taproot, transplant into light rich soil when seedlings are young. The star anise, *Illicium anisatum,* imported from China, belongs to the magnolia family.

THE BASILS

Not without reason called *l'herbe royale,* these versatile herbs have a great affinity for tomatoes, fish and egg dishes, but are good in almost all savory dishes. They darken quickly after cutting. Serve them as they do in Italy—where basil is very popular—in a bouquet of sprigs set in water in a small vase. Be sure to try Pesto, 570, with spaghetti. *Ocinum basilicum,* which grows to 2 feet, dries poorly and should never be dried in heat above 110°. It roots in a few days in water. Make cuttings and pot up before frost in rich soil. It is worth keeping at least one plant over the winter to supply that fresh basil flavor until the new crop is ready. *Ocinum minimum,* dwarf bush basil, less than 1 foot tall, is the sweetest and mildest in flavor and the best for house culture.

THE BAYS

Always use these leaves, fresh or dry, with discretion—only 1/3 of a fresh leaf or 1/6 of a dry leaf in a quart of stew—and only a pinch if in powdered form. But do use them, not only in stuffings but in stocks, sauces and marinades, in the cooking of vegetables and meats, and in a Bouquet Garni, 572. Dry the leaves in August. ➤ Do not confuse the leaves of the edible bay tree, *Laurus nobilis,* highly aromatic when bruised, with those of the poisonous *Prunus laurocerasus,* the cherry laurel leaf of our gardens which is high in prussic acid.

BORAGE

Only good fresh; its flavor vanishes as it dries. Use the leaves wherever you want a cucumber flavor in fish sauces or white aspics. It is traditional in some fruit punches, and the choice blue starlike blooms, 42, are beautiful floated in punches and lemonades or used in food garnishes. Young borage can be cooked like spinach, 326. *Borago officinalis,* which self-seeds, grows to 2½ feet even in poor soil.

BURNET

Sometimes called salad burnet; in fact, Italians say that salad without burnet is like love without a woman. This herb has a haunting cucumberish flavor. It does not dry well, but it keeps green all winter long and can be plucked at any time. Pick the center leaves; the older ones are bitter. Use the leaves, or soak the seeds in vinegar for use in salads.

Poterium sanguisorba, a hardy evergreen perennial growing to 2 feet, is almost fernlike in habit and is easy to germinate in any well-drained soil, in sun.

CAMOMILE

Famous as a tisane, 40. A small quantity is occasionally put into beef stock. Sometimes the fresh leaves are used, but it is the very center of the flower that is most prized. The petals of this tiny daisy are removed after the flower is dried. *Anthemis nobilis,* a creeping perennial, grows to 6 inches in dry light soil.

THE CAPERS AND CAPERLIKE BUDS AND SEEDS

When pickled, these bulletlike buds of the caper bush taste like tiny sharp gherkins. Use them in Tartare Sauce, 364, with fish and wherever you wish a piquant note. *Capparis spinosa* is a 3-foot perennial shrub of southern Europe. ➤ Do not confuse it with the caper spurge, *Euphorbia lathyrum,* which is poisonous. Also pickled are immature or mature seeds and buds of *Tropaeolum minus* or *majus,* the nasturtium; or the buds of *Caltha palustris,* the marsh marigold. Similar in use are Chinese fermented black beans, or *toushi,* which are available in cans; and the pickled green seeds of *Martynia Proboscidea juisieui,* an annual growing to 2½ feet, with dramatic flowers and an evilly horned pod.

CARAWAY

Use the leaves of this herb sparingly in soups and stews. The seeds, similar to cumin in flavor, are classic additions to rye breads, cheeses, stews, marinades, cabbage, sauerkraut, turnips and onions. And they are the basic flavoring of kümmel. If added to borsch or other soups, put them in a bag for the last 30 minutes of cooking only, as protracted heating makes them bitter. Crush them before adding to vegetables or salads, to release their flavor. *Carum carvi* is an easily grown biennial that reaches 2 feet in the second year when the seeds develop.

THE CELERIES

The tender leaves of the celery you grow or buy can be used fresh or dried in almost all foods.

Celery salt is a powdered form combined with salt. But the seeds sold for flavoring are not those of the plant we grow, but those of smallage or wild celery. These seeds, either whole or ground, have a powerful flavor and must be used sparingly: whole in stocks, court bouillon, pickles and salads; or in ground form in salad dressings, seafoods or vegetables. *Apium graveolens* needs rich moist soil and hilling to blanch. For celeriac, see 298.

CHERVIL

One of the famous "fines herbes," this is more delicate and ferny than parsley. The leaf is used with chicken, veal, omelets, green salad and spinach—as a garnish, of course—and always in the making of a Béarnaise Sauce, 359, or Vinaigrette Sauce, 360. It is one of the herbs it pays to grow—for when dried at even as low a temperature as 90°, it is practically without flavor. *Pluches de cerfeuille* are sprigs of fresh or fresh blanched chervil often specified in stocks and stews. *Anthriscus cerefolium* is a self-sowing annual that grows to 2 feet. It needs some shade to keep it from turning purplish and toughening. Sow in place from April to September. Do not transplant, as this forces bolting.

COMFREY

A healing herb—its very name implies a knitting together—comfrey makes a popular tisane, 40. Use its young leaves sparingly, raw in salads, or cook them as for spinach, cutting the leaves before the plant blooms. *Symphytum officinale* is a hardy perennial growing to 3 feet, preferring rich friable lime soil and moisture and shade. Propagate in spring by dividing its long white roots.

CORIANDER

Many of us identify this flavor from childhood with the seed in the heart of a "jaw breaker," in gingerbread, apple pie, sausages and pickles, or as an ingredient of curry. But few of us know the fresh leaves of this plant as Chinese parsley, as the Cilantro of the Caribbean, the Kothamille of Mexico, or the Dhuma of India, where its somewhat fetid odor and taste are much treasured. Use leaves only—no stems—and do not chop. Float the leaves in pea or chicken soups and in stews, place them on top of roasts, or use them in a court bouillon for clams. *Coriandrum sativum,* a 12- to 18-inch plant, grows in moderately heavy soil and, while needing drainage, can take some moisture.

COSTMARY

Used sparingly in sauces, soups and stuffings, this herb is sometimes substituted for mint but has bitter overtones. *Balsamita major,* a perennial, also known as alecost, grows to 4 feet and is not particular as to soil.

CUMIN

This flavor is classic in cheese, sauerkraut and unleavened bread. The seed is also used whole in marinades, chilis and tomato sauces. One of the principal ingredients of a curry, cumin is even incorporated into baked items and eggs as well as bean and rice dishes and Enchiladas, 252. *Cuminum odorum,* an annual growing to 1 foot, needs near-tropical conditions for good growth.

DILL

Both seed and leaf of this feathery, pungent and slightly bitter plant are used in sour cream, fish, bean, cucumber and cabbage dishes as well as in potato salad or on new potatoes. If using dill butter sauce, do not brown the butter. The seed is also good in vinegar. The leaves make a lovely garnish. *Anethum graveolens,* an annual sometimes referred to as dillweed, grows to 3 feet and self-sows. Pull up plants when flower heads brown, and dry over paper so that the easily shattered seeds are not lost.

THE FENNELS

The leaves of common and Florence fennel can be used interchangeably where a slightly vigorous flavor is wanted. In flavoring, both the leaves and seeds are used—as for dill—especially for fat fish and in lentils, rice and potatoes and in apple pies. Fish is sometimes cooked over fennel twigs. But in sauces—as with dill—do not let the leaves cook long enough to wilt, unless they have been previously blanched. The leaves do not retain flavor in drying. *Foeniculum vulgare* and its variant, the bronze fennel, are self-sowing and grow to 5 feet. Plant in well-drained moisture-retaining soil. *F. var. dulce,* the Florence fennel or finocchio, illustrated 276, is used as a vegetable, 304.

FENUGREEK

This has the same odor as celery but a bitterer flavor. Popular as a tisane, 40, it is also used in many African dishes. It constitutes one of the main ingredients of curries and is the base of artificial maple flavor. *Trigonella-Foenum graeca,* which grows to 1 or 2 feet, needs well-drained loam.

GERANIUMS

The sweet-scented many-flavored leaves are used in pound cake, jellies and compotes, or merely as floaters in finger bowls. Use a lime-scented leaf in custard or an apple-flavored one in baked apples. For lime flavor try *Pelargonium nervosum;* for apple, *P. odoratissimum;* for mint, *P. tomentosum;* for rose, *P. graveolens*. These geraniums are tender but grow well in pots under ordinary household conditions.

HOREHOUND

The woolly leaves of this plant are made into an extract which is combined with sugar into confections, 787. *Marrubium vulgare,* a perennial that grows to 3 feet, flourishes in poor soil.

HORSERADISH

Along with coriander, nettle, horehound and lettuce, horseradish is one of the five bitter herbs of the Passover. As the flavor is overpowering, use sparingly, and use it fresh rather than reconstituted if possible. You may grate peeled fresh root into lemon or vinegar. If the ground dried form must be used, ➤ it should be reconstituted not more than 30 minutes before serving; for, once the powder is mixed, its volatile oils are dissipated. To prepare dried ground root: soak 1 tablespoon of dried horseradish in 2 tablespoons of water and add ½ cup heavy cream. Whether fresh, reconstituted or bought jarred—and in this book the term for the latter is "prepared horseradish"—use all horseradish promptly to avoid loss of volatile oils and development of intense bitterness. Horseradish is prized for use with Boiled Beef, 461, and other fatty meats; in cocktail sauces and potato salad; or with cold meats, fish and shellfish. *Armoracia rusticana,* a perennial growing to 2 feet, is propagated from pieces of root and demands rich, moist soil. You may store roots in moist sand for winter use.

HYSSOP

The leaves of this minty, spicy, somewhat bitter herb are used sparingly with salads and fruits. The dried flowers are used in soups and tisanes. *Hyssopus officinalis,* a perennial which grows to 2 feet, prefers dry calcareous soil.

LAVENDER

The leaves and flowers of this highly aromatic plant give a bitter pungency to salads. We prefer to use it as a sachet rather than as a seasoner. But its grayness lends a lovely accent to the herb garden. Grown from cuttings or seed, *Lavandula vera,* a perennial growing to 4 feet, prefers dry lime soil and a warm climate.

LEMON BALM

Use the lemony leaves for tisane or as a garnish in fruit punch or fruit soup. *Melissa officinalis,* a perennial which reaches 2½ feet, grows in sun in any soil.

LEMON VERBENA

This, like lavender, in our opinion is better reserved for sachets or closets than for food; however, it is often used as a lemon substitute in drinks and tisanes. *Lippia citriodora* is a tender perennial growing to 5 feet; it does well in pots.

LOVAGE

The leaves of this bold herb, whose stems can be candied like Angelica, 580, or blanched and eaten like celery, are often used as a celery substitute with stews or tongue. The seeds are sometimes pickled like capers. *Levisticum officinale,* a perennial that grows to 8 feet, is not particular as to soil; it is best divided in spring.

THE MARJORAMS AND OREGANOS

These, whether called sweet or pot marjoram, oregano or oregano dulce or wild, are all very pungent. While similar in their uses, they are not quite the same in their growth habits. Use them in sausages, stews, tomato dishes; with lamb, pork, chicken and goose; with omelets, eggs, pizzas, and cream cheeses; with all of the cabbage family and with green beans; in minestrone and mock turtle soups; and, of course, don't fail to try them fresh and finely chopped for salads.

There is great horticultural confusion in regard to the oreganos of commerce, and seeds ordered under the name origanum vary enormously. *Origanum vulgare* and *O. onite,* or pot marjoram, are hardy perennials to 2 feet. *Origanum marjoram,* sweet marjoram, is a tender perennial growing about a foot high; it prefers alkaline soil.

THE MINTS

We all know peppermint and spearmint. But there are many other mints worth trying, like the curly varieties, and apple, orange and pineapple. These are less penetrating but equally refreshing. Use any of them in fruit cups, with coleslaw peas, zucchini, lamb, veal, cream cheeses; in chocolate combinations, teas, and of course jellies and juleps. These leaves, fresh or candied, see 794, make attractive garnishes. If using fresh leaves, ¼ to ½ teaspoon—crushed just before using—is enough per serving. But in the form of oil, a drop of mint flavoring is often too much—so go easy.

All of the following grow rampant in sun or partial shade, and even in dry but preferably moist soil: *Mentha viridis,* perhaps the most peppery of all; *M. piperita,* the peppermint we know best; *M. spicata* or spearmint and its preferred form *crispa;* and the woolly apple mint, *M. rotundifolia,* frosted in appearance and fine for a drink garnish.

All the mints are perennial and easily raised from root divisions. They reach 1½ to 3 feet. Plant them in areas confined by metal or rock edgings sunk at least 6 inches deep to keep them from invading less sturdy neighbors in the herb garden. Keep them pruned to have bushy tops for beverage garnishes. If your growing area is confined, try *Mentha requienii* or Corsican mint—a tiny-leaved plant only 1 inch high, as discreet as a moss.

And, incidentally, field mice hate mint odor and will stay away from any plant near which it is scattered.

MARIGOLD

The dried centers of pot marigolds are sometimes used as a color substitute for saffron, and the young leaves can be used in salads. The petals are used only when the recipe calls for cooking, as in stews. *Calendula officinalis* is not particular as to soil and grows to 15 inches.

THE MUSTARDS

Mustard fanciers will argue the merits of a mild champagne-based or poupon Dijon type or a Louisiana mix—against the sharp English or the fiery Jamaican or Chinese. There are many ways to prepare mustards from mustard powder, which is the dry residue left after the oil is expressed from the seed. But the freshness of the mix is an important factor. The flavor changes rapidly once moisture is added or once a bottle of prepared mustard is opened. Try keeping it fresh by putting a slice of lemon on top before closing the lid. The lemon needs renewal about once a week. Commercial mustards with their blends of flour and spices—often heavy in turmeric to color them—may be based on water, wine or vinegar. If you want to mix your own, allow 2 to 3 tablespoons liquid to 1/4 cup dry mustard. More details about preparing mustard follow.

Mustard can be added advantageously in small quantities to cheese, seasoned flour, chicken or pot roasts and to sauces, hot or cold. It is classic served with cold meats and for use in pickles—both ground and as seed.

➤ In this book prepared mustard indicates the saucelike mustard. It has about one-third to one-half the strength of dry mustard.

➤ **Hot Mustards** are based on cold liquids—water, vinegar or flat beer. Add 2 to 3 tablespoons liquid to about 1/4 cup dry mustard. If it is too hot, tone it with a little olive or vegetable oil, garlic, tarragon leaves and a pinch of sugar. To make a **Suave Mustard,** put into a heatproof glass double boiler top about 2 ounces of dry mustard. Pour water which has been brought to a rolling boil over it to cover. Place ➤ over, not in, rapidly boiling water for 15 minutes. Before covering see that the mustard has been stirred into a paste but is still covered with the hot liquid. Drain any excess water. You may add 1 teaspoon sugar and 1/4 to 1/2 teaspoon salt. If you want a bright mustard, add 1/4 teaspoon turmeric, vinegar and other spices to your taste. Put mustard in a jar. Let cool uncovered 1 to 2 hours. Then cap tightly. Keep at room temperature. Do not refrigerate.

The dark seeds come from *Brassica nigra,* the white from *Sinapsis alba,* both self-seeding and growing to 3 feet. If seed is desired, plants can tolerate poor soil. If leaves are to be used as a vegetable, *Brassica nigra, Sinapsis alba* and *Brassica juncea* should be grown in rich soil.

NASTURTIUM

Flowers, seeds and leaves are all used as flavorings. The leaves and lovely orange and yellow flowers are fine in salads, and the pickled pods often replace capers. The pods of *Tropaeolum* are best picked just as soon as the blossom drops, and prepared at once. To preserve nasturtium pods, see 845. *Tropaeolum majus* vines to 6 feet; *T. minus* grows to 9 inches.

THE ONIONS

Never since our first encounter with the host of alliums in a bulb catalogue have these lilies lost their allure for us as food or flower—from the thinnest chive to the enormous Schuberti with its choicest florets held captive within a flowered cage. This is a plea not only to use a variety of onions in your cooking, but to grow the perennial ones so you will always have them on hand. We have tried to indicate their use in individual recipes. To cook onions as vegetables, see 311. Nothing can add such subtlety to a dish, yet none is more abused in the cooking than onions. And when we say onions, we mean any of the alliums we list below.

Use onion bulbs fresh or dry, the green tops of onions or leeks in making soups and court bouillon; and don't forget that ➤ a touch of onion freshly added to canned vegetables and soups often disguises the "canned" taste and varies the expected one.

➤ High heat and a too-long cooking period bring out the worst features. ➤ If you scorch onions, they will be bitter. ➤ Yet onions must be cooked long enough to get rid of any rawness. If you want them to taste mild in soups, like Potage St. Germain, 178, or in delicate stews, the flavor of the dish can be improved and the onion odor lessened during cooking if you will follow this procedure. ➤ If they are 1 inch in diameter, parblanch the onions 5 minutes, before adding them to the soup or stew. If you want them ➤ mild in sautéing, cook them only until translucent—tender, but not flabby. If you want them ➤ penetrating, sauté until golden; if ➤ all-pervasive, brown them very slowly, as for an onion soup, 171, or a Lyonnaise, 346. To give color and flavor to a Petite Marmite, see 170.

To shorten cooking time, onions are frequently chopped and minced fine. There are a number of ways to make this process less tearful, see 311. Or when you haven't time to sauté an onion properly, but do not want a raw taste in cold dishes, hot sauces or dressings, use ➤ onion juice. Ream a cut onion on a lemon juicer, or scrape the cut center of the onion with the edge of a spoon.

To make onions milder when serving them in salads, first soak them in milk. Or put slices in a bowl and pour boiling water over them. Let stand 30 to 40 minutes. Drain, then soak them briefly in cold water with a lump of ice to crisp. Drain and serve.

The use of onions for the bacteria-destroying power of their vapor was demonstrated on a large scale in World War II. However, this antibacterial action was present only when the onion was freshly cut. This power disappeared within 10 minutes. Onions deteriorate rapidly once the outer skin is removed and ➤ should not be stored for reuse after cutting.

To rid your breath of onion traces, eat raw parsley. See 73 for a perfect raw onion-parsley canapé. Onion odor on the hands can be rubbed off with salt, vinegar or lemon juice. For onion scent on pots, moisten them, sprinkle generously with salt, let stand, then rinse with very hot water.

➤ All onions are of easy culture. They prefer sandy, moist, rich earth, with shallow planting in sun. The dry ones should all be sun-dried a few days after being dug up. You may braid the tops so the bulbs can be hung in clusters for even air-ing during storage. If the tops are cut, do not crop too close to the neck of the bulb. Store all onions in a cool, dark, dry, well-ventilated place. Below are descriptions of onion types used in cooking.

CHIVES

Chives are shown in bloom, first on the left opposite. Only the leaves are used. Combine them with soft white cheese and with eggs; use in green sauces. Cut and add them to hot and cold food just before serving. ➤ Do not put chives in a cottage cheese or any uncooked dish you plan storing even as long as overnight, as they get unpleasantly strong. To keep plants of *Allium schoenoprasum* looking well, cut a few of the thin tubular leaves low rather than bobbing the top, which will brown where cut. Remember that, like all bulbs, chives rely for plant renewal strength on the leaves—so don't cut any one plant more than 3 or 4 times a season. The leaves are tenderer after each cutting. Also keep the blooms picked low so the tougher stem does not get mixed with the leaves when you use them and so you are not bothered with seeding. About 3 to 6 small bulbs set in humus-filled soil in the fall will make a good cluster 8 to 10 inches high by the following summer. A slightly larger variety, *Sibericum,* with thicker leaves is also hardy.

GARLIC CHIVES

This is a coarser plant, about 15 inches high, seen second on the left, 586, whose flatter, somewhat stronger leaves are used like chives, above. The charming, starry, honeyed white bloom cluster of this perennial can be used as a decorative garnish, or the florets sprinkled over salads. Cultivate *Allium tuberosum* as for chives.

ORIENTAL GARLIC OR AIL

This is perhaps the most controversial addition to food. Balzac, a formidable gastronome, recommended that even the cook should be rubbed with it! We couldn't live without it, and we think we have learned to use it discreetly, for our guests have sometimes been obviously relishing and unawarely eating food with garlic in it—while inveighing loudly against it. If you are fond of it ➤ keep a check on the amount used, for tolerance to it may grow apace, to the discomfort of your friends. The bulb at the base of the plant, shown last on the right, opposite, is the treasure. Note the scalloped form of the bulb indicating the "cloves" within an outer skin. ➤ In this book, when we say 1 clove garlic, it is assumed that the clove is also peeled of its husk. Learn to place slivers of garlic clove on meat before cooking it; to put a clove of garlic on a skewer, cook it in a sauce or stew, and remove it before serving; to rub a salad bowl lightly with a cut clove; or to make chapons, 95. Drop a peeled clove into French dressing 24 hours before serving, but do not leave it in longer, as it deteriorates. Add a small squeeze of garlic juice to sauces. This is easy to do with a garlic press, a handy kitchen utensil shown 337. Should you not own a press, you may use the back of a spoon against a small bowl, or a mortar and pestle, to crush garlic with salt. The salt softens the bulb almost at once, but if you drop a whole clove into a liquid for seasoning ➤ be sure to strain it out before serving. ➤ Never allow garlic to brown. Always use fresh garlic. Powdered and salt forms tend to have rancid overtones. ➤ To blanch garlic, drop the unpeeled cloves into boiling water. Cook for 2 minutes. Drain, peel and simmer slowly in butter about 15 minutes. Mince the blanched buttered garlic and add to sauces.

True garlic bulbs, which grow 1 to 3 feet high, are not hardy. Plant bulbs of *Allium sativum* in light soil in March. They should be ready for lifting in late July. Be sure to sun-dry the cloves until the outer skin is white and parched.

GIANT OR TOPPING GARLIC, OR ROCHAMBOLE

This hardy plant, sketched second from the right, 586, has a beautiful glaucous leaf and an entrancing pointed bud carried on a furled stem. Its unwinding is a source of great pleasure to watch. The edible bulbs that bunch at the top are indistinguishable in taste and form from the tender oriental garlic described above. Cultivate *Allium sorodoprasum* as for Chives, opposite.

SHALLOTS

The shallot, queen of the sauce onions, is not hardy but well worth growing. It is shown first on the left, 586. Shallot flavor is perhaps closer to garlic than to onions, and although it has a much greater delicacy, it must still be used with discretion. Shallots are indispensable in Bercy Butter, 350, where they should be minced simultaneously with the herbs. They taste especially good in wine cookery. In sautéing them, mince fine so as not to subject them to too much heat. ➤ Never let them brown, as they become bitter. ➤ Substitute 3 to 4 shallots for 1 medium-sized onion.

Allium ascalonicum, always grown from sets, should be put in, barely covered, in the early spring. They should be harvested by late June when the leaves are no longer upright—caving in at the neck—but not yet turning in color. Allow them to dry off on the ground for several days and then braid the leaves so the shallots can be hung in strands in a dry place for use as wanted.

TOPPING ONIONS

Use these as you would any medium-sharp onion. *Allium catawissa,* unlike dry onions purchased in markets, is a perennial. It has a fibrous root system, and the onions develop early in the season at the top of the blooming stock. In fact, some even begin to sprout there too, as shown third from the right, 586, and, in turn, produce more onions at the top of the second sprout the same season. The nonsprouting bulblets can be kept for planting the following August or the next spring. The original plants may also be separated. There is really

no excuse for not trying anything that easy. These are similar to the so-called Egyptian topping onion —*Cepa viviparum*—which, surprisingly, does not grow in Egypt and is hardy and has a usable bulb at the base as well.

LEEKS

The leek, the beloved French *poireau*, is king of the soup onions. It also lends itself well to braising. This biennial, *Allium porrum,* sketched second from the right, above, grows its first year with an elongated root and closely interlaced foliage. Leeks are often hilled to keep them white. This practice traps grit unless the leeks are grown with a paper collar. Be sure to rid them of this grit by washing well. They are choice the first year. A leek with a tough, hollow stem—from which the glorious silver-green bloom has been cut from the center of the foliage—and a more bulbous form at the base, is in its second year and will prove too tough to eat. However, the green portion can be utilized in soups and seasonings.

DRY ONIONS

These types, of which an example is pictured second on the left, above, are the onions most available in the market; they vary greatly in flavor, color and shape. On the whole, American *cepa* varieties are smaller, have stronger flavors and keep better than foreign *cepa* types. Good raw and mild in cooking are the big yellow or white Bermudas. Even more so are the flat Spanish reds, a favorite garnish on hamburgers and salads. They mush somewhat in cooking, so if you want a mild red cooker, try the rounder, more elongated Italian redskins. Pearl onions, including the kind you find in the bottom of your Gibson cocktail, are cluster sowings of *cepa* varieties. *Allium cepa* types are biennials; they are planted in sets in February and harvested in July when the browning leaves have died down.

SCALLIONS

Use the leaves as a soup flavoring. The white flesh with about 4 inches of leaf is often braised as for Leeks, 306, and they are eaten raw by self-assertive people. They are the thinnings of *Allium cepa* plantings or are grown from seeds sown close together and harvested before the bulb develops its characteristic shape. See them shown third on the left, above.

WELSH ONION

These are used as a substitute for scallions, described above. See them last on the right, 586. *Allium fistulosum,* known also as the **Japanese bunching onion** or as **Ciboules,** is usually home-grown.

WILD LEEKS, RAMPS OR BROAD-LEAF WOOD ALLIUM

Around the bulbs of *Allium tricoccum,* seen third on the left, 586, revolve many American folk festivals. These and the strong field garlic in your lawn—*Allium vineale*—are not recommended by us, though we frequently hear them praised.

THE PARSLEYS

These plants—root, stem and leaves—have a high vitamin A-carrying factor. They are flavorful in themselves but also valuable as an agent for blending the flavors of other herbs, and have the power to destroy the scent of garlic and onion, see 583. There is practically no salad, meat, or soup in which they cannot be used. But they should be handled with discretion, particularly the root of the Hamburg-type or soup parsley. These roots are sometimes cooked as for Parsnips, 314.

There are at least 37 varieties of curly parsley, varying in strength. In mincing or deep-fat frying, remove the florets from the more strongly scented stems. The stems are used in white stocks and sauces for their strength of flavor and because they do not color the sauce, as does the leaf. *Petroselinum hortense* and its curled *crispum* varieties are the parsleys seen most frequently in the markets. Biennials, they grow to about 1 foot in rich loamy soil and sun. As they often bolt early during the second season, they are best treated as annuals.

To grow from seed, soak in water to cover about 24 hours. The uncurled or Italian type is better for fall use, as its leaves shed the snow and stay green longer. *Carum petroselinum,* a coarser-growing, heavier-rooted biennial, grows to 3 feet. Soak seeds as described above.

THE RED AND GREEN PEPPERS

These plants of the *Capsicum* family are heavy in vitamins A and C. They are also said to have bacteria-deterrent and anti-oxidant qualities that extend the keeping periods of fats, meats, and casseroles which include peppers. Native to the Americas, they are widely grown in Europe and are very different from the white and black peppers from the Orient, 576. The *Capsicums* all have this in common: the ➤ seeds and membranes are irritating and should always be removed if you are using fresh peppers. The condiments from these dried peppers are made both with and without the seeds. ➤ To skin fresh peppers, place them in a 350° oven until the skin is slightly scorched and easily removed; or blanch them for a moment in deep fat at 375°. See various types on 315.

The sweet or broad bell peppers, variety *C. grossum,* are frequently misnamed "mangoes" in the market. These 4- to 5-inch peppers, both green and, in their more ripened state, red, are used for stuffing and are diced for flavoring. Also to this general type belong the bonnet peppers, or *C. tetragonna,* from which paprikas are ground. The mild Hungarian types are seeded and deprived of their stalks before grinding. Paprika is sensitive to heat and should be added toward the end of the cooking period. When added to broiled food for color, paprika browns when scorched.

The longer peppers, variety *C. longum,* which include most of the chili peppers and cayenne, come in many colors, from chartreuse green to yellow to red. There are hundreds of crosses, and in the endless regional recipes for chili or mole powder, as many as 6 or 8 varieties of *Capsicum*

will be indicated, with names like anchos, pasillo, chilpotle.

Cayenne, which comes from *C. annuum L.,* is often adulterated or replaced commercially by *C. fructescens,* a small red, dried tree berry, or *C. croton annuum,* known also as bird peppers. ➤ Cayenne is so very hot, it should be used only in the smallest pinches. Very hot too are the red clustered *C. fasciculatum* varieties, with fruit over 6 inches long, for which the seeds are supposed to have come from Tabasco in Mexico. Grown in southern Louisiana, they constitute the base for hot pepper sauces which are often matured 2 to 3 years. Use gloves when seeding to avoid skin irritation. Red pepper, not so hot as cayenne, is ground from this type.

➤ To prepare dried chili peppers for use in sauces, soak 6 dry chilis in 1 cup water and simmer until tender, about 20 minutes. Drain and reserve the water. When chilis are cool, split them and remove and discard seeds. Scrape the pulp from the skin and add it to the reserved water. For other *Capsicum* recipes see Chili Powder, 571, Chili Vinegar, 527, and Sherry Peppers, 845. ➤ For decorating with pimientos, see Truffle Garnish, 310; or use them in canned form.

ROSEMARY

The stiff resinous leaves of this sub-shrub are extremely pungent and must be handled with caution. In marinades, for which this flavoring is popular, allow about 1/8 to 1/4 teaspoon fresh for 4 servings. Use the lightly crushed leaves sparsely with lamb, duck, partridge, rabbit, capon and veal; and on peas, spinach and pizza. *Rosmarinus officinalis,* depending on the variety, grows from 2 to 6 feet and tolerates drought and lean soil but is not hardy in the North.

RUE

This herb is sometimes suggested as a flavoring for fruit or claret cups. *Ruta graveoleus,* a handsome gray-green perennial, grows to 3 feet and prefers alkaline soil. As many people are allergic to its irritant qualities, which produce symptoms comparable to poison ivy, we do not recommend its use.

SAFFRON

The golden orange stigmas of the autumn crocus, seen 567, are used to both color and flavor cakes, breads, and dressings and are classic in Risottos, 209, and Bouillabaisse, 188. Even a ➤ small amount of saffron has an overpoweringly medicinal flavor, so use only as directed in the recipes. If using mainly for color, just 1/4 teaspoon in 2 tablespoons hot water will suffice for 5 to 6 cups of flour. Use only about 1/8 to 1/4 teaspoon in 2 tablespoons hot water or white wine to season 6 to 8 servings of a sauce. *Crocus sativus* grows in mellow soil, and, as with all bulbous plants, the foliage of this fall-blooming bulb must be allowed to ripen fully if the plant is to prosper.

THE SAGES

"The young sow wild oats; the old grow sage." Sage is perhaps the best known and loved of all American seasonings. Use for fatty meat like pork and sausages; and for duck, goose and rabbit. It is also used in cheese and chowders. There is no comparison between the flavor of the freshly chopped tender leaves and the dried ones, which lose much of their volatile oil. Dry carefully, as the leaves are thick and mold easily. Always use sages sparingly. Fresh clary sage is used in omelets and fritters and is served with lamb. *Salvia officinalis,* a perennial, grows to 2 feet and should be cut back after blooming. But prune lightly, and only on new growth. Many hybrids exist and dwarf forms are available. Clary sage is biennial.

THE SAVORIES

The leaves of winter savory are used in stews, stuffings and meat loaves. *Sauteria montana,* a rather resinous perennial evergreen sub-shrub, grows to 18 inches and tolerates lean soil. Summer savory is a much more delicately flavored herb and has many more uses. It is classic in green beans and green bean salad; in horseradish sauce and lentil soup; and even in deviled eggs. It is also used with fat fish, roast pork, potatoes, tomatoes and French dressing. *Sauteria hortensis,* which grows to 18 inches, needs light, well-composted soil.

THE SORRELS

The elongated leaves of these plants are quite high in oxalic acid. They are used in small amounts to flavor soups, 185, or sauces, or to combine in small quantities with other vegetables—or to use as garnishes for goose or pork. The leaves may be pounded in a mortar with sugar and vinegar to make a tart sauce. The *Rumex* species grow to 3 feet. The so-called French sorrel, *R. scutatus,* is preferred.

SWEET WOODRUFF OR WALDMEISTER

The beautiful dark green starlike whorled fresh leaves of this plant are floated in May Wine, 64, or in other cold punches, but should not be left in longer than about 1/2 hour. *Asperula odorata,* which grows to 1 foot, makes a charming ground cover in shady locations.

SWEET CICELY

The green seeds and fresh leaves of this soft, ferny plant may be used as a garnish in salads and cold vegetables. Use dry seeds in cakes, candies and liqueurs. *Myrrhis odorata,* a perennial growing to 3 feet, prefers partial shade and rich moist soil.

TARRAGON

Called *estragon* by the French, this herb when fresh is one of the luxuries of cooking. The flavor, chemically identical to that of anise, is pretty well lost in drying, when the leaf vein stiffens and does not resoften in cooking. So, if the dry leaf is used, it must be carefully strained out before the food is served. To avoid the need for straining and to retain flavor better than by drying, we hold tarragon in vinegar and remove the leaves as needed. Do not crowd the vinegar bottle, allowing about 3 tablespoons of leaves to 1 quart mild vinegar. This gives enough acid to keep the leaves from spoiling. Always keep them well immersed. The fresh leaves are often blanched for decorations, 154. Although tarragon is too pungent to be cooked in soups, it is good added to practically everything else: eggs, mushrooms, tomatoes, sweetbreads, tartare and mustard sauces, fish or chicken. And in a Béarnaise sauce it is essential.

True tarragon, *Artemisia dracunculus,* is perennial. As it seldom sets seed, it is propagated by cuttings, or by divisions pulled—not cut—from the emerging shoots in early March. A less desirable form called Russian tarragon, *A. gmelinii* or *sacrorum,* or *A. dracunculoides,* can be grown from seed.

THE THYMES

Thymes may be used sparingly with poultry, mutton, veal, pork and rabbit; with creole and gumbo dishes; in brown sauces; with pickled beets and tomatoes; with fat fish, stews, stuffings and most vegetables; and are always found in stocks. They make lovely garnishes for hors d'oeuvre and canapés. Caraway-scented thyme or *Thymus herba-barona* is traditional with a baron of beef. There are so many of these charming *Thymus* species, and their flavors are so varied, that a collection of them makes a garden in itself. The narrow-leaf French with its upright habit and gray-green balsamic foliage; and the glistening, small-bushed, strongly scented lemon variety—*T. serpyllum citriodorus*—are the thymes most frequently found in the market. Thyme varieties, which grow best in sun, are perennial, persisting for years among rocks. Prune after blooming.

ABOUT COLOR IN FOOD

Resist the impulse to add color to food from little bottles or to retain it by the use of chemicals like soda. Instead, determine, in general, to maintain whatever color is inherent in the food itself and to heighten it by skillful cooking and effective contrast. ➤ Recent research indicates that some people are highly allergic to artificial colorings.

First steps begin with the selection of fresh, well-grown foods, properly washed, dried and trimmed, then prepared according to the "pointers" in our individual recipes. ➤ Choose utensils made of materials suitable to the foods cooked in them, 162. If you have done so and are still unhappy with the results, check the kind of water you are using, 519. ➤ Never overcook foods: nothing so irrevocably dulls the kitchen palette.

Here are some further ways to keep foods colorful. While the color of soups and sauces is built into them by the way their stocks are made, see 520, it will be least affected if they are scummed while heating and cooked uncovered. Meats, if light, maintain better color if scummed. If dark, their color will be improved by browning; by greasing during roasting or broiling; by glazing or flambéing. Fish and light meat grills profit in color by a prior dusting of paprika.

Cook variety meats—or vegetables and fruits that discolor on exposure to air—in slightly acidulated water, or à blanc, 447. But first sprinkle the cut surfaces of such foods with a little lemon juice. Or use an Anti-Browning Solution, 124, to prevent the discoloration of fresh fruits peeled slightly in advance of serving. Vent stews by the use of poaching paper, 151. And keep in mind that color in all foods is enhanced if they are not held hot and covered after cooking.

Breads and pastries develop beautiful crust color not only through the use of fat in their doughs, but by the discreet addition of saffron or safflower. And color may also be improved just before baking by butter-brushing, 731, egg-glazing, 731, or sugar-coating. Foods served in light sauces may be gratinéed, 552, or glazed, 367. And sauces may be glamorized with herb chiffonades; tomato or red pepper; lobster coral, 385; Lobster Butter, 351; egg yolks, saffron, meat glaze, mushrooms and browned flour.

If you are faced with really listless-looking vegetables, a green coloring additive may be very quickly made up in a blender: use spinach, parsley, or watercress mixed with a small quantity of stock.

As to color combinations and color contrasts, no one can lay down hard and fast rules, except to say that they need not be spectacular. Even so simple a combination as light and dark lettuces in a salad—or an accent of cress—will make for substantially greater interest. The occasional use of edible garnishes—suggestions for which are scattered throughout this book—will be helpful. Do consider, too, the total background: dishes and colorful tableware, table surface, linens and decor are all part and parcel of satisfactory and colorful food presentation.

ABOUT WEATHER

Weather—moist or dry, hot or cold—plays an important part in cooking. When its role is decisive, it is so noted in individual recipes. Let's review just a few instances. Since flours and cereals tend to dry out in winter, our indications for rice and flour amounts, pages 206 and 546, are more variable than we would like to have them. Damp weather will greatly affect sugars after food is cooked—as in meringues and during candy making, 777. Cold and heat have a tremendous effect on the creaming of butter and sugars and on success with Puff Paste, 643, Anise Wafers, 707, or the rising of bread, 600. Threatening weather will even delay the "making" of butter, 540, and Mayonnaise, 363. In storing foods, note if they are to be kept tightly lidded. It is evident that Mark

Twain was wrong when he complained that nobody did anything about the weather. The circumspect cook takes account of its vagaries and acts accordingly.

ABOUT MEASURING

➤ All recipes in this book are based on standard U.S. containers: the 8-ounce cup and a tablespoon that takes exactly 16 level fillings to fill that cup level. We suggest that you test for size the tablespoon you select for this purpose, because those on sale frequently do not meet standard specifications.

All our recipes, in turn, are based on level measurements, most hedgers like "heaping" or "scant" having been weeded out of our instructions years ago. Until you are experienced, we strongly urge you to make a fetish of the level standard measure.

To prove how very much careful measurement affects quantity, conduct this simple experiment. Dip the standard spoon into flour or baking powder and then level its contents with a knife. Don't shake. Then scoop up a heaping spoonful of the same ingredients without leveling. You will find that lighter materials, if casually taken, often triple or quadruple the amounts indicated in the recipes. Ten to one the cook who prides herself on using nothing but her intuition as a guide to quantity is the same "old hand" who, for years, has used the same bowls, cups and spoons, the same stove, even the same brands of staples, and who, in addition, gets more than her share of lucky breaks. Like as not, too, she doesn't mind variations in her product.

➤ Accuracy in measuring basic ingredients is especially necessary when making bread, pie and cake, and in using recipes which include gelatin. ➤ For dry ingredients, use a cup that measures 1 cup even—with a flush rim for leveling. ➤ No shortcuts should be adopted if the recipe requires the sifting of flour. If they are, the outcome is chancy, to say the least. In fact, frequent sifting after measurement will improve the texture of all cakes. ➤ Sifting salt, leavens and spices with the flour ensures even distribution.

Most cake recipes call for sugar to be sifted before measuring. We confess that, instead, we sometimes short-cut by spooning our granulated sugar lightly into a measuring cup and then leveling it off, see 546. To measure brown sugar, see 557.

The measurement of what we might call side-ingredients, such as flavorings and spices, is important too, but here much depends on individual taste, to say nothing of the age of the spices, and amounts may vary considerably without risking failure. To measure fats, see 539.

ABOUT SUBSTITUTIONS AND EQUIVALENTS

You're a new cook and you run out of granulated sugar. Don't think this doesn't happen to old cooks too! So you just substitute confectioners' sugar. And then when the cake is not so sweet as it should be and the texture is horrid, you wonder what happened.

Good recipes and the reasonable use of standard measures allow you to cook well without knowing that it takes about 2 cups of sugar or butter to make a pound, but that you will need about 4 cups of flour for that same pound. This you discover fast enough if you leave the United States, for almost everyone else cooks by weight, not volume.

Let's look at a few lucky volume-weight relationships that for the moment protect you, as a new cook, from the menace of that old dragon Mathematics—and his allies, Physics, Chemistry and Semantics. Here are some of our victorious, if homely, weapons, tested in many a battle with these old tricksters.

By weight, if not quite by volume, 2 tablespoons butter equal 2 tablespoons butter, melted. But try to incorporate this positive knowledge into a cake and utter failure results. See About Butter or Shortening Cakes, 671, and About Oil Cakes, 683.

By weight, 1 cup 32% whipping cream equals 1 cup 32% cream, whipped. By volume, 1 cup 32% whipping cream equals about 2 cups 32% cream, whipped.

➤ If the recipe calls for whipped cream rather than for whipping cream, you need the airier, drier texture that results from whipping.

Let's take a closer look at sugars.

1 cup granulated weighs about 8 ounces
1 cup confectioners' weighs 4½ ounces
1 cup brown sugar weighs 6 ounces
1 cup molasses, honey or corn syrup weighs 12 ounces

These are only differences in weight. But you also have to reckon with changes in sweetening power and in texture, and—in the case of molasses and honey—with liquids that also have an acid factor. And don't forget about taste, that most important element of all.

If any of the foregoing ingredients are called for in a recipe, the recipe is written to take care of inequalities. But if you are substituting in emergencies, say, sugar for molasses, please read About Molasses first. Some substitutions work fairly well, others only under special circumstances. ➤ But never expect to get the same results from a friend's recipe if she uses one kind of shortening and you use another. Your product may be better or worse than hers, but it won't be the same.

Before leaving you to delve into the tables that follow, like English standard measures versus those of the United States in relation to the complexities of the metric system, we introduce our ➤ multiply-and-conquer principle for fractions.

You are preparing only ⅓ of a given recipe. The recipe calls for ⅓ cup of flour. Well, ⅓ cup of flour equals 5⅓ tablespoons. 1 tablespoon equals 3 teaspoons. So 5⅓ tablespoons equals 16 teaspoons, and, finally, 16 teaspoons divided by 3—you are working for ⅓ of the recipe, remember?—gives you 5⅓ teaspoons. Now maybe you can get this result by leaving out some of these steps, but we can't.

Here is another tried and true kitchen formula—one for proportions. You want to make your grandmother's fruit cake that has a yield of 11 pounds. You'd like only 3 pounds. The recipe calls for 10 cups of flour. How much flour should you use for 3 pounds of cake? Make yourself a formula in simple proportion: 11 pounds of cake is to 3 pounds of cake as 10 cups of flour is to ? or X cups of flour: i.e., 11:3 = 10:X. Multiply the end factors—11 x X—and the inside factors—3 x 10—to get 11X = 30. Divide 30 by 11 to find that X = 2 8/11 or approximately 2¾ cups. If you are in any doubt that 8/11 is close to ¾, divide 8 by 11, finding the decimal closest to the standard measure. It is worth going through the same reducing process for the other basic ingredients such as egg, liquid and fruit—so the cake will hold together. Approximate the spices. But one more caution in changing recipes. ➤ Don't decrease or enlarge recipes by dividing or multiplying by any number larger than 4—purists recommend 2. This sounds and is mysterious. But the fact remains that recipes are just not indefinitely expandable or shrinkable

TABLES OF EQUIVALENTS AND CONVERSIONS

It is most unfortunate that in United States measuring systems the same word may have two meanings. For instance, an ounce may mean 1/16 of a pound or 1/16 of a pint; but the former is strictly a weight measure and the latter a volume measure. See the difference in weights of cups of different kinds of sugar, 589. Except in the case of water, milk or other ingredients of the same "density," a fluid ounce and an ounce of weight are two completely different quantities. Perhaps for this reason most foreign cooks measure solid ingredients by weight. If you intend to use continental recipes frequently, a gram/ounce scale, 825, is a necessity.

UNITED STATES MEASUREMENTS

All these equivalents are based on United States "fluid" measure. In this book, this measure is used not only for liquids such as water and milk, but also for materials such as flour, sugar and shortening, since the volume measure for these is customary in the United States.

LIQUID MEASURE VOLUME EQUIVALENTS

For U.S.-metric fluid volume, see chart opposite.

A few grains	= Less than ⅛ teaspoon
60 drops	= 1 teaspoon
1 teaspoon	= ⅓ tablespoon
1 tablespoon	= 3 teaspoons
2 tablespoons	= 1 fluid ounce
4 tablespoons	= ¼ cup or 2 ounces
5⅓ tablespoons	= ⅓ cup or 2⅔ ounces
8 tablespoons	= ½ cup or 4 ounces
16 tablespoons	= 1 cup or 8 ounces or 2 gills
8 tablespoons	= 1 teacup or 4 ounces
¼ cup	= 4 tablespoons
⅜ cup	= ¼ cup plus 2 tablespoons
⅝ cup	= ½ cup plus 2 tablespoons
⅞ cup	= ¾ cup plus 2 tablespoons
1 cup	= ½ pint or 8 fluid ounces
2 cups	= 1 pint or 16 fluid ounces
1 gill, liquid	= ½ cup or 4 fluid ounces
1 pint, liquid	= 4 gills or 16 fluid ounces
1 quart, liquid	= 2 pints or 4 cups
1 gallon, liquid	= 4 quarts

LINEAR MEASURES

For equipment comparison.

1 centimeter	= 0.394 inch
1 inch	= 2.54 centimeters
1 meter	= 39.37 inches

DRY MEASURE VOLUME EQUIVALENTS

Be careful not to confuse dry measure pints and quarts with liquid measure pints and quarts. The former are about 1/6 larger than the latter. Dry measure is used for raw fruits and vegetables, when dealing with fairly large quantities.

	Dry Pints	Dry Quarts	Pecks	Bushels	Liters
1 Dry Pint	1	½	1/16	1/64	.55
1 Dry Quart	2	1	⅛	1/32	1.1
1 Peck	16	8	1	¼	8.8
1 Bushel	64	32	4	1	35.23
1 Liter	1.82	.91	.114	.028	1

COMPARATIVE U.S. AND BRITISH MEASUREMENTS

Many British or "Imperial" units of measurement have the same names as United States units, but not all are identical. In general, weights are equivalent, but volumes are not. The most important difference for the cook, and one we were slow to realize until we had had consistent failures using English recipes with American measures, is noted below.

Also, the variable sizes of the British teaspoon and tablespoon created a further problem. Confronted with our dilemma, a British friend laughed and told us that there were no standard household British teaspoons and tablespoons. Her own teaspoons and tablespoons had been in the family since the fifteenth century and fit the family recipes perfectly. As a result the best we can recommend is experimentation. Below are differences between U.S. and British measuring cups:

An 8-U.S.-oz. U.S. measuring cup = 2 U.S. gills of 4 U.S. oz. each, or 16 U.S. tablespoons, or 48 U.S. teaspoons.

A 10-Imperial-oz. English measuring cup = 1

English breakfast cup or 2 Imperial English gills of 5 Imperial oz. each, or 20⅘ U.S. tablespoons, or 62½ U.S. teaspoons.

ABOUT METRIC CONVERSION

We all dread change and often fight it. When you look at the seemingly complicated tables below, you probably feel you want to hug to your breast more tightly than ever your good old U.S. measuring spoons and cups. These tables, which convert by both weight and volume, are handy if you want to translate American or Commonwealth recipes into metric measures.

Take heart as we face our own turnover to metric. We can use either the system already described or a much simpler volume conversion. Our food and equipment manufacturers are already planning three sizes of measures and five sizes of spoons that will give us tolerances close to our present recipes. So rest easy; when the great changeover comes, it will not prove as difficult as you may now fear.

The charts below compare common kitchen measures from metric to American Standard and vice versa. To use, we give the following example: To determine the equivalent number of U.S. cups in a recipe which calls for 500 milliliters of liquid, look at the U.S. Metric Fluid Volume chart. Find 1 ml. in the left column; follow across to cups to find .004. Multiply 500 by .004 and you will get the answer—2 cups.

U.S. METRIC FLUID VOLUME

	Fluid Drams	Teaspoons	Tablespoons	Fluid Ounces	¼ Cups	Gills ½ Cups	Cups	Fluid Pints	Fluid Quarts	Gallons	Milliliters	Liters
1 Fluid Dram	1	¾	¼	⅛ .125	1/16 .0625	.03125	.0156	.0078	.0039	1/1024	3.70	.0037
1 Teaspoon	1⅓	1	⅓	1/6	1/12	1/24	1/48	1/96	1/192	1/768	5	.005
1 Tablespoon	4	3	1	½	¼	⅛	1/16	1/32	1/64	1/256	15	.015
1 Fluid Ounce	8	6	2	1	½	¼	⅛	1/16	1/32	1/128	29.56	.030
¼ Cup	16	12	4	2	1	½	¼	⅛	1/16	1/64	59.125	.059
1 Gill ½ Cup	32	24	8	4	2	1	½	¼	⅛	1/32	118.25	.118
1 Cup	64	48	16	8	4	2	1	½	¼	1/16	236	.236
1 Fluid Pint	128	96	32	16	8	4	2	1	½	⅛	473	.473
1 Fluid Quart	256	192	64	32	16	8	4	2	1	¼	946	.946
1 Gallon	1024	768	256	128	64	32	16	8	4	1	3785.4	3.785
1 Milliliter	.270	.203 or 1/5	.068	.034	.017	.008	.004	.002	.001	.0003	1	.001 or 1/1000
1 Liter	270.5	203.04	67.68	33.814	16.906	8.453	4.227	2.113	1.057	.264	1000	1

U.S. METRIC MASS (WEIGHT)

	Grains	Drams	Ounces	Pounds	Milligrams	Grams	Kilograms
1 Grain	1	.004	.002	1/7000	64.7	.064	.0006
1 Dram	27.34	1	1/16	1/256	1770	1.77	.002
1 Ounce	437.5	16	1	1/16	2835	28.35	.028
1 Pound	7000	256	16	1	"Lots"	454	.454
1 Milligram	.015	.0006	1/29,000	1/"Lots"	.1	.001	.000001

U.S. METRIC MASS (WEIGHT) (cont.)

	Grains	Drams	Ounces	Pounds	Milligrams	Grams	Kilograms
1 Gram	15.43	.565	.032	.002	1000	1	.001
1 Kilogram	15,430	564.97	.000032	2.2	1,000,000	1000	1

BRITISH—METRIC FLUID VOLUME

The British are presently using the metric system, but if you wish to use English recipes written before the early 1970s, you may find these tables a great help.

	Fluid Drams	Fluid Ounces	¼ Cups	Gills ½ Cups	Cups	Fluid Pints	Fluid Quarts	Milli-liters	Liters
1 Fluid Dram	1	⅛	1/20 .05	1/40 .025	1/80 .0125	1/160 .006	1/320 .003	3.55	.0035
1 Fluid Ounce	8	1	¼	1/5 .2	1/10	1/20 .05	1/40 .025	28.4	.028
¼ Cup	20	2.5	1	½	¼	⅛	1/16	71	.07
1 Gill—½ Cup	40	5	2	1	½	¼	⅛	142	.14
1 Cup	80	10	4	2	1	½	¼	284	.28
1 Fluid Pint	160	20	8	4	2	1	½	568	.57
1 Fluid Quart	320	40	16	8	4	2	1	1136	1.13
1 Milli-liter	.28	.035	.014	.007	.0035	.0018	.0009	1	.001 or 1/1000
1 Liter	281.5	35.19	14.08	7.04	3.52	1.76	.88	1000	1

APPROXIMATE TEMPERATURE CONVERSIONS

	FAHRENHEIT	CELSIUS or CENTIGRADE
Coldest area of freezer	−10°	−23°
Freezer	0°	−17°
Water freezes	32°	0°
Water simmers	115°	46°
Water scalds	130°	54°
Water boils—at sea level	212°	100°
Soft ball	234°	112°
Firm ball	244°	117°
Hard ball	250°	121°
Very low oven	250°–275°	121°–133°
Low oven	300°–325°	149°–163°
Moderate oven	350°–375°	177°–190°
Hot oven	400°–425°	204°–218°
Very hot oven	450°–475°	232°–246°
Extremely hot oven	500°–525°	260°–274°
Broil	*See Broiling,* 146	

To convert Fahrenheit into Centigrade, subtract 32, multiply by 5, divide by 9. To convert Centigrade into Fahrenheit, go into reverse: Multiply by 9, divide by 5, add 32.

$100°C \times 9 = 900°$
$900° \div 5 = 180°$
$180° + 32 = 212°$

CAN SIZES	CONTENTS	APPROXIMATE CUPS
5-oz.	5 oz.	⅝
8-oz.	8 oz.	1
Picnic	10½ to 12 oz.	1¼
12-oz. vacuum	12 oz.	1½
No. 300	14 to 16 oz.	1¾
No. 303	16 to 17 oz.	2
No. 2	1 lb. 4 oz. or 1 pint 2 fl. oz.	2½
No. 2½	1 lb. 13 oz.	3½
No. 3	46 oz.	5¾
Baby foods	3½ to 8 oz.	
Condensed milk	14 fl. oz.	1⅓
Evaporated milk	5⅓ and 13 fl. oz.	⅔–1⅔

AVERAGE FROZEN FOOD PACKAGES

Vegetables	8 to 16 oz.
Fruits	10 to 16 oz.
Canned frozen fruits	13½ to 16 oz.
Frozen juice concentrates	6 oz.

EQUIVALENTS AND SUBSTITUTIONS FOR COMMON INGREDIENTS

Also check "Abouts" for individual items; see Index for further information. Some foods are sold by weight, but most **Joy** recipes give amounts in number of measuring cups or spoons and are therefore volume measurements, whether liquid or mass.

Almonds		
In shell	3½ lb.	1 lb. shelled
Unblanched, whole	6 oz.	1 cup
Unblanched, ground	1 lb.	2⅔ cups
Unblanched, slivered	1 lb.	5⅔ cups
Blanched, whole	5⅓ oz.	1 cup
Blanched, slivered	4 oz.	1 cup
Ammonium carbonate	¾ teaspoon ground	1 teaspoon baking soda
Apples	1 lb. unpared	3 cups pared, sliced
	3½ to 4 lb. raw	1 lb. dried
	About 10 apples	1 lb. dried
Apricots, fresh	5½ lb.	1 lb. dried
Apricots, dried	1 lb.	3¼ cups
Apricots, cooked, drained	1 lb.	3 cups
Arrowroot as a thickener	1½ teaspoons	1 tablespoon flour
	2 teaspoons	1 tablespoon cornstarch
Baking powder		
rising equivalent	1 teaspoon	¼ teaspoon baking soda plus ⅝ teaspoon cream of tartar
	1 teaspoon	¼ teaspoon baking soda plus ½ cup buttermilk or yogurt
	1 teaspoon	¼ teaspoon baking soda plus ¼ to ½ cup molasses
double-acting, SAS	1 teaspoon	1½ teaspoons phosphate or tartrate baking powder
Bananas	3 to 4 medium-sized	1 lb. or 1¾ cups mashed
Bay leaf	¼ teaspoon, crushed	1 whole bay leaf
Beans, green, fresh	1 lb. = 3 cups	2½ cups cooked
Beans, kidney, dry	1 lb. = 2½ cups	6 cups cooked
Beans, lima, dry	1 lb. = 2½ cups	6 cups cooked
Beans, navy, dry	½ lb. = 1 cup	2½ cups cooked
Brazil nuts	2 lb. in shell	1 lb. shelled—approximately 3 cups
Bread crumbs, dry	¼ cup	1 slice bread
soft	½ cup	1 slice bread
Butter		
1 stick	4 oz.	8 tablespoons or ½ cup
4 sticks	1 lb.	2 cups
	1 cup	1 cup margarine
		⅘ to ⅞ cup clarified bacon fat or drippings
		¾ cup clarified chicken fat
		⅞ cup lard or cottonseed, corn or nut oil, solid or liquid
Butter	8 oz.	7.3 oz. hydrogenated fats, *see* 541
Butter, whipped	1 lb. or 6 sticks	3 cups
Buttermilk	1 cup	1 cup yogurt
Cabbage	½ lb. minced	3 cups packed
	1 lb. (1 head)	4½ cups shredded
Cane syrup, *see* About Liquid Sugars, 557		
Carob powder	3 tablespoons plus 2 tablespoons water	1 oz. chocolate

Carrots, fresh, without tops	1 lb.	3 cups shredded or 2½ cups diced
Cheese, dry	1 lb.	4 cups
Cheese, freshly shredded	¼ lb.	1 cup
Cheese, blue	4 oz.	1 cup crumbled
Cheese, cottage	½ lb.	1 cup
Cheese, cream	3 oz.	6 tablespoons
Chestnuts	35 to 40 large	2½ cups peeled
	1 lb. shelled	1½ lb. in shell
Chocolate	1 oz.	1 square
	1 oz.	4 tablespoons grated
Chocolate, unsweetened	1 oz.	3 tablespoons cocoa plus 1 tablespoon butter or fat
Chocolate, unsweetened	1 oz.	3 tablespoons carob powder plus 2 tablespoons water
Chocolate, unsweetened	1 oz. plus 4 teaspoons sugar	1⅔ oz. semisweet chocolate
Cocoa	1 lb.	4 cups
Cocoa	3 tablespoons plus 1 tablespoon fat	1 oz. unsweetened chocolate
Coconut, fine-grated	3½ oz.	1 cup
Coconut, grated	1 cup	1⅓ cups flaked
Coconut, flaked	3½ oz.	1⅓ cups
Coconut	1 tablespon dried, chopped	1½ tablespoons fresh
Coconut	1 lb.	5 cups shredded, unsweetened
Coconut	1 lb.	4 cups shredded, sweetened
Coconut milk, *see* 566	1 cup	1 cup milk
Coconut cream, *see* 566	1 cup	1 cup cream
Coffee	1 lb.	40 to 50 6-oz. cups
Coffee, instant or powdered	2 oz.	25 6-oz. cups
Coffee, freeze-dried	4 oz.	About 60 6-oz. cups
Corn syrup, *see* About Liquid Sugars, 557		
Cornmeal	1 lb.	3 cups
Cornmeal	1 cup uncooked	4 to 4½ cups cooked
Cornstarch, *see* Flour		
Cracker crumbs	¾ cup	1 cup bread crumbs
Cream, half-and-half, 10 to 12% butterfat	1 cup	1½ tablespoons butter plus about ⅞ cup milk, or ½ cup coffee cream and ½ cup milk
Cream, coffee, at least 20% butterfat	1 cup	3 tablespoons butter, plus about ⅞ cup milk
Cream, whipping, heavy 36 to 40% butterfat	1 cup	⅓ cup butter plus about ¾ cup milk
Cream, whipping	1 cup unwhipped	2 to 2½ cups whipped
Cream, sour, *see* About Sour Cream, 533	1 cup	3 tablespoons butter plus ⅞ cup buttermilk or yogurt
Cream, sour, cultured, *see* About Sour Cream, 533	1 cup	⅓ ~~cup~~ butter plus ¾ cup cultured buttermilk or yogurt
Dates	1 lb.	2½ cups pitted
Eggs, hen, extra large	4	About 1 cup
large, 2 oz.	5	About 1 cup

Eggs, hen (cont.)		
medium	6	About 1 cup
small	7	About 1 cup
Eggs, dried, sifted	1 lb.	5¼ cups
Eggs, dried, sifted	2½ tablespoons beaten with 2½ tablespoons water	1 whole egg
Eggs, frozen	1 lb.	1⅞ cups
Egg whites, extra large	6	About 1 cup
large, 2 oz.	8	About 1 cup
medium	10 to 11	About 1 cup
small	11 to 12	About 1 cup
Egg whites, dried, sifted	1 tablespoon plus 2 tablespoons water	1 egg white
Egg whites, frozen	2 tablespoons thawed	1 egg white
Egg yolks, for thickening	2 yolks	1 whole egg
Egg yolks, extra large	10 to 11	About 1 cup
large, 2 oz.	12	About 1 cup
medium	13 to 14	About 1 cup
small	15 to 16	About 1 cup
Egg yolks, dried, sifted	1½ tablespoons plus 1 tablespoon water	1 egg yolk
Egg yolks, frozen	3½ teaspoons thawed	1 large egg yolk
Eggs, bantam	1	⅔ oz.
Eggs, duck	1	3 oz.
Eggs, goose	1	8 to 10 oz.
Figs, dried	1 lb.	2⅔ cups chopped
Filberts or hazelnuts	2¼ lb. in shell	1 lb. shelled or 3⅓ cups
Flour, *also see* About Flours, 545		
Cake	1 lb.	4¾ cups
Cake	1 cup sifted	⅞ cup sifted all-purpose flour, or 1 cup less 2 tablespoons
White or all-purpose	1 lb.	4 cups
White	4 cups	3½ cups cracked wheat
White	1 cup	1 cup cornmeal ⅝ cup potato flour 1 cup minus 2 tablespoons rice flour 1¼ cups rye flour 13/16 cup gluten flour
Graham, whole-grain or whole wheat	1 lb.	3¾ to 4 cups finely milled
Flours, for thickening	1 tablespoon flour	1½ teaspoons cornstarch, potato starch, rice starch or arrowroot starch 1 tablespoon quick-cooking tapioca 1 tablespoon waxy rice flour 1 tablespoon waxy corn flour
	½ tablespoon flour	1 tablespoon browned flour, 339
Garlic	1 small clove	⅛ teaspoon powder
Gelatin	¼-oz. envelope	About 1 tablespoon
Gelatin	¼-oz. envelope	4 sheets gelatin, 4″ x 9″
Gelatin for 1 pint liquid	¼ oz. or 1 envelope	About 1 tablespoon
Ginger	1 tablespoon candied, washed of sugar, or 1 tablespoon raw	⅛ teaspoon powdered

Gum tragacanth	¼ oz.	1 tablespoon
Hazelnuts	2¼ lb. in shell	1 lb. shelled or 3⅓ cups
Herbs, *see* About Herbs, 577	⅓ to ½ teaspoon dried	1 tablespoon fresh
Honey, *see* About Liquid Sugars, 557	1 lb.	1⅓ cups
Honey	1 cup	1¼ cups sugar plus ¼ cup liquid
Horseradish	1 tablespoon fresh, grated	2 tablespoons bottled
Horseradish	6 tablespoons dried, grated	10 tablespoons bottled
Lard	1 lb.	2 cups
Lemon	1	1 to 3 tablespoons juice, 1 to 1½ teaspoons grated rind
	1 teaspoon juice	½ teaspoon vinegar
	1 teaspoon grated rind	½ teaspoon lemon extract
Lentils	1 lb. or 2¼ cups	5 cups cooked
Lime	1	1½ to 2 tablespoons juice
Macaroni, uncooked	1 lb.	4 to 5 cups
Macaroni, 1-inch pieces	1 cup uncooked	2 to 2¼ cups cooked
Maple sugar, grated and packed	1 tablespoon	1 tablespoon white granulated
Maple sugar	½ cup	1 cup maple syrup
Maple syrup, *see* About Liquid Sugars, 557		
Marshmallows	1 cup cut up	16 large or 160 miniature
Meat		
Beef, cooked	1 lb.	3 cups minced
Beef, uncooked	1 lb.	2 cups ground
Milk, whole	1 cup	½ cup evaporated plus ½ cup water
		¼ cup dry whole milk plus ⅞ cup water
		1 cup reconstituted nonfat dry milk plus 2½ teaspoons butter or margarine
		1 cup soy or almond milk
		1 cup fruit juice or 1 cup potato water in baking
Milk, whole	1 cup	1 cup water plus 1½ teaspoons butter
	1 quart	1 quart skim milk plus 3 tablespoons cream
Milk, skim	1 cup	⅓ cup instant nonfat dry milk plus about ¾ cup water
Milk, whole dry	1 lb.	14 cups reconstituted
Milk, instant nonfat dry	1 lb.	About 5 quarts reconstituted
Milk, to sour	1 cup	Add 1 tablespoon vinegar or lemon juice to 1 cup milk minus 1 tablespoon. Let stand 5 minutes.
Molasses, *see* About Liquid Sugars, 557		
Mushrooms, fresh	8 oz. or about 3 cups	About 1 cup sliced, cooked
Mushrooms, canned	6 oz. drained	½ lb. fresh
Mushrooms, dried	3 oz.	1 lb. fresh

Mustard	1 teaspoon dry or powdered	1 tablespoon prepared mustard
Noodles, uncooked	1 lb.	6 to 8 cups
Noodles, 1-inch pieces	1 cup uncooked	About 1¼ cups cooked
Nuts, *see individual names*	1 lb. in shell	½ lb. kernels, a little less for heavier nuts, a little more for lighter ones
Oatmeal	1 lb.	5⅓ cups uncooked
	1 cup uncooked	1¾ cups cooked
Oil	1 lb. fat	2 cups
Onions, *see* about Onions, 583		
Orange	1 medium-sized	6 to 8 tablespoons juice
Orange	1 medium-sized	¾ cups diced
Orange rind, grated	1 medium-sized	2 to 3 tablespoons
Peaches	1 lb. or 4 medium-sized	2 cups sliced
Peanuts	1½ lb. unshelled	1 lb. shelled, about 3 cups
Pears	1 lb. or 4 medium-sized	2 cups sliced
Peas, dried, split	1 lb. or 2¼ cups	5 cups cooked
Pecans	2½ lb. in shell	1 lb. shelled, about 4¼ cups
Peppers, green	6 oz. or 1 large	1 cup diced
Pistachios, shelled	1 lb.	3⅔ cups
Pomegranate	1 average	½ cup pulpy seeds
Potatoes	1 lb. sliced or diced	3½ to 4 cups raw
Potatoes	1 lb. or 3 medium-sized	2¼ cups cooked or 1¾ cups mashed
Prunes, dried	1 lb.	2¼ cups pitted
Prunes, cooked, drained	1 lb.	2 cups
Raisins		
Seeded, whole	1 lb.	3¼ cups
Seedless, whole	1 lb.	2¾ cups
Rennet	1 tablet	1 tablespoon liquid rennet
Rhubarb	1 lb. fresh	2 cups cooked
Rice	1 lb. or 2 cups uncooked	About 6 cups cooked
Rice, dehydrated or precooked	2 cups	2⅔ cups cooked
Rolled oats	1 lb. or 6¼ cups uncooked	8 cups cooked
Saccharin	¼ grain	1 teaspoon sugar
Sorghum molasses, *see* About Liquid Sugars, 557	1 lb.	1⅓ cups
Spaghetti	1 lb. dry	5 to 6 cups
Spaghetti, 2-inch pieces	1 cup dry	About 1¾ cups cooked
Spaghetti, 12-inch pieces	1 lb. dry	About 6½ cups cooked
Strawberries, fresh	1 quart	4 cups sliced
Sugar, in baking, *see* About Sugars, 556 *and* About Liquid Sugars, 557		
Sugar, granulated	1 lb.	2 cups
Sugar, brown, packed	1 lb.	2¼ cups
Sugar, brown, packed	1 cup	1 cup granulated sugar
Sugar, superfine	1 cup	1 cup granulated sugar
Sugar, confectioners' or powdered	1 lb.	3½ to 4 cups
Sugar, confectioners'	1¾ cups	1 cup granulated sugar
Sweetener—noncaloric solution	⅛ teaspoon	1 teaspoon sugar
Tapioca	1½ to 2 tablespoons quick-cooking	4 tablespoons pearl, soaked

Tapioca, for thickening	1 tablespoon quick-cooking	1 tablespoon flour
Tea	1 lb.	125 cups
Tomatoes	1 cup packed	½ cup tomato sauce plus ½ cup water
Tomato juice	1 cup	½ cup tomato sauce plus ½ cup water
Tomato sauce	2 cups	¾ cup tomato paste plus 1 cup water
Tomato soup	1 can: 10¾ oz.	1 cup tomato sauce plus ¼ cup water
Water	1 lb.	2 cups
Walnuts, English	2 to 2½ lb. in shell	1 lb. shelled, about 4½ cups of halves
Walnuts, black	5½ lb. in shell	1 lb. shelled, about 3 cups broken
Wheat germ	12 oz.	3 cups
Yeast, compressed	1 cake, ⅗ oz.	1 package active dry yeast
Yeast, active dry	1 package	1 tablespoon
Yogurt	1 cup	1 cup buttermilk

ABOUT LEFTOVERS

The minister's bride set her luncheon casserole down with a flourish and waited for grace. "It seems to me," murmured her husband, "that I have blessed a good deal of this material before."

Leftovers can, of course, stand for simple repetition; but they can also stimulate a cook's ingenuity. For our part, we feel positively blessed when we have a tidy store of them garnered away in the refrigerator. So often they give a needed fillip to a dish we are making from scratch. Sometimes they combine to make a vegetable soufflé or to dress up an omelet. And how often they turn a can of soup into a real delicacy!

One secret we have learned is to limit the number of leftover ingredients we are working with so that they retain some semblance of identity. If there is too much of a mishmash, the flavors simply cancel out—as well as the appetite.

Another secret is to watch leftovers for color. Freshen them up by presenting them with the more positive accents of tomatoes or bright greens; or with a color-contrasting sauce.

Still another secret is to be careful that you create some contrast in texture. When leftover mixtures are soft, contrast can be achieved by adding minced celery or peppers, nuts, water chestnuts, crisp bacon or freshly minced herbs.

Consult the Index under the category you wish to utilize, or try one of the following suggestions:

See About Uses for Ready-Baked and Leftover Breads, Cakes and Crackers, 635; also About Crumbs, 551, and Bread Dressing, 370.

For ways to use cooked cereals and pastas, see Cooked-Cereal Muffins, 631, or Garnishes for Soups, 194 and 196. Also see Croquettes, 247, and Griddle Cakes, 235, or Calas, 246.

See About Stocks, 520, and About Soup Meat, 169, for uses of bones, and for meat, fowl, fish and vegetable trimmings.

For cooked meat, fish and vegetable leftovers, see Brunch, Lunch and Supper Dishes, 250, mousses, soufflés, timbales, meat pies, Cases for Food, 250, and Stuffed Vegetables, 280. See also About Economical Use of Large Cuts of Meat, 452 and 453.

For cooked potatoes, see the Index; use in Shepherd's Pie, 262.

Use leftover gravies and savory sauces with vegetables, pastas, meats, and hot sandwiches.

For cheese, see Soufflés, Timbales, Sauces and Au Gratin, 552.

For uses for egg yolks, see Sponge Cakes, 669, Yolk Letter Cookies, 713, Eight-Yolk Cake, 674, salad dressings, custards; and use hard-cooked yolks in sauces or riced as a garnish.

For uses for egg whites, see Angel and White Cakes, 668 and 671, meringues of all kinds, fruit whips, 745, hot and cold dessert soufflés, 739, icings, 721, insulation for pie crusts; and for breading, 552, and Eggs in a Nest, 224.

For citrus peels, see Candies, 795, and Zests, 571.

For uses for sour or buttermilk, see About Sour and Fermented Milks, 533.

For fruit juices, see fruit drinks or gelatins. Use as the liquid in cakes and custards, for meat basting, for sauces or fruit salad dressings.

For uses for leftover coffee, see coffee and mocha desserts and dessert sauces.

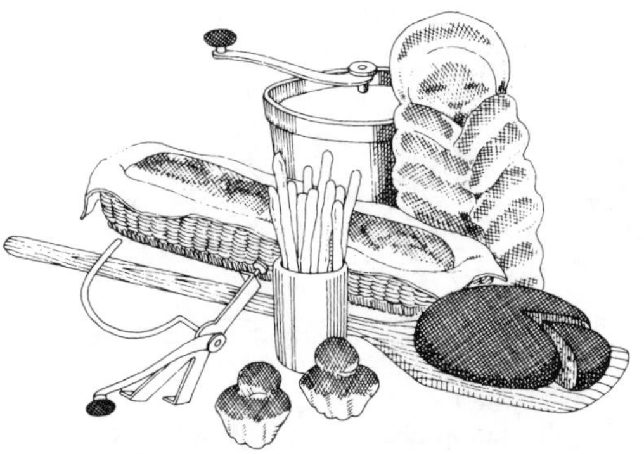

BREADS AND COFFEE CAKES

Once upon a time, when the English language was young, the word from which the modern English "lady" sprang meant "loaf-kneader," and the verb "to knead" has even prehistoric origins! To our own and our families' distinct profit—and with little effort—we housewives can become "ladies" again.

Begin, if you like, with a whole wheat—a flour which requires neither sifting nor kneading—and go on from there to more cunning triumphs. Try a round Swedish rye, 608, or a long crusty French loaf, 605, thin brittle Italian bread sticks, 606, or feather-light brioches, 615, all shown above. Bake quick breads such as biscuits, corn pone and scones. Or fashion a Christmas bambino of yeast bread, see illustration above and 620, kneading it by hand or with the help of an electric or a mechanical dough hook seen above in place at the rear and fully exposed in the foreground. Do become aware of the hearty flavors and varied textures of homemade breads.

ABOUT YEAST BREAD

If you have never made yeast bread, behold one of the great dramas of the kitchen. Every ingredient is a character. As a producer-director, assemble your cast. Yeast is the prima donna. Her volatile temperament is capable of exploitation only within given limits of heat—and does she resent a drafty dressing room! For more intimate details, see About Yeast, 553. Wheat flour is the hero. He has a certain secret something that makes his personality elastic and gives convincing body to his performance. Rice, rye, corn, soy—no other flour can touch him for texture; but he is willing to share the stage with others—if they give him the limelight. For differences in flours, see 545. Water, milk or other liquid ingredients are the intriguers. Any one of them lends steam to the show. For effect of soft and hard water in baking, see 519. As for salt and sugar, they make essential but brief entrances. Too much of either inhibits the range of the other actors. Fat you can enlist or leave. Use him to endow your performance with more tender and more lasting appeal. There are quite a few extras, too, which you can ring in to give depth and variety. Allow some ad-libbing with nuts and raisins, herbs and sprouts, see Additions to Yeast Doughs, 602.

Now, knowing our actors and their quality, "the play's the thing." Let's look into the types, the mixing and the baking of bread.

MIXING BREAD DOUGH

➤ To prepare the leaven, dissolve fresh compressed yeast in liquid at 85°, without stirring, 8 to 10 minutes. If instead the yeast is in active dry form, it will need liquid between 105° and 115° and should dissolve in 3 to 5 minutes. A small quantity of sugar helps activate the yeast, ➤ but do not use more than called for. Formerly milk was always scalded to kill bacteria. Now, with pasteurization, air-dried milk solids and canned milk, this operation is no longer necessary. However, scalding still does save time in dissolving the sugar and melting the fat.

Batters are the simplest of all doughs, requiring little handling. Strong beating to develop the gluten content, best done in an electric mixer, takes the place of kneading. When they come away from the sides of the bowl, these doughs have had enough beating. The breads they make are usually more porous and dry out faster than the kneaded variety. For mixing directions, see Dill Batter Bread, 604.

Sponge breads were favorites in days when yeast strains were poorly controlled. Sponge doughs result in a lighter-textured, coarser-grained loaf or roll than those made with conventional or straight dough. To mix sponge doughs, dissolve the yeast in a larger-than-usual amount of water, to which a portion of the flour is added. When this batter has fermented—and it sometimes takes as long as one hour—it becomes foamy and spongy. Butter and eggs, if called for, additional salt and sugar and the remaining flour are then mixed into the dough with the yeast mixture. See Gluten Bread, 609, for mixing directions.

The **Conventional** or **Straight** dough method, as given for White Bread, 602, is still our favorite for texture, keeping qualities and appearance. Also, and incidentally, we find the required kneading a healthy outlet for frustrations. Use a good-sized bowl, and start stirring the flour into the combined lukewarm liquids, shortening and dissolved yeast mixture. Mix in half the required flour gradually and beat about one minute. Then, as the rest of the flour is added, lay aside the spoon and mix by hand. When the dough begins to leave the sides of the bowl, turn it out onto a lightly floured board or pastry cloth. ➤ To flour a board lightly and evenly, allow about

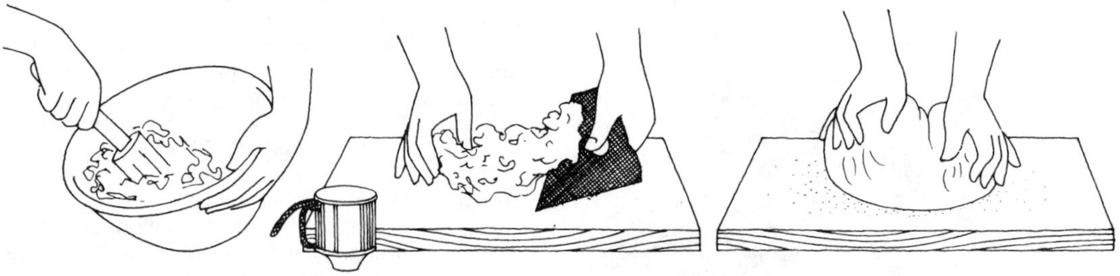

1 tablespoon flour for each cup of flour in the recipe—even less for a very light dough. A damp towel placed under the board will keep it from slipping. Turn the dough several times to make it easier to handle. ➤ Cover the dough with a cloth and let it rest 10 to 15 minutes before kneading.

With the **Mixer** method: using a strong electric mixer, you may shorten preliminary preparation time by blending the active dry yeast at the very outset with part of the flour and other dry ingredients. The liquids and shortening required are heated to 120° to 130°, added to the flour-yeast mixture, and the whole beaten 2 minutes at medium speed. If eggs are called for, add them at this time with an additional cup of flour. Beat ½ minute at low speed, then 3 minutes at high speed. Stir in the remaining ingredients and enough flour to make a soft dough; then proceed as for White Bread Plus, 603.

KNEADING AND PROOFING YEAST DOUGH

Generally speaking, flours vary in moisture content, see 546, and only experience can tell you exactly how much flour to add during the kneading process. Hence, some variations in amounts are indicated in the individual recipes. Grease your fingertips to prevent sticking. When the dough is first turned out on the board it is slightly sticky, as can be seen in the center, above. Then, as the gluten develops in the wheat flour through continued strong, rhythmic kneading, the dough becomes smooth and elastic.

Overkneading and long, slow risings will result in a coarse-textured bread. Using a pastry scraper, see illustration above, will help with soft doughs. The first kneading of about 10 minutes must be thorough, but ➤ the pressure exerted on the dough should be neither heavy nor rough.

Fold the dough over toward you. Then press it away from you with the floured heel of the hand, as shown below; give it a quarter turn, fold it and press away again. More flour may be necessary on your hands and board to overcome stickiness. Repeat this process until the dough becomes smooth, elastic and satiny. Air blisters will appear just under the surface coating or "cloak." Try not to break the coating. The dough at this point should no longer stick to the board or cloth.

If an electric mixer is used, and particularly if you make it a regular practice to bake bread, a bread hook—as illustrated in the chapter heading—is an enormous help. Follow the manufacturer's directions. The right amount of flour has been added when the dough cleans itself from the sides of the bowl. Turn the dough onto a floured board and knead by hand until it is smooth, elastic and satiny.

In both methods, the next step is to grease a large clean bowl evenly, put the dough into it and then turn the dough over ➤ so that the entire surface of the dough will be lightly greased. Cover the bowl with a cloth. Set the dough to rise. This process and the covering step after separating the bread into loaf sizes are shown graphically below to emphasize the importance of these so-called proofing periods. During this resting time, a smooth film again develops over the surface of the dough and makes it much easier to handle.

Yeast dough should rise in a draft-free place at

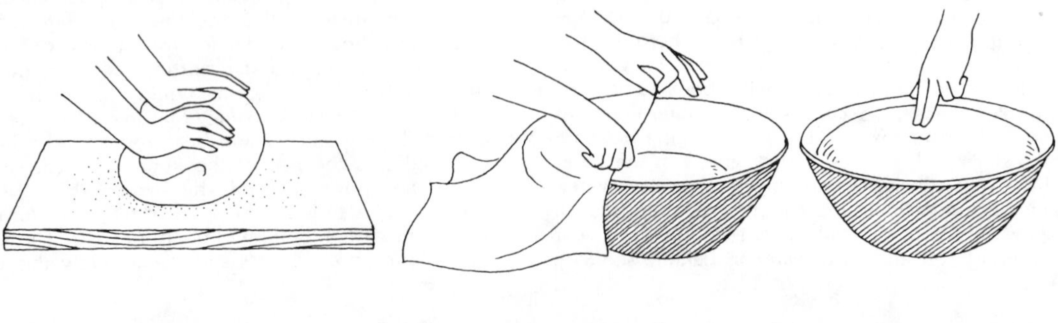

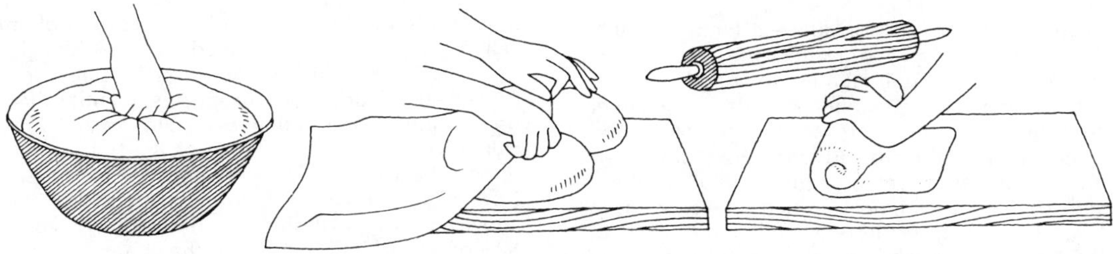

a temperature of about 75° to 85°. If the room is cold, you may place the dough in the bowl on a rack ➤ over a pan of warm water; near, but not on, a convector or radiator; or in an oven heated less than 1 minute, until you can just feel warmth —a quite ideal rising cabinet. Turn the heat off and keep the door closed. ➤ Be sure to remove the bread before preheating the oven to bake it.

The first time the dough rises it should double in bulk, if the loaf is to have a moist crumb. Should the dough rise to more than double its bulk, it will fall back into the bowl. Do not permit this to happen unless the recipe calls for it, as it may result in a coarse, dry bread. To make sure the dough has risen sufficiently, press it well with the fingertips. When it has doubled in bulk, usually in 1 to 2 hours ➤ the imprint of the fingertips will remain in the dough, as shown opposite. Now punch down the dough with a balled hand, as illustrated on the left above. Work the edges to the center and turn the bottom to the top.

▲ Yeast bread dough rises more rapidly at high altitudes and may become overproofed if it is not watched carefully and allowed to rise only until doubled in bulk. For other high-altitude baking hints, see 602.

Now you will be ready for the second kneading, if indicated in the recipe. Its purpose is to give a finer grain. It lasts only a few minutes and may be done in the bowl. Then permit the covered dough to rise again, until it has a second time ➤ almost, but not quite, doubled in bulk.

SHAPING YEAST DOUGHS

Once more, for a final time, punch down the dough and divide it into the number of pieces called for in the recipe. Shape them lightly into mounds; place them on a board, cover with a cloth as shown center above; and allow them to rest 10 minutes.

Meanwhile get your pans ready. Most breads call for a greased pan. To choose an appropriate one, see About Bread Crusts, 602. Begin to form the loaf by throwing down onto the board one of the pieces of dough which has been resting. You may use a rolling pin or your palm to press it evenly first. Professional bakers start with a circle and fold the curved outer segments toward the center to make their rectangle before shaping the loaf. You may prefer to treat yours instead like a thick scroll, as shown, using the heel of your hand to press it together as you complete the roll. Then with your stiffened hands at either end of the roll, compress the short ends and seal the loaf as shown below on the left, folding under any excess as you slide the dough, seam side down, into the greased pan. ➤ It is important that the finished dough contact the short ends of the pan to help support the dough as it rises. When the loaf is in the pan, you may grease its top lightly.

Cover the pan with a cloth. The dough will eventually fill out to the corners of the pan. While it is rising—to almost, but not quite, double in bulk—preheat your oven. When ready to bake, the loaf will be symmetrical, and ➤ a slight impression will remain when you press lightly with your fingers. To bake, see directions in the recipes. For pan placement in the oven, see 159.

To encourage round loaves to rise rather than spread, use round cake pans, or encircle each loaf loosely with 1-inch-high foil. Remove foil after bread has risen about halfway.

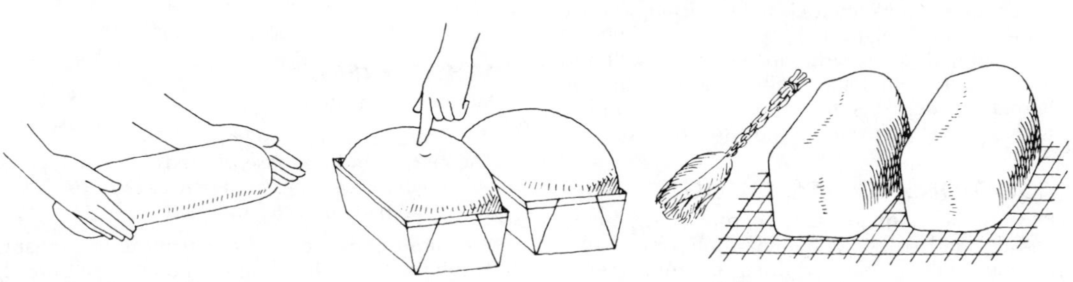

ABOUT BREAD CRUSTS

People have passions for different kinds of crust. ➤ The choice of pan will affect the crust. Glass, darkened tin and dull aluminum will all produce a thick one; but remember ➤ glass and enamel pans require a lower temperature, see 666. Hard rolls, Vienna and rye breads sometimes are baked on a parchment-covered or greased baking sheet sprinkled with cornmeal, which prevents these low-fat breads from sticking. Milk, either used in the recipe or brushed on at the end of the baking period, gives a good all-over brown color. Cream or butter may also be brushed on after baking for color; then the bread is returned to the oven for about 5 to 10 minutes. Setting a pan of warm water in the bottom of the oven during baking will harden crusts—as will brushing them, when partially baked, with salted water. Allow 1 teaspoon salt to ½ cup water.

For a glazed crust, toward the end of baking you may brush the top with an Egg Wash, 731. To keep the crust soft, brush the crust with butter after the bread is baked and out of the pan; then cover it with a damp cloth.

TESTING FOR DONENESS

➤ To test for doneness, notice if the loaf has shrunk from the sides of the pan. Or test by tapping the bottom of the pan to release the loaf and then tapping the bottom of the loaf; if a hollow sound emerges, the bread is done. Otherwise, return the loaf to the pan and bake a few minutes longer.

▲ Baking time at high altitudes usually remains the same, but oven temperatures should be increased slightly, from 10 to 15 degrees.

COOLING AND STORING BREAD

When the bread has finished baking, remove it at once from the pan and place it on its side on a wire rack to cool, as shown on the right, 601. ➤ Keep it away from drafts, which cause shrinkage. Let the bread cool completely before wrapping, storing or freezing. It is best stored in covered tins in which there are a few pinhole-sized openings for ventilation. It is sterile as it comes from the oven, but if it is not cooled sufficiently before wrapping, condensation may cause rapid molding. Keep the bread box away from any heat source. And keep it clean by washing it once a week with a baking soda solution and drying it thoroughly. Most breads can be frozen, 829 and 830, but dry out rapidly after thawing. In hot, humid weather, keep bread refrigerated in a plastic bag to help prevent the growth of mold.

ADDITIONS TO YEAST DOUGHS

Raisins, dates, dried fruits, citron, nuts, hulled sesame and roasted hulled sunflower seeds, slightly sautéed onions, dried or fresh herbs, 579, bean or grain sprouts, toasted wheat germ, milk solids and brewer's yeast—ingredients often called "improvers"—are added to yeast doughs for flavor and increased nutritional values. Improvers are seldom used in greater quantity than up to about one-fourth the weight of the flour called for in the recipe. Some of the flour called for can be used to dust the fruits, to keep them from sticking together. Before adding any of the above improvers, thoroughly mix the first addition of wheat flour to develop the gluten.

Any bread in which wheat or gluten flour is lacking will be deficient in the elasticity that this unique gluten factor of wheat provides. When, therefore, you are mixing flours to substitute for wheat flour in any of our recipes, please note the following: If substituting buckwheat, barley, cornmeal, millet meal, white or brown rice flour, leftover cooked cereal, or a combination of these, use wheat flour or gluten flour for at least half the flour called for; if substituting carob, bran or soy flour, use wheat flour or gluten flour for at least three-fourths the flour called for. Coarser grains like rolled oats, grits or bran can be pulverized in the blender, but whole grains and cracked grains should be cooked before adding to bread.

Recipes for the allergy-prone, omitting wheat and stressing all rye or rice, can be found in this chapter, as well as in the USDA Home and Garden Bulletin No. 147, "Baking for People with Food Allergies."

CORNELL TRIPLE-RICH FLOUR FORMULA

Work accomplished under Dr. Clive McCay at Cornell has done much to raise the standard of nutrition for large segments of the world's population. It was discovered that the addition of certain supplements in their natural forms to unbleached, synthetically enriched bread flours increases significantly their nutritive value. Use this formula in your favorite bread, cookie, muffin or cake recipe. When you measure, put in the bottom of each cup of flour called for:

1 tablespoon soya flour
1 tablespoon dry milk solids
1 teaspoon wheat germ

then fill the cup with sifted unbleached enriched flour.

WHITE BREAD

Wrote Louis Untermeyer:

"Why has our poetry eschewed
The rapture and response of food?
What hymns are sung, what praises said
To home-made miracles of bread?"

Even more constructive than versification, perhaps, are the recipes which follow: home-baked bread, in our view, can best be celebrated by repetition.

Two 5 x 9-Inch Loaves

We are partial to the straight dough or conventional method of making this even-grained all-purpose bread, which stales slowly and cuts well for sandwiches.

Scald:

1 cup milk

Add:

1 cup water
1 tablespoon shortening or lard
1 tablespoon butter
2 tablespoons sugar
1 tablespoon salt

In a separate large bowl, combine:

¼ cup 105°–115° water
1 package active dry yeast

and let dissolve 3 to 5 minutes. If using compressed yeast, crumble 1 cake yeast into ¼ cup 85° water and let stand 8 to 10 minutes. Add the lukewarm milk mixture to the dissolved yeast. Have ready:

6½ cups sifted all-purpose flour

Stir in 3 cups flour, beat 1 minute, then stir or work in remaining flour by tossing the dough on a floured board and kneading well until it is smooth, elastic and full of bubbles. Place the dough in a greased bowl, turn the dough over once and cover with a cloth. Let rise in a warm place until doubled in bulk, at least 1 hour. Punch it down to its original size and, if time permits, allow the dough to rise until double once more. Otherwise, skip the second bowl rising, shape the dough lightly into 2 loaves, and place them in greased pans. Cover and let the dough rise again until almost doubled in bulk.

Preheat oven to 450°.

To achieve the kind of crust you like, see 602. Bake the bread 10 minutes. Reduce heat to 350° and bake about 30 minutes longer. Test for doneness, 602. Remove loaves at once from pans and cool on a rack before storing.

WHITE BREAD PLUS

Three 5 x 9-Inch Loaves

This method of mixing bread dough calls for active dry yeast and an electric mixer. If using compressed yeast, use these same ingredients, but follow the conventional method given for White Bread, above. As this recipe requires less yeast and more sugar than does White Bread, and because this bread, started in a cold oven, has a longer proofing period, less yeast flavor is retained.

In a large mixer bowl, mix together:

3 cups sifted all-purpose flour
½ cup sugar
1 tablespoon salt
1 package active dry yeast

Combine:

2½ cups 120°–130° water
½ cup lard or shortening

The shortening does not need to melt. Gradually add to dry ingredients and beat 2 minutes at medium speed, scraping bowl occasionally. Add to make a thick batter:

1 beaten egg
1 cup sifted all-purpose flour

Beat ½ minute at low speed, then at high speed 3 minutes. Stir in to make a soft dough:

3 to 4 cups sifted all-purpose flour

Turn out onto a lightly floured board and knead until smooth and elastic, about 10 minutes. Allow the bread to rise once in the mixing bowl and once in the baking pan. To bake, place loaves in a cold oven. Turn the heat to 400°. After 15 minutes, reduce heat to 375° and bake 25 minutes longer. Test for doneness, 602. Remove the loaves at once from the pans and cool on a rack before storing.

SOURDOUGH BREAD

Two 5 x 9-Inch Loaves

➤ Please read About Sourdough, 554. A variety of breads can be made by substituting 1 cup wheat germ or cornmeal, etc., for 1 cup of the white flour, or using 3 cups whole-grain flour for 3 cups white flour. About ½ teaspoon baking soda added to the whole-grain flours improves the flavor.

Combine thoroughly and let stand uncovered to ferment overnight in a warm place:

1½ cups 85° water
1 cup Sourdough Starter, 555
4 cups all-purpose flour
2 teaspoons sugar, honey or molasses
2 teaspoons salt

Next morning, after the sponge has risen and fallen, stir down any crust which may have formed. Add:

1 cup all-purpose flour
(2 tablespoons soft butter or shortening)
(1 to 2 beaten eggs)

When thoroughly mixed, turn out onto a board covered with:

1 cup all-purpose flour

Knead in enough of this flour to make the dough smooth and elastic. Shape the dough into 2 loaves, put into bread pans, brush lightly with butter and let rise covered until almost doubled in bulk. Bake in a preheated 400° oven 45 to 50 minutes.

RAISIN, PRUNE OR NUT BREAD

I. Add to any unflavored bread dough:

1 cup drained, cooked, chopped prunes, or 1 cup washed, well-drained seeded raisins, or 1 cup chopped nuts

Sprinkle the above with:

1 tablespoon sifted all-purpose flour
(1 tablespoon cinnamon)

II. Cook over low heat until liquid is almost absorbed:

1½ cups raisins
½ cup water
1 tablespoon cinnamon

Cool and add to the dissolved yeast with:

(1 well-beaten egg)

CINNAMON LOAF

Two 5 x 9-Inch Regular or Three Cylindrical Loaves

Follow recipe for:

White Bread, 602

While dough is rising in bowl, combine:

½ cup sugar
1 tablespoon cinnamon

After dough has been punched down, divided and rolled into two 9 x 14-inch rectangles, brush lightly with:

Melted butter

Sprinkle surfaces with the sugar mixture and roll as for Jelly Roll, 691. Place in greased 5 x 9-inch pans and proceed as for White Bread, 602. If you prefer to use a specially designed hinged or lidded cylindrical pan, it is essential that the cover be firmly bound so the loaf will not distort in the baking. The dough should be put into the cylinder before it rises a second time. This is the pan used for our children's birthday bread horse, shown on 635.

CHEESE BREAD

Two 5 x 9-Inch Loaves

For a pleasant variation, try using whole wheat flour and 2 tablespoons honey instead of the sugar indicated.

Scald:

1½ cups milk

Add to it and cool to about 105°:

⅓ cup sugar
¼ cup butter
1 tablespoon salt

In a large bowl, dissolve for 3 to 5 minutes:

2 packages active dry yeast

in:

½ cup 105°–115° water

Stir in the cooled milk mixture. Add and beat until smooth:

1 well-beaten egg
1½ cups shredded sharp cheddar cheese
(1 teaspoon powdered thyme)
(½ teaspoon powdered marjoram)
(½ cup finely chopped pimiento)

Beat in well:

3 cups sifted all-purpose flour

Add, and then continue beating and stirring until the dough begins to leave the sides of the bowl, about:

3 cups sifted all-purpose flour

Knead the dough about 10 minutes. Allow to rise once in the bowl and once in the pans, covered, until doubled in bulk. Brush the loaves with:

(Melted butter)

Bake in a preheated 375° oven about 30 minutes. To test for doneness, to cool and to store, see 602.

HERB BREADS

If fresh herbs are available, triple the amounts suggested for the dry herbs given below.

Follow the recipe for:

White Bread Plus, 603, or Whole-Grain Bread, 607

For each 5 x 9-inch loaf, add to dough before kneading:

1 teaspoon ground celery seeds
1 teaspoon ground caraway seeds
1 teaspoon ground dill or dillseeds

or add:

½ teaspoon marjoram or basil
¼ teaspoon thyme
1 tablespoon chopped fresh parsley
(½ teaspoon oregano)

or:

¼ teaspoon ginger
1 teaspoon thyme
1 teaspoon summer savory
1 teaspoon rosemary

or:

1 teaspoon nutmeg or cloves
1 teaspoon rosemary
1 teaspoon dill
1 tablespoon chopped fresh sage

DILL BATTER LOAF

Mix together in a large mixer bowl:

1 package active dry yeast
¼ cup sifted all-purpose flour
¼ teaspoon baking soda
2 tablespoons sugar
1 teaspoon salt
2 tablespoons dried minced onions or 2 teaspoons grated onion
1 tablespoon dillseed or dillweed

Combine and gradually add to the yeast mixture:

1 to 2 tablespoons butter
¼ cup 120°–130° water

Beat 2 minutes at medium speed, scraping bowl occasionally. Add:

1 cup lukewarm large-curd cottage cheese
1 lightly beaten egg
½ cup sifted all-purpose flour

Beat at high speed 2 minutes. Beat in to make a stiff batter:

1½ cups sifted all-purpose flour

Cover and let rise until doubled in bulk. Stir down and transfer to a well-greased 1½-quart heatproof casserole. Cover and let rise until doubled in bulk. Bake in a preheated 350° oven 35 to 40 minutes. Top with:

Melted butter
A sprinkling of salt

EGG BREAD OR CHALLAH

2 Braided Loaves

A heavier bread than the following brioche, with good keeping qualities. Combine:

2 packages active dry yeast
1 teaspoon sugar
¼ cup 105°–115° water

Measure into a large bowl:

6 cups sifted all-purpose flour
1 tablespoon salt

Make a deep well, 643, and pour in the yeast. Combine and add to the flour:

2 cups 105° water
3 slightly beaten eggs
¼ cup vegetable shortening or oil
3 tablespoons sugar
(1/16 teaspoon saffron)

Beat well until a ball of dough is formed, then turn out onto a floured board and knead about 10 minutes until smooth and elastic. Place in a greased bowl, turn, cover and allow to rise until doubled in bulk, about 1 hour. Punch down and divide dough into two sections, kneading each for several minutes.

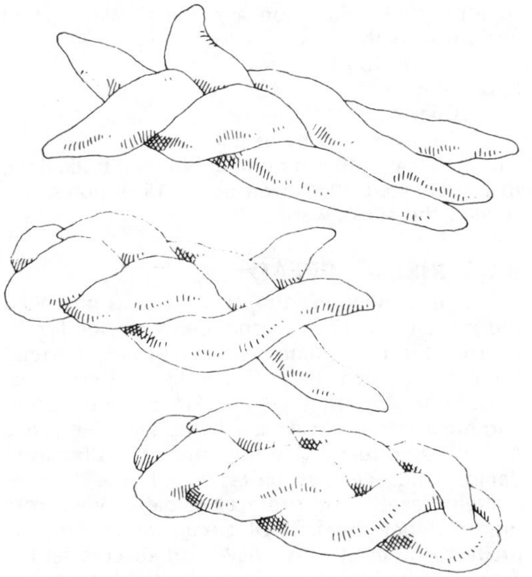

Now, to make the braids. Cut each section of dough into 3 parts and roll between the hands or on a board into long tapered cylinders. With the three ropes of dough lying side by side on a greased floured sheet, start to braid loosely from center to end, then braid the other portion from center to end. Finish the ends by tucking them under. Repeat for the second loaf. Cover and let rise until almost doubled in bulk. Brush tops with:

French Egg Wash, 731

and sprinkle over all:

Poppy seeds

Bake 15 minutes in a preheated 400° oven, then reduce heat to 375° and bake about 45 minutes longer.

BRIOCHE LOAF COCKAIGNE

This light egg loaf has a feathery, tender crumb. While very similar to a true brioche, 615, it is much easier to make. Serve it right out of the oven, if possible. To cut, use an angel cake server, 668, or two forks held back to back, leaving a pulled surface rather than a cut surface. Combine and let stand 3 to 5 minutes:

2 packages active dry yeast
3 tablespoons 105°–115° milk

Beat well:

3 tablespoons sugar
3 eggs

Add:

½ cup soft butter
2 cups sifted all-purpose flour
½ teaspoon salt

Add the yeast mixture to the batter. Beat well 3 minutes. Place in a greased 9-inch tube pan. Let rise in a warm place until doubled in bulk, about 1 hour. Bake in a preheated 450° oven about 15 to 20 minutes. Test for doneness as for cake, 665.

FRENCH BREAD

To an American who travels in France, the commonest of tourist sights at the noon hour is what looks like *tout le monde* coming from the baker, afoot or a-cycle, with a couple or three long loaves of French bread, naked and gloriously unashamed, strapped on behind. French cookbooks ignore French bread, and French housewives leave the making of this characteristic loaf to the commercial baker. Why? Because he alone has the traditional wood-fired stone hearth with its evenly reflected heat, and the skilled hand with sourdough—both of which are necessary to produce the genuine article. We regard French bread as uniquely delicious and consider the closely approximate substitute recipe given below as rather more than well worth following. It was contributed some years ago by Mr. Julian Street.

2 Long Loaves

Scald:

½ cup milk

Add to it:

1 cup boiling water

While this liquid cools to 85°, dissolve:

1 cake compressed yeast

in:

¼ cup 85° water

After the yeast rests 10 minutes, add it to the milk mixture with:

1½ tablespoons melted shortening
1 tablespoon sugar

Measure into a large mixing bowl:

4 cups sifted all-purpose flour
2 teaspoons salt
2 teaspoons sugar

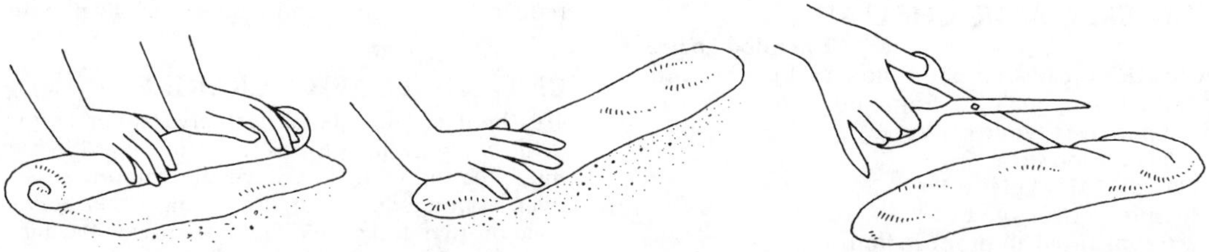

Make a hole in the center of these ingredients. Pour in the liquid mixture. Stir thoroughly, but do not knead. The dough will be soft. Cover with a damp cloth and set in a warm place to rise, allowing about 2 hours. Punch down the dough. Place on a floured board and pat into 2 equal oblongs. Form each into a French loaf by rolling the dough away from you, as shown above. Continue rolling, pressing outward with the hands and tapering the dough toward the ends until a long, thin form results. Place the 2 loaves on a greased baking sheet. Cut diagonal, ¼-inch-deep slits across the tops with sharp-pointed scissors. Set in warm place to rise to ➤ somewhat less than doubled in bulk.

Preheat oven to 400°.

On bottom of oven, place a pan filled with ½ inch boiling water. Bake the bread 15 minutes, then reduce the heat to 350° and bake about 30 minutes longer. Five minutes or so before the bread is finished, brush the loaves with a glazing mixture of:

1 beaten egg white
1 tablespoon cold water

We once received a letter from a gentleman in Junction City, Kansas, which began: "My wife is too old to cook and I am too old to do anything else." It seems that he was an enthusiastic baker of French bread, but he complained that his

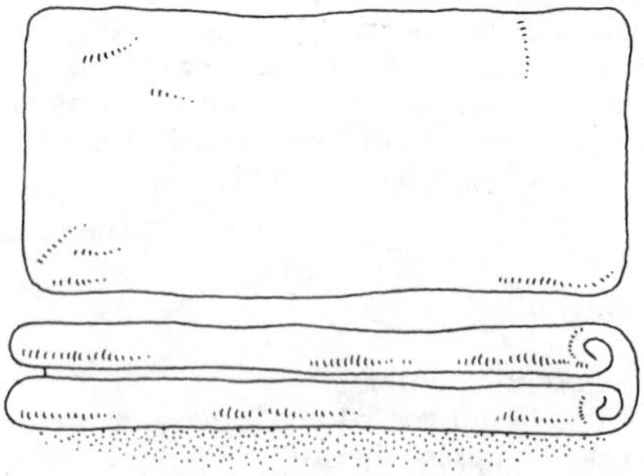

loaves turned out too flat. We suggested that he try shaping them in the following manner: Make a long oblong of the dough, fold over one edge to the center, repeat the operation for the second edge and taper the ends slightly. The bottom of the loaf may be pressed on a board which has been dusted with cornmeal and the loaf then placed on a large greased sheet for baking. This correspondent made several batches of bread and then wrote again: "Your plan works fine in shaping the loaves and I am also using ¼ cup less water. This makes the loaves come up a better shape, although it makes the dough harder to mix thoroughly. I think, however, the bread is just as good, and my French son-in-law says it is the best French bread he has eaten outside of France."

BREAD STICKS OR GRISSINI

Prepare:

French Bread, above

Roll into an oblong about ¼ inch thick, one dimension of which is about 8 inches. Cut into strips 2 inches wide and 8 inches long. Roll them to form sticks. Place on a greased baking sheet and brush with:

Egg Wash, 731

Sprinkle with:

(Coarse salt)
(Caraway, sesame or dill seeds)

Allow to rise until not quite doubled in bulk. Bake in a preheated 400° oven about 15 minutes. Try serving the sticks warm.

SALT-RISING BREAD

This unusually good formula, which has provoked the most dramatic correspondence, relies for its riser on the fermentation of a salt-tolerant bacterium in cornmeal or potato pulp. The cornmeal must be freshly stone ground. Since stone-ground cornmeal is not always available, we give also a potato-based recipe. Do not attempt this bread in damp, cold weather unless the house is adequately heated, and protect the batter well from drafts. Under the best of circumstances, it may prove to be erratic. We have had success setting a covered heavy bowl in water heated by an electric frypan or on a heating tray.

I. Cornmeal Salt-Rising Bread

Three 5 x 9-Inch Loaves

Measure into a large jar or bowl:

½ cup fresh coarse white ➤ stone-ground cornmeal
1 tablespoon sugar

Scald and pour over the cornmeal:

1 cup milk

Let stand overnight or longer, covered, in a warm place, 90° to 95°, until it ferments. By then it should be light and have a number of small cracks over the surface. If it isn't light in texture, it is useless to proceed, as the bread will not rise properly. Scald:

3 cups milk

Pour it over:

2 tablespoons sugar
5 tablespoons lard
1 tablespoon salt

Stir in:

3½ cups sifted all-purpose flour

Stir in the corn mixture. Place the bowl containing these ingredients in a pan of warm water for 1 to 2 hours, until bubbles work up from the bottom. Keep water warm this full length of time. Stir in:

5 cups sifted all-purpose flour

Knead in until smooth, but not stiff, about:

2½ cups sifted all-purpose flour

Place dough in greased pans, cover and let rise until it has doubled in bulk. ➤ Watch it, for if it gets too high, it may sour. Preheat the oven to 400° and bake the bread for 10 minutes. Reduce the heat to 350° and bake 25 to 30 minutes more. To test for doneness, to cool and to store, see 602.

II. Potato Salt-Rising Bread

Three 5 x 9-Inch Loaves

A fan, trapped by her grandchild's measles, sent us a treatise on lessening the fantastic odors of "salt-rising." She says, "Use non-mealy 2½-inch-diameter new red-skinned potatoes for the starter. Place them in a stainless steel bowl. Set bowl in water in an electric dutch oven with heat maintained at about 90° to 95°. Perfect results are produced in 15 hours with only a mild odor—like that of good Italian cheese." As we lived for some years in an apartment with a salt-rising bread addict and shared the endless variety of smells she produced, we would settle any day for a mild cheese aroma.

Pare, then cut into thin slices:

2½ cups new non-mealy potatoes

Sprinkle over them:

1 tablespoon salt
2 teaspoons sugar
2 tablespoons white cornmeal

Add and stir until salt is dissolved:

4 cups boiling water

Let the potato mixture stand, covered with a cloth, 15 hours. Now squeeze out the potatoes. Discard them. Drain the liquid into a bowl and add, stirring until very well blended:

1 teaspoon baking soda
1½ teaspoons salt
5 cups sifted all-purpose flour

Beat and beat "until the arm rebels." Set the sponge in a warm place to rise until light. Bubbles should come to the surface and the sponge should increase its volume by approximately a third. This will take about 1½ hours. Scald:

1 cup milk

When lukewarm, add:

2 tablespoons butter

Add this mixture to the potato sponge with:

5 to 6 cups sifted all-purpose flour

Knead dough about 10 minutes before shaping into 3 loaves. Place in greased pans. Let rise, covered, until ➤ light and not quite doubled in bulk. Bake in a preheated 350° oven about 1 hour.

WHOLE-GRAIN BREAD

Feather-lightness is, of course, by no means a prime objective in making whole-grain breads. Yet such loaves should have substance without high density. If our instructions are closely followed, you will never have occasion to level at us the reproach of Mrs. Burns, who, on viewing an impressive monument to her illustrious son, exclaimed: "Aye Robbie! Ye asked for bread, and they've gien ye a stane."

Three 5 x 9-Inch Loaves

Please read about Whole-Grain Flour, 547. Prepare the yeast as for White Bread, 602. Beat together and add to the yeast mixture:

1 beaten egg
¼ cup melted butter
2½ cups lukewarm water
1½ teaspoons salt
¼ to ½ cup sugar, honey or maple syrup

Add, without sifting, a mixture of:

4 cups whole-grain flour
4 cups all-purpose flour

To mix, knead, proof and shape, follow the arrow symbols and illustrations, 600 and 601, allowing the dough to rise once in the mixing bowl and once in the baking pans. Bake in a 350° oven about 45 minutes. To test for doneness, see 602.

ALL WHOLE-GRAIN BREAD COCKAIGNE

Two 4½ x 8½-Inch Loaves

A heavier, coarser bread which makes a *bonne bouche* with cheese.

Sprinkle:

1 package active dry yeast
1 tablespoon brown sugar

over:

¼ cup 105°–115° water

Measure and combine:

6 cups whole-grain flour
½ cup dry milk solids

Combine:

2 cups warm water or milk
1 tablespoon salt
1 to 3 tablespoons melted bacon fat
4 to 6 tablespoons dark molasses or honey

Combine the yeast and water mixtures. Beat in the flour. Knead briefly, adding flour if necessary. Allow the dough to rise once in the bowl and once in the baking pans. Bake in a 350° oven about 45 minutes. To test for doneness, to cool and to store, see 602.

SPROUTED WHOLE-GRAIN BREAD

Prepare:

Whole-Grain Bread, above

using 2 packages of yeast. Mix with the lukewarm water before adding the other ingredients:

2 cups ground sprouted wheat, soybeans, lentils or chick-peas, 565

SOY WHOLE WHEAT BREAD

Follow directions for:

White Bread, 602

but substitute for 3 cups of the sifted all-purpose flour:

1 cup soy flour
2 cups whole wheat flour

CRACKED-WHEAT BREAD

Two 5 x 9-Inch Loaves

If your cracked wheat is a coarse grind, put it in the blender to get a finer grind. Try making this good bread with cooked cereals other than cracked wheat.

Cook for 10 minutes or until the moisture is absorbed:

1 cup finely ground cracked wheat

in:

3 cups boiling water

Remove from heat and stir in:

2 tablespoons butter or shortening
1 tablespoon salt
3 tablespoons sugar or honey
1 tablespoon molasses
3/4 cup milk

While this mixture is cooling, dissolve for 3 minutes:

2 packages active dry yeast

in:

1/4 cup 105°–115° water

Combine the cooked cereal and yeast mixture, then beat in gradually:

4 cups all-purpose flour
2 cups whole wheat flour

Turn the dough out onto a floured board and knead about 10 minutes. Place in a greased bowl, cover, and let rise in a warm place until doubled in bulk. Punch down, knead a few times and shape dough to fit into 2 greased bread pans to let rise, covered, until again doubled in bulk. Preheat oven to 350°. Bake about 35 to 40 minutes or until done.

OAT BREAD COCKAIGNE

Two 5 x 9-Inch Loaves

Scald:

2 cups milk

and pour it over:

1 cup rolled oats

Add:

2 teaspoons salt
1/4 cup vegetable oil
1/2 cup brown sugar
(1/2 teaspoon ground ginger)

Cool this mixture to lukewarm. Combine:

1/4 cup 105°–115° water
2 packages active dry yeast

Add the yeast solution to the oats, plus:

1 or 2 slightly beaten eggs
1/4 to 1/2 cup wheat germ
1 cup soy flour
2 cups whole wheat or rye flour
3 to 4 cups sifted unbleached all-purpose flour

➤ To knead, proof and shape, follow the arrow symbols and illustrations on 600 and 601, allowing the dough to rise once in the mixing bowl and once in the baking pans. Bake in a preheated 350° oven about 1 hour. To test for doneness, to cool and to store, see 602.

SWEDISH RYE BREAD

2 Loaves

A moist aromatic loaf that keeps well. Combine in a large bowl:

1 1/2 cups 105°–115° water
2 packages active dry yeast

Let rest 3 to 5 minutes until dissolved.

Add:

1/4 cup molasses
1/3 cup sugar
1 tablespoon salt
2 tablespoons grated orange rind
1 tablespoon fennel seed
1 tablespoon anise seed
(2/3 cup chopped raisins)

Stir in:

2 1/2 cups sifted, finely milled rye flour
2 tablespoons softened butter

Beat all these ingredients together until smooth.

Add:

2 1/2 to 3 cups sifted all-purpose flour

If the dough is soft to handle, use the larger amount of flour. ➤ To knead, follow the arrows and illustrations, pages 600 and 601. Allow the dough to rise once in the bowl and once on the baking sheet. To shape, form into two ovals on a greased baking sheet dusted with cornmeal. To prevent spreading, see 601. Cover with a cloth and let rise until almost doubled in bulk, about 1 hour. Make four 1/4-inch-deep diagonal slashes in the tops of the loaves. Bake in a preheated 375° oven 30 to 35 minutes. To test for doneness, to cool and to store, see 602.

ALL-RYE FLOUR BREAD

2 Rather Flat Loaves

Rye flour lacks the gluten of wheat, so a loaf made of all rye has a dense, heavy texture, similar to that of pumpernickel.

Combine:

1/2 cup 105°–115° water
2 packages active dry yeast

Scald:

2 cups milk

As it cools, add:

2 tablespoons butter

1 tablespoon sugar or honey
2 teaspoons salt

Add the yeast mixture and stir in:

2 cups rye flour

Let this sponge rise about 1 hour. Then add slowly, while stirring:

3 cups rye flour
(1 beaten egg)
(2 tablespoons caraway seeds)
(2 tablespoons sesame seeds)

Let rise about 2 hours. Sprinkle a board with:

1 cup rye flour

Knead the dough into it 10 minutes. Divide into 2 parts. To form, see 601. Put on a well-greased baking sheet, grease the tops of the loaves, cover and allow to rise about 2 hours more. Bake in a preheated 350° oven about 1 hour. To test for doneness, to cool and to store, see 602.

SOURDOUGH RYE BREAD

2 Round or 2 Long Loaves

The best-flavored rye breads call for sourdoughs, 554. We love this recipe which comes from Merna Lazier, who has run, among many other successful projects, a bakery of her own. She says: "You may object to the number of stages in this process, but I must say that old-time bakers who were proud of their rye bread really nursed it along—so there must be a reason." For this recipe, on one day you make a sourdough, using ½ cake of yeast. The following day, you make two sponges, using the other ½ cake of yeast.

The first day, prepare the sourdough. Mix in a bowl and work together lightly:

½ cup rye flour
¼ cup water
½ cake compressed yeast

Cover this sourdough tightly so it will not dry out, and keep it in a warm place at about 85° for 24 hours. Then work into it:

¾ cup water
1 cup rye flour

The sourdough should be ready to use after it has fermented, covered, 4 hours longer.

Sponge I. Mix into the above sourdough:

1¾ cups rye flour
⅔ of ½ cake compressed yeast
¼ cup water

Allow this sponge to rise, covered with a damp cloth, at 85° until it doubles in bulk.

Sponge II. Add to Sponge I:

1¾ cups rye flour
1¾ cups all-purpose flour
Remaining ⅓ of ½ cake compressed yeast
1 cup water

Mix until smooth. Cover with a damp cloth and let rise until doubled in bulk. Then add:

1 cup water
1 tablespoon salt
1¾ cups all-purpose flour
1 tablespoon caraway seed

Mix until smooth, then let the mixture rest, covered, 20 minutes. Turn the dough out onto a floured board and mix and knead into it:

1½ to 2 cups all-purpose flour

depending on the flour, until you have a rather firm dough—one that will not flatten or spread. Divide and shape it into 2 long or 2 round loaves. Place them on a greased pan and allow to rise, but not double in bulk. Too much rising will result in a flat loaf.

Preheat oven to 425°.

Place a flat pan containing about one-fourth inch water in the oven. Bake the loaves 50 to 60 minutes. You may have to replenish the water, but ➤ remove the pan after 20 minutes. As soon as the bread is done, spread it with:

Melted butter

or, if you wish a glazed crust, spread with:

Salted water—1 teaspoon salt to ½ cup water

Cool loaves on a rack, away from drafts.

GLUTEN BREAD

Two 5 x 9-Inch Loaves

A boon for those on low-starch diets but overrated for its protein quality, as both wheat flour and the gluten made from it are deficient in lysine. See about incomplete proteins on 2.

Combine:

3 cups 105°–115° water
1 package active dry yeast

After 3 to 5 minutes, when the yeast is dissolved, beat in:

2 cups gluten flour, 548

Let this sponge rise in a warm place until light and foamy. Combine, beat and then stir into the sponge:

1 beaten egg
2 tablespoons melted shortening
½ teaspoon salt
(2 tablespoons sugar)

Stir in:

About 4 cups gluten flour

Use only enough flour to make a dough that will knead well. After kneading, shape into 2 loaves. Let rise until doubled in bulk. Bake in a preheated 350° oven about 1 hour. To test for doneness, to cool and to store, see 602.

FLATBREADS

Two 8-Inch Loaves

Called **Armenian, Peda, Greek, Arab, Syrian, Euphrates Bread,** this dough can be formed into hard rolls, long thin loaves and flat envelopes for stuffing with exotic sandwich fillings. If making small sandwich-sized puffs, divide the dough into 4-inch circles and bake on a greased sheet 7 to 9 minutes until puffed and lightly browned. **Sopaipillas** can be made from this dough. Cut into 3-inch squares after the first rising and deep-fat-fried at 365°, they are seasoned with cinnamon and sugar. For a typical flatbread dough, combine in a mixing bowl and let stand 3 to 5 minutes:

1 package active dry yeast
1 cup 105°–115° water

Add and beat until smooth:

1½ cups sifted all-purpose flour
1 teaspoon salt
(1 tablespoon sugar)
1 tablespoon soft shortening

Add:

1½ cups sifted all-purpose flour

If the dough is too stiff to beat, knead in the flour by hand until it is smooth and elastic, about 5 minutes. Place in a greased bowl, cover and let rise until doubled in bulk, about 45 minutes. Punch down and divide into 2 balls. Flatten the dough evenly in 2 greased 8-inch layer cake pans. Slash a decorative pattern in the dough and brush with:

(Milk)

Sprinkle with:

(Sesame seeds)

Let rise again until almost doubled in bulk, and bake in a preheated 425° oven about 20 minutes. Flatbread is best eaten warm, so reheat before serving.

PIZZAS

Two 14-Inch Pizza Crusts

Who would guess that this popular Italian pie began its career as a leftover improvised from surplus bread dough? In a pinch you might try pie dough or sliced English muffins as a base.

To make pizza dough, mix as for bread, 599, using the following ingredients, but do not let it rise a second time:

4 cups sifted all-purpose flour
1 cake yeast in 1⅓ cups 85° water
2 tablespoons vegetable or olive oil
1 teaspoon salt

Knead 10 minutes. Cover with damp cloth and let rise about 2 hours. Have ready two oiled 14-inch pizza pans. Sprinkle a little cornmeal over all. Pat and stretch the dough in the pans, pinching up a collar around the edge to hold the filling. Prick dough in about 6 places.

Preheat oven to 400°.

Brush each pizza lightly with olive oil to prevent crust from becoming soggy. Spread with your preferred filling and rest it about 10 minutes. At this stage the pizzas may be frozen for at least a week before baking. Bake about 25 minutes until light brown and serve at once.

I. Spread the pizza with:

(Thin slices of cheese)
Thickened Tomato Sauce, 352

Arrange on top:

12 to 14 anchovies or sliced Italian sausage, pepperoni, prosciutto ham or salami

Sprinkle with:

Oregano
Olive oil
Chopped parsley
(Parmesan or Romano cheese)

II. Use a highly seasoned:

Italian Meat Sauce for Pasta, 352, or other meat sauce for pasta

Cover with a layer of:

Fontina or Mozzarella cheese

III. Use as a base:

Thickened Tomato Sauce, 352

Add:

1 cup chopped or sliced mushrooms

IV. Cover the base with:

Lightly sautéed onions
Black olives
Anchovies

Brush with:

Olive oil

ABOUT YEAST ROLLS

There is little difference in bread- and roll-making, so if you are a novice ➤ please read About Yeast Bread, 599. The visual appeal of delicately formed, crusty or glazed rolls is a stimulant to the appetite. For varied shaping suggestions, see the illustrations in this chapter.

Professional cooks weigh the dough to keep the rolls uniform in size for good appearance and even baking. If you do not use muffin pans, place approximately equal-sized shapes of dough at regular intervals over the entire baking sheet. Baking parchment paper saves having a greasy pan to wash and also cuts the grease build-up which results in a discolored pan and uneven browning.

You may use additions to yeast dough, 602, and coffee cake, 621, to vary the flavor. Sprinkle the tops with poppy, celery, fennel, caraway, or lightly toasted sesame seeds, depending on the rest of your menu.

To bake, follow the individual recipes. ➤ Remove the rolls at once from the pan to a cooling rack. ➤ To reheat, sprinkle them lightly with water and heat, covered, in a 400° oven or in the top of a double boiler over hot water. Sometimes the suggestion is made that the rolls be put in a dampened paper bag and heated until the bag dries. We find, however, that some types of bags can transmit a disagreeable flavor.

NO-KNEAD LIGHT ROLLS

Eighteen 2-Inch Rolls

These are the rolls we remember from childhood: light as a feather and served in a special soft linen napkin. Although they require no kneading, they are best chilled at least 2 hours and up to 12. They are not true refrigerator rolls, since this recipe is not heavy enough in sugar to retard the rising

action, and all the dough should be baked after the 2- to 12-hour period.
Combine and let stand 3 to 5 minutes:

¼ cup 105°–115° water
1 package active dry yeast

Place in a separate bowl:

¼ cup butter or shortening
1¼ teaspoons salt
2 tablespoons sugar

Pour over these ingredients and stir until they are dissolved:

1 cup hot water

When they are lukewarm, add the yeast. Beat in:

1 egg

Stir in and beat until blended:

About 2¾ cups sifted all-purpose flour, to make a soft dough

Put dough in a large greased bowl. Either cover with foil and chill from 2 to 12 hours, or place in a greased bowl covered with a cloth until doubled in bulk. Punch it down. Shape the rolls to fill the greased cups in a muffin pan to about one-third. Again let rise until about doubled in bulk. Bake in a preheated 425° oven 15 to 18 minutes. Cool at once.

PARKER HOUSE ROLLS

About Thirty 2-Inch Rolls

This is a basic not-too-sweet dough that can be used for variously shaped dinner rolls.
Scald:

1 cup milk

Add and stir until dissolved:

1 tablespoon sugar
2 tablespoons butter
¾ teaspoon salt

Sprinkle:

1 package active dry yeast

over:

2 tablespoons 105°–115° water

Add the milk mixture when it has cooled to lukewarm. Beat in:

(1 egg)

Sift before measuring:

2⅔ cups all-purpose flour

Stir in part of the flour; knead in the rest. Use only enough flour to form a dough that can be handled easily. Place in a greased bowl. Brush the top with:

Melted butter

Cover and let the dough rise in a warm place until doubled in bulk. Roll it and cut into rounds with a floured biscuit cutter. Dip the handle of a knife in flour and use it to make a deep crease across the middle of each roll. Fold the rolls over on the crease and press the edges together lightly. Place rolls in rows on a greased baking sheet. Let rise in a warm place until light, a matter of 35 minutes or so. Bake in a preheated 425° oven about 20 minutes. Remove at once from pans.

CLOVERLEAF ROLLS

Twenty-Four 2-Inch Rolls

Prepare dough for:

Parker House Rolls, above

After the first rising in the bowl, punch down the dough. Now, fill greased muffin tins about one-third with 3 small balls, as sketched below. Brush the tops with:

Melted butter

Let rise covered in a warm place until about doubled in bulk. Bake in a preheated 425° oven 15 to 18 minutes. Remove at once from pans.

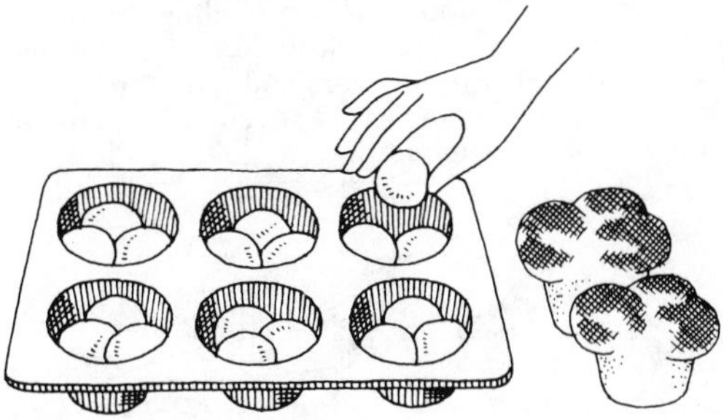

HOT CROSS BUNS

About 18 Buns

Prepare dough for:

Parker House Rolls, above

increasing the sugar to ¼ cup and including the egg. Add to the sugar:

¼ teaspoon cinnamon
⅛ teaspoon nutmeg
¼ cup currants or raisins
2 tablespoons finely chopped citron

After the first rising, shape dough into 18 balls and place in rows on a greased baking sheet. Cover and let rise until almost doubled in bulk. Bake in a preheated 425° oven about 20 minutes, until golden brown. Decorate with the traditional cross, using:

Milk Glaze, 731

PALM LEAF OR SOUR CREAM ROLLS

About 4 Dozen Leaves

Sweet enough for a dessert. Serve with coffee and fruit.
Sprinkle:

1 package active dry yeast

over:

¼ cup 105°–115° water

Sift:

3 cups all-purpose flour
1½ teaspoons salt

Cut in, until reduced to pea-sized bits:

½ cup butter

Blend and add:

2 beaten eggs
1 cup cultured sour cream
1 teaspoon vanilla

and the dissolved yeast. Cover and chill for about 2 hours or more. When ready to bake, sprinkle a board with:

½ cup Vanilla Sugar, 557

or a mixture of:

½ cup sugar
1 teaspoon cinnamon

Roll half the dough into a 6 x 18 x ¼-inch strip. Fold as sketched on the left below, bringing the ends to within about ¾ inch of each other. Repeat this folding as shown in the right foreground and again as shown in the rear. Slice into ¼-inch-thick "palm leaves." Repeat this process with the other half of the dough, first sprinkling the board with the sugar mixture. Put leaves on an ungreased baking sheet. Let rise, covered, about 20 minutes. Bake in a preheated 375° oven until golden brown, about 15 minutes.

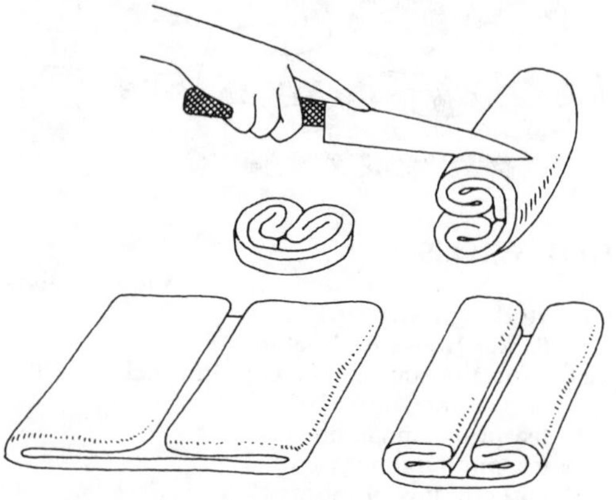

BUTTERMILK ROLLS OR FAN-TANS

About 24 Rolls

Rolls prepared in this way need not be buttered. Fine for a serve-yourself party.

Heat to about 110°:

1½ to 2 cups buttermilk

If the buttermilk is thick, use the lesser amount. In ⅓ cup of the buttermilk, dissolve for 3 to 5 minutes:

1 package active dry yeast

Add the yeast mixture to the remaining buttermilk with:

¼ teaspoon baking soda
2 teaspoons salt
¼ cup sugar

Beat well; then stir in:

2 cups sifted all-purpose flour
2 tablespoons melted butter

Add another:

2 cups sifted all-purpose flour

Place dough in a greased bowl and turn it, so it is lightly greased all over. Cover with a cloth and let rise until more than doubled in bulk. Knead lightly 1 minute. Separate into 2 parts. Roll each part into a square about ⅛ inch thick. Brush the dough with melted butter. Cut into strips 1½ inches wide. Stack them. There should be from 6 to 8 layers of stacked strips. Cut off pieces about 1½ inches wide, with a string, as shown below. Place them in buttered muffin tins, with the cut edges up. Let rise in a warm place until doubled in size. Bake in a preheated 425° oven 15 to 20 minutes until well browned.

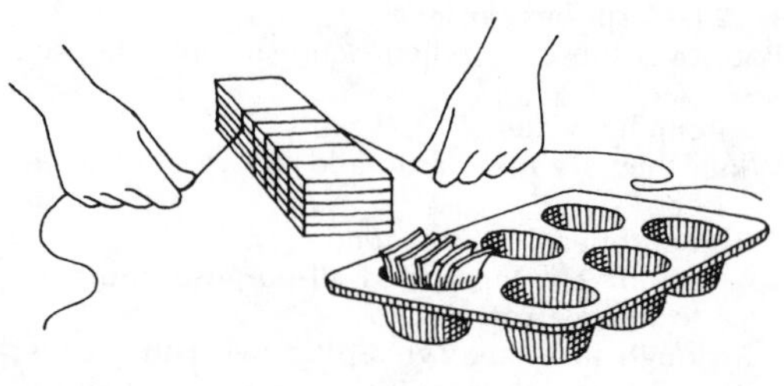

KOLATCHEN

About Thirty-Six 2-Inch Rolls

Prepare the dough for:

Palm Leaf Rolls, 611

When ready to bake, roll the dough into 2-inch balls and place on a greased baking sheet about 2 inches apart. Have ready one or more of the following:

Prune, Apricot, Date or Fig Filling, 622,
jam or chopped fruit

Press an indentation into the center of each roll, leaving a ¼-inch rim. Fill with your chosen fillings, cover and let rise about 40 minutes. Preheat oven to 375°. Bake approximately 20 minutes. Sprinkle with:

(Confectioners' sugar)

OVERNIGHT ROLLS

About 48 Rolls

This is a sweet dough good for rolls and coffee cakes.

Combine and let stand 3 to 5 minutes:

1 package active dry yeast
2 teaspoons sugar
2 tablespoons 105°–115° water

Scald:

1 cup milk

Add and stir in:

7 tablespoons lard

Cool. Combine and beat well:

7 tablespoons sugar
3 beaten eggs
1 teaspoon salt

Stir in the milk and yeast mixtures. Add:

4½ cups sifted all-purpose flour

Beat the dough about 5 minutes. Place in a foil-covered bowl in the refrigerator overnight. Take out just before baking. Divide dough into 3 parts. Roll each part into a circle about 9 inches in diameter. Cut each circle into 16 wedge-shaped pieces. Before rolling further, brush with:

Melted butter
and dust with:
Sugar and cinnamon
or top with a:
Coffee Cake Filling, 621

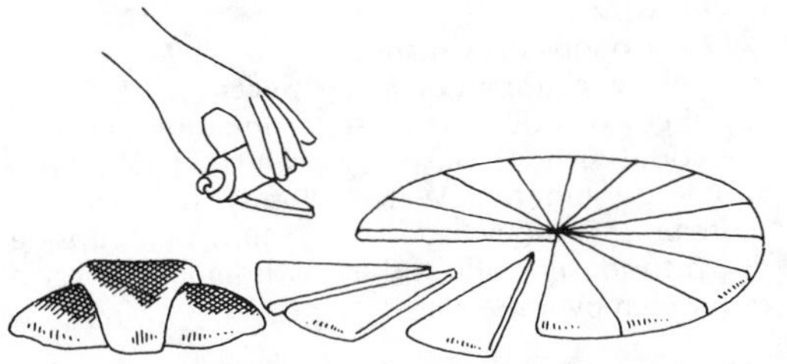

Roll up each piece by beginning at the wide end, stretching the dough a bit as you roll it. Brush with:
Egg Wash, 731
Let rolls rise until doubled in bulk. Bake 15 to 18 minutes on a greased baking sheet in a preheated 425° oven. Take care: they burn easily.

FILLED PINWHEEL ROLLS

About 48 Rolls

Follow the recipe for:
Overnight Rolls, above
Prepare the dough and let rise until doubled in bulk. Roll to ¼-inch thickness. Cut into 4-inch squares. Spread the squares generously with:
Butter
Sugar and cinnamon
Place in the center of each square:
Raisins and nuts or 2 teaspoons apricot or raspberry jam
Cut diagonally into the dough from each corner to within ¾ inch of the center. Fold every other point toward the center, as sketched below, over-

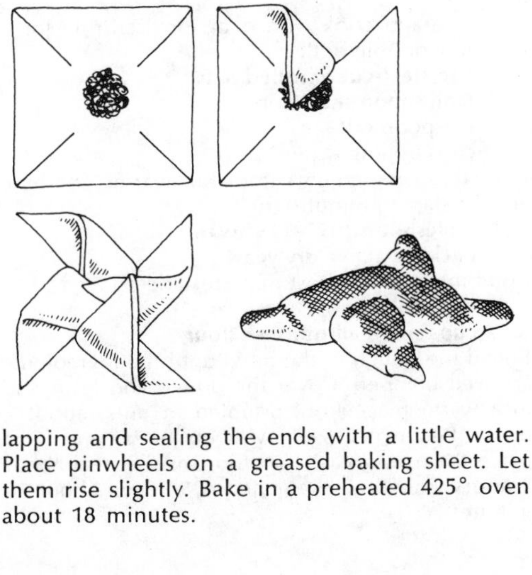

lapping and sealing the ends with a little water. Place pinwheels on a greased baking sheet. Let them rise slightly. Bake in a preheated 425° oven about 18 minutes.

BUTTERMILK-POTATO ROLLS

About 46 Cloverleaf Rolls

Prepare:
¾ cup riced freshly cooked potatoes
While still hot, mix with:
½ cup butter
Heat to 105°–115°:
2 cups buttermilk
Sprinkle into about ½ cup of the buttermilk:
1 package active dry yeast
2 tablespoons sugar
Let stand 3 to 5 minutes. Add the remaining buttermilk and mix with the potatoes. Beat until light and stir in:
2 eggs
1 teaspoon salt
Sift before measuring:
7½ cups all-purpose flour
Stir in 6 cups of the flour. Knead in the rest. Place the dough in a greased bowl and turn it, so that it is greased lightly on all sides. Cover and let rise until doubled in bulk. Punch down. Shape and let rise as for Cloverleaf Rolls, 611. Glaze tops with:
(French Egg Wash, 731)
Sprinkle with:
(Poppy seeds)
Bake in a preheated 425° oven 15 to 18 minutes. Remove at once from pans.

CHEESE ROLLS

Prepare:
Cheese Bread, 604
Shape and bake as for:
Overnight Rolls, 612

LOW-FAT, EGGLESS ROLLS

About 5 Dozen Rolls

You may bake these excellent rolls in advance and reheat before serving; and, after wrapping, keep them in a refrigerator 2 weeks or in a freezer 3 months.
Scald:
2 cups milk
Add:
5 teaspoons salt
¼ cup sugar
Cool this mixture to lukewarm. Combine and let stand 3 to 5 minutes:
1 cup 105°–115° water
2 packages active dry yeast
Combine above ingredients and mix well. Add gradually:
8 to 10 cups all-purpose flour
Knead the dough until smooth and elastic and let it rise, covered, until almost doubled in bulk. Shape the dough as you prefer. Let rolls rise on greased covered baking sheets until again almost doubled in bulk. Bake about 40 minutes in a preheated 275° oven. If storing, leave them in the pans to cool for 20 minutes. When they reach room temperature, wrap well. To serve: if re-

frigerated, reheat on a greased baking sheet about 10 minutes in a 400° oven; if frozen, bring to room temperature before reheating.

CINNAMON SNAILS AND CRISPS

Prepare:

Scandinavian Pastry, 621, omitting the cardamom; or Overnight Rolls, 612

When the dough has doubled in bulk, roll into an oblong on a floured board to the thickness of ¼ inch. Spread generously with:

Melted butter

Sprinkle with:

Cinnamon
Brown sugar

Add:

(Chopped nutmeats)
(Seedless raisins)
(Chopped citron)
(Grated lemon or orange rind)

Roll the dough like a Jelly Roll, 690.

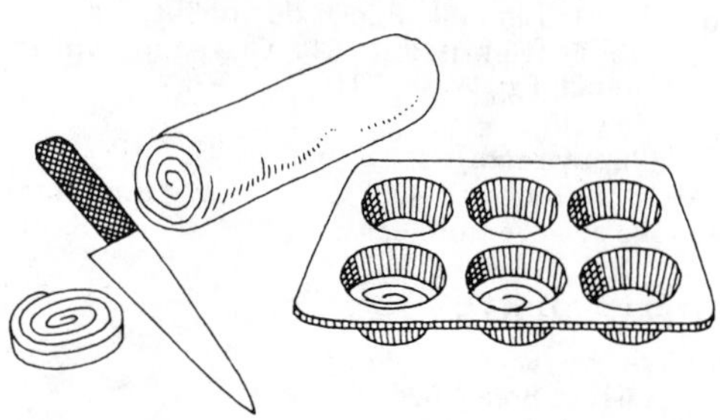

To make snails, cut into 1-inch slices, see above. Rub muffin tins generously with:

Butter

Sprinkle well with:

Brown sugar
(Finely chopped nutmeats)

Place each slice of roll firmly on the bottom of a muffin tin. Let rise in a warm place ½ hour. Bake in a preheated 350° oven about 30 minutes.

For crisps, cut the rolled dough into ⅛-inch slices and place on a greased baking sheet 3 inches or so apart. Flatten to about 3 inches in diameter. Allow to rise approximately 30 minutes. Now cover with waxed paper and roll to about ⅛-inch thickness. Remove paper and brush with:

¼ cup melted butter

Sprinkle with a mixture of:

Sugar and cinnamon
(Crushed nuts)

Roll flat again, using waxed paper, and bake in a preheated 400° oven 10 to 12 minutes.

SCHNECKEN OR CARAMEL BUNS

Prepare rolls as for:

Cinnamon Snails, above

➤ Be sure to use in the filling:

Grated lemon rind
Raisins
Pecans

Roll as for Jelly Roll, 690. Cut into 1½-inch slices. Fill bottom of each muffin tin with a mixture of:

1 teaspoon melted butter
1 teaspoon warmed honey

Cover with:

2 teaspoons brown sugar
A few chopped or whole pecans

Lay slices of dough over sugar mixture. Let rolls rise about ½ hour. Bake in a preheated 350° oven about 20 minutes. Watch closely for signs of scorching. Remove from oven, turn pans upside down to loosen rolls and allow honey mixture to drip down over the rolls.

WHOLE-GRAIN ROLLS

About 40 Rolls

Prepare dough for:

Whole-Grain Bread, 607, or Oat Bread Cockaigne, 608

Shape dough into rolls after the first rising, and let rise again until almost doubled in size. Butter the tops. Sprinkle with:

(Coarse salt, chopped nuts or sesame seeds)

Bake in a preheated 400° oven 15 to 20 minutes.

RYE ROLLS

About 36 Rolls

Prepare:

Swedish Rye Bread, 608

Shape rolls after the first rising. Sprinkle tops with:

Coarse salt

For the crust of your choice, see 602. Bake in a preheated 375° oven about 20 minutes. Remove from pans at once and cool on a rack.

OAT-AND-MOLASSES ROLLS

Thirty-Eight 2-Inch Rolls

An agreeable variation on an old-time favorite formula.

Combine and cook with occasional stirring for 1 hour in a double boiler:

1 cup steel-cut or rolled oats
½ tablespoon shortening
¾ teaspoon salt
1½ cups boiling water

Cool these ingredients until lukewarm. Combine and let stand 5 minutes in:

1 tablespoon 105°–115° water
1 package active dry yeast

Combine oat and yeast mixtures and add:

½ cup molasses
4 cups sifted all-purpose flour

Knead the dough in the bowl until the ingredients are well blended. Cover the dough and let it rise in a warm place until doubled in bulk, about 2 hours. Pinch pieces off with buttered hands and place them in greased muffin tins. Let rise about 2 hours. Bake in a preheated 425° oven about 20 minutes.

BRIOCHE

About 15 Brioches

Due to a number of special circumstances, our recipes for French bread, while not classic, are close approximations. So, for similar reasons, is our recipe for another superb French specialty—the brioche. But we are proud of them both. The method for making brioche is more complicated to describe than to carry out. It involves good coordination between the rising of a small amount of floating yeast paste, or starter, and the working of the rest of the dough. Please read about this process before plunging in.

Cream and set aside:

6 tablespoons butter

Sift and then measure:

2 cups all-purpose flour

Make a well, see 643, with about a fourth of this flour and crumble into it:

1 cake compressed yeast at 70°

➤ Be sure to use no less. A high yeast and butter content distinguishes this dough. Mix the flour and yeast with:

2 tablespoons 85° water

Gradually work the flour into a paste. When it becomes a small soft ball, snip a cross in the top with scissors and then drop it into a 2-quart pan filled with water at 85°. ➤ The ball will sink to the bottom of the pan, so be sure it is not over a burner, where additional heat might kill the yeast. As the yeast develops, the ball of paste, or starter, rises to the surface and doubles in size in about 7 to 8 minutes—if the water temperature is right. If the water chills too much, add hotter water to bring the temperature back to 85°. ➤ When the starter has doubled in bulk, it must be removed from the water. Should this state be reached before you are ready to use it, drain and cover it. Meanwhile, once you have dropped the starter into the water, shape into another well the remaining flour, mixed with:

1 tablespoon sugar
1 teaspoon salt

Break into the center of it:

2 eggs at 70°

Mix them in by gradually drawing the flour from the sides of the well. Also work in:

2 to 3 tablespoons milk

until the ingredients form a sticky but cohesive mass which you continue to work as follows. Use only one hand. Do not try to release it from the dough. Just keep picking up as much as will adhere, and throw it back hard onto the board with a turn of the wrist, gathering more from the board each time. ➤ This rough throwing process develops the gluten and should be repeated about fifty times. By then the dough should be glistening and smooth and your fingers will have become free. At this point, work the butter into the dough. When it is all absorbed, scoop the floating starter out of the water by spreading wide the fingers of one hand and ➤ drain the starter for a moment on a dry towel. Work the starter into the smooth dough, which will remain shining and of about the consistency of whipped cream.

➤ Now, get the dough ready to chill for at least 1 hour. Gather up as much as you can, including what remains on the board, releasing it with a spatula. Put it into a greased or floured bowl and chill, covered. Have ready the classic fluted and flaring brioche forms—or muffin tins. When the dough has chilled, knead it with floured hands. It should be firm enough not to require a floured board. For each brioche, make 2 balls—about 2 tablespoons of dough for one, 1 tablespoon for the other. The first ball is placed in the base of a tin. The smaller ball will form the characteristic topknot.

Mold it into a pear-shaped form. Cut a small gash in the center of the large ball, then 3 more shallow gashes radiating out from the center. Insert the point of the "pear," so it is seated firmly. The brioches should rise until almost doubled in bulk, 15 to 20 minutes. Glaze them with French Egg Wash, 731, ➤ but be sure it does not slip into the crack and bind the topknot to the base—which would keep the topknot from rising properly.

Preheat oven to 450°.

Bake the brioches about 10 minutes, or until the egg-washed portions are a lovely brown. Should the topknots brown too rapidly, cover them loosely with a piece of foil. When baked they should puff to the proportionate size shown in the illustration. Serve at once or release from the tins and cool on a rack. Reheat before serving.

BRIOCHE AU CHOCOLAT

A favorite French after-school treat.

Prepare:

Brioche, above, or Scandinavian Pastry, 621

Cut into 2-inch squares. Roll in each square a generous sliver of:

Semisweet chocolate

Bake as directed for Scandinavian Pastries, 621.

FRENCH CRESCENTS OR CROISSANTS

About 18 Crescents

Rich, somewhat troublesome, but unequaled by any other form of roll.

Scald:

⅞ cup milk

Stir into it, until melted and dissolved:

1 tablespoon lard or vegetable oil
1½ tablespoons sugar
1 teaspoon salt

Cool until lukewarm. Add:

1 package active dry yeast

dissolved in:

⅓ cup 105°–115° water

Stir in or knead in to make a soft sticky dough about:

2½ cups sifted all-purpose flour

Knead on a lightly floured surface, using a pastry scraper to flip the soft dough end over end 10 times. The dough should now hold together. Place it in an ungreased bowl. Cover with a cloth and let rise until doubled in bulk, about 1½ hours. Then cover the dough with a lid and place in the refrigerator until thoroughly chilled, at least 20 minutes. Roll or pat it out on a floured surface into an oblong ¼ inch thick. Now, following the directions for kneading butter and folding the dough as in Puff Paste, 643, knead:

1 cup cold butter

Spread the butter over two-thirds the surface of the dough, leaving an unbuttered border ¼ inch wide. Fold the unbuttered third over the center third. Then, fold the remaining third over the doubled portion. The dough is now in 3 layers. Swing the layered dough a quarter turn—or, directionally speaking, bring east to south. Roll it again into an oblong ¼ inch thick. Fold again in thirds as before. Sprinkle dough lightly with flour, cover with a plastic or waxed wrap and chill 1½ hours. Allow the unwrapped dough to rest on a lightly floured surface about 10 minutes. Twice again, roll into a rectangle and fold in 3 layers. Then, roll it again on a slightly floured surface to the thickness of ¼ inch.

Now, cut off any folded edges which might keep the dough from expanding. Cut the dough into 3-inch squares, and cut the squares on the bias. Roll the triangular pieces, beginning with the wide side and stretching them slightly as you roll. Shape the rolls into crescents, as sketched below.

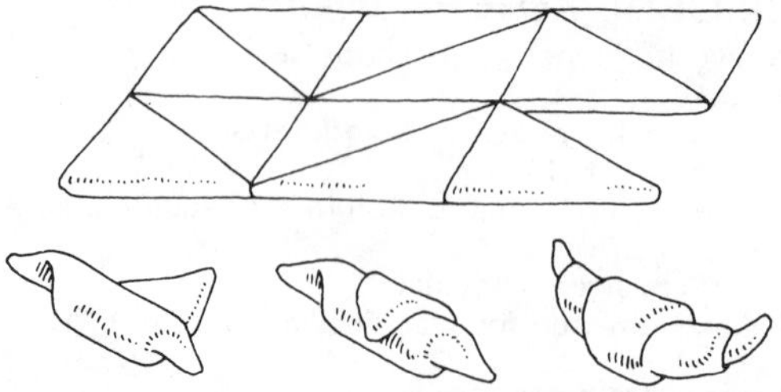

Place them on a baking sheet. Chill at once for ½ hour. Never allow them a final rising, as they will not have the proper flakiness.
Preheat oven to 400°.

Bake the crescents 10 minutes, then reduce the heat to 350° and bake until done—10 to 15 minutes longer.

FILLED SWEET CRESCENTS

About 28 Crescents

Prepare the dough for:

Refrigerator Potato Rolls, 618,
or Scandinavian Pastry, 621

Use for each crescent:

2 teaspoons nut or fruit filling, 622

If using the refrigerator dough, roll out to ¼-inch thickness before chilling and cut into 3-inch squares. If using the Scandinavian dough, shape it after chilling. Cut the squares diagonally. Shape as shown. Place on a greased baking sheet. Let them rise until doubled in bulk. Brush lightly with:

French Egg Wash, 731

Bake in a preheated 375° oven 18 to 20 minutes. Cool on a rack or serve hot.

ORANGE TEA ROLLS

These must be served hot the same day they are baked.

Prepare:

Refrigerator Potato Rolls, 618

Shape them into bite-sized rolls. In the center of each roll, embed:

A section of fresh orange

which has been rolled in:

Brown sugar

Bake in a preheated 400° oven 8 to 10 minutes. If reheating, you may glaze with a mixture of equal parts of:

Sugar, water and Cointreau

HARD OR VIENNA ROLLS

Twelve 3-Inch Rolls

Sift:

4 cups all-purpose flour

Dissolve for 3 to 5 minutes in:

¼ cup 105°–115° water
1 package active dry yeast

Combine:

1 cup warm water
1 tablespoon sugar
1 teaspoon salt
2 tablespoons shortening

and the dissolved yeast mixture. Fold in thoroughly but lightly:

2 stiffly beaten egg whites

Add enough of the sifted flour to make a soft dough. To knead and proof, see 600. Allow the dough to rise twice. After the second rising, punch down and knead about 1 minute, then let rest, covered, about 10 minutes before shaping into 12 oblong pieces. Place them about 3 inches apart on a greased baking sheet. ➤ To ensure a hard crust, have in the oven a 9 x 13-inch pan filled with ½ inch boiling water. Bake at once in a preheated 450° oven about 20 minutes or until golden brown.

ENGLISH OR RAISED MUFFINS

About Twenty 3-Inch Muffins

These are heavenly when eaten fresh and do not taste at all like "store-bought" ones. They do begin to resemble them the second day, however, so freeze leftovers immediately. You may bake these breads with or without muffin rings. The classic size is about 4 inches. We make our own rings from small unlacquered fish cans and deviled-meat cans. The tops and bottoms are removed and the rims thoroughly scrubbed. English muffins are always baked on a greased griddle.

Combine in a mixing bowl:

1 cup water
½ cup scalded milk
2 teaspoons sugar
1 teaspoon salt

Dissolve 3 to 5 minutes in:

2 tablespoons 105°–115° water
1 package active dry yeast

Combine the two mixtures. Sift before measuring:

4 cups all-purpose flour

Beat 2 cups flour gradually into the milk mixture. Cover the bowl with a cloth. Let the sponge rise in a warm place, 85°, about 1½ hours or ➤ until it collapses back into the bowl. Beat in:

3 tablespoons softened butter

Beat or knead in the remaining flour. For the final rising you may put the batter into greased rings, filling the forms to a depth of no more than ½ inch. If not using rings, place the dough on a board lightly floured or sprinkled with cornmeal. Pat or press the dough to a thickness of about ½ inch, and cut it into rounds about 3 inches in diameter. Let them stand on a lightly greased cookie

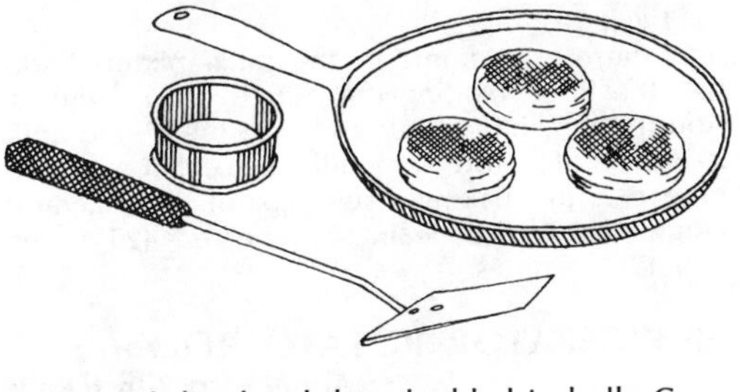

sheet until the dough has doubled in bulk. Carefully slip a pancake turner under the muffin rings or rounds of dough and transfer them to a fairly hot, well-buttered griddle. Remove the rings. Cook until light brown. Turn once while cooking. Cool slightly on a rack. To separate the muffins before the traditional toasting, take 2 forks back to back and pry them open horizontally. Butter generously and toast. The uneven browning gives them great charm. Serve with:

(Marmalade)

CRUMPETS

Crumpets are essentially similar to English muffins, except that greased muffin rings must be used when preparing them, see illustration opposite, as the batter is more liquid. Follow the recipe for English Muffins, above, but increase the milk to 1⅔ cups.

WHITE, WHOLE-GRAIN, GRAHAM OR RYE BREAD STICKS

Pinch off small pieces of:

Bread dough

that has risen once. This may be done with buttered hands. Roll into sticks of pencil thickness. Brush with:

Melted butter or 1 beaten egg

Place the sticks on a buttered baking sheet. Sprinkle with a choice of:

(Coarse salt)
(Poppy seed)
(Fresh celery seed)
(Chopped nutmeats)
(Caraway seed)

Let rise until doubled in bulk. Bake in a 425° oven until brown and crisp.

BAGELS

About 18 Rings

The classic accompaniment is cream cheese and lox or smoked salmon. But try adding to the basic dough, below, spices, raisins, finely chopped nuts or freeze-dried onions.

Combine:

1 cup scalded milk
¼ cup butter
1 tablespoon sugar
1 teaspoon salt

When this mixture is 105°–115°, add and dissolve for 3 minutes:

1 package active dry yeast

Blend in:

1 to 2 eggs
3¾ cups sifted all-purpose flour

Knead this soft dough about 10 minutes, adding more flour if necessary to make it firm enough to handle. Let rise, covered, in a greased bowl until doubled in bulk. Punch down and divide into 18 equal pieces. Roll each piece into a rope about 7 inches long and tapered at the ends. Wet the ends to help seal. Form into doughnut-shaped rings, shown on 618. Let rise, covered, on a floured board about 15 minutes. To help firm the dough, you may chill it 2 hours. Drop rings, one at a time, into a solution of:

2 quarts almost boiling water
1 tablespoon sugar

As the bagels surface, turn them over and cook about 3 minutes longer. Skim out and place on an ungreased baking sheet. Coat with:

Beaten egg white

Bake in a preheated 400° oven 20 to 25 minutes until golden brown and crisp. Very tasty toasted and served with butter.

BREAD PRETZELS OR STICKS

3 Dozen 6-Inch Sticks or Twelve 6-Inch Pretzels

A chewy soft pretzel: the kind that still—praise be!—can occasionally be bought from a street-vendor.

Combine in a mixer bowl:

1 cup 105°–115° water
1 package active dry yeast

When dissolved, add and beat at least 3 minutes:

1½ cups sifted all-purpose flour
2 tablespoons soft butter
½ teaspoon salt
1 tablespoon sugar

Stir in:

1¼ cups sifted all-purpose flour

and knead until the dough loses its stickiness. Let rise in a covered greased bowl until doubled in bulk. Punch down and divide into 12 pieces for pretzels or 36 smaller pieces for sticks. With your

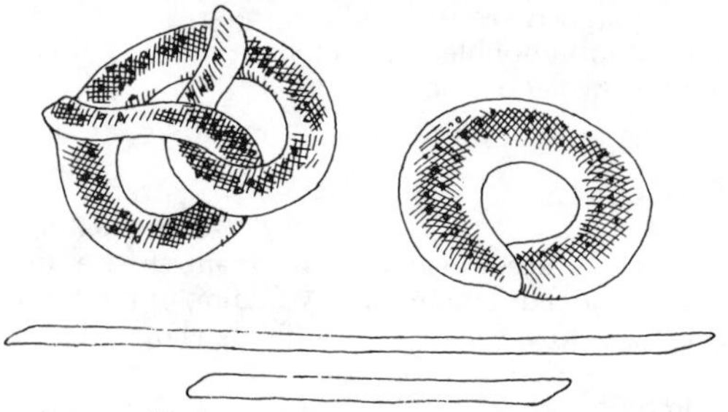

palms, roll the 12 pretzel pieces into 18-inch lengths about pencil thickness, tapering the ends slightly. Loop into a twisted oval as shown above. Place on a greased baking sheet and let rise until almost doubled in bulk. Preheat oven to 475°. Have ready a boiling solution of:

4 cups water
5 teaspoons baking soda

➤ Do not use an aluminum pan for this mixture. With a slotted spoon, carefully lower the pretzels into the water about 1 minute, or until they float to the top. Return them to the greased sheet. Sprinkle with:

Coarse salt

Bake until crispy and browned, about 12 minutes for the pretzels, less for the sticks. They are best served at once, but will keep about one week in an airtight container. Cool before storing.

ABOUT REFRIGERATOR DOUGHS

By "refrigerator," we mean just that—these are not freezer doughs. If it's a freezer product you're after, by all means ➤ bake before freezing for best results. We find the following recipes somewhat limited in use, because ➤ the milk-based ones can be kept chilled only three days and the water-based ones five days. Yeast action is slowed by the cold, but it does continue, so both more fat and more sugar are needed in refrigerator doughs than in other kinds to keep the yeast potent during the refrigerator period. We find that kneading before storage helps to retain rising power.

The advantage of this type of dough, of course, is that you can bake some at once and keep the rest for later. To store for chilling ➤ keep the dough in a greased plastic bag large enough to allow for some small expansion. If it rises in the refrigerator, punch the dough down. Or, place the balled dough in a greased bowl, turn it so the entire surface is evenly coated, cover it closely with waxed paper or foil, and weight it down with a plate.

After removal from refrigeration, always ➤ rest the dough, covered, 30 minutes. Then ➤ punch it down to let the gases escape before further handling. To shape or fill, see previous roll recipes and illustrations. Be sure the dough at least doubles in bulk. Allow ample time for rising because of the chilled condition of the dough. To bake, see the following individual recipes.

NO-KNEAD REFRIGERATOR ROLLS

Eighteen 2½-Inch Rolls

Sift before measuring:

3½ cups all-purpose flour

Scald:

1 cup milk

Stir in until dissolved:

6 tablespoons shortening or butter
6 tablespoons sugar
1 teaspoon salt

Cool to lukewarm. Combine and let stand for 3 to 5 minutes:

½ cup 105°–115° water
1 package active dry yeast

Beat in:

1 egg

Add these ingredients to the milk mixture. Add half the flour, beating the dough for 2 minutes. Add the remaining flour and beat the dough until it blisters. To store for chilling, to shape and to prepare for baking, see About Refrigerator Doughs, above. Bake in a preheated 425° oven about 15 minutes.

REFRIGERATOR POTATO ROLLS

About Forty 2-Inch Rolls

A sweet dough also entirely suitable for coffee cakes.

Prepare:

1 cup freshly cooked riced Boiled Potatoes, 317

Combine and let stand 3 to 5 minutes:

½ cup 105°–115° water
1 package active dry yeast

Place in a separate large bowl:

½ cup lard or shortening

Scald and pour over it:

1 cup milk

Stir until the lard is melted. When the mixture is lukewarm, add the dissolved yeast and the riced potatoes. Add:

3 beaten eggs

¾ cup sugar
2 teaspoons salt

Beat well. Sift before measuring:

5 cups all-purpose flour

Add 4 cups of the flour and beat the batter thoroughly. Stir in the remaining flour, or toss the dough on a board and knead in the flour. To store for chilling, to shape and to prepare for baking, see About Refrigerator Doughs, above. Bake the rolls in a preheated 425° oven about 15 minutes.

REFRIGERATOR WHOLE-GRAIN ROLLS

About Twenty 2-Inch Rolls

Please read About Flours, 545.

Combine and let stand 3 to 5 minutes:

1 cup 105°–115° water
1 package active dry yeast

Beat until creamy:

¼ cup shortening
6 tablespoons sugar

Stir in the yeast mixture. Sift before measuring:

1¾ cups all-purpose flour

Mix in:

1¼ teaspoons salt
1½ cups whole-grain flour

Stir the flour mixture gradually into the yeast mixture. Beat until well blended. To store for chilling, to shape and to prepare for baking, see About Refrigerator Doughs, opposite. Bake in a preheated 425° oven about 15 minutes.

REFRIGERATOR BRAN ROLLS

About Forty-Eight 2-Inch Rolls

These are crisp, crunchy and light.

Combine:

1 cup shortening
¾ cup sugar
1½ to 2 teaspoons salt

Pour over these ingredients and stir until the shortening is melted:

1 cup boiling water

Add:

1 cup bran or bran cereal

In a separate bowl, combine and let stand for 3 to 5 minutes:

1 cup 105°–115° water
2 packages active dry yeast

When the first mixture is lukewarm, add to it:

2 well-beaten eggs

and the dissolved yeast. Add:

6 cups sifted all-purpose flour

Beat the dough well. To store for chilling, to shape and to prepare for baking, see About Refrigerator Doughs, opposite. Bake in a preheated 425° oven about 15 minutes.

ABOUT YEAST COFFEE CAKES

Holidays are an inspiration to bakers. The Portuguese make an Easter bread, hiding within it hard-cooked eggs. Czechoslovakia has **Babka,** which is much like our Panettone, below, baked in a Turk's-head mold pan. And the Russians call our Panettone **Kulich** but bake it in a greased form similar to one of our own 1-pound metal coffee cans.

The following recipes all call for the finest of white flours, but there is no reason why flours of greater nutritional value cannot be substituted. Remember when you are baking bread and rolls that many of these doughs can be made into very acceptable coffee cake and sweet rolls. Try some with the special fillings suggested at the end of this section, 621.

NO-KNEAD YEAST COFFEE CAKE OR PANETTONE

Two 9-Inch Tube Pans

Baked in 1-pound greased coffee cans and attractively packaged, this cake makes wonderful gifts.

Combine and let stand for 3 to 5 minutes:

1 cup 105°–115° water
2 packages active dry yeast

Sift and stir in:

1 cup all-purpose flour

Cover this sponge and let rise about 30 minutes in a warm place. Beat until soft:

½ cup butter

Add gradually and blend until light and creamy:

½ cup sifted sugar

Beat in, one at a time:

2 to 3 eggs

Add:

1 teaspoon salt
2 teaspoons grated lemon rind

Beat in the sponge. Sift and beat in gradually:

3½ cups all-purpose flour

Beat the dough for 5 minutes more. Add:

(⅛ cup chopped citron)
(¼ cup golden raisins or chopped candied pineapple)
(1 cup broken nutmeats)

Cover the bowl with a cloth and let the dough rise about 2 hours or until almost doubled in bulk. Punch down, divide and place in 2 greased tube pans or in greased 1-pound coffee cans and let rise about ½ hour. Lightly brush the tops with:

Melted butter

If no fruit or nutmeats were added to the batter, combine and sprinkle on the dough:

(½ cup shredded blanched almonds)
(¼ cup sugar)

Preheat oven to 350°.

Bake about ½ hour, depending on pan size. If you have omitted the top dressing of almonds and sugar, you may spread on it, after the cake has baked and cooled:

(Milk or Lemon Glaze, 731)

GLAZED FILLED COFFEE CAKE OR BIENENSTICH

A 9 x 12-Inch Cake

Prepare half the recipe for:

Panettone, above

After the first rising, arrange dough in a 9 x 12-inch baking pan and cover with a cooled:

Honey-Bee Glaze, 731

using 1 cup sliced almonds. Let the dough rise until almost doubled, then bake in a preheated 375° oven 15 to 20 minutes. When cool, cut pastry into 3-inch squares. Split each piece and fill with half the recipe for:

Crème Patissière I, 697

★ KNEADED FILLED COFFEE CAKE

Prepare dough for: **2 Loaves**

Buttermilk Potato Rolls, 613,
or White Bread Plus, 603

adding an additional:

¼ cup sugar

To give these breads an interesting color, use the tiniest smidgen of:

Saffron, 587

To let rise and bake, see Stollen, below.

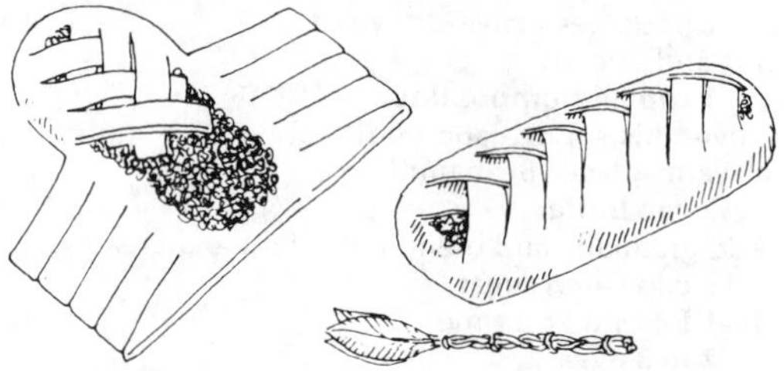

Consider beforehand whether to fashion your cake like a Jelly Roll, 690, to make a filled wreath, 621, or to weave a so-called **alligator,** as shown here. One of the most famous Christmas breads is **Vanocka,** a braided loaf supposed to resemble the Christ Child in swaddling clothes. Ironically enough, the simplified version shown in the chapter heading, 599, can be confected by adapting the "alligator" procedure. To fill, see About Fillings for Coffee Cakes, 621. To glaze, see 731.

★ STOLLEN OR CHRISTMAS LOAF

2 Loaves

Have ready:

6 to 8 cups all-purpose flour

Combine and let stand for 3 to 5 minutes:

1½ cups 105°–115° water or milk
2 packages active dry yeast

Add 1 cup of the flour. Cover this sponge and let it rest in a warm place until light and foamy, about 1 hour. Sprinkle a little of the sifted flour over:

½ lb. raisins
½ lb. chopped blanched almonds
(½ cup chopped candied fruits)

Beat until soft:

1½ cups butter

Add gradually and blend until light and creamy:

¾ cup sifted sugar

Beat in, one at a time:

3 eggs

Add:

¾ teaspoon salt
¾ teaspoon grated lemon rind

Add the sponge and enough flour to knead the dough until smooth and elastic. Cover and let rise until doubled in bulk. Toss it onto a floured board. Knead in the fruit and nuts. Divide the dough into 2 equal pieces. Roll each into an 8 x 15-inch oval. Fold in half lengthwise and place loaves on greased baking sheets. Brush the tops with:

Melted butter

Let the loaves rise, covered, until they again almost double in bulk, about 45 minutes.
Preheat oven to 350°. Bake 30 to 40 minutes or until done. When cool, brush with·

Milk or Lemon Glaze, 731

GUGELHUPF OR BUNDKUCHEN

A true Gugelhupf, shown in the chapter heading, is baked in a fluted tube pan. It is the traditional Name Day cake—not your birthday, but the birthday of the saint for whom you were named. This recipe also makes an excellent Baba or Savarin, 689. For Quick Gugelhupf, see 626.
Have ready:

4 cups all-purpose flour

Scald:

1 cup milk

When cooled to 105°–115°, pour it over:

2 packages active dry yeast

After the yeast has dissolved, beat in 1 cup of the sifted flour. Cover and set the sponge in a warm place until light and frothy, about 1 hour.
Beat until soft:

1 cup butter

Add gradually and blend until light and creamy:

¾ cup sifted sugar

Beat in, one at a time:

5 eggs

Add the sponge, the remaining flour and:

1 teaspoon salt
1 teaspoon grated lemon rind
1 cup seedless raisins

Beat the batter well until smooth and elastic. Spread in the bottom of a greased 10-inch tube pan:

½ cup blanched almonds

Place the dough on top of them and let rise until almost doubled in bulk.
Preheat oven to 350°.
Bake the cake 50 to 60 minutes. The top and sides should be a golden brown. When cool, sprinkle the top with:

Confectioners' sugar

FRUIT-TOPPED YEAST COFFEE CAKE

Four 8-Inch Cakes

For other versions of **Galette,** see 642.
Prepare:

White Bread Plus dough, 603

adding an additional:

¼ cup sugar

After the first rising, pat the dough out thin in the greased pans, prick it well and let it rest. Then make a rim by pinching up the edges all around. Brush the surface with:

Melted butter

or apply a:

French Egg Wash, 731

Although the egg wash always tends to toughen, it does prevent sogginess. Cover the entire surface of the cake with closely placed rows of:

Fruit: sliced pared apples, peeled peaches or plums or seeded cherries

Cover the fruit with:

Streusel, 731, or cinnamon and sugar mixed with butter

Or, after the last rising indicated below, in place of the butter mixture, pour around the fruit the following custard.
Beat:

1 egg yolk
1/4 cup cream

Let the fruit-covered dough rise only half as high as usual for bread.
Preheat oven to 375°.
Bake about 25 minutes, when the fruit should be soft and the cake done.

SCANDINAVIAN COFFEE CAKE OR PASTRY

Two 9-Inch Rings

Call them Danish, Swedish or Norwegian, these light confections fall between rich coffee cakes and rich pastries. The method of folding and rolling the dough, similar to that used in Croissants, 615, accounts for the characteristic flakiness of the superbly light crumb. The basic dough can be used for the ring shown opposite. Fillings and toppings are usually rich in nuts, with a little saffron occasionally added to the flavoring.
Beat well:

2 eggs

Add:

3/4 cup 105°–115° water

Dissolve in this mixture:

1 package active dry yeast

Let all these ingredients rest refrigerated for about 15 minutes. Meanwhile, blend with a pastry blender or by hand:

4 cups sifted all-purpose flour
1 teaspoon salt
2 tablespoons sugar
1/2 cup butter
10 crushed cardamom seeds or
1 1/2 teaspoons powdered cardamom

In a large mixing bowl, make a ring of the blended flour. Pour the chilled yeast mixture into the center and work it gradually into the dry ingredients. Knead until smooth, about 2 minutes. Form the dough into a ball and rest it, covered, about 20 minutes in the refrigerator. Roll out the dough ➤ lightly into an oblong about 3/8 inch thick. Beat until creamy:

1 1/3 to 1 1/2 cups butter

To spread the butter, follow the directions for Croissants, 616, folding and rolling 4 times. Cover and chill the dough at least 2 hours. Then roll it again on a slightly floured surface, to the thickness of 3/8 inch. Cut off any folded edges that might keep the dough from expanding. To shape the ring as shown below, roll it first into an oblong, about 29 x 11 inches. Fill it with any rich filling for coffee cake, below. It is not necessary to shape the roll on a cloth, but you may need to use a spatula or pancake turner to help lift it if the dough should stick to the lightly floured board. Bring the two ends of the roll together, using a little water for glue.

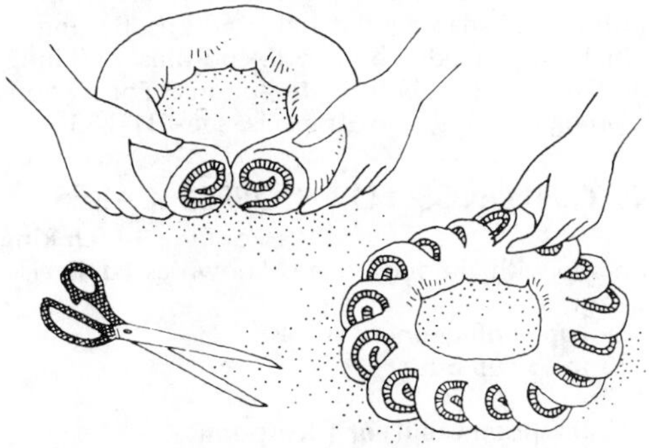

Place the ring on a greased baking sheet. With floured scissors held perpendicular to the roll, cut bias gashes about 1 to 2 inches apart into the upper outer edges of the ring, to within one inch of the inner circle. As you cut, you may turn each partially cut slice flat onto the tin. Sometimes the slices are cut very narrow, and one slice is turned toward the outer rim, the other twisted and turned toward the inner rim; but with these variations, should the filling be generous, it tends to leak and burn on the pan. Wash the top areas with:

French Egg Wash, 731

being careful not to cover the cut portions, as the glaze may harden later too rapidly in baking and inhibit further rising of the dough. Cover the cut ring with a cloth and let rise about 25 minutes, until doubled in bulk.
Preheat the oven to 400° for a ring, to 375° for filled rolls or croissants.
Bake a ring about 25 minutes. Bake rolls about 15 minutes. If a Fruit Glaze, 732, is to be applied, allow the pastry to cool and apply the glaze warm. For other glazes, see 731.

ABOUT SEASONINGS AND FILLINGS FOR COFFEE CAKE

Home cooks often wonder why their coffee cakes and fillings seem insipid in flavor and color when compared with some of the more sophisticated commercial products. First of all, a slight touch of yellow coloring often used in commercial coffee cakes lends them a more convincing "eggy" look. Often, too, for gusto, bakers add to their crumb mixtures crushed macaroons, almond paste, rolled cake crumbs, and finely ground nuts—especially hazelnuts. Sometimes they use pecans, walnuts, almonds and, occasionally, Brazil nuts. Considerably less effective are finely chopped peanuts, coconut and cashews.

The amateur baker may also add distinction to pastry fillings with a small quantity of lemon juice, grated lemon or orange rind, dried currants, a bit of finely chopped citron or finely chopped sweet chocolate. Sometimes they may choose to avoid more solid fillings altogether and substitute a thin layer of jam or marmalade. Fillings are applied during final shaping and before the last rising. A 9-inch ring needs about one-cup-plus of filling, individual rolls about 2 teaspoons. For various Toppings, Glazes, and Streusels, see 731–733.

NUT FILLINGS FOR COFFEE CAKES

I. **For One 9-Inch Ring**

If made with almonds, this is known as **Edelweiss.**
Cream:

½ cup confectioners' sugar
¼ to ½ cup butter

Stir in:

½ teaspoon vanilla or 1 teaspoon grated lemon rind
½ cup shredded or ground blanched almonds or other nuts
(1 egg)

II. **For One 9-Inch Ring**

Combine:

½ cup ground hazelnuts or other nuts
½ cup sugar
2 teaspoons cinnamon
½ teaspoon vanilla
2 tablespoons finely chopped citron or orange peel

Beat well and add:

1 egg

Thin these ingredients with:

Milk

until they are of the right consistency to spread over the dough.

III. **For One 9-Inch Ring**

Chop:

¼ cup each blanched almonds, citron and raisins

Melt:

¼ cup butter, or ⅛ cup butter and ⅛ cup cultured sour cream

After rolling the dough, spread it with the melted butter and the chopped ingredients. Sprinkle with:

(Sugar)
(Cinnamon)

IV. **For Three 9-Inch Rings**

You may buy canned almond paste or make it, 781, for coffee cake fillings. For:

10 oz. almond paste

allow:

1 cup sugar
2 unbeaten egg whites

Work these ingredients in a bowl placed over ice, 205, to keep them cool and to prevent the oil in the almonds from being released.

CRUMB FRUIT FILLING

For One 9-Inch Ring

Mix well:

¾ cup crushed macaroons
3 tablespoons melted butter
2 tablespoons sugar
½ cup raisins or chopped dates, cooked prunes or grated coconut
(¼ cup chopped nuts)

APPLE COFFEE CAKE FILLING

For Two 9-Inch Rings

Combine and boil for 4 minutes:

2½ cups pared and chopped apples
1 cup brown sugar
⅓ cup butter
1 cup raisins
½ teaspoon cinnamon
½ teaspoon salt

Cool slightly and spread over dough.

PRUNE OR APRICOT FILLING FOR COFFEE CAKE AND ROLLS

For One 9-Inch Ring

Combine:

½ cup sweetened puréed prunes or apricots
2 to 4 tablespoons butter
2 teaspoons grated orange or lemon rind
(¼ cup nuts or coconut)

DATE OR FIG FILLING FOR COFFEE CAKE

For One 9-Inch Ring

Melt and simmer about 2 minutes:

¼ cup butter
⅓ cup brown sugar

Remove from heat and stir in:

¾ cup chopped dates or dried figs
¼ cup Almond Paste, 781
½ teaspoon cinnamon
A grating of fresh nutmeg

Cool slightly before using.

POPPY SEED OR MOHN FILLINGS

I. Cockaigne **For One 9-Inch Ring**

This filling is for that special occasion.
Grind or crush in a mortar:

½ cup poppy seeds

Put the poppy seeds in the top of a double boiler and, over direct heat, bring to a boil with:

¼ cup milk

Remove pan from the heat and add:

⅓ cup brown sugar
2 tablespoons butter

Put the pan ➤ over—not in—boiling water and add:

2 egg yolks

Heat until the mixture thickens, stirring constantly. When it has cooled slightly, add:

⅓ cup Almond Paste, 781, or
½ cup ground almonds
(3 tablespoons citron)
(2 teaspoons lemon juice or 1 teaspoon vanilla)

Cool and have ready to add to strudel or use for coffee cake.

II. **For Two 9-Inch Rings**

Mix together well:

¾ cup ground poppy seeds
¼ cup sugar
¼ cup raisins
½ cup sour cream
⅛ teaspoon cinnamon
1 teaspoon grated lemon rind

III. **For Four 9-Inch Rings**

Grind or mash between towels with a wooden mallet:

2 cups poppy seeds

Mix in:

1 egg
⅓ cup honey
1 tablespoon lemon juice
¼ cup chopped nuts

IV. **For One 9-Inch Ring**

Grind or mash between towels with a wooden mallet:

¼ cup poppy seeds

Place the ground seeds in a bowl and add:

About 2 tablespoons milk

just enough to make this mixture feel buttery between your fingers. Then add:

2 tablespoons melted butter
2 tablespoons dry cake crumbs
1 teaspoon cinnamon
1 teaspoon grated lemon rind

POT-CHEESE OR RICOTTA FILLING

For One 9-Inch Coffee Cake Ring

Put through a ricer or a strainer:

1½ cups pot or Ricotta cheese

Mix well with:

¼ cup sugar
1 slightly beaten egg yolk
¼ to ½ cup raisins
2 teaspoons grated lemon rind

Beat until ➤ stiff, but not dry, and fold in:

1 egg white

ABOUT QUICK TEA BREADS AND COFFEE CAKES

These sweet breads are delightful but, with the exception of nut and fruit breads, should be served immediately after baking; they wither young. If you want breads that keep and reheat well, see recipes for yeast breads and yeast coffee cakes. Also see Additions to Yeast Doughs and the Cornell Formula, 602, to enrich these breads.

Nut and fruit breads are attractive baked in 6-oz. metal juice cans so that they slice prettily for tea. If you use cans, do not fill them more than three-fourths full to allow for expansion of the dough, and bake for less time than a loaf. Quick nut and fruit breads slice better if, after baking and cooling, they are wrapped in foil and refrigerated about 12 hours.

▲ When baking quick breads at high altitudes, reduce the baking powder or soda in the recipe by one-fourth. ➤ But do not decrease the soda to less than ½ teaspoon for each cup of sour milk or cream used.

QUICK NUT OR DATE BREAD

A 9 x 5-Inch Loaf

Preheat oven to 350°.
➤ Have all ingredients at about 70°.
Sift into a bowl:

2 cups all-purpose flour
⅓ cup white or ½ cup brown sugar
2 teaspoons double-acting baking powder
1 teaspoon salt

Melt and cool slightly:

2 tablespoons butter

Beat until light:

1 egg

Beat with the egg:

1 cup milk
(½ teaspoon vanilla)

Add the melted butter. Beat the liquid ingredients into the sifted ones until well mixed. Fold in:

¾ cup chopped nutmeats, or part dates and part nutmeats

Place the dough in a greased bread pan and bake about 40 minutes.

QUICK HONEY LOAF

Prepare:

Quick Nut Bread, above

increasing the flour by ½ cup and omitting the sugar. Add:

¾ cup honey
½ teaspoon baking soda

QUICK SALLY LUNN

A 9 x 13-Inch Pan

A light sweet bread. For an even lighter one, try Brioche Loaf Cockaigne, 605, or Brioche, 615.
➤ Have all ingredients at about 70°.
Preheat oven to 425°.
Sift together:

2 cups sifted all-purpose flour
2¼ teaspoons double-acting baking powder
¾ teaspoon salt

Combine and cream well:

½ cup shortening
½ cup sugar

Beat in, one at a time:

3 eggs

Add the sifted ingredients to the batter in about 3 parts, alternately with:

1 cup milk

Stir the batter lightly ➤ until the ingredients are just blended. Bake in a greased pan about 30 minutes. Break the bread into squares. Serve hot.

QUICK PRUNE, APRICOT, APPLE OR CRANBERRY BREAD

A 9 x 5-Inch Loaf

➤ Have all ingredients at about 70°.
Preheat oven to 350°.
Sift together:

1½ cups sifted all-purpose flour
½ teaspoon salt
1 teaspoon baking soda

Add:

1½ cups whole-grain flour

Cream in a large bowl:

¼ cup shortening

with:

½ cup sugar

Beat in:

1 egg

Add:

¾ cup unsweetened, cooked, mashed prune, apricot or cranberry pulp or freshly grated apple
¼ cup prune, apricot or cranberry juice

Add the sifted ingredients alternately to the fruit mixture with:

1 cup buttermilk

Stir the batter ➤ with a few swift strokes, until just blended. Fold in:

1 cup broken nutmeats
(Grated rind of 1 orange)

Place the dough in a greased loaf pan. Bake the bread about 1¼ hours, letting it cool in the pan.

QUICK ORANGE BREAD

Two 8½ x 4½-Inch Loaves

This is an economical, easily made tea bread. If you want a quick treat, break it apart and eat it while hot, with or without lots of good butter. If you intend it for sandwiches, bake it in cans, see About Quick Tea Breads, 623. You'll find it easier to slice on the second day.

➤ Have all ingredients at about 70°.
Preheat oven to 350°.
Sift together into a large bowl:

3 cups sifted all-purpose flour
3 teaspoons double-acting baking powder
½ teaspoon salt

Combine and add:

1 tablespoon grated orange rind
½ to ¾ cup sugar

For a more cakelike result, use the larger amount of sugar. Combine and beat:

1 egg
¼ cup orange juice
1¼ cups milk
2 tablespoons melted shortening

Add:

(1 cup chopped or broken nutmeats)

Pour the liquid mixture into the bowl. Combine all ingredients with a few swift strokes. Stir lightly until barely blended. Bake the bread in two greased loaf pans about 50 minutes or until done.

QUICK BANANA BREAD

An 8½ x 4½-Inch Loaf

➤ Have all ingredients at about 70°.
Preheat oven to 350°.
Sift together:

1¾ cups sifted all-purpose flour
2¼ teaspoons double-acting baking powder
½ teaspoon salt

Blend until creamy:

⅓ cup shortening
⅔ cup sugar
¾ teaspoon grated lemon rind

Beat in:

1 to 2 beaten eggs
1 to 1¼ cups ripe banana pulp

Add the sifted ingredients in about 3 parts to the sugar mixture. Beat the batter after each addition until smooth. Fold in:

(½ cup broken nutmeats)
(¼ cup finely chopped dried apricots)

Place the batter in a greased bread pan. Bake the bread about 1 hour or until done. Cool before slicing.

QUICK BANANA WHEAT-GERM BREAD

Prepare:

Banana Bread, above

Use in all:

1½ cups all-purpose flour

Add:

¼ cup wheat germ

QUICK PUMPKIN BREAD

One 9 x 5-Inch Loaf

Preheat oven to 350°.
Sift together:

1¾ cups sifted all-purpose flour
¼ teaspoon double-acting baking powder
1 teaspoon baking soda
1 teaspoon salt
½ teaspoon cinnamon
¼ teaspoon ground cloves

In a large bowl, beat until light and fluffy:

1⅓ cups sugar
⅓ cup soft shortening
2 eggs

Add and beat in:

1 cup cooked or canned pumpkin

Now add the sifted dry ingredients in 3 additions alternately with:

⅓ cup water or milk
(½ teaspoon vanilla)

Do not overbeat between each addition. Fold in:

½ cup coarsely chopped nuts
⅓ cup raisins or chopped dates

Pour batter into a greased pan and bake about 1 hour or until bread tests done, see 602.

QUICK CARROT-NUT BREAD

One 5 x 9-Inch Loaf

Preheat oven to 350°.
Sift together:

1½ cups sifted all-purpose flour
1½ teaspoons baking soda
¼ teaspoon cinnamon

Add:

¾ cup sugar
2 beaten eggs
½ cup vegetable oil
1 teaspoon vanilla
½ teaspoon salt

Blend in with a few swift strokes:

1½ cups grated carrots
1½ cups ground pecans or walnuts

Bake in a greased pan about 1 hour. Cool in the pan 10 minutes, then turn out onto a rack for further cooling.

double it; subst. nuts w/ raisins & bake in a 9x13 pan, 35-45 min.

QUICK OLIVE-NUT BREAD

One 4½ x 8½-Inch Loaf

Sliced thin, this makes a very good canapé or sandwich base.
Preheat oven to 350°.
Sift together:

1½ cups sifted all-purpose flour
4 teaspoons double-acting baking powder
½ teaspoon salt

Add:

1 cup whole wheat flour

Mix together:

1 beaten egg
1 cup milk
2 tablespoons melted butter

Combine the milk and flour mixtures with a few swift strokes, then add:

1 cup sliced stuffed green olives
1 cup chopped nuts

Bake in a greased pan about 45 minutes.

QUICK IRISH SODA BREAD

An 8-Inch Round Loaf

Preheat oven to 375°.
Sift together in a large bowl:

2 cups sifted all-purpose flour
1½ teaspoons double-acting baking powder
½ teaspoon baking soda
½ teaspoon salt
1 tablespoon sugar

Cut into the flour with a pastry blender, until the mixture has the consistency of coarse cornmeal:

¼ cup chilled shortening

Stir in:

½ to 1 cup raisins or currants
2 teaspoons caraway seeds

Mix together:

1 beaten egg
⅔ cup buttermilk

Add to dry ingredients and stir well. Knead briefly and place in a greased 8-inch round pan. Press down so dough will fill the pan. Cut a bold cross over the top and sides so the bread will not crack in baking. Brush the top with:

Milk

Bake 35 to 40 minutes.
To bake ⊟ outdoors, see Skillet Bread, 627.

QUICK SWEET WHOLE WHEAT BREAD

A 9 x 5-Inch Loaf

A homely coarse sweet bread, delightful served with fruit salads and cottage cheese.
Preheat oven to 375°.
Mix:

2½ cups whole wheat flour
½ teaspoon cinnamon
¼ teaspoon salt
2 teaspoons double-acting baking powder
1 teaspoon baking soda

Combine:

1 beaten egg
½ cup molasses
¼ cup brown sugar
¼ cup vegetable oil
1 teaspoon grated lemon or orange peel

Add the flour mixture, alternately with:

⅔ cup yogurt or buttermilk

to the above ingredients. Pour into a greased pan and bake about 50 minutes.

QUICK BRAN DATE BREAD

Two 8½ x 4½-Inch Loaves

Preheat oven to 350°.
Prepare:

2 cups chopped dates

Pour over them:

2 cups boiling water

In a separate bowl, beat until light:

2 eggs

Add slowly, beating constantly:

¾ cup brown sugar or ½ cup molasses

When these ingredients are creamy, add:

1 cup whole-grain flour
2 teaspoons double-acting baking powder
1 teaspoon baking soda

Add half the date mixture and:

1 cup whole-grain flour
2 cups bran
1 teaspoon vanilla

Add the remaining date mixture and:

1 cup or less chopped nutmeats

Place the dough in lightly greased loaf pans. Bake about 1 hour.

EGGLESS ALL-RYE HONEY CAKE COCKAIGNE

One 7¼ x 3⅝-Inch Loaf

Like a soft, deliciously spiced **Lebkuchen,** this confection keeps for weeks. The dough is stiff to beat and does not make a very high loaf, but it toasts well for tea. Age it three days or more in a plastic bag or tin box before eating.

Preheat oven to 350°.

Heat in the top of a double boiler until small bubbles appear through the mixture:

⅓ cup honey
¾ cup water
½ cup sugar

Remove from heat and beat it into the following mixture:

2 cups very finely milled rye flour
½ teaspoon baking soda
2 teaspoons double-acting baking powder
1 tablespoon cinnamon
½ teaspoon each cloves and allspice
⅛ teaspoon cardamom

Beat 10 minutes with an electric beater. Add:

¼ cup pecans or blanched shredded almonds
1 tablespoon grated orange rind
¼ to ½ cup finely chopped citron

Place a pan of water on the bottom shelf of the oven. Bake the cake in a greased loaf pan about 1 hour.

BAKED BROWN BREAD

One 9 x 5-Inch Loaf

Preheat oven to 350°.

Sift together:

1 cup sifted all-purpose flour
2 tablespoons sugar
¾ teaspoon salt
1 teaspoon baking soda

Stir in:

2 cups graham flour
1 cup buttermilk
1 cup dark molasses

You may add:

1 cup broken nutmeats and/or raisins

Combine all ingredients and bake in a greased 9 x 5-inch loaf pan about 1 hour; or in four 10-ounce buttered molds 30 to 40 minutes.

BOSTON STEAMED BROWN BREAD

Two 1-Pound Loaves or
Two 1-Quart Pudding Molds

➤ Please read About Steamed Puddings, 753.

Combine:

1 cup yellow stone-ground cornmeal
1 cup rye flour
1 cup graham flour
2 teaspoons baking soda
1 teaspoon salt

Combine in a separate bowl:

2 cups buttermilk
¾ cup molasses
1 cup chopped raisins

One of our friends soaks the raisins overnight in brandy! Add the liquid to the dry ingredients. Pour the batter into 2 buttered 1-quart pudding molds or fill 1-pound buttered coffee cans about three-fourths full. Butter the lids before closing molds and tie the lids on, so rising bread does not break the seal. Aluminum foil may be used as a lid; make sure the seal is tight. ➤ Steam 3 hours in 1 inch of water. To cut without crumbling, use a tough string and slice with a sawing motion.

QUICK COFFEE CAKE OR KUCHEN

A 9 x 9-Inch Pan

We prize this coffee cake for a Sunday brunch, topping it with drained sugared blueberries or pitted cherries distributed over the batter before baking.

Preheat oven to 375°.

Sift together:

1½ cups sifted all-purpose flour
¼ teaspoon salt
2 teaspoons double-acting baking powder

Cream until soft in a large bowl:

¼ cup butter

Add gradually and cream until light:

¼ to ½ cup sugar

Beat in:

1 egg
⅔ cup milk

Add the sifted ingredients to the butter mixture. Add:

(¾ teaspoon grated lemon rind or
½ teaspoon vanilla)

Stir the batter until smooth. Spread in a greased pan. Cover with:

Streusel, 731, or
Honey-Bee Glaze, 731

or with fruits mentioned above. Bake about 25 minutes.

QUICK GUGELHUPF

A 7-Inch Tube Pan

➤ Have all ingredients at about 70°.

Preheat oven to 350°.

Sift together:

3½ cups sifted all-purpose flour
3 teaspoons double-acting baking powder
½ teaspoon salt

Cream in a large bowl until soft:

1 cup butter

Add gradually and cream until very light:

1 cup sifted sugar

Beat in, one at a time:

5 eggs

Add the flour mixture in 3 parts, alternately with:

1 cup milk

Stir the batter until smooth after each addition. Add:

1 cup seedless white raisins
1 teaspoon grated lemon rind
1 teaspoon vanilla

Bake the cake in a greased tube pan 45 to 50 minutes. When cool, sprinkle with:

Confectioners' sugar

QUICK SOUR CREAM COFFEE CAKE

A 9 x 9-Inch Pan

Made on a muffin principle, this cake is wonderfully good and easy. When it is served fresh, its smooth texture approximates that of a sourdough coffee cake.

➤ Have all ingredients at about 70°.
Preheat oven to 350°.
Sift together:

1½ cups sifted all-purpose flour
1 cup sugar
2 teaspoons double-acting baking powder
½ teaspoon baking soda
¼ teaspoon salt

Combine and beat well:

1 cup cultured sour cream
2 eggs

Add the sifted ingredients to the cream mixture. Beat until just smooth ➤ as overbeating tends to toughen dough. Spread in a lightly greased pan. Sprinkle with:

Streusel, 731

Bake about 20 minutes.

BISHOP'S BREAD

Prepare the batter for:

Quick Sour Cream Coffee Cake, above

Add:

2 oz. grated unsweetened chocolate
1 cup chopped dates
1 cup chopped nuts

Bake as directed.

QUICK SPICE COFFEE CAKE WITH OIL

An 8 x 8 x 2½-Inch Pan

➤ Have all ingredients at about 70°.
Preheat oven to 350°.
Combine in a mixing bowl:

2 cups sifted all-purpose flour
⅔ cup sugar
¾ teaspoon double-acting baking powder
¾ teaspoon baking soda
½ teaspoon salt
½ teaspoon freshly grated nutmeg
1 teaspoon cinnamon

Combine in another bowl and mix well:

½ cup vegetable oil
1 beaten egg
½ cup buttermilk or yogurt
⅓ cup light or dark corn syrup
¾ cup raisins

Pour this into the flour mixture, stirring rapidly until blended. All the lumps need not have vanished. Pour into a greased pan and cover with:

Streusel I, 731

Bake the cake about 35 minutes.

SKILLET OR GRIDDLE BREADS

Either:

Irish Soda Bread, 625, or
Skillet Corn Bread, 628

will make acceptable, even good, skillet bread on an open fire ⊟ especially over charcoal. But our results on these heats did not compare in quality with those obtained when the same recipes were oven-baked. Bake them covered. If you prefer **Irish Farls,** use the Irish Soda Bread recipe and cut the bread in triangular wedges about 1 inch thick and bake on a griddle heated to about 370° and lightly rubbed with oil. Allow about 10 minutes for one side; turn and allow 10 minutes more.

ABOUT CORN BREADS

Anyone who grew up on southern corn breads hankers for a rich brown crust and a light but slightly gritty bite. We can assure you that without stone-ground cornmeal and a heavy, hot pan, the end product will be pale and lifeless. For a very crisp crust, grease the pan well and heat it in a 425° oven before filling. Whether you bake as muffins, sticks or bread, you may vary the corn and wheat proportion within a 2-cup limit, to your own taste. We like 1¼ cups cornmeal to ¾ cup all-purpose flour. Try, if you like, adding a little minced onion, shredded cheddar cheese, cream-style corn or bits of cooked ham or bacon. Many southern cooks use no sugar, but for a distinctive flavor, try dark brown sugar instead of granulated.

▲ When baking corn breads at high altitudes, reduce the baking powder or soda by one-fourth. ➤ But do not reduce soda to less than ½ teaspoon for each cup of buttermilk or sour cream used.

CORN BREAD, MUFFINS OR STICKS

A 9 x 9-Inch Pan, or
About Fifteen 2-Inch Muffins

➤ Have all ingredients at about 70°.
Preheat oven to 425°.
Grease the pan with butter, oil or bacon drippings. Place it in the oven until sizzling hot.
Sift together:

¾ cup sifted all-purpose flour
2½ teaspoons double-acting baking powder
1 to 2 tablespoons sugar
¾ teaspoon salt

Add:

1¼ cups yellow or white stone-ground cornmeal

Beat in a separate bowl:

1 egg

Beat into it:

2 to 3 tablespoons melted butter or drippings
1 cup milk

Combine all ingredients with a few rapid strokes. Place the batter in the hot pan. Bake sticks about 15 minutes, corn bread and muffins 20 to 25 minutes. Serve immediately.

SKILLET CORN BREAD

Prepare:

Corn Bread, above

⊟ Cook it in a 10-inch covered skillet for about ½ hour or until done. You may add to the dough:

(¼ to ½ cup cooked ham or bacon bits)

BUCKWHEAT CORN BREAD

Prepare:

Corn Bread, above

and substitute for ½ cup of the cornmeal:

½ cup buckwheat flour

and add:

(¼ cup hulled sunflower seeds)

BUTTERMILK CRACKLING CORN BREAD

A 9 x 9-Inch Pan or Twenty 2-Inch Muffins

➤ Have all ingredients at about 70°.

Preheat oven to 425°.

Sift together:

1 cup sifted all-purpose flour
½ teaspoon baking soda
1½ teaspoons double-acting baking powder
1 tablespoon sugar
1 teaspoon salt

Add:

¾ cup yellow stone-ground cornmeal

Combine and beat:

1½ cups buttermilk or yogurt
2 eggs
3 to 4 tablespoons melted butter or fresh bacon drippings

Stir the liquid into the dry ingredients with a few swift strokes. Add:

(¼ cup salt pork cracklings)

Pour the batter into a preheated greased pan. Bake the bread 25 to 30 minutes, muffins 15.

SOURDOUGH CORN BREAD

A 10-Inch Skillet or Two 8-Inch Round Pans

A moist heavy bread, best served hot from the oven.

Preheat oven to 450°.

Thoroughly mix together in a large bowl:

1 cup Sourdough Starter, 555
1½ cups yellow cornmeal
½ teaspoon salt
¾ teaspoon baking soda
2 tablespoons sugar
¼ cup melted butter
1½ cups evaporated milk
2 beaten eggs

Pour into a 10-inch greased skillet or two 8-inch round cake pans and bake 25 to 30 minutes.

CORN ZEPHYRS COCKAIGNE

About Twenty 2-Inch Puffs

In our endless search for the best recipe of its type, we welcomed the offer of a southern acquaintance to send us the Zephyr recipe she was raving about. When it arrived, it turned out to be word for word our own favorite Zephyr recipe in **Joy.** We consider this the highest of compliments. These puffs are delicate and delicious with a salad course or luncheon dish.

Combine:

1 cup white stone-ground cornmeal
1 tablespoon lard

Scald these ingredients by pouring over them:

4 cups boiling water

Add:

1 teaspoon salt

Cook the cornmeal over low heat 30 minutes, stirring frequently. Before cooling it, butter the top slightly to keep it from crusting. Cool.

Preheat oven to 350°.

Whip until stiff:

4 egg whites

Fold them lightly into the cornmeal mixture. Drop the batter from a teaspoon onto a greased baking sheet. Bake about ½ hour.

GOLDEN CORN PUFFS

About Twenty 2-Inch Puffs

Pour:

2¼ cups boiling water

over:

1 cup yellow stone-ground cornmeal

Add:

1 tablespoon sugar
1 teaspoon salt
2 tablespoons butter

Cook and stir over low heat until you obtain a thick mush. Cool and beat well.

Preheat oven to 425°.

Beat in:

2 beaten egg yolks

Beat until stiff, then fold in:

2 egg whites

Drop the batter from a teaspoon onto a hot greased baking sheet. Bake the puffs about 20 minutes.

CORN DODGERS COCKAIGNE

About 24

Preheat oven to 400°.

Combine:

1 cup stone-ground cornmeal
1 teaspoon salt
1½ teaspoons sugar

Pour over the dry ingredients and stir:

1 cup boiling water

Beat in until blended:

2 tablespoons butter or bacon drippings
(1 beaten egg)

Drop the batter from a spoon onto a greased baking sheet; or dip your hand in cold water, fill it with batter and release the batter "splat" onto the sheet. The hand method was learned from our Sarah, who, as a child, helped her father make dodgers at the Kentucky Derby. Bake about 20 minutes.

TORTILLAS

12 Tortillas

Large tortillas are served as a substitute for bread; small ones may be filled, see Tacos, 70. A tortilla press is helpful if you are planning to make them often.

Combine by mixing well with hands:

2 cups corn flour: masa harina
1 to 1⅓ cups warm water
1 teaspoon salt

Dough should be moist but stiff enough to hold its shape. Divide into 12 balls and press each between waxed paper on a tortilla press, or between the palms of your hands, or with a flat plate, until a thin round cake is formed. Peel waxed paper from one side of the tortilla and place dough on a hot ungreased griddle. Remove other piece of waxed paper. Cook one at a time until edges begin to curl and they are very slightly browned. Turn and cook till puffs appear. Wrap in a dampened cloth and foil and keep warm in oven.

CRUSTY SOFT-CENTER SPOON BREAD

4 Servings

Preheat oven to 375°.

Sift together:

¼ cup all-purpose flour
1 tablespoon sugar
1 teaspoon salt
1 teaspoon double-acting baking powder

Add:

¾ cup yellow cornmeal

Stir in until well blended:

1 beaten egg
1 cup milk

Melt in a high-rimmed 8 x 8-inch baking dish:

2 tablespoons butter

Pour in the batter. Pour over the top:

½ cup milk

Bake 45 minutes or more, until good and crusty.

BUTTERMILK SPOON BREAD

4 Servings

Pour:

1½ cups boiling water

over:

1 cup white cornmeal

Mix well and cool slightly.

Preheat oven to 350°.

Beat well before adding:

1 egg
1 tablespoon butter
1 cup buttermilk
1 teaspoon baking soda
¾ teaspoon salt

Pour the batter into a hot, greased 7-inch baking dish. Bake 30 to 40 minutes. If you wish to keep the top soft, add from time to time, while the bread is baking, a few tablespoons of milk. For this purpose, use in all:

½ cup milk or thin cream

This process calls for longer baking than the above, about 1 hour in all.

RICE OR MILLET SPOON BREAD

6 Servings

In Mexico, chopped green chilis or scallions and shredded cheddar cheese are added. In Italy, bits of cooked ham and cooked seafood are incorporated into the batter, which is baked until very crisp.

Preheat oven to 325°.

➤ If you use buttermilk, include the baking soda; otherwise, omit it. Combine in the order given, then stir until blended:

1 cup cooked rice or millet
¼ cup cornmeal
2 cups milk or buttermilk
(½ teaspoon baking soda)
1 teaspoon salt
2 beaten eggs
2 tablespoons melted shortening or butter

Place the batter in a greased ovenproof dish. Bake about 1 hour. The spoon bread may be served with:

Mushroom Sauce, 348, or
Tomatoes Provençale, 332

HUSH PUPPIES

About Twelve 2½-Inch Puppies

Fishermen used to cook these finger-shaped concoctions on the river bank, along with their catch. Rumor has it that they threw a large number to their clamorous dogs with the admonition, "Hush, puppy!" Sometimes we think that is still the best use for them.

Mix together:

1 cup stone-ground cornmeal
1 teaspoon double-acting baking powder
½ teaspoon salt
2 to 3 tablespoons minced onion

Beat together:

1 egg
½ cup milk

Combine with dry ingredients and form into oblong cakes or pones, about 2 x 4 x ¾ inches. Fry in deep fat heated to 370° until golden brown. Drain on paper toweling and serve at once.

ABOUT MUFFINS

Muffin batters are easily made. ➤ To mix, add in a few swift strokes the beaten liquid ingredients to the combined sifted dry ones. ➤ The mixing is held to an absolute minimum, a light stirring of from 10 to 20 seconds, which will leave some lumps. Ignore them. The dough should not be mixed to the point of pouring, ribbonlike, from the spoon, but should break in coarse globs. If the batter has been beaten too long, the gluten in the flour will develop and toughen the dough; and the grain of the muffin will be coarse and full of tunnels, as shown in the cross section on the right below.

Good muffins should be straight-sided and rounded on top, as shown on the left. The grain of the muffin is not fine but uniform and the crumb moist. The center drawings show, first, the weary muffin peak caused by oven heat that is too slow. The next drawing shows the cracked, wobbly-peaked, unsymmetrical shape caused by oven heat that is too high.

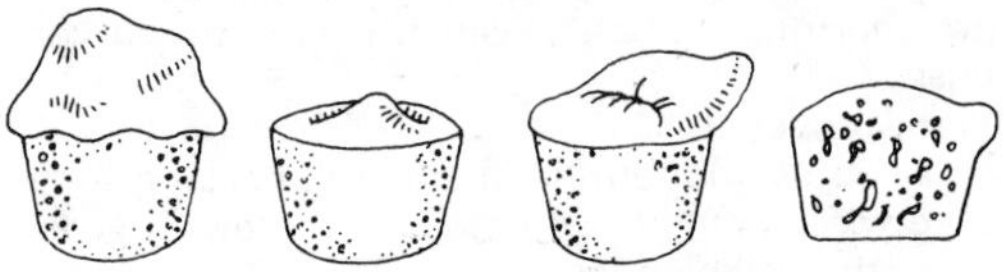

To bake, fill well-greased tins about two-thirds full. Should the dough not fill every muffin cup, put a few tablespoons of water in the empty forms, both to protect the pans and to keep the rest of the muffins moist. Unless a different indication is given in the individual recipe ➤ bake at once in a preheated 400° oven 20 to 25 minutes. ➤ If muffins remain in the tins a few moments after leaving the oven, they will be easier to remove. They are really best eaten very promptly. If you must reheat them, enclose them loosely in foil and heat about 5 minutes in a preheated 450° oven.

ADDITIONS TO MUFFINS

Muffins may be enriched by these additions, but have them all ready and beat them in so that the total beating time agrees exactly with the one described above.

I. Use any of the following as a single ingredient or in combination:

¼ to ½ cup nuts, riced apricots, prunes, dates, figs
½ cup chopped cranberries plus 2 teaspoons grated orange rind
½ cup mashed ripe bananas or chopped apples
½ cup very well drained crushed pineapple
6 to 8 slices cooked bacon, crumbled

II. **Cornell Triple-Rich Formula, 602**

III. **For other suggestions, see Additions to Yeast Doughs, 602**

MUFFINS

About 2 Dozen 2-Inch Muffins

Please read About Muffins, above.
Preheat oven to 400°.
Sift together:
1¾ cups sifted all-purpose flour
¾ teaspoon salt
¼ cup sugar
2 teaspoons double-acting baking powder
Beat in a separate bowl:
2 eggs
Add to the eggs:
2 to 4 tablespoons melted butter
¾ cup milk
Combine the liquid and the dry ingredients with a few swift strokes. Fill well-greased muffin pans two-thirds full and bake 20 to 25 minutes.

SOUR CREAM MUFFINS

About 2 Dozen 2-Inch Muffins

Please read About Muffins, 629.
Preheat oven to 400°.
Sift together:
1¾ cups sifted all-purpose flour
1 teaspoon double-acting baking powder
½ teaspoon salt
2 tablespoons sugar
½ teaspoon baking soda
Beat together:
1 cup cultured sour cream
1 beaten egg
2 tablespoons milk or water
➤ To mix and bake, see Muffins, above.

BUTTERMILK MUFFINS

Prepare:
Sour Cream Muffins, above
Substitute for the sour cream:
1 cup buttermilk
Add to the milk:
3 tablespoons melted butter

WHOLE-GRAIN MUFFINS

Twenty 2-Inch Muffins

Please read About Muffins, 629.
Preheat oven to 400°.
Combine:
⅔ cup sifted all-purpose flour
1⅓ cups whole-grain flour
1 teaspoon salt
2 teaspoons double-acting baking powder
(¼ cup chopped dates, raisins or roasted pumpkin seeds)
Beat in a separate bowl:
1 beaten egg
2 tablespoons molasses or honey
1 cup milk
2 to 3 teaspoons melted butter
➤ To mix and bake, see Muffins, above.

BRAN MUFFINS

About Twenty-Two 2-Inch Muffins

These muffins are rather hefty. Served with cheese, they make excellent picnic companions. Please read About Muffins, 629.
Preheat oven to 350°.
Combine and stir well:
2 cups all-purpose or whole-grain flour
1½ cups bran
2 tablespoons sugar
¼ teaspoon salt

1¼ teaspoons baking soda
(1 to 2 tablespoons grated orange rind)

Beat:

2 cups buttermilk
1 beaten egg
½ cup molasses
2 to 4 tablespoons melted butter

Combine the dry and the liquid ingredients with a few swift strokes. Fold in, before the dry ingredients are entirely moist:

1 cup nutmeats, or nutmeats and raisins combined, or 1 cup chopped dates

Bake about 25 minutes.

RICE FLOUR MUFFINS

About Two Dozen 2-Inch Muffins

Please read ➤ About Rice Flour, 549, and About Muffins, 629. Read the recipe through before mixing.
Preheat oven to 450°.
Measure into a bowl:

1 cup rice flour
½ teaspoon salt
2 teaspoons double-acting baking powder
1 to 2 tablespoons sugar

Melt:

2 tablespoons shortening

and, when slightly cooled, add it to:

1 well-beaten egg
1 cup milk

Mix the dry ingredients well and then with a few light strokes combine with the liquid mixture. About 10 strokes should suffice. The muffins are less crumbly if you add to them, before the dry ingredients are completely moistened:

⅛ cup raisins or 2 tablespoons orange or pineapple marmalade

If you include the marmalade, omit the sugar. Bake 12 to 15 minutes and serve at once.

COOKED-CEREAL MUFFINS

About Thirty 2-Inch Muffins

A good way of utilizing leftover cereals or rice. Please read About Muffins, 629.
Preheat oven to 400°.
Beat:

2 egg yolks

Add:

1 cup cooked rice, oatmeal or cornmeal
1¼ cups milk
2 tablespoons melted butter

Sift together:

1½ cups sifted all-purpose flour
1 tablespoon sugar
½ teaspoon salt
2 teaspoons double-acting baking powder

Beat until stiff ➤ but not dry:

2 egg whites

Combine the liquid and the dry ingredients with a few swift strokes, then fold in the egg whites. To bake, see Muffins, 629.

CHEESE MUFFINS

About Thirty-Two 2-Inch Muffins

Please read About Muffins, 629.
Preheat oven to 350°.
Sift together:

1¾ cups sifted all-purpose flour
3 teaspoons double-acting baking powder
1 tablespoon sugar
½ teaspoon salt

Stir into the sifted ingredients, until all the particles of cheese have been separated:

½ cup grated American cheese

Combine and beat well:

1 egg
1 cup milk
3 tablespoons melted butter

➤ To mix and bake, see Muffins, 629.

PUMPKIN OR YAM MUFFINS

About Twenty-Four 2-Inch Muffins

Prepare:

Muffins, 630

but add to the dry ingredients:

¼ cup additional sugar
1 teaspoon cinnamon
1 teaspoon nutmeg

Add to the milk mixture:

1 cup canned pumpkin or 1 cup cold cooked mashed yams

You may add:

(1 cup chopped pecans)
(2 teaspoons grated orange rind)

Proceed as for Muffins, 630.

BLUEBERRY OR CRANBERRY MUFFINS

About Thirty 2-Inch Muffins

Please read About Muffins, 629.
Prepare:

Muffins, 630

Use in all:

⅓ cup sugar
¼ cup melted butter

Fold into the batter, before the dry ingredients are completely moist:

1 cup fresh blueberries; 1 cup well-drained canned blueberries, lightly floured; or 1 cup chopped cranberries
(1 teaspoon grated orange or lemon rind)

Proceed as for Muffins, 630.

POPOVERS

About 9 Popovers

Everyone enthusiastically gives us a favorite popover recipe, and all are equally enthusiastic, but contradictory, about baking advice. We prefer a preheated oven, but we know that starting with a cold oven also works. Have ready buttered deep muffin or popover tins. If you use highly glazed deep custard cups, grease them lightly and—depending on what you are serving with the popovers—dust the cups with sugar, flour or grated

Parmesan cheese. This will give the batter something to cling to. Have all ingredients at 70°.
Preheat oven to 450°.
Beat just until smooth:

1 cup milk
1 tablespoon melted butter
1 cup sifted all-purpose flour
¼ teaspoon salt

Add, one at a time, but ➤ do not overbeat:

2 beaten eggs

The batter should be no heavier than whipping cream. Fill the buttered baking cups three-fourths full. Don't overload—too much batter in the pans will give a muffinlike texture. ➤ Bake at once. After 15 minutes, lower the heat ➤ without peeping, to 350° and bake about 20 minutes longer. To test for doneness, remove a popover to be sure the side walls are firm. If not cooked long enough, the popovers will collapse. You may want to insert a sharp paring knife gently into the other popovers to allow the steam to escape, after baking.

CHEESE POPOVERS

Preheat oven to 450°.
Prepare:

Popovers, above

Grate into a separate bowl:

½ cup sharp cheddar or Parmesan cheese

Add:

⅛ teaspoon paprika
A few grains cayenne

Pour 1 scant tablespoon of batter into each cup and cover it with a few teaspoons of cheese and another tablespoon of batter. Bake as directed for Popovers, above.

ABOUT HOT BISCUITS

Now, as in pioneer times, biscuits are popular for the speed with which they can be made. A light hand in kneading gives the treasured flaky result. The amount of liquid called for in the recipe determines whether the biscuit is a rolled or dropped type. The shortening is ➤ cut into the dry ingredients with a pastry blender or 2 knives, until the mixture is the consistency of coarse cornmeal. Make a well in the center of these ingredients. ➤ Pour all the milk or milk and water in at once. Stir cautiously until there is no danger of spilling, then stir vigorously until the dough is fairly free from the sides of the bowl. The time for stirring should be a scant ½ minute.

Turn the dough onto a lightly floured board. ➤ Knead it gently and quickly for another scant ½ minute—just long enough so it is neither knobby nor sticky, and the riser is well distributed. If it isn't, or if soda is used in excess, tiny brown spots will show on the surface of the baked biscuits. Roll the dough with a lightly floured rolling pin or pat it gently with the palm of the hand until it has the desired thickness—about ¼ inch is right for the plain biscuit, ½ inch or less for a tea biscuit and 1 inch or more for shortcake. Cut the dough in typical rounds, with a biscuit cutter that has been lightly dipped in flour. ➤ Do not twist the cutter.

There are many other ways to shape biscuit dough. For easy filled biscuits, pat out 2 thin squares of dough. Put a filling on the first. Cover with the second. Glaze the top with milk. Cut into smaller squares. For a breakfast ring, see Quick Drop Biscuits, 633. Make Biscuit Easter Bunnies for the children, 634. You may also place small rounds of dough on top of a casserole. Or cut dough in sticks for hors d'oeuvre or fill as for Pinwheels, 613. Use a spatula to place these on an ungreased baking sheet.

For a brown finish, brush the tops of the biscuits with milk or butter. Place biscuits 1 inch apart if you like them crusty all over, close together if not. Bake in a ➤ 450° preheated oven 12 to 15 minutes, depending on their thickness.

▲ At high altitude, baking powder biscuits should require no adjustment of leavening.

ADDITIONS TO BISCUITS

Biscuit flavors are easily varied to suit the menu. Dust them, before baking, with:

Cinnamon and sugar

or, just before they are finished, with:

Grated Parmesan and paprika

Or, press into the top center:

1 lump sugar

soaked in:

Orange juice

Or incorporate into the dough of any of the following biscuit recipes:

2 tablespoons finely chopped parsley or chives, or 2 teaspoons finely chopped fresh sage, or ⅓ cup crumbled Roquefort or grated cheddar cheese
3 to 6 slices cooked, crumbled bacon, or 3 tablespoons chopped cooked ham, or 4 tablespoons sautéed chopped onions

Prepare them like rissoles, placing between the layers one of the following:

1 cup sugared fresh strawberries, raspberries or blueberries
¼ cup nuts, dates or dried figs
½ cup raisins or currants
1 cup cooked, ground and seasoned poultry, sausage, ham or other meat

ROLLED BISCUITS

About Twenty-Four 1½-Inch Biscuits

➤ Please read About Hot Biscuits, above.
Preheat oven to 450°.
Sift together into a large bowl:

1¾ cups sifted all-purpose flour
½ teaspoon salt
3 teaspoons double-acting baking powder

Add:

4 to 6 tablespoons chilled butter or shortening or a combination of both

Cut solid shortening into dry ingredients as directed above, then make a well in the center. Add, all at once:

¾ cup milk

Stir until the dough is fairly free from the sides of the bowl. Turn the dough onto a lightly floured board. Knead gently and quickly, making about eight to ten folds. Roll with a lightly floured rolling pin, until the dough has the desired thickness. Cut with a biscuit cutter dipped in a very little flour. Brush the tops with:

(Milk or melted butter)

Place on an ungreased baking sheet. Bake until lightly browned—12 to 15 minutes.

QUICK DROP BISCUITS

No kneading or rolling is necessary in these two recipes. The biscuits are very palatable but less shapely, unless you drop them into muffin tins. For a good breakfast ring, prepare I, below. Form the dough into 12 balls; roll them in melted butter. Place them in a 7-inch ring mold, into the bottom of which you have poured Caramel Roll Topping, 731. Bake at 400° about 25 minutes.

I. Preheat oven to 450°.
Prepare:

Rolled Biscuits, above

using in all:

1 cup milk

➤ Stir the dough 1 scant minute. Drop from a spoon onto an ungreased sheet and bake 12 to 15 minutes or until lightly browned.

II. About Twenty-Four 1½-Inch Biscuits

When you are obliged to use oil, it is preferable to flavor the biscuit highly. See Additions to Biscuits, 632.
Preheat oven to 475°.
Sift into a bowl:

2 cups sifted all-purpose flour
3 teaspoons double-acting baking powder
1 teaspoon salt

Pour over the top, all at once, without mixing:

⅓ cup vegetable oil
⅔ cup milk

Stir with a fork until the mixture readily leaves the sides of the bowl. Drop from a spoon onto an ungreased sheet. Bake 10 to 12 minutes.

FLUFFY BISCUITS OR SHORTCAKE DOUGH

About Twenty-Four 1½-Inch Biscuits

For other shortcakes, see Index. ➤ To mix, see About Hot Biscuits, 632.
Prepare:

Rolled Biscuits, above

but add:

1 tablespoon sugar
½ teaspoon salt

and you may use cream instead of milk for added richness.

WHOLE WHEAT BISCUITS

About Twenty-Four 1½-Inch Biscuits

Preheat oven to 400°.
Sift together:

⅞ cup sifted all-purpose flour
2 teaspoons double-acting baking powder
½ teaspoon baking soda
2 teaspoons sugar
¾ teaspoon salt

Add and mix well:

1 cup whole wheat flour

Cut into the flour with a pastry blender:

⅓ cup butter or shortening

When the mixture has a fine-crumb consistency, stir in with a fork:

1 cup cultured sour cream or buttermilk

Turn out onto a floured board and proceed as for Rolled Biscuits, 632.

BISCUIT EASTER BUNNIES

Preheat oven to 425°.
Prepare:

Fluffy Biscuits, opposite

Pat or roll out the dough to the thickness of ½ inch. Cut it out with 3 sizes of cutters: 1—large, about 3 inches; 2—half as large; and 3—one-fourth as large. Assemble your bunnies as sketched below. Use the large biscuit for the body, the second one for the head, and roll the third one into a ball for the tail. Flatten two of the second-size biscuits slightly and shape them into ovals for the ears. Place the bunnies on a greased sheet. Bake about 15 minutes or until done.

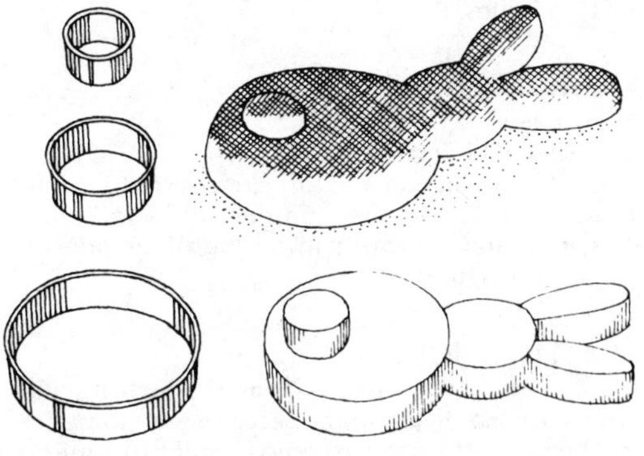

PINWHEEL BISCUITS

Use this same form also for other fillings such as cooked meat or cheese.
Preheat oven to 450°.
Prepare any:

Rolled biscuit dough

Roll it to the thickness of ½ inch. Spread the surface with:

¼ cup soft butter
¾ cup brown sugar
(Chopped nuts)
(Chopped raisins)

Roll the dough like a Jelly Roll, 691, but rather loosely. Cut into 1-inch slices. Lift them carefully with a pancake turner onto a lightly greased cookie sheet. Bake about 12 minutes.

BISCUIT STICKS

Prepare dough for:

Rolled Biscuits, 632

Cut it into sticks ½ x ½ x 3 inches. Brush the sticks with:

Melted butter

Bake as directed but for a shorter period. Then to serve stack them log-cabin fashion.

BUTTERMILK BISCUITS

About Twenty-Four 1½-Inch Biscuits

Because of the sour milk and soda, this recipe has a very tender dough. ➤ To mix, please read About Hot Biscuits, 632.

Preheat oven to 450°.

Sift together into a mixing bowl:

1¾ cups sifted all-purpose flour
½ teaspoon salt
2 teaspoons double-acting baking powder
1 teaspoon sugar
½ teaspoon baking soda

Cut in:

¼ cup lard or 5 tablespoons butter

Add and lightly mix:

¾ cup buttermilk

Turn the dough onto a floured board. Knead it gently for ½ minute. Pat the dough to the thickness of ¼ inch. Cut with a biscuit cutter. Bake 10 to 12 minutes.

⊟ GRIDDLE BISCUITS

Prepare any:

Rolled biscuit dough

Cook the biscuits on a lightly greased hot griddle, 1 inch apart. Brown them on one side 5 to 7 minutes; turn and brown them on the other side for the same length of time.

BEATEN BISCUITS

About Forty-Four 1½-Inch Biscuits

To win unending gratitude, serve to any homesick southerner this classic accompaniment to Virginia ham. The following lines by Miss Howard Weeden in *Bandanna Ballads* sum up in a nutshell the art of making biscuits:

"Of course I'll gladly give de rule
I meks beat biscuit by,
Dough I ain't sure dat you will mek
Dat bread de same as I.

" 'Case cookin's like religion is—
Some's 'lected an' some ain't,
An' rules don't no more mek a cook
Den sermons mek a saint."

Sift 3 times:

1 tablespoon sugar
4 cups all-purpose flour
1 teaspoon salt
(1 teaspoon double-acting baking powder)

Cut into the flour, with a pastry blender or 2 knives:

¼ cup chilled leaf lard

When ingredients are the consistency of cornmeal, add to make a stiff dough:

Equal parts of chilled milk and ice water, approximately 1 cup in all

Beat the dough with a mallet until it is well blistered, or put it 10 times through the coarse chopper of a meat grinder. Fold it over frequently. This is a long process, requiring ½ hour or more.

Miss Weeden's verse goes on to say:

"Two hundred licks is what I gives
For home-folks, never fewer,
An' if I'm 'specting company in,
I gives five hundred sure!"

If you make these often, it might be worth investing in a biscuit machine, available from a bakers' supply company. When the dough is smooth and glossy, roll it to the thickness of ½ inch and cut it with a floured biscuit cutter. Spread the tops with:

Melted butter

Pierce through the biscuits with a fork. Bake about 30 minutes in a preheated 325° oven.

SHIP'S BISCUITS

About Twenty-Four 1½-Inch Biscuits

These are really a simpler version of Beaten Biscuits, above. The longer they are folded and beaten, the better the results, so let the children work out with them.

Preheat oven to 325°.

Mix:

2 cups all-purpose flour
½ teaspoon salt

Work in with the fingertips:

1 teaspoon shortening

Stir in to make a very stiff dough:

About ½ cup water

Beat this dough to a ½-inch thinness with a mallet. Fold it into 6 layers. Beat it thin again and refold 5 or 6 times until the dough is very elastic. Before cutting with a floured biscuit cutter, roll to ½ inch again. Bake about 30 minutes and store tightly covered.

SCONES

About 12 Scones

These are richer than ordinary biscuits because of the addition of cream and eggs. Fine with a light luncheon.

Preheat oven to 450°.

Sift together into a large bowl:

1¾ cups sifted all-purpose flour
2¼ teaspoons double-acting baking powder

1 tablespoon sugar
1/2 teaspoon salt
Cut into these ingredients, until the size of small peas, using a pastry blender or 2 knives:
1/4 cup cold butter
Beat in a separate bowl:
2 eggs
Reserve 2 tablespoons of this mixture. Add to the remainder and beat in:
1/3 cup cream
Make a well in the dry ingredients. Pour the liquid into it. Combine with a few swift strokes. Handle the dough as little as possible. Place it on a lightly floured board. Pat until 3/4 inch thick. Cut with a knife into diamond shapes or Biscuit Sticks, 634. Brush with the reserved egg and sprinkle with:
Salt or sugar
Bake about 15 minutes.

BIRTHDAY BREAD HORSE

As our children have always demanded a piece of their birthday cake for breakfast, we concocted a bread horse to be supplemented later in the day by the candlelighted cake of richer content. This also makes a good Christmas or Fourth of July breakfast decoration.

You will need a well-rounded loaf of bread—a log-shaped Cinnamon Loaf, 604, is fine—plus an oval bun or roll about 2 1/2 x 3 1/2 inches; 2 braided rolls about 1 x 3 1/2 inches; 5 peppermint candy sticks 1 x 8 inches; 2 raisins, 2 almonds and a piece of cherry or a redhot. Use the loaf for the body. Mount it on four of the candy sticks. Break off about a third or less of the fifth candy stick. Use it for the neck. Stick it into one end of the loaf at an angle. Put the oval roll on the other end for the head. Use the braided rolls for the mane and tail, the raisins for eyes, the almonds for ears, and the piece of cherry for the lips. Bed the horse on leaves or grass. Add a ribbon bridle to keep this mad steed under some sort of control.

ABOUT USES FOR READY-BAKED AND LEFTOVER BREADS, CAKES AND CRACKERS

A bread surplus can be put to many good uses—so don't throw a piece away! It can be used for Melba Toast, 636; for Stuffings, 370; as a thickener in soups, see Panades, 179; and for a sauce, see Bread Sauce, 343. For other uses, see About Crumbs, 551; and don't forget good old Bread Pudding, 751.

Many recipes in **Joy** call for dry bread, cracker or cake crumbs. In fact, dry cake crumbs are so prized that commercial bakeries make sheets of cake solely for this purpose.

PUFFED BREAD BLOCKS

About Thirty 1 1/2-Inch Blocks

These may be prepared in advance. Keep at room temperature until soft, then blend well:
1/2 lb. cheddar cheese
1/4 lb. butter: 1 stick
Season palatably with:
Mustard
Curry powder
Caraway or celery seed
Salt and pepper or paprika
Cut into 1 1/2 x 3/4 x 3/4-inch blocks:
Fresh bread
Cover blocks with the cheese spread. Keep them chilled until ready for use. Pop them into a 375° oven. They should brown lightly and puff.

CHEESE OR BUTTER BREAD CUBES

Serve hot as an appetizer. Also good with soup or salads.

I. Preheat oven to 375°.
Beat together:
1 egg
1 1/2 tablespoons melted butter
Cut into cubes or blocks of any size:
Fresh bread
Roll the cubes in the egg mixture, then in:
Finely shredded American cheese
Salt and cayenne or paprika
Toast the cubes on a buttered sheet until the cheese is melted.

II. Preheat oven to 375°.
Spread bread cubes with a paste made of:
Butter
Grated Parmesan cheese
Caraway or celery seed
Salt and a few grains cayenne
(Mustard)
Toast and serve, as above.

MELBA CHEESE ROUNDS

Especially good with Onion Soup, 171.
Spread:
Melba toast rounds, 636

lightly with:

Butter

Sprinkle generously with:

Grated Parmesan cheese

Just before using, run them under a broiler until toasted. Serve at once, floating one or two on top of the soup.

SEEDED CRACKERS

Brush:

Small crisp salt crackers

with:

Melted butter or partially beaten egg white

Sprinkle lightly with:

Caraway, celery or sesame seeds

Toast and serve.

TOASTED BUTTERED BREAD LOAF OR GARLIC BREAD

Preheat oven to 350°.

Slice thick or thin to taste:

A medium-sized loaf of bread or French bread

Do not slice it all the way through; leave the bottom crust intact. With a pastry brush spread the top and sides of each piece, using in all:

½ cup melted butter

The butter may be flavored with:

(A minced clove of garlic)

(Herbs: basil, marjoram, oregano, etc.)

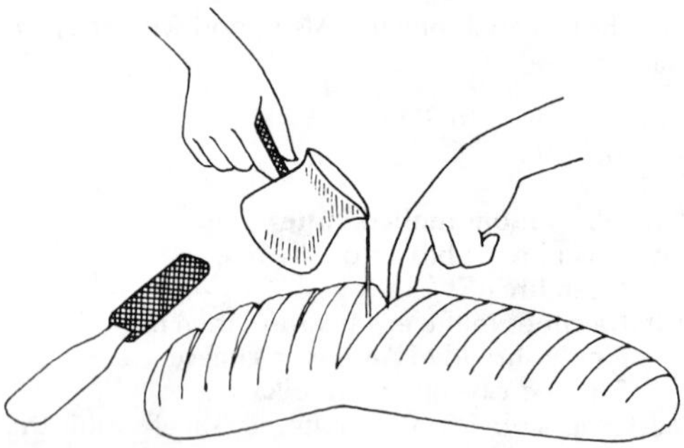

You may also crush 2 cloves of garlic with a little salt, until smooth. Spread a little on each slice. Follow with melted butter as shown above. Separate the slices slightly, so that the butter will be evenly distributed. Cover the loaf with a piece of foil. Place it in the oven until the bread is light brown, about 20 minutes. Serve immediately on a napkined platter.

QUICK CINNAMON LOAF

Slice a loaf of:

French or Vienna bread

and spread it, as illustrated above, with the following mixture, baking 8 minutes in a 400° oven:

⅓ cup melted butter

⅓ cup white or light brown sugar

2 teaspoons cinnamon

A grating of nutmeg

¼ teaspoon grated lemon peel

CINNAMON TOAST OR STICKS

Remove the crusts from bread. Spread the tops of:

Thin bread slices

or spread all 4 sides of:

¾-inch bread sticks

with the mixture for:

Quick Cinnamon Loaf, above

You may sprinkle the bread sticks with:

(Rum)

Place the slices or strips in a 400° oven about 8 minutes. Be sure to toast the sticks on all sides. You may also place them under a broiler to crisp them. Applesauce is a good complement to this dish.

FRENCH TOAST

4 Servings

Beat slightly:

4 eggs

Add:

½ teaspoon salt

1 cup milk

Flavor with:

(½ teaspoon vanilla or 1 tablespoon rum)

Dip into this mixture:

8 slices bread

The bread may be cut in rounds with a doughnut cutter. Brown the bread, each side, on a hot, well-buttered griddle. Serve hot sprinkled with:

Sugar

Cinnamon

Garnish the cooked rounds with:

Bright red jelly

or serve with pie cherries, sweetened, slightly thickened with cornstarch, 548, and flavored with lemon; with applesauce flavored with cinnamon and cloves; or with maple syrup.

MELBA TOAST

Preferable to use dry bread.

Cut into the thinnest possible slices:

White or other bread

Remove crusts. Place bread in a 250° oven. Leave it in until it becomes crisp and a light golden brown and until all the moisture is withdrawn.

HONEY BUTTER TOAST

Prepare:

Honey Butter, 775

Spread it on a slice of bread. Cover with another slice. Cut the bread into 1-inch strips. Toast the strips on both sides under a broiler. Serve sprinkled with:

Cinnamon

ORANGE TOAST

Very nice with tea.

Combine:

Grated rind of 1 orange
¼ cup orange juice
½ cup sugar

Cut:

6 slices of bread

Remove the crusts and toast the bread. Spread it, while hot, with:

Butter

Cover it with the orange mixture. Put the toast in the oven or under a broiler, just long enough to brown the tops lightly.

ZWIEBACK, RUSKS OR TWICE-BAKED BREAD

Bake:

White Bread Plus, 603

using in all 2 eggs. Replace the 2 cups of water with 2 cups of milk. The finished loaf should be just half as high as a normal loaf of bread, so bake in six rather than three pans. Maybe this shape was evolved to suit baby mouths, for no one enjoys this confection more than the very, very young. When the bread is cool, cut it into ½-inch slices and toast as for Melba Toast, above. You may want to glaze it before toasting with:

Lemon Glaze, 731

In the slow heat of the oven, this turns a golden brown.

PIES AND PASTRIES

At home and abroad, Americans boast about pie. It has apparently always been so; way back in the clipper era, sailors brought home not only heart-shaped boxes crusted over with tiny rare shells but the pie-jaggers they had carved to while away the doldrum days in *outre-mer*. These implements of bone, often furnished with as many as three wheels but marvelously precise all the same, sped the fancy cutting of lattice over succulent apple pies such as that shown lower left. Ingenious French cooks form delicate swans, shown both unbaked and assembled, lower right; or the monumental croquembouche shimmering with glaze at the right rear. Whatever the nation, skill in pastry making has been regarded worldwide as a passport to matrimony. In Hungarian villages, for example, no girl was considered eligible until her strudel dough had become so translucent that her beloved could read the newspaper through it.

First let's consider what makes for success with pastry doughs:

➤ Handle pie dough lightly, for two reasons: to incorporate as much air as possible and to inhibit the development of gluten. The aim here is a flaky and tender crust.

➤ Measure carefully—too much flour toughens pastry; too much liquid makes it soggy; too much shortening makes doughs greasy and crumbly.

➤ Chilling pastry dough, covered, up to 12 hours after mixing tenderizes it, keeps it from shrinking during baking, and makes it easier to handle. Be sure to remove the dough from the refrigerator at least one hour before shaping; otherwise you will be obliged to overhandle it. Pinch off just enough dough for one pie shell. Press it into the approximate shape needed. Roll as lightly and as little as possible, following the directions below. Closely covered pie dough will hold for a week or more in the refrigerator.

➤ Choose nonshiny pie pans for good browning. ➤ Always start the baking in a preheated oven. The contrast between the coolness of the dough and the heat of the oven causes rapid air expansion and contributes to the desired lightness of the texture. For various pie doughs, see 640.

▲ In making pies at high altitudes, where evaporation is greater, you may find that you achieve better results if you add a trifle more liquid.

Many pie doughs ❄ freeze well. ➤ It is better to shape them before freezing. See Frozen Baked Pie, 830, and Frozen Unbaked Pie, 829.

ROLLING PIE DOUGH

If the dough has been refrigerated, bring to room temperature before rolling. To make 2 pie shells or a double-crust pie, divide the dough evenly before rolling it. A pastry cloth and roller stocking are highly recommended. They practically do away with sticking and require the use of very little additional flour. Next to the pastry cloth, your best bet is a large wooden board. If you use either of the above methods, flour the rolling surface and the rolling pin lightly.

As to the roller, whether it's a French broomstick-type, a bottle, or the revolving type, as shown in the drawings, the important thing is how you use it. ➤ Roll the dough from the center out. Lift the roller. Do not push it to and fro, which stretches the dough. Roll the dough to a 1/8-inch thickness or less. Should it have a few tears, patch them carefully rather than trying to reroll.

CUTTING AND FORMING PIE DOUGH

To cut pie dough, allow a piece about 2 inches larger than pan dimensions, seen next page, to take care of inevitable shrinkage. It is fun to cut fancy edges on the top crust with a pastry wheel.

To form the crust, have ready a 9-inch pie pan. It's a poor pie crust that requires a greased pan, but buttering will help brown the bottom of the crust. Loosen the pastry from the board, fold it in half, lift it, lay the fold across the center of the pan and unfold it; or, after rolling it around the rolling pin, unroll it onto the pan, seen at right, where this method is being used to form a top crust.

Ease the dough into the pan loosely, but press it in place so that no air will be left between dough and pan to form blisters in baking. You may cut a small square of dough, form it into a ball, dip it in flour and use it to press the dough down and shape it against the pan. Trim off the excess with a knife, using an easy slashing motion against the edge of the pan; or use scissors. Trimmings can be given to the children for play dough or baked up into bits for hors d'oeuvre or small pastries.

ABOUT CRUSTS FOR FILLED PIES

For crusts which are to be baked with fillings, use a deep pie pan with a wide channeled rim to catch any juices. For a one-crust pie, make a fluted edge with the dough that laps over, or build up a rim with a strip of pastry. Full it on by using a fork to press it down; or pinch it with the thumb and forefinger, as shown opposite on the right. This edge is important, as it will help to hold the juices in the pie. Do not prick the lower crust. If the filling for the pie is the juicy kind, first brush the bottom crust lightly with the white of an egg, melted butter or a light sprinkling of flour. Any of these will keep the crust from becoming soggy. Putting the filling in very hot helps, too.

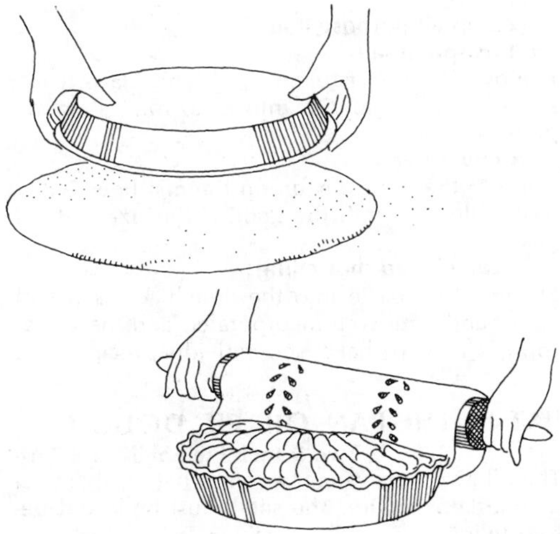

There are many attractive ways to make the lattice. You may cut plain ½-inch strips with a knife or pink them with a jagger. Or you may roll, then twist ½-inch ropelike pieces and weave any of these together or place them crisscross.

To weave, place half of the strips from left to right over the pie about ¾ inch apart. Fold back every other strip halfway, as shown below. Place a strip across the unfolded strips from front to back. Unfold the strips. Fold back the alternates. Place the next strip ¾ inch from the last. Continue until half of the pie is latticed. Then repeat the process, beginning on the other side of the center line.

When the whole pie is latticed, attach the strips to the pie edge loosely to allow for shrinkage. Moisten the ends slightly to make them stick. Cut them off before crimping the pie. We like to sprinkle a tablespoon of granulated sugar over the latticed dough before baking.

For a solid top crust, cut the rolled ⅛-inch-thick dough 1 inch larger than the pan. To allow the steam to escape, prick it with a fork in several places, double it over and gash it along the fold, or make fancy patterns with whatever cutting tool you like. Place the top crust on the pie. Full in the surplus dough and press it down around the edges with a fork. Or you may tuck it under the lower crust and press it around the edge with a fork.

If you prefer, after sealing the edges by pressing with a fork, you may make a vent with a one-inch hollow tube of dough—3 inches high—only partially sunk into a hole in the center of the upper crust. Support it with a round border of fulled-on dough which will hide any discoloration from juices bubbling over when you cut the vent down to the decorative support after the baking. Should any juice spill over onto the oven, sprinkle it with salt to prevent smoke and smell.

For baking filled pies, note directions in each recipe and preheat the oven to the correct temperature. Should the edge of a pie tend to brown too quickly, place a protective rim of foil lightly over it.

ABOUT CRUSTS FOR UNFILLED PIES

If the pie shell is to be baked without filling, or as the English say "blind," ➤ prick the dough generously with a fork after you have placed it in the pie pan, and weight it with dry beans or, as they do in France, with small clean round pebbles. This keeps it from heaving and baking unevenly. Remove the beans or pebbles a few minutes before the baking period is over. To cut a round for a prebaked top crust, prick it and bake it on a baking sheet.

When making individual pies, use an inverted muffin tin or, for deeper shells, inverted custard cups. Cut the rounds of dough 4½ or 5½ inches in diameter and fit them over the cups; or, with the help of foil as a support, create your own fancy shapes—fluted cups, simple tricornes, long barquettes. You may even make your tarts into baskets by forming handles with strips of dough molded over inverted custard cups. When baked, sink the handles into the filling just before serving. ➤ Prick the shells before baking. When you fill baked shells, spoon the filling in carefully.

Unfilled crusts may be protected from overbrowning by setting the pie pan into a larger pan or, as with filled pies, by covering the edge of the dough with a strip of aluminum foil. To glaze pie crust, giving it added flavor or color, see pages 731–732. Keep in mind, however, that glazes also tend to toughen crusts.

Baking time will vary according to the material of which the pan is made. ➤ If it is ovenproof glass or enamelware, cut the baking time indicated by one-fifth to one-fourth. When tins are used, those that are perforated, have lost their shininess, or have a base of screen material are helpful for producing a well-browned crust.

Unfilled shells, whether for individual or big pies, are baked in a preheated 450° oven, unless otherwise noted, 10 to 12 minutes or until lightly browned. Cool them before filling.

BASIC PIE DOUGH

For a double-crust 9-inch, or a single-crust pie with a generous lattice, use the following amounts. For a one-crust 9-inch pie, use half the recipe.

Sift together:

2 cups all-purpose flour
1 teaspoon salt

Measure and combine:

⅔ cup chilled leaf lard or shortening
2 tablespoons chilled butter

Cut half of the shortening into the flour mixture with a pastry blender, or work it in lightly with the tips of your fingers until it has the grain of cornmeal. Cut the remaining half coarsely into the dough until it is pea size. Sprinkle the dough with:

4 tablespoons water

➤ Blend the water lightly into the dough. You may lift the ingredients with a fork, allowing the mixture to spread. If needed to hold the ingredients together, add:

1 teaspoon to 1 tablespoon water

When you can gather the dough up into a tidy ball, as shown 639, stop handling it. To fill and bake, see individual recipes. For a baked shell, see About Crusts for Unfilled Pies, above.

PIE DOUGH COCKAIGNE

A 9-Inch Double-Crust

A dough that refrigerates well after baking and reheats to perfection.

Sift together:

2 cups all-purpose flour
1 teaspoon salt
2 teaspoons sugar

Measure and combine:

¼ cup butter
3 tablespoons shortening

Cut half the shortening into the flour mixture until it has the grain of cornmeal. Cut in the remaining half until it is pea-sized. Sprinkle the dough with:

5 tablespoons water

Proceed as for Basic Pie Dough, above.

MIXER PIE DOUGH

Using the ingredients and proportions for:

Basic Pie Dough, above

place in a large mixer bowl the flour, salt and shortening. Scraping the bowl constantly, blend at low speed 1 minute. Add the water. Mix about 10 seconds longer, or until the dough begins to cling to the beaters. Should the dough be too crumbly, incorporate 1 teaspoon to 1 tablespoon water with your hands so that the dough forms into a ball. To bake, see individual recipes. For a baked shell, see About Crusts for Unfilled Pies, above.

FLOUR PASTE PIE DOUGH

A 9-Inch Double-Crust

Sift into a bowl:

2 cups all-purpose flour
1 teaspoon salt

Remove ⅓ cup of this mixture and place it in a small bowl or cup. Stir into it, to form a smooth paste:

¼ cup water

Cut into the flour mixture in the first bowl with a pastry blender until the grain is the size of small peas:

⅔ cup chilled shortening

Stir the flour paste into the dough. Work it with your hand until well incorporated and the dough forms a ball. To bake, see individual recipes.

PAT-IN-THE-PAN OIL PIE DOUGH

Two 9-Inch Pie Shells or 8 Tarts

The oil gives this variant a somewhat mealy rather than a flaky texture. The shell must be baked before filling.

Sift into a mixing bowl:

2 cups all-purpose flour
1¼ teaspoons salt

Mix in a cup until creamy:

⅔ cup cooking oil
3 tablespoons cold milk

Pour the mixture over the flour all at once. Stir these ingredients lightly with a fork until blended. Form them into a crust, right in the pan, by patting out the dough with a spoon, or you may roll the dough between 2 sheets of waxed paper. When ready, remove the top paper, reverse the crust into the pie pan and then remove the other paper. After pricking sides and bottom, bake 12 to 15 minutes, in a preheated 475° oven. Cool before filling.

WHEATLESS PIE DOUGH

A 9-Inch Single-Crust

This crust must be baked before filling.

➤ Sift 3 times:

½ cup cornstarch
½ cup finely milled rye flour

The repeated sifting is very important. Work the flour mixture as for pastry with:

½ cup fine dry cottage cheese
½ cup chilled butter
½ teaspoon salt

Chill the dough at least 2 hours. Pat into the pan. Prick bottom and sides well and bake in a preheated 425° oven 12 to 15 minutes.

ABOUT PASTRY FOR MEATS

For meat pies, rissoles or turnovers, see About Meat Pies, 449; for Meat en Croûte, see 448; for Crust or Pâte for Pâtés, see 494.

PÂTE BRISÉE

A 9-Inch Pie Shell

This short French pie dough has a remarkable way of withstanding a moist filling, and is best used for meat pies and pâtés. If you want a dessert crust, see Pâte Sucrée, below. The recipe can be doubled or tripled and stored refrigerated for a week or more before baking.

Work:

½ cup chilled butter plus 3 tablespoons lard or vegetable shortening

very lightly into:

2 cups all-purpose flour
½ teaspoon salt

This can be done best by working the flour and butter first with the fingers and then lightly and quickly rotating it between the palms of the hands. Make a well, 643, of the crumbly flour mixture. Pour in gradually:

5 to 6 tablespoons cold water

The index finger is used to stir the liquid ➤ quickly into the flour, in a spiral fashion, beginning at the inside of the well and gradually moving to the outer edge. The dough should be soft enough to gather up into a ball but should not stick to the fingers or the board. ➤ Allow the dough to rest refrigerated from 2 to 36 hours. Cover it with a damp, wrung-out cloth for the shorter period or a piece of foil for the longer one. The resting of the dough breaks any rubbery reactions it might develop when rolled and handled. To roll, shape and bake, see 638.

VIENNA PASTRY

Eight 3-Inch Tarts

Delicious as tart shells, turnovers or thin wafers served with soup or salad. Sift together:

1 cup all-purpose flour
¼ teaspoon salt

Cut into these ingredients with a pastry blender:

½ cup chilled butter
4½ oz. soft cream cheese

When these ingredients are well blended, wrap the dough in foil and refrigerate for at least 12 hours. In readying for use, roll to ⅛-inch thickness, adding as little flour as possible.

I. To use as tarts, form pastry over inverted muffin tins and bake at 450° for about 12 minutes.

II. To use as turnovers, see 251.

III. To use as wafers, roll and cut the dough into rounds or put it directly into a cookie press without rolling. Before baking, dot with sesame or poppy seed. Bake 8 to 10 minutes at 450°.

PASTRY FOR CHEESE STRAWS OR WAFERS

4 Dozen

These keep for weeks in a refrigerator or freezer and are quickly sliced and baked for the unexpected guest. Or just after mixing put the dough in a pastry tube to make straws. Or use the 1½-inch ribbon disk on a cookie press to make ribbons. Cut into 2-inch lengths.

Preheat oven to 425°.

Grate or grind:

¼ to ½ lb. aged cheddar cheese

Combine with:

3 to 4 tablespoons soft butter
¾ cup all-purpose flour
(1 teaspoon Worcestershire sauce)
½ teaspoon salt
Dash of hot pepper sauce

Form the dough into 1-inch rolls. Wrap in foil and refrigerate or freeze till cold enough to slice as thin as possible, under a quarter of an inch. Bake in a preheated 475° oven about 12 minutes.

RICH EGG TART DOUGH, PÂTE SUCRÉE OR MÜRBETEIG

Six 3-Inch Tart Shells

There are many versions of this paste, varying in richness and sweetness. This one makes a very

tender paste for fresh fruit fillings. For a sweeter dough, use Roll Cookie dough, 711.
Combine:

1 cup all-purpose flour
2 tablespoons sugar
½ teaspoon salt

Work into it as you would for pastry, using a pastry blender or the tips of your fingers:

6 tablespoons softened butter

Make a well, 643, and add:

1 egg yolk
½ teaspoon vanilla
1 tablespoon lemon juice or water

Stir with your fingers until the mixture forms one blended ball and no longer adheres to your hands. Cover it and refrigerate for at least 30 minutes. Roll to ⅛-inch thickness as for pie dough, see 639. Line the tart pans with this dough. Prick and weight down with beans or pebbles, see 640. Bake in a 400° oven 7 to 10 minutes or until lightly browned. Unmold the pastry shells and cool on a rack. Fill with fresh fruit. Glaze with:

Melted, cooled Currant or Apricot Glaze, 732

Garnish with:

(Whipped cream)

ABOUT GALETTE DOUGH

Fifty million Frenchmen can't be wrong; but it is hard to get any two of them to agree on the exact formula for this classic pastry. In some regions, galette is almost like a Kuchen dough. Perhaps the most famous is Galette des Rois, served on Twelfth Night. Regardless of the material used, the "Kings' Galette" has a dried bean baked in it, which is expected to bring good fortune to the guest who gets the lucky slice.

Our version of galette which, we hope, will merit majority approval is a well-pricked Rough Puff Paste, 645, rolled to 1-inch thickness and coated with a heavy French Egg Wash glaze, 731. ➤ Keep the glaze on the top surface only, for if it runs over the edge it will solidify early in the baking and prevent the dough from puffing as it should.

An alternative is to use a yeast coffee cake dough. After the last rising, pat it out thin and make a rim by pinching the dough edges all around. Put the fruit in the depression and cover it with a Streusel, 731. Bake as directed for bread. You may, as the cake cools, cover it with Apricot Glaze, 732. A less time-consuming and, we think, quite delicious solution is simply to bake Apple, Peach or Plum Cake Cockaigne, 661.

ABOUT COOKIE AND KUCHEN CRUSTS

If another type of sweet crust is desired, try Roll Cookie dough, 711. There are many, many forms of fruit Kuchen; see Apple, Plum or Peach Cake Cockaigne, 661, French Apple Cake, 661, Quick Sour Cream Coffee Cake, 627. For less sweet versions, try fruit toppings on raised coffee cake doughs, 619–627.

CHEESECAKE CRUSTS

To Line a 10-Inch Pan

This crust works well if filled before baking with dry cheesecake fillings such as Ricotta, 660.
Sift together:

2 cups all-purpose flour
¼ teaspoon salt

Work in with a pastry blender:

½ cup chilled butter

Gradually add:

1½ to 2 tablespoons brandy
4 tablespoons water

Mix as for pie dough, 638. Chill about 30 minutes before rolling to line the pan. Roll about ⅛ inch thick and, after filling, bake as directed under individual cheesecakes, 659–660.

SUGGESTED ADDITIONS TO CRUSTS

Vary your favorite basic pie crust by adding, before rolling, for a double crust, one of the following sweet or savory additions that will enhance the filling:

1 to 3 teaspoons poppy or caraway seed
1 to 3 tablespoons toasted sesame seed
¼ to ½ cup finely chopped nuts
¼ to ⅓ cup grated aged cheese
2 tablespoons confectioners' sugar or 1 tablespoon sugar
¼ to ½ teaspoon cinnamon and/or nutmeg
1 teaspoon grated citrus rind
2 tablespoons cocoa

ABOUT CRUMB CRUSTS

These, mixed and patted into the pan, are a shortcut to pie making. An easy way to form them is first to place the crumb mixture in a pie pan, distributing the crumbs fairly evenly. Now press another pie pan of the same diameter firmly into the dough. When the top pan is removed, presto!—a crust of even thickness underneath. Trim any excess that is forced to the top edge.

Crumb crusts need not be baked before filling ➤ but, if used unbaked, must be first chilled thoroughly or the filling will immediately disintegrate the crust. If baked before filling, they require a 350° oven for about 10 minutes. ➤ It is best to cool the empty baked shell before filling.

Fill a prebaked shell with chiffon fillings, Bavarian creams or gelatin whips topped with sweetened whipped cream, or with custard or fruit filling, which may be covered with a high Meringue, 730.

GRAHAM CRACKER, ZWIEBACK OR COOKIE CRUMB CRUST

A 9-Inch Single-Crust and Topping

Crush or grind fine, or crumb in a ⅄ blender as directed until very fine:

1½ cups crumbs of graham crackers, zwieback, vanilla or chocolate wafers, or gingersnaps, 707

The flavor of the filling should determine which of the above to use. Stir into the crumbs until well blended:

¼ to ½ cup sifted confectioners' sugar
6 tablespoons melted butter
(1 teaspoon cinnamon)

Reserve 2 to 3 tablespoons of the crumb mixture. Pat the rest into the pan or press out to the desired thickness. To form the shell and bake, see About Crumb Crusts, above. When the pie is filled, scatter the reserved crumbs as a topping.

BREAD OR CAKE CRUMB CRUST

A 9-Inch Single-Crust

A good way, this, of utilizing dry bread or cake. To be successful, the crust must be fully baked before filling.

To form the shell and bake, see About Crumb Crusts, 642. Follow the rule for Graham Cracker Crust, above. Substitute for the graham cracker or zwieback crumbs:

1½ cups toasted fine bread or cake crumbs
(6 tablespoons ground unbleached almonds)

If you use cake crumbs, omit sugar.

CEREAL PIE CRUST

A 9-Inch Single-Crust

To form the shell and bake, see About Crumb Crusts, 642. For a quick cereal ring mold, see 690.

Roll or grind:

6 cups flaked- or puffed-type breakfast cereal

There should be 1½ cups after crushing. Combine with:

½ cup melted butter
¼ cup sugar—if the cereal is not presweetened
(½ teaspoon cinnamon)

PUFF PASTE OR PÂTE FEUILLETÉE

Puff paste recipes usually start: "Choose a bright, windy, chilly day . . ." We stand off unfavorable weather with an electric fan, but are careful not to train it on the work surface. If you ask, "What do commercial bakeries do about puff paste and the weather?"—the answer is: they use a highly emulsified, very impervious margarine. To become an amateur champion, keep in mind first and foremost that this most delicate and challenging of pastries must be made the way porcupines make love—that is, very, very carefully. Then shut off the telephone for an hour or two, cut yourself some paper pattern guides to the measurements below and set to work.

➤ It is best to use flour that has a high gluten content, to develop real elasticity—and this is hard to come by. We do succeed, however, with all-purpose flour by using the procedure we describe. To be "puffy" ➤ the paste must be chilled, well-kneaded, and handled in such a way as to trap air, and finally ➤ baked in a hot, thoroughly preheated oven. Then the air inside the dough expands with almost explosive effect. ➤ The surface on which you work—preferably marble—the tools, the ingredients and your fingers should be chilled throughout the operation, as it is necessary to hold the fat, which is in very high proportion to the flour, in constant suspension.

➤ The paste must not absorb undue moisture, but it must never dry out. ➤ It must entirely envelop the butter. Try not to let any cracks or tears develop, as they release the air, which is your only riser. If they do appear, mend them at once to keep the butter encased.

With these ideas firmly in mind, try making this small quantity first. As you become experienced, double or triple the recipe. Knead:

¼ lb. sweet butter

in ice water or under very cold running water. The butter should become soft through kneading, but in no sense soft through melting. Quite the contrary—it must stay soft and chilled at the same time throughout the operation. The final kneading of the butter is best done on a marble slab; or the butter may be patted briskly in the hands until no water flies. Shape it into an oblong about 4 x 6 x ¼ inch. Wrap in foil and chill about 15 minutes.

Weigh, do not measure:

¼ lb. all-purpose flour

On a chilled smooth surface, make a ring with the flour, allowing about a 6-inch hollow center, see below.

Pour into the ring gradually—meanwhile forming the flour into a ball with it—a mixture of:

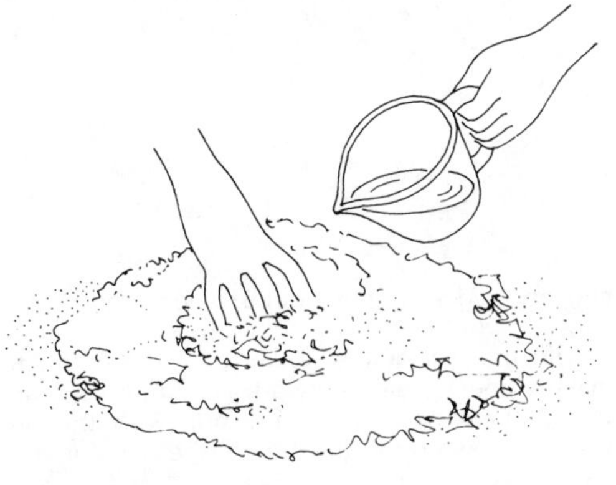

2 to 2½ oz. ice water
(1 teaspoon lemon juice)
¼ teaspoon salt

Knead the dough lightly until smooth. The whole process should take not more than about 2 minutes if you are experienced. Cover the dough carefully and refrigerate it for 15 minutes or so. When you remove the butter and dough from the refrigerator, they should be about the same consistency—chilled but not hard. Roll the dough into a very neat oblong measuring about 6 x 16 inches and less than ⅓ inch thick, as in the following sketch. At this point, the dough is some-

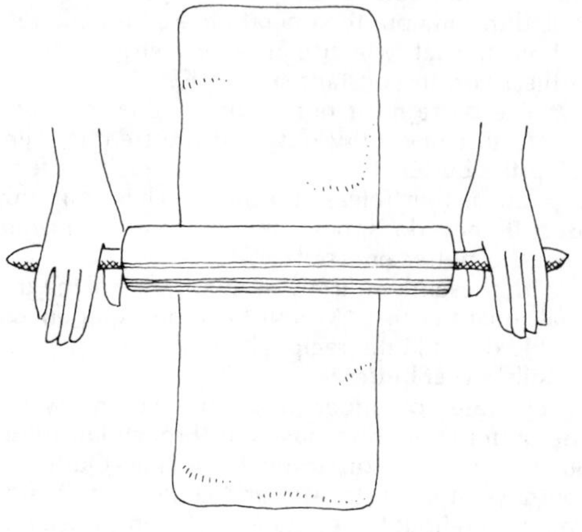

what elastic and may have to be cajoled into the rectangle. Make the edges as even and the thickness as constant as possible. Quickly place the chilled butter pad about 1 inch from a short

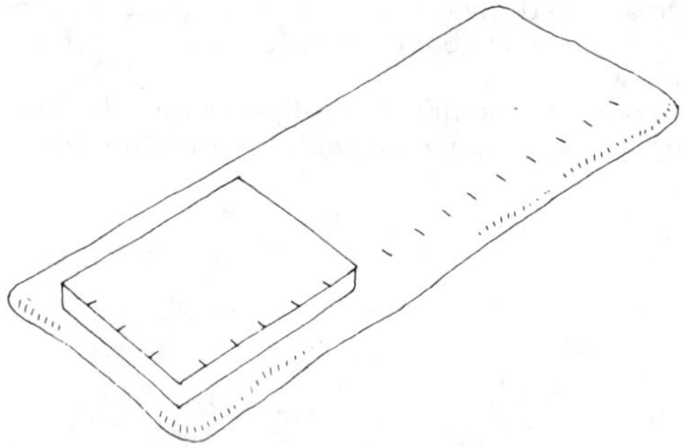

end and sides of the dough oblong, as shown above.

Fold the rest of the dough over the butter to make a pouch. Seal the two layers firmly together on all three open sides, pressing with the fingers, as shown opposite, or with the sides of your hands.

With the narrow dimension always toward you as you work, roll the dough evenly, being careful not to break the layers or force the roller in such a way that the edges of the dough envelope become cracked. Should any opening develop, be sure to patch it at once with a small piece of dough taken from the long sides. Keep the pastry 6 inches in width while rolling, and extend it to about 16 inches in length.

The use of two paper patterns makes this measuring very quick to judge. Fold the pastry into three exact parts, see below.

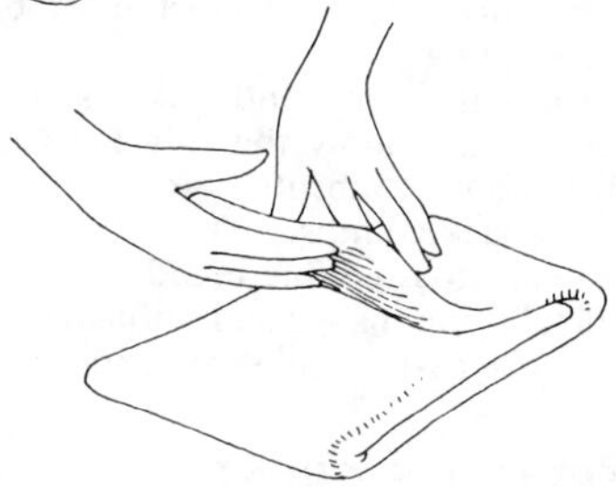

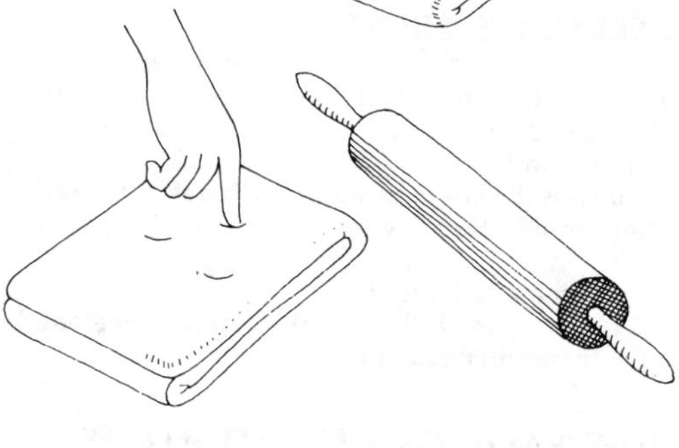

Make sure that the corners match neatly. Compress the pack slightly with the roller. At this point, the dough should have a transparent quality. The yellow of the butter should show through but not break through anywhere. Wrap the dough, now approximately 4 x 6 x 1 inch, in foil and chill for 30 minutes. You have now made your first "turn" and, if you need a reminder, you can professionally make an initial shallow fingertip imprint in one corner before refrigerating. Keep track of your turns by increasing the number of fingerprints after each rolling, as shown above.

When the dough has chilled, remove it from the refrigerator and repeat the rolling. ➤ Always roll with the narrow dimension of the dough toward you as you work. Roll as before, until the dough again measures about 6 x 16 inches. Fold once more into three equal parts. This time, make two fingertip impressions before refrigerating, covered, for 30 minutes. Repeat the turns until you have made five fingerprints. You may store the dough for 24 hours before baking. Wrap it first in foil and then in a dry towel. Refrigerate it.

If you prefer to bake the same day, make a sixth turn and chill the dough 30 minutes to 1½ hours. Then roll it to about 3/16 inch. This paste can be cut into many shapes. ➤ Whichever you choose, be sure to cut off a narrow slice along the folded edges. The folds have the inhibiting character of a selvage on cloth and do not allow the dough to expand evenly and freely.

➤ Always cut puff paste with a very sharp, very thin hot knife, a hot cutter or a sharp hot pastry wheel. Do not let the knife drag, as this will distort the layering.

Since making puff paste is time-consuming, you will want to use every scrap. But never, after cutting, reroll the dough for the same purpose. Get your patty shells and vol-au-vent and other classic shapes, see below, from the first cutting. Make out of rerolled scraps only those related types of pastry—such as flan, barquettes, croissants—for which the puff requirement is less exacting.

To prepare the pan for baking any of the classic shapes, sprinkle it lightly with cold water, but ➤ be sure that the side that was up when cut is now down against the wet baking surface. If properly made and cut, puff paste should rise six to eight times the height of the rolled dough.

Before baking an unsweetened paste, you may give it a lovely color by brushing the top with a combination of egg, salt and milk, see 731. ➤ Do not let this glaze spill over the edge, as the quick setting of the egg will have a deterrent effect on the rising. If the paste is to be used with sweetened food, brush with a combination of sugar and milk. For a really crispy finish, glaze also with a light sugar and water syrup just as the finished product comes from the oven.

To bake ➤ have ready an oven that has been thoroughly preheated to 500° at least 20 minutes. Bake at this temperature 5 minutes, reduce the heat to 375° and bake 25 to 30 minutes more, depending on the size of the pastry. If it colors too rapidly, place a piece of baker's paper or bond over it during the last stages of baking. The pastry is done if very light when lifted. Should it rise unevenly, the fault may lie with uneven rolling or with the uneven heat of the oven. In hot weather it may tend to slide to one side. Nothing can be done about this.

All puff paste recipes are best used fresh, but will keep closely covered and stored in a refrigerator for several days or frozen for a few weeks. For shapes to make with puff paste, see the illustration opposite and some of the following recipes.

Top left shows the cutting of a Vol-au-Vent, 646. It is really a larger version of the bouchée or patty shell illustrated in its dough and baked forms in the first three drawings below it.

At the top right is a Napoleon, 646. The remaining two forms are the baked and unbaked Cream Rolls, 646. ➤ Do not try to make these shapes with the Rough Puff Paste below, which is placed here because it is treated just like puff paste.

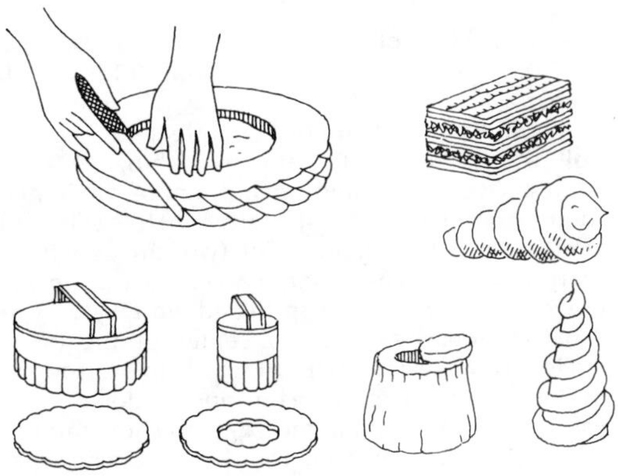

ROUGH OR HALF-PUFF PASTE, OR PÂTE DEMI-FEUILLETÉE

Do not expect this crust to rise even half so high as Puff Paste. It is made from the ingredients described below but is given fewer turns; or it is formed from the rerolled parings of true Puff Paste, when additional handling has driven off some of the trapped air. Use this paste for barquettes or croissants. Prepare:

Puff Paste, 643

using in all:

6 oz. butter

2 oz. water

Give it only 3 or 4 turns. To cut, shape and bake, see Puff Paste, 643.

PALM LEAVES

About 20 Palm Leaves

Roll into a 6 x 18-inch strip, ¼ inch thick:

Puff Paste, 643

To sugar, fold and cut, see Palm Leaf Rolls, 611. Chill and bake as noted opposite.

* PATTY SHELLS OR BOUCHÉES

Ten 4-Inch Shells

Prepare:

Puff Paste, 643, noting ➤ pointers

Roll the chilled paste into an oblong, 7 x 16 inches. Use a hot 3¼-inch cutter on the dough ten times. ➤ Be sure that the cutter is well within the rounded edge of the dough. Using a 2½-inch cutter and centering it in turn on each of the 3¼-inch rounds, make incisions, as shown above, about two-thirds through the dough. To chill, place and bake the dough, see Puff Paste, 643. As soon as the patty shells come from the oven, release the inner circles that were cut two-thirds into the shell. The first third will act as the lid when the shell is filled. The second is usually damp and so is discarded. The third uncut portion forms the base of the shell. These shells are suitable for luncheon entrées. They can be made into much smaller sizes for hors d'oeuvre, when they are called **Petites Bouchées,** or "little mouthfuls."

* VOL-AU-VENT

One 9-Inch Shell

Prepare:

Puff Paste, 643, noting ➤ pointers

Roll the chilled paste into an oblong, 9 x 17 inches. Use the removable bottom of an 8-inch round cake pan, or make an 8-inch cardboard circle as a cutting guide. Cut two circles with a sharp hot knife. Leave one whole. Place it upside down on a baking sheet sprinkled with water. Cut a 5-inch round out of the center of the other circle. Place the 1½-inch rim which this cut forms over the whole circle—again, upside down—and gash it diagonally along the edge, as shown upper left, 645. You may bake the 5-inch circle separately as a lid or cut it into Petites Bouchées, see 645. To chill and bake, see Puff Paste, 643. Fill at once with creamed food and serve, or cool to serve filled with:

Strawberries Romanoff, 133

CREAM ROLLS

8 Rolls

If you visit a Konditorei in Weimar, you will find the cream rolls called Schillerlocken, named for their resemblance to the long curls worn by the renowned romantic German poet. To make them, you need a special cone-shaped form known as a cornet.

Prepare:

Puff Paste, 643, noting ➤ pointers

Roll the chilled paste into an oblong, 12½ x 9 inches. Remove the rolled edges of the paste with a very sharp hot knife or pastry wheel. Cut the dough into eight strips 12 inches long. Roll the strips around the cones, as shown lower right in the illustration, 645. Chill the cornets, covered, at least ½ hour. Glaze the tops of the strips with:

Milk Glaze, 731

Stand the cornets on a baking tin. To bake, see Puff Paste, 643.

NAPOLEONS

About Forty 2 x 3-Inch Bars

Could the Emperor conceivably have had these in mind when he contended that "an army marches on its stomach"?

Prepare:

Puff Paste, 643

Preheat oven to 450°.

Roll the chilled paste into an oblong, 24 x 33 inches, to a thickness of ⅛ inch or less. ➤ Trim all folded edges carefully to a depth of ½ inch. Divide the paste into three 11 x 24-inch oblongs. Place the 3 equal oblongs upside down on baking sheets that have been sprinkled with cold water. Prick them uniformly with a fork. Bake about 25 to 30 minutes, see Puff Paste, 643. When cool, you may glaze the layer reserved for the top with two successive coats of:

(Quick Icing I, 727)

Let the first coat dry before applying the second, or dust the top layer with:

Confectioners' sugar

Stack the 3 layers and cut them into 2 x 3-inch oblongs. Put between the layers:

Sweetened Whipped Cream, 696
or Crème Patissière, 697

The finished pastry is shown at the top right of the illustration on 645.

ABOUT CREAM PUFF SHELLS, PÂTE À CHOUX OR POUF PASTE

Please cease thinking of this basic, quite easy paste as something for adventurous moments only. Use it unsweetened as a base for Gnocchi, 204; for Dauphine Potatoes, 323; as a bland foil for fillings; as soup garnishes or as hors d'oeuvre cases. Pâte à choux, when sweetened, imparts great individuality to the presentation of food. With a pastry tube you can make elegant Éclairs, 647, Beignets, 244, characteristic cabbagy or choux shapes for cream puffs, Swans, 647, dainty choux paste cases, or the towering pyramid, Croquembouche, 647, all illustrated in the chapter heading. If you serve éclair cases filled with ice cream or cream and covered with a sauce, they are called **Profiteroles,** 647.

CREAM PUFF SHELLS

Two Dozen 3-Inch Shells

Preheat oven to 400°.

Have the eggs at room temperature. Sift before measuring:

1 cup all-purpose flour
⅛ teaspoon salt
1 tablespoon sugar, if the puffs are to be used with a sweet filling

Place in a heavy pan:

1 cup water or milk
⅓ cup butter

Bring to a boil, add the flour mixture in one fell swoop and stir quickly with a wooden spoon. It looks rough at first, but suddenly becomes smooth, at which point you stir faster. In a few minutes the paste becomes dry and does not cling to the spoon or the sides of the pan, and when the spoon is pressed on it lightly, it leaves a smooth imprint. ➤ Do not overcook or overstir at this point, for then the dough will fail to puff. ➤ Remove pan from heat for about 2 minutes. It must never be returned to the heat; this is why, to cook properly, ➤ the eggs must be at room temperature. Add one at a time, beating vigorously after each addition:

4 or 5 eggs

Continue to beat each time until the dough no longer looks slippery. The paste is ready to bake when the last egg has been incorporated. The proper consistency has been reached when a small quantity of the dough will stand erect if scooped up on the end of the spoon. It is best to use the dough at once.

A spoon or a pastry bag will serve to form the different shapes. Be sure to press the filled bag until you are rid of all the air in the tube. Allow space for expansion around shapes, as you squeeze them onto the greased pan. To form the puff or characteristic cabbagy, choux shape, hold the tube close to the baking sheet. ➤ Do not move the tube. Simply let the paste bubble up around it until the desired size is reached. To form éclairs, draw the tube along for about 3 to 4 inches while pressing, and always finish with a lifting reverse motion. To form small pastry cups, make one-inch globules. The little point left when you lift the bag can be pressed down with a moistened finger.

Before baking, sprinkle a few drops of water over the shapes on the pan—lightly—as you would sprinkle laundry. Bake cream puff shells and éclairs in a preheated 400° oven for 10 minutes. Reduce the heat to 350° and bake about 25 minutes longer. Do not remove them from the oven until they are quite firm to the touch. Cool the shells away from any draft before filling. For filling, cut them horizontally with a sharp knife. If there are any damp dough filaments inside, be sure to remove them. For suggested cream puff fillings, see below.

CHOUX PASTE SWAN

Prepare paste for:

Cream Puff Shells, above

Use a simple cut-off round tube, see Decorative Icings, 722, to form the head and neck all in one piece. To force a greater quantity of paste for the head, squeeze hard at the inception of the movement, and swing the tube in an arc for the neck, as shown in the chapter heading. Head and neck sections are baked on a greased sheet for only 10 minutes in a 400° oven. For the rest of the swan's anatomy, use a serrated tube to form 3-inch éclairs. Cut them lengthwise. Just before serving, fill the bottom piece with cream. Divide the top piece lengthwise for the wings. Embed them and the neck in the fluffy cream filling. The wings are braced somewhat diagonally to steady the neck. Dust the whole swan lightly with confectioners' sugar. Perfect for a little girl's party!

CHOCOLATE ECLAIRS

To form and bake the shells, see Cream Puff Shells, left. For the characteristic shape, see the elongated éclair in the chapter heading. Gash the shell sufficiently to line it with filling, or squirt the filling in with a pastry tube. Fill the shells as close to serving time as possible with:

Whipped cream, or Custard Chocolate or Coffee Fillings, 697

Cover them with:

A chocolate or caramel icing, 726

Garnish with:

Toasted slivered almonds

PROFITEROLES

To form and bake the shells, see Cream Puff Shells, 646. Divide the shells horizontally and fill as close to serving time as possible with:

Crème Chantilly, 696, or ice cream

Cover with:

Chocolate Sauce, 772

or fill with:

Whipped cream, 531

and serve with a strawberry sauce.

CROQUEMBOUCHE

Serves 10 to 12

This spectacular dessert, shown in the chapter heading, is a structural marvel. It needs considerable organization, for it is best when assembled as close to serving time as possible.

Caramelize:

2 cups sugar, 559

Form on the base of a 9-inch greased pie pan or directly on a footed cake tray a thin layer of caramelized sugar, keeping the rest soft in a 250° oven. When the thin layer has hardened, put it on the platter on which you intend to serve the dessert. Have ready:

Cream puffs under 2 inches in size, made from Cream Puff paste, 646

filled with:

Whipped or flavored cream, 696

Remove the caramel from the oven and work quickly. If the syrup tends to harden, reheat it slowly. ➤ Dip a portion of each filled puff in turn, as you place it in circular layers of decreasing width on the caramel disk. Arrange the puffs on the outer layers so that their tops form the exposed surface. Let additional syrup drip partially over the whole as a final glaze. Serve by pulling apart with 2 forks.

ABOUT FILLINGS FOR CREAM PUFF SHELLS AND ÉCLAIRS

Use Sweetened Whipped Creams, 696, Custards, 734, Crème Patissière, 697, or almost any of the fillings in complete dessert cakes, 687. ➤ Fill as close to serving time as possible to avoid sogginess. In any case, remember ➤ that cream-based and particularly egg-based fillings must be kept refrigerated. Egg fillings, if carelessly stored, are subject to bacterial activity which may be highly toxic, even though they give no evidence of spoilage. For fillings for unsweetened puff shells, see Canapés, 69 and 70.

With a sweetened dough try one of the following:

I. For a marvelous tea-teaser, put in the base of a puff shell a layer of:

Sweetened whipped cream, 696

Lightly insert with the pointed end up:

A flawless ripe strawberry

II. Or fill the puffs with:

Soft cream cheese
A dab of bright jelly

ABOUT STRUDEL

When the last princesse slip was freshly beribboned, our beloved Hungarian laundress sometimes found time to give us a treat. She made strudel. Draping the round dining room table with a fresh cloth, she patiently worked flour into it. Neighborhood small fry gathered on the fringes of the light cast by the Tiffany dome, and their eyes would pop as she rolled the dough, no larger than a softball, into a big thin circle. Then, hands lightly clenched, palms down, working under the sheet of dough and from the center out, she stretched it with the flat planes of the knuckles, as shown below. She would play it out, so to

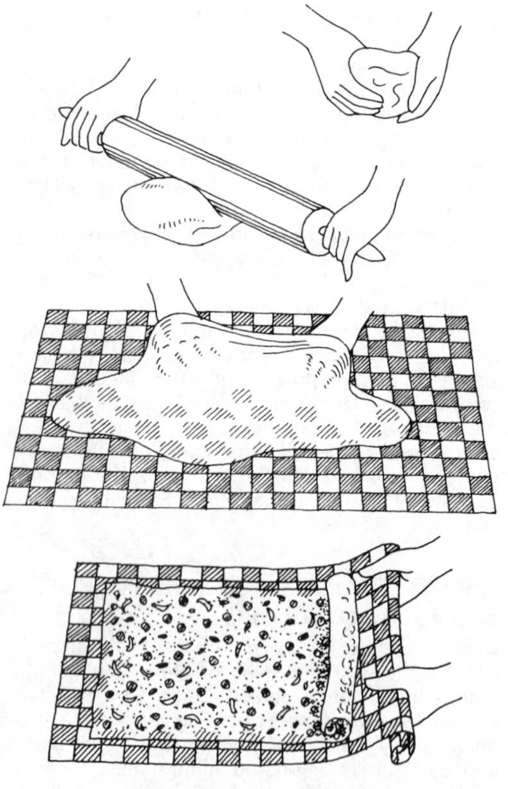

speak, not so much pulling it as coaxing it with long, even friction, moving round and round the table as she worked.

In our household, the filling was invariably apple. But whether you make strudel dough yourself or buy it, or the similar **phyllo**—for it now comes ready to use—there are endless possibilities for "interior decoration": poppy seed, ground meat mixtures, cheese, cherries, or just pepper worked originally into the dough. This last makes an excellent hors d'oeuvre pastry.

Our Janka had organized her filling well in advance. Browned bread crumbs, lemon rind grated into sugar, raisins, currants, very finely sliced apples, almonds and a small pitcher of melted butter were all set out on a tray. These were strewn alternately over the surface of the dough. Then came the forming of the roll. Using both hands, Janka picked up one side of the cloth and, while never actually touching the dough itself, tilted and nudged the cloth and the sheet this way and that until the dough rolled over on itself —jelly-roll fashion—and completely enclosed the filling. Finally, she slid the long cylinder onto a greased baking sheet and curved it into a horseshoe. From beginning to end the process had masterly craftsmanship. Would that we could give you her skill as easily as we give you her recipe. Now are you ready? Prepare the filling ingredients. Do not feel limited by these proportions or materials. See other fillings, 622.

Mix:

1 tablespoon cinnamon

with:

4 to 6 tablespoons browned bread crumbs
1 tablespoon lemon rind

grated into:

1 cup sugar
¾ cup raisins or currants
(½ cup shredded blanched almonds)
6 to 8 cups finely chopped tart apples

For the dough, have ready:

6 tablespoons melted butter

part of which will be incorporated into the flour. Have a cloth ready on a large table-height surface around which you will be able to walk. Work lightly into the cloth:

Flour

Sift onto a board, making a well, as shown on 643:

1½ cups all-purpose flour
¼ teaspoon salt

Pour into the center of the well:

1 well-beaten egg

mixed with:

⅓ to ½ cup tepid water or milk
2 teaspoons melted butter
(⅛ teaspoon vinegar)

Depending on your flour, you may have to add a few tablespoons more of tepid water. Combine the ingredients quickly with your fingers, working from the outside of the well, and when it is consolidated, knead on a board until the dough is pliable and silky and no longer sticks to the board. Brush the surface of the ball with melted butter. Cover the dough with a warm bowl and let it rest 30 minutes to one hour. Roll it out on the board as thin as possible. Move it to the table. Begin to stretch the dough gently from the center out, trying not to tear it, as patching is difficult. If you are skillful, this should stretch to about a square yard. A heavier edge of dough or a border will develop as you work, and whatever remains of this must be cut off with a knife before the filling is spread or the pastry rolled up. Use this excess dough for making patches.

Preheat oven to 400°.

Before filling, brush the dough with some of the melted butter. Sprinkle over the surface the filling mixture above. Dust with:

Cinnamon

Form the roll as described above ➤ not too tightly, as the dough will expand. Slide it onto the greased baking sheet. Brush the surface of the roll with some of the melted butter and sprinkle lightly with water. Bake 20 minutes at 400°, then lower the heat to 350°, brush the strudel again with the remaining butter, and bake about 10 minutes longer, until golden brown. Remove from oven and dust with:

Confectioners' sugar

Cut in wide diagonal slices and serve.

PHYLLO LEAVES

Fila, phyllo, yukka, brik, malsouka—call it what you like—is the tissue-thin pastry sheet used all over the Near East. The simplest of ingredients—flour and water—are so skillfully kneaded, rested and stretched as almost to defy amateur reproduction. In recipes calling for these leaves, we have successfully used our Strudel dough, 648. Phyllo leaves may be purchased in 12 sheets to the half pound. Use at once or freeze. ➤ If frozen, thaw very slowly, still wrapped, and plan to use all exposed sheets immediately.

ABOUT MERINGUE PASTE

There are many variations of meringue—all based on egg white and sugar. Also see Meringue Topping, 730. They include glamorous glacées and vacherins, served with ices or creams, including ice cream; Christmas meringue cookies, of which Cinnamon Stars are, perhaps deservedly, the best beloved; mountainous fluffy pie toppings; more discreet Italian types of meringue used over puddings and tarts; insulating meringues like those prepared for Omelette Soufflée Surprise and Baked Alaska; Swiss Meringue or Royal Glaze. Each calls for special treatment.

In this day of the electric mixer, showy meringue desserts have become effortless to make. They can, however, be made using a large egg whisk, but it takes endurance. ➤ Use glass, stainless steel or copper bowls for whipping the egg whites. See about Beating Eggs, 544. ➤ A word of warning: Do not attempt meringues when the humidity is high.

Ingredients and proportions do not vary. For every 4 egg whites—from 2-ounce eggs—use ½ pound sugar. As you know, sugars of the same weight differ tremendously in volume, see About Solid Sugars, 556. Eggs at about 70° should be opened, separated and whipped just before you are ready to mix the meringue. The baking is more a drying than a heating process. ➤ Use bottom heat only. A preheated 225° oven will give you a soft, crunchy meringue; a preheated 275° oven, a chewy one.

If you wonder about the indestructible meringues served in public places, they are based on confectioners' sugar; the egg whites are heated over hot water as for Génoise, 675; and the meringues are dried overnight in a warming oven, not above 175°. Whichever baking procedure is chosen, the classic confectioner does not allow his meringues to color. ➤ Store meringues immediately, tightly covered, as they absorb moisture and disintegrate easily. Do not try to freeze them.

To form meringue paste, use a spoon and spatula or a pastry bag. ➤ Do not fill meringues until just before serving. Individual kisses or rings filled with ices, ice creams or frozen desserts are called **Meringues Glacées.** Shape the paste into a large nest on a heat-resistant platter and fill it with fruits and cream for **Pinch Pie.** Baked in springform pans in shallow layers, they are called **Schaumtorten.** A **Vacherin Ring** is a flat coil of meringue with a piped edging to hold a filling of sweetened whipped cream—plain or with fruit. The top of the confection is an open meringue crown decorated at the edges with large contiguous baroque dots of meringue that are baked on. For filling suggestions, see 696, and for a cake with batter and meringue baked simultaneously, see Cream Meringue Tart, 689.

MERINGUES

Twelve 3-Inch Meringues or a 9-Inch Pie Shell

Preheat oven to 225°.

➤ Have egg whites at about 70°. Beat until foamy in an electric mixer or by hand:

4 egg whites

Add:

1 teaspoon vanilla

(⅛ teaspoon cream of tartar)

Add, while continuing to beat, 1 tablespoon at a time:

1 cup sifted, finely powdered sugar or
1 cup minus 1 tablespoon sifted sugar

(½ teaspoon cinnamon)

When the mixture stands in stiff peaks on the beater, it is ready for baking. ➤ Do not overbeat. To shape, see above. For a glaze, you may dust the meringues lightly with:

Granulated sugar

Bake on baking sheets covered with parchment paper about 1 hour or longer, depending on the size. The reason for the use of paper is not only to prevent sticking but to diffuse the heat. In some famous kitchens the meringues are baked on a thick board or a pan, both greased and floured. ➤ Do not remove from the oven at once, but turn off the oven, open the door and leave them for at least 5 minutes. Cool gradually, away from a draft. Remove them from the sheet when cool. If kisses are to be filled, crush the bottom lightly with the thumb while still warm. Shortly before serving, fill the hollows with:

Sweetened and flavored whipped cream or a frozen mixture

covered with:

Sweetened crushed fruit, or a chocolate sauce, 772

ABOUT BERRY AND OTHER FRUIT PIES

If you don't find the fruit combination you are looking for in our fruit pie recipes, perhaps you would like to experiment with fillings for yourself. A 9-inch fruit or berry pie needs about 4 cups of fresh fruit or 3 cups of cooked fruit. Each fruit will require its own quota of sweetening, depending on acidity and your personal taste. Four cups of gooseberries, for example, need about 1¾ cups of sugar, while the same amount of blueberries may need no more than ½ cup—plus lemon juice to heighten the flavor.

As to thickening for pie fruit: technically, each batch would require a different amount of thickener, depending on the variety of fruit, degree of ripeness, etc. For practical purposes, an often suggested formula for 4 cups of fruit is:

¼ cup all-purpose flour

However, acid fruits should be thickened with tapioca, cornstarch or arrowroot starch because the acidity of the fruit may neutralize the thickening power of the flour. So for 4 cups of fruit, mix:

2⅔ tablespoons quick-cooking tapioca
⅔ to 1 cup sugar

or mix:

2 tablespoons cornstarch or arrowroot starch

with:

¼ cup water or fruit juice

until very smooth and then blend with:

⅔ to 1 cup sugar

Whether you use tapioca or cornstarch, let the mixture stand for 15 minutes after blending it gently into the fresh fruit. Correct the sweetening, then proceed as directed in Berry Pies, below.

Some suggested proportions are:

½ apple and ½ pear
½ apple and ½ green tomato
½ rhubarb and ½ strawberry
⅓ gooseberry and ⅔ strawberry
½ cherry and ½ rhubarb
⅓ cranberry and ⅔ apple
½ mincemeat, ¼ applesauce and ¼ crushed pineapple
½ fresh strawberries and ½ bananas
⅔ raspberries and ⅓ currants

Fruit pies ✻ freeze well, but ➤ do not freeze those with a custard base.

BERRY PIE WITH FRESH FRUIT

A 9-Inch Double-Crust Pie

Please read About Berry Pies, above. Use:

Gooseberry, currant, blackberry, raspberry, strawberry, blueberry, huckleberry or loganberry

Line a pie pan with:

A pie dough, 640–642

Prepare by picking over and hulling:

4 cups fresh berries

Combine:

⅔ to 1 cup or more sugar
¼ cup all-purpose flour
(1½ tablespoons lemon juice or ½ teaspoon cinnamon)

If the fruit is juicy, add:

(2 teaspoons quick-cooking tapioca)

Sprinkle these ingredients over the berries and stir gently until well blended. Let stand for 15 minutes.

Preheat oven to 450°.

Turn the fruit into the pie shell. Dot with:

1 to 2 tablespoons butter

Cover the pie with a well-pricked top or with a lattice. Bake the pie in a 450° oven 10 minutes. Reduce the heat to 350° and bake 35 to 40 minutes or until golden brown.

BERRY OR CHERRY PIE WITH COOKED OR CANNED FRUIT

A 9-Inch Double-Crust Pie

Allow approximately:

2½ cups sweetened canned or cooked berries or cherries
1 cup fruit juice

Proceed as directed in the above recipe for Berry Pie with Fresh Fruit, but for thickening use:

1½ tablespoons quick-cooking tapioca

and the smaller amount of sugar. For cherry pie, see flavoring in Fresh Cherry Pie, 651. You may bake the filling in the unbaked pie shell as in Berry Pie with Fresh Fruit, or you may thicken the fruit juice by heating it separately with the thickener. Then mix it with the fruit and put it in a baked shell to serve.

BERRY OR CHERRY PIE WITH FROZEN FRUIT

A 9-Inch Double-Crust Pie

Line a pie pan with:

A pie dough, 640–642

Defrost until the fruit separates easily:

Frozen berries or cherries: 20 oz.

Mix fruit with:

3 tablespoons quick-cooking tapioca
1¼ cups sugar
⅛ teaspoon salt
2 tablespoons melted butter

Let stand for 15 minutes before adding to shell.

Preheat oven to 450°.

Cover filling with a pricked top or a lattice and

bake in a 450° oven 10 minutes. Reduce the heat to 350° and bake about 45 minutes or until golden brown.

FRESH CHERRY PIE

A 9-Inch Double-Crust Pie

Line a pie pan with:

A pie dough, 640–642

Wash, drain and pit:

4 cups fresh sour cherries

Combine, then mix gently with cherries:

2⅔ tablespoons quick-cooking tapioca
1⅓ cups sugar
(2 drops almond flavoring or
2 tablespoons kirsch)

Let fruit mixture stand 15 minutes.
Preheat oven to 450°.
Pour fruit into pie shell and dot with:

2 tablespoons butter

Cover with a well-pricked top or a lattice. Bake 10 minutes at 450°, then reduce heat to 350° and bake about 40 minutes longer or until golden brown.

SOUR CREAM CHERRY OR BERRY PIE

A 9-Inch Single-Crust Pie or 4 Tarts

Prepare a pie shell or tart shells, using:

Graham Cracker or Zwieback Crust, 642

Chill the shell, then fill it with the following cherry custard.
Preheat oven to 325°
Beat:

3 eggs

Add:

¾ cup sugar
¾ cup cultured sour cream
2 cups fresh or canned drained cherries or berries

Bake the pie until the custard is firm, about 1 hour. Serve very hot or very cold.

GLAZED BERRY PIE

A 9-Inch Single-Crust Pie

Prepare with a generous high rim:

A baked pie shell, 640

Clean and hull:

1 quart strawberries or red or black raspberries

Reserve and ⅄ blend or sieve 1 cup of the fruit. Combine and cook, stirring until thickened over low heat 10 to 15 minutes:

¾ cup sugar
2½ tablespoons cornstarch
¼ teaspoon salt
1 cup water

Add the blended fruit to give color. Put the whole berries into the baked pie shell, evenly distributed. Pour the syrup over the berries, coating them thoroughly by turning but not displacing them. Chill the pie in the refrigerator at least 4 hours. Serve garnished with:

(Whipped cream)

BLUEBERRY OR HUCKLEBERRY CUSTARD TARTS

Six to Eight 3-Inch Tarts

If seeds are small, it's blueberries you have; if many and large—huckleberries. The flavor is almost identical.
Prepare:

Pâte Sucrée, 641, or Vienna Pastry, 641

Preheat oven to 450°.
Place dough in the tart pans. Bake 8 to 12 minutes. Remove from oven and reduce heat to 375°. Fill tarts with a mixture of:

1 quart blueberries
½ cup sugar
(2 tablespoons lemon juice)

Bake about 10 minutes. Remove from oven. Cook and stir ➤ over—not in—boiling water until thickened:

½ cup cream
3 beaten egg yolks
½ cup sugar
⅛ teaspoon salt

Cool the custard and pour it over the slightly cooled tarts. Continue to cool and top with:

(Whipped Cream, 531)

APPLE PIE

I. A 9-Inch Double-Crust Pie

Call it **à la mode** if you garnish your pie with ice cream—a real inspiration when your apples are tart.
Line a 9-inch pie pan with:

A pie dough, 640–642

Pare, core and thinly slice:

5 to 6 cups apples

If you are using dried apples, allow 1 pound apples to 1 quart water and cook 35 to 45 minutes before proceeding. Combine and sift over the apples:

½ to ⅔ cup white or brown sugar
⅛ teaspoon salt
1 to 1½ tablespoons cornstarch
(¼ teaspoon cinnamon)
(⅛ teaspoon nutmeg)

Only very tart apples require the larger amount of sugar. Only very juicy apples require the larger amount of cornstarch. Stir the apples gently until they are well coated. Place them in layers in the pie shell. Dot with:

1½ tablespoons butter

If the apples are bland or lacking in flavor, sprinkle with:

1 tablespoon lemon juice
½ teaspoon grated lemon rind
(1 teaspoon vanilla)

If you are serving the pie with cheese, omit the above flavors and use:

(1 teaspoon fennel or anise seed)

Should the apples be very dry, add:

(2 tablespoons water or cream)

Preheat oven to 450°

Cover the pie with a pricked upper crust. Bake in a 450° oven 10 minutes. Reduce the heat to 350°. Bake until done, 35 to 45 minutes or until golden brown. For a delicious touch, sprinkle the top crust lightly with sugar and cinnamon as you put the pie into the oven. Some cooks brush it first with milk. Others prefer to finish the pie off, after baking, with:

(1 cup shredded cheese)

Place briefly under a broiler to melt the cheese.

II. A 9-Inch Single-Crust Pie

Follow directions for I above, using a single pie crust recipe. In place of an upper crust, top with a sprinkling of:

Streusel II, 731

Bake as directed. However, if the crumb crust is becoming too brown, protect with a foil covering until apples are tender.

APPLE TARTS

8 Tarts

Preheat oven to 375°.

Line eight shallow 3-inch muffin cups or individual pie pans with:

A pie dough, 640–642

Fill them with:

4 cups pared, thinly sliced apples

Combine and pour over the fruit:

½ cup sugar
2 slightly beaten eggs
2 tablespoons melted butter
1 tablespoon lemon juice
1 cup cream, or ½ cup evaporated milk and ½ cup water
(½ teaspoon cinnamon)
(⅛ teaspoon nutmeg)

Bake about 40 minutes.

PEACH PIE

I. A 9-Inch Single-Crust Pie

Preheat oven to 400°.

Line a pie pan with:

A pie dough, 640–642

Combine and blend well:

1 egg or 2 egg yolks
2 tablespoons flour
⅔ to 1 cup granulated sugar
(⅓ cup melted butter)

Pour this mixture over:

Halves of canned or peeled fresh peaches

that have been placed cut side up in the pie shell. Bake 15 minutes at 400°, then reduce the heat to 300° and bake about 50 minutes longer. Serve hot or, if cold, garnished with:

(Whipped cream)

II. A 9-Inch Double-Crust Pie

Follow the recipe for:

Apple Pie, 651

Substitute for the apples:

5 cups peeled, sliced peaches

Use the smaller amount of sugar.

RHUBARB PIE

I. A 9-Inch Double-Crust Pie

Follow the rule for baking Berry Pie with Fresh Fruit, 650, making a lattice crust for the top. This pie can also be made with half rhubarb and half strawberries.

Use:

4 cups unpeeled, diced young rhubarb stalks
¼ cup all-purpose flour
1¼ to 2 cups sugar
1 tablespoon butter
(1 teaspoon grated orange rind)

II. A 9-Inch Single-Crust Pie

A custardy rhubarb pie. Line a pie pan with:

A pie dough, 640–642

Preheat oven to 400°.

Place in the pie shell:

4 cups diced pink rhubarb

Combine and beat:

1½ cups sugar
3 egg yolks
½ cup all-purpose flour
3 tablespoons milk
(¾ teaspoon nutmeg)

Spread these ingredients over the rhubarb. Bake 20 minutes at 400°, then reduce the heat to 350° and bake another 20 minutes. When pie has cooled, use the 3 egg whites for a:

Meringue, 730

GRAPE PIE

A 9-Inch Double-Crust Pie

Stem:

4 cups blue grapes

Slip the pulp out of the skins. Reserve the skins. Cook the pulp until the seeds loosen. Press through a colander to remove seeds. Combine the pulp, the skins and:

¾ cup sugar
(1½ tablespoons lemon juice)
1 tablespoon grated orange rind
1 tablespoon quick-cooking tapioca

Let these ingredients stand 15 minutes. Line a pie pan with:

A pie dough, 640–642

Preheat oven to 450°.

Fill the shell with the grape mixture and form a lattice over the top, see 639. Bake the pie 10 minutes at 450°, then reduce heat to 350° and bake about 20 minutes.

★ MINCE PIE

A 9-Inch Double-Crust Pie

Preheat oven to 450°.

Line a pie pan with:

A pie dough, 640–642

Fill it with:

Mincemeat, 812, or a 28-oz. jar of mincemeat

Add to the mincemeat:

(2 to 4 tablespoons brandy)

Cover the pie with a pricked top. Bake at 450° 10 minutes, then reduce heat to 350° and bake about 30 minutes.

★ MOCK MINCE PIE

A 9-Inch Double-Crust Pie

Cut into pieces:

1½ cups seeded raisins

Pare, core and slice:

4 medium-sized tart apples or a combination of apples and green tomatoes

Combine the raisins and apples. Add:

Grated rind of 1 orange
Juice of 1 orange
½ cup cider or other fruit juice

Cover these ingredients and simmer until the apples are very soft. Stir in until well blended:

¾ cup sugar
½ teaspoon each cinnamon and cloves
2 or 3 tablespoons finely crushed soda crackers

If the apples are dry, use the smaller amount. This mixture will keep for several days. Shortly before using it, add:

(1 or 2 tablespoons brandy)

Preheat oven to 450°.
Line a pie pan with:

A pie dough, 640–642

Fill it with mock mincemeat. Cover with a pricked upper crust or with a lattice. Bake at 450° ten minutes, then reduce heat to 350° and bake about 20 minutes longer.

PRUNE OR APRICOT PIE

A 9-Inch Single-Crust Pie

Have ready:

A baked pie shell, 640

Preheat oven to 325°.
Put stewed, unsweetened prunes or apricots through a ricer. Combine:

¾ cup prune or apricot pulp
½ teaspoon grated lemon rind
1 tablespoon lemon juice
½ cup sugar

Beat until ➤ stiff, but not dry:

3 egg whites

Beat in very slowly:

½ cup sugar

Fold the egg whites into the fruit mixture. Fill the pie shell. Bake about 20 minutes or until set.

RAISIN PIE

A 9-Inch Single-Crust Pie

Have ready:

A baked pie shell, 640

Heat to the boiling point:

1 cup seedless or seeded white raisins
1 cup water

Add:

½ cup white or brown sugar

Cool ½ cup of this mixture. Stir into it gently:

2 tablespoons butter
2 tablespoons all-purpose flour

Return it to the saucepan. Cook and stir over low heat until the mixture has thickened. Remove pan from heat. Beat in:

2 egg yolks
1 teaspoon grated lemon rind
3 tablespoons lemon juice

Cool the filling. Fill the pie shell. Cover with Meringue I, 730, and bake as directed.

ABOUT TRANSPARENT PIES

There is a whole galaxy of pie fillings based on brown sugar, molasses, and corn or maple syrup. These are thickened usually with egg, but sometimes with a crumb mixture or, as in Shoo-Fly Pie, with a flour base, which gives the dessert a cake-like quality. Some cooks cut the sweetness with tart jellies, lemon or vinegar. Some add butter or cream, spices, nuts and dried fruits. You may top these pies with crumb mixtures, meringues, whipped cream or icing. Some transparents claim southern, some Pennsylvania ancestry; and a few acknowledge their direct descent from English forebears—the traditional Banbury or chess tarts. To test for doneness, read About Custards, 743.

BASIC TRANSPARENT PIE

We have encountered this great southern favorite at all sorts of gatherings, from fiestas to funerals. There are many variations, but we like to use our recipe for Pecan Pie, below, omitting the pecans and replacing the vanilla with:

A grating of nutmeg or 1 tablespoon lemon juice

If you add to the filling or line the crust with ¼ cup of tart jelly, you have **Amber Pie.**

PECAN PIE

A 9-Inch Single-Crust Pie

Black walnuts for pecans makes a piquant substitution.
Preheat oven to 450°.
Line a pan with:

A pie dough, 640–642

and bake it only partially, from 5 to 7 minutes. Allow it to cool. ➤ Reduce oven heat to 375°. Combine and beat thoroughly.

3 eggs
1 cup sugar
½ teaspoon salt
⅓ cup melted butter
1 cup light corn syrup

Stir in:

1 cup pecan halves
1 teaspoon vanilla or 1 tablespoon rum

Fill the shell. Bake the pie 40 to 50 minutes at 375° or until a knife inserted in the filling comes out clean. Serve warm or cold. If you omit the nuts and substitute for the vanilla 3 tablespoons of bourbon whisky, you will have a **Bourbon Pie.**

BANBURY TARTS

About Six 4-Inch Tarts

Have ready:

Individual baked tart crusts, 641

Combine:

1 cup seeded raisins
1 cup sugar
2 tablespoons cracker crumbs
1 well-beaten egg
Grated rind of 1 lemon
1½ tablespoons lemon juice
2 tablespoons butter
¼ cup chopped candied fruits
(2 tablespoons chopped walnuts)

Cook and stir these ingredients over low heat until the mixture begins to thicken. Remove from the heat. Cool. Half fill the tart shells. Top with:

(Whipped cream)

You may use this filling in Turnovers, 251.

JEFFERSON DAVIS PIE

A 9-Inch Single-Crust Pie

Prepare:

A baked pie shell, 640

Preheat oven to 325°.
Cream:

½ cup butter
2 cups packed light brown sugar

Beat in:

4 egg yolks

Mix, then add:

2 tablespoons all-purpose flour
1 teaspoon cinnamon
½ teaspoon allspice
1 teaspoon freshly grated nutmeg

Stir in:

1 cup cream
½ cup chopped dates
½ cup raisins
½ cup broken pecan meats

Fill the shell. Bake the pie until set, about 30 minutes. When cool, top with:

Meringue I, 730

Bake as directed. Without the nuts and spices this becomes **Kentucky Pie.**

CHESS TARTS

Fill:

Baked tart crusts, 641

with filling for:

Jefferson Davis Pie, above

omitting the dates and spices. When cool, cover with:

Whipped cream

CRUMB OR GRAVEL PIE

A 9-Inch Single-Crust Pie

Use a:

Baked pie shell, 640

for this Pennsylvania Dutch specialty. Sprinkle the bottom of shell with:

(½ cup seedless raisins)

Combine and cook in the top of a double boiler or over low heat until thick:

1 cup brown sugar, mild molasses or honey
½ cup hot water
3 beaten eggs

Cool and pour these ingredients into the pie shell.
Preheat oven to 325°
Combine and work like pastry:

1 cup cake or cookie crumbs
⅓ cup all-purpose flour
½ to 1 teaspoon cinnamon
¼ teaspoon nutmeg
⅛ teaspoon ginger
⅓ cup soft butter

Sprinkle this mixture over the filling. To make **Gravel Pie,** don't combine the above ingredients. Instead, sprinkle them alternately over the pie—with the crumbs on top. Bake 20 to 30 minutes. If you bake from three to five of these shells with thin fillings, stack them and top them with Boiled Icing, 721, flavored with lemon, or Caramel Icing, 726, you have a **Stack Pie.**

PUMPKIN OR SQUASH PIE

When Halloween comes 'round, we welcome pumpkins as symbols of harvest and sources of shivery fun. For holiday decorations, why not have each of the children carve his own small pumpkin? Then stack them into a totem pole. Use the topmost cutout as a lid, the rest for ears and noses. Stems make good features, too. Choose pumpkins of varied shapes, as shown on 638, and encourage the sculptors to vary their expressions.

Abroad, we find almost everywhere that a great diversity of puddings like the filling below, soups, 185, breads, 624, and vegetable dishes, 330, are prepared from these members of the squash family. Here in America we restrict their use mostly to pie.

➤ To cook pumpkin, wash and cut it in half crosswise. Remove seeds and strings. Place it in a pan, shell side up, and bake it in a 325° oven for 1 hour or more, depending on size, until it is tender and begins to fall apart. Scrape the pulp from the shell and put it through a ricer or strainer or blender.

I. **A 9-Inch Single-Crust Pie**

Line a pie pan with:

A pie dough, 640–642

Preheat oven to 425°.
Mix until well blended:

2 cups cooked or canned pumpkin or squash
1½ cups undiluted evaporated milk or rich cream
¼ cup brown sugar
½ cup white sugar
½ teaspoon salt
1 teaspoon cinnamon
½ teaspoon ginger
¼ teaspoon nutmeg or allspice

⅛ teaspoon cloves
2 slightly beaten eggs

Pour the mixture into the pie shell. Bake 15 minutes at 425°, then reduce heat to 350° and bake about 45 minutes longer or until an inserted knife comes out clean. Serve with:

Sweetened whipped cream

flavored with:

(2 tablespoons bourbon)

II.

Follow the directions in I, above, omitting the milk and adding:

2 tablespoons molasses
1½ cups sour cream

ABOUT CUSTARD PIES

How many puzzled inquiries we have answered about "Custard, my family's favorite pie"! In a recent one, our correspondent gloomily points out: "My mother thinks it's lumpy because I cook it too long. My husband thinks it gets watery because I put it in the icebox." How right, unfortunately, are both of this bride's critics! ➤ Custard and cream pies, unless eaten almost at once, must be kept well chilled. The lightly cooked eggs are especially subject to adverse bacterial activity, even though they may give no evidence of spoilage. It is Hobson's choice here: eat within 3 hours if the pie is left unrefrigerated or risk wateriness under refrigeration.

Again, pie dough needs a high heat, while the custard itself demands a low one. How to reconcile these contradictions? We find that the easiest way to satisfaction is to prebake crust and filling separately; then, just before serving, to slip the cooled filling into the cooled shell. To prebake

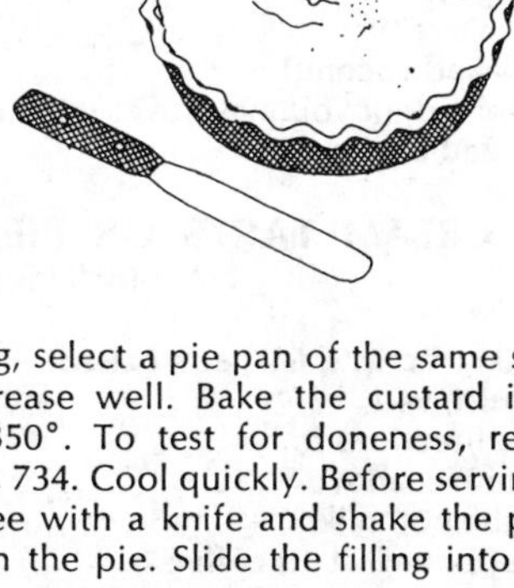

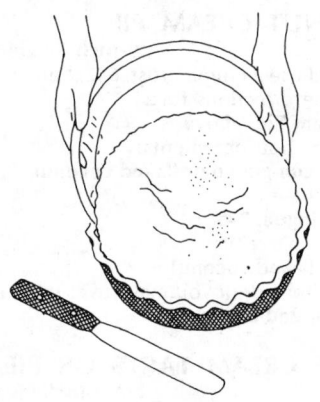

the filling, select a pie pan of the same size as the crust. Grease well. Bake the custard in the pie pan at 350°. To test for doneness, read About Custards, 734. Cool quickly. Before serving, cut the edges free with a knife and shake the pan gently to loosen the pie. Slide the filling into the crust, see below. This method takes a bit of dexterity, but after you get used to it, you will prefer it.

The filling need not even be preformed but, if precooked, can be spooned carefully into the prebaked shell. If you use a topping, see 696, no one but you will be the wiser. Two more important comments about fillings which are precooked, but not preformed, like Rich Custard, 735: ➤ always cook them over—not in—boiling water; and ➤ when they are thickened, beat them until they are cool to allow all the steam to escape. The steam will otherwise condense and thin the filling too much. Mark Twain inelegantly wrote of a frustrated crow that it was "sweating like an ice pitcher," and this is exactly what custard filling will do, unless beaten until cool. Or you may use Baked Custard, 734. When either custard is 70° or cooler, place the filling in the prebaked shell, and the pie is ready to serve.

CUSTARD PIE

A 9-Inch Single-Crust Pie

Preheat oven to 450°.

The partial baking of this pie shell before filling ensures a crisper undercrust. Line a pie pan with:

A pie dough, 640–642

Build up a fluted rim. Prick the bottom and bake it in a 450° oven just 10 minutes. Reduce heat to 325°. Pull the oven rack partway out and pour the following custard into the crust, or remove the crust from the oven only long enough to fill it.

Beat slightly:

3 eggs or 6 egg yolks

Add and stir well:

½ cup sugar
¼ teaspoon salt
2 cups milk, or milk and light cream
1 teaspoon vanilla or 1 tablespoon rum

Sprinkle the top with:

(¼ teaspoon nutmeg)

Bake the pie in the 325° oven about 30 minutes or until firm. Serve plain, with sugared fresh fruit, or garnished with curls of:

(Sweet chocolate)

QUICK CUSTARD TARTS, OR FLAN WITH FRUIT

To be assembled just before serving.

Prepare:

Prebaked tart crusts, 641

Spoon into them:

½-inch layer of Baked Custard, 734

Top the custard with:

Strawberries or other berries, cooked drained apples, drained cherries, peaches, bananas, pineapple or coconut

Coat the fruit with Glaze for Tarts, 732, to which you may add:

(1 tablespoon or more of brandy or rum)

Garnish with:

(Whipped cream)

CARAMEL CUSTARD PIE

A 9-Inch Single-Crust Pie

Prepare:

A baked pie shell, 640

and:

Caramel Custard Pudding, 738

Cool the pudding and fill the slightly cooled pie crust. Garnish with:

Sweetened Whipped Cream II, 696

CREAM PIE

A 9-Inch Single-Crust Pie

Prepare:

A baked pie shell, 640

In top of double boiler combine:

⅔ cup sugar
½ cup all-purpose flour
½ teaspoon salt

Add, stir and cook ➤ over—not in—boiling water 10 minutes or until mixture thickens:

2 cups milk

Remove from heat. Beat slightly:

3 egg yolks

Stirring well, pour half of hot mixture into eggs. When smooth, return eggs to rest of hot mixture and cook until thickened. Remove from heat and add:

2 tablespoons butter
2 teaspoons vanilla

Cool slightly before turning into the crust. Cover with:

Meringue, 730

Brown delicately as directed.

CHOCOLATE CREAM PIE

I. **A 9-Inch Single-Crust Pie**

Follow the directions for:

Cream Pie, above

with the following changes. You may increase the sugar to 1 cup. Melt in the hot milk mixture:

2 oz. cut-up unsweetened chocolate

II.

Or fill the pie crust with half the recipe for:

Pots-de-Crème, 737, or French Chocolate Mousse, 737, or Rum Chocolate Mousse, 738, or Mocha Filling, 697

Garnish with:

Whipped cream

and keep chilled until ready to serve.

FUDGE PIE

An 8-Inch Pie

A crustless pie or cake unexcelled in its delicious and devastatingly rich quality. But do not let a little devastation deter you.

Preheat oven to 325°.

Cream together:

1 cup sugar
½ cup butter

Beat in:

2 egg yolks
2 oz. melted, slightly cooled unsweetened chocolate

Add and beat:

⅓ cup all-purpose flour
1 teaspoon vanilla
1 cup broken nutmeats

Whip until ➤ stiff, but not dry:

2 egg whites
⅛ teaspoon salt

Fold them into the batter. Pour into a greased 8-inch pie pan and bake about 30 minutes. Serve topped with:

Ice cream

BUTTERSCOTCH CREAM PIE

A 9-Inch Single-Crust Pie

Follow the directions for:

Cream Pie, above

but substitute for the granulated sugar:

1 cup brown sugar

and decrease the vanilla to ½ teaspoon. A good addition is:

(½ cup nutmeats or crushed Nut Brittle or Praliné, 789)

Cover with:

Meringue, 730

and bake as directed; or cover with:

Whipped cream, 531

BANANA CREAM PIE

A 9-Inch Single-Crust Pie

Follow the directions for:

Cream Pie, above

Peel and slice thinly:

2 ripe bananas

Place them in the baked pie shell. Pour the cooled filling over them.

COCONUT CREAM PIE

A 9-Inch Single-Crust Pie

You could use a crumb crust, 642, here.

Follow the directions for:

Cream Pie, above

Add to the hot ingredients:

½ to 1 cup grated or flaked coconut

Cover with:

Meringue, 730

and sprinkle over it:

¼ cup flaked coconut

Bake as directed; or you may cover the pie with:

Whipped cream, 531

COFFEE CREAM TARTS OR PIE

A 9-Inch Pie or 6 Tarts

Prepare:

6 baked tart crusts, 641, or a baked pie crust, 640

Follow the directions for:

Cream Pie, above

adding to the hot milk:

3 tablespoons instant coffee

You may substitute for the vanilla:

(2 teaspoons rum)

Top with:

Whipped cream, 531, or
Mocha Marshmallow Cream, 749

STRAWBERRY OR RASPBERRY BAVARIAN PIE

A 9-Inch Single-Crust Pie

Prepare:

A baked pie shell, 640

When cool, fill with:

Bavarian Berry Cream, 747

LEMON MERINGUE PIE

A 9-Inch Single-Crust Pie

Prepare:

A baked pie shell, 640

Sift into a 2- or 3-quart saucepan:

1½ cups sugar
6 tablespoons cornstarch
¼ teaspoon salt

Gradually blend in:

½ cup cold water
½ cup fresh lemon juice

When smooth add, blending thoroughly:

3 well-beaten egg yolks
2 tablespoons butter

Stirring constantly, gradually add:

1½ cups boiling water

Bring the mixture to a full boil, stirring gently. As it begins to thicken, reduce the heat and allow to simmer slowly 1 minute. Remove from heat and stir in:

1 teaspoon grated lemon peel

Pour into the baked pie shell. Cover with:

Meringue, 730

and bake as directed. Serve when cool.

OHIO LEMON PIE

A 9-Inch Double-Crust Pie

A very tart Shaker favorite.
Grate and reserve the yellow peel from:

2 large lemons

With a very sharp knife remove the white inner peel from the lemons and cut them into paper-thin slices. Remove seeds. Combine in a bowl the lemon slices, the grated peel and:

2 cups sugar
1 teaspoon salt

Let stand 2 to 24 hours—the longer the better.
Preheat oven to 425°.
Line a pie pan with:

A pie dough, 640–642

Add to the lemon-and-sugar mixture:

4 well-beaten eggs

After the mixture has been well stirred, pour it into the pastry-lined pan and cover with a top crust, 639. Bake ten minutes. Reduce heat to 325° and bake about 45 minutes longer. If the pie crust edges brown too fast, see 639. Cool pie before serving.

KEY LIME PIE

A 9-Inch Single-Crust Pie

This pie owes its distinctive character to the pungent citrus variety—native to Florida—called the Key lime. It may be used in any other recipe calling for either lemon or lime.
Prepare:

A baked pie shell, 640

Preheat oven to 350°.
Mix together well:

1 can sweetened condensed milk: 15 oz.
1 tablespoon grated Key lime rind
½ cup Key lime juice
¼ teaspoon salt
(2 slightly beaten egg yolks)

Stir until thickened, a result of the reaction of the milk with the citrus juice.
Pour the mixture into the baked crust and cover with a meringue made by beating until ➤ stiff, but not dry:

2 egg whites

to which are gradually added:

2 tablespoons sugar

Bake pie 10 to 15 minutes or until lightly browned.

EGGLESS LEMON OR LIME PIE

A 9-Inch Single-Crust Pie

Prepare:

A baked pie shell, 640

Combine:

1 can sweetened condensed milk: 15 oz.
⅓ cup lime or lemon juice
1 tablespoon grated lime or lemon rind
¼ teaspoon salt

➤ Stir until thickened. The thickening results from the reaction of the milk and citrus juice.
Turn the filling into the crust. Chill about 3 hours.
Serve garnished with:

(Whipped cream)
(Shaved sweet chocolate)

LEMON ANGEL PIE

A 9-Inch Single-Crust Pie

Prepare a shell of:

Meringue Paste, 649

Butter the bottom of a deep 9-inch ovenproof dish and cover with the meringue, making a fluted rim. Bake as directed. Let cool in the oven with the door open. Prepare the following filling in a double boiler ➤ over—not in—boiling water. Beat well:

4 egg yolks

Add:

1 tablespoon all-purpose flour
½ cup sugar
½ cup water
Juice and grated rind of 1 lemon

Cook until thickened, beating constantly. Cool.
Whip:

1 cup whipping cream

Fold in:

½ teaspoon vanilla

Put half the cream in the meringue shell, then the cooked lemon filling. Cover with the remaining cream. Chill before serving.

ABOUT CHIFFON PIES

Many chiffon pies call for raw egg whites, so please see note on uncooked eggs, 743.

Don't neglect the wonderful Bavarian Creams, 746–748, the Gelatin Puddings, 743, and the Fruit Whips, 745. All can be used in a baked pie shell.

LEMON OR LIME CHIFFON PIE

A 9-Inch Single-Crust Pie

Please see note on uncooked eggs, 743. Prepare:

A baked pie shell, 640

Combine in the top of a double boiler:

½ cup sugar
⅔ cup water
4 egg yolks
1 tablespoon gelatin
⅓ cup lemon or lime juice

Cook and stir these ingredients ➤ over—not in—boiling water until thick. Add:

1 tablespoon grated lemon or lime peel

Chill mixture in refrigerator until it forms little mounds when dropped from a spoon. Whip:

4 egg whites

until ➤ stiff, but not dry. Fold in:

⅓ cup sugar

Fold this mixture lightly in turn into the lemon mixture. Fill the pie crust. Chill until set, which may take several hours.

ORANGE CHIFFON PIE

A 9-Inch Single-Crust Pie

Follow directions for:

Lemon Chiffon Pie, above

but substitute a well-flavored orange juice for the water and lemon juice, and orange peel for the lemon peel. Indifferently flavored orange juice may be improved by the addition of 2 teaspoons of vanilla.

CHOCOLATE MOCHA GELATIN CHIFFON PIE

A 9-Inch Single-Crust Pie

Please see note on uncooked eggs, 743.
Prepare:

A baked pie shell, 640

Soak:

1 tablespoon gelatin

in:

¼ cup cold strong coffee

Combine and stir until smooth:

6 tablespoons cocoa or 2 oz. melted unsweetened chocolate
½ cup sugar
½ cup boiling strong coffee

Stir in the soaked gelatin until it is dissolved. Cool slightly and pour these ingredients gently onto:

4 lightly beaten egg yolks

Cook and stir this mixture in a double boiler ➤ over—not in—boiling water until it thickens. Chill until about to set. Beat with a wire whisk until light. Add:

1 teaspoon vanilla
(1 tablespoon brandy)

Whip until ➤ stiff, but not dry:

4 egg whites

Slowly beat in:

½ cup sugar

Fold the egg whites into the chocolate mixture. Fill the pie shell. Chill the pie to set the filling. Spread with:

Whipped cream, 531

RASPBERRY OR STRAWBERRY CHIFFON PIE

A 9-Inch Single-Crust Pie

Prepare:

A baked pie shell, 640

Just before serving, fill with:

Bavarian Berry Cream, 747

and serve covered with:

Glaze for Fruit Pies II, 732

BLACK BOTTOM GELATIN PIE

A Deep 9-Inch Single-Crust Pie

Please see note on uncooked eggs, 743. Prepare:

A baked crumb crust, 642, or baked pie shell, 640

Soak:

1 tablespoon gelatin

in:

¼ cup cold water

Scald:

2 cups rich milk

Combine:

½ cup sugar
4 teaspoons cornstarch

Beat until light:

4 egg yolks

Slowly stir the milk into the eggs. Stir in the sugar mixture. Cook these ingredients ➤ over—not in—boiling water, stirring occasionally, about 20 minutes—or until the custard coats a spoon heavily. Take out 1 cup of the custard. Add to it:

1½ oz. melted unsweetened chocolate

Beat until well blended and cool. Add:

½ teaspoon vanilla

Pour this into the crust. Dissolve the soaked gelatin in the remaining hot custard. Let it cool, but not stiffen. Stir in:

1 tablespoon or more rum

Beat until well blended:

3 egg whites

Add:

¼ teaspoon cream of tartar

Beat the egg whites until ➤ stiff, but not dry. Beat in gradually, a teaspoon at a time:

¼ cup sugar

Fold the egg whites into the custard. Cover the

chocolate custard with the rum-flavored custard. Chill to set. Whip until stiff:

1 cup whipping cream

Add gradually:

2 tablespoons confectioners' sugar

Cover custard with the cream. Top with:

½ oz. shaved semisweet chocolate

MAPLE OR CARAMEL GELATIN CHIFFON PIE

A 9-Inch Single-Crust Pie

Prepare:

A baked pie shell, 640

Follow directions for:

Caramel or Maple Bavarian Cream, 747

reducing the milk to ⅔ cup and folding in before chilling:

2 stiffly beaten egg whites

PUMPKIN GELATIN CHIFFON PIE

A 9-Inch Single-Crust Pie

Please see note on uncooked eggs, 743.

Prepare:

A baked pie shell, 640, or Graham Cracker Crust, 642

Soak:

1 tablespoon gelatin

in:

¼ cup cold water

Beat slightly:

3 egg yolks

Add:

½ cup white or brown sugar
1¼ cups canned or cooked pumpkin
½ cup milk
½ teaspoon salt
¼ teaspoon each cinnamon, nutmeg and ginger

Cook and stir these ingredients ➤ over—not in—boiling water until thick. Stir in the soaked gelatin until dissolved. Chill until mixture begins to set. Whip until ➤ stiff, but not dry:

3 egg whites

Stir in gradually:

½ cup sugar

and fold into the pumpkin mixture. Fill the pie shell. Chill several hours to set. Serve garnished with:

Whipped cream, 531

ABOUT CHEESECAKE

No wonder pictures of leggy starlets are called cheesecake! We think the following recipes are starlets. Take your pick, but remember to ➤ watch temperatures. Cheesecakes are egg-based. They need low heat and are usually left in the turned-off oven with the door open after baking. Expect a slight shrinkage as they cool. If there is great shrinkage, you have baked them at too high heat. They all profit by ➤ thorough chilling before serving, preferably 12 hours. For safe storage, keep refrigerated, lightly covered.

⅄ We have found it a time-saver to put all ingredients together in a blender except the egg whites or whipped cream, which should be folded in just before the mixture is poured into the crust. If smooth cottage cheese is not available, regular curd cottage cheese may be put through a sieve or a ⅄ blender.

A few wine-soaked currants, finely shaved almonds, or tiny pieces of angelica or citron are sometimes mixed with the filling or used as topping. Shaved curled chocolate may be added as a surface garnish. To glaze cheesecakes, see Strawberry Glaze and Apricot Glaze, 732, Sauce Cockaigne, 770, and other fruit sauces.

WHIPPED CREAM CHEESECAKE

I. **16 Servings**

Prepare a double recipe of:

A crumb crust, 642

Reserve ½ cup of this mixture. Press the remainder with a spoon or the palm of the hand on the bottom and sides of a 12-inch spring-form pan. Chill this shell thoroughly.

Preheat oven to 350°.

To make the filling, sift:

1½ cups sugar

Beat until light:

6 eggs

Add the sugar gradually. Beat these ingredients until very light. Add:

⅛ teaspoon salt
2 teaspoons grated lemon rind
1 to 2 tablespoons lemon juice
1 teaspoon vanilla

Blend well and add to the above:

½ cup all-purpose flour
3½ pints smooth cottage cheese: 2¼ lb.

Whip and fold in:

2 cups whipped cream

Fill the pie crust. Sprinkle the reserved crumb mixture over the filling. Bake about 1 hour. Turn off the heat and permit the pie to stand in the oven with the door open for 1 hour longer or until cooled.

II. **10 Servings**

This very delicate pie should be baked in a 2-inch-deep 9-inch pan.

Prepare:

A baked pie shell, 640, or crumb crust, 642

Make enough to also line the sides of the pan.

Preheat oven to 350°.

Combine and beat:

3 cups smooth cottage cheese
3 whole eggs

Add:

¾ cup whipping cream
3 tablespoons melted butter
5 tablespoons sugar
½ teaspoon vanilla, or 1 tablespoon lemon juice plus ½ teaspoon grated lemon rind
(¼ cup chopped blanched almonds)

Bake the pie until the filling is firm, about 45 minutes. Sprinkle it while hot with:

4 tablespoons confectioners' sugar
1 teaspoon cinnamon

SOUR CREAM CHEESECAKE

12 Servings

Using 2 cups crumbs, line a 2½-inch-deep, 9-inch spring mold with:

Zwieback Crust, 642

Chill the crust.
Preheat oven to 375°.
Mix well, then pour into the crust:

2 well-beaten eggs
¾ lb. soft cream cheese
½ cup sugar
1 teaspoon lemon juice or ½ teaspoon vanilla
½ teaspoon salt

Bake about 20 minutes. Remove from oven. Dust the top with:

Cinnamon

Let cool to room temperature. Heat oven to 425°.
Mix well and pour over the cake:

1½ cups thick cultured sour cream
2 tablespoons sugar
½ teaspoon vanilla
⅛ teaspoon salt

Bake about 5 minutes to glaze the cheesecake. Let it cool, then refrigerate from 6 to 12 hours before serving.

RICOTTA CHEESECAKE OR PIE

A 10-Inch Single-Crust Pie

This North Italian delight is a favorite of our friend Jim Beard, who has generously allowed us to include it.
Prepare and line a deep pie pan with:

Cheesecake Crust, 642

Make a fluted edge and bake about 7 minutes at 450°. Cool. Heat oven to 375°.
Have ready:

3 tablespoons toasted pine nuts
2 tablespoons chopped blanched almonds
2 tablespoons chopped citron

and dust with:

1 tablespoon flour

Beat until light and lemony in color:

4 eggs

Gradually add:

1 cup sugar
1½ teaspoons vanilla

Add to the eggs and blend well:

1½ lb. Ricotta cheese

Stir in the nut mixture and pour the filling into the crust. Bake about 40 minutes.

GELATIN CHEESECAKE

A 10-Inch Cake

This handsome and toothsome affair will serve up to 18 persons and may be made a day in advance. Fruit may be incorporated, but if it is, substitute fruit juice for the water and milk. See note on uncooked eggs, 743. Prepare a double recipe of:

Graham Cracker or Zwieback Crumb Crust, 642

Reserve ½ cup crumbs. Spread or pat the rest in a thin layer over the bottom and sides of a 3-inch-deep 10-inch spring mold. Bake the crust about 10 minutes. Cool it. Beat in the top of a double boiler:

4 beaten egg yolks
¾ cup sugar
¼ teaspoon salt
⅓ cup milk

Heat and stir this custard ➤ over—not in—boiling water until it thickens. Soak:

2 tablespoons gelatin

in:

½ cup water

Add the gelatin to the hot custard and stir until dissolved. Cool the custard. Add:

1½ teaspoons vanilla or ⅓ cup lemon juice

Beat until smooth:

1½ lb. soft cream cheese

Gradually beat the custard into the cheese until well blended. Whip until ➤ stiff, but not dry:

4 egg whites

Whip in gradually:

½ cup sugar

Fold this into the custard. Beat until stiff, then fold in:

1 cup whipping cream

Fill the crust with the custard. Sprinkle the reserved crumbs over the top. Chill well in the refrigerator until ready to serve.

ABOUT FRUIT PASTRIES

Here we include **cobblers, deep-dish pies,** fresh **fruit cakes, shortcakes, upside-down cakes, crisps** and **crunches.** Remember that large shortcakes, fresh fruit cakes and crunches lend themselves well to baking for individual servings.

COBBLERS AND DEEP-DISH PIES

A cobbler, first cousin to a deep-dish pie, involves a rich biscuit dough, 632, and fruit. Baked with the fruit either under or over it, it is usually served with rich cream, Hard Sauce, 775, or Sweetened Butters, 775; but try a fresh hot blackberry cobbler with vanilla ice cream.
Preheat oven to 425°.
Combine in a saucepan and heat:

3 cups prepared fruit: apples, peaches, plums, etc.
⅔ cup sugar—depending on sweetness of fruit
1 tablespoon all-purpose flour or 1 beaten egg

If using flour, allow the mixture to boil. If using egg, stir until it thickens somewhat, but do not allow it to boil. Have ready half the recipe for:

Fluffy Biscuit Dough, 633

Place the dough in a greased 8 x 8-inch pan or casserole and cover it closely with the hot fruit; or place the hot fruit in the bottom of an 8-inch baking dish and spoon over it the dough. Dot the fruit with:

2 tablespoons butter

Sprinkle with:

(3/4 teaspoon cinnamon)

Bake the cobbler about 1/2 hour.

APPLE, PEACH OR PLUM CAKE COCKAIGNE

A 9- or 10-Inch Round Pan

Our friend Jane Nickerson, formerly Food Editor of the *New York Times,* suggests using fresh guavas in this dish.

Preheat oven to 425°.

If the fruit used is very juicy, reduce the liquid in the dough by at least 1 tablespoon. Sift together:

1 cup all-purpose flour
1 teaspoon double-acting baking powder
1/4 teaspoon salt
2 tablespoons sugar

Add:

11/2 to 3 tablespoons butter

Work these ingredients like pastry, 639. Beat well in a measuring cup:

1 egg
1/2 teaspoon vanilla

Add:

Enough milk to make a 1/2-cup mixture

Combine with the flour and butter to make a stiff dough. You may pat the dough into the greased pan with your floured palm, or spread it in part with a spoon and then distribute it evenly by pushing it with the fruit sections when you place them closely in overlapping rows. Use about:

4 cups sliced pared apples or peaches or sliced unpared plums, preferably freestone blue

Sprinkle with a mixture of:

1 cup white or brown sugar
2 teaspoons cinnamon
3 tablespoons melted butter

Bake about 25 minutes.

FRENCH APPLE OR PEACH CAKE

A Deep 8-Inch Pie Pan

Sweet and rich.

Preheat oven to 425°.

Grease the pan or ovenproof dish and cover the bottom well with:

2 cups or more peeled sliced apples, peaches or other fruit

Sprinkle the fruit with:

2/3 cup sugar
Cinnamon or nutmeg
Grated rind and juice of 1 lemon

Dredge with:

1 tablespoon all-purpose flour

Pour over surface:

2 to 4 tablespoons melted butter

Prepare the following batter. Sift together:

1 cup all-purpose flour
1/2 cup sugar
1 teaspoon double-acting baking powder
1/4 teaspoon salt

Beat and add:

2 egg yolks
1 tablespoon melted butter
1/4 cup milk

Beat these ingredients with swift strokes until blended. Cover the fruit with the batter. Bake the cake for about 30 minutes. Reverse it on a platter. Cool slightly. Use the egg whites for:

(Meringue II, 730)

and brown as directed.

SKILLET OR UPSIDE-DOWN CAKE

A 9- or 10-Inch Heavy Skillet

Vary this recipe, which conventionally calls for canned pineapple, by using canned or frozen raspberries, peaches or apricots. The last two require only 1/2 cup sugar. Fresh fruit—peaches, cherries, apples, etc.—may require more than 1 cup, depending on the acidity of the fruit.

Preheat oven to 350°.

Melt in a skillet:

1/4 to 1/2 cup butter

Add, cook gently and stir until dissolved:

1/2 to 1 cup packed brown sugar

Remove the pan from the heat and add:

(1 cup pecan meats)

Place over the butter and sugar mixture:

Slices or halves of drained canned fruit: No. 21/2 can

Cover the fruit with the following batter. Sift together:

1 cup cake flour
1 teaspoon double-acting baking powder

Beat in a separate bowl:

4 egg yolks

Add:

1 tablespoon melted butter
1 teaspoon vanilla

Sift in a separate bowl:

1 cup sugar

Whip until stiff ➤ but not dry:

4 egg whites

Fold in the sugar, 1 tablespoon at a time; then fold in the yolk mixture, and finally the sifted flour, 1/4 cup at a time. Bake the cake about 30 minutes. Immediately upon removal from the oven, reverse the cake onto a serving plate. Allow pan to remain over the cake briefly to let brown sugar mixture coat the cake. Remove pan and serve upside down, after sprinkling the fruit with:

(Brandy or rum)

The cake may be garnished with:

(Whipped cream or a dessert sauce)

For individual servings, try this method: Put butter, sugar and fruit in base of custard cups, run batter given above on top of the fruit and bake in a 350° oven until done.

APPLE CRISP OR FRUIT PARADISE

6 Servings

This dessert can be baked in an ovenproof dish from which you may serve at table. Its success,

when made with apples, depends on their flavor. See About Apples, 129.
Preheat oven to 375°.
Pare, core and slice into a 9-inch pie pan or dish:
4 cups tart apples
or use the same amount of:
Peaches, slightly sugared rhubarb or pitted cherries
Season with:
(2 tablespoons lemon juice or kirsch)
Work like pastry with a pastry blender or with the fingertips:
½ cup all-purpose flour
½ cup packed brown sugar
¼ cup butter
½ teaspoon salt, if butter is unsalted
(1 teaspoon cinnamon)
The mixtures must be lightly worked so that it does not become oily. Spread these crumbly ingredients over the apples. Bake about 30 minutes. Serve hot or cold with:
(Sweet or cultured sour cream)

GINGER CRISP

Substitute for the flour in the recipe above:
1½ cups crushed gingersnap cookies
and proceed as directed.

APPLE-MINCE-OAT CRISP

Add to the recipe for Apple Crisp, above:
1 cup moist mincemeat
and reduce the flour to ⅓ cup. Add to the flour mixture:
1 cup rolled oats
¼ teaspoon nutmeg
and proceed as directed above.

QUICK CHERRY CRUNCH

A 9 x 9 x 2-Inch Pan

A well-flavored, easy cherry pastry.
Preheat oven to 350°.
Mix and let stand 15 minutes:
½ cup cherry juice
1½ tablespoons quick-cooking tapioca
Melt in a large pan:
½ cup butter
Mix with it:
1 to 1½ cups packed brown sugar
1 cup all-purpose flour
1 cup quick-cooking oatmeal
¼ teaspoon each double-acting baking powder, salt, and baking soda
Put half of this mixture into the baking pan. Scatter over it:
2 cups drained canned red cherries
and the juice and tapioca mixture. Cover the fruit with the other half of the pastry mixture. Bake 30 to 35 minutes or until brown.

SWEET FRUIT TURNOVERS

To shape these tea pastries, see Filled Cookies, 716. The pastry may be:
Rough Puff Paste, 645
or use any pie dough. After cutting into shapes, place in the center of each pastry 1 teaspoonful or more of one of the following fillings:
Well-flavored applesauce
Preserves or jam
Mincemeat, 812
Banbury Tart Filling, 654
Filled Cookie Filling, 716
Preheat oven to 450°.
Brush the edges lightly with water. Fold the dough over into triangles or crescents and press edges to seal. Brush the tops with:
1 egg yolk diluted with 2 tablespoons cream
Bake about 15 minutes. While still warm dust pastries with:
Powdered sugar

FRUIT DUMPLINGS

4 Dumplings

Prepare:
A pie dough, 640–642, or Biscuit Dough, 632
Chill it. Pare and core:
4 medium-sized apples or 4 peeled, pitted and halved peaches or apricots
If using canned fruit, drain well and sprinkle with:
Lemon juice or rum
and use less sugar. Combine until blended:
¾ cup packed brown sugar
¼ cup soft butter
½ teaspoon salt
½ teaspoon cinnamon
(Grated lemon rind or citron)
Fill the core hollows with this mixture or with:
Raspberry jam
and spread the remainder over the fruit.
Preheat oven to 450°.
Roll out the dough in a thin sheet, ⅛ inch for pastry, ¼ inch for biscuit dough. Cut it into 4 squares, large enough to enclose the apple entirely. Brush squares with the white of an egg to keep the dough from becoming soggy. Place an apple on each square. Bring up the four corners of the dough to cover the apple and press the edges together, using a little water, if necessary, to make them stick. Prick the tops of the dumplings in several places. They may be chilled for several hours or baked at once. Brush the tops with milk. Bake about 10 minutes at 450°, reduce the heat to 350° and bake about 45 minutes longer, until the apples are tender. Test them with a wooden pick. Serve with:
Brown Sugar Butter Sauce, 773
If you wish to bake the dumplings in sauce, combine and simmer 5 minutes:
1 cup water
½ cup sugar
2 tablespoons butter
½ teaspoon cinnamon
For enhanced flavor, if you are using apples, you may simmer the cores and peelings in 1½ cups

water 15 minutes. Drain and use the fruit liquid in place of the water. Pour it boiling hot over the dumplings when they begin to color. Dumplings that are not baked in sauce may be served hot or cold with:

Fluffy Hard Sauce with Rum, 775, Foamy Sauce, 775, Lemon Sauce, 769, or cream

RAISED DUMPLINGS OR DAMPFNUDELN

About 16 Dumplings

It was fun digging into old cookbooks for this recipe, if only because it made us realize that the modern method of writing for cooks is an immense improvement over the old. Our grandmothers had to hack through a labyrinth, undoubtedly armed with a ball of string, plus a rabbit's foot, in order to arrive at their culinary goals. This homely old-time favorite is worth resurrecting. Try it in its modern form. A well-known Cincinnati hostess serves it as a dessert at formal dinners with much success.

Combine:

½ tablespoon active dry yeast
1 tablespoon sugar
1¼ cups all-purpose flour

Add:

½ cup 110°–115° milk

Let this heavy sponge rise, covered with a cloth in a warm place, until light, for about 1 hour.

Cream:

1 tablespoon butter
2 tablespoons sugar
½ teaspoon salt

Beat in and stir until light:

1 whole egg

Add this to the sponge and work in about:

½ cup all-purpose flour

or enough to stiffen, as for yeast cake. Cover the bowl with a cloth. Allow the dough to rise until doubled in bulk. Shape it into about 16 biscuits. They may be rolled out and cut. If you have time, permit them to rise again. From here on, there is a great divergence in treatment. The old method required the use of a Dutch oven, but a covered deep 10-inch ovenproof glass baking dish is preferable, as it enables you to watch the cooking process. Place in it one of the hot liquids indicated below and then the dumplings. If they are to be served with a meat course with lots of gravy, use ½ cup butter and ½ cup milk. If they are to constitute a dessert, use 1½ cups syrup, fruit juice, preserves or stewed fruit.

➤ Cover the pot closely, place it in a 275° oven and cook the dumplings about 1½ hours. If you have not used a glass baker, do not lift the lid, even to peek. Old recipes add that your sense of smell must be your guide as to when to uncover. Do it when the dumplings begin to give off a tempting fragrance of finality and all sizzling noises have ceased, telling you that the liquid has been absorbed. Test the dumplings with a wooden pick to be sure they are dry. Remove them from the pot and serve at once.

An outstanding accompaniment for this dessert is stewed blue plums or prunes. Use part of the syrup in the pot. Serve the dumplings with:

Plums or prunes stewed with part white wine and part water

In addition, it is customary to serve:

Custard Sauce, 771, or Rich Custard, 735

CAKES, CUPCAKES, TORTEN, AND FILLED CAKES

A gaggle of cakes can be oven-ready in short order with the sensitive use of an electric mixer, above. Whip up a Lightning Cake, 681, which should be eaten warm from the oven, with its baked-on garnish of cinnamon, sugar and almonds, or Honey-Bee Glaze, 731. Above center is a perfectly textured Bundkuchen, 620, needing only a dusting of powdered sugar, and in the right foreground a pan for Madeleines, 695, which are perfect unadorned. Bake a fresh Coconut Cake, 673; cut it into a swirl, and highlight it with one tactful candle, as a birthday treat. For other special occasions, you may want to try your hand at a classic Yule Log, 691, or a towering Kransekake, 688.

For all these cakes, start, of course, with high-quality materials. Pay attention to the ➤ measurements and proportions you use, ➤ the temperature of the ingredients, and ➤ the heat of your oven, 666. Most recipes call for ingredients at room temperature. As kitchen temperatures vary, we suggest that ➤ ingredients be about 70°, the ideal recommended by professional bakers. ➤ Pay attention also to the physical states you induce by stirring, creaming and folding. Our drawings and descriptions can do no more than get you off to a flying start. The proper "look" of well-creamed butter and eggs, of batter ready for the oven—these and other critical stages in cake making you will learn to recognize most effectively through practice.

If you are concerned with the amount of sugar in most cakes, we suggest you consider Quick Breads, 623, and muffin recipes, 629. Whole grains, the Cornell Formula, 602, and other substitutions may be used to enrich cakes as well as breads. When using whole wheat flour for cakes, sift to remove the coarse bran Use the bran in cereals or soups.

CAKE TYPES

We divide cakes according to their leavens. If you know what makes them rise, it will help you to safeguard this lifting action during the mixing period. Angel and sponge cakes are sometimes called ➤ foam cakes, because they depend for their leavening exclusively on the expansion of the vapor trapped in their light egg-rich doughs. Egg yolk contains fat; egg white does not. As a consequence, angel cakes are fat-free; ➤ but sponge cakes, though light in texture, contain an appreciable amount of fat by reason of their yolk content, 5.

➤ Butter and shortening cakes need baking powder for proper leavening. We feel that most cakes in this category are more delicious if butter alone is used as the shortening. One exception may be spice cakes, where the strong flavors overwhelm the taste of butter. If you care to use, instead, one of the bland vegetable shortenings now on the market, you will trade distinctive flavor for a measure of economy, a spongier texture and a somewhat greater volume.

In cakes made with ➤ melted butter, such as the classic Génoise, 675, the butter is put in last. In cakes made with oils, special mixing procedures are employed to allow the incorporation of air into the batter.

Torten often depend on egg yolks instead of butter for their fat content and on egg whites for their leavening; ground nuts and bread crumbs replace flour as their base. Our cake recipes are all adjusted in method to the specific demands of the ingredients. So, for success, please follow directions as given.

All these cake types may be ✻ frozen, see 830, but dry out rapidly after thawing.

▲ To bake cakes at high altitude, see 692.

CAKE MIXING

After reading About Leavens, 553, look at the drawing opposite. ➤ To cream, work 70° shortening lightly with the fingertips—or use the back of a wooden spoon. Press the mixture between the back of the spoon and the side of the bowl in a gently gliding motion. Use short rocking strokes over a rather limited area, as shown between the arrows in the sketch. When thoroughly creamed, the sugar mixture should become light in color; smooth, even, and creamy in texture. If it looks curdled and frothy, you have worked it too long; the oil in the butter has separated, and the result will be a coarsely grained cake. In the center, you see how to ➤ stir a batter. Begin at the center of

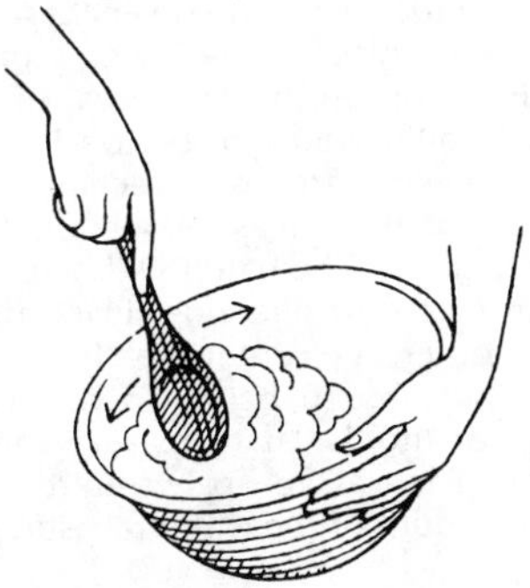

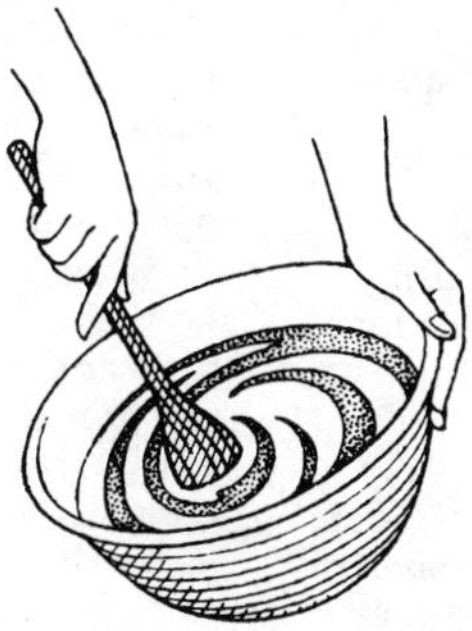

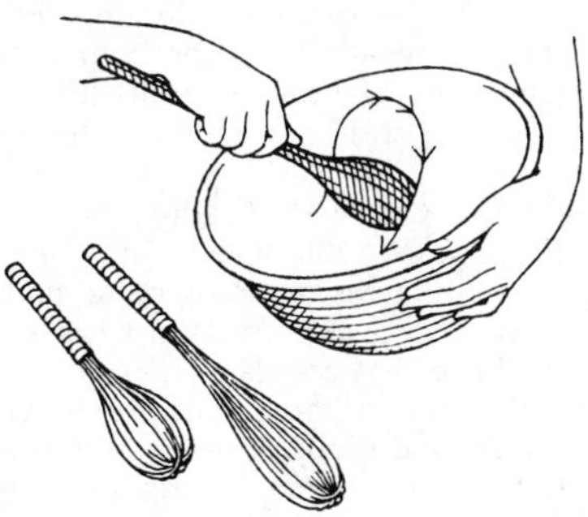

the bowl, using a circular motion; widen the circle as the ingredients become blended. The entire operation of adding and blending the dry and liquid ingredients should take no more than 2 minutes, or the result may be a too finely grained cake. To beat or whip, ➤ use a long, free-swinging, lifting motion, which brings the bottom mass constantly to the top, trapping as much air as possible in the mixture, as shown on the right. A slotted spoon makes the work quicker; a wooden, rather than a metal, spoon keeps the ingredients in the best condition. Whipping is done rapidly with an increasing tempo. For best results in handling egg whites, use a long, thin whip, such as the one shown on the right above or as shown on the right below. For beating cream, use a wider whisk like the one on the left above. In choosing a mechanical mixer, see that the beaters have many wires that are as thin as is consistent with durability.

Folding in is one of the most delicate of cake-making operations: the objective is to blend thoroughly, yet not lose any of the air you have previously worked into your materials.

➤ To fold, first of all have a large enough bowl. A flat whip as shown below is usually recommended, but this tool can be maddening because it cuts through the whites, and its too widely spaced wires allow the heavier substances to fall through. We commonly dispense with tools for this step and use the flat of the hand both to scoop and to slice. Begin by folding into the dough a small quantity of the whites. When thoroughly mixed, fold in the rest of the whites by scooping up some of the more solid material and covering the whites. Then, cut it in with a gentle but determined slicing motion to the base of the mixing bowl. Turn the bowl slightly with the other hand each time you repeat the folding motions. It is surprising how quickly blending is achieved by this simple procedure.

TESTING CAKES FOR DONENESS

Insert a wire cake tester or a wooden pick in the center of the cake; if it emerges perfectly clean, the cake is done. The cake should be lightly browned and beginning to shrink from the sides of the pan. If pressed lightly with a finger, it should at once come back into shape, except in very rich cakes and chocolate cakes, which may dent slightly and still be done.

When removed from the oven, the cake is cooled in the pan on a rack—plain cakes about 5 minutes and rich cakes 10 to 15 minutes—and then cooled out of the pan, on a rack, until all heat has left. For exceptions, see About Angel, 668, Sponge, 669, Génoise, 675, and Fruit Cakes, 682. If cakes are left in pans too long, they become soggy and obstinate. You may set the pan on a cloth wrung out in hot water. This often helps in removing the cake from the pan.

A towel placed on the cooling rack will prevent the wire from indenting the fragile top of the cake when it is turned out of the pan. Do not leave the cake resting on its top, but immediately turn it right side up onto another rack.

ABOUT CAKE PANS

If you want a thin, evenly browned crust, try using ➤ medium-weight shiny metal pans. If you prefer heavier, browner crusts, use glass or enamel pans or those that are dark in color—all of which absorb and hold more heat. Should you choose from the second group ➤ reduce the oven heat by 25°, but use the same baking time. In baking layer cakes, use pans with straight sides. Note also that too-high sides will prevent good browning. But even more important to the crumb and volume of your cake is the relation of dough to the size of the pan. All our cake recipes indicate the proper pan sizes.

If the recipe calls for a greased pan, use solid shortening, but not butter, margarine or oil. Use a pastry brush or waxed paper to apply evenly about ½ tablespoon of shortening to the bottom only of each layer or tube pan. You may dust each greased pan with flour—about ½ tablespoon—and remove any excess by tapping the overturned pan gently. If using nonstick pans, follow the manufacturer's directions. For pan placement in the oven, see 159.

The batter, for a velvety texture, should be at least 1 inch deep in the pan. If the pan is too big, the cake will not rise properly and may brown unevenly. If the pan is too small, the texture will be coarse and the batter may overflow before it sets. If it doesn't overflow, it will probably sink in cooling. Most pans are filled at least half full, but not more than two-thirds. Loaf and tube pans can be filled higher. If you have no pan corresponding to the size called for in the recipe, see the chart below to find the corresponding square-inch area of pan size. Then substitute a pan of that approximate size. For instance, a recipe calls for a 9-inch round pan which has an area of approximately 64 square inches. From the tables you see that you could equally well use an 8 x 8-inch square pan, which offers also an area of 64 square inches. ➤ Note, below, that a round 9-inch-diameter pan equals only about three-fourths the area of a square 9-inch pan. Should your pan be too large, you can reduce the baking area of a rectangular pan by folding a piece of foil as shown in the drawing on the right below. The batter will help to hold the divider in place on one side. Place dry beans or rice on the other, see center sketch.

➤ To determine how much batter to mix for oddly shaped pans or molds, first measure their contents with water. Then make up two-thirds as much dough as the amount of the water measured.

COMPARATIVE PAN SIZES

Cake pans are measured across the top between the inside edges.

ROUND CAKE PANS

8 x 1½	50 sq. inches
9 x 1½	64 sq. inches
10 x 1½	79 sq. inches

SQUARE AND RECTANGULAR CAKE PANS

7¾ x 3⅝ x 2¼	28 sq. inches
8 x 8 x 1½	64 sq. inches
9 x 5 x 2¾	45 sq. inches
9 x 9 x 1½	81 sq. inches
11 x 4½ x 2¾	50 sq. inches
11 x 7 x 1½	77 sq. inches
13 x 9 x 2	117 sq. inches
15 x 10 x 2	150 sq. inches
15½ x 10½ x 1	163 sq. inches
16 x 5 x 4	80 sq. inches

ABOUT CAKES IN A MIXER

Electric mixers are the greatest boon to cake bakers, but, because models vary in speed and efficiency, ➤ be sure to read the manual which comes with your particular appliance. Having an extra mixer bowl is a great convenience if you bake often. The following comments can give only approximate speeds and times. So-called one-bowl cakes can be mixed in as little as three minutes.

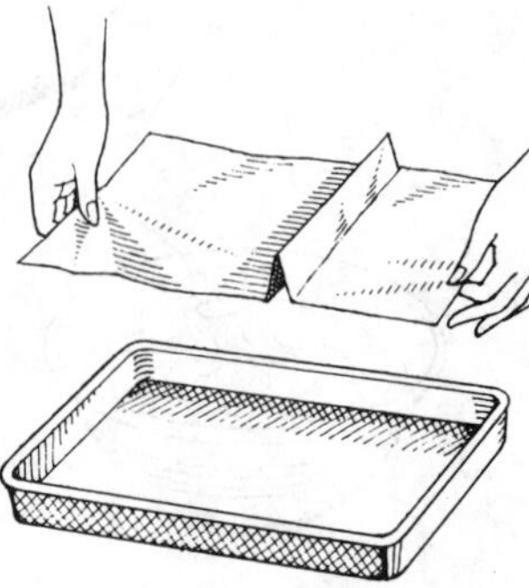

Butter cakes may take as long as 8 to 10 minutes. Basically, you apply the same principles that you use in hand mixing. ➤ Have all ingredients assembled. If chocolate, honey or molasses mixtures are called for, melt or heat them ➤ and cool, before using, to about 70°, which should be the approximate temperature of all your ingredients. Sift and measure the flour; sift it once again with the baking powder, the soda, the spices and the cocoa, if called for. You may then mix just as though you were working by hand, or use the one-bowl method described below. ➤ The main things to observe are the beating speed and the timing of each process. We find it wise to stop the beating during the addition of most ingredients. During these breaks is the time, too, when the sides of the bowl should be scraped down with a rubber or plastic scraper, unless you have a heavy-duty mixer which revolves with an off-center motion, covering every bit of the mixing area.

To mix a typical butter cake, cream the 70° butter until light, at low speed. Then cream it with the sugar at medium speed until the mix is the consistency of whipped cream. If the recipe calls for whole eggs, they may be creamed from the beginning with the sugar and butter. If the eggs are separated, add the yolks at the end of about a 3- to 5-minute creaming period of the butter and sugar. The whites are added later. For descriptions of the textures that these ingredients should have, read about Cake Mixing, 664. Then ➤ using low speed and stopping the mixing between additions, add the flour mixture in 3 parts and the milk in 2 parts. Begin and end with the flour. Mix until just smooth after each addition. The whole operation should not take more than about 2 minutes or you will have a too finely grained cake. If nuts and other lumpy substances are to be added, fold them in lightly with a fork at the end of the mixing period, or briefly use the low speed on the beater.

Be sure ➤ before you begin beating the egg whites that your oven has reached the right temperature and that your pans are greased. Beat the whites, in a grease-free bowl, at medium speed for about ½ minute—until foamy. Now the cream of tartar, if called for, is added. Then beat at high speed for another ½ minute until the whites are ➤ stiff, but not dry, see 545. For the best results from this point on, the beater is no longer used and the beaten whites are folded in by hand, see 665.

To mix so-called one-bowl cakes with unseparated eggs and solid shortenings, put sifted flour, baking powder, spices and cocoa, if called for, the fat and ⅔ of the liquid into the mixer bowl at once. Beat on medium speed about 2 minutes. Add the rest of the liquid. Add, unbeaten, the whole eggs, the yolks, or the whites, as called for in the recipe, and beat for 2 minutes more. ➤ Scrape the bowl several times during this beating period. ➤ Overbeating will reduce the volume and give a too densely grained cake.

ABOUT PACKAGED BAKING MIXES

We know that people think they save time by using mixes—just how much time is a sobering consideration—but we also know they do not save money, nor are they assured of good ingredients and best results. Use mixes, if you must, in emergencies. But consider that, under present distribution methods, the mix you buy may be as old as 2 years—if the store has a slow turnover. Remember that, in contriving the mix originally, everything was done to use ingredients that would keep. Egg whites were used in preference to whole eggs, as the fat from the yolks might turn rancid. For the same reason, non-fat dry milk solids were preferred. Even when the natural moisture content of flour has been greatly lowered, what remains in the packaged mix can still deteriorate baking powders, flavorings and spices. Furthermore, even the most elaborate packaging is not proof, over a protracted storage period, against spoilage by moisture from without. So why not become expert at a few quick cakes and hot breads? Build up your own baking speed, control your ingredients, create really topnotch flavor and save money.

ABOUT WEDDING AND OTHER LARGE CAKES

Be sure for any big cake to ➤ choose a recipe that enlarges successfully, see comment under White Cake I, 671, or use a large fruit-cake recipe. We find that when rather shallow pans are used—not more than 2 inches deep for each layer—the cake bakes more evenly and cuts more attractively. For any large cake, lower the indicated oven temperature by 25°. For more even baking, turn the pans in the oven frequently during the necessarily longer baking period. To help support the tiers of cakes, bake three 1-inch-wide dowels in the lower layers, as long in length as the pan is high. Place the dowels upright within the diameter of the succeeding layer. Test for doneness as you would with any cake, see 665. To ice, see Decorative

Twice-Cooked or Cream Icings, 724, or Royal Glaze, 727. Top the cake with the traditional bride-and-groom figurines, with an icing flower or with a miniature vase of fresh flowers.

After the bride's first slice, whether the wedding cake is round or rectangular, the cutting begins at the lowest tier. To make the cuts even in depth, run a knife perpendicularly through the bottom layer, where it abuts the second layer. Continue this process at each tier. Cut successive slices until a single cylindrical central core remains, crested by the ornate top, as shown on the preceding page. Remove and save this, or freeze it for the first anniversary party. Then finish slicing the central core, beginning at the top.

ABOUT ANGEL CAKES

Laboratory research in some types of recipes—and no cake has a larger bibliography than angel cake—has become so elaborate as to intimidate the housewife, who can rarely know the exact age of the eggs she uses or the precise blend of flour. Yet, working innocently as she must, she can still contrive a glamorous result with a little care. The main risers in angel cake are air and steam, so the egg-white volume is important. See Beating Eggs, 545, for the type of bowl and preparation of equipment.

➤ Have egg whites ready. They should be at least 3 days old, at about 60° to 70°, and separated just before use. These are preferable to leftover egg whites. Divide the beating time into 4 quarters. During the first quarter, beat whites gently ➤ until foamy. Add salt, cream of tartar and liquid flavoring. Be sure the cream of tartar has been stored in a closely covered container. It is added midway during the first quarter of the beating and controls both the stabilizing of the foam and the whiteness of the cake. End the first quarter of the beating with an increasing speed and gradually add, while continuing to beat at high speed, three-fourths of the sugar called for in the recipe. Finely granulated fruit or berry sugar, 556, is best.

If you are using an electric mixer, this sugar addition begins in the second quarter because it guards against overbeating the whites. If you are beating by hand with a flat whip—and this gives the best results—or a rotary one, the gradual addition of sugar is made in the last half of the beating time. In either case, the remaining one-fourth of the sugar is sifted with the cake flour to keep the flour well dispersed when it is folded into the egg and sugar mixture. ➤ The folding should never be done mechanically, unless you are using a mix, in which case follow the package directions. As in all hand-folding, the movement is both gentle and firm but rapid. Avoid breaking down the cellular structure of the egg whites which have trapped air.

The choice of pan and its careful preparation are essential to good results. Choose a tube pan with a removable rim. Since the dough is light, a central tube helps to give it additional support while it rises. ➤ Don't grease the pan. If it has been used for other purposes and any grease remains, the batter will not rise. Wash a suspect pan with detergent, scrubbing well to remove every trace of grease. After putting the batter in the pan, draw a thin spatula gently through the dough to destroy any large air pockets.

Endless experiments have been performed for baking angel cakes—starting with a cold oven and ending with a very hot one. But ➤ the best oven is one that is not so slow that it will dry and toughen the cake and not so hot that it will set the protein of the whites before they can expand to their fullest volume. In other words, the ideal is a preheated moderate oven. We use 350° for about 45 minutes for the recipes given here. Set the pan on a rack placed in the lower third of the oven. When the cake is done ➤ reverse the pan when you remove it from the oven, as shown in the illustration. Use an inverted funnel or a soft-drink bottle to rest the pan on, if the tube is not high enough to keep the cake above the surface of the table. Let the cake hang for about 1½ hours

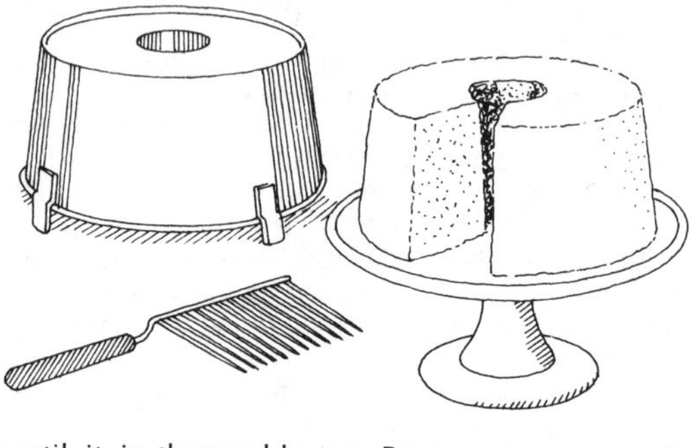

until it is thoroughly set. Be sure to remove it from the pan before storing. Do not cut a fresh angel or sponge cake with a knife, but use a divider such as the one shown on the left, or 2 forks inserted back to back to pry the cake gently apart.

To make an angel cake for a jelly roll, use half the recipe for a 10½ x 15½-inch pan. Here we make an exception and grease the bottom of the roll pan. To fill an angel cake with a secret filling, see About Filled Cakes, 687. Or decorate the cake with one of the Glazes Applied After Baking, 731, or one of the luscious Icings, 721–733.

ANGEL CAKE

I. **A 9-Inch Tube Pan**

Preheat oven to 350°.

Sift twice:

1¼ cups sugar

Sift separately before measuring:

1 cup cake flour

Resift the flour 3 times with ¼ cup of the sifted sugar and:

½ teaspoon salt

Whip until foamy:

1¼ cups egg whites: about 10 egg whites
(2 tablespoons water or 1 tablespoon water and 1 tablespoon lemon juice)

Add:

1 teaspoon cream of tartar

Whip the egg whites ➤ until stiff, but not dry. Fold in:

½ teaspoon vanilla
½ teaspoon almond extract

Gradually whip in, about 1 tablespoon at a time, the remaining sifted sugar. Sift about ¼ cup of the flour and sugar mixture over the batter. Fold it in gently and briefly. Continue until all the mixture is used. Pour the batter into an ungreased tube pan. Bake about 45 minutes. To cool, see About Angel Cakes, 668. Over this cake we like to dribble:

European Chocolate Icing, 728

thinned a bit by an additional tablespoon of whipping cream.

A 10-Inch Tube Pan

II. An electric mixer method.
Preheat oven to 350°.
Sift, then measure:

1 cup cake flour

Add and resift 6 times:

½ cup sugar or confectioners' sugar

Combine:

1½ cups egg whites: 10 to 12 egg whites
2½ tablespoons cold water
1½ teaspoons cream of tartar
¼ teaspoon vanilla
1 teaspoon almond extract or 1 or 2 drops anise flavoring
½ teaspoon salt

Beat ➤ until stiff, but not dry. Stop while the mixture is still glossy. Fold in, about 2 tablespoons at a time:

1 cup sifted sugar

Fold in the flour and sugar mixture lightly, a little at a time. Bake the batter in an ungreased tube pan about 45 minutes. To cool, see About Angel Cakes, 668.

COCOA ANGEL CAKE

A 9-Inch Tube Pan

This cake is incredibly delicate.
Preheat oven to 350°.
Sift before measuring:

¾ cup cake flour

Resift 5 times with:

¼ cup cocoa
¼ cup sugar

Sift separately:

1 cup sugar

Whip until foamy:

1¼ cups egg whites: about 10 egg whites

Add:

1 teaspoon cream of tartar

Whip ➤ until stiff, but not dry. Fold in the sifted sugar, 1 tablespoon at a time. Add:

1 teaspoon vanilla
½ teaspoon lemon extract

Sift a small amount of the flour mixture over the batter and fold it in. Repeat this process until the flour is used up. Bake the cake in an ungreased tube pan about 45 minutes. To cool, see About Angel Cake, 668. Cover the cooled cake with:

Chocolate Coating over Boiled White Icing, 725, or with Coffee Icing, 729

FLAVORED ANGEL CAKE

Try using flavored angel cake batter for cupcakes, 694.
Add to the flour for Angel Cake I or II, above:

1 teaspoon cinnamon
½ teaspoon nutmeg
¼ teaspoon cloves

Or, crush with a rolling pin:

⅓ cup soft peppermint sticks

Fold the candy into the egg and flour mixture. This is good iced with Boiled White Icing, 722, to which you may add more crushed candy for color, or, if using the spiced cake:

(1 to 2 teaspoons instant coffee)

MARBLE ANGEL CAKE

Prepare:

Angel Cake I, opposite

and:

Cocoa Angel Cake, above

Alternate the batters in 2 ungreased 9-inch tube pans. Bake as directed in Angel Cake I.

ABOUT SPONGE CAKES

In true sponge cakes, as in angel cakes, the main riser is air, plus steam, so all the suggestions for trapping air given in About Angel Cakes apply here—with this added admonition: egg yolks beat to a greater volume if they are at about 70°. Beat the yolks until light and foamy; add the sugar gradually, while continuing to beat, until the mixture is pale in color and thick in texture. It has reached proper consistency when a sample dropped from a spoon remains raised for a moment above the rest of the batter and then rather reluctantly settles down to the level in the bowl.

➤ In sponge cakes, an electric or rotary beater gives a better result than a hand whip. You can beat the egg and sugar mixture mechanically as long as 7 minutes with good results for the amounts given in the recipes here. Then stir in the dry ingredients carefully by hand. When they are blended, use the folding technique illustrated on 665. For pan preparation and baking, see About Angel Cakes, 668.

True-blue sponge cake enthusiasts scorn baking powder, but it does give added volume in the basic recipe just below. See Flavored Angel Cake, above, for additions to vary the usual sponge cake.

SPONGE CAKE

A 9-Inch Tube Pan

Economical, if you use the minimum number of eggs. Especially delightful if you vary the flavors. To prepare the pan, bake and cool, see About Angel Cakes, 668.
Preheat oven to 350°.
Grate, then stir:
1 teaspoon lemon or orange rind
into:
1 cup sifted sugar
Beat until very light:
3 to 6 egg yolks
Beat in the sugar gradually. Beat in:
¼ cup boiling water or coffee
When cool, beat in:
1 tablespoon lemon juice or
1 teaspoon vanilla or 3 drops anise oil
Sift before measuring:
1 cup cake flour
Resift with:
1½ teaspoons double-acting baking powder
¼ teaspoon salt
Add the sifted ingredients gradually to the yolk mixture. Stir the batter until blended. Whip ➤ until stiff, but not dry:
3 to 6 egg whites
Fold them lightly into the batter. Bake the cake about 45 minutes.

RICE- OR POTATO-FLOUR SPONGE CAKE

A 9-Inch Round Pan

Because rice and potato flours lack the gluten of wheat, do not expect the same cake texture.
Preheat oven to 325°.
Sift 3 times or more:
1 cup potato or rice flour
Beat until light and creamy:
4 egg yolks
Blend in:
1 cup sugar
Add the sifted flour and:
⅛ teaspoon salt
2 tablespoons lemon juice
1½ teaspoons vanilla
Whip ➤ until stiff, but not dry:
4 egg whites
Fold the egg whites into the batter. Bake in a greased and floured pan 20 minutes at 325°, then 15 minutes longer at 350°.

SUNSHINE CAKE

A 9-Inch Tube Pan

To prepare pan, bake and cool, see About Angel Cakes, 668.
Preheat oven to 350°.
Sift before measuring:
1 cup cake flour
Resift with:
½ teaspoon cream of tartar
Boil to the soft-ball stage, 240°, see 778.
⅓ cup water
1¼ cups sugar
Whip ➤ until stiff, but not dry:
5 to 7 egg whites
Pour the syrup over them in a fine stream. Beat constantly until the mixture is cool. Add:
1 teaspoon vanilla
Beat well and fold in:
5 to 7 egg yolks
Fold in the sifted flour, 1 tablespoon at a time. Bake the cake about 45 minutes.

CHOCOLATE SPONGE CAKE

A 7-Inch Tube Pan

Butterless but rich in taste. To prepare pan, bake and cool, see About Angel Cakes, 668.
Preheat oven to 350°.
Melt:
4 oz. unsweetened chocolate
in a pan with:
1 cup milk
Sift before measuring:
1¼ cups cake flour
Resift with:
2½ teaspoons double-acting baking powder
½ teaspoon salt
When the chocolate mixture is cool, add it to:
4 beaten egg yolks
creamed with:
2 cups sifted confectioners' sugar
1 teaspoon vanilla
Stir in the sifted flour. Beat ➤ until stiff, but not dry:
4 egg whites
Fold the beaten whites into the chocolate mixture. Bake about 50 minutes.

CHOCOLATE DATE CAKE

A 9-Inch Tube Pan

An unusual flavor combination.
Prepare batter for:
Chocolate Sponge Cake, above
but wait to add the beaten egg whites until after incorporating the date mixture below. Sprinkle:
2 tablespoons sifted all-purpose flour
over:
¾ cup chopped dates
1 tablespoon grated orange rind
(½ cup chopped nutmeats)
Stir these ingredients into the cake batter before folding in the egg whites. Bake as directed.
Sprinkle with:
Powdered sugar
We serve this to everybody's intense satisfaction with:
Liqueur Cream Sauce, 775, or
Foamy Sauce, 775

DAFFODIL CAKE

A 9-Inch Tube Pan

A yellow and white marble cake. To prepare pan, bake and cool, see About Angel Cakes, 668.

Preheat oven to 350°.
Sift before measuring:
1⅛ cups cake flour
Resift it twice more. Sift separately:
1¼ cups sugar
Whip until frothy:
10 egg whites
Add:
½ teaspoon salt
1 teaspoon cream of tartar
Whip until egg whites hold a peak. Fold the sifted sugar in gradually. Separate the mixture into halves. Fold into one half, a little at a time, ¾ cup of the sifted flour and:
6 beaten egg yolks
Grated rind of 1 orange
Fold into the other half, a little at a time, the remaining sifted flour and:
1 teaspoon vanilla
Place the batters, a cupful or more at a time, in the ungreased tube pan, alternating the colors. Bake about 45 minutes or until done.

ABOUT BUTTER OR SHORTENING CAKES

For flavor and texture, butter is our strong preference. It is not a very novel one, for way back when the cathedrals were white, one of the spires at Rouen was nicknamed the Butter Tower, having been built, reputedly, with money paid for indulgences permitting the use of butter during Lent.

The butter, margarine or shortening—but not lard, as it is best reserved for pastries—should be at ➤ about 70° when ready to cream. If much cooler, it fails to disperse properly into the other ingredients. If melted, it prevents the proper incorporation of air into the batter. ➤ So don't try to hasten the conditioning of shortenings with heat.

Creaming softens and lightens cake ingredients. If the weather is very hot, cream butter and sugar in a bowl immersed in a pan of 60° water. Add the sugar ➤ gradually, continuing to cream with a light touch.

Add beaten egg yolks gradually, or, as in Quick Cakes, 681, add egg yolks unbeaten, one at a time, beating well after each addition. The sifted dry ingredients and the 70° liquids are added in 3 or more alternating periods, usually beginning with the dry ingredients. After the addition of flour the blending should be gentle so as not to develop the gluten, and continued until the flour is no longer dry. ➤ Overblending will cause too fine a crumb. We suggest, for a cake made with double-acting baking powder, about 200 strokes by hand or 2 minutes at medium speed with an electric mixer; be sure to consult the directions that come with the mixer. If you use other baking powders, they may require about one-third less beating. Just before being incorporated into the batter, the whites are beaten to a state described as "stiff, but not dry." ➤ The whites are then simultaneously folded and cut in gently but quickly, as shown in the illustrations on 665. For a more stable foam, reserve one-fourth of the sugar called for in the recipe and beat it in as described in Fudge Meringue Cake, 676. Bake in a preheated oven. Grease and flour bottoms of pans but ➤ not sides. Use the pan sizes indicated for each recipe or adjust by consulting the Pan Size Chart, 666.

WHITE CAKE

This recipe is amazing: it can be multiplied by 8 and still give as good a result as when made in the smaller quantity below. See hints under About Large Cakes, 667. We once saw a wedding cake made from this recipe which contained 130 eggs and was big enough to serve 400 guests. This formula is also the classic base for Lady Baltimore Cake, below, for which, in the Good Old Days, 5 layers were considered none too many.

I. **Three 8-Inch Round Pans**

Preheat oven to 375°.
➤ Have all ingredients at about 70°
Sift before measuring:
3½ cups cake flour
Resift it twice with:
4 teaspoons double-acting baking powder
½ teaspoon salt
Cream well:
1 cup butter
Add gradually and cream until very light:
2 cups sifted sugar
Add the flour mixture to the butter mixture in 3 parts, alternately with:
1 cup milk
Stir the batter until smooth after each addition. Beat in:
1 teaspoon vanilla
(¼ teaspoon almond extract)
Whip ➤ until stiff, but not dry:
7 or 8 egg whites
Fold them gently into the cake batter. Bake in greased pans about 25 minutes. Spread the cake when cool with:
A choice of Icings, 721 to 733

II. **Two 9-Inch Round Pans**

This batter, which we use for our Easter Bunny, see 672, is enough to fill a 7-cup-capacity mold.
Preheat oven to 375°.
➤ Have all ingredients at about 70°.
Sift before measuring:
2¼ cups cake flour
Resift with:
2½ teaspoons double-acting baking powder
½ teaspoon salt
Cream until fluffy:
1¼ cups sugar
½ cup butter
Combine:
1 cup milk
1 teaspoon vanilla

Add the sifted ingredients to the butter mixture in 3 parts, alternating with the liquid combination. Stir the batter until smooth after each addition. Whip ➤ until stiff, but not dry:

4 egg whites

Fold them lightly into the batter and bake in layers, about 25 minutes. When cool, ice with:

Luscious Orange, 725, or
Quick Chocolate Icing, 728

LADY BALTIMORE CAKE

Prepare the batter for:

White Cake I, 671

Bake it in 3 layers. When cool, place the following filling between the layers. Chop:

6 dried figs
½ cup seeded raisins
1 cup nutmeats

Prepare:

Boiled White Icing, 722, or Seven-Minute White Icing, 725

Reserve a generous portion of this. To the rest, add the nuts, figs and raisins for the filling between the layers. Spread the reserved icing over the top and sides.

MARBLE CAKE

A 9-Inch Tube Pan

This old-fashioned cake is still a great favorite.
Preheat oven to 350°.
Prepare:

White Cake II, 671

Before whipping the egg whites, separate the batter into 2 parts. Add to half the batter:

1½ oz. melted, cooled unsweetened chocolate
1 teaspoon cinnamon
¼ teaspoon cloves
⅛ teaspoon baking soda

Whip the egg whites as directed and fold half into the light and half into the dark batter. Grease the bottom of a tube pan. Place large spoonfuls of batter in it, alternating light and dark batter. Bake about 45 minutes. Spread when cool with:

Boiled White Icing, 722, or
Raisin or Nut Icing, 722

ABOUT TWO-PIECE CAKE MOLDS

To prepare a new cast iron mold, see directions on 162. Lambs, bunnies and Santas need firm, compact batters.
Prepare:

White Cake II, 671

Keep nuts, raisins, etc., for decorations, rather than using them in the batter itself, because these solid ingredients, while they make the cake more interesting, tend to break down the tensile strength of the batter. Ground spices, however, are a good addition. Grease the mold with unsalted fat or oil. Use a pastry brush and be rather lavish. Then dust the greased surface with flour, reversing the mold to get rid of any excess. Fill the face side of the mold with batter. Leftover batter may be used for cupcakes or cake eggs. If the mold has steam vents, fill the solid section with the batter to just below the joint. Using the following directions, we have baked successfully in cake molds even when they had no steam vents. Move a wooden spoon gently through the batter to release any air bubbles. ➤ Be careful not to disturb the greased and floured surface of the mold. You may insert wooden picks into the snout and into the ears where they join the head, ➤ but be sure to remove the picks when you cut the cake. Put the lid on the mold, making sure it locks, and tie or wire together so the steam of the rising batter will not force the two sections apart.

To bake, put the filled mold on a cookie sheet in a 375° preheated oven for about 1 hour. Test as you would for any cake, inserting a thin metal skewer or wooden pick through a steam vent. Put the cake, still in the mold, on a rack for about 15 minutes. Carefully remove the top of the mold. Before you separate the cake from the bottom, let it continue to cool about 5 minutes more to let all steam escape and to allow the cake to firm up a little. After removing, continue to cool on a rack. ➤ Do not try to let it sit upright until it is cold. If the cake has constitutional weaknesses, reinforce it with a wooden or metal skewer before icing. Ice with:

Boiled White Icing, 722, or
Seven-Minute White Icing, 725

As a variation to coat a bunny mold, you may use:

Caramel Icing, 726

Or, if you are in a hurry, try:

French Icing, 727

Increase the recipes by half for a heavy coat. For woolly or angora effects, press into the icing:

½ to 1 cup shredded coconut

To accentuate the features, use:

Raisins, nuts, cherries, citron and gumdrops

Surround your animals with seasonal flowers and ferns. If bunnies or lambs are made for Easter, you may want to confect cake eggs and decorate them with icings of different colors. See Angel Cake Balls, 694.

LADY CAKE

A 9-Inch Tube Pan

Another white cake using egg whites only, this makes a tube or loaf cake or an excellent batter for Petits Fours, see 695. It tastes and looks a lot like a conventional white wedding cake.
Preheat oven to 350°.
Have all ingredients about 70°. Sift before measuring:

1¾ cups cake flour

Resift twice with:

2 teaspoons double-acting baking powder
¼ teaspoon salt

Cream until soft:

¾ cup butter

Add gradually and cream until very light:

1 cup sifted sugar

Add the flour mixture to the butter mixture in 3 parts, alternating with:

½ cup milk

Stir the batter a few minutes after each addition. Add:

1 teaspoon almond extract
Grated rind of 1 lemon

Whip ➤ until stiff, but not dry:

3 egg whites

Fold them lightly into the cake batter. Bake in a greased tube pan about 45 minutes. Sprinkle with:

Powdered sugar

or spread, when cool, with:

Quick Lemon Icing, 727

WHIPPED CREAM CAKE

Two 9-Inch Layers

Preheat oven to 350°.
➤ Have all ingredients except the whipping cream about 70°. Sift before measuring:

2 cups cake flour

Resift twice with:

2¾ teaspoons double-acting baking powder
1⅓ cups sugar
¾ teaspoon salt

Whip until stiff:

1 cup cold whipping cream

and add gradually, stirring gently until smooth:

½ cup water
1½ teaspoons vanilla or almond flavoring

Whip ➤ until stiff, but not dry:

3 egg whites

Combine the cream and the egg whites. Fold the sifted ingredients into the cream mixture, about one-third at a time. Bake in greased layer pans about 25 to 30 minutes. Fill with:

Ginger Fruit Filling, 698

Dust cake with:

Powdered sugar

COCONUT MILK CAKE COCKAIGNE

Three 8-Inch Round Pans

Some years ago we gave a pet recipe to a friend who later presented us with the one which follows —best made with fresh coconut milk. She said that, in her family, whenever a treasured recipe was received, an equally treasured one was given in return. We love this festive adopted child.
Preheat oven to 350°.
➤ Have all ingredients about 70°. Have ready, reserving the coconut milk:

1½ cups freshly grated coconut

Sift before measuring:

3 cups cake flour

Resift it with:

3 teaspoons double-acting baking powder
½ teaspoon salt

Cream well:

¾ cup butter

Add gradually and cream until very light:

1½ cups sifted sugar

Beat in:

3 egg yolks

Add the sifted flour mixture in 3 parts to the butter mixture, alternately with:

¾ cup coconut milk or milk
½ teaspoon vanilla

Stir the batter until smooth after each addition. Then add ¾ cup of the grated coconut. Whip ➤ until stiff, but not dry:

3 egg whites

Fold the egg whites gently into the batter. Bake in greased layer pans about 25 minutes. To serve, spread between the layers:

Currant, strawberry or raspberry jelly

Cover the cake with:

Seven-Minute Sea Foam Icing, 725

Coat it with the remaining ¾ cup grated coconut.

SOUR CREAM CAKE

Two 8-Inch Round Pans

Preheat oven to 375°
➤ Have all ingredients about 70°. Sift before measuring:

1¾ cups cake flour

Resift with:

¼ teaspoon baking soda
1¾ teaspoons double-acting baking powder
¼ teaspoon salt

Cream until soft:

⅓ cup butter

Add gradually and cream until light:

1 cup sifted sugar

Beat in:

2 egg yolks
1 teaspoon vanilla

Add the sifted flour mixture to the butter mixture in 3 parts, alternating with:

⅔ cup yogurt or 1 cup cultured sour cream

Stir the batter after each addition until smooth. Whip until ➤ stiff, but not dry:

2 egg whites
¼ teaspoon salt
Fold them lightly into the batter. Bake in greased pans about 25 minutes. When cool, spread with:
Almond-Fig or Raisin Filling, 698
Cover with:
Boiled White Icing, 722

CAROB CAKE

Two 8-Inch Round Pans

A delicate distinctive flavor resembling chocolate. Please read about Carob Flour, 550.
Prepare the batter for:
Sour Cream Cake, above
Omit ¼ cup of the cake flour and substitute:
¼ cup sifted carob flour
You may use either white or brown sugar. The latter gives the cake a butterscotch flavor.

GOLD LAYER CAKE

Two 8-Inch Round Layers

A delicious way to utilize leftover egg yolks.
Preheat oven to 375°.
➤ Have all ingredients about 70°. Sift before measuring:
2 cups cake flour
Resift with:
2 teaspoons double-acting baking powder
¼ teaspoon salt
Cream until soft:
½ cup butter
Add gradually and cream until light:
1 cup sifted sugar
Beat in:
3 egg yolks
Add:
1 teaspoon vanilla or 1 teaspoon grated lemon rind
Add the flour mixture to the butter mixture in 3 parts, alternating with:
¾ cup milk
Stir the batter until smooth after each addition. Bake in greased layer pans about 25 minutes Spread between the layers, when cool:
Lemon-Orange Custard Filling, 698, or
Lemon Filling, 697
Dust the top with:
Powdered sugar
This cake is also delicious filled with a layer of good raspberry jam.

FOUR-EGG CAKE

Three 9-Inch Round Pans

This is the old-time One-Two-Three-Four Cake, slightly modernized.
Preheat oven to 350°.
➤ Have all ingredients about 70°. Sift before measuring:
2⅔ cups cake flour
Resift with:
2¼ teaspoons double-acting baking powder
½ teaspoon salt
Cream until soft:
1 cup butter
Add gradually and cream until light:
2 cups sifted sugar
Beat in, one at a time:
4 egg yolks
Add:
1½ teaspoons vanilla, or 1 teaspoon vanilla and ½ teaspoon almond extract
Add the flour mixture to the butter mixture in about 3 parts, alternating with:
1 cup milk
Stir the batter until smooth after each addition.
Whip ➤ until stiff, but not dry:
4 egg whites
Fold them lightly into the batter. Bake in greased layer pans from 30 to 35 minutes. Spread the layers, when cool, with:
Ginger Fruit Filling, 698, or
Almond Custard Filling, 699
Cover with:
Whipped cream

COCONUT LOAF OR LAYER CAKE

Follow the recipe for:
Four-Egg Cake, above
Add to the batter, before folding in the egg whites:
¾ cup shredded coconut
1½ teaspoons grated lemon rind
¼ teaspoon salt
Bake in a greased 10-inch tube pan or two 9 x 5-inch loaf pans about 50 minutes.

EIGHT-YOLK CAKE

Three 9-Inch Layers

Bake it as a second cake after making Angel Food Cake with the whites.
Preheat oven to 375°.
➤ Have all ingredients about 70°. Sift before measuring:
2½ cups cake flour
Resift 3 times with:
2½ teaspoons double-acting baking powder
¼ teaspoon salt
Cream until soft:
¾ cup butter
Add gradually and cream until light:
1¼ cups sifted sugar
In a separate bowl, beat until light and lemon colored:
8 egg yolks
Beat them into the butter mixture. Add the flour mixture in 3 parts, alternating with:
¾ cup milk
Stir the batter after each addition. Add and beat 2 minutes:
1 teaspoon vanilla
1 teaspoon lemon juice or grated lemon rind
Bake in greased layer pans about 20 minutes.
Sprinkle with:
Powdered sugar

Or, when cool, spread with:
Quick Orange Icing, 728, or with one of the Seven-Minute Icings, 725

POUND CAKE

Two 9 x 5-Inch Pans or One 10-Inch Tube Pan

An electric mixer is a true aid for creaming this batter. You may add the eggs whole to give the traditional dense pound cake, or separate the yolks and whites for a fluffy texture.
Preheat oven to 325°.
➤ Have all ingredients about 70°.
Cream:
2 cups butter, no substitutes
Add slowly and cream well:
2 cups sugar
Beat in one at a time:
9 egg yolks, see note above
Beat the batter well after each addition. Add:
1 teaspoon vanilla
½ teaspoon mace
You may add:
(2 tablespoons brandy or 8 drops rose water)
Sift before measuring:
4 cups cake flour
Resift with:
½ teaspoon cream of tartar
½ teaspoon salt
Add the sifted ingredients slowly, at lowest speed, mixing only until thoroughly blended. Whip in a separate bowl ➤ until stiff, but not dry, then fold in:
9 egg whites
Pour the batter into a greased tube pan or into 2 greased loaf pans lined with parchment paper as

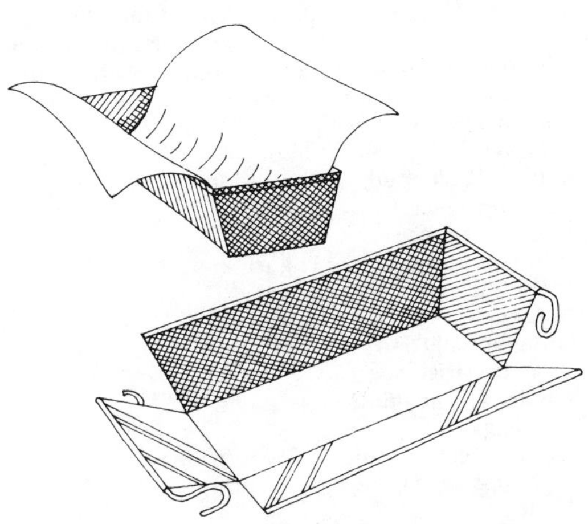

shown or into a greased and floured hinged loaf pan. Bake the cake about 1 hour for pans; 15 minutes longer for tube pan.

Sometimes we add to half the mixture ½ cupful each of candied cherries, pineapple, citron and white raisins—and have a delicious fruit cake.

SEED CAKE

A cake that reminds us of antimacassars and aspidistras.
Prepare:
Pound Cake, above
Add:
2 teaspoons caraway seed
⅓ cup shaved citron or candied orange peel
1 teaspoon grated lemon rind

* GÉNOISE

Two 9-Inch Round Pans

This rich, moist Italian cake, which the French and we have borrowed, has no equal for versatility. It also keeps well and freezes well. If not overbaked it may be used for dessert rolls with cream or jelly fillings, see About Roll Cakes, 690, or Baked Alaska, 742; also with butter icings or as a foil for fruit. You may bake it as Ladyfingers, 695, or in layers. For a very elaborate Génoise, sprinkle it after cooling with Cointreau or kirsch, fill it with Sauce Cockaigne, 770, or cover it with whipped cream or with European Chocolate Icing, 728. For a children's party, bake favors in the cake, see Galette des Rois, 642.
Preheat oven to 350°.
Melt and put aside:
¼ cup butter
Do not let it get cooler than about 80°. Break into the top of a double boiler ➤ over—not in—boiling water until they are lukewarm:
6 eggs
Add:
⅔ cup sugar
Beat with a rotary or electric mixer at medium speed 7 minutes. Add:
⅓ cup sugar
Increase speed and beat 2 minutes longer or until the mixture is lemony in color and has reached the stage known as **au ruban**—like a continuous flat ribbon when dropped from a spoon. Add:
1 teaspoon vanilla
Fold in:
1 cup sifted cake flour
Add the melted butter with a folding motion. Pour the batter into greased and floured pans and bake about 30 to 40 minutes or until done. ➤ Turn out at once onto a rack to cool.

CHOCOLATE CAKE

A 9 x 13-Inch Pan

A mild light chocolate cake known as "Rombauer Special."
Preheat oven to 350°.
➤ Have ingredients about 70°. Sift before measuring:
1¾ cups cake flour
Resift with:
3 teaspoons double-acting baking powder
¼ teaspoon salt
(1 teaspoon cinnamon)
(¼ teaspoon cloves)

(1 cup coarsely chopped nuts)
Melt over hot water:
2 oz. unsweetened chocolate
Add:
5 tablespoons boiling water
Cream until soft:
½ cup butter
Add and cream until light:
1½ cups sifted sugar
Beat in, one at a time:
4 egg yolks
Add the cooled chocolate mixture. Add the flour mixture to the butter mixture in 3 parts, alternating with:
½ cup milk
Stir the batter until smooth after each addition. Add:
1 teaspoon vanilla
Whip ➤ until stiff, but not dry:
4 egg whites
Fold them lightly into the cake batter. Bake in a greased pan about ½ hour. Spread with thick:
Chocolate Coating over Boiled White Icing, 725; or Quick Chocolate Icing with chocolate peppermints, 728

FUDGE MERINGUE CAKE

A 9 x 13-Inch Pan

Preheat oven to 350°.
➤ Have all ingredients about 70°. Sift:
2 cups cake flour
Resift with:
1 tablespoon double-acting baking powder
¼ teaspoon salt
Melt ➤ over—not in—boiling water:
4 oz. unsweetened chocolate
Cream:
¼ cup butter
Add gradually; continue to cream and mix:
1½ cups sugar
Beat in:
3 egg yolks
1 teaspoon vanilla
and the cooled chocolate. Then add the sifted flour in 3 parts, alternating with:
1 cup milk
Stir well after each addition. Whip ➤ until stiff, but not dry:
3 egg whites
Fold in:
½ cup sugar
Beat to a meringue consistency. Fold into batter. Bake about 35 minutes in a greased pan. When cool, ice with:
French Icing, 727

DEVIL'S FOOD CAKE COCKAIGNE

Two 9-Inch Round Pans

The best chocolate cake we know. Whether made with 2 or 4 oz. chocolate, it is wonderfully light, but rich and moist.
Preheat oven to 350°.
Prepare the following custard:
Cook and stir in a double boiler ➤ over—not in—boiling water:
2 to 4 oz. unsweetened chocolate
½ cup milk
1 cup light brown sugar, firmly packed
1 egg yolk
Remove from the heat when thickened. Have other ingredients at about 70°. Sift before measuring:
2 cups cake flour
Resift with:
1 teaspoon baking soda
½ teaspoon salt
Beat until soft:
½ cup butter
Add and cream until light:
1 cup sifted sugar
Beat in, one at a time:
2 egg yolks
Add the flour to the butter mixture in 3 parts, alternating with the following mixture:
¼ cup water
½ cup milk
1 teaspoon vanilla
Stir the batter until smooth after each addition. Stir in the chocolate custard. Whip ➤ until stiff, but not dry:
2 egg whites
Fold them lightly into the cake batter. Bake in greased pans about 25 minutes. Spread when cool with:
Coconut Pecan Icing, 726,
Caramel Icing, 726, or
Chocolate-Fudge Icing, 726

COCOA DEVIL'S FOOD CAKE

One 9-Inch Tube or
Two 9-Inch Round Pans

During wartime shortages, a foreign fan had success with this long-keeping cake using cassava flour when no other flour was available.
➤ Have all ingredients about 70°. Combine, beat until well blended, and set aside:
1 cup sugar
½ cup cocoa
½ cup buttermilk or yogurt
Beat until soft:
½ cup butter
Add gradually and cream until light:
1 cup sifted sugar
Beat in, one at a time:
2 eggs
Beat in cocoa mixture. Sift before measuring:
2 cups cake flour
Resift with:
1 teaspoon baking soda
½ teaspoon salt
Add the flour in 3 parts to the butter mixture, alternately with:
½ cup buttermilk or yogurt
1 teaspoon vanilla

Beat batter after each addition just until smooth. Grease the tube pan and sprinkle sugar over the bottom. Bake the cake about 1 hour in a preheated 350° oven. It may be baked in 2 layer pans about 35 minutes in a 375° oven. Spread the cake with:

A white, 722, or chocolate icing, 728

Add to the icing:

(Nutmeats)

SOURDOUGH CHOCOLATE CAKE

One 9-Inch Square Pan or Two 8-Inch Round Pans

Please read About Sourdough, 554. ➤ Have all ingredients about 70°.
Preheat oven to 350°.
Cream thoroughly:

6 tablespoons butter
1 cup sugar

Add and beat:

2 eggs

Stir in, then beat well:

1 cup Sourdough Starter, 555
¾ cup milk
3 oz. melted semisweet chocolate
1 teaspoon vanilla

Sift together:

1¾ cups sifted all-purpose flour
1 teaspoon baking soda
½ teaspoon salt

Fold the flour mixture into the batter and stir until smooth. Pour into greased pans and bake about 40 minutes for one square pan or 25 minutes for two round pans. Sprinkle over this moist cake.

Sifted powdered sugar

★ OLD-WORLD CHOCOLATE SPICE CAKE WITH CITRON

A 9-Inch Tube Pan

A tempting tube cake with a rather heavy crumb.
Preheat oven to 350°.
➤ Have all ingredients about 70°. Sift before measuring:

2⅓ cups cake flour

Resift with:

1½ teaspoons double-acting baking powder
½ teaspoon cloves
1 teaspoon cinnamon
½ teaspoon freshly grated nutmeg

Cream until soft:

½ cup butter

Add gradually and cream until light:

1½ cups sugar

Beat in, one at a time:

4 eggs

Stir in:

4 oz. grated sweet chocolate
½ cup very finely shaved citron, candied orange or lemon peel

Stir the flour mixture into the butter mixture in about 3 parts, alternating with:

⅞ cup milk

Stir the batter after each addition until smooth. Most European cakes are stirred a long time. This gives them a close, sandy texture. Bake the cake in a greased tube pan or in a loaf pan about 1 hour. When cool, simply dust with:

Powdered sugar

or ice with:

Chocolate Butter Icing, 728

SPICED CHOCOLATE PRUNE CAKE

A 9 x 13-Inch Pan

A moist, fruity loaf cake which makes a delightful dessert when served with whipped cream or pudding sauce.
Preheat oven to 350°.
➤ Have all ingredients about 70°. Cook and cool:

1 cup lightly sweetened drained puréed prunes

➤ Canned puréed prunes will not do, because they are too liquid. Sift before measuring:

1½ cups cake flour

Resift with:

1½ teaspoons double-acting baking powder
¼ teaspoon baking soda
¼ teaspoon salt
(1 teaspoon cinnamon)
(½ teaspoon cloves)

Cream until soft:

⅓ cup butter

Add gradually and cream until light:

¾ cup sifted sugar

Melt and add when cool:

1 oz. unsweetened chocolate

Beat well and add to the butter mixture.

2 eggs

Add the flour mixture to the butter mixture in 3 parts, alternating with:

½ cup milk

Stir the batter until smooth after each addition. Add the prunes and:

½ teaspoon vanilla

Bake in a greased pan about 25 minutes. Spread, when cool, with:

French Icing, 727

CHOCOLATE APRICOT CAKE

Follow the recipe for:

Chocolate Prune Cake, above

Substitute for the prunes:

1 cup cooked, lightly sweetened, well-drained puréed apricots

Omit the spices. Ice, when cool, with:

Whipped cream

or serve with:

Foamy Sauce, 775

HONEY CAKE

A 9 x 9-Inch Square Pan

Well wrapped and kept in a cool place, this cake improves with age. ➤ Have all ingredients about 70°.

Preheat oven to 350°.
Cream thoroughly:
½ cup butter or shortening
½ cup sugar
Add and continue creaming until light and fluffy:
2 eggs
Sift together:
2 cups sifted all-purpose flour
½ teaspoon baking soda
1 teaspoon double-acting baking powder
½ teaspoon cinnamon
¼ teaspoon ginger
¼ teaspoon salt
Add the sifted ingredients to the egg mixture alternately in 3 parts with:
½ cup honey
½ cup cool strong coffee
Stir in:
½ teaspoon vanilla
¾ cup chopped walnuts
(Grated rind of ½ orange)
Pour batter into a greased pan and bake about 30 minutes. Dust with:
Confectioners' sugar
or spread with:
Three-Minute Icing, 727, or
French Icing, 727

VELVET SPICE CAKE

A 9-Inch Tube Pan

This cake has a very delicate consistency. Among spice cakes its flavor is unequaled. ➤ Be sure to bake it in a 9-inch tube pan.
Preheat oven to 350°.
➤ Have all ingredients about 70°. Sift before measuring:
2⅓ cups cake flour
Resift twice with:
1½ teaspoons double-acting baking powder
½ teaspoon baking soda
1 teaspoon freshly grated nutmeg
1 teaspoon cinnamon
½ teaspoon cloves
½ teaspoon salt
Cream:
¾ cup butter or shortening
Add gradually and cream together:
1½ cups sifted sugar
Beat in:
3 egg yolks
Add the sifted ingredients to the butter mixture in 3 parts, alternating with:
⅞ cup yogurt or buttermilk
Stir the batter after each addition until smooth.
Whip ➤ until stiff, but not dry:
3 egg whites
Fold them lightly into the cake batter. Bake in a greased tube pan 1 hour or more. Spread, when cool, with:
Chocolate Butter Icing, 728, or
Boiled White Icing, 722

BROWN-SUGAR SPICE CAKE

Prepare:
Velvet Spice Cake, above
substituting for the granulated sugar:
1½ cups packed brown sugar
and adding to the batter:
2 to 3 teaspoons grated orange rind

BURNT-SUGAR CAKE

Two 9-Inch Round Pans

A caramelized flavor and a taste sensation.
➤ Have all ingredients about 70°. Caramelize, 559:
½ cup sugar
and add ➤ very slowly:
½ cup boiling water
Boil the syrup until it has the consistency of molasses. Cool it.
Preheat oven to 375°.
Sift together:
2½ cups sifted cake flour
2½ teaspoons double-acting baking powder
¼ teaspoon salt
Cream:
½ cup butter
Add gradually and cream until light:
1½ cups sifted sugar
Beat in, one at a time:
2 egg yolks
Add the flour mixture in 3 parts to the butter mixture, alternating with:
1 cup water
Stir the batter after each addition until smooth.
Stir in:
3 tablespoons of the caramelized syrup
1 teaspoon vanilla
Whip ➤ until stiff, but not dry:
2 egg whites
Fold them lightly into the cake batter. Bake in greased pans about 25 minutes. Spread when cool with:
A white icing
In making the icing, flavor it with:
4 teaspoons of the caramelized syrup
in addition to the vanilla.
Place any remaining syrup in a closed jar. It will keep indefinitely.

APPLESAUCE CAKE

A 9-Inch Tube Pan

If someone in your family is allergic to eggs, omit the egg and add an additional teaspoon of soda.
Preheat oven to 350°.
➤ Have all ingredients about 70°. Sift before measuring:
1¾ cups cake flour
Sift a little of the flour over:
1 cup raisins
1 cup currants, nutmeats or dates
Resift the remainder with:
½ teaspoon salt
1 teaspoon baking soda

1 teaspoon cinnamon
½ teaspoon cloves
Cream until soft:
½ cup butter or shortening
Add gradually and cream until light:
1 cup white or packed brown sugar
Beat in:
1 egg
Stir the flour mixture gradually into the butter mixture until the batter is smooth. Add the raisins, nutmeats and:
1 cup thick, lightly sweetened applesauce
Stir it into the batter. Bake in a greased tube pan 50 to 60 minutes. Spread when cool with:
Caramel Icing, 726

FIG SPICE CAKE

A 9-Inch Tube Pan

➤ Have all ingredients about 70°. Cool, drain, then cut into ¼-inch cubes and reserve the syrup:
1 lb. cooked dried figs
There should be 2 cups of figs. Combine:
½ cup fig juice
½ cup buttermilk or yogurt
Preheat oven to 350°.
Sift before measuring:
1½ cups cake flour
Resift with:
1 teaspoon double-acting baking powder
1 teaspoon salt
½ teaspoon cinnamon
¼ teaspoon cloves
½ teaspoon baking soda
Cream until soft:
½ cup butter or shortening
Add gradually and cream until light:
1 cup sifted sugar
Beat in, one at a time:
2 eggs
Add the flour mixture to the butter mixture in 3 parts, alternating with the milk and fig juice. Stir the batter after each addition until smooth. Add the figs and:
1 teaspoon vanilla
(1 cup broken nutmeats or raisins)
Bake in a greased tube pan about 50 minutes. Spread when cool with:
Coffee or Mocha Icing, 729

DATE SPICE CAKE

An 8½ x 4½-Inch Loaf

Preheat oven to 325°.
➤ Have all ingredients about 70°. Cut into small pieces:
1 cup dates
Pour over them:
1 cup boiling water or coffee
Cool these ingredients. Sift before measuring:
1½ cups cake flour
Resift with:
1½ teaspoons double-acting baking powder
¾ teaspoon freshly grated nutmeg
¼ teaspoon salt
¼ teaspoon baking soda
Cream together:
3 tablespoons butter or shortening
1 cup sifted sugar
1 egg
Add the flour mixture to the butter mixture in 3 parts, alternating with the date mixture. Stir the batter well after each addition. Fold in:
1 cup raisins
1 cup broken pecan meats
Bake in a greased loaf pan about 50 minutes. Test for doneness, 665. Dust with:
Powdered sugar

EGGLESS, MILKLESS SPICE CAKE

A 7-Inch Tube Pan

Preheat oven to 325°.
Boil for 3 minutes:
1 cup water or beer
2 cups seeded raisins
1 cup packed brown sugar
⅓ cup butter or shortening
½ teaspoon each cinnamon and allspice
½ teaspoon salt
⅛ teaspoon nutmeg
Cool these ingredients. Sift before measuring:
2 cups cake flour
Resift with:
1 teaspoon double-acting baking powder
1 teaspoon baking soda
Stir the flour gradually into the other ingredients. Stir the batter until smooth. Add:
(1 cup chopped almonds)
By the addition of 1 cup chopped dates, figs and citron, this becomes an acceptable fruit cake. Bake in a greased tube pan for 1 hour or more. Spread with:
Caramel Icing, 726

ROMBAUER JAM CAKE

A 7-Inch Tube Pan

Preheat oven to 350°.
➤ Have all ingredients about 70°. Sift, then measure:
1½ cups all-purpose flour
Resift with:
1 teaspoon double-acting baking powder
½ teaspoon baking soda
½ teaspoon cloves
1 teaspoon each cinnamon and nutmeg
Cream until light:
6 tablespoons butter or shortening
1 cup packed brown sugar
Beat in, one at a time:
2 eggs
Beat in:
3 tablespoons cultured sour cream
Stir the flour mixture into the butter mixture until barely blended. Stir in:
1 cup rather firm raspberry or blackberry jam
(½ cup broken nutmeats)

Pour the batter into a greased tube pan. Bake it about ½ hour or until done. When cool, ice the cake with:

Quick Brown-Sugar Icing, 728

OATMEAL CAKE

A 9 x 13-Inch Pan

Make this cake a day or two before eating. For another oat cake, see Guy Fawkes Day Cake, 682.
Preheat oven to 350°.
➤ Have all ingredients about 70°.
Combine and let stand at least 20 minutes:

1 cup rolled oats
1½ cups boiling water

Cream together:

½ cup butter
1 cup sugar
1 cup packed brown sugar

Add, mixing thoroughly:

2 eggs
1 teaspoon vanilla

and the oat mixture. Sift together:

1⅓ cups all-purpose flour
1 teaspoon baking soda
½ teaspoon salt
1 teaspoon cinnamon
½ teaspoon nutmeg

Stir flour mixture into the egg mixture. Beat about 2 minutes, then turn into a greased cake pan and bake 30 minutes or until done. To ice the warm cake, make up a double portion of:

Broiled Icing, 730

and put under the broiler until light brown.

TOMATO SOUP OR MYSTERY CAKE

A 9-Inch Tube Pan

This curious combination of ingredients makes a surprisingly good cake. But why shouldn't it? The deep secret is tomato, which after all is a fruit.
Preheat oven to 350°.
Have all ingredients about 70°. Sift before measuring:

2 cups all-purpose flour

Resift with:

½ teaspoon salt
1 teaspoon cinnamon
½ teaspoon each nutmeg and cloves
1 teaspoon baking soda

Sift:

1 cup sugar

Cream until soft:

2 tablespoons butter

Add the sifted sugar gradually and cream these ingredients well. Stir the flour mixture in 3 parts into the sugar mixture, alternating with:

1 can condensed tomato soup: 10½ oz.

Stir the batter until smooth after each addition. Fold in:

1 cup nutmeats
1 cup raisins

Bake in a greased tube pan about 45 minutes. Spread, when cool, with:

Boiled White Icing, 722, or Cream Cheese Icing, 727

TUTTI-FRUTTI CAKE

A 9-Inch Tube Pan

A well-flavored summer fruit cake.
Preheat oven to 350°.
➤ Have all ingredients about 70°.
Sift before measuring:

2 cups and 2 tablespoons cake flour

Resift with:

1 teaspoon each cloves, cinnamon, nutmeg
1 teaspoon baking soda
½ teaspoon salt

Cream:

½ cup butter or shortening

Add gradually and cream until light:

1½ cups packed brown sugar

Beat in, one at a time:

2 eggs

Stir the flour mixture into the butter mixture in 3 parts, alternating with:

1 cup lightly drained crushed pineapple

Stir in:

½ cup each raisins and currants
1 cup broken nutmeats

Bake in a greased tube pan about 1 hour.

BANANA CAKE COCKAIGNE

Two 9-Inch Round Pans

Do try this if you like a banana flavor.
Preheat oven to 350°.
➤ Have all ingredients about 70°. Sift before measuring:

2¼ cups cake flour

Resift with:

½ teaspoon double-acting baking powder
¾ teaspoon baking soda
½ teaspoon salt

Cream:

½ cup butter

Add gradually and cream until light:

1½ cups sifted sugar

Beat in, one at a time:

2 eggs

Prepare:

1 cup lightly mashed ripe bananas

Add:

1 teaspoon vanilla
¼ cup yogurt or buttermilk

Add the flour mixture to the butter mixture in 3 parts, alternating with the banana mixture. Stir the batter after each addition until smooth. Bake in greased pans about ½ hour. When cool, place between the layers:

2 sliced ripe bananas

Spread the cake with:

A white icing

If served at once, this cake is good without icing—just sprinkled with:

Powdered sugar

or served with:
Whipped cream, Caramel-Cream Sauce, 774, or Custard Sauce, 771

ABOUT QUICK CAKES

We all want a good cake in a big hurry. But let's not delude ourselves that shortcuts make for the best textures or flavors. Any cake in the following group can be mixed in one bowl and successfully beaten with an electric mixer. However, ➤ never try to use the one-bowl method for just any recipe.

QUICK OR LIGHTNING CAKE

Two 8-Inch Square or Two 8-Inch Round Pans

Vary the flavor of this cake—the German **Blitz-kuchen**—by using the suggestions below.
Preheat oven to 375°.
➤ Have all ingredients about 70°.
If you want a wonderful, thin tea cake, have ready a topping of:
½ cup confectioners' sugar
1 tablespoon cinnamon
¼ cup chopped pecans
and prepare the 8-inch square pans. If you want a thicker layer cake to ice, use the 8-inch round pans and omit the topping. Let soften to the consistency of mayonnaise:
½ cup butter
Sift into a beater bowl:
1¾ cups cake flour
½ teaspoon salt
1 cup sugar
Add:
2 eggs
½ cup plus 2½ teaspoons milk
and the softened butter. Using the ➤ whip attachment of your beater, whip for 1 minute at low speed. Scrape the bowl. Whip for 1½ minutes at slightly higher speed. Scrape the bowl again and fold in:
1½ teaspoons double-acting baking powder
(1 teaspoon vanilla)
Whip for 30 seconds on first speed. Pour the batter into 2 greased pans, sprinkle with the topping and bake 20 minutes.

QUICK CARAMEL CAKE

Prepare:
Quick Cake, above, omitting the topping
Substitute for the white sugar:
1 cup packed brown sugar
You may add to the batter:
(¾ cup nutmeats)
(¾ cup chopped dates)
Spread the cake when cool with:
Caramel Icing, 726

QUICK COCOA CAKE

Prepare:
Quick Cake, above, omitting the topping
Substitute for ¼ cup of the cake flour:
¼ cup Dutch process cocoa
Ice the cake, when cool, with:
European Chocolate Icing, 728

QUICK SPICE CAKE

Prepare:
Quick Cake, above, omitting the topping
Add:
1 teaspoon cinnamon
½ teaspoon cloves
When cool, dust the cake with:
Confectioners' sugar

ONE-EGG CAKE

Two 8-Inch Round Pans

Preheat oven to 375°.
➤ Have all ingredients about 70°. Sift into an electric-mixer bowl:
1¾ cups sifted all-purpose flour
1¼ cups sugar
2½ teaspoons double-acting baking powder
1 teaspoon salt
Add and mix for 2 minutes at medium speed:
⅓ cup soft butter
⅔ cup milk
Add and mix for ➤ 2 minutes more, scraping bowl constantly:
1 egg
⅓ cup milk
1 teaspoon vanilla
Pour the batter into greased pans and bake about 25 minutes. See Quick Icings, 726, for a choice; apply when cake is cool.

GINGERBREAD

A 9 x 9 x 2-Inch Pan

Preheat oven to 350°.
Melt in a heavy pan and let cool:
½ cup butter
Add and beat well:
½ cup sugar
1 egg
Sift together:
2½ cups sifted all-purpose flour
1½ teaspoons baking soda
1 teaspoon each cinnamon and ginger
½ teaspoon salt
Combine:
½ cup light molasses
½ cup honey
1 cup hot water
(1 tablespoon grated orange rind)
Add the sifted and liquid ingredients alternately to the butter mixture until blended. Bake in a greased pan about 1 hour.

WHEATLESS GINGERBREAD

A 9 x 9 x 2-Inch Pan

Unusual, yet perhaps the best of all.
Preheat oven to 325°.
Sift together 6 times:

1¼ cups rye or rice flour
1¼ cups cornstarch
2 teaspoons baking soda
1 teaspoon cinnamon
¼ teaspoon each cloves and ginger
Mix together:
½ cup sugar
1 cup molasses
½ cup soft butter
1 cup boiling water
Add and stir well:
2 well-beaten eggs
Combine all ingredients and beat until thoroughly mixed. Bake in a greased pan 60 to 70 minutes or until it tests done.

GUY FAWKES DAY CAKE

An 8 x 8-Inch Pan

Also called **Parkin**—a not-too-sweet cake.
Preheat oven to 350°.
Heat ➤ over—not in—boiling water, until the butter is melted:
½ cup butter
⅔ cup treacle
Mix in a bowl:
⅔ cup rolled oats
1 cup all-purpose flour
1 tablespoon sugar
½ teaspoon ginger
¼ teaspoon cloves
½ teaspoon salt
½ teaspoon baking soda
(1 teaspoon grated lemon rind)
Add alternately with the melted butter mixture:
⅔ cup milk
Combine until the dry ingredients are just moist. The batter will be thin. Bake in a greased pan about 35 minutes or until the cake begins to pull from the sides of the pan.

ABOUT FRUIT CAKES

Many people feel that these cakes improve greatly with age. When they are well saturated with alcoholic liquors, which raise the spirits and keep down mold, and are buried in powdered sugar in tightly closed tins, they have been enjoyed as long as 25 years after baking.

Fruit cakes are fundamentally butter cakes with just enough batter to bind the fruit. Raisins, figs and dates can be more easily cut if the scissors or knife used is dipped periodically in water. If you do not care for the usual candied fruits, do as one fan wrote us. She cooked chopped dried apricots, dates, raisins and currants in orange juice, used whole wheat flour and added pumpkin and sunflower seeds.

For a 2½-pound cake, use an 8-inch ring mold or a 4½ x 8½-inch loaf pan, either filled to about 2½ inches. To prepare loaf pans, see Pound Cake, 675. To prepare a tube pan, line the bottom with a round of greased parchment paper or foil and cut a straight strip for the sides. Bake as long as indicated in individual recipes or until the cake tests done by pressing lightly with a finger, see 665.

Fruit cakes, still in the pan, are cooled from 20 to 30 minutes on a rack. After removing the cakes from pans, the parchment or foil in which they are baked is carefully peeled away and the cake rack-cooled further until entirely free from heat. To decorate the cakes with candied fruit or nutmeats, dip the undersides of the decorations into a light sugar syrup before applying them, or simply cover the cake with a sugar syrup glaze and arrange the trimming on it.

To store, wrap the loaves or tubes in brandy- or wine-soaked linens. If you prefer, you may make a few fine skewer punctures in the cake and pour over it very slowly, drop by drop, ¼ to 1 cup heated, but not boiling, brandy or wine. However you glaze or soak the cake, wrap it in liquor-soaked linen, then in foil. For very long storage, bury the liquor-soaked cake in powdered sugar. In any case, place it in a tightly covered tin in a cool place.

▲ In baking fruit cakes at high altitude, omit any leavening.

★ FRUIT CAKE COCKAIGNE

Two 4 x 8½-Inch Loaves

Not unlike a pound cake. The fruits stay light in color.
➤ Please review About Butter Cakes, 671, and About Fruit Cakes, above.
Preheat oven to 350°.
➤ Have all ingredients about 70°. Sift before measuring:
4 cups all-purpose flour
Mix ½ cup of the sifted flour with 4 cups nuts and fruits. We particularly like:
1⅓ cups pecans or hickory nuts
1⅓ cups white raisins
1⅓ cups seeded and chopped preserved kumquats or dried apricots
Resift the remainder of the flour with:
1 teaspoon double-acting baking powder
½ teaspoon salt
Cream until light:
¾ cup butter
Then cream it with:
2 cups sugar
Beat in, one at a time:
5 eggs
Add:
1 teaspoon vanilla
and continue to beat until light. Stir the flour mixture into the egg mixture and continue beating until thoroughly mixed. Fold in the reserved floured nuts and fruits. Bake about 1 hour.

★ CURRANT CAKE

Prepare the batter for:
Fruit Cake Cockaigne, above

Add instead of the suggested fruit mixture:
1 to 1½ cups currants
Bake, cool and store as for the above cake.

★ WHITE FRUIT CAKE

Two 4 x 8½-Inch Loaves

Preheat oven to 350°.
Prepare the batter for:
Fruit Cake Cockaigne, above
Substitute for the fruits and nuts:
1 cup chopped nutmeats, preferably blanched, slivered almonds
½ cup finely sliced citron, candied orange or lemon peel
1 cup white raisins
¼ cup chopped candied pineapple
¼ cup chopped candied cherries
(½ cup finely shredded coconut)
Bake about 1 hour. To prepare pans, cool and store, see About Fruit Cakes, above.

★ DARK FRUIT CAKE

I. **Two 4½ x 8-Inch Loaves, plus Two 9-Inch Tube Pans—About 12 Pounds**

➤ Please review About Butter Cakes, 671, and About Fruit Cakes, above.
Preheat oven to 275°.
➤ Have all ingredients about 70°. Sift before measuring:
4 cups all-purpose flour
Reserve 1 cup. Resift the remainder with:
1 tablespoon each of cinnamon, cloves, allspice and nutmeg
½ tablespoon mace
1½ teaspoons salt
Wash:
2½ lb. currants
Cut up:
2½ lb. raisins
1 lb. citron
Break coarsely:
1 lb. pecan meats
Sprinkle these ingredients well with the reserved flour. Sift:
1 lb. brown sugar: 2⅔ cups, packed
Cream until soft:
1 lb. butter
Add the sugar gradually. Cream until very light. Beat in:
15 beaten egg yolks
Add the flour mixture to the butter mixture, alternately with:
¼ cup bourbon whisky and ¼ cup wine, or ½ cup thick fruit juice: prune, apricot or grape
Fold in the floured fruits and nuts. Beat ➤ until stiff, but not dry:
15 egg whites
Fold them into the butter mixture. Bake a 2½-pound cake in prepared pans, for 1½ to 3 hours, depending on pan size. For over 5 pounds, allow at least 5 hours. Place a shallow pan filled with water in the oven. Remove it the last hour of baking. Cool cakes and store.

II. **Two 4½ x 8 x 2½-Inch Loaves, Plus Two 8-Inch Tube Pans—About 11 Pounds**

In this recipe the fruit is preconditioned, so it does not draw moisture from the cake during or after baking. Place and cook in a heavy pot for 5 minutes, stirring constantly:
1½ cups apricot nectar
2½ cups seedless white raisins
2½ cups seedless raisins
1 cup pitted, chopped dates
1 cup diced candied pineapple
2 cups diced candied cherries
1 cup diced candied apricots
Remove from heat, cover and let stand 12 to 15 hours.
➤ Please review About Butter Cakes, 671, and About Fruit Cakes, 682.
➤ Have all ingredients about 70°.
Preheat oven to 300°.
Sift before measuring:
6 cups all-purpose flour
Resift with:
2 teaspoons salt
½ teaspoon baking soda
2 teaspoons cinnamon
1 teaspoon each allspice and nutmeg
½ teaspoon cloves
¼ teaspoon cardamom
Cream until light:
2 cups butter
2 cups sugar
Add and beat in well:
10 beaten eggs
2 tablespoons vanilla
Stir in the sifted flour mixture. Combine the batter with the fruit syrup and fruit and:
3 cups coarsely chopped pecans
until well mixed. Pour into the loaf and tube pans and bake 3 to 3½ hours or until the tests indicate that the cake is done. Cool and store.

ABOUT OIL CAKES

In this book, all cakes made with cooking oil carry the word "oil" in the title. Have all ingredients about 70°. If liquid fats are used in cake mixing, they demand special mixing processes. The egg whites must be beaten so stiff that they begin to lose their gloss.

➤ Olive oil should never be used, because its flavor is too strong. To achieve a light texture, oil cakes often need a disproportionate amount of sugar and egg, and consequently the calorie and saturated-fat content approximates that of butter cakes. Because of the difference in mixing ➤ do not try to substitute oil for solid fats in other cake recipes. You may vary the recipes given for oil cakes, however, by the addition of spices, flavorings, nuts and raisins.

CHIFFON OIL CAKE

A 10-Inch Tube or a 9 x 13-Inch Oblong Pan

Please read About Oil Cakes, above, and ➤ mix exactly as indicated. ➤ Have all ingredients about 70°.

Preheat oven to 325°.

Sift twice and put into a beater bowl:

2¼ cups sifted cake flour
1½ cups sugar
3 teaspoons double-acting baking powder
1 teaspoon salt

Beat until smooth and fold in all at once:

½ cup vegetable oil
5 egg yolks
¾ cup water
1 teaspoon grated lemon rind
1 teaspoon vanilla

Beat until foamy:

6 to 10 egg whites

Add:

½ teaspoon cream of tartar

Now beat until the whites are so stiff that they begin to lose their gloss. Fold the flour, egg and oil mixture gently into the egg whites. Do this by hand, not in the mixer, see 665. Bake the cake in an ungreased tube pan about 1 hour and 10 minutes or in an ungreased 9 x 13-inch pan 30 to 35 minutes. Reverse the tube pan to cool the cake, as shown on 668, or set the oblong pan reversed and supported at the edges by two other pans while the cake cools. Ice with:

Quick Lemon Icing, 727

CHIFFON CHOCOLATE-MOCHA OIL CAKE

A 10-Inch Tube or a 9 x 13-Inch Oblong Pan

Mix and bake as for preceding cake. ➤ Have all ingredients about 70°.

Preheat oven to 325°.

Melt over hot water:

3 oz. unsweetened chocolate

Sift twice and put into a beater bowl:

2¼ cups sifted cake flour
1⅔ cups sugar
3 teaspoons double-acting baking powder
2 teaspoons instant coffee
1 teaspoon salt
¼ teaspoon cinnamon

Beat until smooth and fold in all at once:

½ cup vegetable oil
6 egg yolks
¾ cup milk
1 teaspoon vanilla

and the cooled melted chocolate. Blend well. Beat until frothy:

8 egg whites

Add:

½ teaspoon cream of tartar

Continue to beat until the whites are very stiff. Gently fold the egg whites into the flour, egg and oil mixture. Pour the batter into an ungreased pan and bake as for the cake above. Ice with:

Luscious Orange Icing, 725

CARROT OIL CAKE

One 8-Inch Square Pan

➤ Have all ingredients about 70°.

Preheat oven to 325°.

Sift before measuring:

1 cup all-purpose flour

Resift with:

1 teaspoon baking soda
1 teaspoon double-acting baking powder
1 teaspoon cinnamon
½ teaspoon salt

Mix together and add to flour, stirring well:

⅔ cup vegetable oil
1 cup sugar
2 beaten eggs

Add and blend in well:

½ cup chopped nuts
1½ cups grated carrots

Bake in a greased and floured pan about 1 hour and 25 minutes.

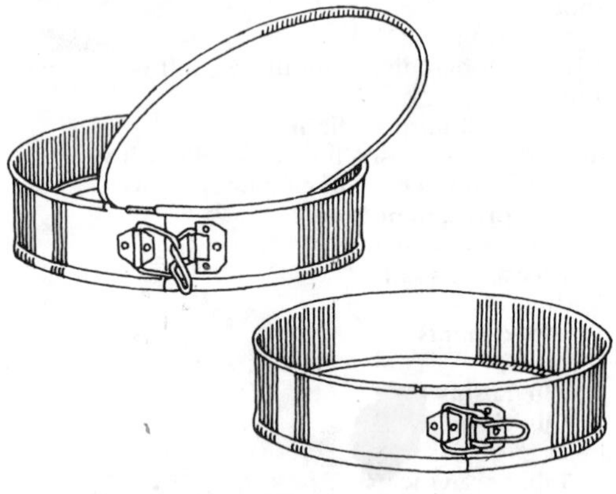

ABOUT TORTEN

So many people speak of baking torten as unattainably difficult, not realizing that mixing a torte is just a matter of replacing the flour in certain recipes with dry bread or cake crumbs and nuts ground to a fine meal. Here are some tricks in making torten: ➤ Do not use ground commercial bread crumbs; they are too fine. Prepare your own, using a medium blade in the meat grinder. ➤ The nuts should never be ground in a meat grinder, which simply crushes them and brings up the oil. A small hand grinder with a sharp cutting edge like the one shown in About Nuts, 562, will produce the light, dry, fluffy particles needed. Or, you may grind nuts at very high speed in the ⅄ blender. Do no more than ¼ cup at a time.

➤ Use a pan with a removable rim—either a

spring-form or a tube from which you can remove the bottom, because this kind of pastry is often too delicate in texture to withstand much handling. The sketch opposite shows you a cross section of the bottom separate and unlocked, the open rim unlocked, and the entire assembly locked into place. If baking in a tube or in layers, use pans with removable rims. ➤ Never grease the pan sides. Torten are good just as baked, with black coffee. But who can possibly object to a whipped cream or fruit-sauce garnish?

* ALMOND TORTE COCKAIGNE

An 8-Inch Removable-Rim Pan or Two 8-Inch Layer Pans

The following recipe is the well-known German **Mandeltorte.**

➤ Please read About Torten, above.

Preheat oven to 350°.

➤ Have all ingredients about 70°. Sift:

1 cup sugar

Beat:

6 egg yolks

Add the sugar gradually and beat until very creamy. Add:

Grated rind and juice of
1 lemon or of 1 small orange
1 teaspoon cinnamon
1 cup ground unblanched almonds
½ cup toasted or dry white bread crumbs
(½ teaspoon almond extract)

Whip ➤ until stiff, but not dry:

6 or 7 egg whites

The extra egg white makes a much lighter cake. Fold them lightly into the batter. Bake about 40 minutes in an ungreased removable-rim pan or loaf pan. Let cool in the pan. Spread with:

Chocolate Butter Icing, 728

Or, bake it about 20 minutes in two 8-inch ungreased layer pans. Spread between the layers:

Lemon Orange Custard Filling, 698

Spread the top with:

Sifted confectioners' sugar

or with one of the fillings suggested on 696. This cake is very light and consequently difficult to remove from the pan, so be careful.

* PECAN TORTE

For a richer, moister cake, prepare.

Almond Torte, above

substituting pecans for the almonds. ➤ Be sure to grind the nuts in a nut grinder.

* BREAD TORTE OR BROTTORTE

A 9-Inch Removable-Rim Pan

In the following recipe for a celebrated German confection, the ingredients differ only slightly from those in the preceding Mandeltorte, but the results, thanks to the wine bath, are gratifyingly different. You might try substituting walnuts for the almonds.

Preheat oven to 350°.

➤ Have all ingredients about 70°. Sift:

1 cup sugar

Beat:

6 egg yolks

Add the sugar gradually. Beat until creamy. Combine and add:

1¼ cups dry bread crumbs
½ teaspoon double-acting baking powder
½ teaspoon cinnamon
2 oz. citron, cut fine
1 cup unblanched almonds, ground in a nut grinder
Grated rind and juice of 1 lemon

Whip ➤ until stiff, but not dry:

6 egg whites

Fold them lightly into the cake batter. Bake 1 hour or more in an ungreased pan Heat but do not boil for about 10 minutes:

¾ cup dry sherry
2 tablespoons water
2 whole cloves
1 stick cinnamon
¼ cup sugar

Strain these ingredients and place the syrup in a small pitcher. Pour it very slowly onto the hot cake. When all the liquid has been absorbed, cool the cake and remove it from the pan. Spread with:

A flavored Crème Patissière, 697

DOBOS OR DRUM TORTE

The many-tiered Hungarian chocolate-filled torte that looks rich, is rich and enriches everyone who eats it. We like to think of it as "drummer's" torte because of its hard glazed top, but it seems its name refers to its creator, a patissier named Dobos.

➤ Have all ingredients about 70°. Prepare:

Génoise, 675

Using well-greased 8-inch cake pans, bake the cake in 9 thin layers, 5 to 9 minutes each. If your oven will not hold so many layers, bake thicker ones and slice them in two, in the professional manner, holding them as shown on 687. Stack them so that the icing is applied to the uncut surfaces. When cool, spread between the layers the following filling. Place in a double boiler ➤ over—not in—boiling water:

½ cup sugar
4 eggs
1-inch vanilla bean

or omit the vanilla bean and add 1 teaspoon vanilla after the filling has cooled. Beat until the eggs begin to thicken. Cool the filling slightly. Cut into pieces and dissolve:

4 oz. unsweetened chocolate

in:

2 tablespoons boiling water

Keep this warm. Cream until light:

⅞ cup butter: 1¾ sticks

Add the chocolate mixture. Beat this into the egg mixture. This filling may also be spread over the top and sides of the cake, but the true Hungarian will spread it between layers only, reserving the best-looking layer for the top. Glaze this chef d'oeuvre with:

½ cup Clear Caramel Glaze, 732

Before the caramel sets, use a hot buttered knife to cut 12 to 18 radial lines into the top glaze, so the cake may be easily sliced. "Rest" the cake in a chilled place 12 hours or more before serving.

* HAZELNUT TORTE

A 10-Inch Removable-Rim Pan

➤ Please read About Torten, 684.
Preheat oven to 350°.
➤ Have all ingredients about 70°. Sift:

1 cup sugar

Beat:

12 egg yolks

Add the sugar gradually. Beat well until ingredients are very creamy. Grind in a nut grinder and add to the yolk mixture:

¼ lb. hazelnuts
¼ lb. pecans or walnuts

Add:

(2 tablespoons bread crumbs)

Whip ➤ until stiff, but not dry:

8 egg whites

Fold them lightly into the other ingredients. Bake the cake in an ungreased pan about 40 minutes. When cool, serve with:

Whipped cream, flavored with vanilla or sweet sherry

or spread the cake with:

(Coffee or Caramel Icing, 726, 729)

CHOCOLATE WALNUT TORTE

A 9-Inch Removable-Rim Pan

➤ Please read about Torten, 684.
Preheat oven to 325°.
➤ Have all ingredients about 70°. Sift:

⅞ cup sugar

Beat until light:

6 egg yolks

Add the sugar gradually. Beat until well blended. Add:

½ cup finely crushed cracker crumbs
¼ cup grated unsweetened chocolate
¾ cup chopped walnut meats
2 tablespoons brandy or rum
½ teaspoon double-acting baking powder
½ teaspoon cinnamon
¼ teaspoon each cloves and nutmeg

Whip ➤ until stiff, but not dry:

6 egg whites

Fold them lightly into the cake batter. Bake in an ungreased pan about 1 hour. Spread with:

Chocolate Butter Icing, 728

or serve with:

Wine Custard, 736

FLOURLESS ANGEL ALMOND CAKE

A 7-Inch Tube Pan

➤ Have all ingredients about 70°.
Preheat oven to 350°.
Blanch, then grind in a nut grinder, 562:

1½ cups almonds

Sift:

1½ cups confectioners' sugar

Beat until stiff:

7 egg whites

Fold in the sugar and almonds. Bake in a greased pan about 45 minutes or until done. To cool, see About Angel Cakes, 668.

* LINZERTORTE

A 9-Inch Pie or Cake

The following is a delicious German "company" cake or pie. It looks like an open jam pie and, being rich, is usually served in thin wedges. It should serve 12.
Have all ingredients about 70°. Sift:

1 cup sugar

Beat until soft:

¾ cup butter

Add the sugar gradually. Blend these ingredients until very light and creamy. Add:

1 teaspoon grated lemon rind

Beat in, one at a time:

2 eggs

Stir in gradually:

1¼ cups sifted all-purpose flour
1 cup unblanched almonds, ground in a nut grinder or a ⅄ blender
½ teaspoon cinnamon
¼ teaspoon cloves
1 tablespoon cocoa
¼ teaspoon salt

The old recipe reads, "Stir for one hour," but of course no high-geared American has time for that. If the dough is very soft, chill it. Pat half the dough into an ovenproof dish to the thickness of ⅛ inch. Rechill it until firm. Cover this part of the cake generously with good-quality:

Raspberry jam or preserves, or apple butter

Preheat oven to 325°.
Place the remaining dough in a pastry tube. Forcing the dough through the bag, form a good edge and lattice. Bake the cake about 50 minutes. Before serving, fill the hollows with additional preserves. You may also dust the top with:

Confectioners' sugar

SACHERTORTE

A 9-Inch Removable-Rim Pan

Frau Sacher, one of the great personalities of Vienna, fed the impoverished Austrian nobility in her famous restaurant long after they had ceased to pay. Today she is remembered throughout the world for her chocolate torte, for which endless recipes, all claiming authenticity, abound. We make no claims but think the following delicious.
➤ Please read about Torten, 684.

➤ Have all ingredients about 70°.
Preheat oven to 325°.
Grate:

5 to 6 oz. semisweet chocolate

Cream well:

½ cup sugar
½ cup butter

Beat in one at a time until mixture is light and fluffy:

6 egg yolks

Add the grated chocolate and:

¾ cup dry bread crumbs
¼ cup finely ground blanched almonds
¼ teaspoon salt

Beat ➤ until stiff, but not dry, and fold in:

6 to 7 egg whites

The extra egg white makes a lighter cake.
Bake in an ungreased removable-rim or springform pan 50 minutes to 1 hour. When well cooled, slice the torte horizontally through the middle. Should the top be mounded, reverse the layers so the finished cake has a flat top. Place between the layers:

1 cup apricot jam or preserves

Cover the cake with:

Chocolate Glaze, 732

which should retain its glossy sheen. For a really Viennese effect, garnish each slice with a great gob of "Schlag" or whipped cream.

ABOUT FILLED CAKES

Filled cakes are especially appropriate for buffets; they serve as complete desserts, combining ice cream and cake, pudding and cake or fruit and cake. They may also be as rich and substantial or as light in texture and calorie content as you choose.

We have assembled in the next pages some individual recipes that we enjoy serving as complete desserts. We also suggest a number of ways that basic cakes can be combined with fillings. Read about Roll Cakes, 690, Torten, 684, Filled Rolled Cookies, 716, and Charlottes, 748. See illustrations for making a secret filling, opposite, lining pudding molds, 743, or turning a simple Baked Alaska into an Omelette Surprise, 742.

If you must, buy your basic angel and sponge cakes, ice cream and ice fillings. But when you combine them, make a delicious sauce of your very own with fresh eggs or fruit and—most important of all—real vanilla, fresh spices and quality spirits. All the recipes for sponge, angel cakes, Génoise, Daffodil Cake, roll cakes, nut torten, ladyfingers and rolled cookies are suitable for mold linings. For additional fillings and combinations, see About Cake Fillings, 696 to 699.

To prepare a tube cake for a secret filling, see the illustrations opposite. Have ready a serrated knife or a long piece of thread. Marking the section to be separated with wooden picks, as shown, cut a 1-inch incision at the pick level all around the cake. Then cut through or if using a thread hold it taut and with a sawing motion cut the 1-inch-high section free. Reserve this top slice for the lid.

Then start to cut a smooth-rimmed channel in the remaining section, to receive the filling. Allow for 1-inch walls by making 2 circular, vertical incisions, to within 1 inch of the base. To remove the cake loosened by these incisions, next insert your knife diagonally, first from the top of the inside of the outer rim to the base cut of the inner rim, and continue to cut diagonally all around through the channel core. Then reverse the action and repeat the cut from the top of the inside of the inner rim to the base cut of the outer rim. Performed with a saw-bladed knife, these two cuts bisect each other in an × operation and give you 3 loose triangular sections which are easily removed. The fourth triangle still attached at the base is then cut free one inch from the base of the cake. A curved knife is a help here. The cake which formed the channel area can be used for Angel Balls, 694, or some of it may be shredded and mixed with the filling. Ladle the filling of your choice into the channel as shown in the center. Replace the lid. Top this whole cake with whipped cream or icing. When you cut the cake, each slice will look like the cross sections sketched on the cake-stand.

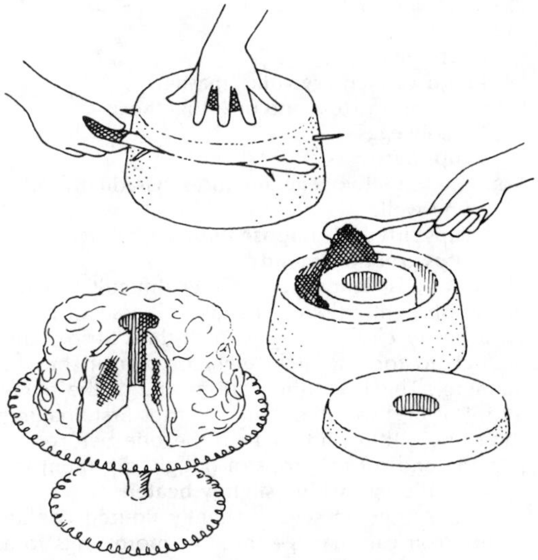

REFRIGERATED FILLED CAKE

Line molds with cakes suggested above, or make a cake with a secret filling, shown above. Fill with:

Bavarians, 746, or mousses, 737
Whipped gelatin puddings, 743
Pastry creams, 697, or Charlotte mixtures, 748
Fillings for cream pie, 656, or chiffon pie, 658
Sweetened whipped creams, 696

Refrigerate at least 6 hours, covered, before serving. Garnish with:

Fruits and nuts

or serve with:

Sauce or whipped cream

Dust with:

Toasted nuts
Shredded coconut or Praliné, 789

* QUICK MOCHA-CHOCOLATE FREEZER CAKE

About 10 to 12 Servings

Cut:

Angel Cake, 668

into 4 layers. Soften:

½ gallon Mocha Ice Cream, 762

Stir in:

3 shaved sweet chocolate and almond bars

Put the ice cream between the layers and cover the cake all over with it. Put into the * freezer and allow to set for about an hour. If you make this the day before and keep it in the freezer, be sure to unfreeze ½ hour before serving.

KRANSEKAKE OR PYRAMID CAKE

A tiered cake usually served at weddings and confirmations in Norway; in America, a spectacular finale to a dinner party; see illustration in chapter heading on 664.

Preheat oven to 375°.

Mix together:

1 cup sugar
4 hard-cooked egg yolks, mashed

Set aside this mixture and beat together:

4 whole eggs
2 cups butter

Combine the two egg mixtures. Gradually add, kneading well:

5 cups sifted all-purpose flour
3 cups ground almonds

The dough is delicate and rather difficult to handle. With lightly floured hands, roll a small lump on a pastry cloth into a ½-inch-thick strip, long enough to form a circle eight or nine inches in diameter. This is for the bottom ring of the pyramid. It is best to roll out all the strips first, making each one a little shorter than the one before. To join the ends of the strips of dough, dip them in:

A little egg white, slightly beaten

Place the rings on several slightly floured cookie sheets. You can manage three or more rings to a sheet. Sprinkle with:

Granulated sugar

Bake about 7 minutes or until light brown. When removed from the oven, immediately place one ring on top of the other so they will stick together. Decorate with:

Lemon Glaze, 731

by piping a thin line of glaze at the point where two rings meet. Then continue in an irregular zigzag fashion all over the cake. This pastry is delightful served with:

Fresh strawberries or other fruit

CASSATA ALLA SICILIANA

Prepare:

Pound Cake, 675

Cut off and reserve crusts for cookie crumbs, 635. Cut the cake horizontally into 4 long even slices. Prepare a filling by mixing in a ⅄ blender until very smooth:

1 lb. Ricotta cheese
2 tablespoons cream
¼ cup sugar
3 tablespoons crème de cacao or Grand Marnier

Fold in:

2 tablespoons coarsely chopped candied orange or lemon peel
2 squares coarsely chopped semisweet chocolate

Divide the filling in about three parts so as to cover all but the top layer. Firm up the filled cake by refrigerating, wrapped, about 2 hours. Depending on how rich a dessert you want, dust with:

(Powdered sugar)

or cover the cake with:

(Chocolate Butter Icing, 728)

using coffee as the liquid.

MOHRENKÖPFE OR MOORS' HEADS

These Moors' heads, along with Individual Nut Tarts, 718, and Macaroon Jam Tarts, 717, were specialties of a famous St. Louis bakery, now extinct, and these cakes graced a thousand Kaffeeklatsches. While the true Mohrenkopf is baked in a special half-round mold, then filled and the halves joined, the full taste effect can be gained by the following method.

Cut in rounds or squares:

Thin Génoise, 675

Make a "sandwich" filling of:

Hazelnut-flavored whipped cream

placed between 2 slices of cake. Ice with:

European Chocolate Icing, 728,
or Chocolate Sauce Cockaigne, 772

TRIFLE OR RASPBERRY RUM CAKE

A good use for dry cake. Combine it with raspberries, which are traditional. But apricot jam or other preserves, thickened pie cherries, or fresh or cooked drained fruit may be substituted.

Place in a deep dish:

Rounds of yellow, sponge or layer cake

You may sprinkle the cake with:

(2 tablespoons rum or sherry)

Spread the pieces with:

½ cup jam or jelly or
1 to 2 cups sweetened fruit
(¼ cup blanched, slivered almonds)

Prepare:

Rich Custard, 735

Pour the custard over the cake. If desired, garnish with:

(Whipped cream)

BABA AU RHUM OR SAVARIN

Beloved by the French, who frequently serve babas with tea. This is an American version. Savarin is really a larger version of Baba au Rhum. The same dough and the same syrup are used, but the Savarin is baked in a ring mold with a rounded base, and it is often flavored with kirsch instead of rum. When it is turned out, the center is filled with fruit. If you fill it with tart red cherry compote, you need hardly be told it will have become **Savarin Montmorency!**
Prepare the dough for:
Bundkuchen, 620, or
Brioche, 615
Place it in a greased 8-inch tube pan. Let rise, and bake as directed. Remove from the pan, cool and return to the pan. Prepare a syrup by boiling for 10 minutes:
½ cup water
1 cup sugar
Cool it to lukewarm. Flavor it generously with:
Dark rum, whisky or kirsch: at least ¼ cup
Place the syrup in a small pitcher. One hour before serving, pour the syrup slowly, drop by drop, onto the baba. Use as much as will be absorbed. Remove the cake from the pan and let it drain on a rack until ready to serve. If it is to be a dessert, top it with:
(Whipped cream or Crème Chantilly, 696)
You may serve individual baba cakes. Bake them in greased muffin or popover tins. Soak them with syrup as directed or cut a slice from the top, hollow the cakes slightly and fill the hollows with the raspberry or apricot jam. Serve with:
Lemon Sauce, 769
Or slice the babas in half. Cover each half with a slice of fresh pineapple and currant jelly, sprinkled with confectioners' sugar and kirsch.

POPPY SEED CUSTARD CAKE COCKAIGNE

Two 9-Inch Round Pans

A delightful filled tea cake.
➤ Have all ingredients about 70°. Combine and soak ➤ 2 hours:
⅔ cup poppy seed
¾ cup milk
Preheat oven to 375°.
Beat until soft:
⅔ cup butter
Add gradually and cream until fluffy:
1½ cups sugar
Sift before measuring:
2 cups cake flour
Resift with:
2½ teaspoons double-acting baking powder
½ teaspoon salt
Combine the poppy seed–milk mixture with:
¼ cup milk
1 teaspoon vanilla
Add the sifted ingredients to the butter mixture in 3 parts, alternating with the liquid ingredients. Beat the batter after each addition until blended. Whip ➤ until stiff, but not dry, then fold in:
4 egg whites
Bake about 20 minutes in pans with greased bottoms. Place between the layers:
Crème Patissière, 697
Dust with:
Powdered sugar
Or serve with:
(Chocolate Sauce Cockaigne, 772)

ORANGE-FILLED CAKE

Three 9-Inch Round Pans

Most recipes for orange cake prove to be disappointing, for upon reading them you find that they are merely sponge or butter cake with an orange filling. This one calls for orange juice in the batter plus orange filling and icing. Earrings for an elephant with no apologies!
Preheat oven to 375°.
➤ Have all ingredients about 70°. Sift before measuring:
3 cups cake flour
Resift with:
¾ teaspoon salt
3½ teaspoons double-acting baking powder
Grate:
Rind of 1 orange
into:
1½ cups sugar
Cream this until light with:
¾ cup butter
Beat in, one at a time:
3 eggs
Measure:
½ cup orange juice
½ cup water
2 tablespoons lemon juice
Add the flour mixture in 3 parts to the butter mixture, alternately with the liquid. Stir the batter after each addition until smooth. Bake the cake about ½ hour in 3 layer pans with greased bottoms. When the cake is cool, spread between the layers:
Orange Cream Filling, 698

BOSTON CREAM PIE OR CAKE

Traditionally called a pie, this is really a 2-layer cake. There are many versions, but the most prevalent one today reads as follows.
Place between 2 layers of:
Gold Layer Cake, 674
a thick coating of:
Crème Patissière, 697
Leave the sides exposed, but cover the top with:
A chocolate icing, 728

CREAM MERINGUE TART COCKAIGNE

Two 8-Inch Layer Pans

The following recipe is not at all difficult to make, yet it is an optical as well as a gastronomic treat.

A cake batter and a meringue are baked at the same time.
Preheat oven to 325°.
➤ Have all ingredients about 70°.
Blanch and shred:
(1/3 cup almonds)
Sift:
1 1/2 cups sugar
Beat until soft:
1/4 cup butter
Add 1/2 cup of the sifted sugar gradually. Blend until light and creamy. Beat in, one at a time:
4 egg yolks
Add:
1/2 teaspoon vanilla
Sift before measuring:
1 cup cake flour
Resift with:
1 teaspoon double-acting baking powder
1/4 teaspoon salt
Add the sifted ingredients to the butter mixture, alternately with:
5 tablespoons cream
Beat the batter until smooth. Spread it in 2 greased pans with 1 1/2-inch sides. Cover it with the following meringue. Whip ➤ until stiff, but not dry:
4 egg whites
Add the remaining cup sifted sugar slowly, about 1 tablespoon at a time. Beat constantly. When all the sugar has been added, continue to beat for several minutes. Fold in:
1 teaspoon vanilla
Spread the meringue lightly over the cake batter in both pans. If using the almonds, stud one meringue with the blanched, shredded almonds, placing the shreds upright and close together. Bake the layers about 40 minutes. Remove them from the oven and let them cool in the pans. Shortly before serving the cake, place the unstudded layer, meringue side down, on a cake plate. Spread one of the following fillings over it, reserving 1/4 cup to garnish the top. Place the almond-studded layer, meringue side up, on the filling and place the reserved filling in the center on top, using:
A cream filling, 697; Sauce Cockaigne, 770; or whipped cream

CARAMEL CORNFLAKE RING

A 7-Inch Ring Mold

Stir and melt in a large saucepan:
1 cup packed brown sugar
3 tablespoons butter
(1/4 teaspoon salt if butter is unsalted)
Fold in until well coated:
4 cups uncrushed cornflakes
Press the mixture lightly into a 7-inch ring mold. Invert the ring onto a platter before the mixture is cold. When set, fill with sweetened fruits and whipped cream, coffee ice cream dribbled with chocolate sauce, or a fruit ice laced with liqueur.

FRUIT SHORTCAKES

Prepare:
Fluffy Biscuit dough, 633, Scone dough, 634, or any of the plain sponge cakes, 670
For small shortcakes, the dough should be baked in 3-inch rounds, split while hot and spread with butter. The sponge cake should be cut to size after baking. For large shortcakes, bake in 2 layers. Place between the layers and over them:
Sugared or cooked fruit
Garnish with:
Whipped cream

ABOUT ROLL CAKES

Any number of batters lend themselves to rolling, see below. For easy removal, they should be baked in sheets, 10 1/2 x 15 1/2 x 1 inch. Grease the baking sheet, then line the bottom with a long strip of parchment paper or foil which extends over the ends of the pan. Grease the paper also and pour in the batter so it covers all corners. Bake in a 375° oven about 12 minutes. Loosen the edges as soon as the cake comes from the oven. Reverse the pan onto a clean towel that has been dusted with:
Sifted confectioners' sugar
Immediately peel off the paper or foil. Trim any crusty edges and roll before the cake cools. If the filling is a perishable one, roll the unfilled cake while it is still hot, with the towel, as shown in the illustration below. Place the cake, still wrapped in the towel, on a rack to cool. Later, when ready to

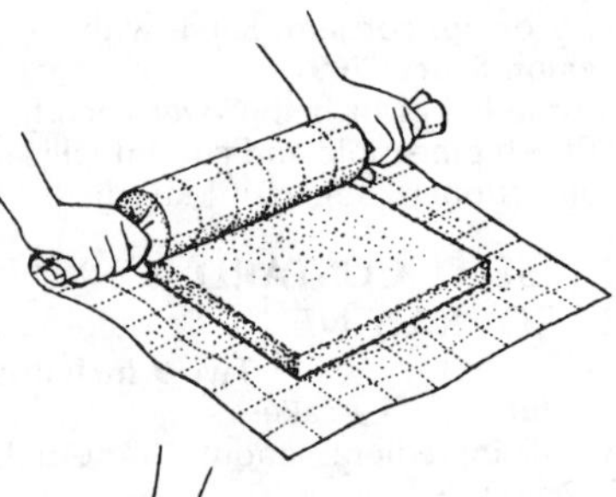

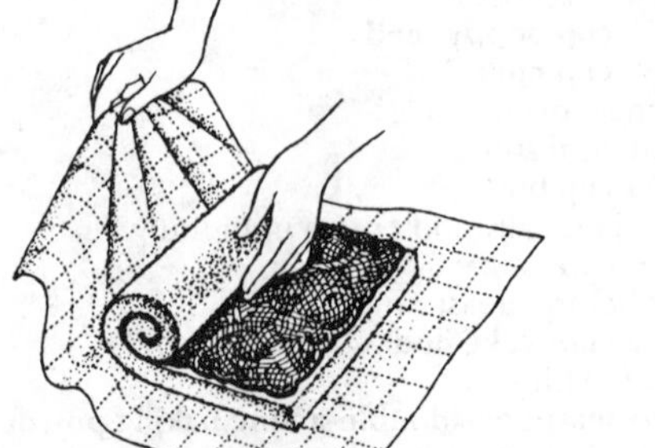

fill, unroll the cake, fill it and use the towel to roll it again, as shown in the lower sketch. If the filling is jam or jelly, it can be put on the warm cake immediately before rolling. When the cake is rolled after filling ➤ place it on the serving plate with the loose edge down.

JELLY ROLL

A 10½ x 15½ x 1-Inch Pan

This standard roll cake, or jelly roll, recipe also bakes well in two 8-inch round layer pans. To prepare pan, bake and roll, see About Roll Cakes, above.

➤ Have all ingredients about 70°.

Preheat oven to 375°.

Sift:

¾ cup sugar

Beat until light:

4 egg yolks

Add the sugar gradually. Beat until creamy. Add:

1 teaspoon vanilla

Sift before measuring:

¾ cup cake flour

Resift with:

¾ teaspoon double-acting baking powder
½ teaspoon salt

Add the flour gradually to the egg mixture. Beat the batter until smooth. Whip ➤ until stiff, but not dry:

4 egg whites

Fold them lightly into the cake batter.

You may add:

(½ cup finely chopped nuts)

Bake about 12 minutes. When cold, spread with at least:

½ cup jelly or tart jam or 1 cup or more cream or custard filling, 697

Or for an unusual touch, try:

Ginger Fruit Filling, 698

LEMON ROLL

Prepare:

Jelly Roll, above

Substitute for the jelly:

Lemon Filling, 697

Roll and fill as directed above.

BUTTERSCOTCH SPICE ROLL

A 10½ x 15½ x 1-Inch Pan

➤ To prepare pan, bake and roll, see About Roll Cakes, above. ➤ Have all ingredients about 70°.

Preheat oven to 400°.

Place in a bowl over hot water:

4 eggs
¼ teaspoon salt

Beat until the eggs are thick and lemon colored.

Beat in gradually:

¾ cup sugar

Remove from the heat. Sift before measuring:

¾ cup cake flour

Resift with:

¾ teaspoon double-acting baking powder
1 teaspoon cinnamon
½ teaspoon cloves

Fold the sifted ingredients into the eggs with:

1 teaspoon vanilla

Bake the batter about 12 minutes. A good filling is:

Butterscotch Filling, 697

ALMOND SPONGE ROLL

A 10½ x 15½ x 1-Inch Pan

➤ To prepare pan, bake and roll, see About Roll Cakes, above. ➤ Have all ingredients about 70°.

Preheat oven to 325°.

Beat until light:

8 egg yolks

Beat in gradually:

½ cup sugar

Add:

½ cup blanched ground almonds

Beat ➤ until stiff, but not dry:

8 egg whites
¼ teaspoon salt

Fold in:

1 teaspoon vanilla

Fold the egg whites into the yolk mixture. Bake about 15 minutes, roll and, when cold, spread with any desired filling, see 696 to 699.

ANGEL CAKE ROLL

A 10½ x 15½ x 1-Inch Pan

To prepare pan, bake and roll, see About Roll Cakes, above. The pan is greased here in order to free the cake intact for rolling.

Prepare half the recipe for:

Angel Cake I, 668

Bake in a 300° oven about 20 minutes. Use any of the fillings suggested for the various Cake Rolls in this chapter. Raspberry or apricot jam and whipped cream are fine.

CHOCOLATE-FILLED ROLL

A 10½ x 15½ x 1-Inch Pan

Prepare:

Jelly Roll, above

When rolled and cooled, spread with:

Chocolate Sauce Cockaigne, 772

Serve with:

Whipped cream

★ CHOCOLATE CREAM ROLL OR BÛCHE DE NOËL

An 8 x 12-Inch Pan

For Christmas this can be made into a Yule Log, shown in the chapter heading. Trim it without the mushrooms for Washington's Birthday. To prepare pan, bake and roll, see About Roll Cakes, 690.

➤ Have all ingredients about 70°.

Preheat oven to 325°.

Sift:

½ cup powdered sugar

Beat until light:

3 to 6 egg yolks

Add the sugar gradually and beat these ingredients until creamy. Add:

1 teaspoon vanilla

Sift and add:

2 to 6 tablespoons cocoa

If you use less than 4 tablespoons cocoa, add:

(2 tablespoons all-purpose flour)

⅛ teaspoon salt

Whip ➤ until stiff, but not dry:

3 to 6 egg whites

½ teaspoon cream of tartar

Fold lightly into the cake batter. Spread the dough in the greased pan to the thickness of ¼ inch. Bake the cake about 25 minutes. Let it cool in the pan 5 minutes before rolling. Fill with:

A sweetened whipped cream, 696

Cover with:

Chocolate Sauce, 772

For the Yule Log, cover with a roughed-up:

Chocolate Butter Icing, 728

sprouting small:

Macaroon mushrooms

▲ ABOUT HIGH-ALTITUDE CAKE BAKING

Cake batters at high altitudes are subject to pixie-like variations that often defy general rules. Read the comments and then launch forth on your own, keeping records at first until you know what gives you the greatest success. On the whole, ➤ cupcakes and layer cakes are better textured than loaf cakes.

Up to 3000 feet, if you reduce the air in the cakes by ➤ not overbeating eggs, you will probably need no adjustment of the cake formula. ➤ Also raise the baking temperature about 25°. In elevations higher than 3000 feet, continue to underbeat the eggs as compared to sea level consistency. Another way to reduce their volume is to keep the eggs refrigerated until almost ready to use.

At around 5000 feet, it will also help to reduce the double-acting baking powder or baking soda by ⅛ to ¼ teaspoon for each teaspoon called for in the recipe. Decrease sugar 1 to 2 tablespoons for each cup called for, and increase liquid 2 to 3 tablespoons for each cup indicated. Raise the baking temperature about 25°.

At 7000 feet, decrease double-acting baking powder or baking soda by ¼ teaspoon for every teaspoon called for. Decrease sugar by 2 to 3 tablespoons for each cup indicated and increase liquid by 3 to 4 tablespoons for each cup in the recipe. Increase the flour 1 tablespoon for each cup called for. Raise the baking temperature about 25°.

At 10,000 feet, decrease the double-acting baking powder or baking soda by ¼ to ½ teaspoon for every teaspoon called for in the recipe, and add an extra egg, but do not overbeat the eggs. Decrease the sugar 2 to 3 tablespoons for each cup in the recipe. Increase the liquid by 3 to 4 tablespoons for each cup liquid indicated. Increase the flour by 1 to 2 tablespoons for each cup called for. Increase the baking temperature about 25°.

Following are some basic high-altitude recipes from government sources. But if you are reluctant to give up your own recipes from home, we also throw in as a talisman the homely formula of a friend who has for years had luck with it at 7000 to 8000 feet, using her old Chicago favorites. She merely uses three-fourths the amount of double-acting baking powder or baking soda called for, adds 1 additional tablespoon flour and 1 extra egg, decreases the butter by a few tablespoons if the recipe is very rich, and increases the oven heat by about 25°.

But whatever formula you use ➤ grease your baking pans well and dust them with flour or line them with parchment paper. For, at high altitudes, cakes have a tendency to stick to the pan. Exceptions are angel and sponge cakes, see recipes below. Fill cake pans only half full of batter, as high-altitude cakes may overflow.

▲ HIGH-ALTITUDE ANGEL CAKE

10-Inch Tube Pan

This recipe is for baking at 5000 feet. If baking at 7000 feet, add 1 tablespoon cake flour and decrease sugar by 2 tablespoons. If baking at 10,000 feet, add 2 tablespoons cake flour and decrease sugar by 4 tablespoons.

➤ Please read About Angel Cakes, 668.

Preheat oven to 375°.

Mix and sift together 3 times:

1 cup plus 2 tablespoons sifted cake flour

½ cup sugar

Keep refrigerated until ready to use:

1½ cups egg whites: 10 to 12 eggs

Beat the egg whites until foamy and add:

1½ teaspoons cream of tartar

½ teaspoon salt

Continue beating until egg whites are glossy and ➤ form peaks which just barely fall over. Fold in, with about 25 strokes:

1 cup sugar

Beat until mixture is fluffy and meringuelike. Beat briefly while adding:

1½ teaspoons vanilla

Add the dry ingredients about one-fourth at a time by sifting them over the egg mixture, using about 15 folding strokes after each addition. After last addition, use about 10 more strokes to blend completely. Pour into ungreased tube pan. Cut through batter with knife to release air bubbles. Bake about 40 minutes. Invert pan, as shown on 668, and allow cake to cool before removing it from the pan.

▲ HIGH-ALTITUDE CHOCOLATE ANGEL CAKE

Prepare:

High-Altitude Angel Cake, above

Use in all 1 cup cake flour and add:

¼ cup cocoa

¼ cup sugar

▲ HIGH-ALTITUDE SPICE ANGEL CAKE

Prepare:

High-Altitude Angel Cake, above

Omit the vanilla and substitute by sifting with dry ingredients:

¼ teaspoon cloves
½ teaspoon nutmeg
1 teaspoon cinnamon

▲ HIGH-ALTITUDE WHITE CAKE

Two 8-Inch Round Pans

This formula is for baking at 5000 feet. If baking at 7500 feet, reduce baking powder by ½ teaspoon. If baking at 10,000 feet, reduce baking powder by 1 teaspoon.

➤ Please read About Butter or Shortening Cakes, 671.

Preheat oven to 375°.

Place in a mixer:

½ cup soft butter

Sift together twice and then sift into the beater bowl with the butter:

2 cups sifted cake flour
2 teaspoons double-acting baking powder
½ teaspoon salt
1 cup sugar

Add and mix 2 minutes:

¾ cup milk
1 teaspoon vanilla

Beat until foamy:

4 egg whites

Add and beat ➤ until stiff, but not dry:

¼ cup sugar

Add this meringue to batter with:

3 tablespoons milk

and beat 1 minute. Grease the pans and dust well with flour or line with foil, pour in the batter and bake about 30 minutes or until done.

▲ HIGH-ALTITUDE FUDGE CAKE

A 9 x 13-Inch Pan

This recipe is for baking at 5000 feet. If baking at 7500 to 10,000 feet, decrease baking powder by 1 teaspoon, and if baking at 10,000, also decrease sugar by ¼ cup.

➤ Please read About Butter or Shortening Cakes, 671.

Preheat oven to 350°.

Melt over hot water:

4 squares unsweetened chocolate

Mix and sift together 3 times:

2 cups sifted cake flour
2 teaspoons double-acting baking powder
1 teaspoon salt

Soften:

½ cup butter

Add slowly to butter, and cream longer than you would at sea level:

2¼ cups sugar

Remove from the refrigerator and separate:

3 eggs

Beat and add the yolks and the cooled melted chocolate. Add alternately by thirds the dry ingredients and:

1½ cups milk
2 teaspoons vanilla

After each addition of flour, beat about 25 strokes. After each addition of liquid, beat about 75 strokes. Whip the egg whites ➤ until stiff, but not dry. Fold them into the batter. Grease pan and dust well with flour or line with foil. Pour in the batter and bake about 45 minutes or until done.

▲ HIGH-ALTITUDE TWO-EGG CAKE

Two 8-Inch Pans

The following high-altitude recipe is for a cake baked at 5000 feet. If baking at 7500 feet, decrease baking powder by ¼ teaspoon and add 2 tablespoons milk. If baking at 10,000 feet, decrease baking powder by ½ teaspoon and add 2 tablespoons milk.

Preheat oven to 375°.

Mix and sift together 3 times.

2 cups sifted cake flour
1½ teaspoons double-acting baking powder
½ teaspoon salt

Cream:

½ cup butter

Add gradually to the butter:

1 cup sugar
1 teaspoon vanilla

Cream until light and fluffy, somewhat longer than you would at sea level. Add to creamed mixture and mix thoroughly:

2 eggs

which were refrigerated until ready to use. Add alternately by thirds the sifted dry ingredients and:

¾ cup plus 1 tablespoon milk

using about 50 strokes each time the liquid is added. Grease the layer pans, dust them well with flour or line them with foil. Release air pockets by cutting through batter 3 or 4 times. Bake about 25 minutes or until done.

▲ HIGH-ALTITUDE SPICED COCOA CAKE

Prepare:

High-Altitude Two-Egg Cake, above

observing the adjustments for the altitude at which you are baking. Add to the dry ingredients before the final sifting:

½ teaspoon nutmeg
¼ teaspoon cloves
1 teaspoon cinnamon

Replace ½ cup cake flour with:

½ cup cocoa

▲ HIGH-ALTITUDE SPONGE CAKE

An 8-Inch Tube Pan

This recipe is for an altitude of 5000 to 7500 feet. If baking at 10,000 feet, add 5 tablespoons sifted cake flour

➤ Please read About Sponge Cakes, 669.
Preheat oven to 350°.
Remove from the refrigerator and separate:

6 eggs

Beat the yolks slightly. Add to them:

1½ tablespoons water
1 teaspoon vanilla
½ teaspoon salt

Continue to beat while adding gradually:

½ cup sugar

Beat until thick and lemon-yellow in color. Beat the egg whites until foamy and add:

½ teaspoon cream of tartar

Then add gradually to egg whites:

½ cup sugar

➤ Beat just until peaks form and fall over slightly when beater is removed from mixture. Fold yolk mixture into the beaten whites. Add one-fourth at a time, using about 15 strokes after each addition:

1¼ cups plus 1 tablespoon sifted cake flour

After fourth addition, mix for about 10 more strokes. Fold in:

1½ tablespoons lemon juice
1 tablespoon grated lemon rind

Bake in an ungreased tube pan 40 to 50 minutes. Invert pan as shown on 668 and allow cake to cool completely before removing from pan.

▲ HIGH-ALTITUDE GINGERBREAD

A 9-Inch Square Pan

This recipe is for baking at 5000 feet. If baking at 7500 feet, decrease baking soda by ¼ teaspoon. If baking at 10,000 feet, reduce soda by ½ teaspoon, sugar by 3 tablespoons and molasses by 2 teaspoons.
Preheat oven to 350°.
Mix and sift together 3 times:

2⅓ cups sifted all-purpose flour
¾ teaspoon baking soda
½ teaspoon salt
¼ teaspoon each cinnamon, nutmeg and allspice
1 teaspoon ginger

Beat:

½ cup soft shortening

Add gradually to shortening, and cream somewhat longer than you would at sea level, until light and fluffy:

½ cup sugar

Add 1 at a time and beat well after each addition:

2 eggs

Add and mix in thoroughly:

¾ cup molasses

Add the dry ingredients alternately by fourths with:

⅔ cup boiling water

Beat about 20 strokes after each addition of flour and 30 strokes after each addition of liquid. Grease and flour the pan well or line with foil, pour in the batter and bake about 45 minutes.

ABOUT CUPCAKES

Nearly all cake batters lend themselves to baking in individual portions; only the baking time will differ, and this depends on the size of cupcakes being made. Bake them in muffin, madeleine or ladyfinger molds. On informal occasions like children's parties, bake and serve in fluted paper baking cups. If the papers are set in muffin tins, the cakes will retain their shape and you do not have to grease the pans. If not using paper cups, grease the pans and fill the molds about halfway. Bake in a 375° preheated oven 20 to 25 minutes. Another suggestion for children: bake in cup-shaped ice cream cones. Fill cones about half with batter. Set them on a baking sheet and bake as for cupcakes.

Cupcakes can be filled and iced, see About Cake Fillings, 696, and About Quick Icings, 726. Or garnish the cakes with nuts, diced dried fruits, or a dusting of powdered sugar.

YELLOW CUPCAKES

About Two Dozen 2-Inch Cakes

See About Cupcakes, above.
Prepare:

Gold Layer Cake, 674, Lightning Cake, 681, or One-Egg Cake, 681

Add to the batter:

(1 cup raisins or washed, dried currants)

When cool, sprinkle the tops with:

Confectioners' sugar

SPONGE CUPCAKES

See About Cupcakes, above.
Prepare:

Any sponge cake, 670

Permit the cakes to cool in the pans, then remove and sprinkle with:

Powdered sugar

ANGEL CUPCAKES OR BALLS

About Sixteen 2½-Inch Cupcakes

See About Cupcakes, above.
Prepare the batter for:

Angel Cake, 668, or Flavored Angel Cake, 669

Place it in deep muffin tins with greased bottoms. Bake about 20 minutes. When cold, split the cupcakes horizontally and fill them. See Filled Cakes, 687, and Torten, 685, for suggestions. For a luxurious tea cake, ice with a rather soft icing and roll in chopped nuts or shredded chopped coconut.

CHOCOLATE CUPCAKES

See About Cupcakes, above.
Prepare any recipe for:

A chocolate cake, 675 to 677

When cool, spread cupcakes with:

Quick White Icing, 727, or Chocolate Butter Icing, 728, or Coffee Icing, 729

CARAMEL CUPCAKES

About Twenty-Four 2-Inch Cakes

See About Cupcakes, 694.
Prepare the batter for:
Quick Caramel Cake, 681
Spread when cool with:
Caramel Icing, 726

SOUR CREAM SPICE CUPCAKES

About Two Dozen 2-Inch Cakes

See About Cupcakes, 694.
Prepare the batter for:
Sour Cream Cake, 673
substituting for the white sugar:
Brown sugar
Add:
½ teaspoon cinnamon
¼ teaspoon cloves
Fold in:
¾ cup nutmeats
Good served plain or iced.

JAM CUPCAKES

About Twenty 2-Inch Cakes

See About Cupcakes, 694.
Prepare the batter for:
Rombauer Jam Cake, 679
Spread over the cooled cupcakes:
Quick Brown Sugar Icing, 728

PEANUT BUTTER CUPCAKES

About Twenty-Two 2-Inch Cakes

Delicate and well flavored. See About Cupcakes, 694. ➤ Have all ingredients about 70°.
Preheat oven to 350°.
Beat until soft:
⅓ cup butter
Add gradually:
1 cup packed brown sugar
When these ingredients are light and fluffy, beat in and blend well:
½ cup peanut butter
Combine and beat until light:
2 eggs
½ cup packed brown sugar
1 teaspoon vanilla
Sift before measuring:
2 cups all-purpose flour
Resift with:
½ teaspoon salt
2 teaspoons double-acting baking powder
Beat the egg mixture into the butter mixture. Add the sifted ingredients in 3 parts alternately with:
¾ cup milk
Bake the cakes about 25 minutes. Ice them with:
Quick Maple Icing, 729

COCONUT CUPCAKES

Three Dozen 2-Inch Cakes

See About Cupcakes, 694.
Prepare batter for:
Coconut Loaf Cake, 674
Serve plain or iced.

* PETITS FOURS

Prepare the batter for:
Lady Cake, 673, or Génoise, 675
Pour the batter into greased pans, so that you can cut the cake into small cubes. You may cut the cubes in half horizontally and apply a filling, 696. To apply Fondant, the traditional icing, see 725 and the illustration below.

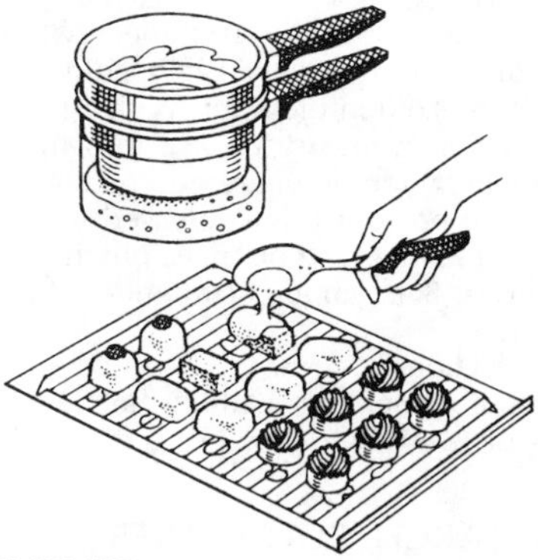

MADELEINES

About 15 Cakes

It was Proust's fortuitous nibble of a madeleine with tea that awakened from the subconscious the sensitive recollections of his childhood in a French provincial town—and from there, the long pageant of *Remembrance*.

These light-as-a-feather French tea cakes are usually baked in greased and lightly floured scalloped madeleine shells or muffin tins, see illustration in chapter heading, 664. Who could guess that their tender crumb results from an overdose of butter? The method of making them is just like that of Génoise, 675.
Preheat oven to 350°.
Melt and allow to cool to lukewarm:
¾ cup clarified butter, 349
Heat until lukewarm in the top of a double boiler ➤ over—not in—boiling water:
2 eggs
1 cup sugar
Stir constantly. Remove from heat and beat until thick but light and creamy, incorporating as much air as possible. When cool, sift and add gradually:
1 cup sifted cake flour
Add the melted butter and:
1 tablespoon rum or brandy
1 teaspoon vanilla or 1 teaspoon grated lemon rind
Bake shell forms about 8 minutes; muffins about 15 minutes, until a delicate brown. Cool on a rack, shell side up.

LADYFINGERS

About 15 Ladyfingers

Preheat oven to 375°.
➤ Have ingredients about 70°. Sift before measuring:

1/3 cup cake flour
Resift it 3 times. Sift:
1/3 cup confectioners' sugar
1/8 teaspoon salt
Beat until thick and lemon colored:
1 whole egg
2 egg yolks
1/2 teaspoon vanilla
Whip until stiff, but not dry:
2 egg whites
Fold the sugar gradually into the egg whites. Beat the mixture until it thickens again. Fold in the egg-yolk mixture. Fold in the flour. With a pastry tube, shape the dough into strips 3 1/2 to 4 inches long by 1 1/4 inches wide on ungreased paper placed on a sheet pan; or pour it into greased ladyfinger or small muffin tins. Or you may put it through a cookie press. Bake about 12 minutes. When cool, dust with:
Confectioners' sugar
Serve plain, or enclose a filling between the flat surfaces of two ladyfingers pressed together.

CORNSTARCH PUFF CAKES

Fifteen Small Cupcakes

Preheat oven to 350°.
Have ingredients about 70°. Cream:
1/2 cup butter
1 cup sifted powdered sugar
Add and beat until light:
4 eggs
1 teaspoon vanilla
Sift before measuring:
1 cup cornstarch
Sift 3 times again, with:
2 teaspoons double-acting baking powder
Combine the creamed and the sifted ingredients until blended. Fill muffin tins with greased bottoms half full and bake about 15 minutes.

ABOUT CAKE FILLINGS

If you happen to be pressed for time or are just plain lazy, you may prefer to buy the "baked goods"—sponge, angel cakes, macaroons, ladyfingers—which make the foundation for many and varied fancy desserts. Such pastries may be filled with seasonally flavored creams, pastry creams, Bavarians, mousses, zabagliones or layers of jam or jelly. Garnish these desserts with candied fruits and creams. Many pie fillings—fruit, custard and chiffon—as well as whipped gelatin puddings also lend themselves to use with cake bases. Thickened fillings, such as those having the word custard in the title, or the heavier nut and fruit fillings can stand somewhat longer storage before serving; but do not hold them more than 24 hours. Should you choose flavored creams and the less-stable fillings such as gelatins or ice creams, add them to your cake just before serving to forestall sogginess. For the same reason, be sure to choose fillings heavy in cream for freezing.

Fillings seem to adhere better if the layers are placed with the bottom crusts facing each other. For a charming but not rich finish, coat filled cakes with a dusting of confectioners' sugar, see 730. Filling yields are given in cups. For approximate coverage, see Icing Yields, 721.

SWEETENED WHIPPED CREAM OR CRÈME CHANTILLY FILLINGS

About 2 1/2 to 3 Cups

I. Whip until stiff, see 531:
1 cup whipping cream
Fold in:
1/2 teaspoon vanilla
(1 to 3 tablespoons sifted confectioners' sugar or 2 teaspoons strained honey)
You may use as is or add any one of the following:

II. Fold into the whipped cream:
1/2 cup walnuts, pecans, pistachios, hazelnuts or blanched, slivered, toasted almonds, or 1/4 cup nut paste

III. 1/2 cup lightly toasted coconut
1 tablespoon rum or crème de cacao

IV. 1/2 cup jam or orange or ginger marmalade

V. 3/4 cup fresh, canned or frozen fruit purée
(2 tablespoons kirsch)

VI. 3/4 cup drained, chopped fresh fruit
Reserve 1/4 cup of perfect berries or fruit slices for garnish.

VII. 1/2 cup crushed soft peppermint stick candy

VIII. 2/3 cup brown sugar or 1/2 cup maple sugar
1 teaspoon vanilla or 1/4 teaspoon nutmeg

IX. 1 teaspoon instant coffee
3/4 cup crushed nut brittle

X. 1/4 cup Almond or Filbert Paste, 780

XI. Prepare an angel or sponge cake shell, see 687. Shred the removed cake. Combine some of it with the whipped cream. Then add:
2 cups drained crushed pineapple
1 cup shredded coconut
(20 diced marshmallows)
2 teaspoons melted semisweet chocolate
2 teaspoons rum or Cointreau
Chill the filled cake 6 hours before serving.

XII. Heat in the top of a double boiler ➤ over—not in—boiling water, 2 tablespoons of the whipped cream and:
1/4 cup sugar
1/8 teaspoon salt
1 oz. unsweetened chocolate, cut in pieces
When the sugar is dissolved and the chocolate melted, beat the filling with a wire whisk until well blended. Cool. Blend in the remainder of the whipped cream.

XIII. Before whipping the cup of cream, mix in:

1/3 cup sifted confectioners' sugar
3 tablespoons cocoa
1/8 teaspoon salt
1/2 teaspoon vanilla

Thoroughly chill 2 to 3 hours, then whip until it holds its shape. You may sprinkle the filling with:

2 tablespoons chopped toasted pistachio or other nuts

CUSTARD CREAM PASTRY FILLING OR CRÈME PATISSIÈRE

About 2 Cups

The custardy pastry fillings below can all be varied. Enrich them by folding in 1/4 to 3/4 cup of whipped cream and/or chopped nuts, candied fruits and liqueur flavorings.

I. Vanilla

Scald:

1 1/2 cups milk
A vanilla bean

Mix in the top of a double boiler ➤ over—not in—boiling water:

1/2 cup sugar
1/4 cup all-purpose flour
3 to 4 well-beaten egg yolks or 2 eggs and 2 yolks

Beat this mixture until light. Now remove the vanilla bean and add the scalded milk gradually. Stir until all is well blended. Cook, stirring constantly, until it begins to thicken. Remove from the heat and continue to stir to release the steam and prevent crusting. Cool mixture before filling pastry.

II. Chocolate

When scalding the milk, above, add to it:

2 to 4 oz. semisweet chocolate

III. Coffee

When scalding the milk, above, add to it:

1 to 2 teaspoons instant coffee
(Ground hazelnuts)

IV. Banana

Before spreading the custard, above, add to it:

2 or more thinly sliced bananas

FRANGIPANE CREAM

Prepare Crème Patissière I, above, but after removing from the heat, beat in:

2 tablespoons butter
1/4 cup crushed macaroons or chopped blanched almonds
2 teaspoons chopped candied nuts

BUTTERSCOTCH FILLING

About 2 Cups

Prepare:

Butterscotch Cream Pie Filling, 656

using in all:

1 1/2 cups milk

CHOCOLATE MOCHA FILLING

About 2 1/2 Cups

Combine, cook and stir in the top of a double boiler ➤ over—not in—boiling water, until smooth:

2 oz. unsweetened chocolate
2/3 cup cream
1 1/3 cups strong coffee

Then add and stir into this mixture a smooth paste of:

3 tablespoons cornstarch
2 tablespoons cold coffee

Stir and cook the filling about 8 minutes. Cover and continue to cook 10 minutes more. Meanwhile, combine and beat:

4 egg yolks
1 egg
1/4 teaspoon salt

Beat in gradually:

1 3/4 cups sugar

Pour some of the hot cornstarch mixture over the egg mixture and then gradually return it to the double boiler. Cook 2 to 3 minutes, stirring lightly. Remove the filling from the heat and stir gently until cool and thickened.

RICOTTA CHOCOLATE FILLING

About 3 1/2 Cups

Combine and beat until light and fluffy:

2 3/4 cups ricotta cheese: 1 1/4 lb.
2 cups sugar
1 teaspoon vanilla
2 tablespoons crème de cacao

Fold in:

2 tablespoons shaved semisweet chocolate
2 tablespoons chopped candied fruit

LEMON FILLING

About 1 1/2 Cups

Mix in the top of a double boiler:

2 1/2 tablespoons cornstarch
3/4 cup sugar
1/4 teaspoon salt

Gradually stir in:

1/2 cup water or orange juice
3 tablespoons lemon juice
1/2 teaspoon grated lemon rind
1 tablespoon butter

Cook ➤ over—not in—boiling water about 5 minutes, stirring constantly. Cover and cook gently 10 minutes longer without stirring. Remove from heat and stir in gently:

3 slightly beaten egg yolks

Return to heat and cook about 2 minutes longer, stirring gently and constantly. Remove the filling from the heat and stir gently until cool.

ORANGE CUSTARD FILLING

About 1 1/2 Cups

Mix in the top of a double boiler ➤ over—not in—boiling water:

1/3 cup sugar

5 tablespoons all-purpose flour
¼ teaspoon salt
Stir in until smooth:
1 cup milk
Then stir in:
½ cup orange juice
Cook about 10 minutes, stirring frequently. Beat slightly:
1 egg
Beat about a third of the sauce into the egg. Return it to the pan. Continue to cook and stir about 2 minutes or until it thickens. Cool the filling before spreading.

ORANGE CREAM FILLING

About 2½ Cups

Soak about 5 minutes:
1 teaspoon gelatin
in:
1 tablespoon water
Combine in the top of a double boiler:
2 tablespoons cornstarch
2 tablespoons all-purpose flour
¾ cup sugar
Add:
¾ cup hot water
Cook these ingredients ➤ over—not in—boiling water 8 to 12 minutes. Stir constantly. ➤ Cover and cook undisturbed 10 minutes more. Add:
1 tablespoon butter
Pour part of this mixture over:
2 beaten egg yolks
Beat and pour back into the double boiler. Cook and stir the custard gently, about 2 minutes, to let the yolks thicken. Add the soaked gelatin. Stir until dissolved. Remove custard from heat. Add:
Grated rind of orange
3 tablespoons each orange and lemon juice
Cool the custard. Beat until stiff:
½ cup whipping cream
Fold it into the custard. Chill 1 hour. If spread between the layers of a cake, ice with:
Luscious Orange Icing, 725

LEMON-ORANGE CUSTARD FILLING

About 1½ Cups

Stir and cook in the top of a double boiler ➤ over—not in—boiling water, until thick:
2½ tablespoons lemon juice
6 tablespoons orange juice
⅓ cup water
½ cup sugar
2 tablespoons all-purpose flour
⅛ teaspoon salt
3 beaten egg yolks or 1 egg and 1 yolk
(½ teaspoon grated lemon or orange rind)
Cool the filling.

APRICOT CUSTARD FILLING

About 2 Cups

Prepare:
Lemon-Orange Custard Filling, above
Add:
½ to ⅔ cup sweetened thick cooked apricot pulp

CHOPPED FRUIT FILLING

About 1¾ Cups

I. Cook in the top of a double boiler ➤ over—not in—boiling water:
¾ cup evaporated milk
¼ cup water
¾ cup sugar
⅛ teaspoon salt
When the sugar is dissolved, add and cook until thick:
¼ cup each chopped dates and figs
Cool these ingredients and add:
1 teaspoon vanilla
½ cup chopped nutmeats

II. **About 2 Cups**
Combine and cook until it thickens:
⅔ cup puréed or mashed cooked apricots
⅔ cup sugar
Remove from the heat and add:
2 tablespoons orange juice
2 tablespoons grated orange rind
¾ cup chopped raisins
¼ cup chopped dates or figs

GINGER FRUIT FILLING

About 1½ Cups

Mix well in the top of a double boiler and cook, stirring constantly ➤ over—not in—boiling water about 8 to 10 minutes or ➤ until the mixture thickens:
¼ cup sifted confectioners' sugar
3 tablespoons cornstarch
½ teaspoon salt
1 cup canned pineapple juice
Cover and cook about 10 minutes longer. Remove from the heat and add:
½ cup mashed banana
½ cup drained canned crushed pineapple
Return to heat 2 minutes, stirring gently. Add:
3 tablespoons finely chopped drained candied ginger
1 teaspoon vanilla
(¼ cup slivered, blanched almonds)

ALMOND AND FIG OR RAISIN FILLING

About 1½ Cups

Blanch, sliver, then toast:
¾ cup almonds
Combine:
½ cup sugar
1 tablespoon grated orange rind
½ cup orange juice
2 tablespoons all-purpose flour
½ cup water
1½ cups chopped or ground dried figs or seeded raisins
⅛ teaspoon salt

Simmer these ingredients 5 minutes. Stir constantly. Add the almonds and:

½ teaspoon vanilla

TOASTED WALNUT OR PECAN FILLING

About ¾ Cup

Combine, stir and heat in the top of a double boiler ➤ over—not in—boiling water until sugar is dissolved:

½ cup packed brown sugar
¼ teaspoon salt
2 tablespoons butter
1 tablespoon water

Stir part of this into:

1 slightly beaten egg yolk

Return it to the double boiler. Stir and cook until the mixture is slightly thickened. Cool. Add:

¾ cup toasted walnuts or pecans
½ teaspoon vanilla
(¼ cup finely flaked coconut)

ALMOND OR HAZELNUT CUSTARD FILLING

About 1½ Cups

Stir and heat in the top of a double boiler ➤ over—not in—boiling water:

1 cup sugar
1 cup cultured sour cream
1 tablespoon all-purpose flour

Pour one-third of this mixture over:

1 beaten egg

Return it to the double boiler. Stir and cook the custard until thick. Add:

1 cup blanched or unblanched, shredded or ground almonds or ground hazelnuts, 562

When the custard is cool, add:

½ teaspoon vanilla or 1 tablespoon liqueur

COOKIES AND BARS

★ ABOUT CHRISTMAS COOKIES

Christmas and cookies are inseparable. Stars, angels, bells, trees, Santas and even pretzels—the pilgrim's token—are memorialized in rich holiday confections. Why not make use of these charming cookie shapes to decorate a small table tree at Christmas, or get a gifted friend to make you a wooden mold of the three kings bearing gifts. To cut your own molds, see Gingerbread Men, 712, and to build a cookie house, see 704. You can bake the strings for hanging right into the cookies. It irks us that such delightful sweets as Christmas cookies should be relegated to a period of a few weeks. In the hope that you will prolong the season, we have marked with this symbol ★ recipes that are generally recognized as traditional, as well as some that have become traditional with us, if for no other reason than that they can be baked in advance of a busy season.

MIXING AND DECORATING COOKIES

If you are planning to bake a number of kinds of cookies, see that they complement each other in texture and flavor and that they use up ingredients economically. Choose shapes that will look attractive on serving dishes. Many of these recipes call for butter as the basic fat. ➤ If you feel that, for reasons of economy, you cannot afford all butter, do try to use at least one-third butter. You will notice a marked superiority in flavor.

The mixing of cookies is usually quick and easy. Some ingredients must be well stirred together; some are creamed like cakes and, abroad, are called biscuits; others are blended like pastry. Use whatever mixing process the recipe calls for.

You may want to combine different flours. If you do so ➤ be sure to see the note on flour substitutions, 602. Because of variations in the size of eggs and in the moisture content of honey, molasses and flour, the consistency of your dough may have to be modified. ➤ Chill cookie doughs well and keep them covered until ready to bake.

▲ In altitudes up to 5000 feet, simple cookies usually need no adjustment. But for cookies rich in chocolate, nuts, or dates, a reduction of about one-half the baking powder or soda may be advisable. And at very high altitudes a slight reduction in sugar may help. ➤ But the soda should not be reduced beyond ½ teaspoon for each cup of sour milk or cream used.

To decorate cookies, dip the garnish before baking into either a simple syrup or unbeaten egg white. Then press the garnish firmly onto the cookie surface. Or dust sugar onto the cookies after placing them on the sheet and press it in with a wide spatula. Try icing cookies with flowers, patterns, names and holiday messages. To color cookies for special occasions, stir ¼ teaspoon water into 1 egg yolk. Divide the mixture into several custard cups and tint each one with a drop of different vegetable food coloring. (The yolk color will affect only the blue, which can be added to the egg white if you wish.) This coloring applied with a soft brush before baking allows you to make elaborate patterns.

BAKING COOKIES

If you wonder why commercial cookies are often large, the answer lies in handling and oven costs. A true sign of home baking is a delicate small cookie. Successful baking depends on the preheating of the oven, as well as on the kind of baking sheet used, its size, the material of which it is made—even its temperature. Choose a heavy flat baking sheet, or use the bottom of a reversed baking pan, as shown illustrated on the left, 711; or if you prefer, cut the cookies on a board and transfer them to the reversed pan bottom. The heat can then circulate directly and evenly over the cookie tops. A pan with high sides will both deflect the heat and make the cookies hard to remove when baked. The very best aluminum sheets have permanently shiny baking surfaces and specially dulled bottoms to produce an even browning. If only dark thin sheets are available, a second empty sheet may be placed under the first while baking.

Grease cookie sheets with unsalted fats, preferably sweet butter or beeswax. Warm the baking sheet and rub a lump of beeswax lightly over the surface. It will eventually acquire a permanent coat of wax and will not require further greasing. ➤ When baking cookies with a large amount of shortening, you may find it unnecessary to grease the cookie sheets. For delicate cookies, use a greased parchment paper or foil liner. They will peel off easily when slightly cooled. ➤ The baking sheet should always be cold when cookies are put on it, so they will not lose their shape. ➤ Always fill out a sheet, placing cookies of even size and thickness about 1 inch apart, unless otherwise indicated. On a partially filled sheet the heat is drawn to the area where the cookies lie, and the batch may burn on the bottom. If you haven't enough dough on your last baking to fill a whole baking sheet, reverse a pie pan or turn a small baking pan upside down.

➤ The placement of the pans during baking is very important. Bake 1 sheet of cookies at a time, at least 2 inches from the oven walls. If using two smaller pans, see that they are spaced evenly from the walls and from each other. Heat should circulate all around the pans. Few ovens are so nearly perfect that they will brown a large sheet evenly. During the baking process, do turn the sheet sometimes to compensate for uneven baking. Oven thermostats are also variable, so watch closely, especially when baking molasses and brown-sugar cookies, which burn easily. When cookies are done, remove them from the baking sheet at once or they will continue to cook. Should they harden on the pan, return the baking sheet for a moment to the oven before trying to remove them. ➤ Always cool cookies on a rack ➤ not overlapping, and store as suggested below.

STORING COOKIES

Most cookies and bars tend to dry out or go limp. To restore freshness, cookies can be heated briefly before serving, but it is wiser to use good storage practices from the start. Keep cookies in tightly covered tins or containers. If for immediate use, store bar cookies in the pan in which they are baked. Cover with aluminum foil. Or store them in an aluminum pan with its own lid, shown on 721. However, to prolong freshness, be sure to wrap these bars individually in foil after cooling and cutting. They are then all ready for serving, freezing, or packing in lunch boxes.

To soften hard dry cookies, put them with a piece of bread or apple into a tightly closed container. Replace the bread or apple every few days, for they mold easily. Another way to restore moisture is to use a dampened paper napkin, wrapped in punctured foil.

If you have frozen baked cookies and want them for immediate consumption ➤ thaw them unwrapped, then heat them for a moment on a cookie sheet in a 300° oven to restore crispness. This is also a good plan for weary "bought" cookies.

If you are sending cookies or cakes to out-of-towners, wrap them individually or put them into a polyethylene bag and bed them down in popcorn. Fill all the crannies of the box with the corn, until it just touches the lid.

We find that egg-white cookies, a natural byproduct of Christmas baking, need special handling. Some of the meringues heavy in nuts, like Cinnamon Stars, 714, keep well if tightly tinned. In packing mixed b
meringue-based c
unwrapped, they
made and stored
may disintegrate

ABOUT SQ

The quickest a
small cakes are squares
greased pans at least 1½ inches dee
serve pan sizes indicated in recipes, because the texture is much affected by thickness. A pan smaller than indicated in the recipes will give a cakey result—not a chewy one. A too large pan will give a dry, brittle result. If your pan is too large, divide it with a piece of foil folded as illustrated on 666. The dough placed on the horizontal lap will help hold the divider in place. Most bars, unless meringue-based, bake about 25 minutes in a preheated 350° oven. To prepare filled bars, line a 9 x 13-inch pan with two-thirds of the dough; spread the filling over it, see Cookie Fillings, 717; and cover the filling with the remaining one-third dough. We suggest the use of muffin tins for individual servings, or pie tins to make larger festive rounds under ice cream. See chart of comparative pan sizes on 666.

Squares or bars of different flavors wrapped in colored foils, or one dull side up and one shiny side up in regular foil, make an attractive dessert to pass at an informal outdoor buffet.

BROWNIES COCKAIGNE

About 30 Brownies

Almost everyone wants to make this classic American confection. Brownies may vary greatly in richness and contain anywhere from 1½ cups of butter and 5 ounces of chocolate to 2 tablespoons of butter and 2 ounces of chocolate for every cup of flour. If you want them chewy and moist, use a 9 x 13-inch pan; if cakey, a 9 x 9-inch pan. We love the following.

Preheat oven to 350°.

Melt in a double boiler:

½ cup butter
4 oz. unsweetened chocolate

➤ Cool this mixture. If you don't, your brownies will be heavy and dry. Beat until light in color and foamy in texture:

4 eggs at 70°
¼ teaspoon salt

Add gradually and continue beating until well creamed:

2 cups sugar
1 teaspoon vanilla

With a few swift strokes, combine the cooled chocolate mixture and the eggs and sugar. ➤ Even if you normally use an electric mixer, do this manually. Before the mixture becomes uniformly colored, fold in, again by hand:

1 cup sifted all-purpose flour

e flour is uniformly colored, stir in

ecan meats

a greased 9 x 13-inch pan about 25 min- Cut when cool, as interiors are still moist n fresh from the oven.

Good ways to serve Brownies are to garnish with whipped cream, ice cream or an icing.

RICE OR POTATO FLOUR BROWNIES

Prepare:

Brownies Cockaigne, above

substituting for the flour:

1 1/3 cups rice or potato flour

Proceed as directed. The baking time may be longer, so watch carefully.

BUTTERSCOTCH BROWNIES

About 16 Thin 2 1/4-Inch Squares

An all-time favorite, easily made.

Preheat oven to 350°.

Melt in a saucepan:

1/4 cup butter

Stir into it until dissolved:

1 cup brown sugar

Cool these ingredients slightly, then beat in well:

1 egg
1 teaspoon vanilla

Sift, then measure:

1/2 cup all-purpose flour

Resift it with:

1 teaspoon double-acting baking powder
1/2 teaspoon salt

Stir these ingredients into the butter mixture. Add:

1/2 to 1 cup finely chopped nuts or
3/4 cup grated coconut

Chopped dates and figs may be substituted for the nuts. Use a little of the flour over them. Pour the batter into a greased 9 x 9-inch pan. Bake about 20 to 25 minutes. Cut into bars when cool.

CAROB BARS

About 16 Thin 2 1/4-Inch Squares

A nonchocolate chocolate bar.

Prepare:

Butterscotch Brownies, above

using either white or brown sugar. Sift into the flour mixture:

3 tablespoons carob powder

and proceed as directed.

RAISIN MOLASSES BARS

About Thirty 2 1/2 x 2-Inch Squares

Preheat oven to 375°.

Melt:

6 tablespoons butter

When cooled slightly, stir in:

1/3 cup sugar
2/3 cup dark molasses
1 slightly beaten egg
1 teaspoon vanilla

Sift together:

1 cup all-purpose flour
1/8 teaspoon each salt and baking soda
1 teaspoon cinnamon
1/8 teaspoon each cloves and ginger

Add to the flour:

1 cup raisins
(1/2 to 1 cup chopped nutmeats)

Combine all ingredients until well blended, then pour into a greased 10 1/2 x 15 1/2-inch cookie sheet and bake about 12 minutes. Cut the cake into bars when cool and dust with a combination of:

2 teaspoons cinnamon
1/3 cup sugar

or cover with:

Lemon Glaze, 731

★ CHRISTMAS CHOCOLATE BARS COCKAIGNE

About 108 Bars, 1 x 2 Inches

Preheat oven to 350°.

Sift:

2 3/4 cups packed brown sugar: 1 lb.

Beat until light:

6 eggs

Add the sugar gradually, beating until well blended. Grate and add:

4 oz. unsweetened chocolate

Combine and sift:

3 cups all-purpose flour
1 tablespoon cinnamon
1 1/2 teaspoons cloves
1/2 teaspoon allspice
1 teaspoon each baking soda and salt

Add the sifted ingredients to the egg mixture, alternately with:

1/2 cup honey or molasses

Chop and add in all:

2 1/2 cups mixed citron, candied lemon, orange, pineapple and nuts—preferably blanched almonds

Spread the dough with a spatula into two 9 x 13-inch greased pans. Bake about 20 minutes. When cool, ice one pan with:

Lemon Glaze, 731

and the other with:

Chocolate Butter Icing, 728

Cut into bars.

CHOCOLATE OAT BARS

About 6 Dozen 1 x 2-Inch Bars

Preheat oven to 350°

Cream together:

1 cup butter
2 cups packed brown sugar

Beat in:

2 eggs
2 teaspoons vanilla

Sift together:

2 1/2 cups sifted all-purpose flour
1 teaspoon baking soda
1 teaspoon salt

Add:

3 cups rolled oats

Over low heat combine:

2 cups semisweet chocolate pieces: 12 oz.
1 can sweetened condensed milk: 14 oz.
2 tablespoons butter
¼ teaspoon salt

Stir until smooth, then add:

1 cup chopped walnuts or pecans
1 teaspoon vanilla

Now combine the egg and flour mixtures and pat about two-thirds of it into a 10½ x 15½-inch cookie sheet. Pour the chocolate mixture over all, then dot with the remaining one-third batter. Bake about 25 minutes.

★ NUT BARS

About Forty-Eight 1 x 2-Inch Sticks

These, like the following Pecan Slices, are made on a rich, sweet pastry base.

Preheat oven to 350°.

Cream until well blended:

½ cup butter
¼ cup sugar

Beat in well:

1 egg
½ teaspoon vanilla

Combine:

1¼ cups sifted all-purpose flour
⅛ teaspoon salt

Add these dry ingredients in about 3 parts to the butter mixture, blending them well. Use your hands to pat the dough evenly in a greased 9 x 12-inch pan. Bake about 15 minutes. In a heavy saucepan, beat until they begin to froth:

4 egg whites

Stir in:

2¼ cups finely chopped pecans
1 cup sugar
1½ teaspoons cinnamon

Cook and stir this mixture over low heat. After the sugar has dissolved, increase the heat slightly. Stir and cook until the mixture leaves the sides of the pan, but remove it from the heat before it is dry. Spread it over the pastry base. Bake the cake about 15 minutes longer. When cool, cut into sticks.

★ PECAN OR ANGEL SLICES

About Forty-Eight 1 x 2-Inch Bars

Many a copy of the **Joy** has been sold on the strength of this recipe. One fan says her family is sure these are the cakes St. Peter gives little children at the Gates of Heaven, to get them over the first pangs of homesickness. Her family has dubbed them Angel Cookies.

Preheat oven to 350°.

Line a pan with dough for:

Nut Bars, above

Bake as directed. Spread with the following mixture:

2 beaten eggs
1½ cups brown sugar
½ cup flaked coconut
1 cup chopped pecan meats
2 tablespoons all-purpose flour
½ teaspoon double-acting baking powder
½ teaspoon salt
1 teaspoon vanilla

If preferred, omit the coconut and use 1½ cups nutmeats instead. Bake the cake about 25 minutes. When cool, ice with:

1½ cups sifted confectioners' sugar

thinned to a good spreading consistency with:

Lemon juice

Cut the cake into oblongs.

APRICOT MERINGUE BARS

About Forty-Eight 1 x 2-Inch Sticks

Preheat oven to 350°.

Line a pan with dough for:

Nut Bars, above

Cover the unbaked batter with:

1 cup apricot preserves

Beat until stiff but not dry:

2 egg whites

Add gradually, continuing to beat:

½ cup sugar

When the mixture stands in peaks, fold in:

½ cup chopped pecans or walnuts

Spread the meringue over the apricot jam and bake 35 to 40 minutes or until firm. Cool slightly before cutting into squares.

DATE BARS COCKAIGNE

About Forty 2-Inch Squares

Preheat oven to 325°.

Cream:

½ cup butter
½ cup packed brown sugar

Add and beat well:

1 egg
6 tablespoons milk
1 cup chopped dates
1 cup chopped pecans

Sift together:

¼ cup sifted all-purpose flour
¼ teaspoon salt
½ teaspoon double-acting baking powder
1 teaspoon cinnamon
¼ teaspoon cloves
½ teaspoon allspice

Add to the sifted ingredients:

¾ cup rolled oats

Combine all ingredients. You may add:

(Juice and grated rind of 1 lemon)

Let dough stand about 15 minutes, then spread it into a 10½ x 15½-inch greased cookie sheet. Bake 15 to 20 minutes or until the dough begins to leave the sides of the pan. Cut into squares.

LEMON CURD SQUARES

About 16 Squares

Preheat oven to 350°.

Sift together:

1 cup sifted all-purpose flour

¼ cup confectioners' sugar
Add and combine:
½ cup melted butter
Press the mixture into an 8 x 8-inch greased baking pan and bake 20 minutes. Meanwhile combine:
1 cup sugar
½ teaspoon double-acting baking powder
2 slightly beaten eggs
2 tablespoons lemon juice
2 teaspoons grated lemon peel
(½ cup flaked coconut)
Pour these ingredients over the baked warm crust and bake 25 minutes. Chill. Before serving, cut into 2-inch squares and sprinkle with:
Confectioners' sugar

★ LEBKUCHEN OR GERMAN HONEY BARS

About One 8 x 8-Inch Cake
Plus One 10½ x 15½-Inch Cake

Honey, like molasses, may be troublesome. Old German cooks used to insist on its being over a year old. Very good cakes are made with fresh honey, but then the amount of flour is a little hard to gauge. If a crisper bar is desired, substitute carbonate of ammonia, 556, for the baking powder and soda given below. Use 1 teaspoon carbonate of ammonia dissolved in 2 tablespoons warm water, rum or wine. These German Honey Bars will keep 6 months in a tightly closed tin, especially if, as our grandmother used to say with a twinkle, "locked up."
Heat slightly in a large saucepan:
1⅓ cups honey or molasses
¾ cup sugar
Add and melt:
3 tablespoons butter
Sift together and add:
About 2 cups sifted all-purpose flour: enough to make a semiliquid dough
1 teaspoon double-acting baking powder
½ teaspoon baking soda
Add:
½ cup blanched almonds
¼ cup each chopped citron and chopped candied orange or lemon peel
¼ teaspoon ginger
½ teaspoon cardamom
2 teaspoons cinnamon
⅛ teaspoon cloves
Add:
1½ to 2 cups more flour
The dough should be sticky to the touch. You may age the dough overnight, refrigerated, in a covered crock, or pat it out at once into a ¼-inch thickness in buttered pans. If you age it, you may find it necessary to heat it slightly before working it into the pans. Bake about 25 minutes in a preheated 350° oven. Cut into squares and ice with:
Lemon Glaze, 731

ABOUT CAKE AND COOKIE HOUSES

No matter how peculiar the medium or incongruous the scale, the instinct to build persists. We have tried and discarded many cake construction methods. Professionals use Pastillage, 791, and Royal Glaze, 727, thus achieving rather cold-looking but clean-cut and intricate models. We prefer a simple approach.
Prepare any close-grained cake such as:
Gingerbread, 681, German Honey Bars, above, or Eggless All-Rye Honey Cake, 626
You will need 2 sheets of cake baked in an 11 x 17-inch pan, and a third sheet if also using cake for the foundation. The baking can be done over a period of days, but cut the cakes while still warm. Either use your own ingenuity or cut a paper pattern as illustrated below.

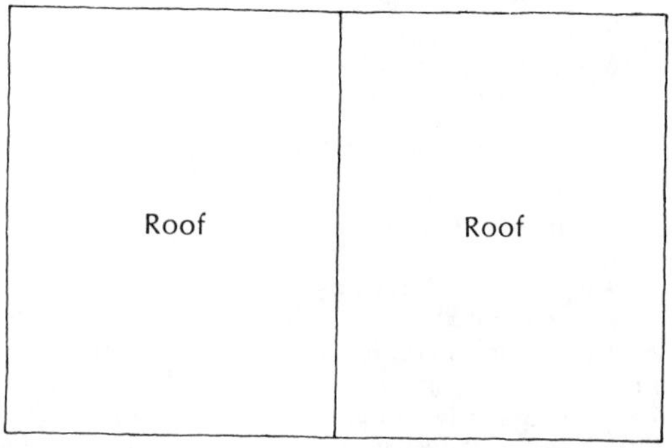

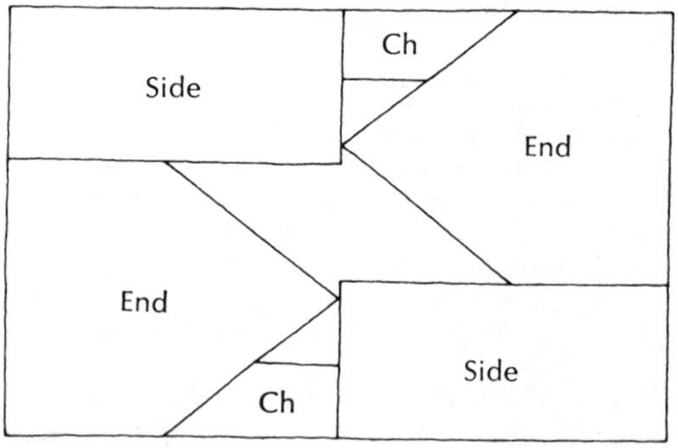

When ready to assemble, find an extra pair of hands, and with the help of plenty of "glue" made of:
Royal Glaze, 727
start to build. This icing, which dries hard and colors easily, makes a perfect bond for the various building elements and whatever decorations you want to add onto the house. Mitre the edges where the walls meet and shamelessly drive wooden pick "nails." ➤ Watch for these when the cake is eaten. When the walls are in place, use slabs for the roof, nailing them again with

picks where they touch the side walls. You could decorate the whole with icing, contrasting color of windows and door, shingle tile, etc. Or build up overlapping roof tiles and make doors and shutters of thin:

Molasses Crisps Cockaigne, 716

Affix these with the glaze. Colored hard candies and gumdrops also make festive decorations for your holiday house.

ABOUT DROP COOKIES

Almost any cookie dough can be baked as a drop cookie if additional liquid is added to the batter. Drop cookie doughs vary in texture. Some fall easily from the spoon and flatten into wafers in baking. Stiffer doughs need a push with a finger or the use of a second spoon to release them, as seen second on the left. To make uniform soft drops, use a measuring teaspoon. When chilled, these doughs may be formed into balls and flattened between palms, as shown on the left. First dust your hands with flour or powdered sugar; or, if the cookies are a dark or chocolate dough, use cocoa for dusting. Or, to flatten the balls, use a glass tumbler greased lightly on the bottom or dusted with flour, powdered sugar or cocoa as shown below, or a spatula dipped in ice water.

To prepare the pans, grease them lightly and dust with flour. For chocolate cookies, dust with cocoa. Shake off excess flour or cocoa.

DROP BUTTER WAFERS

About Forty-Eight 2¼-Inch Wafers

These, when baked, automatically produce a lovely paper-thin brown rim.
Preheat oven to 375°.
Cream until light:

½ cup butter
½ cup sugar

Beat in:

1 egg
1 teaspoon vanilla
¼ teaspoon grated lemon rind

Add:

¾ cup sifted cake flour
(1½ tablespoons poppy seed or
1 teaspoon grated orange rind)

Drop the cookies from a teaspoon ➤ well apart on a greased cookie sheet. Bake about 7 minutes or until the rims brown.

CHOCOLATE-CHIP DROP COOKIES

About Forty-Five 2-Inch Cookies

Preheat oven to 375°.
Cream:

½ cup butter

Add gradually and beat until creamy:

½ cup brown sugar
½ cup white sugar

Beat in:

1 egg
½ teaspoon vanilla

Sift and stir in:

1 cup plus 2 tablespoons sifted all-purpose flour
½ teaspoon salt
½ teaspoon baking soda

Stir in:

½ cup chopped nutmeats
½ cup semisweet chocolate chips

Drop the batter from a teaspoon, well apart, on a greased cookie sheet. Bake about 10 minutes.

SUGAR DROP COOKIES WITH OIL

About 5 Dozen Cookies

Preheat oven to 375°.
Sift together:

2½ cups sifted all-purpose flour
1½ teaspoons double-acting baking powder
¾ teaspoon salt
1 teaspoon cinnamon or ¼ teaspoon freshly grated nutmeg

Combine:

1 cup sugar
¾ cup vegetable oil

Add to this mixture and beat well after each addition:

2 eggs
1 teaspoon vanilla

Add the flour mixture all at once and beat well. Shape the dough into ½-inch balls. Dip the balls in:

Granulated sugar

or, flatten the balls as thin as you can between very lightly floured hands. To give a corrugated effect, score them in parallel lines, as shown below, with a fork dipped in flour. Sprinkle with:

Granulated sugar

Bake about 10 to 12 minutes on a lightly greased cookie sheet.

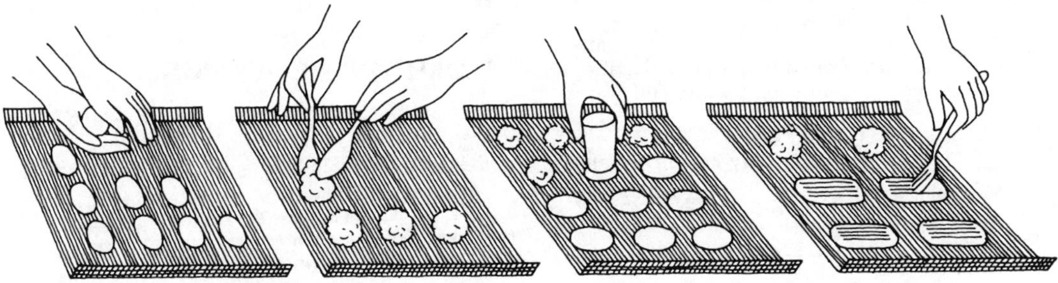

ABOUT NUT DROP COOKIES

The following four recipes, all delicious, may read as though they are much alike, yet they differ greatly when baked. They have in common a brown sugar and egg base ➤ so don't try to bake them in hot humid weather. In such weather, choose, instead, Pecan Puffs or Florentines. To prepare nuts, please read About Nuts, 562.

Most of these cookies are fragile. But if made small, and baked on a beeswaxed sheet, 700, or a foil pan liner, they are easy to remove intact. ➤ Should they harden on the pan, return the baking sheet to the oven for a moment before trying to remove them.

PECAN OR HAZELNUT DROP COOKIES

About Fifty 1½-Inch Wafers

If made with hazelnuts, these are very like **Nürnberger Lebkuchen.**

Preheat oven to 325°.

➤ Read About Nut Drop Cookies, above. Grind in a nut grinder:

1 cup pecan meats

Put through a sieve:

1⅓ cups firmly packed brown sugar

Whip until stiff, but not dry:

3 egg whites

Add the sugar very slowly, beating constantly. Fold in the ground pecans and:

1 teaspoon vanilla

Drop the batter from a teaspoon, well apart, onto a greased and floured cookie sheet. Bake about 15 minutes.

PECAN OR BENNE WAFERS

About Fifty 2½-Inch Wafers

Preheat oven to 375°.

➤ Read About Nut Drop Cookies, above. Whip until light:

2 eggs

Add gradually:

1⅓ cups firmly packed brown sugar

Beat these ingredients until they are well blended. Add:

5 tablespoons all-purpose flour
⅛ teaspoon salt
⅛ teaspoon double-acting baking powder
1 teaspoon vanilla

Beat the batter until smooth, then add:

1 cup broken nutmeats or
½ cup toasted benne seeds

Grease and flour cookie sheets. Drop the batter on them, well apart, from a teaspoon. Bake about 8 minutes. Remove from sheets while still warm.

MOLASSES NUT WAFERS

About Fifty 2½-Inch Wafers

Preheat oven to 375°.

➤ Read About Nut Drop Cookies, above.

Sift:

1 cup firmly packed dark brown sugar

Whip until light:

2 eggs

Add the sugar gradually. Beat these ingredients until well blended. Add:

1 tablespoon dark molasses
¼ teaspoon double-acting baking powder
6 tablespoons all-purpose flour
⅛ teaspoon salt

Beat the batter until smooth. Stir in:

1 cup chopped black or English walnuts, hazelnuts or mixed nutmeats

Drop the batter, well apart, from a teaspoon onto a well-greased cookie sheet. Bake about 8 minutes.

★ FLOURLESS NUT BALLS

About Thirty-Six 1¼-Inch Balls

Preheat oven to 325°.

➤ Read About Nut Drop Cookies, above.

Grind in a nut grinder:

1½ cups almonds or pecans

Combine in a pan with:

1 cup firmly packed brown sugar
1 egg white
1½ teaspoons butter

Stir these ingredients over very low heat until well blended. Cool the mixture. Shape the dough into small balls or roll it out and cut it into shapes. If the dough is hard to handle, dust the hands with a little confectioners' sugar. Place the cookies on a very well-greased cookie sheet. Bake 30 to 40 minutes. Leave on the sheet until cool. Ice with:

Lemon Glaze, 731, or a chocolate icing, 728

PECAN PUFFS

About Forty 1½-Inch Balls

Rich and devastating.

Preheat oven to 300°.

Beat until soft:

½ cup butter

Add and blend until creamy:

2 tablespoons sugar

Add:

1 teaspoon vanilla

Measure, then grind in a nut grinder:

1 cup pecan meats

Sift before measuring:

1 cup cake flour

Stir the pecans and the flour into the butter mixture. Roll the dough into small balls. Place balls on a greased cookie sheet and bake about 30 minutes. Roll while hot in:

Confectioners' sugar

To glaze, put the sheet back into the oven for a minute. Cool and serve.

FLORENTINES COCKAIGNE

About 18 Thin 2½- to 3-Inch Patties

A great European favorite—really choice!

Preheat oven to 350°.

Place in a blender:

4 tablespoons brown sugar
4 tablespoons honey
½ cup slivered almonds

1/8 teaspoon salt
1/2 teaspoon vanilla
Add:
1 1/4 cups packed mixed candied fruits
that have been thoroughly separated by working them over with the hands in:
1/2 cup flour
Blend this mixture until fruits and nuts are about 1/4-inch size. Add:
4 tablespoons melted butter
and reblend briefly, reducing fruits and nuts to about 1/8-inch size. Form dough into 1-inch balls and place on 2 buttered cookie tins. Flatten the balls to 2 1/2- to 3-inch patties. Bake 7 to 8 minutes or until golden brown. Allow the patties to cool very briefly, then turn them onto wire racks. Meanwhile, melt over hot water:
4 ounces semisweet chocolate
and cover the bottoms of the slightly cooled patties with the chocolate. Cool completely and store covered.

OLD-FASHIONED MOLASSES COOKIES

About Forty 2-Inch Cookies

These are highly spiced.
Preheat oven to 350°.
Beat until soft:
1/2 cup butter or shortening
Add gradually and blend until light and creamy:
1/2 cup sugar
Beat in:
1 egg
1/2 cup molasses
Have ready:
1/2 cup buttermilk
Sift together:
2 1/2 cups sifted cake flour
1 teaspoon baking soda
1 teaspoon each cinnamon and ginger
1/4 teaspoon cloves
1/4 teaspoon salt
Add the sifted ingredients in 3 parts to the sugar mixture alternately with the buttermilk. Beat the batter until smooth after each addition. Add:
(1/2 cup chopped raisins)
Drop the batter from a teaspoon onto a greased cookie sheet. Bake 8 to 12 minutes.

GINGERSNAPS

About 10 Dozen 2-Inch Cookies

Like "boughten" ones in texture, but with a dreamy flavor.
Preheat oven to 325°.
Cream together:
3/4 cup butter
2 cups sugar
Stir in:
2 well-beaten eggs
1/2 cup molasses
2 teaspoons vinegar
Sift and add:
3 3/4 cups all-purpose flour
1 1/2 teaspoons baking soda
2 to 3 teaspoons ginger
1/2 teaspoon cinnamon
1/4 teaspoon cloves
Mix ingredients until blended. Form dough into 3/4-inch balls. Bake on a greased cookie sheet about 12 minutes. As the ball melts down during baking, the cookie develops the characteristic crinkled surface. When cool, ice to taste. A topping to delight the children is half a marshmallow, cut side down, on the almost baked cookies. Return to oven about 4 minutes.

★ GINGER THINS

About Three Hundred 3/4-Inch Wafers

Mme. Bu Wei, in her charming book, *How to Cook and Eat in Chinese,* tells us that little cakes served between meals in her native country are called "dot hearts." They should have the diameter of a quarter when baked, for they toughen if they are larger.
Preheat oven to 325°.
Cream:
3/4 cup butter
1 cup brown sugar
1 beaten egg
1/4 cup molasses
Sift together:
1 1/2 cups sifted all-purpose flour
1/4 teaspoon salt
1/2 teaspoon baking soda
1/2 teaspoon each cloves, cinnamon and ginger
Combine the above ingredients and stir until smooth. Puts dots of 1/8 teaspoon of dough 1 inch apart on a greased cookie sheet and bake 5 to 6 minutes. Cool on a rack. Cookies snap off if you twist the sheet slightly.

★ ANISE OR BUTTERLESS DROP COOKIES

About Ninety-Six 1-Inch Cookies

These professional-looking self-glazing cookies with the charming puffed tops are best made in cool weather. They do not turn out well if the humidity is over 50%.
Beat until light:
3 eggs
Add gradually:
1 cup sifted sugar
Beat at least 3 to 5 minutes on medium speed with an electric beater, longer if beating by hand, then add:
1/2 teaspoon vanilla
Sift before measuring:
2 cups all-purpose flour
Resift with:
1 teaspoon double-acting baking powder
Add:
1 1/2 tablespoons crushed anise seed
Add flour ingredients to egg mixture and beat the batter another 5 minutes. Drop 1/2 teaspoon at a

time, well apart, on a cookie sheet lined with foil. The dough should flatten to a 1-inch round but should not spread more. If it does, add a little more flour. Let the drops dry at room temperature 18 hours. Bake the cakes in a preheated 325° oven until they begin to color, about 12 minutes. When done, they will have a puffed meringuelike top on a soft cookie base.

HERMITS

About Fifty 2-Inch Cookies

Preheat oven to 375°.
Beat until soft:
½ cup butter
Add gradually:
1 cup packed brown sugar
Blend until light and creamy. Beat in:
1 egg
½ cup cultured sour cream or buttermilk
Sift before measuring:
1⅓ cups all-purpose flour
Resift with:
¾ teaspoon cinnamon
½ teaspoon cloves
¼ teaspoon baking soda
Add the sifted ingredients to the butter mixture and beat until smooth. Stir in:
½ cup chopped raisins, dates, figs, dried apricots or citron
¼ cup hickory or other nutmeats
(¼ cup coconut)
Drop batter from a teaspoon onto greased cookie sheets. Bake about 15 minutes.

★ PFEFFERNÜSSE

One Hundred Eighty 1-Inch Balls

Sift together:
2 cups plus 2 tablespoons sifted all-purpose flour
¾ teaspoon double-acting baking powder
⅛ teaspoon baking soda
¼ teaspoon salt
¼ teaspoon freshly ground black pepper
Add:
¼ teaspoon each nutmeg and ground cloves
1 teaspoon cinnamon
¼ teaspoon anise seeds or 1 teaspoon crushed cardamom seeds
Cream together:
½ cup butter or shortening
⅓ cup sugar
Add and beat well until light:
1 egg
Add:
¼ cup finely chopped almonds
(1 tablespoon finely chopped citron)
(¼ cup finely chopped candied orange peel)
Add the flour mixture to the above ingredients in thirds, alternately with:
⅓ cup molasses
1 tablespoon corn syrup
⅓ cup brandy
1 teaspoon grated lemon rind
1 tablespoon lemon juice
Beat well, then set aside overnight.
Preheat oven to 350°.
Shape into 1-inch balls and bake on a greased cookie sheet 10 to 15 minutes. Roll while warm in:
Confectioners' sugar

★ GERMAN HONEY COOKIES

About Two Hundred 2½-Inch Cookies

Cut into small pieces and combine:
3 oz. each of citron, candied orange peel and candied lemon peel
Add:
1 cup chopped blanched almonds
1 teaspoon grated lemon rind
3 tablespoons cinnamon
1 tablespoon cloves
3⅓ cups confectioners' sugar
Beat until light and add:
6 eggs
¼ cup orange juice
Bring to the boiling point and cool until lukewarm:
1 pint honey
2 tablespoons hot water
Stir this into the egg mixture with:
5 cups sifted all-purpose flour
1 tablespoon baking soda
Cover the dough and let it stand 12 hours or more.
Preheat oven to 350°.
Drop the dough from a spoon, well apart, onto a greased cookie sheet. Bake about 8 minutes or until light brown. When cool, decorate with:
Lemon Glaze, 731
or decorate before baking with:
Blanched almonds

QUICK OATMEAL OR WHEAT FLAKE COOKIES

About 3 Dozen 2-Inch Cookies

Preheat oven to 350°.
Cream:
½ cup butter
Add and cream well:
½ cup firmly packed brown sugar
½ cup granulated sugar
Combine and beat in until smooth:
1 egg
1 teaspoon vanilla
1 tablespoon milk
Sift together and add to the above ingredients:
1 cup sifted all-purpose flour
½ teaspoon baking soda
½ teaspoon double-acting baking powder
½ teaspoon salt
When beaten smooth, add:
1 cup uncooked quick rolled oats or wheat flakes
For a different flavor or texture, try adding one of the following:
(¾ cup chocolate chips)

(1 teaspoon grated orange rind)
(½ cup raisins)
(1 can flaked coconut)

Beat the mixture well. Drop cookies 2 inches apart on a well-greased cookie sheet and bake 10 to 12 minutes or until light brown.

GLAZED OR FLOURLESS OATMEAL LACE WAFERS

About 8 Dozen 2-Inch Wafers

A pale yellow, crisp yet chewy cookie with a shiny bottom.
Preheat oven to 350°.
Beat:
3 whole eggs
Add gradually, beating constantly:
2 cups sugar
Stir in:
2 tablespoons melted butter
¾ teaspoon vanilla
1 teaspoon salt
1 cup shredded coconut
2 cups uncooked rolled oats
Line cookie sheet with foil. Drop the dough by half-teaspoons 1 inch apart. Bake about 10 minutes or until the edges are lightly browned. Lift foil from pan; cool until wafers can be easily removed.

ORANGE MARMALADE DROPS

About Forty-Eight 2-Inch Cookies

This chewy cookie needs a tart marmalade. It is difficult to prescribe the right amount of flour, as marmalades differ a great deal in consistency. Follow the recipe, then try out 1 or 2 cookies. If they are too dry, add a little more marmalade; if too moist, a little more flour.
Preheat oven to 375°.
Beat until soft:
⅓ cup butter
Add gradually:
⅔ cup sugar
Blend until light and creamy. Beat in:
1 whole egg
6 tablespoons tart orange marmalade
Sift:
1½ cups all-purpose flour
Resift with:
1¼ teaspoons double-acting baking powder
Stir the sifted ingredients into the butter mixture. Drop the batter from a teaspoon, well apart, onto a greased cookie sheet. Bake about 8 minutes.

PUMPKIN COOKIES

About 5 Dozen Cookies

A spicy cookie with a mealy, rather unusual texture.
Preheat oven to 375°.
Cream together:
1 cup butter or shortening
1 cup sugar
Add and mix well:
1 cup cooked pumpkin
1 egg
1 teaspoon vanilla
Sift together and add to above mixture:
2 cups sifted all-purpose flour
1 teaspoon double-acting baking powder
½ teaspoon baking soda
½ teaspoon salt
1 teaspoon cinnamon
½ teaspoon allspice
Stir in:
1 cup chopped nuts
1 cup raisins
Drop cookies onto a well-greased cookie sheet and bake about 15 minutes.

PEANUT BUTTER COOKIES

About Sixty 1½-Inch Cookies

For those who dote on peanut butter cookies, try these rich and crumbly ones. Use the greater amount of flour if your peanut butter is heavy in oil.
Preheat oven to 375°.
Beat until soft:
½ cup butter or shortening
Add gradually and blend until creamy:
½ cup firmly packed brown sugar
½ cup granulated sugar
Beat in:
1 egg
1 cup peanut butter
½ teaspoon salt
½ teaspoon baking soda
½ teaspoon vanilla
Sift before measuring and add:
1 to 1½ cups all-purpose flour
Roll the dough into small balls. Place them on a greased cookie sheet. Press flat with a fork, as illustrated on 705. Bake about 10 to 12 minutes.

BUTTERSCOTCH NUT COOKIES

Preheat oven to 375°.
For flavor, chewiness and ease of making, we suggest using the recipe for:
Butterscotch Brownies, 702
and adding:
2 tablespoons flour
Drop well apart on a greased cookie sheet and bake about 6 minutes.

MACAROONS

About 2 Dozen Cookies

Preheat oven to 325°.
Cut into a bowl thin slices of:
1 cup almond paste: ½ lb.
Gradually knead into the paste:
1 cup sugar
and when the mixture gets too stiff, add in small amounts:
3 unbeaten egg whites

until all the above ingredients are thoroughly mixed, with no lumps remaining. Line a cookie sheet with parchment paper. Put the batter into a pastry bag and squeeze out small thick drops about the size of a half-dollar, 2 inches apart. Bake 25 to 30 minutes. After cooling, dampen the underside of the paper, using a moist cloth. After a few minutes remove the cookies from the paper.

COCONUT MACAROONS

About Twenty 1-Inch Cookies

Preheat oven to 350°.
Have ready in a bowl:

3 cups moist shredded coconut: 8 oz.

Add:

1 teaspoon vanilla or almond extract
1/8 teaspoon salt

Combine these ingredients with:

2/3 cup sweetened condensed milk

to make a thick paste. These cookies are much improved by folding into the batter:

(1 to 2 stiffly beaten egg whites)

Roll the paste into balls or drop it from a teaspoon onto well-greased cookie sheets, about 2 inches apart. Bake 8 to 10 minutes, until edges are lightly browned. They may be rolled in:

Sifted confectioners' sugar

CHOCOLATE COCONUT MACAROONS

Prepare the recipe for:

Coconut Macaroons, above

heating the milk and adding:

2 tablespoons cocoa or
3/4 oz. grated chocolate

Cool the mixture before adding it to the coconut.

★ ALMOND MERINGUE RINGS

About 36 Rings

Decorative in Christmas boxes, but add them at the last minute, because they do not keep well.
Preheat oven to 300°.
Blanch:

1/4 lb. almonds

Cut them lengthwise into thin shreds. Toast lightly. Whip:

2 egg whites

Add gradually, beating constantly:

1 cup sifted confectioners' sugar

Our old recipe says "stir" for 1/2 hour, but of course you won't do that, so whip until you are tired, or use an electric beater. Fold in the almonds and:

1 teaspoon vanilla

Shape the batter into rings on a greased cookie sheet. Bake until the rings just begin to color.

KISSES

About Thirty-Six 1-Inch Kisses

Preheat oven to 375°.
Whip until frothy:

2 egg whites

Continue to beat while adding gradually:

1/2 cup sugar

When the mixture is quite stiff, fold in:

1/2 cup chopped nuts and cinnamon

Drop from a teaspoon onto a greased cookie sheet and put into the oven. ➤ Immediately turn heat off, and do not open oven door for at least 1 1/2 hours, preferably overnight.

COCOA KISSES

About Forty 1-Inch Meringues

Preheat oven to 250°.
Sift:

1 cup sugar

Whip until stiff, but not dry:

3 egg whites
1/8 teaspoon salt

Add gradually half of the sugar. Combine:

2 teaspoons water
1 teaspoon vanilla

Add the liquid, a few drops at a time, alternately with the remaining sugar. Whip constantly. Fold in:

3 tablespoons cocoa
3/4 cup chopped pecans

Drop the batter from a spoon onto a lightly greased cookie sheet and shape into cones. Bake until the kisses are firm to the touch but soft inside. Remove from the pan while hot.

CHOCOLATE CRACKER KISSES

About Sixty 1-Inch Kisses

The only people who will be wise to these ingredients are those who, in adolescence, were addicted to the consumption of thin chocolate candy bars between salted soda crackers.
Preheat oven to 300°.
Beat until frothy:

2 egg whites

Add:

1/4 teaspoon vanilla
1/4 teaspoon cream of tartar

Continue beating while adding:

2/3 cup sugar

When the mixture is quite stiff, fold in gently:

3 tablespoons crushed salted soda crackers
2/3 cup semisweet chocolate chips or peppermint-flavored chocolate morsels

Drop the meringuelike dough, 1 teaspoon at a time, onto a well-greased cookie sheet. Bake about 20 minutes. When cool, store in a tightly closed container.

ABOUT ROLLED AND MOLDED COOKIES

Aunties and grandmothers who roll cookies for and with children are scarce these days. But shaping cookies is such fun that children should be encouraged to learn to make them for themselves. Inexperienced bakers often ruin rolled cookies by using too much flour in the rolling process. To

use as little extra flour as possible ➤ chill the dough at least 1 hour before rolling it, and ➤ use a pastry cloth and rolling pin cover, 639. These practically do away with sticking and require the use of very little additional flour. Grease the pan, but ➤ remember never to use a pan with deep rims for cookie baking. Removing the cookies from such a pan is very difficult.

➤ Use cutters that interlock, as shown above, so that dough need be handled as little as possible. An even easier way to form fancy shapes that will not be distorted by handling: grease the back of a baking pan. Spread dough on pan as shown on left, above. Place cutters for maximum yield. Lift out the dough scraps between the shapes and reroll or re-form them on another pan to make more cookies.

A roller cutter speeds cookie-cutting. Two time-saving molds are an old French one of dovetailed hearts and diamonds, and a wheel cutter, which spins out the shapes shown on the right, with great rapidity. Amusing cutters lurk in antique shops. We wish a designer today would charm us with something contemporary. If you have a yen to do your own, take your designs to a tinsmith or make them from cardboard or plastic. See Gingerbread Men, 712.

ROLL COOKIES

About Forty 2-Inch Cookies

Remarkable for its handling quality, this dough can be shaped into crusts for filled cookies or tarts, as well as cut into intricate patterns.

Cream:

1/2 cup white or brown sugar

with:

1/2 cup butter

Beat in:

1 teaspoon vanilla
2 eggs
2 1/2 cups sifted all-purpose flour
2 teaspoons double-acting baking powder
1/2 teaspoon salt

Chill the dough 3 to 4 hours before rolling.
Preheat oven to 375°.
To roll and cut, see About Rolled Cookies, above.
Place cookies on a greased cookie sheet. You may decorate them with:

(Sugar, sugar and cinnamon, or colored sugar)
(1/2 nutmeat or candied cherry)

Bake 7 to 12 minutes.

RICH ROLL COOKIES

About Sixty 2-Inch Cookies

Just what they are named, and delicious!

Cream:

1 cup butter
2/3 cup sugar

Beat in:

1 egg
1 teaspoon vanilla or almond extract

Combine and add:

2 1/2 cups sifted all-purpose flour
1/2 teaspoon salt
(1/2 teaspoon grated lemon rind, or 1 tablespoon cinnamon, or 2 tablespoons poppy seeds)

Chill dough 3 to 4 hours before rolling.
Preheat oven to 350°.
To roll and cut, see About Rolled Cookies, above.
Bake on a greased cookie sheet 8 to 10 minutes or until slightly colored.

SAND TARTS

About Eighty 1 1/2-Inch Cookies

When touring in Normandy we met up with a famous local specialty which, curiously enough, proved to be our very own sand tarts.

Beat until soft:

3/4 cup butter

Add gradually and blend until creamy:

1 1/4 cups sifted white sugar

Beat in:

1 egg
1 egg yolk
1 teaspoon vanilla
1 teaspoon grated lemon rind

Sift before measuring:

3 cups all-purpose flour

Resift with:

1/4 teaspoon salt

Stir the flour gradually into the butter mixture until well blended. The last of the flour may have to be kneaded in by hand. Chill the dough several hours.
Preheat oven to 400°.
Roll the dough until very thin, see About Rolled

Cookies, 710. Cut into rounds and place on greased cookie sheets. Brush the tops of the cookies with:

The white of an egg

Sprinkle generously with:

Sugar

Garnish with:

(Blanched, split almonds)

Bake about 8 minutes. A good sand tart with a slightly different flavor may be made by following this recipe, but substituting for the white sugar 1⅓ cups firmly packed brown sugar.

WHOLE WHEAT SEED WAFERS

About 5 Dozen Cookies

For best flavor, try storing these cookies a few days—usually a futile effort in our cookie-loving family.

Preheat oven to 350°.

Cream together:

1 cup soft butter or shortening
⅔ cup sifted sugar

Sift together:

2 cups sifted all-purpose flour
1 teaspoon double-acting baking powder
1 teaspoon salt

Add to flour mixture:

1 cup whole wheat flour
(2 teaspoons grated orange or lemon peel)

With a fork or pastry blender, lightly combine the butter and flour mixtures, adding:

6 to 7 tablespoons water

until the dough holds together. Roll it out to ⅛-inch thickness. Have ready a topping made from a mixture of:

2 tablespoons finely ground seeds: anise, coriander, sesame, caraway, hulled sunflower or cardamom
¼ cup sugar

Sprinkle the dough with the topping, pat it in gently with fingers, then cut into individual shapes. Bake on a greased cookie sheet 10 to 12 minutes, until edges are slightly browned.

★ GINGERBREAD MEN

About Eight 5-Inch-Long Fat Men or 16 Thinner Ones

Even quite young children are good at making these if the modeling method suggested below is followed.

Preheat oven to 350°.

Blend until creamy:

¼ cup butter
½ cup white or brown sugar

Beat in:

½ cup dark molasses

Sift:

3½ cups all-purpose flour

Resift with:

1 teaspoon baking soda
¼ teaspoon cloves
½ teaspoon cinnamon
2 teaspoons ginger
½ teaspoon salt

Add the sifted ingredients to the butter mixture in about three parts, alternately with:

¼ cup water if you roll the dough, or
⅓ cup if you model it

You may have to work in the last of the flour mixture with your hands if you are not using an electric mixer. If you are satisfied with a crude approximation, roll a ball for a head, a larger one for the body, and cylinders for the arms and legs. Be sure to overlap and press these dough elements together carefully on the greased pan, so they will stay in one piece after baking. If you want something looking less like Primitive Man, roll the dough first to any thickness you like. A good way to do this is to grease the bottom of a baking sheet and to roll the dough directly onto it. Now, cut out your figures, either by using a floured cookie cutter or by making a pattern of your own, as follows:

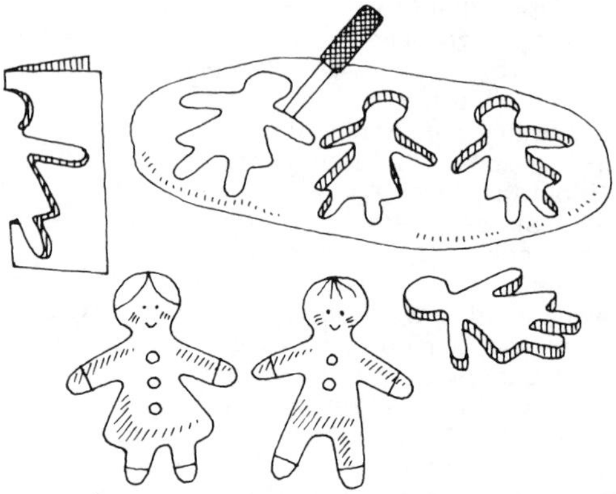

Fold a square of stiff cardboard or light plastic lengthwise and cut it. Unfold it and you have a symmetrical pattern. Grease or flour one side of the pattern and place it on the rolled dough. Cut around the outlines with a sharp knife. Remove the scraps of dough between the figures, using them to make more men. Decorate before baking with small raisins, bits of candied fruits, red-hots, marshmallows and citron, indicating features or buttons. The men may receive further decorations after baking, as described later. Bake the cookies about 8 minutes or longer, according to their thickness. Test for doneness by pressing the dough with your finger. If it springs back after pressing, they are ready to be cooled on a rack. Stir in a small bowl, to make a paste:

¼ cup confectioners' sugar
A few drops water

You may add:

(A drop or two of vegetable coloring)

Apply the icing with a wooden pick or a small knife for additional garnishes—caps, hair, mustaches, belts or shoes.

ALMOND CRESCENTS

About 5 Dozen Cookies

Sift:

¾ cup confectioners' sugar

Add the sugar gradually and cream with:

1 cup butter

Add:

2 teaspoons vanilla
(1 teaspoon cinnamon)
1 cup ground blanched almonds

Knead in by hand until completely mixed:

2½ cups sifted all-purpose flour

Chill the dough and roll it to the thickness of ¼ inch. Cut or form into crescent shapes. Bake the cakes on a greased cookie sheet in a preheated 350° oven, about 15 minutes. When baked, dip them in:

Confectioners' sugar or Vanilla Sugar, 557

★ ALMOND PRETZELS OR MANDELPLÄTTCHEN

About 2 Dozen 2-Inch Pretzels

Beat until soft:

1 cup butter

Add gradually and blend until creamy:

1 cup sifted sugar

Beat in:

1 to 2 egg yolks
2 eggs
¼ cup cultured sour cream

Sift together and stir in:

2½ cups sifted all-purpose flour
1 teaspoon double-acting baking powder
1 teaspoon cinnamon
1 teaspoon grated lemon rind

Chill the dough several hours until easy to handle.
Preheat oven to 375°.
Shape the dough into long thin rolls and twist these into pretzel shape, see 617. Place on a greased cookie sheet. Brush with:

French Egg Wash, 731

Sprinkle the tops with:

Chopped blanched almonds
Sugar

Bake at once 10 to 15 minutes. Do not let the pretzels color.

SCOTCH SHORTBREAD

About 20 Squares

Preheat oven to 325°.
Cream:

1 cup butter

Sift together:

2 cups sifted all-purpose flour
½ cup sifted confectioners' sugar
¼ teaspoon salt

Blend the dry ingredients into the butter. Pat the stiff dough into an ungreased 9 x 9-inch pan and press edges down. Pierce with a fork through the dough every half-inch. Bake 25 to 30 minutes. Cut into squares while warm.

YOLK LETTER COOKIES

About 100 Initials or Thin 1½-Inch Cookies

A great lexicographer said that an expression such as "It's me" was a sturdy indefensible. These cookies are our version of a sturdy indefensible. While not unusual, they use up leftover yolks. They have good tensile strength and make an excellent base for filled nut or jam tarts. We have used them as "initial" cookies for engagement parties.

Beat until soft:

1 cup butter
½ teaspoon salt

Add gradually and blend until creamy:

1 cup sifted sugar

Add:

½ teaspoon grated lemon rind
1½ tablespoons lemon juice

Beat in:

8 egg yolks

Stir in:

4 cups sifted all-purpose flour

Chill the dough 1 hour.
Preheat oven to 375°.
Roll the dough into sticks ¼ inch in diameter. Shape these into letters. Brush them with:

Yolk of an egg

Sprinkle with:

Colored or white sugar

Bake on a greased cookie sheet 6 to 8 minutes.

★ SPRINGERLE

About 5 Dozen Cookies

This recipe produces the well-known German **anise cakes** which are stamped with a wooden mold, shown in the chapter heading, 700, middle right, or roller, into quaint little designs and figures. If you have no mold, cut the dough into ¾ x 2½-inch bars.

Beat until light:

4 eggs

Add gradually and beat until creamy:

2 cups sifted sugar

Sift together and add:

3 cups sifted all-purpose flour
½ teaspoon double-acting baking powder

Sprinkle ½ cup flour on a pastry cloth. Turn the dough onto the cloth and knead in enough flour—about ½ cup more—to stiffen dough. Roll to the dimensions of your mold, ⅓ inch thick. Use the floured springerle board and press it hard upon the dough to get a good imprint. If the dough is too soft, pick it up and add more flour. Separate the squares, place them on a board and let dry 12 hours, uncovered, in a cool dry place.
Preheat oven to 300°.
Grease cookie sheet and sprinkle with:

2 tablespoons crushed anise seed

Place the squares of dough on the pan and bake about 15 minutes or until the lower part is light yellow. To store, see 701.

★ SPECULATIUS

About Twenty-Eight 2 x 4-Inch Thin Cookies

A rich cookie of Danish origin, pressed with carved wooden molds into Santas and Christmas symbols.

Work as for pie dough, until the particles are like coarse cornmeal:

2/3 cup butter
1 cup flour

Cream:

1 egg

with:

1/2 cup firmly packed brown sugar

Add:

1/8 teaspoon cloves or
1/16 teaspoon cardamom
1 teaspoon cinnamon

Combine the egg and butter mixtures well. Spread the dough on a 14 x 17-inch baking sheet. Let it rest chilled 12 hours.

Preheat oven to 350°.

Stamp the figures with the floured molds. Bake about 10 minutes or until done.

COOKIE-PRESS OR SPRITZ COOKIES

About 5 Dozen Cookies

These may also be made in a pastry bag, illustrated 724.

Sift together:

2 1/4 cups all-purpose flour
1/2 teaspoon salt

Cream together:

3/4 cup sugar
1 cup butter

Add:

2 egg yolks
1 teaspoon vanilla or almond extract

Stir in the flour.

Beat well, then chill. Put dough through cookie press onto ➤ an ungreased cookie sheet. ➤ The dough should be pliable, but if it becomes too soft, rechill it slightly. Bake about 10 minutes in a 350° oven until lightly browned.

LANGUE DE CHAT OR CAT'S TONGUE

About 2 Dozen

There are special pans for these ladyfinger-shaped wafers. To turn them into **Maquis,** put between two of these cookies a filling made of 3 parts chocolate icing, 728, and 1 part crushed nut brittle, 788.

Preheat oven to 350°.

Cream:

1/4 cup butter
1/4 cup sifted sugar

Beat in:

2 eggs
1 teaspoon vanilla

Fold in:

1/2 cup sifted all-purpose flour

Bake in greased molds about 15 minutes. You may dip one end of each wafer in:

(European Chocolate Icing, 728)

★ CHOCOLATE ALMOND SHELLS

About Sixty 1 1/2-Inch Cookies

This dough is usually pressed into little wooden molds in the shape of a shell, but any attractive ones like individual butter molds will do. ➤ The batter must stand for 12 hours.

Grind in a nut grinder:

1/2 lb. unblanched almonds

Whip until stiff:

4 egg whites
1/4 teaspoon salt

Add gradually, whipping constantly:

1 cup sifted sugar

Fold in the ground almonds and:

1 1/2 teaspoons cinnamon
1/8 teaspoon cloves
1 teaspoon grated lemon rind
1 tablespoon lemon juice
2 1/2 oz. grated unsweetened chocolate

Let this batter stand uncovered in a cool dry place 12 hours.

Preheat oven to 300°.

Shape the batter into balls. Dredge molds with equal parts of:

Sugar and flour

Press the balls into the molds. Unmold them. Bake on a greased cookie sheet about 30 minutes.

★ CINNAMON STARS

About Forty-Five 1 1/2-Inch Stars

Deservedly one of the most popular Christmas cakes; also one of the most decorative. See About Nut Drop Cookies, 706.

Preheat oven to 300°.

Sift:

2 cups confectioners' sugar

Whip until ➤ stiff but not dry:

5 egg whites
1/8 teaspoon salt

Add the sugar gradually, continuing to whip. Add:

2 teaspoons cinnamon
1 teaspoon grated lemon rind

Whip constantly. Reserve one-third of the mixture. Fold into the remainder:

1 lb. ground unblanched almonds

Dust a board or pastry canvas lightly with confectioners' sugar. Pat the dough to the thickness of 1/3 inch; it is too delicate to roll. If it tends to stick, dust your palms with confectioners' sugar. Cut the cakes with a star or other cutter, or simply mold them into small mounds. Glaze the tops with the reserved mixture. Bake on a greased cookie sheet about 20 minutes.

TEA WAFERS

About 100 Paper-Thin Wafers

Sometimes when a recipe looks as innocuous as this one, it's hard to believe the result can be so outstanding. These tender, crisp squares are literally paper-thin. ➤ As soon as cool, they must be placed in a tightly covered tin. They keep several weeks this way, but we have a hard time hiding them successfully enough to prove it.

Preheat oven to 325°.

Cream:

½ cup butter

Sift, then measure and beat in:

1 cup confectioners' sugar

Beat until smooth. Add:

1 teaspoon vanilla

Sift, then measure:

1¾ cups all-purpose flour

Resift and add to the creamed mixture, alternately with:

½ cup milk

Beat until creamy. Lightly butter a 16½ x 14-inch cookie sheet. Chill the sheet. With a spatula, spread only about 2 tablespoons of the mixture over it as thinly and evenly as possible. You may sprinkle the dough with:

(Chopped nutmeats or cinnamon and sugar or grated lemon rind)

It is well to press the nuts in a bit so that they will stick. Take a sharp knife and mark off the dough in 1½-inch squares. Bake about 5 minutes or until brown. When done, take from oven and, while still hot, quickly cut through the marked squares. Slip a knife under to remove from sheet. The cakes grow crisp as soon as they cool, and they break easily, so you have to work fast.

LEAF WAFERS

Although a metal stencil available at confectionery suppliers is used for these thin crisp cookies, they add great distinction to a tray when dipped like Florentines, 706, in chocolate or in icing or glaze. Place the stencil on a well-greased cookie sheet. Spread the dough over the stencil with a wet spatula. Remove excess dough and lift the stencil. If you have no stencil, spread the dough thinly, using the palm of your hand, onto greased cookie sheets. Score the dough in diamond shapes before baking and cut wafers after baking. Bake at 375° 5 to 7 minutes. Remove from pan while still warm.

I. Black Walnut Leaves

About 60 Thin Leaves

Preheat oven to 375°.

Cream together:

¼ cup butter
1 cup brown sugar

Add and mix well:

1 beaten egg
¼ teaspoon each baking soda, cream of tartar and salt
½ teaspoon vanilla
1¾ cups sifted cake flour

Stir in:

½ cup ground black walnuts

To form and bake, see above.

II. Almond Leaves

About 50 Thin Leaves

Preheat oven to 375°.

Cut into thin slices:

½ lb. almond paste: 1 cup

Knead in gradually and work until the mixture is very smooth:

2 egg whites
1 tablespoon water

Stir in and beat well:

¾ cup sifted confectioners' sugar
¼ cup cake flour

To form and bake, see above.

ABOUT REFRIGERATOR COOKIES

An advantage of these doughs is that they can all be baked as drop cookies, 705, without chilling, if you want to make up a batch immediately. After mixing the dough, form it into a 2-inch-diameter roll on a piece of foil or waxed paper, in which you wrap it securely. Chill the roll 4 to 12 hours, after which time it can be very thinly sliced with a sharp knife. You may hasten the chilling by placing the roll in the freezer. Whole nutmeats may be combined with the dough or used to garnish the slices; or, the entire roll of dough may be rolled in chopped nuts, so as to make a border when the cookie is cut, as shown on the left, below. Two sheets of differently colored dough may be rolled together, see below. These, when sliced, become pinwheel cookies.

Bake the refrigerated cookies on a greased cookie sheet in a 400° oven 8 to 10 minutes, unless otherwise directed. Refrigerator cookies ❄ freeze well baked or unbaked. See Freezing Unbaked Cookies, 829.

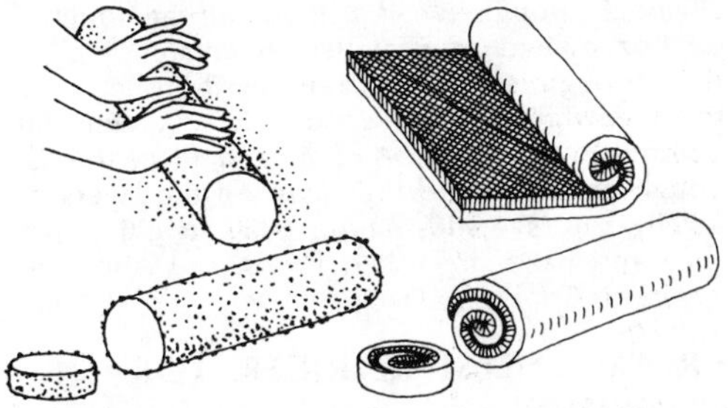

VANILLA REFRIGERATOR COOKIES

About Forty 2-Inch Cookies

This dough makes a good filled cookie, 717, or rich drop cookie if the lesser amount of flour is used.

Beat until soft:

½ cup butter

Add gradually and blend until creamy:

1 cup sifted sugar

Mix in:

1 beaten egg
1 teaspoon vanilla
(½ teaspoon grated lemon rind or cinnamon)

Sift before measuring:

1¼ to 1½ cups all-purpose flour

Resift with:

¼ teaspoon salt

1½ teaspoons double-acting baking powder

Stir the sifted ingredients into the butter mixture. You may add:

(½ cup nutmeats)

To chill, form and bake, see About Refrigerator Cookies, 715. Before baking, sprinkle the cookies with:

(Sugar)

to make them sandy, or with:

(Chopped or half nutmeats)

BUTTERSCOTCH REFRIGERATOR COOKIES

Prepare:

Vanilla Refrigerator Cookies, above

Substitute for the white sugar:

1¼ cups firmly packed brown sugar

You may substitute for the nutmeats:

(1 cup grated coconut)

CHOCOLATE REFRIGERATOR COOKIES

Prepare:

Vanilla Refrigerator Cookies, 715

Melt, then cool and mix into the dough:

2 oz. unsweetened chocolate

(1 tablespoon brandy or rum)

PINWHEEL REFRIGERATOR COOKIES

Prepare:

Vanilla Refrigerator Cookies, 715

Divide the dough in half. Add to half the dough:

1 oz. melted unsweetened chocolate

If the dough is soft, chill until easily rolled. Then roll the white and brown dough separately into oblongs to the thickness of ⅛ inch. Place the dark dough on the light dough and roll the layers like a jelly roll, see illustration, 690. To chill, form, slice and bake the rolled layers, see About Refrigerator Cookies, 715.

CREAM CHEESE REFRIGERATOR COOKIES

About Sixty 2-Inch Cookies

Blend until creamy:

½ cup butter

1 cup sugar

1 well-beaten egg

Soften slightly:

1 package cream cheese: 3 oz.

Beat it into the butter mixture with:

2 tablespoons buttermilk or yogurt

1 teaspoon vanilla

Beat in:

2 cups sifted all-purpose flour

⅛ teaspoon baking soda

½ teaspoon double-acting baking powder

½ teaspoon salt

After being chilled, see About Refrigerator Cookies, 715, this dough may be rolled to paper-thinness, cut into shapes and baked. Sprinkle before baking with:

Sugar and cinnamon

Preheat oven to 350° and bake from 12 to 15 minutes.

MOLASSES CRISPS COCKAIGNE

About 6 Dozen 2 x 3-Inch Cookies

Heat to the boiling point in a double boiler ➤ over, not in, boiling water:

½ cup dark molasses

Remove from heat, add and beat until blended:

¼ cup sugar

6 tablespoons butter

1 tablespoon milk

2 cups all-purpose flour

½ teaspoon salt

½ teaspoon double-acting baking powder

½ teaspoon each fresh ground nutmeg and cloves

2 teaspoons cinnamon

Wrap in foil and cool until firm, see About Refrigerator Cookies, 715. To form, slice very thin and, if necessary, pat thin on a greased cookie sheet with fingers until dough is translucent. Press into the center of each cookie:

½ a pecan or blanched almond

Preheat oven to 325° and bake 10 to 12 minutes.

★ JUBILEE WAFERS

About Seventy 2-Inch Wafers

Good for all those festive anniversaries. Soften and mix in the top of a double boiler ➤ over, not in, boiling water:

⅔ cup honey

1 cup sugar

¼ cup butter

Sift together and add:

2½ cups all-purpose flour

1 teaspoon double-acting baking powder

¼ teaspoon each mace and cardamom

½ teaspoon baking soda

2 teaspoons cinnamon

½ teaspoon cloves

Combine with all the above ingredients:

⅓ cup whisky or brandy

Add:

1 cup grated blanched almonds

2 tablespoons each chopped citron, candied orange and lemon peel

To make into a roll, chill, slice and bake, see About Refrigerator Cookies, 715.

ABOUT FILLED COOKIES

The recipes that follow describe individual ways to shape and fill cookies. But first, look at simple and basic ways to shape and fill them as sketched at right.

Prepare:

Roll Cookies, 711; Vanilla Refrigerator Cookies, 715; Sand Tarts, 711, or Yolk Letter Cookies, 713

Form a ball and make an imprint with your thumb to hold a filling as shown on the left, below. Or roll the dough thin and cut into rounds. For a turnover, use a single round of dough and less than a tablespoon of filling. Fold over and seal edges firmly by pressing with a floured fork. A closed tart takes 2 rounds of dough. Place a tablespoon of filling on one and cover with the other, then seal. For a see-through tart, employ the same bottom round and filling, but cut the top with a doughnut cutter and seal outer edge in the same way.

Here are 4 basic fillings. For others, see Nut Bars, 703, or Pecan Slices, 703; or try Ricotta Chocolate Filling, 697.

I. Raisin, Fig, or Date Cookie Filling

Boil and stir until thick:

1 cup chopped raisins, figs or dates
6 tablespoons sugar
5 tablespoons boiling water
½ teaspoon grated lemon rind
2 teaspoons lemon juice
2 teaspoons butter
⅛ teaspoon salt

II. Apricot-Orange Cookie Filling

Combine and cook until thick:

⅔ cup drained mashed cooked apricots
⅔ cup sugar

Remove from heat and add:

2 tablespoons orange juice
2 tablespoons grated orange rind
½ cup chopped raisins
(¼ cup chopped dates or figs)

III. Coconut Cookie Filling

Combine:

1 slightly beaten egg
½ cup brown sugar
1 tablespoon flour
1½ cups flaked or chopped shredded coconut

IV. ★ Drained Mincemeat, 812

JELLY TOTS

About Forty-Two 1¼-Inch Cookies

You may call these **thimble cookies, Hussar balls, jam cookies, thumbprint cookies, deep-well cookies or pits of love**—the latter borrowed, of course, from the French—but a rose by any other name . . .

Preheat oven to 375°.

Prepare the dough for:

Roll Cookies, 711

Roll the dough into a ball. You may chill it briefly for easier handling. Pinch off pieces, to roll into 1-inch balls. Roll the balls in:

Sugar

Or, for a fancier cookie, roll the balls in:

1 slightly beaten egg white

then in:

1 cup finely chopped nutmeats

Place them on a lightly greased and floured sheet. Bake 5 minutes. Depress the center of each cookie with a thimble or your thumb, as shown in sketch below. Continue baking until done, about 8 minutes. When cool, fill the pits with:

A preserved strawberry, a bit of jelly or jam, a candied cherry or pecan half, or a dab of icing

MACAROON JAM TARTS

About Fourteen 3-Inch Cakes

The star of stars.

Blend until creamy:

2 tablespoons sugar
½ cup butter

Beat in:

1 egg yolk
½ teaspoon grated lemon rind
1½ tablespoons lemon juice

Stir in gradually, until well blended:

1½ cups sifted all-purpose flour

alternately with:

2 tablespoons cold water

Chill the dough 12 hours.

Preheat oven to 325°.

Roll out dough ⅛ inch thick. Cut into 3-inch rounds and place on a greased cookie sheet. Whip until foamy:

3 egg whites

Beat in gradually, until stiff but not dry:

1⅓ cups sifted confectioners' sugar
1 teaspoon vanilla

Fold in:

½ lb. almonds, blanched and ground in a nut grinder

Place mixture around the edge of each cookie,

making a ¾-inch border, and, if you like, add two crossed lines on top, as illustrated on 717. Use a pastry bag, a spatula or spoon, as sketched. Bake 20 minutes or until done. When cool, fill centers with:

A thick jam

INDIVIDUAL NUT TARTS

About 10 to 12 Tarts

Prepare and chill 12 hours:

Vanilla Refrigerator Cookie Dough, 715

Preheat oven to 350°.

Pat or roll the dough until very thin. Line shallow muffin pans with it. Beat until light:

3 egg yolks

Beat in gradually:

1 cup sifted sugar
¼ teaspoon salt

Grind in a nut grinder and add:

1 cup blanched almonds or other nuts

Stir in:

1½ tablespoons lemon juice

Fold in:

3 stiffly beaten egg whites

You may place in the bottom of each tart:

(1 teaspoon Apricot Glaze, 732)

Fill the lined muffin pans with the nut and egg mixture. Bake about 20 minutes.

FILLED PRUNE COOKIE

About Forty 2-Inch Cookies

Have ready a double recipe of:

Prune Filling for Coffee Cakes, 622

Prepare dough for:

Roll Cookies, 711

After chilling, roll to ⅛-inch thickness on a floured board, then cut into 2-inch rounds. Place 1 teaspoon filling on each round. Bring edges together and pinch to form a triangle. Bake 10 to 12 minutes in a 375° oven.

ABOUT CURLED COOKIES

Some curled cookies are simply dropped on a baking sheet; others require a special iron. In either case they are very dressy-looking—whether they make a tube or cornucopia or are just partially curled, after being shaped over a rolling pin or wooden spoon handle while still warm. Filled ➤ just before serving, they make a complete dessert. Use flavored whipped cream fillings, 696, a cake filling, 697, or cream cheese. Serve them as tea cakes with a contrasting butter-cream filling, 775. Dip the ends in:

Ground pistachio or chocolate shot "gimmies"

to lend a most festive look.

SCANDINAVIAN KRUMKAKES

To make these fabulously thin wafers, you will need the inexpensive iron shown below. It fits over a 7-inch surface burner, either gas or electric, and is ➤ always used over moderate heat. For each baking period the iron should be lightly rubbed at the beginning with unsalted butter; but after this initial greasing, nothing more is required. The batter needs a preliminary testing, as it is quite variable, depending on the condition of the flour; so do not add at once all the flour called for in the recipe. Test the batter for consistency by baking 1 teaspoonful first. The iron is geared to use 1 tablespoon of batter for each wafer, and it should spread easily over the whole surface but should not run over when pressed down. If the batter is too thin, add more flour. Should any batter drip over, lift the iron off its frame and cut off the excess batter with a knife run along the edge of the iron. Cook each wafer about 2 minutes on each side or until barely colored. As soon as you remove it from the iron, roll it on a wooden spoon handle or cone form as illustrated and, when cool, fill it. You may prefer to use these cookies as round filled sandwich cookies, see Frankfurter Oblaten, below. For a toasted sesame seed effect, a fan suggests sprinkling ¼ teaspoon sesame seeds over the batter before closing the iron. For suggestions for fillings, see Curled Cookies, above.

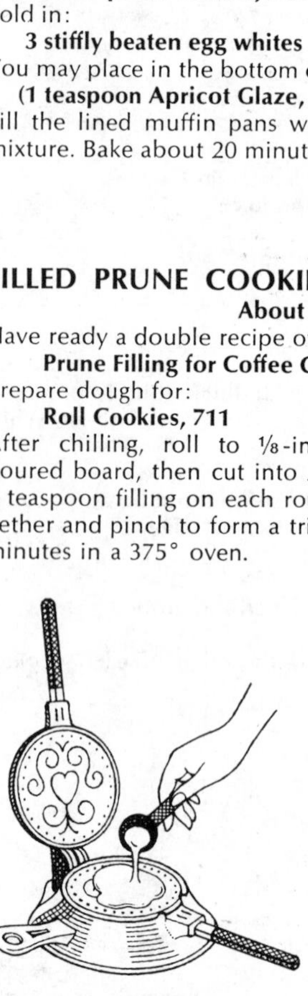

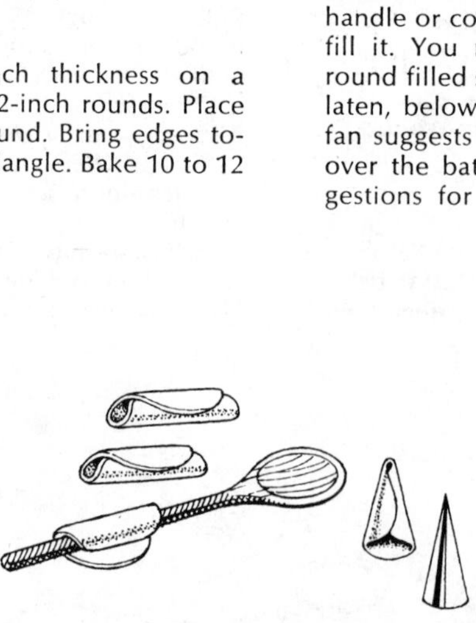

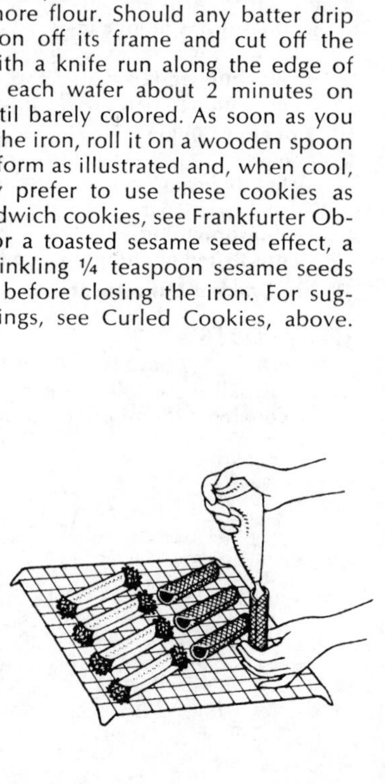

I. Butter Krumkakes

About Thirty 5-Inch Wafers

A teen-age neighbor recommends an ice cream filling. We like cultured sour cream with a spot of tart jelly, or a flavored whipped cream, 696.

Beat until light:

2 eggs

Add slowly and beat until pale yellow:

⅔ cup sugar

Melt and add slowly:

½ cup butter

Stir in until well blended:

1¾ cups sifted all-purpose flour
1 teaspoon vanilla

To bake, form and fill, see Krumkakes, 718.

II. Lemon Krumkakes

About Thirty 5-Inch Wafers

Cream:

1 cup sugar
½ cup butter

Combine and add:

3 beaten eggs
1 cup whipped cream
½ teaspoon grated lemon rind

Add enough flour to make a dough that spreads easily on the iron—not more than:

1½ cups sifted all-purpose flour

To bake, form and fill, see Krumkakes, 718.

III. Almond Krumkakes

About Twelve 5-Inch Wafers

Fortune cookies can be made from this batter, see Almond Curls, below.

Cream and beat well:

¼ cup butter
½ cup sifted confectioners' sugar

Add by degrees:

3 unbeaten egg whites
2 tablespoons ground almonds
½ cup sifted all-purpose flour
1 teaspoon vanilla

To bake, form and fill, see Krumkakes, 718.

FRANKFURTER OBLATEN

Prepare:

Butter Krumkakes, above

Fill in, between two wafers, a thin layer of:

Flavored soft fondant or French Icing, 727

ICE CREAM CONES OR GAUFRETTES

7 Large or 12 Small Cones

If made on a krumkake iron, as illustrated, this dough can be rolled into delicious thin-walled cones. If made on an oblong waffled gaufrette iron, they become the typical French honeycombed wafer or gaufrette so often served with wine or ices.

Preheat the krumkake or gaufrette iron over a moderate surface burner. Melt and let cool:

¼ cup butter

Beat until very stiff:

2 egg whites

Fold in gradually:

¾ cup sifted confectioners' sugar
⅛ teaspoon salt
¼ teaspoon vanilla

Fold in:

½ cup sifted all-purpose flour

Add the cooled butter, folding it in gently. Put 1 tablespoon of this batter into the preheated iron. After about 1½ minutes, turn the iron and bake on the other side until a pale golden beige in color. Remove and use flat or curl the wafer into a cone. When cool, fill and serve. Or serve plain in the French fashion, as described above.

ALMOND CURLS OR FORTUNE COOKIES

About 5 Dozen Cookies

These cookies and Almond Krumkakes, above, may be made into a western version of fortune cookies for a party. Have your remarks printed on thin papers, 3 x ¾ to 1 inch in size. After the cookies are curled, insert a slip in each, letting part of the paper project. Pinch the ends of the roll closed while the cookie is still warm.

Preheat oven to 350°.

Combine and mix until sugar is dissolved:

¾ cup unbeaten egg whites: 5 to 6
1⅔ cups sugar
¼ teaspoon salt

Stir in separately and beat until well blended:

1 cup melted butter
1 cup all-purpose flour
¾ cup finely ground blanched almonds
½ teaspoon vanilla or 1 tablespoon lemon juice

Drop the dough in tablespoonfuls, well apart, onto a greased baking sheet. Bake about 10 minutes or until the edges are a golden brown. Mold cookie over a wooden spoon handle, see 718; see also Curled Caramel Cookies, 720.

BRANDY SNAPS

About Twenty 3½-Inch Cookies

Preheat oven to 300°.

Stir over low heat:

½ cup butter
½ cup sugar, or ¼ cup sugar plus ¼ cup packed, grated maple sugar
⅓ cup dark molasses
¼ teaspoon ginger
½ teaspoon cinnamon
½ teaspoon grated lemon or orange rind

Remove from heat and add:

1 cup sifted all-purpose flour
2 teaspoons brandy

Roll into ¾-inch balls.

Bake on an ungreased cookie sheet about 12 minutes. Remove cookies from pan, after a minute or so, with a spatula. Roll over a spoon handle, see sketch, 718. Store in a tightly covered tin.

MAPLE CURLS

About Fifteen 3-Inch Curls

Preheat oven to 350°.
Bring to a hard boil for about ½ minute:

½ cup maple syrup or maple-blended syrup
¼ cup butter

Remove from heat and add:

½ cup sifted all-purpose flour
¼ teaspoon salt

When well blended, drop the dough onto a greased cookie sheet, 1 tablespoonful at a time, 3 inches apart. Bake from 9 to 12 minutes or until the cookie colors to the shade of maple sugar. Remove pan from oven. When slightly cool, remove cookies with a spatula, roll as shown on 718, and cool on a rack.

CURLED CARAMEL COOKIES

About 24 Cornucopias

Preheat oven to 400°.
Cream well:

¼ cup butter
½ cup firmly packed brown sugar

Beat in:

1 egg

When well blended, beat in:

½ teaspoon vanilla
⅛ teaspoon salt
3 tablespoons all-purpose flour

Stir in:

¼ cup ground or minced nutmeats

Black walnuts or hazelnuts are excellent. Drop the batter from a teaspoon, well apart, on a greased cookie sheet—about 6 to a sheet. Flatten the cookies with the back of a spoon. Bake 8 or 9 minutes. Cool slightly and remove from pan with a small pancake turner. Then roll the cookies over a wooden spoon handle or a rolling pin, or roll them with your hands. If they cool too quickly to manipulate, return them ➤ for a minute to the oven.

CURLED NUT WAFERS

About 20 Wafers

Preheat oven to 375°.
Beat until soft:

2 tablespoons butter
2 tablespoons shortening

Add gradually:

⅔ cup sifted sugar

Blend these ingredients until very light and creamy. Beat in:

1 egg
2 tablespoons milk
½ teaspoon vanilla
¼ teaspoon almond extract

Sift before measuring:

1⅓ cups all-purpose flour

Resift with:

1 teaspoon double-acting baking powder
½ teaspoon salt

Add the sifted ingredients to the butter mixture. Beat batter until smooth. Grease a cookie sheet. Spread the batter evenly, to the thickness of ⅛ inch, over the pan with a spatula. Sprinkle dough with:

½ cup chopped nutmeats

Bake about 12 minutes. Cut the cake into ¾ x 4-inch strips. Shape the strips, while hot, over a rolling pin. If the strips become too brittle before they are shaped, return them to the oven until they become pliable again.

ICINGS, TOPPINGS AND GLAZES

To decorate certain kinds of cake is to gild the lily. If the cake dough is rich and sweet, as in Old-World Spice Cake, 677, or baked in a Bundkuchen mold as shown on 664, a plain dusting of powdered sugar, or a fancy one repeating the pattern of its lace plate doily, shown in the foreground above, is enough. To make such a sugar design, see 729. One form of gilding—for the less self-sufficient kinds of cake—is an ornamental icing whose design indicates portion servings, like the jacquard decoration on the flat loaf-cake shown above, baked in a pan with its own handy storage lid. Or show descending radials such as those on the high loaf-cake on the upper right. Or make the icing delightfully frilly to harmonize by designs sympathetic to the stand; or, as on the Valentine cake, let it capture the gaiety of the occasion.

In the icing operation—if you are working directly on the serving platter—you can cope with the spillage problem by tucking narrow overlapping pieces of waxed paper or foil just under the cake to the edge of the platter, removing them as the icing sets. If you are using a turntable or another work surface, you may place on it several strips of sturdy paper or foil projecting beyond the cake on either side. After the cake has been iced, lift it by the paper strips onto the serving platter; pull out the strips and discard. In both filling and icing, layers should be turned topside down for both a flatter and a rougher surface. If the cake is uneven, you may want to trim it slightly. Use about a fourth to a third of the total icing as filling between the layers. Then, depending on the consistency of your icing, either pour it over the top and smooth with a spatula, correcting the overflow on the sides; or slather the icing around the sides first and then apply to the top.

ABOUT ICING YIELDS

Yields on icing and filling recipes are given in numbers of cups, so you can mix or match your choice according to the size of your cake. For comparative pan sizes and areas, see 666. We consider the following amounts a sufficient coverage but suggest that for fluffy frostings you choose the greater amounts, for butter icings the lesser:

For the top and sides of one 9-inch round layer cake, use ¾ to 1¼ cups.
For the tops and sides of two 9-inch round layers, use 1½ to 2⅔ cups.
For the tops and sides of three 9-inch round layers, use 2¼ to 3 cups.
For the top and sides of a 9½ x 5½ x 3-inch loaf pan, use 1 to 1½ cups.
For a 16 x 5 x 4-inch loaf pan, use 2 to 2½ cups.
For the top and sides of a 9 or 10-inch tube, use 3 cups.
For 16 large or 24 small cupcake tops, use 1½ to 2¼ cups.
For glazing a 9- or 10-inch cake, use 1 cup.
For glazing a 10 x 15-inch sheet, use 1⅓ cups.
For filling a 10 x 15-inch roll, use 2 cups.

ABOUT BOILED ICINGS

Just as in candy making, success with boiled icing depends on favorable weather and the recognition of certain stages in preparing sugar syrup, see 777. If the icing is too soft or too hard, take the corrective steps suggested below. ➤ Never ruin a good cake with a doubtful icing.

Boiled white icings are based on a principle known as Italian meringue—the cooking of egg whites by beating into them ➤ gradually, a hot but not boiling syrup.

For boiled icings ➤ the cake must be cooled before the icing is applied. ➤ Have all utensils absolutely free of grease, and eggs at room temperature. Separate the whites ➤ keeping them absolutely free of yolk, and put them in a large bowl. You may start with unbeaten, frothy, or stiffly whipped whites. ➤ Have available a stabilizer: lemon juice, vinegar, cream of tartar or light corn syrup; and also a small quantity of boiling water—in case the icing tends to harden prematurely.

Cook the syrup to 238° to 240°. It will have gone through a coarse thread stage and, when dropped from the edge of a spoon, will pull out into thickish threads. When the thick thread develops a hairlike appendage that curls back on itself, remove the syrup from the heat. Hold the very hot, but not bubbling, syrup above the bowl and let it drop in a slow and gradual thin stream onto the whites as you beat them. In an electric mixer, this is no trick. If you are beating by hand, you may have to steady your bowl by placing it on a folded wet towel

As the egg whites become cooked by the hot syrup, the beating increases the volume of the icing. By the time the syrup is used up, you should have a creamy mass, almost ready for spreading. At this point, add any of the stabilizers—a few drops of lemon juice or vinegar, a pinch of cream of tartar or a teaspoon or two of light corn syrup. These substances help to keep the icing from sugaring and becoming gritty. Then beat in the flavoring of your choice. When the icing begins to harden at the edges of the bowl, it should be ready to put on the cake. ➤ Do not scrape the bowl.

If the syrup has not been boiled long enough and the icing is somewhat runny, beat it in strong sunlight. If this doesn't do the trick, place the icing in the top of a double boiler or in a heat-proof bowl ➤ over—not in—boiling water, until it reaches the right consistency for spreading. If the syrup has been overcooked and the icing tends to harden too soon, a teaspoon or two of boiling water or a few drops of lemon juice will restore it. If raisins, nutmeats, zest or other ingredients are to be added to the icing, wait until the last moment to incorporate them. They contain oil or acid which will thin the icing.

▲ In high altitudes it helps to add to the sugar 1/8 teaspoon glycerin and to allow a longer cooking period.

BOILED WHITE ICING

About 2 Cups

Stir until the sugar is dissolved and bring to a boil:

2 cups sugar
1 cup water

➤ Cover and cook about 3 minutes, until the steam has washed down any crystals which may have formed on the sides of the pan. ➤ Uncover and cook to 238° to 240°. At that temperature the syrup will spin a very thin thread on the end of a coarser thread. This final thread will almost disappear, like a self-consuming spider web. Whip until frothy:

2 egg whites
1/8 teaspoon salt

Add the syrup in a thin stream, whipping eggs constantly. When these ingredients are all combined, add:

(1/8 teaspoon cream of tartar or a few drops lemon juice)
1 teaspoon vanilla

WHITE-MOUNTAIN ICING

About 1¾ Cups

You need an electric mixer for this recipe. Stir until the sugar is dissolved, then cook covered until the syrup boils rapidly:

1 tablespoon white corn syrup
1 cup sugar
1/3 cup water

Beat about 2 minutes in a small bowl at high speed:

1 egg white

Add 3 tablespoons of the boiling syrup. Let the mixer continue to beat. Meanwhile ➤ cover the remaining syrup and cook covered about 3 minutes, until the steam has washed down from the sides of the pan any crystals which may have formed. ➤ Uncover and cook until the syrup reaches 238° to 240°. Pour the remaining syrup gradually into the egg mixture, while continuing to beat at high speed. While still beating, add:

1 teaspoon vanilla

Now beat the icing until it is ready to spread—4 to 6 minutes.

RAISIN OR NUT ICING

Chop:

1 cup seeded raisins, or 1/2 cup raisins and 1/2 cup nuts

Add them at the last minute to:

Boiled White Icing, above

or sprinkle raisins and nuts on the cake and spread the icing over them.

NUT OR COCONUT ICING

To make a nut or coconut coating, have chopped nuts or fresh or dried shredded or grated coconut ready to press gently into the icing. Or, while the icing is still soft, proceed as follows: hold the cake on the palm of the left hand and, cupping the right hand to the curve of the cake, apply grated coconut or nuts to the icing as shown. Have a bowl underneath to catch the reusable excess. To prepare fresh coconut, see 566. To chop nuts, see 562.

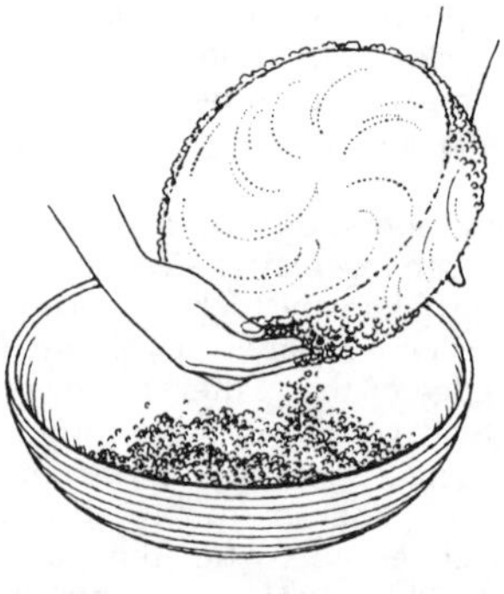

ABOUT DECORATIVE ICINGS

Several types of pastry bags made of canvas or plastic are available in stores. And there is also a rigid metal "bag" on the market. If you choose canvas, be sure to use it with the ragged fabric seam outside. Several metal tips with different patterns are included in pastry bag kits. The most useful have a rose, star and round cutout.

Here's how to make your own decorating bag:

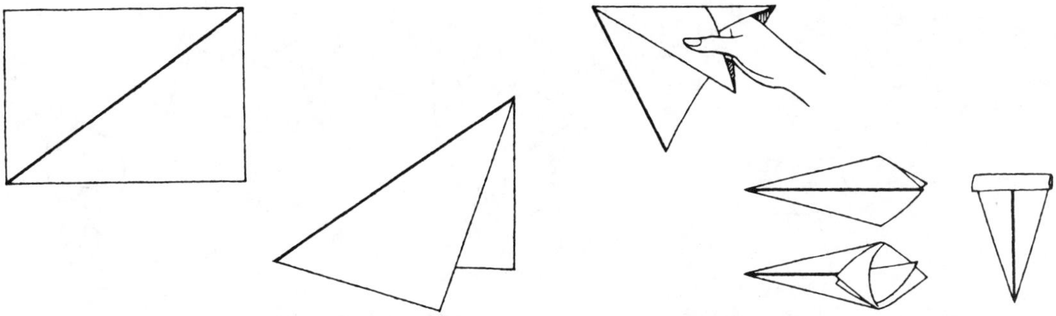

Using heavy bond or bakery paper, cut an oblong about 11 x 15 inches. Fold the oblong diagonally as shown on the left, above. Keep the folded edge away from you. Roll the paper from the right side into a cornucopia with a tight point at the center of the long fold, as seen in upper right of sketch. With the left hand, continue to roll the paper until the cornucopia is complete. Turn it with the seam toward you and the point away from you. The seam should lie in a direct line with the point of one of the highest peaks of the bag, so that, by folding the peaks outward and away from you, you stabilize the shape of the cornucopia and the seam. This is shown by the two horizontal bags illustrated. If you could see through the lower one, you would find the hollow cone ready to receive the icing. The upright bag at the end shows the final double fold that tightly closes the top of the filled bag. The peaks have already been turned inside to help make the cornucopia leakproof at the top when pressure is applied. Before filling, press the tip of the paper bag flat and cut off the end. If you plan to use the metal tips from your pastry bag kit, be sure the opening is large enough to hold the tip, but not so large that it will slip through under pressure. If you plan to use the paper point rather than a metal tip to make the designs, make three paper cornucopias. Cut one point straight across to make a small round opening; clip the others with a single and a double notch, to achieve the star and rose cutouts. These three cuts will make all of the patterns shown in the drawings on 724, depending on the angle at which the bags are held and the amount of pressure applied. You can control the scale of the decoration by the size of the cut.

Now for the actual decorating. You have a choice of three fine icings: Royal Glaze, 727, Decorative Icing, 724, and Creamy Icing, 724. Decorative Icing is tastier but not so easy to handle and does not keep so well as the others. In any case, apply a smooth base coat to the cake. ➤ For Decorative Icing and Royal Glaze you may use a spatula dipped in tepid water for a glossy finish. ➤ Allow the base coat to dry. If using several colors for decoration, divide the icing into small bowls and tint with vegetable paste or liquid vegetable coloring. ➤ Keep the bowls covered with a damp cloth. Never fill the bag to more than two-thirds of its capacity. For colors needed in small quantities, make the bags half size. Use a small spatula to push the icing well down into the point of the bag.

Before beginning any trimming, press the bag to equalize the icing in it and to force any unwanted air toward the tip, so that no bubbles will later destroy the evenness of your decorations. If the bag becomes soft through use or has been unsatisfactorily made, cut a generous piece off the point and press the icing directly into a new bag.

Practice making and filling bags. Then apply the icing on an inverted cake pan. For practice, the icing can be scraped off repeatedly and reused. Make patterns like old-fashioned Spencerian-writing doodles until you have achieved some ease. ➤ Experiment with the feel of the bag, until you can sustain the pressure evenly for linear effects and with varying force for borders, petals and leaves. With the bag in your right hand, you may work with as much freedom as in drawing.

Now you are ready to make the designs. It is a great help if the cake is on a turntable or lazy susan. In any case, when working on the sides, try to have the cake just above elbow level as you work. Pressure and movement, as we said before ➤ are controlled by the right hand. ➤ The left is used only for steadying. As shown in the sketch on 724, grasp the bag lightly but firmly in the palm of the hand ➤ with the thumb resting on top, leaving the fingers free to press the bag as the hand and wrist turn to form the designs.

Sometimes the bag rests in the scissorlike crotch of the first two fingers. At other times the bag is merely guided, as shown in the second to last figure, 724. As the icing diminishes, refold the bag at the top, pushing the icing down.

First shown below left, 724, are forms executed from a bag with simple crosscut at the tip—making a small round opening. The second group was achieved with a notch like a V, and the elaborate composite-type flower needed a double notch, like a W. The decoration on the cake involves the use of all three types of cuts.

As in any work of art, the concept must domi-

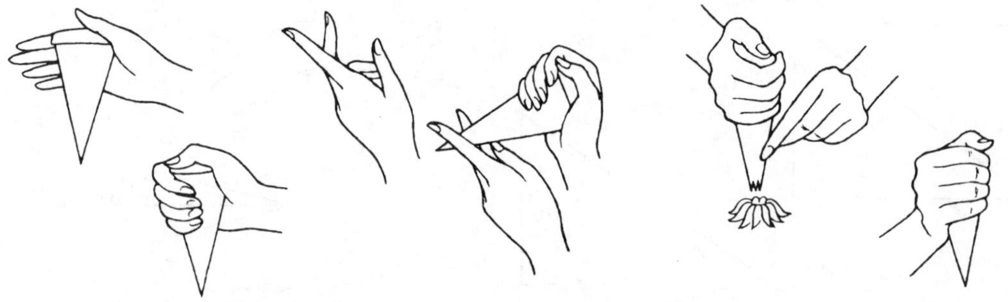

nate the technique. Make a sketch first of what you intend to do, or have it clearly in mind. The patterns shown below are conventional ones; try them, and then develop your own style. We remember a cake that Alexander Calder did for a mutual friend—complete with mobile and showing a clarity of line so characteristic of his talent.

It is a great temptation when decorating cakes to overload them. Try out some asymmetrical compositions. Partially bind the top and sides of the cake with garlands, heavy in relief but light in values, and remember to leave plenty of undecorated space to set them off. At first, you may make some of the more complicated designs separately on a piece of wax paper and let them dry before applying them to the cake. For those items made separately, use as an adhesive a little of the reserved fresh icing.

DECORATIVE ICING OR TWICE-COOKED ICING

About 1¾ Cups

This is a fine recipe for decorative icing. It will keep for a long time without hardening if closely covered with waxed paper. ➤ Please read About Boiled Icings, 721.

Stir until the sugar is dissolved, then boil without stirring:

1 cup sugar
½ cup water

Meanwhile, whip until ➤ stiff, but not dry:

2 egg whites
⅛ teaspoon salt

Sift and add very slowly, whipping constantly:

3 tablespoons sugar

When the syrup begins to fall in heavy drops from a spoon, add a small quantity of it to the eggs and sugar; continue beating. Repeat this process, adding the syrup to the eggs in 4 or 5 parts. If these additions are properly timed, the last of the syrup will have reached the thread stage. Beat the icing constantly. Have a pan ready, partly filled with water. Place it over heat. The bowl in which the icing is being made should fit closely into this pan, so that the bowl will be over—but not in—the water. When the water in the pan begins to boil, add to the icing:

¼ teaspoon icing powder: equal parts of baking powder and tartaric acid

Continue to beat the icing until it sticks to the sides and the bottom of the bowl and holds a point. Remove from heat. Place as much as is required for the decoration, usually about a third, in a small bowl. Cover it closely with waxed paper. To the remainder, add:

1 teaspoon or more hot water

thinning it to the right consistency for spreading. Beat it well and spread it on the cake. To decorate, see About Decorative Icings, above.

CREAMY ICING

A highly manageable icing for intricate, precise decorations that keeps well if stored covered. Enough to frost and lightly decorate a 9-inch cake. Sift:

1 lb. confectioners' sugar

Add and mix well with electric mixer:

½ cup white vegetable shortening
5 to 6 tablespoons milk or cream

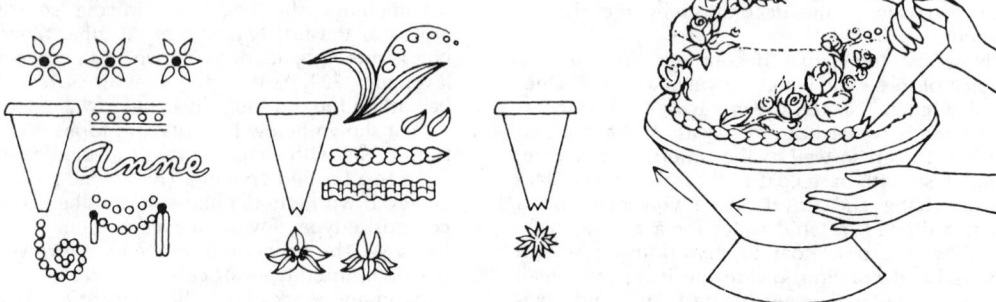

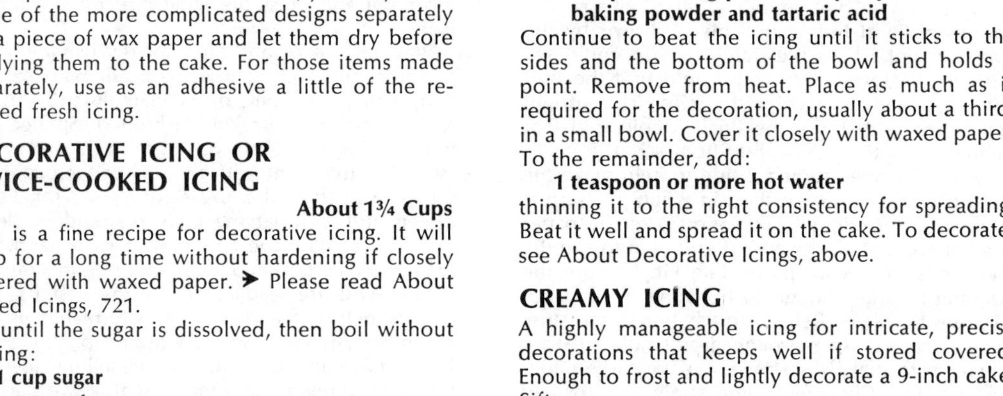

1 teaspoon vanilla, or ½ vanilla and
½ almond extract

Continue beating until icing is evenly smooth. It will be slightly stiff, which is the proper consistency for making decorations.

CHOCOLATE COATING OVER BOILED WHITE ICING

About 2¼ Cups

The supreme touch to something that is already good in itself.

Melt:

2 oz. chocolate

Cool and spread with a broad knife or spatula over:

Boiled White Icing, 721, or
Seven-Minute White Icing, below

This may be done as soon as the white icing is set. Allow several hours for the coating to harden. In summer or in moist weather, add to the chocolate before spreading it:

(¼ teaspoon melted paraffin)

This coating is always thin when applied, and hardens more rapidly if refrigerated. ➤ It is not recommended for use in damp hot weather. Transfer the cake to a fresh plate before serving.

SEVEN-MINUTE WHITE ICING

I. **About 2 Cups**

A very fluffy, delightful icing that never fails. ➤ Please read About Boiled Icings, 721. Place in the top of a double boiler and beat until thoroughly blended:

2 unbeaten egg whites
1½ cups sugar
5 tablespoons cold water
¼ teaspoon cream of tartar
(1½ teaspoons light corn syrup)

Place these ingredients ➤ over rapidly boiling water. Beat them constantly with a rotary beater or with a wire whisk 7 minutes. Remove icing from heat. Add:

1 teaspoon vanilla

Continue beating until the icing is the right consistency for spreading. You may add to it at this point:

(½ cup chopped nutmeats or grated coconut or 1 stick crushed peppermint candy)

II. Made with an electric mixer.

Stir, then boil in a covered pan until the sugar is dissolved:

3 tablespoons hot water
1 cup confectioners' sugar

Place in a small mixing bowl:

1 unbeaten egg white
¼ teaspoon cream of tartar
⅛ teaspoon salt

Add the hot syrup. Beat these ingredients at high speed until the icing is the right consistency to spread, 3 to 4 minutes. Add while beating:

1 teaspoon vanilla

SEVEN-MINUTE LEMON ICING

Prepare:

Seven-Minute White Icing I, above

Use only:

3 tablespoons water

Add:

2 tablespoons lemon juice
¼ teaspoon grated lemon rind

SEVEN-MINUTE ORANGE ICING

About 1½ Cups

Place in the top of a double boiler and beat until thoroughly blended:

1½ cups sugar
2 egg whites
1 tablespoon lemon juice
½ teaspoon orange rind
¼ cup orange juice

Follow the recipe for Seven-Minute White Icing I, above.

SEVEN-MINUTE SEA-FOAM ICING

Cook:

Seven-Minute White Icing I, above

for 8 minutes. Fold in:

4 teaspoons Caramelized Sugar I, 559

Don't forget the vanilla.

FONDANT ICING

About 2 Cups

This is the classic icing for petits fours. It is tricky to apply evenly.

Prepare:

Basic Fondant, 778

Just before you are ready to use it, heat the fondant ➤ over—not in—boiling water, beating it constantly until it melts. Then add any desired flavoring or coloring. Spread at once, as this icing tends to glaze over rapidly and then needs reheating. Let the icing drip across, from one narrow edge of the cake to the other, as shown on 695, repeating until covered. Reheat and reuse any icing that falls onto the sheet below. If you have only a very few cakes to frost, place them one at a time on a slotted pancake turner or spoon held over the pot and ice them individually.

LUSCIOUS ORANGE ICING

About 1½ Cups

This icing becomes firm on the outside and remains soft inside. ➤ Please read About Boiled Icings, 721.

Stir over heat until dissolved:

1 cup granulated sugar
1 tablespoon white corn syrup
⅛ teaspoon cream of tartar
½ cup water

➤ Cover and cook about 3 minutes or until the steam has washed down any crystals that may have formed on the sides of the pan. ➤ Uncover and cook to 238° to 240° without stirring. Pour the syrup in a slow stream over:

2 beaten egg whites

Beat for 10 minutes. Add:

1/4 cup powdered sugar
1 teaspoon grated orange rind
1 tablespoon orange juice or
3/4 teaspoon vanilla

Beat the icing to a spreading consistency.

CARAMEL ICING

About 1 1/2 Cups

➤ Please read About Boiled Icings, 721.

Stir until the sugar is dissolved:

2 cups brown sugar
1 cup cream, or 1/2 cup butter plus
1/2 cup milk

➤ Cover and cook about 3 minutes or until the steam has washed down any crystals that may have formed on the sides of the pan. ➤ Uncover and cook without stirring to 238° to 240°. Add:

3 tablespoons butter

Remove the icing from the heat and cool to 110°. Add:

1 teaspoon vanilla

Beat the icing until thick and creamy. If it becomes too heavy, thin it with a little:

Cream

until it is of spreading consistency. Top with:

(Chopped nuts)

MAPLE SUGAR ICING

About 1 1/2 Cups

➤ Please read About Boiled Icings, 721.

Combine and cook, stirring frequently, until the mixture reaches a boil:

2 cups maple sugar
1 cup cream

Then ➤ cover and cook about 3 minutes or until the steam has washed down any crystals that may have formed on the sides of the pan. ➤ Uncover and cook to 234°. Remove the icing from the heat. Cool to 110°. Beat well until creamy. Fold in:

1/2 cup chopped nutmeats, preferably butternuts or slivered toasted almonds

COCONUT PECAN ICING

About 2 1/2 Cups

Combine in a pan:

2/3 cup sugar
2/3 cup evaporated milk
2 egg yolks
1/3 cup butter
1/2 teaspoon vanilla

Cook and stir constantly over low heat about 10 minutes or until the egg thickens. ➤ Do not boil. Remove from heat and add:

1 1/3 cups flaked coconut
2/3 to 1 cup chopped pecans

CHOCOLATE MARSHMALLOW ICING

About 2 Cups

➤ Please read About Boiled Icings, 721.

Stir until the sugar is dissolved:

1 1/2 cups sugar
1 1/2 cups water

Then ➤ cover and cook about 3 minutes or until the steam washes down any crystals that may have formed on the sides of the pan. ➤ Uncover and cook without stirring to 238° to 240°. Remove from the heat and add:

2 oz. grated unsweetened chocolate
1 dozen large marshmallows, cut into eighths and steamed until soft

Let these ingredients stand until the mixture no longer bubbles. Add:

1/8 teaspoon cream of tartar

Whip until ➤ stiff, but not dry:

2 egg whites
1/8 teaspoon salt

Pour the syrup over the egg whites in a thin stream. Whip constantly, until the icing is of the right consistency for spreading.

CHOCOLATE FUDGE ICING

About 2 Cups

Prepare:

Fudge Cockaigne, 782

Use in all:

1 cup milk

Beat until the icing is of the right consistency to be spread.

BROWN SUGAR MARSHMALLOW ICING

About 1 1/2 Cups

➤ Please read About Boiled Icings, 721.

Cut into small cubes:

12 large marshmallows

Stir over low heat until dissolved:

2 cups brown sugar
1/2 cup milk

➤ Cover the syrup for about 3 minutes or until the steam has washed down any crystals which may have formed on the sides of the pan. ➤ Uncover and cook without stirring to 238°. Remove from the heat and add the marshmallows and:

1/4 cup butter

When these ingredients are melted and the icing has cooled to 110°, beat until it is of a good consistency for spreading. If too heavy, thin with a little:

Cream

Pour the cream a few drops at a time. Add:

(1/2 cup chopped nutmeats)

ABOUT QUICK ICINGS

Most quick icings, unless heavy in butter, are best spread on warm cakes. ➤ Those which have eggs in them, if not consumed the day they are made, should be refrigerated. Recipes calling for confectioners' sugar are tastier when ➤ allowed to stand over—not in—boiling water for 10 to 15 minutes, to cancel out the raw taste of the cornstarch filler. If you don't mind that taste, you can mix these icings more quickly in a ⅄ blender. ➤ Any delicate flavoring should be added after the icing leaves the heat. A glossy finish can be achieved by dipping your spatula frequently in hot water while icing the cake.

QUICK WHITE ICING

I. **About 1 Cup**

See About Quick Icings, above.
Cream together:
2 cups sifted confectioners' sugar
¼ cup soft butter or 3 tablespoons hot whipping cream
Add and beat until smooth:
¼ teaspoon salt
1 teaspoon vanilla
3 to 4 tablespoons milk, dry sherry, rum, or coffee
If the icing is too thin, add more:
Confectioners' sugar
If too thick, add:
A little cream

II. **About ¾ Cup**

Melt and stir in a skillet until golden brown:
6 tablespoons butter
Blend in gradually:
1½ cups confectioners' sugar
Add 1 tablespoon at a time, until the icing is of a good spreading consistency:
Hot water
Flavor with:
1 teaspoon vanilla

ROYAL GLAZE, SWISS MERINGUE OR QUICK DECORATIVE ICING

About 2 Cups

This icing will become very hard. To avoid the naturally grayish tone that develops during preparation, add to portions that you want to keep white a slight amount of blue vegetable coloring. Do not use blue in any icing that you plan to color yellow, orange or any other pale, warm tint.
Sift:
3½ cups confectioners' sugar
Beat until ➤ stiff, but not dry:
2 egg whites
Gradually add the sifted sugar and:
Juice of a lemon
1 to 2 drops glycerin
until it is of a good consistency to spread. Cover with a damp cloth until ready to use.

To apply as piping or for decorative effects, see About Decorative Icing, 722. Should you want the icing stiffer, add a little more sifted sugar. To make it softer, thin it ➤ very, very gradually with lemon juice, more egg white or water.

LEMON TOPPING FOR COOKIES OR BARS

About 1½ Cups

Whip until ➤ stiff, but not dry:
2 egg whites
⅛ teaspoon salt
Sift and add gradually:
2 to 2½ cups confectioners' sugar
Grated rind and juice of 1 lemon

QUICK LEMON ICING

About 1 Cup

Please read About Quick Icings, above.
A very subtle flavor may be obtained by coarsely grating the rind of an orange or lemon, wrapping the rind in a piece of cheesecloth, and wringing the citrus oils onto the sugar before it is blended. Stir the oils into the sugar and allow it to stand 15 minutes or more.
Blend well:
2 cups confectioners' sugar
¼ cup soft butter
Beat in:
1 or more tablespoons cream
If you have not treated the sugar as suggested above, add:
Grated rind and juice of 1 lemon or 3 tablespoons liqueur such as apricot or crème de cacao

THREE-MINUTE ICING

Use this soft icing as a substitute for whipped cream or meringue.
Beat until blended, then place in a double boiler over boiling water:
2 egg whites
½ cup sugar
⅛ teaspoon salt
2 tablespoons cold water
Beat these ingredients with a wire whisk 3 minutes, or until stiff. Remove the icing from the heat.
Add:
1 teaspoon vanilla or almond extract
Beat the icing well. Spread it over jellied fruit, pies or tarts, cakes, etc., that have been cooled
Top it with:
Chopped nutmeats or coconut

FRENCH ICING

About 1½ Cups

See About Quick Icings, 726.
Sift:
2 cups confectioners' sugar
Beat until soft:
¼ cup butter
Add the sugar gradually. Blend these ingredients until creamy. Beat in:
1 egg
1 teaspoon vanilla
Place the mixture ➤ over—not in—boiling water 10 to 15 minutes.

CREAM CHEESE ICING

About ¾ Cup

➤ Please read About Quick Icings, 726.
Sift:
¾ cup confectioners' sugar
Work until soft and fluffy:

3 oz. cream cheese
1½ tablespoons cream or milk
Beat in the sugar gradually. Add:
1½ teaspoons grated lemon or orange rind
or:
1 teaspoon vanilla and
½ teaspoon cinnamon
or:
A good dash liqueur, lemon or orange juice and grated rind

QUICK ORANGE ICING

About 1 Cup

See About Quick Icings, 726.
Place in the top of a double boiler:
2 cups sifted confectioners' sugar
1 tablespoon melted butter
1 tablespoon grated orange rind
¼ cup orange juice, or 3 tablespoons orange juice and 1 tablespoon lemon juice
Place these ingredients ➤ over—not in—boiling water 10 minutes. Then beat the icing until cool and of a good spreading consistency.

BUTTERSCOTCH OR PENUCHE ICING

About 1¼ Cups

Combine, stir and heat in a double boiler until smooth:
¼ cup butter
½ cup brown sugar
⅛ teaspoon salt
⅓ cup light cream or evaporated milk
Cool this slightly. Beat in, to a good spreading consistency:
2 cups, more or less, of confectioners' sugar
You may add:
½ teaspoon vanilla or 1 teaspoon rum
½ cup chopped nutmeats

CHOCOLATE BUTTER ICING

About 1½ Cups

This icing can be used for decorating.
➤ Please read About Quick Icings, 726.
Melt over very low heat:
2 to 3 oz. unsweetened chocolate
Melt in it:
2 teaspoons to 3 tablespoons butter
Remove these ingredients from the heat and add:
¼ cup hot water, cream or coffee
⅛ teaspoon salt
Add gradually:
2 cups, more or less, sifted confectioners' sugar
1 teaspoon vanilla
You may not need quite all the sugar.

QUICK BROWN SUGAR ICING

About ¾ Cup

A quickly made but rather coarse icing.
Combine, stir and cook slowly to the boiling point:
1½ cups brown sugar
5 tablespoons cream
2 teaspoons butter
⅛ teaspoon salt
Remove from the heat. Cool slightly and add:
½ teaspoon vanilla
Beat the icing until it can be spread. You may add:
(½ cup chopped nutmeats)

CHOCOLATE CREAM CHEESE ICING

About 2 Cups

Melt:
3 oz. unsweetened chocolate
Soften:
3 oz. cream cheese
in:
¼ cup milk
Add gradually:
4 cups confectioners' sugar
½ teaspoon salt
Combine this mixture with the melted chocolate and beat until smooth and ready to be spread.

⅄ EUROPEAN CHOCOLATE ICING

About ⅔ Cup

A letter from a homesick American bride made us realize that familiar tastes abroad have an accent as foreign as English words spoken by other nationals. Where to get bitter chocolate for icing, to make it taste the way she thought it should? Chef James Gregory made her feel almost at home with this semisweet answer.
Melt in a double boiler ➤ over—not in—boiling water:
1 tablespoon butter
4 oz. semisweet chocolate
When melted, add and beat well or ⅄ blend:
6 tablespoons whipping cream
Sift and add, until the desired sweetness is reached and the icing is smooth, about:
1½ cups confectioners' sugar
1 teaspoon vanilla
Spread while warm.

QUICK CHOCOLATE ICING

Melt over hot water:
Sweet chocolate bars or chocolate peppermints
Cool slightly, then spread the icing. If the chocolate seems stiff, beat in a little:
Cream
and, to perfect the flavor, add:
Vanilla

CAROB ICING

Prepare:
French Icing, 727
and sift with the confectioners' sugar:
¼ cup carob powder
You may add:
(½ teaspoon instant coffee)
Proceed as for French Icing.

COFFEE OR MOCHA ICING

About 1¼ Cups

Sift:

1⅔ cups confectioners' sugar
1 to 2 tablespoons cocoa

Beat until soft:

¼ to ½ cup butter

Add the sugar gradually. Blend these ingredients until creamy. Add:

⅛ teaspoon salt
3 tablespoons strong hot coffee

Beat for 2 minutes. When the icing is cool, add:

1 teaspoon vanilla, almond flavoring or rum

Let stand 5 minutes. Beat well and spread.

QUICK MAPLE ICING

About 1 Cup

Sift:

2 cups confectioners' sugar

Add and blend:

1 tablespoon butter
¼ teaspoon salt
½ teaspoon vanilla

Add and beat to a good consistency for spreading:

Maple syrup
(½ cup toasted coconut)

QUICK HONEY–PEANUT BUTTER ICING

This appeals mainly to the small fry.
Combine and bring to a boil:

2 tablespoons shortening
2 tablespoons butter
¼ cup honey

Remove from heat and add:

½ cup coarsely ground peanuts

Stir until well blended. Spread on a warm cake. Toast very lightly under a broiler at medium heat; watch carefully.

APRICOT OR PINEAPPLE ICING

About 1 Cup

A soft icing.
Stir until smooth:

½ cup sweetened, cooked dried apricot pulp or drained crushed pineapple

with:

1½ to 2 cups sifted confectioners' sugar

Beat in:

1 to 3 tablespoons soft butter
½ tablespoon lemon juice

Add more confectioners' sugar if needed.

PINEAPPLE ICING

About 1½ Cups

Sift:

2 cups confectioners' sugar

Beat until soft:

¼ cup butter

Add the sugar gradually. Blend until creamy. Beat in:

1 teaspoon lemon juice
⅛ teaspoon salt
½ teaspoon vanilla
½ cup drained crushed pineapple

Let stand 5 minutes. Beat the icing until creamy. Add more sugar, if necessary.

ABOUT ICING SMALL CAKES AND COOKIES

There are a number of ways to ice and garnish small cakes quickly. Some are shown below. **I.** Place on a hot cupcake small bits of semisweet or sweet chocolate. Spread as it melts. **II.** Just before removing cookies from the oven, put on each one a mint-flavored chocolate candy wafer and return the cookie sheet to the oven until the wafer melts. **III.** To ice cupcakes or leaf cookies, dip them quickly into any soft icing. Swirl the cakes as shown. Cookies are most easily iced if impaled on a skewer. **IV.** For cupcakes, sift confectioners' sugar over them through a strainer, as shown below. **V.** Or ice as for Petit Fours, 695.

QUICK LACE TOPPING

A good, quick decorative effect on any cake can be gained with a slightly rough top, see sketch, 730. Place a paper doily or monogrammed cut paper pattern on top of the cake and fill the interstices with sugar. Be sure that the sugar, confectioners' or colored, is dusted lavishly over the doily and filters down into all the voids. Lift the doily or pattern off gingerly, with a straight upward motion, and you will find a clearly marked lacy design on your cake top. Shake into a bowl any surplus sugar left on the pattern. Reserve it for

future use. You may also follow this principle in applying finely grated semisweet chocolate on an iced cake.

HARD-SAUCE TOPPING

Soften slightly, then apply a thin layer of brandied:

Hard Sauce, 775

to any cooled cake or coffee cake.

BAKED ICING

Glaze for an 8 x 8-Inch Cake

This icing is baked at the same time as the cake. Use it on a thin cake only, one that will require 25 minutes of baking or less—such as spice, ginger or coffee cake.

Preheat oven to 375°.

Sift:

½ cup brown sugar

Whip until ➤ stiff, but not dry:

1 egg white
⅛ teaspoon salt

Fold in the sugar or beat it in slowly. For an exciting new taste, fold in:

(2 tablespoons cocoa)

Spread the icing on the cake. Sprinkle it with:

¼ cup broken nutmeats

Bake the cake as indicated in the recipe.

BROILED ICING

For an 8 x 8-Inch Cake

Combine and spread on a cake, coffee cake or cookies, while they are warm, a mixture of:

3 tablespoons melted butter
⅔ cup brown sugar
1 to 2 tablespoons cream
⅛ teaspoon salt
½ cup shredded coconut or nutmeats

Place the cake 3 inches below a broiler, with the heat turned low. Broil the icing until it bubbles all over the surface, but see that it does not burn.

ABOUT MERINGUE TOPPINGS

Pie and pudding meringues are delicate affairs that ➤ are best made and added to pastry shortly before serving. Since meringue is beaten constantly until the moment to spread it, have the ➤ oven preheated to between 325° and 350°. Lower heat will dry the meringue. Higher heat will cause egg protein to shrink or shrivel. The two toppings below differ greatly in volume, texture and method. The first is cooked on the pie or dessert itself. The second is cooked separately and beaten until cool before applying; it may or may not be browned later. As volume in the egg white is essential, please follow these suggestions: ➤ Have the utensils absolutely free of grease, with ➤ egg whites at about 70° and ➤ without a trace of yolk. Add sugar as specified in each recipe. Excess sugar beaten into the meringue will cause gumminess and "beading." If you prefer a topping sweeter than these, you may glaze the surface, after the meringue is in place, by sprinkling it with additional sugar. This also makes the meringue easier to cut cleanly when serving. You may also top it with a sprinkling of coconut or slivered almonds before baking.

Meringue toppings for small tarts may be baked on foil and slipped onto a cooked or fresh pie filling just before serving. For a large pie, spread the meringue lightly from the edges toward the center of the pie. ➤ Should it not adhere well to the edges at all points, it will pull away during the baking. ➤ To avoid shrinkage, cool meringues in a warm place, away from drafts.

MERINGUE TOPPING

I. For a 9-Inch Pie

Preheat oven to 325° to 350°.

Whip until frothy:

2 egg whites

Add:

¼ teaspoon cream of tartar

Whip them until they are ➤ stiff, but not dry; until they stand in peaks that lean over slightly when the beater is removed. Beat in, 1 tablespoon at a time:

3 tablespoons sugar or
4 tablespoons confectioners' sugar

➤ Do not overbeat. Beat in:

½ teaspoon vanilla

Spread on pie and bake 10 to 15 minutes, depending on the thickness of the meringue.

II. About 1¼ Cups

This classic Italian meringue does not require baking, because the egg whites are already cooked by the hot syrup. You may want to brown it lightly in a 350° oven. This meringue is not so stiff as the preceding one.

Heat in a heavy pan and stir until dissolved:

½ cup water
¼ teaspoon cream of tartar
1 cup sugar

When the syrup is boiling ➤ cover and cook about 3 minutes or until the steam has washed down any crystals that may have formed on the sides of the pan. ➤ Uncover and cook without stirring to 238° to 240°. Pour the syrup ➤ very gradually onto:

3 well-beaten egg whites

beating constantly, until this frosting meringue is cool and ready to be spread on the pie fllling or pudding.

STREUSEL AND TOPPINGS APPLIED BEFORE BAKING TO COFFEE CAKES, PIES AND SWEET ROLLS

I. Streusel **For an 8 x 8-Inch Cake**

Prepare:

Any coffee cake dough, 619–621

After spreading it with butter, combine:

2 tablespoons all-purpose or rice flour
2 tablespoons butter
5 tablespoons sugar

Blend these ingredients until they crumble. Add:

½ teaspoon cinnamon

Sprinkle the crumbs over the cake and bake as directed. Add:

(¼ to ½ cup chopped nuts)

II. Streusel **For a 9-Inch Pie**

Frequently called Danish or Swedish and much like the topping for Apple Paradise. This is a crumb topping usually served in place of a top crust on apple or tart fruit pie, but which does well for coffee cakes. Melt:

6 tablespoons butter

Stir in and brown lightly:

1 cup fine dry cake crumbs
¾ teaspoon cinnamon

III. Honey Glaze **For a 9 x 13-Inch Cake**

Cream:

½ cup sugar
¼ cup butter

Blend in:

1 unbeaten egg white

Add:

¼ cup honey
½ cup crushed nutmeats
½ teaspoon cardamom

Spread these ingredients on coffee cakes that are ready to be baked.

IV. Honey-Bee Glaze
For Two 9-Inch Square Cakes

Stir and bring to the boiling point over low heat:

½ cup sugar
¼ cup milk
¼ cup butter
¼ cup honey
½ cup crushed nutmeats

Spread these ingredients on coffee cakes that are ready for baking.

V. Caramel Roll Topping **For 12 Rolls**

This heavy topping is put in the bottom of the pan, and when the cake or rolls are reversed, it becomes the topping.

Melt:

¼ cup butter

Stir in until dissolved:

1 cup packed brown sugar
2 tablespoons honey or corn syrup
1 to 2 teaspoons cinnamon
½ teaspoon chopped lemon rind
½ cup chopped nuts

Add:

(2 tablespoons finely chopped citron)

GLAZES APPLIED BEFORE OR DURING BAKING

I. To give color to yeast dough or pastry, brush with:

Milk or butter or a combination of milk and sugar

II. French Egg Wash or Dorure

To give color and gloss to yeast dough or pastry, brush with:

1 egg yolk diluted with
1 to 2 tablespoons water or milk

III. To sparkle a glaze, sprinkle before baking with:

Granulated sugar

IV. For a clear glaze, just before the pastry has finished baking, apply with brush dipped in:

¼ cup sugar

dissolved in:

¼ cup hot water or strong hot coffee
(½ teaspoon cinnamon)

and return to oven.

V. To give yeast dough or pastry a glow and flavor, brush with sweetened fruit juice and lemon rind.

VI. To gloss and harden crust of yeast dough, brush with a cornstarch and water glaze several times during the baking.

VII. Broiled Icing, 730.

VIII. Baked Icing, 730.

GLAZES APPLIED AFTER BAKING

Just after these glazes are applied, decorate with:

Whole or half nuts, cherries, pineapple bits and citron

When it dries, the glaze will hold the decorations in place on cakes and sweet breads.

I. Milk Glaze **About ⅓ Cup**

This can be used as a substitute on small cakes similar to petits fours, which are classically iced with fondant.

Sift:

½ cup confectioners' sugar

Add:

2 teaspoons hot milk
¼ teaspoon vanilla

II. ★ Lemon Glaze **About ½ Cup**

Enough glaze to cover four 8 x 8-inch cakes. This

glaze needs no heating but is spread directly on warm cakes or Christmas cookies. It is of a fine consistency for imbedding decorative nuts and fruits.
Mix or ⅄ blend:

1¼ cups confectioners' sugar

with:

¼ cup lemon, orange or lime juice
1 teaspoon vanilla

Mix until smooth.

III. Honey Glaze

Combine and bring to a boil:

2 tablespoons sugar
¼ cup honey
1 tablespoon butter

IV. Chocolate Glaze — **About 1¼ Cups**

This retains a glossy sheen.
Melt in a double boiler ➤ over—not in—boiling water:

6 to 7 oz. semisweet chocolate
(1 tablespoon butter)

Cook to the thread stage (230°):

1 cup sugar
⅓ cup water (of which 3 tablespoons may be strong coffee)

Pour the syrup slowly into the chocolate, stirring constantly until the mixture coats the back of the spoon. Pour the glaze over the cake.

V. ⅄ Blender-Whipped Cheese Topping — **About ⅓ Cup**

Soften:

3 oz. cream cheese

with:

1 tablespoon cream
½ teaspoon vanilla

Blend in and cream well:

3 tablespoons confectioners' sugar

VI. Liqueur Glaze — **About ⅔ Cup**

Combine and mix well:

2 cups sifted confectioners' sugar
3 tablespoons liqueur
2 tablespoons melted butter

Spread over cake or cookies.

VII. Glaze for Breads

To make a crisp crust, brush with water immediately when taken from oven.

VIII. Glaze for Puff Paste

For a crisp crust, brush with a light sugar syrup immediately upon removal from oven.

GLAZES FOR FRUIT PIES, TARTS AND COFFEE CAKES

I. Apricot, Peach or Raspberry Glaze — **About 4½ Cups**

For already baked pastries, the simplest glazes are melted preserves or jellies such as currant, quince or apple. Below is a useful glaze to keep on hand in the refrigerator.
Prepare:

3 cups strained apricots, peaches or raspberries

Cook until the sugar is dissolved, with:

1 cup sugar
1 cup light corn syrup

While the mixture is still warm, glaze the cooled pastry.

II. Fruit Glaze — **Sufficient for Glazing 3 Cups of Berries or Fruit**

Boil to the jelly stage, 833, then strain these ingredients:

¼ cup water
1 cup sugar
1 cup cleaned fruit
2 medium-sized chopped apples
A little red vegetable coloring
(1 tablespoon butter)

The butter will keep the glaze supple. Cool. When the jelly is about to set, pour it or spread it over the fruit to be glazed.

III. Strawberry Glaze — **Sufficient for a 9-Inch Pie Shell or Six 2½-Inch Tarts**

Hull and crush:

3 cups strawberries

Strain them first through a ricer, then through a fine sieve. Add to the juice:

⅓ cup sugar
1 tablespoon lemon juice
1 tablespoon cornstarch
A little red vegetable coloring

Cook and stir these ingredients over low heat until thick and transparent. Cool. Spread over the fruit to be glazed.

IV. Thickened Fruit Glaze

Glaze may also be made of canned fruit syrups or of jellies. Boil the syrup or jelly until thick. To each ½ cup, add:

1 teaspoon cornstarch or arrowroot

blended with:

1 tablespoon sugar

The cornstarch will give a smooth glaze, the arrowroot a more transparent and stickier one.

CLEAR CARAMEL GLAZE

About 1 Cup

This brittle topping is used on many European cakes, especially the famous Dobos or Drum Torte, 685.
Place in a large, heavy skillet over low heat:

1 cup sugar

Cook and stir with a wooden spoon, using the same kind of gentle motion you use for scrambling eggs. ➤ Keep agitating the pan to prevent scorching. When the sugar bubbles, remove the pan from the heat. The glaze should be clear, light brown and smooth, and should have reached a temperature of about 310°. Spread it at once with a hot spatula. ➤ If you work quickly, you may score it in patterns for easier cutting later. Use a knife dipped in cold water.

FRESH FLOWERS FOR CAKES

Cake decorations can be made from flowers, if you are sure they were ➤ not sprayed. Place on the cake just before it is served. Choose delicately colored open-petaled flowers like hollyhocks. Remove the stamens. Cut off all but 3/4 inch of the stem. Arrange the flowers on an iced cake. Place a small candle in the center of each one. A hemerocallis wreath is good for daytime decorations but closes at night. Field daisies and African daisies hold up well. ➤ Beware of flowers like lilies of the valley or Star of Bethlehem, which have poisonous properties.

DESSERTS

A family we know had a cook who always urged the children to eat sparingly of the main course, so as to leave a little room for the "hereafter." Desserts can indeed be heavenly. They also give the hostess a chance to build a focal point for a buffet, such as the flambéed plum pudding shown above, or to produce a startling soufflé. Serve a rich chocolate custard in Empire pots-de-crème, 737, as shown in foreground. Remember, too, fruits and fruit fondues, 128, and dessert cheeses, 756. See also Filled Cakes, 687, and Torten, 684, that serve as complete desserts, and Crêpes, 236, and Beignets, 246, and by all means Compotes, 126.

ABOUT CUSTARDS

Custard puddings, sauces and fillings accompany the seven ages of man in sickness and in health. To prepare them in ways that enhance their charm, remember these simple precautions. ➤ When pasteurized milk is used in making custards, it is not necessary to scald it; but scalding does shorten the cooking time. If scalded, cool the milk enough afterward to keep the eggs, when added, from curdling; or temper the beaten eggs by adding a small quantity of the hot liquid to them before gradually adding the eggs to the hot mixture.

For baked custard, simply whip the ingredients together well and pour them into custard cups. We prefer cups of heavy ceramic glaze like those shown on 735, with their pottery tray. Or cups may be set on a rack or on a folded towel in a pan. In either case, pour an inch of hot, but not boiling, water into the cooking container. Bake them 50 to 60 minutes at low heat, around 300°. If you have used homogenized milk, allow about 10 minutes longer. To test for doneness, insert a knife ➤ near the edge of the cup. If the blade comes out clean, the custard will be solid all the way through when cooled. There is sufficient stored heat in the cups to finish the cooking process. Remove the custards from the pan and cool on a rack. ➤ However, should you suspect that they are overcooked, test them at the centers. If they are as well done as at the edges, set the cups in ice water at once to arrest further cooking.

For softer top-of-the-stove custards and sauces, use a double boiler, cooking ➤ over—not in—boiling water. Too high heat will toughen and shrink the albumen in the eggs and keep it from holding the liquid in suspension as it should. Beat the eggs well. Add about 1/4 cup of the hot liquid to them and then slowly add the rest of it, stirring constantly. Cook until the custard is thick enough to coat a spoon. Remove pan from heat. Strain. Then continue stirring to release steam. If the steam is allowed to condense, it may make the custard watery. Should you have reason to believe that the custard has become too hot, turn it into a chilled dish and whisk it quickly, or put it in the blender at high speed to cool rapidly. ➤ Always store custards or custard-based dishes like pies and éclairs covered in the refrigerator, as they are highly susceptible to bacterial activity even though they may give no evidence of spoilage.

CUSTARD

5 Servings

This artless confection, often referred to as "boiled" custard, is badly nicknamed, because ➤ it must not be permitted to boil at any time. It is never so firm as baked custard but is more like a thick custard sauce.

Scald in the top of a double boiler.

2 cups milk

Stir in slowly:

3 or 4 slightly beaten egg yolks
1/4 cup sugar
1/8 teaspoon salt

Place the custard ➤ over—not in—boiling water. Stir it constantly until it begins to thicken. As it cools, beat to release the steam. Add before chilling thoroughly:

1 teaspoon vanilla, rum or dry sherry, or a little grated lemon rind

⅄ BAKED OR CUP CUSTARD

5 Servings

Delicious served in solitary glory. Use it also to top a summer brunch of unsweetened dry cereal and fresh berries; or as a filling in cored pear halves, fresh or stewed, sprinkled with rum and garnished with a stewed pitted prune dusted in cinnamon.

Preheat oven to 300°.

Blend together:

2 cups milk
1/4 to 1/2 cup sugar or 1/4 cup honey
1/8 teaspoon salt

Should the milk be unpasteurized, be sure to see About Custards, above. Add and beat well:

2 whole eggs or 4 egg yolks

If you want to unmold the custard, add an extra

egg. The greater the proportion of yolk, the tenderer the custard will be. If you use 2 egg whites to 1 yolk, quite a stiff custard results. Add:

½ teaspoon vanilla or almond extract, or the scraped seeds from a 1-inch length of vanilla bean

When this is all well beaten, pour it into a baking dish or into individual custard cups. Dust with:

(Nutmeg)

A nutmeg grater is shown at the right, below. Place the molds in a pan of hot water on a rack or in a heavy ceramic baking dish, shown below. Bake an hour or more for the casserole and 50 to 60 minutes for the cups. To test, see About Custards, above. Chill and serve with:

Caramel Syrup, 791, berries, a fruit sauce, or Maple Syrup Sauce, 773

⅄ COFFEE CHOCOLATE CUSTARD

4 Servings

A sophisticated dessert easily made in a blender. Put into blender:

½ to 1 oz. finely cut-up unsweetened chocolate

Pour over it:

1 cup strong, hot coffee

Add:

1 cup milk
4 to 6 tablespoons sugar
⅛ teaspoon salt
2 whole eggs or 3 egg yolks

Blend this mixture. Bake as for Baked Custard, above.

CARAMELIZED CUSTARD OR CRÈME CARAMEL

4 to 5 Servings

Caramelize:

½ cup sugar, see Caramelized Sugar I, 559

Place it in a 7-inch ring mold or custard cups. Turn the mold so the caramel spreads evenly, then push the coating with a wooden spoon until the entire base of the dish is covered. At this point the syrup should be, and should remain, thick if you have caramelized the sugar properly.

Prepare:

Baked Custard, above

Bake as directed in the caramelized mold or cups. Invert it when cold onto a platter. To ensure that the caramel comes out intact, dip the mold to the depth of the caramel ➤ quickly into hot water, as you would in releasing a gelatin. Now the center may be filled with:

(Whipped cream)

Sprinkle the top with:

Shredded toasted almonds or crushed nut brittle

CARAMEL CUSTARD

Prepare:

Baked Custard, above

omitting the sugar. Mix with it:

½ cup Caramelized Sugar I, 559

Bake as directed.

RICH CUSTARD

6 Servings

Mix in the top of a double boiler:

¾ cup sugar
2 tablespoons cornstarch
⅛ teaspoon salt

Gradually stir in:

2 cups milk and cream, mixed

Cook covered ➤ over—not in—boiling water 8 minutes without stirring. Uncover and cook for about 10 minutes more. Add:

4 well-beaten egg yolks
2 tablespoons butter

Continue to cook and stir these ingredients 2 minutes longer. Cool, stirring occasionally to release steam, then add:

1½ teaspoons vanilla

Fold in:

1 cup whipped cream

Chill the custard. It will have the consistency of a heavy whipped cream. It is divine with:

Dampfnudeln, 663, or drained Tutti-Frutti, 840

FLOATING ISLAND

4 Servings

The French call this dish **Oeufs à la Neige** or **Snowy Eggs.**

Whip until stiff:

3 egg whites

Beat in gradually:

¼ cup sugar

Scald:

2 cups milk

Drop the meringue mixture from a tablespoon in rounds onto the milk. Poach them gently, without letting the milk boil, for about 4 minutes, turning them once. Lift them out carefully with a skimmer onto a towel. Use the milk and egg yolks to make:

Custard, 734

Cool the custard. Place the meringues on top. Chill before serving.

Or you may heap the meringue on the cooled custard. Place the custard dish in a pan of ice water and put the whole into the hot oven just long enough to brown the tips of the meringue. Dribble over the tops of the "eggs":

(Caramelized Sugar I, 559)

CRÈME BRÛLÉE

6 Servings

A rich French custard—famous for its hard, caramelized sugar glaze.
Heat in a double boiler until hot:

2 cups whipping cream

Pour it slowly over:

4 well-beaten eggs

Beat constantly while pouring. Return the mixture to the double boiler. Stir in:

(2 tablespoons sugar)

Heat, stirring constantly, until the eggs thicken and the custard coats a spoon heavily. Place the mixture in a greased baking dish or custard cups. Some people insist this custard should be made and chilled the day before it is caramelized. In any case, chill it well. Cover the custard with:

¼- to ⅓-inch layer of sieved light-brown sugar or maple sugar

Be sure to cover the custard with the sugar to the very edges of the dish. To avoid a mess, place a piece of paper under the dish. Place the custard cups or dish in a shallow pan. If the custard has been chilled for 12 hours, put it in a cold oven. Turn the heat to 250° and heat until the sugar is caramelized. If the custard has been chilled a shorter time, put the dish in a shallow pan. Surround it with ice. Place it under a hot broiler just long enough to let the sugar form a crust. Keep the oven door open, and regularly rotate the dish to even the heating. While the sugar caramelizes, watch carefully, because it may scorch. Serve at once. A delicate garnish is:

A compote of greengage plums and apricots

BRÛLÉE CRUST

Making the brûlée crust in advance, separately, relieves tension and assures a professional look. Cut a piece of aluminum foil the exact size of the dish in which you want to serve the brûlée. Grease the foil on one side with:

Butter

Pat onto the buttered side in a firm, lacy disk pattern about ¼ inch thick:

Brown sugar

Put the sugar-covered foil on a cookie sheet. ➤ At this point the operation needs your entire attention. Put the cookie sheet under broiler heat until the sugar is caramelized or glazed. Remove it from the oven and reverse the foil, with the sugar disks, onto a cake rack to cool. When they are slightly cooled, the foil should peel off, leaving a large praline. Place the praline on the custard just before serving. The crust will disintegrate if put on the custard too soon.

ZABAGLIONE OR SABAYON

6 Servings

Served as sauce, dessert or beverage. Marsala is the classic wine, but Madeira or sherry is also used. If for a sauce, you might even try a good dry white wine and a little Cointreau. For Sabayon Sauce, which can be made in advance and held, see 771. Beat until very light:

8 egg yolks
1 cup confectioners' sugar

Place these ingredients in the top of a double boiler ➤ over—not in—boiling water. Beat the custard constantly with a wire beater. When foamy, add gradually:

½ cup dry Marsala, Madeira or sherry

Continue to beat the custard until it doubles in bulk and begins to thicken. Remove it from the heat. If you want a fluffier result, whip until ➤ stiff, but not dry:

(8 egg whites)

Fold into the custard. Serve the Zabaglione at once in sherbet glasses.

WINE CUSTARD OR WEINSCHAUM

6 Servings

Similar to Sabayon, above, but less sweet. Place in the top of a double boiler ➤ over—not in—boiling water:

2 cups dry white wine
½ cup water

Add:

4 unbeaten eggs
½ cup sugar

Beat these ingredients vigorously with a wire whisk. Cook the custard until it thickens, beating it constantly. Serve hot or cold.

ORANGE CUSTARD WITH MERINGUE

6 Servings

Mix together:

2 tablespoons grated orange rind
⅓ cup sugar

Peel:

6 oranges

Separate the sections and remove the membrane as illustrated on 135. Place sections in a baking dish. Scald:

3 cups milk

Pour over:

3 beaten egg yolks

Beat these ingredients until well blended. Combine the sugar with:

2 tablespoons cornstarch
¼ teaspoon salt

Stir this mixture into the custard. Cook and stir in the top of a double boiler until thick, about 7 minutes. Cool. Pour over the oranges.
Preheat oven to 325°.
Top the custard with:

Meringue Topping I, 730

Bake about 15 minutes. Serve chilled.

ABOUT SPONGE CUSTARDS

From a fan came a drawing of an elaborate mold and the question, "Can you tell me how my great-aunt used to make a dessert that had a spongy bottom and a clear quivery top?" Her aunt's creation must have been a sponge custard baked and unmolded. This batter holds together when put into the baking dish, but magically separates while cooking. If you serve it in the dish, the sponge will form a decorative top. If you prefer a meringue-like quality rather than a spongy one, reserve 1/4 cup sugar to beat slowly into the stiff egg whites before folding them into the egg-yolk mixture.

PINEAPPLE SPONGE CUSTARD

4 Servings

Please read About Sponge Custards, above.
Preheat oven to 350°.
Combine and stir in the order given:

5 tablespoons sugar
3 tablespoons all-purpose flour
1/2 cup pineapple syrup
1 teaspoon grated lemon rind
2 tablespoons lemon juice
2 or 3 beaten egg yolks
1/2 cup milk
1 1/2 tablespoons melted butter

Whip until ➤ stiff, but not dry, then fold in:

2 or 3 egg whites

Place in the bottom of a buttered 7-inch ovenproof dish or in four buttered 3 1/2-inch individual ones:

1 1/4 to 1 1/2 cups drained crushed pineapple

Pour the custard mixture over the fruit. Place the dishes on a rack in a pan in 1 inch of hot water. Bake the custard for about 1 hour for the dish and 45 minutes for the cups. Serve hot or cold.

ORANGE OR LEMON SPONGE CUSTARD

4 to 6 Servings

Please read About Sponge Custards, above.
Preheat oven to 350°.
Cream:

3/4 cup sugar
1 1/2 tablespoons butter
1 tablespoon grated orange rind or 2 teaspoons lemon rind

Add and beat well:

2 or 3 egg yolks

Stir in:

3 tablespoons all-purpose flour

alternately with:

1/3 cup orange juice or 1/4 cup lemon juice
1 cup milk

Beat until ➤ stiff, but not dry:

2 or 3 egg whites

Fold them into the yolk mixture. Place the batter in buttered custard cups or in a buttered 7-inch ovenproof dish. Set on a rack in a pan filled with 1 inch of hot water. Bake about 45 minutes for the cups and about 1 hour for the baking dish, or until set. Serve hot or ice cold with:

(Thick cream or raspberry sauce)

CHOCOLATE CUSTARD OR POTS-DE-CRÈME

Some custard recipes are perfect for use in lidded pots-de-crème like those illustrated in the chapter heading. Although the classic procedure is baking, the consistency is simpler to control by this top-of-the-stove method. ➤ Be sure the eggs are at room temperature.

I. **6 Servings**

Combine and cook in the top of a double boiler, over—not in—boiling water:

2 cups milk or cream, or half milk and half cream
5 to 8 oz. best quality sweet chocolate, grated
(2 tablespoons sugar)

Cook and stir these ingredients until they are blended and the milk scalded. Beat lightly:

6 egg yolks

Before adding the eggs to the above mixture, temper them by stirring in about 1/2 cup of the hot milk mixture. Then stir the eggs into the mixture in the double boiler. Add:

1 teaspoon vanilla or grated rind of 1 orange

Continue to stir until the custard begins to thicken. You may strain the custard. Pour into custard cups. Cool uncovered until steam is out, then cover and refrigerate.

II. Pots-de-Crème Café

4 Servings

Cook and serve as above, using:

1/2 cup whipping cream
1/2 cup sugar
1 tablespoon instant coffee
6 egg yolks
1 tablespoon brandy or lemon zest, 571

III. ⅄ Blender Pots-de-Crème

4 Servings

⅄ Blend together:

3/4 cup semisweet chocolate bits
3/4 cup hot milk

Add when the chocolate is melted:

1 egg

Pour into 4 pot-de-crème cups. Chill 2 to 3 hours and serve garnished with:

(Whipped cream)

FRENCH CHOCOLATE MOUSSE

6 Servings

The director of a boys' camp in Maine recently reported to us the crestfallen faces in the dining room when it turned out that the "moose" promised for evening dessert had emerged from the pages of **Joy** instead of from the woods.
Scald and stir in a saucepan over low heat:

2 cups milk
1/4 cup sugar
3 oz. grated sweet chocolate

Pour part of these ingredients over:

4 beaten egg yolks

Return the sauce to the pan. Stir the custard constantly over low heat until it thickens slightly. Do not overcook. You may strain it. Cool by placing the pan in cold water and then in the refrigerator. In a separate bowl, whip until stiff:

¾ cup whipping cream

Add:

1 teaspoon vanilla

Fold the cold custard into the whipped cream mixture until well blended. Fill custard cups with the mousse. Chill thoroughly before serving, but do not expect it to become firm.

RUM CHOCOLATE MOUSSE

8 to 10 Servings

A phenomenally smooth, rich dessert that is quickly confected. A specialty of our friend Chef Pierre Adrian.

Cook over very low heat until dissolved but not brown in color:

¼ cup sugar

2 to 4 tablespoons rum

Melt in a double boiler:

¼ lb. semisweet or sweet chocolate

When the chocolate is melted, stir in:

2 to 3 tablespoons whipping cream

Add the syrup to the melted chocolate and stir until smooth. When the mixture is cool but not chilled, fold into it:

2 stiffly beaten egg whites

and then fold this combination very gently into:

2 cups whipped cream

Chill in sherbet glasses at least 2 hours before serving.

CHESTNUT MOUND OR MONT BLANC

6 Servings

A typical European recipe needing lots of time.

Boil in water 8 minutes:

2 lb. chestnuts, see 563

Remove shells. Cook the shelled nuts until mealy in a double boiler over—not in—boiling water in:

1 quart milk

Drain, discard milk, then cook the drained chestnuts in a sugar syrup made of:

1 cup water

1 cup sugar

until the syrup is reduced by a third. Add:

(¼ cup Almond Paste, 781)

When partially cool, add:

1 teaspoon vanilla or 2 or more tablespoons brandy, curaçao, etc.

Put the mixture through a ricer. Let it fall lightly onto a large service platter into a mound. If necessary to touch it, try to do so very lightly, so that the chestnuts will not pack. Chill well, and when ready to serve, whip until stiff:

1 cup whipping cream

Fold in:

1 teaspoon vanilla

2 tablespoons sifted confectioners' sugar

Place the cream on the mound and let it overflow onto the sides. You may cover the top of the cream with a grating of:

(Sweet chocolate)

CORNSTARCH CUSTARD PUDDING OR BLANCMANGE

8 Servings

To be really good, this pudding needs loving care. For success, see about cornstarch, 548.

Mix in the top of a double boiler:

½ cup sugar

6 tablespoons cornstarch

¼ teaspoon salt

Gradually add while stirring well:

4 cups milk

Place the mixture ➤ over—not in—boiling water and stir constantly 8 to 12 minutes, at which time it should have begun to thicken. Cover and continue to cook for about 10 minutes more. Stir 1 cup of this thickened mixture slowly into:

2 well-beaten eggs

Return it to the milk mixture and continue to cook 2 minutes, stirring constantly. Do not overcook. The pudding will thicken more as it cools. Remove from heat, and when slightly cooled by gentle stirring to release the steam, add:

1 teaspoon vanilla

Place in prepared molds, 743.

CARAMEL CUSTARD CORNSTARCH PUDDING

8 Servings

➤ Please read about cornstarch, 548.

Heat slightly in the top of a double boiler over direct heat:

3 cups milk

Caramelize as in Caramelized Sugar I, 559:

1 cup sugar

Add it gradually to the warm milk and heat to the boiling point. Gradually pour:

1 cup cold milk

over:

4 tablespoons cornstarch

stirring to make a thin paste. When this is smooth, combine the two mixtures by pouring the hot one ➤ gradually into the cold one and stirring until smooth again. Place in the top of the double boiler ➤ over—not in—boiling water and stir constantly 10 minutes until the mixture begins to thicken. Cover and continue to cook for 10 minutes more. Mix 1 cup of this thickened mixture slowly into:

2 well-beaten eggs

Return to the pan and continue to cook 2 minutes, stirring constantly. Then remove pudding from heat. Stir gently until slightly cooled, then add:

1 teaspoon vanilla

Place in prepared molds, 743.

CHOCOLATE CORNSTARCH PUDDING

4 Servings

➤ Please read about cornstarch, 548.
Melt in the top of a double boiler:

1 oz. unsweetened chocolate

Stir in slowly:

½ cup sugar
1¾ cups milk
⅛ teaspoon salt

Heat these ingredients to the boiling point. Dissolve:

3 tablespoons cornstarch

in:

¼ cup milk

Stir the cornstarch slowly into the hot milk mixture. Cook over boiling water for 10 minutes, stirring constantly. Cover and cook 10 to 12 minutes more. Cool by stirring very gently. Add:

1 teaspoon vanilla

Place in prepared molds, 743. Serve with:

Cream

FRIED CREAM OR CRÈME FRITE

Thirty-six 1½-Inch Squares

➤ Please read about cornstarch, 548.
Place in the top of a double boiler:

A 2-inch piece of vanilla bean
1 cinnamon stick
1½ cups milk

Bring to a boil over direct heat and then cool slightly. Mix in a bowl until smooth:

¼ cup sugar
1 tablespoon all-purpose flour
¼ cup cornstarch
½ cup milk

Remove vanilla bean and cinnamon stick from the slightly cooled milk and stir the smooth cornstarch mixture into the milk. ➤ Cook over—not in—boiling water until it begins to thicken—about 10 minutes. Pour some of this mixture over:

3 beaten egg yolks

Return the egg mixture to the pan and ➤ cook, stirring gently, about 3 minutes. Beat in:

1 tablespoon butter
¼ teaspoon salt

Pour the thickened cream into a 9 x 9-inch buttered pan. Cool. Cut into diamonds or squares about 1½ inches long. Beat:

1 egg

Dust cream with:

Finely crushed bread or cake crumbs

Dip the pieces of cream in the egg, then again in the crumbs. Fry in deep fat heated to 370°. Drain and roll in:

Powdered Vanilla Sugar, 557

Serve at once sprinkled with:

Rum

or with:

A fruit sauce, 769

ABOUT DESSERT SOUFFLÉS

If you have never made soufflés before ➤ please read the directions for making and baking them on 228. ➤ To prepare a dish for a sweet soufflé, use a straight-sided ovenproof baker. Butter it and dust the inside with powdered sugar. Or, as an added touch, caramelize sugar in the base of the soufflé dish as for Crème Caramel, 735.

Some fruit and nut soufflés are very close in texture to omelets and whips, having no binding sauce. For such soufflés, the proper beating of the egg whites and the right baking temperatures are more important than ever. If the egg whites are under- or overbeaten or the baking heat is too high, they have the look and texture of an old leather belt. If mixed and baked with care, these same ingredients produce a delicacy and strength that remind us of dandelion seed puffs just before they blow. Some soufflés, like Apricot Omelette Soufflé, 742, are made on choux-paste base.

If you decide to add liqueurs as a flavoring, allow an extra egg yolk for every 2 tablespoons of liqueur. Otherwise, the mixture will be thinned too much.

To glaze a soufflé, dust it with confectioners' sugar 2 or 3 minutes before it is to come from the oven. The soufflé should have doubled in height and be firm before the glaze is applied. Watch it closely with the oven door partially open. The glaçage will remain fairly shiny when the soufflé is served.

Cold soufflés are based on gelatins and resemble mousses or Bavarians, 746.

Note carefully the size of the baking dish indicated, as this affects the lightness and volume of the result. A 7-inch dish should serve 3 to 4; a 10-inch dish, 8 to 10.

VANILLA SOUFFLÉ

A 9-Inch Soufflé Dish

➤ Please read About Dessert Soufflés, above, to prepare a soufflé baker.

This soufflé has a versatile wardrobe and many aliases. You may add a very few drops of oil of anise or a few marrons glacés; or you may replace the sugar with ⅓ to ½ cup of syrup from preserved ginger; also, add about ¼ cup very finely chopped candied fruits that have been soaked in Danziger Goldwasser or kirsch. In the latter guise, it is called **Soufflé Rothschild.** Sift before measuring:

½ cup all-purpose flour

Resift with:

¼ cup sugar
¼ teaspoon salt

Stir in until smooth:

½ cup cold milk

Scald:

2 cups milk

with:

A vanilla bean

Remove the bean and stir in the flour mixture with

a wire whisk. Cook and stir these ingredients over low heat until they thicken. Remove from the heat. Stir in:

¼ cup butter
4 to 5 beaten egg yolks

You may add:

(¾ cup chopped nutmeats)

Cool the mixture.
Preheat oven to 350°.
Whip until ➤ stiff, but not dry:

5 egg whites

Fold them lightly into the batter. Bake soufflé about 25 minutes. Serve with:

A fruit sauce, a rum-flavored sauce, or Maple Syrup Sauce, 773

SOUFFLÉ GRAND MARNIER

An 8-Inch Soufflé Dish

➤ Please read About Dessert Soufflés, 739, to prepare a soufflé baking dish.
Preheat oven to 400°.
Beat in a double boiler over boiling water:

8 lightly beaten egg yolks
⅔ cup sugar

Continue to beat until the mixture forms a broad ribbon as it runs from a lifted spoon. Add:

½ cup Grand Marnier liqueur

To arrest the cooking, transfer the mixture to a bowl and beat it over ice until cooled. Beat until foamy:

10 egg whites

Add:

¼ teaspoon cream of tartar

Continue to beat until ➤ stiff, but not dry. Fold the egg yolk mixture into the whites, see illustration, 665. Mound the mixture in a soufflé dish. Bake 12 to 15 minutes, until firm, and serve at once.

PINEAPPLE SOUFFLÉ

A 7-Inch Soufflé Dish

➤ Please read About Dessert Soufflés, 739, to prepare a soufflé baking dish.
Melt over low heat:

3 tablespoons butter

Stir in:

3 tablespoons all-purpose flour

When blended, stir in:

1 cup drained crushed pineapple

Cook until thick; cool slightly and stir in:

⅔ cup crushed dry macaroons
3 beaten egg yolks

Heat again until the yolks thicken slightly. Cool the mixture.
Preheat oven to 325°.
Beat until ➤ stiff, but not dry:

3 to 4 egg whites

Beat in gradually:

2 tablespoons sugar
½ teaspoon vanilla

Fold this into the soufflé mixture. Bake in a soufflé dish about 30 minutes or until firm.

CHOCOLATE SOUFFLÉ

A 9-Inch Soufflé Dish

➤ Please read About Dessert Soufflés, 739, to prepare a soufflé baking dish.
Melt:

2 tablespoons butter

Stir in until blended:

1 tablespoon all-purpose flour

In a separate saucepan, heat but do not boil:

1 cup milk
1 oz. unsweetened chocolate, cut into pieces
⅓ cup sugar

Slowly add the hot milk mixture to the flour mixture, stirring constantly until well blended. Beat until light:

3 egg yolks

Beat part of the sauce into the yolks, then add the yolk mixture to the rest of the sauce and stir the custard over very low heat until the yolks thicken slightly. Cool the custard well.
Preheat oven to 350°.
Add to the cooled chocolate mixture:

1 teaspoon vanilla

Whip until ➤ stiff, but not dry:

3 egg whites

Fold them lightly into the cooled chocolate mixture. Bake in a soufflé dish set in a pan of hot water about 20 minutes or until firm. Serve at once with:

Cream; Vanilla Sauce, 774; Foamy Sauce, 775; or Weinschaum Sauce, 771

LEMON SOUFFLÉ

An 8-Inch Soufflé Dish

➤ Please read About Dessert Soufflés, 739, to prepare a soufflé baking dish.
Preheat oven to 350°.
Sift:

¾ cup sugar

Beat until very light:

5 egg yolks

Add the sugar gradually. Beat constantly until the eggs are creamy. Add:

1 teaspoon grated lemon rind
¼ cup lemon juice
(½ cup chopped nutmeats)

Whip until ➤ stiff, but not dry:

5 egg whites

Fold them lightly into the yolk mixture. Bake in an ovenproof dish set in a pan of ➤ hot, but not boiling, water about 35 minutes, or until firm. Serve at once with:

Cream

FRESH FRUIT SOUFFLÉ

A 7-Inch Soufflé Baker

➤ Please read About Dessert Soufflés, 739, to prepare a soufflé baker.
Preheat oven to 350°.
Prepare by peeling and mashing ripe fruits to make:

1 cup sweetened fruit pulp: fresh apricots, nectarines, peaches, plums, raspberries or strawberries

Add:

1½ tablespoons lemon juice
4 beaten egg yolks
⅛ teaspoon salt
(1 tablespoon grated orange rind)

Beat until ➤ stiff, but not dry, and fold in:

4 egg whites

Bake the soufflé in a dish set in a pan of ➤ hot, but not boiling, water about 30 minutes or until it is firm. Serve hot with:

Cream

PRUNE OR APRICOT SOUFFLÉ OR WHIP

A 9-Inch Soufflé Baker

➤ Please read About Dessert Soufflés, 739, to prepare a soufflé baker.

Preheat oven to 350°.

Have ready:

1 cup sweetened, thick cooked prune or apricot purée

Whip until ➤ stiff, but not dry:

5 egg whites

Add:

¼ teaspoon cream of tartar

Fold in the prune or apricot pulp and:

(½ cup broken nutmeats)
(1 teaspoon grated lemon rind)

Bake the soufflé in a baking dish set in a pan of ➤ hot, but not boiling, water. Bake about 1 hour or until firm. Serve hot with:

Cream or Custard Sauce, 771

HAZELNUT SOUFFLÉ

An 8-Inch Soufflé Baker

➤ Please read About Dessert Soufflés, 739, to prepare a soufflé baker.

Preheat oven to 350°.

Put through a nut grinder:

¾ cup hazelnuts

Heat to just below the boiling point and pour over the nuts:

1 cup milk

Beat until light:

3 egg yolks

Beat in gradually:

3 tablespoons sugar
3 tablespoons all-purpose flour
⅛ teaspoon salt

Stir a small quantity of the hot mixture into the eggs, then return this combination to the rest of the hot mixture. Stir and cook these ingredients over low heat to let the yolks thicken slightly. Stir in:

3 tablespoons butter

Cool. Beat in:

½ teaspoon vanilla or 1 tablespoon rum

Beat until ➤ stiff, but not dry:

3 egg whites

Fold them into the cooled custard. Bake in a soufflé dish about 30 minutes or until firm. Serve hot with:

1 cup whipped cream

flavored with:

Caramel or coffee

NUT SOUFFLÉ

A 12-Inch Soufflé Baker

➤ Please read About Dessert Soufflés, 739, to prepare a soufflé baker.

Preheat oven to 350°.

Sift:

1 cup confectioners' sugar

Beat until very light:

8 egg yolks

Add the sugar gradually. Beat constantly until the yolks are creamy. Fold in:

2 teaspoons grated lemon rind or
1 teaspoon vanilla
½ lb. ground blanched almonds or walnuts

Whip until ➤ stiff, but not dry:

8 egg whites

Fold them lightly into the yolk mixture. Bake the soufflé in a baking dish set in a pan of ➤ hot, but not boiling, water. Bake until firm, about 45 minutes. Serve with:

Sabayon Sauce, 771, or a fruit sauce, 769

SOUR CREAM APPLE CAKE SOUFFLÉ COCKAIGNE

A 12 x 17-Inch Pan or Ten 4-Inch Round Baking Dishes

The specialty of our great-grandmother, who came from Lübeck. It was once served to us in a pie crust, as a renowned confection of Lyons. We feel the pie shell makes an attractive container. However, the crust does not greatly improve the flavor.

Prepare:

5 to 6 cups pared, cored and sliced tart apples

Melt in a large heavy skillet:

¼ cup butter

Add the apples and cook them uncovered over medium heat, stirring them often until they are tender. Do not let them brown. Combine and pour over the apples:

½ cup cultured sour cream
Grated rind and juice of 1 lemon
1 cup sugar, scant unless apples are very tart
2 tablespoons all-purpose flour
8 beaten egg yolks
(½ cup shredded blanched almonds)

Stir these ingredients over low heat until they thicken. Cool the mixture. Preheat oven to 325°.

Whip until ➤ stiff, but not dry:

8 egg whites

Fold them lightly into the apple mixture. Spread the mixture to a thickness of 1 inch in a large pan or ovenproof dish. Sprinkle the top with a combination of:

¼ cup sugar
1 tablespoon cinnamon
¼ cup dry bread crumbs
¼ cup shredded blanched almonds

Bake about 45 minutes or until firm. The cake may be served hot, but it is best very cold, covered with:

Whipped cream flavored with vanilla, or with Angelica Parfait, 762

OMELETTE AUX CONFITURES

2 Servings

To prepare, please read about French Omelette, 226.

Beat until light:

2 egg yolks

Beat in gradually:

¼ cup confectioners' sugar

Add:

½ teaspoon vanilla or a grating of orange or lemon rind

Whip until ➤ stiff, but not dry:

4 egg whites

Fold them lightly into the yolk mixture.

Melt in a skillet:

2 tablespoons butter

When the butter is very hot, pour in the omelet mixture. To cook and fold, see 226. When done, sprinkle with:

Confectioners' sugar

Serve with:

Preserves or jelly

or fold the omelet and spread with:

Applesauce, prune or apricot pulp, drained canned fruit or sugared berries

BAKED ALASKA

12 Servings

This tour de force speaks several languages and always seems gala. It needs last-minute preparation to be *à point*—the meringue glazed and delicately colored, the ice cream firm, the cake not soggy—in other words, "Just right!" There are individual or large pans, and also ovenproof dishes, shown 769, made especially for this dessert. Or you may also build a similar "cake case" on an oval heatproof dish.

Preheat broiler.

Line the dish with a half-inch layer of:

Génoise, 675, or sponge or angel cake

Three-day-old cake dry enough to absorb any liquid from the ice cream is suggested. You may sprinkle it lightly with:

(Brandy)

Have ready:

¾-inch thick pieces of Génoise, sponge or angel cake to cover the ice cream later

Make a meringue as follows. Beat until frothy:

6 egg whites

Add and beat until almost stiff:

½ teaspoon cream of tartar
¼ teaspoon salt

Beat in, a tablespoon at a time:

¾ cup superfine sugar

Continue to beat and add:

1 teaspoon vanilla

When the meringue is stiff, quickly form on the cake base an oval mound made of:

1½ quarts ice cream

➤ softened just enough so that you can shape it. Cover this melon-mold shape with the cut strips of cake. Cover it at once with the meringue, so the cake surface is entirely coated to at least a three-fourths-inch thickness. Bring the meringue right down to the dish surface. You may use some of the meringue in a pastry bag to pipe on fluted edges and patterns. Accent them with:

(Candied fruit)

Run this meringue-covered confection under a 500° broiler—not more than 3 minutes—to brown. Watch it very closely! Serve at once.

You may like to try out this baked meringue covering by using orange cups instead of cake as a base to hold the ice cream. Bring the meringue well down over the edge of the orange cup.

NORWEGIAN OMELET OR OMELETTE SOUFFLÉE SURPRISE

An unusual meringue because it includes egg yolks. This is another version of Baked Alaska. Prepare the cake and ice cream as directed above, but make the meringue as follows. Beat:

4 egg yolks

Beat in:

¼ cup sugar
½ teaspoon grated lemon rind

Whip until ➤ stiff, but not dry, and fold in:

6 egg whites

Continue as directed for Baked Alaska, above.

APRICOT OMELETTE SOUFFLÉE

6 Servings

Two 9-Inch Round Pans with Removable Rims

Blend together in the top of a double boiler and heat ➤ over—not in—boiling water until the mass leaves the sides of the pan:

¼ cup butter
1 cup all-purpose flour
1 tablespoon sugar
1¼ cups cream
¾ cup milk

Cool the mixture. Preheat oven to 325°. Add one at a time, beating after each addition:

6 egg yolks
1 teaspoon vanilla

Beat until ➤ stiff, but not dry, and fold in:

6 egg whites

Pour the omelette mixture into the pans and bake 25 to 30 minutes. While baking, heat in the top of a double boiler:

1½ cups apricot jam

Have ready a heated serving dish on which to reverse one of the omelette layers. Cover it lightly with the jam. Reverse the second layer over it. Cover second layer with jam and serve at once with:

(Whipped cream)

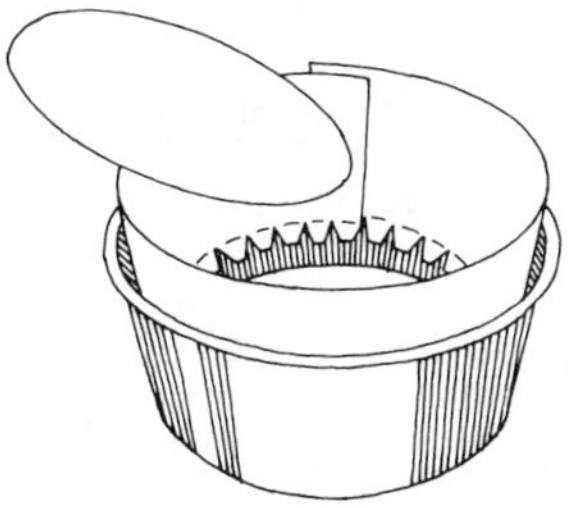

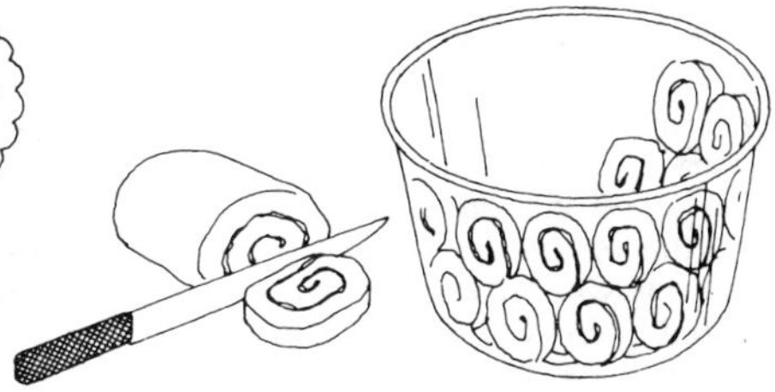

ABOUT DESSERT MOLDS

Almost any bowl that splays out is suitable for a pudding mold. Be sure the slanted sides allow molded ingredients to slide out easily when the mold is inverted. For straight-sided desserts, use spring forms, shown on 684. One of the favorite shapes for Bavarians is the melon mold. To prepare the mold, rinse it out with cold water.

Dessert molds are often cake-lined. To make a pudding mold from a cake itself, see description below and illustration above. If the mold is deep and the pudding or cake surface very tender, always use a paper lining as a safety measure, see above. First cut a piece of paper for the base. Then, for the sides, notch the bottom and fold in at the base line. The simplest cake linings are made with thin sheets of Génoise, 675, or large areas cut from Jelly Rolls, 690, while they are still flat, before filling. Shown on the right is a mold lined with filled jelly roll slices. Macaroons and cookies can also be used in this pattern. In the center, you see ladyfingers, either whole or split, forming the mold. If they are split, be sure to put the curved sides against the form. To make an even top, slice each section to a point by cutting it diagonally, as shown, and placing it with the pointed end toward the middle, until the base of the mold is filled. You may want to cut a small round for the very center.

If the ladyfingers are sparsely sprinkled with a liqueur or a fruit juice after placing, they will soften enough to fill any crevices. If moistened too much, they will disintegrate.

For fillings in such molds, see suggestions on 696. Whatever fillings you choose, be sure to ➤ refrigerate them, preferably 12 hours, before unmolding. Garnish the molded food with flavored creams, sauces or fruit and serve at once.

ABOUT CARAMEL-COATED MOLDS

I. Sprinkle the bottom of a mold with:

Sugar

Heat it in a slow—250° to 300°—oven or over low heat until the sugar is brown and bubbling. This is a simple method to be used if only the top of the custard or pudding is to be caramelized when the mold is reversed.

II. Spread the mold with:

Caramelized Sugar I, 559

before the syrup hardens. If necessary, spread the caramel around with a wooden spoon to coat the sides. Let the caramel harden before adding the filling.

SEMISWEET CHOCOLATE CASES

6 Servings

Melt in the top of a double boiler over hot, not boiling, water:

6 squares semisweet chocolate
1 tablespoon butter

When melted, beat thoroughly. Swirl the mixture into the insides of crinkled paper baking cups. Place cups in muffin tins and chill to allow the chocolate to harden. To serve, carefully remove the paper and fill the chocolate cases with:

Ice Cream or Custard, 734

ABOUT GELATIN PUDDINGS

➤ For details about handling gelatin, see About Gelatin, 560. These desserts vary greatly in texture. Easiest to prepare are the clear jellies, to which you may add fruit and nuts. If you add puréed fruits, you lose clarity at once, and the dessert bears some similarity to a mousse. When gelatins are allowed to set partially until slightly thicker than unbeaten egg whites, and are then beaten or combined with egg whites, they are known as **whips, sponges** or **snows.** Whipped gelatins double in volume; snows and sponges, which include egg white, may triple. We also indicate in Molded Custard, 745, a method whereby you can get a jellied effect in the bottom of the mold and a custard on top.

For very rich gelatin puddings, see Bavarians, 746. For both Bavarians and clear fruit gelatins, you may line the mold with macaroons. Sprinkle them lightly with fruit juice, rum or cordial before adding the pudding or gelatin.

A word of caution: gelatin puddings with uncooked egg whites are often served to children or invalids over protracted periods of time. Since it has been discovered that biotin deficiency is occasionally induced by overproportionate quantities of raw egg white, we suggest varying such diets. Substitute instead some of the puddings we describe in which the egg whites are cooked like meringues.

To get a snow or whip texture, begin as for clear gelatin. Chill to a syrupy consistency. Using an electric mixer, a rotary beater or a ⅄ blender, mix in a ➤ cold bowl or over ice. ➤ If the gelatin is not sufficiently chilled before whipping or before adding the egg white, it may revert to a clear jelly. Gelatins without cream or eggs ➤ must be refrigerated, but cannot be frozen. But Bavarians, mousses and ice creams, rich in cream and eggs, with gelatin as a stabilizer, may be solidified and stored in the freezer ➤ for not longer than 3 or 4 days. The use of gelatin in these puddings prevents the formation of coarse crystals and produces a lovely smooth texture.

LEMON GELATIN

4 Servings

Soak:

1 tablespoon gelatin

in:

¼ cup cold water

Dissolve it in:

1½ cups boiling water

Add and stir until dissolved:

¾ cup sugar
¼ teaspoon salt

Add:

½ cup lemon juice
(1 teaspoon grated lemon rind)

Pour the jelly into a wet mold. ➤ Chill 4 hours or more. Serve with:

Cream or Custard Sauce, 771

ORANGE GELATIN

4 Servings

Soak:

1 tablespoon gelatin

in:

¼ cup cold water

Dissolve it in:

½ cup boiling water

Add and stir until dissolved:

½ cup sugar
¼ teaspoon salt

Add:

6 tablespoons lemon juice
1½ cups orange juice
(1½ teaspoons grated orange rind)

Pour jelly into a wet mold. Chill 4 hours or more. Unmold and serve with:

Cream or Custard Sauce, 771

FRUIT MOLDED INTO LEMON OR ORANGE GELATIN

Prepare:

Lemon or Orange Gelatin, above

➤ Chill it until nearly set. It will fall in sheets from a spoon. Combine it with well-drained:

Cooked or raw fruit

➤ Fresh pineapple must be poached before it is added to any gelatin mixture. Add:

(Nutmeats)
(Marshmallows cut into quarters)

➤ Do not use more than 2 cupfuls of solids in all. Pour jelly into a wet mold and ➤ chill 4 hours or more before serving.

PINEAPPLE GELATIN

8 Servings

➤ Note that fresh pineapple must be poached before it is added to any gelatin. Soak:

2 tablespoons gelatin

in:

1 cup cold water

Dissolve it in:

1½ cups boiling pineapple juice

Add:

1 cup boiling water

Add and stir until dissolved:

¾ cup sugar
⅛ teaspoon salt

➤ Chill the gelatin until it is about to set. It will fall in sheets from a spoon. Add:

2½ cups canned, drained crushed pineapple
3 tablespoons lemon juice

Pour the jelly into a wet mold. ➤ Chill 4 hours or more. Unmold and serve with:

Cream or Custard Sauce, 771

FRUIT JUICE GELATIN

4 Servings

Soak:

1 tablespoon gelatin

in:

¼ cup cold water

Dissolve it in:

¾ cup boiling water

Add:

1 cup sweetened fruit juice: prune, apricot, peach or cooked pineapple
(2 tablespoons lemon juice)

and if not sweet enough, add:

Sugar

When gelatin is ➤ about to set, it will fall in sheets from the spoon. Add:

Drained diced fruit

Pour jelly into a wet mold and chill for 4 hours or more before serving.

QUICK FRUIT GELATIN

4 Servings

Dissolve:

1 package fruit-flavored gelatin

in:

1 cup boiling water

Chill rapidly by adding any but pineapple:

1 can frozen fruit juice: 6 oz.

Pour jelly into sherbet glasses. Chill further until firm.

MOCHA GELATIN

4 Servings

The subtle flavor of this gelatin comes from coffee combined with a syrup from canned fruit. Dress it up if you want with nuts or cream, but we like it served simply with a light custard sauce.
Prepare:

Fruit Juice Gelatin, above

substituting for the water:

1 cup very hot double-strength coffee

Omit the lemon juice. Serve with;

Custard Sauce, 771

WINE GELATIN

8 Servings

The proportions of water, fruit juice and wine may be varied. If the wine is not strong, use less water to dissolve the gelatin and increase the amount of wine accordingly. This makes a soft jelly of a very good consistency, suitable for serving in sherbet glasses or from a bowl. If a stiff jelly is desired for molds, increase the gelatin to 3 tablespoons.
Soak:

2 tablespoons gelatin

in:

¼ cup cold water

Dissolve it in:

¾ cup boiling water

Stir in until dissolved:

½ cup or more sugar

It is difficult to give an accurate sugar measurement. One-half cup is sufficient if both the orange juice and the wine are sweet. Taste the combined ingredients and stir in additional sugar if needed. Cool these ingredients. Add:

1¾ cups orange juice
6 tablespoons lemon juice
1 cup well-flavored wine

Pour the jelly into sherbet glasses. Chill until firm. Serve with:

Cream, whipped cream, or Custard Sauce, 771

BLANCMANGE

8 Servings

Blancmange, in America, is often a cornstarch pudding, see 738, but the true French type is made with almond milk and gelatin.
To prepare **Almond Milk,** pound in a mortar to extract as much flavor as possible from the almonds:

½ lb. blanched almonds

adding gradually:

¼ cup water
½ cup milk

Strain the liquid through a cloth. Soak:

1 tablespoon gelatin

in:

¼ cup water

Heat until scalded:

1 cup cream
½ cup sugar

Dissolve the gelatin in the hot cream mixture. Stir in the almond milk. Add:

1 tablespoon kirsch

➤ Chill it about 4 hours. Serve the pudding in sherbet cups with:

Fresh or stewed fruit

PERSIAN CREAM

6 Servings

Soak:

1 tablespoon gelatin

in:

¼ cup cold milk

Scald:

1½ cups milk

Dissolve the gelatin in it. Beat:

2 egg yolks
⅓ cup sugar

Beat a little of the hot milk into the yolks, then return to saucepan. Cook and stir these ingredients over ➤ very low heat until they begin to thicken. Cool. Add:

1 teaspoon vanilla or rum

Whip until ➤ stiff, but not dry:

2 egg whites

Fold them lightly into the gelatin mixture. Chill for 4 hours or more. Serve very cold with:

Crushed fruit or fruit sauce

MOLDED CUSTARD

8 Servings

Place in the top of a double boiler ➤ over—not in—boiling water:

3 cups milk

Sprinkle over it:

1 tablespoon gelatin
½ cup sugar

Stir until ingredients are dissolved. Beat:

3 egg yolks
¼ teaspoon salt

Pour a small quantity of the hot milk over the eggs to temper them, then add this mixture to the rest of the milk. Cook until thickened somewhat, stirring constantly. Remove from heat and add:

1 teaspoon vanilla

At this point decide if you want a molded custard all of one texture or if you prefer a clear jellied base with an opaque layer at the top of the mold. To get a mold of uniform texture, add while the gelatin mixture is hot:

3 stiffly beaten egg whites

If you prefer the clear jellied base and opaque top, cool the gelatin mixture slightly before adding the stiffly beaten whites. In either case, turn the mixture into a large mold or individual molds that have been rinsed in cold water. When set, unmold and serve with:

A fruit sauce

FRUIT WHIPS

6 to 8 Servings

➤ Please read About Gelatin Puddings, 743. Oranges, raspberries, peaches, strawberries, apricots, prunes, etc.—raw or cooked—may be used alone

or in combination. ➤ If fresh pineapple is preferred, it must be poached before being added to any gelatin mixture.
Stir:
1 teaspoon grated lemon rind
into:
⅞ cup sugar
Soak, according to the juiciness of the fruit:
2½ teaspoons to 1 tablespoon gelatin
in:
¼ cup cold water
Dissolve it in:
¼ cup boiling water
Stir in the sugar until dissolved. Add:
3 tablespoons lemon juice
1 cup crushed or ⅄ blended fruit
Place the pan holding these ingredients in ice water. When they are chilled ➤ to a syrupy consistency, whip them with an eggbeater until frothy. Whip until stiff:
4 egg whites
Whip these ingredients into the gelatin mixture until the jelly holds its shape. Pour it into a wet mold. ➤ Chill 4 hours or more. Serve with:
Cream or Custard Sauce, 771

⅄ BLENDER FRUIT WHIP

4 Servings

Cut into 16 pieces the contents of:
1 package frozen fruit: 10 oz.
Put into an electric blender:
1 tablespoon gelatin
2 tablespoons lemon juice
½ cup boiling water
Cover and blend for 40 seconds. Add:
2 unbeaten egg whites
Cover and blend 10 seconds. Continuing to blend, uncover the container and drop in, a few at a time, the pieces of still frozen fruit until they are all mixed in. Pour into a wet mold and chill 4 hours or more.

MARSHMALLOW PUDDING

6 to 8 Servings

Although this pudding calls for no marshmallows, the consistency is similar.
Sift:
1 cup sugar
Soak:
1½ tablespoons gelatin
in:
½ cup cold water
Dissolve it in:
½ cup boiling water
Cool these ingredients. Whip until stiff:
4 egg whites
Add the gelatin to the egg whites in a slow stream, whipping the pudding constantly. Add the sugar, ½ cupful at a time. Whip well after each addition. Add:
1 teaspoon vanilla
Continue to whip until the pudding thickens. ➤ Chill 4 hours or more. Serve with:
Custard Sauce, 771
Flavor the custard when it is cold with:
Cointreau, rum or sherry
or serve the pudding with:
Crushed sweetened fruit

★ PINEAPPLE SNOW

8 Servings

A refreshing Christmas pudding.
Soak:
1 tablespoon gelatin
in:
¼ cup cold water
Heat:
2 cups canned crushed pineapple
➤ If fresh pineapple is used, be sure it is poached before adding it to the gelatin mixture. Stir in:
1 cup sugar
⅛ teaspoon salt
When these ingredients are boiling, add the soaked gelatin. Remove pan from heat and stir until the gelatin is dissolved. ➤ Chill until it is about to set. Whip until stiff:
1 cup whipping cream
Add:
½ teaspoon vanilla
Fold in the pineapple mixture. Place pudding in a wet mold. Chill 4 hours or longer. Unmold and serve with:
(Maraschino cherries)

ABOUT BAVARIAN CREAMS

You can count on finding eggs combined with gelatin and cream as ingredients in a classic Bavarian. The additions of egg and cream are made when the gelatin mixture mounds slightly if dropped from a spoon. They are then chilled until firm. ➤ If Bavarian puddings are to be unmolded, chill them 12 hours or more. If served in sherbet glasses, chill 4 hours. Bavarians are often called "Cold Soufflés." If very heavy in egg and cream content, they may be frozen for a few days. They are frequently heightened by a collar or band of paper tied around the outside of the dish in which the soufflé is to be served, and extending a few inches above it. Remove the collar just before serving.

CABINET PUDDING OR BAVARIAN DE LUXE

10 Servings

Whose Cabinet? Cabinet de Diplomate. Where else could you find anything so smooth and suave?
Heat in the top of a double boiler ➤ over—not in—boiling water, until lukewarm:
5 eggs
Beat at medium speed for 7 minutes; then beat in:
¼ cup sugar
until a mayonnaise consistency is reached. Beat in an additional:
¼ cup sugar

➤ but do not overbeat or overheat. The somewhat thickened eggs should stand in soft peaks. Dissolve over hot water:

1½ tablespoons gelatin
¼ cup cold water

Fold the cooled gelatin very gently into the egg mixture. Chill the mixture, while you beat over a bowl of ice until stiff:

2 cups whipping cream

➤ Do not overbeat the cream. Let it still have a glistening finish when you combine it with the egg mixture. Dribble onto it:

2 teaspoons vanilla or 1 tablespoon kirsch or Grand Marnier

You may fold into it:

(⅓ cup preserved ginger or ½ cup sliced candied kumquats)

Chill this mixture until it is like heavy cream. Line a mold with:

Ladyfingers, 695

Build layers of rum- or lemon-sprinkled fruits and berries with ladyfinger crumbs, alternating with the Bavarian mixture. Repeat these layers until the mold is complete, with ladyfingers on top. ➤ Refrigerate about 12 hours before unmolding.

NESSELRODE PUDDING

Prepare:

Cabinet Pudding, above

You may use the fruits or not, as you like. Fold into it, after putting through a ricer:

2 cups slightly sweetened Boiled Chestnuts II, 299
5 oz. crumbled Glazed Chestnuts, 796

Serve it garnished with:

Crème Chantilly, 696

BAVARIAN BERRY CREAM

8 Servings

Crush:

1 quart hulled strawberries or raspberries

Add:

1 cup sugar

Let them stand 30 minutes. Soak:

2 teaspoons gelatin

in:

3 tablespoons water

Dissolve it in:

3 tablespoons boiling water

Stir this into the berries. You may add:

(1 tablespoon lemon juice)

Cool the gelatin. When it is about to set, whip and fold in lightly:

1 cup whipping cream

Pour the Bavarian cream into a wet mold. ➤ Chill for 12 hours if you plan to unmold it. Serve with:

Strawberry or Fruit Glaze, 732

HAZELNUT BAVARIAN CREAM

8 Servings

Soak:

1 tablespoon gelatin

in:

2 tablespoons cold water

Scald:

½ cup milk

Beat together:

¼ cup sugar
4 egg yolks
⅛ teaspoon salt

Combine the milk with the egg mixture ➤ by first pouring a little of the hot milk over the mixture and adding the rest gradually. Stir ➤ over—not in—boiling water until the ingredients begin to thicken. Stir in the soaked gelatin until dissolved. Grind and add:

¾ cup hazelnuts

Add:

1 teaspoon vanilla

Chill these ingredients until they are about to set. Whip until stiff:

1 cup whipping cream

Fold into the other ingredients. Place the pudding in the dish from which it is to be served, or in a wet mold. Chill thoroughly if you plan to unmold it—12 hours or more. Serve with:

Raspberry syrup

CARAMEL OR MAPLE BAVARIAN CREAM

8 Servings

Soak:

1 tablespoon gelatin

in:

¼ cup water

Prepare:

¾ cup Caramelized Sugar I, 559, or ½ cup maple syrup

When the sugar is slightly cooled, put it or the maple syrup in the top of a double boiler with:

1 cup hot milk
¼ cup sugar
¼ teaspoon salt

Stir over boiling water until these ingredients are dissolved. Pour part of this over:

3 beaten egg yolks

Return the sweetened yolks to the double boiler. Stir and cook the mixture over boiling water until it coats a spoon heavily. Stir in the soaked gelatin until it is dissolved. Cool the custard. Add:

1 teaspoon vanilla or 1 tablespoon rum

Whip and fold in:

1 cup whipping cream

Place the Bavarian in a wet mold. Chill at least 12 hours if you plan to unmold it.

CHOCOLATE OR COFFEE BAVARIAN

Add to any of the Bavarians calling for scalded milk:

2 oz. melted sweet chocolate and/or 2 teaspoons instant coffee

EGGLESS BAVARIAN CREAM

8 Servings

Not classic, but pleasant, and it will lend itself to all the variations in the previous recipes.
Soak:

1 tablespoon gelatin

in:

2 tablespoons cold water

Scald:

1½ cups milk

If a richer pudding is preferred, use instead ½ cup milk and 1 cup whipping cream. Add:

⅓ to ½ cup sugar
¼ teaspoon salt

Stir the gelatin into this mixture until dissolved. Chill. As it thickens, flavor it with:

1½ teaspoons vanilla
(¼ teaspoon almond extract)

Whip it with a wire whisk until fluffy. Beat until stiff:

1 cup whipping cream

Fold into gelatin mixture. Place pudding in a wet mold. If desired, alternate the pudding mixture in layers with:

6 broken macaroons or ladyfingers soaked in rum or dry sherry and
½ cup ground nutmeats, preferably almonds

➤ Chill the pudding at least 12 hours if you plan to unmold it. Serve with:

Whole or crushed berries or stewed fruit and whipped cream

RENNET PUDDING OR JUNKET

4 Servings

➤ Please read about rennet, 561, before making this favorite English dessert.
Put into the bowl in which the pudding will be served:

2 cups milk

warmed to exactly 98°. Add:

2 teaspoons sugar

Stir in:

2 teaspoons essence of rennet or 1 teaspoon prepared rennet
(2 teaspoons brandy)

Let the pudding stand about 1½ hours until it coagulates. Sprinkle with:

Cinnamon or nutmeg

Serve cold.

MOLDED PINEAPPLE CREAM

4 Servings

Soak:

1 tablespoon gelatin

in:

¼ cup cold water

Combine and stir constantly over very low heat until slightly thickened:

2 egg yolks
½ cup sugar
2 cups unsweetened cooked pineapple juice
⅛ teaspoon salt

Add the soaked gelatin. Stir until dissolved. Pour half of this mixture into a wet mold. Chill it. Chill the remaining gelatin until it begins to set. Then whip and fold in:

½ cup whipping cream

Fill the mold. Chill until firm.

ABOUT CHARLOTTES

How dull seem the charlottes of our youth, with only a cream and a cherry, when compared with those put together in the sophisticated society we now seem to frequent!

Today's fillings include all kinds of creams and Bavarians, nuts, angelica, citron, jams, chestnuts, fruits and ices. Whether the mold is lined with ladyfingers, sponge or Génoise, it may still be called a charlotte. For combinations, see below.

CHARLOTTE RUSSE

6 Servings

Soak:

¾ tablespoon gelatin

in:

¼ cup cold water

Dissolve it in:

⅓ cup scalded milk

Beat in:

⅓ cup powdered sugar

Cool. Flavor with:

2 tablespoons strong coffee

Whip until stiff:

1 cup whipping cream

Fold it lightly into the chilled ingredients. Line a mold with:

Ladyfingers, 695

Pour the pudding into it. Chill thoroughly. Unmold and serve with:

Custard Sauce, 771, flavored with rum

CHOCOLATE CHARLOTTE

Prepare:

French Chocolate Mousse, 737 or Rum Chocolate Mousse, 738

adding:

(¾ cup ground nut meats)

Line a mold as described in About Dessert Molds, 743. Fill the ladyfinger-lined mold with the mousse.

MAPLE CHARLOTTE

10 Servings

Soak:

1 tablespoon gelatin

in:

¼ cup cold water

Dissolve it in:

¾ cup hot maple syrup

Chill until it falls in heavy sheets from a spoon. Whip until the cream holds soft peaks:

2 cups whipping cream

Fold in with a spoon:

(½ cup chopped, blanched almonds)

Fold in the gelatin until well blended. Line a bowl with pieces of:

Sponge Cake, 670, or Ladyfingers, 695

Pour the gelatin into it. Chill until firm. Unmold and serve garnished with:

Whipped cream

MOCHA MARSHMALLOW CREAM

6 Servings

Melt in the top of a double boiler ➤ over—not in—boiling water:

1 lb. diced marshmallows
2 oz. unsweetened chocolate
1 tablespoon sugar

in:

1 cup double-strength coffee

Stir and cook these ingredients until the marshmallows are dissolved. Chill the mixture until it is about to set. Whip and fold in:

1 cup whipping cream

Place in a wet ring mold. Chill at least 4 hours. Invert and cover the top of the cream with:

Slivered toasted Brazil nuts or crushed nut brittle

INDIAN PUDDING

8 Servings

This dish is sometimes made with apples. In that case, add 2 cups thinly sliced apples and use, in all, 2 cups milk.

Preheat oven to 300°.

Boil in the top of a double boiler over direct heat:

4 cups milk

Stir in:

⅓ cup cornmeal

Place these ingredients over boiling water. Cook them for about 15 minutes. Stir into them and cook for about 5 minutes:

¾ cup dark molasses

Remove from heat. Stir in:

¼ cup butter
1 teaspoon salt
1 teaspoon ginger
3 tablespoons sugar
(1 well-beaten egg)
(½ cup raisins)
(½ teaspoon cinnamon)

Pour into a well-greased baking dish. To achieve a soft center, after 1 hour of baking, float over the top without stirring:

(1 cup cold milk)

Bake the pudding from 1½ to 3 hours, the latter if you added milk. Serve pudding hot with:

Hard Sauce, 775, cream or ice cream

FARINA PUDDING

6 Servings

Try this for a finicky breakfaster.

Boil:

2 cups milk
¼ cup sugar

Add:

½ cup farina

Stir and cook the farina over low heat until thick. Add and stir until melted:

1 tablespoon butter

Remove pan from heat. Beat in, one at a time:

2 egg yolks

Cool. Add:

1 teaspoon vanilla
(½ teaspoon grated lemon rind)

Whip until ➤ stiff, but not dry:

(2 egg whites)

Fold into the farina mixture. If used as a dessert, serve the pudding cold with:

Cream, tart fruit juice, stewed fruit, crushed sweetened berries or Hot Wine Sauce, 771, using claret

ROTE GRÜTZE

4 Servings

This good German fruit pudding, Rote Grütze, long popular in our family, is usually made with raspberry juice. It is designed to end a meal; not, like the less sweet Fruit Soups, 128, to begin it. Strawberries, cherries or black currants may be used, but our favorite base is a combination of raspberry and strawberry juice, which may be strengthened with raspberry jelly or red wine. In winter a wonderfully fresh taste may be obtained if you cook frozen raspberries and strawberries and strain off the juice.

I. Bring to a boil:

2 cups fruit juice

Sweeten it palatably with:

Sugar

Season with:

⅛ teaspoon salt

Stir into the boiling juice:

⅓ cup farina

Cook this mixture in the top of a double boiler ➤ over—not in—boiling water about 20 minutes. Stir until it thickens. Pour into individual serving dishes. Chill. Serve very cold with:

Heavy cream

II. Substitute for the farina, above:

2½ tablespoons tapioca

CREAMY RICE PUDDING

12 Servings

This dessert is frequently served in Europe, where rice puddings are highly appreciated. Steam covered in the top of a double boiler over—not in—boiling water about 1 hour:

1 cup short- or medium-grain rice
6 cups hot milk
1 teaspoon salt

Stir frequently and watch that the water in the bottom pan does not boil off. When the rice is tender, cool slightly and add:

2 tablespoons butter

2 teaspoons vanilla, or 1 teaspoon vanilla and 1 teaspoon lemon rind, grated
2 teaspoons sugar

Serve as a pudding, hot or cold, with:

Stewed or canned fruit, crushed sweetened berries or Jelly Sauce, 770, using quince jelly

or serve with a combination of:

4 tablespoons sugar
1 tablespoon cinnamon

RICE PUDDING

6 to 8 Servings

Preheat oven to 325°.
Have ready:

2 cups short- or medium-grain Boiled Rice, 206

Combine, beat well and add:

1 1/3 cups milk
1/8 teaspoon salt
4 to 6 tablespoons sugar or 1/2 cup brown sugar
1 tablespoon soft butter
1 teaspoon vanilla
2 to 4 eggs

Add:

1/2 teaspoon grated lemon rind
1 teaspoon lemon juice
(1/3 cup raisins or dates)

Combine these ingredients lightly with a fork. Grease a baking dish. Cover the bottom and sides with:

(Cake or cookie crumbs)

Put rice in dish and cover top with more crumbs. Bake the pudding until set—about 50 minutes. Serve hot or cold with:

Cream, Fruit Sauce, 769, fruit juice or Hot Wine Sauce, 771

RICE AND FRUIT CREAM

5 Servings

Combine:

1 cup short- or medium-grain Boiled Rice, 206
1 cup drained apricots, pineapple, etc.

Whip until stiff:

1/2 cup whipping cream

Fold in the rice mixture. Add:

(12 diced marshmallows)

Place the cream in individual dishes. Chill thoroughly. You may top it with:

(Crushed nut brittle)

RICE PUDDING WITH WHIPPED CREAM

10 Servings

Have ready:

1 cup short- or medium-grained Boiled Rice, 206

Soak for 5 minutes:

2 teaspoons gelatin

in:

1/4 cup cold water

Dissolve over heat. Add to the rice. Stir in:

6 tablespoons sugar
(1/2 cup shredded blanched almonds)

Chill. Whip until stiff:

2 cups whipping cream

Fold into the cream:

2 teaspoons vanilla

Fold the cream into rice. Place in a wet mold. Chill 4 hours or more. Unmold and serve very cold with:

Cold Jelly Sauce, 770, or hot Butterscotch Sauce, 773

QUICK TAPIOCA CUSTARD

4 Servings

Combine and stir in the top of a double boiler:

3 tablespoons quick-cooking tapioca
1/2 cup sugar
1/4 teaspoon salt
1 or 2 beaten eggs
2 cups milk

Cook these ingredients without stirring ➤ over—not in—rapidly boiling water for 7 minutes. Stir and cook 5 minutes longer. Remove from heat. The tapioca thickens as it cools. Fold in gradually:

1/2 teaspoon vanilla or 1 teaspoon grated orange or lemon rind

Chill. Serve with:

Cream, fresh berries, crushed or canned fruit, or Chocolate Sauce, 772

Additions may be made to this recipe. In that case, the eggs may be omitted. Suggestions:

1/4 cup or more coconut or toasted almonds
1/2 cup or more chopped dates
1 crushed or diced banana
1 cup sliced, drained, cooked apples
1/2 cup fruit, soaked in wine or liqueur

If the eggs are omitted, serve with:

Custard Sauce, 771

BUTTERSCOTCH TAPIOCA CUSTARD

4 Servings

Follow the preceding recipe for:

Quick Tapioca Custard, above

but omit the sugar. Melt:

2 tablespoons butter

Stir in until it melts and bubbles:

1/3 cup packed brown sugar

Add this mixture to the cooked tapioca.

EGGLESS CRUSHED-FRUIT TAPIOCA PUDDING

8 Servings

This may be made with pineapple, prunes, berries, etc.

Boil in the top of a double boiler over direct heat:

2 cups water

Combine and stir in gradually:

1/3 cup quick-cooking tapioca

½ cup sugar
¼ teaspoon salt

When these ingredients are boiling, place them ➤ over—not in—rapidly boiling water. Cook and stir them about 5 minutes. Remove from heat. Cool slightly. Fold in:

2½ cups canned crushed pineapple or 2 cups cooked prune or apricot pulp or 2 cups crushed sweetened berries
2 tablespoons lemon juice

Chill. This may be served in sherbet glasses with:

Whipped cream, plain cream or Custard Sauce, 771

PEARL TAPIOCA PUDDING

8 Servings

Soak overnight, refrigerated:

1 cup pearl tapioca

in:

1 cup milk

Add these ingredients to:

3 cups milk

and cook them 3 hours in a double boiler ➤ over—not in—boiling water. Cool.
Preheat oven to 325°.
Beat and add:

5 egg yolks
Grated rind of 1 lemon
Juice of ½ lemon
¾ cup sugar

Beat until ➤ stiff, but not dry:

5 egg whites

Line a baking dish with a layer of the tapioca mixture, a layer of the egg whites, another layer of tapioca and end with the egg whites on top. Bake about 15 minutes. Serve hot or cold without a sauce, or with one such as:

Hot Fruit Sauce, 769, 770

BREAD PUDDING WITH MERINGUE

6 Servings

Preheat oven to 350°.
Cut bread into slices and trim away crusts. It should be measured lightly, not packed. Soak for 15 minutes:

3 to 5 cups diced fresh bread or 3½ cups stale bread or stale cake

in:

3 cups warm milk, or 2 cups milk and 1 cup fruit juice
¼ teaspoon salt

Combine and beat well:

3 egg yolks
⅓ to ½ cup sugar
1 teaspoon vanilla
(½ teaspoon nutmeg)

Add:

Grated rind and juice of ½ lemon
(¼ cup raisins, dates or nutmeats, or ½ cup drained crushed pineapple, or ¼ cup orange marmalade)

Pour these ingredients over the soaked bread. Stir them lightly with a fork until well blended. If preferred, the meringue may be dispensed with and the stiffly beaten egg whites may be folded in at this time. Bake the pudding in a baking dish set in a pan of hot water about 45 minutes. Cool pudding. Cover with:

(Meringue I, 730)

Bake in a 300° oven until the meringue is set, about 15 minutes. Serve hot with:

Hard Sauce, 775, Jelly Sauce, 770, or cream, fruit juice or dabs of tart jelly

BROWN BETTY

5 Servings

Preheat oven to 350°.
Combine:

1 cup dry bread or graham cracker crumbs
¼ cup melted butter

Line the bottom of a baking dish with one-third of the crumb mixture. Prepare:

2½ cups peeled, diced or sliced apples or peaches; or cherries or cranberries

Sift:

¾ cup packed brown sugar
1 teaspoon cinnamon
¼ teaspoon each nutmeg and cloves
½ teaspoon salt

Add:

1 teaspoon grated lemon rind
(1 teaspoon vanilla)

Place half of the apples in the dish. Cover the layer with half of the sugar mixture. Sprinkle with:

1 tablespoon lemon juice

Add:

2 tablespoons water

Cover the apples with a third of the crumb mixture and:

(¼ cup raisins or currants)

Add the remaining apples and sprinkle them as before with the sugar mixture and:

2 tablespoons lemon juice
2 tablespoons water
(¼ cup raisins or currants)

Place the last third of the crumb mixture on top. Cover the dish and bake about 40 minutes, until the apples are nearly tender. Remove cover, increase heat to 400° and let pudding brown for about 15 minutes. Serve hot with:

Cream, Hard Sauce, 775, or Lemon Sauce, 769

PRUNE OR APRICOT BETTY

Follow the preceding recipe for:

Brown Betty

Use only:

2 tablespoons sugar

Substitute for the apples:

1½ cups stewed, drained, sweetened prunes or apricots

Substitute for the lemon juice and water:

¾ cup prune or apricot juice

BAKED PINEAPPLE BETTY

4 Servings

This may be made in advance. It is equally good served hot or very cold.
Preheat oven to 325°.
Cream until light:
½ cup butter
¾ cup sugar
Beat in:
5 egg yolks
¼ cup dry bread crumbs
1 cup drained crushed pineapple
1 tablespoon lemon juice
Whip until stiff, then fold in:
3 egg whites
Place the mixture in a baking dish. Cover with Meringue I, 730, and bake it, set in a pan of hot water, about 30 minutes. Serve with.
Cream or whipped cream

★ BAKED FIG PUDDING

14 Servings

Preheat oven to 325°.
Beat until soft:
½ cup butter
Add and beat until fluffy:
2 eggs
1 cup molasses
Add:
2 cups finely chopped dried figs
½ teaspoon grated lemon rind
1 cup buttermilk
(½ cup broken black walnut meats)
Sift before measuring:
2½ cups all-purpose flour
Resift with:
½ teaspoon baking soda
2 teaspoons double-acting baking powder
1 teaspoon salt
1 teaspoon cinnamon
½ teaspoon nutmeg
One teaspoon ginger may be substituted for the cinnamon and nutmeg. Stir the sifted ingredients into the pudding mixture. Bake in a greased 9-inch tube pan about 1 hour. Serve hot with:
Brown Sugar Hard Sauce, 775, Sabayon Sauce, 771, or Hot Wine Sauce, 771

★ BAKED DATE RING OR CHRISTMAS WREATH

6 Servings

You may bake this in a ring mold. When cold, unmold it onto a platter, cover it well with whipped cream and stud it with maraschino cherries. Surround it with holly leaves. Although very effective this way, it tastes almost as good baked in a shallow pan, cut into squares and served with Foamy Sauce, 775.
Preheat oven to 350°.
Prepare:
1 cup pitted minced dates
1 cup chopped nutmeats
Combine these ingredients with:
½ cup white or packed brown sugar
1 tablespoon all-purpose flour
1 teaspoon double-acting baking powder
2 beaten egg yolks
1 teaspoon vanilla
Fold in:
2 stiffly beaten egg whites
Bake the pudding in a well-greased 9-inch ring mold about 30 minutes. You may sprinkle over it, while hot, ¼ cup Madeira or sherry or 3 tablespoons brandy or rum. Let it cool in the pan.
Whip until stiff:
1 cup whipping cream
Fold in:
2 teaspoons powdered sugar
1 teaspoon vanilla
Garnish the ring as suggested above.

★ BAKED PLUM PUDDING

10 Servings

Not for Jack Horner's legendary thumb, but a rewarding confection just the same.
Preheat oven to 375°.
Beat until soft:
½ cup butter
Add gradually and cream
1 cup sugar
Beat in, one at a time:
6 eggs
Combine:
1 cup raisins, currants and pecans
Sprinkle lightly with:
Flour
Add these ingredients to the butter mixture. Combine:
2 cups bread crumbs
2 teaspoons cinnamon
½ teaspoon cloves
½ teaspoon allspice
Stir these ingredients into the butter mixture. Bake in a greased pan or baking dish about 30 minutes.
Serve with:
Hard Sauce, 775, Lemon Sauce, 769, or Hot Wine Sauce, 771

COTTAGE PUDDING

6 Servings

Preheat oven to 400°.
Follow the recipe for:
One-Egg Cake, 681
For a new fillip, line a greased 8 x 8-inch pan with:
(1 cup heated marmalade)
Pour the batter over the marmalade. Marmalade or none, bake the pudding about 25 minutes. Serve cut into squares with:
Crushed fruit, stewed fruit, Fluffy Hard Sauce, 775, Raisin Sauce, 770, Coffee Sauce, 774, Hot Wine Sauce, 771, or Hot Brown Sugar Sauce, 773

PANCAKE AND WAFFLE DESSERTS

Serve:

Pancakes or waffles

spread with:

Thick cultured sour cream
Strawberry or other preserves

or serve with:

Crushed sweetened berries or fruit, or with Sauce Cockaigne, 770

CHOCOLATE FEATHER PUDDING

8 Servings

Perhaps this should be placed among the steamed puddings, but they are more troublesome and this one might be neglected in such company. It is an inexpensive and delightful dessert.

Preheat oven to 350°.

Sift:

1 cup sugar

Beat until light:

1 egg

Stir in sugar gradually. When these ingredients are well blended, stir in:

1 cup milk or coffee
1 tablespoon melted butter
1½ oz. melted unsweetened chocolate

Sift:

1½ cups all-purpose flour

Resift with:

¼ teaspoon salt
1½ teaspoons double-acting baking powder

Stir these ingredients into the egg mixture. Add:

½ teaspoon vanilla

Place the batter in well-greased deep custard cups —about two-thirds full. Cover with foil. Steam in the oven by setting cups in a pan of hot water, about 30 minutes, or place pan over low heat on top of stove for same length of time. Remove foil and serve pudding at once with:

Vanilla Sauce, 774

flavored with:

(Rum)

SWEET-POTATO PUDDING

6 Servings

Preheat oven to 350°.

Combine and beat well:

2 cups cooked, mashed sweet potatoes
1 cup sugar
½ cup melted butter
6 beaten egg yolks
1½ teaspoons grated lemon rind
1 cup orange juice
¼ teaspoon nutmeg or 2 tablespoons rum

Fold in:

2 stiffly beaten egg whites

Bake pudding in a greased baking dish about 1 hour. Before baking, the top may be sprinkled with:

(Sliced citron)
(Broken nutmeats)

After the pudding is baked and cooled, it may also be topped with Meringue I, 730, made with the remaining egg whites. Bake in a 325° oven about 15 minutes.

PERSIMMON PUDDING

8 Servings

Best made with the small native *Diospyros virginiana,* which give a waxy but not tough consistency to the pudding. The large Japanese *Diospyros kaki* do not have enough flavor to warrant using.

Preheat oven to 325°.

Put through a colander:

Persimmons

There should be about 2 cups of pulp.

Beat in:

3 eggs
1¼ cups sugar: white or light brown
1 cup all-purpose flour
1 teaspoon double-acting baking powder
1 teaspoon baking soda
½ teaspoon salt
½ cup melted butter
2½ cups light cream
2 teaspoons cinnamon
1 teaspoon ginger
½ teaspoon freshly grated nutmeg

One cupful raisins or nutmeats may be added to the batter. Bake the pudding in a greased 9 x 9-inch baking dish about 1 hour or until firm. Serve with:

Cream or Hard Sauce, 775

UNCOOKED DATE LOAF

12 Servings

Crush:

½ lb. graham crackers

Remove pits and cut into pieces:

1 lb. dates: 2 cups

Cut into pieces:

½ lb. marshmallows

Chop fine:

1 cup pecan meats

Whip until stiff:

1 cup whipping cream

Fold in:

1 teaspoon vanilla

Combine half the cracker crumbs with the dates, marshmallows, nuts and whipped cream. Shape into a roll. Roll it in the remaining cracker crumbs. Chill 12 hours. Cut into slices and serve with:

Cream or whipped cream

ABOUT STEAMED PUDDINGS

To steam pudding mixtures in a steamer, use pudding molds or cans with tightly fitting lids. First, grease insides of molds well, then sprinkle with sugar. Containers should be ➤ only two-thirds full. Place molds on a trivet in a heavy kettle over 1 inch of boiling water. Cover kettle closely. Use high heat at first, then, as the steam begins to escape, low heat for the rest of the cooking.

➤ To steam pudding mixtures in a ⊗ pressure cooker, use tightly lidded molds or cans as described above and ➤ fill only two-thirds full. Place them on a rack in the bottom of the cooker, allowing space between both the molds and the walls of the cooker. Add boiling water ➤ until it is halfway up the sides of the molds.

If the steaming period for a regular steamer is 30 minutes, steam with vent off for 5 minutes, then pressure-cook at 15 pounds for 10 minutes. If steaming for 45 minutes to 1½ hours is called for, steam without closing the vent for 25 minutes, then pressure-cook at 15 pounds pressure for 25 minutes. If steaming for 2 to 4 hours is called for, steam without closing the vent for 30 minutes, then pressure-cook at 15 pounds pressure for 50 minutes. ➤ After steaming, reduce the heat at once. True steamed puddings need complete circulation of steam, so do not expect good results if you use a greased double boiler. Always ➤ before unmolding, take the lid from the mold and allow the pudding to rest long enough to let excess steam escape. The pudding will be less apt to crack in unmolding.

▲ In high altitudes, reduce the leavening by half the required amount.

STEAMED BROWN PUDDING

14 Servings

To steam or ⊗ pressure-cook and unmold, see About Steamed Puddings, above.

Combine and blend well:

1 cup packed brown sugar
½ cup shortening

Add:

1 cup milk
1 cup molasses
1 cup dry bread crumbs
2 beaten eggs
2 cups chopped seeded raisins

Sift before measuring:

2 cups all-purpose flour

Resift with:

2 teaspoons double-acting baking powder
½ teaspoon baking soda
1 teaspoon cinnamon
½ teaspoon each ginger, cloves and grated nutmeg

Add sifted ingredients to the molasses mixture. Pour batter into a well-greased pudding mold. Steam 1½ hours. Serve hot with:

Hard Sauce, 775, or Foamy Sauce, 775

★ STEAMED FRUIT SUET PUDDING

12 Servings

Less cooking is needed here, as the thickener is bread crumbs. To steam or ⊗ pressure-cook and unmold, see About Steamed Puddings, above.

Beat until soft:

1 cup very finely chopped beef suet: ½ lb.

Add gradually:

1 cup sugar

When these ingredients are well blended, beat in:

3 egg yolks

Stir in:

1 cup milk
3 tablespoons brandy

Put through a grinder and add:

1 lb. figs or dates or 2 cups peeled sliced apples
(1 cup chopped pecans or walnuts)

Grate and add:

2 teaspoons orange rind
1 teaspoon freshly ground nutmeg or ginger

Combine and add:

1½ cups dry bread crumbs
2 teaspoons double-acting baking powder

Whip until stiff, then fold in:

3 egg whites

Pour the ingredients into a greased mold. Steam slowly 4 hours. Serve with:

Hot Sabayon Sauce, 771, or Hot Wine Sauce, 771

Flavor the sauce with:

(2 teaspoons or more brandy)

★ STEAMED DATE PUDDING

8 Servings

Not so rich as Steamed Fruit Suet Pudding. To steam or ⊗ pressure-cook and unmold, see About Steamed Puddings, 753.

Sift:

1 cup packed brown sugar

Beat until soft:

¼ cup butter

Add the sugar gradually. Blend these ingredients until they are creamy. Beat in:

1 egg
½ teaspoon vanilla

Sift before measuring:

1¼ cups all-purpose flour

Resift with:

2⅔ teaspoons double-acting baking powder
½ teaspoon salt

Add sifted ingredients to butter mixture in 3 parts, alternately with:

1 cup milk

Beat batter until smooth after each addition. Fold in:

1 cup chopped dates
1 cup broken nutmeats

Pour into a greased pudding mold. Cover closely. Steam 2 hours. Serve hot with:

Foamy Sauce, 775, or Hard Sauce, 775

STEAMED CHOCOLATE PUDDING

6 Servings

This is richer than Chocolate Feather Pudding, which may also be steamed in a mold. To steam or ⊗ pressure-cook and unmold, see About Steamed Puddings, 753.

Beat until light:

6 egg yolks

Beat in gradually:

1 cup sugar

Stir in:

3/4 cup grated unsweetened chocolate
2 tablespoons finely crushed crackers or toasted bread crumbs
1 teaspoon double-acting baking powder
1 teaspoon vanilla
1/2 teaspoon cinnamon
(1/2 cup grated nutmeats)

Beat until ➤ stiff, but not dry:

6 egg whites

Fold them lightly into the batter. Pour into a greased pudding mold. Steam 1 1/2 hours. Serve with:

Hard Sauce, 775, or cream

STEAMED CARAMEL PUDDING

6 Servings

Try this as a company pudding. To steam or ✪ pressure-cook and unmold, see About Steamed Puddings, 753.

Melt in a heavy skillet:

1/3 cup sugar

When it is light brown, stir in ➤ very slowly:

3/4 cup hot milk

Cool this syrup. Beat until soft:

2 tablespoons butter

Beat in one at a time:

5 egg yolks

Add the syrup and:

1 teaspoon vanilla
1 1/2 tablespoons all-purpose flour
1 cup ground unblanched almonds

Beat batter until smooth. Whip ➤ until stiff, but not dry:

5 egg whites

Fold them lightly into the batter. Pour into a greased pudding mold sprinkled with:

Sugar

Cover closely. Steam 1 hour. Serve hot with:

Whipped cream or Sauce Cockaigne, 770

STEAMED APPLE MOLASSES PUDDING

6 Servings

To steam or ✪ pressure-cook and unmold, see About Steamed Puddings, 753.

Cream until fluffy:

1/4 cup butter
1/2 cup packed brown sugar

Beat in:

1 egg
1/2 cup molasses
1 tablespoon grated orange rind

Measure:

1 1/2 cups sifted all-purpose flour

Resift with:

1/2 teaspoon baking soda
1 teaspoon double-acting baking powder
1 teaspoon each ginger and cinnamon

Add these ingredients to the butter mixture, alternately with:

1/2 cup buttermilk

Stir in:

1 cup chopped apples

Place the pudding in a greased mold. Steam it 1 1/2 hours. Serve with:

Lemon Sauce, 769, or Hard Sauce, 775

★ STEAMED PLUM PUDDING

24 Servings

A truly festive Christmas dish that needs patience in the making. ➤ The slow six-hour cooking is necessary, so that all the suet melts before the flour particles burst. If the pudding cooks too fast and the flour grains burst before the fat melts, the pudding will be close and hard. To steam and unmold, see About Steamed Puddings, 753.

Sift:

1 cup all-purpose flour

Prepare and dredge lightly with part of the flour:

1 lb. chopped suet: 2 cups
1 lb. seeded raisins
1 lb. washed dried currants
1/2 lb. chopped citron

Resift the remaining flour with:

1 grated nutmeg
1 tablespoon cinnamon
1/2 tablespoon mace
1 teaspoon salt
6 tablespoons sugar or 1/2 cup packed brown sugar

Combine the dredged and the sifted ingredients. Add:

7 egg yolks
1/4 cup cream
1/2 cup brandy or sherry
3 cups grated dry bread crumbs, white or rye

The bread crumbs help make the pudding light. Whip until stiff:

7 egg whites

Fold them lightly into the raisin mixture. Pour the batter into a covered greased gallon mold and steam 6 hours. Serve with:

Hot Wine Sauce, 771, or Hard Sauce, 775

To store plum pudding for future use, cool, and pour over it:

1/2 cup brandy or applejack

Cover and store. Heat through in double boiler at least an hour before serving.

ABOUT SAVORIES

To most Americans, savories seem curious desserts. Of course, ours must also seem strange to the English—for, to them, the word "dessert" signifies fruit. Their term for our cold desserts is "sweets," and they call our hot ones "puddings."

Traditionally English, savories are a course presented before the fruit or after the sweet to cut the sugar taste before the port is served. They function like an hors d'oeuvre, although they are slightly larger in size. Try oysters or chicken livers in bacon; also sardine, caviar and roe crêpes; or pancakes or a tomato tart; deviled or curried seafood tarts or toasted cheese rolls. If you are serving wine, choose cheese straws or cheese-and-cracker combinations rather than the fishy savories.

ABOUT DESSERT CHEESES

Dessert cheeses may be served after the roast, with the same red wine that has accompanied that course; or after the salad, if, of course, the salad has not been served as a first course. Cheeses may also be served following the sweet or with a suitable dessert fruit such as apples, pears, grapes, cherries, plums or melons. Cheeses should always be served at a temperature of about 70°. Some types which are best when *coulant,* or runny, should be removed from refrigeration 3 to 6 hours before serving.

Usually some pats of sweet butter are added to the cheese-board. Toast, crackers, pumpernickel, crusty French Bread, 605, or Sour Rye, 609, follows the cheese on a separate tray. Salted, toasted or freshly shelled nuts, roasted chestnuts, celery or fennel make pleasant accessories. Try mixing mild cheeses with the more highly ripened aromatic or smoked ones.

Above all, remember that cheeses have their own seasons. And choose varieties that are in season. If you must store them, see 536. Below are listed some favorite dessert cheeses.

Soft types include uncrusted, unripened cheeses like Petit Gervais and Petit Suisse, Ricotta and Coulommiers; as well as those which are ripened and have soft edible crusts, such as Brie, Camembert, Liederkranz and Poona.

Among the semihards are the famous *fromages persilles,* or mold-ripened blue-greens, in which the mold patterns the cream-colored bases in traceries resembling parsley. The interior mold, which contributes to the characteristic flavor, must be distinguished from green mold on the exterior of the cheese, which may be harmless but should be removed.

The famous blues include Stilton, Gorgonzola, Bleu, Dorset Vinney and Roquefort. Other well-known semihard dessert cheeses are Muenster, Port du Salut, Bel Paese and Gammelost.

Hard types, from which come the very best cheeses for cooking, afford many choice ones for dessert: cheddar, Gruyère, Provolone, Gjetost, Emmentaler, Cheshire and Edam, to name a few.

DESSERT CHEESE MIX

Many people like to mix sweet butter with the stronger cheeses in serving them for dessert. The combinations are legion; for others, see 72. This one is a favorite of our friend Helmut Ripperger, who likes to prepare it at the table. However, sometimes these mixtures are made in advance, formed into a large ball, and rolled in toasted bread crumbs or nuts.

➤ Have ingredients at room temperature.

Mix:

2 parts Roquefort cheese
1 part sweet butter

Add enough:

Armagnac or your favorite brandy

to make a spreadable soft paste. Serve with:

Toasted crackers

POTTED CHEESE

About ¾ Cup

If you would like to make up a combination of cheeses to keep, try one based on a mixture of:

4 oz. cheese
2 oz. butter
3 tablespoons port, sherry or brandy

Season to taste with:

Pepper or cayenne
(Mace)

COEUR À LA CRÈME OR FRENCH CHEESE CREAM

6 Servings

When the fruit is prime, this very simple dessert is as good as any elaborate concoction we know of or use.

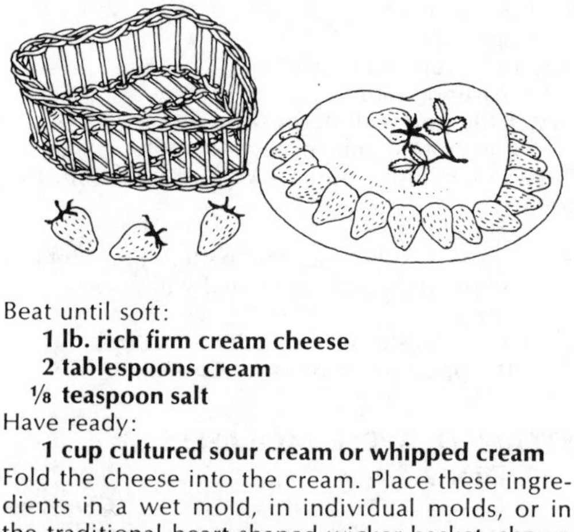

Beat until soft:

1 lb. rich firm cream cheese
2 tablespoons cream
⅛ teaspoon salt

Have ready:

1 cup cultured sour cream or whipped cream

Fold the cheese into the cream. Place these ingredients in a wet mold, in individual molds, or in the traditional heart-shaped wicker basket, shown here, lined with moistened cheesecloth. Chill the cheese thoroughly. Unmold it. Serve with:

Fresh unhulled strawberries, or raspberries or other fresh fruit, or Cherry Sauce, 770

COTTAGE OR CREAM CHEESE OR YOGURT DESSERT

Sweeten:

Cottage or cream cheese or yogurt

with:

White or brown sugar
Vanilla

Sprinkle the top with:

Cinnamon

Serve the mixture very cold with:

Stewed cherries, crushed strawberries, skinned, sliced apricots or peaches, pared apples, pomegranates, green grapes or sliced melon

BAR-LE-DUC

About 1 Cup

A pleasant summer dish. Serve it with toasted crackers.

Stir to a smooth paste:

¾ cup firm cream cheese
1 or 2 tablespoons cream

Fold in:

2 tablespoons currant preserves or Bar-le-Duc Preserves, 838

Refrigerate to firm the dessert, but serve at about 70°.

LIPTAUER CHEESE

About 2 Cups

If you can't buy the real thing, try this savory cheese made by mixing together, until well blended:

½ lb. dry cottage cheese
½ lb. soft butter
½ teaspoon paprika
½ teaspoon caraway seeds
1 teaspoon chopped capers
½ teaspoon anchovy paste
½ teaspoon mild prepared mustard
1 tablespoon chopped chives

Mold. Serve within 6 hours of mixing, as the taste of the chives may grow strong.

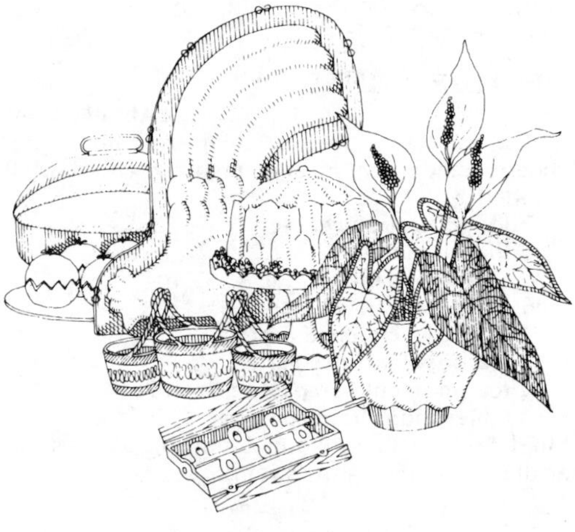

FROZEN DESSERTS AND SWEET SAUCES

Molds, whether of metal—such as the proud rooster and the classic melon on the left—or of ceramic, on the right, do much to enhance bombes, 762, mousses, 764, and Bavarians, 746. Also presented above on a raised milk glass platter is a bombe whose white mold is shown reversed and used as a sympathetic flower container with a white and green arrangement of caladium, calla leaves and spathiphyllum blooms. The antique sauceboat in the left middle-ground holds a variety of sweet sauces. Between the rooster and the melon mold are individual Frozen Orange Surprises, 766. In the foreground lies the dasher from the ice cream freezer shown 760. The texture of frozen desserts depends on how long and at what speed you turn this vital tool.

CHURNED ICE CREAMS AND ICES

A century and a half ago the youthful Stendhal, when he first tasted ice cream, exclaimed: "What a pity this isn't a sin!" Nowadays, with electric churning and plentiful ice, few people recall the shared excitement of the era when making ice cream was a rarely scheduled event. Then the iceman brought to the back door, on special order, a handsome 2-foot-square cube of cold crystal, and everyone in the family took a turn at the crank. The critical question among us children was, of course, who might lick the dasher—that portion of the freezing equipment which defies modernization and which is shown in the foreground above. For no power-driven machine has yet been invented that can achieve a comparable texture. Even French Pot, the very best commercial method for making ice cream, calls for finishing by hand.

Ice creams are based on ➤ carefully cooked ➤ well-chilled syrups and heavy custards, added to ➤ unwhipped cream. ➤ No form of vanilla flavoring can surpass that of vanilla sugar or of the bean itself, steeped in a hot syrup. If sweetened frozen fruits are incorporated into the cream mixture instead of fresh fruits, be sure to adjust sugar content accordingly.

➤ Make up mixtures for churn-frozen ice creams the day before you freeze, to increase yield and to produce a smoother-textured cream. ➤ In churn-freezing ice creams and ices, fill the container only two-thirds full to permit expansion. ➤ To pack the freezer, allow 4 parts chipped or cracked ice to 1 part coarse rock salt. Pack about one-third of the freezer with ice and add layers of salt and ice around the container until the freezer is full. Allow the pack to stand about 3 minutes before you start turning—slowly at first, about 40 revolutions a minute, until a slight pull is felt, then triple speed for 5 or 6 minutes. If any additions, such as finely cut candied or fresh fruits or nuts, are to be made, do so at this point. Then repack and taper off the churning to about 80 revolutions a minute for a few minutes more. The cream should be ready in 10 to 20 minutes, depending on quantity.

If the ice cream or ice is to be used at once, it should be frozen harder than if you plan to serve it later. Should the interval be 2 hours or more, packing will firm it. ➤ To pack, pour off the salt water in the freezer and wipe off the lid. Remove the dasher carefully, making sure that no salt or water gets into the cream container. Scrape the cream down from the sides of the container. Place a cork in the lid and replace the lid. Repack the container in the freezer with additional ice and salt, using the same proportions as before. Cover the freezer with wet newspapers, burlap or other heavy material.

The cream should be smooth when served. If it proves granular, you used too much salt in the packing mixture, overfilled the inner container with the ice cream mixture, or turned too rapidly. ✲ If making a large quantity with the idea of storing some in the deep-freeze, package in sizes you plan serving. Do not store longer than 1 month. Should ice cream be allowed to melt even slightly and then be refrozen, it loses in volume and even more in good texture. As we have said, texture also suffers if you use an electric freezer. If you do so, follow manufacturer's directions.

GARNISHES AND ADDITIONS TO ICE CREAM

You may add to ice cream, when it is in a partially frozen state, allowing the following amounts per quart:

1 cup toasted chopped nuts
1 cup finely crushed Nut Brittle, 788
1/8 cup preserved chopped ginger and 1 tablespoon of the syrup
1 cup crushed chocolate molasses chips
1 cup crushed Macaroons, 709, plus
2 tablespoons sherry or liqueur
1/2 cup Polvo de Amor, 567

For fruit additions, see Fruit Ice Creams, 760.
To garnish ice cream, add just before serving:

Chopped nuts or shredded coconut
Candied violets
Chopped candied citrus peel or other candied fruits
Crystallized angelica, cut in tiny fancy shapes
Decorettes
Shaved or chopped sweet or bitter chocolate
Marzipan fruits or rosettes
Sweet Sauces, 769

VANILLA ICE CREAM I

About 9 Servings

Scald over low heat, but do not boil:
1 cup cream
Stir in, until dissolved:
3/4 cup sugar
1/8 teaspoon salt
If you have a vanilla bean, add to the hot mixture:
Seeds scraped from a 2-inch section of vanilla bean
If you do not have a bean, add after chilling:
1 1/2 teaspoons vanilla
Chill. Add:
3 cups cream
To churn-freeze the ice cream, see 758.
Serve with:
Tutti Frutti, 840, Cherry Jubilee Sauce, 770, a heavy liqueur, or a chocolate sauce, 772

DELMONICO ICE CREAM I, OR CRÊME GLACÉE

About 9 Servings

Scald over low heat, but do not boil:
1 1/2 cups milk
Stir in, until dissolved:
3/4 cup sugar
1/8 teaspoon salt
Pour the milk slowly over:
2 or 3 beaten egg yolks
Beat these ingredients until well blended. Stir and cook in a double boiler ➤ over—not in—boiling water until thick enough to coat the back of a spoon. Chill. Add and fold into the custard:
1 tablespoon vanilla
1 cup whipping cream
1 cup cream
To churn-freeze the ice cream, see 758.
Serve with:
Crushed Nut Brittle, 788

CARAMEL ICE CREAM

Prepare:
Vanilla or Delmonico Ice Cream, above
Add:
2 to 4 tablespoons Caramelized Sugar I, 559
To churn-freeze and serve, see 758.
Garnish with:
Chopped pecans or toasted almonds

PEPPERMINT-STICK ICE CREAM

About 12 Servings

Grind or crush:
1/2 lb. peppermint-stick candy
Soak for 12 hours, refrigerated, in:
2 cups milk
Add:
1 cup cream
1 cup whipping cream
To churn-freeze and serve, see 758.
Serve with:
Shaved sweet chocolate, 566, or Chocolate Sauce Cockaigne, 772

CHOCOLATE ICE CREAM

About 8 Servings

Dissolve in the top of a double boiler ➤ over—not in—boiling water:
2 oz. unsweetened chocolate
in:
2 cups milk
Stir in:
1 cup sugar
1/8 teaspoon salt
Remove from heat. Beat with a wire whisk until cool and fluffy. Add:
1 1/2 teaspoons vanilla
1 cup whipping cream
1 cup cream
To churn-freeze and serve, see 758. You may serve it in:
(Meringues, 649)
with:
(A chocolate sauce, 772)

COFFEE ICE CREAM

About 9 Servings

Scald over low heat, but do not boil:
2 1/2 cups milk
Stir in, until dissolved:
1 1/2 cups sugar
Pour the milk slowly over:
2 beaten eggs
Beat until well blended. Stir and cook in a double boiler ➤ over—not in—boiling water until thick enough to coat the back of a spoon. Chill. Add:
1/2 cup strong cold coffee
1/2 teaspoon salt
1 cup whipping cream
Partly churn-freeze these ingredients, 758, and

when almost frozen, add:

1 teaspoon vanilla
3 tablespoons rum

Finish freezing.
Garnish with:

Shaved sweet chocolate, 566

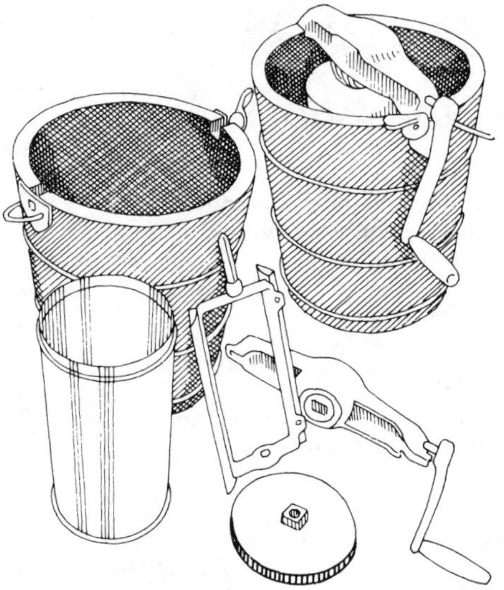

★ PISTACHIO ICE CREAM

About 9 Servings

A pretty Christmas dessert served in a meringue tart garnished with whipped cream and cherries.
Shell and blanch, 562:

4 oz. pistachio nuts

Pound them in a mortar with:

A few drops rose water

Add to them:

¼ cup sugar
¼ cup cream
1 teaspoon vanilla
½ teaspoon almond extract
A little green vegetable coloring

Stir these ingredients until the sugar is dissolved. Heat, but do not boil:

1 cup cream

Add and stir until dissolved:

¾ cup sugar
⅛ teaspoon salt

Chill these ingredients. Add the pistachio mixture and:

2 cups whipping cream
1 cup cream

To churn-freeze and serve, see 758.

FRUIT ICE CREAMS

About 9 Servings

Delicious fruit creams can be made using:

2 cups sweetened puréed or finely sliced fruit—greengage plums, mangoes, peaches, apricots or bananas

Add:

¼ teaspoon salt
Lemon juice to taste
2 cups whipping cream
1 cup cream

To churn-freeze the cream, see 758.

APRICOT OR PEACH ICE CREAM

About 9 Servings

Peel, slice and mash:

4 lb. ripe peaches or apricots

Stir in:

½ to ¾ cup sugar
⅛ teaspoon salt

Cover the fruit closely and keep it refrigerated until the sugar is dissolved. Combine:

1 teaspoon vanilla
½ cup sugar
2 cups cream
2 cups whipping cream

Partly churn-freeze these ingredients, see 758. When half-frozen, add the fruit mixture and finish freezing.

ORANGE ICE CREAM

About 9 Servings

Heat but do not boil:

1½ cups cream

Stir in until dissolved:

1½ cups sugar

Chill. Add:

1½ cups whipping cream

Churn-freeze the cream, see 758, until it has a slushy consistency. Add:

3 tablespoons lemon juice
1¼ cups orange juice

Finish freezing. Serve with:

Polvo de Amor, 567

STRAWBERRY OR RASPBERRY ICE CREAM

About 9 Servings

Hull:

1 quart berries

Sieve them. Stir into the pulpy juice:

⅞ cup sugar

Chill thoroughly. Combine with:

2 cups cream
2 cups whipping cream

To churn-freeze, see 758.

ABOUT STILL-FROZEN ICE CREAMS, ICES, BOMBES, MOUSSES AND PARFAITS

In our family, a richly loaded bombe, even more than a churned ice cream, betokened festivity—the burst of glory that topped off a party dinner. Fancy molds such as those illustrated in the chapter heading, 758, were reserved for these occasions. We children always hoped they might be chilled in the backyard, under snow: such fun finding them!

Then, as now, these still-frozen desserts ➤ needed an emulsifying agent—eggs, cornstarch, gelatin or corn syrup—to keep large crystals from forming during the freezing process. Some classic French recipes specify at least 8 eggs for each cup of sugar syrup to obtain the requisite smoothness. Whatever the proportions, count on a very different texture in these still-frozen desserts from those made by churning.

Here are some good combinations:

Strawberry ice outside, Delmonico with strawberries in kirsch inside
Raspberries and pistachios
Coffee and vanilla praliné
Coffee and banana mousse
Chocolate and angelica
Vanilla, orange and chocolate

➤ To still-freeze creams and ices ➤ whip the cream only to the point where it stands in soft peaks. Any further beating will make the dessert disagreeably buttery. The whipped cream and any solids such as nuts and candied fruits are incorporated when the rest of the mixture is partially frozen, and liqueurs are usually added almost at the end of the freezing period.

Chill the mold before packing. Pack the ice cream firmly so no air spaces remain.

When the mixtures are in the mold, rest them at least 6 hours in the deep freeze on top of other packages, not directly on the freezer shelves. They may be made the day before you plan to use them, but ➤ they do not keep well much longer than this. ➤ Remove them from the freezer about 1/2 hour before use, leaving them in the mold until ready to serve. Then garnish with meringues, fruits, sauces or cakes. ➤ To make ornamental bombes, put the cream into tall fancy or melon molds or in the special ones from which they took their playfully sinister name.

Churn-frozen ices or ice creams may form a single or double outside coating. They are applied as a rather thin layer to the inside surface of the mold, each layer being, in turn, individually frozen, see Gelatin Molds, 560. The softer, still-frozen bombe, mousse or Bavarian mixtures are then filled into the center and the mold covered before placement in the freezer for at least 6 hours. To unmold, let cool water run briefly over the mold, and have a cooled platter ready to receive the molded cream.

To make still-frozen ice cream in freezer trays, prepare as in the following recipes. After about 2 hours of freezing, remove tray from freezer and beat contents well. Return to freezer. Repeat the beating in about 2 hours and again in 2 more hours if crystals appear on the surface. Refreeze after each beating. Cover the tray closely each time with plastic or foil. ➤ Do not store more than 24 hours if you want a satisfactory texture. You may form individual parfaits before the last freezing in stemmed tall parfait glasses, layering the ice creams between preserved fruits and sauces. When serving, top them with freshly whipped cream and a maraschino cherry.

➤ In the absence of a freezer, set the well-covered mold in a bed of cracked ice. Allow from 2 to 4 parts ice to 1 of salt and use a bucket or a pail that will ensure complete coverage—about 3 inches on top, bottom and sides. Chill the cream 4 to 6 hours.

VANILLA ICE CREAM II

About 9 Servings

Soak:

2 teaspoons gelatin

in:

1/4 cup cold water

Scald over low heat but do not boil:

3/4 cup milk

with:

Seeds scraped from a 2-inch section of vanilla bean

Stir into it, until dissolved:

3/4 cup sugar
1/8 teaspoon salt

Stir in the soaked gelatin. Cool and place this mixture in refrigerator trays until thoroughly chilled. Then whip with a wire whisk until thickened, but not stiff:

3 cups whipping cream

Fold cream into the chilled and beaten gelatin mixture. ➤ Still-freeze the dessert in a mold or in a foil-covered refrigerator tray. Serve with:

Chocolate Mint Sauce, 773, or
Maple Sugar Sauce, 773

or cover with:

Shredded coconut
A chocolate sauce, 772

An attractive way to serve vanilla ice cream in summer is to place balls of cream in the center of a large platter and surround them with mounds of red raspberries, black raspberries and fresh pineapple sticks, using green leaves as a garnish. You may also use any of the additions suggested in Vanilla Ice Cream I, 759.

VANILLA ICE CREAM III

4 Servings

Start to make this the day before you need it, as the evaporated milk needs to chill 12 hours. Prepare for whipping by the method on 532:

1 1/4 cups evaporated milk

During the process of evaporating milk, a caramel overtone develops which plays hob with the delicate flavor of vanilla. We prefer to accentuate the caramel by adding:

2 to 4 tablespoons or more Caramel Syrup, 791

Or you may transform the caramel flavor with:

1 to 2 teaspoons instant coffee

To prepare the ice cream, stir over heat, but do not boil:

⅓ to ½ cup sugar
¼ cup cream

Chill. Add:

1½ teaspoons vanilla

Whip the evaporated milk and combine lightly with the sugar mixture. To still-freeze and serve, see 761.

DELMONICO ICE CREAM II

6 Servings

Beat:

2 egg yolks

Beat in until well blended:

½ cup confectioners' sugar
¼ cup cream

Cook and stir in a double boiler ➤ over—not in—boiling water until the mixture coats the back of a spoon. Chill. Add:

1 teaspoon vanilla or 1 tablespoon or more dry sherry

➤ Whip until thickened, but not stiff:

1 cup whipping cream

In a separate bowl, whip until stiff ➤ but not dry:

2 egg whites

Fold the cream and the egg whites into the custard. ➤ Still-freeze the ice cream in a mold or in foil-covered refrigerator trays, see 761. Serve with:

Jelly Sauce, 770

* FROZEN EGGNOG

Prepare:

Delmonico Ice Cream I, 759, or II, above

When almost frozen, make a funnel-shaped hole in the center. Place in it:

Several tablespoons rum, brandy or whisky

Stir the liquor into the ice cream. Let the mixture continue to freeze.

MANGO ICE CREAM

Prepare:

Delmonico Ice Cream I, 759, or II, above

Before freezing, fold in:

2 cups mango purée

Freeze in refrigerator trays, see 761.

DELMONICO BOMBE

About 15 Servings

Soak:

1½ teaspoons gelatin

in:

¼ cup cold water

Stir and bring to the boiling point:

2 cups milk
1½ cups sugar

Dissolve the gelatin in the hot milk. Pour part of this mixture over:

2 beaten egg yolks

Beat until blended, then add the rest of the mixture. Stir and cook in a double boiler ➤ over—not in—boiling water until the custard coats the back of a spoon. Cool. Add:

1 teaspoon vanilla

Chill until about to set. ➤ Whip until thickened, but not stiff:

4 cups whipping cream

In a separate bowl, whip until ➤ stiff, but not dry:

2 egg whites

Fold the cream and the egg whites lightly into the custard. Have ready:

18 Macaroons, 709

Sprinkle them with:

Cointreau or kirsch

Spread them with:

Tart jelly

Place alternate layers of cream and macaroons in a mold or in refrigerator trays. To still-freeze the ice cream, see 761.

BISCUIT TORTONI OR MACAROON BOMBE

4 Servings

Combine:

¾ cup crushed Macaroons, 709
¾ cup cream
¼ cup sifted confectioners' sugar
A few grains salt

Let these ingredients stand 1 hour. ➤ Whip until thickened, but not stiff:

1 cup whipping cream

Fold in the macaroon mixture and:

1 teaspoon vanilla

Place in paper muffin cups set in a refrigerator tray. To still-freeze, see 761. Either before freezing or when partly frozen, decorate tops with:

Candied cherries
Unsalted toasted almonds
Crystallized angelica

ANGELICA PARFAIT

About 12 Servings

Try combining layers of angelica, chocolate and lime sherbet.

Boil to the thread stage, 778:

1½ cups sugar
½ cup water

Whip ➤ until stiff, but not dry:

2 egg whites

Pour syrup over them in a slow stream. Whip constantly. When cool, add:

1 teaspoon vanilla or 1 tablespoon or more Cointreau

➤ Whip until thickened, but not stiff:

3 cups whipping cream

Fold lightly into egg mixture. Still-freeze in a mold or in foil-covered refrigerator trays, see 761. Serve with:

Raspberry syrup, or
A chocolate sauce, 772

MOCHA ICE CREAM

8 Servings

In spite of an almost lifelong prejudice against marshmallows, we give the next two recipes more than grudging approval.

Melt in a double boiler ➤ over—not in—boiling water:

18 average-sized Marshmallows, 781: 1/4 lb.
1/2 lb. semisweet chocolate

Cool slightly and stir in:

2 cups whipping cream
3/4 cup strong coffee

Pour this mixture gradually over:

4 well-beaten egg yolks

➤ Be sure that the mixture is not so hot as to curdle the eggs. To still-freeze and serve, see 761.

CHOCOLATE ICE CREAM II

4 Servings

Chill until ice-cold so it will whip, 532:

1 cup evaporated milk

Combine:

6 tablespoons cocoa or 1 1/2 oz. melted unsweetened chocolate
6 tablespoons sugar
1/4 teaspoon salt

Stir in gradually:

1/2 cup evaporated milk
1/2 cup water

Stir and cook these ingredients in a double boiler ➤ over—not in—boiling water until smooth. Add and stir until melted:

18 average-sized Marshmallows, 781: 1/4 lb.

Cool this mixture. Whip the chilled milk until stiff, then fold it in. To still-freeze the ice cream in a mold or in foil-covered refrigerator trays, see 761.

CHOCOLATE BOMBE

About 10 Servings

Soak:

1 1/2 teaspoons gelatin

in:

1 cup cold water

Stir and bring to the boiling point:

1 cup milk
1 1/2 cups sugar
2 to 4 tablespoons cocoa

Dissolve the gelatin in the mixture. Cool. Add:

1 teaspoon vanilla

Chill until about to set. ➤ Whip until thickened, but not stiff:

2 cups whipping cream

Fold lightly into the gelatin mixture. To still-freeze the bombe in a mold or in foil-covered refrigerator trays, see 761.

BUTTER PECAN ICE CREAM

About 6 Servings

Boil for 2 minutes:

1 cup light brown sugar
1/2 cup water
1/8 teaspoon salt

Beat:

2 eggs

Beat in the syrup slowly. Cook in a double boiler ➤ over—not in—boiling water, stirring constantly until the mixture coats the back of the spoon. Add:

2 tablespoons butter

Cool, then add:

1 cup milk
1 teaspoon vanilla extract
1 tablespoon sherry

Beat until ➤ thickened, but not stiff:

1 cup whipping cream

Fold it into the egg mixture. To still-freeze, see 761. When partially frozen, fold in:

1/2 cup broken toasted pecan meats

If the nuts are salted, a very special piquancy results.

CARAMEL PARFAIT

About 9 Servings

Soak:

1 1/2 teaspoons gelatin

in:

1/2 cup cold water

Prepare:

3/4 cup warm Caramelized Sugar I, 559

Beat:

2 egg yolks

Beat in slowly:

1/2 cup sugar

Beat these ingredients until well blended. Add the caramel mixture. Stir in a double boiler ➤ over—not in—boiling water until the custard coats the back of a spoon. Stir in the soaked gelatin. Cool. Add:

2 teaspoons vanilla

Chill until about to set. ➤ Whip until thickened, but not stiff:

2 cups whipping cream

Fold lightly into the custard. Still-freeze in a mold or in foil-covered refrigerator trays, see 761. Garnish with:

Toasted slivered almonds

BUTTERSCOTCH PARFAIT

About 6 Servings

Stir and melt in a saucepan over low heat, then boil for 1 minute:

2/3 cup brown sugar
2 tablespoons butter
1/8 teaspoon salt

Add:

1/2 cup water

Cook the butterscotch until smooth and syrupy. Beat:

4 egg yolks

Add the cooled syrup slowly, beating constantly. Cook and stir in a double boiler ➤ over—not in—boiling water until the mixture coats the back of a spoon. Whip until fluffy. Chill. ➤ Whip until thickened, but not stiff:

1 cup whipping cream

Add:

2 teaspoons vanilla

Fold into egg mixture. Still-freeze in a mold or in foil-covered refrigerator trays, see 761.

MAPLE PARFAIT

About 9 Servings

Cook and stir ➤ over—not in—boiling water until thick:

6 egg yolks
¾ cup maple syrup
⅛ teaspoon salt

When the custard coats the back of a spoon, remove it from the heat. Pour into a bowl and beat with a wire whisk until cool. ➤ Whip until thickened, but not stiff:

2 cups whipping cream

Fold it lightly into the custard. When partially frozen, add:

(½ cup crushed Nut Brittle, 788)

Still-freeze in a mold or in foil-covered refrigerator trays, see 761.

COFFEE PARFAIT

About 6 Servings

Combine:

2 tablespoons cornstarch
⅔ cup sugar
⅛ teaspoon salt

Stir into this mixture:

2 tablespoons milk

Add:

2 beaten egg yolks
1 cup strong coffee

Stir and cook this custard in a double boiler ➤ over—not in—boiling water until it coats the back of a spoon. Chill. ➤ Whip until thickened, but not stiff, and fold in:

1½ cups whipping cream

To still-freeze in foil-covered refrigerator trays, see 761. Serve in tall glasses, topped with:

Whipped cream
(Grated chocolate)

FRUIT MOUSSE

About 9 Servings

Prepare:

2 cups crushed fruit—peaches, apricots, bananas, strawberries or puréed black or red raspberries

Stir in:

⅛ teaspoon salt
¾ to 1 cup confectioners' sugar

Soak:

1½ teaspoons gelatin

in:

2 tablespoons cold water

Dissolve it in:

¼ cup boiling water

Cool and add:

2 tablespoons lemon juice

Stir into the fruit mixture. ➤ Whip until thickened, but not stiff:

2 cups whipping cream

Fold into the fruit and gelatin mixture. Still-freeze in a mold or in foil-covered refrigerator trays, see 761.

APRICOT MOUSSE

About 6 Servings

Surprisingly good—the fruit flavor being decided enough to disguise the evaporated milk taste. Prepare for whipping, 532:

1¼ cups evaporated milk

Put through a ricer or blender:

¾ cup cooked sweetened drained dried apricots

We do not like to substitute the canned ones, as the flavor is not strong enough. Soak:

1 teaspoon gelatin

in:

2 tablespoons cold apricot juice

Dissolve it in:

2 tablespoons hot apricot juice

Add the gelatin to the apricot purée. Chill until about to set. Whip the chilled evaporated milk and add to it:

½ teaspoon vanilla
⅛ teaspoon salt

Fold lightly into gelatin mixture. To still-freeze in foil-covered refrigerator trays, see 761.

STRAWBERRY OR RASPBERRY BOMBE

Prepare:

Bavarian Berry Cream, 747

using in all:

1½ cups sugar

To still-freeze the ice cream, see 761.

RASPBERRY PARFAIT

About 9 Servings

Crush and strain through two thicknesses of cheesecloth:

1 quart raspberries: about 1 cup juice

Discard the pulp. Boil to the thread stage, 778:

¾ cup water
1 cup sugar

Whip until stiff ➤ but not dry:

3 egg whites

Pour the syrup over them in a slow stream. Whip constantly until cool. Fold in juice. In a separate bowl ➤ whip until thickened, but not stiff:

2 cups whipping cream

Fold lightly into other ingredients. Still-freeze in a mold or in foil-covered refrigerator trays, see 761.

GREENGAGE PLUM ICE CREAM

12 Servings

Drain:

3½ cups canned pitted greengage plums

Put them through a ricer. There should be about 1½ cups of pulp. Soak:

1½ teaspoons gelatin

in:

1/4 cup cold water

Heat to the boiling point:

2 cups milk
3/4 to 1 cup sugar
1/8 teaspoon salt

Dissolve the gelatin in the hot milk. Cool, then add the plum pulp and:

2 tablespoons lemon juice

Chill the mixture until slushy. Whip until thickened, but not stiff, and add to above ingredients:

2 cups whipping cream

Still-freeze the ice cream in a mold or in foil-covered trays, see 761.

PERSIMMON ICE CREAM

About 6 Servings

A California creation.

Put through a ricer:

4 ripe Japanese persimmons

Add:

2 tablespoons sugar
6 tablespoons lemon juice

➤ Whip until thickened, but not stiff, and fold in:

2 cups whipping cream

Still-freeze in a mold or in foil-covered refrigerator trays, see 761.

TUTTI-FRUTTI PARFAIT

About 6 Servings

Cover and soak for several hours:

1 cup chopped candied fruit

in a combination of:

Brandy, rum, liqueur and syrup from canned stewed fruit

Drain well. Reserve liquid for flavoring other puddings. Soak:

1 teaspoon gelatin

in:

2 tablespoons water

Dissolve it over hot water. Boil to the thread stage, 778:

1/2 cup water
1/2 cup sugar

Beat ➤ until stiff, but not dry:

2 egg whites

Pour the syrup over the egg whites in a fine stream, beating constantly. Add the dissolved gelatin and continue beating until mixture thickens somewhat. Beat in drained fruit. ➤ Whip until thickened, but not stiff:

1 cup whipping cream
1 teaspoon vanilla

Fold into fruit and egg mixture. Still-freeze in a mold or in foil-covered refrigerator trays, see 761. Serve topped with:

Whipped cream

FRUIT-BUTTERMILK ICE CREAM

About 5 Servings

For girth-watchers: a quite acceptable low-fat variation.

Combine:

1 cup sweetened fruit purée: apricot, peach or strawberry

with:

3 tablespoons lemon juice
1/8 teaspoon salt
1 1/2 cups buttermilk

To still-freeze, see 761.

ABOUT ICES AND SHERBETS

Ices, or **glaces,** are made simply of fruit juice, sugar and water. Sherbets have variants, like the Italian **Graniti** and French **Sorbets**. These may have added egg white, milk or cream and are generally less sweet. Sherbets may be appropriately served with the meat course, as well as for dessert. Both are best when churn-frozen. Some types may be still-frozen without the addition of gelatin or egg white, but their texture is considerably lighter and less flinty when these modifying ingredients are included.

Freezing diminishes flavoring and sweetening, so sugar your base accordingly. ➤ However, if ices are too sweet they will not freeze. A safe proportion is approximately 1 part sugar to 4 parts liquid. ➤ Stir in any liqueurs after the ices have begun to freeze.

➤ To churn-freeze ices and sherbets, follow the directions for processing ice cream, 758. Like ice creams, they can be molded, after freezing, into attractive shapes like those shown in the chapter heading, 758. Pack a mold in salted ice for 3 hours. Remove the ice or sherbet from it about 5 minutes before serving.

➤ To still-freeze ices and sherbets, put them in a covered mold or a refrigerator tray covered with foil and place them in the freezer. While they are still slushy, they should be stirred or beaten from front to back in the tray to reduce the size of the crystals. Repeated beating at half-hour intervals will give them the consistency of a coarse churn-frozen water ice. ➤ Remove them from freezer to refrigerator about 20 minutes before serving. Ices and sherbets are especially delectable when served in fruit shells—fancy-cut and hollowed-out lemons, tangerines or oranges—garnished with leaves. See also Frozen Orange Surprise, 766.

Of course, meringues topped with whipped cream are containers as wonderful as crystal coupes or frappé goblets. Ices and sherbets lend themselves particularly to combinations with fruits —fresh, poached, preserved and candied; to chestnut garnishes with touches of liqueur; and if you are really professional, to veils of spun sugar.

FRUIT ICE

About 10 Servings

Have ready:

1 cup any sweetened fruit purée

Add to taste:

(Lemon juice)

Combine with:

4 cups water

To churn-freeze, see 758. If adding:

(Liqueur)

➤ have the ice almost completely churned before you do so: the high alcoholic content tends to inhibit freezing.

RASPBERRY OR STRAWBERRY ICE I

About 10 Servings

This method makes delicious linings for bombes. Cook until soft:

2 quarts strawberries or raspberries

Strain the juice through 2 thicknesses of cheesecloth. There should be about 2 cups of thick juice. Combine, stir over heat until the sugar is dissolved, then boil 5 minutes, covered, without stirring, to avoid crystallization:

4 cups water
2 cups sugar

Chill. Add the thick berry juice and:

1 tablespoon lemon juice

To churn-freeze, see 758.

PEACH ICE

About 12 Servings

Combine:

2 cups peach pulp: fresh peaches, peeled and riced
6 tablespoons lemon juice
¾ cup orange juice

Stir over heat until sugar is dissolved:

3 cups water
1 cup sugar

Then boil 5 minutes, covered, without stirring, to avoid crystallization. Chill. Combine with the fruit pulp and juices. To churn-freeze, see 758. Top each serving with:

1 teaspoon cassis or Melba Sauce, 770

APRICOT ICE

About 9 Servings

Put through a ricer or a sieve:

3½ cups drained canned apricots

Add:

2¼ cups orange juice
6 tablespoons lemon juice

Stir in over heat until dissolved:

1 cup sugar

Then boil 5 minutes, covered, without stirring, to avoid crystallization. Chill. To churn-freeze, see 758.

PINEAPPLE ICE

About 9 Servings

Stir over heat until sugar is dissolved:

1 cup sugar
4 cups water

Boil 5 minutes, covered, without stirring, to avoid crystallization. Chill the syrup and add:

1 cup drained canned crushed pineapple
6 tablespoons lemon juice

To churn-freeze, see 758. Garnish with:

Mint leaves

LEMON ICE

About 9 Servings

Grate:

2 teaspoons lemon rind

onto:

2 cups sugar

Add:

4 cups water or tea
¼ teaspoon salt

Stir over heat until sugar is dissolved, then boil 5 minutes, covered, without stirring, to avoid crystallization. Chill. Add:

¾ cup lemon juice

To churn or still-freeze, see 758 or 765. Serve in a mound or ring with:

Fruit or canned fruit used in some attractive combination, flavored with curaçao, Cointreau or rum

LEMON AND ORANGE ICE

About 12 Servings

Combine and stir over heat until sugar is dissolved:

2 teaspoons grated orange rind
2 cups sugar
4 cups water
¼ teaspoon salt

Boil for 5 minutes, covered, without stirring, to avoid crystallization. Chill. Add:

2 cups orange juice
¼ cup lemon juice

To churn-freeze, see 758. Top each serving with:

1 teaspoon rum or orange marmalade

FROZEN ORANGE OR LEMON SURPRISE

This dessert can be made well in advance. If it is removed from the freezer and set in place just before the guests are served, it may even be used as a centerpiece or table decoration, bedded on a shallow tray of cracked ice. Choose:

Navel oranges or heavy-skinned lemons

Cut a fancy opening near the top, which later serves as a lid. ➤ Keep lids and bottoms matched until ready to fill. Hollow out the pulp. Use it for juice or for making fruit ice or sherbet. When ready to fill the orange case, have all ingredients ready so you can work fast to avoid undue melting. Fill the cases with:

Fruit ice or sherbet

or a combination of:

Fruit ice
Ice cream
Partially frozen raspberries, peaches, strawberries
A touch of liqueur

Wrap fruits individually in foil and deep-freeze at once. Depending on the temperature of the room, allow about ½ hour or more to defrost, uncovered, before serving. Garnish the cases with fresh green leaves stuck in the lids and around the bases, see sketch on 758.

RASPBERRY OR STRAWBERRY ICE II

About 4 Servings

This combines well with Angelica Parfait, 762.
Press through a sieve or a ricer:
1 quart strawberries or raspberries
Soak:
1 teaspoon gelatin
in:
1 tablespoon cold water
Stir over heat until sugar is dissolved:
1 cup water or ½ cup water and ½ cup pineapple juice
¾ to 1 cup sugar
Boil 5 minutes, covered, without stirring, to avoid crystallization. Add:
1 to 2 tablespoons lemon juice
Dissolve the gelatin in the hot syrup. Chill. Combine juice with syrup. To still-freeze, see 765.

MINT ICE

About 9 Servings

A refreshing alternate for the mint jelly that traditionally accompanies lamb.
Prepare:
Any orange or lemon ice
After the syrup reaches the boiling point, pour it over:
½ cup chopped fresh mint leaves
Steep 1 to 2 minutes, drain out the mint leaves, and proceed as for the recipe you have chosen.

LEMON SHERBET

About 5 Servings

Soak:
2 teaspoons gelatin
in:
¼ cup cold water
Stir over heat until sugar dissolves:
2¼ cups water
¾ cup sugar
Boil 5 minutes, covered, without stirring, to avoid crystallization. Dissolve gelatin in hot syrup. Chill.
Grate:
1 teaspoon lemon rind
Add:
¾ cup lemon juice
Add these ingredients to the syrup. Beat ➤ until stiff, but not dry, and fold into the chilled mixture:
2 egg whites
To still-freeze, see 765. Serve topped with:
(Finely chopped candied orange or lemon rind)

ORANGE SHERBET

About 5 Servings

Soak:
2 teaspoons gelatin
in:
¼ cup cold water
Stir over heat until sugar dissolves:
1 cup water
⅔ to ¾ cup sugar, depending on sweetness of fruit
Boil 5 minutes, covered, without stirring, to avoid crystallization. Dissolve gelatin in hot syrup. Cool.
Add:
1 teaspoon grated lemon rind
1 teaspoon grated orange rind
1½ cups orange juice
⅓ cup lemon juice
Beat ➤ until stiff, but not dry, and add:
2 egg whites
To still-freeze, see 765. Garnish with:
Fresh pineapple slices

LIME SHERBET

About 6 Servings

Soak:
1¼ teaspoons gelatin
in:
¼ cup cold water
Stir over heat until sugar dissolves:
⅔ cup sugar
1¾ cups water
Boil 5 minutes, covered, without stirring, to avoid crystallization. Add the gelatin mixture. Chill and add:
½ cup lime juice
2 drops green vegetable coloring
Beat until ➤ stiff, but not dry, and add:
2 egg whites
To still-freeze, see 765. Serve in:
Lemon shells
Garnish with:
Green leaves

GRAPEFRUIT SHERBET

About 4 Servings

Soak:
2 teaspoons gelatin
in:
½ cup cold water
Stir over heat until sugar dissolves:
1 cup sugar
1 cup water
Boil 5 minutes, covered, without stirring, to avoid crystallization. Dissolve the gelatin in the hot syrup. Chill. Add:
¼ cup lemon juice
2 cups fresh grapefruit juice
⅓ cup orange juice
¼ teaspoon salt
Beat until ➤ stiff, but not dry, and add:
2 egg whites
To still-freeze, see 765.

RASPBERRY OR STRAWBERRY SHERBET

About 5 Servings

Soak:

2 teaspoons gelatin

in:

¼ cup cold water

Press through a sieve or a ricer:

1 quart fresh berries

Add to them:

¼ cup lemon juice

Stir over heat until sugar dissolves:

1¾ cups water

¾ cup sugar

Boil 5 minutes, covered, without stirring, to avoid crystallization. Dissolve the gelatin in the hot syrup. Cool and add berries. Chill. Beat until ➤ stiff, but not dry, and add:

2 egg whites

To still-freeze, see 765.

BANANA-PINEAPPLE SHERBET

About 8 Servings

Combine and stir until sugar is dissolved:

1½ cups crushed pineapple

¾ cup confectioners' sugar

Add:

1½ cups banana pulp: about 3 large bananas

½ cup orange juice

6 tablespoons lemon juice

Place in refrigerator trays. Freeze until nearly firm. ➤ Beat until stiff, but not dry:

2 egg whites

Add fruit mixture gradually. Beat sherbet until light and fluffy. Return to trays. To still-freeze, see 765.

★ CRANBERRY SHERBET

About 8 Servings

Simmer until soft and ready to pop:

1 quart cranberries

in:

1¾ cups water

Force the berries through a sieve or blend in an electric blender. Add to them and boil, covered, 5 minutes, without stirring:

1¾ cups sugar

1 cup water or pineapple juice

Soak:

2 teaspoons gelatin

in:

¼ cup cold water

Dissolve the gelatin in the hot juice. Chill. Beat until ➤ stiff, but not dry, and add:

2 egg whites

To still-freeze, see 765. Serve in:

Orange cups

WINE SHERBET

About 8 Servings

A dry sherbet—delightful served after roasted meat or as a garnish for a fruit compote.

Soak:

1 tablespoon gelatin

in:

¼ cup cold water

Stir over heat until sugar dissolves:

1 cup water

¾ cup sugar

Boil 5 minutes, covered, without stirring, to avoid crystallization. Dissolve gelatin in hot syrup. Chill. Add:

2 cups dry white wine

1 cup unstrained lime juice

1 tablespoon crème de menthe

Beat until ➤ stiff, but not dry, and fold into this chilled mixture:

1 egg white

To still-freeze, see 765.

CHAMPAGNE SHERBET

About 8 Servings

Stir over heat until sugar dissolves:

1¼ cups sugar

1 cup water

Boil 5 minutes, covered, without stirring, to avoid crystallization. Cool. Stir in:

1½ cups champagne

3 tablespoons lemon juice

Churn-freeze, 758, until almost set. Fold in:

Meringue I, 730

When ready to serve, pour over each portion:

2 tablespoons champagne

LEMON MILK SHERBET

About 9 Servings

Dissolve:

1⅓ cups sugar

in:

7 tablespoons lemon juice

Stir these ingredients slowly into:

3½ cups milk or milk and cream

If the milk curdles, it will not affect texture after freezing. To churn-freeze, see 758.

ORANGE MILK SHERBET

About 10 Servings

Combine and stir:

1½ teaspoons grated orange rind

1½ cups sugar

Stir into:

¼ cup lemon juice

1½ cups orange juice

(1½ bananas, riced)

until sugar is dissolved. Stir these ingredients gradually into:

4 cups very cold milk

If the milk curdles slightly, it will not affect the texture after the sherbet is frozen. To churn-freeze, see 758.

PINEAPPLE MILK SHERBET

About 10 Servings

Combine and stir until sugar is dissolved:

1 cup unsweetened pineapple juice

1 teaspoon grated lemon rind
¼ cup lemon juice
1 cup sugar
⅛ teaspoon salt
Stir these ingredients slowly into:
4 cups chilled milk
To churn-freeze, see 758.

PINEAPPLE BUTTERMILK SHERBET

About 6 Servings

A low-fat version, well worth trying.
Combine:
2 cups buttermilk
½ cup sugar
1 cup crushed pineapple
Freeze these ingredients until they have a slushy consistency. Place them in a chilled bowl. Add:
1 slightly beaten egg white
1½ teaspoons vanilla
Beat until light and fluffy. Return to freezer in foil-covered refrigerator trays. To still-freeze, see 765.

FROZEN SUCKERS

Fourteen 1½-inch Suckers

Quickly made from canned baby fruits, and definitely for the very young.
When these mixtures are partially frozen in a compartmented ice tray or in individual paper cups, insert a looped paraffined string or a paper spoon into each unit to form a handle. Then freeze until hard.

I. Mix and stir well:
2 cups sweetened puréed fruit
1 cup orange juice
2 tablespoons sugar
Freeze as described above.

II. Mix and freeze, as described above:
¾ cup orange or grape juice
1 cup yogurt
½ teaspoon vanilla
(1 tablespoon lemon juice)

SNOW ICE CREAM

The ancestor of all frozen delights and a favorite of small fry.
Arrange attractively in a chilled bowl, trying not to compact it:
Fresh, clean snow
Pour over it:
Sweetened fruit juice or maple syrup
Or, for a gallon of snow, stir in:
1 cup cream
¾ cup sugar
½ teaspoon vanilla
For this kind of frozen delight, as well as for packing frozen desserts in general and for serving them attractively on a dish in thin slabs, the shovel scoop shown at the bottom is useful. A spring-release scoop, also shown, turns out uniform ball-shapes, and is a great help in molding single portions quickly at dessert time, provided the entire utensil is dipped into very hot water between dollops.

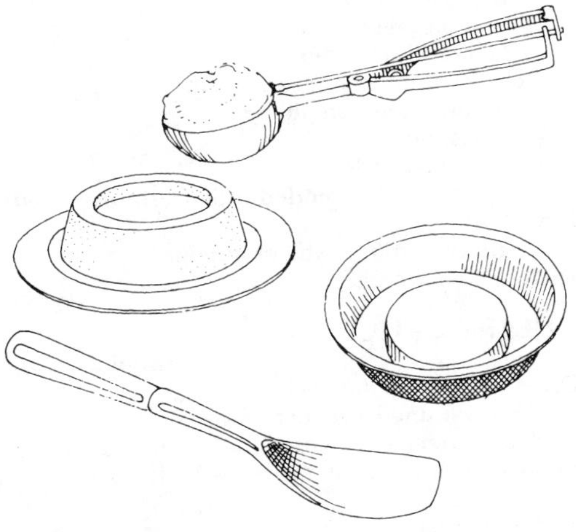

ABOUT SWEET SAUCES

With dessert sauces, "the object all sublime" is to "let the punishment fit the crime." In fact, unless the sauce can complement the dessert, omit it. Should the latter be tart, tone it down with a bland sauce; if bland, use a sauce to which a tablespoon of liqueur imparts the final sprightly touch. Sauces based on sugar are usually very simple to confect. They have distinct family branches similar to those of their unsweetened counterparts. The main things to remember are ➤ don't overbeat cream bases or cream garnishes and ➤ do cook egg sauces over—not in—boiling water. ➤ Be sure that sauces thickened with flour and cornstarch are free from lumps, and cook them thoroughly to avoid any raw taste. See flour paste, 339, and cornstarch, 339. ➤ In preparing heavy syrups, guard against sugaring, see 777.

LEMON, ORANGE OR LIME SAUCE

About 1 Cup

A lovely, translucent foil for puddings and gelatins. Combine and stir in a double boiler ➤ over—not in—boiling water until thickened:
¼ to ½ cup sugar
1 tablespoon cornstarch
1 cup water
Remove sauce from heat. Stir in:
2 to 3 tablespoons butter
½ teaspoon grated lemon or orange rind
1½ tablespoons lemon or lime juice or
3 tablespoons orange juice
⅛ teaspoon salt

FRUIT FONDUE SAUCE

About 1½ Cups

If you omit the crushed fruit, this sauce can serve as a hot sweet fondue sauce for fruits or bits of cake.

Combine and stir in a double boiler over—not in—boiling water until thickened:

1 cup unsweetened fruit juice
½ to ¾ cup sugar
1 tablespoon cornstarch or
2 tablespoons flour

Remove mixture from heat. Stir in:

2 teaspoons lemon juice
(2 tablespoons butter)

Cool. You may add:

(1 cup crushed, shredded fruit, fresh or stewed)

Flavor with:

Sherry or other wine or liqueur

Serve cold or hot.

CHERRY SAUCE

About 2½ Cups

Drain well, reserving juice:

2 cups canned sweet cherries

Add to the cherry syrup and simmer about 10 minutes in the top of a double boiler over direct heat:

¼ cup sugar
¼ cup corn syrup
1 stick cinnamon: 2 inches
1 tablespoon lemon juice

Remove the cinnamon. Mix:

2 teaspoons cornstarch
1 tablespoon cold water

Stir this mixture into the hot cherry juice. Cook ➤ over—not in—boiling water and stir until it thickens. Add the cherries. Serve hot or cold.

CHERRY JUBILEE SAUCE

About 1¼ Cups

This recipe always involves the use of liqueurs. If you do not wish to ignite the brandy, you may soak the cherries in it well ahead of time. If you flambé, be sure that the fruit is at room temperature, and the brandy warm, see 127. Other preserved fruits may be substituted for the cherries. Heat well:

1 cup preserved pitted Bing or other cherries

Add:

¼ cup slightly warmed brandy

Ignite the brandy. When the flame has died down, add:

2 tablespoons kirsch

You may serve the sauce hot on:

Vanilla ice cream

MELBA SAUCE

About 1¾ Cups

Combine and bring to the boiling point in the top of a double boiler over direct heat:

½ cup currant jelly
1 cup sieved raspberries

Mix and add:

1 teaspoon cornstarch
⅛ teaspoon salt
½ cup sugar

Cook ➤ over—not in—boiling water until thick and clear. Chill before using.

⅄ QUICK AMBROSIA SAUCE

About 1¾ Cups

Mix:

¾ cup sweetened puréed apricots
¾ cup sweetened puréed peaches

Add:

¼ cup orange juice
1 teaspoon grated lemon rind
2 tablespoons rum or sloe gin

SAUCE COCKAIGNE

About 8 Cups

A sauce for all seasons—its ingredients are always available. Great with custards, glazed bananas, cottage pudding and waffles, by itself or combined with a little liqueur or whipped cream.

Cook gently in a wide-bottomed covered pan until the fruit is pulpy and disintegrates easily when stirred with a wire whisk:

2 cups dried apricots
1¼ cups water

Add:

1½ cups sugar

Stir until dissolved. Add:

5 cups canned crushed pineapple

Bring the mixture to a boil. Pour into jars and cover. Keep under refrigeration.

RAISIN SAUCE

About 1⅔ Cups

Boil 15 minutes:

1½ cups water
⅓ cup seeded raisins
¼ cup sugar
⅛ teaspoon salt

Melt:

2 tablespoons butter

Stir in, until blended:

1 teaspoon flour

Add the hot sauce slowly. Stir and cook until it boils. Mix in:

A grating of nutmeg or lemon rind

Serve over:

Steamed puddings, 754

JELLY SAUCE

About ¾ Cup

For steamed and cornstarch puddings, or use as a fondue sauce.

Dilute over hot water in double boiler:

¾ cup currant or other jelly

Thin with:

¼ cup boiling water or wine

Serve hot or cold. This sauce may be thickened. Melt:

1 tablespoon butter

Blend in:

1 tablespoon flour

Add the jelly mixture. Stir over low heat until it reaches the consistency desired. You may spice the sauce with:

1 teaspoon cinnamon
1/8 teaspoon ground cloves
1/8 teaspoon grated lemon rind

JAM SAUCE

About 3/4 Cup

Combine in a small saucepan:
1/4 cup raspberry, damson, gooseberry, grape or peach jam
1/2 cup water
Stir and boil these ingredients 2 minutes. Remove from heat and add:
1 teaspoon kirsch or 1/4 teaspoon almond extract
Serve hot or cold. Use on:
Bread, farina and other cereal puddings, 749

CUSTARD SAUCE OR CRÈME ANGLAISE

Prepare:
Custard, 734
using 5 egg yolks and 2/3 cup sugar. You may add:
(1/2 cup slivered almonds)

QUICK FRUIT CUSTARD SAUCE

About 3 Cups

Cream:
1/4 cup butter
Add gradually and beat until fluffy:
1 cup sugar
Beat in, one at a time:
2 eggs
One or two extra eggs will add richness. Beat in slowly and thoroughly and cook in a double boiler ➤ over—not in—boiling water:
1 cup scalded milk
1 teaspoon vanilla
1 teaspoon nutmeg
Fold in:
1 cup crushed berries, sliced peaches, etc.

CLASSIC SABAYON SAUCE

About 3 Cups

Prepare:
Zabaglione or Sabayon, 736
You may omit the egg white if you prefer a richer and denser mixture. If you do, use in all:
1 cup wine

HOT SABAYON SAUCE

About 2 Cups

Excellent with beignets or fruit cake. Marsala is traditional in Italian recipes. We find that it gives the sauce a rather dull color and prefer to use, instead, a sweet white wine—after the French fashion. This mixture should be creamy rather than fluffy. For a fluffy sauce, see the next recipe.
Stir constantly until thick in the top of a double boiler ➤ over—not in—boiling water:
6 egg yolks
1/3 cup sugar
1 cup white wine or 1/2 cup water and 1/2 cup Cointreau or Grand Marnier

COLD SABAYON SAUCE

About 1 1/4 Cups

The advantage of this sauce over the classic version is that it will keep for several days in the refrigerator. Use it over fresh fruits.
Combine, beat and heat in the top of a double boiler ➤ over—not in—boiling water:
4 egg yolks
3/4 cup sugar
3/4 cup dry sherry or other dry wine
Beat with a whisk until very thick. Set the double boiler top in a pan of cracked ice and continue to beat the sauce until cold. Add:
(1/4 cup lightly whipped cream)

WEINSCHAUM SAUCE

Prepare:
Wine Custard or Weinschaum, 736

RUM SAUCE

About 2 1/2 Cups

Beat:
2 egg yolks
Add and beat until dissolved:
1 cup sifted confectioners' sugar
Add slowly:
6 tablespoons rum
Beat these ingredients until well blended. Whip until stiff:
1 cup whipping cream
Fold in:
1 teaspoon vanilla
Fold the egg mixture into the cream.

RED WINE SAUCE

About 2 Cups

Boil for 5 minutes:
1 cup sugar
1/2 cup water
Cool and add to the syrup:
1/4 cup claret or other red wine
1/2 teaspoon grated lemon rind

HOT WINE OR PLUM PUDDING SAUCE

About 1 1/2 Cups

Cream:
1/2 cup butter
1 cup sugar
Beat and add:
1 or 2 eggs
Stir in:
3/4 cup dry sherry, Tokay or Madeira
1 teaspoon grated lemon rind
(1/4 teaspoon nutmeg)
Shortly before serving, beat the sauce over—not in—boiling water in a double boiler. Heat thoroughly.

CRÈME DE MENTHE OR LIQUEUR SAUCE

Allow, for each serving, about:

1½ tablespoons crème de menthe or other liqueur

Pour it over:

Ice cream, ices or lightly sugared fruits

NESSELRODE SAUCE

About 4 Cups

Combine and stir well:

¾ cup chopped maraschino cherries
⅓ cup chopped citron or orange peel

Add:

1 cup orange marmalade
½ cup coarsely chopped candied ginger
2 tablespoons maraschino cherry juice
1 cup chopped Boiled Chestnuts, 298
½ cup or more rum, to make the sauce of a good consistency

Place in jars and seal. Ripen for 2 weeks before serving.

CIDER SAUCE

About 2 Cups

Melt over low heat:

1 tablespoon butter

Blend in and simmer 3 to 5 minutes:

¾ tablespoon flour

Add:

1½ cups cider

Add, if needed:

(Sugar)
(1 teaspoon cinnamon)
(¼ teaspoon cloves)

Stir and boil these ingredients about 2 minutes. Serve hot or cold on a bland pudding.

CHOCOLATE SAUCE COCKAIGNE

About 1¾ Cups

Dreamy on vanilla, coffee or chocolate ice cream. Melt in the top of a double boiler ➤ over—not in—boiling water:

3 oz. unsweetened chocolate

Combine, then stir into the chocolate:

1 well-beaten egg
¾ cup evaporated milk
1 cup sugar

Cook about 20 minutes. Remove from heat and beat with a rotary beater 1 minute or until well blended. Stir in:

1 teaspoon vanilla
(¼ teaspoon cinnamon)

Cool sauce before using. If tightly covered and placed in the refrigerator, it will keep several days.

CHOCOLATE SAUCE

About 1 Cup

Stir until dissolved, then cook, without stirring, to the syrup stage, about 5 minutes:

¾ cup water
½ cup sugar or ⅓ cup honey

Melt in the syrup:

1 to 2 oz. unsweetened chocolate

Cool. Add:

1 teaspoon vanilla

You may add a small amount of:

Cream, dry sherry or brandy

Serve hot. If made in advance, keep the sauce hot in a double boiler.

HOT FUDGE SAUCE

About 1 Cup

The grand kind that, when cooked for the longer period and served hot, grows hard on ice cream and enraptures children.

Melt in a double boiler ➤ over—not in—boiling water:

2 oz. unsweetened chocolate
1 tablespoon butter

Stir and blend well, then add:

⅓ cup boiling water

Stir well and add:

1 cup sugar
2 tablespoons corn syrup

Let the sauce boil readily, but not too furiously, over direct heat. Do not stir. If you wish an ordinary sauce, boil it ➤ covered for about 3 minutes to wash down any crystals which may have formed on the sides of the pan. Uncover, reduce the heat, and cook 2 minutes more without stirring. If you wish a hot sauce that will harden over ice cream ➤ boil it, uncovered, about 3 minutes more. Add just before serving:

1 teaspoon vanilla or 2 teaspoons rum

When cold, this sauce is very thick. It may be reheated over—not in—boiling water.

CHOCOLATE CUSTARD SAUCE

About 2¼ Cups

Heat in a double boiler ➤ over—not in—boiling water until melted:

2 oz. chopped unsweetened chocolate
2 cups milk

Beat well:

4 egg yolks
¾ cup sugar
⅛ teaspoon salt

Beat the hot mixture gradually into the yolks. Return to double boiler. Cook gently, stirring constantly ➤ over—not in—boiling water, about 5 minutes or until thickened. Cool. Add:

1 teaspoon vanilla

Serve hot or cold over:

Puddings, ice ceam, or filled cream puffs

CHOCOLATE NUT-BRITTLE SAUCE

About 1½ Cups

Melt in a double boiler ➤ over—not in—boiling water:

3 oz. sweet chocolate

Stir in slowly:

½ cup boiling water

Add:
1¼ cups crushed nut brittle
Cool slightly. Before serving, add:
1 tablespoon brandy
Serve over:
Ice cream

QUICK CHOCOLATE FONDUE SAUCE

I. **About 1¼ Cups**
Combine and stir in a heavy saucepan over low heat until smooth:
1 cup semisweet chocolate pieces
½ cup evaporated milk
(¼ cup marshmallows)
Keep warm in a fondue pan, 254, and use for dipping fruit: pieces of pineapple, banana or orange, or small squares of cake.

II. **About 1 Cup**
Put into an ⅄ electric blender:
2 squares chopped unsweetened chocolate
½ cup sugar
6 tablespoons warm milk, cream, coffee or sherry
½ teaspoon vanilla or rum
⅛ teaspoon salt
Blend until smooth. Heat in a fondue pan, see I, above.

MOCHA SAUCE

About 1½ Cups
Bring to a boil and cook over moderate heat about 3 minutes, stirring occasionally:
½ cup cocoa
⅛ teaspoon salt
1 cup dark corn syrup
¼ cup sugar or 16 average-sized Marshmallows, 781
¼ cup water
1 teaspoon instant coffee
Swirl in:
2 tablespoons butter
When slightly cool, stir in:
½ teaspoon vanilla
Serve hot or cold.

CHOCOLATE MINT SAUCE

6 Servings
Melt in a double boiler ➤ over—not in—boiling water:
10 large chocolate peppermint creams
Add:
3 tablespoons cream
Stir well.

CHOCOLATE CARAMEL SAUCE

About 1 Cup
Melt over low heat:
4 oz. semisweet chocolate
Stir in and cook until sauce is thick:
1 cup brown sugar
½ cup cream
1 tablespoon butter
Cool slightly and add:
1 teaspoon vanilla

MAPLE SYRUP SAUCE

About ¾ Cup
Heat, but do not boil:
½ cup maple syrup
Add:
½ teaspoon grated lemon peel
¼ teaspoon freshly grated nutmeg or
⅛ teaspoon ginger or cloves
(2 to 3 tablespoons chopped nutmeats)
Chill and serve cold. If you care to serve it hot, swirl in:
1 to 2 tablespoons butter

MAPLE SUGAR SAUCE

About 2 Cups
Stir over low heat until dissolved, then cook to a thin syrup without stirring:
1 lb. maple sugar
½ cup evaporated milk
¼ cup light corn syrup
Add when cooked:
½ teaspoon vanilla
½ cup shredded nutmeats

BUTTERSCOTCH SAUCE

About ¾ Cup
Boil to the consistency of heavy syrup:
⅓ cup light corn syrup
⅝ cup light brown sugar
2 tablespoons butter
⅛ teaspoon salt
Cool these ingredients. Add:
⅓ cup evaporated milk or cream
Serve the sauce hot or cold. It may be reheated in a double boiler.

HOT BROWN-SUGAR SAUCE

About 1½ Cups
Cook 5 minutes, stirring occasionally:
1 cup brown sugar
½ cup water
Pour a little of the syrup in a fine stream over:
1 beaten egg
Beat constantly, adding the rest of the syrup gradually so the egg thickens. Add:
3 tablespoons dry sherry
⅛ teaspoon salt
Serve at once, or hold in a double boiler ➤ over—not in—hot water.

BROWN-SUGAR BUTTER SAUCE

About 1 Cup
Fine with hot puddings or waffles.
Cream in a small saucepan:
¼ cup butter
1 cup brown sugar

Add gradually:

1 cup warm half-and-half or light cream

Stir over low heat until it boils. Remove from heat. Add:

¼ cup bourbon or brandy

Beat with a wire whisk until smooth. Add and mix in:

(⅓ cup chopped nuts)

RICH BROWN-SUGAR SAUCE

About 1½ Cups

Place in a double boiler ➤ over—not in—boiling water:

3 beaten egg yolks
¾ cup cream
¾ teaspoon salt
½ cup brown sugar

Stir and cook until thick and creamy.
Add a little at a time, stirring constantly:

3 tablespoons butter
1½ tablespoons lemon juice

BROWN-SUGAR ORANGE SAUCE

About 1 Cup

Superfine for filling coffee cakes or for pouring over pancakes and waffles.
Combine in a saucepan:

¾ cup brown sugar
¼ cup butter
½ cup orange juice

Stir constantly and heat for 3 minutes, then cool.

CARAMEL MOCHA SAUCE

About 1 Cup

Prepare and cool, so as not to curdle the cream:

½ cup Caramel Syrup, 791

Add:

1 cup cream or strong coffee
1 teaspoon vanilla
⅛ teaspoon salt

If you use coffee instead of cream, swirl in:

2 tablespoons butter

You may keep the sauce hot over hot water.

CARAMEL CREAM SAUCE

About 1½ Cups

Combine and stir in a double boiler ➤ over—not in—boiling water until melted:

½ lb. Caramels, 784
1 cup whipping cream or evaporated milk

COFFEE SAUCE

About 1½ Cups

Beat:

2 eggs

Beat into them, very slowly:

½ cup strong boiling coffee

Add:

¼ cup sugar
⅛ teaspoon salt

Cook ➤ over—not in—boiling water and stir the sauce in the top of a double boiler until it coats a spoon. Chill.
Shortly before serving, fold in:

½ cup whipped cream
(¼ cup chopped candied ginger)

HONEY SAUCE

About 1 Cup

Combine and stir well:

¼ cup hot water
½ cup honey
¼ cup chopped nutmeats
¼ cup minced candied orange or lemon peel or candied ginger

Chill.

HONEY MINT SAUCE

About ¾ Cup

Recommended for fruit compotes.
Combine:

½ cup orange juice
2 tablespoons lemon juice
2 tablespoons honey
⅛ cup finely chopped fresh mint

VANILLA SAUCE

About 1 Cup

Combine and stir in a double boiler over—not in—boiling water until thickened:

¼ cup sugar
1 tablespoon cornstarch
1 cup water

Remove sauce from heat. Stir in:

2 to 3 tablespoons butter
⅛ teaspoon salt
1 to 2 teaspoons vanilla or the seeds scraped from a 2-inch length of vanilla bean, 577, or 1 tablespoon rum

MARSHMALLOW SAUCE

About 2 Cups

Stir over low heat until the sugar is dissolved:

¾ cup sugar
1 tablespoon light corn syrup
¼ cup milk

Bring to a boil, then simmer gently about 5 minutes. Dissolve in top of double boiler by stirring ➤ over—not in—boiling water:

½ lb. Marshmallows, 781
2 tablespoons water

Pour the syrup over the dissolved marshmallows, beating well.
Add:

1 teaspoon vanilla

Serve the sauce hot or cold. It may be reheated in a double boiler. Beat well before serving.

COCONUT DULCIE

About 4½ Cups

Good by itself over fruit puddings, or combined as a sauce with purées of tart fruit such as guava and currant.

Boil to a thick syrup:

4 cups water
3 cups sugar

Add:

1 freshly grated coconut, 566

Cook slowly about 25 minutes until the mixture is translucent. Pour into sterile jars and seal.

SWEETENED BUTTERS

I. **About ¼ Cup**

Cream, then chill:

3 tablespoons butter
½ cup sifted confectioners' sugar
¾ teaspoon cinnamon

II. Honey Butter **About ½ Cup**

Delicious on waffles or toast.

Beat well:

¼ cup honey
2 tablespoons soft butter
2 tablespoons whipping cream

III. See **Butter Sauce for Crêpes Suzette, 237.**

HARD SAUCE

About 1 Cup

Basic ingredients are always the same, although proportions and flavoring may vary. In this recipe, the larger amount of butter is preferable. An attractive way to serve hard sauce on cold cake or pudding is to chill it and mold it with a small fancy cutter—or to put it through the individual butter mold illustrated on 541.

Sift:

1 cup confectioners' sugar

Beat until soft:

2 to 5 tablespoons butter

Add the sugar gradually. Beat these ingredients until well blended and fluffy. Add:

⅛ teaspoon salt
1 teaspoon vanilla or 1 tablespoon coffee, rum, whisky, brandy or lemon juice

You may beat in:

(1 egg or ¼ cup cream)

When the sauce is very smooth, chill thoroughly.

SPICY HARD SAUCE

About 1 Cup

Prepare:

Hard Sauce, above

Beat into it:

½ teaspoon cinnamon
¼ teaspoon cloves
(Liqueur, to taste)

Chill.

BROWN-SUGAR HARD SAUCE

About 1⅔ Cups

Sift:

1½ cups brown sugar

Beat until soft:

½ cup butter

Add the sugar gradually. Beat these ingredients until well blended. Beat in slowly:

⅓ cup cream

Beat in, drop by drop:

2 tablespoons dry wine or
1 teaspoon vanilla

Chill well. Add for garnish:

(¼ cup chopped nuts)

FRUIT HARD SAUCE

About 1⅔ Cups

Sift:

1 cup confectioners' sugar

Beat until soft:

⅓ cup butter

Add the sugar gradually. Beat until well blended. Beat in:

¼ cup cream
⅔ cup crushed strawberries, raspberries, apricots or bananas

Chill thoroughly.

FLUFFY HARD SAUCE

About 1½ Cups

Sift:

1 cup sugar

Beat until soft:

1 tablespoon butter

Add the sugar gradually and:

1 tablespoon cream

Beat until well blended. Whip until stiff:

3 egg whites

Fold them into the sugar mixture. Add:

2 tablespoons cream
1 teaspoon or more vanilla, rum or port

Beat the sauce well. Pile it in a sauceboat. Chill thoroughly.

FOAMY SAUCE

About 2 Cups

Sift:

1 cup confectioners' sugar

Beat until soft:

⅓ to ½ cup butter

Add the sugar slowly. Beat until well blended. Beat in:

1 egg yolk
1 teaspoon vanilla or 2 tablespoons port or
1 tablespoon Grand Marnier

Place the sauce in a double boiler ➤ over—not in—boiling water. Beat and cook until the yolk has thickened slightly. Whip until stiff:

1 egg white

Fold it lightly into the sauce. Serve hot at once, or cold—but do not try to reheat.

LIQUEUR CREAM SAUCE

About 1½ Cups

So zestful that it will glorify the plainest cottage pudding, cake or gingerbread. Less extravagant, too, than it sounds; only a small amount is needed.

Beat until soft in the top of a double boiler ➤ over—not in—boiling water:

⅓ cup butter

Add gradually and beat until creamy:

1 cup sifted confectioners' sugar

Beat in slowly:

3 tablespoons brandy or other liqueur

Beat in, one at a time:

2 egg yolks

Add:

½ cup cream

Cook until slightly thickened.

SOUR CREAM SAUCE

About 1½ Cups

Use as dressing for berries, or combine berries with it and serve over cake or fruit gelatin.

Combine:

1 cup cultured sour cream

½ cup brown sugar

(1 cup berries)

(½ teaspoon vanilla)

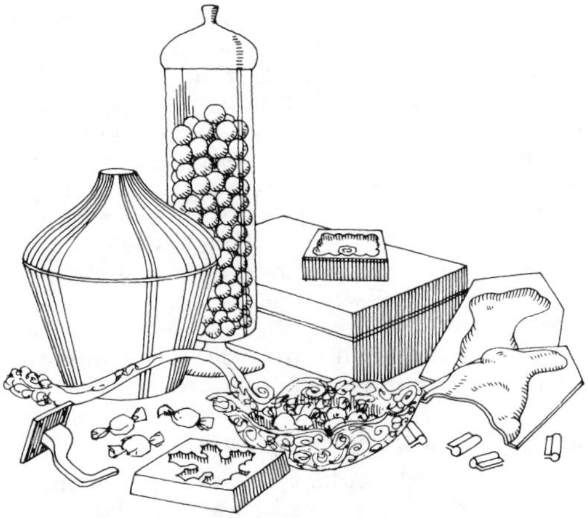

CANDIES AND CONFECTIONS

The fudge pot is responsible for the beginnings of many a good cook. So be tolerant when, some rainy day, your children take an interest in the sweeter side of kitchen life. Weather and altitude play important roles for confectioners, young and old. On humid days, candy requires longer cooking and ingredients must be brought to a heat at least 2 degrees higher than on dry days. In fact, clear, cool weather is a near-precondition for a large group of confections, such as hard candies, glazes, divinities, fondant, nougats and those made with honey.

To avoid a mess ➤ always choose a pan with about four times as great a volume as that of the ingredients used, so that the candy will not boil over. ➤ To keep from burning the candy, see that the pan has a heavy bottom or is lined with a nonstick material. ➤ To keep from burning yourself, use a long wooden spoon that will not heat up during the prolonged cooking period.

Be adventurous about shaping candies. A maple sugar mold and a double chocolate rabbit mold with its clips are shown above. As sugar is highly hygroscopic, be sure to store candies tightly covered in glass, ceramic or tin; or serve candies wrapped as temptingly as possible. The illustration above shows a sumptuous and lighthearted silver bonbonnière, filigreed and spoon-shaped. The utilitarian object in the left foreground is a candy hook for taffy-making, 785.

ABOUT SUGARING IN CANDIES

When we were inexperienced, we were constantly baffled by the tendency of smooth, promising candy syrups to turn with lightning speed into grainy masses. We did not realize that one cause of this calamity was that we had stirred down the sugar crystals that had formed on the sides of the pan into crystals of quite different structure in the liquid below it.

Here are other tips to ward off sugaring. ➤ If the recipe calls for butter—and remember, always use unsalted butter—a good precaution is to grease the sides of the pan with some of it before putting in the other ingredients. Again, in cooking any candy, we achieve never-fail results by adopting the following procedure, adding other ingredients along the way as called for in specific individual recipes. Mix liquid and sugar ➤ stirring until the sugar is dissolved. Place pan on heat. Bring mixture to a boil and ➤ cover it until the candy develops enough steam to wash down crystals from the walls of the pan. This is a matter of 2 or 3 minutes only. Now ➤ uncover the pan to allow for evaporation. ➤ Reduce the heat to medium if the liquid is milk. ➤ Do not stir after uncovering, but continue cooking until the mixture has reached the desired temperature. When you do test for temperature, be sure to use an absolutely clean spoon or thermometer, the reason being, as before, to avoid introducing extraneous sugar crystals. Should the candy start to sugar, add a small quantity of water and begin over again.

Those who make candy frequently will do well to provide themselves for the finishing step with a marble slab of generous proportions. For candies that require rapid cooling, this material absorbs heat quickly and evenly, but not so rapidly as to hasten and so adversely affect crystallization. The next best base is a heavy stoneware platter or a flat pan elevated on a cooling rack so that air can circulate around it. Surfaces should be buttered in advance, except in making fondant.

ABOUT CANDY THERMOMETER TEMPERATURES

Producing varied and distinctive kinds of candy depends entirely on arriving at certain established stages of crystallization; and crystallization, in turn, depends on temperature. For this reason ➤ an accurate professional candy thermometer, properly used, is invaluable. To test your thermometer for accuracy, heat it in water—gradually, to avoid breakage—and keep it in boiling water for 10 minutes. It should register 212°. If there is any variation, add or subtract the number of degrees necessary to correct its reading.

When actually using the thermometer, warm it, as for testing, before inserting it into the candy. Place it near the center of the pan, and do not let the bulb touch the bottom. Also keep it from rolling around in the syrup, for this can trigger crystallization. Have a spoon ready when you remove the thermometer to catch any syrup drops that might fall back into the pan. Clean the thermometer after each use by letting it stand in warm water. Heat rises slowly to 220°, then takes a spurt—so watch carefully. ➤ For true accuracy, read at eye level, which of course means some gymnastics on your part.

If you have no thermometer, practice can make you expert in recognizing the subtle differences in color, bubbling and threading that reveal crucial temperatures. Always remove the pot from the heat while testing so as not to overcook, as a few extra degrees can bring the candy up into the next stage of crystallization. Use fresh chilled water for each test.

THREAD—Begins at 230°
The syrup makes a 2-inch coarse thread when dropped from a spoon.

SOFT BALL—Begins at 234°
A small quantity of syrup dropped into chilled water forms a ball which does not disintegrate but flattens out of its own accord when picked up with the fingers.

FIRM BALL—Begins at 244°
The ball will just hold its shape and will not flatten unless pressed with the fingers.

HARD BALL—Begins at 250°
The ball is more rigid but still pliable.

SOFT CRACK—Begins at 270°
Drop a small quantity of syrup into chilled water. It will separate into hard threads, which, when removed from the water, will bend.

HARD CRACK—Begins at 300°
The syrup separates into threads that are hard and brittle.

CARAMELIZED SUGAR—310° to 338°
Between these temperatures syrup turns dark golden, but it will turn black at 350°.

▲ For each increase of 500 feet above sea level, cook candy syrups 1° lower than indicated in the following recipes. For instance, if 234° is given and you are at 2000 feet, your syrup should be brought to 230°; at 5000 feet, to 224°.

➤ Do not jostle the pan when removing it from heat or during the cooling period. ➤ The candy should never be beaten until it has cooled to 110°. There are two ways of cooling. If you are the impatient type, place the pot gently—the minute you take it from the heat—into a pan of ice-cold water and allow it to remain until you can touch the bottom without discomfort. The other way is to pour the candy onto a marble slab or a heavy buttered platter. If it is taffy, caramel or brittle, hold the pouring edge of the pan away from you and only a few inches above the slab to avoid spattering. With these candies, too, let the mix run out of the pan of its own accord. ➤ To avoid sugaring, do not scrape the dregs from the pan. There is a difference in crystallization rate between the free-flowing portion and the other, near the bottom of the pan, which was exposed to greater heat. If you have neglected to add the called-for butter, you may drop it onto the surface of the hot candy and beat it in after the candy reaches 110°.

These are general principles. For particulars, follow the individual recipes carefully. Should you substitute honey in part for sugar, remember that honey needs a higher degree of heat and longer beating. When used as a candy ingredient, it will attract even more atmospheric moisture than sugar. For this reason honey-based confections must be wrapped with special care.

➤ In gauging yields for the following recipes, we have not included nuts, fruits and other additions where such additions are optional.

ABOUT CANDY WRAPPINGS

For that professional look, wrap candies in attractive foils, or buy, at small cost, fancy fluted foil cups into which you can pour directly. Delight the children by inserting lollipop cords. Or let them form candy chains by cutting 2 long narrow strips of thin self-sealing transparent wrap, laying out squares of candy—rather generously spaced—on one, placing the other neatly on top, then sealing in the candy bits, sausage-fashion. By twisting the wrap between the candy segments, colorful ★ Christmas-tree chains can be made and the links cut apart later for individual distribution.

ABOUT FONDANT AND CREAM CENTERS

One of the charms of fondant is that a batch can be made and ripened and then used at will over a period of weeks, with varying flavors, colors and shapes to suit the occasion. Basic Fondant also lends itself to variations during cooking. You may replace the water in the recipe with strong coffee, or use half white and half brown sugar, or half white and half maple sugar. But in case you don't want to make up a large batch of Basic Fondant, read the alternate processes given after the basic recipe—or use recipes carrying the word "center" in the title.

After removing fondant or centers from refrigeration, cover for several hours to keep them from absorbing atmospheric moisture as they reach room temperature.

BASIC FONDANT

About 1¼ Pounds

Bring to a boil in a large heavy pan:

1 cup water

Remove from heat and stir in until dissolved:

3 cups sugar

Return to heat and have ready:

1/16 teaspoon cream of tartar

More will make the fondant harder to work later. ➤ Just as the syrup comes up to a boil, add the cream of tartar to the mixture by tapping it from the spoon on the edge of the pan. Be ready to stir, as it will tend to make the syrup boil over.

➤ Cover 2 to 3 minutes until the steam can wash down the sides of the pan. Then cook this mixture ➤ uncovered, without stirring, until it reaches the soft-ball stage, 234°. Remove pan gently from heat. Pour syrup onto a marble slab or platter moistened with ice water by snapping the water off your fingers as though you were sprinkling laundry. ➤ Do not scrape pan. ➤ Let the syrup cool at least until it holds a fingerprint momentarily.

Work the syrup with a candy scraper or a wooden spoon by lifting and folding, always from edges to center. When the syrup loses its translucency and begins to become opaque and creamy, knead it well with your hands, dusting them with confectioners' sugar if necessary.

Even experts sometimes cook fondant too hard to knead it. If you have done so, add ⅔ of a cup of water. Melt the mixture very slowly in the top of a double boiler ➤ over—not in—boiling water, stirring constantly until it has thoroughly liquefied. Return it to pan and heat to the boiling point again. Then proceed by covering, letting the steam wash down the sides of the pan and recooking to the soft-ball stage, 234°.

After kneading fondant, put it in a tightly covered container. Allow it to remain in a cool place for from 24 hours to a week or more. To prepare it for shaping, put it in a double boiler ➤ over—not in—hot water. Heat it slowly, with the water at 170° to 180°, until you can shape it, then put it on a slab for forming and cutting.

If you want to color fondant, make a depression in the mass and pour in a few drops of vegetable food coloring. Gash it in several places but not all the way through to the slab—allowing the color to spread through the candy. Continue slashing and folding to complete the spreading process. Flavoring can be worked in in the same way. At this time you may also incorporate chopped or whole nuts, candied fruits, ginger, coconut or jam. The amount of such additions should about equal that of the fondant. Correct to the proper consistency with confectioners' sugar if necessary.

Form fondant by rolling it into ½-inch rods, then cutting them into round or oval pieces. You are now ready to dip them in:

Chocolate Coating, 781

➤ Be sure to have centers at room temperature to keep chocolate from developing gray streaks.

SOFT-CENTER FONDANT

About 1 Pound

The type of fondant often used around a candied cherry in a chocolate coating. It is not allowed to ripen but must be molded and dipped at once. After dipping, the egg white causes it to become liquid inside its coating.

Bring to a boil in a large, heavy pan:

2 cups sugar
1 cup water
¼ teaspoon glycerin
1 tablespoon light corn syrup

Stir these ingredients until the sugar is thoroughly dissolved. Place the pan over low heat. ➤ When the mixture begins to boil, cover it, so that the steam will wash down any crystals that may have formed on the sides of the pan. Cook the syrup about 3 minutes. ➤ Uncover and continue cooking syrup without stirring until it reaches the soft-ball stage, 234°. Remove it gently from heat. Pour onto a wet slab or platter. Cool syrup to 110°. Spread over it with a spatula:

1 well-beaten egg white

To work, flavor, form and dip, see Basic Fondant, above. These processes must be done as quickly as possible.

UNCOOKED FONDANT

About 1½ Pounds

"Candy," as Dorothy Parker reminded us, "is dandy." But the chocolate-coated balls below are nothing short of seditious.

Beat until soft:

½ cup butter

Add very slowly and cream until very light:

1 lb. sifted confectioners' sugar

Add:

¼ cup whipping cream
¾ teaspoon vanilla

Work the fondant well with the hands and shape it into 1-inch balls. To roll the balls, use about:

¼ lb. sifted confectioners' sugar

Raisins, nutmeats or bits of candied fruit may be used as centers. Place balls on foil in the refrigerator, covered, until they harden. To dip, see Chocolate Coating, 781.

When coating has hardened, store balls covered and refrigerated until ready to serve.

CARAMEL FONDANT

About 1¼ Pounds

Heat in a large, heavy pan:

½ cup milk

Remove from heat and stir in until dissolved:

1½ cups sugar
¼ cup butter

Return to heat and bring very slowly to a boil. Meanwhile, caramelize, 559, in a heavy skillet:

½ cup sugar

When the sugar and butter mixture boils, stir in the caramelized sugar very slowly. Boil, then ➤ cover about 3 minutes until any crystals on the sides of the pan have been washed down by the steam. Uncover and cook candy to soft-ball stage, 234°, without stirring. Cool candy to 110°. Beat it until creamy. Pour it into a pan and mark it into squares or form candy into small balls. Place between the squares:

Nutmeats

or dip squares or balls in:

Chocolate Coating, 781

NEWPORT CREAMS OR CENTERS

About 1½ Pounds

Much like an opera cream in texture.

Bring to a boil in a large, heavy pan, stirring until the sugar is dissolved:

⅔ cup light corn syrup
2 cups light brown sugar
6 tablespoons hot water

➤ Cover about 3 minutes until any crystals on the sides of the pan have been washed down by the steam. ➤ Uncover and cook, without stirring, to the thread stage, 230°. Whip until stiff:

1 egg white
A few grains of salt

Pour syrup slowly into the egg white, whipping constantly. Add:

1 teaspoon vanilla
1¼ cups nutmeats

When you can no longer stir the candy, flatten it out on a buttered tin. When cold, cut it into squares.

OPERA CREAMS OR CENTERS

About 1¼ Pounds

Bring to a boil in a large, heavy pan, stirring until the sugar is dissolved:

2 cups sugar
¾ cup whipping cream
1 cup milk
2 tablespoons light corn syrup
⅛ teaspoon salt

➤ Cover and cook about 3 minutes until the steam has washed down any crystals on the sides of the pan. ➤ Uncover and cook over low heat to the soft-ball stage, 234°. Remove from heat. Cool to 110°. Add:

1 teaspoon vanilla

Beat the mixture until creamy. Pour it into special rubber-sheet candy molds or a buttered pan. When cold, cut into squares. Place in an airtight container. This candy improves if aged at least 24 hours. When it has ripened, you may dip it in a:

Chocolate Coating, 781

PEPPERMINT CREAM WAFERS

About 1¼ Pounds

These are delightful decorated or initialed for teas. See About Decorative Icings, 722.

Stir over low heat in a large, heavy pan until the sugar is dissolved:

2 cups sugar
¼ cup light corn syrup
¼ cup milk
¼ teaspoon cream of tartar

Cook and stir these ingredients slowly until they boil. ➤ Cover about 3 minutes until any crystals on the sides of the pan have been washed down by the steam. ➤ Uncover and cook without stirring to the soft-ball stage, 234°. Remove from heat. Cool slightly. Beat until creamy. Flavor with:

8 to 12 drops oil of peppermint

Tint lightly with vegetable coloring if desired. Drop the mixture from a teaspoon onto foil to form patties the size you want.

For more uniform shapes, make use of a wooden-handled funnel. Pouring the hot mixture into the funnel requires two people—one to hold the stopper and funnel, the other to pour. As the funnel is filled, keep the stopper in place. Immerse

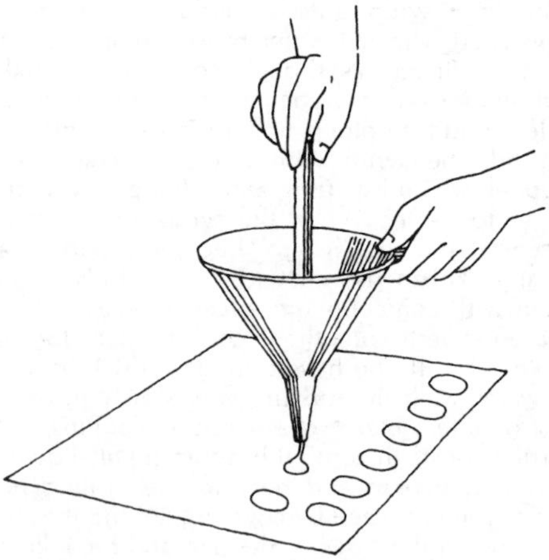

the funnel in hot water just past the neck to avoid chilling and stoppage of the mixture. Then, periodically removing the funnel from the hot water, release the candy onto a wax-paper-covered tray. When an adequate amount has dripped through, as shown, replace the stopper.

MAPLE CREAM CANDY

About 1 Pound

Who would ever suspect this delicious confection to be just plain maple syrup in a more solid—and definitely more delectable—form?

Boil over very low heat without stirring:

2 cups maple syrup

until it reaches about 233°. Pour into a shallow pan and cool to 110°, or lukewarm, without stirring. Beat until it becomes lighter in color and creamy in texture. Pour into a greased pan. This candy dries out on exposure to air, so box tightly as soon as cool.

★ ALMOND OR FILBERT PASTE

About 2 Pounds

In some parts of Europe this almond confection is traditional at Christmas time. It is molded into fancy shapes or into flat cakes that are pie-shaped and elaborately decorated. A thin wedge is served to visitors, together with a glass of dessert wine. You may also prepare filberts this way for cake fillings.

Blanch, 562:

1 lb. almonds or filberts

Grind them. All our other recipes for grinding almonds read: "Put through a nut grinder." This is the only recipe that says: "Put them through a meat grinder." This time you want the nuts to be oily. Use the finest blade and grind the nuts at least 4 times. If you use a ⅄ blender, use the orange juice or kirsch called for to start the blending action. Cook to the end of the soft-ball stage, 240°, in a large heavy pan:

2 cups sugar
1 cup water

Add the ground nuts and:

6 to 8 tablespoons orange juice or kirsch
(A few drops rose water)

Rose water is a traditional flavoring. Stir these ingredients until thoroughly blended and creamy. Let them cool until you can knead them. Here are two things you can do to make kneading easier: put confectioners' sugar on your hands, or cover the paste and allow it to rest about 12 hours. Flatten it on a hard surface dusted with confectioners' sugar, then mold it into any desired shape. Pack in a closely covered tin or jar. Ripen from 6 to 8 days.

Should you buy rather than make almond paste, see that it is marked "genuine." If it is not so marked and has a slightly bitter taste, it may be made of crushed apricot, peach or plum seeds treated to destroy the prussic acid content. Once opened, keep refrigerated.

★ MARZIPAN OR MARCHPANE

About ½ Pound

The Arabs brought this confection to Europe. In tribute to its preciousness, the word which describes it has meant "a seated king," "a little box," "a stamped coin."

Marzipan cake and dessert decorations made in advance are useful to have on hand, and those prepared by the first method can be ✱ frozen for future use.

I. Whip until fluffy:

1 egg white

Work in gradually:

1 cup Almond Paste, above

Add:

1½ cups sifted confectioners' sugar

Use more if necessary to make a paste that is easy to handle. Should it become too thick, work in drop by drop:

Lemon juice

Should it become too oily, work it in a dish over ice. In either case, knead the paste. Mold it into any desired shape. Small fruit shapes are great favorites. If you wish to color it, use a pastry brush with a little diluted vegetable coloring. Glaze the "fruits" with a solution of:

Gum arabic, 794

Also, you may roll the paste in:

Equal parts of cocoa and powdered sugar

or use it as a center for dipping. Wrap each piece separately in foil. Store in a cool place.

II. Use:

Equal parts of almond paste and fondant

Knead, mold and color as above.

MARSHMALLOWS

About 1¾ Pounds

This recipe requires the use of an electric mixer. Results are also much improved if you can get, at a professional outlet, gelatin of 250 bloom—a more concentrated form than that sold to the housewife.

Put in the mixer bowl and let stand for 1 hour:

3 tablespoons gelatin
½ cup cold water

In about ½ hour start to prepare a syrup. Place in a heavy pan over low heat and stir until dissolved:

2 cups sugar
¾ cup light corn syrup
½ cup water
¼ teaspoon salt

When the mixture starts to boil ➤ cover it about 3 minutes to allow any crystals which have formed to be washed down from the sides of the pan. Continue to cook ➤ uncovered and unstirred over high heat to the firm-ball stage, 244°. Overcooking will make marshmallows tough. Remove the mixture from heat and pour slowly over the gelatin, beating constantly. Continue to beat about 15 minutes after all the syrup has been added. When the mixture is thick but still warm add:

2 tablespoons vanilla

Put the mixture into an 8 x 12-inch pan that has been lightly dusted with cornstarch. When it has dried for 12 hours, remove it from the pan, cut it into squares with scissors dusted with cornstarch, and store the fully dusted pieces in a closed tin.

CHOCOLATE COATING

For a long time our attempts to dip candies attractively were not an unqualified success. We finally

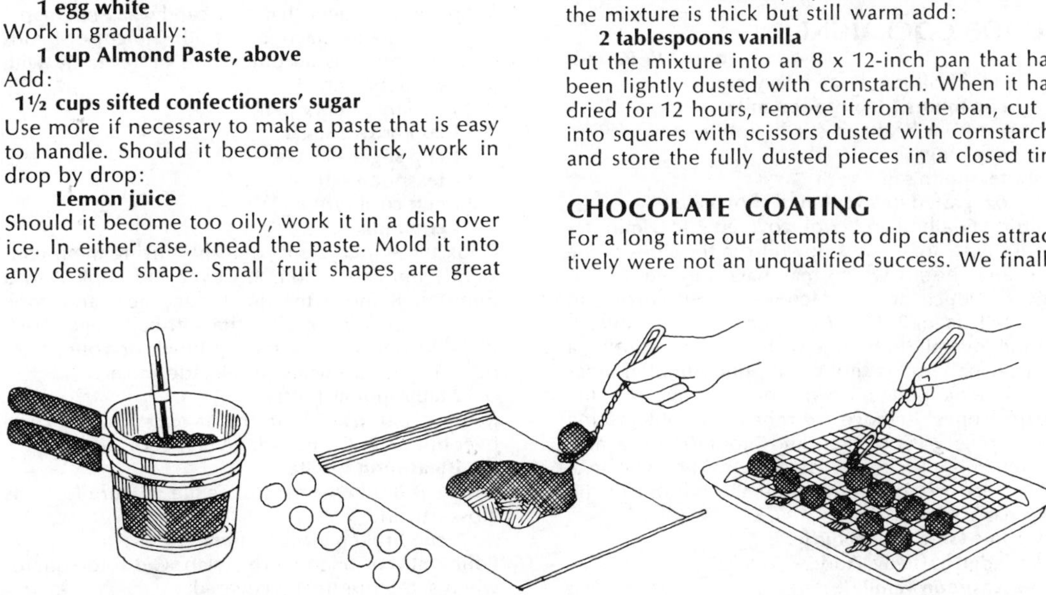

sought the advice of Larry Blumenthal, whose family has been "in chocolate" for generations. He finds our procedure solid, but warns us that when you heat chocolate and cool it to dipping temperature, you have "tempered" it, and that its reactions from this point on are somewhat unpredictable. In the candy trade, dipping is turned over to a "handcoater," who uses no specially processed chocolate, although he may thicken his mix adroitly by adding at just the right moment a few drops of water at 65° to 70°.

➤ Choose crisp dry weather for dipping. ➤ Work in a room where the temperature is 60° to 70°, the humidity below 55 percent, and where there are no drafts.

Grate about:

1 lb. chocolate: sweet, unsweetened, semisweet or milk

Melt it very, very slowly in the top of a 1½-quart double boiler ➤ over—not in—boiling water. ➤ Stir the chocolate until its temperature reaches 130°. If you do not stir constantly at temperatures over 100°, the cocoa butter will separate out. Remove from the heat and cool to about 88°. Heat water to 90° in the bottom of the double boiler. Place chocolate in the upper part.

Before dipping into chocolate, be sure candy centers or fillings are about 70°. Otherwise, the chocolate may streak with gray. Coat the centers one at a time in a small quantity of the chocolate, as shown at center, 781. Lift them out with a fork or a candy-dipping fork onto a ¼-inch wire rack above a pan or tray—to catch chocolate drippings, which may be remelted and reused. There is always a surplus on the dipping fork. This is lifted directly above the candy and dripped to make designs which identify the various fillings.

FUDGE COCKAIGNE

About 1¼ Pounds

Bring to a boil in a large heavy pan:

1 cup minus 1 tablespoon milk

Remove from heat and stir in until dissolved:

2 cups sugar
⅛ teaspoon salt
2 oz. grated unsweetened chocolate

➤ Bring to a boil and cook covered 2 to 3 minutes until the steam washes down from the sides of the pan any crystals which may have formed. ➤ Uncover, reduce heat and cook without stirring to soft-ball stage, 234°. When nearing 234°, there is a fine overall bubbling with, simultaneously, a coarser pattern, as though the fine bubbled areas were being pulled down for quilting into the coarser ones. Remove from heat without jostling or stirring. ➤ Cool the candy to 110°. You may hasten this process by placing the hot pan in a larger pan of cold water until the bottom of the pan has cooled. Add:

2 to 4 tablespoons butter

Beat fudge partially. Add:

1 teaspoon vanilla

Then beat until it begins to lose its sheen. At this point the drip from the spoon, when you flip it over, holds its shape against the bottom of the spoon. Quickly add:

½ to 1 cup broken nutmeats

Pour the fudge into a buttered pan. Cut into squares before it hardens. To use fudge for centers, beat until thick, knead and shape.

COCOA FUDGE OR CENTERS

About 1½ Pounds

An unusually interesting texture for centers.

Melt in a large, heavy pan over medium heat:

¼ cup butter

Add:

1½ cups boiling water

Mix and stir into the hot mixture:

3 cups sugar
⅔ cup cocoa
⅛ teaspoon cream of tartar

➤ Continue to stir until the mixture boils. Cover about 3 minutes to allow steam to wash down any crystals that may have formed on sides of pan. ➤ Uncover, lower heat and cook slowly ➤ without stirring to the soft-ball stage, 234°. Do not stir after removing candy from heat. When the mixture has cooled to 110°, add:

6 tablespoons whole or skim milk solids
1 teaspoon vanilla

Beat until creamy. Pour into an 8 x 8-inch buttered pan. When it becomes firm, cut into squares or knead into 1-inch balls. If it seems too stiff to knead, cover with damp cloth about an hour.

CARAMEL CREAM FUDGE

About 1¼ Pounds

Who would guess that this candy has no maple sugar or maple flavoring at all? Sleight-of-hand? The deception is accomplished more easily with an electric beater.

Put in a large heavy pan:

1 cup brown sugar
1 cup sugar
⅛ teaspoon salt
⅓ cup corn syrup
1 cup milk

Cook these ingredients quickly, stirring them constantly until they boil. ➤ Cover and cook 2 to 3 minutes. Remove the lid, reduce heat and cook until the mixture reaches the soft-ball stage, 234°. Place in bottom of a mixing bowl, or your mixer bowl if you are using an electric mixer:

2 tablespoons butter

Remove pan from heat and at once pour mixture over butter. ➤ Do not stir. When cool, add:

1 teaspoon vanilla

and beat until creamy. Just as the mixture loses its gloss, stir in:

1 cup broken black walnuts

Pour onto an oiled marble slab. Cut into squares when set. Store tightly covered.

COFFEE FUDGE

About 1 Pound

Bring to a boil in a large, heavy pan:

1 cup strong coffee

Remove from heat and stir in until dissolved:

2 cups sugar
1 tablespoon cream
1 tablespoon butter
1/8 teaspoon salt
1/4 teaspoon cream of tartar

Cook these ingredients quickly, stirring them constantly until they boil. ➤ Cover and cook for about 3 minutes, until the steam washes down any crystals which may have formed on the sides of the pan. ➤ Uncover and cook over moderate heat to the soft-ball stage, 234°. Remove from heat. Cool to 110°. Add:

1/2 teaspoon almond extract or 1/2 teaspoon cinnamon

Beat until the mixture begins to solidify. Add:

1 cup broken pecan or hickory nuts

Pour onto a buttered surface. Let the candy cool and harden before cutting it into squares.

COCONUT FUDGE OR CENTERS

About 1 1/4 Pounds

Combine in a deep saucepan:

1 1/2 cups sugar
1/2 cup corn syrup
1/2 cup milk
1/4 cup molasses
(1 tablespoon vinegar)
1/8 teaspoon salt

Stir these ingredients over medium heat until the sugar is dissolved. Bring to a boil and ➤ cook covered for about 3 minutes, until the steam has washed down from the sides of the pan any crystals which may have formed. ➤ Uncover and cook slowly to the soft-ball stage, 234°, without stirring. Remove from heat and stir in:

1 1/4 cups moist shredded coconut
3 tablespoons butter

Pour candy onto a buttered platter. When cool enough to handle, shape into small balls or centers. Place them on foil to dry.

CAROB FUDGE

About 1 Pound

Combine in a saucepan over medium heat:

2 cups brown sugar
6 tablespoons carob powder

Add:

2 tablespoons butter
2/3 cup milk
1/8 teaspoon salt

When the mixture begins to boil ➤ cover and cook 2 or 3 minutes, until the steam washes down any crystals which may have formed on the sides of the pan. ➤ Uncover, reduce heat and cook without stirring to the thread stage, about 230°. Remove from heat and add:

1 1/2 teaspoons vanilla

Beat well and add:

1/2 cup broken nutmeats

Let harden in an 8 x 8-inch buttered pan.

WHITE FUDGE COCKAIGNE

About 1 1/2 Pounds

Stir in a large heavy pan over medium heat until dissolved:

2 1/2 cups sugar
1/2 cup cultured sour cream
1/4 cup milk
1 tablespoon light corn syrup
1/4 teaspoon salt

When the mixture begins to boil ➤ cover and cook for 2 to 3 minutes, until the steam washes down any crystals which may have formed on the sides of the pan. ➤ Uncover, reduce heat and cook without stirring to the soft-ball stage, 234°. Pour at once into an electric mixer bowl. Do not scrape the pan. While the mixture is cooling, float on top:

2 tablespoons butter
1 teaspoon vanilla

In about 1 hour, when cool, beat until the mixture begins to lose its gloss. Quickly beat in:

(3/4 cup broken nutmeats)
(1/4 cup finely cut dried apricots)

Let harden in an 8 x 8-inch buttered pan. Cut into squares. Store tightly covered.

DIVINITY

About 1 1/2 Pounds

Pick a dry day. This candy does not keep well. If you use the brown sugar and vinegar, you may prefer to call this **Sea Foam.** Bring to room temperature:

2 egg whites

Bring to a boil in a heavy pan:

1/2 cup water
1/2 cup light corn syrup

Dissolve in it:

2 cups white or brown sugar
(1 tablespoon vinegar)

When boiling ➤ cover pan and cook about 3 minutes until the steam has washed down any crystals that may have formed on the sides of the pan. ➤ Remove lid and cook over moderate heat, without stirring, to the hard-ball stage, about 250°. While syrup is cooking, beat egg whites in a large bowl until they just hold their shape. When the syrup is ready, pour it slowly over the egg whites in a steady thin stream, whipping slowly at the same time. Toward the end, add the syrup more quickly and whip faster. ➤ Do not scrape pan. After all the syrup has been added, put in:

1 cup broken nutmeats
(1 cup white raisins)

As a variation try omitting nuts and raisins and add:

(1 cup crushed Peppermint Hard Candy, 787)

Beat until candy can be dropped onto a buttered surface into patties which hold their shape.

CARAMEL CREAM DIVINITY

About 2 Pounds

A smooth, rich candy which keeps better than divinity. Bring to a boil in a large heavy pan:

2 cups cream

➤ Remove from heat and stir in:

3 cups sugar

1 cup white corn syrup

Return to heat and cook slowly. When the candy boils ➤ cover and cook about 3 minutes until the steam washes down any crystals which may have formed on the sides of the pan. ➤ Uncover and cook slowly, without stirring, to the soft-ball stage, 234°. Remove syrup from heat. Cool to 110°. Beat until very stiff. Beat in:

1 cup broken pecan meats

Pour the candy into a buttered pan. Cut it when cool.

NOUGAT

About 1¼ Pounds

Southern France and Italy are famous for luscious nougats with distinctive flavors due to regional honey variations. So, why is there no honey in our recipe? For the answer, see About Honey, 558. Pick a dry day. This is a two-part process, and an electric mixer is almost imperative.

First, cook in a 2-quart heavy saucepan:

6 tablespoons sugar

1 tablespoon water

⅓ cup light corn syrup

Blend over low heat and stir until the mixture boils. ➤ Cover and cook about 3 minutes until the steam has washed down any crystals which may have formed on the sides of the pan. Cook ➤ uncovered over medium heat, without stirring, to the soft-ball stage, 234°. Remove pan from heat and let stand while you beat in a mixer until very stiff:

¼ cup egg whites

Add the hot syrup gradually to the whites, continuing to beat at least five minutes until the mass thickens. Blend in a heavy 1-quart pan and stir over low heat to boiling point:

1 cup light corn syrup

1 cup sugar

Stop stirring. ➤ Cover again for 3 minutes, then uncover and boil rapidly, without stirring, to just under the hard-crack stage, about 285°. Remove from heat and let stand until syrup stops bubbling. Now pour the second mixture into the first and beat until well combined. Beat in:

2 tablespoons butter cut into small chunks

Add:

1 cup blanched almonds, 562

½ cup blanched pistachio nuts, 562

(½ cup chopped candied cherries)

Pour into an 8 x 8-inch buttered pan dusted with confectioners' sugar or lined with baker's wafer paper. Let set in a cool place 12 hours. If hard to get out of pan, release sides with a knife. Then hold bottom of pan briefly over heat and reverse the block onto a board for slicing.

VANILLA CREAM CARAMELS

About 2½ Pounds

Dissolve over low heat in a large heavy pan, stirring until the mixture boils:

2 cups sugar

2 cups dark corn syrup

1 cup butter

1 cup cream

Cook over moderate heat, stirring constantly, to just under the firm-ball stage, 244°. Remove from heat and add very gradually:

1 cup cream

Return to heat and cook to the firm-ball stage, 244°. Pour the mixture at once, without stirring, into a buttered pan. When firm, about 3 hours later, invert the candy onto a wooden board and cut into squares with a thin-bladed knife. Use a light sawing motion.

MAPLE CARAMELS

About 1½ Pounds

Stir in a large heavy pan over quick heat until the sugar is dissolved:

2 cups brown sugar

1½ cups maple syrup

½ cup cream

Stir and cook these ingredients slowly to the firm-ball stage, 244°. Add:

1 tablespoon butter

Pour candy onto buttered tin. Cut into squares as it hardens. Nuts may be added to the candy just before removing it from the heat, or they may be sprinkled on the buttered tin before pouring the candy. When cool, about 3 hours later, invert onto a board and cut squares free along lines previously indicated.

CHOCOLATE CARAMELS

About 1½ Pounds

Stir over quick heat until the sugar is dissolved:

3 cups sugar

1 cup light corn syrup

1 cup milk

1½ tablespoons butter

Cut into small pieces and stir in:

3 oz. unsweetened chocolate

Stir and boil these ingredients slowly to the firm-ball stage, 244°. Add:

1 teaspoon vanilla

Pour candy into a lightly buttered 9 x 9-inch tin. When firm—about 3 hours later—invert onto a board and cut into ¾-inch squares.

CHOCOLATE CREAM CARAMELS

About 1 Pound

Stir over high heat until the sugar is dissolved:

1 cup sugar

¾ cup light corn syrup

3 oz. unsweetened chocolate

¼ teaspoon salt

½ cup cream

Bring the ingredients to the soft-ball stage, 234°, over moderate heat. Stir constantly. Add:

½ cup cream

Cook candy until it again reaches the soft-ball stage, 234°. Add:

½ cup cream

Cook to the firm-ball stage, 244°. Remove candy from heat and pour into an 8 x 8-inch buttered pan. Do not scrape pan. When candy is firm, about 3 hours later, invert onto a board and cut into squares.

FILLED CARAMELS COCKAIGNE

Prepare:

Chocolate Cream Caramels, above

Pour half the candy into one 8 x 8-inch buttered pan, the other half into a second buttered pan. When it holds its shape, remove from pans. Slice a ¼-inch layer of:

Basic Fondant, 778

Place it over the surface of one layer. Cover with the other layer. Cut the caramels in ½- or ¾-inch squares, using a sharp knife and a sawing action. Wrap individually.

OLD-FASHIONED BUTTERSCOTCH

About 1 Pound

Place in a heavy pan large enough to allow for foaming:

2 cups brown sugar
¼ cup molasses
½ cup butter
2 tablespoons water
2 tablespoons vinegar

Stir these ingredients over high heat until the sugar is dissolved. Boil quickly—stirring frequently—to the hard-crack stage, 300°. Drop candy from a teaspoon onto a buttered slab or foil to form patties.

BUTTERSCOTCH

About 1¾ Pounds

Stir in a large, heavy saucepan until dissolved:

2 cups sugar
⅔ cup dark corn syrup
¼ cup water
¼ cup cream

Cook these ingredients to just below the hard-ball stage, about 250°, then stir constantly until they almost reach the hard-crack stage, about 300°. Pour candy into a buttered pan. When cool and almost set, mark into squares or bars. When cold, cut or break apart.

COFFEE DROPS

About 1¼ Pounds

Use same ingredients as in above recipe for Butterscotch, but cook to 295°. Have ready an essence made of:

6 to 8 tablespoons instant coffee
3 tablespoons water
1 tablespoon vinegar

Add:

½ teaspoon glycerin

Remove sugar syrup from heat. When it is ready to pour, sprinkle coffee essence over the surface. Stir it in very gently. Drop syrup into ¾-inch patties from the edge of a spoon onto a buttered surface. When cool, wrap individually and store in a tightly covered container.

ABOUT TAFFIES

If you hanker to re-create an old-time candy pull, be sure you have a reasonably stout pair of arms or an adolescent in the family who wants to convert from a puny weakling to a muscle-man. However, should you make taffy-pulling a frequent practice, you may find that a candy hook, shown on 777, is well worth the investment. The hook is normally placed at least 6 feet from the floor. The rope of candy is thrown over it repeatedly, while gravity does the rest.

When syrup for taffy has cooked to the indicated temperature ➤ pour it slowly onto a buttered slab. ➤ Hold the pouring edge of the pan away from you and only a few inches above the slab, so you won't be spattered with the dangerously hot syrup. Allow the syrup to cool briefly. ➤ This is the moment to flavor the taffy. Because of the great heat, use flavoring essences based on essential oils. See flavoring of hard candies, 787. Sprinkle these over the surface of the hot syrup. Go easy, as they are very strong. If chocolate is to be added, grate it on the buttered slab before pouring. Nuts, fruits and coconut can be worked in during the pulling process.

Begin to work the syrup up into a central mass, turning it and working it with a candy scraper

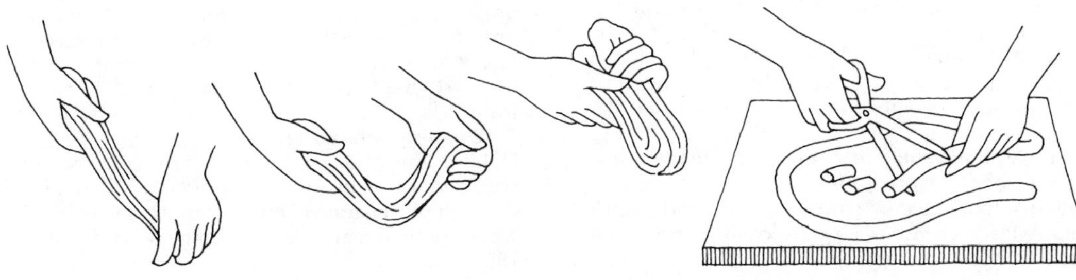

until it is cool enough to handle with your oiled fingertips. ➤ Take care in picking up the mass. It may have cooled on the surface and still be hot enough to burn as you press down into it. Taffy cooked to 270° should be pulled near a source of heat. When you can gather it up, start pulling it with your fingertips, allowing a spread of about 18 inches between your hands. Then fold it back on itself. Repeat this motion rhythmically. As the mass changes from a somewhat sticky, side-whiskered affair to a glistening crystal ribbon, start twisting, while folding and pulling. ➤ Pull until the ridges on the twist begin to hold their shape.

The candy will have become opaque, firm and elastic but will still retain its satiny finish. Depending on proper cooking, the weather and your skill, this pulling process may last from five to twenty minutes.

➤ Have ready a surface dusted with confectioners' sugar or cornstarch. Then form the candy into a ball in your hands and press it into a narrow point at the fingertip end. Grasping the narrow point in one hand, pull it away from the rest of the ball into a long rope about one inch thick. Let the rope fall out onto the dusted board like a snake. With well-buttered shears, cut up into segments of a size you prefer. Let it cool. If you do not want to wrap it separately, put the candy into a tightly covered tin, dusting and all. Some taffies, especially those heavy in cream, will, of their own accord, turn from a pulled chewy consistency to a creamy one. This happens sometimes a few minutes after cutting, sometimes as long as 12 hours later. After creaming takes place, be sure to wrap the taffies in foil and store them in a closed tin, because in this state they dry out readily on exposure to air.

VANILLA TAFFY

About ½ Pound

If you allow this candy to become creamy, it rivals the very rich Cream Pull Candy, next page. Stir over low heat until the sugar is dissolved:

1¼ cups sugar
¼ cup water
2 tablespoons mild vinegar
1½ teaspoons butter

Cook these ingredients quickly, without stirring, to just between the hard-ball and the soft-crack stages, about 265°. Pour candy on buttered platter or marble slab and let cool until a dent can be made in it when pressed with a finger. Gather it into a lump and pull it, as seen 785, with fingertips until porous. Pull into the candy any desired flavoring or coloring, such as:

1 teaspoon vanilla or a few drops peppermint or other flavoring oil

Roll it into long thin strips and cut into 1-inch pieces. Place candy in a tightly covered tin if you want it to become creamy.

MOLASSES TAFFY

About 1 Pound

Stir over high heat until the sugar is dissolved, then stir until the mixture boils:

1 cup molasses
2 teaspoons vinegar
1 cup sugar
⅛ teaspoon salt

➤ Cover pan and, without stirring, cook syrup rather quickly to just below the firm-ball stage, 242°. Add, by dropping in small pieces:

2 tablespoons butter

Boil syrup slowly—just below the soft-crack stage, about 268°. Holding the pouring edge of the pan away from you and a few inches above the slab, allow syrup to spread over slab. ➤ Do not scrape pan. Sprinkle surface of taffy with:

4 drops oil of peppermint

To work, pull and form, see About Taffies, 785. To make chips, pull in long, very thin strips. To cover, see:

Chocolate Coating, 781

PULLED MINTS

About 1 Pound

Like the old-fashioned little cushions we used to buy in tins. Combine in a large, heavy pan and stir until it reaches a boil:

1 cup boiling water
2 cups sugar
¼ teaspoon cream of tartar

➤ Cook covered about 3 minutes until the sides of the pan are washed free of crystals. ➤ Uncover and cook without stirring to mid-hard-ball stage, 262°. Remove from heat and pour onto buttered marble slab. Sprinkle with:

A few drops oil of peppermint

To work, pull, form and cream, see About Taffies, 785.

SALTWATER TAFFY

About 1½ Pounds

Combine and stir over low heat until sugar is dissolved:

2 cups sugar
1½ cups water
1 cup light corn syrup
1½ teaspoons salt
2 teaspoons glycerin

Bring to a boil. Cook covered about 3 minutes until the sides of the pan are washed free of crystals. ➤ Uncover and cook the syrup, without stirring, to the late-hard-ball stage, 265°. Remove from heat. Add:

2 tablespoons butter

Holding the pouring edge of the pan away from you, and a few inches above the oiled slab, allow the syrup to spread. ➤ Do not scrape pan. To work, pull, flavor and form, see About Taffies, 785.

CREAM PULL CANDY

About 1½ Pounds

Do not try this in hot or humid weather.

Combine in a heavy saucepan and stir over low heat until dissolved and boiling:

3 cups sugar
1 cup boiling water
⅛ teaspoon soda
½ teaspoon salt

➤ Cover about 3 minutes until steam has washed crystals from sides of pan. ➤ Uncover and cook without stirring to the soft-ball stage, 234°. ➤ Reduce heat—but not below 225°—while adding almost drop by drop:

1 cup cream
(¼ cup butter cut into small bits)

Cook over moderate heat ➤ without stirring, to 257° and pour syrup at once onto buttered marble slab. Hold the pouring edge away from you and a few inches from the slab. Allow syrup to spread over the slab. ➤ Do not scrape pot. To work, pull, flavor, form and cream, see About Taffies, 785.

HARD CANDY OR LOLLIPOPS

About 1½ Pounds

All hard candies become sticky unless individually wrapped.

Bring to a boil in a large heavy pan:

1 cup water

Remove from heat. Add and stir until dissolved:

2 cups sugar
¾ cup light corn syrup
1 tablespoon butter

Return to heat. When boiling ➤ cover about 3 minutes so the steam can wash down any crystals on the sides of the pan. ➤ Uncover and cook at high heat, without stirring, to the hard-crack stage, 300°. Prepare a slab or molds by brushing them well with butter or oil. If you are going to make lollipops, have stiffened lollipop cords on the oiled slab ready to receive patties. Remove candy mixture from heat and cool to 160°. Add:

A few drops vegetable coloring

Choose a vegetable color suitable to the flavor you have decided to use. An alcohol-based flavor like vanilla will evaporate in the intense heat, so be sure to use a flavor based, instead, on essential oils. For the above recipe, for instance, we suggest one of the following:

¼ teaspoon oil of peppermint, cassia or cinnamon
1 teaspoon oil of orange, lime or wintergreen
⅛ teaspoon oil of anise

To heighten fruit flavors, add:

(1 teaspoon powdered citric acid)

If you have no molds, form into balls by pouring a small amount of the candy onto an oiled slab. Keep the rest in the pan over very low heat. Cut candy on the slab into squares with a scissors and roll quickly into balls. Continue to pour the candy onto the slab as needed, but do not scrape the pan. If you have made lollipops, remove them from the slab just as soon as they are firm so as not to crack them.

ROCK CANDY

Broken into small pieces and piled in an open bowl, this makes a sophisticated-looking sugar substitute for coffee. Small clumps clustered on ⅛-inch dowels make attractive swizzle sticks for drinks. Whether the candy be on sticks or on strings, the process of making it is a fascinating experiment in crystallization. Punch holes at the top edge of a thin 8-inch square pan and lace about seven strings from one side to the other as shown below. Place the laced pan in a pan deep enough to catch any leaking syrup. Dissolve:

2½ cups sugar

in:

1 cup water

and cook without stirring to about hard-ball stage, 247°–252°. Pour syrup into laced pan. It should reach a level about ¾ inch above the strings. Cover the surface with a piece of foil. Watch and wait. The syrup sometimes takes a week to crystallize. Lift out the laced pan. Cut the strings and dislodge the rock candy. Rinse quickly in cold water, and put on racks in a very low oven to dry.

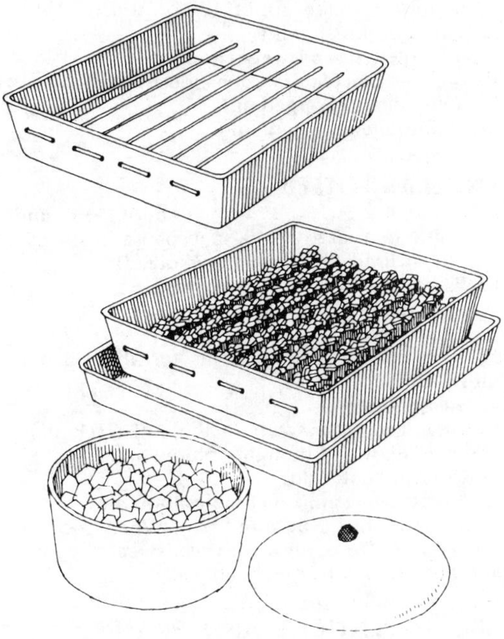

HOREHOUND CANDY

About 2½ Pounds

Make an infusion of:

8 cups boiling water
1½ quarts loosely packed horehound leaves and stems

Steep covered 20 minutes. Drain and discard leaves and stems. To 2 quarts of this bitter dark brew, add:

4 cups sugar
1¼ cups dark cane syrup
1 tablespoon butter
(1 teaspoon cream of tartar)

Cook these ingredients until they reach the hard-crack stage, 300°. Skim off any scum. Pour into a buttered 15 x 10 x 1-inch pan and score into pieces before it sets. Allow to cool.

NUT CRUNCH

About 2 Pounds

Sliver large, dense nuts like almonds and Brazil nuts. Others can be left whole. You may add them at once to the mixture if you like a roasted quality in the nut. If not, spread them on a buttered slab or pan and pour the syrup over them after cooking. Heat in a large, heavy skillet:

1 cup sugar
1 cup butter
3 tablespoons water

Cook rapidly and stir constantly about 10 minutes or until the mixture reaches the hard-crack stage, 300°. Add:

1 to 1½ cups nutmeats

Turn the candy quickly onto the buttered slab. Form into a shape about 1 foot square. When almost cool, brush with:

¼ lb. melted semisweet chocolate

Before the chocolate hardens, dust with:

¼ cup finely chopped nuts

Break into pieces when cold.

ENGLISH TOFFEE

About 1½ Pounds

Combine in a large heavy saucepan and stir over high heat until the sugar is dissolved:

1¾ cups sugar
⅛ teaspoon cream of tartar
1 cup cream

Stir and boil these ingredients for about 3 minutes. Add:

½ cup butter

Cook and stir the syrup to the soft-crack stage, about 270°. It will be light-colored and thick. Remove from heat. Add:

1 teaspoon vanilla or 1 tablespoon rum

Pour candy into a buttered pan. When cool, cut into squares. To cover it with semisweet chocolate and nuts, see Nut Crunch, above.

ABOUT PENUCHE AND PRALINES

The taste of these candies is very similar. Penuche is often cut into squares, like fudge, while pralines are usually made into 3- to 4-inch patties. Why so large, we wonder. We prefer small sugared nuggets made by separating the nuts as the sugar begins to harden. They are best when freshly made with nuts of finest quality. Sometimes coconut or raisins are added. Pralines do not keep well unless wrapped in foil and stored in tightly covered containers.

PENUCHE

About 1 Pound

Dissolve in a large heavy pan and stir constantly until boiling:

3 cups brown sugar
¼ teaspoon salt
1 cup milk or cream

➤ Cover and cook about 3 minutes, until the steam has washed down any crystals from the sides of the pan. ➤ Uncover and cook slowly, without stirring, to the soft-ball stage, 234°. Remove candy from heat and add:

1 to 2 tablespoons butter

Cool to 110°. Beat until smooth and creamy. Add:

1 teaspoon vanilla
1 to 1½ cups nutmeats

In summer try adding instead:

(½ cup grated fresh pineapple)
(1 teaspoon lemon juice)

Pour into a buttered pan and cut into squares.

PLAIN OR SHERRIED PRALINES

About 2 Pounds

Dissolve in a large heavy pan over low heat until boiling:

1⅓ cups sugar
⅔ cup brown sugar
1⅓ cups water or sherry
⅛ teaspoon salt

➤ Cover and cook about 3 minutes to allow the steam to wash down any crystals from the sides of the pan. ➤ Uncover and cook to the soft-ball stage, 234°. Remove pan from heat and cool candy to 110°. Beat until it thickens and begins to lose its gloss. Quickly stir in:

2 to 3 cups pecans

Drop candy in patties from a spoon onto a buttered platter. When hardened, wrap them individually in foil. Or, pour the candy onto a greased sheet, and before it is fully hardened, roll it to separate the nuts. Store tightly closed in glass jars.

PEANUT OR NUT BRITTLE

About 2 Pounds

Have ready a pair of clean white cotton gloves. It is best to use raw nuts and cook them in the syrup. Should only roasted nuts be available, add them after the syrup is cooked. In this case the candy is best if aged 24 hours. If the nuts are salted, rub them between paper towels and omit salt from the recipe. This recipe makes a tender clear brittle. For a porous one, combine ¼ teaspoon cream of tartar with the sugar, and sprinkle ½ teaspoon of soda all over the hot syrup just before pouring. Bring to a boil in a large heavy pan:

1 cup water

➤ Remove from heat and stir in until dissolved:
2 cups sugar
Then add and stir in:
1 cup corn syrup
Cook to hard-ball stage, 250°, then add:
2 cups raw Spanish peanuts, pecans and chopped Brazil nuts, or some other nut combination
1 teaspoon salt
Stir occasionally to submerge any exposed nuts so that they cook thoroughly and so the candy does not burn. Cook to almost hard-crack stage, 295°. Remove from heat. Stir in lightly:
1 to 3 tablespoons butter
¼ teaspoon baking soda
(1 teaspoon vanilla)
Pour onto a well-buttered slab at once, scraping out bottom of pan. Spread mixture rapidly with a spatula. At this point, don the cotton gloves. Loosen the mass from the slab with a scraper, reverse it and, discarding the scraper, stretch and pull the brittle so thin that you can see through it. When cool, crack into eating-size pieces and store at once in a tightly covered tin.

NUT BRITTLE, GLAZED NUTS AND PRALINÉ FOR GARNISH

I. **About ½ Pound**
This clear candy when ground or crushed is called **praliné.** Delicious over ice cream or added to icings and dessert sauces.
Melt in a skillet over low heat:
1 cup sugar
Stir constantly. When the sugar is caramelized, 310°, stir in until well coated:
1 cup toasted almonds or hazelnuts or toasted benne seeds
Pour the candy onto a buttered platter. When cool, crack into pieces.

II. For other syrups to use with nuts, see:
Glazed Fresh Fruits, 794–796

ALMOND CREAMS

Blanch and toast lightly:
Almonds or hazelnuts
Cover them first with:
Basic Fondant, 778, or
Uncooked Fondant, 779
then dip them at once in:
Chocolate Coating, 781
Place them on a wire rack to dry.

SPICED CARAMEL NUTS COCKAIGNE

Have ready:
Toasted blanched almonds, hazelnuts or pecans, 562
Prepare:
Chocolate Cream Caramels, 784
Add to the dissolved ingredients:
1 teaspoon cinnamon
When the candy has cooked almost to the hard-ball stage, 250°, remove it from heat and spread to a ¼-inch thickness on a marble slab. Score the candy in 1-inch squares. Place a whole toasted nut on each square. Before candy hardens, enclose each nut in its candy square, shaping it to the nut.

BURNT ALMONDS AND OTHER NUTS

About 2 Pounds
Cook over low heat, stirring constantly until dissolved:
2 cups sugar
½ cup water
1 teaspoon cinnamon
Boil the syrup rapidly. When it is clear and falls in heavy drops from a spoon, add:
1 lb. unblanched almonds, hazelnuts or peanuts
Stir the nuts until well coated. Remove the mixture from heat and pour onto a marble slab. Stir until nuts are coated and dry. Sift them to remove any superfluous sugar. Put this excess sugar in a pan and add a very little water and:
A few drops of red vegetable coloring
Boil syrup until clear, then add nuts and stir them until they are well coated. Drain and dry.

SPICED NUTS

About ¼ Pound
Preheat oven to 250°.
Sift into a shallow pan:
½ cup sugar
¼ cup cornstarch
⅛ teaspoon salt
1½ teaspoons cinnamon
½ teaspoon allspice
⅓ teaspoon each ginger and nutmeg
Combine and beat slightly:
1 egg white
2 tablespoons cold water
Dip into the liquid:
¼ lb. nutmeats
Drop them one at a time into the sifted dry ingredients. Roll them about lightly. Keep nutmeats separated. Place them on a cookie sheet. Bake at least 1 hour. Remove from oven and shake off excess sugar. Store tightly covered.

CHOCOLATE TRUFFLES

About ⅓ Pound
Definitely a brisk-weather confection.
Coarsely grate:
3 oz. unsweetened chocolate
Melt it with:
¼ cup butter
Add:
2 tablespoons cream
Gradually stir in until lump-free:
7 tablespoons sifted confectioners' sugar
2 tablespoons finely ground hazelnuts
Cover and refrigerate 12 to 24 hours. Make in-

dividual balls by rolling about a teaspoonful of the mixture in the palm of the hand. This friction and warmth will cause the chocolate to melt slightly, so that the final coating will adhere. Roll balls in:

Cinnamon-flavored cocoa, or
Chocolate pastilles or shot

This covering will stick to them very satisfactorily. Keep refrigerated, but for best flavor remove 2 hours before serving.

★ BOURBON BALLS

About 1/3 Pound

Sift together:

2 tablespoons cocoa
1 cup powdered sugar

Combine and stir in:

1/4 cup bourbon whisky
2 tablespoons light corn syrup

Add and mix thorougly:

2 1/2 cups crushed vanilla wafers
1 cup broken pecans

Roll mixture into small balls. Dredge in:

1/2 cup powdered sugar

RUM DROPS, UNCOOKED

About Forty-Five 1-Inch Balls

Fine served with tea or with lemon ice.
Place in a mixing bowl:

2 cups finely sifted crumbs of toasted sponge cake, zwieback or graham crackers

Add:

2 tablespoons cocoa
1 cup sifted confectioners' sugar
1/8 teaspoon salt
1 cup finely chopped nutmeats

Combine:

1 1/2 tablespoons honey or syrup
1/4 cup rum or brandy

Add the liquid ingredients slowly to the crumb mixture. Use your hands in order to tell by the "feel" when the consistency is right. When the ingredients will hold together, stop adding liquid. Roll the mixture into 1-inch balls. Roll them in:

Confectioners' or granulated sugar

Set the drops aside in a tightly covered tin box at least 12 hours to ripen.

HEAVENLY HASH CANDY

About 1 1/4 Pounds

At least a child's idea of heavenly!
Dice:

12 large or 48 miniature marshmallows

Chop:

1 cup nutmeats

Boil water in bottom of a double boiler. Turn off heat. Place in top:

1 lb. milk chocolate

Stir occasionally. Line a tray with waxed paper. Pour in half the chocolate when melted. Cover with marshmallows and nutmeats. Pour rest of chocolate over this. Cool and break candy into pieces.

CHOCOLATE CLUSTERS

About 3/4 Pound

Melt over hot water:

1/2 lb. semisweet chocolate

Stir in slowly:

3/4 cup sweetened condensed milk

When well blended, add:

1 cup nutmeats or unsweetened ready-to-eat cereal, sesame seed or wheat germ

Drop candy from a teaspoon onto foil.

PEANUT BUTTER FUDGE OR CENTERS

About 2 Pounds

Mix and stir until blended:

1 cup peanut butter
1 cup corn syrup
1 1/4 cups nonfat milk solids
1 1/4 cups sifted confectioners' sugar

Mix, then knead. Form into balls.

POPCORN

Kernels of popcorn have been found in the remains of Central American settlements almost 7000 years old, and most archeologists believe that it may have been the earliest variety eaten. Keep unpopped corn tightly covered and refrigerated. ➤ One-half cup corn equals about 1 quart when popped. If popcorn has the right moisture content, you will hear it in a minute—popping gently. It will be completely fluffy and ready in another minute. For best results, never overload the popper. Wire poppers similar to the one seen opposite, used over coals or burner heat, call for no butter or oil before popping, and a drier popcorn results. They will process about 1/4 cup of kernels at a time; a heavy-lidded or electric skillet or a 4-quart pressure pan, 1/2 cup. With an electric popper, follow the manufacturer's directions. Unless you are using a cage-type popper, add to the preheated pan for each cooking:

1 tablespoon vegetable oil

➤ Cook over high heat. ➤ Keep pan moving constantly. When corn stops popping, discard all imperfect kernels. For each 4 cups of hot popcorn, sprinkle with:

1/4 to 1/2 teaspoon salt
2 tablespoons or more melted butter or grated cheese

CANDIED POPCORN

Besides making a tasty confection, candied popcorn lends itself well to large, but largely inedible ★ Christmas decorations. For other seasons, use a well-oiled or -buttered fancy two-piece cake mold such as a lamb or rabbit form, ramming the corn tightly into all the nooks and crannies after you have coated it with one of the syrups below. If you want to color popcorn, use plenty of vegetable coloring to counteract the whiteness of the basic material.

To prepare popcorn for shaping, have ready in a large bowl:

6 cups popped corn, 790

Prepare any of the syrups below. When the liquid has been taken from the heat, pour it over the corn. Stir corn gently with a wooden spoon until

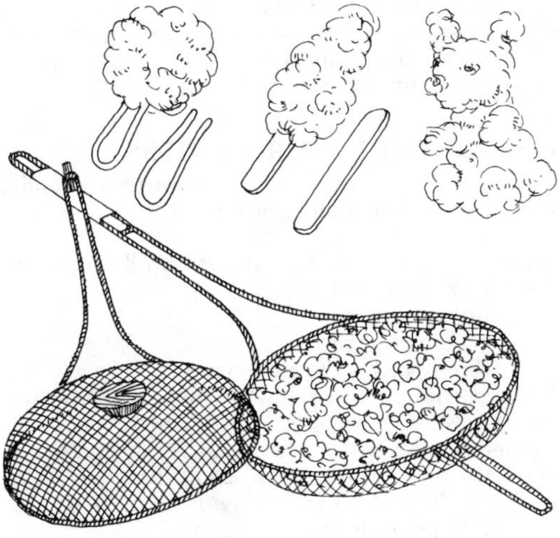

well coated. Then, when you are sure the corn is cool enough to handle with lightly buttered fingers, press it into balls or lollipops with an embedded loop of string or wooden stick as illustrated above.

WHITE SUGAR SYRUP

Stir until the sugar is dissolved:

2/3 cup sugar
1/2 cup water
2 1/2 tablespoons light corn syrup
1/8 teaspoon salt
1/3 teaspoon vinegar

Bring to a boil. ➤ Cook covered for about 3 minutes until steam washes down sides of pan. ➤ Uncover and cook, without stirring, nearly to the hard-crack stage, about 290°.

MOLASSES SYRUP

Melt:

1 tablespoon butter

Add:

1/2 cup molasses
1/4 cup sugar

Stir these ingredients until sugar is dissolved. Bring to a boil. ➤ Cover and cook for about 3 minutes until the steam has washed down the sides of the pan. ➤ Uncover and cook, without stirring, nearly to the hard-crack stage, about 290°.

CARAMEL SYRUP

Melt:

1 1/2 tablespoons butter

Add:

1 1/2 cups brown sugar
6 tablespoons water

Stir these ingredients until sugar is dissolved. Bring to a boil. ➤ Cover and cook for about 3 minutes until the steam has washed down the sides of the pan. ➤ Uncover and cook, without stirring, to the soft-ball stage, 234°.

PASTILLAGE OR GUM PASTE

About 3 Cups

A favorite mixture for decorations, especially on wedding cakes. It makes lovely molded leaves and flowers. The shapes are separately formed and held together later with Quick Decorative Icing, 727. Gum paste can be rolled out like pie crust, but never more at a time than you plan to shape immediately, because it dries rapidly and becomes cracked and grainy.

Dissolve in the top of a double boiler over, not in, boiling water:

1 tablespoon gelatin
1/2 cup water
1 teaspoon cream of tartar
1 tablespoon powdered gum tragacanth

To keep paste white, add:

1 or 2 drops blue vegetable coloring

Mix and knead the mixture with:

4 cups confectioners' sugar

working various vegetable colorings, if you wish, into separate portions of the mix as you complete this operation. Store the paste in a bowl covered with a damp cloth and let it rest at least 1/2 hour. When you are ready to use it, dust a board, a roller and your hands with cornstarch. Roll to the desired thickness as much paste as you will immediately use. Cut into shapes. Large flat ones are allowed to dry on the cornstarch-covered board for at least 24 hours. Cover top surfaces of paste with cornstarch also. Petals, leaves, etc., are shaped and stored in cornstarch or cornmeal until dry and ready to assemble.

TURKISH FRUIT PASTE, TURKISH DELIGHT, OR RAHAT LOUKOUM

I. **About 1 1/2 Pounds**

In the Middle East, this sweet is served with coffee to friends who drop in for a visit. It calls for simultaneous cooking and stirring in 2 pans. ➤ Have everything ready before you turn on the heat.

Put into a very heavy 2-quart pan:

2 tablespoons water
3/4 cup liquid fruit pectin

Stir in:

1/2 teaspoon baking soda

The soda will cause foaming. Do not be alarmed.

Put into another pan:

1 cup light corn syrup
3/4 cup sugar

Put both pans on high heat. Stir alternately 3 to 5 minutes or until foaming has ceased in the pectin pot and boiling is active in the other. Then, still stirring the corn syrup mixture, gradually and steadily pour the pectin mixture into it. Continue stirring and boiling, and add during the next minute:

1/4 cup any jelly: apple, currant, apricot, raspberry, peach or quince

Remove the mixture from heat and stir in:

1 tablespoon lemon juice
(1 teaspoon grated lemon rind)
(1/2 cup broken pistachio or other nutmeats)

Pour into an 8 x 8-inch pan. Let stand at room temperature about 3 hours. When the mixture is very firm, sprinkle with:

Confectioners' sugar

Cut into shapes or squares by pressing down with a buttered or sugared knife. Release the candies onto a sugared tray so all sides become coated. If you plan packing these candies, let them stand sugared 12 hours or more on a rack. Redust on all sides and pack, then store tightly covered. Should you want to dip them in chocolate, remove excess sugar first.

II.

Combine in a measuring cup and let stand at least 5 minutes:

1/3 cup lemon or lemon and lime juice
3 tablespoons cold water
Grated rind of 1 lemon
2 tablespoons gelatin

Place in a large heavy pan over moderate heat:

2/3 cup water
2 cups sugar

Stir until sugar is dissolved. When boiling starts ➤ cover and boil 2 to 3 minutes. Uncover and cook to the soft-ball stage, 234°, without stirring. Remove from heat and add the gelatin mixture. Return to heat and stir until thermometer registers 224°. If you wish, add:

(A few drops vegetable food coloring)

Pour the mixture into a lightly oiled 8 x 8-inch pan in which you have scattered:

(1 cup chopped nuts)

Let stand 12 hours. To cut and store, see I above. You may vary the flavor of fruit paste by using juices other than lemon and lime, such as reduced unsweetened apricot or apple, raspberry or strawberry juice, if the liquid proportions are not altered. You may also replace 1 tablespoon of the cold water used for soaking the gelatin with 1 tablespoon of lemon or lime juice to give additional tartness.

MEXICAN ORANGE DROPS

About 2 Pounds

Heat in the top of a double boiler:

1 cup evaporated milk

Melt in a deep saucepan:

1 cup sugar

When the sugar is a rich brown, stir in slowly:

1/4 cup boiling water or orange juice

Add the hot milk. Stir in until dissolved:

2 cups sugar
1/4 teaspoon salt

➤ Bring to a boil and cook covered 3 minutes until the steam washes down any crystals on the sides of the pan. ➤ Cook uncovered over low heat, without stirring, to the soft-ball stage, 234°. Add:

Grated rind of 2 oranges

Cool these ingredients. Beat until creamy. Stir in:

1 cup broken nutmeats

Drop the candy from a spoon onto foil.

GINGER CANDY OR CENTERS

About 1 3/4 Pounds

Bring to a boil in a large heavy pan:

3/4 cup milk

➤ Remove from heat. Add and stir until dissolved, then cook until boiling:

2 cups white sugar
1 cup brown sugar
2 tablespoons white corn syrup

➤ Cover and cook for about 3 minutes until the steam washes down any crystals which may have formed on the sides of the pan. ➤ Uncover and cook to the soft-ball stage, 234°. Remove from heat and drop on surface of syrup:

2 tablespoons butter

Cool to 110°. Beat until it begins to thicken. Add:

1 teaspoon vanilla
1/4 lb. finely chopped ginger

If preserved ginger is used, drain it well first. If candied ginger is preferred, wash the sugar from it, then dry it in paper towels and chop it. Pour candy onto a buttered platter. Cut into squares before it hardens. These squares may be dipped in:

Chocolate Coating, 781

HAWAIIAN CANDY OR CENTERS

About 1 Pound

A great combination—the tart flavor of pineapple with the spicy taste of ginger.

Bring to a boil in a large heavy pan:

1 cup cream

➤ Remove from heat, add and stir until dissolved:

1/2 cup brown sugar
1 cup sugar
1/2 cup drained crushed pineapple

Bring to a boil, stirring constantly. ➤ Cover and cook for about 3 minutes, until the steam washes down any crystals which may have formed on the sides of the pan. ➤ Uncover and cook over low heat, stirring only if necessary, to the soft-ball stage, 234°. Remove from heat and add:

1 tablespoon butter
1 teaspoon finely chopped preserved ginger
1/2 cup broken pecan meats
1 teaspoon vanilla

Cool to 110°. Beat until creamy. Pour into a shallow buttered pan, and cut into squares before it completely cools.

★ CANDY FRUIT ROLL OR CENTERS

About 5 Pounds

Bring to a boil in a large heavy pan:

1 cup cream
1/4 cup water

➤ Remove from heat and stir in until dissolved:

5 cups light brown sugar
3/4 cup light corn syrup
1 tablespoon butter
1/4 teaspoon salt

Bring these ingredients slowly to a boil, stirring constantly. ➤ Cover and boil about 3 minutes, until the steam has washed down any crystals which may have formed on the sides of the pan. ➤ Uncover and cook without stirring to the soft-ball stage, 234°. Remove from heat and add:

1 lb. blanched shredded almonds
1/4 lb. chopped dried figs
1 lb. seeded chopped raisins

Cool to 110°. Beat mixture until it begins to cream. Shape into a roll. Cover with foil and refrigerate. When cold and firm, remove foil. You may roll it in:

(Melted semisweet chocolate)

★ PERSIAN BALLS OR CENTERS

Put through the coarsest cutter of a meat grinder:

1/2 lb. pitted dates
1 lb. dried figs with stems removed
1 lb. seeded raisins
1 lb. pecan meats
1/2 lb. crystallized ginger or candied orange peel

If the mixture is very stiff, add:

1 or 2 tablespoons lemon juice

Shape these ingredients into balls or centers for dipping, or form them into a roll to be sliced. Coat with:

Confectioners' sugar

then wrap in foil.

★ DATE ROLL OR CENTERS

Boil to the soft-ball stage, 234°:

3 cups sugar
1 cup evaporated milk

Stir in:

1 cup chopped dates
1 cup chopped nutmeats

When cool enough to handle, form these ingredients into a roll with buttered hands. Wrap the roll in foil. Chill and slice later.

★ STUFFED DRIED FRUITS

Steam over hot water in a covered colander for 10 to 20 minutes:

1 lb. apricots, prunes, dates or figs

Stuff fruits as soon as cool with one or two of the following:

Fondant, 778
Hard Sauce, 775
Nutmeats
Candied pineapple
Candied ginger
Marshmallows
Marzipan, 781, and Orange Zest, 571

I. After steaming and stuffing, the fruits may be rolled in:

Granulated or powdered sugar or grated coconut

II. Or you may coat the fruits in a meringue glaze. Preheat oven to 250°. Beat until very stiff:

2 egg whites

Add gradually, beating steadily:

1/2 cup sugar
1/2 teaspoon vanilla

Place the stuffed fruits on a fork. Dip them one by one into the egg mixture until well coated. Place on a wire rack with a baking sheet underneath. Sprinkle tops with:

Grated coconut

Bake about 1/2 hour.

★ APRICOT ORANGE BALLS

About 2 Pounds

Placed in Christmas boxes, these confections keep the tougher cookies from drying out. Use best quality, slightly soft dried apricots. Steam any that seem too hard and dry. Grind twice in a meat grinder using the finest blade:

1 lb. apricots
1 whole seedless orange or 5 seeded preserved kumquats

You may also grind with them a choice of:

(1/4 lb. candied lemon rind)
(1/4 lb. candied citron)
(1/2 cup shredded coconut)
(1/2 cup nutmeats)

Shape the mixture into balls or patties. Dust in:

Granulated sugar

Store closely covered.

★ APRICOT OR PEACH LEATHER

About 2 Pounds

An old-time Southeast Seaboard favorite.

Cover with:

1 cup boiling water

and soak for 12 hours in a glass dish:

1 lb. dried apricots, or 3/4 lb. dried apricots and 1/4 lb. dried peaches

If tenderized fruit is used, omit soaking. Grind fruit with finest blade. Mix in:

(2 teaspoons grated lemon rind)

Sprinkle on a board:

Powdered sugar

You will need about 2 cups sugar in all. Start rolling a small quantity of the fruit pulp with a rolling pin. Sprinkle a little powdered sugar on the surface if the mass sticks. Continue to roll and to add sugar, as necessary, until you have a very thin sheet resembling leather in texture. This amount should make about a 12 x 16-inch sheet, 1/16 inch thick. Cut it into 1¼ x 2-inch strips and roll the powdered strips very tightly. Store closely covered.

BAKLAVA

About 100 2½-Inch-Long Diamonds

A confection prevalent throughout the Near East. Simmer a syrup of:

½ cup sugar or honey
¾ cup water
½ lemon

until it is thick enough to coat the back of a spoon. Remove the lemon. Add:

(1 tablespoon orange blossom water)

and simmer a few minutes longer. Cool and refrigerate.

Prepare a filling of:

1½ cups coarsely chopped nuts: almonds, pistachios and walnuts in any proportion

Sprinkle the nuts with a mixture of:

2 tablespoons sugar
1 teaspoon cinnamon
⅛ teaspoon cloves

Melt:

1 cup sweet butter

Have ready:

24 sheets phyllo, 649: 1 lb.

Layer 12 of them on an 11 x 15-inch buttered baking pan, brushing the sheets of dough with about half the butter. Spread the filling on top and cover with the remaining 12 similarly buttered sheets.

Preheat oven to 350°.

Cut the top layered sheets and filling diagonally into 2-inch-long diamonds, but leave the bottom few layers of sheets uncut. Bake about 30 minutes. Raise oven temperature to 475° and bake about 15 minutes longer or until golden. Remove from oven. Pour the refrigerated syrup over the top of the puffed dough. Cut, using the same diagonals, through the uncut layer of dough and serve the diamond-shaped slices when cooled.

ABOUT CANDIED, CRYSTALLIZED OR GLAZED FRUITS, LEAVES AND BLOSSOMS

There are a number of different methods suggested in the following recipes, and the "keeping" qualities of the product vary. Some fruits and leaves are glazed for temporary decorative effects, which involves a superficially applied covering of syrup or of egg and sugar. Unless used on ➤ very thin leaves and blossoms, they will hold for only a day. If the leaves or flowers are thin and are stored ➤ after thorough drying, in a tightly covered container, they may be kept several months.

The other methods described call for ➤ sugar penetration as well as glazing, and the fruits will keep about 3 months. Different syrup weights and different time intervals of drying are suggested, but the principles in these recipes remain the same.

There is a third method for blossoms, using a syrup much like that for Candied Kumquats, 795—especially for the imported violet, *Viola odorata*. Our native violets are too tender to use.

➤ In every operation, keep the fruit or other material covered with the syrup to avoid any hardening or discoloration. To begin with, the fruit is dropped into a thin syrup which can penetrate the skins and cells. Then the liquid is reduced or is replaced with a heavier one. This also penetrates, after the thin syrup has opened the way, and finally sugars out or dries into a crystal coating.

GLAZED FRESH FRUITS

Enough to Cover About 1 Cup of Solids

The beauty of these sparkling confections depends on sparkling weather and last-minute preparation. They must be eaten the very day they are prepared. Use only fresh fruits that are in prime and perfect condition. If you are covering a large quantity of fruit, divide it into several batches for successive syrup cooking. All fruit must be at room temperature and very dry; orange sections, if used, must be dried for at least 6 hours in advance. Work very quickly to keep the syrup effective. Stir in a heavy saucepan, over low heat, until dissolved:

1 cup sugar
½ to ¾ cup boiling water
1/16 teaspoon cream of tartar

Bring syrup to the boiling point. ➤ Cover and cook, without stirring, about 3 minutes to allow steam to wash down any crystals that may have formed on sides of pan. Uncover, lower heat and cook to the hard-crack stage, 300°. Remove pan from heat and place over hot water. Dip only a few fruits at a time and remove them with a fork. Place them on a wire rack until the coating hardens. Should syrup in the pan begin to solidify, reheat it over hot water and repeat the dipping.

GLAZED MINT LEAVES

Have ready the following solution. Dissolve and cook over low heat until clear:

1 cup sugar
½ cup water

Cool the syrup slightly, before blending in thoroughly:

4 teaspoons powdered acacia

This mixture is called **gum arabic.** ➤ Before using, refrigerate it until chilled. The unsprayed mint leaves should be freshly picked and kept cold, so as not to wilt. Prepare by carefully stripping from the main stem individual leaves, with their small stems attached. Wash and dry thoroughly. Put on a napkin over ice. Dip each leaf in the gum arabic and sugar solution; using your forefinger gently, make a smooth, thin coating. ➤ Be sure every bit of leaf is covered, top and bottom, for any uncoated area will turn brown later. Place leaves carefully on a rack. Turn with a spatula after 12 hours. When the coated leaves become thoroughly dry, store them in tightly covered containers.

CANDIED APPLES

I. Enough for 5 Medium-Sized Apples

Combine in a saucepan:

2 cups sugar
⅔ cup light corn syrup
1 cup water
(A 2-inch piece stick cinnamon)

Stir until dissolved. Bring to a boil. ➤ Cook covered for about 3 minutes until the steam has washed down any crystals that may have formed on the sides of the pan. ➤ Uncover and cook, without stirring, nearly to the hard-crack stage, 290°. Remove cinnamon stick if used. Add:

A few drops of red vegetable coloring

After cooking glaze, keep it in a double boiler ➤ over—not in—boiling water. Now, work quickly. Dip in:

Apples on skewers

Place them on a metal flower holder to harden. Or, to make these lollipops easier to handle after dipping, dust the tops with finely chopped nutmeats or with sugared puffed dry cereals; or arrange on the top of each a trefoil decoration of three pecan or walnut halves, and allow the apples to dry upside down on a piece of foil, as shown.

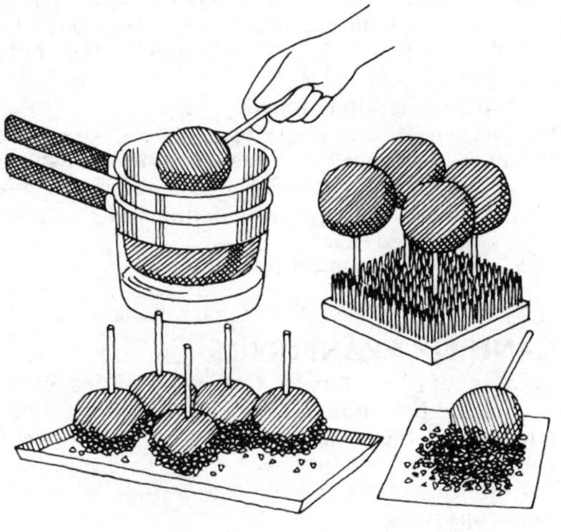

II. Wash, dry and insert a skewer in the stem end of:

5 medium-sized apples

Place in the top of a double boiler:

1 lb. Caramels, 784
2 tablespoons water

Heat and stir these ingredients until they melt into a smooth coating. Dip the skewered apples into the sauce, twirling them until completely coated. Dry as above. If refrigerated, they will harden in a few minutes.

GLAZED PINEAPPLE

Drain and reserve juice from:

3½ cups sliced cooked or canned pineapple

Dry slices with a cloth or paper towel. Add to the juice:

2 cups sugar
⅓ cup light corn syrup

Stir and bring these ingredients to a boil in a large heavy pan. Add the fruit but do not crowd it. Simmer until it is transparent. Lift fruit from syrup. Drain it on racks until thoroughly dry. Place between waxed paper and store tightly covered.

★ CANDIED CITRUS PEEL

This confection may be grated for zest, 571, in cakes and desserts.

I. A moist peel.
Grate fruit slightly to release oil from cells. Cut into thin strips and place in a heavy pan:

2 cups grapefruit, orange, lime or lemon peel

Cover with:

1½ cups cold water

Bring slowly to the boiling point. Simmer 10 minutes or longer if you do not like a rather bitter taste. Drain. Repeat this process 3 to 5 times in all, draining well each time. For each cup of peel, make a syrup of:

¼ cup water
½ cup sugar

Add peel and boil until all syrup is absorbed and the peel is transparent. Roll it in:

Powdered sugar

and spread on racks to dry. When ➤ thoroughly dry, you may dip it into:

(Chocolate Coating, 781)

II. This quicker process makes a softer peel which does not keep as well as the one above.
Cut into strips:

Grapefruit or orange peel

Soak for 24 hours in:

Salt water to cover

Use 1 tablespoon salt to 4 cups water. Drain peel. Rinse and soak for 20 minutes in fresh water. Drain, cover with fresh water and boil 20 minutes. Drain again. Measure in equal parts with the peel:

Sugar

Cook the peel. Add a very little water—but only if necessary—until the peel has absorbed the sugar. Shake the pot as the syrup diminishes, so that the peel does not burn. ➤ Dry thoroughly and store tightly covered.

★ CANDIED OR PRESERVED KUMQUATS OR CALAMONDINS

These miniature oranges should first be washed well in warm soapy water. Rinse, cover with fresh water and boil 15 minutes:

1 lb. kumquats or calamondins
Drain well and repeat twice. Make a syrup of:
1½ cups sugar
4 cups water
Boil 5 minutes. Place drained kumquats in hot syrup and bring syrup to the soft-ball stage, 234° or boil gently until the kumquats are transparent. To plump up the fruit, cover pan just before heat is turned off and allow fruit to remain covered in hot syrup about half an hour. At this point, you have Preserved Kumquats or Calamondins. Pack in sterile jars. Serve as a meat garnish or with desserts. If you chop them, be sure to slit them first and take out the seeds.

To candy the kumquats, remove from syrup and drain. You may prick a hole in the stem end and force out the seeds. Bring to a boil a heavier syrup of:
1 part water to
1 part sugar
(⅛ teaspoon cream of tartar for every quart of liquid)
Reboil the kumquats for 30 minutes. Remove them from heat but allow them to stand in the syrup 24 hours. Bring them to a boil again. Cook for 30 minutes more. Drain, dry on a rack and roll in:
(Granulated sugar)

CANDIED GINGER

5½ Pints Preserved

Our friend Cecily Brownstone has graciously allowed us to use this recipe from her *Associated Press Cook Book*. This is either a single long-day or an intermittent four-day procedure. If you settle for one day, allow several hours between each of the four cookings. ➤ See About Ginger, 576. Scrape and cut into ¼-inch slices enough fresh nonfibrous young:
Gingerroot
to make 1 quart. Put the slices into a large stainless steel pan and cover generously with:
Water
Bring water slowly to a boil and simmer covered until tender, about 20 minutes. Add:
1 cup sugar
and stir until mixture boils. Remove from heat. Cover and let stand overnight at room temperature. Recook, simmering gently for about 15 minutes after the ginger has again come to a boil. Add:
1 seeded sliced lemon
1 cup light corn syrup
Uncover and simmer 15 minutes longer, stirring occasionally. Remove from heat and let stand covered overnight. During the third cooking, the ginger must be stirred often to avoid scorching. Bring the syruped ginger to a boil. Stir in:
1 cup sugar
Simmer 30 minutes. Stir in:
1 cup sugar
and bring mixture again to a boil. Remove from heat. Cover and let stand overnight.

In the fourth cooking, bring the mixture to a boil once more. When the syrup drops heavily from the side of a spoon, 833, and the ginger is translucent, pour the mixture into sterile wide-mouthed jars. Seal, 805. You should now have about 5 cups of **Canton Ginger.** Should you want **Candied Ginger,** drain the ginger after the last cooking. Reserve the syrup for flavoring sauces. Dry the ginger slices on a rack over a tray, uncovered, overnight. When well dried, roll the slices in:
Granulated sugar
Store in tightly covered glass jars.

★ GLAZED CHESTNUTS OR MARRONS GLACÉS

Shell:
Boiled Chestnuts, 563
Soak them overnight, covered with cold water to which you have added:
Juice of 1 lemon
Next morning, drain them and drop into boiling:
Water or milk
Simmer until tender but firm. Drain chestnuts and discard water or milk. For every cup of nuts, make a syrup by cooking to the soft-ball stage, 234°:
1 cup sugar
1 cup water
¼ teaspoon cream of tartar
Drop nuts into boiling syrup and simmer about ten minutes. Remove from heat and let stand, covered, 24 hours. Drain nuts, reserving syrup. While preparing the sauce, put nuts in a 250° oven to dry. Reduce the syrup until very thick. Place nuts in jars. Add to each jar:
1 to 2 tablespoons cognac
Fill jars with the heavy syrup and seal. To candy the nuts, they must be dried not once but three times, dipping them between dryings in the reduced syrup. After the final drying roll them in:
Granulated sugar
Store in tightly covered tins.

CANDIED CRANBERRIES

Because of their innate keeping qualities cranberries can be candied by a rather simple method, after which they will store for 3 months if kept covered.
Stir until dissolved and bring to a boil:
2½ cups sugar
1½ cups water
Have ready in a heat-resistant bowl:
1 quart cranberries
Pour the boiling syrup over the berries. Put the bowl in a steamer, 278, for 45 minutes. Remove and cool without stirring. Leave in a warm, dry room 3 to 4 days. Stir at intervals. When the syrup reaches a jellylike consistency, remove berries and let them dry 3 days longer—out of the syrup. Turn them for uniform drying. When the fruit can be

handled easily, store in a tightly covered container. Use the berries on picks to stud a ham or for other garnishing.

FRUIT PASTE

You find this delicacy in Italy, Spain, the American tropics, and in Germany, where it bears the quaint name of **Quittenbrod** or **Quittenwurst** because quince is a favorite flavor. The trick is to reduce, very radically, equal parts of:

Fruit pulp—guava, quince, apricot, etc.
Sugar

➤ The real trick, of course, is to find the patience and time to watch this mixture so it won't scorch. When it is stiff, spread it to a ½-inch thickness in pans that have been dipped in cold water. Cut into squares and dry on racks in a cool place, turning once a day for 3 to 4 days. Dust the squares with:

Granulated sugar

Or stuff the stiff pulp without drying into cellophane sausage casings. Before pouring or stuffing, you may add at the last minute:

Ground cinnamon, cloves, citron or almonds

The slices or squares look attractive when served on a green leaf.

CANDIED ANGELICA AND OTHER ROOTS AND STALKS

About 1 Pound

Wash:

2 cups edible young roots and stalks such as angelica or Acorus calamus

Place them in a crock. Pour over to cover:

⅓ cup salt
2 cups boiling water

Cover crock and let them soak for 24 hours. Drain, peel and wash in cold water. Cook to the soft-ball stage, 234°:

2 cups sugar
2 cups water

Add the cleaned roots and stems. Cook for 20 minutes. Drain them, but reserve syrup. Put them on a wire rack in a cool, dark place for 4 days. Bring the syrup and roots to 234° and cook 20 minutes or until the syrup candies the roots. Drain on a rack until ➤ thoroughly dry. Store tightly covered.

THE FOODS WE KEEP

As modern living moves many of us farther and farther from primary sources of food, we more easily take for granted the marvels of modern packaging. Gone is the close awareness of growth and decay, of the fragile balance between the heat that halts enzymatic growth and the chill that retards decomposition, of the interaction of humidity and ventilation that discourages molds. No matter what method of preservation we investigate—freezing, canning, salting, smoking, drying, preserving or storing—we still find intricate reactions at work, confronting us with the very same problems that have faced conservers from time immemorial. In the following chapters we give you the safest methods we have found to keep food from season to season. In carrying out these procedures you will experience almost complete success, but unexpected contingencies may lead to a rare and potentially dangerous failure. Such failures may occur in commercial packaging as well. ➤ Whenever kept foods show even the slightest sign of spoilage, such as leakage, off-odor, bulging can ends, or liquid that spurts out when a can is opened, please accept the best advice we know: **If in doubt, throw it out.** Do not even taste the smallest bit of the contents.

Rare is the climate or circumstance that allows man to live the year around on varied, fresh and abundant foodstuffs with bounteous quotas of valuable nutritive elements. So food preservation by home and by commercial methods must loom large on our horizon. As with all foods not eaten when fresh, both processing and storage time usually work against the retention of nutritive values. The following chapters discuss how best to freeze, can, dry, salt, smoke and preserve foods for which we, as housekeepers, must assume the responsibility of safe preparation.

Of all these processes, whether home or commercial, freezing—if its time limitations are observed, 820—seems to give us superior flavor and nutritive values; canning comes in second generally in both flavor and nutrition but wins in superior long-term keeping qualities; while drying, salting and smoking follow in decreasing nutritive and taste values.

In addition to freezing, canning, drying, smoking and salting foods, there are two more recent commercial processes capable of extending shelf life, neither of which can be performed by the householder. One involves commercial dehydration equipment capable of removing 98% of the moisture from a food as opposed to the 25 to 30% extracted in home drying. The **commercially dehydrated foods** resulting are nonfat dried milk, eggs and gelatins; dried soup and cake mixes; dehydrated grains, fruits and vegetables; dried fruit juices, and textured vegetable proteins. As 98% of the moisture is extracted from these commercially dehydrated foods, they shrink in size, and their contracted state helps to protect nutritive values. Extravagant claims are made that commercially dehydrated foods will last fifteen years if properly packaged and stored at proper temperatures. A safer estimate seems to be closer to five years if they are packed in coated cans in a nitrogen atmosphere with less than 2% oxygen.

Compare commercially dehydrated foods with the more expensive, bulkier **freeze-dried foods** for which exorbitant storage claims are also made. Freeze-dried foods result when food sliced or processed prior to immersion in or spraying with a preserving agent is frozen, placed in a vacuum chamber and heated. As the ice crystals in the frozen food melt they are "vacuumed" away, but the cellular structure of the food remains lightweight, porous and ready for quick reconstitution. This freeze-dried process, relatively more expensive than commercial dehydration, retains higher food values during the first six months of storage. Valid total shelf life for freeze-dried foods is estimated at twelve to eighteen months.

Most purchased staples come under state and local sanitary laws, and any that are in interstate commerce are covered by federal food and drug legislation. The integrity of certain additives, like seasonings, salts and flavorings, has been traditionally taken for granted. Since 1960, approved substances "generally recognized as safe" have appeared on the government's so-called GRAS list. Under the Delaney Amendment, however, any substance, new or old, proved to be cancer-inducing may lose its acceptance. This applies, for instance, to sassafras as well as to cyclamates.

A special subject of federal concern is those extra substances that are present in food as a result of the manufacturers' determination to boost nutritive or color content or of special conditions growing out of processing, packaging or storage. An entirely different kind of additive is the unintentional or accidental kind—the one that results from improper processing, contamination, imperfect sealing, or careless keeping. In this area, again, there is a whole series of federal rulings.

A change in the nature of legal concepts during the past decade now puts the burden of proof for the safety of additives on the manufacturer and thus provides more immediate and positive protection for the consumer. It is the business of every one of us to support all legislation controlling amounts and kinds of food additives so that we may be sure they will not increase beyond human tolerance. ➤ Read the labels and carefully note both contents and weight and nutritive claims of all the packaged or preserved food you buy.

For most of us, the responsibility of keeping food in good condition starts as we roll our baskets past the checker. And what a lot we push! In one week, a single normally well fed American uses a minimum of 3½ quarts of milk, ½ pound of fat, 4½ pounds of meat, poultry, fish, cheese, beans or nuts, 3 pounds of cereals and ½ pound of sugar. Add fruits and vegetables and multiply by 52, then by the number of persons in your family. If there are four of you, the total will stand at something like a ton and a half a year. This is an impressive investment in hard currency: an item, in fact, amply huge to warrant protecting your market purchases to the very best of your ability.

But all of us are guilty on occasion of picking up Junior at the tennis club after shopping and getting involved in some friendly gossip—while the lettuces back in the car wilt down and the frozen foods begin disastrously to thaw. Remember that heat and moisture encourage spoilage, bacteria, insect infestation and mold. And sunlight may destroy vitamin content, as in milk; or cause flavor deterioration, as in spices. Keep an insulated cooler in your car to transport purchases that should be kept cold.

Many molds need no light and thrive on acids; some occur only on the surface but give off gases that may adversely affect flavor. ➤ Store most staples in a cool, dark, dry place, preferably with a constant temperature around 70°; or, if indicated, refrigerate. ➤ Any stockpiled food should be kept on a rotating system. Place the new food at the back of the shelves and use the older purchases from the front for the day-to-day needs of the household. ➤ Although we know some stored foods may not spoil for years, flavor and nutritive qualities in all of them are progressively lessened as the months roll by. And if a large portion of your diet comes from freeze-dried or dehydrated foods, be sure to include enough fresh foods high in vitamin C and in essential fatty acids to make up for these losses in processing.

We do urge you to ➤ use a preponderance of fresh foods whenever possible. Build your menus around government "best buys" on produce that appear regularly in the newspapers. These items are apt to be both reasonable in price and fresh, because they are seasonal. After buying, store them in the ways we suggest below, and cook them carefully, following the "pointers" ➤ so as to assure retention of topmost taste and nutritive value.

STOCKING THE KITCHEN

For pots and pans and all the other cooking equipment so necessary to our western culture, see 159, 162, and 163, and the equipment illustrated at the point of use in recipes. Use the following list to stock the larder of a new or second home or to surprise a bride with a basket full of staples. Campers, too, will find the list useful to check before going into the wilderness. Try to buy products that are package-dated: there is no way otherwise to tell how long food has been on a shelf or even before that in a storage warehouse. And be wary of packages bought in obscure places or shops where turnover may be slow.

STAPLES FOR THE AVERAGE FAMILY

Beverages: coffee, tea
Cereals: breakfast foods, rice, macaroni, spaghetti, noodles, farina, cornmeal, tapioca
Cheeses
Chocolate, cocoa
Coconut
Butter, lard, cooking oil or other shortening
Flour: whole-grain, all-purpose, cake
Sugar: granulated, confectioners', brown
Bread, crackers
Fruits: fresh, dried, canned, frozen
Fruit and vegetable juices: frozen, canned
Potatoes: white, sweet
Onions, garlic, shallots, chives
Syrups: corn, molasses, maple
Mayonnaise and French dressing
Salad oils, vinegars
Milk, cream, eggs
Milk solids, evaporated and condensed milk
Frozen and canned meats, fish
Beef, chicken and vegetable cubes
Nuts
Vegetables: fresh, frozen, canned
Honey, preserves, marmalade, jellies
Soups: frozen, canned, dried
Raisins, currants
Peanut butter
Active dried yeast
Worcestershire and hot pepper sauces
Gelatin: flavored, unflavored
Catsup, chili sauce, horseradish
Flavorings: vanilla, almond, etc.
Baking powder, baking soda
Cornstarch
Ground and stick cinnamon
Ground and whole cloves
Ground and crystallized ginger
Allspice
Whole nutmeg

Bay leaves
Salt
Celery seed
Celery salt
Dry and prepared mustard
Black and white peppercorns
Paprika, cayenne
Curry powder
Garlic and onion salt
Chili powder
Dried herbs: tarragon, basil, savory, sage, etc. See Herbs, 579

STORAGE OF PRESERVED FOODS

You may store in an area that ➤ stays around 70° for:

➤ About 5 years: dehydrated foods if properly packaged, see 798.

➤ About 2 years: Salt, sugar, whole pepper.

➤ About 18 months: Canned meat, poultry and vegetables—except sauerkraut and tomatoes—alone or mixed with cereal products. Canned fruit—except citrus fruits and juices and berries. Dried legumes, if stored in stainless steel or aluminum containers, and freeze-dried foods if properly packaged.

➤ About 12 months: Canned fish, hydrogenated fats and oils, flour, ready-to-eat dry cereals stored in stainless or aluminum containers, uncooked cereal in original container, canned nuts, instant puddings, instant dry cream and bouillon products, soda and baking powder.

➤ About 6 months: Evaporated milk, nonfat dry whole milk in metal containers, condensed meat and beef soups, dried fruits in metal container, canned citrus fruits and juices, canned berries. To store water, see 520.

If temperatures are lower than 70° but still above freezing, the permissible storage period for most of these items is longer.

WINTERING FRESH PRODUCE

The earliest agricultural societies realized how urgent it was to protect seed grains from deterioration between harvest and planting time, and they evolved many ingenious methods for storing them against rodents, rain, insect infestation and decay. The same enemies plagued them that plague us in our effort to winter over fresh produce: to find areas cool enough to stave off enzymatic action and ventilated sufficiently to prevent decay. Root cellars with stone walls and earthen floors are now as they were then the most practical solution if the climate is not too cold, too damp, or too dry, since they allow easy access and adequate space in which to segregate fruits from vegetables. When floors and walls are of concrete, produce must be kept free-standing from these surfaces to prevent mildew. Should a basement area be heated, through proximity to a furnace or otherwise, steps must be taken to compensate for this situation; but the precautions necessary depend on so many individual factors that they cannot be spelled out here.

The latest possible mature crops are best for any wintering over, but they should not be overripe. Harvest them on a dry day. Most crops for storage do best if allowed to cool in the field overnight. There are some exceptions: for example, onions need about a week after harvesting to attain regular storage status; with root vegetables like carrots, beets, rutabagas and kohlrabi, be sure to leave on an inch of the tops, discarding the rest.

Unbruised and unblemished produce—no other—may then be stored, for the most part in temperatures between 35° and 40°. Sweet potatoes and yams, however, respond best to somewhat higher temperatures—40° to 50°. They need moderately dry storage, while late cabbage, potatoes, pumpkins, winter squash, root crops, hard apples and pears require moderately moist conditions. Some people prefer to wash vegetables before storing; others refrain, from fear of vitamin loss. In any case, ➤ the surface of the produce should be dry before storage. It can be insulated and kept at more even temperatures if packed in dry sand or sawdust, although we have heard complaints that sand imparts off-flavors. Fruits such as apples and pears may be wrapped separately in paper to keep down contact spoilage from any unnoticed bruises. Whatever material is used, packing should be relegated to the compost heap after one season's use.

Outdoor storage in reinforced sod-house mounds is tricky wherever temperatures average 30° or higher. Fruits and vegetables should be stored in separate structures. In climates where the ground freezes, if the mound does not have an insulated entry door, it should be kept small, because, once opened, the earth covering cannot be made cold-impervious again. Should this happen, all produce should be removed, used quickly and/or, if suitable, refrigerated. Mounds should be located in well-drained areas with a drainage trench dug around the outside. Line the mound bottom with at least 6 inches of straw or dry leaves. To protect produce against rodents, place over the base insulation a piece of hardware cloth which can be shaped up against the sides of the conelike pile of vegetables or fruits you will be placing on it. ➤ Never store fruits and vegetables in the same mound. Then cover the whole with about 6 inches of straw or dry leaves. Shape over this a 6-inch layer of earth, leaving at the top of the cone a chimneylike opening which will allow sufficient ventilation, even when filled with straw and weighted down with a piece of board or metal held in place by a rock. Finally, cover the sides of the produce-cone with one more layer of leaves or straw as further insulation and erosion control.

You may prefer pit rather than mound storage. In a well-drained shady area, dig a hole deep enough to accommodate an 18-inch-diameter by

30-inch-long section of ceramic tile set on a hardware-cloth base, insulating the base beforehand with a layer of straw or dry leaves. Put in the produce. After filling the tile, keep it covered with a thick layer of straw and an outer one of soil and straw, and proceed to make a chimney in the center as described above. Dig a drainage ditch around the finished mound. Whether you use a mound or a pit, if you are in snow country, mark the location of your storage area with a tall pole.

The simplest method of all for storing root-crops, of course, is to leave them in the ground where they were grown and cover them with 15 to 18 inches of straw. This mulch applied on late crops just before frost should keep the ground from freezing hard. Again mark your rows with tall poles and keep a plan of your planting. It is surprising how easy it is to lose the location of the storage rows once the tops have shrunk in colder weather or are snow covered.

CANNING, SALTING, SMOKING AND DRYING

It is a thrill to possess shelves well stocked with home-canned food. In fact, you will find their inspection—often surreptitious—and the pleasure of serving the fruits of your labor comparable only to a clear conscience or a very becoming hat.

In fact, you must carry a clear conscience right with you through the processing itself, making absolutely sure that the food you keep is safe to eat. Great care must be exercised in the canning of all foods to avoid spoilage. Even greater care is required in the canning of nonacid foods—for which pressure-canning is the only recommended process—to prevent the development of Clostridium botulinum, a germ so deadly that "1 oz. could theoretically kill 100 million people." The spores of botulinus may resist 212°, or boiling temperature, even after several hours of processing and may produce a fatal toxin in the canned product. Botulinus poisoning may be present even if no odor, gas, color change or softness in food texture indicates its presence.

Whether or not your suspicions are aroused, ➤ do not test home-canned nonacid food by tasting it out of the container. Instead, before tasting or serving, follow the recommendations of all reputable authorities, and—without exception —cook home-canned vegetables for 15 minutes, meat, poultry and fish for 20 minutes, in boiling liquid, uncovered, stirring closely packed produce to allow heat penetration. By this means, botulinus toxin is positively destroyed.

➤ For maximum nutritional value, only the freshest and best food should be canned. Inspect it with an eagle eye, discarding all blemished or rotted portions and washing or scrubbing the selected remainder to remove spray, soil or insects. Produce that is imperfect before processing may spoil the rest of the food in its container afterward, producing color changes and encouraging the formation of mold or gases. If, as a result of any careless preliminary handling, your jars show evidences of any spoilage or mold, ➤ discard them at once, preferably without opening.

➤ Good organization and proper equipment simplify canning and give you, with a minimum of effort, gay-looking shelves of glistening, jewel-like jars filled with canned fruits and vegetables, all labeled, dated and ready to use.

Seasonal heat and heat from the stove inevitably accompany canning. Hot fluids in hot jars and heavy pans have to be handled carefully.

Seen in the chapter heading are a fruit press, a glazed crock for salting, a wooden sauerkraut fork, a salt container, both narrow and wide-mouthed tempered glass jars, and a wide-mouthed funnel used for filling them. ➤ Plenty of pot holders, strong tongs or jar lifter, 165, and paraffin are added aids. When using special equipment, follow the manufacturer's directions.

CANNING PROCESSES

➤ Remember that all nonacid vegetables and all meats and fish must be pressure-processed, 804.
➤ The boiling-water bath, 804, is not recommended for any nonacid foods.
➤ Oven canning is not recommended under any circumstances. The open-kettle method has been abandoned by officialdom but is still used by some housewives for acid fruits. To can specific foods, see alphabetical listings in this chapter.

In canning, follow these general steps. ➤ Line up your equipment and read below about the type you are using. ➤ Sterilize all equipment and keep it sterile all during the processing. ➤ Should you be using a pressure canner—see illustration, 804—make sure that the jars are the type that can stand 240° or more of heat. Do not use ordinary jars that are not tempered for canning or freezing. ➤ In any case, check all jars against chipping, cracking or other defects. Next, check the closures between the jars and lids. If using screw types, first place them on sound jars without a rubber. Screw them tight. They are usable if it is impossible to insert a thin penknife blade or a thumbnail between the jar and the lid. Unscrew them. Put the rubbers in place and fill the jars with water. Screw down the lids. Invert the jars. If there is no seepage, the jars and lids are safe to use. This test may also be applied to the clamp or wire-bail type of closure, seen in narrow and wide-mouthed styles at either end of the drawing opposite.

Lids are of two main types—those which need separate rubbers and adjustment both before and after processing, and those which have an attached rubberlike sealing compound and are adjusted once before processing and then close automatically by vacuum when cooling. The vacuum types are sketched second and third on the left. The first has a wider mouth and straight sides which make filling and emptying easier than with the shouldered jar shown next. This wide-mouthed jar is recommended for freezing. Lids with attached rubbers should never be sterilized. Merely wash, rinse well and cover with water brought to a simmer, but not to a boil. Remove from heat but leave in hot water until ready to use.

If the lids call for separate rubbers, have clean new rings of the right size. Rubber rings should never be reused. ➤ Unless you are pressure-canning or using a boiling-water bath, jars and lids shown with separate rubbers should be sterilized 15 minutes in boiling water. Also sterilize reused zinc caps. If pressure-canning, wash glass jars and new rubber rings in hot soapy water, rinse well and keep in hot water until ready to fill.

Lids two through five shown below fit on the regular threaded-top canning jars, whether of pint, quart or half-gallon size. The zinc- and glass-disk tops, shown fourth and fifth below, are placed on the rubber ring, screwed clockwise as tightly as possible, and then turned counterclockwise ¼ inch before putting them in the canner.

The jars with the all-glass lids shown next have wire-bail or clamp closures. While processing, the longer wire rests in the groove of the lid. The shorter wire is not snapped down in its final position until after processing. ➤ The slight openings provided by all these adjustments are temporary. They allow excess air to be forced out of the jars during processing, and thus avoid possible explosion. See Sealing Jars, 805.

PREPARING FOOD FOR CANNING

➤ To prepare food for canning, wash, clean, pare and cut up food just as you would if planning to cook it for immediate use. ➤ Remember that vitamins escape quickly, so prepare only small batches of food, about 1 quart at a time. The size in which pieces are cut may depend on convenience in packing.

➤ To blanch or precook foods for canning, put large fruits and all vegetables in a wire basket and immerse them, about 1 quart at a time, in boiling liquid for 5 minutes, counting from the time the water begins to boil again after immersion. Then dip them up and down quickly in cold water 2 or 3 times to reduce the heat. This will keep the food shapely and make handling easier. Blanching shrinks food and drives out air so that produce may be packed more closely. Its most important role, however, is to arrest some undesirable kinds of enzymatic action. ➤ The liquid in which the foods were precooked or steamed should be used to fill the jars, thus saving valuable minerals.

Berries, soft fruits and tomatoes may be canned without blanching. Meat may be partially cooked —about two-thirds done—by simmering or roasting. For more details about meat, see 811.

➤ To steam foods for canning, use a steamer, 804, or steam basket, 278. Steam only a small quantity at a time. ➤ Do not crowd the food, as the steam must penetrate all of it. Use a kettle with a tightly fitting lid. Have in the kettle several inches of boiling water. Close the lid tightly and steam food the length of time given in individual recipes for fruit or vegetables.

PACKING JARS

There are two methods of filling the jars before they go into the pressure canner or boiling-water bath. ➤ With **Cold or Raw Pack,** the hot jars are filled with raw food and covered with boiling syrup, juice or water; they begin their processing treatment in hot, not boiling, water. ➤ With **Hot Pack,** the hot jars are filled with precooked hot food, then processed. More food can be packed into a jar using this method.

➤ In canning, pack jars firmly, but not so tightly that the produce is crushed. ➤ Pack fruits and acid vegetables to within ½ inch of jar tops. Lima beans, dried beans, peas, corn and other low-acid foods which swell considerably more than other vegetables, plus meats canned under pressure, should be packed loosely to within 1 inch of jar tops. Add boiling liquid to completely cover the food solids, but leave headroom for expansion above the liquid, as indicated in individual recipes. You may add salt to meats and vegetables at the rate of 1 teaspoon per quart.

Fill jars of fruit with sugar syrup to within ½

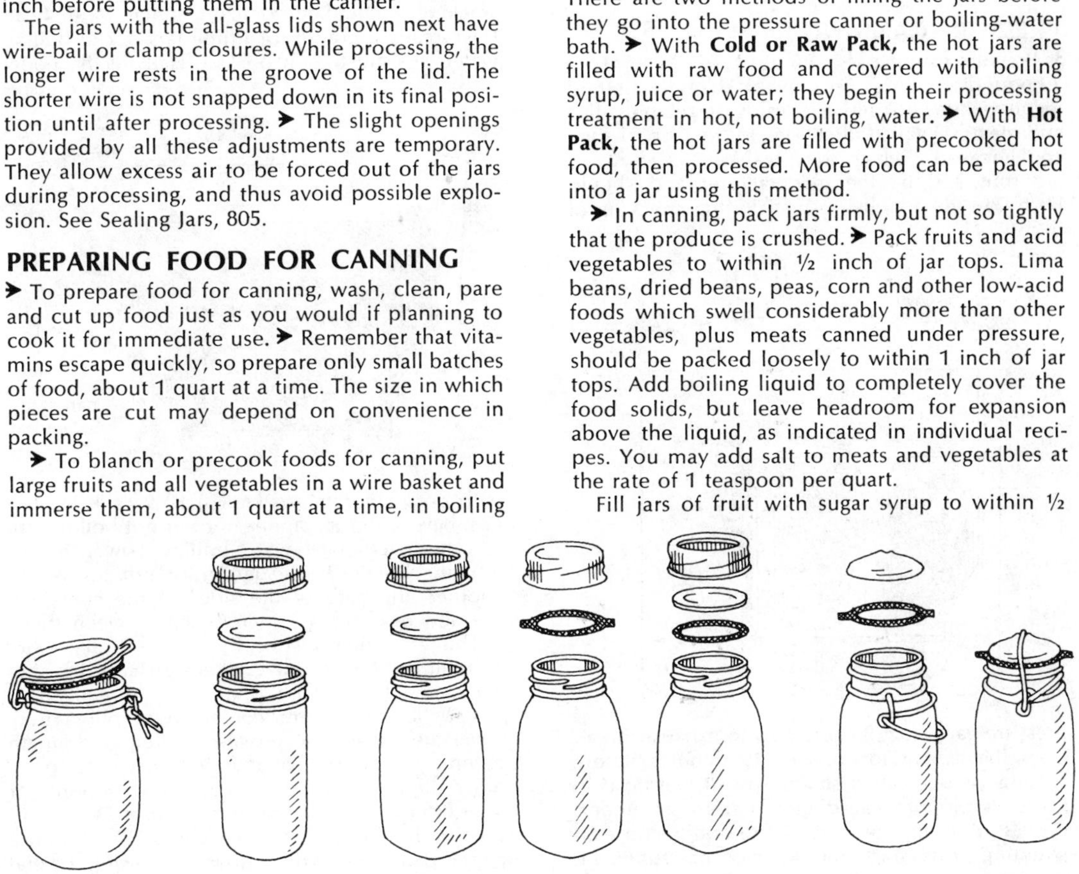

inch of top. For sugar syrup formulas, see 805. ➤ Before putting on lids, make sure that any air that may be trapped in the liquid is expelled. Run a long thin spatula down between the inside of

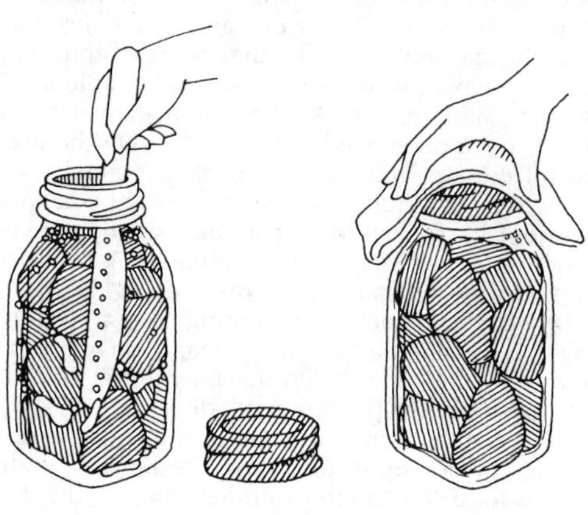

the jar and the produce, changing the position of the contents enough to release any trapped air as shown above. Then carefully wipe the top of the jar before lidding.

PRESSURE-CANNING

➤ Pressure-canning at a temperature of 240° F. at 10 pounds pressure at sea level is the only method recommended for nonacid fruits, vegetables, fish and meats. Detailed directions for the use of such appliances—of which a typical one is shown—are furnished by the manufacturer and should be followed carefully—especially the checking of

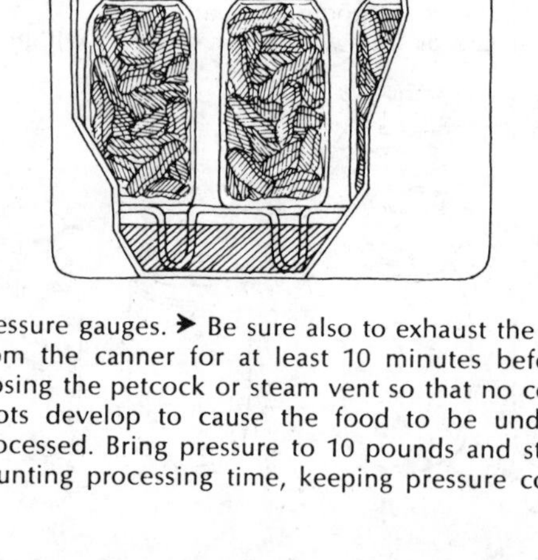

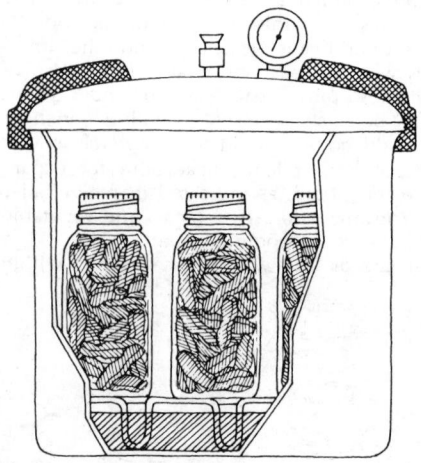

pressure gauges. ➤ Be sure also to exhaust the air from the canner for at least 10 minutes before closing the petcock or steam vent so that no cold spots develop to cause the food to be under-processed. Bring pressure to 10 pounds and start counting processing time, keeping pressure constant. Remove canner from heat and let pressure fall to zero before opening. To remove jars, see directions under Canning in a Boiling-Water Bath, below. ➤ If using a small steam-pressure saucepan, keep the heat constantly at 10 pounds pressure, and be sure to add 20 minutes to the processing time. For vegetable pressure-canning, see 808; and for meats, see 811.

▲ If canning at high altitudes in a pressure canner ➤ add ½ pound to the pressure gauge for each additional 1000 feet. For instance, if processing requires 10 pounds pressure at sea level, use 12 pounds at 4000 feet, 14 pounds at 7500 feet; if 15 pounds at sea level, use 17 pounds at 4000 feet, 19 pounds at 7500 feet.

CANNING IN A BOILING-WATER BATH

➤ The boiling-water-bath process is used only for acid fruits and brined or pickled vegetables. A regular hot-water canner, see below, or a clean washboiler or lard can may be used if it has a tight-fitting lid and enough headroom for briskly boiling water.

An important utensil in canning is a ➤ rack for the bottom of the boiler to keep the jars from cracking when they come in contact with heat. Have ready a holder for lifting jars out of boiling water, see illustration on 165. Half fill the boiler

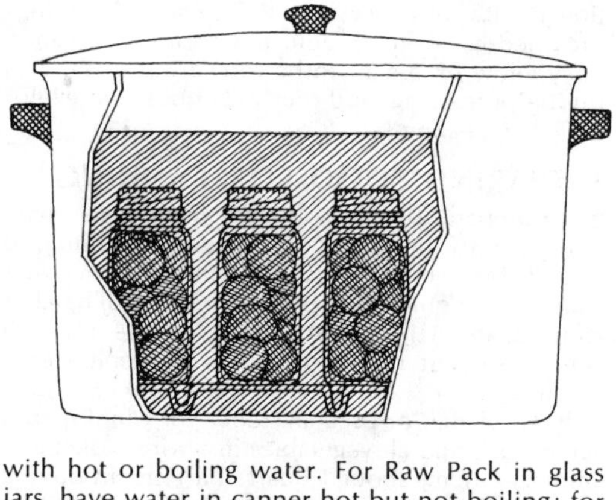

with hot or boiling water. For Raw Pack in glass jars, have water in canner hot but not boiling; for all other packs, have water boiling. Lower the jars into the boiler. ➤ The jars must not touch one another, the base or the sides of the container, see above. Leave a 2-inch space between them. ➤ The jars should rest on the rack. Add more hot or boiling water to cover them at least 2 inches above the tops. Don't pour water directly onto jars. When the water comes to a rolling boil, cover the canner and process the required length of time for the particular food chosen. ➤ To remove the jars from the boiling water, use tongs or a jar lifter as soon as the time is up. ➤ Do not lift the jars by the lids. ➤ Place the jars on wood, a paper pad, or a cloth surface, allowing several inches between them. See that there is no draft on the hot jars, as sudden cooling may cause the glass to crack.

▲ Canning at high altitudes in a boiling-water bath ➤ requires a 1-minute increase in processing time for every 1000 feet above sea level if the total time is 20 minutes or less, and 2 minutes per 1000 feet if the total time is more than 20 minutes.

SEALING, LABELING AND STORING JARS

➤ Seal all jars according to manufacturer's directions. With the types of lids described on 803, the rubber-attached metal lid is self-sealing and is held in place by a metal screw band. This is screwed down completely before processing. The seal automatically tightens itself and should not be touched after processing. After the jar has cooled 12 hours or more, the band may be removed for reuse.

The zinc-screw type and the glass-disk and metal-ring lids should be turned clockwise as far as possible, then loosened 1/4 inch before being processed. Be sure to screw lids with a slow, steady turn, so as not to displace the rubbers. After removal from the canner, tighten the lids or bands again. This is referred to in the recipes as "Complete seals if necessary."

The longer wire on the bail or clamp type should be snapped into place during processing, and the shorter wire snapped down on the shoulder of the jar after removal from the canner.

➤ Whatever type you use, be sure to leave the jars upright and undisturbed for 12 hours. ➤ Do not tighten caps after jars have cooled. While the jars are still hot after sealing, you may see active bubbling going on. This is merely continued boiling caused by the lowered boiling point produced by the vacuum in the jar; it will cease as the contents cool.

➤ Test-seal the metal tops by tapping the lids lightly with a metal spoon or knife. A ringing note indicates a safe seal. If the contents touch the inner side of the lid, the sound may be dull but not hollow. ➤ If the note is both dull and hollow, reprocessing with a new lid is in order. Or, if you prefer, use the food right away.

➤ Label and store jars in a cool, dark, airy place. Storage temperatures between 45° and 60° maintain good color and are generally suitable for all properly heat processed foods.

FRUIT CANNING

All acid fruits should be processed in a hot-water canner, see 804. All nonacid fruits should be pressure-canned, see 804. ➤ Choose fresh, firm fruit that is not overripe. Imperfect fruit may be used, but it must be carefully gone over and all blemishes removed. Wash the fruit. Prepare as for table use. If it is to be pared, it may be dipped in boiling water until the skins loosen, and then dipped for a moment in cold water. It is best to process only enough produce for one canner load at a time.

To keep fruit from discoloring until you can pack it, mist it over with Anti-Browning Solution, below. Leave 1/2 inch headroom in the jars after packing with fruit and syrup. Enough liquid will develop during processing to cover the fruit and prevent darkening.

ANTI-BROWNING SOLUTION FOR CANNING

I. Drop prepared fruit into a solution of 2 tablespoons salt and 2 tablespoons vinegar to 1 gallon water. Do not leave the fruit in the solution longer than 20 minutes, and ➤ rinse before packing.

II. Commercially packaged ascorbic acid—vitamin C—is a concentrated natural constituent of fruit. It should be mixed well with the sugar in the syrup so as not to lose the delicate fruit flavor. Dissolve 1/2 teaspoon crystalline ascorbic acid, or 1500 milligrams in tablet form, in a little water and add to 1 quart syrup.

III. Just before lidding the jar, sprinkle ascorbic acid over the contents. Allow 1/4 teaspoon to each quart of fruit.

APPROXIMATE YIELD OF COMMON FRUITS

	POUNDS PER QUART JAR	QUART JARS PER BUSHEL OR CRATE
Apples	2½–3	16–20
Apricots	2–2½	7–11
Berries	1½–3	12–18
Cherries	2–2½	(unpitted) 22–32
Peaches	2–3	18–24
Pears	2–3	20–25
Plums	1½–2½	24–30
Tomatoes	2½–3½	15–20

SYRUPS FOR CANNING

Sugar helps fruit keep its shape, flavor and color, but you may can fruit without sweetening it. Syrup for canned fruit varies in consistency, depending on the fruit or the use to which it will be put. The following formulas will help you decide on the most appropriate blend of sugar and water. Cook until the sugar dissolves and keep hot until needed. Do not let the syrup boil down. Allow 1 to 1½ cups syrup for each quart of fruit. Light corn syrup or mild-flavored honey may be used to replace up to one-half the specified amount of sugar.

THIN SYRUP

About 5 Cups

2 cups sugar to 4 cups water. Stir well before heating and bring slowly to a boil, 236°. Use for naturally sweet fruits and to approximate the quality of fresh fruits.

MEDIUM SYRUP

About 5½ Cups

3 cups sugar to 4 cups water. Prepare as for thin syrup. Good for canning fruits that are not highly acid.

HEAVY SYRUP

About 6½ Cups

Use 4¾ cups sugar to 4 cups water. ➤ Dissolve and boil very carefully to prevent crystallization and scorching. Use for very sour fruits like rhubarb; also suitable for dessert use. If too heavy a syrup is used the fruit may rise to the top of the jar during processing.

SYNTHETIC SWEETENER

Some artificial sweeteners may be used in canning. Check manufacturer's recommendations and do not use without a doctor's consent.

PROCESSING FRUITS

I. NONACID FRUITS

Use a pressure canner. Place jars as described on 804. Vent canner for 10 minutes. Process fruits 5 minutes at 10 pounds pressure.

II. ACID FRUITS

The following directions are for quart jars processed in a boiling-water bath, 804. Start counting time when the water surrounding the lidded jars reaches a fast boil. Reduce the processing time by 10% if pint jars are used. Increase the processing time by 15 minutes for half-gallon jars. ➤ When fruit is hot-packed, use stainless or enamel pans for the precooking. After removing jars from canner, complete seals if necessary, 805.

III. FRUIT PURÉES AND PASTES

Use ripe, firm, unblemished fruit. Add 1 cup boiling water to each quart fruit. Simmer until it can be forced through a sieve or food mill, shown in chapter heading, 832. If you are using a blender, the fruit should be peeled. You may add sugar to taste, unless you are puréeing tomatoes. Reheat the purée and fill the hot jars, leaving ¼-inch headroom. For acid fruits, seal and process 20 minutes in a boiling-water bath for each half-pint. ➤ For less acid fruits and tomato purées, allow ¼-inch headroom. Pressure-can 15 minutes for each half-pint at 10 pounds pressure.

APPLES

Use Hot Pack, 803. Select firm, sound, tart varieties. Wash, pare and core; cut into quarters or halves. Drop into Anti-Browning Solution, 805. Drain. Boil 5 minutes in thin or medium syrup. Pack in hot jars, cover with boiling syrup and process 20 minutes in boiling-water bath. Apples may also be baked, packed, covered with boiling syrup and processed 15 minutes in boiling-water bath.

APPLE CIDER

Use Raw Pack only. Use a blend of 3 or more varieties of firm, ripe apples, making sure to balance the sweet apples against those that are acid. Because crab apples are astringent, use them in small proportions. After putting apples through a cider mill or fruit press, shown in chapter heading on 802, strain and put into hot sterile jars. Process 30 minutes in hot-water bath at 185° F.

APPLESAUCE

Use Hot Pack, 803. Prepare Applesauce, 131; pack boiling hot. To prevent darkening at top of jar, add 1 teaspoon lemon juice at the last moment before sealing. Process 10 minutes in boiling-water bath.

APRICOTS

Use Raw or Hot Pack, 803. Select ripe, firm fruit. Blanch to remove skins, then heat through and treat to prevent darkening, 805. Drain. Pack whole or in halves into hot jars and cover with boiling medium syrup; process 25 minutes in boiling-water bath for Hot Pack, 30 minutes for Raw Pack.

BERRIES

Use Raw Pack for soft berries: **blackberries, boysenberries, dewberries, loganberries** and **raspberries.** Pick over, wash if gritty, stem, pack closely in hot jars, fill with boiling medium syrup and process 15 minutes in boiling-water bath.

Blueberries should be blanched, 803, and may be packed without sugar, then processed as above.

Use Hot Pack for **currants, elderberries, gooseberries** and **huckleberries.** They should be added to boiling medium or thick syrup for ½ minute, then packed in hot jars. Cover with the boiling syrup and process 15 minutes for all except huckleberries, which need 20 minutes in a boiling-water bath. For **strawberries,** the following more complicated procedure will yield plump, bright-colored fruit. Wash if gritty, then hull. Add 1 cup sugar to each quart prepared berries, placing in alternate layers in shallow pans, and let stand 2 hours. Simmer 5 minutes in the juice they have drawn while standing. Fill hot jars full and add boiling thin syrup if additional liquid is needed. Process 15 minutes in boiling-water bath.

CHERRIES

For Raw Pack, wash and stem. Can whole or pitted. To seed, use a cherry pitter, shown in the heading on 798, or the rounded end of a paper clip. If not seeded, prick with a pin. Use heavy syrup for sour cherries; medium syrup for sweet. Pack, cover with boiling syrup and process 25 minutes in boiling-water bath.

CRANBERRIES

Use Hot Pack. Wash and stem. Boil 3 minutes in heavy syrup. Pack in hot jars. Cover with boiling syrup. Process 10 minutes in boiling-water bath.

CITRUS FRUITS: GRAPEFRUIT, ORANGES
Use Raw Pack only. Prepare sections as shown, 135, and pack in hot jars. Add boiling thin syrup and process 10 minutes in boiling-water bath.

CURRANTS
See berries, above.

FIGS
Use Hot Pack only. Wash ripe, firm figs, leaving peels and stems intact. Let simmer with water to cover 5 minutes. Drain. Pack in hot jars and add boiling thin syrup and ➤ 2 teaspoons lemon juice to each quart to increase acidity. Process 30 minutes in boiling-water bath.

GRAPES
Use Raw or Hot Pack. Use only sound, firm, preferably seedless, grapes. Wash and stem. For Hot Pack bring to a boil in medium syrup. Pack in hot jars. Cover with boiling syrup. Process 20 minutes in boiling-water bath. For Raw Pack, process 30 minutes.

GRAPE JUICE
I. Use Hot Pack only.
Wash sound, ripe grapes. Cover with boiling water and heat slowly to simmering. ➤ Do not boil. Cook slowly until fruit is very soft, then strain through a jelly bag as shown in chapter heading, 832. Let stand 24 hours refrigerated. Strain again. Add ½ cup sugar to each quart juice. Reheat to simmering and pour into hot jars. Process 30 minutes in hot-water bath held at 190°.

OTHER FRUIT JUICES
Use Hot Pack only. Select sound, ripe fruit, crush and heat slowly to simmering point. Strain through several layers of cheesecloth. Add 1 cup sugar to each gallon juice for moderate sweetness. Heat again to about 190° and simmer 10 minutes. ➤ Do not boil, as it ruins the flavor. Pour into hot jars, seal, and process in hot-water bath held at 190° for 30 minutes. Do not allow water to boil.

Juices from uncooked fruit may be pressed out in a cider press and heated to lukewarm before being poured into jars and processed as above. Peach, cherry and apple juice and cider canned this way are less likely to taste flat.

PEACHES
Use Raw or Hot Pack. Use firm, ripe fruit. Scald to remove skins. Halve peaches and discard pits, 139. You may scrape out reddish areas, which brown in canning. Treat to prevent darkening, 805. For Raw Pack, arrange, pit side down, in hot jars, cover with boiling thin or medium syrup and process 30 minutes in boiling-water bath. For Hot Pack, process 25 minutes.

PEARS
Use Raw or Hot Pack. Pare, core and halve, quarter or slice. Treat to prevent darkening, 805. For Hot Pack, boil gently about 5 minutes in thin or medium syrup. Pack into hot jars, cover with boiling syrup and process 25 minutes in boiling-water bath. Hard pears are best if cooked in water only until nearly tender. The sugar is then added to the cooking water in the same proportions as for a medium syrup and the whole brought to a boil. Pack into hot jars, cover with boiling syrup and process 25 minutes in boiling-water bath. For Raw or Cold Pack, process 30 minutes.

PERSIMMONS
Use Hot Pack only. Wash ripe wild persimmons and steam until soft. Put through a colander or food mill. Reheat to boiling and pour into hot jars. Process 20 minutes in boiling-water bath. You may sweeten the pulp before processing if it is to be used as a sauce.

PINEAPPLE
Use Hot Pack only. Slice, pare, core, remove eyes. Shred or cut into cubes. Simmer in light or medium syrup about 5 minutes or until tender. Pack into hot jars and cover with boiling syrup. Process 20 minutes in boiling-water bath.

PINEAPPLE JUICE
Discarded eyes, cores and skins of fresh fruit can be used in making pineapple juice. Cover with cold water. Cook slowly in covered kettle from 30 to 40 minutes. Strain through a jelly bag, shown 832. Measure juice; heat. For each cup of juice add ⅙ cup sugar. Boil rapidly 10 minutes and process 5 minutes in boiling-water bath. Juice may also be extracted from pineapple by putting the pared fruit through the fine blade of a food chopper, with a large bowl beneath to catch the liquid. After sweetening, process as for strained juice above.

PLUMS
Use Raw or Hot Pack method. Use moderately ripe fruit. Meaty instead of juicy plums are best for canning. Wash and prick skins. For Hot Pack, cover with boiling syrup: thin for sweet plums, medium for tart varieties. Cover and let stand 20 to 30 minutes. Pack drained fruit firmly into hot jars, but do not crush. Reheat syrup to boiling and pour over plums. Process 25 minutes in boiling-water bath for Hot Pack, 30 minutes for Cold or Raw Pack.

QUINCES
"Preserved," noted an herbalist optimistically in 1562, "they do mightily prevail against drunkenness." Use well-ripened fruit. Wipe the fuzz from the quince, cut out the stem and blossom ends and cook the fruit gently in several inches of water, covered, 20 minutes. Drain the water and use to make a medium syrup. Pare, or simply cut the fruit from the core unpared. Pack into hot jars, cover with boiling syrup, and process 60 minutes in boiling-water bath.

RHUBARB

Use Hot Pack only. Wash stalks and cut into ½-inch pieces. Add and mix well ½ to 1 cup sugar for each quart fruit. Let stand 3 to 4 hours, then heat slowly to boiling for ½ minute. Pack in hot jars and process 10 minutes in hot-water bath.

TOMATOES

Use Raw or Hot Pack. Use firm, fresh tomatoes. Scald 1 minute and then dip 1 minute into cold water to remove skins. Cut out cores. Halve, quarter, or leave whole. You may add ½ teaspoon salt per quart if desired. If Cold-Packing, press tomatoes gently into hot jars to within ½ inch of top of jar. Add no water. For Hot Pack, place tomatoes in hot jars; fill with boiling water or tomato juice. As it is difficult to judge the acidity of the many new tomato hybrids, we recommend pressure-canning only at 10 pounds pressure for 10 minutes.

TOMATO JUICE

Use Hot Pack only. Use firm, ripe perfect tomatoes. Wash; remove stem ends and cores. Chop or cut into small pieces. Cook gently, covered, until the juice flows freely. Put through a fine sieve or food mill. If there is no residue in the juice, pack into hot jars to within ½ inch of top. Process in boiling-water bath 10 minutes. Flavor just before serving. If some residue remains after straining the juice, we recommend pressure-canning at 10 pounds pressure for 10 minutes.

APPROXIMATE YIELD OF COMMON VEGETABLES

RAW VEGETABLE	POUNDS PER QUART JAR	QUART JARS PER BUSHEL
Beans, lima in the pod	4–5	6–8
Beans, snap	1½–2	15–20
Beets	2½–3	17–20
Carrots	2½–3	16–20
Corn cut off cob	7 ears	8
Greens	2–3	6–9
Okra	1½–2	17
Peas in the pod	2–2½	5–10
Squash, summer	2–2½	16–20
Sweet potatoes	2½–3	18–22
Tomatoes	2½–3½	15–20

VEGETABLE PRESSURE CANNING

➤ Pressure canning, 804, is the only process recommended for vegetables. As with all fruits, vegetables must be very carefully and quickly washed, through several waters if necessary or under running water, to remove all soil. Prepare only one pressure canner load at a time and work quickly. You may add about 1 teaspoon salt to each quart before processing. Pack the vegetable in the water used for blanching or steaming because this contains dissolved vitamins and minerals.

Great care must be exercised in the canning of nonacid foods to prevent the development of Clostridium botulinum, a deadly germ that may be present even though no odor or color change indicates its presence. The U.S. Government warns that all nonacid home-canned vegetables should be boiled in an open pan for 15 minutes before tasting or serving. They should be stirred frequently during cooking.

➤ The following directions are for 1-quart glass jars, unless otherwise specified, processed in a steam pressure canner at 10 pounds pressure at 240° F. One exception is Pickled Beets, which, because of the acidity of the vinegar, may be safely processed in a boiling-water bath. Vegetables may be canned either by Raw Pack or Hot Pack; however, our preference for the recipes below is the Hot Pack method.

The Department of Agriculture does not recommend home canning the following vegetables:

Cabbage, except sauerkraut
Cauliflower
Celery
Cucumbers
Eggplant
Lettuce
Onions
Parsnips
Turnips
Vegetable mixtures

ARTICHOKES

Wash and trim well 2-inch or smaller artichokes. Precook 5 minutes in brine of ¾ cup vinegar or lemon juice and 3 tablespoons salt to 1 gallon water. Pack in hot jars. Fill boiling brine to ½ inch of top. Process 25 minutes at 10 pounds pressure.

ASPARAGUS

Wash; remove loose scales and tough ends. Grade for uniformity. Place upright in wire basket. Hold in boiling water reaching just below tips for 3 minutes. Or cut into 1-inch lengths and boil 2 to 3 minutes. Pack hot jars and cover with boiling water, leaving ½-inch headroom. Process 30 minutes at 10 pounds pressure.

BEANS, GREEN, SNAP OR WAX

Wash; remove strings and tips. Break into small pieces. Precook 5 minutes. Reserve water. Pack hot jars and cover with boiling reserved water, leaving ½-inch headroom. Process 25 minutes at 10 pounds pressure for young tender pods. Old beans should be processed for 40 minutes.

BEANS, FRESH LIMA

Shell, sort and grade for size and age. Boil young beans 5 minutes, older beans 10 minutes. Pack loosely. Cover with boiling water, allowing 1-inch headroom. Process young beans 50 minutes, older beans 60 minutes, at 10 pounds pressure.

BEANS OR PEAS, DRIED
Cover beans or peas with cold water and let stand in a cool place 12 to 18 hours. Boil 30 minutes, then pack into hot jars. Cover with boiling water, leaving 1-inch headroom. Process 90 minutes at 10 pounds pressure.

BEETS
Select and prepare small whole beets with 1-inch stem and all the root. Boil 15 minutes. Trim off roots and stems. Slip off skins. Pack whole, sliced or diced, into hot jars. Add boiling water, leaving ½-inch headroom. Process 35 minutes at 10 pounds pressure.

BEETS, PICKLED
Prepare a boiling pickling syrup of 2 parts vinegar, 2 parts sugar. Dilute with water according to taste. Prepare cooked beets, see above. Fill hot jars and cover with boiling syrup, leaving ½-inch headroom. Process in boiling-water bath 30 minutes.

CARROTS
Sort and grade for uniformity. Wash and scrape. Boil 5 minutes. Reserve water. Slice or pack whole. Fill jars with boiling reserved water, leaving 1-inch headroom. Process 30 minutes at 10 pounds pressure.

CORN, WHOLE-KERNEL
Use tender, freshly gathered corn. Cut from cob. Do not scrape cobs. To each quart of corn add only 2 cups boiling water. Heat to boiling. Pack at once, adding no more water. Leave 1-inch headroom. Process 85 minutes at 10 pounds pressure.

CORN, CREAM-STYLE
Pack in pints only, see Peas, right. Cut off the tops of kernels and scrape cobs with back of knife or corn scraper—see 300—to remove all pulp. To each pint of corn add 1 cup boiling water. Heat to boiling. Pack at once, leaving 1-inch headroom. Process pints 85 minutes at 10 pounds pressure.

GREENS
Use fresh, tender greens. Wash thoroughly; discard any decayed leaves and tough stems. Steam about 8 minutes, or until wilted. Cut through greens several times with a knife. Pack quickly and loosely. Fill jars with boiling water, leaving 1-inch headroom. Process 90 minutes at 10 pounds pressure.

MUSHROOMS
Pack in pints only, see Peas, right. Wash well. Peel if wilted. If old, discard. Let stand 10 minutes in cold water. Wash again. Steam 4 minutes. Pack into hot jars with the hot liquid from the mushrooms and enough added boiling water to cover. Add ½ teaspoon salt and ⅛ teaspoon ascorbic acid to each pint to prevent darkening. Leave 1-inch headroom. Process 30 minutes at 10 pounds pressure.

NUTMEATS
Dry nuts in a 250° oven. Stir occasionally and do not let them brown or scorch. While still hot, fill dry sterilized half-pint or pint self-sealing jars, leaving ½-inch headroom. Process 10 minutes at 5 pounds pressure.

OKRA
Use tender pods only. Wash and remove caps without cutting into pod. Cover with boiling water and bring to a boil for 2 minutes. Pack hot. Cover with boiling liquid, leaving 1-inch headroom. Process 40 minutes at 10 pounds pressure.

PEAS, GREEN OR "ENGLISH"
Pack only in pint jars because they overcook and become mushy if packed in quarts. Shell; sort for size. Cover with boiling water; boil small ones 3 minutes, larger ones 5 minutes. Pack loosely into jars. Cover with boiling cooking liquid to within 1 inch of tops of jars. Process 40 minutes at 10 pounds pressure.

PEAS, BLACKEYE, CROWDER, ETC.
Same as Green Peas, above, but leave 1½-inch headroom.

PEPPERS, GREEN
Wash; remove stems, white cores and seeds. Boil 3 minutes in water. Drain and pack into hot jars. Add 1 tablespoon vinegar or 1½ teaspoons lemon juice. Cover with boiling water, leaving ½-inch headroom. Process 35 minutes at 10 pounds pressure.

PIMIENTOS
Scald in boiling water or roast in a 450° oven until skins can be rubbed off. Remove stem and blossom ends. Pack hot in dry hot half-pint or pint jars. Do not add water. Process 20 minutes at 10 pounds pressure.

POTATOES, WHITE OR IRISH
Wash, pare, and cook in boiling water for 10 minutes. Drain. Pack into hot jars. Add 1 teaspoon salt to each quart. Cover with boiling water, leaving 1-inch headroom. Process 40 minutes at 10 pounds pressure.

PUMPKIN AND WINTER SQUASH
Bake as on 654, or pare and cut into 1-inch cubes. Add enough water to prevent sticking. Cook or steam until tender. Put through food mill or strainer and pack hot into hot jars, leaving 1-inch headroom. Process 80 minutes at 10 pounds pressure.

SQUASH, SUMMER
Wash, but do not pare. Trim ends and cut into small pieces. Steam or boil 3 minutes. Pack loosely into hot jars and cover with boiling water, leaving ½-inch headroom. Process 40 minutes at 10 pounds pressure.

SWEET POTATOES

Wash well and sort for size. Boil or steam slowly about 15 minutes or until skins will slip off easily. Do not pierce with a fork. Skin and cut into pieces. Pack hot. Cover with fresh boiling water or thin or medium syrup, 805, leaving 1-inch headroom. Process 95 minutes at 10 pounds pressure.

TOMATOES

See comments under Tomatoes and Tomato Juice on 808, and Fruit Purées on 806. For Green Tomato Mock Mincemeat, see 844.

PREPARING GAME

The hunter not only must familiarize himself with season, limit and holding laws but must almost of necessity learn how to clean, cut and store his bag, since many states forbid the use of packing plants or butcher shops for this purpose. Quick cooling, scrupulous cleaning and careful preservation greatly enhance that deliciously and legitimately gamy flavor which derives from the fruit, the seeds, the berries or the grasses on which the animal has fed. All too often, gaminess is just the unpleasantly exaggerated result of improper care and manipulation before cooking.

To guard against such diseases as trichinosis, 477, in bear; tularemia, 513, in rabbit; and salmonella, 444, the hunter should wear gloves when handling raw meat. Some of these factors can be counteracted by proper cooking. But whether you go in for little rabbits or big deer, your procedures are basically similar—to bleed, clean, skin, cool, hang or freeze as quickly as possible. It is important, too, to remove the fat of wild animals as soon as possible, as it turns rancid quickly, and to keep any loose hair from the flesh, for the oils in the hair produce off-flavors. Also, in any areas where shot has damaged the flesh, all traces of blood must be removed by scraping or cutting, washing with salted water and drying well. Edible variety meats, 499, should be used at once in camp cooking or should be frozen. For small game like birds, squirrel and rabbit, see 440, 515, and 513. With larger game the logistics of butchering are similar to those for domestic cattle; a careful study of the meat chart on 451 will familiarize you with the bone structure. The ease of further preparation depends somewhat on the skill or luck of your shot.

Immediately after the kill, the animal should be bled. Behead it or cut the jugular vein at the base of the neck, slightly to the left of center. Have a bowl ready underneath to save the blood. You can use it at once or refrigerate it to use later for blood sausage, 497, or as a thickener for gravies, 339. To store see 339.

If the animal is large, place it on a slope with its head at the lowest point. Cut the vein as described above and make sure the blood is flowing freely. Should the animal have been shot in a vital organ, the blood may not be released through the neck but inwardly. It will then be necessary to gut the carcass as quickly and as cleanly as possible to avoid taint from the bullet-ruptured organs. In this case discard the blood. Whatever procedure you use ➤ clean and cool the meat as rapidly as possible.

Leaving the animal with its head lower than the body, you may cut off the feet, pierce the legs and turn it on its back. Tie a rope or wire to each leg and attach them to a shrub or tree nearby, so that when you split the breast bone and cut all the way down the center the animal will be steadied. You may prefer to brace the animal by putting rocks or logs on either side of it.

A good way to start the center cut is to slit the skin for about 3 or 4 inches at the breast bone. Insert your free hand and press the inner organs down out of the way as you continue to cut, now turning the blade of the knife upward so as not to pierce the intestines.

Continue to press downward with your free hand as you go, and cut almost to the end of the gut cavity where the meat of the hindquarters begins. When this long slit is made, roll the skin back about 3 or 4 inches on either side of the cut, keeping the loose hairs away from the flesh. At this point the innards and intestines will be protruding. But before trying to remove them, hold the hind legs apart and continue a skin-deep cut down the center all the way to the anus. If you are working on a buck, cut off the genitals. Then make a very deep cut through the skin all around the anus. Next prepare to remove the lower alimentary canal. This long tract continues from the mouth to the anus. It is more easily taken out if the animal is lying on its side with its legs downhill. Start at the base of the gut cavity near the hindquarters and pull out enough of the intestines to make room for your hand. These are attached only randomly by not very strong tissue. Find and take hold of the large intestine as near as possible to the already loosened anus and pull the tract into and out through the gut cavity past the incision you have made in the abdomen. Care must be taken during this process not to rupture the thin-walled urine sac. Locate this by tracing the tube that leads to the outside. Grasp the tube, pinching it together to close off the bladder, and after further freeing the bladder, retain your grasp on the tube as you ease out the bladder carefully. The alimentary tract is still attached at the upper end, but the lower mass lies outside the carcass. The liver can be found at the upper edges of the stomach toward the back near the thin, tough diaphragm membrane. In animals other than deer, which have no gall, be careful in reconnoitering for the liver not to pierce the gallbladder. Now dispose of all the lower alimentary tract by cutting it loose above the stomach at the base of the thin, tough membrane that forms the diaphragm between the lower cavity and the rib cage. Then remove the diaphragm, heart, lungs and upper alimentary canal. Work if possible in such a way that after the removal of the internal organs you will merely have to wipe the cavity with a dry cloth. But where internal bleeding has taken place and fluids from the organs or blood have touched the flesh, or where the flesh has been bullet-pierced, scrape or cut the areas as clean as possible. Do not allow any blood to remain, as it will produce "fishy" flavors. Wipe such areas with salted water. Dry carefully. If the weather is warm, dust the entire cavity with black pepper or powdered charcoal. To shorten the cooling time of large animals, prop the cavity open with sticks. Skin furry animals as quickly as possible. With deer the musk sacs will pull off with the skin. For other game, see individual recipes.

After cleaning, game and poultry should be cooled to below 40°, preferably for a minimum of 24 hours, before canning. Beef is better if allowed to age for a week or 10 days at 34° to 38°. Large game animals are prepared and processed like beef, small game like poultry. ➤ In processing, use enamel or stainless steel cooking ware.

➤ Spices should be used sparingly in this type of preservation, and vegetables omitted altogether. White pepper retains a better flavor than black pepper in meat products. If you like, you may place 1 teaspoon salt in each empty quart container. This amount flavors but does not help to preserve the meat. ➤ Any canned game should be pressure-processed, see below.

MEAT, POULTRY, GAME AND FISH PRESSURE-CANNING

Methods for canning fish are not given in this book because the various recommended processes are controversial. Government bulletins call for long processing and, in addition, before the food is served, for prolonged cooking of home-canned fish and seafood. This causes great loss of flavor and food value. ➤ The freezing of fish is recommended as an alternative for better retention of both qualities, see 827. But the canning of meats, poultry and game in homes can be both a safe and economical procedure and a much more convenient one than the old-fashioned method of preserving by salting and smoking, although again not nearly so satisfactory as freezing, see 826. **The government warns that all home-canned meats should be boiled in an open pan for 20 minutes before tasting or eating.**

For safe serving of home-canned meat products, process all these nonacid foods in a pressure canner. ➤ Make sure that the temperature reaches at least 240° during processing.

It is best to can only fresh, not brined or salted meats. For brined and salted meats, smoking is considered a more satisfactory method than canning. To butcher meat for canning, see Preparing Game, above.

As the packing of cooked meats involves both cooking them first and processing them the same length of time as for Raw Packed meats, and since both must be boiled in an open pan for 15 minutes again before use, we prefer the Raw Pack method.

➤ To **Raw Pack** fresh meats and poultry, prepare jars, 802. Cut meat from bone. Use bones and scraps to prepare Stock, 520. For chicken, separate pieces at the joints. Trim fat carefully, as it may cause meat to have a strong flavor as well as ruin the sealing rubber of the jar. If necessary, wipe meat clean with a damp cloth. ➤ Do not soak it. Cut meat against the grain into 1-inch strips or chunks. Pack into the sterile jars. Cover with boiling stock or tomato juice. ➤ Never use a thickened gravy. You may add 1 teaspoon salt to each quart for seasoning. Allow 1-inch headroom. Now exhaust the air from the open filled jars by setting them on a rack in a pan of boiling water. Keep water level 2 inches below jar tops. Put a thermometer in the center of a jar, cover the pan and heat the meat slowly to 170° F. If not using a thermometer, heat slowly for 75 minutes. Remove jars from the pan and wipe off tops and threads of jars before lidding, 805. Process in a pressure canner at 10 pounds pressure 75 minutes for pints and 90 minutes for quarts. To remove jars from canner, seal, test closure and store, see 804–805.

PRECOOKING AND PACKING MEATS AND POULTRY FOR CANNING

Roasts, steaks, meatballs or patties and sausage cakes may be processed and canned. Use beef, veal, lamb, mutton, pork, chevon, 471, or venison. To bake, preheat oven to 350°. Cut the meat into pieces about 1 pound each. Remove bones, gristle, and all surface fat. Place in uncovered pans in the oven. Roast until the red or pink color of the meat has almost disappeared at the center, about 20 to 40 minutes. Cut the meat into pieces small enough to fit the jars. Pack closely while still hot into hot, sterile jars, at least 2 pieces to a pint jar. Skim fat from drippings. Add enough boiling water or broth to the drippings to cover the meat, leaving 1-inch headroom. Remove air bubbles, see above. Wipe jar rim carefully to remove any fat. Adjust the lids and pressure-process at 10 pounds pressure, pints 75 minutes, quarts 90 minutes.

To stew, cut meat into uniform pieces about 1 pound each, drop into boiling water and simmer 12 to 20 minutes or until the raw color has disappeared at center. Liver should be simmered about 5 minutes, tongue about 45 minutes, or until skin can be removed. Cut meat into smaller serving pieces. Remove fat and gristle, then salt, pack closely in hot jars and cover with the boiling broth. ➤ To remove air bubbles, see above. Wipe jar rim carefully.

Frying is the least desirable method of precooking. It makes the surface of the meat hard and dry and often gives an undesirable flavor to the finished product.

➤ Meat that is not covered with liquid will discolor and lose some flavor in storage. Depending on the shape of the pieces, 1 to 1½ pounds of meat will fill a pint jar and still remain submerged. ➤ Pint jars are preferable to larger containers, as the heat penetrates more readily to the center of the container. Process pints 75 minutes, quarts 90 minutes at 10 pounds pressure.

To precook chicken, simmer meaty pieces in a broth until medium done. Cover with boiling broth, leaving 1-inch headroom. With bone, process pints 65 minutes, quarts 75 minutes at 10 pounds pressure. Without bone, process 75 and 90 minutes. Gizzards and hearts should be canned together, but separate from the meat, in boiling chicken broth. Process pints 75 minutes at 10 pounds pressure.

★ MINCEMEAT

This is enough filling for about 20 pies. Some of our fans make this recipe for Christmas gifts. It is best if prepared at least 2 weeks before using. Prepare:

9 quarts sliced, peeled apples

Combine with:

4 lb. chopped lean beef or chopped ox heart
2 lb. chopped beef suet
3 lb. sugar
2 quarts cider
4 lb. seeded raisins
3 lb. currants
1½ lb. chopped candied citron
½ lb. dried, chopped, candied orange peel
½ lb. dried, chopped, candied lemon peel
Juice and rind of 1 lemon
1 tablespoon each cinnamon, mace, cloves
1 teaspoon each salt and pepper
2 whole nutmegs, grated
1 gallon sour cherries with juice
2 lb. broken nut meats
(1 teaspoon powdered coriander seed)

Simmer these ingredients about 2 hours. Use an asbestos pad to avoid scorching the mincemeat. Stir frequently. Ladle into hot jars, allowing ½-inch headroom. Process 20 minutes at 10 pounds pressure. If using a boiling-water bath, process 90 minutes. Before serving, season with:

Brandy

SAUSAGE MAKING

There are three major types of sausage: fresh, or "country"; cooked, lightly cured; and partially dried or dry sausage, all described more fully on 496. The preparation for all three types requires using the freshest of meat or game combinations and preferably hard back fat. Best flavor results from the use of a special mechanism whose blades cut and chop rather than grind and crush, as a typical home meat grinder does. Such a machine, seen on 798, is available at butchers' supply houses; and here, too, the blades may be resharpened. This is the place, also, to get special hand stuffers and various sausage casings. For home use, ➤ we do not recommend impervious plastic casings which may allow the development of anerobic organisms, such as those causing botulism. ➤ To avoid trichinosis when making sausage, see 497.

The long natural casings made from the intestines of sheep, hogs and cattle are preferred because they are edible; and more important, because they shrink during smoking so as to adhere to the meat as it dehydrates. These natural casings come dry-salted or brined, if from sheep and hogs; brined only if from beef. ➤ They should be kept refrigerated or frozen until ready to use. Brined casings, however, will not freeze tight because of the strength of the solution. Dry-salted casings should be washed before use; brined casings need not be. All natural casings must be handled with skill and care during the stuffing procedure. While they are available in 1- to 4-inch diameters, we recommend them especially for link sausages.

Sewn casings of unbleached muslin, while not edible, are practical for home preparation of large sausages. These tubular casings, rounded at one end, open at the other, may be stitched together on a sewing machine. For a 2-inch-diameter sausage, tear to size 8-inch strips of unbleached muslin. This width allows for ½-inch seams. Cut the muslin in 9- to 18-inch lengths, depending on the size of your smoker. Cloth casings should be used only after soaking in water and wringing out excess moisture. They usually turn a tawny brown when the sausages have been sufficiently cold-smoked.

➤ Throughout the grinding and mixing process, sausage ingredients should be kept chilled. See the chapter heading on 798, which illustrates the ingredients held over ice. Successful filling depends on the consistency of the sausage mix. If it seems dry, work a little wine or water into the seasoned chopped meat. The trick in stuffing is to keep air from being trapped in the casings, for decay is apt to develop in air pockets. On the other hand, in forcing air out, continuous gentle manipulation is necessary to avoid too great tension in the casings and kinking as the casings fill. Tie off the plumply filled casings in links with string as you fill enough casing for each link, and make the final tie so tight that some of the meat is forced out of the end. Cut this last tie with enough extra cord to make a loop for hanging the sausage during smoking. All these precautions apply to muslin-enclosed sausage, although for larger single units the mix may be somewhat drier.

After stuffing, sausages should hang in a 35° temperature about two days. If using a refrigerator for storage, S-shaped hooks from the shelf grids make a handy means of suspension. If the sausage is to be smoked, allow 12 to 15 hours of cool smoking, 814. During this time it will lose a very appreciable amount of weight. Before eating sausages after smoking, hang them at a 35° temperature at least two weeks to mature. Sausages so prepared may then be kept for many months in a cool, dry, dark place. If a casing mold develops, wipe it off with a vinegar-dampened cloth and discard the casing before serving the sausage.

DRY OR SUMMER SAUSAGE

A great favorite in hot climates. It is called summer sausage even though it is made in winter, because it holds over through the next spring and summer.

Cut into 2-inch cubes:

6 lb. lean beef
2 lb. lean pork

Soak the meat in a 10% brine, 569, in a glass, enamel or stone crock. Weight the meat with a plate held in place with a clean brick or stone, 802, making sure the meat is continually covered with brine. Keep at 35°, stirring every two or three days. Remove the meat after 8 to 12 days; rinse briefly in cold water, and dry; then store refrigerated at 35° on a stainless mesh rack. After four hours or more, when the meat is well dried and chilled, cut it into pieces that will fit your grinder, 812. Add to it:

2 lb. hard back fat

Season with:

3 tablespoons salt
½ teaspoon each cloves, ginger, nutmeg and coriander
2 teaspoons white pepper
2 cups red wine or water

To stuff, hang, smoke and mature, see Sausage Making, above.

DRY-CURING MEAT, GAME AND FOWL

There are two chief ways to salt these meats at home: brining, see Corned Beef, opposite, and dry-curing. When meat is soaked in brines, or, in the more modern technique, unfortunately not practical for home processing, when brine is forced through the arterial system under pressure, temperatures must be very carefully controlled.

Dry-cured meats are more tolerant of fluctuating temperatures under processing than those treated with brine. Ideally, the curing and storing of meats should take place in a 36° to 40° temperature. Even considering the somewhat inconveniently higher temperatures in which most of us are obliged to work, we recommend dry-curing as safer than brining in home-processing. ➤ The three recipes below call for saltpeter, a substance currently questioned by the USDA, but in use to prevent botulism until an effective substitute is available.

➤ To dry-cure, allow the meat to cool as naturally and rapidly as possible after butchering. Spread the pieces out on racks, never allowing them to overlap. Sprinkle them at once ➤ very lightly with salt. Do not blanket them at this time with the salt, as this would retard cooling. When cool, rub them repeatedly with the following salt mixture, being sure to coat the entire surface well in the process. Put the meat into a sterilized crock, being careful not to disturb the salt coating. Cover with a loose-fitting lid or cheesecloth. Six to eight days later resalt the heavier cuts with more of the curing mixture. Allow for every 10 pounds of meat a mixture of:

1 cup salt
¼ cup sugar
2 teaspoons saltpeter, see comment opposite

with:

(2 bay leaves)
(2 coriander seeds)
(3 cloves)
(6 peppercorns)

which you have crushed in a mortar.

To secure effective salt-penetration, cure the salted meat three days for each pound of meat in the piece. Boned hams and other meat and small pieces will of course cure more rapidly. If the temperature should go below 36° at any time, be sure to add an equal length of time to the curing period, as salt-penetration is slowed to a standstill in freezing temperatures. Leave the meat in the curing container even after all surface salt is absorbed. You may turn the meat occasionally and make a second salt application.

When the prescribed time is up, the meat may be left in the dry salt until used, or it may be scrubbed well and hung in a cool ventilated place to dry out before storing or smoking, 814. Hams should be hung at least 25 days before smoking. Smoking gives that wonderful "country" taste to dry-cured and brined foods. If not to be smoked, wrap each piece of meat individually, first in muslin, then in layers of heavy paper. Hang in a dark, cool, well-ventilated room. When properly cured, hams are at their best after a year. But bacon and shoulder meat should be used before hanging that long.

CORNED BEEF

This salted beef actually has nothing to do with corn but got its name in Anglo-Saxon times when a granular salt the size of a kernel of wheat—"corn," of course, to a Briton—was used to process it. To corn, combine:

4 quarts hot water
2 cups coarse salt
¼ cup sugar
2 tablespoons pickling spice
1½ teaspoons saltpeter or sodium nitrate, see comment opposite

When cool, pour over:

A 5-lb. piece of beef: brisket or tongue

which has been placed in a deep enameled pot or stoneware jar. Add:

3 cloves garlic

Weight meat to keep it submerged, and cover pot.

Cure in refrigerator 3 weeks, turning meat every 5 days.

➤ To cook corned beef, see 466. If it is to be stored, wash in lukewarm water, dry thoroughly, then wrap in layers of heavy paper and hang in a cool, dry place.

SALT OR PICKLED PORK

➤ Please read about Pickling Equipment, 841. Known as **white bacon** in some parts of the country, salt pork may be sliced and used as bacon, but it is more often used for seasoning vegetables or for larding roasts.

Cut into pieces 6 inches square:

Fat back or other thin pieces of fat pork

Rub each square well all over with:

Pickling Salt, 569

Pack the salted pork tightly in a clean crock and let stand 12 hours. For each 25 pounds of meat, mix and cool the following brine:

2½ lb. salt
½ oz. saltpeter, see comment 813
4 quarts boiling water

Pour the ➤ cooled brine over the meat to cover. Store the pork ➤ weighted and covered at 35° to 38° until ready to use. Keep refrigerated and use within 3 weeks.

JERKY

Use jerky when backpacking or for high-protein snacking. This chewy well-flavored item is a great extravagance, for you will end up by weight with only one-third the amount of meat you started with. Slice lean meat on the bias 6 inches long, 3 inches wide and ⅛ to ¼ inch thick. This makes drying faster, and the end product is easier to chew or reconstitute in stews. Cut away pieces of fat and any muscle membrane left on the meat. Salt and pepper lightly, or marinate the strips, 528, then hang them from the bars of an oven rack in a 175° oven or on "warm." It is advisable to place aluminum foil on the bottom of the oven to catch any juices. But if the meat is of good quality, there should be none unless marinated. Leave the oven door ajar to allow moisture to escape and to ensure the best drying process. The jerky should be ready in 4 to 5 hours, depending on the thickness and leanness of the meat and the humidity of the environment. Make sure that the jerky is ➤ very dry—not more than 2% moisture—or bacteria will grow. It should be slightly flexible, bending before it breaks. Let cool, place in a lidded dry container and store in a cool area.

ABOUT PREPARING ROE FOR CAVIAR

Remove from very fresh fish as soon as possible:

Roe

Tear the egg masses into small-sized pieces. Work them through a ¼-inch or finer screen to free the eggs from the membrane. Place them for 15 to 20 minutes in a cold-water brine made of:

1⅛ cups Pickling Salt, 569
to every quart of cold water

If you use a salinometer, the reading should be 28.3. There should be twice as much brine as roe in volume. Remove from liquid and drain thoroughly by allowing to drip through a strainer for about 1 hour. Keep refrigerated during this operation. Place in an airtight nonmetal container and store at 34° for 1 to 2 months. Remove, drain and repack, storing at 0° Fahrenheit in the freezer until ready to use.

PRESERVED EGGS

Preserve eggs at home only if you have no alternative. The commonest method is immersion in waterglass or sodium silicate. If possible, use nonfertile eggs that are at least 12 hours old. Do not pack too many layers on top of each other, as the weight might crack those below. Eggs so kept are not good for boiling, as the shells become too fragile—nor do the whites beat well for meringues, or soufflés or for baking cakes dependent on egg alone as a riser.

To preserve 10 dozen eggs, pour 9 quarts of boiling water into a 5-gallon sterile crock. Add 1 quart waterglass, stir thoroughly and add the eggs. The waterglass should cover the eggs 2 inches above the top egg. Cover crock and store in a cool place no longer than 6 months.

SMOKING FOOD

Hot-smoking completely cooks food. **Cold-smoking** preserves the food, often for a considerable time. Both methods add flavor. Cold-smoking is fundamentally a drying process during which brined foods, 569, such as meat, game, fish and fowl are smoked for as short a period as 24 hours or as long as 3 weeks. Length of smoking time depends on the size of the food unit being processed and the steadiness of the temperature. Cold-smoking should never exceed 80° to 85°. If the heat climbs as high as 90°, the fats begin to liquefy and spoilage results. To prepare cured meat, 813, for any smoking process, dry it out first under refrigeration and wipe the surface dry. Hams should be hung to dry out at least 25 days before smoking. Individual taste determines whether to smoke longer than about 72 hours for a ham, 60 hours for a pork shoulder and about 45 hours for a thinner piece of meat like bacon. Food has been sufficiently smoked if it has lost at least one-fourth of its weight during the process. Another test—for unboned meat: a stiff slender wire inserted along the bone to the center of the cut smells sweet when withdrawn.

Hot-smoking is more like a flavorful cooking of brined foods, never producing enough drying to ensure safe keeping qualities. It may last from a very short period to an exposure of 4 to 5 hours, depending again on the size of the unit processed and how steadily the temperature has been maintained. Generally speaking, hot-smoking involves shorter and weaker brining, with temperatures ranging from 250° to 300°.

In another method of hot-smoking, perfected by the Chinese, foods, usually marinated, are cooked in almost sealed smoke pots. A simplified western adaptation is, first, to line a large iron pot generously with foil and sprinkle on it a mixture of brown sugar and condiments. Marinated food is then placed on a rack above the sugar, and the foil closed with a tight seam around the entire contents of the pot—sugar, rack, food and all. After a single tiny hole has been pricked in the top of the foil with a thin skewer, the pot is heated 5 to 7 minutes. As the sugar and spices char, the smoke flavors the food. After smoking, the food is eaten at once. This is the best policy, in fact, with food hot-smoked by any procedure. If not immediately served, the food should be refrigerated without delay. Hot-smoked food—but not that produced by our western version of the Chinese technique—may be kept refrigerated about three weeks. ➤ Freezing is never recommended for any smoked foods.

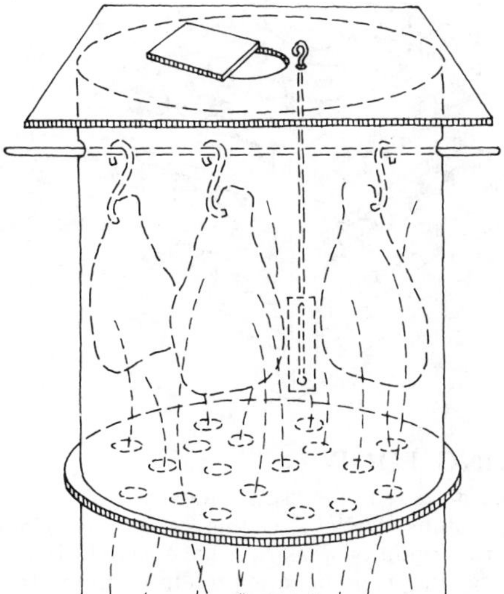

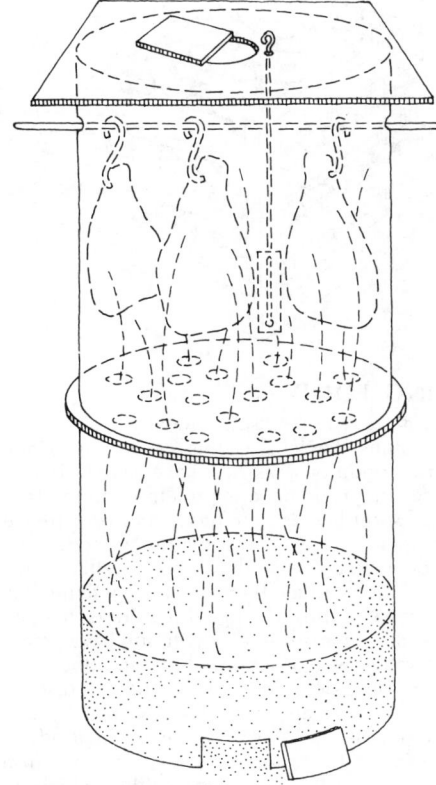

The above equipment may be used for both cold- and hot-smoking. Some cold-smoking enthusiasts build a separate fire pit joined to the smoke chamber by an inclined buried 12-foot length of stove pipe that elbows up into the smoking cavity. This pit is fired with fruitwood, oak, hickory or any other hardwoods or hardwood chips. ➤ Never use a green or a resinous wood. We do not recommend electrical smokers which depend on smoking chemicals and liquids but suggest below a simple device that involves 2 metal drums placed one on top of the other and shown as though the drums were transparent. Remove the bottom of the lower drum and cut a small vent at the base of the side where the fire can be ignited. The strength of the draft can subsequently be controlled by partially closing off the vent with the piece of metal you have removed. The lid of the lower drum is perforated with about fifteen or more 1-inch holes, allowing the smoke to flow up from the lower drum, while it forms a baffle against direct heat. The lower drum itself is kept filled about one-fourth with hardwood sawdust. To replenish sawdust during the smoking period the upper drum and the perforated lid are lifted off. Prepare the second drum by cutting out the bottom and punching holes opposite each other in the sides near the top, to support staggered rods as shown. From these rods the foods to be smoked are suspended on S-shaped hooks so as to keep the food well spaced.

Preheat the lower drum to 85°. Place the upper drum over the baffle and clap a piece of sheet iron over the top of the second drum. This should have a small aperture toward the top center, and smoke emission can be controlled as needed by partial coverage with a small piece of movable metal. In the upper drum on a line with the lowest piece of meat, hang a thermometer near the vent so you can retract it for continual reading. It is also wise during smoking to shift the various meats to give them all fairly uniform smoke exposure.

After smoking, then hanging until cool in temperatures not exceeding 60°—which for large pieces sometimes takes a week or longer, depending on the weather—the food is ready for storing. Should any salt crystals have accumulated on the surface, wipe them off, as this crystallization will reattract moisture. The food should then be wrapped first in parchment and then in muslin and stored in a dark north-facing ventilated area where the temperatures stay between 35° and 60°. Or for more even temperature control, wipe off any crystallization and store the smoked unwrapped food in a wooden box raised off the floor, using cooled wood ashes as the packing medium. To cook smoked meats and other smoked foods, see Index.

PASTRAMI

To convert basic Corned Beef, 813, to pastrami, the meat must be smoked. You may also wish to experiment with a more elaborate marinade, substituting for half the water ingredient a red wine vinegar and adding one or more of the following:

(2 tablespoons ginger)
(1 tablespoon coriander)
(1 tablespoon paprika)
(1 teaspoon pepper)

After marination, commercial pastrami is cooked entirely by **Hot-Smoking,** 814, at 320° for 6 or 7 hours. Because the relatively high heat required is hard to maintain in domestic appliances, one of our correspondents produces pastrami by attaching the marinated meat to a continuously revolving rotisserie and smoking it outdoors over his "char-broil" barbecue grill, using plenty of charcoal and oak and hickory chips. This procedure takes about 10 hours and may or may not meet with complete neighborhood approval.

SMOKING FOWL AND COOKING SMOKED FOWL

To prepare birds for smoking, bleed, 435, cool rapidly and pluck, 435, clean, 436, and wash quickly but thoroughly in running cold water. Dry-cure, 813, or prepare a brine, 569. Chicken and game birds are steeped in the brine 24 to 48 hours, depending on size; ducks and geese for about 3 days, and a 12- to 20-pound turkey for 5 days. Cover the brining birds with a plate weighted with a stone, and check during the brining process to make sure they are brine-covered at all times.

On removal wash quickly in running cold water, wipe well, and further dry by hanging for at least 3 hours in a 38° temperature. If not refrigerated protect from insects. If you wish to serve the meat or fowl at once, roast in a preheated 350° oven about three-fourths the usual roasting time. Remove to a smoke oven and flavor by hot-smoking at 200° to 225° until the skin takes on a pleasing rich color. Although the meat will retain a certain redness, it is done when with gentle twisting you can turn the leg of the fowl in the socket. Before cold-smoking birds which are smoked as for meats, 814, they must be brined, see above. After smoking and before the final cooking, they should be steamed for about 10 minutes to remove excess salt.

SMOKING FISH

Use fat fresh fish, 394, for smoking. Under 3 pounds they may be left whole after cleaning, 395. If you cut the heads off, do so just above the bony collar. It is best to split small fish down the belly side and, before hanging them in the smoker, insert small pointed wooden wedges into the chest cavity to hold it and the split edges below from touching and closing off circulation as the fish smoke. Fish over 3 pounds are best filleted, 396, with the skin left on. Place the fillets ➤ on oiled racks, skin side down, during the entire smoking period.

Whether hot- or cold-smoked, 814, fish must first be brined as for fowl above. Fish under one-fourth pound need 30 minutes, from one to two pounds 2 hours, and four to five pounds 5 hours. Immediately after brining, rinse the fish quickly in cold water. Dry them off carefully and then dry them further, either hung or racked, in a minimum temperature of 38° and, in any case, protected from insects. During this second drying of about 3 hours a shiny hard glaze should form over the entire surface of the fish. Since the flesh of fish is so fragile, we recommend hot-smoking only when the fish is to be eaten at once. The fish is safe to eat when the flesh flakes when pierced with a fork.

Cold-smoking where the temperature must not go over 80° uses the same equipment and fuel described on 814. Smoking time depends on the storage period desired. For 2-week storage, smoke steadily for 24 hours; for 1-year storage, smoke steadily for a week. Cold-smoked fish can be eaten without further cooking. Store at about 35° in nonairtight, nonplastic packaging.

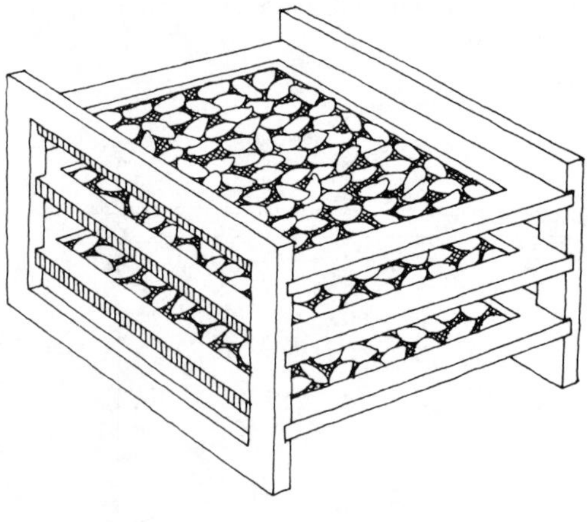

DRYING FOOD

Few climates lend themselves ideally to sun-drying of foodstuffs, ancient as this custom is. Under modern conditions, as we have stated before, freezing and canning are preferred methods of storage. But if harvests are heavy and your freezer and storage space is already preempted, dried foods demand only one-third to one-sixth as much storage space. Albeit there is some vitamin loss due to heat during drying, dried fruits that are eaten without moisture reconstitution have greater caloric value, weight for weight, than either fresh or otherwise processed fruits. In order to discourage spoilage organisms, enzymes, molds, bacteria and yeasts that are present in all foods, at least 80% of the water must be removed from fruit and about 90% from vegetables, which are apt to be less acid. To dry herbs, see 579. Meats and fish which require even greater moisture loss are discussed later. This loss is achieved often by a combination of processes, such as recommended prior steam-blanching, described later; sulfuring, a moot process; and salting, most often in the case of meats and fish, before final drying both in the sun and by other heat means. But home methods never achieve the degree of dryness produced by commercial methods, in which moisture content must measure between 2.5% and 6% in order to qualify for sale as dehydrated.

Steam-blanching, 803, which stops enzymatic action, discourages oxidation, and produces some moisture loss, is ➤ necessary for vegetables but, though recommended, is optional for fruits. Whether or not you steam-blanch fruits, wash them first in cold water. Furthermore, to remove the waxy coatings on fruits like apricots, nectarines, plums and blueberries and to avoid cracking of the skins on berries, cherries, figs and grapes, you may place the fruit in a colander and dip it into rapidly boiling water for about 35 seconds. To test for length of steam-blanching, take a sample from the center of the food. It should be wilted and heated through. Remove the food and let it dry on and covered with paper toweling. It is then ready to be spread on the drying trays.

Whether sun- or heat-drying foods, every effort must be made to hasten matters sufficiently to outrun decomposition, so if your sun source is not steady it must be supplemented by oven or other heat at temperatures below actual cooking or scorching. The heat should never go over 140°. It should be maintained for at least two-thirds of the drying time. The heat buildup should begin slowly from not more than 120° so the outside of the food is not hardened, inhibiting the release of moisture from the center. So for best

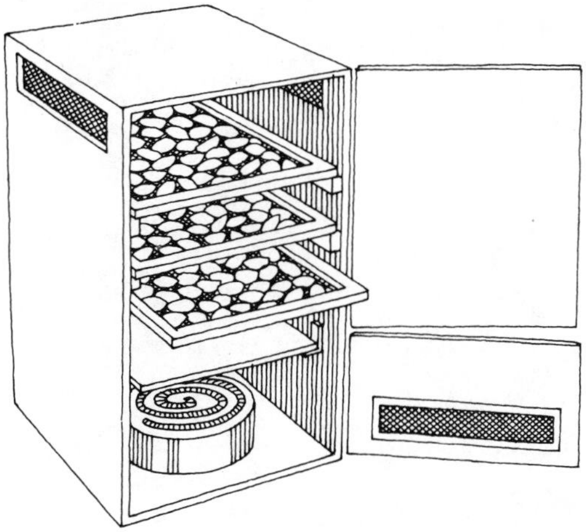

results make your drying racks of such size that they can be moved from sun heat to oven heat as shown above, or, if you are impatient by the limiting size of your oven, make the larger specially constructed drying cabinet described later. To allow for air circulation in the oven, the overall dimension of the trays should be 3 to 4 inches less than the interior of the oven. To dry in larger quantities, build a cabinet such as shown opposite, which can be geared to a hot plate, a cooking gas or electric ring or a small chunk-burning stove. Avoid coal- or oil-burning units because their fumes affect flavor. Venting in the drying cabinet is provided by a 2-inch-wide, 12-inch-long screened slot near the top at the sides of the cabinet. In order to allow air intake at the base, the hinged door has a long 2-inch-high slot at the base. Line the cabinet wall and door to the height of the door with aluminum building paper. Diffused heat is achieved by suspending a metal sheet free from the walls on brackets over the heating element as shown. In both oven and cabinet drying, keep the bottom tray 6 to 8 inches from the heat source.

As in all food-processing, drying demands the utmost cleanliness and selectivity so that no imperfect produce introduces spoilage elements. All food should be cut or sliced as evenly and thinly as practical to hasten drying and should be loosely placed on the drying trays in single layers. These trays should have cloth bottoms of mosquito netting, nylon mesh, or even bed sheeting in preference to any metal except stainless steel screening. Other metals may produce off-flavors. If used out of doors, the sides of the trays should be at least 2 inches high so that the covering protecting the food from insects and airborne detritus can be made taut and will not rest on the food. ➤ Any single trays should be elevated on bricks or boards to allow circulation from underneath. If the trays are tiered, they should be shifted periodically so that heat is equalized. In the oven or in a drying cabinet this should occur about every half hour, and the food should also be turned at those intervals.

For sun-drying, special equipment is shown on 818, covered with a glass cold frame which intensifies the heat. Be sure to provide screening strips top and bottom for ventilation. The equipment itself should be light enough to be shifted during the day to catch the most sun, and the food on the trays should be turned about every hour. With full sun most foods should dry by this method in about 2 days if the humidity is low. With any of these units it is wise to place a candy or dairy thermometer on the lowest rack to make sure the temperature does not exceed 140°. If new loads of food are put in, it is also wise to place them on the top rack where the heat is apt to be less intense. ➤ Any food dried out of doors must be brought indoors at sundown to protect it from night dews. ➤ No food should be dried out of doors in air-polluted areas.

➤ Testing for dryness is a multistaged affair. Fruits are considered dried when they produce no moisture when cut and squeezed and are leathery or resilient in texture. If you wonder how the moist dried fruits you buy are prepared, they contain additives and perhaps sulfur dioxide to protect them from spoilage.

Vegetables are ready when they are brittle and tough and rattle when stirred on the trays. While

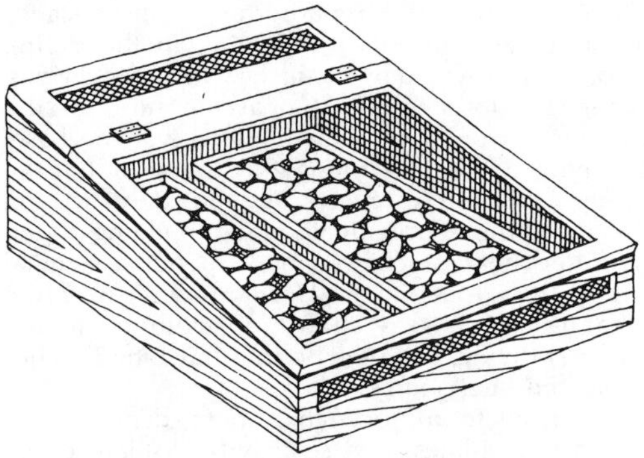

they are still hot the extent of dryness is hard to judge, as the vegetables will seem moister than they really are. So in testing remove a few pieces and allow them to cool before making a final judgment. Once the produce has been sun- or heat-dried sufficiently, it must be conditioned. Cool the food on the trays. Have ready enamel or granite ware or a large crock, but ➤ not an aluminum or galvanized metal container. Pour in the contents of the trays. Keep the container covered with a cloth in a warm, dry, airy room. Stir the food once or twice a day for 10 days to 2 weeks. Remove any pieces that seem limp or moist.

At this point oven pasteurization is recommended for all dried fruits and for finely cut, heat-dried, brittle vegetables that may have dried too fast to kill all spoilage elements. Preheat oven to 175°. Put the food on trays, not more than two at a time, loaded not more than 1 inch deep and loosely arranged. Heat in the oven, allowing for the small vegetables about 10 minutes; for fruits, especially oven-dried, about 15 minutes. Cool the pasteurized produce on paper toweling. Place in small labeled and dated paper or plastic bags and then in airtight containers with insect- or rodent-proof lids. Dried fruits keep well about one year, dried vegetables about four months.

To reconstitute dried fruits, see 125. To reconstitute most dried vegetables, cover with cold water until almost restored to their original texture. Use the soaking water to cook the vegetables. ➤ Never soak greens, but cover with boiling water and simmer until tender.

ABOUT DRYING MUSHROOMS

Steam-blanch, 803, mushrooms 3 to 5 minutes to destroy insects or larvae that might damage them during storage. Dry thoroughly on paper towels. Place them on racks, 816, in a densely shady, dry, airy place. If dried out of doors be sure to bring them in at night. When the mushrooms are thoroughly dry, pack in tightly lidded sterile glass jars and store in a cool dark place. To reconstitute, see 573. To use for seasoning, grind dried mushrooms in a nut grinder, 562, or ⅄ blender and store as above.

FREEZING

We are indebted to an Arctic explorer for the following Eskimo recipe for a frozen dinner: "Kill and gut a medium-sized walrus. Net several flocks of small migrating birds and remove one specific small feather from each wing. Store birds whole in interior of walrus. Sew up walrus and freeze. Two years or so later, find the cache—if you can—notify clan of a feast, partially thaw walrus. Slice and serve." Simplicity itself.

Simple, too, are the mechanics of home freezing, a comparatively easy method of food preservation which has been advertised as all things to all cooks. The result is that some frozen-food enthusiasts toss any type of food into the poor freezer and expect fabulous results. Yes, some foods ➤ but not all foods can be preserved by freezing more successfully than in any other way, but ➤ quality produce comes out only if quality produce goes in. There are other important factors, too. Foods chosen must be given ➤ quick and careful preparation. They must be sealed ➤ in moisture- and vapor-proof wrappings and kept at ➤ constant zero or lower temperatures during storage. Temperatures that fluctuate above and below zero will draw moisture from the food, resulting in loss of quality and nutritive value. Then, of course, the food must be properly thawed and cooked.

Meats, fish, poultry, fruits and precooked foods readily freeze. Vegetables, because of the necessity of blanching, require both more time and more care. But even so, freezing takes a third to half the amount of time and labor involved in canning. And the yields per bushel of produce are about the same, see 805 and 808.

THE FREEZER AND ITS CONTENTS

The economics of keeping a well-stocked freezer presents what we have heard called a "mooty" point. Unless you are a strong-willed planner and dispenser, it may lead to extravagance. When faced with a purely domestic crisis, it is a great temptation to use that choice cut of meat reserved for company, and children love to draw on the seemingly unlimited freezer resources of ice cream and desserts. ➤ It is often only by sharp-eyed scheduling and husbanding of supplies and by raising your own meat and vegetables that you fully realize a freezer's potential for peace of mind and cash savings. ➤ You may also profit, as a quick-witted trader, when markets are glutted with fresh vegetables and fruits or meat and poultry specials. But ➤ avoid bargain frozen foods that have been stored a long time—for they will not have a full complement of vitamins and flavor.

In any case, the freezer is not meant for miserly hoarding. ➤ It should be managed on an overall, continuously shifting plan—a seasonal plan—geared to your family's food needs and preferences. But keep it stocked with favorites, so the family will continue to ask: "What's thawing?"

FILLING THE FREEZER

Space estimates differ, depending on family appetites, but a minimum allowance of 3 cubic feet per person is average if you schedule a turnover every six months.

➤ Neither overload your freezer ➤ nor add, at one time, more than 3 pounds for each cubic foot of freezer space during any 24-hour period. Either procedure will cause the temperature to rise and thus damage the food you are storing. ➤ Until the new packages are frozen, unless the manufacturer directs otherwise, keep them against the freezer plates or the walls of the freezer. ➤ Exceptions are sandwiches and baked items, which, if placed there, attract moisture to themselves. These should be placed on other frozen packages away from the walls.

DEFROSTING THE FREEZER

Your freezer operates most economically if it is located in an area where the temperature is between 50° to 70°. It is hard to specify just how often a manually controlled freezer will need defrosting. The number of times it is opened, how densely it is packed, and how carefully food is wrapped all affect the buildup of condensation. ➤ Defrost whenever there is ½ inch of rime on the plates or sides. If frost has not solidified into ice, scraping with a plastic tool is a good method. ➤ Turn off the current first, though. Remove all food from the freezer and refrigerate it immediately or wrap it with layers of newspaper or blankets for insulation. Pans of hot water are sometimes used to hasten defrosting.

No matter how often you have to defrost ➤ be sure to clean up any spillage when it occurs and ➤ to wipe out your freezer at least once a year with a cloth that has been dipped in a solution of 1 tablespoon baking soda to 1 quart of lukewarm water. ➤ Dry the freezer well with either a cloth or a hair dryer. ➤ Be sure the lining is thoroughly dry before you turn the current on again. It is wise to let the freezer run closed for half an hour before returning food to it.

POWER BREAKS

The seriousness of a power break should not be underestimated, because a 25° rise in temperature over a 24-hour period is ruinous to nutritive values. So, if a prolonged break is indicated, call your local dealer or ice cream company for a source of dry ice. This ice has a temperature of 110° below zero F. If placed in the freezer soon after the electricity fails, a 50-pound cake will prevent thawing for 2 or 3 days if the door is immediately closed and not reopened until 2 or 3 hours after the current is operating. ➤ Handle dry ice with heavy gloves. Do not attempt to chip or cut it, as a stray chip might cause a freeze-burn. In placing the dry ice be sure ➤ a heavy cardboard lies between it and the food. Cover the freezer box with a heavy blanket and pin it so as to expose the motor vents.

Actual thawing, if the box is full and ➤ the freezer is kept closed, is not likely to occur in even 4- to 6-cubic-foot freezers within the first 15 to 20 hours. After 48 hours, the temperature will just reach 40° to 45°—the normal refrigerator range. Food that still retains ice crystals can be refrozen, but meats, poultry and fish registering more than 50° must be cooked and used at once.

ENSURING QUALITY IN THE FREEZING OF FOOD

➤ Quality cannot be created in the freezing process itself. It is sometimes lost even though well-fed animals, and fruits and vegetables from rich soils are used. For example, the keeping qualities of varieties of the same fruit or vegetable differ. Elberta peaches grown in New York are considered tops for freezing, but Elberta peaches grown in Virginia are often reported poor for that purpose. Because new discoveries are being made constantly, it is wise, if you are barging into freezing in a big way, to ➤ consult your county agricultural agent about the best varieties of fruits and vegetables to grow and to buy from your own neighborhood.

Time and conditions of harvest or slaughter are also factors to reckon with. ➤ Crops are prime when they have sunshine just before maturing. Undue rain before harvest may cause the entire pack to be mediocre. Crops such as ➤ early apples, the first asparagus, etc., keep their flavor best.

➤ The retention of nutritional values and flavors depends on the speed with which food can be processed after harvesting. From then on ➤ it must be kept at such favorable temperatures that microbial and enzymatic activities are held to a minimum. Should they have begun before freezing, the freezing process will not destroy the resultant contamination but only arrest it temporarily. Therefore ➤ you are courting danger to allow perishable frozen foods to thaw for any length of time before cooking. Transfer of frozen food packages from retail store to freezer must be effected with all reasonable speed.

➤ Any frozen foods stored in the ice-cube compartment of the refrigerator should be used within a few days, as the temperature range in this section is between 10° and 25° in most refrigerators, not the required 0° or minus of a freezer. You will find a host of frozen items in the many food shops. Among them are potatoes and other watery foods processed with recently developed machinery that removes harmful excess moisture. But such freeze-dry vacuum-processing is beyond the scope of the home-freezing equipment presently available. So are the freeze-dried foods now popular with backpackers.

Beware of using the freezer for certain foods. ➤ Freezing, for example, will ruin gelatins. ➤ In general, most cooked foods can be frozen, but some do not justify the amount of processing required. Always balance original preparation time against the time it takes to prepare properly for freezing, and omit quick broils, quick-cooking pastas or quick sautés. Freezing techniques, as described later, have settled down into a practice as reliable as canning. But keep in mind that the storage life of frozen food is very decidedly shorter than that for the canned product.

WRAPPING, PACKAGING AND SEALING

Since good results depend so much on the speed with which the fresh foods are prepared and put into the freezer, it is wise to have all filling, wrapping and labeling equipment ready at hand. Use proper funnels for filling cartons, to keep liner edges dry for a perfect seal. Choose only those wrappings that are true freezer-wraps—moistureproof and vaporproof—to protect the food from drying out and to keep odors from penetrating into the freezer and causing off-flavors in other food. Air left in the containers dries out the food during storage, drawing moisture from the food itself to form a frost in the package—a frost made from the juices and seasoned with the flavors of the food itself. Dehydration or freezer burn can also occur on the surface of the food if the wrapping does not adhere closely enough. ➤ So always exclude as much air as possible from the package.

➤ Liquids and solid foods with juice must be stored not only in leakproof containers but with enough space left for the expansion of the liquid during the freezing process. Allow ½ inch in pint and 1 inch in quart cartons. If you use glass, allow 1 inch for a pint and 1½ inches for a quart container with a narrow top opening. If the opening is wide, less headroom is needed. Should you be working with dome lids on glass freezer jars, leave the screw bands on until you are ready to use the food.

We prefer cubical containers, as they conserve a good deal more storage space and stack better than cylindrical ones of the same capacity. Meats and irregularly formed foods are best wrapped in aluminum foil, which should have a weight of .0015 or thicker, needs no sealing, and clings to the contour of the food, helping to exclude air. The pack profits from an overwrap of stockinet, which protects against tearing of the foil. For economy, old nylon stockings may be used in place of stockinet. Since laminated plastics and papers vary in quality and require the use of tapes adjusted to low temperatures or equally careful sealing with a medium-hot pressing iron, it is often difficult to judge their effectiveness.

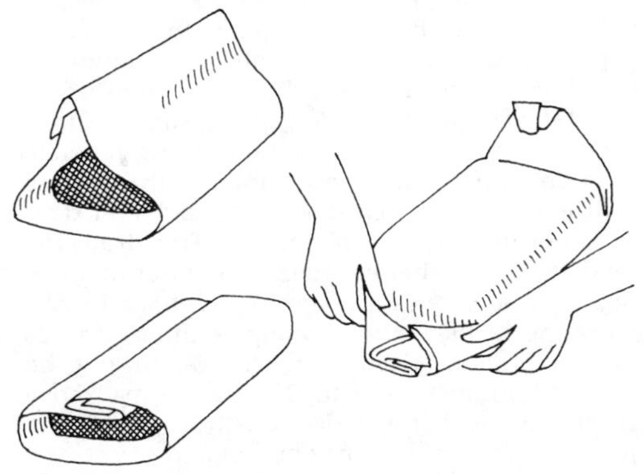

➤ All sheet wrappings should be applied with the lock-seal or drugstore wrap above. To make the drugstore or lock-seal wrap, place the food in the center of a piece of paper large enough so that when the ends are brought together, they can be folded as shown on the left above, and, when brought down taut against the food, make an interlocking seam as shown in the center. Turn over the package, so that the seam lies on the table. Pleat-fold one open end, making an extra fold before pressing the folded end against the package. Spin the package around so that the doubly folded end can be braced against your body, as shown on the right. Now very carefully press any excess air from the package. Then fold the remaining open end. Seal the package with ➤ a tape that is formulated for low temperature.

If the object to be wrapped is bulky, you may have to resort to the less protective butcher wrap which follows.

The food is placed diagonally on a large square of paper. One corner is brought over it generously, as shown on the left at the bottom of the page. The adjoining corners are then folded over, as shown in the center, and the entire package folded over in turn, as shown on the right. Keeping the wrapping taut and flat helps exclude excess air.

Be careful, again, to press out excess air before closing polyethylene bags. Twist the bags tightly into a gooseneck and tie with plastic-covered wires or string. These bags remain pliable even at zero temperature and need no overwrap.

Plastic boxes and heavily waxed cartons are good for liquids, but watch for a tight seal. Both may be used again. Before reusing, wash the wax cartons with a detergent and cold water to keep the wax firm. ➤ Aluminum foil cartons are especially favored. Be extremely careful to seal them tightly. They chill rapidly and can go from freezer to oven without further handling or loss of contents.

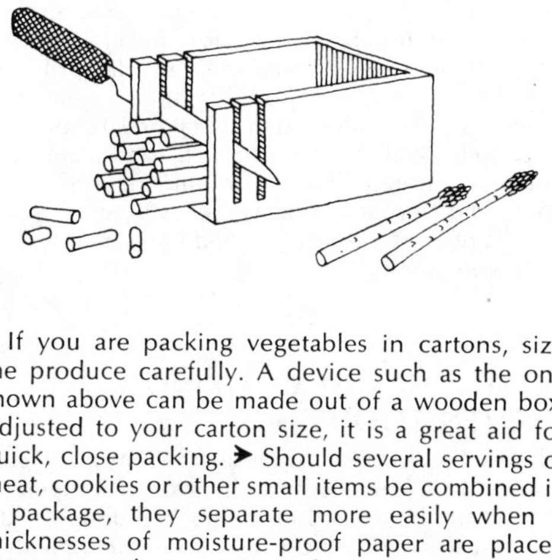

If you are packing vegetables in cartons, size the produce carefully. A device such as the one shown above can be made out of a wooden box. Adjusted to your carton size, it is a great aid for quick, close packing. ➤ Should several servings of meat, cookies or other small items be combined in 1 package, they separate more easily when 2 thicknesses of moisture-proof paper are placed between each 2 units, as shown on the left, or

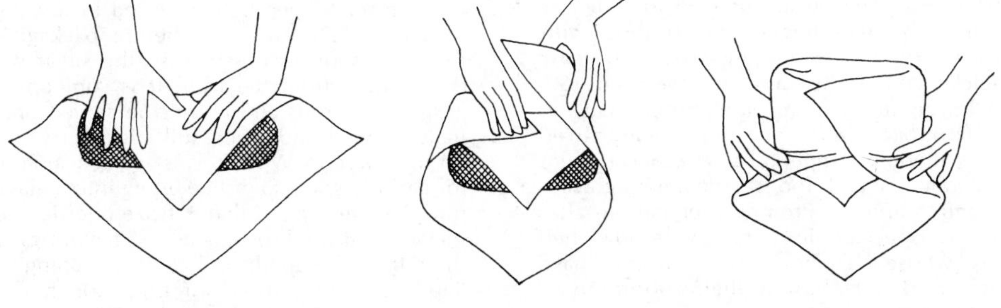

when they are slid into folded foil, as shown on the right below, before the outside wrapping is put on. ➤ Package foods in convenient serving or meal-sized quantities.

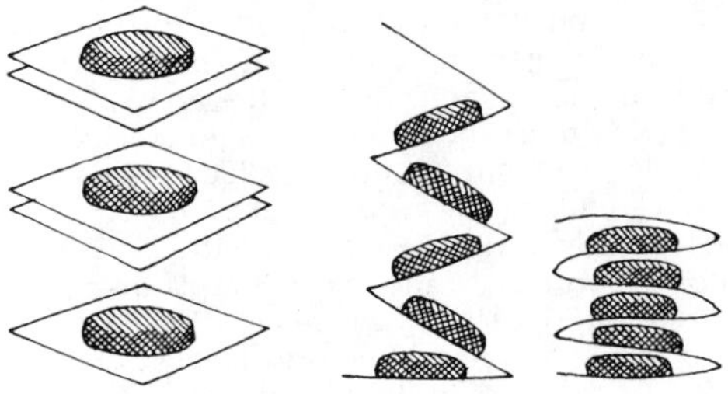

LABELING AND DATING

➤ Keep a master record of dates of freezing, as well as poundage on meats and number of portions of other foods. ➤ Labeling and dating the packages themselves, needless to say, are essential. Soft wax or china marking pencils or marking pens do well for cartons. Different colored labels may be slipped between stockinet and other wrappings or under transparent wrap, for quick identification. While many foods keep satisfactorily for months, there are some exceptions, which are noted in detail later, such as fat meats, poultry, prepared doughs and precooked foods. You may find our storage-limit recommendations short compared to others, but we believe you also prefer optimum standards for food flavor and texture to merely mediocre ones.

THAWING AND COOKING FROZEN FOODS

Always thaw frozen foods in their original containers. It is best to thaw them on a refrigerator shelf, with the exception of unbaked doughs, 829. See Index for thawing instructions for individual foods. For emergencies, if the package is absolutely waterproof, it may be immersed in water that is kept cold. This procedure should be adopted only when you are pressed for time, as the result is poor with fragile foods or those with high water content—like strawberries. To thaw food quickly you may use a microwave oven, 160. Use all frozen items immediately after thawing, for growth of bacteria can occur rapidly in thawed foods left at room temperature, ➤ especially pot pies, TV dinners and foods containing gravies, sauces and stuffings. Prompt preparation after thawing is especially important with blanched products, whose oxygen-resisting enzymes have been destroyed and whose further exposure to air and heat causes rapid adverse changes in quality and nutritional value.

FREEZING FRUITS

Have ready the chilled syrup, 823, and enough ice to wash the fruit in ice-cold water. Choose almost any firm, sound, uniformly sun-ripened fruit. Sort individual pieces carefully and wash well in ice-cold water before removing pits, cores and stems, or paring the fruit if necessary. People who grow their own berries may freeze them successfully without washing—provided they have not been treated with toxic spray. It is safer to wash berries that are not home grown, immersing them briefly but thoroughly in ice-cold water. Drain the fruit well, then spread it out on several thicknesses of paper toweling and cover lightly with additional toweling to absorb as much surface moisture as possible. To avoid crushing or bruising the fruit, use very gentle movements. Large fruits generally pack better if cut into pieces, and less than perfect fruit is best packed crushed or puréed after damaged portions have been removed. Treat fruits that tend to discolor before freezing and during thawing, such as apples, peaches, apricots and pears, with one of the Anti-Browning Solutions on 823, or the solution mixed especially for freezing below. If fruits that tend to discolor are packed in combinations that include citrus fruits, the lemon juice or ascorbic acid may be omitted.

Steam-blanching, 824, is recommended for the following fruits: apple slices and pears, 1½ to 2 minutes; rhubarb, 1 minute; and apricots, ½ minute. ➤ Chill the fruit in ice water before packing.

It is not essential to use sugar in freezing fruit, but it is often preferable, see below. Freshly grated unsweetened coconut may be frozen by adding one part sugar to eight parts coconut. Mix it with its own juice, 566, before freezing. Leftover packaged coconut may also be frozen and used as needed. Mashed bananas for banana bread may be frozen in small containers, and frozen slices of banana make easy additions to cereals and desserts, 132. Unsweetened raspberries, blackberries, etc., may be frozen by the **tray freezing** method, see illustrations on 819. Place them unwrapped, in a single layer, on trays in the freezer until solidly frozen. Then later they can be packaged closely, sealed and stored.

Some fruits keep better packed in dry sugar or in Syrup, 823. Sugar just before packaging and freeze as soon as possible, so the sugar will not draw juices from the fruit. It is sometimes suggested that fruits and berries be served only partially thawed and while still slightly icy, so they do not "weep." While this is a practical approach for garnishes, we so dislike biting into a glassy texture that we suggest that ➤ frozen berries be fully thawed and used for sauces and flavorings, where their taste is superb and their "weeping" not a liability. Thaw fruits on a refrigerator shelf.

ANTI-BROWNING SOLUTION FOR FREEZING

Dissolve ½ to ¾ teaspoon ascorbic acid in a little cold water before adding to 1 quart syrup or 1 quart prepared fruit and use as indicated under packing instructions below. If using lemon juice, which may somewhat alter the flavor of the food, add 1 tablespoon to each quart of syrup.

PACKING FRUITS FOR FREEZING

There are four main ways to freeze and pack fruits. Use the one best suited to your food preferences or dietary needs.

UNSWEETENED DRY PACK

An easy way to freeze the following fruits for pies or jams and preserves, but ➤ not recommended for strawberries. After washing the fruit in ice water where necessary and draining; or peeling, seeding or coring, and conveniently sectioning, place immediately in containers. Shake down to pack closely. Seal and freeze.

*Apples	Elderberries
*Avocados	Loganberries
Blueberries	Melons
Blackberries	Persimmons
Cranberries	Pineapple
Currants	*Plums
*Figs	Prunes
Gooseberries	Raspberries
Grapes	Rhubarb

*Sprinkle the fruit with a solution of dissolved ascorbic acid, see Anti-Browning Solutions, above.

DRY SUGAR PACK

Use this method for quite juicy fruits, washing where necessary, or peeling, coring or seeding, and sectioning. Sprinkle sugar over the fruit on a shallow tray and mix gently until some juice has been drawn out and the sugar is dissolved. Fill containers, shaking to pack closely, and leave ½-inch headroom for pints, ¾-inch for larger containers. Seal and freeze.

For each quart prepared fruit use the amount of sugar indicated

*Apples, ½ cup	Gooseberries, ¾ cup
*Apricots, ½ cup	Loganberries, ¾ cup
*Avocados, 1 cup	Mangoes, ½ cup
Blackberries, ¾ cup	*Nectarines, ⅔ cup
Boysenberries, ¾ cup	*Peaches, ⅔ cup
*Cherries, ¾ cup	*Persimmons, 1 cup
Currants, ¾ cup	*Plums, ½ cup
Dewberries, ¾ cup	Raspberries, ¾ cup
	Strawberries, ¾ cup

*Before adding sugar, sprinkle the fruit with an Anti-Browning Solution, see above.

UNSWEETENED WET PACK

Suitable for naturally sweet fruits and berries. After washing and draining the fruit, pack in leakproof containers, and either crush in its own juice or cover with water to which an Anti-Browning Solution, opposite, has been added. Allow 1-inch headroom. Seal and freeze.

SYRUP PACK

Whole fruits and those that tend to darken are best packed in syrup, as are fruits intended for desserts and compotes.

➤ Syrups for freezing may be made several days in advance and stored in the refrigerator, to be well chilled when combined with their fruit.

For light or 40% syrup, use 1¾ cups sugar to 1 pint water
For medium or 50% syrup, use 2½ cups sugar to 1 pint water
A heavier syrup is not recommended

Some people prefer to combine sugar with corn syrup or honey. If this combination is desired, never use more than ¼ cup corn syrup to ¾ cup sugar. Any of these syrups may be made by merely dissolving the sugar and corn syrup in water, but it is preferable to boil the mixture until the sugar is dissolved. Chill well before using.

If using an Anti-Browning Solution, opposite, add it to the cold syrup just before packing the fruit.

➤ Be sure the syrup covers the fruit completely. When using syrup with small or sliced fruits or berries, allow about 1½ cups of fruit and ⅓ to ½ cup of syrup for a pint container; for halved fruits about 1½ cups of fruit and ¾ to 1 cup of syrup.

If the fruit tends to rise above the syrup after leaving 1-inch headroom, lightly crush a piece of moisture-proof paper and put it on the top to keep the fruit submerged until the expansion of freezing makes the syrup fill the container. Leave the paper in the container.

In the list below, the L stands for light syrup, the M for a medium one. For relative amounts of fruit and syrup, see above.

*†L	Apples
*†L-M	Apricots, peeled or unpeeled
L	Blackberries
L	Blueberries
L-M	Boysenberries
*M	Cherries, sweet
M	Cranberries
M	Currants
M	Dewberries
*L	Figs
L	Fruit cocktail
M	Gooseberries
L	Grapefruit
L	Grapes
L	Guavas
L-M	Loganberries
L	Melons
*L	Nectarines
L	Oranges, sections
L-M	Papayas, ½-inch cubes
*L	Peaches

*†L Pears
L Pineapples
*L-M Plums
L-M Pomegranates
L-M Prunes
L-M Raspberries, whole or crushed
†L Rhubarb
M Strawberries

* Use lemon juice or ascorbic acid, see Anti-Browning Solutions, 823.
† Steam-blanch, see 822.

FREEZING FRUIT PURÉES

Fruits such as plums, prunes, avocados, papayas, mangoes, persimmons and melons keep better in puréed form if left uncooked. To purée, see the food mill illustrated on 832. Applesauce is one of the most delicious of frozen cooked purées, especially if made with early apples. Cooked purées should be used within 4 months. All may, if necessary, be packaged without sugar. Otherwise, allow about 1 cup of sugar per pound of fruit. Fruit sauces or cobbler fillings made from seedy berries, especially blackberries, are smoother if the frozen berries are broken apart and put unthawed through a meat grinder. Use a fine blade.

FREEZING FRUIT JUICES

Juices such as apple, raspberry, plum, cherry and grape, as well as fruit ciders, freeze most satisfactorily. For each gallon of cherry or apple juice, add ½ teaspoon ascorbic acid or 2 teaspoons lemon juice. Peaches for pressing can be steamed to 150° to keep color clear without tasting cooked. Cherries, plums, prunes and grapes have a better flavor if slightly cooked, as some of their characteristic flavor is extracted from the skin. Raspberries are best if the whole berries are mixed with 1 pound of sugar to each 10 pounds of fruit and frozen. Extract the juice when ready to use. In freezing citrus juices, it is difficult to retain their vitamin content without an elaborate vacuum process. Fruit for jelly and jam may be frozen unsugared and the juice extracted later without any cooking. To make the jelly, proceed as usual, see 833.

FREEZING VEGETABLES

Most vegetables take well to freezing. If they are garden-fresh and properly processed, their taste, when served, is hardly distinguishable from that of fresh produce.

Choose young, tender vegetables. Starchy ones such as peas, corn and lima beans are best when slightly immature. If not prepared and frozen at once, vegetables, to retain their freshness, must be kept chilled between harvesting and processing. Wash and prepare them quickly, as for regular cooking. If broccoli or cauliflower is insect-infested, soak ½ hour in a solution of 2 tablespoons salt to 1 gallon water. Rinse well. In order to blanch them evenly and pack efficiently, sort the vegetables for size. Several handy devices for sizing and cutting are available, and a corn scraper, 300, is a great asset for preparing corn cream-style. Better food values and flavor are retained if vegetables are not shredded or frenched. Green peppers do not need to be blanched before freezing if they are diced after the removal of seeds and membranes. Quick-freeze them on shallow trays before packaging.

It is best to fully cook before freezing such vegetables as pumpkin, squash and sweet potatoes. Mushrooms may be sautéed before freezing by heating 2 cups in 1 tablespoon butter in an uncovered pan about 3 minutes. Cool and freeze immediately. Tomatoes to be served raw do not freeze well, but tomatoes for stewing or seasoning may be scalded 2 minutes to loosen skins, then cored and packaged for the freezer without any additional heating. Cook before serving. Tomato juice is heated to boiling, strained and cooled before freezing. Leave at least 1-inch headroom.

BLANCHING VEGETABLES

Except for the varieties specifically noted below, and those above which we recommend processing fully cooked, all vegetables should be blanched before freezing, for enzymes continue to be active in vegetables even after harvesting and, unless arrested, will bring about changes which lead to nutritional loss and off-flavors. Blanching greatly lessens enzymatic activity and for this reason becomes an essential part of the freezing procedure. There are 2 methods of blanching: boiling and steaming. They may be used more or less interchangeably, although steam-blanching takes 30 seconds to 1 minute longer. However, leafy vegetables like spinach must be boil-blanched to allow quick heat-penetration; and watery ones like squashes and cut sweet corn, which lose flavor badly through leaching, if not completely precooked as recommended, should be steamed. Since blanching is not meant to be a cooking process, but merely a preparatory one, it should be carefully timed. Removal of excess moisture after blanching, and proper chilling before packaging, are two extremely important steps.

➤ To **blanch** by boiling, allow at least 1 gallon of boiling water to 1 pound of vegetables. Put the vegetables in a wire basket. Submerge them completely in the boiling water, cover and immediately begin to time the blanching, see below. Shake the wire basket several times during this period to allow even penetration of heat. When finished, lift vegetables from boiling water and put at once into a pan of ice water. Chill until the vegetables are cool to the center. Remove, drain and package.

➤ To **steam-blanch,** bring 2 or 3 inches of water to an active boil in a kettle with a tight lid and a rack. Put the vegetables, not more than a pound at a time, in a wire basket and suspend them above the water. Cover the kettle. When the steam starts to escape under the lid, begin to time for blanching. Shake the basket several times during this period to make sure that all the vege-

tables are uniformly exposed to the steam. Chill at once to stop further softening of the tissues by heat. If your tap water is 50° or less, hold the vegetables under it. If not, immerse them in ice water. Drain the cooled vegetables well and spread them on several thicknesses of paper toweling. Also cover them with paper toweling to absorb as much of the surface moisture as possible before packaging. Except for greens, which should have a 1-inch head space, the containers should be closely and completely filled, but not stuffed. If frozen vegetables toughen consistently, the water used ➤ may be too hard for good results.

▲ At 500 feet or more above sea level, blanch vegetables 1 minute longer than the time specified in the following chart.

BLANCHING CHART FOR VEGETABLES

Vegetable	Minutes to blanch	Minutes to steam-blanch
†Artichoke, whole	8 to 10	
Asparagus, medium-sized	3	4
Bamboo shoots	7 to 13	
Beans, green or wax	2½	3
Beans, lima, medium-sized	1½	2
Beans, shell	1¾	
Beans, soy and broad, in pod	4	
Bean sprouts	4 to 6	
Beet greens	2½	
Beets, small	Until tender	
Broccoli, split	3 to 4½	3 to 5
Brussels sprouts	3 to 4½	3 to 5
Cabbage, leaf or shredded	1½	2
Carrots, sliced	3	3½
Cauliflower, florets		3
Celery, diced	3	3½
Chard	2½	
Chayote, diced	2	2½
Chinese cabbage, shredded	1½	2
Collards	2½	
Corn to be cut, small ears to large	3 to 7	4 to 8
Corn on cob	6 to 10	7 to 11
Dasheen	2½	3
†Eggplant, 1½-inch slices	4	4½
Kale	2½	
Kohlrabi, diced	1	1¾
†Mushrooms, medium, whole	5	
Mustard greens	2½	
Okra, medium, whole	3 to 4	4
Parsnips	2	3
Peas, black-eyed	2	2½
Peas, green	1½ to 2½	2 to 3
Peppers	2	3
†Potatoes, sweet, puréed	Until tender	
Pumpkin, puréed	Until tender	
Rutabaga, diced	2	2½
Spinach	2½	
Squash, winter, puréed	Until tender	
Turnip greens	2½	
Turnips, diced	2	2½
Vegetables, mixed	Blanch separately; combine after chilling.	

†To preserve natural color, soak for 5 minutes in a solution of 1 teaspoon ascorbic acid and 1 quart water before blanching.

THAWING AND COOKING FROZEN VEGETABLES

Most frozen vegetables, because of previous blanching and a tenderizing process induced by temperature changes during storage, cook in from one-third to one-half the time that fresh vegetables require. Uncooked frozen vegetables may be substituted in recipes calling for fresh vegetables, ➤ but shorten their cooking time. Example: add them to stews for the last minutes of cooking. As with fresh vegetables, it is imperative, if flavor and food values are to be retained, not to overcook, especially if you use a pressure pan, see 281.

For table service, cook most vegetables without thawing. Exceptions are broccoli and greens, which profit by partial thawing, and ➤ corn on the cob, which should always be completely thawed, and is delicious if buttered and rewrapped in the aluminum foil in which it was frozen, then baked 20 minutes at 400°. Frozen corn on the cob may also be prepared first by pressure-cooking without previous thawing 1 minute at 15 pounds pressure, cutting off kernels, adding salt and butter and heating 2 minutes in an ovenproof dish under moderate broiler heat.

When cooking unthawed vegetables, break them apart into 4 or 5 chunks, to let the heat penetrate rapidly and evenly. In cooking, use the smallest possible amount of boiling water—¼ cup is enough for most varieties. However, lima beans take almost a cup and soybeans and cauliflower about ½ cup. The vegetables should be ➤ covered immediately with a lid. Once the boiling has begun again ➤ simmer until tender. Because the addition of water in cooking frozen vegetables always to some extent adversely affects flavor, we prefer processing them by steaming or pressure-cooking on a rack over hot water, double-boiler cooking, or baking. This is especially true for corn cut from the cob and for squash.

FREEZING MEATS

Meats, both domestic and game, should be slaughtered, chilled and aged as for canning, 811, after which they may be divided into meal-sized quantities for packaging, see 820. ➤ The reheating of once-thawed and cooked meats does not make for very tasty, nutritious or safe eating. Serve such leftovers cold or heat them in a piquant hot sauce.

The same advice as for all frozen produce applies to the choice of meats: watch quality. Storage at low temperatures does not induce enough change to make tough meats tender. If you usually buy quality cuts over the counter, make sure you can trust a different source which sells in quantity.

Beef, lamb and mutton must be properly aged from 5 to 7 days in a chill-room at 34° before being frozen. ➤ Pork and veal should be frozen as soon as they cool, after slaughtering, to forestall the tendency of the fat to turn rancid.

Although some frozen meats may be held over a year, it is a questionable economic or gastronomic procedure. Hold corn-fed beef, lamb and mutton about 6 to 9 months; pork and veal no longer than 8 to 9 months; variety meats 3 to 4 months; and ground meats and stews only 2 to 3 months. ➤ Do not hold meat loaves more than 3 months, as the seasonings deteriorate. Salted or fat meats, such as fresh sausage, smoked or brined hams and bacon, should never be held longer than a month. ➤ Take extra precautions in wrapping smoked meats ➤ to keep the odor from penetrating other foods. Bones, which add flavor to meats during cooking, take up considerable locker space and may also cause wrappings to tear. Even though removal of bones requires both skill and time, it is worth it. Cook bones, thus removed, with meat trimmings to make a concentrated stock, 520. This is valuable for soups and gravies ➤ or for packaging precooked meats, 820. Freeze stock in ice-cube-sized trays, remove and wrap for storage. These concentrates make quick gravy or soup. Game storage depends in part on the type of game and in part on the laws of your state, which may limit holding time. For large game, see directions for meat above; for birds, see those for poultry below.

THAWING AND COOKING FROZEN MEATS

Frozen meats may be cooked thawed or unthawed. ➤ But partial or complete thawing helps retain juiciness in thick cuts, and they will cook and brown more evenly. Thin cuts and patties may toughen if left frozen. ➤ Variety meats or meats prepared by breading or dredging must be completely thawed. ➤ Always defrost in the original wrappings on a refrigerator shelf. Allow 5 hours for each pound of thick cuts, less for thinner ones.

➤ Cooking unthawed large cuts of meat takes one and a half times as long as fresh ones. Small, thin cuts take one and a quarter times as long. ➤ Thawed cuts are cooked as for fresh ones.

In broiling unthawed meat, regardless of thickness, place it at least 5 to 6 inches below the heat source. Allow one and one-half times the broiling time. ➤ In any roasting process, use only the constant-heat method, see 446. A meat thermometer is a reassuring aid, see 447.

FREEZING AND THAWING POULTRY

Uncooked broilers, fryers and roasting chickens are most desirable for freezing. For stewers, see Freezing and Thawing Precooked Foods, 828. If you raise your own, starve the chickens for 24 hours before slaughtering, but give them plenty of water. Bleed them well. Clean and dress, 418 and 419, immediately. Be careful not to tear or bruise the flesh. Before freezing, chill overnight in the refrigerator or in ice until the birds are no longer stiff and the legs and wings can easily be rotated. ➤ Do not age any poultry unless you are fortunate enough to have wild duck or pheasant, which should be aged 2 or 3 days. For details, see directions listed under recipes for each kind of wild fowl. Remove excess cavity fat. Wrap and seal ➤ being careful to expel as much air as possible from the package. One helpful method is to put the bird in a freezer bag and plunge it quickly into a deep pan of cold water—keeping the top of the bag above the surface of the water. Twist the top and fasten.

When preparing several birds, storage space is saved if chickens are halved or disjointed before packaging. Freeze halves, breasts, thighs and drumsticks separately and wrap with double moisture-proof paper between them or store in cartons. Cook the backbones, wings and necks, remove the meat and freeze in the chicken broth.

Store young frozen chickens no longer than 9 months, older ones 3 to 4 months. Keep ducks and turkeys 6 to 9 months. A slight discoloration of the bones may occur during storage. It is harmless.

➤ Wrap giblets separately in moisture-proof wrappings and keep frozen only 2 to 3 months.

➤ It is not advisable to freeze stuffed poultry, as frequently the stuffing does not freeze fast enough to avoid spoilage. ➤ Freeze the stuffing separately. Poultry is always best when thawed before cooking, unless used for fricassee, 426. The usual method for a bird weighing less than 5 pounds is to thaw in the original wrappings on the refrigerator shelf, allowing two hours per pound. For a faster way, see 418. Cook immediately after thawing. For detailed information about thawing larger birds, see 417. Although we do not recommend it ➤ unthawed fowl needs about one and one-half times as long to cook as nonfrozen fowl. ➤ Treat thawed birds like fresh ones.

FREEZING, THAWING AND COOKING FISH

Fish, shellfish and frog legs keep most successfully when cleaned and frozen at once. If this is impractical, keep fish under refrigeration from catching to freezing, but in no case over 24 hours. Fish weighing 2 pounds or less, minus viscera, head, tails and fins, are frozen whole. For fish weighing 2 to 4 pounds, filleting is advised, 396. Larger fish are usually cut into steaks, 396, but they too may be frozen whole for stuffing later. Separate fillets or steaks with a double thickness of waterproof paper, 820. Try to use frozen fish within 4 months, and fish heavy in fat, like salmon, within 2 months.

Lobster and crab freeze best if cooked first as for the table but without salt. Remove meat from shells and pack dry meat in airtight containers. Shrimp, minus heads, are best frozen uncooked, as they toughen if frozen afterward. In fact, most shellfish are apt to toughen, cooked or uncooked, if held over 2 months. Oysters, clams and scallops should be shelled, and the liquor saved. Scallops may be washed after shelling, but not the other shellfish. Package all of these in their own liquor to cover and freeze or in a brine using 1 tablespoon salt to 3 cups water. Hold no longer than 3 or 4 months.

Fish and shellfish are often packed commercially in an ice glaze or an ice block to seal from oxygen. While this procedure is not easily adapted to home freezing, it is effective and entirely practical. There are two methods. To freeze in an ice block, place several small cleaned fish, steaks, or fillets in a loaf pan, wax carton or coffee tin, cover with water and freeze. When blocks are solid, remove from pan and wrap in freezer packaging material and store. The second method involves an ice glaze and is especially suitable for whole fish. Simply freeze the fish, cleaned but unwrapped, then dip the frozen fish in water just above the freezing point. Return to freezer, then repeat the dipping until a glaze ⅛ to ¼ inch thick has formed. Wrap in moisture-vaporproof material or seal in plastic bag.

Slowly thawed fish loses less juice and is more delicate when cooked than fish quickly thawed. Thaw fish in the original wrappings on a refrigerator shelf and allow about 8 hours per pound. Lobster takes slightly more, scallops, oysters, shellfish and uncooked shrimp slightly less time than given above. Shrimp need not be thawed before cooking, unless it is to be deep-fat-fried. Unthawed fish must be cooked both longer and at much lower temperatures than fresh fish—usually about one and one-quarter times as long.

FREEZING AND THAWING EGGS

Eggs must be removed from the shell before freezing. For short periods, shelled eggs may be frozen individually in an ice-cube tray, then packaged and stored. Usually, however, yolks and whites are stored separately. The whites may be packaged in small vaporproof recipe-sized containers, perhaps in the exact amount for your favorite angel cake. Yolks should be stabilized or they become pasty and hard to mix after freezing. Stabilization is accomplished as follows: If yolks are to be used for unsweetened food, add 1 teaspoon of salt to each pint; if for desserts, add 1 tablespoon of sugar, honey or corn syrup to each pint. Label the yolks accordingly. You will need about 10 whole eggs or 16 whites or 24 yolks for each pint container. To use, ➤ thaw in the refrigerator for 8 to 10 hours.

If you prefer to package whole eggs, stir with 1½ teaspoons sugar or corn syrup or with ½ teaspoon salt to each pint, incorporating as little air as possible. In packaging, allow ½-inch head space for expansion during freezing. Thaw all eggs before using in recipes. To reconstitute a whole egg, use 3 tablespoons thawed whole eggs. To reconstitute a whole egg from your separately packed whites and yolks, allow 1⅓ tablespoons of yolk and 2 tablespoons of white.

FREEZING BUTTER, CREAM AND MILK

Unsalted butter stores well, but if salt is added, 3 months should be the limit of storage. ➤ Cream should be pasteurized first, and may be stored 3 to 6 months. When thawed, the uses for thick cream are limited mainly to making frozen desserts and using small amounts in vegetables and casseroles. Its whipping quality will be impaired, its oil rises on contact with coffee, and the texture is unsatisfactory for use with cereals. If you are making ice cream or frozen desserts for the freezer, choose a recipe that calls for heating the cream first. It is not advisable to freeze light or sour cream. ➤ If milk is frozen, use only pasteurized, homogenized milk. Leave ½-inch headroom when freezing cream or milk. Store only 1 month. To use, ➤ thaw butter about 3 hours on a refrigerator shelf and milk or cream about 4 hours.

FREEZING CHEESES

Cheeses of the hard or cheddar type may be stored 6 months. Cream cheese becomes crumbly when frozen but seems to serve well as an ingredient in sandwiches or dips. Dry cottage cheese can be frozen only before the curds are washed free of whey, see 536. It is again washed after thawing, and drained. To thaw, rest cheese about 3 hours on a refrigerator shelf.

FREEZING AND THAWING PRECOOKED DISHES

The precooked frozen meal, for better or for worse, is a reality. If you should go in extensively for this not very enthusiastically endorsed form of corner-cutting, you may as well take further advantage of it: labor can be saved by baking several pies, cakes or batches of bread at one session and storing the extras; or by doubling a casserole recipe and freezing half. Prepare school lunches in advance. Frozen sandwiches in the lunchbox will be thawed by lunchtime and will keep other foods cool. We urge you, though, to read about the kinds of products really suitable for freezing, 820, and to remember ➤ to cool the cooked dishes you plan to freeze through and through before you pack them. If you do not cool them sufficiently, the outside edges may freeze hard but the interior may not cool quickly enough to prevent spoilage. ➤ Also, do not try to freeze too much at one time, for overloading your freezer raises the temperature to the detriment of your already stored frozen foods. Be just as careful with packaging cooked foods, 820, as with raw ones. Try to use them within 1 month, and in reheating be sure to thaw properly or reheat slowly.

Main dishes of the creamed type, stews, casseroles, meat pies, rissoles, croquettes and spaghetti sauces are among the most convenient of precooked foods for freezing. Fried foods almost without exception tend to rancidity, toughness and dryness when frozen. No appreciable time is gained by freezing such starchy foods as macaroni, noodles or rice. And potatoes should not be frozen.

Prepare main dishes as usual, following your favorite recipes. But, in all instances, undercook the vegetables involved. Chill precooked foods rapidly over ice water and package closely and carefully, see 820, before freezing. Line casserole dishes with foil before filling, then freeze. When frozen solid, remove the foil-wrapped food, seal tightly and freeze. This releases the casserole until you are ready to use the food, at which time you may remove the foil, return the food to the casserole and heat the dish in the oven.

Stewed meats keep best in heavy sauces. If they are to be used for salads, place them in clear concentrated stock. Chill rapidly to room temperature. Cut in meal-sized portions; package closely and freeze. Hold no longer than 1 month. Thaw in original wrappings on a refrigerator shelf, allowing about as much time as for uncooked meats.

Reheat stews and creamed dishes in a double boiler or in the oven at 350° in a heatproof dish that has been placed in hot water. Stir as little as possible. Allow one and one-half times as long as normal to heat a frozen casserole at the usual temperature. Put frozen meat pies into a 350°–375° oven until brown.

Thaw croquettes or ➤ any breaded food that is to be sautéed or deep fried ➤ uncovered and refrigerated, so that moisture does not form. If the food is already fried, thaw ➤ uncovered and refrigerated, and bake in a 400° oven.

Perhaps the most important thing to consider in precooking frozen foods is not to overcook foods that are to be reheated later. ➤ Also, watch seasonings carefully. Baffling changes take place. Onion, pepper, cloves, garlic and synthetic flavorings tend to become strong or bitter; salt tends to vanish, as do herb flavorings, even the indomitable sage; and curry acquires a musty flavor. Sauces have their own peculiar reactions. Avoid freezing all sauces based on egg. Sauces heavy in fat may develop an off-flavor and have a tendency to separate on reheating, but often recombine with stirring; while those with much milk or cheese tend to curdle. Thickened sauces may need thinning.

A number of vegetables such as squash, boiled and candied sweet potatoes, Harvard beets and creamed celery are best cooked before freezing and good to have on hand. See chart, 825, for these and other suggestions. All such vegetables may be heated in a double boiler or in a 400° oven without thawing.

Corn Pudding, 300, was once a seasonal treat but is now available in frozen form at any time. Prepare the pudding as for immediate use. Put it into aluminum cartons; heat it in a moderate oven at 325° for 10 minutes. Cool over cold water. Cover, seal when thoroughly cool and freeze at once. To serve, heat in a 250° oven until thawed, then bake at 325° for about one hour until golden. If you plan keeping the corn longer than 4 months, merely scrape it, heat, chill and seal it as above. Then when ready to serve it, thaw in a 250° oven until soft, add butter, cream and salt and bake at 325° until golden.

➤ Be careful not to stir air into puréed vegetables. Cool quickly and freeze in ice-cube trays first, then place in bags and seal. If packaging in rigid containers, place a piece of plastic film directly on the purée to prevent oxidative changes.

FREEZING CANAPÉS AND SANDWICHES

Canapés and sandwiches should not be stored longer than a few weeks. Make them up quickly to keep the bread from drying out. For mass production methods, see 66. Be sure to spread all bread well and to make the fillings rather heavy in fats, so that the bread will not become saturated. Or you may prefer to prepare and freeze sandwich spreads for use later with fresh bread. As a corollary, bread for canapés can be cut into fancy shapes, frozen and then thawed slightly just before spreading. ➤ In choosing recipes for fillings, avoid mayonnaise and boiled salad dressings, hard-cooked egg whites, jellies and all crisp salad materials. Garnishes like cress, parsley, tomato and cucumber cannot be frozen, so add these the last moment before serving. Ground meats, poultry, fish, butter, cream and cheddar-type cheese, sieved egg yolk, peanut butter, nut meats, dried fruits and olives are all suitable for freezing.

You may freeze canapés on trays first or wrap them carefully and then freeze them. In either case, keep the different kinds separated from one another and away from the interior walls of the freezer, as this contact makes the bread soggy. Canapés and sandwiches should always be thawed in the wrappings. They take from 1 to 2 hours to thaw on a refrigerator shelf and from 15 to 45 minutes at room temperature—depending on size.

FREEZING SOUPS

To freeze soups, prepare them as for immediate use. Chill them rapidly over ice water. Store in any containers suitable for liquids, 820, allowing head space of ½ inch in pint and 1 inch in quart containers. Concentrated meat or fish stock, the stock simmered until reduced to one-half or one-third its original quantity, see Soup Stock, 520, is the most space-saving soup to store. You may freeze them, if you like, in ice-cube trays for additions to gravy and sauces, then put frozen cubes in plastic bags and seal. Another way to freeze liquids is to use a sealed plastic bag inserted in a coffee can with a plastic lid. When the liquid is frozen solid, remove the can. If a soup or chowder calls for potato, it is preferable to add freshly cooked potato just before serving. If you do freeze the potato, undercook it. Fish and meat stock thawed and combined in a ⅄ blender with fresh vegetables make delicate soups in short order. To serve frozen soups, bring them to a boil in a saucepan, unless they are thick or have a cream base, in whicn case a double boiler is necessary. For cold soups, thaw until liquid and serve while still chilled.

FREEZING SALAD INGREDIENTS

The materials that the word salad brings to mind —fresh crisp greens, tomatoes, cucumbers and aspics—are impossible to freeze, but some of the foods traditionally served with them freeze well and will shorten salad preparation time. For instance, frozen precooked meats, poultry and fish —whole, diced or sliced and covered with concentrated stocks—are welcome ingredients for a salad when thawed and drained. Precooked green beans, evenly sized and unsliced, may be packaged, frozen, and later coated with French dressing. And almost any fruit mixture, excluding pears, may be frozen for use in fruit salads later. If using bananas, freeze slices separately.

FREEZING UNBAKED PASTRY, COOKIES AND DOUGHS

➤ Doughs, batters and unbaked pastry on the whole respond less favorably to freezing than do the finished products. ➤ We do not recommend the freezing of cake doughs and batters. For one thing, the spices and condiments used in their preparation have a disconcerting tendency to "zero out" during the freezing process. For another, all leavens are highly variable under frozen storage, particularly those incorporated into the moister kinds of dough.

Unbaked yeast bread dough is most acceptable when frozen and stored for only a week or ten days. It is made up in the usual way, see 599, kneaded and allowed to rise once until doubled in bulk, then kneaded again and shaped before packaging into loaves not more than 2 inches thick. Thin loaves, of course, will thaw with much greater rapidity than thick ones. Frozen bread dough is a notable exception to the rule that frozen foods are best when slowly thawed. Place the dough in a 250° oven for 45 minutes, then bake it as usual, cool and serve. "Serve soon" would be a timelier suggestion, because thawed and baked bread dough dries out very rapidly. Partially baked breads in the brown-and-serve category may be put into the oven without thawing.

Unbaked dough for yeast rolls should not be held frozen for more than one week. Follow the procedure for frozen dough, above. Grease all roll surfaces; freeze them 2 to 4 hours on trays set away from the interior walls of the freezer, and package within 24 hours after freezing. Or, you may wrap the rolls before freezing, separating them with sheets of moisture-vaporproof material. To serve, remove the rolls from the package, cover with a cloth, put them in a warm place to rise until doubled in bulk—2 to 4 hours—and bake as usual.

Unbaked biscuits may also be frozen on trays or packaged before freezing. They, too, rise well and thaw quickly if rolled thin. Thaw them, wrapped, at room temperature for 1 hour and bake as usual. Pastries heavy in fat, like pies, tarts, filled rings and rich cookies, whether frozen baked or unbaked, come through zero storage rather well; but whenever possible, it is good practice to store all the cookies in the same containers in which they will ultimately be baked. If you want to cut cookies before freezing, put them on trays until hard, see tray freezing, 822. Then package for freezing. But if you want to cut them after freezing, make a roll of the dough and wrap it in moisture-vaporproof material in batch sizes and seal. These uncooked cookie doughs keep about 2 months. Bake cookies in a 350°–375° oven 10 to 12 minutes.

FREEZING BAKED PASTRY, CAKES, COOKIES AND DOUGHS

Doughs previously baked are quicker and easier to freeze than the corresponding raw materials and, generally speaking, yield more satisfactory results. Careful packaging for either category is essential. ➤ Always plan to unfreeze just the amount of baked articles needed, for they dry out rapidly after thawing.

Precooked pastries heavy in fats are the most successful "freezers" of all. Their storage limit is about 3 months. Baked yeast bread and rolls have the longest storage potential—6 months or more—but they do begin to lose flavor after eight weeks. Bake all of these varieties in the usual way and, before packaging, let them cool for 3 hours. If bread is to be used for toast, it is not necessary to thaw it. Otherwise thaw it wrapped, at room temperature, for 2 to 3 hours before serving. Freshen it in a 300° oven for 20 minutes. Should you freeze "boughten" bread, leave it in its original wrapper and slip it into a plastic bag or wrap it in foil as well.

➤ Baked cakes will keep 3 to 4 months unfrosted, but only 2 months if frosted. Filled cakes tend to sogginess, and any filling with an egg base is to be avoided. Actually, it is a better policy to wait and add fillings just before serving. Spice cake should not be stored over 6 weeks, as the flavors change in the freezing process. Use a minimum of spices and omit cloves. If frosted cakes are frozen, use icings with a confectioners' sugar and butter base. Brown sugar icings and those containing egg whites or syrups tend to crystallize and freeze poorly. Boiled frosting becomes sticky on thawing. Do not wrap any iced cakes until the icing has been well firmed by chilling, unwrapped, in the freezer. Place waxed paper over iced portions before putting on the outer wrap and sealing. Protect cakes with an extra carton to avoid crushing. Thaw them, unwrapped, in a covered cake dish at room temperature for 2 hours before serving.

➤ When cookies are baked before freezing, they will keep about 3 months. Bake as usual, cool and package closely, separating each cookie with moisture-vaporproof material. To avoid breakage, store in an extra carton after wrapping. Let the cookies thaw, wrapped, in the refrigerator. ➤ Freshen them with a quick run in a 350° oven.

FREEZING UNBAKED PIES

Use foil pans, or pans you can spare, so your pies can be frozen and baked in the same container. You will get better results with frozen pie crust if it has ➤ a high shortening content. Pie crust may be frozen ready for rolling or be rolled and cut ready to be put in the pan, but ➤ unrolled dough must be handled while it is still chilled so it will remain tender. Freeze unfilled shells in the pan, then remove and stack them in a box before wrapping, or store them wrapped in disposable foil pans. Bake, without thawing, at 425° 12 to 15 minutes. In making complete pies for freezing, brush the inside of the bottom crust with shortening to keep it from becoming soggy. After filling, wipe the top crust also with shortening but do not prick until ready to bake. ➤ Never use water, egg or milk for these glazes.

The best pie fillings for freezing are fresh fruits or mincemeat, and their storage limit is 4 to 6 months. Use pumpkin pie within 6 weeks for best flavor. Fruits like peaches and apricots, which darken on exposure to air, should be treated with ascorbic acid, 823, or scalded in syrup, 805, 2 minutes. Cool before using. The fillings for unbaked pies should have about 1½ times more cornstarch or tapioca than usual, or, if possible, use waxy starches, 548. ➤ Never freeze a cream or custard pie.

Allow at least 1 pint of filling for an 8-inch pie. ➤ Freeze the pie before wrapping if the filling is a wobbly one. Then package closely. Seal and protect against weight of other objects in the freezer until frozen hard.

To bake, remove wrappings, cut vent holes in upper crust and place uncooked pies unthawed on the lowest shelf of a 450° preheated oven 15 to 20 minutes. Reduce heat to 375° until done, about 1 hour in all.

FREEZING BAKED PIES

Please read Freezing Unbaked Pies, above. Use foil pans or containers you are willing to spare, so the ➤ pie can be cooked, stored and reheated in the same pan. Cool after baking, then wrap in sheet wrapping, 820, and seal.

➤ Unfilled baked pie shells are one of the most convenient of all frozen items for filling quickly before serving with creamed foods or fruit fillings. Freeze them unwrapped in the pan, then remove and stack them in a box before wrapping or store them wrapped in disposable foil pans. If you are freezing any precooked fillings with starch, be sure to ➤ cook them very thoroughly and, if possible, use waxy starches, 548.

Thaw a baked pie at room temperature for 2 to 3 hours if it is to be served cold. If it is to be served hot, place it unthawed in a 400° preheated oven 30 to 40 minutes, depending on size.

➤ Never freeze a cream or custard pie, and do not freeze pie meringue. Chiffon pies can be frozen in a baked shell if, before freezing, the filling has at least ½ cup of whipping cream incorporated into it. ➤ Defrost unwrapped and refrigerated. Garnish with whipped cream before serving, if preferred.

FREEZING DESSERTS

The same principles apply to desserts made in zero storage cabinets as to those which are still-frozen in refrigerators. Whipped cream, whipped egg white or a gelatin base is necessary to prevent the formation of undesirable graininess or crystals. If these stabilizing ingredients are not used, the dessert mixture must be beaten several times during the freezing to break up these crystals. ➤ Such desserts should be used shortly after being frozen and not stored for any length of time.

Churned ice cream is best for freezing when the recipes call for beating the cream. A final beating and refreezing may be necessary if these creams have been stored longer than 3 weeks. For safety, do not store in the freezer longer than 3 months. Remove all frozen desserts from storage 10 to 15 minutes before serving.

Fruit and steamed puddings may be baked, cooled and then frozen. They may be kept in the freezer as long as one year. Thaw at room temperature, or unwrap and place pudding, unthawed, in a steamer or double boiler. Heat to serving temperature.

FREEZING DRIED FRUITS, NUTS AND JELLIES

Dried fruits and nut meats can be successfully frozen whole, chopped or ground for 6 to 7 months. Wrap them in convenient quantities, taking the usual precautions to exclude air from the packages. Jellies and jams, especially raspberry and strawberry, retain for many months the fresh taste and clear color they attain just after preserving.

JELLIES AND PRESERVES

Have you ever tried to raise money for your church or club at a food stand? It's the homemade breads and old-fashioned cooked-down jellies that get snapped up first, for neither of these is likely to be duplicated commercially.

With jams, jellies and preserves, ➤ flavor is largely a matter of keeping sugar content to a minimum. For this reason we do not give recipes thickened with commercial pectin, as their sugar requirement is very high. Store-bought jellies, according to law, must have at least 45% fruit and 55% sugar. The juice is ordinarily extracted by pressure-cooking; and although as much as one-fourth more juice can be secured in this way than by other methods, the natural pectins in the fruit are destroyed by the high heat involved and must be replaced. ➤ These added pectins, in turn, demand a higher percentage of sugar to fruit to make the juices jell. In fact, pectin manufacturers not uncommonly suggest for the homemade product a proportion as high as 60% sugar to 40% juice or pulp. And they point out as advantages with the use of commercial pectin greater yield, less loss of liquid, and speed of preparation. Only a minute or two of cooking is needed after adding the sugar.

We regard none of these as advantages, or as in any sense comparable with the end product obtained by the open-kettle, cooked-down procedures we advocate, under which fruits low in natural pectins are combined with those having high pectin content, like apples; fruit exceeds sugar, rather than the reverse; and—most important—we wind up with greatly superior flavor.

It has been demonstrated that ➤ cane and beet sugars produce equally good results. But if honey is substituted, there is a distinct and delicious change in flavor. In cooked-down jellies and preserves, honey may replace up to one-half the sugar, but jams and jellies made with honey require longer cooking. If you plan to put up jellies with artificial sweeteners, we suggest you ask your doctor first his opinion of the chemical you propose using; then follow the processor's directions to the letter. You will find the texture of jellies and jams made with such synthetics quite different from—and less interesting than—that of those prepared with sugar or honey.

Jellies, jams, fruit butters, conserves, preserves—just what are the differences among them?

Jelly has great clarity. Two cooking processes are involved. First, the juice alone is extracted from the fruit. Only that portion thin and clear enough to drip through a cloth is cooked with sugar until ➤ sufficiently firm to hold its shape. It is never stiff and never gummy. ➤ **Jams, butters** and **pastes** are purées of progressively increasing density. ➤ **Preserves, marmalades** and **conserves** are bits of fruit cooked to a translucent state in a heavy syrup. These and the jams, all of which need only one cooking, take patience and ➤ careful stirring, so that they reduce without any taint of scorching. For some thicker types, an oven-cooking technique is suggested in the recipes.

Let us come back to the importance of pectins in all jelly and jam making. ➤ With high-pectin fruits such as apples, crab apples, quinces, red currants, gooseberries, plums and cranberries, you need have no worries about jelling. If you should get a syrupy jelly with any of these fruits, either you have used too much sugar or you did not cook the juice long enough after the sugar was added.

Low-pectin fruits—strawberries, blueberries, peaches, apricots, cherries, figs, pears, raspberries, blackberries, grapes and pineapples—or plants such as rhubarb have to be combined either with one of the high-pectin fruits above—or, of course, with commercial pectins.

➤ To determine if fruit juice contains a sufficient amount of pectin to jell, put 1 tablespoon of the cooled fruit juice in a glass. Add the same quantity of grain alcohol and shake gently. The effect of the alcohol is to bring the pectin together in a transparent glob. If a large quantity is present, it will appear in a single mass when poured from the glass. This indicates that equal quantities of sugar and juice should be used. If the pectin does not form a mass, less sugar will be required. If it collects in 2 or 3 masses, use two-thirds to three-fourths as much sugar as juice; if in smaller, even more numerous particles, one-half as much sugar as juice, unless the fruit is very tart.

➤ Get your equipment ready before you begin to cook the jelly or jam. Use a heavy enamel or stainless steel pan with a flat bottom. If you are making jelly, have a bag ready for straining the juice, see Making Juice for Jelly, 833, and the chapter-heading illustration, above. ➤ Have ready too, sterilized jelly glasses. To prepare them, fill glasses or jars three-fourths full of water and place them well apart in a shallow pan partly filled with water. Simmer the water 15 or 20 minutes. Keep the glasses hot until ready to fill. If the lids are placed lightly upon the glasses, they will be sterilized at the same time.

In making jellies and jams, best flavor results if you work with small quantities. ➤ Prepare not more than 6 cups of fruit or juice at a time, preferably only about 4 cups. ➤ If the fruit is one that discolors easily, see Anti-Browning Solutions, 805. Again, to retain flavor, unless fruit is very acid, when sugar can be used cup for cup with fruit ➤ we recommend 3/4 cup sugar to 1 cup fruit or juice. ✽ Jellies and jams may be frozen to advantage, but do not keep them in the refrigerator, as they may "weep." ➤ Store in a cool, dark, dry place. ➤ Discard if they develop mold.

MAKING JUICE FOR JELLY

"Picture-book" jelly takes time. ➤ To prepare juice for jelly by the open-kettle method, wash the fruit well and drain. To accent flavor ➤ add water only if you must. Prick or crush the fruit that forms the bottom layer in the preserving kettle. Less juicy fruits, such as apples and pears, require relatively large amounts of water. Add it to the kettle until you can see it through the top layer of fruit, but ➤ never use enough to float the fruit. Cook over low heat until more moisture is drawn from the fruit and then increase the heat to moderate, continuing to cook ➤ uncovered until the fruit is soft and has begun to lose its color. ➤ Have ready a jelly bag. This should be made of a porous material like unbleached muslin. If well enough sewn, the bag may eventually be suspended; if not, it can be held in a strainer. Wet the bag and wring it out before you pour the jelly into it, as a dry bag can absorb a lot of the precious juice. If you want a sparkling clear and well-flavored jelly ➤ do not squeeze the bag. After using it, rinse the bag in boiling water for subsequent use. See sketch on 832.

If not utilized at once ➤ fruit juice will keep about 6 months and can be made into jelly at your convenience. ✽ You may freeze it, 824, or you may reheat the strained juice, pour it boiling hot into sterilized jars, 802, cover with screw tops and cook in a hot-water bath, 804, at 185° at least 20 minutes. ➤ Seal the jars completely and keep them ➤ stored in a cool dark place.

MAKING JELLY

Measure the strained fruit juice and put it into ➤ a large enamel or stainless steel pan. Simmer the juice, uncovered, about 5 minutes. ➤ Skim off any froth that forms. Measure and add the sugar ➤ stirring until it is dissolved. Because of the addition of the sugar, the boiling point of the mixture will have been raised and the jelly will seem to be boiling at this heat. It should reach 8°F. higher than the boiling point of water in your locality and at this temperature will form a satisfactory jell. For use of a thermometer, see 777.

If you have no jelly thermometer, cook the mix just long enough to bring it to the point of jelling. ➤ Begin to test the juice 10 minutes after the sugar has been added. It is wise to use a timer, illustrated on 832. Place a small amount of jelly in a spoon, cool it slightly and let it drop back into the pan from the side of the spoon.

At first, the drip is light and syrupy. As the syrup thickens, 2 large drops begin to form along the edge of the spoon. ➤ When they come together and fall as a single drop, as shown at the right above, the "sheeting stage," 220° to 222°, has been reached. The jelly is then ready to be taken from the heat. The required time for cooking will range from 8 to 30 minutes, depending on the kind of fruit, the amount of sugar and the amount of juice in each pan.

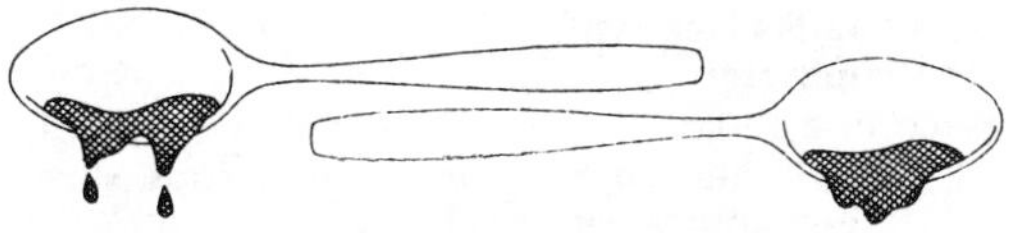

While the juice is cooking, take the jars from the hot water, empty them and reverse them onto a cake cooler. Skim off the foam quickly and pour the jelly into the jars when they are ➤ still hot, but dry. Fill to within 1/2 inch of the top. Cover the jars with 1/8 inch of hot paraffin. If the paraffin becomes very hot, it is apt to pull away from the sides of the jelly glass; so melt the paraffin over hot water in a small metal pitcher as shown in the chapter heading, 832, which can subsequently be covered and stored for the next session. Allow glasses to stand until the paraffin hardens, then cover and store.

If using the jars with a two-piece metal screw-down lid, shown on 803, there is no need to use paraffin. Fill the jars with boiling-hot jelly to within 1/8 inch of the top. Put the rubber on, making sure the top and threads of the jar are clean. Screw the metal band on firmly, then invert the jars for a few seconds to seal completely. Cool the jars in an upright position and store in a cool, dark, dry place.

CURRANT JELLY

➤ Please read about Making Jelly, above.

Wash:

Red, white or black currants

Drain and place in a stainless steel kettle. It is not necessary to stem currants, and they may be cooked with or without water. If water is used, allow about one-fourth as much water as fruit. Otherwise, crush the bottom layer of currants and pile the rest on top of them. Cook the fruit first over low heat about 5 minutes, then over moderate heat until soft and colorless. Strain through a jelly bag, above. Allow to each cup of juice:

3/4 to 1 cup sugar

Cook only 4 cups of juice at a time.

CURRANT AND RASPBERRY JELLY

➤ Please read about Making Jelly, 833.
Prepare currants as for Currant Jelly, 833.
Crush:

Raspberries

Add from 1 to 1⅓ cups raspberries for every cup of currants. Cook the fruit until the currants are soft and colorless. Strain the fruit through a jelly bag, 833. Allow to each cup of juice:

¾ to 1 cup sugar

Cook only 4 cups of juice at a time.

BLACK RASPBERRY AND GOOSEBERRY JELLY

➤ Please read about Making Jelly, 833.
Wash and drain fruit. Place in a saucepan and stew until soft:

4 quarts black raspberries
¼ cup water

Place in a separate saucepan and stew until soft:

2 quarts gooseberries or about 2 cups sliced green apples with peel and core
½ cup water

Combine the fruits and strain through a jelly bag, 833. Allow to each cup of juice:

¾ to 1 cup sugar

Cook only 4 cups of juice at a time.

APPLE, CRAB APPLE OR QUINCE JELLY

Good in itself, especially if made with tart fruit. Apples, crab apples or quinces, as we have indicated, are also extremely useful in combination with fruits whose pectin content is low, such as blueberries, blackberries, elderberries, raspberries and grapes, whether fresh or frozen. In apples, the greatest amount of pectin lies close to the skin. Apple peelings and cores can be cooked up and strained through a jelly bag for addition to low-pectin juices.
➤ Please read about Making Jelly, 833.
Wipe, quarter and remove stems and blossom ends from:

Tart apples, crab apples or quinces

Place in a saucepan. Add water until it can be seen through the top layer of fruit. Cook ➤ uncovered until fruit is soft. Put the juice through a jelly bag, 833. Allow to each cup of juice:

¾ to 1 cup sugar

Cook only 4 cups at a time.

HERB AND SCENTED JELLIES

➤ Please read about Making Jelly, 833.
Prepare:

Apple or Crab Apple Jelly, above

After testing for jelling and before removing the jelly from heat, bruise the leaves and bind together a bunch of one of the following ➤ fresh, unsprayed herbs:

Mint, basil, tarragon, thyme, lemon verbena or rose geranium

Hold the stem ends and pass the leaves through the jelly repeatedly until the desired strength of flavoring is reached. Add a small amount of:

(Vegetable coloring)

PARADISE JELLY

➤ Please read about Making Jelly, 833.
Wash and cut into quarters:

3 quarts apples

Peel and cut into quarters:

3 pints quinces

Remove seeds. Place the apples in a pan with:

1 quart cranberries

Barely cover with water. Boil until soft. Follow the same procedure with the quinces. Strain the juices of all the fruits through a jelly bag. Allow to each cup of juice:

1 cup sugar

Cook only 4 cups at a time.

GRAPE JELLY

➤ Please read about Making Jelly, 833.
Wash:

Slightly underripe Concord or wild grapes

which are preferable to ripe or overripe grapes because of their tart flavor and higher pectin content. Remove stems. Place crushed fruit in a kettle with a small quantity of water—about ½ cup of water to 4 cups of grapes. Add:

1 quartered apple

If you wish to spice the jelly, add at this time:

(⅓ cup vinegar)
(1-inch stick cinnamon)
(½ teaspoon whole cloves without heads)

Boil grapes until soft and beginning to lose color. Strain through a jelly bag. Allow to each cup of juice:

¾ to 1 cup sugar

Cook only 4 cups at a time.

WATERLESS GRAPE OR BERRY JELLY

➤ Please read about Making Jelly, 833.
Try this recipe when slightly underripe fruits are available. It is superlative when it works, but everything depends on the condition of the fruit.
Wash:

Concord or other slip-skin grapes, or berries

Mash them in a large pot. Cook until soft. Strain the juice. Measure it. Bring juice to a rolling boil. Remove from heat. Add 1½ times more:

Sugar

than you have juice. Stir it over heat until dissolved. Pour the jelly into sterilized glasses and seal. ➤ Should the liquid not jell, nothing but time is lost. Allow 1 apple and ¼ cup water to every 4 cups original fruit used. Cook the apple and water until the apple is soft. Strain off the juice, add it to the unjelled jelly, and recook as for any other jelly.

SEA GRAPE JELLY

➤ Please read about Making Jelly, 833.
Wash well:

Sea grapes

Cover with 1½ times as much water as fruit, and cook until the skin and pulp slip from the seeds when pressed. Put the juice through a jelly bag, but do not press. Set this juice aside. Combine the seeds and pulp with an equal amount of water and cook about 15 minutes longer. Drain and combine the juices. Allow to each cup of juice:

1 cup sugar

Cook only 4 cups at a time.

GUAVA JELLY

➤ Please read about Making Jelly, 833.
Wash and cut into quarters:

Slightly underripe guavas

Cover with water and boil, then ➤ simmer about ½ hour. Put the juice through a jelly bag, but do not press, as the juice will become bitter. Allow to each cup of juice:

1 cup sugar

Bring again to a boil and add for each cup of juice:

1 teaspoon lime juice

Cook only 4 cups at a time.

PLUM JELLY

Goose plums make delicious jelly or jam.
➤ Please read about Making Jelly, 833.
Wash:

Small red plums

Place in a saucepan. Add water until it can be seen through the top layer. Boil plums until soft. Put the pulp through a jelly bag. Allow to each cup of juice:

¾ to 1 cup sugar

Boil only 4 cups at a time.

MAKING JAM

Jam is the easiest type to make—and the most economical—as it needs only one cooking step and utilizes the fruit pulp. Measure the fruit; put it into the pan, crushing the lower layers to provide moisture until more is drawn from the fruit by heat; or, if necessary, add about ½ cup of water. ➤ Simmer the fruit uncovered, until soft, before adding the sugar. ➤ Stir until the sugar is dissolved. ➤ Bring the fruit mixture to a boil and continue to stir, making sure no sticking occurs. ➤ Reduce the heat and cook, uncovered, until the mixture thickens, allowing for additional thickening as it cools. If using a thermometer, shown in the chapter heading, 832, cook to a temperature 9°F. higher than the temperature of boiling water in your locality. To keep the heat diffused, you may even want to use an asbestos pad. Sometimes it takes as long as half an hour for jam to thicken.

RED RED STRAWBERRY JAM

➤ Please read about Making Jam, above.
Wash, dry well and stem:

1 quart ➤ perfect strawberries

Put them into a ➤ very heavy 10-inch cooking pot, cutting into a few of the berries to release a little juice. Cover with:

4 cups sugar

Stir the mixture ➤ very gently with a wooden spoon ➤ over low heat until it has "juiced up." Then raise the heat to moderate and stop stirring. When the whole is a bubbling mass, set your timer for exactly 15 minutes—17 if the berries are very ripe. From this point do not disturb. You may take a wooden spoon and streak it slowly through the bottom to make sure there is no sticking. When the timer rings, tilt the pot. You should see in the liquid at the bottom a tendency to set. Slide the pot off the heat. Allow berries to cool ➤ uncovered. Sprinkle surface with:

(Juice of ½ lemon)

When cool, stir the berries lightly and place in sterile jars.

BLUEBERRY JAM

If blueberries are picked early in the day and are only half ripe, at the red instead of blue stage, the result is a jam far more flavorful than usual—almost like the one made with Scandinavian lingonberries.
➤ Please read about Making Jam, above.
Pick over, wash and measure:

Blueberries

Put them in a heavy stainless steel pan. Crush the bottom layer. You may add:

(½ cup water)

Cook over moderate heat, ➤ simmering until almost tender. Add, for each cup of blueberries:

¾ to 1 cup heated sugar

Stir and cook over low heat until a small amount dropped on a plate will stay in place. Place in hot sterilized jars.

SPICED PEAR JAM WITH PINEAPPLE

About 2 Quarts

➤ Please read about Making Jam, above.
As it is hard to gauge the acidity of the pear used, taste the jam as it cooks. Add sugar or lemon juice as needed. Peel and core:

3 lb. firm Bartlett, Kiefer or Seckel pears

Wash well and remove seeds from:

1 orange
1 lemon

Put the fruit through a grinder, using a coarse blade. Save the juices. Add them to the pulp with:

1 cup crushed pineapple
4 to 5 cups sugar

Tie in cheesecloth and add:

3 or 4 whole cloves
6 inches stick cinnamon
A 1-inch piece ginger

Stir the mixture while heating it. Simmer about 30 minutes. Remove spice bag. Pour jam into sterilized hot glasses.

RASPBERRY, BLACKBERRY, GOOSEBERRY, LOGANBERRY OR ELDERBERRY JAM

➤ Please read about Making Jam, 835.
Crushing a few berries, combine:

4 cups raspberries, blackberries, gooseberries, elderberries or loganberries

with:

3 cups sugar

If the berries are tart, use a scant cup of sugar to 1 cup of fruit. These are not high-pectin fruits, so it is wise to add:

1 to 2 apples, cored and cut into small pieces

Stir and cook over low heat until the sugar is dissolved. ➤ Simmer and stir frequently from the bottom to keep jam from sticking. Cook until a small amount dropped on a plate will stay in place. Pack while hot in hot sterilized jars.

FIVE-FRUITS JAM COCKAIGNE

On the whole, we like food to retain its own native flavor. Our sympathy goes out to the cowboy movie actor who is reported to have said, after his first formal dinner: "I et for two hours and I didn't recognize anything I et, except an olive." However, this composite jam is both mysterious and delicious.
➤ Please read about Making Jam, 835.
Hull and place in kettle, in layers:

Strawberries

pound for pound with:

Sugar

End with a layer of sugar on top. Allow this mixture to stand, covered, 12 hours. Now bring strawberries quickly to the boiling point and ➤ simmer with as little stirring as possible until the juice thickens, about 15 minutes. As strawberries usually appear a little in advance of the other fruits, these preserves may be placed in sterilized and sealed fruit jars and set aside until the other 4 fruits are available. Stem and seed:

Cherries

Stem:

Currants

Pick over:

Raspberries

Stem and head:

Gooseberries

The first 4 fruits are best used in equal proportions, but gooseberries have so much character that it is well to use a somewhat smaller amount, or their flavor will predominate. Bring the fruits separately or together to the boiling point. Add to each cup of fruit and juice:

3/4 cup sugar

➤ Simmer the jam until thick, about 30 minutes. Combine with the strawberry preserves which have been reheated to the boiling point.

QUICK APRICOT PINEAPPLE JAM

Prepare Sauce Cockaigne, 770.
Keep under refrigeration.

ROSE-HIP JAM

Wait to collect the hips until after the first frost. Do not use any which have been sprayed with poisonous insecticides.
➤ Please read about Making Jam, 835.
Place in a heavy stainless steel pan and ➤ simmer until fruit is tender, allowing:

1 cup water

to:

1 lb. rose hips

Rub through a fine sieve. Weigh the pulp. Allow, to each pound of pulp:

1 lb. sugar

➤ Simmer until thick.

APPLE BUTTER

About 5 Pints

For best results use Jonathan, Winesap, Wealthy or other well-flavored cooking varieties.
Wash, remove the stems and quarter:

4 lb. apples

Cook slowly until soft in:

2 cups water, cider or cider vinegar

Put fruit through a fine strainer. Add to each cup of pulp:

1/2 cup white or brown sugar

Add to the strained fruit:

1 teaspoon cinnamon
1/2 teaspoon cloves
1/4 teaspoon allspice
(Grated lemon rind and juice)

Cook the fruit butter over low heat, stirring constantly until the sugar is dissolved. Continue to cook, stirring frequently, until the mixture sheets from a spoon. You can also place a small quantity on a plate. When no rim of liquid separates around the edge of the butter, it is done. Pour into hot sterilized jars.

BAKED APPLE BUTTER

About 5 Quarts

A more convenient method than the above, as stirring is not necessary.
Wash and remove cores from:

12 lb. apples: Jonathan, Winesap or McIntosh

Cut them into quarters. Nearly cover with water. Cook gently about 1 1/2 hours. Put the pulp through a fine strainer. Measure it. Allow to each cup of pulp:

1/2 cup sugar

Add to the strained fruit:

Grated rind and juice of 2 lemons
3 teaspoons cinnamon
1 1/2 teaspoons cloves
1/2 teaspoon allspice

Bring these ingredients to the boiling point. Chill. Stir into them:

1 cup port, claret or dry white wine

Place about three-fourths of the purée in a large heat-proof crock. Keep the rest in reserve. Put the crock in a cold oven. Set oven at 300°. Let the apple butter bake until it thickens. As the purée shrinks, fill the crock with reserved apple butter. When the butter is thick, but still moist, put into sterile jars.

PEACH OR APRICOT BUTTER

About 5 Pints

Wash, peel, pit and crush:

4 lb. peaches or apricots

Cook very slowly in their own juice until soft. Stir. Put the fruit through a fine strainer. Add to each cup of pulp:

½ to ⅔ cup sugar

Add to the strained fruit:

2 teaspoons cinnamon
1 teaspoon cloves
½ teaspoon allspice
(Juice and grated rind of 1 lemon)

Cook as for Apple Butter, above.

DAMSON PLUM BUTTER

Wash and quarter:

Damson plums

Put them in a heat-proof crock, in a pan of boiling water, over direct heat. Cover the whole container and cook until the fruit is soft enough to purée. You may use a food mill shown on 832. To each cup purée allow:

1 cup sugar

Place in a heavy pan and ➤ stir over low heat at least 45 minutes or until the fruit butter is quite stiff. Place in hot sterilized jars.

MAKING PRESERVES AND CONSERVES

These, like jams, need only one cooking and can be made by several methods. The fruit may be placed in a crock or stainless steel pan in layers with equal parts of sugar, ending with the sugar layer on top, and allowed to rest covered 24 hours. The mix is then brought slowly to a boil in a pan and ➤ simmered, uncovered, until the fruit is clear. Alternatively, the fruit may be placed in a very small quantity of water in a heavy stainless or enamel pan with sugar, allowing ½ to ¾ cup of sugar per cup of fruit, depending on the sweetness of the fruit. The sugar and fruit are then brought slowly to a boil and ➤ simmered until the fruit is translucent. If using a thermometer, bring syrup to 9°F. higher than the temperature of boiling water in your locality. In either case, should the syrup not be thick enough, the fruit may be drained, put into sterile jars and kept hot while the syrup is simmered, uncovered, to the desired thickness. It is then poured over the fruit. Seal the preserves and store in a dark cool place.

SUNSHINE STRAWBERRY PRESERVES

Like the recipe for Waterless Grape Jelly, 834, this method is risky, but well worth taking the chance if it jells.

Arrange in a large kettle:

2 layers of washed, hulled, perfect strawberries

Sprinkle the layers with an equal amount of:

Sugar

Permit to stand for ½ hour. Heat over low heat until boiling, then ➤ simmer for 15 minutes. Pour the berries onto platters. Cover loosely with a glass or plastic dome, out of the reach of insects. Let the berries stand in the sun 2 or 3 days, until the juice forms a jelly. Turn the berries very gently twice daily. These preserves need not be reheated. Place in hot sterilized glasses and seal.

STRAWBERRY AND PINEAPPLE PRESERVES

➤ Please read about Making Preserves, above.

Combine:

1 quart hulled berries
4 cups sugar
1 cup canned pineapple
Rind and juice of ½ lemon

➤ Simmer these ingredients about 20 minutes. Stir frequently. When thickened, place in sterile jars.

STRAWBERRY AND RHUBARB PRESERVES

➤ Please read about Making Preserves, above.

Cut into small pieces:

1 quart rhubarb

Sprinkle over it:

8 cups sugar

Let these ingredients stand 12 hours. Bring quickly to the boiling point. Wash and hull:

2 quarts strawberries

Add to the rhubarb. ➤ Simmer the preserves until thick, about 15 minutes.

CHERRY PRESERVES

➤ Please read about Making Preserves, above.

Wash, stem, seed and place in pot, in layers:

Cherries

pound for pound with:

Sugar

If cherries are very sweet, ¾ pound sugar will suffice. End with a layer of sugar on top. Let the cherries stand covered 8 to 10 hours. Then bring this mixture slowly to a boil, stirring frequently. ➤ Simmer until tender—about 20 minutes. If the juice seems too thin, skim off the cherries and place them in sterile jars. Simmer juice until it thickens, then pour over cherries.

PEACH OR APRICOT PRESERVES

➤ Please read about Making Preserves, above.

Use firm, slightly underripe, well-flavored fruit. Peel and cut into lengthwise slices:

Peaches or apricots

The fruit may be dipped briefly into boiling water to facilitate the removal of skins. Remove the stones. Measure the fruit. Allow to each cup:

¾ cup sugar
2 tablespoons water
1½ teaspoons lemon juice

Stir this syrup and cook it 5 minutes. Add the fruit. You may omit the water and just pour the sugar over the peaches, letting them stand 2 hours before continuing. ➤ Simmer fruit until transparent. Place in glasses or jars. If the syrup seems too abundant, place the fruit in jars and reduce the syrup until thick. Pour over fruit. Add to the syrup:

(Lemon juice—about 2 teaspoons to every cup of fruit)

DAMSON, ITALIAN PLUM OR GREENGAGE PRESERVES

➤ Please read about Making Preserves, 837.
Wash, cut into halves and remove the seeds from:

Damsons, Italian plums or greengages

Stir into the plums an equal amount of:

Sugar

The sugar may be moistened with a very little water, or the fruit and sugar may be permitted to stand 12 hours before cooking. Bring the preserves to a boil, then ➤ simmer until the syrup is heavy. Add:

(2 minced seeded unpeeled oranges)
(½ lb. chopped walnuts)

QUINCE PRESERVES

➤ Please read about Making Preserves, 837.
Scrub:

Quinces

Slice them into eighths. Core and seed. Pare, reserving fruit, and put the peelings in a pan with just enough water to cover. To each quart of liquid, add:

1 sliced seeded lemon
1 sliced seeded orange

➤ Simmer this mixture until the peelings are soft. Strain, reserving only the liquid. Now weigh and add the quince slices. Weigh same quantity:

Sugar

Bring quince slices to a boil and add the sugar. Bring to a boil again. Then ➤ simmer until the fruit is tender. Place drained fruit in sterile jars. Continue to reduce the syrup until thick. Cover the fruit with the reduced syrup and seal.

HARVEST PRESERVES

➤ Please read about Making Preserves, 837.
Pare, core, seed and quarter equal parts of:

Tart apples
Pears
Plums

Prepare as for Quince Preserves, above.

TOMATO PRESERVES

➤ Please read about Making Preserves, 837.
Scald and skin:

1 lb. tomatoes

Yellow tomatoes may be used with especially fine results. Cover tomatoes with:

An equal amount of sugar

Let stand 12 hours. Drain the juice. Boil it until the syrup falls from a spoon in heavy drops. Add the tomatoes and:

Grated rind and juice of 1 lemon or
2 thinly sliced seeded lemons
2 oz. preserved ginger or
4-inch stick cinnamon

Cook the mixture until thick.

FIG PRESERVES

About 1 Quart

➤ Please read about Making Preserves, 837.
Wash and combine:

1 lb. finely cut unpeeled rhubarb
¼ lb. chopped stemmed figs
3 tablespoons lemon juice

Cover with:

1 lb. sugar

Let stand 24 hours in a cool place. Bring to a boil in a heavy stainless steel pan and ➤ simmer until thickened.

BAR-LE-DUC OR CURRANT PRESERVES

➤ Please read about Making Preserves, 837.
For use with Bar-le-Duc, 757. If you are a classicist, pierce the bottom of each berry and force the seeds through the opening after washing the berries.
Wash and stem:

Red or white currants

For 1 quart currants, cook to the soft-ball stage, 238°:

1½ cups sugar
½ cup honey
1¼ cups water

Drop the berries into the boiling syrup. Bring the syrup to the boiling stage again for 1 minute. Pour into sterilized glasses and seal.

GOOSEBERRY PRESERVES

These, being tart, complement a meat course, soft cream cheese or a sweet cake.
➤ Please read about Making Preserves, 837.
Wash:

1 quart gooseberries

Remove stems and blossom ends. Place in heavy saucepan. Add:

¼ cup water

Place over high heat. Stir. When boiling, add:

3 to 4 cups sugar

➤ Simmer preserves until the berries are clear and the juice thick, about 15 minutes.

KUMQUAT OR CALAMONDIN PRESERVES

About 3 Pints

➤ Please read about Making Preserves, 837.
Weigh:

3 lb. kumquats or calamondins

Separate pulp from skins and reserve it. Cover skins with:

Cold water

Cook until tender. If you do not like the bitter taste, drain several times during this process and replace with fresh water. When tender, drain and slice fine or grind the skins. Meanwhile, cover the pulp with:

3 cups water

and simmer 30 minutes. Strain the pulp and add to the juice:

3 cups water

Discard the pulp. Allow to each cup juice:

¾ cup sugar

Heat the juice and ➤ stir in the sugar until dissolved. Add the cut-up skins and cook until syrup jells.

ORANGE MARMALADE

About 4 Jelly Glasses

➤ Please read about Making Preserves, 837.
Fully ripe oranges may still have a greenish peel, but this has nothing to do with their minimum sugar content. Scrub well, cut into quarters and remove the seeds from:

2 large Valencia oranges
2 large or 3 small lemons

Add and simmer for 5 minutes:

3 cups water

Let stand covered for 12 to 18 hours in a cool place. Remove fruit and cut into very small shreds. Return to the water in which it was soaked. Boil 1 hour. Add for each cup of fruit mixture:

1 cup sugar

Boil the marmalade until the juice forms a jelly when tested, 833.

ORANGE, LEMON AND GRAPEFRUIT MARMALADE

About 18 Jelly Glasses

➤ Please read about Making Preserves, 837.
Scrub, cut into halves, remove the seeds and slice into very small pieces:

1 grapefruit
3 oranges
3 lemons

Measure the fruit and juice and add 3 times the amount of water. Soak 12 hours. ➤ Simmer about 20 minutes. Let stand again 12 hours. For every cup of fruit and juice, add:

¾ cup sugar

Cook these ingredients in small quantities, about 4 to 6 cups at a time, until they form a jelly when tested, 833.

LIME MARMALADE

About 3 Jelly Glasses

➤ Please read about Making Preserves, 837.
Cut the thin outer rind from:

6 small limes
3 lemons

Prepare as for Orange, Lemon and Grapefruit Marmalade, opposite.

TAMARIND MARMALADE

➤ Please read about Making Preserves, 837. Wash:

1 quart tamarinds

Cover with:

1½ cups water

➤ Simmer until soft. Put through sieve to remove fibers and seeds. Heat the pulp and allow for each cup:

1 cup sugar

➤ Simmer, stirring constantly, until the mixture thickens.

BLUE PLUM CONSERVE

About 20 Jelly Glasses

➤ Please read about Making Conserves, 837.
Peel and chop the thin colored rind of:

2 oranges
1 lemon

Add the juice and seeded, chopped pulp of:

3 oranges
1 lemon

and:

1¼ lb. ground seeded raisins
9 cups sugar

Seed and add:

5 lb. blue plums
4 pared, cubed peaches
(1 teaspoon whole cloves)

If you use the cloves, put them in a cheesecloth bag so you can remove them easily later. Cook the conserve slowly until fairly thick. Stir frequently. Add:

½ lb. chopped walnuts

➤ Simmer the conserve 10 minutes longer.

SWEET CHERRY CONSERVE

About 8 Jelly Glasses

➤ Please read about Making Preserves, 837.
Cut into very thin slices:

2 seeded oranges

Barely cover with water, about ¼ cup. Cook until very tender. Stem, seed and add:

1 quart sweet cherries

Add:

6 tablespoons lemon juice
3½ cups sugar
¾ teaspoon cinnamon
(6 cloves)

➤ Simmer the conserve until thick and clear.

SPICED RHUBARB CONSERVE

About 8 Jelly Glasses

➤ Please read about Making Conserves, 837.

Cut into very thin slices:

1 seeded orange
1 seeded lemon

Tie in a small bag:

1 oz. gingerroot
2 whole cloves

Add the spices, including:

¼ lb. cinnamon candy: redhots
¼ teaspoon mace

to the fruit with:

½ cup water
¼ cup vinegar

➤ Simmer these ingredients until the fruit is tender. Add and cook, until the conserve is thick:

1½ cups chopped rhubarb
3 cups sugar
(¼ cup white raisins)

TUTTI-FRUTTI COCKAIGNE, BRANDIED OR CROCKED FRUIT

A sort of liquid hope-chest, the contents of which may be served with a meat course or over puddings or ice cream. Be sure that during its preparation ➤ your container is big enough to hold all the ingredients you plan putting into it and, just as important, that ➤ you can store it in a consistently cool place, not above 45°, to prevent runaway fermentation. Place in a sterile stoneware crock or glass jar with a closely fitting lid:

1 quart brandy

Add, as they come into season, five of the following varieties of fruit—perfect and well-drained fruit only:

1 quart strawberries
1 quart seeded cherries
1 quart raspberries
1 quart currants
1 quart gooseberries
1 quart peeled sliced apricots
1 quart peeled sliced peaches
1 quart peeled sliced pineapple

Avoid apples, as too hard; bananas and pears, as too mushy; blackberries, as too seedy; and seeded grapes, unless skinned, as grape skins become tough. With each addition of fruit, add the same amount of:

Sugar

Stir the tutti-frutti every day with a wooden spoon until the last of the fruit has been added, securing the lid well each time. If you wish to prolong the life of the mixture, for every cup removed, replenish with 1 cup fruit, ¼ cup sugar and ¼ cup brandy.

PICKLES AND RELISHES

Peter Piper proved a pretty pampered pepper picker. Less privileged persons—such as you and we—are expected to pick produce unpickled and process it promptly ourselves. Pickling can be accomplished in several ways, some of them a bit lengthy, but none of them difficult. Granted that a considerable number of vitamins and minerals leach away into liquid residue during the pickling process, it remains a piquant and important method of food preservation.

In spite of the fact that our mothers never did it, it is now a recommended practice ➤ to subject pickles and relishes to a boiling-water bath, 804: 15 minutes for pint jars, 20 minutes for quarts.

PICKLING EQUIPMENT

Please read about care of and filling of jars, and other safety factors in Canning Processes, 802.
➤ Because of the acids involved in pickle making, be sure your equipment for brining is stoneware, pottery or glass, and that your pickling kettles are stainless steel or enamel. For stirring and for transferring the pickles, use a long-handled stainless, enamel-covered or slotted wooden spoon or a glass cup. Pack pickles in unflawed sterile glass jars with lids approved for pickling. All equipment should be absolutely clean and grease-free.

ABOUT PICKLING INGREDIENTS

For best results it is ➤ imperative that vegetables and fruit for pickling are in prime condition and are harvested no more than 24 hours in advance. If cucumbers have been held longer, they tend to become hollow during processing. If fruit or vegetables are very firm or slightly unripe ➤ be sure to cook them a little longer so brine can permeate to their centers. This will help keep fruit from floating to the tops of the jars later and will also discourage spoilage.

Black-spined varieties are the usual choice for cucumber pickles. They may be slightly underripe. ➤ Scrub them well to remove any dirt which might spark subsequent bacterial activity, and trim to retain 1/8 to 1/4 inch of stem.

If using garlic as a seasoning, parblanch 2 minutes before adding it to other ingredients, or remove it from the jar before sealing. ➤ Water used should be soft, 519. If you are in a hard-water area, you may want to use distilled water. If the water contains iron or sulfur compounds, the pickles will become dark.
➤ Use only pickling or dairy salt, free from additives which might deter processing, see About Salt, 568. ➤ Vinegar should test 5% to 6% acetic acid. Distilled white vinegar gives the lightest color. Cider-based malt and herb-flavored vinegars, although they yield a richer flavor, will darken pickles. You may want to make up and have ready to use one of the spice vinegars, 527. Homemade wine vinegars of uncertain strength should not be used, as the vinegar will "mother," 526.

Since spices vary so greatly in strength, 575, the amounts given are only approximate. Taste before bottling and dilute with more vinegar if necessary.
➤ Spices should be both fresh and whole. Ground spices darken the pickle; old spices impart a dusty flavor. Tie spices in a cloth bag for easy removal. If left in, they may cloud the liquid. Distillates, like the oils of cinnamon and of clove, are available at drug stores. They give a clearer pickle than steeped condiments, but the flavor is not so lasting.

➤ To make pickles crisp, wash unsprayed grape or cherry leaves and layer them with the cucumbers during the brining process. Discard leaves when making the pickles. Lime and alum are not recommended for crisping. Just a trifle too much alum may make the pickles bitter.

SHORT-BRINE PICKLING

Pickles produced under **long-brine** procedures, 848, require controlled conditions beyond the reach of the home cook. Accordingly, our recipes for homemade pickles are all of the less exacting **short-brine** type. These pickles are soaked in a salt solution only 24 hours or so. This brining period is sufficiently long to draw out moisture, ➤ but not long enough to induce the fermentation needed for adequate keeping. For this reason, an essential further step, after draining off the brine, is to pour over the produce a hot vinegar solution which penetrates the softened vegetable tissue and so preserves it.

In the short-brine process, pack the produce closely in sterile jars, 803, as soon as the brine is drained off and just before the addition of the vinegar. Heat the vinegar solution to the boiling point and fill the jars, leaving 1/4-inch headroom. Wipe the rims, adjust and seal the lids and process in a boiling-water bath 15 minutes, 804. By this time the interior of the jars should have reached 180°, enough to inhibit destructive enzymes. If a jar shows evidence of leakage or a poor seal, use the contents immediately, or replace the liquid with a fresh boiling pickling solution. Wipe the jars clean, refill them and reprocess 15 minutes in a boiling-water bath. The flavor of almost all pickled produce is improved if it is stored 6 weeks before using.

Keep an eye on your pickles after you have stored them away in a dark, dry, cool place where they cannot freeze; and if you detect evidences of fermentation, a bulging lid, leakage, or other signs of spoilage, do not eat or even taste the product. Destroy it, see 802!

YELLOW CUCUMBER PICKLES

About 14 Quarts

➤ Please read about Pickling Equipment and Ingredients, 841.

The cucumbers used here are simply green ones left on the vine for a spell after ripening. The large, luscious, firm, clear slices of this pickle are served very cold with meat. Pare, cut into strips of about 1½ x 2½ x ¾ inches, and seed:

1 bushel large yellow cucumbers

Soak the strips 12 hours in a:

10% Brine, 569

Drain, rinse and drain again. Sterilize 14 one-quart jars, 832. Place in each one:

A slice of peeled horseradish: 1½ x ⅓ x ⅓ inches
A ½-inch piece long hot red pepper
4 sprigs seeded dill blossoms
1 tablespoon white mustard seed
2 white peppercorns

Combine:

3 cups water
1 cup sugar
1½ gallons distilled white vinegar

Boil about 5 cups of this pickling solution at a time, enough to cover the bottom of a large saucepan to the depth of about ½ inch. Keep several pans going to hasten the process. Immerse in the ➤ boiling vinegar sufficient cucumber strips to cover the bottom of the pan. Let them come to the boiling point. Remove at once to the jars. Do not cook the strips longer, as it will soften them. When a jar is filled with cucumber strips, cover with boiling mixture. Seal and process 20 minutes in a boiling-water bath, 804, for quarts. Let the pickles ripen at least 6 weeks before serving.

SWEET-SOUR YELLOW CUCUMBER PICKLES OR SENFGURKEN

About 9 Quarts

➤ Please read about Pickling Equipment and Ingredients, 841.

Pare, cut into strips about 1½ x 2½ x ¾ inches, and seed:

12 large yellow cucumbers, see above

Soak them for 12 hours in:

10% Brine, 569

Drain, rinse and drain again. Have ready 8 or 10 sterilized quart jars, 832. Prepare the following mixture:

1 gallon pickling vinegar, 841
8 cups sugar
¼ cup mustard seed

Place in a cloth bag and add to this solution:

¾ cup whole mixed spices

➤ Boil about 5 cups of the mixture at a time, enough to cover the bottom of a large stainless steel or enamel pan to a depth of about ½ inch. Place bag of spices in pan. Immerse in the boiling vinegar sufficient cucumber strips to cover the pan bottom. Bring vinegar to boiling point. Remove strips at once. Place them in jars and fill jars with boiling vinegar mixture. Seal and process 20 minutes in a boiling-water bath, 804, for quarts.

SWEET-SOUR SPICED CUCUMBER PICKLES

About 24 Pints

➤ Please read about Pickling Equipment and Ingredients, 841.

These are wonderfully good. Scrub:

20 lb. very small cucumbers

Soak 24 hours in brine made of:

1 cup Pickling Salt, 569
3 quarts water: 12 cups

Remove from brine and add boiling water to cover. Drain quickly in a colander and pack closely while hot in sterilized jars, 832. Cover at once with the following vinegar mixture ➤ just at boiling point:

1 gallon cider vinegar
11 cups sugar

flavored with a spice bag of:

2 oz. whole mixed pickling spices
1 oz. stick cinnamon
1 teaspoon cloves

Seal jars at once. Process 15 minutes in boiling-water bath, 804, for pints.

BREAD AND BUTTER PICKLES

About 12 Pints

➤ Please read about Pickling Equipment and Ingredients, 841.

Wash well:

1 gallon medium-sized cucumbers: 4 quarts
6 to 12 large peeled onions or about 3 cups small white ones
2 green or red peppers, seeds and membrane removed

Proportions for this recipe may vary, as onion fanciers use the larger amount, and even more, of their beloved vegetable. Cut the unpared cucumbers and the peeled onions into the thinnest slices possible. Shred or chop the peppers. Place vegetables in a bowl. Pour over them:

½ cup Pickling Salt, 569

Place in refrigerator 12 hours, covered with weighted lid. Drain vegetables. Rinse in cold water. Drain again thoroughly. A cloth bag similar to a jelly bag is frequently used to let all the moisture drip from them. Prepare the following syrup:

4 cups mild cider vinegar
4 cups white or brown sugar
1½ teaspoons turmeric or allspice
2 tablespoons mustard seed
1½ teaspoons celery seed
½ teaspoon ground cloves or 1-inch stick cinnamon

Bring these ingredients ➤ just to the boiling point. Add vegetables gradually with very little stirring. Heat to the scalding point but do not let them boil. Pour the pickles into hot sterile jars. Seal and process 15 minutes in a boiling-water bath, 804, for pints.

PICKLED GHERKINS OR CORNICHONS

About 3 Pints

Wash thoroughly:
5 dozen very small French gherkins or tiny pickling cucumbers
Dry gherkins and place in glass or enameled bowl. Cover with:
¾ cup Pickling Salt, 569
Let mixture stand 24 hours. Drain and pack in sterile jars filled to 1¼ inch of top. Add to each jar:
5 white peppercorns
½ bay leaf
A few sprigs tarragon
Fill jars with boiling:
White wine vinegar flavored with tarragon
Let jars stand covered overnight, during which period the gherkins will lose their green color. Drain vinegar from jars into an enamel saucepan and add to suit your taste:
Pickling Salt, 569
Bring vinegar to boiling point. Remove liquid from heat; let cool to lukewarm. Pour it over the gherkins which will regain their color. These little pickles may be further flavored by the addition of:
(12 or more Pickled Onions, 845)
Seal jars. Process 15 minutes in a boiling-water bath, 804, for pints.

MUSTARD PICKLE OR CHOW CHOW

About 12 Pints

This formula meets with such enthusiastic approval that we are often tempted to abandon all other mixed pickle recipes.

➤ Please read about Pickling Equipment and Ingredients, 841.

Slice, unpared if tender:
1 quart or more green cucumbers
Cover 12 hours with:
10% Brine, 569
Keep covered until ready to use. Slice to make about 3 quarts of mixed green vegetables:
Green tomatoes, snap beans, green peppers, etc.
Pour over the vegetables to cover:
Boiling salted water: 1 teaspoon salt to 1 quart water
and bring to the boiling point. Drain well and set aside. Peel and slice into a separate bowl:
2 dozen small onions
Break into florets and add:
1 large cauliflower
Slice and add:
2 dozen or more small Pickled Gherkins, above
Pour over them sufficient boiling salted water to cover. Bring to the boiling point. Drain well and combine all vegetables. Have ready the following mustard sauce prepared in an enamel pan.
Combine and stir until smooth:
1½ cups flour
6 tablespoons dry mustard
1½ tablespoons turmeric
2 cups mild cider vinegar
Bring ➤ just to the boiling point:
2 quarts mild cider vinegar
2½ cups sugar
3 tablespoons celery seed
Slowly add the flour mixture, stirring constantly. When the sauce is smooth and boiling, combine it with the well-drained vegetables. Add if needed:
Salt
Place the pickle in sterile jars and seal. Process 15 minutes in boiling-water bath, 804, for pints.

CURRY SAUCE PICKLE

About 16 Pints

➤ Please read about Pickling Equipment and Ingredients, 841.

Pare, core, seed and chop finely:
12 large green cucumbers
Add:
6 finely chopped large onions
2 finely chopped sweet red peppers, seeds and membrane removed
Sprinkle these ingredients with:
¼ cup Pickling Salt, 569
Let stand refrigerated 3 hours. Drain, rinse, and drain again. Peel and cook until soft:
12 large tomatoes
Combine vegetables and tomatoes. Add to the above and ➤ simmer 30 minutes:
4 teaspoons curry powder
2 teaspoons celery seed
2 tablespoons brown sugar
2 cups cider vinegar
Pack the pickle into sterile jars, seal and process 15 minutes in boiling-water bath, 804, for pints.

OLIVE OIL PICKLE

Approximately 6 Pints

Wash:
24 cucumbers, 3 to 4 inches long
Cut them, unpared, into very thin slices. Sprinkle them with:
½ cup Pickling Salt, 569
Let them stand 3 hours. Drain well. Peel, slice very finely and add:

2 small onions
Combine and add:
1 cup white mustard seed
1 tablespoon celery seed
½ cup olive oil
4 cups vinegar
Mix all the ingredients thoroughly. Place them in sterile jars and seal. Process 15 minutes in a boiling-water bath, 804, for pints. The pickle should ripen for 3 weeks.

PICCALILLI

Approximately 10 Pints

➤ Please read about Pickling Equipment and Ingredients, 841.
Cut into very thin slices or dice:
4 quarts small green cucumbers
Seed, remove membrane and slice:
4 medium-sized green peppers
Skin and slice:
4 medium-sized onions
Place these ingredients for 12 hours in:
10% Brine, 569
Drain well. Bring ➤ just to the boiling point:
1 quart cider vinegar
4½ cups sugar
Place in a bag and add:
2½ tablespoons whole mixed spices
½ tablespoon celery seed
½ tablespoon mustard seed
Add the drained vegetables. Bring to the boiling point. Remove spices. Place the pickle in sterile jars, seal and process 15 minutes in boiling-water bath, 804, for pints.

GREEN TOMATO PICKLE OR RELISH

About 12 Pints

➤ Please read about Pickling Equipment and Ingredients, 841.
Wash and cut into thin slices:
1 peck green tomatoes
Peel, cut into thin slices and add:
12 large onions
Sprinkle with:
1 cup Pickling Salt, 569
Let stand refrigerated 12 hours. Rinse in clear water and drain. Heat to the boiling point:
3 quarts cider vinegar
Seed, remove membranes and add to the vinegar:
12 thinly sliced green peppers
6 diced sweet red peppers
Add:
12 minced cloves garlic
4 lb. brown sugar
2 tablespoons dry mustard
1 tablespoon salt
Add the tomatoes and onions. Tie in a cloth bag and add:
2 tablespoons whole cloves
2 sticks cinnamon: 3 inches each
2 tablespoons powdered ginger
1 tablespoon celery seed
➤ Simmer until tomatoes are transparent, about 1 hour. Stir frequently. Place the pickle in sterile jars and seal. Process 15 minutes in a boiling-water bath, 804, for pints. A fan writes that he puts the finished product in his ⅄ blender for a second or two before bottling his favorite relish.

GREEN TOMATO MOCK MINCEMEAT

About 10 Pints

For a meat-based mincemeat, see 812.
Sprinkle and let stand 1 hour:
1 tablespoon salt
over:
20 small cored and chopped green tomatoes
Drain the tomatoes, cover with boiling water and let stand 5 minutes before draining. Grate the rind and chop the pulp of:
1 orange
Mix the orange and tomatoes in a large saucepan and add:
12 medium pared, chopped apples
1 lb. seeded raisins
1½ cups chopped suet
3½ cups firmly packed brown sugar
½ cup vinegar
2 teaspoons cinnamon
1 teaspoon each cloves and nutmeg
½ teaspoon ginger
Cook mixture until boiling hot. Pour into hot sterile jars, leaving 1-inch headroom. Process pints 25 minutes at 10 pounds pressure, 804.

TART CORN RELISH

About 6 Pints

➤ Please read about Pickling Equipment and Ingredients, 841. Also please note: this is an unthickened relish—but a succulent one. If you should hanker after it in winter, use 9 cups canned or frozen kernel corn.
Boil 5 minutes:
18 medium-sized ears corn
Cut the kernels from cobs.
Put through a food grinder:
1 head green cabbage
8 peeled white onions
6 green peppers, seeds and membrane removed
6 small hot red peppers
Combine these ingredients with the corn and:
2 teaspoons celery seed
2 teaspoons mustard seed
2 quarts vinegar
¼ cup salt
2 cups sugar
(⅓ cup minced pimiento)
Bring ➤ just to the boiling point and simmer the relish for 35 minutes. Place in sterile jars, leaving ¼-inch headroom, seal, and process 15 minutes in boiling-water bath, 804, for pints.

PICKLED DILLED BEANS

4 Pints

➤ Please read about Pickling Equipment and Ingredients, 841.

Pack lengthwise in hot sterile jars, leaving ¼-inch headroom:

2 lb. stemmed tender green beans

To each pint jar add:

¼ teaspoon cayenne pepper
1 clove garlic
1 head dill or 1½ tablespoons dill seed

Bring to boil:

2½ cups water
2½ cups vinegar
¼ cup salt

Pour the mixture over the beans, leaving ¼-inch headroom. Seal the jars and process 15 minutes in a boiling-water bath, 804, for pints.

PICKLED CARROT STICKS

2 Pints

Colorful and tasty as an hors d'oeuvre.

Cook in boiling salted water 10 minutes:

1 lb. peeled, thinly sliced carrots

Meanwhile bring to a boil, then simmer 3 minutes:

¾ cup vinegar
¾ cup water
½ cup sugar
1 teaspoon mixed whole pickling spices

Drain the carrots and pack in hot sterilized jars, leaving ½-inch headroom. Cover with the hot pickling liquid, seal and process 15 minutes in a boiling-water bath, 804, for pints.

PICKLED ONIONS

➤ Please read about Pickling Equipment and Ingredients, 841.

To peel, cover with boiling water:

4 quarts small white onions

Let the onions stand for 2 minutes. Drain and dip in cold water, then peel. Soak onions refrigerated for 24 hours in:

10% Brine, 569, to cover

Drain and rinse well. Bring ➤ just to the boiling point:

2 quarts white vinegar
2 cups sugar

Add onions and ➤ simmer for 3 minutes. Place at once in sterile jars. Cover with the vinegar. Add to each quart jar:

½ inch red hot pepper pod
⅛ bay leaf
(3 cloves without heads)

Seal and process 30 minutes in boiling-water bath, 804, for pints.

PICKLED ZUCCHINI

Wash and cut into thin slices:

2 lb. unpeeled small zucchini
2 peeled medium-sized onions

Cover the above with cold water and add:

¼ cup Pickling Salt, 569

Let stand 2 hours, then drain thoroughly. Bring to a boil for 2 minutes:

3 cups cider vinegar
2 cups sugar
1 teaspoon celery seed
2 teaspoons mustard seed
1 teaspoon turmeric

Add the zucchini and onions, remove from heat, and let stand 2 hours. Heat ingredients to the boiling point and cook 5 minutes. Pack in hot jars, leaving ⅛-inch headroom. Seal and process 15 minutes in a boiling-water bath, 804, for pints.

PICKLED NASTURTIUM PODS OR SEEDS

Use these as a variation for capers.

After the blossoms fall, pick off the half-ripened:

Nasturtium seed pods

Continue as your crop develops to drop them into a boiled and strained mixture of:

1 quart white wine vinegar
2 teaspoons Pickling Salt, 569
1 thinly sliced onion
½ teaspoon each allspice, mace and celery seed
3 peppercorns

Keep refrigerated and use as desired.

CHILIS PRESERVED IN SHERRY

Make up this combination and use either the chilis or the sherry for flavoring.

Wash well:

Long thin red, yellow or green chili peppers

Pack tightly into sterile jars. Cover with:

Dry sherry

Cover and store in a cool dark place.

PICKLED WATERMELON RIND

About 10 Pints

More than acceptable in fruit cakes, if drained and finely chopped. ➤ Please read about Pickling Equipment and Ingredients, 841.

Cut before peeling and remove the green skin and pink flesh from:

Rind of 1 large watermelon: about 5 quarts

Dice the rind into 1-inch cubes. Parblanch it, 154, 3 minutes, until it can be pierced with a fork, ➤ but do not overcook. Drain. Make and bring ➤ just to a boil a syrup of:

7 cups sugar
2 cups vinegar
¼ teaspoon oil of cloves
½ teaspoon oil of cinnamon

Pour it over the rind, ➤ just covering it. Let stand overnight. Remove rind. Reboil syrup and pour over rind. Let stand overnight as before. On the third morning, pack the rind in sterile jars. Boil syrup again and pour over rind to overflowing. Seal and process 15 minutes in a boiling-water bath, 804, for pints. The flavor of this pickle may be varied by placing in each jar:

(A star anise)
(1 to 2 teaspoons chopped preserved ginger or Candied Lemon Peel, 795)

PICKLED DUTCH CHERRIES

➤ Please read about Pickling Equipment and Ingredients, 841. During processing this method needs an even temperature under 80°.
Stem, seed and put into a heavy crock:
Sour cherries
Cover with:
Distilled white vinegar
Let stand 24 hours. Drain. Measure cherries and have ready an equal amount of:
Sugar
Arrange in the crock alternate layers of cherries and sugar. Let stand 1 week, covered and weighted. ➤ Stir well daily. Ladle into sterile jars and process 15 minutes in boiling-water bath, 804, for pints. Store in a cool dark place.

SPICED PEARS

About 3 Pints

➤ Please read about Pickling Equipment and Ingredients, 841.

If you are using Bartlett or similar soft pears, choose rather underripe fruit and prepare as for Brandied Peaches, below. If you are using Kiefer, Seckel or other hard pears, prepare as follows.
Wash, peel and core:
3 lb. pears
Cook them ➤ covered until they begin to soften in:
1½ cups boiling water
Tie in a cloth bag:
6 cinnamon sticks: 3 inches long
2 tablespoons whole cloves
2 teaspoons whole ginger
and ➤ simmer for 5 minutes with:
2 cups sugar
1 cup white wine vinegar
Add the partially tenderized pears and the liquid in which they were cooking. Simmer with vinegar syrup 3 minutes. Remove and discard spice bag. Pack fruit into hot sterile jars and cover with the hot syrup. Seal jars and process in boiling-water bath 15 minutes, 804, for pints. Store in a cool dark place.

BRANDIED PEACHES

Select ripe, firm:
Peaches
Weigh them. Rub away fuzz with a coarse towel. Make a thick syrup of equal parts of:
Sugar and water: allow 1 cup sugar and 1 cup water for every lb. of fruit
➤ Simmer the peaches in the syrup 5 minutes. Drain and place in hot sterile jars. Pour over each jar:
2 to 4 tablespoons brandy
Pour the syrup over the fruit, filling the jars. Seal and process in boiling-water bath 15 minutes, 804, for pints. Store in a cool dark place 3 months before using. For other liqueur-flavored fruits, see 127 and 840.

INDIAN RELISH OR BASIC CHUTNEY

About 8 Pints

➤ Please read about Pickling Equipment and Ingredients, 841.
Put through a food chopper or chop until very fine:
12 green tomatoes
12 peeled cored tart apples
3 peeled onions
Boil:
5 cups vinegar
5 cups sugar
1 teaspoon red pepper
3 teaspoons ginger
1 teaspoon turmeric
1 teaspoon salt
Add the chopped ingredients. ➤ Simmer for ½ hour. Pack the relish in sterile jars. Seal and process 15 minutes in boiling-water bath, 804, for pints.

PEACH, MANGO OR KIWI CHUTNEY

12 or 14 Pints

A good way to use up those candied fruits left over from the holiday baking.
➤ Please read about Pickling Equipment and Ingredients, 841.
30 firm peaches
or use a combination of:
15 peeled tropical mangoes or kiwis and
8 medium papayas
Mix with:
3 tablespoons chopped preserved ginger
¾ cup chopped citron
¼ cup chopped candied lemon peel or
½ cup chopped preserved kumquats
Tie in a bag the following whole spices:
2 cinnamon sticks
30 whole cloves
¾ teaspoon coriander seeds
Make a syrup of:
6 cups sugar
4 cups cider vinegar
When the syrup ➤ just boils, add the chopped fresh and candied fruits and the spice bag. Simmer 5 minutes. Remove spice bag. Put mixture into sterile jars, seal and process 15 minutes in boiling-water bath, 804, for pints.

CURRIED APRICOT CHUTNEY

About 2 Pints

Combine and simmer for 30 minutes:
2 cups water
2 cups chopped dried apricots: 11-oz. package
¾ cup finely chopped onions
¼ cup sugar

In a separate pan, cook for 5 minutes:

1½ cups vinegar
1 teaspoon ginger
1½ to 2½ teaspoons curry powder
1 stick cinnamon
½ teaspoon salt

You may remove the stick of cinnamon before combining the apricot and spiced vinegar mixtures. Stir in:

2 cups white raisins: 10-oz. package

Place in sterile jars and process 10 minutes in a boiling-water bath, 804, for pints.

APPLE OR GREEN TOMATO CHUTNEY

I. **About 3 Pints**

➤ Please read about Pickling Equipment and Ingredients, 841.

➤ Simmer at least 2 hours or until the sauce has thickened, stirring frequently:

1 seeded chopped lemon
1 skinned chopped clove garlic
5 cups firm peeled chopped apples or green tomatoes
2¼ cups brown sugar
1½ cups seeded raisins
3 oz. chopped crystallized ginger, or ¼ cup fresh gingerroot
1½ teaspoons salt
¼ teaspoon cayenne
2 cups cider vinegar
(2 chopped red peppers, seeds and membrane removed)

Put the boiling-hot chutney in hot sterile jars and seal. Process 15 minutes in a boiling-water bath, 804, for pints.

II. **About 3 Pints**

Similar to the preceding recipe—but with onions and tomatoes added.

Combine and ➤ simmer slowly for 2 hours or until thickened:

2 cups chopped seeded raisins
2 cups chopped slightly underripe green apples
1 cup minced onion
1½ teaspoons salt
6 medium-sized ripe, skinned, quartered tomatoes
3½ cups brown sugar
1 pint cider vinegar
4 oz. white mustard seed
2 oz. preserved ginger
3 chili peppers

Place hot mixture in hot sterile jars, seal and process 15 minutes in a boiling-water bath, 804, for pints.

CHILI SAUCE

About 8 Pints

➤ Please read about Pickling Equipment and Ingredients, 841.

Wash, peel and quarter:

1 peck ripe tomatoes: 8 quarts

Put through a food grinder:

6 green peppers, seeds and membrane removed
(1 tablespoon dried hot pepper pods)
6 skinned large white onions

Add the tomatoes and:

2 cups brown sugar
3 cups cider vinegar
3 tablespoons coarse salt
1 tablespoon black pepper
1 tablespoon allspice
1 teaspoon ground cloves
1 teaspoon each ginger, cinnamon, nutmeg and celery seed
(2 tablespoons dry mustard)

➤ Simmer these ingredients slowly until very thick, about 3 hours. Stir frequently to prevent scorching. Add salt if needed. Put sauce in ➤ small sterile jars. Seal and process 15 minutes in boiling-water bath, 804, for pints. Store in cool dark place.

TOMATO CATSUP

About 20 Half-Pints

This condiment originated in Malaya, and its name derives from the native word for "taste." No other food so familiar to Americans seems to have so many variations in spelling.

➤ Please read about Pickling Equipment and Ingredients, 841.

Wash and cut into pieces:

1 peck tomatoes: 8 quarts

Add:

8 sliced medium-sized onions
2 long red peppers without seeds or membrane

➤ Simmer these ingredients until soft. Rub through a food mill, see chapter-heading illustration, 841. Add:

¾ cup brown sugar

Tie in a bag and add:

1 tablespoon each whole allspice, cloves, mace, celery seed and peppercorns
2 inches stick cinnamon
½ teaspoon dry mustard
½ clove garlic
1½ bay leaves

The spices may be varied. Boil these ingredients quickly, stirring often. ➤ Continue to stir until the quantity is reduced by one-half. Remove the spice bag. Add:

2 cups cider vinegar
(Cayenne and coarse salt)

➤ Simmer the catsup for 10 minutes longer. Pour at once into sterile jars, leaving ⅛-inch headroom. Seal and process 15 minutes in a boiling-water bath, 804, for half-pints.

GRAPE CATSUP

About 4 Pints

➤ Please read about Pickling Equipment and Ingredients, 841.

Cover:

5 lb. Concord grapes

with:

½ cup water

Bring to a boil. Put the softened grapes through a food mill, colander or sieve and add:

5 cups sugar
2 cups vinegar
1 teaspoon salt

Tie in a bag and add to above:

½ cup mixed pickling spices

Simmer and stir until thick. Remove spice bag and pour the grape mixture into hot sterilized jars. Seal and process 15 minutes in a boiling-water bath, 804, for pints.

WALNUT CATSUP

About 3½ Quarts

➤ Please read about Pickling Equipment and Ingredients, 841.

Pick and bruise:

100 immature green English walnuts

still so soft they can be pierced through with a needle. Put them into a crock with:

2 quarts vinegar
6 oz. salt

Cover, mash and stir daily for 8 days. Drain the liquid and put it into an enamel or stainless steel pan with:

4 oz. finely chopped anchovies
12 finely chopped shallots or
1 clove chopped garlic
½ cup grated fresh horseradish
½ teaspoon each mace, nutmeg, ginger, whole cloves and peppercorns

Cover and bring mixture to a boil, then ➤ simmer gently about 40 minutes. Filter, cool and add:

2 cups Port

Pour into sterile glass bottles. Cork well. Cover the corks with wax. Store in a cool dry place.

PICKLED HORSERADISH

Wash well in hot water:

Horseradish roots

Scrape off the skin. Have ready in a glass or stainless steel bowl a combination of:

2 cups vinegar
1 teaspoon salt

Grate, mince or ⅄ blend the scraped roots and pack into sterile jars. Cover well with the vinegar mixture. Seal and store in refrigerator.

WORCESTERSHIRE SAUCE

About 5 Half-Pints

Put into a jug:

1 quart cider vinegar
6 tablespoons Walnut Catsup, above
5 tablespoons essence of anchovies, or
2 oz. finely chopped anchovies
4 tablespoons Chili Sauce, above
A tiny pinch cayenne
1 teaspoon salt
1 tablespoon sugar

Cork and shake 4 times daily for 2 weeks. Strain into sterile bottles. Cork tightly and store in a cool place.

LONG-BRINE AND SOUR PICKLING

If produce is soaked for long enough period at proper temperatures, a mere brine will suffice to preserve it. The salt solution draws from the vegetables soaked in it both moisture and certain natural sugars, and these combine to form an acid bath which "cures" the produce, making it friendly to beneficial ferments and strong enough to resist the organisms that cause spoilage in food. Pickles subjected to the long-brine process and held at 86° from 2 to 6 weeks turn, after appropriate seasoning, into "dill" types; but see our adaptation below. They may be desalted and further processed in a vinegar solution at 126° for 12 hours to make sour pickles and then in a sugar solution to become sweet-sours.

To learn the details for these long and exacting processes, read "Making Pickles and Relishes at Home" in the U.S.D.A. Home and Garden Bulletin 92.

DILL AND KOSHER DILL PICKLES

About 7 Pints

This procedure bypasses that for long-brined dill pickles. The brine is weaker and the curing more rapid; but the pickles do not keep so well, especially if home-processed. We suggest using a heated brine. Garlic, like all members of the onion family, is very susceptible to bacterial activity, so be sure to remove the garlic cloves before sealing the jars. Wash thoroughly and cut in half lengthwise:

4 lb. cucumbers

Combine and heat to the boiling point:

3 cups white vinegar
3 cups water
⅓ cup Pickling Salt, 569

If you want to create **Kosher Dills**—without benefit of clergy—add:

12 peeled sliced garlic cloves

When the boiling point is reached ➤ remove the garlic cloves. Pack the cucumbers into hot sterile jars. Add to each jar:

2 tablespoons dill seed
3 peppercorns

Fill the jars to within ½ inch of the top with the hot pickling liquid. Immediately adjust lids. ➤ Be sure to use lids recommended for pickling. Seal and process in boiling-water bath 15 minutes, 804, for pints.

BRINING VEGETABLES

If sufficient salt is used to brine vegetables, no fermentation can take place and no further processing is necessary. This is referred to as *dry salting*.

Pack in a crock in very thin layers:

Mushrooms, beans, herbs or other vegetables

well separated with at least ½- to ¾-inch layers of:

Rock salt

Cover the crock tightly and store in a cool dark place. ➤ **Boil the vegetables uncovered 20 minutes before serving.** Stir frequently during this period.

SAUERKRAUT

In brining vegetables with less salt than in the recipe above, it is essential to process them in a boiling-water bath and to observe the cooking period recommended below.

➤ Please read about Pickling Equipment and Ingredients, 841.

A 2-gallon crock holds about 15 pounds of kraut. Choose sound, mature heads of:

Cabbage

Use:

1 lb. salt for 40 lb. cabbage, or 2 teaspoons salt for 1 lb. cabbage

Remove outside leaves, quarter the heads, and cut out cores. Slice the cabbage finely into 1/16-inch shreds and mix with salt. Pack firmly in stone crocks to within 2 inches of top. Cover with a clean cloth and a plate, or any board except pine. Place a weight on the plate—heavy enough to make the brine come up to the cover and wet the cloth. When fermentation begins, remove the scum daily and place a clean cloth over the cabbage, see the chapter-heading illustration, 802. Wash the plate or board daily, too.

The best quality kraut is made at a temperature below 60° and requires at least a month of fermentation. It may be cured in less time at higher temperatures, but the kraut will not be so good. If sauerkraut turns tan, too much juice has been lost in the fermenting process. When fermentation has ceased, store the kraut in a cool place after sealing by either of the following methods: simply pour a layer of hot paraffin over the surface of the crock; or, for greater effectiveness, ➤ heat kraut to simmering temperature, about 180°; pack firmly in hot jars; add sufficient kraut juice or a weak brine—2 tablespoons salt for 1 quart water—to cover, leaving ½-inch head space, and process in boiling-water bath, 804, 25 minutes for pints, 30 minutes for quarts.

➤ **Boil the sauerkraut, uncovered, 20 minutes before serving, see 802.**

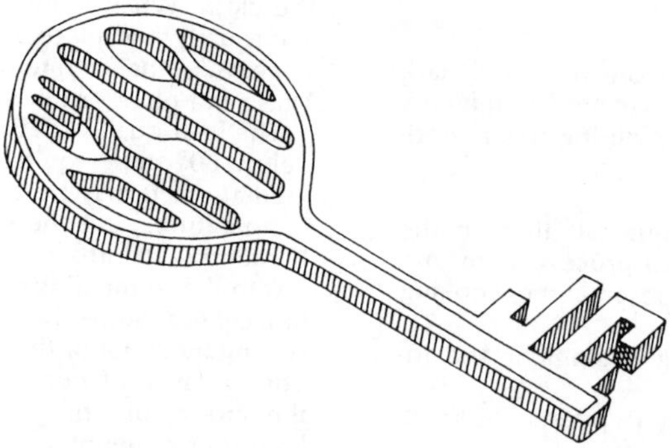

INDEX

"Knowledge," said Dr. Johnson, "is of two kinds. We know a subject as our own, or we know where we can find information on it." Below we put into your hands the second kind of knowledge—a kitchen-door key which will help to open up the first.

If you want information on a certain food, you will find that the initial listing is often an "About," giving characteristics, peculiarities of handling, tests for doneness, storage needs and serving quantities. The titles which follow usually indicate how that particular food may be cooked: Sweetbreads, braised, or Fish, broiled.

In using the Index look for a noun rather than an adjective: Cake, almond, not Almond Cake; unless the modifying term is a foreign one, in which case it will be listed and lead you to an explanation. Foreign terms are frequently translated in an alternate title, thus: Pickled Fish or Escabèche, revealing a process; or, as in Senegalese or Chicken Curry Soup, showing the ingredients mainly responsible for the term. Or the recipe itself will clear your doubts—"à la mode" used with a savory food like beef will describe a stew, whereas with a sweet one, like pie or cake, it will indicate the expected scoop of ice cream. Since cooking terms, both foreign and domestic, are dealt with at the point of use, as described above, we have dispensed with a separate glossary.

Remember, too, that the book as a whole divides into three sections—The Foods We Eat, The Foods We Heat and The Foods We Keep—with Know Your Ingredients at the center of things; and that many "convenience" recipes are grouped under Lunch, Brunch and Supper Dishes. Within chapters, too, initial text or recipes often cover basic methods of preparation, and are followed, as in Fruits, Fish and Vegetables, by alphabetical listings of varieties—from Acerola to Tamarind, Carp to Sea Squab, Artichoke to Zucchini. Under Meats you will find in the Index general comments and processes, with further references to Beef, Veal, Lamb, Pork, Ham, Ground and Variety Meats and Game. In this chapter a further differentiation is made between those cuts cooked by dry heat—often a quick process—and those cooked by moist heat, which, to be effective, is always slower. Note, too, that in the listings below, you can find the illustrations immediately by looking up the boldface numerals.

As you familiarize yourself with the **Joy**, you will need the Index less and less and will become, in the fullest sense of Dr. Johnson's words, a know-it-all. Meanwhile, happy hunting!

A

À blanc, defined, 447
À l'anglaise coating, 552, **552**
À la mode, defined, *see* Apple Pie, 651
  as savory, 460, 461, 509, 514
À l'étouffée, defined, 151
À point, defined, 145
Abalone, about, 383; sautéed, 383
Accessory factors in food, 6
Acerola, 143
Acid foods, canning of, 802–808
Additives, about, 798
African, West, Beef Stew, 462
Agar, 561
Agrodolce Sauce, 354
Ail, 584, **585**
Aioli Sauce, 365
Akee, puréed, 143, **143**
Al burro, defined, 213
Al dente, defined, 213
ALCOHOLIC BEVERAGES, 48–65; *see* Drinks
Ale, about; to serve, 58; glasses, **58**
Allemande Sauce, 345
Allergy substitute flour, 551
Allium, broad-leaf wood, 585, **586**
Allspice, 575
Allumette, defined, 277
Almonds, 563; *also see* Cakes, Cookies
  bitter, 563
  blanching, 154, 562
  burnt, or sugared, 789
  butter, 350
  creams, 789
  crescents, 713
  fillings, 622; custard, 699; fig or raisin, 698
  garnish or Amandine, 553
  leaves, 715
  milk, about, 535; to make, 745
  oil, 563
  paste, 780
  pretzels, 713
  rings, meringue, 710
  sauce, cucumber, 357
  torte Cockaigne, 685
Alternate foods, 535
Amandine Garnish, 553
Amber Pie, *see* Transparent Pie, 653
Ambrosia, 124; sauce, quick, 770
Amino acids, 2
Ammonium bicarbonate, 556
Anchovy, defined, 411
  butter, 350
  caper sauce, 361
  cheese, 81
  cucumber casserole, 302
  dressings, 361; green peppers stuffed with, 316
  hors d'oeuvre, 81, 88
  paste; pesto, 570
  rolls, 88
Anchovy *(cont.)*
  sauce, 343, 361
  seasoning, as; to desalt, 570
  stuffing for tomatoes, 334
Andalouse Sauce, 364
Angelica, herb, 580
  parfait, 762
  roots and stalks, candied, 797
Angel Slices, 703
Angels on Horseback, 76
Anise, 580
  drop cookies, 707
  tisane, 40
Annatto, 575
Anti-Browning Solution, for canning, 805; for freezing, 823; for fresh fruits, 124
Antipasto, about, 78
Apéritifs, about, 56
Appetizer, *see* Canapés; Hors d'Oeuvre
Apple, about, 129; *also see* Fruit
  baked, 130; with sausage, 130, 259
  beets, sweet-sour, 290
  bread, quick, 624
  butters, 836
  cake, sour cream soufflé, Cockaigne, 741
  cake Cockaigne, 661; French, 661
  candied, 795, **795**
  canning, 806
  casserole, and onion, 313
  chutney, 847
  cider, canning, 806
  Cockaigne with cinnamon drops, 131
  crisps, 661, 662
  dressings, 372, 374
  dried, about, 125
  filling for coffee cakes, 622
  glazed, 130; honey, 130
  jelly, 834
  juice, freezing, 824
  pie, 651; deep-dish, 660
  pudding, steamed, molasses, 755
  rings, 129
  salad, 109; molded, 118
  sautéed, and bacon, 130
  strudel, 648
  stuffed with sauerkraut, 131
  and sweet potatoes, 325
  tart, 652
Applejack, 52
Applesauce, 131; canning, 806; freezing, 824
  cake, 678
  and cranberry or other fruit, 131
Apricot, about, 131
  bars, meringue, 703
  Betty, 751
  bread, quick, 624
  butter, 837
  cake, chocolate, 677
  candies, 793

Apricot *(cont.)*
canning, 806
chutney, curried, 846
dressing, 373
dried, cooked, 131
filling, custard, 698; for coffee cake, 622; for cookies, 717
glaze, 732
ice, 766; ice cream, 760
icing, 729
jam, and pineapple, 836
marinade, 529
mousse, 764
pie, 653
preserves, 837
sauce, 356
soufflé or whip, 741; omelette, 742
Aquavit and aquavit cocktails, about, 53
Arab or Armenian Bread, 609
Armadillo, 516
Arrowroot flour or starch, 550
thickener for sauces, 339
Artichokes, about, 282
canning, 808
to eat, 282
globe; uncored, 282, **282;** cored, **282,** 283
hearts, 283
Jerusalem, **276,** 283
salads, 100
stuffed, baked, 283
to wash, 282
Arugula, 93
Asparagus, 283, **284**
aspic with celery, 115
canapés, 73
canning, 808
and creamed eggs Cockaigne, 224
salads, 100
sandwich, 73; and ham, 272
soup, cream of, 182; quick, 191
spears, garnished, 83
timbale, 232
Aspic, *also see* Gelatin
about, 113; additions to, 113
asparagus and celery, 115
cucumber, 114
eggs in, 117
fish in, Cockaigne, 401
garnish, 114
glaze, 368
salads, 113–120; basic, 113
shrimp, glazed, 89
tomato, with tasty centers, 81; canned, 115
tongue in, 508
to unmold, 561, **561**
vegetable juice, 115
wine or liquor in, 113
Attereaux, defined, 147
Au gras, defined, 520
Au gratin, about, 552
Au maigre, defined, 167, 520
Au ruban, defined, *see* Genoise, 675
Aubergine or eggplant, about, 302
Aurore Sauce, 344
Avgolemono, 172
Avocado, about, 131; to slice, **110**
and chutney, 83
cups for salad, 110
dressing, 362
salads, 110, **110;** molded, 117
soup, cream of, chilled, 191
spread or guacamole, 83
to store, 110, 132
stuffed with creamed food, baked, 132

B

Baba au Rhum, 689
Backpacking menu suggestions, 35, **35**
Bacon, about, 485; baked; sautéed, 486
apples, sautéed and, 130
with beans, baked, 259
Canadian, 486
canapés and cheese, 72
cornmeal waffles, 241
and rice custard, 208
rings, eggs baked in, 224
sandwiches, 272–274
sauce, sweet-sour, 354
seasoning, as, 572
white, *see* Salt Pork, 814
Bagels, 617, **618**
Bagna Cauda, 90
Baked Alaska, 742; pan for, 769, **769**
in orange cups, 742
Baking, defined, 146
pan placement, 159, **159**
Baking powder, about; homemade, 555
Baking soda, about, 555
with acid ingredients, 555
Baklava, 794
Bamboo shoots, 276, 284; stuffed, 84
Banana, about, **123,** 132; baked, 132
in blankets, 132
breads, 624
cake, Cockaigne, 680
Caribbean, 132
chocolate-dipped, 132
filling, custard cream, 697
freezing, 132, 822
leaves, stuffed, 153
pie, cream, 656
to ripen, 132; to store, 132
salad, orange and nut, 111
sherbet, pineapple, 768
Banbury Tarts, 654
Barbecue, *also see* Meat, Poultry, Outdoor
about, 146, 158, **158**
coleslaw for, 97
frankfurters, 258
sauces, 354
vegetables for, about, 282
Barding, fowl, 420, **420**
Bar-le-Duc, 757
preserves, 838
Barley, cereal, to cook, 200
flour, 550

Barley *(cont.)*
seeds, 564
soup, 174
Barquettes for Canapés, 69
Bars and Squares, 701–704; *see* Cookies
Basil, 580; Pesto, 570
Basting, 446, **446**
Batter, blooms in, 243
cakes, *see* Pancakes
fritter, about, 242; for fruit, vegetables, meat and fish, 242–243
griddle cakes, or, 236
to mix for cake, 664, 665, **665**
Baumwollsuppe, 172
Bavarian Creams, 746–748
berry, 747
cabinet pudding, 746
caramel or maple, 747
chocolate or coffee, 747
collar for, 746
de luxe, 746
eggless, 748
hazelnut, 747
Nesselrode, 747
pineapple, molded, 748
to unmold, 561, **561,** 746
Bay leaf, 580
BEANS, about, 284, **285**
baked, and bacon or frankfurters, 259
baked; with fruit, 288
boiled, 288
broad, 289
butter, 289
campfire, 288
canning, dried, 809; green, snap or wax, 808
dried, *see* Dried Legumes, 286
dried, casserole, 287
dried, patties, 287
dried, salad, 100
dried, soup, 176
fava, 284, **285**
flour, 550
fresh, about, 285
green, additions to, 285
green, casserole, 285
green, potatoes and smoked meat, 286
green, puréed, 286
green, salads, 101
kidney, canned, and tomatoes, 288
kidney, with rabbit, 515
lima, about, **285,** 289; canning, 808
lima, casserole, 255; and sausage, 260
lima, chili, 289
lima, dried, 286; *see* Dried Legumes
lima, mushrooms and, 290
lima, puréed, 286
marinated, 83
pickled, dilled, 845
pinto, and rice, 288
preprocessed, 286
puréed, 286; dried, 287
refried, or Frijoles Refritos, 287
to roast, 564

BEANS *(cont.)*
salad, Viennese, and herring, 107
snap, 285, **285;** canning, 808
soups, 176–177
soy, *see* Soybeans
soy, edible, 285, **285**
to sprout, 565
sweet-sour, 286
wax, canning, 808
white, 287
Bean sprout, salad, 96; cooked, 286
Bear, 517
Béarnaise Sauce, 359; about, 357; blender, 359
Beating, methods of, 664–665, **665**
Beaver, 516; tail, 516
Béchamel Sauce, *see* White sauce
Beechnuts, 563
BEEF, 453–466; 486–493; *also see* Meat
about, 453
balls, *see* Meatballs
Boeuf Bourguignonne, 460
Boeuf à la Mode, 460, glazed, 461
Boeuf Fondu Bourguignonne, 457
boiled, or Boeuf Bouilli, 461
brisket with sauerkraut, 461
burgers, filled, 488
burgoo, Kentucky, 465
to carve, **454**
casseroled, with fruit, 463
chart of cuts, **451**
chili con carne, 490
chipped, *see* Chipped Beef, 260
chuck, pot roast, 459
chuck roast, in foil, 463
corned, *see* Corned Beef, 466
cuts from 250-pound side of, 452
daube glacé, 461
dried, *see* Chipped Beef, 260
eye of the rib, about, **452,** 453
Filet de Boeuf en Croûte, 455
fillet, Tournedos, defined, 454, **454**
fillet or tenderloin of, about, 454, **454**
Goulash, Gulyàs or Pörkölt, about, 464
ground, 486; *also see* Hamburgers and Meatballs
ground, or biff à la Lindström, 488
ground, canning, 811
hamburgers, filled, 488
hash, with potatoes and mushrooms, 261
hash, red flannel, 466
heart, 508
jerky, 814
juice, 170, 520
kebabs or on skewers, 459
kidney, *see* Kidneys
large cuts, suggested uses, 452, **452,** 453
lifters, 452, **452**
liver, Creole, 501; patties, baked, 489
loaf Cockaigne, 493
marinade for, 529
New England boiled dinner, 466
oxtail, braised or stew, 511
oxtail soup, 179

BEEF *(cont.)*
pot pie, quick, 252
pot roast, 459, 463
ribs, economical use of, 452, **452**
roast, 454, **454;** canning, 811
roast, chuck, 459, 463
roast, in sauce, 262
roast, strip sirloin, 454
rolls, roulades or paupiettes, 465
salad, 109
sandwiches, hot roast, 270
Sauerbraten, 460
short ribs, about, 452, **452,** 464
soup meat, 463
with spaghetti, quick, 217
Spanish casserole with rice, 491
spiced, 463
steak, blade chuck, 456
steak, broiled, 456; pan-broiled, 457
steak, canning, 811
steak, club or minute, 455, **456**
steak, cooking, about, 456; cuts, about, 455
steak, cube, defined, 456
steak, Delmonico, 455, **456**
steak, filet mignon, defined, 454; broiled, 456, 457
steak, fillet, broiled, 456; pan-broiled, 457
steak, fillet, Chateaubriand, defined, 454; broiled, 456, 457
steak, flank, defined, 456; London Broil, 457; with dressing, 464
steak, and green peppers, 464
steak, hamburger, defined, 456
steak-and-kidney pie, 465
steak, for moist heat, 456
steak, peppered or au poivre, 457
steak, planked, 457
steak, porterhouse, 455, **456**
steak, rib or rib eye, 455, **456**
steak, round, 456
steak, rump, 456
steak, Salisbury, defined, 456
steak, sauces, *see* Sauces
steak, short loin cuts, 455, **456**
steak, sirloin cuts, 455, **455**
steak, strip, 455
steak, Swiss, 456, 463
steak, Tartare, or cannibal balls, 86
steak, T-bone, 455, **456**
steak, tournedos, defined, 454, **454**
stew, Belgian or carbonnade flamande, 461
stew, Gaston, 459
stew, Mulligan, 465
stew, West African, 462
stew with kidneys, 506
stew with wine or boeuf Bourguignonne, 460
Stroganoff, 458
sukiyaki, 458; to eat with chopsticks, **459**
tea, 170
tenderloin, 454
tongue, 507, 508
Wellington, 455
yield from side of beef, 452

Beer, about; serving, 58, **58**
bock, 58
in fritter batter, 243; in soup, 168
marinade for beef or pork, 529
sauce, raisin, 356
Beet, cooked, 290; baked, 291
boiled, in sour cream, 290
canning, 809; pickled, 809
casseroled, 290
consommé, jellied, 174
dressing, anchovy and, 361
greens, 291; young beets and leaves, 291
salads, 96, 101; gelatin, 116
soup or borsch, 175
stuffed, Cockaigne, 83
sweet-sour and apple, 290
sweet-sour or Harvard, 290
Beignets or French fritters, 244, 246
Belgian endive, 299
Belgian Stew, or Carbonnade Flamande, 461
Benne seed, 564; wafers, 706
Bercy Butter, 350; kidneys with, 505
Berry, 133; *also see individual fruits*
about, 133; canning, 806
Bavarian cream, 747
Cockaigne, 133
cones, 133, **133**
freezing, 822–823
fresh, self-garnished, 133
jams and preserves, 835–837
jellies, 833–834
pies, 650–651; *see* Pies
Beurre
de Provence, *see* Aioli Sauce, 365
manié, 340
noir, 350
noisette, 349
BEVERAGES, *also see individual names*
alcoholic, *see* Drinks
garnishes for, 42, **42**
juices, about, 42; blended, 44
milk, 42
nonalcoholic, 36–47
party, about, 45
punches, 45, 46
"soft" drinks, about, 46
Bigarade, Duck, 433; Sauce, 355
Birthday Bread Horse, 635, **635**
BISCUIT, 632–634
about; additions to, 632
beaten, 634
buttermilk, 634
drop, quick, 633
Easter bunnies, 633, **633**
fluffy or shortcake dough, 633
griddle, 634
hot, with filling, 270
pinwheel, 633
rolled, 632
scones, 634
ship's, 634
sticks, 634
whole wheat, 633

Biscuit Tortoni, 762
Bishop's Bread, 627
Bisque, defined; see Soups, 174
Black Bottom Gelatin Pie, 658
Black Pudding, 497
Blackberry, 133, 134; canning, 806
jam, 836
pie, 650
Blanchaille, 415
Blanching, about, 154; for canning, 803
chart for freezing, 825
for freezing fruits, 822; vegetables, 824
nuts, 562
Blancmange, 738, 745
Blanquette de Veau, 470
Blender, electric, **336;** *look for blender symbol* ⅄
Blini or Russian Raised Pancakes, 238
Blintzes, 237
Bloaters, defined, 407; grilled or baked, 408
Blood
sausage, 497
as thickener, 339
Blossoms, *also see* Flowers
in batter, 243
candied and glazed, 794
as garnish, **194,** 194–195
Blowfish or sea squab, about, 411
Blueberry, about, 133; canning, 806
freezing, 822–823
jam, 835
muffins, 631
pie, 650; tart, 651
Boar, wild, 517
head, stuffed, **513,** 517; stuffing for, 518
Boeuf Bouilli, 461
Boeuf Bourguignonne, 460
Boeuf Fondu Bourguignonne, 457
Boeuf Miroton, 262
Boeuf à la Mode, 460, 461
Boiling, about, 149; high altitudes, 520
water bath, 804
Bok-choi, 292, **293**
Bologna Cornucopias, 86
Bolognese Pasta Sauce, 353
Bombes, 760–764; see Ice Creams
Bones for Stocks, 521
Bonito, fresh, 415
Bonne Femme, defined, 401
Borage, as vegetable, 580
Bordelaise Sauce, 347
Borsch, 175; blender, 191
Boston Brown Bread, 626
cream pie or cake, 689
Botulinus toxin, about, 802
Bouchées, 645, **645**
Boudin Blanc, 498
Boudin Noir or blood sausage, 497
Bouillabaisse, 188, 189
Bouillon, see Soups, 167
Court; Blanc, 525
Boula-Boula, 178
Bouquets Garnis or Faggots, 572
Bourbon Balls, 790
drinks, 49–51
pie, *see* Pecan Pie, 653
whisky, about, 50
Bourguignonne, Boeuf Fondu, 457
sauce, 350
Boysenberry, 134; canning, 806
Brains, about, 504
baked, and eggs, 504
boiled, 504
fritters, calf, 244
sautéed, 504
Braising, about, 447
Bran, *also see* Bread, Rolls, Muffins
flour, 548
muffins, 630
Brandade de Morue, 405
Brandy and brandy drinks, about, 52
fruit, Tutti-Frutti, 840
glasses for, **57,** 58
snaps, 719
Braunschweiger sandwich, toasted, 272
Brawn, 511
Brazier cooking, foods for, **156,** 157, **157**
BREAD, 599–637
all-rye flour, 608
all-rye honey cake Cockaigne, 626
all-rye sticks, 617
apple or apricot, quick, 624
banana, quick; wheat-germ, 624
bases for canapés, 68
batters, about, 599
birthday horse, to make, 635, **635**
biscuits, *see* Biscuits, 632–634
Bishop's, 627
blocks, cheese or butter, 635; puffed, 635
bran date, quick, 625
breading, 552
brioche loaf Cockaigne, 605
brown, Boston steamed, 626; baked, 626
buckwheat corn, 628
carrot-nut, quick, 625
cases, or croustades, 250
cheese, 604
cinnamon loaf, 604; quick, 636
coating à l'anglaise, 552
cooling and storing, 602
corn, about, 627; *see* Cornmeal Breads
corn, skillet, 628
cornmeal, salt-rising, 606
cracked-wheat, 608
cranberry, quick, 624
croutons, 551
crumbs, *see* Crumbs; about, 551
crusts, about, 602
date, quick, 623
dill batter loaf, 604
dough, additions to, 602
dough, kneading and proofing, 600, **600, 601**
dough, mixer method, 600; mixing, 599
dough, sponge; straight, about, 599
dough, yeast, shaping, 601, **601;**
French dough, 606, **606**

BREAD *(cont.)*
dressing ring with hash, 262
dressings, 370–374
egg or Challah, 605, **605**
fermented milks in, 533
flatbreads, Armenian, Arab, etc., 609
flour, 547
French, **599,** 605, **606**
frozen for canapés, 829
garlic, toasted and buttered, 636, **636**
ginger, *see* Cakes
glaze for, 732
gluten, 609
grissini, **599,** 606
herb, 604; toasted and buttered, 636, **636**
at high altitudes, about quick rising, 601
honey, *see* Cockaigne, 607
honey all-rye eggless, Cockaigne, 626
honey loaf, quick, 623
hook and mixer, **599**
Irish soda, quick, **625**
leftovers, uses for, **635**
loaf with cheese and nuts, 254
melba toast, **636**
nut, 603; quick, 623
oat, Cockaigne, 608
olive-nut, quick, 625
orange, quick, 624
pans, 602
pizzas, 610
popovers, 631–632
potato, salt-rising, 607
pretzels, 618
prune, 603; quick, 624
puddings, *see* Puddings
pumpkin, quick, 624
raisin, 603
rolls, *see* Rolls
rye, sourdough, 609
rye, Swedish, **599,** 608; *also see* Bread, all-rye
rye flour, 608
Sally Lunn, quick, 623
salt-rising, 606
sandwiches, about, 67, **67**
sauce, 343
to serve with soup, 195; with hors d'oeuvre, 79
skillet or griddle, 627–629
sourdough, 603; sourdough rye, 609
soy whole wheat, 608
sponge, 599
spoon, 629
sticks, white, whole-grain, graham or rye, 617
sticks or grissini, **599,** 606
stollen, 620
to substitute for wheat flour, 602
tea, quick, 623–627
temperature for rising, 601
to test for doneness, 602; rising of, **600,** 601, **601**
toasted, 636
torte, 685
white, 602; white plus, 603
whole-grain; all whole-grain Cockaigne, 607
whole-grain, sprouted, 608

BREAD *(cont.)*
whole wheat, sweet, quick, 625; soy, 608
yeast, about, 599–602
zwieback or twice-baked, 637
Breadfruit, 291; seeds, 291
Breading, 552, **552**
Breakfast menus, 25; hunt, 33
Brewers' yeast, 554
Brine, to test for 10% brine, 569
for vegetables, 848
Brining, 569, 813, 841, 848
Brioches, 599, 615, **615**
au chocolat, 615
loaf, Cockaigne, 605
to shape, **615**
yeast starter for, 615
Broccoli, 291, **293**
creamed, quick, 292
deep-fried, 292
timbale, 231
Brochette, *see* Skewer
Broiler, vertical, outdoor, 158, **158**
Broiling, about, 146, 445
outdoor, 156
units, about, 159
Broths, *see* Soups, 167
Brottorte, 685
Brown Betty, 751
Brownies, butterscotch, 702
chocolate, Cockaigne, 701
rice or potato flour, 702
Brûlé, fruit, 127
Brûlée crust, 736
BRUNCH DISHES, Lunch and Supper, 250–275
Brunch Menus, 25
Brunoise, defined, 277
Brunswick Stew, 427
Brussels Sprouts, 292, **293**
baked, and chestnuts, 292
stuffed, 83
with tomatoes, 294
Bûche de Noël, 664, 691
Buckwheat
bread or cornmeal, 628
cakes, 240
cereal, to cook, 200
flour, 550
groats or Kasha, 201
seeds, 564
Buffet Menus, 32; wedding, 33
Buffet Service, 21, **21,** 22, **22,** 77, **77,** 78, **78**
Bulgur cereal, to cook, 200
pilaf, 202
Bundkuchen Coffee Cake, 620, **664**
Buns, *see* Rolls
Burgoo, Kentucky, 465
Burgundy Sauce, 350
Burnet, 580; vinegar, 527
Burns and Burning, about, 165
Butcher wrap, 821
BUTTER, 539, *see also* Seasoned Butters
about, 539
almond, 350

BUTTER *(cont.)*
balls and curls, 540, **541**
blender-made, 540
canapé spreads, 70, 71
to clarify, 542
to churn, 540
drawn or clarified, or ghee, 349
expanded, 540
to freeze, 540, 827
gelatin expanded, 540
kneaded, or Beurre Manié, 340
to measure, 539, **539**
processed, 539
salt, 539; to remove salt, 542
sauce for Crêpes Suzette, 237
sauce, honey, 775
sauce, sweetened, 775
shapes and molds, about, 540, **541**
spreads, 70
to store, 540
sweet, about, 539; churned, 540
swirls, 339
unsalted, in candies, 777
BUTTER, FRUIT, 832–837
defined, 832
apple, 836; baked, 836
apricot; peach; plum, 837
BUTTER, SEASONED, 349–351
and butter sauces, about, 349
anchovy, 350
Bercy, 350
black, or Beurre Noir, 350
brown, or Beurre Noisette, 349
caviar, 350
Colbert, 350
deviled for seafood, 351
garlic, 351
green, 351
herbs, in wine, 71
lemon or Meunière, 350
Maître d'Hôtel, 350
mushroom, blender, 71
nut, 71
seafood, 71
shrimp or lobster, 351
snail, 350
white, 351
Butterklösse, 203
Buttermilk
biscuit, 634
corn bread, crackling, 628
doughnuts, with potatoes, 245
ice cream, fruit, 765
to make, 533
marinade, 528
muffins, 630
pancakes, 239
rolls, potato, 613
rolls or Fan-Tans, 612, **612**
waffles, 241
Butternuts, 564
Butterscotch
brownies, 702
Butterscotch *(cont.)*
cookies, 716
cookies, nut, 709
filling for cakes, 697
icing, 728
old-fashioned, 785
parfait, 763
pie, cream, 656
roll, spice, 691
sauce, 773
tapioca custard, 750

C

Cabbage, about, 292, 293, **293**
baked, 293
celery or Chinese, **93,** 295
creamed with hash, 262
dish and rice, 294
French-fried, 294
leaves, stuffed, 491; baked, 492
leaves for wrap cooking, 152, **152**
mound, spiced, 83
potatoes and ham, 293
red; and chestnuts, 295
salads, 94, 96, 97, *also see* Coleslaw
as sauce container, **77,** 78
sauerkraut, 295, 296; to make, 849
sautéed, 293
scalloped, 294
soup, 175
strudel, savory, 294
stuffed, or Gefüllter Krautkopf, 491
stuffed with corned beef; with ham, 294
with tomatoes, 294
Cabinet Pudding, 746
Café, Caffè, *see* Coffees, 38–39, **39**
Caffeine content of coffee, 37
CAKES, CUPCAKES, TORTEN AND FILLED CAKES, 664–696; *also see* Cakes, High-Altitude
angel, 668, **668,** 669
angel, roll, 691
apple, Cockaigne, 661; French, 661
apple, sour cream, Cockaigne, 741
applesauce, 678
Baba au Rhum or Savarin, 689
banana, Cockaigne, 680
Boston cream pie, 689
brown-sugar spice, 678
burnt-sugar, 678
butter, to mix in mixer, 666
butter or shortening, about, 664, 671
caramel, quick, 681
caramel cornflake ring, 690
carob, 674
Cassata alla Siciliana, 688
cheese, see Cheesecakes, 659–660
chiffon, 684
chocolate, 675; devil's food, 676
chocolate, "Rombauer Special," 675
chocolate, sourdough, 677
chocolate, spice with citron, 677
chocolate apricot, 677; date, 670
chocolate cream roll, **664,** 691

CAKES *(cont.)*
chocolate-filled roll, 691
chocolate mocha oil, 684
chocolate prune, spiced, 677
chocolate sponge, 670
cocoa, quick, 681; angel, 669
coconut loaf or layer, **664,** 674
coconut milk, Cockaigne, 673
coffee, *see* Coffee Cakes
to cool, 665
cornstarch puff, 696
cream meringue tart Cockaigne, 689
cupcakes, about, 694
cupcakes, angel, or balls, 694
cupcakes, caramel, 695
cupcakes, chocolate, 694
cupcakes, coconut, 695
cupcakes, icing, about, 729, **729**
cupcakes, jam, 695
cupcakes, peanut butter, 695
cupcakes, spice, sour cream, 695
cupcakes, sponge, 694
cupcakes, yellow, 694
currant, 682
daffodil, 670
date spice, 679
decorations, fresh flowers, 733
devil's food, Cockaigne, 676
devil's food, cocoa, 676
eggless, milkless, spice, 679
eight-yolk, 674
electric mixer, about, 666
fig spice, 679
filled, about, 687, **687;** *also see* Charlottes, Rolled Cakes, Torten
fillings, 696–699
flour, 547
flourless, angel, almond, 686
four-egg, 674
freezer, mocha, quick, 688
freezing, 830
frozen, about, 830
fruit, about, 682
fruit, Cockaigne, 682
fruit, dark, 683
fruit, white, 683
fruit shortcakes, 690
fudge meringue, 676
Génoise, 675
gingerbread, 681; wheatless, 681
glazes, 731
gold layer, 674
griddle, *see* Griddle Cakes
Guy Fawkes Day or Parkin, 682
honey, 677; eggless all-rye, Cockaigne, 626
houses, and cookie, about, 704, **704**
icings, *see* Icings, 721–733
jam, Rombauer, 679
jelly roll, 691
lady, 673; Baltimore, 672
ladyfingers, 695
lambs, bunnies, and Santas, 672, **672**

CAKES *(cont.)*
leftovers, uses for, 635
lemon roll, 691
lightning or quick, 681
Madeleines, 695
making hints, 664–665, **665**
marble, 672
mixes, about, 667
mixing, to beat and fold, 665, **665**
mocha-chocolate freezer, 688
Mohrenköpfe or Moors' Heads, 688
molds, about, 672, **672**
molds, to line with paper, 743
mystery, 680
oatmeal, 680
oil, about, 683
oil, carrot, 684
oil, chiffon, 684
oil, chocolate-mocha, 684
one-bowl in electric mixer, 667
one-egg, 681
orange-filled, 689
pans, about; sizes, 666, **666**
peach, Cockaigne, 661
peach, French, 661
Petits Fours, 695, **695**
plum, Cockaigne, 661
poppy seed custard, Cockaigne, 689
pound; pans for, 675, **675**
prune, chocolate, spiced, 677
pyramid or Kransekake, **664,** 688
quick, about, 681
quick or lightning, 681
raspberry rum or trifle, 688
refrigerated, filled, 687
roll, about, 690, **690**
seed, 675
shortcakes, 633
skillet or upside-down, 661
small, icing, about, 729, **729**
sour cream, 673
spice, eggless, milkless, 679
spice, quick, 681
spice, velvet, 678
spice roll, butterscotch, 691
sponge, 669, 670
sponge, almond, 691
sponge, chocolate, 670
sponge; rice- or potato-flour, 670
sunshine, 670
to test for doneness, 665
tomato soup or mystery, 680
Torte, bread, or Brottorte, 685
Torten, about, 684
Torten, almond, Cockaigne, 685
Torten, angel almond, flourless, 686
Torten, chocolate walnut, 686
Torten, drum or dobos, 685
Torten, hazelnut, 686
Torten, Linzertorte, 686
Torten, pans for, 684, **684**
Torten, pecan, 685

CAKES *(cont.)*
Torten, Sachertorte, 686
tube, for secret filling, 687, **687**
Tutti-Frutti, 680
types, about, 664
upside-down or skillet, 661
wedding, about, 667, **667**; to cut, 668
whipped cream, 673
white, 671
CAKES, HIGH-ALTITUDE, 692–694
angel; chocolate, 692
angel, spice, 693
baking, about, 692
baking powder in, 692
cocoa, spiced, 693
fruit, 682
fudge, 693
gingerbread, 694
sponge, 693
two-egg, 693
white, 693
CAKE FILLINGS, 696–699, *also see* Coffee Cake Fillings
about, 696
almond and fig or raisin, 698
butterscotch, 697
chocolate mocha, 697
chocolate ricotta, 697
cream, whipped, or Crème Chantilly, 696
custard, almond or hazelnut, 699
custard, apricot, 698
custard, lemon-orange, 698
custard, orange, 697
custard cream or Crème Patissière, 697
Frangipane, cream, 697
fruit, chopped, 698
ginger, fruit, 698
lemon, 697
orange cream, 698
pecan, toasted, 699
raisin, 698
Ricotta chocolate, 697
walnut, toasted, 699
Calamondins, 135; preserves, 839
candied or preserved, 795
Calas or Rice Crullers, 246
Calf, brain, fritters, 244
feet, jellied, 511
head, 510
liver, 500; *also see* Liver
sweetbreads, 502
Cali, *see* Ham
Calories, about, 2
protein relationship, 8
values, 8–14
Calvados, 52
Camomile, 580
Camp Cooking, backpacking, outdoor, 155
Campfire vegetables, about, 282
Can openers, 164
Can sizes, commercial, 592
Canadian Bacon, 486
CANAPÉS, 66-76, *also see* Sandwiches
defined, 66
amounts and ways to serve, 66, 77, **77**
angels on horseback, 76
asparagus, rolled, 73
bacon and cheese, 72
barquettes for, 69
bases for, 68
butters and butter spreads, 70, 71
caviar and cucumber, 74; and onion, 74
cheese dreams, 72
cheese puff, 71
cheese rolls or logs, toasted, 72
cheese spreads, 72
chicken salad, 74
chicken spread, deviled or potted, 74
Christmas, 68
chutney and cheese, 72
clam puffs, 75
crab puff ball, 75
cream cheese spread for, 71
cucumber, 73
cucumber cream cheese spread, 71
egg spreads, 73
fillings for pastry, 70
flower, 67
foie gras for, 75
freezing and thawing, 829
fried pies, 69
glazed, 70
ham salad for, 74
ham spread, deviled or potted, 74
herbs, dried, for butter spreads, 71
herring, marinated, 75
liver sausage, 75
lobster, 75
lobster puff ball, 75
mushroom, 73
mushroom butter, 71
nut butters, 71
onion and parsley, 73
pastry, fillings for, 70
pepper slices with fillings, 103
pizza, small, 74
puff paste or pâté shells, stuffed, 69
quiche, cocktail, 69
radish, black, 73
ribbon, 67
rissoles or empañadas, 69
rolled, 67
Roquefort spread, 71
Roquefort sticks, puffed, 72
rye loaf container, 68, **68**
salmon, smoked, 76
sandwich loaf, 68, **68**
sardine rolls, 76
seafood, creamed, 75
seafood butter, 71
shapes of, 66, **66,** 67, **67**
shrimp puffs, 75
snails, 69
spreads, sweet tea, 72

CANAPÉS *(cont.)*
tacos, 70
tart, cocktail, 69
tarts and tartlets, 68, 69
tomato, 73
tongue, smoked, 74
turnovers, 69
zoo sandwiches, 68, **68**
CANDIES AND CONFECTIONS, 777–797
almond creams, 789
almond or filbert paste, 780
almonds, burnt, 789
apples, candied, 795, **795**
apricot leather, 793
apricot orange balls, 793
Baklava, 794
bourbon balls, 790
butterscotch; old-fashioned, 785
calamondins, candied or preserved, 795
caramel fondant, 779
caramels, chocolate; chocolate cream, 784
caramels, filled, Cockaigne, 785
caramels, vanilla cream; maple, 784
chestnuts, glazed, or Marrons Glacés, 796
chocolate clusters, 790
chocolate coating and dipping, 781, **781**
citrus peel, candied, 795
coffee drops, 785
cranberries, candied, 796
date roll or centers, 793
divinity, caramel cream, 784
divinity, or sea foam, 783
fondant, basic, 778
fondant, caramel, 779
fondant, to color, 779
fondant, soft-center, 779
fondant, uncooked, 779
fondant and cream centers, about, 778
fruit, dried, stuffed, 793
fruit, fresh, glazed, 794
fruit leather, 793
fruit paste, 797; Turkish Delight or Rahat Loukoum, 791
fruit roll, or centers, 793
fruits, candied, crystallized or glazed, about, 794
fudge, caramel, cream, 782
fudge, carob, 783
fudge, Cockaigne, 782
fudge, cocoa, or centers, 782
fudge, coconut, or centers, 783
fudge, coffee, 783
fudge, peanut butter, or centers, 790
fudge, white, Cockaigne, 783
ginger, candied, 796
ginger, or centers, 792
hard or lollipops, 787
Hawaiian, or centers, 792
Heavenly Hash, 790
high-altitude effect, 778
hook, **777**
horehound, 787
kumquats, candied or preserved, 795
CANDIES AND CONFECTIONS *(cont.)*
making, marble slab for, 777
maple cream, 780
marshmallows, 781
Marzipan or Marchpane, 781
mint leaves, glazed, 794
mints, pulled, 786
molds, **777**
Newport creams or centers, 779
nougat, 784
nut brittle, 788; for garnish, 789
nut crunch, 788
nuts, glazed, for garnish, 789
nuts, spiced, 789; caramel Cockaigne, 789
opera creams or centers, 780
orange drops, Mexican, 792
Pastillage or gum paste, 791
peach leather, 793
peanut brittle, 788
peanut butter fudge, or centers, 790
penuche, 788
peppermint cream wafers, 780, **780**
Persian balls or centers, 793
pineapple, glazed, 795
popcorn, 790, **791;** candied, 790
praliné, 789; pralines, 788
pull, cream, 787
rock, 787, **787**
roots and stalks, candied or crystallized, 797
rum drops, uncooked, 790
sea foam or divinity, 783
sugaring in, about, 777
syrups, caramel, molasses, white sugar, 791
syrups, stages of, 778
taffy, about, 785, **785**
taffy, saltwater; molasses, 786
taffy, vanilla, 786
thermometer temperatures, about, 777
toffee, English, 788
truffles, chocolate, 789
Turkish fruit paste, Turkish Delight or Rahat Loukoum, 791
wrappings, about, 778
Cane Syrup, 559
Cannelloni or Manicotti, 216
fillings, 219
Cannibal Balls and mounds, 86
CANNING, 802–818; *also see individual names of:* Fruits, Vegetables, Meat, Poultry and Game
anti-browning solutions for, 805
blanching foods for, 803
boiling-water bath, 804, **804**
botulism, warning, 802
canning equipment, 802–804, **802, 803, 804**
cold or raw pack, 803
fish, 811
fruit, 805–808
fruit purées and pastes, 806
game, 811
high-altitude, pressure-canning, 804; boiling-water bath, 805
hot pack, 803

CANNING *(cont.)*
jars, about, 803, **803, 804,** 805
meat; poultry, 811
preparing food for, 803
pressure-canning, 804, **804**
processes, about, 802
rubbers, to test, 802
steaming foods for, 803
synthetic sweetener for, 806
syrups for, 805
tomato purée, 806
vegetables, about, 808; yields, 808
Canteloupes, 138, **138,** *also see* Melons
Canton ginger, 576
Capers and caperlike buds and seeds, 580
Capon, defined, 422
Carambola, 123, 143
Caramel, Bavarian Cream, 747
cake, quick, 681
candies, *see* Candy
coating for dessert molds, about, 743
coloring, to make, 559
cookies, curled, 720
cornflake ring, 690
cupcakes, 695
custards, 735; cornstarch pudding, 738
glaze, clear, 732
ice cream, 759; parfait, 763
icing, 726
pie, custard, 656; gelatin chiffon, 659
pudding, steamed, 755
rolls, 614
sauces, 774; chocolate, 773
syrup, for candy, 791
topping for rolls, 731
Caramelized custard 735
sugar, 559
sweet potatoes, 325
Caraway, 580; sauce, 355
Carbohydrates, about, 5
Carbonnade Flamande, 461
Cardamom, 575
Cardoons, 296
Carob, bars, 702; cake, 674
flour or powder, 550
fudge, 783
icing, 728
Carp, about, 404
Carrogeenan, 561
Carrots, 296, **296;** baked, 297
in bunches, 296
bread, and nut, quick, 625
cake, oil, 684
canning, 809
marinated, 84
mashed, or carrot ring, 296
and peas, 315
pickled, sticks, 845
salad, with raisins and nuts, 101
Vichy, 297
Carving, fowl, 421, **421;** beef, **454;** lamb, **471;** pork, **477**
sharpening knives for, 449
Cases, bread, 250
chocolate, semisweet, 743
for food, 250
timbale, 247
tomato, cold, 105, **105**
vegetable, to cut, 98, **99**
Cashew nuts, 563
Cassata alla Siciliana, 688
CASSEROLES, *also see* Stews, Chicken, Fish and Shellfish
defined; true, mock, 151
bean, dried, 287
bean, green, 285
bean, lima or soybean, 255
beef with fruit, 463
beet, 290
cheese, 253
chicken, French, 426
chicken or turkey with vegetables, 263
chipped beef and sweet potato, 260
covered, **417**
cucumber anchovy; Creole, 302
eggplant, or Ratatouille Provençale, 304
frankfurter-sauerkraut, 499
fruit, nut and rice, 210
to glaze a sauce, 368
ham noodles, 214
ham slices, 485
Hasenpfeffer, 514
hominy grits, cheese, 201
jambalaya, 211
lamb and eggplant, 491
lamb and spinach, 256
lentil or lima bean and sausage, 260
noodle dish, leftover, 215
noodle and pork, Romanian, 215
octopus, 409
onion and apple, 313
paella, 210
pilaf, 209
rabbit, sausage, 514
rice baked in chicken stock, 207
rice loaf, 210
sauerkraut and tomato, 296
sausage meat, sweet potato and fruit, 498
sausage and millet, **250,** 259
seafood, in Creole sauce, 265
seafood and tomato, 268
shrimp, with snail butter, 391
Spanish, with rice, 491
squid, 409
summer squash, Cockaigne, 330
tomato olive, 332
tuna, noodle, and mushroom soup, 215
tuna, West African, 265
turkey mole, 428
veal kidney, 506
veal with sour cream, 470

CASSEROLES *(cont.)*
veal and spinach, 256
vegetable and hard-cooked egg, 224
Casseroling, about, 151
Cassoulet, 475
Castor sugar, 556
Catfish, Southern-fried, 404
Catsup, grape; tomato; walnut, 847, 848
Cauliflower, 293, deep-fried, 297
mushrooms and, in cheese sauce, 297
sautéed, 297
soup, cream of, 182; quick, 192
steamed, 297
timbale, 231
Caviar, about, 87; server, **77**
butter, 350
canapés, 74
dip, 90
molded egg salad, 106
preparing roe for, 814
sauce, 357
Cayenne, *see* Peppers
Celeri-Rave Rémoulade, 102
Celeriac or Celeri-Rave, 276; to cook, 298
ring mold timbale, 232
salad, 101, 102
Celery, 297; as an herb, 580
aspic with asparagus, 115
braised or glazed, 298
curls, 84, **84**
salad, cooked, 101
salad ring and grapes, 118
for salads, 94
seed dressing, 362
soup, cream of, 182
stuffed, 84
Celery cabbage, salad, 101
Celery root, salad, 101; to cook, 298
Celtuce, 93
CEREALS, 198; *also see individual names*
about, 198; cooking, 199, 200
granola, 198
gruel, to make, 199
mixed whole-grain, cold, 198
muffins, 631
Müsli or Swiss oatmeal, 199
pie crust, 643
puffed, for cocktails, 80
snacks, 198, 199
substitute for flour, 551
to thicken soups, 168
Ceriman, 143, **143**
Chafing dish, 77
Challah, or egg bread, 605, **605**
Champagne, about, 56, **56**
cocktail, 52
cup, 63
punch, 63
glasses for, 57, **57,** 58
sauce, 344
sherbet, 768
Chantilly, Crème, 696
defined, 318
mayonnaise, 365
potatoes, 318
Chapon for salads, 95
Chard, Swiss, 298
Charlottes, 748
Chateaubriand, 454, **454**
Chaud-Froid, chicken breasts, 430
defined, 368
sauce, 369; quick pink, 369;
decorations for, 369
Chausseur Sauce, 347
Chayotes, 298
CHEESE, about, 536
balls, 81, 82; pastry, 82; Florentine, 82
balls for soup, 197
Bar-le-Duc, 757
bread, 604
burgers, 488
cake, *see* Cheesecake
canapés, 71, 72
casserole, 253; and hominy, 201
cheddaring, 539
Coeur à la Crème, 756, **756**
cottage, *see* Cottage Cheese
cream, *see* Cream Cheese
croquettes Cockaigne, 248
dessert, about, 756
dips, 90
dreams, 72; fried, 82
dumplings, 203
flan, 255
fondue, about, 254, 254
freezing, 828
hard, to make, 537
for hors d'oeuvre, 81, 82
Liptauer, 757
loaf, with noodles in quantity, 215
loaf with seafood, 267
logs or rolls toasted, 72
making, 536–539; **538**
mix for dessert, 756
muffins, 631
new, about, 539
nut loaf, 254
pie, custard, 255
potted, 756
quiche, 254, 255
rarebits, 252, 253
rice, 208; ring, 207
rolls, 613
salad ring, 119
sandwiches, 269–275
sauces, *see* Sauces
soufflés, 229
soup, quick, 192
spreads, 71, 72
straws or wafers, 641
timbale or crustless quiche, 232
yogurt, 533

Cheesecake, about, 659
crusts for, 642
gelatin, 660
Ricotta, 660
sour cream, 660
whipped cream, 659
Cherimoya, 143, **143**
Cherry, about, 134
canning, 806
conserve, sweet, 839
crunch, quick, 662
fruit soup, 128
pickled Dutch, 846
pies, *see* Pies
pitter, **798**
poached, 135
preserves, 837
salad with hazelnuts, 111
sauce, Jubilee, 770
sauce, savory, 356
Chervil, 581
Chess Tarts, 654
Chestnuts, 563; baked, 299
boiled, 298
Brussels sprouts, baked, 292
dressing for game, 372
glazed, 796
mound or Mont Blanc, 738
prunes and, 142
red cabbage and, 295
rice, and spinach, 208
ring mold, 234
roasted, 79, **80**
skewered, 79
soup, 182
steamed, 299, **299**
water, 335, 563
Chevon, defined, 471
Chick-Peas, 287; *also see* Hummus, 90
CHICKEN, about, 422; *also see* Poultry
aspic, luncheon, 116
baked in foil, 422
barbecued; curried, 423
in batter, 424
bits, sherried, 86
boned, stuffed, 431
braised, with fruit, 425
braised in wine, or Coq au Vin, 425
breasts, brandied, 430
breasts, Chaud-Froid, 430
breasts, creamed, quick, 430
breasts, in quantity, 429; Cockaigne, 429
breasts, stir-fried, 430
breasts, stuffed, 429
broiled, 423; marinated, 423
broth, 169; with clam, quick, 193
broth with egg, 170
Cacciatore or Hunter's, **417,** 427
à la Campagne, 428
casserole, French, 426
casserole, with vegetables, 263
cockscombs, 512
CHICKEN *(cont.)*
Coq au Vin, 425
Country Captain, 428
creamed, 263
Creole, quick, 263
croquettes; and oyster, 248
curry, East India, 428
curry or Senegalese soup, 176
Divan, 264
farce or forcemeat, 374
freezing and thawing, 826
fricassee, 426
giblets, 418, **418;** stew, 512
gravy, pan, 341
gumbo, 176
hash, 263
Jambalaya, 211
kebabs, 431
Kiev, 429
à la King, 263
liver, sautéed, 500
liver pâté, 495; souffléed, Cockaigne, 496
liver timbales, 233
liver topping for pastas, 219
livers, skewered, 501
livers in batter, 502
livers as hors d'oeuvre, 81, 86
livers à la King, 502; in sour cream sauce, 502
loaf, cooked; quantity, 264
Marengo, 427
marinade for, 529
Maryland, 424
mousse, jellied, 120
oven-fried; with fruit, 424
paella, 210
pan-fried or sautéed, 424
paprika, 425
patties, 488
Persian, 425
Polynesian, 257
pot pie, quick, 252
ring mold with mushrooms, 234
roast, 422
rotisserie or spit cooking, **158**
salad, hot, 264; in aspic, 117
salad spread, 74
salads, 108; in quantity, 108
sandwiches, 274
smothered, 425
soufflé, 230
soup, cream of, 182; quick, 192
spread for canapés, 74
stew, Brunswick, 427
stew, or fricassee, 426
sweetbreads and, 430
Tahiti, 424
Teriyaki marinade, 529
Tetrazzini, 218
timbales, 232
Chicory, 299; in coffee, 37
beetroot salad and, 96
witloof, **93,** 299

Chiffonade of fresh herbs, 571; for soups, 195
Chili
con carne, 490
peppers, about, 315, **315;** preserved in sherry, 845
powder, 571
sauce, 847
vinegar, 527
Chinese or celery cabbage, 293, 295
Chinese
egg rolls, 250
firepot, **145,** 462
meatballs, 489
red stews, 447
rice, fried, 208
sauce for vegetables, 349
spinach, 331
Chipped Beef Cornucopias, 86
Chipped Beef, in canned soup, 260
creamed, 260
sandwich and cheese, 270
in sauce, cheese; Creole, 260
sweet potato and, 260
Chips, fish and, 404
potato or Saratoga, 323
Chitterlings, sautéed, 512
Chives, 584, **585;** garlic, 584, **586**
CHOCOLATE, about, 565, 566
banana dipped in, 132
Bavarian cream, 747
beverages, about, 41
bombe, 763
Brazilian, 41
cakes, *see* Cakes
candy, *see* Candy
cases, semisweet, 743
Charlotte, 748
clusters, 790
coating and dipping, 781, **781**
coating over icing, 725
cookies, *see* Cookies
cupcakes, 694
curls, to make, 566
custard, café, blender, 737
custard, coffee, 735
doughnuts, 246
filling, custard cream, 697
filling, mocha, 697
filling, Ricotta, 697
fudge, *see* Cakes, Candies
glaze, 732
hot, 41; handy, 42
ice cream, 759, 763
iced, 41
icing, *see* Icings
malt or shake syrup, 41, 42
mousses, 737; rum, 738
pies, *see* Pies
puddings, 739, 753, 754
sauces, 772, 773
soufflé, 740
syrup, 41
CHOCOLATE *(cont.)*
Torten, 686
waffles, 242
white, 566
Cholesterol, 5; in fats, 539
Chop Suey, 257
Chopsticks, to eat with, 459, **459**
Choux Paste, canapé, 69
to form, **638,** 647
fritters, unsweetened, 243
garnish for soup, 195
swan, **638,** 647
Chow Chow, 843
Chow Mein, 257
Chowders, defined, 167; *see* Soups
Christmas Loaf, 620
Christmas Wreath Pudding, 752
Chutney, *also see* Pickles
apple or green tomato, 847
apricot, curried, 846
avocado and, 83
basic, or Indian relish, 846
canapés and cheese, 72
dressing, 361
peach, mango or kiwi, 846
Cider, apple, canning, 806
hot or mulled, 44
press, **802**
sauce, 772; raisin, 356
vinegar, 526
Cinnamon, about, 575
loaf, 604; quick, 636
stars, 714
sugar, 557
toast or sticks, 636
Citron, 136
Citrus fruits, about, 135
canning, 807
garnishes, to cut, **571**
juice, 571
juice medley, 44
peel, candied, 795; for drinks, **42,** 571
rinds, to grate, 571
salad, 111
zests, juices and garnishes, 571
City Chicken, 469
Clabber, 533
Clams, 87; about, 379; to open, **379**
bisque, with mushrooms, 187
broiled on the half shell, 381
broth, or soup, 186; with chicken, quick, 193
cakes, 267
chowder, Manhattan; New England, 190
clambake, about, 380; pit-cooking, 155, 156
dip, 91
fried, 381
hard-shell, about, 380
juice, 43
in mushrooms, 309
puff, canapé, 75
ring, jellied, 116
sauce for pasta, 354

Clams *(cont.)*
soft-shell, to open, 379, **379;** baked, 381
soft-shell, steamed, with broth, 381
surf, 380
Clostridium botulinum, 802
Cloves, 575
Cobbler, cherry, crunch, quick, 662
fruit, 660
Cockaigne, *see* Foreword
Cockles, about, **87,** 379
Cockscombs, 512
Cocktail and Buffet Menus, 32
Cocktails, 48–53; *also see* Drinks
bar equipment, 48, **48**
glasses, 49, **49;** to sugar-frost, 51
measurements, about, 49
sauce, 352
shellfish, about, 375
sugar syrup for, 48
Cocoa, about, 565–566
beverages, about, 41
butter, 565
cakes, 669, 681, 693
Dutch, 566
hot, 41; handy, 42
kisses, 710
syrup for shakes, 42
Cocomoka, cold, 46; hot, 46
Coconuts, about; to open, 566
butter, to make, 567
cakes, **664,** 673, 674
cookie filling, 717
cream, to make, 566
cream pie, 656
cupcakes, 695
extravaganza, 60, **60**
fudge or centers, 783
to grate, 566, **566**
icings, 722, **722,** 726
macaroons, 710
milks, about, 534, 566
Polvo de Amor, 567
sauce, Dulcie, 774
shells as containers, 566, **567**
to substitute flakes for grated, 567
to toast, 567
Cod, about, 404
balls or cakes, 405
Brandade de Morue, 405
fresh, Boulangère, 406
fresh, à la Portugaise, 405
scalloped, 405
scrod, fresh, broiled, 406
sounds and tongues, 405
Coeur à la Crème, 756, **756**
COFFEE, 36–39; *also see* Mocha
Bavarian Creams, 747, 748
Café au Lait, 38
Café Brûlot, Diable or Royal, 38, **39**
Café Continental, 39
Capuccino, 38
chicory in, 37
COFFEE *(cont.)*
cream tarts or pie, 656
custard cream filling, 697
decaffeinated, 37
drip or Café Filtré, 37
drops, 785
equipment, 36, **37;** grinder, **36**
Espresso, **37,** 38
frozen, blender, 39
ice cream, 759
iced, 39; Viennoise, 39
icing, 729
instant, 38
Irish, 39
in quantity, 37
parfait, 764
percolated, 37
sauce, 774
steeped, 37
Turkish, **37,** 38
vacuum-method, 37, **37**
COFFEE CAKES, 619–627, **620, 621**
about yeast, 619
Bishop's Bread, 627
Bundkuchen or Gugelhupf, 620
fillings, seasonings, toppings, 621–623
fruit-topped yeast, 620
glazed filled or Bienenstich, 619
Gugelhupf, quick, 626
kneaded filled, 620, **620**
leftovers, uses for, 635
no-knead yeast, or Panettone, 619
quick, about, 623
quick, or Kuchen, 626, 627
Scandinavian or Danish, 621, **621**
sour cream, quick, 627
spice, with oil, quick, 627
stollen or Christmas loaf, 620
streusel or toppings for, 731
Coffee Cake Fillings, 621–623
apple, 622
apricot, 622
crumb fruit, 622
date, 622
fig, 622
nut, 622
poppyseed Cockaigne, 622
poppyseed or Mohn, 622
pot-cheese or Ricotta, 623
prune, 622
Colas, *see* Soft Drinks, 46
Colbert Butter, 350
Cold-smoking, 814
Coleslaw, 96, 97; blender, 97
de luxe, for barbecue, 97
hot with apple; Roquefort, 97
Collards, *see* About Cabbage, 292, **293**
Color in food, about, 588
caramelized sugar, 559
for sauces, 337; for soup, 168
Comfrey, 581

Compote, fruit, baked, 126
kumquat, 136
Compôte Composée, defined, 123
Conch chowder, 190
Cones, ice cream, or Gaufrettes, **718,** 719
Confections, *see* Candy
Confit d'Oie, or potted goose, 434
Conserves, about, 832; making, 837
cherry, sweet, 839
plum, blue, 839
rhubarb, spiced, 839
Tutti-Frutti Cockaigne, 840
Consommé, 167, 169; *also see* Soups
Brunoise, 169
double-strength, *see* Clarifying Stock II, 522
Madrilène, 169
Conversions and Equivalents, 590–598
temperatures, 592
COOKIE FILLINGS
apricot-orange, 717
coconut; date, 717
fig; raisin, 717
mincemeat, 717
COOKIES, 700–720; about, 700–701
almond crescents, 713
almond meringue rings, 710
almond pretzels or Mandelplättchen, 713
angel slices, 703
anise butterless drop, 707
apricot meringue bars, 703
bars, 701–704
brandy snaps, 719
brownies, butterscotch, 702
brownies, Cockaigne, 701
brownies, rice or potato flour, 702
butter wafers, drop, 705
butterscotch nut, 709
butterscotch refrigerator, 716
caramel, curled, 720
carob bars, 702
chocolate almond shells, 714
chocolate chip drop, 705
chocolate oat bars, 702
chocolate refrigerator, 716
Christmas, about, 700; *also see Christmas symbol* ★
Christmas chocolate bars, Cockaigne, 702
cinnamon stars, 714
cookie-press or Spritz, 714
cream cheese refrigerator, 716
crusts, about, 642
curled, about, 718, **718**
curled, iron for, 718, **718**
cutters for, 711, **711**
date bars Cockaigne, 703
drop, or hand-shaped, about, 705, **705**
egg white in, 701
filled, about, 716, **717;** *see* Cookie Fillings
filled, to shape, 717, **717**
Florentines, 706
flourless oatmeal, 709; nut, 706
fortune, or almond curls, 719

COOKIES *(cont.)*
Frankfurter Oblaten, 719
freezing and thawing, 830
Gaufrettes, 719
ginger thins, 707
gingerbread men, **700,** 712, **712**
gingersnaps, 707
hazelnut, drop, 706
hermits, 708
high-altitude, 700
honey, German, 708; bars, 704
houses, about, **700,** 704, **704**
icing, about, 729, **729**
jelly tots, 717, **717**
Jubilee wafers, 716
kisses, chocolate cracker, 710
kisses, cocoa, 710
Krumkakes, Scandinavian, 718, **718**
Langue de Chat or Cat's Tongue, 714
leaf wafers, 715
Lebkuchen, 704
lemon curd squares, 703
macaroon jam tarts, 717, **717**
macaroons, 709; coconut, 710
macaroons, chocolate coconut, 710
maple curls, 720
Maquis, 714
molasses, old-fashioned, 707
molasses crisps Cockaigne, 716
molasses nut wafers, 706
nut balls, flourless, 706
nut bars, 703
nut drop, about, 706
nut tarts, individual, 718
nut wafers, curled, 720
oatmeal or wheat flake, quick, 708
oatmeal wafers, glazed or flourless, 709
orange marmalade drops, 709
peanut butter, 709
pecan or angel slices, 703
pecan or benne wafers, 706
pecan drop; puffs, 706
Pfeffernüsse, 708
pinwheel, refrigerator, 716
prune, filled, 718
pumpkin, 709
raisin molasses bars, 702
refrigerator, 715, **715,** 716
rolled and molded, about, 710, **711**
sand tarts, 711
Scotch shortbread, 713
Speculatius, 714
Springerle, 713
squares and bars, about, 701
sugar drop, with oil, 705
tea wafers, 714
unbaked, freezing and thawing, 829
vanilla, refrigerator, 715
whole wheat seed wafers, 712
yolk letter, 713
Cooking, about, 145–166
outdoor, 155–159

Cooking *(cont.)*
processes, *see* Foods We Heat
utensils, 162
Coots or mudhens, about, 440
Coq au Vin, 425
Coquina broth, 186
Cordials, about, 58; glasses for, **57**
Cordon Bleu, *see* Veal Scallops with Ham, 469
Coriander, 581
Corn, about, 299
bread or cakes, *see* Cornmeal below
canning, 809
chowder, 183; tomato, 192
on the cob; off the cob, cooked, 300
cracked, as cereal, 200
Creole, 301
croquettes, and ham, 248
flour; waxy, *see* Cornstarch, 548
fritters, 301; and ham, 244
grilled or roasted, 300
grits, *see* Hominy, 200
husks, stuffed, **152,** 153
à la King, green peppers stuffed with, 316
oysters, 302
popped, 790
pudding, Cockaigne, 300
pudding, souffléed, 301
relish, tart, 844
salad or mâche, 93, **93**
scalloped, 301
scraper, **300**
soup, cream of, 182
succotash, 301
syrup, 557
tamales, 201
tomatoes stuffed with, 334
Corned Beef, about, 813; to make, 813
in canned soup, 260
to cook; and cabbage, 466
hash, cabbage, stuffed with, 294
hash patties; and potatoes, 261
salad, 109
sandwich, and cheese, 270
sandwich, Reuben, 272
Cornell Flour Formula, 602
Cornichons, pickled, 843
Cornish Hens, about, 434
rice dressing, 373
roast, 434
Cornmeal, as cereal, 200
bread, and buckwheat, 628
bread, buttermilk crackling, 628
bread, muffins or sticks, 627–628
bread, salt-rising, 606
bread, skillet, 628
bread, sourdough, 628
bread Tamale pie, 252
dodgers, Cockaigne, 628
dumplings, 203
flapjacks, crisp, 239
as flour, 549
griddle cakes, rice, 239
Cornmeal *(cont.)*
hush puppies, 629
mush, 201
pancakes, 239
Polenta, 201
puffs, golden, 628
spoon bread, buttermilk, 629
spoon bread, crusty, soft center, 629
tamales, 201
tortillas, 629
waffles, bacon, 241
zephyrs Cockaigne, 628
Cornstarch, about, 548
puddings and custards, 738–739
puff cakes, 696
thickener for sauces, 339
Cos, 93, **93**
Costmary, 581
Cottage cheese, to make, 536
dessert, 756
pancakes or blintzes, 237
salad, 97
Cottage Pudding, 752
Cottonseed flour, 550
Country ham, 483; smoking, 814
Country sausage, 497
Court Bouillon, about; blanc; for fish, 525
Couscous, 476, **476**
CRAB, 383–385
about, types, 383, 384; to clean, **384**
cakes, 267
canapé, puff ball, 75
deviled, 266
gumbo, 188
hard-shell, poached or "boiled," 384
Louis salad, 107
meat custard, 266
meat dip, 91
meat Mongole, quick, 266; soup, 194
meat and prosciutto, 268
meat salad, 106, 107, 121, 122
meat sandwich with cheese, 274
soft-shell, broiled, 384
soft-shell, deep-fat-fried, 384
soft-shell, sautéed, 384
soup, 187
Crackers for hors d'oeuvre, 79
leftovers, uses for, 635
meal dumpling, 203
seeded, 636
Cracklings, 542
as garnish, 572
Cranberry, bread, quick, 624
candied, 796
canning, 806
glaze for fowl, 368
jelly, 133; spiced, 134
juice, 44; hot, 44
muffins, 631
relish, uncooked, 134
salads, 118

Cranberry *(cont.)*
sauce, 133; whole, 134
sherbet, 768
Crayfish or crawfish, about, 391, **392**
bisque, 187
CREAM, 529–534; *also see* Milk and Sour Cream
Bavarians, 746–748
cakes, *see* Cakes
candy, *see* Candies
cereal, 531
cheese, *see* Cream Cheese
coconut, 566
coffee or table, 531
to cream, *see* Cake Mixing, 664
Crème Chantilly, 696
Crème Fleurette, 532
Crème Fraîche, 534
Devonshire or clotted, 534
dressing; horseradish, 357
dressing, sweet-sour, 355
fermented, about, 533
filling, whipped, sweetened, 696
freezing, 827
fried, 739
half-and-half, 531
imitation, 534
light, 531
mayonnaise, 365
mocha marshmallow, 749
pasteurization of, 530
Persian, 745
pies, *see* Pies
pineapple, molded, 748
puff, fillings for, 647
puff shells, **645,** 646
rice and fruit, 750
sauces, *see* Sauces
soups, *see* Soups
sour, 533; *also see* Sour Cream
sour, cultured or dairy, 534
sour, substitutes, 534
substitutions, 532
sweet, about, 531
tart, meringue, Cockaigne, 689
whipped, 531; substitutes for, 532
whipping, 531
Cream Cheese
cookies, 716
dessert, 756
dressing, French, 361
dressing for fruit salad, 367
French, or Coeur à la Crème, 756, **756**
icing, 727
rich, to make, 537
with scrambled eggs, 223
spreads, 71, 72
topping, blender-whipped, 732
Crème Anglaise, 771
Crème Brûlée, 736
Crème Caramel, 735
Crème Chantilly, 532, 696
Crème de Menthe Sauce, 772
Crème Fleurette, 532
Crème Fraîche, 534
Crème Frite or fried cream, 739
Crème Glacée, 759
Crème Patissière, 697
Creole Cucumber Casserole, 302
Creole Sauce, 348; quick, 352
Crêpes
gâteau, 237
pan set, **235**
Suzette, 237; sauce for, 237
Crescents, filled sweet, 616, **616**
French or Croissants, 615, **616**
Cress, garden, 94
Croissants, or crescents, 615, **616**
Croquant, 559
Croque Monsieur Sandwich, 271
Croquembouche, 638, 647
CROQUETTES, 247–249
about, 247
cheese, Cockaigne, 248
chicken or veal, 248
ham and corn, 248
meat, fish, fowl or vegetables, 247
mushroom, 248
oyster and chicken, 248
rice, sweet, 248
salmon, 249
Croustades, 250
Croutons, to make, 551
soup, 197, 551
Crudités Vinaigrette, 83
Crullers, 244, 246
rice or Calas, 246
Crumbs, about, 551, **551;** crumbing, 552, **552**
au gratins, 552
bread, browned or buttered, 551
bread, dry; soft, 551, **551**
crusts for pie, 642, 643
pie, 654
sauce, browned, 351
seasoned, 552
Crumpets, 617
Crustaceans, *see* Shellfish
Cucumbers, about, 302
aspic, 114
canapés, 73, 74
casserole, anchovy, 302
casserole, Creole, 302
lily hors d'oeuvre, 84
mousse, 120
mulled, 302
pickles, 842
salad with tomato, 106, **106**
salads; cold stuffed, 102, **102**
sauce, almond, 357
soup, Bulgarian, cold, 183
soup, Cockaigne, quick, 192
soup, herb, cream of, 183
soup, quick cold, 192
yogurt dressing, low-calorie, 367
Cumberland Sauce, 356

Cumin, 581
Cupcakes, 694–695; *see* Cakes
Curlews, 440
Currant, about, 134
cake, 682
canning, 806
jellies, 833, 834; preserves, 838
pie, 650
Curry, 575
dressing for fruit salad, 367
egg, 224
fondue, fruit, 128
lamb with rice, 475
lobster or seafood, 388
mayonnaise, 365
rice, 208; Rijsttafel, 211
sauce, 345
sauce, pickle, 843
veal or lamb and rice, 256
CUSTARD, 734–739; *also see* Puddings
about, 734, **735**
baked or cup, 734, **735**
"boiled," 734
Brûlée, crust for, 736
cake, poppy seed, Cockaigne, 689
caramel, 735
caramel, cornstarch, 738
caramelized, or Crème Caramel, 735
cheese pie, 255
chestnut mound or Mont Blanc, 738
chocolate, coffee, 735
chocolate cornstarch, 739
chocolate or Pots-de-Crème, 737
cornstarch, or blancmange, 738
crab meat, 266
Crème Brûlée, 736
fillings, pastries and cakes, 697–699
Floating Island, 735
fried cream or Crème Frite, 739
molded, 745
mousse, French chocolate, 737
mousse, rum chocolate, 738
orange, with meringue, 736
orange or lemon sponge, 737
pies, 655, **655,** 656
rich, 735
sauce, 771
soup, or Royale, 172
sponge, 736, 737
tapioca, 750
tart, with fruit, 655
for timbales, 231
tomato, 333
wine or Weinschaum, 736
Zabaglione or Sabayon, 736
Cyclamates, 560

D

Dampfnudeln, or Raised Dumplings, 663
Dandelion, 94
Darnes, 396, 410
Dasheen, or taro, about, 331
Date, about, **123,** 136; to store, 137
bars, Cockaigne, 703
bread, quick, 623; with bran, 625
cake, spice, 679; chocolate, 670
cookies, 717
doughnuts, 246
filling for coffee cake, 622; for cookies, 717
loaf, uncooked, 753
pudding, steamed, 754
ring, baked, 752
roll or centers, 793
Daube Glacé, 461
Day lily blossoms, 235, 243
Decreasing and increasing recipes, 589
Deep-fat frying, about, 147, **147**
fats for, 148
frozen foods, 148
at high altitudes, 148
hors d'oeuvre, 82
Deep-well cooking, 151–152
Deer, *see* Venison
Deglazing, sauces, 340; with wine, 526
Degreasing, sauces, 340; in soups, 168
Dehydrated foods, about, 798
Delmonico, Bombe, 762; ice cream, 759, 762
Demerara sugar, 557
Desalting ham and other cured meats, 482
DESSERT, 734–757
Bavarian creams, 746–748
bombes, 760, 762, 763
cakes, 664–699
candies and confections, 777–797
Charlottes, 748
cheese, 756, **756,** 757
cookies, 700–720
creams or crèmes, 746–751
crêpes, 236; Suzette, 237
crullers, beignets and doughnuts, 244–246
custards, 734–739
dumplings, sweet, 662, 663
to freeze and thaw, 831
frozen, 758–769
frozen, storage, 761; to prevent graininess in, 761
fruit salad with cream, 122
fruits, 123–144
gelatin, 743–746
ices, ice cream, sherbets, 758–769
molds, 743, **743, 758;** to unmold, 561, 743
molds, caramel-coated, about, 743
molds, chocolate cases, 743
molds, lined with cake, 743, **743**
mousses, about, 760
omelets, sweet, 227, 742
pancakes and waffles, 753
parfaits, about, 760
pies and pastries, 638–663
Pots-de-Crème, **734**
puddings, **734,** 734–739, 748–755
sauces, 769–776
savories, about, 755

DESSERT *(cont.)*
souffles, sweet, 739–742
Torten, 684
Deviled, butter for seafood, 351
crab, 266
eggs; in sauce, 225
ham sandwich and cheese, 272
Devonshire cream, 534
Dewberries, 134; canning, 806
Dijonnaise Sauce, 342
Dill, beans, pickled, 845
leaves and seeds, 581
loaf, batter, 604
pickles, 848
seeds, 581
Dinner Menus, 29; formal, 33
Dips for hors d'oeuvre, 83, 89, 90, 91
Divan, chicken or turkey, 264; seafood, 265
Divinity, 783, 784
Dobos Torte, 685
Dolmas, 492
Dorure or French Egg Wash, 731
Double-boiler cooking, about, 153
Dough, bread, 599–602
to freeze and thaw, 829, 830
pie, 639–643
puff paste, 643
refrigerator, about, 618
sour, 554
Doughnuts, about, 244; to fry, 147, **147**
buttermilk-potato, 245
chocolate; drop, 246
high-altitude, 245
jelly or Berlin, 245
orange, 246
pecan or date, 246
sour cream, 245
sweet milk, 245
variations, 245
yeast, 245
Doves, 440, 441
Dredging, defined, 552, **552**
Dresden Sauce, 356
DRESSING, 370–374; *also see* Salad Dressings
apple, 372; prune or onion and, 372
apricot or prune, 373
bread, for fish, 371
bread, with mushrooms, oysters, nuts, giblets, etc., 370
chestnut, for game, 372
chicken farce or forcemeat, 374
for crown roast of pork, 371
dry, 370
fennel, 372
green, for fish or fowl, 371
ham, for turkey, 372
liver, 373
onion; and apple; and sage, 372
oyster bread, 371
rice, 373
rice for Cornish hen or pigeon, 373
rice with tangerine or pineapple Cockaigne, 373
sauerkraut, for game, 374
DRESSING *(cont.)*
sausage, 371
seafood, 371
sherry bread, 371
spoilage, to avoid, 370
sweet potato and apple; sausage, 374
wild rice, for game, 373
Dried Beef, *see* Chipped Beef
DRINKS, alcoholic, 48–65; *also see* Beverages, nonalcoholic
ale, about, 58
Alexander, 49
Aquavit, about; cocktails, 53
bar equipment, 48, **48**
Bénédictine, 51
Bloody Mary, 53
Bobbie Burns, 51
Bowle, 63
brandy, and brandy cocktails, 52
brandy, sour, 49
Bronx, 49
champagne cocktail, 52; cup, 63
champagne fountain, 56, **56**
champagne punch, 63
claret cup, 64
cocktails, about, 48
cocktail glasses, **49**
Coconut Extravaganza, 60, **60**
Cooler, 59
cordials, about, 58
Cuba Libre, 60
Cubana, 51
Curaçao cocktail, 52
daiquiri, 51; blender frozen, 52
eggnog, 61; in quantity, 64
El Presidente, 52
Fish House Punch, 63
flip, 62
fruit, plugged, about, 60, **60**
Gibson, 50
Gimlet, 49
Gin Fizz, 59
gin and gin cocktails, 49
glasses, for brandy, **57;** champagne fountain, **56;** cocktails, **49;** liqueur and cordials, **57;** mixed drinks, **59;** wine, 57, **57,** 58
glasses, to sugar-frost, 51
glogg, 65
grog, 61
highballs, 59
Horse's Neck, 59
ice; decorative cubes, 42; molds, 62, **62**
Irish coffee, 39
Jack Rose, 52
Knickerbocker, 52
liqueurs, about, 58
Mai Tai, 52
Manhattan, 51
Margarita, 53
martinis, 50
May wine, 64
measurements, about, 49
mint julep, 59, **59, 60**

DRINKS *(cont.)*
mixed, about, 59
Negus in quantity, 65
Old-Fashioned, 51
Orange Blossom, 49
party, about, 62
Pineapple Tropic, 61
Pink Lady, 50
Planter's Punch, 63
punch bowl, ice, to make, 62, **63**
punches and toddies, 61–65
Rhine wine cup, 64
rickey, 59
Rob Roy, 51
Ruddy Mary, 53
rum, about, 51; cocktails, 51
rum, hot buttered, 61
rum, mapled, 60
rum cassis cup, 64
rum sour, 49
Sangria, 62
Sazerac, 51
Scarlett O'Hara, 52
Screwdriver, 53
short, about, 61
Sidecar, 52
Silver Fizz, 59
Spritzer, 59
Stinger, 52
sugar syrup for, 48
Syllabub or milk punch, 62
tall, about, 59
tequila and tequila cocktails, 53
toddy, 61
Tom Collins, 59
Tom and Jerry, hot, 61; in quantity, 65
tonic, 60
Tovarich, 53
Vermouth Cassis, 59
Vin Brûlé, 61
vodka and vodka cocktails, 53
vodka martini, 50
wassail, 65
whisky or brandy cup, 64
whisky bitter, 49
whisky and cocktails, 50
whisky sour, 49
White Lady, 50
wine, mulled, in quantity, 65
wines, 53–58
Drippings, about, 542
Drugstore wrap for freezing, 821, **821**
Dry-curing meat, game, and fowl, 813
Dry-salting vegetables, 848
Drying foods, 816–818; equipment, **816, 817, 818**
mushrooms, about, 818
oven pasteurization, 818
sun-drying, 817, **818**
Duck, 432; *also see* Poultry
fruit and honey-glazed, 433
Pilaf, 433
pressed, equipment, **417**
roast, 432; Bigarade, 433
Duck *(cont.)*
Rouennaise, 433
wild, about, 437
wild, braised; broiled or barbecued; roast, 437
Dumplings, about, 202, **202**
butter or Butterklösse, 203
cheese, 203
cornmeal, 203
farina balls Cockaigne, 203
fruit, 662
German egg, Spatzen or Spätzle, 205
gnocchi, 204
liver, or Leberklösse, 196
liver sausage, 196
matzo or cracker meal, 203
Nockerln, 203
potato or Kartoffelklösse, 204
quenelles, 205, **205**
raised or Dampfnudeln, 663
Durian, 143
Duxelles, 573

E

Earthenware, 162
Éclair, chocolate, **638,** 647
fillings for, 647
Ecological awareness, or ecology in food, 4
Écrevisses, about, 391, **392**
Edam cheese, filled, 81; nuggets, 81
Eel, about, 406; smoked, rolls, 88
EGG AND EGG DISHES
about, 543–545; dishes, 220–234
in aspic; Cockaigne, 117
baked, additions to, 223
baked, in bacon rings, 224
baked or shirred, 223
baked on toast, 223
beating, 544, **544**
Benedict, 222
bread or Challah, 605, **605**
coddled, 220
to condition or temper, 543
cooking, about, 543
cowboy or Huevos Rancheros, 222
cream sauce, 345
creamed, and asparagus, Cockaigne, 224
creamed, au gratin, 225
curried, 224
deviled or stuffed, 225; in sauce, 225
dried, to reconstitute, 543
drops, hard-cooked, 172
drops for clear soups, 171, **172**
Florentine, 221
Fooyoung, 228
freezing and thawing, 827
freshness test, 543, **543**
fried or sautéed, 220; additions, 221
Frittata, 228
garnishes, 82, **82;** for soup, 171, 172, **172**
glaze, for baking, 731
ham cakes and, 224
ham and sautéed, 485
hard-cooked, 220; to test, 545

EGG AND EGG DISHES *(cont.)*
hard-cooked, spreads, 73
hard-cooked, white sauce, 342
for hors d'oeuvre, about, 82, **82**
masked, 225
to measure, 543, **543**
in a nest, 224
omelets, 226–228; *see* Omelets
painted, **220**
poached, additions to, 221
poached, Blackstone, 222
poached, in soup; in wine; Mornay, 221
to preserve at home, 814
ring, molded, 117
roll, Chinese, 250
salad, asparagus and, 100
salad, molded, and caviar, 106
sandwich with cheese and tomato sauce, 273
sauces, *see* Sauces
Scotch Woodcock, 223
scrambled, 222; additions to, 223
to separate, beat and fold, 544, **544**
shirred, or en Cocotte, 223
smoked salmon and, 222
soft-cooked, 220
soufflé dish, **220**
soufflées, 228–231
spreads, hard-cooked, 73
stains, to remove, 545
to store, 545
stuffed or deviled, 225
stuffed on rosettes with sauce, 225
to thicken soups, 168
thickened sauces, about, 357
timbales, 231–234
tree, **220**
vegetable casserole, and, 224
whites, to beat, 544, **544;** with electric mixer for cakes, 667
whites, to fold, 545, 665, **665**
whites, stiff, but not dry, 545
whites, uncooked, about, 743
yolk, to add to hot liquid, 543
yolks as sauce thickener, 339
Eggless, Bavarian cream, 748
cakes, 679; honey-rye, 626
cookies, 704, 706, 712, 713, 714, 716, 719, 720
pie, lemon or lime, 657
Eggnog, 61
frozen, 762
milk, 42
pineapple or orange, 45
in quantity, 64
Eggplant, about, 302
casserole, or Ratatouille, 304
casserole with lamb, 491
discoloration, to avoid, 302
fritters, 244
halves, baked, 303
moisture, to rid of excess, 302
scalloped, 303
slices, baked; deep-fried; and sautéed, 303
Eggplant *(cont.)*
stuffed or Farcie; Creole, 304, **304**
timbale, 232
Elderberry, 134; blossoms, **235**
canning, 806
jam, 836
Elk, *see* Venison
Empañadas, 69
Enamelware, 162
En croûte cookery, meat, 448; pâté, 494
En papillote, cooking, 153, **153**
Enchiladas, 252
Endive, Belgian, French or witloof, 93, **93,** 299
braised or glazed, 298
salad, cooked, 101
stuffed, 84
Engineered foods, 535
English muffins, 617, **617**
ENTERTAINING, 15–24
cooking, outdoor, about, 155–159
cooking for large parties, 23
Entrées, defined, 17
Entremets, about, 18
Equipment, cooking, indoor, about, 159–165
kitchen, basic, 163
EQUIVALENTS AND SUBSTITUTIONS, about, 589–592; for common ingredients, 593–598
Escabèche, 402
Escalope de Veau Orloff, 468
Escarole, 93, **93;** soup, cream of, 185
Espresso equipment, 36, **37**
Euphrates Bread, 609
Extracts used with sweets, 577

F

Faggots, 572
Fan-Tans, or buttermilk rolls, 612, **612**
Farce of Lamb, 473
Farces, *see* Dressings, 370–374
Farci, 467
Farina, 547
balls Cockaigne, or dumplings, 203
cereal, 200
gnocchi, 204
pudding, 749
Farls, Irish, *see* Skillet Bread, 627
FATS AND OILS, *also see individual names*
about, 5, **5;** 539–542
absorption in frying, 147
butter, about, 539
cholesterol, about, 5
clarifying, about, 542
cracklings, 542
for deep-frying, 148
drippings, about, 542
lard, about, 542
margarine, about, 541
measuring bulk fats, 539, **539**
pork, about, 542
poultry, about, 542
to remove salt, 542
to remove from soup, 168, **168**
rendering or trying out, 542

FATS AND OILS *(cont.)*
saturated or polyunsaturated, 5, 539
shortenings, about, 148
smoking points of, 148
solid, to measure, 539, **539**
vegetable shortenings, about, 541
Fecula, sauce thickener, 339
Feijoa, 144
Fennel, about, 304; as seasoning, 581
dressing, 372
Florence, **276**
stuffed, 84
tisane, 40
Fenugreek, 581
Fermented milks and creams, about, 533
Fern shoots, 304
Fettucine, or noodle dough, 213, **213**
al burro, 214
Fig, about, **129,** 137; dried, 125
cake, spice, 679
canning, 807
filling, and almond, 698; for coffee cake, 622; for cookie, 717
fresh, stuffed, 137
poached, 137
preserves, 838
pudding, baked, 752
Figpeckers, about, 440
Filberts, 563; paste, 780
Filé powder, 340
Filet de Boeuf en Croûte, 455
Filet Mignon, 454, **454**
Fillets, *see* Beef, Fish
Fillings, *see names of; also see:*
Biscuit fillings, 270
Bread roll, 270
Coffee cake fillings, 621–623
Cookie fillings, 716–718
Pasta fillings, 218
Tomato, fillings for, 105, 333
Fines herbes, 572
Finger bowl service, 20, **20**
Finnan Haddie, about, 406
baked, 407; creamed, 407
Finocchio or fennel, 276, 304; stuffed, 84
Fire, charcoal hazard, 156
grease, 147
outdoor, about, 155
Fireless cooking, 151
Firepot, Chinese, 145, 462
First aid for burns, 165
FISH, 394–416; also see Seafood, Shellfish
about, 394; cooking, **394,** 397
in aspic, Cockaigne, 401
baked, stuffed, 398, unstuffed, 398
baked in clay, 399; in foil, 399
baked in covered dish, 399
baked with sour cream, 399
baker, **394**
balls or cakes, 266, 405
balls or rolls, 88, 89
au bleu trout, 414
bloaters, grilled or baked, 408

FISH *(cont.)*
blowfish, about, 411
boiled or poached, 400, 525
bonito, fresh, 415
braising, about, 400
broiled on skewers, 403
broiling, about, **394;** 402, **403;** types for, 403
cake, emergency, 266
canapés, 75, 76
canning, 811
carp, about, 404
catfish, Southern-fried, 404
caviar, about, 87
Chinese firepot cooking, 462
and chips, 404
chowder, 190, 194
cleaning and preparing, 395–397, **395–397**
cod, about, 404; scalloped, 405
cod, Brandade de Morue, 405
cod, fresh, Boulangère, 406
cod, fresh, à la Portugaise, 405
cod sounds and tongues, 405
codfish balls or cakes, 405
court bouillon, 525
creamed molded, 121
croquettes, 247
cured, about, 407
deep-fat-fried, 403, 404; marinated, 404
dishes for lunch, supper, 264–269
dressings or stuffings, 371
dumplings, *see* Quenelles, 206
eel, about, 406
Escabèche, 88
to fillet, 396–397; **396–397**
fillets, baked, 399; quick, 400
fillets, baked, small, or sticks au gratin, 400
fillets, baked, Spencer, 399
fillets, Florentine; Marguéry, 400
fillets, molded, filled, 400
fillets, sautéed, amandine, 404
fillets, sautéed, Palm Beach, 404
fillets, sole Ambassador, 413; Duglèré, 414
fillets, sole Florentine, 414; Véronique, 413
fillets Bonne Femme, 401
Finnan Haddie, baked; creamed, 407
fishy taste, to minimize, 397
flat, to fillet, 397, **397**
flounder fillets, marinated, 406
freezing, thawing and cooking, 827
fritters, batter for, 243
frozen, 397
fumet or stock, 524
Gefilte, 402
haddock, about, 406
haddock, fillets baked in sauce, 406
haddock, fillets baked with mushrooms and tomatoes, 407
herring, about, 407; marinated, 408
herring, baked, and potatoes, 408
herring, Scotch-fried, 408; salads, 107
herring, sweet and sour, 408
hors d'oeuvre, 87–91
jambalaya, 211

FISH *(cont.)*
kebabs, 403
to keep warm, 397
kippers, grilled or baked, 408
large, preparing, 395
loaf, quick, 266
lox, defined, 410
mackerel, broiled, fresh, 410; salt, 410
mackerel, salt, boiled, 410
marinade for, 528
mousse or timbale, 233
octopus, about, 408, **409;** casseroled, 409
odors, to remove, 397
Paupiettes, 400
pickled, or Escabèche, 402
pie, individual, 266
planked, 398
poaching, **394,** 400
pompano en papillote, 410
quenelles, baked or poached, 206
raw, *see* Seviche, 88
red snapper baked with sauce, 413
roe and milt, about, 87, 411
roe, canned, creamed, broiled, 268; in ramekins, 269
roe, shad, baked; broiled, 412
roe, shad, parboiled, 411
roe, shad, sautéed, 412
salads, 106–108
salmon, about, 410; cold, glazed, 411
salmon steaks, or darnes, broiled, 410
sardines, about, 411
sauces, *see* Sauces
sautéed or pan-fried, 403
scrod, about, 405; broiled, 406
sea, about, 394; tidbits, 87, **87**
sea squab, about, 411
to serve, 18, 19; to serve cold, 397
Seviche, 88
shad, baked, with creamed roe, 412
shad, boning and carving, 412
shark, about, 412
small, butterfly-filleted, 395
small, preparing, 395
smelts, 412
smoking, 816
soufflé, 230
soups, 186–190; quick, 193–194
squid, about, 408, **409;** casseroled, 409
squid, fried, 409; stuffed, 409
squid, in ink sauce, 410
steaks, Marguéry, 400; poached, 401
steaks, or darnes, preparing, 396, **396**
steaming, about, **394,** 400
stews, 188–190
sticks, au gratin, 400
stock or fumet, 524
swordfish steaks, 414
to test for doneness, 397
timbale, 233
trout, blue, or Truite au Bleu, 414
trout, brook, Meunière, 414
trout, lake, broiled, 414

FISH *(cont.)*
tuna, about, 415
turbot, poached, 415
whitebait, or Blanchaille, 415
whitefish, broiled, 414
Five-Spices Powder, 572
Flambéing or flaming, 155
fruits, 127
Flameproof ware, 162
Flan with fruit, 655; with cheese, 255
Flapjacks, *see* Pancakes
Flavors, about, 567–577
used with sweets, 577
Floating Island, 735
Florentine, defined, 326
Florentine Sauce, 342
Florentines, 706
Flounder fillets, marinated, 406
Flour, about, 545
all-purpose, 547
arrowroot or starch, 550
barley, 550
bean, 550
bran, 548
bread, 547
browned, thickening power, 339
buckwheat, 550
cake, 547
carob, 550
cereal substitute, 551
corn, 548; cornmeal, 549
Cornell Triple-Rich Formula, 602
cornstarch; waxy, 548
cottonseed, 550
cracked wheat, 548
farina, 547
to flour foods, 552, **552**
gluten, 548
graham, 547
instant, 547
measuring, 546, **546**
milo maize, 550
moisture-content, 546
nonwheat, about, 548
nut meal, 550
oat and oatmeal, 550
oats, rolled, 550
paste, sauce thickener, 339
pastry, 547
peanut, 550
phosphated, 547
potato, 550
presifted, 547
rice, 549
rye; rye meal, 549
seasoned for flouring, 552
self-rising, 547
semolina, 547
sifting, 546, **546**
sorghum, 550
soy; soy meal, 549
to store, 546
substitutions, *see individual flours*

Flour *(cont.)*
sweet or Mochika, 549
tapioca, 550
triticale, 548
unbleached, 547
wheat, about, 546, **547**
wheat, cracked, 548
wheat allergy substitute, 551
wheat-germ, 548
whole-grain, 547
whole wheat or graham, 547
Flowers, *also see* Blossoms
decorations for cakes, 733
table arrangements, 15–16, **16, 22, 23, 25**
Foie Gras, for canapés, 75
Foil cookery, 153
Fondant, 778–780; icing, 725
Fonds or stock bases, 520
Fondue, Bagna Cauda, 90
bay scallops, 382
Boeuf Bourguignonne, 457
cheese, 254, **254**
chocolate-dipped bananas, 132
curried fruit, 128
savory consommé Cockaigne, quick, 191
sweet, *see* Sweet sauces, 769–776
vegetable, 280
Food mill, 832, 841
FOODS WE EAT, 1–14
accessory factors, 6
calories, about, 2; values, 8–14
carbohydrates, about, 5
daily needs, 6
fats, about, 5, **5**
imitation foods, about, 7
natural poisons in, 7
nutrition, about, 1
product labeling, 7
proteins, about, 2; values, 8–14
FOODS WE HEAT, 145–166
about; dry, 146–149; moist, 149–155
baking, 146; pan placement, 159, **159**
barbecueing, **156,** 156–158, **157, 158**
blanching, 154
boiling, 149
brazier cooking, 156–158
broiling, 146
broiling units, 159
casseroling, 151
deep-fat frying, about, 147, **147**
double-boiler cooking, 153
en papillote cooking, 153, **153**
fireless cooking, 151
flaming or flambéing, 155
foil cookery, 153
grilling, 156–158
high-altitude, 145
indoor cooking equipment, 159–165
kitchen equipment, basic, 163
microwave cooking, 160
outdoor cooking, 155–159
parblanching; parboiling; parsteaming, 154
partial heat processes, 154
FOODS WE HEAT *(cont.)*
pit-cooking, 155
planking, 154
poaching, 150
pressure cooking, 150
reducing liquids, 154
reheating foods, 161
rotisserie cooking, 158, **158**
sautéing or pan-frying, 149
scalding, 155
serving temperatures, 161
simmering, 150
spit cooking, 158
skewer cooking, 146
steam-blanching, 154
steaming, 154
steeping, 154
stir-frying, skillet-panning or shallow frying, 149
time element, 161
toasting, 154
utensils, 162, 163
wrap cookery, 152
FOODS WE KEEP, 798–801
additives, about, 798
brining, 813–814
canning, 802–818
dehydrated, 798
drying, 816–818
freeze-dried, 798
freezing, 819–831
jellies and preserves, 832–840
pickles and relishes, 841–849
preserved foods, storage of, 800
salting or dry-curing, 813–814
smoking, 814–816
spoilage, about, 798, 799
staples for average family, 799
to stock the kitchen, 799
storage, about, 799
wintering fresh produce, 800
Fools, fruit, 124
Forcemeat, 370-374, *see* Dressing
Formal entertaining; place settings, 17–20, **18, 19, 20**
Four Spices, 572
Foyot sauce, 359
Fowl, *also see* Poultry and Wildfowl
barbecue sauce for, 354
croquettes, 247
dry-curing, 813
rotisserie or spit-cooking, **158**
smoking and cooking, 816
stock, 523
Frangipane Cream, filling, 697
Frankfurters, baked beans and, 259
barbecued, 258; kebabs, 259
Oblaten, 719
in sauce, 259
sauerkraut casserole, 499
Freezer, contents and management, 819
power breaks, 820
Freezing, *see* Frozen foods
French Egg Wash, 731

French Toast, 636; cheese or tomato, 273
sandwich, 271; waffles, 242
Fricassee, chicken or turkey, 426
Fried Pies, canapé, 69
Fries, lamb, 510
Frijoles Refritos, 287
Frittata, 228
Fritter, batter, about, 242; for fruit, 243; meat; vegetables; fish, 243; blossoms, 243
calf brain, 244
cassolettes, 242
choux paste, unsweetened, 243
corn, 301; and ham, 244
eggplant, 244
French or Beignets, 246
Fritto Misto, 243
garnish for soups, 196
high-altitude, 242
meat, cooked, 244
rice, 244
vegetable, puréed, 243
Fritto Misto, defined, 243
Frog legs, braised, 415
deep-fat-fried, 415
Forestière, 416
in mushroom sauce, 416
FROZEN DESSERTS, 758–769; *also see individual names*
FROZEN FOODS, 819-831; *see individual names; watch for symbol* ❄
anti-browning solution for, 823
blanching, 824; equipment, 825, **825**
commercial package sizes, 592
cooked in foil, 153
cooking, about, 822
economic advantages of, 819
freeze-dried foods, about, 798
freezing on trays, **819,** 822
freezing principles, 819
labeling and dating, 822
precooked, freezing and thawing, 828
retaining nutrition of, 820
thawing and cooking, 822, 825–827
types suitable for freezing, 820, 823, 824, 826, 827, 828
vegetable sizing box, **821**
wrapping, packaging and sealing, 820, **821, 822**
FRUIT, 123–144; *also see individual names*
ambrosia, 124
anti-browning solution for: fresh, 124; canning, 805; freezing, 823
baked, additions to, 127
baked, stuffed, 127
baked as meat garnish, 127
beverages, about, 42
blanching for freezing, 822, **825**
broiled, 127
Brûlé, 127
cakes, 682-683; *also see* Cakes
cakes, to decorate; to store, 682
candied, crystallized and glazed, about, 794
candy roll or centers, 793
canned, spiced syrup for, 126
FRUIT *(cont.)*
canning, about, 805–808
casserole with beef, 463
casserole with nuts and rice, 210
cobbler or deep-dish pie, 660
compote, fresh, baked, 126
compôte composée, 123
cooked, about, 125
crisps, 661, 662
crocked, or Tutti-Frutti, 840
crumb fillings for coffee cakes, 622, 623
cups, 124
curried, fondue, 128
dried, about, 816; to cook, 125
dried, freezing, 831
dried, to plump, 125; to store, 125
dried, stuffed, appetizer, 80; candy, 793
dumplings, 662
fillings, chopped; ginger, 698
flambéed, 127
fools, 124
freezing, 822–824
fresh, about, 123
fritter or Fritto Misto, 243
as garnish; garnishes for drinks, 42, **42**
gelatin, quick, 744
glaze, 732; and honey, 433
glazed fresh, 794
ice creams, 760, 762, 764, 765
ices, 765–769
juice gelatin, 744
juice for jelly making, 833
juice twosomes, 44
juices, about, 42
juices, canning, 807; freezing, 824
kebabs, 127
Macédoine, 124
for meats and entrées, about, 128
mousse, 764
-nut pemmican, 125
pancake, 237
paradise, or crisp, 661
pared, poached or "stewed," 126
passion, 144
paste, 797; Turkish, 791
pastries, 660–663
plugged, about, 60, **60**
poached, 126
puddings, steamed, 754, 755
puréed, about, 127; freezing, 824
puréed, garnishes for, 127
to ripen, 123
salads, 109–112; gelatin, 117–122
sauces, sweet, 769–776
sautéed, 128
seeds, danger in, 124
to serve, 123
shortcakes, 690
sherbets, 765–769
shrubs or vinegars, 44
soufflé, fresh, 740
soufflé with sweet potato, 230
soup, cherry; orange, 128; rose hip, 129

FRUIT *(cont.)*
spiked, 60, **60**
"stewed," 126
sticks, 274
to store, 123
sugars, 557
sweet potatoes, and, 325
syrups for, 126
as a table arrangement, **15**
tropical, exotic, **123, 129,** 143, **143**
turnovers, sweet, 662
to wash, 124
whips, 745, 746
Frying or sautéing, 149; *also see* Deep-fat frying
Fudge, cakes, *see* Cakes
caramel cream, 782
carob, 783; coffee, 783
Cockaigne, 782; white, 783
cocoa, or centers, 782
coconut, or centers, 783
pie, 656
sauce, hot, 772
Fumet, fowl, rabbit or game, 523; fish, 524

G

Galantine of turkey, 431, **432**
Galette dough, about, 642
Gallinule, 440
GAME, 513–518; *see individual names*
to bleed and hang, 810
canning, about, 811
to clean, cut and store, 810, 811
dressings, 370–374
diseases, to guard against, 810
dry-curing, 813
large, about, **516**
marinades for, 528, 529
preparing, about, 810
saddles of, 517
small, about, 513
stock, 523
tularemia warning, 513
GAME BIRDS, *also see* Wildfowl
small, barding; braised; broiled; roasted, 440
small, skewered, 440
Gänseklein, 434
Garbure, or Bean Soup, 177
Garlic or ail, about; types, 584
to blanch, 584
bread, 636, **636**
butter, 351
giant or topping, 584, **586**
oriental, 584, **585**
to press, 584
for salads, 95
sauce, 365
vinegar, 527
Garnishes, almond or amandine, 553
aspic, 114
au gratin, 552
for beverages, 42, **42**
citrus fruit, 571, **571**
cracklings or grattons, 572
Garnishes *(cont.)*
croutons, buttered crumbs, 551
eggs, 82, **82**
fruit, baked, for meats, 127
for ice cream, 758
mushrooms as, 307, **307**
nuts, glazed, or praliné, 789
Polvo de Amor, 567
for puréed fruit, 127
quenelles, 205
for salads, 98, 99, **99**
Sicilian, 366
for soup, 194–197, **194**
truffles as, 310
Gâteau Crêpe, 237
Gaufrettes or ice cream cones, 719
Gazpacho, 171; blender, 191
Gefilte fish, 402
Gefüllter Krautkopf, 491
GELATIN, 743–746; *also see* Aspic
about, 560, 561; **561**
blancmange, 745
cheesecake, 660
custard, molded, 745
fruit, for desserts, 744–746
fruit, for salads, 117–120
fruit juice, 744
fruit molded in, about, 744
fruit whips, 745, 746
mayonnaise, 368
mocha, 745
molds, fancy, to make, 560, 561, **561**
pies, *see* Pies, 658, 659
puddings, 743–748
salads, 113–120; basic, 113
wine, 745
Gelatinous thickeners, 561
Genip, 144
Génoise, 675
Geranium leaves, 581
Ghee, 349
Gherkins, pickled, 843
Giblets, about, 418, **418**
chicken, stew, 512
dressing, 370
Gin, about, 49
drinks, 49, 50, 59
Ginger, Canton, 576
candied, 796
candy or centers, 792
crisp, 662
snaps, 707; thins, 707
vinegar, 528
Gingerbread, 681; wheatless, 681
high-altitude, 694
men, 712, **712**
Glaçage, about, 367
Glace de Viande, 368
Glaces, defined, 765
Glasses, beer and ale, 58, **58**
champagne fountain, **56**
cocktail, 49, **49**
frosted for mint julep, 60

Glasses *(cont.)*
highball, **59**
mixed drinks, 59, **59**
placement, filling, **16,** 16-21, **18, 19, 20**
sugar-frosted, 51
water, 16–21, **16, 18, 19, 20**
wine, brandy and liqueur, 57, **57,** 58
GLAZE, savory, 367–369; sweet, 731–733
about, 367
applying, 731
apricot, peach, or raspberry, 732
aspic, 368
for breads, 731, 732
for canapés, 70
caramel, clear, 732
caramelized sugar, 559
casserole, on, 368
chocolate, 732
Chaud-Froid sauce, 369
cranberry, for fowl, 368
for fruits, fresh, 794
for fruits, leaves and blossoms, to candy, 794
French egg wash or Dorure, 731
fruit; thickened, 732
fruit and honey, 433
to give color to dough, 731
honey for coffeecakes, 731–732
honey, for meat or onions, 368
lemon, 731
liqueur, 732
Mayonnaise Collée or gelatin, 368
meat or Glace de Viande, 368
milk, 731
for pies, tarts and coffee cakes, 732
for puff paste, 732
to reduce, 522
Royal Glaze or decorative icing, 727
spirit for ham, 368
strawberry, 732
for vegetables, 280
Glazed Boeuf à la Mode, 461
Gluten bread, 609; flour, 548
Gnocchi, 204, **204**
Goat meat, about, 471
Goetta, 499
Golden Syrup, 559
Good Friday Noodles, 214
Goose, about, 433
braised trimmings or Gänseklein, 434
liver, 502; as hors d'oeuvre, 86
potted or Confit d'Oie, 434
roast, about, 432
wild, 438
Gooseberries, about, 134; canning, 806
Chinese, 144
jam, 836; preserves, 838
jelly, and raspberry, 834
pie, 650
Gouda cheese, filled, 81
Goulash, about, 464; à blanc, 475
beef, 465
pork and veal sauerkraut, 481
Graham, *also see* Whole wheat
cracker crust, 642
flour, 547
Grains, about, 564; to sprout, 565
Granadilla, purple, 144
Grand Marnier Soufflé, 740
Graniti, defined, 765
Granola, 198
Grape, about, 137; canning, 807
catsup, 847
jellies, 834, 835
juice, canning, 807
leaves, stuffed, 492; or Dolmas, 152, **152**
pie, 652
salads, 111, 112, 118
Grapefruit, about, 136; to peel and section, 135, **135**
aspic with sherry, 118
canning, 807
cups, 136
juice and pineapple, 44
salads, 111, 118
sherbet, 767
sweetened, 136
Grater, 336
Gratins, about, 552
Grattons, 572
Gravies, 340, 341; *also see* Sauces
boats or dishes for, **340**
pan, meat; poultry, 341
Grease, fire warning, 147
to remove from stock, 521
Greek flat bread, 609
Greek Salad, *see* Combination I, 98
Green Goddess Dressing, 364
Greens, cultivated, about, 305; for salad, 92–94, **93**
canning, 809
to wash and dry, 94, **94, 95**
wild, for salads, 94; for vegetable, 305
wilted, salad, 96
Gremolata, 572
Grenache, mayonnaise, 363
Gribiche Sauce, 365
Griddle, biscuit, 634; breads, 617, 627–629
cake pans, **235**
cakes, *see* Pancakes, 235
soapstone, **235**
Grill or brazier, 156, **156,** 157, **157**
English mixed, 473
foods for, 157
sandwiches, 269
vegetable, mixed, 256
Grissini, 599, 606
Grits, corn or hominy, 200
Groats, buckwheat, 201; cereal, to cook, 200
Grog, 61
Groundnut Soup, 180
Grouse, roasted, 439
Gruel, 199
Guacamole, 83
Guava, about, 137; pineapple, 144
jelly, 835
Gugelhopf Coffee Cake, 620; quick, 626

Guinea fowl, about, 434
breasts of; roast, 434
Gulyàs, about, 464
Gum Arabic, defined, 794
Gum paste, 791
Gum tragacanth, 561
Gumbo, chicken, 176

H

Haddock, about, 406
fillets baked in cheese sauce, 406
fillets baked with mushrooms and tomatoes, 407
Finnan Haddie baked, or creamed, 407
HAM, 482–485
about, 482
baked, 483, 484; with tomatoes and cheese, 485
broiled, 484
butt, shank, or picnic, 485
cabbage, potatoes and, 293
cakes and eggs, 224
cakes with pineapple and sweet potatoes, 258
cakes with potato, 258
canned, about, 483
to carve, **484**
country, to cook, 484
country, defined, 483
croquettes, and corn, 248
cuts of, 483
to decorate, **484**
desalting, about, 482
deviled, sandwich, 272
dressing for turkey, 372
dry-curing, 813
fresh, defined, 483; roast, 478
fritters and corn, 244
"fully cooked" or "ready to eat," about, 484
glaze for, spirit, 368
ground, on pineapple slices, 258
hocks with sauerkraut, 485
hors d'oeuvre, 80, 81
à la King, 258
large cuts, suggested uses, 453
loaf, cooked ground, 257
loaf, raw smoked, 493
mousse, jellied, 120
noodles, 214
processing of, 482–483
prosciutto and Westphalian, *see* About Hams, 482–483
ring and rice, 207
rolls, stuffed, 257
salad, 109
sandwiches, 271–272
sautéed, and eggs, 485
seasoning, as, 572
slices, casseroled, 485
slices, with fruit, 485
smoked, about, 482
smoking, 814, **815**
spreads for canapés, 74
to store, 483
stuffed in cabbage, 294
Ham *(cont.)*
timbales, 232
trichinosis in, 477
Virginia, Smithfield or Kentucky, 484
with veal scallops, 469
HAMBURGER, 486–493
additions to, 487
Biff à la Lindström, 488
broiled, 487
cheeseburgers, 488
filled beef, 488
freezing, 826; to wrap, **822**
grilled, 487
Porcupines, 490
sautéed, 487
Sloppy Joes, 490
venison, 517
Hard Sauce, 775; topping, 730
Hare, see Rabbit, 513–515
Harusame, or "Long Rice," 212
Hasenpfeffer Casserole, 513, 514
Hash, about, 261; to reheat, 162
beef, with potatoes and mushrooms, 261
in bread dressing ring, 262
browned or sautéed, 261
chicken or turkey, 263
corned beef patties, 261
corned beef and potatoes, 261
in creamed cabbage, 262
heavenly, 790
quick, 262
red flannel, 466
shepherd's pie, 262
vegetables, with, 262
Hazelnuts, 563
Bavarian cream, 747
cookies, 706
custard filling, 699
soufflé, 741
torte, 686
Hawaiian, candy or centers, 792
meatballs, 490
toast sandwich, with bacon, 271
Head, calf or lamb, 510
Head cheese or brawn, 511
Heart, about, 508
baked, stuffed, 508
braised slices in sour sauce, 508
Hearts of palm, about, 313
HEAT, *also see* Foods We Heat
cooking equipment, indoor, 159–165, **159, 164**
cooking equipment, outdoor, 155–159, **156, 157, 158**
deep-fat frying, 147, **147**
dry, about, 146
moist, about, 149
outdoor cooking, 155–159
partial, processes, about, 154
placement of oven racks, 159
poaching paper, to prepare, 151
pressure cooking, 150
skewer cooking, 146
slow cooking, 151

HEAT *(cont.)*
spit and rotisserie cooking, 156–158, **156, 157, 158**
Heatproof ware, 162
Hemerocallis blossoms, 235
HERBS, 577–588; *also see individual names*
about, 577–579
bouquets garnis or faggots, 572
bread, 604
butters, seasoned, 349
chiffonade of, 571; for soups, 195
culinary, growing, 577
cultivation, 577
dried, to reconstitute, 580
dried and fresh, to substitute, 579
drying, 579, **579**
fines herbes, 572
freezing, 579
to garnish beverages, 42, **42**
harvesting, 579
jellies, 834
loaf, toasted and buttered, 636, **636**
planting patterns, **578**
to preserve with salt, 570
salts, to make, 570
for tisanes, 40
using, 579
vinegars, 527
Hermits, 708
Herring, about, 407
baked, and potatoes, 408
Bismarck, defined, 408
canapés, marinated, 75
hors d'oeuvre, 88
marinated, 408
Rollmops, 88
salad with potato, 104
salads, 107
Scotch fried, 408
sweet and sour, 408
Hibachi grill, 156, **156**
Hickory nuts, 564
HIGH-ALTITUDE COOKING, *watch for symbol* ▲
about, 145
baking powder, baking soda, about, 555
batters, fritter, 242
blanching vegetables for freezing, 825
bread, 601; quick, 623
cakes, 692–694
candy making, 778
canning, pressure, 804; boiling-water bath, 805
chart, boiling points of water, 145
coffee cakes, quick, 623
cookies, 700
cornstarch, 549
deep-fat frying, 148
doughnuts, about, 245
icings, 722
meat cooking, 448
pancakes, 235
pies, 638
pressure cooking, 150
pudding, steamed, 754
HIGH-ALTITUDE COOKING *(cont.)*
soups, 167
steamed puddings, 754
waffle batter, 241
water, 520
Highballs, 59
Himmel und Erde, 334
Holiday menus, 33
Hollandaise Sauce, 357, 358, **358**
Hominy, baked, 200
cakes, 239
grits, as cereal, 200
grits cheese casserole, 201
pancakes, 239
to prepare from corn, 200
Honey, about, 558; to reliquify, 558
apples, 130
butter, 775; toast, 636
cake, 677; eggless all-rye, Cockaigne, 626
in candy making, 558, 778
cookies, German, 708; bars, 704
dressing, 361
glaze, 731, 732; and fruit, 433
glaze for meat or onions, 368
loaf, quick, 623
icing, with peanut butter, 729
sauce, 774; butter, 775; mint, 774
Hopping John, 287
Horehound, 581; candy, 787
HORS D'OEUVRE, 77–91
about, 77
anchovy cheese or Kleiner Liptauer, **81**
anchovy rolls, 88
antipasto, about, 78
asparagus spears, garnished, 83
aspic, tomato, 81
avocado and chutney, 83
avocado spread or Guacamole, 83
Bagna Cauda, 90
bamboo shoots, stuffed, 84
beans, marinated, 83
beets, stuffed, Cockaigne, 83
bologna cornucopia, 86
breads to serve with, about, 79
Brussels sprouts, stuffed, 83
cabbage mound, spiced, **77,** 83
cannibal balls, or mound, 86
carrots, marinated, 84
caviar and other roes, about, 87; dip, **77,** 90
celeriac rémoulade, 102
celery, stuffed, 84
celery curls, 84, **84**
cereals, puffed, 80
cheese balls Florentine, 82; nut, 81; pastry, 82
cheese carrots, 82
cheese dreams, fried, 82
chestnuts, roasted, 79, **80;** skewered, 79
chicken bits, sherried, 86
chicken and goose livers as, about; chopped, 86
chipped beef cornucopia, 86
crackers and breads to serve with, 79
cucumber lily, 84
deep-fat-fried, about, 82

HORS D'OEUVRE *(cont.)*
dips, 89–91
Edam or Gouda cheese, filled, 81
Edam nuggets, 81
eel rolls, smoked, 88
eggs as, about, 82, **82**
endive, French, stuffed, 84
Escabèche, 88
finocchio, stuffed, 84
fish balls, 88
fondue, *see* Bagna Cauda, 90
fruit, dried, stuffed, 80
Guacamole, or avocado spread, 83
herring, 88
hummus, 90
Kleiner Liptauer, 81
leeks, stuffed, 84
marrow, 85
meatballs, 86
mushrooms, marinated, 84
mussel, cold, **87,** 89
nut creams, 82
nuts, 79; curried, 79
olives, about, 85; garlic, 85; pastry-wrapped, 85
onions, marinated, 85
oyster, cold, 89; pickled, 89
peas, podded, stuffed, 85
peppers, sweet, 85
pheasant, smoked, 87
popcorn, seasoned, 80
prosciutto and fruit, 80
radish; black, 84, **84**
ribs, glazed cocktail, 85
roes, about, 87
Rollmops, 88
Rumaki, 81
salmon roll, smoked, 88
sardine, 88
sausages, broiled, 86
seeds, toasted, 80
serving dishes, **77**
Seviche, 88
shrimp, aspic-glazed, 89
shrimp, broiled, Cockaigne, 89; pickled, 89
shrimp balls, fried, 89
smorgasbord, about, 79
steak Tartare, 86
tarama, 87
tidbits, seaside, 87, **87**
tidbits, skewered, 80
tomato, cherry, stuffed, 84
tongue cornucopias, 86
turkey, galantine of, 431, **432**
turkey, smoked, 87
vegetables, raw, marinated, 83
Vicksburg cheese roll or ball, 81
ways to serve, 77, **77,** 78, **78**
wild rice, popped, 80
Horseradish, about, 581
dressing, 362; cream, 357; sour cream, 356
dried, to reconstitute, 582
pickled, 848
sauce, 343; frozen, 357
Hot cross buns, 611
Hot dog, *see* Frankfurter
Hot-smoking, 814
Huckleberry, 133
canning, 806; custard tart, 651; pie, 650
Huevos Rancheros, or cowboy eggs, 222
Hummus dip, 90
Hunter's Chicken, 427
sauce, 347
Hush Puppies, 629
Hydrogenated fats, 148, 541
Hyssop, 582

I

Ice, cubes, flavored, 42
molds, decorative, 62, **62**
punch bowl, 62, **63**
ICE CREAM, CHURNED, 758–760
about, 758, **760**
additions and garnishes, 758
apricot, 760
caramel, 759
chocolate, 759
coffee, 759
cones or Gaufrettes, 719
Delmonico I or Crème Glacée, 759
freezer, to pack, 758
French Pot, 758
fruit, 760
orange, 760
peach, 760
peppermint-stick, 759
pistachio, 760
raspberry, 760
strawberry, 760
vanilla I, 759
ICE CREAM, STILL-FROZEN, 760–765
about, 760
apricot mousse, 764
biscuit Tortoni, 762
bombes, about; to make, 760; mold, **758**
butter pecan, 763
chocolate bombe, 763
chocolate II, 763
combinations of, 761
Delmonico bombe, 762
Delmonico II, 762
eggnog, frozen, 762
fruit-buttermilk, 765
fruit mousse, 764
greengage plum, 764
macaroon bombe, 762
mango, 762
mocha, 762
parfaits, *see* Parfaits
persimmon, 765
snow, 769
storage period, 761
strawberry or raspberry bombe, 764
vanilla II, 761; vanilla III, with evaporated milk, 761
ICES, 765–769, *also see* Sherbets
about, 765

ICES *(cont.)*
apricot, 766
fruit, 765; as containers, surprise, 766
lemon, 766; and orange, 766
mint, 767
orange or lemon surprise, frozen, 766
peach, 766
pineapple, 766
raspberry or strawberry I, 766; II, 767
snow ice cream, 769
suckers, frozen, 769
tomato, *see* Avocado Cup IV, 111
ICINGS, 721–733
apricot, 729
baked, 730
boiled, about; thread stage defined, 721, 722
broiled, 730
brown sugar, quick, 728
brown sugar marshmallow, 726
butterscotch, 728
cakes, small, 729, **729**
caramel, 726; roll topping, 731
carob, 728
chocolate, European, 728
chocolate, quick, 728
chocolate butter, 728
chocolate coating over white, 725
chocolate cream cheese, 728
chocolate fudge, 726
chocolate marshmallow, 726
coconut, 722, **722**
coconut pecan, 726
coffee or mocha, 729
cream cheese, 727
cream cheese, blender-whipped, 732
creamy, 724
cupcakes, decorating, 729, **729**
decorations, **721**
decorative, 722–724, **723, 724**
decorative, quick, Royal Glaze or Swiss Meringue, 727
fondant, to apply, **695,** 725
freezing, 830
French, 727
glazes, 731–732
hard-sauce topping, 730
high-altitude, about, 722
honey glaze topping, 731
honey-peanut butter, quick, 729
lace topping, quick, 729, **730**
lemon, quick, 727
lemon topping for cookies or bars, 727
maple, quick, 729; sugar, 726
meringue topping, about, 730
nut, raisin, 722, **722**
orange, luscious, 725; quick, 728
penuche, 728
pineapple, 729
quick, about, 726
raisin, 722
seven-minute; lemon; orange; seafoam, 725
small cakes and cookies, about, 729, **729**
substitutes for, *see* Cake fillings, 696
ICINGS *(cont.)*
three-minute, 727
toppings, applied before, during and after baking, 731–732
white, boiled, 722
white, quick, 727
White Mountain, 722
yields, about, 721
Increasing and decreasing recipes, 589
Indian, nuts, 564
pudding, 749
relish, 846
Indienne Sauce, 344
Informal entertaining, 20, 22, **22,** 23, **23**
INGREDIENTS, 519–598; *see individual names;*
optional, *watch for symbol* ( )
Inkfish, defined, 408
Irish Farls, *see* Skillet breads, 627, 628
Irish moss, 561
Iron utensils, 162

J

JAM, 835–837
apricot pineapple, quick, 836
berry, 836
blueberry, 835
cake Rombauer, 679; cupcakes, 695
defined, 832; making, 835
elderberry, 836
five-fruits Cockaigne, 836
loganberry, 836
pear with pineapple, spiced, 835
rose-hip, 836
sauce, 771
strawberry, red red, 835
tarts, macaroon, 717
Jambalaya, 211
Jardinière, defined, 277
Jars, canning, to pack, 802–805, **803, 804**
for pickles, 841
for pressure canner, 804
for storage, **519**
JELLY, 832–835
about, 832
apple, 834
bag, to prepare, **832,** 833
berry, waterless, 834
black raspberry and gooseberry, 834
crab apple, 834
cranberry, 133; spiced, 134
currant, 833
currant and raspberry, 834
doughnuts, 245
equipment for making, 832, **832**
freezing, 831, 833
fruit juice for, 833
glasses, to sterilize, 832; to paraffin, 833
grape; waterless, 834
guava, 835
herb and scented, 834
making, about, 833
Paradise, 834
pectin, to test for, 832

JELLY *(cont.)*
plum, 835
quince, 834
raspberry and currant, 834
roll cake, **690,** 691; to line a mold, 743, **743**
sauce for desserts, 770
sea grape, 835
to store, 833
sugar, proportions in, 832
sweeteners for, 832
to test for doneness, 833, **833**
Tots, 717
Jerky, 814
Jicama, 306
Johnnycakes, 239
Jubilee Wafers, 716
Juices, about, 42
blended, about, 44
clam, 43
fruit, 42–46; citrus, 571
fruit, canning, 807
fruit, freezing, 824
fruit for jelly, 833
Julienne, defined, 277; to cut, **296**
Juniper berries, 576
Junket, 748

K

Kale, 292; sea, 94
Kartoffelklösse, 204
Kasha, to cook, 200; 201
Kebabs, about, 473; *also see* Skewer cooking
beef, 459; frankfurters, 259
chicken, 431
fish, 403; scallop, 382
fresh fruit, 127
lamb, 473
pan, **145;** hibachi, **156**
Kedgeree of lobster, or fish, 265
Keeping foods, 798–801
Kefir, 533
Kettle, cast iron, **145**
Kid, or chevon, about, 471
Kidneys, about, 504
beef stew, 506
en brochette, 506
fat, 505, 148
nuggets, 505
pie, steak-and-, 465
sautéed or Bercy, 505
veal, baked, 505; casserole, 506
Kipper, defined, 407; grilled or baked, 408
Kitchen equipment, basic, 163
hints, 165
ranges, 159; shears, **568;** utensils, 162
Kiwi, 144; chutney, 846; compote, **123**
Kleiner Liptauer, 81
Knives, paring, **571;** to sharpen, 449, **449, 450**
Kohlrabi, 276, 306
Kolatchen, 612
Königsberger Klops, 489
Kosher, defined, 443
pickles, dill, 848; salt, 569
Kothamille or coriander, 581
Kransekake, or pyramid cake, **664,** 688
Kreplach, dough for, *see* Noodles, 213
to form, **173**
soup, 172
Krumkakes, 718, **718**
Kuchen crusts, about, 642
Kumiss, 533
Kumquat, 129, 135
candied or preserved, 795
compote, 136
preserves, 839

L

Lady, cake, 673; Baltimore, 672
fingers, 695; to line a mold, 743, **743**
LAMB, 471–476; 488–491
about, 471; to carve, 471
burgers or patties, filled, 488
butterfly, barbecued leg of, 472
casserole and eggplant, 491
Cassoulet, 475
chops, about, 472; braised, 473
chops, broiled and pan-broiled, 472
Couscous, 476, **476**
crown roast of, **442,** 472
curried, with rice, 475; cooked, 256
cuts, commercial and retail, 450–453, **451**
farce of, 473
Forestière or mock venison, 474
fries, 510
goulash à blanc, 475
grape leaves stuffed with, 492
grill, English mixed, 473
head, 510
kebabs, 473
kidney, *see* Kidney
lamburgers, 488
large cuts, suggested uses, 453
leg of, roast, 471, **471;** barbecued, 472
marinades for, 528
mint sauce for, 355
Moussaka or eggplant casserole, 491
patties, 488
rack of, 472
sandwich, 274
shanks or trotters, braised, 474
shoulder of, braised; stuffed, or farce of, 473
shoulder roast, 472
spareribs, *see* pork spareribs, 481
spinach casserole, and, 256
stew, Irish, 475
stew or Navarin Printanière, 474
stuffed grape leaves or Dolmas, 492
terrapin, 257
Langouste, *see* About lobsters, 385, **385**
Lard, about, 148, 542
seasoned, 572
Larding, about, 444
lardoons or cracklings, 445, 542
Larks, 440
Lasagne, 215
Lavender, 582

Laver, 87, 88
Leaf Wafers, 715
Leavens, about, 553
Leaves, candied, glazed, crystallized, about, 794
  mint, glazed, 794
  for wrap cooking, 152, **152**
Leberklösse or Liver Dumplings, 196
Lebkuchen, 704
Leeks, about, 306, 585, **585**
  pie, 255
  purée of, 306
  seasoning, 585, **585**
  soup, Cock-a-Leekie, 180
  soup, potato, 184
  stuffed, 84
  wild, 585, **585**
Leftovers, about, 598
  in bacon, 257
  breads, cakes and crackers, about, 635
  noodle dish, 215
  potatoes, 324
  veal, creamed, 256
Legumes, dried, about, 286
  dried, danger of pressure cooking, 150
  dried, purée, 287
  soups, about, 176
Lemon, about, 135, 571
  balm, 582
  butter, 350
  curd squares, 703
  custard, sponge, 737
  filling, pastry, 697; orange custard, 698
  garnishes, to make, 571, **571**
  gelatin, 744
  glaze, 731
  ice, 766
  icings, 725, 727
  orange custard filling, 698
  peel, and juices for zests, 571
  pie, *see* Pies
  roll cake, 691
  sauce, dessert, 769
  sherbet, milk, 768
  soufflé, 740
  soup, Greek, 172
  sponge custard, 737
  sugar, 557
  surprise, 766
  verbena, 582; tisane, 40
Lemonade, quantity, 45; syrup for, 45
Lentils, 289
  casserole, and sausage, 260
  and prunes, 289
  purée of, 287
  soup, 177
Lettuce, cooked, 306
  dish and rice, 294
  to dry and store, 94, **95**
  green peas, and, 314
  leaves, stuffed, 152
  leaves for wrap cooking, 152, **152**
  rolls, stuffed, 106
  soup, cream of, 185
Lettuce *(cont.)*
  varieties of, 92–94, **93**
  to wash, 94, **94**
Lima beans, *see* Beans
Lime, about, 135
  juice and orange, 43
  marmalade, 839
  pie, *see* Pies
  sauce, 769
  sherbet, 767
  Spanish, 144
Limeade, 45
Limpet, 87
Linzertorte, 686
Liptauer cheese, 81, 757
Liqueurs, about, 58
  glasses for, **57,** 58
  glaze, 732
  sauce, 772; cream, 775
Liquid, measure, volume, 590–592
  reducing, 154, 339
Litchi, 123, 138
Liver, *also see* Beef, Calf, etc.
  about, 499; canapé, 75
  about chicken and goose as hors d'oeuvre, 86
  beef, Creole, 501
  braised, with vegetables, 500; with wine, Cockaigne, 501
  broiled, 500
  calf or chicken Lyonnaise, 500
  chicken, in batter, 502
  chicken, à la king, 502
  chicken, skewered, 501
  chicken, in sour cream sauce, 502
  chicken or goose, chopped, 86
  dressing, 373
  dumplings or Leberklösse, 196
  goose, 502
  loaf, 493
  pâté, chicken, 495; souffléed, 496
  patties, baked, 489
  pepper, onions and olives on skewers, 501
  sausage, canapés, 75
  sausage dumplings, 196
  sautéed or Lyonnaise, 500
  spaghetti sauce with, 353
Lobsters, about types, 385, **385;** to eat, 385–386
  Americaine or Armoricaine, 387
  bisque, 187
  "boiled" or poached, 385
  broiled, 386; to prepare, 386, **386**
  butter, 351
  canapés, 75
  chowder, quick, 194
  curry, 388
  to eat, 386, **386,** 387, **387**
  kedgeree of, etc., 265
  mold, 107
  Mongole, quick, 266; soup, quick, 194
  mousse, 121
  Newburg, 388
  parfait, 389
  potted, 390

Lobsters *(cont.)*
prosciutto and, 268
puffball canapé, 75
ring, hot, 389
salad, 106; to cook for, 386
sandwiches, 275
stew, 188
to store, live, 385
stuffed, baked, 388
Supreme, quick, 194
tails, grilled, 387; to prepare, 387, **388**
thermidor, 388
Loganberry, 134; canning, 806
jam, 836
pie, 650
Lollipops, 787
London Broil Steak, 457
"Long rice" or Harusame, 212
Loquat, 144
Lorenzo Dressing, 360
Lotus, 276, 306; root salad, 102
Louis, Sauce, 365
Lovage, 582
Lox, defined, 410
Luau pit, 156
Luncheon Menus, 26; formal, 33
Lyonnaise, Liver, 500
sauce, 346
potatoes, 320

M

Macadamia nuts, 564
Macaroni, baked, 217; boiled, 213
cooking, **213**
salad, 106
with shellfish, 217
with tomatoes, livers, mushrooms and cheese, 217
Macaroons, 709
bombe, 762
chocolate coconut, 710
coconut, 710
tarts, 717, **717**
Mace, 576
Macédoine, defined, 277; of fresh fruits, 124
Mâche, 93
Mackerel, broiled fresh, 410; salt, 410
Madeira Sauce, 346
Madeleines, 695; pan, **664**
Madrilène, consommé, 169; ring with shad roe Cockaigne, 115
Maître d'Hôtel Butter, 350
Malt beverages, 41, 42
Maltaise Sauce, 359
Mandarin, 135
Mändelplattchen, 713
Mandeltorte or Almond Tart, 685
Mango, 129, 138; chutney, 846
ice cream, 762
Mangosteen, 143, 144
Manhattan Clam Chowder, 190
Manicotti or cannelloni, 216
Maple, Bavarian creams, 747; caramels, 784
Charlotte, 748
cream, 559; cream candy, 780
curls, 720
icing, quick, 729
parfait, 764
to substitute for sugar, 558
sugar, 559; sugar icing, 726; sauce, 773
syrup, about; to make, 558
tapping a tree, **558**
Marchand de Vin Sauce, 347
Marchpane or Marzipan, 781
Margarines, about, 541
Marigold, 582
Marinades, about, 528
apricot or sassaties, 529
beer, for beef or pork, 529
for chicken, 529; for wildfowl, 436
for fish or lamb or game, 528, 529
pork, 529
Teriyaki, for chicken and steak, 529
for vegetables, 528
yogurt or buttermilk, 528
Marinara Sauce, 353
Marjorams, 582
Marmalade, about, 832
lime, 839
orange, 839; with lemon and grapefruit, 839
tamarind, 839
Marmite, Petite, 170
Marrons, about, 563; roaster, **80**
Glacés, 796
Marrow, about, 512
balls for soup, 196
bones, baked, or Osso Buco, 471
hors d'oeuvre, 85
vegetable, 328
Marshmallows, 781
cream, mocha, 749
icing, brown sugar; chocolate, 726
pudding, 746
sauce, 774
Martynia, capers, 580
Marzipan or Marchpane, 781
Mask, defined, *see* Mayonnaise Collée, 368
Matelote, 189
Matignon, 572
Matjes, defined, 408
Matzo Meal Dumplings, 203
Maurice Salad, 98
May wine, 64
Mayonnaise, 363
blender, 363
Chaud-Froid, 368
Collée or gelatin, 368
cream or Chantilly, 365
curry, 365
dressings, cold, 363–366; hot, 359; herb, 364
fruit-salad, 365
Grenache, 363
hard-cooked egg, 365
low-calorie; eggless, mock, 366
Russian, 364

Mayonnaise *(cont.)*
sauce, souffléd, 359
Sauce Verte, 364
storage of, 363
Measuring, about, 589; metric, 591–592
can sizes, 592
comparative U.S. and British, 590
for drinks, 49
fractions in recipes, 589
frozen food packages, 592
substitutions and equivalents, 593
volume-weight relationship, 589; U.S., 590
MEAT, 442–512; *also see* Beef, Ham, Lamb, Pork, Veal, etc
about, to buy and serve, 442, 443
amount to buy and serve, 443
ball hors d'oeuvre, 86
balls, Chinese, 489
balls, German or Königsberger Klops, 489
balls, Hawaiian, 490
balls, Italian, 489
balls, sauerkraut, 490
balls, Swedish, 489
balls for soup, 196
basting, 446, **446**
braising, about, 447
broiling, 445; fat-free, 445
cabbage, stuffed, or Gefüllter Krautkopf, 491
cabbage leaves, stuffed, 492
canning, 811
carving, roast beef, **454;** lamb, mutton, kid and goat, **471;** crown roast of pork, **477;** whole ham, **484**
Chinese Firepot, 462
color in, 588
cooked, fritters, 244
Couscous, 476, **476**
cracklings, 542
croquettes, 247
en croûte cooking, 448
crust, or pâte for pâté, 494
cuts, identifying, 450–452, **450, 451**
dressings and stuffings, 370-374
drippings, about, 542
dry-curing, 813
English mixed grill, 473
freezing; thawing and cooking frozen, 826
frill for shank bone, to make, 450
fritters, batter for, 243
fruits, for, about, 128
game, *see* Game *and individual names*
glazes, 367, 368
goulash, Gulyàs or Pörkölt, about, 464
grades, about, 442
gravies, 341
green peppers stuffed with; and rice, 316
grilling, 156, **156, 157**
grinding and mincing, 444
ground, 486–493; uncooked, to store, 443
ground, additions to, 487
high-altitude cooking, 448
inspection of, 442
Jambalaya, 211

MEAT *(cont.)*
Jerky, 814
Kentucky Burgoo, 465
Kosher, 443
larding, about, 444, **445**
lardoons, or cracklings, 445
large cuts, about, 452; suggestions for use of, 452, **452,** 453
leftover, *see* Brunch, 250
loaf, about, 492; additions to, 487
marinade, about, 528
marinating, 445
moist heat processes, 149, 442
pan-broiling, 445
pastries, about, 449
pâté, 495
patties, variety, 506
pie roll, or pinwheels, 251
pie with spaghetti, quick, 217
pie topping, 449
porcupines, 490
pork balls in tomato sauce, 490
pot-roasting, about, 447
pounding and macerating, 444, **444**
pressure cooked, 150, 448
reheating, 449
roasting, 446
salad, 108, 109
salted, about, 482
sausage, about, 496
sautéeing or pan-frying, 445
seasoning, 443
sharpening knives, on stone, 449, **449;** on steel, **450**
smoked, green beans, and potatoes, 286
soufflé, 230
for soup, about, 169
steaks, *see* Beef and Salmon steaks
stewing, about, 447
stock making, 520
storing, cooked, 449; raw, 443
to stretch, 487
tenderizing of, 444, **444**
terrines, 494
timing and doneness, 447
tough, cooking, about, 444
turnover, Piroshki or roll, filled, 251
variety, about, 499, **500;** patties, 506
and vegetable timbale, 232
yield, about, 443; cuts from side of beef, 452
Medlar, 138
Melba Sauce, 770
toast, 636
Melon, about, 138; ballers, 541, **541**
aspic-filled, 119
baskets or fruit cups, 138, **138**
mold, **758**
rounds, filled, 139
salad, 111
soup, 185
spiked, 139
winter, 138
Ménagère Stew, 469

MENUS, 25–35
afternoon tea, 32
backpacking, 35, **35**
breakfast, hunt, 33
breakfast and brunch, 25–26
cocktail and buffet, 32
dinners for family or friends, 29
formal, 33
holiday, 33
participatory, 34
picnic, 34
Meringue, about, paste, 649
cake, fudge, 676
glacées, 649
Italian, topping, 730
rings, almond, 710
substitute for, 744
Swiss, 727
tart, cream Cockaigne, 689
topping, Italian, 730
toppings, about, 730; Italian, 730
to store, 649
Metric conversions, 591
Meunière or lemon butter, 350
Mexican, orange drops, 792
sauce, tomato, 352
veal steak, 470
Microwave cooking, 160, 161
MILK, 529–535; *also see* Cream, Sour cream
almond, 535; to make, 745
beverages, 41, 42
buttermilk, *also see* Buttermilk, 533
coconut, 566
condensed, 531
daily requirement, 530
evaporated, 531; frozen desserts, 761, 763
evaporated, to whip, 532
fermented, about, 533
filled, 532
freezing, 827
glaze, 731
homogenized, 530
imitation, 534
nut, 534
pasteurization of, 530
punch or syllabub, 62
scalding, 530
shake, fruit, 42; malt, chocolate, 41
skim, non-fat; low-fat, 531
solids, dry, 531; to whip, 532
sour, 533; *also see* Sour milk
to sour; to substitute, 532
soybean, 535
to store, 530
substitutions, 532
sweet, about, 530
toast or soup, 186
vegetable, about, 534
whole, 530
Millet Casserole with sausage, 259
cereal, to cook, 199, 200
Milo maize, 550
Milt, about 411; defined, 408
Mincemeat, 812; green tomato mock, 844
apple, oat, crisp, 662
pie, 652; mock, 653
Minerals, 1
Minestrone, 177
Mint, candy, pulled, 786
gelatin for fruit salads, 117
herb, 582
ice, 767
julep, 59, **59,** 60, **60**
leaves, glazed, 794
sauce, 355; chocolate, 773
Mirepoix, 572; defined, 277
Miroton Boeuf, 262
Miso, 169
Mixer, electric for cakes, **664,** 666
Mocha, about, 576
cake, chiffon, chocolate, oil, 684
cake, quick, chocolate, freezer, 688
cream, marshmallow, 749
filling, chocolate, 697
gelatin, 745
ice cream, 762–763
icing, 729
pie, chocolate gelatin, chiffon, 658
sauce, 773; caramel, 774
Mochika, 549
Mohn or Poppy Seed Filling, 622, 623
Mohrenköpfe or Moors' Heads Cake, 688
Molasses, about, 559; to substitute, 559
bars, raisin, 702
blackstrap, 559
cookies, old-fashioned, 707; nut wafers, 706
crisps Cockaigne, 716
pudding, apple, steamed, 755
syrup, for candy, 791
Mold, in canning, 802, 833; in cheese, 539, 756; in peanuts, 564; in sprouts, 565
Molds, bombe, **758**
cake, two-piece, about, 672, **672**
caramel-coated, about, 743
celeriac ring, 232
chestnut ring, 234
desserts, about, 743, **743, 758**
fish and seafood, 106, 107; jellied and creamed, 115, 116
gelatin, fancy, to make, 560, 561, **561**
gelatin, fruit, to make, 117–122, 743–746
ice, decorative, to make, 62, **62**
to line with macaroons, ladyfingers, jelly roll slices, 743, **743**
melon, **758**
mushroom ring with sweetbreads or chicken, 234
rice, 207
salad, about, 112–122, **112**
timbale, 231
Mole, turkey, 428
Mollusks and crustaceans, *see* Shellfish
Mongole, crab meat or lobster, quick, 266; soup, 194
Monosodium glutamate, 570
Monstera, 143, **143**

Mont Blanc, or chestnut mound, 738
Moorhens, 440
Moors' Heads or Mohrenköpfe, 688
Moose, *see* Venison, 516
Mornay Sauce, 342
Mortar and pestle, 579, **579**
Morue, Brandade de, 405
Mostaccioli, 218
Moules Marinière, or steamed mussels, 379
Moussaka, 491
Mousse, about, dessert, 760; savory, 120
apricot, 764
chicken, jellied, 120
cucumber, 120
French chocolate, 737
fruit, 764
fruit salad, chilled, 122
ham, jellied, 120
lobster, 121
mousseline of shellfish 122
mushroom ring, or, 309
rum chocolate, 738
savory, *see* Timbales, 231; about, 120
seafood, 121
veal, jellied, 120
Mousseline, defined, 120; of shellfish, 122
sauce, 359
MUFFINS, 629–631
about, 629, **630**
additions to, 630
blueberry, 631
bran, 630
buttermilk, 630
cheese, 631
cooked-cereal, 631
corn, 627
cranberry, 631
English, 617
pumpkin, 631
rice flour, 631
sour cream, 630
whole-grain, 630
yam, 631
Mulberry, 134
Mulled cider, 44; wine, 65
Mulligan stew, defined, 465
Mulligatawny Soup, 178
Mürbeteig, 641
Mush, cornmeal, 201
Mushrooms, about, 306, **306, 307**
bisque with clams, 187
broiled, 308
broth, 171
butter, blender, 71
canapés, 73
canning, 809
cauliflower, and, in cheese sauce, 297
creamed, 308
croquettes, 248
dressing, 370
to dry, 573, 818; to reconstitute, 573
duxelles or seasoning, 573
Mushrooms *(cont.)*
Florentine, 309
frozen, to cook, 825
garnish, 307
lima beans and, 290
marinated, 84
onions in wine, and, 309
peas, and, 315
rice ring, 207
ring mold with sweetbreads or chicken, 234
ring or mousse, 309
sauce, quick, 348; wine, 347
sausage and, 259
sautéed, 308
à la Schoener, 308
seasoning, as, 573
slicing and channeling, 307, **307**
soup, cream of, 183; quick, 193
spores, 573
steamed, 307
stuffed, broiled, Cockaigne, 308
stuffed with clams or oysters, 309
stuffed with oysters, 378
stuffed with seafood or snails, 309, 393
timbale, 231
on toast, and puffed cheese, 273
under glass, 310
Muskmelon, 138
Muskrat, 516
Müsli, or Swiss oatmeal, 199
Mussels, about, 379
baked, buttered, 379
hors d'oeuvre, cold, 89
steamed, or Moules Marinière, 379
stew, 188
Mustard, 582
hot, 583
pickle, 843
sauce, cold, 357; hot, 345
sauce, sweet-sour, 355
suave, 583
types, seasoning, 582
white for salads, 94
MUTTON, 471–476; *also see* Lamb
about, 471
Couscous, 476, **476**
leg of, roast, 471; to carve, **471**
stew, Irish, 475
Mystery Cake, 680

N

Nantua Sauce, 343
Napoleons, 645
Nasturtium, 583; pod or seeds, pickled, 845
Natal plum, 141
Navarin Printanière, 474
Nectarine, about, 139
Negus, or mulled wine, 65
Nesselrode Pudding, 747; sauce, 772
Nettle Soup, 180
New England Boiled Dinner, 466
New England Clam Chowder, 190

Newburg, lobster or seafood, 388
sauce, 359
shrimp, 390
Newport Creams or centers, 779
Niçoise Salads, 103, 104
Nockerln, or Austrian Pancakes, 238
for soup or stew, 203
Noisette, defined, 278
NOODLES, *also see* Pastas
baskets, 214
bean thread or dried cellophane, 212
boiled, 213
casserole, tuna, mushroom soup, 215
cooking, **213;** cutting, **213**
dish, leftover, 215
dough, to make, 213, **213**
dough, white or green or Fettucine, 213
fried, 214
Good Friday, 214
ham, 214
lasagne, 215
loaf and cheese, quantity, 215
mostaccioli, 218
rings, 214
Romanian and pork casserole, 215
with Welsh rarebit, 214
Nori, *see* Laver
Nougat, 784
NUTS, *also see individual names*
about blanching; to chop and grind, 562, **562**
balls, flourless, 706
bars, 703
bread, 603; quick, 623
brittle, 788; for garnish, 789
brittle and chocolate sauce, 772
butter, seasoned, 71
canning, 809
caramel, spiced, Cockaigne, 789
cheese balls, 81
cookies, see Cookies
creams, hors d'oeuvre, 82; candy, 789
crunch, candy, 788
curried, 79
dressing, 370
fillings for coffee cakes, 622, 623
freezing, 831
glazed, for garnish, 789
hors d'oeuvre, as, 79
icing, 722, **722;** raisin and, 722
loaf, cheese and bread, 254; and rice, 210
meal, 550
milks, 534
pemmican, fruit, 125
roasting or toasting and salting, 562
soufflé, 741
spiced, 789
tarts, 718
wafers, curled, 720; molasses, 706
waffle, 241
Nutcracker, 562
Nutmeg, 576; grater, **735**
Nutrient retention, vegetables, 278
Nutrition, 1–8
Nutritional yeast, 554

O

Oat, apple-mince crisp, 662
bars, chocolate, 702
bread, Cockaigne, 608
cereal, to cook, 200
flour, 550
rolled, 550
rolls, molasses, 614
Oatmeal, 550
cake, 680
cookies, quick, 708
griddle cakes, 240
lace wafers, glazed or flourless, 709
Swiss or Müsli, 199
Octopus, about, 408, **409**
casseroled, 409
pasta sauce, 353
Oeufs à la Neige, 735
en Gelée, 117
Oils, about, 541; *also see individual names*
almond, 563
for deep-frying, 148
salad, about, 95
to store, 542
to substitute in baking, 542
Okra, about, **276,** 310
canning, 809
salad, 103
sautéed, 311
stewed, 310
Olives, about, 85
bread, and nut, quick, 625
garlic, 85
oil, pickle, 843
pastry-wrapped, 85
stuffings for, 85
tomato casserole, 332
Olivette, defined, 278
Olla Podrida, defined, 465
Omelet, about, 226, **226**
eggs Fooyoung with shrimp, 228
firm, 227
fluffy or souffléed, 227
French, 226, **226**
Frittata or Italian, 228
Norwegian, 742
piperade, or Basque, 228
Soufflé Surprise, 742
soufflés, dessert, 739–742
Spanish, 228
sweet, 227
Omelette aux Confitures, 742
Onions, about, 311, **311,** 583–585, **585**
baked, whole, 312
braised, small, 312
canapés, and parsley, 73
casserole, and apple, 313
creamed, 312
cultivation of, 583
to destroy bacteria, 583

Onions *(cont.)*
dicing, 311, **311**
dressings, 372
dry, 583, **585**
glazed, 312
green peppers and, 315
green or scallions, 312
to make milder, 583
marinated, 85
mushrooms and, in wine, 309
pickled, 845
pie, or leek, 255
rings, French-fried, 313
salad, with tomato, 106, **106**
sauce, brown, or Lyonnaise, 346
sauce, white, or Soubise, 344
sausage and, 259
sautéed, 312
scalloped with cheese, 313
as seasoning, 583
shortcake, 255
soufflé, 230
soup, 171
soup, cream of, or velouté, 184
soup, quick, 193
steamed, 312
to store, 583
stuffed, 313
stuffed with sauerkraut, 313
tomatoes filled with, and anchovies, 334
topping, 584, **586**
Welsh or Japanese bunching, 585, **586**
Opera creams, 780
Opossum, 515
Orange, 135
balls, and apricot, 793
bitter or Seville, 135
bread, quick, 624
cake, filled, 689
canning, 807
cookie filling, apricot, 717
cream, filling, 698
custard, filling, 697
custard, sponge, 737
custard with meringue, 736
doughnuts, 246
drops, Mexican, 792
eggnog, 45
fruit soup, 128
gelatin, 744
ice cream, 760
ices, 766
icings, 725, 728
in syrup, 136
juice, frozen, about, 136
juice and lime, 43
juice and tomato, 43
lemon custard filling, 698
marmalade, 839
marmalade drops, 709
Murcott, 135
to peel and section, 135, **135**
pie, chiffon, 658
Orange *(cont.)*
rolls, tea, 616
salad with banana and nut, 111
salads, 111
sauce, 769
sauce, brown-sugar, 774
sauce, sweet-sour for duck or goose, 355
Seville or bitter, 135
sherbet, 767; milk, 768
surprise, **758,** 766
Temple, 135
toast, 637
Orangeade, 45
Oreganos, 582
Oriental Dip, 90
sauce, sweet-sour, 355
Ortolans, 440
Osso Buco, 471
OUTDOOR COOKING AND EQUIPMENT, 155–159; *watch for symbol* ⊟
backpacking, 35, **35**
Oven, commercial, 159
convector, **161**
microwave, 160
placement of racks, 159, **159**
thermostats, 159
Ovenproof ware, defined, 162
Oxtails, braised or stew, 511
soup, 179; with wine, quick, 193
Oysters, about, 375, **376**
baked, creamed, and seafood, 378
Benedict, 222
bisque, 188
bread dressing, 370, 371
broiled, 376
cakes, 267
canapés, 69, 76
Casino, 378
crabs, 384
creamed; with celery, 377
creamed, stuffed with green peppers, 316
croquettes, and chicken, 248
deep-fat-fried, 376
Eastern and Pacific, **87**
grilled, 376
gumbo, shrimp and crab, 188
on the half shell, 376; baked, 377
hors d'oeuvre, cold, 89
in mushrooms, 309; au gratin, 378
pickled, 89
rarebit, 378
Rockefeller, 378
sauce for fish, 343
sautéed, 377; scalloped, 377
soufflé, 231
stew, 188
Oyster plant or salsify, about, 326

P

Paella, 210
Palm, hearts of, 313
salad, 103
Palm Leaf or sour cream rolls, 611, **612**

Palm Leaves, 645
Panades, 179
Pancakes, 235–240, **236**
about, 235
additions to, 235
Austrian or Nockerln, 238
Blini or Russian raised, 238
blintzes or cottage cheese, 237
buckwheat, 240
buttermilk, 239
cornmeal, 239
Crêpes Suzette, 237
as dessert, 236–238, 753
flapjacks, crisp corn, 239
French; stuffed, 236
fruit, 237
Gâteau Crêpe, 237
German or Pfannkuchen, 238
hominy, 239
Johnnycakes, 239
oatmeal, 240
potato, 321
rice-corn meal, 239
rice flour, 239
soy, 236
spinach in, 327
whole-grain, 236
Panettone, 619
Pan-frying, or sautéing, 149
Pans, about, 162, 163; glass, 666
bread, **601,** 602
cake, about; comparative sizes, 666, **666**
Madeleine, **664**
omelet, about, 226, **226**
placement in oven, 159, **159**
scorched, 163
springform, 684, **684**
Papain for meats, 444
Papaya, 123, 139, 528
chutney, 846 (*see* Peach Chutney)
leaves, stuffed, 153
Paper, parchment, en papillote, 153
Papillote, 153, **153**
Paprika, see Red peppers
sauce, 344
Paradise Jelly, 834
Paraffin for jelly glasses, 833
Parblanching, 154
Parboiling, 154
Parfait, about, 760
angelica, 762
butterscotch, 763
caramel, 763
coffee, 764
to freeze, 760
lobster, 389
maple, 764
raspberry, 764
Tutti-Frutti, 765
Parisienne, defined, 278; spice, 572
Parmigiana, veal, 468
Parsley, about, 314, 586
Chinese, *see* Coriander, 581
Parsley *(cont.)*
deep-fried, 314
seasoning, 586
Parsnips, 314
Parsteaming, 154
Parties, *see* Entertaining, 15–24; Beverages, 36–47; Drinks, 48–65
beverages for, about, 45
drinks for, about, 62
Partridge, about, 439
Passion Fruit, 143, 144
Pasta, about, 198–219
boiled, 213
cooking, about, 212, **213**
with egg and cheese, 216
fillings and toppings, 218
jars, **198**
sauces, 351–354; suggestions, 219
scoop, **198**
server, **198**
toppings, 219
Paste, almond or filbert, 780
choux, 646
fruit, 797; defined, 832
fruit, canning, 806
gum or pastillage, 791
liver, 75
meringue, 649
puff, 643, **643, 644;** half or rough, 645
tomato, Italian, 574; velvet, 573
Turkish fruit, or Turkish Delight, 791
Pasteurization of milk and cream, 530
Pastillage, or gum paste, 791
Pastrami, 815
PASTRIES, 638–663
beignets, 246
canapé, fillings, 70; shells, 69
cheese straws or wafers, 641
choux paste swan, to make, **638,** 647
cream puff shells, **645,** 646
cream rolls, **645,** 646
Croquembouche, **638,** 647
cups, *see* Cream puff shells, 646
cups, to form, 647
dough, frozen, about, 829
dough for meats, 448; toppings, 449
éclair, chocolate, **638,** 647
fillings for, about, 647
fillings for, 621–623, 696–699
for meats, about, 641
freezing and thawing, 829–830
fruit, 660–663
meat-filled, 251
meringues, 649
Napoleons, **645,** 646
palm leaves, 645
Pâte à Choux, cream puff shells, about, **645,** 646
Pâte Brisée, 641
patty shells or Bouchées, 645, **645**
phyllo leaves, 649
Pouf Paste, about, 646
profiteroles, 647
Scandinavian, 621, **621**

PASTRIES *(cont.)*
Streudel, about, 648, **648**
tarts, *see* Tarts
turnover, 69; sweet, 662
Vienna, 641
Vol-au-Vent, **645,** 646
Pâte à Choux, about, **645,** 646
Brisée, 641
crust for pâte, 494
Demi-Feuilletée, 645
Feuilletée, 643, **643, 644, 645**
Sucrée, 641
Pâté, about, 494, 495
en croûte, about, 494
de Foie Gras, defined, 494
de Foie de Volaille, or chicken liver, 495
liver souffléed, Cockaigne, 496
mold, to line and fill, 494, **495**
Patties
beef, ground, 487, 488
chicken, veal, or lamb, 488
sausage meat, sautéed, 498
shells, or Bouchées, 645, **645**
variety meat, 506
Paupiettes, 400, 465, 469
Pawpaw, 139
Peas, black-eyed, Hopping John, 287
canning, 809
carrots and, 315
chick-, 287: *also see* Hummus, 90
green, 314; and lettuce, 314
green, soup, or Potage St. Germain, 178
mushrooms, and, 315
podded or snow, 315; stuffed, 85
purée of, 315
puréed, 286
to roast, 564
soup, quick, 192
soup, split, 177–178; au maigre, 178;
blender, 178
to sprout, 565
Peach, about, 139
brandied, 846
butter, 837
cake, Cockaigne, 661; French, 661
canning, 807
chutney, 846
filled, 139
glaze, 732
ice, 766
ice cream, 760
leather, 793
to peel by blanching, 154
pie, 652
preserves, 837
salad, 109; and cheese, 111
sauce, 356
stuffed, 139
Peanut, 564
brittle, 788
flour, 550
sauce, and pepper, 346
soup, Ghanian, 180
Peanut butter, 564
cookies, 709
cupcakes, 695
fudge or centers, 790
honey icing, 729
sandwiches, 273
Pear, about, **123,** 139
canning, 807
in liqueur, 140
jam, with pineapple, spiced, 835
prickly, 142
salads, 109, 112
spiced, 846
stuffed, 140
Pearls, vegetable, defined, 277
Pecan, 564; cookies, 706
doughnuts, 246
filling, toasted, 699
ice cream, butter, 763
icing, and coconut, 726
pie, 653
puffs, 706
slices, 703
torte, 685
wafers, 706
Peccary, 517
Pectins, in jellies, 832
Peda, 609
Pemmican, fruit-nut, 125
Penuche, 788
icing, 728
Pepper, about, 576
for ancho, 315
black and white, 576
Cayenne, about, **315,** 587
grinder or mill, **92**
pot soup, 179
sauce, as base for chili, 587
sauce or Poivrade, 347
white, in meat canning, 811
Peppermint Cream Wafers, 780
stick ice cream, 759
Peppers, about, 315; to peel, 315, 586
canning, green, 809
chili, dried, 586
chili, as seasoning, 586
green, onions and, 315
green, sauce, and peanuts, 346
green, stuffed, about, 316
green in sauce, 315
Japanese Santaka, **315**
red and green, about, 586
to remove seeds and membranes, 315, 586
slices with fillings, salad, 103
sweet, green, globe, or bell, **315**
sweet, hors d'oeuvre, 85
sweet, or pimientos, as seasoning, 586
for paprika, **315**
tabasco, **315**
vitamin C content, 315
Périgourdine, defined, 310
Perigueux Sauce, 347
Periwinkles, about, **87,** 379

Persian, balls or centers, 793
chicken, 425
cream, 745
Persimmon, 140
canning, 807
ice cream, 765
Japanese, **123**
oriental, 140
pudding, 753
salad, Japanese, 112
Pesto, anchovy and basil, 570
Petite Marmite, 170
Petits Fours, 695, **695**
Pfannkuchen, or German Pancakes, 238
Pfeffernüsse, 708
Pheasant, about, 438
braised, 438
in game sauce, 439
roast, 438
Smitane, 439
smoked for hors d'oeuvre, 87
Phyllo leaves, about, 649
Piccalilli, 844
PICKLE AND RELISH, 841–849, *also see* Chutney
boiling water bath for, 841
bread and butter, 842
brine, 841
chilis in sherry, 845
cucumber, sweet-sour, spiced, 842
cucumber, yellow, 842; sweet-sour, 842
curry sauce, 843
dill and Kosher, 848
equipment for, 841, **841**
gherkins, pickled, or cornichons, 843
ingredients, about, 841
Kosher dill, 848
long-brined, about, 848
to make crisp, 841
mustard or chow-chow, 843
olive oil, 843
piccalilli, 844
relish, corn, 844
relish, Indian, or basic chutney, 846
salt for, 569, 841
Senfgurken, 842
short-brined, about, 841
to store, 842
tomato, green, 844
vinegar for, 841
Pickled, beans, dilled, 845
carrot sticks, 845
fruits, *see individual fruits*
horseradish, 848
nasturtium pods, or seeds, 845
onions, 845
pork, 814
watermelon rind, 845
zucchini, 845
Picnic Menu Suggestions, 34
PIES, 638–663; *also see* Pastries
amber, *see* Transparent pie, 653
angel, 657
apple, 651
PIES *(cont.)*
apricot, 653
banana cream, 656
berry, glazed, 651
berry, sour cream, 651
berry, with cooked or canned fruit, 650
berry, with fresh fruit, 650
berry, with frozen fruit, 650
berry and fruit, about, 650
Black Bottom, gelatin, 658
Boston cream, 689
bourbon, *see* Pecan pie, 653
butterscotch cream, 656
caramel custard, 656
caramel gelatin chiffon, 659
cheese, 255
cheese custard, 255
cherry, with cooked fruit, 650
cherry, fresh, 651
cherry, with frozen fruit, 650
cherry, sour cream, 651
chess, 654
chiffon, about, 658; to freeze and thaw, 831
chocolate cream, 656
chocolate mocha gelatin chiffon, 658
coconut cream, 656
coffee cream, 656
cream, 656
crumb or gravel, 654
crusts, about, for filled pies, 639
crusts, additions to, 642
crusts, cereal, 643
crusts, cheesecake, 642
crusts, cookie and Kuchen, 642
crusts, crumb, about, 642
crusts, crumb, bread or cake, 643
crusts, frozen, unfilled, 830
crusts, graham cracker, zwieback or cookie crumb, 642
crusts, half-puff paste, or Pâte Demi-Feuilletée, 645
crusts, meringue paste, 649
crusts, puff paste or Pâte Feuilletée, 643, **643, 644, 645**
crusts, unfilled pies, about, 640
custard, about, 655, **655**
deep-dish, 660
dough, basic, 640
dough, Cockaigne, 640
dough, for cheese straws or wafers, 641
dough, flour paste, 640
dough, frozen, baked and unbaked, about, 829–830
dough, galette, about, 642
dough, handling, 638, **638,** 639, **639**
dough, to keep, 638
dough, lattices of, 639, **639**
dough, for meats, about, 641; toppings, 449
dough, mixer, 640
dough, Pâte Brisée, 641
dough, pat-in-the-pan oil, 640
dough, rich egg tart, Pâte Sucrée or Mürbeteig, 641

PIES *(cont.)*
dough, Vienna pastry, 641
dough, wheatless, 641
fish, individual, 266
freezing and thawing, 830
fried, as canapés, 69
frozen, fillings, glazes, 830
fruit, about, 650; deep-dish, 660
fruit, thickening for, 650
fudge, 656
grape, 652
high altitude, making at, 638
Jefferson Davis, 654
Kentucky, *see* Jefferson Davis Pie, 654
lemon, Ohio, 657
lemon angel, 657
lemon or lime, eggless, 657
lemon or lime chiffon, 658
lemon meringue, 657
lime, Key, 657
maple gelatin chiffon, 659
meringue paste, about, 649
mince, 652
mince, mock, 653
à la mode, *see* Apple pie, 651
onion or leek, 255
orange chiffon, 658
peach, 652
pecan, 653
pinch, 649
pizza, 610
pot, chicken or beef, 252
pot, seafood, 267
prune, 653
pumpkin, 654
pumpkin gelatin chiffon, 659
raisin, 653
raspberry Bavarian, 657
raspberry chiffon, 658
rhubarb, 652
Ricotta, 660
shells, individual, to form, 640
Shepherd's, 262
squash, 654
stack, 654
steak-and-kidney, 465
strawberry Bavarian, 657
strawberry chiffon, 658
tarts, *see* Tarts
toppings for, 730–732
transparent, about, 653; basic, 653
veal and pork, 470
Piémontaise, defined, 310
Pig, roast suckling, 478
Pigs' ears, 512
feet, jellied, 511; stewed, 511
knuckles and sauerkraut, 511
tails, 511
Pigs in Potatoes, 260
Pigeon, 441; rice dressing for, 373
Pilaf, 209
bulgur, 202
duck, 433
Pilchard, defined, 411
Pimientos, about, 315, **315**
canning, 809
salad, filled, 103
Pine nuts, 564
Pineapple, about, 140
Betty, baked, 752
cakes with ham and sweet potatoes, 258
canning, 807
as case or container, **78, 109, 141**
cream, molded, 748
cup, 141
custard, sponge, 737
effect on gelatins, 117
eggnog, 45
filled, 141
fresh, to cut, **140;** ways to serve, 140**, 141**
gelatin, 744
glazed, 795
grilled, 141
and ground ham, 258
ice, 766
icings, 729
jam, 835, 836
jam, and apricot, 836
juice, canning, 807
juice, fresh, 43
juice and grapefruit, 44
juice and tomato, 43
plugged, **60**
preserves, and strawberries, 837
punch, 45, 46
receptacle for hors d'oeuvre, **78**
rice, baked, 208
rice dressing Cockaigne, 373
ring, molded, salad, 119
salad, 112, 115, 119
sandwich with ham, 271
sherbet, banana, 768
sherbet, buttermilk, 769; milk, 768
snow, 746
soufflé, 740
tidbits, 140
tomatoes stuffed with, 333
Tropic, **60,** 61
Pinwheel, 251; biscuits, 633
cookies, 716
rolls, filled, 613, **613**
Piperade, *see* Spanish Omelet, 228
Piroshki, 251
Pistachio Ice Cream, 760
nuts, 564
Pit-cooking, 155, 156
Pizza, 610
small, for canapés, 74
Planking, 154
Plantain, 317; *also see* Bananas, 132
Plover, 440
Plum, about, 141
butter, Damson, 837
cake, Cockaigne, 661
canning, 807
conserve, 839

Plum *(cont.)*
ice cream, greengage, 764
jelly, 835
preserves, 838
pudding, baked, 752; flambéed, **734**
pudding, sauce, or hot wine, 771
pudding, steamed, 755
sauce, 356
Poaching, about, 150
paper, to make, 151, **151**
Poi, 331
Pointers to success, *watch for symbol* ➤
Poireaux, *see* Leeks
Poivrade Sauce, 347
Polenta, 201
Polonaise Sauce, 351
Polvo de Amor, 567
Polynesian Pork or Chicken, 257
Pomegranate, 129, 142
Pommes Anglaise, 317
Pompano en Papillote, 410
Pop, *see* Beverages, 46
Popcorn, 790; candied, 790, **791**
seasoned, hors d'oeuvre, 80
Popover, 631; cheese, 632
Poppy seed, 564
cake, custard Cockaigne, 689
fillings, 622–623
Porcupine, 515
meatballs, 490
PORK, 476–486
about, 476
bacon, *see* Bacon
balls, *see* Meatballs
balls, in tomato sauce, 490
birds, 480
casserole, Romanian with noodles, 215
cassoulet, 475
chitterlings, 512; sautéed, 512
chops, 479; baked, 479
chops, braised, Creole, 480
chops, braised, deviled, 480
chops, braised, with fruit, 479
chops, braised, with sauerkraut, 480
chops, braised, stuffed, Cockaigne, 479
chops, breaded, 479
chops, sautéed, 479
city chicken, 469
crown roast, 477, **477**
fat, about, 542
Goulash à Blanc, 475
goulash with sauerkraut and veal, 481
ham, *see* Ham, 482
hocks, stewed, 482
large cuts, suggested uses, 452–453
marinade for, 529
need for thorough cooking, 477
neck bones, stewed, 482
pickled, to make, 814
pie, and veal, 470
pigs' ears, 512
pigs' feet, jellied, 511; stewed, 511
pigs' knuckles and sauerkraut, 511
PORK *(cont.)*
pigtails, 511
Polynesian, 257
roast, 477; dressing for, 371
roast, leg or fresh ham, 478
roast, stuffed with sauerkraut, 478
roast suckling pig, **442,** 478
salt, to make, 814
salt, in milk gravy, 482
salt, as seasoning, 572
sausage, *see* Sausage
scrapple or Goetta, 499
spareribs, about, 481
spareribs, baked, with apple-onion dressing, 481
spareribs, barbecued, 481
spareribs, boiled, 482
spareribs, sweet-sour, 481
sweet and sour, 480
tenderloin, 478; Frenched, 479
tenderloin with mushrooms and olives, 479
trichinosis warning, 477
Pörkölt, about, 464
Pot pies, meat, about, 449
meat or poultry, 251, 252; steak and kidney, 465
seafood, 267
Pot roast, beef, 459
Potages, defined, 174; see Soups
Germiny, 185
St. Germain, 178
POTATO, about, 317
Anna, 320, **320**
baked, 319, 320
balls, fried, 323
baskets, 323
boiled, mature, 317
boiled, new, 317
bread, salt-rising, 607
browned or Franconia, 320
cabbage, and ham, 293
cakes with ham, 258
canning, 809
Chantilly, 318
chips, Saratoga, 323
cooked in resin, 319
creamed, 319
Dauphine, 323
doughnuts, buttermilk, 245
Duchess, 323
dumplings, 204
flour, brownies, 702
flour sponge cake, 670
flour or starch, 550
French-fried, oven, 322
French fries, never fail, 322
fried, 320
grated, pan-broiled, 321
green beans, smoked meat, and, 286
hash and corned beef, 261
hash brown, 321
leftover, about, 324; au gratin, 324
leftover, cakes, 324; German-fried, 324
leftover, O'Brien, 324
Lorette, 323

POTATO *(cont.)*
Lyonnaise or Pan-Fried, 320
mashed, 318; to keep warm, 318
mashed, cheese puffs, 318
nutrients, 317
pancakes, 321
pigs in, 260
poisonous, sprouts, 317
puffs, 323
riced, 318
rolls, buttermilk, 613; refrigerator, 618
salads, 103, 104
sautéed, tiny new, 318
scalloped, 319
shoestring, 322
soufflé or puffed, 321, **322**
soup, 184; with leeks, 184
soup with tomatoes, 184
starch as sauce thickener, 339
stuffed, 319, 320
sweet, about, 324; *also see* Yams
sweet, baked, 324; boiled, 324
sweet, candied; caramelized, 325
sweet, canning, 810
sweet, casserole, and chipped beef, 260
sweet, deep-fried, 325
sweet, dressing and apple, 374
sweet, dressing and sausage, 374
sweet, fruit and, 325
sweet, with ham cakes and pineapple, 258
sweet, mashed, 324
sweet, pudding, 753
sweet, puffs, 325
sweet, soufflé with pineapple or applesauce, 230
sweet, stuffed, 325
sweet, stuffing and sausage, 374
water, 317
Pot-au-Feu, 170
Pots-de-Crème, 737; Café, 737; blender, 737
utensils for, **734**
Poule-au-Pot, 170
POULTRY, 417–435; *also see* Chicken, Turkey, Duck, *etc.*
about, 417
barding, 420, **420**
to bleed, 810
boning, 420
canning, 811
carving, 421, **421**
cooked, to store, 417
Cornish hens, guineas and squabs, about, 434
cutting a drawn bird, 419, **419**
drawing and dressing, 418, **418**
dressings for, 370–374
dry-curing, 813
fats, about, 542
federal inspection stamp, 417
freezing and thawing, 826
fresh, to store, 417
frozen, about, 417
giblets, about preparing, 418
to grill out of doors, 158, **158**
plucking and singeing, about, 418
POULTRY *(cont.)*
relative cost of, 417
roasting, 421; in foil, 422
smoking and cooking, 816
spit-cooking, **158**
stock, 523
stuffing and trussing, 419, **420**
tendons, to remove, 418, **418**
to test for doneness, 421
Pound Cake, 675
Prairie Chicken, roasted, 439
Praliné for garnish, 789
Pralines, 788; *see* Brûlée Crust, 736
sherried, 788
PRESERVES, 837–839; defined, 832
apricot, 837
Bar-le-Duc or currant, 838
calamondin, 839
cherry, 837
fig, 838
gooseberry, 838
harvest, 838
kumquat, 839
making, 837
peach, 837
plum, Damson, Italian or greengage, 838
quince, 838
strawberry and pineapple, 837
strawberry and rhubarb, 837
strawberry, sunshine, 837
tomato, 838
Tutti-Frutti Cockaigne, 840
Pressure canning, 804, **804**
low-acid foods, 804
meat, poultry, game and fish, 811
vegetables, 808
Pressure cooking, about, 150; *also watch for symbol* ✪
at high altitudes, 150, 804
steamed puddings, 754
vegetables, 278
Pretzels, 618, **618**
almond, 713
Prickly pear, 129, 142
Printanière, defined, 277
Profiteroles, 647; defined, 646
Prosciutto, and fruit for hors d'oeuvre, 80
with lobster or crab, 268
Proteins, about, 2
complete and incomplete, 2
daily requirements, 3
production requisites, 4
textured vegetable, 535
value in relation to casein, 8
values, 3; in average servings, 8–14
vegetable combinations, 3
Prune, defined, 141
Betty, 751
bread, 603; quick, 624
cake, spiced chocolate, 677
chestnuts and, 142
cookie, filled, 718
dressing, 373

Prune *(cont.)*
filling for coffee cake, 622
lentils, and, 289
pickled, 142
pie, 653
soufflé or whip, 741
stewed, 141
in wine, 141
Ptarmigan, roasted, 439
PUDDING, SWEET, 734–755, *also see* Custard Bavarians
apple molasses, steamed, 755
Bavarian creams, 746–748
Betty, pineapple, 752
Betty, prune or apricot, 751
bread, with meringue, 751
brown Betty, 751
cabinet or Bavarian de luxe, 746
caramel custard, cornstarch, 738
Charlotte russe, chocolate; maple, 748
chocolate feather, 753
cornstarch, 738–739
cornstarch custard or blancmange, 738
cottage, 752
cream, fried, or crème frite, 739
date loaf, uncooked, 753
date ring, or Christmas wreath, 752
farina, 749
fig, baked, 752
gelatin, about, 743
gelatin, texture, about, 744
Indian, 749
marshmallow, 746
mocha marshmallow cream, 749
molds, **743,** 743–745
Nesselrode, 747
persimmon, 753
plum, baked, **734,** 752; steamed, 755
rennet, or junket, 748
rice, 750
rice and fruit, 750
rice, creamy, 749
rice with whipped cream, 750
Rote Grütze, 749
sauces, 769–776
steamed, about, 753
steamed brown, 754
steamed caramel, 755
steamed chocolate, 754
steamed date, 754
steamed fruit suet, 754
steamed high-altitude, 754
steamed in pressure cooker, 754
steamed plum, **734,** 755
steaming period, 754
sweet potato, 753
tapioca, 750, 751
tapioca, crushed fruit, eggless, 750
tapioca, pearl, 751
to unmold, 561, 743
PUDDINGS, SAVORY, about, 755
corn, fresh, Cockaigne, 300
corn, souffléed, 301
PUDDINGS, SAVORY *(cont.)*
tomato Cockaigne, 333
Yorkshire, 206
Puff, canapés, 75
corn, golden, 628
cream, fillings for, 647
potato, 321, **322,** 323
salmon, 267
shells, cream, **645,** 646
sweet potato, 325
Puff paste, 643, **643, 644, 645**
canapé, 69
cream rolls, **645,** 646
glaze for, 732
half or rough or Pâte Demi-Feuilletée, 645
Napoleons, **645,** 646
palm leaves, 645
patty shells or Bouchées, 645, **645**
shapes, to make, 645, **645**
Vol-au-Vent, **645,** 646
Puffballs, mushroom, **306,** 307
Pumpkin, 330; to bake, 654
bread, quick, 624
canning, 809
cookies, 709
muffin, 631
pie, 654
pie, gelatin chiffon, 659
seeds, 564
soup, 185
Punch, alcoholic, 61–65; nonalcoholic, 44–46
bowl, ice, to make, 62, **63**
bowle, 63
champagne, 63
claret cup, 64
cocomoka, hot; cold, 46
eggnog in quantity, 64
Fish House, 63
fruit, 46; in quantity, 46
Glogg, 65
May wine, 64
milk, or Syllabub, 62
mulled wine or Negus, 65
pineapple, 45
Planter's, 63
Rhine wine cup, 64
rum cassis cup, 64
Sangria, 62
strawberry fruit, 46
Tom and Jerry, in quantity, 65
tomato, gala, 45
Vin Brûlé, 61
wassail, 65
whisky or brandy cup, 64
Purée, canning, 806
defined, 174
Purslane, soup, cream of, 185

Q

Quail, 441, about, 440
Quantity cooking, about, 23
Quatre Épices or spices, 572

Quenelles, about, 205
as hors d'oeuvre, **77**
poached or baked, 206
Quiche, about, 254
Alsacienne, or Lorraine, **250,** 255; defined, 254
canapé, 69
crustless, 232
Quince, 129, **129**
baked, 142
canning, 807
jelly, 834; preserves, 838
paste, or quittenwürst, 797

R

Rabbit and hare, about, 513; to serve, **513**
braised with onions, 514
with chili beans, 515
fricassee, 513
à la mode or jugged hare, 514
mold for cakes, about, 672, **672**
roast, 513
sausage casserole, and, 514
sautéed, 513
to skin, 513, **514**
stock, 523
Raccoon, 515
Radish, canapés, 73
cooked, 325
hors d'oeuvre, 84; rose, 84, **84**
Ragoût Fin, 503
Ragoûts, *see* Stews
Rahat Loukoum or Turkish Delight, 791
Rails, *see* Small Game Birds, 440
Raisin, about, 125, 137
bread, 603
filling, 698; cookie, 717
icing, 722
pie, 653
sauce, 356; cider or beer, 356
sauce, sweet, 770
Ramekins, *see* Custard cups, **735**
Ramps, 585, **586**
Rarebit, oyster, 378
tomato or woodchuck, 253
Welsh, 252; noodles and, 214
Raspberry, about, 134; *also see* Berries
bombe, 764
cake, rum or trifle, 688
canning, 806
cooler, 45
glaze, 732
ice, 766, 767; sherbet, 768
ice cream, 760; parfait, 764
jam, 836
jelly, 834; currant and; gooseberry and, 834
in melon round, 139
pie, 650, 651
pie, Bavarian, 657; chiffon, 658
vinegar, Cockaigne, 527
Ratatouille Provençale, 304
Ravigote Sauce, 345
Ravioli, 216, **216;** dough for, 213
roller for, **198**
Red Flannel Hash, 466
Red snapper baked with sauce, 413
Reduction, liquids, 154
sauces, roux-based, 339
stocks or glazes, 522
Reed birds, 440
Refiner's Syrup, 559
Reheating food, 161
frozen dishes, 828
meats, 449
Relevés, defined, 17
Relish, *see* Pickle
cranberry, uncooked, 134
Rémoulade, celeriac, 102
sauce, 364
turnips, 102
Rendering fats, 542
Rennet, about, 561; pudding, 748
Reuben Sandwich, 272
Rhubarb, about, 142; canning, 808
baked and jam, 142
conserve, spiced, 839
leaves, oxalic acid in, 142
pie, 652
poached, 142
preserves, strawberry and, 837
salad molds, and strawberries, 120
RICE, 206–212; about, 206
baked, pineapple and, 208
baked in chicken stock, 207
beans, pinto, and, 288
boiled, 206
cheese, 208
croquettes, sweet, 248
curried, 208
custard and bacon, 208
dish, cabbage or lettuce and, 294
dish, Rombauer, 209
dressings, 373
flour, 549; waxy, 549
flour brownies, 702
flour griddle cakes, 239
flour muffins, 631
flour sponge cake, 670
fried, Chinese, 208
fritters, 244
fruit and nut casserole, 210
green, baked, 208
griddle cakes, cornmeal, 239
Italian, or Risotto alla Milanese, 209
Jambalaya, chicken, meat or fish, 211
loaf, and nut, 210
loaf or casserole, 210
long or Harusame, 212
paella, 210
peppers, green, stuffed with, 316
pilaf, 209
puddings, 749, 750
ring, and ham, 207; mushroom, 207
ring or mold, **198,** 207; and cheese, 207
salad, 104
Spanish, 209
spinach and chestnuts with, 208

RICE *(cont.)*
table or Rijsttafel, 211
vegetable, or Jambalaya, 211
wild, *see* Wild rice
Ricer, 204
Ricotta, cheesecake or pie, 660
filling, chocolate, 697
filling for coffee cakes, 623
Rickeys, 59
Rijsttafel or rice table, 211
Risotto alla Milanese, 209
Rissoles, as canapés, 69
Rochambole garlic, 584, **586**
Rock Candy, 787, **787**
Rock Cornish hen, 434
Roe, about, 87, 411
lobster coral, 385
preparing for caviar, 814
shad, baked, 412; broiled, 412; parboiled, 411; sautéed, 412
Tarama, 87
Rollmops, defined, 408
hors d'oeuvre, 88
ROLLS AND BUNS, 610–619
bagels, 617, **618**
beef, 465
bread sticks, 617
brioches, **599,** 615, **615;** au chocolat, 615
buttermilk or Fan-Tans, 612, **612**
buttermilk-potato, 613
caramel or Schnecken, 614
cases for food, 250
cheese, 613
cinnamon snails and crisps, 614, **614**
cloverleaf, 611, **611**
cream, **645,** 646
crescents, filled, sweet, 616
crescents, French, or croissants, 616, **616**
crumpets, 617
doughs, refrigerator, about, 618
egg, Chinese, 250
English or raised muffins, 617, **617**
fillings, savory, for, 270
ham, stuffed, 257
hard or Vienna, 616
hot cross, 611
Kolatchen, 612
low-fat, eggless, 613
meat pie or pinwheels, 251
no-knead, light, 610
oat-and-molasses, 614
orange tea, 616
overnight, 612, **613**
palm leaf, 611, **612**
Parker House, 611
pinwheel, filled, 613, **613**
pretzel, 617, **617**
refrigerator, bran, 619
refrigerator, no-knead, 618
refrigerator, potato, 618
refrigerator, whole-grain, 619
rye, 614
sour cream or palm leaf, 611, **612**

ROLLS AND BUNS *(cont.)*
toppings, sweet, for, 731
whole-grain, 614
yeast, about, 610; to reheat, 610
Romaine, 93, **93**
Romanian Noodle and Pork Casserole, 215
Root cellars, 800
Roots, candied, 797; wild, to cook, 305
Roquefort, canapés, 71, 72
coleslaw, 97
dressings, 361; sour cream, 367
Roquette, for salads, 93, **93**
Rose hips, fruit soup, 129; jam, 836
Roselle Sauce, 139
Rosemary, 587
sauce, wine, 347
Rosettes, 246; iron for, **235**
and stuffed eggs with sauce, 225
Rote Grütze, 749
Rotisserie cooking, 158, **158**
Rouille Sauce, 366; Mock, 366
Roulades, 465
Roux, 338
Royal Glaze, 727
Rue, about, 587
Rum, and rum cocktails, about, 51
Baba au or Savarin, 689
drinks, 51, 52, 60, 61, 63, 64, 65
drops, uncooked, 790
mousse, chocolate, 738
punch, 64
sauce, 771
Rumaki, 81
Rusks, 637
Rutabaga or Swedes, boiled, 326
Rye, bread, sourdough, 609; Swedish, 608
cake, honey, eggless, 626
flour, 549; meal, 549
rolls, 614
whisky, about, 50

S

Sabayon, 736; sauces, 771
Saccharin, 560
Sachertorte, 686
Safflower oil, 95
Saffron, 567, 587
Sage, 587; in tisanes, 40
Sago, 550
St. John's Bread, *see* Carob
SALAD, 92–122
about, 92; bowl for, **92,** 95
apple, 109
artichoke hearts, 100; stuffed, 100
asparagus, 100; and celery aspic, 115; and egg, 100; and green pepper, 100
aspic, about, 113; basic, 113; varieties, 113–120
aspic, luncheon, 116; garnish, 114
aspic, tomato or vegetable juice, 115
avocado, 110, **110;** molded, 117
avocado cups, slices, 110; and fruit, 110, **110**
banana, orange and nut, 111
bean, dried, 100

SALAD *(cont.)*
bean, green, 101; hot, 101
bean sprout, oriental, 96
bean, Viennese and herring, 107
beef, 109
beet, pickled, 101; gelatin, 116
beet cups, cold, 101
beetroot and chicory, 96
Bird of Paradise, 109, **109**
buffet, **98**
Caesar, 96
calico, 106
carrot, with raisins and nuts, 101
cases, vegetables, 98, **99**
celeriac or celery root, 101, 102
Celeri-rave Rémoulade, 102
celery, cooked, 101
celery cabbage, 101
chapons for, 95
cheese ring, 119
cherry and hazelnut, 111
chicken, 108; in quantity, 108; variations,
chicken, hot, 264
chicken in aspic, 117
chicken breasts for, 429
chicken mousse, jellied, 120
chicory and beetroot, 96
Christmas, 103
citrus fruit, 111
clam ring, jellied, 116
coleslaw, 96; blender, 97; deluxe, 97
coleslaw, for barbecue, 97
coleslaw, Roquefort, 97
combination, 98
condiments for, 95
corn or field, 93
corned beef, 109
crab, 106
crab Louis, 107
cranberry, molded, 118; and apple, 118
cranberry sauces, 133–134
cucumber, 102, **102**
cucumber, aspic, 114
cucumber, mousse, 120
cucumber, stuffed, cold, 102
cucumber, wilted, 102
dressings, about, 92
dressings for, 360–367; *also see* Salad dressings
egg, in aspic, 117; Cockaigne, 117
egg and caviar, molded, 106
egg ring, molded, 117
endive, cooked, 101
fish, 106–108
fish, creamed, molded, 121
fisherman's, 108
freezing ingredients, 829; thawing, 829
fruit, 109–112
fruit, with cream, 24-hour, 122
fruit, gelatin for, 117
fruit, molded, with cheese balls, 119
fruit, mousse, chilled, 122
garlic for, 95
garnishes, 99, **99**

SALAD *(cont.)*
gelatin, basic, 113; for fruit, 117
gelatin, golden glow, 115
gelatin, mint for fruit, 117
ginger ale gelatin, 118
gingham, with cottage cheese, 97
grape, about, 111
grape and celery ring, 118
grape and pear, 112
grapefruit, 111; orange, 111
grapefruit and sherry aspic, 118
Greek, *see* Combination I, 98
greens, cultivated, 92, **93;** *also see individual names*
greens, for picnic, 95
greens, to wash, 94, **94;** to dry, 94, **95**
greens, wild, about, 94
greens, wilted, 96
ham, 109; mousse, jellied, 120
herring, Christmas, 107; Viennese bean and, 107
herring and potato, 104
lettuce, about, 93
lettuce rolls, stuffed, 106
lobster, 106; mold, 107
lobster mousse, 121
lotus root, 102
macaroni, spaghetti, or calico, 106
Madrilène ring with shad roe Cockaigne, 115
Maurice, 98
meat, 108–109
melon, 111; aspic-filled, 119
molded, about, 112, **112;** additions to, 113
mousseline of shellfish, 122
mousses, 120–122
Niçoise, 103
oils, about, 95
okra, 103
orange, banana and nut, 111
orange and onion, 111
palm, hearts of, 103
peach, 109; fresh, with cheese, 111
pear, 109; and grape, 112
pepper slices with fillings, 103
persimmon, Japanese, 112
pimientos, filled, 103
pineapple, 112; ring, molded, 119
potato, 103; German, hot, 104
potato, Niçoise, 104
potato and herring, 104
rhubarb and strawberry molds, 120
rice, 104
Russian, 99
salmagundi, 103
seafood, jellied, 116; mousse, 121
seasonings for, 95
to serve, 19, 92
shad roe, 108; jellied, 115
shrimp, 108; mold, 107
slaw, hot, with apple, 97
spaghetti or macaroni, 106
strawberry and rhubarb molds, 120
tomato, about, 104
tomato, canned, 105

SALAD *(cont.)*
tomato, French, 105
tomato aspic, 114; canned juice, 115
tomato and onion or cucumber, 106, **106**
tomatoes, stuffed, about, 105, **105**
tossed, about, 94; additions to, 95
tossed, combination, about, 98
tuna fish, 108
turnips Rémoulade, 102
veal, 109
veal mousse, jellied, 120
veal stock, jellied, 114
vegetable cases and garnishes, 98, **99**
vegetable gelatine, molded, 115
vegetables for, 99
Waldorf, 109
western, 96
SALAD DRESSING, 360–367; *also see* Sauces
about, 360
anchovy, 361
anchovy and beet; and Roquefort, blender, 361
anchovy caper, or Salsa Verde, 361
Andalouse, 364
avocado, 362
boiled, 366
celery seed, 362
chiffonade, 360
Chinese low-calorie, Cockaigne, 362
chutney, 361
commercial, fat content, 360
cream or Chantilly, 365
cream cheese for fruit, 367
curry, for fruit, 367
French, with cream cheese, 361
French, for fruit salad, 361
French, herbed, 360
French, low-calorie, 362
French, Roquefort or blue cheese, 361
French, or sauce Vinaigrette, 360
garlic seasoning for, or chapon, 95
Green Goddess, 364
half-and-half, 365
honey, 361
horseradish, 362
Italian, 361
Lorenzo, 360
low-calorie, 360, 362, 364, 366, 367
mayonnaise, blender, 363
mayonnaise, cream or Chantilly, 365
mayonnaise, curry, 365
mayonnaise, for fruit, 365
mayonnaise, green, or Sauce Verte, 364
mayonnaise, Grenache, 363
mayonnaise, herb, 364
mayonnaise, mock, 366
Rémoulade, 364
Roquefort or blue cheese, French, 361
Roquefort sour cream, 367
Russian, or Russian mayonnaise, 364
Salsa Verde, 361
sour cream for vegetables, 367
spinach, 360
sweet-sour, low-calorie, 362
SALAD DRESSING *(cont.)*
Thousand Island; low-calorie, mock, 364
tomato low-calorie, 362
watercress, 360; blender, 360
yogurt, 367
yogurt and cucumber, low-calorie, 367
Salamander, 145
Sally Lunn, quick, 623
Salmagundi, 103
Salmi of wildfowl, 436
Salmon, about, 410
cakes, 267; croquettes, 249
glazed, cold, 411
puffs, 267
smoked, with eggs, 222
smoked canapés, 76; hors d'oeuvre, 88
with spaghetti, quick, 217
steaks or darnes, broiled, 410
Salmonella, meat, 444; eggs, 543
Salpicon, defined, 277
Salsify or oyster plant, 326
SALT, about, types, 568–569
brine, 569
brining; corned beef, 813; vegetables, 848
coarse or Kosher, 569
cooking or table, 569
dry-curing meat, game and fowl, 813
effect on foods, 569
foods heavy in, 569
free-flowing, 569
herb, to make, 570
iodized, 569
monosodium glutamate, 570
pickling or dairy, 569
to remove from fats, 542
rock, 570
sea, 569
seasoned, to make, 570
smoked, 570; smoky mixture, 570
sour, 570
substitute, 570
vegetable, 570
Salt pork, to make, 814
in milk gravy, 482
as seasoning, 572
Salt Water Taffy, 786
Salt-Rising Bread, cornmeal, 606
potato, 607
Samovar, 36
Samp, as cereal, 200
Sand Tarts, 711
SANDWICH, 269–275; *also see* Canapés
about, 269; tea and canapé, 66, **67**
asparagus, rolled, 73
bacon and cheese, 272
bases for small, 68
braunschweiger, 272
bread for, about, 67
butter spreads for, 70
cheese, puffed, with mushrooms, 273
cheese with chipped or corned beef, 270
cheese with mushroom sauce, 273
cheese spreads for, 72

SANDWICH *(cont.)*
chicken, 274; hot, 274
chicken and cream cheese, 274
chicken salad, 74
club, 274
corned beef or chipped beef, 270
Croque Madame; Monsieur, 271
cucumber, 73
deviled ham and cheese, 272
egg and cheese with sauce, 273
egg spreads, 73
freezing and thawing, 829
French toast, ham and pineapple, 271
French toast and cheese, 273
French toast and tomato, 273
fruit sticks, 274
glazed, 70
grilled or sautéed, 269
ham, tomato and egg, 272
ham salad, 74, 271
Hawaiian toast with bacon, 271
hero, 272
lamb, 274
loaf, 68, **68**
lobster, 275
to make in quantity, 66, **67**
meal-in-one, 270
open-faced, 269, **270**
peanut butter and bacon, 273
peanut butter and tomato, 273
poor boy, submarine or hero, 272
preparing and keeping, 66
Reuben, 272
ribbon, 67, **67**
roast beef, hot, 270
rolled, 67, **67**
Savoyarde, 271
shapes of, 66, **66,** 67, **67**
shrimp, with cheese sauce, 275
sprouted cress and mustard, 565
sweet tea spreads, 72
tea, 66–76
to toast, 67
toasted, 269
toasted rolls with crab meat and cheese, 274
toasted rolls with ham and asparagus, 272
tomato, 73
tongue salad, 271
waffle, 269
western, 271
zoo, 68, **68**
Sapodilla, 144
Sapote, 144
Saratoga Chips, 323
Sardines, about, 411
canapés, 76
hors d'oeuvre, 88
Sassaties Marinade, 529
SAUCE, 336–369; *also see* Sauces, sweet or dessert; Salad dressings
Agrodolce, 354
aioli or garlic, 365
Allemande or thickened Velouté, 345

SAUCE *(cont.)*
almond butter, 350
anchovy, 343; butter, 350
anchovy caper or Salsa Verde, 361
Andalouse, 364
arrowroot thickener, 339
aspic glaze, 368
Aurore, 344
barbecue, 354; for fowl, 354
Béarnaise, 359; about, 357; blender, 359
Béchamel, or white, 341
beer raisin or cider, 356
Bercy butter, 350
Bigarade, 355
blood thickener, 339
Bolognese pasta, 353
Bordelaise, 347
Bourguignonne, 350
bread, 343
brown, quick, 348
brown butter or Beurre Noisette, 349
brown or Sauce Espagñole, 346
Burgundy or Bourguignonne, 350
butter, black, or Beurre Noir, 350
butter, for canned or cooked vegetables, 351
butter, for Crêpes Suzette, 237
butter, drawn or clarified, 349
butter, kneaded, or Beurre Manié, 340
butter, and seasoned butters, about, 349
butter, to serve, 349
butter swirls, 339
caper, *see* Allemande, 345
caraway, 355
caviar, 357; butter, 350
champagne, 344
Chasseur, 347
Chaud-Froid, 369; quick pink, 369; decorations for, 369
cheese, 342
cherry, 356
chili, 847
Chinese, for vegetables, 349
Choron, 359
cider or beer raisin, 356
cocktail, 352
Colbert butter, 350
color in, 337; from aluminum pans, 343, *see* Velouté
commercial, about, 574
containers for, **340, 758**
cornstarch thickener, 339
cranberry, 133; whole, 134
cranberry glaze for fowl, 368
cream, *see* white, 341
Creole, 348; quick, 352
cucumber, almond, 357
Cumberland, 356
curdling, to avoid, 337
curry, 345
deglazing and degreasing, 340
demi-glaze, 346
deviled butter, for seafood, 351
Dijonnaise, 342

SAUCE *(cont.)*
doubling of, 338
Dresden, for fish, 356
egg yolk, as thickener, 339
egg-thickened, about, 357
Filé powder, thickener, 340
Florentine, 342
flour, browned, as thickener, 339
flour paste as thickener, 339
Foyot, 359
freezing, 338
garlic or Beurre de Provence, 365
garlic butter, 351
garnishes for, 551–553, 571
glazes and glaçage, 367–369
gravy, pan, meat; poultry, 341
green butter, 351
Green Goddess, 364
Gribiche, 365
holding, heated, 161–162
Hollandaise, about, 357, **358;** blender, 358; variations, 358
Hollandaise, whole-egg, quick, 358
honey glaze for meat or onions, 368
horseradish, or Albert, 343
horseradish, frozen, 357
horseradish, sour cream, 356
horseradish dressing, cream, 357
Hunter's or Chasseur, 347
Indienne, 344
Italian meat, 352
to keep, 338
à la king, quick, 348
lemon butter, 350
lobster butter, 351
Lorenzo, 360
Louis, 365
Lyonnaise or brown onion, 346
Madeira, 346
Maître d'Hôtel butter, 350
Maltaise, 359
Marchand de Vin, 347
marinades, 528–529
Marinara, 353
mayonnaise, 363–366; hot, 359
Mayonnaise Collée, or gelatin, 368
mayonnaise, eggless mock, 366
mayonnaise, low-calorie, mock, 366
mayonnaise, souffléd, for fish, 359
meat glaze, or Glaçe de Viande, 368
Meunière or lemon butter, 350
Mexican tomato, 352
mint, 355
Mornay, 342
Mousseline, 359
mushroom, quick, 348; wine, 347
mustard, cold, 357; hot, 345
Nantua or shrimp, 343
Newburg, 359
octopus pasta, 353
onion, brown, or Lyonnaise, 346
onion, white, or Soubise, 344
orange, for duck or goose, 355

SAUCE *(cont.)*
oyster, for fish, 343
paprika or Hungarian, 344
pasta, suggestions, 219
peanut pepper, 346
pepper or Poivrade, 347
Périgueux, 347
pink, for seafood, 367
piquant, 347
plum, peach, or apricot, 356
Polonaise or browned butter crumb, 351
potato starch or fecula thickener, 339
Poulette, *see* Allemande, 345
in quantity, 338
raisin, 356; cider or beer, 356
Ravigote, 345
reduction, to thicken by, 339
Rémoulade, 364
to retain texture, 337
Robert, 347
roselle, 134
rosemary wine, 347
Rouille, 366; mock, 366
roux, as thickener for, 338; to keep, 338
Salsa Verde, 361
Sassaties or marinade, 529
savory, cold, about, 360; hot, 337
savory, defined, 336
savory, ingredients, about, 338
seafood, pink, 367; spaghetti, 349
to serve attractively, 340, **340**
shrimp butter, 351
shrimp and clam for pasta, 354
Sicilian garnish, 366
Skordalia, 365
Smitane, 345
snail butter, 350
Soubise or white onion, 344
soup, canned, quick, 348
soup, dried, 349
sour cream, for baked potatoes, 357
soy, 574
spaghetti with liver, 353
spaghetti seafood, 349
stocks for, 338
Suprême, 344
sweet-sour, bacon, 354
sweet-sour, cream dressing, 355
sweet-sour, mustard, 355
sweet-sour, orange, 355
sweet-sour, oriental, 355
Tabasco, 574
Tartare, 364
to temper, defined, 336
thickeners for, about, 338
thinning, to avoid, 337
tomato, blender, 352
tomato, low-calorie, 354
tomato, Mexican, 352
tomato, quick, 352
tomato, shrimp, 343
tomato, thickened, 352; unthickened, 351
tomato cheese, quick, 349

SAUCE *(cont.)*
tools, about, 336, **337**
Velouté, egg-thickened, 345
watercress, or au Cresson, 365
white I, or Béchamel, 341
white II, or heavy Béchamel, 341
white III, or binding Béchamel, 341
white IV, or enriched Béchamel, 341
white, butter, 351
white, with hard-cooked egg, 342
white, low-fat, 343
white, quick, 342
white, with stock, or Sauce Velouté, 343
wildfowl, for, 345
wine in, 338; when to add, 337
wine, white, for fish, 342, 345
wine, white, for light meats, 345
Worcestershire, 574; to make, 848
SAUCE, SWEET OR DESSERT, 769–776
about, 769
ambrosia, quick, 770
brown sugar, hot, 773; rich, 774
brown sugar, orange, 774
brown sugar butter, 773
butters, sweetened, 775
butterscotch, 773
caramel cream, 774
caramel mocha, 774
cherry, 770; cherry Jubilee, 770
chocolate, 772; chocolate, Cockaigne, 772
chocolate caramel, 773
chocolate custard, 772
chocolate fondue, quick, 773
chocolate mint, 773
chocolate nut-brittle, 772
cider, 772
Cockaigne, 770
coconut Dulcie, 774
coffee, 774
Crème de Menthe, 772
custard, or Crème Anglaise, 771
custard, fruit, quick, 771
foamy, 775
fruit custard, quick, 771
fruit fondue, 769
fudge, hot, 772
hard, 775; fluffy, 775
hard, brown sugar, 775
hard, fruit, 775; spicy, 775
hard, topping, 730
honey, 774; mint, 774
honey butter, 775
jam, 771
jelly, 770
lemon, 769
lime, 769
liqueur, 772; cream, 775
maple sugar, 773; syrup, 773
marshmallow, 774
melba, 770
mocha, 773
Nesselrode, 772
orange, 769
SAUCE, SWEET OR DESSERT *(cont.)*
plum pudding, 771
preserves, 837–839
raisin, 770
rum, 771
Sabayon, classic, 771; hot and cold, 771
sour cream, 776
vanilla, 774
Weinschaum, 771
wine, hot, or plum pudding, 771
wine, red, 771
Zabaglioni, 736, 771
Sauerbraten, 460
Sauerkraut, 295; to make, 849
apples stuffed with, 131
balls, 490
beef brisket with, 461
dressing for game, 374
frankfurter casserole, 499
juice, 43
onions stuffed with, 313
pork chops with, 480
pork and veal goulash with, 481
soup, 180
tomato and, casserole, 296
SAUSAGE, 258–260; 496–499
about, 496
apples, filled with, 130
baked with apples, 259
balls for soup, 196
blood, or black pudding, 497
boiled, 499
broiled, tiny, 86
canapés, 75
canning, 811
casings for, **798,** 812
casserole, sweet potato and fruit, 498
casserole with lentil or lima beans, 260
casserole with millet, 259
country, 497; defined, 496
dressing, 371
dry or summer, defined, 497
dry or summer, to make, 813
frankfurter-sauerkraut casserole, 499
fresh, danger of trichinosis, 497
liver, *see* Liver
to make, about, **798,** 812
mushrooms and, 259
onions and, 259
pan-broiled, 498
patties, sautéed, 498
Pigs in Potatoes, 260
ring, baked, 498
roll, apple, stuffed, 499
in sauce, 259
scrapple or Goetta, 499
to store, 497
stuffing, with sweet potatoes, **374**
Toad-in-the-Hole, 498
USDA labeling, 497
white or Boudin Blanc, 498
Sautéing or pan-frying, 149
Sautoir, defined, 151

Savarin, 689; *also see* Bundkuchen
Savories, 587
Savory, about, 755; herb, 587
sauces, cold, about, 360
Savoy, 293
Savoyarde sandwich, 271
Scalding, 155; milk, 530
Scallions, 312, 585, **585**
Scallopini, veal, 467; with tomatoes, 468
Scallops, about, 381, **382**
deep-fat-fried, 382
Fondu Bourguignonne, 382
kebabs, 382; Meunière, 382
poached, 382; in wine, 382
scalloped or Mornay, 383
Scandinavian Krumkakes, 718
Schaumtorten, 649
Schmierkase, 536
Schnecken, 614
Schnitzels, defined, 467
paprika, 468
Wiener, 468
Scones, 634
Scorzonera or salsify, 326
Scotch broth, 174
herring, fried, 408
shortbread, 713
whisky, about, 50
Woodcock, 223
Scrapple, 499
Scrod, defined, 405
fresh, broiled, 406
Sea grape jelly, 835
Sea kale, 94
Sea squab or blowfish, about, 411
Sea tidbits, 87, **87**
Sea urchin, 87, 88
Seaweed, 561
SEAFOOD, *also see* Fish and Shellfish
baked with oysters, 378
butter, 71, 351
cakes, with potato, 267
canapés, creamed, 75
casserole, in Creole sauce, 265
color and flavor, to add, 375
creamed, 264; au gratin, 265
creamed with vegetables, 265
curry, 388
dips, 91
Divan, quick, 265
dressing, 371
hors d'oeuvre, 87–89
à la king, 264
loaf, and cheese, 267
mold, jellied, 116
mousse, 121
in mushrooms, 309
Newburg, 388
pot pie, 267
in rice or noodle ring, 268
salads, 106–108, 116, 121, 122
sauce, quick pink Chaud-Froid, 369; with spaghetti, 349
SEAFOOD *(cont.)*
scalloped with tomatoes, 268
Tetrazzini, 218
tomatoes stuffed with, 334
tureen, quick, 194
Searing or browning, 447
grilling, 157
Seasonings, 567–588, *also see individual names*
about, 567, **567**
to chop and mince, **568**
citrus, 571
correcting, 567
meats, about, 443
mushroom or Duxelles, 573
salts, 568–570
for soups, 167; stocks, 521
Soyer's Universal Devil, 574
spices, 572, 574–577
zests, 571
Seed, about, 564
cake, 675
fruit, danger in, 124
sesame or benne, 564
to sprout, 565
toasted, 80
Semolina flour, 547
Senegalese Soup, 176
Senfgurken, 842
Seviche, 88
Shad, baked, with creamed roe, 412
boning and carving, 412
Shad Roe, *also see* Roe
broiled, 268
creamed, 268
salad, 108, 115
timbale, 234
Shakes, syrup for, 41, 42
Shallots, 584, **586**
Shallow-frying, 149
Shark, 412
SHELLFISH, 375–393; *also see individual names*
abalone, 383
clams, 379–381; **379**
cockles, 379
cocktails, about, 375
color and flavor, to add, 375
crabs, **375, 384,** 383–385
crayfish, crawfish or Écrevisses, 391, **392**
dips, 91
freezing, thawing and cooking, 827
gumbo, 188
hors d'oeuvre, 87–91, **87**
Jambalaya, 211
lobsters, 385–389, **385, 386, 387, 388**
with macaroni, 217
Mousseline of, 122
mussels, 379
oysters, 375–379, **376**
periwinkles, 379
scallops, **375,** 381–383, **382**
seaside tidbits, about, 87, **87**
shrimps, **375,** 389–391, **389**
snails, **375,** 392

SHELLFISH *(cont.)*
soup with spinach, 186
soups, 186–190; quick, 193, 194
turtles and terrapin, 393
ways to serve, 375, **375**
wine additions, 375
Shepherd's Pie, 262
Sherbet, churned, about, 765
champagne, 768
milks, lemon, orange, pineapple, 768
Sherbet, still-frozen, about, 765
banana-pineapple, 768
cranberry, 768
grapefruit, 767
lemon, 767
lime, 767
orange, 767
pineapple buttermilk, 769
raspberry or strawberry, 768
wine, 768
Sherry, *see* Wine, 53–58
bread dressing, 371
Ship's Biscuits, 634
Shish Kebab, *see* Kebab, 473
Shoots, wild, to cook, 305
Shortbread, Scotch, 713
Shortcake, dough, 633
fruit, 690
onion, 255
Shortening, about, 539–542; to cut in, 640
Shrimp, about, 389
aspic-glazed, 89
balls, fried, 89
Bisque, 188
broiled, Cockaigne, 89
butter, 351
butterfly, 389, **389,** 391
canned, about, 390
casserole with snail butter, 391
deep-fat-fried, 391
dip, 91
eggs Fooyoung, 228
fried in batter, 391
frozen, to cook, 390
gumbo, with crab and oyster, 188
mold, 107, 390
New Orleans, 390
Newburg, 390
pickled, 89
poached, 390
potted, 390
to prepare, 389, **389**
puffs, canapé, 75
salads, 107, 108
sandwich, with cheese sauce, 275
sauce, or Nantua, 343
sauce, and tomato, 343
sauce for pasta and clams, 354
stuffed, deep-fat-fried, 391
Tempura, 391
Teriyaki, 390
Shrubs, fruit, or vinegars, 44
Silver trays, to protect, 78
Simmering, 150
Skewer cooking, 146, **156;** *also see* Kebabs *and outdoor symbol* ⊟
chicken or goose livers, 501
liver, pepper, onions and olives, 501
sweetbreads, 503
tidbits, cold, 80; hot, 80
Skillet, electric, **145**
panning, 149
Skimming, defined, 168
Skirret, 326
Skordalia Sauce, 365
Slaw, *see* Coleslaw, 96, 97
Sloppy Joes, 490
Slow cooking, 151
Smelts, 412
Smitane, Pheasant, 439
sauce, 345
Smoke cooking, 814–816, **815**
fish, 816
fowl, 816
sausage making, about, **798,** 812
Smorgasbord, about, 79
Snacks, cereal, 198, 199
Snails, 375; about, 392
butter, 350
canned, to prepare, 392
cinnamon, 614, **614**
in mushrooms, 309
mushrooms stuffed with, 393
in shells, 392
Snipe, about, 440, 441
Snows, defined, 743; pineapple, 746
Sofrito, 572
Sole, Ambassadeur, 413
Dugléré, 414
fillet of, about, 413
fillets, Florentine, 414
Véronique, 413
Sopaipilla, 609
Sorbets, defined, 765
Sorghum, flour, 550
syrup, 559
Sorrel, 326, 587
soup, cream of, 185
Soubise, *also see* Veal scallop, 468
sauce, 344
SOUFFLÉ, 228–231; *also see* Dessert soufflés
about, 228; container, **220**
baking dish, to prepare, 229
cheese, additions to, 229
cheese, blender, 229
cheese, Cockaigne, 229
chicken, 230
corn pudding, 301
crown, to make, 229
meat or fish, 230
onion, 230
oyster, 231
sweet potato and pineapple or applesauce, 230
vegetable, 229
SOUFFLÉ, DESSERT, 739–742
about, 739

SOUFFLÉ, DESSERT *(cont.)*
apricot, 741; omelette, 742
baked Alaska, 742
chocolate, 740
cold, *see* Bavarians, 746
collar for, 746
fruit, fresh, 740
to glaze, 739
Grand Marnier, 740
hazelnut, 741
lemon, 740
nut, 741
omelet, Norwegian, 742
Omelette aux Confitures, 742
Omelette Soufflé Surprise, 742
pineapple, 740
prune, 741
Rothschild, *see* Vanilla, 739
sour cream apple cake Cockaigne, 741
vanilla, 739
SOUP, 167–197; *also see* Stock
about, 167; additions to, 194–197, **194**
asparagus, cream of, 182; quick, 191
avocado, cream of, chilled, 191
barley, 174
bean, black, 177
bean, dried; U.S. Senate, 176
bean with vegetables, 177
beef tea, 170
beet or Borsch, 175; blender, 191
beet consommé, jellied, 174
bisque, defined, 167, 174
Bouillabaisse, 188–189
bouillon, 170; court, 525
bouillon, chicken, with egg, 170
bouillon, tomato, 170; jellied, 174
Boula-Boula, 178
breads to serve with, 195
broth, chicken, 169
broth, clam and chicken, quick, 193
broth, clear, 169
broth, coquina, 186
broth, mushroom, 171
broth, on the rocks, 170
broth, turkey, 169
broth, vegetable, 170
bunch, 521
cabbage, 175
canned, for quick sauces, 348
canning stock and broths, 811
cauliflower, cream of, 182; quick, 192
celery, cream of, 182
cheese, quick, 192
cheese balls for, 197
chestnut, 182
chicken, cream of, 182; quick, 192
chicken broth, 169
chicken broth with egg, 170
chicken curry or Senegalese, 176
chicken gumbo, 176
chiffonade of herbs for, 195
choux paste, garnish for, 195
chowder, clam, Manhattan, 190
SOUP *(cont.)*
chowder, clam, New England, 190
chowder, conch, 190
chowder, corn, 183
chowder, lobster, quick, 194
chowder, tomato, corn, quick, 192
chowder, vegetable, 175
clam broth, 186; bisque, 187
clear, about, 169
Cock-a-Leekie, 180
cold, about, to prepare quickly, 167
coloring, about, 168
consommé, 169; canned, quick, 191
consommé Brunoise, 169
consommé fondue Cockaigne, quick, 191
consommé Madrilène, 169
corn, cream of, 182
crab gumbo, 188; she-crab, 187
crab or lobster Mongole, quick, 194
crawfish bisque, 187
cream, about, 181; defined, 174
croutons for, 197; 551
cucumber, Bulgarian cold, 183
cucumber, Cockaigne, quick, 192
cucumber, cold, quick, 192
cucumber, cream of, herb, chilled, 183
custard or Royale, 172
dried, for sauces, 349
dumplings, 202–206; butter, 203
dumplings, liver or Leberklösse, 196
dumplings, liver sausage, 196
egg drops for, 171, **172**
egg drops, hard-cooked, 172
escarole, cream of, 185
farina balls, Cockaigne, 203
fish, about, 186
fish stews, about, 188
freezing and thawing, 829
fritter garnish for, 196
fruit, 128, 129
Garbure, 177
garnishes for, 194–197, **194**
Gazpacho, 171; blender, 191
gnocchi for, 204, **204**
green kern, 175
groundnut, 180
gumbos, 176, 188
high-altitude cooking, 167
jellied, 167; clear, about, 173
kettle or pot, **167, 521**
Kreplach, 172
leek-potato, 184
legume, about, 176; to bind, 169
lemon, Greek, 172
lentil, 177
lettuce, cream of, 185
lobster bisque, 187; Mongole, 194
lobster stew, 188
lobster Supreme, quick, 194
marrow balls, for, 196
Matelote, 189
meat, about, 169; to serve, 463
meatballs for, 196

SOUP *(cont.)*
melon, winter, 185
milk toast, 186
minestrone, 177
miso, thickener, 169
Mulligatawny, 178
mushroom, cream of, 183; quick, 193
mushroom broth, 171
mushroom and clam bisque, 187
mussel stew, 188
nettle, 180
New Year's, 181
Nockerln for, 203
noodle dough, white or green, 213
onion, 171; quick, 193
onion, cream of, 184
oxtail, 179; with wine, quick, 193
oyster gumbo, 188
oyster stews and bisques, 188
Panades, 179
Paysanne, 175
pea, green, or Potage St. Germain, 178
pea, quick, 192
pea, split, 177; blender, 178
pea, split, au maigre, 178
peanut or Ghanian groundnut, 180
pepper pot, 179
Petite Marmite, 170
poached egg in, 221
potages, defined, 174
potato, 184; with tomatoes, 184
Pot-au-Feu or Poule-au-Pot, 170
pumpkin, 185
purée, defined, 174
purslane, cream of, 185
quenelles for, 205, **205**
quick, about, 190
to reheat, 162
to remove fat from, 168, **168**
rose hip, 129
Royale or custard, 172
sauerkraut, 180
sausage balls for, 196
Scotch broth, 174
seafood tureen, quick, 194
seasonings, for, 521; about, 167
Senegalese, 176
to serve, 19
servings for, 167; bowls, **194;** tureen, **167**
she-crab, 187
shellfish gumbo, 188
shrimp bisque, 188; gumbo, 188
sorrel, cream of, 185
Spatzen for, 205
spinach, 180; cream of, 185; quick, 193
spinach, shellfish, 186
stocks, *see* Stocks, 520
thick, about, 174
thickenings for, 168
tomato, cold, 171
tomato, cream of, 185; chilled, 193
tomato, quick, 193
turkey broth, 169

SOUP *(cont.)*
turtle, green, 181; mock, 181
types, 167
vegetable, 175; quick, 191
vegetable, blender, 175; cream of, 191
vegetable chowder, 175
vegetables for, 524
Velouté, defined, 174
Vichyssoise, 184
watercress, clear, 171; cream of, 185
wine in, 526
winter melon, 185
Won Ton, 173

Sour cream, about, 533
apple cake soufflé Cockaigne, 741
cake, 673
cheesecake, 660
coffee cake, quick, 627
cultured or dairy, 534
cupcakes, spice, 695
dips, 89
doughnuts, 245
dressings, 367; horseradish, 356
muffins, 630
pie, cherry or berry, 651
rolls, 611, **612**
sauce for baked potatoes, 357
sauce for desserts, 776
substitute, 534
waffles, 241

Sour milk, 533; substitutions, 532

Sourdough, about, 554; to make, 555
bread, 603; rye, 609
cake, chocolate, 677
corn bread, 628
to substitute for yeast, 555

Soursop, 143

Soy, bread, whole wheat, 608
flour, 549; meal, 549
milk, 535
sauce, 574

Soybean, 285; *also see* Alternate foods
cakes, 256
casserole, 255
curd or Tofu, 535
flour, low-fat, 549
green, 286
paste or extender, 535
to roast, 564

Soyer's Devil Seasoning, 574

Spaghetti, about; to cook, 212, **213**
boiled, 213, **213**
meat pie, quick, 217
salad, 106
sauce with liver, 353
sauce with seafood, 349
squash, 330
Tetrazzini, 218
toppings for, 218–219
with tuna, salmon or beef, quick, 217

Spareribs, 481–482, *see* Pork
cocktail, glazed, 85
grilled, 158

Spareribs *(cont.)*
lamb, *see* pork, 481
spit-cooking, 158, **158**
Spatzen or Spätzle, 204, 205
Spearmint, 582
Speculatius, 714
Spices, *see individual names*
about, 574–579, **579;** jar, bags, **579**
cakes, *see* Cakes, Coffee cakes, Cupcakes
to cook with, 575
épices composes, 572
five-spices powder, 572
four-spices or Parisienne, 572
in frozen precooked dishes, 828
for pickling, 841
in quantity cooking, 575
to store, 575
Spinach, about, 326
boiled, 326
canapé tart, 69
Chinese, 331
creamed, 327
dressing, 360
loaf, tomato and cheese, 327
oysters Rockefeller, 378
pancakes, in, 327
panned or Sicilian, 327
with rice and chestnuts, 208
salads, for, 94
soup, 180; cream of, 185; quick, 193
soup with shellfish, 186
timbale, 231
tomatoes, with, 327
Spirit Glaze for Ham, 368
Spirits, for cooking, about, 525
Spit-cooking, 156, 157, **158**
Spoilage in foods, about, 798, 799
Sponge, defined, 743
cakes, *see* Cakes, Cupcakes
custard, about, 736
custard, orange, lemon; pineapple, 737
Spoon breads, 629
Sprats, defined, 411
Spreads, *see* Canapés and Sandwiches
Springerle, 713
Sprouting grains, beans and peas, **519,** 565
Squabs, about, 434
braised; broiled, 435
roast, 434
Squares, cookies and bar, about, 701
Squash, about, 328
blossoms, stuffed, 329
canning, summer, 809; winter, 809
pie, 654
pumpkin, 330
seeds, 564
spaghetti, 330
summer, about, 328, **328**
summer, baked, 329
summer, Cockaigne casserole, 330
summer, Creole, 330
summer, sauteed, 329
summer, steamed, 328
Squash *(cont.)*
summer, stuffed, baked or steamed, 329; raw, 329
varieties of, **328**
vegetable marrow, 328
winter, about, 328, **328**
winter, baked; mashed; stuffed, 330
zucchini, deep-fried, 330
Squid, about, 408, **409**
casseroled, 409
fried, 409
in ink sauce, 410
stuffed, 409
Squirrel, about, 515; to skin, **515**
Stain removal, 165
Staples, household, 799; storage of, 800
Steaks, *see* Beef, Salmon, Venison, etc.
Tartare, 86
Starches, *see* Cornstarch
waxy, in frozen pies, 830
Steaming, about 154; blanching, 154
for canning, 803, **825**
desserts, pressure-cooked, 754
puddings, 753–755
vegetables, 278
Steeping, 154
STEWS, MEAT, *also see* Fish and Shellfish
about, 447
beef, Belgian, or Carbonnade Flamande, 461
beef, Gaston, 459
beef, kidney, 506
beef, West African, 462
beef with wine or Boeuf Bourguignonne, 460
Blanquette de Veau, 470
Brunswick, 427
Burgoo, Kentucky, 465
Cassoulet, 475
Chicken, 426; giblet, 512
Chinese Firepot, 462
corned beef and cabbage, 466
Couscous, 476
dumplings, for, 202–206
fisherman's, about, 188–190
fricassee of rabbit or hare, 513
goulash, beef, 465
goulash, lamb or pork, à blanc, 475
goulash, pork and veal with sauerkraut, 481
gumbos, 176, 188
Hasenpfeffer, 514
Irish, 475
jugged hare or rabbit à la mode, 514
lamb or Navarin Printanière, 474
lamb shanks or trotters, braised, 474
lobster, 188
Mulligan, *see* burgoo, 465
mussel, 188
New England boiled dinner, 466
oxtail, 511
pigs' feet, 511; pigtails, 511
pigs' knuckles and sauerkraut, 511
pork hocks, 482
pork neck bones, 482

STEWS, MEAT *(cont.)*
red, Chinese, 447
Rombauer rice dish, 209
turkey, 426
veal Ménagère, 469
Stir-frying, 149; vegetables, 279
STOCK, 520–525; *also see* Soup
brown, 522
clarifying, 522
concentrates, frozen, 829
court bouillons, 525
double strength for consommé, 522
faggots for seasoning, 572
fish or Fumet, 524
flavoring, to retain, 521
fowl, rabbit, game, 523
grease, to remove, 521
homemade, about, 167
household, quick, 523
light, from poultry, 523
light, with veal, 522
making, meat, 520
making, vegetable, 524
poultry, light, 523
pressure-cooked, quick, 523
to reduce, 522
reinforcers, 525
seasoning for, 521
skimming, 521
stockpot, 520, **521**
to store, 521
veal; jellied, 114
vegetable, 524
Stollen, 620
Storage of food, 799–801
Stove, camp, 155
household, 146, 159
oven rack placement, 159, **159**
solar heat, 155
top burners, 160
Strawberry, about, 133; *also see* Berries
bombe, 764
canning, 806
fresh, variations, 133
glaze, 732
ice, 766, 767
ice cream, 760
jam, red red, 835
melon rounds, in, 139
pie, 650, 651
pie, Bavarian, 657
pie, chiffon, 658
preserves, 837
punch, 46
Romanoff, 133
salad molds, and rhubarb, 120
sherbet, 768
Stroganoff, Beef, 458
Strudel, about, 648, **648**
cabbage or savory, 294
Stuffings, 370–374, *see* Dressing
SUBSTITUTIONS AND EQUIVALENTS, about, 589; 593–598; *see individual names*
Succotash, 301
Suet Pudding, fruit, steamed, 754
SUGAR, 556–560
apple or sweetsop, 143
berry, 556
brown or Barbados, 557; to measure, **557**
brown, icing, quick, 728
brown, icing, and marshmallow, 726
brown, sauces, 773, 774, 775
brown, to unlump, 557
cane syrup, 559
caramelized, for glazing and coloring, 559
castor, 556
confectioners', 556
confectioners' lace topping, 729, **730**
cookies, *see* Cookies
corn, 557; corn syrup, 557
crystallized; rock candy, 787
Demerara, 557
equivalents, 589, 597
fruit, 557
granulated, 556
honey, 558
icing or European or English, 556
in jelly and jam, 832
liquid, about, 557
lump or loaf, 556
maple, 557; maple syrup, 558
to measure, 556, 557
molasses, 559
powdered, 556
raw, 557
seasoned, about, 557
to sieve, **556**
solid, about, 556
sorghum, 559
to substitute, 589, 597
superfine, 556
synthetic or non-nutritive sweeteners, 560
syrup, white, 791
syrup for canning, 805
syrup for drinks, 48
syrup for freezing fruits, 823
syrup for fruits, 126
treacle, golden or refiner's, 559
Turbinado, 557
types in diet, 5
Sukiyaki, 458; with chopsticks, 459, **459**
Summer sausage, defined, 497
Sunflower seeds, 564
Suprême, defined, 426
sauce, 344
Swan Pastry from choux paste, **638,** 647
Swedes or rutabaga, boiled, 326
Sweet Cicely, 587
Sweet potatoes, 324–325; *see* Potatoes
Sweet woodruff or waldmeister, 587
Sweetbreads, about, 502
broiled, 503

Sweetbreads *(cont.)*
chicken, and, 430
creamed, tomatoes stuffed with, 334
glazed, 503
poached, sauced, 502
Ragoût Fin, 503
ring mold with mushrooms, 234
sautéed, 502
on skewers, 503
Sweeteners, synthetic or non-nutritive, 560
Sweetsop or sugar apple, 143
Sweet-sour, beans, 286
dressing, cream, 355; low-calorie, 362
pork, 480
sauces, 354–355
Swiss chard, 293, 298
Swiss Meringue, 727
Swiss Steak, 463
Swordfish Steaks, 414
Syllabub, 62
Symbols, XII
Syrian Bread, 609
Syrup, caramel, for candy, 791
molasses, for candy, 791
sugar, for canning, 805
sugar, for drinks, 48
sugar, for freezing fruits, 823
sugar, for fruits, 126
sugar, for lemonade, 45
sugar, white, 791

T

Tabasco sauce, 574
Table décor and service, 15–24, **15, 16**
Tacos, 70
Taffy, 785–787, **785;** saltwater, 786
Tahin, 564; *also see* Seeds
Tamales, 201; pie, corn bread, 252
Tamarind, 143, 144; marmalade, 839
Tampala or Chinese spinach, 331
Tangelo, about, 136
Tangerine, 135; rice dressing Cockaigne, 373
Tapioca, about, 550; flour, 550
custard, 750, 751
Tarama, 87
Taro or dasheen, about, 331
Tarragon, 587; vinegar, 527
to store in vinegar, 588
Tart, apple, 652
Banbury, 654
blueberry or huckleberry custard, 651
canapés, tartlets for, 68, 69
chess, 654
coffee cream, 656
cream meringue, Cockaigne, 689
crust for, 640, 641
custard, with fruit, 655
glaze for, 732
macaroon jam, 717, **717**
nut, 718
quiche, 69
sand, 711
tomato, 333; quick, 252
TEA, 39–40
about, 39
beef, 170
breads, quick, 623–627
cakes, *see* Cakes, Cupcakes
iced, 40; flavorings for, 40
menus, afternoon, 32
sandwiches, 66–76
service, about, 22, **23**
spiced, 40
spreads, sweet, 72
tisanes and infusions, 40
wafers, 714
Temperature conversions, 592
foods, holding, 161
Tempura, batter for, 243
shrimp, 391
Tenderloin, *also see* Beef, Pork
pork, 478; Frenched, 479
pork, with mushrooms and olives, 479
Tequila drinks, about, 53
Teriyaki, marinade for chicken and steaks, 529
shrimp, 390
Terrapin, about, 393; lamb, 257
Terrines, about, 494
potted shrimp or lobster, 390
of veal, 496
Tetrazzini, chicken; turkey; seafood, 218
Textured vegetable proteins, 535
Thermometer, candy, 777
deep-fat, 147
meat, 447
to test, 777
Thermostats, oven, about, 159
Thickenings, *also see* Flour
for sauces, 338–340
for soups, 168
Thrushes, 440
Thymes, 588
TIMBALE, 231–234
about, 231
asparagus, 232
broccoli, 231
cases for food, 247
cauliflower, 231
celeriac ring mold, 232
cheese, or crustless quiche, 232
chestnut ring mold, 234
chicken or ham, 232
chicken liver, 233
custard, basic, 231
eggplant, 232
fish, 233
irons, **235**
meat-and-vegetable, 232
mushroom, 231; ring mold, 234
ring mold, about, 231
shad roe, 234
spinach, 231
veal, 233
vegetable, 231

Tinware, 162
Tisanes and infusions, 40
Toad-in-the-Hole, 498
Toast, bread loaf, buttered, 636
cinnamon, or sticks, 636
French, 636
French, tomato or cheese, 273
Hawaiian, with bacon, 271
honey butter, 636
melba, 636; baskets, 250
melba, cheese rounds, 635
milk, 186
orange, 637
sandwiches, 269
waffles, French, 242
zwieback, 637
Toasting, partial heat process, 154
Toddy, 61
Toffee, English, 788
Tofu, to make, 535; dressing, 369
Tomalley, lobster liver, 385
TOMATO, about, 331; for salads, 104
aspic, 114, 115
aspic, with tasty centers, 81
bouillon, 170; jellied, 174
with Brussels sprouts, 294
with cabbage, 294
canapés, 73
canning, 808; purée, 806
catsup, 847
cherry, stuffed, 84
chowder, with corn, quick, 192
chutney, green, 847
cream, chilled, 43
creamed, canned, 332
Creole, 332
custard, 333
fillings for, 105
French toast, 273
green, 332, 844, 846, 847
green, pie, with apple, 650
grilled, 332
ice, 111, *see* Avocado salad cups
juice, aspic, canned, 115
juice, canning, 808
juice, cucumber and, 43
juice, fresh; canned, 43
juice, orange and; pineapple and, 43
kidney beans and, 288
loaf, spinach and cheese, 327
mystery or tomato soup cake, 680
olive casserole, 332
paste, Italian, 574; velvet, 573
pickle, green, 844
preserves, 838
Provençale, 332
pudding Cockaigne, 333
punch, 45
Rarebit or Woodchuck, 253
relish, green, 844
salads, 105, **105,** 106, 114, 115; to cut for, 106, **106**
sandwiches, 73, 272, 273
TOMATO *(cont.)*
sauce, *also see* Sauces
sauce, blender, 352
sauce, low-calorie, 354
sauce, Mexican, 352
sauce, quick, 352; and cheese, 349
sauce, shrimp and, 343
sauce, thickened, 352; unthickened, 351
sauerkraut and, casserole, 296
scalloped, 333
as seasoning, 573
seeds, to remove, **331**
to skin, 105
soup, cold, or Gazpacho, 171
soup, cream of, 185
soup, cream, chilled, quick, 193
soup, potato and, 184
soup, quick, 193
with spinach, 327
stewed, 331
stewed green, 332
stuffed, cold, 105, **105**
stuffed, hot, 333–334
stuffed cherry, 84
tart, 69, 333; quick, 252
Tongue, about, 507
in aspic, 508
baked in Creole sauce, 507
beef, boiled, 507
beef, with raisin sauce, 507
canapés, smoked, 74
corned or pickled, boiled, 507
cornucopias, 86
salad sandwich, 271
smoked, boiled, 507
TOPPINGS, *also see* Icings, Garnishes, Pie or Meat Toppings and Glazes
casseroles, 368, 369
for coffee cakes, pies, rolls, 731–733
hard-sauce, 730
lace, quick, 729, **730**
for pastas, 218–219
Torten, 684–686; *see* Cakes
Tortillas, 629
Tournedos, 454, **454**
Toushi, *see* Capers, 580
Tray freezing, 822
Treacle or golden syrup, 559
Trichinosis, 477, 513, 810
Trifle, 688
Tripe, about, 509
cooked, fresh, 509
fried, 509
à la Mode de Caen, 509
Spanish, 510
Triticale, flour, 548
to cook, 200
Trotters, lamb, braised, 474
Trout, blue, or Truite au Bleu, 414
brook, Meunière, 414
lake, broiled, 414

Truffles, about, 310
chocolate, 789
for garnish, 310
Truite au Bleu, 414
Trying out fats, 542
Tuna fish, about, 415
casserole, with noodle and mushroom soup, 215
casserole, West African, 265
dips, 91
fresh, 415
salad, 108
with spaghetti, quick, 217
Turbot, poached, 415
Turkey, *also see* Poultry
about, 422
baked in foil, 422
breast, roasted, 423
broth, 169
à la Campagne, 428
to carve, 421, **421**
casserole, Mole, 428
casserole, with vegetables, 263
Divan, 264
dressings for, 370–374
galantine of, 431, **432**
hash, 263
loaf, cooked, 264
roast, 422
smoked, for hors d'oeuvre, 87
soup, 523
stew or fricassee, 426
Tetrazzini, 218
wild, 438
Turkish Fruit Paste or Turkish Delight, 791
Turmeric, 576
Turnips, about, 334; cooked, 335; to pare, 335, **335**
cups, stuffed, 335
glazed, 335
Rémoulade, 102
scalloped, 335
"yellow," 326
Turnovers, 251
for canapés, 69
fruit, sweet, 662
Turtles and terrapins, about, 393; to cook, 393
soups, green and mock, 181
Tutti-Frutti, cake, 680
conserve Cockaigne, 840
parfait, 765

U

Ugli, about, 136
Upside-Down Cake, 661
Utensils, about, 162
camping, 35, **35**
cleaning scorched, 163
tea, Japanese, **36**

V

Vacherin Rings, *see* Meringue Paste, 649
Vanilla, bean and extract, 577
cookies, refrigerator, 715
custard cream filling, 697
Vanilla *(cont.)*
ice cream, 759, 761
sauce, 774
soufflé, 739
sugar, 557
VARIETY MEATS, 499–512; *see individual names*
about, 499, **500**
patties, 506
VEAL, 466–471; 488–496
about, 466
balls, *see* Meatballs
birds or paupiettes, 469
Blanquette de Veau, 470
calves' feet, jellied, 511
chops, braised, 469
city chicken, 469
creamed, 263
croquettes, 248
curried, and rice, 256
cutlet or Scallopini, 467
cutlet or Schnitzel, paprika, 468
cutlets, about, 467; breaded, 468
goulash with sauerkraut and pork, 481
and kidney casserole, 506
kidneys, *see* Kidneys
large cuts, suggested uses, 453
leftover, creamed, 256
loaf, 493; cooked, 264
marrowbones, baked, 471
mousse, jellied, 120
Osso Buco, 471
Parmigiana, 468
patties, 488
pie, and pork, 470
roast, 467
roast, stuffed, or Farci, 467
salad, 109; with herring, 107
scallop, about, 467
scallop, with ham, or Cordon Bleu, 469
scallop or Escalope de Veau Orloff, 468
Scallopini with tomatoes, 468
sour cream casserole, with, 470
and spinach casserole, 256
steak, Mexican, with noodles, 470
stew, and rice, Rombauer, 209
stew, Ménagère, 469
stock, jellied, 114
stock, light, 522
terrine of, with chicken, ham, or pork, 496
timbale, 233
Wiener Schnitzel or breaded veal cutlet, 468
VEGETABLE, 276–335; *also see individual names*
about, 276–280; high-altitude cooking, 282
for barbecue, about, 282
blanching for freezing, 824, **825**
braised or skillet-panned, 279
brining or dry-salted, 848
broth, 170
campfire, about, 282
canned, about, 281
canning, about, 808–810; pressure, 808
cases and garnishes for salads, 98, **99**

VEGETABLE *(cont.)*
casserole, eggs and, 224
Chinese style, 279
chowder, 175
cleaning and preparing, 277
color retention, 278
creamed, buttered and sauced, about, 280
croquettes, 247
deep-fat frying, 279
dried, about, 816
flavor retention, 278
fondues, about, 280
freezing, about, 824–825; blanching chart, 825
freezing, to size for, **821**
fritter batter for, 243; puréed, 243
Fritto Misto, 279
frozen, cooking and thawing, 281, 825
garnishes for salad, 98, 99, **99**
to glaze, 367
greens, collecting, 276
à la Grecque, about, 281
grill, mixed, 256
with hash, 262
juice, about, 42; juice aspic, 115
marinade for, 528
marrow, 328
microwave cooking, 282
milks, 534
nutritional values, to keep, 278
oils, 541
pot liquors, 524
potatoes stuffed with, 320
pressure cooking and steaming, 278, **278**
proteins, textured, 535
puréed, blended, about, 280
raw, marinated, or Crudités Vinaigrette, 83
reheated, about, 281
for a roast, about, 280
root, glazed, 280
for salads, 99
salads, gelatin, 115, 116
salt, when to, 278; salts, 570
scraper, **296**
seasonings, 572–574; *also see* Mirepoix, Matignon
shortenings, about, 541
skillet-panning, 279, **279**
slicing and chopping, 277, **277**
soufflé, 229
soup, 175; quick, 191
for soup, 524
soup, blender, 175; cream of, 191
soup with beans, 177
steaming, 278, **278**
stir-frying, 279, **279**
stock; stock-making, 524
to store, 277
stuffed, about, 280
Tempura, 243
timbales, 231
water-soluble vitamins, about, 6
yields in canning, 808

Velouté, about, as soups, 174, 181
sauces, 343, 345
Venison, about, 516
braised, 517
hamburger, 517
meat loaf, 517
mouffle, 516
roast; leg of, 517
saddle of, 517
steaks, sautéed, 517
Vichyssoise, 184
Vinaigrette Sauce, 360
Vinegar, about, 526
chili, 527
cider and malt-based, 526
fruit shrubs, 44
garlic, 527
ginger, 528
herb, fresh, 527; quick, 527
for pickling, 841
red raspberry Cockaigne, 527
spiced, 527
tarragon or burnet, 527
white; distilled, 526; wine, 526
Vitamins, retention of, 6; in fruit, 123
Vodka drinks, about, 53
Vol-au-Vent, 645, 646

W

Wafers, *see* Cookies
Waffles, about, 240
bacon, cornmeal, 241
buttermilk, 241
chocolate, 242
desserts, as, 753
French toast, 242
iron, care of, 240, **240**
sour cream, 241
yam, golden, or squash, 241
Waldmeister or sweet woodruff, 587
Walnut, 564
catsup, 848
filling, toasted, 699
leaves or cookies, 715
Wassail, 65
Water, about, 519
acidulated, 520
for cooking, 519
daily intake, 6
high-altitude usage, 520; boiling point, 145
purification, 520
Water chestnuts, 335, 563
Watercress, 93, **93,** 335
dressing, 360; blender, 360
sauce, 365
soup, clear, 171; cream of, 185
Watermelon, 123, 138
plugged, 60, **60**
rind, pickled, 845
Weather, effect on candy making, 777
effect on cooking, 588
effect on smoking, 815

Wedding Buffet Menus, 33
Weinschaum Custard, 736; sauce, 771
Welsh Rarebit, 252; with noodles, 214
West African Beef Stew, 462
Wheat, breads, *see* Breads
to cook as cereal, 200
flake cookie, 708
flour allergy substitute, 551
flours and grains, 547–548, **547**
germ flour, 548
Whips, defined, 743
fruit, 741, 745, 746
prune or apricot, 741
Whips for egg beating, 665
Whisky, about, types, 50
drinks, 49–51; 59–64
glasses, 49, **49**
White sausage, 498
Whitebait or Blanchaille, 415
Whitefish, broiled, 414
Whole-grain, breads, *see* Breads and Rolls
cereal snacks, 198, 199
cereals, to cook, 200
flour, 547
griddle cakes, 236
Whole wheat flour, 547
Wiener Schnitzel, 468
WILDFOWL, 435–441, *see names of*
about, 435
barding, 436
carrying strap, **417**
marinated, 436
potted, 438
salmi of, about, 436
to test for doneness, 436
WILD rice, 212; ring, 212
dressing for game, 373
popped for hors d'oeuvre, 80
WINES, about, 53–58; vintages, 54
apéritifs, 56
for aspics and jellies, 526
body, defined, 54
bottles for serving, **48**
champagne, about, 56
champagne fountain, 56, **56**
chart for food and, 57, **57**
chilling, 57
classifications, 54
for cooking, 525
cups, 64
custard, 736
dry, defined, 54
food combinations with, 525
formal pouring of, 57
fortified, defined, 56
gelatin, 745
glasses for, 57, **57**
labels, about, 54
May wine, 64
mulled, or Negus, in quantity, 65
Sangria, 62
sauce, Marchand de Vin, 347
sauce, red, dessert; hot, 771
WINES *(cont.)*
sauce, white, for fish, 342
sauce, white for light meats, 345
in sauces, 337
seasoning for shellfish, 375
to serve, 56, 57; amounts, 57, **57**
serving chart, 58, **58**
sherbet, 768
for soups, 167
to store, 57
varietals, about, 55
Vin Brûlé, 61
vinegars, 526
vintages, about, 54
wassail, 65
Wineberry, 134
Winkle or periwinkle, 88
Winter cress, 94
Wintergreen, for tisanes, 40
Witloof endive or chicory, 299
Wok cookery, 149, **279**
Won Ton, dough for, *see* Noodles, 213
soup, 173, **173**
Wood pigeons, 441
Woodchuck, 516
Woodchuck or Tomato Rarebit, 253
Woodcock, 441; about, 440
Worcestershire sauce, 574; to make, 848
Wrap cookery, 152, **152**

Y

Yakitori, 431
Yam, 324–325; *see* Potato, sweet
muffins, 631
waffles, golden, 241
Yeast, about, 553
active dry, 554; compressed, 554
breads, 602--619
brewers' or nutritional, 554
in coffee cakes, 619–621
compressed, 554
doughnuts, 245
doughs, additions to, 602
paste for brioche, 615
rolls and buns, 610–619
to substitute, 554
Yiro, 158, **158**
Yogurt, dessert, 756
dressings, 367
to make, 533; to make cheese, 533
marinade, 528
Yorkshire Pudding Cockaigne, 206

Z

Zabaglione, 736
Zephyrs, corn, Cockaigne, 628
Zests as flavoring, 571, **571**
Zucchini, 328, 328–330; *see* Summer squash
deep-fat-fried, 330
pickled, 845
Zwieback, 637
crusts for pies, 642